MW01614449

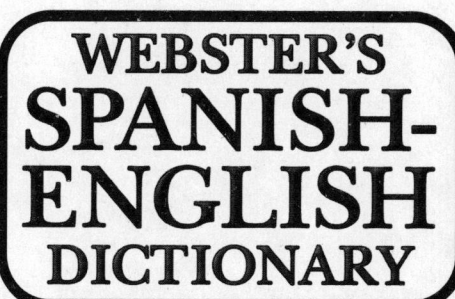

WEBSTER'S SPANISH-ENGLISH DICTIONARY

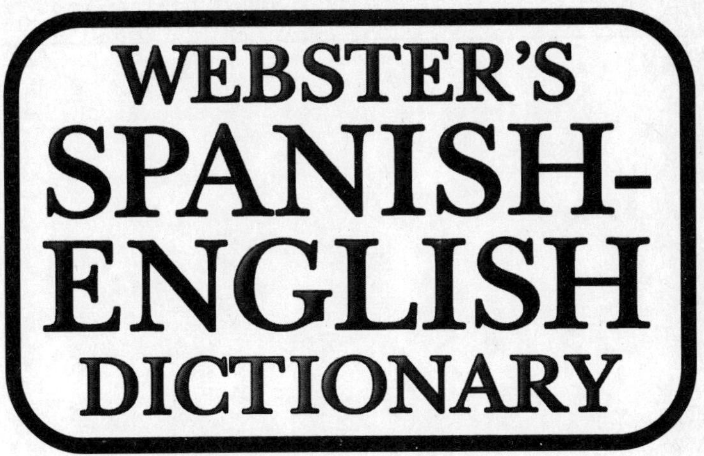

Created in Cooperation with
the Editors of
Merriam-Webster

Federal Street Press is a trademark of Federal Street Press,
a division of Merriam-Webster, Incorporated.

This 2003 edition published by Barnes & Noble, Inc.
by arrangement with Federal Street Press,
a Division of Merriam-Webster, Incorporated

2003 Barnes & Noble Books

ISBN 0-7607-4294-4

Printed in the United States of America

03 04 05 06 07 5 4 3 2

Contents | Índice

Preface

WEBSTER'S SPANISH-ENGLISH DICTIONARY is a completely new dictionary designed to meet the needs of English and Spanish speakers in a time of ever-expanding communication among the countries of the Western Hemisphere. It is intended for language learners, teachers, office workers, tourists, business travelers—anyone who needs to communicate effectively in the Spanish and English languages as they are spoken and written in the Americas. This new dictionary provides accurate and up-to-date coverage of current vocabulary in both languages, as well as abundant examples of words used in context to illustrate idiomatic usage. The selection of Spanish words and idioms was based on evidence drawn from a wide variety of modern Latin-American sources and interpreted by trained Merriam-Webster bilingual lexicographers. The English entries were chosen by Merriam-Webster editors from the most recent Merriam-Webster dictionaries, and they represent the current basic vocabulary of American English.

All of this material is presented in a format that emphasizes convenience and ease of use, clarity and conciseness of the information presented, precise discrimination of senses, and frequent inclusion of example phrases showing words in actual use. Also included are pronunciations (in the International Phonetic Alphabet) for all English words, full coverage of irregular verbs in both languages, a section on basic Spanish grammar, a table of the most common Spanish abbreviations, and a detailed Explanatory Notes section that answers any questions the reader might have concerning the use of this book.

Eileen M. Haraty
Editor

Explanatory Notes

Entries

1. Main Entries

A boldface letter, word, or phrase appearing flush with the left-hand margin of each column of type is a main entry or entry word. The main entry may consist of letters set solid, of letters joined by a hyphen, or of letters separated by a space:

cafetalero[1], **-ra** *adj*. . .
eye–opener. . . *n*. . .
walk out *vi* . . .

The main entry, together with the material that follows it on the same line and succeeding indented lines, constitutes a dictionary entry.

2. Order of Main Entries

Alphabetical order throughout the book follows the order of the English alphabet, with one exception: words beginning with the Spanish letter *ñ* follow all entries for the letter *n*. The main entries follow one another alphabetically letter by letter without regard to intervening spaces or hyphens; for example, *shake-up* follows *shaker.*

Homographs (words with the same spelling) having different parts of speech are usually given separate dictionary entries. These entries are distinguished by superscript numerals following the entry word:

hail[1]. . . *vt*. . .

hail[2] *n*. . .

hail[3] *interj*. . .

madrileño[1], **-ña** *adj*. . .

madrileño[2], **-ña** *n*. . .

Numbered homograph entries are listed in the following order: verb, adverb, adjective, noun, conjunction, preposition, pronoun, interjection, article.

Homographs having the same part of speech are normally included at the same dictionary entry, without regard to their different semantic origins. On the English-to-Spanish side, however, separate entries are made if the homographs have distinct inflected forms or if they have distinct pronunciations.

3. Guide Words

A pair of guide words is printed at the top of each page, indicating the first and last main entries that appear on that page:

fregar • fuego

4. Variants

When a main entry is followed by the word *or* and another spelling, the two spellings are variants. Both are standard, and either one may be used according to personal inclination:

jailer *or* **jailor**. . . *n*. . .
quizá *or* **quizás** *adv*. . .

Occasionally, a variant spelling is used only for a particular sense of a word. In these cases, the variant spelling is listed after the sense number of the sense to which it pertains:

electric. . . *adj* **1** *or* **electrical**. . .

Sometimes the entry word is used interchangeably with a longer phrase containing the entry word. For the purposes of this dictionary, such phrases are considered variants of the headword:

bunk[2] *n* **1** *or* **bunk bed**. . .

angina *nf* **1** *or* **angina de pecho** **:** angina . . .

Variant wordings of boldface phrases may also be shown:

> **madera** *nf*. . . **3 madera dura** *or* **madera noble**. . .
>
> **atención**[1] *nf*. . . **2 poner atención** *or* **prestar atención**. . .

5. Run-On Entries

A main entry may be followed by one or more derivatives or by a homograph with a different functional label. These are run-on entries. Each is introduced by a boldface dash and each has a functional label. They are not defined, however, since their equivalents can be readily derived by adding the corresponding foreign-language suffix to the terms used to define the entry word or, in the case of homographs, simply substituting the appropriate part of speech:

> **illegal**. . . *adj* **:** ilegal **— illegally** *adv*
> (the Spanish adverb is *ilegalmente*)
>
> **transferir**. . . *vt* TRASLADAR **:** to transfer **— transferible** *adj*
> (the English adjective is **transferable**)
>
> **Bosnian** *n* **:** bosnio *m,* -nia *f* **— Bosnian** *adj*
> (the Spanish adjective is *bosnio, -nia*)

On the Spanish side of the book, reflexive verbs are sometimes run on undefined:

> **enrollar** *vt* **:** to roll up, to coil **— enrollarse** *vr*

The absence of a definition means that *enrollarse* has the simple reflexive meaning "to become rolled up or coiled," "to roll itself up."

6. Bold Notes

A main entry may be followed by one or more phrases containing the entry word or an inflected form of the entry word. These are bold notes. Each bold note is defined at its own numbered sense:

> **álamo** *nm* **1 :** poplar **2 álamo temblón :** aspen
>
> **hold**[1]. . . *vi*. . . **4 to hold to :**. . . **5 to hold with :**. . .

If the bold note consists only of the entry word and a single preposition, the entry word is represented by a boldface swung dash **~**.

> **pegar** . . . *vi* . . . **3 ~ con :** to match, to go with . . .

The same bold note phrase may appear at two or more senses if it has more than one distinct meaning:

> **wear**[1]. . . *vt*. . . **3 to wear out :** gastar <he wore out his shoes. . . > **4 to wear out** EXHAUST **:** agotar, fatigar <to wear oneself out . . .> . . .
>
> **estar** . . . *vi* . . . **15 ~ por :** to be in favor of **16 ~ por :** to be about to <está por cerrar . . .> . . .

If the use of the entry word is commonly restricted to one particular phrase, then a bold note may be given as the entry word's only sense:

> **ward**[1]. . . *vt* **to ward off :**. . .

Pronunciation

1. Pronunciation of English Entry Words

The matter between a pair of brackets [ ] following the entry word of an English-to-Spanish entry indicates the pronunciation. The symbols used are explained in the International Phonetic Alphabet chart on page 25a.

The presence of variant pronunciations indicates that not all educated speakers pronounce words the same way. A second-place variant is not to be regarded as less acceptable than the pronunciation that is given first. It may, in fact, be used by as many educated speakers as the first variant, but the requirements of the printed page are such that one must precede the other:

tomato [tə'meɪto, -'mɑ-] . . .

When a compound word has less than a full pronunciation, the missing part is to be supplied from the pronunciation at the entry for the unpronounced element of the compound:

gamma ray ['gæmə]. . .

ray ['reɪ]. . .

smoke[1] ['smo:k]. . .

smoke detector [dɪ'tɛktər]. . .

In general, no pronunciation is given for open compounds consisting of two or more English words that are main entries at their own alphabetical place:

water lily *n* **:** nenúfar *m*

Only the first entry in a series of numbered homographs is given a pronunciation if their pronunciations are the same:

dab[1] ['dæb] *vt*. . .

dab[2] *n*. . .

No pronunciation is shown for principal parts of verbs that are formed by regular suffixation, nor for other derivative words formed by common suffixes.

2. Pronunciation of Spanish Entry Words

Spanish pronunciation is highly regular, so no pronunciations are given for most Spanish-to-English entries. Exceptions have been made for certain words (such as foreign borrowings) whose Spanish pronunciations are not evident from their spellings:

pizza ['pitsa, 'pisa] . . .

footing ['fu,tɪŋ]. . .

Functional Labels

An italic label indicating a part of speech or some other functional classification follows the pronunciation or, if no pronunciation is given, the main entry. The eight traditional parts of speech, adjective, adverb, conjunction, interjection, noun, preposition, pronoun, and verb, are indicated as follows:

daily[2] *adj*. . .

vagamente *adv*. . .

and. . . *conj*. . .

huy *interj*. . .

jackal. . . *n*. . .

para *prep*. . .

neither[3] *pron*. . .

leer. . . *v*. . .

Verbs that are intransitive are labeled *vi,* and verbs that are transitive are labeled *vt.* Entries for verbs that are both transitive and intransitive are labeled *v;* if such an entry includes irregular verb inflections, it is labeled *v* immediately after the main entry, with the labels *vi* and *vt* serving to introduce transitive and intransitive subdivisions when both are present:

deliberar *vi* **:** to deliberate

necessitate. . . *vt* **-tated; -tating :** necesitar, requerir

satisfy. . . *v* **-fied; -fying** *vt*. . . —*vi*. . .

Two other labels are used to indicate functional classifications of verbs: *v aux* (auxiliary verb) and *v impers* (impersonal verb).

may. . . *v aux, past* **might**. . .

haber[1]. . . *v aux* **1 :** have. . . —*v impers* **1 hay :** there is, there are. . .

Gender Labels

In Spanish-to-English noun entries, the gender of the entry word is indicated by an italic *m* (masculine), *f* (feminine), or *mf* (masculine or feminine), immediately following the functional label:

magnesio *nm*. . .

galaxia *nf*. . .

turista *nmf*. . .

If both the masculine and feminine forms are shown for a noun referring to a person, the label is simply *n:*

director, -tora *n*. . .

Spanish noun equivalents of English entry words are also labeled for gender:

amnesia. . . *n* **:** amnesia *f*

earache. . . *n* **:** dolor *m* de oído

gamekeeper. . . *n* **:** guardabosque *mf*

Inflected Forms

1. Nouns

The plurals of nouns are shown in this dictionary when they are irregular, when plural suffixation brings about a change in accentuation or in the spelling of the root word, when an English noun ends in a consonant plus *-o* or in *-ey,* when an English noun ends in *-oo,* when an English noun is a compound that pluralizes any element but the last, when a noun has variant plurals, or whenever the dictionary user might have reasonable doubts regarding the spelling of a plural:

> **tooth**. . . *n, pl* **teeth**. . .
>
> **garrafón** *nm, pl* **-fones**. . .
>
> **potato**. . . *n, pl* **-toes**. . .
>
> **abbey**. . . *n, pl* **-beys**. . .
>
> **cuckoo**[2] *n, pl* **-oos**. . .
>
> **brother–in–law**. . . *n, pl* **brothers–in–law** . . .
>
> **quail**[2] *n, pl* **quail** *or* **quails**. . .
>
> **hábitat** *nm, pl* **-tats**. . .
>
> **tahúr** *nm, pl* **tahúres**. . .

Cutback inflected forms are used for most nouns on the English-to-Spanish side, regardless of the number of syllables. On the Spanish-to-English side, cutback inflections are given for nouns that have three or more syllables; plurals for shorter words are written out in full:

> **shampoo**[2] *n, pl* **-poos**. . .
>
> **calamity** . . . *n, pl* **-ties**. . .
>
> **mouse** . . . *n, pl* **mice**. . .
>
> **sartén** *nmf, pl* **sartenes**. . .
>
> **hámster** *nm, pl* **hámsters**. . .
>
> **federación** *nf, pl* **-ciones**. . .

If only one gender form has a plural which is irregular, that plural form will be given with the appropriate label:

> **campeón, -ona** *n, mpl* **-ones** : champion

The plurals of nouns are usually not shown when the base word is unchanged by the addition of the regular plural suffix or when the noun is unlikely to occur in the plural:

apple. . . *n* **:** manzana *f*

inglés[3] *nm* **:** English (language)

Nouns that are plural in form and that regularly occur in plural constructions are labeled as *npl* (for English nouns), *nmpl* (for Spanish masculine nouns), or *nfpl* (for Spanish feminine nouns):

knickers. . . *npl*. . .

enseres *nmpl*. . .

mancuernas *nfpl*. . .

Entry words that are unchanged in the plural are labeled *ns & pl* (for English nouns), *nms & pl* (for Spanish masculine nouns), *nfs & pl* (for Spanish feminine nouns), and *nmfs & pl* (for Spanish gender-variable nouns):

deer. . . *ns & pl* . . .

lavaplatos *nms & pl*. . .

tesis *nfs & pl* . . .

rompehuelgas *nmfs & pl* . . .

2. Verbs

ENGLISH VERBS

The principal parts of verbs are shown in English-to-Spanish entries when they are irregular, when suffixation brings about a change in spelling of the root word, when the verb ends in *-ey,* when there are variant inflected forms, or whenever it is believed that the dictionary user might have reasonable doubts about the spelling of an inflected form:

break[1]. . . *v* **broke**. . . ; **broken**. . . ; **breaking**. . .

drag[1]. . . *v* **dragged; dragging**. . .

monkey[1]. . . *vi* **-keyed; -keying**. . .

label[1]. . . *vt* **-beled** *or* **-belled; -beling** *or* **-belling**. . .

imagine. . . *vt* **-ined; -ining**. . .

Cutback inflected forms are usually used when the verb has two or more syllables:

multiply. . . *v* **-plied; -plying**. . .

bevel[1]. . . *v* **-eled** *or* **-elled; -eling** *or* **-elling**. . .

forgo *or* **forego**. . . *vt* **-went; -gone; -going**. . .

commit . . . *vt* **-mitted; -mitting** . . .

The principal parts of an English verb are not shown when the base word is unchanged by suffixation:

delay[1]. . . *vt*

pitch[1]. . . *vt*

SPANISH VERBS

Entries for irregular Spanish verbs are cross-referenced by number to the model conjugations appearing in the Conjugation of Spanish Verbs section:

abnegarse {49} *vr*. . .

volver {89} *vi*. . .

Entries for Spanish verbs with regular conjugations are not cross-referenced; however, model conjugations for regular Spanish verbs are included in the Conjugation of Spanish Verbs section beginning on page 44a.

Adverbs and Adjectives

The comparative and superlative forms of English adjective and adverb main entries are shown when suffixation brings about a change in spelling of the root word, when the inflection is irregular, and when there are variant inflected forms:

wet[2] *adj* **wetter; wettest**. . .

good[2] *adj* **better**. . . ; **best**. . .

evil[1]. . . *adj* **eviler** *or* **eviller; evilest** *or* **evillest**. . .

The superlative forms of adjectives and adverbs of two or more syllables are usually cut back; the superlative is shown in full, however, when it is desirable to indicate the pronunciation of the inflected form:

early[1]. . . *adv* **earlier; -est**. . .

gaudy. . . *adj* **gaudier; -est**. . .

secure[2] *adj* **-curer; -est**. . .

but

young[1]. . . *adj* **younger** [ˈjʌŋgər]; **youngest** [-gəst]. . .

At a few entries only the superlative form is shown:

mere *adj, superlative* **merest**. . .

The absence of the comparative form indicates that there is no evidence of its use.

The comparative and superlative forms of adjectives and adverbs are usually not shown when the base word is unchanged by suffixation:

quiet[3] *adj* **1**. . .

Usage

1. Usage Labels

Two types of usage labels are used in this dictionary—regional and stylistic. Spanish words that are limited in use to a specific area or areas of Latin America, or to Spain, are given labels indicating the countries in which they are most commonly used:

guarachear *vi Cuba, PRi fam*. . .

bucket. . . *n* **:**. . . cubeta *f Mex*

The following regional labels are used in this book: *Arg* (Argentina), *Bol* (Bolivia), *CA* (Central America), *Car* (Caribbean), *Chile* (Chile), *Col* (Colombia), *CoRi* (Costa Rica), *Cuba* (Cuba), *DomRep* (Dominican Republic), *Ecua* (Ecuador), *Sal* (El Salvador), *Guat* (Guatemala), *Hond* (Honduras), *Mex* (Mexico), *Nic* (Nicaragua), *Pan* (Panama), *Par* (Paraguay), *Peru* (Peru), *PRi* (Puerto Rico), *Spain* (Spain), *Uru* (Uruguay), *Ven* (Venezuela).

Since this book focuses on the Spanish spoken in Latin America, only the most common regionalisms from Spain have been included in order to allow for more thorough coverage of Latin-American forms.

A number of Spanish words are given a *fam* (familiar) label as well, indicating that these words are suitable for informal contexts but would not normally be used in formal writing or speaking. The stylistic label *usu considered vulgar* is added for a word which is usually considered vulgar or offensive but whose widespread use justifies its inclusion in this book. The label is intended to warn the reader that the word in question may be inappropriate in polite conversation.

2. Usage Notes

Definitions are sometimes preceded by parenthetical usage notes that give supplementary semantic information:

not. . . *adv* **1** (*used to form a negative*) **:** no. . .

within[2] *prep* . . . **2** (*in expressions of distance*) **:**. . . **3** (*in expressions of time*) **:** . . .

> **e**[2] *conj* (*used instead of* **y** *before words beginning with i or hi*) **:**. . .
>
> **poder**[1]. . . *v aux*. . . **2** (*expressing possibility*) **:**. . . **3** (*expressing permission*) **:**. . .

Additional semantic orientation is also sometimes given in the form of parenthetical notes appearing within the definition:

> **calibrate**. . . *vt*. . . **:** calibrar (armas), graduar (termómetros)
>
> **palco** *nm* **:** box (in a theater or stadium)

Occasionally a usage note is used in place of a definition. This is usually done when the entry word has no single foreign-language equivalent. This type of usage note will be accompanied by examples of common use:

> **shall**. . . *v aux*. . . **1** (*used to express a command*) <you shall do as I say **:** harás lo que te digo> . . .

3. Illustrations of Usage

Definitions are sometimes followed by verbal illustrations that show a typical use of the word in context or a common idiomatic usage. These verbal illustrations include a translation and are enclosed in angle brackets:

> **lejos** *adv* **1 :** far away, distant <a lo lejos **:** in the distance, far off> . . .
>
> **make**[1]. . . **9** . . .**:** ganar <to make a living **:** ganarse la vida> . . .

Sense Division

A boldface colon is used to introduce a definition:

> **fable**. . . *n* **:** fábula *f*

Boldface Arabic numerals separate the senses of a word that has more than one sense:

> **laguna** *nf* **1 :** lagoon **2 :** lacuna, gap

Whenever some information (such as a synonym, a boldface word or phrase, a usage note, a cross-reference, or a label) follows a sense number, it applies only to that specific numbered sense and not to any other boldface numbered senses:

> **abanico** *nm*. . . **2** GAMA **:**. . .
>
> **tonic²** *n*. . . **2** *or* **tonic water :**. . .
>
> **grillo** *nm*. . . **2 grillos** *nmpl* **:**. . .
>
> **fairy**. . . *n, pl* **fairies**. . . **2 fairy tale :**. . .
>
> **myself**. . . *pron* **1** (*used reflexively*) **:**. . .
>
> **pike**. . . *n*. . . **3 → turnpike**
>
> **atado²** *nm*. . . **2** *Arg* **:**. . .

Cross-References

Three different kinds of cross-references are used in this dictionary: synonymous, cognate, and inflectional. In each instance the cross-reference is readily recognized by the boldface arrow following the entry word.

Synonymous and cognate cross-references indicate that a definition at the entry cross-referred to can be substituted for the entry word:

> **scapula**. . . **→ shoulder blade**
>
> **amuck**. . . **→ amok**

An inflectional cross-reference is used to identify the entry word as an inflected form of another word (as a noun or verb):

> **fue, etc. → ir, ser**
>
> **mice → mouse**

Synonyms

At many entries or senses in this book, a synonym in small capital letters is provided before the boldface colon and the following defining text. These synonyms are all main entries or bold notes elsewhere in the book. They serve as a helpful guide to the meaning of the entry or sense and also give the reader an additional term that might be substituted in a similar context. On the English-to-Spanish side synonyms are particularly abundant, since special care has been taken to guide the English speaker—by means of synonyms, verbal illustrations, or usage notes—to the meaning of the Spanish terms at each sense of a multisense entry.

Abbreviations in this Work

adj	adjective
adv	adverb
Arg	Argentina
Bol	Bolivia
Brit	British
CA	Central America
Car	Caribbean region
Col	Colombia
conj	conjuction
CoRi	Costa Rica
DomRep	Dominican Republic
Ecua	Ecuador
esp	especially
f	feminine
fam	familiar or colloquial
fpl	feminine plural
Guat	Guatemala
Hond	Honduras
interj	interjection
m	masculine
Mex	Mexico
mf	masculine or feminine
mpl	masculine plural
n	noun
nf	feminine noun
nfpl	feminine plural noun
nfs & pl	invariable singular or plural feminine noun
Nic	Nicaragua
nm	masculine noun
nmf	masculine or feminine noun
nmfpl	plural noun invariable for gender
nmfs & pl	noun invariable for both gender and number
nmpl	masculine plural noun
nms & pl	invariable singular or plural masculine noun
npl	plural noun
ns & pl	noun invariable for plural
Pan	Panama
Par	Paraguay
pl	plural
pp	past participle
prep	preposition
PRi	Puerto Rico
pron	pronoun
s	singular
Sal	El Salvador
Uru	Uruguay
usu	usually
v	verb (transitive and intransitive)
v aux	auxiliary verb
Ven	Venezuela
vi	intransitive verb
v impers	impersonal verb
vr	reflexive verb
vt	transitive verb

Pronunciation Symbols

VOWELS

æ **a**sk, b**a**t, gl**a**d
ɑ c**o**t, b**o**mb
a *New England* **au**nt, *British* **a**sk, gl**a**ss, *Spanish* c**a**s**a**
e *Spanish* p**e**so, j**e**f**e**
ɛ **e**gg, b**e**t, f**e**d
ə **a**bout, jav**e**lin, Al**a**bam**a**
ə when italicized as in *ə*l, *ə*m, *ə*n, indicates a syllabic pronunciation of the consonant as in bott**le**, pris**m**, butt**on**
i ver**y**, an**y**, thirt**y**, *Spanish* p**i**ña
iː **ea**t, b**ea**d, b**ee**
ɪ **i**d, b**i**d, p**i**t
o **O**hio, yell**o**wer, potat**o**, *Spanish* **ó**val**o**
oː **oa**ts, **ow**n, z**o**ne, bl**ow**
ɔ **aw**l, m**au**l, c**au**ght, p**aw**
ʊ s**u**re, sh**ou**ld, c**ou**ld
u *Spanish* **u**va, c**u**lpa
uː b**oo**t, f**ew**, c**oo**
ʌ **u**nder, p**u**tt, b**u**d
eɪ **ei**ght, w**a**de, b**ay**
aɪ **i**ce, b**i**te, t**ie**
aʊ **ou**t, g**ow**n, pl**ow**
ɔɪ **oy**ster, c**oi**l, b**oy**
ɒ *British* b**o**nd, g**o**d
ø *French* d**eu**x, *German* H**öh**le
œ *French* b**œ**uf, *German* H**ö**lle
y *French* l**u**ne, *German* f**üh**len
ʏ *German* f**ü**llt
~ (tilde as in ã, ɔ̃, ɛ̃) *French* v**in**, b**on**, bi**en**
ː indicates that the preceding vowel is long. Long vowels are almost always diphthongs in English, but not in Spanish.

STRESS MARKS

ˈ high stress **pen**manship
ˌ low stress penman**ship**

CONSONANTS

b **b**a**b**y, la**b**or, ca**b**
β *Spanish* ca**b**o, ó**v**alo
d **d**ay, rea**d**y, ki**d**
dʒ **j**ust, ba**dg**er, fu**dg**e
ð **th**en, ei**th**er, ba**th**e
f **f**oe, tou**gh**, bu**ff**
g **g**o, bi**gg**er, ba**g**
ɣ *Spanish* tra**g**ar, da**g**a
h **h**ot, a**h**a
j **y**es, vine**y**ard
ʲ marks palatalization as in *French* digne [dinʲ]
k **c**at, **k**eep, la**cqu**er, flo**ck**
l **l**aw, ho**ll**ow, boi**l**
m **m**at, he**m**p, ha**mm**er, ri**m**
n **n**ew, te**n**t, te**n**or, ru**n**
ŋ ru**ng**, ha**ng**, swi**ng**er
ɲ *Spanish* caba**ñ**a, pi**ñ**a
p **p**ay, la**p**se, to**p**
r **r**ope, bu**r**n, ta**r**
s **s**ad, mi**s**t, ki**ss**
ʃ **sh**oe, mi**ss**ion, slu**sh**
t **t**oe, bu**tt**on, ma**t**
t̬ indicates that some speakers of English pronounce this as a voiced alveolar flap [ɾ], as in la**t**er, ca**tt**y, ba**tt**le
tʃ **ch**oose, ba**tch**
θ **th**in, e**th**er, ba**th**
v **v**at, ne**v**er, ca**v**e
w **w**et, soft**w**are
x *German* Ba**ch**, *Scots* lo**ch**, *Spanish* **g**ente, **j**efe
z **z**oo, ea**s**y, bu**zz**
ʒ **j**aborandi, a**z**ure, bei**g**e
ʔ indicates a glottal stop, the sound beginning the syllables in **uh-oh**
h, k, p, t when italicized indicate sounds which are present in the pronunciation of some speakers of English but absent in that of others, so that *whence* [ˈ*h*wɛn*t*s] can be pronounced as [ˈwɛns], [ˈhwɛns], [ˈwɛnts], or [ˈhwɛnts]

Spanish Grammar

Accentuation

Spanish word stress is generally determined according to the following rules:

- Words ending in a vowel, or in *-n* or *-s,* are stressed on the penultimate syllable (*za**pa**to, **lla**man*).

- Words ending in a consonant other than *-n* or *-s* are stressed on the last syllable (*per**diz**, curiosi**dad***).

Exceptions to these rules have a written accent mark over the stressed vowel (***fá**cil, habla**rá**, **úl**timo*). There are also a few words which take accent marks in order to distinguish them from homonyms (*si, sí; que, qué; el, él;* etc.).

Adverbs ending in *-mente* have two stressed syllables since they retain both the stress of the root word and of the *-mente* suffix (***len**ta**men**te, di**fí**cil**men**te*). Many compounds also have two stressed syllables (***lim**piapara**bri**sas*).

Punctuation and Capitalization

Questions and exclamations in Spanish are preceded by an inverted question mark ¿ and an inverted exclamation mark ¡, respectively:

¿Cuándo llamó Ana?
Y tú, ¿qué piensas?

¡No hagas eso!
Pero, ¡qué lástima!

In Spanish, unlike English, the following words are not capitalized:

- Names of days, months, and languages (*jueves, octubre, español*).
- Spanish adjectives or nouns derived from proper nouns (*los nicaragüenses, una teoría marxista*).

Articles

1. Definite Article

Spanish has five forms of the definite article: *el* (masculine singular), *la* (feminine singular), *los* (masculine plural), *las* (feminine plural), and *lo* (neuter). The first four agree in gender and number with the nouns they limit (*el carro,* the car; *las tijeras,* the scissors), although the form *el* is used with feminine singular nouns beginning with a stressed *a-* or *ha-* (*el águila, el hambre*).

The neuter article *lo* is used with the masculine singular form of an adjective to express an abstract concept (*lo mejor de este método,* the best thing about this method; *lo meticuloso de su trabajo,* the meticulousness of her work; *lo mismo para mí,* the same for me).

Whenever the masculine article *el* immediately follows the words *de* or *a,* it combines with them to form the contractions *del* and *al,* respectively (*viene* ***del*** *campo, vi* ***al*** *hermano de Roberto*).

The use of *el, la, los,* and *las* in Spanish corresponds largely to the use of *the* in English; some exceptions are noted below.

The definite article is used:

- When referring to something as a class (*los gatos son ágiles,* cats are agile; *me gusta el café,* I like coffee).
- In references to meals and in most expressions of time (*¿comiste el almuerzo?,* did you eat lunch?; *vino el año pasado,* he came last year; *son las dos,* it's two o'clock; *prefiero el verano,* I prefer summer; *la reunión es el lunes,*

the meeting is on Monday; but: *hoy es lunes,* today is Monday).

- Before titles (except *don, doña, san, santo, santa, fray,* and *sor*) in third-person references to people (*la señora Rivera llamó,* Mrs. Rivera called; but: *hola, señora Rivera,* hello, Mrs. Rivera).
- In references to body parts and personal possessions (*me duele la cabeza,* my head hurts; *dejó el sombrero,* he left his hat).
- To mean "the one" or "the ones" when the subject is already understood (*la de madera,* the wooden one; *los que vi ayer,* the ones I saw yesterday).

The definite article is omitted:

- Before a noun in apposition, if the noun is not modified (*Caracas, capital de Venezuela;* but: *Pico Bolívar, la montaña más alta de Venezuela*).
- Before a number in a royal title (*Carlos Quinto,* Charles the Fifth).

2. Indefinite Article

The forms of the indefinite article in Spanish are *un* (masculine singular), *una* (feminine singular), *unos* (masculine plural), and *unas* (feminine plural). They agree in number and gender with the nouns they limit (*una mesa,* a table; *unos platos,* some plates), although the form *un* is used with feminine singular nouns beginning with a stressed *a-* or *ha-* (*un ala, un hacha*).

The use of *un, una, unos,* and *unas* in Spanish corresponds largely to the use of *a, an,* and *some* in English, with some exceptions:

- Indefinite articles are generally omitted before nouns identifying someone or something as a member of a class or category (*Paco es profesor/católico,* Paco is a professor/Catholic; *se llama páncreas,* it's called a pancreas).

- They are also often omitted in instances where quantity is understood from context (*vine sin chaqueta,* I came without a jacket; *no tengo carro,* I don't have a car).

Nouns

1. Gender

Nouns in Spanish are either masculine or feminine. A noun's gender can often be determined according to the following guidelines:

- Nouns ending in *-aje, -o,* or *-or* are usually masculine (*el traje, el libro, el sabor*), with some exceptions (*la mano, la foto, la labor,* etc.).
- Nouns ending in *-a, -dad, -ión, -tud,* or *-umbre* are usually feminine (*la alfombra, la capacidad, la excepción, la juventud, la certidumbre*). Exceptions include: *el día, el mapa,* and many learned borrowings ending in *-ma* (*el idioma, el tema*).

Most nouns referring to people or animals agree in gender with the subject (*el hombre, la mujer; el hermano, la hermana; el perro, la perra*). However, some nouns referring to people, including those ending in *-ista,* use the same form for both sexes (*el artista, la artista; el modelo, la modelo;* etc.).

A few names of animals exist in only one gender form (*la jirafa, el sapo,* etc.). In these instances, the adjectives *macho* and *hembra* are sometimes used to distinguish males and females (*una jirafa macho,* a male giraffe).

2. Pluralization

Plurals of Spanish nouns are formed as follows:

- Nouns ending in an unstressed vowel or an accented *-é* are pluralized by adding *-s* (*la vaca, las vacas; el café, los cafés*).

- Nouns ending in a consonant other than *-s,* or in a stressed vowel other than *-é,* are generally pluralized by adding *-es* (*el papel, los papeles; el rubí, los rubíes*). Exceptions include *papá* (*papás*) and *mamá* (*mamás*).

- Nouns with an unstressed final syllable ending in *-s* usually have a zero plural (*la crisis, las crisis; el jueves, los jueves*). Other nouns ending in *-s* add *-es* to form the plural (*el mes, los meses; el país, los países*).

- Nouns ending in *-z* are pluralized by changing the *-z* to *-c* and adding *-es* (*el lápiz, los lápices; la vez, las veces*).

- Many compound nouns have a zero plural (*el paraguas, los paraguas; el aguafiestas, los aguafiestas*).

- The plurals of *cualquiera* and *quienquiera* are *cualesquiera* and *quienesquiera,* respectively.

Adjectives

1. Gender and Number

Most adjectives agree in gender and number with the nouns they modify (un chico *alto,* una chica *alta,* unos chicos *altos,* unas chicas *altas*). Some adjectives, including those ending in *-e* and *-ista* (*fuerte, altruista*) and comparative adjectives ending in *-or* (*mayor, mejor*), vary only for number.

Adjectives whose masculine singular forms end in *-o* generally change the *-o* to *-a* to form the feminine (*pequeño* → *pequeña*). Masculine adjectives ending in *-án, -ón,* or *-dor,* and masculine adjectives of nationality which end in a consonant, usually add *-a* to form the feminine (*holgazán* → *holgazana*; *llorón* → *llorona*; *trabajador* → *trabajadora*; *irlandés* → *irlandesa*).

Adjectives are pluralized in much the same manner as nouns:

- The plurals of adjectives ending in an unstressed vowel or an accented *-é* are formed by adding an *-s* (un postre *rico,* unos postres *ricos;* una camisa *café,* unas camisas *cafés*).

- Adjectives ending in a consonant, or in a stressed vowel other than *-é,* are generally pluralized by adding *-es* (un niño *cortés,* unos niños *corteses;* una persona *iraní,* unas personas *iraníes*).
- Adjectives ending in *-z* are pluralized by changing the *-z* to *-c* and adding *-es* (una respuesta *sagaz*, unas respuestas *sagaces*).

2. Shortening

- The following masculine singular adjectives drop their final *-o* when they occur before a masculine singular noun: *bueno* (*buen*), *malo* (*mal*), *uno* (*un*), *alguno* (*algún*), *ninguno* (*ningún*), *primero* (*primer*), *tercero* (*tercer*).
- *Grande* shortens to *gran* before any singular noun.
- *Ciento* shortens to *cien* before any noun.
- The title *Santo* shortens to *San* before all masculine names except those beginning with *To-* or *Do-* (*San Juan, Santo Tomás*).

3. Position

Descriptive adjectives generally follow the nouns they modify (*una cosa útil, un actor famoso*). However, adjectives that express an inherent quality often precede the noun (*la blanca nieve*).

Some adjectives change meaning depending on whether they occur before or after the noun: *un pobre niño,* a poor (pitiable) child; *un niño pobre,* a poor (not rich) child; *un gran hombre,* a great man; *un hombre grande,* a big man; *el único libro,* the only book; *el libro único,* the unique book, etc.

4. Comparative and Superlative Forms

The comparative of Spanish adjectives is generally rendered as *más . . . que* (more . . . than) or *menos . . . que* (less . . . than): *soy más alta que él,* I'm taller than he; *son menos inteligentes que tú,* they're less intelligent than you.

The superlative of Spanish adjectives usually follows the formula *definite article* + (*noun* +) *más/menos* + *adjective: ella es la estudiante más trabajadora,* she is the hardest-working student; *él es el menos conocido,* he's the least known.

A few Spanish adjectives have irregular comparative and superlative forms:

Adjective	Comparative/Superlative
bueno (good)	**mejor** (better, best)
malo (bad)	**peor** (worse, worst)
grande[1] (big, great), **viejo** (old)	**mayor** (greater, older; greatest, oldest)
pequeño[1] (little), **joven** (young)	**menor** (lesser, younger; least, youngest)
mucho (much), **muchos** (many)	**más** (more, most)
poco (little), **pocos** (few)	**menos** (less, least)

[1]These words have regular comparative and superlative forms when used in reference to physical size: *él es más grande que yo; nuestra casa es la más pequeña.*

ABSOLUTE SUPERLATIVE

The absolute superlative is formed by placing *muy* before the adjective, or by adding the suffix *-ísimo* (*ella es muy simpática* or *ella es simpatiquísima,* she is very nice). The absolute superlative using *-ísimo* is formed according to the following rules:

- Adjectives ending in a consonant other than *-z* simply add the *-ísimo* ending (*fácil* → *facilísimo*).
- Adjectives ending in *-z* change this consonant to *-c* and add *-ísimo* (*feliz* → *felicísimo*).
- Adjectives ending in a vowel or diphthong drop the vowel or diphthong and add *-ísimo* (*claro* → *clarísimo; amplio* → *amplísimo*).

- Adjectives ending in *-co* or *-go* change these endings to *qu* and *gu*, respectively, and add *-ísimo* (*rico* → *riquísimo; largo* → *larguísimo*).
- Adjectives ending in *-ble* change this ending to *-bil* and add *-ísimo* (*notable* → *notabilísimo*).
- Adjectives containing the stressed diphthong *ie* or *ue* will sometimes change these to *e* and *o*, respectively (*ferviente* → *fervientísimo* or *ferventísimo; bueno* → *buenísimo* or *bonísimo*).

Adverbs

Adverbs can be formed by adding the adverbial suffix *-mente* to virtually any adjective (*fácil* → *fácilmente*). If the adjective varies for gender, the feminine form is used as the basis for forming the adverb (*rápido* → *rápidamente*).

Pronouns

1. Personal Pronouns

The personal pronouns in Spanish are:

Person	Singular		Plural	
FIRST	**yo**	I	**nosotros, nosotras**	we
SECOND	**tú**	you (familiar)	**vosotros**[2], **vosotras**[2]	you, all of you
	vos[1]	you		
	usted	you (formal)	**ustedes**[3]	you, all of you
THIRD	**él**	he	**ellos, ellas**	they
	ella	she		
	ello	it (neuter)		

[1] Familiar form used in addition to *tú* in South and Central America.
[2] Familiar form used in Spain.
[3] Formal form used in Spain; familiar and formal form used in Latin America.

FAMILIAR VS. FORMAL

The second person personal pronouns exist in both familiar and formal forms. The familiar forms are generally used when addressing relatives, friends, and children, although usage varies considerably from region to region; the formal forms are used in other contexts to show courtesy, respect, or emotional distance.

In Spain and in the Caribbean, *tú* is used exclusively as the familiar singular "you." In South and Central America, however, *vos* either competes with *tú* to varying degrees or replaces it entirely. (For a more detailed explanation of *vos* and its corresponding verb forms, refer to the Conjugation of Spanish Verbs section.)

The plural familiar form *vosotros, -as* is used only in Spain, where *ustedes* is reserved for formal contexts. In Latin America, *vosotros, -as* is not used, and *ustedes* serves as the all-purpose plural "you."

It should be noted that while *usted* and *ustedes* are regarded as second person pronouns, they take the third person form of the verb.

USAGE

In Spanish, personal pronouns are generally omitted (*voy al cine,* I'm going to the movies; *¿llamaron?,* did they call?), although they are sometimes used for purposes of emphasis or clarity (*se lo diré yo,* I will tell them; *vino ella, pero él se quedó,* she came, but he stayed behind). The forms *usted* and *ustedes* are usually included out of courtesy (*¿cómo está usted?,* how are you?).

Personal pronouns are not generally used in reference to inanimate objects or living creatures other than humans; in these instances, the pronoun is most often omitted (*¿es nuevo? no, es viejo,* is it new? no, it's old).

The neuter third person pronoun *ello* is reserved for indefinite subjects (as abstract concepts): *todo ello implica . . . ,* all of this implies . . . ; *por si ello fuera poco . . . ,* as if that weren't enough . . . . It most commonly appears in formal writing and speech. In less formal contexts, *ello* is often either omitted or replaced with *esto, eso,* or *aquello.*

2. Prepositional Pronouns

Prepositional pronouns are used as the objects of prepositions (*¿es para mí?,* is it for me?; *se lo dio a ellos,* he gave it to them).

The prepositional pronouns in Spanish are:

Singular		Plural	
mí	me	**nosotros, nosotras**	us
ti	you	**vosotros**[1]**, vosotras**[1]	you
usted	you (formal)	**ustedes**	you
él	him	**ellos, ellas**	them
ella	her		
ello	it (neuter)		
sí	yourself, himself, herself, itself, oneself	**sí**	yourselves, themselves

[1]Used primarily in Spain.

When the preposition *con* is followed by *mí, ti,* or *sí,* both words are replaced by *conmigo, contigo,* and *consigo,* respectively (*¿vienes conmigo?,* are you coming with me?; *habló contigo,* he spoke with you; *no lo trajo consigo,* she didn't bring it with her).

3. Object Pronouns

DIRECT OBJECT PRONOUNS

Direct object pronouns represent the primary goal or result of the action of a verb. The direct object pronouns in Spanish are:

Singular		Plural	
me	me	**nos**	us
te	you	**os**[1]	you
le[2]	you, him	**les**[2]	you, them
lo	you, him, it	**los**	you, them
la	you, her, it	**las**	you, them

[1]Used only in Spain.
[2]Used mainly in Spain.

Agreement

The third person forms agree in both gender and number with the nouns they replace or the people they refer to (*pintó las paredes,* she painted the walls → *las pintó,* she painted them; *visitaron al señor Juárez*, they visited Mr. Juárez → *lo visitaron*, they visited him). The remaining forms vary only for number.

Position

Direct object pronouns are normally affixed to the end of an affirmative command, a simple infinitive, or a present participle (*¡hazlo!,* do it!; *es difícil hacerlo,* it's difficult to do it; *haciéndolo, aprenderás,* you'll learn by doing it). With constructions involving an auxiliary verb and an infinitive or present participle, the pronoun may occur either immediately before the construction or suffixed to it (*lo voy a hacer* or *voy a hacerlo,* I'm going to do it; *estoy haciéndolo* or *lo estoy haciendo,* I'm doing it). In all other cases, the pronoun immediately precedes the conjugated verb (*no lo haré,* I won't do it).

Regional Variation

In Spain and in a few areas of Latin America, *le* and *les* are used in place of *lo* and *los* when referring to or addressing people (*le vieron,* they saw him; *les vistió,* she dressed them). In most parts of Latin America, however, *los* and *las* are used for the second person plural in both formal and familiar contexts.

The second person plural familiar form *os* is restricted to Spain.

INDIRECT OBJECT PRONOUNS

Indirect object pronouns represent the secondary goal of the action of a verb (*me dio el regalo,* he gave me the gift; *les dije que no,* I told them no). The indirect object pronouns in Spanish are:

Singular		Plural	
me	(to, for, from) me	**nos**	(to, for, from) us
te	(to, for, from) you	**os**[1]	(to, for, from) you
le	(to, for, from) you, him, her, it	**les**	(to, for, from) you, them
se[2]		**se**[2]	

[1]Used only in Spain.
[2]See explanation below.

Position

Indirect object pronouns follow the same rules as direct object pronouns with regard to their position in relation to verbs. When they occur with direct object pronouns, the indirect object pronoun always precedes (*nos lo dio,* she gave it to us; *estoy trayéndotela,* I'm bringing it to you).

Use of *Se*

When the indirect object pronouns *le* or *les* occur before any direct object pronoun beginning with an *l-*, the indirect object pronouns *le* and *les* convert to *se* (*les mandé la carta,* I sent them the letter → *se la mandé,* I sent it to them; *vamos a comprarle los aretes,* let's buy her the earrings → *vamos a comprárselos,* let's buy them for her).

4. Reflexive Pronouns

Reflexive pronouns are used to refer back to the subject of the verb (*me hice daño,* I hurt myself; *se vistieron,* they got dressed, they dressed themselves; *nos lo compramos,* we bought it for ourselves).

The reflexive pronouns in Spanish are:

Singular		Plural	
me	myself	**nos**	ourselves
te	yourself	**os**[1]	yourselves
se	yourself, himself, herself, itself	**se**	yourselves, themselves

[1]Used only in Spain.

Reflexive pronouns are also used:

- When the verb describes an action performed to one's own body, clothing, etc. (*me quité los zapatos,* I took off my shoes; *se arregló el pelo,* he fixed his hair).

- In the plural, to indicate reciprocal action (*se hablan con frecuencia,* they speak with each other frequently).
- In the third person singular and plural, as an indefinite subject reference (*se dice que es verdad,* they say it's true; *nunca se sabe,* one never knows; *se escribieron miles de páginas,* thousands of pages were written).

It should be noted that many verbs which take reflexive pronouns in Spanish have intransitive equivalents in English (*ducharse,* to shower; *quejarse,* to complain; etc.).

5. Relative Pronouns

Relative pronouns introduce subordinate clauses acting as nouns or modifiers (*el libro que escribió . . . ,* the book that he wrote . . . ; *las chicas a quienes conociste . . . ,* the girls whom you met . . .). In Spanish, the relative pronouns are:

que (that, which, who, whom)

quien, quienes (who, whom, that, whoever, whomever)

el cual, la cual, los cuales, las cuales (which, who)

el que, la que, los que, las que (which, who, whoever)

lo cual (which)

lo que (what, which, whatever)

cuanto, cuanta, cuantos, cuantas (all those that, all that, whatever, whoever, as much as, as many as)

Relative pronouns are not omitted in Spanish as they often are in English: *el carro que vi ayer,* the car (that) I saw yesterday. When relative pronouns are used with prepositions, the preposition precedes the clause (*la película sobre la cual le hablé,* the film I spoke to you about).

The relative pronoun *que* can be used in reference to both people and things. Unlike other relative pronouns, *que* does not take the personal *a* when used as a direct object referring to a person (*el hombre que llamé,* the man that I called; but: *el hombre a quien llamé,* the man whom I called).

Quien is used only in reference to people. It varies in number with the explicit or implied antecedent (*las mujeres con quienes charlamos . . .,* the women we chatted with; *quien lo hizo pagará,* whoever did it will pay).

El cual and *el que* vary for both number and gender, and are therefore often used in situations where *que* or *quien(es)* might create ambiguity: *nos contó algunas cosas sobre los libros, las cuales eran interesantes,* he told us some things about the books which (the things) were interesting.

Lo cual and *lo que* are used to refer back to a whole clause, or to something indefinite (*dijo que iría, lo cual me alegró,* he said he would go, which made me happy; *pide lo que quieras,* ask for whatever you want).

Cuanto varies for both number and gender with the implied antecedent: *conté a cuantas (personas) pude,* I counted as many (people) as I could. If an indefinite mass quantity is referred to, the masculine singular form is used (*anoté cuanto decía,* I jotted down whatever he said).

Possessives

1. Possessive Adjectives

UNSTRESSED FORMS

Singular		Plural	
mi(s)	my	**nuestro(s), nuestra(s)**	our
tu(s)	your	**vuestro(s)**[1], **vuestra(s)**[1]	your
su(s)	your, his, her, its	**su(s)**	your, their

[1]Used only in Spain.

STRESSED FORMS

Singular		Plural	
mío(s), mía(s)	my, mine, of mine	**nuestro(s), nuestra(s)**	our, ours, of ours
tuyo(s), tuya(s)	your, yours, of yours	**vuestro(s)[1], vuestra(s)[1]**	your, yours, of yours
suyo(s), suya(s)	your, yours, of yours; his, of his; her, hers, of hers; its, of its	**suyo(s), suya(s)**	your, yours, of yours; their, theirs, of theirs

[1]Used only in Spain.

The unstressed forms of possessive adjectives precede the nouns they modify (*mis zapatos,* my shoes; *nuestra escuela,* our school).

The stressed forms occur after the noun and are often used for purposes of emphasis (*el carro tuyo,* your car; *la pluma es mía,* the pen is mine; *unos amigos nuestros,* some friends of ours).

All possessive adjectives agree with the noun in number. The stressed forms, as well as the unstressed forms *nuestro* and *vuestro,* also vary for gender.

2. Possessive Pronouns

The possessive pronouns have the same forms as the stressed possessive adjectives (see table above). They are always preceded by the definite article, and they agree in number and gender with the nouns they replace (*las llaves mías,* my keys → *las mías,* mine; *los guantes nuestros,* our gloves → *los nuestros,* ours).

Demonstratives

1. Demonstrative Adjectives

The demonstrative adjectives in Spanish are:

Singular		Plural	
este, esta	this	**estos, estas**	these
ese, esa	that	**esos, esas**	those
aquel, aquella	that	**aquellos, aquellas**	those

Demonstrative adjectives agree with the nouns they modify in gender and number (*esta chica, aquellos árboles*). They normally precede the noun, but may occasionally occur after for purposes of emphasis or to express contempt: *en la época aquella de cambio,* in that era of change; *el perro ese ha ladrado toda la noche,* that (awful, annoying, etc.) dog barked all night long.

The forms *aquel, aquella, aquellos,* and *aquellas* are generally used in reference to people and things that are relatively distant from the speaker in space or time: *ese libro,* that book (a few feet away); *aquel libro,* that book (way over there).

2. Demonstrative Pronouns

The demonstrative pronouns in Spanish are orthographically identical to the demonstrative adjectives except that they take an accent mark over the stressed vowel (*éste, ése, aquél,* etc.). In addition, there are three neuter forms—*esto, eso,* and *aquello*—which are used when referring to abstract ideas or unidentified things (*¿te dijo eso?,* he said that to you?; *¿qué es esto?,* what is this?; *tráeme todo aquello,* bring me all that stuff).

Except for the neuter forms, demonstrative pronouns agree in gender and number with the nouns they replace (*esta silla,* this chair → *ésta,* this one; *aquellos vasos,* those glasses → *aquéllos,* those ones).

Spanish Numbers

Cardinal Numbers

1	uno	33	treinta y tres
2	dos	34	treinta y cuatro
3	tres	35	treinta y cinco
4	cuatro	36	treinta y seis
5	cinco	37	treinta y siete
6	seis	38	treinta y ocho
7	siete	39	treinta y nueve
8	ocho	40	cuarenta
9	nueve	41	cuarenta y uno
10	diez	50	cincuenta
11	once	60	sesenta
12	doce	70	setenta
13	trece	80	ochenta
14	catorce	90	noventa
15	quince	100	cien
16	dieciséis	101	ciento uno
17	diecisiete	102	ciento dos
18	dieciocho	200	doscientos
19	diecinueve	300	trescientos
20	veinte	400	cuatrocientos
21	veintiuno	500	quinientos
22	veintidós	600	seiscientos
23	veintitrés	700	setecientos
24	veinticuatro	800	ochocientos
25	veinticinco	900	novecientos
26	veintiséis	1,000	mil
27	veintisiete	1,001	mil uno
28	veintiocho	2,000	dos mil
29	veintinueve	100,000	cien mil
30	treinta	1,000,000	un millón
31	treinta y uno	1,000,000,000	mil millones
32	treinta y dos		

Ordinal Numbers

1st	primero, -ra	18th	decimoctavo, -va
2nd	segundo, -da	19th	decimonoveno, -na; *or* decimonono, -na
3rd	tercero, -ra		
4th	cuarto, -ta	20th	vigésimo, -ma
5th	quinto, -ta	21st	vigésimoprimero, vigésimaprimera
6th	sexto, -ta		
7th	séptimo, -ma	22nd	vigésimosegundo, vigésimasegunda
8th	octavo, -va		
9th	noveno, -na	30th	trigésimo, -ma
10th	décimo, -ma	40th	cuadragésimo, -ma
11th	undécimo, -ma	50th	quincuagésimo, -ma
12th	duodécimo, -ma	60th	sexagésimo, -ma
13th	decimotercero, -ra	70th	septuagésimo, -ma
14th	decimocuarto, -ta	80th	octogésimo, -ma
15th	decimoquinto, -ta	90th	nonagésimo, -ma
16th	decimosexto, -ta	100th	centésimo, -ma
17th	decimoséptimo, -ma		

Conjugation of Spanish Verbs

Simple Tenses

TENSE	REGULAR VERBS ENDING IN **-AR** hablar	
PRESENT INDICATIVE	hablo	hablamos
	hablas	habláis
	habla	hablan
PRESENT SUBJUNCTIVE	hable	hablemos
	hables	habléis
	hable	hablen
PRETERIT INDICATIVE	hablé	hablamos
	hablaste	hablasteis
	habló	hablaron
IMPERFECT INDICATIVE	hablaba	hablábamos
	hablabas	hablabais
	hablaba	hablaban
IMPERFECT SUBJUNCTIVE	hablara	habláramos
	hablaras	hablarais
	hablara	hablaran
	or	
	hablase	hablásemos
	hablases	hablaseis
	hablase	hablasen
FUTURE INDICATIVE	hablaré	hablaremos
	hablarás	hablaréis
	hablará	hablarán
FUTURE SUBJUNCTIVE	hablare	habláremos
	hablares	hablareis
	hablare	hablaren
CONDITIONAL	hablaría	hablaríamos
	hablarías	hablaríais
	hablaría	hablarían
IMPERATIVE		hablemos
	habla	hablad
	hable	hablen
PRESENT PARTICIPLE (GERUND)	hablando	
PAST PARTICIPLE	hablado	

REGULAR VERBS ENDING IN -ER		REGULAR VERBS ENDING IN -IR	
	comer		vivir
como	comemos	vivo	vivimos
comes	coméis	vives	vivís
come	comen	vive	viven
coma	comamos	viva	vivamos
comas	comáis	vivas	viváis
coma	coman	viva	vivan
comí	comimos	viví	vivimos
comiste	comisteis	viviste	vivisteis
comió	comieron	vivió	vivieron
comía	comíamos	vivía	vivíamos
comías	comíais	vivías	vivíais
comía	comían	vivía	vivían
comiera	comiéramos	viviera	viviéramos
comieras	comierais	vivieras	vivierais
comiera	comieran	viviera	vivieran
or		*or*	
comiese	comiésemos	viviese	viviésemos
comieses	comieseis	vivieses	vivieseis
comiese	comiesen	viviese	viviesen
comeré	comeremos	viviré	viviremos
comerás	comeréis	vivirás	viviréis
comerá	comerán	vivirá	vivirán
comiere	comiéremos	viviere	viviéremos
comieres	comiereis	vivieres	viviereis
comiere	comieren	viviere	vivieren
comería	comeríamos	viviría	viviríamos
comerías	comeríais	vivirías	viviríais
comería	comerían	viviría	vivirían
	comamos		vivamos
come	comed	vive	vivid
coma	coman	viva	vivan
comiendo		viviendo	
comido		vivido	

Compound Tenses

1. Perfect Tenses

The perfect tenses are formed with *haber* and the past participle:

PRESENT PERFECT

he hablado, etc. (*indicative*);
haya hablado, etc. (*subjunctive*)

PAST PERFECT

había hablado, etc. (*indicative*);
hubiera hablado, etc. (*subjuntive*)
or
hubiese hablado, etc. (*subjunctive*)

PRETERIT PERFECT

hube hablado, etc. (*indicative*)

FUTURE PERFECT

habré hablado, etc. (*indicative*)

CONDITIONAL PERFECT

habría hablado, etc. (*indicative*)

2. Progressive Tenses

The progressive tenses are formed with *estar* and the present participle:

PRESENT PROGRESSIVE

estoy llamando, etc. (*indicative*);
esté llamando, etc. (*subjunctive*)

IMPERFECT PROGRESSIVE

estaba llamando, etc. (*indicative*);
estuviera llamando, etc. (*subjunctive*)
or
estuviese llamando, etc. (*subjunctive*)

PRETERIT PROGRESSIVE

estuve llamando, etc. (*indicative*)

FUTURE PROGRESSIVE

estaré llamando, etc. (*indicative*)

CONDITIONAL PROGRESSIVE

estaría llamando, etc. (*indicative*)

PRESENT PERFECT PROGRESSIVE

he estado llamando, etc. (*indicative*);
haya estado llamando, etc. (*subjunctive*)

PAST PERFECT PROGRESSIVE

había estado llamando, etc. (*indicative*);
hubiera estado llamando, etc. (*subjunctive*)
or
hubiese estado llamando, etc. (*subjunctive*)

Use of *Vos*

In parts of South and Central America, *vos* often replaces or competes with *tú* as the second person familiar personal pronoun. It is particularly well established in the Río de la Plata region and much of Central America.

The pronoun *vos* often takes a distinct set of verb forms, usually in the present tense and the imperative. These vary widely from region to region; examples of the most common forms are shown below.

INFINITIVE FORM	hablar	comer	vivir
PRESENT INDICATIVE	vos hablás	vos comés	vos vivís
PRESENT SUBJUNCTIVE	vos hablés	vos comás	vos vivás
IMPERATIVE	hablá	comé	viví

In some areas, *vos* may take the *tú* or *vosotros* forms of the verb, while in others (as Uruguay), *tú* is combined with the *vos* verb forms.

Irregular Verbs

The *imperfect subjunctive,* the *future subjunctive,* the *conditional,* and the remaining forms of the *imperative* are not included in the model conjugations list, but can be derived as follows:

The *imperfect subjunctive* and the *future subjunctive* are formed from the third person plural form of the preterit tense by removing the last syllable (*-ron*) and adding the appropriate suffix:

PRETERIT INDICATIVE, THIRD PERSON PLURAL (querer)	quisieron
IMPERFECT SUBJUNCTIVE (querer)	quisiera, quisieras, etc. *or* quisiese, quisieses, etc.
FUTURE SUBJUNCTIVE (querer)	quisiere, quisieres, etc.

The conditional uses the same stem as the future indicative:

FUTURE INDICATIVE (poner)	pondré, pondrás, etc.
CONDITIONAL (poner)	pondría, pondrías, etc.

The third person singular, first person plural, and third person plural forms of the *imperative* are the same as the corresponding forms of the present subjunctive.

The second person plural *(vosotros)* form of the *imperative* is formed by removing the final *-r* of the infinitive form and adding a *-d* (ex.: *oír* → *oíd).*

Model Conjugations of Irregular Verbs

The model conjugations below include the following simple tenses: the *present indicative* (*IND*), the *present subjunctive* (*SUBJ*), the *preterit indicative* (*PRET*), the *imperfect indicative* (*IMPF*), the *future indicative* (*FUT*), the second person singular form of the *imperative* (*IMPER*), the *present participle* or *gerund* (*PRP*), and the *past participle* (*PP*). Each set of conjugations is preceded by the corresponding infinitive form of the verb, shown in bold type. Only tenses containing irregularities are listed, and the irregular verb forms within each tense are displayed in bold type.

49a Conjugation of Spanish Verbs

Each irregular verb entry in the Spanish-English section of this dictionary is cross-referred by number to one of the following model conjugations. These cross-reference numbers are shown in curly braces { } immediately following the entry's functional label.

1 **abolir** *(defective verb)* **:** IND abolimos, abolís *(other forms not used);* SUBJ *(not used);* IMPER *(only second person plural is used)*

2 **abrir :** PP abierto

3 **actuar :** IND **actúo**, **actúas**, **actúa**, actuamos, actuáis, **actúan;** SUBJ **actúe, actúes, actúe,** actuemos, actuéis, **actúen;** IMPER **actúa**

4 **adquirir :** IND **adquiero, adquieres, adquiere,** adquirimos, adquirís, **adquieren;** SUBJ **adquiera, adquieras, adquiera,** adquiramos, adquiráis, **adquieran;** IMPER **adquiere**

5 **airar :** IND **aíro, aíras, aíra,** airamos, airáis, **aíran;** SUBJ **aíre, aíres, aíre,** airemos, airéis, **aíren;** IMPER **aíra**

6 **andar :** PRET **anduve, anduviste, anduvo, anduvimos, anduvisteis, anduvieron**

7 **asir :** IND **asgo,** ases, ase, asimos, asís, asen; SUBJ **asga, asgas, asga, asgamos, asgáis, asgan**

8 **aunar :** IND **aúno, aúnas, aúna,** aunamos, aunáis, **aúnan;** SUBJ **aúne, aúnes, aúne,** aunemos, aunéis, **aúnen;** IMPER **aúna**

9 **avergonzar :** IND **avergüenzo, avergüenzas, avergüenza,** avergonzamos, avergonzáis, **avergüenzan;** SUBJ **avergüence, avergüences, avergüence, avergoncemos, avergoncéis, avergüencen;** PRET **avergoncé;** IMPER **avergüenza**

10 **averiguar :** SUBJ **averigüe, averigües, averigüe, averigüemos, averigüéis, averigüen;** PRET **averigüé,** averiguaste, averiguó, averiguamos, averiguasteis, averiguaron

11 **bendecir :** IND **bendigo, bendices, bendice,** bendecimos, bendecís, **bendicen;** SUBJ **bendiga, bendigas, bendiga, bendigamos, bendigáis, bendigan;** PRET **bendije, bendijiste, bendijo, bendijimos, bendijisteis, bendijeron;** IMPER **bendice**

12 **caber** : *IND* **quepo,** cabes, cabe, cabemos, cabéis, caben; *SUBJ* **quepa, quepas, quepa, quepamos, quepáis, quepan;** *PRET* **cupe, cupiste, cupo, cupimos, cupisteis, cupieron;** *FUT* **cabré, cabrás, cabrá, cabremos, cabréis, cabrán**

13 **caer** : *IND* **caigo,** caes, cae, caemos, caéis, caen; *SUBJ* **caiga, caigas, caiga, caigamos, caigáis, caigan;** *PRET* caí, **caíste, cayó, caímos, caísteis, cayeron;** *PRP* **cayendo;** *PP* **caído**

14 **cocer** : *IND* **cuezo, cueces, cuece,** cocemos, cocéis, **cuecen;** *SUBJ* **cueza, cuezas, cueza, cozamos, cozáis, cuezan;** *IMPER* **cuece**

15 **coger** : *IND* **cojo,** coges, coge, cogemos, cogéis, cogen; *SUBJ* **coja, cojas, coja, cojamos, cojáis, cojan**

16 **colgar** : *IND* **cuelgo, cuelgas, cuelga,** colgamos, colgáis, **cuelgan;** *SUBJ* **cuelgue, cuelgues, cuelgue, colguemos, colguéis, cuelguen;** *PRET* **colgué,** colgaste, colgó, colgamos, colgasteis, colgaron; *IMPER* **cuelga**

17 **concernir** *(defective verb; used only in the third person singular and plural of the present indicative, present subjunctive, and imperfect subjunctive) see* 25 **discernir**

18 **conocer** : *IND* **conozco,** conoces, conoce, conocemos, conocéis, conocen; *SUBJ* **conozca, conozcas, conozca, conozcamos, conozcáis, conozcan**

19 **contar** : *IND* **cuento, cuentas, cuenta,** contamos, contáis, **cuentan;** *SUBJ* **cuente, cuentes, cuente,** contemos, contéis, **cuenten;** *IMPER* **cuenta**

20 **creer** : *PRET* creí, **creíste, creyó, creímos, creísteis, creyeron;** *PRP* **creyendo;** *PP* **creído**

21 **cruzar** : *SUBJ* **cruce, cruces, cruce, crucemos, crucéis, crucen;** *PRET* **crucé,** cruzaste, cruzó, cruzamos, cruzasteis, cruzaron

22 **dar** : *IND* **doy,** das, da, damos, **dais,** dan; *SUBJ* **dé,** des, **dé,** demos, **deis,** den; *PRET* **di, diste, dio, dimos, disteis, dieron**

23 **decir** : *IND* **digo, dices, dice,** decimos, decís, **dicen;** *SUBJ* **diga, digas, diga, digamos, digáis, digan;** *PRET* **dije, dijiste, dijo,**

dijimos, dijisteis, dijeron; *FUT* **diré, dirás, dirá, diremos, diréis, dirán;** *IMPER* **di;** *PRP* **diciendo;** *PP* **dicho**

24 **delinquir :** *IND* **delinco,** delinques, delinque, delinquimos, delinquís, delinquen; *SUBJ* **delinca, delincas, delinca, delincamos, delincáis, delincan**

25 **discernir :** *IND* **discierno, disciernes, discierne,** discernimos, discernís, **disciernen;** *SUBJ* **discierna, disciernas, discierna,** discernamos, discernáis, **disciernan;** *IMPER* **discierne**

26 **distinguir :** *IND* **distingo,** distingues, distingue, distinguimos, distinguís, distinguen; *SUBJ* **distinga, distingas, distinga, distingamos, distingáis, distingan**

27 **dormir :** *IND* **duermo, duermes, duerme,** dormimos, dormís, **duermen;** *SUBJ* **duerma, duermas, duerma, durmamos, durmáis, duerman;** *PRET* dormí, dormiste, **durmió,** dormimos, dormisteis, **durmieron;** *IMPER* **duerme;** *PRP* **durmiendo**

28 **elegir :** *IND* **elijo, eliges, elige,** elegimos, elegís, **eligen;** *SUBJ* **elija, elijas, elija, elijamos, elijáis, elijan;** *PRET* elegí, elegiste, **eligió,** elegimos, elegisteis, **eligieron;** *IMPER* **elige;** *PRP* **eligiendo**

29 **empezar :** *IND* **empiezo, empiezas, empieza,** empezamos, empezáis, **empiezan;** *SUBJ* **empiece, empieces, empiece, empecemos, empecéis, empiecen;** *PRET* **empecé,** empezaste, empezó, empezamos, empezasteis, empezaron; *IMPER* **empieza**

30 **enraizar :** *IND* **enraízo, enraízas, enraíza,** enraizamos, enraizáis, **enraízan;** *SUBJ* **enraíce, enraíces, enraíce, enraicemos, enraicéis, enraícen;** *PRET* **enraicé,** enraizaste, enraizó, enraizamos, enraizasteis, enraizaron; *IMPER* **enraíza**

31 **erguir :** *IND* **irgo** *or* **yergo, irgues** *or* **yergues, irgue** *or* **yergue,** erguimos, erguís, **irguen** *or* **yerguen;** *SUBJ* **irga** *or* **yerga, irgas** *or* **yergas, irga** *or* **yerga, irgamos, irgáis, irgan** *or* **yergan;** *PRET* erguí, erguiste, **irguió,** erguimos, erguisteis, **irguieron;** *IMPER* **irgue** *or* **yergue;** *PRP* **irguiendo**

32 **errar :** *IND* **yerro, yerras, yerra,** erramos, erráis, **yerran;** *SUBJ* **yerre, yerres, yerre,** erremos, erréis, **yerren;** *IMPER* **yerra**

33 **escribir :** *PP* **escrito**

34 **estar :** *IND* **estoy, estás, está,** estamos, estáis, **están;** *SUBJ* **esté, estés, esté,** estemos, estéis, **estén;** *PRET* **estuve, estuviste, estuvo, estuvimos, estuvisteis, estuvieron;** *IMPER* **está**

35 **exigir :** *IND* **exijo,** exiges, exige, exigimos, exigís, exigen; *SUBJ* **exija, exijas, exija, exijamos, exijáis, exijan**

36 **forzar :** *IND* **fuerzo, fuerzas, fuerza,** forzamos, forzáis, **fuerzan;** *SUBJ* **fuerce, fuerces, fuerce, forcemos, forcéis, fuercen;** *PRET* **forcé,** forzaste, forzó, forzamos, forzasteis, forzaron; *IMPER* **fuerza**

37 **freír :** *IND* **frío, fríes, fríe, freímos,** freís, **fríen;** *SUBJ* **fría, frías, fría, friamos, friáis, frían;** *PRET* freí, **freíste, frió, freímos, freísteis, frieron;** *IMPER* **fríe;** *PRP* **friendo;** *PP* **frito**

38 **gruñir :** *PRET* gruñí, gruñiste, **gruñó,** gruñimos, gruñisteis, **gruñeron;** *PRP* **gruñendo**

39 **haber :** *IND* **he, has, ha, hemos,** habéis, **han;** *SUBJ* **haya, hayas, haya, hayamos, hayáis, hayan;** *PRET* **hube, hubiste, hubo, hubimos, hubisteis, hubieron;** *FUT* **habré, habrás, habrá, habremos, habréis, habrán;** *IMPER* **he**

40 **hacer :** *IND* **hago,** haces, hace, hacemos, hacéis, hacen; *SUBJ* **haga, hagas, haga, hagamos, hagáis, hagan;** *PRET* **hice, hiciste, hizo, hicimos, hicisteis, hicieron;** *FUT* **haré, harás, hará, haremos, haréis, harán;** *IMPER* **haz;** *PP* **hecho**

41 **huir :** *IND* **huyo, huyes, huye,** huimos, huís, **huyen;** *SUBJ* **huya, huyas, huya, huyamos, huyáis, huyan;** *PRET* huí, huiste, **huyó,** huimos, huisteis, **huyeron;** *IMPER* **huye;** *PRP* **huyendo**

42 **imprimir :** *PP* **impreso**

43 **ir :** *IND* **voy, vas, va, vamos, vais, van;** *SUBJ* **vaya, vayas, vaya, vayamos, vayáis, vayan;** *PRET* **fui, fuiste, fue, fuimos, fuisteis, fueron;** *IMPF* **iba, ibas, iba, íbamos, ibais, iban;** *IMPER* **ve;** *PRP* **yendo;** *PP* **ido**

44 **jugar :** *IND* **juego, juegas, juega,** jugamos, jugáis, **juegan;** *SUBJ* **juegue, juegues, juegue, juguemos, juguéis, jueguen;** *PRET* **jugué,** jugaste, jugó, jugamos, jugasteis, jugaron; *IMPER* **juega**

45 **lucir :** IND **luzco,** luces, luce, lucimos, lucís, lucen; SUBJ **luzca, luzcas, luzca, luzcamos, luzcáis, luzcan**

46 **morir :** IND **muero, mueres, muere,** morimos, morís, **mueren;** SUBJ **muera, mueras, muera, muramos, muráis, mueran;** PRET morí, moriste, **murió,** morimos, moristeis, **murieron;** IMPER **muere;** PRP **muriendo;** PP **muerto**

47 **mover :** IND **muevo, mueves, mueve,** movemos, movéis, **mueven;** SUBJ **mueva, muevas, mueva,** movamos, mováis, **muevan;** IMPER **mueve**

48 **nacer :** IND **nazco,** naces, nace, nacemos, nacéis, nacen; SUBJ **nazca, nazcas, nazca, nazcamos, nazcáis, nazcan**

49 **negar :** IND **niego, niegas, niega,** negamos, negáis, **niegan;** SUBJ **niegue, niegues, niegue, neguemos, neguéis, nieguen;** PRET **negué,** negaste, negó, negamos, negasteis, negaron; IMPER **niega**

50 **oír :** IND **oigo, oyes, oye, oímos,** oís, **oyen;** SUBJ **oiga, oigas, oiga, oigamos, oigáis, oigan;** PRET oí, **oíste, oyó, oímos, oísteis, oyeron;** IMPER **oye;** PRP **oyendo;** PP **oído**

51 **oler :** IND **huelo, hueles, huele,** olemos, oléis, **huelen;** SUBJ **huela, huelas, huela,** olamos, oláis, **huelan;** IMPER **huele**

52 **pagar :** SUBJ **pague, pagues, pague, paguemos, paguéis, paguen;** PRET **pagué,** pagaste, pagó, pagamos, pagasteis, pagaron

53 **parecer :** IND **parezco,** pareces, parece, parecemos, parecéis, parecen; SUBJ **parezca, parezcas, parezca, parezcamos, parezcáis, parezcan**

54 **pedir :** IND **pido, pides, pide,** pedimos, pedís, **piden;** SUBJ **pida, pidas, pida, pidamos, pidáis, pidan;** PRET pedí, pediste, **pidió,** pedimos, pedisteis, **pidieron;** IMPER **pide;** PRP **pidiendo**

55 **pensar :** IND **pienso, piensas, piensa,** pensamos, pensáis, **piensan;** SUBJ **piense, pienses, piense,** pensemos, penséis, **piensen;** IMPER **piensa**

56 **perder :** IND **pierdo, pierdes, pierde,** perdemos, perdéis, **pierden;** SUBJ **pierda, pierdas, pierda,** perdamos, perdáis, **pierdan;** IMPER **pierde**

57 **placer :** *IND* **plazco,** places, place, placemos, placéis, placen; *SUBJ* **plazca, plazcas, plazca, plazcamos, plazcáis, plazcan;** *PRET* plací, placiste, plació *or* **plugo,** placimos, placisteis, placieron *or* **pluguieron**

58 **poder :** *IND* **puedo, puedes, puede,** podemos, podéis, **pueden;** *SUBJ* **pueda, puedas, pueda,** podamos, podáis, **puedan;** *PRET* **pude, pudiste, pudo, pudimos, pudisteis, pudieron;** *FUT* **podré, podrás, podrá, podremos, podréis, podrán;** *IMPER* **puede;** *PRP* **pudiendo**

59 **podrir** *or* **pudrir :** *PP* **podrido** *(all other forms based on* pudrir*)*

60 **poner :** *IND* **pongo,** pones, pone, ponemos, ponéis, ponen; *SUBJ* **ponga, pongas, ponga, pongamos, pongáis, pongan;** *PRET* **puse, pusiste, puso, pusimos, pusisteis, pusieron;** *FUT* **pondré, pondrás, pondrá, pondremos, pondréis, pondrán;** *IMPER* **pon;** *PP* **puesto**

61 **producir :** *IND* **produzco,** produces, produce, producimos, producís, producen; *SUBJ* **produzca, produzcas, produzca, produzcamos, produzcáis, produzcan;** *PRET* **produje, produjiste, produjo, produjimos, produjisteis, produjeron**

62 **prohibir :** *IND* **prohíbo, prohíbes, prohíbe,** prohibimos, prohibís, **prohíben;** *SUBJ* **prohíba, prohíbas, prohíba,** prohibamos, prohibáis, **prohíban;** *IMPER* **prohíbe**

63 **proveer :** *PRET* proveí, **proveíste, proveyó, proveímos, proveísteis, proveyeron;** *PRP* **proveyendo;** *PP* **provisto**

64 **querer :** *IND* **quiero, quieres, quiere,** queremos, queréis, **quieren;** *SUBJ* **quiera, quieras, quiera,** queramos, queráis, **quieran;** *PRET* **quise, quisiste, quiso, quisimos, quisisteis, quisieron;** *FUT* **querré, querrás, querrá, querremos, querréis, querrán;** *IMPER* **quiere**

65 **raer :** *IND* rao *or* **raigo** *or* **rayo,** raes, rae, raemos, raéis, raen; *SUBJ* **raiga** *or* **raya, raigas** *or* **rayas, raiga** *or* **raya, raigamos** *or* **rayamos, raigáis** *or* **rayáis, raigan** *or* **rayan;** *PRET* **raí, raíste, rayó, raímos, raísteis, rayeron;** *PRP* **rayendo;** *PP* **raído**

66 **reír :** *IND* **río, ríes, ríe, reímos,** reís, **ríen;** *SUBJ* **ría, rías, ría, riamos, riáis, rían;** *PRET* reí, **reíste, rió, reímos, reísteis, rieron;** *IMPER* **ríe;** *PRP* **riendo;** *PP* **reído**

67 **reñir :** *IND* **riño, riñes, riñe,** reñimos, reñís, **riñen;** *SUBJ* **riña, riñas, riña, riñamos, riñáis, riñan;** *PRET* reñí, reñiste, **riñó,** reñimos, reñisteis, **riñeron;** *PRP* **riñendo**

68 **reunir :** *IND* **reúno, reúnes, reúne,** reunimos, reunís, **reúnen;** *SUBJ* **reúna, reúnas, reúna,** reunamos, reunáis, **reúnan;** *IMPER* **reúne**

69 **roer :** *IND* roo *or* **roigo** *or* **royo,** roes, roe, roemos, roéis, roen; *SUBJ* roa *or* **roiga** *or* **roya,** roas *or* **roigas** *or* **royas,** roa *or* **roiga** *or* **roya,** roamos *or* **roigamos** *or* **royamos,** roáis *or* **roigáis** *or* **royáis,** roan *or* **roigan** *or* **royan;** *PRET* roí, **roíste, royó, roímos, roísteis, royeron;** *PRP* **royendo;** *PP* **roído**

70 **romper :** *PP* **roto**

71 **saber :** *IND* **sé,** sabes, sabe, sabemos, sabéis, saben; *SUBJ* **sepa, sepas, sepa, sepamos, sepáis, sepan;** *PRET* **supe, supiste, supo, supimos, supisteis, supieron;** *FUT* **sabré, sabrás, sabrá, sabremos, sabréis, sabrán**

72 **sacar :** *SUBJ* **saque, saques, saque, saquemos, saquéis, saquen;** *PRET* **saqué,** sacaste, sacó, sacamos, sacasteis, sacaron

73 **salir :** *IND* **salgo,** sales, sale, salimos, salís, salen; *SUBJ* **salga, salgas, salga, salgamos, salgáis, salgan;** *FUT* **saldré, saldrás, saldrá, saldremos, saldréis, saldrán;** *IMPER* **sal**

74 **satisfacer :** *IND* **satisfago,** satisfaces, satisface, satisfacemos, satisfacéis, satisfacen; *SUBJ* **satisfaga, satisfagas, satisfaga, satisfagamos, satisfagáis, satisfagan;** *PRET* **satisfice, satisficiste, satisfizo, satisficimos, satificisteis, satisficieron;** *FUT* **satisfaré, satisfarás, satisfará, satisfaremos, satisfaréis, satisfarán;** *IMPER* **satisfaz** *or* **satisface;** *PP* **satisfecho**

75 **seguir :** *IND* **sigo, sigues, sigue,** seguimos, seguís, **siguen;** *SUBJ* **siga, sigas, siga, sigamos, sigáis, sigan;** *PRET* seguí, seguiste, **siguió,** seguimos, seguisteis, **siguieron;** *IMPER* **sigue;** *PRP* **siguiendo**

76 **sentir :** *IND* **siento, sientes, siente,** sentimos, sentís, **sienten;** *SUBJ* **sienta, sientas, sienta, sintamos, sintáis, sientan;** *PRET* sentí, sentiste, **sintió,** sentimos, sentisteis, **sintieron;** *IMPER* **siente;** *PRP* **sintiendo**

77 **ser :** *IND* **soy, eres, es, somos, sois, son;** *SUBJ* **sea, seas, sea, seamos, seáis, sean;** *PRET* **fui, fuiste, fue, fuimos, fuisteis, fueron;** *IMPF* **era, eras, era, éramos, erais, eran;** *IMPER* **sé;** *PRP* **siendo;** *PP* **sido**

78 **soler** *(defective verb; used only in the present, preterit, and imperfect indicative, and the present and imperfect subjunctive) see* 47 **mover**

79 **tañer :** *PRET* tañí, tañiste, **tañó,** tañimos, tañisteis, **tañeron;** *PRP* **tañendo**

80 **tener :** *IND* **tengo, tienes, tiene,** tenemos, tenéis, **tienen;** *SUBJ* **tenga, tengas, tenga, tengamos, tengáis, tengan;** *PRET* **tuve, tuviste, tuvo, tuvimos, tuvisteis, tuvieron;** *FUT* **tendré, tendrás, tendrá, tendremos, tendréis, tendrán;** *IMPER* **ten**

81 **traer :** *IND* **traigo,** traes, trae, traemos, traéis, traen; *SUBJ* **traiga, traigas, traiga, traigamos, traigáis, traigan;** *PRET* **traje, trajiste, trajo, trajimos, trajisteis, trajeron;** *PRP* **trayendo;** *PP* **traído**

82 **trocar :** *IND* **trueco, truecas, trueca,** trocamos, trocáis, **truecan;** *SUBJ* **trueque, trueques, trueque, troquemos, troquéis, truequen;** *PRET* **troqué,** trocaste, trocó, trocamos, trocasteis, trocaron; *IMPER* **trueca**

83 **uncir :** *IND* **unzo,** unces, unce, uncimos, uncís, uncen; *SUBJ* **unza, unzas, unza, unzamos, unzáis, unzan**

84 **valer :** *IND* **valgo,** vales, vale, valemos, valéis, valen; *SUBJ* **valga, valgas, valga, valgamos, valgáis, valgan;** *FUT* **valdré, valdrás, valdrá, valdremos, valdréis, valdrán**

85 **variar :** *IND* **varío, varías, varía,** variamos, variáis, **varían;** *SUBJ* **varíe, varíes, varíe,** variemos, variéis, **varíen;** *IMPER* **varía**

86 **vencer :** *IND* **venzo,** vences, vence, vencemos, vencéis, vencen; *SUBJ* **venza, venzas, venza, venzamos, venzáis, venzan**

87 **venir :** *IND* **vengo, vienes, viene,** venimos, venís, **vienen;** *SUBJ* **venga, vengas, venga, vengamos, vengáis, vengan;** *PRET* **vine, viniste, vino, vinimos, vinisteis, vinieron;** *FUT* **vendré, vendrás, vendrá, vendremos, vendréis, vendrán;** *IMPER* **ven;** *PRP* **viniendo**

88 **ver :** *IND* veo, **ves, ve, vemos, veis, ven;** *PRET* **vi, viste, vio, vimos, visteis, vieron;** *IMPER* **ve;** *PRP* **viendo;** *PP* **visto**

89 **volver :** *IND* **vuelvo, vuelves, vuelve,** volvemos, volvéis, **vuelven;** *SUBJ* **vuelva, vuelvas, vuelva,** volvamos, volváis, **vuelvan;** *IMPER* **vuelve;** *PP* **vuelto**

90 **yacer :** *IND* **yazco** *or* **yazgo** *or* **yago,** yaces, yace, yacemos, yacéis, yacen; *SUBJ* **yazca** *or* **yazga** *or* **yaga, yazcas** *or* **yazgas** *or* **yagas, yazca** *or* **yazga** *or* **yaga, yazcamos** *or* **yazgamos** *or* **yagamos, yazcáis** *or* **yazgáis** *or* **yagáis, yazcan** *or* **yazgan** *or* **yagan;** *IMPER* yace *or* **yaz**

Spanish–English Dictionary

A

a[1] *nf* **:** first letter of the Spanish alphabet

a[2] *prep* **1 :** to <nos vamos a México : we're going to Mexico> **2** (*used before direct or indirect objects referring to persons*) <¿llamaste a tu papá? : did you call your dad?> <como a usted le guste : as you wish> **3 :** in the manner of <papas a la francesa : french fries> **4 :** on, by means of <a pie : on foot> **5 :** per, each <tres pastillas al día : three pills per day> **6** (*with infinitive*) <enséñales a leer : teach them to read> <problemas a resolver : problems to be solved>

ábaco *nm* **:** abacus

abad *nm* **:** abbot

abadesa *nf* **:** abbess

abadía *nf* **:** abbey

abajo *adv* **1 :** down <póngalo más abajo : put it further down> <arriba y abajo : up and down> **2 :** downstairs **3 :** under, beneath <el abajo firmante : the undersigned> **4 :** down with <¡abajo la inflación! : down with inflation!> **5 ~ de :** under, beneath **6 de ~ :** bottom <el cajón de abajo : the bottom drawer> **7 hacia ~** *or* **para ~ :** downwards **8 cuesta abajo :** downhill **9 río abajo :** downstream

abalanzarse {21} *vr* **:** to hurl oneself, to rush

abanderado, -da *n* **:** standard-bearer

abandonado, -da *adj* **1 :** abandoned, deserted **2 :** neglected **3 :** slovenly, unkempt

abandonar *vt* **1** DEJAR **:** to abandon, to leave **2 :** to give up, to quit <abandonaron la búsqueda : they gave up the search> **— abandonarse** *vr* **1 :** to neglect oneself **2 ~ a :** to succumb to, to give oneself over to

abandono *nm* **1 :** abandonment **2 :** neglect **3 :** withdrawal <ganar por abandono : to win by default>

abanicar {72} *vt* **:** to fan **— abanicarse** *vr*

abanico *nm* **1 :** fan **2** GAMA **:** range, gamut

abaratamiento *nm* **:** price reduction

abaratar *vt* **:** to lower the price of **— abaratarse** *vr* **:** to go down in price

abarcar {72} *vt* **1 :** to cover, to include, to embrace **2 :** to undertake **3 :** to monopolize

abaritonado, -da *adj* **:** baritone

abarrotado, -da *adj* **:** packed, crammed

abarrotar *vt* **:** to fill up, to pack

abarrotería *nf CA, Mex* **:** grocery store

abarrotero, -ra *n Col, Mex* **:** grocer

abarrotes *nmpl* **1 :** groceries, supplies **2 tienda de abarrotes :** general store, grocery store

abastecedor, -dora *n* **:** supplier

abastecer {53} *vt* **:** to supply, to stock **— abastecerse** *vr* **:** to stock up

abastecimiento → abasto

abasto *nm* **:** supply, supplying <no da abasto : there isn't enough for all>

abatido, -da *adj* **:** dejected, depressed

abatimiento *nm* **1 :** drop, reduction **2 :** dejection, depression

abatir *vt* **1** DERRIBAR **:** to demolish, to knock down **2 :** to shoot down **3** DEPRIMIR **:** to depress, to bring low **— abatirse** *vr* **1** DEPRIMIRSE **:** to get depressed **2 ~ sobre :** to swoop down on

abdicación *nf, pl* **-ciones :** abdication

abdicar {72} *vt* **:** to relinquish, to abdicate

abdomen *nm, pl* **-dómenes :** abdomen

abdominal *adj* **:** abdominal

abecé *nm* **:** ABC

abecedario *nm* ALFABETO **:** alphabet

abedul *nm* **:** birch (tree)

abeja *nf* **:** bee

abejorro *nm* **:** bumblebee

aberración *nf, pl* **-ciones :** aberration

aberrante *adj* **:** aberrant, perverse

abertura *nf* **1 :** aperture, opening **2** AGUJERO **:** hole **3 :** slit (in a skirt, etc.) **4** GRIETA **:** crack

abeto *nm* **:** fir (tree)

abierto[1] *pp* **→ abrir**

abierto[2]**, -ta** *adj* **1 :** open **2 :** candid, frank **3 :** generous **— abiertamente** *adv*

abigarrado, -da *adj* **:** multicolored, variegated

abigeato *nm* **:** rustling (of livestock)

abismal *adj* **:** abysmal, vast

abismo *nm* **:** abyss, chasm <al borde del abismo : on the brink of ruin>

abjurar *vi* **~ de :** to abjure **— abjuración** *nf*

ablandamiento *nm* **:** softening, moderation

ablandar *vt* **1** SUAVIZAR **:** to soften **2** CALMAR **:** to soothe, to appease **—** *vi* **:** to moderate, to get milder **— ablandarse** *vr* **1 :** to become soft, to soften **2** CEDER **:** to yield, to relent

ablución *nf, pl* **-ciones :** ablution

abnegación *nf, pl* **-ciones :** abnegation, self-denial

abnegado, -da *adj* **:** self-sacrificing, selfless

abnegarse {49} *vr* **:** to deny oneself

abobado, -da *adj* **1 :** silly, stupid **2 :** bewildered

abocarse {72} *vr* **1** DIRIGIRSE **:** to head, to direct oneself **2** DEDICARSE **:** to dedicate oneself

abochornar *vt* AVERGONZAR **:** to embarrass, to shame **— abochornarse** *vr*

abofetear *vt* **:** to slap

abogacía *nf* **:** law, legal profession

abogado, -da *n* **:** lawyer, attorney

abogar {52} *vi* **~ por :** to plead for, to defend, to advocate

abolengo *nm* LINAJE **:** lineage, ancestry

abolición *nf, pl* **-ciones :** abolition

abolir {1} *vt* DEROGAR **:** to abolish, to repeal

abolladura *nf* **:** dent

abollar *vt* **:** to dent

abombar *vt* **:** to warp, to cause to bulge — **abombarse** *vr* **:** to decompose, to go bad

abominable *adj* ABORRECIBLE **:** abominable

abominación *nf, pl* **-ciones :** abomination

abominar *vt* ABORRECER **:** to abominate, to abhor

abonado, -da *n* **:** subscriber

abonar *vt* **1 :** to pay **2** FERTILIZAR **:** to fertilize — **abonarse** *vr* **:** to subscribe

abono *nm* **1 :** payment, installment **2** FERTILIZANTE **:** fertilizer **3 :** season ticket

abordaje *nm* **:** boarding

abordar *vt* **1 :** to address, to broach **2 :** to accost, to waylay **3 :** to come on board

aborigen¹ *adj, pl* **-rígenes :** aboriginal, native

aborigen² *nmf, pl* **-rígenes :** aborigine, indigenous inhabitant

aborrecer {53} *vt* ABOMINAR, ODIAR **:** to abhor, to detest, to hate

aborrecible *adj* ABOMINABLE, ODIOSO **:** abominable, detestable

aborrecimiento *nm* **:** abhorrence, loathing

abortar *vi* **:** to have an abortion — *vt* **1 :** to abort **2 :** to quash, to suppress

abortista *nmf* **:** abortionist

abortivo, -va *adj* **:** abortive

aborto *nm* **1 :** abortion **2 :** miscarriage

abotonar *vt* **:** to button — **abotonarse** *vr* **:** to button up

abovedado, -da *adj* **:** vaulted

abrasador, -dora *adj* **:** burning, scorching

abrasar *vt* QUEMAR **:** to burn, to sear, to scorch

abrasivo¹, -va *adj* **:** abrasive

abrasivo² *nm* **:** abrasive

abrazadera *nf* **:** clamp, brace

abrazar {21} *vt* **:** to hug, to embrace — **abrazarse** *vr*

abrazo *nm* **:** hug, embrace

abrebotellas *nms & pl* **:** bottle opener

abrelatas *nms & pl* **:** can opener

abrevadero *nm* BEBEDERO **:** watering trough

abreviación *nf, pl* **-ciones :** abbreviation

abreviar *vt* **1 :** to abbreviate **2 :** to shorten, to cut short

abreviatura *nf* → **abreviación**

abridor *nm* **:** bottle opener, can opener

abrigadero *nm* **:** shelter, windbreak

abrigado, -da *adj* **1 :** sheltered **2 :** warm, wrapped up (with clothing)

abrigar {52} *vt* **1 :** to shelter, to protect **2 :** to keep warm, to dress warmly **3 :** to cherish, to harbor <abrigar esperanzas : to cherish hopes> — **abrigarse** *vr* **:** to dress warmly

abrigo *nm* **1 :** coat, overcoat **2 :** shelter, refuge

abril *nm* **:** April

abrillantador *nm* **:** polish

abrillantar *vt* **:** to polish, to shine

abrir {2} *vt* **1 :** to open **2 :** to unlock, to undo **3 :** to turn on (a tap or faucet) — *vi* **:** to open, to open up — **abrirse** *vr* **1 :** to open up **2 :** to clear (of the skies)

abrochar *vt* **:** to button, to fasten — **abrocharse** *vr* **:** to fasten, to hook up

abrogación *nf, pl* **-ciones :** abrogation, annulment, repeal

abrogar {52} *vt* **:** to abrogate, to annul, to repeal

abrojo *nm* **:** bur (of a plant)

abrumador, -dora *adj* **:** crushing, overwhelming

abrumar *vt* **1** AGOBIAR **:** to overwhelm **2** OPRIMIR **:** to oppress, to burden

abrupto, -ta *adj* **1 :** abrupt **2** ESCARPADO **:** steep — **abruptamente** *adv*

absceso *nm* **:** abscess

absolución *nf, pl* **-ciones 1 :** absolution **2 :** acquittal

absolutismo *nm* **:** absolutism

absoluto, -ta *adj* **1 :** absolute, unconditional **2 en ~ :** not at all <no me gustó en absoluto : I did not like it at all> — **absolutamente** *adv*

absolver {89} *vt* **1 :** to absolve **2 :** to acquit

absorbente *adj* **1 :** absorbent **2 :** absorbing, engrossing

absorber *vt* **1 :** to absorb, to soak up **2 :** to occupy, to take up, to engross

absorción *nf, pl* **-ciones :** absorption

absorto, -ta *adj* **:** absorbed, engrossed

abstemio¹, -mia *adj* **:** abstemious, teetotal

abstemio², -mia *n* **:** teetotaler

abstención *nf, pl* **-ciones :** abstention

abstenerse {80} *vr* **:** to abstain, to refrain

abstinencia *nf* **:** abstinence

abstracción *nf, pl* **-ciones :** abstraction

abstracto, -ta *adj* **:** abstract

abstraer {81} *vt* **:** to abstract — **abstraerse** *vr* **:** to lose oneself in thought

abstraído, -da *adj* **:** preoccupied, withdrawn

abstruso, -sa *adj* **:** abstruse

abstuvo, etc. → **abstenerse**

absuelto *pp* → **absolver**

absurdo¹, -da *adj* DISPARATADO, RIDÍCULO **:** absurd, ridiculous — **absurdamente** *adv*

absurdo² *nm* **:** absurdity

abuchear *vt* **:** to boo, to jeer

abucheo *nm* **:** booing, jeering

abuela *nf* **1 :** grandmother **2 :** old woman **3 ¡tu abuela!** *fam* **:** no way!, forget about it!

abuelo *nm* **1 :** grandfather **2 :** old man **3 abuelos** *nmpl* **:** grandparents, ancestors
abulia *nf* **:** apathy, lethargy
abúlico, -ca *adj* **:** lethargic, apathetic
abultado, -da *adj* **:** bulging, bulky
abultar *vi* **:** to bulge — *vt* **:** to enlarge, to expand
abundancia *nf* **:** abundance
abundante *adj* **:** abundant, plentiful — **abundantemente** *adv*
abundar *vi* **1 :** to abound, to be plentiful **2 ~ en :** to be in agreement with
aburrido, -da *adj* **1 :** bored, tired, fed up **2** TEDIOSO **:** boring, tedious
aburrimiento *nm* **:** boredom, weariness
aburrir *vt* **:** to bore, to tire — **aburrirse** *vr* **:** to get bored
abusado, -da *adj Mex fam* **:** sharp, on the ball
abusador, -dora *n* **:** abuser
abusar *vi* **1 :** to go too far, to do something to excess **2 ~ de :** to abuse (as drugs) **3 ~ de :** to take unfair advantage of
abusivo, -va *adj* **1 :** abusive **2 :** outrageous, excessive
abuso *nm* **1 :** abuse **2 :** injustice, outrage
abyecto, -ta *adj* **:** despicable, contemptible
acá *adv* AQUÍ **:** here, over here <¡ven acá! : come here!>
acabado[1], -da *adj* **1 :** finished, done, completed **2 :** old, worn-out
acabado[2] *nm* **:** finish <un acabado brillante : a glossy finish>
acabar *vi* **1** TERMINAR **:** to finish, to end **2 ~ de :** to have just (done something) <acabo de ver a tu hermano : I just saw your brother> **3 ~ con :** to put an end to, to stamp out — *vt* TERMINAR **:** to finish — **acabarse** *vr* TERMINARSE **:** to come to an end, to run out <se me acabó el dinero : I ran out of money>
academia *nf* **:** academy
académico[1], -ca *adj* **:** academic, scholastic — **académicamente** *adv*
académico[2], -ca *n* **:** academic, academician
acaecer {53} *vi* (*3rd person only*) **:** to happen, to take place
acalambrarse *vr* **:** to cramp up, to get a cramp
acallar *vt* **:** to quiet, to silence
acalorado, -da *adj* **:** emotional, heated
acaloramiento *nm* **1 :** heat **2 :** ardor, passion
acalorar *vt* **:** to heat up, to inflame — **acalorarse** *vr* **:** to get upset, to get worked up
acampada *nf* **:** camp, camping <ir de acampada : to go camping>
acampar *vi* **:** to camp
acanalar *vt* **1 :** to groove, to furrow **2 :** to corrugate
acantilado *nm* **:** cliff
acanto *nm* **:** acanthus
acantonar *vt* **:** to station, to quarter
acaparador, -dora *adj* **:** greedy, selfish
acaparar *vt* **1 :** to stockpile, to hoard **2 :** to monopolize
acápite *nm* **:** paragraph
acariciar *vt* **:** to caress, to stroke, to pet
ácaro *nm* **:** mite
acarrear *vt* **1 :** to haul, to carry **2 :** to bring, to give rise to <los problemas que acarrea : the problems that come along with it>
acarreo *nm* **:** transport, haulage
acartonarse *vr* **1 :** to stiffen **2 :** to become wizened
acaso *adv* **1 :** perhaps, by any chance **2 por si acaso :** just in case
acatamiento *nm* **:** compliance, observance
acatar *vt* **:** to comply with, to respect
acaudalado, -da *adj* RICO **:** wealthy, rich
acaudillar *vt* **:** to lead, to command
acceder *vi* **~ a 1 :** to accede to, to agree to **2 :** to assume (a position) **3 :** to gain access to
accesar *vt* **:** to access (on a computer)
accesibilidad *nf* **:** accessibility
accesible *adj* ASEQUIBLE **:** accessible, attainable
acceso *nm* **1 :** access **2 :** admittance, entrance
accesorio[1], -ria *adj* **1 :** accessory **2 :** incidental
accesorio[2] *nm* **1 :** accessory **2 :** prop (in the theater)
accidentado[1], -da *adj* **1 :** eventful, turbulent **2 :** rough, uneven **3 :** injured
accidentado[2], -da *n* **:** accident victim
accidental *adj* **:** accidental, unintentional — **accidentalmente** *adv*
accidentarse *vr* **:** to have an accident
accidente *nm* **1 :** accident **2 :** unevenness **3 accidente geográfico :** geographical feature
acción *nf, pl* **acciones 1 :** action **2** ACTO **:** act, deed **3 :** share, stock
accionamiento *nm* **:** activation
accionar *vt* **:** to put into motion, to activate — *vi* **:** to gesticulate
accionario, -ria *adj* **:** stock <mercado accionario : stock market>
accionista *nmf* **:** stockholder, shareholder
acebo *nm* **:** holly
acechar *vt* **1 :** to watch, to spy on **2 :** to stalk, to lie in wait for
acecho *nm* **al acecho :** lying in wait
acedera *nf* **:** sorrel (herb)
acéfalo, -la *adj* **:** leaderless
aceitar *vt* **:** to oil
aceite *nm* **1 :** oil **2 aceite de ricino :** castor oil **3 aceite de oliva :** olive oil
aceitera *nf* **1 :** cruet (for oil) **2 :** oilcan **3** *Mex* **:** oil refinery
aceitoso, -sa *adj* **:** oily
aceituna *nf* OLIVA **:** olive
aceituno *nm* OLIVO **:** olive tree

aceleración *nf, pl* **-ciones** : acceleration, speeding up

acelerado, -da *adj* : accelerated, speedy

acelerador *nm* : accelerator

aceleramiento *nm* → **aceleración**

acelerar *vt* **1** : to accelerate, to speed up **2** AGILIZAR : to expedite — *vi* : to accelerate (of an automobile) — **acelerarse** *vr* : to hasten, to hurry up

acelga *nf* : chard, Swiss chard

acendrado, -da *adj* : pure, unblemished

acendrar *vt* : to purify, to refine

acento *nm* **1** : accent **2** : stress, emphasis

acentuación *nf, pl* **-ciones** : accentuation

acentuado, -da *adj* : marked, pronounced

acentuar {3} *vt* **1** : to accent **2** : to emphasize, to stress — **acentuarse** *vr* : to become more pronounced

acepción *nf, pl* **-ciones** SIGNIFICADO : sense, meaning

aceptabilidad *nf* : acceptability

aceptable *adj* : acceptable

aceptación *nf, pl* **-ciones** **1** : acceptance **2** APROBACIÓN : approval

aceptar *vt* **1** : to accept **2** : to approve

acequia *nf* **1** : irrigation ditch **2** *Mex* : sewer

acera *nf* : sidewalk

acerado, -da *adj* **1** : made of steel **2** : steely, tough

acerbo, -ba *adj* **1** : harsh, cutting <comentarios acerbos : cutting remarks> **2** : bitter — **acerbamente** *adv*

acerca *prep* **~ de** : about, concerning

acercamiento *nm* : rapprochement, reconciliation

acercar {72} *vt* APROXIMAR, ARRIMAR : to bring near, to bring closer — **acercarse** *vr* APROXIMARSE, ARRIMARSE : to approach, to draw near

acería *nf* : steel mill

acerico *nm* : pincushion

acero *nm* : steel <acero inoxidable : stainless steel>

acérrimo, -ma *adj* **1** : staunch, steadfast **2** : bitter <un acérrimo enemigo : a bitter enemy>

acertado, -da *adj* CORRECTO : accurate, correct, on target — **acertadamente** *adv*

acertante[1] *adj* : winning

acertante[2] *nmf* : winner

acertar {55} *vt* : to guess correctly — *vi* ATINAR : to be accurate, to be on target

acertijo *nm* ADIVINANZA : riddle

acervo *nm* **1** : pile, heap **2** : wealth, heritage <el acervo artístico del instituto : the artistic treasures of the institute>

acetato *nm* : acetate

acético, -ca *adj* : acetic <ácido acético : acetic acid>

acetileno *nm* : acetylene

acetona *nf* **1** : acetone **2** : nail-polish remover

achacar {72} *vt* : to attribute, to impute <te achaca todos sus problemas : he blames all his problems on you>

achacoso, -sa *adj* : frail, sickly

achaparrado, -da *adj* : stunted, scrubby <árboles achaparrados : scrubby trees>

achaque *nm* DOLENCIA : ailment, malady, discomfort

achatar *vt* : to flatten

achicar {72} *vt* **1** REDUCIR : to make smaller, to reduce **2** : to intimidate **3** : to bail out (water) — **achicarse** *vr* : to become intimidated

achicharrar *vt* : to scorch, to burn to a crisp

achicoria *nf* : chicory

achispado, -da *adj fam* : tipsy

achote *or* **achiote** *nm* : annatto seed

achuchón *nm, pl* **-chones** **1** : push, shove **2** *fam* : squeeze, hug **3** *fam* : mild illness

aciago, -ga *adj* : fateful, unlucky

acicalar *vt* **1** PULIR : to polish **2** : to dress up, to adorn — **acicalarse** *vr* : to get dressed up

acicate *nm* **1** : spur **2** INCENTIVO : incentive, stimulus

acidez *nf, pl* **-deces** **1** : acidity **2** : sourness **3** **acidez estomacal** : heartburn

acidificar {72} *vt* : to acidify

ácido[1], **-da** *adj* AGRIO : acid, sour

ácido[2] *nm* : acid

acierto *nm* **1** : correct answer, right choice **2** : accuracy, skill, deftness

acimut *nm* : azimuth

acitronar *vt Mex* : to fry until crisp

aclamación *nf, pl* **-ciones** : acclaim, acclamation

aclamar *vt* : to acclaim, to cheer, to applaud

aclaración *nf, pl* **-ciones** CLARIFICACIÓN : clarification, explanation

aclarar *vt* **1** CLARIFICAR : to clarify, to explain, to resolve **2** : to lighten **3** **aclarar la voz** : to clear one's throat — *vi* **1** : to get light, to dawn **2** : to clear up — **aclararse** *vr* : to become clear

aclaratorio, -ria *adj* : explanatory

aclimatar *vt* : to acclimatize — **aclimatarse** *vr* **~ a** : to get used to — **aclimatación** *nf*

acné *nm* : acne

acobardar *vt* INTIMIDAR : to frighten, to intimidate — **acobardarse** *vr* : to be frightened, to cower

acodarse *vr* **~ en** : to lean (one's elbows) on

acogedor, -dora *adj* : cozy, warm, friendly

acoger {15} *vt* **1** REFUGIAR : to take in, to shelter **2** : to receive, to welcome — **acogerse** *vr* **1** REFUGIARSE : to take refuge **2** **~ a** : to resort to, to avail oneself of

acogida *nf* 1 AMPARO, REFUGIO : refuge, protection 2 RECIBIMIENTO : reception, welcome
acolchar *vt* 1 : to pad (a wall, etc.) 2 : to quilt
acólito *nm* 1 MONAGUILLO : altar boy 2 : follower, helper, acolyte
acomedido, -da *adj* : helpful, obliging
acometer *vt* 1 ATACAR : to attack, to assail 2 EMPRENDER : to undertake, to begin — *vi* ~ **contra** : to rush against
acometida *nf* ATAQUE : attack, assault
acomodado, -da *adj* 1 : suitable, appropriate 2 : well-to-do, prosperous
acomodador, -dora *n* : usher, usherette *f*
acomodar *vt* 1 : to accommodate, to make room for 2 : to adjust, to adapt — **acomodarse** *vr* 1 : to settle in 2 ~ **a** : to adapt to
acomodaticio, -cia *adj* : accommodating, obliging
acomodo *nm* 1 : job, position 2 : arrangement, placement 3 : accommodation, lodging
acompañamiento *nm* : accompaniment
acompañante *nmf* 1 COMPAÑERO : companion 2 : accompanist
acompañar *vt* : to accompany, to go with
acompasado, -da *adj* : rhythmic, regular, measured
acomplejado, -da *adj* : full of complexes, neurotic
acondicionado, -da *adj* 1 : equipped, fitted-out 2 **bien acondicionado** : in good shape, in a fit state
acondicionador *nm* 1 : conditioner 2 **acondicionador de aire** : air conditioner
acondicionar *vt* 1 : to condition 2 : to fit out, to furnish
acongojado, -da *adj* : distressed, upset
acongojarse *vr* : to grieve, to become distressed
aconsejable *adj* : advisable
aconsejar *vt* : to advise, to counsel
acontecer {53} *vi* (*3rd person only*) : to occur, to happen
acontecimiento *nm* SUCESO : event
acopiar *vt* : to gather, to collect, to stockpile
acopio *nm* : collection, stock
acoplamiento *nm* : connection, coupling
acoplar *vt* : to couple, to connect — **acoplarse** *vr* : to fit together
acoquinar *vt* : to intimidate
acorazado[1], -da *adj* BLINDADO : armored
acorazado[2] *nm* : battleship
acordado, -da *adj* : agreed upon
acordar {19} *vt* 1 : to agree on 2 OTORGAR : to award, to bestow — **acordarse** *vr* RECORDAR : to remember, to recall
acorde[1] *adj* 1 : in agreement, in accordance 2 ~ **con** : in keeping with
acorde[2] *nm* : chord
acordeón *nm, pl* **-deones** : accordion — **acordeonista** *nmf*
acordonar *vt* 1 : to cordon off 2 : to lace up 3 : to mill (coins)
acorralar *vt* ARRINCONAR : to corner, to hem in, to corral
acortar *vt* : to shorten, to cut short — **acortarse** *vr* 1 : to become shorter 2 : to end early
acosar *vt* PERSEGUIR : to pursue, to hound, to harass
acoso *nm* ASEDIO : harassment <acoso sexual : sexual harassment>
acostar {19} *vt* 1 : to lay (something) down 2 : to put to bed — **acostarse** *vr* 1 : to lie down 2 : to go to bed
acostumbrado, -da *adj* 1 HABITUADO : accustomed 2 HABITUAL : usual, customary
acostumbrar *vt* : to accustom — *vi* : to be accustomed, to be in the habit — **acostumbrarse** *vr*
acotación *nf, pl* **-ciones** 1 : marginal note 2 : stage direction
acotado, -da *adj* : enclosed
acotamiento *nm Mex* : shoulder (of a road)
acotar *vt* 1 ANOTAR : to note, to annotate 2 DELIMITAR : to mark off (land), to demarcate
acre[1] *adj* 1 : acrid, pungent 2 MORDAZ : caustic, biting
acre[2] *nm* : acre
acrecentamiento *nm* : growth, increase
acrecentar {55} *vt* AUMENTAR : to increase, to augment
acreditación *nf, pl* **-ciones** : accreditation
acreditado, -da *adj* 1 : accredited, authorized 2 : reputable
acreditar *vt* 1 : to accredit, to authorize 2 : to credit 3 : to prove, to verify — **acreditarse** *vr* : to gain a reputation
acreedor[1], -dora *adj* : deserving, worthy
acreedor[2], -dora *n* : creditor
acribillar *vt* 1 : to riddle, to pepper (with bullets, etc.) 2 : to hound, to harass
acrílico *nm* : acrylic
acrimonia *nf* 1 : pungency 2 : acrimony
acrimonioso, -sa *adj* : acrimonious
acriollarse *vr* : to adopt local customs, to go native
acritud *nf* 1 : pungency, bitterness 2 : intensity, sharpness 3 : harshness, asperity
acrobacia *nf* : acrobatics
acróbata *nmf* : acrobat
acrónimo *nm* : acronym
acta *nf* 1 : document, certificate <acta de nacimiento : birth certificate> 2 **actas** *nfpl* : minutes (of a meeting)
actitud *nf* 1 : attitude 2 : posture, position

activación *nf, pl* **-ciones 1 :** activation, stimulation **2** ACELERACIÓN **:** acceleration, speeding up

activar *vt* **1 :** to activate **2 :** to stimulate, to energize **3 :** to speed up

actividad *nf* **:** activity

activista *nmf* **:** activist

activo[1], -va *adj* **:** active — **activamente** *adv*

activo[2] *nm* **:** assets *pl* <activo y pasivo : assets and liabilities>

acto *nm* **1** ACCIÓN **:** act, deed **2 :** act (in a play) **3 el acto sexual :** sexual intercourse **4 en el acto :** right away, on the spot **5 acto seguido :** immediately after

actor *nm* ARTISTA **:** actor

actriz *nf, pl* **actrices** ARTISTA **:** actress

actuación *nf, pl* **-ciones 1 :** performance **2 actuaciones** *nfpl* DILIGENCIAS **:** proceedings

actual *adj* PRESENTE **:** present, current

actualidad *nf* **1 :** present time <en la actualidad : at present> **2 actualidades** *nfpl* **:** current affairs

actualización *nf, pl* **-ciones :** updating, modernization

actualizar {21} *vt* **:** to modernize, to bring up to date

actualmente *adv* **:** at present, nowadays

actuar {3} *vi* **:** to act, to perform

actuarial *adj* **:** actuarial

actuario, -ria *n* **:** actuary

acuarela *nf* **:** watercolor

acuario *nm* **:** aquarium

Acuario *nmf* **:** Aquarius, Aquarian

acuartelar *vt* **:** to quarter (troops)

acuático, -ca *adj* **:** aquatic, water

acuchillar *vt* APUÑALAR **:** to knife, to stab

acuciante *adj* **:** pressing, urgent

acucioso, -sa → **acuciante**

acudir *vi* **1 :** to go, to come (someplace for a specific purpose) <acudió a la puerta : he went to the door> <acudimos en su ayuda : we came to her aid> **2 :** to be present, to show up <acudí a la cita : I showed up for the appointment> **3 ~ a :** to turn to, to have recourse to <hay que acudir al médico : you must consult the doctor>

acueducto *nm* **:** aqueduct

acuerdo *nm* **1 :** agreement **2 estar de acuerdo :** to agree **3 de acuerdo con :** in accordance with **4 de ~ :** OK, all right

acuicultura *nf* **:** aquaculture

acullá *adv* **:** yonder, over there

acumulación *nf, pl* **-ciones :** accumulation

acumulador *nm* **:** storage battery

acumular *vt* **:** to accumulate, to amass — **acumularse** *vr* **:** to build up, to pile up

acumulativo, -va *adj* **:** cumulative — **acumulativamente** *adv*

acunar *vt* **:** to rock, to cradle

acuñar *vt* **:** to coin, to mint

acuoso, -sa *adj* **:** aqueous, watery

acupuntura *nf* **:** acupuncture

acurrucarse {72} *vr* **:** to cuddle, to nestle, to curl up

acusación *nf, pl* **-ciones 1 :** accusation, charge **2 la acusación :** the prosecution

acusado[1], -da *adj* **:** prominent, marked

acusado[2], -da *n* **:** defendant

acusador, -dora *n* **1 :** accuser **2** FISCAL **:** prosecutor

acusar *vt* **1 :** to accuse, to charge **2 :** to reveal, to betray <sus ojos acusaban la desconfianza : his eyes revealed distrust> — **acusarse** *vr* **:** to confess

acusatorio, -ria *adj* **:** accusatory

acuse *nm* **acuse de recibo :** acknowledgment of receipt

acústica *nf* **:** acoustics

acústico, -ca *adj* **:** acoustic

adagio *nm* **1** REFRÁN **:** adage, proverb **2 :** adagio

adalid *nm* **:** leader, champion

adaptable *adj* **:** adaptable — **adaptabilidad** *nf*

adaptación *nf, pl* **-ciones :** adaptation, adjustment

adaptado, -da *adj* **:** suited, adapted

adaptador *nm* **:** adapter (in electricity)

adaptar *vt* **1** MODIFICAR **:** to adapt **2 :** to adjust, to fit — **adaptarse** *vr* **:** to adapt oneself, to conform

adecentar *vt* **:** to tidy up

adecuación *nf, pl* **-ciones** ADAPTACIÓN **:** adaptation

adecuadamente *adv* **:** adequately

adecuado, -da *adj* **1** IDÓNEO **:** suitable, appropriate **2 :** adequate

adecuar {8} *vt* **:** to adapt, to make suitable — **adecuarse** *vr* **~ a :** to be appropriate for, to fit in with

adefesio *nm* **:** eyesore, monstrosity

adelantado, -da *adj* **1 :** advanced, ahead **2 :** fast (of a clock or watch) **3 por ~ :** in advance

adelantamiento *nm* **1 :** advancement **2 :** speeding up

adelantar *vt* **1 :** to advance, to move forward **2 :** to overtake, to pass **3 :** to reveal (information) in advance **4 :** to advance, to lend (money) — **adelantarse** *vr* **1 :** to advance, to get in front **2 ~ a :** to forestall, to preempt

adelante *adv* **1 :** ahead, in front, forward **2 más adelante :** further on, later on **3 ¡adelante! :** come in!

adelanto *nm* **1 :** advance, progress **2 :** advance payment **3 :** earliness <llevamos una hora de adelanto : we're running an hour ahead of time>

adelfa *nf* **:** oleander

adelgazar {21} *vt* **:** to thin, to reduce — *vi* **:** to lose weight

ademán *nm, pl* **-manes 1** GESTO **:** gesture **2 ademanes** *nmpl* **:** manners

además *adv* **1 :** besides, furthermore **2 ~ de :** in addition to, as well as

adenoides *nfpl* : adenoids
adentrarse *vr* ~ **en** : to go into, to penetrate
adentro *adv* : inside, within
adentros *nmpl* **decirse para sus adentros** : to say to oneself <me dije para mis adentros que nunca regresaría : I told myself that I'd never go back>
adepto[1], -ta *adj* : supportive <ser adepto a : to be a follower of>
adepto[2], -ta *n* PARTIDARIO : follower, supporter
aderezar {21} *vt* **1** SAZONAR : to season, to dress (salad) **2** : to embellish, to adorn
aderezo *nm* **1** : dressing, seasoning **2** : adornment, embellishment
adeudar *vt* **1** : to debit **2** DEBER : to owe
adeudo *nm* **1** DÉBITO : debit **2** *Mex* : debt, indebtedness
adherencia *nf* **1** : adherence, adhesiveness **2** : appendage, accretion
adherente *adj* : adhesive, sticky
adherirse {76} *vr* : to adhere, to stick
adhesión *nf, pl* **-siones 1** : adhesion **2** : attachment, commitment (to a cause, etc.)
adhesivo[1], -va *adj* : adhesive
adhesivo[2] *nm* : adhesive
adicción *nf, pl* **-ciones** : addiction
adición *nf, pl* **-ciones** : addition
adicional *adj* : additional — **adicionalmente** *adv*
adicionar *vt* : to add
adicto[1], -ta *adj* **1** : addicted **2** : devoted, dedicated
adicto[2], -ta *n* **1** : addict **2** PARTIDARIO : supporter, advocate
adiestrador, -dora *n* : trainer
adiestramiento *nm* : training
adiestrar *vt* : to train
adinerado, -da *adj* : moneyed, wealthy
adiós *nm, pl* **adioses 1** DESPEDIDA : farewell, good-bye **2 ¡adiós!** : good-bye!
aditamento *nm* : attachment, accessory
aditivo *nm* : additive
adivinación *nf, pl* **-ciones 1** : guess **2** : divination, prediction
adivinanza *nf* ACERTIJO : riddle
adivinar *vt* **1** : to guess **2** : to foretell, to predict
adivino, -na *n* : fortune-teller
adjetivo[1], -va *adj* : adjectival
adjetivo[2] *nm* : adjective
adjudicación *nf, pl* **-ciones 1** : adjudication **2** : allocation, awarding, granting
adjudicar {72} *vt* **1** : to adjudge, to adjudicate **2** : to assign, to allocate <adjudicar la culpa : to assign the blame> **3** : to award, to grant
adjuntar *vt* : to enclose, to attach
adjunto[1], -ta *adj* : enclosed, attached
adjunto[2], -ta *n* : deputy, assistant
adjunto[3] *nm* : adjunct
administración *nf, pl* **-ciones 1** : administration, management **2 administración de empresas** : business administration
administrador, -dora *n* : administrator, manager
administrar *vt* : to administer, to manage, to run
administrativo, -va *adj* : administrative
admirable *adj* : admirable, impressive — **admirablemente** *adv*
admiración *nf, pl* **-ciones** : admiration
admirador, -dora *n* : admirer
admirar *vt* **1** : to admire **2** : to amaze, to astonish — **admirarse** *vr* : to be amazed
admirativo, -va *adj* : admiring
admisibilidad *nf* : admissibility
admisible *adj* : admissible, allowable
admisión *nf, pl* **-siones** : admission, admittance
admitir *vt* **1** : to admit, to let in **2** : to acknowledge, to concede **3** : to allow, to make room for <la ley no admite cambios : the law doesn't allow for changes>
admonición *nf, pl* **-ciones** : admonition, warning
admonitorio, -ria *adj* : admonitory
ADN *nm* : DNA
adobar *vt* : to marinate
adobe *nm* : adobe
adobo *nm* **1** : marinade, seasoning **2** *Mex* : spicy marinade used for cooking pork
adoctrinamiento *nm* : indoctrination
adoctrinar *vt* : to indoctrinate
adolecer {53} *vi* PADECER : to suffer <adolece de timidez : he suffers from shyness>
adolescencia *nf* : adolescence
adolescente[1] *adj* : adolescent, teenage
adolescente[2] *nmf* : adolescent, teenager
adonde *conj* : where <el lugar adonde vamos es bello : the place where we're going is beautiful>
adónde *adv* : where <¿adónde vamos? : where are we going?>
adondequiera *adv* : wherever, anywhere <adondequiera que vayas : anywhere you go>
adopción *nf, pl* **-ciones** : adoption
adoptar *vt* **1** : to adopt (a measure), to take (a decision) **2** : to adopt (children)
adoptivo, -va *adj* **1** : adopted (children, country) **2** : adoptive (parents)
adoquín *nm, pl* **-quines** : paving stone, cobblestone
adorable *adj* : adorable, lovable
adoración *nf, pl* **-ciones** : adoration, worship
adorador[1], -dora *adj* : adoring, worshipping
adorador[2], -dora *n* : worshipper
adorar *vt* : to adore, to worship
adormecer {53} *vt* **1** : to make sleepy, to lull to sleep **2** : to numb — **ador-**

mecerse *vr* **1 :** to doze off **2 :** to go numb
adormecimiento *nm* **1** SUEÑO **:** drowsiness, sleepiness **2** INSENSIBILIDAD **:** numbness
adormilarse *vr* **:** to doze, to drowse
adornar *vt* DECORAR **:** to decorate, to adorn
adorno *nm* **:** ornament, decoration
adquirido, -da *adj* **1 :** acquired **2 mal adquirido :** ill-gotten
adquirir {4} *vt* **1 :** to acquire, to gain **2** COMPRAR **:** to purchase
adquisición *nf, pl* **-ciones 1 :** acquisition **2** COMPRA **:** purchase
adquisitivo, -va *adj* **poder adquisitivo :** purchasing power
adrede *adv* **:** intentionally, on purpose
adrenalina *nf* **:** adrenaline
adscribir {33} *vt* **:** to assign, to appoint — **adscribirse** *vr* **~ a :** to become a member of
adscripción *nf, pl* **-ciones :** assignment, appointment
adscrito *pp* → **adscribir**
aduana *nf* **:** customs, customs office
aduanero¹, -ra *adj* **:** customs
aduanero², -ra *n* **:** customs officer
aducir {61} *vt* **:** to adduce, to offer as proof
adueñarse *vr* **~ de :** to take possession of, to take over
adulación *nf, pl* **-ciones :** adulation, flattery
adulador¹, -dora *adj* **:** flattering
adulador², -dora *n* **:** flatterer, toady
adular *vt* LISONJEAR **:** to flatter
adulteración *nf, pl* **-ciones :** adulteration
adulterar *vt* **:** to adulterate
adulterio *nm* **:** adultery
adúltero¹, -ra *adj* **:** adulterous
adúltero², -ra *n* **:** adulterer
adultez *nf* **:** adulthood
adulto, -ta *adj & n* **:** adult
adusto, -ta *adj* **:** harsh, severe
advenedizo, -za *n* **1 :** upstart, parvenu **2 :** newcomer
advenimiento *nm* **:** advent
adventicio, -cia *adj* **:** adventitious
adverbio *nm* **:** adverb — **adverbial** *adj*
adversario¹, -ria *adj* **:** opposing, contrary
adversario², -ria *n* OPOSITOR **:** adversary, opponent
adversidad *nf* **:** adversity
adverso, -sa *adj* DESFAVORABLE **:** adverse, unfavorable — **adversamente** *adv*
advertencia *nf* AVISO **:** warning
advertir {76} *vt* **1** AVISAR **:** to warn **2 :** to notice, to tell <no advertí que estuviera enojada : I couldn't tell she was angry>
adviento *nm* **:** Advent
adyacente *adj* **:** adjacent
aéreo, -rea *adj* **1 :** aerial, air **2 correo aéreo :** airmail
aeróbic *nm* **:** aerobics
aeróbico, -ca *adj* **:** aerobic
aerobio, -bia *adj* **:** aerobic
aerodinámica *nf* **:** aerodynamics
aerodinámico, -ca *adj* **:** aerodynamic, streamlined
aeródromo *nm* **:** airfield
aeroespacial *adj* **:** aerospace
aerolínea *nf* **:** airline
aeromozo, -za *n* **:** flight attendant, steward *m*, stewardess *f*
aeronáutica *nf* **:** aeronautics
aeronáutico, -ca *adj* **:** aeronautical
aeronave *nf* **:** aircraft
aeropostal *adj* **:** airmail
aeropuerto *nm* **:** airport
aerosol *nm* **:** aerosol, aerosol spray
aeróstata *nmf* **:** baloonist
aerotransportado, -da *adj* **:** airborne
aerotransportar *vt* **:** to airlift
afabilidad *nf* **:** affability
afable *adj* **:** affable — **afablemente** *adv*
afamado, -da *adj* **:** well-known, famous
afán *nm, pl* **afanes 1** ANHELO **:** eagerness, desire **2** EMPEÑO **:** effort, determination
afanador, -dora *n Mex* **:** cleaning person, cleaner
afanarse *vr* **:** to toil, to strive
afanosamente *adv* **:** zealously, industriously, busily
afanoso, -sa *adj* **1 :** eager, industrious **2 :** arduous, hard
afear *vt* **:** to make ugly, to disfigure
afección *nf, pl* **-ciones 1 :** fondness, affection **2 :** illness, complaint
afectación *nf, pl* **-ciones :** affectation
afectado, -da *adj* **1 :** affected, mannered **2 :** influenced **3 :** afflicted **4 :** feigned
afectar *vt* **1 :** to affect **2 :** to upset **3 :** to feign, to pretend
afectísimo, -ma *adj* **suyo afectísimo :** yours truly
afectivo, -va *adj* **:** emotional
afecto¹, -ta *adj* **1 :** affected, afflicted **2 :** fond, affectionate
afecto² *nm* CARIÑO **:** affection
afectuoso, -sa *adj* CARIÑOSO **:** affectionate, caring
afeitar *vt* RASURAR **:** to shave — **afeitarse** *vr*
afelpado, -da *adj* **:** plush
afeminado, -da *adj* **:** effeminate
aferrado, -da *adj* **:** obstinate, stubborn
aferrarse {55} *vr* **:** to cling, to hold on
AFI *nm* (*Alfabeto Fonético Internacional*) **:** IPA
affidávit *nm, pl* **-dávits :** affidavit
afgano, -na *adj & n* **:** Afghan
afianzar {21} *vt* **1 :** to secure, to strengthen **2 :** to guarantee, to vouch for — **afianzarse** *vr* ESTABLECERSE **:** to establish oneself
afiche *nm* **:** poster
afición *nf, pl* **-ciones 1 :** enthusiasm, penchant, fondness <afición al de-

porte : love of sports> 2 PASATIEMPO : hobby
aficionado[1], -da *adj* ENTUSIASTA : enthusiastic, keen
aficionado[2], -da *n* **1** ENTUSIASTA : enthusiast, fan **2** : amateur
áfido *nm* : aphid
afiebrado, -da *adj* : feverish
afilado, -da *adj* **1** : sharp **2** : long, pointed <una nariz afilada : a sharp nose>
afilador *nm* : sharpener
afilalápices *nms & pl* : pencil sharpener
afilar *vt* : to sharpen
afiliación *nf, pl* **-ciones** : affiliation
afiliado[1], -da *adj* : affiliated
afiliado[2], -da *n* : member
afiliarse *vr* : to become a member, to join, to affiliate
afín *adj, pl* **afines 1** PARECIDO : related, similar <la biología y disciplinas afines : biology and related disciplines> **2** PRÓXIMO : adjacent, nearby
afinación *nf, pl* **-ciones 1** : tune-up **2** : tuning (of an instrument)
afinador, -dora *n* : tuner (of musical instruments)
afinar *vt* **1** : to perfect, to refine **2** : to tune (an instrument) — *vi* : to sing or play in tune
afincarse {72} *vr* : to establish oneself, to settle in
afinidad *nf* : affinity, similarity
afirmación *nf, pl* **-ciones 1** : statement **2** : affirmation
afirmar *vt* **1** : to state, to affirm **2** REFORZAR : to make firm, to strengthen
afirmativo, -va *adj* : affirmative — **afirmativamente** *adj*
aflicción *nf, pl* **-ciones** DESCONSUELO, PESAR : grief, sorrow
afligido, -da *adj* : grief-stricken, sorrowful
afligir {35} *vt* **1** : to distress, to upset **2** : to afflict — **afligirse** *vr* : to grieve
aflojar *vt* **1** : to loosen, to slacken **2** *fam* : to pay up, to fork over — *vi* : to slacken, to ease up — **aflojarse** *vr* : to become loose, to slacken
afloramiento *nm* : outcropping, emergence
aflorar *vi* : to come to the surface, to emerge
afluencia *nf* **1** : flow, influx **2** : abundance, plenty
afluente *nm* : tributary
afluir {41} *vi* **1** : to flock <la gente afluía a la frontera : people were flocking to the border> **2** : to flow
aforismo *nm* : aphorism
aforo *nm* **1** : appraisal, assessment **2** : maximum capacity (of a theater, highway, etc.)
afortunado, -da *adj* : fortunate, lucky — **afortunadamente** *adv*
afrecho *nm* : bran, mash
afrenta *nf* : affront, insult
afrentar *vt* : to affront, to dishonor, to insult
africano, -na *adj & n* : African
afroamericano, -na *adj & n* : Afro-American
afrodisiaco *or* **afrodisíaco** *nm* : aphrodisiac
afrontamiento *nm* : confrontation
afrontar *vt* : to confront, to face up to
afrutado, -da *adj* : fruity
afuera *adv* **1** : out <¡afuera! : get out!> **2** : outside, outdoors
afueras *nfpl* ALEDAÑOS : outskirts
agachadiza *nf* : snipe (bird)
agachar *vt* : to lower (a part of the body) <agachar la cabeza : to bow one's head> — **agacharse** *vr* : to crouch, to stoop, to bend down
agalla *nf* **1** BRANQUIA : gill **2 tener agallas** *fam* : to have guts, to have courage
agarradera *nf* ASA, ASIDERO : handle, grip
agarrado, -da *adj fam* : cheap, stingy
agarrar *vt* **1** : to grab, to grasp **2** : to catch, to take — *vi* **agarrar y** *fam* : to do (something) abruptly <el día siguiente agarró y se fue : the next day he up and left> — **agarrarse** *vr* **1** : to hold on, to cling **2** *fam* : to get into a fight <se agarraron a golpes : they came to blows>
agarre *nm* : grip, grasp
agasajar *vt* : to fête, to wine and dine
agasajo *nm* : lavish attention
ágata *nf* : agate
agave *nm* : agave
agazaparse *vr* **1** AGACHARSE : to crouch **2** : to hide
agencia *nf* : agency, office
agenciar *vt* : to obtain, to procure — **agenciarse** *vr* : to manage, to get by
agenda *nf* **1** : agenda **2** : appointment book
agente *nmf* **1** : agent **2 agente de viajes** : travel agent **3 agente de bolsa** : stockbroker **4 agente de tráfico** : traffic officer
agigantado, -da *adj* GIGANTESCO : gigantic
agigantar *vt* **1** : to increase greatly, to enlarge **2** : to exaggerate
ágil *adj* **1** : agile, nimble **2** : sharp, lively (of a response, etc.) — **ágilmente** *adv*
agilidad *nf* : agility, nimbleness
agilizar {21} *vt* ACELERAR : to expedite, to speed up
agitación *nf, pl* **-ciones 1** : agitation **2** NERVIOSISMO : nervousness
agitado, -da *adj* **1** : agitated, excited **2** : choppy, rough, turbulent
agitador, -dora *n* PROVOCADOR : agitator
agitar *vt* **1** : to agitate, to shake **2** : to wave, to flap **3** : to stir up — **agitarse** *vr* **1** : to toss about, to flap around **2** : to get upset

aglomeración *nf, pl* **-ciones 1** : conglomeration, mass **2** GENTÍO : crowd
aglomerar *vt* : to cluster, to amass — **aglomerarse** *vr* : to crowd together
aglutinar *vt* : to bring together, to bind
agnóstico, -ca *adj & n* : agnostic
agobiado, -da *adj* : weary, worn-out, weighted-down
agobiante *adj* **1** : exhausting, overwhelming **2** : stifling, oppressive
agobiar *vt* **1** OPRIMIR : to oppress, to burden **2** ABRUMAR : to overwhelm **3** : to wear out, to exhaust
agonía *nf* : agony, death throes
agonizante *adj* : dying
agonizar {21} *vi* **1** : to be dying **2** : to be in agony **3** : to dim, to fade
agorero, -ra *adj* : ominous
agostar *vt* **1** : to parch **2** : to wither — **agostarse** *vr*
agosto *nm* **1** : August **2 hacer uno su agosto** : to make a fortune, to make a killing
agotado, -da *adj* **1** : exhausted, used up **2** : sold out **3** FATIGADO : worn-out, tired
agotador, -dora *adj* : exhausting
agotamiento *nm* FATIGA : exhaustion
agotar *vt* **1** : to exhaust, to use up **2** : to weary, to wear out — **agotarse** *vr*
agraciado¹, -da *adj* **1** : attractive **2** : fortunate
agraciado², -da *n* : winner
agradable *adj* GRATO, PLACENTERO : pleasant, agreeable — **agradablemente** *adv*
agradar *vi* : to be pleasing <nos agradó mucho el resultado : we were very pleased with the result>
agradecer {53} *vt* **1** : to be grateful for **2** : to thank
agradecido, -da *adj* : grateful, thankful
agradecimiento *nm* : gratitude, thankfulness
agrado *nm* **1** GUSTO : taste, liking <no es de su agrado : it's not to his liking> **2** : graciousness, agreeableness **3 con ~** : with pleasure, willingly <lo haré con agrado : I will be happy to do it>
agrandar *vt* **1** : to exaggerate **2** : to enlarge — **agrandarse** *vr*
agrario, -ria *adj* : agrarian, agricultural
agravación *nf, pl* **-ciones** : aggravation, worsening
agravante *adj* : aggravating
agravar *vt* **1** : to increase (weight), to make heavier **2** EMPEORAR : to aggravate, to worsen — **agravarse** *vr*
agraviar *vt* INJURIAR, OFENDER : to offend, to insult
agravio *nm* INJURIA : affront, offense, insult
agredir {1} *vt* : to assail, to attack
agregado¹, -da *n* **1** : attaché **2** : assistant professor
agregado² *nm* **1** : aggregate **2** AÑADIDURA : addition, something added
agregar {52} *vt* **1** AÑADIR : to add, to attach **2** : to appoint — **agregarse** *vr* : to join
agresión *nf, pl* **-siones 1** : aggression **2** ATAQUE : attack
agresividad *nf* : aggressiveness, aggression
agresivo, -va *adj* : aggressive — **agresivamente** *adv*
agresor¹, -sora *adj* : hostile, attacking
agresor², -sora *n* **1** : aggressor **2** : assailant, attacker
agreste *adj* **1** CAMPESTRE : rural **2** : wild, untamed
agriar *vt* **1** : to sour, to make sour **2** : to embitter — **agriarse** *vr* : to turn sour
agrícola *adj* : agricultural
agricultor, -tora *n* : farmer, grower
agricultura *nf* : agriculture, farming
agridulce *adj* **1** : bittersweet **2** : sweet-and-sour
agrietar *vt* : to crack — **agrietarse** *vr* **1** : to crack **2** : to chap
agrimensor, -sora *n* : surveyor
agrimensura *nf* : surveying
agrio, agria *adj* **1** ÁCIDO : sour **2** : caustic, acrimonious
agriparse *vr* : to catch the flu
agroindustria *nf* : agribusiness
agronomía *nf* : agronomy
agropecuario, -ria *adj* : pertaining to livestock and agriculture
agrupación *nf, pl* **-ciones** GRUPO : group, association
agrupamiento *nm* : grouping, concentration
agrupar *vt* : to group together
agua *nf* **1** : water **2 agua oxigenada** : hydrogen peroxide **3 aguas negras** *or* **aguas residuales** : sewage **4 como agua para chocolate** *Mex fam* : furious **5 echar aguas** *Mex fam* : to keep an eye out, to be on the lookout
aguacate *nm* : avocado
aguacero *nm* : shower, downpour
aguado, -da *adj* **1** DILUIDO : watered-down, diluted **2** *CA, Col, Mex fam* : soft, flabby **3** *Mex, Peru fam* : dull, boring
aguafiestas *nmfs & pl* : killjoy, stick-in-the-mud, spoilsport
aguafuerte *nm* : etching
aguamanil *nm* : ewer, pitcher
aguanieve *nf* : sleet <caer aguanieve : to be sleeting>
aguantar *vt* **1** SOPORTAR : to bear, to tolerate, to withstand **2** : to hold **3 aguantar las ganas** : to resist an urge <no pude aguantar las ganas de reír : I couldn't keep myself from laughing> — *vi* : to hold out, to last — **aguantarse** *vr* **1** : to resign oneself **2** : to restrain oneself
aguante *nm* **1** TOLERANCIA : tolerance, patience **2** RESISTENCIA : endurance, strength
aguar {10} *vt* **1** : to water down, to dilute **2 aguar la fiesta** *fam* : to spoil the party

aguardar *vt* ESPERAR **:** to wait for, to await — *vi* **:** to be in store
aguardiente *nm* **:** clear brandy
aguarrás *nm* **:** turpentine
agudeza *nf* **1 :** keenness, sharpness **2 :** shrillness **3 :** witticism
agudizar {21} *vt* **:** to intensify, to heighten
agudo, -da *adj* **1 :** acute, sharp **2 :** shrill, high-pitched **3** PERSPICAZ **:** clever, shrewd
agüero *nm* AUGURIO, PRESAGIO **:** augury, omen
aguijón *nm, pl* **-jones 1 :** stinger (of a bee, etc.) **2 :** goad
aguijonear *vt* **:** to goad
águila *nf* **1 :** eagle **2 águila o sol** *Mex* **:** heads or tails
aguileño, -ña *adj* **:** aquiline
aguilera *nf* **:** aerie, eagle's nest
aguilón *nm, pl* **-lones :** gable
aguinaldo *nm* **1 :** Christmas bonus, year-end bonus **2** *PRi, Ven* **:** Christmas carol
agüitarse *vr Mex fam* **:** to have the blues, to feel discouraged
aguja *nf* **1 :** needle **2 :** steeple, spire
agujerear *vt* **:** to make a hole in, to pierce
agujero *nm* **1 :** hole **2 agujero negro :** black hole (in astronomy)
agujeta *nf* **1** *Mex* **:** shoelace **2 agujetas** *nfpl* **:** muscular soreness or stiffness
agusanado, -da *adj* **:** worm-eaten
aguzar {21} *vt* **1 :** to sharpen <aguzar el ingenio : to sharpen one's wits> **2 aguzar el oído :** to prick up one's ears
ahí *adv* **1 :** there <ahí está : there it is> **2 por ~ :** somewhere, thereabouts **3 de ahí que :** with the result that, so that
ahijado, -da *n* **:** godchild, godson *m*, goddaughter *f*
ahijar {5} *vt* **:** to adopt (a child)
ahínco *nm* **:** eagerness, zeal
ahogar {52} *vt* **1 :** to drown **2 :** to smother **3 :** to choke back, to stifle — **ahogarse** *vr*
ahogo *nm* **:** breathlessness, suffocation
ahondar *vt* **:** to deepen — *vi* **:** to elaborate, to go into detail
ahora *adv* **1 :** now **2 ahora mismo :** right now **3 hasta ~ :** so far **4 por ~ :** for the time being
ahorcar {72} *vt* **:** to hang, to kill by hanging — **ahorcarse** *vr*
ahorita *adv fam* **:** right now, right away
ahorquillado, -da *adj* **:** forked
ahorrador, -dora *adj* **:** thrifty
ahorrar *vt* **1 :** to save (money) **2 :** to spare, to conserve — *vi* **:** to save up — **ahorrarse** *vr* **:** to spare oneself
ahorrativo, -va *adj* **:** thrifty, frugal
ahorro *nm* **:** saving <cuenta de ahorros : savings account>
ahuecar {72} *vt* **1 :** to hollow out **2 :** to cup (one's hands) **3 :** to plump up, to fluff up
ahuizote *nm Mex fam* **:** annoying person, pain in the neck
ahumar {8} *vt* **:** to smoke, to cure
ahuyentar *vt* **1 :** to scare away, to chase away **2 :** to banish, to dispel <ahuyentar las dudas : to dispel doubts>
airado, -da *adj* FURIOSO **:** angry, irate
airar {5} *vt* **:** to make angry, to anger
aire *nm* **1 :** air **2 aire acondicionado :** air-conditioning **3 darse aires :** to give oneself airs
airear *vt* **:** to air, to air out — **airearse** *vr* **:** to get some fresh air
airoso, -sa *adj* **1 :** elegant, graceful **2 salir airoso :** to come out winning
aislacionismo *nm* **:** isolationism
aislacionista *adj & nmf* **:** isolationist
aislado, -da *adj* **:** isolated, alone
aislamiento *nm* **1 :** isolation **2 :** insulation
aislante *nm* **:** insulator, nonconductor
aislar {5} *vt* **1 :** to isolate **2 :** to insulate
ajado, -da *adj* **1 :** worn, shabby **2 :** wrinkled, crumpled
ajar *vt* **:** to wear out, to spoil
ajardinado, -da *adj* **:** landscaped
ajedrecista *nmf* **:** chess player
ajedrez *nm, pl* **-dreces 1 :** chess **2 :** chess set
ajeno, -na *adj* **1 :** alien **2 :** of another, of others <propiedad ajena : somebody else's property> **3 ~ a :** foreign to **4 ~ de :** devoid of, free from
ajetreado, -da *adj* **:** hectic, busy
ajetrearse *vr* **:** to bustle about, to rush around
ajetreo *nm* **:** hustle and bustle, fuss
ají *nm, pl* **ajíes :** chili pepper
ajo *nm* **:** garlic
ajonjolí *nm, pl* **-líes :** sesame
ajuar *nm* **:** trousseau
ajustable *adj* **:** adjustable
ajustado, -da *adj* **1** CEÑIDO **:** tight, tight-fitting **2 :** reasonable, fitting
ajustar *vt* **1 :** to adjust, to adapt **2 :** to take in (clothing) **3 :** to settle, to resolve — **ajustarse** *vr* **:** to fit, to conform
ajuste *nm* **1 :** adjustment **2 :** tightening
ajusticiar *vt* EJECUTAR **:** to execute, to put to death
al (*contraction of* **a** *and* **el**) → **a**[2]
ala *nf* **1 :** wing **2 :** brim (of a hat)
Alá *nm* **:** Allah
alabanza *nf* ELOGIO **:** praise
alabar *vt* **:** to praise — **alabarse** *vr* **:** to boast
alabastro *nm* **:** alabaster
alabear *vt* **:** to warp — **alabearse** *vr*
alabeo *nm* **:** warp, warping
alacena *nf* **:** cupboard, larder
alacrán *nm, pl* **-cranes** ESCORPIÓN **:** scorpion
alado, -da *adj* **:** winged
alambique *nm* **:** still (to distill alcohol)
alambre *nm* **1 :** wire **2 alambre de púas :** barbed wire

alameda *nf* **1 :** poplar grove **2 :** tree-lined avenue
álamo *nm* **1 :** poplar **2 álamo temblón :** aspen
alar *nm* **:** eaves *pl*
alarde *nm* **1 :** show, display **2 hacer alarde de :** to make show of, to boast about
alardear *vi* PRESUMIR **:** to boast, to brag
alargado, -da *adj* **:** elongated, slender
alargamiento *nm* **:** lengthening, extension, elongation
alargar {52} *vt* **1 :** to extend, to lengthen **2** PROLONGAR **:** to prolong — **alargarse** *vr*
alarido *nm* **:** howl, shriek
alarma *nf* **:** alarm
alarmante *adj* **:** alarming — **alarmantemente** *adv*
alarmar *vt* **:** to alarm
alazán *nm, pl* **-zanes :** sorrel (color or animal)
alba *nf* AMANECER **:** dawn, daybreak
albacea *nmf* TESTAMENTARIO **:** executor, executrix *f*
albahaca *nf* **:** basil
albanés, -nesa *adj & n, mpl* **-neses :** Albanian
albañil *nmf* **:** bricklayer, mason
albañilería *nf* **:** bricklaying, masonry
albaricoque *nm* **:** apricot
albatros *nm* **:** albatross
albedrío *nm* **:** will <libre albedrío : free will>
alberca *nf* **1 :** reservoir, tank **2** *Mex* **:** swimming pool
albergar {52} *vt* ALOJAR **:** to house, to lodge, to shelter
albergue *nm* **1 :** shelter, refuge **2 :** hostel
albino, -na *adj & n* **:** albino — **albinismo** *nm*
albóndiga *nf* **:** meatball
albor *nm* **1 :** dawning, beginning **2** BLANCURA **:** whiteness
alborada *nf* **:** dawn
alborear *v impers* **:** to dawn
alborotado, -da *adj* **1 :** excited, agitated **2 :** rowdy, unruly
alborotador[1], -dora *adj* **1 :** noisy, boisterous **2 :** rowdy, unruly
alborotador[2], -dora *n* **:** agitator, troublemaker, rioter
alborotar *vt* **1 :** to excite, to agitate **2 :** to incite, to stir up — **alborotarse** *vr* **:** to riot
alboroto *nm* **1 :** disturbance, ruckus **2** MOTÍN **:** riot
alborozado, -da *adj* **:** jubilant
alborozar {21} *vt* **:** to gladden, to cheer
alborozo *nm* **:** joy, elation
álbum *nm* **:** album <álbum de recortes : scrapbook>
albúmina *nf* **:** albumin
albur *nm* **1 :** chance, risk **2** *Mex* **:** pun
alca *nf* **:** auk
alcachofa *nf* **:** artichoke
alcahuete, -ta *n* CHISMOSO **:** gossip
alcaide *nm* **:** warden (in a prison)
alcalde, -desa *n* **:** mayor
alcaldía *nf* **1 :** mayoralty **2** AYUNTAMIENTO **:** city hall
álcali *nm* **:** alkali
alcalino, -na *adj* **:** alkaline — **alcalinidad** *nf*
alcance *nm* **1 :** reach **2 :** range, scope
alcancía *nf* **1 :** piggy bank, money box **2 :** collection box (for alms, etc.)
alcanfor *nm* **:** camphor
alcantarilla *nf* CLOACA **:** sewer, drain
alcanzar {21} *vt* **1 :** to reach **2 :** to catch up with **3** LOGRAR **:** to achieve, to attain — *vi* **1** DAR **:** to suffice, to be enough **2 ~ a :** to manage to
alcaparra *nf* **:** caper
alcapurria *nf PRi* **:** stuffed fritter made with taro and green banana
alcaravea *nf* **:** caraway
alcatraz *nm, pl* **-traces :** gannet
alcázar *nm* **:** fortress, castle
alce[1], etc. → **alzar**
alce[2] *nm* **:** moose, European elk
alcoba *nf* **:** bedroom
alcohol *nm* **:** alcohol
alcohólico, -ca *adj & n* **:** alcoholic
alcoholismo *nm* **:** alcoholism
alcoholizarse {21} *vr* **:** to become an alcoholic
alcornoque *nm* **1 :** cork oak **2** *fam* **:** idiot, fool
alcurnia *nf* **:** ancestry, lineage
aldaba *nf* **:** door knocker
aldea *nf* **:** village
aldeano[1], -na *adj* **:** village, rustic
aldeano[2], -na *n* **:** villager
aleación *nf, pl* **-ciones :** alloy
alear *vt* **:** to alloy
aleatorio, -ria *adj* **:** random, fortuitous — **aleatoriamente** *adv*
alebrestar *vt* **:** to excite, to make nervous — **alebrestarse** *vr*
aledaño, -ña *adj* **:** bordering, neighboring
aledaños *nmpl* AFUERAS **:** outskirts, surrounding area
alegar {52} *vt* **:** to assert, to allege — *vi* DISCUTIR **:** to argue
alegato *nm* **1 :** allegation, claim **2** *Mex* **:** argument, summation (in law) **3 :** argument, dispute
alegoría *nf* **:** allegory
alegórico, -ca *adj* **:** allegorical
alegrar *vt* **:** to make happy, to cheer up — **alegrarse** *vr* **:** to be glad, to rejoice
alegre *adj* **1 :** glad, cheerful **2 :** colorful, bright **3** *fam* **:** tipsy
alegremente *adv* **:** happily, cheerfully
alegría *nf* **:** joy, cheer, happiness
alejado, -da *adj* **:** remote
alejamiento *nm* **1 :** removal, separation **2 :** estrangement
alejar *vt* **1 :** to remove, to move away **2 :** to estrange, to alienate — **alejarse** *vr* **1 :** to move away, to stray **2 :** to drift apart
alelado, -da *adj* **1 :** bewildered, stupefied **2 :** foolish, stupid
aleluya *interj* **:** hallelujah!, alleluia!

alemán[1], **-mana** *adj & n, mpl* **-manes** : German
alemán[2] *nm* : German (language)
alentador, -dora *adj* : encouraging
alentar {55} *vt* : to encourage, to inspire — *vi* : to breathe
alerce *nm* : larch
alérgeno *nm* : allergen
alergia *nf* : allergy
alérgico, -ca *adj* : allergic
alergista *nmf* : allergist
alero *nm* **1** : eaves *pl* **2** : forward (in basketball)
alerón *nm, pl* **-rones** : aileron
alerta[1] *adv* : on the alert
alerta[2] *nf* : alert, alarm
alertar *vt* : to alert
alerto, -ta *adj* : alert, watchful
aleta *nf* **1** : fin **2** : flipper **3** : small wing
aletargado, -da *adj* : lethargic, sluggish, torpid
aletargarse {52} *vr* : to feel drowsy, to become lethargic
aleteo *nm* : flapping, flutter
alevosía *nf* **1** : treachery **2** : premeditation
alevoso, -sa *adj* : treacherous
alfabético, -ca *adj* : alphabetical — **alfabéticamente** *adv*
alfabetismo *nm* : literacy
alfabetizado, -da *adj* : literate
alfabetizar {21} *vt* : to alphabetize
alfabeto *nm* : alphabet
alfalfa *nf* : alfalfa
alfanje *nm* : cutlass, scimitar
alfarería *nf* : pottery
alfarero, -ra *n* : potter
alféizar *nm* : sill, windowsill
alfeñique *nm fam* : wimp, weakling
alférez *nmf, pl* **-reces 1** : second lieutenant **2** : ensign
alfiler *nm* **1** : pin **2** BROCHE : brooch
alfiletero *nm* : pincushion
alfombra *nf* : carpet, rug
alfombrado *nm* : carpeting
alfombrar *vt* : to carpet
alfombrilla *nf* : small rug, mat
alforfón *nm, pl* **-fones** : buckwheat
alforja *nf* : saddlebag
alforza *nf* : pleat, tuck
alga *nf* **1** : aquatic plant, alga **2** : seaweed
algáceo, -cea *adj* : algal
algarabía *nf* **1** : gibberish, babble **2** : hubbub, uproar
álgebra *nf* : algebra
algebraico, -ca *adj* : algebraic
álgido, -da *adj* **1** : critical, decisive **2** : icy cold
algo[1] *adv* : somewhat, rather <es simpático, pero algo tacaño : he's nice but rather stingy>
algo[2] *pron* **1** : something **2 ~ de** : some, a little <tengo algo de dinero : I've got some money>
algodón *nm, pl* **-dones** : cotton
algoritmo *nm* : algorithm
alguacil *nm* : constable
alguien *pron* : somebody, someone
alguno[1], **-na** *adj* (**algún** *before masculine singular nouns*) **1** : some, any <algún día : someday, one day> **2** (*in negative constructions*) : not any, not at all <no tengo noticia alguna : I have no news at all> **3 algunas veces** : sometimes
alguno[2], **-na** *pron* **1** : one, someone, somebody <alguno de ellos : one of them> **2 algunos, -nas** *pron pl* : some, a few <algunos quieren trabajar : some want to work>
alhaja *nf* : jewel, gem
alhajar *vt* : to adorn with jewels
alharaca *nf* : fuss
alhelí *nm* : wallflower
aliado[1], **-da** *adj* : allied
aliado[2], **-da** *n* : ally
alianza *nf* : alliance
aliarse {85} *vr* : to form an alliance, to ally oneself
alias *adv & nm* : alias
alicaído, -da *adj* : depressed, discouraged
alicates *nmpl* PINZAS : pliers
aliciente *nm* **1** INCENTIVO : incentive **2** ATRACCIÓN : attraction
alienación *nf, pl* **-ciones** : alienation, derangement
alienar *vt* ENAJENAR : to alienate
aliento *nm* **1** : breath **2** : courage, strength **3 dar aliento a** : to encourage
aligerar *vt* **1** : to lighten **2** ACELERAR : to hasten, to quicken
alijo *nm* : cache, consignment (of contraband)
alimaña *nf* : pest, vermin
alimentación *nf, pl* **-ciones** NUTRICIÓN : nutrition, nourishment
alimentar *vt* **1** NUTRIR : to feed, to nourish **2** MANTENER : to support (a family) **3** FOMENTAR : to nurture, to foster — **alimentarse** *vr* **~ con** : to live on
alimentario, -ria → **alimenticio**
alimenticio, -cia *adj* **1** : nutritional, food, dietary **2** : nutritious, nourishing
alimento *nm* : food, nourishment
alineación *nf, pl* **-ciones 1** : alignment **2** : lineup (in sports)
alineamiento *nm* : alignment
alinear *vt* **1** : to align **2** : to line up — **alinearse** *vr* **1** : to fall in, to line up **2 ~ con** : to align oneself with
aliño *nm* : seasoning, dressing
alipús *nm, pl* **-puses** *Mex fam* : booze, drink
alisar *vt* : to smooth
aliso *nm* : alder
alistamiento *nm* : enlistment, recruitment
alistar *vt* **1** : to recruit **2** : to make ready — **alistarse** *vr* : to join up, to enlist
aliteración *nf, pl* **-ciones** : alliteration
aliterado, -da *adj* : alliterative

aliviar *vt* MITIGAR **:** to relieve, to alleviate, to soothe — **aliviarse** *vr* **:** to recover, to get better

alivio *nm* **:** relief

aljaba *nf* **:** quiver (for arrows)

aljibe *nm* **:** cistern, well

allá *adv* **1 :** there, over there **2 más allá :** farther away **3 más allá de :** beyond **4 allá tú :** that's up to you

allanamiento *nm* **1 :** (police) raid **2 allanamiento de morada :** breaking and entering

allanar *vt* **1 :** to raid, to search **2 :** to resolve, to solve **3 :** to smooth, to level out

allegado[1], -da *adj* **:** close, intimate

allegado[2], -da *n* **:** close friend, relation <parientes y allegados : friends and relations>

allegar {52} *vt* **:** to gather, to collect

allende[1] *adv* **:** beyond, on the other side

allende[2] *prep* **:** beyond <allende las montañas : beyond the mountains>

allí *adv* **:** there, over there <allí mismo : right there> <hasta allí : up to that point>

alma *nf* **1 :** soul **2 :** person, human being **3 no tener alma :** to be pitiless **4 tener el alma en un hilo :** to have one's heart in one's mouth

almacén *nm, pl* **-cenes 1** BODEGA **:** warehouse, storehouse **2** TIENDA **:** shop, store **3 gran almacén** *Spain* **:** department store

almacenaje → **almacenamiento**

almacenamiento *nm* **:** storage <almacenamiento de datos : data storage>

almacenar *vt* **:** to store, to put in storage

almacenero, -ra *n* **:** shopkeeper

almacenista *nm* MAYORISTA **:** wholesaler

almádena *nf* **:** sledgehammer

almanaque *nm* **:** almanac

almeja *nf* **:** clam

almendra *nf* **1 :** almond **2 :** kernel

almendro *nm* **:** almond tree

almiar *nm* **:** haystack

almíbar *nm* **:** syrup

almidón *nm, pl* **-dones :** starch

almidonar *vt* **:** to starch

alminar *nm* MINARETE **:** minaret

almirante *nm* **:** admiral

almizcle *nm* **:** musk

almohada *nf* **:** pillow

almohadilla *nf* **1 :** small pillow, cushion **2 :** bag, base (in baseball)

almohadón *nm, pl* **-dones :** bolster, cushion

almohazar {21} *vt* **:** to curry (a horse)

almoneda *nf* SUBASTA **:** auction

almorranas *nfpl* HEMORROIDES **:** hemorrhoids, piles

almorzar {36} *vi* **:** to have lunch — *vt* **:** to have for lunch

almuerzo *nm* **:** lunch

alocado, -da *adj* **1 :** crazy **2 :** wild, reckless **3 :** silly, scatterbrained

alocución *nf, pl* **-ciones :** speech, address

áloe *or* **aloe** *nm* **:** aloe

alojamiento *nm* **:** lodging, accommodations *pl*

alojar *vt* ALBERGAR **:** to house, to lodge — **alojarse** *vr* **:** to lodge, to room

alondra *nf* **:** lark, skylark

alpaca *nf* **:** alpaca

alpinismo *nm* **:** mountain climbing, mountaineering

alpinista *nmf* **:** mountain climber

alpino, -na *adj* **:** Alpine, alpine

alpiste *nm* **:** birdseed

alquilar *vt* ARRENDAR **:** to rent, to lease

alquiler *nm* ARRENDAMIENTO **:** rent, rental

alquimia *nf* **:** alchemy

alquimista *nmf* **:** alchemist

alquitrán *nm, pl* **-tranes** BREA **:** tar

alquitranar *vt* **:** to tar, to cover with tar

alrededor[1] *adv* **1 :** around, about <todo temblaba alrededor : all around things were shaking> **2 ~ de :** around, approximately <alrededor de quince personas : around fifteen people>

alrededor[2] *prep* **~ de :** around, about <corrió alrededor de la casa : she ran around the house> <llegaré alrededor de diciembre : I will get there around December>

alrededores *nmpl* ALEDAÑOS **:** surroundings, outskirts

alta *nf* **1 :** admission, entry, enrollment **2 dar de alta :** to release, to discharge (a patient)

altanería *nf* ALTIVEZ, ARROGANCIA **:** arrogance, haughtiness

altanero, -ra *adj* ALTIVO, ARROGANTE **:** arrogant, haughty — **altaneramente** *adv*

altar *nm* **:** altar

altavoz *nm, pl* **-voces** ALTOPARLANTE **:** loudspeaker

alteración *nf, pl* **-ciones 1** MODIFICACIÓN **:** alteration, modification **2** PERTURBACIÓN **:** disturbance, disruption

alterado, -da *adj* **:** upset

alterar *vt* **1** MODIFICAR **:** to alter, to modify **2** PERTURBAR **:** to disturb, to disrupt — **alterarse** *vr* **:** to get upset, to get worked up

altercado *nm* DISCUSIÓN, DISPUTA **:** altercation, argument, dispute

alternador *nm* **:** alternator

alternancia *nf* **:** alternation, rotation

alternar *vi* **1 :** to alternate **2 :** to mix, to socialize — *vt* **:** to alternate — **alternarse** *vr* **:** to take turns

alternativa *nf* OPCIÓN **:** alternative, option

alternativo, -va *adj* **1 :** alternating **2 :** alternative — **alternativamente** *adv*

alterno, -na *adj* **:** alternate <corriente alterna : alternating current>

alteza *nf* **1 :** loftiness, lofty height **2 Alteza :** Highness

altibajos *nmpl* **1 :** unevenness (of terrain) **2 :** ups and downs
altímetro *nm* **:** altimeter
altiplano *nm* **:** high plateau
altisonante *adj* **1 :** pompous, affected (of language) **2** *Mex* **:** rude, obscene (of language)
altitud *nf* **:** altitude
altivez *nf, pl* **-veces** ALTANERÍA, ARROGANCIA **:** arrogance, haughtiness
altivo, -va *adj* ALTANERO, ARROGANTE **:** arrogant, haughty
alto[1] *adv* **1 :** high **2 :** loud, loudly
alto[2], -ta *adj* **1 :** tall, high **2 :** loud <en voz alta : aloud, out loud>
alto[3] *nm* **1** ALTURA **:** height, elevation **2 :** stop, halt **3 altos** *nmpl* **:** upper floors
alto[4] *interj* **:** halt!, stop!
altoparlante *nm* ALTAVOZ **:** loudspeaker
altozano *nm* **:** hillock
altruismo *nm* **:** altruism
altruista[1] *adj* **:** altruistic
altruista[2] *nmf* **:** altruist
altura *nf* **1 :** height **2 :** altitude **3 :** loftiness, nobleness **4 a la altura de :** near, up by <en la avenida San Antonio a la altura de la Calle Tres : on San Antonio Avenue up near Third Street> **5 a estas alturas :** at this point, at this stage of the game
alubia *nf* **:** kidney bean
alucinación *nf, pl* **-ciones :** hallucination
alucinante *adj* **:** hallucinatory
alucinar *vi* **:** to hallucinate
alucinógeno[1], -na *adj* **:** hallucinogenic
alucinógeno[2] *nm* **:** hallucinogen
alud *nm* AVALANCHA **:** avalanche, landslide
aludido, -da *n* **1 :** person in question <el aludido : the aforesaid> **2 darse por aludido :** to take personally
aludir *vi* **:** to allude, to refer
alumbrado *nm* ILUMINACIÓN **:** lighting
alumbramiento *nm* **1 :** lighting **2 :** childbirth
alumbrar *vt* **1** ILUMINAR **:** to light, to illuminate **2 :** to give birth to
alumbre *nm* **:** alum
aluminio *nm* **:** aluminum
alumnado *nm* **:** student body
alumno, -na *n* **1 :** pupil, student **2 ex–alumno, -na :** alumnus, alumna *f* **3 ex–alumnos, -nas** *npl* **:** alumni, alumnae *f*
alusión *nf, pl* **-siones :** allusion, reference
alusivo, -va *adj* **1 :** allusive **2 ~ a :** in reference to, regarding
aluvión *nm, pl* **-viones :** flood, barrage
alza *nf* SUBIDA **:** rise <precios en alza : rising prices>
alzamiento *nm* LEVANTAMIENTO **:** uprising, insurrection
alzar {21} *vt* **1** ELEVAR, LEVANTAR **:** to lift, to raise **2 :** to erect — **alzarse** *vr* LEVANTARSE **:** to rise up
ama *nf* → **amo**
amabilidad *nf* **:** kindness
amable *adj* **:** kind, nice — **amablemente** *adv*
amado[1], -da *adj* **:** beloved, darling
amado[2], -da *n* **:** sweetheart, loved one
amaestrar *vt* **:** to train (animals)
amafiarse *vr Mex fam* **:** to conspire, to be in cahoots
amagar {52} *vt* **1 :** to show signs of (an illness, etc.) **2 :** to threaten — *vi* **1 :** to be imminent, to threaten **2 :** to feint, to dissemble
amago *nm* **1** AMENAZA **:** threat **2 :** sign, hint
amainar *vi* **:** to abate, to ease up, to die down
amalgama *nf* **:** amalgam
amalgamar *vt* **:** to amalgamate, to unite
amamantar *v* **:** to breast-feed, to nurse, to suckle
amanecer[1] {53} *v impers* **1 :** to dawn **2 :** to begin to show, to appear **3 :** to wake up (in the morning)
amanecer[2] *nm* ALBA **:** dawn, daybreak
amanerado, -da *adj* **:** affected, mannered
amansar *vt* **1 :** to tame **2 :** to soothe, to calm down — **amansarse** *vr*
amante[1] *adj* **:** loving, fond
amante[2] *nmf* **:** lover
amañar *vt* **:** to rig, to fix, to tamper with — **amañarse** *vr* **amañárselas :** to manage
amaño *nm* **1 :** skill, dexterity **2 :** trick, ruse
amapola *nf* **:** poppy
amar *vt* **:** to love — **amarse** *vr*
amargado, -da *adj* **:** embittered, bitter
amargar {52} *vt* **:** to make bitter, to embitter — *vi* **:** to taste bitter
amargo[1], -ga *adj* **:** bitter — **amargamente** *adv*
amargo[2] *nm* **:** bitterness, tartness
amargura *nf* **1 :** bitterness **2 :** grief, sorrow
amarilis *nf* **:** amaryllis
amarillear *vi* **:** to yellow, to turn yellow
amarillento, -ta *adj* **:** yellowish
amarillismo *nm* **:** yellow journalism, sensationalism
amarillo[1], -lla *adj* **:** yellow
amarillo[2] *nm* **:** yellow
amarra *nf* **1 :** mooring, mooring line **2 soltar las amarras de :** to loosen one's grip on
amarrar *vt* **1 :** to moor (a boat) **2** ATAR **:** to fasten, to tie up, to tie down
amartillar *vt* **:** to cock (a gun)
amasar *vt* **1 :** to amass **2 :** to knead **3 :** to mix, to prepare
amasijo *nm* **:** jumble, hodgepodge
amasio, -sia *n* **:** lover, paramour
amateur *adj & nmf* **:** amateur — **amateurismo** *nm*
amatista *nf* **:** amethyst
amatorio, -ria *adj* **:** amatory, love

amazona *nf* **1 :** Amazon (in mythology) **2 :** horsewoman

amazónico, -ca *adj* **:** amazonian

ambages *mpl* **sin ~ :** without hesitation, straight to the point

ámbar *nm* **1 :** amber **2 ámbar gris :** ambergris

ambición *nf, pl* **-ciones :** ambition

ambicionar *vt* **:** to aspire to, to seek

ambicioso, -sa *adj* **:** ambitious — **ambiciosamente** *adv*

ambidextro, -tra *adj* **:** ambidextrous

ambientación *nf, pl* **-ciones :** setting, atmosphere

ambiental *adj* **:** environmental — **ambientalmente** *adv*

ambientalista *nmf* **:** environmentalist

ambientar *vt* **:** to give atmosphere to, to set (in literature and drama) — **ambientarse** *vr* **:** to adjust, to get one's bearings

ambiente *nm* **1 :** atmosphere **2 :** environment **3 :** surroundings *pl*

ambigüedad *nf* **:** ambiguity

ambiguo, -gua *adj* **:** ambiguous

ámbito *nm* **:** domain, field, area

ambivalencia *nf* **:** ambivalence

ambivalente *adj* **:** ambivalent

ambos, -bas *adj & pron* **:** both

ambulancia *nf* **:** ambulance

ambulante *adj* **1 :** traveling, itinerant **2 vendedor ambulante :** street vendor

ameba *nf* **:** amoeba

amedrentar *vt* **:** to frighten, to intimidate — **amedrentarse** *vr*

amén *nm* **1 :** amen **2 ~ de :** in addition to, besides **3 en un decir amén :** in an instant

amenaza *nf* **:** threat, menace

amenazador, -dora *adj* **:** threatening, menacing

amenazante → **amenazador**

amenazar {21} *v* **:** to threaten

amenguar {10} *vt* **1 :** to diminish **2 :** to belittle, to dishonor

amenidad *nf* **:** pleasantness, amenity

amenizar {21} *vt* **1 :** to make pleasant **2 :** to brighten up, to add life to

ameno, -na *adj* **:** agreeable, pleasant

amento *nm* **:** catkin

americano, -na *adj & n* **:** American

amerindio, -dia *adj & n* **:** Amerindian

ameritar *vt* MERECER **:** to deserve

ametralladora *nf* **:** machine gun

amianto *nm* **:** asbestos

amiba *nf* → **ameba**

amigable *adj* **:** friendly, amicable — **amigablemente** *adv*

amígdala *nf* **:** tonsil

amigdalitis *nf* **:** tonsilitis

amigo[1], -ga *adj* **:** friendly, close

amigo[2], -ga *n* **:** friend

amigote *nm* **:** crony, pal

amilanar *vt* **1 :** to frighten **2 :** to daunt, to discourage — **amilanarse** *vr* **:** to lose heart

aminoácido *nm* **:** amino acid

aminorar *vt* **:** to reduce, to lessen — *vi* **:** to diminish

amistad *nf* **:** friendship

amistoso, -sa *adj* **:** friendly — **amistosamente** *adv*

amnesia *nf* **:** amnesia

amnésico, -ca *adj & n* **:** amnesiac, amnesic

amnistía *nf* **:** amnesty

amnistiar {85} *vt* **:** to grant amnesty to

amo, ama *n* **1 :** master *m,* mistress *f* **2 :** owner, keeper (of an animal) **3 ama de casa :** housewife **4 ama de llaves :** housekeeper

amodorrado, -da *adj* **:** drowsy

amolar {19} *vt* **1 :** to grind, to sharpen **2 :** to pester, to annoy

amoldable *adj* **:** adaptable

amoldar *vt* **1 :** to mold **2 :** to adapt, to adjust — **amoldarse** *vr*

amonestación *nf, pl* **-ciones 1** APERCIBIMIENTO **:** admonition, warning **2** AMONESTACIONES *nfpl* **:** banns

amonestar *vt* APERCIBIR **:** to admonish, to warn

amoníaco *or* **amoniaco** *nm* **:** ammonia

amontonamiento *nm* **:** accumulation, piling up

amontonar *vt* **1** APILAR **:** to pile up, to heap up **2 :** to collect, to gather **3 :** to hoard — **amontonarse** *vr*

amor *nm* **1 :** love **2 :** loved one, beloved **3 amor propio :** self-esteem **4 hacer el amor :** to make love

amoral *adj* **:** amoral

amoratado, -da *adj* **:** black-and-blue, bruised, livid

amordazar {21} *vt* **1 :** to gag, to muzzle **2 :** to silence

amorfo, -fa *adj* **:** shapeless, amorphous

amorío *nm* **:** love affair, fling

amoroso, -sa *adj* **1 :** loving, affectionate **2 :** amorous <una mirada amorosa : an amorous glance> **3 :** charming, cute — **amorosamente** *adv*

amortiguación *nf* **:** cushioning, absorption

amortiguador *nm* **:** shock absorber

amortiguar {10} *vt* **:** to soften (an impact)

amortizar {21} *vt* **:** to amortize, to pay off — **amortización** *nf*

amotinado[1], -da *adj* **:** rebellious, insurgent, mutinous

amotinado[2], -da *n* **:** rebel, insurgent, mutineer

amotinamiento *nm* **:** uprising, rebellion

amotinar *vt* **:** to incite (to riot), to agitate — **amotinarse** *vr* **1 :** to riot, to rebel **2 :** to mutiny

amparar *vt* **:** to safeguard, to protect — **ampararse** *vr* **1 ~ de :** to take shelter from **2 ~ en :** to have recourse to

amparo *nm* ACOGIDA, REFUGIO **:** protection, refuge

amperímetro *nm* **:** ammeter

amperio *nm* : ampere
ampliable *adj* : expandable, enlargeable, extendible
ampliación *nf, pl* **-ciones** : expansion, extension
ampliar {85} *vt* **1** : to expand, to extend **2** : to widen **3** : to enlarge (photographs) **4** : to elaborate on, to develop (ideas)
amplificador *nm* : amplifier
amplificar {72} *vt* : to amplify — **amplificación** *nf*
amplio, -plia *adj* : broad, wide, ample — **ampliamente** *adj*
amplitud *nf* **1** : breadth, extent **2** : spaciousness
ampolla *nf* **1** : blister **2** : vial, ampoule
ampollar *vt* : to blister — **ampollarse** *vr*
ampolleta *nf* **1** : small vial **2** : hourglass **3** *Chile* : light bulb
ampulosidad *nf* : pompousness, bombast
ampuloso, -sa *adj* GRANDILOCUENTE : pompous, bombastic — **ampulosamente** *adv*
amputar *vt* : to amputate — **amputación** *nf*
amueblar *vt* : to furnish
amuleto *nm* TALISMÁN : amulet, charm
amurallar *vt* : to wall in, to fortify
anacardo *nm* : cashew nut
anaconda *nf* : anaconda
anacrónico, -ca *adj* : anachronistic
anacronismo *nm* : anachronism
ánade *nmf* **1** : duck **2** **ánade real** : mallard
anagrama *nm* : anagram
anal *adj* : anal
anales *nmpl* : annals
analfabetismo *nm* : illiteracy
analfabeto, -ta *adj & n* : illiterate
analgésico[1], -ca *adj* : analgesic, painkilling
analgésico[2] *nm* : painkiller, analgesic
análisis *nm* : analysis
analista *nmf* **1** : analyst **2** : annalist
analítico, -ca *adj* : analytical, analytic — **analíticamente** *adv*
analizar {21} *vt* : to analyze
analogía *nf* : analogy
analógico, -ca *adj* **1** : analogical **2** : analog <computadora analógica : analog computer>
análogo, -ga *adj* : analogous, similar
ananá *or* **ananás** *nm, pl* **-nás** : pineapple
anaquel *nm* REPISA : shelf
anaranjado[1], -da *adj* NARANJA : orange-colored
anaranjado[2] *nm* NARANJA : orange (color)
anarquía *nf* : anarchy
anárquico, -ca *adj* : anarchic
anarquismo *nm* : anarchism
anarquista *adj & nmf* : anarchist
anatema *nm* : anathema
anatomía *nf* : anatomy — **anatomista** *nmf*
anatómico, -ca *adj* : anatomical — **anatómicamente** *adv*
anca *nm* **1** : haunch, hindquarter **2** **ancas de rana** : frogs' legs
ancestral *adj* **1** : ancient, traditional **2** : ancestral
ancestro *nm* ASCENDIENTE : ancestor, forefather *m*
ancho[1], -cha *adj* **1** : wide, broad **2** : ample, loose-fitting
ancho[2] *nm* : width, breadth
anchoa *nf* : anchovy
anchura *nf* : width, breadth
ancianidad *nf* SENECTUD : old age
anciano[1], -na *adj* : aged, old, elderly
anciano[2], -na *n* : elderly person
ancla *nf* : anchor
ancladero *nm* → **anclaje**
anclaje *nm* : anchorage
anclar *v* FONDEAR : to anchor
andadas *nfpl* **1** : tracks **2** **volver a las andadas** : to go back to one's old ways, to backslide
andador[1] *nm* **1** : walker, baby walker **2** *Mex* : walkway
andador[2], -dora *n* : walker, one who walks
andadura *nf* : course, journey <su agotadora andadura al campeonato : his exhausting journey to the championship>
andaluz, -luza *adj & n, mpl* **-luces** : Andalusian
andamiaje *nm* **1** : scaffolding **2** ESTRUCTURA : structure, framework
andamio *nm* : scaffold
andanada *nf* **1** : volley, broadside **2** **soltar una andanada a** : to reprimand
andanzas *nfpl* : adventures
andar[1] {6} *vi* **1** CAMINAR : to walk **2** IR : to go, to travel **3** FUNCIONAR : to run, to function <el auto anda bien : the car runs well> **4** : to ride <andar a caballo : to ride on horseback> **5** : to be <anda sin dinero : he's broke> — *vt* : to walk, to travel
andar[2] *nm* : walk, gait
andas *nfpl* : stand (for a coffin), bier
andén *nm, pl* **andenes** **1** : (train) platform **2** *CA, Col* : sidewalk
andino, -na *adj* : Andean
andorrano, -na *adj & n* : Andorran
andrajos *nmpl* : rags, tatters
andrajoso, -sa *adj* : ragged, tattered
andrógino, -na *adj* : androgynous
andurriales *nmpl* : remote place
anea *nf* : cattail
anduvo, etc. → **andar**
anécdota *nf* : anecdote
anecdótico, -ca *adj* : anecdotal
anegar {52} *vt* **1** INUNDAR : to flood **2** AHOGAR : to drown **3** : to overwhelm — **anegarse** *vr* : to be flooded
anejo *nm* → **anexo[2]**
anemia *nf* : anemia
anémico, -ca *adj* : anemic
anémona *nf* : anemone
anestesia *nf* : anesthesia

anestesiar *vt* : to anesthetize

anestésico[1], -ca *adj* : anesthetic

anestésico[2] *nm* : anesthetic

anestesista *nmf* : anesthetist

aneurisma *nmf* : aneurism

anexar *vt* : to annex, to attach

anexión *nf, pl* **-xiones** : annexation

anexo[1], -xa *adj* : attached, joined, annexed

anexo[2] *nm* **1** : annex **2** : supplement (to a book), appendix

anfetamina *nf* : amphetamine

anfibio[1], -bia *adj* : amphibious

anfibio[2] *nm* : amphibian

anfiteatro *nm* **1** : amphitheater **2** : lecture hall

anfitrión, -triona *n, mpl* **-triones** : host, hostess *f*

ánfora *nf* **1** : amphora **2** *Mex, Peru* : ballot box

ángel *nm* : angel

angelical *adj* : angelic, angelical

angina *nf* **1** *or* **angina de pecho** : angina **2** *Mex* : tonsil

anglicano, -na *adj & n* : Anglican

angloparlante[1] *adj* : English-speaking

angloparlante[2] *nmf* : English speaker

anglosajón, -jona *adj & n, mpl* **-jones** : Anglo-Saxon

angoleño, -ña *adj & n* : Angolan

angora *nf* : angora

angostar *vt* : to narrow — **angostarse** *vr*

angosto, -ta *adj* : narrow

angostura *nf* : narrowness

anguila *nf* : eel

angular *adj* : angular — **angularidad** *nf*

ángulo *nm* **1** : angle **2** : corner **3 ángulo muerto** : blind spot

anguloso, -sa *adj* : angular, sharp <una cara angulosa : an angular face> — **angulosidad** *nf*

angustia *nf* **1** CONGOJA : anguish, distress **2** : anxiety, worry

angustiar *vt* **1** : to anguish, to distress **2** : to worry — **angustiarse** *vr*

angustioso, -sa *adj* **1** : anguished, distressed **2** : distressing, worrisome

anhelante *adj* : yearning, longing

anhelar *vt* : to yearn for, to crave

anhelo *nm* : longing, yearning

anidar *vi* **1** : to nest **2** : to make one's home, to dwell — *vt* : to shelter

anillo *nm* SORTIJA : ring

ánima *n* ALMA : soul

animación *nf, pl* **-ciones** **1** : animation **2** VIVEZA : liveliness

animado, -da *adj* **1** : animated, lively **2** : cheerful — **animadamente** *adv*

animador, -dora *n* **1** : (television) host **2** : cheerleader

animadversión *nf, pl* **-siones** ANIMOSIDAD : animosity, antagonism

animal[1] *adj* **1** : animal **2** ESTÚPIDO : stupid, idiotic **3** : rough, brutish

animal[2] *nm* : animal

animal[3] *nmf* **1** IDIOTA : idiot, fool **2** : brute, beastly person

animar *vt* **1** ALENTAR : to encourage, to inspire **2** : to animate, to enliven **3** : to brighten up, to cheer up — **animarse** *vr*

anímico, -ca *adj* : mental <estado anímico : state of mind>

ánimo *nm* **1** ALMA : spirit, soul **2** : mood, spirits *pl* **3** : encouragement **4** PROPÓSITO : intention, purpose <sociedad sin ánimo de lucro : nonprofit organization> **5** : energy, vitality

animosidad *nf* ANIMADVERSIÓN : animosity, ill will

animoso, -sa *adj* : brave, spirited

aniñado, -da *adj* : childlike

aniquilación *nf* → **aniquilamiento**

aniquilamiento *nm* : annihilation, extermination

aniquilar *vt* **1** : to annihilate, to wipe out **2** : to overwhelm, to bring to one's knees — **aniquilarse** *vr*

anís *nm* **1** : anise **2 semilla de anís** : aniseed

aniversario *nm* : anniversary

ano *nm* : anus

anoche *adv* : last night

anochecer[1] {53} *v impers* : to get dark

anochecer[2] *nm* : dusk, nightfall

anodino, -na *adj* : insipid, dull

ánodo *nm* : anode

anomalía *nf* : anomaly

anómalo, -la *adj* : anomalous

anonadado, -da *adj* : dumbfounded, speechless

anonadar *vt* : to dumbfound, to stun

anonimato *nm* : anonymity

anónimo, -ma *adj* : anonymous — **anónimamente** *adv*

anorexia *nf* : anorexia

anoréxico, -ca *adj* : anorexic

anormal *adj* : abnormal — **anormalmente** *adv*

anormalidad *nf* : abnormality

anotación *nf, pl* **-ciones** **1** : annotation, note **2** : scoring (in sports) <lograron una anotación : they managed to score a goal>

anotar *vt* **1** : to annotate **2** APUNTAR, ESCRIBIR : to write down, to jot down **3** : to score (in sports) — *vi* : to score

anquilosado, -da *adj* **1** : stiff-jointed **2** : stagnated, stale

anquilosamiento *nm* **1** : stiffness (of joints) **2** : stagnation, paralysis

anquilosarse *vr* **1** : to stagnate **2** : to become stiff or paralyzed

anquilostoma *nm* : hookworm

ánsar *nm* : goose

ansarino *nm* : gosling

ansia *nf* **1** INQUIETUD : apprehensiveness, uneasiness **2** ANGUSTIA : anguish, distress **3** ANHELO : longing, yearning

ansiar {85} *vt* : to long for, to yearn for

ansiedad *nf* : anxiety

ansioso, -sa *adj* **1** : anxious, worried **2** : eager — **ansiosamente** *adv*

antagónico, -ca *adj* : conflicting, opposing

antagonismo *nm* : antagonism

antagonista[1] *adj* : antagonistic
antagonista[2] *nmf* : antagonist, opponent
antaño *adv* : yesteryear, long ago
antártico, -ca *adj* **1** : antarctic **2 círculo antártico** : antarctic circle
ante[1] *nm* **1** : elk, moose **2** : suede
ante[2] *prep* **1** : before, in front of **2** : considering, in view of **3 ante todo** : first and foremost, above all
anteanoche *adv* : the night before last
anteayer *adv* : the day before yesterday
antebrazo *nm* : forearm
antecedente[1] *adj* : previous, prior
antecedente[2] *nm* **1** : precedent **2 antecedentes** *nmpl* : record, background
anteceder *v* : to precede
antecesor, -sora *n* **1** ANTEPASADO : ancestor **2** PREDECESOR : predecessor
antedicho, -cha *adj* : aforesaid, above
antelación *nf, pl* **-ciones 1** : advance notice **2 con ~** : in advance, beforehand
antemano *adv* **de ~** : in advance <se lo agradezco de antemano : I thank you in advance>
antena *nf* : antenna
antenoche → **anteanoche**
anteojera *nf* **1** : eyeglass case **2 anteojeras** *nfpl* : blinders
anteojos *nmpl* GAFAS : glasses, eyeglasses
antepasado[1], **-da** *adj* : before last <el domingo antepasado : the Sunday before last>
antepasado[2], **-da** *n* ANTECESOR : ancestor
antepecho *nm* **1** : guardrail **2** : ledge, sill
antepenúltimo, -ma *adj* : third from last
anteponer {60} *vt* **1** : to place before <anteponer al interés de la nación el interés de la comunidad : to place the interests of the community before national interest> **2** : to prefer
anteproyecto *nm* **1** : draft, proposal **2 anteproyecto de ley** : bill
antera *nf* : anther
anterior *adj* **1** : previous **2** : earlier <tiempos anteriores : earlier times> **3** : anterior, forward, front
anterioridad *nf* **1** : priority **2 con ~** : beforehand, in advance
anteriormente *adv* : previously, beforehand
antes *adv* **1** : before, earlier **2** : formerly, previously **3** : rather, sooner <antes prefiero morir : I'd rather die> **4 ~ de** : before, previous to <antes de hoy : before today> **5 antes que** : before <antes que llegue Luis : before Luis arrives> **6 cuanto antes** : as soon as possible **7 antes bien** : on the contrary
antesala *nf* **1** : anteroom, waiting room, lobby **2** : prelude, prologue
antiaborto, -ta *adj* : antiabortion
antiácido *nm* : antacid
antiadherente *adj* : nonstick
antiaéreo, -rea *adj* : antiaircraft
antiamericano, -na *adj* : anti-American
antibalas *adj* : bulletproof
antibiótico[1], **-ca** *adj* : antibiotic
antibiótico[2] *nm* : antibiotic
antichoque *adj* : shockproof
anticipación *nf, pl* **-ciones 1** : expectation, anticipation **2 con ~** : in advance
anticipado, -da *adj* **1** : advance, early **2 por ~** : in advance
anticipar *vt* **1** : to anticipate, to forestall, to deal with in advance **2** : to pay in advance — **anticiparse** *vr* **1** : to be early **2** ADELANTARSE : to get ahead
anticipo *nm* **1** : advance (payment) **2** : foretaste, preview
anticlerical *adj* : anticlerical
anticlimático, -ca : anticlimatic
anticlímax *nm* : anticlimax
anticomunismo *nm* : anticommunism
anticomunista *adj & nmf* : anticommunist
anticoncepción *nf, pl* **-ciones** : birth control, contraception
anticonceptivo *nm* : contraceptive
anticongelante *nm* : antifreeze
anticuado, -da *adj* : antiquated, outdated
anticuario[1], **-ria** *adj* : antique, antiquarian
anticuario[2], **-ria** *n* : antiquarian, antiquary
anticuario[3] *nm* : antique shop
anticuerpo *nm* : antibody
antidemocrático, -ca *adj* : antidemocratic
antideportivo, -va *adj* : unsportsmanlike
antidepresivo *nm* : antidepressant
antídoto *nm* : antidote
antidrogas *adj* : antidrug
antier → **anteayer**
antiestético, -ca *adj* : unsightly, unattractive
antifascista *adj & nmf* : antifascist
antifaz *nm, pl* **-faces** : mask
antifeminista *adj & nmf* : antifeminist
antífona *nf* : anthem
antígeno *nm* : antigen
antigualla *nf* **1** : antique **2** : relic, old thing
antiguamente *adv* **1** : formerly, once **2** : long ago
antigüedad *nf* **1** : antiquity **2** : seniority **3** : age <con siglos de antigüedad : centuries-old> **4 antigüedades** *nfpl* : antiques
antiguo, -gua *adj* **1** : ancient, old **2** : former **3** : old-fashioned <a la antigua : in the old-fashioned way>
antihigiénico, -ca *adj* INSALUBRE : unhygienic, unsanitary
antihistamínico *nm* : antihistamine
antiimperialismo *nm* : anti-imperialism

antiimperialista *adj & nmf* : anti-imperialist

antiinflacionario, -ria *adj* : anti-inflationary

antiinflamatorio, -ria *adj* : anti-inflammatory

antillano[1], -na *adj* CARIBEÑO : Caribbean, West Indian

antillano[2], -na *n* : West Indian

antílope *nm* : antelope

antimilitarismo *nm* : antimilitarism

antimilitarista *adj & nmf* : antimilitarist

antimonio *nm* : antimony

antimonopolista *adj* : antimonopoly, antitrust

antinatural *adj* : unnatural, perverse

antipatía *nf* : aversion, dislike

antipático, -ca *adj* : obnoxious, unpleasant

antipatriótico, -ca *adj* : unpatriotic

antirrábico, -ca *adj* : antirabies <vacuna antirrábica : rabies vaccine>

antirreglamentario, -ria *adj* **1** : unlawful, illegal **2** : foul (in sports)

antirrevolucionario, -ria *adj & n* : antirevolutionary

antirrobo, -ba *adj* : antitheft

antisemita *adj* : anti-Semitic

antisemitismo *nm* : anti-Semitism

antiséptico[1], -ca *adj* : antiseptic

antiséptico[2] *nm* : antiseptic

antisocial *adj* : antisocial

antitabaco *adj* : antismoking

antiterrorista *adj* : antiterrorist

antítesis *nf* : antithesis

antitoxina *nf* : antitoxin

antitranspirante *nm* : antiperspirant

antojadizo, -za *adj* CAPRICHOSO : capricious

antojarse *vr* **1** APETECER : to be appealing, to be desirable <se me antoja un helado : I feel like having ice cream> **2** : to seem, to appear <los árboles se antojaban fantasmas : the trees seemed like ghosts>

antojitos *nmpl Mex* : traditional Mexican snack foods

antojo *nm* **1** CAPRICHO : whim **2** : craving

antología *nf* **1** : anthology **2 de ~** *fam* : fantastic, incredible

antónimo *nm* : antonym

antonomasia *nf* **por ~** : par excellence

antorcha *nf* : torch

antracita *nf* : anthracite

antro *nm* **1** : cave, den **2** : dive, seedy nightclub

antropofagia *nf* CANIBALISMO : cannibalism

antropófago[1], -ga *adj* : cannibalistic

antropófago[2], -ga *n* CANÍBAL : cannibal

antropoide *adj & nmf* : anthropoid

antropología *nf* : anthropology

antropológico, -ca *adj* : anthropological

antropólogo, -ga *n* : anthropologist

anual *adj* : annual, yearly — **anualmente** *adv*

anualidad *nf* : annuity

anuario *nm* : yearbook, annual

anudar *vt* : to knot, to tie in a knot — **anudarse** *vr*

anuencia *nf* : consent

anulación *nf, pl* **-ciones** : annulment, nullification

anular *vt* : to annul, to cancel

anunciador, -dora *n* → **anunciante**

anunciante *nmf* : advertiser

anunciar *vt* **1** : to announce **2** : to advertise

anuncio *nm* **1** : announcement **2** : advertisement, commercial

anzuelo *nm* **1** : fishhook **2 morder el anzuelo** : to take the bait

añadido *nm* : addition

añadidura *nf* **1** : additive, addition **2 por ~** : in addition, furthermore

añadir *vt* **1** AGREGAR : to add **2** AUMENTAR : to increase

añejar *vt* : to age, to ripen

añejo, -ja *adj* **1** : aged, vintage **2** : age-old, musty, stale

añicos *nmpl* : smithereens, bits <hacer(se) añicos : to shatter>

añil *nm* **1** : indigo **2** : bluing

año *nm* **1** : year <en el año 1990 : in (the year) 1990> <tiene diez años : she is ten years old> **2** : grade <cuarto año : fourth grade> **3 año bisiesto** : leap year **4 año luz** : light-year **5 Año Nuevo** : New Year

añoranza *nf* : longing, yearning

añorar *vt* **1** DESEAR : to long for **2** : to grieve for, to miss — *vi* : to mourn, to grieve

añoso, -sa *adj* : aged, old

aorta *nf* : aorta

apabullante *adj* : overwhelming, crushing

apabullar *vt* : to overwhelm

apacentar {55} *vt* : to pasture, to put to pasture

apache *adj & nmf* : Apache

apachurrado, -da *adj fam* : depressed, down

apachurrar *vt* : to crush, to squash

apacible *adj* : gentle, mild, calm — **apaciblemente** *adv*

apaciguador, -dora *adj* : calming

apaciguamiento *nm* : appeasement

apaciguar {10} *vt* APLACAR : to appease, to pacify — **apaciguarse** *vr* : to calm down

apadrinar *vt* **1** : to be a godparent to **2** : to sponsor, to support

apagado, -da *adj* **1** : off, out <la luz está apagada : the light is off> **2** : dull, subdued

apagador *nm Mex* : switch

apagar {52} *vt* **1** : to turn off, to shut off **2** : to extinguish, to put out — **apagarse** *vr* **1** : to go out, to fade **2** : to wane, to die down

apagón *nm, pl* **-gones** : blackout (of power)

apalancamiento *nm* : leverage
apalancar {72} *vt* **1** : to jack up **2** : to pry open
apalear *vt* : to beat up, to thrash
apantallar *vt Mex* : to dazzle, to impress
apañar *vt* **1** : to seize, to grasp **2** : to repair, to mend — **apañarse** *vr* : to manage, to get along
apaño *nm fam* **1** : patch **2** HABILIDAD : skill, knack
apapachar *vt Mex fam* : to cuddle, to caress — **apapacharse** *vr*
aparador *nm* **1** : sideboard, cupboard **2** ESCAPARATE, VITRINA : shop window
aparato *nm* **1** : machine, appliance, apparatus <aparato auditivo : hearing aid> <aparato de televisión : television set> **2** : system <aparato digestivo : digestive system> **3** : display, ostentation <sin aparato : without ceremony> **4 aparatos** *nmpl* : braces (for the teeth)
aparatoso, -sa *adj* **1** : ostentatious **2** : spectacular
aparcamiento *nm Spain* **1** : parking **2** : parking lot
aparcar {72} *v Spain* : to park
aparcero, -ra *n* : sharecropper
aparear *vt* **1** : to mate (animals) **2** : to match up — **aparearse** *vr* : to mate
aparecer {53} *vi* **1** : to appear **2** PRESENTARSE : to show up **3** : to turn up, to be found — **aparecerse** *vr* : to appear
aparejado, -da *adj* **1 ir aparejado con** : to go hand in hand with **2 llevar aparejado** : to entail
aparejar *vt* **1** PREPARAR : to prepare, to make ready **2** : to harness (a horse) **3** : to fit out (a ship)
aparejo *nm* **1** : equipment, gear **2** : harness, saddle **3** : rig, rigging (of a ship)
aparentar *vt* **1** : to seem, to appear <no aparentas tu edad : you don't look your age> **2** FINGIR : to feign, to pretend
aparente *adj* **1** : apparent **2** : showy, striking — **aparentemente** *adv*
aparición *nf, pl* **-ciones** **1** : appearance **2** PUBLICACIÓN : publication, release **3** FANTASMA : apparition, vision
apariencia *nf* **1** ASPECTO : appearance, look **2 en ~** : seemingly, apparently
apartado *nm* **1** : section, paragraph **2 apartado postal** : post office box
apartamento *nm* DEPARTAMENTO : apartment
apartar *vt* **1** ALEJAR : to move away, to put at a distance **2** : to put aside, to set aside, to separate — **apartarse** *vr* **1** : to step aside, to move away **2** DESVIARSE : to stray
aparte[1] *adv* **1** : apart, aside <modestia aparte : if I say so myself> **2** : separately **3 ~ de** : apart from, besides
aparte[2] *adj* : separate, special
aparte[3] *nm* : aside (in theater)
apartheid *nm* : apartheid
apasionado, -da *adj* : passionate, enthusiastic — **apasionadamente** *adv*
apasionante *adj* : fascinating, exciting
apasionar *vt* : to enthuse, to excite — **apasionarse** *vr*
apatía *nf* : apathy
apático, -ca *adj* : apathetic
apearse *vr* **1** DESMONTAR : to dismount **2** : to get out of or off (a vehicle)
apedrear *vt* : to stone, to throw stones at
apegado, -da *adj* : attached, close, devoted <es muy apegado a su familia : he is very devoted to his family>
apegarse {52} *vr* **~ a** : to become attached to, to grow fond of
apego *nm* AFICIÓN : attachment, fondness, inclination
apelación *nf, pl* **-ciones** : appeal (in court)
apelar *vi* **1** : to appeal **2 ~ a** : to resort to
apelativo *nm* APELLIDO : last name, surname
apellidarse *vr* : to have for a last name <¿cómo se apellida? : what is your last name?>
apellido *nm* : last name, surname
apelotonar *vt* : to roll into a ball, to bundle up
apenar *vt* : to aggrieve, to sadden — **apenarse** *vr* **1** : to be saddened **2** : to become embarrassed
apenas[1] *adv* : hardly, scarcely
apenas[2] *conj* : as soon as
apéndice *nm* **1** : appendix **2** : appendage
apendicectomía *nf* : appendectomy
apendicitis *nf* : appendicitis
apercibimiento *nm* **1** : preparation **2** AMONESTACIÓN : warning
apercibir *vt* **1** DISPONER : to prepare, to make ready **2** AMONESTAR : to warn **3** OBSERVAR : to observe, to perceive — **apercibirse** *vr* **1** : to get ready **2 ~ de** : to notice
aperitivo *nm* **1** : appetizer **2** : aperitif
apero *nm* : tool, implement
apertura *nf* **1** : opening, aperture **2** : commencement, beginning **3** : openness
apesadumbrar *vt* : to distress, to sadden — **apesadumbrarse** *vr* : to be weighed down
apestar *vt* **1** : to infect with the plague **2** : to corrupt — *vi* : to stink
apestoso, -sa *adj* : stinking, foul
apetecer {53} *vt* **1** : to crave, to long for <apeteció la fama : he longed for fame> **2** : to appeal to <me apetece un bistec : I feel like having a steak> <¿cuándo te apetece ir? : when do you want to go?> — *vi* : to be appealing
apetecible *adj* : appetizing, appealing
apetito *nm* : appetite
apetitoso, -sa *adj* : appetizing
apiario *nm* : apiary
ápice *nm* **1** : apex, summit **2** PIZCA : bit, smidgen

apicultor, -tora *n* **:** beekeeper
apicultura *nf* **:** beekeeping
apilar *vt* AMONTONAR **:** to heap up, to pile up — **apilarse** *vr*
apiñado, -da *adj* **:** jammed, crowded
apiñar *vt* **:** to pack, to cram — **apiñarse** *vr* **:** to crowd together, to huddle
apio *nm* **:** celery
apisonadora *nf* **:** steamroller
apisonar *vt* **:** to pack down, to tamp
aplacamiento *nm* **:** appeasement
aplacar {72} *vt* APACIGUAR **:** to appease, to placate — **aplacarse** *vr* **:** to calm down
aplanadora *nf* **:** steamroller
aplanar *vt* **:** to flatten, to level
aplastante *adj* **:** crushing, overwhelming
aplastar *vt* **:** to crush, to squash
aplaudir *v* **:** to applaud
aplauso *nm* **1 :** applause, clapping **2 :** praise, acclaim
aplazamiento *nm* **:** postponement
aplazar {21} *vt* **:** to postpone, to defer
aplicable *adj* **:** applicable — **aplicabilidad** *nf*
aplicación *nf, pl* **-ciones 1 :** application **2 :** diligence, dedication
aplicado, -da *adj* **:** diligent, industrious
aplicador *nm* **:** applicator
aplicar {72} *vt* **:** to apply — **aplicarse** *vr* **:** to apply oneself
aplique *or* **apliqué** *nm* **:** appliqué
aplomar *vt* **:** to plumb, to make vertical
aplomo *nm* **:** aplomb, composure
apocado, -da *adj* **:** timid
apocalipsis *nms & pl* **:** apocalypse <el Libro del Apocalipsis **:** the Book of Revelation>
apocalíptico, -ca *adj* **:** apocalyptic
apocamiento *nm* **:** timidity
apocarse {72} *vr* **1 :** to shy away, to be intimidated **2 :** to humble oneself, to sell oneself short
apócrifo, -fa *adj* **:** apocryphal
apodar *vt* **:** to nickname, to call — **apodarse** *vr*
apoderado, -da *n* **:** proxy, agent
apoderar *vt* **:** to authorize, to empower — **apoderarse** *vr* **~ de :** to seize, to take over
apodo *nm* SOBRENOMBRE **:** nickname
apogeo *nm* **:** acme, peak, zenith
apología *nf* **:** defense, apology
apoplejía *nf* **:** apoplexy, stroke
apoplético, -ca *adj* **:** apoplectic
aporrear *vt* **:** to bang on, to beat, to bludgeon
aportación *nf, pl* **-ciones :** contribution
aportar *vt* CONTRIBUIR **:** to contribute, to provide
aporte *nm* → **aportación**
apostador, -dora *n* **:** bettor, better
apostar {19} *v* **:** to bet, to wager <I bet he's not coming **:** apuesto que no viene>
apostasía *nf* **:** apostasy
apóstata *nmf* **:** apostate
apostilla *nf* **:** note
apostillar *vt* **:** to annotate
apóstol *nm* **:** apostle
apostólico, -ca *adj* **:** apostolic
apóstrofe *nmf* **:** apostrophe
apostura *nf* **:** elegance, gracefulness
apoyacabezas *nms & pl* **:** headrest
apoyapiés *nms & pl* **:** footrest
apoyar *vt* **1 :** to support, to back **2 :** to lean, to rest — **apoyarse** *vr* **1 ~ en :** to lean on **2 ~ en :** to be based on, to rest on
apoyo *nm* **:** support, backing
apreciable *adj* **:** appreciable, substantial, considerable
apreciación *nf, pl* **-ciones 1 :** appreciation **2 :** appraisal, evaluation
apreciar *vt* **1** ESTIMAR **:** to appreciate, to value **2** EVALUAR **:** to appraise, to assess — **apreciarse** *vr* **:** to appreciate, to increase in value
aprecio *nm* **1** ESTIMO **:** esteem, appreciation **2** EVALUACIÓN **:** appraisal, assessment
aprehender *vt* **1 :** to apprehend, to capture **2 :** to conceive of, to grasp
aprehensión *nf, pl* **-siones :** apprehension, capture, arrest
apremiante *adj* **:** pressing, urgent
apremiar *vt* INSTAR **:** to pressure, to urge — *vi* URGIR **:** to be urgent <el tiempo apremia **:** time is of the essence>
apremio *nm* **:** pressure, urgency
aprender *v* **:** to learn — **aprenderse** *vr*
aprendiz, -diza *n, mpl* **-dices :** apprentice, trainee
aprendizaje *nm* **:** apprenticeship
aprensión *nf, pl* **-siones :** apprehension, dread
aprensivo, -va *adj* **:** apprehensive, worried
apresamiento *nm* **:** seizure, capture
apresar *vt* **:** to capture, to seize
aprestar *vt* **:** to make ready, to prepare — **aprestarse** *vr* **:** to get ready
apresuradamente *adv* **1 :** hurriedly **2 :** hastily, too fast
apresurado, -da *adj* **:** hurried, in a rush
apresuramiento *nm* **:** hurry, haste
apresurar *vt* **:** to quicken, to speed up — **apresurarse** *vr* **:** to hurry up, to make haste
apretado, -da *adj* **1 :** tight **2** *fam* **:** cheap, tightfisted — **apretadamente** *adv*
apretar {55} *vt* **1 :** to press, to push (a button) **2 :** to tighten **3 :** to squeeze — *vi* **1 :** to press, to push **2 :** to fit tightly, to be too tight <los zapatos me aprietan **:** my shoes are tight>
apretón *nm, pl* **-tones 1 :** squeeze **2 apretón de manos :** handshake

apretujar *vt* **:** to squash, to squeeze — **apretujarse** *vr*
aprieto *nm* APURO **:** predicament, difficulty <estar en un aprieto : to be in a fix>
aprisa *adv* **:** quickly, hurriedly
aprisionar *vt* **1 :** to imprison **2 :** to trap, to box in
aprobación *nf, pl* **-ciones :** approval, endorsement
aprobar {19} *vt* **1 :** to approve of **2 :** to pass (a law, an exam) — *vi* **:** to pass (in school)
aprobatorio, -ria *adj* **:** approving
apropiación *nf, pl* **-ciones :** appropriation
apropiado, -da *adj* **:** appropriate, proper, suitable — **apropiadamente** *adv*
apropiarse *vr* **~ de :** to take possession of, to appropriate
aprovechable *adj* **:** usable
aprovechado[1], -da *adj* **1 :** diligent, hardworking **2 :** pushy, opportunistic
aprovechado[2], -da *n* **:** pushy person, opportunist
aprovechamiento *nm* **:** use, exploitation
aprovechar *vt* **:** to take advantage of, to make good use of — *vi* **1 :** to be of use **2 :** to progress, to improve — **aprovecharse** *vr* **~ de :** to take advantage of, to exploit
aprovisionamiento *nm* **:** provisions *pl*, supplies *pl*
aprovisionar *vt* **:** to provide, to supply (with provisions)
aproximación *nf, pl* **-ciones 1 :** approximation, estimate **2 :** rapprochement
aproximado, -da *adj* **:** approximate, estimated — **aproximadamente** *adv*
aproximar *vt* ACERCAR, ARRIMAR **:** to approximate, to bring closer — **aproximarse** *vr* ACERCARSE, ARRIMARSE **:** to approach, to move closer
aptitud *nf* **:** aptitude, capability
apto, -ta *adj* **1 :** suitable, suited, fit **2** HÁBIL **:** capable, competent
apuesta *nf* **:** bet, wager
apuesto, -ta *adj* **:** elegant, good-looking
apuntador, -dora *n* **:** prompter
apuntalar *vt* **:** to prop up, to shore up
apuntar *vt* **1 :** to aim, to point **2** ANOTAR **:** to write down, to jot down **3** INDICAR, SEÑALAR **:** to point to, to point out **4 :** to prompt (in the theater) — *vi* **1 :** to take aim **2 :** to become evident — **apuntarse** *vr* **1 :** to sign up, to enroll **2 :** to score, to chalk up
apunte *nm* **:** note
apuñalar *vt* **:** to stab
apuradamente *adv* **1 :** with difficulty **2 :** hurriedly, hastily
apurado, -da *adj* **1** APRESURADO **:** rushed, pressured **2 :** poor, needy **3 :** difficult, awkward **4 :** embarrassed
apurar *vt* **1** APRESURAR **:** to hurry, to rush **2 :** to use up, to exhaust **3 :** to trouble — **apurarse** *vr* **1** APRESURARSE **:** to hurry up **2** PREOCUPARSE **:** to worry
apuro *nm* **1** APRIETO **:** predicament, jam **2 :** rush, hurry **3 :** embarrassment
aquejar *vt* **:** to afflict
aquel, aquella *adj, mpl* **aquellos :** that, those
aquél, aquélla *pron, mpl* **aquéllos 1 :** that (one), those (ones) **2 :** the former
aquello *pron* (*neuter*) **:** that, that matter, that business <aquello fue algo serio : that was something serious>
aquí *adv* **1 :** here **2 :** now <de aquí en adelante : from now on> **3 por ~ :** around here, hereabouts
aquiescencia *nf* **:** acquiescence, approval
aquietar *vt* **:** to allay, to calm — **aquietarse** *vr* **:** to calm down
aquilatar *vt* **1 :** to assay **2 :** to assess, to size up
ara *nf* **1 :** altar **2 en aras de :** in the interests of, for the sake of
árabe[1] *adj & nmf* **:** Arab, Arabian
árabe[2] *nm* **:** Arabic (language)
arabesco *nm* **:** arabesque — **arabesco, -ca** *adj*
arábigo, -ga *adj* **1 :** Arabic, Arabian **2 número arábigo :** Arabic numeral
arable *adj* **:** arable
arado *nm* **:** plow
aragonés, -nesa *adj & n, mpl* **-neses :** Aragonese
arancel *nm* **:** tariff, duty
arándano *nm* **:** blueberry
arandela *nf* **:** washer (for a faucet, etc.)
araña *nf* **1 :** spider **2 :** chandelier
arañar *v* **:** to scratch, to claw
arañazo *nm* **:** scratch
arar *v* **:** to plow
arbitraje *nm* **1 :** arbitration **2 :** refereeing (in sports)
arbitrar *v* **1 :** to arbitrate **2 :** to referee, to umpire
arbitrariedad *nf* **1 :** arbitrariness **2** INJUSTICIA **:** injustice, wrong
arbitrario, -ria *adj* **1 :** arbitrary **2 :** unfair, unjust — **arbitrariamente** *adv*
arbitrio *nm* **1** ALBEDRÍO **:** will **2** JUICIO **:** judgment
árbitro, -tra *n* **1 :** arbitrator, arbiter **2 :** referee, umpire
árbol *nm* **1 :** tree **2 árbol genealógico :** family tree
arbolado[1], -da *adj* **:** wooded
arbolado[2] *nm* **:** woodland
arboleda *nf* **:** grove, wood
arbóreo, -rea *adj* **:** arboreal
arbusto *nm* **:** shrub, bush, hedge
arca *nf* **1 :** ark **2 :** coffer, chest
arcada *nf* **1 :** arcade, series of arches **2 arcadas** *nfpl* **:** retching <hacer arcadas : to retch>
arcaico, -ca *adj* **:** archaic
arcángel *nm* **:** archangel
arcano, -na *adj* **:** arcane

arce *nm* : maple tree

arcén *nm, pl* **arcenes** : hard shoulder, berm

archidiócesis *nfs & pl* : archdiocese

archipiélago *nm* : archipelago

archivador *nm* : filing cabinet

archivar *vt* **1** : to file **2** : to archive

archivista *nmf* : archivist

archivo *nm* **1** : file **2** : archive, archives *pl*

arcilla *nf* : clay

arco *nm* **1** : arch, archway **2** : bow (in archery) **3** : arc **4** : wicket (in croquet) **5** PORTERÍA : goal, goalposts *pl* **6 arco iris** : rainbow

arder *vi* **1** : to burn <el bosque está ardiendo : the forest is in flames> <arder de ira : to burn with anger, to be seething> **2** : to smart, to sting, to burn <le ardía el estómago : he had heartburn>

ardid *nm* : scheme, ruse

ardiente *adj* **1** : burning **2** : ardent, passionate — **ardientemente** *adv*

ardilla *nf* **1** : squirrel **2** *or* **ardilla listada** : chipmunk

ardor *nm* **1** : heat **2** : passion, ardor

ardoroso, -sa *adj* : heated, impassioned

arduo, -dua *adj* : arduous, grueling — **arduamente** *adv*

área *nf* : area

arena *nf* **1** : sand <arena movediza : quicksand> **2** : arena

arenga *nf* : harangue, lecture

arengar {52} *vt* : to harangue, to lecture

arenilla *nf* **1** : fine sand **2 arenillas** *nfpl* : kidney stones

arenisca *nf* : sandstone

arenoso, -sa *adj* : sandy, gritty

arenque *nm* : herring

arepa *nf* : cornmeal bread

arete *nm* : earring

argamasa *nf* : mortar (cement)

argelino, -na *adj & n* : Algerian

argentino, -na *adj & n* : Argentinian, Argentine

argolla *nf* : hoop, ring

argón *nm* : argon

argot *nm* : slang

argucia *nf* : sophistry, subtlety

argüir {41} *vi* : to argue — *vt* **1** ARGUMENTAR : to contend, to argue **2** INFERIR : to deduce **3** PROBAR : to prove

argumentación *nf, pl* **-ciones** : line of reasoning, argument

argumentar *vt* : to argue, to contend

argumento *nm* **1** : argument, reasoning **2** : plot, story line

aria *nf* : aria

aridez *nf, pl* **-deces** : aridity, dryness

árido, -da *adj* : arid, dry

Aries *nmf* : Aries

ariete *nm* : battering ram

arisco, -ca *adj* : surly, sullen, unsociable

arista *nf* **1** : ridge, edge **2** : beard (of a plant) **3 aristas** *nfpl* : rough edges, complications, problems

aristocracia *nf* : aristocracy

aristócrata *nmf* : aristocrat

aristocrático, -ca *adj* : aristocratic

aritmética *nf* : arithmetic

aritmético, -ca *adj* : arithmetic, arithmetical — **aritméticamente** *adv*

arlequín *nm, pl* **-quines** : harlequin

arma *nf* **1** : weapon **2 armas** *nfpl* : armed forces **3 arma de fuego** : firearm

armada *nf* : navy, fleet

armadillo *nm* : armadillo

armado, -da *adj* **1** : armed **2** : assembled, put together **3** *PRi* : obstinate, stubborn

armador, -dora *n* : shipowner

armadura *nf* **1** : armor **2** ARMAZÓN : skeleton, framework

armamento *nm* : armament, arms *pl*, weaponry

armar *vt* **1** : to assemble, to put together **2** : to create, to cause <armar un escándalo : to cause a scene> **3** : to arm — **armarse** *vr* **armarse de valor** : to steel oneself

armario *nm* **1** CLÓSET, ROPERO : closet **2** ALACENA : cupboard

armatoste *nm fam* : monstrosity, contraption

armazón *nmf, pl* **-zones** **1** ESQUELETO : framework, skeleton <armazón de acero : steel framework> **2** : frames *pl* (of eyeglasses)

armenio, -nia *adj & n* : Armenian

armería *nf* **1** : armory **2** : arms museum **3** : gunsmith's shop **4** : gunsmith's craft

armiño *nm* : ermine

armisticio *nm* : armistice

armonía *nf* : harmony

armónica *nf* : harmonica

armónico, -ca *adj* **1** : harmonic **2** : harmonious — **armónicamente** *adv*

armonioso, -sa *adj* : harmonious — **armoniosamente** *adv*

armonizar {21} *vt* **1** : to harmonize **2** : to reconcile — *vi* : to harmonize, to blend together

arnés *nm, pl* **arneses** : harness

aro *nm* **1** : hoop **2** : napkin ring **3** *Arg, Chile, Uru* : earring

aroma *nm* : aroma, scent

aromático, -ca *adj* : aromatic

arpa *nf* : harp

arpegio *nm* : arpeggio

arpía *nf* : shrew, harpy

arpista *nmf* : harpist

arpón *nm, pl* **arpones** : harpoon — **arponear** *vt*

arquear *vt* : to arch, to bend — **arquearse** *vr* : to bend, to bow

arqueología *nf* : archaeology

arqueológico, -ca *adj* : archaeological

arqueólogo, -ga *n* : archaeologist

arquero, -ra *n* **1** : archer **2** PORTERO : goalkeeper, goalie

arquetípico, -ca *adj* : archetypal
arquetipo *nm* : archetype
arquitecto, -ta *n* : architect
arquitectónico, -ca *adj* : architectural — **aquitectónicamente** *adv*
arquitectura *nf* : architecture
arrabal *nm* **1** : slum **2 arrabales** *nmpl* : outskirts, outlying area
arracada *nf* : hoop earring
arracimarse *vr* : to cluster together
arraigado, -da *adj* : deep-seated, ingrained
arraigar {52} *vi* : to take root, to become established — **arraigarse** *vr*
arraigo *nm* : roots *pl* <con mucho arraigo : deep-rooted>
arrancar {72} *vt* **1** : to pull out, to tear out **2** : to pick, to pluck (a flower) **3** : to start (an engine) **4** : to boot (a computer) — *vi* **1** : to start an engine **2** : to get going — **arrancarse** *vr* : to pull out, to pull off
arrancón *nm, pl* **-cones** *Mex* **1** : sudden loud start (of a car) **2 carrera de arrancones** : drag race
arranque *nm* **1** : starter (of a car) **2** ARREBATO : outburst, fit **3 punto de arranque** : beginning, starting point
arrasar *vt* **1** : to level, to smooth **2** : to devastate, to destroy **3** : to fill to the brim
arrastrar *vt* **1** : to drag, to tow **2** : to draw, to attract — *vi* : to hang down, to trail — **arrastrarse** *vr* **1** : to crawl **2** : to grovel
arrastre *nm* **1** : dragging **2** : pull, attraction **3 red de arrastre** : dragnet, trawling net
arrayán *nm, pl* **-yanes 1** MIRTO : myrtle **2 arrayán brabántico** : bayberry, wax myrtle
arrear *vt* : to urge on, to drive — *vi* : to hurry along
arrebatado, -da *adj* **1** PRECIPITADO : impetuous, hotheaded, rash **2** : flushed, blushing
arrebatar *vt* **1** : to snatch, to seize **2** CAUTIVAR : to captivate — **arrebatarse** *vr* : to get carried away (with anger, etc.)
arrebato *nm* ARRANQUE : fit, outburst
arreciar *vi* : to intensify, to worsen
arrecife *nm* : reef
arreglado, -da *adj* **1** : fixed, repaired **2** : settled, sorted out **3** : neat, tidy **4** : smart, dressed-up
arreglar *vt* **1** COMPONER : to repair, to fix **2** : to tidy up <arregla tu cuarto : pick up your room> **3** : to solve, to work out <quiero arreglar este asunto : I want to settle this matter> — **arreglarse** *vr* **1** : to get dressed (up) <arreglarse el pelo : to get one's hair done> **2 arreglárselas** *fam* : to get by, to manage
arreglo *nm* **1** : repair **2** : arrangement **3** : agreement, understanding
arrellanarse *vr* : to settle (in a chair)
arremangarse {52} *vr* : to roll up one's sleeves
arremeter *vi* EMBESTIR : to attack, to charge
arremetida *nf* EMBESTIDA : attack, onslaught
arremolinarse *vr* **1** : to crowd around, to mill about **2** : to swirl (about)
arrendador, -dora *n* **1** : landlord, landlady *f* **2** : tenant, lessee
arrendajo *nm* : jay
arrendamiento *nm* **1** ALQUILER : rental, leasing **2 contrato de arrendamiento** : lease
arrendar {55} *vt* ALQUILAR : to rent, to lease
arrendatario, -ria *n* : tenant, lessee, renter
arreos *nmpl* GUARNICIONES : tack, harness, trappings
arrepentido, -da *adj* : repentant, remorseful
arrepentimiento *nm* : regret, remorse, repentance
arrepentirse {76} *vr* **1** : to regret, to be sorry **2** : to repent
arrestar *vt* DETENER : to arrest, to detain
arresto *nm* **1** DETENCIÓN : arrest **2 arrestos** *nmpl* : boldness, daring
arriate *nm Mex, Spain* : bed (for plants), border
arriba *adv* **1** : up, upwards **2** : above, overhead **3** : upstairs **4 ~ de** : more than **5 de arriba abajo** : from top to bottom, from head to foot
arribar *vi* **1** : to arrive **2** : to dock, to put into port
arribista *nmf* : parvenu, upstart
arribo *nm* : arrival
arriendo *nm* ARRENDAMIENTO : rent, rental
arriero, -ra *n* : mule driver, muleteer
arriesgado, -da *adj* **1** : risky **2** : bold, daring
arriesgar {52} *vt* : to risk, to venture — **arriesgarse** *vr* : to take a chance
arrimado, -da *n Mex fam* : sponger, freeloader
arrimar *vt* ACERCAR, APROXIMAR : to bring closer, to draw near — **arrimarse** *vr* ACERCARSE, APROXIMARSE : to approach, to get close
arrinconar *vt* **1** ACORRALAR : to corner, to box in **2** : to push aside, to abandon
arroba *nf* : arroba (Spanish unit of measurement)
arrobamiento *nm* : rapture, ecstasy
arrobar *vt* : to enrapture, to enchant — **arrobarse** *vr*
arrocero[1], -ra *adj* : rice
arrocero[2], -ra *n* : rice grower
arrodillarse *vr* : to kneel (down)
arrogancia *nf* ALTANERÍA, ALTIVEZ : arrogance, haughtiness
arrogante *adj* ALTANERO, ALTIVO : arrogant, haughty
arrogarse {52} *vr* : to usurp, to arrogate

arrojado, -da *adj* **:** daring, fearless

arrojar *vt* **1 :** to hurl, to cast, to throw **2 :** to give off, to spew out **3 :** to yield, to produce **4** *fam* **:** to vomit — **arrojarse** *vr* PRECIPITARSE **:** to throw oneself, to leap

arrojo *nm* **:** boldness, fearlessness

arrollador, -dora *adj* **:** sweeping, overwhelming

arrollar *vt* **1 :** to sweep away, to carry away **2 :** to crush, to overwhelm **3 :** to run over (with a vehicle)

arropar *vt* **:** to clothe, to cover (up) — **arroparse** *vr*

arrostrar *vt* **:** to confront, to face (up to)

arroyo *nm* **1** RIACHUELO **:** brook, creek, stream **2 :** gutter

arroz *nm, pl* **arroces :** rice

arrozal *nm* **:** rice field, rice paddy

arruga *nf* **:** wrinkle, fold, crease

arrugado, -da *adj* **:** wrinkled, creased, lined

arrugar {52} *vt* **:** to wrinkle, to crease, to pucker — **arrugarse** *vr*

arruinar *vt* **:** to ruin, to wreck — **arruinarse** *vr* **1 :** to be ruined **2 :** to fall into ruin, to go bankrupt

arrullar *vt* **:** to lull to sleep — *vi* **:** to coo

arrullo *nm* **1 :** lullaby **2 :** coo (of a dove)

arrumaco *nm fam* **:** kissing, cuddling

arrumbar *vt* **1 :** to lay aside, to put away **2 :** to floor, to leave speechless

arsenal *nm* **:** arsenal

arsénico *nm* **:** arsenic

arte *nmf* (*usually m in singular, f in plural*) **1 :** art <artes y oficios : arts and crafts> <bellas artes : fine arts> **2** HABILIDAD **:** skill **3 :** cunning, cleverness

artefacto *nm* **1 :** artifact **2** DISPOSITIVO **:** device

artemisa *nf* **:** sagebrush

arteria *nf* **:** artery — **arterial** *adj*

arteriosclerosis *nf* **:** arteriosclerosis, hardening of the arteries

artero, -ra *adj* **:** wily, crafty

artesanal *adj* **:** pertaining to crafts or craftsmanship, handmade

artesanía *nm* **1 :** craftsmanship **2 :** handicrafts *pl*

artesano, -na *n* **:** artisan, craftsman *m,* craftsperson

artesiano, -na *adj* **:** artesian <pozo artesiano : artesian well>

ártico, -ca *adj* **:** arctic

articulación *nf, pl* **-ciones 1 :** articulation, pronunciation **2** COYUNTURA **:** joint

articular *vt* **1 :** to articulate, to utter **2 :** to connect with a joint **3 :** to coordinate, to orchestrate

articulista *nmf* **:** columnist

artículo *nm* **1 :** article, thing **2 :** item, feature, report **3 artículo de comercio :** commodity **4 artículos de primera necesidad :** essentials **5 artículos de tocador :** toiletries

artífice *nmf* **1** ARTESANO **:** artisan **2 :** mastermind, architect

artificial *adj* **1 :** artificial, man-made **2 :** feigned, false — **artificialmente** *adv*

artificio *nm* **1** HABILIDAD **:** skill **2** APARATO **:** device, appliance **3** ARDID **:** artifice, ruse

artificioso, -sa *adj* **1 :** skillful **2 :** cunning, deceptive

artillería *nf* **:** artillery

artillero, -ra *n* **:** artilleryman *m,* gunner

artilugio *nm* **:** gadget, contraption

artimaña *nf* **:** ruse, trick

artista *nmf* **1 :** artist **2** ACTOR, ACTRIZ **:** actor, actress *f*

artístico, -ca *adj* **:** artistic — **artísticamente** *adv*

artrítico, -ca *adj* **:** arthritic

artritis *nms & pl* **:** arthritis

artrópodo *nm* **:** arthropod

arveja *nf* GUISANTE **:** pea

arzobispado *nm* **:** archbishopric

arzobispo *nm* **:** archbishop

as *nm* **:** ace

asa *nf* AGARRADERA, ASIDERO **:** handle, grip

asado[1], -da *adj* **:** roasted, grilled, broiled

asado[2] *nm* **1 :** roast **2 :** barbecued meat **3 :** barbecue, cookout

asador *nm* **:** spit, rotisserie

asaduras *nfpl* **:** entrails, offal

asalariado[1], -da *adj* **:** wage-earning, salaried

asalariado[2], -da *n* **:** wage earner

asaltante *nmf* **1 :** mugger, robber **2 :** assailant

asaltar *vt* **1 :** to assault **2 :** to mug, to rob **3 asaltar al poder :** to seize power

asalto *nm* **1 :** assault **2 :** mugging, robbery **3 :** round (in boxing) **4 asalto al poder :** coup d'etat

asamblea *nf* **:** assembly, meeting

asambleísta *nmf* **:** assemblyman *m,* assemblywoman *f*

asar *vt* **:** to roast, to grill — **asarse** *vr fam* **:** to roast, to be dying from heat

asbesto *nm* **:** asbestos

ascendencia *nf* **1 :** ancestry, descent **2 ~ sobre :** influence over

ascendente *adj* **:** ascending, upward <un curso ascendente : an upward trend>

ascender {56} *vi* **1 :** to ascend, to rise up **2 :** to be promoted <ascendió a gerente : she was promoted to manager> **3 ~ a :** to amount to, to reach <las deudas ascienden a 20 millones de pesos : the debt amounts to 20 million pesos> — *vt* **:** to promote

ascendiente[1] *nmf* ANCESTRO **:** ancestor

ascendiente[2] *nm* INFLUENCIA **:** influence, ascendancy

ascensión *nf, pl* **-siones 1 :** ascent, rise **2 Fiesta de la Ascensión :** Ascension Day
ascenso *nm* **1 :** ascent, rise **2 :** promotion
ascensor *nm* ELEVADOR **:** elevator
asceta *nmf* **:** ascetic
ascético, -ca *adj* **:** ascetic
ascetismo *nm* **:** asceticism
asco *nm* **1 :** disgust <¡qué asco! : that's disgusting!, how revolting!> **2 darle asco (a alguien) :** to sicken, to revolt **3 estar hecho un asco :** to be filthy **4 hacerle ascos a :** to turn up one's nose at
ascua *nf* **1** BRASA **:** ember **2 estar en ascuas** *fam* **:** to be on edge
asear *vt* **1 :** to wash, to clean **2 :** to tidy up — **asearse** *vr*
asechanza *nf* **:** snare, trap
asechar *vt* **:** to set a trap for
asediar *vt* **1** SITIAR **:** to besiege **2** ACOSAR **:** to harass
asedio *nm* **1 :** siege **2** ACOSO **:** harassment
asegurador¹, -dora *adj* **1 :** insuring, assuring **2 :** pertaining to insurance
asegurador², -dora *n* **:** insurer, underwriter
aseguradora *nf* **:** insurance company
asegurar *vt* **1 :** to assure **2 :** to secure **3 :** to insure — **asegurarse** *vr* **1** CERCIORARSE **:** to make sure **2 :** to take out insurance, to insure oneself
asemejar *vt* **1 :** to make similar <ese bigote te asemeja a tu abuelo : that mustache makes you look like your grandfather> **2** *Mex* **:** to be similar to, to resemble — **asemejarse** *vr* **~ a :** to be look like, to resemble
asentaderas *nfpl fam* **:** bottom, buttocks *pl*
asentado, -da *adj* **:** settled, established
asentamiento *nm* **:** settlement
asentar {55} *vt* **1 :** to lay down, to set down, to place **2 :** to settle, to establish **3** *Mex* **:** to state, to affirm — **asentarse** *vr* **1 :** to settle **2** ESTABLECERSE **:** to settle down, to establish oneself
asentimiento *nm* **:** assent, consent
asentir {76} *vi* **:** to consent, to agree
aseo *nm* **:** cleanliness
aséptico, -ca *adj* **:** aseptic, germ-free
asequible *adj* ACCESIBLE **:** accessible, attainable
aserción *nf* → **aserto**
aserradero *nm* **:** sawmill
aserrar {55} *vt* **:** to saw
aserrín *nm, pl* **-rrines :** sawdust
aserto *nm* **:** assertion, affirmation
asesinar *vt* **1 :** to murder **2 :** to assassinate
asesinato *nm* **1 :** murder **2 :** assassination
asesino¹, -na *adj* **:** murderous, homicidal
asesino², -na *n* **1 :** murderer, killer **2 :** assassin
asesor, -sora *n* **:** advisor, consultant
asesoramiento *nm* **:** advice, counsel
asesorar *vt* **:** to advise, to counsel — **asesorarse** *vr* **~ de :** to consult
asesoría *nf* **1 :** consulting, advising **2 :** consultant's office
asestar {55} *vt* **1 :** to aim, to point (a weapon) **2 :** to deliver, to deal (a blow)
aseveración *nf, pl* **-ciones :** assertion, statement
aseverar *vt* **:** to assert, to state
asexual *adj* **:** asexual — **asexualmente** *adv*
asfaltado¹, -da *adj* **:** asphalted, paved
asfaltado² *nm* PAVIMENTO **:** pavement, asphalt
asfaltar *vt* **:** to pave, to blacktop
asfalto *nm* **:** asphalt
asfixia *nf* **:** asphyxia, asphyxiation, suffocation
asfixiar *vt* **:** to asphyxiate, to suffocate, to smother — **asfixiarse** *vr*
asga, etc. → **asir**
así¹ *adv* **1 :** like this, like that **2 :** so, thus <así sea : so be it> **3 ~ de :** so, about so <una caja así de grande : a box about so big> **4 así que :** so, therefore **5 ~ como :** as well as **6 así así :** so-so, fair
así² *adj* **:** such, such a <un talento así es inestimable : a talent like that is priceless>
así³ *conj* AUNQUE **:** even if, even though <no irá, así le paguen : he won't go, even if they pay him>
asiático¹, -ca *adj* **:** Asian, Asiatic
asiático², -ca *n* **:** Asian
asidero *nm* **1** AGARRADA, ASA **:** grip, handle **2** AGARRE **:** grip, hold
asiduamente *adv* **:** regularly, frequently
asiduidad *nf* **1 :** assiduousness **2 :** regularity, frequency
asiduo, -dua *adj* **1 :** assiduous **2 :** frequent, regular
asiento *nm* **1 :** seat, chair <asiento trasero : back seat> **2 :** location, site
asignación *nf, pl* **-ciones 1 :** allocation **2 :** appointment, designation **3 :** allowance, pay **4** *PRi* **:** homework, assignment
asignar *vt* **1 :** to assign, to allocate **2 :** to appoint
asignatura *nf* MATERIA **:** subject, course
asilado, -da *n* **:** exile, refugee
asilo *nm* **:** asylum, refuge, shelter
asimetría *nf* **:** asymmetry
asimétrico, -ca *adj* **:** asymmetrical, asymmetric
asimilación *nf, pl* **-ciones :** assimilation
asimilar *vt* **:** to assimilate — **asimilarse** *vr* **~ a :** to be similar to, to resemble
asimismo *adv* **1** IGUALMENTE **:** similarly, likewise **2** TAMBIÉN **:** as well, also

asir {7} *vt* **:** to seize, to grasp — **asirse** *vr* **~ a :** to cling to
asistencia *nf* **1 :** attendance **2 :** assistance **3 :** assist (in sports)
asistente[1] *adj* **:** attending, in attendance
asistente[2] *nmf* **1 :** assistant **2 los asistentes :** those present, those in attendance
asistir *vi* **:** to attend, to be present <asistir a clase : to attend class> — *vt* **:** to aid, to assist
asma *nf* **:** asthma
asmático, -ca *adj* **:** asthmatic
asno *nm* BURRO **:** ass, donkey
asociación *nf, pl* **-ciones 1 :** association, relationship **2 :** society, group, association
asociado[1], **-da** *adj* **:** associate, associated
asociado[2], **-da** *n* **:** associate, partner
asociar *vt* **1 :** to associate, to connect **2 :** to pool (resources) **3 :** to take into partnership — **asociarse** *vr* **1 :** to become partners **2 ~ a :** to join, to become a member of
asolar {19} *vt* **:** to devastate, to destroy
asoleado, -da *adj* **:** sunny
asolear *vt* **:** to put in the sun — **asolearse** *vr* **:** to sunbathe
asomar *vt* **:** to show, to stick out — *vi* **:** to appear, to become visible — **asomarse** *vr* **1 :** to show, to appear **2 :** to lean out, to look out <se asomó por la ventana : he leaned out the window>
asombrar *vt* MARAVILLAR **:** to amaze, to astonish — **asombrarse** *vr* **:** to marvel, to be amazed
asombro *nm* **:** amazement, astonishment
asombroso, -sa *adj* **:** amazing, astonishing — **asombrosamente** *adv*
asomo *nm* **1 :** hint, trace **2 ni por asomo :** by no means
aspa *nf* **:** blade (of a fan or propeller)
aspaviento *nm* **:** exaggerated movement, fuss, flounce
aspecto *nm* **1 :** aspect **2** APARIENCIA **:** appearance, look
aspereza *nf* RUDEZA **:** roughness, coarseness
áspero, -ra *adj* **:** rough, coarse, abrasive — **ásperamente** *adv*
aspersión *nf, pl* **-siones :** sprinkling
aspersor *nm* **:** sprinkler
aspiración *nf, pl* **-ciones 1 :** inhalation, breathing in **2** ANHELO **:** aspiration, desire
aspiradora *nf* **:** vacuum cleaner
aspirante *nmf* **:** applicant, candidate
aspirar *vi* **~ a :** to aspire to — *vt* **:** to inhale, to breathe in
aspirina *nf* **:** aspirin
asquear *vt* **:** to sicken, to disgust
asquerosidad *nf* **:** filth, foulness
asqueroso, -sa *adj* **:** disgusting, sickening, repulsive — **asquerosamente** *adv*
asta *nf* **1 :** flagpole <a media asta : at half-mast> **2 :** horn, antler **3 :** shaft (of a weapon)
ástaco *nm* **:** crayfish
astado, -da *adj* **:** horned
áster *nm* **:** aster
asterisco *nm* **:** asterisk
asteroide *nm* **:** asteroid
astigmatismo *nm* **:** astigmatism
astil *nm* **:** shaft (of an arrow or feather)
astilla *nf* **1 :** splinter, chip **2 de tal palo, tal astilla :** like father, like son
astillar *vt* **:** to splinter — **astillarse** *vr*
astillero *nm* **:** dry dock, shipyard
astral *adj* **:** astral
astringente *adj & nm* **:** astringent — **astringencia** *nf*
astro *nm* **1 :** heavenly body **2 :** star
astrología *nf* **:** astrology
astrológico, -ca *adj* **:** astrological
astrólogo, -ga *n* **:** astrologer
astronauta *nmf* **:** astronaut
astronáutica *nf* **:** astronautics
astronautico, -ca *adj* **:** astronautic, astronautical
astronave *nf* **:** spaceship
astronomía *nf* **:** astronomy
astronómico, -ca *adj* **:** astronomical — **astronómicamente** *adv*
astrónomo, -ma *n* **:** astronomer
astroso, -sa *adj* DESALIÑADO **:** slovenly, untidy
astucia *nf* **1 :** astuteness, shrewdness **2 :** cunning, guile
astuto, -ta *adj* **1 :** astute, shrewd **2 :** crafty, tricky — **astutamente** *adv*
asueto *nm* **:** time off, break
asumir *vt* **1 :** to assume, to take on <asumir el cargo : to take office> **2** SUPONER **:** to assume, to suppose
asunción *nf, pl* **-ciones :** assumption
asunto *nm* **1** CUESTIÓN, TEMA **:** affair, matter, subject **2 asuntos** *nmpl* **:** affairs, business
asustadizo, -za *adj* **:** nervous, jumpy, skittish
asustado, -da *adj* **:** frightened, afraid
asustar *vt* ESPANTAR **:** to scare, to frighten — **asustarse** *vr*
atacante *nmf* **:** assailant, attacker
atacar {72} *v* **:** to attack
atado[1], **-da** *adj* **:** shy, inhibited
atado[2] *nm* **1 :** bundle, bunch **2** *Arg* **:** pack (of cigarettes)
atadura *nf* LIGADURA **:** tie, bond
atajar *vt* **1** IMPEDIR **:** to block, to stop **2** INTERRUMPIR **:** to interrupt, to cut off **3** CONTENER **:** to hold back, to restrain — *vi* **~ por :** to take a shortcut through
atajo *nm* **:** shortcut
atalaya *nf* **1 :** watchtower **2 :** vantage point
atañer {79} *vi* (*3rd person only*) **:** to concern, to have to do with <eso no me atañe : that does not concern me>
ataque *nm* **1 :** attack, assault **2 :** fit <ataque de risa : fit of laughter> **3 ataque de nervios :** nervous break-

down **4 ataque cardíaco** *or* **ataque al corazón :** heart attack

atar *vt* AMARRAR **:** to tie, to tie up, to tie down — **atarse** *vr*

atarantado, -da *adj fam* **1 :** restless **2 :** dazed, stunned

atarantar *vt fam* **:** to daze, to stun

atarazana *nf* **:** shipyard

atardecer¹ {53} *v impers* **:** to get dark

atardecer² *v impers* **:** late afternoon, dusk

atareado, -da *adj* **:** busy, overworked

atascar {72} *vt* **1** ATORAR **:** to block, to clog, to stop up **2 :** to hinder — **atascarse** *vr* **1 :** to become obstructed **2 :** to get bogged down **3** PARARSE **:** to stall

atasco *nm* **1 :** blockage **2** EMBOTELLAMIENTO **:** traffic jam

ataúd *nm* **:** coffin, casket

ataviar {85} *vt* **:** to dress, to clothe — **ataviarse** *vr* **:** to dress up

atavío *nm* ATUENDO **:** dress, attire

ateísmo *nm* **:** atheism

atemorizar {21} *vt* **:** to frighten, to intimidate — **atemorizarse** *vr*

atemperar *vt* **:** to temper, to moderate

atención¹ *nf, pl* **-ciones 1 :** attention **2 poner atención** *or* **prestar atención :** to pay attention **3 llamar la atención :** to attract attention **4 en atención a :** in view of

atención² *interj* **1 :** attention! **2 :** watch out!

atender {56 } *vt* **1 :** to help, to wait on **2 :** to look after, to take care of **3 :** to heed, to listen to — *vi* **:** to pay attention

atenerse {80} *vr* **:** to abide <tendrás que atenerte a las reglas **:** you will have to abide by the rules>

atentado *nm* **:** attack, assault

atentamente *adv* **1 :** attentively, carefully **2** (*used in correspondence*) **:** sincerely, sincerely yours

atentar {55} *vi* **~ contra :** to make an attempt on, to threaten <atentaron contra su vida **:** they made an attempt on his life>

atento, -ta *adj* **1 :** attentive, mindful **2** CORTÉS **:** courteous

atenuación *nf, pl* **-ciones 1 :** lessening **2 :** understatement

atenuante¹ *adj* **:** extenuating, mitigating

atenuante² *nmf* **:** extenuating circumstance, excuse

atenuar {3} *vt* **1** MITIGAR **:** to extenuate, to mitigate **2 :** to dim (light), to tone down (colors) **3 :** to minimize, to lessen

ateo¹, atea *adj* **:** atheistic

ateo², atea *n* **:** atheist

aterciopelado, -da *adj* **:** velvety, downy

aterido, -da *adj* **:** freezing, frozen

aterrador, -dora *adj* **:** terrifying

aterrar {55} *vt* **:** to terrify, to frighten

aterrizaje *nm* **:** landing (of a plane)

aterrizar {21} *vi* **:** to land, to touch down

aterrorizar {21} *vt* **1 :** to terrify **2 :** to terrorize — **aterrorizarse** *vr* **:** to be terrified

atesorar *vt* **:** to hoard, to amass

atestado, -da *adj* **:** crowded, packed

atestar {55} *vt* **1** ATIBORRAR **:** to crowd, to pack **2 :** to witness, to testify to — *vi* **:** to testify

atestiguar {10} *vt* **:** to testify to, to bear witness to — *vi* DECLARAR **:** to testify

atiborrar *vt* **:** to pack, to crowd — **atiborrarse** *vr* **:** to stuff oneself

ático *nm* **1 :** penthouse **2** BUHARDILLA, DESVÁN **:** attic

atigrado, -da *adj* **:** tabby (of cats), striped (of fur)

atildado, -da *adj* **:** smart, neat, dapper

atildar *vt* **1 :** to put a tilde over **2 :** to clean up, to smarten up — **atildarse** *vr* **:** to get spruced up

atinar *vi* ACERTAR **:** to be accurate, to be on target

atingencia *nf* **:** bearing, relevance

atípico, -ca *adj* **:** atypical

atiplado, -da *adj* **:** shrill, high-pitched

atirantar *vt* **:** to make taut, to tighten

atisbar *vt* **1 :** to spy on, to watch **2 :** to catch a glimpse of, to make out

atisbo *nm* **:** glimpse, sign, hint

atizador *nm* **:** poker (for a fire)

atizar {21} *vt* **1 :** to poke, to stir, to stoke (a fire) **2 :** to stir up, to rouse **3** *fam* **:** to give, to land (a blow)

atlántico, -ca *adj* **:** Atlantic

atlas *nm* **:** atlas

atleta *nmf* **:** athlete

atlético, -ca *adj* **:** athletic

atletismo *nm* **:** athletics

atmósfera *nf* **:** atmosphere

atmosférico, -ca *adj* **:** atmospheric

atole *nm Mex* **1 :** thick hot beverage prepared with corn flour **2 darle atole con el dedo (a alguien) :** to string (someone) along

atollarse *vr* **:** to get stuck, to get bogged down

atolón *nm, pl* **-lones :** atoll

atolondrado, -da *adj* **1** ATURDIDO **:** bewildered, dazed **2** DESPISTADO **:** scatterbrained, absentminded

atómico, -ca *adj* **:** atomic

atomizador *nm* **:** atomizer

atomizar {21} *vt* FRAGMENTAR **:** to fragment, to break into bits

átomo *nm* **:** atom

atónito, -ta *adj* **:** astonished, amazed

atontar *vt* **1 :** to stupefy **2 :** to bewilder, to confuse

atorar *vt* ATASCAR **:** to block, to clog — **atorarse** *vr* **1** ATASCARSE **:** to get stuck **2** ATRAGANTARSE **:** to choke

atormentador, -dora *n* **:** tormenter

atormentar *vt* **:** to torment, to torture — **atormentarse** *vr* **:** to torment oneself, to agonize

atornillar *vt* **:** to screw (in, on, down)

atorrante *nmf Arg* **:** bum, loafer

atosigar {52} *vt* **:** to harass, to annoy

atracadero *nm* **:** dock, pier

atracador, -dora *n* **:** robber, mugger

atracar {72} *vi* **:** to dock, to land — *vt* **:** to hold up, to rob, to mug — **atracarse** *vr fam* **~ de :** to gorge oneself with

atracción *nf, pl* **-ciones :** attraction

atraco *nm* **:** holdup, robbery

atractivo[1], **-va** *adj* **:** attractive

atractivo[2] *nm* **:** attraction, appeal, charm

atraer {81} *vt* **:** to attract — **atraerse** *vr* **1 :** to attract (each other) **2** GANARSE **:** to gain, to win

atragantarse *vr* **:** to choke (on food)

atrancar {72} *vt* **:** to block, to bar — **atrancarse** *vr*

atrapada *nf* **:** catch

atrapar *vt* **:** to trap, to capture

atrás *adv* **1** DETRÁS **:** back, behind <se quedó atrás : he stayed behind> **2** ANTES **:** ago <mucho tiempo atrás : long ago> **3 para ~** *or* **hacia ~ :** backwards, toward the rear **4 ~ de :** in back of, behind

atrasado, -da *adj* **1 :** late, overdue **2 :** backwards **3 :** old-fashioned **4 :** slow (of a clock or watch)

atrasar *vt* **:** to delay, to put off — *vi* **:** to lose time — **atrasarse** *vr* **:** to fall behind

atraso *nm* **1** RETRASO **:** lateness, delay <llegó con 20 minutos de atraso : he was 20 minutes late> **2 :** backwardness **3 atrasos** *nmpl* **:** arrears

atravesar {55} *vt* **1** CRUZAR **:** to cross, to go across **2 :** to pierce **3 :** to lay across **4 :** to go through (a situation or crisis) — **atravesarse** *vr* **1 :** to be in the way <se me atravesó : it blocked my path> **2 :** to interfere, to meddle

atrayente *adj* **:** attractive

atreverse *vr* **1 :** to dare **2 :** to be insolent

atrevido, -da *adj* **1 :** bold, daring **2 :** insolent

atrevimiento *nm* **1 :** daring, boldness **2 :** insolence

atribución *nf, pl* **-ciones :** attribution

atribuible *adj* IMPUTABLE **:** attributable, ascribable

atribuir {41} *vt* **1 :** to attribute, to ascribe **2 :** to grant, to confer — **atribuirse** *vr* **:** to take credit for

atribular *vt* **:** to afflict, to trouble — **atribularse** *vr*

atributo *nm* **:** attribute

atril *nm* **:** lectern, stand

atrincherar *vt* **:** to entrench — **atrincherarse** *vr* **1 :** to dig in, to entrench oneself **2 ~ en :** to hide behind

atrio *nm* **1 :** atrium **2 :** portico

atrocidad *nf* **:** atrocity

atrofia *nf* **:** atrophy

atrofiar *v* **:** to atrophy

atronador, -dora *adj* **:** thunderous, deafening

atropellado, -da *adj* **1 :** rash, hasty **2 :** brusque, abrupt

atropellamiento *nm* → **atropello**

atropellar *vt* **1 :** to knock down, to run over **2 :** to violate, to abuse — **atropellarse** *vr* **:** to rush through (a task), to trip over one's words

atropello *nm* **:** abuse, violation, outrage

atroz *adj, pl* **atroces :** atrocious, appalling — **atrozamente** *adv*

atuendo *nm* ATAVÍO **:** attire, costume

atufar *vt* **:** to vex, to irritate — **atufarse** *vr* **1 :** to get angry **2 :** to smell bad, to stink

atún *nm, pl* **atunes :** tuna fish, tuna

aturdimiento *nm* **:** bewilderment, confusion

aturdir *vt* **1 :** to stun, to shock **2 :** to bewilder, to confuse, to stupefy

atuvo, etc. → **atenerse**

audacia *nf* OSADÍA **:** boldness, audacity

audaz *adj, pl* **audaces :** bold, audacious, daring — **audazmente** *adv*

audible *adj* **:** audible

audición *nf, pl* **-ciones 1 :** hearing **2 :** audition

audiencia *nf* **:** audience

audífono *nm* **1 :** hearing aid **2 audífonos** *nmpl* **:** headphones, earphones

audio *nm* **:** audio

audiovisual *adj* **:** audiovisual

auditar *vt* **:** to audit

auditivo, -va *adj* **:** auditory, hearing, aural <aparato auditivo : hearing aid>

auditor, -tora *n* **:** auditor

auditoría *nf* **:** audit

auditorio *nm* **1 :** auditorium **2 :** audience

auge *nm* **1 :** peak, height **2 :** boom, upturn

augurar *vt* **:** to predict, to foretell

augurio *nm* AGÜERO, PRESAGIO **:** augury, omen

augusto, -ta *adj* **:** august

aula *nf* **:** classroom

aullar {8} *vi* **:** to howl, to wail

aullido *nm* **:** howl, wail

aumentar *vt* ACRECENTAR **:** to increase, to raise — *vi* **:** to rise, to increase, to grow

aumento *nm* INCREMENTO **:** increase, rise

aun *adv* **1 :** even <ni aun en coche llegaría a tiempo : I wouldn't arrive on time even if I drove> **2 aun así :** even so **3 aun más :** even more

aún *adv* **1** TODAVÍA **:** still, yet <¿aún no ha llegado el correo? : the mail still hasn't come?> **2 más aún :** furthermore

aunar {8} *vt* **:** to join, to combine — **aunarse** *vr* **:** to unite

aunque *conj* **1 :** though, although, even if, even though **2 aunque sea :** at least

aura *nf* **1 :** aura **2 :** turkey buzzard

áureo, -rea *adj* **:** golden

aureola *nf* **1 :** halo **2 :** aura (of power, fame, etc.)
aurícula *nf* **:** auricle
auricular *nm* **:** telephone receiver
aurora *nf* **1 :** dawn **2 aurora boreal :** aurora borealis
ausencia *nf* **:** absence
ausentarse *vr* **1 :** to leave, to go away **2 ~ de :** to stay away from
ausente[1] *adj* **:** absent, missing
ausente[2] *nmf* **1 :** absentee **2 :** missing person
auspiciar *vt* **1** PATROCINAR **:** to sponsor **2** FOMENTAR **:** to foster, to promote
auspicios *nmpl* **:** sponsorship, auspices
austeridad *nf* **:** austerity
austero, -ra *adj* **:** austere
austral[1] *adj* **:** southern
austral[2] *nm* **:** former monetary unit of Argentina
australiano, -na *adj & n* **:** Australian
austriaco *or* **austríaco, -ca** *adj & n* **:** Austrian
autenticar {72} *vt* **:** to authenticate — **autenticación** *nf*
autenticidad *nf* **:** authenticity
auténtico, -ca *adj* **:** authentic — **auténticamente** *adv*
autentificar {72} *vt* **:** to authenticate — **autentificación** *nf*
autismo *nm* **:** autism
autista *adj* **:** autistic
auto *nm* **:** auto, car
autoayuda *nf* **:** self-help
autobiografía *nf* **:** autobiography
autobiográfico, -ca *adj* **:** autobiographical
autobús *nm, pl* **-buses :** bus
autocompasión *nf* **:** self-pity
autocontrol *nm* **:** self-control
autocracia *nf* **:** autocracy
autócrata *nmf* **:** autocrat
autocrático, -ca *adj* **:** autocratic
autóctono, -na *adj* **:** indigenous, native <arte autóctono : indigenous art>
autodefensa *nf* **:** self-defense
autodestrucción *nf* **:** self-destruction — **autodestructivo, -va** *adj*
autodeterminación *nf* **:** self-determination
autodidacta *adj* **:** self-taught
autodisciplina *nf* **:** self-discipline
autoestima *nf* **:** self-esteem
autogobierno *nm* **:** self-government
autografiar *vt* **:** to autograph
autógrafo *nm* **:** autograph
autoinfligido, -da *adj* **:** self-inflicted
automación *nf* → **automatización**
autómata *nm* **:** automaton
automático, -ca *adj* **:** automatic — **automáticamente** *adv*
automatización *nf* **:** automation
automatizar {21} *vt* **:** to automate
automotor, -tora *adj* **1 :** self-propelled **2 :** automotive, car
automotriz[1] *adj, pl* **-trices :** automotive, car
automotriz[2] *nf, pl* **-trices :** car dealership
automóvil *nm* **:** automobile
automovilista *nmf* **:** motorist
automovilístico, -ca *adj* **:** automobile, car <accidente automovilístico : automobile accident>
autonombrado, -da *adj* **:** self-appointed
autonomía *nf* **:** autonomy
autónomo, -ma *adj* **:** autonomous — **autónomamente** *adv*
autopista *nf* **:** expressway, highway
autopropulsado, -da *adj* **:** self-propelled
autopsia *nf* **:** autopsy
autor, -tora *n* **1 :** author **2 :** perpetrator
autoría *nf* **:** authorship
autoridad *nf* **:** authority
autoritario, -ria *adj* **:** authoritarian
autorización *nf, pl* **-ciones :** authorization
autorizado, -da *adj* **1 :** authorized **2 :** authoritative
autorizar {21} *vt* **:** to authorize, to approve
autorretrato *nm* **:** self-portrait
autoservicio *nm* **1 :** self-service restaurant **2** SUPERMERCADO **:** supermarket
autostop *nm* **1 :** hitchhiking **2 hacer autostop :** to hitchhike
autostopista *nmf* **:** hitchhiker
autosuficiencia *nf* **:** self-sufficiency — **autosuficiente** *adj*
auxiliar[1] *vt* **:** to aid, to assist
auxiliar[2] *adj* **:** assistant, auxiliary
auxiliar[3] *nmf* **1 :** assistant, helper **2 auxiliar de vuelo :** flight attendant
auxilio *nm* **1 :** aid, assistance **2 primeros auxilios :** first aid
aval *nm* **:** guarantee, endorsement
avalancha *nf* ALUD **:** avalanche
avalar *vt* **:** to guarantee, to endorse
avaluar {3} *vt* **:** to evaluate, to appraise
avalúo *nm* **:** appraisal, evaluation
avance *nm* ADELANTO **:** advance
avanzado, -da *adj* **1 :** advanced **2 :** progressive
avanzar {21} *v* **:** to advance, to move forward
avaricia *nf* CODICIA **:** greed, avarice
avaricioso, -sa *adj* **:** avaricious, greedy
avaro[1]**, -ra** *adj* **:** miserly, greedy
avaro[2]**, -ra** *n* **:** miser
avasallador, -dora *adj* **:** overwhelming
avasallamiento *nm* **:** subjugation, domination
avasallar *vt* **:** to overpower, to subjugate
ave *nf* **1 :** bird **2 aves de corral :** poultry **3 ave rapaz** *or* **ave de presa :** bird of prey
avecinarse *vr* **:** to approach, to come near
avecindarse *vr* **:** to settle, to take up residence
avellana *nf* **:** hazelnut, filbert
avena *nf* **1 :** oat, oats *pl* **2 :** oatmeal

avenencia *nf* **:** agreement, pact

avenida *nf* **:** avenue

avenir {87} *vt* **:** to reconcile, to harmonize — **avenirse** *vr* **1 :** to agree, to come to terms **2 :** to get along

aventajado, -da *adj* **:** outstanding

aventajar *vt* **1 :** to be ahead of, to lead **2 :** to surpass, to outdo

aventar {55} *vt* **1 :** to fan **2 :** to winnow **3** *Col, Mex* **:** to throw, to toss — **aventarse** *vr* **1** *Col, Mex* **:** to hurl oneself **2** *Mex fam* **:** to dare, to take a chance

aventón *nm, pl* **-tones** *Col, Mex fam* **:** ride, lift

aventura *nf* **1 :** adventure **2** RIESGO **:** venture, risk **3 :** love affair

aventurado, -da *adj* **:** hazardous, risky

aventurar *vt* **:** to venture, to risk — **aventurarse** *vr* **:** to take a risk

aventurero[1]**, -ra** *adj* **:** adventurous

aventurero[2]**, -ra** *n* **:** adventurer

avergonzado, -da *adj* **1 :** ashamed **2 :** embarrassed

avergonzar {9} *vt* APENAR **:** to shame, to embarrass — **avergonzarse** *vr* APENARSE **:** to be ashamed, to be embarrassed

avería *nf* **1 :** damage **2 :** breakdown, malfunction

averiado, -da *adj* **1 :** damaged, faulty **2 :** broken down

averiar {85} *vt* **:** to damage — **averiarse** *vr* **:** to break down

averiguación *nf, pl* **-ciones :** investigation, inquiry

averiguar {10} *vt* **1 :** to find out, to ascertain **2 :** to investigate

aversión *nf, pl* **-siones :** aversion, dislike

avestruz *nm, pl* **-truces :** ostrich

avezado, -da *adj* **:** seasoned, experienced

aviación *nf, pl* **-ciones :** aviation

aviador, -dora *n* **:** aviator, flyer

aviar {85} *vt* **1 :** to prepare, to make ready **2 :** to tidy up **3 :** to equip, to supply

avicultor, -tora *n* **:** poultry farmer

avicultura *nf* **:** poultry farming

avidez *nf, pl* **-deces :** eagerness

ávido, -da *adj* **:** eager, avid — **ávidamente** *adv*

avieso, -sa *adj* **1 :** twisted, distorted **2 :** wicked, depraved

avinagrado, -da *adj* **:** vinegary, sour

avío *nm* **1 :** preparation, provision **2 :** loan (for agriculture or mining) **3 avíos** *nmpl* **:** gear, equipment

avión *nm, pl* **aviones :** airplane

avioneta *nf* **:** light airplane

avisar *vt* **1 :** to notify, to inform **2 :** to advise, to warn

aviso *nm* **1 :** notice **2 :** advertisement, ad **3** ADVERTENCIA **:** warning **4 estar sobre aviso :** to be on the alert

avispa *nf* **:** wasp

avispado, -da *adj fam* **:** clever, sharp

avispero *nm* **:** wasps' nest

avispón *nm, pl* **-pones :** hornet

avistar *vt* **:** to sight, to catch sight of

avituallar *vt* **:** to suppy with food, to provision

avivar *vt* **1 :** to enliven, to brighten **2 :** to strengthen, to intensify

avizorar *vt* **1** ACECHAR **:** to spy on, to watch **2 :** to observe, to perceive <se avizoran dificultades **:** difficulties are expected>

axila *nf* **:** underarm, armpit

axioma *nm* **:** axiom

axiomático, -ca *adj* **:** axiomatic

ay *interj* **1 :** oh! **2 :** ouch!, ow!

ayer[1] *adv* **:** yesterday

ayer[2] *nm* ANTAÑO **:** yesteryear, days gone by

ayote *nm CA, Mex* **:** squash, pumpkin

ayuda *nf* **1 :** help, assistance **2 ayuda de cámara :** valet

ayudante *nmf* **:** helper, assistant

ayudar *vt* **:** to help, to assist — **ayudarse** *vr* **~ de :** to make use of

ayunar *vi* **:** to fast

ayunas *nfpl* **en ~ :** fasting <este medicamento ha de tomarse en ayunas **:** this medication should be taken on an empty stomach>

ayuno *nm* **:** fast

ayuntamiento *nm* **1 :** town hall, city hall **2 :** town or city council

azabache *nm* **:** jet <negro azabache **:** jet black>

azada *nf* **:** hoe

azafata *nf* **1 :** stewardess *f* **2 :** hostess *f* (on a TV show)

azafrán *nm, pl* **-franes 1 :** saffron **2 :** crocus

azahar *nm* **:** orange blossom

azalea *nf* **:** azalea

azar *nm* **1 :** chance <juegos de azar **:** games of chance> **2 :** accident, misfortune **3 al azar :** at random, randomly

azaroso, -sa *adj* **1 :** perilous, hazardous **2 :** turbulent, eventful

azimut *nm* **:** azimuth

azogue *nm* **:** mercury, quicksilver

azorar *vt* **1 :** to alarm, to startle **2 :** to fluster, to embarrass — **azorarse** *vr* **:** to get embarrassed

azotar *vt* **1 :** to whip, to flog **2 :** to lash, to batter **3 :** to devastate, to afflict

azote *nm* **1** LÁTIGO **:** whip, lash **2** *fam* **:** spanking, licking **3 :** calamity, scourge

azotea *nf* **:** flat roof, terraced roof

azteca *adj & nmf* **:** Aztec

azúcar *nmf* **:** sugar — **azucarar** *vt*

azucarado, -da *adj* **:** sweetened, sugary

azucarera *nf* **:** sugar bowl

azucarero, -ra *adj* **:** sugar <industria azucarera **:** sugar industry>

azucena *nf* **:** white lily

azuela *nf* **:** adz

azufre *nm* **:** sulphur — **azufroso, -sa** *adj*

azul *adj & nm* : blue
azulado, -da *adj* : bluish
azulejo *nm* : ceramic tile, floor tile
azulete *nm* : bluing
azuloso, -sa *adj* : bluish
azur[1] *adj* CELESTE : azure
azur[2] *n* CELESTE : azure, sky blue
azuzar {21} *vt* : to incite, to egg on

B

b *nf* : second letter of the Spanish alphabet
baba *nf* **1** : spittle, saliva **2** : dribble, drool (of a baby) **3** : slime, ooze
babear *vi* **1** : to drool, to slobber **2** : to ooze
babel *nf* : babel, chaos, bedlam
babero *nm* : bib
babor *nm* : port, port side
babosa *nf* : slug (mollusk)
babosada *nf CA, Mex* : silly act or remark
baboso, -sa *adj* **1** : drooling, slobbering **2** : slimy **3** *CA, Mex fam* : silly, dumb
babucha *nf* : slipper
babuino *nm* : baboon
bacalao *nm* : cod (fish)
bache *nm* **1** : pothole **2** *PRi* : deep puddle **3** : bad period, rough time <bache económico : economic slump>
bachiller *nmf* : high school graduate
bachillerato *nm* : high school diploma
bacilo *nm* : bacillus
backgammon *nm* : backgammon
bacon *nm Spain* : bacon
bacteria *nf* : bacterium
bacteriano, -na *adj* : bacterial
bacteriología *nf* : bacteriology
bacteriológico, -ca *adj* : bacteriologic, bacteriological
bacteriólogo, -ga *n* : bacteriologist
báculo *nm* **1** : staff, stick **2** : comfort, support
badajo *nm* : clapper (of a bell)
badén *nm, pl* **badenes 1** : (paved) ford, channel **2** : dip, ditch (in a road)
bádminton *nm* : badminton
bafle *or* **baffle** *nm* **1** : baffle **2** : speaker, loudspeaker
bagaje *nm* **1** EQUIPAJE : baggage, luggage **2** : background <bagaje cultural : cultural baggage>
bagatela *nf* : trifle, trinket
bagre *nm* : catfish
bahía *nf* : bay
bailar *vt* : to dance — *vi* **1** : to dance **2** : to spin **3** : to be loose, to be too big
bailarín[1], **-rina** *adj, mpl* **-rines 1** : dancing **2** : fond of dancing
bailarín[2], **-rina** *n, mpl* **-rines 1** : dancer **2** : ballet dancer, ballerina *f*
baile *nm* **1** : dance **2** : dance party, ball **3 llevarse al baile a** *Mex fam* : to take for a ride, to take advantage of
baja *nf* **1** DESCENSO : fall, drop **2** : slump, recession **3** : loss, casualty **4 dar de baja** : to discharge, to dismiss **5 darse de baja** : to withdraw, to drop out
bajada *nf* **1** : descent **2** : dip, slope **3** : decrease, drop
bajar *vt* **1** DESCENDER : to lower, to let down, to take down **2** REDUCIR : to reduce (prices) 3 INCLINAR : to lower, to bow (the head) **4** : to go down, to descend **5 bajar de categoría** : to downgrade — *vi* **1** : to drop, to fall **2** : to come down, to go down **3** : to ebb (of tides) — **bajarse** *vr* **~ de** : to get off, to get out of (a vehicle)
bajeza *nf* **1** : low or despicable act **2** : baseness
bajío *nm* **1** : lowland **2** : shoal, sandbank, shallows
bajista *nmf* : bass player, bassist
bajo[1] *adv* **1** : down, low **2** : softly, quietly <habla más bajo : speak more softly>
bajo[2], **-ja** *adj* **1** : low **2** : short (of stature) **3** : soft, faint, deep (of sounds) **4** : lower <el bajo Amazonas : the lower Amazon> **5** : lowered <con la mirada baja : with lowered eyes> **6** : base, vile **7 los bajos fondos** : the underworld
bajo[3] *nm* **1** : bass (musical instrument) **2** : first floor, ground floor **3** : hemline
bajo[4] *prep* : under, beneath, below
bajón *nm, pl* **bajones** : sharp drop, slump
bajorrelieve *m* : bas-relief
bala *nf* **1** : bullet **2** : bale
balacera *nf* TIROTEO : shoot-out, gunfight
balada *nf* : ballad
balance *nm* **1** : balance **2** : balance sheet
balancear *vt* **1** : to balance **2** : to swing (one's arms, etc.) **3** : to rock (a boat) — **balancearse** *vr* **1** OSCILAR : to swing, to sway, to rock **2** VACILAR : to hesitate, to vacillate
balanceo *nm* **1** : swaying, rocking **2** : vacillation
balancín *nm, pl* **-cines 1** : rocking chair **2** SUBIBAJA : seesaw
balandra *nf* : sloop
balanza *nf* BÁSCULA : scales *pl,* balance
balar *vi* : to bleat
balaustrada *nf* : balustrade
balaustre *nm* : baluster
balazo *nm* **1** TIRO : shot, gunshot **2** : bullet wound
balboa *nf* : balboa (monetary unit of Panama)

balbucear *vi* **1 :** to mutter, to stammer **2 :** to prattle, to babble <los niños están balbuceando : the children are prattling away>
balbuceo *nm* **:** mumbling, stammering
balbucir → **balbucear**
balcánico, -ca *adj* **:** Balkan
balcón *nm, pl* **balcones :** balcony
balde *nm* **1** CUBO **:** bucket, pail **2 en ~ :** in vain, to no avail
baldío¹, -día *adj* **1 :** fallow, uncultivated **2 :** useless, vain
baldío² *nm* **1 :** wasteland **2** *Mex* **:** vacant lot
baldosa *nf* LOSETA **:** floor tile
balear *vt* **:** to shoot, to shoot at
balero *nm* **1** *Mex* **:** ball bearing **2** *Mex, PRi* **:** cup-and-ball toy
balido *nm* **:** bleat
balín *nm, pl* **balines :** pellet
balística *nf* **:** ballistics
balístico, -ca *adj* **:** ballistic
baliza *nf* **1 :** buoy **2 :** beacon (for aircraft)
ballena *nf* **:** whale
ballenero¹, -ra *adj* **:** whaling
ballenero², -ra *n* **:** whaler
ballenero³ *nm* **:** whaleboat, whaler
ballesta *nf* **1 :** crossbow **2 :** spring (of an automobile)
ballet *nm* **:** ballet
balneario *nm* **:** spa, bathing resort
balompié *nm* FUTBOL **:** soccer
balón *nm, pl* **balones :** ball
baloncesto *nm* BASQUETBOL **:** basketball
balsa *nf* **1 :** raft **2 :** balsa
balsámico, -ca *adj* **:** soothing
bálsamo *nm* **:** balsam, balm
báltico, -ca *adj* **:** Baltic
baluarte *nm* BASTIÓN **:** bulwark, bastion
bambolear *vi* **1 :** to sway, to swing **2 :** to wobble — **bambolearse** *vr*
bamboleo *nm* **1 :** swaying, swinging **2 :** wobbling
bambú *nm, pl* **bambúes** *or* **bambús :** bamboo
banal *adj* **:** banal, trivial
banalidad *nf* **:** banality
banana *nf* **:** banana
bananero¹, -ra *adj* **:** banana
bananero² *nm* **:** banana tree
banano *nm* **1 :** banana tree **2** *CA,Col* **:** banana
banca *nf* **1 :** banking **2** BANCO **:** bench
bancada *nf* **1 :** group, faction **2 :** workbench
bancal *nm* **1 :** terrace (in agriculture) **2 :** plot (of land)
bancario, -ria *adj* **:** bank, banking
bancarrota *nf* QUIEBRA **:** bankruptcy
banco *nm* **1 :** bank <banco central : central bank> <banco de datos : data bank> <banco de arena : sandbank> <banco de sangre : blood bank> **2** BANCA **:** stool, bench **3 :** pew **4 :** school (of fish)
banda *nf* **1 :** band, strip **2** *Mex* **:** belt <banda transportadora : conveyor belt> **3 :** band (of musicians) **4 :** gang (of persons), flock (of birds) **5 banda de rodadura :** tread (of a tire, etc.) **6 banda sonora** *or* **banda de sonido :** sound track
bandada *nf* **:** flock (of birds), school (of fish)
bandazo *nm* **:** swerving, lurch
bandearse *vr* **:** to look after oneself, to cope
bandeja *nf* **:** tray, platter
bandera *nf* **:** flag, banner
banderazo *nm* **:** starting signal (in sports)
banderilla *nf* **:** banderilla, dart (in bullfighting)
banderín *nm, pl* **-rines :** pennant, small flag
bandidaje *nm* **:** banditry
bandido, -da *n* BANDOLERO **:** bandit, outlaw
bando *nm* **1** FACCIÓN **:** faction, side **2** EDICTO **:** proclamation
bandolerismo *nm* **:** banditry
bandolero, -ra *n* BANDIDO **:** bandit, outlaw
banjo *nm* **:** banjo
banquero, -ra *n* **:** banker
banqueta *nf* **1 :** footstool, stool, bench **2** *Mex* **:** sidewalk
banquete *nm* **:** banquet
banquetear *v* **:** to feast
banquillo *nm* **1 :** bench (in sports) **2 :** dock, defendant's seat
bañadera *nf* → **bañera**
bañar *vt* **1 :** to bathe, to wash **2 :** to immerse, to dip **3 :** to coat, to cover <bañado en lágrimas : bathed in tears> — **bañarse** *vr* **1 :** to take a bath, to bathe **2 :** to go for a swim
bañera *nf* TINA **:** bathtub
bañista *nmf* **:** bather
baño *nm* **1 :** bath **2 :** swim, dip **3 :** bathroom **4 baño María :** double-boiler
baqueta *nf* **1 :** ramrod **2 baquetas** *nfpl* **:** drumsticks
bar *nm* **:** bar, tavern
baraja *nf* **:** deck of cards
barajar *vt* **1 :** to shuffle (cards) **2 :** to consider, to toy with
baranda *nf* **:** rail, railing
barandal *nm* **1 :** rail, railing **2 :** bannister, handrail
barandilla *nf Spain* **:** bannister, handrail, railing
barata *nf* **1** *Mex* **:** sale, bargain **2** *Chile* **:** cockroach
baratija *nf* **:** bauble, trinket
baratillo *nm* **:** rummage sale, flea market
barato¹ *adv* **:** cheap, cheaply <te lo vendo barato : I'll sell it to you cheap>
barato², -ta *adj* **:** cheap, inexpensive
baratura *nf* **1 :** cheapness **2 :** cheap thing
barba *nf* **1 :** beard, stubble **2 :** chin
barbacoa *nf* **:** barbecue

bárbaramente *adv* : barbarously
barbaridad *nf* **1** : barbarity, atrocity **2** **¡qué barbaridad!** : that's outrageous!
barbarie *nf* : barbarism, savagery
bárbaro[1] *adv fam* : wildly <anoche lo pasamos bárbaro : we had a wild time last night>
bárbaro[2], **-ra** *adj* **1** : barbarous, wild, uncivilized **2** *fam* : great, fantastic
bárbaro[3], **-ra** *n* : barbarian
barbecho *nm* : fallow land <dejar en barbecho : to leave fallow>
barbero, -ra *n* : barber
barbilla *nf* MENTÓN : chin
barbitúrico *nm* : barbiturate
barbudo[1], **-da** *adj* : bearded
barbudo[2] *nm* : bearded man
barca *nf* **1** : boat **2** **barca de pasaje** : ferryboat
barcaza *nf* : barge
barcia *nf* : chaff
barco *nm* **1** BARCA : boat **2** BUQUE, NAVE : ship
bardo *nm* : bard
bario *nm* : barium
barítono *nm* : baritone
barlovento *nm* : windward
barman *nm* : bartender
barniz *nm, pl* **barnices** **1** LACA : varnish, lacquer **2** : glaze (on ceramics, etc.)
barnizar {21} *vt* **1** : to varnish **2** : to glaze
barométrico, -ca *adj* : barometric
barómetro *nm* : barometer
barón *nm, pl* **barones** : baron
baronesa *nf* : baroness
baronet *nm* : baronet
barquero, -ra : boatman *m,* boatwoman *f*
barquillo *nm* : wafer, thin cookie or cracker
barra *nf* : bar
barraca *nf* **1** CABAÑA, CHOZA : hut, cabin **2** : booth, stall
barracuda *nf* : barracuda
barranca *nf* **1** : hillside, slope **2** → **barranco**
barranco *nm* : ravine, gorge
barredora *nf* : street sweeper (machine)
barrena *nf* **1** TALADRO : drill, auger, gimlet **2** : tailspin
barrenar *vt* **1** : to drill **2** : to undermine
barrendero, -ra *n* : sweeper, street cleaner
barrer *v* : to sweep — **barrerse** *vr* : to slide (in sports)
barrera *nf* OBSTÁCULO : barrier, obstacle <barrera de sonido : sound barrier>
barreta *nf* : crowbar
barriada *nf* **1** : district, quarter **2** : slums *pl*
barrica *nf* BARRIL, TONEL : barrel, cask, keg
barricada *nf* : barricade
barrida *nf* **1** : sweep **2** : slide (in sports)
barrido *nm* : sweeping
barriga *nf* PANZA : belly, paunch
barrigón, -gona *adj, mpl* **-gones** *fam* : potbellied, paunchy
barril *nm* **1** BARRICA : barrel, keg **2** **cerveza de barril** : draft beer
barrio *nm* **1** : neighborhood, district **2** **barrios bajos** : slums *pl*
barro *nm* **1** LODO : mud **2** ARCILLA : clay **3** ESPINILLA, GRANO : pimple, blackhead
barroco, -ca *adj* : baroque
barroso, -sa *adj* ENLODADO : muddy
barrote *nm* : bar (on a window)
barrunto *nm* **1** SOSPECHA : suspicion **2** INDICIO : sign, indication, hint
bártulos *nmpl* : things, belongings <liar los bártulos : to pack one's things>
barullo *nm* BULLA : racket, ruckus
basa *nf* : base, pedestal
basalto *nm* : basalt
basar *vt* FUNDAR : to base — **basarse** *vr* FUNDARSE **~ en** : to be based on
báscula *nf* BALANZA : balance, scales *pl*
base *nf* **1** : base, bottom **2** : base (in baseball) **3** FUNDAMENTO : basis, foundation **4** **base de datos** : database **5** **a base de** : based on, by means of **6** **en base a** : based on, on the basis of
básico, -ca *adj* FUNDAMENTAL : basic — **básicamente** *adv*
basílica *nf* : basilica
basquetbol *or* **básquetbol** *nm* BALONCESTO : basketball
basset *nm* : basset hound
bastante[1] *adv* **1** : enough, sufficiently <he trabajado bastante : I have worked enough> **2** : fairly, rather, quite <llegaron bastante temprano : they arrived quite early>
bastante[2] *adj* : enough, sufficient
bastante[3] *pron* : enough <hemos visto bastante : we have seen enough>
bastar *vi* : to be enough, to suffice
bastardilla *nf* CURSIVA : italic type, italics *pl*
bastardo, -da *adj & n* : bastard
bastidor *nm* **1** : framework, frame **2** : wing (in theater) <entre bastidores : backstage, behind the scenes>
bastilla *nf* : hem
bastión *nf, pl* **bastiones** BALUARTE : bastion, bulwark
basto, -ta *adj* : coarse, rough
bastón *nm, pl* **bastones** **1** : cane, walking stick **2** : baton **3** **bastón de mando** : staff (of authority)
basura *nf* DESECHOS : garbage, waste, refuse
basurero[1], **-ra** *n* : garbage collector
basurero[2] *nm Mex* : garbage can
bata *nf* **1** : bathrobe, housecoat **2** : smock, coverall, lab coat
batalla *nf* **1** : battle **2** : fight, struggle **3** **de ~** : ordinary, everyday <mis

zapatos de batalla : my everyday shoes>
batallar *vi* LIDIAR, LUCHAR : to battle, to fight
batallón *nm, pl* **-llones** : battalion
batata *nf* : yam, sweet potato
batazo *nm* HIT : hit (in baseball)
bate *nm* : baseball bat
batea *nf* **1** : tray, pan **2** : flat-bottomed boat, punt
bateador, -dora *n* : batter, hitter
batear *vi* : to bat — *vt* : to hit
batería *nf* **1** PILA : battery **2** : drum kit, drums *pl* **3** : artillery **4 batería de cocina** : kitchen utensils *pl*
baterista *nmf* : drummer
batido *nm* LICUADO : milk shake
batidor *nm* : eggbeater, whisk, mixer
batidora *nf* : (electric) mixer
batir *vt* **1** GOLPEAR : to beat, to hit **2** VENCER : to defeat **3** REVOLVER : to mix, to beat **4** : to break (a record) — **batirse** *vr* : to fight
batista *nf* : batiste, cambric
batuta *nf* **1** : baton **2 llevar la batuta** : to be the leader, to call the tune
baúl *nm* : trunk, chest
bautismal *adj* : baptismal
bautismo *nm* : baptism, christening
bautista *adj & nmf* : Baptist
bautizar {21} *vt* : to baptize, to christen
bautizo *nm* → **bautismo**
bávaro, -ra *adj & n* : Bavarian
baya *nf* **1** : berry **2 baya de saúco** : elderberry
bayeta *nf* : cleaning cloth
bayoneta *nf* : bayonet
baza *nf* **1** : trick (in card games) **2 meter baza en** : to butt in on
bazar *nm* : bazaar
bazo *nm* : spleen
bazofia *nf* **1** : table scraps *pl* **2** : slop, swill **3** : hogwash, rubbish
bazuca *nf* : bazooka
beagle *nm* : beagle
beatificar {72} *vt* : to beatify — **beatificación** *nf*
beatífico, -ca *adj* : beatific
beatitud *nf* : beatitude
beato, -ta *adj* **1** : blessed **2** : pious, devout **3** : sanctimonious, overly devout
bebé *nm* : baby
bebedero *nm* **1** ABREVADERO : watering trough **2** *Mex* : drinking fountain
bebedor, -dora *n* : drinker
beber *v* TOMAR : to drink
bebida *nf* : drink, beverage
beca *nf* : grant, scholarship
becado, -da *n* : scholar, scholarship holder
becerro, -rra *n* : calf
begonia *nf* : begonia
beige *adj & nm* : beige
beisbol *or* **béisbol** *nm* : baseball
beisbolista *nmf* : baseball player
beldad *nf* BELLEZA, HERMOSURA : beauty
belén *nf, pl* **belenes** NACIMIENTO : Nativity scene
belga *adj & nmf* : Belgian
beliceño, -ña *adj & n* : Belizean
belicista[1] *adj* : militaristic
belicista[2] *nmf* : warmonger
bélico, -ca *adj* GUERRERO : war, fighting <esfuerzos bélicos : war efforts>
belicosidad *nf* : bellicosity
belicoso, -sa *adj* **1** : warlike, martial **2** : aggressive, belligerent
beligerancia *nf* : belligerence
beligerante *adj & nmf* : belligerent
bellaco[1], **-ca** *adj* : sly, cunning
bellaco[2], **-ca** *n* : rogue, scoundrel
belleza *nf* BELDAD, HERMOSURA : beauty
bello, -lla *adj* **1** HERMOSO : beautiful **2 bellas artes** : fine arts
bellota *nf* : acorn
bemol *nm* : flat (in music) — **bemol** *adj*
benceno *nm* : benzene
bendecir {11} *vt* **1** CONSAGRAR : to bless, to consecrate **2** ALABAR : to praise, to extol **3 bendecir la mesa** : to say grace
bendición *nf, pl* **-ciones** : benediction, blessing
bendiga, bendijo, etc. → **bendecir**
bendito, -ta *adj* **1** : blessed, holy **2** : fortunate **3** : silly, simple-minded
benedictino, -na *adj & n* : Benedictine
benefactor[1], **-tora** *adj* : beneficent
benefactor[2], **-tora** *n* : benefactor, benefactress *f*
beneficencia *nf* : beneficence, charity
beneficiar *vt* : to benefit, to be of assistance to — **beneficiarse** *vr* : to benefit, to profit
beneficiario, -ria *n* : beneficiary
beneficio *nm* **1** GANANCIA, PROVECHO : gain, profit **2** : benefit
beneficioso, -sa *adj* PROVECHOSO : beneficial
benéfico, -ca *adj* : charitable, beneficent
benemérito, -ta *adj* : meritorious, worthy
beneplácito *nm* : approval, consent
benevolencia *nf* BONDAD : benevolence, kindness
benévolo, -la *adj* BONDADOSO : benevolent, kind, good
bengala *nf* **luz de bengala 1** : flare (signal) **2** : sparkler
bengalí[1] *adj & nmf* : Bengali
bengalí[2] *nm* : Bengali (language)
benignidad *nf* : mildness, kindness
benigno, -na *adj* : benign, mild
beninés, -nesa *adj & n* : Beninese
benjamín, -mina *n, mpl* **-mines** : youngest child
beodo[1], **-da** *adj* : drunk, inebriated
beodo[2], **-da** *n* : drunkard
berberecho *nm* : cockle
berbiquí *nm* : brace (in carpentry)
berenjena *nf* : eggplant
bergantín *nm, pl* **-tines** : brig (ship)
berilo *nm* : beryl

bermudas *nfpl* **:** Bermuda shorts

berrear *vi* **1 :** to bellow, to low **2 :** to bawl, to howl

berrido *nm* **1 :** bellowing **2 :** howl, scream

berrinche *nm fam* **:** tantrum, conniption

berro *nm* **:** watercress

berza *nf* **:** cabbage

besar *vt* **:** to kiss

beso *nm* **:** kiss

bestia[1] *adj* **1 :** ignorant, stupid **2 :** boorish, rude

bestia[2] *nf* **:** beast, animal

bestia[3] *nmf* **1** IGNORANTE **:** ignoramus **2 :** brute

bestial *adj* **1 :** bestial, beastly **2** *fam* **:** huge, enormous <hace un frío bestial : it's terribly cold> **3** *fam* **:** great, fantastic

besuquear *vt fam* **:** to cover with kisses — **besuquearse** *vr fam* **:** to neck, to smooch

betabel *nm Mex* **:** beet

betún *nm, pl* **betunes 1 :** shoe polish **2** *Mex* **:** icing

bianual *adj* **:** biannual

biatlón *nm, pl* **-lones :** biathlon

biberón *nm, pl* **-rones :** baby's bottle

biblia *nf* **1 :** bible **2 la Biblia :** the Bible

bíblico, -ca *adj* **:** biblical

bibliografía *nf* **:** bibliography

bibliográfico, -ca *adj* **:** bibliographic, bibliographical

bibliógrafo, -fa *n* **:** bibliographer

biblioteca *nf* **:** library

bibliotecario, -ria *n* **:** librarian

bicameral *adj* **:** bicameral

bicarbonato *nm* **1 :** bicarbonate **2 bicarbonato de soda :** sodium bicarbonate, baking soda

bicentenario *nm* **:** bicentennial

bíceps *nms & pl* **:** biceps

bicho *nm* **:** small animal, bug, insect

bici *nf fam* **:** bike

bicicleta *nf* **:** bicycle

bicolor *adj* **:** two-tone

bicúspide *adj* **:** bicuspid

bidón *nm, pl* **bidones :** large can, (oil) drum

bien[1] *adv* **1 :** well <¿dormiste bien? : did you sleep well?> **2** CORRECTAMENTE **:** correctly, properly, right <hay que hacerlo bien : it must be done correctly> **3 :** very, quite <el libro era bien divertido : the book was very amusing> **4 :** easily <bien puede acabarlo en un día : he can easily finish it in a day> **5 :** willingly, readily <bien lo aceptaré : I'll gladly accept it> **6 bien que :** although **7 más bien :** rather

bien[2] *adj* **1 :** well, OK, all right <¿te sientes bien? : are you feeling all right?> **2 :** pleasant, agreeable <las flores huelen bien : the flowers smell very nice> **3 :** satisfactory **4 :** correct, right

bien[3] *nm* **1 :** good <el bien y el mal : good and evil> **2 bienes** *nmpl* **:** property, goods, possessions

bienal *adj & nf* **:** biennial — **bienalmente** *adv*

bienaventurado, -da *adj* **1 :** blessed **2 :** fortunate, happy

bienaventuranzas *nfpl* **:** Beatitudes

bienestar *nm* **1 :** welfare, well-being **2** CONFORT **:** comfort

bienhechor[1], **-chora** *adj* **:** beneficent, benevolent

bienhechor[2], **-chora** *n* **:** benefactor, benefactress *f*

bienintencionado, -da *adj* **:** well-meaning

bienvenida *nf* **1 :** welcome **2 dar la bienvenida a :** to welcome

bienvenido, -da *adj* **:** welcome

bies *nm* **:** bias (in sewing)

bife *nm Arg, Chile, Uru* **:** steak

bífido, -da *adj* **:** forked

bifocal *adj* **:** bifocal

bifocales *nmpl* **:** bifocals

bifurcación *nf, pl* **-ciones :** fork (in a river or road)

bifurcarse {72} *vr* **:** to fork

bigamia *nf* **:** bigamy

bígamo, -ma *n* **:** bigamist

bigote *nm* **1 :** mustache **2 :** whisker (of an animal)

bigotudo, -da *adj* **:** mustached, having a big mustache

bikini *nm* **:** bikini

bilateral *adj* **:** bilateral — **bilateralmente** *adv*

bilingüe *adj* **:** bilingual

bilioso, -sa *adj* **1 :** bilious **2 :** irritable

bilis *nf* **:** bile

billar *nm* **:** pool, billiards

billete *nm* **1 :** bill <un billete de cinco dólares : a five-dollar bill> **2** BOLETO **:** ticket <billete de ida y vuelta : round-trip ticket>

billetera *nf* **:** billfold, wallet

billón *nm, pl* **billones 1 :** billion (Great Britain) **2 :** trillion (U.S.A.)

bimestral *adj* **:** bimonthly — **bimestralmente** *adv*

bimotor *adj* **:** twin-engined

binacional *adj* **:** binational

binario, -ria *adj* **:** binary

binocular *adj* **:** binocular

binoculares *nmpl* **:** binoculars

binomio *nm* **:** binomial

biodegradable *adj* **:** biodegradable

biodegradarse *vr* **:** to biodegrade

biodiversidad *nf* **:** biodiversity

biofísica *nf* **:** biophysics

biofísico[1], **-ca** *adj* **:** biophysical

biofísico[2], **-ca** *n* **:** biophysicist

biografía *nf* **:** biography

biográfico, -ca *adj* **:** biographical

biógrafo, -fa *n* **:** biographer

biología *nf* **:** biology

biológico, -ca *adj* **:** biological, biologic — **biológicamente** *adv*

biólogo, -ga *n* **:** biologist

biombo *nm* MAMPARA : folding screen, room divider

biomecánica *nf* : biomechanics

biopsia *nf* : biopsy

bioquímica *nf* : biochemistry

bioquímico[1], **-ca** *adj* : biochemical

bioquímico[2], **-ca** *n* : biochemist

biosfera *or* **biósfera** *nf* : biosphere

biotecnología *nf* : biotechnology

biótico, -ca *adj* : biotic

bipartidismo *nm* : two-party system

bipartidista *adj* : bipartisan

bípedo *nm* : biped

birlar *vt fam* : to swipe, to pinch

birmano, -na *adj & n* : Burmese

bis[1] *adv* **1** : twice, again (in music) **2** : a, A <artículo 47 bis : Article 47A> <calle Bolívar, número 70 bis : Bolívar Street, number 70A>

bis[2] *nm* : encore

bisabuelo, -la *n* : great-grandfather *m,* great-grandmother *f,* great-grandparent

bisagra *nf* : hinge

bisbisar *vt fam* : to mutter, to mumble

bisecar {72} *vt* : bisect — **bisección** *nf*

bisel *nm* : bevel

biselar *vt* : to bevel

bisexual *adj* : bisexual

bisiesto *adj* **año bisiesto** : leap year

bismuto *nm* : bismuth

bisnieto, -ta *n* : great-grandson *m,* great-granddaughter *f,* great-grandchild

bisonte *nm* : bison, buffalo

bisoñé *nm* : hairpiece, toupee

bisoño[1], **-ña** *adj* : inexperienced, green

bisoño[2], **-ña** *n* : rookie, greenhorn

bistec *nm* : steak, beefsteak

bisturí *nm* ESCALPELO : scalpel

bisutería *nf* : costume jewelry

bit *nm* : bit (unit of information)

bituminoso, -sa *adj* : bituminous

bivalvo *nm* : bivalve

bizarría *nf* **1** : courage, gallantry **2** : generosity

bizarro, -rra *adj* **1** VALIENTE : courageous, valiant **2** GENEROSO : generous

bizco, -ca *adj* : cross-eyed

bizcocho *nm* **1** : sponge cake **2** : biscuit **3** *Mex* : breadstick

bizquera *nf* : crossed eyes, squint

blanco[1], **-ca** *adj* : white

blanco[2], **-ca** *n* : white person

blanco[3] *nm* **1** : white **2** : target, bull's-eye <dar en el blanco : to hit the target, to hit the nail on the head> **3** : blank space, blank <un cheque en blanco : a blank check>

blancura *nf* : whiteness

blancuzco, -ca *adj* **1** : whitish, off-white **2** PÁLIDO : pale

blandir {1} *vt* : to wave, to brandish

blando, -da *adj* **1** SUAVE : soft, tender **2** : weak (in character) **3** : lenient

blandura *nf* **1** : softness, tenderness **2** : leniency

blanqueador *nm* : bleach, whitener

blanquear *vt* **1** : to whiten, to bleach **2** : to shut out (in sports) **3** : to launder (money) — *vi* : to turn white

blanquillo *nm CA, Mex* : egg

blasfemar *vi* : to blaspheme

blasfemia *nf* : blasphemy

blasfemo, -ma *adj* : blasphemous

blazer *nm* : blazer

bledo *nm* **no me importa un bledo** *fam* : I couldn't care less, I don't give a damn

blindado, -da *adj* ACORAZADO : armored

blindaje *nm* **1** : armor, armor plating **2** : shield (for cables, machinery, etc.)

bloc *nm, pl* **blocs** : writing pad, pad of paper

blof *nm Col, Mex* : bluff

blofear *vi Col, Mex* : to bluff

blondo, -da *adj* : blond, flaxen

bloque *nm* **1** : block **2** GRUPO : bloc <el bloque comunista : the Communist bloc>

bloquear *vt* **1** OBSTRUIR : to block, to obstruct **2** : to blockade

bloqueo *nm* **1** OBSTRUCCIÓN : blockage, obstruction **2** : blockade

blusa *nf* : blouse

blusón *nm, pl* **blusones** : loose shirt, smock

boa *nf* : boa

boato *nm* : ostentation, show

bobada *nf* : folly, nonsense

bobalicón, -cona *adj, mpl* **-cones** *fam* : silly, stupid

bobina *nf* CARRETE : bobbin, reel

bobo[1], **-ba** *adj* : silly, stupid

bobo[2], **-ba** *n* : fool, simpleton

boca *nf* **1** : mouth **2** **boca arriba** : face up, on one's back **3** **boca abajo** : face down, prone **4** **boca de riego** : hydrant **5** **en boca de** : according to

bocacalle *nf* : entrance to a street <gire a la última bocacalle : take the last turning>

bocadillo *nm Spain* : sandwich

bocado *nm* **1** : bite, mouthful **2** FRENO : bit (of a bridle)

bocajarro *nm* **a ~** : point-blank, directly

bocallave *nf* : keyhole

bocanada *nf* **1** : swig, swallow **2** : puff, mouthful (of smoke) **3** : gust (of air) **4** : stream (of people)

boceto *nm* : sketch, outline

bochinche *nm fam* : ruckus, uproar

bochorno *nm* **1** VERGÜENZA : embarrassment **2** : hot and humid weather **3** : hot flash

bochornoso, -sa *adj* **1** EMBARAZOSO : embarrassing **2** : hot and muggy

bocina *nf* **1** : horn, trumpet **2** : automobile horn **3** : mouthpiece (of a telephone) **4** *Mex* : loudspeaker

bocinazo *nm* : honk (of a horn)

bocio *nm* : goiter

bocón, -cona *n, mpl* **bocones** *fam* : blabbermouth, loudmouth

boda *nf* : wedding

bodega *nf* **1** : wine cellar **2** *Chile, Col, Mex* : storeroom, warehouse **3** (*in various countries*) : grocery store

bofetada *nf* CACHETADA : slap on the face

bofetear *vt* CACHETEAR : to slap

bofetón *nm* → **bofetada**

bofo, -fa *adj* : flabby

boga *nf* : fashion, vogue <estar en boga : to be in style>

bogotano[1], -na *adj* : of or from Bogotá

bogotano[2], -na *n* : person from Bogotá

bohemio, -mia *adj & n* : bohemian, Bohemian

boicot *nm, pl* **boicots** : boycott

boicotear *vt* : to boycott

boina *nf* : beret

boiserie *nf* : wood paneling, wainscoting

boj *nm, pl* **bojes** : box (plant), boxwood

bola *nf* **1** : ball <bola de nieve : snowball> **2** *fam* : lie, fib **3** *Mex fam* : bunch, group <una bola de rateros : a bunch of thieves> **4** *Mex* : uproar, tumult

bolear *vt Mex* : to polish (shoes)

bolera *nf* : bowling alley

bolero *nm* : bolero

boleta *nf* **1** : ballot **2** : ticket **3** : receipt

boletería *nf* TAQUILLA : box office, ticket office

boletín *nm, pl* **-tines 1** : bulletin **2** : journal, review **3 boletín de prensa** : press release

boleto *nm* BILLETE : ticket

boliche *nm* **1** BOLOS : bowling **2** *Arg* : bar, tavern

bolígrafo *nm* : ballpoint pen

bolillo *nm* **1** : bobbin **2** *Mex* : roll, bun

bolívar *nm* : bolivar (monetary unit of Venezuela)

boliviano[1], -na *adj & n* : Bolivian

boliviano[2] *nm* : boliviano (monetary unit of Bolivia)

bollo *nm* : bun, sweet roll

bolo *nm* : bowling pin, tenpin

bolos *nmpl* BOLICHE : bowling

bolsa *nf* **1** : bag, sack **2** *Mex* : pocketbook, purse **3** *Mex* : pocket **4 la Bolsa** : the stock market, the stock exchange **5 bolsa de trabajo** : employment agency

bolsear *vi Mex* : to pick pockets

bolsillo *nm* **1** : pocket **2 dinero de bolsillo** : pocket change, loose change

bolso *nm* : pocketbook, handbag

bomba *nf* **1** : bomb **2** : bubble **3** : pump <bomba de gasolina : gas pump>

bombachos *nmpl* : baggy pants, bloomers

bombardear *vt* **1** : to bomb **2** : to bombard

bombardeo *nm* **1** : bombing, shelling **2** : bombardment

bombardero *nm* : bomber (airplane)

bombástico, -ca *adj* : bombastic

bombear *vt* : to pump

bombero, -ra *n* : firefighter, fireman *m*

bombilla *nf* : lightbulb

bombillo *nm CA, Col, Ven* : lightbulb

bombo *nm* **1** : bass drum **2** *fam* : exaggerated praise, hype <con bombos y platillos : with great fanfare>

bombón *nm, pl* **bombones 1** : bonbon, chocolate **2** *Mex* : marshmallow

bonachón[1], -chona *adj, mpl* **-chones** *fam* : good-natured, kindhearted

bonachón[2], -chona *n, mpl* **-chones** *fam* BUENAZO : kindhearted person

bonaerense[1] *adj* : of or from Buenos Aires

bonaerense[2] *nmf* : person from Buenos Aires

bonanza *nf* **1** PROSPERIDAD : prosperity <bonanza económica : economic boom> **2** : calm weather **3** : rich ore deposit, bonanza

bondad *nf* BENEVOLENCIA : goodness, kindness <tener la bondad de hacer algo : to be kind enough to do something>

bondadoso, -sa *adj* BENÉVOLO : kind, kindly, good — **bondadosamente** *adv*

bonete *nm* : cap, mortarboard

boniato *nm* : sweet potato

bonificación *nf, pl* **-ciones 1** : discount **2** : bonus, extra

bonito[1] *adv* : nicely, well <¡qué bonito canta tu hermana! : your sister sings wonderfully!>

bonito[2], -ta *adj* LINDO : pretty, lovely <tiene un apartamento bonito : she has a nice apartment>

bonito[3] *nm* : bonito (tuna)

bono *nm* **1** : bond <bono bancario : bank bond> **2** : voucher

boqueada *nf* : gasp <to give one's last gasp : dar la última boqueada>

boquear *vi* **1** : to gasp **2** : to be dying

boquete *nm* : gap, opening, breach

boquiabierto, -ta *adj* : open-mouthed, speechless, agape

boquilla *nf* : mouthpiece (of a musical instrument)

borbollar *vi* : to bubble

borbotar *or* **borbotear** *vi* : to boil, to bubble, to gurgle

borboteo *nm* : bubbling, gurgling

borda *nf* : gunwale

bordado *nm* : embroidery, needlework

bordar *v* : to embroider

borde *nm* **1** : border, edge **2 al borde de** : on the verge of <estoy al borde de la locura : I'm about to go crazy>

bordear *vt* **1** : to border, to skirt <el Río Este bordea Manhattan : the East River borders Manhattan> **2** : to border on <bordea la irrealidad : it borders on unreality> **3** : to line <una calle bordeada de árboles : a street lined with trees>

bordillo *nm* : curb

bordo *nm* **a ~** : aboard, on board

boreal *adj* : northern

borgoña *nf* : burgundy

bórico, -ca *adj* **:** boric <ácido bórico : boric acid>
boricua *adj & nmf fam* **:** Puerto Rican
borinqueño, -ña → **boricua**
borla *nf* **1 :** pom-pom, tassel **2 :** powder puff
boro *nm* **:** boron
borrachera *nf* **:** drunkenness <agarró una borrachera : he got drunk>
borrachín, -china *n, mpl* **-chines** *fam* **:** lush, drunk
borracho[1], **-cha** *adj* EBRIO **:** drunk, intoxicated
borracho[2], **-cha** *n* **:** drunk, drunkard
borrador *nm* **1 :** rough copy, first draft <en borrador : in the rough> **2 :** eraser
borrar *vt* **:** to erase, to blot out — **borrarse** *vr* **1 :** to fade, to fade away **2 :** to resign, to drop out **3** *Mex fam* **:** to split, to leave <me borro : I'm out of here>
borrascoso, -sa *adj* **:** gusty, blustery
borrego, -ga *n* **1 :** lamb, sheep **2 :** simpleton, fool
borrico *nm* → **burro**
borrón *nm, pl* **borrones :** smudge, blot <borrón y cuenta nueva : let's start on a clean slate, let's start over again>
borronear *vt* **:** to smudge, to blot
borroso, -sa *adj* **1 :** blurry, smudgy **2** CONFUSO **:** unclear, confused
boscoso, -sa *adj* **:** wooded
bosnio, -nia *adj & n* **:** Bosnian
bosque *nm* **:** woods, forest
bosquecillo *nm* **:** grove, copse, thicket
bosquejar *vt* ESBOZAR **:** to outline, to sketch
bosquejo *nm* **1** TRAZADO **:** outline, sketch **2 :** draft
bostezar {21} *vi* **:** to yawn
bostezo *nm* **:** yawn
bota *nf* **1 :** boot **2 :** wineskin
botana *nf Mex* **:** snack, appetizer
botanear *vi Mex* **:** to have a snack
botánica *nf* **:** botany
botánico[1], **-ca** *adj* **:** botanical
botánico[2], **-ca** *n* **:** botanist
botar *vt* **1** ARROJAR **:** to throw, to fling, to hurl **2** TIRAR **:** to throw out, to throw away **3 :** to launch (a ship)
bote *nm* **1 :** small boat <bote de remos : rowboat> **2 :** can, jar **3 :** jump, bounce **4** *Mex fam* **:** jail
botella *nf* **:** bottle
botica *nf* FARMACIA **:** drugstore, pharmacy
boticario, -ria *n* FARMACÉUTICO **:** pharmacist, druggist
botín *nm, pl* **botines 1 :** baby's bootee **2 :** ankle boot **3 :** booty, plunder
botiquín *nm, pl* **-quines 1 :** medicine cabinet **2 :** first-aid kit
botón *nm, pl* **botones 1 :** button **2 :** bud **3** INSIGNIA **:** badge
botones *nmfs & pl* **:** bellhop
botulismo *nm* **:** botulism
boulevard [ˌbuleˈvar] *nm* → **bulevar**
bouquet *nm* **1 :** fragrance, bouquet (of wine) **2** RAMILLETE **:** bouquet (of flowers)
boutique *nf* **:** boutique
bóveda *nf* **1 :** vault, dome **2** CRIPTA **:** crypt
bovino, -na *adj* **:** bovine
box *nm, pl* **boxes 1 :** pit (in auto racing) **2** *Mex* **:** boxing
boxeador, -dora *n* **:** boxer
boxear *vi* **:** to box
boxeo *nm* **:** boxing
boya *nf* **:** buoy
boyante *adj* **1 :** buoyant **2 :** prosperous, thriving
bozal *nm* **1 :** muzzle **2 :** halter (for a horse)
bracear *vi* **1 :** to wave one's arms **2 :** to make strokes (in swimming)
bracero, -ra *n* **:** migrant worker, day laborer
braguero *nm* **:** truss (in medicine)
bragueta *nf* **:** fly, pants zipper
braille *adj & nm* **:** braille
bramante *nm* **:** twine, string
bramar *vi* **1** RUGIR **:** to roar, to bellow **2 :** to howl (of the wind)
bramido *nm* **:** bellowing, roar
brandy *nm* **:** brandy
branquia *nf* AGALLA **:** gill
brasa *nf* ASCUA **:** ember, live coal
brasero *nm* **:** brazier
brasier *nm Col, Mex* **:** brassiere, bra
brasileño, -ña *adj & n* **:** Brazilian
bravata *nf* **1** JACTANCIA **:** boast, bravado **2** AMENAZA **:** threat
bravo, -va *adj* **1** FEROZ **:** ferocious, fierce <un perro bravo : a ferocious dog> **2** EXCELENTE **:** excellent, great <¡bravo! : bravo!, well done!> **3 :** rough, rugged, wild **4 :** annoyed, angry
bravucón, -cona *n, mpl* **-cones :** bully
bravuconadas *nfpl* **:** bravado
bravura *nf* **1** FEROCIDAD **:** fierceness, ferocity **2** VALENTÍA **:** bravery
braza *nf* **1 :** breaststroke **2 :** fathom (unit of length)
brazada *nf* **:** stroke (in swimming)
brazalete *nm* PULSERA **:** bracelet, bangle
brazo *nm* **1 :** arm **2 brazo derecho :** right-hand man **3 brazos** *nmpl* **:** hands, laborers
brea *nf* ALQUITRÁN **:** tar, pitch
brebaje *nm* **:** potion, brew
brecha *nf* **1 :** gap, breach <estar siempre en la brecha : to be always there when needed, to stay in the thick of things> **2 :** gash
brécol *nm* **:** broccoli
brega *nf* **1** LUCHA **:** struggle, fight **2 :** hard work
bregar {52} *vi* **1** LUCHAR **:** to struggle **2 :** to toil, to work hard **3 ~ con :** to deal with
brete *nm* **:** jam, tight spot
breve *adj* **1** CORTO **:** brief, short **2 en ~ :** shortly, in short — **brevemente** *adv*
brevedad *nf* **:** brevity, shortness
breviario *nm* **:** breviary

brezal *nm* **:** heath, moor
brezo *nm* **:** heather
bribón, -bona *n, mpl* **bribones :** rascal, scamp
bricolaje *or* **bricolage** *nm* **:** do-it-yourself
brida *nf* **:** bridle
brigada *nf* **1 :** brigade **2 :** gang, team, squad
brigadier *nm* **:** brigadier
brillante[1] *adj* **:** brilliant, bright — **brillantemente** *adv*
brillante[2] *nm* DIAMANTE **:** diamond
brillantez *nf* **:** brilliance, brightness
brillar *vi* **:** to shine, to sparkle
brillo *nm* **1** LUSTRE **:** luster, shine **2 :** brilliance
brilloso, -sa *adj* LUSTROSO **:** lustrous, shiny
brincar {72} *vi* **1** SALTAR **:** to jump around, to leap about **2 :** to frolic, to gambol
brinco *nm* **1** SALTO **:** jump, leap, skip **2 pegar un brinco :** to give a start, to jump
brindar *vi* **:** to drink a toast <brindó por los vencedores : he toasted the victors> — *vt* OFRECER, PROPORCIONAR **:** to offer, to provide — **brindarse** *vr* **:** to offer one's assistance, to volunteer
brindis *nm* **:** toast, drink <hacer un brindis : to drink a toast>
brinque, etc. → **brincar**
brío *nm* **1 :** force, determination **2 :** spirit, verve
brioso, -sa *adj* **:** spirited, lively
briqueta *nf* **:** briquette
brisa *nf* **:** breeze
británico[1]**, -ca** *adj* **:** British
británico[2]**, -ca** *n* **1 :** British person **2 los británicos :** the British
brizna *nf* **1 :** strand, thread **2 :** blade (of grass)
brocado *nm* **:** brocade
brocha *nf* **:** paintbrush
broche *nm* **1** ALFILER **:** brooch **2 :** fastener, clasp **3 broche de oro :** finishing touch
brocheta *nf* **:** skewer
brócoli *nm* **:** broccoli
broma *nf* **1** CHISTE **:** joke, prank **2 :** fun, merriment **3 en ~ :** in jest, jokingly
bromear *vi* **:** to joke, to fool around <sólo estaba bromeando : I was only kidding>
bromista[1] *adj* **:** fun-loving, joking
bromista[2] *nmf* **:** joker, prankster
bromo *nm* **:** bromine
bronca *nf fam* **:** fight, quarrel, fuss
bronce *nm* **:** bronze
bronceado[1]**, -da** *adj* **1 :** tanned, suntanned **2 :** bronze
bronceado[2] *nm* **1 :** suntan, tan **2 :** bronzing
broncearse *vr* **:** to get a suntan
bronco, -ca *adj* **1 :** harsh, rough **2 :** untamed, wild
bronquial *adj* **:** bronchial
bronquio *nm* **:** bronchial tube, bronchus
bronquitis *nf* **:** bronchitis
broqueta *nf* **:** skewer
brotar *vi* **1 :** to bud, to sprout **2 :** to spring up, to stream, to gush forth **3 :** to break out, to appear
brote *nm* **1 :** outbreak **2 :** sprout, bud, shoot
broza *nf* **1 :** brushwood **2** MALEZA **:** scrub, undergrowth
brujería *nf* HECHICERÍA **:** witchcraft, sorcery
brujo[1]**, -ja** *adj* **:** bewitching
brujo[2]**, -ja** *n* **:** warlock *m,* witch *f,* sorcerer
brújula *nf* **:** compass
bruma *nf* **:** haze, mist
brumoso, -sa *adj* **:** hazy, misty
bruñir {38} *vt* **:** to burnish, to polish (metals)
brusco, -ca *adj* **1** SÚBITO **:** sudden, abrupt **2 :** curt, brusque — **bruscamente** *adv*
brusquedad *nf* **1 :** abruptness, suddenness **2 :** brusqueness
brutal *adj* **1 :** brutal **2** *fam* **:** incredible, terrific — **brutalmente** *adv*
brutalidad *nf* CRUELDAD **:** brutality
brutalizar {21} *vt* **:** to brutalize, to maltreat
bruto[1]**, -ta** *adj* **1 :** gross <peso bruto : gross weight> <ingresos brutos : gross income> **2 :** unrefined <petróleo bruto : crude oil> **3 :** brutish, stupid
bruto[2]**, -ta** *n* **1 :** brute **2 :** dunce, blockhead
bucal *adj* **:** oral
bucanero *nm* **:** buccaneer, pirate
buccino *nm* **:** whelk
buceador, -dora *n* **:** diver, scuba diver
bucear *vi* **1 :** to dive, to swim underwater **2 :** to explore, to delve
buceo *nm* **1 :** diving, scuba diving **2 :** exploration, searching
buche *nm* **1 :** crop (of a bird) **2** *fam* **:** belly, gut **3 :** mouthful <hacer buches : to rinse one's mouth>
bucle *nm* **1 :** curl, ringlet **2 :** loop
bucólico, -ca *adj* **:** bucolic
budín *nm, pl* **budines :** pudding
budismo *nm* **:** Buddhism
budista *adj & nmf* **:** Buddhist
buen → **bueno**[1]
buenamente *adv* **1 :** easily **2 :** willingly
buenaventura *nf* **1 :** good luck **2 :** fortune, future <le dijo la buenaventura : she told his fortune>
buenazo, -za *n fam* BONACHÓN **:** kindhearted person
bueno[1]**, -na** *adj* (**buen** *before masculine singular nouns*) **1 :** good <una buena idea : a good idea> **2** BONDADOSO **:** nice, kind **3** APROPIADO **:** proper, appropriate **4** SANO **:** well, healthy **5 :** considerable, goodly <una buena cantidad : a lot> **6 buenos días**

: hello, good day **7 buenas tardes** : good afternoon **8 buenas noches** : good evening, good night
bueno[2] *interj* **1 :** OK!, all right! **2** *Mex* **:** hello! (on the telephone)
buey *nm* **:** ox, steer
búfalo *nm* **1 :** buffalo **2 búfalo de agua :** water buffalo
bufanda *nf* **:** scarf, muffler
bufar *vi* **:** to snort
bufet *or* **bufé** *nm* **:** buffet-style meal
bufete *nm* **1 :** law firm, law office **2 :** writing desk
bufido *nm* **:** snort
bufo, -fa *adj* **:** comic
bufón, -fona *n, mpl* **bufones :** clown, buffoon, jester
bufonada *nf* **1 :** jest, buffoonery **2 :** sarcasm
buhardilla *nf* **1** ÁTICO, DESVÁN **:** attic **2 :** dormer window
búho *nm* **1 :** owl **2** *fam* **:** hermit, recluse
buhonero, -ra *n* MERCACHIFLE **:** peddler
buitre *nm* **:** vulture
bujía *nf* **:** spark plug
bulbo *nm* **:** bulb
bulboso, -sa *adj* **:** bulbous
bulevar *nm* **:** boulevard
búlgaro, -ra *adj & n* **:** Bulgarian
bulla *nf* BARULLO **:** racket, rowdiness
bullicio *nm* **1 :** ruckus, uproar **2 :** hustle and bustle
bullicioso, -sa *adj* **:** noisy, busy, turbulent
bullir {38} *vi* **1** HERVIR **:** to boil **2** MOVERSE **:** to stir, to bustle about
bulto *nm* **1 :** package, bundle **2 :** piece of luggage, bag **3 :** size, bulk, volume **4 :** form, shape **5 :** lump (on the body), swelling, bulge
bumerán *nm, pl* **-ranes :** boomerang
búnker *nm, pl* **búnkers :** bunker
búnquer *nm* → **búnker**
buñuelo *nm* **:** fried pastry
buque *nm* BARCO **:** ship, vessel
burbuja *nf* **:** bubble, blister (on a surface)
burbujear *vi* **1 :** to bubble **2 :** to fizz
burbujeo *nm* **:** bubbling
burdel *nm* **:** brothel, whorehouse
burdo, -da *adj* **1 :** coarse, rough **2 :** crude, clumsy <una burda mentira : a clumsy lie> — **burdamente** *adj*
burgués, -guesa *adj & n, mpl* **burgueses :** bourgeois
burguesía *nf* **:** bourgeoisie, middle class
burla *nf* **1 :** mockery, ridicule **2 :** joke, trick **3 hacer burla de :** to make fun of, to mock
burlar *vt* ENGAÑAR **:** to trick, to deceive — **burlarse** *vr* **~ de :** to make fun of, to ridicule
burlesco, -ca *adj* **:** burlesque, comic
burlón[1]**, -lona** *adj, mpl* **burlones :** joking, mocking
burlón[2]**, -lona** *n, mpl* **burlones :** joker
burocracia *nf* **:** bureaucracy
burócrata *nmf* **:** bureaucrat
burocrático, -ca *adj* **:** bureaucratic
burrada *nf fam* **:** stupid act, nonsense
burrito *nm* **:** burrito
burro[1]**, -rra** *adj fam* **:** dumb, stupid
burro[2]**, -rra** *n* **1** ASNO **:** donkey, ass **2** *fam* **:** dunce, poor student
burro[3] *nm* **1 :** sawhorse **2** *Mex* **:** ironing board **3** *Mex* **:** stepladder
bursátil *adj* **:** stock-market
burundés, -desa *adj & n* **:** Burundian
bus *nm* **:** bus
busca *nf* **:** search
buscador, -dora *n* **:** hunter (for treasure, etc.), prospector
buscapleitos *nmfs & pl* **:** troublemaker
buscar {72} *vt* **1 :** to look for, to seek **2 :** to pick up, to collect **3 :** to provoke — *vi* **:** to look, to search <buscó en los bolsillos : he searched through his pockets>
buscavidas *nmfs & pl* **1 :** busybody **2 :** go-getter
busque, etc. → **buscar**
búsqueda *nf* **:** search
busto *nm* **:** bust
butaca *nf* **1** SILLÓN **:** armchair **2 :** seat (in a theatre) **3** *Mex* **:** pupil's desk
butano *nm* **:** butane
buzo[1]**, -za** *adj Mex fam* **:** smart, astute <¡ponte buzo! : get with it!, get on the ball!>
buzo[2] *nm* **:** diver, scuba diver
buzón *nm, pl* **buzones :** mailbox
byte *nm* **:** byte

C

c *nf* **:** third letter of the Spanish alphabet
cabal *adj* **1 :** exact, correct **2 :** complete **3 :** upright, honest
cabales *nmpl* **no estar en sus cabales :** not to be in one's right mind
cabalgar {52} *vi* **:** to ride (on horseback)
cabalgata *nf* **:** cavalcade, procession
cabalidad *nf* **a ~ :** thoroughly, conscientiously
caballa *nf* **:** mackerel
caballada *nf* **1 :** herd of horses **2** *fam* **:** nonsense, stupidity, outrageousness
caballar *adj* EQUINO **:** horse, equine
caballeresco, -ca *adj* **:** gallant, chivalrous
caballería *nf* **1 :** cavalry **2 :** horse, mount **3 :** knighthood, chivalry
caballeriza *nf* **:** stable
caballero[1] → **caballeroso**
caballero[2] *nm* **1 :** gentleman **2 :** knight

caballerosidad *nf* : chivalry, gallantry

caballeroso, -sa *adj* : gentlemanly, chivalrous

caballete *nm* **1** : ridge **2** : easel **3** : trestle (for a table, etc.) **4** : bridge (of the nose) **5** : sawhorse

caballista *nmf* : horseman *m,* horsewoman *f*

caballito *nm* **1** : rocking horse **2 caballito de mar** : seahorse **3 caballitos** *nmpl* : merry-go-round

caballo *nm* **1** : horse **2** : knight (in chess) **3 caballo de fuerza** *or* **caballo de vapor** : horsepower

cabalmente *adv* : fully, exactly

cabaña *nf* CHOZA : cabin, hut

cabaret *nm, pl* **-rets** : nightclub, cabaret

cabecear *vt* : to head (in soccer) — *vi* **1** : to nod one's head **2** : to lurch, to pitch

cabecera *nf* **1** : headboard **2** : head <cabecera de la mesa : head of the table> **3** : heading, headline **4** : headwaters *pl* **5 médico de cabecera** : family doctor **6 cabecera municipal** *CA, Mex* : downtown area

cabecilla *nmf* : ringleader, kingpin

cabellera *nf* : head of hair, mane

cabello *nm* : hair

cabelludo, -da *adj* **1** : hairy **2 cuero cabelludo** : scalp

caber {12} *vi* **1** : to fit, to go <no sé si cabremos todos en el coche : I don't know if we'll all fit in the car> **2** : to be possible <no cabe duda alguna : there's no doubt about it> <cabe que llegue mañana : he may come tomorrow>

cabestro *nm* : halter (for an animal)

cabeza *nf* **1** : head **2 cabeza hueca** : scatterbrain **3 de ~** : head first **4 dolor de cabeza** : headache

cabezada *nf* **1** : butt, blow with the head **2** : nod <echar una cabezada : to take a nap, to doze off>

cabezal *nm* : bolster

cabezazo *nm* : butt, blow with the head

cabezón, -zona *adj, mpl* **-zones** *fam* **1** : having a big head **2** : pigheaded, stubborn

cabida *nf* **1** : room, space, capacity **2 dar cabida a** : to accomodate, to hold

cabildear *vi* : to lobby

cabildeo *nm* : lobbying

cabildero, -ra *n* : lobbyist

cabildo *nm* AYUNTAMIENTO **1** : town or city hall **2** : town or city council

cabina *nf* **1** : cabin **2** : booth **3** : cab (of a truck), cockpit (of an airplane)

cabizbajo, -ja *adj* : dejected, downcast

cable *nm* : cable

cableado *nm* : wiring

cabo *nm* **1** : end <al cabo de dos semanas : at the end of two weeks> **2** : stub, end piece **3** : corporal **4** : cape, headland <el Cabo Cañaveral : Cape Canaveral> **5 al fin y al cabo** : after all, in the end **6 llevar a cabo** : to carry out, to do

caboverdiano, -na *adj & n* : Cape Verdean

cabrá, etc. → **caber**

cabra *nf* : goat

cabrestante *nm* : windlass

cabrío, -ría *adj* : goat, caprine

cabriola *nf* **1** : skip, jump **2 hacer cabriolas** : to prance

cabriolar *vi* : to prance

cabrito *nm* : kid, baby goat

cabús *nm, pl* **cabuses** *Mex* : caboose

cacahuate *or* **cacahuete** *nm* : peanut

cacalote *nm Mex* : crow

cacao *nm* : cacao, cocoa bean

cacarear *vi* : to crow, to cackle, to cluck — *vt fam* : to boast about, to crow about <cacarear un huevo : to brag about an accomplishment>

cacatúa *nf* : cockatoo

cace, etc. → **cazar**

cacería *nf* **1** CAZA : hunt, hunting **2** : hunting party

cacerola *nf* : pan, saucepan

cacha *nf* : butt (of a gun)

cachar *vt fam* : to catch

cacharro *nm* **1** *fam* : thing, piece of junk **2** *fam* : jalopy **3 cacharros** *nmpl* : pots and pans

cache *nm* : cache, cache memory

cachear *vt* : to search, to frisk

cachemir *nm* : cashmere

cachetada *nf* BOFETADA : slap on the face

cachete *nm* : cheek

cachetear *vt* BOFETEAR : to slap

cachiporra *nf* : bludgeon, club, blackjack

cachirul *nm Mex fam* : cheating <hacer cachirul : to cheat>

cachivache *nm fam* : thing <mete tus cachivaches en el maletero : put your stuff in the trunk>

cacho *nm fam* : piece, bit

cachorro, -rra *n* **1** : cub **2** PERRITO : puppy

cachucha *nf Mex* : cap, baseball cap

cacique *nm* **1** : chief (of a tribe) **2** : boss (in politics)

cacofonía *nf* : cacophony

cacofónico, -ca *adj* : cacophonous

cacto *nm* : cactus

cactus *nm* → **cacto**

cada *adj* **1** : each <cuestan diez pesos cada una : they cost ten pesos each> **2** : every <cada vez : every time> **3** : such, some <sales con cada historia : you come up with such crazy stories> **4 cada vez más** : more and more, increasingly **5 cada vez menos** : less and less

cadalso *nm* : scaffold, gallows

cadáver *nm* : corpse, cadaver

cadavérico, -ca *adj* **1** : cadaverous **2** PÁLIDO : deathly pale

caddie *or* **caddy** *nmf, pl* **caddies** : caddy

cadena *nf* **1 :** chain **2 :** network, channel **3 cadena de montaje :** assembly line **4 cadena perpetua :** life sentence

cadencia *nf* **:** cadence, rhythm

cadencioso, -sa *adj* **:** rhythmic, rhythmical

cadera *nf* **:** hip

cadete *nmf* **:** cadet

cadmio *nm* **:** cadmium

caducar {72} *vi* **:** to expire

caducidad *nf* **:** expiration

caduco, -ca *adj* **1 :** outdated, obsolete **2 :** deciduous

caer {13} *vi* **1 :** to fall, to drop **2 :** to collapse **3 :** to hang (down) **4 caer bien** *fam* **:** to be pleasant, to be likeable <me caes bien : I like you> **5 caer mal** *or* **caer gordo** *fam* **:** to be unpleasant, to be unlikeable — **caerse** *vr* **:** to fall down

café[1] *adj* **:** brown <ojos cafés : brown eyes>

café[2] *nm* **1 :** coffee **2 :** café

cafeína *nf* **:** caffeine

cafetal *nm* **:** coffee plantation

cafetalero[1], -ra *adj* **:** coffee <cosecha cafetalera : coffee harvest>

cafetalero[2], -ra *n* **:** coffee grower

cafetera *nf* **:** coffeepot, coffeemaker

cafetería *nf* **1 :** coffee shop, café **2 :** lunchroom, cafeteria

cafetero[1], -ra *adj* **:** coffee-producing

cafetero[2], -ra *n* **:** coffee grower

cafeticultura *nf Mex* **:** coffee industry

caguama *nf* **1 :** large Caribbean turtle **2** *Mex* **:** large bottle of beer

caída *nf* **1** BAJA, DESCENSO **:** fall, drop **2 :** collapse, downfall

caiga, etc. → **caer**

caimán *nm, pl* **caimanes :** alligator, caiman

caimito *nm* **:** star apple

caja *nf* **1 :** box, case **2 :** cash register, checkout counter **3 :** bed (of a truck) **4** *fam* **:** coffin **5 caja fuerte** *or* **caja de caudales :** safe **6 caja de seguridad :** safe-deposit box **7 caja torácica :** rib cage

cajero, -ra *n* **1 :** cashier **2 :** teller **3 cajero automático :** automated teller machine, ATM

cajeta *nf Mex* **:** a sweet carmel-flavored spread

cajetilla *nf* **:** pack (of cigarettes)

cajón *nm, pl* **cajones 1 :** drawer, till **2 :** crate, case **3 cajón de estacionamiento** *Mex* **:** parking space

cajuela *nf Mex* **:** trunk (of a car)

cal *nf* **:** lime, quicklime

cala *nf* **:** cove, inlet

calabacín *nm, pl* **-cines :** zucchini

calabacita *nf Mex* **:** zucchini

calabaza *nf* **1 :** pumpkin, squash **2 :** gourd **3 dar calabazas a :** to give the brush-off to, to jilt

calabozo *nm* **1 :** prison **2 :** jail cell

calado[1], -da *adj* **1 :** drenched **2 :** openworked

calado[2] *nm* **1 :** draft (of a ship) **2 :** openwork

calafatear *vt* **:** to caulk

calamar *nm* **1 :** squid **2 calamares** *nmpl* **:** calamari

calambre *nm* **1** ESPASMO **:** cramp **2 :** electric shock, jolt

calamidad *nf* DESASTRE **:** calamity, disaster

calamina *nf* **:** calamine

calamitoso, -sa *adj* **:** calamitous, disastrous

calaña *nf* **:** ilk, kind, sort <una persona de mala calaña : a bad sort>

calar *vt* **1 :** to soak through **2 :** to pierce, to penetrate — *vi* **:** to catch on — **calarse** *vr* **:** to get drenched

calavera[1] *nf* **1 :** skull **2** *Mex* **:** taillight

calavera[2] *nm* **:** rake, rogue

calcar {72} *vt* **1 :** to trace **2 :** to copy, to imitate

calce, etc. → **calzar**

calceta *nf* **:** knee-high stocking

calcetería *nf* **:** hosiery

calcetín *nm, pl* **-tines :** sock

calcificar {72} *v* **:** to calcify — **calcificarse** *vr*

calcinar *vt* **:** to char, to burn

calcio *nm* **:** calcium

calco *nm* **1 :** transfer, tracing **2 :** copy, image

calcomanía *nf* **:** decal, transfer

calculador, -dora *adj* **:** calculating

calculadora *nf* **:** calculator

calcular *vt* **1 :** to calculate, to estimate **2 :** to plan, to scheme

cálculo *nm* **1 :** calculation, estimation **2 :** calculus **3 :** plan, scheme **4 cálculo biliar :** gallstone **5 hoja de cálculo :** spreadsheet

caldas *nfpl* **:** hot springs

caldear *vt* **:** to heat, to warm — **caldearse** *vr* **1 :** to heat up **2 :** to become heated, to get tense

caldera *nf* **1 :** cauldron **2 :** boiler

caldo *nm* **1** CONSOMÉ **:** broth, stock **2 caldo de cultivo :** culture medium, breeding ground

caldoso, -sa *adj* **:** watery

calefacción *nf, pl* **-ciones :** heating, heat

calefactor *nm* **:** heater

caleidoscopio *nm* → **calidoscopio**

calendario *nm* **1 :** calendar **2 :** timetable, schedule

caléndula *nf* **:** marigold

calentador *nm* **:** heater

calentamiento *nm* **1 :** heating, warming **2 :** warm-up (in sports)

calentar {55} *vt* **1 :** to heat, to warm **2** *fam* **:** to annoy, to anger **3** *fam* **:** to excite, to turn on — **calentarse** *vr* **1 :** to get warm, to heat up **2 :** to warm up (in sports) **3** *fam* **:** to become sexually aroused **4** *fam* **:** to get mad

calentura *nf* **1** FIEBRE **:** temperature, fever **2 :** cold sore

calibrador *nm* **:** gauge, calipers *pl*

calibrar *vt* : to calibrate — **calibración** *nf*
calibre *nm* **1** : caliber, gauge **2** : importance, excellence **3** : kind, sort <un problema de grueso calibre : a serious problem>
calidad *nf* **1** : quality, grade **2** : position, status **3 en calidad de** : as, in the capacity of
cálido, -da *adj* **1** : hot <un clima cálido : a hot climate> **2** : warm <una cálida bienvenida : a warm welcome>
calidoscopio *nm* : kaleidoscope
caliente *adj* **1** : hot, warm <mantenerse caliente : to stay warm> **2** : heated, fiery <una disputa caliente : a heated argument> **3** *fam* : sexually excited, horny
califa *nm* : caliph
calificación *nf, pl* **-ciones 1** NOTA : grade (for a course) **2** : rating, score **3** CLASIFICACIÓN : qualification, qualifying <ronda de calificación : qualifying round>
calificar {72} *vt* **1** : to grade **2** : to describe, to rate <la calificaron de buena alumna : they described her as a good student> **3** : to qualify, to modify (in grammar)
calificativo[1], -va *adj* : qualifying
calificativo[2] *nm* : qualifier, epithet
caligrafía *nf* **1** ESCRITURA : handwriting **2** : calligraphy
calistenia *nf* : calisthenics
cáliz *nm, pl* **cálices 1** : chalice, goblet **2** : calyx
caliza *nf* : limestone
callado, -da *adj* : quiet, silent — **calladamente** *adv*
callar *vi* : to keep quiet, to be silent — *vt* **1** : to silence, to hush <¡calla a los niños! : keep the children quiet!> **2** : to keep secret — **callarse** *vr* : to remain silent <¡cállate! : be quiet!, shut up!>
calle *nf* : street, road
callejear *vi* : to wander about the streets, to hang out
callejero, -ra *adj* : street <perro callejero : stray dog>
callejón *nm, pl* **-jones 1** : alley **2 callejón sin salida** : dead-end street
callo *nm* : callus, corn
calloso, -sa *adj* : callous
calma *nf* : calm, quiet
calmante[1] *adj* : calming, soothing
calmante[2] *nm* : tranquilizer, sedative
calmar *vt* TRANQUILIZAR : to calm, to soothe — **calmarse** *vr* : to calm down
calmo, -ma *adj* TRANQUILO : calm, tranquil
calmoso, -sa *adj* **1** TRANQUILO : calm, quiet **2** LENTO : slow, sluggish
calor *nm* **1** : heat <hace calor : it's hot outside> <tener calor : to feel hot> **2** : warmth, affection **3** : ardor, passion
caloría *nf* : calorie
calórico, -ca *adj* : caloric
calque, etc. → **calcar**
calumnia *nf* : slander, libel — **calumnioso, -sa** *adj*
calumniar *vt* : to slander, to libel
caluroso, -sa *adj* **1** : hot **2** : warm, enthusiastic
calva *nf* : bald spot, bald head
calvario *nm* **1** : Calvary **2** : Stations of the Cross *pl* **3 vivir un calvario** : to suffer great adversity
calvicie *nf* : baldness
calvo[1], -va *adj* : bald
calvo[2], -va *n* : bald person
calza *nf* : block, wedge
calzada *nf* : roadway, avenue
calzado *nm* : footwear
calzador *nm* : shoehorn
calzar {21} *vt* **1** : to wear (shoes) <¿de cuál calza? : what is your shoe size?> <siempre calzaban tenis : they always wore sneakers> **2** : to provide with shoes
calzo *nm* : chock, wedge
calzoncillos *nmpl* : underpants, briefs
calzones *nmpl* : underpants, panties
cama *nf* **1** : bed **2 cama elástica** : trampoline
camada *nf* : litter, brood
camafeo *nm* : cameo
camaleón *nm, pl* **-leones** : chameleon
cámara *nf* **1** : camera **2** : chamber, room **3** : house (in government) **4** : inner tube
camarada *nmf* **1** : comrade, companion **2** : colleague
camaradería *nf* : camaraderie
camarero, -ra *n* **1** MESERO : waiter, waitress *f* **2** : bellboy *m*, chambermaid *f* (in a hotel) **3** : steward *m*, stewardess *f* (on a ship, etc.)
camarilla *nf* : political clique
camarógrafo, -fa *n* : cameraman *m*, camerawoman *f*
camarón *nm, pl* **-rones 1** : shrimp **2** : prawn
camarote *nm* : cabin, stateroom
camastro *nm* : small hard bed, pallet
cambalache *nm fam* : swap
cambiante *adj* **1** : changing **2** VARIABLE : changeable, variable
cambiar *vt* **1** ALTERAR, MODIFICAR : to change **2** : to exchange, to trade — *vi* **1** : to change **2 cambiar de velocidad** : to shift gears — **cambiarse** *vr* **1** : to change (clothing) **2** MUDARSE : to move (to a new address)
cambio *nm* **1** : change, alteration **2** : exchange **3** : change (money) **4 en cambio** : instead **5 en cambio** : however, on the other hand
cambista *nmf* : exchange broker
camboyano, -na *adj & n* : Cambodian
cambur *nm Ven* : banana
camelia *nf* : camellia
camello *nm* : camel
camellón *nm, pl* **-llones** *Mex* : traffic island
camerino *nm* : dressing room
camerunés, -nesa *adj, mpl* **-neses** : Cameroonian

camilla *nf* : stretcher

camillero, -ra *n* : orderly (in a hospital)

caminante *nmf* : wayfarer, walker

caminar *vi* ANDAR : to walk, to move — *vt* : to walk, to cover (a distance)

caminata *nf* : hike, long walk

camino *nm* **1** : path, road **2** : journey <ponerse en camino : to set off> **3** : way <a medio camino : halfway there>

camión *nm, pl* **camiones 1** : truck **2** *Mex* : bus

camionero, -ra *n* **1** : truck driver **2** *Mex* : bus driver

camioneta *nm* : light truck, van

camisa *nf* **1** : shirt **2 camisa de fuerza** : straitjacket

camiseta *nf* **1** : T-shirt **2** : undershirt

camisón *nm, pl* **-sones** : nightshirt, nightgown

camorra *nf fam* : fight, trouble <buscar camorra : to pick a fight>

camote *nm* **1** : root vegetable similar to the sweet potato **2 hacerse camote** *Mex fam* : to get mixed up

campal *adj* : pitched, fierce <batalla campal : pitched battle>

campamento *nm* : camp

campana *nf* : bell

campanada *nf* TAÑIDO : stroke (of a bell), peal

campanario *nm* : bell tower, belfry

campanilla *nf* **1** : small bell, handbell **2** : uvula

campante *adj* : nonchalant, smug <seguir tan campante : to go on as if nothing had happened>

campaña *nf* **1** CAMPO : countryside, country **2** : campaign **3 tienda de campaña** : tent

campañol *nm* : vole

campechana *nf Mex* : puff pastry

campechanía *nf* : geniality

campechano, -na *adj* : open, cordial, friendly

campeón, -peona *n, mpl* **-peones** : champion

campeonato *nm* : championship

cámper *nm* : camper (vehicle)

campero, -ra *adj* : country, rural

campesino, -na *n* : peasant, farm laborer

campestre *adj* : rural, rustic

camping *nm* **1** : camping **2** : campsite

campiña *nf* CAMPO : countryside, country

campista *nmf* : camper

campo *nm* **1** CAMPAÑA : countryside, country **2** : field <campo de aviación : airfield> <su campo de responsabilidad : her field of responsibility>

camposanto *nm* : graveyard, cemetery

campus *nms & pl* : campus

camuflaje *nm* : camouflage

camuflajear *vt* : to camouflage

camuflar → **camuflajear**

can *nm* : hound, dog

cana *nf* **1** : gray hair **2 salirle canas** : to go gray, to get gray hair **3 echar una cana al aire** : to let one's hair down

canadiense *adj & nmf* : Canadian

canal[1] *nm* **1** : canal **2** : channel

canal[2] *nmf* : gutter, groove

canalé *nm* : rib, ribbing (in fabric)

canaleta *nf* : gutter

canalete *nm* : paddle

canalizar {21} *vt* : to channel

canalla[1] *adj fam* : low, rotten

canalla[2] *nmf fam* : bastard, swine

canapé *nm* **1** : hors d'oeuvre, canapé **2** SOFÁ : couch, sofa

canario[1], **-ria** *adj* : of or from the Canary Islands

canario[2], **-ria** *n* : Canarian, Canary Islander

canario[3] *nm* : canary

canasta *nf* **1** : basket **2** : canasta (card game)

cancel *nm* **1** : sliding door **2** : partition

cancelación *nf, pl* **-ciones 1** : cancellation **2** : payment in full

cancelar *vt* **1** : to cancel **2** : to pay off, to settle

cáncer *nm* : cancer

Cáncer *nmf* : Cancer

cancerígeno[1], **-na** *adj* : carcinogenic

cancerígeno[2] *nm* : carcinogen

canceroso, -sa *adj* : cancerous

cancha *nf* : court, field (for sports)

canciller *nm* : chancellor

cancillería *nf* : chancellery, ministry

canción *nf, pl* **canciones 1** : song **2 canción de cuna** : lullaby

cancionero[1] *nm* : songbook

cancionero[2], **-ra** *n Mex* : songster, songstress *f*

candado *nm* : padlock

candela *nf* **1** : flame, fire **2** : candle

candelabro *nm* : candelabra

candelero *nm* **1** : candlestick **2 estar en el candelero** : to be the center of attention

candente *adj* : red-hot

candidato, -ta *n* : candidate, applicant

candidatura *nf* : candidacy

candidez *nf* **1** : simplicity **2** INGENUIDAD : naïveté, ingenuousness

cándido, -da *adj* **1** : simple, unassuming **2** INGENUO : naive, ingenuous

candil *nm* : oil lamp

candilejas *nfpl* : footlights

candor *nm* : naïveté, innocence

candoroso, -sa *adj* : naive, innocent

canela *nf* : cinnamon

canesú *nm* : yoke (of clothing)

cangrejo *nm* JAIBA : crab

canguro *nm* **1** : kangaroo **2 hacer de canguro** *Spain* : to baby-sit

caníbal[1] *adj* : cannibalistic

caníbal[2] *nmf* ANTROPÓFAGO : cannibal

canibalismo *nm* ANTROPOFAGIA : cannibalism

canibalizar {21} *vt* : to cannibalize

canica *nf* **1** : marble **2 canicas** *nfpl* : marbles (toys)

caniche *nm* : poodle

canijo, -ja *adj* **1** *fam* **:** puny, weak **2** *Mex fam* **:** tough, hard <un examen muy canijo : a very tough exam>

canilla *nf* **1 :** shin, shinbone **2** *Arg, Uru* **:** faucet

canino[1], **-na** *adj* **:** canine

canino[2] *nm* **1** COLMILLO **:** canine (tooth) **2 :** dog, canine

canje *nm* INTERCAMBIO **:** exchange, trade

canjear *vt* INTERCAMBIAR **:** to exchange, to trade

cannabis *nm* **:** cannabis

cano, -na *adj* **:** gray <un hombre de pelo cano : a gray-haired man>

canoa *nf* **:** canoe

canon *nm, pl* **cánones :** canon

canónico, -ca *adj* **1 :** canonical **2 derecho canónico :** canon law

canonizar {21} *vt* **:** to canonize — **canonización** *nf*

canoso, -sa → **cano**

cansado, -da *adj* **1 :** tired <estar cansado : to be tired> **2 :** tiresome, wearying <ser cansado : to be tiring>

cansancio *nm* FATIGA **:** fatigue, weariness

cansar *vt* FATIGAR **:** to wear out, to tire — *vi* **:** to be tiresome — **cansarse** *vr* **1 :** to wear oneself out **2 :** to get bored

cansino, -na *adj* **:** slow, weary, lethargic

cantaleta *nf fam* **:** nagging <la misma cantaleta : the same old story>

cantalupo *nm* **:** cantaloupe

cantante *nmf* **:** singer

cantar[1] *v* **:** to sing

cantar[2] *nm* **:** song, ballad

cántaro *nm* **1 :** pitcher, jug **2 llover a cántaros** *fam* **:** to rain cats and dogs

cantata *nf* **:** cantata

cantera *nf* **:** quarry <cantera de piedra : stone quarry>

cántico *nm* **:** canticle, chant

cantidad[1] *adv fam* **:** really <ese carro me costó cantidad : that car cost me plenty>

cantidad[2] *nf* **1 :** quantity **2 :** sum, amount (of money) **3** *fam* **:** a lot, a great many <había cantidad de niños en el parque : there were tons of kids in the park>

cantimplora *nf* **:** canteen, water bottle

cantina *nf* **1 :** tavern, bar **2 :** canteen, mess, dining quarters *pl*

cantinero, -ra *n* **:** bartender

canto *nm* **1 :** singing **2 :** chant <canto gregoriano : Gregorian chant> **3 :** song (of a bird) **4 :** edge, end <de canto : on end, sideways> **5 canto rodado :** boulder

cantón *nm, pl* **cantones 1 :** canton **2** *Mex fam* **:** place, home

cantor[1], **-tora** *adj* **1 :** singing **2 pájaro cantor :** songbird

cantor[2], **-tora** *n* **1 :** singer **2 :** cantor

caña *nf* **1 :** cane <caña de azúcar : sugarcane> **2 :** reed **3 caña de pescar :** fishing rod **4 caña del timón :** tiller (of a boat)

cañada *nf* **:** ravine, gully

cáñamo *nm* **:** hemp

cañaveral *nm* **:** sugarcane field

cañería *nf* TUBERÍA **:** pipes *pl*, piping

caño *nm* **1 :** pipe **2 :** spout **3 :** channel (for navigation)

cañón *nm, pl* **cañones 1 :** cannon **2 :** barrel (of a gun) **3 :** canyon

cañonear *vt* **:** to shell, to bombard

cañoneo *nm* **:** shelling, bombardment

cañonero *nm* **:** gunboat

caoba *nf* **:** mahogany

caos *nm* **:** chaos

caótico, -ca *adj* **:** chaotic

capa *nf* **1 :** cape, cloak **2 :** coating **3 :** layer, stratum **4 :** (social) class, stratum

capacidad *nf* **1 :** capacity **2 :** capability, ability

capacitación *nf, pl* **-ciones :** training

capacitar *vt* **:** to train, to qualify

caparazón *nm, pl* **-zones :** shell, carapace

capataz *nmf, pl* **-taces :** foreman *m*, forewoman *f*

capaz *adj, pl* **capaces 1** APTO **:** capable, able **2** COMPETENTE **:** competent **3 :** spacious <capaz para : with room for>

capcioso, -sa *adj* **:** cunning, deceptive <pregunta capciosa : trick question>

capea *nf* **:** amateur bullfight

capear *vt* **1 :** to make a pass with the cape (in bullfighting) **2 :** to dodge, to weather <capear el temporal : to ride out the storm>

capellán *nm, pl* **-llanes :** chaplain

capilar *nm* **:** capillary — **capilar** *adj*

capilla *nf* **:** chapel

capirotada *nf Mex* **:** traditional bread pudding

capirotazo *nm* **:** flip, flick

capital[1] *adj* **1 :** capital **2 :** chief, principal

capital[2] *nm* **:** capital <capital de riesgo : venture capital>

capital[3] *nf* **:** capital, capital city

capitalino[1], **-na** *adj* **:** of or from a capital city

capitalino[2], **-na** *n* **:** inhabitant of a capital city

capitalismo *nm* **:** capitalism

capitalista *adj & nmf* **:** capitalist

capitalizar {21} *vt* **:** to capitalize — **capitalización** *nf*

capitán, -tana *n, mpl* **-tanes :** captain

capitanear *vt* **:** to captain, to command

capitanía *nf* **:** captaincy

capitel *nm* **:** capital (of a column)

capitolio *nm* **:** capitol

capitulación *nf, pl* **-ciones :** capitulation

capitular *vi* **:** to capitulate, to surrender

capítulo *nm* **1 :** chapter, section **2 :** matter, subject

capó *nm* **:** hood (of a car)

capón *nm, pl* **capones :** capon

caporal *nm* **1 :** chief, leader **2 :** foreman (on a ranch)

capota *nf* **:** top (of a convertible)

capote *nm* **1 :** cloak, overcoat **2 :** bullfighter's cape **3** *Mex* COFRE **:** hood (of a car)

capricho *nm* ANTOJO **:** whim, caprice

caprichoso, -sa *adj* ANTOJADIZO **:** capricious, fickle

Capricornio *nmf* **:** Capricorn

cápsula *nf* **:** capsule

captar *vt* **1 :** to catch, to grasp **2 :** to gain, to attract **3 :** to harness, to collect (waters)

captor, -tora *n* **:** captor

captura *nf* **:** capture, seizure

capturar *vt* **:** to capture, to seize

capucha *nf* **:** hood, cowl

capuchina *nf* **:** nasturtium

capuchino *nm* **1 :** Capuchin (monk) **2 :** capuchin (monkey) **3 :** cappuccino

capullo *nm* **1 :** cocoon **2 :** bud (of a flower)

caqui *adj & nm* **:** khaki

cara *nf* **1 :** face **2** ASPECTO **:** look, appearance <¡qué buena cara tiene ese pastel! : that cake looks delicious!> **3** *fam* **:** nerve, gall **4 ~ a** *or* **de cara a :** facing **5 de cara a :** in view of, in the light of

carabina *nf* **:** carbine

caracol *nm* **1 :** snail **2** CONCHA **:** conch, seashell **3 :** cochlea **4 :** ringlet

caracola *nf* **:** conch

carácter *nm, pl* **caracteres 1** ÍNDOLE **:** character, kind, nature **2** TEMPERAMENTO **:** disposition, temperament **3 :** letter, symbol <caracteres chinos : Chinese characters>

característica *nf* RASGO **:** trait, feature, characteristic

característico, -ca *adj* **:** characteristic — **característicamente** *adv*

caracterizar {21} *vt* **:** to characterize — **caracterización** *nf*

caramba *interj* **:** darn!, heck!

carámbano *nm* **:** icicle

carambola *nf* **1 :** carom **2 :** ruse, trick <por carambola : by a lucky chance>

caramelo *nm* **1 :** caramel **2** DULCE **:** candy

caramillo *nm* **1 :** pipe, small flute **2 :** heap, pile

caraqueño[1], -ña *adj* **:** of or from Caracas

caraqueño[2], -ña *n* **:** person from Caracas

carátula *nf* **1 :** title page **2 :** cover, dust jacket **3** CARETA **:** mask **4** *Mex* **:** face, dial (of a clock or watch)

caravana *nf* **1 :** caravan **2 :** convoy, motorcade **3** REMOLQUE **:** trailer

caray → **caramba**

carbohidrato *nm* **:** carbohydrate

carbón *nm, pl* **carbones 1 :** coal **2 :** charcoal

carbonatado, -da *adj* **:** carbonated

carbonato *nm* **:** carbonate

carboncillo *nm* **:** charcoal

carbonera *nf* **:** coal cellar, coal bunker (on a ship)

carbonero, -ra *adj* **:** coal

carbonizar {21} *vt* **:** to carbonize, to char

carbono *nm* **:** carbon

carbunco *or* **carbunclo** *nm* **:** carbuncle

carburador *nm* **:** carburetor

carca *nmf fam* **:** old fogy

carcacha *nf fam* **:** jalopy, wreck

carcaj *nm* **:** quiver (for arrows)

carcajada *nf* **:** loud laugh, guffaw <reírse a carcajadas : to roar with laughter>

carcajearse *vr* **:** to roar with laughter, to be in stitches

cárcel *nf* PRISIÓN **:** jail, prison

carcelero, -ra *n* **:** jailer

carcinogénico, -ca *adj* **:** carcinogenic

carcinógeno *nm* CANCERÍGENO **:** carcinogen

carcinoma *nm* **:** carcinoma

carcomer *vt* **:** to eat away at, to consume

carcomido, -da *adj* **1 :** worm-eaten **2 :** decayed, rotten

cardán *nm, pl* **cardanes :** universal joint

cardar *vt* **:** to card, to comb

cardenal *nm* **1 :** cardinal (in religion) **2 :** bruise

cardíaco *or* **cardiaco, -ca** *adj* **:** cardiac, heart

cárdigan *nm, pl* **-gans :** cardigan

cardinal *adj* **:** cardinal

cardiología *nf* **:** cardiology

cardiólogo, -ga *n* **:** cardiologist

cardiovascular *adj* **:** cardiovascular

cardo *nm* **:** thistle

cardumen *nm* **:** school of fish

carear *vt* **:** to bring face-to-face

carecer {53} *vi* **~ de :** to lack <el cheque carecía de fondos : the check lacked funds>

carencia *nf* **1** FALTA **:** lack **2** ESCASEZ **:** shortage **3** DEFICIENCIA **:** deficiency

carente *adj* **~ de :** lacking (in)

carero, -ra *adj fam* **:** pricey

carestía *nf* **1 :** rise in cost <la carestía de la vida : the high cost of living> **2 :** dearth, scarcity

careta *nf* MÁSCARA **:** mask

carey *nm* **1 :** hawksbill turtle, sea turtle **2 :** tortoiseshell

carga *nf* **1 :** loading **2 :** freight, load, cargo **3 :** burden, responsibility **4 :** charge <carga eléctrica : electrical charge> **5 :** attack, charge

cargado, -da *adj* **1 :** loaded **2 :** bogged down, weighted down **3 :** close, stuffy **4 :** charged <cargado de tensión : charged with tension> **5** FUERTE **:** strong <café cargado : strong coffee> **6 cargado de hombros :** stoop-shouldered

cargador[1], -dora *n* **:** longshoreman *m*, longshorewoman *f*

cargador[2] *nm* **1 :** magazine (for a firearm) **2 :** charger (for batteries)

cargamento *nm* **:** cargo, load

cargar {52} *vt* **1 :** to carry **2 :** to load, to fill **3 :** to charge — *vi* **1 :** to load **2 :** to rest (in architecture) **3 ~ sobre :** to fall upon

cargo *nm* **1 :** burden, load **2 :** charge <a cargo de : in charge of> **3 :** position, office

cargue, etc. → **cargar**

carguero[1], **-ra** *adj* **:** freight, cargo <tren carguero : freight train>

carguero[2] *nm* **:** freighter, cargo ship

cariarse *vr* **:** to decay (of teeth)

caribe *adj* **:** Caribbean <el mar caribe : the Caribbean Sea>

caribeño, -ña *adj* **:** Caribbean

caribú *nm* **:** caribou

caricatura *nf* **1 :** caricature **2 :** cartoon

caricaturista *nmf* **:** caricaturist, cartoonist

caricaturizar {21} *vt* **:** to caricature

caricia *nf* **1 :** caress **2 hacer caricias :** to pet, to stroke

caridad *nf* **1 :** charity **2** LIMOSNA **:** alms *pl*

caries *nfs & pl* **:** cavity (in a tooth)

carillón *nm, pl* **-llones 1 :** carillon **2 :** glockenspiel

cariño *nm* AFECTO **:** affection, love

cariñoso, -sa *adj* AFECTUOSO **:** affectionate, loving — **cariñosamente** *adv*

carioca[1] *adj* **:** of or from Rio de Janeiro

carioca[2] *nmf* **:** person from Rio de Janeiro

carisma *nf* **:** charisma

carismático, -ca *adj* **:** charismatic

carita *adj Mex fam* **:** cute (said of a man) <tu primo se cree muy carita : your cousin thinks he's gorgeous>

caritativo, -va *adj* **:** charitable

cariz *nm, pl* **carices :** appearance, aspect

carmesí *adj & nm* **:** crimson

carmín *nm, pl* **carmines 1 :** carmine **2 carmín de labios :** lipstick

carnada *nf* CEBO **:** bait

carnal *adj* **1 :** carnal **2 primo carnal :** first cousin

carnaval *nm* **:** carnival

carnaza *nf* **:** bait

carne *nf* **1 :** meat <carne molida : ground beef> **2 :** flesh <carne de gallina : goose bumps>

carné *nm* → **carnet**

carnero *nm* **1 :** ram, sheep **2 :** mutton

carnet *nm* **1 :** identification card, ID **2 :** membership card **3 carnet de conducir** *Spain* **:** driver's license

carnicería *nf* **1 :** butcher shop **2** MATANZA **:** slaughter, carnage

carnicero, -ra *n* **:** butcher

carnívoro[1], **-ra** *adj* **:** carnivorous

carnívoro[2] *nm* **:** carnivore

carnoso, -sa *adj* **:** fleshy, meaty

caro[1] *adv* **:** dearly, a lot <pagué caro : I paid a high price>

caro[2], **-ra** *adj* **1 :** expensive, dear **2** QUERIDO **:** dear, beloved

carpa *nf* **1 :** carp **2 :** big top (of a circus) **3 :** tent

carpelo *nm* **:** carpel

carpeta *nf* **:** folder, binder, portfolio (of drawings, etc.)

carpetazo *nm* **dar carpetazo a :** to shelve, to defer

carpintería *nf* **1 :** carpentry **2 :** carpenter's workshop

carpintero, -ra *n* **:** carpenter

carraspear *vi* **:** to clear one's throat

carraspera *nf* **:** hoarseness <tener carraspera : to have a frog in one's throat>

carrera *nf* **1 :** run, running <a la carrera : at full speed> <de carrera : hastily> **2 :** race **3 :** course of study **4 :** career, profession **5 :** run (in baseball)

carreta *nf* **:** cart, wagon

carrete *nm* **1** BOBINA **:** reel, spool **2 :** roll of film

carretel *nm* → **carrete**

carretera *nf* **:** highway, road <carretera de peaje : turnpike>

carretero, -ra *adj* **:** highway <el sistema carretero nacional : the national highway system>

carretilla *nf* **1 :** wheelbarrow **2 carretilla elevadora :** forklift

carril *nm* **1 :** lane <carretera de doble carril : two-lane highway> **2 :** rail (on a railroad track)

carrillo *nm* **:** cheek, jowl

carrito *nm* **:** cart <carrito de compras : shopping cart>

carrizo *nm* JUNCO **:** reed

carro *nm* **1** COCHE **:** car **2 :** cart **3** *Chile, Mex* **:** coach (of a train) **4 carro alegórico :** float (in a parade)

carrocería *nf* **:** bodywork

carroña *nf* **:** carrion

carroñero, -ra *n* **:** scavenger (animal)

carroza *nf* **1 :** carriage **2 :** float (in a parade)

carruaje *nm* **:** carriage

carrusel *nm* **1 :** merry-go-round **2 :** carousel <carrusel de equipaje : luggage carousel>

carta *nf* **1 :** letter **2** NAIPE **:** playing card **3 :** charter, constitution **4** MENÚ **:** menu **5 :** map, chart **6 tomar cartas en :** to intervene in

cártamo *nm* **:** safflower

cartearse *vr* ESCRIBIRSE **:** to write to one another, to correspond

cartel *nm* **:** sign, poster

cártel *or* **cartel** *nm* **:** cartel

cartelera *nf* **1 :** billboard **2 :** marquee

cartera *nf* **1** BILLETERA **:** wallet, billfold **2** BOLSO **:** pocketbook, purse **3 :** portfolio <cartera de acciones : stock portfolio>

carterista *nmf* **:** pickpocket

cartero, -ra *n* **:** letter carrier, mailman *m*

cartilaginoso, -sa *adj* : cartilaginous, gristly

cartílago *nm* : cartilage

cartilla *nf* **1** : primer, reader **2** : booklet <cartilla de ahorros : bankbook>

cartografía *nf* : cartography

cartógrafo, -fa *n* : cartographer

cartón *nm, pl* **cartones 1** : cardboard <cartón madera : fiberboard> **2** : carton

cartucho *nm* : cartridge

cartulina *nf* : poster board, cardboard

carúncula *nf* : wattle (of a bird)

casa *nf* **1** : house, building **2** HOGAR : home **3** : household, family **4** : company, firm **5 echar la casa por la ventana** : to spare no expense

casaca *nf* : jacket

casado[1], -da *adj* : married

casado[2], -da *n* : married person

casamentero, -ra *n* : matchmaker

casamiento *nm* **1** : marriage **2** BODA : wedding

casar *vt* : to marry — *vi* : to go together, to match up — **casarse** *vr* **1** : to get married **2 ~ con** : to marry

casateniente *nmf Mex* : landlord, landlady *f*

cascabel[1] *nm* : small bell

cascabel[2] *nf* : rattlesnake

cascada *nf* CATARATA, SALTO : waterfall, cascade

cascajo *nm* **1** : pebble, rock fragment **2** *fam* : piece of junk

cascanueces *nms & pl* : nutcracker

cascar {72} *vt* : to crack (a shell) — **cascarse** *vr* : to crack, to chip

cáscara *nf* **1** : skin, peel, rind, husk **2** : shell (of a nut or egg)

cascarón *nm, pl* **-rones 1** : eggshell **2** *Mex* : shell filled with confetti

cascarrabias *nmfs & pl fam* : grouch, crab

casco *nm* **1** : helmet **2** : hull **3** : hoof **4** : fragment, shard **5** : center (of a town) **6** *Mex* : empty bottle **7 cascos** *nmpl* : headphones

caserío *nm* **1** : country house **2** : hamlet

casero[1], -ra *adj* **1** : domestic, household **2** : homemade

casero[2], -ra *n* DUEÑO : landlord *m,* landlady *f*

caseta *nf* : booth, stand, stall <caseta telefónica : telephone booth>

casete *nmf* → **cassette**

casi *adv* **1** : almost, nearly, virtually **2** (*in negative phrases*) : hardly <casi nunca : hardly ever>

casilla *nf* **1** : booth **2** : pigeonhole **3** : box (on a form)

casino *nm* **1** : casino **2** : (social) club

caso *nm* **1** : case **2 en caso de** : in case of, in the event of **3 hacer caso de** : to pay attention to, to notice **4 hacer caso omiso de** : to ignore, to take no notice of **5 no venir al caso** : to be beside the point

caspa *nf* : dandruff

casque, etc. → **cascar**

casquete *nm* **1** : skullcap **2 casquete glaciar** : ice cap **3 casquete corto** *Mex* : crew cut

cassette *nmf* : cassette

casta *nf* **1** : caste **2** : lineage, stock <de casta : thoroughbred, purebred> **3 sacar la casta** *Mex* : to come out ahead

castaña *nf* : chestnut

castañetear *vi* : to chatter (of teeth)

castaño[1], -ña *adj* : chestnut, brown

castaño[2], -ña *nm* **1** : chestnut tree **2** : chestnut, brown

castañuela *nf* : castanet

castellano[1], -na *adj & n* : Castilian

castellano[2] *nm* ESPAÑOL : Spanish, Castilian (language)

castidad *nf* : chastity

castigar {52} *vt* : to punish

castigo *nm* : punishment

castillo *nm* **1** : castle **2 castillo de proa** : forecastle

casto, -ta *adj* : chaste, pure — **castamente** *adv*

castor *nm* : beaver

castración *nf, pl* **-ciones** : castration

castrar *vt* **1** : to castrate, to spay, to neuter, to geld **2** DEBILITAR : to weaken, to debilitate

castrense *adj* : military

casual *adj* **1** FORTUITO : fortuitous, accidental **2** *Mex* : casual (of clothing)

casualidad *nf* **1** : chance **2 por ~** *or* **de ~** : by chance, by any chance

casualmente *adv* : accidentally, by chance

casucha *or* **casuca** *nf* : shanty, hovel

cataclismo *nm* : cataclysm

catacumbas *nfpl* : catacombs

catador, -dora *n* : wine taster

catalán[1], -lana *adj & n, mpl* **-lanes** : Catalan

catalán[2] *nm* : Catalan (language)

catálisis *nm* : catalysis

catalítico, -ca *adj* : catalytic

catalizador *nm* **1** : catalyst **2** : catalytic converter

catalogar {52} *vt* : to catalog, to classify

catálogo *nm* : catalog

catamarán *nm, pl* **-ranes** : catamaran

cataplasma *nf* : poultice

catapulta *nf* : catapult

catapultar *vt* : to catapult

catar *vt* **1** : to taste, to sample **2** : to look at, to examine

catarata *nf* **1** CASCADA, SALTO : waterfall **2** : cataract

catarro *nm* RESFRIADO : cold, catarrh

catarsis *nf* : catharsis

catártico, -ca *adj* : cathartic

catástrofe *nf* DESASTRE : catastrophe, disaster

catastrófico, -ca *adj* DESASTROSO : catastrophic, disastrous

catcher *nmf* : catcher (in baseball)

catecismo *nm* : catechism

cátedra *nf* **1** : chair, professorship **2** : subject, class **3 libertad de cátedra** : academic freedom
catedral *nf* : cathedral
catedrático, -ca *n* PROFESOR : professor
categoría *nf* **1** CLASE : category **2** RANGO : rank, standing **3 categoría gramatical** : part of speech **4 de ~** : first-rate, outstanding
categórico, -ca *adj* : categorical, unequivocal — **categóricamente** *adv*
catéter *nm* : catheter
cátodo *nm* : cathode
catolicismo *nm* : Catholicism
católico, -ca *adj & n* : Catholic
catorce *adj & nm* : fourteen
catorceavo *nm* : fourteenth
catre *nm* : cot
catsup *nm* : ketchup
caucásico, -ca *adj & n* : Caucasian
cauce *nm* **1** LECHO : riverbed **2** : means *pl,* channel
caucho *nm* **1** GOMA : rubber **2** : rubber tree **3** *Ven* : tire
caución *nf, pl* **cauciones** FIANZA : bail, security
caudal *nm* **1** : volume of water **2** RIQUEZA : capital, wealth **3** ABUNDANCIA : abundance
caudillaje *nm* : leadership
caudillo *nm* : leader, commander
causa *nf* **1** MOTIVO : cause, reason, motive <a causa de : because of> **2** IDEAL : cause <morir por una causa : to die for a cause> **3** : lawsuit
causal[1] *adj* : causal
causal[2] *nm* : cause, grounds *pl*
causalidad *nf* : causality
causante[1] *adj* **~ de** : causing, responsible for
causante[2] *nmf Mex* : taxpayer
causar *vt* **1** : to cause **2** : to provoke, to arouse <eso me causa gracia : that strikes me as being funny>
cáustico, -ca *adj* : caustic
cautela *nf* : caution, prudence
cautelar *adj* : precautionary, preventive
cauteloso, -sa *adj* : cautious, prudent — **cautelosamente** *adv*
cauterizar {21} *vt* : to cauterize
cautivador, -dora *adj* : captivating
cautivar *vt* HECHIZAR : to captivate, to charm
cautiverio *nm* : captivity
cautivo, -va *adj & n* : captive
cauto, -ta *adj* : cautious, careful
cavar *vt* : to dig — *vi* **~ en** : to delve into, to probe
caverna *nf* : cavern, cave
cavernoso, -sa *adj* **1** : cavernous **2** : deep, resounding
caviar *nm* : caviar
cavidad *nf* : cavity
cavilar *vi* : to ponder, to deliberate
cayado *nm* : crook, staff, crosier
cayena *nf* : cayenne pepper
cayó, etc. → **caer**
caza[1] *nf* **1** CACERÍA : hunt, hunting **2** : game
caza[2] *nm* : fighter plane
cazador, -dora *n* **1** : hunter **2 cazador furtivo** : poacher
cazar {21} *vt* **1** : to hunt **2** : to catch, to bag **3** *fam* : to land (a job, a spouse) — *vi* : to go hunting
cazatalentos *nmfs & pl* : talent scout
cazo *nm* **1** : saucepan, pot **2** CUCHARÓN : ladle
cazuela *nf* **1** : pan, saucepan **2** : casserole
cazurro, -ra *adj* : sullen, surly
CD *nm* : CD, compact disk
cebada *nf* : barley
cebar *vt* **1** : to bait **2** : to feed, to fatten **3** : to prime (a pump, etc.) — **cebarse** *vr* **~ en** : to take it out on
cebo *nm* **1** CARNADA : bait **2** : feed **3** : primer (for firearms)
cebolla *nf* : onion
cebolleta *nf* : scallion, green onion
cebollino *nm* **1** : chive **2** : scallion
cebra *nf* : zebra
cebú *nm, pl* **cebús** *or* **cebúes** : zebu (cattle)
cecear *vi* : to lisp
ceceo *nm* : lisp
cecina *nf* : dried beef, beef jerky
cedazo *nm* : sieve
ceder *vi* **1** : to yield, to give way **2** : to diminish, to abate **3** : to give in, to relent — *vt* : to cede, to hand over
cedro *nm* : cedar
cédula *nf* : document, certificate
céfiro *nm* : zephyr
cegador, -dora *adj* : blinding
cegar {49} *vt* **1** : to blind **2** : to block, to stop up — *vi* : to be blinded, to go blind
cegatón, -tona *adj, mpl* **-tones** *fam* : blind as a bat
ceguera *nf* : blindness
ceiba *nf* : ceiba, silk-cotton tree
ceja *nf* **1** : eyebrow <fruncir las cejas : to knit one's brows> **2** : flange, rim
cejar *vi* : to give in, to back down
celada *nf* : trap, ambush
celador, -dora *n* GUARDIA : guard, warden
celda *nf* : cell (of a jail)
celebración *nf, pl* **-ciones** : celebration
celebrado, -da *adj* CÉLEBRE, FAMOSO : famous, celebrated
celebrante *nmf* OFICIANTE : celebrant
celebrar *vt* **1** FESTEJAR : to celebrate **2** : to hold (a meeting) **3** : to say (Mass) **4** : to welcome, to be happy about — *vi* : to be glad — **celebrarse** *vr* **1** : to be celebrated, to fall **2** : to be held, to take place
célebre *adj* CELEBRADO, FAMOSO : celebrated, famous
celebridad *nf* **1** : celebrity **2** FAMA : fame, renown
celeridad *nf* : celerity, swiftness
celeste[1] *adj* **1** : celestial **2** : sky blue, azure

celeste² *nm* : sky blue
celestial *adj* : heavenly, celestial
celibato *nm* : celibacy
célibe *adj & nmf* : celibate
cello *nm* : cello
celo *nm* **1** : zeal, fervor **2** : heat (of females), rut (of males) **3 celos** *nmpl* : jealousy <tenerle celos a alguien : to be jealous of someone>
celofán *nm, pl* **-fanes** : cellophane
celosía *nf* **1** : lattice window **2** : latticework, trellis
celoso, -sa *adj* **1** : jealous **2** : zealous — **celosamente** *adv*
celta¹ *adj* : Celtic
celta² *nmf* : Celt
célula *nf* : cell
celular *adj* : cellular
celuloide *nm* **1** : celluloid **2** : film, cinema
celulosa *nf* : cellulose
cementar *vt* : to cement
cementerio *nm* : cemetery
cemento *nm* : cement
cena *nf* : supper, dinner
cenador *nm* : arbor
cenagal *nm* : bog, quagmire
cenagoso, -sa *adj* : swampy
cenar *vi* : to have dinner, to have supper — *vt* : to have for dinner or supper <anoche cenamos tamales : we had tamales for supper last night>
cencerro *nm* : cowbell
cenicero *nm* : ashtray
ceniciento, -ta *adj* : ashen
cenit *nm* : zenith, peak
ceniza *nf* **1** : ash **2 cenizas** *nfpl* : ashes (of a deceased person)
cenizo, -za *n* : jinx
cenote *nm Mex* : natural deposit of spring water
censar *vt* : to take a census of
censo *nm* : census
censor, -sora *n* : censor, critic
censura *nf* **1** : censorship **2** : censure, criticism
censurable *adj* : reprehensible, blameworthy
censurar *vt* **1** : to censor **2** : to censure, to criticize
centauro *nm* : centaur
centavo *nm* **1** : cent (in English-speaking countries) **2** : unit of currency in various Latin-American countries
centella *nf* **1** : lightning flash **2** : spark
centellear *vi* **1** : to twinkle **2** : to gleam, to sparkle
centelleo *nm* : twinkling, sparkle
centenar *nm* **1** : hundred **2 a centenares** : by the hundreds
centenario¹, -ria *adj & n* : centenarian
centenario² *nm* : centennial
centeno *nm* : rye
centésimo¹, -ma *adj* : hundredth
centésimo² *nm* : hundredth
centígrado *adj* : centigrade, Celsius
centigramo *nm* : centigram
centímetro *nm* : centimeter
centinela *nmf* : sentinel, sentry
central¹ *adj* **1** : central **2** PRINCIPAL : main, principal
central² *nf* **1** : main office, headquarters **2 central camionera** *Mex* : bus terminal
centralita *nf* : switchboard
centralizar {21} *vt* : to centralize — **centralización** *nf*
centrar *vt* **1** : to center **2** : to focus — **centrarse** *vr* **~ en** : to focus on, to concentrate on
céntrico, -ca *adj* : central
centrífugo, -ga *adj* : centrifugal
centrípeto, -ta *adj* : centripetal
centro¹ *nmf* : center (in sports)
centro² *nm* **1** MEDIO : center <centro de atención : center of attention> <centro de gravedad : center of gravity> **2** : downtown **3 centro de mesa** : centerpiece
centroamericano, -na *adj & n* : Central American
ceñido, -da *adj* AJUSTADO : tight, tight-fitting
ceñir {67} *vt* **1** : to encircle, to surround **2** : to hug, to cling to <me ciñe demasiado : it's too tight on me> — **ceñirse** *vr* **~ a** : to restrict oneself to, to stick to
ceño *nm* **1** : frown, scowl **2 fruncir el ceño** : to frown, to knit one's brows
cepa *nf* **1** : stump (of a tree) **2** : stock (of a vine) **3** LINAJE : ancestry, stock
cepillar *vt* **1** : to brush **2** : to plane (wood) — **cepillarse** *vr*
cepillo *nm* **1** : brush <cepillo de dientes : toothbrush> **2** : plane (for woodworking)
cepo *nm* : trap (for animals)
cera *nf* **1** : wax <cera de abejas : beeswax> **2** : polish
cerámica *nf* **1** : ceramics *pl* **2** : pottery
cerámico, -ca *adj* : ceramic
ceramista *nmf* ALFARERO : potter
cerca¹ *adv* **1** : close, near, nearby **2 ~ de** : nearly, almost
cerca² *nf* **1** : fence **2** : (stone) wall
cercado *nm* : enclosure
cercanía *nf* **1** PROXIMIDAD : proximity, closeness **2 cercanías** *nfpl* : outskirts, suburbs
cercano, -na *adj* : near, close
cercar {72} *vt* **1** : to fence in, to enclose **2** : to surround
cercenar *vt* **1** : to cut off, to amputate **2** : to diminish, to curtail
cerceta *nf* : teal (duck)
cerciorarse *vr* ASEGURARSE **~ de** : to make sure of, to verify
cerco *nm* **1** : siege **2** : cordon, circle **3** : fence
cerda *nf* **1** : bristle **2** : sow
cerdo *nm* **1** : pig, hog **2 carne de cerdo** : pork
cereal *nm* : cereal — **cereal** *adj*
cerebelo *nm* : cerebellum
cerebral *adj* : cerebral
cerebro *nm* : brain

ceremonia *nf* : ceremony — **ceremonial** *adj*

ceremonioso, -sa *adj* : ceremonious

cereza *nf* : cherry

cerezo *nm* : cherry tree

cerilla *nf* **1** : match **2** : earwax

cerillo *nm* (*in various countries*) : match

cerner {56} *vt* : to sift — **cernerse** *vr* **1** : to hover **2** ~ **sobre** : to loom over, to threaten

cernidor *nm* : sieve

cernir → **cerner**

cero *nm* : zero

ceroso, -sa *adj* : waxy

cerque, etc. → **cercar**

cerquita *adv fam* : very close, very near

cerrado, -da *adj* **1** : closed, shut **2** : thick, broad <tiene un acento cerrado : she has a thick accent> **3** : cloudy, overcast **4** : quiet, reserved **5** : dense, stupid

cerradura *nf* : lock

cerrajería *nf* : locksmith's shop

cerrajero, -ra *n* : locksmith

cerrar {55} *vt* **1** : to close, to shut **2** : to turn off **3** : to bring to an end — *vi* **1** : to close up, to lock up **2** : to close down — **cerrarse** *vr* **1** : to close **2** : to fasten, to button up **3** : to conclude, to end

cerrazón *nf, pl* **-zones** : obstinacy, stubbornness

cerro *nm* COLINA, LOMA : hill

cerrojo *nm* PESTILLO : bolt, latch

certamen *nm, pl* **-támenes** : competition, contest

certero, -ra *adj* : accurate, precise — **certeramente** *adv*

certeza *nf* : certainty

certidumbre *nf* : certainty

certificable *adj* : certifiable

certificación *nf, pl* **-ciones** : certification

certificado[1], -da *adj* **1** : certified **2** : registered (of mail)

certificado[2] *nm* **1** : certificate **2** : registered letter

certificar {72} *vt* **1** : to certify **2** : to register (mail)

cervato *nm* : fawn

cervecería *nf* **1** : brewery **2** : beer hall, bar

cerveza *nf* : beer <cerveza de barril : draft beer>

cervical *adj* : cervical

cerviz *nf, pl* **cervices** : nape of the neck, cervix

cesación *nf, pl* **-ciones** : cessation, suspension

cesante *adj* : laid off, unemployed

cesantía *nf* : unemployment

cesar *vi* : to cease, to stop — *vt* : to dismiss, to lay off

cesárea *nf* : cesarean, C-section

cese *nm* **1** : cessation, stop <cese del fuego : cease-fire> **2** : dismissal

cesio *nm* : cesium

cesión *nf, pl* **cesiones** : transfer, assignment <cesión de bienes : transfer of property>

césped *nm* : lawn, grass

cesta *nf* **1** : basket **2** : jai alai racket

cesto *nm* **1** : hamper **2** : basket (in basketball) **3 cesto de (la) basura** : wastebasket

cetrería *nf* : falconry

cetrino, -na *adj* : sallow

cetro *nm* : scepter

chabacano[1], -na *adj* : tacky, tasteless

chabacano[2] *nm Mex* : apricot

chacal *nm* : jackal

cháchara *nf fam* **1** : small talk, chatter **2 cháchara** *nfpl* : trinkets, junk

chacharear *vi fam* : to chatter, to gab

chacra *nf Arg, Chile, Peru* : small farm

chadiano, -na *adj & n* : Chadian

chal *nm* MANTÓN : shawl

chalado[1], -da *adj fam* : crazy, nuts

chalado[2], -da *n* : nut, crazy person

chalán *nm, pl* **chalanes** *Mex* : barge

chalé *nm* → **chalet**

chaleco *nm* : vest

chalet *nm Spain* : house

chalupa *nf* **1** : small boat **2** *Mex* : small stuffed tortilla

chamaco, -ca *n Mex fam* : kid, boy *m*, girl *f*

chamarra *nf* **1** : sheepskin jacket **2** : poncho, blanket

chamba *nf Mex, Peru fam* : job, work

chambear *vi Mex, Peru fam* : to work

chamo -ma *n Ven fam* **1** : kid, boy *m*, girl *f* **2** : buddy, pal

champaña *or* **champán** *nm* : champagne

champiñón *nm, pl* **-ñones** : mushroom

champú *nm, pl* **-pus** *or* **-púes** : shampoo

champurrado *nm Mex* : hot chocolate thickened with cornstarch

chamuco *nm Mex fam* : devil

chamuscar {72} *vt* : to singe, to scorch — **chamuscarse** *vr*

chamusquina *nf* : scorch

chance *nm* OPORTUNIDAD : chance, opportunity

chancho[1], -cha *adj fam* : dirty, filthy, gross

chancho[2], -cha *n* **1** : pig, hog **2** *fam* : slob

chanchullero, -ra *adj fam* : shady, crooked

chanchullo *nm fam* : shady deal, scam

chancla *nf* **1** : thong sandal, slipper **2** : old shoe

chancleta *nf* → **chancla**

chanclo *nm* **1** : clog **2 chanclos** *nmpl* : overshoes, galoshes, rubbers

chancro *nm* : chancre

changarro *nm Mex* : small shop, stall

chango, -ga *n Mex* : monkey

chantaje *nm* : blackmail

chantajear *vt* : to blackmail

chantajista *nmf* : blackmailer

chanza *nf* **1** : joke, jest **2** *Mex fam* : chance, opportunity

chapa *nf* **1** : sheet, panel, veneer **2** : lock **3** : badge
chapado, -da *adj* **1** : plated **2 chapado a la antigua** : old-fashioned
chapar *vt* **1** : to veneer **2** : to plate (metals)
chaparrón *nm, pl* **-rrones 1** : downpour **2** : great quantity, torrent
chapeado, -da *adj Col, Mex* : flushed
chapopote *nm Mex* : tar, blacktop
chapotear *vi* : to splash about
chapucero¹, -ra *adj* **1** : crude, shoddy **2** *Mex fam* : dishonest
chapucero², -ra *n* **1** : sloppy worker, bungler **2** *Mex fam* : cheat, swindler
chapulín *nm, pl* **-lines** *CA, Mex* : grasshopper, locust
chapuza *nf* **1** : botched job **2** *Mex fam* : fraud, trick <hacer chapuzas : to cheat>
chapuzón *nm, pl* **-zones** : dip, swim <darse un chapuzón : to go for a quick dip>
chaqueta *nf* : jacket
charada *nf* : charades (game)
charango *nm* : traditional Andean stringed instrument
charca *nf* : pond, pool
charco *nm* : puddle, pool
charcutería *nf* : delicatessen
charla *nf* : chat, talk
charlar *vi* : to chat, to talk
charlatán¹, -tana *adj* : talkative, chatty
charlatán², -tana *n, mpl* **-tanes 1** : chatterbox **2** FARSANTE : charlatan, phony
charlatanear *vi* : to chatter away
charol *nm* **1** : lacquer, varnish **2** : patent leather **3** : tray
charola *nf Bol, Mex, Peru* : tray
charreada *nf Mex* : charro show, rodeo
charretera *nf* : epaulet
charro¹, -rra *adj* **1** : gaudy, tacky **2** *Mex* : pertaining to charros
charro², -rra *n Mex* : charro (Mexican cowboy or cowgirl)
chascarrillo *nm fam* : joke, funny story
chasco *nm* **1** BROMA : trick, joke **2** DECEPCIÓN, DESILUSIÓN : disillusionment, disappointment
chasis *or* **chasís** *nm* : chassis
chasquear *vt* **1** : to click (the tongue, fingers, etc.) **2** : to snap (a whip)
chasquido *nm* **1** : click (of the tongue or fingers) **2** : snap, crack
chatarra *nf* : scrap metal
chato, -ta *adj* **1** : pug-nosed **2** : flat
chauvinismo *nm* : chauvinism
chauvinista¹ *adj* : chauvinistic
chauvinista² *nmf* : chauvinist
chaval, -vala *n fam* : kid, boy *m,* girl *f*
chavo¹, -va *adj Mex fam* : young
chavo², -va *n Mex fam* : kid, boy *m,* girl *f*
chavo³ *nm fam* : cent, buck <no tengo un chavo : I'm broke>
chayote *nm* : chayote (plant, fruit)
checar {72} *vt Mex* : to check, to verify
checo¹, -ca *adj & n* : Czech
checo² *nm* : Czech (language)
checoslovaco, -ca *adj & n* : Czechoslovakian
chef *nm* : chef
chelín *nm, pl* **chelines** : shilling
cheque¹, etc. → **checar**
cheque² *nm* **1** : check **2 cheque de viajero** : traveler's check
chequear *vt* **1** : to check, to verify **2** : to check in (baggage)
chequeo *nm* **1** INSPECCIÓN : check, inspection **2** : checkup, examination
chequera *nf* : checkbook
chévere *adj fam* : great, fantastic
chic *adj & nm* : chic
chica → **chico**
chicano, -na *adj & n* : Chicano, Chicana *f*
chicha *nf* : fermented alcoholic beverage made from corn
chícharo *nm* : pea
chicharra *nf* **1** CIGARRA : cicada **2** : buzzer
chicharrón *nm, pl* **-rrones 1** : pork rind **2 darle chicharrón a** *Mex fam* : to get rid of
chichón *nm, pl* **chichones** : bump, swelling
chicle *nm* : chewing gum
chicloso *nm Mex* : taffy
chico¹, -ca *adj* **1** : little, small **2** : young
chico², -ca *n* **1** : child, boy *m,* girl *f* **2** : young man *m,* young woman *f*
chicote *nm* LÁTIGO : whip, lash
chiffon *nm* → **chifón**
chiflado¹, -da *adj fam* : nuts, crazy
chiflado², -da *n fam* : crazy person, lunatic
chiflar *vi* : to whistle — *vt* : to whistle at, to boo — **chiflarse** *vr fam* **~ por** : to be crazy about
chiflido *nm* : whistle, whistling
chiflón *nm, pl* **chiflones** : draft (of air)
chifón *nm, pl* **chifones** : chiffon
chilango¹, -ga *adj Mex fam* : of or from Mexico City
chilango², -ga *n Mex fam* : person from Mexico City
chilaquiles *nmpl Mex* : shredded tortillas in sauce
chile *nm* : chili pepper
chileno, -na *adj & n* : Chilean
chillar *vi* **1** : to squeal, to screech **2** : to scream, to yell **3** : to be gaudy, to clash
chillido *nm* **1** : scream, shout **2** : squeal, screech, cry (of an animal)
chillo *nm PRi* : red snapper
chillón, -llona *adj, mpl* **chillones 1** : piercing, shrill **2** : loud, gaudy
chilpayate *nmf Mex fam* : child, little kid
chimenea *nf* **1** : chimney **2** : fireplace
chimichurri *nm Arg* : traditional hot sauce

chimpancé *nm* : chimpanzee
china *nf* **1** : pebble, small stone **2** *PRi* : orange
chinchar *vt fam* : to annoy, to pester — **chincharse** *vr fam* : to put up with something, to grin and bear it
chinchayote *nm Mex* : chayote root
chinche[1] *nf* **1** : bedbug **2** *Ven* : ladybug **3** : thumbtack
chinche[2] *nmf fam* : nuisance, pain in the neck
chinchilla *nf* : chinchilla
chino[1], **-na** *adj* **1** : Chinese **2** *Mex* : curly, kinky
chino[2], **-na** *n* : Chinese person
chino[3] *nm* : Chinese (language)
chip *nm, pl* **chips** : chip <chip de memoria : memory chip>
chipote *nm Mex fam* : bump (on the head)
chipotle *nm Mex* : type of chili pepper
chipriota *adj & nmf* : Cypriot
chiquear *vt Mex* : to spoil, to indulge
chiquero *nm* POCILGA : pigpen, pigsty
chiquillada *nf* : childish prank
chiquillo[1], **-lla** *adj* : very young, little
chiquillo[2], **-lla** *n* : kid, youngster
chiquito[1], **-ta** *adj* : tiny
chiquito[2], **-ta** *n* : little one, baby
chiribita *nf* **1** : spark **2** **chiribitas** *nfpl* : spots before the eyes
chiribitil *nm* **1** DESVÁN : attic, garret **2** : cubbyhole
chirigota *nf fam* : joke
chirimía *nf* : traditional reed pipe
chirimoya *nf* : cherimoya, custard apple
chiripa *nf* **1** : fluke **2** **de ~** : by sheer luck
chirivía *nf* : parsnip
chirona *nf fam* : slammer, jail
chirriar {85} *vi* **1** : to squeak, to creak **2** : to screech — **chirriante** *adj*
chirrido *nm* **1** : squeak, squeaking **2** : screech, screeching
chirrión *nm, pl* **chirriones** *Mex* : whip, lash
chisme *nm* **1** : gossip, tale **2** *Spain fam* : gadget, thingamajig
chismear *vi* : to gossip
chismoso[1], **-sa** *adj* : gossipy, gossiping
chismoso[2], **-sa** *n* **1** : gossiper, gossip **2** *Mex fam* : tattletale
chispa[1] *adj* **1** *Mex fam* : lively, vivacious <un perrito chispa : a frisky puppy> **2** *Spain fam* : tipsy
chispa[2] *nf* **1** : spark **2** **echar chispas** : to be furious
chispeante *adj* : sparkling, scintillating
chispear *vi* **1** : to give off sparks **2** : to sparkle
chisporrotear *vi* : to crackle, to sizzle
chiste *nm* **1** : joke, funny story **2** **tener chiste** : to be funny **3** **tener su chiste** *Mex* : to be tricky
chistoso[1], **-sa** *adj* **1** : funny, humorous **2** : witty
chistoso[2], **-sa** *n* : wit, joker
chivas *nfpl Mex fam* : stuff, odds and ends
chivo[1], **-va** *n* **1** : kid, young goat **2** **chivo expiatorio** : scapegoat
chivo[2] *nm* **1** : billy goat **2** : fit of anger
chocante *adj* **1** : shocking **2** : unpleasant, rude
chocar {72} *vi* **1** : to crash, to collide **2** : to clash, to conflict **3** : to be shocking <le chocó : he was shocked> **4** *Mex, Ven fam* : to be unpleasant or obnoxious <me choca tu jefe : I can't stand your boss> — *vt* **1** : to shake (hands) **2** : to clink glasses
chochear *vi* **1** : to be senile **2** **~ por** : to dote on, to be soft on
chochín *nm, pl* **-chines** : wren
chocho, -cha *adj* **1** : senile **2** : doting
choclo *nm* **1** : ear of corn, corncob **2** : corn **3** **meter el choclo** *Mex fam* : to make a mistake
chocolate *nm* **1** : chocolate **2** : hot chocolate, cocoa
chofer *or* **chófer** *nm* **1** : chauffeur **2** : driver
choke *nm* : choke (of an automobile)
chole *interj Mex fam* **¡ya chole!** : enough!, cut it out!
cholo, -la *adj & n* : mestizo
cholla *nf fam* : head
chollo *nm Spain fam* : bargain
chongo *nm Mex* **1** : bun (chignon) **2** **chongos** *nmpl Mex* : dessert made with fried bread
choque[1], **etc.** → **chocar**
choque[2] *nm* **1** : crash, collision **2** : clash, conflict **3** : shock
chorizo *nm* : chorizo, sausage
chorrear *vi* **1** : to drip **2** : to pour out, to gush out
chorrito *nm* : squirt, splash
chorro *nm* **1** : flow, stream, jet **2** *Mex fam* : heap, ton
choteado, -da *adj Mex fam* : worn-out, stale <esa canción está bien choteada : that song's been played to death>
chotear *vt* : to make fun of
choteo *nm* : joking around, kidding
chovinismo, chovinista → **chauvinismo, chauvinista**
choza *nf* BARRACA, CABAÑA : hut, shack
chubasco *nm* : downpour, storm
chuchería *nf* : knickknack, trinket
chueco, -ca *adj* **1** : crooked, bent **2** *Chile, Mex fam* : dishonest, shady
chulada *nf Mex, Spain fam* : cute or pretty thing <¡qué chulada de vestido! : what a lovely dress!>
chulear *vt Mex fam* : to compliment
chuleta *nf* : cutlet, chop
chulo[1], **-la** *adj* **1** *fam* : cute, pretty **2** *Spain fam* : cocky, arrogant
chulo[2] *nm Spain* : pimp
chupada *nf* **1** : suck, sucking **2** : puff, drag (on a cigarette)
chupado, -da *adj fam* **1** : gaunt, skinny **2** : plastered, drunk
chupaflor *nm* COLIBRÍ : hummingbird
chupamirto *nm Mex* : hummingbird

chupar *vt* **1 :** to suck **2 :** to absorb **3 :** to puff on **4** *fam* **:** to drink, to guzzle — *vi* **:** to suckle — **chuparse** *vr* **1 :** to waste away **2** *fam* **:** to put up with **3 ¡chúpate esa!** *fam* **:** take that!
chupete *nm* **1 :** pacifier **2** *Chile, Peru* **:** lollipop
chupetear *vt* **:** to suck (at)
chupón *nm, pl* **chupones 1 :** sucker (of a plant) **2 :** baby bottle, pacifier
churrasco *nm* **1 :** steak **2 :** barbecued meat
churro *nm* **1 :** fried dough **2** *fam* **:** botch, mess **3** *fam* **:** attractive person, looker
chusco, -ca *adj* **:** funny, amusing
chusma *nf* GENTUZA **:** riffraff, rabble
chutar *vi* **:** to shoot (in soccer)
chute *nm* **:** shot (in soccer)
cianuro *nm* **:** cyanide
cibernética *nf* **:** cybernetics
cicatriz *nf, pl* **-trices :** scar
cicatrizarse {21} *vr* **:** to form a scar, to heal
cíclico, -ca *adj* **:** cyclical
ciclismo *nm* **:** bicycling
ciclista *nmf* **:** bicyclist
ciclo *nm* **:** cycle
ciclomotor *nm* **:** moped
ciclón *nm, pl* **ciclones :** cyclone
cicuta *nf* **:** hemlock
cidra *nf* **:** citron (fruit)
ciega, ciegue, etc. → **cegar**
ciego[1], -ga *adj* **1** INVIDENTE **:** blind **2 a ciegas :** blindly **3 quedarse ciego :** to go blind — **ciegamente** *adv*
ciego[2], -ga *n* INVIDENTE **:** blind person
cielo *nm* **1 :** sky **2 :** heaven **3 :** ceiling
ciempiés *nms & pl* **:** centipede
cien[1] *adj* **1 :** a hundred, hundred <las primeras cien páginas : the first hundred pages> **2 cien por cien** *or* **cien por ciento :** a hundred percent, through and through, wholeheartedly
cien[2] *nm* **:** one hundred
ciénaga *nf* **:** swamp, bog
ciencia *nf* **1 :** science **2 :** learning, knowledge **3 a ciencia cierta :** for a fact, for certain
cieno *nm* **:** mire, mud, silt
científico[1], -ca *adj* **:** scientific — **científicamente** *adv*
científico[2], -ca *n* **:** scientist
ciento[1] *adj* (*used in compound numbers*) **:** one hundred <ciento uno : one hundred and one>
ciento[2] *nm* **1 :** hundred, group of a hundred **2 por ~ :** percent
cierne, etc. → **cerner**
cierra, etc. → **cerrar**
cierre *nm* **1 :** closing, closure **2 :** fastener, clasp, zipper
cierto, -ta *adj* **1 :** true, certain, definite <lo cierto es que... : the fact is that...> **2 :** certain, one <cierto día de verano : one summer day> <bajo ciertas circunstancias : under certain circumstances> **3 por ~ :** in fact, as a matter of fact — **ciertamente** *adv*
ciervo, -va *n* **:** deer, stag *m,* hind *f*
cifra *nf* **1 :** figure, number **2 :** quantity, amount **3** CLAVE **:** code, cipher
cifrar *vt* **1 :** to write in code **2 :** to place, to pin <cifró su esperanza en la lotería : he pinned his hopes on the lottery> — **cifrarse** *vr* **:** to amount <la multa se cifra en millares : the fine amounts to thousands>
cigarra *nf* CHICHARRA **:** cicada
cigarrera *nf* **:** cigarette case
cigarrillo *nm* **:** cigarrette
cigarro *nm* **1 :** cigarette **2** PURO **:** cigar
cigoto *nm* **:** zygote
cigüeña *nf* **:** stork
cilantro *nm* **:** cilantro, coriander
cilíndrico, -ca *adj* **:** cylindrical
cilindro *nm* **:** cylinder
cima *nf* CUMBRE **:** peak, summit, top
cimarrón, -rrona *adj, mpl* **-rrones :** untamed, wild
címbalo *nm* **:** cymbal
cimbel *nm* **:** decoy
cimbrar *vt* **:** to shake, to rock — **cimbrarse** *vr* **:** to sway, to swing
cimentar {55} *vt* **1 :** to lay the foundation of, to establish **2 :** to strengthen, to cement
cimientos *nmpl* **:** base, foundation(s)
cinc *nm* **:** zinc
cincel *nm* **:** chisel
cincelar *vt* **1 :** to chisel **2 :** to engrave
cincha *nf* **:** cinch, girth
cinchar *vt* **:** to cinch (a horse)
cinco *adj & nm* **:** five
cincuenta *adj & nm* **:** fifty
cincuentavo[1], -va *adj* **:** fiftieth
cincuentavo[2] *nm* **:** fiftieth (fraction)
cine *nm* **1 :** cinema, movies *pl* **2 :** movie theater
cineasta *nmf* **:** filmmaker
cinematográfico, -ca *adj* **:** movie, film, cinematic <la industria cinematográfica : the film industry>
cingalés[1], -lesa *adj & n* **:** Sinhalese
cingalés[2] *nm* **:** Sinhalese (language)
cínico[1], -ca *adj* **1 :** cynical **2 :** shameless, brazen — **cínicamente** *adv*
cínico[2], -ca *n* **:** cynic
cinismo *nm* **:** cynicism
cinta *nf* **1 :** ribbon **2 :** tape <cinta métrica : tape measure> **3 :** strap, belt <cinta transportadora : conveyor belt>
cinto *nm* **:** strap, belt
cintura *nf* **1 :** waist, waistline **2 meter en cintura** *fam* **:** to bring into line, to discipline
cinturón *nm, pl* **-rones 1 :** belt **2 cinturón de seguridad :** seat belt
ciñe, etc. → **ceñir**
ciprés *nm, pl* **cipreses :** cypress
circo *nm* **:** circus
circón *nm, pl* **circones :** zircon
circonio *nm* **:** zirconium
circuitería *nf* **:** circuitry
circuito *nm* **:** circuit
circulación *nf, pl* **-ciones 1 :** circulation **2 :** movement **3 :** traffic

circular[1] *vi* **1 :** to circulate **2 :** to move along **3 :** to drive
circular[2] *adj* **:** circular
circular[3] *nf* **:** circular, flier
circulatorio, -ria *adj* **:** circulatory
círculo *nm* **1 :** circle **2 :** club, group
circuncidar *vt* **:** to circumcise
circuncisión *nf, pl* **-siones :** circumcision
circundar *vt* **:** to surround — **circundante** *adj*
circunferencia *nf* **:** circumference
circunflejo, -ja *adj* **acento circunflejo :** circumflex
circunlocución *nf, pl* **-ciones :** circumlocution
circunloquio *nm* → **circunlocución**
circunnavegar {52} *vt* **:** to circumnavigate — **circunnavegación** *nf*
circunscribir {33} *vt* **:** to circumscribe, to constrict, to limit — **circunscribirse** *vr*
circunscripción *nf, pl* **-ciones 1 :** limitation, restriction **2 :** constituency
circunscrito *pp* → **circunscribir**
circunspección *nf, pl* **-ciones :** circumspection, prudence
circunspecto, -ta *adj* **:** circumspect, prudent
circunstancia *nf* **:** circumstance
circunstancial *adj* **:** circumstantial, incidental
circunstante *nmf* **1 :** onlooker, bystander **2 los circunstantes :** those present
circunvalación *nf, pl* **-ciones :** surrounding, encircling <carretera de circunvalación : bypass, beltway>
circunvecino, -na *adj* **:** surrounding, neighboring
cirio *nm* **:** large candle
cirro *nm* **:** cirrus (cloud)
cirrosis *nf* **:** cirrhosis
ciruela *nf* **1 :** plum **2 ciruela pasa :** prune
cirugía *nf* **:** surgery
cirujano, -na *n* **:** surgeon
cisma *nm* **:** schism, rift
cisne *nm* **:** swan
cisterna *nf* **:** cistern, tank
cita *nf* **1 :** quote, quotation **2 :** appointment, date
citable *adj* **:** quotable
citación *nf, pl* **-ciones** EMPLAZAMIENTO **:** summons, subpoena
citadino[1]**, -na** *adj* **:** of the city, urban
citadino[2]**, -na** *n* **:** city dweller
citado, -da *adj* **:** said, aforementioned
citar *vt* **1 :** to quote, to cite **2 :** to make an appointment with **3 :** to summon (to court), to subpoena — **citarse** *vr* **~ con :** to arrange to meet (someone)
cítara *nf* **:** zither
citatorio *nm* **:** subpoena
citoplasma *nm* **:** cytoplasm
cítrico[1]**, -ca** *adj* **:** citric
cítrico[2] *nm* **:** citrus fruit
ciudad *nf* **1 :** city, town **2 ciudad universitaria :** college or university campus **3 ciudad perdida** *Mex* **:** shantytown
ciudadanía *nf* **1 :** citizenship **2 :** citizenry, citizens *pl*
ciudadano[1]**, -na** *adj* **:** civic, city
ciudadano[2]**, -na** *n* **1** NACIONAL **:** citizen **2** HABITANTE **:** resident, city dweller
ciudadela *nf* **:** citadel, fortress
cívico, -ca *adj* **1 :** civic **2 :** public-spirited
civil[1] *adj* **1 :** civil **2 :** civilian
civil[2] *nmf* **:** civilian
civilidad *nf* **:** civility, courtesy
civilización *nf, pl* **-ciones :** civilization
civilizar {21} *vt* **:** to civilize
civismo *nm* **:** community spirit, civic-mindedness, civics
cizaña *nf* **:** discord, rift
clamar *vi* **:** to clamor, to raise a protest — *vt* **:** to cry out for
clamor *nm* **:** clamor, outcry
clamoroso, -sa *adj* **:** clamorous, resounding, thunderous
clan *nm* **:** clan
clandestinidad *nf* **:** secrecy <en la clandestinidad : underground>
clandestino, -na *adj* **:** clandestine, secret
clara *nf* **:** egg white
claraboya *nf* **:** skylight
claramente *adv* **:** clearly
clarear *v impers* **1 :** to clear, to clear up **2 :** to get light, to dawn — *vi* **:** to go gray, to turn white
claridad *nf* **1** NITIDEZ **:** clarity, clearness **2 :** brightness, light
clarificación *nf, pl* **-ciones** ACLARACIÓN **:** clarification, explanation
clarificar {72} *vt* ACLARAR **:** to clarify, to explain
clarín *nm, pl* **clarines :** bugle
clarinete *nm* **:** clarinet
clarividencia *nf* **1 :** clairvoyance **2 :** perspicacity, discernment
clarividente[1] *adj* **1 :** clairvoyant **2 :** perspicacious, discerning
clarividente[2] *nmf* **:** clairvoyant
claro[1] *adv* **1 :** clearly <habla más claro : speak more clearly> **2 :** of course, surely <¡claro!, ¡claro que sí! : absolutely!, of course!> <claro que entendió : of course she understood>
claro[2]**, -ra** *adj* **1 :** bright, clear **2 :** pale, fair, light **3 :** clear, evident
claro[3] *nm* **1 :** clearing **2 claro de luna :** moonlight
clase *nf* **1 :** class **2** ÍNDOLE, TIPO **:** sort, kind, type
clasicismo *nm* **:** classicism
clásico[1]**, -ca** *adj* **1 :** classic **2 :** classical
clásico[2] *nm* **:** classic
clasificación *nf, pl* **-ciones 1 :** classification, sorting out **2 :** rating **3** CALIFICACIÓN **:** qualification (in competitions)
clasificado, -da *adj* **:** classified <aviso clasificado : classified ad>
clasificar {72} *vt* **1 :** to classify, to sort out **2 :** to rate, to rank — *vi* CALIFICAR

: to qualify (in competitions) — **clasificarse** *vr*

claudicación *nf, pl* **-ciones** : surrender, abandonment of one's principles

claudicar {72} *vi* : to back down, to abandon one's principles

claustro *nm* : cloister

claustrofobia *nf* : claustrophobia

claustrofóbico, -ca *adj* : claustrophobic

cláusula *nf* : clause

clausura *nf* **1** : closure, closing **2** : closing ceremony **3** : cloister

clausurar *vt* **1** : to close, to bring to a close **2** : to close down

clavadista *nmf* : diver

clavado[1], -da *adj* **1** : nailed, fixed, stuck **2** *fam* : punctual, on the dot **3** *fam* : identical <es clavado a su padre : he's the image of his father>

clavado[2] *nm* : dive

clavar *vt* **1** : to nail, to hammer **2** HINCAR : to plunge, to stick **3** : to fix (one's eyes) on — **clavarse** *vr* : to stick oneself (with a sharp object)

clave[1] *adj* : key, essential

clave[2] *nf* **1** CIFRA : code **2** : key <la clave del misterio : the key to the mystery> **3** : clef **4** : keystone

clavel *nm* : carnation

clavelito *nm* : pink (flower)

clavicémbalo *nm* : harpsichord

clavícula *nf* : collarbone

clavija *nf* **1** : plug **2** : peg, pin

clavo *nm* **1** : nail <clavo grande : spike> **2** : clove **3 dar en el clavo** : to hit the nail on the head

claxon *nm, pl* **cláxones** : horn (of an automobile)

clemencia *nf* : clemency, mercy

clemente *adj* : merciful

cleptomanía *nf* : kleptomania

cleptómano, -na *n* : kleptomaniac

clerecía *nf* : ministry, ministers *pl*

clerical *adj* : clerical

clérigo, -ga *n* : cleric, member of the clergy

clero *nm* : clergy

cliché *nm* **1** : cliché **2** : stencil **3** : negative (of a photograph)

cliente, -ta *n* : customer, client

clientela *nf* : clientele, customers *pl*

clima *nm* **1** : climate **2** AMBIENTE : atmosphere, ambience

climático, -ca *adj* : climatic

climatización *nf, pl* **-ciones** : air-conditioning

climatizar {21} *vt* : to air-condition — **climatizado, -da** *adj*

clímax *nm* : climax

clínica *nf* : clinic

clínico, -ca *adj* : clinical — **clínicamente** *adv*

clip *nm* **1** : clip **2** : paper clip

clítoris *nms & pl* : clitoris

cloaca *nf* ALCANTARILLA : sewer

clocar {82} *vi* : to cluck

cloche *nm CA, Car, Col, Ven* : clutch (of an automobile)

clon *nm* : clone

cloqué, etc. → **clocar**

cloquear *vi* : to cluck

clorar *vt* : to chlorinate — **cloración** *nf*

cloro *nm* : chlorine

clorofila *nf* : chlorophyll

cloroformo *nm* : chloroform

cloruro *nm* : chloride

clóset *nm, pl* **clósets 1** : closet **2** : cupboard

club *nm* : club

clueca, clueque, etc. → **clocar**

coa *nf Mex* : hoe

coacción *nf, pl* **-ciones** : coercion, duress

coaccionar *vt* : to coerce

coactivo, -va *adj* : coercive

coagular *v* : to clot, to coagulate — **coagulación** *nf*

coágulo *nm* : clot

coalición *nf, pl* **-ciones** : coalition

coartada *nf* : alibi

coartar *vt* : to restrict, to limit

cobalto *nm* : cobalt

cobarde[1] *adj* : cowardly

cobarde[2] *nmf* : coward

cobardía *nf* : cowardice

cobaya *nf* : guinea pig

cobertizo *nm* : shed, shelter

cobertor *nm* COLCHA : bedspread, quilt

cobertura *nf* **1** : coverage **2** : cover, collateral

cobija *nf* FRAZADA, MANTA : blanket

cobijar *vt* : to shelter — **cobijarse** *vr* : to take shelter

cobra *nf* : cobra

cobrador, -dora *n* **1** : collector **2** : conductor (of a bus or train)

cobrar *vt* **1** : to charge **2** : to collect, to draw, to earn **3** : to acquire, to gain **4** : to recover, to retrieve **5** : to cash (a check) **6** : to claim, to take (a life) **7** : to shoot (game), to bag — *vi* **1** : to be paid **2 llamar por cobrar** *Mex* : to call collect

cobre *nm* : copper

cobro *nm* : collection (of money), cashing (of a check)

coca *nf* **1** : coca **2** *fam* : coke, cocaine

cocaína *nf* : cocaine

cocal *nm* : coca plantation

cocción *nf, pl* **cocciones** : cooking

cocear *vi* : to kick (of an animal)

cocer {14} *vt* **1** COCINAR : to cook **2** HERVIR : to boil

cochambre *nmf fam* : filth, grime

cochambroso, -sa *adj* : filthy, grimy

coche *nm* **1** : car, automobile **2** : coach, carriage **3 coche cama** : sleeping car **4 coche fúnebre** : hearse

cochecito *nm* : baby carriage, stroller

cochera *nf* : garage, carport

cochinada *nf fam* **1** : filthy language **2** : disgusting behavior **3** : dirty trick

cochinillo *nm* : suckling pig, piglet

cochino[1], -na *adj* **1** : dirty, filthy, disgusting **2** *fam* : rotten, lousy

cochino[2], -na *n* : pig, hog

cocido[1], -da *adj* **1 :** boiled, cooked **2 bien cocido :** well-done
cocido[2] *nm* ESTOFADO, GUISADO **:** stew
cociente *nm* **:** quotient
cocimiento *nm* **:** cooking, baking
cocina *nf* **1 :** kitchen **2 :** stove **3 :** cuisine, cooking
cocinar *v* **:** to cook
cocinero, -ra *n* **:** cook, chef
cocineta *nf Mex* **:** kitchenette
coco *nm* **1 :** coconut **2** *fam* **:** head **3** *fam* **:** bogeyman
cocoa *nf* **:** cocoa, hot chocolate
cocodrilo *nm* **:** crocodile
cocotero *nm* **:** coconut palm
coctel *or* **cóctel** *nm* **1 :** cocktail **2 :** cocktail party
coctelera *nf* **:** cocktail shaker
codazo *nm* **1 darle un codazo a :** to elbow, to nudge **2 abrirse paso a codazos :** to elbow one's way through
codearse *vr* **:** to rub elbows, to hobnob
códice *nm* **:** codex, manuscript
codicia *nf* AVARICIA **:** avarice, covetousness
codiciar *vt* **:** to covet
codicilo *nm* **:** codicil
codicioso, -sa *adj* **:** avaricious, covetous
codificación *nf, pl* **-ciones 1 :** codification **2 :** coding, encoding
codificar {72} *vt* **1 :** to codify **2 :** to code, to encode
código *nm* **1 :** code **2 código postal :** zip code **3 código morse :** Morse code
codo[1], -da *adj Mex* **:** cheap, stingy
codo[2], -da *n Mex* **:** tightwad, cheapskate
codo[3] *nm* **:** elbow
codorniz *nf, pl* **-nices :** quail
coeficiente *nm* **1 :** coefficient **2 coeficiente intelectual :** IQ, intelligence quotient
coexistir *vi* **:** to coexist — **coexistencia** *nf*
cofa *nm* **:** crow's nest
cofre *nm* **1** BAÚL **:** trunk, chest **2** *Mex* CAPOTE **:** hood (of a car)
coger {15} *vt* **1 :** to seize, to take hold of **2 :** to catch **3 :** to pick up **4 :** to gather, to pick **5 :** to gore — **cogerse** *vr* AGARRARSE **:** to hold on
cogida *nf* **1 :** gathering, harvest **2 :** goring
cognición *nf, pl* **-ciones :** cognition
cognitivo, -va *adj* **:** cognitive
cogollo *nm* **1 :** heart (of a vegetable) **2 :** bud, bulb **3 :** core, crux <el cogollo de la cuestión : the heart of the matter>
cogote *nm* **:** scruff, nape
cohabitar *vi* **:** to cohabit — **cohabitación** *nf*
cohechar *vt* SOBORNAR **:** to bribe
cohecho *nm* SOBORNO **:** bribe, bribery
coherencia *nf* **:** coherence — **coherente** *adj*
cohesión *nf, pl* **-siones :** cohesion
cohesivo, -va *adj* **:** cohesive
cohete *nm* **:** rocket
cohibición *nf, pl* **-ciones 1 :** (legal) restraint **2** INHIBICIÓN **:** inhibition
cohibido, -da *adj* **:** inhibited, shy
cohibir {62} *vt* **:** to inhibit, to make self-conscious — **cohibirse** *vr* **:** to feel shy or embarrassed
cohorte *nf* **:** cohort
coima *nf Arg, Chile, Peru* **:** bribe
coimear *vt Arg, Chile, Peru* **:** to bribe
coincidencia *nf* **:** coincidence
coincidir *vi* **1 :** to coincide **2 :** to agree
coito *nm* **:** sexual intercourse, coitus
coja, etc. → **coger**
cojear *vi* **1 :** to limp **2 :** to wobble, to rock **3 cojear del mismo pie :** to be two of a kind
cojera *nf* **:** limp
cojín *nm, pl* **cojines :** cushion, throw pillow
cojinete *nm* **1 :** bearing, bushing **2 cojinete de bola :** ball bearing
cojo[1], -ja *adj* **1 :** limping, lame **2 :** wobbly **3 :** weak, ineffectual
cojo[2], -ja *n* **:** lame person
cojones *nmpl usu considered vulgar* **1 :** testicles *pl* **2 :** guts *pl,* courage
col *nf* **1** REPOLLO **:** cabbage **2 col de Bruselas :** Brussels sprout **3 col rizada :** kale
cola *nf* **1** RABO **:** tail <cola de caballo : ponytail> **2** FILA **:** line (of people) <hacer cola : to wait in line> **3 :** cola, drink **4 :** train (of a dress) **5 :** tails *pl* (of a tuxedo) **6** PEGAMENTO **:** glue **7** *fam* **:** buttocks *pl,* rear end
colaboracionista *nmf* **:** collaborator, traitor
colaborador, -dora *n* **1 :** contributor (to a periodical) **2 :** collaborator
colaborar *vi* **:** to collaborate — **colaboración** *nf*
colación *nf, pl* **-ciones 1 :** light meal **2 :** comparison, collation <sacar a colación : to bring up, to broach> **3 :** conferral (of a degree)
colador *nm* **1 :** colander, strainer **2** *PRi* **:** small coffeepot
colapso *nm* **1 :** collapse **2 :** standstill
colar {19} *vt* **:** to strain, to filter — **colarse** *vr* **1 :** to sneak in, to cut in line, to gate-crash **2 :** to slip up, to make a mistake
colateral[1] *adj* **:** collateral — **colateralmente** *adv*
colateral[2] *nm* **:** collateral
colcha *nf* COBERTOR **:** bedspread, quilt
colchón *nm, pl* **colchones 1 :** mattress **2 :** cushion, padding, buffer
colchoneta *nf* **:** mat (for gymnastic sports)
colear *vi* **1 :** to wag its tail **2 vivito y coleando** *fam* **:** alive and kicking
colección *nf, pl* **-ciones :** collection
coleccionar *vt* **:** to collect, to keep a collection of
coleccionista *nmf* **:** collector
colecta *nf* **:** collection (of donations)

colectar *vt* : to collect
colectividad *nf* : community, group
colectivo[1], -va *adj* : collective — **colectivamente** *adv*
colectivo[2] *nm* **1** : collective **2** *Arg, Bol, Peru* : city bus
colector[1], -tora *n* : collector <colector de impuestos : tax collector>
colector[2] *nm* **1** : sewer **2** : manifold (of an engine)
colega *nmf* **1** : colleague **2** HOMÓLOGO : counterpart **3** *fam* : buddy
colegiado[1], -da *adj* : collegiate
colegiado[2], -da *n* **1** ÁRBITRO : referee **2** : member (of a professional association)
colegial[1], -giala *adj* **1** : school, collegiate **2** *Mex fam* : green, inexperienced
colegial[2], -giala *n* : schoolboy *m*, schoolgirl *f*
colegiatura *nf Mex* : tuition
colegio *nm* **1** : school **2** : college <colegio electoral : electoral college> **3** : professional association
colegir {28} *vt* **1** JUNTAR : to collect, to gather **2** INFERIR : to infer, to deduce
cólera[1] *nm* : cholera
cólera[2] *nf* FURIA, IRA : anger, rage
colérico, -ca *adj* **1** FURIOSO : angry **2** IRRITABLE : irritable
colesterol *nm* : cholesterol
coleta *nf* **1** : ponytail **2** : pigtail
coletazo *nm* : lash, flick (of a tail)
colgado, -da *adj* **1** : hanging, hanged **2** : pending **3 dejar colgado a** : to disappoint, to let down
colgante[1] *adj* : hanging, dangling
colgante[2] *nm* : pendant, charm (on a bracelet)
colgar {16} *vt* **1** : to hang (up), to put up **2** AHORCAR : to hang (someone) **3** : to hang up (a telephone) **4** *fam* : to fail (an exam) — **colgarse** *vr* **1** : to hang, to be suspended **2** AHORCARSE : to hang oneself **3** : to hang up a telephone
colibrí *nm* CHUPAFLOR : hummingbird
cólico *nm* : colic
coliflor *nf* : cauliflower
colilla *nf* : butt (of a cigarette)
colina *nf* CERRO, LOMA : hill
colindante *adj* CONTIGUO : adjacent, neighboring
colindar *vi* : to adjoin, to be adjacent
coliseo *nm* : coliseum
colisión *nf, pl* **-siones** : collision
colisionar *vi* : to collide
collage *nm* : collage
collar *nm* **1** : collar (for an animal) **2** : necklace <collar de perlas : string of pearls>
colmado, -da *adj* : heaping
colmar *vt* **1** : to fill to the brim **2** : to fulfill, to satisfy **3** : to heap, to shower <me colmaron de regalos : they showered me with gifts>
colmena *nf* : beehive
colmenar *nm* APIARIO : apiary
colmillo *nm* **1** CANINO : canine (tooth), fang **2** : tusk
colmilludo, -da *adj Mex, PRi* : astute, shrewd, crafty
colmo *nm* : height, extreme, limit <el colmo de la locura : the height of folly> <¡eso es el colmo! : that's the last straw!>
colocación *nf, pl* **-ciones 1** : placement, placing **2** : position, job **3** : investment
colocar {72} *vt* **1** PONER : to place, to put **2** : to find a job for **3** : to invest — **colocarse** *vr* **1** SITUARSE : to position oneself **2** : to get a job
colofón *nm, pl* **-fones 1** : ending, finale **2** : colophon
colofonia *nf* : rosin
colombiano, -na *adj & n* : Colombian
colon *nm* : (intestinal) colon
colón *nm, pl* **colones** : Costa Rican and Salvadoran unit of currency
colonia *nf* **1** : colony **2** : cologne **3** *Mex* : residential area, neighborhood
colonial *adj* : colonial
colonización *nf, pl* **-ciones** : colonization
colonizador[1], -dora *adj* : colonizing
colonizador[2], -dora *n* : colonizer, colonist
colonizar {21} *vt* : to colonize, to settle
colono, -na *n* **1** : settler, colonist **2** : tenant farmer
coloquial *adj* : colloquial
coloquio *nm* **1** : discussion, talk **2** : conference, symposium
color *nm* **1** : color **2** : paint, dye **3 colores** *nmpl* : colored pencils
coloración *nf, pl* **-ciones** : coloring, coloration
colorado[1], -da *adj* **1** ROJO : red **2 ponerse colorado** : to blush **3 chiste colorado** *Mex* : off-color joke
colorado[2] *nm* ROJO : red
colorante *nm* : coloring <colorante de alimentos : food coloring>
colorear *vt* : to color — *vi* **1** : to redden **2** : to ripen
colorete *nm* : rouge, blusher
colorido *nm* : color, coloring
colorín *nm, pl* **-rines 1** : bright color **2** : goldfinch
colosal *adj* : colossal
coloso *nm* : colossus
coludir *vi* : to be in collusion, to conspire
columna *nf* **1** : column **2 columna vertebral** : spine, backbone
columnata *nf* : colonnade
columnista *nmf* : columnist
columpiar *vt* : to push (on a swing) — **columpiarse** *vr* : to swing
columpio *nm* : swing
colusión *nf, pl* **-siones** : collusion
colza *nf* : rape (plant)
coma[1] *nm* : coma
coma[2] *nf* : comma
comadre *nf* **1** : godmother of one's child **2** : mother of one's godchild **3**

fam : neighbor, female friend **4** *fam* : gossip
comadrear *vi fam* : to gossip
comadreja *nf* : weasel
comadrona *nf* : midwife
comanche *nmf* : Comanche
comandancia *nf* **1** : command headquarters **2** : command
comandante *nmf* **1** : commander, commanding officer **2** : major
comandar *vt* : to command, to lead
comando *nm* **1** : commando **2** : command (for computers)
comarca *nf* REGIÓN : region
comarcal *adj* REGIONAL : regional, local
combar *vt* : to bend, to curve — **combarse** *vr* **1** : to bend, to buckle **2** : to warp, to bulge, to sag
combate *nm* **1** : combat **2** : fight, boxing match
combatiente *nmf* : combatant, fighter
combatir *vt* : to combat, to fight against — *vi* : to fight
combatividad *nf* : fighting spirit
combativo, -va *adj* : combative, spirited
combinación *nf, pl* **-ciones 1** : combination **2** : connection (in travel)
combinar *vt* **1** UNIR : to combine, to mix together **2** : to match, to put together — **combinarse** *vr* : to get together, to conspire
combo *nm* **1** : (musical) band **2** *Chile, Peru* : sledgehammer **3** *Chile, Peru* : punch
combustible[1] *adj* : combustible
combustible[2] *nm* : fuel
combustión *nf, pl* **-tiones** : combustion
comedero *nm* : trough, feeder
comedia *nf* : comedy
comediante *nmf* : actor, actress *f*
comedido, -da *adj* MESURADO : moderate, restrained
comediógrafo, -fa *n* : playwright
comedor *nm* : dining room
comején *nm, pl* **-jenes** : termite
comelón[1], **-lona** *adj, mpl* **-lones** *fam* : gluttonous
comelón[2] **-lona** *n, pl* **-lones** *fam* : big eater, glutton
comensal *nmf* : dinner guest
comentador, -dora *n* → **comentarista**
comentar *vt* **1** : to comment on, to discuss **2** : to mention, to remark
comentario *nm* **1** : comment, remark <sin comentarios : no comment> **2** : commentary
comentarista *nmf* : commentator
comenzar {29} *v* EMPEZAR : to begin, to start
comer[1] *vt* **1** : to eat **2** : to consume, to eat up, to eat into — *vi* **1** : to eat **2** CENAR : to have a meal **3** **dar de comer** : to feed — **comerse** *vr* : to eat up
comer[2] *nm* : eating, dining
comercial *adj & nm* : commercial — **comercialmente** *adv*
comercializar {21} *vt* **1** : to commercialize **2** : to market
comerciante *nmf* : merchant, dealer
comerciar *vi* : to do business, to trade
comercio *nm* **1** : commerce, trade **2** NEGOCIO : business, place of business
comestible *adj* : edible
comestibles *nmpl* VÍVERES : groceries, food
cometa[1] *nm* : comet
cometa[2] *nf* : kite
cometer *vt* **1** : to commit **2** **cometer un error** : to make a mistake
cometido *nm* : assignment, task
comezón *nf, pl* **-zones** PICAZÓN : itchiness, itching
comible *adj fam* : eatable, edible
comic *or* **cómic** *nm* : comic strip, comic book
comicastro, -tra *n* : second-rate actor, ham
comicidad *nf* HUMOR : humor, wit
comicios *nmpl* : elections, voting
cómico[1], **-ca** *adj* : comic, comical
cómico[2], **-ca** *n* HUMORISTA : comic, comedian, comedienne *f*
comida *nf* **1** : food **2** : meal **3** : dinner **4** **comida basura** : junk food **5** **comida rápida** : fast food
comidilla *nf* : talk, gossip
comienzo *nm* **1** : start, beginning **2** **al comienzo** : at first **3** **dar comienzo** : to begin
comillas *nfpl* : quotation marks <entre comillas : in quotes>
comilón, -lona → **comelón, -lona**
comilona *nf fam* : feast
comino *nm* **1** : cumin **2** **me vale un comino** *fam* : not to matter to someone <no me importa un comino : I couldn't care less>
comisaría *nf* : police station
comisario, -ria *n* : commissioner
comisión *nf, pl* **-siones 1** : commission, committing **2** : committee **3** : percentage, commission <comisión sobre las ventas : sales commission>
comisionado[1], **-da** *adj* : commissioned, entrusted
comisionado[2], **-da** *n* → **comisario**
comisionar *vt* : to commission
comité *nm* : committee
comitiva *nf* : retinue, entourage
como[1] *adv* **1** : around, about <cuesta como 500 pesos : it costs around 500 pesos> **2** : kind of, like <tengo como mareos : I'm kind of dizzy>
como[2] *conj* **1** : how, as <hazlo como dijiste que lo harías : do it the way you said you would> **2** : since, given that <como estaba lloviendo, no salí : since it was raining, I didn't go out> **3** : if <como lo vuelva a hacer lo arrestarán : if he does that again he'll be arrested> **4** **como quiera** : in any way

como[3] *prep* **1 :** like, as <ligero como una pluma : light as a feather> **2 así como :** as well as

cómo *adv* **:** how <¿cómo estás? : how are you?> <¿a cómo están las manzanas? : how much are the apples?> <¿cómo? : excuse me?, what was that?> <¿se puede? ¡cómo no! : may I? please do!>

cómoda *nf* **:** bureau, chest of drawers

comodidad *nf* **1 :** comfort **2 :** convenience

comodín *nm, pl* **-dines 1 :** joker, wild card **2 :** all-purpose word or thing **3 :** pretext, excuse

cómodo, -da *adj* **1** CONFORTABLE **:** comfortable **2 :** convenient — **cómodamente** *adv*

comodoro *nm* **:** commodore

comoquiera *adv* **1 :** in any way **2 comoquiera que :** in whatever way, however <comoquiera que sea eso : however that may be>

compa *nm fam* **:** buddy, pal

compactar *vt* **:** to compact, to compress

compacto, -ta *adj* **:** compact

compadecer {53} *vt* **:** to sympathize with, to feel sorry for — **compadecerse** *vr* **1 ~ de :** to take pity on, to commiserate with **2 ~ con :** to fit, to accord (with)

compadre *nm* **1 :** godfather of one's child **2 :** father of one's godchild **3** *fam* **:** buddy, pal

compaginar *vt* **1** COORDINAR **:** to combine, to coordinate **2 :** to collate

compañerismo *nm* **:** comradeship, camaraderie

compañero, -ñera *n* **:** companion, mate, partner

compañía *nf* **1 :** company <llegó en compañía de su madre : he arrived with his mother> **2** EMPRESA, FIRMA **:** firm, company

comparable *adj* **:** comparable

comparación *nf, pl* **-ciones :** comparison

comparado, -da *adj* **:** comparative <literatura comparada : comparative literature>

comparar *vt* **:** to compare

comparativo[1], **-va** *adj* **:** comparative, relative — **comparativamente** *adv*

comparativo[2] *nm* **:** comparative degree or form

comparecencia *nf* **1 :** appearance (in court) **2 orden de comparecencia :** subpoena, summons

comparecer {53} *vi* **:** to appear (in court)

compartimiento *or* **compartimento** *nm* **:** compartment

compartir *vt* **:** to share

compás *nm, pl* **-pases 1 :** beat, rhythm, time **2 :** compass

compasión *nf, pl* **-siones :** compassion, pity

compasivo, -va *adj* **:** compassionate, sympathetic

compatibilidad *nf* **:** compatibility

compatible *adj* **:** compatible

compatriota *nmf* PAISANO **:** compatriot, fellow countryman

compeler *vt* **:** to compel

compendiar *vt* **:** to summarize, to condense

compendio *nm* **:** summary

compenetración *nf, pl* **-ciones :** rapport, mutual understanding

compenetrarse *vr* **1 :** to understand each other **2 ~ con :** to identify oneself with

compensación *nf, pl* **-ciones :** compensation

compensar *vt* **:** to compensate for, to make up for — *vi* **:** to be worth one's while

compensatorio, -ria *adj* **:** compensatory

competencia *nf* **1 :** competition, rivalry **2 :** competence

competente *adj* **:** competent, able — **competentemente** *adv*

competición *nf, pl* **-ciones :** competition

competidor[1], **-dora** *adj* RIVAL **:** competing, rival

competidor[2], **-dora** *n* RIVAL **:** competitor, rival

competir {54} *vi* **:** to compete

competitividad *nf* **:** competitiveness

competitivo, -va *adj* **:** competitive — **competitivamente** *adv*

compilar *vt* **:** to compile — **compilación** *nf*

compinche *nmf fam* **1 :** buddy, pal **2 :** partner in crime, accomplice

complacencia *nf* **:** pleasure, satisfaction

complacer {57} *vt* **:** to please — **complacerse** *vr* **~ en :** to take pleasure in

complaciente *adj* **:** obliging, eager to please

complejidad *nf* **:** complexity

complejo[1], **-ja** *adj* **:** complex

complejo[2] *nm* **:** complex

complementar *vt* **:** to complement, to supplement — **complementarse** *vr*

complementario, -ria *adj* **:** complementary

complemento *nm* **1 :** complement, supplement **2 :** supplementary pay, allowance

completamente *adv* **:** completely, totally

completar *vt* TERMINAR **:** to complete, to finish

completo, -ta *adj* **1 :** complete **2 :** perfect, absolute **3 :** full, detailed — **completamente** *adv*

complexión *nf, pl* **-xiones :** (physical) constitution

complicación *nf, pl* **-ciones :** complication

complicado, -da *adj* **:** complicated

complicar {72} *vt* **1 :** to complicate **2 :** to involve — **complicarse** *vr*
cómplice *nmf* **:** accomplice
complicidad *nf* **:** complicity
complot *nm, pl* **complots** CONFABULACIÓN, CONSPIRACIÓN **:** conspiracy, plot
componenda *nf* **:** shady deal, scam
componente *adj & nm* **:** component, constituent
componer {60} *vt* **1** ARREGLAR **:** to fix, to repair **2** CONSTITUIR **:** to make up, to compose **3 :** to compose, to write **4 :** to set (a bone) — **componerse** *vr* **1 :** to improve, to get better **2 ~ de :** to consist of
comportamiento *nm* CONDUCTA **:** behavior, conduct
comportarse *vr* **:** to behave, to conduct oneself
composición *nf, pl* **-ciones 1** OBRA **:** composition, work **2 :** makeup, arrangement
compositor, -tora *n* **:** composer, songwriter
compostura *nf* **1 :** composure **2 :** mending, repair
compra *nf* **1 :** purchase **2 ir de compras :** to go shopping **3 orden de compra :** purchase order
comprador, -dora *n* **:** buyer, shopper
comprar *vt* **:** to buy, to purchase
compraventa *nf* **:** buying and selling
comprender *vt* **1** ENTENDER **:** to comprehend, to understand **2** ABARCAR **:** to cover, to include — *vi* **:** to understand <¡ya comprendo! : now I understand!>
comprensible *adj* **:** understandable — **comprensiblemente** *adv*
comprensión *nf, pl* **-siones 1 :** comprehension, understanding, grasp **2 :** understanding, sympathy
comprensivo, -va *adj* **:** understanding
compresa *nf* **1 :** compress **2** *or* **compresa higiénica :** sanitary napkin
compresión *nf, pl* **-siones :** compression
compresor *nm* **:** compressor
comprimido *nm* PÍLDORA, TABLETA **:** pill, tablet
comprimir *vt* **:** to compress
comprobable *adj* **:** verifiable, provable
comprobación *nf, pl* **-ciones :** verification, confirmation
comprobante *nm* **1 :** proof <comprobante de identidad : proof of identity> **2 :** voucher, receipt <comprobante de ventas : sales slip>
comprobar {19} *vt* **1 :** to verify, to check **2 :** to prove
comprometedor, -dora *adj* **:** compromising
comprometer *vt* **1 :** to compromise **2 :** to jeopardize **3 :** to commit, to put under obligation — **comprometerse** *vr* **1 :** to commit oneself **2 ~ con :** to get engaged to
comprometido, -da *adj* **1 :** compromising, awkward **2 :** committed, obliged **3 :** engaged (to be married)
compromiso *nm* **1 :** obligation, commitment **2 :** engagement <anillo de compromiso : engagement ring> **3 :** agreement **4 :** awkward situation, fix
compuerta *nf* **:** floodgate
compuesto[1] *pp* → **componer**
compuesto[2], **-ta** *adj* **1 :** fixed, repaired **2 :** compound, composite **3 :** decked out, spruced up **4 ~ de :** made up of, consisting of
compuesto[3] *nm* **:** compound
compulsión *nf, pl* **-siones :** compulsion
compulsivo, -va *adj* **1 :** compelling, urgent **2 :** compulsive — **compulsivamente** *adv*
compungido, -da *adj* **:** contrite, remorseful
compungirse {35} *vr* **:** to feel remorse
compuso, etc. → **componer**
computación *nf, pl* **-ciones :** computing, computers *pl*
computador *nm* → **computadora**
computadora *nf* **1 :** computer **2 computadora portátil :** laptop computer
computar *vt* **:** to compute, to calculate
computarizar {21} *vt* **:** to computerize
cómputo *nm* **:** computation, calculation
comulgar {52} *vi* **:** to receive Communion
común *adj, pl* **comunes 1 :** common **2 común y corriente :** ordinary, regular **3 por lo común :** generally, as a rule
comuna *nf* **:** commune
comunal *adj* **:** communal
comunicación *nf, pl* **-ciones 1 :** communication **2 :** access, link **3 :** message, report
comunicado *nm* **1 :** communiqué **2 comunicado de prensa :** press release
comunicar {72} *vt* **1 :** to communicate, to convey **2 :** to notify — **comunicarse** *vr* **~ con 1 :** to contact, to get in touch with **2 :** to be connected to
comunicativo, -va *adj* **:** communicative, talkative
comunidad *nf* **:** community
comunión *nf, pl* **-niones 1 :** communion, sharing **2 :** Communion
comunismo *nm* **:** communism, Communism
comúnmente *adv* **:** commonly
con *prep* **1 :** with <vengo con mi padre : I'm going with my father> <¿con quién hablas? : who are you speaking to?> **2 :** in spite of <con todo : in spite of it all> **3 :** to, towards <ella es amable con los niños : she is kind to the children> **4 :** by <con llegar temprano : by arriving early> **5 con (tal) que :** as long as, so long as
conato *nm* **:** attempt, effort <conato de robo : attempted robbery>

cóncavo, -va *adj* : concave

concebible *adj* : conceivable

concebir {54} *vt* **1** : to conceive **2** : to conceive of, to imagine — *vi* : to conceive, to become pregnant

conceder *vt* **1** : to grant, to bestow **2** : to concede, to admit

concejal, -jala *n* : councilman *m,* councilwoman *f,* alderman *m,* alderwoman *f*

concejo *nm* : council <concejo municipal : town council>

concentración *nf, pl* **-ciones** : concentration

concentrado *nm* : concentrate

concentrar *vt* : to concentrate — **concentrarse** *vr*

concéntrico, -ca *adj* : concentric

concepción *nf, pl* **-ciones** : conception

concepto *nm* NOCIÓN : concept, idea, opinion

conceptuar {3} *vt* : to regard, to judge

concernir {17} *vi* : to be of concern

concertar {55} *vt* **1** : to arrange, to set up **2** : to agree on, to settle **3** : to harmonize — *vi* : to be in harmony

concesión *nf, pl* **-siones 1** : concession **2** : awarding, granting

concha *nf* : conch, seashell

conciencia *nf* **1** : conscience **2** : consciousness, awareness

concientizar {21} *vt* : to make aware — **concientizarse** *vr* **~ de** : to realize, to become aware of

concienzudo, -da *adj* : conscientious

concierto *nm* **1** : concert **2** : agreement **3** : concerto

conciliador[1], **-dora** *adj* : conciliatory

conciliador[2], **-dora** *n* : arbitrator, peacemaker

conciliar *vt* : to conciliate, to reconcile — **conciliación** *nf*

concilio *nm* : (church) council

conciso, -sa *adj* : concise — **concisión** *nf*

conciudadano, -na *n* : fellow citizen

cónclave *nm* : conclave, private meeting

concluir {41} *vt* **1** TERMINAR : to conclude, to finish **2** DEDUCIR : to deduce, to infer — *vi* : to end, to conclude

conclusión *nf, pl* **-siones** : conclusion

concluyente *adj* : conclusive

concomitante *adj* : concomitant

concordancia *nf* : agreement, accordance

concordar {19} *vi* : to agree, to coincide — *vt* : to reconcile

concordia *nf* : concord, harmony

concretar *vt* **1** : to pinpoint, to specify **2** : to fulfill, to realize — **concretarse** *vr* : to become real, to take shape

concretizar → **concretar**

concreto[1], **-ta** *adj* **1** : concrete, actual **2** : definite, specific <en concreto : specifically> — **concretamente** *adv*

concreto[2] *nm* HORMIGÓN : concrete

concubina *nf* : concubine

concurrencia *nf* **1** : audience, turnout **2** : concurrence

concurrente *adj* : concurrent — **concurrentemente** *adv*

concurrido, -da *adj* : busy, crowded

concurrir *vi* **1** : to converge, to come together **2** : to concur, to agree **3** : to take part, to participate **4** : to attend, to be present <concurrir a una reunión : to attend a meeting> **5 ~ a** : to contribute to

concursante *nmf* : contestant, competitor

concursar *vt* : to compete in — *vi* : to compete, to participate

concurso *nm* **1** : contest, competition **2** : concurrance, coincidence **3** : crowd, gathering **4** : cooperation, assistance

condado *nm* **1** : county **2** : earldom

conde, -desa *n* : count *m,* earl *m,* countess *f*

condecoración *nf, pl* **-ciones** : decoration, medal

condecorar *vt* : to decorate, to award (a medal)

condena *nf* **1** REPROBACIÓN : disapproval, condemnation **2** SENTENCIA : sentence, conviction

condenación *nf, pl* **-ciones 1** : condemnation **2** : damnation

condenado[1], **-da** *adj* **1** : fated, doomed **2** : convicted, sentenced **3** *fam* : darn, damned

condenado[2], **-da** *n* : convict

condenar *vt* **1** : to condemn **2** : to sentence **3** : to board up, to wall up — **condenarse** *vr* : to be damned

condensación *nf, pl* **-ciones** : condensation

condensar *vt* : to condense

condesa *nf* → **conde**

condescendencia *nf* : condescension

condescender {56} *vi* **1** : to condescend **2** : to agree, to acquiesce

condición *nf, pl* **-ciones 1** : condition, state **2** : capacity, position **3 condiciones** *nfpl* : conditions, circumstances <condiciones de vida : living conditions>

condicional *adj* : conditional — **condicionalmente** *adv*

condicionamiento *nm* : conditioning

condicionar *vt* **1** : to condition, to determine **2 ~ a** : to be contingent on, to depend on

condimentar *vt* SAZONAR : to season, to spice

condimento *nm* : condiment, seasoning, spice

condolencia *nf* : condolence, sympathy

condolerse {47} *vr* : to sympathize

condominio *nm* : condominium, condo

condón *nm, pl* **condones** : condom

cóndor *nm* : condor

conducción *nf, pl* **-ciones 1** : conduction (of electricity, etc.) **2** DIRECCIÓN : management, direction

conducir {61} *vt* **1** DIRIGIR, GUIAR **:** to direct, to lead **2** MANEJAR **:** to drive (a vehicle) — *vi* **1 :** to drive a vehicle **2** **~ a :** to lead to — **conducirse** *vr* PORTARSE **:** to behave, to conduct oneself
conducta *nf* COMPORTAMIENTO **:** conduct, behavior
conducto *nm* **:** conduit, channel, duct
conductor¹, -tora *adj* **:** conducting, leading
conductor², -tora *n* **:** driver
conductor³ *nm* **:** conductor (of electricity, etc.)
conectar *vt* **:** to connect — *vi* **~ con :** to link up with, to communicate with
conector *nm* **:** connector
conejera *nf* **:** rabbit hutch
conejillo *nm* **conejillo de Indias :** guinea pig
conejo, -ja *n* **:** rabbit
conexión *nf, pl* **-xiones :** connection
confabulación *nf, pl* **-ciones** COMPLOT, CONSPIRACIÓN **:** plot, conspiracy
confabularse *vr* **:** to plot, to conspire
confección *nf, pl* **-ciones 1 :** preparation **2 :** tailoring, dressmaking
confeccionar *vt* **:** to make, to produce, to prepare
confederación *nf, pl* **-ciones :** confederation
confederarse *vr* **:** to confederate, to form a confederation
conferencia *nf* **1** REUNIÓN **:** conference, meeting **2 :** lecture
conferenciante *nmf* **:** lecturer
conferencista *nmf* → **conferenciante**
conferir {76} *vt* **:** to confer, to bestow
confesar {55} *v* **:** to confess — **confesarse** *vr* **:** to go to confession
confesión *nf, pl* **-siones 1 :** confession **2 :** creed, denomination
confesionario *nm* **:** confessional
confesor *nm* **:** confessor
confeti *nm* **:** confetti
confiable *adj* **:** trustworthy, reliable
confiado, -da *adj* **1 :** confident, self-confident **2 :** trusting — **confiadamente** *adv*
confianza *nf* **1 :** trust <de poca confiaza : untrustworthy> **2 :** confidence, self-confidence
confianzudo, -da *adj* **:** forward, presumptuous
confiar {85} *vi* **:** to have trust, to be trusting — *vt* **1 :** to confide **2 :** to entrust — **confiarse** *vr* **1 :** to be overconfident **2 ~ a :** to confide in
confidencia *nf* **:** confidence, secret
confidencial *adj* **:** confidential — **confidencialmente** *adv*
confidencialidad *nf* **:** confidentiality
confidente *nmf* **1 :** confidant, confidante *f* **2 :** informer
configuración *nf, pl* **-ciones :** configuration, shape
configurar *vt* **:** to shape, to form
confín *nm, pl* **confines :** boundary, limit
confinamiento *nm* **:** confinement
confinar *vt* **1 :** to confine, to limit **2 :** to exile — *vi* **~ con :** to border on
confirmación *nf, pl* **-ciones :** confirmation
confirmar *vt* **:** to confirm, to substantiate
confiscar {72} *vt* DECOMISAR **:** to confiscate, to seize
confitado, -da *adj* **:** candied
confite *nm* **:** comfit, candy
confitería *nm* **1** DULCERÍA **:** candy store, confectionery **2 :** tearoom, café
confitero, -ra *n* **:** confectioner
confitura *nf* **:** preserves, jam
conflagración *nf, pl* **-ciones 1 :** conflagration, fire **2 :** war
conflictivo, -va *adj* **1 :** troubled **2 :** controversial
conflicto *nm* **:** conflict
confluencia *nf* **:** junction, confluence
confluir {41} *vi* **1 :** to converge, to join **2 :** to gather, to assemble
conformar *vt* **1 :** to form, to create **2 :** to constitute, to make up — **conformarse** *vr* **1** RESIGNARSE **:** to resign oneself **2 :** to comply, to conform **3 ~ con :** to content oneself with, to be satisfied with
conforme¹ *adj* **1 :** content, satisfied **2 ~ a :** in accordance with
conforme² *conj* **:** as <entreguen sus tareas conforme vayan saliendo : hand in your homework as you leave>
conformidad *nf* **1 :** agreement, consent **2 :** resignation
confort *nm* **:** comfort
confortable *adj* CÓMODO **:** comfortable
confortar *vt* CONSOLAR **:** to comfort, to console
confraternidad *nf* **:** brotherhood, fraternity
confrontación *nf, pl* **-ciones :** confrontation
confrontar *vt* **1** ENCARAR **:** to confront **2 :** to compare **3 :** to bring face-to-face — *vi* **:** to border — **confrontarse** *vr* **~ con :** to face up to
confundir *vt* **:** to confuse, to mix up — **confundirse** *vr* **:** to make a mistake, to be confused <confundirse de número : to get the wrong number>
confusión *nf, pl* **-siones :** confusion
confuso, -sa *adj* **1 :** confused, mixed-up **2 :** obscure, indistinct
congelación *nf, pl* **-ciones 1 :** freezing **2 :** frostbite
congelado, -da *adj* HELADO **:** frozen
congelador *nm* HELADORA **:** freezer
congelamiento *nm* → **congelación**
congelar *vt* **:** to freeze — **congelarse** *vr*
congeniar *vi* **:** to get along (with someone)
congénito, -ta *adj* **:** congenital
congestión *nf, pl* **-tiones :** congestion
congestionado, -da *adj* **:** congested
congestionamiento *nm* → **congestión**

congestionarse *vr* **1 :** to become flushed **2 :** to become congested
conglomerado[1], **-da** *adj* **:** conglomerate, mixed
conglomerado[2] *nm* **:** conglomerate, conglomeration
congoja *nf* ANGUSTIA **:** anguish, grief
congoleño, -ña *adj & n* **:** Congolese
congraciarse *vr* **:** to ingratiate oneself
congratular *vt* FELICITAR **:** to congratulate
congregación *nf, pl* **-ciones :** congregation, gathering
congregar {52} *vt* **:** to bring together — **congregarse** *vr* **:** to congregate, to assemble
congresista *nmf* **:** congressman *m,* congresswoman *f*
congreso *nm* **:** congress, conference
congruencia *nf* **1 :** congruence **2** COHERENCIA **:** coherence — **congruente** *adj*
cónico, -ca *adj* **:** conical, conic
conífera *nf* **:** conifer
conífero, -ra *adj* **:** coniferous
conjetura *nf* **:** conjecture, guess
conjeturar *vt* **:** to guess, to conjecture
conjugación *nf, pl* **-ciones :** conjugation
conjugar {52} *vt* **1 :** to conjugate **2 :** to combine
conjunción *nf, pl* **-ciones :** conjunction
conjuntivo, -va *adj* **:** connective <tejido conjuntivo : connective tissue>
conjunto[1], **-ta** *adj* **:** joint
conjunto[2] *nm* **1 :** collection, group **2 :** ensemble, outfit <conjunto musical : musical ensemble> **3 :** whole, entirety <en conjunto : as a whole, altogether>
conjurar *vt* **1 :** to exorcise **2 :** to avert, to ward off — *vi* CONSPIRAR **:** to conspire, to plot
conjuro *nm* **1 :** exorcism **2 :** spell
conllevar *vt* **1 :** to bear, to suffer **2** IMPLICAR **:** to entail, to involve
conmemorar *vt* **:** to commemorate — **conmemoración** *nf*
conmemorativo, -va *adj* **:** commemorative, memorial
conmigo *pron* **:** with me <habló conmigo : he talked with me>
conminar *vt* AMENAZAR **:** to threaten, to warn
conmiseración *nf, pl* **-ciones :** pity, conmiseration
conmoción *nf, pl* **-ciones 1 :** shock, upheaval **2** *or* **conmoción cerebral :** concussion
conmocionar *vt* **:** to shake, to shock
conmovedor, -dora *adj* EMOCIONANTE **:** moving, touching
conmover {47} *vt* **1** EMOCIONAR **:** to move, to touch **2 :** to shake up — **conmoverse** *vr*
conmutador *nm* **1 :** switch **2 :** switchboard
connivencia *nf* **:** connivance
connotación *nf, pl* **-ciones :** connotation
connotar *vt* **:** to connote, to imply
cono *nm* **:** cone
conocedor[1], **-dora** *adj* **:** knowledgeable
conocedor[2], **-dora** *n* **:** connoisseur, expert
conocer {18} *vt* **1 :** to know, to be acquainted with <ya la conocí : I've already met him> **2 :** to meet **3** RECONOCER **:** to recognize — **conocerse** *vr* **1 :** to know each other **2 :** to meet **3 :** to know oneself
conocido[1], **-da** *adj* **1 :** familiar **2 :** well-known, famous
conocido[2], **-da** *n* **:** acquaintance
conocimiento *nm* **1 :** knowledge **2** SENTIDO **:** consciousness
conque *conj* **:** so, so then, and so <¡ah, conque esas tenemos! : oh, so that's what's going on!>
conquista *nf* **:** conquest
conquistador[1], **-dora** *adj* **:** conquering
conquistador[2], **-dora** *n* **:** conqueror
conquistar *vt* **:** to conquer
consabido, -da *adj* **:** usual, typical
consagración *nf, pl* **-ciones :** consecration
consagrar *vt* **1 :** to consecrate **2** DEDICAR **:** to dedicate, to devote
consciencia *nf* → **conciencia**
consciente *adj* **:** conscious, aware — **conscientemente** *adv*
conscripción *nf, pl* **-ciones :** conscription, draft
conscripto, -ta *n* **:** conscript, inductee
consecución *nf, pl* **-ciones :** attainment
consecuencia *nf* **1 :** consequence, result <a consecuencia de : as a result of> **2 en ~ :** accordingly
consecuente *adj* **:** consistent — **consecuentemente** *adv*
consecutivo, -va *adj* **:** consecutive, successive — **consecutivamente** *adv*
conseguir {75} *vt* **1 :** to get, to obtain **2 :** to achieve, to attain **3 :** to manage to <consiguió acabar el trabajo : she managed to finish the job>
consejero, -ra *n* **:** adviser, counselor
consejo *nm* **1 :** advice, counsel **2 :** council <consejo de guerra : court-martial>
consenso *nm* **:** consensus
consentido, -da *adj* **:** spoiled, pampered
consentimiento *nm* **:** consent, permission
consentir {76} *vt* **1** PERMITIR **:** to consent to, to allow **2** MIMAR **:** to pamper, to spoil — *vi* **~ en :** to agree to, to approve of
conserje *nmf* **:** custodian, janitor, caretaker
conserva *nf* **1 :** preserve(s), jam **2 conservas** *nfpl* **:** canned goods
conservación *nf, pl* **-ciones :** conservation, preservation

conservacionista *nmf* : conservationist

conservador[1], -dora *adj & n* : conservative

conservador[2] *nm* : preservative

conservadurismo *nf* : conservatism

conservante *nm* : preservative

conservar *vt* **1** : to preserve **2** GUARDAR : to keep, to conserve

conservatorio *nm* : conservatory

considerable *adj* : considerable — **considerablemente** *adv*

consideración *nf, pl* **-ciones** **1** : consideration **2** : respect **3 de ~** : considerable, important

considerado, -da *adj* **1** : considerate, thoughtful **2** : respected

considerar *vt* **1** : to consider, to think over **2** : to judge, to deem **3** : to treat with respect

consigna *nf* **1** ESLOGAN : slogan **2** : assignment, orders *pl* **3** : checkroom

consignar *vt* **1** : to consign **2** : to record, to write down **3** : to assign, to allocate

consigo *pron* : with her, with him, with you, with oneself <se llevó las llaves consigo : she took the keys with her>

consiguiente *adj* **1** : resulting, consequent **2 por ~** : consequently, as a result

consistencia *nf* : consistency

consistente *adj* **1** : firm, strong, sound **2** : consistent — **consistentemente** *adv*

consistir *vi* **1 ~ en** : to consist of **2 ~ en** : to lie in, to consist in

consola *nf* : console

consolación *nf, pl* **-ciones** : consolation <premio de consolación : consolation prize>

consolar {19} *vt* CONFORTAR : to console, to comfort

consolidar *vt* : to consolidate — **consolidación** *nf*

consomé *nm* CALDO : consommé, clear soup

consonancia *nf* **1** : consonance, harmony **2 en consonancia con** : in accordance with

consonante[1] *adj* : consonant, harmonious

consonante[2] *nf* : consonant

consorcio *nm* : consortium

consorte *nmf* : consort, spouse

conspicuo, -cua *adj* : eminent, famous

conspiración *nf, pl* **-ciones** COMPLOT, CONFABULACIÓN : conspiracy, plot

conspirador, -dora *n* : conspirator

conspirar *vi* CONJURAR : to conspire, to plot

constancia *nf* **1** PRUEBA : proof, certainty **2** : record, evidence <que quede constancia : for the record> **3** : perseverance, constancy

constante[1] *adj* : constant — **constantemente** *adv*

constante[2] *nm* : constant

constar *vi* **1** : to be evident, to be on record <que conste : believe me, have no doubt> **2 ~ de** : to consist of

constatación *nf, pl* **-ciones** : confirmation, proof

constatar *vt* **1** : to verify **2** : to state

constelación *nf, pl* **-ciones** : constellation

consternación *nf, pl* **-ciones** : consternation, dismay

consternar *vt* : to dismay, to appall

constipación *nf, pl* **-ciones** : constipation

constipado[1], -da *adj* **estar constipado** : to have a cold

constipado[2] *nm* RESFRIADO : cold

constiparse *vr* : to catch a cold

constitución *nf, pl* **-ciones** : constitution — **constitucional** *adj* — **constitucionalmente** *adv*

constitucionalidad *nf* : constitutionality

constituir {41} *vt* **1** FORMAR : to constitute, to make up, to form **2** FUNDAR : to establish, to set up — **constituirse** *vr* **~ en** : to set oneself up as, to become

constitutivo, -va *adj* : constituent, component

constituyente *adj & nmf* : constituent

constreñir {67} *vt* **1** FORZAR, OBLIGAR : to constrain, to oblige **2** LIMITAR : to restrict, to limit

construcción *nf, pl* **-ciones** : construction, building

constructivo, -va *adj* : constructive — **constructivamente** *adv*

constructor, -tora *n* : builder

constructora *nf* : construction company

construir {41} *vt* : to build, to construct

consuelo *nm* : consolation, comfort

consuetudinario, -ria *adj* **1** : customary, habitual **2 derecho consuetudinario** : common law

cónsul *nmf* : consul — **consular** *adj*

consulado *nm* : consulate

consulta *nf* **1** : consultation **2** : inquiry

consultar *vt* : to consult

consultor[1], -tora *adj* : consulting <firma consultora : consulting firm>

consultor[2], -tora *n* : consultant

consultorio *nm* : office (of a doctor or dentist)

consumación *nf, pl* **-ciones** : consummation

consumado, -da *adj* : consummate, perfect

consumar *vt* **1** : to consummate, to complete **2** : to commit, to carry out

consumible *adj* : consumable

consumición *nf, pl* **-ciones** **1** : consumption **2** : drink (in a restaurant)

consumido, -da *adj* : thin, emaciated

consumidor, -dora *n* : consumer

consumir *vt* : to consume — **consumirse** *vr* : to waste away

consumo *nm* : consumption

contabilidad *nf* **1** : accounting, bookkeeping **2** : accountancy
contabilizar {21} *vt* : to enter, to record (in accounting)
contable[1] *adj* : countable
contable[2] *nmf Spain* : accountant, bookkeeper
contactar *vt* : to contact — *vi* **~ con** : to get in touch with, to contact
contacto *nm* : contact
contado[1], **-da** *adj* **1** : counted <tenía los días contados : his days were numbered> **2** : rare, scarce <en contadas ocasiones : on rare occasions>
contado[2] *nm* **al contado** : cash <pagar al contado : to pay in cash>
contador[1], **-dora** *n* : accountant
contador[2] *nm* : meter <contador de agua : water meter>
contaduría *nf* **1** : accounting office **2** CONTABILIDAD : accountancy
contagiar *vt* **1** : to infect **2** : to transmit (a disease) — **contagiarse** *vr* **1** : to be contagious **2** : to become infected
contagio *nm* : contagion, infection
contagioso, -sa *adj* : contagious, catching
contaminación *nf, pl* **-ciones** : contamination, pollution
contaminante *nm* : pollutant, contaminant
contaminar *vt* : to contaminate, to pollute
contar {19} *vt* **1** : to count **2** : to tell **3** : to include — *vi* **1** : to count (up) **2** : to matter, to be of concern <eso no cuenta : that doesn't matter> **3 ~ con** : to rely on, to count on — **contarse** *vr* **~ entre** : to be numbered among
contemplación *nf, pl* **-ciones** : contemplation — **contemplativo, -va** *adj*
contemplar *vt* **1** : to contemplate, to ponder **2** : to gaze at, to look at
contemporáneo, -nea *adj & n* : contemporary
contención *nf, pl* **-ciones** : containment, holding
contencioso, -sa *adj* : contentious
contender {56} *vi* **1** : to contend, to compete **2** : to fight
contendiente *nmf* : contender
contenedor *nm* **1** : container, receptacle **2** : Dumpster™
contener {80} *vt* **1** : to contain, to hold **2** ATAJAR : to restrain, to hold back — **contenerse** *vr* : to restrain oneself
contenido[1], **-da** *adj* : restrained, reserved
contenido[2] *nm* : contents *pl,* content
contentar *vt* : to please, to make happy — **contentarse** *vr* : to be satisfied, to be pleased
contento[1], **-ta** *adj* : contented, glad, happy
contento[2] *nm* : joy, happiness
contestación *nf, pl* **-ciones 1** : answer, reply **2** : protest
contestar *vt* RESPONDER : to answer — *vi* **1** RESPONDER : to answer, to reply **2** REPLICAR : to answer back
contexto *nm* : context
contienda *nf* **1** : dispute, conflict **2** : contest, competition
contigo *pron* : with you <voy contigo : I'm going with you>
contiguo, -gua *adj* COLINDANTE : contiguous, adjacent
continencia *nf* : continence
continente *nm* : continent — **continental** *adj*
contingencia *nf* : contingency, eventuality
contingente *adj & nm* : contingent
continuación *nf, pl* **-ciones 1** : continuation **2 a ~** : next <lo demás sigue a continuación : the rest follows> **3 a continuación de** : after, following
continuar {3} *v* : to continue
continuidad *nf* : continuity
continuo, -nua *adj* : continuous, steady, constant — **continuamente** *adv*
contonearse *vr* : to sway one's hips
contoneo *nm* : swaying, wiggling (of the hips)
contorno *nm* **1** : outline **2 contornos** *nmpl* : outskirts
contorsión *nf, pl* **-siones** : contortion
contra[1] *nf* **1** *fam* : difficulty, snag **2 llevar la contra a** : to oppose, to contradict
contra[2] *nm* : con <los pros y los contras : the pros and cons>
contra[3] *prep* : against
contraalmirante *nm* : rear admiral
contraatacar {72} *v* : to counterattack — **contraataque** *nm*
contrabajo *nm* : double bass
contrabalancear *vt* : to counterbalance — **contrabalanza** *nf*
contrabandear *v* : to smuggle
contrabandista *nmf* : smuggler, black marketeer
contrabando *nm* **1** : smuggling **2** : contraband
contracción *nf, pl* **-ciones** : contraction
contracepción *nf, pl* **-ciones** : contraception
contrachapado *nm* : plywood
contraconceptivo *nm* ANTICONCEPTIVO : contraceptive — **contracepción** *nf*
contracorriente *nf* **1** : crosscurrent **2 ir a contracorriente** : to go against the tide
contractual *adj* : contractual
contradecir {11} *vt* DESMENTIR : to contradict — **contradecirse** *vr* DESDECIRSE : to contradict oneself
contradicción *nf, pl* **-ciones** : contradiction
contradictorio, -ria *adj* : contradictory
contraer {81} *vt* **1** : to contract (a disease) **2** : to establish by contract

<contraer matrimonio : to get married> **3** : to tighten, to contract — **contraerse** *vr* : to contract, to tighten up
contrafuerte *nm* : buttress
contragolpe *nm* **1** : counterblow **2** : backlash
contrahecho, -cha *adj* : deformed, hunchbacked
contraindicado, -da *adj* : contraindicated — **contraindicación** *nf*
contralor, -lora *n* : comptroller
contralto *nmf* : contralto
contramaestre *nm* **1** : boatswain **2** : foreman
contramandar *vt* : to countermand
contramano *nm* **a ~** : the wrong way (on a street)
contramedida *nf* : countermeasure
contraorden *nf* : countermand
contraparte *nf* **1** : counterpart **2 en ~** : on the other hand
contrapartida *nf* : compensation
contrapelo *nm* **a ~** : in the wrong direction, against the grain
contrapeso *nm* : counterbalance
contraponer {60} *vt* **1** : to counter, to oppose **2** : to contrast, to compare
contraposición *nf, pl* **-ciones** : comparison
contraproducente *adj* : counterproductive
contrapunto *nm* : counterpoint
contrariar {85} *vt* **1** : to contradict, to oppose **2** : to vex, to annoy
contrariedad *nf* **1** : setback, obstacle **2** : vexation, annoyance
contrario, -ria *adj* **1** : contrary, opposite <al contrario : on the contrary> **2** : conflicting, opposed
contrarrestar *vt* : to counteract
contrarrevolución *nf, pl* **-ciones** : counterrevolution — **contrarrevolucionario, -ria** *adj & n*
contrasentido *nm* : contradiction
contraseña *nf* : password
contrastante *adj* : contrasting
contrastar *vt* **1** : to resist **2** : to check, to confirm — *vi* : to contrast
contraste *nm* : contrast
contratar *vt* **1** : to contract for **2** : to hire, to engage
contratiempo *nm* **1** PERCANCE : mishap, accident **2** DIFICULTAD : setback, difficulty
contratista *nmf* : contractor
contrato *nm* : contract
contravenir {87} *vt* : to contravene, to infringe
contraventana *nf* : shutter
contribución *nf, pl* **-ciones** : contribution
contribuidor, -dora *n* : contributor
contribuir {41} *vt* **1** APORTAR : to contribute **2** : to pay (in taxes) — *vi* **1** : contribute, to help out **2** : to pay taxes
contribuyente[1] *adj* : contributing
contribuyente[2] *nmf* : taxpayer
contrición *nf, pl* **-ciones** : contrition
contrincante *nmf* : rival, opponent
contrito, -ta *adj* : contrite, repentant
control *nm* **1** : control **2** : inspection, check **3** : checkpoint, roadblock
controlador, -dora *n* : controller <controlador aéreo : air traffic controller>
controlar *vt* **1** : to control **2** : to monitor, to check
controversia *nf* : controversy
controversial → **controvertido**
controvertido, -da *adj* : controversial
controvertir {76} *vt* : to dispute, to argue about — *vi* : to argue, to debate
contubernio *nm* : conspiracy
contumacia *nf* : obstinacy, stubbornness
contumaz *adj, pl* **-maces** : obstinate, stubbornly disobedient
contundencia *nf* **1** : forcefulness, weight **2** : severity
contundente *adj* **1** : blunt <un objeto contundente : a blunt instrument> **2** : forceful, convincing — **contundentemente** *adv*
contusión *nf, pl* **-siones** : bruise, contusion
contuvo, etc. → **contener**
convalecencia *nf* : convalescence
convalecer {53} *vi* : to convalesce, to recover
convaleciente *adj & nmf* : convalescent
convección *nf, pl* **-ciones** : convection
convencer {86} *vt* : to convince, to persuade — **convencerse** *vr*
convencimiento *nm* : belief, conviction
convención *nf, pl* **-ciones** **1** : convention, conference **2** : pact, agreement **3** : convention, custom
convencional *adj* : conventional — **convencionalmente** *adv*
convencionalismo *nm* : conventionality
conveniencia *nf* **1** : convenience **2** : fitness, suitability, advisability
conveniente *adj* **1** : convenient **2** : suitable, advisable
convenio *nm* PACTO : agreement, pact
convenir {87} *vi* **1** : to be suitable, to be advisable **2** : to agree
convento *nm* **1** : convent **2** : monastery
convergencia *nf* : convergence
convergente *adj* : convergent, converging
converger {15} *vi* **1** : to converge **2 ~ en** : to concur on
conversación *nf, pl* **-ciones** : conversation
conversador, -dora *n* : conversationalist, talker
conversar *vi* : to converse, to talk
conversión *nf, pl* **-siones** : conversion
converso, -sa *n* : convert
convertible *adj & nm* : convertible
convertidor *nm* : converter

convertir {76} *vt* **1 :** to convert **2 :** to transform, to change **3 :** to exchange (money) — **convertirse** *vr* **~ en :** to turn into
convexo, -xa *adj* **:** convex
convicción *nf, pl* **-ciones :** conviction
convicto¹, -ta *adj* **:** convicted
convicto², -ta *n* **:** convict, prisoner
convidado, -da *n* **:** guest
convidar *vt* **1** INVITAR **:** to invite **2 :** to offer
convincente *adj* **:** convincing — **convincentemente** *adv*
convivencia *nf* **1 :** coexistence **2 :** cohabitation
convivir *vi* **1 :** to coexist **2 :** to live together
convocación *nf, pl* **-ciones :** convocation
convocar {72} *vt* **:** to convoke, to call together
convocatoria *nf* **:** summons, call
convoy *nm* **:** convoy
convulsión *nf, pl* **-siones 1 :** convulsion **2 :** agitation, upheaval
convulsivo, -va *adj* **:** convulsive
conyugal *adj* **:** conjugal
cónyuge *nmf* **:** spouse, partner
coñac *nm* **:** cognac, brandy
cooperación *nf, pl* **-ciones :** cooperation
cooperador, -dora *adj* **:** cooperative
cooperar *vi* **:** to cooperate
cooperativa *nf* **:** cooperative, co-op
cooperativo, -va *adj* **:** cooperative
cooptar *vt* **:** to co-opt
coordenada *nf* **:** coordinate
coordinación *nf, pl* **-ciones :** coordination
coordinador, -dora *n* **:** coordinator
coordinar *vt* COMPAGINAR **:** to coordinate, to combine
copa *nf* **1 :** wineglass, goblet **2 :** drink <irse de copas : to go out drinking> **3 :** cup, trophy
copar *vt* **1 :** to take <ya está copado el puesto : the job is already taken> **2 :** to fill, to crowd
copartícipe *nmf* **:** joint partner
copete *nm* **1 :** tuft (of hair) **2 estar hasta el copete :** to be completely fed up
copia *nf* **1 :** copy **2 :** imitation, replica
copiadora *nf* **:** photocopier
copiar *vt* **:** to copy
copiloto *nmf* **:** copilot
copioso, -sa *adj* **:** copious, abundant
copla *nf* **1 :** popular song or ballad **2 :** couplet, stanza
copo *nm* **1 :** snowflake **2 copos de avena :** rolled oats **3 copos de maíz :** cornflakes
copra *nf* **:** copra
cópula *nf* **:** copulation
copular *vi* **:** to copulate
coque *nm* **:** coke (fuel)
coqueta *nf* **:** dressing table
coquetear *vi* **:** to flirt
coqueteo *nm* **:** flirting, coquetry
coqueto¹, -ta *adj* **:** flirtatious, coquettish
coqueto², -ta *n* **:** flirt
coraje *nm* **1** VALOR **:** valor, courage **2** IRA **:** anger <darle coraje a alguien : to make someone angry>
coral¹ *nm* **1 :** coral **2 :** chorale
coral² *nf* **:** choir
Corán *nm* **el Corán :** the Koran
coraza *nf* **1 :** armor, armor plating **2 :** shell (of an animal)
corazón *nm, pl* **-zones 1 :** heart <de todo corazón : wholeheartedly> <de buen corazón : kindhearted> **2 :** core **3 :** darling, sweetheart
corazonada *nf* **:** hunch, impulse
corbata *nf* **:** tie, necktie
corcel *nm* **:** steed, charger
corchete *nm* **1 :** hook and eye, clasp **2 :** square bracket
corcho *nm* **:** cork
corcholata *nf Mex* **:** cap, bottle top
corcovear *vi* **:** to buck
cordel *nm* **:** cord, string
cordero *nm* **:** lamb
cordial¹ *adj* **:** cordial, affable — **cordialmente** *adv*
cordial² *nm* **:** cordial (liqueur)
cordialidad *nf* **:** cordiality, warmth
cordillera *nf* **:** mountain range
córdoba *nf* **:** Nicaraguan unit of currency
cordón *nm, pl* **cordones 1 :** cord <cordón umbilical : umbilical cord> **2 :** cordon
cordura *nf* **1 :** sanity **2 :** prudence, good judgment
coreano¹, -na *adj & n* **:** Korean
coreano² *nm* **:** Korean (language)
corear *vt* **:** to chant, to chorus
coreografía *nf* **:** choreography
coreografiar {85} *vt* **:** to choreograph
coreográfico, -ca *adj* **:** choreographic
coreógrafo, -fa *n* **:** choreographer
cormorán *nm, pl* **-ranes :** cormorant
cornada *nf* **:** goring, butt (with the horns)
córnea *nf* **:** cornea
cornear *vt* **:** to gore
cornejo *nm* **:** dogwood (tree)
corneta *nf* **:** bugle, horn, cornet
cornisa *nf* **:** cornice
cornudo, -da *adj* **:** horned
coro *nm* **1 :** choir **2 :** chorus
corola *nf* **:** corolla
corolario *nm* **:** corollary
corona *nf* **1 :** crown **2 :** wreath, garland **3 :** corona (in astronomy)
coronación *nf, pl* **-ciones :** coronation
coronar *vt* **1 :** to crown **2 :** to reach the top of, to culminate
coronel, -nela *n* **:** colonel
coronilla *nf* **1 :** crown (of the head) **2 estar hasta la coronilla :** to be completely fed up
corpiño *nm* **1 :** bodice **2** *Arg* **:** brassiere, bra
corporación *nf, pl* **-ciones :** corporation

corporal *adj* **:** corporal, bodily
corporativo, -va *adj* **:** corporate
corpóreo, -rea *adj* **:** corporeal, physical
corpulencia *nf* **:** corpulence, stoutness, sturdiness
corpulento, -ta *adj* ROBUSTO **:** robust, stout, sturdy
corpúsculo *nm* **:** corpuscle
corral *nm* **1 :** farmyard **2 :** corral, pen, stockyard **3** *or* **corralito :** playpen
correa *nf* **:** strap, belt
correcaminos *nms & pl* **:** roadrunner
corrección *nf, pl* **-ciones 1 :** correction **2 :** correctness, propriety **3 :** rebuke, reprimand **4 corrección de pruebas :** proofreading
correccional *nm* REFORMATORIO **:** reformatory
correctivo, -va *adj* **:** corrective <lentes correctivos : corrective lenses>
correcto, -ta *adj* **1 :** correct, right **2 :** courteous, polite — **correctamente** *adv*
corrector, -tora *n* **:** proofreader
corredizo, -za *adj* **:** sliding <puerta corrediza : sliding door>
corredor[1], -dora *n* **1 :** runner, racer **2 :** agent, broker <corredor de bolsa : stockbroker>
corredor[2] *nm* PASILLO **:** corridor, hallway
correduría *nf* → **corretaje**
corregir {28} *vt* **1** ENMENDAR **:** to correct, to emend **2 :** to reprimand **3 corregir pruebas :** to proofread — **corregirse** *vr* **:** to reform, to mend one's ways
correlación *nf, pl* **-ciones :** correlation
correo *nm* **1 :** mail <correo aéreo : airmail> **2 :** post office
correoso, -sa *adj* **:** leathery, rough
correr *vi* **1 :** to run, to race **2 :** to rush **3 :** to flow — *vt* **1 :** to travel over, to cover **2 :** to move, to slide, to roll, to draw (curtains) **3 correr un riesgo :** to run a risk — **correrse** *vr* **1 :** to move along **2 :** to run, to spill over
correspondencia *nf* **1 :** correspondence, mail **2 :** equivalence **3 :** connection, interchange
corresponder *vi* **1 :** to correspond **2 :** to pertain, to belong **3 :** to be appropriate, to fit **4 :** to reciprocate — **corresponderse** *vr* **:** to write to each other
correspondiente *adj* **:** corresponding, respective
corresponsal *nmf* **:** correspondent
corretaje *nm* **:** brokerage
corretear *vi* **1** VAGAR **:** to loiter, to wander about **2 :** to run around, to scamper about — *vt* **:** to pursue, to chase
corrida *nf* **1 :** run, dash **2 :** bullfight
corrido[1], -da *adj* **1 :** straight, continuous **2 :** wordly, experienced
corrido[2] *nm* **:** Mexican narrative folk song
corriente[1] *adj* **1 :** common, everyday **2 :** current, present **3** *Mex* **:** cheap, trashy **4 perro corriente** *Mex* **:** mutt
corriente[2] *nf* **1 :** current <corriente alterna : alternating current> <direct current : corriente continua> **2 :** draft **3** TENDENCIA **:** tendency, trend
corrillo *nm* **:** small group, clique
corro *nm* **:** ring, circle (of people)
corroborar *vt* **:** to corroborate
corroer {69} *vt* **1 :** to corrode **2 :** to erode, to wear away
corromper *vt* **1 :** to corrupt **2 :** to rot — **corromperse** *vr*
corrompido, -da *adj* CORRUPTO **:** corrupt, rotten
corrosión *nf, pl* **-siones :** corrosion
corrosivo, -va *adj* **:** corrosive
corrugar {52} *vt* **:** to corrugate — **corrugación** *nf*
corrupción *nf, pl* **-ciones 1 :** decay **2 :** corruption
corruptela *nf* **:** corruption, abuse of power
corrupto, -ta *adj* CORROMPIDO **:** corrupt
corsario *nm* **:** privateer
corsé *nm* **:** corset
cortada *nf* **:** cut, gash
cortador, -dora *n* **:** cutter
cortadora *nf* **:** cutter, slicer
cortadura *nm* **:** cut, slash
cortafuego *nm* **:** firebreak
cortante *adj* **:** cutting, sharp
cortar *vt* **1 :** to cut, to slice, to trim **2 :** to cut out, to omit **3 :** to cut off, to interrupt **4 :** to block, to close off **5 :** to curdle (milk) — *vi* **1 :** to cut **2 :** to break up **3 :** to hang up (the telephone) — **cortarse** *vr* **1 :** to cut oneself <cortarse el pelo : to cut one's hair> **2 :** to be cut off **3 :** to sour (of milk)
cortauñas *nms & pl* **:** nail clippers
corte[1] *nm* **1 :** cut, cutting <corte de pelo : haircut> **2 :** style, fit
corte[2] *nf* **1 :** court <corte suprema : supreme court> **2 hacer la corte a :** to court, to woo
cortejar *vt* GALANTEAR **:** to court, to woo
cortejo *nm* **1** GALANTEO **:** courtship **2 :** retinue, entourage
cortés *adj* **:** courteous, polite — **cortésmente** *adv*
cortesano[1], -na *adj* **:** courtly
cortesano[2], -na *n* **:** courtier
cortesía *nf* **1 :** courtesy, politeness **2 de ~ :** complimentary, free
corteza *nf* **1 :** bark **2 :** crust **3 :** peel, rind **4 :** cortex <corteza cerebral : cerebral cortex>
cortijo *nm* **:** farmhouse
cortina *nm* **:** curtain
cortisona *nf* **:** cortisone
corto, -ta *adj* **1 :** short (in length or duration) **2 :** scarce **3 :** timid, shy **4 corto de vista :** nearsighted
cortocircuito *nm* **:** short circuit
corvo, -va *adj* **:** curved, bent

cosa *nf* **1 :** thing, object **2 :** matter, affair **3 otra cosa :** anything else, something else
cosecha *nf* **:** harvest, crop
cosechador, -dora *n* **:** harvester, reaper
cosechadora *nf* **:** harvester (machine)
cosechar *vt* **1 :** to harvest, to reap **2 :** to win, to earn, to garner — *vi* **:** to harvest
coser *vt* **1 :** to sew **2 :** to stitch up — *vi* **:** to sew
cosmético¹, -ca *adj* **:** cosmetic
cosmético² *nm* **:** cosmetic
cósmico, -ca *adj* **:** cosmic
cosmonauta *nmf* **:** cosmonaut
cosmopolita *adj & nmf* **:** cosmopolitan
cosmos *nm* **:** cosmos
cosquillas *nfpl* **1 :** tickling **2 hacer cosquillas :** to tickle
cosquilleo *nm* **:** tickling sensation, tingle
cosquilloso, -sa *adj* **:** ticklish
costa *nf* **1 :** coast, shore **2 :** cost <a toda costa : at all costs>
costado *nm* **1 :** side **2 al costado :** alongside
costar {19} *v* **:** to cost <¿cuánto cuesta? : how much does it cost?>
costarricense *adj & nmf* **:** Costa Rican
costarriqueño, -ña → **costarricense**
coste *nm* → **costo**
costear *vt* **:** to pay for, to finance
costero, -ra *adj* **:** coastal, coast
costilla *nf* **1 :** rib **2 :** chop, cutlet **3** *fam* **:** better half, wife
costo *nm* **1 :** cost, price **2 costo de vida :** cost of living
costoso, -sa *adj* **:** costly, expensive
costra *nf* **1 :** crust **2** POSTILLA **:** scab
costumbre *nf* **1 :** custom **2** HÁBITO **:** habit
costura *nf* **1 :** seam **2 :** sewing, dressmaking **3 alta costura :** haute couture
costurera *nf* **:** seamstress *f*
cotejar *vt* **:** to compare, to collate
cotejo *nm* **:** comparison, collation
cotidiano, -na *adj* **:** daily, everyday <la vida cotidiana : daily life>
cotización *nf, pl* **-ciones 1 :** market price **2 :** quote, estimate
cotizado, -da *adj* **:** in demand, sought after
cotizar {21} *vt* **:** to quote, to value — **cotizarse** *vr* **:** to be worth
coto *nm* **1 :** enclosure, reserve **2 poner coto a :** to put a stop to
cotorra *nf* **1 :** small parrot **2** *fam* **:** chatterbox, windbag
cotorrear *vi fam* **:** to chatter, to gab, to blab
cotorreo *nm fam* **:** chatter, prattle
coyote *nm* **1 :** coyote **2** *Mex fam* **:** smuggler (of illegal immigrants)
coyuntura *nf* **1** ARTICULACIÓN **:** joint **2 :** occasion, moment
coz *nm, pl* **coces :** kick (of an animal)
crac *nm, pl* **cracs :** crash (of the stock market)
cozamos, etc. → **cocer**
craneal *adj* **:** cranial
cráneo *nf* **:** cranium, skull — **craneano, -na** *adj*
cráter *nm* **:** crater
creación *nf, pl* **-ciones :** creation
creador¹, -dora *adj* **:** creative, creating
creador², -dora *n* **:** creator
crear *vt* **1 :** to create, to cause **2 :** to originate
creatividad *nf* **:** creativity
creativo, -va *adj* **:** creative
crecer {53} *vi* **1 :** to grow **2 :** to increase
crecida *nf* **:** flooding, floodwater
crecido, -da *adj* **1 :** grown, grown-up **2 :** large (of numbers)
creciente *adj* **1 :** growing, increasing **2 luna creciente :** waxing moon
crecientemente *adv* **:** increasingly
crecimiento *nm* **1 :** growth **2 :** increase
credencial *adj* **cartas credenciales :** credentials
credenciales *nfpl* **:** documents, documentation, credentials
credibilidad *nf* **:** credibility
crédito *nm* **:** credit
credo *nm* **:** creed, credo
credulidad *nf* **:** credulity
crédulo, -la *adj* **:** credulous, gullible
creencia *nf* **:** belief
creer {20} *v* **1 :** to believe **2 :** to suppose, to think <creo que sí : I think so> — **creerse** *vr* **1 :** to believe, to think **2 :** to regard oneself as <se cree guapísimo : he thinks he's so handsome>
creíble *adj* **:** believable, credible
creído, -da *adj* **1** *fam* **:** conceited **2 :** confident, sure
crema *nf* **1 :** cream **2 la crema y nata :** the pick of the crop
cremación *nf, pl* **-ciones :** cremation
cremallera *nf* **:** zipper
cremar *vt* **:** to cremate
cremoso, -sa *adj* **:** creamy
crepa *nf Mex* **:** crepe (pancake)
crepe *or* **crep** *nmf* **:** crepe (pancake)
crepé *nm* **1** → **crespón 2 papel crepé :** crepe paper
crepitar *vi* **:** to crackle
crepúsculo *nm* **:** twilight
crescendo *nm* **:** crescendo
crespo, -pa *adj* **:** curly, frizzy
crespón *nm, pl* **crespones :** crepe (fabric)
cresta *nf* **1 :** crest **2 :** comb (of a rooster)
creta *nf* **:** chalk (mineral)
cretino, -na *n* **:** cretin
creyente *nmf* **:** believer
creyó, etc. → **creer**
crezca, etc. → **crecer**
cría *nf* **1 :** breeding, rearing **2 :** young **3 :** litter
criadero *nm* **:** hatchery
criado¹, -da *adj* **1 :** raised, brought up **2 bien criado :** well-bred
criado², -da *n* **:** servant, maid *f*
criador, -dora *n* **:** breeder

crianza *nf* : upbringing, rearing

criar {85} *vt* **1** : to breed **2** : to bring up, to raise

criatura *nf* **1** : baby, child **2** : creature

criba *nf* : sieve, screen

cribar *vt* : to sift

cric *nm, pl* **crics** : jack

crimen *nm, pl* **crímenes** : crime

criminal *adj & nmf* : criminal

crin *nf* **1** : mane **2** : horsehair

criollo[1], -lla *adj* **1** : Creole **2** : native, national <comida criolla : native cuisine>

criollo[2], -lla *n* : Creole

criollo[3] *nm* : Creole (language)

cripta *nf* : crypt

críptico, -ca *adj* **1** : cryptic, coded **2** : enigmatic, cryptic

criptón *nm* : krypton

críquet *nm* : cricket (game)

crisálida *nf* : chrysalis, pupa

crisantemo *nm* : chrysanthemum

crisis *nf* **1** : crisis **2 crisis nerviosa** : nervous breakdown

crisma *nf fam* : head <romperle la crisma a alguien : to knock someone's block off>

crisol *nm* **1** : crucible **2** : melting pot

crispar *vt* **1** : to cause to contract **2** : to irritate, to set on edge <eso me crispa : that gets on my nerves> — **crisparse** *vr* : to tense up

cristal *nm* **1** VIDRIO : glass, piece of glass **2** : crystal

cristalería *nf* **1** : glassware shop <como chivo en cristalería : like a bull in a china shop> **2** : glassware, crystal

cristalino[1], -na *adj* : crystalline, clear

cristalino[2] *nm* : lens (of the eye)

cristalizar {21} *vi* : to crystallize — **cristalización** *nf*

cristianismo *nm* : Christianity

cristiano, -na *adj & n* : Christian

criterio *nm* **1** : criterion **2** : judgment, sense

crítica *nf* **1** : criticism **2** : review, critique

criticar {72} *vt* : to criticize

crítico[1], -ca *adj* : critical — **críticamente** *adv*

crítico[2], -ca *n* : critic

criticón[1], -cona *adj, mpl* **-cones** *fam* : hypercritical, captious

criticón[2], -cona *n, mpl* **-cones** *fam* : faultfinder, critic

croar *vi* : to croak

croata *adj & nmf* : Croatian

crocante *adj* : crunchy

croché *or* **crochet** *nm* : crochet

cromático, -ca *adj* : chromatic

cromo *nm* **1** : chromium, chrome **2** : picture card, sports card

cromosoma *nm* : chromosome

crónica *nf* **1** : news report **2** : chronicle, history

crónico, -ca *adj* : chronic

cronista *nmf* **1** : reporter, newscaster **2** HISTORIADOR : chronicler, historian

cronología *nf* : chronology

cronológico, -ca *adj* : chronological — **cronológicamente** *adv*

cronometrador, -dora *n* : timekeeper

cronometrar *vt* : to time, to clock

cronómetro *nm* : chronometer

croquet *nm* : croquet

croqueta *nf* : croquette

croquis *nm* : rough sketch

cruce[1], etc. → **cruzar**

cruce[2] *nm* **1** : crossing, cross **2** : crossroads, intersection <cruce peatonal : crosswalk>

crucero *nm* **1** : cruise **2** : cruiser, warship **3** *Mex* : intersection

crucial *adj* : crucial — **crucialmente** *adv*

crucificar {72} *vt* : to crucify

crucifijo *nm* : crucifix

crucifixión *nf, pl* **-xiones** : crucifixion

crucigrama *nm* : crossword puzzle

crudo[1], -da *adj* **1** : raw **2** : crude, harsh

crudo[2] *nm* : crude oil

cruel *adj* : cruel — **cruelmente** *adv*

crueldad *nf* : cruelty

cruento, -ta *adj* : bloody

crujido *nm* **1** : rustling **2** : creaking **3** : crackling (of a fire) **4** : crunching

crujiente *adj* : crunchy, crisp

crujir *vi* **1** : to rustle **2** : to creak, to crack **3** : to crunch

crup *nm* : croup

crustáceo *nm* : crustacean

crutón *nm, pl* **crutones** : crouton

cruz *nf, pl* **cruces** : cross

cruza *nf* : cross (hybrid)

cruzada *nf* : crusade

cruzado[1], -da *adj* : crossed <espadas cruzadas : crossed swords>

cruzado[2] *nm* **1** : crusader **2** : Brazilian unit of currency

cruzar {21} *vt* **1** : to cross **2** : to exchange (words, greetings) **3** : to cross, to interbreed — **cruzarse** *vr* **1** : to intersect **2** : to meet, to pass each other

cuaderno *nm* LIBRETA : notebook

cuadra *nf* **1** : city block **2** : stable

cuadrado[1], -da *adj* : square

cuadrado[2] *nm* : square <elevar al cuadrado : to square (a number)>

cuadragésimo[1] *adj* : fortieth, forty-

cuadragésimo[2], -ma *n* : fortieth, forty- (in a series)

cuadrante *nm* **1** : quadrant **2** : dial

cuadrar *vi* : to conform, to agree — *vt* : to square — **cuadrarse** *vr* : to stand at attention

cuadriculado *nm* : grid (on a map, etc.)

cuadrilátero *nm* **1** : quadrilateral **2** : ring (in sports)

cuadrilla *nf* : gang, team, group

cuadro *nm* **1** : square <una blusa a cuadros : a checkered blouse> **2** : painting, picture **3** : baseball diamond, infield **4** : panel, board, cadre

cuadrúpedo *nm* : quadruped

cuadruple *adj* : quadruple

cuadruplicar {72} *vt* : to quadruple — **cuadruplicarse** *vr*

cuajada *nf* : curd

cuajar *vi* **1** : to curdle **2** COAGULAR : to clot, to coagulate **3** : to set, to jell **4** : to be accepted <su idea no cuajó : his idea didn't catch on> — *vt* **1** : to curdle **2** : to adorn

cual[1] *prep* : like, as

cual[2] *pron* **1 el cual, la cual, los cuales, las cuales** : who, whom, which <la razón por la cual lo dije : the reason I said it> **2 lo cual** : which <se rió, lo cual me dio rabia : he laughed, which made me mad> **3 cada cual** : everyone, everybody

cuál[1] *adj* : which, what <¿cuáles libros? : which books?>

cuál[2] *pron* **1** (*in questions*) : which (one), what (one) <¿cuál es el mejor? : which one is the best?> <¿cuál es tu apellido? : what is your last name?> **2 cuál más, cuál menos** : some more, some less

cualidad *nf* : quality, trait

cualitativo, -va *adj* : qualitative — **cualitativamente** *adv*

cualquier → **cualquiera**[1]

cualquiera[1] (**cualquier** *before nouns*) *adj, pl* **cualesquiera 1** : any, whichever <cualquier persona : any person> **2** : everyday, ordinary <un hombre cualquiera : an ordinary man>

cualquiera[2] *pron, pl* **cualesquiera 1** : anyone, anybody, whoever **2** : whatever, whichever

cuán *adv* : how <¡cuán risible fue todo eso! : how funny it all was!>

cuando[1] *conj* **1** : when <cuando llegó : when he arrived> **2** : since, if <cuando lo dices : if you say so> **3 cuando más** : at the most **4 de vez en cuando** : from time to time

cuando[2] *prep* : during, at the time of <cuando la guerra : during the war>

cuándo *adv & conj* **1** : when <¿cuándo llegará? : when will she arrive?> <no sabemos cuándo será : we don't know when it will be> **2 ¿de cuándo acá?** : since when?, how come?

cuantía *nf* **1** : quantity, extent **2** : significance, import

cuántico, -ca *adj* : quantum <teoría cuántica : quantum theory>

cuantioso, -sa *adj* **1** : abundant, considerable **2** : heavy, grave <cuantiosos daños : heavy damage>

cuantitativo, -va *adj* : quantitative — **cuantitativamente** *adv*

cuanto[1] *adv* **1** : as much as <come cuanto puedas : eat as much as you can> **2 cuanto antes** : as soon as possible **3 en ~** : as soon as **4 en cuanto a** : as for, as regards

cuanto[2], **-ta** *adj* : as many, whatever <llévate cuantas flores quieras : take as many flowers as you wish>

cuanto[3], **-ta** *pron* **1** : as much as, all that, everything <tengo cuanto deseo : I have all that I want> **2 unos cuantos, unas cuantas** : a few

cuánto[1] *adv* : how much, how many <¿a cuánto están las manzanas? : how much are the apples?> <no sé cuánto desean : I don't know how much they want>

cuánto[2], **-ta** *adj* : how much, how many <¿cuántos niños tiene? : how many children do you have?>

cuánto[3] *pron* : how much, how many <¿cuántos quieren participar? : how many want to take part?> <¿cuánto cuesta? : how much does it cost?>

cuarenta *adj & nm* : forty

cuarentavo[1] *adj* : fortieth

cuarentavo[2] *nm* : fortieth (fraction)

cuarentena *nf* **1** : group of forty **2** : quarantine

Cuaresma *nf* : Lent

cuartear *vt* **1** : to quarter **2** : to divide up — **cuartearse** *vr* AGRIETARSE : to crack, to split

cuartel *nm* **1** : barracks, headquarters **2** : mercy <una guerra sin cuartel : a merciless war>

cuartelazo *nm* : coup d'état

cuarteto *nm* : quartet

cuartilla *nf* : sheet (of paper)

cuarto[1], **-ta** *adj* : fourth

cuarto[2], **-ta** *n* : fourth (in a series)

cuarto[3] *nm* **1** : quarter, fourth <cuarto de galón : quart> **2** HABITACIÓN : room

cuarzo *nm* : quartz

cuate, -ta *n Mex* **1** : twin **2** *fam* : buddy, pal

cuatrero, -ra *n* : rustler

cuatrillizo, -za *n* : quadruplet

cuatro *adj & nm* : four

cuatrocientos[1], **-tas** *adj* : four hundred

cuatrocientos[2] *nms & pl* : four hundred

cuba *nf* BARRÍL : cask, barrel

cubano, -na *adj & n* : Cuban

cubertería *nf* : flatware, silverware

cubeta *nf* **1** : keg, cask **2** : bulb (of a thermometer) **3** *Mex* : bucket, pail

cúbico, -ca *adj* : cubic, cubed

cubículo *nm* : cubicle

cubierta *nf* **1** : covering **2** FORRO : cover, jacket (of a book) **3** : deck

cubierto[1] *pp* → **cubrir**

cubierto[2] *nm* **1** : cover, shelter <bajo cubierto : under cover> **2** : table setting **3** : utensil, piece of silverware

cubil *nm* : den, lair

cúbito *nm* : ulna

cubo *nm* **1** : cube **2** BALDE : pail, bucket, can <cubo de basura : garbage can> **3** : hub (of a wheel)

cubrecama *nm* COLCHA : bedspread

cubrir {2} *vt* : to cover — **cubrirse** *vr*

cucaracha *nf* : cockroach, roach

cuchara *nf* : spoon

cucharada *nf* : spoonful

cucharilla *or* **cucharita** *nf* : teaspoon

cucharón *nf, pl* **-rones** : ladle

cuchichear *vi* : to whisper

cuchicheo *nm* : whisper

cuchilla *nf* **1 :** kitchen knife, cleaver **2 :** blade <cuchilla de afeitar : razor blade> **3 :** crest, ridge
cuchillada *nf* **:** stab, knife wound
cuchillo *nm* **:** knife
cuclillas *nfpl* **en ~ :** squatting, crouching
cuco[1], -ca *adj fam* **:** pretty, cute
cuco[2] *nm* **:** cuckoo
cuece, cueza, etc. → cocer
cuela, etc. → colar
cuelga, cuelgue, etc. → colgar
cuello *nm* **1 :** neck **2 :** collar (of a shirt) **3 cuello del útero :** cervix
cuenca *nf* **1 :** river basin **2 :** eye socket
cuenco *nm* **:** bowl, basin
cuenta[1], etc. → contar
cuenta[2] *nf* **1 :** calculation, count **2 :** account **3 :** check, bill **4 darse cuenta :** to realize **5 tener en cuenta :** to bear in mind
cuentagotas *nfs & pl* **1 :** dropper **2 con ~ :** little by little
cuentista *nmf* **1 :** short story writer **2** *fam* **:** liar, fibber
cuento *nm* **1 :** story, tale **2 cuento de hadas :** fairy tale **3 sin ~ :** countless
cuerda *nf* **1 :** cord, rope, string **2 cuerdas vocales :** vocal cords **3 darle cuerda a :** to wind up (a clock, a toy, etc.)
cuerdo, -da *adj* **:** sane, sensible
cuerno *nm* **1 :** horn, antler **2 :** cusp (of the moon) **3 :** horn (musical instrument)
cuero *nm* **1 :** leather, hide **2 cuero cabelludo :** scalp
cuerpo *nm* **1 :** body **2 :** corps
cuervo *nm* **:** crow, raven
cuesta[1], etc. → costar
cuesta[2] *nf* **1 :** slope <cuesta arriba : uphill> **2 a cuestas :** on one's back
cuestión *nf, pl* **-tiones** ASUNTO, TEMA **:** matter, affair
cuestionable *adj* **:** questionable, dubious
cuestionar *vt* **:** to question
cuestionario *nm* **1 :** questionnaire **2 :** quiz
cueva *nf* **:** cave
cuidado *nm* **1 :** care **2 :** worry, concern **3 tener cuidado :** to be careful **4 ¡cuidado! :** watch out!, be careful!
cuidadoso, -sa *adj* **:** careful, attentive — **cuidadosamente** *adv*
cuidar *vt* **1 :** to take care of, to look after **2 :** to pay attention to — *vi* **1 ~ de :** to look after **2 cuidar de que :** to make sure that — **cuidarse** *vr* **:** to take care of oneself
culata *nf* **:** butt (of a gun)
culatazo *nf* **:** kick, recoil
culebra *nf* SERPIENTE **:** snake
culi *nmf* **:** coolie
culinario, -ria *adj* **:** culinary
culminante *adj* **punto culminante :** peak, high point, climax
culminar *vi* **:** to culminate — **culminación** *nf*
culo *nm* **1** *fam* **:** backside, behind **2 :** bottom (of a glass)
culpa *nf* **1 :** fault, blame <echarle la culpa a alguien : to blame someone> **2 :** sin
culpabilidad *nf* **:** guilt
culpable[1] *adj* **:** guilty
culpable[2] *nmf* **:** culprit, guilty party
culpar *vt* **:** to blame
cultivado, -da *adj* **1 :** cultivated, farmed **2 :** cultured
cultivador, -dora *n* **:** cultivator
cultivar *vt* **1 :** to cultivate **2 :** to foster
cultivo *nm* **1 :** cultivation, farming **2 :** crop
culto[1], -ta *adj* **:** cultured, educated
culto[2] *nm* **1 :** worship **2 :** cult
cultura *nf* **:** culture
cultural *adj* **:** cultural — **culturalmente** *adv*
cumbre *nf* CIMA **:** top, peak, summit
cumpleaños *nms & pl* **:** birthday
cumplido[1], -da *adj* **1 :** complete, full **2 :** courteous, correct
cumplido[2] *nm* **:** compliment, courtesy <por cumplido : out of courtesy> <andarse con cumplidos : to stand on ceremony, to be formal>
cumplimentar *vt* **1 :** to congratulate **2 :** to carry out, to perform
cumplimiento *nm* **1 :** completion, fulfillment **2 :** performance
cumplir *vt* **1 :** to accomplish, to carry out **2 :** to comply with, to fulfill **3 :** to attain, to reach <su hermana cumple los 21 el viernes : her sister will be 21 on Friday> — *vi* **1 :** to expire, to fall due **2 :** to fulfill one's obligations <cumplir con el deber : to do one's duty> <cumplir con la palabra : to keep one's word> — **cumplirse** *vr* **1 :** to come true, to be fulfilled <se cumplieron sus sueños : her dreams came true> **2 :** to run out, to expire
cúmulo *nm* **1** MONTÓN **:** heap, pile **2 :** cumulus
cuna *nf* **1 :** cradle **2 :** birthplace <Puerto Rico es la cuna de la música salsa : Puerto Rico is the birthplace of salsa music>
cundir *vi* **1 :** to propagate, to spread <cundió el pánico en el vecindario : panic spread throughout the neighborhood> **2 :** to progress, to make headway
cuneta *nf* **:** ditch (in a road), gutter
cuña *nf* **:** wedge
cuñado, -da *n* **:** brother-in-law *m,* sister-in-law *f*
cuño *nm* **:** die (for stamping)
cuota *nf* **1 :** fee, dues **2 :** quota, share **3 :** installment, payment
cupé *nm* **:** coupe
cupo[1], etc. → caber
cupo[2] *nm* **1 :** quota, share **2 :** capacity, room
cupón *nm, pl* **cupones 1 :** coupon, voucher **2 cupón federal :** food stamp
cúpula *nf* **:** dome, cupola

cura[1] *nm* : priest
cura[2] *nf* **1** CURACIÓN, TRATAMIENTO : cure, treatment **2** : dressing, bandage
curación *nf, pl* **-ciones** CURA, TRATAMIENTO : cure, treatment
curandero, -ra *nm* **1** : witch doctor **2** : quack, charlatan
curar *vt* **1** : to cure, to heal **2** : to treat, to dress **3** CURTIR : to tan **4** : to cure (meat) — *vi* : to get well, to recover — **curarse** *vr*
curativo, -va *adj* : curative, healing
curiosear *vi* **1** : to snoop, to pry **2** : to browse — *vt* : to look over, to check
curiosidad *nf* **1** : curiosity **2** : curio
curioso, -sa *adj* **1** : curious, inquisitive **2** : strange, unusual, odd — **curiosamente** *adv*
currículo *nm* → **currículum**
currículum *nm, pl* **-lums 1** : résumé, curriculum vitae **2** : curriculum, course of study
curry ['kurri] *nm, pl* **-rries 1** : curry powder **2** : curry (dish)
cursar *vt* **1** : to attend (school), to take (a course) **2** : to dispatch, to pass on
cursi *adj fam* : affected, pretentious
cursilería *nf* **1** : vulgarity, poor taste **2** : pretentiousness
cursiva *nf* BASTARDILLA : italic type, italics *pl*
curso *nm* **1** : course, direction **2** : school year **3** : course, subject (in school)
cursor *nm* : cursor
curtido, -da *adj* : weather-beaten, leathery (of skin)
curtidor, -dora *n* : tanner
curtiduría *nf* : tannery
curtir *vt* **1** : to tan **2** : to harden, to weather — **curtirse** *vr*
curva *nf* : curve, bend
curvar *vt* : to bend
curvatura *nf* : curvature
curvilíneo, -nea *adj* : curvaceous, shapely
curvo, -va *adj* : curved, bent
cúspide *nf* : zenith, apex, peak
custodia *nf* : custody
custodiar *vt* : to guard, to look after
custodio, -dia *n* : keeper, guardian
cúter *nm* : cutter (boat)
cutícula *nf* : cuticle
cutis *nms & pl* : skin, complexion
cuyo, -ya *adj* **1** : whose, of whom, of which **2 en cuyo caso** : in which case

D

d *nf* : fourth letter of the Spanish alphabet
dable *adj* : feasible, possible
dactilar *adj* **huellas dactilares** : fingerprints
dádiva *nf* : gift, handout
dadivoso, -sa *adj* : generous
dado, -da *adj* **1** : given **2 dado que** : given that, since
dador, -dora *n* : giver, donor
dados *nmpl* : dice
daga *nf* : dagger
dalia *nf* : dahlia
dálmata *nm* : dalmatian
daltónico, -ca *adj* : color-blind
daltonismo *nm* : color blindness
dama *nf* **1** : lady **2 damas** *nfpl* : checkers
damasco *nm* : damask
damisela *nf* : damsel
damnificado, -da *n* : victim (of a disaster)
damnificar {72} *vt* : to damage, to injure
dance, etc. → **danzar**
dandi *nm* : dandy, fop
danés[1], **-nesa** *adj* : Danish
danés[2], **-nesa** *n, mpl* **daneses** : Dane, Danish person
danza *nf* : dance, dancing <danza folklórica : folk dance>
danzante, -ta *n* BAILARÍN : dancer
danzar {21} *v* BAILAR : to dance
dañar *vt* **1** : to damage, to spoil **2** : to harm, to hurt — **dañarse** *vr*
dañino, -na *adj* : harmful
daño *nm* **1** : damage **2** : harm, injury **3 hacer daño a** : to harm, to damage **4 daños y perjuicios** : damages
dar {22} *vt* **1** : to give **2** ENTREGAR : to deliver, to hand over **3** : to hit, to strike **4** : to yield, to produce **5** : to perform **6** : to give off, to emit **7 ~ como** *or* **~ por** : to regard as, to consider — *vi* **1** ALCANZAR : to suffice, to be enough <no me da para dos pasajes : I don't have enough for two fares> **2 ~ a** *or* **~ sobre** : to overlook, to look out on **3 ~ con** : to run into **4 ~ con** : to hit upon (an idea) **5 dar de sí** : to give, to stretch — **darse** *vr* **1** : to give in, to surrender **2** : to occur, to arise **3** : to grow, to come up **4 ~ con** *or* **~ contra** : to hit oneself against **5 dárselas de** : to boast about <se las da de muy listo : he thinks he's very smart>
dardo *nm* : dart
datar *vt* : to date — *vi* **~ de** : to date from, to date back to
dátil *nm* : date (fruit)
dato *nm* **1** : fact, piece of information **2 datos** *nmpl* : data, information
dé → **dar**
de *prep* **1** : of <la casa de Pepe : Pepe's house> <un niño de tres años : a three-year-old boy> **2** : from <es de Managua : she's from Managua> <salió del edificio : he left the building> **3** : in, at <a las tres de la mañana

: at three in the morning> <salen de noche : they go out at night> **4** : than <más de tres : more than three>

deambular *vi* : to wander, to roam

debajo *adv* **1** : underneath, below, on the bottom **2** ~ **de** : under, underneath **3 por** ~ : below, beneath

debate *nm* : debate

debatir *vt* : to debate, to discuss — **debatirse** *vr* : to struggle

debe *nm* : debit column, debit

deber[1] *vt* : to owe — *v aux* **1** : must, have to <debo ir a la oficina : I must go to the office> **2** : should, ought to <deberías buscar trabajo : you ought to look for work> **3** (*expressing probability*) : must <debe ser mexicano : he must be Mexican> — **deberse** *vr* ~ **a** : to be due to

deber[2] *nm* **1** OBLIGACIÓN : duty, obligation **2 deberes** *nmpl Spain* : homework

debidamente *adv* : properly, duly

debido, -da *adj* **1** : right, proper, due **2** ~ **a** : due to, owing to

débil *adj* : weak, feeble — **débilmente** *adv*

debilidad *nf* : weakness, debility, feebleness

debilitamiento *nm* : debilitation, weakening

debilitar *vt* : to debilitate, to weaken — **debilitarse** *vr*

debilucho[1], **-cha** *adj* : weak, frail

debilucho[2], **-cha** *n* : weakling

debitar *vt* : to debit

débito *nm* **1** DEUDA : debt **2** : debit

debut [deˈbut] *nm, pl* **debuts** : debut

debutante[1] *nmf* : beginner, newcomer

debutante[2] *nf* : debutante *f*

debutar *vi* : to debut, to make a debut

década *nf* DECENIO : decade

decadencia *nf* **1** : decadence **2** : decline

decadente *adj* **1** : decadent **2** : declining

decaer {13} *vi* **1** : to decline, to decay, to deteriorate **2** FLAQUEAR : to weaken, to flag

decaiga, etc. → **decaer**

decano, -na *n* **1** : dean **2** : senior member

decantar *vt* : to decant

decapitar *vt* : to decapitate, to behead

decayó, etc. → **decaer**

decena *nf* : group of ten

decencia *nf* : decency

decenio *nm* DÉCADA : decade

decente *adj* : decent — **decentemente** *adv*

decepción *nf, pl* **-ciones** : disappointment, letdown

decepcionante *adj* : disappointing

decepcionar *vt* : to disappoint, to let down — **decepcionarse** *vr*

deceso *nm* DEFUNCIÓN : death, passing

dechado *nm* **1** : sampler (of embroidery) **2** : model, paragon

decibelio *or* **decibel** *nm* : decibel

decidido, -da *adj* : decisive, determined, resolute — **decididamente** *adv*

decidir *vt* **1** : to decide, to determine <no he decidido nada : I haven't made a decision> **2** : to persuade, to decide <su padre lo decidió a estudiar : his father persuaded him to study> — *vi* : to decide — **decidirse** *vr* : to make up one's mind

decimal *adj* : decimal

décimo, -ma *adj* : tenth — **décimo, -ma** *n*

decimoctavo[1], **-va** *adj* : eighteenth

decimoctavo[2], **-va** *nm* : eighteenth (in a series)

decimocuarto[1], **-ta** *adj* : fourteenth

decimocuarto[2], **-ta** *nm* : fourteenth (in a series)

decimonoveno[1], **-na** *or* **decimonono, -na** *adj* : nineteenth

decimonoveno[2], **-na** *or* **decimonono, -na** *nm* : nineteenth (in a series)

decimoquinto[1], **-ta** *adj* : fifteenth

decimoquinto[2], **-ta** *nm* : fifteenth (in a series)

decimoséptimo[1], **-ma** *adj* : seventeenth

decimoséptimo[2], **-ma** *nm* : seventeenth (in a series)

decimosexto[1], **-ta** *adj* : sixteenth

decimosexto[2], **-ta** *nm* : sixteenth (in a series)

decimotercero[1], **-ra** *adj* : thirteenth

decimotercero[2], **-ra** *nm* : thirteenth (in a series)

decir[1] {23} *vt* **1** : to say <dice que no quiere ir : she says she doesn't want to go> **2** : to tell <dime lo que estás pensando : tell me what you're thinking> **3** : to speak, to talk <no digas tonterías : don't talk nonsense> **4** : to call <me dicen Rosy : they call me Rosy> **5 es decir** : that is to say **6 querer decir** : to mean — **decirse** *vr* **1** : to say to oneself **2** : to be said <¿cómo se dice ''lápiz'' en francés? : how do you say ''pencil'' in French?>

decir[2] *nm* DICHO : saying, expression

decisión *nf, pl* **-siones** : decision, choice

decisivo, -va *adj* : decisive, conclusive — **decisivamente** *adv*

declamar *vi* : to declaim — *vt* : to recite

declaración *nf, pl* **-ciones** **1** : declaration, statement **2** TESTIMONIO : deposition, testimony **3 declaración de derechos** : bill of rights **4 declaración jurada** : affidavit

declarado, -da *adj* : professed, open — **declaradamente** *adv*

declarar *vt* : to declare, to state — *vi* ATESTIGUAR : to testify — **declararse** *vr* **1** : to declare oneself, to make a statement **2** : to confess one's love **3**

: to plead (in court) <declararse inocente : to plead not guilty>
declinación *nf, pl* **-ciones 1 :** drop, downward trend **2 :** declination **3 :** declension (in grammar)
declinar *vt* **:** to decline, to turn down — *vi* **1 :** to draw to a close **2 :** to diminish, to decline
declive *nm* **1** DECADENCIA **:** decline **2 :** slope, incline
decodificador *nm* **:** decoder
decolar *vi Chile, Col, Ecua* **:** to take off (of an airplane)
decolorar *vt* **:** to bleach — **decolorarse** *vr* **:** to fade
decomisar *vt* CONFISCAR **:** to seize, to confiscate
decomiso *nm* **:** seizure, confiscation
decoración *nf, pl* **-ciones 1 :** decoration **2 :** decor **3 :** stage set, scenery
decorado *nm* **:** stage set, scenery
decorador, -dora *n* **:** decorator
decorar *vt* ADORNAR **:** to decorate, to adorn
decorativo, -va *adj* **:** decorative, ornamental
decoro *nm* **:** decorum, propriety
decoroso, -sa *adj* **:** decent, proper, respectable
decrecer {53} *vi* **:** to decrease, to wane, to diminish — **decreciente** *adj*
decrecimiento *nm* **:** decrease, decline
decrépito, -ta *adj* **:** decrepit
decretar *vt* **:** to decree, to order
decreto *nm* **:** decree
decúbito *nm* **:** horizontal position <en decúbito prono : prone> <en decúbito supino : supine>
dedal *nm* **:** thimble
dedalera *nf* DIGITAL **:** foxglove
dedicación *nf, pl* **-ciones :** dedication, devotion
dedicar {72} *vt* CONSAGRAR **:** to dedicate, to devote — **dedicarse** *vr* **~ a :** to devote oneself to, to engage in
dedicatoria *nf* **:** dedication (of a book, song, etc.)
dedo *nm* **1 :** finger <dedo meñique : little finger> **2 dedo del pie :** toe
deducción *nf, pl* **-ciones :** deduction
deducible *adj* **1 :** deducible, inferable **2 :** deductible
deducir {61} *vt* **1** INFERIR **:** to deduce **2** DESCONTAR **:** to deduct
defecar {72} *vi* **:** to defecate — **defecación** *nf*
defecto *nm* **1 :** defect, flaw, shortcoming **2 en su defecto :** lacking that, in the absence of that
defectuoso, -sa *adj* **:** defective, faulty
defender {56} *vt* **:** to defend, to protect — **defenderse** *vr* **1 :** to defend oneself **2 :** to get by, to know the basics <su inglés no es perfecto pero se defiende : his English isn't perfect but he gets by>
defendible *adj* **:** defensible, tenable
defensa[1] *nf* **:** defense
defensa[2] *nmf* **:** defender, back (in sports)
defensiva *nf* **:** defensive, defense
defensivo, -va *adj* **:** defensive — **defensivamente** *adv*
defensor[1], **-sora** *adj* **:** defending, defense
defensor[2], **-sora** *n* **1 :** defender, advocate **2 :** defense counsel
defeño, -ña *n* **:** person from the Federal District (Mexico City)
deficiencia *nf* **:** deficiency, flaw
deficiente *adj* **:** deficient
déficit *nm, pl* **-cits 1 :** deficit **2 :** shortage, lack
definición *nf, pl* **-ciones :** definition
definido, -da *adj* **:** definite, well-defined
definir *vt* **1 :** to define **2 :** to determine
definitivamente *adv* **1 :** finally **2 :** permanently, for good **3 :** definitely, absolutely
definitivo, -va *adj* **1 :** definitive, conclusive **2 en definitiva :** all in all, on the whole **3 en definitiva** *Mex* **:** permanently, for good
deflación *nf, pl* **-ciones :** deflation
deforestación *nf, pl* **-ciones :** deforestation
deformación *nf, pl* **-ciones 1 :** deformation **2 :** distortion
deformar *vt* **1 :** to deform, to disfigure **2 :** to distort — **deformarse** *vr*
deforme *adj* **:** deformed, misshapen
deformidad *nf* **:** deformity
defraudación *nf, pl* **-ciones :** fraud
defraudar *vt* **1** ESTAFAR **:** to defraud, to cheat **2 :** to disappoint
defunción *nf, pl* **-ciones** DECESO **:** death, passing
degeneración *nf, pl* **-ciones 1 :** degeneration **2 :** degeneracy, depravity
degenerado, -da *adj* DEPRAVADO **:** degenerate
degenerar *vi* **:** to degenerate
degenerativo, -va *adj* **:** degenerative
degollar {19} *vt* **1 :** to slit the throat of, to slaughter **2** DECAPITAR **:** to behead **3 :** to ruin, to destroy
degradación *nf, pl* **-ciones 1 :** degradation **2 :** demotion
degradar *vt* **1 :** to degrade, to debase **2 :** to demote
degustación *nf, pl* **-ciones :** tasting, sampling
degustar *vt* **:** to taste
deidad *nf* **:** deity
deificar {72} *vt* **:** to idolize, to deify
dejado, -da *adj* **1 :** slovenly **2 :** careless, lazy
dejar *vt* **1 :** to leave **2** ABANDONAR **:** to abandon, to forsake **3 :** to let be, to let go **4** PERMITIR **:** to allow, to permit — *vi* **~ de :** to stop, to quit <dejar de fumar : to quit smoking> — **dejarse** *vr* **1 :** to let oneself be <se deja insultar : he lets himself be insulted> **2 :** to forget, to leave <me dejé las llaves en el carro : I left the keys in

the car> **3 :** to neglect oneself, to let oneself go **4 :** to grow <nos estamos dejando el pelo largo : we're growing our hair long>

dejo *nm* **1 :** aftertaste **2 :** touch, hint **3 :** (regional) accent

delación *nf, pl* **-ciones :** denunciation, betrayal

delantal *nm* **1 :** apron **2 :** pinafore

delante *adv* **1** ENFRENTE **:** ahead, in front **2 ~ de :** before, in front of

delantera *nf* **1 :** front, front part, front row <tomar la delantera : to take the lead> **2 :** forward line (in sports)

delantero[1], -ra *adj* **1 :** front, forward **2 tracción delantera :** front-wheel drive

delantero[2], -ra *n* **:** forward (in sports)

delatar *vt* **1 :** to betray, to reveal **2 :** to denounce, to inform against

delegación *nf, pl* **-ciones :** delegation

delegado, -da *n* **:** delegate, representative

delegar {52} *vt* **:** to delegate

deleitar *vt* **:** to delight, to please — **deleitarse** *vr*

deleite *nm* **:** delight, pleasure

deletrear *vi* **:** to spell <¿como se deletrea? : how do you spell it?>

deleznable *adj* **1 :** brittle, crumbly **2 :** slippery **3 :** weak, fragile <una excusa deleznable : a weak excuse>

delfín *nm, pl* **delfines 1 :** dolphin **2 :** dauphin, heir apparent

delgadez *nf* **:** thinness, skinniness

delgado, -da *adj* **1** FLACO **:** thin, skinny **2** ESBELTO **:** slender, slim **3** DELICADO **:** delicate, fine **4** AGUDO **:** sharp, clever

deliberación *nf, pl* **-ciones :** deliberation

deliberado, -da *adj* **:** deliberate, intentional — **deliberadamente** *adv*

deliberar *vi* **:** to deliberate

deliberativo, -va *adj* **:** deliberative

delicadeza *nf* **1 :** delicacy, fineness **2 :** gentleness, softness **3 :** tact, discretion, consideration

delicado, -da *adj* **1 :** delicate, fine **2 :** sensitive, frail **3 :** difficult, tricky **4 :** fussy, hard to please **5 :** tactful, considerate

delicia *nf* **:** delight

delicioso, -sa *adj* **1** RICO **:** delicious **2 :** delightful

delictivo, -va *adj* **:** criminal

delictuoso, -sa → delictivo

delimitación *nf, pl* **-ciones 1 :** demarcation **2 :** defining, specifying

delimitar *vt* **1 :** to demarcate **2 :** to define, to specify

delincuencia *nf* **:** delinquency, crime

delincuente[1] *adj* **:** delinquent

delincuente[2] *nmf* CRIMINAL **:** delinquent, criminal

delinear *vt* **1 :** to delineate, to outline **2 :** to draft, to draw up

delinquir {24} *vi* **:** to break the law

delirante *adj* **:** delirious

delirar *vi* DESVARIAR **1 :** to be delirious **2 :** to rave, to talk nonsense

delirio *nm* **1** DESVARÍO **:** delirium **2** DISPARATE **:** nonsense, ravings *pl* <delirios de grandeza : delusions of grandeur> **3** FRENESÍ **:** mania, frenzy <¡fue el delirio! : it was wild!>

delito *nm* **:** crime, offense

delta *nm* **:** delta

demacrado, -da *adj* **:** emaciated, gaunt

demagogia *nf* **:** demagogy

demagógico, -ca *adj* **:** demagogic, demagogical

demagogo, -ga *n* **:** demagogue

demanda *nf* **1 :** demand <la oferta y la demanda : supply and demand> **2 :** petition, request **3 :** lawsuit

demandado, -da *n* **:** defendant

demandante *nmf* **:** plaintiff

demandar *vt* **1 :** to demand **2** REQUERIR **:** to call for, to require **3 :** to sue, to file a lawsuit against

demarcar {72} *vt* **:** to demarcate — **demarcación** *nf*

demás[1] *adj* **:** remaining <acabó las demás tareas : she finished the rest of the chores>

demás[2] *pron* **1 lo (la, los, las) demás :** the rest, everyone else, everything else <Pepe, Rosa, y los demás : Pepe, Rosa, and everybody else> **2 estar por demás :** to be of no use, to be pointless <no estaría por demás : it couldn't hurt, it's worth a try> **3 por demás :** extremely **4 por lo demás :** otherwise **5 y demás :** and so on, et cetera

demasía *nf* **en ~ :** excessively, in excess

demasiado[1] *adv* **1 :** too <vas demasiado aprisa : you're going too fast> **2 :** too much <estoy comiendo demasiado : I'm eating too much>

demasiado[2], -da *adj* **:** too much, too many, excessive

demencia *nf* **1 :** dementia **2** LOCURA **:** madness, insanity

demente[1] *adj* **:** insane, mad

demente[2] *nmf* **:** insane person

demeritar *vt* **1 :** to detract from **2 :** to discredit

demérito *nm* **1 :** fault **2 :** discredit, disrepute

democracia *nf* **:** democracy

demócrata[1] *adj* **:** democratic

demócrata[2] *nmf* **:** democrat

democrático, -ca *adj* **:** democratic — **democráticamente** *adv*

democratizar {21} *vt* **:** to democratize, to make democratic

demografía *nf* **:** demography

demográfico, -ca *adj* **:** demographic

demoledor, -dora *adj* **:** devastating

demoler {47} *vt* DERRIBAR, DERRUMBAR **:** to demolish, to destroy

demolición *nf, pl* **-ciones :** demolition

demonio *nm* DIABLO **:** devil, demon

demora *nf* **:** delay

demorar *vt* **1** RETRASAR **:** to delay **2** TARDAR **:** to take, to last <la reparación demorará varios días : the repair will take several days> — *vi* **:** to delay, to linger — **demorarse** *vr* **1 :** to be slow, to take a long time **2 :** to take too long

demostración *nf, pl* **-ciones :** demonstration

demostrar {19} *vt* **:** to demonstrate, to show

demostrativo, -va *adj* **:** demonstrative

demudar *vt* **:** to change, to alter — **demudarse** *vr* **:** to change one's expression

denegación *nf, pl* **-ciones :** denial, refusal

denegar {49} *vt* **:** to deny, to turn down

denigrante *adj* **:** degrading, humiliating

denigrar *vt* **1** DIFAMAR **:** to denigrate, to disparage **2 :** to degrade, to humiliate

denodado, -da *adj* **:** bold, dauntless

denominación *nf, pl* **-ciones 1 :** name, designation **2 :** denomination (of money)

denominador *nm* **:** denominator

denominar *vt* **:** to designate, to name

denostar {19} *vt* **:** to revile

denotar *vt* **:** to denote, to show

densidad *nf* **:** density, thickness

denso, -sa *adj* **:** dense, thick — **densamente** *adv*

dentado, -da *adj* SERRADO **:** serrated, jagged

dentadura *nf* **1 :** teeth *pl* **2 dentadura postiza :** dentures *pl*

dental *adj* **:** dental

dentellada *nf* **1 :** bite **2 :** tooth mark

dentera *nf* **1 :** envy, jealousy **2 dar dentera :** to set one's teeth on edge

dentición *nf, pl* **-ciones 1 :** teething **2 :** dentition, set of teeth

dentífrico *nm* **:** toothpaste

dentista *nmf* **:** dentist

dentro *adv* **1 :** in, inside **2 :** indoors **3 ~ de :** within, inside, in **4 dentro de poco :** soon, shortly **5 dentro de todo :** all in all, all things considered **6 por ~ :** inwardly, inside

denuedo *nm* **:** valor, courage

denuesto *nm* **:** insult

denuncia *nf* **1 :** denunciation, condemnation **2 :** police report

denunciante *nmf* **:** accuser (of a crime)

denunciar *vt* **1 :** to denounce, to condemn **2 :** to report (to the authorities)

deparar *vt* **:** to have in store for, to provide with <no sabemos lo que nos depara el destino : we don't know what fate has in store for us>

departamental *adj* **1 :** departmental **2 tienda departamental** *Mex* **:** department store

departamento *nm* **1 :** department **2** APARTAMENTO **:** apartment

departir *vi* **:** to converse

dependencia *nf* **1 :** dependence, dependency <dependencia emocional : emotional dependence> <dependencia del alcohol : dependence on alcohol> **2 :** agency, branch office

depender *vi* **1 :** to depend **2 ~ de :** to depend on **3 ~ de :** to be subordinate to

dependiente[1] *adj* **:** dependent

dependiente[2], **-ta** *n* **:** clerk, salesperson

deplorable *adj* **:** deplorable

deplorar *vt* **1 :** to deplore **2** LAMENTAR **:** to regret

deponer {60} *vt* **1 :** to depose, to overthrow **2 :** to abandon (an attitude or stance) **3 deponer las armas :** to lay down one's arms — *vi* **1** TESTIFICAR **:** to testify, to make a statement **2** EVACUAR **:** to defecate

deportación *nf, pl* **-ciones :** deportation

deportar *vt* **:** to deport

deporte *nm* **:** sport, sports *pl* <hacer deporte : to engage in sports>

deportista[1] *adj* **1 :** fond of sports **2 :** sporty

deportista[2] *nmf* **1 :** sports fan **2 :** athlete, sportsman *m,* sportswoman *f*

deportividad *nf Spain* **:** sportsmanship

deportivo, -va *adj* **1 :** sports, sporting <artículos deportivos : sporting goods> **2 :** sporty

deposición *nf, pl* **-ciones 1 :** statement, testimony **2 :** removal from office

depositante *nmf* **:** depositor

depositar *vt* **1 :** to deposit, to place **2 :** to store — **depositarse** *vr* **:** to settle

depósito *nm* **1 :** deposit **2 :** warehouse, storehouse

depravado, -da *adj* DEGENERADO **:** depraved, degenerate

depravar *vt* **:** to deprave, to corrupt

depreciación *nf, pl* **-ciones :** depreciation

depreciar *vt* **:** to depreciate, to reduce the value of — **depreciarse** *vr* **:** to lose value

depredación *nf* SAQUEO **:** depredation, plunder

depredador[1], **-dora** *adj* **:** predatory

depredador[2] *nm* **1 :** predator **2** SAQUEADOR **:** plunderer

depresión *nf, pl* **-siones 1 :** depression **2 :** hollow, recess **3 :** drop, fall **4 :** slump, recession

depresivo[1], **-va** *adj* **1 :** depressive **2 :** depressant

depresivo[2] *nm* **:** depressant

deprimente *adj* **:** depressing

deprimir *vt* **1 :** to depress **2 :** to lower — **deprimirse** *vr* ABATIRSE **:** to get depressed

depuesto *pp* → **deponer**

depuración *nf, pl* **-ciones 1** PURIFICACIÓN **:** purification **2** PURGA **:** purge **3 :** refinement, polish

depurar *vt* **1** PURIFICAR **:** to purify **2** PURGAR **:** to purge

depuso, etc. → **deponer**

derecha *nf* **1 :** right **2 :** right hand, right side **3 :** right wing, right (in politics)

derechazo *nm* **1 :** pass with the cape on the right hand (in bullfighting) **2 :** right (in boxing) **3 :** forehand (in tennis)
derechista[1] *adj* **:** rightist, right-wing
derechista[2] *nmf* **:** right-winger
derecho[1] *adv* **1 :** straight **2 :** upright **3 :** directly
derecho[2], **-cha** *adj* **1 :** right **2 :** right-hand **3 :** RECTO **:** straight, upright, erect
derecho[3] *nm* **1 :** right <derechos humanos : human rights> **2 :** law <derecho civil : civil law> **3 :** right side (of cloth or clothing)
deriva *nf* **1 :** drift **2 a la deriva :** adrift
derivación *nf, pl* **-ciones :** derivation
derivar *vi* **1 :** to drift **2 ~ de :** to come from, to derive from **3 ~ en :** to result in — *vt* **:** to steer, to direct <derivó la discusión hacia la política : he steered the discussion over to politics> — **derivarse** *vr* **:** to be derived from, to arise from
dermatología *nf* **:** dermatology
dermatológico, -ca *adj* **:** dermatological
dermatólogo, -ga *n* **:** dermatologist
derogación *nf, pl* **-ciones :** abolition, repeal
derogar {52} *vt* ABOLIR **:** to abolish, to repeal
derramamiento *nm* **1 :** spilling, overflowing **2 derramamiento de sangre :** bloodshed
derramar *vt* **1 :** to spill **2 :** to shed (tears, blood) — **derramarse** *vr* **1 :** to spill over **2 :** to scatter
derrame *nm* **1 :** spilling, shedding **2 :** leakage, overflow **3 :** discharge, hemorrhage
derrapar *vi* **:** to skid
derrape *nm* **:** skid
derredor *nm* **al derredor** *or* **en derredor :** around, round about
derrengado, -da *adj* **1 :** bent, twisted **2 :** exhausted
derretir {54} *vt* **:** to melt, to thaw — **derretirse** *vr* **1 :** to melt, to thaw **2 ~ por** *fam* **:** to be crazy about
derribar *vt* **1** DEMOLER, DERRUMBAR **:** to demolish, to knock down **2 :** to shoot down, to bring down (an airplane) **3** DERROCAR **:** to overthrow
derribo *nm* **1 :** demolition, razing **2 :** shooting down **3 :** overthrow
derrocamiento *nm* **:** overthrow
derrocar {72} *vt* DERRIBAR **:** to overthrow, to topple
derrochador[1], **-dora** *adj* **:** extravagant, wasteful
derrochador[2], **-dora** *n* **:** spendthrift
derrochar *vt* **:** to waste, to squander
derroche *nm* **:** extravagance, waste
derrota *nf* **1 :** defeat, rout **2 :** course (at sea)
derrotar *vt* **:** to defeat
derrotero *nm* RUTA **:** course
derrotista *adj & nmf* **:** defeatist
derruir {41} *vt* **:** to demolish, to tear down
derrumbamiento *nm* **:** collapse
derrumbar *vt* **1** DEMOLER, DERRIBAR **:** to demolish, to knock down **2** DESPEÑAR **:** to cast down, to topple — **derrumbarse** *vr* DESPLOMARSE **:** to collapse, to break down
derrumbe *nm* **1** DESPLOME **:** collapse, fall <el derrumbe del comunismo : the fall of Communism> **2 :** landslide
desabastecimiento *nm* **:** shortage, scarcity
desabasto *nm Mex* **:** shortage, scarcity
desabrido, -da *adj* **:** tasteless, bland
desabrigar {52} *vt* **1 :** to undress **2 :** to uncover **3 :** to deprive of shelter
desabrochar *vt* **:** to unbutton, to undo — **desabrocharse** *vr* **:** to come undone
desacato *nm* **1 :** disrespect **2 :** contempt (of court)
desacelerar *vi* **:** to decelerate, to slow down
desacertado, -da *adj* **1 :** mistaken **2 :** unwise
desacertar {55} *vi* ERRAR **:** to err, to be mistaken
desacierto *nm* ERROR **:** error, mistake
desaconsejado, -da *adj* **:** ill-advised, unwise
desacorde *adj* **1 :** conflicting **2 :** discordant
desacostumbrado, -da *adj* **:** unaccustomed, unusual
desacreditar *vt* DESPRESTIGIAR **:** to discredit, to disgrace
desactivar *vt* **:** to deactivate, to defuse
desacuerdo *nm* **:** disagreement
desafiante *adj* **:** defiant
desafiar {85} *vt* RETAR **:** to defy, to challenge
desafilado, -da *adj* **:** blunt
desafinado, -da *adj* **:** out-of-tune, off-key
desafinarse *vr* **:** to go out of tune
desafío *nm* **1** RETO **:** challenge **2** RESISTENCIA **:** defiance
desafortunado, -da *adj* **:** unfortunate, unlucky — **desafortunadamente** *adv*
desafuero *nm* ABUSO **:** injustice, outrage
desagradable *adj* **:** unpleasant, disagreeable — **desagradablemente** *adv*
desagradar *vi* **:** to be unpleasant, to be disagreeable
desagradecido, -da *adj* **:** ungrateful
desagrado *nm* **1 :** displeasure **2 con ~ :** reluctantly
desagravio *nm* **1 :** apology **2 :** amends, reparation
desagregarse {52} *vr* **:** to break up, to disintegrate
desaguar {10} *vi* **:** to drain, to empty
desagüe *nm* **1 :** drain **2 :** drainage
desahogado, -da *adj* **1 :** well-off, comfortable **2 :** spacious, roomy

desahogar {52} *vt* **1 :** to relieve, to ease **2 :** to give vent to — **desahogarse** *vr* **1 :** to recover, to feel better **2 :** to unburden oneself, to let off steam
desahogo *nm* **1 :** relief, outlet **2 con ~ :** comfortably
desahuciar *vt* **1 :** to deprive of hope **2 :** to evict — **desahuciarse** *vr* **:** to lose all hope
desahucio *nm* **:** eviction
desairar {5} *vt* **:** to snub, to rebuff
desaire *nm* **:** rebuff, snub, slight
desajustar *vt* **1 :** to disarrange, to put out of order **2 :** to upset (plans)
desajuste *nm* **1 :** maladjustment **2 :** imbalance **3 :** upset, disruption
desalentar {55} *vt* DESANIMAR **:** to discourage, to dishearten — **desalentarse** *vr*
desaliento *nm* **:** discouragement
desaliñado, -da *adj* **:** slovenly, untidy
desalmado, -da *adj* **:** heartless, callous
desalojar *vt* **1 :** to remove, to clear **2** EVACUAR **:** to evacuate, to vacate **3 :** to evict
desalojo *nm* **1 :** removal, expulsion **2 :** evacuation **3 :** eviction
desamor *nm* **1** FRIALDAD **:** indifference **2** ENEMISTAD **:** dislike, enmity
desamparado, -da *adj* DESVALIDO **:** helpless, destitute
desamparar *vt* **:** to abandon, to forsake
desamparo *nm* **1 :** abandonment, neglect **2 :** helplessness
desamueblado, -da *adj* **:** unfurnished
desandar {6} *vt* **:** to go back, to return to the starting point
desangelado, -da *adj* **:** dull, lifeless
desangrar *vt* **:** to bleed, to bleed dry — **desangrarse** *vr* **1 :** to be bleeding **2 :** to bleed to death
desanimar *vt* DESALENTAR **:** to discourage, to dishearten — **desanimarse** *vr*
desánimo *nm* DESALIENTO **:** discouragement, dejection
desanudar *vt* **:** to untie, to disentangle
desapacible *adj* **:** unpleasant, disagreeable
desaparecer {53} *vt* **:** to cause to disappear — *vi* **:** to disappear, to vanish
desaparecido[1], -da *adj* **1 :** late, deceased **2 :** missing
desaparecido[2], -da *n* **:** missing person
desaparición *nf, pl* **-ciones :** disappearance
desapasionado, -da *adj* **:** dispassionate, impartial — **desapasionadamente** *adv*
desapego *nm* **:** coolness, indifference
desapercibido, -da *adj* **1 :** unnoticed **2** DESPREVENIDO **:** unprepared, off guard
desaprobación *nf, pl* **-ciones :** disapproval
desaprobar {19} *vt* REPROBAR **:** to disapprove of
desaprovechar *vt* MALGASTAR **:** to waste, to misuse — *vi* **:** to lose ground, to slip back
desarmador *nm Mex* **:** screwdriver
desarmar *vt* **1 :** to disarm **2** DESMONTAR **:** to disassemble, to take apart
desarme *nm* **:** disarmament
desarraigado, -da *adj* **:** rootless
desarraigar {52} *vt* **:** to uproot, to root out
desarreglado, -da *adj* **:** untidy, disorganized
desarreglar *vt* **1 :** to mess up **2 :** to upset, to disrupt
desarreglo *nm* **1 :** untidiness **2 :** disorder, confusion
desarrollar *vt* **:** to develop — **desarrollarse** *vr* **:** to take place
desarrollo *nm* **:** development
desarticulación *nf, pl* **-ciones 1 :** dislocation **2 :** breaking up, dismantling
desarticular *vt* **1** DISLOCAR **:** to dislocate **2 :** to break up, to dismantle
desaseado, -da *adj* **1 :** dirty **2 :** messy, untidy
desastre *nm* CATÁSTROFE **:** disaster
desastroso, -sa *adj* **:** disastrous, catastrophic
desatar *vt* **1 :** to undo, to untie **2 :** to unleash **3 :** to trigger, to precipitate — **desatarse** *vr* **:** to break out, to erupt
desatascar {72} *vt* **:** to unblock, to clear
desatención *nf, pl* **-ciones 1 :** absentmindedness, distraction **2 :** discourtesy
desatender {56} *vt* **1 :** to disregard **2 :** to neglect
desatento, -ta *adj* **1** DISTRAÍDO **:** absentminded **2** GROSERO **:** discourteous, rude
desatinado, -da *adj* **:** foolish, silly
desatino *nm* **:** folly, mistake
desautorizar {21} *vt* **:** to deprive of authority, to discredit
desavenencia *nf* DISCORDANCIA **:** disagreement, dispute
desayunar *vi* **:** to have breakfast — *vt* **:** to have for breakfast
desayuno *nm* **:** breakfast
desazón *nf, pl* **-zones** INQUIETUD **:** uneasiness, anxiety
desbalance *nm* **:** imbalance
desbancar {72} *vt* **:** to displace, to oust
desbandada *nf* **:** scattering, dispersal
desbarajuste *nm* DESORDEN **:** disarray, disorder, mess
desbaratar *vt* **1** ARRUINAR **:** to destroy, to ruin **2** DESCOMPONER **:** to break, to break down — **desbaratarse** *vr* **:** to fall apart
desbloquear *vt* **1 :** to open up, to clear, to break through **2 :** to free, to release
desbocado, -da *adj* **:** unbridled, rampant
desbocarse {72} *vr* **:** to run away, to bolt
desbordamiento *nm* **:** overflowing
desbordante *adj* **:** overflowing, bursting <desbordante de energía : bursting with energy>
desbordar *vt* **1 :** to overflow, to spill over **2 :** to surpass, to exceed **3 :** to

burst with, to brim with — **desbordarse** *vr*
descabellado, -da *adj* : outlandish, ridiculous
descafeinado, -da *adj* : decaffeinated
descalabrar *vt* : to hit on the head — **descalabrarse** *vr*
descalabro *nm* : setback, misfortune, loss
descalificar {72} *vt* : to disqualify — **descalificarse** *vr*
descalzarse {21} *vr* : take off one's shoes
descalzo, -za *adj* : barefoot
descansado, -da *adj* **1** : rested, refreshed **2** : restful, peaceful
descansar *vi* : to rest, to relax — *vt* : to rest <descansar la vista : to rest one's eyes>
descansillo *nm* : landing (of a staircase)
descanso *nm* **1** : rest, relaxation **2** : break **3** : landing (of a staircase) **4** : intermission
descapotable *adj & nm* : convertible
descarado, -da *adj* : brazen, impudent — **descaradamente** *adv*
descarga *nf* **1** : discharge **2** : unloading
descargar {52} *vt* **1** : to discharge **2** : to unload **3** : to release, to free **4** : to take out, to vent (anger, etc.) — **descargarse** *vr* **1** : to unburden oneself **2** : to quit **3** : to lose power
descargo *nm* **1** : unloading **2** : defense <testigo de descargo : witness for the defense>
descarnado, -da *adj* : scrawny, gaunt
descaro *nm* : audacity, nerve
descarriado, -da *adj* : lost, gone astray
descarrilar *vi* : to derail — **descarrilarse** *vr*
descartar *vt* : to rule out, to reject — **descartarse** *vr* : to discard
descascarar *vt* : to peel, to shell, to husk — **descascararse** *vr* : to peel off, to chip
descendencia *nf* **1** : descendants *pl* **2** LINAJE : descent, lineage
descendente *adj* : downward, descending
descender {56} *vt* **1** : to descend, to go down **2** BAJAR : to lower, to take down, to let down — *vi* **1** : to descend, to come down **2** : to drop, to fall **3** ~ **de** : to be a descendant of
descendiente *adj & nm* : descendant
descenso *nm* **1** : descent **2** BAJA, CAÍDA : drop, fall
descentralizar {21} *vt* : to decentralize — **descentralizarse** *vr* — **descentralización** *nf*
descifrable *adj* : decipherable
descifrar *vt* : to decipher, to decode
descolgar {16} *vt* **1** : to take down, to let down **2** : to pick up, to answer (the telephone)
descollar {19} *vi* SOBRESALIR : to stand out, to be outstanding, to excel
descolorarse *vr* : to fade
descolorido, -da *adj* : discolored, faded
descomponer {60} *vt* **1** : to rot, to decompose **2** DESBARATAR : to break, to break down — **descomponerse** *vr* **1** : to break down **2** : to decompose
descomposición *nf, pl* **-ciones** **1** : breakdown, decomposition **2** : decay
descompresión *nf* : decompression
descompuesto[1] *pp* → **descomponer**
descompuesto[2], **-ta** *adj* **1** : broken down, out of order **2** : rotten, decomposed
descomunal *adj* **1** ENORME : enormous, huge **2** EXTRAORDINARIO : extraordinary
desconcertante *adj* : disconcerting
desconcertar {55} *vt* : to disconcert — **desconcertarse** *vr*
desconchar *vt* : to chip — **desconcharse** *vr* : to chip off, to peel
desconcierto *nm* : uncertainty, confusion
desconectar *vt* **1** : to disconnect, to switch off **2** : to unplug
desconfiado, -da *adj* : distrustful, suspicious
desconfianza *nf* RECELO : distrust, suspicion
desconfiar {85} *vi* ~ **de** : to distrust, to be suspicious of
descongelar *vt* **1** : to thaw **2** : to defrost **3** : to unfreeze (assets) — **descongelarse** *vr*
descongestionante *adj & nm* : decongestant
desconocer {18} *vt* **1** IGNORAR : to be unaware of **2** : to fail to recognize
desconocido[1], **-da** *adj* : unknown, unfamiliar
desconocido[2], **-da** *n* EXTRAÑO : stranger
desconocimiento *nm* : ignorance
desconsiderado, -da *adj* : inconsiderate, thoughtless — **desconsideradamente** *adj*
desconsolado, -da *adj* : disconsolate, heartbroken
desconsuelo *nm* AFLICCIÓN : grief, distress, despair
descontaminar *vt* : to decontaminate — **descontaminación** *nf*
descontar {19} *vt* **1** : to discount, to deduct **2** EXCEPTUAR : to except, to exclude
descontento[1], **-ta** *adj* : discontented, dissatisfied
descontento[2] *nm* : discontent, dissatisfaction
descontrol *nm* : lack of control, disorder, chaos
descontrolarse *vr* : to get out of control, to be out of hand
descorazonado, -da *adj* : disheartened, discouraged
descorrer *vt* : to draw back
descortés *adj, pl* **-teses** : discourteous, rude
descortesía *nf* : discourtesy, rudeness

descrédito *nm* DESPRESTIGIO **:** discredit

descremado, -da *adj* **:** nonfat, skim

describir {33} *vt* **:** to describe

descripción *nf, pl* **-ciones :** description

descriptivo, -va *adj* **:** descriptive

descrito *pp* → **describir**

descuartizar {21} *vt* **1 :** to cut up, to quarter **2 :** to tear to pieces

descubierto[1] *pp* → **descubrir**

descubierto[2], **-ta** *adj* **1 :** exposed, revealed **2 al descubierto :** out in the open

descubridor, -dora *n* **:** discoverer, explorer

descubrimiento *nm* **:** discovery

descubrir {2} *vt* **1** HALLAR **:** to discover, to find out **2** REVELAR **:** to uncover, to reveal — **descubrirse** *vr*

descuento *nm* REBAJA **:** discount

descuidado, -da *adj* **1 :** neglectful, careless **2 :** neglected, unkempt

descuidar *vt* **:** to neglect, to overlook — *vi* **:** to be careless — **descuidarse** *vr* **1 :** to be careless, to drop one's guard **2 :** to let oneself go

descuido *nm* **1 :** carelessness, negligence **2 :** slip, oversight

desde *prep* **1 :** from **2 :** since **3 desde ahora :** from now on **4 desde entonces :** since then **5 desde hace :** for, since (a time) <ha estado nevando desde hace dos días **:** it's been snowing for two days> **6 desde luego :** of course **7 desde que :** since, ever since **8 desde ya :** right now, immediately

desdecir {11} *vi* **~ de 1 :** to be unworthy of **2 :** to clash with — **desdecirse** *vr* **1** CONTRADECIRSE **:** to contradict oneself **2** RETRACTARSE **:** to go back on one's word

desdén *nm, pl* **desdenes** DESPRECIO **:** disdain, scorn

desdentado, -da *adj* **:** toothless

desdeñar *vt* DESPRECIAR **:** to disdain, to scorn, to despise

desdeñoso, -sa *adj* **:** disdainful, scornful — **desdeñosamente** *adv*

desdibujar *vt* **:** to blur — **desdibujarse** *vr*

desdicha *nf* **1 :** misery **2 :** misfortune

desdichado[1], **-da** *adj* **1 :** unfortunate **2 :** miserable, unhappy

desdichado[2], **-da** *n* **:** wretch

desdicho *pp* → **desdecir**

desdiga, desdijo, etc. → **desdecir**

desdoblar *vt* DESPLEGAR **:** to unfold

deseable *adj* **:** desirable

desear *vt* **1 :** to wish <te deseo buena suerte **:** I wish you good luck> **2** QUERER **:** to want, to desire

desechable *adj* **:** disposable

desechar *vt* **1 :** to discard, to throw away **2** RECHAZAR **:** to reject

desecho *nm* **1 :** reject **2 desechos** *nmpl* RESIDUOS **:** rubbish, waste

desembarazarse {21} *vr* **~ de :** to get rid of

desembarcadero *nm* **:** jetty, landing pier

desembarcar {72} *vi* **:** to disembark — *vt* **:** to unload

desembarco *nm* **1 :** landing, arrival **2 :** unloading

desembarque *nm* → **desembarco**

desembocadura *nf* **1 :** mouth (of a river) **2 :** opening, end (of a street)

desembocar {72} *vi* **~ en** *or* **~ a 1 :** to flow into, to join **2 :** to lead to, to result in

desembolsar *vt* PAGAR **:** to disburse, to pay out

desembolso *nm* PAGO **:** disbursement, payment

desempacar {72} *v* **:** to unpack

desempate *nm* **:** tiebreaker, play-off

desempeñar *vt* **1 :** to play (a role) **2 :** to fulfill, to carry out **3 :** to redeem (from a pawnshop) — **desempeñarse** *vr* **:** to function, to act

desempeño *nm* **1 :** fulfillment, carrying out **2 :** performance

desempleado[1], **-da** *adj* **:** unemployed

desempleado[2], **-da** *n* **:** unemployed person

desempleo *nm* **:** unemployment

desempolvar *vt* **1 :** to dust off **2 :** to resurrect, to revive

desencadenar *vt* **1 :** to unchain **2 :** to trigger, to unleash — **desencadenarse** *vr*

desencajar *vt* **1 :** to dislocate **2 :** to disconnect, to disengage

desencantar *vt* **:** to disenchant, to disillusion — **desencantarse** *vr*

desencanto *nm* **:** disenchantment, disillusionment

desenchufar *vt* **:** to disconnect, to unplug

desenfadado, -da *adj* **1 :** uninhibited, carefree **2 :** confident, self-assured

desenfado *nm* **1** DESENVOLTURA **:** self-assurance, confidence **2 :** naturalness, ease

desenfrenadamente *adv* **:** wildly, with abandon

desenfrenado, -da *adj* **:** unbridled, unrestrained

desenfreno *nm* **:** abandon, unrestraint

desenganchar *vt* **:** to unhitch, to uncouple

desengañar *vt* **:** to disillusion, to disenchant — **desengañarse** *vr*

desengaño *nm* **:** disenchantment, disillusionment

desenlace *nm* **:** ending, outcome

desenlazar {21} *vt* **1 :** to untie **2 :** to clear up, to resolve

desenmarañar *vt* **:** to disentangle, to unravel

desenmascarar *vt* **:** to unmask, to expose

desenredar *vt* **:** to untangle, to disentangle

desenrollar *vt* **:** to unroll, to unwind

desentenderse {56} *vr* **~ de 1 :** to want nothing to do with, to be uninterested in **2 :** to pretend ignorance of

desenterrar {55} *vt* **1** EXHUMAR **:** to exhume **2 :** to unearth, to dig up

desentonar *vi* **1 :** to clash, to conflict **2 :** to be out of tune, to sing off-key

desentrañar *vt* **:** to get to the bottom of, to unravel

desenvainar *vt* **:** to draw, to unsheathe (a sword)

desenvoltura *nf* **1** DESENFADO **:** confidence, self-assurance **2** ELOCUENCIA **:** eloquence, fluency

desenvolver {89} *vt* **:** to unwrap, to open — **desenvolverse** *vr* **1 :** to unfold, to develop **2 :** to manage, to cope

desenvuelto[1] *pp* → **desenvolver**

desenvuelto[2], **-ta** *adj* **:** confident, relaxed, self-assured

deseo *nm* **:** wish, desire

deseoso, -sa *adj* **:** eager, anxious

desequilibrar *vt* **:** to unbalance, to throw off balance — **desequilibrarse** *vr*

desequilibrio *nm* **:** imbalance

deserción *nf, pl* **-ciones :** desertion, defection

desertar *vi* **1 :** to desert, to defect **2 ~ de :** to abandon, to neglect

desertor, -tora *n* **:** deserter, defector

desesperación *nf, pl* **-ciones :** desperation, despair

desesperado, -da *adj* **:** desperate, despairing, hopeless — **desesperadamente** *adv*

desesperanza *nf* **:** despair, hopelessness

desesperar *vt* **:** to exasperate — *vi* **:** to despair, to lose hope — **desesperarse** *vr* **:** to become exasperated

desestimar *vt* **1 :** to reject, to disallow **2 :** to have a low opinion of

desfachatez *nf, pl* **-teces :** audacity, nerve, cheek

desfalcador, -dora *n* **:** embezzler

desfalcar {72} *vt* **:** to embezzle

desfalco *nm* **:** embezzlement

desfallecer {53} *vi* **1 :** to weaken **2 :** to faint

desfallecimiento *nm* **1 :** weakness **2 :** fainting

desfasado, -da *adj* **1 :** out of sync **2 :** out of step, behind the times

desfase *nm* **:** gap, lag <desfase horario : jet lag>

desfavorable *adj* **:** unfavorable, adverse — **desfavorablemente** *adv*

desfavorecido, -da *adj* **:** underprivileged

desfigurar *vt* **1 :** to disfigure, to mar **2 :** to distort, to misrepresent

desfiladero *nm* **:** narrow gorge, defile

desfilar *vi* **:** to parade, to march

desfile *nm* **:** parade, procession

desfogar {52} *vt* **1 :** to vent **2** *Mex* **:** to unclog, to unblock — **desfogarse** *vr* **:** to vent one's feelings, to let off steam

desforestación *nf, pl* **-ciones :** deforestation

desgajar *vt* **1 :** to tear off **2 :** to break apart — **desgajarse** *vr* **:** to come apart

desgana *nf* **1** INAPETENCIA **:** lack of appetite **2** APATÍA **:** apathy, unwillingness, reluctance

desgano *nm* → **desgana**

desgarbado, -da *adj* **:** ungainly

desgarrador, -dora *adj* **:** heartrending, heartbreaking

desgarradura *nf* **:** tear, rip

desgarrar *vt* **1 :** to tear, to rip **2 :** to break (one's heart) — **desgarrarse** *vr*

desgarre *nm* → **desgarro**

desgarro *nm* **:** tear

desgarrón *nm, pl* **-rrones :** rip, tear

desgastar *vt* **1 :** to use up **2 :** to wear away, to wear down

desgaste *nm* **:** deterioration, wear and tear

desglosar *vt* **:** to break down, to itemize

desglose *nm* **:** breakdown, itemization

desgobierno *nm* **:** anarchy, disorder

desgracia *nf* **1 :** misfortune **2 :** disgrace **3 por ~ :** unfortunately

desgraciadamente *adv* **:** unfortunately

desgraciado[1], **-da** *adj* **1 :** unfortunate, unlucky **2 :** vile, wretched

desgraciado[2], **-da** *n* **:** unfortunate person, wretch

desgranar *vt* **:** to shuck, to shell

deshabitado, -da *adj* **:** unoccupied, uninhabited

deshacer {40} *vt* **1 :** to destroy, to ruin **2** DESATAR **:** to undo, to untie **3 :** to break apart, to crumble **4 :** to dissolve, to melt **5 :** to break, to cancel — **deshacerse** *vr* **1 :** to fall apart, to come undone **2 ~ de :** to get rid of

deshecho[1] *pp* → **deshacer**

deshecho[2], **-cha** *adj* **1 :** destroyed, ruined **2 :** devastated, shattered **3 :** undone, untied

desherbar {55} *vt* **:** to weed

desheredado, -da *adj* MARGINADO **:** dispossessed, destitute

desheredar *vt* **:** to disinherit

deshicieron, etc. → **deshacer**

deshidratar *vt* **:** to dehydrate — **deshidratación** *nf*

deshielo *nm* **:** thaw, thawing

deshilachar *vt* **:** to fray — **deshilacharse** *vr*

deshizo → **deshacer**

deshonestidad *nf* **:** dishonesty

deshonesto, -ta *adj* **:** dishonest

deshonra *nf* **:** dishonor, disgrace

deshonrar *vt* **:** to dishonor, to disgrace

deshonroso, -sa *adj* **:** dishonorable, disgraceful

deshuesar *vt* **1 :** to pit (a fruit, etc.) **2 :** to bone, to debone

deshumanizar {21} *vt* **:** to dehumanize — **deshumanización** *nf*

desidia *nf* **1** APATÍA **:** apathy, indolence **2** NEGLIGENCIA **:** negligence, sloppiness

desierto[1], **-ta** *adj* **:** deserted, uninhabited

desierto[2] *nm* : desert
designación *nf, pl* **-ciones** NOMBRAMIENTO : appointment, naming (to an office, etc.)
designar *vt* NOMBRAR : to designate, to appoint, to name
designio *nm* : plan
desigual *adj* **1** : unequal **2** DISPAREJO : uneven
desigualdad *nf* **1** : inequality **2** : unevenness
desilusión *nf, pl* **-siones** DESENCANTO, DESENGAÑO : disillusionment, disenchantment
desilusionar *vt* DESENCANTAR, DESENGAÑAR : to disillusion, to disenchant — **desilusionarse** *vr*
desinfectante *adj & nm* : disinfectant
desinfectar *vt* : to disinfect — **desinfección** *nf*
desinflar *vt* : to deflate — **desinflarse** *vr*
desinhibido, -da *adj* : unihibited, unrestrained
desintegración *nf, pl* **-ciones** : disintegration
desintegrar *vt* : to disintegrate, to break up — **desintegrarse** *vr*
desinterés *nm* **1** : lack of interest, indifference **2** : unselfishness
desinteresado, -da *adj* GENEROSO : unselfish
desintoxicar {72} *vt* : to detoxify, to detox
desistir *vi* **1** : to desist, to stop **2** **~ de** : to give up, to relinquish
deslave *nm Mex* : landslide
desleal *adj* INFIEL : disloyal — **deslealmente** *adv*
deslealtad *nf* : disloyalty
desleír {66} *vt* : to dilute, to dissolve
desligar {52} *vt* **1** : to separate, to undo **2** : to free (from an obligation) — **desligarse** *vr* **~ de** : to extricate oneself from
deslindar *vt* **1** : to mark the limits of, to demarcate **2** : to define, to clarify
deslinde *nm* : demarcation
desliz *nm, pl* **deslices** : error, mistake, slip <desliz de la lengua : slip of the tongue>
deslizar {21} *vt* **1** : to slide, to slip **2** : to slip in — **deslizarse** *vr* **1** : to slide, to glide **2** : to slip away
deslucido, -da *adj* **1** : unimpressive, dull **2** : faded, dingy, tarnished
deslucir {45} *vt* **1** : to spoil **2** : to fade, to dull, to tarnish **3** : to discredit
deslumbrar *vt* : to dazzle — **deslumbrante** *adj*
deslustrado, -da *adj* : dull, lusterless
deslustrar *vt* : to tarnish, to dull
deslustre *nm* : tarnish
desmán *nm, pl* **desmanes** **1** : outrage, abuse **2** : misfortune
desmandarse *vr* : to behave badly, to get out of hand
desmantelar *vt* DESMONTAR : to dismantle
desmañado, -da *adj* : clumsy, awkward
desmayado, -da *adj* **1** : fainting, weak **2** : dull, pale
desmayar *vi* : to lose heart, to falter — **desmayarse** *vr* DESVANECERSE : to faint, to swoon
desmayo *nm* **1** : faint, fainting **2** **sufrir un desmayo** : to faint
desmedido, -da *adj* DESMESURADO : excessive, undue
desmejorar *vt* : to weaken, to make worse — *vi* : to decline (in health), to get worse
desmembramiento *nm* : dismemberment
desmembrar {55} *vt* **1** : to dismember **2** : to break up
desmemoriado, -da *adj* : absent-minded, forgetful
desmentido *nm* : denial
desmentir {76} *vt* **1** NEGAR : to deny, to refute **2** CONTRADECIR : to contradict
desmenuzar {21} *vt* **1** : to break down, to scrutinize **2** : to crumble, to shred — **desmenuzarse** *vr*
desmerecer {53} *vt* : to be unworthy of — *vi* **1** : to decline in value **2** **~ de** : to compare unfavorably with
desmesurado, -da *adj* DESMEDIDO : excessive, inordinate — **desmesuradamente** *adv*
desmigajar *vt* : to crumble — **desmigajarse** *vr*
desmilitarizado, -da *adj* : demilitarized
desmontar *vt* **1** : to clear, to level off **2** DESMANTELAR : to dismantle, to take apart — *vi* : to dismount
desmonte *nm* : clearing, leveling
desmoralizador, -dora *adj* : demoralizing
desmoralizar {21} *vt* DESALENTAR : to demoralize, to discourage
desmoronamiento *nm* : crumbling, falling apart
desmoronar *vt* : to wear away, to erode — **desmoronarse** *vr* : to crumble, to deteriorate, to fall apart
desmotadora *nf* : gin, cotton gin
desmovilizar {21} *vt* : to demobilize — **desmovilización** *nf*
desnaturalizar {21} *vt* **1** : to denature **2** : to distort, to alter
desnivel *nm* **1** : disparity, difference **2** : unevenness (of a surface) **3** **paso a desnivel** *Mex* : underpass
desnivelado, -da *adj* **1** : uneven **2** : unbalanced
desnudar *vt* **1** : to undress **2** : to strip, to lay bare — **desnudarse** *vr* : to undress, to strip off one's clothing
desnudez *nf, pl* **-deces** : nudity, nakedness
desnudismo *nm* → **nudismo**
desnudista → **nudista**
desnudo[1], **-da** *adj* : nude, naked, bare
desnudo[2] *nm* : nude

desnutrición *nf, pl* **-ciones** : MALNUTRICIÓN : malnutrition, undernourishment

desnutrido, -da *adj* MALNUTRIDO : malnourished, undernourished

desobedecer {53} *v* : to disobey

desobediencia *nf* : disobedience — **desobediente** *adj*

desocupación *nf, pl* **-ciones** : unemployment

desocupado, -da *adj* **1** : vacant, empty **2** : free, unoccupied **3** : unemployed

desocupar *vt* **1** : to empty **2** : to vacate, to move out of — **desocuparse** *vr* : to leave, to quit (a job)

desodorante *adj & nm* : deodorant

desolación *nf, pl* **-ciones** : desolation

desolado, -da *adj* **1** : desolate **2** : devastated, distressed

desolador, -dora *adj* **1** : devastating **2** : bleak, desolate

desollar *vt* : to skin, to flay

desorbitado, -da *adj* **1** : excessive, exorbitant **2 con los ojos desorbitados** : with eyes popping out of one's head

desorden *nm, pl* **desórdenes 1** DESBARAJUSTE : disorder, mess **2** : disorder, disturbance, upset

desordenado, -da *adj* **1** : untidy, messy **2** : disorderly, unruly

desorganización *nf, pl* **-ciones** : disorganization

desorganizar {21} *vt* : to disrupt, to disorganize

desorientación *nf, pl* **-ciones** : disorientation, confusion

desorientar *vt* : to disorient, to mislead, to confuse — **desorientarse** *vr* : to become disoriented, to lose one's way

desovar *vi* : to spawn

despachar *vt* **1** : to complete, to conclude **2** : to deal with, to take care of, to handle **3** : to dispatch, to send off **4** *fam* : to finish off, to kill — **despacharse** *vr fam* : to gulp down, to polish off

despacho *nm* **1** : dispatch, shipment **2** OFICINA : office, study

despacio *adv* LENTAMENTE, LENTO : slowly, slow <¡despacio! : take it easy!, easy does it!>

desparasitar *vt* : to worm (an animal), to delouse

desparpajo *nm* **1** *fam* : self-confidence, nerve **2** *CA fam* : confusion, muddle

desparramar *vt* **1** : to spill, to splatter **2** : to spread, to scatter

despatarrarse *vr* : to sprawl (out)

despavorido, -da *adj* : terrified, horrified

despecho *nm* **1** : spite **2 a despecho de** : despite, in spite of

despectivo, -va *adj* **1** : contemptuous, disparaging **2** : derogatory, pejorative

despedazar {21} *vt* : to cut to pieces, to tear apart

despedida *nf* **1** : farewell, good-bye **2 despedida de soltera** : bridal shower

despedir {54} *vt* **1** : to see off, to show out **2** : to dismiss, to fire **3** EMITIR : to give off, to emit <despedir un olor : to give off an odor> — **despedirse** *vr* : to take one's leave, to say good-bye

despegado, -da *adj* **1** : separated, detached **2** : cold, distant

despegar {52} *vt* : to remove, to detach — *vi* : to take off, to lift off, to blast off

despegue *nm* : takeoff, liftoff

despeinado, -da *adj* : disheveled, tousled <estoy despeinada : my hair's a mess>

despejado, -da *adj* **1** : clear, fair **2** : alert, clear-headed **3** : uncluttered, unobstructed

despejar *vt* **1** : to clear, to free **2** : to clarify — *vi* **1** : to clear up **2** : to punt (in sports)

despeje *nm* **1** : clearing **2** : punt (in sports)

despellejar *vt* : to skin (an animal)

despenalizar {21} *vt* : to legalize — **despenalización** *nf*

despensa *nf* **1** : pantry, larder **2** PROVISIONES : provisions *pl*, supplies *pl*

despeñar *vt* : to hurl down

despepitar *vt* : to seed, to remove the seeds from

desperdiciar *vt* **1** DESAPROVECHAR, MALGASTAR : to waste **2** : to miss, to miss out on

desperdicio *nm* **1** : waste **2 desperdicios** *nmpl* RESIDUOS : refuse, scraps, rubbish

desperdigar {52} *vt* DISPERSAR : to disperse, to scatter

desperfecto *nm* **1** DEFECTO : flaw, defect **2** : damage

despertador *nm* : alarm clock

despertar {55} *vi* : to awaken, to wake up — *vt* **1** : to arouse, to wake **2** EVOCAR : to elicit, to evoke — **despertarse** *vr* : to wake (oneself) up

despiadado, -da *adj* CRUEL : cruel, merciless, pitiless — **despiadadamente** *adv*

despido *nm* : dismissal, layoff

despierto, -ta *adj* **1** : awake, alert **2** LISTO : clever, sharp <con la mente despierta : with a sharp mind>

despilfarrador[1], -dora *adj* : extravagant, wasteful

despilfarrador[2], -dora *n* : spendthrift, prodigal

despilfarrar *vt* MALGASTAR : to squander, to waste

despilfarro *nm* : extravagance, wastefulness

despintar *vt* : to strip the paint from — **despintarse** *vr* : to fade, to wash off, to peel off

despistado[1], -da *adj* **1** DISTRAÍDO : absentminded, forgetful **2** CONFUSO : confused, bewildered

despistado[2], -da *n* : scatterbrain, absentminded person

despistar *vt* : to throw off the track, to confuse — **despistarse** *vr*

despiste *nm* **1** : absentmindedness **2** : mistake, slip

desplantador *nm* : garden trowel

desplante *nm* : insolence, rudeness

desplazamiento *nm* **1** : movement, displacement **2** : journey

desplazar {21} *vt* **1** : to replace, to displace **2** TRASLADAR : to move, to shift

desplegar {49} *vt* **1** : to display, to show, to manifest **2** DESDOBLAR : to unfold, to unfurl **3** : to spread (out) **4** : to deploy

despliegue *nm* **1** : display **2** : deployment

desplomarse *vr* **1** : to plummet, to fall **2** DERRUMBARSE : to collapse, to break down

desplome *nm* **1** : fall, drop **2** : collapse

desplumar *vt* : to pluck (a chicken, etc.)

despoblado[1], -da *adj* : uninhabited, deserted

despoblado[2] *nm* : open country, deserted area

despoblar {19} *vt* : to depopulate

despojar *vt* **1** : to strip, to clear **2** : to divest, to deprive — **despojarse** *vr* **1** **~ de** : to remove (clothing) **2** **~ de** : to relinquish, to renounce

despojos *nmpl* **1** : remains, scraps **2** : plunder, spoils

desportilladura *nf* : chip, nick

desportillar *vt* : to chip — **desportillarse** *vr*

desposeer {20} *vt* : to dispossess

déspota *nmf* : despot, tyrant

despotismo *nm* : despotism — **despótico, -ca** *adj*

despotricar {72} *vi* : to rant and rave, to complain excessively

despreciable *adj* **1** : despicable, contemptible **2** : negligible <nada despreciable : not inconsiderable, significant>

despreciar *vt* DESDEÑAR, MENOSPRECIAR : to despise, to scorn, to disdain

despreciativo, -va *adj* : scornful, disdainful

desprecio *nm* DESDÉN, MENOSPRECIO : disdain, contempt, scorn

desprender *vt* **1** SOLTAR : to detach, to loosen, to unfasten **2** EMITIR : to emit, to give off — **desprenderse** *vr* **1** : to come off, to come undone **2** : to be inferred, to follow **3** **~ de** : to part with, to get rid of

desprendido, -da *adj* : generous, unselfish, disinterested

desprendimiento *nm* **1** : detachment **2** GENEROSIDAD : generosity **3 desprendimiento de tierras** : landslide

despreocupación *nf, pl* **-ciones** : indifference, lack of concern

despreocupado, -da *adj* : carefree, easygoing, unconcerned

desprestigiar *vt* DESACREDITAR : to discredit, to disgrace — **desprestigiarse** *vr* : to lose prestige

desprestigio *nm* DESCRÉDITO : discredit, disrepute

desprevenido, -da *adj* DESAPERCIBIDO : unprepared, off guard, unsuspecting

desproporción *nf, pl* **-ciones** : disproportion, disparity

desproporcionado, -da : out of proportion

despropósito *nm* : piece of nonsense, absurdity

desprotegido, -da *adj* : unprotected, vulnerable

desprovisto, -ta *adj* **~ de** : devoid of, lacking in

después *adv* **1** : afterward, later **2** : then, next **3** **~ de** : after, next after <después de comer : after eating> **4** **después (de) que** : after <después que lo acabé : after I finished it> **5** **después de todo** : after all **6** **poco después** : shortly after, soon thereafter

despuntado, -da *adj* : blunt, dull

despuntar *vt* : to blunt — *vi* **1** : to dawn **2** : to sprout **3** : to excel, to stand out

desquiciar *vt* **1** : to unhinge (a door) **2** : to drive crazy — **desquiciarse** *vr* : to go crazy

desquitarse *vr* **1** : to get even, to retaliate **2** **~ con** : to take it out on

desquite *nm* : revenge

desregulación *nf, pl* **-ciones** : deregulation

desregular *vt* : to deregulate

destacadamente *adv* : outstandingly, prominently

destacado, -da *adj* **1** : outstanding, prominent **2** : stationed, posted

destacar {72} *vt* **1** ENFATIZAR, SUBRAYAR : to emphasize, to highlight, to stress **2** : to station, to post — *vi* : to stand out

destajo *nm* **1** : piecework **2 a ~** : by the item, by the job

destapador *nm* : bottle opener

destapar *vt* **1** : to open, to take the top off **2** DESCUBRIR : to reveal, to uncover **3** : to unblock, to unclog

destape *nm* : uncovering, revealing

destartalado, -da *adj* : dilapidated, tumbledown

destellar *vi* **1** : to sparkle, to flash, to glint **2** : to twinkle

destello *nm* **1** : flash, sparkle, twinkle **2** : glimmer, hint

destemplado, -da *adj* **1** : out of tune **2** : irritable, out of sorts **3** : unpleasant (of weather)

desteñir {67} *vi* : to run, to fade — **desteñirse** DESCOLORARSE : to fade

desterrado[1], -da *adj* : banished, exiled

desterrado[2], -da *n* : exile

desterrar {55} *vt* **1** EXILIAR **:** to banish, to exile **2** ERRADICAR **:** to eradicate, to do away with

destetar *vt* **:** to wean

destiempo *adv* **a ~ :** at the wrong time

destierro *nm* EXILIO **:** exile

destilación *nf, pl* **-ciones :** distillation

destilador, -dora *n* **:** distiller

destilar *vt* **1 :** to exude **2 :** to distill

destilería *nf* **:** distillery

destinación *nf, pl* **-ciones** DESTINO **:** destination

destinado, -da *adj* **:** destined, bound

destinar *vt* **1 :** to appoint, to assign **2** ASIGNAR **:** to earmark, to allot

destinatario, -ria *n* **1 :** addressee **2 :** payee

destino *nm* **1 :** destiny, fate **2** DESTINACIÓN **:** destination **3 :** use **4 :** assignment, post

destitución *nf, pl* **-ciones :** dismissal, removal from office

destituir {41} *vt* **:** to dismiss, to remove from office

destorcer {14} *vt* **:** to untwist

destornillador *nm* **:** screwdriver

destornillar *vt* **:** to unscrew

destrabar *vt* **1 :** to untie, to undo, to ease up **2 :** to separate

destreza *nf* HABILIDAD **:** dexterity, skill

destronar *vt* **:** to depose, to dethrone

destrozado, -da *adj* **1 :** ruined, destroyed **2 :** devastated, brokenhearted

destrozar {21} *vt* **1 :** to smash, to shatter **2 :** to destroy, to wreck — **destrozarse** *vr*

destrozo *nm* **1** DAÑO **:** damage **2 :** havoc, destruction

destrucción *nf, pl* **-ciones :** destruction

destructivo, -va *adj* **:** destructive

destructor[1]**, -tora** *adj* **:** destructive

destructor[2] *nm* **:** destroyer (ship)

destruir {41} *vt* **:** to destroy — **destruirse** *vr*

desubicado, -da *adj* **1 :** out of place **2 :** confused, disoriented

desunión *nf, pl* **-niones :** disunity

desunir *vt* **:** to split, to divide

desusado, -da *adj* **1** INSÓLITO **:** unusual **2** OBSOLETO **:** obsolete, disused, antiquated

desuso *nm* **:** disuse, obsolescence <caer en desuso : to fall into disuse>

desvaído, -da *adj* **1 :** pale, washed-out **2 :** vague, blurred

desvainar *vt* **:** to shell

desvalido, -da *adj* DESAMPARADO **:** destitute, helpless

desvalijar *vt* **1 :** to ransack **2 :** to rob

desvalorización *nf, pl* **-ciones 1** DEVALUACIÓN **:** devaluation **2 :** depreciation

desvalorizar {21} *vt* **:** to devalue

desván *nm, pl* **desvanes** ÁTICO, BUHARDILLA **:** attic

desvanecer {53} *vt* **1** DISIPAR **:** to make disappear, to dispel **2 :** to fade, to blur — **desvanecerse** *vr* **1 :** to vanish, to disappear **2 :** to fade **3** DESMAYARSE **:** to faint, to swoon

desvanecimiento *nm* **1 :** disappearance **2** DESMAYO **:** faint **3 :** fading

desvariar {85} *vi* **1** DELIRAR **:** to be delirious **2 :** to rave, to talk nonsense

desvarío *nm* DELIRIO **:** delirium

desvelado, -da *adj* **:** sleepless

desvelar *vt* **1 :** to keep awake **2** REVELAR **:** to reveal, to disclose — **desvelarse** *vr* **1 :** to stay awake **2 :** to do one's utmost

desvelo *nm* **1 :** sleeplessness **2 desvelos** *nmpl* **:** efforts, pains

desvencijado, -da *adj* **:** dilapidated, rickety

desventaja *nf* **:** disadvantage, drawback

desventajoso, -sa *adj* **:** disadvantageous, unfavorable

desventura *nf* INFORTUNIO **:** misfortune

desventurado, -da *adj* **:** unfortunate, ill-fated

desvergonzado, -da *adj* **:** shameless, impudent

desvergüenza *nf* **:** shamelessness, impudence

desvestir {54} *vt* **:** to undress — **desvestirse** *vr* **:** to get undressed

desviación *nf, pl* **-ciones 1 :** deviation, departure **2 :** detour, diversion

desviar {85} *vt* **1 :** to change the course of, to divert **2 :** to turn away, to deflect — **desviarse** *vr* **1 :** to branch off **2** APARTARSE **:** to stray

desvinculación *nf, pl* **-ciones :** dissociation

desvincular *vt* **~ de :** to separate from, to dissociate from — **desvincularse** *vr*

desvío *nm* **1 :** diversion, detour **2 :** deviation

desvirtuar {3} *vt* **1 :** to impair, to spoil **2 :** to detract from **3 :** to distort, to misrepresent

detalladamente *adv* **:** in detail, at great length

detallar *vt* **:** to detail

detalle *nm* **1 :** detail **2 al detalle :** retail

detallista[1] *adj* **1 :** meticulous **2 :** retail

detallista[2] *nmf* **1 :** perfectionist **2 :** retailer

detección *nf, pl* **-ciones :** detection

detectar *vt* **:** to detect — **detectable** *adj*

detective *nmf* **:** detective

detector *nm* **:** detector <detector de mentiras : lie detector>

detención *nf, pl* **-ciones 1** ARRESTO **:** detention, arrest **2 :** stop, halt **3 :** delay, holdup

detener {80} *vt* **1** ARRESTAR **:** to arrest, to detain **2** PARAR **:** to stop, to halt **3 :** to keep, to hold back — **detenerse** *vr* **1 :** to stop **2 :** to delay, to linger

detenidamente *adv* **:** thoroughly, at length

detenimiento *nm* **con ~ :** carefully, in detail

detentar *vt* : to hold, to retain
detergente *nm* : detergent
deteriorado, -da *adj* : damaged, worn
deteriorar *vt* ESTROPEAR : to damage, to spoil — **deteriorarse** *vr* **1** : to get damaged, to wear out **2** : to deteriorate, to worsen
deterioro *nm* **1** : deterioration, wear **2** : worsening, decline
determinación *nf, pl* **-ciones 1** : determination, resolve **2 tomar una determinación** : to make a decision
determinado, -da *adj* **1** : certain, particular **2** : determined, resolute
determinante[1] *adj* : determining, deciding
determinante[2] *nm* : determinant
determinar *vt* **1** : to determine **2** : to cause, to bring about — **determinarse** *vr* : to make up one's mind, to decide
detestar *vt* : to detest — **detestable** *adj*
detonación *nf, pl* **-ciones** : detonation
detonador *nm* : detonator
detonante[1] *adj* : detonating, explosive
detonante[2] *nm* **1** → **detonador 2** : catalyst, cause
detonar *vi* : to detonate, to explode
detractor, -tora *n* : detractor, critic
detrás *adv* **1** : behind **2 ~ de** : in back of **3 por ~** : from behind
detuvo, etc. → **detener**
deuda *nf* **1** DÉBITO : debt **2 en deuda con** : indebted to
deudo, -da *n* : relative
deudor[1], **-dora** *adj* : indebted
deudor[2], **-dora** *n* : debtor
devaluación *nf, pl* **-ciones** DESVALORIZACIÓN : devaluation
devaluar {3} *vt* : to devalue — **devaluarse** *vr* : to depreciate
devanarse *vr* **devanarse los sesos** : to rack one's brains
devaneo *nm* **1** : flirtation, fling **2** : idle pursuit
devastador, -dora *adj* : devastating
devastar *vt* : to devastate — **devastación** *nf*
devenir {87} *vi* **1** : to come about **2 ~ en** : to become, to turn into
devoción *nf, pl* **-ciones** : devotion
devolución *nf, pl* **-ciones** REEMBOLSO : return, refund
devolver {89} *vt* **1** : to return, to give back **2** REEMBOLSAR : to refund, to pay back **3** : to vomit, to bring up — *vi* : to vomit, to throw up — **devolverse** *vr* : to return, to come back, to go back
devorar *vt* **1** : to devour **2** : to consume
devoto[1], **-ta** *adj* : devout — **devotamente** *adv*
devoto[2], **-ta** *n* : devotee, admirer
di → **dar, decir**
día *nm* **1** : day <todos los días : every day> **2** : daytime, daylight <de día : by day, in the daytime> <en pleno día : in broad daylight> **3 al día** : up-to-date **4 en su día** : in due time
diabetes *nf* : diabetes
diabético, -ca *adj & n* : diabetic
diablillo *nm* : little devil, imp
diablo *nm* DEMONIO : devil
diablura *nf* **1** : prank **2 diabluras** *nfpl* : mischief
diabólico, -ca *adj* : diabolical, diabolic, devilish
diaconisa *nf* : deaconess
diácono *nm* : deacon
diadema *nf* : diadem, crown
diáfano, -na *adj* : diaphanous
diafragma *nm* : diaphragm
diagnosticar {72} *vt* : to diagnose
diagnóstico[1], **-ca** *adj* : diagnostic
diagnóstico[2] *nm* : diagnosis
diagonal *adj & nf* : diagonal — **diagonalmente** *adv*
diagrama *nm* **1** : diagram **2 diagrama de flujo** ORGANIGRAMA : flowchart
dialecto *nm* : dialect
dialogar {52} *vi* : to have a talk, to converse
diálogo *nm* : dialogue
diamante *nm* : diamond
diametral *adj* : diametric, diametrical — **diametralmente** *adv*
diámetro *nm* : diameter
diana *nf* **1** : target, bull's-eye **2** *or* **toque de diana** : reveille
diapositiva *nf* : slide, transparency
diario[1] *adv Mex* : every day, daily
diario[2], **-ria** *adj* : daily, everyday — **diariamente** *adv*
diario[3] *nm* **1** : diary **2** PERIÓDICO : newspaper
diarrea *nf* : diarrhea
diatriba *nf* : diatribe, tirade
dibujante *nmf* **1** : draftsman *m,* draftswoman *f* **2** CARICATURISTA : cartoonist
dibujar *vt* **1** : to draw, to sketch **2** : to portray, to depict
dibujo *nm* **1** : drawing **2** : design, pattern **3 dibujos animados** : (animated) cartoons
dicción *nf, pl* **-ciones** : diction
diccionario *nm* : dictionary
dícese → **decir**
dicha *nf* **1** SUERTE : good luck **2** FELICIDAD : happiness, joy
dicho[1] *pp* → **decir**
dicho[2], **-cha** *adj* : said, aforementioned
dicho[3] *nm* DECIR : saying, proverb
dichoso, -sa *adj* **1** : blessed **2** FELIZ : happy **3** AFORTUNADO : fortunate, lucky
diciembre *nm* : December
diciendo → **decir**
dictado *nm* : dictation
dictador, -dora *n* : dictator
dictadura *nf* : dictatorship
dictamen *nm, pl* **dictámenes 1** : report **2** : judgment, opinion
dictaminar *vt* : to report — *vi* : to give an opinion, to pass judgment
dictar *vt* **1** : to dictate **2** : to pronounce (a judgment) **3** : to give, to deliver <dictar una conferencia : to give a lecture>
dictatorial *adj* : dictatorial

didáctico, -ca *adj* **:** didactic

diecinueve *adj & nm* **:** nineteen

diecinueveavo[1], **-va** *adj* **:** nineteenth

diecinueveavo[2] *nm* **:** nineteenth (fraction)

dieciocho *adj & nm* **:** eighteen

dieciochoavo[1], **-va** *or* **dieciochavo, -va** *adj* **:** eighteenth

dieciochoavo[2] *or* **dieciochavo** *nm* **:** eighteenth (fraction)

dieciséis *adj & nm* **:** sixteen

dieciseisavo[1], **-va** *adj* **:** sixteenth

dieciseisavo[2] *nm* **:** sixteenth (fraction)

diecisietaeavo[1], **-va** *adj* **:** seventeenth

diecisietaeavo[2] *nm* **:** seventeenth (fraction)

diecisiete *adj & nm* **:** seventeen

diecisieteavo[1], **-va** *adj* **:** seventeenth

diecisieteavo[2] *nm* **:** seventeenth

diente *nm* **1 :** tooth <diente canino : eyetooth, canine tooth> **2 :** tusk, fang **3 :** prong, tine **4 diente de león :** dandelion

dieron, etc. → **dar**

diesel [ˈdisɛl] *nm* **:** diesel

diestra *nf* **:** right hand

diestramente *adv* **:** skillfully, adroitly

diestro[1], **-tra** *adj* **1 :** right **2 :** skillful, accomplished

diestro[2] *nm* **:** bullfighter, matador

dieta *nf* **:** diet

dietética *nf* **:** dietetics

dietético, -ca *adj* **:** dietetic

dietista *nmf* **:** dietitian

diez *adj & nm, pl* **dieces :** ten

difamación *nf, pl* **-ciones :** defamation, slander

difamar *vt* **:** to defame, to slander

difamatorio, -ria *adj* **:** slanderous, defamatory, libelous

diferencia *nf* **1 :** difference **2 a diferencia de :** unlike, in contrast to

diferenciación *nf, pl* **-ciones :** differentiation

diferenciar *vt* **:** to differentiate between, to distinguish — **diferenciarse** *vr* **:** to differ

diferendo *nm* **:** dispute, conflict

diferente *adj* DISTINTO **:** different — **diferentemente** *adv*

diferir {76} *vt* DILATAR, POSPONER **:** to postpone, to put off — *vi* **:** to differ

difícil *adj* **:** difficult, hard

difícilmente *adv* **1 :** with difficulty **2 :** hardly

dificultad *nf* **:** difficulty

dificultar *vt* **:** to make difficult, to obstruct

dificultoso, -sa *adj* **:** difficult, hard

difteria *nf* **:** diphtheria

difundir *vt* **1 :** to diffuse, to spread out **2 :** to broadcast, to spread

difunto, -ta *adj & n* FALLECIDO **:** deceased

difusión *nf, pl* **-siones 1 :** spreading **2 :** diffusion (of heat, etc.) **3 :** broadcast, broadcasting <los medios de difusión : the media>

difuso, -sa *adj* **:** diffuse, widespread

diga, etc. → **decir**

digerir {76} *vt* **:** to digest — **digerible** *adj*

digestión *nf, pl* **-tiones :** digestion

digestivo, -va *adj* **:** digestive

digital[1] *adj* **:** digital — **digitalmente** *adv*

digital[2] *nm* **1** DEDALERA **:** foxglove **2 :** digitalis

dígito *nm* **:** digit

dignarse *vr* **:** to deign, to condescend <no se dignó contestar : he didn't deign to answer>

dignatario, -ria *n* **:** dignitary

dignidad *nf* **1 :** dignity **2 :** dignitary

dignificar {72} *vt* **:** to dignify

digno, -na *adj* **1** HONORABLE **:** honorable **2 :** worthy — **dignamente** *adv*

digresión *nf, pl* **-ciones :** digression

dije *nm* **:** charm (on a bracelet)

dijo, etc. → **decir**

dilación *nf, pl* **-ciones :** delay

dilapidar *vt* **:** to waste, to squander

dilatar *vt* **1 :** to dilate, to widen, to expand **2** DIFERIR, POSPONER **:** to put off, to postpone — **dilatarse** *vr* **1 :** to expand (of gases, metals, etc.) **2** *Mex* **:** to take long, to be long

dilatorio, -ria *adj* **:** dilatory, delaying

dilema *nm* **:** dilemma

diligencia *nf* **1 :** diligence, care **2 :** promptness, speed **3 :** action, step **4 :** task, errand **5 :** stagecoach **6 diligencias** *nfpl* **:** judicial procedures, formalities

diligente *adj* **:** diligent — **diligentemente** *adv*

dilucidar *vt* **:** to elucidate, to clarify

diluir {41} *vt* **:** to dilute

diluviar *v impers* **:** to pour (with rain), to pour down

diluvio *nm* **1 :** flood **2 :** downpour

dimensión *nf, pl* **-siones :** dimension — **dimensional** *adj*

dimensionar *vt* **:** to measure, to gauge

diminuto, -ta *adj* **:** minute, tiny

dimisión *nf, pl* **-siones :** resignation

dimitir *vi* **:** to resign, to step down

dimos → **dar**

dinámica *nf* **:** dynamics

dinámico, -ca *adj* **:** dynamic — **dinámicamente** *adv*

dinamita *nf* **:** dynamite

dinamitar *vt* **:** to dynamite

dínamo *or* **dinamo** *nm* **:** dynamo

dinastía *nf* **:** dynasty

dineral *nm* **:** fortune, large sum of money

dinero *nm* **:** money

dinosaurio *nm* **:** dinosaur

dintel *nm* **:** lintel

dio, etc. → **dar**

diocesano, -na *adj* **:** diocesan

diócesis *nfs & pl* **:** diocese

dios, diosa *n* **:** god, goddess *f*

Dios *nm* **:** God

diploma *nm* **:** diploma

diplomacia *nf* **:** diplomacy

diplomado[1], **-da** *adj* : qualified, trained
diplomado[2] *nm Mex* : seminar
diplomático[1], **-ca** *adj* : diplomatic — **diplomáticamente** *adv*
diplomático[2], **-ca** *n* : diplomat
diputación *nf, pl* **-ciones** : deputation, delegation
diputado, -da *n* : delegate, representative
dique *nm* : dike
dirá, etc. → **decir**
dirección *nf, pl* **-ciones 1** : address **2** : direction **3** : management, leadership **4** : steering (of an automobile)
direccional[1] *adj* : directional
direccional[2] *nf* : directional, turn signal
directa *nf* : high gear
directamente *adv* : straight, directly
directiva *nf* **1** ORDEN : directive **2** DIRECTORIO, JUNTA : board of directors
directivo[1], **-va** *adj* : executive, managerial
directivo[2], **-va** *n* : executive, director
directo, -ta *adj* **1** : direct, straight, immediate **2 en ~** : live (in broadcasting)
director, -tora *n* **1** : director, manager, head **2** : conductor (of an orchestra)
directorial *adj* : managing, executive
directorio *nm* **1** : directory **2** DIRECTIVA, JUNTA : board of directors
directriz *nf, pl* **-trices** : guideline
dirigencia *nf* : leaders *pl*, leadership
dirigente[1] *adj* : directing, leading
dirigente[2] *nmf* : director, leader
dirigible *nm* : dirigible, blimp
dirigir {35} *vt* **1** : to direct, to lead **2** : to address **3** : to aim, to point **4** : to conduct (music) — **dirigirse** *vr* **~ a 1** : to go towards **2** : to speak to, to address
dirimir *vt* **1** : to resolve, to settle **2** : to annul, to dissolve (a marriage)
discapacidad *nf* MINUSVALÍA : disability, handicap
discapacitado[1], **-da** *adj* : disabled, handicapped
discapacitado[2], **-da** *n* : disabled person, handicapped person
discernimiento *nm* : discernment
discernir {25} *v* : to discern, to distinguish
disciplina *nf* : discipline
disciplinar *vt* : to discipline — **disciplinario, -ria** *adj*
discípulo, -la *n* : disciple, follower
disc jockey [ˌdiskˈjoke, -ˈdʒo-] *nmf* : disc jockey
disco *nm* **1** : phonograph record **2** : disc, disk <disco compacto : compact disc> **3** : discus
díscolo, -la *adj* : unruly, disobedient
disconforme *adj* : in disagreement
discontinuidad *nf* : discontinuity
discontinuo, -nua *adj* : discontinuous
discordancia *nf* DESAVENENCIA : conflict, disagreement
discordante *adj* **1** : discordant **2** : conflicting
discordia *nf* : discord
discoteca *nf* **1** : disco, discotheque **2** *CA, Mex* : record store
discreción *nf, pl* **-ciones** : discretion
discrecional *adj* : discretionary
discrepancia *nf* : discrepancy
discrepar *vi* **1** : to disagree **2** : to differ
discreto, -ta *adj* : discreet — **discretamente** *adv*
discriminación *nf, pl* **-ciones** : discrimination
discriminar *vt* **1** : to discriminate against **2** : to distinguish, to differentiate
discriminatorio, -ria *adj* : discriminatory
disculpa *nf* **1** : apology **2** : excuse
disculpable *adj* : excusable
disculpar *vt* : to excuse, to pardon — **disculparse** *vr* : to apologize
discurrir *vi* **1** : to flow **2** : to pass, to go by **3** : to ponder, to reflect
discurso *nm* **1** ORACIÓN : speech, address **2** : discourse, treatise
discusión *nf, pl* **-siones 1** : discussion **2** ALTERCADO, DISPUTA : argument
discutible *adj* : arguable, debatable
discutidor, -dora *adj* : argumentative
discutir *vt* **1** : to discuss **2** : to dispute — *vi* ALTERCAR : to argue, to quarrel
disecar {72} *vt* **1** : to dissect **2** : to stuff (for preservation)
disección *nf, pl* **-ciones** : dissection
diseminación *nf, pl* **-ciones** : dissemination, spreading
diseminar *vt* : to disseminate, to spread
disensión *nf, pl* **-siones** : dissension, disagreement
disentería *nf* : dysentery
disentir {76} *vi* : to dissent, to disagree
diseñador, -dora *n* : designer
diseñar *vt* **1** : to design, to plan **2** : to lay out, to outline
diseño *nm* : design
disertación *nf, pl* **-ciones 1** : lecture, talk **2** : dissertation
disertar *vi* : to lecture, to give a talk
disfraz *nm, pl* **disfraces 1** : disguise **2** : costume **3** : front, pretense
disfrazar {21} *vt* **1** : to disguise **2** : to mask, to conceal — **disfrazarse** *vr* : to wear a costume, to be in disguise
disfrutar *vt* : to enjoy — *vi* : to enjoy oneself, to have a good time
disfrute *nm* : enjoyment
disfunción *nf, pl* **-ciones** : dysfunction — **disfuncional** *adj*
disgresión *nf* → **digresión**
disgustar *vt* : to upset, to displease, to make angry — **disgustarse** *vr*
disgusto *nm* **1** : annoyance, displeasure **2** : argument, quarrel **3** : trouble, misfortune
disidencia *nf* : dissidence, dissent
disidente *adj & nmf* : dissident
disímbolo, -la *adj Mex* : dissimilar

disímil *adj* **:** dissimilar
disimulado, -da *adj* **1 :** concealed, disguised **2 :** furtive, sly
disimular *vi* **:** to dissemble, to pretend — *vt* **:** to conceal, to hide
disimulo *nm* **1 :** dissembling, pretense **2 :** slyness, furtiveness **3 :** tolerance
disipar *vt* **1 :** to dissipate **2 :** to dispel — **disiparse** *vr*
diskette [di'skɛt] *nm* **:** floppy disk, diskette
dislocar {72} *vt* **:** to dislocate — **dislocación** *nf*
disminución *nf, pl* **-ciones :** decrease, drop, fall
disminuir {41} *vt* REDUCIR **:** to reduce, to decrease, to lower — *vi* **1 :** to lower **2 :** to drop, to fall
disociación *nf, pl* **-ciones :** dissociation
disociar *vt* **:** to dissociate, to separate
disolución *nf, pl* **-ciones 1 :** dissolution, dissolving **2 :** breaking up **3 :** dissipation
disoluto, -ta *adj* **:** dissolute, dissipated
disolver {89} *vt* **1 :** to dissolve **2 :** to break up — **disolverse** *vr*
disonancia *nf* **:** dissonance — **disonante** *adj*
disparado, -da *adj* **salir disparado** *fam* **:** to take off in a hurry, to rush away
disparar *vi* **1 :** to fire (a gun) **2** *Mex fam* **:** to pay — *vt* **1 :** to shoot **2 :** to rush off **3** *Mex fam* **:** to treat to, to buy — **dispararse** *vr* **:** to shoot up, to skyrocket
disparatado, -da *adj* ABSURDO, RIDÍCULO **:** absurd, ridiculous, crazy
disparate *nm* **:** silliness, stupidity <decir disparates : to talk nonsense>
disparejo, -ja *adj* DESIGUAL **:** uneven
disparidad *nf* **:** disparity
disparo *nm* TIRO **:** shot
dispendio *nm* **:** wastefulness, extravagance
dispendioso, -sa *adj* **:** wasteful, extravagant
dispensa *nf* **:** dispensation
dispensable *adj* **1 :** dispensable **2 :** excusable
dispensar *vt* **1 :** to dispense, to give, to grant **2** EXCUSAR **:** to excuse, to forgive **3** EXIMIR **:** to exempt
dispensario *nm* **1 :** dispensary, clinic **2** *Mex* **:** dispenser
dispersar *vt* DESPERDIGAR **:** to disperse, to scatter
dispersión *nf, pl* **-siones :** dispersion
disperso, -sa *adj* **:** dispersed, scattered
displicencia *nf* **:** indifference, coldness, disdain
displicente *adj* **:** indifferent, cold, disdainful
disponer {60} *vt* **1 :** to arrange, to lay out **2 :** to stipulate, to order **3 :** to prepare — *vi* **~ de :** to have at one's disposal — **disponerse** *vr* **~ a :** to prepare to, to be about to
disponibilidad *nf* **:** availability
disponible *adj* **:** available
disposición *nf, pl* **-ciones 1 :** disposition **2 :** aptitude, talent **3 :** order, arrangement **4 :** willingness, readiness **5 última disposición :** last will and testament
dispositivo *nm* **1** APARATO, MECANISMO **:** device, mechanism **2 :** force, detachment
dispuesto[1] *pp* → **disponer**
dispuesto[2], -ta *adj* PREPARADO **:** ready, prepared, disposed
dispuso, etc. → **disponer**
disputa *nf* ALTERCADO, DISCUSIÓN **:** dispute, argument
disputar *vi* **:** to argue, to contend, to vie — *vt* **:** to dispute, to question — **disputarse** *vr* **:** to be in competition for <se disputan la corona : they're fighting for the crown>
disquera *nf* **:** record label, recording company
disquete *nm* → **diskette**
disquisición *nf, pl* **-ciones 1 :** formal discourse **2 disquisiciones** *nfpl* **:** digressions
distancia *nf* **:** distance
distanciamiento *nm* **1 :** distancing **2 :** rift, estrangement
distanciar *vt* **1 :** to space out **2 :** to draw apart — **distanciarse** *vr* **:** to grow apart, to become estranged
distante *adj* **1 :** distant, far-off **2 :** aloof
distar *vi* **~ de :** to be far from <dista de ser perfecto : he is far from perfect>
diste → **dar**
distender {56} *vt* **:** to distend, to stretch
distensión *nf, pl* **-siones :** distension
distinción *nf, pl* **-ciones :** distinction
distinguido, -da *adj* **:** distinguished, refined
distinguir {26} *vt* **1 :** to distinguish **2 :** to honor — **distinguirse** *vr*
distintivo, -va *adj* **:** distinctive, distinguishing
distinto, -ta *adj* **1** DIFERENTE **:** different **2** CLARO **:** distinct, clear, evident
distorsión *nf, pl* **-siones :** distortion
distorsionar *vt* **:** to distort
distracción *nf, pl* **-ciones 1 :** distraction, amusement **2 :** forgetfulness **3 :** oversight
distraer {81} *vt* **1 :** to distract **2** ENTRETENER **:** to entertain, to amuse — **distraerse** *vr* **1 :** to get distracted **2 :** to amuse oneself
distraídamente *adv* **:** absentmindedly
distraído[1] *pp* → **distraer**
distraído[2], -da *adj* **1 :** distracted, preoccupied **2** DESPISTADO **:** absentminded
distribución *nf, pl* **-ciones :** distribution
distribuidor, -dora *n* **:** distributor
distribuir {41} *vt* **:** to distribute
distrital *adj* **:** district, of the district

distrito *nm* : district
distrofia *nf* : dystrophy <distrofia muscular : muscular dystrophy>
disturbio *nm* : disturbance
disuadir *vt* : to dissuade, to discourage
disuasión *nf, pl* **-siones** : dissuasion
disuasorio, -ria *adj* : discouraging
disuelto *pp* → **disolver**
disyuntiva *nf* : dilemma
diurético¹, -ca *adj* : diuretic
diurético² *nm* : diuretic
diurno, -na *adj* : day, daytime
diva *nf* → **divo**
divagar {52} *vi* : to digress
diván *nm, pl* **divanes** : divan
divergencia *nf* : divergence, difference
divergente *adj* : divergent, differing
divergir {35} *vi* **1** : to diverge **2** : to differ, to disagree
diversidad *nf* : diversity, variety
diversificación *nf, pl* **-ciones** : diversification
diversificar {72} *vt* : to diversify
diversión *nf, pl* **-siones** ENTRETENIMIENTO : fun, amusement, diversion
diverso, -sa *adj* : diverse, various
divertido, -da *adj* **1** : amusing, funny **2** : entertaining, enjoyable
divertir {76} *vt* ENTRETENER : to amuse, to entertain — **divertirse** *vr* : to have fun, to have a good time
dividendo *nm* : dividend
dividir *vt* **1** : to divide, to split **2** : to distribute, to share out — **dividirse** *vr*
divieso *nm* : boil
divinidad *nf* : divinity
divino, -na *adj* : divine
divisa *nf* **1** : currency **2** LEMA : motto **3** : emblem, insignia
divisar *vt* : to discern, to make out
divisible *adj* : divisible
división *nf, pl* **-siones** : division
divisionismo *nm* : factionalism
divisivo, -va *adj* : divisive
divisor *nm* : denominator
divisorio, -ria *adj* : dividing
divo, -va *n* **1** : prima donna **2** : celebrity, star
divorciado¹, -da *adj* **1** : divorced **2** : split, divided
divorciado², -da *n* : divorcé *m*, divorcée *f*
divorciar *vt* : to divorce — **divorciarse** *vr* : to get a divorce
divorcio *nm* : divorce
divulgación *nf, pl* **-ciones 1** : spreading, dissemination **2** : popularization
divulgar {52} *vt* **1** : to spread, to circulate **2** REVELAR : to divulge, to reveal **3** : to popularize — **divulgarse** *vr*
dizque *adv* : supposedly, apparently
dobladillar *vt* : to hem
dobladillo *nm* : hem
doblar *vt* **1** : to double **2** PLEGAR : to fold, to bend **3** : to turn <doblar la esquina : to turn the corner> **4** : to dub — *vi* **1** : to turn **2** : to toll, to ring —
doblarse *vr* **1** : to fold up, to double over **2** : to give in, to yield
doble¹ *adj* : double — **doblemente** *adv*
doble² *nm* **1** : double **2** : toll (of a bell), knell
doble³ *nmf* : stand-in, double
doblegar {52} *vt* **1** : to fold, to crease **2** : to force to yield — **doblegarse** *vr* : to yield, to bow
doblez¹ *nm, pl* **dobleces** : fold, crease
doblez² *nmf* : duplicity, deceitfulness
doce *adj & nm* : twelve
doceavo¹, -va *adj* : twelfth
doceavo² *nm* : twelfth (fraction)
docena *nf* **1** : dozen **2 docena de fraile** : baker's dozen
docencia *nf* : teaching
docente¹ *adj* : educational, teaching
docente² *n* : teacher, lecturer
dócil *adj* : docile — **dócilmente** *adv*
docilidad *nf* : docility
docto, -ta *adj* : learned, erudite
doctor, -tora *n* : doctor
doctorado *nm* : doctorate
doctrina *nf* : doctrine — **doctrinal** *adj*
documentación *nf, pl* **-ciones** : documentation
documental *adj & nm* : documentary
documentar *vt* : to document
documento *nm* : document
dogma *nm* : dogma
dogmático, -ca *adj* : dogmatic
dogmatismo *nm* : dogmatism
dólar *nm* : dollar
dolencia *nf* : ailment, malaise
doler {47} *vi* **1** : to hurt, to ache **2** : to grieve — **dolerse** *vr* **1** : to be distressed **2** : to complain
doliente *nmf* : mourner, bereaved
dolor *nm* **1** : pain, ache <dolor de cabeza : headache> **2** PENA, TRISTEZA : grief, sorrow
dolorido, -da *adj* **1** : sore, aching **2** : hurt, upset
doloroso, -sa *adj* **1** : painful **2** : distressing — **dolorosamente** *adv*
doloso, -sa *adj* : fraudulent — **dolosamente** *adv*
domador, -dora *n* : tamer
domar *vt* : to tame, to break in
domesticado, -da *adj* : domesticated, tame
domesticar {72} *vt* : to domesticate, to tame
doméstico, -ca *adj* : domestic, household
domiciliado, -da *adj* : residing
domiciliario, -ria *adj* **1** : home **2 arresto domiciliario** : house arrest
domiciliarse *vr* RESIDIR : to reside
domicilio *nm* : home, residence <cambio de domicilio : change of address>
dominación *nf, pl* **-ciones** : domination
dominancia *nf* : dominance
dominante *adj* **1** : dominant **2** : domineering

dominar *vt* **1 :** to dominate **2 :** to master, to be proficient at — *vi* **:** to predominate, to prevail — **dominarse** *vr* **:** to control oneself
domingo *nm* **:** Sunday
dominical *adj* **:** Sunday <periódico dominical : Sunday newspaper>
dominicano, -na *adj & n* **:** Dominican
dominio *nm* **1 :** dominion, power **2 :** mastery **3 :** domain, field
dominó *nm, pl* **-nós 1 :** domino (tile) **2 :** dominoes *pl* (game)
domo *nm* **:** dome
don[1] *nm* **1 :** gift, present **2 :** talent
don[2] *nm* **1 :** title of courtesy preceding a man's first name **2 don nadie :** nobody, insignificant person
dona *nf Mex* **:** doughnut, donut
donación *nf, pl* **-ciones :** donation
donador, -dora *n* **:** donor
donaire *nm* **1** GARBO **:** grace, poise **2 :** witticism
donante *nf* → **donador**
donar *vt* **:** to donate
donativo *nm* **:** donation
doncella *nf* **:** maiden, damsel
doncellez *nf* **:** maidenhood
donde[1] *conj* **:** where, in which <el pueblo donde vivo : the town where I live>
donde[2] *prep* **:** over by <lo encontré donde la silla : I found it over by the chair>
dónde *adv* **:** where <¿dónde está su casa? : where is your house?>
dondequiera *adv* **1 :** anywhere, no matter where **2 dondequiera que :** wherever, everywhere
doña *nf* **:** title of courtesy preceding a woman's first name
doquier *adv* **por ~ :** everywhere, all over
dorado[1], **-da** *adj* **:** gold, golden
dorado[2], **-da** *nm* **:** gilt
dorar *vt* **1 :** to gild **2 :** to brown
dormido, -da *adj* **1 :** asleep **2 :** numb <tiene el pie dormido : her foot's numb, her foot's gone to sleep>
dormilón, -lona *n* **:** sleepyhead, late riser
dormir {27} *vt* **:** to put to sleep — *vi* **:** to sleep — **dormirse** *vr* **:** to fall asleep
dormitar *vi* **:** to snooze, to doze
dormitorio *nm* **1 :** bedroom **2 :** dormitory
dorsal[1] *adj* **:** dorsal
dorsal[2] *nm* **:** number (worn in sports)
dorso *nm* **1 :** back <el dorso de la mano : the back of the hand> **2** *Mex* **:** backstroke
dos *adj & nm* **:** two
doscientos[1], **-tas** *adj* **:** two hundred
doscientos[2] *nms & pl* **:** two hundred
dosel *nm* **:** canopy
dosificación *nf, pl* **-ciones :** dosage
dosis *nfs & pl* **1 :** dose **2 :** amount, quantity
dotación *nf, pl* **-ciones 1 :** endowment, funding **2 :** staff, personnel
dotado, -da *adj* **1 :** gifted **2 ~ de :** endowed with, equipped with
dotar *vt* **1 :** to provide, to equip **2 :** to endow
dote *nf* **1 :** dowry **2 dotes** *nfpl* **:** talent, gift
doy → **dar**
draga *nf* **:** dredge
dragado *nm* **:** dredging
dragar {52} *vt* **:** to dredge
dragón *nm, pl* **dragones 1 :** dragon **2 :** snapdragon
drague, etc. → **dragar**
drama *nm* **:** drama
dramático, -ca *adj* **:** dramatic — **dramáticamente** *adv*
dramatizar {21} *vt* **:** to dramatize — **dramatización** *nf*
dramaturgo, -ga *n* **:** dramatist, playwright
drástico, -ca *adj* **:** drastic — **drásticamente** *adv*
drenaje *nm* **:** drainage
drenar *vt* **:** to drain
drene *nm Mex* **:** drain
driblar *vi* **:** to dribble (in basketball)
drible *nm* **:** dribble (in basketball)
droga *nf* **:** drug
drogadicción *nf, pl* **-ciones :** drug addiction
drogadicto, -ta *n* **:** drug addict
drogar {52} *vt* **:** to drug — **drogarse** *vr* **:** to take drugs
drogue, etc. → **drogar**
droguería *nf* FARMACIA **:** drugstore
dual *adj* **:** dual
dualidad *nf* **:** duality
dualismo *nm* **:** dualism
ducha *nf* **:** shower <darse una ducha : to take a shower>
ducharse *vr* **:** to take a shower
ducho, -cha *adj* **:** experienced, skilled, expert
ducto *nm* **1 :** duct, shaft **2 :** pipeline
duda *nf* **:** doubt <no cabe duda : there's no doubt about it>
dudar *vt* **:** to doubt — *vi* **~ en :** to hesitate to <no dudes en pedirme ayuda : don't hesitate to ask me for help>
dudoso, -sa *adj* **1 :** doubtful **2 :** dubious, questionable — **dudosamente** *adv*
duele, etc. → **doler**
duelo *nm* **1 :** duel **2** LUTO **:** mourning
duende *nm* **1 :** elf, goblin **2** ENCANTO **:** magic, charm <una bailarina que tiene duende : a dancer with a certain magic>
dueño, -na *nmf* **1 :** owner, proprietor, proprietress *f* **2 :** landlord, landlady *f*
duerme, etc. → **dormir**
dueto *nm* **:** duet
dulce[1] *adv* **:** sweetly, softly
dulce[2] *adj* **1 :** sweet **2 :** mild, gentle, mellow — **dulcemente** *adv*
dulce[3] *nm* **:** candy, sweet

dulcería *nf* : candy store
dulcificante *nm* : sweetener
dulzura *nf* **1** : sweetness **2** : gentleness, mellowness
duna *nf* : dune
dúo *nm* : duo, duet
duodécimo[1], **-ma** *adj* : twelfth
duodécimo[2], **-ma** *nm* : twelfth (in a series)
dúplex *nms & pl* : duplex apartment
duplicación *nf, pl* **-ciones** : duplication, copying
duplicado *nm* : duplicate, copy
duplicar {72} *vt* **1** : to double **2** : to duplicate, to copy
duplicidad *nf* : duplicity
duque *nm* : duke
duquesa *nf* : duchess
durabilidad *nf* : durability
durable → **duradero**
duración *nf, pl* **-ciones** : duration, length
duradero, -ra *adj* : durable, lasting
duramente *adv* **1** : harshly, severely **2** : hard
durante *prep* : during <durante todo el día : all day long> <trabajó durante tres horas : he worked for three hours>
durar *vi* : to last, to endure
durazno *nm* **1** : peach **2** : peach tree
dureza *nf* **1** : hardness, toughness **2** : severity, harshness
durmiente[1] *adj* : sleeping
durmiente[2] *nmf* : sleeper
durmió, etc. → **dormir**
duro[1] *adv* : hard <trabajé tan duro : I worked so hard>
duro[2], -ra *adj* **1** : hard, tough **2** : harsh, severe

E

e[1] *nf* : fifth letter of the Spanish alphabet
e[2] *conj* (*used instead of* **y** *before words beginning with i or hi*) : and
ebanista *nmf* : cabinetmaker
ebanistería *nf* : cabinetmaking
ébano *nm* : ebony
ebriedad *nf* EMBRIAGUEZ : inebriation, drunkenness
ebrio, -bria *adj* EMBRIAGADO : inebriated, drunk
ebullición *nf, pl* **-ciones** : boiling
eccéntrico → **excéntrico**
echar *vt* **1** LANZAR : to throw, to cast, to hurl **2** EXPULSAR : to throw out, to expel **3** EMITIR : to emit, give off **4** BROTAR : to sprout, to put forth **5** DESPEDIR : to fire, to dismiss **6** : to put in, to add **7 echar a perder** : to spoil, to ruin **8 echar de menos** : to miss <echan de menos a su madre : they miss their mother> — *vi* **1** : to start off **2 ~ a** : to begin to — **echarse** *vr* **1** : to throw oneself **2** : to lie down **3** : to put on **4 ~ a** : to start to **5 echarse a perder** : to go bad, to spoil **6 echárselas de** : to pose as
ecléctico, -ca *adj* : eclectic
eclesiástico[1], **-ca** *adj* : ecclesiastical, ecclesiastic
eclesiástico[2] *nm* CLÉRIGO : cleric, clergyman
eclipsar *vt* **1** : to eclipse **2** : to outshine, to surpass
eclipse *nm* : eclipse
eco *nm* : echo
ecografía *nf* : ultrasound scanning
ecología *nf* : ecology
ecológico, -ca *adj* : ecological — **ecológicamente** *adv*
ecologista *nmf* : ecologist, environmentalist
ecólogo, -ga *n* : ecologist
economía *nf* **1** : economy **2** : economics
económicamente *adv* : financially
económico, -ca *adj* : economic, economical
economista *nmf* : economist
economizar {21} *vt* : to save, to economize on — *vi* : to save up, to be frugal
ecosistema *nm* : ecosystem
ecuación *nf, pl* **-ciones** : equation
ecuador *nm* : equator
ecuánime *adj* **1** : even-tempered **2** : impartial
ecuanimidad *nf* **1** : equanimity **2** : impartiality
ecuatorial *adj* : equatorial
ecuatoriano, -na *adj & n* : Ecuadorian
ecuestre *adj* : equestrian
ecuménico, -ca *adj* : ecumenical
eczema *nm* : eczema
edad *nf* **1** : age <¿qué edad tiene? : how old is she?> **2** ÉPOCA, ERA : epoch, era
edema *nm* : edema
Edén *nm, pl* **Edenes** : Eden, paradise
edición *nf, pl* **-ciones 1** : edition **2** : publication, publishing
edicto *nm* : edict, proclamation
edificación *nf, pl* **-ciones 1** : edification **2** : construction, building
edificante *adj* : edifying
edificar {72} *vt* **1** : to edify **2** CONSTRUIR : to build, to construct
edificio *nm* : building, edifice
editar *vt* **1** : to edit **2** PUBLICAR : to publish
editor[1], **-tora** *adj* : publishing <casa editora : publishing house>
editor[2], **-tora** *n* **1** : editor **2** : publisher
editora *nf* : publisher, publishing company
editorial[1] *adj* **1** : publishing **2** : editorial
editorial[2] *nm* : editorial
editorial[3] *nf* : publishing house

editorializar {21} *vi* **:** to editorialize

edredón *nm, pl* **-dones** COBERTOR, COLCHA **:** comforter, eiderdown, quilt

educable *adj* **:** educable, teachable

educación *nf, pl* **-ciones 1** ENSEÑANZA **:** education **2 :** manners *pl* — **educacional** *adj*

educado, -da *adj* **:** polite, well-mannered

educador, -dora *n* **:** educator

educando, -da *n* ALUMNO, PUPILO **:** pupil, student

educar {72} *vt* **1 :** to educate **2** CRIAR **:** to bring up, to raise **3 :** to train — **educarse** *vr* **:** to be educated

educativo, -va *adj* **:** educational

efectista *adj* **:** dramatic, sensational

efectivamente *adv* **:** really, actually

efectividad *nf* **:** effectiveness

efectivo[1], **-va** *adj* **1 :** effective **2 :** real, actual **3 :** permanent, regular (of employment)

efectivo[2] *nm* **:** cash

efecto *nm* **1 :** effect **2 en ~ :** actually, in fact **3 efectos** *nmpl* **:** goods, property <efectos personales : personal effects>

efectuar {3} *vt* **:** to carry out, to bring about

efervescencia *nf* **1 :** effervescence **2 :** vivacity, high spirits *pl*

efervescente *adj* **1 :** effervescent **2 :** vivacious

eficacia *nf* **1 :** effectiveness, efficacy **2 :** efficiency

eficaz *adj, pl* **-caces 1 :** effective **2** EFICIENTE **:** efficient — **eficazmente** *adv*

eficiencia *nf* **:** efficiency

eficiente *adj* EFICAZ **:** efficient — **eficientemente** *adv*

eficientizar {21} *vt Mex* **:** to streamline, to make more efficient

efigie *nf* **:** effigy

efímera *nf* **:** mayfly

efímero, -ra *adj* **:** ephemeral

efusión *nf, pl* **-siones 1 :** effusion **2 :** warmth, effusiveness **3 con ~ :** effusively

efusivo, -va *adj* **:** effusive — **efusivamente** *adv*

egipcio, -cia *adj & n* **:** Egyptian

eglefino *nm* **:** haddock

ego *nm* **:** ego

egocéntrico, -ca *adj* **:** egocentric, self-centered

egoísmo *nm* **:** selfishness, egoism

egoísta[1] *adj* **:** selfish, egoistic

egoísta[2] *nmf* **:** egoist, selfish person

egotismo *nm* **:** egotism, conceit

egotista[1] *adj* **:** egotistic, egotistical, conceited

egotista[2] *nmf* **:** egotist, conceited person

egresado, -da *n* **:** graduate

egresar *vi* **:** to graduate

egreso *nm* **1 :** graduation **2 ingresos y egresos :** income and expenditure

eje *nm* **1 :** axle **2 :** axis

ejecución *nf, pl* **-ciones :** execution

ejecutante *nmf* **:** performer

ejecutar *vt* **1 :** to execute, to put to death **2 :** to carry out, to perform

ejecutivo, -va *adj & n* **:** executive

ejecutor, -tora *n* **:** executor

ejemplar[1] *adj* **:** exemplary, model

ejemplar[2] *nm* **1 :** copy (of a book, magazine, etc.) **2 :** specimen, example

ejemplificar {72} *vt* **:** to exemplify, to illustrate

ejemplo *nm* **1 :** example **2 por ~ :** for example **3 dar ejemplo :** to set an example

ejercer {86} *vi* **~ de :** to practice as, to work as — *vt* **1 :** to practice **2 :** exercise (a right) **3 :** to exert

ejercicio *nm* **1 :** exercise **2 :** practice

ejercitar *vt* **1 :** to exercise **2** ADIESTRAR **:** to drill, to train

ejército *nm* **:** army

ejidal *adj Mex* **:** cooperative

ejido *nm* **1 :** common land **2** *Mex* **:** cooperative

ejote *nm Mex* **:** green bean

el[1] *pron* (*referring to masculine nouns*) **1 :** the one <tengo mi libro y el tuyo : I have my book and yours> <de los cantantes me gusta el de México : I prefer the singer from México> **2 el que :** he who, whoever, the one that <el que vino ayer : the one who came yesterday> <el que trabaja duro estará contento : he who works hard will be happy>

el[2], **la** *art, pl* **los, las :** the <los niños están en la casa : the boys are in the house> <me duele el pie : my foot hurts>

él *pron* **:** he, him <él es mi amigo : he's my friend> <hablaremos con él : we will speak with him>

elaboración *nf, pl* **-ciones 1** PRODUCCIÓN **:** production, making **2 :** preparation, devising

elaborado, -da *adj* **:** elaborate

elaborar *vt* **1 :** to make, to produce **2 :** to devise, to draw up

elasticidad *nf* **:** elasticity

elástico[1], **-ca** *adj* **1** FLEXIBLE **:** flexible **2 :** elastic

elástico[2] *nm* **1 :** elastic (material) **2 :** rubber band

elección *nf, pl* **-ciones 1** SELECCIÓN **:** choice, selection **2 :** election

electivo, -va *adj* **:** elective

electo, -ta *adj* **:** elect <el presidente electo : the president-elect>

elector, -tora *n* **:** elector, voter

electorado *nm* **:** electorate

electoral *adj* **:** electoral, election

electricidad *nf* **:** electricity

electricista *nmf* **:** electrician

eléctrico, -ca *adj* **:** electric, electrical

electrificar {72} *vt* **:** to electrify — **electrificación** *nf*

electrizar {21} *vt* **:** to electrify, to thrill — **electrizante** *adj*

electrocardiógrafo *nm* : electrocardiograph
electrocardiograma *nm* : electrocardiogram
electrocutar *vt* : to electrocute — **electrocución** *nf*
electrodo *nm* : electrode
electrodoméstico *nm* : electric appliance
electroimán *nm, pl* **-manes** : electromagnet
electrólisis *nfs & pl* : electrolysis
electrolito *nm* : electrolyte
electromagnético, -ca *adj* : electromagnetic
electromagnetismo *nm* : electromagnetism
electrón *nm, pl* **-trones** : electron
electrónica *nf* : electronics
electrónico, -ca *adj* : electronic — **electrónicamente** *adv*
elefante, -ta *n* : elephant
elegancia *nf* : elegance
elegante *adj* : elegant, smart — **elegantemente** *adv*
elegía *nf* : elegy
elegíaco, -ca *adj* : elegiac
elegibilidad *nf* : eligibility
elegible *adj* : eligible
elegido, -da *adj* **1** : chosen, selected **2** : elected
elegir {28} *vt* **1** ESCOGER, SELECCIONAR : to choose, to select **2** : to elect
elemental *adj* **1** : elementary, basic **2** : fundamental, essential
elemento *nm* : element
elenco *nm* : cast (of actors)
elepé *nm* : long-playing record
elevación *nf, pl* **-ciones** : elevation, height
elevado, -da *adj* **1** : elevated, lofty **2** : high
elevador *nm* ASCENSOR : elevator
elevar *vt* **1** ALZAR : to raise, to lift **2** AUMENTAR : to raise, to increase **3** : to elevate (in a hierarchy), to promote **4** : to present, to submit — **elevarse** *vr* : to rise
elfo *nm* : elf
eliminación *nf, pl* **-ciones** : elimination, removal
eliminar *vt* **1** : to eliminate, to remove **2** : to do in, to kill
elipse *nf* : ellipse
elipsis *nf* : ellipsis
elíptico, -ca *adj* : elliptical, elliptic
elite *or* **élite** *nf* : elite
elixir *or* **elíxir** *nm* : elixir
ella *pron* : she, her <ella es mi amiga : she is my friend> <nos fuimos con ella : we left with her>
ello *pron* : it <es por ello que me voy : that's why I'm going>
ellos, ellas *pron pl* **1** : they, them **2 de ellos, de ellas** : theirs
elocución *nf, pl* **-ciones** : elocution
elocuencia *nf* : eloquence
elocuente *adj* : eloquent — **elocuentemente** *adv*
elogiar *vt* ENCOMIAR : to praise
elogio *nm* : praise
elote *nm* **1** *Mex* : corn, maize **2** *CA, Mex* : corncob
elucidación *nf, pl* **-ciones** ESCLARECIMIENTO : elucidation
elucidar *vt* ESCLARECER : to elucidate
eludir *vt* EVADIR : to evade, to avoid, to elude
emanación *nf, pl* **-ciones** : emanation
emanar *vi* **~ de** : to emanate from — *vt* : to exude
emancipar *vt* : to emancipate — **emancipación** *nf*
embadurnar *vt* EMBARRAR : to smear, to daub
embajada *nf* : embassy
embajador, -dora *n* : ambassador
embalaje *nm* : packing, packaging
embalar *vt* EMPAQUETAR : to pack
embaldosar *vt* : to tile, to pave with tiles
embalsamar *vt* : to embalm
embalsar *vt* : to dam, to dam up
embalse *nm* : dam, reservoir
embarazada *adj* ENCINTA, PREÑADA : pregnant, expecting
embarazar {21} *vt* **1** : to obstruct, to hamper **2** PREÑAR : to make pregnant
embarazo *nm* : pregnancy
embarazoso, -sa *adj* : embarrassing, awkward
embarcación *nf, pl* **-ciones** : boat, craft
embarcadero *nm* : wharf, pier, jetty
embarcar {72} *vi* : to embark, to board — *vt* : to load
embarco *nm* : embarkation
embargar {52} *vt* **1** : to seize, to impound **2** : to overwhelm
embargo *nm* **1** : seizure **2** : embargo **3 sin ~** : however, nevertheless
embarque *nm* **1** : embarkation **2** : shipment
embarrancar {72} *vi* **1** : to run aground **2** : to get bogged down
embarrar *vt* **1** : to cover with mud **2** EMBADURNAR : to smear
embarullar *vt fam* : to muddle, to confuse — **embarullarse** *vr fam* : to get mixed up
embate *nm* **1** : onslaught **2** : battering (of waves or wind)
embaucador, -dora *n* : swindler, deceiver
embaucar {72} *vt* : to trick, to swindle
embeber *vt* : to absorb, to soak up — *vi* : to shrink
embelesado, -da *adj* : spellbound
embelesar *vt* : to enchant, to captivate
embellecer {53} *vt* : to embellish, to beautify
embellecimiento *nm* : beautification, embellishment
embestida *nf* **1** : charge (of a bull) **2** ARREMETIDA : attack, onslaught
embestir {54} *vt* : to hit, to run into, to charge at — *vi* ARREMETER : to charge, to attack

emblanquecer {53} *vt* BLANQUEAR : to bleach, to whiten — **emblanquecerse** *vr* : to turn white
emblema *nm* : emblem
emblemático, -ca *adj* : emblematic
embolia *nf* : embolism
émbolo *nm* : piston
embolsarse *vr* **1** : to pocket (money) **2** : to collect (payment)
emborracharse *vr* EMBRIAGARSE : to get drunk
emborronar *vt* **1** : to blot, to smudge **2** GARABATEAR : to scribble
emboscada *nf* : ambush
emboscar {72} *vt* : to ambush — **emboscarse** *vr* : to lie in ambush
embotadura *nf* : bluntness, dullness
embotar *vt* **1** : to dull, to blunt **2** : to weaken, to enervate
embotellamiento *nm* ATASCO : traffic jam
embotellar *vt* ENVASAR : to bottle
embragar {52} *vi* : to engage the clutch
embrague *nm* : clutch
embravecerse {53} *vr* **1** : to get furious **2** : to get rough <el mar se embraveció : the sea became tempestuous>
embriagado, -da *adj* : inebriated, drunk
embriagador, -dora *adj* : intoxicating
embriagarse {52} *vr* EMBORRACHARSE : to get drunk
embriaguez *nf* EBRIEDAD : drunkenness, inebriation
embrión *nm, pl* **embriones** : embryo
embrionario, -ria *adj* : embryonic
embrollo *nm* ENREDO : imbroglio, confusion
embrujar *vt* HECHIZAR : to bewitch
embrujo *nm* : spell, curse
embudo *nm* : funnel
embuste *nm* **1** MENTIRA : lie, fib **2** ENGAÑO : trick, hoax
embustero[1], **-ra** *adj* : lying, deceitful
embustero[2], **-ra** *n* : liar, cheat
embutido *nm* **1** : sausage **2** : inlaid work
embutir *vt* **1** : to cram, to stuff, to jam **2** : to inlay
emergencia *nf* **1** : emergency **2** : emergence
emergente *adj* **1** : emergent **2** : consequent, resultant
emerger {15} *vi* : to emerge, to surface
emético[1], **-ca** *adj* : emetic
emético[2] *nm* : emetic
emigración *nf, pl* **-ciones 1** : emigration **2** : migration
emigrante *adj & nmf* : emigrant
emigrar *vi* **1** : to emigrate **2** : to migrate
eminencia *nf* : eminence
eminente *adj* : eminent, distinguished
eminentemente *adv* : basically, essentially
emisario[1], **-ria** *n* : emissary
emisario[2] *nm* : outlet (of a body of water)
emisión *nf, pl* **-siones 1** : emission **2** : broadcast **3** : issue <emisión de acciones : stock issue>
emisor *nm* TRANSMISOR : television or radio transmitter
emisora *nf* : radio station
emitir *vt* **1** : to emit, to give off **2** : to broadcast **3** : to issue **4** : to cast (a vote)
emoción *nf, pl* **-ciones** : emotion — **emocional** *adj* — **emocionalmente** *adv*
emocionado, -da *adj* **1** : moved, affected by emotion **2** ENTUSIASMADO : excited
emocionante *adj* **1** CONMOVEDOR : moving, touching **2** EXCITANTE : exciting, thrilling
emocionar *vt* **1** CONMOVER : to move, to touch **2** : to excite, to thrill — **emocionarse** *vr*
emotivo, -va *adj* : emotional, moving
empacador, -dora *n* : packer
empacar {72} *vt* **1** EMPAQUETAR : to pack **2** : to bale — *vi* : to pack — **empacarse** *vr* **1** : to balk, to refuse to budge **2** *Col, Mex fam* : to eat ravenously, to devour
empachar *vt* **1** ESTORBAR : to obstruct **2** : to give indigestion to **3** DISFRAZAR : to disguise, to mask — **empacharse** *vr* **1** INDIGESTARSE : to get indigestion **2** AVERGONZARSE : to be embarrassed
empacho *nm* **1** INDIGESTIÓN : indigestion **2** VERGÜENZA : embarrassment **3** **no tener empacho en** : to have no qualms about
empadronarse *vr* : to register to vote
empalagar {52} *vt* **1** : to cloy, to surfeit **2** FASTIDIAR : to annoy, to bother
empalagoso, -sa *adj* MELOSO : cloying, excessively sweet
empalar *vt* : to impale
empalizada *nf* : palisade (fence)
empalmar *vt* **1** : to splice, to link **2** : to combine — *vi* : to meet, to converge
empalme *nm* **1** CONEXIÓN : connection, link **2** : junction
empanada *nf* : pie, turnover
empanadilla *nf* : meat or seafood pie
empanar *vt* : to bread
empantanado, -da *adj* : bogged down, delayed
empañar *vt* **1** : to steam up **2** : to tarnish, to sully
empapado, -da *adj* : soggy, sodden
empapar *vt* MOJAR : to soak, to drench — **empaparse** *vr* **1** : to get soaking wet **2** **~ de** : to absorb, to be imbued with
empapelar *vt* : to wallpaper
empaque *nm fam* **1** : presence, bearing **2** : pomposity **3** DESCARO : impudence, nerve
empaquetar *vt* EMBALAR : to pack, to package — **empaquetarse** *vr fam* : to dress up

emparedado *nm* : sandwich

emparedar *vt* : to wall in, to confine

emparejar *vt* **1** : to pair, to match up **2** : to make even — *vi* : to catch up — **emparejarse** *vr* : to pair up

emparentado, -da *adj* : related

emparentar {55} *vi* : to become related by marriage

emparrillado *nm Mex* : gridiron (in football)

empastar *vt* **1** : to fill (a tooth) **2** : to bind (a book)

empaste *nm* : filling (of a tooth)

empatar *vt* : to tie, to connect — *vi* : to result in a draw, to be tied — **empatarse** *vr Ven* : to hook up, to link together

empate *nm* : draw, tie

empatía *nf* : empathy

empecinado, -da *adj* TERCO : stubborn

empecinarse *vr* OBSTINARSE : to be stubborn, to persist

empedernido, -da *adj* INCORREGIBLE : hardened, inveterate

empedrado *nm* : paving, pavement

empedrar {55} *vt* : to pave (with stones)

empeine *nm* : instep

empellón *nm, pl* **-llones** : shove, push

empelotado, -da *adj* **1** *Mex fam* : madly in love **2** *fam* : stark naked

empeñado, -da *adj* : determined, committed

empeñar *vt* **1** : to pawn **2** : to pledge, to give (one's word) — **empeñarse** *vr* **1** : to insist stubbornly **2** : to make an effort

empeño *nm* **1** : pledge, commitment **2** : insistence **3** ESFUERZO : effort, determination **4** : pawning <casa de empeños : pawnshop>

empeoramiento *nm* : worsening, deterioration

empeorar *vi* : to deteriorate, to get worse — *vt* : to make worse

empequeñecer {53} *vi* : to diminish, to become smaller — *vt* : to minimize, to make smaller

emperador *nm* : emperor

emperatriz *nf, pl* **-trices** : empress

empero *conj* : however, nevertheless

empezar {29} *v* COMENZAR : to start, to begin

empinado, -da *adj* : steep

empinar *vt* ELEVAR : to lift, to raise — **empinarse** *vr* : to stand on tiptoe

empírico, -ca *adj* : empirical — **empíricamente** *adv*

emplasto *nm* : poultice, dressing

emplazamiento *nm* **1** : location, site **2** CITACIÓN : summons, subpoena

emplazar {21} *vt* **1** CONVOCAR : to convene, to summon **2** : to subpoena **3** UBICAR : to place, to position

empleado, -da *n* : employee

empleador, -dora *n* PATRÓN : employer

emplear *vt* **1** : to employ **2** USAR : to use — **emplearse** *vr* **1** : to get a job **2** : to occupy oneself

empleo *nm* **1** OCUPACIÓN : employment, occupation, job **2** : use, usage

empobrecer {53} *vt* : to impoverish — *vi* : to become poor — **empobrecerse** *vr*

empobrecimiento *nm* : impoverishment

empollar *vi* : to brood eggs — *vt* : to incubate

empolvado, -da *adj* **1** : dusty **2** : powdered, powdery

empolvar *vt* **1** : to cover with dust **2** : to powder — **empolvarse** *vr* **1** : to gather dust **2** : to powder one's face

emporio *nm* **1** : center, capital, empire <un emporio cultural : a cultural center> <un emporio financiero : a financial empire> **2** : department store

empotrado, -da *adj* : built-in <armarios empotrados : built-in cabinets>

empotrar *vt* : to build into, to embed

emprendedor, -dora *adj* : enterprising

emprender *vt* : to undertake, to begin

empresa *nf* **1** COMPAÑÍA, FIRMA : company, corporation, firm **2** : undertaking, venture

empresariado *nm* **1** : business world **2** : management, managers *pl*

empresarial *adj* : business, managerial, corporate

empresario, -ria *n* **1** : manager **2** : businessman *m*, businesswoman *f* **3** : impresario

empujar *vi* : to push, to shove — *vt* **1** : to push **2** PRESIONAR : to spur on, to press

empuje *nm* : impetus, drive

empujón *nm, pl* **-jones** : push, shove

empuñadura *nf* MANGO : hilt, handle

empuñar *vt* **1** ASIR : to grasp **2 empuñar las armas** : to take up arms

emú *nm* : emu

emular *vt* IMITAR : to emulate — **emulación** *nf*

emulsión *nf, pl* **-siones** : emulsion

emulsionante *nm* : emulsifier

emulsionar *vt* : to emulsify

en *prep* **1** : in <en el bolsillo : in one's pocket> <en una semana : in a week> **2** : on <en la mesa : on the table> **3** : at <en casa : at home> <en el trabajo : at work> <en ese momento : at that moment>

enagua *nf* : petticoat, slip

enajenación *nf, pl* **-ciones** **1** : transfer (of property) **2** : alienation **3** : absentmindedness

enajenado, -da *adj* : out of one's mind

enajenar *vt* **1** : to transfer (property) **2** : to alienate **3** : to enrapture — **enajenarse** *vr* **1** : to become estranged **2** : to go mad

enaltecer {53} *vt* : to praise, to extol

enamorado[1]**, -da** *adj* : in love

enamorado[2]**, -da** *n* : lover, sweetheart

enamoramiento *nm* : infatuation, crush

enamorar *vt* **:** to enamor, to win the love of — **enamorarse** *vr* **:** to fall in love
enamoriscarse {72} *vr fam* **:** to have a crush, to be infatuated
enamorizado, -da *adj* **:** amorous, passionate
enano[1], **-na** *adj* **:** tiny, minute
enano[2], **-na** *n* **:** dwarf, midget
enarbolar *vt* **1 :** to hoist, to raise **2 :** to brandish
enarcar {72} *vt* **:** to arch, to raise
enardecer {53} *vt* **1 :** to arouse (anger, passions) **2 :** to stir up, to excite — **enardecerse** *vr*
encabezado *nm Mex* **:** headline
encabezamiento *nm* **1 :** heading **2 :** salutation, opening
encabezar {21} *vt* **1 :** to head, to lead **2 :** to put a heading on
encabritarse *vr* **1 :** to rear up **2** *fam* **:** to get angry
encadenar *vt* **1 :** to chain **2 :** to connect, to link **3** INMOVILIZAR **:** to immobilize
encajar *vi* **:** to fit, to fit together, to fit in — *vt* **1 :** to insert, to stick **2 :** to take, to cope with <encajó el golpe : he withstood the blow>
encaje *nm* **1 :** lace **2 :** financial reserve
encajonar *vt* **1 :** to box, to crate **2 :** to cram in
encalar *vt* **:** to whitewash
encallar *vi* **1 :** to run aground **2 :** to get stuck
encallecido, -da *adj* **:** callused
encamar *vt* **:** to confine to a bed
encaminado, -da *adj* **1 :** on the right track **2 ~ a :** aimed at, designed to
encaminar *vt* **1 :** to direct, to channel **2 :** to head in the right direction — **encaminarse** *vr* **~ a :** to head for, to aim at
encandilar *vt* **:** to dazzle
encanecer {53} *vi* **:** to gray, to go gray
encantado, -da *adj* **1 :** charmed, bewitched **2 :** delighted
encantador[1], **-dora** *adj* **:** charming, delightful
encantador[2], **-dora** *n* **:** magician
encantamiento *nm* **:** enchantment, spell
encantar *vt* **1 :** to enchant, to bewitch **2 :** to charm, to delight <me encanta esta canción : I love this song>
encanto *nm* **1 :** charm, fascination **2** HECHIZO **:** spell **3 :** delightful person or thing
encañonar *vt* **:** to point (a gun) at, to hold up
encapotado, -da *adj* **:** cloudy, overcast
encapotarse *vr* **:** to cloud over, to become overcast
encaprichado, -da *adj* **:** infatuated
encaprichamiento *nm* **:** infatuation
encapuchado, -da *adj* **:** hooded
encarado, -da *adj* **estar mal encarado** *fam* **:** to be ugly-looking, to look mean
encaramar *vt* **:** to raise, to lift up — **encaramarse** *vr* **:** to perch
encarar *vt* CONFRONTAR **:** to face, to confront
encarcelación *nf* → **encarcelamiento**
encarcelamiento *nm* **:** incarceration, imprisonment
encarcelar *vt* **:** to incarcerate, to imprison
encarecer {53} *vt* **1 :** to increase, to raise (price, value) **2 :** to beseech, to entreat — **encarecerse** *vr* **:** to become more expensive
encarecidamente *adv* **:** insistently, urgently
encarecimiento *nm* **:** increase, rise (in price)
encargado[1], **-da** *adj* **:** in charge
encargado[2], **-da** *n* **:** manager, person in charge
encargar {52} *vt* **1 :** to put in charge of **2 :** to recommend, to advise **3 :** to order, to request — **encargarse** *vr* **~ de :** to take charge of
encargo *nm* **1 :** errand **2 :** job assignment **3 :** order <hecho de encargo : custom-made, made to order>
encariñarse *vr* **~ con :** to become fond of, to grow attached to
encarnación *nf, pl* **-ciones :** incarnation, embodiment
encarnado[1], **-da** *adj* **1 :** incarnate **2 :** flesh-colored **3 :** red **4 :** ingrown
encarnado[2] *nm* **:** red
encarnar *vt* **:** to incarnate, to embody — **encarnarse** *vr* **encarnarse una uña :** to have an ingrown nail
encarnizado, -da *adj* **1 :** bloodshot, inflamed **2 :** fierce, bloody
encarnizar {21} *vt* **:** to enrage, to infuriate — **encarnizarse** *vr* **:** to be brutal, to attack viciously
encarrilar *vt* **:** to guide, to put on the right track
encasillar *vt* CLASIFICAR **:** to classify, to pigeonhole, to categorize
encausar *vt* **:** to prosecute, to charge
encauzar {21} *vt* **:** to channel, to guide — **encauzarse** *vr*
encebollado, -da *adj* **:** cooked with onions
encefalitis *nms & pl* **:** encephalitis
encendedor *nm* **:** lighter
encender {56} *vi* **:** to light — *vt* **1 :** to light, to set fire to **2** PRENDER **:** to switch on **3 :** to start (a motor) **4 :** to arouse, to kindle — **encenderse** *vr* **1 :** to get excited **2 :** to blush
encendido[1], **-da** *adj* **1 :** burning **2 :** flushed **3 :** fiery, passionate
encendido[2] *nm* **:** ignition
encerado *nm* **1 :** waxing, polishing **2 :** blackboard
encerar *vt* **:** to wax, to polish
encerrar {55} *vt* **1 :** to lock up, to shut away **2 :** to contain, to include **3 :** to involve, to entail
encerrona *nf* **1** TRAMPA **:** trap, setup **2** **prepararle una encerrona a alguien**

: to set a trap for someone, to set someone up

encestar *vi* : to make a basket (in basketball)

enchapado *nm* : plating, coating (of metal)

encharcamiento *nm* : flood, flooding

encharcar {72} *vt* : to flood, to swamp — **encharcarse** *vr*

enchilada *nf* : enchilada

enchilar *vt Mex* : to season with chili

enchuecar {72} *vt Chile, Mex fam* : to make crooked, to twist

enchufar *vt* **1** : to plug in **2** : to connect, to fit together

enchufe *nm* **1** : connection **2** : plug, socket

encía *nf* : gum (tissue)

encíclica *nf* : encyclical

enciclopedia *nf* : encyclopedia

enciclopédico, -ca *adj* : encyclopedic

encierro *nm* **1** : confinement **2** : enclosure

encima *adv* **1** : on top, above **2** ADEMÁS : as well, besides **3 ~ de** : on, on top of, over **4 por encima de** : above, beyond <por encima de la ley : above the law> **5 echarse encima** : to take upon oneself **6 estar encima de** *fam* : to nag, to criticize **7 quitarse de encima** : to get rid of

encina *nf* : evergreen oak

encinta *adj* EMBARAZADA, PREÑADA : pregnant, expecting

enclaustrado, -da *adj* : cloistered, shut away

enclavado, -da *adj* : buried

enclenque *adj* : weak, sickly

encoger {15} *vt* **1** : to shrink, to make smaller **2** : to intimidate — *vi* : to shrink, to contract — **encogerse** *vr* **1** : to shrink **2** : to be intimidated, to cower, to cringe **3 encogerse de hombros** : to shrug <one's shoulders>

encogido, -da *adj* **1** : shriveled, shrunken **2** TÍMIDO : shy, inhibited

encogimiento *nm* **1** : shrinking, shrinkage **2** : shrug **3** TIMIDEZ : shyness

encolar *vt* : to paste, to glue

encolerizar {21} *vt* ENFURECER : to enrage, to infuriate — **encolerizarse** *vr*

encomendar {55} *vt* CONFIAR : to entrust, to commend — **encomendarse** *vr*

encomiable *adj* : commendable, praiseworthy

encomiar *vt* ELOGIAR : to praise, to pay tribute to

encomienda *nf* **1** : charge, mission **2** : royal land grant **3** : parcel

encomio *nm* : praise, eulogy

encomioso, -sa *adj* : eulogistic, laudatory

enconar *vt* **1** : to irritate, to anger **2** : to inflame — **enconarse** *vr* **1** : to become heated **2** : to fester

encono *nm* **1** RENCOR : animosity, rancor **2** : inflamation, infection

encontrado, -da *adj* : contrary, opposing

encontrar {19} *vt* **1** HALLAR : to find **2** : to encounter, to meet — **encontrarse** *vr* **1** REUNIRSE : to meet **2** : to clash, to conflict **3** : to be <su abuelo se encuentra mejor : her grandfather is doing better>

encorvar *vt* : to bend, to curve — **encorvarse** *vr* : to hunch over, to stoop

encrespar *vt* **1** : to curl, to ruffle, to ripple **2** : to annoy, to irritate — **encresparse** *vr* **1** : to curl one's hair **2** : to become choppy **3** : to get annoyed

encrucijada *nf* : crossroads

encuadernación *nf, pl* **-ciones** : bookbinding

encuadernar *vt* EMPASTAR : to bind (a book)

encuadrar *vt* **1** ENMARCAR : to frame **2** ENCAJAR : to fit, to insert **3** COMPRENDER : to contain, to include

encubierto *pp* → **encubrir**

encubrimiento *nm* : cover-up

encubrir {2} *vt* : to cover up, to conceal

encuentro *nm* **1** : meeting, encounter **2** : conference, congress

encuerado, -da *adj fam* : naked

encuerar *vt fam* : to undress

encuesta *nf* **1** INVESTIGACIÓN, PESQUISA : inquiry, investigation **2** SONDEO : survey

encuestador, -dora *n* : pollster

encuestar *vt* : to poll, to take a survey of

encumbrado, -da *adj* **1** : lofty, high **2** : eminent, distinguished

encumbrar *vt* **1** : to exalt, to elevate **2** : to extol — **encumbrarse** *vr* : to reach the top

encurtir *vt* ESCABECHAR : to pickle

ende *adv* **por ~** : therefore, consequently

endeble *adj* : feeble, weak

endeblez *nf* : weakness, frailty

endémico, -ca *adj* : endemic

endemoniado, -da *adj* : fiendish, diabolical

endentecer {53} *vi* : to teethe

enderezar {21} *vt* **1** : to straighten (out) **2** : to stand on end, to put upright

endeudado, -da *adj* : in debt, indebted

endeudamiento *nm* : indebtedness

endeudarse *vr* **1** : to go into debt **2** : to feel obliged

endiabladamente *adv* : extremely, diabolically

endiablado, -da *adj* **1** : devilish, diabolical **2** : complicated, difficult

endibia *or* **endivia** *nm* : endive

endilgar {52} *vt fam* : to spring, to foist <me endilgó la responsabilidad : he saddled me with the responsibility>

endocrino, -na *adj* : endocrine

endogamia *nf* : inbreeding

endosar *vt* : to endorse

endoso *nm* : endorsement

endulzante *nm* : sweetener

endulzar {21} *vt* **1** : to sweeten **2** : to soften, to mellow — **endulzarse** *vr*

endurecer {53} *vt* : to harden, to toughen — **endurecerse** *vr*

enebro *nm* : juniper

eneldo *nm* : dill

enema *nm* : enema

enemigo, -ga *adj & n* : enemy

enemistad *nf* : enmity, hostility

enemistar *vt* : to make enemies of — **enemistarse** *vr* **~ con** : to fall out with

energía *nf* : energy

enérgico, -ca *adj* **1** : energetic, vigorous **2** : forceful, emphatic — **enérgicamente** *adv*

energúmeno, -na *n fam* : lunatic, crazy person

enero *nm* : January

enervar *vt* **1** : to enervate **2** *fam* : to annoy, to get on one's nerves — **enervante** *adj*

enésimo, -ma *adj* : umpteenth, nth

enfadar *vt* **1** : to annoy, to make angry **2** *Mex fam* : to bore — **enfadarse** *vr* : to get angry, to get annoyed

enfado *nm* : anger, annoyance

enfadoso, -sa *adj* : irritating, annoying

enfardar *vt* : to bale

énfasis *nms & pl* : emphasis

enfático, -ca *adj* : emphatic — **enfáticamente** *adv*

enfatizar {21} *vt* DESTACAR, SUBRAYAR : to emphasize

enfermar *vt* : to make sick — *vi* : to fall ill, to get sick — **enfermarse** *vr*

enfermedad *nf* **1** INDISPOSICIÓN : sickness, illness **2** : disease

enfermería *nf* : infirmary

enfermero, -ra *n* : nurse

enfermizo, -za *adj* : sickly

enfermo[1], **-ma** *adj* : sick, ill

enfermo[2], **-ma** *n* **1** : sick person, invalid **2** PACIENTE : patient

enfilar *vt* **1** : to take, to go along <enfiló la carretera de Montevideo : she went up the road to Montevideo> **2** : to line up, to put in a row **3** : to string, to thread **4** : to aim, to direct — *vi* : to make one's way

enflaquecer {53} *vi* : to lose weight, to become thin — *vt* : to emaciate

enfocar {72} *vt* **1** : to focus (on) **2** : to consider, to look at

enfoque *nm* : focus

enfrascamiento *nm* : immersion, absorption

enfrascarse {72} *vr* **~ en** : to immerse oneself in, to get caught up in

enfrentamiento *nm* : clash, confrontation

enfrentar *vt* : to confront, to face — **enfrentarse** *vr* **1 ~ con** : to clash with **2 ~ a** : to face up to

enfrente *adv* **1** DELANTE : in front **2** : opposite

enfriamiento *nm* **1** CATARRO : chill, cold **2** : cooling off, damper

enfriar {85} *vt* **1** : to chill, to cool **2** : to cool down, to dampen — *vi* : to get cold — **enfriarse** *vr* : to get chilled, to catch a cold

enfundar *vt* : to sheathe, to encase

enfurecer {53} *vt* ENCOLERIZAR : to infuriate — **enfurecerse** *vr* : to fly into a rage

enfurecido, -da *adj* : furious, raging

enfurruñarse *vr fam* : to sulk

engalanar *vt* : to decorate, to deck out — **engalanarse** *vr* : to dress up

enganchar *vt* **1** : to hook, to snag **2** : to attach, to hitch up — **engancharse** *vr* **1** : to get snagged, to get hooked **2** : to enlist

enganche *nm* **1** : hook **2** : coupling, hitch **3** *Mex* : down payment

engañar *vt* **1** EMBAUCAR : to trick, to deceive, to mislead **2** : to cheat on, to be unfaithful to — **engañarse** *vr* **1** : to be mistaken **2** : to deceive oneself

engaño *nm* **1** : deception, trick **2** : fake, feint (in sports)

engañoso, -sa *adj* **1** : deceitful **2** : misleading, deceptive

engarrotarse *vr* : to stiffen up, to go numb

engatusamiento *nm* : cajolery

engatusar *vt* : to coax, to cajole

engendrar *vt* **1** : to beget, to father **2** : to give rise to, to engender

engentarse *vr Mex* : to be in a daze

englobar *vt* : to include, to embrace

engomar *vt* : to glue

engordar *vt* : to fatten, to fatten up — *vi* : to gain weight

engorro *nm* : nuisance, bother

engorroso, -sa *adj* : bothersome

engranaje *nm* : gears *pl*, cogs *pl*

engranar *vt* : to mesh, to engage — *vi* : to mesh gears

engrandecer {53} *vt* **1** : to enlarge **2** : to exaggerate **3** : to exalt

engrandecimiento *nm* **1** : enlargement **2** : exaggeration **3** : exaltation

engrane *nm Mex* : cogwheel

engrapadora *nf* : stapler

engrapar *vt* : to staple

engrasar *vt* : to grease, to lubricate

engrase *nm* : greasing, lubrication

engreído, -da *adj* PRESUMIDO, VANIDOSO : vain, conceited, stuck-up

engreimiento *nm* ARROGANCIA : arrogance, conceit

engreír {66} *vt* ENVANECER : to make vain — **engreírse** *vr* : to become conceited

engrosar {19} *vt* : to enlarge, to increase, to swell — *vi* ENGORDAR : to gain weight

engrudo *nm* : paste

engullir {38} *vt* : to gulp down, to gobble up — **engullirse** *vr*

enharinar *vt* : to flour

enhebrar *vt* ENSARTAR : to string, to thread

enhiesto, -ta *adj* **1 :** erect, upright **2 :** lofty, towering
enhilar *vt* **:** to thread (a needle, etc.)
enhorabuena *nf* FELICIDADES **:** congratulations *pl*
enigma *nm* **:** enigma, mystery
enigmático, -ca *adj* **:** enigmatic — **enigmáticamente** *adv*
enjabonar *vt* **:** to soap up, to lather — **enjabonarse** *vr*
enjaezar {21} *vt* **:** to harness
enjalbegar {52} *vt* **:** to whitewash
enjambrar *vi* **:** to swarm
enjambre *nm* **1 :** swarm **2** MUCHEDUMBRE **:** crowd, mob
enjaular *vt* **1 :** to cage **2** *fam* **:** to jail, to lock up
enjuagar {52} *vt* **:** to rinse — **enjuagarse** *vr* **:** to rinse out
enjuague *nm* **1 :** rinse **2 enjuague bucal :** mouthwash
enjugar {52} *vt* **:** to wipe away (tears)
enjuiciar *vt* **1 :** to indict, to prosecute **2** JUZGAR **:** to try
enjundioso, -sa *adj* **:** substantial, weighty
enjuto, -ta *adj* **:** lean, gaunt
enlace *nm* **1 :** bond, link, connection **2 :** liaison
enladrillado *nm* **:** brick paving
enladrillar *vt* **:** to pave with bricks
enlatar *vt* ENVASAR **:** to can
enlazar {21} *v* **:** to join, to link, to fit together
enlistar *vt* **:** to list — **enlistarse** *vr* **:** to enlist
enlodado, -da *adj* BARROSO **:** muddy
enlodar *vt* **1 :** to cover with mud **2 :** to stain, to sully — **enlodarse** *vr*
enlodazar → **enlodar**
enloquecedor, -dora *adj* **:** maddening
enloquecer {53} *vt* ALOCAR **:** to drive crazy — **enloquecerse** *vr* **:** to go crazy
enlosado *nm* **:** flagstone pavement
enlosar *vt* **:** to pave with flagstone
enlutarse *vr* **:** to go into mourning
enmaderado *nm* **1 :** wood paneling **2 :** hardwood floor
enmarañar *vt* **1 :** to tangle **2 :** to complicate **3 :** to confuse, to mix up — **enmarañarse** *vr*
enmarcar {72} *vt* **1** ENCUADRAR **:** to frame **2 :** to provide the setting for
enmascarar *vt* **:** to mask, to disguise
enmasillar *vt* **:** to putty, to caulk
enmendar {55} *vt* **1 :** to amend **2** CORREGIR **:** to emend, to correct **3** COMPENSAR **:** to compensate for — **enmendarse** *vr* **:** to mend one's ways
enmienda *nf* **1 :** amendment **2 :** correction, emendation
enmohecerse {53} *vr* **1 :** to become moldy **2** OXIDARSE **:** to rust, to become rusty
enmudecer {53} *vt* **:** to mute, to silence — *vi* **:** to fall silent
enmugrar *vt* **:** to soil, to make dirty — **enmugrarse** *vr* **:** to get dirty
ennegrecer {53} *vt* **:** to blacken, to darken — **ennegrecerse** *vr*
ennoblecer {53} *vt* **1 :** to ennoble **2 :** to embellish
enojadizo, -za *adj* IRRITABLE **:** irritable, cranky
enojado, -da *adj* **1 :** annoyed **2 :** angry, mad
enojar *vt* **1 :** to anger **2 :** to annoy, to upset — **enojarse** *vr*
enojo *nm* **1** CÓLERA **:** anger **2 :** annoyance
enojón, -jona *adj, pl* **-jones** *Chile, Mex fam* **:** irritable, cranky
enojoso, -sa *adj* FASTIDIOSO, MOLESTOSO **:** annoying, irritating
enorgullecer {53} *vt* **:** to make proud — **enorgullecerse** *vr* **:** to pride oneself
enorme *adj* INMENSO **:** enormous, huge — **enormemente** *adv*
enormidad *nf* **1 :** enormity, seriousness **2 :** immensity, hugeness
enraizado, -da *adj* **:** deep-seated, deeply rooted
enraizar {30} *vi* **:** to take root
enramada *nf* **:** arbor, bower
enramar *vt* **:** to cover with branches
enrarecer {53} *vt* **:** to rarefy — **enrarecerse** *vr*
enredadera *nf* **:** climbing plant, vine
enredar *vt* **1 :** to tangle up, to entangle **2 :** to confuse, to complicate **3 :** to involve, to implicate — **enredarse** *vr*
enredo *nm* **1** EMBROLLO **:** muddle, confusion **2** MARAÑA **:** tangle
enredoso, -sa *adj* **:** complicated, tricky
enrejado *nm* **1 :** railing **2 :** grating, grille **3 :** trellis, lattice
enrevesado, -da *adj* **:** complicated, involved
enriquecer {53} *vt* **:** to enrich — **enriquecerse** *vr* **:** to get rich
enriquecido, -da *adj* **:** enriched
enriquecimiento *nm* **:** enrichment
enrojecer {53} *vt* **:** to make red, to redden — **enrojecerse** *vr* **:** to blush
enrolar *vt* RECLUTAR **:** to recruit — **enrolarse** *vr* INSCRIBIRSE **:** to enlist, to sign up
enrollar *vt* **:** to roll up, to coil — **enrollarse** *vr*
enronquecerse {53} *vr* **:** to become hoarse
enroscar {72} *vt* TORCER **:** to twist — **enroscarse** *vr* **:** to coil, to twine
ensacar {72} *vt* **:** to bag (up)
ensalada *nf* **:** salad
ensaladera *nf* **:** salad bowl
ensalmo *nm* **:** incantation, spell
ensalzar {21} *vt* **1 :** to praise, to extol **2** EXALTAR **:** to exalt
ensamblaje *nm* **:** assembly
ensamblar *vt* **1 :** to assemble **2 :** to join, to fit together
ensanchar *vt* **1 :** to widen **2 :** to expand, to extend — **ensancharse** *vr*
ensanche *nm* **1 :** widening **2 :** expansion, development

ensangrentado, -da *adj* : bloody, bloodstained

ensañarse *vr* : to act cruelly, to be merciless

ensartar *vt* **1** ENHEBRAR : to string, to thread **2** : to skewer, to pierce

ensayar *vi* : to rehearse — *vt* **1** : to try out, to test **2** : to assay

ensayista *nmf* : essayist

ensayo *nm* **1** : essay **2** : trial, test **3** : rehearsal **4** : assay (of metals)

enseguida *adv* INMEDIATAMENTE : right away, immediately, at once

ensenada *nf* : cove, inlet

enseña *nf* **1** INSIGNIA : emblem, insignia **2** : standard, banner

enseñanza *nf* **1** EDUCACIÓN : education **2** : teaching

enseñar *vt* **1** : to teach **2** MOSTRAR : to show, to display — **enseñarse** *vr* **~ a** : to learn to, to get used to

enseres *nmpl* : equipment, furnishings *pl* <enseres domésticos : household goods>

ensillar *vt* : to saddle (up)

ensimismado, -da *adj* : absorbed, engrossed

ensimismarse *vr* : to lose oneself in thought

ensoberbecerse {53} *vr* : to become haughty

ensombrecer {53} *vt* : to cast a shadow over, to darken — **ensombrecerse** *vr*

ensoñación *nf, pl* **-ciones** : fantasy

ensopar *vt* **1** : to drench **2** : to dunk, to dip

ensordecedor, -dora *adj* : deafening, thunderous

ensordecer {53} *vt* : to deafen — *vi* : to go deaf

ensuciar *vt* : to soil, to dirty — **ensuciarse** *vr*

ensueño *nm* **1** : daydream, revery **2** FANTASÍA : illusion, fantasy

entablar *vt* **1** : to cover with boards **2** : to initiate, to enter into, to start

entallar *vt* AJUSTAR : to tailor, to fit, to take in — *vi* QUEDAR : to fit

ente *nm* **1** : being, entity **2** : body, organization <ente rector : ruling body> **3** *fam* : eccentric, crackpot

enteco, -ca *adj* : gaunt, frail

entenado, -da *n Mex* : stepchild, stepson *m,* stepdaughter *f*

entender[1] {56} *vt* **1** COMPRENDER : to understand **2** OPINAR : to think, to believe **3** QUERER : to mean, to intend **4** DEDUCIR : to infer, to deduce — *vi* **1** : to understand <¡ya entiendo! : now I understand!> **2 ~ de** : to know about, to be good at **3 ~ en** : to be in charge of — **entenderse** *vr* **1** : to be understood **2** : to get along well, to understand each other **3 ~ con** : to deal with

entender[2] *nm* **a mi entender** : in my opinion

entendible *adj* : understandable

entendido[1], **-da** *adj* **1** : skilled, expert **2 tener entendido** : to understand, to be under the impression <teníamos entendido que vendrías : we were under the impression you would come> **3 darse por entendido** : to go without saying

entendido[2] *nm* : expert, authority, connoisseur

entendimiento *nm* **1** : intellect, mind **2** : understanding, agreement

enterado, -da *adj* : aware, well-informed <estar enterado de : to be privy to>

enteramente *adv* : entirely, completely

enterar *vt* INFORMAR : to inform — **enterarse** *vr* INFORMARSE : to find out, to learn

entereza *nf* **1** INTEGRIDAD : integrity **2** FORTALEZA : fortitude **3** FIRMEZA : resolve

enternecedor, -dora *adj* CONMOVEDOR : touching, moving

enternecer {53} *vt* CONMOVER : to move, to touch

entero[1], **-ra** *adj* **1** : entire, whole **2** : complete, absolute **3** : intact — **enteramente** *adv*

entero[2] *nm* **1** : integer, whole number **2** : point (in finance)

enterramiento *nm* : burial

enterrar {55} *vt* : to bury

entibiar *vt* : to cool (down) — **entibiarse** *vr* : to become lukewarm

entidad *nf* **1** ENTE : entity **2** : body, organization **3** : firm, company **4** : importance, significance

entierro *nm* **1** : burial **2** : funeral

entintar *vt* : to ink

entoldado *nm* : awning

entomología *nf* : entomology

entomólogo, -ga *n* : entomologist

entonación *nf, pl* **-ciones** : intonation

entonar *vi* : to be in tune — *vt* **1** : to intone **2** : to tone up

entonces *adv* **1** : then **2 desde ~** : since then **3 en aquel entonces** : in those days

entornado, -da *adj* ENTREABIERTO : half-closed, ajar

entornar *vt* ENTREABRIR : to leave ajar

entorno *nm* : surroundings *pl,* environment

entorpecer {53} *vt* **1** : to hinder, to obstruct **2** : to dull — **entorpecerse** *vr* : to dull the senses

entrada *nf* **1** : entrance, entry **2** : ticket, admission **3** : beginning, onset **4** : entrée **5** : cue (in music) **6 entradas** *nfpl* : income <entradas y salidas : income and expenditures> **7 tener entradas** : to have a receding hairline

entrado, -da *adj* **entrado en años** : elderly

entramado *nm* : framework

entrampar *vt* **1** ATRAPAR : to entrap, to ensnare **2** ENGAÑAR : to deceive, to trick

entrante *adj* **1 :** next, upcoming <el año entrante : next year> **2 :** incoming, new <el presidente entrante : the president elect>

entraña *nf* **1** MEOLLO **:** core, heart, crux **2 entrañas** *nfpl* VÍSCERAS **:** entrails

entrañable *adj* **:** close, intimate

entrañar *vt* **:** to entail, to involve

entrar *vi* **1 :** to enter, to go in, to come in **2 :** to begin — *vt* **1 :** to bring in, to introduce **2 :** to access

entre *prep* **1 :** between **2 :** among

entreabierto[1] *pp* → **entreabrir**

entreabierto[2]**, -ta** *adj* ENTORNADO **:** half-open, ajar

entreabrir {2} *vt* ENTORNAR **:** to leave ajar

entreacto *nm* **:** intermission, interval

entrecano, -na *adj* **:** grayish, graying

entrecejo *nm* **fruncir el entrecejo :** to knit one's brows

entrecomillar *vt* **:** to place in quotation marks

entrecortado, -da *adj* **1 :** labored, difficult <respiración entrecortada : shortness of breath> **2 :** faltering, hesitant <con la voz entrecortada : with a catch in his voice>

entrecruzar {21} *vt* ENTRELAZAR **:** to interweave, to intertwine — **entrecruzarse** *vr*

entredicho *nm* **1** DUDA **:** doubt, question **2 :** prohibition

entrega *nf* **1 :** delivery **2 :** handing over, surrender **3 :** installment <entrega inicial : down payment>

entregar {52} *vt* **1 :** to deliver **2** DAR **:** to give, to present **3 :** to hand in, to hand over — **entregarse** *vr* **1 :** to surrender, to give in **2 :** to devote oneself

entrelazar {21} *vt* ENTRECRUZAR **:** to interweave, to intertwine

entremedias *adv* **1 :** in between, halfway **2 :** in the meantime

entremés *nm, pl* **-meses 1** APERITIVO **:** appetizer, hors d'oeuvre **2 :** interlude, short play

entremeterse → **entrometerse**

entremetido *nm* → **entrometido**

entremezclar *vt* **:** to intermingle

entrenador, -dora *n* **:** trainer, coach

entrenamiento *nm* **:** training, drill, practice

entrenar *vt* **:** to train, to drill, to practice — **entrenarse** *vr* **:** to train, to spar (in boxing)

entreoír {50} *vt* **:** to hear indistinctly

entrepierna *nf* **1 :** inner thigh **2 :** crotch **3 :** inseam

entrepiso *nm* ENTRESUELO **:** mezzanine

entresacar {72} *vt* **1** SELECCIONAR **:** to pick out, to select **2 :** to thin out

entresuelo *nm* ENTREPISO **:** mezzanine

entretanto[1] *adv* **:** meanwhile

entretanto[2] *nm* **en el entretanto :** in the meantime

entretejer *vt* **:** to interweave

entretela *nf* **:** facing (of a garment)

entretener {80} *vt* **1** DIVERTIR **:** to entertain, to amuse **2** DISTRAER **:** to distract **3** DEMORAR **:** to delay, to hold up — **entretenerse** *vr* **1 :** to amuse oneself **2 :** to dally

entretenido, -da *adj* DIVERTIDO **:** entertaining, amusing

entretenimiento *nm* **1 :** entertainment, pastime **2** DIVERSIÓN **:** fun, amusement

entrever {88} *vt* **1 :** to catch a glimpse of **2 :** to make out, to see indistinctly

entreverar *vt* **:** to mix, to intermingle

entrevero *nm* **:** confusion, disorder

entrevista *nf* **:** interview

entrevistador, -dora *n* **:** interviewer

entrevistar *vt* **:** to interview — **entrevistarse** *vr* REUNIRSE **~ con :** to meet with

entristecer {53} *vt* **:** to sadden

entrometerse *vr* **:** to interfere, to meddle

entrometido, -da *n* **:** meddler, busybody

entroncar {72} *vt* RELACIONAR **:** to establish a relationship between, to conncct — *vi* **1 :** to be related **2 :** to link up, to be connected

entronque *nm* **1 :** kinship **2** VÍNCULO **:** link, connection

entuerto *nm* **:** wrong, injustice

entumecer {53} *vt* **:** to make numb, to be numb — **entumecerse** *vr* **:** to go numb, to fall asleep

entumecido, -da *adj* **1 :** numb **2 :** stiff (of muscles, joints, etc.)

entumecimiento *nm* **:** numbness

enturbiar *vt* **1 :** to cloud **2 :** to confuse — **enturbiarse** *vr*

entusiasmar *vt* **:** to excite, to fill with enthusiasm — **entusiasmarse** *vr* **:** to get excited

entusiasmo *nm* **:** enthusiasm

entusiasta[1] *adj* **:** enthusiastic

entusiasta[2] *nmf* AFICIONADO **:** enthusiast

enumerar *vt* **:** to enumerate — **enumeración** *nf*

enunciación *nf, pl* **-ciones :** enunciation, statement

enunciar *vt* **:** to enunciate, to state

envainar *vt* **:** to sheathe

envalentonar *vt* **:** to make bold, to encourage — **envalentonarse** *vr*

envanecer {53} *vt* ENGREÍR **:** to make vain — **envanecerse** *vr*

envasar *vt* **1** EMBOTELLAR **:** to bottle **2** ENLATAR **:** to can **3 :** to pack in a container

envase *nm* **1 :** packaging, packing **2 :** container **3** LATA **:** can **4 :** empty bottle

envejecer {53} *vt* **:** to age, to make look old — *vi* **:** to age, to grow old

envejecido, -da *adj* **:** aged, old-looking

envejecimiento *nm* **:** aging

envenenamiento *nm* **:** poisoning

envenenar *vt* **1 :** to poison **2 :** to embitter

envergadura *nf* **1 :** span, breadth, spread **2 :** importance, scope

envés *nm, pl* **enveses :** reverse, opposite side

enviado, -da *n* **:** envoy, correspondent

enviar {85} *vt* **1 :** to send **2 :** to ship

envidia *nf* **:** envy, jealousy

envidiar *vt* **:** to envy — **envidiable** *adj*

envidioso, -sa *adj* **:** envious, jealous

envilecer {53} *vt* **:** to degrade, to debase

envilecimiento *nm* **:** degradation, debasement

envío *nm* **1 :** shipment **2 :** remittance

enviudar *vi* **:** to be widowed, to become a widower

envoltorio *nm* **1 :** bundle, package **2 :** wrapping, wrapper

envoltura *nf* **:** wrapper, wrapping

envolver {89} *vt* **1 :** to wrap **2 :** to envelop, to surround **3 :** to entangle, to involve — **envolverse** *vr* **1 :** to become involved **2 :** to wrap oneself (up)

envuelto *pp* → **envolver**

enyerbar *vt Mex* **:** to bewitch

enyesar *vt* **1 :** to plaster **2** ESCAYOLAR **:** to put in a plaster cast

enzima *nf* **:** enzyme

éon *nm, pl* **eones :** aeon

eperlano *nm* **:** smelt (fish)

épico, -ca *adj* **:** epic

epicúreo[1], -rea *adj* **:** epicurean

epicúreo[2], -rea *n* **:** epicure

epidemia *nf* **:** epidemic

epidémico, -ca *adj* **:** epidemic

epidermis *nf* **:** epidermis

epifanía *nf* **:** feast of the Epiphany (January 6th)

epigrama *nm* **:** epigram

epilepsia *nf* **:** epilepsy

epiléptico, -ca *adj & n* **:** epileptic

epílogo *nm* **:** epilogue

episcopal *adj* **:** episcopal

episcopalista *adj & nmf* **:** Episcopalian

episódico, -ca *adj* **:** episodic

episodio *nm* **:** episode

epístola *nf* **:** epistle

epitafio *nm* **:** epitaph

epíteto *nm* **:** epithet, name

epítome *nm* **:** summary, abstract

época *nf* **1** EDAD, ERA, PERÍODO **:** epoch, age, period **2 :** time of year, season **3 de ~ :** vintage, antique

epopeya *nf* **:** epic poem

equidad *nf* JUSTICIA **:** equity, justice, fairness

equilátero, -ra *adj* **:** equilateral

equilibrado, -da *adj* **:** well-balanced

equilibrar *vt* **:** to balance — **equilibrarse** *vr*

equilibrio *nm* **1 :** balance, equilibrium <perder el equilibrio : to lose one's balance> <equilibrio político : balance of power> **2 :** poise, aplomb

equilibrista *nmf* ACRÓBATA, FUNÁMBULO **:** acrobat, tightrope walker

equino, -na *adj* **:** equine

equinoccio *nm* **:** equinox

equipaje *nm* BAGAJE **:** baggage, luggage

equipamiento *nm* **:** equipping, equipment

equipar *vt* **:** to equip — **equiparse** *vr*

equiparable *adj* **:** comparable

equiparar *vt* **1** IGUALAR **:** to put on a same level, to make equal **2** COMPARAR **:** to compare

equipo *nm* **1 :** team, crew **2 :** gear, equipment

equitación *nf, pl* **-ciones :** horseback riding, horsemanship

equitativo, -va *adj* JUSTO **:** equitable, fair, just — **equitativamente** *adv*

equivalencia *nf* **:** equivalence

equivalente *adj & nm* **:** equivalent

equivaler {84} *vi* **:** to be equivalent

equivocación *nf, pl* **-ciones** ERROR **:** error, mistake

equivocado, -da *adj* **:** mistaken, wrong — **equivocadamente** *adv*

equivocar {72} *vt* **:** to mistake, to confuse — **equivocarse** *vr* **:** to make a mistake, to be wrong

equívoco[1], -ca *adj* AMBIGUO **:** ambiguous, equivocal

equívoco[2] *nm* **:** misunderstanding

era[1], etc. → **ser**

era[2] *nf* EDAD, ÉPOCA **:** era, age

erario *nm* **:** public treasury

erección *nf, pl* **-ciones :** erection, raising

eremita *nmf* ERMITAÑO **:** hermit

ergonomía *nf* **:** ergonomic

erguido, -da *adj* **:** erect, upright

erguir {31} *vt* **:** to raise, to lift up — **erguirse** *vr* **:** to straighten up

erial *nm* **:** uncultivated land

erigir {35} *vt* **:** to build, to erect — **erigirse** *vr* **~ en :** to set oneself up as

erizado, -da : bristly

erizarse {21} *vr* **:** to bristle, to stand on end

erizo *nm* **1 :** hedgehog **2 erizo de mar :** sea urchin

ermitaño[1], -ña *n* EREMITA **:** hermit, recluse

ermitaño[2] *nm* **:** hermit crab

erogación *nf, pl* **-ciones :** expenditure

erogar {52} *vt* **1 :** to pay out **2 :** to distribute

erosión *nf, pl* **-siones :** erosion

erosionar *vt* **:** to erode

erótico, -ca *adj* **:** erotic

erotismo *nm* **:** eroticism

errabundo, -da *adj* ERRANTE, VAGABUNDO **:** wandering

erradicar {72} *vt* **:** to eradicate — **erradicación** *nf*

errado, -da *adj* **:** wrong, mistaken

errante *adj* ERRABUNDO, VAGABUNDO **:** errant, wandering

errar {32} *vt* FALLAR **:** to miss — *vi* **1** DESACERTAR **:** to be wrong, to be mistaken **2** VAGAR **:** to wander

errata *nf* **:** misprint, error

errático, -ca *adj* : erratic — **erráticamente** *adv*
erróneo, -nea *adj* EQUIVOCADO : erroneous, wrong — **erróneamente** *adv*
error *nm* EQUIVOCACIÓN : error, mistake
eructar *vi* : to belch, to burp
eructo *nm* : belch, burp
erudición *nf, pl* **-ciones** : erudition, learning
erudito[1], -ta *adj* LETRADO : erudite, learned
erudito[2], -ta *n* : scholar
erupción *nf, pl* **-ciones 1** : eruption **2** SARPULLIDO : rash
eruptivo, -va *adj* : eruptive
es → **ser**
esbelto, -ta *adj* DELGADO : slender, slim
esbirro *nm* : henchman
esbozar {21} *vt* BOSQUEJAR : to sketch, to outline
esbozo *nm* **1** : sketch **2** : rough draft
escabechar *vt* **1** ENCURTIR : to pickle **2** *fam* : to kill, to rub out
escabeche *nm* : brine (for pickling)
escabechina *nf* MASACRE : massacre, bloodbath
escabel *nm* : footstool
escabroso, -sa *adj* **1** : rugged, rough **2** : difficult, tough **3** : risqué
escabullirse {38} *vr* : to slip away, to escape
escala *nf* **1** : scale **2** ESCALERA : ladder **3** : stopover
escalada *nf* : ascent, climb
escalador, -dora *n* ALPINISTA : mountain climber
escalafón *nm, pl* **-fones 1** : list of personnel **2** : salary scale, rank
escalar *vt* : to climb, to scale — *vi* **1** : to go climbing **2** : to escalate
escaldar *vt* : to scald
escalera *nf* **1** : ladder <escalera de tijera : stepladder> **2** : stairs *pl*, staircase **3 escalera mecánica** : escalator
escalfador *nm* : chafing dish
escalfar *vt* : to poach (eggs)
escalinata *nf* : flight of stairs
escalofriante *adj* : horrifying, bloodcurdling
escalofrío *nm* : shiver, chill, shudder
escalón *nm, pl* **-lones 1** : echelon **2** : step, rung
escalonado, -da *adj* GRADUAL : gradual, staggered
escalonar *vt* **1** : to terrace **2** : to stagger, to alternate
escalpelo *nm* BISTURÍ : scalpel
escama *nf* **1** : scale (of fish or reptiles) **2** : flake (of skin)
escamar *vt* **1** : to scale (fish) **2** : to make suspicious
escamocha *nf Mex* : fruit salad
escamoso, -sa *adj* : scaly
escamotear *vt* **1** : to palm, to conceal **2** *fam* : to lift, to swipe **3** : to hide, to cover up
escandalizar {21} *vt* : to shock, to scandalize — *vi* : to make a fuss — **escandalizarse** *vr* : to be shocked
escándalo *nm* **1** : scandal **2** : scene, commotion
escandaloso, -sa *adj* **1** : shocking, scandalous **2** RUIDOSO : noisy, rowdy **3** : flagrant, outrageous — **escandalosamente** *adv*
escandinavo, -va *adj & n* : Scandinavian
escandir *vt* : to scan (poetry)
escáner *nm* : scanner, scan
escaño *nm* **1** : seat (in a legislative body) **2** BANCO : bench
escapada *nf* HUIDA : flight, escape
escapar *vi* HUIR : to escape, to flee, to run away — **escaparse** *vr* : to escape notice, to leak out
escaparate *nm* **1** : shop window **2** : showcase
escapatoria *nf* **1** : loophole, excuse, pretext <no tener escapatoria : to have no way out> **2** ESCAPADA : escape, flight
escape *nm* **1** FUGA : escape **2** : exhaust (from a vehicle)
escapismo *nm* : escapism
escápula *nm* OMÓPLATO : scapula, shoulder blade
escapulario *nm* : scapular
escarabajo *nm* : beetle
escaramuza *nf* **1** : skirmish **2** : scrimmage
escaramuzar {21} *vi* : to skirmish
escarapela *nf* : rosette (ornament)
escarbar *vt* **1** : to dig, to scratch up **2** : to poke, to pick **3 ~ en** : to investigate, to pry into
escarcha *nf* **1** : frost **2** *Mex, PRi* : glitter
escarchar *vt* **1** : to frost (a cake) **2** : to candy (fruit)
escardar *vt* **1** : to weed, to hoe **2** : to weed out
escariar *vt* : to ream
escarlata *adj & nf* : scarlet
escarlatina *nf* : scarlet fever
escarmentar {55} *vt* : to punish, to teach a lesson to — *vi* : to learn one's lesson
escarmiento *nm* **1** : lesson, warning **2** CASTIGO : punishment
escarnecer {53} *vt* RIDICULIZAR : to ridicule, to mock
escarnio *nm* : ridicule, mockery
escarola *nf* : escarole
escarpa *nf* : escarpment, steep slope
escarpado, -da *adj* : steep, sheer
escarpia *nf* : hook, spike
escasamente *adv* : scarcely, barely
escasear *vi* : to be scarce, to run short
escasez *nf, pl* **-seces** : shortage, scarcity
escaso, -sa *adj* **1** : scarce, scant **2 ~ de** : short of
escatimar *vt* : to skimp on, to be sparing with <no escatimar esfuerzos : to spare no effort>
escayola *nf* **1** : plaster (for casts) **2** : plaster cast
escayolar *vt* : to put in a plaster cast

escena *nf* **1 :** scene **2 :** stage
escenario *nm* **1** ESCENA **:** stage **2 :** setting, scene <el escenario del crimen : the scene of the crime>
escénico, -ca *adj* **1 :** scenic **2 :** stage
escenificar {72} *vt* **:** to stage, to dramatize
escepticismo *nm* **:** skepticism
escéptico¹, -ca *adj* **:** skeptical
escéptico², -ca *n* **:** skeptic
escindirse *vr* **1 :** to split **2 :** to break away
escisión *nf, pl* **-siones 1 :** split, division **2 :** excision
esclarecer {53} *vt* **1** ELUCIDAR **:** to elucidate, to clarify **2** ILUMINAR **:** to illuminate, to light up
esclarecimiento *nm* ELUCIDACIÓN **:** elucidation, clarification
esclavitud *nf* **:** slavery
esclavización *nf, pl* **-ciones :** enslavement
esclavizar {21} *vt* **:** to enslave
esclavo, -va *n* **:** slave
esclerosis *nf* **esclerosis múltiple :** multiple sclerosis
esclusa *nf* **:** floodgate, lock (of a canal)
escoba *nf* **:** broom
escobilla *nf* **:** small broom, brush, whisk broom
escobillón *nm, pl* **-llones :** swab
escocer {14} *vi* ARDER **:** to smart, to sting **— escocerse** *vr* **:** to be sore
escocés¹, -cesa *adj, mpl* **-ceses 1 :** Scottish **2 :** tartan, plaid
escocés², -cesa *n, mpl* **-ceses :** Scottish person, Scot
escocés³ *nm* **1 :** Scots (language) **2** *pl* **-ceses :** Scotch (whiskey)
escofina *nf* **:** file, rasp
escoger {15} *vt* ELEGIR, SELECCIONAR **:** to choose, to select
escogido, -da *adj* **:** choice, select
escolar¹ *adj* **:** school
escolar² *nmf* **:** student, pupil
escolaridad *nf* **:** schooling <escolaridad obligatoria : compulsory education>
escolarización *nf, pl* **-ciones :** education, schooling
escollo *nm* **1 :** reef **2** OBSTÁCULO **:** obstacle
escolta *nmf* **:** escort
escoltar *vt* **:** to escort, to accompany
escombro *nm* **1 :** debris, rubbish **2 escombros** *nmpl* **:** ruins, rubble
esconder *vt* OCULTAR **:** to hide, to conceal
escondidas *nfpl* **1 :** hide-and-seek **2 a ~ :** secretly, in secret
escondimiento *nm* **:** concealment
escondite *nm* **1** ENCONDRIJO **:** hiding place **2** ESCONDIDAS **:** hide-and-seek
escondrijo *nm* ESCONDITE **:** hiding place
escopeta *nf* **:** shotgun
escoplear *vt* **:** to chisel (out)
escoplo *nm* **:** chisel
escora *nf* **:** list, heeling
escorar *vi* **:** to list, to heel (of a boat)
escorbuto *nm* **:** scurvy
escoria *nf* **1 :** slag, dross **2** HEZ **:** dregs *pl,* scum <la escoria de la sociedad : the dregs of society>
Escorpio *or* **Escorpión** *nmf* **:** Scorpio
escorpión *nm, pl* **-piones** ALACRÁN **:** scorpion
escote *nm* **1 :** low neckline **2 pagar a escote :** to go dutch
escotilla *nf* **:** hatch, hatchway
escotillón *nf, pl* **-llones :** trapdoor
escozor *nm* **:** smarting, stinging
escriba *nm* **:** scribe
escribano, -na *n* **1 :** court clerk **2** NOTARIO **:** notary public
escribir {33} *v* **1 :** to write **2 :** to spell **— escribirse** *vr* CARTEARSE **:** to write to one another, to correspond
escrito¹ *pp* **→ escribir**
escrito², -ta *adj* **:** written
escrito³ *nm* **1 :** written document **2 escritos** *nmpl* **:** writings, works
escritor, -tora *n* **:** writer
escritorio *nm* **:** desk
escritorzuelo, -la *n* **:** hack (writer)
escritura *nf* **1 :** writing, handwriting **2 :** deed
escroto *nm* **:** scrotum
escrúpulo *nm* **:** scruple
escrupuloso, -sa *adj* **1 :** scrupulous **2** METICULOSO **:** exact, meticulous **— escrupulosamente** *adv*
escrutador, -dora *adj* **:** penetrating, searching
escrutar *vt* ESCUDRIÑAR **:** to scrutinize, to examine closely
escrutinio *nm* **:** scrutiny
escuadra *nf* **1 :** square (instrument) **2 :** fleet, squadron
escuadrilla *nf* **:** squadron, formation, flight
escuadrón *nm, pl* **-drones :** squadron
escuálido, -da *adj* **1 :** skinny, scrawny **2** INMUNDO **:** filthy, squalid
escuchar *vt* **1 :** to listen to **2 :** to hear **—** *vi* **:** to listen **— escucharse** *vr*
escudar *vt* **:** to shield **— escudarse** *vr* **~ en :** to hide behind
escudero *nm* **:** squire
escudo *nm* **1 :** shield **2 escudo de armas :** coat of arms
escudriñar *vt* **1** ESCRUTAR **:** to scrutinize **2 :** to inquire into, to investigate
escuela *nf* **:** school
escueto, -ta *adj* **1 :** plain, simple **2 :** succinct, concise **— escuetamente** *adv*
escuincle, -cla *n Mex fam* **:** child, kid
esculcar {72} *vt* **:** to search
esculpir *vt* **1 :** to sculpt **2 :** to carve, to engrave **—** *vi* **:** to sculpt
escultor, -tora *n* **:** sculptor
escultórico, -ca *adj* **:** sculptural
escultura *nf* **:** sculpture
escultural *adj* **:** statuesque
escupidera *nf* **:** spittoon, cuspidor
escupir *v* **:** to spit
escupitajo *nm* **:** spit
escurridizo, -za *adj* **:** slippery, elusive

escurridor *nm* **1** : dish rack **2** : colander
escurrir *vt* **1** : to wring out **2** : to drain — *vi* **1** : to drain **2** : to drip, to drip-dry — **escurrirse** *vr* : to slip away
ese, esa *adj, mpl* **esos** : that, those
ése, ésa *pron, mpl* **ésos** : that one, those ones *pl*
esencia *nf* : essence
esencial *adj* : essential — **esencialmente** *adv*
esfera *nf* **1** : sphere **2** : face, dial (of a watch)
esférico[1], **-ca** *adj* : spherical
esférico[2] *nm* : ball (in sports)
esfinge *nf* : sphinx
esforzado, -da *adj* **1** : energetic, vigorous **2** VALIENTE : courageous, brave
esforzar {36} *vt* : to strain — **esforzarse** *vr* : to make an effort
esfuerzo *nm* **1** : effort **2** ÁNIMO, VIGOR : spirit, vigor **3 sin ~** : effortlessly
esfumar *vt* : to tone down, to soften — **esfumarse** *vr* **1** : to fade away, to vanish **2** *fam* : to take off, to leave
esgrima *nf* : fencing (sport)
esgrimidor, -dora *n* : fencer
esgrimir *vt* **1** : to brandish, to wield **2** : to use, to resort to — *vi* : to fence
esguince *nm* : sprain, strain (of a muscle)
eslabón *nm, pl* **-bones** : link
eslabonar *vt* : to link, to connect, to join
eslavo[1], **-va** *adj* : Slavic
eslavo[2], **-va** *n* : Slav
eslogan *nm, pl* **-lóganes** : slogan
eslovaco, -ca *adj & n* : Slovakian, Slovak
esloveno, -na *adj & nm* : Slovene, Slovenian
esmaltar *vt* : to enamel
esmalte *nm* **1** : enamel **2 esmalte de uñas** : nail polish
esmerado, -da *adj* : careful, painstaking
esmeralda *nf* : emerald
esmerarse *vr* : to take great pains, to do one's utmost
esmeril *nm* : emery
esmero *nm* : meticulousness, great care
esmoquin *nm, pl* **-quins** : tuxedo
esnob[1] *adj, pl* **esnobs** : snobbish
esnob[2] *nmf, pl* **esnobs** : snob
esnobismo *nm* : snobbery, snobbishness
eso *pron* (*neuter*) **1** : that <eso no me gusta : I don't like that> **2 ¡eso es!** : that's it!, that's right! **3 a eso de** : around <a eso de las tres : around three o'clock> **4 en ~** : at that point, just then
esófago *nm* : esophagus
esos → **ese**
ésos → **ése**
esotérico, -ca *adj* : esoteric — **esotéricamente** *adv*
espabilado, -da *adj* : bright, smart
espabilarse *vr* **1** : to awaken **2** : to get a move on **3** : to get smart, to wise up
espacial *adj* **1** : space **2** : spatial
espaciar *vt* DISTANCIAR : to space out, to spread out
espacio *nm* **1** : space, room **2** : period, length (of time) **3 espacio exterior** : outer space
espacioso, -sa *adj* : spacious, roomy
espada[1] *nf* **1** : sword **2 espadas** *nfpl* : spades (in playing cards)
espada[2] *nm* MATADOR, TORERO : bullfighter, matador
espadaña *nf* **1** : belfry **2** : cattail
espadilla *nf* : scull, oar
espagueti *nm or* **espaguetis** *nmpl* : spaghetti
espalda *nf* **1** : back **2 espaldas** *nfpl* : shoulders, back **3 por la espalda** : from behind
espaldarazo *nm* **1** : recognition, support **2** : slap on the back
espaldera *nf* : trellis
espantajo *nm* : scarecrow
espantapájaros *nms & pl* : scarecrow
espantar *vt* ASUSTAR : to scare, to frighten — **espantarse** *vr*
espanto *nm* : fright, fear, horror
espantoso, -sa *adj* **1** : frightening, terrifying **2** : frightful, dreadful
español[1], **-ñola** *adj* : Spanish
español[2], **-ñola** *n* : Spaniard
español[3] *nm* CASTELLANO : Spanish (language)
esparadrapo *nm* : adhesive bandage, Band-Aid™
esparcimiento *nm* **1** DIVERSIÓN, RECREO : entertainment, recreation **2** DESCANSO : relaxation **3** DISEMINACIÓN : dissemination, spreading
esparcir {83} *vt* DISPERSAR : to scatter, to spread — **esparcirse** *vr* **1** : to spread out **2** DESCANSARSE : to take it easy **3** DIVERTIRSE : to amuse oneself
espárrago *nm* : asparagus
espartano, -na *adj* : severe, austere
espasmo *nm* : spasm
espasmódico, -ca *adj* : spasmodic
espástico, -ca *adj* : spastic
espátula *nf* : spatula
especia *nf* : spice
especial *adj & nm* : special
especialidad *nf* : specialty
especialista *nmf* : specialist, expert
especializarse {21} *vr* : to specialize
especialmente *adv* : especially, particularly
especie *nf* **1** : species **2** CLASE, TIPO : type, kind, sort
especificación *nf, pl* **-ciones** : specification
especificar {72} *vt* : to specify
específico, -ca *adj* : specific — **específicamente** *adv*
espécimen *nm, pl* **especímenes** : specimen
especioso, -sa *adj* : specious
espectacular *adj* : spectacular — **espectacularmente** *adv*

espectáculo *nm* **1 :** spectacle, sight **2 :** show, performance

espectador, -dora *n* **:** spectator, onlooker

espectro *nm* **1 :** ghost, specter **2 :** spectrum

especulación *nf, pl* **-ciones :** speculation

especulador, -dora *n* **:** speculator

especular *vi* **:** to speculate

especulativo, -va *adj* **:** speculative

espejismo *nm* **1 :** mirage **2 :** illusion

espejo *nm* **:** mirror

espejuelos *nmpl* ANTEOJOS **:** spectacles, glasses

espeluznante *adj* **:** hair-raising, terrifying

espera *nf* **:** wait

esperanza *nf* **:** hope, expectation

esperanzado, -da *adj* **:** hopeful

esperanzador, -dora *adj* **:** encouraging, promising

esperanzar {21} *vt* **:** to give hope to

esperar *vt* **1** AGUARDAR **:** to wait for, to await **2 :** to expect **3 :** to hope <espero poder trabajar **:** I hope to be able to work> <espero que sí **:** I hope so> — *vi* **:** to wait — **esperarse** *vr* **1 :** to expect, to be hoped <como podría esperarse **:** as would be expected> **2 :** to hold on, to hang on <espérate un momento **:** hold on a minute>

esperma *nmf* **:** sperm

esperpéntico, -ca *adj* GROTESCO **:** grotesque

esperpento *nm fam* MAMARRACHO **:** sight, fright <voy hecha un esperpento **:** I really look a sight>

espesante *nm* **:** thickener

espesar *vt* **:** to thicken — **espesarse** *vr*

espeso, -sa *adj* **:** thick, heavy, dense

espesor *nm* **:** thickness, density

espesura *nf* **1 :** thickness **2 :** thicket

espetar *vt* **1 :** to blurt out **2 :** to skewer

espía *nmf* **:** spy

espiar {85} *vt* **:** to spy on, to observe — *vi* **:** to spy

espiga *nf* **1 :** ear (of wheat) **2 :** spike (of flowers)

espigado, -da *adj* **:** willowy, slender

espigar {52} *vt* **:** to glean, to gather — **espigarse** *vr* **:** to grow quickly, to shoot up

espigón *nm, pl* **-gones :** breakwater

espina *nf* **1 :** thorn **2 :** spine <espina dorsal **:** spinal column> **3 :** fish bone

espinaca *nf* **1 :** spinach (plant) **2 espinacas** *nfpl* **:** spinach (food)

espinal *adj* **:** spinal

espinazo *nm* **:** backbone

espineta *nf* **:** spinet

espinilla *nf* **1** BARRO, GRANO **:** pimple **2 :** shin

espino *nm* **:** hawthorn

espinoso, -sa *adj* **1 :** thorny, prickly **2 :** bony (of fish) **3 :** knotty, difficult

espionaje *nm* **:** espionage

espiración *nf, pl* **-ciones :** exhalation

espiral *adj & nf* **:** spiral

espirar *vt* EXHALAR **:** to breathe out, to give off — *vi* **:** to exhale

espiritismo *nm* **:** spiritualism

espiritista *nmf* **:** spiritualist

espíritu *nm* **1 :** spirit **2** ÁNIMO **:** state of mind, spirits *pl* **3 el Espíritu Santo :** the Holy Ghost

espiritual *adj* **:** spiritual — **espiritualmente** *adv*

espiritualidad *nf* **:** spirituality

espita *nf* **:** spigot, tap

esplendidez *nf, pl* **-deces** ESPLENDOR **:** magnificence, splendor

espléndido, -da *adj* **1 :** splendid, magnificent **2 :** generous, lavish — **espléndidamente** *adv*

esplendor *nm* ESPLENDIDEZ **:** splendor

esplendoroso, -sa *adj* MAGNÍFICO **:** magnificent, grand

espliego *nm* LAVANDA **:** lavender

espolear *vt* **:** to spur on

espoleta *nf* **1** DETONADOR **:** detonator, fuse **2 :** wishbone

espolón *nm, pl* **-lones :** spur (of poultry), fetlock (of a horse)

espolvorear *vt* **:** to sprinkle, to dust

esponja *nf* **1 :** sponge **2 tirar la esponja :** to throw in the towel

esponjado, -da *adj* **:** spongy

esponjoso, -sa *adj* **1 :** spongy **2 :** soft, fluffy

esponsales *nmpl* **:** betrothal, engagement

espontaneidad *nf* **:** spontaneity

espontáneo, -nea *adj* **:** spontaneous — **espontáneamente** *adv*

espora *nf* **:** spore

esporádico, -ca *adj* **:** sporadic — **esporádicamente** *adv*

esposar *vt* **:** to handcuff

esposas *nfpl* **:** handcuffs

esposo, -sa *n* **:** spouse, wife *f,* husband *m*

esprint *nm* **:** sprint

esprintar *vi* **:** to sprint

esprinter *nmf* **:** sprinter

espuela *nf* **:** spur

espuerta *nf* **:** two-handled basket

espulgar {52} *vt* **1 :** to delouse **2 :** to scrutinize

espuma *nf* **1 :** foam **2 :** lather **3 :** froth, head (on beer)

espumar *vi* **:** to foam, to froth — *vt* **:** to skim off

espumoso, -sa *adj* **:** foamy, frothy

espurio, -ria *adj* **:** spurious

esputar *v* **:** to expectorate, to spit

esputo *nm* **:** spit, sputum

esqueje *nm* **:** cutting (from a plant)

esquela *nf* **1 :** note **2 :** notice, announcement

esquelético, -ca *adj* **:** emaciated, skeletal

esqueleto *nm* **1 :** skeleton **2** ARMAZÓN **:** framework

esquema *nf* BOSQUEJO **:** outline, sketch, plan

esquemático, -ca *adj* **:** schematic

esquí *nm* **1 :** ski **2 esquí acuático :** water ski, waterskiing

esquiador, -dora *n* **:** skier

esquiar {85} *vi* **:** to ski

esquife *nm* **:** skiff

esquila *nf* **1** CENCERRO **:** cowbell **2 :** shearing

esquilar *vt* TRASQUILAR **:** to shear

esquimal *adj & nmf* **:** Eskimo

esquina *nf* **:** corner

esquinazo *nm* **1 :** corner **2 dar esquinazo a** *fam* **:** to stand up, to give the slip to

esquirla *nf* **:** splinter (of bone, glass, etc.)

esquirol *nm* ROMPEHUELGAS **:** strikebreaker, scab

esquisto *nm* **:** shale

esquivar *vt* **1** EVADIR **:** to dodge, to evade **2** EVITAR **:** to avoid

esquivez *nf, pl* **-veces 1 :** aloofness **2** TIMIDEZ **:** shyness

esquivo, -va *adj* **1** HURAÑO **:** aloof, unsociable **2 :** shy **3 :** elusive, evasive

esquizofrenia *nf* **:** schizophrenia

esquizofrénico, -ca *adj & n* **:** schizophrenic

esta → **este**[1]

ésta → **éste**

estabilidad *nf* **:** stability

estabilización *nf, pl* **-ciones :** stabilization

estabilizador *nm* **:** stabilizer

estabilizar {21} *vt* **:** to stabilize — **estabilizarse** *vr*

estable *adj* **:** stable, steady

establecer {53} *vt* FUNDAR, INSTITUIR **:** to establish, to found, to set up — **establecerse** *vr* INSTALARSE **:** to settle, to establish oneself

establecimiento *nm* **1 :** establishing **2 :** establishment, institution, office

establo *nm* **:** stable

estaca *nf* **:** stake, picket, post

estacada *nf* **1 :** picket fence **2 :** stockade

estacar {72} *vt* **1 :** to stake out **2 :** to fasten down with stakes — **estacarse** *vr* **:** to remain rigid

estación *nf, pl* **-ciones 1 :** station <estación de servicio : service station, gas station> **2 :** season

estacional *adj* **:** seasonal

estacionamiento *nm* **1 :** parking **2 :** parking lot

estacionar *vt* **1 :** to place, to station **2 :** to park — **estacionarse** *vr* **1 :** to park **2 :** to remain stationary

estacionario, -ria *adj* **1 :** stationary **2 :** stable

estada *nf* **:** stay

estadía *nf* ESTANCIA **:** stay, sojourn

estadio *nm* **1 :** stadium **2 :** phase, stage

estadista *nmf* **:** statesman

estadística *nf* **1 :** statistic, figure **2 :** statistics

estadístico[1], **-ca** *adj* **:** statistical — **estadísticamente** *adv*

estadístico[2], **-ca** *n* **:** statistician

estado *nm* **1 :** state **2 :** status <estado civil : marital status> **3** CONDICIÓN **:** condition

estadounidense *adj & nmf* AMERICANO, NORTEAMERICANO **:** American

estafa *nf* **:** swindle, fraud

estafador, -dora *n* **:** cheat, swindler

estafar *vt* DEFRAUDAR **:** to swindle, to defraud

estalactita *nf* **:** stalactite

estalagmita *nf* **:** stalagmite

estallar *vi* **1** REVENTAR **:** to burst, to explode, to erupt **2 :** to break out

estallido *nm* **1** EXPLOSIÓN **:** explosion **2 :** report (of a gun) **3 :** outbreak, outburst

estambre *nm* **1 :** worsted (fabric) **2 :** stamen

estampa *nf* **1** ILUSTRACIÓN, IMAGEN **:** printed image, illustration **2** ASPECTO **:** appearance, demeanor

estampado[1], **-da** *adj* **:** patterned, printed

estampado[2] *nm* **:** print, pattern

estampar *vt* **:** to stamp, to print, to engrave

estampida *nf* **:** stampede

estampilla *nf* **1 :** rubber stamp **2** SELLO, TIMBRE **:** postage stamp

estancado, -da *adj* **:** stagnant

estancamiento *nm* **:** stagnation

estancar {72} *vt* **1 :** to dam up, to hold back **2 :** to bring to a halt, to deadlock — **estancarse** *vr* **1 :** to stagnate **2 :** to be brought to a standstill, to be deadlocked

estancia *nf* **1** ESTADÍA **:** stay, sojourn **2 :** ranch, farm

estanciero, -ra *n* **:** rancher, farmer

estanco, -ca *adj* **:** watertight

estándar *adj & nm* **:** standard

estandarización *nf, pl* **-ciones :** standardization

estandarizar {21} *vt* **:** to standardize

estandarte *nm* **:** standard, banner

estanque *nm* **1 :** pool, pond **2 :** tank, reservoir

estante *nm* REPISA **:** shelf

estantería *nf* **:** shelves *pl,* bookcase

estaño *nm* **:** tin

estaquilla *nf* **1 :** peg **2** ESPIGA **:** spike

estar {34} *v aux* **:** to be <estoy aprendiendo inglés : I'm learning English> <está terminado : it's finished> — *vi* **1** (*indicating a state or condition*) **:** to be <está muy alto : he's so tall, he's gotten very tall><¿ya estás mejor? : are you feeling better now?> <estoy casado : I'm married> **2** (*indicating location*) **:** to be <están en la mesa : they're on the table> <estamos en la página 2 : we're on page 2> **3 :** to be at home <¿está María? : is Maria in?> **4 :** to remain <estaré aquí 5 días : I'll be here for 5 days> **5 :** to be ready, to be done <estará para las diez : it will be ready by ten o'clock> **6 :** to agree <¿estamos? : are we in agreement?> <estoy contigo : I'm with you> **7**

¿cómo estás? : how are you? **8 ¡está bien!** : all right!, that's fine! **9 ~ a** : to cost **10 ~ a** : to be <¿a qué dia estamos? : what's today's date?> **11 ~ con** to have <está con fiebre : she has a fever> **12 ~ de** : to be <estoy de vacaciones : I'm on vacation> <está de director hoy : he's acting as director today> **13 estar bien (mal)** : to be well (sick) **14 ~ para** : to be in the mood for **15 ~ por** : to be in favor of **16 ~ por** : to be about to <está por cerrar : it's on the verge of closing> **17 estar de más** : to be unnecessary **18 estar que** : to be (in a state or condition) <está que echa chispas : he's hopping mad> — **estarse** *vr* QUEDARSE : to stay, to remain <¡estáte quieto! : be still!>

estarcir {83} *vt* : to stencil
estatal *adj* : state, national
estática *nf* : static
estático, -ca *adj* : static
estatizar {21} *vt* : to nationalize — **estatización** *nf*
estatua *nf* : statue
estatuilla *nf* : statuette, figurine
estatura *nf* : height, stature <de mediana estatura : of medium height>
estatus *nm* : status, prestige
estatutario, -ria *adj* : statutory
estatuto *nm* : statute
este[1], esta *adj, mpl* **estos** : this, these
este[2] *adj* : eastern, east
este[3] *nm* **1** ORIENTE : east **2** : east wind **3 el Este** : the East, the Orient
éste, ésta *pron, mpl* **éstos 1** : this one, these ones *pl* **2** : the latter
estela *nf* **1** : wake (of a ship) **2** RASTRO : trail (of dust, smoke, etc.)
estelar *adj* : stellar
estelarizar {21} *vt Mex* : to star in, to be the star of
esténcil *nm* : stencil
estentóreo, -rea *adj* : loud, thundering
estepa *nf* : steppe
éster *nf* : ester
estera *nf* : mat
estercolero *nm* : dunghill
estéreo *adj & nm* : stereo
estereofónico, -ca *adj* : stereophonic
estereotipado, -da *adj* : stereotyped
estereotipar *vt* : to stereotype
estereotipo *nm* : stereotype
estéril *adj* **1** : sterile, germ-free **2** : infertile, barren **3** : futile, vain
esterilidad *nf* **1** : sterility **2** : infertility
esterilizar {21} *vt* **1** : to sterilize, to disinfect **2** : to sterilize (a person), to spay (an animal) — **esterilización** *nf*
esterlina *adj* : sterling
esternón *nm, pl* **-nones** : sternum
estero *nm* : estuary
estertor *nm* : death rattle
estética *nf* : aesthetics
estético, -ca *adj* : aesthetic — **estéticamente** *adv*
estetoscopio *nm* : stethoscope
estibador, -dora *n* : longshoreman, stevedore
estibar *vt* : to load (freight)
estiércol *nm* : dung, manure
estigma *nm* : stigma
estigmatizar {21} *vt* : to stigmatize, to brand
estilarse *vr* : to be in fashion
estilete *nm* : stiletto
estilista *nmf* : stylist
estilizar {21} *vt* : to stylize
estilo *nm* **1** : style **2** : fashion, manner **3** : stylus
estima *nf* ESTIMACIÓN : esteem, regard
estimable *adj* **1** : considerable **2** : estimable, esteemed
estimación *nf, pl* **-ciones 1** ESTIMA : esteem, regard **2** : estimate
estimado, -da *adj* : esteemed, dear <Estimado señor Ortiz : Dear Mr. Ortiz>
estimar *vt* **1** APRECIAR : to esteem, to respect **2** EVALUAR : to estimate, to appraise **3** OPINAR : to consider, to deem
estimulación *nf, pl* **-ciones** : stimulation
estimulante[1] *adj* : stimulating
estimulante[2] *nm* : stimulant
estimular *vt* **1** : to stimulate **2** : to encourage
estímulo *nm* **1** : stimulus **2** INCENTIVO : incentive, encouragement
estío *nm* : summertime
estipendio *nm* **1** : salary **2** : stipend, remuneration
estipular *vt* : to stipulate — **estipulación** *nf*
estirado, -da *adj* **1** : stretched, extended **2** PRESUMIDO : stuck-up, conceited
estiramiento *nm* **1** : stretching **2 estiramiento facial** : face-lift
estirar *vt* : to stretch (out), to extend — **estirarse** *vr*
estirón *nm, pl* **-rones 1** : pull, tug **2 dar un estirón** : to grow quickly, to shoot up
estirpe *nf* LINAJE : lineage, stock
estival *adj* VERANIEGO : summer
esto *pron* (*neuter*) **1** : this <¿qué es esto? : what is this?> **2 en ~** : at this point **3 por ~** : for this reason
estocada *nf* **1** : final thrust (in bullfighting) **2** : thrust, lunge (in fencing)
estofa *nf* CLASE : class, quality <de baja estofa : low-class, poor-quality>
estofado *nm* COCIDO, GUISADO : stew
estofar *vt* GUISAR : to stew
estoicismo *nm* : stoicism
estoico[1], -ca *adj* : stoic, stoical
estoico[2], -ca *n* : stoic
estola *nf* : stole
estomacal *adj* GÁSTRICO : stomach, gastric
estómago *nm* : stomach
estoniano, -na *adj & n* : Estonian
estopa *nf* **1** : tow (yarn or cloth) **2** : burlap

estopilla *nf* : cheesecloth
estoque *nm* : rapier, sword
estorbar *vt* OBSTRUIR : to obstruct, to hinder — *vi* : to get in the way
estorbo *nm* **1** : obstacle, hindrance **2** : nuisance
estornino *nm* : starling
estornudar *vi* : to sneeze
estornudo *nm* : sneeze
estos → **este**[1]
éstos → **éste**
estoy → **estar**
estrabismo *nm* : squint
estrado *nm* **1** : dais, platform, bench (of a judge) **2** ESTRADOS *nmpl* : courts of law
estrafalario, -ria *adj* ESTRAMBÓTICO, EXCÉNTRICO : eccentric, bizarre
estragar {52} *vt* DEVASTAR : to ruin, to devastate
estragón *nm* : tarragon
estragos *nmpl* **1** : ravages, destruction, devastation <los estragos de la guerra : the ravages of war> **2 hacer estragos en** *or* **causar estragos entre** : to play havoc with
estrambótico, -ca *adj* ESTRAFALARIO, EXCÉNTRICO : eccentric, bizarre
estrangulamiento *nm* : strangling, strangulation
estrangular *vt* AHOGAR : to strangle — **estrangulación** *nf*
estratagema *nf* ARTIMAÑA : stratagem, ruse
estratega *nmf* : strategist
estrategia *nf* : strategy
estratégico, -ca *adj* : strategic, tactical — **estratégicamente** *adv*
estratificación *nf, pl* **-ciones** : stratification
estratificado, -da *adj* : stratified
estrato *nm* : stratum, layer
estratosfera *nf* : stratosphere
estratosférico, -ca *adj* **1** : stratospheric **2** : astronomical, exorbitant
estrechamiento *nm* **1** : narrowing **2** : narrow point **3** : tightening, strengthening (of relations)
estrechar *vt* **1** : to narrow **2** : to tighten, to strengthen (a bond) **3** : to hug, to embrace **4 estrechar la mano de** : to shake hands with — **estrecharse** *vr*
estrechez *nf, pl* **-checes 1** : tightness, narrowness **2 estrecheces** *nfpl* : financial problems
estrecho[1], **-cha** *adj* **1** : tight, narrow **2** ÍNTIMO : close — **estrechamente** *adv*
estrecho[2] *nm* : strait, narrows
estrella *nf* **1** ASTRO : star <estrella fugaz : shooting star> **2** : destiny <tener buena estrella : to be born lucky> **3** : movie star **4 estrella de mar** : starfish
estrellado, -da *adj* **1** : starry **2** : star-shaped **3 huevos estrellados** : fried eggs
estrellamiento *nm* : crash, collision
estrellar *vt* : to smash, to crash — **estrellarse** *vr* : to crash, to collide
estrellato *nm* : stardom
estremecedor, -dora *adj* : horrifying
estremecer {53} *vt* : to cause to shake — *vi* : to tremble, to shake — **estremecerse** *vr* : to shudder, to shiver (with emotion)
estremecimiento *nm* : trembling, shaking, shivering
estrenar *vt* **1** : to use for the first time **2** : to premiere, to open — **estrenarse** *vr* : to make one's debut
estreno *nm* DEBUT : debut, premiere
estreñimiento *nm* : constipation
estreñirse {67} *vr* : to be constipated
estrépito *nm* ESTRUENDO : clamor, din
estrepitoso, -sa *adj* : clamorous, noisy — **estrepitosamente** *adv*
estrés *nm, pl* **estreses** : stress
estresante *adj* : stressful
estresar *vt* : to stress, to stress out
estría *nf* : fluting, groove
estribación *nf, pl* **-ciones 1** : spur, ridge **2 estribaciones** *nfpl* : foothills
estribar *vi* FUNDARSE **~ en** : to be due to, to stem from
estribillo *nm* : refrain, chorus
estribo *nm* **1** : stirrup **2** : abutment, buttress **3 perder los estribos** : to lose one's temper
estribor *nm* : starboard
estricnina *nf* : strychnine
estricto, -ta *adj* SEVERO : strict, severe — **estrictamente** *adv*
estridente *adj* : strident, shrill, loud — **estridentemente** *adv*
estrofa *nf* : stanza, verse
estrógeno *nm* : estrogen
estropajo *nm* : scouring pad
estropear *vt* **1** ARRUINAR : to ruin, to spoil **2** : to break, to damage — **estropearse** *vr* **1** : to spoil, to go bad **2** : to break down
estropicio *nm* DAÑO : damage, breakage
estructura *nf* : structure, framework
estructuración *nf, pl* **-ciones** : structuring, structure
estructural *adj* : structural — **estructuralmente** *adv*
estructurar *vt* : to structure, to organize
estruendo *nm* ESTRÉPITO : racket, din, roar
estruendoso, -sa *adj* : resounding, thunderous
estrujar *vt* APRETAR : to press, to squeeze
estuario *nm* : estuary
estuche *nm* : kit, case
estuco *nm* : stucco
estudiado, -da *adj* : affected, mannered
estudiantado *nm* : student body, students *pl*
estudiante *nmf* : student
estudiantil *adj* : student <la vida estudiantil : student life>

estudiar *v* : to study
estudio *nm* **1** : study **2** : studio **3 estudios** *nmpl* : studies, education
estudioso, -sa *adj* : studious
estufa *nf* **1** : stove, heater **2** *Col, Mex* : cooking stove, range
estupefacción *nf, pl* **-ciones** : stupefaction, astonishment
estupefaciente[1] *adj* : narcotic
estupefaciente[2] *nm* DROGA, NARCÓTICO : drug, narcotic
estupefacto, -ta *adj* : astonished, stunned
estupendo, -da *adj* MARAVILLOSO : stupendous, marvelous — **estupendamente** *adv*
estupidez *nf, pl* **-deces 1** : stupidity **2** : nonsense
estúpido[1], **-da** *adj* : stupid — **estúpidamente** *adj*
estúpido[2], **-da** *n* IDIOTA : idiot, fool
estupor *nm* **1** : stupor **2** : amazement
esturión *nm, pl* **-riones** : sturgeon
estuvo, etc. → **estar**
etano *nm* : ethane
etanol *nm* : ethanol
etapa *nf* FASE : stage, phase
etcétera[1] : et cetera, and so on
etcétera[2] *nmf* : etcetera
éter *nm* : ether
etéreo, -rea *adj* : ethereal, heavenly
eternidad *nf* : eternity
eternizar {21} *vt* PERPETUAR : to make eternal, to perpetuate — **eternizarse** *vr fam* : to take forever
eterno, -na *adj* : eternal, endless — **eternamente** *adv*
ética *nf* : ethics
ético, -ca *adj* : ethical — **éticamente** *adv*
etimología *nf* : etymology
etimológico, -ca *adj* : etymological
etimólogo, -ga *n* : etymologist
etíope *adj & nmf* : Ethiopian
etiqueta *nf* **1** : etiquette **2** : tag, label **3 de ~** : formal, dressy
etiquetar *vt* : to label
étnico, -ca *adj* : ethnic
etnología *nf* : ethnology
etnólogo, -ga *n* : ethnologist
eucalipto *nm* : eucalyptus
Eucaristía *nf* : Eucharist, communion
eucarístico, -ca *adj* : eucharistic
eufemismo *nm* : euphemism
eufemístico, -ca *adj* : euphemistic
eufonía *nf* : euphony
eufónico, -ca *adj* : euphonious
euforia *nf* : euphoria, joyousness
eufórico, -ca *adj* : euphoric, exuberant, joyous — **eufóricamente** *adv*
eunuco *nm* : eunuch
europeo, -pea *adj & n* : European
euskera *nm* : Basque (language)
eutanasia *nf* : euthanasia
evacuación *nf, pl* **-ciones** : evacuation
evacuar *vt* **1** : to evacuate, to vacate **2** : to carry out — *vi* : to have a bowel movement
evadir *vt* ELUDIR : to evade, to avoid — **evadirse** *vr* : to escape, to slip away
evaluación *nf, pl* **-ciones** : assessment, evaluation
evaluar {3} *vt* : to evaluate, to assess, to appraise
evangélico, -ca *adj* : evangelical — **evangélicamente** *adv*
evangelio *nm* : gospel
evangelismo *nm* : evangelism
evangelista *nm* : evangelist
evangelizador, -dora *n* : evangelist, missionary
evaporación *nf, pl* **-ciones** : evaporation
evaporar *vt* : to evaporate — **evaporarse** *vr* ESFUMARSE : to disappear, to vanish
evasión *nf, pl* **-siones 1** : escape, flight **2** : evasion, dodge
evasiva *nf* : excuse, pretext
evasivo, -va *adj* : evasive
evento *nm* : event
eventual *adj* **1** : possible **2** : temporary <trabajadores eventuales : temporary workers> — **eventualmente** *adv*
eventualidad *nf* : possibility, eventuality
evidencia *nf* **1** : evidence, proof **2 poner en evidencia** : to demonstrate, to make clear
evidenciar *vt* : to demonstrate, to show — **evidenciarse** *vr* : to be evident
evidente *adj* : evident, obvious, clear — **evidentemente** *adv*
eviscerar *vt* : to eviscerate
evitable *adj* : avoidable, preventable
evitar *vt* **1** : to avoid **2** PREVENIR : to prevent **3** ELUDIR : to escape, to elude
evocación *nf, pl* **-ciones** : evocation
evocador, -dora *adj* : evocative
evocar {72} *vt* **1** : to evoke **2** RECORDAR : to recall
evolución *nf, pl* **-ciones 1** : evolution **2** : development, progress
evolucionar *vi* **1** : to evolve **2** : to change, to develop
evolutivo, -va *adj* : evolutionary
exabrupto *nm* : pointed remark
exacción *nf, pl* **-ciones** : levying, exaction
exacerbar *vt* **1** : to exacerbate, to aggravate **2** : to irritate, to exasperate
exactamente *adv* : exactly
exactitud *nf* PRECISIÓN : accuracy, precision, exactitude
exacto, -ta *adj* PRECISO : accurate, precise, exact
exageración *nf, pl* **-ciones** : exaggeration
exagerado, -da *adj* **1** : exaggerated **2** : excessive — **exageradamente** *adv*
exagerar *v* : to exaggerate
exaltación *nf, pl* **-ciones 1** : exaltation **2** : excitement, agitation
exaltado[1], **-da** *adj* : excitable, hotheaded
exaltado[2], **-da** *n* : hothead

exaltar *vt* **1** ENSALZAR : to exalt, to extol **2 :** to excite, to agitate — **exaltarse** *vr* ACALORARSE : to get overexcited
ex–alumno → **alumno**
examen *nm, pl* **exámenes 1 :** examination, test **2 :** consideration, investigation
examinar *vt* **1 :** to examine **2** INSPECCIONAR : to inspect — **examinarse** *vr* : to take an exam
exánime *adj* **1 :** lifeless **2 :** exhausted
exasperar *vt* IRRITAR : to exasperate, to irritate — **exasperación** *nf*
excavación *nf, pl* **-ciones :** excavation
excavadora *nf* : excavator
excavar *v* : to excavate, to dig
excedente[1] *adj* **1 :** excessive **2 :** excess, surplus
excedente[2] *nm* : surplus, excess
exceder *vt* : to exceed, to surpass — **excederse** *vr* : to go too far
excelencia *nf* **1 :** excellence **2 :** excellency <Su Excelencia : His Excellency>
excelente *adj* : excellent — **excelentemente** *adv*
excelso, -sa *adj* : lofty, sublime
excentricidad *nf* : eccentricity
excéntrico, -ca *adj & n* : eccentric
excepción *nf, pl* **-ciones :** exception
excepcional *adj* EXTRAORDINARIO : exceptional, extraordinary, rare
excepto *prep* SALVO : except
exceptuar {3} *vt* EXCLUIR : to except, to exclude
excesivo, -va *adj* : excessive — **excesivamente** *adv*
exceso *nm* **1 :** excess **2 excesos** *nmpl* : excesses, abuses **3 exceso de velocidad :** speeding
excitabilidad *nf* : excitability
excitación *nf, pl* **-ciones :** excitement
excitante *adj* : exciting
excitar *vt* : to excite, to arouse — **excitarse** *vr*
exclamación *nf, pl* **-ciones :** exclamation
exclamar *v* : to exclaim
excluir {41} *vt* EXCEPTUAR : to exclude, to leave out
exclusión *nf, pl* **-siones :** exclusion
exclusividad *nf* **1 :** exclusiveness **2** : exclusive rights *pl*
exclusivo, -va *adj* : exclusive — **exclusivamente** *adv*
excomulgar {52} *vt* : to excommunicate
excomunión *nf, pl* **-niones :** excommunication
excreción *nf, pl* **-ciones :** excretion
excremento *nm* : excrement
excretar *vt* : to excrete
exculpar *vt* : to exonerate, to exculpate — **exculpación** *nf*
excursión *nf, pl* **-siones :** excursion, outing
excursionista *nmf* **1 :** sightseer, tourist **2 :** hiker
excusa *nf* **1** PRETEXTO : excuse **2** DISCULPA : apology
excusar *vt* **1 :** to excuse **2 :** to exempt — **excusarse** *vr* : to apologize, to send one's regrets
execrable *adj* : detestable, abominable
exención *nf, pl* **-ciones :** exemption
exento, -ta *adj* **1 :** exempt, free **2 exento de impuestos :** tax-exempt
exequias *nfpl* FUNERALES : funeral rites
exhalar *vt* ESPIRAR : to exhale, to give off
exhaustivo, -va *adj* : exhaustive — **exhaustivamente** *adv*
exhausto, -ta *adj* AGOTADO : exhausted, worn-out
exhibición *nf, pl* **-ciones 1 :** exhibition, show **2 :** showing
exhibir *vt* : to exhibit, to show, to display — **exhibirse** *vr*
exhortación *nf, pl* **-ciones :** exhortation
exhortar *vt* : to exhort
exhumar *vt* DESENTERRAR : to exhume — **exhumación** *nf*
exigencia *nf* : demand, requirement
exigente *adj* : demanding, exacting
exigir {35} *vt* **1 :** to demand, to require **2 :** to exact, to levy
exiguo, -gua *adj* : meager
exiliado[1], **-da** *adj* : exiled, in exile
exiliado[2], **-da** *n* : exile
exiliar *vt* DESTERRAR : to exile, to banish — **exiliarse** *vr* : to go into exile
exilio *nm* DESTIERRO : exile
eximio, -mia *adj* : distinguished, eminent
eximir *vt* EXONERAR : to exempt
existencia *nf* **1 :** existence **2 existencias** *nfpl* MERCANCÍA : goods, stock
existente *adj* **1 :** existing, in existence **2 :** in stock
existir *vi* : to exist
éxito *nm* **1** TRIUNFO : success, hit **2 tener éxito :** to be successful
exitoso, -sa *adj* : successful — **exitosamente** *adv*
éxodo *nm* : exodus
exoneración *nf, pl* **-ciones** EXENCIÓN : exoneration, exemption
exonerar *vt* **1** EXIMIR : to exempt, to exonerate **2** DESPEDIR : to dismiss
exorbitante *adj* : exorbitant
exorcismo *nm* : exorcism — **exorcista** *nmf*
exorcizar {21} *vt* : to exorcize
exótico, -ca *adj* : exotic
expandir *vt* EXPANSIONAR : to expand — **expandirse** *vr* : to spread
expansión *nf, pl* **-siones 1 :** expansion, spread **2** DIVERSIÓN : recreation, relaxation
expansionar *vt* EXPANDIR : to expand — **expansionarse** *vr* **1 :** to expand **2** DIVERTIRSE : to amuse oneself, to relax
expansivo, -va *adj* : expansive
expatriado, -da *adj & n* : expatriate
expatriarse {85} *vr* **1** EMIGRAR : to emigrate **2 :** to go into exile

expectación *nf, pl* **-ciones** : expectation, anticipation
expectante *adj* : expectant
expectativa *nf* **1** : expectation, hope **2** **expectativas** *nfpl* : prospects
expedición *nf, pl* **-ciones** : expedition
expediente *nm* **1** : expedient, means **2** ARCHIVO : file, dossier, record
expedir {54} *vt* **1** EMITIR : to issue **2** DESPACHAR : to dispatch, to send
expedito, -ta *adj* **1** : free, clear **2** : quick, easy
expeler *vt* : to expel, to eject
expendedor, -dora *n* : dealer, seller
expendio *nm* TIENDA : store, shop
expensas *nfpl* **1** : expenses, costs **2** **a expensas de** : at the expense of
experiencia *nf* **1** : experience **2** EXPERIMENTO : experiment
experimentación *nf, pl* **-ciones** : experimentation
experimental *adj* : experimental
experimentar *vi* : to experiment — *vt* **1** : to experiment with, to test out **2** : to experience
experimento *nm* EXPERIENCIA : experiment
experto, -ta *adj & n* : expert
expiación *nf, pl* **-ciones** : expiation, atonement
expiar {85} *vt* : to expiate, to atone for
expiración *nf, pl* **-ciones** VENCIMIENTO : expiration
expirar *vi* **1** FALLECER, MORIR : to pass away, to die **2** : to expire
explanada *nf* : esplanade, promenade
explayar *vt* : to extend — **explayarse** *vr* : to expound, to speak at length
explicable *adj* : explicable, explainable
explicación *nf, pl* **-ciones** : explanation
explicar {72} *vt* : to explain — **explicarse** *vr* : to understand
explicativo, -va *adj* : explanatory
explicitar *vt* : to state explicitly, to specify
explícito, -ta *adj* : explicit — **explícitamente** *adv*
exploración *nf, pl* **-ciones** : exploration
explorador, -dora *n* : explorer, scout
explorar *vt* : to explore — **exploratorio, -ria** *adj*
explosión *nf, pl* **-siones** **1** ESTALLIDO : explosion **2** : outburst <una explosión de ira : an outburst of anger>
explosivo, -va *adj* : explosive
explotación *nf, pl* **-ciones** **1** : exploitation **2** : operation, running
explotar *vt* **1** : to exploit **2** : to operate, to run — *vi* ESTALLAR, REVENTAR : to explode
exponente *nm* : exponent
exponential *adj* : exponential — **exponentialmente** *adv*
exponer {60} *vt* **1** : to exhibit, to show, to display **2** : to explain, to present, to set forth **3** : to expose, to risk — *vi* : to exhibit
exportación *nf, pl* **-ciones** **1** : exportation **2** **exportaciones** *nfpl* : exports
exportador, -dora *n* : exporter
exportar *vt* : to export — **exportable** *adj*
exposición *nf, pl* **-ciones** **1** EXHIBICIÓN : exposition, exhibition **2** : exposure **3** : presentation, statement
expositor, -tora *n* **1** : exhibitor **2** : exponent
exprés *nms & pl* **1** : express, express train **2** : espresso
expresamente *adv* : expressly, on purpose
expresar *vt* : to express — **expresarse** *vr*
expresión *nf, pl* **-siones** : expression
expresivo, -va *adj* **1** : expressive **2** CARIÑOSO : affectionate — **expresivamente** *adv*
expreso[1], **-sa** *adj* : express, specific
expreso[2] *nm* : express train, express
exprimidor *nm* : squeezer, juicer
exprimir *vt* **1** : to squeeze **2** : to exploit
expropiar *vt* : to expropriate, to commandeer — **expropiación** *nf*
expuesto[1] *pp* → **exponer**
expuesto[2], **-ta** *adj* **1** : exposed **2** : hazardous, risky
expulsar *vt* : to expel, to eject
expulsión *nf, pl* **-siones** : expulsion
expurgar {52} *vt* : to expurgate
expuso, etc. → **exponer**
exquisitez *nf, pl* **-teces** **1** : exquisiteness, refinement **2** : delicacy, special dish
exquisito, -ta *adj* **1** : exquisite **2** : delicious
extasiarse {85} *vr* : to be in ecstasy, to be enraptured
éxtasis *nms & pl* : ecstasy, rapture
extático, -ta *adj* : ecstatic
extemporáneo, -nea *adj* **1** : unseasonable **2** : untimely
extender {56} *vt* **1** : to spread out, to stretch out **2** : to broaden, to expand <extender la influencia : to broaden one's influence> **3** : to draw up (a document), to write out (a check) — **extenderse** *vr* **1** : to spread **2** : to last
extendido, -da *adj* **1** : outstretched **2** : widespread
extensamente *adv* : extensively, at length
extensible *adj* : extensible, extendable
extensión *nf, pl* **-siones** **1** : extension, stretching **2** : expanse, spread **3** : extent, range **4** : length, duration
extenso, -sa *adj* **1** : extensive, detailed **2** : spacious, vast
extenuar {3} *vt* : to exhaust, to tire out — **extenuarse** *vr* — **extenuante** *adj*
exterior[1] *adj* **1** : exterior, external **2** : foreign <asuntos exteriores : foreign affairs>
exterior[2] *nm* **1** : outside **2** : abroad
exteriorizar {21} *vt* : to express, to reveal
exteriormente *adv* : outwardly

exterminar *vt* : to exterminate — **exterminación** *nf*
exterminio *nm* : extermination
externar *vt Mex* : to express, to display
externo, -na *adj* : external, outward
extinción *nf, pl* **-ciones** : extinction
extinguidor *nm* : fire extinguisher
extinguir {26} *vt* **1** APAGAR : to extinguish, to put out **2** : to wipe out — **extinguirse** *vr* **1** APAGARSE : to go out, to fade out **2** : to die out, to become extinct
extinto, -ta *adj* : extinct
extintor *nm* : extinguisher
extirpación *n, pl* **-ciones** : removal, excision
extirpar *vt* : to eradicate, to remove, to excise — **extirparse** *vr*
extorsión *nf, pl* **-siones** **1** : extortion **2** : harm, trouble
extorsionar *vt* : to extort
extra[1] *adv* : extra
extra[2] *adj* **1** : additional, extra **2** : superior, top-quality
extra[3] *nmf* : extra (in movies)
extra[4] *nm* : extra expense <paga extra : bonus>
extracción *nf, pl* **-ciones** : extraction
extracto *nm* **1** : extract <extracto de vainilla : vanilla extract> **2** : abstract, summary
extradición *nf, pl* **-ciones** : extradition
extraditar *vt* : to extradite
extraer {81} *vt* : to extract
extraído *pp* → **extraer**
extrajudicial *adj* : out-of-court
extramatrimonial *adj* : extramarital
extranjerizante *adj* : foreign-sounding, foreign-looking
extranjero[1], **-ra** *adj* : foreign
extranjero[2], **-ra** *n* : foreigner
extranjero[3] *nm* : foreign countries *pl* <viajó al extranjero : he traveled abroad> <trabajan en el extranjero : they work overseas>
extrañamente *adv* : strangely, oddly
extrañamiento *nm* ASOMBRO : amazement, surprise, wonder
extrañar *vt* : to miss (someone) — **extrañarse** *vr* : to be surprised
extrañeza *nf* **1** : strangeness, oddness **2** : surprise
extraño[1], **-ña** *adj* **1** RARO : strange, odd **2** EXTRANJERO : foreign
extraño[2], **-ña** *n* DESCONOCIDO : stranger
extraoficial *adj* OFICIOSO : unofficial — **extraoficialmente** *adv*
extraordinario, -ria *adj* EXCEPCIONAL : extraordinary — **extraordinariamente** *adv*
extrasensorial *adj* : extrasensory <percepción extrasensorial : extrasensory perception>
extraterrestre *adj & nmf* : extraterrestrial, alien
extravagancia *nf* : extravagance, outlandishness, flamboyance
extravagante *adj* : extravagant, outrageous, flamboyant
extraviar {85} *vt* **1** : to mislead, to lead astray **2** : to misplace, to lose — **extraviarse** *vr* : to get lost, to go astray
extravío *nm* **1** PÉRDIDA : loss, misplacement **2** : misconduct
extremado, -da *adj* : extreme — **extremadamente** *adv*
extremar *vt* : to carry to extremes — **extremarse** *vr* : to do one's utmost
extremidad *nf* **1** : extremity, tip, edge **2** **extremidades** *nfpl* : extremities
extremista *adj & nmf* : extremist
extremo[1], **-ma** *adj* **1** : extreme, utmost **2** EXCESIVO : excessive **3 en caso extremo** : as a last resort
extremo[2] *nm* **1** : extreme, end **2 al extremo de** : to the point of **3 en ~** : in the extreme
extrovertido[1] **-da** *adj* : extroverted, outgoing
extrovertido[2], **-da** *n* : extrovert
extrudir *vt* : to extrude
exuberancia *nf* **1** : exuberance **2** : luxuriance, lushness
exuberante *adj* : exuberant, luxuriant — **exuberantemente** *adv*
exudar *vt* : to exude
exultación *nf, pl* **-ciones** : exultation, elation
exultante *adj* : exultant, elated — **exultantemente** *adv*
exultar *vi* : to exult, to rejoice
eyacular *vi* : to ejaculate — **eyaculación** *nf*
eyección *nf, pl* **-ciones** : ejection, expulsion
eyectar *vt* : to eject, to expel — **eyectarse** *vr*

F

f *nf* : sixth letter of the Spanish alphabet
fábrica *nf* FACTORÍA : factory
fabricación *nf, pl* **-ciones** : manufacture
fabricante *nmf* : manufacturer
fabricar {72} *vt* MANUFACTURAR : to manufacture, to make
fabril *adj* INDUSTRIAL : industrial, manufacturing
fábula *nf* **1** : fable **2** : fabrication, fib
fabuloso, -sa *adj* **1** : fabulous, fantastic **2** : mythical, fabled
facción *nf, pl* **facciones** **1** : faction **2** **facciones** *nfpl* RASGOS : features
faccioso, -sa *adj* : factious
faceta *nf* : facet
facha *nf* : appearance, look <estar hecho una facha : to look a sight>
fachada *nf* : facade

facial *adj* **:** facial
fácil *adj* **1 :** easy **2 :** likely, probable <es fácil que no pase : it probably won't happen>
facilidad *nf* **1 :** facility, ease **2 facilidades** *nfpl* **:** facilities, services **3 facilidades** *nfpl* **:** opportunities
facilitar *vt* **1 :** to facilitate **2 :** to provide, to supply
fácilmente *adv* **:** easily, readily
facsímil *or* **facsímile** *nm* **1 :** facsimile, copy **2 :** fax
facsimilar *adj* **:** facsimile
factibilidad *nf* **:** feasibility
factible *adj* **:** feasible, practicable
facticio, -cia *adj* **:** artificial, factitious
factor[1], -tora *n* **1 :** agent, factor **2 :** baggage clerk
factor[2] *nm* ELEMENTO **:** factor, element
factoría *nf* FÁBRICA **:** factory
factótum *nm* **:** factotum
factura *nf* **1 :** making, manufacturing **2 :** bill, invoice
facturación *nf, pl* **-ciones 1 :** invoicing, billing **2 :** check-in
facturar *vt* **1 :** to bill, to invoice **2 :** to register, to check in
facultad *nf* **1 :** faculty, ability <facultades mentales : mental faculties> **2 :** authority, power **3 :** school (of a university) <facultad de derecho : law school>
facultar *vt* **:** to authorize, to empower
facultativo, -va *adj* **1** OPTATIVO **:** voluntary, optional **2 :** medical <informe facultativo : medical report>
faena *nf* **:** task, job, work <faenas domésticas : housework>
faenar *vi* **1 :** to work, to labor **2** PESCAR **:** to fish
fagot *nm* **:** bassoon
faisán *nm, pl* **faisanes :** pheasant
faja *nf* **1 :** sash, belt **2 :** girdle **3 :** strip (of land)
fajar *vt* **1 :** to wrap (a sash or girdle) around **2 :** to hit, to thrash — **fajarse** *vr* **1 :** to put on a sash or girdle **2 :** to come to blows
fajo *nm* **:** bundle, sheaf <un fajo de billetes : a wad of cash>
falacia *nf* **:** fallacy
falaz, -laza *adj, mpl* **falaces** FALSO **:** fallacious, false
falda *nf* **1 :** skirt <falda escocesa : kilt> **2** REGAZO **:** lap (of the body) **3** VERTIENTE **:** side, slope
falible *adj* **:** fallible
fálico, -ca *adj* **:** phallic
falla *nf* **1 :** flaw, defect **2 :** (geological) fault **3 :** fault, failing
fallar *vi* **1** FRACASAR **:** to fail, to go wrong **2 :** to rule (in a court of law) — *vt* **1** ERRAR **:** to miss (a target) **2 :** to pronounce judgment on
fallecer {53} *vi* MORIR **:** to pass away, to die
fallecido, -da *adj & n* DIFUNTO **:** deceased
fallecimiento *nm* **:** demise, death
fallido, -da *adj* **:** failed, unsuccessful
fallo *nm* **1** SENTENCIA **:** sentence, judgment, verdict **2 :** error, fault
falo *nm* **:** phallus, penis
falsamente *adv* **:** falsely
falsear *vt* **1 :** to falsify, to fake **2 :** to distort — *vi* **1** CEDER **:** to give way **2 :** to be out of tune
falsedad *nf* **1 :** falseness, hypocrisy **2** MENTIRA **:** falsehood, lie
falsete *nm* **:** falsetto
falsificación *nf, pl* **-ciones 1 :** counterfeit, forgery **2 :** falsification
falsificador, -dora *n* **:** counterfeiter, forger
falsificar {72} *vt* **1 :** to counterfeit, to forge **2 :** to falsify
falso, -sa *adj* **1** FALAZ **:** false, untrue **2 :** counterfeit, forged
falta *nf* **1** CARENCIA **:** lack <hacer falta : to be lacking, to be needed> **2** DEFECTO **:** defect, fault, error **3 :** offense, misdemeanor **4 :** foul (in basketball), fault (in tennis)
faltar *vi* **1 :** to be lacking, to be needed <me falta ayuda : I need help> **2 :** to be absent, to be missing **3** QUEDAR **:** to remain, to be left <faltan pocos días para la fiesta : the party is just a few days away> **4 ¡no faltaba más! :** don't mention it!, you're welcome!
falto, -ta *adj* **~ de :** lacking (in), short of
fama *nf* **1 :** fame **2** REPUTACIÓN **:** reputation **3 de mala fama :** disreputable
famélico, -ca *adj* HAMBRIENTO **:** starving, famished
familia *nf* **1 :** family **2 familia política :** in-laws
familiar[1] *adj* **1** CONOCIDO **:** familiar **2 :** familial, family **3** INFORMAL **:** informal
familiar[2] *nmf* PARIENTE **:** relation, relative
familiaridad *nf* **1 :** familiarity **2 :** informality
familiarizarse {21} *vr* **~ con :** to familiarize oneself with
famoso[1], -sa *adj* CÉLEBRE **:** famous
famoso[2], -sa *n* **:** celebrity
fanal *nm* **1 :** beacon, signal light **2** *Mex* **:** headlight
fanático, -ca *adj & n* **:** fanatic
fanatismo *nm* **:** fanaticism
fandango *nm* **:** fandango
fanfarria *nf* **1 :** (musical) fanfare **2 :** pomp, ceremony
fanfarrón[1], -rrona *adj, mpl* **-rrones** *fam* **:** bragging, boastful
fanfarrón[2], -rrona *n, mpl* **-rrones** *fam* **:** braggart
fanfarronada *nf* **:** boast, bluster
fanfarronear *vi* **:** to brag, to boast
fango *nm* LODO **:** mud, mire
fangosidad *nf* **:** muddiness
fangoso, -sa *adj* LODOSO **:** muddy
fantasear *vi* **:** to fantasize, to daydream
fantasía *nf* **1 :** fantasy **2 :** imagination

fantasma *nm* : ghost, phantom
fantasmal *adj* : ghostly
fantástico, -ca *adj* **1** : fantastic, imaginary, unreal **2** *fam* : great, fantastic
faquir *nm* : fakir
farándula *nf* : show business, theater
faraón *nm, pl* **faraones** : pharaoh
fardo *nm* **1** : bale **2** : bundle
farfulla *nf* : jabbering
farfullar *v* : to jabber, to gabble
faringe *nf* : pharynx
faríngeo, -gea *adj* : pharyngeal
fariña *nf* : coarse manioc flour
farmacéutico[1]**, -ca** *adj* : pharmaceutical
farmacéutico[2]**, -ca** *n* : pharmacist
farmacia *nf* : drugstore, pharmacy
fármaco *nm* : medicine, drug
farmacodependencia *nf* : drug addiction
farmacología *nf* : pharmacology
faro *nm* **1** : lighthouse **2** : headlight
farol *nm* **1** : streetlight **2** : lantern, lamp **3** *fam* : bluff **4** *Mex* : headlight
farola *nf* **1** : lamppost **2** : streetlight
farolero, -ra *n fam* : bluffer
farra *nf* : spree, revelry
fárrago *nm* REVOLTIJO : hodgepodge, jumble
farsa *nf* **1** : farce **2** : fake, sham
farsante *nmf* CHARLATÁN : charlatan, fraud, phony
fascículo *nm* : fascicle, part (of a publication)
fascinación *nf, pl* **-ciones** : fascination
fascinante *adj* : fascinating
fascinar *vt* **1** : to fascinate **2** : to charm, to captivate
fascismo *nm* : fascism
fascista *adj & nmf* : fascist
fase *nf* : phase, stage
fastidiar *vt* **1** MOLESTAR : to annoy, to bother, to hassle **2** ABURRIR : to bore — *vi* : to be annoying or bothersome
fastidio *nm* **1** MOLESTIA : annoyance, nuisance, hassle **2** ABURRIMIENTO : boredom
fastidioso, -sa *adj* **1** MOLESTO : annoying, bothersome **2** ABURRIDO : boring
fatal *adj* **1** MORTAL : fatal **2** *fam* : awful, terrible **3** : fateful, unavoidable
fatalidad *nf* **1** : fatality **2** DESGRACIA : misfortune, bad luck
fatalismo *nm* : fatalism
fatalista[1] *adj* : fatalistic
fatalista[2] *nmf* : fatalist
fatalmente *adv* **1** : unavoidably **2** : unfortunately
fatídico, -ca *adj* : fateful, momentous
fatiga *nf* CANSANCIO : fatigue
fatigado, -da *adj* AGOTADO : weary, tired
fatigar {52} *vt* CANSAR : to fatigue, to tire — **fatigarse** *vr* : to wear oneself out
fatigoso, -sa *adj* : fatiguing, tiring
fatuidad *nf* **1** : fatuousness **2** VANIDAD : vanity, conceit
fatuo, -tua *adj* **1** : fatuous **2** PRESUMIDO : vain
fauces *nfpl* : jaws *pl,* maw
faul *nm, pl* **fauls** : foul, foul ball
fauna *nf* : fauna
fausto *nm* : splendor, magnificence
favor *nm* **1** : favor **2 a favor de** : in favor of **3 por ~** : please
favorable *adj* : favorable — **favorablemente** *adv*
favorecedor, -dora *adj* : becoming, flattering
favorecer {53} *vt* **1** : to favor **2** : to look well on, to suit
favorecido, -da *adj* **1** : flattering **2** : fortunate
favoritismo *nm* : favoritism
favorito, -ta *adj & n* : favorite
fax *nm* : fax, facsimile
fayuca *nf Mex* **1** : contraband **2** : black market
fayuquero *nm Mex* : smuggler, black marketeer
faz *nf* **1** : face, countenance <la faz de la tierra : the face of the earth> **2** : side (of coins, fabric, etc.)
fe *nf* **1** : faith **2** : assurance, testimony <dar fe de : to bear witness to> **3** : intention, will <de buena fe : bona fide, in good faith>
fealdad *nf* : ugliness
febrero *nm* : February
febril *adj* : feverish — **febrilmente** *adv*
fecal *adj* : fecal
fecha *nf* **1** : date **2 fecha de caducidad** *or* **fecha de vencimiento** : expiration date **3 fecha límite** : deadline
fechar *vt* : to date, to put a date on
fechoría *nf* : misdeed
fécula *nf* : starch
fecundar *vt* : to fertilize (an egg) — **fecundación** *nf*
fecundidad *nf* **1** : fecundity, fertility **2** : productiveness
fecundo, -da *adj* FÉRTIL : fertile, fecund
federación *nf, pl* **-ciones** : federation
federal *adj* : federal
federalismo *nm* : federalism
federalista *adj & nmf* : federalist
federar *vt* : to federate
fehaciente *adj* : reliable, irrefutable — **fehacientemente** *adv*
feldespato *nm* : feldspar
felicidad *nf* **1** : happiness **2 ¡felicidades!** : best wishes!, congratulations!, happy birthday!
felicitación *nf, pl* **-ciones 1** : congratulation <¡felicitaciones! : congratulations!> **2** : greeting card
felicitar *vt* CONGRATULAR : to congratulate — **felicitarse** *vr* : to be glad about
feligrés, -gresa *n, mpl* **-greses** : parishioner
feligresía *nf* : parish
felino, -na *adj & n* : feline
feliz *adj, pl* **felices 1** : happy **2 Feliz Navidad** : Merry Christmas

felizmente *adv* **1** : happily **2** : fortunately, luckily
felonía *nf* : felony
felpa *nf* **1** : terry cloth **2** : plush
felpudo *nm* : doormat
femenil *adj* : women's, girls' <futbol femenil : women's soccer>
femenino, -na *adj* **1** : feminine **2** : women's <derechos femeninos : women's rights> **3** : female
femineidad *nf* : femininity
feminidad *nf* : femininity
feminismo *nm* : feminism
feminista *adj & nmf* : feminist
femoral *adj* : femoral
fémur *nm* : femur, thighbone
fenecer {53} *vi* **1** : to die, to pass away **2** : to come to an end, to cease
fénix *nm* : phoenix
fenomenal *adj* **1** : phenomenal **2** *fam* : fantastic, terrific — **fenomenalmente** *adv*
fenómeno *nm* **1** : phenomenon **2** : prodigy, genius
feo[1] *adv* : badly, bad
feo[2], **fea** *adj* **1** : ugly **2** : unpleasant, nasty
féretro *nm* ATAÚD : coffin, casket
feria *nf* **1** : fair, market **2** : festival, holiday **3** *Mex* : change (money)
feriado, -da *adj* **día feriado** : public holiday
ferial *nm* : fairground
fermentar *v* : to ferment — **fermentación** *nf*
fermento *nm* : ferment
ferocidad *nf* : ferocity, fierceness
feroz *adj, pl* **feroces** FIERO : ferocious, fierce — **ferozmente** *adv*
férreo, -rrea *adj* **1** : iron **2** : strong, steely <una voluntad férrea : an iron will> **3** : strict, severe **4** **vía férrea** : railroad track
ferretería *nf* **1** : hardware store **2** : hardware **3** : foundry, ironworks
férrico, -ca *adj* : ferric
ferrocarril *nm* : railroad, railway
ferrocarrilero → **ferroviario**
ferroso, -sa *adj* : ferrous
ferroviario, -ria *adj* : rail, railroad
ferry *nm, pl* **ferrys** : ferry
fértil *adj* FECUNDO : fertile, fruitful
fertilidad *nf* : fertility
fertilizante[1] *adj* : fertilizing <droga fertilizante : fertility drug>
fertilizante[2] *nm* ABONO : fertilizer
fertilizar *vt* ABONAR : to fertilize — **fertilización** *nf*
ferviente *adj* FERVOROSO : fervent
fervor *nm* : fervor, zeal
fervoroso, -sa *adj* FERVIENTE : fervent, zealous
festejar *vt* **1** CELEBRAR : to celebrate **2** AGASAJAR : to entertain, to wine and dine **3** *Mex fam* : to thrash, to beat
festejo *nm* : celebration, festivity
festín *nm, pl* **festines** : banquet, feast
festinar *vt* : to hasten, to hurry up
festival *nm* : festival
festividad *nf* **1** : festivity **2** : (religious) feast, holiday
festivo, -va *adj* **1** : festive **2** **día festivo** : holiday — **festivamente** *adv*
fetal *adj* : fetal
fetiche *nm* : fetish
fétido, -da *adj* : fetid, foul
feto *nm* : fetus
feudal *adj* : feudal — **feudalismo** *nm*
feudo *nm* **1** : fief **2** : domain, territory
fiabilidad *nf* : reliability, trustworthiness
fiable *adj* : trustworthy, reliable
fiado, -da *adj* : on credit
fiador, -dora *n* : bondsman, guarantor
fiambrería *nf* : delicatessen
fiambres *nfpl* : cold cuts
fianza *nf* **1** CAUCIÓN : bail, bond **2** : surety, deposit
fiar {85} *vt* **1** : to sell on credit **2** : to guarantee — **fiarse** *vr* **~ de** : to place trust in
fiasco *nm* FRACASO : fiasco, failure
fibra *nf* **1** : fiber **2** **fibra de vidrio** : fiberglass
fibrilar *vi* : to fibrillate — **fibrilación** *nf*
fibroso, -sa *adj* : fibrous
ficción *nf, pl* **ficciones** **1** : fiction **2** : fabrication, lie
ficha *nf* **1** : index card **2** : file, record **3** : token **4** : domino, checker, counter, poker chip
fichar *vt* **1** : to open a file on **2** : to sign up — *vi* : to punch in, to punch out
fichero *nm* **1** : card file **2** : filing cabinet
ficticio, -cia *adj* : fictitious
fidedigno, -na *adj* FIABLE : reliable, trustworthy
fideicomisario, -ria *n* : trustee
fideicomiso *nm* : trusteeship, trust <guardar en fideicomiso : to hold in trust>
fidelidad *nf* : fidelity, faithfulness
fideo *nm* : noodle
fiduciario[1], **-ria** *adj* : fiduciary
fiduciario[2], **-ria** *n* : trustee
fiebre *nf* **1** CALENTURA : fever, temperature <fiebre amarilla : yellow fever> <fiebre palúdica : malaria> **2** : fever, excitement
fiel[1] *adj* **1** : faithful, loyal **2** : accurate — **fielmente** *adv*
fiel[2] *nm* **1** : pointer (of a scale) **2** **los fieles** : the faithful
fieltro *nm* : felt
fiera *nf* **1** : wild animal, beast **2** : fiend, demon <una fiera para el trabajo : a demon for work>
fiero, -ra *adj* FEROZ : fierce, ferocious
fierro *nm* HIERRO : iron
fiesta *nf* **1** : party, fiesta **2** : holiday, feast day
figura *nf* **1** : figure **2** : shape, form **3** **figura retórica** : figure of speech
figurado, -da *adj* : figurative — **figuradamente** *adv*

figurar *vi* **1 :** to figure, to be included <Rivera figura entre los más grandes pintores de México : Rivera is among Mexico's greatest painters> **2 :** to be prominent, to stand out — *vt* **:** to represent <esta línea figura el horizonte : this line represents the horizon> — **figurarse** *vr* **:** to imagine, to think <¡figúrate el lío en que se metió! : imagine the mess she got into!>

fijación *nf, pl* **-ciones 1 :** fixation, obsession **2 :** fixing, establishing **3 :** fastening, securing

fijador *nm* **1 :** fixative **2 :** hair spray

fijamente *adv* **:** fixedly

fijar *vt* **1 :** to fasten, to affix **2** ESTABLECER **:** to establish, to set up **3** CONCRETAR **:** to set, to fix <fijar la fecha : to set the date> — **fijarse** *vr* **1 :** to settle, to become fixed **2 ~ en :** to notice, to pay attention to

fijeza *nf* **1 :** firmness (of convictions) **2 :** persistence, constancy <mirar con fijeza a : to stare at>

fijiano, -na *adj & n* **:** Fijian

fijo, -ja *adj* **1 :** fixed, firm, steady **2** PERMANENTE **:** permanent

fila *nf* **1** HILERA **:** line, file <ponerse en fila : to get in line> **2 :** rank, row **3 filas** *nfpl* **:** ranks <cerrar filas : to close ranks>

filamento *nm* **:** filament

filantropía *nf* **:** philanthropy

filantrópico, -ca *adj* **:** philanthropic

filántropo, -pa *n* **:** philanthropist

filatelia *nf* **:** philately, stamp collecting

filatelista *nmf* **:** stamp collector, philatelist

filete *nm* **1 :** fillet **2** SOLOMILLO **:** sirloin **3 :** thread (of a screw)

filiación *nf, pl* **-ciones 1 :** affiliation, connection **2 :** particulars *pl,* (police) description

filial[1] *adj* **:** filial

filial[2] *nf* **:** affiliate, subsidiary

filibustero *nm* **:** freebooter, pirate

filigrana *nf* **1 :** filigree **2 :** watermark (on paper)

filipino, -na *adj & n* **:** Filipino

filmación *nf, pl* **-ciones :** filming, shooting

filmar *vt* **:** to film, to shoot

filme *or* **film** *nm* PELÍCULA **:** film, movie

filmina *nf* **:** slide, transparency

filo *nm* **1 :** cutting edge, blade **2 :** edge <al filo del escritorio : at the edge of the desk> <al filo de la medianoche : at the stroke of midnight>

filología *nf* **:** philology

filólogo, -ga *n* **:** philologist

filón *nm, pl* **filones 1 :** seam, vein (of minerals) **2** *fam* **:** successful business, gold mine

filoso, -sa *adj* **:** sharp

filosofar *vi* **:** to philosophize

filosofía *nf* **:** philosophy

filosófico, -ca *adj* **:** philosophic, philosophical — **filosóficamente** *adv*

filósofo, -fa *n* **:** philosopher

filtración *nf* **:** seepage, leaking

filtrar *v* **:** to filter — **filtrarse** *vr* **:** to seep through, to leak

filtro *nm* **:** filter

filudo, -da *adj* **:** sharp

fin *nm* **1 :** end **2 :** purpose, aim, objective **3 en ~ :** in short **4 fin de semana :** weekend **5 por ~ :** finally, at last

finado, -da *adj & n* DIFUNTO **:** deceased

final[1] *adj* **:** final, ultimate — **finalmente** *adv*

final[2] *nm* **1 :** end, conclusion, finale **2 finales** *nmpl* **:** play-offs

finalidad *nf* **1 :** purpose, aim **2 :** finality

finalista *nmf* **:** finalist

finalización *nf* **:** completion, end

finalizar {21} *v* **:** to finish, to end

financiación *nf, pl* **-ciones :** financing, funding

financiamiento *nm* → **financiación**

financiar *vt* **:** to finance, to fund

financiero[1], **-ra** *adj* **:** financial

financiero[2], **-ra** *n* **:** financier

financista *nmf* **:** financier

finanzas *nfpl* **:** finances, finance <altas finanzas : high finance>

finca *nf* **1 :** farm, ranch **2 :** country house

fineza *nf* FINURA, REFINAMIENTO **:** refinement

fingido, -da *adj* **:** false, feigned

fingimiento *nm* **:** pretense

fingir {35} *v* **:** to feign, to pretend

finiquitar *vt* **1 :** to settle (an account) **2 :** to conclude, to bring to an end

finiquito *nm* **:** settlement (of an account)

finito, -ta *adj* **:** finite

finja, etc. → **fingir**

finlandés, -desa *adj & n* **:** Finnish

fino, -na *adj* **1 :** fine, excellent **2 :** delicate, slender **3** REFINADO **:** refined **4 :** sharp, acute <olfato fino : keen sense of smell> **5 :** subtle

finta *nf* **:** feint

fintar *or* **fintear** *vi* **:** to feint

finura *nf* **1 :** fineness, high quality **2** FINEZA, REFINAMIENTO **:** refinement

fiordo *nm* **:** fjord

fique *nm* **:** sisal

firma *nf* **1 :** signature **2 :** signing **3** EMPRESA **:** firm, company

firmamento *nm* **:** firmament, sky

firmante *nmf* **:** signer, signatory

firmar *v* **:** to sign

firme *adj* **1 :** firm, resolute **2 :** steady, stable

firmemente *adv* **:** firmly

firmeza *nf* **1 :** firmness, stability **2 :** strength, resolve

firuletes *nmpl* **:** frills, adornments

fiscal[1] *adj* **:** fiscal — **fiscalmente** *adv*

fiscal[2] *nmf* **:** district attorney, prosecutor

fiscalizar {21} *vt* **1 :** to audit, to inspect **2 :** to oversee **3 :** to criticize

fisco *nm* **:** national treasury, exchequer

fisgar {52} *vt* HUSMEAR : to pry into, to snoop on
fisgón, -gona *n, mpl* **fisgones** : snoop, busybody
fisgonear *vi* : to snoop, to pry
fisgue, etc. → **fisgar**
física *nf* : physics
físico¹, -ca *adj* : physical — **físicamente** *adv*
físico², -ca *n* : physicist
físico³ *nm* : physique, figure
fisiología *nf* : physiology
fisiológico, -ca *adj* : physiological, physiologic
fisiólogo, -ga *n* : physiologist
fisión *nf, pl* **fisiones** : fission — **fisionable** *adj*
fisionomía *nf* → **fisonomía**
fisioterapeuta *nmf* : physical therapist
fisioterapia *nf* : physical therapy
fisonomía *nf* : physiognomy, features *pl*
fistol *nm Mex* : tie clip
fisura *nf* : fissure, crevasse
fláccido, -da *or* **flácido, -da** *adj* : flaccid, flabby
flaco, -ca *adj* **1** DELGADO : thin, skinny **2** : feeble, weak <una excusa flaca : a feeble excuse>
flagelar *vt* : to flagellate — **flagelación** *nf*
flagelo *nm* **1** : scourge, whip **2** : calamity
flagrante *adj* : flagrant, glaring, blatant — **flagrantemente** *adv*
flama *nf* LLAMA : flame
flamante *adj* **1** : bright, brilliant **2** : brand-new
flamear *vi* **1** LLAMEAR : to flame, to blaze **2** ONDEAR : to flap, to flutter
flamenco¹, -ca *adj* **1** : flamenco **2** : Flemish
flamenco², -ca *n* : Fleming, Flemish person
flamenco³ *nm* **1** : Flemish (language) **2** : flamingo **3** : flamenco (music or dance)
flanco *nm* : flank, side
flanquear *vt* : to flank
flaquear *vi* DECAER : to flag, to weaken
flaqueza *nf* **1** DEBILIDAD : frailty, feebleness **2** : thinness **3** : weakness, failing
flato *nm* : gloom, melancholy
flatulento, -ta *adj* : flatulent — **flatulencia** *nf*
flauta *nf* **1** : flute **2 flauta dulce** : recorder
flautín *nm, pl* **flautines** : piccolo
flautista *nmf* : flute player, flutist
flebitis *nf* : phlebitis
flecha *nf* : arrow
fleco *nm* **1** : bangs *pl* **2** : fringe
flema *nf* : phlegm
flemático, -ca *adj* : phlegmatic, stolid, impassive
flequillo *nm* : bangs *pl*
fletar *vt* **1** : to charter, to hire **2** : to load (freight)
flete *nm* **1** : charter fee **2** : shipping cost **3** : freight, cargo
fletero *nm* : shipper, carrier
flexibilidad *nf* : flexibility
flexibilizar {21} *vt* : to make more flexible
flexible¹ *adj* : flexible
flexible² *nm* **1** : flexible electrical cord **2** : soft hat
flirtear *vi* : to flirt
flojear *vi* **1** DEBILITARSE : to weaken, to flag **2** : to idle, to loaf around
flojedad *nf* : weakness
flojera *nf fam* **1** : lethargy, feeling of weakness **2** : laziness
flojo, -ja *adj* **1** SUELTO : loose, slack **2** : weak, poor <está flojo en las ciencias : he's weak in science> **3** PEREZOSO : lazy
flor *nf* **1** : flower **2 flor de Pascua** : poinsettia
flora *nf* : flora
floración *nf* : flowering <en plena floración : in full bloom>
floral *adj* : floral
floreado, -da *adj* : flowered, flowery
florear *vi* FLORECER : to flower, to bloom — *vt* **1** : to adorn with flowers **2** *Mex* : to flatter, to compliment
florecer {53} *vi* **1** : to bloom, to blossom **2** : to flourish, to thrive
floreciente *adj* **1** : flowering **2** PROSPERO : flourishing, thriving
florecimiento *nm* : flowering
floreo *nm* : flourish
florería *nf* : flower shop, florist's
florero¹, -ra *n* : florist
florero² *nm* JARRÓN : vase
floresta *nf* **1** : glade, grove **2** BOSQUE : woods
florido, -da *adj* **1** : full of flowers **2** : florid, flowery <escritos floridos : flowery prose>
florista *nmf* : florist
floritura *nf* : frill, embellishment
flota *nf* : fleet
flotabilidad *nf* : buoyancy
flotación *nf, pl* **-ciones** : flotation
flotador *nm* **1** : float **2** : life preserver
flotante *adj* : floating, buoyant
flotar *vi* : to float
flote *nm* **a ~** : afloat
flotilla *nf* : flotilla, fleet
fluctuar {3} *vi* **1** : to fluctuate **2** VACILAR : to vacillate — **fluctuación** *nf* — **fluctuante** *adj*
fluidez *nf* **1** : fluency **2** : fluidity
fluido¹, -da *adj* **1** : flowing **2** : fluent **3** : fluid
fluido² *nm* : fluid
fluir {41} *vi* : to flow
flujo *nm* **1** : flow **2** : discharge
flúor *nm* : fluorine
fluoración *nf, pl* **-ciones** : fluoridation
fluorescencia *nf* : fluorescence — **fluorescente** *adj*
fluorizar {21} *vt* : to fluoridate
fluoruro *nm* : fluoride
fluvial *adj* : fluvial, river

fluye, etc. → **fluir**

fobia *nf* **:** phobia

foca *nf* **:** seal (animal)

focal *adj* **:** focal

focha *nf* **:** coot

foco *nm* **1 :** focus **2 :** center, pocket **3 :** lightbulb **4 :** spotlight **5 :** headlight

fofo, -fa *adj* **1** ESPONJOSO **:** soft, spongy **2 :** flabby

fogaje *nm* **1** FUEGO **:** skin eruption, cold sore **2** BOCHORNO **:** hot and humid weather

fogata *nf* **:** bonfire

fogón *nm, pl* **fogones :** bonfire

fogonazo *nm* **:** flash, explosion

fogonero, -ra *n* **:** stoker (of a furnace), fireman

fogoso, -sa *adj* ARDIENTE **:** ardent

foguear *vt* **:** to inure, to accustom

foja *nf* **:** sheet (of paper)

folículo *nm* **:** follicle

folio *nm* **:** folio, leaf

folklore *nm* **:** folklore

folklórico, -ca *adj* **:** folk, traditional

follaje *nm* **:** foliage

folleto *nm* **:** pamphlet, leaflet, circular

fomentar *vt* **1 :** to foment, to stir up **2** PROMOVER **:** to promote, to foster

fomento *nm* **:** promotion, encouragement

fonda *nf* **1** POSADA **:** inn **2 :** small restaurant

fondeado, -da *adj fam* **:** rich, in the money

fondear *vt* **1 :** to sound **2 :** to sound out, to examine **3** *Mex* **:** to fund, to finance — *vi* ANCLAR **:** to anchor — **fondearse** *vr fam* **:** to get rich

fondeo *nm* **1 :** anchoring **2** *Mex* **:** funding, financing

fondillos *mpl* **:** seat, bottom (of clothing)

fondo *nm* **1 :** bottom **2 :** rear, back, end **3 :** depth **4 :** background **5 :** sea bed **6 :** fund <fondo de inversiones : investment fund> **7** *Mex* **:** slip, petticoat **8 fondos** *nmpl* **:** funds, resources <cheque sin fondos : bounced check> **9 a ~ :** thoroughly, in depth **10 en ~ :** abreast

fonema *nm* **:** phoneme

fonética *nf* **:** phonetics

fonético, -ca *adj* **:** phonetic

fontanería *nf* PLOMERÍA **:** plumbing

fontanero, -ra *n* PLOMERO **:** plumber

footing [ˈfuˌtɪŋ] *nm* **:** jogging <hacer footing : to jog>

foque *nm* **:** jib

forajido, -da *n* **:** bandit, fugitive, outlaw

foráneo, -nea *adj* **:** foreign, strange

forastero, -ra *n* **:** stranger, outsider

forcejear *vi* **:** to struggle

forcejeo *nm* **:** struggle

fórceps *nms & pl* **:** forceps *pl*

forense *adj* **:** forensic, legal

forestal *adj* **:** forest

forja *nf* FRAGUA **:** forge

forjar *vt* **1 :** to forge **2 :** to shape, to create <forjar un compromiso : to hammer out a compromise> **3 :** to invent, to concoct

forma *nf* **1 :** form, shape **2** MANERA, MODO **:** manner, way **3 :** fitness <estar en forma : to be fit, to be in shape> **4 formas** *nfpl* **:** appearances, conventions

formación *nf, pl* **-ciones 1 :** formation **2 :** training <formación profesional : vocational training>

formal *adj* **1 :** formal **2 :** serious, dignified **3 :** dependable, reliable

formaldehído *nm* **:** formaldehyde

formalidad *nf* **1 :** formality **2 :** seriousness, dignity **3 :** dependability, reliability

formalizar {21} *vt* **:** to formalize, to make official

formalmente *adv* **:** formally

formar *vt* **1 :** to form, to make **2** CONSTITUIR **:** to constitute, to make up **3 :** to train, to educate — **formarse** *vr* **1** DESARROLLARSE **:** to develop, to take shape **2** EDUCARSE **:** to be educated

formatear *vt* **:** to format

formativo, -va *adj* **:** formative

formato *nm* **:** format

formidable *adj* **1 :** formidable, tremendous **2** *fam* **:** fantastic, terrific

formón *nm, pl* **formones :** chisel

fórmula *nf* **:** formula

formulación *nf, pl* **-ciones :** formulation

formular *vt* **1 :** to formulate, to draw up **2 :** to make, to lodge (a protest or complaint)

formulario *nm* **:** form <rellenar un formulario : to fill out a form>

fornicar {72} *vi* **:** to fornicate — **fornicación** *nf*

fornido, -da *adj* **:** well-built, burly, hefty

foro *nm* **1 :** forum **2 :** public assembly, open discussion

forraje *nm* **1 :** forage, fodder **2 :** foraging **3** *fam* **:** hodgepodge

forrajear *vi* **:** to forage

forrar *vt* **1 :** to line (a garment) **2 :** to cover (a book)

forro *nm* **1 :** lining **2** CUBIERTA **:** book cover

forsitia *nf* **:** forsythia

fortachón, -chona *adj, pl* **-chones** *fam* **:** brawny, strong, tough

fortalecer {53} *vt* **:** to strengthen, to fortify — **fortalecerse** *vr*

fortalecimiento *nm* **1 :** strengthening, fortifying **2 :** fortifications

fortaleza *nf* **1 :** fortress **2** FUERZA **:** strength **3 :** resolution, fortitude

fortificación *nf, pl* **-ciones :** fortification

fortificar {72} *vt* **1 :** to fortify **2 :** to strengthen

fortín *nm, pl* **fortines :** small fort

fortuito, -ta *adj* **:** fortuitous

fortuna *nf* **1** SUERTE **:** fortune, luck **2** RIQUEZA **:** wealth, fortune
forzar {36} *vt* **1** OBLIGAR **:** to force, to compel **2 :** to force open **3 :** to strain <forzar los ojos : to strain one's eyes>
forzosamente *adv* **1 :** forcibly, by force **2 :** necessarily, inevitably <forzosamente tendrán que pagar : they'll have no choice but to pay>
forzoso, -sa *adj* **1 :** forced, compulsory **2 :** necessary, inevitable
fosa *nf* **1 :** ditch, pit <fosa séptica : septic tank> **2** TUMBA **:** grave **3 :** cavity <fosas nasales : nasal cavities, nostrils>
fosfato *nm* **:** phosphate
fosforescencia *nf* **:** phosphorescence — **fosforescente** *adj*
fósforo *nm* **1** CERILLA **:** match **2 :** phosphorus
fósil¹ *adj* **:** fossilized, fossil
fósil² *nm* **:** fossil
fosilizarse {21} *vr* **:** to fossilize, to become fossilized
foso *nm* **1** FOSA, ZANJA **:** ditch **2 :** pit (of a theater) **3 :** moat
foto *nf* **:** photo, picture
fotocopia *nf* **:** photocopy — **fotocopiar** *vt*
fotocopiadora *nf* COPIADORA **:** photocopier
fotoeléctrico, -ca *adj* **:** photoelectric
fotogénico, -ca *adj* **:** photogenic
fotografía *nf* **1 :** photograph **2 :** photography
fotografiar {85} *vt* **:** to photograph
fotográfico, -ca *adj* **:** photographic — **fotográficamente** *adv*
fotógrafo, -fa *n* **:** photographer
fotosíntesis *nf* **:** photosynthesis
fotosintético, -ca *adj* **:** photosynthetic
fracasado¹, -da *adj* **:** unsuccessful, failed
fracasado², -da *n* **:** failure
fracasar *vi* **1** FALLAR **:** to fail **2 :** to fall through
fracaso *nm* FIASCO **:** failure
fracción *nf, pl* **fracciones 1 :** fraction **2 :** part, fragment **3 :** faction, splinter group
fraccionamiento *nm* **1 :** division, breaking up **2** *Mex* **:** residential area, housing development
fraccionar *vt* **:** to divide, to break up
fractura *nf* **1 :** fracture **2 fractura complicada :** compound fracture
fracturarse *vr* QUEBRARSE, ROMPERSE **:** to fracture, to break <fracturarse el brazo : to break one's arm>
fragancia *nf* **:** fragrance, scent
fragante *adj* **:** fragrant
fragata *nf* **:** frigate
frágil *adj* **1 :** fragile **2 :** frail, delicate
fragilidad *nf* **1 :** fragility **2 :** frailty, delicacy
fragmentar *vt* **:** to fragment — **fragmentación** *nf*
fragmentario, -ria *adj* **:** fragmentary, sketchy
fragmento *nm* **1 :** fragment, shard **2 :** bit, snippet **3 :** excerpt, passage
fragor *nm* **:** clamor, din, roar
fragoroso, -sa *adj* **:** thunderous, deafening
fragoso, -sa *adj* **1 :** rough, uneven **2 :** thick, dense
fragua *nf* FORJA **:** forge
fraguar {10} *vt* **1 :** to forge **2 :** to conceive, to concoct, to hatch — *vi* **:** to set, to solidify
fraile *nm* **:** friar, monk
frambuesa *nf* **:** raspberry
francamente *adv* **1 :** frankly, candidly **2** REALMENTE **:** really <es francamente admirable : it's really impressive>
francés¹, -cesa *adj, mpl* **franceses :** French
francés², -cesa *n, mpl* **franceses :** French person, Frenchman *m,* Frenchwoman *f*
francés³ *nm* **:** French (language)
franciscano, -na *adj & n* **:** Franciscan
francmasón, -sona *n, mpl* **-sones :** Freemason — **francmasonería** *nf*
franco¹, -ca *adj* **1** CÁNDIDO **:** frank, candid **2** PATENTE **:** clear, obvious **3 :** free <franco a bordo : free on board>
franco² *nm* **:** franc
francotirador, -dora *n* **:** sniper
franela *nf* **:** flannel
franja *nf* **1 :** stripe, band **2 :** border, fringe
franquear *vt* **1 :** to clear **2** ATRAVESAR **:** to cross, to go through **3 :** to pay the postage on
franqueo *nm* **:** postage
franqueza *nf* **:** frankness
franquicia *nf* **1** EXENCIÓN **:** exemption **2 :** franchise
frasco *nm* **:** small bottle, flask, vial
frase *nf* **1 :** phrase **2** ORACIÓN **:** sentence
frasear *vt* **:** to phrase
fraternal *adj* **:** fraternal, brotherly
fraternidad *nf* **1 :** brotherhood **2 :** fraternity
fraternizar {21} *vi* **:** to fraternize — **fraternización** *nf*
fraterno, -na *adj* **:** fraternal, brotherly
fratricida *adj* **:** fratricidal
fratricidio *nm* **:** fratricide
fraude *nm* **:** fraud
fraudulento, -ta *adj* **:** fraudulent — **fraudulentamente** *adv*
fray *nm* **:** brother (title of a friar) <Fray Bartolomé : Brother Bartholomew>
frazada *nf* COBIJA, MANTA **:** blanket
frecuencia *nf* **:** frequency
frecuentar *vt* **:** to frequent, to haunt
frecuente *adj* **:** frequent — **frecuentemente** *adv*
fregadera *nf fam* **:** hassle, pain in the neck
fregadero *nm* **:** kitchen sink
fregado¹, -da *adj fam* **:** annoying, bothersome
fregado² *nm* **1 :** scrubbing, scouring **2** *fam* **:** mess, muddle

fregar {49} *vt* **1 :** to scrub, to scour, to wash <fregar los trastes : to do the dishes> <fregar el suelo : to scrub the floor> **2** *fam* **:** to annoy — *vi* **1 :** to wash the dishes **2 :** to clean, to scrub **3** *fam* **:** to be annoying

freidera *nf Mex* **:** frying pan

freír {37} *vt* **:** to fry — **freírse** *vr*

frenar *vt* **1 :** to brake **2** DETENER **:** to curb, to check — *vi* **:** to apply the brakes — **frenarse** *vr* **:** to restrain oneself

frenesí *nm* **:** frenzy

frenético, -ca *adj* **:** frantic, frenzied — **frenéticamente** *adv*

freno *nm* **1 :** brake **2 :** bit (of a bridle) **3 :** check, restraint **4 frenos** *nmpl Mex* **:** braces (for teeth)

frente[1] *nm* **1 :** front <al frente de : at the head of> <en frente : in front, opposite> **2 :** facade **3 :** front line, sphere of activity **4 :** front (in meteorology) <frente frío : cold front> **5 hacer frente a :** to face up to, to brave

frente[2] *nf* **1 :** forehead, brow **2 frente a frente :** face to face

fresa *nf* **1 :** strawberry **2 :** drill (in dentistry)

fresco[1], -ca *adj* **1 :** fresh **2 :** cool **3** *fam* **:** insolent, nervy

fresco[2] *nm* **1 :** coolness **2 :** fresh air <al fresco : in the open air, outdoors> **3 :** fresco

frescor *nm* **:** cool air <el frescor de la noche : the cool of the evening>

frescura *nf* **1 :** freshness **2 :** coolness **3 :** calmness **4** DESCARO **:** nerve, audacity

fresno *nm* **:** ash (tree)

freza *nf* **:** spawn, roe

frezar {21} *vi* DESOVAR **:** to spawn

friable *adj* **:** friable

frialdad *nf* **1 :** coldness **2** INDIFERENCIA **:** indifference, unconcern

fríamente *adv* **:** coldly, indifferently

fricasé *nm* **:** fricassee

fricción *nf, pl* **fricciones 1 :** friction **2 :** rubbing, massage **3 :** discord, disagreement <fricción entre los hermanos : friction between the brothers>

friccionar *vt* **1** FROTAR **:** to rub **2 :** to massage

friega[1], friegue, etc. → **fregar**

friega[2] *nf* **1** FRICCIÓN **:** rubdown, massage **2 :** annoyance, bother

frigidez *nf* **:** (sexual) frigidity

frigorífico *nm Spain* **:** refrigerator

frijol *nm* **:** bean <frijoles refritos : refried beans>

frío[1], fría *adj* **1 :** cold **2** INDIFERENTE **:** cool, indifferent

frío[2] *nm* **1 :** cold <hace mucho frío esta noche : it's very cold tonight> **2** INDIFERENCIA **:** coldness, indifference **3 tener frío :** to feel cold <tengo frío : I'm cold> **4 tomar frío** RESFRIARSE **:** to catch a cold

friolento, -ta *adj* **:** sensitive to cold

friolera *nf* (*used ironically or humorously*) **:** trifling amount <una friolera de mil dólares : a mere thousand dollars>

friso *nm* **:** frieze

fritar *vt* **:** to fry

frito[1] *pp* → **freír**

frito[2], -ta *adj* **1 :** fried **2** *fam* **:** worn-out, fed up <tener frito a alguien : to get on someone's nerves> **3** *fam* **:** fast asleep <se quedó frito en el sofá : she fell asleep on the couch>

fritura *nf* **1 :** frying **2 :** fried food

frivolidad *nf* **:** frivolity

frívolo, -la *adj* **:** frivolous — **frívolamente** *adv*

fronda *nf* **1 :** frond **2 frondas** *nfpl* **:** foliage

frondoso, -sa *adj* **:** leafy, luxuriant

frontal *adj* **:** frontal, head-on <un choque frontal : a head-on collision>

frontalmente *adv* **:** head-on

frontera *nf* **:** border, frontier

fronterizo, -za *adj* **:** border, on the border <estados fronterizos : neighboring states>

frotar *vt* **1 :** to rub **2 :** to strike (a match) — **frotarse** *vr* **:** to rub (together)

frote *nm* **:** rubbing, rub

fructífero, -ra *adj* **:** fruitful, productive

fructificar {72} *vi* **1 :** to bear or produce fruit **2 :** to be productive

fructuoso, -sa *adj* **:** fruitful

frugal *adj* **:** frugal, thrifty — **frugalmente** *adv*

frugalidad *adj* **:** frugality

frunce *nm* **:** gather (in cloth), pucker

fruncido *nm* **:** gathering, shirring

fruncir {83} *vt* **1 :** to gather, to shirr **2 fruncir el ceño :** to knit one's brow, to frown **3 fruncir la boca :** to pucker up, to purse one's lips

frunza, etc. → **fruncir**

frustración *nf, pl* **-ciones :** frustration

frustrado, -da *adj* **1 :** frustrated **2 :** failed, unsuccessful

frustrante *adj* **:** frustrating

frustrar *vt* **:** to frustrate, to thwart — **frustrarse** *vr* FRACASAR **:** to fail, to come to nothing <se frustraron sus esperanzas : his hopes were dashed>

fruta *nf* **:** fruit

frutal[1] *adj* **:** fruit, fruit-bearing

frutal[2] *nm* **:** fruit tree

frutilla *nf* **:** South American strawberry

fruto *nm* **1 :** fruit, agricultural product <los frutos de la tierra : the fruits of the earth> **2 :** result, consequence <los frutos de su trabajo : the fruits of his labor>

fucsia *adj & nm* **:** fuchsia

fue, etc. → **ir, ser**

fuego *nm* **1 :** fire **2 :** light <¿tienes fuego? : have you got a light?> **3 :** flame, burner (on a stove) **4 :** ardor, passion **5** FOGAJE **:** skin eruption, cold sore **6 fuegos artificiales** *nmpl* **:** fireworks

fuelle *nm* **:** bellows

fuente *nf* **1** MANANTIAL **:** spring **2 :** fountain **3** ORIGEN **:** source <fuentes informativas : sources of information> **4 :** platter, serving dish

fuera *adv* **1 :** outside, out **2 :** abroad, away **3 ~ de :** outside of, out of, beyond **4 ~ de :** besides, in addition to <fuera de eso : aside from that> **5 fuera de lugar :** out of place, amiss

fuerce, fuerza, etc. → forzar

fuero *nm* **1** JURISDICCIÓN **:** jurisdiction **2 :** privilege, exemption **3 fuero interno :** conscience, heart of hearts

fuerte[1] *adv* **1 :** strongly, tightly, hard **2 :** loudly **3 :** abundantly

fuerte[2] *adj* **1 :** strong **2 :** intense <un fuerte dolor : an intense pain> **3 :** loud **4 :** extreme, excessive

fuerte[3] *nm* **1 :** fort, stronghold **2 :** forte, strong point

fuerza *nf* **1 :** strength, vigor <fuerza de voluntad : willpower> **2 :** force <fuerza bruta : brute force> **3 :** power, might <fuerza de brazos : manpower> **4 fuerzas** *nfpl* **:** forces <fuerzas armadas : armed forces> **5 a fuerza de :** by, by dint of

fuetazo *nm* **:** lash

fuga *nf* **1** HUIDA **:** flight, escape **2 :** fugue **3 :** leak <fuga de gas : gas leak>

fugarse {52} *vr* **1 :** to escape **2** HUIR **:** to flee, to run away **3 :** to elope

fugaz *adj, pl* **fugaces :** brief, fleeting

fugitivo, -va *adj & n* **:** fugitive

fulana *nf* **:** hooker, slut

fulano, -na *n* **:** so-and-so, what's-his-name, what's-her-name <fulano, mengano, y zutano : Tom, Dick, and Harry> <señora fulana de tal : Mrs. so-and-so>

fulcro *nm* **:** fulcrum

fulgor *nm* **:** brilliance, splendor

fulgurar *vi* **:** to shine brightly, to gleam, to glow

fulminante *adj* **1 :** fulminating, explosive **2 :** devastating, terrible <una mirada fulminante : a withering look>

fulminar *vt* **1 :** to strike with lightning **2 :** to strike down <fulminar a alguien con la mirada : to look daggers at someone>

fumador, -dora *n* **:** smoker

fumar *v* **:** to smoke

fumble *nm* **:** fumble (in football)

fumblear *vt* **:** to fumble (in football)

fumigante *nm* **:** fumigant

fumigar {52} *vt* **:** to fumigate **— fumigación** *nf*

funámbulo, -la *n* EQUILIBRISTA **:** tightrope walker

función *nf, pl* **funciones 1 :** function **2 :** duty **3 :** performance, show

funcional *adj* **:** functional **— funcionalmente** *adv*

funcionamiento *nm* **1 :** functioning **2 en ~ :** in operation

funcionar *vi* **1 :** to function **2 :** to run, to work

funcionario, -ria *n* **:** civil servant, official

funda *nf* **1 :** case, cover, sheath **2 :** pillowcase

fundación *nf, pl* **-ciones :** foundation, establishment

fundado, -da *adj* **:** well-founded, justified

fundador, -dora *n* **:** founder

fundamental *adj* BÁSICO **:** fundamental, basic **— fundamentalmente** *adv*

fundamentar *vt* **1 :** to lay the foundations for **2 :** to support, to back up **3 :** to base, to found

fundamento *nm* **:** basis, foundation, groundwork

fundar *vt* **1** ESTABLECER, INSTITUIR **:** to found, to establish **2** BASAR **:** to base **— fundarse** *vr* **~ en :** to be based on, to stem from

fundición *nf, pl* **-ciones 1 :** founding, smelting **2 :** foundry

fundir *vt* **1 :** to melt down, to smelt **2 :** to fuse, to merge **3 :** to burn out (a lightbulb) **— fundirse** *vr* **1 :** to fuse together, to blend, to merge **2 :** to melt, to thaw **3 :** to fade (in television or movies)

fúnebre *adj* **1 :** funeral, funereal **2** LÚGUBRE **:** gloomy, mournful

funeral[1] *adj* **:** funeral, funerary

funeral[2] *nm* **1 :** funeral **2 funerales** *nmpl* EXEQUIAS **:** funeral rites

funeraria *nf* **1 :** funeral home, funeral parlor **2 director de funeraria :** funeral director, undertaker

funerario, -ria *adj* **:** funeral

funesto, -ta *adj* **:** terrible, disastrous <consecuencias funestas : disastrous consequences>

fungicida[1] *adj* **:** fungicidal

fungicida[2] *nm* **:** fungicide

fungir {35} *vi* **:** to act, to function <fungir de asesor : to act as a consultant>

fungoso, -sa *adj* **:** fungous

funja, etc. → fungir

furgón *nm, pl* **furgones 1 :** van, truck **2 :** freight car, boxcar **3 furgón de cola :** caboose

furgoneta *nf* **:** van

furia *nf* **1** CÓLERA, IRA **:** fury, rage **2 :** violence, fury <la furia de la tormenta : the fury of the storm>

furibundo, -da *adj* **:** furious

furiosamente *adv* **:** furiously, frantically

furioso, -sa *adj* **1** AIRADO **:** furious, irate **2 :** intense, violent

furor *nm* **1 :** fury, rage **2 :** violence (of the elements) **3 :** passion, frenzy **4 :** enthusiasm <hacer furor : to be all the rage>

furtivo, -va *adj* **:** furtive **— furtivamente** *adv*

furúnculo *nm* DIVIESO : boil
fuselaje *nm* : fuselage
fusible *nm* : (electrical) fuse
fusil *nm* : rifle
fusilar *vt* **1** : to shoot, to execute (by firing squad) **2** *fam* : to plagiarize, to pirate
fusilería *nf* **1** : rifles *pl*, rifle fire **2** **descarga de fusilería** : fusillade
fusión *nf*, *pl* **fusiones** **1** : fusion **2** : union, merger
fusionar *vt* **1** : to fuse **2** : to merge, to amalgamate — **fusionarse** *vr*
fusta *nf* : riding crop
fustigar {52} *vt* **1** AZOTAR : to whip, to lash **2** : to upbraid, to berate
futbol *or* **fútbol** *nm* **1** : soccer **2** **futbol americano** : football
futbolista *nmf* : soccer player
futesa *nf* **1** : small thing, trifle **2** **futesas** *nfpl* : small talk
fútil *adj* : trifling, trivial
futurista *adj* : futuristic
futuro[1], **-ra** *adj* : future
futuro[2] *nm* PORVENIR : future

G

g *nf* : seventh letter of the Spanish alphabet
gabán *nm*, *pl* **gabanes** : topcoat, overcoat
gabardina *nf* **1** : gabardine **2** : trench coat, raincoat
gabarra *nf* : barge
gabinete *nm* **1** : cabinet (in government) **2** : study, office (in the home) **3** : (professional) office
gablete *nm* : gable
gabonés, -nesa *adj & n*, *mpl* **-neses** : Gabonese
gacela *nf* : gazelle
gaceta *nf* : gazette, newspaper
gachas *nfpl* : porridge
gacho, -cha *adj* **1** : drooping, turned downward **2** *Mex fam* : nasty, awful **3** **ir a gachas** *fam* : to go on all fours
gaélico[1], **-ca** *adj* : Gaelic
gaélico[2] *nm* : Gaelic (language)
gafas *nfpl* ANTEOJOS : eyeglasses, glasses
gaita *nf* : bagpipes *pl*
gajes *nmpl* **gajes del oficio** : occupational hazards
gajo *nm* **1** : broken branch (of a tree) **2** : cluster, bunch (of fruit) **3** : segment (of citrus fruit)
gala *nf* **1** : gala <vestido de gala : formal dress> <tener algo a gala : to be proud of something> **2** **galas** *nfpl* : finery, attire
galáctico, -ca *adj* : galactic
galán *nm*, *pl* **galanes** **1** : ladies' man, gallant **2** : leading man, hero **3** : boyfriend, suitor
galano, -na *adj* **1** : elegant **2** *Mex* : mottled
galante *adj* : gallant, attentive — **galantemente** *adv*
galantear *vt* **1** CORTEJAR : to court, to woo **2** : to flirt with
galanteo *nm* **1** CORTEJO : courtship **2** : flirtation, flirting
galantería *nf* **1** : gallantry, attentiveness **2** : compliment
galápago *nm* : aquatic turtle
galardón *nm*, *pl* **-dones** : award, prize
galardonado, -da *adj* : prize-winning
galardonar *vt* : to give an award to
galaxia *nf* : galaxy
galeno *nm fam* : physician, doctor
galeón *nm*, *pl* **galeones** : galleon
galera *nf* : galley
galería *nf* **1** : gallery, balcony (in a theater) <galería comercial : shopping mall> **2** : corridor, passage
galerón *nm*, *pl* **-rones** *Mex* : large hall
galés[1], **-lesa** *adj* : Welsh
galés[2], **-lesa** *n*, *mpl* **galeses** **1** : Welshman *m*, Welshwoman *f* **2** **los galeses** : the Welsh
galés[3] *nm* : Welsh (language)
galgo *nm* : greyhound
galimatías *nms & pl* : gibberish, nonsense
galio *nm* : gallium
gallardete *nm* : pennant, streamer
gallardía *nf* **1** VALENTÍA : bravery **2** APOSTURA : elegance, gracefulness
gallardo, -da *adj* **1** VALIENTE : brave **2** APUESTO : elegant, graceful
gallear *vi* : to show off, to strut around
gallego[1], **-ga** *adj* **1** : Galician **2** *fam* : Spanish
gallego[2], **-ga** *n* **1** : Galician **2** *fam* : Spaniard
galleta *nf* **1** : cookie **2** : cracker
gallina *nf* **1** : hen **2** **gallina de Guinea** : guinea fowl
gallinazo *nm* : vulture, buzzard
gallinero *nm* : chicken coop, henhouse
gallito, -ta *adj fam* : cocky, belligerent
gallo *nm* **1** : rooster, cock **2** *fam* : squeak or crack in the voice **3** *Mex* : serenade **4** **gallo de pelea** : gamecock
galo[1], **-la** *adj* **1** : Gaulish **2** : French
galo[2], **-la** *n* : Frenchman *m*, Frenchwoman *f*
galocha *nf* : galosh
galón *nm*, *pl* **galones** **1** : gallon **2** : stripe (military insignia)
galopada *nf* : gallop
galopante *adj* : galloping <inflación galopante : galloping inflation>
galopar *vi* : to gallop
galope *nm* : gallop

galpón *nm, pl* **galpones** : shed, storehouse

galvanizar {21} *vt* : to galvanize — **galvanización** *nf*

gama *nf* **1** : range, spectrum, gamut **2** → **gamo**

gamba *nf* : large shrimp, prawn

gameto *nm* : gamete

gamo, -ma *n* : fallow deer

gamuza *nf* **1** : suede **2** : chamois

gana *nf* **1** : desire, inclination **2 de buena gana** : willingly, readily, gladly **3 de mala gana** : reluctantly, half-heartedly **4 tener ganas de** : to feel like, to be in the mood for <tengo ganas de bailar : I feel like dancing> **5 ponerle ganas a algo** : to put effort into something

ganadería *nf* **1** : cattle raising, stockbreeding **2** : cattle ranch **3** GANADO : cattle *pl,* livestock

ganadero[1], **-ra** *adj* : cattle, ranching

ganadero[2], **-ra** *n* : rancher, stockbreeder

ganado *nm* **1** : cattle *pl,* livestock **2 ganado ovino** : sheep *pl* **3 ganado porcino** : swine *pl*

ganador[1], **-dora** *adj* : winning

ganador[2], **-dora** *n* : winner

ganancia *nf* **1** : profit **2 ganancias** *nfpl* : winnings, gains

ganancioso, -sa *adj* : profitable

ganar *vt* **1** : to win **2** : to gain <ganar tiempo : to buy time> **3** : to earn <ganar dinero : to make money> **4** : to acquire, to obtain — *vi* **1** : to win **2** : to profit <salir ganando : to come out ahead> — **ganarse** *vr* **1** : to gain, to win <ganarse a alguien : to win someone over> **2** : to earn <ganarse la vida : to make a living> **3** : to deserve

gancho *nm* **1** : hook **2** : clothes hanger **3** : hairpin, bobby pin **4** *Col* : safety pin

gandul[1] *nm CA, Car, Col* : pigeon pea

gandul[2], **-dula** *n fam* : idler, lazybones

gandulear *vi* : to idle, to loaf, to lounge about

ganga *nf* : bargain

ganglio *nm* **1** : ganglion **2** : gland

gangrena *nf* : gangrene — **gangrenoso, -sa** *adj*

gángster *nmf, pl* **gángsters** : gangster

gansada *nf* : silly thing, nonsense

ganso, -sa *n* **1** : goose, gander *m* **2** : idiot, fool

gañido *nm* : yelp (of a dog)

gañir {38} *vi* : to yelp

garabatear *v* : to scribble, to scrawl, to doodle

garabato *nm* **1** : doodle **2 garabatos** *nmpl* : scribble, scrawl

garaje *nm* : garage

garante *nmf* : guarantor

garantía *nf* **1** : guarantee, warranty **2** : security <garantía de trabajo : job security>

garantizar {21} *vt* : to guarantee

garapiña *nf* : pineapple drink

garapiñar *vt* : to candy

garbanzo *nm* : chickpea, garbanzo

garbo *nm* **1** DONAIRE : grace, poise **2** : jauntiness

garboso, -sa *adj* **1** : graceful **2** : elegant, stylish

garceta *nf* : egret

gardenia *nf* : gardenia

garfio *nm* : hook, gaff, grapnel

gargajo *nm* : phlegm

garganta *nf* **1** : throat **2** : neck (of a person or a bottle) **3** : ravine, narrow pass

gargantilla *nf* : choker, necklace

gárgara *nf* **1** : gargle, gargling **2 hacer gárgaras** : to gargle

gargarizar *vi* : to gargle

gárgola *nf* : gargoyle

garita *nf* **1** : cabin, hut **2** : sentry box, lookout post

garoso, -sa *adj Col, Ven* : gluttonous, greedy

garra *nf* **1** : claw **2** : hand, paw **3 garras** *nfpl* : claws, clutches <caer en las garras de alguien : to fall into someone's clutches>

garrafa *nf* : decanter, carafe

garrafal *adj* : terrible, monstrous

garrafón *nm, pl* **-fones** : large decanter, large bottle

garrapata *nf* : tick

garrobo *nm CA* : large lizard, iguana

garrocha *nf* **1** PICA : lance, pike **2** : pole <salto con garrocha : pole vault>

garrotazo *nm* : blow (with a club)

garrote *nm* **1** : club, stick **2** *Mex* : brake

garúa *nf* : drizzle

garuar {3} *v impers* LLOVIZNAR : to drizzle

garza *nf* : heron

gas *nm* : gas, vapor, fumes *pl* <gas lagrimógeno : tear gas>

gasa *nf* : gauze

gasear *vt* **1** : to gas **2** : to aerate (a liquid)

gaseosa *nf* REFRESCO : soda, soft drink

gaseoso, -sa *adj* **1** : gaseous **2** : carbonated, fizzy

gasoducto *nm* : gas pipeline

gasolina *nf* : gasoline, gas

gasolinera *nf* : gas station, service station

gastado, -da *adj* **1** : spent **2** : worn, worn-out

gastador[1], **-dora** *adj* : extravagant, spendthrift

gastador[2], **-dora** *n* : spendthrift

gastar *vt* **1** : to spend **2** CONSUMIR : to consume, to use up **3** : to squander, to waste **4** : to wear <gasta un bigote : he sports a mustache> — **gastarse** *vr* **1** : to spend, to expend **2** : to run down, to wear out

gasto *nm* **1** : expense, expenditure **2** DETERIORO : wear **3 gastos generales** *or* **gastos indirectos** : overhead

gástrico, -ca *adj* : gastric

gastritis *nf* : gastritis

gastronomía *nf* : gastronomy
gastronómico, -ca *adj* : gastronomic
gastrónomo, -ma *n* : gourmet
gatas *adv* **andar a gatas** : to crawl, to go on all fours
gatear *vi* **1** : to crawl **2** : to climb, to clamber (up)
gatillero *nm Mex* : gunman
gatillo *nm* : trigger
gatito, -ta *n* : kitten
gato[1], -ta *n* : cat
gato[2] *nm* : jack (for an automobile)
gauchada *nf Arg, Uru* : favor, kindness
gaucho *nm* : gaucho
gaveta *nf* **1** CAJÓN : drawer **2** : till
gavilla *nf* **1** : gang, band **2** : sheaf
gaviota *nf* : gull, seagull
gay ['ge, 'gai] *adj* : gay (homosexual)
gaza *nf* : loop
gazapo *nm* **1** : young rabbit **2** : misprint, error
gazmoñería *nf* MOJIGATERÍA : prudery, primness
gazmoño[1], -ña *adj* : prudish, prim
gazmoño[2], -ña *n* MOJIGATO : prude, prig
gaznate *nm* : throat, gullet
gazpacho *nm* : gazpacho
géiser *or* **géyser** *nm* : geyser
gel *nm* : gel
gelatina *nf* : gelatin
gélido, -da *adj* : icy, freezing cold
gelificarse *vr* : to jell
gema *nf* : gem
gemelo[1], -la *adj & n* MELLIZO : twin
gemelo[2] *nm* **1** : cuff link **2 gemelos** *nmpl* BINOCULARES : binoculars
gemido *nm* : moan, groan, wail
Géminis *nmf* : Gemini
gemir {54} *vi* : to moan, to groan, to wail
gen *or* **gene** *nm* : gene
gendarme *nmf* POLICÍA : police officer, policeman *m*, policewoman *f*
gendarmería *nf* : police
genealogía *nf* : genealogy
genealógico, -ca *adj* : genealogical
generación *nf, pl* **-ciones 1** : generation <tercera generación : third generation> **2** : generating, creating **3** : class <la generación del '97 : the class of '97>
generacional *adj* : generation, generational
generador *nm* : generator
general[1] *adj* **1** : general **2 en ~** *or* **por lo general** : in general, generally
general[2] *nmf* **1** : general **2 general de división** : major general
generalidad *nf* **1** : generality, generalization **2** : majority
generalización *nf, pl* **-ciones 1** : generalization **2** : escalation, spread
generalizado, -da *adj* : generalized, widespread
generalizar {21} *vi* : to generalize — *vt* : to spread, to spread out — **generalizarse** *vr* : to become widespread
generalmente *adv* : usually, generally
generar *vt* : to generate — **generarse** *vr*
genérico, -ca *adj* : generic
género *nm* **1** : genre, class, kind <el género humano : the human race, mankind> **2** : gender (in grammar) **3 géneros** *nmpl* : goods, commodities
generosidad *nf* : generosity
generoso, -sa *adj* **1** : generous, unselfish **2** : ample — **generosamente** *adv*
genética *nf* : genetics
genético, -ca *adj* : genetic — **genéticamente** *adv*
genetista *nmf* : geneticist
genial *adj* **1** AGRADABLE : genial, pleasant **2** : brilliant <una obra genial : a work of genius> **3** *fam* FORMIDABLE : fantastic, terrific
genialidad *nf* **1** : genius **2** : stroke of genius **3** : eccentricity
genio *nm* **1** : genius **2** : temper, disposition <de mal genio : bad-tempered> **3** : genie
genital *adj* : genital
genitales *nmpl* : genitals, genitalia
genocidio *nm* : genocide
genotipo *nm* : genotype
gente *nf* **1** : people **2** : relatives *pl*, folks *pl* **3 gente menuda** *fam* : children, kids *pl* **4 ser buena gente** : to be nice, to be kind
gentil[1] *adj* **1** AMABLE : kind **2** : gentile
gentil[2] *nmf* : gentile
gentileza *nf* **1** AMABILIDAD : kindness **2** CORTESÍA : courtesy
gentilicio, -cia *adj* **1** : national, tribal **2** : family
gentío *nm* MUCHEDUMBRE, MULTITUD : crowd, mob
gentuza *nf* CHUSMA : riffraff, rabble
genuflexión *nf, pl* **-xiones 1** : genuflection **2 hacer una genuflexión** : to genuflect
genuino, -na *adj* : genuine — **genuinamente** *adv*
geofísica *nf* : geophysics
geofísico, -ca *adj* : geophysical
geografía *nf* : geography
geográfico, -ca *adj* : geographic, geographical — **geográficamente** *adv*
geógrafo, -fa *n* : geographer
geología *nf* : geology
geológico, -ca *adj* : geologic, geological — **geológicamente** *adv*
geólogo, -ga *n* : geologist
geometría *nf* : geometry
geométrico, -ca *adj* : geometric, geometrical — **geométricamente** *adv*
geopolítica *nf* : geopolitics
geopolítico, -ca *adj* : geopolitical
georgiano, -na *adj & n* : Georgian
geranio *nm* : geranium
gerbo *nm* : gerbil
gerencia *nf* : management, administration
gerencial *adj* : managerial
gerente *nmf* : manager, director
geriatría *nf* : geriatrics

geriátrico, -ca *adj* : geriatric
germanio *nm* : germanium
germano, -na *adj* : Germanic, German
germen *nm, pl* **gérmenes** : germ
germicida *nf* : germicide
germinación *nf, pl* **-ciones** : germination
germinar *vi* : to germinate, to sprout
gerontología *nf* : gerontology
gerundio *nm* : gerund
gesta *nf* : deed, exploit
gestación *nf, pl* **-ciones** : gestation
gesticulación *nf, pl* **-ciones** : gesturing, gesticulation
gesticular *vi* : to gesticulate, to gesture
gestión *nf, pl* **gestiones 1** TRÁMITE : procedure, step **2** ADMINISTRACIÓN : management **3 gestiones** *nfpl* : negotiations
gestionar *vt* **1** : to negotiate, to work towards **2** ADMINISTRAR : to manage, to handle
gesto *nm* **1** ADEMÁN : gesture **2** : facial expression **3** MUECA : grimace
gestor[1], -tora *adj* : facilitating, negotiating, managing
gestor[2], -tora *n* : facilitator, manager
géyser *nm* → **géiser**
ghanés, -nesa *adj & n, mpl* **ghaneses** : Ghanaian
ghetto → **gueto**
giba *nf* **1** : hump (of an animal) **2** : hunchback (of a person)
gibón *nm, pl* **gibones** : gibbon
giboso[1], -sa *adj* : hunchbacked, humpbacked
giboso[2], -sa *n* : hunchback, humpback
gigante[1] *adj* : giant, gigantic
gigante[2], -ta *n* : giant
gigantesco, -ca *adj* : gigantic, huge
gime, etc. → **gemir**
gimnasia *nf* : gymnastics
gimnasio *nm* : gymnasium, gym
gimnasta *nmf* : gymnast
gimnástico, -ca *adj* : gymnastic
gimotear *vi* LLORIQUEAR : to whine, to whimper
gimoteo *nm* : whimpering
ginebra *nf* : gin
ginecología *nf* : gynecology
ginecológico, -ca *adj* : gynecologic, gynecological
ginecólogo, -ga *n* : gynecologist
gira *nf* : tour
giralda *nf* : weather vane
girar *vi* **1** : to turn around, to revolve **2** : to swing around, to swivel — *vt* **1** : to turn, to twist, to rotate **2** : to draft (checks) **3** : to transfer (funds)
girasol *nm* MIRASOL : sunflower
giratorio, -ria *adj* : revolving
giro *nm* **1** VUELTA : turn, rotation **2** : change of direction <giro de 180 grados : U-turn, about-face> **3 giro bancario** : bank draft **4 giro postal** : money order
giroscopio *or* **giróscopo** *nm* : gyroscope
gis *nm Mex* : chalk
gitano, -na *adj & n* : Gypsy
glacial *adj* : glacial, icy — **glacialmente** *adv*
glaciar *nm* : glacier
gladiador *nm* : gladiator
gladiolo *or* **gladíolo** *nm* : gladiolus
glándula *nf* : gland — **glandular** *adj*
glaseado *nm* : glaze, icing
glasear *vt* : to glaze
glaucoma *nm* : glaucoma
glicerina *nf* : glycerin, glycerol
glicinia *nf* : wisteria
global *adj* **1** : global, worldwide **2** : full, comprehensive **3** : total, overall
globalizar {21} *vt* **1** ABARCAR : to include, to encompass **2** : to extend worldwide
globalmente *adv* : globally, as a whole
globo *nm* **1** : globe, sphere **2** : balloon **3 globo ocular** : eyeball
glóbulo *nm* **1** : globule **2** : blood cell, corpuscle
gloria *nf* **1** : glory **2** : fame, renown **3** : delight, enjoyment **4** : star, legend <las glorias del cine : the great names in motion pictures>
glorieta *nf* **1** : rotary, traffic circle **2** : bower, arbor
glorificar {72} *vt* ALABAR : to glorify — **glorificación** *nf*
glorioso, -sa *adj* : glorious — **gloriosamente** *adv*
glosa *nf* **1** : gloss **2** : annotation, commentary
glosar *vt* **1** : to gloss **2** : to annotate, to comment on (a text)
glosario *nm* : glossary
glotis *nf* : glottis
glotón[1], -tona *adj, mpl* **glotones** : gluttonous
glotón[2], -tona *n, mpl* **glotones** : glutton
glotón[3] *nm, pl* **glotones** : wolverine
glotonería *nf* GULA : gluttony
glucosa *nf* : glucose
glutinoso, -sa *adj* : glutinous
gnomo *nm* : gnome
gobernación *nf, pl* **-ciones** : governing, government
gobernador, -dora *n* : governor
gobernante[1] *adj* : ruling, governing
gobernante[2] *nmf* : ruler, leader, governor
gobernar {55} *vt* **1** : to govern, to rule **2** : to steer, to sail (a ship) — *vi* **1** : to govern **2** : to steer
gobierno *nm* : government
goce[1], etc. → **gozar**
goce[2] *nm* **1** PLACER : enjoyment, pleasure **2** : use, possession
gol *nm* : goal (in soccer)
golear *vt* : to rout, to score many goals against (in soccer)
goleta *nf* : schooner
golf *nm* : golf
golfista *nmf* : golfer
golfo *nm* : gulf, bay
golondrina *nf* **1** : swallow (bird) **2 golondrina de mar** : tern

golosina *nf* **:** sweet, snack

goloso, -sa *adj* **:** fond of sweets <ser goloso : to have a sweet tooth>

golpazo *nm* **:** heavy blow, bang, thump

golpe *nm* **1 :** blow <caerle a golpes a alguien : to give someone a beating> **2 :** knock **3 de ~ :** suddenly **4 de un golpe :** all at once, in one fell swoop **5 golpe de estado :** coup, coup d'etat **6 golpe de suerte :** stroke of luck

golpeado, -da *adj* **1 :** beaten, hit **2 :** bruised (of fruit) **3 :** dented

golpear *vt* **1 :** to beat (up), to hit **2 :** to slam, to bang, to strike — *vi* **1 :** to knock (at a door) **2 :** to beat <la lluvia golpeaba contra el tejado : the rain beat against the roof> — **golpearse** *vr*

golpetear *v* **:** to knock, to rattle, to tap

golpeteo *nm* **:** banging, knocking, tapping

goma *nf* **1 :** gum <goma de mascar : chewing gum> **2** CAUCHO **:** rubber <goma espuma : foam rubber> **3** PEGAMENTO **:** glue **4 :** rubber band **5** *Arg* **:** tire **6** *or* **goma de borrar :** eraser

gomita *nf* **:** rubber band

gomoso, -sa *adj* **:** gummy, sticky

góndola *nf* **:** gondola

gong *nm* **:** gong

gonorrea *nf* **:** gonorrhea

gorda *nf Mex* **:** thick corn tortilla

gordinflón[1], -flona *adj, mpl* **-flones** *fam* **:** chubby, pudgy

gordinflón[2], -flona *n, mpl* **-flones** *fam* **:** chubby person

gordo[1], -da *adj* **1 :** fat **2 :** thick **3 :** fatty, greasy, oily **4 :** unpleasant <me cae gorda tu tía : I can't stand your aunt>

gordo[2], -da *n* **:** fat person

gordo[3] *nm* **1** GRASA **:** fat **2 :** jackpot

gordura *nf* **:** fatness, flab

gorgojo *nm* **:** weevil

gorgotear *vi* **:** to gurgle, to bubble

gorgoteo *nm* **:** gurgle

gorila *nm* **:** gorilla

gorjear *vi* **1 :** to chirp, to tweet, to warble **2 :** to gurgle

gorjeo *nm* **1 :** chirping, warbling **2 :** gurgling

gorra *nf* **1 :** bonnet **2 :** cap **3 de ~** *fam* **:** for free, at someone else's expense <vivir de gorra : to sponge, to freeload>

gorrear *vt fam* **:** to bum, to scrounge — *vi fam* **:** to freeload

gorrero, -ra *n fam* **:** freeloader, sponger

gorrión *nm, pl* **gorriones :** sparrow

gorro *nm* **1 :** cap **2 estar hasta el gorro :** to be fed up

gorrón, -rrona *n fam, mpl* **gorrones :** freeloader, scrounger

gorronear *vt fam* **:** to bum, to scrounge — *vi fam* **:** to freeload

gota *nf* **1 :** drop <una gota de sudor : a bead of sweat> <como dos gotas de agua : like two peas in a pod> <sudar la gota gorda : to sweat buckets, to work very hard> **2 :** gout

gotear *v* **1 :** to drip **2 :** to leak — *v impers* LLOVIZNAR **:** to drizzle

goteo *nm* **:** drip, dripping

gotera *nf* **1 :** leak **2 :** stain (from dripping water)

gotero *nm* **:** (medicine) dropper

gótico, -ca *adj* **:** Gothic

gourmet *nmf* **:** gourmet

gozar {21} *vi* **1 :** to enjoy oneself, to have a good time **2 ~ de :** to enjoy, to have, to possess <gozar de buena salud : to enjoy good health> **3 ~ con :** to take delight in

gozne *nm* BISAGRA **:** hinge

gozo *nm* **1 :** joy **2** PLACER **:** enjoyment, pleasure

gozoso, -sa *adj* **:** joyful

grabación *nf, pl* **-ciones :** recording

grabado *nm* **1 :** engraving **2 grabado al aguafuerte :** etching

grabador, -dora *n* **:** engraver

grabadora *nf* **:** tape recorder

grabar *vt* **1 :** to engrave **2 :** to record, to tape — *vi* **grabar al aguafuerte :** to etch — **grabarse** *vr* **grabársele a alguien en la memoria :** to become engraved on someone's mind

gracia *nf* **1 :** grace **2 :** favor, kindness **3 :** humor, wit <su comentario no me hizo gracia : I wasn't amused by his remark> **4 gracias** *nfpl* **:** thanks <¡gracias! : thank you!> <dar gracias : to give thanks>

grácil *adj* **1 :** graceful **2 :** delicate, slender, fine

gracilidad *nm* **:** gracefulness

gracioso, -sa *adj* **1** CHISTOSO **:** funny, amusing **2 :** cute, attractive

grada *nf* **1 :** harrow **2** PELDAÑO **:** step, stair **3 gradas** *nfpl* **:** bleachers, grandstand

gradación *nf, pl* **-ciones :** gradation, scale

gradar *vt* **:** to harrow, to hoe

gradería *nf* **:** tiers *pl,* stands *pl,* rows *pl* (in a theater)

gradiente *nf* **:** gradient, slope

grado *nm* **1 :** degree (in meteorology and mathematics) <grado centígrado : degree centigrade> **2 :** extent, level, degree <en grado sumo : greatly, to the highest degree> **3** RANGO **:** rank **4 :** year, class (in education) **5 de buen grado :** willingly, readily

graduable *adj* **:** adjustable

graduación *nf, pl* **-ciones 1 :** graduation (from a school) **2** GRADO **:** rank **3 :** alcohol content, proof

graduado[1], -da *adj* **1 :** graduated **2 lentes graduados :** prescription lenses

graduado[2], -da *n* **:** graduate

gradual *adj* **:** gradual — **gradualmente** *adv*

graduar {3} *v* **1 :** to regulate, to adjust **2** CALIBRAR **:** to calibrate, to gauge —

graduarse *vr* : to graduate (from a school)
gráfica *nf* → **gráfico²**
gráfico¹, -ca *adj* : graphic — **gráficamente** *adv*
gráfico² *nm* **1** : graph, chart **2** : graphic (for a computer, etc.) **3 gráfico de barras** : bar graph
grafismo *nm* : graphics *pl*
grafito *nm* : graphite
gragea *nf* **1** : coated pill or tablet **2 grageas** *nfpl* : sprinkles, jimmies
grajo *nm* : rook (bird)
grama *nf* : grass
gramática *nf* : grammar
gramatical *adj* : grammatical — **gramaticalmente** *adv*
gramo *nm* : gram
gran → **grande**
grana *nf* : scarlet, deep red
granada *nf* **1** : pomegranate **2** : grenade <granada de mano : hand grenade>
granadero *nm* **1** : grenadier **2 granaderos** *nmpl Mex* : riot squad
granadino, -na *adj & n* : Grenadian
granado, -da *adj* **1** DISTINGUIDO : distinguished **2** : choice, select
granate *nm* **1** : garnet **2** : deep red, maroon
grande *adj* (**gran** *before singular nouns*) **1** : large, big <un libro grande : a big book> **2** ALTO : tall **3** NOTABLE : great <un gran autor : a great writer> **4** (*indicating intensity*) : great <con gran placer : with great pleasure> **5** : old, grown-up <hijos grandes : grown children>
grandeza *nf* **1** MAGNITUD : greatness, size **2** : nobility **3** : generosity, graciousness **4** : grandeur, magnificence
grandilocuencia *nf* : grandiloquence — **grandilocuente** *adj*
grandiosidad *nf* : grandeur
grandioso, -sa *adj* **1** MAGNÍFICO : grand, magnificent **2** : grandiose
granel *adv* **1 a ∼** : galore, in great quantities **2 a ∼** : in bulk <vender a granel : to sell in bulk>
granero *nm* : barn, granary
granito *nm* : granite
granizada *nf* : hailstorm
granizar {21} *v impers* : to hail
granizo *nm* : hail
granja *nf* : farm
granjear *vt* : to earn, to win — **granjearse** *vr* : to gain, to earn
granjero, -ra *n* : farmer
grano *nm* **1** PARTÍCULA : grain, particle <un grano de arena : a grain of sand> **2** : grain (of rice, etc.), bean (of coffee), seed **3** : grain (of wood or rock) **4** BARRO, ESPINILLA : pimple **5 ir al grano** : to get to the point
granuja *nmf* PILLUELO : rascal, urchin
granular¹ *vt* : to granulate — **granularse** *vr* : to break out in spots
granular² *adj* : granular, grainy
granza *nf* : chaff
grapa *nf* **1** : staple **2** : clamp
grapadora *nf* ENGRAPADORA : stapler
grapar *vt* ENGRAPAR : to staple
grasa *nf* **1** : grease **2** : fat **3** *Mex* : shoe polish
grasiento, -ta *adj* : greasy, oily
graso, -sa *adj* **1** : fatty **2** : greasy, oily
grasoso, -sa *adj* GRASIENTO : greasy, oily
gratificación *nf, pl* **-ciones 1** SATISFACCIÓN : gratification **2** : bonus **3** RECOMPENSA : recompense, reward
gratificar {72} *vt* **1** SATISFACER : to satisfy, to gratify **2** RECOMPENSAR : to reward **3** : to give a bonus to
gratinado, -da *adj* : au gratin
gratis¹ *adv* GRATUITAMENTE : free, for free, gratis
gratis² *adj* GRATUITO : free, gratis
gratitud *nf* : gratitude
grato, -ta *adj* AGRADABLE, PLACENTERO : pleasant, agreeable — **gratamente** *adv*
gratuitamente *adv* **1** : gratuitously **2** GRATIS : free, for free, gratis
gratuito, -ta *adj* **1** : gratuitous, unwarranted **2** GRATIS : free, gratis
grava *nf* : gravel
gravamen *nm, pl* **-vámenes 1** : burden, obligation **2** : (property) tax
gravar *vt* **1** : to burden, to encumber **2** : to levy (a tax)
grave *adj* **1** : grave, important **2** : serious, somber **3** : serious (of an illness)
gravedad *nf* **1** : gravity <centro de gravedad : center of gravity> **2** : seriousness, severity
gravemente *adv* : gravely, seriously
gravilla *nf* : (fine) gravel
gravitación *nf, pl* **-ciones** : gravitation
gravitar *vi* **1** : to gravitate **2 ∼ sobre** : to rest on **3 ∼ sobre** : to loom over
gravoso, -sa *adj* **1** ONEROSO : burdensome, onerous **2** : costly
graznar *vi* : to caw, to honk, to quack, to squawk
graznido *nm* : cawing, honking, quacking, squawking
gregario, -ria *adj* : gregarious
gregoriano, -na *adj* : Gregorian
gremial *adj* SINDICAL : union, labor
gremio *nm* SINDICATO : union, guild
greña *nf* **1** : mat, tangle **2 greñas** *nfpl* MELENAS : shaggy hair, mop
greñudo, -da *n* HIPPIE, MELENUDO : long-hair, hippie
grey *nf* : congregation, flock
griego¹, -ga *adj & n* : Greek
griego² *nm* : Greek (language)
grieta *nf* : crack, crevice
grifo *nm* **1** : faucet <agua del grifo : tap water> **2** : griffin
grillete *nm* : shackle
grillo *nm* **1** : cricket **2 grillos** *nmpl* : fetters, shackles
grima *nf* **1** : disgust, uneasiness **2 darle grima a alguien** : to get on someone's nerves

gringo, -ga *adj & n* YANQUI : Yankee, gringo

gripa *nf Col, Mex* : flu

gripe *nf* : flu

gris *adj* **1** : gray **2** : overcast, cloudy

grisáceo, -cea *adj* : grayish

gritar *v* : to shout, to scream, to cry

gritería *nf* : shouting, clamor

grito *nm* : shout, scream, cry <a grito pelado : at the top of one's voice>

groenlandés, -desa *adj & n* : Greenlander

grogui *adj fam* : dazed, groggy

grosella *nf* **1** : currant **2 grosella espinosa** : gooseberry

grosería *nf* **1** : insult, coarse language **2** : rudeness, discourtesy

grosero[1], -ra *adj* **1** : rude, fresh **2** : coarse, vulgar

grosero[2], -ra *n* : rude person

grosor *nm* : thickness

grosso *adj* **a grosso modo** : roughly, broadly, approximately

grotesco, -ca *adj* : grotesque, hideous

grúa *nf* **1** : crane (machine) **2** : tow truck

gruesa *nf* : gross

grueso[1], -sa *adj* **1** : thick, bulky **2** : heavy, big **3** : heavyset, stout

grueso[2] *nm* **1** : thickness **2** : main body, mass **3 en ~** : in bulk

grulla *nf* : crane (bird)

grumo *nm* : lump, glob

gruñido *nm* : growl, grunt

gruñir {38} *vi* **1** : to growl, to grunt **2** : to grumble

gruñón[1], -ñona *adj, mpl* **gruñones** *fam* : grumpy, crabby

gruñón[2], -ñona *n, mpl* **gruñones** *fam* : grumpy person, nag

grupa *nf* : rump, hindquarters *pl*

grupo *nm* : group

gruta *nf* : grotto, cave

guacal *nm Col, Mex, Ven* : crate

guacamayo *nm* : macaw

guacamole *or* **guacamol** *nm* : guacamole

guacamote *nm Mex* : yuca, cassava

guachinango → huachinango

guacho, -cha *adj* **1** *Arg, Col, Chile, Peru* : orphaned **2** *Chile, Peru* : odd, unmatched

guadaña *nf* : scythe

guagua *nf* **1** *Arg, Col, Chile, Peru* : baby **2** *Cuba, PRi* : bus

guaira *nf* **1** *CA* : traditional flute **2** *Peru* : smelting furnace

guajiro, -ra *n Cuba* : peasant

guajolote *nm Mex* : turkey

guanábana *nf* : guanabana, soursop (fruit)

guanaco *nm* : guanaco

guandú *nm CA, Car, Col* : pigeon pea

guango, -ga *adj Mex* **1** : loose-fitting, baggy **2** : slack, loose

guano *nm* : guano

guante *nm* **1** : glove <guante de boxeo : boxing glove> **2 arrojarle el guante (a alguien)** : to throw down the gauntlet (to someone)

guantelete *nm* : gauntlet

guapo, -pa *adj* **1** : handsome, good-looking, attractive **2** : elegant, smart **3** *fam* : bold, dashing

guapura *nf fam* : handsomeness, attractiveness, good looks *pl* <¡qué guapura! : what a vision!>

guarache → huarache

guarachear *vi Cuba, PRi fam* : to go on a spree, to go out on the town

guaraní[1] *adj & nmf* : Guarani

guaraní[2] *nm* : Guarani (language of Paraguay)

guarda *nmf* **1** GUARDIÁN : security guard **2** : keeper, custodian

guardabarros *nms & pl* : fender, mudguard

guardabosque *nmfs & pl* : forest ranger, gamekeeper

guardacostas[1] *nmfs & pl* : coastguardsman

guardacostas[2] *nms & pl* : coast guard vessel

guardaespaldas *nmfs & pl* : bodyguard

guardafangos *nms & pl* : fender, mudguard

guardameta *nmf* ARQUERO, PORTERO : goalkeeper, goalie

guardapelo *nm* : locket

guardapolvo *nm* **1** : dustcover **2** : duster, housecoat

guardar *vt* **1** : to guard **2** : to maintain, to preserve **3** CONSERVAR : to put away **4** RESERVAR : to save **5** : to keep (a secret or promise) — **guardarse** *vr* **1 ~ de** : to refrain from **2 ~ de** : to guard against, to be careful not to

guardarropa *nm* **1** : cloakroom, checkroom **2** ARMARIO : closet, wardrobe

guardería *nf* : nursery, day-care center

guardia[1] *nf* **1** : guard, defense **2** : guard duty, watch **3 en ~** : on guard

guardia[2] *nmf* **1** : sentry, guardsman, guard **2** : police officer, policeman *m*, policewoman *f*

guardián, -diana *n, mpl* **guardianes 1** GUARDA : security guard, watchman **2** : guardian, keeper **3 perro guardián** : watchdog

guarecer {53} *vt* : to shelter, to protect — **guarecerse** *vr* : to take shelter

guarida *nf* **1** : den, lair **2** : hideout

guarismo *nm* : figure, numeral

guarnecer {53} *vt* **1** : to adorn **2** : to garnish **3** : to garrison

guarnición *nf, pl* **-ciones 1** : garnish **2** : garrison **3** : decoration, trimming, setting (of a jewel)

guaro *nm CA* : liquor distilled from sugarcane

guasa *nf fam* **1** : joking, fooling around **2 de ~** : in jest, as a joke

guasón[1], -sona *adj, mpl* **guasones** *fam* : funny, witty

guasón[2], **-sona** *n, mpl* **guasones** *fam* : joker, clown
guatemalteco, -ca *adj & n* : Guatemalan
guau *interj* : wow!
guayaba *nf* : guava (fruit)
gubernamental *adj* : governmental
gubernativo, -va → **gubernamental**
gubernatura *nf Mex* : governing body
guepardo *nm* : cheetah
güero, -ra *adj Mex* : blond, fair
guerra *nf* **1** : war <declarar la guerra : to declare war> <guerra sin cuartel : all-out war> **2** : warfare **3** LUCHA : conflict, struggle
guerrear *vi* : to wage war
guerrero[1], **-ra** *adj* **1** : war, fighting **2** : warlike
guerrero[2], **-ra** *n* : warrior
guerrilla *nf* : guerrilla warfare
guerrillero, -ra *adj & n* : guerrilla
gueto *nm* : ghetto
guía[1] *nf* **1** : directory, guidebook **2** ORIENTACIÓN : guidance, direction <la conciencia me sirve como guía : conscience is my guide>
guía[2] *nmf* : guide, leader <guía de turismo : tour guide>
guiar {85} *vt* **1** : to guide, to lead **2** CONDUCIR : to manage — **guiarse** *vr* : to be guided by, to go by
guija *nf* : pebble
guijarro *nm* : pebble
guillotina *nf* : guillotine — **guillotinar** *vt*
guinda[1] *adj & nm Mex* : burgundy (color)
guinda[2] *nf* : morello (cherry)
guineo *nm Car* : banana
guinga *nf* : gingham
guiñada → **guiño**
guiñar *vi* : to wink
guiño *nm* : wink
guión *nm, pl* **guiones** **1** : script, screenplay **2** : hyphen, dash **3** ESTANDARTE : standard, banner
guirnalda *nf* : garland
guisa *nf* **1** : manner, fashion **2 a guisa de** : like, by way of **3 de tal guisa** : in such a way
guisado ESTOFADO *nm* : stew
guisante *nm* : pea
guisar *vt* **1** ESTOFAR : to stew **2** *Spain* : to cook
guiso *nm* **1** : stew **2** : casserole
güisqui → **whisky**
guita *nf* : string, twine
guitarra *nf* : guitar
guitarrista *nmf* : guitarist
gula *nf* GLOTONERÍA : gluttony, greed
gusano *nm* **1** LOMBRIZ : worm, earthworm <gusano de seda : silkworm> **2** : caterpillar, maggot, grub
gustar *vt* **1** : to taste **2** : to like <¿gustan pasar? : would you like to come in?> — *vi* **1** : to be pleasing <me gustan los dulces : I like sweets> <a María le gusta Carlos : Maria is attracted to Carlos> <no me gusta que me griten : I don't like to be yelled at> **2 ~ de** : to like, to enjoy <no gusta de chismes : she doesn't like gossip> **3 como guste** : as you wish, as you like
gustativo, -va *adj* : taste <papilas gustativas : taste buds>
gusto *nm* **1** : flavor, taste **2** : taste, style **3** : pleasure, liking **4** : whim, fancy <a gusto : at will> **5 a ~** : comfortable, at ease **6 al gusto** : to taste, as one likes **7 mucho gusto** : pleased to meet you
gustosamente *adv* : gladly
gustoso, -sa *adj* **1** : willing, glad <nuestra empresa participará gustosa : our company will be pleased to participate> **2** : zesty, tasty
gutural *adj* : guttural

H

h *nf* : eighth letter of the Spanish alphabet
ha → **haber**
haba *nf* : broad bean
habanero[1], **-ra** *adj* : of or from Havana
habanero[2], **-ra** *n* : native or resident of Havana
haber[1] {39} *v aux* **1** : have, has <no ha llegado el envío : the shipment hasn't arrived> **2 ~ de** : must <ha de ser tarde : it must be late> — *v impers* **1 hay** : there is, there are <hay dos mensajes : there are two messages> <¿qué hay de nuevo? : what's new?> **2 hay que** : it is necessary <hay que trabajar más rápido : you have to work faster>
haber[2] *nm* **1** : assets *pl* **2** : credit, credit side **3 haberes** *nmpl* : salary, income, remuneration
habichuela *nf* **1** : bean, kidney bean **2** : green bean
hábil *adj* **1** : able, skillful **2** : working <días hábiles : working days>
habilidad *nf* CAPACIDAD : ability, skill
habilidoso, -sa *adj* : skillful, clever
habilitación *nf, pl* **-ciones** **1** : authorization **2** : furnishing, equipping
habilitar *vt* **1** : to enable, to authorize, to empower **2** : to equip, to furnish
hábilmente *adv* : skillfully, expertly
habitable *adj* : habitable, inhabitable
habitación *nf, pl* **-ciones** **1** CUARTO : room **2** DORMITORIO : bedroom **3** : habitation, occupancy

habitante *nmf* : inhabitant, resident

habitar *vt* : to inhabit — *vi* : to reside, to dwell

hábitat *nm, pl* **-tats** : habitat

hábito *nm* **1** : habit, custom **2** : habit (of a monk or nun)

habitual *adj* : habitual, customary — **habitualmente** *adv*

habituar {3} *vt* : to accustom, to habituate — **habituarse** *vr* **~ a** : to get used to, to grow accustomed to

habla *nf* **1** : speech **2** : language, dialect **3 de ~** : speaking <de habla inglesa : English-speaking>

hablado, -da *adj* **1** : spoken **2 mal hablado** : foulmouthed

hablador[1], -dora *adj* : talkative

hablador[2], -dora *n* : chatterbox

habladuría *nf* **1** : rumor **2 habladurías** *nfpl* : gossip, scandal

hablante *nmf* : speaker

hablar *vi* **1** : to speak, to talk <hablar en broma : to be joking> **2 ~ de** : to mention, to talk about **3 dar que hablar** : to make people talk — *vt* **1** : to speak (a language) **2** : to talk about, to discuss <háblalo con tu jefe : discuss it with your boss> — **hablarse** *vr* **1** : to speak to each other, to be on speaking terms **2 se habla inglés (etc.)** : English (etc.) spoken

habrá, etc. → **haber**

hacedor, -dora *n* : creator, maker, doer

hacendado, -da *n* : landowner

hacer {40} *vt* **1** : to make **2** : to do, to perform **3** : to force, to oblige <los hice esperar : I made them wait> — *vi* : to act <haces bien : you're doing the right thing> — *v impers* **1** (*referring to weather*) <hacer frío : to be cold> <hace viento : it's windy> **2 hace** : ago <hace mucho tiempo : a long time ago, for a long time> **3 no le hace** : it doesn't matter, it makes no difference **4 hacer falta** : to be necessary, to be needed — **hacerse** *vr* **1** : to become **2** : to pretend, to act, to play <hacerse el tonto : to play dumb> **3** : to seem <el examen se me hizo difícil : the exam seemed difficult to me> **4** : to get, to grow <se hace tarde : it's growing late>

hacha *nf* : hatchet, ax

hachazo *nm* : blow, chop (with an ax)

hachís *nm* : hashish

hacia *prep* **1** : toward, towards <hacia abajo : downward> <hacia adelante : forward> **2** : near, around, about <hacia las seis : about six o'clock>

hacienda *nf* **1** : estate, ranch, farm **2** : property **3** : livestock **4 la Hacienda** : department of revenue, tax office

hacinar *vt* **1** : to pile up, to stack **2** : to overcrowd — **hacinarse** *vr* : to crowd together

hada *nf* : fairy

hado *nm* : destiny, fate

haga, etc. → **hacer**

haitiano, -na *adj & n* : Haitian

halagador[1], -dora *adj* : flattering

halagador[2], -dora *n* : flatterer

halagar {52} *vt* : to flatter, to compliment

halago *nm* : flattery, praise

halagüeño, -ña *adj* **1** : flattering **2** : encouraging, promising

halcón *nm, pl* **halcones** : hawk, falcon

halibut *nm, pl* **-buts** : halibut

hálito *nm* **1** : breath **2** : gentle breeze

hallar *vt* **1** ENCONTRAR : to find **2** DESCUBRIR : to discover, to find out — **hallarse** *vr* **1** : to be situated, to find oneself **2** : to feel <no se halla bien : he doesn't feel comfortable, he feels out of place>

hallazgo *nm* **1** : discovery **2** : find <¡es un verdadero hallazgo! : it's a real find!>

halo *nm* **1** : halo **2** : aura

halógeno *nm* : halogen

hamaca *nf* : hammock

hambre *nf* **1** : hunger **2** : starvation **3 tener hambre** : to be hungry **4 dar hambre** : to make hungry

hambriento, -ta *adj* : hungry, starving

hambruna *nf* : famine

hamburguesa *nf* : hamburger

hampa *nf* : criminal underworld

hampón, -pona *n, mpl* **hampones** : criminal, thug

hámster *nm, pl* **hámsters** : hamster

han → **haber**

handicap *or* **hándicap** [ˈhandiˌkap] *nm, pl* **-caps** : handicap (in sports)

hangar *nm* : hangar

hará, etc. → **hacer**

haragán[1], -gana *adj, mpl* **-ganes** : lazy, idle

haragán[2], -gana *n, mpl* **-ganes** HOLGAZÁN : slacker, good-for-nothing

haraganear *vi* : to be lazy, to waste one's time

haraganería *nf* : laziness

harapiento, -ta *adj* : ragged, tattered

harapos *nmpl* ANDRAJOS : rags, tatters

hardware [ˈhardˌwɛr] *nm* : computer hardware

harén *nm, pl* **harenes** : harem

harina *nf* **1** : flour **2 harina de maíz** : cornmeal

hartar *vt* **1** : to glut, to satiate **2** FASTIDIAR : to tire, to irritate, to annoy — **hartarse** *vr* : to be weary, to get fed up

harto[1] *adv* : most, extremely, very

harto[2], -ta *adj* **1** : full, satiated **2** : fed up

hartura *nf* **1** : surfeit **2** : abundance, plenty

has → **haber**

hasta[1] *adv* : even

hasta[2] *prep* **1** : until, up until <hasta entonces : until then> <¡hasta luego! : see you later!> **2** : as far as <nos fuimos hasta Managua : we went all the way to Managua> **3** : up to <hasta cierto punto : up to a certain point> **4 hasta que** : until

hastiar {85} *vt* **1 :** to make weary, to bore **2 :** to disgust, to sicken — **hastiarse** *vr* **~ de :** to get tired of

hastío *nm* **1** TEDIO **:** tedium **2** REPUGNANCIA **:** disgust

hato *nm* **1 :** flock, herd **2 :** bundle (of possessions)

hawaiano, -na *adj & n* **:** Hawaiian

hay → **haber**

haya[1], **etc.** → **haber**

haya[2] *nf* **:** beech (tree and wood)

hayuco *nm* **:** beechnut

haz[1] → **hacer**

haz[2] *nm, pl* **haces 1** FARDO **:** bundle **2 :** beam (of light)

haz[3] *nf, pl* **haces 1 :** face **2 haz de la tierra :** surface of the earth

hazaña *nf* PROEZA **:** feat, exploit

hazmerreír *nm fam* **:** laughingstock

he[1] {39} → **haber**

he[2] *v impers* **he aquí :** here is, here are, behold

hebilla *nf* **:** buckle, clasp

hebra *nf* **:** strand, thread

hebreo[1], **-brea** *adj & n* **:** Hebrew

hebreo[2] *nm* **:** Hebrew (language)

hecatombe *nm* **1** MATANZA **:** massacre **2 :** disaster

heces → **hez**

hechicería *nf* **1** BRUJERÍA **:** sorcery, witchcraft **2 :** curse, spell

hechicero[1], **-ra** *adj* **:** bewitching, enchanting

hechicero[2], **-ra** *n* **:** sorcerer, sorceress *f*

hechizar {21} *vt* **1** EMBRUJAR **:** to bewitch **2** CAUTIVAR **:** to charm

hechizo *nm* **1** SORTILEGIO **:** spell, enchantment **2** ENCANTO **:** charm, fascination

hecho[1] *pp* → **hacer**

hecho[2], **-cha** *adj* **1 :** made, done **2 :** ready-to-wear **3 :** complete, finished <hecho y derecho : full-fledged>

hecho[3] *nm* **1 :** fact **2 :** event <hechos históricos : historic events> **3 :** act, action **4 de ~ :** in fact, in reality

hechura *nf* **1 :** style **2 :** craftsmanship, workmanship **3 :** product, creation

hectárea *nf* **:** hectare

heder {56} *vi* **:** to stink, to reek

hediondez *nf* **:** stink, stench

hediondo, -da *adj* MALOLIENTE **:** foul-smelling, stinking

hedor *nm* **:** stench, stink

hegemonía *nf* **1 :** dominance **2 :** hegemony (in politics)

helada *nf* **:** frost (in meteorology)

heladería *nf* **:** ice-cream parlor, ice-cream stand

helado[1], **-da** *adj* **1** GÉLIDO **:** icy, freezing cold **2** CONGELADO **:** frozen

helado[2] *nm* **:** ice cream

heladora *nf* CONGELADOR **:** freezer

helar {55} *v* CONGELAR **:** to freeze — *v impers* **:** to produce frost <anoche heló : there was frost last night> — **helarse** *vr*

helecho *nm* **:** fern, bracken

hélice *nf* **1 :** spiral, helix **2 :** propeller

helicóptero *nm* **:** helicopter

helio *nm* **:** helium

helipuerto *nm* **:** heliport

hembra *adj & nf* **:** female

hemisférico, -ca *adj* **:** hemispheric, hemispherical

hemisferio *nm* **:** hemisphere

hemofilia *nf* **:** hemophilia

hemofílico, -ca *adj & n* **:** hemophiliac

hemoglobina *nf* **:** hemoglobin

hemorragia *nf* **1 :** hemorrhage **2 hemorragia nasal :** nosebleed

hemorroides *nfpl* ALMORRANAS **:** hemorrhoids, piles

hemos → **haber**

henchido, -da *adj* **:** swollen, bloated

henchir {54} *vt* **1 :** to stuff, to fill **2 :** to swell, to swell up — **henchirse** *vr* **:** to stuff oneself **2** LLENARSE **:** to fill up, to be full

hender {56} *vt* **:** to cleave, to split

hendidura *nf* **:** crack, crevice, fissure

henequén *nm, pl* **-quenes :** sisal hemp

heno *nm* **:** hay

hepatitis *nf* **:** hepatitis

heráldica *nf* **:** heraldry

heráldico, -ca *adj* **:** heraldic

heraldo *nm* **:** herald

herbario, -ria *adj* **:** herbal

herbicida *nm* **:** herbicide, weed killer

herbívoro[1], **-ra** *adj* **:** herbivorous

herbívoro[2] *nm* **:** herbivore

herbolario, -ria *n* **:** herbalist

hercúleo, -lea *adj* **:** herculean

heredar *vt* **:** to inherit

heredero, -ra *n* **:** heir, heiress *f*

hereditario, -ria *adj* **:** hereditary

hereje *nmf* **:** heretic

herejía *nf* **:** heresy

herencia *nf* **1 :** inheritance **2 :** heritage **3 :** heredity

herético, -ca *adj* **:** heretical

herida *nf* **:** injury, wound

herido[1], **-da** *adj* **1 :** injured, wounded **2 :** hurt, offended

herido[2], **-da** *n* **:** injured person, casualty

herir {76} *vt* **1 :** to injure, to wound **2 :** to hurt, to offend

hermafrodita *nmf* **:** hermaphrodite

hermanar *vt* **1 :** to unite, to bring together **2 :** to match up, to twin (cities)

hermanastro, -tra *n* **:** half brother *m*, half sister *f*

hermandad *nf* **1** FRATERNIDAD **:** brotherhood <hermandad de mujeres : sisterhood, sorority> **2 :** association

hermano, -na *n* **:** sibling, brother *m*, sister *f*

hermético, -ca *adj* **:** hermetic, watertight — **herméticamente** *adv*

hermoso, -sa *adj* BELLO **:** beautiful, lovely — **hermosamente** *adv*

hermosura *nf* BELLEZA **:** beauty, loveliness

hernia *nf* **:** hernia

héroe *nm* **:** hero

heroicidad *nf* **:** heroism, heroic deed

heroico, -ca *adj* : heroic — **heroicamente** *adv*
heroína *nf* **1** : heroine **2** : heroin
heroísmo *nm* : heroism
herpes *nms & pl* **1** : herpes **2** : shingles
herradura *nf* : horseshoe
herraje *nm* : ironwork
herramienta *nf* : tool
herrar {55} *vt* : to shoe (a horse)
herrería *nf* : blacksmith's shop
herrero, -ra *n* : blacksmith
herrumbre *nf* ORÍN : rust
herrumbroso, -sa *adj* OXIDADO : rusty
hertzio *nm* : hertz
hervidero *nm* **1** : mass, swarm **2** : hotbed (of crime, etc.)
hervidor *nm* : kettle
hervir {76} *vi* **1** BULLIR : to boil, to bubble **2** ~ **de** : to teem with, to be swarming with — *vt* : to boil
hervor *nm* **1** : boiling **2** : fervor, ardor
heterogeneidad *nf* : heterogeneity
heterogéneo, -nea *adj* : heterogeneous
heterosexual *adj & nmf* : heterosexual
heterosexualidad *nf* : heterosexuality
hexágono *nm* : hexagon — **hexagonal** *adj*
hez *nf, pl* **heces** **1** ESCORIA : scum, dregs *pl* **2** : sediment, lees *pl* **3** **heces** *nfpl* : feces, excrement
hiato *nm* : hiatus
hibernar *vi* : to hibernate — **hibernación** *nf*
híbrido[1], -da *adj* : hybrid
híbrido[2] *nm* : hybrid
hicieron, etc. → **hacer**
hidalgo, -ga *n* : nobleman *m,* noblewoman *f*
hidrante *nm CA, Col* : hydrant
hidratar *vt* : to moisturize — **hidratante** *adj*
hidrato *nm* **1** : hydrate **2** **hidrato de carbono** : carbohydrate
hidráulico, -ca *adj* : hydraulic
hidroavión *nm, pl* **-viones** : seaplane
hidrocarburo *nm* : hydrocarbon
hidroeléctrico, -ca *adj* : hydroelectric
hidrofobia *nf* RABIA : hydrophobia, rabies
hidrófugo, -ga *adj* : water-repellent
hidrógeno *nm* : hydrogen
hidroplano *nm* : hydroplane
hiede, etc. → **heder**
hiedra *nf* **1** : ivy **2** **hiedra venenosa** : poison ivy
hiel *nf* **1** BILIS : bile **2** : bitterness
hiela, etc. → **helar**
hielo *nm* **1** : ice **2** : coldness, reserve <romper el hielo : to break the ice>
hiena *nf* : hyena
hiende, etc. → **hender**
hierba *nf* **1** : herb **2** : grass **3** **mala hierba** : weed
hierbabuena *nf* : mint, spearmint
hiere, etc. → **herir**
hierra, etc. → **herrar**
hierro *nm* **1** : iron <hierro fundido : cast iron> **2** : branding iron
hierve, etc. → **hervir**
hígado *nm* : liver
higiene *nf* : hygiene
higiénico, -ca *adj* : hygienic — **higiénicamente** *adv*
higienista *nmf* : hygienist
higo *nm* **1** : fig **2** **higo chumbo** : prickly pear (fruit)
higrómetro *nm* : hygrometer
higuera *nf* : fig tree
hijastro, -tra *n* : stepson *m,* stepdaughter *f*
hijo, -ja *n* **1** : son *m,* daughter *f* **2** **hijos** *nmpl* : children, offspring
híjole *interj Mex* : wow!, good grief!
hilacha *nf* **1** : ravel, loose thread **2** **mostrar la hilacha** : to show one's true colors
hilado *nm* **1** : spinning **2** HILO : yarn, thread
hilar *vt* **1** : to spin (thread) **2** : to consider, to string together (ideas) — *vi* **1** : to spin **2** **hilar delgado** : to split hairs
hilarante *adj* **1** : humorous, hilarious **2** **gas hilarante** : laughing gas
hilaridad *nf* : hilarity
hilera *nf* FILA : file, row, line
hilo *nm* **1** : thread <colgar de un hilo : to hang by a thread> <hilo dental : dental floss> **2** LINO : linen **3** : (electric) wire **4** : theme, thread (of a discourse) **5** : trickle (of water, etc.)
hilvanar *vt* **1** : to baste, to tack **2** : to piece together
himnario *nm* : hymnal
himno *nm* **1** : hymn **2** **himno nacional** : national anthem
hincapié *nm* **hacer hincapié en** : to emphasize, to stress
hincar {72} *vt* CLAVAR : to stick, to plunge — **hincarse** *vr* **hincarse de rodillas** : to kneel down, to fall to one's knees
hinchado, -da *adj* **1** : swollen, inflated **2** : pompous, overblown
hinchar *vt* **1** INFLAR : to inflate **2** : to exaggerate — **hincharse** *vr* **1** : to swell up **2** : to become conceited, to swell with pride
hinchazón *nf, pl* **-zones** : swelling
hinche, etc. → **henchir**
hindú *adj & nmf* : Hindu
hinduismo *nm* : Hinduism
hiniesta *nf* : broom (plant)
hinojo *nm* **1** : fennel **2** **de hinojos** : on bended knee
hinque, etc. → **hincar**
hipar *vi* : to hiccup
hiperactividad *nf* : hyperactivity
hiperactivo, -va *adj* : hyperactive, overactive
hipérbole *nf* : hyperbole
hiperbólico, -ca *adj* : hyperbolic, exaggerated
hipercrítico, -ca *adj* : hypercritical
hipermetropía *nf* : farsightedness
hipersensibilidad *nf* : hypersensitivity
hipersensible *adj* : hypersensitive

hipertensión *nf, pl* **-siones** : hypertension, high blood pressure
hípico, -ca *adj* : equestrian <concurso hípico : horse show>
hipil *nm* → **huipil**
hipnosis *nfs & pl* : hypnosis
hipnótico, -ca *adj* : hypnotic
hipnotismo *nm* : hypnotism
hipnotizador[1], **-dora** *adj* **1** : hypnotic **2** : spellbinding, mesmerizing
hipnotizador[2], **-dora** *n* : hypnotist
hipnotizar {21} *vt* : to hypnotize
hipo *nm* : hiccup, hiccups *pl*
hipocampo *nm* : sea horse
hipocondría *nf* : hypochondria
hipocondríaco, -ca *adj & n* : hypochondriac
hipocresía *nf* : hypocrisy
hipócrita[1] *adj* : hypocritical — **hipócritamente** *adv*
hipócrita[2] *nmf* : hypocrite
hipodérmico, -ca *adj* **aguja hipodérmica** : hypodermic needle
hipódromo *nm* : racetrack
hipopótamo *nm* : hippopotamus
hipoteca *nf* : mortgage
hipotecar {72} *vt* **1** : to mortgage **2** : to compromise, to jeopardize
hipotecario, -ria *adj* : mortgage
hipotensión *nf* : low blood pressure
hipotenusa *nf* : hypotenuse
hipótesis *nfs & pl* : hypothesis
hipotético, -ca *adj* : hypothetical — **hipotéticamente** *adv*
hippie *or* **hippy** [ˈhipi] *nmf, pl* **hippies** [-pis] : hippie
hiriente *adj* : hurtful, offensive
hirió, etc. → **herir**
hirsuto, -ta *adj* **1** : hirsute, hairy **2** : bristly, wiry
hirviente *adj* : boiling
hirvió, etc. → **hervir**
hisopo *nm* **1** : hyssop **2** : cotton swab
hispánico, -ca *adj & n* : Hispanic
hispano[1], **-na** *adj* : Hispanic <de habla hispana : Spanish-speaking>
hispano[2], **-na** *n* : Hispanic (person)
hispanoamericano[1], **-na** *adj* LATINOAMERICANO : Latin-American
hispanoamericano[2], **-na** *n* LATINOAMERICANO : Latin American
hispanohablante[1] *adj* : Spanish-speaking
hispanohablante[2] *nmf* : Spanish speaker
histerectomía *nf* : hysterectomy
histeria *nf* **1** : hysteria **2** : hysterics
histérico, -ca *adj* : hysterical — **histéricamente** *adv*
histerismo *nm* **1** : hysteria **2** : hysterics
historia *nf* **1** : history **2** NARRACIÓN, RELATO : story
historiador, -dora *n* : historian
historial *nm* **1** : record, document **2** CURRÍCULUM : résumé, curriculum vitae
histórico, -ca *adj* **1** : historical **2** : historic, important — **históricamente** *adv*
historieta *nf* : comic strip
histrionismo *nm* : histrionics, acting
hit [ˈhit] *nm, pl* **hits 1** ÉXITO : hit, popular song **2** : hit (in baseball)
hito *nm* : milestone, landmark
hizo → **hacer**
hobby [ˈhɔbi] *nm, pl* **hobbies** [-bis] : hobby
hocico *nm* : snout, muzzle
hockey [ˈhɔke, -ki] *nm* : hockey
hogar *nm* **1** : home **2** : hearth, fireplace
hogareño, -ña *adj* **1** : home-loving **2** : domestic, homelike
hogaza *nf* : large loaf (of bread)
hoguera *nf* **1** FOGATA : bonfire **2 morir en la hoguera** : to burn at the stake
hoja *nf* **1** : leaf, petal, blade (of grass) **2** : sheet (of paper), page (of a book) <hoja de cálculo : spreadsheet> **3** FORMULARIO : form <hoja de pedido : order form> **4** : blade (of a knife) <hoja de afeitar : razor blade>
hojalata *nf* : tinplate
hojaldra *or* **hojaldre** *nm* : puff pastry
hojarasca *nf* : fallen leaves *pl*
hojear *vt* : to leaf through (a book or magazine)
hojuela *nf* **1** : leaflet, young leaf **2** : flake
hola *interj* : hello!, hi!
holandés[1], **-desa** *adj, mpl* **-deses** : Dutch
holandés[2], **-desa** *n, mpl* **-deses** : Dutch person, Dutchman *m*, Dutchwoman *f* <los holandeses : the Dutch>
holandés[3] *nm* : Dutch (language)
holgadamente *adv* : comfortably, easily <vivir holgadamente : to be well-off>
holgado, -da *adj* **1** : loose, baggy **2** : at ease, comfortable
holganza *nf* : leisure, idleness
holgazán[1], **-zana** *adj, mpl* **-zanes** : lazy
holgazán[2], **-zana** *n, mpl* **-zanes** HARAGÁN : slacker, idler
holgazanear *vi* HARAGANEAR : to laze around, to loaf
holgazanería *nf* PEREZA : idleness, laziness
holgura *nf* **1** : looseness **2** COMODIDAD : comfort, ease
holístico, -ca *adj* : holistic
hollar {19} *vt* : to tread on, to trample
hollín *nm, pl* **hollines** TIZNE : soot
holocausto *nm* : holocaust
holograma *nm* : hologram
hombre *nm* **1** : man <el hombre : man, mankind> **2 hombre de estado** : statesman **3 hombre de negocios** : businessman **4 hombre lobo** : werewolf
hombrera *nf* **1** : shoulder pad **2** : epaulet
hombría *nf* : manliness
hombro *nm* : shoulder <encogerse de hombros : to shrug one's shoulders>
hombruno, -na *adj* : mannish

homenaje *nm* : homage, tribute <rendir homenaje a : to pay tribute to>

homenajear *vt* : to pay homage to, to honor

homeopatía *nf* : homeopathy

homicida[1] *adj* : homicidal, murderous

homicida[2] *nmf* ASESINO : murderer

homicidio *nm* ASESINATO : homicide, murder

homilía *nf* : homily, sermon

homófono *nm* : homophone

homogeneidad *nf* : homogeneity

homogeneización *nf* : homogenization

homogeneizar {21} *vt* : to homogenize

homogéneo, -nea *adj* : homogeneous

homógrafo *nm* : homograph

homologación *nf, pl* **-ciones 1** : sanctioning, approval **2** : parity

homologar {52} *vt* **1** : to sanction **2** : to bring into line

homólogo[1], **-ga** *adj* : homologous, equivalent

homólogo[2], **-ga** *n* : counterpart

homónimo[1], **-ma** *n* TOCAYO : namesake

homónimo[2] *nm* : homonym

homosexual *adj & nmf* : homosexual

homosexualidad *nf* : homosexuality

honda *nf* : sling

hondo[1] *adv* : deeply

hondo[2], **-da** *adj* PROFUNDO : deep <en lo más hondo de : in the depths of> — **hondamente** *adv*

hondonada *nf* **1** : hollow, depression **2** : ravine, gorge

hondura *nf* : depth

hondureño, -ña *adj & n* : Honduran

honestidad *nf* **1** : decency, modesty **2** : honesty, uprightness

honesto, -ta *adj* **1** : decent, virtuous **2** : honest, honorable — **honestamente** *adv*

hongo *nm* **1** : fungus **2** : mushroom

honor *nm* **1** : honor <en honor a la verdad : to be quite honest> **2 honores** *nmpl* : honors <hacer los honores : to do the honors>

honorable *adj* HONROSO : honorable — **honorablemente** *adv*

honorario, -ria *adj* : honorary

honorarios *nmpl* : payment, fees (for professional services)

honorífico, -ca *adj* : honorary <mención honorífica : honorable mention>

honra *nf* **1** : dignity, self-respect <tener a mucha honra : to take great pride in> **2** : good name, reputation

honradamente *adv* : honestly, decently

honradez *nf, pl* **-deces** : honesty, integrity, probity

honrado, -da *adj* **1** HONESTO : honest, upright **2** : honored

honrar *vt* **1** : to honor **2** : to be a credit to <su generosidad lo honra : his generosity does him credit>

honroso, -sa *adj* HONORABLE : honorable — **honrosamente** *adv*

hora *nf* **1** : hour <media hora : half an hour> <a la última hora : at the last minute> <a la hora en punto : on the dot> <horas de oficina : office hours> **2** : time <¿qué hora es? : what time is it?> **3** CITA : appointment

horario *nm* : schedule, timetable, hours *pl* <horario de visita : visiting hours>

horca *nf* **1** : gallows *pl* **2** : pitchfork

horcajadas *nfpl* **a ~** : astride, astraddle

horcón *nm, pl* **horcones** : wooden post, prop

horda *nf* : horde

horizontal *adj* : horizontal — **horizontalmente** *adv*

horizonte *nm* : horizon, skyline

horma *nf* **1** : shoe tree **2** : shoemaker's last

hormiga *nf* : ant

hormigón *nm, pl* **-gones** CONCRETO : concrete

hormigonera *nf* : cement mixer

hormigueo *nm* **1** : tingling, pins and needles *pl* **2** : uneasiness

hormiguero *nm* **1** : anthill **2** : swarm (of people)

hormona *nf* : hormone — **hormonal** *adj*

hornacina *nf* : niche, recess

hornada *nf* : batch

hornear *vt* : to bake

hornilla *nf* : burner (of a stove)

horno *nm* **1** : oven <horno crematorio : crematorium> <horno de microondas : microwave oven> **2** : kiln

horóscopo *nm* : horoscope

horqueta *nf* **1** : fork (in a river or road) **2** : crotch (in a tree) **3** : small pitchfork

horquilla *nf* **1** : hairpin, bobby pin **2** : pitchfork

horrendo, -da *adj* : horrendous, horrible

horrible *adj* : horrible, dreadful — **horriblemente** *adv*

horripilante *adj* : horrifying, hair-raising

horripilar *vt* : to horrify, to terrify

horror *nm* : horror, dread

horrorizado, -da *adj* : terrified

horrorizar {21} *vt* : to horrify, to terrify — **horrorizarse** *vr*

horroroso, -sa *adj* **1** : horrifying, terrifying **2** : dreadful, bad

hortaliza *nf* **1** : vegetable **2 hortalizas** *nfpl* : garden produce

hortera *adj Spain fam* : tacky, gaudy

hortícola *adj* : horticultural

horticultor, -ra *n* : horticulturist

horticultura *nf* : horticulture

hosco, -ca *adj* : sullen, gloomy

hospedaje *nm* : lodging, accomodations *pl*

hospedar *vt* : to provide with lodging, to put up — **hospedarse** *vr* : to stay, to lodge

hospicio *nm* : orphanage
hospital *nm* : hospital
hospitalario, -ria *adj* : hospitable
hospitalidad *nf* : hospitality
hospitalización *nf, pl* **-ciones** : hospitalization
hospitalizar {21} *vt* : to hospitalize — **hospitalizarse** *vr*
hostería *nf* POSADA : inn
hostia *nf* : host, Eucharist
hostigamiento *nm* : harassment
hostigar {52} *vt* ACOSAR, ASEDIAR : to harass, to pester
hostil *adj* : hostile
hostilidad *nf* **1** : hostility, antagonism **2 hostilidades** *nfpl* : (military) hostilities
hostilizar {21} *vt* : to harass
hotel *nm* : hotel
hotelero[1], -ra *adj* : hotel <la industria hotelera : the hotel business>
hotelero[2], -ra *n* : hotel manager, hotelier
hoy *adv* **1** : today <hoy mismo : right now, this very day> **2** : now, nowadays <de hoy en adelante : from now on>
hoyo *nm* AGUJERO : hole
hoyuelo *nm* : dimple
hoz *nf, pl* **hoces** : sickle
hozar {21} *vi* : to root (of a pig)
huachinango *nm Mex* : red snapper
huarache *nm* : huarache sandal
hubo, etc. → **haber**
hueco[1], -ca *adj* **1** : hollow, empty **2** : soft, spongy **3** : hollow-sounding, resonant **4** : proud, conceited **5** : superficial
hueco[2] *nm* **1** : hole, hollow, cavity **2** : gap, space **3** : recess, alcove
huele, etc. → **oler**
huelga *nf* **1** PARO : strike **2 hacer huelga** : to strike, to go on strike
huelguista *nmf* : striker
huella[1], etc. → **hollar**
huella[2] *nf* **1** : footprint <seguir las huellas de alguien : to follow in someone's footsteps> **2** : mark, impact <dejar huella : to leave one's mark> <sin dejar huella : without a trace> **3 huella digital** *or* **huella dactilar** : fingerprint
huérfano[1], -na *adj* **1** : orphan, orphaned **2** : defenseless **3 ~ de** : lacking, devoid of
huérfano[2], -na *n* : orphan
huerta *nf* **1** : large vegetable garden, truck farm **2** : orchard **3** : irrigated land
huerto *nm* **1** : vegetable garden **2** : orchard
hueso *nm* **1** : bone **2** : pit, stone (of a fruit)
huésped[1], -peda *n* INVITADO : guest
huésped[2] *nm* : host <organismo huésped : host organism>
huestes *nfpl* **1** : followers **2** : troops, army
huesudo, -da *adj* : bony
hueva *nf* : roe, spawn
huevo *nm* : egg <huevos revueltos : scrambled eggs>
huida *nf* : flight, escape
huidizo, -za *adj* **1** ESCURRIDIZO : elusive, slippery **2** : shy, evasive
huipil *nm CA, Mex* : traditional sleeveless blouse or dress
huir {41} *vi* **1** ESCAPAR : to escape, to flee **2 ~ de** : to avoid
huiro *nm Chile, Peru* : seaweed
huizache *nm* : huisache, acacia
hule *nm* **1** : oilcloth, oilskin **2** *Mex* : rubber **3 hule espuma** *Mex* : foam rubber
humanidad *nf* **1** : humanity, mankind **2** : humaneness **3 humanidades** *nfpl* : humanities *pl*
humanismo *nm* : humanism
humanista *nmf* : humanist
humanístico, -ca *adj* : humanistic
humanitario, -ria *adj & n* : humanitarian
humano[1], -na *adj* **1** : human **2** BENÉVOLO : humane , benevolent — **humanamente** *adv*
humano[2] *nm* : human being, human
humareda *nf* : cloud of smoke
humeante *adj* **1** : smoky **2** : smoking, steaming
humear *vi* **1** : to smoke **2** : to steam
humectante[1] *adj* : moisturizing
humectante[2] *nm* : moisturizer
humedad *nf* **1** : humidity **2** : dampness, moistness
humedecer {53} *vt* **1** : to humidify **2** : to moisten, to dampen
húmedo, -da *adj* **1** : humid **2** : moist, damp
humidificador *nm* : humidifier
humidificar {72} *vt* : to humidify
humildad *nf* **1** : humility **2** : lowliness
humilde *adj* **1** : humble **2** : lowly <gente humilde : poor people>
humildemente *adv* : meekly, humbly
humillación *nf, pl* **-ciones** : humiliation
humillante *adj* : humiliating
humillar *vt* : to humiliate — **humillarse** *vr* : to humble oneself <humillarse a hacer algo : to stoop to doing something>
humo *nm* **1** : smoke, steam, fumes **2 humos** *nmpl* : airs *pl,* conceit
humor *nm* **1** : humor **2** : mood, temper <está de buen humor : she's in a good mood>
humorada *nf* **1** BROMA : joke, witticism **2** : whim, caprice
humorismo *nm* : humor, wit
humorista *nmf* : humorist, comedian, comedienne *f*
humorístico, -ca *adj* : humorous — **humorísticamente** *adv*
humoso, -sa *adj* : smoky, steamy
humus *nm* : humus
hundido, -da *adj* **1** : sunken **2** : depressed

hundimiento *nm* **1** : sinking **2** : collapse, ruin
hundir *vt* **1** : to sink **2** : to destroy, to ruin — **hundirse** *vr* **1** : to sink down **2** : to cave in **3** : to break down, to go to pieces
húngaro[1], **-ra** *adj & n* : Hungarian
húngaro[2] *nm* : Hungarian (language)
huracán *nm, pl* **-canes** : hurricane
huraño, -ña *adj* **1** : unsociable, aloof **2** : timid, skittish (of an animal)
hurgar {52} *vt* : to poke, to jab, to rake (a fire) — *vi* **~ en** : to rummage in, to poke through
hurgue, etc. → **hurgar**
hurón *nm, pl* **hurones** : ferret
huronear *vi* : to pry, to snoop
hurra *interj* : hurrah!, hooray!
hurtadillas *nfpl* **a ~** : stealthily, on the sly
hurtar *vt* ROBAR : to steal
hurto *nm* **1** : theft, robbery **2** : stolen property, loot
husmear *vt* **1** : to follow the scent of, to track **2** : to sniff out, to pry into — *vi* **1** : to pry, to snoop **2** : to sniff around (of an animal)
huso *nm* **1** : spindle **2 huso horario** : time zone
huy *interj* : ow!, ouch!
huye, etc. → **huir**

I

i *nf* : ninth letter of the Spanish alphabet
iba, etc. → **ir**
ibérico, -ca *adj* : Iberian
ibero, -ra *or* **íbero, -ra** *adj & n* : Iberian
iberoamericano, -na *adj* HISPANOAMERICANO, LATINOAMERICANO : Latin-American
ibis *nfs & pl* : ibis
ice, etc. → **izar**
iceberg *nm, pl* **icebergs** : iceberg
icono *nm* : icon
iconoclasia *nf* : iconoclasm
iconoclasta *nmf* : iconoclast
ictericia *nf* : jaundice
ida *nf* **1** : going, departure **2 ida y vuelta** : round-trip **3 idas y venidas** : comings and goings
idea *nf* **1** : idea, notion **2** : opinion, belief **3** PROPÓSITO : intention
ideal *adj & nm* : ideal — **idealmente** *adv*
idealismo *nm* : idealism
idealista[1] *adj* : idealistic
idealista[2] *nmf* : idealist
idealizar {21} *vt* : to idealize — **idealización** *nf*
idear *vt* : to devise, to think up
ideario *nm* : ideology
ídem *nm* : idem, the same, ditto
idéntico, -ca *adj* : identical, alike — **idénticamente** *adv*
identidad *nf* : identity
identificable *adj* : identifiable
identificación *nf, pl* **-ciones 1** : identification, identifying **2** : identification document, ID
identificar {72} *vt* : to identify — **identificarse** *vr* **1** : to identify oneself **2 ~ con** : to identify with
ideología *nf* : ideology — **ideológicamente** *adv*
ideológico, -ca *adj* : ideological
idílico, -ca *adj* : idyllic
idilio *nm* : idyll
idioma *nm* : language <el idioma inglés : the English language>
idiomático, -ca *adj* : idiomatic — **idiomáticamente** *adv*
idiosincrasia *nf* : idiosyncrasy
idiosincrásico, -ca *adj* : idiosyncratic
idiota[1] *adj* : idiotic, stupid, foolish
idiota[2] *nmf* : idiot, foolish person
idiotez *nf, pl* **-teces 1** : idiocy **2** : idiotic act or remark <¡no digas idioteces! : don't talk nonsense!>
ido *pp* → **ir**
idólatra[1] *adj* : idolatrous
idólatra[2] *nmf* : idolater
idolatrar *vt* : to idolize
idolatría *nf* : idolatry
ídolo *nm* : idol
idoneidad *nf* : suitability
idóneo, -nea *adj* ADECUADO : suitable, fitting
iglesia *nf* : church
iglú *nm* : igloo
ignición *nf, pl* **-ciones** : ignition
ignífugo, -ga *adj* : fire-resistant, fireproof
ignominia *nf* : ignominy, disgrace
ignominioso, -sa *adj* : ignominious, shameful
ignorancia *nf* : ignorance
ignorante[1] *adj* : ignorant
ignorante[2] *nmf* : ignorant person, ignoramus
ignorar *vt* **1** : to ignore **2** DESCONOCER : to be unaware of <lo ignoramos por absoluto : we have no idea>
ignoto, -ta *adj* : unknown
igual[1] *adv* **1** : in the same way **2 por ~** : equally
igual[2] *adj* **1** : equal **2** IDÉNTICO : the same, alike **3** : even, smooth **4** SEMEJANTE : similar **5** CONSTANTE : constant
igual[3] *nmf* : equal, peer
igualación *nf* **1** : equalization **2** : leveling, smoothing **3** : equating (in mathematics)
igualado, -da *adj* **1** : even (of a score) **2** : level **3** *Mex* : disrespectful
igualar *vt* **1** : to equalize **2** : to tie <igualar el marcador : to even the score>

igualdad *nf* **1** : equality **2** UNIFORMIDAD : evenness, uniformity
igualmente *adv* **1** : equally **2** ASIMISMO : likewise
iguana *nf* : iguana
ijada *nf* : flank, loin, side
ijar *nm* → **ijada**
ilegal[1] *adj* : illegal, unlawful — **ilegalmente** *adv*
ilegal[2] *nmf CA, Mex* : illegal alien
ilegalidad *nf* : illegality, unlawfulness
ilegibilidad *nf* : illegibility
ilegible *adj* : illegible — **ilegiblemente** *adv*
ilegitimidad *nf* : illegitimacy
ilegítimo, -ma *adj* : illegitimate, unlawful
ileso, -sa *adj* : uninjured, unharmed
ilícito, -ta *adj* : illicit — **ilícitamente** *adv*
ilimitado, -da *adj* : unlimited
ilógico, -ca *adj* : illogical — **ilógicamente** *adv*
iluminación *nf, pl* **-ciones 1** : illumination **2** ALUMBRADO : lighting
iluminado, -da *adj* : illuminated, lighted
iluminar *vt* **1** : to illuminate, to light (up) **2** : to enlighten
ilusión *nf, pl* **-siones 1** : illusion, delusion **2** ESPERANZA : hope <hacerse ilusiones : to get one's hopes up>
ilusionado, -da *adj* ESPERANZADO : hopeful, eager
ilusionar *vt* : to build up hope, to excite — **ilusionarse** *vr* : to get one's hopes up
iluso[1], **-sa** *adj* : naive, gullible
iluso[2], **-sa** *n* SOÑADOR : dreamer, visionary
ilusorio, -ria *adj* ENGAÑOSO : illusory, misleading
ilustración *nf, pl* **-ciones 1** : illustration **2** : erudition, learning <la Ilustración : the Enlightenment>
ilustrado, -da *adj* **1** : illustrated **2** DOCTO : learned, erudite
ilustrador, -dora *n* : illustrator
ilustrar *vt* **1** : to illustrate **2** ACLARAR, CLARIFICAR : to explain
ilustrativo, -va *adj* : illustrative
ilustre *adj* : illustrious, eminent
imagen *nf, pl* **imágenes** : image, picture
imaginable *adj* : imaginable, conceivable
imaginación *nf, pl* **-ciones** : imagination
imaginar *vt* : to imagine — **imaginarse** *vr* **1** : to suppose, to imagine **2** : to picture
imaginario, -ria *adj* : imaginary
imaginativo, -va *adj* : imaginative — **imaginativamente** *adv*
imán *nm, pl* **imanes** : magnet
imantar *vt* : to magnetize
imbatible *adj* : unbeatable
imbécil[1] *adj* : stupid, idiotic
imbécil[2] *nmf* **1** : imbecile **2** *fam* : idiot, dope
imborrable *adj* : indelible
imbuir {41} *vt* : to imbue — **imbuirse** *vr*
imitación *nf, pl* **-ciones 1** : imitation **2** : mimicry, impersonation
imitador[1], **-dora** *adj* : imitative
imitador[2], **-dora** *n* **1** : imitator **2** : mimic
imitar *vt* **1** : to imitate, to copy **2** : to mimic, to impersonate
impaciencia *nf* : impatience
impacientar *vt* : to make impatient, to exasperate — **impacientarse** *vr*
impaciente *adj* : impatient — **impacientemente** *adv*
impactado, -da *adj* : shocked, stunned
impactante *adj* **1** : shocking **2** : impressive, powerful
impactar *vt* **1** GOLPEAR : to hit **2** IMPRESIONAR : to impact, to affect — **impactarse** *vr*
impacto *nm* **1** : impact, effect **2** : shock, collision
impagable *adj* **1** : unpayable **2** : priceless
impago *nm* : nonpayment
impalpable *adj* INTANGIBLE : impalpable, intangible
impar[1] *adj* : odd <números impares : odd numbers>
impar[2] *nm* : odd number
imparable *adj* : unstoppable
imparcial *adj* : impartial — **imparcialmente** *adv*
imparcialidad *nf* : impartiality
impartir *vt* : to impart, to give
impasible *adj* : impassive, unmoved — **impasiblemente** *adv*
impasse *nm* : impasse
impávido, -da *adj* : undaunted, unperturbed
impecable *adj* INTACHABLE : impeccable, faultless — **impecablemente** *adv*
impedido, -da *adj* : disabled, crippled
impedimento *nm* **1** : impediment, obstacle **2** : disability
impedir {54} *vt* **1** : to prevent, to block **2** : to impede, to hinder
impeler *vt* **1** : to drive, to propel **2** : to impel
impenetrable *adj* : impenetrable — **impenetrabilidad** *nf*
impenitente *adj* : unrepentant, impenitent
impensable *adj* : unthinkable
impensado, -da *adj* : unforeseen, unexpected
imperante *adj* : prevailing
imperar *vi* **1** : to reign, to rule **2** PREDOMINAR : to prevail
imperativo[1], **-va** *adj* : imperative
imperativo[2] *nm* : imperative
imperceptible *adj* : imperceptible — **imperceptiblemente** *adv*
imperdible *Spain nm* : safety pin

imperdonable *adj* **:** unpardonable, unforgivable

imperecedero, -ra *adj* **1 :** imperishable **2** INMORTAL **:** immortal, everlasting

imperfección *nf, pl* **-ciones 1 :** imperfection **2** DEFECTO **:** defect, flaw

imperfecto[1], -ta *adj* **:** imperfect, flawed

imperfecto[2] *nm* **:** imperfect tense

imperial *adj* **:** imperial

imperialismo *nm* **:** imperialism

imperialista *adj & nmf* **:** imperialist

impericia *nf* **:** lack of skill, incompetence

imperio *nm* **:** empire

imperioso, -sa *adj* **1 :** imperious **2 :** pressing, urgent — **imperiosamente** *adv*

impermeabilizante *adj* **:** water-repellent

impermeabilizar {21} *vt* **:** to waterproof

impermeable[1] *adj* **1 :** impervious **2 :** impermeable, waterproof

impermeable[2] *nm* **:** raincoat

impersonal *adj* **:** impersonal — **impersonalmente** *adv*

impertinencia *nf* INSOLENCIA **:** impertinence, insolence

impertinente *adj* **1** INSOLENTE **:** impertinent, insolent **2** INOPORTUNO **:** inappropriate, uncalled-for **3** IRRELEVANTE **:** irrelevant

imperturbable *adj* **:** imperturbable, impassive, stolid

ímpetu *nm* **1 :** impetus, momentum **2 :** vigor, energy **3 :** force, violence

impetuoso, -sa *adj* **:** impetuous, impulsive — **impetuosamente** *adv*

impiedad *nf* **:** impiety

impío, -pía *adj* **:** impious, ungodly

implacable *adj* **:** implacable, relentless — **implacablemente** *adv*

implantación *nf, pl* **-ciones 1 :** implantation **2** ESTABLECIMIENTO **:** establishment, introduction

implantado, -da *adj* **:** well-established

implantar *vt* **1 :** to implant **2** ESTABLECER **:** to establish, to introduce — **implantarse** *vr*

implante *nm* **:** implant

implementar *vt* **:** to implement — **implementarse** *vr* — **implementación** *nf*

implemento *nm* **:** implement, tool

implicación *nf, pl* **-ciones :** implication

implicar {72} *vt* **1** ENREDAR, ENVOLVER **:** to involve, to implicate **2 :** to imply

implícito, -ta *adj* **:** implied, implicit — **implícitamente** *adv*

implorar *vt* **:** to implore

implosión *nf, pl* **-siones :** implosion — **implosivo, -va** *adj*

implosionar *vi* **:** to implode

imponderable *adj & nm* **:** imponderable

imponente *adj* **:** imposing, impressive

imponer {60} *vt* **1 :** to impose **2 :** to confer — *vi* **:** to be impressive, to command respect — **imponerse** *vr* **1 :** to take on (a duty) **2 :** to assert oneself **3 :** to prevail

imponible *adj* **:** taxable

impopular *adj* **:** unpopular — **impopularidad** *nf*

importación *nf, pl* **-ciones 1 :** importation **2 importaciones** *nfpl* **:** imports

importado, -da *adj* **:** imported

importador[1], -dora *adj* **:** importing

importador[2], -dora *n* **:** importer

importancia *nf* **:** importance

importante *adj* **:** important — **importantemente** *adv*

importar *vi* **:** to matter, to be important <no le importa lo que piensen : she doesn't care what they think> — *vt* **:** to import

importe *nm* **1 :** price, cost **2 :** sum, amount

importunar *vt* **:** to bother, to inconvenience — *vi* **:** to be inconvenient

importuno, -na *adj* **1 :** inopportune, inconvenient **2 :** bothersome, annoying

imposibilidad *nf* **:** impossibility

imposibilitado, -da *adj* **1 :** disabled, crippled **2 verse imposibilitado :** to be unable (to do something)

imposibilitar *vt* **1 :** to make impossible **2 :** to disable, to incapacitate — **imposibilitarse** *vr* **:** to become disabled

imposible *adj* **:** impossible

imposición *nf, pl* **-ciones 1 :** imposition **2** EXIGENCIA **:** demand, requirement **3 :** tax **4 :** deposit

impositivo, -va *adj* **:** tax <tasa impositiva : tax rate>

impostor, -tora *n* **:** impostor

impotencia *nf* **1 :** impotence, powerlessness **2 :** impotence (in medicine)

impotente *adj* **1 :** powerless **2 :** impotent

impracticable *adj* **:** impracticable

imprecisión *nf, pl* **-siones 1 :** imprecision, vagueness **2 :** inaccuracy

impreciso, -sa *adj* **1 :** imprecise, vague **2 :** inaccurate

impredecible *adj* **:** unpredictable

impregnar *vt* **:** to impregnate

imprenta *nf* **1 :** printing **2 :** printing shop, press

imprescindible *adj* **:** essential, indispensable

impresentable *adj* **:** unpresentable, unfit

impresión *nf, pl* **-siones 1 :** print, printing **2 :** impression, feeling

impresionable *adj* **:** impressionable

impresionante *adj* **:** impressive, incredible, amazing — **impresionantemente** *adv*

impresionar *vt* **1 :** to impress, to strike **2 :** to affect, to move — *vi* **:** to make an impression — **impresionarse** *vr* **:** to be affected, to be removed

impresionismo *nm* **:** impressionism

impresionista[1] *adj* : impressionist, impressionistic
impresionista[2] *nmf* : impressionist
impreso[1] *pp* → **imprimir**
impreso[2], **-sa** *adj* : printed
impreso[3] *nm* PUBLICACIÓN : printed matter, publication
impresor, -sora *n* : printer
impresora *nf* : (computer) printer
imprevisible *adj* : unforeseeable
imprevisión *nf, pl* **-siones** : lack of foresight, thoughtlessness
imprevisto[1], **-ta** *adj* : unexpected, unforeseen
imprevisto[2] *nm* : unexpected occurrence, contingency
imprimir {42} *vt* **1** : to print **2** : to imprint, to stamp, to impress
improbabilidad *nf* : improbability
improbable *adj* : improbable, unlikely
improcedente *adj* **1** : inadmissible **2** : inappropriate, improper
improductivo, -va *adj* : unproductive
improperio *nm* : affront, insult
impropio, -pia *adj* **1** : improper, incorrect **2** INADECUADO : unsuitable, inappropriate
improvisación *nf, pl* **-ciones** : improvisation, ad-lib
improvisado, -da *adj* : improvised, ad-lib
improvisar *v* : to improvise, to ad-lib
improviso *adj* **de ~** : all of a sudden, unexpectedly
imprudencia *nf* INDISCRECIÓN : imprudence, indiscretion
imprudente *adj* INDISCRETO : imprudent, indiscreet — **imprudentemente** *adv*
impúdico, -ca *adj* : shameless, indecent
impuesto[1] *pp* → **imponer**
impuesto[2] *nm* : tax
impugnar *vt* : to challenge, to contest
impulsar *vt* : to propel, to drive
impulsividad *nf* : impulsiveness
impulsivo, -va *adj* : impulsive — **impulsivamente** *adv*
impulso *nm* **1** : drive, thrust **2** : impulse, urge
impune *adj* : unpunished
impunemente *adv* : with impunity
impunidad *nf* : impunity
impureza *nf* : impurity
impuro, -ra *adj* : impure
impuso, etc. → **imponer**
imputable *adj* ATRIBUIBLE : attributable
imputación *nf, pl* **-ciones** **1** : attribution, imputation **2** : accusation
imputar *vt* ATRIBUIR : to impute, to attribute
inacabable *adj* : endless
inacabado, -da *adj* INCONCLUSO : unfinished
inaccesibilidad *nf* : inaccessibility
inaccesible *adj* **1** : inaccessible **2** : unattainable
inacción *nf, pl* **-ciones** : inactivity, inaction
inaceptable *adj* : unacceptable
inactividad *nf* : inactivity, idleness
inactivo, -va *adj* : inactive, idle
inadaptado[1], **-da** *adj* : maladjusted
inadaptado[2], **-da** *n* : misfit
inadecuación *nf, pl* **-ciones** : inadequacy
inadecuado, -da *adj* **1** : inadequate **2** IMPROPIO : inappropriate — **inadecuadamente** *adv*
inadmisible *adj* **1** : inadmissible **2** : unacceptable
inadvertencia *nf* : oversight
inadvertidamente *adv* : inadvertently
inadvertido, -da *adj* **1** : unnoticed <pasar inadvertido : to go unnoticed> **2** DESPISTADO, DISTRAÍDO : inattentive, distracted
inagotable *adj* : inexhaustible
inaguantable *adj* INSOPORTABLE : insufferable, unbearable
inalámbrico, -ca *adj* : wireless, cordless
inalcanzable *adj* : unreachable, unattainable
inalienable *adj* : inalienable
inalterable *adj* **1** : unalterable, unchangeable **2** : impassive **3** : colorfast
inamovible *adj* : immovable, fixed
inanición *nf, pl* **-ciones** : starvation
inanimado, -da *adj* : inanimate
inapelable *adj* : indisputable
inapetencia *nf* : lack of appetite
inaplicable *adj* : inapplicable
inapreciable *adj* **1** : imperceptible, negligible **2** : invaluable
inapropiado, -da *adj* : inappropriate, unsuitable
inarticulado, -da *adj* : inarticulate, unintelligible — **inarticuladamente** *adv*
inasequible *adj* : unattainable, inaccessible
inasistencia *nf* AUSENCIA : absence
inatacable *adj* : unassailable, indisputable
inaudible *adj* : inaudible
inaudito, -ta *adj* : unheard-of, unprecedented
inauguración *nf, pl* **-ciones** : inauguration
inaugural *adj* : inaugural, opening
inaugurar *vt* **1** : to inaugurate **2** : to open
inca *adj & nmf* : Inca
incalculable *adj* : incalculable
incalificable *adj* : indescribable
incandescencia *nf* : incandescence — **incandescente** *adj*
incansable *adj* INFATIGABLE : tireless — **incansablemente** *adv*
incapacidad *nf* **1** : inability, incapacity **2** : disability, handicap
incapacitado, -da *adj* **1** : disqualified **2** : disabled, handicapped
incapacitar *vt* **1** : to incapacitate, to disable **2** : to disqualify
incapaz *adj, pl* **-paces** **1** : incapable, unable **2** : incompetent, inept

incautación *nf, pl* **-ciones** : seizure, confiscation
incautar *vt* CONFISCAR : to confiscate, to seize — **incautarse** *vr*
incauto, -ta *adj* : unwary, unsuspecting
incendiar *vt* : to set fire to, to burn (down) — **incendiarse** *vr* : to catch fire
incendiario[1], **-ria** *adj* : incendiary, inflammatory
incendiario[2], **-ria** *n* : arsonist
incendio *nm* **1** : fire **2 incendio premeditado** : arson
incentivar *vt* : to encourage, to stimulate
incentivo *nm* : incentive
incertidumbre *nf* : uncertainty, suspense
incesante *adj* : incessant — **incesantemente** *adv*
incesto *nm* : incest
incidencia *nf* **1** : incident **2** : effect, impact **3 por ~** : by chance, accidentally
incidental *adj* : incidental
incidentalmente *adv* : by chance
incidente *nm* : incident, occurrence
incidir *vi* **1 ~ en** : to fall into, to enter into <incidimos en el mismo error : we fell into the same mistake> **2 ~ en** : to affect, to influence, to have a bearing on
incienso *nm* : incense
incierto, -ta *adj* **1** : uncertain **2** : untrue **3** : unsteady, insecure
incineración *nf, pl* **-ciones 1** : incineration **2** : cremation
incinerador *nm* : incinerator
incinerar *vt* **1** : to incinerate **2** : to cremate
incipiente *adj* : incipient
incisión *nf, pl* **-siones** : incision
incisivo[1], **-va** *adj* : incisive
incisivo[2] *nm* : incisor
inciso *nm* : digression, aside
incitación *nf, pl* **-ciones** : incitement
incitante *adj* : provocative
incitar *vt* : to incite, to rouse
incivilizado, -da *adj* : uncivilized
inclemencia *nf* : inclemency, severity
inclemente *adj* : inclement
inclinación *nf, pl* **-ciones 1** PROPENSIÓN : inclination, tendency **2** : incline, slope
inclinado, -da *adj* **1** : sloping **2** : inclined, apt
inclinar *vt* : to tilt, to lean, to incline <inclinar la cabeza : to bow one's head> — **inclinarse** *vr* **1** : to lean, to lean over **2 ~ a** : to be inclined to
incluir {41} *vt* : to include
inclusión *nf, pl* **-siones** : inclusion
inclusive *adv* : inclusively, up to and including
inclusivo, -va *adj* : inclusive
incluso *adv* **1** AUN : even, in fact <es importante e incluso crucial : it is important and even crucial> **2** : inclusively
incógnita *nf* **1** : unknown quantity (in mathematics) **2** : mystery
incógnito, -ta *adj* **1** : unknown **2 de incógnito** : incognito
incoherencia *nf* : incoherence
incoherente *adj* : incoherent — **incoherentemente** *adv*
incoloro, -ra *adj* : colorless
incombustible *adj* : fireproof
incomible *adj* : inedible
incomodar *vt* **1** : to make uncomfortable **2** : to inconvenience — **incomodarse** *vr* : to put oneself out, to take the trouble
incomodidad *nf* **1** : discomfort, awkwardness **2** MOLESTIA : inconvenience, bother
incómodo, -da *adj* **1** : uncomfortable, awkward **2** INCONVENIENTE : inconvenient
incomparable *adj* : incomparable
incompatibilidad *nf* : incompatibility
incompatible *adj* : incompatible, uncongenial
incompetencia *nf* : incompetence
incompetente *adj & nmf* : incompetent
incompleto, -ta *adj* : incomplete
incomprendido, -da *adj* : misunderstood
incomprensible *adj* : incomprehensible
incomprensión *nf, pl* **-siones** : lack of understanding, incomprehension
incomunicación *nf, pl* **-ciones** : lack of communication
incomunicado, -da *adj* **1** : cut off, isolated **2** : in solitary confinement
inconcebible *adj* : inconceivable, unthinkable — **inconcebiblemente** *adv*
inconcluso, -sa *adj* INACABADO : unfinished
incondicional *adj* : unconditional — **incondicionalmente** *adv*
inconexo, -xa *adj* : unconnected, disconnected
inconfesable *adj* : unspeakable, shameful
inconforme *adj & nmf* : nonconformist
inconformidad *nf* : nonconformity
inconformista *adj & nmf* : nonconformist
inconfundible *adj* : unmistakable, obvious — **inconfundiblemente** *adv*
incongruencia *nf* : incongruity
incongruente *adj* : incongruous
inconmensurable *adj* : vast, immeasurable
inconquistable *adj* : unyielding
inconsciencia *nf* **1** : unconsciousness, unawareness **2** : irresponsibility
inconsciente[1] *adj* **1** : unconscious, unaware **2** : reckless, needless — **inconscientemente** *adv*
inconsciente[2] *n* **el inconsciente** : the unconscious

inconsecuente *adj* : inconsistent — **inconsecuencia** *nf*
inconsiderado, -da *adj* : inconsiderate, thoughtless
inconsistencia *nf* : inconsistency
inconsistente *adj* **1** : weak, flimsy **2** : watery, runny (of a sauce, etc.) **3** : inconsistent, weak (of an argument)
inconsolable *adj* : inconsolable — **inconsolablemente** *adv*
inconstancia *nf* : inconstancy
inconstante *adj* : inconstant, fickle, changeable
inconstitucional *adj* : unconstitutional
inconstitucionalidad *nf* : unconstitutionality
incontable *adj* INNUMERABLE : countless, innumerable
incontenible *adj* : uncontrollable, unstoppable
incontestable *adj* INCUESTIONABLE, INDISCUTIBLE : irrefutable, indisputable
incontinencia *nf* : incontinence — **incontinente** *adj*
incontrolable *adj* : uncontrollable
incontrolado, -da *adj* : uncontrolled, out of control
incontrovertible *adj* : indisputable
inconveniencia *nf* **1** : inconvenience, trouble **2** : unsuitability, inappropriateness **3** : tactless remark
inconveniente¹ *adj* **1** INCÓMODO : inconvenient **2** INAPROPIADO : improper, unsuitable
inconveniente² *nm* : obstacle, problem, snag <no tengo inconveniente en hacerlo : I don't mind doing it>
incorporación *nf, pl* **-ciones** : incorporation
incorporar *vt* **1** : to incorporate **2** : to add, to include — **incorporarse** *vr* **1** : to sit up **2** ~ **a** : to join
incorpóreo, -rea *adj* : incorporeal, bodiless
incorrección *n, pl* **-ciones** : impropriety, improper word or action
incorrecto, -ta *adj* : incorrect — **incorrectamente** *adv*
incorregible *adj* : incorrigible — **incorregibilidad** *nf*
incorruptible *adj* : incorruptible
incredulidad *nf* : incredulity, skepticism
incrédulo¹, -la *adj* : incredulous, skeptical
incrédulo², -la *n* : skeptic
increíble *adj* : incredible, unbelievable — **increíblemente** *adv*
incrementar *vt* : to increase — **incrementarse** *vr*
incremento *nm* AUMENTO : increase
incriminar *vt* : to incriminate — **incriminación** *nf*
incruento, -ta *adj* : bloodless
incrustación *nf, pl* **-ciones** : inlay
incrustar *vt* **1** : to embed **2** : to inlay — **incrustarse** *vr* : to become embedded
incubación *nf, pl* **-ciones** : incubation
incubadora *nf* : incubator
incubar *v* : to incubate
incuestionable *adj* INCONTESTABLE, INDISCUTIBLE : unquestionable, indisputable — **incuestionablemente** *adv*
inculcar {72} *vt* : to inculcate, to instill
inculpar *vt* ACUSAR : to accuse, to charge
inculto, -ta *adj* **1** : uncultured, ignorant **2** : uncultivated, fallow
incumbencia *nf* : obligation, responsibility
incumbir *vi* (*3rd person only*) ~ **a** : to be incumbent upon, to be of concern to <a mí no me incumbe : it's not my concern>
incumplido, -da *adj* : irresponsible, unreliable
incumplimiento *nm* **1** : nonfulfillment, neglect **2 incumplimiento de contrato** : breach of contract
incumplir *vt* : to fail to carry out, to break (a promise, a contract)
incurable *adj* : incurable
incurrir *vi* **1** ~ **en** : to incur <incurrir en gastos : to incur expenses> **2** ~ **en** : to fall into, to commit <incurrió en un error : he made a mistake>
incursión *nf, pl* **-siones** : incursion, raid
incursionar *vi* **1** : to raid **2** ~ **en** : to go into, to enter <el actor incursionó en el baile : the actor worked in dance for a while>
indagación *nf, pl* **-ciones** : investigation, inquiry
indagar {52} *vt* : to inquire into, to investigate
indebido, -da *adj* : improper, undue — **indebidamente** *adv*
indecencia *nf* : indecency, obscenity
indecente *adj* : indecent, obscene
indecible *adj* : indescribable, inexpressible
indecisión *nf, pl* **-siones** : indecision
indeciso, -sa *adj* **1** IRRESOLUTO : indecisive **2** : undecided
indeclinable *adj* : unavoidable
indecoro *nm* : impropriety, indecorousness
indecoroso, -sa *adj* : indecorous, unseemly
indefectible *adj* : unfailing, sure
indefendible *adj* : indefensible
indefenso, -sa *adj* : defenseless, helpless
indefinido, -da *adj* **1** : undefined, vague **2** INDETERMINADO : indefinite — **indefinidamente** *adv*
indeleble *adj* : indelible — **indeleblemente** *adv*
indelicado, -da *adj* : indelicate, tactless
indemnización *nf, pl* **-ciones** **1** : indemnity **2 indemnización por despido** : severance pay
indemnizar {21} *vt* : to indemnify, to compensate
independencia *nf* : independence

independiente *adj* : independent — **independientemente** *adv*
independizarse {21} *vr* : to become independent, to gain independence
indescifrable *adj* : indecipherable
indescriptible *adj* : indescribable — **indescriptiblemente** *adv*
indeseable *adj & nmf* : undesirable
indestructible *adj* : indestructible
indeterminación *nf, pl* **-ciones** : indeterminacy
indeterminado, -da *adj* **1** INDEFINIDO : indefinite **2** : indeterminate
indexar *vt* INDICIAR : to index (wages, prices, etc.)
indicación *nf, pl* **-ciones 1** : sign, signal **2** : direction, instruction **3** : suggestion, hint
indicado, -da *adj* **1** APROPIADO : appropriate, suitable **2** : specified, indicated <al día indicado : on the specified day>
indicador *nm* **1** : gauge, dial, meter **2** : indicator <indicadores económicos : economic indicators>
indicar {72} *vt* **1** SEÑALAR : to indicate **2** ENSEÑAR, MOSTRAR : to show
indicativo[1], **-va** *adj* : indicative
indicativo[2] *nm* : indicative (mood)
índice *nm* **1** : index **2** : index finger, forefinger **3** INDICIO : indication
indiciar *vt* : to index (prices, wages, etc.)
indicio *nm* : indication, sign
indiferencia *nf* : indifference
indiferente *adj* **1** : indifferent, unconcerned **2 ser indiferente** : to be of no concern <me es indiferente : it doesn't matter to me>
indígena[1] *adj* : indigenous, native
indígena[2] *nmf* : native
indigencia *nf* MISERIA : poverty, destitution
indigente *adj & nmf* : indigent
indigestarse *vr* **1** EMPACHARSE : to have indigestion **2** *fam* : to nauseate, to disgust <ese tipo se me indigesta : that guy makes me sick>
indigestión *nf, pl* **-tiones** EMPACHO : indigestion
indigesto, -ta *adj* : indigestible, difficult to digest
indignación *nf, pl* **-ciones** : indignation
indignado, -da *adj* : indignant
indignante *adj* : outrageous, infuriating
indignar *vt* : to outrage, to infuriate — **indignarse** *vr*
indignidad *nf* : indignity
indigno, -na *adj* : unworthy
indio[1], **-dia** *adj* **1** : American Indian, Indian, Amerindian **2** : Indian (from India)
indio[2], **-dia** *n* **1** : American Indian **2** : Indian (from India)
indirecta *nf* **1** : hint, innuendo **2 echar indirectas** *or* **lanzar indirectas** : to drop a hint, to insinuate
indirecto, -ta *adj* : indirect — **indirectamente** *adv*
indisciplina *nf* : indiscipline, unruliness
indisciplinado, -da *adj* : undisciplined, unruly
indiscreción *nf, pl* **-ciones 1** IMPRUDENCIA : indiscretion **2** : tactless remark
indiscreto, -ta *adj* IMPRUDENTE : indiscreet, imprudent — **indiscretamente** *adv*
indiscriminado, -da *adj* : indiscriminate — **indiscriminadamente** *adv*
indiscutible *adj* INCONTESTABLE, INCUESTIONABLE : indisputable, unquestionable — **indiscutiblemente** *adv*
indispensable *adj* : indispensable — **indispensablemente** *adv*
indisponer {60} *vt* **1** : to spoil, to upset **2** : to make ill — **indisponerse** *vr* **1** : to become ill **2 ~ con** : to fall out with
indisposición *nf, pl* **-ciones** : indisposition, illness
indispuesto, -ta *adj* : unwell, indisposed
indistinguible *adj* : indistinguishable
indistintamente *adv* **1** : indistinctly **2** : indiscriminately
indistinto, -ta *adj* : indistinct, vague, faint
individual *adj* : individual — **individualmente** *adv*
individualidad *nf* : individuality
individualismo *nm* : individualism
individualista[1] *adj* : individualistic
individualista[2] *nmf* : individualist
individualizar {21} *vt* : to individualize
individuo *nm* : individual, person
indivisible *adj* : indivisible — **indivisibilidad** *nf*
indocumentado, -da *n* : illegal immigrant
índole *nf* **1** : nature, character **2** CLASE, TIPO : sort, kind
indolencia *nf* : indolence, laziness
indolente *adj* : indolent, lazy
indoloro, -ra *adj* : painless
indomable *adj* **1** : indomitable **2** : unruly, unmanageable
indómito, -ta *adj* : indomitable
indonesio, -sia *adj & n* : Indonesian
inducción *nf, pl* **-ciones** : induction
inducir {61} *vt* **1** : to induce, to cause **2** : to infer, to deduce
inductivo, -va *adj* : inductive
indudable *adj* : unquestionable, beyond doubt
indudablemente *adv* : undoubtedly, unquestionably
indulgencia *nf* **1** : indulgence, leniency **2** : indulgence (in religion)
indulgente *adj* : indulgent, lenient
indultar *vt* : to pardon, to reprieve
indulto *nm* : pardon, reprieve
indumentaria *nf* : clothing, attire
industria *nf* : industry
industrial[1] *adj* : industrial

industrial[2] *nmf* : industrialist, manufacturer
industrialización *nf, pl* **-ciones** : industrialization
industrializar {21} *vt* : to industrialize
industrioso, -sa *adj* : industrious
inédito, -ta *adj* **1** : unpublished **2** : unprecedented
inefable *adj* : ineffable
ineficacia *nf* **1** : inefficiency **2** : ineffectiveness
ineficaz *adj, pl* **-caces 1** : inefficient **2** : ineffective — **ineficazmente** *adv*
ineficiencia *nf* : inefficiency
ineficiente *adj* : inefficient — **ineficientemente** *adv*
inelegancia *nf* : inelegance — **inelegante** *adj*
inelegible *adj* : ineligible — **inelegibilidad** *nf*
ineludible *adj* : inescapable, unavoidable — **ineludiblemente** *adv*
ineptitud *nf* : ineptitude, incompetence
inepto, -ta *adj* : inept, incompetent
inequidad *nf* : inequity
inequitativo, -va *adj* : inequitable
inequívoco, -ca *adj* : unequivocal, unmistakable — **inequívocamente** *adv*
inercia *nf* **1** : inertia **2** : apathy, passivity **3 por ~** : out of habit
inerme *adj* : unarmed, defenseless
inerte *adj* : inert
inescrupuloso, -sa *adj* : unscrupulous
inescrutable *adj* : inscrutable
inesperado, -da *adj* : unexpected — **inesperadamente** *adv*
inestabilidad *nf* : instability, unsteadiness
inestable *adj* : unstable, unsteady
inestimable *adj* : inestimable, invaluable
inevitabilidad *nf* : inevitability
inevitable *adj* : inevitable, unavoidable — **inevitablemente** *adv*
inexactitud *nf* : inaccuracy
inexacto, -ta *adj* : inexact, inaccurate
inexcusable *adj* : inexcusable, unforgivable
inexistencia *nf* : lack, nonexistence
inexistente *adj* : nonexistent
inexorable *adj* : inexorable — **inexorablemente** *adv*
inexperiencia *nf* : inexperience
inexperto, -ta *adj* : inexperienced, unskilled
inexplicable *adj* : inexplicable — **inexplicablemente** *adv*
inexplorado, -da *adj* : unexplored
inexpresable *adj* : inexpressible
inexpresivo, -va *adj* : inexpressive, expressionless
inextinguible *adj* **1** : inextinguishable **2** : unquenchable
inextricable *adj* : inextricable — **inextricablemente** *adv*
infalible *adj* : infallible — **infaliblemente** *adv*
infame *adj* **1** : infamous **2** : loathsome, vile <tiempo infame : terrible weather>
infamia *nf* : infamy, disgrace
infancia *nf* **1** NIÑEZ : infancy, childhood **2** : children *pl* **3** : beginnings *pl*
infante *nm* **1** : infante, prince **2** : infantryman
infantería *nf* : infantry
infantil *adj* **1** : childish, infantile **2** : child's, children's
infarto *nm* : heart attack
infatigable *adj* : indefatigable, tireless — **infatigablemente** *adv*
infección *nf, pl* **-ciones** : infection
infeccioso, -sa *adj* : infectious
infectar *vt* : to infect — **infectarse** *vr*
infecto, -ta *adj* **1** : infected **2** : repulsive, sickening
infecundidad *nf* : infertility
infecundo, -da *adj* : infertile, barren
infelicidad *nf* : unhappiness
infeliz[1] *adj, pl* **-lices 1** : unhappy **2** : hapless, unfortunate, wretched
infeliz[2] *nmf, pl* **-lices** : wretch
inferior[1] *adj* : inferior, lower
inferior[2] *nmf* : inferior, underling
inferioridad *nf* : inferiority
inferir {76} *vt* **1** DEDUCIR : to infer, to deduce **2** : to cause (harm or injury), to inflict
infernal *adj* : infernal, hellish
infestación *n, pl* **-ciones** : infestation
infestar *vt* **1** : to infest **2** : to overrun, to invade
infición *nf, pl* **-ciones** *Mex* : pollution
infidelidad *nf* : unfaithfulness, infidelity
infiel[1] *adj* : unfaithful, disloyal
infiel[2] *nmf* : infidel, heathen
infierno *nm* **1** : hell **2 el quinto infierno** : the middle of nowhere
infiltrar *vt* : to infiltrate — **infiltrarse** *vr* — **infiltración** *nf*
infinidad *nf* **1** : infinity **2** SINFÍN : great number, huge quantity <una infinidad de veces : countless times>
infinitesimal *adj* : infinitesimal
infinitivo *nm* : infinitive
infinito[1] *adv* : infinitely, vastly
infinito[2], **-ta** *adj* **1** : infinite **2** : limitless, endless **3 hasta lo infinito** : ad infinitum — **infinitamente** *adv*
infinito[3] *nm* : infinity
inflable *adj* : inflatable
inflación *nf, pl* **-ciones** : inflation
inflacionario, -ria *adj* : inflationary
inflamable *adj* : flammable
inflamación *nf, pl* **-ciones** : inflammation
inflamar *vt* : to inflame
inflamatorio, -ria *adj* : inflammatory
inflar *vt* HINCHAR : to inflate — **inflarse** *vr* **1** : to swell **2** : to become conceited
inflexibilidad *nf* : inflexibility
inflexible *adj* : inflexible, unyielding
inflexión *nf, pl* **-xiones** : inflection
infligir {35} *vt* : to inflict
influencia *nf* INFLUJO : influence

influenciable *adj* : easily influenced, suggestible

influenciar *vt* : to influence

influenza *nf* : influenza

influir {41} *vt* : to influence — *vi* ~ **en** *or* ~ **sobre** : to have an influence on, to affect

influjo *nm* INFLUENCIA : influence

influyente *adj* : influential

información *nf, pl* **-ciones 1** : information **2** INFORME : report, inquiry **3** NOTICIAS : news

informado, -da *adj* : informed <bien informado : well-informed>

informador, -dora *n* : informer, informant

informal *adj* **1** : unreliable (of persons) **2** : informal, casual — **informalmente** *adv*

informalidad *nf* : informality

informante *nmf* : informant

informar *vt* ENTERAR : to inform — *vi* : to report — **informarse** *vr* ENTERARSE : to get information, to find out

informática *nf* : computer science, computing

informativo[1], -va *adj* : informative

informativo[2] *nm* : news program, news

informatización *nf, pl* **-ciones** : computerization

informatizar {21} *vt* : to computerize

informe[1] *adj* AMORFO : shapeless, formless

informe[2] *nm* **1** : report **2** : reference (for employment) **3** INFORMES *nmpl* : information, data

infortunado, -da *adj* : unfortunate, unlucky

infortunio *nm* **1** DESGRACIA : misfortune **2** CONTRATIEMPO : mishap

infracción *nf, pl* **-ciones** : violation, offense, infraction

infractor, -tora *n* : offender

infraestructura *nf* : infrastructure

infrahumano, -na *adj* : subhuman

infranqueable *adj* **1** : impassable **2** : insurmountable

infrarrojo, -ja *adj* : infrared

infrecuente *adj* : infrequent

infringir {35} *vt* : to infringe, to breach

infructuoso, -sa *adj* : fruitless — **infructuosamente** *adv*

ínfulas *nfpl* **1** : conceit **2 darse ínfulas** : to put on airs

infundado, -da *adj* : unfounded, baseless

infundio *nm* : false story, lie, tall tale <todo eso son infundios : that's a pack of lies>

infundir *vt* **1** : to instill **2 infundir ánimo a** : to encourage **3 infundir miedo a** : to intimidate

infusión *nf, pl* **-siones** : infusion

ingeniar *vt* : to devise, to think up — **ingeniarse** *vr* : to manage, to find a way

ingeniería *nf* : engineering

ingeniero, -ra *n* : engineer

ingenio *nm* **1** : ingenuity **2** CHISPA : wit, wits **3** : device, apparatus **4 ingenio azucarero** : sugar refinery

ingenioso, -sa *adj* **1** : ingenious **2** : clever, witty — **ingeniosamente** *adv*

ingente *adj* : huge, enormous

ingenuidad *nf* : naïveté, ingenuousness

ingenuo[1], -nua *adj* CÁNDIDO : naive — **ingenuamente** *adv*

ingenuo[2], -nua *n* : naive person

ingerencia → **injerencia**

ingerir {76} *vt* : to ingest, to consume

ingestión *nf, pl* **-tiones** : ingestion

ingle *nf* : groin

inglés[1], -glesa *adj, mpl* **ingleses** : English

inglés[2], -glesa *n, mpl* **ingleses** : Englishman *m*, Englishwoman *f*

inglés[3] *nm* : English (language)

inglete *nm* : miter joint

ingobernable *adj* : ungovernable, lawless

ingratitud *nf* : ingratitude

ingrato[1], -ta *adj* **1** : ungrateful **2** : thankless

ingrato[2], -ta *n* : ingrate

ingrediente *nm* : ingredient

ingresar *vt* **1** : to admit <ingresaron a Luis al hospital : Luis was admitted into the hospital> **2** : to deposit — *vi* **1** : to enter, to go in **2** ~ **en** : to join, to enroll in

ingreso *nm* **1** : entrance, entry **2** : admission **3 ingresos** *nmpl* : income, earnings *pl*

íngrimo, -ma *adj* : all alone, all by oneself

inhábil *adj* : unskillful, clumsy

inhabilidad *nf* **1** : unskillfulness **2** : unfitness

inhabilitar *vt* **1** : to disqualify, to bar **2** : to disable

inhabitable *adj* : uninhabitable

inhabituado, -da *adj* ~ **a** : unaccustomed to

inhalante *nm* : inhalant

inhalar *vt* : to inhale — **inhalación** *nf*

inherente *adj* : inherent

inhibición *nf, pl* **-ciones** COHIBICIÓN : inhibition

inhibir *vt* : to inhibit — **inhibirse** *vr*

inhóspito, -ta *adj* : inhospitable

inhumación *nf, pl* **-ciones** : interment, burial

inhumanidad *nf* : inhumanity

inhumano, -na *adj* : inhuman, cruel, inhumane

inhumar *vt* : to inter, to bury

iniciación *nf, pl* **-ciones 1** : initiation **2** : introduction

iniciado, -da *n* : initiate

iniciador[1], -dora *adj* : initiatory

iniciador[2], -dora *n* : initiator, originator

inicial[1] *adj* : initial, original — **inicialmente** *adv*

inicial[2] *nf* : initial (letter)

iniciar *vt* COMENZAR : to initiate, to begin — **iniciarse** *vr*
iniciativa *nf* : initiative
inicio *nm* COMIENZO : beginning
inicuo, -cua *adj* : iniquitous, wicked
inigualado, -da *adj* : unequaled
inimaginable *adj* : unimaginable
inimitable *adj* : inimitable
ininteligible *adj* : unintelligible
ininterrumpido, -da *adj* : uninterrupted, continuous — **ininterrumpidamente** *adv*
iniquidad *nf* : iniquity, wickedness
injerencia *nf* : interference
injerirse {76} *vr* ENTROMETERSE, INMISCUIRSE : to meddle, to interfere
injertar *vt* : to graft
injerto *nm* : graft <injerto de piel : skin graft>
injuria *nf* AGRAVIO : affront, insult
injuriar *vt* INSULTAR : to insult, to revile
injurioso, -sa *adj* : insulting, abusive
injusticia *nf* : injustice, unfairness
injustificable *adj* : unjustifiable
injustificadamente *adv* : unjustifiably, unfairly
injustificado, -da *adj* : unjustified, unwarranted
injusto, -ta *adj* : unfair, unjust — **injustamente** *adv*
inmaculado, -da *adj* : immaculate, spotless
inmadurez *nf, pl* **-reces** : immaturity
inmaduro, -ra *adj* **1** : immature **2** : unripe
inmediaciones *nfpl* : environs, surrounding area
inmediatamente *adv* ENSEGUIDA : immediately
inmediatez *nf, pl* **-teces** : immediacy
inmediato, -ta *adj* **1** : immediate **2** CONTIGUO : adjoining **3 de ~** : immediately, right away **4 ~ a** : next to, close to
inmejorable *adj* : excellent, unbeatable
inmensidad *nf* : immensity, vastness
inmenso, -sa *adj* ENORME : immense, huge, vast — **inmensamente** *adv*
inmensurable *adj* : boundless, immeasurable
inmerecido, -da *adj* : undeserved — **inmerecidamente** *adv*
inmersión *nf, pl* **-siones** : immersion
inmerso, -sa *adj* **1** : immersed **2** : involved, absorbed
inmigración *nf, pl* **-ciones** : immigration
inmigrado, -da *adj & n* : immigrant
inmigrante *adj & nmf* : immigrant
inmigrar *vi* : to immigrate
inminencia *nf* : imminence
inminente *adj* : imminent — **inminentemente** *adv*
inmiscuirse {41} *vr* ENTROMETERSE, INJERIRSE : to meddle, to interfere
inmobiliario, -ria *adj* : real estate, property
inmoderación *n, pl* **-ciones** : immoderation, intemperance
inmoderado, -da *adj* : immoderate, excessive — **inmoderamente** *adv*
inmodestia *nf* : immodesty — **inmodesto, -ta** *adj*
inmolar *vt* : to immolate — **inmolación** *nf*
inmoral *adj* : immoral
inmoralidad *nf* : immorality
inmortal *adj & nmf* : immortal
inmortalidad *nf* : immortality
inmortalizar {21} *vt* : to immortalize
inmotivado, -da *adj* **1** : unmotivated **2** : groundless
inmovible *adj* : immovable, fixed
inmóvil *adj* **1** : still, motionless **2** : steadfast
inmovilidad *nf* : immobility
inmovilizar {21} *vt* : to immobilize
inmueble *nm* : building, property
inmundicia *nf* : dirt, filth, trash
inmundo, -da *adj* : dirty, filthy, nasty
inmune *adj* : immune
inmunidad *nf* : immunity
inmunizar {21} *vt* : to immunize — **inmunización** *nf*
inmunología *nf* : immunology
inmunológico, -ca *adj* : immune <sistema inmunológico : immune system>
inmutabilidad *nf* : immutability
inmutable *adj* : immutable, unchangeable
innato, -ta *adj* : innate, inborn
innecesario, -ria *adj* : unnecessary — **innecesariamente** *adv*
innegable *adj* : undeniable
innoble *adj* : ignoble — **innoblemente** *adv*
innovación *nf, pl* **-ciones** : innovation
innovador, -dora *adj* : innovative
innovar *vt* : to introduce — *vi* : to innovate
innumerable *adj* INCONTABLE : innumerable, countless
inobjetable *adj* : indisputable, unobjectionable
inocencia *nf* : innocence
inocente[1] *adj* **1** : innocent **2** INGENUO : naive — **inocentemente** *adv*
inocente[2] *nmf* : innocent person
inocentón[1], **-tona** *adj, mpl* **-tones** : naive, gullible
inocentón[2], **-tona** *n, mpl* **-tones** : simpleton, dupe
inocuidad *nf* : harmlessness
inocular *vt* : to inoculate, to vaccinate — **inoculación** *nf*
inocuo, -cua *adj* : innocuous, harmless
inodoro[1], **-ra** *adj* : odorless
inodoro[2] *nm* : toilet
inofensivo, -va *adj* : inoffensive, harmless
inolvidable *adj* : unforgettable
inoperable *adj* : inoperable
inoperante *adj* : ineffective, inoperative

inopinado, -da *adj* : unexpected — **inopinadamente** *adv*
inoportuno, -na *adj* : untimely, inopportune, inappropriate
inorgánico, -ca *adj* : inorganic
inoxidable *adj* **1** : rustproof **2 acero inoxidable** : stainless steel
inquebrantable *adj* : unshakable, unwavering
inquietante *adj* : disturbing, worrisome
inquietar *vt* PREOCUPAR : to disturb, to upset, to worry — **inquietarse** *vr*
inquieto, -ta *adj* **1** : anxious, uneasy, worried **2** : restless
inquietud *nf* **1** : anxiety, uneasiness, worry **2** AGITACIÓN : restlessness
inquilinato *nm* : tenancy
inquilino, -na *n* : tenant, occupant
inquina *nf* **1** : aversion, dislike **2** : ill will <tener inquina a alguien : to have a grudge against someone>
inquirir {4} *vi* : to make inquiries — *vt* : to investigate
inquisición *nf, pl* **-ciones** : investigation, inquiry
inquisidor, -dora *adj* : inquisitive
inquisitivo, -va *adj* : inquisitive, curious — **inquisitivamente** *adv*
insaciable *adj* : insatiable
insalubre *adj* **1** : unhealthy **2** ANTIHIGIÉNICO : unsanitary
insalubridad *nf* : unhealthiness
insalvable *adj* : insuperable, insurmountable
insano, -na *adj* **1** LOCO : insane, mad **2** INSALUBRE : unhealthy
insatisfacción *nf, pl* **-ciones** : dissatisfaction
insatisfactorio *nm* : unsatisfactory
insatisfecho, -cha *adj* **1** : dissatisfied **2** : unsatisfied
inscribir {33} *vt* **1** MATRICULAR : to enroll, to register **2** GRABAR : to engrave — **inscribirse** *vr* : to register, to sign up
inscripción *nf, pl* **-ciones 1** MATRÍCULA : enrollment, registration **2** : inscription
inscrito *pp* → **inscribir**
insecticida[1] *adj* : insecticidal
insecticida[2] *nm* : insecticide
insecto *nm* : insect
inseguridad *nf* **1** : insecurity **2** : lack of safety **3** : uncertainty
inseguro, -ra *adj* **1** : insecure **2** : unsafe **3** : uncertain
inseminar *vt* : to inseminate — **inseminación** *nf*
insensatez *nf, pl* **-teces** : foolishness, stupidity
insensato[1], **-ta** *adj* : foolish, senseless
insensato[2], **-ta** *n* : fool
insensibilidad *nf* : insensitivity
insensible *adj* : insensitive, unfeeling
inseparable *adj* : inseparable — **inseparablemente** *adv*
inserción *nf, pl* **-ciones** : insertion
insertar *vt* : to insert
inservible *adj* INÚTIL : useless, unusable
insidia *nf* **1** : snare, trap **2** : malice
insidioso, -sa *adj* : insidious
insigne *adj* : noted, famous
insignia *nf* ENSEÑA : insignia, emblem, badge
insignificancia *nf* **1** : insignificance **2** NIMIEDAD : trifle, triviality
insignificante *adj* : insignificant
insincero, -ra *adj* : insincere — **insinceridad** *nf*
insinuación *nf, pl* **-ciones** : insinuation, hint
insinuante *adj* : suggestive
insinuar {3} *vt* : to insinuate, to hint at — **insinuarse** *vr* **1 ~ a** : to make advances to **2 ~ en** : to worm one's way into
insipidez *nf, pl* **-deces** : insipidness, blandness
insípido, -da *adj* : insipid, bland
insistencia *nf* : insistence
insistente *adj* : insistent — **insistentemente** *adv*
insistir *v* : to insist
insociable *adj* : unsociable
insolación *nf, pl* **-ciones** : sunstroke
insolencia *nf* IMPERTINENCIA : insolence
insolente *adj* IMPERTINENTE : insolent
insólito, -ta *adj* : rare, unusual
insoluble *adj* : insoluble — **insolubilidad** *nf*
insolvencia *nf* : insolvency, bankruptcy
insolvente *adj* : insolvent, bankrupt
insomne *adj & nmf* : insomniac
insomnio *nm* : insomnia
insondable *adj* : fathomless, deep
insonorizado, -da *adj* : soundproof
insoportable *adj* INAGUANTABLE : unbearable, intolerable
insoslayable *adj* : unavoidable, inescapable
insospechado, -da *adj* : unexpected, unforeseen
insostenible *adj* : untenable
inspección *nf, pl* **-ciones** : inspection
inspeccionar *vt* : to inspect
inspector, -tora *n* : inspector
inspiración *nf, pl* **-ciones 1** : inspiration **2** INHALACIÓN : inhalation
inspirador, -dora *adj* : inspiring
inspirar *vt* : to inspire — *vi* INHALAR : to inhale
instalación *nf, pl* **-ciones** : installation
instalar *vt* **1** : to install **2** : to instate — **instalarse** *vr* ESTABLECERSE : to settle, to establish oneself
instancia *nf* **1** : petition, request **2 en última instancia** : as a last resort
instantánea *nf* : snapshot
instantáneo, -nea *adj* : instantaneous — **instantáneamente** *adv*
instante *nm* **1** : instant, moment **2 al instante** : immediately **3 a cada instante** : frequently, all the time **4 por instantes** : constantly, incessantly

instar *vt* APREMIAR : to urge, to press — *vi* URGIR : to be urgent or pressing <insta que vayamos pronto : it is imperative that we leave soon>
instauración *nf, pl* **-ciones** : establishment
instaurar *vt* : to establish
instigador, -dora *n* : instigator
instigar {52} *vt* : to instigate, to incite
instintivo, -va *adj* : instinctive — **instintivamente** *adv*
instinto *nm* : instinct
institución *nf, pl* **-ciones** : institution
institucional *adj* : institutional — **institucionalmente** *adv*
institucionalización *nf, pl* **-ciones** : institutionalization
institucionalizar {21} *vt* : to institutionalize
instituir {41} *vt* ESTABLECER, FUNDAR : to institute, to establish, to found
instituto *nm* : institute
institutriz *nf, pl* **-trices** : governess *f*
instrucción *nf, pl* **-ciones 1** EDUCACIÓN : education **2 instrucciones** *nfpl* : instructions, directions
instructivo, -va *adj* : instructive, educational
instructor, -tora *n* : instructor
instruir {41} *vt* **1** ADIESTRAR : to instruct, to train **2** ENSEÑAR : to educate, to teach
instrumentación *nf, pl* **-ciones** : orchestration
instrumental *adj* : instrumental
instrumentar *vt* : to orchestrate
instrumentista *nmf* : instrumentalist
instrumento *nm* : instrument
insubordinado, -da *adj* : insubordinate — **insubordinación** *nf*
insubordinarse *vr* : to rebel
insuficiencia *nf* **1** : insufficiency, inadequacy **2 insuficiencia cardíaca** : heart failure
insuficiente *adj* : insufficient, inadequate — **insuficientemente** *adv*
insufrible *adj* : insufferable
insular *adj* : insular
insulina *nf* : insulin
insulso, -sa *adj* **1** INSÍPIDO : insipid, bland **2** : dull
insultante *adj* : insulting
insultar *vt* : to insult
insulto *nm* : insult
insumos *nmpl* : supplies <insumos agrícolas : agricultural supplies>
insuperable *adj* : insuperable, insurmountable
insurgente *adj & nmf* : insurgent — **insurgencia** *nf*
insurrección *nf, pl* **-ciones** : insurrection, uprising
insustancial *adj* : insubstantial, flimsy
insustituible *adj* : irreplaceable
intachable *adj* : irreproachable, faultless
intacto, -ta *adj* : intact
intangible *adj* IMPALPABLE : intangible, impalpable
integración *nf, pl* **-ciones** : integration
integral *adj* **1** : integral, essential **2 pan integral** : whole grain bread
integrante[1] *adj* : integrating, integral
integrante[2] *nmf* : member
integrar *vt* : to make up, to compose — **integrarse** *vr* : to integrate, to fit in
integridad *nf* **1** RECTITUD : integrity, honesty **2** : wholeness, completeness
integrismo *nm* : fundamentalism
integrista *adj & nmf* : fundamentalist
íntegro, -gra *adj* **1** : honest, upright **2** ENTERO : whole, complete **3** : unabridged
intelecto *nm* : intellect
intelectual *adj & nmf* : intellectual — **intelectualmente** *adv*
intelectualidad *nf* : intelligentsia
inteligencia *nf* : intelligence
inteligente *adj* : intelligent — **inteligentemente** *adv*
inteligible *adj* : intelligible — **inteligibilidad** *nf*
intemperancia *adj* : intemperance, excess
intemperie *nf* **1** : bad weather, elements *pl* **2 a la intemperie** : in the open air, outside
intempestivo, -va *adj* : inopportune, untimely — **intempestivamente** *adv*
intención *nf, pl* **-ciones** : intention, plan
intencional *adj* : intentional — **intencionalmente** *adv*
intendencia *nf* : management, administration
intendente *nmf* : quartermaster
intensidad *nf* : intensity
intensificar {72} *vt* : to intensify — **intensificarse** *vr*
intensivo, -va *adj* : intensive — **intensivamente** *adv*
intenso, -sa *adj* : intense — **intensamente** *adv*
intentar *vt* : to attempt, to try
intento *nm* **1** PROPÓSITO : intent, intention **2** TENTATIVA : attempt, try
interacción *nf, pl* **-ciones** : interaction
interactivo, -va *adj* : interactive
interactuar {3} *vi* : to interact
intercalar *vt* : to intersperse, to insert
intercambiable *adj* : interchangeable
intercambiar *vt* CANJEAR : to exchange, to trade
intercambio *nm* CANJE : exchange, trade
interceder *vi* : to intercede
intercepción *nf, pl* **-ciones** : interception
interceptar *vt* **1** : to intercept, to block **2 interceptar las líneas** : to wiretap
intercesión *nf, pl* **-siones** : intercession
intercomunicación *nf, pl* **-ciones** : intercommunication
interconexión *nf, pl* **-xiones** : interconnection
interconfesional *adj* : interdenominational

interdependencia *nf* : interdependence — **interdependiente** *adj*

interdicción *nf, pl* **-ciones** : interdiction, prohibition

interés *nm, pl* **-reses** : interest

interesado, -da *adj* **1** : interested **2** : selfish, self-seeking

interesante *adj* : interesting

interesar *vt* : to interest — *vi* : to be of interest, to be interesting — **interesarse** *vr*

interestatal *adj* : interstate <autopista interestatal : interstate highway>

interestelar *adj* : interstellar

interfaz *nf, pl* **-faces** : interface

interferencia *nf* : interference, static

interferir {76} *vi* : to interfere, to meddle — *vt* : to interfere with, to obstruct

interín[1] *or* **ínterin** *adv* : meanwhile

interín[2] *or* **ínterin** *nm, pl* **-rines** : meantime, interim <en el interín : in the meantime>

interinamente *adv* : temporarily

interino, -na *adj* : acting, temporary, interim

interior[1] *adj* : interior, inner

interior[2] *nm* **1** : interior, inside **2** : inland region

interiormente *adv* : inwardly

interjección *nf, pl* **-ciones** : interjection

interlocutor, -tora *n* : interlocutor, speaker

intermediario, -ria *adj & n* : intermediary, go-between

intermedio[1], **-dia** *adj* : intermediate

intermedio[2] *nm* **1** : intermission **2 por intermedio de** : by means of

interminable *adj* : interminable, endless — **interminablemente** *adv*

intermisión *nf, pl* **-siones** : intermission, pause

intermitente[1] *adj* **1** : intermittent **2 luz intermitente** : strobe light — **intermitentemente** *adv*

intermitente[2] *nm* : blinker, turn signal

internacional *adj* : international — **internacionalmente** *adv*

internacionalismo *nm* : internationalism

internacionalizar {21} *vt* : to internationalize

internado *nm* : boarding school

internar *vt* : to commit, to confine — **internarse** *vr* **1** : to penetrate, to advance into **2 ~ en** : to go into, to enter

internista *nmf* : internist

interno[1], **-na** *adj* : internal — **internamente** *adv*

interno[2], **-na** *n* **1** : intern **2** : inmate, internee

interpelación *nf, pl* **-ciones** : appeal, plea

interpelar *vt* : to question (formally)

interpolar *vt* : to insert, to interpolate

interponer {60} *vt* : to interpose — **interponerse** *vr* : to intervene

interpretación *nf, pl* **-ciones** : interpretation

interpretar *vt* **1** : to interpret **2** : to play, to perform

interpretativo, -va *adj* : interpretive

intérprete *nmf* **1** TRADUCTOR : interpreter **2** : performer

interpuesto *pp* → **interponer**

interracial *adj* : interracial

interrelación *nf, pl* **-ciones** : interrelationship

interrelacionar *vi* : to interrelate

interrogación *nf, pl* **-ciones 1** : interrogation, questioning **2 signo de interrogación** : question mark

interrogador, -dora *n* : interrogator, questioner

interrogante[1] *adj* : questioning

interrogante[2] *nm* **1** : question mark **2** : query

interrogar {52} *vt* : to interrogate, to question

interrogativo, -va *adj* : interrogative

interrogatorio *nm* : interrogation, questioning

interrumpir *v* : to interrupt

interrupción *nf, pl* **-ciones** : interruption

interruptor *nm* **1** : (electrical) switch **2** : circuit breaker

intersección *nf, pl* **-ciones** : intersection

intersticio *nm* : interstice — **intersticial** *adj*

intervalo *nm* : interval

intervención *nf, pl* **-ciones 1** : intervention **2** : audit **3 intervención quirúrgica** : operation

intervencionista *adj & nmf* : interventionist

intervenir {87} *vi* **1** : to take part **2** INTERCEDER : to intervene, to intercede — *vt* **1** : to control, to supervise **2** : to audit **3** : to operate on **4** : to tap (a telephone)

interventor, -tora *n* **1** : inspector **2** : auditor, comptroller

intestado, -da *adj* : intestate

intestinal *adj* : intestinal

intestino *nm* : intestine

intimar *vi* **~ con** : to become friendly with — *vt* : to require, to call on

intimidación *nf, pl* **-ciones** : intimidation

intimidad *nf* **1** : intimacy **2** : privacy, private life

intimidar *vt* ACOBARDAR : to intimidate

íntimo, -ma *adj* **1** : intimate, close **2** PRIVADO : private — **íntimamente** *adv*

intitular *vt* : to entitle, to title

intocable *adj* : untouchable

intolerable *adj* : intolerable, unbearable

intolerancia *nf* : intolerance

intolerante[1] *adj* : intolerant

intolerante[2] *nmf* : intolerant person, bigot

intoxicación *nf, pl* **-ciones** : poisoning

intoxicante *nm* : poison

intoxicar {72} *vt* **:** to poison
intranquilidad *nf* PREOCUPACIÓN **:** worry, anxiety
intranquilizar {21} *vt* **:** to upset, to make uneasy — **intranquilizarse** *vr* **:** to get worried, to be anxious
intranquilo, -la *adj* PREOCUPADO **:** uneasy, worried
intransigencia *nf* **:** intransigence
intransigente *adj* **:** intransigent, unyielding
intransitable *adj* **:** impassable
intransitivo, -va *adj* **:** intransitive
intrascendente *adj* **:** unimportant, insignificant
intratable *adj* **1 :** intractable **2 :** awkward **3 :** unsociable
intravenoso, -sa *adj* **:** intravenous
intrepidez *nf* **:** fearlessness
intrépido, -da *adj* **:** intrepid, fearless
intriga *nf* **:** intrigue
intrigante *nmf* **:** schemer
intrigar {52} *v* **:** to intrigue — **intrigante** *adj*
intrincado, -da *adj* **:** intricate, involved
intrínseco, -ca *adj* **:** intrinsic — **intrínsecamente** *adv*
introducción *nf, pl* **-ciones :** introduction
introducir {61} *vt* **1 :** to introduce **2 :** to bring in **3 :** to insert **4 :** to input, to enter — **introducirse** *vr* **:** to penetrate, to get into
introductorio, -ria *adj* **:** introductory
intromisión *nf, pl* **-siones :** interference, meddling
introspección *nf, pl* **-ciones :** introspection
introspectivo, -va *adj* **:** introspective
introvertido¹, -da *adj* **:** introverted
introvertido², -da *n* **:** introvert
intrusión *nf, pl* **-siones :** intrusion
intruso¹, -sa *adj* **:** intrusive
intruso², -sa *n* **:** intruder
intuición *nf, pl* **-ciones :** intuition
intuir {41} *vt* **:** to intuit, to sense
intuitivo, -va *adj* **:** intuitive — **intuitivamente** *adv*
inundación *nf, pl* **-ciones :** flood, inundation
inundar *vt* **:** to flood, to inundate
inusitado, -da *adj* **:** unusual, uncommon — **inusitadamente** *adv*
inusual *adj* **:** unusual, uncommon — **inusualmente** *adv*
inútil¹ *adj* INSERVIBLE **:** useless — **inútilmente** *adv*
inútil² *nmf* **:** good-for-nothing
inutilidad *nf* **:** uselessness
inutilizar {21} *vt* **1 :** to make useless **2** INCAPACITAR **:** to disable, to put out of commission
invadir *vt* **:** to invade
invalidar *vt* **:** to nullify, to invalidate
invalidez *nf, pl* **-deces 1 :** invalidity **2 :** disablement
inválido, -da *adj & n* **:** invalid
invariable *adj* **:** invariable — **invariablemente** *adv*
invasión *nf, pl* **-siones :** invasion
invasivo, -va *adj* **:** invasive
invasor¹, -sora *adj* **:** invading
invasor², -sora *n* **:** invader
invectiva *nf* **:** invective, abuse
invencible *adj* **1 :** invincible **2 :** insurmountable
invención *nf, pl* **-ciones 1** INVENTO **:** invention **2** MENTIRA **:** fabrication, lie
inventar *vt* **1 :** to invent **2 :** to fabricate, to make up
inventariar {85} *vt* **:** to inventory
inventario *nm* **:** inventory
inventiva *nf* **:** ingenuity, inventiveness
inventivo, -va *adj* **:** inventive
invento *nm* INVENCIÓN **:** invention
inventor, -tora *n* **:** inventor
invernadero *nm* **:** greenhouse, hothouse
invernal *adj* **:** winter, wintry
invernar {55} *vi* **1 :** to spend the winter **2** HIBERNAR **:** to hibernate
inverosímil *adj* **:** unlikely, farfetched
inversión *nf, pl* **-siones 1 :** inversion **2 :** investment
inversionista *nmf* **:** investor
inverso¹, -sa *adj* **1 :** inverse, inverted **2** CONTRARIO **:** opposite **3 a la inversa :** on the contrary, vice versa **4 en orden inverso :** in reverse order — **inversamente** *adv*
inverso² *n* **:** inverse
inversor, -sora *n* **:** investor
invertebrado¹, -da *adj* **:** invertebrate
invertebrado² *nm* **:** invertebrate
invertir {76} *vt* **1 :** to invert, to reverse **2 :** to invest — *vi* **:** to make an investment — **invertirse** *vr* **:** to be reversed
investidura *nf* **:** investiture, inauguration
investigación *nf, pl* **-ciones 1** ENCUESTA, INDAGACIÓN **:** investigation, inquiry **2 :** research
investigador¹, -dora *adj* **:** investigative
investigador², -dora *n* **1 :** investigator **2 :** researcher
investigar {52} *vt* **1** INDAGAR **:** to investigate **2 :** to research — *vi* **~ sobre :** to do research into
investir {54} *vt* **1 :** to empower **2 :** to swear in, to inaugurate
inveterado, -da *adj* **:** inveterate, deep-seated
invicto, -ta *adj* **:** undefeated
invidente¹ *adj* CIEGO **:** blind, sightless
invidente² *nmf* CIEGO **:** blind person
invierno *nm* **:** winter, wintertime
inviolable *adj* **:** inviolable — **inviolabilidad** *nf*
inviolado, -da *adj* **:** inviolate, pure
invisibilidad *nf* **:** invisibility
invisible *adj* **:** invisible — **invisiblemente** *adv*
invitación *nf, pl* **-ciones :** invitation
invitado, -da *n* **:** guest

invitar *vt* : to invite
invocación *nf, pl* **-ciones** : invocation
invocar {72} *vt* : to invoke, to call on
involucramiento *nm* : involvement
involucrar *vt* : to implicate, to involve — **involucrarse** *vr* : to get involved
involuntario, -ria *adj* : involuntary — **involuntariamente** *adv*
invulnerable *adj* : invulnerable
inyección *nf, pl* **-ciones** : injection, shot
inyectado, -da *adj* **ojos inyectados** : bloodshot eyes
inyectar *vt* : to inject
ion *nm* : ion
ionizar {21} *vt* : to ionize — **ionización** *nf*
ionosfera *nf* : ionosphere
ir {43} *vi* **1** : to go <ir a pie : to go on foot, to walk> <ir a caballo : to ride horseback> <ir a casa : to go home> **2** : to lead, to extend, to stretch <el camino va de Cali a Bogotá : the road goes from Cali to Bogotá> **3** FUNCIONAR : to work, to function <esta computadora ya no va : this computer doesn't work anymore> **4** : to get on, to get along <¿cómo te va? : how are you?, how's it going?> <el negocio no va bien : the business isn't doing well> **5** : to suit <ese vestido te va bien : that dress really suits you> **6** ~ **con** : to be <ir con prisa : to be in a hurry> **7** ~ **por** : to follow, to go along <fueron por la costa : they followed the shoreline> **8 dejarse ir** : to let oneself go **9 ir a parar** : to end up **10 vamos a ver** : let's see — *v aux* **1** (*with present participle*) <ir caminando : to walk> <¡voy corriendo! : I'll be right there!> **2** ~ **a** : to be going to <voy a hacerlo : I'm going to do it> <el avión va a despegar : the plane is about to take off> — **irse** *vr* **1** : to leave, to go <¡vámonos! : let's go!> <todo el mundo se fue : everyone left> **2** ESCAPARSE : to leak **3** GASTARSE : to be used up, to be gone
ira *nf* CÓLERA, FURIA : wrath, anger
iracundo, -da *adj* : irate, angry
iraní *adj & nmf* : Iranian
iraquí *adj & nmf* : Iraqi
irascible *adj* : irascible, irritable — **irascibilidad** *nf*
irga, irgue, etc. → **erguir**
iridio *nm* : iridium
iridiscencia *nf* : iridescence — **iridiscente** *adj*
iris *nms & pl* **1** : iris **2 arco iris** : rainbow
irlandés[1], -desa *adj, mpl* **-deses** : Irish
irlandés[2], -desa *n, pl* **-deses** : Irish person, Irishman *m,* Irishwoman *f*
irlandés[3] *nm* : Irish (language)
ironía *nf* : irony
irónico, -ca *adj* : ironic, ironical — **irónicamente** *adv*
irracional *adj* : irrational — **irracionalmente** *adv*
irracionalidad *nf* : irrationality
irradiar *vt* : to radiate, to irradiate
irrazonable *adj* : unreasonable
irreal *adj* : unreal
irrebatible *adj* : unanswerable, irrefutable
irreconciliable *adj* : irreconcilable
irreconocible *adj* : unrecognizable
irrecuperable *adj* : irrecoverable, irretrievable
irredimible *adj* : irredeemable
irreductible *adj* : unyielding
irreemplazable *adj* : irreplaceable
irreflexión *nf, pl* **-xiones** : thoughtlessness, impetuosity
irreflexivo, -va *adj* : rash, unthinking — **irreflexivamente** *adv*
irrefrenable *adj* : uncontrollable, unstoppable <un impulso irrefrenable : an irresistable urge>
irrefutable *adj* : irrefutable
irregular *adj* : irregular — **irregularmente** *adv*
irregularidad *nf* : irregularity
irrelevante *adj* : irrelevant — **irrelevancia** *nf*
irreligioso, -sa *adj* : irreligious
irremediable *adj* : incurable — **irremediablemente** *adv*
irreparable *adj* : irreparable
irreprimible *adj* : irrepressible
irreprochable *adj* : irreproachable
irresistible adj : irresistible — **irresistiblemente** adv
irresolución *nf, pl* **-ciones** : indecision, hesitation
irresoluto, -ta *adj* INDECISO : undecided
irrespeto *nm* : disrespect
irrespetuoso, -sa *adj* : disrespectful — **irrespetuosamente** *adv*
irresponsabilidad *nf* : irresponsibility
irresponsable *adj* : irresponsible — **irresponsablemente** *adv*
irrestricto, -ta *adj* : unrestricted, unconditional <apoyo irrestricto : unconditional support>
irreverencia *nf* : disrespect
irreverente *adj* : disrespectful
irreversible *adj* : irreversible
irrevocable *adj* : irrevocable — **irrevocablemente** *adv*
irrigar {52} *vt* : to irrigate — **irrigación** *nf*
irrisible *adj* : laughable
irrisión *nf, pl* **-siones** : derision, ridicule
irrisorio, -ria *adj* RISIBLE : ridiculous, ludicrous
irritabilidad *nf* : irritability
irritable *adj* : irritable
irritación *nf, pl* **-ciones** : irritation
irritante *adj* : irritating
irritar *vt* : to irritate — **irritación** *nf*
irrompible *adj* : unbreakable
irrumpir *vi* ~ **en** : to burst into
irrupción *nf, pl* **-ciones 1** : irruption **2** : invasion
isla *nf* : island

islámico, -ca *adj* : Islamic, Muslim
islandés[1], **-desa** *adj, mpl* **-deses** : Icelandic
islandés[2], **-desa** *n, mpl* **-deses** : Icelander
islandés[3] *nm* : Icelandic (language)
isleño, -ña *n* : islander
islote *nm* : islet
isometría *nfs & pl* : isometrics
isométrico, -ca *adj* : isometric
isósceles *adj* : isosceles <triángulo isósceles : isosceles triangle>
isótopo *nm* : isotope
israelí *adj & nmf* : Israeli
istmo *nm* : isthmus
itacate *nm Mex* : pack, provisions *pl*
italiano[1], **-na** *adj & n* : Italian
italiano[2] *nm* : Italian (language)
iterbio *nm* : ytterbium
itinerante *adj* AMBULANTE : traveling, itinerant
itinerario *nm* : itinerary, route
itrio *nm* : yttrium
izar {21} *vt* : to hoist, to raise <izar la bandera : to raise the flag>
izquierda *nf* : left
izquierdista *adj & nmf* : leftist
izquierdo, -da *adj* : left

J

j *nf* : tenth letter of the Spanish alphabet
jabalí *nm* : wild boar
jabalina *nf* : javelin
jabón *nm, pl* **jabones** : soap
jabonar *vt* ENJABONAR : to soap up, to lather — **jabonarse** *vr*
jabonera *nf* : soap dish
jabonoso, -sa *adj* : soapy
jaca *nf* **1** : pony **2** YEGUA : mare
jacal *nm Mex* : shack, hut
jacinto *nm* : hyacinth
jactancia *nf* **1** : boastfulness **2** : boasting, bragging
jactancioso[1], **-sa** *adj* : boastful
jactancioso[2], **-sa** *n* : boaster, braggart
jactarse *vr* : to boast, to brag
jade *nm* : jade
jadear *vi* : to pant, to gasp, to puff — **jadeante** *adj*
jadeo *nm* : panting, gasping, puffing
jaez *nm, pl* **jaeces 1** : harness **2** : kind, sort, ilk **3 jaeces** *nmpl* : trappings
jaguar *nm* : jaguar
jai alai *nm* : jai alai
jaiba *nf* CANGREJO : crab
jalapeño *nm Mex* : jalapeño pepper
jalar *vt* **1** : to pull, to tug **2** *fam* : to attract, to draw in <las ideas nuevas lo jalan : new ideas appeal to him> — *vi* **1** : to pull, to pull together **2** *fam* : to hurry up, to get going **3** *Mex fam* : to be in working order <esta máquina no jala : this machine doesn't work>
jalbegue *nm* : whitewash
jalea *nf* : jelly
jalear *vt* : to encourage, to urge on
jaleo *nm fam* **1** : uproar, ruckus, racket **2** *fam* : confusion, hassle **3** : cheering and clapping (for a dance)
jalón *nm, pl* **jalones 1** : milestone, landmark **2** TIRÓN : pull, tug
jalonar *vt* : to mark, to stake out
jalonear *vt Mex, Peru fam* : to tug at — *vi* **1** *fam* : to pull, to tug **2** *CA fam* : to haggle
jamaica *nf* : hibiscus
jamaicano, -na → **jamaiquino**
jamaiquino, -na *adj & n* : Jamaican
jamás *adv* **1** NUNCA : never **2 nunca jamás** *or* **jamás de los jamases** : never ever **3 para siempre jamás** : for ever and ever
jamba *nf* : jamb
jamelgo *nm* : nag (horse)
jamón *nm, pl* **jamones** : ham
Januká *nmf* : Hanukkah
japonés, -nesa *adj & n, mpl* **-neses** : Japanese
jaque *nm* **1** : check (in chess) <jaque mate : checkmate> **2 tener en jaque** : to intimidate, to bully
jaqueca *nf* : headache, migraine
jarabe *nm* **1** : syrup **2** : Mexican folk dance
jarana *nf* **1** *fam* : revelry, partying, spree **2** *fam* : joking, fooling around **3** : small guitar
jaranear *vi fam* : to go on a spree, to party
jarcia *nf* **1** : rigging **2** : fishing tackle
jardín *nm, pl* **jardines 1** : garden **2 jardín de niños** : kindergarten **3 los jardines** *nmpl* : the outfield
jardinería *nf* : gardening
jardinero, -ra *n* **1** : gardener **2** : outfielder (in baseball)
jarra *nf* **1** : pitcher, jug **2** : stein, mug **3 de jarras** *or* **en jarras** : akimbo
jarrete *nm* **1** : back of the knee **2** : hock (of an animal)
jarro *nm* **1** : pitcher, jug **2** : mug
jarrón *nm, pl* **jarrones** FLORERO : vase
jaspe *nm* : jasper
jaspeado, -da *adj* **1** VETEADO : streaked, veined **2** : speckled, mottled
jaula *nf* : cage
jauría *nf* : pack of hounds
javanés, -nesa *adj & n* : Javanese
jazmín *nm, pl* **jazmines** : jasmine
jazz ['jas, 'dʒas] *nm* : jazz
jeans ['jins, 'dʒins] *nmpl* : jeans
jeep ['jip, 'dʒip] *nm, pl* **jeeps** : jeep
jefatura *nf* **1** : leadership **2** : headquarters <jefatura de policía : police headquarters>
jefe, -fa *n* **1** : chief, head, leader <jefe de bomberos : fire chief> **2** : boss
Jehová *nm* : Jehovah

jején *nm, pl* **jejenes** : gnat, small mosquito

jengibre *nm* : ginger

jeque *nm* : sheikh, sheik

jerarca *nmf* : leader, chief

jerarquía *nf* **1** : hierarchy **2** RANGO : rank

jerárquico, -ca *adj* : hierarchical

jerbo *nm* : gerbil

jerez *nm, pl* **jereces** : sherry

jerga *nf* **1** : jargon, slang **2** : coarse cloth

jerigonza *nf* GALIMATÍAS : mumbo jumbo, gibberish

jeringa *nf* : syringe

jeringar {52} *vt* **1** : to inject **2** *fam* JOROBAR : to annoy, to pester — *vi fam* JOROBAR : to be annoying, to be a nuisance

jeringuear → **jeringar**

jeringuilla *nf* → **jeringa**

jeroglífico *nm* : hieroglyphic

jersey *nm, pl* **jerseys 1** : jersey (fabric) **2** *Spain* : sweater

jesuita *adj & nm* : Jesuit

Jesús *nm* : Jesus

jeta *nf* **1** : snout **2** *fam* : face, mug

jíbaro, -ra *adj* **1** : Jivaro **2** : rustic, rural

jibia *nf* : cuttlefish

jícama *nf* : jicama

jícara *nf Mex* : calabash

jilguero *nm* : European goldfinch

jinete *nmf* : horseman, horsewoman *f*, rider

jinetear *vt* **1** : to ride, to perform (on horseback) **2** DOMAR : to break in (a horse) — *vi* CABALGAR : to ride horseback

jingoísmo [ˌjɪŋgoˈizmo, ˌdʒɪŋ-] *nm* : jingoism

jingoísta *adj* : jingoist, jingoistic

jiote *nm Mex* : rash

jira *nf* : outing, picnic

jirafa *nf* **1** : giraffe **2** : boom microphone

jirón *nm, pl* **jirones** : shred, rag <hecho jirones : in tatters>

jitomate *nm Mex* : tomato

jockey [ˈjɔki, ˈdʒɔ-] *nmf, pl* **jockeys** [-kis] : jockey

jocosidad *nf* : humor, jocularity

jocoso, -sa *adj* : playful, jocular — **jocosamente** *adv*

jofaina *nf* : washbowl

jogging [ˈjɔgɪŋ, ˈdʒɔ-] *nm* : jogging

jolgorio *nm* : merrymaking, fun

jonrón *nm, pl* **jonrones** : home run

jordano, -na *adj & n* : Jordanian

jornada *nf* **1** : expedition, day's journey **2 jornada de trabajo** : working day **3 jornadas** *nfpl* : conference, congress

jornal *nm* **1** : day's pay **2 a ~** : by the day

jornalero, -ra *n* : day laborer

joroba *nf* **1** GIBA : hump **2** *fam* : nuisance, pain in the neck

jorobado[1], -da *adj* GIBOSO : hunchbacked, humpbacked

jorobado[2], -da *n* GIBOSO : hunchback, humpback

jorobar *vt fam* JERINGAR : to bother, to annoy — *vi fam* JERINGAR : to be annoying, to be a nuisance

jorongo *nm Mex* : full-length poncho

jota *nf* **1** : jot, bit <no entiendo ni jota : I don't understand a word of it> <no se ve ni jota : you can't see a thing> **2** : jack (in playing cards)

joven[1] *adj, pl* **jóvenes 1** : young **2** : youthful

joven[2] *nmf, pl* **jóvenes** : young man *m*, young woman *f*, young person

jovial *adj* : jovial, cheerful — **jovialmente** *adv*

jovialidad *nf* : joviality, cheerfulness

joya *nf* **1** : jewel, piece of jewelry **2** : treasure, gem <la nueva empleada es una joya : the new employee is a real gem>

joyería *nf* **1** : jewelry store **2** : jewelry **3 joyería de fantasía** : costume jewelry

joyero, -ra *n* : jeweler

juanete *nm* : bunion

jubilación *nf, pl* **-ciones 1** : retirement **2** PENSIÓN : pension

jubilado[1], -da *adj* : retired, in retirement

jubilado[2], -da *nmf* : retired person, retiree

jubilar *vt* **1** : to retire, to pension off **2** *fam* : to get rid of, to discard — **jubilarse** *vr* : to retire

jubileo *nm* : jubilee

júbilo *nm* : jubilation, joy

jubiloso, -sa *adj* : jubilant, joyous

judaico, -ca *adj* : Judaic, Jewish

judaísmo *nm* : Judaism

judía *nf* **1** : bean **2** *or* **judía verde** : green bean, string bean

judicatura *nf* **1** : judiciary, judges *pl* **2** : office of judge

judicial *adj* : judicial — **judicialmente** *adv*

judío[1], -día *adj* : Jewish

judío[2], -día *n* : Jewish person, Jew

judo [ˈjuðo, ˈdʒu-] *nm* : judo

juega, juegue, etc. → **jugar**

juego *nm* **1** : play, playing <poner en juego : to bring into play> **2** : game, sport <juego de cartas : card game> <Juegos Olímpicos : Olympic Games> **3** : gaming, gambling <estar en juego : to be at stake> **4** : set <un juego de llaves : a set of keys> **5 hacer juego** : to go together, to match **6 juego de manos** : conjuring trick, sleight of hand

juerga *nf* : partying, binge <irse de juerga : to go on a spree>

juerguista *nmf* : reveler, carouser

jueves *nms & pl* : Thursday

juez *nmf, pl* **jueces 1** : judge **2** ÁRBITRO : umpire, referee

jugada *nf* **1 :** play, move **2 :** trick <hacer una mala jugada : to play a dirty trick>
jugador, -dora *n* **1 :** player **2 :** gambler
jugar {44} *vi* **1 :** to play <jugar a la pelota : to play ball> **2** APOSTAR **:** to gamble, to bet **3 :** to joke, to kid — *vt* **1 :** to play <jugar un papel : to play a role> <jugar una carta : to play a card> **2 :** to bet — **jugarse** *vr* **1 :** to risk, to gamble away <jugarse la vida : to risk one's life> **2 jugarse el todo por el todo :** to risk everything
jugarreta *nf fam* **:** prank, dirty trick
juglar *nm* **:** minstrel
jugo *nm* **1 :** juice **2 :** substance, essence <sacarle el jugo a algo : to get the most out of something>
jugosidad *nf* **:** juiciness, succulence
jugoso, -sa *adj* **:** juicy
juguete *nm* **:** toy
juguetear *vi* **1 :** to play, to cavort, to frolic **2 :** to toy, to fiddle
juguetería *nf* **:** toy store
juguetón, -tona *adj, mpl* **-tones :** playful — **juguetonamente** *adv*
juicio *nm* **1 :** good judgment, reason, sense **2 :** opinion <a mi juicio : in my opinion> **3 :** trial <llevar a juicio : to take to court>
juicioso, -sa *adj* **:** judicious, wise — **juiciosamente** *adv*
julio *nm* **:** July
juncia *nf* **:** sedge
junco *nm* **1 :** reed, rush **2 :** junk (boat)
jungla *nf* **:** jungle
junio *nm* **:** June
junquillo *nm* **:** jonquil
junta *nf* **1 :** board, committee <junta directiva : board of directors> **2** REUNIÓN **:** meeting, session **3 :** junta **4 :** joint, gasket
juntamente *adv* **1 :** jointly, together <juntamente con : together with> **2 :** at the same time
juntar *vt* **1** UNIR **:** to unite, to combine, to put together **2** REUNIR **:** to collect, to gather together, to assemble **3 :** to close partway <juntar la puerta : to leave the door ajar> — **juntarse** *vr* **1 :** to join together **2 :** to socialize, to get together
junto, -ta *adj* **1** UNIDO **:** joined, united **2 :** close, adjacent <colgaron los dos retratos juntos : they hung the two paintings side by side> **3** (*used adverbially*) **:** together <llegamos juntos : we arrived together> **4 ~ a :** next to, alongside of **5 ~ con :** together with, along with
juntura *nf* **:** joint, coupling
Júpiter *nm* **:** Jupiter
jura *nf* **:** oath, pledge <jura de bandera : pledge of allegiance>
jurado[1] *nm* **:** jury
jurado[2], **-da** *n* **:** juror
juramento *nm* **1 :** oath <juramento hipocrático : Hippocratic oath> **2 :** swearword, oath
jurar *vt* **1 :** to swear <jurar lealtad : to swear loyalty> **2 :** to take an oath <el alcalde juró su cargo : the mayor took the oath of office> — *vi* **:** to curse, to swear
jurídico, -ca *adj* **:** legal
jurisdicción *nf, pl* **-ciones :** jurisdiction
jurisdiccional *adj* **:** jurisdictional, territorial
jurisprudencia *nf* **:** jurisprudence, law
justa *nf* **1 :** joust **2** TORNEO **:** tournament, competition
justamente *adv* **1** PRECISAMENTE **:** precisely, exactly **2 :** justly, fairly
justar *vi* **:** to joust
justicia *nf* **1 :** justice, fairness <hacerle justicia a : to do justice to> <ser de justicia : to be only fair> **2 la justicia :** the law <tomarse la justicia por su mano : to take the law into one's own hands>
justiciero, -ra *adj* **:** righteous, avenging
justificable *adj* **:** justifiable
justificación *nf, pl* **-ciones :** justification
justificante *nm* **1 :** justification **2 :** proof, voucher
justificar {72} *vt* **1 :** to justify **2 :** to excuse, to vindicate
justo[1] *adv* **1 :** justly **2 :** right, exactly <justo a tiempo : just in time> **3 :** tightly
justo[2], **-ta** *adj* **1 :** just, fair **2 :** right, exact **3 :** tight <estos zapatos me quedan muy justos : these shoes are too tight>
justo[3], **-ta** *n* **:** just person <los justos : the just>
juvenil *adj* **1 :** juvenile, young, youthful **2** ADOLESCENTE **:** teenage
juventud *nf* **1 :** youth **2 :** young people
juzgado *nm* TRIBUNAL **:** court, tribunal
juzgar {52} *vt* **1 :** to try, to judge (a case in court) **2 :** to pass judgment on **3** CONSIDERAR **:** to consider, to deem
juzgue, etc. → **juzgar**

K

k *nf* **:** eleventh letter of the Spanish alphabet
kaki *adj & nm* → **caqui**
kaleidoscopio *nm* → **caleidoscopio**
kamikaze *adj & nm* **:** kamikaze
kampucheano, -na *adj & n* **:** Kampuchean
kan *nm* **:** khan
karaoke *nm* **:** karaoke
karate *or* **kárate** *nm* **:** karate

kayac *or* **kayak** *nm, pl* **kayacs** *or* **kayaks** : kayak

keniano, -na *adj & n* : Kenyan

kepí *nm* : kepi

kermesse *or* **kermés** [kɛr'mɛs] *nf, pl* **kermesses** *or* **kermeses** [-'mɛsɛs] : charity fair, bazaar

kerosene *or* **kerosén** *or* **keroseno** *nm* : kerosene, paraffin

kilo *nm* **1** : kilo, kilogram **2** *fam* : large amount

kilobyte [ˌkilo'bait] *nm* : kilobyte

kilociclo *nm* : kilocycle

kilogramo *nm* : kilogram

kilohertzio *nm* : kilohertz

kilometraje *nm* : distance in kilometers, mileage

kilométrico, -ca *adj fam* : endless, very long

kilómetro *nm* : kilometer

kilovatio *nm* : kilowatt

kimono *nm* : kimono

kinder ['kɪndɛr] *nm* → **kindergarten**

kindergarten [ˌkɪndɛr'gartɛn] *nm, pl* **kindergartens** [-tɛns] : kindergarten, nursery school

kinesiología *nf* : physical therapy

kinesiólogo, -ga *n* : physical therapist

kiosco *nm* → **quiosco**

kit *nm, pl* **kits** : kit

kiwi ['kiwi] *nm* **1** : kiwi (bird) **2** : kiwifruit

klaxon *nm* → **claxon**

knockout [nɔ'kaut] *nm* → **nocaut**

koala *nm* : koala bear

kriptón *nm* : krypton

kurdo[1], -da *adj* : Kurdish

kurdo[2], -da *n* : Kurd

kuwaití [kuˌwai'ti] *adj & nmf* : Kuwaiti

L

l *nf* : twelfth letter of the Spanish alphabet

la[1] *pron* **1** : her, it <llámala hoy : call her today> <sacó la botella y la abrió : he took out the bottle and opened it> **2** (*formal*) : you <no la vi a usted, Señora Díaz : I didn't see you, Mrs. Díaz> **3** : the one <mi casa y la de la puerta roja : my house and the one with the red door> **4 la que** : the one who

la[2] *art* → **el[2]**

laberíntico, -ca *adj* : labyrinthine

laberinto *nm* : labyrinth, maze

labia *nf fam* : gift of gab <tu amigo tiene labia : your friend has a way with words>

labial *adj* : labial, lip <lápiz labial : lipstick>

labio *nm* **1** : lip **2 labio leporino** : harelip

labor *nf* : work, labor

laborable *adj* **1** : arable **2 día laborable** : workday, business day

laboral *adj* **1** : work, labor <costos laborales : labor costs> **2 estancia laboral** : workstation

laborar *vi* : to work

laboratorio *nm* : laboratory, lab

laboriosidad *nf* : industriousness, diligence

laborioso, -sa *adj* **1** : laborious, hard **2** : industrious, hard-working

labrado[1], -da *adj* **1** : cultivated, tilled **2** : carved, wrought

labrado[2] *nm* : cultivated field

labrador, -dora *n* : farmer

labranza *nf* : farming

labrar *vt* **1** : to carve, to work (metal) **2** : to cultivate, to till **3** : to cause, to bring about

laca *nf* **1** : lacquer, shellac **2** : hair spray **3 laca de uñas** : nail polish

lacayo *nm* : lackey

lace, etc. → **lazar**

lacear *vt* : to lasso

laceración *nf, pl* **-ciones** : laceration

lacerante *adj* : hurtful, wounding

lacerar *vt* **1** : to lacerate, to cut **2** : to hurt, to wound (one's feelings)

lacio, -cia *adj* **1** : limp, lank **2 pelo lacio** : straight hair

lacónico, -ca *adj* : laconic — **lacónicamente** *adv*

lacra *nf* **1** : scar, mark (on the skin) **2** : stigma, blemish

lacrar *vt* : to seal (with wax)

lacrimógeno, -na *adj* **gas lacrimógeno** : tear gas

lacrimoso, -sa *adj* : tearful, moving

lactancia *nf* **1** : lactation **2** : breast-feeding

lactante *nmf* : nursing infant, suckling

lactar *v* : to breast-feed

lácteo, -tea *adj* **1** : dairy **2 Vía Láctea** : Milky Way

láctico, -ca *adj* : lactic

lactosa *nf* : lactose

ladeado, -da *adj* : crooked, tilted, lopsided

ladear *vt* : to tilt, to tip — **ladearse** *vr* : to bend (over)

ladera *nf* : slope, hillside

ladino[1], -na *adj* **1** : cunning, shrewd **2** *CA, Mex* : mestizo

ladino[2], -na *n* **1** : trickster **2** *CA, Mex* : Spanish-speaking Indian **3** *CA, Mex* : mestizo

lado *nm* **1** : side **2** PARTE : place <miró por todos lados : he looked everywhere> **3 al lado de** : next to, beside **4 de ~** : tilted, sideways <está de lado : it's lying on its side> **5 hacerse a un lado** : to step aside **6 lado a lado** : side by side **7 por otro lado** : on the other hand

ladrar *vi* : to bark

ladrido *nm* : bark (of a dog), barking

ladrillo *nm* : brick
ladrón, -drona *n, mpl* **ladrones** : robber, thief, burglar
lagartija *nf* : small lizard
lagarto *nm* **1** : lizard **2 lagarto de Indias** : alligator
lago *nm* : lake
lágrima *nf* : tear, teardrop
lagrimear *vi* **1** : to water (of eyes) **2** : to weep easily
laguna *nf* **1** : lagoon **2** : lacuna, gap
laicado *nm* : laity
laico[1], **-ca** *adj* : lay, secular
laico[2], **-ca** *n* : layman *m*, laywoman *f*
laja *nf* : slab
lama[1] *nf* : slime, ooze
lama[2] *nm* : lama
lamber *vt* : to lick
lamentable *adj* **1** : unfortunate, lamentable **2** : pitiful, sad
lamentablemente *adv* : unfortunately, regrettably
lamentación *nf, pl* **-ciones** : lamentation, groaning, moaning
lamentar *vt* **1** : to lament **2** : to regret <lo lamento : I'm sorry> — **lamentarse** *vr* : to grumble, to complain
lamento *nm* : lament, groan, cry
lamer *vt* **1** : to lick **2** : to lap against
lamida *nf* : lick
lámina *nf* **1** PLANCHA : sheet, plate **2** : plate, illustration
laminado[1], **-da** *adj* : laminated
laminado[2] *nm* : laminate
laminar *vt* : to laminate — **laminación** *nf*
lámpara *nf* : lamp
lampiño, -ña *adj* : hairless
lamprea *nf* : lamprey
lana *nf* **1** : wool <lana de acero : steel wool> **2** *Mex fam* : money, dough
lance[1], **etc.** → **lanzar**
lance[2] *nm* **1** INCIDENTE : event, incident **2** RIÑA : quarrel **3** : throw, cast (of a net, etc.) **4** : move, play (in a game), throw (of dice)
lancear *vt* : to spear
lanceta *nf* : lancet
lancha *nf* **1** : small boat, launch **2 lancha motora** : motorboat, speedboat
langosta *nf* **1** : lobster **2** : locust
langostino *nm* : prawn, crayfish
languidecer {53} *vi* : to languish
languidez *nf, pl* **-deces** : languor, listlessness
lánguido, -da *adj* : languid, listless — **lánguidamente** *adv*
lanolina *nf* : lanolin
lanudo, -da *adj* : woolly
lanza *nf* : spear, lance
lanzadera *nf* **1** : shuttle (for weaving) **2 lanzadera espacial** : space shuttle
lanzado, -da *adj* **1** : impulsive, brazen **2** : forward, determined <ir lanzado : to hurtle along>
lanzador, -dora *n* : thrower, pitcher
lanzallamas *nms & pl* : flamethrower
lanzamiento *nm* **1** : throw **2** : pitch (in baseball) **3** : launching, launch
lanzar {21} *vt* **1** : to throw, to hurl **2** : to pitch **3** : to launch — **lanzarse** *vr* **1** : to throw oneself (at, into) **2 ~ a** : to embark upon, to undertake
laosiano, -na *adj & n* : Laotian
lapicero *nm* **1** : mechanical pencil **2** *CA, Peru* : ballpoint pen
lápida *nf* : marker, tombstone
lapidar *vt* APEDREAR : to stone
lapidario, -ria *adj & n* : lapidary
lápiz *nm, pl* **lápices 1** : pencil **2 lápiz de labios** *or* **lápiz labial** : lipstick
lapón, -pona *adj & n, mpl* **lapones** : Lapp
lapso *nm* : lapse, space (of time)
lapsus *nms & pl* : error, slip
laquear *vt* : to lacquer, to varnish, to shellac
largamente *adv* **1** : at length, extensively **2** : easily, comfortably **3** : generously
largar {52} *vt* **1** SOLTAR : to let loose, to release **2** AFLOJAR : to loosen, to slacken **3** *fam* : to give, to hand over **4** *fam* : to hurl, to let fly (insults, etc.) — **largarse** *vr fam* : to scram, to beat it
largo[1], **-ga** *adj* **1** : long **2 a lo largo** : lengthwise **3 a lo largo de** : along **4 a la larga** : in the long run
largo[2] *nm* : length <tres metros de largo : three meters long>
largometraje *nm* : feature film
largue, etc. → **largar**
larguero *nm* : crossbeam
largueza *nf* : generosity, largesse
larguirucho, -cha *adj fam* : lanky
largura *nf* : length
laringe *nf* : larynx
laringitis *nfs & pl* : laryngitis
larva *nf* : larva — **larval** *adj*
las → **el**[2], **los**[1]
lasaña *nf* : lasagna
lasca *nf* : chip, chipping
lascivia *nf* : lasciviousness, lewdness
lascivo, -va *adj* : lascivious, lewd — **lascivamente** *adv*
láser *nm* : laser
lasitud *nf* : lassitude, weariness
laso, -sa *adj* : languid, weary
lástima *nf* **1** : compassion, pity **2** PENA : shame, pity <¡qué lástima! : what a shame!>
lastimadura *nf* : injury, wound
lastimar *vt* **1** DAÑAR, HERIR : to hurt, to injure **2** AGRAVIAR : to offend — **lastimarse** *vr* : to hurt oneself
lastimero, -ra *adj* : pitiful, wretched
lastimoso, -sa *adj* **1** : shameful **2** : pitiful, terrible
lastrar *vt* **1** : to ballast **2** : to burden, to encumber
lastre *nm* **1** : burden **2** : ballast
lata *nf* **1** : tinplate **2** : tin can **3** *fam* : pest, bother, nuisance **4 dar lata** *fam* : to bother, to annoy
latencia *nf* : latency
latente *adj* : latent

lateral[1] *adj* **1 :** lateral, side **2 :** indirect — **lateralmente** *adv*
lateral[2] *nm* **:** end piece, side
látex *nms & pl* **:** latex
latido *nm* **:** beat, throb <latido del corazón : heartbeat>
latifundio *nm* **:** large estate
latigazo *nm* **:** lash (with a whip)
látigo *nm* AZOTE **:** whip
latín *nm* **:** Latin (language)
latino[1], **-na** *adj* **1 :** Latin **2** *fam* **:** Latin-American
latino[2], **-na** *n fam* **:** Latin American
latinoamericano[1], **-na** *adj* HISPANOAMERICANO **:** Latin American
latinoamericano, -na *n* **:** Latin American
latir *vi* **1 :** to beat, to throb **2 latirle a uno** *Mex fam* **:** to have a hunch <me late que no va a venir : I have a feeling he's not going to come>
latitud *nf* **1 :** latitude **2 :** breadth
lato, -ta *adj* **1 :** extended, lengthy **2 :** broad (in meaning)
latón *nm, pl* **latones :** brass
latoso[1], **-sa** *adj fam* **:** annoying, bothersome
latoso[2], **-sa** *n fam* **:** pest, nuisance
latrocinio *nm* **:** larceny
laúd *nm* **:** lute
laudable *adj* **:** laudable, praiseworthy
laudo *nm* **:** findings, decision
laureado, -da *adj & n* **:** laureate
laurear *vt* **:** to award, to honor
laurel *nm* **1 :** laurel **2 :** bay leaf **3 dormirse en sus laureles :** to rest on one's laurels
lava *nf* **:** lava
lavable *adj* **:** washable
lavabo *nm* **1** LAVAMANOS **:** sink, washbowl **2 :** lavatory, toilet
lavadero *nm* **:** laundry room
lavado *nm* **1 :** laundry, wash **2 :** laundering <lavado de dinero : money laundering>
lavadora *nf* **:** washing machine
lavamanos *nms & pl* LAVABO **:** sink, washbowl
lavanda *nf* ESPLIEGO **:** lavender
lavandería *nf* **:** laundry (service)
lavandero, -ra *n* **:** launderer, laundress *f*
lavaplatos *nms & pl* **1 :** dishwasher **2** *Chile, Col, Mex* **:** kitchen sink
lavar *vt* **1 :** to wash, to clean **2 :** to launder (money) **3 lavar en seco :** to dry-clean — **lavarse** *vr* **1 :** to wash oneself **2 lavarse las manos de :** to wash one's hands of
lavativa *nf* **:** enema
lavatorio *nm* **:** lavatory, washroom
lavavajillas *nms & pl* **:** dishwasher
laxante *adj & nm* **:** laxative
laxitud *nf* **:** laxity, slackness
laxo, -xa *adj* **:** lax, slack
lazada *nf* **:** bow, loop
lazar {21} *vt* **:** to rope, to lasso
lazo *nm* **1** VÍNCULO **:** link, bond **2 :** bow, ribbon **3 :** lasso, lariat
le *pron* **1 :** to her, to him, to it <¿qué le dijiste? : what did you tell him?> **2 :** from her, from him, from it <el ladrón le robó la cartera : the thief stole his wallet> **3 :** for her, for him, for it <cómprale flores a tu mamá : buy your mom some flowers> **4** (*formal*) **:** to you, for you <le traje un regalo : I brought you a gift>
leal *adj* **:** loyal, faithful — **lealmente** *adv*
lealtad *nf* **:** loyalty, allegiance
lebrel *nm* **:** hound
lección *nf, pl* **lecciones :** lesson
lechada *nf* **1 :** whitewash **2 :** grout
lechal *adj* **:** suckling, unweaned <cordero lechal : suckling lamb>
leche *nf* **1 :** milk <leche en polvo : powdered milk> <leche de magnesia : milk of magnesia> **2 :** milky sap
lechera *nf* **1 :** milk jug **2 :** dairymaid *f*
lechería *nf* **:** dairy store
lechero[1], **-ra** *adj* **:** dairy
lechero[2], **-ra** *n* **:** milkman *m,* milk dealer
lecho *nm* **1 :** bed <un lecho de rosas : a bed of roses> <lecho de muerte : deathbed> **2 :** riverbed **3 :** layer, stratum (in geology)
lechón, -chona *n, mpl* **lechones :** suckling pig
lechoso, -sa *adj* **:** milky
lechuga *nf* **:** lettuce
lechuza *nf* BÚHO **:** owl, barn owl
lectivo, -va *adj* **:** school <año lectivo : school year>
lector[1], **-tora** *adj* **:** reading <nivel lector : reading level>
lector[2], **-tora** *n* **:** reader
lector[3] *nm* **:** scanner, reader <lector óptico : optical scanner>
lectura *nf* **1 :** reading **2 :** reading matter
leer {20} *v* **:** to read
legación *nf, pl* **-ciones :** legation
legado *nm* **1 :** legacy, bequest **2 :** legate, emissary
legajo *nm* **:** dossier, file
legal *adj* **:** legal, lawful — **legalmente** *adv*
legalidad *nf* **:** legality, lawfulness
legalizar {21} *vt* **:** to legalize — **legalización** *nf*
legar {52} *vt* **1 :** to bequeath, to hand down **2** DELEGAR **:** to delegate
legendario, -ria *adj* **:** legendary
legible *adj* **:** legible
legión *nf, pl* **legiones :** legion
legionario, -ria *n* **:** legionnaire
legislación *nf* **1 :** legislation, lawmaking **2 :** laws *pl,* legislation
legislador[1], **-dora** *adj* **:** legislative
legislador[2], **-dora** *n* **:** legislator
legislar *vi* **:** to legislate
legislativo, -va *adj* **:** legislative
legislatura *nf* **1 :** legislature **2 :** term of office
legitimar *vt* **1 :** to legitimize **2 :** to authenticate — **legitimación** *nf*

legitimidad *nf* : legitimacy
legítimo, -ma *adj* **1** : legitimate **2** : genuine, authentic — **legítimamente** *adv*
lego[1], -ga *adj* **1** : secular, lay **2** : uninformed, ignorant
lego[2], -ga *n* : layperson, layman *m,* laywoman *f*
legua *nf* **1** : league **2 notarse a leguas** : to be very obvious <se notaba a leguas : you could tell from a mile away>
legue, etc. → **legar**
legumbre *nf* **1** HORTALIZA : vegetable **2** : legume
leíble *adj* : readable
leída *nf* : reading, read <de una leída : in one reading, at one go>
leído[1] *pp* → **leer**
leído[2], -da *adj* : well-read
lejanía *nf* : remoteness, distance
lejano, -na *adj* : remote, distant, far away
lejía *nf* **1** : lye **2** : bleach
lejos *adv* **1** : far away, distant <a lo lejos : in the distance, far off> <desde lejos : from a distance> **2** : long ago, a long way off <está lejos de los 50 años : he's a long way from 50 years old> **3 de ~** : by far <esta decisión fue de lejos la más fácil : this decision was by far the easiest> **4 ~ de** : far from <lejos de ser reprobado, recibió una nota de B : far from failing, he got a B>
lelo, -la *adj* : silly, stupid
lema *nm* : motto, slogan
lencería *nf* : lingerie
lengua *nf* **1** : tongue <morderse la lengua : to bite one's tongue> **2** IDIOMA : language <lengua materna : mother tongue, native language> <lengua muerta : dead language>
lenguado *nm* : sole, flounder
lenguaje *nm* **1** : language, speech **2 lenguaje gestual** *or* **lenguaje de gestos** : sign language **3 lenguaje de programación** : programming language
lengüeta *nf* **1** : tongue (of a shoe), tab, flap **2** : reed (of a musical instrument) **3** : barb, point
lengüetada *nf* **beber a lengüetadas** : to lap (up)
lenidad *nf* : leniency
lenitivo, -va *adj* : soothing
lente *nmf* **1** : lens <lentes de contacto : contact lenses> **2 lentes** *nmpl* ANTEOJOS : eyeglasses <lentes de sol : sunglasses>
lenteja *nf* : lentil
lentejuela *nf* : sequin, spangle
lentitud *nf* : slowness
lento[1] *adv* DESPACIO : slowly
lento[2], -ta *adj* **1** : slow **2** : slow-witted, dull — **lentamente** *adv*
leña *nf* : wood, firewood
leñador, -dora *n* : lumberjack, woodcutter
leñera *nf* : woodshed
leño *nm* : log
leñoso, -sa *adj* : woody
Leo *nmf* : Leo
león, -ona *n, mpl* **leones 1** : lion, lioness *f* **2** (*in various countries*) : puma, cougar
leonado, -da *adj* : tawny
leonino, -na *adj* **1** : leonine **2** : one-sided, unfair
leopardo *nm* : leopard
leotardo *nm* MALLA : leotard, tights *pl*
leperada *nf Mex* : obscenity
lépero, -ra *adj Mex* : vulgar, coarse
lepra *nf* : leprosy
leproso[1], -sa *adj* : leprous
leproso[2], -sa *n* : leper
lerdo, -da *adj* **1** : clumsy **2** : dull, oafish, slow-witted
les *pron* **1** : to them <dales una propina : give them a tip> **2** : from them <se les privó de su herencia : they were deprived of their inheritance> **3** : for them <les hice sus tareas : I did their homework for them> **4** : to you *pl*, for you *pl* <les compré un regalo : I bought you all a present>
lesbiana *nf* : lesbian — **lesbiano, -na** *adj*
lesbianismo *nm* : lesbianism
lesión *nf, pl* **lesiones** HERIDA : lesion, wound, injury <una lesión grave : a serious injury>
lesionado, -da *adj* HERIDO : injured, wounded
lesionar *vt* : to injure, to wound — **lesionarse** *vr* : to hurt oneself
lesivo, -va *adj* : harmful, damaging
letal *adj* MORTÍFERO : deadly, lethal — **letalmente** *adv*
letanía *nf* **1** : litany **2** *fam* : spiel, song and dance
letárgico, -ca *adj* : lethargic
letargo *nm* : lethargy, torpor
letón[1], -tona *adj & n, mpl* **letones** : Latvian
letón[2] *nm* : Latvian (language)
letra *nf* **1** : letter **2** CALIGRAFÍA : handwriting, lettering **3** : lyrics *pl* **4 al pie de la letra** : word for word, by the book **5 letras** *nfpl* : arts (in education)
letrado[1], -da *adj* ERUDITO : learned, erudite
letrado[2], -da *n* : attorney-at-law, lawyer
letrero *nm* RÓTULO : sign, notice
letrina *nf* : latrine
letrista *nmf* : lyricist, songwriter
leucemia *nf* : leukemia
levadizo, -za *adj* **1** : liftable **2 puente levadizo** : drawbridge
levadura *nf* **1** : yeast, leavening **2 levadura en polvo** : baking powder
levantamiento *nm* **1** ALZAMIENTO : uprising **2** : raising, lifting <levantamiento de pesas : weight lifting>
levantar *vt* **1** ALZAR : to lift, to raise **2** : to put up, to erect **3** : to call off, to adjourn **4** : to give rise to, to arouse

<levantar sospechas : to arouse suspicion> — **levantarse** *vr* **1 :** to rise, to stand up **2 :** to get out of bed

levar *vt* **levar anclas :** to weigh anchor

leve *adj* **1 :** light, slight **2 :** trivial, unimportant — **levemente** *adv*

levedad *nf* **:** lightness

levemente *adv* LIGERAMENTE **:** lightly, softly

léxico[1], -ca *adj* **:** lexical

léxico[2] *nm* **:** lexicon, glossary

lexicografía *nf* **:** lexicography

lexicográfico, -ca *adj* **:** lexicographical, lexicographic

lexicógrafo, -fa *n* **:** lexicographer

ley *nf* **1 :** law <fuera de la ley : outside the law> <la ley de gravedad : the law of gravity> **2 :** purity (of metals) <oro de ley : pure gold>

leyenda *nf* **1 :** legend **2 :** caption, inscription

leyó, etc. → **leer**

liar {85} *vt* **1** ATAR **:** to bind, to tie (up) **2 :** to roll (a cigarette) **3 :** to confuse — **liarse** *vr* **:** to get mixed up

libanés, -nesa *adj & n, mpl* **-neses :** Lebanese

libar *vt* **1 :** to suck (nectar) **2 :** to sip, to swig (liquor, etc.)

libelo *nm* **1 :** libel, lampoon **2 :** petition (in court)

libélula *nf* **:** dragonfly

liberación *nf, pl* **-ciones :** liberation, deliverance <liberación de la mujer : women's liberation>

liberado, -da *adj* **1 :** liberated <una mujer liberada : a liberated woman> **2 :** freed, delivered

liberal *adj & nmf* **:** liberal

liberalidad *nf* **:** generosity, liberality

liberalismo *nm* **:** liberalism

liberalizar {21} *vt* **:** to liberalize — **liberalización** *nf*

liberar *vt* **:** to liberate, to free — **liberarse** *vr* **:** to get free of

liberiano, -na *adj & n* **:** Liberian

libertad *nf* **1 :** freedom, liberty <tomarse la libertad de : to take the liberty of> **2 libertad bajo fianza :** bail **3 libertad condicional :** parole

libertador[1], -dora *adj* **:** liberating

libertador[2], -dora *n* **:** liberator

libertar *vt* LIBRAR **:** to set free

libertario, -ria *adj & n* **:** libertarian

libertinaje *nm* **:** licentiousness, dissipation

libertino[1], -na *adj* **:** licentious, dissolute

libertino[2], -na *n* **:** libertine

libidinoso, -sa *adj* **:** lustful, lewd

libido *nf* **:** libido

libio, -bia *adj & n* **:** Libyan

libra *nf* **1 :** pound **2 libra esterlina :** pound sterling

Libra *nmf* **:** Libra

libramiento *nm* **1 :** liberating, freeing **2** LIBRANZA **:** order of payment **3** *Mex* **:** beltway

libranza *nf* **:** order of payment

librar *vt* **1** LIBERTAR **:** to deliver, to set free **2 :** to wage <librar batalla : to do battle> **3 :** to issue <librar una orden : to issue an order> — **librarse** *vr* **~ de :** to free oneself from, to get out of

libre *adj* **1 :** free <un país libre : a free country> <libre de : free from, exempt from> <libre albedrío : free will> **2** DESOCUPADO **:** vacant **3 día libre :** day off

librea *nf* **:** livery

librecambio *nm* **:** free trade

libremente *adv* **:** freely

librería *nf* **:** bookstore

librero[1], -ra *n* **:** bookseller

librero[2] *nm Mex* **:** bookcase

libresco, -ca *adj* **:** bookish

libreta *nf* CUADERNO **:** notebook

libreto *nm* **:** libretto, script

libro *nm* **1 :** book <libro de texto : textbook> **2 libros** *nmpl* **:** books (in bookkeeping), accounts <llevar los libros : to keep the books>

licencia *nf* **1 :** permission **2 :** leave, leave of absence **3 :** permit, license <licencia de conducir : driver's license>

licenciado, -da *n* **1 :** university graduate **2** ABOGADO **:** lawyer

licenciar *vt* **1 :** to license, to permit, to allow **2 :** to discharge **3 :** to grant a university degree to — **licenciarse** *vr* **:** to graduate

licenciatura *nf* **1 :** college degree **2 :** course of study (at a college or university)

licencioso, -sa *adj* **:** licentious, lewd

liceo *nm* **:** secondary school, high school

licitación *nf, pl* **-ciones :** bid, bidding

licitar *vt* **:** to bid on

lícito, -ta *adj* **1 :** lawful, licit **2** JUSTO **:** just, fair

licor *nm* **1 :** liquor **2 :** liqueur

licorera *nf* **:** decanter

licuado *nm* BATIDO **:** milk shake

licuadora *nf* **:** blender

licuar {3} *vt* **:** to liquefy — **licuarse** *vr*

lid *nf* **1 :** fight, combat **2 :** argument, dispute **3 lides** *nfpl* **:** matters, affairs **4 en buena lid :** fair and square

líder[1] *adj* **:** leading, foremost

líder[2] *nmf* **:** leader

liderar *vt* DIRIGIR **:** to lead, to head

liderato *nm* **:** leadership, leading

liderazgo *nm* → **liderato**

lidiar *vt* **:** to fight — *vi* BATALLAR, LUCHAR **:** to struggle, to battle, to wrestle

liebre *nf* **:** hare

liendre *nf* **:** nit

lienzo *nm* **1 :** linen **2 :** canvas, painting **3 :** stretch of wall or fencing

liga *nf* **1** ASOCIACIÓN **:** league **2** GOMITA **:** rubber band **3 :** garter

ligado, -da *adj* **:** linked, connected

ligadura *nf* **1** ATADURA **:** tie, bond **2 :** ligature

ligamento *nm* **:** ligament

ligar {52} *vt* **:** to bind, to tie (up)

ligeramente *adv* **1 :** slightly **2** LEVEMENTE **:** lightly, gently **3 :** casually, flippantly
ligereza *nf* **1 :** lightness **2 :** flippancy **3 :** agility
ligero, -ra *adj* **1 :** light, lightweight **2 :** slight, minor **3 :** agile, quick **4 :** lighthearted, superficial
ligue, etc. → **ligar**
lija *nf or* **papel de lija :** sandpaper
lijar *vt* **:** to sand
lila[1] *adj* **:** lilac, light purple
lila[2] *nf* **:** lilac
lima *nf* **1 :** lime (fruit) **2 :** file <lima de uñas : nail file>
limadora *nf* **:** polisher
limar *vt* **1 :** to file **2 :** to polish, to put the final touch on **3 :** to smooth over <limar las diferencias : to iron out differences>
limbo *nm* **1 :** limbo **2 :** limb (in botany and astronomy)
limeño[1], **-ña** *adj* **:** of or from Lima, Peru
limeño[2], **-ña** *n* **:** person from Lima, Peru
limero *nm* **:** lime tree
limitación *nf, pl* **-ciones 1 :** limitation **2 :** limit, restriction <sin limitación : unlimited>
limitado, -da *adj* **1** RESTRINGIDO **:** limited **2 :** dull, slow-witted
limitar *vt* RESTRINGIR **:** to limit, to restrict — *vi* **~ con :** to border on — **limitarse** *vr* **~ a :** to limit oneself to
límite *nm* **1 :** boundary, border **2 :** limit <el límite de mi paciencia : the limit of my patience> <límite de velocidad : speed limit> **3 fecha límite :** deadline
limítrofe *adj* LINDANTE, LINDERO **:** bordering, adjoining
limo *nm* **:** slime, mud
limón *nm, pl* **limones 1 :** lemon **2 :** lemon tree **3 limón verde** *Mex* **:** lime
limonada *nf* **:** lemonade
limosna *nf* **:** alms, charity
limosnear *vi* **:** to beg (for alms)
limosnero, -ra *n* MENDIGO **:** beggar
limoso, -sa *adj* **:** slimy
limpiabotas *nmfs & pl* **:** bootblack
limpiador[1], **-dora** *adj* **:** cleaning
limpiador[2], **-dora** *n* **:** cleaning person, cleaner
limpiamente *adv* **:** cleanly, honestly, fairly
limpiaparabrisas *nms & pl* **:** windshield wiper
limpiar *vt* **1 :** to clean, to cleanse **2 :** to clean up, to remove defects **3** *fam* **:** to clean out (in a game) **4** *fam* **:** to swipe, to pinch — *vi* **:** to clean — **limpiarse** *vr*
limpiavidrios *nmfs & pl Mex* **:** windshield wiper
límpido, -da *adj* **:** limpid
limpieza *nf* **1 :** cleanliness, tidiness **2 :** cleaning **3** HONRADEZ **:** integrity, honesty **4** DESTREZA **:** skill, dexterity
limpio[1] *adv* **:** fairly
limpio[2], **-pia** *adj* **1 :** clean, neat **2 :** honest <un juego limpio : a fair game> **3 :** free <limpio de impurezas : pure, free from impurities> **4 :** clear, net <ganancia limpia : clear profit>
limusina *nf* **:** limousine
linaje *nm* ABOLENGO **:** lineage, ancestry
linaza *nf* **:** linseed
lince *nm* **:** lynx
linchamiento *nm* **:** lynching
linchar *vt* **:** to lynch
lindante *adj* LIMÍTROFE, LINDERO **:** bordering, adjoining
lindar *vi* **1 ~ con :** to border, to skirt **2 ~ con** BORDEAR **:** to border on, to verge on
linde *nmf* **:** boundary, limit
lindero[1], **-ra** *adj* LIMÍTROFE, LINDANTE **:** bordering, adjoining
lindero[2] *nm* **:** boundary, limit
lindeza *nf* **1 :** prettiness **2 :** clever remark **3 lindezas** *nfpl* (*used ironically*) **:** insults
lindo[1] *adv* **1 :** beautifully, wonderfully <canta lindo tu mujer : your wife sings beautifully> **2 de lo lindo :** a lot, a great deal <los zancudos nos picaban de lo lindo : the mosquitoes were biting away at us>
lindo[2], **-da** *adj* **1** BONITO **:** pretty, lovely **2** MONO **:** cute
línea *nf* **1 :** line <línea divisoria : dividing line> <línea de banda : sideline> **2 :** line, course, position <línea de conducta : course of action> <en líneas generales : in general terms, along general lines> **3 :** line, service <línea aérea : airline> <línea telefónica : telephone line>
lineal *adj* **:** linear
linfa *nf* **:** lymph
linfático, -ca *adj* **:** lymphatic
lingote *nm* **:** ingot
lingüista *nmf* **:** linguist
lingüística *nf* **:** linguistics
lingüístico, -ca *adj* **:** linguistic
linimento *nm* **:** liniment
lino *nm* **1 :** linen **2 :** flax
linóleo *nm* **:** linoleum
linterna *nf* **1 :** lantern **2 :** flashlight
lío *nm fam* **1 :** confusion, mess **2 :** hassle, trouble, jam <meterse en un lío : to get into a jam> **3 :** affair, liason
liofilizar {21} *vt* **:** to freeze-dry
lioso, -sa *adj fam* **1 :** confusing, muddled **2 :** troublemaking
liquen *nm* **:** lichen
liquidación *nf, pl* **-ciones 1 :** liquidation **2 :** clearance sale **3 :** settlement, payment
liquidar *vt* **1 :** to liquefy **2 :** to liquidate **3 :** to settle, to pay off **4** *fam* **:** to rub out, to kill
liquidez *nf, pl* **-deces :** liquidity

líquido[1], -da *adj* **1 :** liquid, fluid **2 :** net <ingresos líquidos : net income>

líquido[2] *nm* **1 :** liquid, fluid <líquido de frenos : brake fluid> **2 :** ready cash, liquid assets

lira *nf* **:** lyre

lírica *nf* **:** lyric poetry

lírico, -ca *adj* **:** lyric, lyrical

lirio *nm* **1 :** iris **2 lirio de los valles** MUGUETE **:** lily of the valley

lirismo *nm* **:** lyricism

lirón *nm, pl* **lirones :** dormouse

lisiado[1], -da *adj* **:** disabled, crippled

lisiado[2], -da *n* **:** disabled person, cripple

lisiar *vt* **:** to cripple, to disable — **lisiarse** *vr*

liso, -sa *adj* **1 :** smooth **2 :** flat **3 :** straight <pelo liso : straight hair> **4 :** plain, unadorned <liso y llano : plain and simple>

lisonja *nf* **:** flattery

lisonjear *vt* ADULAR **:** to flatter

lista *nf* **1 :** list **2 :** roster, roll <pasar lista : to take attendance> **3 :** stripe, strip **4 :** menu

listado[1], -da *adj* **:** striped

listado[2] *nm* **:** listing

listar *vt* **:** to list

listeza *nf* **:** smartness, alertness

listo, -ta *adj* **1** DISPUESTO, PREPARADO **:** ready <¿estás listo? : are you ready?> **2 :** clever, smart

listón *nm, pl* **listones 1 :** ribbon **2 :** strip (of wood), lath **3 :** high bar (in sports)

lisura *nf* **:** smoothness

litera *nf* **:** bunk bed, berth

literal *adj* **:** literal — **literalmente** *adv*

literario, -ria *adj* **:** literary

literato, -ta *n* **:** writer, author

literatura *nf* **:** literature

litigante *adj & nmf* **:** litigant

litigar {52} *vi* **:** to litigate, to be in litigation

litigio *nm* **1 :** litigation, lawsuit **2 en ~ :** in dispute

litigioso, -sa *adj* **:** litigious

litio *nm* **:** lithium

litografía *nf* **1 :** lithography **2 :** lithograph

litógrafo, -fa *n* **:** lithographer

litoral[1] *adj* **:** coastal

litoral[2] *nm* **:** shore, seaboard

litosfera *nf* **:** lithosphere

litro *nm* **:** liter

lituano[1], -na *adj & n* **:** Lithuanian

lituano[2] *nm* **:** Lithuanian (language)

liturgia *nf* **:** liturgy

litúrgico, -ca *adj* **:** liturgical — **litúrgicamente** *adv*

liviandad *nf* LIGEREZA **:** lightness

liviano, -na *adj* **1 :** light, slight **2** INCONSTANTE **:** fickle

lividez *nf* PALIDEZ **:** pallor

lívido, -da *adj* **1** AMORATADO **:** livid **2** PÁLIDO **:** pallid, extremely pale

living *nm* **:** living room

llaga *nf* **:** sore, wound

llama *nf* **1 :** flame **2 :** llama

llamada *nf* **:** call <llamada a larga distancia : long-distance call> <llamada al orden : call to order>

llamado[1], -da *adj* **:** named, called <una mujer llamada Rosa : a woman called Rosa>

llamado[2] → **llamamiento**

llamador *nm* **:** door knocker

llamamiento *nm* **:** call, appeal

llamar *vt* **1 :** to name, to call **2 :** to call, to summon **3 :** to phone, to call up — **llamarse** *vr* **:** to be called, to be named <¿cómo te llamas? : what's your name?>

llamarada *nf* **1 :** flare-up, sudden blaze **2 :** flushing (of the face)

llamativo, -va *adj* **:** flashy, showy, striking

llameante *adj* **:** flaming, blazing

llamear *vi* **:** to flame, to blaze

llana *nf* **1 :** trowel **2** → **llano[2]**

llanamente *adv* **:** simply, plainly, straightforwardly

llaneza *nf* **:** simplicity, naturalness

llano[1], -na *adj* **1 :** even, flat **2 :** frank, open **3** LISO **:** plain, simple

llano[2] *nm* **:** plain

llanta *nf* **1** NEUMÁTICO **:** tire **2 :** rim

llantén *nm, pl* **llantenes :** plantain (weed)

llanto *nm* **:** crying, weeping

llanura *nf* **:** plain, prairie

llave *nf* **1 :** key **2 :** faucet **3** INTERRUPTOR **:** switch **4 :** brace (punctuation mark) **5 llave inglesa :** monkey wrench

llavero *nm* **:** key chain, key ring

llegada *nf* **:** arrival

llegar {52} *vi* **1 :** to arrive, to come **2 ~ a :** to arrive at, to reach, to amount to **3 ~ a :** to manage to <llegó a terminar la novela : she managed to finish the novel> **4 llegar a ser :** to become <llegó a ser un miembro permanente : he became a permanent member>

llegue, etc. → **llegar**

llenar *vt* **1 :** to fill, to fill up, to fill in **2 :** to meet, to fulfill <los regalos no llenaron sus expectativas : the gifts did not meet her expectations> — **llenarse** *vr* **:** to fill up, to become full

llenito, -ta *adj fam* REGORDETE **:** chubby, plump

lleno[1], -na *adj* **1 :** full, filled **2 de ~ :** completely, fully **3 estar lleno de sí mismo :** to be full of oneself

lleno[2] *nm* **1** *fam* **:** plenty, abundance **2 :** full house, sellout

llevadero, -ra *adj* **:** bearable

llevar *vt* **1 :** to take away, to carry <me gusta, me lo llevo : I like it, I'll take it> **2 :** to wear **3 :** to take, to lead <llevamos a Pedro al cine : we took Pedro to the movies> **4 llevar a cabo :** to carry out **5 llevar adelante :** to carry on, to keep going — *vi* **:** to lead <un problema lleva al otro : one problem leads to another> — *v aux* **:** to have <llevo mucho tiempo buscándolo : I've been looking for it for a long time> <lleva leído medio libro : he's halfway through the book> — **llevarse** *vr* **1** : to take away, to carry off **2** : to get along <siempre nos llevábamos bien : we always got along well>

llorar *vi* : to cry, to weep — *vt* : to mourn, to bewail

lloriquear *vi* : to whimper, to whine

lloriqueo *nm* : whimpering, whining

llorón, -rona *n, mpl* **llorones** : crybaby, whiner

lloroso, -sa *adj* : tearful, sad

llovedizo, -za *adj* : rain <agua llovediza : rainwater>

llover {47} *v impers* : to rain <está lloviendo : it's raining> <llover a cántaros : to rain cats and dogs> — *vi* : to rain down, to shower <le llovieron regalos : he was showered with gifts>

llovizna *nf* : drizzle, sprinkle

lloviznar *v impers* : to drizzle, to sprinkle

llueve, etc. → **llover**

lluvia *nf* **1** : rain, rainfall **2** : barrage, shower

lluvioso, -sa *adj* : rainy

lo[1] *pron* **1** : him, it <lo vi ayer : I saw him yesterday> <lo entiendo : I understand it> <no lo creo : I don't believe so> **2** (*formal, masculine*) : you <disculpe, señor, no lo oí : excuse me sir, I didn't hear you> **3 lo que** : what, that which <eso es lo que más le gusta : that's what he likes the most>

lo[2] *art* **1** : the <lo mejor : the best, the best thing> **2** : how <sé lo bueno que eres : I know how good you are>

loa *nf* : praise

loable *adj* : laudable, praiseworthy — **loablemente** *adv*

loar *vt* : to praise, to laud

lobato, -ta *n* : wolf cub

lobby *nm* : lobby, pressure group

lobo, -ba *n* : wolf

lóbrego, -ga *adj* SOMBRÍO : gloomy, dark

lobulado, -da *adj* : lobed

lóbulo *nm* : lobe <lóbulo de la oreja : earlobe>

locación *nf, pl* **-ciones 1** : location (in moviemaking) **2** *Mex* : place

local[1] *adj* : local — **localmente** *adv*

local[2] *nm* : premises *pl*

localidad *nf* : town, locality

localización *nf, pl* **-ciones 1** : locating, localization **2** : location

localizar {21} *vt* **1** UBICAR : to locate, to find **2** : to localize — **localizarse** *vr* UBICARSE : to be located <se localiza en el séptimo piso : it is located on the seventh floor>

locatario, -ria *n* : tenant

loción *nf, pl* **lociones** : lotion

lócker *nm, pl* **lóckers** : locker

loco[1], **-ca** *adj* **1** DEMENTE : crazy, insane, mad **2 a lo loco** : wildly, recklessly **3 volverse loco** : to go mad

loco[2], **-ca** *n* **1** : crazy person, lunatic **2 hacerse el loco** : to act the fool

locomoción *nf, pl* **-ciones** : locomotion

locomotor, -tora *adj* : locomotive

locomotora *nf* **1** : locomotive **2** : driving force

locuacidad *nf* : loquacity, talkativeness

locuaz *adj, pl* **locuaces** : loquacious, talkative

locución *nf, pl* **-ciones** : locution, phrase <locución adverbial : adverbial phrase>

locura *nf* **1** : insanity, madness **2** : crazy thing, folly

locutor, -tora *n* : announcer

lodazal *nm* : bog, quagmire

lodo *nm* BARRO : mud, mire

lodoso, -sa *adj* : muddy

logaritmo *nm* : logarithm

logia *nf* : lodge <logia masónica : Masonic lodge>

lógica *nf* : logic

lógico, -ca *adj* : logical — **lógicamente** *adv*

logística *nf* : logistics *pl*

logístico, -ca *adj* : logistic, logistical

logo *nm* → **logotipo**

logotipo *nm* : logo

logrado, -da *adj* : successful, well done

lograr *vt* **1** : to get, to obtain **2** : to achieve, to attain — **lograrse** *vr* : to be successful

logro *nm* : achievement, attainment

loma *nf* : hill, hillock

lombriz *nf, pl* **lombrices** : worm <lombriz de tierra : earthworm, night crawler> <lombriz solitaria : tapeworm> <tener lombrices : to have worms>

lomo *nm* **1** : back (of an animal) **2** : loin <lomo de cerdo : pork loin> **3** : spine (of a book) **4** : blunt edge (of a knife)

lona *nf* : canvas

loncha *nf* LONJA, REBANADA : slice

lonche *nm* **1** ALMUERZO : lunch **2** *Mex* : submarine sandwich

lonchería *nf Mex* : luncheonette

londinense[1] *adj* : of or from London

londinense[2] *nmf* : Londoner

longaniza *nf* : spicy pork sausage

longevidad *nf* : longevity

longevo, -va *adj* : long-lived

longitud *nf* **1** LARGO : length <longitud de onda : wavelength> **2** : longitude

longitudinal *adj* : longitudinal

lonja *nf* LONCHA, REBANADA : slice

lontananza *nf* : background <en lontananza : in the distance, far away>

lord *nm, pl* **lores** (*title in England*) : lord

loro *nm* : parrot

los[1], **las** *pron* **1** : them <hice galletas y se las di a los nuevos vecinos : I made cookies and gave them to the

new neighbors> **2 :** you <voy a llevarlos a los dos **:** I am going to take both of you> **3 los que, las que :** those, who, the ones <los que van a cantar deben venir temprano **:** those who are singing must come early> **4** (*used with* **haber**) <los hay en varios colores **:** they come in various colors>

los[2] → **el**[2]

losa *nf* **:** flagstone, paving stone

loseta *nf* BALDOSA **:** floor tile

lote *nm* **1 :** part, share **2 :** batch, lot **3 :** plot of land, lot

lotería *nf* **:** lottery

loto *nm* **:** lotus

loza *nf* **1 :** crockery, earthenware **2 :** china

lozanía *nf* **1 :** healthiness, robustness **2 :** luxuriance, lushness

lozano, -na *adj* **1 :** robust, healthy-looking <un rostro lozano **:** a smooth, fresh face> **2 :** lush, luxuriant

lubricante[1] *adj* **:** lubricating

lubricante[2] *nm* **:** lubricant

lubricar {72} *vt* **:** to lubricate, to oil — **lubricación** *nf*

lucero *nm* **:** bright star <lucero del alba **:** morning star>

lucha *nf* **1 :** struggle, fight **2 :** wrestling

luchador, -dora *n* **1 :** fighter **2 :** wrestler

luchar *vi* **1 :** to fight, to struggle **2 :** to wrestle

luchón, -chona *adj, mpl* **luchones** *Mex* **:** industrious, hardworking

lucidez *nf, pl* **-deces :** lucidity, clarity

lucido, -da *adj* MAGNÍFICO **:** magnificent, splendid

lúcido, -da *adj* **:** lucid

luciérnaga *nf* **:** firefly, glowworm

lucimiento *nm* **1 :** brilliance, splendor, sparkle **2 :** triumph, success <salir con lucimiento **:** to succeed with flying colors>

lucio *nm* **:** pike (fish)

lucir {45} *vi* **1 :** to shine **2 :** to look good, to stand out **3 :** to seem, to appear <ahora luce contento **:** he looks happy now> — *vt* **1 :** to wear, to sport **2 :** to flaunt, to show off — **lucirse** *vr* **1 :** to distinguish oneself, to excel **2 :** to show off

lucrarse *vr* **:** to make a profit

lucrativo, -va *adj* **:** lucrative, profitable — **lucrativamente** *adv*

lucro *nm* GANANCIA **:** profit, gain

luctuoso, -sa *adj* **:** mournful, tragic

luego[1] *adv* **1** DESPUÉS **:** then, afterwards **2 :** later (on) **3 desde ~ :** of course **4 ¡hasta luego! :** see you later! **5 luego que :** as soon as **6 luego luego** *Mex fam* **:** right away, immediately

luego[2] *conj* **:** therefore <pienso, luego existo **:** I think, therefore I am>

lugar *nm* **1 :** place, position <se llevó el primer lugar en su división **:** she took first place in her division> **2** ESPACIO **:** space, room **3 dar lugar a :** to give rise to, to lead to **4 en lugar de :** instead of **5 lugar común :** cliché, platitude **6 tener lugar :** to take place

lugareño[1], **-ña** *adj* **:** village, rural

lugareño[2], **-ña** *n* **:** villager

lugarteniente *nmf* **:** lieutenant, deputy

lúgubre *adj* **:** gloomy, lugubrious

lujo *nm* **1 :** luxury **2 de ~ :** deluxe

lujoso, -sa *adj* **:** luxurious

lujuria *nf* **:** lust, lechery

lujurioso, -sa *adj* **:** lustful, lecherous

lumbar *adj* **:** lumbar

lumbre *nf* **1** FUEGO **:** fire **2 :** brilliance, splendor **3 poner en la lumbre :** to put on the stove, to warm up

lumbrera *nf* **1 :** skylight **2 :** vent, port **3 :** brilliant person, luminary

luminaria *nf* **1 :** altar lamp **2** LUMBRERA **:** luminary, celebrity

luminiscencia *nf* **:** luminescence — **luminiscente** *adj*

luminosidad *nf* **:** luminosity, brightness

luminoso, -sa *adj* **:** shining, luminous

luna *nf* **1 :** moon **2 luna de miel :** honeymoon

lunar[1] *adj* **:** lunar

lunar[2] *nm* **1 :** mole, beauty spot **2 :** defect, blemish **3 :** polka dot

lunático, -ca *adj & n* **:** lunatic

lunes *nms & pl* **:** Monday

luneta *nf* **1 :** lens (of eyeglasses) **2 :** windshield (of an automobile) **3 :** crescent

lupa *nf* **:** magnifying glass

lúpulo *nm* **:** hops (plant)

lustrar *vt* **:** to shine, to polish

lustre *nm* **1** BRILLO **:** luster, shine **2 :** glory, distinction

lustroso, -sa *adj* BRILLOSO **:** lustrous, shiny

luto *nm* **:** mourning <estar de luto **:** to be in mourning>

luz *nf, pl* **luces 1 :** light **2 :** lighting **3** *fam* **:** electricity **4 :** window, opening **5 :** light, lamp **6 :** span, spread (between supports) **7 a la luz de :** in light of **8 dar a luz :** to give birth **9 traje de luces :** matador's costume

luzca, etc. → **lucir**

M

m *nf* **:** thirteenth letter of the Spanish alphabet

macabro, -bra *adj* **:** macabre

macaco[1], **-ca** *adj* **:** ugly, misshapen

macaco[2], **-ca** *n* **:** macaque

macadán *nm, pl* **-danes :** macadam

macana *nf* **1 :** club, cudgel **2** *fam* **:** nonsense, silliness **3** *fam* **:** lie, fib

macanudo, -da *adj fam* **:** great, fantastic

macarrón *nm, pl* **-rrones 1 :** macaroon **2 macarrones** *nmpl* **:** macaroni
maceta *nf* **1 :** flowerpot **2 :** mallet **3** *Mex fam* **:** head
machacar {72} *vt* **1 :** to crush, to grind **2 :** to beat, to pound — *vi* **:** to insist, to go on (about)
machacón, -cona *adj, mpl* **-cones :** insistent, tiresome
machete *nm* **:** machete
machetear *vt* **:** to hack with a machete — *vi Mex fam* **:** to plod, to work tirelessly
machismo *nm* **1 :** machismo **2 :** male chauvinism
machista *nm* **:** male chauvinist
macho¹ *adj* **1 :** male **2 :** macho, virile, tough
macho² *nm* **1 :** male **2 :** he-man
machote *nm* **1** *fam* **:** tough guy, he-man **2** *CA, Mex* **:** rough draft, model **3** *Mex* **:** blank form
machucar {72} *vt* **1 :** to pound, to beat, to crush **2 :** to bruise
machucón *nm, pl* **-cones 1** MORETÓN **:** bruise **2 :** smashing, pounding
macilento, -ta *adj* **:** gaunt, wan
macis *nm* **:** mace (spice)
macizo, -za *adj* **1 :** solid <oro macizo **:** solid gold> **2 :** strong, strapping **3 :** massive
macrocosmo *nm* **:** macrocosm
mácula *nf* **:** blemish, stain
madeja *nf* **1 :** skein, hank **2 :** tangle (of hair)
madera *nf* **1 :** wood **2 :** lumber, timber **3 madera dura** *or* **madera noble :** hardwood
maderero, -ra *adj* **:** timber, lumber
madero *nm* **:** piece of lumber, plank
madrastra *nf* **:** stepmother
madrazo *nm Mex fam* **:** punch, blow <se agarraron a madrazos **:** they beat each other up>
madre *nf* **1 :** mother **2 madre política :** mother-in-law **3 la Madre Patria :** the mother country (said of Spain)
madrear *vt Mex fam* **:** to beat up
madreperla *nf* NÁCAR **:** mother-of-pearl
madreselva *nf* **:** honeysuckle
madriguera *nf* **:** burrow, den, lair
madrileño¹, -ña *adj* **:** of or from Madrid
madrileño², -ña *n* **:** person from Madrid
madrina *nf* **1 :** godmother **2 :** bridesmaid **3 :** sponsor
madrugada *nf* **1 :** early morning, wee hours **2** ALBA **:** dawn, daybreak
madrugador, -dora *n* **:** early riser
madrugar {52} *vi* **1 :** to get up early **2 :** to get a head start
madurar *v* **1 :** to ripen **2 :** to mature
madurez *nf, pl* **-reces 1 :** maturity **2 :** ripeness
maduro, -ra *adj* **1 :** mature **2 :** ripe
maestría *nf* **1 :** mastery, skill **2 :** master's degree
maestro¹, -tra *adj* **1 :** masterly, skilled **2 :** chief, main **3 :** trained <un elefante maestro **:** a trained elephant>
maestro², -tra *n* **1 :** teacher (in grammar school) **2 :** expert, master **3 :** maestro
Mafia *nf* **:** Mafia
mafioso, -sa *n* **:** mafioso, gangster
magdalena *nf* **:** bun, muffin
magenta *adj & n* **:** magenta
magia *nf* **:** magic
mágico, -ca *adj* **:** magic, magical — **mágicamente** *adv*
magisterio *nm* **1 :** teaching **2 :** teachers *pl,* teaching profession
magistrado, -da *n* **:** magistrate, judge
magistral *adj* **1 :** masterful, skillful **2 :** magisterial
magistralmente *adv* **:** masterfully, brilliantly
magistratura *nf* **:** judgeship, magistracy
magma *nm* **:** magma
magnanimidad *nf* **:** magnanimity
magnánimo, -ma *adj* GENEROSO **:** magnanimous — **magnánimamente** *adv*
magnate *nmf* **:** magnate, tycoon
magnesia *nf* **:** magnesia
magnesio *nm* **:** magnesium
magnético, -ca *adj* **:** magnetic
magnetismo *nm* **:** magnetism
magnetizar {21} *vt* **:** to magnetize
magnetófono *nm* **:** tape recorder
magnetofónico, -ca *adj* **cinta magnetofónica :** magnetic tape
magnificar {72} *vt* **1 :** to magnify **2** EXAGERAR **:** to exaggerate **3** ENSALZAR **:** to exalt, to extol, to praise highly
magnificencia *nf* **:** magnificence, splendor
magnífico, -ca *adj* ESPLENDOROSO **:** magnificent, splendid — **magníficamente** *adv*
magnitud *nf* **:** magnitude
magnolia *nf* **:** magnolia (flower)
magnolio *nm* **:** magnolia (tree)
mago, -ga *n* **1 :** magician **2 :** wizard (in folk tales, etc.) **3 los Reyes Magos :** the Magi
magro, -gra *adj* **1 :** lean (of meat) **2 :** meager
maguey *nm* **:** maguey
magulladura *nf* MORETÓN **:** bruise
magullar *vt* **:** to bruise — **magullarse** *vr*
mahometano¹, -na *adj* ISLÁMICO **:** Islamic, Muslim
mahometano², -na *n* **:** Muslim
mahonesa *nf* → **mayonesa**
maicena *nf* **:** cornstarch
maíz *nm* **:** corn, maize
maizal *nm* **:** cornfield
maja *nf* **:** pestle
majadería *nf* **1** TONTERÍA **:** stupidity, foolishness **2** *Mex* LEPERADA **:** insult, obscenity
majadero¹, -ra *adj* **1 :** foolish, silly **2** *Mex* LÉPERO **:** crude, vulgar

majadero[2], -ra *n* **1** TONTO : fool **2** *Mex* : rude person, boor
majar *vt* : to crush, to mash
majestad *nf* : majesty <Su Majestad : Your Majesty>
majestuosamente *adv* : majestically
majestuosidad *nf* : majesty, grandeur
majestuoso, -sa *adj* : majestic, stately
majo, -ja *adj Spain* **1** : nice, likeable **2** GUAPO : attractive, good-looking
mal[1] *adv* **1** : badly, poorly <baila muy mal : he dances very badly> **2** : wrong, incorrectly <me entendió mal : she misunderstood me> **3** : with difficulty, hardly <mal puedo oírte : I can hardly hear you> **4 de mal en peor** : from bad to worse **5 menos mal** : it could have been worse
mal[2] *adj* → **malo**
mal[3] *nm* **1** : evil, wrong **2** DAÑO : harm, damage **3** DESGRACIA : misfortune **4** ENFERMEDAD : illness, sickness
malabar *adj* **juegos malabares** : juggling
malabarista *nmf* : juggler
malaconsejado, -da *adj* : ill-advised
malacostumbrado, -da *adj* CONSENTIDO : spoiled, pampered
malacostumbrar *vt* : to spoil
malagradecido, -da *adj* INGRATO : ungrateful
malaisio → **malasio**
malaquita *nf* : malachite
malaria *nf* PALUDISMO : malaria
malasio, -sia *adj & n* : Malaysian
malaventura *nf* : misadventure, misfortune
malaventurado, -da *adj* MALHADADO : ill-fated, unfortunate
malayo, -ya *adj & n* : Malay, Malayan
malbaratar *vt* **1** MALGASTAR : to squander **2** : to undersell
malcriado[1], -da *adj* **1** : ill-bred, bad-mannered **2** : spoiled, pampered
malcriado[2], -da *n* : spoiled brat
maldad *nf* **1** : evil, wickedness **2** : evil deed
maldecir {11} *vt* : to curse, to damn — *vi* **1** : to curse, to swear **2 ~ de** : to speak ill of, to slander, to defame
maldición *nf, pl* **-ciones** : curse
maldiga, maldijo, etc. → **maldecir**
maldito, -ta *adj* **1** : cursed, damned <¡maldita sea! : damn it all!> **2** : wicked
maldoso, -sa *adj Mex* : mischievous
maleable *adj* : malleable
maleante *nmf* : crook, thug
malecón *nm, pl* **-cones** : jetty, breakwater
maleducado, -da *adj* : ill-mannered, rude
maleficio *nm* : curse, hex
maléfico, -ca *adj* : evil, harmful
malentender {56} *vt* : to misunderstand
malentendido *nm* : misunderstanding
malestar *nm* **1** : discomfort **2** IRRITACIÓN : annoyance **3** INQUIETUD : uneasiness, unrest
maleta *nf* : suitcase, bag <haz tus maletas : pack your bags>
maletero[1], -ra *n* : porter
maletero[2] *nm* : trunk (of an automobile)
maletín *nm, pl* **-tines** **1** PORTAFOLIO : briefcase **2** : overnight bag, satchel
malevolencia *nf* : malevolence, wickedness
malévolo, -la *adj* : malevolent, wicked
maleza *nf* **1** : thicket, underbrush **2** : weeds *pl*
malformación *nf, pl* **-ciones** : malformation
malgache *adj & nmf* : Madagascan
malgastar *vt* : to squander (resources), to waste (time, effort)
malhablado, -da *adj* : foul-mouthed
malhadado, -da *adj* MALAVENTURADO : ill-fated
malhechor, -chora *n* : criminal, delinquent, wrongdoer
malherir {76} *vt* : to injure seriously
malhumor *nm* : bad mood, sullenness
malhumorado, -da *adj* : bad-tempered, cross
malicia *nf* **1** : wickedness, malice **2** : mischief, naughtiness **3** : cunning, craftiness
malicioso, -sa *adj* **1** : malicious **2** PÍCARO : mischievous
malignidad *nf* **1** : malignancy **2** MALDAD : evil
maligno, -na *adj* **1** : malignant <un tumor maligno : a malignant tumor> **2** : evil, harmful, malign
malinchismo *nm Mex* : preference for foreign goods or people — **malinchista** *adj*
malintencionado, -da *adj* : malicious, spiteful
malinterpretar *vt* : to misinterpret
malla *nf* **1** : mesh **2** LEOTARDO : leotard, tights *pl* **3 malla de baño** : bathing suit
mallorquín, -quina *adj & n* : Majorcan
malnutrición *nf, pl* **-ciones** DESNUTRICIÓN : malnutrition
malnutrido, -da *adj* DESNUTRIDO : malnourished, undernourished
malo[1], -la *adj* (**mal** *before masculine singular nouns*) **1** : bad <mala suerte : bad luck> **2** : wicked, naughty **3** : cheap, poor (quality) **4** : harmful <malo para la salud : bad for one's health> **5** (*using the form* **mal**) : unwell <estar mal del corazón : to have heart trouble> **6 estar de malas** : to be in a bad mood
malo[2], -la *n* : villain, bad guy (in novels, movies, etc.)
malogrado, -da *adj* : failed, unsuccessful
malograr *vt* **1** : to spoil, to ruin **2** : to waste (an opportunity, time) — **mal-**

ograrse *vr* **1** FRACASAR **:** to fail **2 :** to die young
malogro *nm* **1 :** untimely death **2** FRACASO **:** failure
maloliente *adj* HEDIONDO **:** foul-smelling, smelly
malparado, -da *adj* **salir malparado** *or* **quedar malparado :** to come out of (something) badly, to end up in a bad state
malpensado, -da *adj* **:** distrustful, suspicious, nasty-minded
malquerencia *nf* AVERSIÓN **:** ill will, dislike
malquerer {64} *vt* **:** to dislike
malquiso, etc. → **malquerer**
malsano, -na *adj* **:** unhealthy
malsonante *adj* **:** rude, offensive <palabras malsonantes **:** foul language>
malta *nf* **:** malt
malteada *nf* **:** malted milk <malteada de chocolate **:** chocolate malt>
maltés, -tesa *adj & n, mpl* **malteses :** Maltese
maltratar *vt* **1 :** to mistreat, to abuse **2 :** to damage, to spoil
maltrato *nm* **:** mistreatment, abuse
maltrecho, -cha *adj* **:** battered, damaged
malucho, -cha *adj fam* **:** sick, under the weather
malva *adj & nm* **:** mauve
malvado[1], -da *adj* **:** evil, wicked
malvado[2], -da *n* **:** evildoer, wicked person
malvavisco *nm* **:** marshmallow
malvender *vt* **:** to sell at a loss
malversación *nf, pl* **-ciones :** misappropriation (of funds), embezzlement
malversador, -dora *n* **:** embezzler
malversar *vt* **:** to embezzle
malvivir *vi* **:** to live badly, to just scrape by
mamá *nf fam* **:** mom, mama
mamar *vi* **1 :** to suckle **2 darle de mamar a :** to breast-feed — *vt* **1 :** to suckle, to nurse **2 :** to learn from childhood, to grow up with — **mamarse** *vr fam* **:** to get drunk
mamario, -ria *adj* **:** mammary
mamarracho *nm fam* **1** ESPERPENTO **:** mess, sight **2 :** laughingstock, fool **3 :** rubbish, junk
mambo *nm* **:** mambo
mami *nf fam* **:** mommy
mamífero[1], -ra *adj* **:** mammalian
mamífero[2] *nm* **:** mammal
mamila *nf* **1 :** nipple **2** *Mex* **:** baby bottle, pacifier
mamografía *nf* **:** mammogram
mamola *nf* **:** pat, chuck under the chin
mamotreto *nm fam* **1 :** huge book, tome **2** ARMATOSTE **:** hulk, monstrosity
mampara *nf* BIOMBO **:** screen, room divider
mamparo *nm* **:** bulkhead
mampostería *nf* **:** masonry, stonemasonery
mampostero *nm* **:** mason, stonemason
mamut *nm, pl* **mamuts :** mammoth
maná *nm* **:** manna
manada *nf* **1 :** flock, herd, pack **2** *fam* **:** horde, mob <llegaron en manada **:** they came in droves>
manantial *nm* **1** FUENTE **:** spring **2 :** source
manar *vi* **1 :** to flow **2 :** to abound
manatí *nm* **:** manatee
mancha *nf* **1 :** stain, spot, mark <mancha de sangre **:** bloodstain> **2 :** blemish, blot <una mancha en su reputación **:** a blemish on his reputation> **3 :** patch
manchado, -da *adj* **:** stained
manchar *vt* **1** ENSUCIAR **:** to stain, to soil **2** DESHONRAR **:** to sully, to tarnish — **mancharse** *vr* **:** to get dirty
mancillar vt **:** to sully, to besmirch
manco, -ca *adj* **:** one-armed, one-handed
mancomunar *vt* **:** to combine, to pool — **mancomunarse** *vr* **:** to unite, to join together
mancomunidad *nf* **1 :** commonwealth **2 :** association, confederation
mancuernas *nfpl* **:** cuff links
mancuernillas *nf Mex* **:** cuff links
mandadero, -ra *n* **:** errand boy *m,* errand girl *f,* messenger
mandado *nm* **1 :** order, command **2 :** errand <hacer los mandados **:** to run errands, to go shopping>
mandamás *nmf, pl* **-mases** *fam* **:** boss, bigwig, honcho
mandamiento *nm* **1 :** commandment **2 :** command, order, warrant <mandamiento judicial **:** warrant, court order>
mandar *vt* **1** ORDENAR **:** to command, to order **2** ENVIAR **:** to send <te manda saludos **:** he sends you his regards> **3** ECHAR **:** to hurl, to throw **4 ¿mande?** *Mex* **:** yes?, pardon? — *vi* **:** to be the boss, to be in charge — **mandarse** *vr Mex* **:** to take liberties, to take advantage
mandarina *nf* **:** mandarin orange, tangerine
mandatario, -ria *n* **1 :** leader (in politics) <primer mandatario **:** head of state> **2 :** agent (in law)
mandato *nm* **1 :** term of office **2 :** mandate
mandíbula *nf* **1 :** jaw **2 :** mandible
mandil *nm* **1** DELANTAL **:** apron **2 :** horse blanket
mandilón *nm, pl* **-lones** *fam* **:** wimp, coward
mandioca *nf* **1 :** manioc, cassava **2 :** tapioca
mando *nm* **1 :** command, leadership **2 :** control (for a device) <mando a distancia **:** remote control> **3 al mando de :** in charge of **4 al mando de :** under the command of
mandolina *nf* **:** mandolin
mandón, -dona *adj, mpl* **mandones :** bossy, domineering

mandonear *vt fam* MANGONEAR : to boss around
mandrágora *nf* : mandrake
manecilla *nf* : hand (of a clock), pointer
manejable *adj* **1** : manageable **2** : docile, easily led
manejar *vt* **1** CONDUCIR : to drive (a car) **2** OPERAR : to handle, to operate **3** : to manage **4** : to manipulate (a person) — *vi* : to drive — **manejarse** *vr* **1** COMPORTARSE : to behave **2** : to get along, to manage
manejo *nm* **1** : handling, operation **2** : management
manera *nf* **1** MODO : way, manner, fashion **2 de cualquier manera** *or* **de todas maneras** : anyway, anyhow **3 de manera que** : so, in order that **4 de ninguna manera** : by no means, absolutely not **5 manera de ser** : personality, demeanor
manga *nf* **1** : sleeve **2** MANGUERA : hose
manganeso *nm* : manganese
mangle *nm* : mangrove
mango *nm* **1** : hilt, handle **2** : mango
mangonear *vt fam* : to boss around, to bully — *vi* **1** : to be bossy **2** : to loaf, to fool around
mangosta *nf* : mongoose
manguera *nf* : hose
maní *nm, pl* **maníes** : peanut
manía *nf* **1** OBSESIÓN : mania, obsession **2** : craze, fad **3** : odd habit, peculiarity **4** : dislike, aversion
maníaco¹, -ca *adj* : maniacal
maníaco², -ca *n* : maniac
maniatar *vt* : to tie the hands of, to manacle
maniático¹, -ca *adj* **1** MANÍACO : maniacal **2** : obsessive **3** : fussy, finicky
maniático², -ca *n* **1** MANÍACO : maniac, lunatic **2** : obsessive person, fanatic **3** : eccentric, crank
manicomio *nm* : insane asylum, madhouse
manicura *nf* : manicure
manicuro, -ra *n* : manicurist
manido, -da *adj* : hackneyed, stale, trite
manifestación *nf, pl* **-ciones 1** : manifestation, sign **2** : demonstration, rally
manifestante *nmf* : demonstrator
manifestar {55} *vt* **1** : to demonstrate, to show **2** : to declare — **manifestarse** *vr* **1** : to be or become evident **2** : to state one's position <se han manifestado a favor del acuerdo : they have declared their support for the agreement> **3** : to demonstrate, to rally
manifiesto¹, -ta *adj* : manifest, evident, clear — **manifiestamente** *adv*
manifiesto² *nm* : manifesto
manija *nf* MANGO : handle
manilla *nf* → **manecilla**
manillar *nm* : handlebars *pl*
maniobra *nf* : maneuver, stratagem
maniobrar *v* : to maneuver
manipulación *nf, pl* **-ciones** : manipulation
manipulador¹, -dora *adj* : manipulating, manipulative
manipulador², -dora *n* : manipulator
manipular *vt* **1** : to manipulate **2** MANEJAR : to handle
maniquí¹ *nmf, pl* **-quíes** : mannequin, model
maniquí² *nm, pl* **-quíes** : mannequin, dummy
manirroto¹, -ta *adj* : extravagant
manirroto², -ta *n* : spendthrift
manivela *nf* : crank
manjar *nm* : delicacy, special dish
mano¹ *nf* **1** : hand **2** : coat (of paint or varnish) **3 a ~** : by hand **4 a ~** *or* **a la mano** : handy, at hand, nearby **5 darse la mano** : to shake hands **6 de la mano** : hand in hand <la política y la economía van de la mano : politics and economics go hand in hand> **7 de primera mano** : firsthand, at firsthand **8 de segunda mano** : secondhand <ropa de segunda mano : secondhand clothing> **9 mano a mano** : one-on-one **10 mano de obra** : labor, manpower **11 mano de mortero** : pestle **12 echar una mano** : to lend a hand **13** *Mex fam* **mano negra** : shady dealings *pl*
mano², -na *n Mex fam* : buddy, pal <¡oye, mano! : hey man!>
manojo *nm* PUÑADO : handful, bunch
manopla *nf* **1** : mitten, mitt **2** : brass knuckles *pl*
manosear *vt* **1** : to handle or touch excessively **2** ACARICIAR : to fondle, to caress
manotazo *nm* : slap, smack, swipe
manotear *vi* : to wave one's hands, to gesticulate
mansalva *adv* **a ~** : at close range
mansarda *nf* BUHARDILLA : attic
mansedumbre *nf* **1** : gentleness, meekness **2** : tameness
mansión *nf, pl* **-siones** : mansion
manso, -sa *adj* **1** : gentle, meek **2** : tame — **mansamente** *adv*
manta *nf* **1** COBIJA, FRAZADA : blanket **2** : poncho **3** *Mex* : coarse cotton fabric
manteca *nf* **1** GRASA : lard, fat **2** : butter
mantecoso, -sa *adj* : buttery
mantel *nm* **1** : tablecloth **2** : altar cloth
mantelería *nf* : table linen
mantener {80} *vt* **1** SUSTENTAR : to support, to feed <mantener uno su familia : to support one's family> **2** CONSERVAR : to keep, to preserve **3** CONTINUAR : to keep up, to sustain <mantener una correspondencia : to keep up a correspondence> **4** AFIRMAR : to maintain, to affirm — **mantenerse** *vr* **1** : to support oneself, to subsist **2 mantenerse firme** : to hold one's ground
mantenimiento *nm* **1** : maintenance, upkeep **2** : sustenance, food **3** : preservation

mantequera *nf* **1** : churn **2** : butter dish
mantequería *nf* **1** : creamery, dairy **2** : grocery store
mantequilla *nf* : butter
mantilla *nf* : mantilla
manto *nm* **1** : cloak **2** : mantle (in geology)
mantón *nm, pl* **-tones** CHAL : shawl
mantuvo, etc. → **mantener**
manual[1] *adj* **1** : manual <trabajo manual : manual labor> **2** : handy, manageable — **manualmente** *adv*
manual[2] *nm* : manual, handbook
manualidades *nfpl* : handicrafts (in schools)
manubrio *nm* **1** : handle, crank **2** : handlebars *pl*
manufactura *nf* **1** FABRICACIÓN : manufacture **2** : manufactured item, product **3** FÁBRICA : factory
manufacturar *vt* FABRICAR : to manufacture
manufacturero[1], **-ra** *adj* : manufacturing
manufacturero[2], **-ra** *n* FABRICANTE : manufacturer
manuscrito[1], **-ta** *adj* : handwritten
manuscrito[2] *nm* : manuscript
manutención *nf, pl* **-ciones** : maintenance, support
manzana *nf* **1** : apple **2** CUADRA : block (enclosed by streets or buildings) **3** *or* **manzana de Adán** : Adam's apple
manzanal *nm* **1** : apple orchard **2** MANZANO : apple tree
manzanar *nm* : apple orchard
manzanilla *nf* **1** : chamomile **2** : chamomile tea
manzano *nm* : apple tree
maña *nf* **1** : dexterity, skill **2** : cunning, guile **3 mañas** *or* **malas mañas** *nfpl* : bad habits, vices
mañana *nf* **1** : morning **2** : tomorrow
mañanero, -ra *adj* MATUTINO : morning <rocío mañanero : morning dew>
mañanitas *nfpl Mex* : birthday serenade
mañoso, -sa *adj* **1** HÁBIL : skillful **2** ASTUTO : cunning, crafty **3** : fussy, finicky
mapa *nm* CARTA : map
mapache *nm* : raccoon
mapamundi *nm* : map of the world
maqueta *nf* : model, mock-up
maquillador, -dora *n* : makeup artist
maquillaje *nm* : makeup
maquillarse *vr* : to put on makeup, to make oneself up
máquina *nf* **1** : machine <máquina de coser : sewing machine> <máquina de escribir : typewriter> **2** LOCOMOTORA : engine, locomotive **3** : machine (in politics) **4 a toda máquina** : at full speed
maquinación *nf, pl* **-ciones** : machination, scheme, plot
maquinal *adj* : mechanical, automatic — **maquinalmente** *adv*
maquinar *vt* : to plot, to scheme
maquinaria *nf* **1** : machinery **2** : mechanism, works *pl*
maquinilla *nf* **1** : small machine or device **2** *CA, Car* : typewriter
maquinista *nmf* **1** : machinist **2** : railroad engineer
mar *nmf* **1** : sea <un mar agitado : a rough sea> <hacerse a la mar : to set sail> **2 alta mar** : high seas
maraca *nf* : maraca
maraña *nf* **1** : thicket **2** ENREDO : tangle, mess
marasmo *nm* : paralysis, stagnation
maratón *nm, pl* **-tones** : marathon
maravilla *nf* **1** : wonder, marvel <a las mil maravillas : wonderfully, marvelously> <hacer maravillas : to work wonders> **2** : marigold
maravillar *vt* ASOMBRAR : to astonish, to amaze — **maravillarse** *vr* : to be amazed, to marvel
maravilloso, -sa *adj* ESTUPENDO : wonderful, marvelous — **maravillosamente** *adv*
marbete *nm* **1** ETIQUETA : label, tag **2** *PRi* : registration sticker (of a car)
marca *nf* **1** : mark **2** : brand, make **3** : trademark <marca registrada : registered trademark> **4** : record (in sports) <batir la marca : to beat the record>
marcado, -da *adj* : marked <un marcado contraste : a marked contrast>
marcador *nm* **1** TANTEADOR : scoreboard **2** : marker, felt-tipped pen **3 marcador de libros** : bookmark
marcaje *nm* **1** : scoring (in sports) **2** : guarding (in sports)
marcapasos *nms & pl* : pacemaker
marcar {72} *vt* **1** : to mark **2** : to brand (livestock) **3** : to indicate, to show **4** RESALTAR : to emphasize **5** : to dial (a telephone) **6** : to guard (an opponent) **7** ANOTAR : to score (a goal, a point) — *vi* **1** ANOTAR : to score **2** : to dial
marcha *nf* **1** : march **2** : hike, walk <ir de marcha : to go hiking> **3** : pace, speed <a toda marcha : at top speed> **4** : gear (of an automobile) <marcha atrás : reverse, reverse gear> **5 en ~** : in motion, in gear, under way
marchar *vi* **1** IR : to go, to travel **2** ANDAR : to walk **3** FUNCIONAR : to work, to go **4** : to march — **marcharse** *vr* : to leave
marchitar *vi* : to make wither, to wilt — **marchitarse** *vr* **1** : to wither, to shrivel up, to wilt **2** : to languish, to fade away
marchito, -ta *adj* : withered, faded
marcial *adj* : martial, military
marco *nm* **1** : frame, framework **2** : goalposts *pl* **3** AMBIENTE : setting, atmosphere **4** : mark (unit of currency)
marea *nf* : tide
mareado, -da *adj* **1** : dizzy, lightheaded **2** : queasy, nauseous **3** : seasick

marear *vt* **1 :** to make sick <los gases me marearon : the fumes made me sick> **2 :** to bother, to annoy — **marearse** *vr* **1 :** to get sick, to become nauseated **2 :** to feel dizzy **3 :** to get tipsy

marejada *nf* **1 :** surge, swell (of the sea) **2 :** undercurrent, ferment, unrest

maremoto *nm* **:** tidal wave

mareo *nm* **1 :** dizzy spell **2 :** nausea **3 :** seasickness, motion sickness **4 :** annoyance, vexation

marfil *nm* **:** ivory

margarina *nf* **:** margarine

margarita *nf* **1 :** daisy **2 :** margarita (cocktail)

margen[1] *nf, pl* **márgenes :** bank (of a river), side (of a street)

margen[2] *nm, pl* **márgenes 1 :** edge, border **2 :** margin <margen de ganancia : profit margin>

marginación *nf, pl* **-ciones :** marginalization, exclusion

marginado[1], **-da** *adj* **1** DESHEREDADO **:** outcast, alienated, dispossessed **2 clases marginadas :** underclass

marginado[2], **-da** *n* **:** outcast, misfit

marginal *adj* **:** marginal, fringe

marginalidad *nf* **:** marginality

marginar *vt* **:** to ostracize, to exclude

mariachi *nm* **:** mariachi musician or band

maridaje *nm* **:** marriage, union

maridar *vt* UNIR **:** to marry, to unite

marido *nm* ESPOSO **:** husband

marihuana *or* **mariguana** *or* **marijuana** *nf* **:** marihuana

marimacho *nmf fam* **1 :** mannish woman **2 :** tomboy

marimba *nf* **:** marimba

marina *nf* **1 :** coast, coastal area **2 :** navy, fleet <marina mercante : merchant marine>

marinada *nf* **:** marinade

marinar *vt* **:** to marinate

marinero[1], **-ra** *adj* **1 :** seaworthy **2 :** sea, marine

marinero[2] *nm* **:** sailor

marino[1], **-na** *adj* **:** marine, sea

marino[2] *nm* **:** sailor, seaman

marioneta *nf* TÍTERE **:** puppet, marionette

mariposa *nf* **1 :** butterfly **2 mariposa nocturna :** moth

mariquita[1] *nf* **:** ladybug

mariquita[2] *nm fam* **:** sissy, wimp

mariscal *nm* **1 :** marshal **2 mariscal de campo :** field marshal (in the military), quarterback (in football)

marisco *nm* **1 :** shellfish **2 mariscos** *nmpl* **:** seafood

marisma *nf* **:** marsh, salt marsh

marital *adj* **:** marital, married <la vida marital : married life>

marítimo, -ma *adj* **:** maritime, shipping <la industria marítima : the shipping industry>

marmita *nf* **:** (cooking) pot

mármol *nm* **:** marble

marmóreo, -rea *adj* **:** marble, marmoreal

marmota *nf* **1 :** marmot **2 marmota de América :** woodchuck, groundhog

maroma *nf* **1 :** rope **2 :** acrobatic stunt **3** *Mex* **:** somersault

marque, etc. → **marcar**

marqués, -quesa *n, mpl* **marqueses :** marquis *m,* marquess *m,* marquise *f,* marchioness *f*

marquesina *nf* **:** marquee, canopy

marqueta *nf Mex* **:** block (of chocolate), lump (of sugar or salt)

marranada *nf* **1 :** disgusting thing **2 :** dirty trick

marrano[1], **-na** *adj* **:** filthy, disgusting

marrano[2], **-na** *n* **1** CERDO **:** pig, hog **2 :** dirty pig, slob

marrar *vt* **:** to miss (a target) — *vi* **:** to fail, to go wrong

marras *adv* **1 :** long ago **2 de ~ :** said, aforementioned <el individuo de marras : the individual in question>

marrasquino *nm* **:** maraschino

marrón *adj & nm, pl* **marrones** CASTAÑO **:** brown

marroquí *adj & nmf, pl* **-quíes :** Moroccan

marsopa *nf* **:** porpoise

marsupial *nm* **:** marsupial

marta *nf* **1 :** marten **2 marta cebellina :** sable (animal)

Marte *nm* **:** Mars

martes *nms & pl* **:** Tuesday

martillar *v* **:** to hammer

martillazo *nm* **:** blow with a hammer

martillo *nm* **1 :** hammer **2 martillo neumático :** jackhammer

martinete *nm* **1 :** heron **2 :** pile driver

mártir *nmf* **:** martyr

martirio *nm* **1 :** martyrdom **2 :** ordeal, torment

martirizar {21} *vt* **1 :** to martyr **2** ATORMENTAR **:** to torment

marxismo *nm* **:** Marxism

marxista *adj & nmf* **:** Marxist

marzo *nm* **:** March

mas *conj* PERO **:** but

más[1] *adv* **1 :** more <¿hay algo más grande? : is there anything bigger?> **2 :** most <Luis es el más alto : Luis is the tallest> **3 :** longer <el sabor dura más : the flavor lasts longer> **4 :** rather <más querría andar : I would rather walk> **5 a ~ :** besides, in addition **6 más allá :** further **7 qué . . . más . . . :** what . . ., what a . . . <¡qué día más bonito! : what a beautiful day!>

más[2] *adj* **1 :** more <dáme dos kilos más : give me two more kilos> **2 :** most <la que ganó más dinero : the one who earned the most money> **3 :** else <¿quién más quiere vino? : who else wants wine?>

más[3] *n* **:** plus sign

más[4] *prep* **:** plus <tres más dos es igual a cinco : three plus two equals five>

más[5] *pron* **1 :** more <¿tienes más? : do you have more?> **2 a lo más :** at most **3 de ~ :** extra, excess **4 más o menos :** more or less, approximately **5 por más que :** no matter how much <por más que corras no llegarás a tiempo : no matter how fast you run you won't arrive on time>
masa *nf* **1 :** mass, volume <masa atómica : atomic mass> <producción en masa : mass production> **2 :** dough, batter **3 masas** *nfpl* **:** people, masses <las masas populares : the common people> **4 masa harina** *Mex* **:** corn flour (for tortillas, etc.)
masacrar *vt* **:** to massacre
masacre *nf* **:** massacre
masaje *nm* **:** massage
masajear *vt* **:** to massage
masajista *nmf* **:** masseur *m,* masseuse *f*
mascar {72} *v* MASTICAR **:** to chew
máscara *nf* **1** CARETA **:** mask **2 :** appearance, pretense
mascarada *nf* **:** masquerade
mascarilla *nf* **1 :** mask (in medicine) <mascarilla de oxígeno : oxygen mask> **2 :** facial mask (in cosmetology)
mascota *nf* **:** mascot
masculinidad *nf* **:** masculinity
masculino, -na *adj* **1 :** masculine, male **2 :** manly **3 :** masculine (in grammar)
mascullar *v* **:** to mumble, to mutter
masificado, -da *adj* **:** overcrowded
masilla *nf* **:** putty
masivamente *adv* **:** en masse
masivo, -va *adj* **:** mass <comunicación masiva : mass communication>
masón *nm, pl* **masones** FRANCMASÓN **:** Mason, Freemason
masonería *nf* FRANCMASONERÍA **:** Masonry, Freemasonry
masónico, -ca *adj* **:** Masonic
masoquismo *nm* **:** masochism
masoquista[1] *adj* **:** masochistic
masoquista[2] *nmf* **:** masochist
masque, etc. → **mascar**
masticar {72} *v* MASCAR **:** to chew, to masticate
mástil *nm* **1 :** mast **2** ASTA **:** flagpole **3 :** neck (of a stringed instrument)
mastín *nm, pl* **mastines :** mastiff
mástique *nm* **:** putty, filler
mastodonte *nm* **:** mastodon
masturbación *nf, pl* **-ciones :** masturbation
masturbarse *vr* **:** to masturbate
mata *nf* **1** ARBUSTO **:** bush, shrub **2 :** plant <mata de tomate : tomato plant> **3 :** sprig, tuft **4 mata de pelo :** mop of hair
matadero *nm* **:** slaughterhouse, abattoir
matado, -da *adj Mex* **:** strenuous, exhausting
matador *nm* TORERO **:** matador, bullfighter
matamoscas *nms & pl* **:** flyswatter
matanza *nf* MASACRE **:** slaughter, butchering
matar *vt* **1 :** to kill **2 :** to slaughter, to butcher **3** APAGAR **:** to extinguish, to put out (fire, light) **4 :** to tone down (colors) **5 :** to pass, to waste (time) **6 :** to trump (in card games) — *vi* **:** to kill — **matarse** *vr* **1 :** to be killed **2** SUICIDARSE **:** to commit suicide **3** *fam* **:** to exhaust oneself <se mató tratando de terminarlo : he knocked himself out trying to finish it>
matasanos *nms & pl fam* **:** quack
matasellar *vt* **:** to cancel (a stamp), to postmark
matasellos *nms & pl* **:** postmark
matatena *nf Mex* **:** jacks
mate[1] *adj* **:** matte, dull
mate[2] *nm* **1 :** maté **2 jaque mate :** checkmate <darle mate a *or* darle jaque mate a : to checkmate>
matemática → **matemáticas**
matemáticas *nfpl* **:** mathematics, math
matemático[1]**, -ca** *adj* **:** mathematical — **matemáticamente** *adv*
matemático[2]**, -ca** *n* **:** mathematician
materia *nf* **1 :** matter <materia gris : gray matter> **2 :** material <materia prima : raw material> **3 :** (academic) subject **4 en materia de :** on the subject of, concerning
material[1] *adj* **1 :** material, physical, real **2 daños materiales :** property damage
material[2] *nm* **1 :** material <material de construcción : building material> **2** EQUIPO **:** equipment, gear
materialismo *nm* **:** materialism
materialista[1] *adj* **:** materialistic
materialista[2] *nmf* **1 :** materialist **2** *Mex* **:** truck driver
materializar {21} *vt* **:** to bring to fruition, to realize — **materializarse** *vr* **:** to materialize, to come into being
materialmente *adv* **1 :** materially, physically <materialmente imposible : physically impossible> **2 :** really, absolutely
maternal *adj* **:** maternal, motherly
maternidad *nf* **1 :** maternity, motherhood **2 :** maternity hospital, maternity ward
materno, -na *adj* **:** maternal
matinal *adj* MATUTINO **:** morning <la pálida luz matinal : the pale morning light>
matinée *or* **matiné** *nf* **:** matinee
matiz *nm, pl* **matices 1 :** hue, shade **2 :** nuance
matización *nf, pl* **-ciones 1 :** tinting, toning, shading **2 :** clarification (of a statement)
matizar {21} *vt* **1 :** to tinge, to tint (colors) **2 :** to vary, to modulate (sounds) **3 :** to qualify (statements)
matón *nm, pl* **matones :** thug, bully
matorral *nm* **1 :** thicket **2 :** scrub, scrubland

matraca *nf* **1** : rattle, noisemaker **2 dar la matraca a** : to pester, to nag
matriarca *nf* : matriarch
matriarcado *nm* : matriarchy
matrícula *nf* **1** : list, roll, register **2** INSCRIPCIÓN : registration, enrollment **3** : license plate, registration number
matriculación *nf, pl* **-ciones** : matriculation, registration
matricular *vt* **1** INSCRIBIR : to enroll, to register (a person) **2** : to register (a vehicle) — **matricularse** *vr* : to matriculate
matrimonial *adj* : marital, matrimonial <la vida matrimonial : married life>
matrimonio *nm* **1** : marriage, matrimony **2** : married couple
matriz *nf, pl* **matrices 1** : uterus, womb **2** : original, master copy **3** : main office, headquarters **4** : stub (of a check) **5** : matrix <matriz de puntos : dot matrix>
matrona *nf* : matron
matronal *adj* : matronly
matutino[1], -na *adj* : morning <la edición matutina : the morning edition>
matutino[2] *nm* : morning paper
maullar {8} *vi* : to meow
maullido *nm* : meow
mauritano, -na *adj & n* : Mauritanian
mausoleo *nm* : mausoleum
maxilar *nm* : jaw, jawbone
máxima *nf* : maxim
máxime *adv* ESPECIALMENTE : especially, principally
maximizar {21} *vt* : to maximize
máximo[1], -ma *adj* : maximum, greatest, highest
máximo[2] *nm* **1** : maximum **2 al máximo** : to the utmost **3 como ~** : at the most, at the latest
maya[1] *adj & nmf* : Mayan
maya[2] *nmf* : Maya, Mayan
mayo *nm* : May
mayonesa *nf* : mayonnaise
mayor[1] *adj* **1** (*comparative of* **grande**) : bigger, larger, greater, elder, older **2** (*superlative of* **grande**) : biggest, largest, greatest, eldest, oldest **3** : grown-up, mature **4** : main, major **5 mayor de edad** : of (legal) age **6 al por mayor** *or* **por ~** : wholesale
mayor[2] *nmf* **1** : major (in the military) **2** : adult
mayoral *nm* CAPATAZ : foreman, overseer
mayordomo *nm* : butler, majordomo
mayoreo *nm* : wholesale
mayores *nmpl* : grown-ups, elders
mayoría *nf* **1** : majority **2 en su mayoría** : on the whole
mayorista[1] *adj* ALMACENISTA : wholesale
mayorista[2] *nmf* : wholesaler
mayoritariamente *adv* : primarily, chiefly
mayoritario, -ria *adj & n* : majority <un consenso mayoritario : a majority consensus>
mayormente *adv* : primarily, chiefly
mayúscula *nf* : capital letter
mayúsculo, -la *adj* **1** : capital, uppercase **2** : huge, terrible <un problema mayúsculo : a huge problem>
maza *nf* **1** : mace (weapon) **2** : drumstick **3** *fam* : bore, pest
mazacote *nm* **1** : concrete **2** : lumpy mess (of food) **3** : eyesore, crude work of art
mazapán *nm, pl* **-panes** : marzipan
mazmorra *nf* CALABOZO : dungeon
mazo *nm* **1** : mallet **2** : pestle **3** MANOJO : handful, bunch
mazorca *nf* **1** CHOCLO : cob, ear of corn **2 pelar la mazorca** *Mex fam* : to smile from ear to ear
me *pron* **1** : me <me vieron : they saw me> **2** : to me, for me, from me <dame el libro : give me the book> <me lo compró : he bought it for me> <me robaron la cartera : they stole my pocketbook> **3** : myself, to myself, for myself, from myself <me preparé una buena comida : I cooked myself a good dinner> <me equivoqué : I made a mistake>
mecánica *nf* : mechanics
mecánico[1], -ca *adj* : mechanical — **mecánicamente** *adv*
mecánico[2], -ca *n* **1** : mechanic **2** : technician <mecánico dental : dental technician>
mecanismo *nm* : mechanism
mecanización *nf, pl* **-ciones** : mechanization
mecanizar {21} *vt* : to mechanize
mecanografía *nf* : typing
mecanografiar {85} *vt* : to type
mecanógrafo, -fa *n* : typist
mecate *nm CA, Mex, Ven* : rope, twine, cord
mecedor *nm* : glider (seat)
mecedora *nf* : rocking chair
mecenas *nmfs & pl* : patron (of the arts), sponsor
mecenazgo *nm* PATROCINIO : sponsorship, patronage
mecer {86} *vt* **1** : to rock **2** COLUMPIAR : to push (on a swing) — **mecerse** *vr* : to rock, to swing, to sway
mecha *nf* **1** : fuse **2** : wick **3 mechas** *nfpl* : highlights (in hair)
mechero *nm* **1** : burner **2** *Spain* : lighter
mechón *nm, pl* **mechones** : lock (of hair)
medalla *nf* : medal, medallion
medallista *nmf* : medalist
medallón *nm, pl* **-llones 1** : medallion **2** : locket
media *nf* **1** CALCETÍN : sock **2** : average, mean **3 medias** *nfpl* : stockings, hose, tights **4 a medias** : by halves, half and half, halfway <ir a medias : to go

halves> <verdad a medias : half-truth>

mediación *nf, pl* **-ciones** : mediation

mediado, -da *adj* **1** : half full, half empty, half over **2** : halfway through <mediada la tarea : halfway through the job>

mediador, -dora *n* : mediator

mediados *nmpl* **a mediados de** : halfway through, in the middle of <a mediados del mes : towards the middle of the month, mid-month>

medialuna *nf* **1** : crescent **2** : croissant, crescent roll

medianamente *adv* : fairly, moderately

medianero, -ra *adj* **1** : dividing **2** : mediating

medianía *nf* **1** : middle position **2** : mediocre person, mediocrity

mediano, -na *adj* **1** : medium, average <la mediana edad : middle age> **2** : mediocre

medianoche *nf* : midnight

mediante *prep* : through, by means of <Dios mediante : God willing>

mediar *vi* **1** : to mediate **2** : to be in the middle, to be halfway through **3** : to elapse, to pass <mediaron cinco años entre el inicio de la guerra y el armisticio : five years passed between the start of the war and the armistice> **4** : to be a consideration <media el hecho de que cuesta mucho : one must take into account that it is costly> **5** : to come up, to happen <medió algo urgente : something pressing came up>

mediatizar {21} *vt* : to influence, to interfere with

medicación *nf, pl* **-ciones** : medication, treatment

medicamento *nm* : medication, medicine, drug

medicar {72} *vt* : to medicate — **medicarse** *vr* : to take medicine

medicina *nf* : medicine

medicinal *adj* **1** : medicinal **2** : medicated

medicinar *vt* : to give medication to, to dose

medición *nf, pl* **-ciones** : measuring, measurement

médico[1], -ca *adj* : medical <una receta médica : a doctor's prescription>

médico[2], -ca *n* DOCTOR : doctor, physician

medida *nf* **1** : measurement, measure <hecho a medida : custom-made> **2** : measure, step <tomar medidas : to take steps> **3** : moderation, prudence <sin medida : immoderately> **4** : extent, degree <en gran medida : to a great extent>

medidor *nm* : meter, gauge

medieval *adj* : medieval — **medievalista** *nmf*

medievo *nm* → **medioevo**

medio[1] *adv* **1** : half <está medio dormida : she's half asleep> **2** : rather, kind of <está medio aburrida esta fiesta : this party is rather boring>

medio[2], -dia *adj* **1** : half <una media hora : half an hour> <medio hermano : half brother> <a media luz : in the half-light> <son las tres y media : it's half past three, it's three-thirty> **2** : midway, halfway <a medio camino : halfway there> **3** : middle <la clase media : the middle class> **4** : average <la temperatura media : the average temperature>

medio[3] *nm* **1** CENTRO : middle, center <en medio de : in the middle of, amid> **2** AMBIENTE : milieu, environment **3** : medium, spiritualist **4** : means *pl,* way <por medio de : by means of> <los medios de comunicación : the media> **5 medios** *nmpl* : means, resources

mediocre *adj* : mediocre, average

mediocridad *nf* : mediocrity

mediodía *nm* : noon, midday

medioevo *nm* : Middle Ages

medir {54} *vt* **1** : to measure **2** : to weigh, to consider <medir los riesgos : to weigh the risks> — *vi* : to measure — **medirse** *vr* : to be moderate, to exercise restraint

meditabundo, -da *adj* PENSATIVO : pensive, thoughtful

meditación *nf, pl* **-ciones** : meditation, thought

meditar *vi* : to meditate, to think <meditar sobre la vida : to contemplate life> — *vt* **1** : to think over, to consider **2** : to plan, to work out

meditativo, -va *adj* : pensive

mediterráneo, -nea *adj* : Mediterranean

medrar *vi* **1** PROSPERAR : to prosper, to thrive **2** AUMENTAR : to increase, to grow

medro *nm* PROSPERIDAD : prosperity, growth

medroso, -sa *adj* : fainthearted, fearful

médula *nf* **1** : marrow, pith **2 médula espinal** : spinal cord

medular *adj* : fundamental, core <el punto medular : the crux of the matter>

medusa *nf* : jellyfish, medusa

megabyte *nm* : megabyte

megáfono *nm* : megaphone

megahertzio *nm* : megahertz

megatón *nm, pl* **-tones** : megaton

megavatio *nm* : megawatt

mejicano → **mexicano**

mejilla *nf* : cheek

mejillón *nm, pl* **-llones** : mussel

mejor[1] *adv* **1** : better <Carla cocina mejor que Ana : Carla cooks better than Ana> **2** : best <ella es la que lo hace mejor : she's the one who does it best> **3** : rather <mejor morir que rendirme : I'd rather die than give up> **4** : it's better that . . . <mejor te

vas : you'd better go> **5 a lo mejor** : maybe, perhaps

mejor[2] *adj* **1** (*comparative of* **bueno**) : better <a falta de algo mejor : for lack of something better> **2** (*comparative of* **bien**) : better <está mucho mejor : he's much better> **3** (*superlative of* **bueno**) : best, the better <mi mejor amigo : my best friend> **4** (*superlative of* **bien**) : best, the better <duermo mejor en un clima seco : I sleep best in a dry climate> **5** PREFERIBLE : preferable, better **6 lo mejor** : the best thing, the best part

mejor[3] *nmf* (*with definite article*) : the better (one), the best (one)

mejora *nf* : improvement

mejoramiento *nm* : improvement

mejorana *nf* : marjoram

mejorar *vt* : to improve, to make better — *vi* : to improve, to get better — **mejorarse** *vr*

mejoría *nf* : improvement, betterment

mejunje *nm* : concoction, brew

melancolía *nf* : melancholy, sadness

melancólico, -ca *adj* : melancholy, sad

melanoma *nm* : melanoma

melaza *nf* : molasses

maleficio *nm* : curse, spell

melena *nf* **1** : mane **2** : long hair **3 melenas** *nfpl* GREÑAS : shaggy hair, mop

melenudo[1], **-da** *adj fam* : longhaired

melenudo[2], **-da** *n* GREÑUDO : longhair, hippie

melindres *nmpl* **1** : affectation, airs *pl* **2** : finickiness

melindroso[1], **-sa** *adj* **1** : affected **2** : fussy, finicky

melindroso[2], **-sa** *n* : finicky person, fussbudget

melisa *nf* : lemon balm

mella *nf* **1** : dent, nick **2 hacer mella en** : to have an effect on, to make an impression on

mellado, -da *adj* **1** : chipped, dented **2** : gap-toothed

mellar *vt* : to dent, to nick

mellizo, -za *adj & n* GEMELO : twin

melocotón *nm, pl* **-tones** : peach

melodía *nf* : melody, tune

melódico, -ca *adj* : melodic

melodioso, -sa *adj* : melodious

melodrama *nm* : melodrama

melodramático, -ca *adj* : melodramatic

melón *nm, pl* **melones** : melon, cantaloupe

meloso, -sa *adj* **1** : honeyed, sweet **2** EMPALAGOSO : cloying, saccharine

membrana *nf* **1** : membrane **2 membrana interdigital** : web, webbing (of a bird's foot) — **membranoso, -sa** *adj*

membresía *nf*: membership, members *pl*

membrete *nm* : letterhead, heading

membrillo *nm* : quince

membrudo, -da *adj* FORNIDO : muscular, well-built

memez *nf, pl* **memeces** : stupid thing

memo, -ma *adj* : silly, stupid

memorabilia *nf* : memorabilia

memorable *adj* : memorable

memorándum *or* **memorando** *nm, pl* **-dums** *or* **-dos 1** : memorandum, memo **2** : memo book, appointment book

memoria *nf* **1** : memory <de memoria : by heart> <hacer memoria : to try to remember> <traer a la memoria : to call to mind> **2** RECUERDO : remembrance, memory <su memoria perdurará para siempre : his memory will live forever> **3** : report <memoria anual : annual report> **4 memorias** *nfpl* : memoirs

memorizar {21} *vt* : to memorize — **memorización** *nf*

mena *nf* : ore

menaje *nm* : household goods *pl*, furnishings *pl*

mención *nf, pl* **-ciones** : mention

mencionar *vt* : to mention, to refer to

mendaz *adj, pl* **mendaces** : mendacious, lying

mendicidad *nf* : begging

mendigar {52} *vi* : to beg — *vt* : to beg for

mendigo, -ga *n* LIMOSNERO : beggar

mendrugo *nm* : crust (of bread)

menear *vt* **1** : to shake (one's head) **2** : to sway, to wiggle (one's hips) **3** : to wag (a tail) **4** : to stir (a liquid) — **menearse** *vr* **1** : to wiggle one's hips **2** : to fidget

meneo *nm* **1** : movement **2** : shake, toss **3** : swaying, wagging, wiggling **4** : stir, stirring

menester *nm* **1** : activity, occupation, duties *pl* **2 ser menester** : to be necessary <es menester que vengas : you must come>

mengano, -na *n* → **fulano**

mengua *nf* **1** : decrease, decline **2** : lack, want **3** : discredit, dishonor

menguar *vt* : to diminish, to lessen — *vi* **1** : to decline, to decrease **2** : to wane — **menguante** *adj*

meningitis *nf* : meningitis

menisco *nm* : meniscus, cartilage

menjurje *nm* → **mejunje**

menopausia *nf* : menopause

menor[1] *adj* **1** (*comparative of* **pequeño**) : smaller, lesser, younger **2** (*superlative of* **pequeño**) : smallest, least, youngest **3** : minor **4 al por menor** : retail **5 ser menor de edad** : to be a minor, to be underage

menor[2] *nmf* : minor, juvenile

menos[1] *adv* **1** : less <llueve menos en agosto : it rains less in August> **2** : least <el coche menos caro : the least expensive car> **3 ~ de** : less than, fewer than

menos[2] *adj* **1** : less, fewer <tengo más trabajo y menos tiempo : I have more

work and less time> **2 :** least, fewest <la clase que tiene menos estudiantes : the class that has the fewest students>

menos[3] *prep* **1** SALVO, EXCEPTO **:** except **2 :** minus <quince menos cuatro son once : fifteen minus four is eleven>

menos[4] *pron* **1 :** less, fewer <no deberías aceptar menos : you shouldn't accept less> **2 al menos** *or* **por lo menos :** at least **3 a menos que :** unless

menoscabar *vt* **1 :** to lessen, to diminish **2 :** to disgrace, to discredit **3** PERJUDICAR **:** to harm, to damage

menoscabo *nm* **1 :** lessening, diminishing **2 :** disgrace, discredit **3 :** harm, damage

menospreciar *vt* **1** DESPRECIAR **:** to scorn, to look down on **2 :** to underestimate, to undervalue

menosprecio *nm* DESPRECIO **:** contempt, scorn

mensaje *nm* **:** message

mensajero, -ra *n* **:** messenger

menso, -sa *adj Mex fam* **:** foolish, stupid

menstrual *adj* **:** menstrual

menstruar {3} *vi* **:** to menstruate — **menstruación** *nf*

mensual *adj* **:** monthly

mensualidad *nf* **1 :** monthly payment, installment **2 :** monthly salary

mensualmente *adv* **:** every month, monthly

mensurable *adj* **:** measurable

menta *nf* **1 :** mint, peppermint **2 menta verde :** spearmint

mentado, -da *adj* **1 :** aforementioned **2** FAMOSO **:** renowned, famous

mental *adj* **:** mental, intellectual — **mentalmente** *adv*

mentalidad *nf* **:** mentality

mentar {55} *vt* **1 :** to mention, to name **2 mentar la madre a** *fam* **:** to insult, to swear at

mente *nf* **:** mind <tener en mente : to have in mind>

mentecato[1], **-ta** *adj* **:** foolish, simple

mentecato[2], **-ta** *n* **:** fool, idiot

mentir {76} *vi* **:** to lie

mentira *nf* **:** lie

mentiroso[1], **-sa** *adj* EMBUSTERO **:** lying, untruthful

mentiroso[2], **-sa** *n* EMBUSTERO **:** liar

mentís *nm, pl* **mentises :** denial, repudiation <dar el mentís a : to deny, to refute>

mentol *nm* **:** menthol

mentón *nm, pl* **mentones** BARBILLA **:** chin

mentor *nm* **:** mentor, counselor

menú *nm, pl* **menús :** menu

menudear *vi* **:** to occur frequently — *vt* **:** to do repeatedly

menudencia *nf* **1 :** trifle **2 menudencias** *nfpl* **:** giblets

menudeo *nm* **:** retail, retailing

menudillos *nmpl* **:** giblets

menudo[1], **-da** *adj* **1 :** minute, small **2 a ~** FRECUENTEMENTE **:** often, frequently

menudo[2] *nm* **1** *Mex* **:** tripe stew **2 menudos** *nmpl* **:** giblets

meñique *nm or* **dedo meñique :** little finger, pinkie

meollo *nm* **1** MÉDULA **:** marrow **2** SESO **:** brains *pl* **3** ENTRAÑA **:** essence, core <el meollo del asunto : the heart of the matter>

mequetrefe *nm fam* **:** good-for-nothing

mercachifle *nm* **:** peddler, hawker

mercadeo *nm* **:** marketing

mercadería *nf* **:** merchandise, goods *pl*

mercado *nm* **:** market <mercado de trabajo *or* mercado laboral : labor market> <mercado de valores *or* mercado bursátil : stock market>

mercadotecnia *nf* **:** marketing

mercancía *nf* **:** merchandise, goods *pl*

mercante *nmf* **:** merchant, dealer

mercantil *adj* COMERCIAL **:** commercial, mercantile

merced *nf* **1 :** favor **2 ~ a :** thanks to, due to **3 a merced de :** at the mercy of

mercenario, -ria *adj & n* **:** mercenary

mercería *nf* **:** notions store

mercurio *nm* **:** mercury

Mercurio *nm* **:** Mercury (planet)

merecedor, -dora *adj* **:** deserving, worthy

merecer {53} *vt* **:** to deserve, to merit — *vi* **:** to be worthy

merecidamente *adv* **:** rightfully, deservedly

merecido *nm* **:** something merited, due <recibieron su merecido : they got their just deserts>

merecimiento *nm* **:** merit, worth

merendar {55} *vi* **:** to have an afternoon snack — *vt* **:** to have as an afternoon snack

merendero *nm* **1 :** lunchroom, snack bar **2 :** picnic area

merengue *nm* **1 :** meringue **2 :** merengue (dance)

meridiano[1], **-na** *adj* **1 :** midday **2 :** crystal clear

meridiano[2] *nm* **:** meridian

meridional *adj* SUREÑO **:** southern

merienda *nf* **:** afternoon snack, tea

mérito *nm* **:** merit

meritorio[1], **-ria** *adj* **:** deserving, meritorious

meritorio[2], **-ria** *n* **:** intern, trainee

merluza *nf* **:** hake

merma *nf* **1 :** decrease, cut **2 :** waste, loss

mermar *vi* **:** to decrease, to diminish — *vt* **:** to reduce, to cut down

mermelada *nf* **:** marmalade, jam

mero[1], **-ra** *adv Mex fam* **1 :** nearly, almost <ya mero me caí : I almost fell> **2 :** just, exactly <aquí mero : right here>

mero², **-ra** *adj* **1** : mere, simple **2** *Mex fam* (*used as an intensifier*) : very <en el mero centro : in the very center of town>
mero³ *nm* : grouper
merodeador, **-dora** *n* **1** : marauder **2** : prowler
merodear *vi* **1** : to maraud, to pillage **2** : to prowl around, to skulk
mes *nm* : month
mesa *nf* **1** : table **2** : committee, board
mesada *nf* : allowance, pocket money
mesarse *vr* : to pull at <mesarse los cabellos : to tear one's hair>
mesero, **-ra** *n* CAMARERO : waiter, waitress *f*
meseta *nf* : plateau, tableland
Mesías *nm* : Messiah
mesón *nm, pl* **mesones** : inn
mesonero, **-ra** *nm* : innkeeper
mestizo¹, **-za** *adj* **1** : of mixed ancestry **2** HÍBRIDO : hybrid
mestizo², **-za** *n* : person of mixed ancestry
mesura *nf* **1** MODERACIÓN : moderation, discretion **2** CORTESÍA : courtesy **3** GRAVEDAD : seriousness, dignity
mesurado, **-da** *adj* COMEDIDO : moderate, restrained
mesurar *vt* : to moderate, to restrain, to temper — **mesurarse** *vr* : to restrain oneself
meta *nf* : goal, objective
metabólico, **-ca** *adj* : metabolic
metabolismo *nm* : metabolism
metabolizar {21} *vt* : to metabolize
metafísica *nf* : metaphysics
metafísico, **-ca** *adj* : metaphysical
metáfora *nf* : metaphor
metafórico, **-ca** *adj* : metaphoric, metaphorical
metal *nm* **1** : metal **2** : brass section (in an orchestra)
metálico, **-ca** *adj* : metallic, metal
metalistería *nf* : metalworking
metalurgia *nf* : metallurgy
metalúrgico¹, **-ca** *adj* : metallurgical
metalúrgico², **-ca** *n* : metallurgist
metamorfosis *nfs & pl* : metamorphosis
metano *nm* : methane
meteórico, **-ca** *adj* : meteoric
meteorito *nm* : meteorite
meteoro *nm* : meteor
meteorología *nf* : meteorology
meteorológico, **-ca** *adj* : meteorologic, meteorological
meteorólogo, **-ga** *n* : meteorologist
meter *vt* **1** : to put (in) <metieron su dinero en el banco : they put their money in the bank> **2** : to fit, to squeeze <puedes meter dos líneas más en esa página : you can fit two more lines on that page> **3** : to place (in a job) <lo metieron de barrendero : they got him a job as a street sweeper> **4** : to involve <lo metió en un buen lío : she got him in an awful mess> **5** : to make, to cause <meten demasiado ruido : they make too much noise> **6** : to spread (a rumor) **7** : to strike (a blow) **8** : to take up, to take in (clothing) **9 a todo meter** : at top speed — **meterse** *vr* **1** : to get into, to enter **2** *fam* : to meddle <no te metas en lo que no te importa : mind your own business> **3 ~ con** *fam* : to pick a fight with, to provoke <no te metas conmigo : don't mess with me>
metiche¹ *adj Mex fam* : nosy
metiche² *nmf Mex fam* : busybody
meticulosidad *nf* : thoroughness, meticulousness
meticuloso, **-sa** *adj* : meticulous, thorough — **meticulosamente** *adv*
metida *nf* **metida de pata** *fam* : blunder, gaffe, blooper
metódico, **-ca** *adj* : methodical — **metódicamente** *adv*
metodista *adj & nmf* : Methodist
método *nm* : method
metodología *nf* : methodology
metomentodo *nmf fam* : busybody
metralla *nf* : shrapnel
metralleta *nf* : submachine gun
métrico, **-ca** *adj* **1** : metric **2 cinta métrica** : tape measure
metro *nm* **1** : meter **2** : subway
metrónomo *nm* : metronome
metrópoli *nf or* **metrópolis** *nfs & pl* : metropolis
metropolitano, **-na** *adj* : metropolitan
mexicanismo *nm* : Mexican word or expression
mexicano, **-na** *adj & n* : Mexican
mexicoamericano, **-na** *adj & n* : Mexican-American
meza, **etc.** → **mecer**
mezcla *nf* **1** : mixing **2** : mixture, blend **3** : mortar (masonry material)
mezclar *vt* **1** : to mix, to blend **2** : to mix up, to muddle **3** INVOLUCRAR : to involve — **mezclarse** *vr* **1** : to get mixed up (in) **2** : to mix, to mingle (socially)
mezclilla *nf Chile, Mex* : denim <pantalones de mezclilla : jeans>
mezcolanza *nf* : jumble, hodgepodge
mezquindad *nf* **1** : meanness, stinginess **2** : petty deed, mean action
mezquino¹, **-na** *adj* **1** : mean, petty **2** : stingy **3** : paltry
mezquino² *nm Mex* : wart
mezquita *nf* : mosque
mezquite *nm* : mesquite
mi *adj* : my
mí *pron* **1** : me <es para mí : it's for me> <a mí no me importa : it doesn't matter to me> **2 mí mismo, mí misma** : myself
miasma *nm* : miasma
miau *nm* : meow
mica *nf* : mica
mico *nm* : monkey, long-tailed monkey
micra *nf* : micron
microbio *nm* : microbe, germ
microbiología *nf* : microbiology

microbiólogico, -ca *adj* : microbiological
microbús *nm, pl* **-buses** : minibus
microcomputadora *nf* : microcomputer
microcosmos *nms & pl* : microcosm
microficha *nf* : microfiche
microfilm *nm, pl* **-films** : microfilm
micrófono *nm* : microphone
micrómetro *nm* : micrometer
microonda *nf* : microwave
microondas *nms & pl* : microwave, microwave oven
microordenador *nm Spain* : microcomputer
microorganismo *nm* : microorganism
microprocesador *nm* : microprocessor
microscópico, -ca *adj* : microscopic
microscopio *nm* : microscope
mide, etc. → **medir**
miedo *nm* **1** TEMOR : fear <le tiene miedo al perro : he's scared of the dog> <tenían miedo de hablar : they were afraid to speak> **2 dar miedo** : to frighten
miedoso, -sa *adj* TEMEROSO : fearful
miel *nf* : honey
miembro *nm* **1** : member **2** EXTREMIDAD : limb, extremity
mienta, etc. → **mentar**
miente, etc. → **mentir**
mientras[1] *adv* **1** *or* **mientras tanto** : meanwhile, in the meantime **2 mientras más** : the more <mientras más como, más quiero : the more I eat, the more I want>
mientras[2] *conj* **1** : while, as <roncaba mientras dormía : he snored while he was sleeping> **2** : as long as <luchará mientras pueda : he will fight as long as he is able> **3 mientras que** : while, whereas <él es alto mientras que ella es muy baja : he is tall, whereas she is very short>
miércoles *nms & pl* : Wednesday
miga *nf* **1** : crumb **2 hacer buenas (malas) migas con** : to get along well (poorly) with
migaja *nf* **1** : crumb **2 migajas** *nfpl* SOBRAS : leftovers, scraps
migración *nf, pl* **-ciones** : migration
migrante *nmf* : migrant
migraña *nf* : migraine
migratorio, -ria *adj* : migratory
mijo *nm* : millet
mil[1] *adj* : thousand
mil[2] *nm* : one thousand, a thousand
milagro *nm* : miracle <de milagro : miraculously>
milagroso, -sa *adj* : miraculous, marvelous — **milagrosamente** *adv*
milenio *nm* : millennium
milésimo, -ma *adj* : thousandth — **milésimo** *n*
milicia *nf* **1** : militia **2** : military service
miligramo *nm* : milligram
mililitro *nm* : milliliter
milímetro *nm* : millimeter
militancia *nf* : militancy
militante[1] *adj* : militant
militante[2] *nmf* : militant, activist
militar[1] *vi* **1** : to serve (in the military) **2** : to be active (in politics)
militar[2] *adj* : military
militar[3] *nmf* SOLDADO : soldier
militarizar {21} *vt* : to militarize
milla *nf* : mile
millar *nm* : thousand
millón *nm, pl* **millones** : million
millonario, -ria *n* : millionaire
millonésimo[1], **-ma** *adj* : millionth
millonésimo[2] *nm* : millionth
mil millones *nms & pl* : billion
milpa *nf CA, Mex* : cornfield
milpiés *nms & pl* : millipede
mimar *vt* CONSENTIR : to pamper, to spoil
mimbre *nm* : wicker
mimeógrafo *nm* : mimeograph
mímica *nf* **1** : mime, sign language **2** IMITACIÓN : mimicry
mimo *nm* **1** : pampering, indulgence <hacerle mimos a alguien : to pamper someone> **2** : mime
mimoso, -sa *adj* **1** : fussy, finicky **2** : affectionate, clinging
mina *nf* **1** : mine **2** : lead (for pencils)
minar *vt* **1** : to mine **2** DEBILITAR : to undermine
minarete *nm* ALMINAR : minaret
mineral *adj & nm* : mineral
minería *nf* : mining
minero[1], **-ra** *adj* : mining
minero[2], **-ra** *n* : miner, mine worker
miniatura *nf* : miniature
minicomputadora *nf* : minicomputer
minifalda *nf* : miniskirt
minifundio *nm* : small farm
minimizar {21} *vt* : to minimize
mínimo[1], **-ma** *adj* **1** : minimum <salario mínimo : minimum wage> **2** : least, smallest **3** : very small, minute
mínimo[2] *nm* **1** : minimum, least amount **2** : modicum, small amount **3 como ~** : at least
minino, -na *n fam* : pussy, pussycat
miniserie *nf* : miniseries
ministerial *adj* : ministerial
ministerio *nm* : ministry, department
ministro, -tra *n* : minister, secretary <primer ministro : prime minister> <Ministro de Defensa : Secretary of Defense>
minivan [ˌmini'ban, -'van] *nf, pl* **-vanes** : minivan
minoría *nf* : minority
minorista[1] *adj* : retail
minorista[2] *nmf* : retailer
minoritario, -ria *adj* : minority
mintió, etc. → **mentir**
minuciosamente *adv* **1** : minutely **2** : in great detail **3** : thoroughly, meticulously
minucioso, -sa *adj* **1** : minute **2** DETALLADO : detailed **3** : thorough, meticulous
minué *nm* : minuet

minúsculo, -la *adj* DIMINUTO : tiny, miniscule

minusvalía *nf* : disability, handicap

minusválido[1], -da *adj* : handicapped, disabled

minusválido[2], -da *n* : handicapped person

minuta *nf* **1** BORRADOR : rough draft **2** : bill, fee

minutero *nm* : minute hand

minuto *nm* : minute

mío[1], mía *adj* **1** : my, of mine <¡Dios mío! : my God!, good heavens!> <una amiga mía : a friend of mine> **2** : mine <es mío : it's mine>

mío[2], mía *pron* (*with definite article*) : mine, my own <tus zapatos son iguales a los míos : your shoes are just like mine>

miope *adj* : nearsighted, myopic

miopía *nf* : myopia, nearsightedness

mira *nf* **1** : sight (of a firearm or instrument) **2** : aim, objective <con miras a : with the intention of, with a view to> <de amplias miras : broad-minded> <poner la mira en : to aim at, to aspire to>

mirada *nf* **1** : look, glance, gaze **2** EXPRESIÓN : look, expression <una mirada de sorpresa : a look of surprise>

mirado, -da *adj* **1** : cautious, careful **2** : considerate **3 bien mirado** : well thought of **4 mal mirado** : disliked, disapproved of

mirador *nm* : balcony, lookout, vantage point

miramiento *nm* **1** CONSIDERACIÓN : consideration, respect **2 sin miramientos** : without due consideration, carelessly

mirar *vt* **1** : to look at **2** OBSERVAR : to watch **3** REFLEXIONAR : to consider, to think over — *vi* **1** : to look **2** : to face, to overlook **3 ~ por** : to look after, to look out for — **mirarse** *vr* **1** : to look at oneself **2** : to look at each other

mirasol *nm* GIRASOL : sunflower

miríada *nf* : myriad

mirlo *nm* : blackbird

mirra *nf* : myrrh

mirto *nm* ARRAYÁN : myrtle

misa *nf* : Mass

misantropía *nf* : misanthropy

misantrópico, -ca *adj* : misanthropic

misántropo, -pa *n* : misanthrope

miscelánea *nf* : miscellany

misceláneo, -nea *adj* : miscellaneous

miserable *adj* **1** LASTIMOSO : miserable, wretched **2** : paltry, meager **3** MEZQUINO : stingy, miserly **4** : despicable, vile

miseria *nf* **1** POBREZA : poverty **2** : misery, suffering **3** : pittance, meager amount

misericordia *nf* COMPASIÓN : mercy, compassion

misericordioso, -sa *adj* : merciful

mísero, -ra *adj* **1** : wretched, miserable **2** : stingy **3** : paltry, meager

misil *nm* : missile

misión *nf, pl* **misiones** : mission

misionero, -ra *adj & n* : missionary

misiva *nf* : missive, letter

mismísimo, -ma *adj* (*used as an intensifier*) : very, selfsame <el mismísimo día : that very same day>

mismo[1] *adv* (*used as an intensifier*) : right, exactly <hazlo ahora mismo : do it right now> <te llamará hoy mismo : he'll definitely call you today>

mismo[2], -ma *adj* **1** : same **2** (*used as an intensifier*) : very <en ese mismo momento : at that very moment> **3** : oneself <lo hizo ella misma : she made it herself> **4 por lo mismo** : for that reason

misoginia *nf* : misogyny

misógino *nm* : misogynist

misterio *nm* : mystery

misterioso, -sa *adj* : mysterious — **misteriosamente** *adv*

misticismo *nm* : mysticism

místico[1], -ca *adj* : mystic, mystical

místico[2], -ca *n* : mystic

mitad *nf* **1** : half <mitad y mitad : half and half> **2** MEDIO : middle <a mitad de : halfway through> <por la mitad : in half>

mítico, -ca *adj* : mythical, mythic

mitigar {52} *vt* ALIVIAR : to mitigate, to alleviate — **mitigación** *nf*

mitin *nm, pl* **mítines** : (political) meeting, rally

mito *nm* LEYENDA : myth, legend

mitología *nm* : mythology

mitológico, -ca *adj* : mythological

mitosis *nfs & pl* : mitosis

mitra *nf* : miter (bishop's hat)

mixto, -ta *adj* **1** : mixed, joint **2** : coeducational

mixtura *nf* : mixture, blend

mnemónico, -ca *adj* : mnemonic

mobiliario *nm* : furniture

mocasín *nm, pl* **-sines** : moccasin

mocedad *nf* **1** JUVENTUD : youth **2** : youthful prank

mochila *nf* MORRAL : backpack, knapsack

moción *nf, pl* **-ciones** **1** MOVIMIENTO : motion, movement **2** : motion (to a court or assembly)

moco *nm* **1** : mucus **2** *fam* : snot <limpiarse los mocos : to wipe one's (runny) nose>

mocoso, -sa *n* : kid, brat

moda *nf* **1** : fashion, style **2 a la moda** *or* **de ~** : in style, fashionable **3 moda pasajera** : fad

modales *nmpl* : manners

modalidad *nf* **1** CLASE : kind, type **2** MANERA : way, manner

modelar *vt* : to model, to mold — **modelarse** *vr* : to model oneself after, to emulate

modelo[1] *adj* : model <una casa modelo : a model home>
modelo[2] *nm* : model, example, pattern
modelo[3] *nmf* : model, mannequin
módem *or* **modem** [ˈmoðɛm] *nm* : modem
moderación *nf, pl* **-ciones** MESURA : moderation
moderado, -da *adj & n* : moderate — **moderadamente** *adv*
moderador, -dora *n* : moderator, chair
moderar *vt* **1** TEMPERAR : to temper, to moderate **2** : to curb, to reduce <moderar gastos : to curb spending> **3** PRESIDIR : to chair (a meeting) — **moderarse** *vr* **1** : to restrain oneself **2** : to diminish, to calm down
modernidad *nf* **1** : modernity, modernness **2** : modern age
modernismo *nm* : modernism
modernista[1] *adj* : modernist, modernistic
modernista[2] *nmf* : modernist
modernizar {21} *vt* : to modernize — **modernización** *nf*
moderno, -na *adj* : modern, up-to-date
modestia *nf* : modesty
modesto, -ta *adj* : modest — **modestamente** *adv*
modificación *nf, pl* **-ciones** : alteration
modificante *nm* : modifier
modificar {72} *vt* ALTERAR : to modify, to alter, to adapt
modismo *nm* : idiom
modista *nmf* **1** : dressmaker **2** : fashion designer
modo *nm* **1** MANERA : way, manner, mode <de un modo u otro : one way or another> <a mi modo de ver : to my way of thinking> **2** : mood (in grammar) **3** : mode (in music) **4** **a modo de** : by way of, in the manner of, like <a modo de ejemplo : by way of example> **5** **de cualquier modo** : in any case, anyway **6** **de modo que** : so, in such a way that **7** **de todos modos** : in any case, anyway **8** **en cierto modo** : in a way, to a certain extent
modorra *nf* : drowsiness, lethargy
modular[1] *v* : to modulate — **modulación** *nf*
modular[2] *adj* : modular
módulo *nm* : module, unit
mofa *nf* **1** : mockery, ridicule **2** **hacer mofa de** : to make fun of, to ridicule
mofarse *vr* ~ **de** : to scoff at, to make fun of
mofeta *nf* ZORRILLO : skunk
mofle *nm CA, Mex* : muffler (of a car)
moflete *nm fam* : fat cheek
mofletudo, -da *adj fam* : fat-cheeked, chubby
mohín *nm, pl* **mohines** : grimace, face
mohino, -na *adj* : gloomy, melancholy
moho *nm* **1** : mold, mildew **2** : rust
mohoso, -sa *adj* **1** : moldy **2** : rusty
moisés *nm, pl* **moiseses** : bassinet, cradle
mojado[1], **-da** *adj* : wet
mojado[2], **-da** *n Mex fam* : illegal immigrant
mojar *vt* **1** : to wet, to moisten **2** : to dunk — **mojarse** *vr* : to get wet
mojigatería *nf* **1** : hypocrisy **2** GAZMOÑERÍA : primness, prudery
mojigato[1], **-ta** *adj* : prudish, prim — **mojigatamente** *adv*
mojigato[2], **-ta** *n* : prude, prig
mojón *nm, pl* **mojones** : boundary stone, marker
molar *nm* MUELA : molar
molcajete *nm Mex* : mortar
molde *nm* **1** : mold, form **2** **letras de molde** : printing, block lettering
moldear *vt* **1** FORMAR : to mold, to shape **2** : to cast
moldura *nf* : molding
mole[1] *nm Mex* **1** : spicy sauce made with chilies and usually chocolate **2** : meat served with mole sauce
mole[2] *nf* : mass, bulk
molécula *nf* : molecule — **molecular** *adj*
moler {47} *vt* **1** : to grind, to crush **2** CANSAR : to exhaust, to wear out
molestar *vt* **1** FASTIDIAR : to annoy, to bother **2** : to disturb, to disrupt — *vi* : to be a nuisance — **molestarse** *vr* ~ **en** : to take the trouble to
molestia *nf* **1** FASTIDIO : annoyance, bother, nuisance **2** : trouble <se tomó la molestia de investigar : she took the trouble to investigate> **3** MALESTAR : discomfort
molesto, -ta *adj* **1** ENOJADO : bothered, annoyed **2** FASTIDIOSO : bothersome, annoying
molestoso, -sa *adj* : bothersome, annoying
molido, -da *adj* **1** MACHACADO : ground, crushed **2** **estar molido** : to be exhausted
molinero, -ra *n* : miller
molinillo *nm* : grinder, mill <molinillo de café : coffee grinder>
molino *nm* **1** : mill **2** **molino de viento** : windmill
molla *nf* : soft fleshy part, flesh (of fruit), lean part (of meat)
molleja *nf* : gizzard
molusco *nm* : mollusk
momentáneamente *adv* : momentarily
momentáneo, -nea *adj* **1** : momentary **2** TEMPORARIO : temporary
momento *nm* **1** : moment, instant <espera un momentito : wait just a moment> **2** : time, period of time <momentos difíciles : hard times> **3** : present, moment <los atletas del momento : the athletes of the moment, today's popular athletes> **4** : momentum **5** **al momento** : right away, at once **6** **de** ~ : at the moment, for the moment **7** **de un momento a otro** : any time now **8** **por momentos** : at times

momia *nf* : mummy
monaguillo *nm* ACÓLITO : altar boy
monarca *nmf* : monarch
monarquía *nf* : monarchy
monárquico, -ca *n* : monarchist
monasterio *nm* : monastery
monástico, -ca *adj* : monastic
mondadientes *nms & pl* PALILLO : toothpick
mondar *vt* : to peel
mondongo *nm* ENTRAÑAS : innards *pl,* insides *pl,* guts *pl*
moneda *nf* **1** : coin **2** : money, currency
monedero *nm* : change purse
monetario, -ria *adj* : monetary, financial
mongol, -gola *adj & n* : Mongol, Mongolian
monitor[1], **-tora** *n* : instructor (in sports)
monitor[2] *nm* : monitor <monitor de televisión : television monitor>
monitorear *vt* : to monitor
monja *nf* : nun
monje *nm* : monk
mono[1], **-na** *adj fam* : lovely, pretty, cute, darling
mono[2], **-na** *n* : monkey
monóculo *nm* : monocle
monogamia *nf* : monogamy
monógamo -ma *adj* : monogamous
monografía *nf* : monograph
monograma *nm* : monogram
monolingüe *adj* : monolingual
monolítico, -ca *adj* : monolithic
monolito *nm* : monolith
monólogo *nm* : monologue
monomanía *nf* : obsession
monopatín *nm, pl* **-tines** : scooter
monopolio *nm* : monopoly
monopolizar {21} *vt* : to monopolize — **monopolización** *nf*
monosilábico, -ca *adj* : monosyllabic
monosílabo *nm* : monosyllable
monoteísmo *nm* : monotheism
monoteísta[1] *adj* : monotheistic
monoteísta[2] *nmf* : monotheist
monotonía *nf* **1** : monotony **2** : monotone
monótono, -na *adj* : monotonous — **monótonamente** *adv*
monóxido *nm* : monoxide <monóxido de carbono : carbon monoxide>
monserga *nf* : gibberish, drivel
monstruo *nm* : monster
monstruosidad *nf* : monstrosity
monstruoso, -sa *adj* : monstrous — **monstruosamente** *adv*
monta *nf* **1** : sum, total **2** : importance, value <de poca monta : unimportant, insignificant>
montaje *nm* **1** : assembling, assembly **2** : montage
montante *nm* : transom, fanlight
montaña *nf* **1** MONTE : mountain **2 montaña rusa** : roller coaster
montañero, -ra *n* : mountaineer, mountain climber
montañoso, -sa *adj* : mountainous
montar *vt* **1** : to mount **2** ESTABLECER : to set up, to establish **3** ARMAR : to assemble, to put together **4** : to edit (a film) **5** : to stage, to put on (a show) **6** : to cock (a gun) **7 montar en bicicleta** : to get on a bicycle **8 montar a caballo** CABALGAR : to ride horseback
monte *nm* **1** MONTAÑA : mountain, mount **2** : woodland, scrubland <monte bajo : underbrush> **3** : outskirts (of a town), surrounding country **4 monte de piedad** : pawnshop
montés *adj, pl* **monteses** : wild (of animals or plants)
montículo *nm* **1** : mound, heap **2** : hillock, knoll
monto *nm* : amount, total
montón *nm, pl* **-tones 1** : heap, pile **2** *fam* : ton, load <un montón de preguntas : a ton of questions> <montones de gente : loads of people>
montura *nf* **1** : mount (horse) **2** : saddle, tack **3** : setting, mounting (of jewelry) **4** : frame (of glasses)
monumental *adj fam* **1** : tremendous, terrific **2** : massive, huge
monumento *nm* : monument
monzón *nm, pl* **monzones** : monsoon
moño *nm* **1** : bun (chignon) **2** LAZO : bow, knot <corbata de moño : bow tie>
moquear *vi* : to snivel
moquillo *nm* : distemper
mora *nf* **1** : blackberry **2** : mulberry
morada *nf* RESIDENCIA : dwelling, abode
morado[1], **-da** *adj* : purple
morado[2] *nm* : purple
morador, -dora *n* : dweller, inhabitant
moral[1] *adj* : moral — **moralmente** *adv*
moral[2] *nf* **1** MORALIDAD : ethics, morality, morals *pl* **2** ÁNIMO : morale, spirits *pl*
moraleja *nf* : moral (of a story)
moralidad *nf* : morality
moralista[1] *adj* : moralistic
moralista[2] *nmf* : moralist
morar *vi* : to dwell, to reside
moratoria *nf* : moratorium
morboso, -sa *adj* : morbid — **morbosidad** *nf*
morcilla *nf* : blood sausage, blood pudding
mordacidad *nf* : bite, sharpness
mordaz *adj* : caustic, scathing
mordaza *nf* **1** : gag **2** : clamp
mordedura *nf* : bite (of an animal)
morder {47} *v* : to bite
mordida *nf* **1** : bite **2** *CA, Mex* : bribe, payoff
mordisco *nm* : bite, nibble
mordisquear *vt* : to nibble (on), to bite
morena *nf* **1** : moraine **2** : moray (eel)
moreno[1], **-na** *adj* **1** : brunette **2** : dark, dark-skinned
moreno[2], **-na** *n* **1** : brunette **2** : dark-skinned person

moretón *nm, pl* **-tones** : bruise
morfina *nf* : morphine
morfología *nf* : morphology
morgue *nf* : morgue
moribundo[1], **-da** *adj* : dying, moribund
moribundo[2], **-da** *n* : dying person
morillo *nm* : andiron
morir {46} *vi* **1** FALLECER : to die **2** APAGARSE : to die out, to go out
mormón, -mona *adj & n, pl* **mormones** : Mormon
moro[1], **-ra** *adj* : Moorish
moro[2], **-ra** *n* **1** : Moor **2** : Muslim
morosidad *nf* **1** : delinquency (in payment) **2** : slowness
moroso, -sa *adj* **1** : delinquent, in arrears <cuentas morosas : delinquent accounts> **2** : slow, sluggish
morral *nm* MOCHILA : backpack, knapsack
morralla *nf* **1** : small fish **2** : trash, riffraff **3** *Mex* : small change
morriña *nf* : homesickness
morro *nm* HOCICO : snout
morsa *nf* : walrus
morse *nm* : Morse code
mortaja *nf* SUDARIO : shroud
mortal[1] *adj* **1** : mortal **2** FATAL : fatal, deadly — **mortalmente** *adv*
mortal[2] *nmf* : mortal
mortalidad *nf* : mortality
mortandad *nf* **1** : loss of life, death toll **2** : carnage, slaughter
mortero *nm* : mortar (bowl, cannon, or building material)
mortífero, -ra *adj* LETAL : deadly, fatal
mortificación *nf, pl* **-ciones 1** : mortification **2** TORMENTO : anguish, torment
mortificar {72} *vt* **1** : to mortify **2** TORTURAR : to trouble, to torment — **mortificarse** *vr* : to be mortified, to feel embarrassed
mosaico *nm* : mosaic
mosca *nf* **1** : fly **2 mosca común** : housefly
moscada *adj* **nuez moscada** : nutmeg
moscovita *adj & nmf* : Muscovite
mosquearse *vr* **1** : to become suspicious **2** : to take offense
mosquete *nm* : musket
mosquetero *nm* : musketeer
mosquitero *nm* : mosquito net
mosquito *nm* ZANCUDO : mosquito
mostachón *nm, pl* **-chones** : macaroon
mostaza *nf* : mustard
mostrador *nm* : counter (in a store)
mostrar {19} *vt* **1** : to show **2** EXHIBIR : to exhibit, to display — **mostrarse** *vr* : to show oneself, to appear
mota *nf* **1** : fleck, speck **2** : defect, blemish
mote *nm* SOBRENOMBRE : nickname
moteado, -da *adj* : dotted, spotted, dappled
motel *nm* : motel
motín *nm, pl* **motines 1** : riot **2** : rebellion, mutiny
motivación *nf, pl* **-ciones** : motivation — **motivacional** *adj*
motivar *vt* **1** CAUSAR : to cause **2** IMPULSAR : to motivate
motivo *nm* **1** MÓVIL : motive **2** CAUSA : cause, reason **3** TEMA : theme, motif
moto *nf* : motorcycle, motorbike
motocicleta *nf* : motorcycle
motociclismo *nm* : motorcycling
motociclista *nmf* : motorcyclist
motor[1], **-ra** *adj* MOTRIZ : motor
motor[2] *nm* **1** : motor, engine **2** : driving force, cause
motorista *nmf* : motorist
motriz *adj, pl* **motrices** : driving
motu proprio *adv* **de motu proprio** [deˈmotuˈproprio] : voluntarily, of one's own accord
mousse [ˈmus] *nm* : mousse
mover {47} *vt* **1** TRASLADAR : to move, to shift **2** AGITAR : to shake, to nod (the head) **3** ACCIONAR : to power, to drive **4** INDUCIR : to provoke, to cause **5** : to excite, to stir — **moverse** *vr* **1** : to move, to move over **2** : to hurry, to get a move on **3** : to get moving, to make an effort
movible *adj* : movable
movida *nf* : move (in a game)
móvil[1] *adj* : mobile
móvil[2] *nm* **1** MOTIVO : motive **2** : mobile
movilidad *nf* : mobility
movilizar {21} *vt* : to mobilize — **movilización** *nf*
movimiento *nm* : movement, motion <movimiento del cuerpo : bodily movement> <movimiento sindicalista : labor movement>
mozo[1], **-za** *adj* : young, youthful
mozo[2], **-za** *n* **1** JOVEN : young man *m*, young woman *f*, youth **2** : helper, servant
mucamo, -ma *n* : servant, maid *f*
muchacha *nf* : maid
muchacho, -cha *n* **1** : kid, boy *m*, girl *f* **2** JOVEN : young man *m*, young woman *f*
muchedumbre *nf* MULTITUD : crowd, multitude
mucho[1] *adv* **1** : much, a lot <mucho más : much more> <le gusta mucho : he likes it a lot> **2** : long, a long time <tardó mucho en venir : he was a long time getting here> **3 por mucho que** : no matter how much
mucho[2], **-cha** *adj* **1** : a lot of, many, much <mucha gente : a lot of people> <hace mucho tiempo que no lo veo : I haven't seen him in ages> **2 muchas veces** : often
mucho[3], **-cha** *pron* **1** : a lot, many, much <hay mucho que hacer : there is a lot to do> <muchas no vinieron : many didn't come> **2 cuando ~** *or* **como ~** : at most **3 con ~** : by far **4 ni mucho menos** : not at all, far from it
mucílago *nm* : mucilage
mucosidad *nf* : mucus

mucoso, -sa *adj* : mucous, slimy

muda *nf* **1** : change <muda de ropa : change of clothes> **2** : molt, molting

mudanza *nf* **1** CAMBIO : change **2** TRASLADO : move, moving

mudar *v* **1** CAMBIAR : to change **2** : to molt, to shed — **mudarse** *vr* **1** TRASLADARSE : to move (one's residence) **2** : to change (clothes)

mudo[1], -da *adj* **1** SILENCIOSO : silent <el cine mudo : silent films> **2** : mute, dumb

mudo[2], -da *n* : mute

mueble *nm* **1** : piece of furniture **2 muebles** *nmpl* : furniture, furnishings

mueblería *nf* : furniture store

mueca *nf* : grimace, face

muela *nf* **1** : tooth, molar <dolor de muelas : toothache> <muela de juicio : wisdom tooth> **2** : millstone **3** : whetstone

muele, etc. → **moler**

muelle[1] *adj* : soft, comfortable, easy

muelle[2] *nm* **1** : wharf, dock **2** RESORTE : spring

muérdago *nm* : mistletoe

muerde, etc. → **morder**

muere, etc. → **morir**

muerte *nf* : death

muerto[1] *pp* → **morir**

muerto[2], -ta *adj* **1** : dead **2** : lifeless, flat, dull **3 ~ de** : dying of <estoy muerto de hambre : I'm dying of hunger>

muerto[3], -ta *nm* DIFUNTO : dead person, deceased

muesca *nf* : nick, notch

muestra[1], etc. → **mostrar**

muestra[2] *nf* **1** : sample **2** SEÑAL : sign, show <una muestra de respeto : a show of respect> **3** EXPOSICIÓN : exhibition, exposition **4** : pattern, model

mueve, etc. → **mover**

mugido *nm* : moo, lowing, bellow

mugir {35} *vi* : to moo, to low, to bellow

mugre *nf* SUCIEDAD : grime, filth

mugriento, -ta *adj* : filthy

muguete *nm* : lily of the valley

muja, etc. → **mugir**

mujer *nf* **1** : woman **2** ESPOSA : wife

mulato, -ta *adj & n* : mulatto

muleta *nf* : crutch

mullido, -da *adj* **1** : soft, fluffy **2** : spongy, springy

mulo, -la *n* : mule

multa *nf* : fine

multicolor *adj* : multicolored

multicultural *adj* : multicultural

multidisciplinario, -ria *adj* : multidisciplinary

multifacético, -ca *adj* : multifaceted

multifamiliar *adj* : multifamily

multilateral *adj* : multilateral

multimedia *nf* : multimedia

multimillonario, -ria *n* : multimillionaire

multinacional *adj* : multinational

múltiple *adj* : multiple

multiplicación *nf, pl* **-ciones** : multiplication

multiplicar {72} *v* **1** : to multiply **2** : to increase — **multiplicarse** *vr* : to multiply, to reproduce

multiplicidad *nf* : multiplicity

múltiplo *nm* : multiple

multitud *nf* MUCHEDUMBRE : crowd, multitude

multiuso, -sa *adj* : multipurpose

multivitamínico, -ca *adj* : multivitamin

mundano, -na *adj* : worldly, earthly

mundial *adj* : world, worldwide

mundialmente *adv* : worldwide, all over the world

mundo *nm* **1** : world **2 todo el mundo** : everyone, everybody

municiones *nfpl* : ammunition, munitions

municipal *adj* : municipal

municipio *nm* **1** : municipality **2** AYUNTAMIENTO : town council

muñeca *nf* **1** : doll **2** MANIQUÍ : mannequin **3** : wrist

muñeco *nm* **1** : doll, boy doll **2** MARIONETA : puppet

muñon *nm, pl* **muñones** : stump (of an arm or leg)

mural *adj & nm* : mural

muralista *nmf* : muralist

muralla *nf* : rampart, wall

murciélago *nm* : bat (animal)

murga *nf* : band of street musicians

murió, etc. → **morir**

murmullo *nm* **1** : murmur, murmuring **2** : rustling, rustle <el murmullo de las hojas : the rustling of the leaves>

murmurar *vt* **1** : to murmur, to mutter **2** : to whisper (gossip) — *vi* **1** : to murmur **2** CHISMEAR : to gossip

muro *nm* : wall

musa *nf* : muse

musaraña *nf* : shrew

muscular *adj* : muscular

musculatura *nf* : muscles *pl,* musculature

músculo *nm* : muscle

musculoso, -sa *adj* : muscular, brawny

muselina *nf* : muslin

museo *nm* : museum

musgo *nm* : moss

musgoso, -sa *adj* : mossy

música *nf* : music

musical *adj* : musical — **musicalmente** *adv*

músico[1], -ca *adj* : musical

músico[2], -ca *n* : musician

musitar *vt* : to mumble, to murmur

muslo *nm* : thigh

musulmán, -mana *adj & n, mpl* **-manes** : Muslim

mutación *nf, pl* **-ciones** : mutation

mutante *adj & nm* : mutant

mutar *v* : to mutate

mutilar *vt* : to mutilate — **mutilación** *nf*

mutis *nm* **1** : exit (in theater) **2** : silence

mutual *adj* : mutual

mutuo, -tua *adj* : mutual, reciprocal — **mutuamente** *adv*
muy *adv* **1** : very, quite <es muy inteligente : she's very intelligent> <muy bien : very well, fine> <eso es muy americano : that's typically American> **2** : too <es muy grande para él : it's too big for him>

N

n *nf* : fourteenth letter of the Spanish alphabet
nabo *nm* : turnip
nácar *nm* MADREPERLA : nacre, mother-of-pearl
nacarado, -da *adj* : pearly
nacer {48} *vi* **1** : to be born <nací en Guatemala : I was born in Guatemala> <no nació ayer : he wasn't born yesterday> **2** : to hatch **3** : to bud, to sprout **4** : to rise, to originate **5 nacer para algo** : to be born to be something **6 volver a nacer** : to have a lucky escape
nacido¹, -da *adj* **1** : born **2 recién nacido** : newborn
nacido², -da *n* **1 los nacidos** : those born (at a particular time) **2 recién nacido** : newborn baby
naciente *adj* **1** : newfound, growing **2** : rising <el sol naciente : the rising sun>
nacimiento *nm* **1** : birth **2** : source (of a river) **3** : beginning, origin **4** BELÉN : Nativity scene, crèche
nación *nf, pl* **naciones** : nation, country, people (of a country)
nacional¹ *adj* : national
nacional² *nmf* CIUDADANO : national, citizen
nacionalidad *nf* : nationality
nacionalismo *nm* : nationalism
nacionalista¹ *adj* : nationalist, nationalistic
nacionalista² *nmf* : nationalist
nacionalización *nf, pl* **-ciones 1** : nationalization **2** : naturalization
nacionalizar {21} *vt* **1** : to nationalize **2** : to naturalize (as a citizen) — **nacionalizarse** *vr*
naco, -ca *adj Mex* : trashy, vulgar, common
nada¹ *adv* : not at all, not in the least <no estamos nada cansados : we are not at all tired>
nada² *nf* **1** : nothingness **2** : smidgen, bit <una nada le disgusta : the slightest thing upsets him>
nada³ *pron* **1** : nothing <no estoy haciendo nada : I'm not doing anything> **2 casi nada** : next to nothing **3 de ~** : you're welcome **4 dentro de nada** : very soon, in no time **5 nada más** : nothing else, nothing more
nadador, -dora *n* : swimmer
nadar *vi* **1** : to swim **2 ~ en** : to be swimming in, to be rolling in — *vt* : to swim
nadería *nf* : small thing, trifle
nadie *pron* : nobody, no one <no vi a nadie : I didn't see anyone>
nadir *nm* : nadir
nado *nm* **1** *Mex* : swimming **2 a ~** : swimming <cruzó el río a nado : he swam across the river>
nafta *nf* **1** : naphtha **2** (*in various countries*) : gasoline
naftalina *nf* : naphthalene, mothballs *pl*
náhuatl¹ *adj & nmf, pl* **nahuas** : Nahuatl
náhuatl² *nm* : Nahuatl (language)
nailon → **nilón**
naipe *nm* : playing card
nalga *nf* **1** : buttock **2 nalgas** *nfpl* : buttocks, bottom
nalgada *nf* : smack on the bottom, spanking
namibio, -bia *adj & n* : Namibian
nana *nf* **1** : lullaby **2** *fam* : grandma **3** *CA, Col, Mex, Ven* : nanny
nanay *interj fam* : no way!, not likely!
naranja¹ *adj & nm* : orange (color)
naranja² *nf* : orange (fruit)
naranjal *nm* : orange grove
naranjo *nm* : orange tree
narcisismo *nm* : narcissism
narcisista¹ *adj* : narcissistic
narcisista² *nmf* : narcissist
narciso *nm* : narcissus, daffodil
narcótico¹, -ca *adj* : narcotic
narcótico² *nm* : narcotic
narcotizar {21} *vt* : to drug, to dope
narcotraficante *nmf* : drug trafficker
narcotráfico *nm* : drug trafficking
narigón, -gona *adj, mpl* **-gones** : big-nosed
narigudo → **narigón**
nariz *nf, pl* **narices 1** : nose <sonar(se) la nariz : to blow one's nose> **2** : sense of smell
narración *nf, pl* **-ciones** : narration, account
narrador, -dora *n* : narrator
narrar *vt* : to narrate, to tell
narrativa *nf* : narrative, story
narrativo, -va *adj* : narrative
narval *nm* : narwhal
nasa *nf* : creel
nasal *adj* : nasal
nata *nf* **1** : cream <nata batida : whipped cream> **2** : skin (on boiled milk)
natación *nf, pl* **-ciones** : swimming
natal *adj* : native, natal
natalicio *nm* : birthday <el natalicio de George Washington : George Washington's birthday>
natalidad *nf* : birthrate

natillas *nfpl* : custard

natividad *nf* : birth, nativity

nativo, -va *adj & n* : native

natural[1] *adj* **1** : natural **2** : normal <como es natural : naturally, as expected> **3 ~ de** : native of, from **4 de tamaño natural** : life-size

natural[2] *nm* **1** CARÁCTER : disposition, temperament **2** : native <un natural de Venezuela : a native of Venezuela>

naturaleza *nf* **1** : nature <la madre naturaleza : mother nature> **2** ÍNDOLE : nature, disposition, constitution <la naturaleza humana : human nature> **3 naturaleza muerta** : still life

naturalidad *nf* : simplicity, naturalness

naturalismo *nm* : naturalism

naturalista[1] *adj* : naturalistic

naturalista[2] *nmf* : naturalist

naturalización *nf, pl* **-ciones** : naturalization

naturalizar {21} *vt* : to naturalize — **naturalizarse** *vr* NACIONALIZARSE : to become naturalized

naturalmente *adv* **1** : naturally, inherently **2** : of course

naufragar {52} *vi* **1** : to be shipwrecked **2** FRACASAR : to fail, to collapse

naufragio *nm* **1** : shipwreck **2** FRACASO : failure, collapse

náufrago[1], -ga *adj* : shipwrecked, castaway

náufrago[2], -ga *n* : shipwrecked person, castaway

náusea *nf* **1** : nausea **2 dar náuseas** : to nauseate, to disgust **3 náuseas matutinas** : morning sickness

nauseabundo, -da *adj* : nauseating, sickening

náutica *nf* : navigation

náutico, -ca *adj* : nautical

nautilo *nm* : nautilus

navaja *nf* **1** : pocketknife, penknife <navaja de muelle : switchblade> **2 navaja de afeitar** : straight razor, razor blade

navajo, -ja *adj & n* : Navajo

naval *adj* : naval

nave *nf* **1** : ship <nave capitana : flagship> <nave espacial : spaceship> **2** : nave <nave lateral : aisle> **3 quemar uno sus naves** : to burn one's bridges

navegabilidad *nf* : navigability

navegable *adj* : navigable

navegación *nf, pl* **-ciones** : navigation

navegante[1] *adj* : sailing, seafaring

navegante[2] *nmf* : navigator

navegar {52} *v* : to navigate, to sail

Navidad *nf* : Christmas, Christmastime <Feliz Navidad : Merry Christmas>

navideño, -ña *adj* : Christmas

naviero, -ra *adj* : shipping

náyade *nf* : naiad

nazca, etc. → **nacer**

nazi *adj & nmf* : Nazi

nazismo *nm* : Nazism

nébeda *nf* : catnip

neblina *nf* : light fog, mist

neblinoso, -sa *adj* : misty, foggy

nebulosa *nf* : nebula

nebulosidad *nf* : mistiness, haziness

nebuloso, -sa *adj* **1** : hazy, misty **2** : nebulous, vague

necedad *nf* : stupidity, foolishness <decir necedades : to talk nonsense>

necesariamente *adv* : necessarily

necesario, -ria *adj* **1** : necessary **2 si es necesario** : if need be **3 hacerse necesario** : to be required

neceser *nm* : toilet kit, vanity case

necesidad *nf* **1** : need, necessity **2** : poverty, want **3 necesidades** *nfpl* : hardships **4 hacer sus necesidades** : to relieve oneself

necesitado, -da *adj* : needy

necesitar *vt* **1** : to need **2** : to necessitate, to require — *vi* **~ de** : to have need of

necio[1], -cia *adj* **1** : foolish, silly, dumb **2** *fam* : naughty

necio[2], -cia *n* ESTÚPIDO : fool, idiot

necrología *nf* : obituary

necrópolis *nfs & pl* : cemetery

néctar *nm* : nectar

nectarina *nf* : nectarine

neerlandés[1], -desa *adj, mpl* **-deses** HOLANDÉS : Dutch

neerlandés[2], -desa *n, mpl* **-deses** HOLANDÉS : Dutch person, Dutchman *m*

nefando, -da *adj* : unspeakable, heinous

nefario, -ria *adj* : nefarious

nefasto, -ta *adj* **1** : ill-fated, unlucky **2** : disastrous, terrible

negación *nf, pl* **-ciones 1** : negation, denial **2** : negative (in grammar)

negar {49} *vt* **1** : to deny **2** REHUSAR : to refuse **3** : to disown — **negarse** *vr* **1** : to refuse **2** : to deny oneself

negativa *nf* **1** : denial **2** : refusal

negativo[1], -va *adj* : negative

negativo[2] *nm* : negative (of a photograph)

negligé *nm* : negligee

negligencia *nf* : negligence

negligente *adj* : neglectful, negligent — **negligentemente** *adv*

negociable *adj* : negotiable

negociación *nf, pl* **-ciones 1** : negotiation **2 negociación colectiva** : collective bargaining

negociador, -dora *n* : negotiator

negociante *nmf* : businessman *m*, businesswoman *f*

negociar *vt* : to negotiate — *vi* : to deal, to do business

negocio *nm* **1** : business, place of business **2** : deal, transaction **3 negocios** *nmpl* : commerce, trade, business

negrero, -ra *n* **1** : slave trader **2** *fam* : slave driver, brutal boss

negrita *nf* : boldface (type)

negro[1], **-gra** *adj* **1 :** black, dark **2** BRONCEADO **:** suntanned **3 :** gloomy, awful, desperate <la cosa se está poniendo negra : things are looking bad> **4 mercado negro :** black market
negro[2], **-gra** *n* **1 :** dark-skinned person, black person **2** *fam* **:** darling, dear
negro[3] *nm* **:** black (color)
negrura *nf* **:** blackness
negruzco, -ca *adj* **:** blackish
nene, -na *n* **:** baby, small child
nenúfar *nm* **:** water lily
neocelandés → **neozelandés**
neoclasicismo *nm* **:** neoclassicism
neoclásico, -ca *adj* **:** neoclassical
neófito, -ta *n* **:** neophyte, novice
neologismo *nm* **:** neologism
neón *nm, pl* **neones :** neon
neoyorquino[1], **-na** *adj* **:** of or from New York
neoyorquino[2], **-na** *n* **:** New Yorker
neozelandés[1], **-desa** *adj, mpl* **-deses :** of or from New Zealand
neozelandés[2], **-desa** *n, mpl* **-deses :** New Zealander
nepalés, -lesa *adj & n, mpl* **-leses :** Nepali
nepotismo *nm* **:** nepotism
neptunio *nm* **:** neptunium
Neptuno *nm* **:** Neptune
nervio *nm* **1 :** nerve **2 :** tendon, sinew, gristle (in meat) **3 :** energy, drive **4 :** rib (of a vault) **5 nervios** *nmpl* **:** nerves <estar mal de los nervios : to be a bundle of nerves> <ataque de nervios : nervous breakdown>
nerviosamente *adv* **:** nervously
nerviosidad *nf* → **nerviosismo**
nerviosismo *nf* **:** nervousness, anxiety
nervioso, -sa *adj* **1 :** nervous, nerve <sistema nervioso : nervous system> **2 :** high-strung, restless, anxious <ponerse nervioso : to get nervous> **3 :** vigorous, energetic
nervudo, -da *adj* **:** sinewy, wiry
neta *nf Mex fam* **:** truth <la neta es que me cae mal : the truth is, I don't like her>
netamente *adv* **:** clearly, obviously
neto, -ta *adj* **1 :** net <peso neto : net weight> **2 :** clear, distinct
neumático[1], **-ca** *adj* **:** pneumatic
neumático[2] *nm* LLANTA **:** tire
neumonía *nf* PULMONÍA **:** pneumonia
neural *adj* **:** neural
neuralgia *nf* **:** neuralgia
neuritis *nf* **:** neuritis
neurología *nf* **:** neurology
neurológico, -ca *adj* **:** neurological, neurologic
neurólogo, -ga *n* **:** neurologist
neurosis *nfs & pl* **:** neurosis
neurótico, -ca *adj & n* **:** neurotic
neutral *adj* **:** neutral
neutralidad *nf* **:** neutrality
neutralizar {21} *vt* **:** to neutralize — **neutralización** *nf*
neutro, -tra *adj* **1 :** neutral **2 :** neuter
neutrón *nm, pl* **neutrones :** neutron
nevada *nf* **:** snowfall
nevado, -da *adj* **1 :** snowcapped **2 :** snow-white
nevar {55} *v impers* **:** to snow
nevasca *nf* **:** snowstorm, blizzard
nevera *nf* REFRIGERADOR **:** refrigerator
nevería *nf Mex* **:** ice cream parlor
nevisca *nf* **:** light snowfall, flurry
nevoso, -sa *adj* **:** snowy
nexo *nm* VÍNCULO **:** link, connection, nexus
ni *conj* **1 :** neither, nor <afuera no hace ni frío ni calor : it's neither cold nor hot outside> **2 ni que :** not even if, not as if <ni que me pagaran : not even if they paid me> <ni que fuera (yo) su madre : it's not as if I were his mother> **3 ni siquiera :** not even <ni siquiera nos llamaron : they didn't even call us>
nicaragüense *adj & nmf* **:** Nicaraguan
nicho *nm* **:** niche
nicotina *nf* **:** nicotine
nido *nm* **1 :** nest **2 :** hiding place, den
niebla *nf* **:** fog, mist
niega, niegue, etc. → **negar**
nieto, -ta *n* **1 :** grandson *m,* granddaughter *f* **2 nietos** *nmpl* **:** grandchildren
nieva, etc. → **nevar**
nieve *nf* **1 :** snow **2** *Cuba, Mex, PRi* **:** sherbet
nigeriano, -na *adj & n* **:** Nigerian
nigua *nf* **:** sand flea, chigger
nihilismo *nm* **:** nihilism
nilón *or* **nilon** *nm, pl* **nilones :** nylon
nimbo *nm* **1 :** halo **2 :** nimbus
nimiedad *nf* INSIGNIFICANCIA **:** trifle, triviality
nimio, -mia *adj* INSIGNIFICANTE **:** insignificant, trivial
ninfa *nf* **:** nymph
ningunear *vt Mex fam* **:** to disrespect
ninguno[1], **-na** (**ningún** *before masculine singular nouns*) *adj, mpl* **ningunos :** no, none <no es ninguna tonta : she's no fool> <no debe hacerse en ningún momento : that should never be done>
ninguno[2], **-na** *pron* **1 :** neither, none <ninguno de los dos ha vuelto aún : neither one has returned yet> **2 :** no one, no other <te quiero más que a ninguna : I love you more than any other>
niña *nf* **1** PUPILA **:** pupil (of the eye) **2 la niña de los ojos :** the apple of one's eye
niñada *nf* **1 :** childishness **2 :** trifle, silly thing
niñería *nf* → **niñada**
niñero, -ra *n* **:** baby-sitter, nanny
niñez *nf, pl* **niñeces** INFANCIA **:** childhood
niño, -ña *n* **:** child, boy *m,* girl *f*
niobio *nm* **:** niobium
nipón, -pona *adj & n, mpl* **nipones** JAPONÉS **:** Japanese
níquel *nm* **:** nickel

nitidez *nf, pl* **-deces** CLARIDAD : clarity, vividness, sharpness
nítido, -da *adj* CLARO : clear, vivid, sharp
nitrato *nm* : nitrate
nítrico, -ca *adj* **ácido nítrico** : nitric acid
nitrito *nm* : nitrite
nitrógeno *nm* : nitrogen
nitroglicerina *nf* : nitroglycerin
nivel *nm* **1** : level, height <nivel del mar : sea level> **2** : level, standard <nivel de vida : standard of living>
nivelar *vt* : to level (out)
nixtamal *nm Mex* : limed corn used for tortillas
no *adv* **1** : no <¿quieres ir al mercado? no, voy más tarde : do you want to go shopping? no, I'm going later> **2** : not <¡no hagas eso! : don't do that!> <creo que no : I don't think so> **3** : non- <no fumador : non-smoker> **4** **¡como no!** : of course! **5** **no bien** : as soon as, no sooner
nobelio *nm* : nobelium
noble[1] *adj* : noble — **noblemente** *adv*
noble[2] *nmf* : nobleman *m*, noblewoman *f*
nobleza *nf* **1** : nobility **2** HONRADEZ : honesty, integrity
nocaut *nm* : knockout, KO
noche *nf* **1** : night, nighttime, evening **2** **buenas noches** : good evening, good night **3** **de noche** *or* **por la noche** : at night **4** **hacerse de noche** : to get dark
Nochebuena *nf* : Christmas Eve
nochecita *nf* : dusk
Nochevieja *nf* : New Year's Eve
noción *nf, pl* **nociones** **1** CONCEPTO : notion, concept **2** **nociones** *nfpl* : smattering, rudiments *pl*
nocivo, -va *adj* DAÑINO : harmful, noxious
noctámbulo, -la *n* **1** : sleepwalker **2** : night owl
nocturno[1], **-na** *adj* : night, nocturnal
nocturno[2] *nm* : nocturne
nodriza *nf* : wet nurse
nódulo *nm* : nodule
nogal *nm* **1** : walnut tree **2** *Mex* : pecan tree **3** **nogal americano** : hickory
nómada[1] *adj* : nomadic
nómada[2] *nmf* : nomad
nomás *adv* : only, just <lo hice nomás porque sí : I did it just because> <nomás de recordarlo me enojo : I get angry just remembering it> <nomás faltan dos semanas para Navidad : there are only two weeks left till Christmas>
nombradía *nf* RENOMBRE : fame, renown
nombrado, -da *adj* : famous, well-known
nombramiento *nm* : appointment, nomination
nombrar *vt* **1** : to appoint **2** : to mention, to name
nombre *nm* **1** : name <nombre de pluma : pseudonym, pen name> <en nombre : on behalf of> <sin nombre : nameless> **2** : noun <nombre propio : proper noun> **3** : fame, renown
nomenclatura *nf* : nomenclature
nomeolvides *nmfs & pl* : forget-me-not
nómina *nf* : payroll
nominación *nf, pl* **-ciones** : nomination
nominal *adj* : nominal — **nominalmente** *adv*
nominar *vt* : to nominate
nominativo[1], **-va** *adj* : nominative
nominativo[2] *nm* : nominative (case)
nomo *nm* : gnome
non[1] *adj* IMPAR : odd, not even
non[2] *nm* : odd number
nonagésimo[1], **-ma** *adj* : ninetieth, ninety-
nonagésimo[2], **-ma** *n* : ninetieth, ninety- (in a series)
nono, -na *adj* : ninth — **nono** *nm*
nopal *nm* : nopal, cactus
nopalitos *nmpl Mex* : pickled cactus leaves
noquear *vt* : to knock out, to KO
norcoreano, -na *adj & n* : North Korean
nordeste[1] *or* **noreste** *adj* **1** : northeastern **2** : northeasterly
nordeste[2] *or* **noreste** *nm* : northeast
nórdico, -ca *adj & n* ESCANDINAVO : Scandinavian
noreste → **nordeste**
noria *nf* **1** : waterwheel **2** : Ferris wheel
norirlandés[1], **-desa** *adj, mpl* **-deses** : Northern Irish
norirlandés[2], **-desa** *n, mpl* **-deses** : person from Northern Ireland
norma *nf* **1** : rule, regulation **2** : norm, standard
normal *adj* **1** : normal, usual **2** : standard **3** **escuela normal** : teacher-training college
normalidad *nf* : normality, normalcy
normalización *nf, pl* **-ciones** *nf* **1** REGULARIZACIÓN : normalization **2** ESTANDARIZACIÓN : standardization
normalizar {21} *vt* **1** REGULARIZAR : to normalize **2** ESTANDARIZAR : to standardize — **normalizarse** *vr* : to return to normal
normalmente *adv* GENERALMENTE : ordinarily, generally
noroeste[1] *adj* **1** : northwestern **2** : northwesterly
noroeste[2] *nm* : northwest
norte[1] *adj* : north, northern
norte[2] *nm* **1** : north **2** : north wind **3** META : aim, objective
norteamericano, -na *adj & n* **1** : North American **2** AMERICANO, ESTADOUNIDENSE : American, native or inhabitant of the United States
norteño[1], **-ña** *adj* : northern
norteño[2], **-ña** *n* : Northerner

noruego[1], -ga *adj & n* : Norwegian

noruego[2] *nm* : Norwegian (language)

nos *pron* **1** : us <nos enviaron a la frontera : they sent us to the border> **2** : ourselves <nos divertimos muchísimo : we enjoyed ourselves a great deal> **3** : each other, one another <nos vimos desde lejos : we saw each other from far away> **4** : to us, for us, from us <nos lo dio : he gave it to us> <nos lo compraron : they bought it from us>

nosotros, -tras *pron* **1** : we <nosotros llegamos ayer : we arrived yesterday> **2** : us <ven con nosotros : come with us> **3 nosotros mismos** : ourselves <lo arreglamos nosotros mismos : we fixed it ourselves>

nostalgia *nf* **1** : nostalgia, longing **2** : homesickness

nostálgico, -ca *adj* **1** : nostalgic **2** : homesick

nota *nf* **1** : note, message **2** : announcement <nota de prensa : press release> **3** : grade, mark (in school) **4** : characteristic, feature, touch **5** : note (in music) **6** : bill, check (in a restaraunt)

notable *adj* **1** : notable, noteworthy **2** : outstanding

notar *vt* **1** : to notice <hacer notar algo : to point out something> **2** : to tell <la diferencia se nota inmediatamente : you can tell the difference right away> — **notarse** *vr* **1** : to be evident, to show **2** : to feel, to seem

notario, -ria *n* : notary, notary public

noticia *nf* **1** : news item, piece of news **2 noticias** *nfpl* : news

noticiero *nm* : news program, newscast

noticioso, -sa *adj* : news <agencia noticiosa : news agency>

notificación *nf, pl* **-ciones** : notification

notificar {72} *vt* : to notify, to inform

notoriedad *nf* **1** : knowledge, obviousness **2** : fame, notoriety

notorio, -ria *adj* **1** OBVIO : obvious, evident **2** CONOCIDO : well-known

novato[1], -ta *adj* : inexperienced, new

novato[2], -ta *n* : beginner, novice

novecientos[1], -tas *adj* : nine hundred

novecientos[2] *nms & pl* : nine hundred

novedad *nf* **1** : newness, novelty **2** : innovation

novedoso, -sa *adj* : original, novel

novel *adj* NOVATO : inexperienced, new

novela *nf* **1** : novel **2** : soap opera

novelar *vt* : to fictionalize, to make a novel out of

novelesco, -ca *adj* **1** : fictional **2** : fantastic, fabulous

novelista *nmf* : novelist

novena *nf* : novena

noveno, -na *adj* : ninth — **noveno, -na** *n*

noventa *adj & nm* : ninety

noventavo[1], -va *adj* : ninetieth

noventavo[2] *nm* : ninetieth (fraction)

noviazgo *nm* **1** : courtship, relationship **2** : engagement, betrothal

novicio, -cia *n* **1** : novice (in religion) **2** PRINCIPIANTE : novice, beginner

noviembre *nm* : November

novilla *nf* : heifer

novillada *nf* : bullfight featuring young bulls

novillero, -ra *n* : apprentice bullfighter

novillo *nm* : young bull

novio, -via *n* **1** : boyfriend *m,* girlfriend *f* **2** PROMETIDO : fiancé *m,* fiancée *f* **3** : bridegroom *m,* bride *f*

novocaína *nf* : novocaine

nubarrón *nm, pl* **-rrones** : storm cloud

nube *nf* **1** : cloud <andar en las nubes : to have one's head in the clouds> <por las nubes : sky-high> **2** : cloud (of dust), swarm (of insects, etc.)

nublado[1], -da *adj* **1** NUBOSO : cloudy, overcast **2** : clouded, dim

nublado[2] *nm* **1** : storm cloud **2** AMENAZA : menace, threat

nublar *vt* **1** : to cloud **2** OSCURECER : to obscure — **nublarse** *vr* : to get cloudy

nubosidad *nf* : cloudiness

nuboso, -sa *adj* NUBLADO : cloudy

nuca *nf* : nape, back of the neck

nuclear *adj* : nuclear

núcleo *nm* **1** : nucleus **2** : center, heart, core

nudillo *nm* : knuckle

nudismo *nm* : nudism

nudista *adj & nmf* : nudist

nudo *nm* **1** : knot <square knot : nudo de rizo> <un nudo en la garganta : a lump in one's throat> **2** : node **3** : junction, hub <nudo de comunicaciones : communication center> **4** : crux, heart (of a problem, etc.)

nudoso, -sa *adj* : knotty, gnarled

nuera *nf* : daughter-in-law

nuestro[1], -tra *adj* : our

nuestro[2], -tra *pron* (*with definite article*) : ours, our own <el nuestro es más grande : ours is bigger> <es de los nuestros : it's one of ours>

nuevamente *adv* : again, anew

nuevas *nfpl* : tidings *pl*

nueve *adj & nm* : nine

nuevecito, -ta *adj* : brand-new

nuevo, -va *adj* **1** : new <una casa nueva : a new house> <¿qué hay de nuevo? : what's new?> **2 de ~** : again, once more

nuez *nf, pl* **nueces 1** : nut **2** : walnut **3** *Mex* : pecan **4 nuez de Adán** : Adam's apple **5 nuez moscada** : nutmeg

nulidad *nf* **1** : nullity **2** : incompetent person <¡es una nulidad! : he's hopeless!>

nulo, -la *adj* **1** : null, null and void **2** INEPTO : useless, inept <es nula para la cocina : she's hopeless at cooking>

numen *nm* : poetic muse, inspiration

numerable *adj* : countable

numeración *nf, pl* **-ciones 1 :** numbering **2 :** numbers *pl,* numerals *pl* <numeración romana : Roman numerals>

numerador *nm* **:** numerator

numeral *adj* **:** numeral

numerar *vt* **:** to number

numerario, -ria *adj* **:** long-standing, permanent <profesor numerario : tenured professor>

numérico, -ca *adj* **:** numerical — **numéricamente** *adv*

número *nm* **1 :** number <número impar : odd number> <número ordinal : ordinal number> <número arábico : Arabic numeral> <número quebrado : fraction> **2 :** issue (of a publication) **3 sin ~ :** countless

numeroso, -sa *adj* **:** numerous

numismática *nf* **:** numismatics

nunca *adv* **1 :** never, ever <nunca es tarde : it's never too late> <no trabaja casi nunca : he hardly ever works> **2 nunca más :** never again **3 nunca jamás :** never ever

nuncio *nm* **:** harbinger, herald

nupcial *adj* **:** nuptial, wedding

nupcias *nfpl* **:** nuptials *pl,* wedding

nutria *nf* **1 :** otter **2 :** nutria

nutrición *nf, pl* **-ciones :** nutrition, nourishment

nutrido, -da *adj* **1 :** nourished <mal nutrido : undernourished, malnourished> **2 :** considerable, abundant <de nutrido : full of, abounding in>

nutriente *nm* **:** nutrient

nutrimento *nm* **:** nutriment

nutrir *vt* **1** ALIMENTAR **:** to feed, to nourish **2 :** to foster, to provide

nutritivo, -va *adj* **:** nourishing, nutritious

nylon *nm* → **nilón**

ñ *nf* **:** fifteenth letter of the Spanish alphabet

ñame *nm* **:** yam

ñandú *nm* **:** rhea

ñapa *nf* **:** extra amount <de ñapa : for good measure>

ñoñear *vi fam* **:** to whine

ñoño, -ña *adj fam* **:** whiny, fussy <no seas tan ñoño : don't be such a wimp>

ñoquis *nmpl* **:** gnocchi *pl*

ñu *nm* **:** gnu, wildebeest

O

o[1] *nf* **:** sixteenth letter of the Spanish alphabet

o[2] *conj* (**u** *before words beginning with o- or ho-*) **1 :** or <¿vienes con nosotros o te quedas? : are you coming with us or staying?> **2 :** either <o vienes con nosotros o te quedas : either you come with us or you stay> **3 o sea :** that is to say, in other words

oasis *nms & pl* **:** oasis

obcecado, -da *adj* **1 :** blinded <obcecado por la ira : blinded by rage> **2 :** stubborn, obstinate

obcecar {72} *vt* **:** to blind (by emotions) — **obcecarse** *vr* **:** to become stubborn

obedecer {53} *vt* **:** to obey <obedecer órdenes : to obey orders> <obedece a tus padres : obey your parents> — *vi* **1 :** to obey **2 ~ a :** to respond to **3 ~ a :** to be due to, to result from

obediencia *nf* **:** obedience

obediente *adj* **:** obedient — **obedientemente** *adv*

obelisco *nm* **:** obelisk

obertura *nf* **:** overture

obesidad *nf* **:** obesity

obeso, -sa *adj* **:** obese

óbice *nm* **:** obstacle, impediment

obispado *nm* DIÓCESIS **:** bishopric, diocese

obispo *nm* **:** bishop

obituario *nm* **:** obituary

objeción *nf, pl* **-ciones :** objection <ponerle objeciones a algo : to object to something>

objetar *v* **:** to object <no tengo nada que objetar : I have no objections>

objetividad *nf* **:** objectivity

objetivo[1]**, -va** *adj* **:** objective — **objetivamente** *adv*

objetivo[2] *nm* **1** META **:** objective, goal, target **2 :** lens

objeto *nm* **1** COSA **:** object, thing **2** OBJETIVO **:** objective, purpose <con objeto de : in order to, with the aim of> **3 objeto volador no identificado :** unidentified flying object

objetor, -tora *n* **:** objector <objetor de conciencia : conscientious objector>

oblea *nf* **1 :** wafer **2 hecho una oblea** *fam* **:** skinny as a rail

oblicuo, -cua *adj* **:** oblique — **oblicuamente** *adv*

obligación *nf, pl* **-ciones 1** DEBER **:** obligation, duty **2 :** bond, debenture

obligado, -da *adj* **1 :** obliged **2 :** obligatory, compulsory **3 :** customary

obligar {52} *vt* **:** to force, to require, to oblige — **obligarse** *vr* **:** to commit oneself, to undertake (to do something)

obligatorio, -ria *adj* : mandatory, required, compulsory

obliterar *vt* : to obliterate, to destroy — **obliteración** *nf*

oblongo, -ga *adj* : oblong

obnubilación *nf, pl* **-ciones** : bewilderment, confusion

obnubilar *vt* : to daze, to bewilder

oboe[1] *nm* : oboe

oboe[2] *nmf* : oboist

obra *nf* **1** : work <obra de arte : work of art> <obra de teatro : play> <obra de consulta : reference work> **2** : deed <una buena obra : a good deed> **3** : construction work **4 obra maestra** : masterpiece **5 obras públicas** : public works **6 por obra de** : thanks to, because of

obrar *vt* : to work, to produce <obrar milagros : to work miracles> — *vi* **1** : to act, to behave <obrar con cautela : to act with caution> **2 obrar en poder de** : to be in possession of

obrero[1], -ra *adj* : working <la clase obrera : the working class>

obrero[2], -ra *n* : worker, laborer

obscenidad *nf* : obscenity

obsceno, -na *adj* : obscene

obscurecer, obscuridad, obscuro → **oscurecer, oscuridad, oscuro**

obsequiar *vt* REGALAR : to give, to present <lo obsequiaron con una placa : they presented him with a plaque>

obsequio *nm* REGALO : gift, present

obsequiosidad *nf* : attentiveness, deference

obsequioso, -sa *adj* : obliging, attentive

observación *nf, pl* **-ciones 1** : observation, watching **2** : remark, comment

observador[1], -dora *adj* : observant

observador[2], -dora *n* : observer, watcher

observancia *nf* : observance

observar *vt* **1** : to observe, to watch <estábamos observando a los niños : we were watching the children> **2** NOTAR : to notice **3** ACATAR : to obey, to abide by **4** COMENTAR : to remark, to comment

observatorio *nm* : observatory

obsesión *nf, pl* **-siones** : obsession

obsesionar *vt* : to obsess, to preoccupy excessively — **obsesionarse** *vr*

obsesivo, -va *adj* : obsessive

obseso, -sa *adj* : obsessed

obsolescencia *nf* DESUSO : obsolescence — **obsolescente** *adj*

obsoleto, -ta *adj* DESUSADO : obsolete

obstaculizar {21} *vt* IMPEDIR : to obstruct, to hinder

obstáculo *nm* IMPEDIMENTO : obstacle

obstante[1] *conj* **no obstante** : nevertheless, however

obstante[2] *prep* **no obstante** : in spite of, despite <mantuvo su inocencia no obstante la evidencia : he maintained his innocence in spite of the evidence>

obstar *v impers* **~ a** *or* **~ para** : to hinder, to prevent <eso no obsta para que me vaya : that doesn't prevent me from leaving>

obstetra *nmf* TOCÓLOGO : obstetrician

obstetricia *nf* : obstetrics

obstétrico, -ca *adj* : obstetric, obstetrical

obstinación *nf, pl* **-ciones 1** TERQUEDAD : obstinacy, stubbornness **2** : perseverance, tenacity

obstinado, -da *adj* **1** TERCO : obstinate, stubborn **2** : persistent — **obstinadamente** *adv*

obstinarse *vr* EMPECINARSE : to be obstinate, to be stubborn

obstrucción *nf, pl* **-ciones** : obstruction, blockage

obstruccionismo *nm* : obstructionism, filibustering

obstructor, -tora *adj* : obstructive

obstruir {41} *vt* BLOQUEAR : to obstruct, to block, to clog — **obstruirse** *vr*

obtención *nf* : obtaining, procurement

obtener {80} *vt* : to obtain, to secure, to get — **obtenible** *adj*

obturador *nm* : shutter (of a camera)

obtuso, -sa *adj* : obtuse

obtuvo, etc. → **obtener**

obviar *vt* : to get around (a difficulty), to avoid

obvio, -via *adj* : obvious — **obviamente** *adv*

oca *nf* : goose

ocasión *nf, pl* **-siones 1** : occasion, time **2** : opportunity, chance **3** : bargain **4 de ~** : secondhand **5 aviso de ocasión** *Mex* : classified ad

ocasional *adj* **1** : occasional **2** : chance, fortuitous

ocasionalmente *adv* **1** : occasionally **2** : by chance

ocasionar *vt* CAUSAR : to cause, to occasion

ocaso *nm* **1** ANOCHECER : sunset, sundown **2** DECADENCIA : decline, fall

occidental *adj* : western, occidental

occidente *nm* **1** OESTE, PONIENTE : west **2 el Occidente** : the West

oceánico, -ca *adj* : oceanic

océano *nm* : ocean

oceanografía *nf* : oceanography

oceanográfico, -ca *adj* : oceanographic

ocelote *nm* : ocelot

ochenta *adj & nm* : eighty

ochentavo[1], -va *adj* : eightieth

ochentavo[2] *nm* : eightieth (fraction)

ocho *adj & nm* : eight

ochocientos[1], -tas *adj* : eight hundred

ochocientos[2] *nms & pl* : eight hundred

ocio *nm* **1** : free time, leisure **2** : idleness

ociosidad *nf* : idleness, inactivity

ocioso, -sa *adj* **1** INACTIVO **:** idle, inactive **2** INÚTIL **:** pointless, useless

ocre *nm* **:** ocher

octágono *nm* **:** octagon — **octagonal** *adj*

octava *nf* **:** octave

octavo, -va *adj* **:** eighth — **octavo, -va** *n*

octeto *nm* **1 :** octet **2 :** byte

octogésimo[1], -ma *adj* **:** eightieth, eighty-

octogésimo[2], -ma *n* **:** eightieth, eighty- (in a series)

octubre *nm* **:** October

ocular *adj* **1 :** ocular, eye <músculos oculares : eye muscles> **2 testigo ocular :** eyewitness

oculista *nmf* **:** oculist, opthalmologist

ocultación *nf, pl* **-ciones :** concealment

ocultar *vt* ESCONDER **:** to conceal, to hide — **ocultarse** *vr*

oculto, -ta *adj* **1** ESCONDIDO **:** hidden, concealed **2 :** occult

ocupación *nf, pl* **-ciones 1 :** occupation, activity **2 :** occupancy **3** EMPLEO **:** employment, job

ocupacional *adj* **:** occupational, job-related

ocupado, -da *adj* **1 :** busy **2 :** taken <este asiento está ocupado : this seat is taken> **3 :** occupied <territorios ocupados : occupied territories> **4 señal de ocupado :** busy signal

ocupante *nmf* **:** occupant

ocupar *vt* **1 :** to occupy, to take possession of **2 :** to hold (a position) **3 :** to employ, to keep busy **4 :** to fill (space, time) **5 :** to inhabit (a dwelling) **6 :** to bother, to concern — **ocuparse** *vr* **~ de 1 :** to be concerned with **2 :** to take care of

ocurrencia *nf* **1 :** occurrence, event **2 :** witticism **3 :** bright idea

ocurrente *adj* **1 :** witty **2 :** clever, sharp

ocurrir *vi* **:** to occur, to happen — **ocurrirse** *vr* **~ a :** to occur to, to strike <se me ocurrió una mejor idea : a better idea occurred to me>

oda *nf* **:** ode

odiar *vt* ABOMINAR, ABORRECER **:** to hate

odio *nm* **:** hate, hatred

odioso, -sa *adj* ABOMINABLE, ABORRECIBLE **:** hateful, detestable

odisea *nf* **:** odyssey

odontología *nf* **:** dentistry, dental surgery

odontólogo, -ga *n* **:** dentist, dental surgeon

oeste[1] *adj* **1 :** west, western <la región oeste : the western region> **2 :** westerly

oeste[2] *nm* **1 :** west, West **2 :** west wind

ofender *vt* AGRAVIAR **:** to offend, to insult — *vi* **:** to offend, to be insulting — **ofenderse** *vr* **:** to take offense

ofensa *nf* **:** offense, insult

ofensiva *nf* **:** offensive <pasar a la ofensiva : to go on the offensive>

ofensivo, -va *adj* **:** offensive, insulting

ofensor, -sora *n* **:** offender

oferente *nmf* **1 :** supplier **2** FUENTE **:** source <un oferente no identificado : an unidentified source>

oferta *nf* **1 :** offer **2 :** sale, bargain <las camisas están en oferta : the shirts are on sale> **3 oferta y demanda :** supply and demand

ofertar *vt* OFRECER **:** to offer

oficial[1] *adj* **:** official — **oficialmente** *adv*

oficial[2] *nmf* **1 :** officer, police officer, commissioned officer (in the military) **2 :** skilled worker

oficializar {21} *vt* **:** to make official

oficiante *nmf* **:** celebrant

oficiar *vt* **1 :** to inform officially **2 :** to officiate at, to celebrate (Mass) — *vi* **~ de :** to act as

oficina *nf* **:** office

oficinista *nmf* **:** office worker

oficio *nm* **1 :** trade, profession <es electricista de oficio : he's an electrician by trade> **2 :** function, role **3 :** official communication **4 :** experience <tener oficio : to be experienced> **5 :** religious ceremony

oficioso, -sa *adj* **1** EXTRAOFICIAL **:** unofficial **2 :** officious — **oficiosamente** *adv*

ofrecer {53} *vt* **1 :** to offer **2 :** to provide, to give **3 :** to present (an appearance, etc.) — **ofrecerse** *vr* **1 :** to offer oneself, to volunteer **2 :** to open up, to present itself

ofrecimiento *nm* **:** offer, offering

ofrenda *nf* **:** offering

oftalmología *nf* **:** ophthalmology

oftalmólogo, -ga *n* **:** ophthalmologist

ofuscación *nf, pl* **-ciones :** blindness, confusion

ofuscar {72} *vt* **1 :** to blind, to dazzle **2** CONFUNDIR **:** to bewilder, to confuse — **ofuscarse** *vr* **~ con :** to be blinded by

ogro *nm* **:** ogre

ohm *nm, pl* **ohms :** ohm

ohmio *nm* → **ohm**

oídas *nfpl* **de ~ :** by hearsay

oído *nm* **1 :** ear <oído interno : inner ear> **2 :** hearing <duro de oído : hard of hearing> **3 tocar de oído :** to play by ear

oiga, etc. → **oír**

oír {50} *vi* **:** to hear — *vt* **1 :** to hear **2** ESCUCHAR **:** to listen to **3 :** to pay attention to, to heed **4 ¡oye!** *or* **¡oiga! :** listen!, excuse me!, look here!

ojal *nm* **:** buttonhole

ojalá *interj* **1 :** I hope so!, if only!, God willing! **2 :** I hope, I wish, hopefully <¡ojalá que le vaya bien! : I hope things go well for her!> <¡ojalá no llueva! : hopefully it won't rain!>

ojeada *nf* **:** glimpse, glance <echar una ojeada : to have a quick look>

ojear *vt* **:** to eye, to have a look at

ojete *nm* **:** eyelet

ojiva *nf* : warhead

ojo *nm* **1** : eye **2** : judgment, sharpness <tener buen ojo para : to be a good judge of, to have a good eye for> **3** : hole (in cheese), eye (in a needle), center (of a storm) **4** : span (of a bridge) **5 a ojos vistas** : openly, publicly **6 andar con ojo** : to be careful **7 ojo de agua** *Mex* : spring, source **8 ¡ojo!** : look out!, pay attention!

ola *nf* **1** : wave **2 ola de calor** : heat wave

oleada *nf* : swell, wave <una oleada de protestas : a wave of protests>

oleaje *nm* : waves *pl*, surf

óleo *nm* **1** : oil **2** : oil painting

oleoducto *nm* : oil pipeline

oleoso, -sa *adj* : oily

oler {51} *vt* **1** : to smell **2** INQUIRIR : to pry into, to investigate **3** AVERIGUAR : to smell out, to uncover — *vi* **1** : to smell <huele mal : it smells bad> **2 ~ a** : to smell like, to smell of <huele a pino : it smells like pine> — **olerse** *vr* : to have a hunch, to suspect

olfatear *vt* **1** : to sniff **2** : to sense, to sniff out

olfativo, -va *adj* : olfactory

olfato *nm* **1** : sense of smell **2** : nose, instinct

oligarquía *nf* : oligarchy

olimpiada *or* **olimpíada** *nf* : Olympics *pl*, Olympic Games *pl*

olímpico, -ca *adj* : Olympic

olisquear *vt* : to sniff at

oliva *nf* ACEITUNA : olive <aceite de oliva : olive oil>

olivo *nm* : olive tree

olla *nf* **1** : pot <olla de presión : pressure cooker> **2 olla podrida** : Spanish stew

olmeca *adj & nmf* : Olmec

olmo *nm* : elm

olor *nm* : smell, odor

oloroso, -sa *adj* : scented, fragrant

olote *nm Mex* : cob, corncob

olvidadizo, -za *adj* : forgetful, absent-minded

olvidar *vt* **1** : to forget, to forget about <olvida lo que pasó : forget about what happened> **2** : to leave behind <olvidé mi chequera en la casa : I left my checkbook at home> — **olvidarse** *vr* : to forget <se me olvidó mi cuaderno : I forgot my notebook> <se le olvidó llamarme : he forgot to call me>

olvido *nm* **1** : forgetfulness **2** : oblivion **3** DESCUIDO : oversight

omaní *adj & nmf* : Omani

ombligo *nm* : navel, belly button

ombudsman *nmfs & pl* : ombudsman

omelette *nmf* : omelet

ominoso, -sa *adj* : ominous — **ominosamente** *adv*

omisión *nf, pl* **-siones** : omission, neglect

omiso, -sa *adj* **1** NEGLIGENTE : neglectful **2 hacer caso omiso de** : to ignore

omitir *vt* **1** : to omit, to leave out **2** : to fail to <omitió dar su nombre : he failed to give his name>

ómnibus *n, pl* **-bus** *or* **-buses** : bus, coach

omnipotencia *nf* : omnipotence

omnipotente *adj* TODOPODEROSO : omnipotent, almighty

omnipresencia *nf* : ubiquity, omnipresence

omnipresente *adj* : ubiquitous, omnipresent

omnisciente *adj* : omniscient — **omnisciencia** *nf*

omnívoro, -ra *adj* : omnivorous

omóplato *or* **omoplato** *nm* : shoulder blade

once *adj & nm* : eleven

onceavo[1], -va *adj* : eleventh

onceavo[2] *nm* : eleventh (fraction)

onda *nf* **1** : wave, ripple, undulation <onda sonora : sound wave> **2** : wave (in hair) **3** : scallop (on clothing) **4** *fam* : wavelength, understanding <agarrar la onda : to get the point> <en la onda : on the ball, with it> **5 ¿qué onda?** *fam* : what's happening?, what's up?

ondear *vi* : to ripple, to undulate, to flutter

ondulación *nf, pl* **-ciones** : undulation

ondulado, -da *adj* **1** : wavy <pelo ondulado : wavy hair> **2** : undulating

ondular *vt* : to wave (hair) — *vi* : to undulate, to ripple

oneroso, -sa *adj* GRAVOSO : onerous, burdensome

ónix *nm* : onyx

onza *nf* : ounce

opacar {72} *vt* **1** : to make opaque or dull **2** : to outshine, to overshadow

opacidad *nf* **1** : opacity **2** : dullness

opaco, -ca *adj* **1** : opaque **2** : dull

ópalo *nm* : opal

opción *nf, pl* **opciones 1** ALTERNATIVA : option, choice **2** : right, chance <tener opción a : to be eligible for>

opcional *adj* : optional — **opcionalmente** *adv*

ópera *nf* : opera

operación *nf, pl* **-ciones 1** : operation **2** : transaction, deal

operacional *adj* : operational

operador, -dora *n* **1** : operator **2** : cameraman, projectionist

operante *adj* : operating, working

operar *vt* **1** : to produce, to bring about **2** INTERVENIR : to operate on **3** *Mex* : to operate, to run (a machine) — *vi* **1** : to operate, to function **2** : to deal, to do business — **operarse** *vr* **1** : to come about, to take place **2** : to have an operation

operario, -ria *n* : laborer, worker

operático, -ca → **operístico**

operativo[1], -va *adj* **1** : operating <capacidad operativa : operating capacity> **2** : operative

operativo[2] *nm* : operation <operativo militar : military operation>

opereta *nf* : operetta

operístico, -ca *adj* : operatic

opiato *nm* : opiate

opinable *adj* : arguable

opinar *vi* **1** : to think, to have an opinion **2** : to express an opinion **3 opinar bien de** : to think highly of — *vt* : to think <opinamos lo mismo : we're of the same opinion, we're in agreement>

opinión *nf, pl* **-niones** : opinion, belief

opio *nm* : opium

oponente *nmf* : opponent

oponer {60} *vt* **1** CONTRAPONER : to oppose, to place against **2 oponer resistencia** : to resist, to put up a fight — **oponerse** *vr* **~ a** : to object to, to be against

oporto *nm* : port (wine)

oportunamente *adv* **1** : at the right time, opportunely **2** : appropriately

oportunidad *nf* : opportunity, chance

oportunismo *nm* : opportunism

oportunista[1] *adj* : opportunistic

oportunista[2] *nmf* : opportunist

oportuno, -na *adj* **1** : opportune, timely **2** : suitable, appropriate

oposición *nf, pl* **-ciones** : opposition

opositor, -tora *n* ADVERSARIO : opponent

oposum *nm* ZARIGÜEYA : opossum

opresión *nf, pl* **-siones 1** : oppression **2 opresión de pecho** : tightness in the chest

opresivo, -va *adj* : oppressive

opresor[1], **-sora** *adj* : oppressive

opresor[2], **-sora** *n* : oppressor

oprimir *vt* **1** : to oppress **2** : to press, to squeeze <oprima el botón : push the button>

oprobio *nm* : opprobrium, shame

optar *vi* **1 ~ por** : to opt for, to choose **2 ~ a** : to aspire to, to apply for <dos candidatos optan a la presidencia : two candidates are running for president>

optativo, -va *adj* FACULTATIVO : optional

óptica *nf* **1** : optics **2** : optician's shop **3** : viewpoint

óptico[1], **-ca** *adj* : optical, optic

óptico[2], **-ca** *n* : optician

optimismo *nm* : optimism

optimista[1] *adj* : optimistic

optimista[2] *nmf* : optimist

óptimo, -ma *adj* : optimum, optimal

optometría *nf* : optometry — **optometrista** *nmf*

opuesto[1] *pp* → **oponer**

opuesto[2] *adj* **1** : opposite, contrary **2** : opposed

opulencia *nf* : opulence — **opulento, -ta** *adj*

opus *nm* : opus

opuso, etc. → **oponer**

ora *conj* : now <los matices eran variados, ora verdes, ora ocres : the hues were varied, now green, now ocher>

oración *nf, pl* **-ciones 1** DISCURSO : oration, speech **2** PLEGARIA : prayer **3** FRASE : sentence, clause

oráculo *nm* : oracle

orador, -dora *n* : speaker, orator

oral *adj* : oral — **oralmente** *adv*

órale *interj Mex fam* **1** : sure!, OK! <¿los dos por cinco pesos? ¡órale! : both for five pesos? you've got a deal!> **2** : come on! <¡órale, vámonos! : come on, let's go!>

orangután *nm, pl* **-tanes** : orangutan

orar *vi* REZAR : to pray

oratoria *nf* : oratory

oratorio *nm* **1** CAPILLA : oratory, chapel **2** : oratorio

orbe *nm* **1** : orb, sphere **2** GLOBO : globe, world

órbita *nf* **1** : orbit **2** : eye socket **3** ÁMBITO : sphere, field

orbitador *nm* : space shuttle, orbiter

orbital *adj* : orbital

orden[1] *nm, pl* **órdenes 1** : order <todo está en orden : everything's in order> <por orden cronológico : in chronological order> **2 orden del día** : agenda (at a meeting) **3 orden público** : law and order

orden[2] *nf, pl* **órdenes 1** : order <una orden religiosa : a religious order> <una orden de tacos : an order of tacos> **2 orden de compra** : purchase order **3 estar a la orden del día** : to be the order of the day, to be prevalent

ordenación *nf, pl* **-ciones 1** : ordination **2** : ordering, organizing

ordenadamente *adv* : in an orderly fashion, neatly

ordenado, -da *adj* : orderly, neat

ordenador *nm Spain* : computer

ordenamiento *nm* **1** : ordering, organizing **2** : code (of laws)

ordenanza[1] *nf* REGLAMENTO : ordinance, regulation

ordenanza[2] *nm* : orderly (in the armed forces)

ordenar *vt* **1** MANDAR : to order, to command **2** ARREGLAR : to put in order, to arrange **3** : to ordain (a priest)

ordeñar *vt* : to milk

ordeño *nm* : milking

ordinal *nm* : ordinal (number)

ordinariamente *adv* **1** : usually **2** : coarsely

ordinariez *nf* : coarseness, vulgarity

ordinario, -ria *adj* **1** : ordinary **2** : coarse, common, vulgar **3 de ~** : usually

orear *vt* : to air

orégano *nm* : oregano

oreja *nf* : ear

orfanato *nm* : orphanage

orfanatorio *nm Mex* : orphanage

orfebre *nmf* : goldsmith, silversmith

orfebrería *nf* : articles of gold or silver

orfelinato *nm* : orphanage
orgánico, -ca *adj* : organic — **orgánicamente** *adv*
organigrama *nm* : organization chart, flowchart
organismo *nm* **1** : organism **2** : agency, organization
organista *nmf* : organist
organización *nf, pl* **-ciones** : organization
organizador[1], **-dora** *adj* : organizing
organizador[2], **-dora** *n* : organizer
organizar {21} *vt* : to organize, to arrange — **organizarse** *vr* : to get organized
organizativo, -va *adj* : organizational
órgano *nm* : organ
orgasmo *nm* : orgasm
orgía *nf* : orgy
orgullo *nm* : pride
orgulloso, -sa *adj* : proud — **orgullosamente** *adv*
orientación *nf, pl* **-ciones 1** : orientation **2** DIRECCIÓN : direction, course **3** GUÍA : guidance, direction
oriental[1] *adj* **1** : eastern **2** : oriental **3** *Arg, Uru* : Uruguayan
oriental[2] *nmf* **1** : Easterner **2** : Oriental **3** *Arg, Uru* : Uruguayan
orientar *vt* **1** : to orient, to position **2** : to guide, to direct — **orientarse** *vr* **1** : to orient oneself, to get one's bearings **2 ~ hacia** : to turn towards, to lean towards
oriente *nm* **1** : east, East **2 el Oriente** : the Orient
orífice *nmf* : goldsmith
orificio *nm* : orifice, opening
origen *nm, pl* **orígenes 1** : origin **2** : lineage, birth **3 dar origen a** : to give rise to **4 en su origen** : originally
original *adj & nm* : original — **originalmente** *adv*
originalidad *nf* : originality
originar *vt* : to originate, to give rise to — **originarse** *vr* : to originate, to begin
originario, -ria *adj* **~ de** : native of
originariamente *adv* : originally
orilla *nf* **1** BORDE : border, edge **2** : bank (of a river) **3** : shore
orillar *vt* **1** : to skirt, to go around **2** : to trim, to edge (cloth) **3** : to settle, to wind up **4** *Mex* : to pull over (a vehicle)
orín *nm* **1** HERRUMBRE : rust **2 orines** *nmpl* : urine
orina *nf* : urine
orinación *nf* : urination
orinal *nm* : urinal (vessel)
orinar *vi* : to urinate — **orinarse** *vr* : to wet oneself
oriol *nm* OROPÉNDOLA : oriole
oriundo, -da *adj* **~ de** : native of
orla *nf* : border, edging
orlar *vt* : to edge, to trim
ornamentación *nf, pl* **-ciones** : ornamentation
ornamental *adj* : ornamental
ornamentar *vt* ADORNAR : to ornament, to adorn
ornamento *nm* : ornament, adornment
ornar *vt* : to adorn, to decorate
ornitología *nf* : ornithology
ornitólogo, -ga *n* : ornithologist
ornitorrinco *nm* : platypus
oro *nm* : gold
orondo, -da *adj* **1** : rounded, potbellied (of a container) **2** *fam* : smug, self-satisfied
oropel *nm* : glitz, glitter, tinsel
oropéndola *nf* : oriole
orquesta *nf* : orchestra — **orquestal** *adj*
orquestar *vt* : to orchestrate — **orquestación** *nf*
orquídea *nf* : orchid
ortiga *nf* : nettle
ortodoncia *nf* : orthodontics
ortodoncista *nmf* : orthodontist
ortodoxia *nf* : orthodoxy
ortodoxo, -xa *adj* : orthodox
ortografía *nf* : orthography, spelling
ortográfico, -ca *adj* : orthographic, spelling
ortopedia *nf* : orthopedics
ortopedista *nmf* : orthopedist
oruga *nf* **1** : caterpillar **2** : track (of a tank, etc.)
orzuelo *nm* : sty, stye (in the eye)
os *pron pl* (*objective form of* **vosotros**) *Spain* **1** : you, to you **2** : yourselves, to yourselves **3** : each other, to each other
osa *nf* → **oso**
osadía *nf* **1** VALOR : boldness, daring **2** AUDACIA : audacity, nerve
osado, -da *adj* **1** : bold, daring **2** : audacious, impudent — **osadamente** *adv*
osamenta *nf* : skeletal remains *pl*, bones *pl*
osar *vi* : to dare
oscilación *nf, pl* **-ciones 1** : oscillation **2** : fluctuation **3** : vacillation, wavering
oscilar *vi* **1** BALANCEARSE : to swing, to sway, to oscillate **2** FLUCTUAR : to fluctuate **3** : to vacillate, to waver
oscuramente *adv* : obscurely
oscurecer {53} *vt* **1** : to darken **2** : to obscure, to confuse, to cloud **3 al oscurecer** : at dusk, at nightfall — *v impers* : to grow dark, to get dark — **oscurecerse** *vr* : to darken, to dim
oscuridad *nf* **1** : darkness **2** : obscurity
oscuro, -ra *adj* **1** : dark **2** : obscure **3 a oscuras** : in the dark, in darkness
óseo, ósea *adj* : skeletal, bony
ósmosis *or* **osmosis** *nf* : osmosis
oso, osa *n* **1** : bear **2 Osa Mayor** : Big Dipper **3 Osa Menor** : Little Dipper **4 oso blanco** : polar bear **5 oso hormiguero** : anteater **6 oso de peluche** : teddy bear
ostensible *adj* : ostensible, apparent — **ostensiblemente** *adv*
ostentación *nf, pl* **-ciones** : ostentation, display

ostentar *vt* **1 :** to display, to flaunt **2** POSEER **:** to have, to hold <ostenta el récord mundial : he holds the world record>
ostentoso, -sa *adj* **:** ostentatious, showy — **ostentosamente** *adv*
osteópata *nmf* **:** osteopath
osteopatía *n* **:** osteopathy
osteoporosis *nf* **:** osteoporosis
ostión *nm, pl* **ostiones 1** *Mex* **:** oyster **2** *Chile* **:** scallop
ostra *nf* **:** oyster
ostracismo *nm* **:** ostracism
otear *vt* **:** to scan, to survey, to look over
otero *nm* **:** knoll, hillock
otomana *nf* **:** ottoman
otoñal *adj* **:** autumn, autumnal
otoño *nm* **:** autumn, fall
otorgamiento *nm* **:** granting, awarding
otorgar {52} *vt* **1 :** to grant, to award **2 :** to draw up, to frame (a legal document)
otro[1], otra *adj* **1 :** other **2 :** another <en otro juego, ellos ganaron : in another game, they won> **3 otra vez :** again **4 de otra manera :** otherwise **5 otra parte :** elsewhere **6 en otro tiempo :** once, formerly
otro[2], otra *pron* **1 :** another one <dame otro : give me another> **2 :** other one <el uno o el otro : one or the other> **3 los otros, las otras :** the others, the rest <me dio una y se quedó con las otras : he gave me one and kept the rest>
ovación *nf, pl* **-ciones :** ovation
ovacionar *vt* **:** to cheer, to applaud
oval → ovalado
ovalado, -da *adj* **:** oval
óvalo *nm* **:** oval
ovárico, -ca *adj* **:** ovarian
ovario *nm* **:** ovary
oveja *nf* **1 :** sheep, ewe **2 oveja negra :** black sheep
overol *nm* **:** overalls *pl*
ovillar *vt* **:** to roll into a ball
ovillo *nm* **1 :** ball (of yarn) **2 :** tangle
ovni *or* **OVNI** *nm* (*objeto volador no identificado*) **:** UFO
ovoide *adj* **:** ovoid, ovoidal
ovulación *nf, pl* **-ciones :** ovulation
ovular *vi* **:** to ovulate
óvulo *nm* **:** ovum
oxidación *nf, pl* **-ciones 1 :** oxidation **2 :** rusting
oxidado, -da *adj* **:** rusty
oxidar *vt* **1 :** to cause to rust **2 :** to oxidize — **oxidarse** *vr* **:** to rust, to become rusty
óxido *nm* **1** HERRUMBRE, ORÍN **:** rust **2 :** oxide
oxigenar *vt* **1 :** to oxygenate **2 :** to bleach (hair)
oxígeno *nm* **:** oxygen
oxiuro *nm* **:** pinworm
oye, etc. → oír
oyente *nmf* **1 :** listener **2 :** auditor, auditing student
ozono *nm* **:** ozone

P

p *nf* **:** seventeenth letter of the Spanish alphabet
pabellón *nm, pl* **-llones 1 :** pavilion **2 :** summerhouse, lodge **3 :** flag (of a vessel)
pabilo *nm* MECHA **:** wick
paca *nf* FARDO **:** bale
pacana *nf* **:** pecan
pacer {48} *v* **:** to graze, to pasture
paces → paz
pachanga *nf fam* **:** party, bash
paciencia *nf* **:** patience
paciente *adj & nmf* **:** patient — **pacientemente** *adv*
pacificación *nf, pl* **-ciones :** pacification
pacíficamente *adv* **:** peacefully, peaceably
pacificar {72} *vt* **:** to pacify, to calm — **pacificarse** *vr* **:** to calm down, to abate
pacífico, -ca *adj* **:** peaceful, pacific
pacifismo *nm* **:** pacifism
pacifista *adj & nmf* **:** pacifist
pacotilla *nf* **de ~ :** shoddy, trashy
pactar *vt* **:** to agree on — *vi* **:** to come to an agreement
pacto *nm* CONVENIO **:** pact, agreement
padecer {53} *vt* **:** to suffer, to endure — *vi* ADOLECER **~ de :** to suffer from
padecimiento *nm* **1 :** suffering **2 :** ailment, condition
padrastro *nm* **1 :** stepfather **2 :** hangnail
padre[1] *adj Mex fam* **:** fantastic, great
padre[2] *nm* **1 :** father **2 padres** *nmpl* **:** parents
padrenuestro *nm* **:** Lord's Prayer, paternoster
padrino *nm* **1 :** godfather **2 :** best man **3 :** sponsor, patron
padrón *nm, pl* **padrones :** register, roll <padrón municipal : city register>
paella *nf* **:** paella
paga *nf* **1 :** payment **2 :** pay, wages *pl*
pagadero, -ra *adj* **:** payable
pagado, -da *adj* **1 :** paid **2 pagado de sí mismo :** self-satisfied, smug
pagador, -dora *n* **:** payer
paganismo *nm* **:** paganism
pagano, -na *adj & n* **:** pagan
pagar {52} *vt* **:** to pay, to pay for, to repay — *vi* **:** to pay
pagaré *nm* VALE **:** promissory note, IOU
página *nf* **:** page

pago *nm* **1 :** payment **2 en pago de :** in return for
pagoda *nf* **:** pagoda
pague, etc. → **pagar**
país *nm* **1** NACIÓN **:** country, nation **2** REGIÓN **:** region, territory
paisaje *nm* **:** scenery, landscape
paisano, -na *n* COMPATRIOTA **:** compatriot, fellow countryman
paja *nf* **1 :** straw **2** *fam* **:** trash, tripe
pajar *nm* **:** hayloft, haystack
pajarera *nf* **:** aviary
pájaro *nm* **:** bird <pájaro cantor : songbird> <pájaro bobo : penguin> <pájaro carpintero : woodpecker>
pajita *nf* **:** (drinking) straw
pajote *nm* **:** straw, mulch
pala *nf* **1 :** shovel, spade **2 :** blade (of an oar or a rotor) **3 :** paddle, racket
palabra *nf* **1** VOCABLO **:** word **2** PROMESA **:** word, promise <un hombre de palabra : a man of his word> **3** HABLA **:** speech **4 :** right to speak <tener la palabra : to have the floor>
palabrería *nf* **:** empty talk
palabrota *nf* **:** swearword
palacio *nm* **1 :** palace, mansion **2 palacio de justicia :** courthouse
paladar *nm* **1 :** palate **2** GUSTO **:** taste
paladear *vt* SABOREAR **:** to savor
paladín *nm, pl* **-dines :** champion, defender
palanca *nf* **1 :** lever, crowbar **2** *fam* **:** leverage, influence **3 palanca de cambio** *or* **palanca de velocidad :** gearshift
palangana *nf* **:** washbowl
palanqueta *nf* **:** jimmy, small crowbar
palco *nm* **:** box (in a theater or stadium)
palear *vt* **1 :** to shovel **2 :** to paddle
palenque *nm* **1** ESTACADA **:** stockade, palisade **2 :** arena, ring
paleontología *nf* **:** paleontology
paleontólogo, -ga *n* **:** paleontologist
palestino, -na *adj & n* **:** Palestinian
palestra *nf* **:** arena <salir a la palestra : to join the fray>
paleta *nf* **1 :** palette **2 :** trowel **3 :** spatula **4 :** blade, vane **5 :** paddle **6** *CA, Mex* **:** lollipop, Popsicle—
paletilla *nf* **:** shoulder blade
paliar *vt* MITIGAR **:** to alleviate, to palliate
paliativo[1], -va *adj* **:** palliative
paliativo[2] *nm* **:** palliative
palidecer {53} *vi* **:** to turn pale
palidez *nf, pl* **-deces :** paleness, pallor
pálido, -da *adj* **:** pale
palillo *nm* **1** MONDADIENTES **:** toothpick **2 palillos** *nmpl* **:** chopsticks **3 palillo de tambor :** drumstick
paliza *nf* **:** beating, pummeling <darle una paliza a : to beat, to thrash>
palma *nf* **1 :** palm (of the hand) **2 :** palm (tree or leaf) **3 batir palmas :** to clap, to applaud **4 llevarse la palma** *fam* **:** to take the cake
palmada *nf* **1 :** pat **2 :** slap **3 :** clap
palmarés *nm* **:** record (of achievements)
palmario, -ria *adj* MANIFIESTO **:** clear, manifest
palmeado, -da *adj* **:** webbed
palmear *vt* **:** to slap on the back — *vi* **:** to clap, to applaud
palmera *nf* **:** palm tree
palmo *nm* **1 :** span, small amount **2 palmo a palmo :** bit by bit, inch by inch **3 dejar con un palmo de narices :** to disappoint
palmotear *vi* **:** to applaud
palmoteo *nm* **:** clapping, applause
palo *nm* **1 :** stick, pole, post **2 :** shaft, handle <palo de escoba : broomstick> **3 :** mast, spar **4 :** wood **5 :** blow (with a stick) **6 :** suit (of cards)
paloma *nf* **1 :** pigeon, dove **2 paloma mensajera :** carrier pigeon
palomilla *nf* **:** moth
palomitas *nfpl* **:** popcorn
palpable *adj* **:** palpable, tangible
palpar *vt* **:** to feel, to touch
palpitación *nf, pl* **-ciones :** palpitation
palpitar *vi* **:** to palpitate, to throb — **palpitante** *adj*
palta *nf* **:** avocado
paludismo *nm* MALARIA **:** malaria
palurdo, -da *n* **:** boor, yokel, bumpkin
pampa *nf* **:** pampa
pampeano, -na *adj* **:** pampean, pampas
pampero → **pampeano**
pan *nm* **1 :** bread **2 :** loaf of bread **3 :** cake, bar <pan de jabón : bar of soap> **4 pan dulce** *CA, Mex* **:** traditional pastry **5 pan tostado :** toast **6 ser pan comido** *fam* **:** to be a piece of cake, to be a cinch
pana *nf* **:** corduroy
panacea *nf* **:** panacea
panadería *nf* **:** bakery, bread shop
panadero, -ra *n* **:** baker
panal *nm* **:** honeycomb
panameño, -ña *adj & n* **:** Panamanian
pancarta *nf* **:** placard, sign
pancita *nf Mex* **:** tripe
páncreas *nms & pl* **:** pancreas
panda *nmf* **:** panda
pandeado, -da *adj* **:** warped
pandearse *vr* **1 :** to warp **2 :** to bulge, to sag
pandemonio *or* **pandemónium** *nm* **:** pandemonium
pandereta *nf* **:** tambourine
pandero *nm* **:** tambourine
pandilla *nf* **1 :** group, clique **2 :** gang
panecito *nm* **:** roll, bread roll
panegírico[1], -ca *adj* **:** eulogistic, panegyrical
panegírico[2] *nm* **:** eulogy, panegyric
panel *nm* **:** panel — **panelista** *nmf*
panera *nf* **:** bread box
panfleto *nm* **:** pamphlet
pánico *nm* **:** panic
panorama *nm* **1** VISTA **:** panorama, view **2 :** scene, situation <el pa-

norama nacional : the national scene> **3** PERSPECTIVA : outlook

panorámico, -ca *adj* : panoramic

panqueque *nm* : pancake

pantaletas *nfpl* : panties

pantalla *nf* **1** : screen, monitor **2** : lampshade **3** : fan

pantalón *nm, pl* **-lones 1** : pants *pl,* trousers *pl* **2 pantalones vaqueros** : jeans **3 pantalones de mezclilla** *Chile, Mex* : jeans **4 pantalones de montar** : jodhpurs

pantano *nm* **1** : swamp, marsh, bayou **2** : reservoir **3** : obstacle, difficulty

pantanoso, -sa *adj* **1** : marshy, swampy **2** : difficult, thorny

panteón *nm, pl* **-teones 1** CEMENTERIO : cemetery **2** : pantheon, mausoleum

pantera *nf* : panther

pantimedias *nfpl Mex* : panty hose

pantomima *nf* : pantomime

pantorrilla *nf* : calf (of the leg)

pantufla *nf* ZAPATILLA : slipper

panza *nf* BARRIGA : belly, paunch

panzón, -zona *adj, mpl* **panzones** : potbellied, paunchy

pañal *nm* : diaper

pañería *nf* **1** : cloth, material **2** : fabric store

pañito *nm* : doily

paño *nm* **1** : cloth **2** : rag, dust cloth **3 paño de cocina** : dishcloth **4 paño higiénico** : sanitary napkin

pañuelo *nm* **1** : handkerchief **2** : scarf

papa[1] *nm* : pope

papa[2] *nf* **1** : potato **2 papa dulce** : sweet potato **3 papas fritas** : potato chips, french fries **4 papas a la francesa** *Mex* : french fries

papá *nm fam* **1** : dad, pop **2 papás** *nmpl* : parents, folks

papada *nf* **1** : double chin, jowl **2** : dewlap

papagayo *nm* LORO : parrot

papal *adj* : papal

papalote *nm Mex* : kite

papaya *nf* : papaya

papel *nm* **1** : paper, piece of paper **2** : role, part **3 papel de estaño** : tinfoil **4 papel de empapelar** *or* **papel pintado** : wallpaper **5 papel higiénico** : toilet paper **6 papel de lija** : sandpaper

papeleo *nm* : paperwork, red tape

papelera *nf* : wastebasket

papelería *nf* : stationery store

papelero, -ra *adj* : paper

papeleta *nf* **1** : ballot **2** : ticket, slip

paperas *nfpl* : mumps

papi *nm fam* : daddy, papa

papilla *nf* **1** : pap, mash **2 hacer papilla** : to beat to a pulp

papiro *nm* : papyrus

paquete *nm* BULTO : package, parcel

paquistaní *adj & nmf* : Pakistani

par[1] *adj* : even (in number)

par[2] *nm* **1** : pair, couple **2** : equal, peer <sin par : matchless, peerless> **3** : par (in golf) **4** : rafter **5 de par en par** : wide open

par[3] *nf* **1** : par <por encima de la par : above par> **2 a la par que** : at the same time as, as well as <interesante a la par que instructivo : both interesting and informative>

para *prep* **1** : for <para ti : for you> <alta para su edad : tall for her age> <una cita para el lunes : an appointment for Monday> **2** : to, towards <para la derecha : to the right> <van para el río : they're heading towards the river> **3** : to, in order to <lo hace para molestarte : he does it to annoy you> **4** : around, by (a time) <para mañana estarán listos : they'll be ready by tomorrow> **5 para adelante** : forwards **6 para atrás** : backwards **7 para que** : so, so that, in order that <te lo digo para que sepas : I'm telling you so you'll know>

parabién *nm, pl* **-bienes** : congratulations *pl*

parábola *nf* **1** : parable **2** : parabola

parabrisas *nms & pl* : windshield

paracaídas *nms & pl* : parachute

paracaidista *nmf* **1** : parachutist **2** : paratrooper

parachoques *nms & pl* : bumper

parada *nf* **1** : stop <parada de autobús : bus stop> **2** : catch, save, parry (in sports) **3** DESFILE : parade

paradero *nm* : whereabouts

paradigma *nm* : paradigm

parado, -da *adj* **1** : motionless, idle, stopped **2** : standing (up) **3** : confused, bewildered **4 bien (mal) parado** : in good (bad) shape <salió bien parado : it turned out well for him>

paradoja *nf* : paradox

paradójico, -ca *adj* : paradoxical

parafernalia *nf* : paraphernalia

parafina *nf* : paraffin

parafrasear *vt* : to paraphrase

paráfrasis *nfs & pl* : paraphrase

paraguas *nms & pl* : umbrella

paraguayo, -ya *adj & n* : Paraguayan

paraíso *nm* **1** : paradise, heaven **2 paraíso fiscal** : tax shelter

paraje *nm* : spot, place

paralelismo *nm* : parallelism, similarity

paralelo[1], **-la** *adj* : parallel

paralelo[2] *nm* : parallel

paralelogramo *nm* : parallelogram

parálisis *nfs & pl* **1** : paralysis **2** : standstill **3 parálisis cerebral** : cerebral palsy

paralítico, -ca *adj & n* : paralytic

paralizar {21} *vt* **1** : to paralyze **2** : to bring to a standstill — **paralizarse** *vr*

parámetro *nm* : parameter

páramo *nm* : barren plateau, moor

parangón *nm, pl* **-gones 1** : comparison **2 sin ~** : incomparable

paraninfo *nm* : auditorium, assembly hall

paranoia *nf* : paranoia
paranoico, -ca *adj & n* : paranoid
parapeto *nm* : parapet, rampart
parapléjico, -ca *adj & n* : paraplegic
parar *vt* **1** DETENER : to stop **2** : to stand, to prop — *vi* **1** CESAR : to stop **2** : to stay, to put up **3 ir a parar** : to end up, to wind up — **pararse** *vr* **1** : to stop **2** ATASCARSE : to stall (out) **3** : to stand up, to get up
pararrayos *nms & pl* : lightning rod
parasitario, -ria *adj* : parasitic
parasitismo *nm* : parasitism
parásito *nm* : parasite
parasol *nm* SOMBRILLA : parasol
parcela *nf* : parcel, tract of land
parcelar *vt* : to parcel (land)
parchar *vt* : to patch, to patch up
parche *nm* : patch
parcial *adj* : partial — **parcialmente** *adv*
parcialidad *nf* : partiality, bias
parco, -ca *adj* **1** : sparing, frugal **2** : moderate, temperate
pardo, -da *adj* : brownish grey
pardusco → **pardo**
parecer[1] {53} *vi* **1** : to seem, to look, to appear to be <parece bien fácil : it looks very easy> <así parece : so it seems> <pareces una princesa : you look like a princess> **2** : to think, to have an opinion <me parece que sí : I think so> **3** : to like, to be in agreement <si te parece : if you like, if it's all right with you> — **parecerse** *vr* **~ a** : to resemble
parecer[2] *nm* **1** OPINIÓN : opinion **2** ASPECTO : appearance <al parecer : apparently>
parecido[1], **-da** *adj* **1** : similar, alike **2 bien parecido** : good-looking
parecido[2] *nm* : resemblance, similarity
pared *nf* : wall
pareja *nf* **1** : couple, pair **2** : partner, mate
parejo, -ja *adj* **1** : even, smooth, level **2** : equal, similar
parentela *nf* : relations *pl*, kinfolk
parentesco *nm* : relationship, kinship
paréntesis *nms & pl* **1** : parenthesis **2** : digression
parentético, -ca *adj* : parenthetic, parenthetical
paria *nmf* : pariah, outcast
paridad *nf* : parity, equality
pariente *nmf* : relative, relation
parir *vi* : to give birth — *vt* : to give birth to, to bear
parking *nm* : parking lot
parlamentar *vi* : to talk, to parley
parlamentario[1], **-ria** *adj* : parliamentary
parlamentario[2], **-ria** *n* : member of parliament
parlamento *nm* **1** : parliament **2** : negotiations *pl*, talks *pl*
parlanchín[1], **-china** *adj*, *mpl* **-chines** : chatty, talkative
parlanchín[2], **-china** *n*, *mpl* **-chines** : chatterbox
parlante *nm* ALTOPARLANTE : loudspeaker
parlotear *vi fam* : to gab, to chat, to prattle
parloteo *nm fam* : prattle, chatter
paro *nm* **1** HUELGA : strike **2** : stoppage, stopping **3 paro forzoso** : layoff
parodia *nf* : parody
parodiar *vt* : to parody
parpadear *vi* **1** : to blink **2** : to flicker
parpadeo *nm* **1** : blink, blinking **2** : flickering
párpado *nm* : eyelid
parque *nm* **1** : park **2 parque de atracciones** : amusement park
parquear *vt* : to park — **parquearse** *vr*
parqueo *nm* : parking
parquet *or* **parqué** *nm* : parquet
parquímetro *nm* : parking meter
parra *nf* : vine, grapevine
párrafo *nm* : paragraph
parranda *nf fam* : party, spree
parrilla *nf* **1** : broiler, grill **2** : grate
parrillada *nf* BARBACOA : barbecue
párroco *nm* : parish priest
parroquia *nf* **1** : parish **2** : parish church **3** : customers *pl*, clientele
parroquial *adj* : parochial
parroquiano, -na *nm* **1** : parishioner **2** : customer, patron
parsimonia *nf* **1** : calm **2** : parsimony, thrift
parsimonioso, -sa *adj* **1** : calm, unhurried **2** : parsimonious, thrifty
parte[1] *nm* : report, dispatch
parte[2] *nf* **1** : part, share **2** : part, place <en alguna parte : somewhere> <por todas partes : everywhere> **3** : party (in negotiations, etc.) **4 de parte de** : on behalf of **5 ¿de parte de quién?** : may I ask who's calling? **6 tomar parte** : to take part
partero, -ra *n* : midwife
partición *nf*, *pl* **-ciones** : division, sharing
participación *nf*, *pl* **-ciones 1** : participation **2** : share, interest **3** : announcement, notice
participante *nmf* **1** : participant **2** : competitor, entrant
participar *vi* **1** : to participate, to take part **2 ~ en** : to have a share in — *vt* : to announce, to notify
partícipe *nmf* : participant
participio *nm* : participle
partícula *nf* : particle
particular[1] *adj* **1** : particular, specific **2** : private, personal **3** : special, unique
particular[2] *nm* **1** : matter, detail **2** : individual
particularidad *nf* : characteristic, peculiarity
particularizar {21} *vt* **1** : to distinguish, to characterize **2** : to specify

partida *nf* **1 :** departure **2 :** item, entry **3 :** certificate <partida de nacimiento : birth certificate> **4 :** game, match, hand **5 :** party, group
partidario, -ria *n* **:** follower, supporter
partido *nm* **1 :** (political) party **2 :** game, match <partido de futbol : soccer game> **3** APOYO **:** support, following **4** PROVECHO **:** profit, advantage <sacar partido de : to profit from>
partir *vt* **1 :** to cut, to split **2 :** to break, to crack **3 :** to share (out), to divide — *vi* **1 :** to leave, to depart **2 ~ de :** to start from **3 a partir de :** as of, from <a partir de hoy : as of today> — **partirse** *vr* **1 :** to smash, to split open **2 :** to chap
partisano, -na *adj & n* **:** partisan
partitura *nf* **:** (musical) score
parto *nm* **1 :** childbirth, delivery, labor <estar de parto : to be in labor> **2 :** product, creation, brainchild
parvulario *nm* **:** nursery school
párvulo, -la *n* **:** toddler, preschooler
pasa *nf* **1 :** raisin **2 pasa de Corinto :** currant
pasable *adj* **:** passable, tolerable — **pasablemente** *adv*
pasada *nf* **1 :** passage, passing **2 :** pass, wipe, coat (of paint) **3 de ~ :** in passing **4 mala pasada :** dirty trick
pasadizo *nm* **:** passageway, corridor
pasado[1], -da *adj* **1 :** past <el año pasado : last year> <pasado mañana : the day after tomorrow> <pasadas las siete : after seven o'clock> **2 :** stale, bad, overripe **3 :** old-fashioned, out-of-date **4 :** overripe, slightly spoiled
pasado[2] *nm* **:** past
pasador *nm* **1 :** bolt, latch **2 :** barrette **3** *Mex* **:** bobby pin
pasaje *nm* **1 :** ticket (for travel) **2** TARIFA **:** fare **3 :** passageway **4 :** passengers *pl*
pasajero[1], -ra *adj* **:** passing, fleeting
pasajero[2], -ra *n* **:** passenger
pasamanos *nms & pl* **1 :** handrail **2 :** banister
pasante *nmf* **:** assistant
pasaporte *nm* **:** passport
pasar *vi* **1 :** to pass, to go by, to come by **2 :** to come in, to enter <¿se puede pasar? : may we come in?> **3 :** to happen <¿qué pasa? : what's happening?, what's going on?> **4 :** to manage, to get by **5 :** to be over, to end **6 ~ de :** to exceed, to go beyond **7 ~ por :** to pretend to be — *vt* **1 :** to pass, to give <¿me pasas la sal? : would you pass me the salt?> **2 :** to pass (a test) **3 :** to go over, to cross **4 :** to spend (time) **5 :** to tolerate **6 :** to go through, to suffer **7 :** to show (a movie, etc.) **8 :** to overtake, to pass, to surpass **9 :** to pass over, to wipe up **10 pasarlo bien** *or* **pasarla bien :** to have a good time **11 pasarlo mal** *or* **pasarla mal :** to have a bad time, to have a hard time **12 pasar por alto :** to overlook, to omit — **pasarse** *vr* **1 :** to move, to pass, to go away **2 :** to slip one's mind, to forget **3 :** to go too far
pasarela *nf* **1 :** gangplank **2 :** footbridge **3 :** runway, catwalk
pasatiempo *nm* **:** pastime, hobby
Pascua *nf* **1 :** Easter **2 :** Passover **3 :** Christmas **4 Pascuas** *nfpl* **:** Christmas season
pase *nm* **1** PERMISO **:** pass, permit **2 pase de abordar** *Mex* **:** boarding pass
pasear *vi* **:** to take a walk, to go for a ride — *vt* **1 :** to take for a walk **2 :** to parade around, to show off — **pasearse** *vr* **:** to walk around
paseo *nm* **1 :** walk, stroll **2 :** ride **3** EXCURSIÓN **:** outing, trip
pasiflora *nf* **:** passionflower
pasillo *nm* CORREDOR **:** hallway, corridor, aisle
pasión *nf, pl* **pasiones :** passion
pasional *adj* **:** passionate <crimen pasional : crime of passion>
pasionaria *nf* → **pasiflora**
pasivo[1], -va *adj* **:** passive — **pasivamente** *adv*
pasivo[2] *nm* **1 :** liability <activos y pasivos : assets and liabilities> **2 :** debit side (of an account)
pasmado, -da *adj* **:** stunned, flabbergasted
pasmar *vt* **:** to amaze, to stun — **pasmarse** *vr*
pasmo *nm* **1 :** shock, astonishment **2 :** wonder, marvel
pasmoso, -sa *adj* **:** incredible, amazing — **pasmosamente** *adv*
paso[1], -sa *adj* **:** dried <ciruela pasa : prune>
paso[2] *nm* **1 :** passage, passing <de paso : in passing, on the way> **2 :** way, path <abrirse paso : to make one's way> **3 :** crossing <paso de peatones : crosswalk> <paso a desnivel : underpass> <paso elevado : overpass> **4 :** step <paso a paso : step by step> **5 :** pace, gait <a buen paso : quickly, at a good rate>
pasta *nf* **1 :** paste <pasta de dientes *or* pasta dental : toothpaste> **2 :** pasta **3 :** pastry dough **4 libro en pasta dura :** hardcover book **5 tener pasta de :** to have the makings of
pastar *vi* **:** to graze — *vt* **:** to put to pasture
pastel[1] *adj* **:** pastel
pastel[2] *nm* **1 :** cake <pastel de cumpleaños : birthday cake> **2 :** pie, turnover **3 :** pastel
pastelería *nf* **:** pastry shop
pasteurización *nf, pl* **-ciones :** pasteurization
pasteurizar {21} *vt* **:** to pasteurize
pastilla *nf* **1** COMPRIMIDO, PÍLDORA **:** pill, tablet **2 :** lozenge <pastilla para la tos

: cough drop> **3** : cake (of soap), bar (of chocolate)

pastizal *nm* : pasture, grazing land

pasto *nm* **1** : pasture **2** HIERBA : grass, lawn

pastor, -tora *n* **1** : shepherd, shepherdess *f* **2** : minister, pastor

pastoral *adj & nf* : pastoral

pastorear *vt* : to shepherd, to tend

pastorela *nf* **1** : pastoral, pastourelle **2** *Mex* : a traditional Christmas play

pastoso, -sa *adj* **1** : pasty, doughy **2** : smooth, mellow (of sounds)

pata *nf* **1** : paw, leg (of an animal) **2** : foot, leg (of furniture) **3 patas de gallo** : crow's-feet **4 meter la pata** *fam* : to put one's foot in it, to make a blunder

patada *nf* **1** PUNTAPIÉ : kick **2** : stamp (of the foot)

patalear *vi* **1** : to kick **2** : to stamp one's feet

pataleta *nf fam* : tantrum

patán[1] *adj, pl* **patanes** : boorish, crude

patán[2] *nm, pl* **patanes** : boor, lout

patata *nf Spain* : potato

patear *vt* : to kick — *vi* : to stamp one's foot

patentar *vt* : to patent

patente[1] *adj* EVIDENTE : obvious, patent — **patentemente** *adv*

patente[2] *nf* : patent

paternal *adj* : fatherly, paternal

paternidad *nf* **1** : fatherhood, paternity **2** : parenthood **3** : authorship

paterno, -na *adj* : paternal <abuela paterna : paternal grandmother>

patético, -ca *adj* : pathetic, moving

patetismo *nm* : pathos

patíbulo *nm* : gallows, scaffold

patillas *nfpl* : sideburns

patín *nm, pl* **patines** : skate <patín de ruedas : roller skate>

patinador, -dora *n* : skater

patinaje *nm* : skating

patinar *vi* **1** : to skate **2** : to skid, to slip **3** *fam* : to slip up, to blunder

patinazo *nm* **1** : skid **2** *fam* : blunder, slipup

patineta *nf* **1** : scooter **2** : skateboard

patinete *nm* : scooter

patio *nm* **1** : courtyard, patio **2 patio de recreo** : playground

patito, -ta *n* : duckling

pato, -ta *n* **1** : duck **2 pato real** : mallard **3 pagar el pato** *fam* : to take the blame

patología *nf* : pathology

patológico, -ca *adj* : pathological

patólogo, -ga *n* : pathologist

patraña *nf* : tall tale, humbug, nonsense

patria *nf* : native land

patriarca *nm* : patriarch — **patriarcal** *adj*

patriarcado *nm* : patriarchy

patrimonio *nm* : patrimony, legacy

patrio, -tria *adj* **1** : native, home <suelo patrio : native soil> **2** : paternal

patriota[1] *adj* : patriotic

patriota[2] *nmf* : patriot

patriotería *nf* : jingoism, chauvinism

patriotero[1]**, -ra** *adj* : jingoistic, chauvinistic

patriotero[2]**, -ra** *n* : jingoist, chauvinist

patriótico, -ca *adj* : patriotic

patriotismo *nm* : patriotism

patrocinador, -dora *n* : sponsor, patron

patrocinar *vt* : to sponsor

patrocinio *nm* : sponsorship, patronage

patrón[1]**, -trona** *n, mpl* **patrones 1** JEFE : boss **2** : patron saint

patrón[2] *nm, pl* **patrones 1** : standard **2** : pattern (in sewing)

patronal *adj* **1** : management, employers' <sindicato patronal : employers' association> **2** : pertaining to a patron saint <fiesta patronal : patron saint's day>

patronato *nm* **1** : board, council **2** : foundation, trust

patrono, -na *n* **1** : employer **2** : patron saint

patrulla *nf* **1** : patrol **2** : police car, cruiser

patrullar *v* : to patrol

patrullero *nm* **1** : police car **2** : patrol boat

paulatino, -na *adj* : gradual

paupérrimo, -ma *adj* : destitute, poverty-stricken

pausa *nf* : pause, break

pausado[1] *adv* : slowly, deliberately <habla más pausado : speak more slowly>

pausado[2]**, -da** *adj* : slow, deliberate — **pausadamente** *adv*

pauta *nf* **1** : rule, guideline **2** : lines *pl* (on paper)

pava *nf Arg, Bol, Chile* : kettle

pavimentar *vt* : pave

pavimento *nm* : pavement

pavo, -va *n* **1** : turkey **2 pavo real** : peacock **3 comer pavo** : to be a wallflower

pavón *nm, pl* **pavones** : peacock

pavonearse *vr* : to strut, to swagger

pavoneo *nm* : strut, swagger

pavor *nm* TERROR : dread, terror

pavoroso, -sa *adj* ATERRADOR : dreadful, terrifying

payasada *nf* BUFONADA : antic, buffoonery

payasear *vi* : to clown around

payaso, -sa *n* : clown

paz *nf, pl* **paces 1** : peace **2 dejar en paz** : to leave alone **3 hacer las paces** : to make up, to reconcile

pazca, etc. → **pacer**

PC *nmf* : PC, personal computer

peaje *nm* : toll

peatón *nm, pl* **-tones** : pedestrian

peca *nf* : freckle

pecado *nm* : sin

pecador[1], -dora *adj* : sinful, sinning

pecador[2], -dora *n* : sinner

pecaminoso, -sa *adj* : sinful

pecar {72} *vi* **1 :** to sin **2 ~ de :** to be too much (something) <no pecan de amabilidad : they're not overly friendly>

pécari *or* **pecarí** *nm* : peccary

pececillo *nm* : small fish

pecera *nf* : fishbowl, fish tank

pecho *nm* **1 :** chest **2** SENO **:** breast, bosom **3 :** heart, courage **4 dar el pecho :** to breast-feed **5 tomar a pecho :** to take to heart

pechuga *nf* : breast (of fowl)

pecoso, -sa *adj* : freckled

pectoral *adj* : pectoral

peculado *nm* : embezzlement

peculiar *adj* **1** CARACTERÍSTICO **:** particular, characteristic **2** RARO **:** peculiar, uncommon

peculiaridad *nf* : peculiarity

pecuniario, -ria *adj* : pecuniary

pedagogía *nf* : pedagogy

pedagógico, -ca *adj* : pedagogic, pedagogical

pedagogo, -ga *n* : educator, pedagogue

pedal *nm* : pedal

pedalear *vi* : to pedal

pedante[1] *adj* : pedantic

pedante[2] *nmf* : pedant

pedantería *nf* : pedantry

pedazo *nm* TROZO : piece, bit, chunk <caerse a pedazos : to fall to pieces> <hacer pedazos : to tear into shreds, to smash to pieces>

pedernal *nm* : flint

pedestal *nm* : pedestal

pedestre *adj* : commonplace, pedestrian

pediatra *nmf* : pediatrician

pediatría *nf* : pediatrics

pediátrico, -ca *adj* : pediatric

pedido *nm* **1 :** order (of merchandise) **2 :** request

pedigrí *nm* : pedigree

pedir {54} *vt* **1 :** to ask for, to request <le pedí un préstamo a Claudia : I asked Claudia for a loan> **2 :** to order (food, merchandise) **3 pedir disculpas** *or* **pedir perdón :** to apologize — *vi* **1 :** to order **2 :** to beg

pedrada *nf* **1 :** blow (with a rock or stone) <la ventana se quebró de una pedrada : the window was broken by a rock> **2** *fam* **:** cutting remark, dig

pedregal *nm* : rocky ground

pedregoso, -sa *adj* : rocky, stony

pedrera *nf* CANTERA : quarry

pedrería *nf* : precious stones *pl*, gems *pl*

pegado, -da *adj* **1 :** glued, stuck, stuck together **2 ~ a :** right next to

pegajoso, -sa *adj* **1 :** sticky, gluey **2 :** catchy <una tonada pegajosa : a catchy tune>

pegamento *nm* : adhesive, glue

pegar {52} *vt* **1 :** to glue, to stick, to paste **2 :** to attach, to sew on **3 :** to infect with, to give <me pegó el resfriado : he gave me his cold> **4** GOLPEAR **:** to hit, to deal, to strike <me pegaron un puntapié : they gave me a kick> **5 :** to give (out with) <pegó un grito : she let out a yell> — *vi* **1 :** to adhere, to stick **2 ~ en :** to hit, to strike (against) **3 ~ con :** to match, to go with — **pegarse** *vr* **1** GOLPEARSE **:** to hit oneself, to hit each other **2 :** to stick, to take hold **3 :** to be contagious **4** *fam* **:** to tag along, to stick around

pegote *nm* **1 :** sticky mess **2** *Mex* **:** sticker, adhesive label

pegue, etc. → **pegar**

peinado *nm* : hairstyle, hairdo

peinador, -dora *n* : hairdresser

peinar *vt* : to comb — **peinarse** *vr*

peine *nm* : comb

peineta *nf* : ornamental comb

peladez *nf, pl* **-deces** *Mex fam* : obscenity, bad language

pelado, -da *adj* **1 :** bald, hairless **2 :** peeled **3 :** bare, barren **4 :** broke, penniless **5** *Mex fam* **:** coarse, crude

pelador *nm* : peeler

pelagra *nf* : pellagra

pelaje *nm* : coat (of an animal), fur

pelar *vt* **1 :** to peel, to shell **2 :** to skin **3 :** to pluck **4 :** to remove hair from **5** *fam* **:** to clean out (of money) — **pelarse** *vr* **1 :** to peel **2** *fam* **:** to get a haircut **3** *Mex fam* **:** to split, to leave

peldaño *nm* **1 :** step, stair **2 :** rung

pelea *nf* **1** LUCHA **:** fight **2 :** quarrel

pelear *vi* **1** LUCHAR **:** to fight **2** DISPUTAR **:** to quarrel — **pelearse** *vr*

peleón, -ona *adj, mpl* **-ones** *Spain* : quarrelsome, argumentative

peleonero, -ra *adj Mex* : quarrelsome

peletería *nf* **1 :** fur shop **2 :** fur trade

peletero, -ra *n* : furrier

peliagudo, -da *adj* : tricky, difficult, ticklish

pelícano *nm* : pelican

película *nf* **1 :** movie, film **2 :** (photographic) film **3 :** thin covering, layer

peligrar *vi* : to be in danger

peligro *nm* **1 :** danger, peril **2 :** risk <correr peligro de : to run the risk of>

peligroso, -sa *adj* : dangerous, hazardous

pelirrojo[1], -ja *adj* : red-haired, redheaded

pelirrojo[2], -ja *n* : redhead

pellejo *nm* **1 :** hide, skin **2 salvar el pellejo :** to save one's neck

pellizcar {72} *vt* **1 :** to pinch **2 :** to nibble on

pellizco *nm* : pinch

pelo *nm* **1 :** hair **2 :** fur **3 :** pile, nap **4 a pelo :** bareback **5 con pelos y señales :** in great detail **6 no tener pelos en la lengua :** to not mince words, to be blunt **7 tomarle el pelo a alguien :** to tease someone, to pull someone's leg

pelón, -lona *adj, mpl* **pelones 1 :** bald **2** *fam* **:** broke **3** *Mex fam* **:** tough, difficult

pelota *nf* **1 :** ball **2** *fam* **:** head **3 en pelotas** *fam* **:** naked **4 pelota vasca :** jai alai **5 pasar la pelota** *fam* **:** to pass the buck

pelotón *nm, pl* **-tones :** squad, detachment

peltre *nm* **:** pewter

peluca *nf* **:** wig

peluche *nm* **:** plush (fabric)

peludo, -da *adj* **:** hairy, shaggy, bushy

peluquería *nf* **1 :** hairdresser's, barber shop **2 :** hairdressing

peluquero, -ra *n* **:** barber, hairdresser

peluquín *nm, pl* **-quines** TUPÉ **:** hairpiece, toupee

pelusa *nf* **:** lint, fuzz

pélvico, -ca *adj* **:** pelvic

pelvis *nfs & pl* **:** pelvis

pena *nf* **1** CASTIGO **:** punishment, penalty <pena de muerte : death penalty> **2** AFLICCIÓN **:** sorrow, grief <morir de pena : to die of a broken heart> <¡que pena! : what a shame!, how sad!> **3** DOLOR **:** pain, suffering **4** DIFICULTAD **:** difficulty, trouble <a duras penas : with great difficulty> **5** VERGÜENZA **:** shame, embarrassment **6 valer la pena :** to be worthwhile

penacho *nm* **1 :** crest, tuft **2 :** plume (of feathers)

penal[1] *adj* **:** penal

penal[2] *nm* CÁRCEL **:** prison, penitentiary

penalidad *nf* **1 :** hardship **2 :** penalty, punishment

penalizar {21} *vt* **:** to penalize

penalty *nm* **:** penalty (in sports)

penar *vt* **:** to punish, to penalize — *vi* **:** to suffer, to grieve

pendenciero, -ra *adj* **:** argumentative, quarrelsome

pender *vi* **1 :** to hang **2 :** to be pending

pendiente[1] *adj* **1 :** pending **2 estar pendiente de :** to be watchful of, to be on the lookout for

pendiente[2] *nm Spain* **:** earring

pendiente[3] *nf* **:** slope, incline

pendón *nm, pl* **pendones :** banner

péndulo *nm* **:** pendulum

pene *nm* **:** penis

penetración *nf, pl* **-ciones 1 :** penetration **2 :** insight

penetrante *adj* **1 :** penetrating, piercing **2 :** sharp, acute **3 :** deep (of a wound)

penetrar *vi* **1 :** to penetrate, to sink in **2 ~ por** *or* **~ en :** to pierce, to go in, to enter into <el frío penetra por la ventana : the cold comes right in through the window> — *vt* **1 :** to penetrate, to permeate **2 :** to pierce <el dolor penetró su corazón : sorrow pierced her heart> **3 :** to fathom, to understand

penicilina *nf* **:** penicillin

península *nf* **:** peninsula — **peninsular** *adj*

penitencia *nf* **:** penance, penitence

penitenciaría *nf* **:** penitentiary

penitente *adj & nmf* **:** penitent

penol *nm* **:** yardarm

penoso, -sa *adj* **1 :** painful, distressing **2 :** difficult, arduous **3 :** shy, bashful

pensado, -da *adj* **1 bien pensado :** well thought-out **2 en el momento menos pensado :** when least expected **3 poco pensado :** badly thought-out **4 mal pensado :** evil-minded

pensador, -dora *n* **:** thinker

pensamiento *nm* **1 :** thought **2 :** thinking **3 :** pansy

pensar {55} *vi* **1 :** to think **2 ~ en :** to think about — *vt* **1 :** to think **2 :** to think about **3 :** to intend, to plan on — **pensarse** *vr* **:** to think over

pensativo, -va *adj* **:** pensive, thoughtful

pensión *nf, pl* **pensiones 1** JUBILACIÓN **:** pension **2 :** boarding house **3 pensión alimenticia :** alimony

pensionado, -da *n* → **pensionista**

pensionista *nmf* **1** JUBILADO **:** pensioner, retiree **2 :** boarder, lodger

pentágono *nm* **:** pentagon — **pentagonal** *adj*

pentagrama *nm* **:** staff (in music)

penúltimo, -ma *adj* **:** next to last, penultimate

penumbra *nf* **:** semidarkness

penuria *nf* **1** ESCASEZ **:** shortage, scarcity **2 :** poverty

peña *nf* **:** rock, crag

peñasco *nm* **:** crag, large rock

peñón *nm* → **peñasco**

peón *nm, pl* **peones 1 :** laborer, peon **2 :** pawn (in chess)

peonía *nf* **:** peony

peor[1] *adv* **1** (*comparative of* **mal**) **:** worse <se llevan peor que antes : they get along worse than before> **2** (*superlative of* **mal**) **:** worst <me fue peor que a nadie : I did the worst of all>

peor[2] *adj* **1** (*comparative of* **malo**) **:** worse <es peor que el original : it's worse than the original> **2** (*superlative of* **malo**) **:** worst <el peor de todos : the worst of all>

pepa *nf* **:** seed, pit (of a fruit)

pepenador, -dora *n CA, Mex* **:** scavenger

pepenar *vt CA, Mex* **:** to scavenge, to scrounge

pepinillo *nm* **:** pickle, gherkin

pepino *nm* **:** cucumber

pepita *nf* **1 :** seed, pip **2 :** nugget **3** *Mex* **:** dried pumpkin seed

peque, etc. → **pecar**

pequeñez *nf, pl* **-ñeces 1 :** smallness **2 :** trifle, triviality **3 pequeñez de espíritu :** pettiness

pequeño[1], **-ña** *adj* **1 :** small, little <un libro pequeño : a small book> **2 :** young **3** BAJO **:** short

pequeño[2], **-ña** *n* **:** child, little one

pera *nf* : pear

peraltar *vt* : to bank (a road)

perca *nf* : perch (fish)

percal *nm* : percale

percance *nm* : mishap, misfortune

percatarse *vr* **~ de** : to notice, to become aware of

percebe *nm* : barnacle

percepción *nf, pl* **-ciones 1** : perception **2** : idea, notion **3** COBRO : receipt (of payment), collection

perceptible *adj* : perceptible, noticeable — **perceptiblemente** *adv*

percha *nf* **1** : perch **2** : coat hanger **3** : coatrack, coat hook

perchero *nm* : coatrack

percibir *vt* **1** : to perceive, to notice, to sense **2** : to earn, to draw (a salary)

percudido, -da *adj* : grimy

percudir *vt* : to make grimy — **percudirse** *vr*

percusión *nf, pl* **-siones** : percussion

percusor *or* **percutor** *nm* : hammer (of a firearm)

perdedor[1], -dora *adj* : losing

perdedor[2], -dora *n* : loser

perder {56} *vt* **1** : to lose **2** : to miss <perdimos la oportunidad : we missed the opportunity> **3** : to waste (time) — *vi* : to lose — **perderse** *vr* EXTRAVIARSE : to get lost, to stray

perdición *nf, pl* **-ciones** : perdition, damnation

pérdida *nf* **1** : loss **2 pérdida de tiempo** : waste of time

perdidamente *adv* : hopelessly

perdido, -da *adj* **1** : lost **2** : inveterate, incorrigible <es un caso perdido : he's a hopeless case> **3** : in trouble, done for **4 de ~** *Mex fam* : at least

perdigón *nm, pl* **-gones** : shot, pellet

perdiz *nf, pl* **perdices** : partridge

perdón[1] *nm, pl* **perdones** : forgiveness, pardon

perdón[2] *interj* : excuse me!, sorry!

perdonable *adj* : forgivable

perdonar *vt* **1** DISCULPAR : to forgive, to pardon **2** : to exempt, to excuse

perdurable *adj* : lasting

perdurar *vi* : to last, to endure, to survive

perecedero, -ra *adj* : perishable

perecer {53} *vi* : to perish, to die

peregrinación *nf, pl* **-ciones** : pilgrimage

peregrinaje *nm* → **peregrinación**

peregrino[1], -na *adj* **1** : unusual, odd **2** MIGRATORIO : migratory

peregrino[2], -na *n* : pilgrim

perejil *nm* : parsley

perenne *adj* : perennial

pereza *nf* FLOJERA, HOLGAZANERÍA : laziness, idleness

perezoso[1], -sa *adj* FLOJO, HOLGAZÁN : lazy

perezoso[2] *nm* : sloth (animal)

perfección *nf, pl* **-ciones** : perfection

perfeccionamiento *nm* : perfecting, refinement

perfeccionar *vt* : to perfect, to refine

perfeccionismo *nm* : perfectionism

perfeccionista *nmf* : perfectionist

perfecto, -ta *adj* : perfect — **perfectamente** *adv*

perfidia *nf* : perfidy, treachery

pérfido, -da *adj* : perfidious

perfil *nm* **1** : profile **2 de ~** : sideways, from the side **3 perfiles** *nmpl* RASGOS : features, characteristics

perfilar *vt* : to outline, to define — **perfilarse** *vr* **1** : to be outlined, to be silhouetted **2** : to take shape

perforación *nf, pl* **-ciones 1** : perforation **2** : drilling

perforar *vt* **1** : to perforate, to pierce **2** : to drill, to bore

perfumar *vt* : to perfume, to scent — **perfumarse** *vr*

perfume *nm* : perfume, scent

pergamino *nm* : parchment

pérgola *nf* : pergola, arbor

pericia *nf* : skill, expertise

pericial *adj* : expert <testigo pericial : expert witness>

perico *nm* COTORRA : small parrot

periferia *nf* : periphery

periférico[1], -ca *adj* : peripheral

periférico[2] *nm* **1** *CA, Mex* : beltway **2** : peripheral

perilla *nf* **1** : goatee **2** : pommel (on a saddle) **3** *Col, Mex* : knob, handle **4 perilla de la oreja** : earlobe **5 de perillas** *fam* : handy, just right

perímetro *nm* : perimeter

periódico[1], -ca *adj* : periodic — **periódicamente** *adv*

periódico[2] *nm* DIARIO : newspaper

periodismo *nm* : journalism

periodista *nmf* : journalist

periodístico, -ca *adj* : journalistic, news

período *or* **periodo** *nm* : period

peripecia *nf* VICISITUD : vicissitude, reversal <las peripecias de su carrera : the ups and downs of her career>

periquito *nm* **1** : parakeet **2 periquito australiano** : budgerigar

periscopio *nm* : periscope

perito, -ta *adj & n* : expert

perjudicar {72} *vt* : to harm, to be detrimental to

perjudicial *adj* : harmful, detrimental

perjuicio *nm* **1** : harm, damage **2 en perjuicio de** : to the detriment of

perjurar *vi* : to perjure oneself

perjurio *nm* : perjury

perjuro, -ra *n* : perjurer

perla *nf* **1** : pearl **2 de perlas** *fam* : wonderfully <me viene de perlas : it suits me just fine>

permanecer {53} *vi* **1** QUEDARSE : to remain, to stay **2** SEGUIR : to remain, to continue to be

permanencia *nf* **1** : permanence, continuance **2** ESTANCIA : stay

permanente[1] *adj* **1** : permanent **2** : constant — **permanentemente** *adv*

permanente[2] *nf* : permanent (wave)

permeabilidad *nf* **:** permeability
permeable *adj* **:** permeable
permisible *adj* **:** permissible, allowable
permisividad *nf* **:** permissiveness
permisivo, -va *adv* **:** permissive
permiso *nm* **1 :** permission **2 :** permit, license **3 :** leave, furlough **4 con ~ :** excuse me, pardon me
permitir *vt* **:** to permit, to allow — **permitirse** *vr*
permuta *nf* **:** exchange
permutar *vt* INTERCAMBIAR **:** to exchange
pernicioso, -sa *adj* **:** pernicious, destructive
pernil *nm* **1 :** haunch (of an animal) **2 :** leg (of meat), ham **3 :** trouser leg
perno *nm* **:** bolt, pin
pernoctar *vi* **:** to stay overnight, to spend the night
pero[1] *nm* **1 :** fault, defect <ponerle peros a : to find fault with> **2 :** objection
pero[2] *conj* **:** but
perogrullada *nf* **:** truism, platitude, cliché
peroné *nm* **:** fibula
perorar *vi* **:** to deliver a speech
perorata *nf* **:** oration, long-winded speech
peróxido *nm* **:** peroxide
perpendicular *adj & nf* **:** perpendicular
perpetrar *vt* **:** to perpetrate
perpetuar {3} *vt* ETERNIZAR **:** to perpetuate
perpetuidad *nf* **:** perpetuity
perpetuo, -tua *adj* **:** perpetual — **perpetuamente** *adv*
perplejidad *nf* **:** perplexity
perplejo, -ja *adj* **:** perplexed, puzzled
perrada *nf fam* **:** dirty trick
perrera *nf* **:** kennel, dog pound
perrero, -ra *n* **:** dogcatcher
perrito, -ta *n* CACHORRO **:** puppy, small dog
perro, -rra *n* **1 :** dog, bitch *f* **2 perro caliente :** hot dog **3 perro salchicha :** dachsund **4 perro faldero :** lapdog **5 perro cobrador :** retriever
persa *adj & nmf* **:** Persian
persecución *nf, pl* **-ciones 1 :** pursuit, chase **2 :** persecution
perseguidor, -dora *n* **1 :** pursuer **2 :** persecutor
perseguir {75} *vt* **1 :** to pursue, to chase **2 :** to persecute **3 :** to pester, to annoy
perseverancia *nf* **:** perseverance
perseverar *vi* **:** to persevere
persiana *nf* **:** blind, venetian blind
persignarse *vr* SANTIGUARSE **:** to cross oneself, to make the sign of the cross
persistir *vi* **:** to persist — **persistencia** *nf* — **persistente** *adj*
persona *nf* **:** person
personaje *nm* **1 :** character (in drama or literature) **2 :** personage, celebrity
personal[1] *adj* **:** personal — **personalmente** *adv*
personal[2] *nm* **:** personnel, staff
personalidad *nf* **:** personality
personalizar {21} *vt* **:** to personalize
personificar {72} *vi* **:** to personify — **personificación** *nf*
perspectiva *nf* **1 :** perspective, view **2 :** prospect, outlook
perspicacia *nf* **:** shrewdness, perspicacity, insight
perspicaz *adj, pl* **-caces :** shrewd, perspicacious
persuadir *vt* **:** to persuade — **persuadirse** *vr* **:** to become convinced
persuasión *nf, pl* **-siones :** persuasion
persuasivo, -va *adj* **:** persuasive
pertenecer {53} *vi* **:** to belong
perteneciente *adj* **~ a :** belonging to
pertenencia *nf* **1 :** membership **2 :** ownership **3 pertenencias** *nfpl* **:** belongings, possessions
pértiga *nf* GARROCHA **:** pole <salto de pértiga : pole vault>
pertinaz *adj, pl* **-naces 1** OBSTINADO **:** obstinate **2** PERSISTENTE **:** persistent
pertinencia *nf* **:** pertinence, relevance — **pertinente** *adj*
pertrechos *nmpl* **:** equipment, gear
perturbación *nf, pl* **-ciones :** disturbance, disruption
perturbador, -dora *adj* **1** INQUIETANTE **:** disturbing, troubling **2 :** disruptive
perturbar *vt* **1 :** to disturb, to trouble **2 :** to disrupt
peruano, -na *adj & n* **:** Peruvian
perversidad *nf* **:** perversity, depravity
perversión *nf, pl* **-siones :** perversion
perverso, -sa *adj* **:** wicked, depraved
pervertido[1]**, -da** *adj* DEPRAVADO **:** perverted, depraved
pervertido[2]**, -da** *n* **:** pervert
pervertir {76} *vt* **:** to pervert, to corrupt
pesa *nf* **1 :** weight **2 levantamiento de pesas :** weightlifting
pesadamente *adv* **1 :** heavily **2 :** slowly, clumsily
pesadez *nf, pl* **-deces 1 :** heaviness **2 :** slowness **3 :** tediousness
pesadilla *nf* **:** nightmare
pesado[1]**, -da** *adj* **1 :** heavy **2 :** slow **3 :** irritating, annoying **4 :** tedious, boring **5 :** tough, difficult
pesado[2]**, -da** *n fam* **:** bore, pest
pesadumbre *nf* AFLICCIÓN **:** grief, sorrow, sadness
pésame *nm* **:** condolences *pl* <mi más sentido pésame : my heartfelt condolences>
pesar[1] *vt* **1 :** to weigh **2** EXAMINAR **:** to consider, to think over — *vi* **1 :** to weigh <¿cuánto pesa? : how much does it weigh?> **2 :** to be heavy **3 :** to weigh heavily, to be a burden <no le pesa : it's not a burden on him> <pesa sobre mi corazón : it weighs upon my heart> **4** INFLUIR **:** to carry weight, to have bearing **5** (*with personal pro-*

nouns) : to grieve, to sadden <me pesa mucho : I'm very sorry> **6 pese a** : in spite of, despite

pesar[2] *nm* **1** AFLICCIÓN, PENA : sorrow, grief **2** REMORDIMIENTO : remorse **3 a pesar de** : in spite of, despite

pesaroso, -sa *adj* **1** : sad, mournful **2** ARREPENTIDO : sorry, regretful

pesca *nf* : fishing

pescadería *nf* : fish market

pescado *nm* : fish (as food)

pescador, -dora *n* : fisherman *m*, fisherwoman *f*

pescar {72} *vt* **1** : to fish for **2** : to catch **3** *fam* : to get a hold of, to land — *vi* : to fish, to go fishing

pescuezo *nm* : neck

pesebre *nm* : manger

pesera *nf Mex* : minibus

peseta *nf* : peseta (Spanish unit of currency)

pesimismo *nm* : pessimism

pesimista[1] *adj* : pessimistic

pesimista[2] *nmf* : pessimist

pésimo, -ma *adj* : dreadful, abominable

peso *nm* **1** : weight, heaviness **2** : burden, responsibility **3** : weight (in sports) **4** BÁSCULA : scales *pl* **5** : peso

pesque, etc. → **pescar**

pesquería *nf* : fishery

pesquero[1], **-ra** *adj* : fishing <pueblo pesquero : fishing village>

pesquero[2] *nm* : fishing boat

pesquisa *nf* INVESTIGACIÓN : inquiry, investigation

pestaña *nf* **1** : eyelash **2** : flange, rim

pestañear *vi* : to blink

pestañeo *nm* : blink

peste *nf* **1** : plague, pestilence **2** : stench, stink **3** : nuisance, pest

pesticida *nm* : pesticide

pestilencia *nf* **1** : stench, foul odor **2** : pestilence

pestilente *adj* **1** : foul, smelly **2** : pestilent

pestillo *nm* CERROJO : bolt, latch

petaca *nf* **1** *Mex* : suitcase **2 petacas** *nfpl Mex fam* : bottom, behind

pétalo *nm* : petal

petardear *vi* : to backfire

petardeo *nm* : backfiring

petardo *nm* : firecracker

petate *nm Mex* : mat

petición *nf, pl* **-ciones** : petition, request

peticionar *vt* : to petition

peticionario, -ria *n* : petitioner

petirrojo *nm* : robin

peto *nm* : bib (of clothing)

pétreo, -trea *adj* : stone, stony

petrificar {72} *vt* : to petrify

petróleo *nm* : oil, petroleum

petrolero[1], **-ra** *adj* : oil <industria petrolera : oil industry>

petrolero[2] *nm* : oil tanker

petulancia *nf* INSOLENCIA : insolence, petulance

petulante *adj* INSOLENTE : insolent, petulant — **petulantemente** *adv*

petunia *nf* : petunia

peyorativo, -va *adj* : pejorative

pez[1] *nm, pl* **peces 1** : fish **2 pez de colores** : goldfish **3 pez espada** : swordfish **4 pez gordo** : big shot

pez[2] *nf, pl* **peces** : pitch, tar

pezón *nm, pl* **pezones** : nipple

pezuña *nf* : hoof <pezuña hendida : cloven hoof>

pi *nf* : pi

piadoso, -sa *adj* **1** : compassionate, merciful **2** DEVOTO : pious, devout

pianista *nmf* : pianist, piano player

piano *nm* : piano

piar {85} *vi* : to chirp, to cheep, to tweet

pibe, -ba *n Arg, Uru fam* : kid, child

pica *nf* **1** : pike, lance **2** : goad (in bullfighting) **3** : spade (in playing cards)

picada *nf* **1** : bite, sting (of an insect) **2** : sharp descent

picadillo *nm* **1** : minced meat, hash **2 hacer picadillo a** : to beat to a pulp

picado, -da *adj* **1** : perforated **2** : minced, chopped **3** : decayed (of teeth) **4** : choppy, rough **5** *fam* : annoyed, miffed

picador *nm* : picador

picadura *nf* **1** : sting, bite **2** : prick, puncture **3** : decay, cavity

picaflor *nm* COLIBRÍ : hummingbird

picana *nf* : goad, prod

picante[1] *adj* **1** : hot, spicy **2** : sharp, cutting **3** : racy, risqué

picante[2] *nm* **1** : spiciness **2** : hot spices *pl*, hot sauce

picaporte *nm* **1** : latch **2** : door handle **3** ALDABA : door knocker

picar {72} *vt* **1** : to sting, to bite **2** : to peck at **3** : to nibble on **4** : to prick, to puncture, to punch (a ticket) **5** : to grind, to chop **6** : to goad, to incite **7** : to pique, to provoke — *vi* **1** : to itch **2** : to sting **3** : to be spicy **4** : to nibble **5** : to take the bait **6 ~ en** : to dabble in **7 picar muy alto** : to aim too high — **picarse** *vr* **1** : to get a cavity, to decay **2** : to get annoyed, to take offense

picardía *nf* **1** : cunning, craftiness **2** : prank, dirty trick

picaresco, -ca *adj* **1** : picaresque **2** : rascally, roguish

pícaro[1], **-ra** *adj* **1** : mischievous **2** : cunning, sly **3** : off-color, risqué

pícaro[2], **-ra** *n* **1** : rogue, scoundrel **2** : rascal

picazón *nf, pl* **-zones** COMEZÓN : itch

picea *nf* : spruce (tree)

pichel *nm* : pitcher, jug

pichón, -chona *n, mpl* **pichones 1** : young pigeon, squab **2** *Mex fam* : novice, greenhorn

picnic *nm* : picnic

pico *nm* **1** : peak **2** : point, spike **3** : beak, bill **4** : pick, pickax **5 y pico**

: and a little, and a bit <las siete y pico : a little after seven> <dos metros y pico : a bit over two meters>
picor *nm* : itch, irritation
picoso, -sa *adj Mex* : very hot, spicy
picota *nf* **1** : pillory, stock **2 poner a alguien en la picota** : to put someone on the spot
picotada *nf* → **picotazo**
picotazo *nm* : peck (of a bird)
picotear *vt* : to peck — *vi* : to nibble, to pick
pictórico, -ca *adj* : pictorial
picudo, -da *adj* **1** : pointy, sharp **2 ~ para** *Mex fam* : clever at, good at
pide, etc. → **pedir**
pie *nm* **1** : foot <a pie : on foot> <de pie : on one's feet, standing> **2** : base, bottom, stem, foot <pie de la cama : foot of the bed> <pie de una lámpera : base of a lamp> <pie de la escalera : bottom of the stairs> <pie de una copa : stem of a glass> **3** : foot (in measurement) <pie cuadrado : square foot> **4** : cue (in theater) **5 dar pie a** : to give cause for, to give rise to **6 en pie de igualidad** : on equal footing
piedad *nf* **1** COMPASIÓN : mercy, pity **2** DEVOCIÓN : piety, devotion
piedra *nf* **1** : stone **2** : flint (of a lighter) **3** : hailstone **4 piedra de afilar** : whetstone, grindstone **5 piedra angular** : cornerstone **6 piedra arenisca** : sandstone **7 piedra caliza** : limestone **8 piedra imán** : lodestone **9 piedra de molino** : millstone **10 piedra de toque** : touchstone
piel *nf* **1** : skin **2** CUERO : leather, hide <piel de venado : deerskin> **3** : fur, pelt **4** CÁSCARA : peel, skin **5 piel de gallina** : goose bumps *pl* <me pone la piel de gallina : it gives me goose bumps>
piélago *nm* **el piélago** : the deep, the ocean
piensa, etc. → **pensar**
pienso *nm* : feed, fodder
pierde, etc. → **perder**
pierna *nf* : leg
pieza *nf* **1** ELEMENTO : piece, part, component <vestido de dos piezas : two-piece dress> <pieza de recambio : spare part> <pieza clave : key element> **2** : piece (in chess) **3** OBRA : piece, work <pieza de teatro : play> **4** : room, bedroom
pifia *nf fam* : goof, blunder
pigargo *nm* : osprey
pigmentación *nf, pl* **-ciones** : pigmentation
pigmento *nm* : pigment
pigmeo, -mea *adj & n* : pygmy, Pygmy
pijama *nm* : pajamas *pl*
pila *nf* **1** BATERÍA : battery <pila de linterna : flashlight battery> **2** MONTÓN : pile, heap **3** : sink, basin, font <pila bautismal : baptismal font> <pila para pájaros : birdbath>
pilar *nm* **1** : pillar, column **2** : support, mainstay
píldora *nf* PASTILLA : pill
pillaje *nm* : pillage, plunder
pillar *vt fam* **1** : to catch <¡cuidado! ¡nos pillarán! : watch out! they'll catch us!> **2** : to grasp, to catch on <¿no lo pillas? : don't you get it?>
pillo¹, -lla *adj* : cunning, crafty
pillo², -lla *n* **1** : rascal, brat **2** : rogue, scoundrel
pilluelo, -la *n* : urchin
pilotar *vt* : to pilot, to drive
pilote *nm* : pile (stake)
pilotear → **pilotar**
piloto *nm* **1** : pilot, driver **2** : pilot light
piltrafa *nf* **1** : poor quality meat **2** : wretch **3 piltrafas** *nfpl* : food scraps
pimentero *nm* : pepper shaker
pimentón *nm, pl* **-tones 1** : paprika **2** : cayenne pepper
pimienta *nf* **1** : pepper (condiment) **2 pimienta de Jamaica** : allspice
pimiento *nm* : pepper (fruit) <pimiento verde : green pepper>
pináculo *nm* **1** : pinnacle (of a building) **2** : peak, acme
pincel *nm* : paintbrush
pincelada *nf* **1** : brushstroke **2 últimas pinceladas** : final touches
pinchar *vt* **1** PICAR : to puncture (a tire) **2** : to prick, to stick **3** : to goad, to tease, to needle — *vi* **1** : to be prickly **2** : to get a flat tire **3** *fam* : to get beaten, to lose out — **pincharse** *vr* : to give oneself an injection
pinchazo *nm* **1** : prick, jab **2** : puncture, flat tire
pingüe *adj* **1** : rich, huge (of profits) **2** : lucrative
pingüino *nm* : penguin
pininos *or* **pinitos** *nmpl* : first steps <hacer pininos : to take one's first steps, to toddle>
pino *nm* : pine, pine tree
pinta *nf* **1** : dot, spot **2** : pint **3** *fam* : aspect, appearance <las peras tienen buena pinta : the pears look good> **4 pintas** *nfpl Mex* : graffiti
pintadas *nfpl* : graffiti
pintar *vt* **1** : to paint **2** : to draw, to mark **3** : to describe, to depict — *vi* **1** : to paint, to draw **2** : to look <no pinta bien : it doesn't look good> **3** *fam* : to count <aquí no pinta nada : he has no say here> — **pintarse** *vr* **1** MAQUILLARSE : to put on makeup **2 pintárselas solo** *fam* : to manage by oneself, to know it all
pintarrajear *vt* : to daub (with paint)
pinto, -ta *adj* : speckled, spotted
pintor, -tora *n* **1** : painter **2 pintor de brocha gorda** : housepainter, dauber
pintoresco, -ca *adj* : picturesque, quaint
pintura *nf* **1** : paint **2** : painting (art, work of art)

pinza *nf* **1** : clothespin **2** : claw, pincer **3** : pleat, dart **4 pinzas** *nfpl* : tweezers **5 pinzas** *nfpl* ALICATES : pliers, pincers
pinzón *nm, pl* **pinzones** : finch
piña *nf* **1** : pineapple **2** : pine cone
piñata *nf* : piñata
piñón *nm, pl* **piñones 1** : pine nut **2** : pinion
pío[1], pía *adj* **1** DEVOTO : pious, devout **2** : piebald, pied, dappled
pío[2] *nm* : peep, tweet, cheep
piocha *nf* **1** : pickax **2** *Mex* : goatee
piojo *nm* : louse
piojoso, -sa *adj* **1** : lousy **2** : filthy
pionero[1], -ra *adj* : pioneering
pionero[2], -ra *n* : pioneer
pipa *nf* : pipe (for smoking)
pipián *nm, pl* **pipianes** *Mex* : a spicy sauce or stew
pipiolo, -la *n fam* **1** : greenhorn, novice **2** : kid, youngster
pique[1], etc. → **picar**
pique[2] *nm* **1** : pique, resentment **2** : rivalry, competition **3 a pique de** : about to, on the verge of **4 irse a pique** : to sink, to founder
piqueta *nf* : pickax
piquete *nm* **1** : picketers *pl*, picket line **2** : squad, detachment **3** *Mex* : prick, jab
piquetear *vt* **1** : to picket **2** *Mex* : to prick, to jab
pira *nf* : pyre
piragua *nf* : canoe — **piragüista** *nmf*
pirámide *nf* : pyramid
piraña *nf* : piranha
pirata[1] *adj* : bootleg, pirated
pirata[2] *nmf* **1** : pirate **2** : bootlegger **3 pirata aéreo** : hijacker
piratear *vt* **1** : to hijack, to commandeer **2** : to bootleg, to pirate
piratería *nf* : piracy, bootlegging
piromanía *nf* : pyromania
pirómano, -na *n* : pyromaniac
piropo *nm* : flirtatious compliment
pirotecnia *nf* : fireworks *pl*, pyrotechnics *pl*
pirotécnico, -ca *adj* : fireworks, pyrotechnic
pírrico, -ca *adj* : Pyrrhic
pirueta *nf* : pirouette
pirulí *nm* : cone-shaped lollipop
pisada *nf* **1** : footstep **2** HUELLA : footprint
pisapapeles *nms & pl* : paperweight
pisar *vt* **1** : to step on, to set foot in **2** : to walk all over, to mistreat — *vi* : to step, to walk, to tread
piscina *nf* **1** : swimming pool **2** : fish pond
Piscis *nmf* : Pisces
piso *nm* **1** PLANTA : floor, story **2** SUELO : floor **3** *Spain* : apartment
pisotear *vt* **1** : to stamp on, to trample **2** PISAR : to walk all over **3** : to flout, to disregard
pisotón *nm, pl* **-tones** : stamp, step <sufrieron empujones y pisotones : they were pushed and stepped on>
pista *nf* **1** RASTRO : trail, track <siguen la pista de los sospechosos : they're on the trail of the suspects> **2** : clue **3** CAMINO : road, trail **4** : track, racetrack **5** : ring, arena, rink **6 pista de aterrizaje** : runway, airstrip **7 pista de baile** : dance floor
pistacho *nm* : pistachio
pistilo *nm* : pistil
pistola *nf* **1** : pistol, handgun **2** : spray gun
pistolera *nf* : holster
pistolero *nm* : gunman
pistón *nm, pl* **pistones** : piston
pita *nf* **1** : agave **2** : pita fiber **3** : twine
pitar *vi* **1** : to blow a whistle **2** : to whistle, to boo **3** : to beep, to honk, to toot — *vt* : to whistle at, to boo
pitido *nm* **1** : whistle, whistling **2** : beep, honk, toot
pito *nm* **1** SILBATO : whistle **2 no me importa un pito** *fam* : I don't give a damn
pitón *nm, pl* **pitones** *nm* **1** : python **2** : point of a bull's horn
pituitario, -ria *adj* : pituitary
pívot *nmf, pl* **pívots** : center (in basketball)
pivote *nm* : pivot
piyama *nmf* : pajamas *pl*
pizarra *nf* **1** : slate **2** : blackboard **3** : scoreboard
pizarrón *nm, pl* **-rrones** : blackboard, chalkboard
pizca *nf* **1** : pinch <una pizca de canela : a pinch of cinnamon> **2** : speck, trace <ni pizca : not a bit> **3** *Mex* : harvest
pizcar {72} *vt Mex* : to harvest
pizque, etc. → **pizcar**
pizza ['pitsa, 'pisa] *nf* : pizza
pizzería *nf* : pizzeria, pizza parlor
placa *nf* **1** : sheet, plate **2** : plaque, nameplate **3** : plate (in photography) **4** : badge, insignia **5 placa de matrícula** : license plate, tag **6 placa dental** : plaque, tartar
placebo *nm* : placebo
placenta *nf* : placenta, afterbirth
placentero, -ra *adj* AGRADABLE, GRATO : pleasant, agreeable
placer[1] {57} *vi* GUSTAR : to be pleasing <hazlo como te plazca : do it however you please>
placer[2] *nm* **1** : pleasure, enjoyment **2 a ~** : as much as one wants
plácido, -da *adj* TRANQUILO : placid, calm
plaga *nf* **1** : plague, infestation, blight **2** CALAMIDAD : disaster, scourge
plagado, -da *adj* **~ de** : filled with, covered with
plagar {52} *vt* : to plague
plagiar *vt* **1** : to plagiarize **2** SECUESTRAR : to kidnap, to abduct

plagiario, -ria *n* **1 :** plagiarist **2** SECUESTRADOR **:** kidnapper, abductor
plagio *nm* **1 :** plagiarism **2** SECUESTRO **:** kidnapping, abduction
plague, etc. → **plagar**
plan *nm* **1 :** plan, strategy, program <plan de inversiones : investment plan> <plan de estudios : curriculum> **2** PLANO **:** plan, diagram **3 :** attitude, intent, purpose <ponte en plan serio : be serious> <estamos en plan de divertirnos : we're looking to have some fun>
plana *nf* **1 :** page <noticias en primera plana : front-page news> **2 plana mayor :** staff (in the military)
plancha *nf* **1 :** iron, ironing **2 :** grill, griddle <a la plancha : grilled> **3 :** sheet, plate <plancha para hornear : baking sheet> **4** *fam* **:** blunder, blooper
planchada *nf* **:** ironing, pressing
planchado *nm* → **planchada**
planchar *v* **:** to iron
planchazo *nm fam* **:** goof, blunder
plancton *nm* **:** plankton
planeación *nf* → **planeamiento**
planeador *nm* **:** glider (aircraft)
planeamiento *nm* **:** plan, planning
planear *vt* **:** to plan — *vi* **:** to glide (in the air)
planeo *nm* **:** gliding, soaring
planeta *nm* **:** planet
planetario[1], -ria *adj* **1 :** planetary **2 :** global, worldwide
planetario[2] *nm* **:** planetarium
planicie *nf* **:** plain
planificación *nf* **:** planning <planificación familiar : family planning>
planificar {72} *vt* **:** to plan
planilla *nf* **1** LISTA **:** list **2** NÓMINA **:** payroll **3** TABLA **:** chart, table **4** *Mex* **:** slate, ticket (of candidates) **5 planilla de cálculo** *Arg, Chile* **:** spreadsheet
plano[1], -na *adj* **:** flat, level, plane
plano[2] *nm* **1** PLAN **:** map, plan **2 :** plane (surface) **3** NIVEL **:** level <en un plano personal : on a personal level> **4 :** shot (in photography) **5 de ~ :** flatly, outright, directly <se negó de plano : he flatly refused>
planta *nf* **1 :** plant <planta de interior : houseplant> **2** FÁBRICA **:** plant, factory **3** PISO **:** floor, story **4 :** staff, employees *pl* **5 :** sole (of the foot)
plantación *nf, pl* **-ciones 1 :** plantation **2 :** planting
plantar *vt* **1 :** to plant, to sow **2 :** to put in, to place **3** *fam* **:** to plant, to land <plantar un beso : to plant a kiss> **4** *fam* **:** to leave, to jilt — **plantarse** *vr* **1 :** to stand firm **2** *fam* **:** to arrive, to show up **3** *fam* **:** to balk
planteamiento *nm* **1 :** approach, position <el planteamiento feminista : the feminist viewpoint> **2 :** explanation, exposition **3 :** proposal, suggestion, plan
plantear *vt* **1 :** to set forth, to bring up, to suggest **2 :** to establish, to set up **3 :** to create, to pose (a problem) — **plantearse** *vr* **1 :** to think about **2 :** to arise
plantel *nm* **1 :** educational institution **2 :** staff, team
planteo *nm* → **planteamiento**
plantilla *nf* **1 :** insole **2 :** pattern, template, stencil **3** *Mex, Spain* **:** staff, roster of employees
plantío *nm* **:** field (planted with a crop)
plantón *nm, pl* **plantones 1 :** seedling **2 :** long wait <darle a alguien un plantón : to stand someone up>
plañidero[1], -ra *adj* **:** mournful
plañidero[2], -ra *nf* **:** hired mourner
plañir {38} *v* **:** to mourn, to lament
plasma *nm* **:** plasma
plasmar *vt* **:** to express, to give form to — **plasmarse** *vr*
plasta *nf* **:** soft mass, lump
plástica *nf* **:** modeling, sculpture
plasticidad *nf* **:** plasticity
plástico[1], -ca *adj* **:** plastic
plástico[2] *nm* **:** plastic
plastificar {72} *vt* **:** to laminate
plata *nf* **1 :** silver **2 :** money
plataforma *nf* **1** ESTRADO, TARIMA **:** platform, dais **2 :** platform (in politics) **3 :** springboard, stepping stone **4 plataforma continental :** continental shelf **5 plataforma de lanzamiento :** launchpad **6 plataforma petrolífera :** oil rig (at sea)
platal *nm* **:** large sum of money, fortune
platanal *nm* **:** banana plantation
platanero[1], -ra *adj* **:** banana, banana-producing
platanero[2], -ra *n* **:** banana grower
plátano *nm* **1 :** banana **2 :** plantain **3 plátano macho** *Mex* **:** plantain
platea *nf* **:** orchestra, pit (in a theater)
plateado, -da *adj* **1 :** silver, silvery **2 :** silver-plated
plática *nf* **1 :** talk, lecture **2 :** chat, conversation
platicar {72} *vi* **:** to talk, to chat — *vt* *Mex* **:** to tell, to say
platija *nf* **:** flatfish, flounder
platillo *nm* **1 :** saucer <platillo volador : flying saucer> **2 :** cymbal **3** *Mex* **:** dish <platillos típicos : local dishes>
platino *nm* **:** platinum
plato *nm* **1 :** plate, dish <lavar los platos : to do the dishes> **2 :** serving, helping **3 :** course (of a meal) **4 :** dish <plato típico : typical dish> **5 :** home plate (in baseball) **6 plato hondo :** soup bowl
plató *nm* **:** set (in the movies)
platónico, -ca *adj* **:** platonic
playa *nf* **:** beach, seashore
playera *nf* **1 :** canvas sneaker **2** *CA, Mex* **:** T-shirt
plaza *nf* **1 :** square, plaza **2 :** marketplace **3 :** room, space, seat (in a vehicle) **4 :** post, position **5 plaza fuerte**

: stronghold, fortified city **6 plaza de toros** : bullring

plazca, etc. → **placer**

plazo *nm* **1** : period, term <un plazo de cinco días : a period of five days> <a largo plazo : long-term> **2** ABONO : installment <pagar a plazos : to pay in installments>

pleamar *nf* : high tide

plebe *nf* : common people, masses *pl*

plebeyo[1], -ya *adj* : plebeian

plebeyo[2], -ya *n* : plebeian, commoner

plegable *adj* : folding, collapsible

plegadizo → **plegable**

plegar {49} *vt* DOBLAR : to fold, to bend — **plegarse** *vr* : to give in, to yield

plegaria *nf* ORACIÓN : prayer

pleito *nm* **1** : lawsuit **2** : fight, argument, dispute

plenamente *adv* COMPLETAMENTE : fully, completely

plenario, -ria *adj* : plenary, full

plenilunio *nm* : full moon

plenipotenciario, -ria *n* : plenipotentiary

plenitud *nf* : fullness, abundance

pleno, -na *adj* COMPLETO (*often used as an intensifier*) : full, complete <en pleno uso de sus facultades : in full command of his faculties> <en plena noche : in the middle of the night> <en pleno corazón de la ciudad : right in the heart of the city>

plétora *nf* : plethora

pleuresía *nf* : pleurisy

pliega, pliegue, etc. → **plegar**

pliego *nm* **1** HOJA : sheet of paper **2** : sealed document

pliegue *nm* **1** DOBLEZ : crease, fold **2** : pleat

plisar *vt* : to pleat

plomada *nf* **1** : plumb line **2** : sinker

plomería *nf* FONTANERÍA : plumbing

plomero, -ra *n* FONTANERO : plumber

plomizo, -za *adj* : leaden

plomo *nm* **1** : lead **2** : plumb line **3** : fuse **4** *fam* : bore, drag **5 a ~** : plumb, straight

plugo, etc. → **placer**

pluma *nf* **1** : feather **2** : pen **3 pluma fuente** : fountain pen

plumaje *nm* : plumage

plumero *nm* : feather duster

plumilla *nf* : nib

plumón *nm, pl* **plumones** : down

plumoso, -sa *adj* : feathery, downy

plural *adj & nm* : plural

pluralidad *nf* : plurality

pluralizar {21} *vt* : to pluralize

pluriempleado, -da *adj* : holding more than one job

pluriempleo *nm* : moonlighting

plus *nm* : bonus

plusvalía *nf* : appreciation, capital gain

Plutón *nm* : Pluto

plutocracia *nf* : plutocracy

plutonio *nm* : plutonium

población *nf, pl* **-ciones 1** : population **2** : city, town, village

poblado[1], -da *adj* **1** : inhabited, populated **2** : full, thick <cejas pobladas : bushy eyebrows>

poblado[2] *nm* : village, settlement

poblador, -dora *n* : settler

poblar {19} *vt* **1** : to populate, to inhabit **2** : to settle, to colonize **3 ~ de** : to stock with, to plant with — **poblarse** *vr* : to fill up, to become crowded

pobre[1] *adj* **1** : poor, impoverished **2** : unfortunate <¡pobre de mí! : poor me!> **3** : weak, deficient <una dieta pobre : a poor diet>

pobre[2] *nmf* : poor person <los pobres : the poor> <¡pobre! : poor thing!>

pobremente *adv* : poorly

pobreza *nf* : poverty

pocilga *nf* CHIQUERO : pigsty, pigpen

pocillo *nm* : small coffee cup, demitasse

poción *nf, pl* **pociones** : potion

poco[1] *adv* **1** : little, not much <poco probable : not very likely> <come poco : he doesn't eat much> **2** : a short time, a while <tardaremos poco : we won't be very long> **3 poco antes** : shortly before **4 poco después** : shortly after

poco[2], -ca *adj* **1** : little, not much, (a) few <tengo poco dinero : I don't have much money> <en no pocas ocasiones : on more than a few occasions> <poca gente : few people> **2 pocas veces** : rarely

poco[3], -ca *pron* **1** : little, few <le falta poco para terminar : he's almost finished> <uno de los pocos que quedan : one of the remaining few> **2 un poco** : a little, a bit <un poco de vino : a little wine> <un poco extraño : a bit strange> **3 a ~** *Mex* (*used to express disbelief*) <¿a poco no se te hizo difícil? : you mean you didn't find it difficult?> **4 de a poco** : little by little **5 hace poco** : not long ago **6 poco a poco** : little by little **7 dentro de poco** : shortly, in a little while **8 por ~** : nearly, almost

podar *vt* : to prune, to trim

poder[1] {58} *v aux* **1** : to be able to, can <no puede hablar : he can't speak> **2** (*expressing possibility*) : might, may <puede llover : it may rain at any moment> <¿cómo puede ser? : how can that be?> **3** (*expressing permission*) : can, may <¿puedo ir a la fiesta? : can I go to the party?> <¿se puede? : may I come in?> — *vi* **1** : to beat, to defeat <cree que le puede a cualquiera : he thinks he can beat anyone> **2** : to be possible <¿crees que vendrán? — puede (que sí) : do you think they'll come? — maybe> **3 ~ con** : to cope with, to manage <¡no puedo con estos niños! : I can't handle these children!> **4 no poder más** : to have had enough <no puede más : she can't take anymore> **5 no poder menos**

que : to not be able to help <no pudo menos que asombrarse : she couldn't help but be amazed>

poder[2] *nm* **1** : control, power <poder adquisitivo : purchasing power> **2** : authority <el poder legislativo : the legislature> **3** : possession <está en mi poder : it's in my hands> **4** : strength, force <poder militar : military might>

poderío *nm* **1** : power **2** : wealth, influence

poderoso, -sa *adj* **1** : powerful **2** : wealthy, influential **3** : effective

podiatría *nf* : podiatry

podio *nm* : podium

pódium *nm* → **podio**

podología *nf* : podiatry, chiropody

podólogo, -ga *n* : podiatrist, chiropodist

podrá, etc. → **poder**

podredumbre *nf* **1** : decay, rottenness **2** : corruption

podrido, -da *adj* **1** : rotten, decayed **2** : corrupt

podrir → **pudrir**

poema *nm* : poem

poesía *nf* **1** : poetry **2** POEMA : poem

poeta *nmf* : poet

poético, -ca *adj* : poetic, poetical

pogrom *nm* : pogrom

póker *or* **poker** *nm* : poker (card game)

polaco[1], **-ca** *adj* : Polish

polaco[2], **-ca** *n* : Pole, Polish person

polaco[3] *nm* : Polish (language)

polar *adj* : polar

polarizar {21} *vt* : to polarize — **polarizarse** *vr* — **polarización** *nf*

polea *nf* : pulley

polémica *nf* CONTROVERSIA : controversy, polemics

polémico, -ca *adj* CONTROVERTIDO : controversial, polemical

polen *nm, pl* **pólenes** : pollen

policía[1] *nf* : police

policía[2] *nmf* : police officer, policeman *m*, policewoman *f*

policíaco, -ca *or* **policiaco, -ca** *adj* : police <novela policíaca : detective story>

policial *adj* : police

poliéster *nm* : polyester

poligamia *nf* : polygamy

polígamo[1], **-ma** *adj* : polygamous

polígamo[2], **-ma** *n* : polygamist

polígono *nm* : polygon — **polígonal** *adj*

poliinsaturado, -da *adj* : polyunsaturated

polilla *nf* : moth

polimerizar {21} *vt* : to polymerize

polímero *nm* : polymer

polinesio, -sia *adj & n* : Polynesian

polinizar {21} *vt* : to pollinate — **polinización** *nf*

polio *nf* : polio

poliomielitis *nf* : poliomyelitis, polio

polisón *nm, pl* **-sones** : bustle (on clothing)

politécnico, -ca *adj* : polytechnic

politeísmo *nm* : polytheism — **politeísta** *adj & nmf*

política *nf* **1** : politics **2** : policy

políticamente *adv* : politically

político[1], **-ca** *adj* **1** : political **2** : tactful, politic **3** : by marriage <padre político : father-in-law>

político[2], **-ca** *n* : politician

póliza *nf* : policy <póliza de seguros : insurance policy>

polizón *nm, pl* **-zones** : stowaway <viajar de polizón : to stow away>

polla *nf* APUESTA : bet

pollera *nf* **1** : chicken coop **2** : skirt

pollero, -ra *n* **1** : poulterer **2** : poultry farm **3** *Mex fam* COYOTE : smuggler of illegal immigrants

pollito, -ta *n* : chick, young bird, fledgling

pollo, -lla *n* **1** : chicken **2** POLLITO : chick **3** JOVEN : young man *m*, young lady *f*

polluelo *nm* → **pollito**

polo *nm* **1** : pole <el Polo Norte : the North Pole> <polo negativo : negative pole> **2** : polo (sport) **3** : polo shirt **4** : focal point, center **5** **polo opuesto** : exact opposite

polución *nf, pl* **-ciones** CONTAMINACIÓN : pollution

polvareda *nf* **1** : cloud of dust **2** : uproar, fuss

polvera *nf* : compact (for face powder)

polvo *nm* **1** : dust **2** : powder **3** **polvos** *nmpl* : face powder **4** **polvos de hornear** : baking powder **5** **hacer polvo** *fam* : to crush, to shatter <vas a hacer polvo el reloj : you're going to destroy your watch>

pólvora *nf* **1** : gunpowder **2** : fireworks *pl*

polvoriento, -ta *adj* : dusty, powdery

polvorín *nm, pl* **-rines** : magazine, storehouse (for explosives)

pomada *nf* : ointment, cream

pomelo *nm* : grapefruit

pómez *nm or* **piedra pómez** : pumice

pomo *nm* **1** : pommel (on a sword) **2** : knob, handle **3** : perfume bottle

pompa *nf* **1** : bubble **2** : pomp, splendor **3** **pompas fúnebres** : funeral

pompón *nm, pl* **pompones** BORLA : pom-pom

pomposidad *nf* **1** : pomp, splendor **2** : pomposity, ostentation

pomposo, -sa *adj* : pompous — **pomposamente** *adv*

pómulo *nm* : cheekbone

pon → **poner**

ponchadura *nf Mex* : puncture, flat (tire)

ponchar *vt* **1** : to strike out (in baseball) **2** *Mex* : to puncture — **poncharse** *vr* **1** *Col, Ven* : to strike out (in baseball) **2** *Mex* : to blow out (of a tire)

ponche *nm* **1 :** punch (drink) **2 ponche de huevo :** eggnog

poncho *nm* **:** poncho

ponderación *nf, pl* **-ciones 1 :** consideration, deliberation **2 :** high praise

ponderar *vt* **1 :** to weigh, to consider **2 :** to speak highly of

pondrá, etc. → **poner**

ponencia *nf* **1** DISCURSO **:** paper, presentation, address **2** INFORME **:** report

ponente *nmf* **:** speaker, presenter

poner {60} *vt* **1** COLOCAR **:** to put, to place <pon el libro en la mesa : put the book on the table> **2** AGREGAR, AÑADIR **:** to put in, to add **3 :** to put on (clothes) **4** CONTRIBUIR **:** to contribute **5** ESCRIBIR **:** to put in writing <no le puso su nombre : he didn't put his name on it> **6** IMPONER **:** to set, to impose **7** EXPONER **:** to put, to expose <lo puso en peligro : she put him in danger> **8 :** to prepare, to arrange <poner la mesa : to set the table> **9 :** to name <le pusimos Ana : we called her Ana> **10** ESTABLECER **:** to set up, to establish <puso un restaurante : he opened up a restaurant> **11** INSTALAR **:** to install, to put in **12** (*with an adjective or adverb*) **:** to make <siempre lo pones de mal humor : you always put him in a bad mood> **13 :** to turn on, to switch on **14** SUPONER **:** to suppose <pongamos que no viene : supposing he doesn't come> **15 :** to lay (eggs) **16 ~ a :** to start (someone doing something) <lo puse a trabajar : I put him to work> **17 ~ de :** to place as <la pusieron de directora : they made her director> **18 ~ en :** to put in (a state or condition) <poner en duda : to call into question — *vi* **1 :** to contribute **2 :** to lay eggs — **ponerse** *vr* **1 :** to move (into a position) <ponerse de pie : to stand up> **2 :** to put on, to wear **3 :** to become, to turn <se puso colorado : he turned red> **4 :** to set (of the sun or moon)

poni *or* **poney** *nm* **:** pony

ponga, etc. → **poner**

poniente *nm* **1** OCCIDENTE **:** west **2 :** west wind

ponqué *nm Col, Ven* **:** cake

pontifical *adj* **:** pontifical

pontificar {72} *vi* **:** to pontificate

pontífice *nm* **:** pontiff, pope

pontón *nm, pl* **pontones :** pontoon

ponzoña *nf* VENENO **:** poison — **ponzoñoso, -sa** *adj*

popa *nf* **1 :** stern **2 a ~ :** astern, abaft, aft

popelín *nm, pl* **-lines :** poplin

popelina *nf* **:** poplin

popote *nm Mex* **:** (drinking) straw

populachero, -ra *adj* **:** common, popular, vulgar

populacho *nm* **:** rabble, masses *pl*

popular *adj* **1 :** popular **2 :** traditional **3 :** colloquial

popularidad *nf* **:** popularity

popularizar {21} *vt* **:** to popularize — **popularizarse** *vr*

populista *adj & nmf* **:** populist — **populismo** *nm*

populoso, -sa *adj* **:** populous

popurrí *nm* **:** potpourri

por *prep* **1 :** for, during <se quedaron allí por la semana : they stayed there during the week> <por el momento : for now, at the moment> **2 :** around, during <por noviembre empieza a nevar : around November it starts to snow> <por la mañana : in the morning> **3 :** around (a place) <debe estar por allí : it must be over there> <por todas partes : everywhere> **4 :** by, through, along <por la puerta : through the door> <pasé por tu casa : I stopped by your house> <por la costa : along the coast> **5 :** for, for the sake of <lo hizo por su madre : he did it for his mother> <¡por Dios! : for heaven's sake!> **6 :** because of, on account of <llegué tarde por el tráfico : I arrived late because of the traffic> <dejar por imposible : to give up as impossible> **7 :** per <60 millas por hora : 60 miles per hour> <por docena : by the dozen> **8 :** for, in exchange for, instead of <su hermana habló por él : his sister spoke on his behalf> **9 :** by means of <hablar por teléfono : to talk on the phone> <por escrito : in writing> **10 :** as for <por mí : as far as I'm concerned> **11 :** times <tres por dos son seis : three times two is six> **12** SEGÚN **:** from, according to <por lo que dices : judging from what you're telling me> **13 :** as, for <por ejemplo : for example> **14 :** by <hecho por mi abuela : made by my grandmother> <por correo : by mail> **15 :** for, in order to <lucha por ganar su respeto : he struggles to win her respect> **16 estar por :** to be about to **17 por ciento :** percent **18 por favor :** please **19 por lo tanto :** therefore, consequently **20 ¿por qué? :** why? **21 por que** → **porque 22 por . . . que :** no matter how <por mucho que intente : no matter how hard I try> **23 por si** *or* **por si acaso :** just in case

porcelana *nf* **:** china, porcelain

porcentaje *nm* **:** percentage

porche *nm* **:** porch

porción *nf, pl* **porciones 1 :** portion **2** PARTE **:** part, share **3** RACIÓN **:** serving, helping

pordiosear *vi* MENDIGAR **:** beg

pordiosero, -ra *n* MENDIGO **:** beggar

porfiado, -da *adj* OBSTINADO, TERCO **:** obstinate, stubborn — **: porfiadamente** *adv*

porfiar {85} *vi* **:** to insist, to persist

pormenor *nm* DETALLE **:** detail

pormenorizar {21} *vi* **:** to go into detail — *vt* **:** to tell in detail

pornografía *nf* **:** pornography

pornográfico, -ca *adj* : pornographic
poro *nm* : pore
poroso, -sa *adj* : porous — **porosidad** *nf*
poroto *nm Arg, Chile, Uru* : bean
porque *conj* **1** : because **2** *or* **por que** : in order that
porqué *nm* : reason, cause
porquería *nf* **1** SUCIEDAD : dirt, filth **2** : nastiness, vulgarity **3** : worthless thing, trifle **4** : junk food
porra *nf* **1** : nightstick, club **2** *Mex* : cheer, yell <los aficionados le echaban porras : the fans cheered him on>
porrazo *nm* **1** : blow, whack **2 de golpe y porrazo** : suddenly
porrista *nmf* **1** : cheerleader **2** : fan, supporter
portaaviones *nms & pl* : aircraft carrier
portada *nf* **1** : title page **2** : cover **3** : facade, front
portador, -dora *n* : carrier, bearer
portafolio *or* **portafolios** *nm, pl* **-lios 1** MALETÍN : briefcase **2** : portfolio (of investments)
portal *nm* **1** : portal, doorway **2** VESTÍBULO : vestibule, hall
portar *vt* **1** : to carry, to bear **2** : to wear — **portarse** *vr* CONDUCIRSE : to behave <pórtate bien : behave yourself>
portátil *adj* : portable
portaviandas *nms & pl* : lunch box
portaviones *nm* → **portaaviones**
portavoz *nmf, pl* **-voces** : spokesperson, spokesman *m*, spokeswoman *f*
portazo *nm* : slam (of a door)
porte *nm* **1** ASPECTO : bearing, demeanor **2** TRANSPORTE : transport, carrying <porte pagado : postage paid>
portento *nm* MARAVILLA : marvel, wonder
portentoso, -sa *adj* MARAVILLOSO : marvelous, wonderful
porteño, -ña *adj* : of or from Buenos Aires
portería *nf* **1** ARCO : goal, goalposts *pl* **2** : superintendent's office
portero, -ra *n* **1** ARQUERO : goalkeeper, goalie **2** : doorman *m* **3** : janitor, superintendent
pórtico *nm* : portico
portilla *nf* : porthole
portón *nm, pl* **portones 1** : main door **2** : gate
portugués[1], -guesa *adj & n, mpl* **-gueses** : Portuguese
portugués[2] *nm* : Portuguese (language)
porvenir *nm* FUTURO : future
pos *adv* **en pos de** : in pursuit of
posada *nf* **1** : inn **2** *Mex* : Advent celebration
posadero, -ra *n* : innkeeper
posar *vi* : to pose — *vt* : to place, to lay — **posarse** *vr* **1** : to land, to light, to perch **2** : to settle, to rest
posavasos *nms & pl* : coaster (for drinks)
posdata *nf* → **postdata**
pose *nf* : pose
poseedor, -dora *n* : possessor, holder
poseer {20} *vt* : to possess, to hold, to have
poseído, -da *adj* : possessed
posesión *nf, pl* **-siones** : possession
posesionarse *vr* **~ de** : to take possession of, to take over
posesivo[1], -va *adj* : possessive
posesivo[2] *nm* : possessive case
posguerra *nf* : postwar period
posibilidad *nf* **1** : possibility **2 posibilidades** *nfpl* : means, income
posibilitar *vt* : to make possible, to permit
posible *adj* : possible — **posiblemente** *adv*
posición *nf, pl* **-ciones 1** : position, place **2** : status, standing **3** : attitude, stance
posicionar *vt* **1** : to position, to place **2** : to establish — **posicionarse** *vr*
positivo[1], -va *adj* : positive
positivo[2] *nm* : print (in photography)
poso *nm* **1** : sediment, dregs *pl* **2** : grounds *pl* (of coffee)
posoperatorio, -ria *adj* : postoperative
posponer {60} *vt* **1** : to postpone **2** : to put behind, to subordinate
pospuso, etc. → **posponer**
posta *nf* : relay race
postal[1] *adj* : postal
postal[2] *nm* : postcard
postdata *nf* : postscript
poste *nm* : post, pole <poste de teléfonos : telephone pole>
póster *or* **poster** *nm, pl* **pósters** *or* **posters** : poster, placard
postergación *nf, pl* **-ciones** : postponement, deferring
postergar {52} *vt* **1** : to delay, to postpone **2** : to pass over (an employee)
posteridad *nf* : posterity
posterior *adj* **1** ULTERIOR : later, subsequent **2** TRASERO : back, rear
postgrado *nm* : graduate course
postgraduado, -da *n* : graduate student, postgraduate
postigo *nm* **1** CONTRAVENTANA : shutter **2** : small door, wicket gate
postilla *nf* : scab
postizo, -za *adj* : artificial, false <dentadura postiza : dentures>
postnatal *adj* : postnatal
postor, -tora *n* : bidder <mejor postor : highest bidder>
postración *nf, pl* **-ciones 1** : prostration **2** ABATIMIENTO : depression
postrado, -da *adj* **1** : prostrate **2 postrado en cama** : bedridden
postrar *vt* DEBILITAR : to debilitate, to weaken — **postrarse** *vr* : to prostrate oneself
postre *nm* : dessert

postrero, -ra *adj* (**postrer** *before masculine singular nouns*) ÚLTIMO : last
postulación *nf, pl* **-ciones 1** : collection **2** : nomination (of a candidate)
postulado *nm* : postulate, assumption
postulante, -ta *n* **1** : postulant **2** : candidate, applicant
postular *vt* **1** : to postulate **2** : to nominate **3** : to propose — **postularse** *vr* : to run, to be a candidate
póstumo, -ma *adj* : posthumous — **póstumamente** *adv*
postura *nf* **1** : posture, position (of the body) **2** ACTITUD, POSICIÓN : position, stance
potable *adj* : drinkable, potable
potaje *nm* : thick vegetable soup, pottage
potasa *nf* : potash
potasio *nm* : potassium
pote *nm* **1** OLLA : pot **2** : jar, container
potencia *nf* **1** : power <potencias extranjeras : foreign powers> <elevado a la tercera potencia : raised to the third power> **2** : capacity, potency
potencial *adj & nm* : potential
potenciar *vt* : to promote, to foster
potenciómetro *nm* : dimmer, dimmer switch
potentado, -da *n* **1** SOBERANO : potentate, sovereign **2** MAGNATE : tycoon, magnate
potente *adj* **1** : powerful, strong **2** : potent, virile
potestad *nf* **1** AUTORIDAD : authority, jurisdiction **2 patria potestad** : custody, guardianship
potrero *nm* **1** : field, pasture **2** : cattle ranch
potro[1], -tra *n* : colt *m,* filly *f*
potro[2] *nm* **1** : rack (for torture) **2** : horse (in gymnastics)
pozo *nm* **1** : well <pozo de petróleo : oil well> **2** : deep pool (in a river) **3** : mine shaft **4** *Arg, Par, Uru* : pothole **5 pozo séptico** : cesspool
pozole *nm Mex* : spicy stew made with pork and hominy
práctica *nf* **1** : practice, experience **2** EJERCICIO : exercising <la práctica de la medicina : the practice of medicine> **3** APLICACIÓN : application, practice <poner en práctica : to put into practice> **4 prácticas** *nfpl* : training
practicable *adj* : practicable, feasible
prácticamente *adv* : practically
practicante[1] *adj* : practicing <católicos practicantes : practicing Catholics>
practicante[2] *nmf* : practicer, practitioner
practicar {72} *vt* **1** : to practice **2** : to perform, to carry out **3** : to exercise (a profession) — *vi* : to practice
práctico, -ca *adj* : practical, useful
pradera *nf* : grassland, prairie
prado *nm* **1** CAMPO : field, meadow **2** : park
pragmático, -ca *adj* : pragmatic — **pragmáticamente** *adv*
pragmatismo *nm* : pragmatism
preámbulo *nm* **1** INTRODUCCIÓN : preamble, introduction **2** RODEO : evasion <gastar preámbulos : to beat around the bush>
prebélico, -ca *adj* : antebellum
prebenda *nf* : privilege, perquisite
precalentar {55} *vt* : to preheat
precariedad *nf* : precariousness
precario, -ria *adj* : precarious — **precariamente** *adv*
precaución *nf, pl* **-ciones 1** : precaution <medidas de precaución : precautionary measures> **2** PRUDENCIA : caution, care <con precaución : cautiously>
precautorio, -ria *adj* : precautionary
precaver *vt* PREVENIR : to prevent, to guard against — **precaverse** *vr* PREVENIRSE : to take precautions, to be on guard
precavido, -da *adj* CAUTELOSO : cautious, prudent
precedencia *nf* : precedence, priority
precedente[1] *adj* : preceding, previous
precedente[2] *nm* : precedent
preceder *v* : to precede
precepto *nm* : rule, precept
preciado, -da *adj* : esteemed, prized, valuable
preciarse *vr* **1** JACTARSE : to boast, to brag **2 ~ de** : to pride oneself on
precinto *nm* : seal
precio *nm* **1** : price **2** : cost, sacrifice <a cualquier precio : whatever the cost>
preciosidad *nf* : beautiful thing <este vestido es una preciosidad : this dress is lovely>
precioso, -sa *adj* **1** HERMOSO : beautiful, exquisite **2** VALIOSO : precious, valuable
precipicio *nm* **1** : precipice **2** RUINA : ruin
precipitación *nf, pl* **-ciones 1** PRISA : haste, hurry, rush **2** : precipitation, rain, snow
precipitado, -da *adj* **1** : hasty, sudden **2** : rash — **precipitadamente** *adv*
precipitar *vt* **1** APRESURAR : to hasten, to speed up **2** ARROJAR : to hurl, to throw — **precipitarse** *vr* **1** APRESURARSE : to rush **2** : to act rashly **3** ARROJARSE : to throw oneself
precisamente *adv* JUSTAMENTE : precisely, exactly
precisar *vt* **1** : to specify, to determine exactly **2** NECESITAR : to need, to require — *vi* : to be necessary
precisión *nf, pl* **-siones 1** EXACTITUD : precision, accuracy **2** CLARIDAD : clarity (of style, etc.) **3** NECESIDAD : necessity <tener precisión de : to have need of>
preciso, -sa *adj* **1** EXACTO : precise **2** : very, exact <en ese preciso instante : at that very instant> **3** NECESARIO : necessary

precocidad *nf* **:** precocity
precocinar *vt* **:** to precook
preconcebir {54} *vt* **:** to preconceive
precondición *nf, pl* **-ciones :** precondition
preconizar {21} *vt* **1 :** to recommend, to advocate **2 :** to extol
precoz *adj, pl* **precoces 1 :** precocious **2 :** early, premature — **precozmente** *adv*
precursor, -sora *n* **:** forerunner, precursor
predecesor, -sora *n* ANTECESOR **:** predecessor
predecir {11} *vt* **:** to foretell, to predict
predestinado, -da *adj* **:** predestined, fated
predestinar *vt* **:** to predestine — **predestinación** *nf*
predeterminar *vt* **:** to predetermine
prédica *nf* SERMÓN **:** sermon
predicado *nm* **:** predicate
predicador, -dora *n* **:** preacher
predicar {72} *v* **:** to preach
predicción *nf, pl* **-ciones 1 :** prediction **2** PRONÓSTICO **:** forecast <predicción del tiempo : weather forecast>
prediga, predijo, etc. → **predecir**
predilección *nf, pl* **-ciones :** predilection, preference
predilecto, -ta *adj* **:** favorite
predio *nm* **:** property, piece of land
predisponer {60} *vt* **1 :** to predispose, to incline **2 :** to prejudice, to bias
predisposición *nf, pl* **-ciones 1 :** predisposition, tendency **2 :** prejudice, bias
predominante *adj* **:** predominant — **predominantemente** *adv*
predominar *vi* PREVALECER **:** to predominate, to prevail
predominio *nm* **:** predominance, prevalence
preeminente *adj* **:** preeminent — **preeminencia** *nf*
preescolar *adj & nm* **:** preschool
preestreno *nm* **:** preview
prefabricado, -da *adj* **:** prefabricated
prefacio *nm* **:** preface
prefecto *nm* **:** prefect
preferencia *nf* **1 :** preference **2** PRIORIDAD **:** priority **3 de ~ :** preferably
preferencial *adj* **:** preferential
preferente *adj* **:** preferential, special <trato preferente : special treatment>
preferentemente *adv* **:** preferably
preferible *adj* **:** preferable
preferido, -da *adj & n* **:** favorite
preferir {76} *vt* **:** to prefer
prefijo *nm* **:** prefix
pregonar *vt* **1 :** to proclaim, to announce **2 :** to hawk (merchandise) **3 :** to extol **4 :** to reveal, to disclose
pregunta *nf* **1 :** question **2 hacer una pregunta :** to ask a question
preguntar *vt* **:** to ask, to question — *vi* **:** to ask, to inquire — **preguntarse** *vr* **:** to wonder
preguntón, -tona *adj, mpl* **-tones :** inquisitive
prehistórico, -ca *adj* **:** prehistoric
prejuicio *nm* **:** prejudice
prejuzgar {52} *vt* **:** to prejudge
prelado *nm* **:** prelate
preliminar *adj & nm* **:** preliminary
preludio *nm* **:** prelude
prematrimonial *adj* **:** premarital
prematuro, -ra *adj* **:** premature
premeditación *nf, pl* **-ciones :** premeditation
premeditar *vt* **:** to premeditate, to plan
premenstrual *adj* **:** premenstrual
premiado, -da *adj* **:** winning, prizewinning
premiar *vt* **1 :** to award a prize to **2 :** to reward
premier *nmf* **:** premier, prime minister
premio *nm* **1 :** prize <premio gordo : grand prize, jackpot> **2 :** reward **3 :** premium
premisa *nf* **:** premise, basis
premolar *nm* **:** bicuspid (tooth)
premonición *nf, pl* **-ciones :** premonition
premura *nf* **:** haste, urgency
prenatal *adj* **:** prenatal
prenda *nf* **1 :** piece of clothing **2 :** security, pledge
prendar *vt* **1 :** to charm, to captivate **2 :** to pawn, to pledge — **prendarse** *vr* **~ de :** to fall in love with
prendedor *nm* **:** brooch, pin
prender *vt* **1** SUJETAR **:** to pin, to fasten **2** APRESAR **:** to catch, to apprehend **3 :** to light (a cigarette, a match) **4 :** to turn on <prende la luz : turn on the light> **5 prender fuego a :** to set fire to — *vi* **1 :** to take root **2 :** to catch fire **3 :** to catch on
prensa *nf* **1 :** printing press **2 :** press <conferencia de prensa : press conference>
prensar *vt* **:** to press
prensil *adj* **:** prehensile
preñado, -da *adj* **1 :** pregnant **2 ~ de :** filled with
preñar *vt* EMBARAZAR **:** to make pregnant
preñez *nf, pl* **preñeces :** pregnancy
preocupación *nf, pl* **-ciones** INQUIETUD **:** worry, concern
preocupante *adj* **:** worrisome
preocupar *vt* INQUIETAR **:** to worry, to concern — **preocuparse** *vr* APURARSE **:** to worry, to be concerned
preparación *nf, pl* **-ciones 1 :** preparation, readiness **2 :** education, training **3 :** (medicinal) preparation
preparado¹, -da *adj* **1 :** ready, prepared **2 :** trained
preparado² *nm* **:** preparation, mixture
preparar *vt* **1 :** to prepare, to make ready **2 :** to teach, to train, to coach — **prepararse** *vr*
preparativos *nmpl* **:** preparations
preparatoria *nf Mex* **:** high school
preparatorio, -ria *adj* **:** preparatory

preponderante *adj* : preponderant, predominant — **preponderancia** *nf* — **preponderantemente** *adv*

preposición *nf, pl* **-ciones** : preposition — **preposicional** *adj*

prepotente *adj* : arrogant, domineering, overbearing — **prepotencia** *nf*

prerrogativa *nf* : prerogative, privilege

presa *nf* **1** : capture, seizure <hacer presa de : to seize> **2** : catch, prey <presa de : prey to, seized with> **3** : claw, fang **4** DIQUE : dam **5** : morsel, piece (of food)

presagiar *vt* : to presage, to portend

presagio *nm* : omen, portent

presbiterio *nm* : presbytery, sanctuary (of a church)

presbítero *nm* : presbyter

presciencia *nf* : prescience

prescindir *vi* **~ de 1** : to do without, to dispense with **2** DESATENDER : to ignore, to disregard **3** OMITIR : to omit, to skip

prescribir {33} *vt* : to prescribe

prescripción *nf, pl* **-ciones** : prescription

prescrito *pp* → **prescribir**

presencia *nf* **1** : presence **2** ASPECTO : appearance

presenciar *vt* : to be present at, to witness

presentación *nf, pl* **-ciones 1** : presentation **2** : introduction **3** : appearance

presentador, -dora *n* : newscaster, anchorman *m,* anchorwoman *f*

presentar *vt* **1** : to present, to show **2** : to offer, to give **3** : to submit (a document), to launch (a product) **4** : to introduce (a person) — **presentarse** *vr* **1** : to show up, to appear **2** : to arise, to come up **3** : to introduce oneself

presente[1] *adj* **1** : present, in attendance **2** : present, current **3 tener presente** : to keep in mind

presente[2] *nm* **1** : present (time, tense) **2** : one present <entre los presentes se encontraban . . . : those present included . . .>

presentimiento *nm* : premonition, hunch, feeling

presentir {76} *vt* : to sense, to intuit <presentía lo que iba a pasar : he sensed what was going to happen>

preservación *nf, pl* **-ciones** : preservation

preservar *vt* **1** : to preserve **2** : to protect

preservativo *nm* CONDÓN : condom

presidencia *nf* **1** : presidency **2** : chairmanship

presidencial *adj* : presidential

presidente, -ta *n* **1** : president **2** : chair, chairperson **3** : presiding judge

presidiario, -ria *n* : convict, prisoner

presidio *nm* : prison, penitentiary

presidir *vt* **1** MODERAR : to preside over, to chair **2** : to dominate, to rule over

presilla *nf* : eye, loop, fastener

presión *nf, pl* **presiones 1** : pressure **2 presión arterial** : blood pressure

presionar *vt* **1** : to pressure **2** : to press, to push — *vi* : to put on the pressure

preso[1], **-sa** *adj* : imprisoned

preso[2], **-sa** *n* : prisoner

prestado, -da *adj* **1** : borrowed, on loan **2 pedir prestado** : to borrow

prestamista *nmf* : moneylender, pawnbroker

préstamo *nm* : loan

prestar *vt* **1** : to lend, to loan **2** : to render (a service), to give (aid) **3 prestar atención** : to pay attention **4 prestar juramento** : to take an oath — **prestarse** *vr* : to lend oneself <se presta a confusiones : it lends itself to confusion>

prestatario, -ria *n* : borrower

presteza *nf* : promptness, speed

prestidigitación *nf, pl* **-ciones** : sleight of hand, prestidigitation

prestidigitador, -dora *n* : conjurer, magician

prestigio *nm* : prestige — **prestigioso, -sa** *adj*

presto[1] *adv* : promptly, at once

presto[2], **-ta** *adj* **1** : quick, prompt **2** DISPUESTO, PREPARADO : ready

presumido, -da *adj* VANIDOSO : conceited, vain

presumir *vt* SUPONER : to presume, to suppose — *vi* **1** ALARDEAR : to boast, to show off **2 ~ de** : to consider oneself <presume de inteligente : he thinks he's intelligent>

presunción *nf, pl* **-ciones 1** SUPOSICIÓN : presumption, supposition **2** VANIDAD : conceit, vanity

presunto, -ta *adj* : presumed, supposed, alleged — **presuntamente** *adv*

presuntuoso, -sa *adj* : conceited

presuponer {60} *vt* : to presuppose

presupuestal *adj* : budget, budgetary

presupuestar *vi* : to budget — *vt* : to budget for

presupuestario, -ria *adj* : budget, budgetary

presupuesto *nm* **1** : budget, estimate **2** : assumption, supposition

presurizar {21} *vt* : to pressurize

presuroso, -sa *adj* : hasty, quick

pretencioso, -sa *adj* : pretentious

pretender *vt* **1** INTENTAR : to attempt, to try <pretendo estudiar : I'm trying to study> **2** AFIRMAR : to claim <pretende ser pobre : he claims he's poor> **3** : to seek, to aspire to <¿qué pretendes tú? : what are you after?> **4** CORTEJAR : to court **5 pretender que** : to expect <¿pretendes que lo crea? : do you expect me to believe you?>

pretendiente[1] *nmf* **1** : candidate, applicant **2** : pretender, claimant (to a throne, etc.)

pretendiente[2] *nm* : suitor

pretensión *nf, pl* **-siones 1 :** intention, hope, plan **2 :** pretension <sin pretensiones : unpretentious>
pretexto *nm* EXCUSA **:** pretext, excuse
pretil *nm* **:** parapet, railing
prevalecer {53} *vi* **:** to prevail, to triumph
prevaleciente *adj* **:** prevailing, prevalent
prevalerse {84} *vr* **~ de :** to avail oneself of, to take advantage of
prevención *nf, pl* **-ciones 1 :** prevention **2 :** preparation, readiness **3 :** precautionary measure **4 :** prejudice, bias
prevenido, -da *adj* **1** PREPARADO **:** prepared, ready **2** ADVERTIDO **:** forewarned **3** CAUTELOSO **:** cautious
prevenir {87} *vt* **1 :** to prevent **2 :** to warn — **prevenirse** *vr* **~ contra** *or* **~ de :** to take precautions against
preventivo, -va *adj* **:** preventive, precautionary
prever {88} *vt* ANTICIPAR **:** to foresee, to anticipate
previo, -via *adj* **1 :** previous, prior **2 :** after, upon <previo pago : after paying, upon payment>
previsible *adj* **:** foreseeable
previsión *nf, pl* **-siones 1 :** foresight **2 :** prediction, forecast **3 :** precaution
previsor, -sora *adj* **:** farsighted, prudent
prieto, -ta *adj* **1 :** blackish, dark **2 :** dark-skinned, swarthy **3 :** tight, compressed
prima *nf* **1 :** premium **2 :** bonus **3** → **primo**
primacía *nf* **1 :** precedence, priority **2 :** superiority, supremacy
primado *nm* **:** primate (bishop)
primario, -ria *adj* **:** primary
primate *nm* **:** primate
primavera *nf* **1 :** spring (season) **2** PRÍMULA **:** primrose
primaveral *adj* **:** spring, springlike
primero[1] *adv* **1 :** first **2 :** rather, sooner
primero[2]**, -ra** *adj* (**primer** *before masculine singular nouns*) **1 :** first **2 :** top, leading **3 :** fundamental, basic **4 de primera :** first-rate
primero[3]**, -ra** *n* **:** first
primicia *nf* **1 :** first fruits **2 :** scoop, exclusive
primigenio, -nia *adj* **:** original, primary
primitivo, -va *adj* **1 :** primitive **2** ORIGINAL **:** original
primo, -ma *n* **:** cousin
primogénito, -ta *adj & n* **:** firstborn
primor *nm* **1 :** skill, care **2 :** beauty, elegance
primordial *adj* **1 :** primordial **2 :** basic, fundamental
primoroso, -sa *adj* **1 :** exquisite, fine, delicate **2 :** skillful
prímula *nf* **:** primrose
princesa *nf* **:** princess
principado *nm* **:** principality
principal[1] *adj* **1 :** main, principal **2 :** foremost, leading
principal[2] *nm* **:** capital, principal
príncipe *nm* **:** prince
prinipesco, -ca *adj* **:** princely
principiante[1] *adj* **:** beginning
principiante[2] *nmf* **:** beginner, novice
principiar *vt* EMPEZAR **:** to begin
principio *nm* **1** COMIENZO **:** beginning **2 :** principle **3 al principio :** at first **4 a principios de :** at the beginning of <a principios de agosto : at the beginning of August> **5 en ~ :** in principle
pringar {52} *vt* **1 :** to dip (in grease) **2 :** to soil, to spatter (with grease) — **pringarse** *vr*
pringoso, -sa *adj* **:** greasy
pringue[1]**, etc.** → **pringar**
pringue[2] *nm* **:** grease, drippings *pl*
prior, priora *n* **:** prior *m,* prioress *f*
priorato *nm* **:** priory
prioridad *nf* **:** priority, precedence
prisa *nf* **1 :** hurry, rush **2 a ~** *or* **de ~ :** quickly, fast **3 a toda prisa :** as fast as possible **4 darse prisa :** to hurry **5 tener prisa :** to be in a hurry
prisión *nf, pl* **prisiones 1** CÁRCEL **:** prison, jail **2** ENCARCELAMIENTO **:** imprisonment
prisionero, -ra *n* **:** prisoner
prisma *nf* **:** prism
prismáticos *nmpl* **:** binoculars
prístino, -na *adj* **:** pristine
privacidad *nf* **:** privacy
privación *nf, pl* **-ciones 1 :** deprivation **2 :** privation, want
privado, -da *adj* **:** private — **privadamente** *adv*
privar *vt* **1** DESPOJAR **:** to deprive **2 :** to stun, to knock out — **privarse** *vr* **:** to deprive oneself
privativo, -va *adj* **:** exclusive, particular
privilegiado, -da *adj* **:** privileged
privilegiar *vt* **:** to grant a privilege to, to favor
privilegio *nm* **:** privilege
pro[1] *nm* **1 :** pro, advantage <los pros y contras : the pros and cons> **2 en pro de :** for, in favor of
pro[2] *prep* **:** for, in favor of <grupos pro derechos humanos : groups supporting human rights>
proa *nf* **:** bow, prow
probabilidad *nf* **:** probability
probable *adj* **:** probable, likely
probablemente *adv* **:** probably
probar {19} *vt* **1 :** to demonstrate, to prove **2 :** to test, to try out **3 :** to try on (clothing) **4 :** to taste, to sample — *vi* **:** to try — **probarse** *vr* **:** to try on (clothing)
probeta *nf* **:** test tube
probidad *nf* **:** probity
problema *nm* **:** problem
problemática *nf* **:** set of problems <la problemática que debemos enfrentar : the problems we must face>
probóscide *nf* **:** proboscis

problemático, -ca *adj* : problematic
procaz *adj, pl* **procaces 1** : insolent, impudent **2** : indecent
procedencia *nf* : origin, source
procedente *adj* **1** : proper, fitting **2** ~ **de** : coming from
proceder *vi* **1** AVANZAR : to proceed **2** : to act, to behave **3** : to be appropriate, to be fitting **4** ~ **de** : to originate from, to come from
procedimiento *nm* : procedure, process
prócer *nmf* : eminent person, leader
procesado, -da *n* : accused, defendant
procesador *nm* : processor <procesador de textos : word processor>
procesamiento *nm* : processing <procesamiento de datos : data processing>
procesar *vt* **1** : to prosecute, to try **2** : to process
procesión *nf, pl* **-siones** : procession
proceso *nm* **1** : process **2** : trial, proceedings *pl*
proclama *nf* : proclamation
proclamación *nf, pl* **-ciones** : proclamation
proclamar *vt* : to proclaim — **proclamarse** *vr*
proclive *adj* ~ **a** : inclined to, prone to
proclividad *nf* : proclivity, inclination
procrear *vi* : to procreate — **procreación** *nf*
procurador, -dora *n* ABOGADO : attorney
procurar *vt* **1** INTENTAR : to try, to endeavor **2** CONSEGUIR : to obtain, to procure **3 procurar hacer** : to manage to do
prodigar {52} *vt* : to lavish, to be generous with
prodigio *nm* : wonder, marvel
prodigioso, -sa *adj* : prodigious, marvelous
pródigo[1], -ga *adj* **1** : generous, lavish **2** : wasteful, prodigal
pródigo[2], -ga *n* : spendthrift, prodigal
producción *nf, pl* **-ciones 1** : production **2 producción en serie** : mass production
producir {61} *vt* **1** : to produce, to make, to manufacture **2** : to cause, to bring about **3** : to bear (interest) — **producirse** *vr* : to take place, to occur
productividad *nf* : productivity
productivo, -va *adj* **1** : productive **2** LUCRATIVO : profitable
producto *nm* **1** : product **2** : proceeds *pl*, yield
productor, -tora *n* : producer
proeza *nf* HAZAÑA : feat, exploit
profanar *vt* : to profane, to desecrate — **profanación** *nf*
profano[1], -na *adj* **1** : profane **2** : worldly, secular
profano[2], -na *n* : nonspecialist
profecía *nf* : prophecy
proferir {76} *vt* **1** : to utter **2** : to hurl (insults)
profesar *vt* **1** : to profess, to declare **2** : to practice, to exercise
profesión *nf, pl* **-siones** : profession
profesional *adj & nmf* : professional — **profesionalmente** *adv*
profesionalismo *nm* : professionalism
profesionalizar {21} *vt* : to professionalize
profesionista *nmf Mex* : professional
profesor, -sora *n* **1** MAESTRO : teacher **2** : professor
profesorado *nm* **1** : faculty **2** : teaching profession
profeta *nm* : prophet
profético, -ca *adj* : prophetic
profetisa *nf* : prophetess, prophet
profetizar {21} *vt* : to prophesy
prófugo, -ga *adj & n* : fugitive
profundidad *nf* : depth, profundity
profundizar {21} *vt* **1** : to deepen **2** : to study in depth — *vi* ~ **en** : to go deeply into, to study in depth
profundo, -da *adj* **1** HONDO : deep **2** : profound — **profundamente** *adv*
profusión *nf, pl* **-siones** : abundance, profusion
profuso, -sa *adj* : profuse, abundant, extensive
progenie *nf* : progeny, offspring
progenitor, -tora *n* ANTEPASADO : ancestor, progenitor
prognóstico *nm* : prognosis
programa *nm* **1** : program **2** : plan **3 programa de estudios** : curriculum
programable *adj* : programmable
programación *nf, pl* **-ciones 1** : programming **2** : planning
programador, -dora *n* : programmer
programar *vt* **1** : to schedule, to plan **2** : to program (a computer, etc.)
progresar *vi* : to progress, to make progress
progresista *adj & nmf* : progressive
progresivo, -va *adj* : progressive, gradual
progreso *nm* : progress
prohibición *nf, pl* **-ciones** : ban, prohibition
prohibir {62} *vt* : to prohibit, to ban, to forbid
prohibitivo, -va *adj* : prohibitive
prohijar {5} *vt* ADOPTAR : to adopt
prójimo *nm* : neighbor, fellow man
prole *nf* : offspring, progeny
proletariado *nm* : proletariat, working class
proletario, -ria *adj & n* : proletarian
proliferar *vi* : to proliferate — **proliferación** *nf*
prolífico, -ca *adj* : prolific
prolijo, -ja *adj* : wordy, long-winded
prólogo *nm* : prologue, preface, foreword
prolongación *nf, pl* **-ciones** : extension, lengthening

prolongar {52} *vt* **1 :** to prolong **2 :** to extend, to lengthen — **prolongarse** *vr* CONTINUAR **:** to last, to continue
promediar *vt* **1 :** to average **2 :** to divide in half — *vi* **:** to be half over
promedio *nm* **1 :** average **2 :** middle, mid-point
promesa *nf* **:** promise
prometedor, -dora *adj* **:** promising, hopeful
prometer *vt* **:** to promise — *vi* **:** to show promise — **prometerse** *vr* COMPROMETERSE **:** to get engaged
prometido[1], **-da** *adj* **:** engaged
prometido[2], **-da** *n* NOVIO **:** fiancé *m,* fiancée *f*
prominente *adj* **:** prominent — **prominencia** *nf*
promiscuo, -cua *adj* **:** promiscuous — **promiscuidad** *nf*
promisorio, -ria *adj* **1 :** promising **2 :** promissory
promoción *nf, pl* **-ciones 1 :** promotion **2 :** class, year **3 :** play-off (in soccer)
promocionar *vt* **:** to promote — **promocional** *adj*
promontorio *nm* **:** promontory, headland
promotor, -tora *n* **:** promoter
promover {47} *vt* **1 :** to promote, to advance **2** FOMENTAR **:** to foster, to encourage **3** PROVOCAR **:** to provoke, to cause
promulgación *nf, pl* **-ciones 1 :** enactment **2 :** proclamation, enactment
promulgar {52} *vt* **1 :** to promulgate, to proclaim **2 :** to enact (a law or decree)
prono, -na *adj* **:** prone
pronombre *nm* **:** pronoun
pronosticar {72} *vt* **:** to predict, to forecast
pronóstico *nm* **1** PREDICCIÓN **:** forecast, prediction **2 :** prognosis
prontitud *nf* **1** PRESTEZA **:** promptness, speed **2 con ~ :** promptly, quickly
pronto[1] *adv* **1 :** quickly, promptly **2 :** soon **3 de ~ :** suddenly **4 lo más pronto posible :** as soon as possible **5 tan pronto como :** as soon as
pronto[2], **-ta** *adj* **1** RÁPIDO **:** quick, speedy, prompt **2** PREPARADO **:** ready
pronunciación *nf, pl* **-ciones :** pronunciation
pronunciado, -da *adj* **1 :** pronounced, sharp, steep **2 :** marked, noticeable
pronunciar *vt* **1 :** to pronounce, to say **2 :** to give, to deliver (a speech) **3 pronunciar un fallo :** to pronounce sentence — **pronunciarse** *vr* **:** to declare oneself
propagación *nf, pl* **-ciones :** propagation, spreading
propaganda *nf* **1 :** propaganda **2** PUBLICIDAD **:** advertising
propagar {52} *vt* **1 :** to propagate **2 :** to spread, to disseminate — **propagarse** *vr*
propalar *vt* **1 :** to divulge **2 :** to spread
propano *nm* **:** propane
propasarse *vr* **:** to go too far, to overstep one's bounds
propensión *nf, pl* **-siones** INCLINACIÓN **:** inclination, propensity
propenso, -sa *adj* **:** prone, susceptible
propiamente *adv* **1 :** properly, correctly **2 :** exactly, precisely <propiamente dicho : strictly speaking>
propiciar *vt* **1 :** to propitiate **2 :** to favor, to foster
propicio, -cia *adj* **:** favorable, propitious
propiedad *nf* **1 :** property <propiedad privada : private property> **2 :** ownership **3** CUALIDAD **:** property, quality **4 :** suitability, appropriateness
propietario[1], **-ria** *adj* **:** proprietary
propietario[2], **-ria** *n* DUEÑO **:** owner, proprietor
propina *nf* **:** tip, gratuity
propinar *vt* **:** to give, to strike <propinar una paliza : to give a beating>
propio, -pia *adj* **1 :** own <su propia casa : his own house> <sus recursos propios : their own resources> **2** APROPIADO **:** appropriate, suitable **3** CARACTERÍSTICO **:** characteristic, typical **4** MISMO **:** oneself <el propio director : the director himself>
proponer {60} *vt* **1 :** to propose, to suggest **2 :** to nominate — **proponerse** *vr* **:** to intend, to plan, to set out <lo que se propone lo cumple : he does what he sets out to do>
proporción *nf, pl* **-ciones 1 :** proportion **2 :** ratio (in mathematics) **3 proporciones** *nfpl* **:** proportions, size <de grandes proporciones : very large>
proporcionado, -da *adj* **1 :** proportionate **2 :** proportioned <bien proporcionado : well-proportioned> — **proporcionadamente** *adv*
proporcional *adj* **:** proportional — **proporcionalmente** *adv*
proporcionar *vt* **1 :** to provide, to give **2 :** to proportion, to adapt
proposición *nf, pl* **-ciones :** proposal, proposition
propósito *nm* **1** INTENCIÓN **:** purpose, intention **2 a ~ :** by the way **3 a ~ :** on purpose, intentionally
propuesta *nf* PROPOSICIÓN **:** proposal
propulsar *vt* **1** IMPULSAR **:** to propel, to drive **2** PROMOVER **:** to promote, to encourage
propulsión *nf, pl* **-siones :** propulsion
propulsor *nm* **:** propellant
propuso, etc. → **proponer**
prorrata *nf* **1 :** share, quota **2 a ~ :** pro rata, proportionately
prórroga *nf* **1 :** extension, deferment **2 :** overtime (in sports)
prorrogar {52} *vt* **1 :** to extend (a deadline) **2 :** to postpone
prorrumpir *vi* **:** to burst forth, to break out <prorrumpí en lágrimas : I burst into tears>
prosa *nf* **:** prose

prosaico, -ca *adj* : prosaic, mundane
proscribir {33} *v* **1** PROHIBIR : to prohibit, to ban, to proscribe **2** DESTERRAR : to banish, to exile
proscripción *nf, pl* **-ciones 1** PROHIBICIÓN : ban, proscription **2** DESTIERRO : banishment
proscrito[1] *pp* → **proscribir**
proscrito[2], **-ta** *n* **1** DESTERRADO : exile **2** : outlaw
prosecución *nf, pl* **-ciones 1** : continuation **2** : pursuit
proseguir {75} *vt* **1** CONTINUAR : to continue **2** : to pursue (studies, goals) — *vi* : to continue, to go on
prosélito, -ta *n* : proselyte
prospección *nf, pl* **-ciones** : prospecting, exploration
prospectar *vi* : to prospect
prospecto *nm* : prospectus, leaflet, brochure
prosperar *vi* : to prosper, to thrive
prosperidad *nf* : prosperity
próspero, -ra *adj* : prosperous, flourishing
próstata *nf* : prostate
prostitución *nf, pl* **-ciones** : prostitution
prostituir {41} *vt* : to prostitute — **prostituirse** *vr* : to prostitute oneself
prostituto, -ta *n* : prostitute
protagonista *nmf* **1** : protagonist, main character **2** : leader
protagonizar {21} *vt* : to star in
protección *nf, pl* **-ciones** : protection
protector[1], **-tora** *adj* : protective
protector[2], **-tora** *n* **1** : protector, guardian **2** : patron
protector[3] *nm* : protector, guard <chaleco protector : chest protector>
protectorado *nm* : protectorate
proteger {15} *vt* : to protect, to defend — **protegerse** *vr*
protegido, -da *n* : protégé
proteína *nf* : protein
prótesis *nfs & pl* : prosthesis
protesta *nf* **1** : protest **2** *Mex* : promise, oath
protestante *adj & nmf* : Protestant
protestantismo *nm* : Protestantism
protestar *vi* : to protest, to object — *vt* **1** : to protest, to object to **2** : to declare, to profess
protocolo *nm* : protocol
protón *nm, pl* **protones** : proton
protoplasma *nm* : protoplasm
prototipo *nm* : prototype
protozoario *or* **protozoo** *nm* : protozoan
protuberancia *nf* : protuberance — **protuberante** *adj*
provecho *nm* : benefit, advantage
provechoso, -sa *adj* BENEFICIOSO : beneficial, profitable, useful — **provechosamente** *adv*
proveedor, -dora *n* : provider, supplier
proveer {63} *vt* : to provide, to supply — **proveerse** *vr* **~ de** : to obtain, to supply oneself with
provenir {87} *vi* **~ de** : to come from
provenzal[1] *adj* : Provençal
provenzal[2] *nmf* : Provençal
provenzal[3] *nm* : Provençal (language)
proverbio *nm* REFRÁN : proverb — **proverbial** *adj*
providencia *nf* **1** : providence, foresight **2** : Providence, God **3 providencias** *nfpl* : steps, measures
providencial *adj* : providential
provincia *nf* : province — **provincial** *adj*
provinciano, -na *adj* : provincial, unsophisticated
provisión *nf, pl* **-siones** : provision
provisional *adj* : provisional, temporary
provisionalmente *adv* : provisionally, tentatively
provisorio, -ria *adj* : provisional, temporary
provisto *pp* → **proveer**
provocación *nf, pl* **-ciones** : provocation
provocador[1], **-dora** *adj* : provocative, provoking
provocador[2], **-dora** *n* AGITADOR : agitator
provocar {72} *vt* **1** CAUSAR : to provoke, to cause **2** IRRITAR : to provoke, to pique
provocativo, -va *adj* : provocative
proxeneta *nmf* : pimp *m*
próximamente *adv* : shortly, soon
proximidad *nf* **1** : nearness, proximity **2 proximidades** *nfpl* : vicinity
próximo, -ma *adj* **1** : near, close <la Navidad está próxima : Christmas is almost here> **2** SIGUIENTE : next, following <la próxima semana : the following week>
proyección *nf, pl* **-ciones 1** : projection **2** : showing, screening (of a film) **3** : range, influence, diffusion
proyectar *vt* **1** : to plan **2** LANZAR : to throw, to hurl **3** : to project, to cast (light or shadow) **4** : to show, to screen (a film)
proyectil *nm* : projectile, missile
proyecto *nm* **1** : plan, project **2 proyecto de ley** : bill
proyector *nm* **1** : projector **2** : spotlight
prudencia *nf* : prudence, care, discretion
prudente *adj* : prudent, sensible, reasonable
prueba[1], **etc.** → **probar**
prueba[2] *nf* **1** : proof, evidence **2** : trial, test **3** : proof (in printing or photography) **4** : event, qualifying round (in sports) **5 a prueba de agua** : waterproof **6 prueba de fuego** : acid test **7 poner a prueba** : to put to the test
prurito *nm* **1** : itching **2** : desire, urge
psicoanálisis *nm* : psychoanalysis — **psicoanalista** *nmf*

psicoanalítico, -ca *adj* : psychoanalytic

psicoanalizar {21} *vt* : to psychoanalyze

psicología *nf* : psychology

psicológico, -ca *adj* : psychological — **psicológicamente** *adv*

psicólogo, -ga *n* : psychologist

psicópata *nmf* : psychopath

psicopático, -ca *adj* : psycopathic

psicosis *nfs & pl* : psychosis

psicosomático, -ca *adj* : psychosomatic

psicoterapeuta *nmf* : psychotherapist

psicoterapia *nf* : psychotherapy

psicótico, -ca *adj & n* : psychotic

psique *nf* : psyche

psiquiatra *nmf* : psychiatrist

psiquiatría *nf* : psychiatry

psiquiátrico[1], -ca *adj* : psychiatric

psiquiátrico[2] *nm* : mental hospital

psíquico, -ca *adj* : psychic

psiquis *nfs & pl* : psyche

psoriasis *nf* : psoriasis

ptomaína *nf* : ptomaine

púa *nf* **1** : barb <alambre de púas : barbed wire> **2** : tooth (of a comb) **3** : quill, spine

pubertad *nf* : puberty

pubiano → **púbico**

púbico, -ca *adj* : pubic

publicación *nf, pl* **-ciones** : publication

publicar {72} *vt* **1** : to publish **2** DIVULGAR : to divulge, to disclose

publicidad *nf* **1** : publicity **2** : advertising

publicista *nmf* : publicist

publicitar *vt* **1** : to publicize **2** : to advertise

publicitario, -ria *adj* : advertising, publicity <agencia publicitaria : advertising agency>

público[1], -ca *adj* : public — **públicamente** *adv*

público[2] *nm* **1** : public **2** : audience, spectators *pl*

puchero *nm* **1** : pot **2** : stew **3** : pout <hacer pucheros : to pout>

pucho *nm* **1** : waste, residue **2** : cigarette butt **3 a puchos** : little by little, bit by bit

púdico, -ca *adj* : chaste, modest

pudiente *adj* **1** : powerful **2** : rich, wealthy

pudín *nm, pl* **pudines** BUDÍN : pudding

pudo, etc. → **poder**

pudor *nm* : modesty, reserve

pudoroso, -sa *adj* : modest, reserved, shy

pudrir {59} *vt* **1** : to rot **2** *fam* : to annoy, to upset — **pudrirse** *vr* **1** : to rot **2** : to languish

pueblerino, -na *adj* : provincial, countrified

puebla, etc. → **poblar**

pueblo *nm* **1** NACIÓN : people **2** : common people **3** ALDEA, POBLADO : town, village

puede, etc. → **poder**

puente *nm* **1** : bridge <puente levadizo : drawbridge> **2** : denture, bridge **3 puente aéreo** : airlift

puerco[1], -ca *adj* : dirty, filthy

puerco[2], -ca *n* **1** CERDO, MARRANO : pig, hog **2** : pig, dirty or greedy person **3 puerco espín** : porcupine

pueril *adj* : childish, puerile

puerro *nm* : leek

puerta *nf* **1** : door, entrance, gate **2 a puerta cerrada** : behind closed doors

puerto *nm* **1** : port, harbor **2** : mountain pass **3 puerto marítimo** : seaport

puertorriqueño, -ña *adj & n* : Puerto Rican

pues *conj* **1** : since, because, for <no puedo ir, pues no tengo plata : I can't go, since I don't have any money> <lo hace, pues a él le gusta : he does it because he likes to> **2** (*used interjectionally*) : well, then <¡pues claro que sí! : well, of course!> <¡pues no voy! : well then, I'm not going!>

puesta *nf* **1** : setting <puesta del sol : sunset> **2** : laying (of eggs) **3 puesta a punto** : tune-up **4 puesta en marcha** : start, starting up

puestero, -ra *n* : seller, vendor

puesto[1] *pp* → **poner**

puesto[2], -ta *adj* : dressed <bien puesto : well-dressed>

puesto[3] *nm* **1** LUGAR, SITIO : place, position **2** : position, job **3** : kiosk, stand, stall **4 puesto que** : since, given that

pugilato *nm* BOXEO : boxing, pugilism

pugilista *nm* BOXEADOR : boxer, pugilist

pugna *nf* **1** CONFLICTO, LUCHA : conflict, struggle **2 en ~** : at odds, in conflict

pugnar *vi* LUCHAR : to fight, to strive, to struggle

pugnaz *adj* : pugnacious

pujante *adj* : mighty, powerful

pujanza *nf* : strength, vigor <pujanza económica : economic strength>

pulcritud *nf* **1** : neatness, tidiness **2** ESMERO : meticulousness

pulcro, -cra *adj* **1** : clean, neat **2** : exquisite, delicate, refined

pulga *nf* **1** : flea **2 tener malas pulgas** : to be bad-tempered

pulgada *nf* : inch

pulgar *nm* **1** : thumb **2** : big toe

pulir *vt* **1** : to polish, to shine **2** REFINAR : to refine, to perfect

pulla *nf* **1** : cutting remark, dig, gibe **2** : obscenity

pulmón *nm, pl* **pulmones** : lung

pulmonar *adj* : pulmonary

pulmonía *nf* NEUMONÍA : pneumonia

pulpa *nf* : pulp, flesh

pulpería *nf* : small grocery store

púlpito *nm* : pulpit

pulpo *nm* : octopus

pulsación *nf, pl* **-ciones 1** : beat, pulsation, throb **2** : keystroke

pulsar *vt* **1** APRETAR : to press, to push **2** : to strike (a key) **3** : to assess — *vi* : to beat, to throb

pulsera *nf* : bracelet
pulso *nm* **1** : pulse <tomarle el pulso a alguien : to take someone's pulse> <tomarle el pulso a la opinión : to sound out opinion> **2** : steadiness (of hand) <dibujo a pulso : freehand sketch>
pulular *vi* ABUNDAR : to abound, to swarm <en el río pululan los peces : the river is teeming with fish>
pulverizador *nm* **1** : atomizer, spray **2** : spray gun
pulverizar {21} *vt* **1** : to pulverize, to crush **2** : to spray
puma *nf* : cougar, puma
puna *nf* : bleak Andean tableland
punción *nf, pl* **punciones** : puncture
punible *adj* : punishable
punitivo, -va *adj* : punitive
punce, etc. → **punzar**
punta *nf* **1** : tip, end <punta del dedo : fingertip> <en la punta de la lengua : at the tip of one's tongue> **2** : point (of a weapon or pencil) <punta de lanza : spearhead> **3** : point, headland **4** : bunch, lot <una punta de ladrones : a bunch of thieves> **5 a punta de** : by, by dint of
puntada *nf* **1** : stitch (in sewing) **2** PUNZADA : sharp pain, stitch, twinge **3** *Mex* : witticism, quip
puntal *nm* **1** : prop, support **2** : stanchion
puntapié *nm* PATADA : kick
puntazo *nm* CORNADA : wound (from a goring)
puntear *vt* **1** : to pluck (a guitar) **2** : to lead (in sports)
puntería *nf* : aim, marksmanship
puntero *nm* **1** : pointer **2** : leader
puntiagudo, -da *adj* : sharp, pointed
puntilla *nf* **1** : lace edging **2** : dagger (in bullfighting) **3 de puntillas** : on tiptoe
puntilloso, -sa *adj* : punctilious
punto *nm* **1** : dot, point **2** : period (in punctuation) **3** : item, question **4** : spot, place **5** : moment, stage, degree **6** : point (in a score) **7** : stitch **8 en ~** : on the dot, sharp <a las dos en punto : at two o'clock sharp> **9 al punto** : at once **10 a punto fijo** : exactly, certainly **11 dos puntos** : colon **12 hasta cierto punto** : up to a point **13 punto decimal** : decimal point **14 punto de vista** : point of view **15 punto y coma** : semicolon **16 y punto** : period <es el mejor que hay y punto : it's the best there is, period> **17 puntos cardinales** : points of the compass
puntuación *nf, pl* **-ciones 1** : punctuation **2** : scoring, score, grade
puntual *adj* **1** : prompt, punctual **2** : exact, accurate — **puntualmente** *adv*
puntualidad *nf* **1** : promptness, punctuality **2** : exactness, accuracy
puntualizar {21} *vt* **1** : to specify, to state **2** : to point out
puntuar {3} *vt* : to punctuate — *vi* : to score points
punzada *nf* : sharp pain, twinge, stitch
punzante *adj* **1** : sharp **2** CÁUSTICO : biting, caustic
punzar {21} *vt* : to pierce, to puncture
punzón *nm, pl* **punzones 1** : awl **2** : hole punch
puñado *nm* **1** : handful **2 a puñados** : lots of, by the handful
puñal *nm* DAGA : dagger
puñalada *nf* : stab, stab wound
puñetazo *nm* : punch (with the fist)
puño *nm* **1** : fist **2** : handful, fistful **3** : cuff (of a shirt) **4** : handle, hilt
pupila *nf* : pupil (of the eye)
pupilo, -la *n* **1** : pupil, student **2** : ward, charge
pupitre *nm* : writing desk
puré *nm* : purée <puré de papas : mashed potatoes>
pureza *nf* : purity
purga *nf* **1** : laxative **2** : purge
purgante *adj & nm* : laxative, purgative
purgar {52} *vt* **1** : to purge, to cleanse **2** : to liquidate (in politics) **3** : to give a laxative to — **purgarse** *vr* **1** : to take a laxative **2 ~ de** : to purge oneself of
purgatorio *nm* : purgatory
purgue, etc. → **purgar**
purificador *nm* : purifier
purificar {72} *vt* : to purify — **purificación** *nf*
puritano[1], -na *adj* : puritanical, puritan
puritano[2], -na *n* **1** : Puritan **2** : puritan
puro[1] *adv* : sheer, much <de puro terco : out of sheer stubbornness>
puro[2], -ra *adj* **1** : pure <aire puro : fresh air> **2** : plain, simple, sheer <por pura curiosidad : from sheer curiosity> **3** : only, just <emplean puras mujeres : they only employ women> **4 pura sangre** : Thoroughbred horse
puro[3] *nm* : cigar
púrpura *nf* : purple
purpúreo, -rea *adj* : purple
purpurina *nf* : glitter (for decoration)
pus *nm* : pus
pusilánime *adj* COBARDE : pusillanimous, cowardly
puso, etc. → **poner**
pústula *nf* : pustule, pimple
puta *nf* : whore, slut
putrefacción *nf, pl* **-ciones** : putrefaction
putrefacto, -ta *adj* **1** PODRIDO : putrid, rotten **2** : decayed
pútrido, -da *adj* : putrid, rotten
puya *nf* **1** : point (of a lance) **2 lanzar una puya** : to gibe, to taunt

Q

q *nf* **:** eighteenth letter of the Spanish alphabet

que[1] *conj* **1 :** that <dice que está listo **:** he says that he's ready> <espero que lo haga **:** I hope that he does it> **2 :** than <más que nada **:** more than anything> **3** (*implying permission or desire*) <¡que entre! **:** send him in!> <¡que te vaya bien! **:** I wish you well!> **4** (*indicating a reason or cause*) <¡cuidado, que te caes! **:** be careful, you're about to fall!> <no provoques al perro, que te va a morder **:** don't provoke the dog or (else) he'll bite> **5 es que :** the thing is that, I'm afraid that **6 yo que tú :** if I were you

que[2] *pron* **1 :** who, that <la niña que viene **:** the girl who is coming> **2 :** whom, that <los alumnos que enseñé **:** the students that I taught> **3 :** that, which <el carro que me gusta **:** the car that I like> **4 el** (**la, lo, las, los**) **que** → **el[1], la[1], lo[1], los[1]**

qué[1] *adv* **:** how, what <¡qué bonito! **:** how pretty!>

qué[2] *adj* **:** what, which <¿qué hora es? **:** what time is it?>

qué[3] *pron* **:** what <¿qué quieres? **:** what do you want?>

quebracho *nm* **:** quebracho (tree)

quebrada *nf* DESFILADERO **:** ravine, gorge

quebradizo, -za *adj* FRÁGIL **:** breakable, delicate, fragile

quebrado[1], -da *adj* **1 :** bankrupt **2 :** rough, uneven **3** ROTO **:** broken

quebrado[2] *nm* **:** fraction

quebrantamiento *nm* **1 :** breaking **2 :** deterioration, weakening

quebrantar *vt* **1 :** to break, to split, to crack **2 :** to weaken **3 :** to violate (a law or contract)

quebranto *nm* **1 :** break, breaking **2** AFLICCIÓN **:** affliction, grief **3** PÉRDIDA **:** loss

quebrar {55} *vt* **1** ROMPER **:** to break **2** DOBLAR **:** to bend, to twist — *vi* **1 :** to go bankrupt **2 :** to fall out, to break up — **quebrarse** *vr*

queda *nf* **:** curfew

quedar *vi* **1** PERMANECER **:** to remain, to stay **2 :** to be <quedamos contentos con las mejoras **:** we were pleased with the improvements> **3 :** to be situated <queda muy lejos **:** it's very far, it's too far away> **4 :** to be left <quedan sólo dos alternativas **:** there are only two options left> **5 :** to fit, to suit <estos zapatos no me quedan **:** these shoes don't fit> **6 quedar bien (mal) :** to turn out well (badly) **7 ~ en :** to agree, to arrange <¿en qué quedamos? **:** what's the arrangement, then?> — **quedarse** *vr* **1 :** to stay <se quedó en casa **:** she stayed at home> **2 :** to keep on <se quedó esperando **:** he kept on waiting> **3 quedarse atrás :** to stay behind <no quedarse atrás **:** to be no slouch> **4 ~ con :** to remain <me quedé con hambre después de comer **:** I was still hungry after I ate>

quedo[1] *adv* **:** softly, quietly

quedo[2], -da *adj* **:** quiet, still

quehacer *nm* **1 :** work **2 quehaceres** *nmpl* **:** chores

queja *nf* **:** complaint

quejarse *vr* **1 :** to complain **2 :** to groan, to moan

quejido *nm* **1 :** groan, moan **2 :** whine, whimper

quejoso, -sa *adj* **:** complaining, whining

quejumbroso, -sa *adj* **:** querulous, whining

quema *nf* **1** FUEGO **:** fire **2 :** burning

quemado, -da *adj* **1 :** burned, burnt **2 :** annoyed **3 :** burned-out

quemador *nm* **:** burner

quemadura *nf* **:** burn

quemar *vt* **:** to burn, to set fire to — *vi* **:** to be burning hot — **quemarse** *vr*

quemarropa *nf* **a ~ :** point-blank

quemazón *nf, pl* **-zones 1 :** burning **2 :** intense heat **3 :** itch **4 :** cutting remark

quena *nf* **:** Peruvian reed flute

quepa, etc. → **caber**

querella *nf* **1 :** complaint **2 :** lawsuit

querellante *nmf* **:** plaintiff

querellarse *vr* **~ contra :** to bring suit against, to sue

querer[1] {64} *vt* **1** DESEAR **:** to want, to desire <quiere ser profesor **:** he wants to be a teacher> <¿cuánto quieres por esta computadora? **:** how much do you want for this computer?> **2 :** to love, to like, to be fond of <te quiero **:** I love you> **3** (*indicating a request*) <¿quieres pasarme la leche? **:** please pass the milk> **4 querer decir :** to mean **5 sin ~ :** unintentionally — *vi* **:** like, want <si quieras **:** if you like>

querer[2] *nm* **:** love, affection

querido[1], -da *adj* **:** dear, beloved

querido[2], -da *n* **:** dear, sweetheart

queroseno *nm* **:** kerosene

querúbico, -ca *adj* **:** cherubic

querrá, etc. → **querer**

querubín *nm, pl* **-bines :** cherub

quesadilla *nf* **:** quesadilla

quesería *nf* **:** cheese shop

queso *nm* **:** cheese

quetzal *nm* **1 :** quetzal (bird) **2 :** monetary unit of Guatemala

quicio *nm* **1 estar fuera de quicio :** to be beside oneself **2 sacar de quicio :** to exasperate, to drive crazy

quid *nm* **:** crux, gist <el quid de la cuestión **:** the crux of the matter>

quiebra[1], etc. → **quebrar**

quiebra[2] *nf* **1 :** break, crack **2** BANCARROTA **:** failure, bankruptcy
quien *pron, pl* **quienes 1 :** who, whom <no sé quien ganará : I don't know who will win> <las personas con quienes trabajo : the people with whom I work> **2 :** whoever, whomever <quien quiere salir que salga : whoever wants to can leave> **3 :** anyone, some people <hay quienes no están de acuerdo : some people don't agree>
quién *pron, pl* **quiénes 1 :** who, whom <¿quién sabe? : who knows?> <¿con quién hablo? : with whom am I speaking?> **2 de ~ :** whose <¿de quién es este libro? : whose book is this?>
quienquiera *pron, pl* **quienesquiera :** whoever, whomever
quiere, etc. → **querer**
quieto, -ta *adj* **1 :** calm, quiet **2** INMÓVIL **:** still
quietud *nf* **1 :** calm, tranquility **2** INMOVILIDAD **:** stillness
quijada *nf* **:** jaw, jawbone
quijotesco, -ca *adj* **:** quixotic
quilate *nm* **:** karat
quilla *nf* **:** keel
quimera *nf* **:** chimera, illusion
quimérico, -ca *adj* **:** chimeric, fanciful
química *nf* **:** chemistry
químico[1], **-ca** *adj* **:** chemical
químico[2], **-ca** *n* **:** chemist
quimioterapia *nf* **:** chemotherapy
quimono *nm* **:** kimono
quince *adj & nm* **:** fifteen
quinceañero, -ra *n* **:** fifteen-year-old, teenager
quinceavo[1], **-va** *adj* **:** fifteenth
quinceavo[2] *nm* **:** fifteenth (fraction)
quincena *nf* **:** two week period, fortnight
quincenal *adj* **:** bimonthly, twice a month
quingombó *nm* **:** okra
quincuagésimo[1], **-ma** *adj* **:** fiftieth, fifty-
quincuagésimo[2], **-ma** *n* **:** fiftieth, fifty- (in a series)
quiniela *nf* **:** sports lottery
quinientos[1], **-tas** *adj* **:** five hundred
quinientos[2] *nms & pl* **:** five hundred
quinina *nf* **:** quinine
quino *nm* **:** cinchona
quinqué *nm* **:** oil lamp
quinquenal *adj* **:** five-year <un plan quinquenal : a five-year plan>
quinta *nf* **:** country house, villa
quintaesencia *nf* **:** quintessence — **quintaesencial** *adj*
quintal *nm* **:** hundredweight
quinteto *nm* **:** quintet
quintillizo, -za *n* **:** quintuplet
quinto, -ta *adj* **:** fifth — **quinto, -ta** *n*
quíntuplo, -la *adj* **:** quintuple, fivefold
quiosco *nm* **1 :** kiosk **2 :** newsstand **3 quiosco de música :** bandstand
quirófano *nm* **:** operating room
quiromancia *nf* **:** palmistry
quiropráctica *nf* **:** chiropractic
quiropráctico, -ca *n* **:** chiropractor
quirúrgico, -ca *adj* **:** surgical — **quirúrgicamente** *adv*
quiso, etc. → **querer**
quisquilloso[1], **-sa** *adj* **:** fastidious, fussy
quisquilloso[2], **-sa** *n* **:** fussy person, fussbudget
quiste *nm* **:** cyst
quitaesmalte *nm* **:** nail polish remover
quitamanchas *nms & pl* **:** stain remover
quitanieves *nms & pl* **:** snowplow
quitar *vt* **1 :** to remove, to take away **2 :** to take off (clothes) **3 :** to get rid of, to relieve — **quitarse** *vr* **1 :** to withdraw, to leave **2 :** to take off (one's clothes) **3 ~ de :** to give up (a habit) **4 quitar de encima :** to get rid of
quitasol *nm* **:** parasol
quiteño[1], **-ña** *adj* **:** of or from Quito
quiteño[2], **-ña** *n* **:** person from Quito
quizá *or* **quizás** *adv* **:** maybe, perhaps
quórum *nm, pl* **quórums :** quorum

R

r *nf* **:** nineteenth letter of the Spanish alphabet
rábano *nm* **1 :** radish **2 rábano picante :** horseradish
rabí *nmf, pl* **rabíes :** rabbi
rabia *nf* **1** HIDROFOBIA **:** rabies, hydrophobia **2 :** rage, anger
rabiar *vi* **1 :** to rage, to be furious **2 :** to be in great pain **3 a ~** *fam* **:** like crazy, like mad
rabieta *nf* BERRINCHE **:** tantrum
rabino, -na *n* **:** rabbi
rabioso, -sa *adj* **1 :** enraged, furious **2 :** rabid
rabo *nm* **1** COLA **:** tail **2 el rabo del ojo :** the corner of one's eye
racha *nf* **1 :** gust of wind **2 :** run, series, string <racha perdedora : losing streak>
racheado, -da *adj* **:** gusty, windy
racial *adj* **:** racial
racimo *nm* **:** bunch, cluster <un racimo de uvas : a bunch of grapes>
raciocinio *nm* **:** reason, reasoning
ración *nf, pl* **raciones 1 :** share, ration **2** PORCIÓN **:** portion, helping
racional *adj* **:** rational, reasonable — **racionalmente** *adv*
racionalidad *nf* **:** rationality

racionalización *nf, pl* **-ciones :** rationalization
racionalizar {21} *vt* **1 :** to rationalize **2 :** to streamline
racionamiento *nm* **:** rationing
racionar *vt* **:** to ration
racismo *nm* **:** racism
racista *adj & nmf* **:** racist
radar *nm* **:** radar
radiación *nf, pl* **-ciones :** radiation, irradiation
radiactividad *nf* **:** radioactivity
radiactivo, -va *adj* **:** radioactive
radiador *nm* **:** radiator
radial *adj* **1 :** radial **2 :** radio, broadcasting <emisora radial : radio transmitter>
radiante *adj* **:** radiant
radiar *vt* **1 :** to radiate **2 :** to irradiate **3 :** to broadcast (on the radio)
radical[1] *adj* **:** radical, extreme — **radicalmente** *adv*
radical[2] *nmf* **:** radical
radicalismo *nm* **:** radicalism
radicar {72} *vi* **1 :** to be found, to lie **2** ARRAIGAR **:** to take root — **radicarse** *vr* **:** to settle, to establish oneself
radio[1] *nm* **1 :** radius **2 :** radium
radio[2] *nmf* **:** radio
radioactividad *nf* **:** radioactivity
radioactivo, -va *adj* **:** radioactive
radioaficionado, -da *n* **:** ham radio operator
radiodifusión *nf, pl* **-siones :** radio broadcasting
radiodifusora *nf* **:** radio station
radioemisora *nf* **:** radio station
radiofaro *nm* **:** radio beacon
radiofónico, -ca *adj* **:** radio <estación radiofónica pública : public radio station>
radiofrecuencia *nf* **:** radio frequency
radiografía *nf* **:** X ray (photograph)
radiografiar {85} *vt* **:** to x-ray
radiología *nf* **:** radiology
radiólogo, -ga *n* **:** radiologist
radón *nm* **:** radon
raer {65} *vt* RASPAR **:** to scrape, to scrape off
ráfaga *nf* **1 :** gust (of wind) **2 :** flash, burst <una ráfaga de luz : a flash of light>
raid *nm CA, Mex fam* **:** lift, ride
raído, -da *adj* **:** worn, shabby
raiga, etc. → **raer**
raíz *nf, pl* **raíces 1 :** root **2 :** origin, source **3 a raíz de :** following, as a result of **4 echar raíces :** to take root
raja *nf* **1 :** crack, slit **2 :** slice, wedge
rajá *nm* **:** raja
rajadura *nf* **:** crack, split
rajar *vt* HENDER **:** to crack, to split — *vi* **1** *fam* **:** to chatter **2** *fam* **:** to boast, to brag — **rajarse** *vr* **1 :** to crack, to split open **2** *fam* **:** to back out
rajatabla *adv* **a ~ :** strictly, to the letter
ralea *nf* **:** kind, sort, ilk <son de la misma valea : they're two of a kind>
ralentí *nm* **dejar al ralentí :** to leave (a motor) idling
rallado, -da *adj* **1 :** grated **2 pan rallado :** bread crumbs *pl*
rallador *nm* **:** grater
rallar *vt* **:** to grate
ralo, -la *adj* **:** sparse, thin
rama *nf* **:** branch
ramaje *nm* **:** branches *pl*
ramal *nm* **1 :** branchline **2 :** halter, strap
ramera *nf* **:** harlot, prostitute
ramificación *nf, pl* **-ciones :** ramification
ramificarse {72} *vr* **:** to branch out, to divide into branches
ramillete *nm* **1** RAMO **:** bouquet **2 :** select group, cluster
ramo *nm* **1 :** branch **2** RAMILLETE **:** bouquet **3 :** division (of science or industry) **4 Domingo de Ramos :** Palm Sunday
rampa *nf* **:** ramp, incline
rana *nf* **1 :** frog **2 rana toro :** bullfrog
ranchera *nf Mex* **:** traditional folk song
ranchería *nf* **:** settlement
ranchero, -ra *n* **:** rancher, farmer
rancho *nm* **1 :** ranch, farm **2 :** hut **3 :** settlement, camp **4 :** food, mess (for soldiers, etc.)
rancio, -cia *adj* **1 :** aged, mellow (of wine) **2 :** ancient, old **3 :** rancid
rango *nm* **1 :** rank, status **2 :** high social standing **3 :** pomp, splendor
ranúnculo *nm* **:** buttercup
ranura *nf* **:** groove, slot
rapacidad *nf* **:** rapacity
rapar *vt* **1 :** to crop **2 :** to shave
rapaz[1] *adj, pl* **rapaces :** rapacious, predatory
rapaz[2]**, -paza** *n, mpl* **rapaces :** youngster, child
rape *nm* **:** close haircut
rapé *nm* **:** snuff
rapidez *nf* **:** rapidity, speed
rápido[1] *adv* **:** quickly, fast <¡manejas tan rápido! : you drive so fast!>
rápido[2]**, -da** *adj* **:** rapid, quick — **rápidamente** *adv*
rápido[3] *nm* **1 :** express train **2 rápidos** *nmpl* **:** rapids
rapiña *nf* **1 :** plunder, pillage **2 ave de rapiña :** bird of prey
raposa *nf* **:** vixen (fox)
rapsodia *nf* **:** rhapsody
raptar *vt* SEQUESTRAR **:** to abduct, to kidnap
rapto *nm* **1** SECUESTRO **:** kidnapping, abduction **2** ARREBATO **:** fit, outburst
raptor, -tora *n* SECUESTRADOR **:** kidnapper
raque *nm* **:** beachcombing
raquero, -ra *n* **:** beachcomber
raqueta *nf* **1 :** racket (in sports) **2 :** snowshoe
raquítico, -ca *adj* **1 :** scrawny, weak **2 :** measly, skimpy
raquitismo *nm* **:** rickets
raramente *adv* **:** seldom, rarely

rareza *nf* **1** : rarity **2** : peculiarity, oddity

raro, -ra *adj* **1** EXTRAÑO : odd, strange, peculiar **2** : unusual, rare **3** : exceptional **4 rara vez** : seldom, rarely

ras *nm* **a ras de** : level with

rasar *vt* **1** : to skim, to graze **2** : to level

rascacielos *nms & pl* : skyscraper

rascar {72} *vt* **1** : to scratch **2** : to scrape — **rascarse** *vr* : to scratch an itch

rasgadura *nf* : tear, rip

rasgar {52} *vt* : to rip, to tear — **rasgarse** *vr*

rasgo *nm* **1** : stroke (of a pen) <a grandes rasgos : in broad outlines> **2** CARACTERÍSTICA : trait, characteristic **3** : gesture, deed **4 rasgos** *nmpl* FACCIONES : features

rasgón *nm, pl* **rasgones** : rip, tear

rasgue, etc. → **rasgar**

rasguear *vt* : to strum

rasguñar *vt* **1** : to scratch **2** : to sketch, to outline

rasguño *nm* **1** : scratch **2** : sketch

raso[1], -sa *adj* **1** : level, flat **2 soldado raso** : private (in the army) <los soldados rasos : the ranks>

raso[2] *nm* : satin

raspadura *nf* **1** : scratching, scraping **2 raspaduras** *nfpl* : scrapings

raspar *vt* **1** : to scrape **2** : to file down, to smooth — *vi* : to be rough

rasque, etc. → **rascar**

rastra *nf* **1** : harrow **2 a rastras** : by dragging, unwillingly

rastrear *vt* **1** : to track, to trace **2** : to comb, to search **3** : to trawl

rastrero, -ra *adj* **1** : creeping, crawling **2** : vile, despicable

rastrillar *vt* : to rake, to harrow

rastrillo *nm* **1** : rake **2** *Mex* : razor

rastro *nm* **1** PISTA : trail, track **2** VESTIGIO : trace, sign

rastrojo *nm* : stubble (of plants)

rasurar *vt* AFEITAR : to shave — **rasurarse** *vr*

rata[1] *nm fam* : pickpocket, thief

rata[2] *nf* **1** : rat **2** *Col, Pan, Peru* : rate, percentage

ratear *vt* : to pilfer, to steal

ratero, -ra *n* : petty thief

ratificación *nf, pl* **-ciones** : ratification

ratificar {72} *vt* **1** : to ratify **2** : to confirm

rato *nm* **1** : while **2 pasar el rato** : to pass the time **3 a cada rato** : all the time, constantly <les sacaba dinero a cada rato : he was always taking money from them> **4 al poco rato** : later, shortly after

ratón[1], -tona *n, mpl* **ratones 1** : mouse **2 ratón de biblioteca** *fam* : bookworm

ratón[2] *nm, pl* **ratones 1** : (computer) mouse **2** *CoRi* : biceps

ratonera *nf* : mousetrap

raudal *nm* **1** : torrent **2 a raudales** : in abundance

raya[1], etc. → **raer**

raya[2] *nf* **1** : line **2** : stripe **3** : skate, ray **4** : part (in the hair) **5** : crease (in clothing)

rayar *vt* **1** ARAÑAR : to scratch **2** : to scrawl on, to mark up <rayaron las paredes : they covered the walls with graffiti> — *vi* **1** : to scratch **2** AMANECER : to dawn, to break <al rayar el alba : at break of day> **3 ~ con** : to be adjacent to, to be next to **4 ~ en** : to border on, to verge on <su respuesta raya en lo ridículo : his answer borders on the ridiculous> — **rayarse** *vr*

rayo *nm* **1** : ray, beam <rayo láser : laser beam> <rayo de gamma : gamma ray> <rayo de sol : sunbeam> **2** RELÁMPAGO : lightning bolt **3 rayo X** : X ray

rayón *nm, pl* **rayones** : rayon

raza *nf* **1** : race <raza humana : human race> **2** : breed, strain **3 de ~** : thoroughbred, pedigreed

razón *nf, pl* **razones 1** MOTIVO : reason, motive <en razón de : by reason of, because of> **2** JUSTICIA : rightness, justice <tener razón : to be right> **3** : reasoning, sense <perder la razón : to lose one's mind> **4** : ratio, proportion

razonable *adj* : reasonable — **razonablemente** *adv*

razonado, -da *adj* : itemized, detailed

razonamiento *nm* : reasoning

razonar *v* : to reason, to think

reabastecimiento *nm* : replenishment

reabierto *pp* → **reabrir**

reabrir {2} *vt* : to reopen — **reabrirse** *vr*

reacción *nf, pl* **-ciones 1** : reaction **2 motor a reacción** : jet engine

reaccionar *vi* : to react, to respond

reaccionario, -ria *adj & n* : reactionary

reacio, -cia *adj* : resistant, opposed

reacondicionar *vt* : to recondition

reactor *nm* **1** : reactor <reactor nuclear : nuclear reactor> **2** : jet engine **3** : jet airplane, jet

reafirmar *vt* : to reaffirm, to assert, to strengthen

reajustar *vt* : to readjust, to adjust

reajuste *nm* : readjustment <reajuste de precios : price increase>

real *adj* **1** : real, true **2** : royal

realce *nm* **1** : embossing, relief **2 dar realce** : to highlight, to bring out

realeza *nf* : royalty

realidad *nf* **1** : reality **2 en ~** : in truth, actually

realinear *vt* : to realign

realismo *nm* **1** : realism **2** : royalism

realista[1] *adj* **1** : realistic **2** : realist **3** : royalist

realista[2] *nmf* **1** : realist **2** : royalist

realización *nf, pl* **-ciones** : execution, realization

realizar {21} *vt* **1** : to carry out, to execute **2** : to produce, to direct (a film or play) **3 :** to fulfill, to achieve **4 :** to realize (a profit) — **realizarse** *vr* **1 :** to come true **2 :** to fulfill oneself

realmente *adv* **:** really, in reality

realzar {21} *vt* **1 :** to heighten, to raise **2 :** to highlight, to enhance

reanimación *nf, pl* **-ciones :** revival, resuscitation

reanimar *vt* **1 :** to revive, to restore **2 :** to resuscitate — **reanimarse** *vr* **:** to come around, to recover

reanudar *vt* **:** to resume, to renew — **reanadarse** *vr* **:** to resume, to continue

reaparecer {53} *vi* **1 :** to reappear **2 :** to make a comeback

reaparición *nf, pl* **-ciones :** reappearance

reapertura *nf* **:** reopening

reata *nf* **1 :** rope **2** *Mex* **:** lasso, lariat **3 de ~ :** single file

reavivar *vt* **:** to revive, to reawaken

rebaja *nf* **1 :** reduction **2** DESCUENTO **:** discount **3 rebajas** *nfpl* **:** sale

rebajar *vt* **1 :** to reduce, to lower **2 :** to lessen, to diminish **3 :** to humiliate — **rebajarse** *vr* **: 1 :** to humble oneself **2 rebajarse a :** to stoop to

rebanada *nf* **:** slice

rebañar *vt* **:** to mop up, to sop up

rebaño *nm* **1 :** flock **2 :** herd

rebasar *vt* **1 :** to surpass, to exceed **2** *Mex* **:** to pass, to overtake

rebatiña *nf* **:** scramble, fight (over something)

rebatir *vt* REFUTAR **:** to refute

rebato *nm* **1 :** surprise attack **2 tocar a rebato :** to sound the alarm

rebelarse *vr* **:** to rebel

rebelde[1] *adj* **:** rebellious, unruly

rebelde[2] *nmf* **1 :** rebel **2 :** defaulter

rebeldía *nf* **1 :** rebelliousness **2 en ~ :** in default

rebelión *nf, pl* **-liones :** rebellion

rebobinar *vt* **:** to rewind

reborde *nm* **:** border, flange, rim

rebosante *adj* **:** brimming, overflowing <rebosante de salud : brimming with health>

rebosar *vi* **1 :** to overflow **2 ~ de :** to abound in, to be bursting with — *vt* **:** to radiate

rebotar *vi* **1 :** to bounce **2 :** to ricochet, to rebound

rebote *nm* **1 :** bounce **2 :** rebound, ricochet

rebozar {21} *vt* **:** to coat in batter

rebozo *nm* **1 :** shawl, wrap **2 sin ~ :** frankly, openly

rebullir {38} *v* **:** to move, to stir — **rebullirse** *vr*

rebuscado, -da *adj* **:** affected, pretentious

rebuscar {72} *vi* **:** to search thoroughly

rebuznar *vi* **:** to bray

rebuzno *nm* **:** bray, braying

recabar *vt* **1 :** to gather, to obtain, to collect **2 recabar fondos :** to raise money

recado *nm* **1 :** message <mandar recado : to send word> **2** *Spain* **:** errand

recaer {13} *vi* **1 :** to relapse **2 ~ en** *or* **~ sobre :** to fall on, to fall to

recaída *nf* **:** relapse

recaiga, etc. → **recaer**

recalar *vi* **:** to arrive

recalcar {72} *vt* **:** to emphasize, to stress

recalcitrante *adj* **:** recalcitrant

recalentar {55} *vt* **1 :** to reheat, to warm up **2 :** to overheat

recámara *nf* **1** *Col, Mex, Pan* **:** bedroom **2 :** chamber (of a firearm)

recamarera *nf Mex* **:** chambermaid

recambio *nm* **1 :** spare part **2 :** refill (for a pen, etc.)

recapacitar *vi* **1 :** to reconsider **2 ~ en :** to reflect on, to weigh

recapitular *v* **:** to recapitulate — **recapitulación** *nf*

recargable *adj* **:** rechargeable

recargado, -da *adj* **:** overly elaborate or ornate

recargar {52} *vt* **1 :** to recharge **2 :** to overload

recargo *nm* **:** surcharge

recatado, -da *adj* MODESTO **:** modest, demure

recato *nm* PUDOR **:** modesty

recaudación *nf, pl* **-ciones 1 :** collection **2 :** earnings *pl*, takings *pl*

recaudador, -dora *n* **recaudador de impuestos :** tax collector

recaudar *vt* **:** to collect

recaudo *nm* **:** safe place <a (buen) recaudo : in safe keeping>

recayó, etc. → **recaer**

rece, etc. → **rezar**

recelo *nm* **:** distrust, suspicion

receloso, -sa *adj* **:** distrustful, suspicious

recepción *nf, pl* **-ciones :** reception

recepcionista *nmf* **:** receptionist

receptáculo *nm* **:** receptacle

receptividad *nf* **:** receptivity, receptiveness

receptivo, -va *adj* **:** receptive

receptor[1]**, -tora** *adj* **:** receiving

receptor[2]**, -tora** *n* **1 :** recipient **2 :** catcher (in baseball), receiver (in football)

receptor[3] *nm* **:** receiver <receptor de televisión : television set>

recesión *nf, pl* **-siones :** recession

recesivo, -va *adj* **:** recessive

receso *nm* **:** recess, adjournment

receta *nf* **1 :** recipe **2 :** prescription

recetar *vt* **:** to prescribe (medications)

rechazar {21} *vt* **1 :** to reject **2 :** to turn down, to refuse

rechazo *nm* **:** rejection, refusal

rechifla *nf* **:** booing, jeering

rechinar *vi* **1 :** to squeak **2 :** to grind, to gnash <hacer rechinar los dientes : to grind one's teeth>
rechoncho, -cha *adj fam* **:** chubby, squat
recibidor *nm* **:** vestibule, entrance hall
recibimiento *nm* **:** reception, welcome
recibir *vt* **1 :** to receive, to get **2 :** to welcome — *vi* **:** to receive visitors — **recibirse** *vr* **~ de :** to qualify as
recibo *nm* **:** receipt
reciclable *adj* **:** recyclable
reciclado *nm* → **reciclaje**
reciclaje *nm* **1 :** recycling **2 :** retraining
reciclar *vt* **1 :** to recycle **2 :** to retrain
recién *adv* **1 :** newly, recently <recién nacido : newborn> <recién casados : newlyweds> <recién llegado : newcomer> **2 :** just, only just <recién ahora me acordé : I just now remembered>
reciente *adj* **:** recent — **recientemente** *adv*
recinto *nm* **1 :** enclosure **2 :** site, premises *pl*
recio[1] *adv* **1 :** strongly, hard **2 :** loudly, loud
recio[2], **-cia** *adj* **1 :** severe, harsh **2 :** tough, strong
recipiente[1] *nm* **:** container, receptacle
recipiente[2] *nmf* **:** recipient
reciprocar {72} *vi* **:** to reciprocate
reciprocidad *nf* **:** reciprocity
recíproco, -ca *adj* **:** reciprocal, mutual
recitación *nf, pl* **-ciones :** recitation, recital
recital *nm* **:** recital
recitar *vt* **:** to recite
reclamación *nf, pl* **-ciones 1 :** claim, demand **2** QUEJA **:** complaint
reclamar *vt* **1** EXIGIR **:** to demand, to require **2 :** to claim — *vi* **:** to complain
reclamo *nm* **1 :** bird call, lure **2 :** lure, decoy **3 :** inducement, attraction **4 :** advertisement **5 :** complaint
reclinar *vt* **:** to rest, to lean — **reclinarse** *vr* **:** to recline, to lean back
recluir {41} *vt* **:** to confine, to lock up — **recluirse** *vr* **:** to shut oneself up, to withdraw
reclusión *nf, pl* **-siones :** imprisonment
recluso, -sa *n* **1 :** inmate, prisoner **2** SOLITARIO **:** recluse
recluta *nmf* **:** recruit, draftee
reclutamiento *nm* **:** recruitment, recruiting
reclutar *vt* ENROLAR **:** to recruit, to enlist
recobrar *vt* **:** to recover, to regain — **recobrarse** *vr* **:** to recover, to recuperate
recocer {14} *vt* **:** to overcook, to cook again
recodo *nm* **:** bend
recogedor *nm* **:** dustpan
recoger {15} *vt* **1 :** to collect, to gather **2 :** to get, to retrieve, to pick up **3 :** to clean up, to tidy (up)
recogido, -da *adj* **:** quiet, secluded
recogimiento *nm* **1 :** collecting, gathering **2 :** withdrawal **3 :** absorption, concentration
recolección *nf, pl* **-ciones 1 :** collection <recolección de basura : trash pickup> **2 :** harvest
recolectar *vt* **1 :** to gather, to collect **2 :** to harvest, to pick
recomendable *adj* **:** advisable, recommended
recomendación *nf, pl* **-ciones :** recommendation
recomendar {55} *vt* **1 :** to recommend **2** ACONSEJAR **:** to advise
recompensa *nf* **:** reward, recompense
recompensar *vt* **1** PREMIAR **:** to reward **2 :** to compensate
reconciliación *nf, pl* **-ciones :** reconciliation
reconciliar *vt* **:** to reconcile — **reconciliarse** *vr*
recóndito, -ta *adj* **1 :** remote, isolated **2 :** hidden, recondite **3 en lo más recóndito de :** in the depths of
reconfortar *vt* **:** to comfort — **reconfortante** *adj*
reconocer {18} *vt* **1 :** to recognize **2 :** to admit **3 :** to examine
reconocible *adj* **:** recognizable
reconocido, -da *adj* **1 :** recognized, accepted **2 :** grateful
reconocimiento *nm* **1 :** acknowledgment, recognition, avowal **2 :** (medical) examination **3 :** reconnaissance
reconsiderar *vt* **:** to reconsider — **reconsideración** *nf*
reconstrucción *nf, pl* **-ciones :** reconstruction
reconstruir {41} *vt* **:** to rebuild, to reconstruct
reconversión *nf, pl* **-siones :** restructuring
reconvertir {76} *vt* **1 :** to restructure **2 :** to retrain
recopilación *nf, pl* **-ciones 1 :** summary **2 :** collection, compilation
recopilar *vt* **:** to compile, to collect
récord *or* **record** [ˈrɛkɔr] *nm, pl* **récords** *or* **records** [-kɔrs] **:** record <record mundial : world record> — **récord** *or* **record** *adj*
recordar {19} *vt* **1 :** to recall, to remember **2 :** to remind — *vi* **1** ACORDARSE **:** to remember **2** DESPERTAR **:** to wake up
recordatorio[1], **-ria** *adj* **:** commemorative
recordatorio[2] *nm* **:** reminder
recorrer *vt* **1 :** to travel through, to tour **2 :** to cover (a distance) **3 :** to go over, to look over
recorrido *nm* **1 :** journey, trip **2 :** path, route, course **3 :** round (in golf)
recortar *vt* **1 :** to cut, to reduce **2 :** to cut out **3 :** to trim, to cut off **4 :** to outline — **recortarse** *vr* **:** to stand out <los árboles se recortaban en el horizonte : the trees were silhouetted against the horizon>

recorte *nm* **1 :** cut, reduction **2 :** clipping <recortes de periódicos : newspaper clippings>
recostar {19} *vt* **:** to lean, to rest — **recostarse** *vr* **:** to lie down, recline
recoveco *nm* **1** VUELTA **:** bend, turn **2 :** nook, corner **3 recovecos** *nmpl* **:** intricacies, ins and outs
recreación *nf, pl* **-ciones 1 :** re-creation **2** DIVERSIÓN **:** recreation, entertainment
recrear *vt* **1 :** to re-create **2 :** to entertain, to amuse — **recrearse** *vr* **:** to enjoy oneself
recreativo, -va *adj* **:** recreational
recreo *nm* **1** DIVERSIÓN **:** entertainment, amusement **2 :** recess, break
recriminación *nf, pl* **-ciones :** reproach, recrimination
recriminar *vt* **:** to reproach — *vi* **:** to recriminate — **recriminarse** *vr*
recrudecer {53} *v* **:** to intensify, to worsen — **recrudecerse** *vr*
rectal *adj* **:** rectal
rectangular *adj* **:** rectangular
rectángulo *nm* **:** rectangle
rectificación *nf, pl* **-ciones :** rectification, correction
rectificar {72} *vt* **1 :** to rectify, to correct **2 :** to straighten (out)
rectitud *nf* **1 :** straightness **2 :** honesty, rectitude
recto[1] *adv* **:** straight
recto[2], **-ta** *adj* **1 :** straight **2 :** upright, honorable **3 :** sound
recto[3] *nm* **:** rectum
rector[1], **-tora** *adj* **:** governing, managing
rector[2], **-tora** *n* **:** rector
rectoría *nf* **:** rectory
recubierto *pp* → **recubrir**
recubrir {2} *vt* **:** to cover, to coat
recuento *nm* **:** recount, count <un recuento de los votos : a recount of the votes>
recuerdo *nm* **1 :** memory **2 :** souvenir, memento **3 recuerdos** *nmpl* **:** regards
recuperación *nf, pl* **-ciones 1 :** recovery, recuperation **2 recuperación de datos :** data retrieval
recuperar *vt* **1 :** to recover, to get back, to retrieve **2 :** to recuperate **3 :** to make up for <recuperar el tiempo perdido : to make up for lost time> — **recuperarse** *vr* **~ de :** to recover from, to get over
recurrente *adj* **:** recurrent, recurring
recurrir *vi* **1 ~ a :** to turn to, to appeal to **2 ~ a :** to resort to **3 :** to appeal (in law)
recurso *nm* **1 :** recourse <el último recurso : the last resort> **2 :** appeal (in law) **3 recursos** *nmpl* **:** resources, means <recursos naturales : natural resources>
red *nf* **1 :** net, mesh **2 :** network, system, chain **3 :** trap, snare
redacción *nf, pl* **-ciones 1 :** writing, composition **2 :** editing
redactar *vt* **1 :** to write, to draft **2 :** to edit
redactor, -tora *n* **:** editor
redada *nf* **1 :** raid **2 :** catch, haul
redefinir *vt* **:** to redefine — **redefinición** *nf*
redención *nf, pl* **-ciones :** redemption
redentor[1], **-tora** *adj* **:** redeeming
redentor[2], **-tora** *n* **:** redeemer
redescubierto *pp* → **redescubrir**
redescubrir {2} *vt* **:** to rediscover
redicho, -cha *adj fam* **:** affected, pretentious
redil *nm* **1 :** sheepfold **2 volver al redil :** to return to the fold
redimir *vt* **:** to redeem, to deliver (from sin)
rediseñar *vt* **:** to redesign
redistribuir {41} *vt* **:** to redistribute — **redistribución** *nf*
rédito *nm* **:** return, yield
redituar {3} *vt* **:** to produce, to yield
redoblar *vt* **:** to redouble, to strengthen — **redoblado, -da** *adj*
redomado, -da *adj* **1 :** sly, crafty **2 :** utter, out-and-out
redonda *nf* **1 :** region, surrounding area **2 a la redonda** ALREDEDOR **:** around <de diez millas a la redonda : for ten miles around>
redondear *vt* **:** to round off, to round out
redondel *nm* **1 :** ring, circle **2 :** bullring, arena
redondez *nf* **:** roundness
redondo, -da *adj* **1 :** round <mesa redonda : round table> **2 :** great, perfect <un negocio redondo : an excellent deal> **3 :** straightforward, flat <un rechazo redondo : a flat refusal> **4** *Mex* **:** round-trip **5 en ~ :** around
reducción *nf, pl* **-ciones :** reduction, decrease
reducido, -da *adj* **1 :** reduced, limited **2 :** small
reducir {61} *vt* **1** DISMINUIR **:** to reduce, to decrease, to cut **2 :** to subdue **3 :** to boil down — **reducirse** *vr* **~ a :** to come down to, to be nothing more than
redundancia *nf* **:** reduncancy
redundante *adj* **:** redundant
reedición *nf, pl* **-ciones :** reprint
reelegir {28} *vt* **:** to reelect — **reelección** *nf*
reembolsable *adj* **:** refundable
reembolsar *vt* **1 :** to refund, to reimburse **2 :** to repay
reembolso *nm* **:** refund, reimbursement
reemplazable *adj* **:** replaceable
reemplazar {21} *vt* **:** to replace, to substitute
reemplazo *nm* **:** replacement, substitution
reencarnación *nf, pl* **-ciones :** reincarnation
reencuentro *nm* **:** reunion
reestablecer {53} *vt* **:** to reestablish

reestructurar *vt* : to restructure
reexaminar *vt* : to reexamine
refaccionar *vt* : to repair, to renovate
refacciones *nfpl* : repairs, renovations
referencia *nf* **1** : reference **2 hacer referencia a** : to refer to
referendo *nm* → **referéndum**
referéndum *nm, pl* **-dums** : referendum
referente *adj* **~ a** : concerning
réferi *or* **referi** ['rɛfɛri] *nmf* : referee
referir {76} *vt* **1** : to relate, to tell **2** : to refer <nos refirió al diccionario : she referred us to the dictionary> — **referirse** *vr* **1 ~ a** : to refer to **2 ~ a** : to be concerned, to be in reference to <en lo que se refiere a la educación : as far as education is concerned>
refinado¹, -da *adj* : refined
refinado² *nm* : refining
refinamiento *nm* **1** : refining **2** FINURA : refinement
refinanciar *vt* : to refinance
refinar *vt* : to refine
refinería *nf* : refinery
reflectante *adj* : reflective, reflecting
reflector¹, -tora *adj* : reflecting
reflector² *nm* **1** : spotlight, searchlight **2** : reflector
reflejar *vt* : to reflect — **reflejarse** *vr* : to be reflected <la decepción se refleja en su rostro : the disappointment shows on her face>
reflejo *nm* **1** : reflection **2** : reflex **3 reflejos** *nmpl* : highlights, streaks (in hair)
reflexión *nf, pl* **-xiones** : reflection, thought
reflexionar *vi* : to reflect, to think
reflexivo, -va *adj* **1** : reflective, thoughtful **2** : reflexive
reflujo *nm* : ebb, ebb tide
reforma *nf* **1** : reform **2** : alteration, renovation
reformador, -dora *n* : reformer
reformar *vt* **1** : to reform **2** : to change, to alter **3** : to renovate, to repair — **reformarse** *vr* : to mend one's ways
reformatorio *nm* : reformatory
reformular *vt* : to reformulate — **reformulación** *nf*
reforzar {36} *vt* **1** : to reinforce, to strengthen **2** : to encourage, to support
refracción *nf, pl* **-ciones** : refraction
refractar *vt* : to refract — **refractarse** *vr*
refractario, -ria *adj* : refractory, obstinate
refrán *nm, pl* **refranes** ADAGIO : proverb, saying
refregar {49} *vt* : to scrub
refrenar *vt* **1** : to rein in (a horse) **2** : to restrain, to check — **refrenarse** *vr* : to restrain oneself
refrendar *vt* **1** : to countersign, to endorse **2** : to stamp (a passport)
refrescante *adj* : refreshing
refrescar {72} *vt* **1** : to refresh, to cool **2** : to brush up (on) **3 refrescar la memoria** : to refresh one's memory — *vi* : to turn cooler
refresco *nm* : refreshment, soft drink
refriega *nf* : skirmish, scuffle
refrigeración *nf, pl* **-ciones 1** : refrigeration **2** : air-conditioning
refrigerador *nmf* NEVERA : refrigerator
refrigeradora *nf Col, Peru* : refrigerator
refrigerante *nm* : coolant
refrigerar *vt* **1** : to refrigerate **2** : to air-condition
refrigerio *nm* : snack, refreshments *pl*
refrito¹, -ta *adj* : refried
refrito² *nm* : rehash
refuerzo *nm* : reinforcement, support
refugiado, -da *n* : refugee
refugiar *vt* : to shelter — **refugiarse** *vr* ACOGERSE : to take refuge
refugio *nm* : refuge, shelter
refulgencia *nf* : brilliance, splendor
refulgir {35} *vi* : to shine brightly
refundir *vt* **1** : to recast (metals) **2** : to revise, to rewrite
refunfuñar *vi* : to grumble, to groan
refutar *vt* : to refute — **refutación** *nf*
regadera *nf* **1** : watering can **2** : shower head, shower **3** : sprinkler
regaderazo *nm Mex* : shower
regalar *vt* **1** OBSEQUIAR : to present (as a gift), to give away **2** : to regale, to entertain **3** : to flatter, to make a fuss over — **regalarse** *vr* : to pamper oneself
regalía *nf* : royalty, payment
regaliz *nm, pl* **-lices** : licorice
regalo *nm* **1** OBSEQUIO : gift, present **2** : pleasure, comfort **3** : treat
regañadientes *mpl* **a ~** : reluctantly, unwillingly
regañar *vt* : to scold, to give a talking to — *vi* **1** QUEJARSE : to grumble, to complain **2** REÑIR : to quarrel, to argue
regaño *nm fam* : scolding
regañon, -ñona *adj, mpl* **-ñones** *fam* : grumpy, irritable
regar {49} *vt* **1** : to irrigate **2** : to water **3** : to wash, to hose down **4** : to spill, to scatter
regata *nf* : regatta, yacht race
regate *nm* : dodge, feint
regatear *vt* **1** : to haggle over **2** ESCATIMAR : to skimp on, to be sparing with — *vi* : to bargain, to haggle
regateo *nm* : bargaining, haggling
regatón *nm, pl* **-tones** : ferrule, tip
regazo *nm* : lap (of a person)
regencia *nf* : regency
regenerar *vt* : to regenerate — **regenerarse** *vr* — **regeneración** *nf*
regentar *vt* : to run, to manage
regente *nmf* : regent
regidor, -dora *n* : town councillor
régimen *nm, pl* **regímenes 1** : regime **2** : diet **3** : regimen, rules *pl* <régimen de vida : lifestyle>
regimiento *nm* : regiment

regio, -gia *adj* **1 :** great, magnificent **2 :** regal, royal

región *nf, pl* **regiones :** region, area

regional *adj* **:** regional — **regionalmente** *adv*

regir {28} *vt* **1 :** to rule **2 :** to manage, to run **3 :** to control, to govern <las costumbres que rigen la conducta : the customs which govern behavior> — *vi* **:** to apply, to be in force <las leyes rigen en los tres países : the laws apply in all three countries> — **regirse** *vr* **~ por :** to go by, to be guided by

registrador[1], -dora *adj* **caja registradora :** cash register

registrador[2], -dora *n* **:** registrar, recorder

registrar *vt* **1 :** to register, to record **2** GRABAR **:** to record, to tape **3 :** to search, to examine — **registrarse** *vr* **1** INSCRIBIRSE **:** to register **2** OCURRIR **:** to happen, to occur

registro *nm* **1 :** register **2 :** registration **3 :** registry, record office **4 :** range (of a voice or musical instrument) **5 :** search

regla *nf* **1** NORMA **:** rule, regulation **2 :** ruler <regla de cálculo : slide rule> **3** MENSTRUACIÓN **:** period, menstruation

reglamentación *nf, pl* **-ciones 1 :** regulation **2 :** rules *pl*

reglamentar *vt* **:** to regulate, to set rules for

reglamentario, -ria *adj* **:** regulation, official <equipo reglamentario : standard equipment>

reglamento *nm* **:** regulations *pl*, rules *pl* <reglamento de tráfico : traffic regulations>

regocijar *vt* **:** to gladden, to delight — **regocijarse** *vr* **:** to rejoice

regocijo *nm* **:** delight, rejoicing

regordete *adj fam* LLENITO **:** chubby

regresar *vt* DEVOLVER **:** to give back — *vi* **:** to return, to come back, to go back

regresión *nf, pl* **-siones :** regression, return

regresivo, -va *adj* **:** regressive

regreso *nm* **1 :** return **2 estar de regreso :** to be back, to be home

reguero *nm* **1 :** irrigation ditch **2 :** trail, trace **3 propagarse como reguero de pólvora :** to spread like wildfire

regulable *adj* **:** adjustable

regulación *nf, pl* **-ciones :** regulation, control

regulador[1], -dora *adj* **:** regulating, regulatory

regulador[2] *nm* **1 :** regulator, governor **2 regulador de tiro :** damper (in a chimney)

regular[1] *vt* **:** to regulate, to control

regular[2] *adj* **1 :** regular **2 :** fair, OK, so-so **3 :** medium, average **4 por lo regular :** in general, generally

regularidad *nf* **:** regularity

regularización *nf, pl* **-ciones** NORMALIZACIÓN **:** normalization

regularizar {21} *vt* NORMALIZAR **:** to normalize, to make regular

regularmente *adv* **:** regularly

rehabilitar *vt* **1 :** to rehabilitate **2 :** to reinstate **3 :** renovate, to restore — **rehabilitación** *nf*

rehacer {40} *vt* **1 :** to redo **2 :** to remake, to repair, to renew — **rehacerse** *vr* **1 :** to recover **2 ~ de :** to get over

rehecho *pp* → **rehacer**

rehén *nm, pl* **rehenes :** hostage

rehicieron, etc. → **rehacer**

rehizo → **rehacer**

rehuir {41} *vt* **:** to avoid, to shun

rehusar {8} *v* **:** to refuse

reimprimir *vt* **:** to reprint

reina *nf* **:** queen

reinado *nm* **:** reign

reinante *adj* **1 :** reigning **2 :** prevailing, current

reinar *vi* **1 :** to reign **2 :** to prevail

reincidencia *nf* **:** recidivism, relapse

reincidente *nmf* **:** backslider, recidivist

reincidir *vi* **:** to backslide, to retrogress

reincorporar *vt* **:** to reinstate — **reincorporarse** *vr* **~ a :** to return to, to rejoin

reino *nm* **:** kingdom, realm <reino animal : animal kingdom>

reinstalar *vt* **1 :** to reinstall **2 :** to reinstate

reintegrar *vt* **1 :** to reintegrate, reinstate **2 :** to refund, to reimburse — **reintegrarse** *vr* **~ a :** to return to, to rejoin

reír {66} *vi* **:** to laugh — *vt* **:** to laugh at — **reírse** *vr*

reiteración *nf, pl* **-ciones :** reiteration, repetition

reiterado, -da *adj* **:** repeated <lo explicó en reiteradas ocasiones : he explained it repeatedly> — **reiteradamente** *adv*

reiterar *vt* **:** to reiterate, to repeat

reiterativo, -va *adj* **:** repetitive, repetitious

reivindicación *nf, pl* **-ciones 1 :** demand, claim **2 :** vindication

reivindicar {72} *vt* **1 :** to vindicate **2 :** to demand, to claim **3 :** to restore

reja *nf* **1 :** grill, grating <entre rejas : behind bars> **2 :** plowshare

rejilla *nf* **:** grille, grate, screen

rejuvenecer {53} *vt* **:** to rejuvenate — *vi* **:** to be rejuvenated — **rejuvenecerse** *vr*

rejuvencimiento *m* **:** rejuvenation

relación *nf, pl* **-ciones 1 :** relation, connection, relevance **2 :** relationship **3** RELATO **:** account **4** LISTA **:** list **5 con relación a** *or* **en relación con :** in relation to, concerning **6 relaciones públicas :** public relations

relacionar *vt* **:** to relate, to connect — **relacionarse** *vr* **~ con :** to be connected to, to be linked with

relajación *nf, pl* **-ciones :** relaxation
relajado, -da *adj* **1 :** relaxed, loose **2 :** dissolute, depraved
relajar *vt* **:** to relax, to slacken — *vi* **:** to be relaxing — **relajarse** *vr*
relajo *nm* **1 :** commotion, ruckus **2 :** joke, laugh <lo hizo de relajo : he did it for a laugh>
relamerse *vr* **:** to smack one's lips, to lick one's chops
relámpago *nm* **:** flash of lightning
relampaguear *vi* **:** to flash
relanzar {21} *vt* **:** to relaunch
relatar *vt* **:** to relate, to tell
relativo, -va *adj* **1 :** relative **2 en lo relativo a :** with regard to, concerning — **relativamente** *adv*
relato *nm* **1 :** story, tale **2 :** account
releer {20} *vt* **:** to reread
relegar {52} *vt* **1 :** to relegate **2 relegar al olvido :** to consign to oblivion
relevante *adj* **:** outstanding, important
relevar *vt* **1 :** to relieve, to take over from **2 ~ de :** to exempt from — **relevarse** *vr* **:** to take turns
relevo *nm* **1 :** relief, replacement **2 :** relay <carrera de relevos : relay race>
relicario *nm* **1 :** reliquary **2 :** locket
relieve *nm* **1 :** relief, projection <mapa en relieve : relief map> <letras en relieve : embossed letters> **2 :** prominence, importance **3 poner en relieve :** to highlight, to emphasize
religión *nf, pl* **-giones :** religion
religiosamente *adv* **:** religiously, faithfully
religioso[1], **-sa** *adj* **:** religious
religioso[2], **-sa** *n* **:** monk *m,* nun *f*
relinchar *vi* **:** to neigh, to whinny
relincho *nm* **:** neigh, whinny
reliquia *nf* **1 :** relic **2 reliquia de familia :** family heirloom
rellenar *vt* **1 :** to refill **2 :** to stuff, to fill **3 :** to fill out
relleno[1], **-na** *adj* **:** stuffed, filled
relleno[2] *nm* **:** stuffing, filling
reloj *nm* **1 :** clock **2 :** watch **3 reloj de arena :** hourglass **4 reloj de pulsera :** wristwatch **5 como un reloj :** like clockwork
relojería *nf* **1 :** watchmaker's shop **2 :** watchmaking, clockmaking
reluciente *adj* **:** brilliant, shining
relucir {45} *vi* **1 :** to glitter, to shine **2 salir a relucir :** to come to the surface **3 sacar a relucir :** to bring up, to mention
relumbrante *adj* **:** dazzling
relumbrar *vi* **:** to shine brightly
relumbrón *nm, pl* **-brones 1 :** flash, glare **2 de ~ :** flashy, showy
remachar *vt* **1 :** to rivet **2 :** to clinch (a nail) **3 :** to stress, to drive home — *vi* **:** to smash, to spike (a ball)
remache *nm* **1 :** rivet **2 :** smash, spike (in sports)
remanente *nm* **1 :** remainder, balance **2 :** surplus
remanso *nm* **:** pool
remar *vi* **1 :** to row, to paddle **2 :** to struggle, to toil
remarcar {72} *vt* **:** to emphasize, to stress
rematado, -da *adj* **:** utter, complete
rematador, -dora *n* **:** auctioneer
rematar *vt* **1 :** to finish off **2 :** to auction — *vi* **1 :** to shoot **2 :** to end
remate *nm* **1 :** shot (in sports) **2 :** auction **3 :** end, conclusion **4 como ~ :** to top it off **5 de ~ :** completely, utterly
remecer {86} *vt* **:** to sway, to swing
remedar *vt* **1** IMITAR **:** to imitate, to copy **2 :** to mimic, to ape
remediar *vt* **1 :** to remedy, to repair **2 :** to help out, to assist **3** EVITAR **:** to prevent, to avoid
remedio *nm* **1 :** remedy, cure **2 :** solution **3 :** option <no me quedó más remedio : I had no other choice> <no hay remedio : it can't be helped> **4 poner remedio a :** to put a stop to **5 sin ~ :** unavoidable, inevitable
remedo *nm* **:** imitation
rememorar *vi* **:** to recall <rememorar los viejos tiempos : to reminisce>
remendar {55} *vt* **1 :** to mend, to patch, to darn **2 :** to correct
remero, -ra *n* **:** rower
remesa *nf* **1 :** remittance **2 :** shipment
remezón *nm, pl* **-zones :** mild earthquake, tremor
remiendo *nm* **1 :** patch **2 :** correction
remilgado, -da *adj* **1 :** prim, prudish **2 :** affected
remilgo *nm* **:** primness, affectation
reminiscencia *nf* **:** reminiscence
remisión *nf, pl* **-siones 1** ENVÍO **:** sending, delivery **2 :** remission **3 :** reference, cross-reference
remiso, -sa *adj* **1 :** lax, remiss **2 :** reluctant
remitente[1] *nm* **:** return address
remitente[2] *nmf* **:** sender (of a letter, etc.)
remitir *vt* **1 :** to send, to remit **2 ~ a :** to refer to, to direct to <nos remitió al diccionario : he referred us to the dictionary> — *vi* **:** to subside, to let up
remo *nm* **1 :** paddle, oar **2 :** rowing (sport)
remoción *nf, pl* **-ciones 1 :** removal **2 :** dismissal
remodelación *nf, pl* **-ciones 1 :** remodeling **2 :** reorganization, restructuring
remodelar *vt* **1 :** to remodel **2 :** to restructure
remojar *vt* **1 :** to soak, to steep **2 :** to dip, to dunk **3 :** to celebrate with a drink
remojo *nm* **1 :** soaking, steeping **2 poner en remojo :** to soak, to leave soaking
remolacha *nf* **:** beet
remolcador *nm* **:** tugboat
remolcar {72} *vt* **:** to tow, to haul

remolino *nm* **1 :** whirlwind **2 :** eddy, whirlpool **3 :** crowd, throng **4 :** cowlick

remolque *nm* **1 :** towing, tow **2 :** trailer **3 a ~ :** in tow

remontar *vt* **1 :** to overcome **2** SUBIR **:** to go up — **remontarse** *vr* **1 :** to soar **2 ~ a :** to date from, to go back to

rémora *nf* **:** obstacle, hindrance

remorder {47} *vt* INQUIETAR **:** to trouble, to distress

remordimiento *nm* **:** remorse

remotamente *adv* **:** remotely, vaguely

remoto, -ta *adj* **1 :** remote, unlikely <hay una posibilidad remota : there is a slim possibility> **2 :** distant, far-off

remover {47} *vt* **1 :** to stir **2 :** to move around, to turn over **3 :** to stir up **4 :** to remove **5 :** to dismiss

remozamiento *nm* **:** renovation

remozar {21} *vt* **1 :** to renew, to brighten up **2 :** to redo, to renovate

remuneración *nf, pl* **-ciones :** remuneration, pay

remunerar *vt* **:** to pay, to remunerate

remunerativo, -va *adj* **:** remunerative

renacer {48} *vi* **:** to be reborn, to revive

renacimiento *nm* **1 :** rebirth, revival **2 el Renacimiento :** the Renaissance

renacuajo *nm* **:** tadpole, pollywog

renal *adj* **:** renal, kidney

rencilla *nf* **:** quarrel

renco, -ca *adj* **:** lame

rencor *nm* **1 :** rancor, enmity, hostility **2 guardar rencor :** to hold a grudge

rencoroso, -sa *adj* **:** resentful, rancorous

rendición *nf, pl* **-ciones 1 :** surrender, submission **2 :** yield, return

rendido, -da *adj* **1 :** submissive **2 :** worn-out, exhausted **3 :** devoted

rendija *nf* GRIETA **:** crack, split

rendimiento *nm* **1 :** performance **2 :** yield

rendir {54} *vt* **1 :** to render, to give <rendir las gracias : to give thanks> <rendir homenaje a : to pay homage to> **2 :** to yield **3** CANSAR **:** to exhaust — *vi* **1** CUNDIR **:** to progress, to make headway **2 :** to last, to go a long way — **rendirse** *vr* **:** to surrender, to give up

renegado, -da *n* **:** renegade

renegar {49} *vi* **1 ~ de :** to renounce, to disown, to give up **2 ~ de :** to complain about — *vt* **1 :** to deny vigorously **2 :** to abhor, to hate

renegociar *vt* **:** to renegotiate — **renegociación** *nf*

renglón *nm, pl* **renglones 1 :** line (of writing) **2 :** merchandise, line (of products)

rengo, -ga *adj* **:** lame

renguear *vi* **:** to limp

reno *nm* **:** reindeer

renombrado, -da *adj* **:** renowned, famous

renombre *nm* NOMBRADÍA **:** renown, fame

renovable *adj* **:** renewable

renovación *nf, pl* **-ciones 1 :** renewal <renovación de un contrato : renewal of a contract> **2 :** change, renovation

renovar {19} *vt* **1 :** to renew, to restore **2 :** to renovate

renquear *vi* **:** to limp, to hobble

renquera *nf* COJERA **:** limp, lameness

renta *nf* **1 :** income **2 :** rent **3 impuesto sobre la renta :** income tax

rentable *adj* **:** profitable

rentar *vt* **1 :** to produce, to yield **2** ALQUILAR **:** to rent

renuencia *nf* **:** reluctance, unwillingness

renuente *adj* **:** reluctant, unwilling

renuncia *nf* **1 :** resignation **2 :** renunciation **3 :** waiver

renunciar *vi* **1 :** to resign **2 ~ a :** to renounce, to relinquish <renunció al título : he relinquished the title>

reñido, -da *adj* **1 :** tough, hard-fought **2 :** at odds, on bad terms

reñir {67} *vi* **1 :** to argue **2 ~ con :** to fall out with, to go up against — *vt* **:** to scold, to reprimand

reo, rea *n* **1 :** accused, defendant **2 :** offender, culprit

reojo *nm* **de ~ :** out of the corner of one's eye <una mirada de reojo : a sidelong glance>

reorganizar {21} *vt* **:** to reorganize — **reorganización** *nf*

repantigarse {52} *vr* **:** to slouch, to loll about

reparación *nf, pl* **-ciones 1 :** reparation, amends **2 :** repair

reparar *vt* **1 :** to repair, to fix, to mend **2 :** to make amends for **3 :** to correct **4 :** to restore, to refresh — *vi* **1 ~ en :** to observe, to take notice of **2 ~ en :** to consider, to think about

reparo *nm* **1 :** repair, restoration **2 :** reservation, qualm <no tuvieron reparos en decírmelo : they didn't hesitate to tell me> **3 poner reparos a :** to find fault with, to object to

repartición *nf, pl* **-ciones 1 :** distribution **2 :** department, division

repartidor[1], -dora *adj* **:** delivery <camión repartidor : delivery truck>

repartidor[2], -dora *n* **:** delivery person, distributor

repartimiento *nm* → **repartición**

repartir *vt* **1 :** to allocate **2** DISTRIBUIR **:** to distribute, to hand out **3 :** to spread

reparto *nm* **1 :** allocation **2 :** distribution **3 :** cast (of characters)

repasar *vt* **1 :** to pass by again **2 :** to review, to go over **3 :** to mend

repaso *nm* **1 :** review **2 :** mending **3 :** checkup, overhaul

repatriar {85} *vt* **:** to repatriate — **repatriación** *nf*

repavimentar *vt* **:** to resurface

repelente[1] *adj* **:** repellent, repulsive

repelente[2] *nm* : repellent <repelente de insectos : insect repellent>

repeler *vt* **1** : to repel, to resist, to repulse **2** : to reject **3** : to disgust <el sabor me repele : I find the taste repulsive>

repensar {55} *v* : to rethink, to reconsider

repente *nm* **1** : sudden movement, start <de repente : suddenly> **2** : fit, outburst <un repente de ira : a fit of anger>

repentino, -na *adj* : sudden — **repentinamente** *adv*

repercusión *nf, pl* **-siones** : repercussion

repercutir *vi* **1** : to reverberate, to echo **2 ~ en** : to have effects on, to have repercussions on

repertorio *nm* : repertoire

repetición *nf, pl* **-ciones 1** : repetition **2** : rerun, repeat

repetidamente *adv* : repeatedly

repetido, -da *adj* **1** : repeated, numerous **2 repetidas veces** : repeatedly, time and again

repetir {54} *vt* **1** : to repeat **2** : to have a second helping of — **repetirse** *vr* **1** : to repeat oneself **2** : to recur

repetitivo, -va *adj* : repetitive, repetitious

repicar {72} *vt* : to ring — *vi* : to ring out, to peal

repique *nm* : ringing, pealing

repisa *nf* : shelf, ledge <repisa de chimenea : mantelpiece> <repisa de ventana : windowsill>

replantear *vt* : to redefine, to restate — **replantearse** *vr* : to reconsider

replegar {49} *vt* : to fold — **replegarse** *vr* RETIRARSE : to retreat, to withdraw

repleto, -ta *adj* **1** : replete, full **2 ~ de** : packed with, crammed with

réplica *nf* **1** : reply **2** : replica, reproduction **3** *Chile, Mex* : aftershock

replicación *nf, pl* **-ciones** : replication

replicar {72} *vi* **1** : to reply, to retort **2** : to argue, to answer back

repliegue *nm* **1** : fold **2** : retreat, withdrawal

repollo *nm* COL : cabbage

reponer {60} *vt* **1** : to replace, to put back **2** : to reinstate **3** : to reply — **reponerse** *vr* : to recover

reportaje *nm* : article, story, report

reportar *vt* **1** : to check, to restrain **2** : to bring, to carry, to yield <me reportó numerosos beneficios : it brought me many benefits> **3** : to report — **reportarse** *vr* **1** CONTENERSE : to control oneself **2** PRESENTARSE : to report, to show up

reporte *nm* : report

reportear *vt* : to report on, to cover

reportero, -ra *n* **1** : reporter **2 reportero gráfico** : photojournalist

reposado, -da *adj* : calm

reposar *vi* **1** : to rest, to repose **2** : to stand, to settle <deje reposar la masa media hora : let the dough stand for half an hour> **3** : to lie, to be buried — **reposarse** *vr* : to settle

reposición *nf, pl* **-ciones 1** : replacement **2** : reinstatement **3** : revival

repositorio *nm* : repository

reposo *nm* : repose, rest

repostar *vi* **1** : to stock up **2** : to refuel

repostería *nf* **1** : confectioner's shop **2** : pastry-making

repostero, -ra *n* : confectioner

repreguntar *vt* : to cross-examine

repreguntas *nfpl* : cross-examination

reprender *vt* : to reprimand, to scold

reprensible *adj* : reprehensible

represa *nf* : dam

represalia *nf* **1** : reprisal, retaliation **2 tomar represalias** : to retaliate

represar *vt* : to dam

representación *nf, pl* **-ciones 1** : representation **2** : performance **3 en representación de** : on behalf of

representante *nmf* **1** : representative **2** : performer

representar *vt* **1** : to represent, to act for **2** : to perform **3** : to look, to appear as **4** : to symbolize, to stand for **5** : to signify, to mean — **representarse** *vr* : to imagine, to picture

representativo, -va *adj* : representative

represión *nf, pl* **-siones** : repression

represivo, -va *adj* : repressive

reprimenda *nf* : reprimand

reprimir *vt* **1** : to repress **2** : to suppress, to stifle

reprobable *adj* : reprehensible, culpable

reprobación *nf* : disapproval

reprobar {19} *vt* **1** DESAPROBAR : to condemn, to disapprove of **2** : to fail (a course)

reprobatorio, -ria *adj* : disapproving, admonitory

reprochar *vt* : to reproach — **reprocharse** *vr*

reproche *nm* : reproach

reproducción *nf, pl* **-ciones** : reproduction

reproducir {61} *vt* : to reproduce — **reproducirse** *vr* **1** : to breed, to reproduce **2** : to recur

reproductor, -tora *adj* : reproductive

reptar *vi* : to crawl, to slither

reptil[1] *adj* : reptilian

reptil[2] *nm* : reptile

república *nf* : republic

republicanismo *nm* : republicanism

republicano, -na *adj & n* : republican

repudiar *vt* : to repudiate — **repudiación** *nf*

repudio *nm* : repudiation

repuesto[1] *pp* → **reponer**

repuesto[2] *nm* **1** : spare part **2 de ~** : spare <rueda de repuesto : spare wheel>

repugnancia *nf* : repugnance

repugnante *adj* : repulsive, repugnant, revolting
repugnar *vt* : to cause repugnance, to disgust — **repugnarse** *vr*
repujar *vt* : to emboss
repulsivo, -va *adj* : repulsive
repuntar *vt Arg, Chile* : to round up (cattle) — *vi* : to begin to appear — **repuntarse** *vr* : to fall out, to quarrel
repuso, etc. → **reponer**
reputación *nf, pl* **-ciones** : reputation
reputar *vt* : to consider, to deem
requerir {76} *vt* **1** : to require, to call for **2** : to summon, to send for
requesón *nm, pl* **-sones** : curd cheese, cottage cheese
réquiem *nm* : requiem
requisa *nf* **1** : requisition **2** : seizure **3** : inspection
requisar *vt* **1** : to requisition **2** : to seize **3** INSPECCIONAR : to inspect
requisito *nm* **1** : requirement **2 requisito previo** : prerequisite
res *nf* **1** : beast, animal **2** *CA, Mex* : beef **3 reses** *nfpl* : cattle <60 reses : 60 head of cattle>
resabio *nm* **1** VICIO : bad habit, vice **2** DEJO : aftertaste
resaca *nf* **1** : undertow **2** : hangover
resaltar *vi* **1** SOBRESALIR : to stand out **2 hacer resaltar** : to bring out, to highlight — *vt* : to stress, to emphasize
resarcimiento *nm* **1** : compensation **2** : reimbursement
resarcir {83} *vt* : to compensate, to indemnify — **resarcirse** *vr* **~ de** : to make up for
resbaladizo, -za *adj* **1** RESBALOSO : slippery **2** : tricky, ticklish, delicate
resbalar *vi* **1** : to slip, to slide **2** : to slip up, to make a mistake **3** : to skid — **resbalarse** *vr*
resbalón *nm, pl* **-lones** : slip
resbaloso, -sa *adj* : slippery
rescatar *vt* **1** : to rescue, to save **2** : to recover, to get back
rescate *nm* **1** : rescue **2** : recovery **3** : ransom
rescindir *vt* : to rescind, to annul, to cancel
rescisión *nf, pl* **-siones** : annulment, cancelation
rescoldo *nm* : embers *pl*
resecar {72} *vt* : to make dry, to dry up — **resecarse** *vr* : to dry up
reseco, -ca *adj* : dry, dried-up
resentido, -da *adj* : resentful
resentimiento *nm* : resentment
resentirse {76} *vr* **1** : to suffer, to be weakened **2** OFENDERSE : to be upset <se resintió porque la insultaron : she got upset when they insulted her, she resented being insulted> **3 ~ de** : to feel the effects of
reseña *nf* **1** : report, summary, review **2** : description
reseñar *vt* **1** : to review **2** DESCRIBIR : to describe
reserva *nf* **1** : reservation **2** : reserve **3** : confidence, privacy <con la mayor reserva : in strictest confidence> **4 de ~** : spare, in reserve **5 reservas** *nfpl* : reservations, doubts
reservación *nf, pl* **-ciones** : reservation
reservado, -da *adj* **1** : reserved, reticent **2** : confidential
reservar *vt* : to reserve — **reservarse** *vr* **1** : to save oneself **2** : to conceal, to keep to oneself
reservorio *nm* : reservoir, reserve
resfriado *nm* CATARRO : cold
resfriar {85} *vt* : to cool — **resfriarse** *vr* **1** : to cool off **2** : to catch a cold
resfrío *nm* : cold
resguardar *vt* : to safeguard, to protect — **resguardarse** *vr*
resguardo *nm* **1** : safeguard, protection **2** : receipt, voucher **3** : border guard, coast guard
residencia *nf* **1** : residence **2** : boarding house
residencial *adj* : residential
residente *adj & nmf* : resident
residir *vi* **1** VIVIR : to reside, to dwell **2 ~ en** : to lie in, to consist of
residual *adj* : residual
residuo *nm* **1** : residue **2** : remainder **3 residuos** *nmpl* : waste <residuos nucleares : nuclear waste>
resignación *nf, pl* **-ciones** : resignation
resignar *vt* : to resign — **resignarse** *vr* **~ a** : to resign oneself to
resina *nf* **1** : resin **2 resina epoxídica** : epoxy
resistencia *nf* **1** : resistance **2** AGUANTE : endurance, strength, stamina
resistente *adj* **1** : resistant **2** : strong, tough
resistir *vt* **1** : to stand, to bear, to tolerate **2** : to withstand — *vi* : to resist <resistió hasta el último minuto : he held out until the last minute> — **resistirse** *vr* **~ a** : to be resistent to, to be reluctant
resollar {19} *vi* : to breathe heavily, to wheeze
resolución *nf, pl* **-ciones 1** : resolution, settlement **2** : decision **3** : determination, resolve
resolver {89} *vt* **1** : to resolve, to settle **2** : to decide — **resolverse** *vr* : to make up one's mind
resonancia *nf* **1** : resonance **2** : impact, repercussions *pl*
resonante *adj* **1** : resonant **2** : tremendous, resounding <un éxito resonante : a resounding success>
resonar {19} *vi* : to resound, to ring
resoplar *vi* **1** : to puff, to pant **2** : to snort
resoplo *nm* **1** : puffing, panting **2** : snort
resorte *nm* **1** MUELLE : spring **2** : elasticity **3** : influence, means *pl* <tocar resortes : to pull strings>
resortera *nf Mex* : slingshot

respaldar *vt* **:** to back, to support, to endorse — **respaldarse** *vr* **:** to lean back

respaldo *nm* **1 :** back (of an object) **2 :** support, backing

respectar *vt* **:** to concern, to relate to <por lo que a mí respecta : as far as I'm concerned>

respectivo, -va *adj* **:** respective — **respectivamente** *adv*

respecto *nm* **1 ~ a :** in regard to, concerning **2 al respecto :** on this matter, in this respect

respetable *adj* **:** respectable — **respetabilidad** *nf*

respetar *vt* **:** to respect

respeto *nm* **1 :** respect, consideration **2 respetos** *nmpl* **:** respects <presentar sus respetos : to pay one's respects>

respetuosidad *nf* **:** respectfulness

respetuoso, -sa *adj* **:** respectful — **respetuosamente** *adv*

respingo *nm* **:** start, jump

respiración *nf, pl* **-ciones :** respiration, breathing

respiradero *nm* **:** vent, ventilation shaft

respirador *nm* **:** respirator

respirar *v* **:** to breathe

respiratorio, -ria *adj* **:** respiratory

respiro *nm* **1 :** breath **2 :** respite, break

resplandecer {53} *vi* **1 :** to shine **2 :** to stand out

resplandeciente *adj* **1 :** resplendent, shining **2 :** radiant

resplandor *nm* **1 :** brightness, brilliance, radiance **2 :** flash

responder *vt* **:** to answer — *vi* **1 :** to answer, to reply, to respond **2 ~ a :** to respond to <responder al tratamiento : to respond to treatment> **3 ~ de :** to answer for, to vouch for (something) **4 ~ por :** to vouch for (someone)

responsabilidad *nf* **:** responsibility

responsable *adj* **:** responsible — **responsablemente** *adv*

respuesta *nf* **:** answer, response

resquebrajar *vt* **:** to split, to crack — **resquebrajarse** *vr*

resquemor *nm* **:** resentment, bitterness

resquicio *nm* **1 :** crack **2 :** opportunity, chance **3 :** trace <sin un resquicio de remordimiento : without a trace of remorse> **4 resquicio legal :** loophole

resta *nf* SUSTRACCIÓN **:** subtraction

restablecer {53} *vt* **:** to reestablish, to restore — **restablecerse** *vr* **:** to recover

restablecimiento *nm* **1 :** reestablishment, restoration **2 :** recovery

restallar *vi* **:** to crack, to crackle, to click

restallido *nm* **:** crack, crackle

restante *adj* **1 :** remaining **2 lo restante, los restantes :** the rest

restañar *vt* **:** to stanch

restar *vt* **1 :** to deduct, to subtract <restar un punto : to deduct a point> **2 :** to minimize, to play down — *vi* **:** to remain, to be left

restauración *nf, pl* **-ciones 1 :** restoration **2 :** catering, food service

restaurante *nm* **:** restaurant

restaurar *vt* **:** to restore

restitución *nf, pl* **-ciones :** restitution, return

restituir {41} *vt* **:** to return, to restore, to reinstate

resto *nm* **1 :** rest, remainder **2 restos** *nmpl* **:** remains <restos de comida : leftovers> <restos arqueológicos : archeological ruins> **3 restos mortales :** mortal remains

restorán *nm, pl* **-ranes :** restaurant

restregadura *nf* **:** scrub, scrubbing

restregar {49} *vt* **1 :** to rub **2 :** to scrub — **restregarse** *vr*

restricción *nf, pl* **-ciones :** restriction, limitation

restrictivo, -va *adj* **:** restrictive

restringido, -da *adj* LIMITADO **:** limited, restricted

restringir {35} *vt* LIMITAR **:** to restrict, to limit

restructuración *nf* **:** restructuring

restructurar *vt* **:** to restructure

resucitación *nf* **:** resuscitation <resucitación cardiopulmonar : CPR, cardiopulmonary resuscitation>

resucitar *vt* **1 :** to resuscitate, to revive, to resurrect **2 :** to revitalize

resuello *nm* **1 :** puffing, heavy breathing, wheezing **2 :** break, breather

resuelto[1] *pp* → **resolver**

resuelto[2], **-ta** *adj* **:** determined, resolved, resolute

resulta *nf* **1 :** consequence, result **2 a resultas de** *or* **de resultas de :** as a result of

resultado *nm* **:** result, outcome

resultante *adj & nf* **:** resultant

resultar *vi* **1 :** to work, to work out <mi idea no resultó : my idea didn't work out> **2 :** to prove, to turn out to be <resultó bien simpático : he turned out to be very nice> **3 ~ en :** to lead to, to result in **4 ~ de :** to be the result of

resumen *nm, pl* **-súmenes 1 :** summary, summation **2 en ~ :** in summary, in short

resumidero *nm* **:** drain

resumir *v* **:** to summarize, to sum up

resurgimiento *nm* **:** resurgence

resurgir {35} *vi* **:** to reappear, to revive

resurrección *nf, pl* **-ciones :** resurrection

retablo *nm* **1 :** tableau **2 :** altarpiece

retador, -dora *n* **:** challenger (in sports)

retaguardia *nf* **:** rear guard

retahíla *nf* **:** string, series <una retahíla de insultos : a volley of insults>

retaliación *nf, pl* **-ciones :** retaliation

retama *nf* **:** broom (plant)

retar *vt* DESAFIAR **:** to challenge, to defy

retardante *adj* **:** retardant

retardar *vt* **1** RETRASAR **:** to delay, to retard **2 :** to postpone

retazo *nm* **1 :** remnant, scrap **2 :** fragment, piece <retazos de su obra : bits and pieces from his writings>

retención *nf, pl* **-ciones 1 :** retention **2 :** deduction, withholding

retener {80} *vt* **1 :** to retain, to keep **2 :** to withhold **3 :** to detain

retentivo, -va *adj* **:** retentive

reticencia *nf* **1 :** reluctance, reticence **2 :** insinuation

reticente *adj* **1 :** reluctant, reticent **2 :** insinuating, misleading

retina *nf* **:** retina

retintín *nm, pl* **-tines 1 :** jingle, jangle **2 con ~ :** sarcastically

retirada *nf* **1 :** retreat <batirse en retirada : to withdraw, to beat a retreat> **2 :** withdrawl (of funds) **3 :** retirement **4 :** refuge, haven

retirado, -da *adj* **1 :** remote, distant, far off **2 :** secluded, quiet

retirar *vt* **1 :** to remove, to take away, to recall **2 :** to withdraw, to take out — **retirarse** *vr* **1** REPLEGARSE **:** to retreat, to withdraw **2** JUBILARSE **:** to retire

retiro *nm* **1** JUBILACIÓN **:** retirement **2 :** withdrawal, retreat **3 :** seclusion

reto *nm* DESAFÍO **:** challenge, dare

retocar {72} *vt* **:** to touch up

retoñar *vi* **:** to sprout

retoño *nm* **:** sprout, shoot

retoque *nm* **:** retouching

retorcer {14} *vt* **1 :** to twist **2 :** to wring — **retorcerse** *vr* **1 :** to get twisted, to get tangled up **2 :** to squirm, to writhe, to wiggle about

retorcijón *nm, pl* **-jones :** cramp, sharp pain

retorcimiento *nm* **1 :** twisting, wringing **2 :** deviousness

retórica *nf* **:** rhetoric

retórico, -ca *adj* **:** rhetorical — **retóricamente** *adv*

retornar *v* **:** to return

retorno *nm* **:** return

retozar {21} *vi* **:** to frolic, to romp

retozo *nm* **:** frolicking

retozón, -zona *adj, mpl* **-zones :** playful

retracción *nf, pl* **-ciones :** retraction, withdrawal

retractable *adj* **:** retractable

retractación *nf, pl* **-ciones :** retraction (of a statement, etc.)

retractarse *vr* **1 :** to withdraw, to back down **2 ~ de :** to take back, to retract

retraer {81} *vt* **1 :** to bring back **2 :** to dissuade — **retraerse** *vr* **1** RETIRARSE **:** to withdraw, to retire **2** REFUGIARSE **:** to take refuge

retraído, -da *adj* **:** withdrawn, retiring, shy

retraimiento *nm* **1 :** shyness, timidity **2 :** withdrawal

retrasado, -da *adj* **1 :** retarded, mentally slow **2 :** behind, in arrears **3 :** backward (of a country) **4 :** slow (of a watch)

retrasar *vt* **1** DEMORAR, RETARDAR **:** to delay, to hold up **2 :** to put off, to postpone — **retrasarse** *vr* **1 :** to be late **2 :** to fall behind

retraso *nm* **1** ATRASO **:** delay, lateness **2 retraso mental :** mental retardation

retratar *vt* **1 :** to portray, to depict **2 :** to photograph **3 :** to paint a portrait of

retrato *nm* **1 :** depiction, portrayal **2 :** portrait, photograph

retrete *nm* **:** restroom, toilet

retribución *nf, pl* **-ciones 1 :** pay, payment **2 :** reward

retribuir {41} *vt* **1 :** to pay **2 :** to reward

retroactivo, -va *adj* **:** retroactive — **retroactivamente** *adv*

retroalimentación *nf, pl* **-ciones :** feedback

retroceder *vi* **1 :** to move back, to turn back **2 :** to back off, to back down **3 :** to recoil (of a firearm)

retroceso *nm* **1 :** backward movement **2 :** backing down **3 :** setback, relapse **4 :** recoil

retrógrado, -da *adj* **1 :** reactionary **2 :** retrograde

retropropulsión *nf* **:** jet propulsion

retrospectiva *nf* **:** retrospective, hindsight

retrospectivo, -va *adj* **1 :** retrospective **2 mirada retrospectiva :** backward glance

retrovisor *nm* **:** rearview mirror

retruécano *nm* **:** pun, play on words

retumbar *vi* **1 :** to boom, to thunder **2 :** to resound, to reverberate

retumbo *nm* **:** booming, thundering, roll

retuvo, etc. → **retener**

reubicar {72} *vt* **:** to relocate — **reubicación** *nf*

reuma *or* **reúma** *nmf* → **reumatismo**

reumático, -ca *adj* **:** rheumatic

reumatismo *nm* **:** rheumatism

reunión *nf, pl* **-niones 1 :** meeting **2 :** gathering, reunion

reunir {68} *vt* **1 :** to unite, to join, to bring together **2 :** to have, to possess <reunieron los requisitos necesarios : they fulfilled the necessary requirements> **3 :** to gather, to collect, to raise (funds) — **reunirse** *vr* **:** to meet

reutilizable *adj* **:** reusable

reutilizar {21} *vt* **:** to recycle, to reuse

revalidar *vt* **1 :** to confirm, to ratify **2 :** to defend (a title)

revaluar {3} *vt* **:** to reevaluate — **revaluación** *n*

revancha *nf* **1** DESQUITE **:** revenge, requital **2 :** rematch

revelación *nf, pl* **-ciones :** revelation

revelado *nm* **:** developing (of film)

revelador[1], **-dora** *adj* **:** revealing

revelador[2] *nm* **:** developer

revelar *vt* **1 :** to reveal, to disclose **2 :** to develop (film)
revendedor, -dora *n* **1 :** scalper **2** DETALLISTA **:** retailer
revender *vt* **1 :** to resell **2 :** to scalp
reventa *nf* **1 :** resale **2 :** scalping
reventar {55} *vi* **1** ESTALLAR, EXPLOTAR **:** to burst, to blow up **2 ~ de :** to be bursting with — *vt* **1 :** to burst **2** *fam* **:** to annoy, to rile
reventón *nm, pl* **-tones 1 :** burst, bursting **2 :** blowout, flat tire **3** *Mex fam* **:** bash, party
reverberar *vi* **:** to reverberate — **reverberación** *nf*
reverdecer {53} *vi* **1 :** to grow green again **2 :** to revive
reverencia *nf* **1 :** reverence **2 :** bow, curtsy
reverenciar *vt* **:** to revere, to venerate
reverendo[1], -da *adj* **1 :** reverend **2** *fam* **:** total, absolute <es un reverendo imbécil : he is a complete idiot>
reverendo[2], -da *n* **:** reverend
reverente *adj* **:** reverent
reversa *nf Col, Mex* **:** reverse (gear)
reversible *adj* **:** reversible
reversión *nf, pl* **-siones :** reversion
reverso *nm* **1 :** back, other side **2 el reverso de la medalla :** the complete opposite
revertir {76} *vi* **1 :** to revert, to go back **2 ~ en :** to result in, to end up as
revés *nm, pl* **reveses 1 :** back, wrong side **2 :** setback, reversal **3 :** backhand (in sports) **4 al revés :** the other way around, upside down, inside out **5 al revés de :** contrary to
revestimiento *nm* **:** covering, facing (of a building)
revestir {54} *vt* **1 :** to coat, to cover, to surface **2 :** to conceal, to disguise **3 :** to take on, to assume <la reunión revistió gravedad : the meeting took on a serious note>
revisar *vt* **1 :** to examine, to inspect, to check **2 :** to check over, to overhaul (machinery) **3 :** to revise
revisión *nf, pl* **-siones 1 :** revision **2 :** inspection, check
revisor, -sora *n* **1 :** inspector **2 :** conductor (on a train)
revista *nf* **1 :** magazine, journal **2 :** revue **3 pasar revista :** to review, to inspect
revistar *vt* **:** to review, to inspect
revitalizar {21} *vt* **:** to revitalize — **revitalización** *nf*
revivir *vi* **:** to revive, to come alive again — *vt* **:** to relive
revocación *nf, pl* **-ciones :** revocation, repeal
revocar {72} *vt* **1 :** to revoke, to repeal **2 :** to plaster (a wall)
revolcar {82} *vt* **:** to knock over, to knock down — **revolcarse** *vr* **:** to roll around, to wallow
revolcón *nm, pl* **-cones** *fam* **:** tumble, fall
revolotear *vi* **:** to flutter around, to flit
revoloteo *nm* **:** fluttering, flitting
revoltijo *nm* **1** FÁRRAGO **:** mess, jumble **2** *Mex* **:** traditional seafood dish
revoltoso, -sa *adj* **:** unruly, rebellious
revolución *nf, pl* **-ciones :** revolution
revolucionar *vt* **:** to revolutionize
revolucionario, -ria *adj & n* **:** revolutionary
revolver {89} *vt* **1 :** to move about, to mix, to shake, to stir **2 :** to upset (one's stomach) **3 :** to mess up, to rummage through <revolver la casa : to turn the house upside down> — **revolverse** *vr* **1 :** to toss and turn **2** VOLVERSE **:** to turn around
revólver *nm* **:** revolver
revoque *nm* **:** plaster
revuelo *nm* **1 :** fluttering **2 :** commotion, stir
revuelta *nf* **:** uprising, revolt
revuelto[1] *pp* → **revolver**
revuelto[2], -ta *adj* **1 :** choppy, rough <mar revuelto : rough sea> **2 :** untidy **3 huevos revueltos :** scrambled eggs
rey *nm* **:** king
reyerta *nf* **:** brawl, fight
rezagado, -da *n* **:** straggler, latecomer
rezagar {52} *vt* **1 :** to leave behind **2 :** to postpone — **rezagarse** *vr* **:** to fall behind, to lag
rezar {21} *vi* **1 :** to pray **2 :** to say <como reza el refrán : as the saying goes> **3 ~ con :** to concern, to have to do with — *vt* **:** to say, to recite <rezar un Ave María : to say a Hail Mary>
rezo *nm* **:** prayer, praying
rezongar {52} *vi* **:** to gripe, to grumble
rezumar *v* **:** to ooze, to leak
ría[1], etc. → **reír**
ría[2] *nf* **:** estuary
riachuelo *nm* ARROYO **:** brook, stream
riada *nf* **:** flood
ribera *nf* **:** bank, shore
ribete *nm* **1 :** border, trim **2 :** frill, adornment **3 ribetes** *nmpl* **:** hint, touch <tiene sus ribetes de genio : there's a touch of genius in him>
ribetear *vt* **:** to border, to edge, to trim
ricamente *adv* **:** richly, splendidly
rice, etc. → **rizar**
rico[1], -ca *adj* **1 :** rich, wealthy **2 :** fertile **3 :** luxurious, valuable **4 :** delicious **5 :** adorable, lovely **6 :** great, wonderful
rico[2], -ca *n* **:** rich person
ridiculez *nf, pl* **-leces :** ridiculousness, absurdity
ridiculizar {21} *vt* **:** to ridicule
ridículo[1], -la *adj* ABSURDO, DISPARATADO **:** ridiculous, ludicrous — **ridículamente** *adv*
ridículo[2], -la *n* **1 hacer el ridículo :** to make a fool of oneself **2 poner en ridículo :** to ridicule
ríe, etc. → **reír**
riega, riegue, etc. → **regar**
riego *nm* **:** irrigation

riel *nm* **:** rail, track

rienda *nf* **1 :** rein **2 dar rienda suelta a :** to give free rein to **3 llevar las riendas :** to be in charge **4 tomar las riendas :** to take control

riesgo *nm* **:** risk

riesgoso, -sa *adj* **:** risky

rifa *nf* **:** raffle

rifar *vt* **:** to raffle — *vi* **:** to quarrel, to fight

rifle *nm* **:** rifle

rige, rija, etc. → **regir**

rigidez *nf, pl* **-deces 1 :** rigidity, stiffness <rigidez cadavérica : rigor mortis> **2 :** inflexibility

rígido, -da *adj* **1 :** rigid, stiff **2 :** strict — **rígidamente** *adv*

rigor *nm* **1 :** rigor, harshness **2 :** precision, meticulousness **3 de ~ :** usual <la respuesta de rigor : the standard reply> **4 de ~ :** essential, obligatory **5 en ~ :** strictly speaking, in reality

riguroso, -sa *adj* **:** rigorous — **rigurosamente** *adv*

rima *nf* **1 :** rhyme **2 rimas** *nfpl* **:** verse, poetry

rimar *vi* **:** to rhyme

rimbombante *adj* **1 :** grandiose, showy **2 :** bombastic, pompous

rímel *or* **rimel** *nm* **:** mascara

rin *nm Col, Mex* **:** wheel, rim (of a tire)

rincón *nm, pl* **rincones :** corner, nook

rinde, etc. → **rendir**

rinoceronte *nm* **:** rhinoceros

riña *nf* **1 :** fight, brawl **2 :** dispute, quarrel

riñe, etc. → **reñir**

riñón *nm, pl* **riñones :** kidney

río[1] → **reír**

río[2] *nm* **1 :** river **2 :** torrent, stream <un río de lágrimas : a flood of tears>

ripio *nm* **1 :** debris, rubble **2 :** gravel

riqueza *nf* **1 :** wealth, riches *pl* **2 :** richness **3 riquezas naturales :** natural resources

risa *nf* **1 :** laughter, laugh **2 dar risa :** to make laugh <me dio mucha risa : I found it very funny> **3** *fam* **morirse de la risa :** to die laughing, to crack up

risco *nm* **:** crag, cliff

risible *adj* IRRISORIO **:** ludicrous, laughable

risita *nf* **:** giggle, titter, snicker

risotada *nf* **:** guffaw

ristra *nf* **:** string, series *pl*

risueño, -ña *adj* **1 :** cheerful, pleasant **2 :** promising

rítmico, -ca *adj* **:** rhythmical, rhythmic — **rítmicamente** *adv*

ritmo *nm* **1 :** rhythm **2 :** pace, tempo <trabajó a ritmo lento : she worked at a slow pace>

rito *nm* **:** rite, ritual

ritual *adj & nm* **:** ritual — **ritualmente** *adv*

rival *adj & nmf* COMPETIDOR **:** rival

rivalidad *nf* **:** rivalry, competition

rivalizar {21} *vi* **~ con :** to rival, to compete with

rizado, -da *adj* **1 :** curly **2 :** ridged **3 :** ripply, undulating

rizar {21} *vt* **1 :** to curl **2 :** to ripple, to ruffle (a surface) **3 :** to crumple, to fold — **rizarse** *vr* **1 :** to frizz **2 :** to ripple

rizo *nm* **1 :** curl **2 :** loop (in aviation)

robalo *or* **róbalo** *nm* **:** sea bass

robar *vt* **1 :** to steal **2 :** to rob, to burglarize **3** SECUESTRAR **:** to abduct, to kidnap **4 :** to captivate — *vi* **~ en :** to break into

roble *nm* **:** oak

robo *nm* **:** robbery, theft

robot *nm, pl* **robots :** robot

robótica *nf* **:** robotics

robustecer {53} *vt* **:** to grow stronger, to strengthen

robustez *nf* **:** sturdiness, robustness

robusto, -ta *adj* **:** robust, sturdy

roca *nf* **:** rock, boulder

roce[1], **etc.** → **rozar**

roce[2] *nm* **1 :** rubbing, chafing **2 :** brush, graze, touch **3 :** close contact, familiarity **4 :** friction, disagreement

rociador *nm* **:** sprinkler

rociar {85} *vt* **:** to spray, to sprinkle

rocío *nm* **1 :** dew **2 :** shower, light rain

rocola *nf* **:** jukebox

rocoso, -sa *adj* **:** rocky

rodada *nf* **:** track (of a tire), rut

rodado, -da *adj* **1 :** wheeled **2 :** dappled (of a horse)

rodaja *nf* **:** round, slice

rodaje *nm* **1 :** filming, shooting **2 :** breaking in (of a vehicle)

rodamiento *nm* **1 :** bearing <rodamiento de bolas : ball bearings> **2 :** rolling

rodar {19} *vi* **1 :** to roll, to roll down, to roll along <rodé por la escalera : I tumbled down the stairs> <todo rodaba bien : everthing was going along well> **2** GIRAR **:** to turn, to go around **3 :** to move about, to travel <andábamos rodando por todas partes : we drifted along from place to place> — *vt* **1 :** to film, to shoot **2 :** to break in (a new vehicle)

rodear *vt* **1 :** to surround **2 :** to round up (cattle) — *vi* **1 :** to go around **2 :** to beat around the bush — **rodearse** *vr* **~ de :** to surround oneself with

rodeo *nm* **1 :** rodeo, roundup **2** DESVÍO **:** detour **3 :** evasion <andar con rodeos : to beat around the bush> <sin rodeos : without reservations>

rodilla *nf* **:** knee

rodillo *nm* **1 :** roller **2 :** rolling pin

rododendro *nm* **:** rhododendron

roedor[1], **-dora** *adj* **:** gnawing

roedor[2] *nm* **:** rodent

roer {69} *vt* **1 :** to gnaw **2 :** to eat away at, to torment

rogar {16} *vt* **:** to beg, to request — *vi* **1 :** to beg, to plead **2 :** to pray

rojez *nf* **:** redness

roiga, etc. → **roer**

rojizo, -za *adj* : reddish

rojo[1], -ja *adj* **1** : red **2 ponerse rojo** : to blush

rojo[2] *nm* : red

rol *nm* **1** : role **2** : list, roll

rollo *nm* **1** : roll, coil <un rollo de cinta : a roll of tape> <en rollo : rolled up> **2** *fam* : roll of fat **3** *fam* : boring speech, lecture

romance *nm* **1** : Romance language **2** : ballad **3** : romance **4 en buen romance** : simply stated, simply put

romano, -na *adj & n* : Roman

romanticismo *nm* : romanticism

romántico, -ca *adj* : romantic — **románticamente** *adv*

rombo *nm* : rhombus

romería *nf* **1** : pilgrimage, procession **2** : crowd, gathering

romero[1], -ra *n* PEREGRINO : pilgrim

romero[2] *nm* : rosemary

romo, -ma *adj* : blunt, dull

rompecabezas *nms & pl* : puzzle, riddle

rompehielos *nms & pl* : icebreaker (ship)

rompehuelgas *nmfs & pl* ESQUIROL : strikebreaker, scab

rompenueces *nms & pl* : nutcracker

rompeolas *ns & pl* : breakwater, jetty

romper {70} *vt* **1** : to break, to smash **2** : to rip, to tear **3** : to break off (relations), to break (a contract) **4** : to break through, to break down **5** GASTAR : to wear out — *vi* **1** : to break <al romper del día : at the break of day> **2 ~ a** : to begin to, to burst out with <romper a llorar : to burst into tears> **3 ~ con** : to break off with

rompope *nm CA, Mex* : drink similar to eggnog

ron *nm* : rum

roncar {72} *vi* **1** : to snore **2** : to roar

ronco, -ca *adj* **1** : hoarse **2** : husky (of the voice) — **roncamente** *adv*

ronda *nf* **1** : beat, patrol **2** : round (of drinks, of negotiations, of a game)

rondar *vt* **1** : to patrol **2** : to hang around <siempre está rondando la calle : he's always hanging around the street> **3** : to be approximately <debe rondar los cincuenta : he must be about 50> — *vi* **1** : to be on patrol **2** : to prowl around, to roam about

ronque, etc. → **roncar**

ronquera *nf* : hoarseness

ronquido *nm* **1** : snore **2** : roar

ronronear *vi* : to purr

ronroneo *nm* : purr, purring

ronzal *nm* : halter (for an animal)

ronzar {21} *v* : to munch, to crunch

roña *nf* **1** : mange **2** : dirt, filth **3** *fam* : stinginess

roñoso, -sa *adj* **1** : mangy **2** : dirty **3** *fam* : stingy

ropa *nf* **1** : clothes *pl,* clothing **2 ropa interior** : underwear

ropaje *nm* : apparel, garments *pl,* regalia

ropero *nm* ARMARIO, CLÓSET : wardrobe, closet

rosa[1] *adj* : rose-colored, pink

rosa[2] *nm* : rose, pink (color)

rosa[3] *nf* : rose (flower)

rosáceo, -cea *adj* : pinkish

rosado[1], -da *adj* **1** : pink **2 vino rosado** : rosé

rosado[2] *nm* : pink (color)

rosal *nm* : rosebush

rosario *nm* **1** : rosary **2** : series <un rosario de islas : a string of islands>

rosbif *nm* : roast beef

rosca *nf* **1** : thread (of a screw) <una tapa a rosca : a screw top> **2** : ring, coil

roseta *nf* : rosette

rosquilla *nf* : ring-shaped pastry, doughnut

rostro *nm* : face, countenance

rotación *nf, pl* **-ciones** : rotation

rotar *vt* : to rotate, to turn — *vi* : to turn, to spin

rotativo[1], -va *adj* : rotary

rotativo[2] *nm* : newspaper

rotatorio, -ria → **rotativo[1]**

roto[1] *pp* → **romper**

roto[2], -ta *adj* **1** : broken **2** : ripped, torn

rotonda *nf* **1** : traffic circle, rotary **2** : rotunda

rotor *nm* : rotor

rótula *nf* : kneecap

rotular *vt* **1** : to head, to entitle **2** : to label

rótulo *nm* **1** : heading, title **2** : label, sign

rotundo, -da *adj* **1** REDONDO : round **2** : categorical, absolute <un éxito rotundo : a resounding success> — **rotundamente** *adv*

rotura *nf* : break, tear, fracture

roya *nf* : plant rust

roya, etc. → **roer**

rozado, -da *adj* GASTADO : worn

rozadura *nf* **1** : scratch, abrasion **2** : rubbed spot, sore

rozar {21} *vt* **1** : to chafe, to rub against **2** : to border on, to touch on **3** : to graze, to touch lightly — **rozarse** *vr* **~ con** *fam* : to rub shoulders with

ruandés, -desa *adj & n* : Rwandan

ruano, -na *adj* : roan

rubí *nm, pl* **rubíes** : ruby

rubio, -bia *adj & n* : blond

rublo *nm* : ruble

rubor *nm* **1** : flush, blush **2** : rouge, blusher

ruborizarse {21} *vr* : to blush

rubrica *nf* : title, heading

rubricar {72} *vt* **1** : sign with a flourish <firmado y rubricado : signed and sealed> **2** : to endorse, to sanction

rubro *nm* **1** : heading, title **2** : line, area (in business)

rudeza *nf* ASPEREZA : roughness, coarseness

rudimentario, -ria *adj* **:** rudimentary — **rudimentariamente** *adv*
rudimento *nm* **:** rudiment, basics *pl*
rudo, -da *adj* **1 :** rough, harsh **2 :** coarse, unpolished — **rudamente** *adv*
rueda[1], etc. → **rodar**
rueda[2] *nf* **1 :** wheel **2** RODAJA **:** round slice **3 :** circle, ring **4 rueda de andar :** treadmill **5 rueda de prensa :** press conference **6 ir sobre ruedas :** to go smoothly
ruedita *nf* **:** caster (on furniture)
ruedo *nm* **1 :** bullring, arena **2 :** rotation, turn **3 :** hem
ruega, ruegue, etc. → **rogar**
ruego *nm* **:** request, appeal, plea
rugido *nm* **:** roar
rugir {35} *vi* **:** to roar
ruibarbo *nm* **:** rhubarb
ruido *nm* **:** noise, sound
ruidoso, -sa *adj* **:** loud, noisy — **ruidosamente** *adv*
ruin *adj* **1 :** base, despicable **2 :** mean, stingy
ruina *nf* **1 :** ruin, destruction **2 :** downfall, collapse **3 ruinas** *nfpl* **:** ruins, remains
ruinoso, -sa *adj* **1 :** run-down, dilapidated **2 :** ruinous, disasterous
ruiseñor *nm* **:** nightingale
ruja, etc. → **rugir**
ruleta *nf* **:** roulette
rulo *nm* **:** curler, roller
rumano, -na *n* **:** Romanian, Rumanian
rumbo *nm* **1 :** direction, course <con rumbo a : bound for, heading for> <perder el rumbo : to go off course, to lose one's bearings> <sin rumbo : aimless, aimlessly> **2 :** ostentation, pomp **3 :** lavishness, generosity
rumiante *adj & nm* **:** ruminant
rumiar *vt* **:** to ponder, to mull over — *vi* **1 :** to chew the cud **2 :** to ruminate, to ponder
rumor *nm* **1 :** rumor **2 :** murmur
rumorearse *or* **rumorarse** *vr* **:** to be rumored <se rumorea que se va : rumor has it that she's leaving>
rumoroso, -sa *adj* **:** murmuring, babbling <un arroyo rumoroso : a babbling brook>
rupia *nf* **:** rupee
ruptura *nf* **1 :** break **2 :** breaking, breach (of a contract) **3 :** breaking off, breakup
rural *adj* **:** rural
ruso[1], -sa *adj & n* **:** Russian
ruso[2] *nm* **:** Russian (language)
rústico[1], -ca *adj* **:** rural, rustic
rústico[2], -ca *n* **:** rustic, country dweller
ruta *nf* **:** route
rutina *nf* **:** routine, habit
rutinario, -ria *adj* **:** routine, ordinary <visita rutinaria : routine visit> — **rutinariamente** *adv*

S

s *nf* **:** twentieth letter of the Spanish alphabet
sábado *nm* **1 :** Saturday **2 :** Sabbath
sábalo *nm* **:** shad
sabana *nf* **:** savanna
sábana *nf* **:** sheet, bedsheet
sabandija *nf* BICHO **:** bug, small reptile, pesky creature
sabático, -ca *adj* **:** sabbatical
sabedor, -dora *adj* **:** aware, informed
sabelotodo *nmf fam* **:** know-it-all
saber[1] {71} *vt* **1 :** to know **2 :** to know how to, to be able to <sabe tocar el violín : she can play the violin> **3 :** to learn, to find out **4 a ~ :** to wit, namely — *vi* **1 :** to know, to suppose **2 :** to be informed <supimos del desastre : we heard about the disaster> **3 :** to taste <esto no sabe bien : this doesn't taste right> **4 ~ a :** to taste like <sabe a naranja : it tastes like orange> — **saberse** *vr* **:** to know <ese chiste no me lo sé : I don't know that joke>
saber[2] *nm* **:** knowledge, learning
sabiamente *adv* **:** wisely
sabido, -da *adj* **:** well-known
sabiduría *nf* **1 :** wisdom **2 :** learning, knowledge
sabiendas *adv* **1 a ~ :** knowingly **2 a sabiendas de que :** knowing full well that
sabio[1], -bia *adj* **1** PRUDENTE **:** wise, sensible **2** DOCTO **:** learned
sabio[2], -bia *n* **1 :** wise person **2 :** savant, learned person
sable *nm* **:** saber, cutlass
sablear *vt fam* **:** to scrounge, to cadge
sabor *nm* **1 :** flavor, taste **2 sin ~ :** flavorless
saborear *vt* **1 :** to taste, to savor **2 :** to enjoy, to relish
sabotaje *nm* **:** sabotage
saboteador, -dora *n* **:** saboteur
sabotear *vt* **:** to sabotage
sabrá, etc. → **saber**
sabroso, -sa *adj* **1** RICO **:** delicious, tasty **2** AGRADABLE **:** pleasant, nice, lovely
sabueso *nm* **1 :** bloodhound **2** *fam* **:** detective, sleuth
sacacorchos *nms & pl* **:** corkscrew
sacapuntas *nms & pl* **:** pencil sharpener
sacar {72} *vt* **1 :** to pull out, to take out <saca el pollo del congelador : take the chicken out of the freezer> **2 :** to get, to obtain <saqué un 100 en el examen : I got 100 on the exam> **3 :** to get out, to extract <le saqué la infor-

mación : I got the information from him> **4 :** to stick out <sacar la lengua : to stick out one's tongue> **5 :** to bring out, to introduce <sacar un libro : to publish a book> <sacaron una moda nueva : they introduced a new style> **6 :** to take (photos) **7 :** to make (copies) — *vi* **1 :** to kick off (in soccer or football) **2 :** to serve (in sports)
sacarina *nf* **:** saccharin
sacarosa *nf* **:** sucrose
sacerdocio *nm* **:** priesthood
sacerdotal *adj* **:** priestly
sacerdote, -tisa *n* **:** priest *m,* priestess *f*
saciar *vt* **1** HARTAR **:** to sate, to satiate **2** SATISFACER **:** to satisfy
saciedad *nf* **:** satiety
saco *nm* **1 :** bag, sack **2 :** sac **3 :** jacket, sport coat
sacramento *nm* **:** sacrament — **sacramental** *adj*
sacrificar {72} *vt* **:** to sacrifice — **sacrificarse** *vr* **:** to sacrifice oneself, to make sacrifices
sacrificio *nm* **:** sacrifice
sacrilegio *nm* **:** sacrilege
sacrílego, -ga *adj* **:** sacrilegious
sacristán *nm, pl* **-tanes :** sexton, sacristan
sacristía *nf* **:** sacristy, vestry
sacro, -cra *adj* SAGRADO **:** sacred <arte sacro : sacred art>
sacrosanto, -ta *adj* **:** sacrosanct
sacudida *nf* **1 :** shaking **2 :** jerk, jolt, shock **3 :** shake-up, upheaval
sacudir *vt* **1 :** to shake, to beat **2 :** to jerk, to jolt **3 :** to dust off **4** CONMOVER **:** to shake up, to shock — **sacudirse** *vr* **:** to shake off
sacudón *nm, pl* **-dones :** intense jolt or shake-up
sádico[1], -ca *adj* **:** sadistic
sádico[2], -ca *n* **:** sadist
sadismo *nm* **:** sadism
safari *nm* **:** safari
saga *nf* **:** saga
sagacidad *nf* **:** sagacity, shrewdness
sagaz *adj, pl* **sagaces** PERSPICAZ **:** shrewd, discerning, sagacious
Sagitario *nmf* **:** Sagittarius, Sagittarian
sagrado, -da *adj* **:** sacred, holy
sainete *nm* **:** comedy sketch, one-act farce <este proceso es un sainete : these proceedings are a farce>
sajar *vt* **:** to lance, to cut open
sal[1] → **salir**
sal[2] *nf* **1 :** salt **2** *CA, Mex* **:** misfortune, bad luck
sala *nf* **1 :** living room **2 :** room, hall <sala de conferencias : lecture hall> <sala de urgencias : emergency room> <sala de baile : ballroom>
salado, -da *adj* **1 :** salty **2 agua salada :** salt water
salamandra *nf* **:** salamander
salami *nm* **:** salami
salar *vt* **1 :** to salt **2 :** to spoil, to ruin **3** *CoRi, Mex* **:** to jinx, to bring bad luck
salarial *adj* **:** salary, salary-related
salario *nm* **1 :** salary **2 salario mínimo :** minimum wage
salaz *adj, pl* **salaces :** salacious, lecherous
salchicha *nf* **1 :** sausage **2 :** frankfurter, wiener
salchichón *nf, pl* **-chones :** a type of deli meat
salchichonería *nf Mex* **1 :** delicatessen **2 :** cold cuts *pl*
saldar *vt* **:** to settle, to pay off <saldar una cuenta : to settle an account>
saldo *nm* **1 :** settlement, payment **2 :** balance <saldo de cuenta : account balance> **3 :** remainder, leftover merchandise
saldrá, etc. → **salir**
salero *nm* **1 :** saltshaker **2 :** wit, charm
salga, etc. → **salir**
salida *nf* **1 :** exit <salida de emergencia : emergency exit> **2 :** leaving, departure **3** SOLUCIÓN **:** way out, solution **4 :** start (of a race) **5** OCURRENCIA **:** wisecrack, joke **6 salida del sol :** sunrise
saliente[1] *adj* **1 :** departing, outgoing **2 :** projecting **3** DESTACADO **:** salient, prominent
saliente[2] *nm* **1 :** projection, protrusion **2 ventana en saliente :** bay window
salinidad *nf* **:** salinity, saltiness
salino, -na *adj* **:** saline <solución salina : saline solution>
salir {73} *vi* **1 :** to go out, to come out, to get out <salimos todas las noches : we go out every night> <su libro acaba de salir : her book just came out> **2** PARTIR **:** to leave, to depart **3** APARECER **:** to appear <salió en todos los diarios : it came out in all the papers> **4 :** to project, to stick out **5 :** to cost, to come to **6** RESULTAR **:** to turn out, to prove **7 :** to come up, to occur <salga lo que salga : whatever happens> <salió una oportunidad : an opportunity came up> **8 ~ a :** to take after, to look like, to resemble **9 ~ con :** to go out with, to date — **salirse** *vr* **1 :** to escape, to get out, to leak out **2 :** to come loose, to come off **3 salirse con la suya :** to get one's own way
saliva *nf* **:** saliva
salivar *vi* **:** to salivate
salmo *nm* **:** psalm
salmón[1] *adj* **:** salmon-colored
salmón[2] *nm, pl* **salmones :** salmon
salmuera *nf* **:** brine
salobre *adj* **:** brackish, briny
salón *nm, pl* **salones 1 :** hall, large room <salón de clase : classroom> <salón de baile : ballroom> **2 :** salon <salón de belleza : beauty salon> **3 :** parlor, sitting room
salpicadera *nf Mex* **:** fender
salpicadura *nf* **:** spatter, splash

salpicar {72} *vt* **1 :** to spatter, to splash **2 :** to sprinkle, to scatter about

salpimentar {55} *vt* **1 :** to season (with salt and pepper) **2 :** to spice up

salsa *nf* **1 :** sauce <salsa picante : hot sauce> <salsa inglesa : Worcestershire sauce> <salsa tártara : tartar sauce> **2 :** gravy **3 :** salsa (music) **4 salsa mexicana :** salsa (sauce)

salsero, -ra *n* **:** salsa musician

saltador, -dora *n* **:** jumper

saltamontes *nms & pl* **:** grasshopper

saltar *vi* **1** BRINCAR **:** to jump, to leap **2 :** to bounce **3 :** to come off, to pop out **4 :** to shatter, to break **5 :** to explode, to blow up — *vt* **1 :** to jump, to jump over **2 :** to skip, to miss — **saltarse** *vr* OMITIR **:** to skip, to omit <me salté ese capítulo : I skipped that chapter>

saltarín, -rina *adj, mpl* **-rines :** leaping, hopping <frijol saltarín : jumping bean>

salteado, -da *adj* **1 :** sautéed **2 :** jumbled up <los episodios se transmitieron salteados : the episodes were broadcast in random order>

salteador *nm* **:** highwayman

saltear *vt* **1** SOFREÍR **:** to sauté **2 :** to skip around, to skip over

saltimbanqui *nmf* **:** acrobat

salto *nm* **1** BRINCO **:** jump, leap, skip **2 :** jump, dive (in sports) **3 :** gap, omission **4 dar saltos :** to jump up and down **5** *or* **salto de agua** CATARATA **:** waterfall

saltón, -tona *adj, mpl* **saltones :** bulging, protruding

salubre *adj* **:** healthful, salubrious

salubridad *nf* **:** healthfulness, health

salud *nf* **1 :** health <buena salud : good health> **2 ¡salud! :** bless you! (when someone sneezes) **3 ¡salud! :** cheers!, to your health!

saludable *adj* **1** SALUBRE **:** healthful **2** SANO **:** healthy, well

saludar *vt* **1 :** to greet, to say hello to **2 :** to salute — **saludarse** *vr*

saludo *nm* **1 :** greeting, regards *pl* **2 :** salute

salutación *nf, pl* **-ciones :** salutation

salva *nf* **1 :** salvo, volley **2 salva de aplausos :** round of applause

salvación *nf, pl* **-ciones 1 :** salvation **2** RESCATE **:** rescue

salvado *nm* **:** bran

salvador, -dora *n* **1 :** savior, rescuer **2 el Salvador :** the Savior

salvadoreño, -ña *adj & n* **:** Salvadoran, El Salvadoran

salvaguardar *vt* **:** to safeguard

salvaguardia *or* **salvaguarda** *nf* **:** safeguard, defense

salvajada *nf* ATROCIDAD **:** atrocity, act of savagery

salvaje¹ *adj* **1 :** wild <animales salvajes : wild animals> **2 :** savage, cruel **3 :** primitive, uncivilized

salvaje² *nmf* **:** savage

salvajismo *nm* **:** savagery

salvamento *nm* **1 :** rescuing, lifesaving **2 :** salvation **3 :** refuge

salvar *vt* **1 :** to save, to rescue **2 :** to cover (a distance) **3 :** to get around (an obstacle), to overcome (a difficulty) **4 :** to cross, to jump across **5 salvando :** except for, excluding — **salvarse** *vr* **1 :** to survive, to escape **2 :** to save one's soul

salvavidas¹ *nms & pl* **1 :** life preserver **2 bote salvavidas :** lifeboat

salvavidas² *nmf* **:** lifeguard

salvedad *nf* **1** EXCEPCIÓN **:** exception **2 :** proviso, stipulation

salvia *nf* **:** sage (plant)

salvo¹, -va *adj* **1 :** unharmed, sound <sano y salvo : safe and sound> **2 a ~ :** safe from danger

salvo² *prep* **1** EXCEPTO **:** except (for), save <todos asistirán salvo Jaime : all will attend except for Jaime> **2 salvo que :** unless <salvo que llueva : unless it rains>

salvoconducto *nm* **:** safe-conduct

samba *nf* **:** samba

San → **santo¹**

sanar *vt* **:** to heal, to cure — *vi* **:** to get well, to recover

sanatorio *nm* **1 :** sanatorium **2 :** clinic, private hospital

sanción *nf, pl* **sanciones :** sanction

sancionar *vt* **1 :** to penalize, to impose a sanction on **2 :** to sanction, to approve

sancochar *vt* **:** to parboil

sandalia *nf* **:** sandal

sándalo *nm* **:** sandalwood

sandez *nf, pl* **sandeces** ESTUPIDEZ **:** nonsense, silly thing to say

sandía *nf* **:** watermelon

sandwich [ˈsandwitʃ, ˈsaŋgwitʃ] *nm, pl* **sandwiches** [-dwitʃɛs, -gwi-] EMPAREDADO **:** sandwich

saneamiento *nm* **1 :** cleaning up, sanitation **2 :** reorganizing, streamlining

sanear *vt* **1 :** to clean up, to sanitize **2 :** to reorganize, to streamline

sangrante *adj* **1 :** bleeding **2 :** flagrant, blatant

sangrar *vi* **:** to bleed — *vt* **:** to indent (a paragraph, etc.)

sangre *nf* **1 :** blood **2 a sangre fría :** in cold blood **3 a sangre y fuego :** by violent force **4 pura sangre :** thoroughbred

sangría *nf* **1 :** bloodletting **2 :** sangria (wine punch) **3 :** drain, draining <una sangría fiscal : a financial drain> **4 :** indentation, indenting

sangriento, -ta *adj* **1 :** bloody **2 :** cruel

sanguijuela *nf* **1 :** leech, bloodsucker **2 :** sponger, leech

sanguinario, -ria *adj* **:** bloodthirsty

sanguíneo, -nea *adj* **1 :** blood <vaso sanguíneo : blood vessel> **2 :** sanguine, ruddy

sanidad *nf* **1 :** health **2 :** public health, sanitation

sanitario[1], **-ria** *adj* **1** : sanitary **2** : health <centro sanitario : health center>
sanitario[2], **-ria** *n* : sanitation worker
sanitario[3] *nm Col, Mex, Ven* : toilet <los sanitarios : the toilets, the restroom>
sano, -na *adj* **1** SALUDABLE : healthy **2** : wholesome **3** : whole, intact
santiaguino, -na *adj* : of or from Santiago, Chile
santiamén *nm* **en un santiamén** : in no time at all
santidad *nf* : holiness, sanctity
santificar {72} *vt* : to sanctify, to consecrate, to hallow
santiguarse {10} *vr* PERSIGNARSE : to cross oneself
santo[1], **-ta** *adj* **1** : holy, saintly <el Santo Padre : the Holy Father> <una vida santa : a saintly life> **2 Santo, Santa** (**San** *before names of masculine saints except those beginning with D or T*) : Saint <Santa Clara : Saint Claire> <Santo Tomás : Saint Thomas> <San Francisco : Saint Francis>
santo[2], **-ta** *n* : saint
santo[3] *nm* **1** : saint's day **2** CUMPLEAÑOS : birthday
santuario *nm* : sanctuary
santurrón, -rrona *adj, mpl* **-rrones** : overly pious, sanctimonious — **santurronamente** *adv*
saña *nf* **1** : fury, rage **2** : viciousness <con saña : viciously>
sapo *nm* : toad
saque[1], **etc.** → **sacar**
saque[2] *nm* **1** : kick-off (in soccer or football) **2** : serve, service (in sports)
saqueador, -dora *n* DEPREDADOR : plunderer, looter
saquear *vt* : to sack, to plunder, to loot
saqueo *nm* DEPREDACIÓN : sacking, plunder, looting
sarampión *nm* : measles *pl*
sarape *nm CA, Mex* : serape, blanket
sarcasmo *nm* : sarcasm
sarcástico, -ca *adj* : sarcastic
sarcófago *nm* : sarcophagus
sardina *nf* : sardine
sardónico, -ca *adj* : sardonic
sarga *nf* : serge
sargento *nmf* : sergeant
sarna *nf* : mange
sarnoso, -sa *adj* : mangy
sarpullido *nm* ERUPCIÓN : rash
sarro *nm* **1** : deposit, coating **2** : tartar, plaque
sartén *nmf, pl* **sartenes 1** : frying pan **2 tener la sartén por el mango** : to call the shots, to be in control
sasafrás *nm* : sassafras
sastre, -tra *n* : tailor
sastrería *nf* **1** : tailoring **2** : tailor's shop
Satanás *or* **Satán** *nm* : Satan, the devil
satánico, -ca *adj* : satanic
satélite *nm* : satellite
satín *or* **satén** *nm, pl* **satines** *or* **satenes** : satin
satinado, -da *adj* : satiny, glossy
sátira *nf* : satire
satírico, -ca *adj* : satirical, satiric
satirizar {21} *vt* : to satirize
sátiro *nm* : satyr
satisfacción *nf, pl* **-ciones** : satisfaction
satisfacer {74} *vt* **1** : to satisfy **2** : to fulfill, to meet **3** : to pay, to settle — **satisfacerse** *vr* **1** : to be satisfied **2** : to take revenge
satisfactorio, -ria *adj* : satisfactory — **satisfactoriamente** *adv*
satisfecho, -cha *adj* : satisfied, content, pleased
saturación *nf, pl* **-ciones** : saturation
saturar *vt* **1** : to saturate, to fill up **2** : to satiate, to surfeit
saturnismo *nm* : lead poisoning
Saturno *nm* : Saturn
sauce *nm* : willow
saúco *nm* : elder (tree)
saudí *or* **saudita** *adj & nmf* : Saudi, Saudi Arabian
sauna *nmf* : sauna
savia *nf* : sap
saxofón *nm, pl* **-fones** : saxophone
sazón[1] *nf, pl* **sazones 1** : flavor, seasoning **2** : ripeness, maturity <en sazón : in season, ripe> **3 a la sazón** : at that time, then
sazón[2] *nmf, pl* **sazones** *Mex* : flavor, seasoning
sazonar *vt* CONDIMENTAR : to season, to spice
sé → **saber, ser**
se *pron* **1** : to him, to her, to you, to them <se los daré a ella : I'll give them to her> **2** : each other, one another <se abrazaron : they hugged each other> **3** : himself, herself, itself, yourself, yourselves, themselves <se afeitó antes de salir : he shaved before leaving> **4** (*used in passive constructions*) <se dice que es hermosa : they say she's beautiful> <se habla inglés : English spoken>
sea, etc. → **ser**
sebo *nm* **1** : grease, fat **2** : tallow **3** : suet
secado *nm* : drying
secador *nm* : hair dryer
secadora *nf* **1** : dryer, clothes dryer **2** *Mex* : hair dryer
secante *nm* : blotting paper, blotter
secar {72} *v* : to dry — **secarse** *vr* **1** : to get dry **2** : to dry up
sección *nf, pl* **secciones 1** : section <sección transversal : cross section> **2** : department, division
seco, -ca *adj* **1** : dry **2** DISECADO : dried <fruta seca : dried fruit> **3** : thin, lean **4** : curt, brusque **5** : sharp <un golpe seco : a sharp blow> **6 a secas** : simply, just <se llama Chico, a secas : he's just called Chico> **7 en ~**

: abruptly, suddenly <frenar en seco : to make a sudden stop>
secoya *nf* : sequoia, redwood
secreción *nf, pl* **-ciones** : secretion
secretar *vt* : to secrete
secretaría *nf* **1** : secretariat, administrative department **2** *Mex* : ministry, cabinet office
secretariado *nm* **1** : secretariat **2** : secretarial profession
secretario, -ria *n* : secretary — **secretarial** *adj*
secreto¹, -ta *adj* **1** : secret **2** : secretive — **secretamente** *adv*
secreto² *nm* **1** : secret **2** : secrecy
secta *nf* : sect
sectario, -ria *adj & n* : sectarian
sector *nm* : sector
secuaz *nmf, pl* **secuaces** : follower, henchman, underling
secuela *nf* : consequence, sequel <las secuelas de la guerra : the aftermath of the war>
secuencia *nf* : sequence
secuestrador, -dora *n* **1** : kidnapper, abductor **2** : hijacker
secuestrar *vt* **1** RAPTAR : to kidnap, to abduct **2** : to hijack, to commandeer **3** CONFISCAR : to confiscate, to seize
secuestro *nm* **1** RAPTO : kidnapping, abduction **2** : hijacking **3** : seizure, confiscation
secular *adj* : secular — **secularismo** *nm* — **secularización** *nf*
secundar *vt* : to support, to second
secundaria *nf* **1** : secondary education, high school **2** *Mex* : junior high school, middle school
secundario, -ria *adj* : secondary
secuoya *nf* : sequoia
sed *nf* **1** : thirst <tener sed : to be thirsty> **2 tener sed de** : to hunger for, to thirst for
seda *nf* : silk
sedación *nf, pl* **-ciones** : sedation
sedal *nm* : fishing line
sedán *nm, pl* **sedanes** : sedan
sedante *adj & nm* CALMANTE : sedative
sedar *vt* : to sedate
sede *nf* **1** : seat, headquarters **2** : venue, site **3 la Santa Sede** : the Holy See
sedentario, -ria *adj* : sedentary
sedición *nf, pl* **-ciones** : sedition — **sedicioso, -sa** *adj*
sediento, -ta *adj* : thirsty, thirsting
sedimentación *nf, pl* **-ciones** : sedimentation
sedimentario, -ria *adj* : sedimentary
sedimento *nm* : sediment
sedoso, -sa *adj* : silky, silken
seducción *nf, pl* **-ciones** : seduction
seducir {61} *vt* **1** : to seduce **2** : to captivate, to charm
seductivo, -va *adj* : seductive
seductor¹, -tora *adj* **1** SEDUCTIVO : seductive **2** ENCANTADOR : charming, alluring
seductor², -tora *n* : seducer
segar {49} *vt* **1** : to reap, to harvest, to cut **2** : to sever abruptly <una vida segada por la enfermedad : a life cut short by illness>
seglar¹ *adj* LAICO : lay, secular
seglar² *nm* LAICO : layperson, layman *m,* laywoman *f*
segmentación *nm, pl* **-ciones** : segmentation
segmentado, -da *adj* : segmented
segmento *nm* : segment
segregar {52} *vt* **1** : to segregate **2** SECRETAR : to secrete
seguida *nf* **en ~** : right away, immediately <vuelvo en seguida : I'll be right back>
seguidamente *adv* **1** : next, immediately after **2** : without a break, continuously
seguido¹ *adv* **1** RECTO : straight, straight ahead **2** : often, frequently
seguido², -da *adj* **1** CONSECUTIVO : consecutive, successive <tres días seguidos : three days in a row> **2** : straight, unbroken **3 ~ por** *or* **~ de** : followed by
seguidor, -dora *n* : follower, supporter
seguimiento *nm* **1** : following, pursuit **2** : continuation **3** : tracking, monitoring
seguir {75} *vt* **1** : to follow <el sol sigue la lluvia : sunshine follows the rain> <seguiré tu consejo : I'll follow your advice> <me siguieron con la mirada : they followed me with their eyes> **2** : to go along, to keep on <seguimos toda la carretera panamericana : we continued along the Pan-American Highway> <siguió hablando : he kept on talking> <seguir el curso : to stay on course> **3** : to take (a course, a treatment) — *vi* **1** : to go on, to keep going <sigue adelante : keep going, carry on> **2** : to remain, to continue to be <¿todavía sigues aquí? : you're still here?> <sigue con vida : she's still alive> **3** : to follow, to come after <la frase que sigue : the following sentence>
según¹ *adv* : it depends <según y como : it all depends on>
según² *conj* **1** COMO, CONFORME : as, just as <según lo dejé : just as I left it> **2** : depending on how <según se vea : depending on how one sees it>
según³ *prep* **1** : according to <según los rumores : according to the rumors> **2** : depending on <según los resultados : depending on the results>
segundo¹, -da *adj* : second <el segundo lugar : second place>
segundo², -da *n* **1** : second (in a series) **2** : second (person), second-in-command
segundo³ *nm* : second <sesenta segundos : sixty seconds>
seguramente *adv* **1** : for sure, surely **2** : probably

seguridad *nf* **1** : safety, security **2** : (financial) security <seguridad social : Social Security> **3** CERTEZA : certainty, assurance <con toda seguridad : with complete certainty> **4** : confidence, self-confidence
seguro[1] *adv* : certainly, definitely <va a llover, seguro : it's going to rain for sure> <¡seguro que sí! : of course!>
seguro[2], **-ra** *adj* **1** : safe, secure **2** : sure, certain <estoy segura que es él : I'm sure that's him> **3** : reliable, trustworthy **4** : self-assured
seguro[3] *nm* **1** : insurance <seguro de vida : life insurance> **2** : fastener, clasp **3** *Mex* : safety pin
seis *adj & nm* : six
seiscientos[1], **-tas** *adj* : six hundred
seiscientos[2] *nms & pl* : six hundred
selección *nf, pl* **-ciones 1** ELECCIÓN : selection, choice **2 selección natural** : natural selection
seleccionar *vt* ELEGIR : to select, to choose
selectivo, -va *adj* : selective — **selectivamente** *adv*
selecto, -ta *adj* **1** : choice, select **2** EXCLUSIVO : exclusive
selenio *nm* : selenium
sellar *vt* **1** : to seal **2** : to stamp
sello *nm* **1** : seal **2** ESTAMPILLA, TIMBRE : postage stamp **3** : hallmark, characteristic
selva *nf* **1** BOSQUE : woods *pl,* forest <selva húmeda : rain forest> **2** JUNGLA : jungle
selvático, -ca *adj* **1** : forest, jungle <sendero selvático : jungle path> **2** : wild
semáforo *nm* **1** : traffic light **2** : stop signal
semana *nf* : week
semanal *adj* : weekly — **semanalmente** *adv*
semanario *nm* : weekly (publication)
semántica *nf* : semantics
semántico, -ca *adj* : semantic
semblante *nm* **1** : countenance, face **2** : appearance, look
semblanza *nf* : biographical sketch, profile
sembrado *nm* : cultivated field
sembrador, -dora *n* : planter, sower
sembradora *nf* : seeder (machine)
sembrar {55} *vt* **1** : to plant, to sow **2** : to scatter, to strew <sembrar el pánico : to spread panic>
semejante[1] *adj* **1** PARECIDO : similar, alike **2** TAL : such <nunca he visto cosa semejante : I have never seen such a thing>
semejante[2] *nm* PRÓJIMO : fellowman
semejanza *nf* PARECIDO : similarity, resemblance
semejar *vi* : to resemble, to look like — **semejarse** *vr* : to be similar, to look alike
semen *nm* : semen
semental *nm* : stud (animal) <caballo semental : stallion>
semestre *nm* : semester
semicírculo *nm* : semicircle, half circle
semiconductor *nm* : semiconductor
semidiós *nm, pl* **-dioses** : demigod *m*
semifinal *nf* : semifinal
semifinalista[1] *adj* : semifinal
semifinalista[2] *nmf* : semifinalist
semiformal *adj* : semiformal
semilla *nf* : seed
semillero *nm* **1** : seedbed **2** : hotbed, breeding ground
seminario *nm* **1** : seminary **2** : seminar, graduate course
seminarista *nm* : seminarian
semiprecioso, -sa *adj* : semiprecious
semita[1] *adj* : Semitic
semita[2] *nmf* : Semite
sémola *nf* : semolina
sempiterno, -na *adj* ETERNO : eternal, everlasting
senado *nm* : senate
senador, -dora *n* : senator
sencillamente *adv* : simply, plainly
sencillez *nf* : simplicity
sencillo[1], **-lla** *adj* **1** : simple, easy **2** : plain, unaffected **3** : single
sencillo[2] *nm* **1** : single (recording) **2** : small change (coins) **3** : one-way ticket
senda *nf* CAMINO, SENDERO : path, way
sendero *nm* CAMINO, SENDA : path, way
sendos, -das *adj pl* : each, both <llevaban sendos vestidos nuevos : they were each wearing a new dress>
senectud *nf* ANCIANIDAD : old age
senegalés, -lesa *adj & n, mpl* **-leses** : Senegalese
senil *adj* : senile — **senilidad** *nf*
seno *nm* **1** : breast, bosom <los senos : the breasts> <el seno de la familia : the bosom of the family> **2** : sinus **3 seno materno** : womb
sensación *nf, pl* **-ciones 1** IMPRESIÓN : feeling <tener la sensación : to have a feeling> **2** : sensation <causar sensación : to cause a sensation>
sensacional *adj* : sensational
sensacionalista *adj* : sensationalistic, lurid
sensatez *nf* **1** : good sense **2 con ~** : sensibly
sensato, -ta *n* : sensible, sound — **sensatamente** *adv*
sensibilidad *nf* **1** : sensitivity, sensibility **2** SENSACIÓN : feeling
sensibilizar {21} *vt* : to sensitize
sensible *adj* **1** : sensitive **2** APRECIABLE : considerable, significant
sensiblemente *adv* : considerably, significantly
sensiblería *nf* : sentimentality, mush
sensiblero, -ra *adj* : mawkish, sentimental, mushy
sensitivo, -va *adj* **1** : sense <órganos sensitivos : sense organs> **2** : sentient, capable of feeling
sensor *nm* : sensor

sensorial *adj* **:** sensory
sensual *adj* **:** sensual, sensuous — **sensualmente** *adv*
sensualidad *nf* **:** sensuality
sentado, -da *adj* **1 :** sitting, seated **2 :** established, settled <dar por sentado : to take for granted> <dejar sentado : to make clear> **3 :** sensible, steady, judicious
sentar {55} *vt* **1 :** to seat, to sit **2 :** to establish, to set — *vi* **1 :** to suit <ese color te sienta : that color suits you> **2 :** to agree with (of food or drink) <las cebollas no me sientan : onions don't agree with me> **3 :** to please <le sentó mal el paseo : she didn't enjoy the trip> — **sentarse** *vr* **:** to sit, to sit down <siéntese, por favor : please have a seat>
sentencia *nf* **1 :** sentence, judgment **2 :** maxim, saying
sentenciar *vt* **:** to sentence
sentido¹, -da *adj* **1 :** heartfelt, sincere <mi más sentido pésame : my sincerest condolences> **2 :** touchy, sensitive **3 :** offended, hurt
sentido² *nm* **1 :** sense <sentido común : common sense> <los cinco sentidos : the five senses> <sin sentido : senseless> **2** CONOCIMIENTO **:** consciousness **3** SIGNIFICADO **:** meaning, sense <doble sentido : double entendre> **4 :** direction <calle de sentido único : one-way street>
sentimental¹ *adj* **1 :** sentimental **2 :** love, romantic <vida sentimental : love life>
sentimental² *nmf* **:** sentimentalist
sentimentalismo *nm* **:** sentimentality, sentimentalism
sentimiento *nm* **1 :** feeling, emotion **2** PESAR **:** regret, sorrow
sentir {76} *vt* **1 :** to feel, to experience <no siento nada de dolor : I don't feel any pain> <sentía sed : he was feeling thirsty> <sentir amor : to feel love> **2** PERCIBIR **:** to perceive, to sense <sentir un ruido : to hear a noise> **3** LAMENTAR **:** to regret, to feel sorry for <lo siento mucho : I'm very sorry> — *vi* **1 :** to have feeling, to feel **2 sin ~ :** without noticing, inadvertently — **sentirse** *vr* **1 :** to feel <¿te sientes mejor? : are you feeling better?> **2** *Chile, Mex* **:** to take offense
seña *nf* **1 :** sign, signal **2 dar señas de :** to show signs of
señal *nf* **1 :** signal **2 :** sign <señal de tráfico : traffic sign> **3** INDICIO **:** indication <en señal de : as a token of> **4** VESTIGIO **:** trace, vestige **5 :** scar, mark **6 :** deposit, down payment
señalado, -da *adj* **:** distinguished, notable
señalador *nm* **:** marker <señalador de libros : bookmark>
señalar *vt* **1** INDICAR **:** to indicate, to show **2 :** to mark **3 :** to point out, to stress **4 :** to fix, to set — **señalarse** *vr* **:** to distinguish oneself
señor, -ñora *n* **1 :** gentleman *m,* man *m,* lady *f,* woman *f,* wife *f* **2 :** Sir *m,* Madam *f* <estimados señores : Dear Sirs> **3 :** Mr. *m,* Mrs. *f* **4 :** lord *m,* lady *f* <el Señor : the Lord>
señoría *nf* **1 :** lordship **2 Su Señoría :** Your Honor
señorial *adj* **:** stately, regal
señorío *nm* **1 :** manor, estate **2 :** dominion, power **3 :** elegance, class
señorita *nf* **1 :** young lady, young woman **2 :** Miss
señuelo *nm* **1 :** decoy **2 :** bait
sépalo *nm* **:** sepal
sepa, etc. → **saber**
separación *nf, pl* **-ciones 1 :** separation, division **2 :** gap, space
separadamente *adv* **:** separately, apart
separado, -da *adj* **1 :** separated **2 :** separate <vidas separadas : separate lives> **3 por ~ :** separately
separar *vt* **1 :** to separate, to divide **2 :** to split up, to pull apart — **separarse** *vr*
sepelio *nm* **:** interment, burial
sepia¹ *adj & nm* **:** sepia
sepia² *nf* **:** cuttlefish
septentrional *adj* **:** northern
séptico, -ca *adj* **:** septic
septiembre *nm* **:** September
séptimo¹, -ma *adj* **:** seventh
séptimo² *nm* **:** seventh
septuagésimo¹, -ma *adj* **:** seventieth
septuagésimo² *nm* **:** seventieth
sepulcral *adj* **1 :** sepulcral **2 :** dismal, gloomy
sepulcro *nm* TUMBA **:** tomb, sepulchre
sepultar *vt* ENTERRAR **:** to bury
sepultura *nf* **1 :** burial **2** TUMBA **:** grave, tomb
seque, etc. → **secar**
sequedad *nf* **1 :** dryness **2 :** brusqueness, curtness
sequía *nf* **:** drought
séquito *nm* **:** retinue, entourage
ser¹ {77} *vi* **1 :** to be <él es mi hermano : he is my brother> <Camila es linda : Camila is pretty> **2 :** to exist, to live <ser, o no ser : to be or not to be> **3 :** to take place, to occur <el concierto es el domingo : the concert is on Sunday> **4** (*used with expressions of time, date, season*) <son las diez : it's ten o'clock> <hoy es el 9 : today's the 9th> **5 :** to cost, to come to <¿cuánto es? : how much is it?> **6** (*with the future tense*) **:** to be able to be <¿será posible? : can it be possible?> **7 ~ de :** to come from <somos de Managua : we're from Managua> **8 ~ de :** to belong to <ese lápiz es de Juan : that's Juan's pencil> **9 es que :** the thing is that <es que no lo conozco : it's just that I don't know him> **10 ¡sea! :** agreed!, all right! **11 sea . . . sea :** either . . . or — *v aux* (*used in passive constructions*) **:** to be <la cuenta

ha sido pagada : the bill has been paid> <él fue asesinado : he was murdered>

ser[2] *nm* : being <ser humano : human being>

seráfico, -ca *adj* : angelic, seraphic

serbio[1], **-bia** *adj & n* : Serb, Serbian

serbio[2] *nm* : Serbian (language)

serbocroata[1] *adj* : Serbo-Croatian

serbocroata[2] *nm* : Serbo-Croatian (language)

serenar *vt* : to calm, to soothe — **serenarse** *vr* CALMARSE : to calm down

serenata *nf* : serenade

serendipia *nf* : serendipity

serenidad *nf* : serenity, calmness

sereno[1], **-na** *adj* **1** SOSEGADO : serene, calm, composed **2** : fair, clear (of weather) **3** : calm, still (of the sea) — **serenamente** *adv*

sereno[2] *nm* : night watchman

seriado, -da *adj* : serial

serial *nm* : serial (on radio or television)

seriamente *adv* : seriously

serie *nf* **1** : series **2** SERIAL : serial **3** **fabricación en serie** : mass production **4** **fuera de serie** : extraordinary, amazing

seriedad *nf* **1** : seriousness, earnestness **2** : gravity, importance

serio, -ria *adj* **1** : serious, earnest **2** : reliable, responsible **3** : important **4** **en ~** : seriously, in earnest — **seriamente** *adv*

sermón *nm, pl* **sermones** **1** : sermon **2** *fam* : harangue, lecture

sermonear *vt fam* : to harangue, to lecture

serpentear *vi* : to twist, to wind — **serpenteante** *adj*

serpentina *nf* : paper streamer

serpiente *nf* : serpent, snake

serrado, -da *adj* DENTADO : serrated

serranía *nf* : mountainous area

serrano, -na *adj* : from the mountains

serrar {55} *vt* : to saw

serrín *nm, pl* **serrines** : sawdust

serruchar *vt* : to saw up

serrucho *nm* : saw, handsaw

servicentro *nm Peru* : gas station

servicial *adj* : obliging, helpful

servicio *nm* **1** : service **2** SAQUE : serve (in sports) **3** **servicios** *nmpl* : restroom

servidor, -dora *n* **1** : servant **2** **su seguro servidor** : yours truly (in correspondence)

servidumbre *nf* **1** : servitude **2** : help, servants *pl*

servil *adj* **1** : servile, subservient **2** : menial

servilismo *nm* : servility, subservience

servilleta *nf* : napkin

servir {54} *vt* **1** : to serve, to be of use to **2** : to serve, to wait **3** SURTIR : to fill (an order) — *vi* **1** : to work <mi radio no sirve : my radio isn't working> **2** : to be of use, to be helpful <esa computadora no sirve para nada : that computer's perfectly useless> — **servirse** *vr* **1** : to help oneself to **2** : to be kind enough <sírvase enviarnos un catálogo : please send us a catalog>

sésamo *nm* AJONJOLÍ : sesame, sesame seeds *pl*

sesenta *adj & nm* : sixty

sesentavo[1], **-va** *adj* : sixtieth

sesentavo[2] *n* : sixtieth (fraction)

sesgado, -da *adj* **1** : inclined, tilted **2** : slanted, biased

sesgar {52} *vt* **1** : to cut on the bias **2** : to tilt **3** : to bias, to slant

sesgo *nm* : bias

sesgue, etc. → **sesgar**

sesión *nf, pl* **sesiones** **1** : session **2** : showing, performance

sesionar *vi* REUNIRSE : to meet, to be in session

seso *nm* **1** : brains, intelligence **2** **sesos** *nmpl* : brains (as food)

sesudo, -da *adj* **1** : prudent, sensible **2** : brainy

set *nm, pl* **sets** : set (in tennis)

seta *nf* : mushroom

setecientos[1], **-tas** *adj* : seven hundred

setecientos[2] *nms & pl* : seven hundred

setenta *adj & nm* : seventy

setentavo[1], **-va** *adj* : seventieth

setentavo[2] *nm* : seventieth

setiembre *nm* → **septiembre**

seto *nm* **1** : fence, enclosure **2** **seto vivo** : hedge

seudónimo *nm* : pseudonym

severidad *nf* **1** : harshness, severity **2** : strictness

severo, -ra *adj* **1** : harsh, severe **2** ESTRICTO : strict — **severamente** *adv*

sexagésimo[1], **-ma** *adj* : sixtieth, sixty-

sexagésimo[2], **-ma** *n* : sixtieth, sixty- (in a series)

sexismo *nm* : sexism — **sexista** *adj & nmf*

sexo *nm* : sex

sextante *nm* : sextant

sexteto *nm* : sextet

sexto, -ta *adj* : sixth — **sexto, -ta** *n*

sexual *adj* : sexual, sex <educación sexual : sex education> — **sexualmente** *adv*

sexualidad *nf* : sexuality

sexy *adj, pl* **sexy** *or* **sexys** : sexy

shock [ˈʃɔk, ˈtʃɔk] *nm* : shock <estado de shock : state of shock>

short *nm, pl* **shorts** : shorts *pl*

show *nm, pl* **shows** : show

si *conj* **1** : if <lo haré si me pagan : I'll do it if they pay me> <si lo supiera te lo diría : if I knew it I would tell you> **2** : whether, if <no importa si funciona o no : it doesn't matter whether it works (or not)> **3** (*expressing desire, protest, or surprise*) <si supiera la verdad : if only I knew the truth> <¡si no quiero! : but I don't want to!> **4** **si bien** : although <si bien se ha progresado : although progress has been made> **5** **si no** : otherwise, or else <si no, no voy : otherwise I won't go>

sí[1] *adv* **1 :** yes <sí, gracias : yes, please> <creo que sí : I think so> **2 sí que :** indeed, absolutely <esta vez sí que ganaré : this time I'm sure to win> **3 porque sí** *fam* **:** because, just because <lo hizo porque sí : she did it just because>

sí[2] *nm* **:** yes <dar el sí : to say yes, to express consent>

sí[3] *pron* **1 de por sí** *or* **en sí :** by itself, in itself, per se **2 fuera de sí :** beside oneself **3 para sí (mismo) :** to himself, to herself, for himself, for herself **4 entre ~ :** among themselves

siamés, -mesa *adj & n, mpl* **siameses :** Siamese

sibilante *adj & nf* **:** sibilant

siciliano, -na *adj & n* **:** Sicilian

sico- → **psico-**

sicomoro *or* **sicómoro** *nm* **:** sycamore

SIDA *or* **sida** *nm* **:** AIDS

siderurgia *nf* **:** iron and steel industry

siderúrgico, -ca *adj* **:** steel, iron <the steel industry : la industria siderúrgica>

sidra *nf* **:** hard cider

siega[1], siegue, etc. → **segar**

siega[2] *nf* **1 :** harvesting **2 :** harvest time **3 :** harvested crop

siembra[1], etc. → **sembrar**

siembra[2] *nf* **1 :** sowing **2 :** sowing season **3** SEMBRADO **:** cultivated field

siempre *adv* **1 :** always <siempre tienes hambre : you're always hungry> **2 :** still <¿siempre te vas? : are you still going?> **3** *Mex* **:** after all <siempre no fui : I didn't go after all> **4 siempre que :** whenever, every time <siempre que pasa : every time he walks by> **5 para ~ :** forever, for good **6 siempre y cuando :** provided that

sien *nf* **:** temple (on the forehead)

sienta, etc. → **sentar**

siente, etc. → **sentir**

sierpe *nf* **:** serpent, snake

sierra[1], etc. → **serrar**

sierra[2] *nf* **1 :** saw <sierra de vaivén : jigsaw> **2** CORDILLERA **:** mountain range **3 :** mountains *pl* <viven en la sierra : they live in the mountains>

siervo, -va *n* **1 :** slave **2 :** serf

siesta *nf* **:** nap, siesta

siete *adj & nm* **:** seven

sífilis *nf* **:** syphilis

sifón *nm, pl* **sifones :** siphon

siga, sigue, etc. → **seguir**

sigilo *nm* **:** secrecy, stealth

sigiloso, -sa *adj* FURTIVO **:** furtive, stealthy — **sigilosamente** *adv*

sigla *nf* **:** acronym, abbreviation

siglo *nm* **1 :** century **2 :** age <el Siglo de Oro : the Golden Age> <hace siglos que no te veo : I haven't seen you in ages> **3 :** world, secular life

signar *vt* **:** to sign (a treaty or agreement)

signatario, -ria *n* **:** signatory

significación *nf, pl* **-ciones 1 :** significance, importance **2 :** signification, meaning

significado *nm* **1 :** sense, meaning **2 :** significance

significante *adj* **:** significant

significar {72} *vt* **1 :** to mean, to signify **2 :** to express, to make known — **significarse** *vr* **1 :** to draw attention, to become known **2 :** to take a stance

significativo, -va *adj* **1 :** significant, important **2 :** meaningful — **significativamente** *adv*

signo *nm* **1 :** sign <signo de igual : equal sign> <un signo de alegría : a sign of happiness> **2 :** (punctuation) mark <signo de interrogación : question mark> <signo de admiración : exclamation point> <signo de intercalación : caret>

siguiente *adj* **:** next, following

sílaba *nf* **:** syllable

silábico, -ca *adj* **:** syllabic

silbar *v* **:** to whistle

silbato *nm* PITO **:** whistle

silbido *nm* **:** whistle, whistling

silenciador *nm* **1 :** muffler (of an automobile) **2 :** silencer

silenciar *vt* **1 :** to silence **2 :** to muffle

silencio *nm* **1 :** silence, quiet <¡silencio! : be quiet!> **2 :** rest (in music)

silencioso, -sa *adj* **:** silent, quiet — **silenciosamente** *adv*

sílice *nf* **:** silica

silicio *nm* **:** silicon

silla *nf* **1 :** chair **2 silla de ruedas :** wheelchair

sillón *nm, pl* **sillones :** armchair, easy chair

silo *nm* **:** silo

silueta *nf* **1 :** silhouette **2 :** figure, shape

silvestre *adj* **:** wild <flor silvestre : wildflower>

silvicultor, -tora *n* **:** forester

silvicultura *nf* **:** forestry

sima *nf* ABISMO **:** chasm, abyss

simbólico, -ca *adj* **:** symbolic — **simbólicamente** *adj*

simbolismo *nm* **:** symbolism

simbolizar {21} *vt* **:** to symbolize

símbolo *nm* **:** symbol

simetría *nf* **:** symmetry

simétrico, -ca *adj* **:** symmetrical, symmetric

simiente *nf* **:** seed

símil *nm* **1 :** simile **2 :** analogy, comparison

similar *adj* SEMEJANTE **:** similar, alike

similitud *nf* **:** similarity, resemblance

simio *nm* **:** ape

simpatía *nf* **1 :** liking, affection <tomarle simpatía a : to take a liking to> **2 :** warmth, friendliness **3 :** support, solidarity

simpático, -ca *adj* **:** nice, friendly, likeable

simpatizante *nf* **:** sympathizer, supporter

simpatizar {21} *vi* **1 :** to get along, to hit it off <simpaticé mucho con él : I really liked him> **2 ~ con :** to sympathize with, to support

simple[1] *adj* **1** SENCILLO **:** plain, simple, easy **2 :** pure, mere <por simple vanidad : out of pure vanity> **3 :** simpleminded, foolish

simple[2] *n* **:** fool, simpleton

simplemente *adv* **:** simply, merely, just

simpleza *nf* **1 :** foolishness, simpleness **2** NECEDAD **:** nonsense

simplicidad *nf* **:** simplicity

simplificar {72} *vt* **:** to simplify — **simplificación** *nf*

simposio *or* **simposium** *nm* **:** symposium

simulación *nf, pl* **-ciones :** simulation

simulacro *nm* **:** imitation, sham <simulacro de juicio : mock trial>

simular *vt* **1 :** to simulate **2 :** to feign, to pretend

simultáneo, -nea *adj* **:** simultaneous — **simultáneamente** *adv*

sin *prep* **1 :** without <sin querer : unintentionally> <sin refinar : unrefined> **2 sin que :** without <lo hicimos sin que él se diera cuenta : we did it without him noticing>

sinagoga *nf* **:** synagogue

sinceridad *nf* **:** sincerity

sincero, -ra *adj* **:** sincere, honest, true — **sinceramente** *adv*

síncopa *nf* **:** syncopation

sincopar *vt* **:** to syncopate

sincronizar {21} *vt* **:** to synchronize — **sincronización** *nf*

sindical *adj* GREMIAL **:** union, labor <representante sindical : union representative>

sindicalización *nf, pl* **-ciones :** unionizing, unionization

sindicalizar {21} *vt* **:** to unionize — **sindicalizarse** *vr* **1 :** to form a union **2 :** to join a union

sindicar → **sindicalizar**

sindicato *nm* GREMIO **:** union, guild

síndrome *nm* **:** syndrome

sinecura *nf* **:** sinecure

sinfín *nm* **:** endless number <un sinfín de problemas : no end of problems>

sinfonía *nf* **:** symphony

sinfónica *nf* **:** symphony orchestra

sinfónico, -ca *adj* **:** symphonic, symphony

singular[1] *adj* **1 :** singular, unique **2** PARTICULAR **:** peculiar, odd **3 :** singular (in grammar) — **singularmente** *adv*

singular[2] *nm* **:** singular

singularidad *nf* **:** uniqueness, singularity

singularizar {21} *vt* **:** to make unique or distinct — **singularizarse** *vr* **:** to stand out, to distinguish oneself

siniestrado, -da *adj* **:** damaged, wrecked <zona siniestrada : disaster zone>

siniestro[1]**, -tra** *adj* **1** IZQUIERDO **:** left, left-hand **2** MALVADO **:** sinister, evil

siniestro[2] *nm* **:** accident, disaster

sinnúmero → **sinfín**

sino *conj* **1 :** but, rather <no será hoy, sino mañana : it won't be today, but tomorrow> **2** EXCEPTO **:** but, except <no hace sino despertar suspicacias : it does nothing but arouse suspicion>

sinónimo[1]**, -ma** *adj* **:** synonymous

sinónimo[2] *nm* **:** synonym

sinopsis *nfs & pl* RESUMEN **:** synopsis, summary

sinrazón *nf, pl* **-zones :** wrong, injustice

sinsabores *nmpl* **:** woes, troubles

sinsonte *nm* **:** mockingbird

sintáctico, -ca *adj* **:** syntactic, syntactical

sintaxis *nfs & pl* **:** syntax

síntesis *nfs & pl* **1 :** synthesis, fusion **2** SINOPSIS **:** synopsis, summary

sintético, -ca *adj* **:** synthetic — **sintéticamente** *adv*

sintetizar {21} *vt* **1 :** to synthesize **2** RESUMIR **:** to summarize

sintió, etc. → **sentir**

síntoma *nm* **:** symptom

sintomático, -ca *adj* **:** symptomatic

sintonía *nf* **1 :** tuning in (of a radio) **2 en sintonía con :** in tune with, attuned to

sintonizador *nm* **:** tuner, knob for tuning (of a radio, etc.)

sintonizar {21} *vt* **:** to tune (in) to — *vi* **1 :** to tune in **2 ~ con :** to be in tune with, to empathize with

sinuosidad *nf* **:** sinuosity

sinuoso, -sa *adj* **1 :** winding, sinuous **2 :** devious

sinvergüenza[1] *adj* **1** DESCARADO **:** shameless, brazen, impudent **2** TRAVIESO **:** naughty

sinvergüenza[2] *nmf* **1 :** rogue, scoundrel **2 :** brat, rascal

sionista *adj & nmf* **:** Zionist — **sionismo** *nm*

siqui- → **psiqui-**

siquiera *adv* **1 :** at least <dame siquiera un poquito : at least give me a little bit> **2** (*in negative constructions*) **:** not even <ni siquiera nos saludaron : they didn't even say hello to us>

sirena *nf* **1 :** mermaid **2 :** siren <sirena de niebla : foghorn>

sirio, -ria *adj & n* **:** Syrian

sirope *nm* **:** syrup

sirve, etc. → **servir**

sirviente, -ta *n* **:** servant, maid *f*

sisal *nm* **:** sisal

sisear *vi* **:** to hiss

siseo *nm* **:** hiss

sísmico, -ca *adj* **:** seismic

sismo *nm* **1** TERREMOTO **:** earthquake **2** TEMBLOR **:** tremor

sismógrafo *nm* **:** seismograph

sistema *nm* **:** system

sistemático, -ca *adj* **:** systematic — **sistemáticamente** *adv*

sistematizar {21} *vt* **:** to systematize

sistémico, -ca *adj* **:** systemic

sitiar *vt* ASEDIAR **:** to besiege

sitio *nm* **1** LUGAR **:** place, site <vámonos a otro sitio : let's go somewhere else> **2** ESPACIO **:** room, space <hacer sitio a : to make room for> **3 :** siege <estado de sitio : state of siege> **4** *Mex* **:** taxi stand

situación *nf, pl* **-ciones :** situation

situado, -da *adj* **:** situated, placed

situar {3} *vt* UBICAR **:** to situate, to place, to locate — **situarse** *vr* **1 :** to be placed, to be located **2 :** to make a place for oneself, to do well

sketch *nm* **:** sketch, skit

slip *nm* **:** briefs *pl*, underpants *pl*

smog *nm* **:** smog

smoking *nm* ESMOQUIN **:** tuxedo

snob → **esnob**

so *prep* **:** under <so pena de : under penalty of>

sobaco *nm* **:** armpit

sobado, -da *adj* **1 :** worn, shabby **2 :** well-worn, hackneyed

sobar *vt* **1 :** to finger, to handle **2 :** to knead **3 :** to rub, to massage **4** *fam* **:** to beat, to pummel

soberanía *nf* **:** sovereignty

soberano, -na *adj & n* **:** sovereign

soberbia *nf* **1** ORGULLO **:** pride, arrogance **2** MAGNIFICENCIA **:** magnificence

soberbio, -bia *adj* **1 :** proud, arrogant **2 :** grand, magnificent

sobornable *adv* **:** venal, bribable

sobornar *vt* **:** to bribe

soborno *nm* **1 :** bribery **2 :** bribe

sobra *nf* **1 :** excess, surplus **2 de ~ :** extra, to spare **3 sobras** *nfpl* **:** leftovers, scraps

sobrado, -da *adj* **:** abundant, excessive, more than enough

sobrante[1] *adj* **:** remaining, superfluous

sobrante[2] *nm* **:** remainder, surplus

sobrar *vi* **:** to be in excess, to be superfluous <más vale que sobre a que falte : it's better to have too much than not enough>

sobre[1] *nm* **1 :** envelope **2 :** packet <un sobre de sazón : a packet of seasoning>

sobre[2] *prep* **1 :** on, on top of <sobre la mesa : on the table> **2 :** over, above **3 :** about <¿tiene libros sobre Bolivia? : do you have books on Bolivia?> **4 sobre todo :** especially, above all

sobrealimentar *vt* **:** to overfeed

sobrecalentar {55} *vt* **:** to overheat — **sobrecalentarse** *vr*

sobrecama *nmf* **:** bedspread

sobrecargar {52} *vt* **:** to overload, to overburden, to weigh down

sobrecoger {15} *vt* **1 :** to surprise, to startle **2 :** to scare — **sobrecogerse** *vr*

sobrecubierta *nf* **:** dust jacket

sobredosis *nfs & pl* **:** overdose

sobreentender {56} *vt* **:** to infer, to understand

sobreestimar *vt* **:** to overestimate, to overrate

sobreexitado, -da *adj* **:** overexcited

sobreexponer {60} *vt* **:** to overexpose

sobregirar *vt* **:** to overdraw

sobregiro *nm* **:** overdraft

sobrehumano, -na *adj* **:** superhuman

sobrellevar *vt* **:** to endurc, to bear

sobremanera *adv* **:** exceedingly

sobremesa *nf* **:** after-dinner conversation

sobrenatural *adj* **:** supernatural

sobrenombre *nm* APODO **:** nickname

sobrentender → **sobreentender**

sobrepasar *vt* **:** to exceed, to surpass — **sobrepasarse** *vr* PASARSE **:** to go too far

sobrepelliz *nf, pl* **-pellices :** surplice

sobrepeso *nm* **1 :** excess weight **2 :** overweight, obesity

sobrepoblación, sobrepoblado → **superpoblación, superpoblado**

sobreponer {60} *vt* **1** SUPERPONER **:** to superimpose **2** ANTEPONER **:** to put first, to give priority to — **sobreponerse** *vr* **1 :** to pull oneself together **2 ~ a :** to overcome

sobreprecio *nm* **:** surcharge

sobreproducción *nf, pl* **-ciones :** overproduction

sobreproducir {61} *vt* **:** to overproduce

sobreprotector, -tora *adj* **:** overprotective

sobreproteger {15} *vt* **:** to overprotect

sobresaliente[1] *adj* **1 :** protruding, projecting **2 :** outstanding, noteworthy **3 :** significant, salient

sobresaliente[2] *nmf* **:** understudy

sobresalir {73} *vi* **1 :** to protrude, to jut out, to project **2 :** to stand out, to excel

sobresaltar *vt* **:** to startle, to frighten — **sobresaltarse** *vr*

sobresalto *nm* **:** start, fright

sobresueldo *nm* **:** bonus, additional pay

sobretasa *nf* **:** surcharge <sobretasa a la gasolina : gas tax>

sobretodo *nm* **:** overcoat

sobrevalorar *or* **sobrevaluar** {3} *vt* **:** to overvalue, to overrate

sobrevender *vt* **:** to oversell

sobrevenir {87} *vi* ACAECER **:** to take place, to come about <podrían sobrevenir complicaciones : complications could occur>

sobrevivencia *nf* → **supervivencia**

sobreviviente → **superviviente**

sobrevivir *vi* **:** to survive — *vt* **:** to outlive, to outlast

sobrevolar {19} *vt* **:** to fly over, to overfly

sobriedad *nf* **:** sobriety, moderation

sobrino, -na *n* **:** nephew *m*, niece *f*

sobrio, -bria *adj* **:** sober — **sobriamente** *adv*

socarrón, -rrona *adj, mpl* **-rrones 1** : sly, cunning **2** : sarcastic

socavar *vt* : to undermine

sociabilidad *nf* : sociability

sociable *adj* : sociable

social *adj* : social — **socialmente** *adv*

socialista *adj & nmf* : socialist — **socialismo** *nm*

sociedad *nf* **1** : society **2** : company, enterprise **3 sociedad anónima** : incorporated company

socio, -cia *n* **1** : member **2** : partner

socioeconómico, -ca *adj* : socioeconomic

sociología *nf* : sociology

sociológico, -ca *adj* : sociological — **sociológicamente** *adv*

sociólogo, -ga *n* : sociologist

socorrer *vt* : to assist, to come to the aid of

socorrido, -da *adj* ÚTIL : handy, practical

socorrista *nmf* **1** : rescue worker **2** : lifeguard

socorro *nm* AUXILIO **1** : aid, help <equipo de socorro : rescue team> **2** **¡socorro!** : help!

soda *nf* : soda, soda water

sodio *nf* : sodium

soez *adj, pl* **soeces** GROSERO : rude, vulgar — **soezmente** *adv*

sofá *nm* : couch, sofa

sofistería *nf* : sophistry — **sofista** *nmf*

sofisticación *nf, pl* **-ciones** : sophistication

sofisticado, -da *adj* : sophisticated

sofocante *adj* : suffocating, stifling

sofocar {72} *vt* **1** AHOGAR : to suffocate, to smother **2** EXTINGUIR : to extinguish, to put out (a fire) **3** APLASTAR : to crush, to put down <sofocar una rebelión : to crush a rebellion> — **sofocarse** *vr* **1** : to suffocate **2** *fam* : to get upset, to get mad

sofreír {66} *vt* : to sauté

sofrito[1], -ta *adj* : sautéed

sofrito[2] *nm* : seasoning sauce

softbol *nm* : softball

software *nm* : software

soga *nf* : rope

soja *nf* → **soya**

sojuzgar *vt* : to subdue, to conquer, to subjugate

sol *nm* **1** : sun **2** : Peruvian unit of currency

solamente *adv* SÓLO : only, just

solapa *nf* **1** : lapel (of a jacket) **2** : flap (of an envelope)

solapado, -da *adj* : secret, underhanded

solapar *vt* : to cover up, to keep secret — **solaparse** *vr* : to overlap

solar[1] {19} *vt* : to floor, to tile

solar[2] *adj* : solar, sun

solar[3] *nm* **1** TERRENO : lot, piece of land, site **2** *Cuba, Peru* : tenement building

solariego, -ga *adj* : ancestral

solaz *nm, pl* **solaces 1** CONSUELO : solace, comfort **2** DESCANSO : relaxation, recreation

solazarse {21} *vr* : to relax, to enjoy oneself

soldado *nm* **1** : soldier **2 soldado raso** : private, enlisted man

soldador[1], -dora *n* : welder

soldador[2] *nm* : soldering iron

soldadura *nf* **1** : welding **2** : soldering, solder

soldar {19} *vt* **1** : to weld **2** : to solder

soleado, -da *adj* : sunny

soledad *nf* : loneliness, solitude

solemne *adj* : solemn — **solemnemente** *adv*

solemnidad *nf* : solemnity

soler {78} *vi* : to be in the habit of, to tend to <solía tomar café por la tarde : she usually drank coffee in the afternoon> <eso suele ocurrir : that frequently happens>

solera *nf* **1** : prop, support **2** : tradition

solicitante *nmf* : applicant

solicitar *vt* **1** : to request, to solicit **2** : to apply for <solicitar empleo : to apply for employment>

solícito, -ta *adj* : solicitous, attentive, obliging

solicitud *nf* **1** : solicitude, concern **2** : request **3** : application

solidaridad *nf* : solidarity

solidario, -ria *adj* : supportive, united in support <se declararon solidarios con la nueva ley : they declared their support for the new law> <espíritu solidario : spirit of solidarity>

solidarizar {21} *vi* : to be in solidarity <solidarizamos con la huelga : we support the strike>

solidez *nf* **1** : solidity, firmness **2** : soundness (of an argument, etc.)

solidificar {72} *vt* : to solidify, to make solid — **solidificarse** *vr* — **solidificación** *nf*

sólido[1], -da *adj* **1** : solid, firm **2** : sturdy, well-made **3** : sound, well-founded — **sólidamente** *adv*

sólido[2] *nm* : solid

soliloquio *nm* : soliloquy

solista *nmf* : soloist

solitaria *nf* TENIA : tapeworm

solitario[1], -ria *adj* **1** : lonely **2** : lone, solitary **3** DESIERTO : deserted, lonely <una calle solitaria : a deserted street>

solitario[2], -ria *n* : recluse, loner

solitario[3] *nm* : solitaire

sollozar {21} *vi* : to sob

sollozo *nm* : sob

solo[1], -la *adj* **1** : alone, by oneself **2** : lonely **3** ÚNICO : only, sole, unique <hay un solo problema : there's only one problem> **4 a solas** : alone

solo[2] *nm* : solo

sólo *adv* SOLAMENTE : just, only <sólo quieren comer : they just want to eat>

solomillo *nm* : sirloin, loin

solsticio *nm* : solstice

soltar {19} *vt* **1 :** to let go of, to drop **2 :** to release, to set free **3** AFLOJAR **:** to loosen, to slacken

soltería *nf* **:** bachelorhood, spinsterhood

soltero[1], -ra *adj* **:** single, unmarried

soltero[2], -ra *n* **1 :** bachelor *m,* single man *m,* single woman *f* **2 apellido de soltera :** maiden name

soltura *nf* **1 :** looseness, slackness **2 :** fluency (of language) **3 :** agility, ease of movement

soluble *adj* **:** soluble — **solubilidad** *nf*

solución *nf, pl* **-ciones 1 :** solution (in a liquid) **2 :** answer, solution

solucionar *vt* RESOLVER **:** to solve, to resolve — **solucionarse** *vr*

solvencia *nf* **1 :** solvency **2 :** settling, payment (of debts) **3 :** reliability <solvencia moral : trustworthiness>

solvente[1] *adj* **1 :** solvent **2 :** reliable, trustworthy

solvente[2] *nm* **:** solvent

somalí *adj & nmf* **:** Somalian

sombra *nf* **1 :** shadow **2 :** shade **3 sombras** *nfpl* **:** darkness, shadows *pl* **4 sin sombra de duda :** without a shadow of a doubt

sombreado, -da *adj* **1 :** shady **2 :** shaded, darkened

sombrear *vt* **:** to shade

sombrerero, -ra *n* **:** milliner, hatter

sombrero *nm* **1 :** hat **2 sin ~ :** bareheaded **3 sombrero hongo :** derby

sombrilla *nf* **:** parasol, umbrella

sombrío, -bría *adj* LÓBREGO **:** dark, somber, gloomy — **sombríamente** *adv*

someramente *adv* **:** cursorily, summarily

somero, -ra *adj* **:** superficial, cursory, shallow

someter *vt* **1 :** to subjugate, to conquer **2 :** to subordinate **3 :** to subject (to treatment or testing) **4 :** to submit, to present — **someterse** *vr* **1 :** to submit, to yield **2 :** to undergo

sometimiento *nm* **1 :** submission, subjection **2 :** presentation

somnífero[1], -ra *adj* **:** soporific

somnífero[2] *nm* **:** sleeping pill

somnolencia *nf* **:** drowsiness, sleepiness

somnoliento, -ta *adj* **:** drowsy, sleepy

somorgujo *or* **somormujo** *nm* **:** loon, grebe

somos → **ser**

son[1] → **ser**

son[2] *nm* **1 :** sound <al son de la trompeta : at the sound of the trumpet> **2 :** news, rumor **3 en son de :** as, in the manner of, by way of <en son de broma : as a joke> <en son de paz : in peace>

sonado, -da *adj* **:** celebrated, famous, much-discussed

sonaja *nf* **:** rattle

sonajero *nm* **:** rattle (toy)

sonámbulo, -la *n* **:** sleepwalker

sonar[1] {19} *vi* **1 :** to sound <suena bien : it sounds good> **2 :** to ring (bells) **3 :** to look or sound familiar <me suena ese nombre : that name rings a bell> **4 ~ a :** to sound like — *vt* **1 :** to ring **2 :** to blow (a trumpet, a nose) — **sonarse** *vr* **:** to blow one's nose

sonar[2] *nm* **:** sonar

sonata *nf* **:** sonata

sonda *nf* **1 :** sounding line **2 :** probe **3** CATÉTER **:** catheter

sondar *vt* **1 :** to sound, to probe (in medicine, drilling, etc.) **2 :** to probe, to explore (outer space)

sondear *vt* **1 :** to sound **2 :** to probe **3 :** to sound out, to test (opinions, markets)

sondeo *nm* **1 :** sounding, probing **2 :** drilling **3** ENCUESTA **:** survey, poll

soneto *nm* **:** sonnet

sónico, -ca *adj* **:** sonic

sonido *nm* **:** sound

sonoridad *nf* **:** sonority, resonance

sonoro, -ra *adj* **1 :** resonant, sonorous, voiced (in linguistics) **2 :** resounding, loud **3 banda sonora :** soundtrack

sonreír {66} *vi* **:** to smile

sonriente *adj* **:** smiling

sonrisa *nf* **:** smile

sonrojar *vt* **:** to cause to blush — **sonrojarse** *vr* **:** to blush

sonrojo *nm* RUBOR **:** blush

sonrosado, -da *adj* **:** rosy, pink

sonsacar {72} *vt* **:** to wheedle, to extract

sonsonete *nm* **1 :** tapping **2 :** drone **3 :** mocking tone

soñador[1], -dora *adj* **:** dreamy

soñador[2], -dora *n* **:** dreamer

soñar {19} *v* **1 :** to dream **2 ~ con :** to dream about **3 soñar despierto :** to daydream

soñoliento, -ta *adj* **:** sleepy, drowsy

sopa *nf* **1 :** soup **2 estar hecho una sopa :** to be soaked to the bone

sopera *nf* **:** soup tureen

sopesar *vt* **:** to weigh, to evaluate

soplar *vi* **:** to blow — *vt* **:** to blow on, to blow out, to blow off

soplete *nm* **:** blowtorch

soplido *nm* **:** puff

soplo *nm* **:** puff, gust

soplón, -plona *n, mpl* **soplones** *fam* **:** tattletale, sneak

sopor *nm* SOMNOLENCIA **:** drowsiness, sleepiness

soporífero, -ra *adj* **:** soporific

soportable *adj* **:** bearable, tolerable

soportar *vt* **1** SOSTENER **:** to support, to hold up **2** RESISTIR **:** to withstand, to resist **3** AGUANTAR **:** to bear, to tolerate

soporte *nm* **:** base, stand, support

soprano *nmf* **:** soprano

sor *nf* **:** Sister (religious title)

sorber *vt* **1 :** to sip, to suck in **2 :** to absorb, to soak up

sorbete *nm* **:** sherbet

sorbo *nm* **1 :** sip, gulp, swallow **2 beber a sorbos :** to sip

sordera *nf* : deafness
sordidez *nf, pl* **-deces** : sordidness, squalor
sórdido, -da *adj* : sordid, dirty, squalid
sordina *nf* : mute (for a musical instrument)
sordo, -da *adj* **1** : deaf **2** : muted, muffled
sordomudo, -da *n* : deaf-mute
sorgo *nm* : sorghum
soriasis *nfs & pl* : psoriasis
sorna *nf* : sarcasm, mocking tone
sorprendente *adj* : surprising — **sorprendentemente** *adv*
sorprender *vt* : to surprise — **sorprenderse** *vr*
sorpresa *nf* : surprise
sorpresivo, -va *adj* **1** : surprising, surprise **2** IMPREVISTO : sudden, unexpected
sortear *vt* **1** RIFAR : to raffle, to draw lots for **2** : to dodge, to avoid
sorteo *nm* : drawing, raffle
sortija *nf* **1** ANILLO : ring **2** : curl, ringlet
sortilegio *nm* **1** HECHIZO : spell, charm **2** HECHICERÍA : sorcery
SOS *nm* : SOS
sosegado, -da *adj* SERENO : calm, tranquil, serene
sosegar {49} *vt* : to calm, to pacify — **sosegarse** *vr*
sosiego *nm* : tranquillity, serenity, calm
soslayar *vt* ESQUIVAR : to dodge, to evade
soslayo *nm* **de ~** : obliquely, sideways <mirar de soslayo : to look askance>
soso, -sa *adj* **1** INSÍPIDO : bland, flavorless **2** ABURRIDO : dull, boring
sospecha *nf* : suspicion
sospechar *vt* : to suspect — *vi* : to be suspicious
sospechosamente *adv* : suspiciously
sospechoso[1], **-sa** *adj* : suspicious, suspect
sospechoso[2], **-sa** *n* : suspect
sostén *nm, pl* **sostenes 1** APOYO : support **2** : sustenance **3** : brassiere, bra
sostener {80} *vt* **1** : to support, to hold up **2** : to hold <sostenme la puerta : hold the door for me> <sostener una conversación : to hold a conversation> **3** : to sustain, to maintain — **sostenerse** *vr* **1** : to stand, to hold oneself up **2** : to continue, to remain
sostenible *adj* : sustainable, tenable
sostenido[1], **-da** *adj* **1** : sustained, prolonged **2** : sharp (in music)
sostenido[2] *nm* : sharp (in music)
sostuvo, etc. → **sostener**
sotana *nf* : cassock
sótano *nm* : basement
sotavento *nm* : lee <a sotavento : leeward>
soterrar {55} *vt* **1** : to bury **2** : to conceal, to hide away
soto *nm* : grove, copse
souvenir *nm, pl* **-nirs** RECUERDO : souvenir, memento
soviético, -ca *adj* : Soviet
soy → **ser**
soya *nf* : soy, soybean
spaghetti *nm* → **espagueti**
sport [ɛ'spor] *adj* : sport, casual
sprint [ɛ'sprin, -'sprint] *nm* : sprint — **sprinter** *nmf*
squash [ɛ'skwaʃ, -'skwatʃ] *nm* : squash (sport)
Sr. *nm* : Mr.
Sra. *nf* : Mrs., Ms.
Srta. *or* **Srita.** *nf* : Miss, Ms.
standard → **estándar**
stress *nm* → **estrés**
su *adj* **1** : his, her, its, their, one's <su libro : her book> <sus consecuencias : its consequences> **2** (*formal*) : your <tómese su medicina, señor : take your medicine, sir>
suave *adj* **1** BLANDO : soft **2** LISO : smooth **3** : gentle, mild **4** *Mex fam* : great, fantastic
suavemente *adj* : smoothly, gently, softly
suavidad *nf* : softness, smoothness, mellowness
suavizante *nm* : softener, fabric softener
suavizar {21} *vt* **1** : to soften, to smooth out **2** : to tone down — **suavizarse** *vr*
subacuático, -ca *adj* : underwater
subalterno[1], **-na** *adj* **1** SUBORDINADO : subordinate **2** SECUNDARIO : secondary
subalterno[2], **-na** *n* SUBORDINADO : subordinate
subarrendar {55} *vt* : to sublet
subasta *nf* : auction
subastador, -dora *n* : auctioneer
subastar *vt* : to auction, to auction off
subcampeón, -peona *n, mpl* **-peones** : runner-up
subcomité *nm* : subcommittee
subconsciente *adj & nm* : subconscious — **subconscientemente** *adv*
subcontratar *vt* : to subcontract
subcontratista *nmf* : subcontractor
subcultura *nf* : subculture
subdesarrollado, -da *adj* : underdeveloped
subdirector, -tora *n* : assistant manager
súbdito, -ta *n* : subject (of a monarch)
subdividir *vt* : to subdivide
subdivisión *nf, pl* **-siones** : subdivision
subestimar *vt* : to underestimate, to undervalue
subexponer {60} *vt* : to underexpose
subexposición *nf, pl* **-ciones** : underexposure
subgrupo *nm* : subgroup
subibaja *nm* : seesaw
subida *nf* **1** : ascent, climb **2** : rise, increase **3** : slope, hill <ir de subida : to go uphill>

subido, -da *adj* **1 :** intense, strong <amarillo subido : bright yellow> **2** **subido de tono :** risqué
subir *vt* **1 :** to bring up, to take up **2 :** to climb, to go up **3 :** to raise — *vi* **1 :** to go up, to come up **2 :** to rise, to increase **3 :** to be promoted **4 ~ a :** to get on, to mount <subir a un tren : to get on a train> — **subirse** *vr* **1 :** to climb (up) **2 :** to pull up (clothing) **3** **subirse a la cabeza :** to go to one's head
súbito, -ta *adj* **1** REPENTINO **:** sudden **2** **de ~ :** all of a sudden, suddenly — **súbitamente** *adv*
subjetivo, -va *adj* **:** subjective — **subjetivamente** *adv* — **subjetividad** *nf*
subjuntivo¹, -va *adj* **:** subjunctive
subjuntivo² *nm* **:** subjunctive
sublevación *nf, pl* **-ciones** ALZAMIENTO **:** uprising, rebellion
sublevar *vt* **:** to incite to rebellion — **sublevarse** *vr* **:** to rebel, to rise up
sublimar *vt* **:** to sublimate — **sublimación** *nf*
sublime *adj* **:** sublime
submarinismo *nm* **:** scuba diving
submarinista *nmf* **:** scuba diver
submarino¹, -na *adj* **:** submarine, undersea
submarino² *nm* **:** submarine
suboficial *nmf* **:** noncommissioned officer, petty officer
subordinado, -da *adj & n* **:** subordinate
subordinar *vt* **:** to subordinate — **subordinarse** *vr* — **subordinación** *nf*
subproducto *nm* **:** by-product
subrayar *vt* **1 :** to underline, to underscore **2** ENFATIZAR **:** to highlight, to emphasize
subrepticio, -cia *adj* **:** surreptitious — **subrepticiamente** *adv*
subsahariano, -na *adj* **:** sub-Saharan
subsanar *vt* **1** RECTIFICAR **:** to rectify, to correct **2 :** to overlook, to excuse **3** **:** to make up for
subscribir → **suscribir**
subsecretario, -ria *n* **:** undersecretary
subsecuente *adj* **:** subsequent — **subsecuentemente** *adv*
subsidiar *vt* **:** to subsidize
subsidiaria *nf* **:** subsidiary
subsidio *nm* **:** subsidy
subsiguiente *adj* **:** subsequent
subsistencia *nf* **1 :** subsistence **2 :** sustenance
subsistir *vi* **1 :** to subsist, to live **2 :** to endure, to survive
substancia *nf* → **sustancia**
subteniente *nmf* **:** second lieutenant
subterfugio *nm* **:** subterfuge
subterráneo¹, -nea *adj* **:** underground, subterranean
subterráneo² *nm* **1 :** underground passage, tunnel **2** *Arg, Uru* **:** subway
subtítulo *nm* **:** subtitle, subheading
subtotal *nm* **:** subtotal
suburbano, -na *adj* **:** suburban
suburbio *nm* **1 :** suburb **2 :** slum (outside a city)
subvención *nf, pl* **-ciones :** subsidy, grant
subvencionar *vt* **:** to subsidize
subversivo, -va *adj & n* **:** subversive — **subversión** *nf*
subvertir {76} *vt* **:** to subvert
subyacente *adj* **:** underlying
subyugar {52} *vt* **:** to subjugate — **subyugación** *nf*
succión *nf, pl* **succiones :** suction
succionar *vt* **:** to suck up, to draw in
sucedáneo *nm* **:** substitute <sucedáneo de azucar : sugar substitute>
suceder *vi* **1** OCURRIR **:** to happen, to occur <¿qué sucede? : what's going on?> <suceda lo que suceda : come what may> **2 ~ a :** to follow, to succeed <suceder al trono : to succeed to the throne> <a la primavera sucede el verano : summer follows sping>
sucesión *nf, pl* **-siones 1 :** succession **2** **:** sequence, series **3 :** issue, heirs *pl*
sucesivamente *adv* **:** successively, consecutively <y así sucesivamente : and so on>
sucesivo, -va *adj* **:** successive <en los días sucesivos : in the days that followed>
suceso *nm* **1 :** event, happening, occurrence **2 :** incident, crime
sucesor, -sora *n* **:** successor
suciedad *nf* **1 :** dirtiness, filthiness **2** MUGRE **:** dirt, filth
sucinto, -ta *adj* CONCISO **:** succinct, concise — **sucintamente** *adv*
sucio, -cia *adj* **:** dirty, filthy
sucre *nm* **:** Ecuadoran unit of currency
suculento, -ta *adj* **:** succulent
sucumbir *vi* **:** to succumb
sucursal *nf* **:** branch (of a business)
sudadera *nf* **:** sweatshirt
sudado, -da → **sudoroso**
sudafricano, -na *adj & n* **:** South African
sudamericano, -na *adj & n* **:** South American
sudanés, -nesa *adj & n, mpl* **-neses** **:** Sudanese
sudar *vi* TRANSPIRAR **:** to sweat, to perspire
sudario *nm* **:** shroud
sudeste → **sureste**
sudoeste → **suroeste**
sudor *nm* TRANSPIRACIÓN **:** sweat, perspiration
sudoroso, -sa *adj* **:** sweaty
sueco¹, -ca *adj* **:** Swedish
sueco², -ca *n* **:** Swede
sueco³ *nm* **:** Swedish (language)
suegro, -gra *n* **1 :** father-in-law *m,* mother-in-law *f* **2** **suegros** *nmpl* **:** in-laws
suela *nf* **:** sole (of a shoe)
suelda, etc. → **soldar**
sueldo *nm* **:** salary, wage
suele, etc. → **soler**

suelo *nm* **1 :** ground <caerse al suelo : to fall down, to hit the ground> **2 :** floor, flooring **3** TIERRA **:** soil, land
suelta, etc. → **soltar**
suelto[1], -ta *adj* **:** loose, free, unattached
suelto[2] *nm* **:** loose change
suena, etc. → **sonar**
sueña, etc. → **soñar**
sueño *nm* **1 :** dream **2 :** sleep <perder el sueño : to lose sleep> **3 :** sleepiness <tener sueño : to be sleepy>
suero *nm* **1 :** serum **2 :** whey
suerte *nf* **1** FORTUNA **:** luck, fortune <tener suerte : to be lucky> <por suerte : luckily> **2** DESTINO **:** fate, destiny, lot **3** CLASE, GÉNERO **:** sort, kind <toda suerte de cosas : all kinds of things>
suertudo, -da *adj fam* **:** lucky
suéter *nm* **:** sweater
suficiencia *nf* **1 :** adequacy, sufficiency **2 :** competence, fitness **3 :** smugness, self-satisfaction
suficiente *adj* **1** BASTANTE **:** enough, sufficient <tener suficiente : to have enough> **2 :** suitable, fit **3 :** smug, complacent
suficientemente *adv* **:** sufficiently, enough
sufijo *nm* **:** suffix
suflé *nm* **:** soufflé
sufragar {52} *vt* **1** AYUDAR **:** to help out, to support **2 :** to defray (costs) — *vi* **:** to vote
sufragio *nm* **:** suffrage, vote
sufrido, -da *adj* **1 :** long-suffering, patient **2 :** sturdy, serviceable (of clothing)
sufrimiento *nm* **:** suffering
sufrir *vt* **1 :** to suffer <sufrir una pérdida : to suffer a loss> **2 :** to tolerate, to put up with <ella no lo puede sufrir : she can't stand him> — *vi* **:** to suffer
sugerencia *nf* **:** suggestion
sugerir {76} *vt* **1** PROPONER, RECOMENDAR **:** to suggest, to recommend, to propose **2 :** to suggest, to bring to mind
sugestión *nf, pl* **-tiones :** suggestion, prompting <poder de sugestión : power of suggestion>
sugestionable *adj* **:** suggestible, impressionable
sugestionar *vt* **:** to influence, to sway — **sugestionarse** *vr* **~ con :** to talk oneself into, to become convinced of
sugestivo, -va *adj* **1 :** suggestive **2 :** interesting, stimulating
suicida[1] *adj* **:** suicidal
suicida[2] *nmf* **:** suicide victim, suicide
suicidarse *vr* **:** to commit suicide
suicidio *nm* **:** suicide
suite *nf* **:** suite
suizo, -za *adj & n* **:** Swiss
sujeción *nf, pl* **-ciones 1 :** holding, fastening **2 :** subjection
sujetador *nm* **1 :** fastener **2 :** holder <sujetador de tazas : cup holder>
sujetalibros *nms & pl* **:** bookend
sujetapapeles *nms & pl* CLIP **:** paper clip
sujetar *vt* **1 :** to hold on to, to steady, to hold down **2** FIJAR **:** to fasten, to attach **3** DOMINAR **:** to subdue, to conquer — **sujetarse** *vr* **1 :** to hold on, to hang on **2 ~ a :** to abide by
sujeto[1], -ta *adj* **1 :** secure, fastened **2 ~ a :** subject to
sujeto[2] *nm* **1** INDIVIDUO **:** individual, character **2 :** subject (in grammar)
sulfúrico, -ca *adj* **:** sulfuric
sulfuro *nm* **:** sulfur
sultán *nm, pl* **sultanes :** sultan
suma *nf* **1** CANTIDAD **:** sum, quantity **2 :** addition
sumamente *adv* **:** extremely, exceedingly
sumar *vt* **1 :** to add, to add up **2 :** to add up to, to total — *vi* **:** to add up — **sumarse** *vr* **~ a :** to join
sumario[1], -ria *adj* SUCINTO **:** succinct, summary — **sumariamente** *adv*
sumario[2] *nm* **:** summary
sumergir {35} *vt* **:** to submerge, to immerse, to plunge — **sumergirse** *vr*
sumersión *nf, pl* **-siones :** submersion, immersion
sumidero *nm* **:** drain, sewer
suministrar *vt* **:** to supply, to provide
suministro *nm* **:** supply, provision
sumir *vt* SUMERGIR **:** to plunge, to immerse, to sink — **sumirse** *vr*
sumisión *nf, pl* **-siones 1 :** submission **2 :** submissiveness
sumiso, -sa *adj* **:** submissive, acquiescent, docile
sumo, -ma *adj* **1 :** extreme, great, high <la suma autoridad : the highest authority> **2 a lo sumo :** at the most — **sumamente** *adv*
suntuoso, -sa *adj* **:** sumptuous, lavish — **suntuosamente** *adv*
supeditar *vt* SUBORDINAR **:** to subordinate — **supeditación** *nf*
super[1] *or* **súper** *adj fam* **:** super, great
super[2] *nm* SUPERMERCADO **:** market, supermarket
superable *adj* **:** surmountable
superabundancia *nf* **:** overabundance, superabundance — **superabundante** *adj*
superar *vt* **1 :** to surpass, to exceed **2 :** to overcome, to surmount — **superarse** *vr* **:** to improve oneself
superávit *nm, pl* **-vit** *or* **-vits :** surplus
supercheria *nf* **:** trickery, fraud
superestructura *nf* **:** superstructure
superficial *adj* **:** superficial — **superficialmente** *adv*
superficialidad *nf* **:** superficiality
superficie *nf* **1 :** surface **2 :** area <el superficie de un triángulo : the area of a triangle>
superfluidad *nf* **:** superfluity
superfluo, -flua *adj* **:** superfluous
superintendente *nmf* **:** supervisor, superintendent

superior[1] *adj* **1 :** superior **2 :** upper <nivel superior : upper level> **3 :** higher <educación superior : higher education> **4 ~ a :** above, higher than, in excess of
superior[2] *nm* **:** superior
superioridad *nf* **:** superiority
superlativo[1], **-va** *adj* **:** superlative
superlativo[2] *nm* **:** superlative
supermercado *nm* **:** supermarket
superpoblación *nf, pl* **-ciones :** overpopulation
superpoblado, -da *adj* **:** overpopulated
superponer {60} *vt* **:** to superimpose
superpotencia *nf* **:** superpower
superproducción *nf* → **sobreproducción**
supersónico, -ca *adj* **:** supersonic
superstición *nf, pl* **-ciones :** superstition
supersticioso, -sa *adj* **:** superstitious
supervisar *vt* **:** to supervise, to oversee
supervisión *nf, pl* **-siones :** supervision
supervisor, -sora *n* **:** supervisor, overseer
supervivencia *nf* **:** survival
superviviente *nmf* **:** survivor
supino, -na *adj* **:** supine
suplantar *vt* **:** to supplant, to replace
suplemental → **suplementario**
suplementario, -ria *adj* **:** supplementary, additional, extra
suplemento *nm* **:** supplement
suplencia *nf* **:** substitution, replacement
suplente *adj & nmf* **:** substitute <equipo suplente : replacement team>
supletorio, -ria *adj* **:** extra, additional <teléfono supletorio : extension phone> <cama supletoria : spare bed>
súplica *nf* **:** plea, entreaty
suplicar {72} *vt* IMPLORAR, ROGAR **:** to entreat, to implore, to supplicate
suplicio *nm* TORMENTO **:** ordeal, torture
suplir *vt* **1** COMPENSAR **:** to make up for, to compensate for **2** REEMPLAZAR **:** to replace, to substitute
supo, etc. → **saber**
suponer {60} *vt* **1** PRESUMIR **:** to suppose, to assume <supongo que sí : I guess so, I suppose so> <se supone que van a llegar mañana : they're supposed to arrive tomorrow> **2 :** to imply, to suggest **3 :** to involve, to entail <el éxito supone mucho trabajo : success involves a lot of work>
suposición *nf, pl* **-ciones** PRESUNCIÓN **:** supposition, assumption
supositorio *nm* **:** suppository
supremacía *nf* **:** supremacy
supremo, -ma *adj* **:** supreme
supresión *nf, pl* **-siones 1 :** suppression, elimination **2 :** deletion
suprimir *vt* **1 :** to suppress, to eliminate **2 :** to delete
supuestamente *adv* **:** supposedly, allegedly
supuesto, -ta *adj* **1 :** supposed, alleged **2 por ~ :** of course, absolutely
supurar *vi* **:** to ooze, to discharge
supuso, etc. → **suponer**
sur[1] *adj* **:** southern, southerly, south
sur[2] *nm* **1 :** south, South **2 :** south wind
surafricano, -na → **sudafricano**
suramericano, -na → **sudamericano**
surcar {72} *vt* **1 :** to plow (through) **2 :** to groove, to score, to furrow
surco *nm* **:** groove, furrow, rut
sureño[1], **-ña** *adj* **:** southern, Southern
sureño[2], **-ña** *n* **:** Southerner
sureste[1] *adj* **1 :** southeast, southeastern **2 :** southeasterly
sureste[2] *nm* **:** southeast, Southeast
surf *nm* **:** surfing
surfear *vi* **:** to surf
surfing *nm* → **surf**
surfista *nmf* **:** surfer
surgimiento *nm* **:** rise, emergence
surgir {35} *vi* **:** to rise, to arise, to emerge
suroeste[1] *adj* **1 :** southwest, southwestern **2 :** southwesterly
suroeste[2] *nm* **:** southwest, Southwest
surtido[1], **-da** *adj* **1 :** assorted, varied **2 :** stocked, provisioned
surtido[2] *nm* **:** assortment, selection
surtidor *nm* **1 :** jet, spout **2** *Arg, Chile, Spain* **:** gas pump
surtir *vt* **1 :** to supply, to provide <surtir un pedido : to fill an order> **2 surtir efecto :** to have an effect — *vi* **:** to spout, to spurt up — **surtirse** vr **:** to stock up
susceptible *adj* **:** susceptible, sensitive — **susceptibilidad** *nf*
suscitar *vt* **:** to provoke, to give rise to
suscribir {33} *vt* **1 :** to sign (a formal document) **2 :** to endorse, to sanction — **suscribirse** *vr* **~ a :** to subscribe to
suscripción *nf, pl* **-ciones 1 :** subscription **2 :** endorsement, sanction **3 :** signing
suscriptor, -tora *n* **:** subscriber
susodicho, -cha *adj* **:** aforementioned, aforesaid
suspender *vt* **1** COLGAR **:** to suspend, to hang **2 :** to suspend, to discontinue **3 :** to suspend, to dismiss
suspensión *nf, pl* **-siones :** suspension
suspenso *nm* **:** suspense
suspicacia *nf* **:** suspicion, mistrust
suspicaz *adj, pl* **-caces** DESCONFIADO **:** suspicious, wary
suspirar *vi* **:** to sigh
suspiro *nm* **:** sigh
surque, etc. → **surcar**
suscrito *pp* → **suscribir**
sustancia *nf* **1 :** substance **2 sin ~ :** shallow, lacking substance
sustancial *adj* **1 :** substantial **2** ESENCIAL, FUNDAMENTAL **:** essential, fundamental — **sustancialmente** *adv*

sustancioso, -sa *adj* **1** NUTRITIVO **:** hearty, nutritious **2 :** substantial, solid
sustantivo *nm* **:** noun
sustentación *nf, pl* **-ciones** SOSTÉN **:** support
sustentar *vt* **1 :** to support, to hold up **2 :** to sustain, to nourish **3 :** to maintain, to hold (an opinion) — **sustentarse** *vr* **:** to support oneself
sustento *nm* **1 :** means of support, livelihood **2 :** sustenance, food
sustitución *nf, pl* **-ciones :** replacement, substitution
sustituir {41} *vt* **1 :** to replace, to substitute for **2 :** to stand in for
sustituto, -ta *n* **:** substitute, stand-in
susto *nm* **:** fright, scare
sustracción *nf, pl* **-ciones 1** RESTA **:** subtraction **2 :** theft
sustraer {81} *vt* **1 :** to remove, to take away **2** RESTAR **:** to subtract **3 :** to steal — **sustraerse** *vr* **~ a :** to avoid, to evade
susurrar *vi* **1 :** to whisper **2 :** to murmur **3 :** to rustle (leaves, etc.) — *vt* **:** to whisper
susurro *nm* **1 :** whisper **2 :** murmur **3 :** rustle, rustling
sutil *adj* **1 :** delicate, thin, fine **2 :** subtle
sutileza *nf* **1 :** delicacy **2 :** subtlety
sutura *nf* **:** suture
suturar *vt* **:** to suture
suyo[1], -ya *adj* **1 :** his, her, its, theirs <los libros suyos : his books> <un amigo suyo : a friend of hers> <esta casa es suya : this house is theirs> **2** (*formal*) **:** yours <¿este abrigo es suyo, señor? : is this your coat, sir?>
suyo[2], -ya *pron* **1 :** his, hers, theirs <mi guitarra y la suya : my guitar and hers> <ellos trajeron las suyas : they brought theirs, they brought their own> **2** (*formal*) **:** yours <usted olvidó la suya : you forgot yours>
switch *nm* **:** switch

T

t *nf* **:** twenty-first letter of the Spanish alphabet
taba *nf* **:** anklebone
tabacalero[1], -ra *adj* **:** tobacco <industria tabacalera : tobacco industry>
tabacalero[2], -ra *n* **:** tobacco grower
tabaco *nm* **:** tobacco
tábano *nm* **:** horsefly
taberna *nf* **:** tavern, bar
tabernáculo *nm* **:** tabernacle
tabicar {72} *vt* **:** to wall up
tabique *nm* **:** thin wall, partition
tabla *nf* **1 :** table, list <tabla de multiplicar : multiplication table> **2 :** board, plank, slab <tabla de planchar : ironing board> **3 :** plot, strip (of land) **4 tablas** *nfpl* **:** stage, boards *pl*
tablado *nm* **1 :** flooring, floorboards **2 :** platform, scaffold **3 :** stage
tablero *nm* **1 :** bulletin board **2 :** board (in games) <tablero de ajedrez : chessboard> <tablero de damas : checkerboard> **3** PIZARRA **:** blackboard **4 :** switchboard **5 tablero de instrumentos :** dashboard, instrument panel
tableta *nf* **1** COMPRIMIDO, PÍLDORA **:** tablet, pill **2 :** bar (of chocolate)
tabletear *vi* **:** to rattle, to clack
tableteo *nm* **:** clack, rattling
tablilla *nf* **1 :** small board or tablet **2 :** bulletin board **3 :** splint
tabloide *nm* **:** tabloid
tablón *nm, pl* **tablones 1 :** plank, beam **2 tablón de anuncios :** bulletin board
tabú[1] *adj* **:** taboo
tabú[2] *nm, pl* **tabúes** or **tabús :** taboo
tabulador *nm* **:** tabulator
tabular[1] *vt* **:** to tabulate
tabular[2] *adj* **:** tabular
taburete *nm* **:** footstool, stool
tacañería *nf* **:** miserliness, stinginess
tacaño[1], -na *adj* MEZQUINO **:** stingy, miserly
tacaño[2], -ña *n* **:** miser, tightwad
tacha *nf* **1 :** flaw, blemish, defect **2 poner tacha a :** to find fault with **3 sin ~ :** flawless
tachadura *nf* **:** erasure, correction
tachar *vt* **1 :** to cross out, to delete **2 ~ de :** to accuse of, to label as <lo tacharon de mentiroso : they accused him of being a liar>
tachón *nm, pl* **tachones :** stud, hobnail
tachonar *vt* **:** to stud
tachuela *nf* **:** tack, hobnail, stud
tácito, -ta *adj* **:** tacit, implicit — **tácitamente** *adv*
taciturno, -na *adj* **1 :** taciturn **2 :** sullen, gloomy
tacle *nm* **:** tackle
taclear *vt* **:** to tackle (in football)
taco *nm* **1 :** wad, stopper, plug **2 :** pad (of paper) **3 :** cleat **4 :** heel (of a shoe) **5 :** cue (in billiards) **6 :** light snack, bite **7 :** taco
tacón *nm, pl* **tacones :** heel (of a shoe) <de tacón alto : high-heeled>
táctica *nf* **:** tactic, tactics *pl*
táctico[1], -ca *adj* **:** tactical
táctico[2], -ca *n* **:** tactician
táctil *adj* **:** tactile
tacto *nm* **1 :** touch, touching, feel **2** DELICADEZA **:** tact
tafetán *nm, pl* **-tanes :** taffeta
tahúr *nm, pl* **tahúres :** gambler
tailandés[1], -desa *adj & n, pl* **-deses :** Thai
tailandés[2] *nm* **:** Thai (language)

taimado, -da *adj* **1 :** crafty, sly **2** *Chile* **:** sullen, sulky

tajada *nf* **1 :** slice **2 sacar tajada** *fam* **:** to get one's share

tajante *adj* **1 :** cutting, sharp **2 :** decisive, categorical

tajantemente *adj* **:** emphatically, categorically

tajar *vt* **:** to cut, to slice

tajo *nm* **1 :** cut, slash, gash **2** ESCARPA **:** steep cliff

tal[1] *adv* **1 :** so, in such a way **2 tal como :** just as <tal como lo hice : just the way I did it> **3 con tal que :** provided that, as long as **4 ¿qué tal? :** how are you?, how's it going?

tal[2] *adj* **1 :** such, such a **2 tal vez :** maybe, perhaps

tal[3] *pron* **1 :** such a one, someone **2 :** such a thing, something **3 tal para cual :** two of a kind

tala *nf* **:** felling (of trees)

taladrar *vt* **:** to drill

taladro *nm* **:** drill, auger <taladro eléctrico : power drill>

talante *nm* **1** HUMOR **:** mood, disposition **2** VOLUNTAD **:** will, willingness

talar *vt* **1 :** to cut down, to fell **2** DEVASTAR **:** to devastate, to destroy

talco *nm* **1 :** talc **2 :** talcum powder

talego *nm* **:** sack

talento *nm* **:** talent, ability

talentoso, -sa *adj* **:** talented, gifted

talismán *nm, pl* **-manes** AMULETO **:** talisman, charm

talla *nf* **1** ESTATURA **:** height **2 :** size (in clothing) **3 :** stature, status **4 :** sculpture, carving

tallar *vt* **1 :** to sculpt, to carve **2 :** to measure (someone's height) **3 :** to deal (cards)

tallarín *nf, pl* **-rines :** noodle

talle *nm* **1 :** size **2 :** waist, waistline **3 :** figure, shape

taller *nm* **1 :** shop, workshop **2 :** studio (of an artist)

tallo *nm* **:** stalk, stem <tallo de maíz : cornstalk>

talón *nm, pl* **talones 1 :** heel (of the foot) **2 :** stub (of a check) **3 talón de Aquiles :** Achilles' heel

talud *nm* **:** slope, incline

tamal *nm* **:** tamale

tamaño[1], **-ña** *adj* **:** such a big <¿crees tamaña mentira? : do you believe such a lie?>

tamaño[2] *nm* **1 :** size **2 de tamaño natural :** life-size

tamarindo *nm* **:** tamarind

tambalearse *vr* **1 :** to teeter **2 :** to totter, to stagger, to sway — **tambaleante** *adj*

tambaleo *nm* **:** staggering, lurching, swaying

también *adv* **:** too, as well, also

tambor *nm* **:** drum

tamborilear *vi* **:** to drum, to tap

tamborileo *nm* **:** tapping, drumming

tamiz *nm* **:** sieve

tamizar {21} *vt* **:** to sift

tampoco *adv* **:** neither, not either <ni yo tampoco : me neither>

tampón *nm, pl* **tampones 1 :** ink pad **2 :** tampon

tam–tam *nm* **:** tom-tom

tan *adv* **1 :** so, so very <no es tan difícil : it is not that difficult> **2 :** as <tan pronto como : as soon as> **3 tan siquiera :** at least, at the least **4 tan sólo :** only, merely

tanda *nf* **1 :** turn, shift **2 :** batch, lot, series

tándem *nm* **1 :** tandem (bicycle) **2 :** duo, pair

tangente *adj & nf* **:** tangent — **tangencial** *adj*

tangible *adj* **:** tangible

tango *nm* **:** tango

tanino *nm* **:** tannin

tanque *nm* **1 :** tank, reservoir **2 :** tanker, tank (vehicle)

tanteador *nm* MARCADOR **:** scoreboard

tantear *vt* **1 :** to feel, to grope **2 :** to size up, to weigh — *vi* **1 :** to keep score **2 :** to feel one's way

tanteo *nm* **1 :** estimate, rough calculation **2 :** testing, sizing up **3 :** scoring

tanto[1] *adv* **1 :** so much <tanto mejor : so much the better> **2 :** so long <¿por qué te tardaste tanto? : why did you take so long?>

tanto[2], **-ta** *adj* **1 :** so much, so many, such <no hagas tantas preguntas : don't ask so many questions> <tiene tanto encanto : he has such charm, he's so charming> **2 :** as much, as many <come tantos dulces como yo : she eats as many sweets as I do> **3 :** odd, however many <cuarenta y tantos años : forty-odd years>

tanto[3] *nm* **1 :** certain amount **2 :** goal, point (in sports) **3 al tanto :** abreast, in the picture **4 un tanto :** somewhat, rather <un tanto cansado : rather tired>

tanto[4], **-ta** *pron* **1 :** so much, so many <tiene tanto que hacer : she has so much to do> <¡no me des tantos! : don't give me so many!> **2 entre ~ :** meanwhile **3 por lo tanto :** therefore

tañer {79} *vt* **1 :** to ring (a bell) **2 :** to play (a musical instrument)

tañido *nm* **1** CAMPANADA **:** ring, peal, toll **2 :** sound (of an instrument)

tapa *nf* **1 :** cover, top, lid **2** *Spain* **:** bar snack

tapacubos *nms & pl* **:** hubcap

tapadera *nf* **1 :** cover, lid **2 :** front, cover (for an organization or person)

tapar *vt* **1** CUBRIR **:** to cover, to cover up **2** OBSTRUIR **:** to block, to obstruct — **taparse** *vr*

tapete *nm* **1 :** small rug, mat **2 :** table cover **3 poner sobre el tapete :** to bring up for discussion

tapia *nf* **:** (adobe) wall, garden wall

tapiar *vt* **1 :** to wall in **2 :** to enclose, to block off

tapicería *nf* **1 :** upholstery **2** TAPIZ **:** tapestry
tapicero, -ra *n* **:** upholsterer
tapioca *nf* **:** tapioca
tapir *nm* **:** tapir
tapiz *nm, pl* **tapices :** tapestry
tapizar {21} *vt* **1 :** to upholster **2 :** to cover, to carpet
tapón *nm, pl* **tapones 1 :** cork **2 :** bottle cap **3 :** plug, stopper
tapujo *nm* **1 :** deceit, pretension **2 sin tapujos :** openly, frankly
taquigrafía *nf* **:** stenography, shorthand
taquigráfico, -ca *adj* **:** stenographic
taquígrafo, -fa *n* **:** stenographer
taquilla *nf* **1 :** box office, ticket office **2 :** earnings *pl*, take
taquillero, -ra *adj* **:** box-office, popular <un éxito taquillero : a box-office success>
tarántula *nf* **:** tarantula
tararear *vt* **:** to hum
tardanza *nf* **:** lateness, delay
tardar *vi* **1 :** to delay, to take a long time **2 :** to be late **3 a más tardar :** at the latest — *vt* DEMORAR **:** to take (time) <tarda una hora : it takes an hour>
tarde[1] *adv* **1 :** late **2 tarde o temprano :** sooner or later
tarde[2] *nf* **1 :** afternoon, evening **2 ¡buenas tardes! :** good afternoon!, good evening! **3 en la tarde** *or* **por la tarde :** in the afternoon, in the evening
tardío, -día *adj* **:** late, tardy
tardo, -da *adj* **:** slow
tarea *nf* **1 :** task, job **2 :** homework
tarifa *nf* **1 :** rate <tarifas postales : postal rates> **2 :** fare (for transportation) **3 :** price list **4** ARANCEL **:** duty
tarima *nf* PLATAFORMA **:** dais, platform, stage
tarjeta *nf* **:** card <tarjeta de crédito : credit card> <tarjeta postal : postcard>
tarro *nm* **1 :** jar, pot **2** *Arg, Chile* **:** can, tin
tarta *nf* **1 :** tart **2 :** cake
tartaleta *nf* **:** tart
tartamudear *vi* **:** to stammer, to stutter
tartamudeo *nm* **:** stutter, stammer
tartán *nm, pl* **tartanes :** tartan, plaid
tártaro *nm* **:** tartar <cream of tartar : crémor, tártaro>
tasa *nf* **1 :** rate <tasa de desempleo : unemployment rate> **2 :** tax, fee **3 :** appraisal, valuation
tasación *nf, pl* **-ciones :** appraisal, assessment
tasador, -dora *n* **:** assessor, appraiser
tasar *vt* **1** VALORAR **:** to appraise, to value **2 :** to set the price of **3 :** to ration, to limit
tasca *nf* **:** cheap bar, dive
tatuaje *nm* **:** tattoo, tattooing
tatuar {3} *vt* **:** to tattoo
taurino, -na *adj* **:** bull, bullfighting
Tauro *nmf* **:** Taurus
tauromaquia *nf* **:** (art of) bullfighting
taxi *nm, pl* **taxis :** taxi, taxicab
taxidermia *nf* **:** taxidermy
taxidermista *nmf* **:** taxidermist
taxímetro *nm* **:** taximeter
taxista *nmf* **:** taxi driver
taza *nf* **1 :** cup **2 :** cupful **3 :** (toilet) bowl **4 :** basin (of a fountain)
tazón *nm, pl* **tazones 1 :** bowl **2 :** large cup, mug
te *pron* **1 :** you <te quiero : I love you> **2 :** for you, to you, from you <me gustaría dártelo : I would like to give it to you> **3 :** yourself, for yourself, to yourself, from yourself <¡cálmate! : calm yourself!> <¿te guardaste uno? : did you keep one for yourself?> **4 :** thee
té *nm* **1 :** tea **2 :** tea party
tea *nf* **:** torch
teatral *adj* **:** theatrical — **teatralmente** *adv*
teatro *nm* **1 :** theater **2 hacer teatro :** to put on an act, to exaggerate
teca *nf* **:** teak
techado *nm* **1 :** roof **2 bajo techado :** under cover, indoors
techar *vt* **:** to roof, to shingle
techo *nm* **1** TEJADO **:** roof **2 :** ceiling **3 :** upper limit, ceiling
techumbre *nf* **:** roofing
tecla *nf* **1 :** key (of a musical instrument or a machine) **2 dar en la tecla :** to hit the nail on the head
teclado *nm* **:** keyboard
teclear *vt* **:** to type in, to enter
técnica *nf* **1 :** technique, skill **2 :** technology
técnico[1], **-ca** *adj* **:** technical — **técnicamente** *adv*
técnico[2], **-ca** *n* **:** technician, expert, engineer
tecnología *nf* **:** technology
tecnológico, -ca *adj* **:** technological — **tecnológicamente** *adv*
tecolote *nm Mex* **:** owl
tedio *nm* **:** tedium, boredom
tedioso, -sa *adj* **:** tedious, boring — **tediosamente** *adv*
teja *nf* **:** tile
tejado *nm* TECHO **:** roof
tejedor, -dora *n* **:** weaver
tejer *vt* **1 :** to knit, to crochet **2 :** to weave **3** FABRICAR **:** to concoct, to make up, to fabricate
tejido *nm* **1** TELA **:** fabric, cloth **2 :** weave, texture **3 :** tissue <tejido muscular : muscle tissue>
tejo *nm* **:** yew
tejón *nm, pl* **tejones :** badger
tela *nf* **1 :** fabric, cloth, material **2 tela de araña :** spiderweb **3 poner en tela de juicio :** to call into question, to doubt
telar *nm* **:** loom
telaraña *nf* **:** spiderweb, cobweb
tele *nf fam* **:** TV, television
telecomunicación *nf, pl* **-ciones :** telecommunication

teleconferencia *nf* **:** teleconference
teledifusión *nf, pl* **-siones :** television broadcasting
teledirigido, -da *adj* **:** remote-controlled
telefonear *v* **:** to telephone, to call
telefónico, -ca *adj* **:** phone, telephone <llamada telefónica : phone call>
telefonista *nmf* **:** telephone operator
teléfono *nm* **1 :** telephone **2 llamar por teléfono :** to telephone, to make a phone call
telegrafiar {85} *v* **:** to telegraph
telegráfico, -ca *adj* **:** telegraphic
telégrafo *nm* **:** telegaph
telegrama *nm* **:** telegram
telenovela *nf* **:** soap opera
telepatía *nf* **:** telepathy
telepático, -ca *adj* **:** telepathic — **telepáticamente** *adv*
telescópico, -ca *adj* **:** telescopic
telescopio *nm* **:** telescope
telespectador, -dora *n* **:** television viewer
telesquí *nm, pl* **-squís :** ski lift
televidente *nmf* **:** television viewer
televisar *vt* **:** to televise
televisión *nf, pl* **-siones :** television, TV
televisivo, -va *adj* **:** television <serie televisiva : television series>
televisor *nm* **:** television set
telón *nm, pl* **telones 1 :** curtain (in theater) **2 telón de fondo :** backdrop, background
tema *nm* **1** ASUNTO **:** theme, topic, subject **2** MOTIVO **:** motif, central theme
temario *nm* **1 :** set of topics (for study) **2 :** agenda
temática *nf* **:** subject matter
temático, -ca *adj* **:** thematic
temblar {55} *vi* **1 :** to tremble, to shake, to shiver <le temblaban las rodillas : his knees were shaking> **2 :** to shudder, to be afraid <tiemblo con sólo pensarlo : I shudder to think of it>
temblor *nm* **1 :** shaking, trembling **2 :** tremor, earthquake
tembloroso, -sa *adj* **:** tremulous, trembling, shaking <con la voz temblorosa : with a shaky voice>
temer *vt* **:** to fear, to dread — *vi* **:** to be afraid
temerario, -ria *adj* **:** reckless, rash — **temerariamente** *adv*
temeridad *nf* **1 :** temerity, recklessness, rashness **2 :** rash act
temeroso, -sa *adj* MIEDOSO **:** fearful, frightened
temible *adj* **:** fearsome, dreadful
temor *nm* MIEDO **:** fear, dread
témpano *nm* **:** ice floe
temperamento *nm* **:** temperament — **temperamental** *adj*
temperancia *nf* **:** temperance
temperar *vt* MODERAR **:** to temper, to moderate — *vi* **:** to have a change of air
temperatura *nf* **:** temperature
tempestad *nf* **1 :** storm, tempest **2 tempestad de arena :** sandstorm
tempestuoso, -sa *adj* **:** tempestuous, stormy
templado, -da *adj* **1 :** temperate, mild **2 :** moderate, restrained **3 :** warm, lukewarm **4** VALIENTE **:** courageous, bold
templanza *nf* **1 :** temperance, moderation **2 :** mildness (of weather)
templar *vt* **1 :** to temper (steel) **2 :** to restrain, to moderate **3 :** to tune (a musical instrument) **4 :** to warm up, to cool down — **templarse** *vr* **1 :** to be moderate **2 :** to warm up, to cool down
temple *nm* **1 :** temper (of steel, etc.) **2** HUMOR **:** mood <de buen temple : in a good mood> **3 :** tuning **4** VALOR **:** courage
templo *nm* **1 :** temple **2 :** church, chapel
tempo *nm* **:** tempo (in music)
temporada *nf* **1 :** season, time <temporada de béisbol : baseball season> **2 :** period, spell <por temporadas : on and off>
temporal[1] *adj* **1 :** temporal **2 :** temporary
temporal[2] *nm* **1 :** storm **2 capear el temporal :** to weather the storm
temporalmente *adv* **:** temporarily
temporario, -ria *adj* **:** temporary — **temporariamente** *adv*
temporero[1], **-ra** *adj* **:** temporary, seasonal
temporero[2], **-ra** *n* **:** temporary or seasonal worker
temporizador *nm* **:** timer
tempranero, -ra *adj* **1 :** early **2 :** early-rising
temprano[1] *adv* **:** early <lo más temprano posible : as soon as possible>
temprano[2], **-na** *adj* **:** early <la parte temprana del siglo : the early part of the century>
ten → **tener**
tenacidad *nf* **:** tenacity, perseverance
tenaz *adj, pl* **tenaces 1 :** tenacious, persistent **2 :** strong, tough
tenaza *nf or* **tenazas** *nfpl* **1 :** pliers, pincers **2 :** tongs **3 :** claw (of a crustacean)
tenazmente *adv* **:** tenaciously
tendedero *nm* **:** clothesline
tendencia *nf* **1** PROPENSIÓN **:** tendency, inclination **2 :** trend
tendencioso, -sa *adj* **:** tendencious, biased
tendente → **tendiente**
tender {56} *vt* **1** EXTENDER **:** to spread out, to lay out **2 :** to hang out (clothes) **3 :** to lay (cables, etc.) **4 :** to set (a trap) — *vi* **~ a :** to tend to, to have a tendency towards — **tenderse** *vr* **:** to stretch out, to lie down
tendero, -ra *n* **:** shopkeeper, storekeeper

tendido *nm* **1 :** laying (of cables, etc.) **2 :** seats *pl,* section (at a bullfight)

tendiente *adj* **~ a :** aimed at, designed to

tendón *nm, pl* **tendones :** tendon

tenebrosidad *nf* **:** darkness, gloom

tendrá, etc. → **tener**

tenebroso, -sa *adj* **1** OSCURO **:** gloomy, dark **2** SINIESTRO **:** sinister

tenedor[1], -dora *n* **1 :** holder **2 tenedor de libros, tenedora de libros :** bookkeeper

tenedor[2] *nm* **:** table fork

tenencia *nf* **1 :** possession, holding **2 :** tenancy **3 :** tenure

tener {80} *vt* **1 :** to have <tiene ojos verdes : she has green eyes> <tengo mucho que hacer : I have a lot to do> <tiene veinte años : he's twenty years old> <tiene un metro de largo : it's one meter long> **2 :** to hold <ten esto un momento : hold this for a moment> **3 :** to feel, to make <tengo frío : I'm cold> <eso nos tiene contentos : that makes us happy> **4 ~ por :** to think, to consider <me tienes por loco : you think I'm crazy> — *v aux* **1 tener que :** to have to <tengo que salir : I have to leave> <tiene que estar aquí : it has to be here, it must be here> **2** (*with past participle*) <tenía pensado escribirte : I've been thinking of writing to you> — **tenerse** *vr* **1 :** to stand up **2 ~ por :** to consider oneself <me tengo por afortunado : I consider myself lucky>

tenería *nf* CURTIDURÍA **:** tannery

tenga, etc. → **tener**

tenia *nf* SOLITARIA **:** tapeworm

teniente *nmf* **1 :** lieutenant **2 teniente coronel :** lieutenant colonel

tenis *nms & pl* **1 :** tennis **2 tenis** *nmpl* **:** sneakers *pl*

tenista *nmf* **:** tennis player

tenor *nm* **1 :** tenor **2 :** tone, sense

tensar *vt* **1 :** to tense, to make taut **2 :** to draw (a bow) — **tensarse** *vr* **:** to become tense

tensión *nf, pl* **tensiones 1 :** tension, tautness **2 :** stress, strain **3 tensión arterial :** blood pressure

tenso, -sa *adj* **:** tense

tentación *nf, pl* **-ciones :** temptation

tentáculo *nm* **:** tentacle, feeler

tentador[1], -dora *adj* **:** tempting

tentador[2], -dora *n* **:** tempter, temptress *f*

tentar {55} *vt* **1** TOCAR **:** to feel, to touch **2** PROBAR **:** to test, to try **3** ATRAER **:** to tempt, to entice

tentativa *nf* **:** attempt, try

tentempié *nm fam* **:** snack, bite

tenue *adj* **1 :** tenuous **2 :** faint, weak, dim **3 :** light, fine **4 :** thin, slender

teñir {67} *vt* **1 :** to dye **2 :** to stain

teodolito *nm* **:** theodolite, transit (for surveying)

teología *nf* **:** theology

teológico, -ca *adj* **:** theological

teólogo, -ga *n* **:** theologian

teorema *nm* **:** theorem

teoría *nf* **:** theory

teórico[1], -ca *adj* **:** theoretical — **teóricamente** *adv*

teórico[2], -ca *n* **:** theorist

teorizar {21} *vi* **:** to theorize

tepe *nm* **:** sod, turf

teponaztle *nm Mex* **:** traditional drum

tequila *nm* **:** tequila

terapeuta *nmf* **:** therapist

terapéutica *nf* **:** therapeutics

terapéutico, -ca *adj* **:** therapeutic

terapia *nf* **1 :** therapy **2 terapia intensiva :** intensive care

tercer → **tercero**

tercermundista *adj* **:** third-world

tercero[1], -ra *adj* (**tercer** *before masculine singular nouns*) **1 :** third **2 el Tercer Mundo :** the Third World

tercero[2], -ra *n* **:** third (in a series)

terciar *vt* **1 :** to place diagonally **2 :** to divide into three parts — *vi* **1 :** to mediate **2 ~ en :** to take part in

terciario, -ria *adj* **:** tertiary

tercio[1], -cia → **tercero**

tercio[2] *nm* **:** third <dos tercios : two thirds>

terciopelo *nm* **:** velvet

terco, -ca *adj* OBSTINADO **:** obstinate, stubborn

tergiversación *nf, pl* **-ciones :** distortion

tergiversar *vt* **:** to distort, to twist

termal *adj* **:** thermal, hot

termas *nfpl* **:** hot springs

térmico, -ca *adj* **:** thermal, heat <energía térmica : thermal energy>

terminación *nf, pl* **-ciones :** termination, conclusion

terminal[1] *adj* **:** terminal — **terminalmente** *adv*

terminal[2] *nm* (*in some regions f*) **:** (electric or electronic) terminal

terminal[3] *nf* (*in some regions m*) **:** terminal, station

terminante *adj* **:** final, definitive, categorical — **terminantemente** *adv*

terminar *vt* **1** CONCLUIR **:** to end, to conclude **2** ACABAR **:** to complete, to finish off — *vi* **1 :** to finish **2 :** to stop, to end — **terminarse** *vr* **1 :** to run out **2 :** to come to an end

término *nm* **1** CONCLUSIÓN **:** end, conclusion **2 :** term, expression **3 :** period, term of office **4 término medio :** happy medium **5 términos** *nmpl* **:** terms, specifications <los términos del acuerdo : the terms of the agreement>

terminología *nf* **:** terminology

termita *nf* **:** termite

termo *nm* **:** thermos

termodinámica *nf* **:** thermodynamics

termómetro *nm* **:** thermometer

termóstato *nm* **:** thermostat

ternera *nf* **:** veal

ternero, -ra *n* **:** calf

terno *nm* **1 :** set of three **2 :** three-piece suit

ternura *nf* **:** tenderness

terquedad *nf* OBSTINACIÓN **:** obstinacy, stubbornness

terracota *nf* **:** terra-cotta

terraplén *nm, pl* **-plenes :** terrace, embankment

terráqueo, -quea *adj* **1 :** earth **2 globo terráqueo :** the earth, globe (of the earth)

terrateniente *nmf* **:** landowner

terraza *nf* **1 :** terrace, veranda **2 :** balcony (in a theater) **3 :** terrace (in agriculture)

terremoto *nm* **:** earthquake

terrenal *adj* **:** worldly, earthly

terreno *nm* **1 :** terrain **2** SUELO **:** earth, ground **3 :** plot, tract of land **4 perder terreno :** to lose ground **5 preparar el terreno :** to pave the way

terrestre *adj* **:** terrestrial

terrible *adj* **:** terrible, horrible — **terriblemente** *adv*

terrier *nmf* **:** terrier

territorial *adj* **:** territorial

territorio *nm* **:** territory

terrón *nm, pl* **terrones 1 :** clod (of earth) **2 terrón de azúcar :** lump of sugar

terror *nm* **:** terror

terrorífico, -ca *adj* **:** horrific, terrifying

terrorismo *nm* **:** terrorism

terrorista *adj & nmf* **:** terrorist

terroso, -sa *adj* **:** earthy <colores terrosos : earthy colors>

terruño *nm* **:** native land, homeland

terso, -sa *adj* **1 :** smooth **2 :** glossy, shiny **3 :** polished, flowing (of a style)

tersura *nf* **1 :** smoothness **2 :** shine

tertulia *nf* **:** gathering, group <tertulia literaria : literary circle>

tesauro *nm* **:** thesaurus

tesis *nfs & pl* **:** thesis

tesón *nm* **:** persistence, tenacity

tesonero, -ra *adj* **:** persistent, tenacious

tesorería *nf* **:** treasurer's office

tesorero, -ra *n* **:** treasurer

tesoro *nm* **1 :** treasure **2 :** thesaurus

testaferro *nm* **:** figurehead

testamentario[1], -ria *adj* **:** testamentary

testamentario[2], -ria *n* ALBACEA **:** executor, executrix *f*

testamento *nm* **:** testament, will

testar *vi* **:** to draw up a will

testarudo, -da *adj* **:** stubborn, pigheaded

testículo *nm* **:** testicle

testificar {72} *v* **:** to testify

testigo *nmf* **:** witness

testimonial *adj* **1 :** testimonial **2 :** token

testimoniar *vi* **:** to testify

testimonio *nm* **:** testimony, statement

teta *nf* **:** teat

tétano *or* **tétanos** *nm* **:** tetanus, lockjaw

tetera *nf* **1 :** teapot **2 :** teakettle

tetilla *nf* **1 :** teat **2 :** nipple

tetina *nf* **:** nipple (on a bottle)

tétrico, -ca *adj* **:** somber, gloomy

textil *adj & nm* **:** textile

texto *nm* **:** text

textual *adj* **:** literal, exact — **textualmente** *adv*

textura *nf* **:** texture

tez *nf, pl* **teces :** complexion, coloring

ti *pron* **1 :** you <es para ti : it's for you> **2 ti mismo, ti misma :** yourself **3 :** thee

tía → **tío**

tiamina *nf* **:** thiamine

tianguis *nm Mex* **:** open-air market

tibetano, -na *adj & n* **:** Tibetan

tibia *nf* **:** tibia

tibieza *nf* **1 :** tepidness **2 :** halfheartedness

tibio, -bia *adj* **1 :** lukewarm, tepid **2 :** cool, unenthusiastic

tiburón *nm, pl* **-rones 1 :** shark **2 :** raider (in finance)

tic *nm* **1 :** click, tick **2 tic nervioso :** tic

tico, -ca *adj & n fam* **:** Costa Rican

tiembla, etc. → **temblar**

tiempo *nm* **1 :** time <justo a tiempo : just in time> <perder tiempo : to waste time> <tiempo libre : spare time> **2 :** period, age <en los tiempos que corren : nowadays> **3 :** season, moment <antes de tiempo : prematurely> **4 :** weather <hace buen tiempo : the weather is fine, it's nice outside> **5 :** tempo (in music) **6 :** half (in sports) **7 :** tense (in grammar)

tienda *nf* **1 :** store, shop **2** *or* **tienda de campaña :** tent

tiende, etc. → **tender**

tiene, etc. → **tener**

tienta[1], etc. → **tentar**

tienta[2] *nf* **andar a tientas :** to feel one's way, to grope around

tiernamente *adv* **:** tenderly

tierno, -na *adj* **1 :** affectionate, tender **2 :** tender, young

tierra *nf* **1 :** land **2** SUELO **:** ground, earth **3 :** country, homeland, soil **4 tierra natal :** native land **5 la Tierra :** the Earth

tieso, -sa *adj* **1 :** stiff, rigid **2 :** upright, erect

tiesto *nm* **1 :** potsherd **2** MACETA **:** flowerpot

tiesura *nf* **:** stiffness, rigidity

tifoidea *nf* **:** typhoid

tifoideo, -dea *adj* **:** typhoid <fiebre tifoidea : typhoid fever>

tifón *nm, pl* **tifones :** typhoon

tifus *nm* **:** typhus

tigre, -gresa *n* **1 :** tiger, tigress *f* **2 :** jaguar

tijera *nf* **1** *or* **tijeras** *nfpl* **:** scissors **2 de ~ :** folding <escalera de tijera : stepladder>

tijereta *nf* **:** earwig

tijeretada *nf or* **tijeretazo** *nm* **:** cut, snip

tildar *vt* **~ de** : to brand as, to call <lo tildaron de traidor : they branded him as a traitor>
tilde *nf* **1** : accent mark **2** : tilde (accent over *ñ*)
tilo *nm* : linden (tree)
timador, -dora *n* : swindler
timar *vt* : to swindle, to cheat
timbal *nm* **1** : kettledrum **2 timbales** *nmpl* : timpani
timbre *nm* **1** : bell <tocar el timbre : to ring the doorbell> **2** : tone, timbre **3** SELLO : seal, stamp **4** *CA, Mex* : postage stamp
timidez *nf* : timidity, shyness
tímido, -da *adj* : timid, shy — **tímidamente** *adv*
timo *nm fam* : swindle, trick, hoax
timón *nm, pl* **timones** : rudder <estar al timón : to beat the helm>
timonel *nm* : helmsman, coxwain
timorato, -ta *adj* **1** : timorous **2** : sanctimonious
tímpano *nm* **1** : eardrum **2 tímpanos** *nmpl* : timpani, kettledrums
tina *nf* **1** BAÑERA : tub, bathtub **2** : vat
tinaco *nm Mex* : water tank
tinieblas *nfpl* **1** OSCURIDAD : darkness **2** : ignorance
tino *nm* **1** : good judgment, sense **2** : tact, sensitivity, insight
tinta *nf* : ink
tinte *nm* **1** : dye, coloring **2** : overtone <tintes raciales : racial overtones>
tintero *nm* **1** : inkwell **2 quedarse en el tintero** : to remain unsaid
tintinear *vt* : to jingle, to clink, to tinkle
tintineo *nm* : clink, jingle, tinkle
tinto, -ta *adj* **1** : dyed, stained <tinto en sangre : bloodstained> **2** : red (of wine)
tintorería *nf* : dry cleaner (service)
tintura *nf* **1** : dye, tint **2** : tincture <tintura de yodo : tincture of iodine>
tiña *nf* : ringworm
tiñe, etc. → **teñir**
tío, tía *n* : uncle *m,* aunt *f*
tiovivo *nm* : merry-go-round
tipi *nm* : tepee
típico, -ca *adj* : typical — **típicamente** *adv*
tipificar {72} *vt* **1** : to classify, to categorize **2** : to typify
tiple *nm* : soprano
tipo[1] *nm* **1** CLASE : type, kind, sort **2** : figure, build, appearance **3** : rate <tipo de interés : interest rate> **4** : (printing) type, typeface **5** : style, model <un vestido tipo 60's : a 60's-style dress>
tipo[2]**, -pa** *n fam* : guy *m,* gal *f,* character
tipografía *nf* : typography, printing
tipográfico, -ca *adj* : typographic, typographical
tipográfo, -fa *n* : printer, typographer
tique *or* **tiquet** *nm* **1** : ticket **2** : receipt
tira *nf* **1** : strip, strap **2 tira cómica** : comic, comic strip
tirabuzón *nf, pl* **-zones** : corkscrew
tirada *nf* **1** : throw **2** : distance, stretch **3** IMPRESIÓN : printing, issue
tiradero *nm Mex* **1** : dump **2** : mess, clutter
tirador[1] *nm* : handle, knob
tirador[2]**, -dora** *n* : marksman *m,* markswoman *f*
tiragomas *nms & pl* : slingshot
tiranía *nf* : tyranny
tiránico, -ca *adj* : tyrannical
tiranizar {21} *vt* : to tyrannize
tirano[1]**, -na** *adj* : tyrannical, despotic
tirano[2]**, -na** *n* : tyrant
tirante[1] *adj* **1** : tense, strained **2** : taut
tirante[2] *nm* **1** : shoulder strap **2 tirantes** *nmpl* : suspenders
tirantez *nf* **1** : tautness **2** : tension, friction, strain
tirar *vt* **1** : to throw, to hurl, to toss **2** BOTAR : to throw away, to throw out, to waste **3** DERRIBAR : to knock down **4** : to shoot, to fire, to launch **5** : to take (a photo) **6** : to print, to run off — *vi* **1** : to pull, to draw **2** : to shoot **3** : to attract **4** : to get by, to manage <va tirando : he's getting along, he's managing> **5 ~ a** : to tend towards, to be rather <tira a picante : it's a bit spicy> — **tirarse** *vr* **1** : to throw oneself **2** *fam* : to spend (time)
tiritar *vi* : to shiver, to tremble
tiro *nm* **1** BALAZO, DISPARO : shot, gunshot **2** : shot, kick (in sports) **3** : flue **4** : team (of horses, etc.) **5 a ~** : within range **6 al tiro** : right away **7 tiro de gracia** : coup de grace, death blow
tiroideo, -dea *adj* : thyroid
tiroides *nmf* : thyroid, thyroid gland — **tiroides** *adj*
tirolés, -lesa *adj* : Tyrolean
tirón *nm, pl* **tirones 1** : pull, tug, yank **2 de un tirón** : all at once, in one go
tiroteo *nm* **1** : shooting **2** : gunfight, shoot-out
tirria *nf fam* **tener tirria a** : to have a grudge against
titánico, -ca *adj* : titanic, huge
titanio *nm* : titanium
títere *nm* : puppet
tití *nm* : marmoset
titilar *vi* : to twinkle, to flicker
titileo *nm* : twinkle, flickering
titiritero, -ra *n* **1** : puppeteer **2** : acrobat
titubear *vi* **1** : to hesitate **2** : to stutter, to stammer — **titubeante** *adj*
titubeo *nm* **1** : hesitation **2** : stammering
titulado, -da *adj* **1** : titled, entitled **2** : qualified
titular[1] *vt* : to title, to entitle — **titularse** *vr* **1** : to be called, to be entitled **2** : to receive a degree
titular[2] *adj* : titular, official

titular[3] *nm* : headline

titular[4] *nmf* **1** : owner, holder **2** : officeholder, incumbent

título *nm* **1** : title **2** : degree, qualification **3** : security, bond **4 a título de** : by way of, in the capacity of

tiza *nf* : chalk

tiznar *vt* : to blacken (with soot, etc.)

tizne *nm* HOLLÍN : soot

tiznón *nm, pl* **tiznones** : stain, smudge

tlapalería *nf Mex* : hardware store

TNT *nm* : TNT

toalla *nf* : towel

toallita *nf* : washcloth

tobillo *nm* : ankle

tobogán *nm, pl* **-ganes 1** : toboggan, sled **2** : slide, chute

tocadiscos *nms & pl* : record player, phonograph

tocado[1], **-da** *adj* **1** : bad, bruised (of fruit) **2** *fam* : touched, not all there

tocado[2] *nm* : headdress

tocador[1] *nm* **1** : dressing table, vanity table **2 artículos de tocador** : toiletries

tocador[2], **-dora** *n* : player (of music)

tocante *adj* **~ a** : with regard to, regarding

tocar {72} *vt* **1** : to touch, to feel, to handle **2** : to touch on, to refer to **3** : to concern, to affect **4** : to play (a musical instrument) — *vi* **1** : to knock, to ring <tocar a la puerta : to rap on the door> **2 ~ en** : to touch on, to border on <eso toca en lo ridículo : that's almost ludicrous> **3 tocarle a** : to fall to, to be up to, to be one's turn <¿a quién le toca manejar? : whose turn is it to drive?>

tocayo, -ya *n* : namesake

tocineta *nf Col, Ven* : bacon

tocino *nm* **1** : bacon **2** : salt pork

tocología *nf* OBSTETRICIA : obstetrics

tocólogo, -ga *n* OBSTETRA : obstetrician

tocón *nm, pl* **tocones** CEPA : stump (of a tree)

todavía *adv* **1** AÚN : still, yet <todavía puedes verlo : you can still see it> **2** : even <todavía más rápido : even faster> **3 todavía no** : not yet

todo[1], **-da** *adj* **1** : all, whole, entire <con toda sinceridad : with all sincerity> <toda la comunidad : the whole community> **2** : every, each <a todo nivel : at every level> **3** : maximum <a toda velocidad : at top speed> **4 todo el mundo** : everyone, everybody

todo[2] *nm* : whole

todo[3], **-da** *pron* **1** : everything, all, every bit <lo sabe todo : he knows it all> <es todo un soldado : he's every inch a soldier> **2 todos, -das** *pl* : everybody, everyone, all

todopoderoso, -sa *adj* OMNIPOTENTE : almighty, all-powerful

toga *nf* **1** : toga **2** : gown, robe (for magistrates, etc.)

toldo *nm* : awning, canopy

tolerable *adj* : tolerable — **tolerablemente** *adv*

tolerancia *nf* : tolerance, toleration

tolerante *adj* : tolerant — **tolerantemente** *adv*

tolerar *vt* : to tolerate

tolete *nm* : oarlock

tolva *nf* : hopper (container)

toma *nf* **1** : taking, seizure, capture **2** DOSIS : dose **3** : take, shot **4 toma de corriente** : wall socket, outlet **5 toma y daca** : give-and-take

tomar *vt* **1** : to take <tomé el libro : I took the book> <tomar un taxi : to take a taxi> <tomar una foto : to take a photo> <toma dos años : it takes two years> <tomaron medidas drásticas : they took drastic measures> **2** BEBER : to drink **3** CAPTURAR : to capture, to seize **4 tomar el sol** : to sunbathe **5 tomar tierra** : to land — *vi* : to drink (alcohol) — **tomarse** *vr* **1** : to take <tomarse la molestia de : to take the trouble to> **2** : to drink, to eat, to have

tomate *nm* : tomato

tomillo *nm* : thyme

tomo *nm* : volume, tome

ton *nm* **sin ton ni son** : without rhyme or reason

tonada *nf* **1** : tune, song **2** : accent

tonalidad *nf* : tonality

tonel *nm* BARRICA : barrel, cask

tonelada *nf* : ton

tonelaje *nm* : tonnage

tónica *nf* **1** : tonic (water) **2** : tonic (in music) **3** : trend, tone <dar la tónica : to set the tone>

tónico[1], **-ca** *adj* : tonic

tónico[2] *nm* : tonic <tónico capilar : hair tonic>

tono *nm* **1** : tone <tono muscular : muscle tone> **2** : shade (of colors) **3** : key (in music)

tontamente *adv* : foolishly, stupidly

tontear *vi* **1** : to fool around, to play the fool **2** : to flirt

tontería *nf* **1** : foolishness **2** : stupid remark or action **3 decir tonterías** : to talk nonsense

tonto[1], **-ta** *adj* **1** : dumb, stupid **2** : silly **3 a tontas y a locas** : without thinking, haphazardly

tonto[2], **-ta** *n* : fool, idiot

topacio *nm* : topaz

toparse *vr* **~ con** : to bump into, to run into, to come across <me topé con algunas dificultades : I ran into some problems>

tope *nm* **1** : limit, end <hasta el tope : to the limit, to the brim> **2** : stop, check, buffer <tope de puerta : doorstop> **3** : bump, collision **4** *Mex* : speed bump

tópico[1], **-ca** *adj* **1** : topical, external **2** : trite, commonplace

tópico[2] *nm* **1** : topic, subject **2** : cliché, trite expression

topo *nm* **1** : mole (animal) **2** *fam* : clumsy person, blunderer
topografía *nf* : topography
topográfico, -ca *adj* : topographic, topographical
topógrafo, -fa *n* : topographer
toque[1], **etc.** → **tocar**
toque[2] *nm* **1** : touch <el último toque : the finishing touch> <un toque de color : a touch of color> **2** : ringing, peal, chime **3** *Mex* : shock, jolt **4** **toque de queda** : curfew **5** **toque de diana** : reveille
toquetear *vt* : to touch, to handle, to finger
tórax *nm* : thorax
torbellino *nm* : whirlwind
torcedura *nf* **1** : twisting, buckling **2** : sprain
torcer {14} *vt* **1** : to bend, to twist **2** : to sprain **3** : to turn (a corner) **4** : to wring, to wring out **5** : to distort — *vi* : to turn — **torcerse** *vr*
torcido, -da *adj* **1** : twisted, crooked **2** : devious
tordo *nm* ZORZAL : thrush
torear *vt* **1** : to fight (bulls) **2** : to dodge, to sidestep
toreo *nm* : bullfighting
torero, -ra *n* MATADOR : bullfighter, matador
tormenta *nf* **1** : storm <tormenta de nieve : snowstorm> **2** : turmoil, frenzy
tormento *nm* **1** : torment, anguish **2** : torture
tormentoso, -sa *adj* : stormy, turbulent
tornado *nm* : tornado
tornamesa *nmf* : turntable
tornar *vt* **1** : to return, to give back **2** : to make, to render — *vi* : to go back — **tornarse** *vr* : to become, to turn into
tornasol *nm* **1** : reflected light **2** : sunflower **3** : litmus
tornear *vt* : to turn (in carpentry)
torneo *nm* : tournament
tornillo *nm* **1** : screw **2** **tornillo de banco** : vise
torniquete *nm* **1** : tourniquet **2** : turnstile
torno *nm* **1** : lathe **2** : winch **3** **torno de banco** : vise **4** **en torno a** : around, about <en torno a este asunto : about this issue> <en torno suyo : around him>
toro *nm* : bull
toronja *nf* : grapefruit
toronjil *nm* : balm, lemon balm
torpe *adj* **1** DESMAÑADO : clumsy, awkward **2** : stupid, dull — **torpemente** *adv*
torpedear *vt* : to torpedo
torpedo *nm* : torpedo
torpeza *nf* **1** : clumsiness, awkwardness **2** : stupidity **3** : blunder
torre *nf* **1** : tower <torre de perforación : oil rig> **2** : turret **3** : rook, castle (in chess)
torrencial *adj* : torrential — **torrencialmente** *adv*
torrente *nm* **1** : torrent **2** **torrente sanguíneo** : bloodstream
torreón *nm, pl* **-rreones** : tower (of a castle)
torreta *nf* : turret (of a tank, ship, etc.)
tórrido, -da *adj* : torrid
torsión *nf, pl* **torsiones** : torsion — **torsional** *adj*
torso *nm* : torso, trunk
torta *nf* **1** : torte, cake **2** *Mex* : sandwich
tortazo *nm fam* : blow, wallop
tortilla *nf* **1** : tortilla **2** *or* **tortilla de huevo** : omelet
tórtola *nf* : turtledove
tortuga *nf* **1** : turtle, tortoise **2** **tortuga de agua dulce** : terrapin **3** **tortuga boba** : loggerhead
tortuoso, -sa *adj* : tortuous, winding
tortura *nf* : torture
torturador, -dora *n* : torturer
torturar *vt* : to torture, to torment
torvo, -va *adj* : grim, stern, baleful
torzamos, etc. → **torcer**
tos *nf* **1** : cough **2** **tos ferina** : whooping cough
tosco, -ca *adj* : rough, coarse
toser *vi* : to cough
tosquedad *nf* : crudeness, coarseness, roughness
tostada *nf* **1** : piece of toast **2** : tostada
tostador *nm* **1** : toaster **2** : roaster (for coffee)
tostar {19} *vt* **1** : to toast **2** : to roast (coffee) **3** : to tan — **tostarse** *vr* : to get a tan
tostón *nm, pl* **tostones** *Car* : fried plantain chip
total[1] *adv* : in the end, so <total, que no fui : in short, I didn't go>
total[2] *adj & nm* : total — **totalmente** *adv*
totalidad *nf* : totality, whole
totalitario, -ria *adj & n* : totalitarian
totalitarismo *nm* : totalitarianism
totalizar {21} *vt* : total, to add up to
tótem *nm, pl* **tótems** : totem
totopo *nm CA, Mex* : tortilla chip
totuma *nf* : calabash
tour [ˈtur] *nm, pl* **tours** : tour, excursion
toxicidad *nf* : toxicity
tóxico[1], **-ca** *adj* : toxic, poisonous
tóxico[2] *nm* : poison
toxicomanía *nf* : drug addiction
toxicómano, -na *n* : drug addict
toxina *nf* : toxin
tozudez *nf* : stubbornness, obstinancy
tozudo, -da *adj* : stubborn, obstinate — **tozudamente** *adv*
traba *nf* **1** : tie, bond **2** : obstacle, hinderance
trabajador[1], **-dora** *adj* : hard-working
trabajador[2], **-dora** *n* : worker

trabajar *vi* **1 :** to work <trabaja mucho : he works hard> <trabajo de secretaria : I work as a secretary> **2 :** to strive <trabajan por mejores oportunidades : they're striving for better opportunities> **3 :** to act, to perform <trabajar en una película : to be in a movie> — *vt* **1 :** to work (metal) **2 :** to knead **3 :** to till **4 :** to work on <tienes que trabajar el español : you need to work on your Spanish>

trabajo *nm* **1 :** work, job **2** LABOR **:** labor, work <tengo mucho trabajo : I have a lot of work to do> **3** TAREA **:** task **4** ESFUERZA **:** effort **5 costar trabajo :** to be difficult **6 tomarse el trabajo :** to take the trouble **7 trabajo en equipo :** teamwork **8 trabajos** *nmpl* **:** hardships, difficulties

trabajoso, -sa *adj* LABORIOSO **:** laborious — **trabajosamente** *adv*

trabalenguas *nms & pl* **:** tongue twister

trabar *vt* **1 :** to join, to connect **2 :** to impede, to hold back **3 :** to strike up (a conversation), to form (a friendship) **4 :** to thicken (sauces) — **trabarse** *vr* **1 :** to jam **2 :** to become entangled **3 :** to be tongue-tied, to stammer

trabucar {72} *vt* **:** to confuse, to mix up

trabuco *nm* **:** blunderbuss

tracalero, -ra *adj Mex* **:** dishonest, tricky

tracción *nf* **:** traction

trace, etc. → **trazar**

tracto *nm* **:** tract

tractor *nm* **:** tractor

tradición *nf, pl* **-ciones :** tradition

tradicional *adj* **:** traditional — **tradicionalmente** *adv*

traducción *nf, pl* **-ciones :** translation

traducible *adj* **:** translatable

traducir {61} *vt* **1 :** to translate **2 :** to convey, to express — **traducirse** *vr* **~ en :** to result in

traductor, -dora *n* **:** translator

traer {81} *vt* **1 :** to bring <trae una ensalada : bring a salad> **2** CAUSAR **:** to cause, to bring about <el problema puede traer graves consecuencias : the problem could have serious consequences> **3 :** to carry, to have <todos los periódicos traían las mismas noticias : all of the newspapers carried the same news> **4** LLEVAR **:** to wear — **traerse** *vr* **1 :** to bring along **2 traérselas :** to be difficult

traficante *nmf* **:** dealer, trafficker

traficar {72} *vi* **1 :** to trade, to deal **2 ~ en :** to traffic in

tráfico *nm* **1 :** trade **2 :** traffic

tragaluz *nf, pl* **-luces :** skylight, fanlight

tragar {52} *v* **:** to swallow — **tragarse**

tragedia *nf* **:** tragedy

trágico, -ca *adj* **:** tragic — **trágicamente** *adv*

trago *nm* **1 :** swallow, swig **2 :** drink, liquor **3 trago amargo :** hard time

trague, etc. → **tragar**

traición *nf, pl* **traiciones 1 :** treason **2 :** betrayal, treachery

traicionar *vt* **:** to betray

traicionero, -ra → **traidor**

traidor[1], -dora *adj* **:** traitorous, treasonous

traidor[2], -dora *n* **:** traitor

traiga, etc. → **traer**

tráiler *or* **trailer** *nm* **:** trailer

traílla *nf* **1 :** leash **2 :** harrow

traje *nm* **1 :** suit **2 :** dress **3 :** costume **4 traje de baño :** bathing suit

trajín *nm, pl* **trajines 1 :** transport 2 *fam* **:** hustle and bustle

trajinar *vt* **:** to transport, to carry — *vi* **:** to rush around

trajo, etc. → **traer**

trama *nf* **1 :** plot **2 :** weave, weft (fabric)

tramar *vt* **1 :** to plot, to plan **2 :** to weave

tramitar *vt* **:** to transact, to negotiate, to handle

trámite *nm* **:** procedure, step

tramo *nm* **1 :** stretch, section **2 :** flight (of stairs)

trampa *nf* **1 :** trap **2 hacer trampas :** to cheat

trampear *vt* **:** to cheat

trampero, -ra *n* **:** trapper

trampilla *nf* **:** trapdoor

trampolín *nm, pl* **-lines 1 :** diving board **2 :** trampoline **3 :** springboard <un trampolín al éxito : a springboard to success>

tramposo[1], -sa *adj* **:** crooked, cheating

tramposo[2], -sa *n* **:** cheat, swindler

tranca *nf* **1 :** stick, club **2 :** bar, crossbar

trancar {72} *vt* **:** to bar (a door or window)

trancazo *nm* GOLPE **:** blow, hit

trance *nm* **1 :** critical juncture, tough time **2 :** trance **3 en trance de :** in the process of <en trance de extinción : on the verge of extinction>

tranco *nm* **1 :** stride **2** UMBRAL **:** threshold

tranque, etc. → **trancar**

tranquilidad *nf* **:** tranquility, peace

tranquilizador, -dora *adj* **1 :** soothing **2 :** reassuring

tranquilizante[1] *adj* **1 :** reassuring **2 :** tranquilizing

tranquilizante[2] *nm* **:** tranquilizer

tranquilizar {21} *vt* CALMAR **:** to calm down, to soothe <tranquilizar la conciencia : to ease the conscience> — **tranquilizarse** *vr*

tranquilo, -la *adj* CALMO **:** calm, tranquil <una vida tranquila : a quiet life> — **tranquilamente** *adv*

transacción *nf, pl* **-ciones :** transaction

transar *vi* TRANSIGIR **:** to give way, to compromise — *vt* **:** to buy and sell

transatlántico[1], -ca *adj* **:** transatlantic

transatlántico[2] *nm* **:** ocean liner

transbordador *nm* **1 :** ferry **2 transbordador espacial :** space shuttle

transbordar *v* **:** to transfer

transbordo *nm* **:** transfer

transcendencia *nf* → **trascendencia**

transcender → **trascender**

transcribir {33} *vt* **:** to transcribe

transcrito *pp* → **transcribir**

transcripción *nf, pl* **-ciones :** transcription

transcurrir *vi* **:** to elapse, to pass

transcurso *nm* **:** course, progression <en el transcurso de cien años : over the course of a hundred years>

transeúnte *nmf* **1 :** passerby **2 :** transient

transferencia *nf* **:** transfer, transference

transferir {76} *vt* TRASLADAR **:** to transfer — **transferible** *adj*

transfigurar *vt* **:** to transfigure, to transform — **transfiguración** *nf*

transformación *nf, pl* **-ciones :** transformation, conversion

transformador *nm* **:** transformer

transformar *vt* **1** CONVERTIR **:** to convert **2 :** to transform, to change, to alter — **transformarse** *vr*

transfusión *nf, pl* **-siones :** transfusion

transgredir {1} *vt* **:** to transgress — **transgresión** *nf*

transgresor, -sora *n* **:** transgressor

transición *nf, pl* **-ciones :** transition <período de transición : transition period>

transido, -da *adj* **:** overcome, beset <transido de dolor : racked with pain>

transigir {35} *vi* **1 :** to give in, to compromise **2 ~ con :** to tolerate, to put up with

transistor *nm* **:** transistor

transitable *adj* **:** passable

transitar *vi* **:** to go, to pass, to travel <transitar por la ciudad : to travel through the city>

transitivo, -va *adj* **:** transitive

tránsito *nm* **1** TRÁFICO **:** traffic <hora de máximo tránsito : rush hour> **2 :** transit, passage, movement **3 :** death, passing

transitorio, -ria *adj* **1 :** transitory **2 :** provisional, temporary — **transitoriamente** *adv*

translúcido, -da *adj* **:** translucent

translucir → **traslucir**

transmisión *nf, pl* **-siones 1 :** transmission, broadcast **2 :** transfer **3 :** transmission (of an automobile)

transmisor *nm* **:** transmitter

transmitir *vt* **1 :** to transmit, to broadcast **2 :** to pass on, to transfer — *vi* **:** to transmit, to broadcast

transparencia *nf* **:** transparency

transparentar *vt* **:** to reveal, to betray — **transparentarse** *vr* **1 :** to be transparent **2 :** to show through

transparente[1] *adj* **:** transparent — **transparentemente** *adv*

transparente[2] *nm* **:** shade, blind

transpiración *nf, pl* **-ciones** SUDOR **:** perspiration, sweat

transpirado, -da *adj* **:** sweaty

transpirar *vi* **1** SUDAR **:** to perspire, to sweat **2 :** to transpire

transplantar, transplante → **trasplantar, trasplante**

transponer {60} *vt* **1 :** to transpose, to move about **2** TRASPLANTAR **:** to transplant — **transponerse** *vr* **1** OCULTARSE **:** to hide **2** PONERSE **:** to set, to go down (of the sun or moon) **3** DORMITAR **:** to doze off

transportación *nf, pl* **-ciones :** transportation

transportador *nm* **1 :** protractor **2 :** conveyor

transportar *vt* **1 :** to transport, to carry **2 :** to transmit **3 :** to transpose (music) — **transportarse** *vr* **:** to get carried away

transporte *nm* **:** transport, transportation

transportista *nmf* **:** hauler, carrier, trucker

transpuso, etc. → **transponer**

transversal *adj* **:** transverse, cross <corte transversal : cross section>

transversalmente *adv* **:** obliquely

transverso, -sa *adj* **:** transverse

tranvía *nm* **:** streetcar, trolley

trapeador *nm* **:** mop

trapear *vt* **:** to mop

trapecio *nm* **1 :** trapezoid **2 :** trapeze

trapezoide *nm* **:** trapezoid

trapo *nm* **1 :** cloth, rag <trapo de polvo : dust cloth> **2 soltar el trapo :** to burst into tears **3 trapos** *nmpl fam* **:** clothes

tráquea *nf* **:** trachea, windpipe

traquetear *vi* **:** to clatter, to jolt

traqueteo *nm* **1 :** jolting **2 :** clattering, clatter

tras *prep* **1 :** after <día tras día : day after day> <uno tras otro : one after another> **2 :** behind <tras la puerta : behind the door>

trasbordar, trasbordo → **transbordar, transbordo**

trascendencia *nf* **1 :** importance, significance **2 :** transcendence

trascendental *adj* **1 :** transcendental **2 :** important, momentous

trascendente *adj* **1 :** important, significant **2 :** transcendent

trascender {56} *vi* **1 :** to leak out, to become known **2 :** to spread, to have a wide effect **3 ~ a :** to smell of <la casa trascendía a flores : the house smelled of flowers> **4 ~ de :** to transcend, to go beyond — *vt* **:** to transcend

trasero[1], **-sa** *adj* POSTERIOR **:** rear, back

trasero[2] *nm* **:** buttocks

trasfondo *nm* **1 :** background, backdrop **2 :** undertone, undercurrent

trasformación *nf* → **transformación**

trasgo *nm* **:** goblin, imp

trasgredir → **transgredir**
trasladar *vt* **1** TRANSFERIR **:** to transfer, to move **2** POSPONER **:** to postpone **3** TRADUCIR **:** to translate **4** COPIAR **:** to copy, to transcribe — **trasladarse** *vr* MUDARSE **:** to move, to relocate
traslado *nm* **1 :** transfer, move **2 :** copy
traslapar *vt* **:** to overlap — **traslaparse** *vr*
traslapo *nm* **:** overlap
traslúcido, -da → **translúcido**
traslucir {45} *vi* **:** to reveal, to show — **traslucirse** *vr* **:** to show through
trasmano *nm* **a ~ :** out of the way, out of reach
trasmisión, trasmitir → **transmisión, transmitir**
trasnochar *vi* **:** to stay up all night
trasparencia *nf,* **trasparente** → **transparencia, transparente**
traspasar *vt* **1** PERFORAR **:** to pierce, to go through **2 :** to go beyond <traspasar los límites : to overstep the limits> **3** ATRAVESAR **:** to cross, to go across **4 :** to sell, to transfer
traspaso *nm* **:** transfer, sale
traspié *nm* **1 :** stumble **2 :** blunder
traspiración *nf* → **transpiración**
trasplantar *vt* **:** to transplant
trasplante *nm* **:** transplant
trasponer → **transponer**
trasportar → **transportar**
trasquilar *vt* ESQUILAR **:** to shear
traste *nm* **1 :** fret (on a guitar) **2** *CA, Mex, PRi* **:** kitchen utensil <lavar los trastes : to do the dishes> **3 dar al traste con :** to ruin, to destroy **4 irse al traste :** to fall through
trastornar *vt* **:** to disturb, to upset, to disrupt — **trastornarse** *vr*
trastorno *nm* **1 :** disorder <trastorno mental : mental disorder> **2 :** disturbance, upset
trastos *nmpl* **1 :** implements, utensils **2** *fam* **:** pieces of junk, stuff
trasunto *nm* **:** image, likeness
tratable *adj* **1 :** friendly, sociable **2 :** treatable
tratado *nm* **1 :** treatise **2 :** treaty
tratamiento *nm* **:** treatment
tratante *nmf* **:** dealer, trader
tratar *vi* **1 ~ con :** to deal with, to have contact with <no trato mucho con los clientes : I don't have much contact with customers> **2 ~ de :** to try to <estoy tratando de comer : I am trying to eat> **3 ~ de** *or* **~ sobre :** to be about, to concern <el libro trata de las plantas : the book is about plants> **4 ~ en :** to deal in <trata en herramientas : he deals in tools> — *vt* **1 :** to treat <tratan bien a sus empleados : they treat their employees well> **2 :** to handle <trató el tema con delicadeza : he handled the subject tactfully> — **tratarse** *vr* **~ de :** to be about, to concern
trato *nm* **1 :** deal, agreement **2 :** relationship, dealings *pl* **3 :** treatment <malos tratos : ill-treatment>
trauma *nm* **:** trauma
traumático, -ca *adj* **:** traumatic — **traumáticamente** *adv*
traumatismo *nm* **:** injury <traumatismo cervical : whiplash>
través *nm* **1 a través de :** across, through **2 al través :** crosswise, across **3 de través :** sideways
travesaño *nm* **1 :** crossbar **2 :** crossbeam, crosspiece, transom (of a window)
travesía *nf* **:** voyage, crossing (of the sea)
travesura *nf* **1 :** prank, mischievous act **2 travesuras** *nfpl* **:** mischief
travieso, -sa *adj* **:** mischievous, naughty — **traviesamente** *adv*
trayecto *nm* **1 :** journey **2 :** route **3 :** trajectory, path
trayectoria *nf* **:** course, path, trajectory
trayendo → **traer**
traza *nf* **1** DISEÑO **:** design, plan **2 :** appearance
trazado *nm* **1** BOSQUEJO **:** outline, sketch **2** PLAN **:** plan, layout
trazar {21} *vt* **1 :** to trace **2 :** to draw up, to devise **3 :** to outline, to sketch
trazo *nm* **1 :** stroke, line **2 :** sketch, outline
trébol *nm* **1 :** clover, shamrock **2 :** club (playing card)
trece *adj & nm* **:** thirteen
treceavo[1]**, -va** *adj* **:** thirteenth
treceavo[2] *nm* **:** thirteenth (fraction)
trecho *nm* **1 :** stretch, period <de trecho en trecho : at intervals> **2 :** distance, space
tregua *nf* **1 :** truce **2 :** lull, respite **3 sin ~ :** relentless, unrelenting
treinta *adj & nm* **:** thirty
treintavo[1]**, -va** *adj* **:** thirtieth
treintavo[2] *nm* **:** thirtieth (fraction)
tremendo, -da *adj* **1 :** tremendous, enormous **2 :** terrible, dreadful **3** *fam* **:** great, super
trementina *nf* AGUARRÁS **:** turpentine
trémulo, -la *adj* **1 :** trembling, shaky **2 :** flickering
tren *nm* **1 :** train **2 :** set, assembly <tren de aterrizaje : landing gear> **3 :** speed, pace <a todo tren : at top speed>
trence, etc. → **trenzar**
trenza *nf* **:** braid, pigtail
trenzar {21} *vt* **:** to braid — **trenzarse** *vr* **:** to get involved
trepador, -dora *adj* **:** climbing <rosal trepador : rambling rose>
trepadora *nf* **1 :** climbing plant, climber **2 :** nuthatch
trepar *vi* **1 :** to climb <trepar a un árbol : to climb up a tree> **2 :** to creep, to spread (of a plant)
trepidación *nf, pl* **-ciones :** vibration
trepidante *adj* **1 :** vibrating **2 :** fast, frantic

trepidar *vi* **1 :** to shake, to vibrate **2 :** to hesitate, to waver

tres *adj & nm* **:** three

trescientos[1], **-tas** *adj* **:** two hundred

trescientos[2] *nms & pl* **:** three hundred

treta *nf* **:** trick, ruse

tríada *nf* **:** triad

triángulo *nm* **:** triangle — **triangular** *adj*

tribal *adj* **:** tribal

tribu *nf* **:** tribe

tribulación *nf, pl* **-ciones :** tribulation

tribuna *nf* **1 :** dais, platform **2 :** stands *pl,* bleachers *pl,* grandstand

tribunal *nm* **:** court, tribunal

tributar *vt* **:** to pay, to render — *vi* **:** to pay taxes

tributario[1], **-ria** *adj* **:** tax <evasión tributaria : tax evasion>

tributario[2] *nm* **:** tributary

tributo *nm* **1 :** tax **2 :** tribute

triciclo *nm* **:** tricycle

tricolor *adj* **:** tricolor, tricolored

tridente *nm* **:** trident

tridimensional *adj* **:** three-dimensional, 3-D

trienal *adj* **:** triennial

trifulca *nf fam* **:** row, ruckus

trigésimo[1], **-ma** *adj* **:** thirtieth, thirty-

trigésimo[2], **-ma** *n* **:** thirtieth, thirty- (in a series)

trigo *nm* **1 :** wheat **2 trigo rubión :** buckwheat

trigonometría *nf* **:** trigonometry

trigueño, -ña *adj* **1 :** light brown (of hair) **2** MORENO **:** dark, olive-skinned

trillado, -da *adj* **:** trite, hackneyed

trilladora *nf* **:** thresher, threshing machine

trillar *vt* **:** to thresh

trillizo, -za *n* **:** triplet

trilogía *nf* **:** trilogy

trimestral *adj* **:** quarterly — **trimestralmente** *adv*

trinar *vi* **1 :** to thrill **2 :** to warble

trinchar *vt* **:** to carve, to cut up

trinchera *nf* **1 :** trench, ditch **2 :** trench coat

tridente *nm* **:** trident

trineo *nm* **:** sled, sleigh

trinidad *nf* **la Trinidad :** the Trinity

trino *nm* **:** trill, warble

trinquete *nm* **:** ratchet

trío *nm* **:** trio

tripa *nf* **1** INTESTINO **:** gut, intestine **2 tripas** *nfpl fam* **:** belly, tummy, insides *pl* <dolerle a uno las tripas : to have a stomach ache>

tripartito, -ta *adj* **:** tripartite

triple *adj & nm* **:** triple

triplicado *nm* **:** triplicate

triplicar {72} *vt* **:** to triple, to treble

trípode *nm* **:** tripod

tripulación *nf, pl* **-ciones :** crew

tripulante *nmf* **:** crew member

tripular *vt* **:** to man

tris *nm* **estar en un tris de :** to be within an inch of, to be very close to

triste *adj* **1 :** sad, gloomy <ponerse triste : to become sad> **2 :** desolate, dismal <una perspectiva triste : a dismal outlook> **3 :** sorry, sorry-looking <la triste verdad : the sorry truth>

tristeza *nf* DOLOR **:** sadness, grief

tristón, -tona *adj, mpl* **-tones :** melancholy, downhearted

tritón *nm, pl* **tritones :** newt

triturar *vt* **:** to crush, to grind

triunfal *adj* **:** triumphal, triumphant — **triunfalmente** *adv*

triunfante *adj* **:** triumphant, victorious

triunfar *vi* **:** to triumph, to win

triunfo *nm* **1 :** triumph, victory **2** ÉXITO **:** success **3 :** trump (in card games)

triunvirato *nm* **:** triumvirate

trivial *adj* **1 :** trivial **2 :** trite, commonplace

trivialidad *nf* **:** triviality

triza *nf* **1 :** shred, bit **2 hacer trizas :** to tear into shreds, to smash to pieces

trocar {82} *vt* **1** CAMBIAR **:** to exchange, to trade **2** CAMBIAR **:** to change, to alter, to transform **3** CONFUNDIR **:** to confuse, to mix up

trocha *nf* **:** path, trail

troce, etc. → **trozar**

trofeo *nm* **:** trophy

tromba *nf* **1 :** whirlwind **2 tromba de agua :** downpour, cloudburst

trombón *nm, pl* **trombones 1 :** trombone **2 :** trombonist — **trombonista** *nmf*

trombosis *nf* **:** thrombosis

trompa *nf* **1 :** trunk (of an elephant), proboscis (of an insect) **2 :** horn <trompa de caza : hunting horn> **3 :** tube, duct (in the body)

trompada *nf fam* **1 :** punch, blow **2 :** bump, collision (of persons)

trompeta *nf* **:** trumpet

trompetista *nmf* **:** trumpet player, trumpeter

trompo *nm* **:** spinning top

tronada *nf* **:** thunderstorm

tronar {19} *vi* **1 :** to thunder, to roar **2 :** to be furious, to rage **3** *CA, Mex fam* **:** to shoot — *v impers* **:** to thunder <está tronando : it's thundering>

tronchar *vt* **1 :** to snap, to break off **2 :** to cut off (relations)

tronco *nm* **1 :** trunk (of a tree) **2 :** log **3 :** torso

trono *nm* **1 :** throne **2** *fam* **:** toilet

tropa *nf* **1 :** troop, soldiers *pl* **2 :** crowd, mob **3 :** herd (of livestock)

tropel *nm* **:** mob, swarm

tropezar {29} *vi* **1 :** to trip, to stumble **2 :** to slip up, to blunder **3 ~ con :** to run into, to bump into **4 ~ con :** to come up against (a problem)

tropezón *nm, pl* **-zones 1 :** stumble **2 :** mistake, slip

tropical *adj* **:** tropical

trópico *nm* **1 :** tropic <trópico de Cáncer : tropic of Cancer> **2 el trópico :** the tropics

tropiezo *nm* **1** CONTRATIEMPO : snag, setback **2** EQUIVOCACIÓN : mistake, slip
troqué, etc. → **trocar**
troquel *nm* : die (for stamping)
trotamundos *nmf* : globe-trotter
trotar *vi* **1** : to trot **2** : to jog **3** *fam* : to rush about
trote *nm* **1** : trot **2** *fam* : rush, bustle **3 de ~** : durable, for everyday use
trovador, -dora *n* : troubadour
trozar {21} *vt* : to cut up, to dice
trozo *nm* **1** PEDAZO : piece, bit, chunk **2** : passage, extract
trucha *nf* : trout
truco *nm* **1** : trick **2** : knack
truculento, -ta *adj* : horrifying, gruesome
trueca, trueque, etc. → **trocar**
truena, etc. → **tronar**
trueno *nm* : thunder
trueque *nm* : barter, exchange
trufa *nf* : truffle
truncar {72} *vt* **1** : to truncate, to cut short **2** : to thwart, to frustrate <truncó sus esperanzas : she shattered their hopes>
trunco, -ca *adj* **1** : truncated **2** : unfinished, incomplete
trunque, etc. → **truncar**
tu *adj* **1** : your <tu vestido : your dress> <toma tus vitaminas : take your vitamins> **2** : thy
tú *pron* **1** : you <tú eres mi hijo : you are my son> **2** : thou
tuba *nf* : tuba
tubérculo *nm* : tuber
tuberculosis *nf* : tuberculosis
tuberculoso, -sa *adj* : tuberculous, tubercular
tubería *nf* : pipes *pl*, tubing
tuberoso, -sa *adj* : tuberous
tubo *nm* **1** : tube <tubo de ensayo : test tube> **2** : pipe <tubo de desagüe : drainpipe> **3 tubo digestivo** : alimentary canal
tubular *adj* : tubular
tuerca *nf* : nut <tuercas y tornillos : nuts and bolts>
tuerce, etc. → **torcer**
tuerto, -ta *adj* : one-eyed, blind in one eye
tuerza, etc. → **torcer**
tuesta, etc. → **tostar**
tuétano *nm* : marrow
tufo *nm* **1** : fume, vapor **2** *fam* : stench, stink
tugurio *nm* : hovel
tulipán *nm, pl* **-panes** : tulip
tumba *nf* **1** SEPULCRO : tomb **2** FOSA : grave **3** : felling of trees
tumbar *vt* **1** : to knock down **2** : to fell, to cut down — *vi* : to fall down — **tumbarse** *vr* ACOSTARSE : to lie down
tumbo *nm* **1** : tumble, fall **2 dar tumbos** : to jolt, to bump around
tumor *nm* : tumor
túmulo *nm* : burial mound
tumulto *nm* **1** ALBOROTO : commotion, tumult **2** MOTÍN : riot **3** MULTITUD : crowd
tumultuoso, -sa *adj* : tumultuous
tuna *nf* : prickly pear (fruit)
tundra *nf* : tundra
tunecino, -na *adj & n* : Tunisian
túnel *nm* : tunnel
tungsteno *nm* : tungsten
túnica *nf* : tunic
tupé *nm* PELUQUÍN : toupee
tupido, -da *adj* **1** DENSO : dense, thick **2** OBSTRUIDO : obstructed, blocked up
turba *nf* **1** : peat **2** : mob, throng
turbación *nf, pl* **-ciones 1** : disturbance **2** : alarm, concern **3** : confusion
turbante *nm* : turban
turbar *vt* **1** : to disturb, to disrupt **2** : to worry, to upset **3** : to confuse
turbina *nf* : turbine
turbio, -bia *adj* **1** : cloudy, murky, turbid **2** : dim, blurred **3** : shady, crooked
turbopropulsor *nm* : turboprop
turborreactor *nm* : turbojet
turbulencia *nf* : turbulence
turbulento, -ta *adj* : turbulent
turco[1], -ca *adj* : Turkish
turco[2], -ca *n* : Turk
turgente *adj* : turgid, swollen
turismo *nm* : tourism, tourist industry
turista *nmf* : tourist, vacationer
turístico, -ca *adj* : tourist, travel
turnar *vi* : to take turns, to alternate
turno *nm* **1** : turn <ya te tocará tu turno : you'll get your turn> **2** : shift, duty <turno de noche : night shift> **3 por turno** : alternately
turón *nm, pl* **turones** : polecat
turquesa *nf* : turquoise
turrón *nm, pl* **turrones** : nougat
tusa *nf* : corn husk
tutear *vt* : to address as *tú*
tutela *nf* **1** : guardianship **2** : tutelage, protection
tuteo *nm* : addressing as *tú*
tutor, -tora *n* **1** : tutor **2** : guardian
tuvo, etc. → **tener**
tuyo[1], -ya *adj* : yours, of yours <un amigo tuyo : a friend of yours> <¿es tuya esta casa? : is this house yours?>
tuyo[2], -ya *pron* **1** : yours <ése es el tuyo : that one is yours> <trae la tuya : bring your own> **2 los tuyos** : your relations, your friends <¿vendrán los tuyos? : are your folks coming?>
tweed [ˈtwið] *nm* : tweed

U

u[1] *nf* : twenty-second letter of the Spanish alphabet

u[2] *conj* (*used instead of* **o** *before words beginning with o- or ho-*) : or

ualabí *nm* : wallaby

uapití *nm* : American elk, wapiti

ubicación *nf, pl* **-ciones** : location, position

ubicar {72} *vt* **1** SITUAR : to place, to put, to position **2** LOCALIZAR : to locate, to find — **ubicarse** *vr* **1** LOCALIZARSE : to be placed, to be located **2** SITUARSE : to position oneself

ubicuidad *nf* OMNIPRESENCIA : ubiquity

ubicuo, -cua *adj* OMNIPRESENTE : ubiquitous

ubre *nf* : udder

ucraniano, -na *adj & n* : Ukranian

Ud., Uds. → **usted**

ufanarse *vr* **~ de** : to boast about, to pride oneself on

ufano, -na *adj* **1** ORGULLOSO : proud **2** : self-satisfied, smug

ugandés, -desa *adj & n, mpl* **-deses** : Ugandan

ukelele *nm* : ukulele

úlcera *nf* : ulcer — **ulceroso, -sa** *adj*

ulcerar *vt* : to ulcerate — **ulcerarse** *vr* — **ulceración** *nf*

ulceroso, -sa *adj* : ulcerous

ulterior *adj* : later, subsequent — **ulteriormente** *adv*

últimamente *adv* : lately, recently

ultimar *vt* **1** CONCLUIR : to complete, to finish, to finalize **2** MATAR : to kill

ultimátum *nm, pl* **-tums** : ultimatum

último, -ma *adj* **1** : last, final <la última galleta : the last cookie> <en último caso : as a last resort> **2** : last, latest, most recent <su último viaje a España : her last trip to Spain> <en los últimos años : in recent years> **3 por ~** : finally

ultrajar *vt* INSULTAR : to offend, to outrage, to insult

ultraje *nm* INSULTO : outrage, insult

ultramar *nm* **de ~** *or* **en ~** : overseas, abroad

ultranza *nf* **a ~ 1** : to the extreme <lo defendió a ultranza : she defended him fiercely> **2** : extreme, out-and-out <perfeccionismo a ultranza : rabid perfectionism>

ultrarrojo, -ja *adj* : infrared

ultravioleta *adj* : ultraviolet

ulular *vi* **1** : to hoot **2** : to howl, to wail

ululato *nm* : hoot (of an owl), wail (of a person)

umbilical *adj* : umbilical <cordón umbilical : umbilical cord>

umbral *nm* : threshold, doorstep

un[1] → **uno**[1]

un[2], **una** *art, mpl* **unos 1** : a, an **2 unos** *or* **unas** *pl* : some, a few <hace unas semanas : a few weeks ago> **3 unos** *or* **unas** *pl* : about, approximately <unos veinte años antes : about twenty years before>

unánime *adj* : unanimous — **unánimemente** *adv*

unanimidad *nf* **1** : unanimity **2 por ~** : unanimously

unción *nf, pl* **-ciones** : unction

uncir {83} *vt* : to yoke

undécimo[1], **-ma** *adj* : eleventh

undécimo[2], **-ma** *n* : eleventh (in a series)

ungir {35} *vt* : to anoint

ungüento *nm* : ointment, salve

únicamente *adv* : only, solely

unicelular *adj* : unicellular

único[1], **-ca** *adj* **1** : only, sole **2** : unique, extraordinary

único[2], **-ca** *n* : only one <los únicos que vinieron : the only ones who showed up>

unicornio *nm* : unicorn

unidad *nf* **1** : unity **2** : unit

unidireccional *adj* : unidirectional

unido, -da *adj* **1** : joined, united **2** : close <unos amigos muy unidos : very close friends>

unificar {72} *vt* : to unify — **unificación** *nf*

uniformado, -da *adj* : uniformed

uniformar *vt* ESTANDARIZAR : to standardize, to make uniform

uniforme[1] *adj* : uniform — **uniformemente** *adv*

uniforme[2] *nm* : uniform

uniformidad *nf* : uniformity

unilateral *adj* : unilateral — **unilateralmente** *adv*

unión *nf, pl* **uniones 1** : union **2** JUNTURA : joint, coupling

unir *vt* **1** JUNTAR : to unite, to join, to link **2** COMBINAR : to combine, to blend — **unirse** *vr* **1** : to join together **2** : to combine, to mix together **3 ~ a** : to join <se unieron al grupo : they joined the group>

unísono *nm* : unison <al unísono : in unison>

unitario, -ria *adj* : unitary, unit <precio unitario : unit price>

universal *adj* : universal — **universalmente** *adv*

universidad *nf* : university

universitario[1], **-ria** *adj* : university, college

universitario[2], **-ria** *n* : university student, college student

universo *nm* : universe

unja, etc. → **ungir**

uno[1], **una** *adj* (**un** *before masculine singular nouns*) : one <una silla : one chair> <tiene treinta y un años : he's thirty-one years old> <el tomo uno : volume one>

uno[2] *nm* : one, number one

uno[3], **una** *pron* **1** : one (number) <uno por uno : one by one> <es la una : it's

one o'clock> **2 :** one (person or thing) <una es mejor que las otras : one (of them) is better than the others> <hacerlo uno mismo : to do it oneself> **3 unos, unas** *pl* **:** some (ones), some people **4 uno y otro :** both **5 unos y otros :** all of them **6 el uno al otro :** one another, each other <se enseñaron los unos a los otros : they taught each other>

untar *vt* **1 :** to anoint **2 :** to smear, to grease **3 :** to bribe

unza, etc. → **uncir**

uña *nf* **1 :** fingernail, toenail **2 :** claw, hoof, stinger

uranio *nm* **:** uranium

Urano *nm* **:** Uranus

urbanidad *nf* **:** urbanity, courtesy

urbanización *nf, pl* **-ciones :** housing development, residential area

urbano, -na *adj* **1 :** urban **2** CORTÉS **:** urbane, polite

urbe *nf* **:** large city, metropolis

urdimbre *nf* **:** warp (in a loom)

uretra *nf* **:** urethra

urgencia *nf* **1 :** urgency **2** EMERGENCIA **:** emergency

urgente *adj* **:** urgent — **urgentemente** *adv*

urgir {35} *v impers* **:** to be urgent, to be pressing <me urge localizarlo : I urgently need to find him> <el tiempo urge : time is running out>

urinario[1], -ria *adj* **:** urinary

urinario[2] *nm* **:** urinal (place)

urja, etc. → **urgir**

urna *nf* **1 :** urn **2 :** ballot box <acudir a las urnas : to go to the polls>

urogallo *nm* **:** grouse (bird)

urraca *nf* **1 :** magpie **2 urraca de América :** blue jay

urticaria *nf* **:** hives

uruguayo, -ya *adj & n* **:** Uruguayan

usado, -da *adj* **1 :** used, secondhand **2 :** worn, worn-out

usanza *nf* **:** custom, usage

usar *vt* **1** EMPLEAR, UTILIZAR **:** to use, to make use of **2** CONSUMIR **:** to consume, to use (up) **3** LLEVAR **:** to wear **4 de usar y tirar :** disposable — **usarse 1 :** to be used **2 :** to be in fashion

uso *nm* **1** EMPLEO, UTILIZACIÓN **:** use <de uso personal : for personal use> <hacer uso de : to make use of> **2 :** wear <uso y desgaste : wear and tear> **3** USANZA **:** custom, usage, habit <al uso de : in the manner of, in the style of>

usted *pron* **1** (*formal form of address in most countries; often written as* **Ud.** *or* **Vd.**) **:** you **2 ustedes** *pl* (*often written as* **Uds.** *or* **Vds.**) **:** you, all of you

usual *adj* **:** usual, common, normal <poco usual : not very common> — **usualmente** *adv*

usuario, -ria *n* **:** user

usura *nf* **:** usury — **usurario, -ria** *adj*

usurero, -ra *n* **:** usurer

usurpador, -dora *n* **:** usurper

usurpar *vt* **:** to usurp — **usurpación** *nf*

utensilio *nm* **:** utensil, tool

uterino, -na *adj* **:** uterine

útero *nm* **:** uterus, womb

útil *adj* **:** useful, handy, helpful

útiles *nmpl* **:** implements, tools

utilidad *nf* **1 :** utility, usefulness **2 utilidades** *nfpl* **:** profits

utilitario, -ria *adj* **:** utilitarian

utilizable *adj* **:** usable, fit for use

utilización *nf, pl* **-ciones :** utilization, use

utilizar {21} *vt* **:** to use, to utilize

útilmente *adv* **:** usefully

utopía *nf* **:** utopia

utópico, -ca *adj* **:** utopian

uva *nf* **:** grape

uvular *adj* **:** uvular

V

v *nf* **:** twenty-third letter of the Spanish alphabet

va → **ir**

vaca *nf* **:** cow

vacación *nf, pl* **-ciones 1 :** vacation <dos semanas de vacaciones : two weeks of vacation> **2 estar de vacaciones :** to be on vacation **3 irse de vacaciones :** to go on vacation

vacacionar *vi Mex* **:** to vacation

vacacionista *nmf CA, Mex* **:** vacationer

vacante[1] *adj* **:** vacant, empty

vacante[2] *nf* **:** vacancy (for a job)

vaciado *nm* **:** cast, casting <vaciado de yeso : plaster cast>

vaciar {85} *vt* **1 :** to empty, to empty out, to drain **2** AHUECAR **:** to hollow out **3 :** to cast (in a mold) — *vi* **~ en :** to flow into, to empty into

vacilación *nf, pl* **-ciones :** hesitation, vacillation

vacilante *adj* **1 :** hesitant, unsure **2 :** shaky, unsteady **3 :** flickering

vacilar *vi* **1 :** to hesitate, to vacillate, to waver **2 :** to be unsteady, to wobble **3 :** to flicker **4** *fam* **:** to joke, to fool around

vacío[1], -cía *adj* **1 :** vacant **2 :** empty **3 :** meaningless

vacío[2] *nm* **1 :** emptiness, void **2 :** space, gap **3 :** vacuum **4 hacerle el vacío a alguien :** to ostracize someone, to give someone the cold shoulder

vacuidad *nf* **:** vacuity, vacuousness

vacuna *nf* **:** vaccine

vacunación *nf, pl* **-ciones** INOCULACIÓN **:** vaccination, inoculation

vacunar *vt* INOCULAR **:** to vaccinate, to inoculate

vacuno[1], -na *adj* **:** bovine <ganado vacuno : beef cattle>

vacuno[2] *nm* **:** bovine

vacuo, -cua *adj* **:** empty, shallow, inane

vadear *vt* **:** to ford, to wade across

vado *nm* **:** ford

vagabundear *vi* **:** to wander, to roam about

vagabundo[1], -da *adj* **1** ERRANTE **:** wandering **2 :** stray

vagabundo[2], -da *n* **:** vagrant, bum, vagabond

vagamente *adv* **:** vaguely

vagancia *nf* **1 :** vagrancy **2** PEREZA **:** laziness, idleness

vagar {52} *vi* ERRAR **:** to roam, to wander

vagina *nf* **:** vagina — **vaginal** *adj*

vago[1], -ga *adj* **1 :** vague **2** PEREZOSO **:** lazy, idle

vago[2], -ga *n* **1 :** idler, loafer **2** VAGABUNDO **:** vagrant, bum

vagón *nm, pl* **vagones :** car (of a train)

vague, etc. → **vagar**

vaguear *vi* **1 :** to loaf, to lounge around **2** VAGAR **:** to wander

vaguedad *nf* **:** vagueness

vahído *nm* **:** dizzy spell

vaho *nm* **1 :** breath **2 :** vapor, steam (on glass, etc.)

vaina *nf* **1 :** sheath, scabbard **2 :** pod (of a pea or bean) **3** *fam* **:** nuisance, bother

vainilla *nf* **:** vanilla

vaivén *nm, pl* **vaivenes 1 :** swinging, swaying, rocking **2 :** change, fluctuation <los vaivenes de la vida : life's ups and downs>

vajilla *nf* **:** dishes *pl*, set of dishes

valdrá, etc. → **valer**

vale *nm* **1 :** voucher **2** PAGARÉ **:** promissory note, IOU

valedero, -ra *adj* **:** valid

valentía *nf* **:** courage, valor

valer {84} *vt* **1 :** to be worth <valen una fortuna : they're worth a fortune> <no vale protestar : there's no point in protesting> <valer la pena : to be worth the trouble> **2 :** to cost <¿cuánto vale? : how much does it cost?> **3 :** to earn, to gain <le valió una reprimenda : it earned him a reprimand> **4 :** to protect, to aid <¡válgame Dios! : God help me!> **5 :** to be equal to — *vi* **1 :** to have value <sus consejos no valen para nada : his advice is worthless> **2 :** to be valid, to count <¡eso no vale! : that doesn't count!> **3 hacerse valer :** to assert oneself **4 más vale :** it's better <más vale que te vayas : you'd better go> — **valerse** *vr* **1 ~ de :** to take advantage of **2 valerse solo** *or* **valerse por sí mismo :** to look after oneself **3** *Mex* **:** to be fair <no se vale : it's not fair>

valeroso, -sa *adj* **:** brave, valiant

valet [ˈbalɛt, -ˈle] *nm* **:** jack (in playing cards)

valga, etc. → **valer**

valía *nf* **:** value, worth

validar *vt* **:** to validate — **validación** *nf*

validez *nf* **:** validity

válido, -da *adj* **:** valid

valiente *adj* **1 :** brave, valiant **2** (*used ironically*) **:** fine, great <¡valiente amiga! : what a fine friend!> — **valientemente** *adv*

valija *nf* **:** suitcase, valise

valioso, -sa *adj* PRECIOSO **:** valuable, precious

valla *nf* **1 :** fence, barricade **2 :** hurdle (in sports) **3 :** obstacle, hindrance

vallar *vt* **:** to fence, to put a fence around

valle *nm* **:** valley, vale

valor *nm* **1 :** value, worth, importance **2** CORAJE **:** courage, valor **3 valores** *nmpl* **:** values, principles **4 valores** *nmpl* **:** securities, bonds **5 sin ~ :** worthless

valoración *nf, pl* **-ciones 1** EVALUACIÓN **:** valuation, appraisal, assessment **2** APRECIACIÓN **:** appreciation

valorar *vt* **1** EVALUAR **:** to evaluate, to appraise, to assess **2** APRECIAR **:** to value, to appreciate

valorizarse {21} *vr* **:** to appreciate, to increase in value — **valorización** *nf*

vals *nm* **:** waltz

valsar *vi* **:** to waltz

valuación *nf, pl* **-ciones :** valuation, appraisal

valuar {3} *vt* **:** to value, to appraise, to assess

válvula *nf* **1 :** valve **2 válvula reguladora :** throttle

vamos → **ir**

vampiro *nm* **:** vampire

van → **ir**

vanadio *nm* **:** vanadium

vanagloriarse *vr* **:** to boast, to brag

vanamente *adv* **:** vainly, in vain

vandalismo : vandalism

vándalo *nm* **:** vandal — **vandalismo** *nm*

vanguardia *nf* **1 :** vanguard **2 :** avant-garde **3 a la vanguardia :** at the forefront

vanidad *nf* **:** vanity

vanidoso, -sa *adj* PRESUMIDO **:** vain, conceited

vano, -na *adj* **1** INÚTIL **:** vain, useless **2 :** vain, worthless <vanas promesas : empty promises> **3 en ~ :** in vain, of no avail

vapor *nm* **1 :** vapor, steam **2 :** steamer, steamship **3 al vapor :** steamed

vaporizador *nm* **:** vaporizer

vaporizar {21} *vt* **:** to vaporize — **vaporizarse** *vr* — **vaporización** *nf*

vaporoso, -sa *adj* **1 :** vaporous **2 :** sheer, airy

vapulear *vt* **:** to beat, to thrash

vaquero[1], **-ra** *adj* **:** cowboy <pantalón vaquero : jeans>
vaquero[2], **-ra** *n* **:** cowboy *m,* cowgirl *f*
vaqueros *nmpl* JEANS **:** jeans
vaquilla *nf* **:** heifer
vara *nf* **1 :** pole, stick, rod **2 :** staff (of office) **3 :** lance, pike (in bullfighting) **4 :** yardstick **5 vara de oro :** goldenrod
varado, -da *adj* **1 :** beached, aground **2 :** stranded
varar *vt* **:** to beach (a ship), to strand — *vi* **:** to run aground
variable *adj & nf* **:** variable — **variabilidad** *nf*
variación *nf, pl* **-ciones :** variation
variado, -da *adj* **:** varied, diverse
variante *adj & nf* **:** variant
varianza *nf* **:** variance
variar {85} *vt* **1 :** to change, to alter **2 :** to diversify — *vi* **1 :** to vary, to change **2 variar de opinión :** to change one's mind
varicela *nf* **:** chicken pox
varices *or* **várices** *nfpl* **:** varicose veins
varicoso, -sa *adj* **:** varicose
variedad *nf* DIVERSIDAD **:** variety, diversity
varilla *nf* **1 :** rod, bar **2 :** spoke (of a wheel) **3 :** rib (of an umbrella)
vario, -ria *adj* **1 :** varied, diverse **2 :** variegated, motley **3 :** changeable **4 varios, varias** *pl* **:** various, several
variopinto, -ta *adj* **:** diverse, assorted, motley
varita *nf* **:** wand <varita mágica : magic wand>
varón *nm, pl* **varones 1** HOMBRE **:** man, male **2** NIÑO **:** boy
varonil *adj* **1 :** masculine, manly **2 :** mannish
vas → **ir**
vasallo *nm* **:** vassal — **vasallaje** *nm*
vasco[1], **-ca** *adj & n* **:** Basque
vasco[2] *nm* **:** Basque (language)
vascular *adj* **:** vascular
vasija *nf* **:** container, vessel
vaso *nm* **1 :** glass, tumbler **2 :** glassful **3 :** vessel <vaso sanguíneo : blood vessel>
vástago *nm* **1 :** offspring, descendent **2 :** shoot (of a plant)
vastedad *nf* **:** vastness, immensity
vasto, -ta *adj* **:** vast, immense
vataje *nm* **:** wattage
vaticinar *vt* **:** to predict, to foretell
vaticinio *nm* **:** prediction, prophecy
vatio *nm* **:** watt
vaya, etc. → **ir**
Vd., Vds. → **usted**
ve, etc. → **ir, ver**
vea, etc. → **ver**
vecinal *adj* **:** local
vecindad *nf* **1 :** neighborhood, vicinity **2 casa de vecindad :** tenement
vecindario *nm* **1 :** neighborhood, area **2 :** residents *pl*
vecino, -na *n* **1 :** neighbor **2 :** resident, inhabitant
veda *nf* **1** PROHIBICIÓN **:** prohibition **2 :** closed season (for hunting or fishing)
vedar *vt* **1 :** to prohibit, to ban **2** IMPEDIR **:** to impede, to prevent
vega *nf* **:** fertile lowland
vegetación *nf, pl* **-ciones 1 :** vegetation **2 vegetaciones** *nfpl* **:** adenoids
vegetal *adj & nm* **:** vegetable, plant
vegetar *vi* **:** to vegetate
vegetarianismo *nm* **:** vegetarianism
vegetariano, -na *adj & n* **:** vegetarian
vegetativo, -va *adj* **:** vegetative
vehemente *adj* **:** vehement — **vehemencia** *nf*
vehículo *nm* **:** vehicle — **vehicular** *adj*
veía, etc. → **ver**
veinte *adj & nm* **:** twenty
veinteavo[1], **-va** *adj* **:** twentieth
veinteavo[2] *nm* **:** twentieth (fraction)
veintena *nf* **:** group of twenty, score <una veintena de participantes : about twenty participants>
vejación *nf, pl* **-ciones :** ill-treatment, humiliation
vejar *vt* **:** to mistreat, to ridicule, to harass
vejete *nm* **:** old fellow, codger
vejez *nf* **:** old age
vejiga *nf* **1 :** bladder **2** AMPOLLA **:** blister
vela *nf* **1** VIGILIA **:** wakefulness <pasé la noche en vela : I stayed awake all night> **2 :** watch, vigil, wake **3 :** candle **4 :** sail
velada *nf* **:** evening party, soirée
velado, -da *adj* **1 :** veiled, hidden **2 :** blurred **3 :** muffled
velador[1], **-dora** *n* **:** guard, night watchman
velador[2] *nm* **1 :** candlestick **2 :** night table
velar *vt* **1 :** to hold a wake over **2 :** to watch over, to sit up with **3 :** to blur, to expose (a photo) **4 :** to veil, to conceal — *vi* **1 :** to stay awake **2 ~ por :** to watch over, to look after
velatorio *nm* VELORIO **:** wake (for the dead)
veleidad *nf* **1 :** fickleness **2 :** whim, caprice
veleidoso, -sa : fickle, capricious
velero *nm* **1 :** sailing ship **2 :** sailboat
veleta *nf* **:** weather vane
vello *nm* **1 :** body hair **2 :** down, fuzz
vellocino *nm* **:** fleece
vellón *nm, pl* **vellones 1 :** fleece, sheepskin **2** *PRi* **:** nickel (coin)
vellosidad *nf* **:** downiness, hairiness
velloso, -sa *adj* **:** downy, fluffy, hairy
velo *nm* **:** veil
velocidad *nf* **1 :** speed, velocity <velocidad máxima : speed limit> **2** MARCHA **:** gear (of an automobile)
velocímetro *nm* **:** speedometer
velocista *nmf* **:** sprinter
velorio *nm* VELATORIO **:** wake (for the dead)
velour *nm* **:** velour, velours

veloz *adj, pl* **veloces :** fast, quick, swift — **velozmente** *adv*

ven → **venir**

vena *nf* **1 :** vein <vena yugular : jugular vein> **2 :** vein, seam, lode **3 :** grain (of wood) **4 :** style <en vena lírica : in a lyrical vein> **5 :** strain, touch <una vena de humor : a touch of humor> **6 :** mood

venado *nm* **1 :** deer **2 :** venison

venal *adj* **:** venal — **venalidad** *nf*

vencedor, -dora *n* **:** winner, victor

vencejo *nm* **:** swift (bird)

vencer {86} *vt* **1** DERROTAR **:** to vanquish, to defeat **2** SUPERAR **:** to overcome, to surmount — *vi* **1** GANAR **:** to win, to triumph **2** CADUCAR **:** to expire <el plazo vence el jueves : the deadline is Thursday> **3 :** to fall due, to mature — **vencerse** *vr* **1** DOMINARSE **:** to control oneself **2 :** to break, to collapse

vencido, -da *adj* **1 :** defeated **2 :** expired **3 :** due, payable **4 darse por vencido :** to give up

vencimiento *nm* **1 :** defeat **2 :** expiration **3 :** maturity (of a loan)

venda *nf* **:** bandage

vendaje *nm* **:** bandage, dressing

vendar *vt* **1 :** to bandage **2 vendar los ojos :** to blindfold

vendaval *nm* **:** gale, strong wind

vendedor, -dora *n* **:** salesperson, salesman *m,* saleswoman *f*

vender *vt* **1 :** to sell **2 :** to sell out, to betray — **venderse 1 :** to be sold <se vende : for sale> **2 :** to sell out

vendetta *nf* **:** vendetta

vendible *adj* **:** salable, marketable

vendimia *nf* **:** grape harvest

vendrá, etc. → **venir**

veneno *nm* **1 :** poison **2 :** venom

venenoso, -sa *adj* **:** poisonous, venomous

venerable *adj* **:** venerable

veneración *nf, pl* **-ciones :** veneration, reverence

venerar *vt* **:** to venerate, to revere

venéreo, -rea *adj* **:** venereal

venero *nm* **1** VENA **:** seam, lode, vein **2** MANANTIAL **:** spring **3** FUENTE **:** origin, source

venezolano, -na *adj & n* **:** Venezuelan

venga, etc. → **venir**

vengador, -dora *n* **:** avenger

venganza *nf* **:** vengeance, revenge

vengar {52} *vt* **:** to avenge — **vengarse** *vr* **:** to get even, to revenge oneself

vengativo, -va *adj* **:** vindictive, vengeful

vengue, etc. → **vengar**

venia *nf* **1** PERMISO **:** permission, leave **2** PERDÓN **:** pardon **3 :** bow (of the head)

venial *adj* **:** venial

venida *nf* **1** LLEGADA **:** arrival, coming **2** REGRESO **:** return **3 idas y venidas :** comings and goings

venidero, -ra *adj* **:** coming, future

venir {87} *vi* **1 :** to come <lo vi venir : I saw him coming> <¡venga! : come on!> **2 :** to arrive <vinieron en coche : they came by car> **3 :** to come, to originate <sus zapatos vienen de Italia : her shoes are from Italy> **4 :** to come, to be available <viene envuelto en plástico : it comes wrapped in plastic> **5 :** to come back, to return **6 :** to affect, to overcome <me vino un vahído : a dizzy spell came over me> **7 :** to fit <te viene un poco grande : it's a little big for you> **8** (*with the present participle*) **:** to have been <viene entrenando diariamente : he's been training daily> **9 ~ a** (*with the infinitive*) **:** to end up, to turn out <viene a ser lo mismo : it comes out the same> **10 que viene :** coming, next <el año que viene : next year> **11 venir bien :** to be suitable, to be just right — **venirse** *vr* **1 :** to come, to arrive **2 :** to come back **3 venirse abajo :** to fall apart, to collapse

venta *nf* **1 :** sale **2 venta al por menor** *or* **venta al detalle :** retail sales

ventaja *nf* **1 :** advantage **2 :** lead, head start **3 ventajas** *nfpl* **:** perks, extras

ventajoso, -sa *adj* **1 :** advantageous **2 :** profitable — **ventajosamente** *adv*

ventana *nf* **1 :** window (of a building) **2 ventana de la nariz :** nostril

ventanal *nm* **:** large window

ventanilla *nf* **1 :** window (of a vehicle or airplane) **2 :** ticket window, box office

ventero, -ra *n* **:** innkeeper

ventilación *nf, pl* **-ciones :** ventilation

ventilador *nm* **1 :** ventilator **2 :** fan

ventilar *vt* **1 :** to ventilate, to air out **2 :** to air, to discuss **3 :** to make public, to reveal — **ventilarse** *vr* **:** to get some air

ventisca *nf* **:** snowstorm, blizzard

ventisquero *nm* **:** snowdrift

ventosear *vi* **:** to break wind

ventosidad *nf* **:** wind, flatulence

ventoso, -sa *adj* **:** windy

ventrículo *nm* **:** ventricle

ventrílocuo, -cua *n* **:** ventriloquist

ventriloquia *nf* **:** ventriloquism

ventura *nf* **1 :** fortune, luck, chance **2 :** happiness **3 a la ventura :** at random, as it comes

venturoso, -sa *adj* **1** AFORTUNADO **:** fortunate, lucky **2 :** successful

Venus *nm* **:** Venus

venza, etc. → **vencer**

ver[1] {88} *vt* **1 :** to see <vimos la película : we saw the movie> **2** ENTENDER **:** to understand <ya lo veo : now I get it> **3** EXAMINAR **:** to examine, to look into <lo veré : I'll take a look at it> **4** JUZGAR **:** to see, to judge <a mi manera de ver : to my way of thinking> **5** VISITAR **:** to meet with, to visit **6** AVERIGUAR **:** to find out **7 a ver** *or* **vamos a ver :** let's see — *vi* **1 :** to see **2** ENTERARSE **:** to learn, to find out **3**

ENTENDER : to understand — **verse** *vr* **1** HALLARSE : to find oneself **2** PARECER : to look, to appear **3** ENCONTRARSE : to see each other, to meet

ver[2] *nm* **1** : looks *pl*, appearance **2** : opinion <a mi ver : in my view>

vera *nf* : side <a la vera del camino : alongside the road>

veracidad *nf* : truthfulness, veracity

veranda *nf* : veranda

veraneante *nmf* : summer vacationer

veranear *vi* : to spend the summer

veraniego, -ga *adj* **1** ESTIVAL : summer <el sol veraniego : the summer sun> **2** : summery

verano *nm* : summer

veras *nfpl* **de ~** : really, truly

veraz *adj, pl* **veraces** : truthful, veracious

verbal *adj* : verbal — **verbalmente** *adv*

verbalizar {21} *vt* : to verbalize, to express

verbena *nf* **1** FIESTA : festival, fair **2** : verbena, vervain

verbigracia *adv* : for example

verbo *nm* : verb

verborrea *nf* : verbiage

verbosidad *nf* : verbosity, wordiness

verboso, -sa *adj* : verbose, wordy

verdad *nf* **1** : truth **2 de ~** : really, truly **3 ¿verdad?** : right?, isn't that so?

verdaderamente *adv* : really, truly

verdadero, -dera *adj* **1** REAL, VERÍDICO : true, real **2** AUTÉNTICO : genuine

verde[1] *adj* **1** : green (in color) **2** : green, unripe **3** : inexperienced, green **4** : dirty, risqué

verde[2] *nm* : green

verdear *vi* : to turn green, to become verdant

verdín *nm, pl* **verdines** : slime, scum

verdor *nm* **1** : greenness **2** : verdure

verdoso, -sa *adj* : greenish

verdugo *nm* **1** : executioner, hangman **2** : tyrant

verdugón *nm, pl* **-gones** : welt, wheal

verdura *nf* : vegetable(s), green(s)

vereda *nf* **1** SENDA : path, trail **2** : sidewalk, pavement

veredicto *nm* : verdict

verga *nf* : spar, yard (of a ship)

vergonzoso, -sa *adj* **1** : disgraceful, shameful **2** : bashful, shy — **vergonzosamente** *adv*

vergüenza *nf* **1** : disgrace, shame **2** : embarrassment **3** : bashfulness, shyness

vericueto *nm* : rough terrain

verídico, -ca *adj* **1** REAL, VERDADERO : true, real **2** VERAZ : truthful

verificación *nf, pl* **-ciones 1** : verification **2** : testing, checking

verificador, -dora *n* : inspector, tester

verificar {72} *vt* **1** : to verify, to confirm **2** : to test, to check **3** : to carry out, to conduct — **verificarse** *vr* **1** : to take place, to occur **2** : to come true

verja *nf* **1** : rails *pl* (of a fence) **2** : grating, grille **3** : gate

vermut *nm, pl* **vermuts** : vermouth

vernáculo, -la *adj* : vernacular

vernal *adj* : vernal, spring

verosímil *adj* **1** : probable, likely **2** : credible, realistic

verosimilitud *nf* **1** : probability, likeliness **2** : verisimilitude

verraco *nm* : boar

verruga *nf* : wart

versado, -da *adj* **~ en** : versed in, knowledgeable about

versar *vi* **~ sobre** : to deal with, to be about

versátil *adj* **1** : versatile **2** : fickle

versatilidad *nf* **1** : versatility **2** : fickleness

versículo *nm* : verse (in the Bible)

versión *nf, pl* **versiones 1** : version **2** : translation

verso *nm* : verse

versus *prep* : versus, against

vértebra *nf* : vertebra — **vertebral** *adj*

vertebrado[1], **-da** *adj* : vertebrate

vertebrado[2] *nm* : vertebrate

vertedero *nm* **1** : garbage dump **2** DESAGÜE : drain, outlet

verter {56} *vt* **1** : to pour **2** : to spill, to shed **3** : to empty out **4** : to express, to voice **5** : to translate, to render — *vi* : to flow

vertical *adj & nf* : vertical — **verticalmente** *adv*

vértice *nm* : vertex, apex

vertido *nm* : spilling, spill

vertiente *nf* **1** : slope **2** : aspect, side, element

vertiginoso, -sa *adj* : vertiginous — **vertiginosamente** *adv*

vértigo *nm* : vertigo, dizziness

vesícula *nf* **1** : vesicle **2 vesícula biliar** : gallbladder

vesicular *adj* : vesicular

vestíbulo *nm* : vestibule, hall, lobby, foyer

vestido *nm* **1** : dress, costume, clothes *pl* **2** : dress (garment)

vestidor *nm* : dressing room

vestiduras *nfpl* **1** : clothing, raiment, regalia **2** *or* **vestiduras sacerdotales** : vestments

vestigio *nm* : vestige, sign, trace

vestimenta *nf* ROPA : clothing, clothes *pl*

vestir {54} *vt* **1** : to dress, to clothe **2** LLEVAR : to wear **3** ADORNAR : to decorate, to dress up — *vi* **1** : to dress <vestir bien : to dress well> **2** : to look good, to suit the occasion — **vestirse** *vr* **1** : to get dressed **2 ~ de** : to dress up as <se vistieron de soldados : they dressed up as soldiers> **3 ~ de** : to wear, to dress in

vestuario *nm* **1** : wardrobe **2** : dressing room, locker room

veta *nf* **1** : grain (in wood) **2** : vein, seam, lode **3** : trace, streak <una veta de terco : a stubborn streak>

vetar *vt* : to veto

veteado, -da *adj* : streaked, veined

veterano, -na *adj & n* : veteran

veterinaria *nf* : veterinary medicine

veterinario[1], -ria *adj* : veterinary

veterinario[2], -ria *n* : veterinarian

veto *nm* : veto

vetusto, -ta *adj* ANTIGUO : ancient, very old

vez *nf, pl* **veces 1** : time, occasion <a la vez : at the same time> <a veces : at times, occasionally> <de vez en cuando : from time to time> **2** (*with numbers*) : time <una vez : once> <de una vez : all at once> <de una vez para siempre : once and for all> <dos veces : twice> **3** : turn <a su vez : in turn> <en vez de : instead of> <hacer las veces de : to act as, to stand in for>

vía[1] *nf* **1** RUTA, CAMINO : road, route, way <Vía Láctea : Milky Way> **2** MEDIO : means, way <por vía oficial : through official channels> **3** : track, line (of a railroad) **4** : tract, passage <por vía oral : orally> **5 en vías de** : in the process of <en vías de solución : on the road to a solution> **6 por ~** : by (in transportation) <por vía aérea : by air, airmail>

vía[2] *prep* : via

viable *adj* : viable, feasible — **viabilidad** *nf*

viaducto *nm* : viaduct

viajante *mf* : traveling salesman, traveling saleswoman

viajar *vi* : to travel, to journey

viaje *nm* : trip, journey <viaje de negocios : business trip>

viajero[1], -ra *adj* : traveling

viajero[2], -ra *n* **1** : traveler **2** PASAJERO : passenger

vial *adj* : road, traffic

viático *nm* : travel allowance, travel expenses *pl*

víbora *nf* : viper

vibración *nf, pl* **-ciones** : vibration

vibrador *nm* : vibrator

vibrante *adj* **1** : vibrant **2** : vibrating

vibrar *vi* : to vibrate

vibratorio, -ria *adj* : vibratory

vicario, -ria *n* : vicar

vicealmirante *nmf* : vice admiral

vicepresidente, -ta *n* : vice president — **vicepresidencia** *nf*

viceversa *adv* : vice versa, conversely

viciado, -da *adj* : stuffy, close

viciar *vt* **1** : to corrupt **2** : to invalidate **3** FALSEAR : to distort **4** : to pollute, to adulterate

vicio *nm* **1** : vice, depravity **2** : bad habit **3** : defect, blemish

vicioso, -sa *adj* : depraved, corrupt

vicisitud *nf* : vicissitude

víctima *nf* : victim

victimario, -ria *n* ASESINO : killer, murderer

victimizar {21} *vt Arg, Mex* : to victimize

victoria *nf* : victory — **victorioso, -sa** *adj* — **victoriosamente** *adv*

victoriano, -na *adj* : Victorian

vid *nf* : vine, grapevine

vida *nf* **1** : life <la vida cotidiana : everyday life> **2** : life span, lifetime **3** BIOGRAFÍA : biography, life **4** : way of life, lifestyle **5** : livelihood <ganarse la vida : to earn one's living> **6** VIVEZA : liveliness **7 media vida** : half-life

vidente *nmf* **1** : psychic, clairvoyant **2** : sighted person

video *or* **vídeo** *nm* : video

videocasete *or* **videocasette** *nm* : videocassette

videocasetera *or* **videocasettera** *nf* : videocassette recorder, VCR

videocinta *nf* : videotape

videograbar *vt* : to videotape

vidriado *nm* : glaze

vidriar *vt* : to glaze (pottery, tile, etc.)

vidriera *nf* **1** : stained-glass window **2** : glass door or window **3** : store window

vidriero, -ra *n* : glazier

vidrio *nm* **1** : glass, piece of glass **2** : windowpane

vidrioso, -sa *adj* **1** : brittle, fragile **2** : slippery **3** : glassy, glazed (of eyes) **4** : touchy, delicate

vieira *nf* **1** : scallop **2** : scallop shell

viejo[1], -ja *adj* **1** ANCIANO : old, elderly **2** ANTIGUO : former, longstanding <viejas tradiciones : old traditions> <viejos amigos : old friends> **3** GASTADO : old, worn, worn-out

viejo[2], -ja *n* ANCIANO : old man *m*, old woman *f*

viene, etc. → **venir**

viento *nm* **1** : wind **2 hacer viento** : to be windy **3 contra viento y marea** : against all odds **4 viento en popa** : splendidly, successfully

vientre *nm* **1** : abdomen, belly **2** : womb **3** : bowels *pl*

viernes *nms & pl* : Friday

vierte, etc. → **verter**

vietnamita *adj & nmf* : Vietnamese

viga *nf* **1** : beam, rafter, girder **2 viga voladiza** : cantilever

vigencia *nf* **1** : validity **2** : force, effect <entrar en vigencia : to go into effect>

vigente *adj* : valid, in force

vigésimo[1], -ma *adj* : twentieth, twenty- <la vigésima segunda edición : the twenty-second edition>

vigésimo[2], -ma *n* : twentieth, twenty- (in a series)

vigía *nmf* : lookout

vigilancia *nf* : vigilance, watchfulness <bajo vigilancia : under surveillance>

vigilante[1] *adj* : vigilant, watchful

vigilante[2] *nmf* : watchman, guard

vigilar *vt* **1** CUIDAR : to look after, to keep an eye on **2** GUARDAR : to watch over, to guard — *vi* **1** : to be watchful **2** : to keep watch

vigilia *nf* **1** VELA **:** wakefulness **2 :** night work **3 :** vigil (in religion)
vigor *nm* **1 :** vigor, energy, strength **2** VIGENCIA **:** force, effect
vigorizante *adj* **:** envigorating
vigorizar {21} *vt* **:** to strengthen, to invigorate
vigoroso, -sa *adj* **:** vigorous — **vigorosamente** *adv*
VIH *nm* **:** HIV
vil *adj* **:** vile, dispicable
vileza *nf* **1 :** vileness **2 :** despicable action, villainy
vilipendiar *vt* **:** to vilify, to revile
villa *nf* **1 :** town, village **2 :** villa
villancico *nm* **:** carol, Christmas carol
villano, -na *n* **1 :** villain **2 :** peasant
vilo *nm* **en ~ 1 :** in the air **2 :** uncertain, in suspense
vinagre *nm* **:** vinegar
vinagrera *nf* **:** cruet (for vinegar)
vinatería *nf* **:** wine shop
vinculación *nf, pl* **-ciones 1 :** linking **2** RELACIÓN **:** bond, link, connection
vincular *vt* CONECTAR, RELACIONAR **:** to tie, to link, to connect
vínculo *nm* LAZO **:** tie, link, bond
vindicación *nf, pl* **-ciones :** vindication
vindicar *vt* **1 :** to vindicate **2 :** to avenge
vinilo *nm* **:** vinyl
vino[1]**, etc.** → **venir**
vino[2] *nm* **:** wine
viña *nf* **:** vineyard
viñedo *nm* **:** vineyard
vio, etc. → **ver**
viola *nf* **:** viola
violación *nf, pl* **-ciones 1 :** violation, offense **2 :** rape
violador[1]**, -dora** *n* **:** violator, offender
violador[2] *nm* **:** rapist
violar *vt* **1 :** to rape **2 :** to violate (a law or right) **3** PROFANAR **:** to desecrate
violencia *nf* **:** violence
violentamente *adv* **:** by force, violently
violentar *vt* **1** FORZAR **:** to break open, to force **2 :** to distort (words or ideas) — **violentarse** *vr* **:** to force oneself
violento, -ta *adj* **1 :** violent **2** EMBARAZOSO, INCÓMODO **:** awkward, embarassing
violeta[1] *adj & nm* **:** violet (color)
violeta[2] *nf* **:** violet (flower)
violín *nm, pl* **-lines :** violin
violinista *nmf* **:** violinist
violonchelista *nmf* **:** cellist
violonchelo *nm* **:** cello, violoncello
VIP *nmf, pl* **VIPs :** VIP
vira *nf* **:** welt (of a shoe)
virago *nf* **:** virago, shrew
viraje *nm* **1 :** turn, swerve **2 :** change
viral *adj* **:** viral
virar *vi* **:** to tack, to turn, to veer
virgen[1] *adj* **:** virgin <lana virgen : virgin wool>
virgen[2] *nmf, pl* **vírgenes :** virgin <la Santísima Virgen : the Blessed Virgin>
virginal *adj* **:** virginal, chaste
virginidad *nf* **:** virginity
Virgo *nmf* **:** Virgo
vírico, -ca *adj* **:** viral
viril *adj* **:** virile — **virilidad** *nf*
virrey, -rreina *n* **:** viceroy *m,* vicereine *f*
virtual *adj* **:** virtual — **virtualmente** *adv*
virtud *nf* **1 :** virtue **2 en virtud de :** by virtue of
virtuosismo *nm* **:** virtuosity
virtuoso[1]**, -sa** *adj* **:** virtuous — **virtuosamente** *adv*
virtuoso[2]**, -sa** *n* **:** virtuoso
viruela *nf* **1 :** smallpox **2 :** pockmark
virulencia *nf* **:** virulence
virulento, -ta *adj* **:** virulent
virus *nm* **:** virus
viruta *nf* **:** shaving
visa *nf* **:** visa
visado *nm Spain* **:** visa
visaje *nm* **:** face, grimace <hacer visajes : to make faces>
visceral *adj* **:** visceral
vísceras *nfpl* **:** viscera, entrails
visconde, -desa *n* **:** viscount *m,* viscountess *f*
viscosidad *nf* **:** viscosity
viscoso, -sa *adj* **:** viscous
visera *nf* **:** visor
visibilidad *nf* **:** visibility
visible *adj* **:** visible — **visiblemente** *adv*
visión *nf, pl* **visiones 1 :** vision, eyesight **2 :** view, perspective **3 :** vision, illusion <ver visiones : to be seeing things>
visionario, -ria *adj & n* **:** visionary
visita *nf* **1 :** visit, call **2 :** visitor **3 ir de visita :** to go visiting
visitador, -dora *n* **:** visitor, frequent caller
visitante[1] *adj* **:** visiting
visitante[2] *nmf* **:** visitor
visitar *vt* **:** to visit
vislumbrar *vt* **1 :** to discern, to make out **2 :** to begin to see, to have an inkling of
vislumbre *nf* **:** glimmer, gleam
viso *nm* **1** APARIENCIA **:** appearance <tener visos de : to seem, to show signs of> **2** DESTELLO **:** glint, gleam **3 :** sheen, iridescence
visón *nm, pl* **visones :** mink
víspera *nf* **1 :** eve, day before **2 vísperas** *nfpl* **:** vespers
vista *nf* **1** VISIÓN **:** vision, eyesight **2** MIRADA **:** look, gaze, glance **3** PANORAMA **:** view, vista, panorama **4 :** hearing (in court) **5 a primera vista :** at first sight **6 en vista de :** in view of **7 hacer la vista gorda :** to turn a blind eye **8 ¡hasta la vista! :** so long!, see you! **9 perder de vista :** to lose sight of **10 punto de vista :** point of view
vistazo *nm* **:** glance, look
viste, etc. → **ver, vestir**

visto[1] *pp* → **ver**
visto[2], **-ta** *adj* **1 :** obvious, clear **2 :** in view of, considering **3 estar bien visto :** to be approved of **4 estar mal visto :** to be frowned upon **5 por lo visto :** apparently **6 nunca visto :** unheard-of **7 visto que :** since, given that
visto[3] *nm* **visto bueno :** approval
vistoso, -sa *adj* **:** colorful, bright
visual *adj* **:** visual — **visualmente** *adv*
visualización *nf, pl* **-ciones :** visualization
visualizar {21} *vt* **1 :** to visualize **2 :** to display (on a screen)
vital *adj* **1 :** vital **2 :** lively, dynamic
vitalicio, -cia *adj* **:** life, lifetime
vitalidad *nf* **:** vitality
vitamina *nf* **:** vitamin
vitamínico, -ca *adj* **:** vitamin <complejos vitamínicos : vitamin compounds>
vitorear *vt* **:** to cheer, to acclaim
vitral *nm* **:** stained-glass window
vítreo, -rea *adj* **:** vitreous, glassy
vitrina *nf* **1 :** showcase, display case **2 :** store window
vitriolo *nm* **:** vitriol
vituperar *vt* **:** to condemn, to vituperate against
vituperio *nm* **:** vituperation, censure
viudez *nf* **:** widowerhood, widowhood
viudo, -da *n* **:** widower *m,* widow *f*
vivacidad *nf* VIVEZA **:** vivacity, liveliness
vivamente *adv* **1 :** in a lively manner **2 :** vividly **3 :** strongly, acutely <lo recomendamos vivamente : we strongly recommend it>
vivaque *nm* **:** bivouac
vivaquear *vi* **:** to bivouac
vivar *vi* **:** to cheer
vivaz *adj, pl* **vivaces 1 :** lively, vivacious **2 :** clever, sharp **3 :** perennial
víveres *nmpl* **:** provisions, supplies, food
vivero *nm* **1 :** nursery (for plants) **2 :** hatchery, fish farm
viveza *nf* **1** VIVACIDAD **:** liveliness **2** BRILLO **:** vividness, brightness **3** ASTUCIA **:** cleverness, sharpness
vívido, -da *adj* **:** vivid, lively
vividor, -dora *n* **:** sponger, parasite
vivienda *nf* **1 :** housing **2** MORADA **:** dwelling, home
viviente *adj* **:** living
vivificar {72} *vt* **:** to vivify, to give life to
vivir[1] *vi* **1 :** to live, to be alive **2** SUBSISTIR **:** to subsist, to make a living **3** RESIDIR **:** to reside **4 :** to spend one's life <vive para trabajar : she lives to work> **5 ~ de :** to live on — *vt* **1 :** to live <vivir su vida : to live one's life> **2** EXPERIMENTAR **:** to go through, to experience
vivir[2] *nm* **1 :** life, lifestyle **2 de mal vivir :** disreputable
vivisección *nf, pl* **-ciones :** vivisection
vivo, -va *adj* **1 :** alive **2** INTENSO **:** vivid, bright, intense **3** ANIMADO **:** lively, vivacious **4** ASTUTO **:** sharp, clever **5 en ~ :** live <transmisión en vivo : live broadcast> **6 al rojo vivo :** red-hot
vizconde, -desa *n* **:** viscount *m,* viscountess *f*
vocablo *nm* PALABRA **:** word
vocabulario *nm* **:** vocabulary
vocación *nf, pl* **-ciones :** vocation
vocacional *adj* **:** vocational
vocal[1] *adj* **:** vocal
vocal[2] *nmf* **:** member (of a committee, board, etc.)
vocal[3] *nf* **:** vowel
vocalista *nmf* CANTANTE **:** singer, vocalist
vocalizar {21} *vi* **:** to vocalize
vocear *v* **:** to shout
vocerío *nm* **:** clamor, shouting
vocero, -ra *n* PORTAVOZ **:** spokesperson, spokesman *m,* spokeswoman *f*
vociferante *adj* **:** vociferous
vociferar *vi* GRITAR **:** to shout, to yell
vodevil *nm* **:** vaudeville
vodka *nm* **:** vodka
voladizo[1], **-za** *adj* **:** projecting
voladizo[2] *nm* **:** projection
volador, -dora *adj* **:** flying
volando *adv* **:** quickly, in a hurry
volante[1] *adj* **:** flying
volante[2] *nm* **1 :** steering wheel **2** FOLLETO **:** flier, circular **3 :** shuttlecock **4 :** flywheel **5 :** balance wheel (of a watch) **6 :** ruffle, flounce
volar {19} *vi* **1 :** to fly **2** CORRER **:** to hurry, to rush <el tiempo vuela : time flies> <pasar volando : to fly past> **3** DIVULGARSE **:** to spread <unos rumores volaban : rumors were spreading around> **4** DESAPARECER **:** to disappear <el dinero ya voló : the money's already gone> — *vt* **1 :** to blow up, to demolish **2 :** to irritate
volátil *adj* **:** volatile — **volatilidad** *nf*
volatilizar {21} *vt* **:** to volatize — **volatilizarse** *vr*
volcán *nm, pl* **volcanes :** volcano
volcánico, -ca *adj* **:** volcanic
volcar {82} *vt, pl* **volcanes 1 :** to upset, to knock over, to turn over **2 :** to empty out **3 :** to make dizzy **4 :** to cause a change of mind in **5 :** to irritate — *vi* **1 :** to overturn, to tip over **2 :** to capsize — **volcarse** *vr* **1 :** to overturn **2 :** to do one's utmost
volea *nf* **:** volley (in sports)
volear *vi* **:** to volley (in sports)
voleibol *nm* **:** volleyball
voleo *nm* **al voleo :** haphazardly, at random
volframio *nm* **:** wolfram, tungsten
volición *nf, pl* **-ciones :** volition
volqué, etc. → **volcar**
voltaje *nm* **:** voltage
voltear *vt* **1 :** to turn over, to turn upside down **2 :** to reverse, to turn inside out **3 :** to turn <voltear la cara : to turn one's head> **4 :** to knock

down — *vi* **1** : to roll over, to do somersaults **2** : to turn <volteó a la izquierda : he turned left> — **voltearse** *vr* **1** : to turn around **2** : to change one's allegiance

voltereta *nf* : somersault, tumble

voltio *nm* : volt

volubilidad *nf* : fickleness, changeableness

voluble *adj* : fickle, changeable

volumen *nm, pl* **-lúmenes 1** TOMO : volume, book **2** : capacity, size, bulk **3** CANTIDAD : amount <el volumen de ventas : the volume of sales> **4** : volume, loudness

voluminoso, -sa *adj* : voluminous, massive, bulky

voluntad *nf* **1** : will, volition **2** DESEO : desire, wish **3** INTENCIÓN : intention **4 a voluntad** : at will **5 buena voluntad** : good will **6 mala voluntad** : ill will **7 fuerza de voluntad** : willpower

voluntario[1], -ria *adj* : voluntary — **voluntariamente** *adv*

voluntario[2], -ria *n* : volunteer

voluntarioso, -sa *adj* **1** : stubborn **2** : willing, eager

voluptuosidad *nf* : voluptuousness

voluptuoso, -sa *adj* : voluptuous — **voluptuosamente** *adv*

voluta *nf* : spiral, column (of smoke)

volver {89} *vi* **1** : to return, to come or go back <volver a casa : to return home> **2** : to revert <volver al tema : to get back to the subject> **3 ~ a** : to do again <volvieron a llamar : they called again> **4 volver en sí** : to come to, to regain consciousness — *vt* **1** : to turn, to turn over, to turn inside out **2** : to return, to repay, to restore **3** : to cause, to make <la volvía loca : it was driving her crazy> — **volverse** *vr* **1** : to become <se volvió deprimido : he became depressed> **2** : to turn around

vomitar *vi* : to vomit — *vt* **1** : to vomit **2** : to spew out (lava, etc.)

vómito *nm* **1** : vomiting **2** : vomit

voracidad *nf* : voracity

vorágine *nf* : whirlpool, maelstrom

voraz *adj, pl* **voraces** : voracious — **vorazmente** *adv*

vórtice *nm* **1** : whirlpool, vortex **2** TORBELLINO : whirlwind

vos *pron* (*in some regions of Latin America*) : you

vosear *vt* : to address as *vos*

vosotros, -tras *pron pl Spain* **1** : you, yourselves **2** : ye

votación *nf, pl* **-ciones** : vote, voting

votante *nmf* : voter

votar *vi* : to vote — *vt* : to vote for

votivo, -va *adj* : votive

voto *nm* **1** : vote **2** : vow (in religion) **3 votos** *nmpl* : good wishes

voy → **ir**

voz *nf, pl* **voces 1** : voice **2** : opinion, say **3** GRITO : shout, yell **4** : sound **5** VOCABLO : word, term **6** : rumor **7 a voz en cuello** : at the top of one's lungs **8 dar voces** : to shout **9 en voz alta** : aloud, in a loud voice **10 en voz baja** : softly, in a low voice

vudú *nm* : voodoo

vuelco *nm* : upset, overturning <me dio un vuelco el corazón : my heart skipped a beat>

vuela, etc. → **volar**

vuelca, vuelque, etc. → **volcar**

vuelo *nm* **1** : flight, flying <alzar el vuelo : to take flight> **2** : flight (of an aircraft) <vuelo espacial : space flight> **3** : flare, fullness (of clothing) **4 al vuelo** : on the wing

vuelta *nf* **1** GIRO : turn <se dio la vuelta : he turned around> **2** REVOLUCIÓN : circle, revolution <dio la vuelta al mundo : she went around the world> <las ruedas daban vueltas : the wheels were spinning> **3** : flip, turn <le dio la vuelta : she flipped it over> **4** : bend, curve <a la vuelta de la esquina : around the corner> **5** REGRESO : return <de ida y vuelta : round trip> <a vuelta de correo : return mail> **6** : round, lap (in sports or games) **7** PASEO : walk, drive, ride <dio una vuelta : he went for a walk> **8** DORSO, REVÉS : back, other side <a la vuelta : on the back> **9** : cuff (of pants) **10 darle vueltas** : to think over **11 estar de vuelta** : to be back

vuelto *pp* → **volver**

vuelve, etc. → **volver**

vuestro[1], -stra *adj Spain* : your, of yours <vuestros coches : your cars> <una amiga vuestra : a friend of yours>

vuestro[2], -stra *pron Spain* (*with definite article*) : yours <la vuestra es más grande : yours is bigger> <esos son los vuestros : those are yours>

vulcanizar {21} *vt* : to vulcanize

vulgar *adj* **1** : common **2** : vulgar

vulgaridad *nf* : vulgarity

vulgarismo *nm* : vulgarism

vulgarizar {21} *vt* : to vulgarize, to popularize

vulgarmente *adv* : vulgarly, popularly

vulgo *nm* **el vulgo** : the masses, common people

vulnerable *adj* : vulnerable — **vulnerabilidad** *nf*

vulnerar *vt* **1** : to injure, to damage (one's reputation or honor) **2** : to violate, to break (a law or contract)

W

w *nf* **:** twenty-fourth letter of the Spanish alphabet
wafle *nm* **:** waffle
waflera *nf* **:** waffle iron
wapití *nm* **:** wapiti, elk
whisky *nm, pl* **whiskys** *or* **whiskies** **:** whiskey
wigwam *nm* **:** wigwam

X

x *nf* **:** twenty-fifth letter of the Spanish alphabet
xenofobia *nf* **:** xenophobia
xenófobo[1], -ba *adj* **:** xenophobic
xenófobo[2], -ba *n* **:** xenophobe
xenón *nm* **:** xenon
xerocopiar *vt* **:** to photocopy, to xerox
xilófono *nm* **:** xylophone

Y

y[1] *nf* **:** twenty-sixth letter of the Spanish alphabet
y[2] *conj* **1 :** and <mi hermano y yo : my brother and I> <¿y los demás? : and (what about) the others?> **2** (*used in numbers*) <cincuenta y cinco : fifty-five> **3** *fam* **:** well <y por supuesto : well, of course>
ya[1] *adv* **1 :** already <ya terminó : she's finished already> **2 :** now, right now <¡hazlo ya! : do it now!> <ya mismo : right away> **3 :** later, soon <ya iremos : we'll go later on> **4 :** no longer, anymore <ya no fuma : he no longer smokes> **5** (*used for emphasis*) **:** <¡ya lo sé! : I know!> <ya lo creo : of course> **6 no ya :** not only <no ya lloran sino gritan : they're not only crying but screaming> **7 ya que :** now that, since <ya que sabe la verdad : now that she knows the truth>
ya[2] *conj* **ya . . . ya :** whether . . . or, first . . . then <ya le gusta, ya no : first he likes it, then he doesn't>
yac *nm* **:** yak
yacer {90} *vi* **:** to lie <en esta tumba yacen sus abuelos : his grandparents lie in this grave>
yacimiento *nm* **:** bed, deposit <yacimiento petrolífero : oil field>
yaga, etc. → **yacer**
yanqui *adj & nmf* **:** Yankee
yarda *nf* **:** yard
yate *nm* **:** yacht
yaz, yazca, yazga, etc. → **yacer**
yedra *nf* **:** ivy
yegua *nf* **:** mare
yelmo *nm* **:** helmet
yema *nf* **1 :** bud, shoot **2 :** yolk (of an egg) **3 yema del dedo :** fingertip
yemenita *adj & nmf* **:** Yemenite
yendo → **ir**
yerba *nf* **1** *or* **yerba mate :** maté **2** → **hierba**
yerga, yergue, etc. → **erguir**
yermo[1], -ma *adj* **:** barren, deserted
yermo[2] *nm* **:** wasteland
yerno *nm* **:** son-in-law
yerra, etc. → **errar**
yerro *nm* **:** blunder, mistake
yerto, -ta *adj* **:** rigid, stiff
yesca *nf* **:** tinder
yeso *nm* **1 :** plaster **2 :** gypsum
yo[1] *nm* **:** ego, self
yo[2] *pron* **1 :** I **2 :** me <todos menos yo : everyone except me> <tan bajo como yo : as short as me> **3 soy yo :** it is I, it's me
yodado, -da *adj* **:** iodized
yodo *nm* **:** iodine
yoduro *nm* **:** iodide
yoga *nm* **:** yoga
yogui *nm* **:** yogi
yogurt *or* **yogur** *nm* **:** yogurt
yola *nf* **:** yawl
yoyo *or* **yoyó** *nm* **:** yo-yo
yuca *nf* **1 :** yucca (plant) **2 :** cassava, manioc
yucateco[1], -ca *adj* **:** of or from the Yucatán
yucateco[2], -ca *n* **:** person from the Yucatán
yudo → **judo**
yugo *nm* **:** yoke
yugoslavo, -va *adj & n* **:** Yugoslavian
yugular *adj* **:** jugular <vena yugular : jugular vein>
yungas *nfpl Bol, Chile, Peru* **:** warm tropical valleys
yunque *nm* **:** anvil
yunta *nf* **:** yoke, team (of oxen)
yute *nm* **:** jute
yuxtaponer {60} *vt* **:** to juxtapose — **yuxtaposición** *nf*

Z

z *nf* **:** twenty-seventh letter of the Spanish alphabet
zacate *nm CA, Mex* **1 :** grass, forage **2 :** hay
zafacón *nm, pl* **-cones :** wastebasket
zafar *vt* **:** to loosen, to untie — **zafarse** *vr* **1 :** to loosen up, to come undone **2 :** to get free of
zafio, -fia *adj* **:** coarse, crude
zafiro *nm* **:** sapphire
zaga *nf* **1 :** defense (in sports) **2 a la zaga** *or* **en ~ :** behind, in the rear
zagual *nm* **:** paddle (of a canoe)
zaguán *nm, pl* **zaguanes :** front hall, vestibule
zaherir {76} *vt* **1 :** to criticize sharply **2 :** to wound, to mortify
zahones *nmpl* **:** chaps
zaino, -na *adj* **:** chestnut (color)
zalamería *nf* **:** flattery, sweet talk
zalamero¹, -ra *adj* **:** flattering, fawning
zalamero², -ra *n* **:** flatterer
zambiano, -na *adj & nmf* **:** Zambian
zambullida *nf* **:** dive, plunge
zambullirse {38} *vr* **:** to dive, to plunge
zanahoria *nf* **:** carrot
zancada *nf* **:** stride, step
zancadilla *nf* **1 :** trip, stumble **2** *fam* **:** trick, ruse
zancos *nmpl* **:** stilts
zancuda *nf* **:** wading bird
zancudo *nm* MOSQUITO **:** mosquito
zángano *nm* **:** drone, male bee
zanja *nf* **:** ditch, trench
zanjar *vt* ACLARAR **:** to settle, to clear up, to resolve
zapallo *nm Arg, Chile, Peru, Uru* **:** pumpkin
zapapico *nm* **:** pickax
zapata *nf* **:** brake shoe
zapatería *nf* **1 :** shoemaker's, shoe factory **2 :** shoe store
zapatero¹, -ra *adj* **:** dry, tough, poorly cooked
zapatero², -ra *n* **:** shoemaker, cobbler
zapatilla *nf* **1** PANTUFLA **:** slipper **2** *or* **zapatilla de deporte :** sneaker
zapato *nm* **:** shoe
zar, zarina *n* **:** czar *m,* czarina *f*
zarandear *vt* **1 :** to sift, to sieve **2 :** to shake, to jostle, to jiggle
zarapito *nm* **:** curlew
zarcillo *nm* **1 :** earring **2 :** tendril (of a plant)
zarigüeya *nf* **:** opossum
zarista *adj & nmf* **:** czarist
zarpa *nf* **:** paw
zarpar *vi* **:** to set sail, to raise anchor
zarza *nf* **:** bramble, blackberry bush
zarzamora *nf* **1 :** blackberry **2 :** bramble, blackberry bush
zarzaparrilla *nf* **:** sarsaparilla
zepelín *nm, pl* **-lines :** zeppelin
zigoto *nm* **:** zygote
zigzag *nm, pl* **zigzags** *or* **zigzagues :** zigzag
zigzaguear *vi* **:** to zigzag
zimbabuense *adj & nmf* **:** Zimbabwean
zinc *nm* **:** zinc
zinnia *nf* **:** zinnia
zíper *nm CA, Mex* **:** zipper
zircón *nm, pl* **zircones :** zircon
zócalo *nm Mex* **:** main square
zodíaco *nm* **:** zodiac — **zodíacal** *adj*
zombi *or* **zombie** *nmf* **:** zombie
zona *nf* **:** zone, district, area
zonzo¹, -za *adj* **:** stupid, silly
zonzo², -za *n* **:** idiot, nitwit
zoo *nm* **:** zoo
zoología *nf* **:** zoology
zoológico¹, -ca *adj* **:** zoological
zoológico² *nm* **:** zoo
zoólogo, -ga *n* **:** zoologist
zoom *nm* **:** zoom lens
zopilote *nm CA, Mex* **:** buzzard
zoquete *nmf fam* **:** oaf, blockhead
zorrillo *nm* MOFETA **:** skunk
zorro¹, -rra *adj* **:** sly, crafty
zorro², -rra *n* **1 :** fox, vixen **2 :** sly crafty person
zorzal *nm* **:** thrush
zozobra *nf* **:** anxiety, worry
zozobrar *vi* **:** to capsize
zueco *nm* **:** clog (shoe)
zulú¹ *adj & nmf* **:** Zulu
zulú² *nm* **:** Zulu (language)
zumaque *nm* **:** sumac
zumbar *vi* **:** to buzz, to hum — *vt fam* **1 :** to hit, to thrash **2 :** to make fun of
zumbido *nm* **:** buzzing, humming
zumo *nf* JUGO **:** juice
zurcir {83} *vt* **:** to darn, to mend
zurdo¹, -da *adj* **:** left-handed
zurdo², -da *n* **:** left-handed person
zurza, etc. → zurcir
zutano, -na → fulano

English–Spanish Dictionary

A

a[1] [ˈeɪ] *n, pl* **a's** *or* **as** [ˈeɪz] **:** primera letra del alfabeto inglés

a[2] [ə, ˈeɪ] *art* (**an** [ən, ˈæn] *before vowel or silent h*) **1 :** un *m,* una *f* <a house : una casa> <half an hour : media hora> <what a surprise! : ¡qué sorpresa!> **2** PER **:** por, a la, al <30 kilometers an hour : 30 kilómetros por hora> <twice a month : dos veces al mes>

aardvark [ˈɑrd͵vɑrk] *n* **:** oso *m* hormiguero

aback [əˈbæk] *adv* **1 :** por sorpresa **2 to be taken aback :** quedarse desconcertado

abacus [ˈæbəkəs] *n, pl* **abaci** [ˈæbə͵saɪ, -͵kiː] *or* **abacuses :** ábaco *m*

abaft [əˈbæft] *adv* **:** a popa

abalone [͵æbəˈloːni] *n* **:** abulón *m,* oreja *f* marina

abandon[1] [əˈbændən] *vt* **1** DESERT, FORSAKE **:** abandonar, desamparar (a alguien), desertar de (algo) **2** GIVE UP, SUSPEND **:** renunciar a, suspender <he abandoned the search : suspendió la búsqueda> **3** EVACUATE, LEAVE **:** abandonar, evacuar, dejar <to abandon ship : abandonar el buque> **4 to abandon oneself :** entregarse, abandonarse

abandon[2] *n* **:** desenfreno *m* <with wild abandon : desenfrenadamente>

abandoned [əˈbændənd] *adj* **1** DESERTED **:** abandonado **2** UNRESTRAINED **:** desenfrenado, desinhibido

abandonment [əˈbændənmənt] *n* **:** abandono *m,* desamparo *m*

abase [əˈbeɪs] *vt* **abased; abasing :** degradar, humillar, rebajar

abash [əˈbæʃ] *vt* **:** avergonzar, abochornar

abashed [əˈbæʃt] *adj* **:** avergonzado

abate [əˈbeɪt] *vi* **abated; abating :** amainar, menguar, disminuir

abattoir [ˈæbə͵twɑr] *n* **:** matadero *m*

abbess [ˈæbɪs, -͵bɛs, -bəs] *n* **:** abadesa *f*

abbey [ˈæbi] *n, pl* **-beys :** abadía *f*

abbot [ˈæbət] *n* **:** abad *m*

abbreviate [əˈbriːvi͵eɪt] *vt* **-ated; -ating :** abreviar

abbreviation [ə͵briːviˈeɪʃən] *n* **:** abreviación *f,* abreviatura *f*

abdicate [ˈæbdɪ͵keɪt] *v* **-cated; -cating :** abdicar

abdication [͵æbdɪˈkeɪʃən] *n* **:** abdicación *f*

abdomen [ˈæbdəmən, æbˈdoːmən] *n* **:** abdomen *m,* vientre *m*

abdominal [æbˈdɑmənəl] *adj* **:** abdominal — **abdominally** *adv*

abduct [æbˈdʌkt] *vt* **:** raptar, secuestrar

abduction [æbˈdʌkʃən] *n* **:** rapto *m,* secuestro *m*

abductor [æbˈdʌktər] *n* **:** raptor *m,* -tora *f;* secuestrador *m,* -dora *f*

abed [əˈbɛd] *adv & adj* **:** en cama

aberrant [æˈbɛrənt, ˈæbərənt] *adj* **1** ABNORMAL **:** anormal, aberrante **2** ATYPICAL **:** anómalo, atípico

aberration [͵æbəˈreɪʃən] *n* **1 :** aberración *f* **2** DERANGEMENT **:** perturbación *f* mental

abet [əˈbɛt] *vt* **abetted; abetting** ASSIST **:** ayudar <to aid and abet : ser cómplice de>

abeyance [əˈbeɪən*t*s] *n* **:** desuso *m,* suspensión *f*

abhor [əbˈhɔr, æb-] *vt* **-horred; -horring :** abominar, aborrecer

abhorrence [əbˈhɔrən*t*s, æb-] *n* **:** aborrecimiento *m,* odio *m*

abhorrent [əbˈhɔrənt, æb-] *adj* **:** abominable, aborrecible, odioso

abide [əˈbaɪd] *v* **abode** [əˈboːd] *or* **abided; abiding** *vt* STAND **:** soportar, tolerar <I can't abide them : no los puedo ver> — *vi* **1** ENDURE **:** quedar, permanecer **2** DWELL **:** morar, residir **3 to abide by :** atenerse a

ability [əˈbɪləṭi] *n, pl* **-ties 1** CAPABILITY **:** aptitud *f,* capacidad *f,* facultad *f* **2** COMPETENCE **:** competencia *f* **3** TALENT **:** talento *m,* don *m,* habilidad *f*

abject [ˈæb͵dʒɛkt, æbˈ-] *adj* **1** WRETCHED **:** miserable, desdichado **2** HOPELESS **:** abatido, desesperado **3** SERVILE **:** servil <abject flattery : halagos serviles> — **abjectly** *adv*

ablaze [əˈbleɪz] *adj* **1** BURNING **:** ardiendo, en llamas **2** RADIANT **:** resplandeciente, radiante

able [ˈeɪbəl] *adj* **abler; ablest 1** CAPABLE **:** capaz, hábil **2** COMPETENT **:** competente

ablution [əˈbluːʃən] *n* **:** ablución *f* <to perform one's ablutions : lavarse>

ably [ˈeɪbəli] *adv* **:** hábilmente, eficientemente

abnormal [æbˈnɔrməl] *adj* **:** anormal — **abnormally** *adv*

abnormality [͵æbnərˈmæləṭi, -nɔr-] *n, pl* **-ties :** anormalidad *f*

aboard[1] [əˈbord] *adv* **:** a bordo

aboard[2] *prep* **:** a bordo de

abode[1] → **abide**

abode[2] [əˈboːd] *n* **:** morada *f,* residencia *f,* vivienda *f*

abolish [əˈbɑlɪʃ] *vt* **:** abolir, suprimir

abolition [͵æbəˈlɪʃən] *n* **:** abolición *f,* supresión *f*

abominable [əˈbɑmənəbəl] *adj* DETESTABLE **:** abominable, aborrecible, espantoso

abominate [əˈbɑmə͵neɪt] *vt* **-nated; -nating :** abominar, aborrecer

abomination [ə͵bɑməˈneɪʃən] *n* **:** abominación *f*

aboriginal [͵æbəˈrɪdʒənəl] *adj* **:** aborigen, indígena

aborigine [ˌæbəˈrɪdʒəni] *n* NATIVE : aborigen *mf,* indígena *mf*

abort [əˈbɔrt] *vt* **1** : abortar (en medicina) **2** CALL OFF : suspender, abandonar — *vi* : abortar, hacerse un aborto

abortion [əˈbɔrʃən] *n* : aborto *m*

abortive [əˈbɔrtɪv] *adj* UNSUCCESSFUL : fracasado, frustrado, malogrado

abound [əˈbaʊnd] *vi* **to abound in** : abundar en, estar lleno de

about¹ [əˈbaʊt] *adv* **1** APPROXIMATELY : aproximadamente, casi, más o menos **2** AROUND : por todas partes, alrededor <the children are running about : los niños están corriendo por todas partes> **3 to be about to** : estar a punto de **4 to be up and about** : estar levantado

about² *prep* **1** AROUND : alrededor de **2** CONCERNING : de, acerca de, sobre <he always talks about politics : siempre habla de política>

above¹ [əˈbʌv] *adv* **1** OVERHEAD : por encima, arriba **2** : más arriba <as stated above : como se indica más arriba>

above² *adj* : anterior, antedicho <for the above reasons : por las razones antedichas>

above³ *prep* **1** OVER : encima de, arriba de, sobre **2** : superior a, por encima de <he's above those things : él está por encima de esas cosas> **3** : más de, superior a <he earns above $50,000 : gana más de $50,000> <a number above 10 : un número superior a 10> **4 above all** : sobre todo

aboveboard¹ [əˈbʌvˈbord, -ˌbord] *adv* **open and aboveboard** : sin tapujos

aboveboard² *adj* : legítimo, sincero

abrade [əˈbreɪd] *vt* **abraded; abrading 1** ERODE : erosionar, corroer **2** SCRAPE : escoriar, raspar

abrasion [əˈbreɪʒən] *n* **1** SCRAPE, SCRATCH : raspadura *f,* rasguño *m* **2** EROSION : erosión *f*

abrasive¹ [əˈbreɪsɪv] *adj* **1** ROUGH : abrasivo, áspero **2** BRUSQUE, IRRITATING : brusco, irritante

abrasive² *n* : abrasivo *m*

abreast [əˈbrɛst] *adv* **1** : en fondo, al lado <to march three abreast : marchar de tres en fondo> **2 to keep abreast** : mantenerse al día

abridge [əˈbrɪdʒ] *vt* **abridged; abridging** : compendiar, resumir

abridgment *or* **abridgement** [əˈbrɪdʒmənt] *n* : compendio *m,* resumen *m*

abroad [əˈbrɔd] *adv* **1** ABOUT, WIDELY : por todas partes, en todas direcciones <the news spread abroad : la noticia corrió por todas partes> **2** OVERSEAS : en el extranjero, en el exterior

abrupt [əˈbrʌpt] *adj* **1** SUDDEN : abrupto, repentino, súbito **2** BRUSQUE, CURT : brusco, cortante — **abruptly** *adv*

abscess [ˈæbˌsɛs] *n* : absceso *m*

abscond [æbˈskɑnd] *vi* : huir, fugarse

absence [ˈæbsənts] *n* **1** : ausencia *f* (de una persona) **2** LACK : falta *f,* carencia *f*

absent¹ [æbˈsɛnt] *vt* **to absent oneself** : ausentarse

absent² [ˈæbsənt] *adj* : ausente

absentee [ˌæbsənˈtiː] *n* : ausente *mf*

absentminded [ˌæbsəntˈmaɪndəd] *adj* : distraído, despistado

absentmindedly [ˌæbsəntˈmaɪndədli] *adv* : distraídamente

absentmindedness [ˌæbsəntˈmaɪndədnəs] *n* : distracción *f,* despiste *m*

absolute [ˈæbsəˌluːt, ˌæbsəˈluːt] *adj* **1** COMPLETE, PERFECT : completo, pleno, perfecto **2** UNCONDITIONAL : absoluto, incondicional **3** DEFINITE : categórico, definitivo

absolutely [ˈæbsəˌluːtli, ˌæbsəˈluːtli] *adv* **1** COMPLETELY : completamente, absolutamente **2** CERTAINLY : desde luego <do you agree? absolutely! : ¿estás de acuerdo? ¡desde luego!>

absolution [ˌæbsəˈluːʃən] *n* : absolución *f*

absolve [əbˈzɑlv, æb-, -ˈsɑlv] *vt* **-solved; -solving** : absolver, perdonar

absorb [əbˈzɔrb, æb-, -ˈsɔrb] *vt* **1** : absorber, embeber (un líquido), amortiguar (un golpe, la luz) **2** ENGROSS : absorber **3** ASSIMILATE : asimilar

absorbed [əbˈzɔrbd, æb-, -ˈsɔrbd] *adj* ENGROSSED : absorto, ensimismado

absorbency [əbˈzɔrbəntsi, æb-, -ˈsɔr-] *n* : absorbencia *f*

absorbent [əbˈzɔrbənt, æb-, -ˈsɔr-] *adj* : absorbente

absorbing [əbˈzɔrbɪŋ, æb-, -ˈsɔr-] *adj* : absorbente, fascinante

absorption [əbˈzɔrpʃən, æb-, -ˈsɔrp-] *n* **1** : absorción *f* **2** CONCENTRATION : concentración *f*

abstain [əbˈsteɪn, æb-] *vi* : abstenerse

abstainer [əbˈsteɪnər, æb-] *n* : abstemio *m,* -mia *f*

abstemious [æbˈstiːmiəs] *adj* : abstemio, sobrio — **abstemiously** *adv*

abstention [əbˈstɛntʃən, æb-] *n* : abstención *f*

abstinence [ˈæbstənənts] *n* : abstinencia *f*

abstract¹ [æbˈstrækt, ˈæbˌ-] *vt* **1** EXTRACT : abstraer, extraer **2** SUMMARIZE : compendiar, resumir

abstract² *adj* : abstracto — **abstractly** [æbˈstræktli, ˈæbˌ-] *adv*

abstract³ [ˈæbˌstrækt] *n* : resumen *m,* compendio *m,* sumario *m*

abstraction [æbˈstrækʃən] *n* **1** : abstracción *f,* idea *f* abstracta **2** ABSENTMINDEDNESS : distracción *f*

abstruse [əbˈstruːs, æb-] *adj* : abstruso, recóndito — **abstrusely** *adv*

absurd [əbˈsərd, -ˈzərd] *adj* : absurdo, ridículo, disparatado — **absurdly** *adv*

absurdity [əbˈsərdəti, -ˈzər-] *n, pl* **-ties 1** : absurdo *m* **2** NONSENSE : disparate *m,* despropósito *m*

abundance [ə'bʌndənts] *n* : abundancia *f*

abundant [ə'bʌndənt] *adj* : abundante, cuantioso, copioso

abundantly [ə'bʌndəntli] *adv* : abundantemente, en abundancia

abuse[1] [ə'bju:z] *vt* **abused; abusing 1** MISUSE : abusar de **2** MISTREAT : maltratar **3** REVILE : insultar, injuriar, denostar

abuse[2] [ə'bju:s] *n* **1** MISUSE : abuso *m* **2** MISTREATMENT : abuso *m,* maltrato *m* **3** INSULTS : insultos *mpl,* improperios *mpl* <a string of abuse : una serie de improperios>

abuser [ə'bju:zər] *n* : abusador *m,* -dora *f*

abusive [ə'bju:sɪv] *adj* **1** ABUSING : abusivo **2** INSULTING : ofensivo, injurioso, insultante — **abusively** *adv*

abut [ə'bʌt] *v* **abutted; abutting** *vt* : bordear — *vi* **to abut on** : colindar con

abutment [ə'bʌtmənt] *n* **1** BUTTRESS : contrafuerte *m,* estribo *m* **2** CLOSENESS : contigüidad *f*

abysmal [ə'bɪzməl] *adj* **1** DEEP : abismal, insondable **2** TERRIBLE : atroz, desastroso

abysmally [ə'bɪzməli] *adv* : desastrosamente, terriblemente

abyss [ə'bɪs, 'æbɪs] *n* : abismo *m,* sima *f*

acacia [ə'keɪʃə] *n* : acacia *f*

academic[1] [ˌækə'dɛmɪk] *adj* **1** : académico **2** THEORETICAL : teórico — **academically** [-mɪkli] *adv*

academic[2] *n* : académico *m,* -ca *f*

academy [ə'kædəmi] *n, pl* **-mies** : academia *f*

accede [æk'si:d] *vi* **-ceded; -ceding 1** AGREE : acceder, consentir **2** ASCEND : subir, acceder <he acceded to the throne : subió al trono>

accelerate [ɪk'sɛləˌreɪt, æk-] *v* **-ated; -ating** *vt* : acelerar, apresurar — *vi* : acelerar (dícese de un carro)

acceleration [ɪkˌsɛlə'reɪʃən, æk-] *n* : aceleración *f*

accelerator [ɪk'sɛləˌreɪt̬ər, æk-] *n* : acelerador *m*

accent[1] ['ækˌsɛnt, æk'sɛnt] *vt* : acentuar

accent[2] ['ækˌsɛnt, -sənt] *n* **1** : acento *m* **2** EMPHASIS, STRESS : énfasis *m,* acento *m*

accentuate [ɪk'sɛntʃʊˌeɪt, æk-] *vt* **-ated; -ating** : acentuar, poner énfasis en

accept [ɪk'sɛpt, æk-] *vt* **1** : aceptar **2** ACKNOWLEDGE : admitir, reconocer

acceptability [ɪkˌsɛptə'bɪlət̬i, æk-] *n* : aceptabilidad *f*

acceptable [ɪk'sɛptəbəl, æk-] *adj* : aceptable, admisible — **acceptably** [-bli] *adv*

acceptance [ɪk'sɛptənts, æk-] *n* : aceptación *f,* aprobación *f*

access[1] ['ækˌsɛs] *vt* : obtener acceso a, entrar a

access[2] *n* : acceso *m*

accessible [ɪk'sɛsəbəl, æk-] *adj* : accesible, asequible

accession [ɪk'sɛʃən, æk-] *n* **1** : ascenso *f,* subida *f* (al trono, etc.) **2** ACQUISITION : adquisición *f*

accessory[1] [ɪk'sɛsəri, æk-] *adj* : auxiliar

accessory[2] *n, pl* **-ries 1** : accesorio *m,* complemento *m* **2** ACCOMPLICE : cómplice *mf*

accident ['æksədənt] *n* **1** MISHAP : accidente *m* **2** CHANCE : casualidad *f*

accidental [ˌæksə'dɛntəl] *adj* : accidental, casual, imprevisto, fortuito

accidentally [ˌæksə'dɛntəli, -'dɛntli] *adv* **1** BY CHANCE : por casualidad **2** UNINTENTIONALLY : sin querer, involuntariamente

acclaim[1] [ə'kleɪm] *vt* : aclamar, elogiar

acclaim[2] *n* : aclamación *f,* elogio *m*

acclamation [ˌæklə'meɪʃən] *n* : aclamación *f*

acclimate ['ækləˌmeɪt, ə'klaɪmət] → **acclimatize**

acclimatize [ə'klaɪməˌtaɪz] *v* **-tized; -tizing** *vt* **1** : aclimatar **2 to acclimatize oneself** : aclimatarse

accolade ['ækəˌleɪd, -ˌlɑd] *n* **1** PRAISE : elogio *m* **2** AWARD : galardón *m*

accommodate [ə'kɑməˌdeɪt] *vt* **-dated; -dating 1** ADAPT : acomodar, adaptar **2** SATISFY : tener en cuenta, satisfacer **3** HOLD : dar cabida a, tener cabida para

accommodation [əˌkɑmə'deɪʃən] *n* **1** : adaptación *f,* adecuación *f* **2 accommodations** *npl* LODGING : alojamiento *m,* hospedaje *m*

accompaniment [ə'kʌmpənəmənt, -'kɑm-] *n* : acompañamiento *m*

accompanist [ə'kʌmpənɪst, -'kɑm-] *n* : acompañante *mf*

accompany [ə'kʌmpəni, -'kɑm-] *vt* **-nied; -nying** : acompañar

accomplice [ə'kɑmpləs, -'kʌm-] *n* : cómplice *mf*

accomplish [ə'kɑmplɪʃ, -'kʌm-] *vt* : efectuar, realizar, lograr, llevar a cabo

accomplished [ə'kɑmplɪʃt, -'kʌm-] *adj* : consumado, logrado

accomplishment [ə'kɑmplɪʃmənt, -'kʌm-] *n* **1** ACHIEVEMENT : logro *m,* éxito *m* **2** SKILL : destreza *f,* habilidad *f*

accord[1] [ə'kɔrd] *vt* GRANT : conceder, otorgar — *vi* **to accord with** : concordar con, conformarse con

accord[2] *n* **1** AGREEMENT : acuerdo *m,* convenio *m* **2** VOLITION : voluntad *f* <on one's own accord : voluntariamente, de motu proprio>

accordance [ə'kɔrdənts] *n* **1** ACCORD : acuerdo *m,* conformidad *f* **2 in ac-**

cordance with : conforme a, según, de acuerdo con
accordingly [ə'kɔrdɪŋli] *adv* **1** CORRESPONDINGLY : en consecuencia **2** CONSEQUENTLY : por consiguiente, por lo tanto
according to [ə'kɔrdɪŋ] *prep* : según, de acuerdo con, conforme a
accordion [ə'kɔrdiən] *n* : acordeón *m*
accordionist [ə'kɔrdiənɪst] *n* : acordeonista *mf*
accost [ə'kɔst] *vt* : abordar, dirigirse a
account[1] [ə'kaʊnt] *vt* : considerar, estimar <he accounts himself lucky : se considera afortunado> — *vi* **to account for** : dar cuenta de, explicar
account[2] *n* **1** : cuenta *f* <savings account : cuenta de ahorros> **2** EXPLANATION : versión *f,* explicación *f* **3** REPORT : relato *m,* informe *m* **4** IMPORTANCE : importancia *f* <to be of no account : no tener importancia> **5 on account of** BECAUSE OF : a causa de, debido a, por **6 on no account** : de ninguna manera
accountability [ə,kaʊntə'bɪləṭi] *n* : responsabilidad *f*
accountable [ə'kaʊntəbəl] *adj* : responsable
accountant [ə'kaʊntənt] *n* : contador *m,* -dora *f;* contable *mf Spain*
accounting [ə'kaʊntɪŋ] *n* : contabilidad *f*
accoutrements *or* **accouterments** [ə'kuːtrəmənts, -'kuːtər-] *npl* **1** EQUIPMENT : equipo *m,* avíos *mpl* **2** ACCESSORIES : accesorios *mpl* **3** TRAPPINGS : símbolos *mpl* <the accoutrements of power : los símbolos del poder>
accredit [ə'krɛdət] *vt* : acreditar, autorizar
accreditation [ə,krɛdə'teɪʃən] *n* : acreditación *f,* homologación *f*
accrual [ə'kruːəl] *n* : incremento *m,* acumulación *f*
accrue [ə'kruː] *vi* **-crued; -cruing** : acumularse, aumentarse
accumulate [ə'kjuːmjə,leɪt] *v* **-lated; -lating** *vt* : acumular, amontonar — *vi* : acumularse, amontonarse
accumulation [ə,kjuːmjə'leɪʃən] *n* : acumulación *f,* amontonamiento *m*
accuracy ['ækjərəsi] *n* : exactitud *f,* precisión *f*
accurate ['ækjərət] *adj* : exacto, correcto, fiel, preciso — **accurately** *adv*
accusation [,ækjə'zeɪʃən] *n* : acusación *f*
accuse [ə'kjuːz] *vt* **-cused; -cusing** : acusar, delatar, denunciar
accused [ə'kjuːzd] *ns & pl* DEFENDANT : acusado *m,* -da *f*
accuser [ə'kjuːzər] *n* : acusador *m,* -dora *f*
accustom [ə'kʌstəm] *vt* : acostumbrar, habituar
ace ['eɪs] *n* : as *m*
acerbic [ə'sərbɪk, æ-] *adj* : acerbo, mordaz
acetate ['æsə,teɪt] *n* : acetato *m*
acetylene [ə'sɛṭələn, -ṭə,liːn] *n* : acetileno *m*
ache[1] ['eɪk] *vi* **ached; aching 1** : doler **2 to ache for** : anhelar, ansiar
ache[2] *n* : dolor *m*
achieve [ə'tʃiːv] *vt* **achieved; achieving** : lograr, alcanzar, conseguir, realizar
achievement [ə'tʃiːvmənt] *n* : logro *m,* éxito *m,* realización *f*
acid[1] ['æsəd] *adj* **1** SOUR : ácido, agrio **2** CAUSTIC, SHARP : acerbo, mordaz — **acidly** *adv*
acid[2] *n* : ácido *m*
acidic [ə'sɪdɪk, æ-] *adj* : ácido
acidity [ə'sɪdəṭi, æ-] *n, pl* **-ties** : acidez *f*
acknowledge [ɪk'nɑlɪdʒ, æk-] *vt* **-edged; -edging 1** ADMIT : reconocer, admitir **2** RECOGNIZE : reconocer **3 to acknowledge receipt of** : acusar recibo de
acknowledgment [ɪk'nɑlɪdʒmənt, æk-] *n* **1** RECOGNITION : reconocimiento *m* **2** THANKS : agradecimiento *m*
acme ['ækmi] *n* : colmo *m,* apogeo *m,* cúspide *f*
acne ['ækni] *n* : acné *m*
acorn ['eɪ,kɔrn, -kərn] *n* : bellota *f*
acoustic [ə'kuːstɪk] *or* **acoustical** [-stɪkəl] *adj* : acústico — **acoustically** *adv*
acoustics [ə'kuːstɪks] *ns & pl* : acústica *f*
acquaint [ə'kweɪnt] *vt* **1** INFORM : enterar, informar **2** FAMILIARIZE : familiarizar **3 to be acquainted with** : conocer a (una persona), estar al tanto de (un hecho)
acquaintance [ə'kweɪntənts] *n* **1** KNOWLEDGE : conocimiento *m* **2** : conocido *m,* -da *f* <friends and acquaintances : amigos y conocidos>
acquiesce [,ækwi'ɛs] *vi* **-esced; -escing** : consentir, conformarse
acquiescence [,ækwi'ɛsənts] *n* : consentimiento *m,* aquiescencia *f*
acquire [ə'kwaɪr] *vt* **-quired; -quiring** : adquirir, obtener
acquisition [,ækwə'zɪʃən] *n* : adquisición *f*
acquisitive [ə'kwɪzəṭɪv] *adj* : adquisitivo, codicioso
acquit [ə'kwɪt] *vt* **-quitted; -quitting 1** : absolver, exculpar **2 to acquit oneself** : comportarse, defenderse
acquittal [ə'kwɪṭəl] *n* : absolución *f,* exculpación *f*
acre ['eɪkər] *n* : acre *m*
acreage ['eɪkərɪdʒ] *n* : superficie *f* en acres
acrid ['ækrəd] *adj* **1** BITTER : acre **2** CAUSTIC : acre, mordaz — **acridly** *adv*
acrimonious [,ækrə'moːniəs] *adj* : áspero, cáustico, sarcástico
acrimony ['ækrə,moːni] *n, pl* **-nies** : acrimonia *f*

acrobat ['ækrə,bæt] *n* **:** acróbata *mf,* satimbanqui *mf*

acrobatic [,ækrə'bæṱɪk] *adj* **:** acrobático

acronym ['ækrə,nɪm] *n* **:** acrónimo *m*

across[1] [ə'krɔs] *adv* **1** CROSSWISE **:** al través **2 :** a través, del otro lado <he's already across : ya está del otro lado> **3 :** de ancho <40 feet across : 40 pies de ancho>

across[2] *prep* **1 :** al otro lado de <across the street : al otro lado de la calle> **2 :** a través de <a log across the road : un tronco a través del camino>

acrylic [ə'krɪlɪk] *n* **:** acrílico *m*

act[1] ['ækt] *vi* **1** PERFORM **:** actuar, interpretar **2** FEIGN, PRETEND **:** fingir, simular **3** BEHAVE **:** comportarse **4** FUNCTION **:** actuar, servir, funcionar **5 :** tomar medidas <he acted to save the business : tomó medidas para salvar el negocio> **6 to act as :** servir de, hacer de

act[2] *n* **1** DEED **:** acto *m,* hecho *m,* acción *f* **2** DECREE **:** ley *f,* decreto *m* **3 :** acto *m* (en una obra de teatro), número *m* (en un espectáculo) **4** PRETENSE **:** fingimiento *m*

action ['ækʃən] *n* **1** DEED **:** acción *f,* acto *m,* hecho *m* **2** BEHAVIOR **:** actuación *f,* comportamiento *m* **3** LAWSUIT **:** demanda *f* **4** MOVEMENT **:** movimiento *m* **5** COMBAT **:** combate *m* **6** PLOT **:** acción *f,* trama *f* **7** MECHANISM **:** mecanismo *m*

activate ['æktə,veɪt] *vt* **-vated; -vating :** activar

active ['æktɪv] *adj* **1** MOVING **:** activo, en movimiento **2** LIVELY **:** vigoroso, enérgico **3 :** en actividad <an active volcano : un volcán en actividad> **4** OPERATIVE **:** vigente

actively ['æktɪvli] *adv* **:** activamente, enérgicamente

activity [æk'tɪvəṱi] *n, pl* **-ties 1** MOVEMENT **:** actividad *f,* movimiento *m* **2** VIGOR **:** vigor *m,* energía *f* **3** OCCUPATION **:** actividad *f,* ocupación *f*

actor ['æktər] *n* **:** actor *m,* artista *mf*

actress ['æktrəs] *n* **:** actriz *f*

actual ['æktʃʊəl] *adj* **:** real, verdadero

actuality [,æktʃʊ'æləṱi] *n, pl* **-ties :** realidad *f*

actually ['æktʃʊəli, -ʃəli] *adv* **:** realmente, en realidad

actuary ['æktʃʊ,ɛri] *n, pl* **-aries :** actuario *m,* -ria *f* de seguros

acumen [ə'kju:mən] *n* **:** perspicacia *f*

acupuncture ['ækjʊ,pʌŋktʃər] *n* **:** acupuntura *f*

acute [ə'kju:t] *adj* **acuter; acutest 1** SHARP **:** agudo **2** PERCEPTIVE **:** perspicaz, sagaz **3** KEEN **:** fino, muy desarrollado, agudo <an acute sense of smell : un fino olfato> **4** SEVERE **:** grave **5 acute angle :** ángulo *m* agudo

acutely [ə'kju:tli] *adv* **:** intensamente <to be acutely aware : estar perfectamente consciente>

acuteness [ə'kju:tnəs] *n* **:** agudeza *f*

ad ['æd] → **advertisement**

adage ['ædɪdʒ] *n* **:** adagio *m,* refrán *m,* dicho *m*

adamant ['ædəmənt, -,mænt] *adj* **:** firme, categórico, inflexible — **adamantly** *adv*

Adam's apple ['ædəmz] *n* **:** nuez *f* de Adán

adapt [ə'dæpt] *vt* **:** adaptar, ajustar — *vi* **:** adaptarse

adaptability [ə,dæptə'bɪləṱi] *n* **:** adaptabilidad *f,* flexibilidad *f*

adaptable [ə'dæptəbəl] *adj* **:** adaptable, amoldable

adaptation [,æ,dæp'teɪʃən, -dəp-] *n* **1 :** adaptación *f,* modificación *f* **2** VERSION **:** versión *f*

adapter [ə'dæptər] *n* **:** adaptador *m*

add ['æd] *vt* **1 :** añadir, agregar <to add a comment : añadir una observación> **2 :** sumar <add these numbers : suma estos números> — *vi* **:** sumar (en total)

adder ['ædər] *n* **:** víbora *f*

addict[1] [ə'dɪkt] *vt* **:** causar adicción en

addict[2] ['ædɪkt] *n* **1 :** adicto *m,* -ta *f* **2 drug addict :** drogadicto *m,* -ta *f;* toxicómano *m,* -na *f*

addiction [ə'dɪkʃən] *n* **1 :** adicción *f,* dependencia *f* **2 drug addiction :** drogadicción *f*

addictive [ə'dɪktɪv] *adj* **:** adictivo

addition [ə'dɪʃən] *n* **1 :** adición *f,* añadidura *f* **2 in ~ :** además, también

additional [ə'dɪʃənəl] *adj* **:** extra, adicional, de más

additionally [ə'dɪʃənəli] *adv* **:** además, adicionalmente

additive ['ædəṱɪv] *n* **:** aditivo *m*

addle ['ædəl] *vt* **-dled; -dling :** confundir, enturbiar

address[1] [ə'drɛs] *vt* **1 :** dirigirse a, pronunciar un discurso ante <to address a jury : dirigirse a un jurado> **2 :** dirigir, ponerle la dirección a <to address a letter : dirigir una carta>

address[2] [ə'drɛs, 'æ,drɛs] *n* **1** SPEECH **:** discurso *m,* alocución *f* **2 :** dirección *f* (de una residencia, etc.)

adenoids ['æd,nɔɪd, -dən,ɔɪd] *npl* **:** adenoides *fpl*

adept [ə'dɛpt] *adj* **:** experto, hábil — **adeptly** *adv*

adequacy ['ædɪkwəsi] *n, pl* **-cies :** cantidad *f* suficiente

adequate ['ædɪkwət] *adj* **1** SUFFICIENT **:** adecuado, suficiente **2** ACCEPTABLE, PASSABLE **:** adecuado, aceptable

adequately ['ædɪkwətli] *adv* **:** suficientemente, apropiadamente

adhere [æd'hɪr, əd-] *vi* **-hered; -hering 1** STICK **:** pegarse, adherirse **2 to adhere to :** adherirse a (una política, etc.), cumplir con (una promesa)

adherence [æd'hɪrənts, əd-] *n* : adhesión *f,* adherencia *f,* observancia *f* (de una ley, etc.)
adherent[1] [æd'hɪrənt, əd-] *adj* : adherente, adhesivo, pegajoso
adherent[2] *n* : adepto *m,* -ta *f;* partidario *m,* -ria *f*
adhesive[1] [æd'hi:sɪv, əd-, -zɪv] *adj* : adhesivo
adhesive[2] *n* : adhesivo *m,* pegamento *m*
adjacent [ə'dʒeɪsənt] *adj* : adyacente, colindante, contiguo
adjective ['ædʒɪktɪv] *n* : adjetivo *m* — **adjectival** [ˌædʒɪk'taɪvəl] *adj*
adjoin [ə'dʒɔɪn] *vt* : lindar con, colindar con
adjoining [ə'dʒɔɪnɪŋ] *adj* : contiguo, colindante
adjourn [ə'dʒərn] *vt* : levantar, suspender <the meeting is adjourned : se levanta la sesión> — *vi* : aplazarse
adjournment [ə'dʒərnmənt] *n* : suspensión *f,* aplazamiento *m*
adjudicate [ə'dʒu:dɪˌkeɪt] *vt* **-cated; -cating** : juzgar, arbitrar
adjunct ['æˌdʒʌŋkt] *n* : adjunto *m,* complemento *m*
adjust [ə'dʒʌst] *vt* : ajustar, arreglar, regular — *vi* **to adjust to** : adaptarse a
adjustable [ə'dʒʌstəbəl] *adj* : ajustable, regulable, graduable
adjustment [ə'dʒʌstmənt] *n* : ajuste *m,* modificación *f*
ad–lib[1] ['æd'lɪb] *v* **-libbed; -libbing** : improvisar
ad–lib[2] *adj* : improvisado
administer [æd'mɪnəstər, əd-] *vt* : administrar
administration [ædˌmɪnə'streɪʃən, əd-] *n* **1** MANAGING : administración *f,* dirección *f* **2** GOVERNMENT, MANAGEMENT : administración *f,* gobierno *m*
administrative [æd'mɪnəˌstreɪtɪv, əd-] *adj* : administrativo — **administratively** *adv*
administrator [æd'mɪnəˌstreɪtər, əd-] *n* : administrador *m,* -dora *f*
admirable ['ædmərəbəl] *adj* : admirable, loable — **admirably** *adv*
admiral ['ædmərəl] *n* : almirante *mf*
admiration [ˌædmə'reɪʃən] *n* : admiración *f*
admire [æd'maɪr] *vt* **-mired; -miring** : admirar
admirer [æd'maɪrər] *n* : admirador *m,* -dora *f*
admiring [æd'maɪrɪŋ] *adj* : admirativo, de admiración
admiringly [æd'maɪrɪŋli] *adv* : con admiración
admissible [æd'mɪsəbəl] *adj* : admisible, aceptable
admission [æd'mɪʃən] *n* **1** ADMITTANCE : entrada *f,* admisión *f* **2** ACKNOWLEDGMENT : reconocimiento *m,* admisión *f*
admit [æd'mɪt, əd-] *vt* **-mitted; -mitting 1** : admitir, dejar entrar <the museum admits children : el museo deja entrar a los niños> **2** ACKNOWLEDGE : reconocer, admitir
admittance [æd'mɪtənts, əd-] *n* : admisión *f,* entrada *f,* acceso *m*
admittedly [æd'mɪtədli, əd-] *adv* : la verdad es que, lo cierto es que <admittedly we went too fast : la verdad es que fuimos demasiado de prisa>
admonish [æd'mɑnɪʃ, əd-] *vt* : amonestar, reprender
admonition [ˌædmə'nɪʃən] *n* : admonición *f*
ado [ə'du:] *n* **1** FUSS : ruido *m,* alboroto *m* **2** TROUBLE : dificultad *f,* lío *m* **3 without further ado** : sin más preámbulos
adobe [ə'do:bi] *n* : adobe *m*
adolescence [ˌædəl'ɛsənts] *n* : adolescencia *f*
adolescent[1] [ˌædəl'ɛsənt] *adj* : adolescente, de adolescencia
adolescent[2] *n* : adolescente *mf*
adopt [ə'dɑpt] *vt* : adoptar
adoption [ə'dɑpʃən] *n* : adopción *f*
adorable [ə'dorəbəl] *adj* : adorable, encantador
adorably [ə'dorəbli] *adv* : de manera adorable
adoration [ˌædə'reɪʃən] *n* : adoración *f*
adore [ə'dor] *vt* **adored; adoring 1** WORSHIP : adorar **2** LOVE : querer, adorar **3** LIKE : encantarle (algo a uno), gustarle mucho (algo a uno) <I adore your new dress : me encanta tu vestido nuevo>
adorn [ə'dɔrn] *vt* : adornar, ornar, engalanar
adornment [ə'dɔrnmənt] *n* : adorno *m,* decoración *f*
adrift [ə'drɪft] *adj & adv* : a la deriva
adroit [ə'drɔɪt] *adj* : diestro, hábil — **adroitly** *adv*
adroitness [ə'drɔɪtnəs] *n* : destreza *f,* habilidad *f*
adult[1] [ə'dʌlt, 'æˌdʌlt] *adj* : adulto
adult[2] *n* : adulto *m,* -ta *f*
adulterate [ə'dʌltəˌreɪt] *vt* **-ated; -ating** : adulterar
adulterous [ə'dʌltərəs] *adj* : adúltero
adultery [ə'dʌltəri] *n, pl* **-teries** : adulterio *m*
adulthood [ə'dʌltˌhʊd] *n* : adultez *f,* edad *f* adulta
advance[1] [æd'vænts, əd-] *v* **-vanced; -vancing** *vt* **1** : avanzar, adelantar <to advance troops : avanzar las tropas> **2** PROMOTE : ascender, promover **3** PROPOSE : proponer, presentar **4** : adelantar, anticipar <they advanced me next month's salary : me adelantaron el sueldo del próximo mes> — *vi* **1** PROCEED : avanzar, adelantarse **2** PROGRESS : progresar
advance[2] *adj* : anticipado <advance notice : previo aviso>
advance[3] *n* **1** PROGRESSION : avance *m* **2** PROGRESS : adelanto *m,* mejora *f,* pro-

greso *m* **3** RISE **:** aumento *m,* alza *f* **4** LOAN **:** anticipo *m,* préstamo *m* **5 in ~ :** por adelantado

advanced [æd'væntst, əd-] *adj* **1** DEVELOPED **:** avanzado, desarrollado **2** PRECOCIOUS **:** adelantado, precoz **3** HIGHER **:** superior

advancement [æd'væntsmənt, əd-] *n* **1** FURTHERANCE **:** fomento *m,* adelantamiento *m,* progreso *m* **2** PROMOTION **:** ascenso *m*

advantage [əd'væntɪdʒ, æd-] *n* **1** SUPERIORITY **:** ventaja *f,* superioridad *f* **2** GAIN **:** provecho *m,* partido *m* **3 to take advantage of :** aprovecharse de

advantageous [ˌædˌvæn'teɪdʒəs, -vən-] *adj* **:** ventajoso, provechoso — **advantageously** *adv*

advent ['ædˌvɛnt] *n* **1 Advent :** Adviento *m* **2** ARRIVAL **:** advenimiento *m,* venida *f*

adventure [æd'vɛntʃər, əd-] *n* **:** aventura *f*

adventurer [æd'vɛntʃərər, əd-] *n* **:** aventurero *m,* -ra *f*

adventurous [æd'vɛntʃərəs, əd-] *adj* **1 :** intrépido, aventurero <an adventurous traveler **:** un viajero intrépido> **2** RISKY **:** arriesgado, aventurado

adverb ['ædˌvərb] *n* **:** adverbio *m* — **adverbial** [æd'vərbiəl] *adj*

adversary ['ædvərˌsɛri] *n, pl* **-saries :** adversario *m,* -ria *f*

adverse [æd'vərs, 'æd-ˌ] *adj* **1** OPPOSING **:** opuesto, contrario **2** UNFAVORABLE **:** adverso, desfavorable — **adversely** *adv*

adversity [æd'vərsət̬i, əd-] *n, pl* **-ties :** adversidad *f*

advertise ['ædvərˌtaɪz] *v* **-tised; -tising** *vt* **:** anunciar, hacerle publicidad a — *vi* **:** hacer publicidad, hacer propaganda

advertisement ['ædvərˌtaɪzmənt; æd'vərt̬əzmənt] *n* **:** anuncio *m*

advertiser ['ædvərˌtaɪzər] *n* **:** anunciante *mf*

advertising ['ædvərˌtaɪzɪŋ] *n* **:** publicidad *f,* propaganda *f*

advice [æd'vaɪs] *n* **:** consejo *m,* recomendación *f* <take my advice **:** sigue mis consejos>

advisability [ædˌvaɪzə'bɪlət̬i, əd-] *n* **:** conveniencia *f*

advisable [æd'vaɪzəbəl, əd-] *adj* **:** aconsejable, recomendable, conveniente

advise [æd'vaɪz, əd-] *v* **-vised; -vising** *vt* **1** COUNSEL **:** aconsejar, asesorar **2** RECOMMEND **:** recomendar **3** INFORM **:** informar, notificar — *vi* **:** dar consejo

adviser *or* **advisor** [æd'vaɪzər, əd-] *n* **:** consejero *m,* -ra *f;* asesor *m,* -sora *f*

advisory [æd'vaɪzəri, əd-] *adj* **1 :** consultivo **2 in an advisory capacity :** como asesor

advocacy ['ædvəkəsi] *n* **:** promoción *f,* apoyo *m*

advocate¹ ['ædvəˌkeɪt] *vt* **-cated; -cating :** recomendar, abogar por, ser partidario de

advocate² ['ædvəkət] *n* **:** defensor *m,* -sora *f;* partidario *m,* -ria *f*

adze ['ædz] *n* **:** azuela *f*

aeon ['i:ən, 'i:ˌɑn] *n* **:** eón *m,* siglo *m,* eternidad *f*

aerate ['ærˌeɪt] *vt* **-ated; -ating :** gasear (un líquido), oxigenar (la sangre)

aerial¹ ['æriəl] *adj* **:** aéreo

aerial² *n* **:** antena *f*

aerie ['æri, 'ɪri, 'eɪəri] *n* **:** aguilera *f*

aerobic [ˌær'o:bɪk] *adj* **:** aerobio, aeróbico <aerobic exercises **:** ejercicios aeróbicos>

aerobics [ˌær'o:bɪks] *ns & pl* **:** aeróbic *m*

aerodynamic [ˌæro:daɪ'næmɪk] *adj* **:** aerodinámico — **aerodynamically** [-mikli] *adv*

aerodynamics [ˌæro:daɪ'næmɪks] *n* **:** aerodinámica *f*

aeronautical [ˌærə'nɔt̬ɪkəl] *adj* **:** aeronáutico

aeronautics [ˌærə'nɔt̬ɪks] *n* **:** aeronáutica *f*

aerosol ['ærəˌsɔl] *n* **:** aerosol *m*

aerospace¹ ['æroˌspeɪs] *adj* **:** aeroespacial

aerospace² *n* **:** espacio *m*

aesthetic [ɛs'θɛt̬ɪk] *adj* **:** estético — **aesthetically** [-t̬ɪkli] *adv*

aesthetics [ɛs'θɛt̬ɪks] *n* **:** estética *f*

afar [ə'fɑr] *adv* **:** lejos, a lo lejos

affability [ˌæfə'bɪlət̬i] *n* **:** afabilidad *f*

affable ['æfəbəl] *adj* **:** afable — **affably** *adv*

affair [ə'fær] *n* **1** MATTER **:** asunto *m,* cuestión *f,* caso *m* **2** EVENT **:** ocasión *f,* acontecimiento *m* **3** LIAISON **:** amorío *m,* aventura *f* **4 business affairs :** negocios *mpl* **5 current affairs :** actualidades *fpl*

affect [ə'fɛkt, æ-] *vt* **1** INFLUENCE, TOUCH **:** afectar, tocar **2** FEIGN **:** fingir

affectation [ˌæˌfɛk'teɪʃən] *n* **:** afectación *f*

affected [ə'fɛktəd, æ-] *adj* **1** FEIGNED **:** afectado, fingido **2** MOVED **:** conmovido

affecting [ə'fɛktɪŋ, æ-] *adj* **:** conmovedor

affection [ə'fɛkʃən] *n* **:** afecto *m,* cariño *m*

affectionate [ə'fɛkʃənət] *adj* **:** afectuoso, cariñoso — **affectionately** *adv*

affidavit [ˌæfə'deɪvət, 'æfəˌ-] *n* **:** declaración *f* jurada, affidávit *m*

affiliate¹ [ə'fɪliˌeɪt] *v* **-ated; -ating** *vt* **:** afiliar, asociar <to be affiliated with **:** estar afiliado a>

affiliate² [ə'fɪliət] *n* **:** afiliado *m,* -da *f* (persona), filial *f* (organización)

affiliation [əˌfɪli'eɪʃən] *n* **:** afiliación *f,* filiación *f*

affinity [ə'fɪnət̬i] *n, pl* **-ties :** afinidad *f*

affirm [ə'fərm] *vt* **:** afirmar, aseverar, declarar

affirmation [ˌæfər'meɪʃən] *n* **:** afirmación *f,* aserto *m,* declaración *f*

affirmative[1] [ə'fərmət̬ɪv] *adj* **:** afirmativo <affirmative action : acción afirmativa>

affirmative[2] *n* **1 :** afirmativa *f* **2 to answer in the affirmative :** responder afirmativamente, dar una respuesta afirmativa

affix [ə'fɪks] *vt* **:** fijar, poner, pegar

afflict [ə'flɪkt] *vt* **1 :** afligir, aquejar **2 to be afflicted with :** padecer de, sufrir de

affliction [ə'flɪkʃən] *n* **1** TRIBULATION **:** aflicción *f,* tribulación *f* **2** AILMENT **:** enfermedad *f,* padecimiento *m*

affluence ['æˌflu:ən*t*s; æ'flu:-, ə-] *n* **:** afluencia *f,* abundancia *f,* prosperidad *f*

affluent ['æˌflu:ənt; æ'flu:-, ə-] *adj* **:** próspero, adinerado

afford [ə'ford] *vt* **1 :** tener los recursos para, permitirse el lujo de <I can afford it : puedo permitírmelo, tengo con que comprarlo> **2** PROVIDE **:** ofrecer, proporcionar, dar

affront[1] [ə'frʌnt] *vt* **:** afrentar, insultar, ofender

affront[2] *n* **:** afrenta *f,* insulto *m,* ofensa *f*

Afghan ['æfˌgæn, -gən] *n* **:** afgano *m,* -na *f* **— Afghan** *adj*

afire [ə'faɪr] *adj* **:** ardiendo, en llamas

aflame [ə'fleɪm] *adj* **:** llameante, en llamas

afloat [ə'flo:t] *adv & adj* **:** a flote

afoot [ə'fʊt] *adj* **1** WALKING **:** a pie, andando **2** UNDER WAY **:** en marcha <something suspicious is afoot : algo sospechoso se está tramando>

aforesaid [ə'forˌsɛd] *adj* **:** antes mencionado, antedicho

afraid [ə'freɪd] *adj* **1 to be afraid :** tener miedo **2 to be afraid that :** temerse que <I'm afraid not : me temo que no>

afresh [ə'frɛʃ] *adv* **1 :** de nuevo, otra vez **2 to start afresh :** volver a empezar

African ['æfrɪkən] *n* **:** africano *m,* -na *f* **— African** *adj*

Afro–American[1] [ˌæfroə'mɛrɪkən] *adj* **:** afroamericano *m,* -na *f*

Afro–American[2] *n* **:** afroamericano

aft ['æft] *adv* **:** a popa

after[1] ['æftər] *adv* **1** AFTERWARD **:** después **2** BEHIND **:** detrás, atrás

after[2] *adj* **:** posterior, siguiente <in after years : en los años posteriores>

after[3] *conj* **:** después de, después de que <after we ate : después de que comimos, después de comer>

after[4] *prep* **1** FOLLOWING **:** después de, tras <after Saturday : después del sábado> <day after day : día tras día> **2** BEHIND **:** tras de, después de <I ran after the dog : corrí tras del perro> **3** CONCERNING **:** por <they asked after you : preguntaron por ti> **4 after all :** después de todo

aftereffect ['æftərɪˌfɛkt] *n* **:** efecto *m* secundario

afterlife ['æftərˌlaɪf] *n* **:** vida *f* venidera, vida *f* después de la muerte

aftermath ['æftərˌmæθ] *n* **:** consecuencias *fpl,* resultados *mpl*

afternoon [ˌæftər'nu:n] *n* **:** tarde *f*

afterthought ['æftərˌθɔt] *n* **:** ocurrencia *f* tardía, idea *f* tardía

afterward ['æftərwərd] *or* **afterwards** [-wərdz] *adv* **:** después, luego <soon afterward : poco después>

again [ə'gɛn, -'gɪn] *adv* **1** ANEW, OVER **:** de nuevo, otra vez **2** BESIDES **:** además **3 then again :** por otra parte <I may stay, then again I may not : puede ser que me quede, por otra parte, puede que no>

against [ə'gɛn*t*st, -'gɪn*t*st] *prep* **1** TOUCHING **:** contra <against the wall : contra la pared> **2** OPPOSING **:** contra, en contra de <I will vote against the proposal : votaré en contra de la propuesta> <against the grain : a contrapelo>

agape [ə'geɪp] *adj* **:** boquiabierto

agate ['ægət] *n* **:** ágata *f*

age[1] ['eɪdʒ] *vi* **aged; aging :** envejecer, madurar

age[2] *n* **1 :** edad *f* <ten years of age : diez años de edad> <to be of age : ser mayor de edad> **2** PERIOD **:** era *f,* siglo *m,* época *f* **3 old age :** vejez *f* **4 ages** *npl* **:** siglos *mpl,* eternidad *f*

aged *adj* **1** ['eɪdʒəd, 'eɪdʒd] OLD **:** anciano, viejo, vetusto **2** ['eɪdʒd] (*indicating a specified age*) <a girl aged 10 : una niña de 10 años de edad>

ageless ['eɪdʒləs] *adj* **1** YOUTHFUL **:** eternamente joven **2** TIMELESS **:** eterno, perenne

agency ['eɪdʒən*t*si] *n, pl* **-cies 1 :** agencia *f,* oficina *f* <travel agency : agencia de viajes> **2 through the agency of :** a través de, por medio de

agenda [ə'dʒɛndə] *n* **:** agenda *f,* orden *m* del día

agent ['eɪdʒənt] *n* **1** MEANS **:** agente *m,* medio *m,* instrumento *m* **2** REPRESENTATIVE **:** agente *mf,* representante *mf*

aggravate ['ægrəˌveɪt] *vt* **-vated; -vating 1** WORSEN **:** agravar, empeorar **2** ANNOY **:** irritar, exasperar

aggravation [ˌægrə'veɪʃən] *n* **1** WORSENING **:** empeoramiento *m* **2** ANNOYANCE **:** molestia *f,* irritación *f,* exasperación *f*

aggregate[1] ['ægrɪˌgeɪt] *vt* **-gated; -gating :** juntar, sumar

aggregate[2] ['ægrɪgət] *adj* **:** total, global, conjunto

aggregate[3] ['ægrɪgət] *n* **1** CONGLOMERATE **:** agregado *m,* conglomerado *m* **2** WHOLE **:** total *m,* conjunto *m*

aggression [ə'grɛʃən] *n* **1** ATTACK : agresión *f* **2** AGGRESSIVENESS : agresividad *f*

aggressive [ə'grɛsɪv] *adj* : agresivo — **aggressively** *adv*

aggressiveness [ə'grɛsɪvnəs] *n* : agresividad *f*

aggressor [ə'grɛsər] *n* : agresor *m*, -sora *f*

aggrieved [ə'gri:vd] *adj* : ofendido, herido

aghast [ə'gæst] *adj* : espantado, aterrado, horrorizado

agile ['ædʒəl] *adj* : ágil

agility [ə'dʒɪləṱi] *n, pl* **-ties** : agilidad *f*

agitate ['ædʒə,teɪt] *v* **-tated; -tating** *vt* **1** SHAKE : agitar **2** UPSET : inquietar, perturbar — *vi* **to agitate against** : hacer campaña en contra de

agitation [,ædʒə'teɪʃən] *n* : agitación *f*, inquietud *f*

agitator ['ædʒə,teɪṱər] *n* : agitador *m*, -dora *f*

agnostic [æg'nɑstɪk] *n* : agnóstico *m*, -ca *f*

ago [ə'go:] *adv* : hace <two years ago : hace dos años> <long ago : hace tiempo, hace mucho tiempo>

agog [ə'gɑg] *adj* : ansioso, curioso

agonize ['ægə,naɪz] *vi* **-nized; -nizing** : tormentarse, angustiarse

agonizing ['ægə,naɪzɪŋ] *adj* : angustioso, terrible — **agonizingly** [-zɪŋli] *adv*

agony ['ægəni] *n, pl* **-nies 1** PAIN : dolor *m* **2** ANGUISH : angustia *f*

agrarian [ə'grɛriən] *adj* : agrario

agree [ə'gri:] *v* **agreed; agreeing** *vt* ACKNOWLEDGE : estar de acuerdo <he agreed that I was right : estuvo de acuerdo en que tenía razón> — *vi* **1** CONCUR : estar de acuerdo **2** CONSENT : ponerse de acuerdo **3** TALLY : concordar **4 to agree with** : sentarle bien (a alguien) <this climate agrees with me : este clima me sienta bien>

agreeable [ə'gri:əbəl] *adj* **1** PLEASING : agradable, simpático **2** WILLING : dispuesto **3** AGREEING : de acuerdo, conforme

agreeably [ə'gri:əbli] *adv* : agradablemente

agreement [ə'gri:mənt] *n* **1** : acuerdo *m*, conformidad *f* <in agreement with : de acuerdo con> **2** CONTRACT, PACT : acuerdo *m*, pacto *m*, convenio *m* **3** CONCORD, HARMONY : concordia *f*

agriculture ['ægrɪ,kʌltʃər] *n* : agricultura *f* — **agricultural** [,ægrɪ'kʌltʃərəl] *adj*

aground [ə'graʊnd] *adj* : encallado, varado

ahead [ə'hɛd] *adv* **1** : al frente, delante, adelante <he walked ahead : caminó delante> **2** BEFOREHAND : por adelantado, con antelación **3** LEADING : a la delantera **4 to get ahead** : adelantar, progresar

ahead of *prep* **1** : al frente de, delante de, antes de **2 to get ahead of** : adelantarse a

ahoy [ə'hɔɪ] *interj* **ship ahoy!** : ¡barco a la vista!

aid[1] ['eɪd] *vt* : ayudar, auxiliar

aid[2] *n* **1** HELP : ayuda *f*, asistencia *f* **2** ASSISTANT : asistente *mf*

aide ['eɪd] *n* : ayudante *mf*

AIDS ['eɪdz] *n* : SIDA *m*, sida *m*

ail ['eɪl] *vt* : molestar, afligir — *vi* : sufrir, estar enfermo

aileron ['eɪlə,rɑn] *n* : alerón *m*

ailment ['eɪlmənt] *n* : enfermedad *f*, dolencia *f*, achaque *m*

aim[1] ['eɪm] *vt* **1** : apuntar (un arma), dirigir (una observación) **2** INTEND : proponerse, querer <he aims to do it tonight : se propone hacerlo esta noche> — *vi* **1** POINT : apuntar **2 to aim at** : aspirar a

aim[2] *n* **1** MARKSMANSHIP : puntería *f* **2** GOAL : propósito *m*, objetivo *m*, fin *m*

aimless ['eɪmləs] *adj* : sin rumbo, sin objeto

aimlessly ['eɪmləsli] *adv* : sin rumbo, sin objeto

air[1] ['ær] *vt* **1** : airear, ventilar <to air out a mattress : airear un colchón> **2** EXPRESS : airear, manifestar, comunicar **3** BROADCAST : transmitir, emitir

air[2] *n* **1** : aire *m* **2** MELODY : aire *m* **3** APPEARANCE : aire *m*, aspecto *m* **4 airs** *npl* : aires *mpl*, afectación *f* **5 by ~** : por avión (dícese de una carta), en avión (dícese de una persona) **6 to be on the air** : estar en el aire, estar emitiendo

airborne ['ær,born] *adj* **1** : aerotransportado <airborne troops : tropas aerotransportadas> **2** FLYING : volando, en el aire

air–condition [,ærkən'dɪʃən] *vt* : climatizar, condicionar con el aire

air conditioner [,ærkən'dɪʃənər] *n* : acondicionador *m* de aire

air–conditioning [,ærkən'dɪʃənɪŋ] *n* : aire *m* acondicionado

aircraft ['ær,kræft] *ns & pl* **1** : avión *m*, aeronave *f* **2 aircraft carrier** : portaaviones *m*

airfield ['ær,fi:ld] *n* : aeródromo *m*, campo *m* de aviación

air force *n* : fuerza *f* aérea

airlift ['ær,lɪft] *n* : puente *m* aéreo, transporte *m* aéreo

airline ['ær,laɪn] *n* : aerolínea *f*, línea *f* aérea

airliner ['ær,laɪnər] *n* : avión *m* de pasajeros

airmail[1] ['ær,meɪl] *vt* : enviar por vía aérea

airmail[2] *n* : correo *m* aéreo

airman ['ærmən] *n, pl* **-men** [-mən, -,mɛn] **1** AVIATOR : aviador *m*, -dora *f* **2** : soldado *m* de la fuerza aérea

airplane ['ær,pleɪn] *n* : avión *m*

airport ['ær,port] *n* : aeropuerto *m*

airship [ˈærˌʃɪp] *n* : dirigible *m*, zepelín *m*
airstrip [ˈærˌstrɪp] *n* : pista *f* de aterrizaje
airtight [ˈærˈtaɪt] *adj* : hermético, herméticamente cerrado
airwaves [ˈærˌweɪvz] *npl* : radio *m*, televisión *f*
airy [ˈæri] *adj* **airier** [-iər]; **-est 1** DELICATE, LIGHT : delicado, ligero **2** BREEZY : aireado, bien ventilado
aisle [ˈaɪl] *n* : pasillo *m*, nave *f* lateral (de una iglesia)
ajar [əˈdʒɑr] *adj* : entreabierto, entornado
akimbo [əˈkɪmbo] *adj & adv* : en jarras
akin [əˈkɪn] *adj* **1** RELATED : emparentado **2** SIMILAR : semejante, parecido
alabaster [ˈæləˌbæstər] *n* : alabastro *m*
alacrity [əˈlækrət̬i] *n* : presteza *f*, prontitud *f*
alarm[1] [əˈlɑrm] *vt* **1** WARN : alarmar, alertar **2** FRIGHTEN : asustar
alarm[2] *n* **1** WARNING : alarma *f*, alerta *f* **2** APPREHENSION, FEAR : aprensión *f*, inquietud *f*, temor *m* **3 alarm clock** : despertador *m*
alas [əˈlæs] *interj* : ¡ay!
Albanian [ælˈbeɪniən] *n* : albanés *m*, -nesa *f* — **Albanian** *adj*
albatross [ˈælbəˌtrɔs] *n, pl* **-tross** *or* **-trosses** : albatros *m*
albeit [ɔlˈbiːət, æl-] *conj* : aunque
albino [ælˈbaɪno] *n, pl* **-nos** : albino *m*, -na *f*
album [ˈælbəm] *n* : álbum *m*
albumen [ælˈbjuːmən] *n* **1** : clara *f* de huevo **2** → **albumin**
albumin [ælˈbjuːmən] *n* : albúmina *f*
alcohol [ˈælkəˌhɔl] *n* **1** ETHANOL : alcohol *m*, etanol *m* **2** LIQUOR : alcohol *m*, bebidas *fpl* alcohólicas
alcoholic[1] [ˌælkəˈhɔlɪk] *adj* : alcohólico
alcoholic[2] *n* : alcohólico *m*, -ca *f*
alcoholism [ˈælkəhɔˌlɪzəm] *n* : alcoholismo *m*
alcove [ˈælˌkoːv] *n* : nicho *m*, hueco *m*
alderman [ˈɔldərmən] *n, pl* **-men** [-mən, -ˌmɛn] : concejal *mf*
ale [ˈeɪl] *n* : cerveza *f*
alert[1] [əˈlərt] *vt* : alertar, poner sobre aviso
alert[2] *adj* **1** WATCHFUL : alerta, vigilante **2** QUICK : listo, vivo
alert[3] *n* : alerta *f*, alarma *f*
alertly [əˈlərtli] *adv* : con listeza
alertness [əˈlərtnəs] *n* **1** WATCHFULNESS : vigilancia *f* **2** ASTUTENESS : listeza *f*, viveza *f*
alfalfa [ælˈfælfə] *n* : alfalfa *f*
alga [ˈælgə] *n, pl* **-gae** [ˈælˌdʒiː] : alga *f*
algebra [ˈældʒəbrə] *n* : álgebra *m*
algebraic [ˌældʒəˈbreɪɪk] *adj* : algebraico — **algebraically** [-ɪkli] *adv*
Algerian [ælˈdʒɪriən] *n* : argelino *m*, -na *f* — **Algerian** *adj*
alias[1] [ˈeɪliəs] *adv* : alias
alias[2] *n* : alias *m*
alibi[1] [ˈæləˌbaɪ] *vi* : ofrecer una coartada
alibi[2] *n* **1** : coartada *f* **2** EXCUSE : pretexto *m*, excusa *f*
alien[1] [ˈeɪliən] *adj* **1** STRANGE : ajeno, extraño **2** FOREIGN : extranjero, foráneo **3** EXTRATERRESTRIAL : extraterrestre
alien[2] *n* **1** FOREIGNER : extranjero *m*, -ra *f*; forastero *m*, -ra *f* **2** EXTRATERRESTRIAL : extraterrestre *mf*
alienate [ˈeɪliəˌneɪt] *vt* **-ated; -ating 1** ESTRANGE : alienar, enajenar **2 to alienate oneself** : alejarse, distanciarse
alienation [ˌeɪliəˈneɪʃən] *n* : alienación *f*, enajenación *f*
alight [əˈlaɪt] *vi* **1** DISMOUNT : bajarse, apearse **2** LAND : posarse, aterrizar
align [əˈlaɪn] *vt* : alinear
alignment [əˈlaɪnmənt] *n* : alineación *f*, alineamiento *m*
alike[1] [əˈlaɪk] *adv* : igual, del mismo modo
alike[2] *adj* : igual, semejante, parecido
alimentary [ˌæləˈmɛntəri] *adj* **1** : alimenticio **2 alimentary canal** : tubo *m* digestivo
alimony [ˈæləˌmoːni] *n, pl* **-nies** : pensión *f* alimenticia
alive [əˈlaɪv] *adj* **1** LIVING : vivo, viviente **2** LIVELY : animado, activo **3** ACTIVE : vigente, en uso **4** AWARE : consciente <alive to the danger : consciente del peligro>
alkali [ˈælkəˌlaɪ] *n, pl* **-lies** [-ˌlaɪz] *or* **-lis** [-ˌlaɪz] : álcali *m*
alkaline [ˈælkələn, -ˌlaɪn] *adj* : alcalino
all[1] [ˈɔl] *adv* **1** COMPLETELY : todo, completamente **2** : igual <the score is 14 all : es 14 iguales, están empatados a 14> **3 all the better** : tanto mejor **4 all the more** : aún más, todavía más
all[2] *adj* : todo <all the children : todos los niños> <in all likelihood : con toda probabilidad, con la mayor probabilidad>
all[3] *pron* **1** : todo, -da <they ate it all : lo comieron todo> <that's all : eso es todo> <enough for all : suficiente para todos> **2 all in all** : en general **3 not at all** (*in negative constructions*) : en absoluto, para nada
Allah [ˈɑlɑ, ɑˈlɑ] *n* : Alá *m*
all–around [ˌɔləˈraʊnd] *adj* : completo, amplio
allay [əˈleɪ] *vt* **1** ALLEVIATE : aliviar, mitigar **2** CALM : aquietar, calmar
allegation [ˌælɪˈgeɪʃən] *n* : alegato *m*, acusación *f*
allege [əˈlɛdʒ] *vt* **-leged; -leging 1** : alegar, afirmar **2 to be alleged** : decirse, pretenderse <she is alleged

to be wealthy : se dice que es adinerada>

alleged [ə'lɛdʒd, ə'lɛdʒəd] *adj* : presunto, supuesto

allegedly [ə'lɛdʒədli] : *adv* : supuestamente, según se alega

allegiance [ə'liːdʒənts] *n* : lealtad *f,* fidelidad *f*

allegorical [ˌælə'gɔrɪkəl] *adj* : alegórico

allegory ['æləˌgori] *n, pl* **-ries** : alegoría *f*

alleluia [ˌɑlə'luːjə, ˌæ-] → **hallelujah**

allergic [ə'lərdʒɪk] *adj* : alérgico

allergy ['ælərdʒi] *n, pl* **-gies** : alergia *f*

alleviate [ə'liːviˌeɪt] *vt* **-ated; -ating** : aliviar, mitigar, paliar

alleviation [əˌliːvi'eɪʃən] *n* : alivio *m*

alley ['æli] *n, pl* **-leys 1** : callejón *m* **2 bowling alley** : bolera *f*

alliance [ə'laɪənts] *n* : alianza *f,* coalición *f*

alligator ['æləˌgeɪtər] *n* : caimán *m*

alliteration [əˌlɪtə'reɪʃən] *n* : aliteración *f*

allocate ['æləˌkeɪt] *vt* **-cated; -cating** : asignar, adjudicar

allocation [ˌælə'keɪʃən] *n* : asignación *f,* reparto *m,* distribución *f*

allot [ə'lɑt] *vt* **-lotted; -lotting** : repartir, distribuir, asignar

allotment [ə'lɑtmənt] *n* : reparto *m,* asignación *f,* distribución *f*

allow [ə'laʊ] *vt* **1** PERMIT : permitir, dejar **2** ALLOT : conceder, dar **3** ADMIT, CONCEDE : admitir, conceder — *vi* **to allow for** : tener en cuenta

allowable [ə'laʊəbəl] *adj* **1** PERMISSIBLE : permisible, lícito **2** : deducible <allowable expenditure : gasto deducible>

allowance [ə'laʊənts] *n* **1** : complemento *m* (para gastos, etc.), mesada *f* (para niños) **2 to make allowance(s)** : tener en cuenta, disculpar

alloy ['æˌlɔɪ] *n* : aleación *f*

all right[1] *adv* **1** YES : sí, por supuesto **2** WELL : bien <I did all right : me fue bien> **3** DEFINITELY : bien, ciertamente, sin duda <he's sick all right : está bien enfermo>

all right[2] *adj* **1** OK : bien <are you all right? : ¿estás bien?> **2** SATISFACTORY : bien, bueno <your work is all right : tu trabajo es bueno>

all–round [ˌɔl'raʊnd] → **all–around**

allspice ['ɔlspaɪs] *n* : pimienta *f* de Jamaica

allude [ə'luːd] *vi* **-luded; -luding** : aludir, referirse

allure[1] [ə'lʊr] *vt* **-lured; -luring** : cautivar, atraer

allure[2] *n* : atractivo *m,* encanto *m*

allusion [ə'luːʒən] *n* : alusión *f*

ally[1] [ə'laɪ, 'æˌlaɪ] *vi* **-lied; -lying** : aliarse

ally[2] ['æˌlaɪ, ə'laɪ] *n* : aliado *m,* -da *f*

almanac ['ɔlməˌnæk, 'æl-] *n* : almanaque *m*

almighty [ɔl'maɪti] *adj* : omnipotente, todopoderoso

almond ['ɑmənd, 'ɑl-, 'æ-, 'æl-] *n* : almendra *f*

almost ['ɔlˌmoːst, ɔl'moːst] *adv* : casi, prácticamente

alms ['ɑmz, 'ɑlmz, 'ælmz] *ns & pl* : limosna *f,* caridad *f*

aloft [ə'lɔft] *adv* : en alto, en el aire

alone[1] [ə'loːn] *adv* : sólo, solamente, únicamente

alone[2] *adj* : solo <they're alone in the house : están solos en la casa>

along[1] [ə'lɔŋ] *adv* **1** FORWARD : adelante <farther along : más adelante> <move along! : ¡circulen, por favor!> **2 to bring along** : traer **3 ~ with** : con, junto con **4 all along** : desde el principio

along[2] *prep* **1** : por, a lo largo de <along the coast : a lo largo de la costa> **2** : en, en el curso de, por <along the way : en el curso del viaje>

alongside[1] [əˌlɔŋ'saɪd] *adv* : al costado, al lado

alongside[2] *or* **alongside of** *prep* : junto a, al lado de

aloof [ə'luːf] *adj* : distante, reservado

aloofness [ə'luːfnəs] *n* : reserva *f,* actitud *f* distante

aloud [ə'laʊd] *adv* : en voz alta

alpaca [æl'pækə] *n* : alpaca *f*

alphabet ['ælfəˌbɛt] *n* : alfabeto *m*

alphabetical [ˌælfə'bɛtɪkəl] *or* **alphabetic** [-'bɛtɪk] *adj* : alfabético — **alphabetically** [-tɪkli] *adv*

alphabetize ['ælfəbəˌtaɪz] *vt* **-ized; -izing** : alfabetizar, poner en orden alfabético

already [ɔl'rɛdi] *adv* : ya

also ['ɔlˌsoː] *adv* : también, además

altar ['ɔltər] *n* : altar *m*

alter ['ɔltər] *vt* : alterar, cambiar, modificar

alteration [ˌɔltə'reɪʃən] *n* : alteración *f,* cambio *m,* modificación *f*

altercation [ˌɔltər'keɪʃən] *n* : altercado *m,* disputa *f*

alternate[1] ['ɔltərˌneɪt] *v* **-nated; -nating** : alternar

alternate[2] ['ɔltərnət] *adj* **1** : alterno <alternate cycles of inflation and depression : ciclos alternos de inflación y depresión> **2** : uno sí y uno no <he cooks on alternate days : cocina un día sí y otro no>

alternate[3] ['ɔltərnət] *n* : suplente *mf;* sustituto *m,* -ta *f*

alternately ['ɔltərnətli] *adv* : alternativamente, por turno

alternating current ['ɔltərˌneɪtɪŋ] *n* : corriente *f* alterna

alternation [ˌɔltər'neɪʃən] *n* : alternancia *f,* rotación *f*

alternative[1] [ɔl'tərnətɪv] *adj* : alternativo

alternative[2] *n* : alternativa *f*
alternator [ˈɔltərˌneɪt̬ər] *n* : alternador *m*
although [ɔlˈðoː] *conj* : aunque, a pesar de que
altitude [ˈæltəˌtuːd, -ˌtjuːd] *n* : altitud *f,* altura *f*
alto [ˈælˌtoː] *n, pl* **-tos** : alto *mf,* contralto *mf*
altogether [ˌɔltəˈgɛðər] *adv* **1** COMPLETELY : completamente, totalmente, del todo **2** ON THE WHOLE : en suma, en general
altruism [ˈæltrʊˌɪzəm] *n* : altruismo *m*
altruistic [ˌæltrʊˈɪstɪk] *adj* : altruista — **altruistically** [-tɪkli] *adv*
alum [ˈæləm] *n* : alumbre *m*
aluminum [əˈluːmənəm] *n* : aluminio *m*
alumna [əˈlʌmnə] *n, pl* **-nae** [-ˌniː] : ex-alumna *f*
alumnus [əˈlʌmnəs] *n, pl* **-ni** [-ˌnaɪ] : ex-alumno *m*
always [ˈɔlwiz, -ˌweɪz] *adv* **1** INVARIABLY : siempre, invariablemente **2** FOREVER : para siempre
am → **be**
amalgam [əˈmælgəm] *n* : amalgama *f*
amalgamate [əˈmælgəˌmeɪt] *vt* **-ated; -ating** : amalgamar, unir, fusionar
amalgamation [əˌmælgəˈmeɪʃən] *n* : fusión *f,* unión *f*
amaryllis [ˌæməˈrɪləs] *n* : amarilis *f*
amass [əˈmæs] *vt* : amasar, acumular
amateur [ˈæmətʃər, -tər, -ˌtʊr, -ˌtjʊr] *n* **1** : amateur *mf* **2** BEGINNER : principiante *mf;* aficionado *m,* -da *f*
amateurish [ˈæməˌtʃərɪʃ, -ˌtər-, -ˌtʊr-, -ˌtjʊr-] *adj* : amateur, inexperto
amaze [əˈmeɪz] *vt* **amazed; amazing** : asombrar, maravillar, pasmar
amazement [əˈmeɪzmənt] *n* : asombro *m,* sorpresa *f*
amazing [əˈmeɪzɪŋ] *adj* : asombroso, sorprendente — **amazingly** [-zɪŋli] *adv*
ambassador [æmˈbæsədər] *n* : embajador *m,* -dora *f*
amber [ˈæmbər] *n* : ámbar *m*
ambergris [ˈæmbərˌgrɪs, -ˌgriːs] *n* : ámbar *m* gris
ambidextrous [ˌæmbɪˈdɛkstrəs] *adj* : ambidextro — **ambidextrously** *adv*
ambience *or* **ambiance** [ˈæmbiənts, ˈɑmbiˌɑnts] *n* : ambiente *m,* atmósfera *f*
ambiguity [ˌæmbəˈgjuːət̬i] *n, pl* **-ties** : ambigüedad *f*
ambiguous [æmˈbɪgjʊəs] *adj* : ambiguo
ambition [æmˈbɪʃən] *n* : ambición *f*
ambitious [æmˈbɪʃəs] *adj* : ambicioso — **ambitiously** *adv*
ambivalence [æmˈbɪvələnts] *n* : ambivalencia *f*
ambivalent [æmˈbɪvələnt] *adj* : ambivalente
amble[1] [ˈæmbəl] *vi* **-bled; -bling** : ir tranquilamente, pasearse despreocupadamente
amble[2] *n* : paseo *m* tranquilo
ambulance [ˈæmbjələnts] *n* : ambulancia *f*
ambush[1] [ˈæmˌbʊʃ] *vt* : emboscar
ambush[2] *n* : emboscada *f,* celada *f*
ameliorate [əˈmiːljəˌreɪt] *v* **-rated; -rating** IMPROVE : mejorar
amelioration [əˌmiːljəˈreɪʃən] *n* : mejora *f*
amen [ˈeɪˈmɛn, ˈɑ-] *interj* : amén
amenable [əˈmiːnəbəl, -ˈmɛ-] *adj* RESPONSIVE : susceptible, receptivo, sensible
amend [əˈmɛnd] *vt* **1** IMPROVE : mejorar, enmendar **2** CORRECT : enmendar, corregir
amendment [əˈmɛndmənt] *n* : enmienda *f*
amends [əˈmɛndz] *ns & pl* : compensación *f,* reparación *f,* desagravio *m*
amenity [əˈmɛnət̬i, -ˈmiː-] *n, pl* **-ties 1** PLEASANTNESS : lo agradable, amenidad *f* **2 amenities** *npl* : servicios *mpl*, comodidades *fpl*
American [əˈmɛrɪkən] *n* : americano *m,* -na *f* — **American** *adj*
American Indian *n* : indio *m* (americano), india *f* (americana)
amethyst [ˈæməθəst] *n* : amatista *f*
amiability [ˌeɪmiːəˈbɪlət̬i] *n* : amabilidad *f,* afabilidad *f*
amiable [ˈeɪmiːəbəl] *adj* : amable, afable — **amiably** [-bli] *adv*
amicable [ˈæmɪkəbəl] *adj* : amigable, amistoso, cordial — **amicably** [-bli] *adv*
amid [əˈmɪd] *or* **amidst** [əˈmɪdst] *prep* : en medio de, entre
amino acid [əˈmiːno] *n* : aminoácido *m*
amiss[1] [əˈmɪs] *adv* : mal, fuera de lugar <to take amiss : tomar a mal, llevar a mal>
amiss[2] *adj* **1** WRONG : malo, inoportuno **2 there's something amiss** : pasa algo, algo anda mal
ammeter [ˈæˌmiːt̬ər] *n* : amperímetro *m*
ammonia [əˈmoːnjə] *n* : amoníaco *m*
ammunition [ˌæmjəˈnɪʃən] *n* **1** : municiones *fpl* **2** ARGUMENTS : argumentos *mpl*
amnesia [æmˈniːʒə] *n* : amnesia *f*
amnesty [ˈæmnəsti] *n, pl* **-ties** : amnistía *f*
amoeba [əˈmiːbə] *n, pl* **-bas** *or* **-bae** [-ˌbiː] : ameba *f*
amoebic [əˈmiːbɪk] *adj* : amébico
amok [əˈmʌk, -ˈmɑk] *adv* **to run amok** : correr a ciegas, enloquecerse, desbocarse (dícese de la economía, etc.)
among [əˈmʌŋ] *prep* : entre
amorous [ˈæmərəs] *adj* **1** PASSIONATE : enamoradizo, apasionado **2** ENAM-

ORED : enamorado 3 LOVING : amoroso, cariñoso
amorously [ˈæmərəsli] *adv* : con cariño
amorphous [əˈmɔrfəs] *adj* : amorfo, informe
amortize [ˈæmərˌtaɪz, əˈmɔr-] *vt* **-tized; -tizing** : amortizar
amount[1] [əˈmaʊnt] *vi* **to amount to 1** : equivaler a, significar <that amounts to treason : eso equivale a la traición> **2** : ascender (a) <my debts amount to $2000 : mis deudas ascienden a $2000>
amount[2] *n* : cantidad *f,* suma *f*
ampere [ˈæmˌpɪr] *n* : amperio *m*
ampersand [ˈæmpərˌsænd] *n* : el signo &
amphibian [æmˈfɪbiən] *n* : anfibio *m*
amphibious [æmˈfɪbiəs] *adj* : anfibio
amphitheater [ˈæmfəˌθiːət̬ər] *n* : anfiteatro *m*
ample [ˈæmpəl] *adj* **-pler; -plest 1** LARGE, SPACIOUS : amplio, extenso, grande **2** ABUNDANT : abundante, generoso
amplifier [ˈæmpləˌfaɪər] *n* : amplificador *m*
amplify [ˈæmpləˌfaɪ] *vt* **-fied; -fying** : amplificar
amply [ˈæmpli] *adv* : ampliamente, abundantemente, suficientemente
amputate [ˈæmpjəˌteɪt] *vt* **-tated; -tating** : amputar
amputation [ˌæmpjəˈteɪʃən] *n* : amputación *f*
amuck [əˈmʌk] → **amok**
amulet [ˈæmjələt] *n* : amuleto *m,* talismán *m*
amuse [əˈmjuːz] *vt* **amused; amusing 1** ENTERTAIN : entretener, distraer **2** : hacer reír, divertir <the joke amused us : la broma nos hizo reír>
amusement [əˈmjuːzmənt] *n* **1** ENTERTAINMENT : diversión *f,* entretenimiento *m,* pasatiempo *m* **2** LAUGHTER : risa *f*
an → **a**[2]
anachronism [əˈnækrəˌnɪzəm] *n* : anacronismo *m*
anachronistic [əˌnækrəˈnɪstɪk] *adj* : anacrónico
anaconda [ˌænəˈkɑndə] *n* : anaconda *f*
anagram [ˈænəˌgræm] *n* : anagrama *m*
anal [ˈeɪnəl] *adj* : anal
analgesic [ˌænəlˈdʒiːzɪk, -sɪk] *n* : analgésico *m*
analogical [ˌænəˈlɑdʒɪkəl] *adj* : analógico — **analogically** [-kli] *adv*
analogous [əˈnæləgəs] *adj* : análogo
analogy [əˈnælədʒi] *n, pl* **-gies** : analogía *f*
analysis [əˈnæləsəs] *n, pl* **-yses** [-ˌsiːz] **1** : análisis *m* **2** PSYCHOANALYSIS : psicoanálisis *m*
analyst [ˈænəlɪst] *n* **1** : analista *mf* **2** PSYCHOANALYST : psicoanalista *mf*
analytic [ˌænəˈlɪt̬ɪk] *or* **analytical** [-tɪkəl] *adj* : analítico — **analytically** [-t̬ɪkli] *adv*
analyze [ˈænəˌlaɪz] *vt* **-lyzed; -lyzing** : analizar
anarchic [æˈnɑrkɪk] *adj* : anárquico — **anarchically** [-kɪkli] *adv*
anarchism [ˈænərˌkɪzəm, -nɑr-] *n* : anarquismo *m*
anarchist [ˈænərkɪst, -nɑr-] *n* : anarquista *mf*
anarchy [ˈænərki, -nɑr-] *n* : anarquía *f*
anathema [əˈnæθəmə] *n* : anatema *m*
anatomic [ˌænəˈtɑmɪk] *or* **anatomical** [-mɪkəl] *adj* : anatómico — **anatomically** [-mɪkli] *adv*
anatomy [əˈnæt̬əmi] *n, pl* **-mies** : anatomía *f*
ancestor [ˈænˌsɛstər] *n* : antepasado *m,* -da *f;* antecesor *m,* -sora *f*
ancestral [ænˈsɛstrəl] *adj* : ancestral, de los antepasados
ancestry [ˈænˌsɛstri] *n* **1** DESCENT : ascendencia *f,* linaje *m,* abolengo *m* **2** ANCESTORS : antepasados *mpl,* -das *fpl*
anchor[1] [ˈæŋkər] *vt* **1** MOOR : anclar, fondear **2** FASTEN : sujetar, asegurar, fijar
anchor[2] *n* **1** : ancla *f* **2** : presentador *m,* -dora *f* (en televisión)
anchorage [ˈæŋkərɪdʒ] *n* : anclaje *m*
anchovy [ˈænˌtʃoːvi, ænˈtʃoː-] *n, pl* **-vies** *or* **-vy** : anchoa *f*
ancient [ˈeɪntʃənt] *adj* **1** : antiguo <ancient history : historia antigua> **2** OLD : viejo
ancients [ˈeɪntʃənts] *npl* : los antiguos *mpl*
and [ˈænd] *conj* **1** : y (e *before words beginning with i- or hi-*) **2** : con <ham and eggs : huevos con jamón> **3** : a <go and see : ve a ver> **4** : de <try and finish it soon : trata de terminarlo pronto>
andiron [ˈænˌdaɪərn] *n* : morillo *m*
Andorran [ænˈdɔrən] *n* : andorrano *m,* -na *f* — **Andorran** *adj*
androgynous [ænˈdrɑdʒənəs] *adj* : andrógino
anecdotal [ˌænɪkˈdoːt̬əl] *adj* : anecdótico
anecdote [ˈænɪkˌdoːt] *n* : anécdota *f*
anemia [əˈniːmiə] *n* : anemia *f*
anemic [əˈniːmɪk] *adj* : anémico
anemone [əˈnɛməni] *n* : anémona *f*
anesthesia [ˌænəsˈθiːʒə] *n* : anestesia *f*
anesthetic[1] [ˌænəsˈθɛt̬ɪk] *adj* : anestésico
anesthetic[2] *n* : anestésico *m*
anesthetist [əˈnɛsθətɪst] *n* : anestesista *mf*
anesthetize [əˈnɛsθəˌtaɪz] *vt* **-tize; -tized** : anestesiar
anew [əˈnuː, -ˈnjuː] *adv* : de nuevo, otra vez, nuevamente
angel [ˈeɪndʒəl] *n* : ángel *m*

angelic [æn'dʒɛlɪk] *or* **angelical** [-lɪkəl] *adj* : angélico — **angelically** [-lɪkli] *adv*

anger[1] ['æŋgər] *vt* : enojar, enfadar

anger[2] *n* : enojo *m,* enfado *m,* ira *f,* cólera *f,* rabia *f*

angina [æn'dʒaɪnə] *n* : angina *f*

angle[1] ['æŋgəl] *v* **angled; angling** *vt* DIRECT, SLANT : orientar, dirigir — *vi* FISH : pescar (con caña)

angle[2] *n* **1** : ángulo *m* **2** POINT OF VIEW : perspectiva *f,* punto *m* de vista

angler ['æŋglər] *n* : pescador *m,* -dora *f*

Anglo–Saxon[1] [ˌæŋglo'sæksən] *adj* : anglosajón

Anglo–Saxon[2] *n* : anglosajón *m,* -jona *f*

Angolan [æŋ'goːlən, æn-] *n* : angoleño *m,* -ña *f* — **Angolan** *adj*

angora [æŋ'gorə, æn-] *n* : angora *f*

angrily ['æŋgrəli] *adv* : furiosamente, con ira

angry ['æŋgri] *adj* **-grier; -est** : enojado, enfadado, furioso

anguish ['æŋgwɪʃ] *n* : angustia *f,* congoja *f*

anguished ['æŋgwɪʃt] *adj* : angustiado, acongojado

angular ['æŋgjələr] *adj* : angular (dícese de las formas), anguloso (dícese de las caras)

animal ['ænəməl] *n* **1** : animal *m* **2** BRUTE : bruto *m,* -ta *f*

animate[1] ['ænəˌmeɪt] *vt* **-mated; -mating** : animar

animate[2] ['ænəmət] *adj* : animado

animated ['ænəˌmeɪtəd] *adj* **1** LIVELY : animado, vivo, vivaz **2 animated cartoon** : dibujos *mpl* animados

animation [ˌænə'meɪʃən] *n* : animación *f*

animosity [ˌænə'mɑsəti] *n, pl* **-ties** : animosidad *f,* animadversión *f*

anise ['ænəs] *n* : anís *m*

aniseed ['ænəsˌsiːd] *n* : anís *m,* semilla *f* de anís

ankle ['æŋkəl] *n* : tobillo *m*

anklebone ['æŋkəlˌboːn] *n* : taba *f*

annals ['ænəlz] *npl* : anales *mpl,* crónica *f*

anneal [ə'niːl] *vt* **1** TEMPER : templar **2** STRENGTHEN : fortalecer

annex[1] [ə'nɛks, 'æˌnɛks] *vt* : anexar

annex[2] ['æˌnɛks, -nɪks] *n* : anexo *m,* anejo *m*

annexation [ˌæˌnɛk'seɪʃən] *n* : anexión *f*

annihilate [ə'naɪəˌleɪt] *vt* **-lated; -lating** : aniquilar

annihilation [əˌnaɪə'leɪʃən] *n* : aniquilación *f,* aniquilamiento *m*

anniversary [ˌænə'vərsəri] *n, pl* **-ries** : aniversario *m*

annotate ['ænəˌteɪt] *vt* **-tated; -tating** : anotar

annotation [ˌænə'teɪʃən] *n* : anotación *f*

announce [ə'naʊnts] *vt* **-nounced; -nouncing** : anunciar

announcement [ə'naʊntsmənt] *n* : anuncio *m*

announcer [ə'naʊntsər] *n* : anunciador *m,* -dora *f;* comentarista *mf;* locutor *m,* -tora *f*

annoy [ə'nɔɪ] *vt* : molestar, fastidiar, irritar

annoyance [ə'nɔɪənts] *n* **1** IRRITATION : irritación *f,* fastidio *m* **2** NUISANCE : molestia *f,* fastidio *m*

annoying [ə'nɔɪɪŋ] *adj* : molesto, fastidioso, engorroso — **annoyingly** [-ɪŋli] *adv*

annual[1] ['ænjʊəl] *adj* : anual — **annually** *adv*

annual[2] *n* **1** : planta *f* anual **2** YEARBOOK : anuario *m*

annuity [ə'nuːəti] *n, pl* **-ties** : anualidad *f*

annul [ə'nʌl] *vt* **anulled; anulling** : anular, invalidar

annulment [ə'nʌlmənt] *n* : anulación *f*

anode ['æˌnoːd] *n* : ánodo

anoint [ə'nɔɪnt] *vt* : ungir

anomalous [ə'nɑmələs] *adj* : anómalo

anomaly [ə'nɑməli] *n, pl* **-lies** : anomalía *f*

anonymity [ˌænə'nɪməti] *n* : anonimato *m*

anonymous [ə'nɑnəməs] *adj* : anónimo — **anonymously** *adv*

another[1] [ə'nʌðər] *adj* : otro

another[2] *pron* : otro, otra

answer[1] ['æntsər] *vt* **1** : contestar (a), responder (a) <to answer the telephone : contestar el teléfono> **2** FULFILL : satisfacer **3 to answer for** : ser responsable de, pagar por <she'll answer for that mistake : pagará por ese error> — *vi* : contestar, responder

answer[2] *n* **1** REPLY : respuesta *f,* contestación *f* **2** SOLUTION : solución *f*

answerable ['æntsərəbəl] *adj* : responsable

ant ['ænt] *n* : hormiga *f*

antagonism [æn'tægəˌnɪzəm] *n* : antagonismo *m,* hostilidad *f*

antagonist [æn'tægənɪst] *n* : antagonista *mf*

antagonistic [ænˌtægə'nɪstɪk] *adj* : antagonista, hostil

antagonize [æn'tægəˌnaɪz] *vt* **-nized; -nizing** : antagonizar

antarctic [ænt'ɑrktɪk, -'ɑrtɪk] *adj* : antártico

antarctic circle *n* : círculo *m* antártico

antebellum [ˌæntɪ'bɛləm] *adj* : prebélico

antecedent[1] [ˌæntə'siːdənt] *adj* : antecedente, precedente

antecedent[2] *n* : antecedente *mf;* precursor *m,* -sora *f*

antelope ['æntəlˌoːp] *n, pl* **-lope** *or* **-lopes** : antílope *m*

antenna [æn'tɛnə] *n, pl* **-nae** [-ˌniː, -ˌnaɪ] *or* **-nas** : antena *f*

anterior [æn'tɪriər] *adj* : anterior

anthem ['ænθəm] *n* : himno *m* <national anthem : himno nacional>

anther [ˈænθər] *n* : antera *f*
anthill [ˈænt,hɪl] *n* : hormiguero *m*
anthology [ænˈθɑlədʒi] *n, pl* **-gies** : antología *f*
anthracite [ˈænθrə,saɪt] *n* : antracita *f*
anthropoid[1] [ˈænθrə,pɔɪd] *adj* : antropoide
anthropoid[2] *n* : antropoide *mf*
anthropological [,ænθrəpəˈlɑdʒɪkəl] *adj* : antropológico
anthropologist [,ænθrəˈpɑlədʒɪst] *n* : antropólogo *m*, -ga *f*
anthropology [,ænθrəˈpɑlədʒi] *n* : antropología *f*
antiabortion [,æntiəˈbɔrʃən, ,æntaɪ-] *adj* : antiaborto
antiaircraft [,æntiˈær,kræft, ,æntaɪ-] *adj* : antiaéreo
anti–American [,æntiəˈmɛrɪkən, ,æntaɪ-] *adj* : antiamericano
antibiotic[1] [,æntibaɪˈɑtɪk, ,æntaɪ-, -bi-] *adj* : antibiótico
antibiotic[2] *n* : antibiótico *m*
antibody [ˈænti,bɑdi] *n, pl* **-bodies** : anticuerpo *m*
antic[1] [ˈæntɪk] *adj* : extravagante, juguetón
antic[2] *n* : payasada *f*, travesura *f*
anticipate [ænˈtɪsə,peɪt] *vt* **-pated; -pating 1** FORESEE : anticipar, prever **2** EXPECT : esperar, contar con
anticipation [æn,tɪsəˈpeɪʃən] *n* **1** FORESIGHT : previsión *f* **2** EXPECTATION : anticipación *f*, expectación *f*, esperanza *f*
anticipatory [ænˈtɪsəpə,tori] *adj* : en anticipación, en previsión
anticlimactic [,æntiklaɪˈmæktɪk] *adj* : anticlimático, decepcionante
anticlimax [,æntiˈklaɪ,mæks] *n* : anticlímax *m*
anticommunism [,æntiˈkɑmjə,nɪzəm, ,æntaɪ-] *n* : anticomunismo *m*
anticommunist[1] [,æntiˈkɑmjənɪst, ,æntaɪ-] *adj* : anticomunista
anticommunist[2] *n* : anticomunista *mf*
antidemocratic [,ænti,dɛməˈkrætɪk, ,æntaɪ-] *adj* : antidemocrático
antidote [ˈæntɪ,doːt] *n* : antídoto *m*
antidrug [,æntiˈdrʌg, ,æntaɪ-; ˈænti,drʌg, ˈæntaɪ-] *adj* : antidrogas
antifascist [,æntiˈfæʃɪst, ,æntaɪ-] *adj* : antifascista
antifeminist [,æntiˈfɛmənɪst, ,æntaɪ-] *adj* : antifeminista
antifreeze [ˈænti,friːz] *n* : anticongelante *m*
anti–imperialism [,æntiɪmˈpɪriə,lɪzəm, ,æntaɪ-] *n* : antiimperialismo *m*
anti–imperialist [,æntiɪmˈpɪriəlɪst, ,æntaɪ-] *adj* : antiimperialista
anti–inflationary [,æntiɪnˈfleɪʃə,nɛri, ,æntaɪ-] *adj* : antiinflacionario
antimony [ˈæntə,moːni] *n* : antimonio *m*
antipathy [ænˈtɪpəθi] *n, pl* **-thies** : antipatía *f*, aversión *f*
antiperspirant [,æntiˈpərspərənt, ,æntaɪ-] *n* : antitranspirante *m*
antiquarian[1] [,æntəˈkwɛriən] *adj* : antiguo, anticuario <an antiquarian book : un libro antiguo>
antiquarian[2] *n* : anticuario *m*, -ria *f*
antiquary [ˈæntə,kwɛri] → **antiquarian**[2]
antiquated [ˈæntə,kweɪtəd] *adj* : anticuado, pasado de moda
antique[1] [ænˈtiːk] *adj* **1** OLD : antiguo, de época <an antique mirror : un espejo antiguo> **2** OLD-FASHIONED : anticuado, pasado de moda
antique[2] *n* : antigüedad *f*
antiquity [ænˈtɪkwəti] *n, pl* **-ties** : antigüedad
antirevolutionary [,ænti,rɛvəˈluːʃə,nɛri, ,æntaɪ-] *adj* : antirrevolucionario
anti–Semitic [,æntisəˈmɪtɪk, ,æntaɪ-] *adj* : antisemita
anti–Semitism [,æntiˈsɛmə,tɪzəm, ,æntaɪ-] *n* : antisemitismo *m*
antiseptic[1] [,æntəˈsɛptɪk] *adj* : antiséptico — **antiseptically** [-tɪkli] *adv*
antiseptic[2] *n* : antiséptico *m*
antismoking [,æntiˈsmoːkɪŋ, ,æntaɪ-] *adj* : antitabaco
antisocial [,æntiˈsoːʃəl, ,æntaɪ-] *adj* **1** : antisocial **2** UNSOCIABLE : poco sociable
antitheft [,æntiˈθɛft, ,æntaɪ-] *adj* : antirrobo
antithesis [ænˈtɪθəsɪs] *n, pl* **-eses** [-,siːz] : antítesis *f*
antitoxin [,æntiˈtɑksən, ,æntaɪ-] *n* : antitoxina *f*
antitrust [,æntiˈtrʌst, ,æntaɪ-] *adj* : antimonopolista
antler [ˈæntlər] *n* : asta *f*, cuerno *m*
antonym [ˈæntə,nɪm] *n* : antónimo *m*
anus [ˈeɪnəs] *n* : ano *m*
anvil [ˈænvəl, -vɪl] *n* : yunque *m*
anxiety [æŋkˈzaɪəti] *n, pl* **-eties 1** UNEASINESS : inquietud *f*, preocupación *f*, ansiedad *f* **2** APPREHENSION : ansiedad *f*, angustia *f*
anxious [ˈæŋkʃəs] *adj* **1** WORRIED : inquieto, preocupado, ansioso **2** WORRISOME : preocupante, inquietante **3** EAGER : ansioso, deseoso
anxiously [ˈæŋkʃəsli] *adv* : con inquietud, con ansiedad
any[1] [ˈɛni] *adv* **1** : algo <is it any better? : ¿está (algo) mejor?> **2** : para nada <it is not any good : no sirve para nada>
any[2] *adj* **1** : alguno <is there any doubt? : ¿hay alguna duda?> <call me if you have any questions : llámeme si tiene alguna pregunta> **2** : cualquier <I can answer any question : puedo responder a cualquier pregunta> **3** : todo <in any case : en todo caso> **4** : ningún <he would not accept it under any circumstances : no lo aceptaría bajo ninguna circunstancia>
any[3] *pron* **1** : alguno *m*, -na *f* <are there any left? : ¿queda alguno?> **2** : nin-

guno *m,* -na *f* <I don't want any : no quiero ninguno>

anybody [ˈɛniˌbʌdi, -ˌbɑ-] → **anyone**

anyhow [ˈɛniˌhaʊ] *adv* **1** HAPHAZARDLY : de cualquier manera **2** IN ANY CASE : de todos modos, en todo caso

anymore [ˌɛniˈmor] *adv* **1 :** ya, ya más <he doesn't dance anymore : ya no baila más> **2 :** todavía <do they sing anymore? : ¿cantan todavía?>

anyone [ˈɛniˌwʌn] *pron* **1 :** alguien <is anyone here? : ¿hay alguien aquí?> <if anyone wants to come : si alguno quiere venir> **2 :** cualquiera <anyone can play : cualquiera puede jugar> **3 :** nadie <I don't want anyone here : no quiero a nadie aquí>

anyplace [ˈɛniˌpleɪs] → **anywhere**

anything [ˈɛniˌθɪŋ] *pron* **1 :** algo, alguna cosa <do you want anything? : ¿quieres algo?, ¿quieres alguna cosa?> **2 :** nada <hardly anything : casi nada> **3 :** cualquier cosa <I eat anything : como de todo>

anytime [ˈɛniˌtaɪm] *adv* **:** en cualquier momento, a cualquier hora, cuando sea

anyway [ˈɛniˌweɪ] → **anyhow**

anywhere [ˈɛniˌ*h*wɛr] *adv* **1 :** en algún sitio, en alguna parte <do you see it anywhere? : ¿lo ves en alguna parte?> **2 :** en ningún sitio, por ninguna parte <I can't find it anywhere : no puedo encontrarlo por ninguna parte> **3 :** en cualquier parte, dondequiera, donde sea <put it anywhere : ponlo dondequiera>

aorta [eɪˈɔrt̬ə] *n, pl* **-tas** *or* **-tae** [-t̬i, -taɪ] **:** aorta *f*

apart [əˈpɑrt] *adv* **1** SEPARATELY **:** aparte, separadamente **2** ASIDE **:** aparte, a un lado **3 to fall apart :** deshacerse, hacerse pedazos **4 to take apart :** desmontar, desmantelar

apartheid [əˈpɑrˌteɪt, -ˌtaɪt] *n* **:** apartheid *m*

apartment [əˈpɑrtmənt] *n* **:** apartamento *m,* departamento *m,* piso *m Spain*

apathetic [ˌæpəˈθɛt̬ɪk] *adj* **:** apático, indiferente — **apathetically** [-tɪkli] *adv*

apathy [ˈæpəθi] *n* **:** apatía *f,* indiferencia *f*

ape[1] [ˈeɪp] *vt* **aped; aping :** imitar, remedar

ape[2] *n* **:** simio *m;* mono *m,* -na *f*

aperture [ˈæpərtʃər, -ˌtʃʊr] *n* **:** abertura *f,* rendija *f,* apertura *f* (en fotografía)

apex [ˈeɪˌpɛks] *n, pl* **apexes** *or* **apices** [ˈeɪpəˌsiːz, ˈæ-] **:** ápice *m,* cúspide *f,* cima *f*

aphid [ˈeɪfɪd, ˈæ-] *n* **:** áfido *m*

aphorism [ˈæfəˌrɪzəm] *n* **:** aforismo *m*

aphoristic [ˌæfəˈrɪstɪk] *adj* **:** aforístico

aphrodisiac [ˌæfrəˈdiːziˌæk, -ˈdɪ-] *n* **:** afrodisíaco *m*

apiary [ˈeɪpiˌɛri] *n, pl* **-aries :** apiario *m,* colmenar *m*

apiece [əˈpiːs] *adv* **:** cada uno

aplenty [əˈplɛnti] *adj* **:** en abundancia

aplomb [əˈplɑm, -ˈplʌm] *n* **:** aplomo *m*

apocalypse [əˈpɑkəˌlɪps] *n* **:** apocalipsis *m*

apocalyptic [əˌpɑkəˈlɪptɪk] *adj* **:** apocalíptico

apocrypha [əˈpɑkrəfə] *n* **:** textos *mpl* apócrifos

apocryphal [əˈpɑkrəfəl] *adj* **:** apócrifo

apologetic [əˌpɑləˈdʒɛt̬ɪk] *adj* **:** lleno de disculpas

apologetically [əˌpɑləˈdʒɛt̬ɪkli] *adv* **:** disculpándose, con aire de disculpas

apologize [əˈpɑləˌdʒaɪz] *vi* **-gized; -gizing :** disculparse, pedir perdón

apology [əˈpɑlədʒi] *n, pl* **-gies :** disculpa *f,* excusa *f*

apoplectic [ˌæpəˈplɛktɪk] *adj* **:** apopléctico

apoplexy [ˈæpəˌplɛksi] *n* **:** apoplejía *f*

apostasy [əˈpɑstəsi] *n, pl* **-sies :** apostasía *f*

apostate [əˈpɑsˌteɪt] *n* **:** apóstata *mf*

apostle [əˈpɑsəl] *n* **:** apóstol *m*

apostleship [əˈpɑsəlʃɪp] *n* **:** apostolado *m*

apostolic [ˌæpəˈstɑlɪk] *adj* **:** apostólico

apostrophe [əˈpɑstrəˌfiː] *n* **:** apóstrofo *m*

apothecary [əˈpɑθəˌkɛri] *n, pl* **-caries :** boticario *m,* -ria *f*

appall [əˈpɔl] *vt* **:** consternar, horrorizar

apparatus [ˌæpəˈræt̬əs, -ˈreɪ-] *n, pl* **-tuses** *or* **-tus :** aparato *m,* equipo *m*

apparel [əˈpærəl] *n* **:** atavío *m,* ropa *f*

apparent [əˈpærənt] *adj* **1** VISIBLE **:** visible **2** OBVIOUS **:** claro, evidente, manifiesto **3** SEEMING **:** aparente, ostensible

apparently [əˈpærəntli] *adv* **:** aparentemente, al parecer

apparition [ˌæpəˈrɪʃən] *n* **:** aparición *f,* visión *f*

appeal[1] [əˈpiːl] *vt* **1 :** apelar <to appeal a decision : apelar contra una decisión> — *vi* **1 to appeal for :** pedir, solicitar **2 to appeal to :** atraer a <that doesn't appeal to me : eso no me atrae>

appeal[2] *n* **1 :** apelación *f* (en derecho) **2** PLEA **:** ruego *m,* súplica *f* **3** ATTRACTION **:** atracción *f,* atractivo *m,* interés *m*

appear [əˈpɪr] *vi* **1 :** aparecer, aparecerse, presentarse <he suddenly appeared : apareció de repente> **2** COME OUT **:** aparecer, salir, publicarse **3 :** comparecer (ante el tribunal), actuar (en el teatro) **4** SEEM **:** parecer

appearance [əˈpɪrən*t*s] *n* **1** APPEARING **:** aparición *f,* presentación *f,* comparecencia *f* (ante un tribunal), publicación *f* (de un libro) **2** LOOK **:** apariencia *f,* aspecto *m*

appease [ə'piːz] *vt* **-peased; -peasing** **1** CALM, PACIFY : aplacar, apaciguar, sosegar **2** SATISFY : satisfacer, mitigar
appeasement [ə'piːzmənt] *n* : aplacamiento *m,* apaciguamiento *m*
append [ə'pɛnd] *vt* : agregar, añadir, adjuntar
appendage [ə'pɛndɪdʒ] *n* **1** ADDITION : apéndice *m,* añadidura *f* **2** LIMB : miembro *m,* extremidad *f*
appendectomy [ˌæpən'dɛktəmi] *n, pl* **-mies** : apendicectomía *f*
appendicitis [əˌpɛndə'saɪt̬əs] *n* : apendicitis *f*
appendix [ə'pɛndɪks] *n, pl* **-dixes** *or* **-dices** [-dəˌsiːz] : apéndice *m*
appetite ['æpəˌtaɪt] *n* **1** CRAVING : apetito *m,* deseo *m,* ganas *fpl* **2** PREFERENCE : gusto *m,* preferencia *f* <the cultural appetites of today : los gustos culturales de hoy>
appetizer ['æpəˌtaɪzər] *n* : aperitivo *m,* entremés *m,* botana *f Mex,* tapa *f Spain*
appetizing ['æpəˌtaɪzɪŋ] *adj* : apetecible, apetitoso — **appetizingly** [-zɪŋli] *adv*
applaud [ə'plɔd] *v* : aplaudir
applause [ə'plɔz] *n* : aplauso *m*
apple ['æpəl] *n* : manzana *f*
appliance [ə'plaɪənts] *n* **1** : aparato *m* **2** **household appliance** : electrodoméstico *m,* aparato *m* electrodoméstico
applicability [ˌæplɪkə'bɪlət̬i, əˌplɪkə-] *n* : aplicabilidad *f*
applicable ['æplɪkəbəl, ə'plɪkə-] *adj* : aplicable, pertinente
applicant ['æplɪkənt] *n* : solicitante *mf,* aspirante *mf,* postulante *mf;* candidato *m,* -ta *f*
application [ˌæplə'keɪʃən] *n* **1** USE : aplicación *f,* empleo *m,* uso *m* **2** DILIGENCE : aplicación *f,* diligencia *f,* dedicación *f* **3** REQUEST : solicitud *f,* petición *f,* demanda *f*
applicator ['æpləˌkeɪt̬ər] *n* : aplicador *m*
appliqué¹ [ˌæplə'keɪ] *vt* : decorar con apliques
appliqué² *n* : aplique *m*
apply [ə'plaɪ] *v* **-plied; -plying** *vt* **1** : aplicar (una sustancia, los frenos, el conocimiento) **2** **to apply oneself** : dedicarse, aplicarse — *vi* **1** : aplicarse, referirse <the rules apply to everyone : las reglas se aplican a todos> **2** **to apply for** : solicitar, pedir
appoint [ə'pɔɪnt] *vt* **1** NAME : nombrar, designar **2** FIX, SET : fijar, señalar, designar <to appoint a date : fijar una fecha> **3** EQUIP : equipar <a well-appointed office : una oficina bien equipada>
appointee [əˌpɔɪn'tiː, ˌæ-] *n* : persona *f* designada
appointment [ə'pɔɪntmənt] *n* **1** APPOINTING : nombramiento *m,* designación *f* **2** ENGAGEMENT : cita *f,* hora *f* **3** POST : puesto *m*
apportion [ə'porʃən] *vt* : distribuir, repartir
apportionment [ə'porʃənmənt] *n* : distribución *f,* repartición *f,* reparto *m*
apposite ['æpəzət] *adj* : apropiado, oportuno, pertinente — **appositely** *adv*
appraisal [ə'preɪzəl] *n* : evaluación *f,* valoración *f,* tasación *f,* apreciación *f*
appraise [ə'preɪz] *vt* **-praised; -praising** : evaluar, valorar, tasar, apreciar
appraiser [ə'preɪzər] *n* : tasador *m,* -dora *f*
appreciable [ə'priːʃəbəl, -'prɪʃiə-] *adj* : apreciable, sensible, considerable — **appreciably** [-bli] *adv*
appreciate [ə'priːʃiˌeɪt, -'prɪ-] *v* **-ated; -ating** *vt* **1** VALUE : apreciar, valorar **2** : agradecer <we appreciate his frankness : agradecemos su franqueza> **3** UNDERSTAND : darse cuenta de, entender — *vi* : apreciarse, valorizarse
appreciation [əˌpriːʃi'eɪʃən, -ˌprɪ-] *n* **1** GRATITUDE : agradecimiento *m,* reconocimiento *m* **2** VALUING : apreciación *f,* valoración *f,* estimación *f* <art appreciation : apreciación artística> **3** UNDERSTANDING : comprensión *f,* entendimiento *m*
appreciative [ə'priːʃət̬ɪv, -'prɪ-; ə'priːʃiˌeɪ-] *adj* **1** : apreciativo <an appreciative audience : un público apreciativo> **2** GRATEFUL : agradecido **3** ADMIRING : de admiración
apprehend [ˌæprɪ'hɛnd] *vt* **1** ARREST : aprehender, detener, arrestar **2** DREAD : temer **3** COMPREHEND : comprender, entender
apprehension [ˌæprɪ'hɛntʃən] *n* **1** ARREST : arresto *m,* detención *f,* aprehensión *f* **2** ANXIETY : aprensión *f,* ansiedad *f,* temor *m* **3** UNDERSTANDING : comprensión *f,* percepción *f*
apprehensive [ˌæprɪ'hɛntsɪv] *adj* : aprensivo, inquieto — **apprehensively** *adv*
apprentice¹ [ə'prɛntɪs] *vt* **-ticed; -ticing** : colocar de aprendiz
apprentice² *n* : aprendiz *m,* -diza *f*
apprenticeship [ə'prɛntɪsˌʃɪp] *n* : aprendizaje *f*
apprise [ə'praɪz] *vt* **-prised; -prising** : informar, avisar
approach¹ [ə'proːtʃ] *vt* **1** NEAR : acercarse a **2** APPROXIMATE : aproximarse a **3** : abordar, dirigirse a <I approached my boss with the proposal : me dirigí a mi jefe con la propuesta> **4** TACKLE : abordar, enfocar, considerar — *vi* : acercarse, aproximarse
approach² *n* **1** NEARING : acercamiento *m,* aproximación *f* **2** POSITION : enfoque *m,* planteamiento *m* **3** OFFER : propuesta *f,* oferta *f* **4** ACCESS : acceso *m,* vía *f* de acceso
approachable [ə'proːtʃəbəl] *adj* : accesible, asequible

approbation [ˌæprəˈbeɪʃən] *n* : aprobación *f*

appropriate[1] [əˈproːpriˌeɪt] *vt* **-ated; -ating 1** SEIZE : apropiarse de **2** ALLOCATE : destinar, asignar

appropriate[2] [əˈproːpriət] *adj* : apropiado, adecuado, idóneo — **appropriately** *adv*

appropriateness [əˈproːpriətnəs] *n* : idoneidad *f,* propiedad *f*

appropriation [əˌproːpriˈeɪʃən] *n* **1** SEIZURE : apropiación *f* **2** ALLOCATION : asignación *f*

approval [əˈpruːvəl] *n* **1** : aprobación *f,* visto *m* bueno **2 on approval** : a prueba

approve [əˈpruːv] *vt* **-proved; -proving 1** : aprobar, sancionar, darle el visto bueno a **2 to approve of** : consentir en, aprobar <he doesn't approve of smoking : está en contra del tabaco>

approximate[1] [əˈprɑksəˌmeɪt] *vt* **-mated; -mating** : aproximarse a, acercarse a

approximate[2] [əˈprɑksəmət] *adj* : aproximado

approximately [əˈprɑksəmətli] *adv* : aproximadamente, más o menos

approximation [əˌprɑksəˈmeɪʃən] *n* : aproximación *f*

appurtenance [əˈpərtənən*t*s] *n* : accesorio *m*

apricot [ˈæprəˌkɑt, ˈeɪ-] *n* : albaricoque *m,* chabacano *m Mex*

April [ˈeɪprəl] *n* : abril *m*

apron [ˈeɪprən] *n* : delantal *m,* mandil *m*

apropos[1] [ˌæprəˈpoː, ˈæprəˌpoː] *adv* : a propósito

apropos[2] *adj* : pertinente, oportuno, acertado

apropos of *prep* : a propósito de

apt [ˈæpt] *adj* **1** FITTING : apto, apropiado, acertado, oportuno **2** LIABLE : propenso, inclinado **3** CLEVER, QUICK : listo, despierto

aptitude [ˈæptəˌtuːd, -ˌtjuːd] *n* **1** : aptitud *f,* capacidad *f* <aptitude test : prueba de aptitud> **2** TALENT : talento *m,* facilidad *f*

aptly [ˈæptli] *adv* : acertadamente

aqua [ˈækwə, ˈɑ-] *n* : color *m* aguamarina

aquarium [əˈkwæriəm] *n, pl* **-iums** *or* **-ia** [-iə] : acuario *m*

Aquarius [əˈkwæriəs] *n* : Acuario *mf*

aquatic [əˈkwɑt̬ɪk, -ˈkwæ-] *adj* : acuático

aqueduct [ˈækwəˌdʌkt] *n* : acueducto *m*

aquiline [ˈækwəˌlaɪn, -lən] *adj* : aguileño

Arab[1] [ˈærəb] *adj* : árabe

Arab[2] *n* : árabe *mf*

arabesque [ˌærəˈbɛsk] *n* : arabesco *m*

Arabian[1] [əˈreɪbiən] *adj* : árabe

Arabian[2] *n* → **Arab**[2]

Arabic[1] [ˈærəbɪk] *adj* : árabe

Arabic[2] *n* : árabe *m* (idioma)

arable [ˈærəbəl] *adj* : arable, cultivable

arbiter [ˈɑrbət̬ər] *n* : árbitro *m,* -tra *f*

arbitrary [ˈɑrbəˌtrɛri] *adj* : arbitrario — **arbitrarily** [ˌɑrbəˈtrɛrəli] *adv*

arbitrate [ˈɑrbəˌtreɪt] *v* **-trated; -trating** : arbitrar

arbitration [ˌɑrbəˈtreɪʃən] *n* : arbitraje *m*

arbitrator [ˈɑrbəˌtreɪt̬ər] *n* : árbitro *m,* -tra *f*

arbor [ˈɑrbər] *n* : cenador *m,* pérgola *f*

arboreal [ɑrˈboriəl] *adj* : arbóreo

arc[1] [ˈɑrk] *vi* **arced; arcing** : formar un arco

arc[2] *n* : arco *m*

arcade [ɑrˈkeɪd] *n* **1** ARCHES : arcada *f* **2** MALL : galería *f* comercial

arcane [ɑrˈkeɪn] *adj* : arcano, secreto, misterioso

arch[1] [ˈɑrtʃ] *vt* : arquear, enarcar — *vi* : formar un arco, arquearse

arch[2] *adj* **1** CHIEF : principal **2** MISCHIEVOUS : malicioso, pícaro

arch[3] *n* : arco *m*

archaeological [ˌɑrkiəˈlɑdʒɪkəl] *adj* : arqueológico

archaeologist [ˌɑrkiˈɑlədʒɪst] *n* : arqueólogo *m,* -ga *f*

archaeology *or* **archeology** [ˌɑrkiˈɑlədʒi] *n* : arqueología *f*

archaic [ɑrˈkeɪɪk] *adj* : arcaico — **archaically** [-ɪkli] *adv*

archangel [ˈɑrkˌeɪndʒəl] *n* : arcángel *m*

archbishop [ɑrtʃˈbɪʃəp] *n* : arzobispo *m*

archdiocese [ɑrtʃˈdaɪəsəs, -ˌsiːz, -ˌsiːs] *n* : archidiócesis *f*

archer [ˈɑrtʃər] *n* : arquero *m,* -ra *f*

archery [ˈɑrtʃəri] *n* : tiro *m* al arco

archetype [ˈɑrkɪˌtaɪp] *n* : arquetipo *m*

archipelago [ˌɑrkəˈpɛləˌgoː, ˌɑrtʃə-] *n, pl* **-goes** *or* **-gos** [-goːz] : archipiélago *m*

architect [ˈɑrkəˌtɛkt] *n* : arquitecto *m,* -ta *f*

architectural [ˌɑrkəˈtɛk*t*ʃərəl] *adj* : arquitectónico — **architecturally** *adv*

architecture [ˈɑrkəˌtɛk*t*ʃər] *n* : arquitectura *f*

archives [ˈɑrˌkaɪvz] *npl* : archivo *m*

archivist [ˈɑrkəvɪst, -ˌkaɪ-] *n* : archivero *m,* -ra *f;* archivista *mf*

archway [ˈɑrtʃˌweɪ] *n* : arco *m,* pasadizo *m* abovedado

arctic [ˈɑrktɪk, ˈɑrt̬-] *adj* **1** : ártico <arctic regions : zonas árticas> **2** FRIGID : glacial

arctic circle *n* : círculo *m* ártico

ardent [ˈɑrdənt] *adj* **1** PASSIONATE : ardiente, fogoso, apasionado **2** FERVENT : ferviente, fervoroso — **ardently** *adv*

ardor [ˈɑrdər] *n* : ardor *m,* pasión *f,* fervor *m*

arduous [ˈɑrdʒʊəs] *adj* : arduo, duro, riguroso — **arduously** *adv*

arduousness [ˈɑrdʒʊəsnəs] *n* **:** dureza *f,* rigor *m*

are → **be**

area [ˈæriə] *n* **1** SURFACE **:** área *f,* superficie *f* **2** REGION **:** área *f,* región *f,* zona *f* **3** FIELD **:** área *f,* terreno *m,* campo *m* (de conocimiento)

area code *n* **:** código *m* de la zona, prefijo *m Spain*

arena [əˈriːnə] *n* **1 :** arena *f,* estadio *m* <sports arena : estadio deportivo> **2 :** arena *f,* ruedo *m* <the political arena : el ruedo político>

Argentine [ˈɑrdʒən,taɪn, -,tiːn] *or* **Argentinean** *or* **Argentinian** [,ɑrdʒənˈtɪniən] *n* **:** argentino *m,* -na *f* — **Argentine** *or* **Argentinean** *or* **Argentinian** *adj*

argon [ˈɑr,gɑn] *n* **:** argón *m*

argot [ˈɑrgət, -,goː] *n* **:** argot *m*

arguable [ˈɑrgjʊəbəl] *adj* **:** discutible

argue [ˈɑr,gjuː] *v* **-gued; -guing** *vi* **1** REASON **:** argüir, argumentar, razonar **2** DISPUTE **:** discutir, pelear(se), alegar — *vt* **1** SUGGEST **:** sugerir **2** MAINTAIN **:** alegar, argüir, sostener **3** DISCUSS **:** discutir, debatir

argument [ˈɑrgjəmənt] *n* **1** REASONING **:** argumento *m,* razonamiento *m* **2** DISCUSSION **:** discusión *f,* debate *m* **3** QUARREL **:** pelea *f,* riña *f,* disputa *f*

argumentative [,ɑrgjəˈmɛntət̬ɪv] *adj* **:** discutidor

argyle [ˈɑr,gaɪl] *n* **:** diseño *m* de rombos

aria [ˈɑriə] *n* **:** aria *f*

arid [ˈærəd] *adj* **:** árido

aridity [əˈrɪdət̬i, æ-] *n* **:** aridez *f*

Aries [ˈɛriːz, -i,iːz] *n* **:** Aries *mf*

arise [əˈraɪz] *vi* **arose** [əˈroːz]; **arisen** [əˈrɪzən]; **arising 1** ASCEND **:** ascender, subir, elevarse **2** ORIGINATE **:** originarse, surgir, presentarse **3** GET UP **:** levantarse

aristocracy [,ærəˈstɑkrəsi] *n, pl* **-cies :** aristocracia *f*

aristocrat [əˈrɪstə,kræt] *n* **:** aristócrata *mf*

aristocratic [ə,rɪstəˈkræt̬ɪk] *adj* **:** aristocrático, noble

arithmetic¹ [,ærɪθˈmɛt̬ɪk] *or* **arithmetical** [-t̬ɪkəl] *adj* **:** aritmético

arithmetic² [əˈrɪθmə,tɪk] *n* **:** aritmética

ark [ˈɑrk] *n* **:** arca *f*

arm¹ [ˈɑrm] *vt* **:** armar — *vi* **:** armarse

arm² *n* **1 :** brazo *m* (del cuerpo o de un sillón), manga *f* (de una prenda) **2** BRANCH **:** rama *f,* sección *f* **3** WEAPON **:** arma *f* <to take up arms : tomar las armas> **4 coat of arms :** escudo *m* de armas

armada [ɑrˈmɑdə, -ˈmeɪ-] *n* **:** armada *f,* flota *f*

armadillo [,ɑrməˈdɪlo] *n, pl* **-los :** armadillo *m*

armament [ˈɑrməmənt] *n* **:** armamento *m*

armed [ˈɑrmd] *adj* **1 :** armado <armed robbery : robo a mano armada> **2 armed forces :** fuerzas *fpl* armadas

Armenian [ɑrˈmiːniən] *n* **:** armenio *m,* -nia *f* — **Armenian** *adj*

armistice [ˈɑrməstɪs] *n* **:** armisticio *m*

armor [ˈɑrmər] *n* **:** armadura *f,* coraza *f*

armored [ˈɑrmərd] *adj* **:** blindado, acorazado

armory [ˈɑrməri] *n, pl* **-mories :** arsenal *m* (almacén), armería *f* (museo), fábrica *f* de armas

armpit [ˈɑrm,pɪt] *n* **:** axila *f,* sobaco *m*

army [ˈɑrmi] *n, pl* **-mies 1 :** ejército *m* (militar) **2** MULTITUDE **:** legión *f,* multitud *f,* ejército *m*

aroma [əˈroːmə] *n* **:** aroma *f*

aromatic [,ærəˈmæt̬ɪk] *adj* **:** aromático

around¹ [əˈraʊnd] *adv* **1 :** de circunferencia <a tree three feet around : un árbol de tres pies de circunferencia> **2 :** alrededor, a la redonda <for miles around : por millas a la redonda> <all around : por todos lados, todo alrededor> **3 :** por ahí <they're somewhere around : deben estar por ahí> **4** APPROXIMATELY **:** más o menos, aproximadamente <around 5 o'clock : a eso de las 5> **5 to turn around :** darse la vuelta, voltearse

around² *prep* **1** SURROUNDING **:** alrededor de, en torno a **2** THROUGH **:** por, en <he traveled around Mexico : viajó por México> <around the house : en casa> **3 :** a la vuelta de <around the corner : a la vuelta de la esquina> **4** NEAR **:** alrededor de, cerca de

arousal [əˈraʊzəl] *n* **:** excitación *f*

arouse [əˈraʊz] *vt* **aroused; arousing 1** AWAKE **:** despertar **2** EXCITE **:** despertar, suscitar, excitar

arraign [əˈreɪn] *vt* **:** hacer comparecer (ante un tribunal)

arraignment [əˈreɪnmənt] *n* **:** orden *m* de comparecencia, acusación *f*

arrange [əˈreɪndʒ] *vt* **-ranged; -ranging 1** ORDER **:** arreglar, poner en orden, disponer **2** SETTLE **:** arreglar, fijar, concertar **3** ADAPT **:** arreglar, adaptar

arrangement [əˈreɪndʒmənt] *n* **1** ORDER **:** arreglo *m,* orden *m* **2** ARRANGING **:** disposición *f* <floral arrangement : arreglo floral> **3** AGREEMENT **:** arreglo *m,* acuerdo *m,* convenio *m* **4 arrangements** *npl* **:** preparativos *mpl,* planes *mpl*

array¹ [əˈreɪ] *vt* **1** ORDER **:** poner en orden, presentar, formar **2** GARB **:** vestir, ataviar, engalanar

array² *n* **1** ORDER **:** orden *m,* formación *f* **2** ATTIRE **:** atavío *m,* galas *mpl* **3** RANGE, SELECTION **:** selección *f,* serie *f,* gama *f* <an array of problems : una serie de problemas>

arrears [əˈrɪrz] *npl* **:** atrasos *mpl* <to be in arrears : estar atrasado en los pagos>

arrest[1] [ə'rɛst] *vt* **1** APPREHEND : arrestar, detener **2** CHECK, STOP : detener, parar

arrest[2] *n* **1** APPREHENSION : arresto *m*, detención *f* <under arrest : detenido> **2** STOPPING : paro *m*

arrival [ə'raɪvəl] *n* : llegada *f*, venida *f*, arribo *m*

arrive [ə'raɪv] *vi* **-rived; -riving 1** COME : llegar, arribar **2** SUCCEED : triunfar, tener éxito

arrogance ['ærəgənts] *n* : arrogancia *f*, soberbia *f*, altanería *f*, altivez *f*

arrogant ['ærəgənt] *adj* : arrogante, soberbio, altanero, altivo — **arrogantly** *adv*

arrogate ['ærə,geɪt] *vt* **-gated; -gating to arrogate to oneself** : arrogarse

arrow ['æro] *n* : flecha *f*

arrowhead ['æro,hɛd] *n* : punta *f* de flecha

arroyo [ə'rɔɪo] *n* : arroyo *m*

arsenal ['ɑrsənəl] *n* : arsenal *m*

arsenic ['ɑrsənɪk] *n* : arsénico *m*

arson ['ɑrsən] *n* : incendio *m* premeditado

arsonist *n* ['ɑrsənɪst] : incendiario *m*, -ria *f*; pirómano *m*, -na *f*

art ['ɑrt] *n* **1** : arte *m* **2** SKILL : destreza *f*, habilidad *f*, maña *f* **3 arts** *npl* : letras *fpl* (en la educación) **4 fine arts** : bellas artes *fpl*

arterial [ɑr'tɪriəl] *adj* : arterial

arteriosclerosis [ɑr,tɪriosklə'ro:sɪs] *n* : arteriosclerosis *f*

artery ['ɑrtəri] *n, pl* **-teries 1** : arteria *f* **2** THOROUGHFARE : carretera *f* principal, arteria *f*

artesian well [ɑr'ti:ʒən] *n* : pozo *m* artesiano

artful ['ɑrtfəl] *adj* **1** INGENIOUS : ingenioso, diestro **2** CRAFTY : astuto, taimado, ladino, artero — **artfully** *adv*

arthritic [ɑr'θrɪtɪk] *adj* : artrítico

arthritis [ɑr'θraɪtəs] *n, pl* **-tides** [ɑr'θrɪtə,di:z] : artritis *f*

arthropod ['ɑrθrə,pɑd] *n* : artrópodo *m*

artichoke ['ɑrtə,tʃo:k] *n* : alcachofa *f*

article ['ɑrtɪkəl] *n* **1** ITEM : artículo *m*, objeto *m* **2** ESSAY : artículo *m* **3** CLAUSE : artículo *m*, cláusula *f* **4** : artículo *m* <definite article : artículo determinado>

articulate[1] [ɑr'tɪkjə,leɪt] *vt* **-lated; -lating 1** UTTER : articular, enunciar, expresar **2** CONNECT : articular (en anatomía)

articulate[2] [ɑr'tɪkjələt] *adj* **to be articulate** : poder articular palabras, expresarse bien

articulately [ɑr'tɪkjələtli] *adv* : elocuentemente, con fluidez

articulateness [ɑr'tɪkjələtnəs] *n* : elocuencia *f*, fluidez *f*

articulation [ɑr,tɪkjə'leɪʃən] *n* **1** JOINT : articulación *f* **2** UTTERANCE : articulación *f*, declaración *f* **3** ENUNCIATION : articulación *f*, pronunciación *f*

artifact ['ɑrtə,fækt] *n* : artefacto *m*

artifice ['ɑrtəfəs] *n* : artificio *m*

artificial [,ɑrtə'fɪʃəl] *adj* **1** SYNTHETIC : artificial, sintético **2** FEIGNED : artificial, falso, afectado

artificially [,ɑrtə'fɪʃəli] *adv* : artificialmente, con afectación

artillery [ɑr'tɪləri] *n, pl* **-leries** : artillería *f*

artisan ['ɑrtəzən, -sən] *n* : artesano *m*, -na *f*

artist ['ɑrtɪst] *n* : artista *mf*

artistic [ɑr'tɪstɪk] *adj* : artístico — **artistically** [-tɪkli] *adv*

artistry ['ɑrtəstri] *n* : maestría *f*, arte *m*

artless ['ɑrtləs] *adj* : sencillo, natural, ingenuo, cándido — **artlessly** *adv*

artlessness ['ɑrtləsnəs] *n* : ingenuidad *f*, candidez *f*

arty ['ɑrti] *adj* **artier; -est** : pretenciosamente artístico

as[1] ['æz] *adv* **1** : tan, tanto <this one's not as difficult : éste no es tan difícil> **2** : como <some trees, as oak and pine : algunos árboles, como el roble y el pino>

as[2] *conj* **1** LIKE : como, igual que **2** WHEN, WHILE : cuando, mientras, a la vez que **3** BECAUSE : porque **4** THOUGH : aunque, por más que <strange as it may appear : por extraño que parezca> **5 as is** : tal como está

as[3] *prep* **1** : de <I met her as a child : la conocí de pequeña> **2** LIKE : como <behave as a man : compórtate como un hombre>

as[4] *pron* : que <in the same building as my brother : en el mismo edificio que mi hermano>

asbestos [æz'bɛstəs, æs-] *n* : asbesto *m*, amianto *m*

ascend [ə'sɛnd] *vi* : ascender, subir — *vt* : subir, subir a, escalar

ascendancy [ə'sɛndəntsi] *n* : ascendiente *m*, predominio *m*

ascendant[1] [ə'sɛndənt] *adj* **1** RISING : ascendente **2** DOMINANT : superior, dominante

ascendant[2] *n* **to be in the ascendant** : estar en alza, ir ganando predominio

ascension [ə'sɛntʃən] *n* : ascensión *f*

ascent [ə'sɛnt] *n* **1** RISE : ascensión *f*, subida *f*, ascenso *m* **2** SLOPE : cuesta *f*, pendiente *f*

ascertain [,æsər'teɪn] *vt* : determinar, establecer, averiguar

ascertainable [,æsər'teɪnəbəl] *adj* : determinable, averiguable

ascetic[1] [ə'sɛtɪk] *adj* : ascético

ascetic[2] *n* : asceta *mf*

asceticism [ə'sɛtə,sɪzəm] *n* : ascetismo *m*

ascribable [ə'skraɪbəbəl] *adj* : atribuible, imputable

ascribe [ə'skraɪb] *vt* **-cribed; -cribing** : atribuir, imputar

aseptic [eɪ'sɛptɪk] *adj* : aséptico

as for *prep* CONCERNING : en cuanto a, respecto a, para

ash [ˈæʃ] *n* **1 :** ceniza *f* <to reduce to ashes : reducir a cenizas> **2 :** fresno *m* (árbol)

ashamed [əˈʃeɪmd] *adj* **:** avergonzado, abochornado, apenado — **ashamedly** [əˈʃeɪmədli] *adv*

ashen [ˈæʃən] *adj* **:** lívido, ceniciento, pálido

ashore [əˈʃor] *adv* **1 :** en tierra **2 to go ashore :** desembarcar

ashtray [ˈæʃˌtreɪ] *n* **:** cenicero *m*

Asian[1] [ˈeɪʒən, -ʃən] *adj* **:** asiático

Asian[2] *n* **:** asiático *m,* -ca *f*

aside [əˈsaɪd] *adv* **1 :** a un lado <to step aside : hacerse a un lado> **2 :** de lado, aparte <jesting aside : bromas aparte> **3 to set aside :** guardar, apartar, reservar

aside from *prep* **1** BESIDES **:** además de **2** EXCEPT **:** aparte de, menos

as if *conj* **:** como si

asinine [ˈæsənˌaɪn] *adj* **:** necio, estúpido

ask [ˈæsk] *vt* **1 :** preguntar <ask him if he's coming : pregúntale si viene> **2** REQUEST **:** pedir, solicitar <to ask a favor : pedir un favor> **3** INVITE **:** invitar — *vi* **1** INQUIRE **:** preguntar <I asked about her children : pregunté por sus niños> **2** REQUEST **:** pedir <we asked for help : pedimos ayuda>

askance [əˈskænts] *adv* **1** SIDELONG **:** de reojo, de soslayo **2** SUSPICIOUSLY **:** con recelo, con desconfianza

askew [əˈskjuː] *adj* **:** torcido, ladeado

asleep [əˈsliːp] *adj* **1 :** dormido, durmiendo **2 to fall asleep :** quedarse dormido

as of *prep* **:** desde, a partir de

asparagus [əˈspærəgəs] *n* **:** espárrago *m*

aspect [ˈæˌspɛkt] *n* **:** aspecto *m*

aspen [ˈæspən] *n* **:** álamo *m* temblón

asperity [æˈspɛrət̬i, ə-] *n, pl* **-ties :** aspereza *f*

aspersion [əˈspərʒən] *n* **:** difamación *f,* calumnia *f*

asphalt [ˈæsˌfɔlt] *n* **:** asfalto *m*

asphyxia [æˈsfɪksiə, ə-] *n* **:** asfixia *f*

asphyxiate [æˈsfɪksiˌeɪt] *v* **-ated; -ating** *vt* **:** asfixiar — *vi* **:** asfixiarse

asphyxiation [æˌsfɪksiˈeɪʃən] *n* **:** asfixia *f*

aspirant [ˈæspərənt, əˈspaɪrənt] *n* **:** aspirante *mf,* pretendiente *mf*

aspiration [ˌæspəˈreɪʃən] *n* **1** DESIRE **:** aspiración *f,* anhelo *m,* ambición *f* **2** BREATHING **:** aspiración *f*

aspire [əˈspaɪr] *vi* **-pired; -piring :** aspirar

aspirin [ˈæsprən, ˈæspə-] *n, pl* **aspirin** *or* **aspirins :** aspirina *f*

ass [ˈæs] *n* **1 :** asno *m* **2** IDIOT **:** imbécil *mf,* idiota *mf*

assail [əˈseɪl] *vt* **:** atacar, asaltar

assailant [əˈseɪlənt] *n* **:** asaltante *mf,* atacante *mf*

assassin [əˈsæsən] *n* **:** asesino *m,* -na *f*

assassinate [əˈsæsənˌeɪt] *vt* **-nated; -nating :** asesinar

assassination [əˌsæsənˈeɪʃən] *n* **:** asesinato *m*

assault[1] [əˈsɔlt] *vt* **:** atacar, asaltar, agredir

assault[2] *n* **:** ataque *m,* asalto *m,* agresión *f*

assay[1] [æˈseɪ, ˈæˌseɪ] *vt* **:** ensayar

assay[2] [ˈæˌseɪ, æˈseɪ] *n* **:** ensayo *m*

assemble [əˈsɛmbəl] *v* **-bled; -bling** *vt* **1** GATHER **:** reunir, recoger, juntar **2** CONSTRUCT **:** ensamblar, montar, construir — *vi* **:** reunirse, congregarse

assembly [əˈsɛmbli] *n, pl* **-blies 1** MEETING **:** reunión *f* **2** CONSTRUCTING **:** ensamblaje *m,* montaje *m*

assemblyman [əˈsɛmblimən] *n, pl* **-men** [-mən, -ˌmɛn] **:** asambleísta *m*

assemblywoman [əˈsɛmbliˌwʊmən] *n, pl* **-women** [-ˌwɪmən] **:** asambleísta *f*

assent[1] [əˈsɛnt] *vi* **:** asentir, consentir

assent[2] *n* **:** asentimiento *m,* aprobación *f*

assert [əˈsərt] *vt* **1** AFFIRM **:** afirmar, aseverar, mantener **2 to assert oneself :** imponerse, hacerse valer

assertion [əˈsərʃən] *n* **:** afirmación *f,* aseveración *f,* aserto *m*

assertive [əˈsərt̬ɪv] *adj* **:** firme, enérgico

assertiveness [əˈsərt̬ɪvnəs] *n* **:** seguridad *f* en sí mismo

assess [əˈsɛs] *vt* **1** IMPOSE **:** gravar (un impuesto), imponer **2** EVALUATE **:** evaluar, valorar, aquilatar

assessment [əˈsɛsmənt] *n* **:** evaluación *f,* valoración *f*

assessor [əˈsɛsər] *n* **:** evaluador *m,* -dora *f;* tasador *m,* -dora *f*

asset [ˈæˌsɛt] *n* **1 :** ventaja *f,* recurso *m* **2 assets** *npl* **:** bienes *mpl,* activo *m* <assets and liabilities : activo y pasivo>

assiduous [əˈsɪdʒʊəs] *adj* **:** diligente, aplicado, asiduo — **assiduously** *adv*

assign [əˈsaɪn] *vt* **1** APPOINT **:** designar, nombrar **2** ALLOT **:** asignar, señalar **3** ATTRIBUTE **:** atribuir, dar, conceder

assignment [əˈsaɪnmənt] *n* **1** TASK **:** función *f,* tarea *f,* misión *f* **2** HOMEWORK **:** tarea *f,* asignación *f PRi,* deberes *mpl Spain* **3** APPOINTMENT **:** nombramiento *m* **4** ALLOCATION **:** asignación *f*

assimilate [əˈsɪməˌleɪt] *v* **-lated; -lating** *vt* **:** asimilar — *vi* **:** adaptarse, integrarse

assimilation [əˌsɪməˈleɪʃən] *n* **:** asimilación *f*

assist[1] [əˈsɪst] *vt* **:** asistir, ayudar

assist[2] *n* **:** asistencia *f,* contribución *f*

assistance [əˈsɪstənts] *n* **:** asistencia *f,* ayuda *f,* auxilio *m*

assistant [əˈsɪstənt] *n* **:** ayudante *mf,* asistente *mf*

associate[1] [əˈsoːʃiˌeɪt, -si-] *v* **-ated; -ating** *vt* **1** CONNECT, RELATE **:** asociar, relacionar **2 to be associated with**

: estar relacionado con, estar vinculado a — *vi* **to associate with** : relacionarse con, frecuentar
associate[2] [ə'soːʃiət, -siət] *n* : asociado *m*, -da *f;* colega *mf;* socio *m*, -cia *f*
association [ə,soːʃi'eɪʃən, -si-] *n* **1** ORGANIZATION : asociación *f*, sociedad *f* **2** RELATIONSHIP : asociación *f*, relación *f*
as soon as *conj* : en cuanto, tan pronto como
assorted [ə'sɔrtəd] *adj* : surtido
assortment [ə'sɔrtmənt] *n* : surtido *m*, variedad *f*, colección *f*
assuage [ə'sweɪdʒ] *vt* **-suaged; -suaging 1** EASE : aliviar, mitigar **2** CALM : calmar, aplacar **3** SATISFY : saciar, satisfacer
assume [ə'suːm] *vt* **-sumed; -suming 1** SUPPOSE : suponer, asumir **2** UNDERTAKE : asumir, encargarse de **3** TAKE ON : adquirir, adoptar, tomar <to assume importance : tomar importancia> **4** FEIGN : adoptar, afectar, simular
assumption [ə'sʌmpʃən] *n* : asunción *f*, presunción *f*
assurance [ə'ʃʊrən*t*s] *n* **1** CERTAINTY : certidumbre *f*, certeza *f* **2** CONFIDENCE : confianza *f*, aplomo *m*, seguridad *f*
assure [ə'ʃʊr] *vt* **-sured; -suring** : asegurar, garantizar <I assure you that I'll do it : te aseguro que lo haré>
assured [ə'ʃʊrd] *adj* **1** CERTAIN : seguro, asegurado **2** CONFIDENT : confiado, seguro de sí mismo
aster ['æstər] *n* : áster *m*
asterisk ['æstə,rɪsk] *n* : asterisco *m*
astern [ə'stərn] *adv* **1** BEHIND : detrás, a popa **2** BACKWARDS : hacia atrás
asteroid ['æstə,rɔɪd] *n* : asteroide *m*
asthma ['æzmə] *n* : asma *m*
asthmatic [æz'mæt̬ɪk] *adj* : asmático
as though → **as if**
astigmatism [ə'stɪgmə,tɪzəm] *n* : astigmatismo *m*
as to *prep* **1** ABOUT : sobre, acerca de **2** → **according to**
astonish [ə'stɑnɪʃ] *vt* : asombrar, sorprender, pasmar
astonishing [ə'stɑnɪʃɪŋ] *adj* : asombroso, sorprendente, increíble — **astonishingly** *adv*
astonishment [ə'stɑnɪʃmənt] *n* : asombro *m*, estupefacción *f*, sorpresa *f*
astound [ə'staʊnd] *vt* : asombrar, pasmar, dejar estupefacto
astounding [ə'staʊndɪŋ] *adj* : asombroso, pasmoso — **astoundingly** *adv*
astraddle [ə'strædəl] *adv* : a horcajadas
astral ['æstrəl] *adj* : astral
astray [ə'streɪ] *adv & adj* : perdido, extraviado, descarriado
astride [ə'straɪd] *adv* : a horcajadas
astringency [ə'strɪndʒən*t*si] *n* : astringencia *f*
astringent[1] [ə'strɪndʒənt] *adj* : astringente
astringent[2] *n* : astringente *m*
astrologer [ə'strɑlədʒər] *n* : astrólogo *m*, -ga *f*
astrological [,æstrə'lɑdʒɪkəl] *adj* : astrológico
astrology [ə'strɑlədʒi] *n* : astrología *f*
astronaut ['æstrə,nɔt] *n* : astronauta *mf*
astronautic [,æstrə'nɔt̬ɪk] *or* **astronautical** [-t̬ɪkəl] *adj* : astronáutico
astronautics [,æstrə'nɔt̬ɪks] *ns & pl* : astronáutica *f*
astronomer [ə'strɑnəmər] *n* : astrónomo *m*, -ma *f*
astronomical [,æstrə'nɑmɪkəl] *adj* **1** : astronómico **2** ENORMOUS : astronómico, enorme, gigantesco
astronomy [ə'strɑnəmi] *n, pl* **-mies** : astronomía *f*
astute [ə'stuːt, -'stjuːt] *adj* : astuto, sagaz, perspicaz — **astutely** *adv*
astuteness [ə'stuːtnəs, -'stjuːt-] *n* : astucia *f*, sagacidad *f*, perspicacia *f*
asunder [ə'sʌndər] *adv* : en dos, en pedazos <to tear asunder : hacer pedazos>
as well as[1] *conj* : tanto como
as well as[2] *prep* BESIDES : además de, aparte de
as yet *adv* : aún, todavía
asylum [ə'saɪləm] *n* **1** REFUGE : refugio *m*, santuario *m*, asilo *m* **2 insane asylum** : manicomio *m*
asymmetrical [,eɪsə'mɛtrɪkəl] *or* **asymmetric** [-'mɛtrɪk] *adj* : asimétrico
asymmetry [,eɪ'sɪmətri] *n* : asimetría *f*
at ['æt] *prep* **1** : en <at the top : en lo alto> <at peace : en paz> <at Ana's house : en casa de Ana> **2** : a <at the rear : al fondo> <at 10 o'clock : a las diez> **3** : por <at last : por fin> <to be surprised at something : sorprenderse por algo> **4** : de <he's laughing at you : está riéndose de ti> **5** : para <you're good at this : eres bueno para esto>
at all *adv* : en absoluto, para nada
ate → **eat**
atheism *n* ['eɪθi,ɪzəm] : ateísmo *m*
atheist ['eɪθiɪst] *n* : ateo *m*, atea *f*
atheistic [,eɪθi'ɪstɪk] *adj* : ateo
athlete ['æθ,liːt] *n* : atleta *mf*
athletic [æθ'lɛt̬ɪk] *adj* : atlético
athletics [æθ'lɛt̬ɪks] *ns & pl* : atletismo *m*
atlas ['ætləs] *n* : atlas *m*
atmosphere ['ætmə,sfɪr] *n* **1** AIR : atmósfera *f*, aire *m* **2** AMBIENCE : ambiente *m*, atmósfera *f*, clima *m*
atmospheric [,ætmə'sfɪrɪk, -'sfɛr-] *adj* : atmosférico — **atmospherically** [-ɪkli] *adv*
atoll ['æ,tɔl, 'eɪ-, -,tɑl] *n* : atolón *m*
atom ['æt̬əm] *n* **1** : átomo *m* **2** SPECK : ápice *m*, pizca *f*
atomic [ə'tɑmɪk] *adj* : atómico

atomic bomb *n* **:** bomba *f* atómica
atomizer [ˈætəˌmaɪzər] *n* **:** atomizador *m,* pulverizador *m*
atone [əˈtoːn] *vt* **atoned; atoning to atone for :** expiar
atonement [əˈtoːnmənt] *n* **:** expiación *f,* desagravio *m*
atop[1] [əˈtɑp] *adj* **:** encima
atop[2] *prep* **:** encima de, sobre
atrium [ˈeɪtriəm] *n, pl* **atria** [-triə] *or* **atriums 1 :** atrio *m* **2 :** aurícula *f* (del corazón)
atrocious [əˈtroːʃəs] *adj* **:** atroz — **atrociously** *adv*
atrocity [əˈtrɑsət̬i] *n, pl* **-ties :** atrocidad *f*
atrophy[1] [ˈætrəfi] *vt* **-phied; -phying :** atrofiar
atrophy[2] *n, pl* **-phies :** atrofia *f*
atropine [ˈætrəˌpiːn] *n* **:** atropina *f*
attach [əˈtætʃ] *vt* **1** FASTEN **:** sujetar, atar, amarrar, pegar **2** JOIN **:** juntar, adjuntar **3** ATTRIBUTE **:** dar, atribuir <I attached little importance to it **:** le di poca importancia> **4** SEIZE **:** embargar **5 to become attached to someone :** encariñarse con alguien
attaché [ˌæt̬əˈʃeɪ, ˌæˌtæ-, əˌtæ-] *n* **:** agregado *m,* -da *f*
attachment [əˈtætʃmənt] *n* **1** ACCESSORY **:** accesorio *m* **2** CONNECTION **:** conexión *f,* acoplamiento *m* **3** FONDNESS **:** apego *m,* cariño *m,* afición *f*
attack[1] [əˈtæk] *vt* **1** ASSAULT **:** atacar, asaltar, agredir **2** TACKLE **:** acometer, combatir, enfrentarse con
attack[2] *n* **1 :** ataque *m,* asalto *m,* acometida *f* <to launch an attack **:** lanzar un ataque> **2 :** ataque *m,* crisis *f* <heart attack **:** ataque cardíaco, infarto> <attack of nerves **:** crisis nerviosa>
attacker [əˈtækər] *n* **:** asaltante *mf*
attain [əˈteɪn] *vt* **1** ACHIEVE **:** lograr, conseguir, alcanzar, realizar **2** REACH **:** alcanzar, llegar a
attainable [əˈteɪnəbəl] *adj* **:** alcanzable, realizable, asequible
attainment [əˈteɪnmənt] *n* **:** logro *m,* consecución *f,* realización *f*
attempt[1] [əˈtɛmpt] *vt* **:** intentar, tratar de
attempt[2] *n* **:** intento *m,* tentativa *f*
attend [əˈtɛnd] *vt* **1 :** asistir a <to attend a meeting **:** asistir a una reunión> **2 :** atender, ocuparse de, cuidar <to attend a patient **:** atender a un paciente> **3** HEED **:** atender a, hacer caso de **4** ACCOMPANY **:** acompañar
attendance [əˈtɛndənts] *n* **1** ATTENDING **:** asistencia *f* **2** TURNOUT **:** concurrencia *f*
attendant[1] [əˈtɛndənt] *adj* **:** concomitante, inherente
attendant[2] *n* **:** asistente *mf,* acompañante *mf,* guarda *mf*
attention [əˈtɛntʃən] *n* **1 :** atención *f* **2 to pay attention :** prestar atención, hacer caso **3 to stand at attention :** estar firme
attentive [əˈtɛntɪv] *adj* **:** atento — **attentively** *adv*
attentiveness [əˈtɛntɪvnəs] *n* **1** THOUGHTFULNESS **:** cortesía *f,* consideración *f* **2** CONCENTRATION **:** atención *f,* concentración *f*
attest [əˈtɛst] *vt* **:** atestiguar, dar fe de
attestation [ˌæˌtɛsˈteɪʃən] *n* **:** testimonio *m*
attic [ˈætɪk] *n* **:** ático *m,* desván *m,* buhardilla *f*
attire[1] [əˈtaɪr] *vt* **-tired; -tiring :** ataviar
attire[2] *n* **:** atuendo *m,* atavío *m*
attitude [ˈætəˌtuːd, -ˌtjuːd] *n* **1** FEELING **:** actitud *f* **2** POSTURE **:** postura *f*
attorney [əˈtərni] *n, pl* **-neys :** abogado *m,* -da *f*
attract [əˈtrækt] *vt* **1 :** atraer **2 to attract attention :** llamar la atención
attraction [əˈtrækʃən] *n* **:** atracción *f,* atractivo *m*
attractive [əˈtræktɪv] *adj* **:** atractivo, atrayente
attractively [əˈtræktɪvli] *adv* **:** de manera atractiva, de buen gusto, hermosamente
attractiveness [əˈtræktɪvnəs] *n* **:** atractivo *m*
attributable [əˈtrɪbjʊt̬əbəl] *adj* **:** atribuible, imputable
attribute[1] [əˈtrɪˌbjuːt] *vt* **-tributed; -tributing :** atribuir
attribute[2] [ˈætrəˌbjuːt] *n* **:** atributo *m,* cualidad *f*
attribution [ˌætrəˈbjuːʃən] *n* **:** atribución *f*
attune [əˈtuːn, -ˈtjuːn] *vt* **-tuned; -tuning 1** ADAPT **:** adaptar, adecuar **2 to be attuned to :** estar en armonía con
auburn [ˈɔbərn] *adj* **:** castaño rojizo
auction[1] [ˈɔkʃən] *vt* **:** subastar, rematar
auction[2] *n* **:** subasta *f,* remate *m*
auctioneer [ˌɔkʃəˈnɪr] *n* **:** subastador *m,* -dora *f;* rematador *m,* -dora *f*
audacious [ɔˈdeɪʃəs] *adj* **:** audaz, atrevido
audacity [ɔˈdæsət̬i] *n, pl* **-ties :** audacia *f,* atrevimiento *m,* descaro *m*
audible [ˈɔdəbəl] *adj* **:** audible — **audibly** [-bli] *adv*
audience [ˈɔdiənts] *n* **1** INTERVIEW **:** audiencia *f* **2** PUBLIC **:** audiencia *f,* público *m,* auditorio *m,* espectadores *mpl*
audio[1] [ˈɔdiˌoː] *adj* **:** de sonido, de audio
audio[2] *n* **:** audio *m*
audiovisual [ˌɔdioˈvɪʒʊəl] *adj* **:** audiovisual
audit[1] [ˈɔdət] *vt* **1 :** auditar (finanzas) **2 :** asistir como oyente a (una clase o un curso)
audit[2] *n* **:** auditoría *f*
audition[1] [ɔˈdɪʃən] *vi* **:** hacer una audición
audition[2] *n* **:** audición *f*

auditor [ˈɔdəṭər] *n* **1** : auditor *m,* -tora *f* (de finanzas) **2** STUDENT : oyente *mf*
auditorium [ˌɔdəˈtoriəm] *n, pl* **-riums** *or* **-ria** [-riə] : auditorio *m,* sala *f*
auditory [ˈɔdəˌtori] *adj* : auditivo
auger [ˈɔgər] *n* : taladro *m,* barrena *f*
augment [ɔgˈmɛnt] *vt* : aumentar, incrementar
augmentation [ˌɔgmənˈteɪʃən] *n* : aumento *m,* incremento *m*
augur[1] [ˈɔgər] *vt* : augurar, presagiar — *vi* **to augur well** : ser de buen agüero
augur[2] *n* : augur *m*
augury [ˈɔgjʊri, -gər-] *n, pl* **-ries** : augurio *m,* presagio *m,* agüero *m*
august [ɔˈgʌst] *adj* : augusto
August [ˈɔgəst] *n* : agosto *m*
auk [ˈɔk] *n* : alca *f*
aunt [ˈænt, ˈant] *n* : tía *f*
aura [ˈɔrə] *n* : aura *f*
aural [ˈɔrəl] *adj* : auditivo
auricle [ˈɔrɪkəl] *n* : aurícula *f*
aurora borealis [əˈrorəˌboriˈæləs] *n* : aurora *f* boreal
auspices [ˈɔspəsəz, -ˌsiːz] *npl* : auspicios *mpl*
auspicious [ɔˈspɪʃəs] *adj* : prometedor, propicio, de buen augurio
austere [ɔˈstɪr] *adj* : austero, severo, adusto — **austerely** *adv*
austerity [ɔˈstɛrəṭi] *n, pl* **-ties** : austeridad *f*
Australian [ɔˈstreɪljən] *n* : australiano *m,* -na *f* — **Australian** *adj*
Austrian [ˈɔstriən] *n* : austriaco *m,* -ca *f* — **Austrian** *adj*
authentic [əˈθɛntɪk, ɔ-] *adj* : auténtico, genuino — **authentically** [-tɪkli] *adv*
authenticate [əˈθɛntɪˌkeɪt, ɔ-] *vt* **-cated; -cating** : autenticar, autentificar
authenticity [ɔˌθɛnˈtɪsəṭi] *n* : autenticidad *f*
author [ˈɔθər] *n* **1** WRITER : escritor *m,* -tora *f;* autor *m,* -tora *f* **2** CREATOR : autor *m,* -tora *f;* creador *m,* -dora *f;* artífice *mf*
authoritarian [ɔˌθɔrəˈtɛriən, ə-] *adj* : autoritario
authoritative [əˈθɔrəˌteɪṭɪv, ɔ-] *adj* **1** RELIABLE : fidedigno, autorizado **2** DICTATORIAL : autoritario, dictatorial, imperioso
authoritatively [əˈθɔrəˌteɪṭɪvli, ɔ-] *adv* **1** RELIABLY : con autoridad **2** DICTATORIALLY : de manera autoritaria
authority [əˈθɔrəṭi, ɔ-] *n, pl* **-ties 1** EXPERT : autoridad *f;* experto *m,* -ta *f* **2** POWER : autoridad *f,* poder *m* **3** AUTHORIZATION : autorización *f,* licencia *f* **4 the authorities** : las autoridades *fpl* **5 on good authority** : de buena fuente
authorization [ˌɔθərəˈzeɪʃən] *n* : autorización *f*
authorize [ˈɔθəˌraɪz] *vt* **-rized; -rizing** : autorizar, facultar
authorship [ˈɔθərˌʃɪp] *n* : autoría *f*
auto [ˈɔṭo] → **automobile**
autobiographical [ˌɔṭoˌbaɪəˈgræfɪkəl] *adj* : autobiográfico
autobiography [ˌɔṭobaɪˈɑgrəfi] *n, pl* **-phies** : autobiografía *f*
autocracy [ɔˈtɑkrəsi] *n, pl* **-cies** : autocracia *f*
autocrat [ˈɔṭəˌkræt] *n* : autócrata *mf*
autocratic [ˌɔṭəˈkræṭɪk] *adj* : autocrático — **autocratically** [-ṭɪkli] *adv*
autograph[1] [ˈɔṭəˌgræf] *vt* : autografiar
autograph[2] *n* : autógrafo *m*
automate [ˈɔṭəˌmeɪt] *vt* **-mated; -mating** : automatizar
automatic [ˌɔṭəˈmæṭɪk] *adj* : automático — **automatically** [-ṭɪkli] *adv*
automation [ˌɔṭəˈmeɪʃən] *n* : automatización *f*
automaton [ɔˈtɑməˌtɑn] *n, pl* **-atons** *or* **-ata** [-ṭə, -ˌtɑ] : autómata *m*
automobile [ˌɔṭəmoˈbiːl, -ˈmoːˌbiːl] *n* : automóvil *m,* auto *m,* carro *m,* coche *m*
automotive [ˌɔṭəˈmoːṭɪv] *adj* : automotor
autonomous [ɔˈtɑnəməs] *adj* : autónomo — **autonomously** *adv*
autonomy [ɔˈtɑnəmi] *n, pl* **-mies** : autonomía *f*
autopsy [ˈɔˌtɑpsi, -təp-] *n, pl* **-sies** : autopsia *f*
autumn [ˈɔṭəm] *n* : otoño *m*
autumnal [ɔˈtʌmnəl] *adj* : otoñal
auxiliary[1] [ɔgˈzɪljəri, -ˈzɪləri] *adj* : auxiliar
auxiliary[2] *n, pl* **-ries** : auxiliar *mf,* ayudante *mf*
avail[1] [əˈveɪl] *vt* **to avail oneself** : aprovecharse, valerse
avail[2] *n* **1** : provecho *m,* utilidad *f* **2 to no avail** : en vano **3 to be of no avail** : no servir de nada, ser inútil
availability [əˌveɪləˈbɪləṭi] *n, pl* **-ties** : disponibilidad *f*
available [əˈveɪləbəl] *adj* : disponible
avalanche [ˈævəˌlæntʃ] *n* : avalancha *f,* alud *m*
avarice [ˈævərəs] *n* : avaricia *f,* codicia *f*
avaricious [ˌævəˈrɪʃəs] *adj* : avaricioso, codicioso
avenge [əˈvɛndʒ] *vt* **avenged; avenging** : vengar
avenger [əˈvɛndʒər] *n* : vengador *m,* -dora *f*
avenue [ˈævəˌnuː, -ˌnjuː] *n* **1** : avenida *f* **2** MEANS : vía *f,* camino *m*
average[1] [ˈævrɪdʒ, ˈævə-] *vt* **-aged; -aging 1** : hacer un promedio de <he averages 8 hours a day : hace un promedio de 8 horas diarias> **2** : calcular el promedio de, promediar (en matemáticas)
average[2] *adj* **1** MEAN : medio <the average temperature : la temperatura media> **2** ORDINARY : común, ordinario <the average man : el hombre común>

average[3] *n* : promedio *m*

averse [ə'vərs] *adj* : reacio, opuesto

aversion [ə'vərʒən] *n* : aversión *f*

avert [ə'vərt] *vt* **1** : apartar, desviar <he averted his eyes from the scene : apartó los ojos de la escena> **2** AVOID, PREVENT : evitar, prevenir

aviary ['eɪvi,ɛri] *n, pl* **-aries** : pajarera *f*

aviation [,eɪvi'eɪʃən] *n* : aviación *f*

aviator ['eɪvi,eɪt̬ər] *n* : aviador *m,* -dora *f*

avid ['ævɪd] *adj* **1** GREEDY : ávido, codicioso **2** ENTHUSIASTIC : ávido, entusiasta, ferviente — **avidly** *adv*

avocado [,ævə'kɑdo, ,ɑvə-] *n, pl* **-dos** : aguacate *m,* palta *f*

avocation [,ævə'keɪʃən] *n* : pasatiempo *m,* afición *f*

avoid [ə'vɔɪd] *vt* **1** SHUN : evitar, eludir **2** FORGO : evitar, abstenerse de <I always avoided gossip : siempre evitaba los chismes> **3** EVADE : evitar <if I can avoid it : si puedo evitarlo>

avoidable [ə'vɔɪdəbəl] *adj* : evitable

avoidance [ə'vɔɪdənts] *n* : el evitar

avoirdupois [,ævərdə'pɔɪz] *n* : sistema *m* inglés de pesos y medidas

avow [ə'vaʊ] *vt* : reconocer, confesar

avowal [ə'vaʊəl] *n* : reconocimiento *m,* confesión *f*

await [ə'weɪt] *vt* : esperar

awake[1] [ə'weɪk] *v* **awoke** [ə'wo:k]; **awoken** [ə'wo:kən] *or* **awaked; awaking** : despertar

awake[2] *adj* : despierto

awaken [ə'weɪkən] → **awake**[1]

award[1] [ə'wɔrd] *vt* : otorgar, conceder, conferir

award[2] *n* **1** PRIZE : premio *m,* galardón *m* **2** MEDAL : condecoración *f*

aware [ə'wær] *adj* : consciente <to be aware of : darse cuenta de, estar consciente de>

awareness [ə'wærnəs] *n* : conciencia *f,* conocimiento *m*

awash [ə'wɔʃ] *adj* : inundado

away[1] [ə'weɪ] *adv* **1** : de aquí <go away! : ¡fuera de aquí!, ¡vete!> **2** : de distancia <10 miles away : 10 millas de distancia, queda a 10 millas> **3 far away** : lejos, a lo lejos **4 right away** : en seguida, ahora mismo **5 to be away** : estar ausente, estar de viaje **6 to give away** : regalar (una posesión), revelar (un secreto) **7 to go away** : irse, largarse **8 to put away** : guardar **9 to turn away** : volver la cara

away[2] *adj* **1** ABSENT : ausente <away for the week : ausente por la semana> **2 away game** : partido *m* que se juega fuera

awe[1] ['ɔ] *vt* **awed; awing** : abrumar, asombrar, impresionar

awe[2] *n* : asombro *m*

awesome ['ɔsəm] *adj* **1** IMPOSING : imponente, formidable **2** AMAZING : asombroso

awestruck ['ɔ,strʌk] *adj* : asombrado

awful ['ɔfəl] *adj* **1** AWESOME : asombroso **2** DREADFUL : horrible, terrible, atroz **3** ENORMOUS : enorme, tremendo <an awful lot of people : muchísima gente, la mar de gente>

awfully ['ɔfəli] *adv* **1** EXTREMELY : terriblemente, extremadamente **2** BADLY : muy mal, espantosamente

awhile [ə'*h*waɪl] *adv* : un rato, algún tiempo

awkward ['ɔkwərd] *adj* **1** CLUMSY : torpe, desmañado **2** EMBARRASSING : embarazoso, delicado — **awkwardly** *adv*

awkwardness ['ɔkwərdnəs] *n* **1** CLUMSINESS : torpeza *f* **2** INCONVENIENCE : incomodidad *f*

awl ['ɔl] *n* : punzón *m*

awning ['ɔnɪŋ] *n* : toldo *m*

awry [ə'raɪ] *adj* 1 ASKEW : torcido **2 to go awry** : salir mal, fracasar

ax *or* **axe** ['æks] *n* : hacha *m*

axiom ['æksiəm] *n* : axioma *m*

axiomatic [,æksiə'mæt̬ɪk] *adj* : axiomático

axis ['æksɪs] *n, pl* **axes** [-,si:z] : eje *m*

axle ['æksəl] *n* : eje *m*

aye[1] ['aɪ] *adv* : sí

aye[2] *n* : sí *m*

azalea [ə'zeɪljə] *n* : azalea *f*

azimuth ['æzəməθ] *n* : azimut *m,* acimut *m*

azure[1] ['æʒər] *adj* : azur, celeste

azure[2] *n* : azur *m*

B

b ['bi:] *n, pl* **b's** *or* **bs** ['bi:z] : segunda letra del alfabeto inglés

babble[1] ['bæbəl] *vi* **-bled; -bling 1** PRATTLE : balbucear **2** CHATTER : charlatanear, parlotear *fam* **3** MURMUR : murmurar

babble[2] *n* : balbuceo *m* (de bebé), parloteo *m* (de adultos), murmullo *m* (de voces, de un arroyo)

babe ['beɪb] → **baby**[3]

babel ['beɪbəl, 'bæ-] *n* : babel *f,* caos *m*

baboon [bæ'bu:n] *n* : babuino *m*

baby[1] ['beɪbi] *vt* **-bied; -bying** : mimar, consentir

baby[2] *adj* **1** : de niño <a baby carriage : un cochecito> <baby talk : habla infantil> **2** TINY : pequeño, minúsculo

baby[3] *n, pl* **-bies** : bebé *m;* niño *m,* -ña *f*

babyhood ['beɪbi,hʊd] *n* : niñez *f,* primera infancia *f*

babyish ['beɪbiɪʃ] *adj* : infantil, pueril

baby–sit ['beɪbiˌsɪt] *vi* **-sat** [-ˌsæt]; **-sitting** : cuidar niños, hacer de canguro *Spain*

baby–sitter ['beɪbiˌsɪt̬ər] *n* : niñero *m,* -ra *f;* canguro *mf Spain*

baccalaureate [ˌbækə'lɔriət] *n* : licenciatura *f*

bachelor ['bætʃələr] *n* **1** : soltero *m* **2** : licenciado *m,* -da *f* <bachelor of arts degree : licenciatura en filosofía y letras>

bacillus [bə'sɪləs] *n, pl* **-li** [-ˌlaɪ] : bacilo *m*

back[1] ['bæk] *vt* **1** *or* **to back up** SUPPORT : apoyar, respaldar **2** *or* **to back up** REVERSE : darle marcha atrás a (un vehículo) **3** : estar detrás de, formar el fondo de <trees back the garden : unos árboles están detrás del jardín> — *vi* **1** *or* **to back up** : retroceder **2** **to back away** : echarse atrás **3** **to back down** *or* **to back out** : volverse atrás, echarse para atrás

back[2] *adv* **1** : atrás, hacia atrás, detrás <to move back : moverse atrás> <back and forth : de acá para allá> **2** AGO : atrás, antes, ya <some years back : unos años atrás, ya unos años> <10 months back : hace diez meses> **3** : de vuelta, de regreso <we're back : estamos de vuelta> <she ran back : volvió corriendo> <to call back : llamar de nuevo>

back[3] *adj* **1** REAR : de atrás, posterior, trasero **2** OVERDUE : atrasado **3** **back pay** : atrasos *mpl*

back[4] *n* **1** : espalda *f* (de un ser humano), lomo *m* (de un animal) **2** : respaldo *m* (de una silla), espalda *f* (de ropa) **3** REVERSE : reverso *m,* dorso *m,* revés *m* **4** REAR : fondo *m,* parte *f* de atrás **5** : defensa *mf* (en deportes)

backache ['bækˌeɪk] *n* : dolor *m* de espalda

backbite ['bækˌbaɪt] *v* **-bit** [-ˌbɪt]; **-bitten** [-ˌbɪtən]; **-biting** *vt* : calumniar, hablar mal de — *vi* : murmurar

backbiter ['bækˌbaɪt̬ər] *n* : calumniador *m,* -dora *f*

backbone ['bækˌboːn] *n* **1** : columna *f* vertebral **2** FIRMNESS : firmeza *f,* carácter *m*

backdrop ['bækˌdrɑp] *n* : telón *m* de fondo

backer ['bækər] *n* **1** SUPPORTER : partidario *m,* -ria *f* **2** SPONSOR : patrocinador *m,* -dora *f*

backfire[1] ['bækˌfaɪr] *vi* **-fired; -firing** **1** : petardear (dícese de un automóvil) **2** FAIL : fallar, salir el tiro por la culata

backfire[2] *n* : petardeo *m,* explosión *f*

background ['bækˌgraʊnd] *n* **1** : fondo *m* (de un cuadro, etc.), antecedentes *mpl* (de una situación) **2** EXPERIENCE, TRAINING : experiencia *f* profesional, formación *f*

backhand[1] ['bækˌhænd] *adv* : de revés, con el revés

backhand[2] *n* : revés *m*

backhanded ['bækˌhændəd] *adj* **1** : dado con el revés, de revés **2** INDIRECT : indirecto, ambiguo

backing ['bækɪŋ] *n* **1** SUPPORT : apoyo *m,* respaldo *m* **2** REINFORCEMENT : refuerzo *m* **3** SUPPORTERS : partidarios *mpl,* -rias *fpl*

backlash ['bækˌlæʃ] *n* : reacción *f* violenta

backlog ['bækˌlɔg] *n* : atraso *m,* trabajo *m* acumulado

backpack[1] ['bækˌpæk] *vi* : viajar con mochila

backpack[2] *n* : mochila *f*

backrest ['bækˌrɛst] *n* : respaldo *m*

backslide ['bækˌslaɪd] *vi* **-slid** [-ˌslɪd]; **-slid** *or* **-slidden** [-ˌslɪdən]; **-sliding** : recaer, reincidir

backstage [ˌbæk'steɪdʒ, 'bækˌ-] *adv & adj* : entre bastidores

backtrack ['bækˌtræk] *vi* : dar marcha atrás, volverse atrás

backup ['bækˌʌp] *n* **1** SUPPORT : respaldo *m,* apoyo *m* **2** : copia *f* de seguridad (para computadoras)

backward[1] ['bækwərd] *or* **backwards** [-wərdz] *adv* **1** : hacia atrás **2** : de espaldas <he fell backwards : se cayó de espaldas> **3** : al revés <you're doing it backwards : lo estás haciendo al revés> **4** **to bend over backwards** : hacer todo lo posible

backward[2] *adj* **1** : hacia atrás <a backward glance : una mirada hacia atrás> **2** RETARDED : retrasado **3** SHY : tímido **4** UNDERDEVELOPED : atrasado

backwardness ['bækwərdnəs] *n* : atraso *m* (dícese de una región), retraso *m* (dícese de una persona)

backwoods [ˌbæk'wʊdz] *npl* : monte *m,* región *f* alejada

bacon ['beɪkən] *n* : tocino *m,* tocineta *f Col, Ven,* bacon *m Spain*

bacterial [bæk'tɪriəl] *adj* : bacteriano

bacteriologist [bækˌtɪri'ɑlədʒɪst] *n* : bacteriólogo *m,* -ga *f*

bacteriology [bækˌtɪri'ɑlədʒi] *n* : bacteriología *f*

bacterium [bæk'tɪriəm] *n, pl* **-ria** [-iə] : bacteria *f*

bad[1] ['bæd] *adv* → **badly**

bad[2] *adj* **1** : malo **2** ROTTEN : podrido **3** SERIOUS, SEVERE : grave **4** DEFECTIVE : defectuoso <a bad check : un cheque sin fondos> **5** HARMFUL : perjudicial **6** CORRUPT, EVIL : malo, corrompido **7** NAUGHTY : travieso **8** **from bad to worse** : de mal en peor **9** **too bad!** : ¡qué lástima!

bad[3] *n* : lo malo <the good and the bad : lo bueno y lo malo>

bade → **bid**

badge ['bædʒ] *n* : insignia *f,* botón *m,* chapa *f*

badger[1] ['bædʒər] *vt* : fastidiar, acosar, importunar

badger[2] *n* : tejón *m*

badly [ˈbædli] *adv* **1** : mal **2** URGENTLY : mucho, con urgencia **3** SEVERELY : gravemente
badminton [ˈbæd,mɪntən, -,mɪt-] *n* : bádminton *m*
badness [ˈbædnəs] *n* : maldad *f*
baffle¹ [ˈbæfəl] *vi* **-fled; -fling 1** PERPLEX : desconcertar, confundir **2** FRUSTRATE : frustrar
baffle² *n* : deflector *m,* bafle *m* (acústico)
bafflement [ˈbæfəlmənt] *n* : desconcierto *m,* confusión *f*
bag¹ [ˈbæg] *v* **bagged; bagging** *vi* SAG : formar bolsas — *vt* **1** : ensacar, poner en una bolsa **2** : cobrar (en la caza), cazar
bag² *n* **1** : bolsa *f,* saco *m* **2** HANDBAG : cartera *f,* bolso *m,* bolsa *f Mex* **3** SUITCASE : maleta *f,* valija *f*
bagatelle [,bægəˈtɛl] *n* : bagatela *f*
bagel [ˈbeɪgəl] *n* : rosquilla *f* de pan
baggage [ˈbægɪdʒ] *n* : equipaje *m*
baggy [ˈbægi] *adj* **-gier; -est** : holgado, ancho
bagpipe [ˈbæg,paɪp] *n* : gaita *f*
bail¹ [ˈbeɪl] *vt* **1** : achicar (agua de un bote) **2 to bail out** : poner en libertad (de una cárcel) bajo fianza **3 to bail out** EXTRICATE : sacar de apuros
bail² *n* : fianza *f,* caución *f*
bailiff [ˈbeɪləf] *n* : aguacil *mf*
bailiwick [ˈbeɪli,wɪk] *n* : dominio *m*
bailout [ˈbeɪl,aʊt] *n* : rescate *m* (financial)
bait¹ [ˈbeɪt] *vt* **1** : cebar (un anzuelo o cepo) **2** HARASS : acosar
bait² *n* : cebo *m,* carnada *f*
bake¹ [ˈbeɪk] *vt* **baked; baking** : hornear, hacer al horno
bake² *n* : fiesta con platos hechos al horno
baker [ˈbeɪkər] *n* : panadero *m,* -ra *f*
baker's dozen *n* : docena *f* de fraile
bakery [ˈbeɪkəri] *n, pl* **-ries** : panadería *f*
bakeshop [ˈbeɪk,ʃɑp] *n* : pastelería *f,* panadería *f*
baking powder *n* : levadura *f* en polvo
baking soda → **sodium bicarbonate**
balance¹ [ˈbælənts] *v* **-anced; -ancing** *vt* **1** : hacer el balance de (una cuenta) <to balance the books : cuadrar las cuentas> **2** EQUALIZE : balancear, equilibrar **3** HARMONIZE : armonizar — *vi* : balancearse
balance² *n* **1** SCALES : balanza *f,* báscula *f* **2** COUNTERBALANCE : contrapeso *m* **3** EQUILIBRIUM : equilibrio *m* **4** REMAINDER : balance *m,* resto *m*
balanced [ˈbæləntst] *adj* : equilibrado, balanceado
balcony [ˈbælkəni] *n, pl* **-nies 1** : balcón *m,* terraza *f* (de un edificio) **2** : galería *f* (de un teatro)
bald [ˈbɔld] *adj* **1** : calvo, pelado, pelón **2** PLAIN : simple, puro <the bald truth : la pura verdad>
balding [ˈbɔldɪŋ] *adj* : quedándose calvo
baldly [ˈbɔldli] *adv* : sin reparos, sin rodeos, francamente
baldness [ˈbɔldnəs] *n* : calvicie *f*
bale¹ [ˈbeɪl] *vt* **baled; baling** : empacar, hacer balas de
bale² *n* : bala *f,* fardo *m,* paca *f*
baleful [ˈbeɪlfəl] *adj* **1** DEADLY : mortífero **2** SINISTER : siniestro, funesto, torvo <a baleful glance : una mirada torva>
balk¹ [ˈbɔk] *vt* : obstaculizar, impedir — *vi* **1** : plantarse *fam* (dícese de un caballo, etc.) **2 to balk at** : resistarse a, mostrarse reacio a
balk² *n* : obstáculo *m*
Balkan [ˈbɔlkən] *adj* : balcánico
balky [ˈbɔki] *adj* **balkier; -est** : reacio, obstinado, terco
ball¹ [ˈbɔl] *vt* : apelotonar, ovillar
ball² *n* **1** : pelota *f,* bola *f,* balón *m,* ovillo *m* (de lana) **2** : juego *m* con pelota o bola **3** DANCE : baile *m,* baile *m* de etiqueta
ballad [ˈbæləd] *n* : romance *m,* balada *f*
balladeer [,bæləˈdɪr] *n* : cantante *mf* de baladas
ballast¹ [ˈbæləst] *vt* : lastrear
ballast² *n* : lastre *m*
ball bearing *n* : cojinete *m* de bola
ballerina [,bæləˈriːnə] *n* : bailarina *f*
ballet [bæˈleɪ, ˈbæ,leɪ] *n* : ballet *m*
ballistic [bəˈlɪstɪk] *adj* : balístico
ballistics [bəˈlɪstɪks] *ns & pl* : balística *f*
balloon¹ [bəˈluːn] *vi* **1** : viajar en globo **2** SWELL : hincharse, inflarse
balloon² *n* : globo *m*
balloonist [bəˈluːnɪst] *n* : aeróstata *mf*
ballot¹ [ˈbælət] *vi* : votar
ballot² *n* **1** : papeleta *f* (de voto) **2** BALLOTING : votación *f* **3** VOTE : voto *m*
ballpoint pen [ˈbɔl,pɔɪnt] *n* : bolígrafo *m*
ballroom [ˈbɔl,ruːm, -,rʊm] *n* : sala *f* de baile
ballyhoo [ˈbæli,huː] *n* : propaganda *f,* publicidad *f,* bombo *m fam*
balm [ˈbɑm, ˈbɑlm] *n* : bálsamo *m,* ungüento *m*
balmy [ˈbɑmi, ˈbɑl-] *adj* **balmier; -est 1** MILD : templado, agradable **2** SOOTHING : balsámico **3** CRAZY : chiflado *fam,* chalado *fam*
baloney [bəˈloːni] *n* NONSENSE : tonterías *fpl,* estupideces *fpl*
balsa [ˈbɔlsə] *n* : balsa *f*
balsam [ˈbɔlsəm] *n* **1** : bálsamo *m* **2** *or* **balsam fir** : abeto *m* balsámico
baluster [ˈbæləstər] *n* : balaustre *m*
balustrade [ˈbælə,streɪd] *n* : balaustrada *f*
bamboo [bæmˈbuː] *n* : bambú *m*
bamboozle [bæmˈbuːzəl] *vt* **-zled; -zling** : engañar, embaucar
ban¹ [ˈbæn] *vt* **banned; banning** : prohibir, proscribir

ban[2] *n* : prohibición *f,* proscripción *f*

banal [bəˈnɑl, bəˈnæl, ˈbeɪnəl] *adj* : banal, trivial

banality [bəˈnæləṭi] *n, pl* **-ties** : banalidad *f,* trivialidad *f*

banana [bəˈnænə] *n* : banano *m,* plátano *m,* banana *f,* cambur *m Ven,* guineo *m Car*

band[1] [ˈbænd] *vt* **1** BIND : fajar, atar **2 to band together** : unirse, juntarse

band[2] *n* **1** STRIP : banda *f,* cinta *f* (de un sombrero, etc.) **2** STRIPE : franja *f* **3** : banda *f* (de radiofrecuencia) **4** RING : anillo *m* **5** GROUP : banda *f,* grupo *m,* conjunto *m* <jazz band : conjunto de jazz>

bandage[1] [ˈbændɪdʒ] *vt* **-daged; -daging** : vendar

bandage[2] *n* : vendaje *m,* venda *f*

bandanna *or* **bandana** [bænˈdænə] *n* : pañuelo *m* (de colores)

bandit [ˈbændət] *n* : bandido *m,* -da *f;* bandolero *m,* -ra *f*

banditry [ˈbændətri] *n* : bandolerismo *m,* bandidaje *m*

bandstand [ˈbændˌstænd] *n* : quiosco *m* de música

bandwagon [ˈbændˌwægən] *n* **1** : carroza *f* de músicos **2 to jump on the bandwagon** : subirse al carro, seguir la moda

bandy[1] [ˈbændi] *vt* **-died; -dying 1** EXCHANGE : intercambiar **2 to bandy about** : circular, propagar

bandy[2] *adj* : arqueado, torcido <bandy-legged : de piernas arqueadas>

bane [ˈbeɪn] *n* **1** POISON : veneno *m* **2** RUIN : ruina *f,* pesadilla *f*

baneful [ˈbeɪnfəl] *adj* : nefasto, funesto

bang[1] [ˈbæŋ] *vt* **1** STRIKE : golpear, darse <he banged his elbow against the door : se dio con el codo en la puerta> **2** SLAM : cerrar (la puerta) con un portazo — *vi* **1** SLAM : cerrarse de un golpe **2 to bang on** : aporrear, golpear <she was banging on the table : aporreaba la mesa>

bang[2] *adv* : directamente, exactamente

bang[3] *n* **1** BLOW : golpe *m,* porrazo *m,* trancazo *m* **2** EXPLOSION : explosión *f,* estallido *m* **3** SLAM : portazo *m* **4 bangs** *npl* : flequilla *f,* fleco *m*

Bangladeshi [ˌbɑŋgləˈdɛʃi, ˌbæŋ-, ˌbʌŋ-, -ˈdeɪ-] *n* : bangladesí *mf* — **Bangladeshi** *adj*

bangle [ˈbæŋgəl] *n* : brazalete *m,* pulsera *f*

banish [ˈbænɪʃ] *vt* **1** EXILE : desterrar, exiliar **2** EXPEL : expulsar

banishment [ˈbænɪʃmənt] *n* **1** EXILE : destierro *m,* exilio *m* **2** EXPULSION : expulsión *f*

banister [ˈbænəstər] *n* **1** BALUSTER : balaustre *m* **2** HANDRAIL : pasamanos *m,* barandilla *f,* barandal *m*

banjo [ˈbænˌdʒoː] *n, pl* **-jos** : banjo *m*

bank[1] [ˈbæŋk] *vt* **1** TILT : peraltar (una carretera), ladear (un avión) **2** HEAP : amontonar **3** : cubrir (un fuego) **4** : depositar (dinero en un banco) — *vi* **1** : ladearse (dícese de un avión) **2** : tener una cuenta (en un banco) **3 to bank on** : contar con

bank[2] *n* **1** MASS : montón *m,* montículo *m,* masa *f* **2** : orilla *f,* ribera *f* (de un río) **3** : peralte *m* (de una carretera) **4** : banco *m* <World Bank : Banco Mundial> <banco de sangre : blood bank>

bankbook [ˈbæŋkˌbʊk] *n* : libreta *f* bancaria, libreta *f* de ahorros

banker [ˈbæŋkər] *n* : banquero *m,* -ra *f*

bankrupt[1] [ˈbæŋˌkrʌpt] *vt* : hacer quebrar, llevar a la quiebra, arruinar

bankrupt[2] *adj* **1** : en bancarrota, en quiebra **2 ~ of** LACKING : carente de, falto de

bankrupt[3] *n* : fallido *m,* -da *f;* quebrado *m,* -da *f*

bankruptcy [ˈbæŋˌkrʌptsi] *n, pl* **-cies** : ruina *f,* quiebra *f,* bancarrota *f*

banner[1] [ˈbænər] *adj* : excelente

banner[2] *n* : estandarte *m,* bandera *f*

banns [ˈbænz] *npl* : amonestaciones *fpl*

banquet[1] [ˈbæŋkwət] *vi* : celebrar un banquete

banquet[2] *n* : banquete *m*

banter[1] [ˈbæntər] *vi* : bromear, hacer bromas

banter[2] *n* : bromas *fpl*

baptism [ˈbæpˌtɪzəm] *n* : bautismo *m*

baptismal [bæpˈtɪzməl] *adj* : bautismal

baptize [bæpˈtaɪz, ˈbæpˌtaɪz] *vt* **-tized; -tizing** : bautizar

bar[1] [ˈbɑr] *vt* **barred; barring 1** OBSTRUCT : obstruir, bloquear **2** EXCLUDE : excluir **3** PROHIBIT : prohibir **4** SECURE : atrancar, asegurar <bar the door! : ¡atranca la puerta!>

bar[2] *n* **1** : barra *f,* barrote *m* (de una ventana), tranca *f* (de una puerta) **2** BARRIER : barrera *f,* obstáculo *m* **3** LAW : abogacía *f* **4** STRIPE : franja *f* **5** COUNTER : mostrador *m,* barra *f* **6** TAVERN : bar *m,* taberna *f*

bar[3] *prep* **1** : excepto, con excepción de **2 bar none** : sin excepción

barb [ˈbɑrb] *n* **1** POINT : púa *f,* lengüeta *f* **2** GIBE : pulla *f*

barbarian[1] [bɑrˈbæriən] *adj* **1** : bárbaro **2** CRUDE : tosco, bruto

barbarian[2] *n* : bárbaro *m,* -ra *f*

barbaric [bɑrˈbærɪk] *adj* **1** PRIMITIVE : primitivo **2** CRUEL : brutal, cruel

barbarity [bɑrˈbærəṭi] *n, pl* **-ties** : barbaridad *f*

barbarous [ˈbɑrbərəs] *adj* **1** UNCIVILIZED : bárbaro **2** MERCILESS : despiadado, cruel

barbarously [ˈbɑrbərəsli] *adv* : bárbaramente

barbecue[1] [ˈbarbɪˌkjuː] *vt* **-cued; -cuing** : asar a la parrilla
barbecue[2] *n* : barbacoa *f,* parrillada *f*
barber [ˈbarbər] *n* : barbero *m,* -ra *f*
barbiturate [barˈbɪtʃərət] *n* : barbitúrico *m*
bard [ˈbard] *n* : bardo *m*
bare[1] [ˈbær] *vt* **bared; baring** : desnudar
bare[2] *adj* **1** NAKED : desnudo **2** EXPOSED : descubierto, sin protección **3** EMPTY : desprovisto, vacío **4** MINIMUM : mero, mínimo <the bare necessities : las necesidades mínimas> **5** PLAIN : puro, sencillo
bareback [ˈbærˌbæk] *or* **barebacked** [-ˌbækt] *adv & adj* : a pelo
barefaced [ˈbærˌfeɪst] *adj* : descarado
barefoot [ˈbærˌfʊt] *or* **barefooted** [-ˌfʊtəd] *adv & adj* : descalzo
bareheaded [ˈbærˈhɛdəd] *adv & adj* : sin sombrero, con la cabeza descubierta
barely [ˈbærli] *adv* : apenas, por poco
bareness [ˈbærnəs] *n* : desnudez *f*
bargain[1] [ˈbargən] *vi* HAGGLE : regatear, negociar — *vt* BARTER : trocar, cambiar
bargain[2] *n* **1** AGREEMENT : acuerdo *m,* convenio *m* <to strike a bargain : cerrar un trato> **2** : ganga *f* <bargain price : precio de ganga>
barge[1] [ˈbardʒ] *vi* **barged; barging 1** : mover con torpeza **2 to barge in** : entrometerse, interrumpir
barge[2] *n* : barcaza *f,* gabarra *f*
bar graph *n* : gráfico *m* de barras
baritone [ˈbærəˌtoːn] *n* : barítono *m*
barium [ˈbæriəm] *n* : bario *m*
bark[1] [ˈbark] *vi* : ladrar — *vt or* **to bark out** : gritar <to bark out an order : dar una orden a gritos>
bark[2] *n* **1** : ladrido *m* (de un perro) **2** : corteza *f* (de un árbol) **3** *or* **barque** : tipo de embarcación con velas de proa y popa
barley [ˈbarli] *n* : cebada *f*
barn [ˈbarn] *n* : granero *m* (para cosechas), establo *m* (para ganado)
barnacle [ˈbarnɪkəl] *n* : percebe *m*
barnyard [ˈbarnˌjard] *n* : corral *m*
barometer [bəˈramət̬ər] *n* : barómetro *m*
barometric [ˌbærəˈmɛtrɪk] *adj* : barométrico
baron [ˈbærən] *n* **1** : barón *m* **2** TYCOON : magnate *mf*
baroness [ˈbærənɪs, -nəs, -ˌnɛs] *n* : baronesa *f*
baronet [ˌbærəˈnɛt, ˈbærənət] *n* : baronet *m*
baronial [bəˈroːniəl] *adj* **1** : de barón **2** STATELY : señorial, majestuoso
baroque [bəˈroːk, -ˈrak] *adj* : barroco
barracks [ˈbærəks] *ns & pl* : cuartel *m*
barracuda [ˌbærəˈkuːdə] *n, pl* **-da** *or* **-das** : barracuda *f*
barrage [bəˈraʒ, -ˈradʒ] *n* **1** : descarga *f* (de artillería) **2** DELUGE : aluvión *m* <a barrage of questions : un aluvión de preguntas>
barred [ˈbard] *adj* : excluido, prohibido
barrel[1] [ˈbærəl] *v* **-reled** *or* **-relled; -reling** *or* **-relling** *vt* : embarrilar — *vi* : ir disparado
barrel[2] *n* **1** : barril *m,* tonel *m* **2** : cañón *m* (de un arma de fuego), cilindro *m* (de una cerradura)
barren [ˈbærən] *adj* **1** STERILE : estéril (dícese de las plantas o la mujer), árido (dícese del suelo) **2** DESERTED : yermo, desierto
barrette [baˈrɛt, bə-] *n* : pasador *m,* broche *m* para el cabello
barricade[1] [ˈbærəˌkeɪd, ˌbærəˈ-] *vt* **-caded; -cading** : cerrar con barricadas
barricade[2] *n* : barricada *f*
barrier [ˈbæriər] *n* **1** : barrera *f* **2** OBSTACLE : obstáculo *m,* impedimento *m*
barring [ˈbarɪŋ] *prep* : excepto, salvo, a excepción de
barrio [ˈbario, ˈbær-] *n* : barrio *m*
barroom [ˈbarˌruːm, -ˌrʊm] *n* : bar *m*
barrow [ˈbærˌoː] → **wheelbarrow**
bartender [ˈbarˌtɛndər] *n* : camarero *m,* -ra *f;* barman *m*
barter[1] [ˈbart̬ər] *vt* : cambiar, trocar
barter[2] *n* : trueque *m,* permuta *f*
basalt [bəˈsɔlt, ˈbeɪˌ-] *n* : basalto *m*
base[1] [ˈbeɪs] *vt* **based; basing** : basar, fundamentar, establecer
base[2] *adj* **baser; basest 1** : de baja ley (dícese de un metal) **2** CONTEMPTIBLE : vil, despreciable
base[3] *n, pl* **bases** : base *f*
baseball [ˈbeɪsˌbɔl] *n* : beisbol *m,* béisbol *m*
baseless [ˈbeɪsləs] *adj* : infundado
basely [ˈbeɪsli] *adv* : vilmente
basement [ˈbeɪsmənt] *n* : sótano *m*
baseness [ˈbeɪsnəs] *n* : vileza *f,* bajeza *f*
bash[1] [ˈbæʃ] *vt* : golpear violentamente
bash[2] *n* **1** BLOW : golpe *m,* porrazo *m,* madrazo *m Mex fam* **2** PARTY: fiesta *f,* juerga *f fam*
bashful [ˈbæʃfəl] *adj* : tímido, vergonzoso, penoso
bashfulness [ˈbæʃfəlnəs] *n* : timidez *f*
basic [ˈbeɪsɪk] *adj* **1** FUNDAMENTAL : básico, fundamental **2** RUDIMENTARY : básico, elemental **3** : básico (en química)
basically [ˈbeɪsɪkli] *adv* : fundamentalmente
basil [ˈbeɪzəl, ˈbæzəl] *n* : albahaca *f*
basilica [bəˈsɪlɪkə] *n* : basílica *f*
basin [ˈbeɪsən] *n* **1** WASHBOWL : palangana *f,* lavamanos *m,* lavabo *m* **2** : cuenca *f* (de un río)
basis [ˈbeɪsəs] *n, pl* **bases** [-ˌsiːz] **1** BASE : base *f,* pilar *m* **2** FOUNDATION : fundamento *m,* base *f* **3 on a weekly basis** : semanalmente

bask [ˈbæsk] *vi* **:** disfrutar, deleitarse <to bask in the sun : disfrutar del sol>

basket [ˈbæskət] *n* **:** cesta *f,* cesto *m,* canasta *f*

basketball [ˈbæskətˌbɔl] *n* **:** baloncesto *m,* basquetbol *m*

bas–relief [ˌbɑrɪˈliːf] *n* **:** bajorrelieve *m*

bass[1] [ˈbæs] *n, pl* **bass** *or* **basses** **:** róbalo *m* (pesca)

bass[2] [ˈbeɪs] *n* **:** bajo *m* (tono, voz, cantante)

bass drum *n* **:** bombo *m*

basset hound [ˈbæsətˌhaʊnd] *n* **:** basset *m*

bassinet [ˌbæsəˈnɛt] *n* **:** moisés *m,* cuna *f*

bassoon [bəˈsuːn, bæ-] *n* **:** fagot *m*

bass viol [ˈbeɪsˈvaɪəl, -ˌoːl] → **double bass**

bastard[1] [ˈbæstərd] *adj* **:** bastardo

bastard[2] *n* **:** bastardo *m,* -da *f*

bastardize [ˈbæstərˌdaɪz] *vt* **-ized; -izing** DEBASE **:** degradar, envilecer

baste [ˈbeɪst] *vt* **basted; basting 1** STITCH **:** hilvanar **2 :** bañar (con su jugo durante la cocción)

bastion [ˈbæstʃən] *n* **:** bastión *m,* baluarte *m*

bat[1] [ˈbæt] *vt* **batted; batting 1** HIT **:** batear **2 without batting an eye :** sin pestañear

bat[2] *n* **1 :** murciélago *m* (animal) **2 :** bate *m* <baseball bat : bate de beisbol>

batch [ˈbætʃ] *n* **:** hornada *f,* tanda *f,* grupo *m,* cantidad *f*

bate [ˈbeɪt] *vt* **bated; bating 1 :** aminorar, reducir **2 with bated breath :** con ansiedad, aguantando la respiración

bath [ˈbæθ, ˈbaθ] *n, pl* **baths** [ˈbæðz, ˈbæθs, ˈbaðz, ˈbaθs] **1** BATHING **:** baño *m* <to take a bath : bañarse> **2 :** baño *m* (en fotografía, etc.) **3** BATHROOM **:** baño *m,* cuarto *m* de baño **4** SPA **:** balneario *m* **5** LOSS **:** pérdida *f*

bathe [ˈbeɪð] *v* **bathed; bathing** *vt* **1** WASH **:** bañar, lavar **2** SOAK **:** poner en remojo **3** FLOOD **:** inundar <to bathe with light : inundar de luz> — *vi* **:** bañarse, ducharse

bather [ˈbeɪðər] *n* **:** bañista *mf*

bathrobe [ˈbæθˌroːb] *n* **:** bata *f* (de baño)

bathroom [ˈbæθˌruːm, -ˌrʊm] *n* **:** baño *m,* cuarto *m* de baño

bathtub [ˈbæθˌtʌb] *n* **:** bañera *f,* tina *f* (de baño)

batiste [bəˈtiːst] *n* **:** batista *f*

baton [bəˈtɑn] *n* **:** batuta *f,* bastón *m*

battalion [bəˈtæljən] *n* **:** batallón *m*

batten [ˈbætən] *vt* **to batten down the hatches :** cerrar las escotillas

batter[1] [ˈbæt̬ər] *vt* **1** BEAT **:** aporrear, golpear **2** MISTREAT **:** maltratar

batter[2] *n* **1 :** masa *f* para rebozar **2** HITTER **:** bateador *m,* -dora *f*

battering ram *n* **:** ariete *m*

battery [ˈbæt̬əri] *n, pl* **-teries 1 :** lesiones *fpl* <assault and battery : agresión con lesiones> **2** ARTILLERY **:** batería *f* **3 :** batería *f,* pila *f* (de electricidad) **4** SERIES **:** serie *f*

batting [ˈbæt̬ɪŋ] *n* **1** *or* **cotton batting :** algodón *m* en láminas **2 :** bateo *m* (en beisbol)

battle[1] [ˈbæt̬əl] *vi* **-tled; -tling :** luchar, pelear

battle[2] *n* **:** batalla *f,* lucha *f,* pelea *f*

battle–ax [ˈbæt̬əlˌæks] *n* **:** hacha *f* de guerra

battlefield [ˈbæt̬əlˌfiːld] *n* **:** campo *m* de batalla

battlements [ˈbæt̬əlmənts] *npl* **:** almenas *fpl*

battleship [ˈbæt̬əlˌʃɪp] *n* **:** acorazado *m*

batty [ˈbæt̬i] *adj* **-tier; -est :** chiflado *fam,* chalado *fam*

bauble [ˈbɔbəl] *n* **:** chuchería *f,* baratija *f*

bawdiness [ˈbɔdinəs] *n* **:** picardía *f*

bawdy [ˈbɔdi] *adj* **bawdier; -est :** subido de tono, verde, colorado *Mex*

bawl[1] [ˈbɔl] *vi* **:** llorar a gritos

bawl[2] *n* **:** grito *m,* alarido *m*

bawl out *vt* SCOLD **:** regañar

bay[1] [ˈbeɪ] *vi* HOWL **:** aullar

bay[2] *adj* **:** castaño, zaino (dícese de los caballos)

bay[3] *n* **1 :** bahía *f* <Bay of Campeche : Bahía de Campeche> **2** *or* **bay horse :** caballo *m* castaño **3** LAUREL **:** laurel *m* **4** HOWL **:** aullido *m* **5 :** saliente *m* <bay window : ventana en saliente> **6** COMPARTMENT **:** área *f,* compartimento *m* **7 at ~ :** acorralado

bayberry [ˈbeɪˌbɛri] *n, pl* **-ries :** arrayán *m* brabántico

bayonet[1] [ˌbeɪəˈnɛt, ˈbeɪəˌnɛt] *vt* **-neted; -neting :** herir (*o* matar) con bayoneta

bayonet[2] *n* **:** bayoneta *f*

bayou [ˈbaɪˌuː, -ˌoː] *n* **:** pantano *m*

bazaar [bəˈzɑr] *n* **1 :** bazar *m* **2** SALE **:** venta *f* benéfica

bazooka [bəˈzuːkə] *n* **:** bazuca *f*

BB [ˈbiːbi] *n* **:** balín *m*

be [ˈbiː] *v* **was** [ˈwəz, ˈwɑz], **were** [ˈwər]; **been** [ˈbɪn]; **being; am** [ˈæm], **is** [ˈɪz], **are** [ˈɑr] *vi* **1** (*expressing equality*) **:** ser <José is a doctor : José es doctor> <I'm Ana's sister : soy la hermana de Ana> **2** (*expressing quality*) **:** ser <the tree is tall : el árbol es alto> <you're silly! : ¡eres tonto!> **3** (*expressing origin or possession*) **:** ser <she's from Managua : es de Managua> <it's mine : es mío> **4** (*expressing location*) **:** estar <my mother is at home : mi madre está en casa> <the cups are on the table : las tazas están en la mesa> **5** (*expressing existence*) **:** ser, existir <to be or not to be : ser, o no ser> <I think, therefore I am : pienso, luego existo> **6** (*expressing a state of being*)

: estar, tener <how are you? : ¿cómo estás?> <I'm cold : tengo frío> <she's 10 years old : tiene 10 años> <they're both sick : están enfermos los dos> — *v impers* **1** (*indicating time*) : ser <it's eight o'clock : son las ocho> <it's Friday : hoy es viernes> **2** (*indicating a condition*) : hacer, estar <it's sunny : hace sol> <it's very dark outside : está bien oscuro afuera> — *v aux* **1** (*expressing progression*) : estar <what are you doing? —I'm working : ¿qué haces? —estoy trabajando> **2** (*expressing occurrence*) : ser <it was finished yesterday : fue acabado ayer, se acabó ayer> <it was cooked in the oven : se cocinó en el horno> **3** (*expressing possibility*) : poderse <can she be trusted? : ¿se puede confiar en ella?> **4** (*expressing obligation*) : deber <you are to stay here : debes quedarte aquí> <he was to come yesterday : se esperaba que viniese ayer>

beach[1] [ˈbiːtʃ] *vt* : hacer embarrancar, hacer varar, hacer encallar

beach[2] *n* : playa *f*

beachcomber [ˈbiːtʃˌkoːmər] *n* : raquero *m*, -ra *f*

beachhead [ˈbiːtʃˌhɛd] *n* : cabeza *f* de playa

beacon [ˈbiːkən] *n* : faro *m*

bead[1] [ˈbiːd] *vi* : formarse en gotas

bead[2] *n* **1** : cuenta *f* **2** DROP : gota *f* **3** **beads** *npl* NECKLACE : collar *m*

beady [ˈbiːdi] *adj* **beadier; -est** **1** : de forma de cuenta **2** **beady eyes** : ojos *mpl* pequeños y brillantes

beagle [ˈbiːgəl] *n* : beagle *m*

beak [ˈbiːk] *n* : pico *m*

beaker [ˈbiːkər] *n* **1** CUP : taza *f* alta **2** : vaso *m* de precipitados (en un laboratorio)

beam[1] [ˈbiːm] *vi* **1** SHINE : brillar **2** SMILE : sonreír radiantemente — *vt* BROADCAST : transmitir, emitir

beam[2] *n* **1** : viga *f*, barra *f* **2** RAY : rayo *m*, haz *m* de luz **3** : haz *m* de radiofaro (para guiar pilotos, etc.)

bean [ˈbiːn] *n* **1** : habichuela *f*, frijol *m* **2** **broad bean** : haba *f* **3** **string bean** : judía *f*

bear[1] [ˈbær] *v* **bore** [ˈbor]; **borne** [ˈbɔrn]; **bearing** *vt* **1** CARRY : llevar, portar **2** : dar a luz a (un niño) **3** PRODUCE : dar (frutas, cosechas) **4** ENDURE, SUPPORT : soportar, resistir, aguantar — *vi* **1** TURN : doblar, dar la vuelta <bear right : doble a la derecha> **2** **to bear up** : resistir

bear[2] *n, pl* **bears** *or* **bear** : oso *m*, osa *f*

bearable [ˈbærəbəl] *adj* : soportable

beard [ˈbɪrd] *n* **1** : barba *f* **2** : arista *f* (de plantas)

bearded [ˈbɪrdəd] *adj* : barbudo, de barba

bearer [ˈbærər] *n* : portador *m*, -dora *f*

bearing [ˈbærɪŋ] *n* **1** CONDUCT, MANNERS : comportamiento *m*, modales *mpl* **2** SUPPORT : soporte *f* **3** SIGNIFICANCE : relacíon *f*, importancia *f* <to have no bearing on : no tener nada que ver con> **4** : cojinete *m*, rodamiento *m* (de una máquina) **5** COURSE, DIRECTION : dirección *f*, rumbo *m* <to get one's bearings : orientarse>

beast [ˈbiːst] *n* **1** : bestia *f*, fiera *f* <beast of burden : animal de carga> **2** BRUTE : bruto *m*, -ta *f*; bestia *mf*

beastly [ˈbiːstli] *adj* : detestable, repugnante

beat[1] [ˈbiːt] *v* **beat; beaten** [ˈbiːtən] *or* **beat; beating** *vt* **1** STRIKE : golpear, pegar, darle una paliza (a alguien) **2** DEFEAT : vencer, derrotar **3** AVOID : anticiparse a, evitar <to beat the crowd : evitar el gentío> **4** MASH, WHIP : batir — *vi* THROB : palpitar, latir

beat[2] *adj* EXHAUSTED : derrengado, muy cansado <I'm beat! : ¡estoy molido!>

beat[3] *n* **1** : golpe *m*, redoble *m* (de un tambor), latido *m* (del corazón) **2** RHYTHM : ritmo *m*, tiempo *m*

beater [ˈbiːtər] *n* **1** : batidor *m*, -dora *f* **2** EGGBEATER : batidor *m*

beatific [ˌbiːəˈtɪfɪk] *adj* : beatífico

beatitude [biˈætəˌtuːd] *n* **1** : beatitud *f* **2** **the Beatitudes** : las bienaventuranzas

beau [ˈboː] *n, pl* **beaux** *or* **beaus** : pretendiente *m*, galán *m*

beautification [ˌbjuːtəfəˈkeɪʃən] *n* : embellecimiento *m*

beautiful [ˈbjuːtɪfəl] *adj* : hermoso, bello, lindo, precioso

beautifully [ˈbjuːtɪfəli] *adv* **1** ATTRACTIVELY : hermosamente **2** EXCELLENTLY : maravillosamente, excelentemente

beauty [ˈbjuːti] *n, pl* **-ties** : belleza *f*, hermosura *f*, beldad *f*

beauty shop *or* **beauty salon** *n* : salón *m* de belleza

beaver [ˈbiːvər] *n* : castor *m*

because [bɪˈkʌz, -ˈkɔz] *conj* : porque

because of *prep* : por, a causa de, debido a

beck [ˈbɛk] *n* **to be at the beck and call of** : estar a la entera disposición de, estar sometido a la voluntad de

beckon [ˈbɛkən] *vi* **to beckon to someone** : hacerle señas a alguien

become [bɪˈkʌm] *v* **-came** [-ˈkeɪm]; **-come; -coming** *vi* : hacerse, volverse, ponerse <he became famous : se hizo famoso> <to become sad : ponerse triste> <to become accustomed to : acostumbrarse a> — *vt* **1** BEFIT : ser apropiado para **2** SUIT : favorecer, quedarle bien (a alguien) <that dress becomes you : ese vestido te favorece>

becoming [bɪˈkʌmɪŋ] *adj* **1** SUITABLE : apropiado **2** FLATTERING : favorecedor

bed[1] [ˈbɛd] *v* **bedded; bedding** *vt* : acostar — *vi* : acostarse

bed[2] *n* **1** : cama *f*, lecho *m* **2** : cauce *m* (de un río), fondo *m* (del mar) **3**

: arriate *m* (para plantas) **4** LAYER, STRATUM : estrato *m,* capa *f*
bedbug ['bɛd,bʌg] *n* : chinche *f*
bedclothes ['bɛd,klo:ðz, -,klo:z] *npl* : ropa *f* de cama, sábanas *fpl*
bedding ['bɛdɪŋ] *n* **1** → **bedclothes 2** : cama *f* (para animales)
bedeck [bɪ'dɛk] *vt* : adornar, engalanar
bedevil [bɪ'dɛvəl] *vt* **-iled** *or* **-illed; -iling** *or* **-illing** : acosar, plagar
bedlam ['bɛdləm] *n* : locura *f,* caos *m,* alboroto *m*
bedraggled [bɪ'drægəld] *adj* : desaliñado, despeinado
bedridden ['bɛd,rɪdən] *adj* : postrado en cama
bedrock ['bɛd,rɑk] *n* : lecho *m* de roca
bedroom ['bɛd,ru:m, -,rʊm] *n* : dormitorio *m,* habitación *f,* pieza *f,* recámara *f Col, Mex, Pan*
bedspread ['bɛd,sprɛd] *n* : cubrecama *m,* colcha *f,* cobertor *m*
bee ['bi:] *n* **1** : abeja *f* (insecto) **2** GATHERING : círculo *m,* reunión *f*
beech ['bi:tʃ] *n, pl* **beeches** *or* **beech** : haya *f*
beechnut ['bi:tʃ,nʌt] *n* : hayuco *m*
beef[1] ['bi:f] *vt* **to beef up** : fortalecer, reforzar — *vi* COMPLAIN : quejarse
beef[2] *n, pl* **beefs** ['bi:fs] *or* **beeves** ['bi:vz] : carne *f* de vaca, carne *f* de res *CA, Mex*
beefsteak ['bi:f,steɪk] *n* : filete *m,* bistec *m*
beehive ['bi:,haɪv] *n* : colmena *f*
beekeeper ['bi:,ki:pər] *n* : apicultor *m,* -tora *f*
beeline ['bi:,laɪn] *n* **to make a beeline for** : ir derecho a, ir directo hacia
been → **be**
beep[1] ['bi:p] *v* : pitar
beep[2] *n* : pitido *m*
beeper ['bi:pər] *n* : busca *m,* buscapersonas *m*
beer ['bɪr] *n* : cerveza *f*
beeswax ['bi:z,wæks] *n* : cera *f* de abejas
beet ['bi:t] *n* : remolacha *f,* betabel *m Mex*
beetle ['bi:təl] *n* : escarabajo *m*
befall [bɪ'fɔl] *v* **-fell** [-'fɛl]; **-fallen** [-'fɔlən] *vt* : sucederle a, acontecerle a — *vi* : acontecer
befit [bɪ'fɪt] *vt* **-fitted; -fitting** : convenir a, ser apropiado para
before[1] [bɪ'for] *adv* **1** : antes <before and after : antes y después> **2** : anterior <the month before : el mes anterior>
before[2] *conj* : antes que <he would die before surrendering : moriría antes que rendirse>
before[3] *prep* **1** : antes de <before eating : antes de comer> **2** : delante de, ante <I stood before the house : estaba parada delante de la casa> <before the judge : ante el juez>
beforehand [bɪ'for,hænd] *adv* : antes, por adelantado, de antemano, con anticipación
befriend [bɪ'frɛnd] *vt* : hacerse amigo de
befuddle [bɪ'fʌdəl] *vt* **-dled; -dling** : aturdir, ofuscar, confundir
beg ['bɛg] *v* **begged; begging** *vt* : pedir, mendigar, suplicar <I begged him to go : le supliqué que fuera> — *vi* : mendigar, pedir limosna
beget [bɪ'gɛt] *vt* **-got** [-'gɑt]; **-gotten** [-'gɑtən] *or* **-got; -getting** : engendrar
beggar ['bɛgər] *n* : mendigo *m,* -ga *f;* pordiosero *m,* -ra *f*
begin [bɪ'gɪn] *v* **-gan** [-'gæn]; **-gun** [-'gʌn]; **-ginning** *vt* : empezar, comenzar, iniciar — *vi* **1** START : empezar, comenzar, iniciarse **2** ORIGINATE : nacer, originarse **3 to begin with** : en primer lugar, para empezar
beginner [bɪ'gɪnər] *n* : principiante *mf*
beginning [bɪ'gɪnɪŋ] *n* : principio *m,* comienzo *m*
begone [bi'gɔn] *interj* : ¡fuera de aquí!
begonia [bɪ'go:njə] *n* : begonia *f*
begrudge [bɪ'grʌdʒ] *vt* **-grudged; -grudging 1** : dar de mala gana **2** ENVY : envidiar, resentir
beguile [bɪ'gaɪl] *vt* **-guiled; -guiling 1** DECEIVE : engañar **2** AMUSE : divertir, entretener
behalf [bɪ'hæf, -'haf] *n* **1** : favor *m,* beneficio *m,* parte *f* **2 on behalf of** *or* **in behalf of** : de parte de, en nombre de
behave [bɪ'heɪv] *vi* **-haved; -having** : comportarse, portarse
behavior [bɪ'heɪvjər] *n* : comportamiento *m,* conducta *f*
behead [bɪ'hɛd] *vt* : decapitar
behest [bɪ'hɛst] *n* **1** : mandato *m,* orden *f* **2 at the behest of** : a instancia de
behind[1] [bɪ'haɪnd] *adv* : atrás, detrás <to fall behind : quedarse atrás>
behind[2] *prep* **1** : atrás de, detrás de, tras <behind the house : detrás de la casa> <one behind another : uno tras otro> **2** : atrasado con, después de <behind schedule : atrasado con el trabajo> <I arrived behind the others : llegué después de los otros> **3** SUPPORTING : en apoyo de, detrás
behold [bɪ'ho:ld] *vt* **-held; -holding** : contemplar
beholder [bɪ'ho:ldər] *n* : observador *m,* -dora *f*
behoove [bɪ'hu:v] *vt* **-hooved; -hooving** : convenirle a, corresponderle a <it behooves us to help him : nos conviene ayudarlo>
beige[1] ['beɪʒ] *adj* : beige
beige[2] *n* : beige *m*
being ['bi:ɪŋ] *n* **1** EXISTENCE : ser *m,* existencia *f* **2** CREATURE : ser *m,* ente *m*
belabor [bɪ'leɪbər] *vt* **to belabor the point** : extenderse sobre el tema

belated [bɪˈleɪt̬əd] *adj* : tardío, retrasado

belch[1] [ˈbɛltʃ] *vi* **1** BURP : eructar **2** EXPEL : expulsar, arrojar

belch[2] *n* : eructo *m*

beleaguer [bɪˈliːgər] *vt* **1** BESIEGE : asediar, sitiar **2** HARASS : fastidiar, molestar

belfry [ˈbɛlfri] *n, pl* **-fries** : campanario *m*

Belgian [ˈbɛldʒən] *n* : belga *mf* — **Belgian** *adj*

belie [bɪˈlaɪ] *vt* **-lied; -lying 1** MISREPRESENT : falsear, ocultar **2** CONTRADICT : contradecir, desmentir

belief [bəˈliːf] *n* **1** TRUST : confianza *f* **2** CONVICTION : creencia *f,* convicción *f* **3** FAITH : fe *f*

believable [bəˈliːvəbəl] *adj* : verosímil, creíble

believe [bəˈliːv] *v* **-lieved; -lieving** : creer

believer [bəˈliːvər] *n* **1** : creyente *mf* **2** : partidario *m,* -ria *f;* entusiasta *mf* <she's a great believer in vitamins : ella es una gran partidaria de las vitaminas>

belittle [bɪˈlɪt̬əl] *vt* **-littled; -littling 1** DISPARAGE : menospreciar, denigrar, rebajar **2** MINIMIZE : minimizar, quitar importancia a

Belizean [bəˈliːziən] *n* : beliceño *m,* -ña *f* — **Belizean** *adj*

bell[1] [ˈbɛl] *vt* : ponerle un cascabel a

bell[2] *n* : campana *f,* cencerro *m* (para una vaca o cabra), cascabel *m* (para un gato), timbre *m* (de teléfono, de la puerta)

belladonna [ˌbɛləˈdɑnə] *n* : belladona *f*

belle [ˈbɛl] *n* : belleza *f,* beldad *f*

bellhop [ˈbɛlˌhɑp] *n* : botones *m*

bellicose [ˈbɛlɪˌkoːs] *adj* : belicoso *m* — **bellicosity** [ˌbɛlɪˈkɑsət̬i] *n*

belligerence [bəˈlɪdʒərən*t*s] *n* : agresividad *f,* beligerancia *f*

belligerent[1] [bəˈlɪdʒərənt] *adj* : agresivo, beligerante

belligerent[2] *n* : beligerante *mf*

bellow[1] [ˈbɛˌloː] *vi* : bramar, mugir — *vt* : gritar

bellow[2] *n* : bramido *m,* grito *m*

bellows [ˈbɛˌloːz] *ns & pl* : fuelle *m*

bellwether [ˈbɛlˌwɛðər] *n* : líder *mf*

belly[1] [ˈbɛli] *vi* **-lied; -lying** SWELL : hincharse, inflarse

belly[2] *n, pl* **-lies** : abdomen *m,* vientre *m,* barriga *f,* panza *f*

belong [bɪˈlɔŋ] *vi* **1** : pertenecer (a), ser propiedad (de) <it belongs to her : pertenece a ella, es suyo, es de ella> **2** : ser parte (de), ser miembro (de) <he belongs to the club : es miembro del club> **3** : deber estar, ir <your coat belongs in the closet : tu abrigo va en el ropero>

belongings [bɪˈlɔŋɪŋz] *npl* : pertenencias *fpl,* efectos *mpl* personales

beloved[1] [bɪˈlʌvəd, -ˈlʌvd] *adj* : querido, amado

beloved[2] *n* : amado *m,* -da *f;* enamorado *m,* -da *f;* amor *m*

below[1] [bɪˈloː] *adv* : abajo

below[2] *prep* **1** : abajo de, debajo de <below the window : debajo de la ventana> **2** : por debajo de, bajo <below average : por debajo del promedio> <5 degrees below zero : 5 grados bajo cero>

belt[1] [ˈbɛlt] *vt* **1** : ceñir con un cinturón, ponerle un cinturón a **2** THRASH : darle una paliza a, darle un trancazo a

belt[2] *n* **1** : cinturón *m,* cinto *m* (para el talle) **2** BAND, STRAP : cinta *f,* correa *f,* banda *f Mex* **3** AREA : frente *m,* zona *f*

bemoan [bɪˈmoːn] *vt* : lamentarse de

bemuse [bɪˈmjuːz] *vt* **-mused; -musing 1** BEWILDER : confundir, desconcertar **2** ENGROSS : absorber

bench [ˈbɛntʃ] *n* **1** SEAT : banco *m,* escaño *m,* banca *f* **2** : estrado *m* (de un juez) **3** COURT : tribunal *m*

bend[1] [ˈbɛnd] *v* **bent** [ˈbɛnt]; **bending** *vt* : torcer, doblar, curvar, flexionar — *vi* **1** : torcerse, agacharse <to bend over : inclinarse> **2** TURN : torcer, hacer una curva

bend[2] *n* **1** TURN : vuelta *f,* recodo *m* **2** CURVE : curva *f,* ángulo *m,* codo *m*

beneath[1] [bɪˈniːθ] *adv* : bajo, abajo, debajo

beneath[2] *prep* : bajo de, abajo de, por debajo de

benediction [ˌbɛnəˈdɪkʃən] *n* : bendición *f*

benefactor [ˈbɛnəˌfæktər] *n* : benefactor *m,* -tora *f*

beneficence [bəˈnɛfəsən*t*s] *n* : beneficencia *f*

beneficent [bəˈnɛfəsənt] *adj* : benéfico, caritativo

beneficial [ˌbɛnəˈfɪʃəl] *adj* : beneficioso, provechoso — **beneficially** *adv*

beneficiary [ˌbɛnəˈfɪʃiˌɛri, -ˈfɪʃəri] *n, pl* **-ries** : beneficiario *m,* -ria *f*

benefit[1] [ˈbɛnəfɪt] *vt* : beneficiar — *vi* : beneficiarse

benefit[2] *n* **1** ADVANTAGE : beneficio *m,* ventaja *f,* provecho *m* **2** AID : asistencia *f,* beneficio *m* **3** : función *f* benéfica (para recaudar fondos)

benevolence [bəˈnɛvələn*t*s] *n* : bondad *f,* benevolencia *f*

benevolent [bəˈnɛvələnt] *adj* : benévolo, bondadoso — **benevolently** *adv*

Bengali [bɛnˈgɔli, bɛŋ-] *n* **1** : bengalí *mf* **2** : bengalí *m* (idioma) — **Bengali** *adj*

benign [bɪˈnaɪn] *adj* **1** GENTLE, KIND : benévolo, amable **2** FAVORABLE : propicio, favorable **3** MILD : benigno <a benign tumor : un tumor benigno>

Beninese [bə͵nɪ'ni:z, -͵ni:-, -'ni:s; ͵bɛnɪ'-] *n* : beninés *m,* -nesa *f* — **Beninese** *adj*
bent ['bɛnt] *n* : aptitud *f,* inclinación *f*
benumb [bɪ'nʌm] *vt* : entumecer
benzene ['bɛn͵zi:n] *n* : benceno *m*
bequeath [bɪ'kwi:θ, -'kwi:ð] *vt* : legar, dejar en testamento
bequest [bɪ'kwɛst] *n* : legado *m*
berate [bɪ'reɪt] *vt* **-rated; -rating** : reprender, regañar
bereaved[1] [bɪ'ri:vd] *adj* : que está de luto, afligido (por la muerte de alguien)
bereaved[2] *n* **the bereaved** : los deudos del difunto (o de la difunta)
bereavement [bɪ'ri:vmənt] *n* **1** SORROW : dolor *m,* pesar *m* **2** LOSS : pérdida *f*
bereft [bɪ'rɛft] *adj* : privado, desprovisto
beret [bə'reɪ] *n* : boina *f*
beriberi [͵bɛri'bɛri] *n* : beriberi *m*
berm ['bərm] *n* : arcén *m*
berry ['bɛri] *n, pl* **-ries** : baya *f*
berserk [bər'sərk, -'zərk] *adj* **1** : enloquecido **2 to go beserk** : volverse loco
berth[1] ['bərθ] *vi* : atracar
berth[2] *n* **1** DOCK : atracadero *m* **2** ACCOMMODATION : litera *f,* camarote *m* **3** POSITION : trabajo *m,* puesto *m*
beryl ['bɛrəl] *n* : berilo *m*
beseech [bɪ'si:tʃ] *vt* **-sought** [-'sɔt] *or* **-seeched; -seeching** : suplicar, implorar, rogar
beset [bɪ'sɛt] *vt* **-set; -setting 1** HARASS : acosar **2** SURROUND : rodear
beside [bɪ'saɪd] *prep* : al lado de, junto a
besides[1] [bɪ'saɪdz] *adv* **1** ALSO : además, también, aparte **2** MOREOVER : además, por otra parte
besides[2] *prep* **1** : además de, aparte de <six others besides you : seis otros además de ti> **2** EXCEPT : excepto, fuera de, aparte de
besiege [bɪ'si:dʒ] *vt* **-sieged; -sieging** : asediar, sitiar, cercar
besmirch [bɪ'smərtʃ] *vt* : ensuciar, mancillar
best[1] ['bɛst] *vt* : superar, ganar a
best[2] *adv* (*superlative of* **well**) : mejor <as best I can : lo mejor que puedo>
best[3] *adj* (*superlative of* **good**) : mejor <my best friend : mi mejor amigo>
best[4] *n* **1 the best** : lo mejor, el mejor, la mejor, los mejores, las mejores **2 at ~** : a lo más **3 to do one's best** : hacer todo lo posible
bestial ['bɛstʃəl, 'bi:s-] *adj* **1** : bestial **2** BRUTISH : brutal, salvaje
best man *n* : padrino *m*
bestow [bɪ'sto:] *vt* : conferir, otorgar, conceder
bestowal [bɪ'sto:əl] *n* : concesión *f,* otorgamiento *m*
bet[1] ['bɛt] *v* **bet; betting** *vt* : apostar — *vi* **to bet on** : apostarle a
bet[2] *n* : apuesta *f*
betoken [bɪ'to:kən] *vt* : denotar, ser indicio de
betray [bɪ'treɪ] *vt* **1** : traicionar <to betray one's country : traicionar uno a su patria> **2** DIVULGE, REVEAL : delatar, revelar <to betray a secret : revelar un secreto>
betrayal [bɪ'treɪəl] *n* : traición *f,* delación *f,* revelación *f* <betrayal of trust : abuso de confianza>
betrothal [bɪ'tro:ðəl, -'trɔ-] *n* : esponsales *mpl,* compromiso *m*
betrothed [bɪ'tro:ðd, -'trɔθt] *n* FIANCÉ : prometido *m,* -da *f*
better[1] ['bɛt̬ər] *vt* **1** IMPROVE : mejorar **2** SURPASS : superar
better[2] *adv* (*comparative of* **well**) **1** : mejor **2** MORE : más <better than 50 miles : más de 50 millas>
better[3] *adj* (*comparative of* **good**) **1** : mejor <the weather is better today : hace mejor tiempo hoy> <I was sick, but now I'm better : estuve enfermo, pero ahora estoy mejor> **2** : mayor <the better part of a month : la mayor parte de un mes>
better[4] *n* **1** : el mejor, la mejor <the better of the two : el mejor de los dos> **2 to get the better of** : vencer a, quedar por encima de, superar
betterment ['bɛt̬ərmənt] *n* : mejoramiento *m,* mejora *f*
bettor *or* **better** ['bɛt̬ər] *n* : apostador *m,* -dora *f*
between[1] [bɪ'twi:n] *adv* **1** : en medio, por lo medio **2 in ~** : intermedio
between[2] *prep* : entre
bevel[1] ['bɛvəl] *v* **-eled** *or* **-elled; -eling** *or* **-elling** *vt* : biselar — *vi* INCLINE : inclinarse
bevel[2] *n* : bisel *m*
beverage ['bɛvrɪdʒ, 'bɛvə-] *n* : bebida *f*
bevy ['bɛvi] *n, pl* **bevies** : grupo *m* (de personas), bandada *f* (de pájaros)
bewail [bɪ'weɪl] *vt* : lamentarse de, llorar
beware [bɪ'wær] *vi* **to beware of** : tener cuidado con <beware of the dog! : ¡cuidado con el perro!> — *vt* : guardarse de, cuidarse de
bewilder [bɪ'wɪldər] *vt* : desconcertar, dejar perplejo
bewilderment [bɪ'wɪldərmənt] *n* : desconcierto *m,* perplejidad *f*
bewitch [bɪ'wɪtʃ] *vt* **1** : hechizar, embrujar **2** CHARM : cautivar, encantar
bewitchment [bɪ'wɪtʃmənt] *n* : hechizo *m*
beyond[1] [bi'jɑnd] *adv* **1** FARTHER, LATER : más allá, más lejos (en el espacio), más adelante (en el tiempo) **2** MORE : más <$50 and beyond : $50 o más>
beyond[2] *n* **the beyond** : el más allá, lo desconocido
beyond[3] *prep* **1** : más allá de <beyond the frontier : más allá de la frontera>

2 : fuera de <beyond one's reach : fuera de su alcance> 3 BESIDES : además de

biannual [ˌbaɪˈænjʊəl] *adj* : bianual — **biannually** *adv*

bias[1] [ˈbaɪəs] *vt* **-ased** *or* **-assed; -asing** *or* **-assing 1 :** predisponer, sesgar, influir en, afectar **2 to be biased against :** tener prejuicio contra

bias[2] *n* **1 :** sesgo *m*, bies *m* (en la costura) **2** PREJUDICE **:** prejuicio *m* **3** TENDENCY **:** inclinación *f*, tendencia *f*

biased [ˈbaɪəst] *adj* **:** tendencioso, parcial

bib [ˈbɪb] *n* **1 :** peto *m* **2 :** babero *m* (para niños)

Bible [ˈbaɪbəl] *n* **:** Biblia *f*

biblical [ˈbɪblɪkəl] *adj* **:** bíblico

bibliographer [ˌbɪbliˈɑgrəfər] *n* **:** bibliógrafo *m*, -fa *f*

bibliographic [ˌbɪbliəˈgræfɪk] *adj* **:** bibliográfico

bibliography [ˌbɪbliˈɑgrəfi] *n, pl* **-phies :** bibliografía *f*

bicameral [ˌbaɪˈkæmərəl] *adj* **:** bicameral

bicarbonate [ˌbaɪˈkɑrbənət, -ˌneɪt] *n* **:** bicarbonato *m*

bicentennial [ˌbaɪsɛnˈtɛniəl] *n* **:** bicentenario *m*

biceps [ˈbaɪˌsɛps] *ns & pl* **:** bíceps *m*

bicker[1] [ˈbɪkər] *vi* **:** pelear, discutir, reñir

bicker[2] *n* **:** pelea *f*, riña *f*, discusión *f*

bicuspid [baɪˈkʌspɪd] *n* **:** premolar *m*, diente *m* bicúspide

bicycle[1] [ˈbaɪsɪkəl, -ˌsɪ-] *vi* **-cled; -cling :** ir en bicicleta

bicycle[2] *n* **:** bicicleta *f*

bicycling [ˈbaɪsɪkəlɪŋ] *n* **:** ciclismo *m*

bicyclist [ˈbaɪsɪkəlɪst] *n* **:** ciclista *mf*

bid[1] [ˈbɪd] *vt* **bade** [ˈbæd, ˈbeɪd] *or* **bid; bidden** [ˈbɪdən] *or* **bid; bidding 1** ORDER **:** pedir, mandar **2** INVITE **:** invitar **3** SAY **:** dar, decir <to bid good evening : dar las buenas noches> <to bid farewell to : decir adiós a> **4 :** ofrecer (en una subasta), declarar (en juegos de cartas)

bid[2] *n* **1** OFFER **:** oferta *f* (en una subasta), declaración *f* (en juegos de cartas) **2** INVITATION **:** invitación *f* **3** ATTEMPT **:** intento *m*, tentativa *f*

bidder [ˈbɪdər] *n* **:** postor *m*, -tora *f*

bide [ˈbaɪd] *v* **bode** [ˈboːd] *or* **bided; bided; biding** *vt* **:** esperar, aguardar <to bide one's time : esperar el momento oportuno> — *vi* DWELL **:** morar, vivir

biennial [baɪˈɛniəl] *adj* **:** bienal — **biennially** *adv*

bier [ˈbɪr] *n* **1** STAND **:** andas *fpl* **2** COFFIN **:** ataúd *m*, féretro *m*

bifocals [ˈbaɪˌfoːkəlz] *npl* **:** lentes *mpl* bifocales, bifocales *mpl*

big [ˈbɪg] *adj* **bigger; biggest 1** LARGE **:** grande **2** PREGNANT **:** embarazada **3** IMPORTANT, MAJOR **:** importante, grande <a big decision : una gran decisión> **4** POPULAR **:** popular, famoso, conocido

bigamist [ˈbɪgəmɪst] *n* **:** bígamo *m*, -ma *f*

bigamous [ˈbɪgəməs] *adj* **:** bígamo

bigamy [ˈbɪgəmi] *n* **:** bigamia *f*

Big Dipper → dipper

bighorn [ˈbɪgˌhɔrn] *n, pl* **-horn** *or* **-horns** *or* **bighorn sheep :** oveja *f* salvaje de las montañas

bight [ˈbaɪt] *n* **:** bahía *f*, ensenada *f*, golfo *m*

bigot [ˈbɪgət] *n* **:** intolerante *mf*

bigoted [ˈbɪgət̮əd] *adj* **:** intolerante, prejuiciado, fanático

bigotry [ˈbɪgətri] *n, pl* **-tries :** intolerancia *f*, fanaticismo *m*

big shot *n* **:** pez *m* gordo *fam*, mandamás *mf*

bigwig [ˈbɪgˌwɪg] **→ big shot**

bike [ˈbaɪk] *n* **1 :** bicicleta *f*, bici *f fam* **2 :** motocicleta *f*, moto *f*

bikini [bəˈkiːni] *n* **:** bikini *m*

bilateral [baɪˈlæt̮ərəl] *adj* **:** bilateral — **bilaterally** *adv*

bile [ˈbaɪl] *n* **1 :** bilis *f* **2** IRRITABILITY **:** mal genio *m*

bilingual [baɪˈlɪŋgwəl] *adj* **:** bilingüe

bilious [ˈbɪliəs] *adj* **1 :** bilioso **2** IRRITABLE **:** bilioso, colérico

bilk [ˈbɪlk] *vt* **:** burlar, estafar, defraudar

bill[1] [ˈbɪl] *vt* **:** pasarle la cuenta a — *vi* **:** acariciar <to bill and coo : acariciarse>

bill[2] *n* **1** LAW **:** proyecto *m* de ley, ley *f* **2** INVOICE **:** cuenta *f*, factura *f* **3** POSTER **:** cartel *m* **4** PROGRAM **:** programa *m* (del teatro) **5 :** billete *m* <a five-dollar bill : un billete de cinco dólares> **6** BEAK **:** pico *m*

billboard [ˈbɪlˌbɔrd] *n* **:** cartelera *f*

billet[1] [ˈbɪlət] *vt* **:** acuartelar, alojar

billet[2] *n* **:** alojamiento *m*

billfold [ˈbɪlˌfoːld] *n* **:** billetera *f*, cartera *f*

billiards [ˈbɪljərdz] *n* **:** billar *m*

billion [ˈbɪljən] *n, pl* **billions** *or* **billion :** mil millones *mpl*

billow[1] [ˈbɪlo] *vi* **:** hincharse, inflarse

billow[2] *n* **1** WAVE **:** ola *f* **2** CLOUD **:** nube *f* <a billow of smoke : un nube de humo>

billowy [ˈbɪlowi] *adj* **:** ondulante

billy goat [ˈbɪliˌgoːt] *n* **:** macho *m* cabrío

bin [ˈbɪn] *n* **:** cubo *m*, cajón *m*

binary [ˈbaɪnəri, -ˌnɛri] *adj* **:** binario *m*

bind [ˈbaɪnd] *vt* **bound** [ˈbaʊnd]; **binding 1** TIE **:** atar, amarrar **2** OBLIGATE **:** obligar **3** UNITE **:** aglutinar, ligar, unir **4** BANDAGE **:** vendar **5 :** encuadernar (un libro)

binder [ˈbaɪndər] *n* **1** FOLDER **:** carpeta *f* **2 :** encuadernador *m*, -dora *f* (de libros)

binding [ˈbaɪndɪŋ] *n* **1 :** encuadernación *f* (de libros) **2** COVER **:** cubierta *f*, forro *m*

binge ['bɪndʒ] *n* : juerga *f*, parranda *f* *fam*
bingo ['bɪŋ,goː] *n, pl* **-gos** : bingo *m*
binocular [baɪ'nɑkjələr, bə-] *adj* : binocular
binoculars [bə'nɑkjələrz, baɪ-] *npl* : binoculares *mpl*
biochemical[1] [,baɪo'kɛmɪkəl] *adj* : bioquímico
biochemical[2] *n* : bioquímico *m*
biochemist [,baɪo'kɛmɪst] *n* : bioquímico *m*, -ca *f*
biochemistry [,baɪo'kɛməstri] *n* : bioquímica *f*
biodegradable [,baɪodɪ'greɪdəbəl] *adj* : biodegradable
biodegradation [,baɪodɛgrə'deɪʃən] *n* : biodegradación *f*
biodegrade [,baɪodɪ'greɪd] *vi* **-graded; -grading** : biodegradarse
biographer [baɪ'ɑgrəfər] *n* : biógrafo *m*, -fa *f*
biographical [,baɪə'græfɪkəl] *adj* : biográfico
biography [baɪ'ɑgrəfi, biː-] *n, pl* **-phies** : biografía *f*
biologic [,baɪə'lɑdʒɪk] *or* **biological** [-dʒɪkəl] *adj* : biológico
biologist [baɪ'ɑlədʒɪst] *n* : biólogo *m*, -ga *f*
biology [baɪ'ɑlədʒi] *n* : biología *f*
biophysical [,baɪo'fɪzɪkəl] *adj* : biofísico
biophysicist [,baɪo'fɪzəsɪst] *n* : biofísico *m*, -ca *f*
biophysics [,baɪo'fɪzɪks] *ns & pl* : biofísica *f*
biopsy ['baɪ,ɑpsi] *n, pl* **-sies** : biopsia *f*
biotechnology [,baɪotɛk'nɑlədʒi] *n* : biotecnología *f*
biotic [baɪ'ɑtɪk] *adj* : biótico
bipartisan [baɪ'pɑrṭəzən, -sən] *adj* : bipartidista, de dos partidas
biped ['baɪ,pɛd] *n* : bípedo *m*
birch ['bərtʃ] *n* : abedul *m*
bird ['bərd] *n* : pájaro *m* (pequeño), ave *f* (grande)
birdbath ['bərd,bæθ, -,baθ] *n* : pila *f* para pájaros
bird dog *n* : perro *m*, -rra *f* de caza
bird of prey *n* : ave *f* rapaz, ave *f* de presa
birdseed ['bərd,siːd] *n* : alpiste *m*
bird's–eye ['bərdz,aɪ] *adj* **1** : visto desde arriba <bird's-eye view : vista aérea> **2** CURSORY : rápido, somero
birth ['bərθ] *n* **1** : nacimiento *m*, parto *m* **2** ORIGIN : origen *m*, nacimiento *m*
birthday ['bərθ,deɪ] *n* : cumpleaños *m*, aniversario *m*
birthmark ['bərθ,mɑrk] *n* : mancha *f* de nacimiento
birthplace ['bərθ,pleɪs] *n* : lugar *m* de nacimiento
birthrate ['bərθ,reɪt] *n* : índice *m* de natalidad
birthright ['bərθ,raɪt] *n* : derecho *m* de nacimiento
biscuit ['bɪskət] *n* : bizcocho *m*
bisect ['baɪ,sɛkt, ,baɪ'-] *vt* : bisecar
bisector ['baɪ,sɛktər, ,baɪ'-] *n* : bisectriz *f*
bishop ['bɪʃəp] *n* : obispo *m*
bismuth ['bɪzməθ] *n* : bismuto *m*
bison ['baɪzən, -sən] *ns & pl* : bisonte *m*
bistro ['biːstro, 'bɪs-] *n, pl* **-tros** : bar *m*, restaurante *m* pequeño
bit ['bɪt] *n* **1** FRAGMENT, PIECE : pedazo *m*, trozo *m* <a bit of luck : un poco de suerte> **2** : freno *m*, bocado *m* (de una brida) **3** : broca *f* (de un taladro) **4** : bit *m* (de información)
bitch[1] ['bɪtʃ] *vi* COMPLAIN : quejarse, reclamar
bitch[2] *n* : perra *f*
bite[1] ['baɪt] *v* **bit** ['bɪt]; **bitten** ['bɪtən]; **biting** *vt* **1** : morder **2** STING : picar **3** PUNCTURE : punzar, pinchar **4** GRIP : agarrar — *vi* **1** : morder <that dog bites : ese perro muerde> **2** STING : picar (dícese de un insecto), cortar (dícese del viento) **3** : picar <the fish are biting now : ya están picando los peces> **4** GRAB : agarrarse
bite[2] *n* **1** BITING : mordisco *m*, dentellada *f* **2** SNACK : bocado *m* <a bite to eat : algo de comer> **3** : picadura *f* (de un insecto), mordedura *f* (de un animal) **4** SHARPNESS : mordacidad *f*, penetración *f*
biting *adj* **1** PENETRATING : cortante, penetrante **2** CAUSTIC : mordaz, sarcástico
bitter ['bɪṭər] *adj* **1** ACRID : amargo, acre **2** PENETRATING : cortante, penetrante <bitter cold : frío glacial> **3** HARSH : duro, amargo <to the bitter end : hasta el final> **4** INTENSE, RELENTLESS : intenso, extremo, implacable <bitter hatred : odio implacable>
bitterly ['bɪṭərli] *adv* : amargamente
bittern ['bɪṭərn] *n* : avetoro *m* común
bitterness ['bɪṭərnəs] *n* : amargura *f*
bituminous coal [bə'tuːmənəs, -'tjuː-] *n* : carbón *m* bituminoso
bivalve ['baɪ,vælv] *n* : bivalvo *m* — **bivalve** *adj*
bivouac[1] ['bɪvə,wæk, 'bɪv,wæk] *vi* **-ouacked; -ouacking** : acampar, vivaquear
bivouac[2] *n* : vivaque *m*
bizarre [bə'zɑr] *adj* : extraño, singular, estrafalario, estrambótico — **bizarrely** *adv*
blab ['blæb] *vi* **blabbed; blabbing** : parlotear *fam*, cotorrear *fam*
black[1] ['blæk] *vt* : ennegrecer
black[2] *adj* **1** : negro (color, raza) **2** SOILED : sucio **3** DARK : oscuro, negro **4** WICKED : malvado, perverso, malo **5** GLOOMY : negro, sombrío, deprimente
black[3] *n* **1** : negro *m* (color) **2** : negro *m*, -gra *f* (persona)
black–and–blue [,blækən'bluː] *adj* : amoratado

blackball ['blæk,bɔl] *vt* **1** OSTRACIZE : hacerle el vacío a, aislar **2** BOYCOTT : boicotear
blackberry ['blæk,bɛri] *n, pl* **-ries** : mora *f*
blackbird ['blæk,bərd] *n* : mirlo *m*
blackboard ['blæk,bɔrd] *n* : pizarra *f,* pizarrón *m*
blacken ['blækən] *vt* **1** BLACK : ennegrecer **2** DEFAME : deshonrar, difamar, manchar
blackhead ['blæk,hɛd] *n* : espinilla *f,* punto *m* negro
black hole *n* : agujero *m* negro
blackjack ['blæk,jæk] *n* **1** : cachiporra *f* (arma) **2** : veintiuna *f* (juego de cartas)
blacklist[1] ['blæk,lɪst] *vt* : poner en la lista negra
blacklist[2] *n* : lista *f* negra
blackmail[1] ['blæk,meɪl] *vt* : chantajear, hacer chantaje a
blackmail[2] *n* : chantaje *m*
blackmailer ['blæk,meɪlər] *n* : chantajista *mf*
blackout ['blæk,aʊt] *n* **1** : apagón *m* (de poder eléctrico) **2** FAINT : desmayo *m,* desvanecimiento *m*
black out *vt* : dejar sin luz — *vi* FAINT : perder el conocimiento, desmayarse
blacksmith ['blæk,smɪθ] *n* : herrero *m*
blacktop ['blæk,tɑp] *n* : asfalto *m*
bladder ['blædər] *n* : vejiga *f*
blade ['bleɪd] *n* : hoja *f* (de un cuchillo), cuchilla *f* (de un patín), pala *f* (de un remo o una hélice), brizna *f* (de hierba)
blamable ['bleɪməbəl] *adj* : culpable
blame[1] ['bleɪm] *vt* **blamed; blaming** : culpar, echar la culpa a
blame[2] *n* : culpa *f*
blameless ['bleɪmləs] *adj* : intachable, sin culpa, inocente — **blamelessly** *adv*
blameworthiness ['bleɪm,wərðinəs] *n* : culpa *f,* culpabilidad *f*
blameworthy ['bleɪm,wərði] *adj* : culpable, reprochable, censurable
blanch ['blæntʃ] *vt* WHITEN : blanquear — *vi* PALE : palidecer
bland ['blænd] *adj* : soso, insulso, desabrido <a bland smile : una sonrisa insulsa> <a bland diet : una dieta fácil de digerir>
blandishments ['blændɪʃmənts] *npl* : lisonjas *fpl,* halagos *mpl*
blandly ['blændli] *adv* : de manera insulsa
blandness ['blændnəs] *n* : lo insulso, lo desabrido
blank[1] ['blæŋk] *vt* OBLITERATE : borrar
blank[2] *adj* **1** DAZED : perplejo, desconcertado **2** EXPRESSIONLESS : sin expresión, inexpresivo **3** : en blanco (dícese de un papel), liso (dícese de una pared) **4** EMPTY : vacío, en blanco <a blank stare : una mirada vacía> <his mind went blank : se quedó en blanco>
blank[3] *n* **1** SPACE : espacio *m* en blanco **2** FORM : formulario *m* **3** CARTRIDGE : cartucho *m* de fogueo **4** *or* **blank key** : llave *f* ciega
blanket[1] [blæŋkət] *vt* : cubrir
blanket[2] *adj* : global
blanket[3] *n* : manta *f,* cobija *f,* frazada *f*
blankly ['blænkli] *adv* : sin comprender
blankness ['blænknəs] *n* **1** PERPLEXITY : desconcierto *m,* perplejidad *f* **2** EMPTINESS : vacío *m,* vacuidad *f*
blare[1] ['blær] *vi* **blared; blaring** : resonar
blare[2] *n* : estruendo *m*
blarney ['blɑrni] *n* : labia *f fam*
blasé [blɑ'zeɪ] *adj* : displicente, indiferente
blaspheme [blæs'fi:m, 'blæs,-] *vi* **-phemed; -pheming** : blasfemar
blasphemer [blæs'fi:mər, 'blæs,-] *n* : blasfemo *m,* -ma *f*
blasphemous ['blæsfəməs] *adj* : blasfemo
blasphemy ['blæsfəmi] *n, pl* **-mies** : blasfemia *f*
blast[1] ['blæst] *vt* **1** BLOW UP : volar, hacer volar **2** ATTACK : atacar, arremeter contra
blast[2] *n* **1** GUST : ráfaga *f* **2** EXPLOSION : explosión *f*
blast-off ['blæst,ɔf] *n* : despegue *m*
blast off *vi* : despegar
blatant ['bleɪtənt] *adj* : descarado — **blatantly** ['bleɪtəntli] *adv*
blaze[1] ['bleɪz] *v* **blazed; blazing** *vi* SHINE : arder, brillar, resplandecer — *vt* MARK : marcar, señalar <to blaze a trail : abrir un camino>
blaze[2] *n* **1** FIRE : fuego *m* **2** BRIGHTNESS : resplandor *m,* brillantez *f* **3** OUTBURST : arranque *m* <a blaze of anger : un arranque de cólera> **4** DISPLAY : alarde *m,* llamarada *f* <a blaze of color : un derroche de color>
blazer ['bleɪzər] *n* : chaqueta *f* deportiva, blazer *m*
bleach[1] ['bli:tʃ] *vt* : blanquear, decolorar
bleach[2] *n* : lejía *f,* blanqueador *m*
bleachers ['bli:tʃərz] *ns & pl* : gradas *fpl,* tribuna *f* descubierta
bleak ['bli:k] *adj* **1** DESOLATE : inhóspito, sombrío, desolado **2** DEPRESSING : deprimente, triste, sombrío
bleakly ['bli:kli] *adv* : sombríamente
bleakness ['bli:knəs] *n* : lo inhóspito, lo sombrío
blear ['blɪr] *adj* : empañado, nublado
bleary ['blɪri] *adj* **1** : adormilado, fatigado **2** **bleary–eyed** : con los ojos nublados
bleat[1] ['bli:t] *vi* : balar
bleat[2] *n* : balido *m*
bleed ['bli:d] *v* **bled** ['blɛd]; **bleeding** *vi* **1** : sangrar **2** GRIEVE : sufrir, afligirse **3** EXUDE : exudar (dícese de una planta), correrse (dícese de los colo-

res) — *vt* **1 :** sangrar (a una persona), purgar (frenos) **2 to bleed someone dry :** sacarle todo el dinero a alguien

blemish[1] [ˈblɛmɪʃ] *vt* **:** manchar, marcar

blemish[2] *n* **:** imperfección *f,* mancha *f,* marca *f*

blend[1] [ˈblɛnd] *vt* **1** MIX **:** mezclar **2** COMBINE **:** combinar, aunar

blend[2] *n* **:** mezcla *f,* combinación *f*

blender [ˈblɛndər] *n* **:** licuadora *f*

bless [ˈblɛs] *vt* **blessed** [ˈblɛst]; **blessing 1** CONSECRATE **:** bendecir, consagrar **2 :** bendecir <may God bless you! : ¡que Dios te bendiga!> **3 to bless with :** dotar de **4 to bless oneself :** santiguarse

blessed [ˈblɛsəd] *or* **blest** [ˈblɛst] *adj* **:** bienaventurado, bendito, dichoso

blessedly [ˈblɛsədli] *adv* **:** felizmente, alegremente, afortunadamente

blessing [ˈblɛsɪŋ] *n* **1 :** bendición *f* **2** APPROVAL **:** aprobación *f,* consentimiento *m*

blew → **blow**

blight[1] [ˈblaɪt] *vt* **:** arruinar, infestar

blight[2] *n* **1 :** añublo *m* **2** PLAGUE **:** peste *f,* plaga *f* **3** DECAY **:** deterioro *m,* ruina *f*

blimp [ˈblɪmp] *n* **:** dirigible *m*

blind[1] [ˈblaɪnd] *vt* **1 :** cegar, dejar ciego **2** DAZZLE **:** deslumbrar

blind[2] *adj* **1** SIGHTLESS **:** ciego **2** INSENSITIVE **:** ciego, insensible, sin razón **3** CLOSED **:** sin salida <blind alley : callejón sin salida>

blind[3] *n* **1 :** persiana *f* (para una ventana) **2** COVER **:** escondite *m,* escondrijo *m*

blindfold[1] [ˈblaɪnd,foːld] *vt* **:** vendar los ojos

blindfold[2] *n* **:** venda *f* (para los ojos)

blindly [ˈblaɪndli] *adv* **:** a ciegas, ciegamente

blindness [ˈblaɪndnəs] *n* **:** ceguera *f*

blink[1] [ˈblɪŋk] *vi* **1** WINK **:** pestañear, parpadear **2 :** brillar intermitentemente

blink[2] *n* **:** pestañeo *m,* parpadeo *m*

blinker [ˈblɪŋkər] *n* **:** intermitente *m,* direccional *f*

bliss [ˈblɪs] *n* **1** HAPPINESS **:** dicha *f,* felicidad *f* absoluta **2** PARADISE **:** paraíso *m*

blissful [ˈblɪsfəl] *adj* **:** dichoso, feliz — **blissfully** *adv*

blister[1] [ˈblɪstər] *vi* **:** ampollarse

blister[2] *n* **:** ampolla *f* (en la piel o una superficie), burbuja *f* (en una superficie)

blithe [ˈblaɪθ, ˈblaɪð] *adj* **blither; blithest 1** CAREFREE **:** despreocupado **2** CHEERFUL **:** alegre, risueño — **blithely** *adv*

blitz[1] [ˈblɪts] *vt* **1** BOMBARD **:** bombardear **2 :** atacar con rapidez

blitz[2] *n* **1 :** bombardeo *m* aéreo **2** CAMPAIGN **:** ataque *m,* acometida *f*

blizzard [ˈblɪzərd] *n* **:** tormenta *f* de nieve, ventisca *f*

bloat [ˈbloːt] *vi* **:** hincharse, inflarse

blob [ˈblɑb] *n* **:** gota *f,* mancha *f,* borrón *m*

bloc [ˈblɑk] *n* **:** bloque *m*

block[1] [ˈblɑk] *vt* **1** OBSTRUCT **:** obstruir, bloquear **2** CLOG **:** atascar, atorar

block[2] *n* **1** PIECE **:** bloque *m* <building blocks : cubos de construcción> <auction block : plataforma de subastas> <starting block : taco de salida> **2** OBSTRUCTION **:** obstrucción *f,* bloqueo *m* **3 :** cuadra *f,* manzana *f* (de edificios) <to go around the block : dar la vuelta a la cuadra> **4** BUILDING **:** edificio *m* (de apartamentos, oficinas, etc.) **5** GROUP, SERIES **:** serie *f,* grupo *m* <a block of tickets : una serie de entradas> **6 block and tackle :** aparejo *m* de poleas

blockade[1] [blɑˈkeɪd] *vt* **-aded; -ading :** bloquear

blockade[2] *n* **:** bloqueo *m*

blockage [ˈblɑkɪdʒ] *n* **:** bloqueo *m,* obstrucción *f*

blockhead [ˈblɑk,hɛd] *n* **:** bruto *m,* -ta *f;* estúpido *m,* -da *f*

blond[1] *or* **blonde** [ˈblɑnd] *adj* **:** rubio, güero *Mex,* claro (dícese de la madera)

blond[2] *or* **blonde** *n* **:** rubio *m,* -bia *f;* güero *m,* -ra *f Mex*

blood [ˈblʌd] *n* **1 :** sangre *f* **2** LIFEBLOOD **:** vida *f,* alma *f* **3** LINEAGE **:** linaje *m,* sangre *f*

blood bank *n* **:** banco *m* de sangre

bloodcurdling [ˈblʌd,kərdəlɪŋ] *adj* **:** espeluznante, aterrador

blooded [ˈblʌdəd] *adj* **:** de sangre <cold-blooded animal : animal de sangre fría>

bloodhound [ˈblʌd,haʊnd] *n* **:** sabueso *m*

bloodless [ˈblʌdləs] *adj* **1 :** incruento, sin derramamiento de sangre **2** LIFELESS **:** desanimado, insípido, sin vida

bloodmobile [ˈblʌdmo,biːl] *n* **:** unidad *f* móvil para donantes de sangre

blood pressure *n* **:** tensión *f,* presión *f* (arterial)

bloodshed [ˈblʌd,ʃɛd] *n* **:** derramamiento *m* de sangre

bloodshot [ˈblʌd,ʃɑt] *adj* **:** inyectado de sangre

bloodstain [ˈblʌd,steɪn] *n* **:** mancha *f* de sangre

bloodstained [ˈblʌd,steɪnd] *adj* **:** manchado de sangre

bloodstream [ˈblʌd,striːm] *n* **:** torrente *m* sanguíneo, corriente *f* sanguínea

bloodsucker [ˈblʌd,sʌkər] *n* **:** sanguijuela *f*

bloodthirsty [ˈblʌd,θərsti] *adj* **:** sanguinario

blood vessel *n* **:** vaso *m* sanguíneo

bloody [ˈblʌdi] *adj* **bloodier; -est :** ensangrentado, sangriento

bloom[1] [ˈbluːm] *vi* **1** FLOWER : florecer **2** MATURE : madurar

bloom[2] *n* **1** FLOWER : flor *f* <to be in bloom : estar en flor> **2** FLOWERING : floración *f* <in full bloom : en plena floración> **3** : rubor *m* (de la tez) <in the bloom of youth : en plena juventud, en la flor de la vida>

bloomers [ˈbluːmərz] *npl* : bombachos *mpl*

blooper [ˈbluːpər] *n* : metedura *f* de pata *fam*

blossom[1] [ˈblɑsəm] *vi* : florecer, dar flor

blossom[2] *n* : flor *f*

blot[1] [ˈblɑt] *vt* **blotted; blotting 1** SPOT : emborronar, borronear **2** DRY : secar

blot[2] *n* **1** STAIN : mancha *f,* borrón *m* **2** BLEMISH : mancha *f,* tacha *f*

blotch[1] [ˈblɑtʃ] *vt* : emborronar, borronear

blotch[2] *n* : mancha *f,* borrón *m*

blotchy [ˈblɑtʃi] *adj* **blotchier; -est** : lleno de manchas

blotter [ˈblɑt̬ər] *n* : hoja *f* de papel secante, secante *m*

blouse [ˈblaʊs, ˈblaʊz] *n* : blusa *f*

blow[1] [ˈbloː] *v* **blew** [ˈbluː]; **blown** [ˈbloːn]; **blowing** *vi* **1** : soplar, volar <the wind is blowing hard : el viento está soplando con fuerza> <it blew out the door : voló por la puerta> <the window blew shut : se cerró la ventana> **2** SOUND : sonar <the whistle blew : sonó el silbato> **3 to blow out** : fundirse (dícese de un fusible eléctrico), reventarse (dícese de una llanta) — *vt* **1** : soplar, echar <to blow smoke : echar humo> **2** SOUND : tocar, sonar **3** SHAPE : soplar, dar forma a <to blow glass : soplar vidrio> **4** BUNGLE : echar a perder

blow[2] *n* **1** PUFF : soplo *m,* soplido *m* **2** GALE : vendaval *f* **3** HIT, STROKE : golpe *m* **4** CALAMITY : golpe *m,* desastre *m* **5 to come to blows** : llegar a las manos

blower [ˈbloːər] *n* FAN : ventilador *m*

blowout [ˈbloːˌaʊt] *n* : reventón *m*

blowtorch [ˈbloːˌtɔrtʃ] *n* : soplete *m*

blow up *vi* EXPLODE : estallar, hacer explosión — *vt* BLAST : volar, hacer volar

blubber[1] [ˈblʌbər] *vi* : lloriquear

blubber[2] *n* : esperma *f* de ballena

bludgeon [ˈblʌdʒən] *vt* : aporrear

blue[1] [ˈbluː] *adj* **bluer; bluest 1** : azul **2** MELANCHOLY : melancólico, triste

blue[2] *n* : azul *m*

blueberry [ˈbluːˌbɛri] *n, pl* **-ries** : arándano *m*

bluebird [ˈbluːˌbərd] *n* : azulejo *m*

blue cheese *n* : queso *m* azul

blueprint [ˈbluːˌprɪnt] *n* **1** : plano *m,* proyecto *m,* cianotipo *m* **2** PLAN : anteproyecto *m,* programa *m*

blues [ˈbluːz] *npl* **1** DEPRESSION : depresión *f,* melancolía *f* **2** : blues *m* <to sing the blues : cantar blues>

bluff[1] [ˈblʌf] *vi* : hacer un farol, blofear *Col, Mex*

bluff[2] *adj* **1** STEEP : escarpado **2** FRANK : campechano, franco, directo

bluff[3] *n* **1** : farol *m,* blof *m Col, Mex* **2** CLIFF : acantilado *m,* risco *m*

bluffer [ˈblʌfər] *n* : farolero *m,* -ra *f fam;* blofeador *m,* -dora *f Col, Mex*

bluing *or* **blueing** [ˈbluːɪŋ] *n* : añil *m,* azulete *m*

bluish [ˈbluːɪʃ] *adj* : azulado

blunder[1] [ˈblʌndər] *vi* **1** STUMBLE : tropezar, dar traspiés **2** ERR : cometer un error, tropezar, meter la pata *fam*

blunder[2] *n* : error *m,* fallo *m* garrafal, metedura *f* de pata *fam*

blunderbuss [ˈblʌndərˌbʌs] *n* : trabuco *m*

blunt[1] [ˈblʌnt] *vt* : despuntar (aguja o lápiz), desafilar (cuchillo o tijeras), suavizar (crítica)

blunt[2] *adj* **1** DULL : desafilado, despuntado **2** DIRECT : directo, franco, categórico

bluntly [ˈblʌntli] *adv* : sin rodeos, francamente, bruscamente

bluntness [ˈblʌntnəs] *n* **1** DULLNESS : falta *f* de filo, embotadura *f* **2** FRANKNESS : franqueza *f*

blur[1] [ˈblər] *vt* **blurred; blurring** : desdibujar, hacer borroso

blur[2] *n* **1** SMEAR : mancha *f,* borrón *m* **2** : aspecto *m* borroso <everything was just a blur : todo se volvió borroso>

blurb [ˈblərb] *n* : propaganda *f,* nota *f* publicitaria

blurt [ˈblərt] *vt* : espetar, decir impulsivamente

blush[1] [ˈblʌʃ] *vi* : ruborizarse, sonrojarse, hacerse colorado

blush[2] *n* : rubor *m,* sonrojo *m*

bluster[1] [ˈblʌstər] *vi* **1** BLOW : soplar con fuerza **2** BOAST : fanfarronear, echar bravatas

bluster[2] *n* : fanfarronada *f,* bravata *f*

blustery [ˈblʌstəri] *adj* : borrascoso, tempestuoso

boa [ˈboːə] *n* : boa *f*

boar [ˈbor] *n* : cerdo *m* macho, verraco *m*

board[1] [ˈbord] *vt* **1** : embarcarse en, subir a bordo de (una nave o un avión), subir a (un tren o carro) **2** LODGE : hospedar, dar hospedaje con comidas a **3 to board up** : cerrar con tablas

board[2] *n* **1** PLANK : tabla *f,* tablón *m* **2** : tablero *m* <chessboard : tablero de ajedrez> **3** MEALS : comida *f* <board and lodging : comida y alojamiento> **4** COMMITTEE, COUNCIL : junta *f,* consejo *m*

boarder [ˈbordər] *n* LODGER : huésped *m,* -peda *f*

boardinghouse [ˈbordɪŋˌhaʊs] *n* : casa *f* de huéspedes

boarding school *n* : internado *m*

boardwalk ['bord,wɔk] *n* : paseo *m* marítimo entablado
boast[1] ['bo:st] *vi* : alardear, presumir, jactarse
boast[2] *n* : jactancia *f,* alarde *m*
boaster ['bo:stər] *n* : presumido *m,* -da *f;* fanfarrón *m,* -rrona *f fam*
boastful ['bo:stfəl] *adj* : jactancioso, fanfarrón *fam*
boastfully ['bo:stfəli] *adv* : de manera jactanciosa
boat[1] ['bo:t] *vt* : transportar en barco, poner a bordo
boat[2] *n* : barco *m,* embarcación *f,* bote *m,* barca *f*
boatman ['bo:tmən] *n, pl* **-men** [-mən, -,mɛn] : barquero *m*
boatswain ['bo:sən] *n* : contramaestre *m*
bob[1] ['bɑb] *v* **bobbed; bobbing** *vi* **1** : balancearse, mecerse <to bob up and down : subir y bajar> **2** *or* **to bob up** APPEAR : presentarse, surgir — *vt* **1** : inclinar (la cabeza o el cuerpo) **2** CUT : cortar, recortar <she bobbed her hair : se cortó el pelo>
bob[2] *n* **1** : inclinación *f* (de la cabeza, del cuerpo), sacudida *f* **2** FLOAT : flotador *m,* corcho *m* (de pesca) **3** : pelo *m* corto
bobbin ['bɑbən] *n* : bobina *f,* carrete *m*
bobby pin ['bɑbi,pɪn] *n* : horquilla *f*
bobcat ['bɑb,kæt] *n* : lince *m* rojo
bobolink ['bɑbə,lɪŋk] *n* : tordo *m* arrocero
bobsled ['bɑb,slɛd] *n* : bobsleigh *m*
bobwhite ['bɑb'*h*waɪt] *n* : codorniz *m* (del Nuevo Mundo)
bode[1] ['bo:d] *v* **boded; boding** *vt* : presagiar, augurar — *vi* **to bode well** : ser de buen agüero
bode[2] → **bide**
bodice ['bɑdəs] *n* : corpiño *m*
bodied ['bɑdid] *adj* : de cuerpo <lean-bodied : de cuerpo delgado> <able-bodied : no discapacitado>
bodiless ['bɑdiləs, 'bɑdələs] *adj* : incorpóreo
bodily[1] ['bɑdəli] *adv* : en peso <to lift someone bodily : levantar a alguien en peso>
bodily[2] *adj* : corporal, del cuerpo <bodily harm : daños corporales>
body ['bɑdi] *n, pl* **bodies 1** : cuerpo *m,* organismo *m* **2** CORPSE : cadáver *m* **3** PERSON : persona *f,* ser *m* humano **4** : nave *f* (de una iglesia), carrocería (de un automóvil), fuselaje *m* (de un avión), casco *m* (de una nave) **5** COLLECTION, MASS : conjunto *m,* grupo *m,* masa *f* <in a body : todos juntos, en masa> **6** ORGANIZATION : organismo *m,* organización *f*
bodyguard ['bɑdi,gɑrd] *n* : guardaespaldas *mf*
bog[1] ['bɑg, 'bɔg] *vt* **bogged; bogging** : empantanar, inundar <to get bogged down : empantanarse>
bog[2] *n* : lodazal *m,* ciénaga *f,* cenagal *m*
bogey ['bʊgi, 'bo:-] *n, pl* **-geys** : terror *m,* coco *m fam*
boggle ['bɑgəl] *vi* **-gled; -gling** : quedarse atónito, quedarse pasmado <the mind boggles! : ¡es increíble!>
boggy ['bɑgi, 'bɔ-] *adj* **boggier; -est** : cenagoso
bogus ['bo:gəs] *adj* : falso, fingido, falaz
bohemian [bo:'hi:miən] *n* : bohemio *m,* -mia *f* — **bohemian** *adj*
boil[1] ['bɔɪl] *vi* **1** : hervir **2 to make one's blood boil** : hervirle la sangre a uno — *vt* **1** : hervir, hacer hervir <to boil water : hervir agua> **2** : cocer, hervir <to boil potatoes : cocer papas>
boil[2] *n* **1** BOILING : hervor *m* **2** : furúnculo *m,* divieso *m* (in medicine)
boiler ['bɔɪlər] *n* : caldera *f*
boisterous ['bɔɪstərəs] *adj* : bullicioso, escandaloso — **boisterously** *adv*
bold ['bo:ld] *adj* **1** COURAGEOUS : valiente **2** INSOLENT : insolente, descarado **3** DARING : atrevido, audaz — **boldly** *adv*
boldface ['bo:ld,feɪs] *n or* **boldface type** : negrita *f*
boldness ['bo:ldnəs] *n* **1** COURAGE : valor *m,* coraje *m* **2** INSOLENCE : atrevimiento *m,* insolencia *f,* descaro *m* **3** DARING : audacia *f*
bolero [bə'lɛro] *n, pl* **-ros** : bolero *m*
Bolivian [bə'lɪviən] *n* : boliviano *m,* -na *f* — **Bolivian** *adj*
boll ['bo:l] *n* : cápsula *f* (del algodón)
boll weevil *n* : gorgojo *m* del algodón
bologna [bə'lo:ni] *n* : salchicha *f* ahumada
bolster[1] ['bo:lstər] *vt* **-stered; -stering** : reforzar, reafirmar <to bolster morale : levantar la moral>
bolster[2] *n* : cabezal *m,* almohadón *m*
bolt[1] ['bo:lt] *vt* **1** atornillar, sujetar con pernos <bolted to the floor : sujetado con pernos al suelo> **2** : cerrar con pestillo, echar el cerrojo a <to bolt the door : echar el cerrojo a la puerta> **3 to bolt down** : engullir <she bolted down her dinner : engulló su comida> — *vi* : echar a correr, salir corriendo <he bolted from the room : salió corriendo de la sala>
bolt[2] *n* **1** LATCH : pestillo *m,* cerrojo *m* **2** : tornillo *m,* perno *m* <nuts and bolts : tuercas y tornillos> **3** : rollo *m* <a bolt of cloth : un rollo de tela> **4 lightning bolt** : relámpago *m,* rayo *m*
bomb[1] ['bɑm] *vt* : bombardear
bomb[2] *n* : bomba *f*
bombard [bɑm'bɑrd, bəm-] *vt* : bombardear
bombardier [,bɑmbə'dɪr] *n* : bombardero *m,* -ra *f*
bombardment [bɑm'bɑrdmənt] *n* : bombardeo *m*

bombast [ˈbɑm͵bæst] *n* : grandilocuencia *f*, ampulosidad *f*

bombastic [bɑmˈbæstɪk] *adj* : grandilocuente, ampuloso, bombástico

bomber [ˈbɑmər] *n* : bombardero *m*

bombproof [ˈbɑm͵pruːf] *adj* : a prueba de bombas

bombshell [ˈbɑm͵ʃɛl] *n* : bomba *f* <a political bombshell : una bomba política>

bona fide [ˈboːnə͵faɪd, ˈbɑ-; ͵boːnəˈfaɪdi] *adj* **1** : de buena fe <a bona fide offer : una oferta de buena fe> **2** GENUINE : genuino, auténtico

bonanza [bəˈnænzə] *n* : bonanza *f*

bonbon [ˈbɑn͵bɑn] *n* : bombón *m*

bond[1] [ˈbɑnd] *vt* **1** INSURE : dar fianza a, asegurar **2** STICK : adherir, pegar — *vi* : adherirse, pegarse

bond[2] *n* **1** LINK, TIE : vínculo *m*, lazo *m* **2** BAIL : fianza *f*, caución *f* **3** : bono *m* <stocks and bonds : acciones y bonos> **4 bonds** *npl* FETTERS : cadenas *fpl*

bondage [ˈbɑndɪdʒ] *n* : esclavitud *f*

bondholder [ˈbɑnd͵hoːldər] *n* : tenedor *m*, -dora *f* de bonos

bondsman [ˈbɑndzmən] *n*, *pl* **-men** [-mən, -͵mɛn] **1** SLAVE : esclavo *m* **2** SURETY : fiador *m*, -dora *f*

bone[1] [ˈboːn] *vt* **boned; boning** : deshuesar

bone[2] *n* : hueso *m*

boneless [ˈboːnləs] *adj* : sin huesos, sin espinas

boner [ˈboːnər] *n* : metedura *f* de pata, metida *f* de pata

bonfire [ˈbɑn͵faɪr] *n* : hoguera *f*, fogata *f*, fogón *m*

bonito [bəˈniːt̬o] *n*, *pl* **-tos** *or* **-to** : bonito *m*

bonnet [ˈbɑnət] *n* : sombrero *m* (de mujer), gorra *f* (de niño)

bonus [ˈboːnəs] *n* **1** : prima *f*, bonificación *f* (pagado al empleado) **2** ADVANTAGE, BENEFIT : beneficio *m*, provecho *m*

bony [ˈboːni] *adj* **bonier; -est** : huesudo, osudo

boo[1] [ˈbuː] *vt* : abuchear

boo[2] *n*, *pl* **boos** : abucheo *m*

booby [ˈbuːbi] *n*, *pl* **-bies** : bobo *m*, -ba *f*; tonto *m*, -ta *f*

book[1] [ˈbʊk] *vt* : reservar <to book a flight : reservar un vuelo>

book[2] *n* **1** : libro *m* **2 the Book** : la Biblia **3 by the book** : según las reglas

bookcase [ˈbʊk͵keɪs] *n* : estantería *f*, librero *m* *Mex*

bookend [ˈbʊk͵ɛnd] *n* : sujetalibros *m*

bookie [ˈbʊki] → **bookmaker**

bookish [ˈbʊkɪʃ] *adj* : libresco

bookkeeper [ˈbʊk͵kiːpər] *n* : tenedor *m*, -dora *f* de libros; contable *mf* *Spain*

bookkeeping [ˈbʊk͵kiːpɪŋ] *n* : contabilidad *f*, teneduría *f* de libros

booklet [ˈbʊklət] *n* : folleto *m*

bookmaker [ˈbʊk͵meɪkər] *n* : corredor *m*, -dora *f* de apuestas

bookmark [ˈbʊk͵mɑrk] *n* : señalador *m* de libros, marcador *m* de libros

bookseller [ˈbʊk͵sɛlər] *n* : librero *m*, -ra *f*

bookshelf [ˈbʊk͵ʃɛlf] *n*, *pl* **-shelves 1** : estante *m* **2 bookshelves** *npl* : estantería *f*

bookstore [ˈbʊk͵stor] *n* : librería *f*

bookworm [ˈbʊk͵wərm] *n* : ratón *m* de biblioteca *fam*

boom[1] [ˈbuːm] *vi* **1** THUNDER : tronar, resonar **2** FLOURISH, PROSPER : estar en auge, prosperar

boom[2] *n* **1** BOOMING : bramido *m*, estruendo *m* **2** FLOURISHING : auge *m* <population boom : auge de población>

boomerang [ˈbuːmə͵ræŋ] *n* : bumerán *m*

boon[1] [ˈbuːn] *adj* **boon companion** : amigo *m*, -ga *f* del alma

boon[2] *n* : ayuda *f*, beneficio *m*, adelanto *m*

boondocks [ˈbuːn͵dɑks] *npl* : area *f* rural remota, región *f* alejada

boor [ˈbʊr] *n* : grosero *m*, -ra *f*

boorish [ˈbʊrɪʃ] *adj* : grosero

boost[1] [ˈbuːst] *vt* **1** LIFT : levantar, alzar **2** INCREASE : aumentar, incrementar **3** PROMOTE : promover, fomentar, hacer publicidad por

boost[2] *n* **1** THRUST : impulso *m*, empujón *m* **2** ENCOURAGEMENT : estímulo *m*, aliento *m* **3** INCREASE : aumento *m*, incremento *m*

booster [ˈbuːstər] *n* **1** SUPPORTER : partidario *m*, -ria *f* **2 booster rocket** : cohete *m* propulsor **3 booster shot** : vacuna *f* de refuerzo

boot[1] [ˈbuːt] *vt* KICK : dar una patada a, patear

boot[2] *n* **1** : bota *f*, botín *m* **2** KICK : puntapié *m*, patada *f*

bootee *or* **bootie** [ˈbuːt̬i] *n* : botita *f*, botín *m*

booth [ˈbuːθ] *n*, *pl* **booths** [ˈbuːðz, ˈbuːθs] : cabina *f* (de teléfono, de votar), caseta *f* (de información), barraca *f* (a una feria)

bootlegger [ˈbuːt͵lɛgər] *n* : contrabandista *mf* del alcohol

booty [ˈbuːt̬i] *n*, *pl* **-ties** : botín *m*

booze [ˈbuːz] *n* : trago *m*, bebida *f* (alcohólica)

borax [ˈbɔr͵æks] *n* : bórax *m*

border[1] [ˈbɔrdər] *vt* **1** EDGE : ribetear, bordear **2** BOUND : limitar con, lindar con — *vi* VERGE : rayar, lindar <that borders on absurdity : eso raya en el absurdo>

border[2] *n* **1** EDGE : borde *m*, orilla *f* **2** TRIM : ribete *m* **3** FRONTIER : frontera *f*

bore[1] [ˈbor] *vt* **bored; boring 1** PIERCE : taladrar, perforar <to bore metals : taladrar metales> **2** OPEN : hacer, abrir <to bore a tunnel : abrir un túnel> **3** WEARY : aburrir

bore[2] → **bear**[1]

bore[3] *n* **1** : pesado *m,* -da *f* (persona aburrida) **2** TEDIOUSNESS : pesadez *f,* lo aburrido **3** DIAMETER : calibre *m*

boredom [ˈbordəm] *n* : aburrimiento *m*

boring [ˈborɪŋ] *adj* : aburrido, pesado

born [ˈbɔrn] *adj* **1** : nacido **2** : nato <she's a born singer : es una cantante nata> <he's a born leader : nació para mandar>

borne → **bear**[1]

boron [ˈborˌɑn] *n* : boro *m*

borough [ˈbəro] *n* : distrito *m* municipal

borrow [ˈbɑro] *vt* **1** : pedir prestado, tomar prestado **2** APPROPRIATE : apropiarse de, adoptar

Bosnian [ˈbɑzniən, ˈbɔz-] *n* : bosnio *m,* -nia *f* — **Bosnian** *adj*

bosom[1] [ˈbʊzəm, ˈbuː-] *adj* : íntimo

bosom[2] *n* **1** CHEST : pecho *m* **2** BREAST : pecho *m,* seno *m* **3** CLOSENESS : seno *m* <in the bosom of her family : en el seno de su familia>

bosomed [ˈbʊzəmd, ˈbuː-] *adj* : con busto <big-bosomed : con mucho busto>

boss[1] [ˈbɔs] *vt* **1** SUPERVISE : dirigir, supervisar **2 to boss around** : mandonear *fam,* mangonear *fam*

boss[2] *n* : jefe *m,* -fa *f;* patrón *m,* -trona *f*

bossy [ˈbɔsi] *adj* **bossier; -est** : mandón *fam,* autoritario, dominante

botanist [ˈbɑtənɪst] *n* : botánico *m,* -ca *f*

botany [ˈbɑtəni] *n* : botánica *f* — **botanical** [bəˈtænɪkəl] *adj*

botch[1] [ˈbɑtʃ] *vt* : hacer una chapuza de, estropear

botch[2] *n* : chapuza *f*

both[1] [ˈboːθ] *adj* : ambos, los dos, las dos <both books : ambos libros, los dos libros>

both[2] *conj* : tanto como <both Ana and her mother are tall : tanto Ana como su madre son altas>

both[3] *pron* : ambos *m,* -bas *f;* los dos, las dos

bother[1] [ˈbɑðər] *vt* **1** IRK : preocupar <nothing's bothering me : nada me preocupa> <what's bothering him? : ¿qué le pasa?> **2** PESTER : molestar, fastidiar — *vi* **to bother to** : molestarse en, tomar la molestia de

bother[2] *n* **1** TROUBLE : molestia *f,* problemas *mpl* **2** ANNOYANCE : molestia *f,* fastidio *m*

bothersome [ˈbɑðərsəm] *adj* : molesto, fastidioso

bottle[1] [ˈbɑtəl] *vt* **bottled; bottling** : embotellar, envasar

bottle[2] *n* : botella *f,* frasco *m*

bottleneck [ˈbɑtəlˌnɛk] *n* **1** : cuello *m* de botello (en un camino) **2** : embotellamiento *m,* atasco *m* (de tráfico) **3** OBSTACLE : obstáculo *m*

bottom[1] [ˈbɑtəm] *adj* : más bajo, inferior, de abajo

bottom[2] *n* **1** : fondo *m* (de una caja, de una taza, del mar), pie *m* (de una escalera, una página, una montaña), asiento *m* (de una silla), parte *f* de abajo (de una pila) **2** CAUSE : origen *m,* causa *f* <to get to the bottom of : llegar al fondo de> **3** BUTTOCKS : trasero *m,* nalgas *fpl*

bottomless [ˈbɑtəmləs] *adj* : sin fondo, sin límites

botulism [ˈbɑtʃəˌlɪzəm] *n* : botulismo *m*

boudoir [bəˈdwɑr, bʊ-; ˈbuːˌ-, ˈbʊ-] *n* : tocador *m*

bough [ˈbaʊ] *n* : rama *f*

bought → **buy**[1]

bouillon [ˈbuːˌjɑn; ˈbʊlˌjɑn, -jən] *n* : caldo *m*

boulder [ˈboːldər] *n* : canto *m* rodado, roca *f* grande

boulevard [ˈbʊləˌvɑrd, ˈbuː-] *n* : bulevar *m,* boulevard *m*

bounce[1] [ˈbaʊnts] *v* **bounced; bouncing** *vt* : hacer rebotar — *vi* : rebotar

bounce[2] *n* : rebote *m*

bouncy [ˈbaʊntsi] *adj* **bouncier; -est 1** LIVELY : vivo, exuberante, animado **2** RESILIENT : elástico, flexible **3** : que rebota (dícese de una pelota)

bound[1] [ˈbaʊnd] *vt* : delimitar, rodear — *vi* LEAP : saltar, dar brincos

bound[2] *adj* **1** OBLIGED : obligado **2** : encuadernado, empastado <a book bound in leather : un libro encuadernado en cuero> **3** DETERMINED : decidido, empeñado **4 to be bound to** : ser seguro que, tener que, no caber duda que <it was bound to happen : tenía que suceder> **5 bound for** : con rumbo a <bound for Chicago : con rumbo a Chicago> <to be homeward bound : ir camino a casa>

bound[3] *n* **1** LIMIT : límite *m* **2** LEAP : salto *m,* brinco *m*

boundary [ˈbaʊndri, -dəri] *n, pl* **-aries** : límite *m,* línea *f* divisoria, linde *mf*

boundless [ˈbaʊndləs] *adj* : sin límites, infinito

bounteous [ˈbaʊntiəs] *adj* **1** GENEROUS : generoso **2** ABUNDANT : copioso, abundante — **bounteously** *adv*

bountiful [ˈbaʊntɪfəl] *adj* **1** GENEROUS, LIBERAL : munificente, pródigo, generoso **2** ABUNDANT : copioso, abundante

bounty [ˈbaʊnti] *n, pl* **-ties 1** GENEROSITY : generosidad *f,* munificiencia *f* **2** REWARD : recompensa *f*

bouquet [boːˈkeɪ, buː-] *n* **1** : ramo *m,* ramillete *m* **2** FRAGRANCE : bouquet *m,* aroma *m*

bourbon [ˈbərbən, ˈbʊr-] *n* : bourbon *m,* whiskey *m* americano

bourgeois[1] [ˈbʊrʒˌwɑ, bʊrʒˈwɑ] *adj* : burgués

bourgeois[2] *n* : burgués *m,* -guesa *f*

bourgeoisie [ˌbʊrʒˌwɑˈzi] *n* : burguesía *f*

bout ['baʊt] *n* **1** : encuentro *m,* combate *m* (en deportes) **2** ATTACK : ataque *m* (de una enfermedad) **3** PERIOD, SPELL : período *m* (de actividad)

boutique [buː'tiːk] *n* : boutique *f*

bovine[1] ['boːˌvaɪn, -ˌviːn] *adj* : bovino, vacuno

bovine[2] *n* : bovino *m*

bow[1] ['baʊ] *vi* **1** : hacer una reverencia, inclinarse **2** SUBMIT : ceder, resignarse, someterse — *vt* **1** LOWER : inclinar, bajar **2** BEND : doblar

bow[2] ['baʊː] *n* **1** BOWING : reverencia *f,* inclinación *f* **2** : proa *f* (de un barco)

bow[3] ['boː] *vi* CURVE : arquearse, doblarse

bow[4] ['boː] *n* **1** ARCH, CURVE : arco *m,* curva *f* **2** : arco *m* (arma o vara para tocar varios instrumentos de música) **3** : lazo *m,* moño *m* <to tie a bow : hacer un moño>

bowels ['baʊəls] *npl* **1** INTESTINES : intestinos *mpl* **2** : entrañas *fpl* <in the bowels of the earth : en las entrañas de la tierra>

bower ['baʊər] *n* : enramada *f*

bowl[1] ['boːl] *vi* : jugar a los bolos

bowl[2] *n* : tazón *m,* cuenco *m*

bowler ['boːlər] *n* : jugador *m,* -dora *f* de bolos

bowling ['boːlɪŋ] *n* : bolos *mpl*

box[1] ['bɑks] *vt* **1** PACK : empaquetar, embalar, encajonar **2** SLAP : bofetear, cachetear — *vi* : boxear

box[2] *n* **1** CONTAINER : caja *f,* cajón *m* **2** COMPARTMENT : compartimento *m,* palco *m* (en el teatro) **3** SLAP : bofetada *f,* cachetada *f* **4** : boj *m* (planta)

boxcar ['bɑksˌkɑr] *n* : vagón *m* de carga, furgón *m*

boxer ['bɑksər] *n* : boxeador *m,* -dora *f*

boxing ['bɑksɪŋ] *n* : boxeo *m*

box office *n* : taquilla *f,* boletería *f*

boxwood ['bɑksˌwʊd] *n* : boj *m*

boy ['bɔɪ] *n* : niño *m,* chico *m*

boycott[1] ['bɔɪˌkɑt] *vt* : boicotear

boycott[2] *n* : boicot *m*

boyfriend ['bɔɪˌfrɛnd] *n* **1** FRIEND : amigo *m* **2** SWEETHEART : novio *m*

boyhood ['bɔɪˌhʊd] *n* : niñez *f*

boyish ['bɔɪɪʃ] *adj* : de niño, juvenil

bra ['brɑ] → **brassiere**

brace[1] ['breɪs] *v* **braced; bracing** *vt* **1** PROP UP, SUPPORT : apuntalar, apoyar, sostener **2** INVIGORATE : vigorizar **3** REINFORCE : reforzar — *vi* **to brace oneself** PREPARE : prepararse

brace[2] *n* **1** : berbiquí *m* <brace and bit : berbiquí y barrena> **2** CLAMP, REINFORCEMENT : abrazadera *f,* refuerzo *m* **3** : llave *f* (signo de puntuación) **4 braces** *npl* : aparatos *mpl* (de ortodoncia), frenos *mpl Mex*

bracelet ['breɪslət] *n* : brazalete *m,* pulsera *f*

bracken ['brækən] *n* : helecho *m*

bracket[1] ['brækət] *vt* **1** SUPPORT : asegurar, apuntalar **2** : poner entre corchetes **3** CATEGORIZE, GROUP : catalogar, agrupar

bracket[2] *n* **1** SUPPORT : soporte *m* **2** : corchete *m* (marca de puntuación) **3** CATEGORY, CLASS : clase *f,* categoría *f*

brackish ['brækɪʃ] *adj* : salobre

brad ['bræd] *n* : clavo *m* con cabeza pequeña, clavito *m*

brag[1] ['bræg] *vi* **bragged; bragging** : alardear, fanfarronear, jactarse

brag[2] *n* : alarde *m,* jactancia *f,* fanfarronada *f*

braggart ['brægərt] *n* : fanfarrón *m,* -rrona *f fam;* jactancioso *m,* -sa *f*

braid[1] ['breɪd] *vt* : trenzar

braid[2] *n* : trenza *f*

braille ['breɪl] *n* : braille *m*

brain[1] ['breɪn] *vt* : romper la crisma a, aplastar el cráneo a

brain[2] *n* **1** : cerebro *m* **2 brains** *npl* INTELLECT : inteligencia *f,* sesos *mpl*

brainless ['breɪnləs] *adj* : estúpido, tonto

brainstorm ['breɪnˌstɔrm] *n* : idea *f* brillante, idea *f* genial

brainy ['breɪni] *adj* **brainier; -est** : inteligente, listo

braise ['breɪz] *vt* **braised; braising** : cocer a fuego lento, estofar

brake[1] ['breɪk] *v* **braked; braking** : frenar

brake[2] *n* : freno *m*

bramble ['bræmbəl] *n* : zarza *f,* zarzamora *f*

bran ['bræn] *n* : salvado *m*

branch[1] ['bræntʃ] *vi* **1** : echar ramas (dícese de una planta) **2** DIVERGE : ramificarse, separarse

branch[2] *n* **1** : rama *f* (de una planta) **2** EXTENSION : ramal *m* (de un camino, un ferrocarril, un río), rama *f* (de una familia o un campo de estudiar), sucursal *f* (de una empresa), agencia *f* (del gobierno)

brand[1] ['brænd] *vt* **1** : marcar (ganado) **2** LABEL : tachar, tildar <they branded him as a liar : lo tacharon de mentiroso>

brand[2] *n* **1** : marca *f* (de ganado) **2** STIGMA : estigma *m* **3** MAKE : marca *f* <brand name : marca de fábrica>

brandish ['brændɪʃ] *vt* : blandir

brand–new ['brænd'nuː, -'njuː] *adj* : nuevo, flamante

brandy ['brændi] *n, pl* **-dies** : brandy *m*

brash ['bræʃ] *adj* **1** IMPULSIVE : impulsivo, impetuoso **2** BRAZEN : excesivamente desenvuelto, descarado

brass ['bræs] *n* **1** : latón *m* **2** GALL, NERVE : descaro *m,* cara *f fam* **3** OFFICERS : mandamases *mpl fam*

brassiere [brə'zɪr, brɑ-] *n* : sostén *m,* brasier *m Col, Mex*

brassy ['bræsi] *adj* **brassier; -est** : dorado

brat ['bræt] *n* : mocoso *m,* -sa *f;* niño *m* mimado, niña *f* mimada

bravado [brə'vɑdo] *n, pl* **-does** *or* **-dos** : bravuconadas *fpl*, bravatas *fpl*
brave[1] ['breɪv] *vt* **braved; braving** : afrontar, hacer frente a
brave[2] *adj* **braver; bravest** : valiente, valeroso — **bravely** *adv*
brave[3] *n* : guerrero *m* indio
bravery ['breɪvəri] *n* : valor *m,* valentía *f*
bravo ['brɑ,voː] *n, pl* **-vos** : bravo *m*
brawl[1] ['brɔl] *vi* : pelearse, pegarse
brawl[2] *n* : pelea *f,* reyerta *f*
brawn ['brɔn] *n* : fuerza *f* muscular
brawny ['brɔni] *adj* **brawnier; -est** : musculoso
bray[1] ['breɪ] *vi* : rebuznar
bray[2] *n* : rebuzno *m*
brazen ['breɪzən] *adj* **1** : de latón **2** BOLD : descarado, directo
brazenly ['breɪzənli] *adv* : descaradamente, insolentemente
brazenness ['breɪzənnəs] *n* : descaro *m,* atrevimiento *m*
brazier ['breɪʒər] *n* : brasero *m*
Brazilian [brə'zɪljən] *n* : brasileño *m,* -ña *f* — **Brazilian** *adj*
Brazil nut [brə'zɪl,nʌt] *n* : nuez *f* de Brasil
breach[1] ['briːtʃ] *vt* **1** PENETRATE : abrir una brecha en, penetrar **2** VIOLATE : infringir, violar
breach[2] *n* **1** VIOLATION : infracción *f,* violación *f* <breach of trust : abuso de confianza> **2** GAP, OPENING : brecha *f*
bread[1] ['brɛd] *vt* : empanar
bread[2] *n* : pan *m*
breadth ['brɛtθ] *n* : ancho *m,* anchura *f*
breadwinner ['brɛd,wɪnər] *n* : sostén *m* de la familia
break[1] ['breɪk] *v* **broke** ['broːk]; **broken** ['broːkən]; **breaking** *vt* **1** SMASH : romper, quebrar **2** VIOLATE : infringir, violar, romper **3** SURPASS : batir, superar **4** CRUSH, RUIN : arruinar, deshacer, destrozar <to break one's spirit : quebrantar su espíritu> **5** : dar, comunicar <to break the news : dar las noticias> **6** INTERRUPT : cortar, interrumpir — *vi* **1** : romperse, quebrarse <my calculator broke : se me rompió la calculadora> **2** DISPERSE : dispersarse, despejarse **3** : estallar (dícese de una tormenta), romper (dícese del día) **4** CHANGE : cambiar (dícese del tiempo o de la voz) **5** DECREASE : bajar <my fever broke : me bajó la fiebre> **6** : divulgarse, revelarse <the news broke : la noticia se divulgó> **7 to break into** : forzar, abrir **8 to break out of** : escaparse de **9 to break through** : penetrar
break[2] *n* **1** : ruptura *f,* rotura *f,* fractura *f* (de un hueso), claro *m* (entre las nubes), cambio *m* (del tiempo) **2** CHANCE : oportunidad *f* <a lucky break : un golpe de suerte> **3** REST : descanso *m* <to take a break : tomar(se) un descanso>
breakable ['breɪkəbəl] *adj* : quebradizo, frágil
breakage ['breɪkɪdʒ] *n* **1** BREAKING : rotura *f* **2** DAMAGE : destrozos *mpl*, daños *mpl*
breakdown ['breɪk,daʊn] *n* **1** : avería *f* (de máquinas), interrupción *f* (de comunicaciones), fracaso *m* (de negociaciones) **2** ANALYSIS : análisis *m,* desglose *m* **3** *or* **nervous breakdown** : crisis *f* nerviosa
break down *vi* **1** : estropearse, descomponerse <the machine broke down : la máquina se descompuso> **2** FAIL : fracasar **3** CRY : echarse a llorar — *vt* **1** DESTROY : derribar, echar abajo **2** OVERCOME : vencer (la resistencia), disipar (sospechas) **3** ANALYZE : analizar, descomponer
breaker ['breɪkər] *n* **1** WAVE : ola *f* grande **2** : interruptor *m* automático (de electricidad)
breakfast[1] ['brɛkfəst] *vi* : desayunar
breakfast[2] *n* : desayuno *m*
breakneck ['breɪk,nɛk] *adj* **at breakneck speed** : a una velocidad vertiginosa
break out *vi* **1** : salirse <she broke out in spots : le salieron granos> **2** ERUPT : estallar (dícese de una guerra, la violencia, etc.) **3** ESCAPE : fugarse, escaparse
break up *vt* **1** DIVIDE : dividir **2** : disolver (una muchedumbre, una pelea, etc.) — *vi* **1** BREAK : romperse **2** SEPARATE : deshacerse, separarse <I broke up with him : terminé con él>
breast ['brɛst] *n* **1** : pecho *m,* seno *m* (de una mujer) **2** CHEST : pecho *m*
breastbone ['brɛst,boːn] *n* : esternón *m*
breast–feed ['brɛst,fiːd] *vt* **-fed** [-,fɛd]; **-feeding** : amamantar, darle de mamar (a un niño)
breath ['brɛθ] *n* **1** BREATHING : aliento *m* <to hold one's breath : aguantar la respiración>**2** BREEZE : soplo *m* <a breath of fresh air : un soplo de aire freso>
breathe ['briːð] *v* **breathed; breathing** *vi* **1** : respirar **2** LIVE : vivir, respirar — *vt* **1** : respirar, aspirar <to breathe fresh air : respirar el aire fresco> **2** UTTER : decir <I won't breathe a word of this : no diré nada de esto>
breathless ['brɛθləs] *adj* : sin aliento, jadeante
breathlessly ['brɛθləsli] *adv* : entrecortadamente, jadeando
breathlessness ['brɛθləsnəs] *n* : dificultad *f* al respirar
breathtaking ['brɛθ,teɪkɪŋ] *adj* IMPRESSIVE : impresionante, imponente
breeches ['brɪtʃəz, 'briː-] *npl* : pantalones *mpl*, calzones *mpl*, bombachos *mpl*
breed[1] ['briːd] *v* **bred** ['brɛd]; **breeding** *vt* **1** : criar (animales) **2** ENGENDER

: engendrar, producir <familiarity breeds contempt : la confianza hace perder el respeto> **3** RAISE, REAR : criar, educar — *vi* REPRODUCE : reproducirse

breed[2] *n* **1** : variedad *f* (de plantas), raza *f* (de animales) **2** CLASS : clase *f,* tipo *m*

breeder ['bri:dər] *n* : criador *m,* -dora *f* (de animales); cultivador *m,* -dora *f* (de plantas)

breeze[1] ['bri:z] *vi* **breezed; breezing** : pasar con ligereza <to breeze in : entrar como si nada>

breeze[2] *n* : brisa *f,* soplo *m* (de aire)

breezy ['bri:zi] *adj* **breezier; -est 1** AIRY, WINDY : aireado, ventoso **2** LIVELY : animado, alegre **3** NONCHALANT : despreocupado

brethren → **brother**

brevity ['brɛvəti] *n, pl* **-ties** : brevedad *f,* concisión *f*

brew[1] ['bru:] *vt* **1** : fabricar, elaborar (cerveza) **2** FOMENT : tramar, maquinar, fomentar — *vi* **1** : fabricar cerveza **2** : amenazar <a storm is brewing : una tormenta amenaza>

brew[2] *n* **1** BEER : cerveza *f* **2** POTION : brebaje *m*

brewer ['bru:ər] *n* : cervecero *m,* -ra *f*

brewery ['bru:əri, 'brʊri] *n, pl* **-eries** : cervecería *f*

briar ['braɪər] → **brier**

bribe[1] ['braɪb] *vt* **bribed; bribing** : sobornar, cohechar, coimear *Arg, Chile, Peru*

bribe[2] *n* : soborno *m,* cohecho *m,* coima *f Arg, Chile, Peru,* mordida *f CA, Mex*

bribery ['braɪbəri] *n, pl* **-eries** : soborno *m,* cohecho *m,* coima *f,* mordida *f CA, Mex*

bric-a-brac ['brɪkə,bræk] *npl* : baratijas *fpl,* chucherías *fpl*

brick[1] ['brɪk] *vt* **to brick up** : tabicar, tapiar

brick[2] *n* : ladrillo *m*

bricklayer ['brɪk,leɪər] *n* : albañil *mf*

bricklaying ['brɪk,leɪɪŋ] *n* : albañilería *f*

bridal ['braɪdəl] *adj* : nupcial, de novia

bride ['braɪd] *n* : novia *f*

bridegroom ['braɪd,gru:m] *n* : novio *m*

bridesmaid ['braɪdz,meɪd] *n* : dama *f* de honor

bridge[1] ['brɪdʒ] *vt* **bridged; bridging 1** : tender un puente sobre **2 to bridge the gap** : salvar las diferencias

bridge[2] *n* **1** : puente *m* **2** : caballete *m* (de la nariz) **3** : puente *m* de mando (de un barco) **4** DENTURE : puente *m* (dental) **5** : bridge *m* (juego de naipes)

bridle[1] ['braɪdəl] *v* **-dled; -dling** *vt* **1** : embridar (un caballo) **2** RESTRAIN : refrenar, dominar, contener — *vi* **to bridle at** : molestarse por, picarse por

bridle[2] *n* : brida *f*

brief[1] ['bri:f] *vt* : dar órdenes a, instruir

brief[2] *adj* : breve, sucinto, conciso

brief[3] *n* : resumen *m,* sumario *m*

briefcase ['bri:f,keɪs] *n* : portafolio *m,* maletín *m*

briefly ['bri:fli] *adv* : brevemente, por poco tiempo <to speak briefly : discursar en pocas palabras>

brier ['braɪər] *n* **1** BRAMBLE : zarza *f,* rosal *m* silvestre **2** HEATH : brezo *m* veteado

brig ['brɪg] *n* **1** : bergantín *m* (barco) **2** : calabozo *m* (en un barco)

brigade [brɪ'geɪd] *n* : brigada *f*

brigadier general [,brɪgə'dɪr] *n* : general *m* de brigada

brigand ['brɪgənd] *n* : bandolero *m,* -ra *f;* forajido *m,* -da *f*

bright ['braɪt] *adj* **1** : brillante (dícese del sol, de los ojos), vivo (dícese de un color), claro, fuerte **2** CHEERFUL : alegre, animado <bright and early : muy temprano> **3** INTELLIGENT : listo, inteligente <a bright idea : una idea luminosa>

brighten ['braɪtən] *vt* **1** ILLUMINATE : iluminar **2** ENLIVEN : alegrar, animar — *vi* **1** : hacerse más brillante **2 to brighten up** : animarse, alegrarse, mejorar

brightly ['braɪtli] *adv* : vivamente, intensamente, alegremente

brightness ['braɪtnəs] *n* **1** LUMINOSITY : luminosidad *f,* brillantez *f,* resplandor *m,* brillo *m* **2** CHEERFULNESS : alegría *f,* ánimo *m*

brilliance ['brɪljənts] *n* **1** BRIGHTNESS : resplandor *m,* fulgor *m,* brillo *m,* brillantez *f* **2** INTELLIGENCE : inteligencia *f,* brillantez *f*

brilliancy ['brɪljəntsi] → **brilliance**

brilliant ['brɪljənt] *adj* : brillante

brilliantly ['brɪljəntli] *adv* : brillantemente, con brillantez

brim[1] ['brɪm] *vi* **brimmed; brimming 1** *or* **to brim over** : desbordarse, rebosar **2 to brim with tears** : llenarse de lágrimas

brim[2] *n* **1** : ala *f* (de un sombrero) **2** : borde *m* (de una taza o un vaso)

brimful ['brɪm'fʊl] *adj* : lleno hasta el borde, repleto, rebosante

brimless ['brɪmləs] *adj* : sin ala

brimstone ['brɪm,sto:n] *n* : azufre *m*

brindled ['brɪndəld] *adj* : manchado, pinto

brine ['braɪn] *n* **1** : salmuera *f,* escabeche *m* (para encurtir) **2** OCEAN : océano *m,* mar *m*

bring ['brɪŋ] *vt* **brought** ['brɔt]; **bringing 1** CARRY : traer <bring me some coffee : tráigame un café> **2** PRODUCE : traer, producir, conseguir <his efforts will bring him success : sus esfuerzos le conseguirán el éxito> **3** PERSUADE : convencer, persuadir **4** YIELD : rendir, alcanzar, venderse por <to bring a good price : alcanzar un

precio alto> **5 to bring to an end** : terminar (con) **6 to bring to light** : sacar a la luz
bring about *vt* : ocasionar, provocar, determinar
bring forth *vt* PRODUCE : producir
bring out *vt* : sacar, publicar (un libro, etc.)
bring to *vt* REVIVE : resucitar
bring up *vt* **1** REAR : criar **2** MENTION : sacar, mencionar
brininess ['braɪninəs] *n* : salinidad *f*
brink ['brɪŋk] *n* : borde *m*
briny ['braɪni] *adj* **brinier; -est** : salobre
briquette *or* **briquet** [brɪ'kɛt] *n* : briqueta *f*
brisk ['brɪsk] *adj* **1** LIVELY : rápido, enérgico, brioso **2** INVIGORATING : fresco, estimulante
brisket ['brɪskət] *n* : falda *f*
briskly ['brɪskli] *adv* : rápidamente, enérgicamente, con brío
briskness ['brɪsknəs] *n* : brío *m,* rapidez *f*
bristle[1] ['brɪsəl] *vi* **-tled; -tling 1** : erizarse, ponerse de punta **2** : enfurecerse, enojarse <she bristled at the suggestion : se enfureció ante tal sugerencia> **3** : estar plagado, estar repleto <a city bristling with tourists : una ciudad repleta de turistas>
bristle[2] *n* : cerda *f* (de un animal), pelo *m* (de una planta)
bristly ['brɪsəli] *adj* **bristlier; -est** : erizado, cerdoso, hirsuto
British[1] ['brɪṭɪʃ] *adj* : británico
British[2] *n* **the British** *npl* : los británicos
brittle ['brɪtəl] *adj* **-tler; -tlest** : frágil, quebradizo
brittleness ['brɪtəlnəs] *n* : fragilidad *f*
broach ['bro:tʃ] *vt* BRING UP : mencionar, abordar, sacar
broad ['brɔd] *adj* **1** WIDE : ancho **2** SPACIOUS : amplio, extenso **3** FULL : pleno <in broad daylight : en pleno día> **4** OBVIOUS : claro, evidente **5** TOLERANT : tolerante, liberal **6** GENERAL : general **7** ESSENTIAL : principal, esencial <the broad outline : los rasgos esenciales>
broadcast[1] ['brɔd,kæst] *vt* **-cast; -casting 1** SCATTER : esparcir, diseminar **2** CIRCULATE, SPREAD : divulgar, difundir, propagar **3** TRANSMIT : transmitir, emitir
broadcast[2] *n* **1** TRANSMISSION : transmisión *f,* emisión *f* **2** PROGRAM : programa *m,* emisión *f*
broadcaster ['brɔd,kæstər] *n* : presentador *m,* -dora *f;* locutor *m,* -tora *f*
broadcloth ['brɔd,klɔθ] *n* : paño *m* fino
broaden ['brɔdən] *vt* : ampliar, ensanchar — *vi* : ampliarse, ensancharse
broadloom ['brɔd,lu:m] *adj* : tejido en telar ancho
broadly ['brɔdli] *adv* **1** GENERALLY : en general, aproximadamente **2** WIDELY : extensivamente
broad-minded ['brɔd'maɪndəd] *adj* : tolerante, de amplias miras
broad-mindedness [brɔd'maɪndədnəs] *n* : tolerancia *f*
broadside ['brɔd,saɪd] *n* **1** VOLLEY : andanada *f* **2** ATTACK : ataque *m,* invectiva *f,* andanada *f*
brocade [bro'keɪd] *n* : brocado *m*
broccoli ['brɑkəli] *n* : brócoli *m,* brécol *m*
brochure [bro'ʃʊr] *n* : folleto *m*
brogue ['bro:g] *n* : acento *m* irlandés
broil[1] ['brɔɪl] *vt* : asar a la parrilla
broil[2] *n* : asado *m*
broiler ['brɔɪlər] *n* **1** GRILL : parrilla *f* **2** : pollo *m* para asar
broke[1] ['bro:k] → **break**[1]
broke[2] *adj* : pelado, arruinado <to go broke : arruinarse, quebrar>
broken ['bro:kən] *adj* **1** DAMAGED, SHATTERED : roto, quebrado, fracturado **2** IRREGULAR, UNEVEN : accidentado, irregular, recortado **3** VIOLATED : roto, quebrantado **4** INTERRUPTED : interrumpido, descontinuo **5** CRUSHED : abatido, quebrantado <a broken man : un hombre destrozado> **6** IMPERFECT : mal <to speak broken English : hablar el inglés con dificultad>
brokenhearted [,bro:kən'hɑrṭəd] *adj* : descorazonado, desconsolado
broker[1] ['bro:kər] *vt* : hacer corretaje de
broker[2] *n* **1** : agente *mf;* corredor *m,* -dora *f* **2** → **stockbroker**
brokerage ['bro:kərɪdʒ] *n* : corretage *m,* agencia *f* de corredores
bromine ['bro:,mi:n] *n* : bromo *m*
bronchitis [brɑn'kaɪṭəs, brɑŋ-] *n* : bronquitis *f*
bronze[1] ['brɑnz] *vt* **bronzed; bronzing** : broncear
bronze[2] *n* : bronce *m*
brooch ['bro:tʃ, 'bru:tʃ] *n* : broche *m,* prendedor *m*
brood[1] ['bru:d] *vt* **1** INCUBATE : empollar, incubar **2** PONDER : sopesar, considerar — *vi* **1** INCUBATE : empollar **2** REFLECT : rumiar, reflexionar **3** WORRY : ponerse melancólico, inquietarse
brood[2] *adj* : de cría
brood[3] *n* : nidada *f* (de pájaros), camada *f* (de mamíferos)
brooder ['bru:dər] *n* **1** THINKER : pensador *m,* -dora *f* **2** INCUBATOR : incubadora *f*
brook[1] ['brʊk] *vt* TOLERATE : tolerar, admitir
brook[2] *n* : arroyo *m*
broom ['bru:m, 'brʊm] *n* **1** : retama *f,* hiniesta *f* **2** : escoba *f* (para barrer)
broomstick ['bru:m,stɪk, 'brʊm-] *n* : palo *m* de escoba
broth ['brɔθ] *n, pl* **broths** ['brɔθs, 'brɔðz] : caldo *m*

brothel [ˈbrɑθəl, ˈbrɔ-] *n* : burdel *m*

brother [ˈbrʌðər] *n, pl* **brothers** *also* **brethren** [ˈbrɛðrən, -ðərn] **1** : hermano *m* **2** KINSMAN : pariente *m,* familiar *m*

brotherhood [ˈbrʌðərˌhʊd] *n* **1** FELLOWSHIP : fraternidad *f* **2** ASSOCIATION : hermandad *f*

brother–in–law [ˈbrʌðərɪnˌlɔ] *n, pl* **brothers–in–law:** cuñado *m*

brotherly [ˈbrʌðərli] *adj* : fraternal

brought → **bring**

brow [ˈbraʊ] *n* **1** EYEBROW : ceja *f* **2** FOREHEAD : frente *f* **3** : cima *f* <the brow of a hill : la cima de una colina>

browbeat [ˈbraʊˌbiːt] *vt* **-beat; -beaten** [-ˌbiːtən] *or* **-beat; -beating** : intimidar

brown[1] [ˈbraʊn] *vt* **1** : dorar (en cocinar) **2** TAN : broncear — *vi* **1** : dorarse (en cocinar) **2** TAN : broncearse

brown[2] *adj* : marrón, café, castaño (dícese del pelo), moreno (dícese de la piel)

brown[3] *n* : marrón *m,* café *m*

brownish [ˈbraʊnɪʃ] *adj* : pardo

browse [ˈbraʊz] *vi* **browsed; browsing** **1** GRAZE : pacer **2** LOOK : mirar, echar un vistazo

bruin [ˈbruːɪn] *n* BEAR : oso *m*

bruise[1] [ˈbruːz] *vt* **bruised; bruising** **1** : contusionar, machucar, magullar (a una persona) **2** DAMAGE : magullar, dañar (frutas) **3** CRUSH : majar **4** HURT : herir (los sentimientos)

bruise[2] *n* : moretón *m,* cardenal *m,* magulladura *f* (dícese de frutas)

brunch [ˈbrʌntʃ] *n* : combinación *f* de desayuno y almuerzo

brunet[1] *or* **brunette** [bruːˈnɛt] *adj* : moreno

brunet[2] *or* **brunette** *n* : moreno *m,* -na *f*

brunt [ˈbrʌnt] *n* **to bear the brunt of** : llevar el peso de, aguantar el mayor impacto de

brush[1] [ˈbrʌʃ] *vt* **1** : cepillar <to brush one's teeth : cepillarse uno los dientes> **2** SWEEP : barrer, quitar con un cepillo **3** GRAZE : rozar **4** **to brush off** DISREGARD : hacer caso omiso de, ignorar — *vi* **to brush up on** : repasar, refrescar, dar un repaso a

brush[2] *n* **1** *or* **brushwood** [ˈbrʌʃˌwʊd] : broza *f* **2** SCRUB, UNDERBRUSH : maleza *f* **3** : cepillo *m,* pincel *m* (de artista), brocha *f* (de pintor) **4** TOUCH : roce *m* **5** SKIRMISH : escaramuza *f*

brush–off [ˈbrʌʃˌɔf] *n* **to give the brush–off to** : dar calabazas a

brusque [ˈbrʌsk] *adj* : brusco — **brusquely** *adv*

brussels sprout [ˈbrʌsəlzˌspraʊt] *n* : col *f* de Bruselas

brutal [ˈbruːtəl] *adj* : brutal, cruel, salvaje — **brutally** *adv*

brutality [bruːˈtæləti] *n, pl* **-ties** : brutalidad *f*

brutalize [ˈbruːtəlˌaɪz] *vt* **-ized; -izing** : brutalizar, maltratar

brute[1] [ˈbruːt] *adj* : bruto <brute force : fuerza bruta>

brute[2] *n* **1** BEAST : bestia *f,* animal *m* **2** : bruto *m,* -ta *f;* bestia *mf* (persona)

brutish [ˈbruːtɪʃ] *adj* **1** : de animal **2** CRUEL : brutal, salvaje **3** STUPID : bruto, estúpido

bubble[1] [ˈbʌbəl] *vi* **-bled; -bling** : burbujear <to bubble over with joy : rebosar de alegría>

bubble[2] *n* : burbuja *f*

bubbly [ˈbʌbəli] *adj* **bubblier; -est** **1** BUBBLING : burbujeante **2** LIVELY : vivaz, lleno de vida

bubonic plague [buːˈbɑnɪk, ˈbjuː-] *n* : peste *f* bubónica

buccaneer [ˌbʌkəˈnɪr] *n* : bucanero *m*

buck[1] [ˈbʌk] *vi* **1** : corcovear (dícese de un caballo o un burro) **2** JOLT : dar sacudidas **3** **to buck against** : resistirse a, rebelarse contra **4** **to buck up** : animarse, levantar el ánimo — *vt* OPPOSE : oponerse a, ir en contra de

buck[2] *n, pl* **buck** *or* **bucks** **1** : animal *m* macho, ciervo *m* (macho) **2** DOLLAR : dólar *m* **3** **to pass the buck** *fam* : pasar la pelota *fam*

bucket [ˈbʌkət] *n* : balde *m,* cubo *m,* cubeta *f Mex*

bucketful [ˈbʌkətˌfʊl] *n* : balde *m* lleno

buckle[1] [ˈbʌkəl] *v* **-led; -ling** *vt* **1** FASTEN : abrochar **2** BEND, TWIST : combar, torcer — *vi* **1** BEND, TWIST : combarse, torcerse, doblarse (dícese de las rodillas) **2** **to buckle down** : ponerse a trabajar con esmero **3** **to buckle up** : abrocharse

buckle[2] *n* **1** : hebilla *f* **2** TWISTING : torcedura *f*

buckshot [ˈbʌkˌʃɑt] *n* : perdigón *m*

buckskin [ˈbʌkˌskɪn] *n* : gamuza *f*

bucktooth [ˈbʌkˌtuːθ] *n* : diente *m* saliente, diente *m* salido

buckwheat [ˈbʌkˌhwiːt] *n* : trigo *m* rubión, alforfón *m*

bucolic [bjuːˈkɑlɪk] *adj* : bucólico

bud[1] [ˈbʌd] *v* **budded; budding** *vt* GRAFT : injertar — *vi* : brotar, hacer brotes

bud[2] *n* : brote *m,* yema *f,* capullo *m* (de una flor)

Buddhism [ˈbuːˌdɪzəm, ˈbʊ-] *n* : Budismo *m*

Buddhist [ˈbuːdɪst, ˈbʊ-] *n* : budista *mf* — **Buddhist** *adj*

buddy [ˈbʌdi] *n, pl* **-dies** : amigo *m,* -ga *f;* compinche *mf fam;* cuate *m,* -ta *f Mex fam*

budge [ˈbʌdʒ] *vi* **budged; budging** **1** MOVE : moverse, desplazarse **2** YIELD : ceder

budget[1] [ˈbʌdʒət] *vt* : presupuestar (gastos), asignar (dinero) — *vi* : presupuestar, planear el presupuesto

budget[2] *n* : presupuesto

budgetary [ˈbʌdʒəˌtɛri] *adj* : presupuestario

buff[1] [ˈbʌf] *vt* POLISH : pulir, sacar brillo a, lustrar

buff[2] *adj* : beige, amarillento

buff[3] *n* **1** : beige *m,* amarillento *m* **2** ENTHUSIAST : aficionado *m,* -da *f;* entusiasta *mf*

buffalo [ˈbʌfəˌloː] *n, pl* **-lo** *or* **-loes 1** : búfalo *m* **2** BISON : bisonte *m*

buffer [ˈbʌfər] *n* **1** BARRIER : barrera *f* <buffer state : estado tapón> **2** SHOCK ABSORBER : amortiguador *m*

buffet[1] [ˈbʌfət] *vt* : golpear, zarandear, sacudir

buffet[2] *n* BLOW : golpe *m*

buffet[3] [ˌbʌˈfeɪ, ˌbuː-] *n* **1** : bufete *m,* bufé *m* (comida) **2** SIDEBOARD : aparador *m*

buffoon [ˌbʌˈfuːn] *n* : bufón *m,* -fona *f;* payaso *m,* -sa *f*

buffoonery [ˌbʌˈfuːnəri] *n, pl* **-eries** : bufonada *f,* payasada *f*

bug[1] [ˈbʌg] *vt* **bugged; bugging 1** PESTER : fastidiar, molestar **2** : ocultar micrófonos en

bug[2] *n* **1** INSECT : bicho *m,* insecto *m* **2** DEFECT : defecto *m,* falla *f,* problema *m* **3** GERM : microbio *m,* virus *m* **4** MICROPHONE : micrófono *m*

bugaboo [ˈbʌgəˌbuː] → **bogey**

bugbear [ˈbʌgˌbær] *n* : pesadilla *f,* coco *m*

buggy [ˈbʌgi] *n, pl* **-gies** : calesa *f* (tirada por caballos), cochecito *m* (para niños)

bugle [ˈbjuːgəl] *n* : clarín *m,* corneta *f*

bugler [ˈbjuːgələr] *n* : corneta *mf*

build[1] [ˈbɪld] *v* **built** [ˈbɪlt]; **building** *vt* **1** CONSTRUCT : construir, edificar, ensamblar, levantar **2** DEVELOP : desarrollar, elaborar, forjar **3** INCREASE : incrementar, aumentar — *vi* **to build up** : aumentar, intensificar

build[2] *n* PHYSIQUE : físico *m,* complexión *f*

builder [ˈbɪldər] *n* : constructor *m,* -tora *f;* contratista *mf*

building [ˈbɪldɪŋ] *n* **1** EDIFICE : edificio *m* **2** CONSTRUCTION : construcción *f*

built-in [ˈbɪltˈɪn] *adj* **1** : empotrado <built-in cabinets : armarios empotrados> **2** INHERENT : incorporado, intrínseco

bulb [ˈbʌlb] *n* **1** : bulbo *m* (de una planta), cabeza *f* (de ajo), cubeta *f* (de un termómetro) **2** LIGHTBULB : bombilla *f,* foco *m,* bombillo *m CA, Col, Ven*

bulbous [ˈbʌlbəs] *adj* : bulboso

Bulgarian [bʌlˈgæriən, bʊl-] *n* **1** : búlgaro *m,* -ra *f* **2** : búlgaro *m* (idioma) — **Bulgarian**

bulge[1] [ˈbʌldʒ] *vi* **bulged; bulging** : abultar, sobresalir

bulge[2] *n* : bulto *m,* protuberancia *f*

bulk[1] [ˈbʌlk] *vt* : hinchar — *vi* EXPAND, SWELL : ampliarse, hincharse

bulk[2] *n* **1** SIZE, VOLUME : volumen *m,* tamaño *m* **2** FIBER : fibra *f* **3** MASS : mole *f* **4 the bulk of** : la mayor parte de **5 in ~** : en grandes cantidades

bulkhead [ˈbʌlkˌhɛd] *n* : mamparo *m*

bulky [ˈbʌlki] *adj* **bulkier; -est** : voluminoso, grande

bull[1] [ˈbʊl] *adj* : macho

bull[2] *n* **1** : toro *m,* macho *m* (de ciertas especies) **2** : bula *f* (papal) **3** DECREE : decreto *m,* edicto *m*

bulldog [ˈbʊlˌdɔg] *n* : buldog *m*

bulldoze [ˈbʊlˌdoːz] *vt* **-dozed; -dozing 1** LEVEL : nivelar (el terreno), derribar (un edificio) **2** FORCE : forzar <he bulldozed his way through : se abrió paso a codazos>

bulldozer [ˈbʊlˌdoːzər] *n* : bulldozer *m*

bullet [ˈbʊlət] *n* : bala *f*

bulletin [ˈbʊlətən, -lətən] *n* **1** NOTICE : comunicado *m,* anuncio *m,* boletín *m* **2** NEWSLETTER : boletín *m* (informativo)

bulletin board *n* : tablón *m* de anuncios

bulletproof [ˈbʊlətˌpruːf] *adj* : antibalas, a prueba de balas

bullfight [ˈbʊlˌfaɪt] *n* : corrida *f* (de toros)

bullfighter [ˈbʊlˌfaɪtər] *n* : torero *m,* -ra *f;* matador *m*

bullfrog [ˈbʊlˌfrɔg] *n* : rana *f* toro

bullheaded [ˈbʊlˈhɛdəd] *adj* : testarudo

bullion [ˈbʊljən] *n* : oro *m* en lingotes, plata *f* en lingotes

bullock [ˈbʊlək] *n* **1** STEER : buey *m,* toro *m* castrado **2** : toro *m* joven, novillo *m*

bull's–eye [ˈbʊlzˌaɪ] *n, pl* **bull's–eyes** : diana *f,* blanco *m*

bully[1] [ˈbʊli] *vt* **-lied; -lying** : intimidar, amendrentar, mangonear

bully[2] *n, pl* **-lies** : matón *m;* bravucón *m,* -cona *f*

bulrush [ˈbʊlˌrʌʃ] *n* : especie *f* de junco

bulwark [ˈbʊlˌwərk, -ˌwɔrk; ˈbʌlˌwərk] *n* : baluarte *m,* bastión *f*

bum[1] [ˈbʌm] *v* **bummed; bumming** *vi* **to bum around** : vagabundear, vagar — *vt* : gorronear *fam,* sablear *fam*

bum[2] *adj* : inútil, malo <a bum rap : una acusación falsa>

bum[3] *n* **1** LOAFER : vago *m,* -ga *f* **2** HOBO, TRAMP : vagabundo *m,* -da *f*

bumblebee [ˈbʌmbəlˌbiː] *n* : abejorro *m*

bump[1] [ˈbʌmp] *vt* : chocar contra, golpear contra, dar <to bump one's head : darse (un golpe) en la cabeza> — *vi* **to bump into** MEET : encontrarse con, tropezarse con

bump[2] *n* **1** BULGE : bulto *m,* protuberancia *f* **2** IMPACT : golpe *m,* choque *m* **3** JOLT : sacudida *f*

bumper[1] [ˈbʌmpər] *adj* : extraordinario, récord <a bumper crop : una cosecha abundante>

bumper[2] *n* **:** parachoques *mpl*
bumpkin ['bʌmpkən] *n* **:** palurdo *m*, -da *f*
bumpy ['bʌmpi] *adj* **bumpier; -est :** desigual, lleno de baches (dícese de un camino), agitado (dícese de un vuelo en avión)
bun ['bʌn] *n* **:** bollo *m*
bunch[1] ['bʌntʃ] *vt* **:** agrupar, amontonar — *vi* **to bunch up :** amontarse, agruparse, fruncirse (dícese de una tela)
bunch[2] *n* **:** grupo *m*, montón *m*, ramo *m* (de flores)
bundle[1] ['bʌndəl] *vt* **-dled; -dling :** liar, atar
bundle[2] *n* **1 :** fardo *m*, atado *m*, bulto *m*, haz *m* (de palos) **2** PARCEL **:** paquete *m* **3** LOAD **:** montón *m* <a bundle of money : un montón de dinero>
bungalow ['bʌŋgə,lo:] *n* **:** tipo de casa de un solo piso
bungle[1] ['bʌŋgəl] *vt* **-gled; -gling :** echar a perder, malograr
bungle[2] *n* **:** chapuza *f*, desatino *m*
bungler ['bʌŋgələr] *n* **:** chapucero *m*, -ra *f;* inepto *m*, -ta *f*
bunion ['bʌnjən] *n* **:** juanete *m*
bunk[1] ['bʌŋk] *vi* **:** dormir (en una litera)
bunk[2] *n* **1** *or* **bunk bed :** litera *f* **2** NONSENSE **:** tonterías *fpl*, bobadas *fpl*
bunker ['bʌŋkər] *n* **1 :** carbonera *f* (en un barco) **2** SHELTER **:** búnker *m*
bunny ['bʌni] *n, pl* **-nies :** conejo *m*, -ja *f*
buoy[1] ['bu:i, 'bɔɪ] *vt* **to buoy up 1 :** mantener a flote **2** CHEER, HEARTEN **:** animar, levantar el ánimo a
buoy[2] *n* **:** boya *f*
buoyancy ['bɔɪən*t*si, 'bu:jən-] *n* **1 :** flotabilidad *f* **2** OPTIMISM **:** confianza *f*, optimismo *m*
buoyant ['bɔɪənt, 'bu:jənt] *adj* **:** boyante, flotante
bur *or* **burr** ['bər] *n* **:** abrojo *m* (de una planta)
burden[1] ['bərdən] *vt* **:** cargar, oprimir
burden[2] *n* **:** carga *f*, peso *m*
burdensome ['bərdənsəm] *adj* **:** oneroso
burdock ['bər,dɑk] *n* **:** bardana *f*
bureau ['bjʊro] *n* **1** CHEST OF DRAWERS **:** cómoda *f* **2** DEPARTMENT **:** departamento *m* (del gobierno) **3** AGENCY **:** agencia *f* <travel bureau : agencia de viajes>
bureaucracy [bjʊ'rɑkrəsi] *n, pl* **-cies :** burocracia *f*
bureaucrat ['bjʊrə,kræt] *n* **:** burócrata *mf*
bureaucratic [,bjʊrə'kræṭɪk] *adj* **:** burocrático
burgeon ['bərdʒən] *vi* **:** florecer, retoñar, crecer
burglar ['bərglər] *n* **:** ladrón *m*, -drona *f*
burglarize ['bərglə,raɪz] *vt* **-ized; -izing :** robar
burglary ['bərgləri] *n, pl* **-glaries :** robo *m*
burgle ['bərgəl] *vt* **-gled; -gling :** robar
burgundy ['bərgəndi] *n, pl* **-dies :** borgoña *m*, vino *m* de Borgoña
burial ['bɛriəl] *n* **:** entierro *m*, sepelio *m*
burlap ['bər,læp] *n* **:** arpillera *f*
burlesque[1] [bər'lɛsk] *vt* **-lesqued; -lesquing :** parodiar
burlesque[2] *n* **1** PARODY **:** parodia *f* **2** REVUE **:** revista *f* (musical)
burly ['bərli] *adj* **-lier; -liest :** fornido, corpulento, musculoso
burn[1] ['bərn] *v* **burned** ['bərnd, 'bərnt] *or* **burnt** ['bərnt]; **burning** *vt* **1 :** quemar, incendiar <to burn a building : incendiar un edificio> <I burned my hand : me quemé la mano> **2** CONSUME **:** usar, gastar, consumir — *vi* **1 :** arder (dícese de un fuego o un edificio), quemarse (dícese de la comida, etc.) **2 :** estar prendido, estar encendido <we left the lights burning : dejamos las luces encendidas> **3 to burn out :** consumirse, apagarse **4 to burn with :** arder de <he was burning with jealousy : ardía de celos>
burn[2] *n* **:** quemadura *f*
burner ['bərnər] *n* **:** quemador *m*
burnish ['bərnɪʃ] *vt* **:** bruñir
burp[1] ['bərp] *vi* **:** eructar — *vt* **:** hacer eructar
burp[2] *n* **:** eructo *m*
burr → **bur**
burro ['bəro, 'bʊr-] *n, pl* **-os :** burro *m*
burrow[1] ['bəro] *vi* **1 :** cavar, hacer una madriguera **2 to burrow into :** hurgar en — *vt* **:** cavar, excavar
burrow[2] *n* **:** madriguera *f*, conejera *f* (de un conejo)
bursar ['bərsər] *n* **:** administrador *m*, -dora *f*
bursitis [bər'saɪṭəs] *n* **:** bursitis *f*
burst[1] ['bərst] *v* **burst** *or* **bursted; bursting** *vi* **1 :** reventarse (dícese de una llanta o un globo), estallar (dícese de obuses o fuegos artificiales), romperse (dícese de un dique) **2 to burst in :** irrumpir en **3 to burst into :** empezar a, echar a <to burst into tears : echarse a llorar> — *vt* **:** reventar
burst[2] *n* **1** EXPLOSION **:** estallido *m*, explosión *f*, reventón *m* (de una llanta) **2** OUTBURST **:** arranque *m* (de actividad, de velocidad), arrebato *m* (de ira), salva *f* (de aplausos)
Burundian [bʊ'ru:ndiən, -'rʊn-] *n* **:** burundés *m*, -desa *f* — **Burundian** *adj*
bury ['bɛri] *vt* **buried; burying 1** INTER **:** enterrar, sepultar **2** HIDE **:** esconder, ocultar **3 to bury oneself in :** enfrascarse en
bus[1] ['bʌs] *v* **bused** *or* **bussed** ['bʌst]; **busing** *or* **bussing** ['bʌsɪŋ] *vt* **:** trans-

portar en autobús — *vi* : viajar en autobús

bus[2] *n* : autobús *m,* bus *m,* camión *m Mex,* colectivo *m Arg, Bol, Peru*

busboy [ˈbʌs,bɔɪ] *n* : ayudante *mf* de camarero

bush [ˈbʊʃ] *n* **1** SHRUB : arbusto *m,* mata *f* **2** THICKET : maleza *f,* matorral *m*

bushel [ˈbʊʃəl] *n* : medida de áridos igual a 35.24 litros

bushing [ˈbʊʃɪŋ] *n* : cojinete *m*

bushy [ˈbʊʃi] *adj* **bushier; -est** : espeso, poblado <bushy eyebrows : cejas pobladas>

busily [ˈbɪzəli] *adv* : afanosamente, diligentemente

business [ˈbɪznəs, -nəz] *n* **1** OCCUPATION : ocupación *f,* oficio *m* **2** DUTY, MISSION : misión *f,* deber *m,* responsabilidad *f* **3** ESTABLISHMENT, FIRM : empresa *f,* firma *f,* negocio *m,* comercio *m* **4** COMMERCE : negocios *mpl,* comercio *m* **5** AFFAIR, MATTER : asunto *m,* cuestión *f,* cosa *f* <it's none of your business : no es asunto tuyo>

businessman [ˈbɪznəs,mæn, -nəz-] *n, pl* **-men** [-mən, -,mɛn] : empresario *m,* hombre *m* de negocios

businesswoman [ˈbɪznəs,wʊmən, -nəz-] *n, pl* **-women** [-,wɪmən] : empresaria *f,* mujer *f* de negocios

bust[1] [ˈbʌst] *vt* **1** BREAK, SMASH : romper, estropear, destrozar **2** TAME : domar, amansar (un caballo) — *vi* : romperse, estropearse

bust[2] *n* **1** : busto *m* (en la escultura) **2** BREASTS : pecho *m,* senos *mpl,* busto *m*

bustle[1] [ˈbʌsəl] *vi* **-tled; -tling to bustle about** : ir y venir, trajinar, ajetrearse

bustle[2] *n* **1** *or* **hustle and bustle** : bullicio *m,* ajetreo *m* **2** : polisón *m* (en la ropa feminina)

busy[1] [ˈbɪzi] *vt* **busied; busying to busy oneself with** : ocuparse con, ponerse a, entretenerse con

busy[2] *adj* **busier; -est 1** OCCUPIED : ocupado, atareado <he's busy working : está ocupado en su trabajo> <the telephone was busy : el teléfono estaba ocupado> **2** BUSTLING : concurrido, animado <a busy street : una calle concurrida, una calle con mucho tránsito>

busybody [ˈbɪzi,bɑdi] *n, pl* **-bodies** : entrometido *m,* -da *f;* metiche *mf fam;* metomentodo *mf*

but[1] [ˈbʌt] *conj* **1** THAT : que <there is no doubt but he is lazy : no cabe duda que sea perezoso> **2** WITHOUT : sin que **3** NEVERTHELESS : pero, no obstante, sin embargo <I called her but she didn't answer : la llamé pero no contestó> **4** YET : pero <he was poor but proud : era pobre pero orgulloso>

but[2] *prep* EXCEPT : excepto, menos <everyone but Carlos : todos menos Carlos> <the last but one : el penúltimo>

butcher[1] [ˈbʊtʃər] *vt* **1** SLAUGHTER : matar (animales) **2** KILL : matar, asesinar, masacrar **3** BOTCH : estropear, hacer una chapuza

butcher[2] *n* **1** : carnicero *m,* -ra *f* **2** KILLER : asesino *m,* -na *f* **3** BUNGLER : chapucero *m,* -ra *f*

butler [ˈbʌtlər] *n* : mayordomo *m*

butt[1] [ˈbʌt] *vt* **1** : embestir (con los cuernos), darle un cabezazo a **2** ABUT : colindar con, bordear — *vi* **to butt in 1** INTERRUPT : interrumpir **2** MEDDLE : entrometerse, meterse

butt[2] *n* **1** BUTTING : embestida *f* (de cuernos), cabezazo *m* **2** TARGET : blanco *m* <the butt of their jokes : el blanco de sus bromas> **3** BOTTOM, END : extremo *m,* culata *f* (de un rifle), colilla *f* (de un cigarillo)

butte [ˈbjuːt] *n* : colina *f* empinada y aislada

butter[1] [ˈbʌtər] *vt* **1** : untar con mantequilla **2 to butter up** : halagar

butter[2] *n* : mantequilla *f*

buttercup [ˈbʌt̬ər,kʌp] *n* : ranúnculo *m*

butterfat [ˈbʌt̬ər,fæt] *n* : grasa *f* de la leche

butterfly [ˈbʌt̬ər,flaɪ] *n, pl* **-flies** : mariposa *f*

buttermilk [ˈbʌt̬ər,mɪlk] *n* : suero *m* de la leche

butternut [ˈbʌt̬ər,nʌt] *n* : nogal *m* ceniciento (árbol)

butterscotch [ˈbʌt̬ər,skɑtʃ] *n* : caramelo *m* duro hecho con mantequilla

buttery [ˈbʌt̬əri] *adj* : mantecoso

buttocks [ˈbʌt̬əks, -,tɑks] *npl* : nalgas *fpl,* trasero *m*

button[1] [ˈbʌtən] *vt* : abrochar, abotonar — *vi* : abrocharse, abotonarse

button[2] *n* : botón *m*

buttonhole[1] [ˈbʌtən,hoːl] *vt* **-holed; -holing** : acorralar

buttonhole [2] *n* : ojal *m*

buttress[1] [ˈbʌtrəs] *vt* : apoyar, reforzar

buttress[2] *n* **1** : contrafuerte *m* (en la arquitectura) **2** SUPPORT : apoyo *m,* sostén *m*

buxom [ˈbʌksəm] *adj* : con mucho busto, con mucho pecho

buy[1] [ˈbaɪ] *vt* **bought** [ˈbɔt]; **buying** : comprar

buy[2] *n* BARGAIN : compra *f,* ganga *f*

buyer [ˈbaɪər] *n* : comprador *m,* -dora *f*

buzz[1] [ˈbʌz] *vi* : zumbar (dícese de un insecto), sonar (dícese de un teléfono o un despertador)

buzz[2] *n* **1** : zumbido *m* (de insectos) **2** : murmullo *m,* rumor *m* (de voces)

buzzard [ˈbʌzərd] *n* VULTURE : buitre *m,* zopilote *m CA, Mex*

buzzer [ˈbʌzər] *n* : timbre *m,* chicharra *f*

buzzword [ˈbʌz,wərd] *n* : palabra *f* de moda

by[1] [ˈbaɪ] *adv* **1** NEAR : cerca <he lives close by : vive muy cerca> **2 to stop**

by : pasar por casa, hacer una visita **3 to go by :** pasar <they rushed by : pasaron corriendo> **4 to put by :** reservar, poner a un lado **5 by and by :** poco después, dentro de poco **6 by and large :** en general

by² *prep* **1** NEAR **:** cerca de, al lado de, junto a **2** VIA **:** por <she left by the door : salió por la puerta> **3** PAST **:** por, por delante de <they walked by him : pasaron por delante de él> **4** DURING **:** de, durante <by night : de noche> **5** (*in expressions of time*) **:** para <we'll be there by ten : estaremos allí para las diez> <by then : para entonces> **6** (*indicating cause or agent*) **:** por, de, a <built by the Romans : construido por los romanos> <a book by Borges : un libro de Borges> <made by hand : hecho a mano>

by and by *adv* **:** dentro de poco

bygone¹ [ˈbaɪˌgɔn] *adj* **:** pasado

bygone² *n* **let bygones be bygones :** lo pasado, pasado está

bylaw *or* **byelaw** [ˈbaɪˌlɔ] *n* **:** norma *f*, reglamento *m*

by–line [ˈbaɪˌlaɪn] *n* **:** data *f*

bypass¹ [ˈbaɪˌpæs] *vt* **:** evitar

bypass² *n* **:** carretera *f* de circunvalación, desvío *m*

by–product [ˈbaɪˌprɑdəkt] *n* **:** subproducto *m*, producto *m* derivado

bystander [ˈbaɪˌstændər] *n* **:** espectador *m*, -dora *f*

byway [ˈbaɪˌweɪ] *n* **:** camino *m* (apartado), carretera *f* secundaria

byword [ˈbaɪˌwərd] *n* **1** PROVERB **:** proverbio *m*, refrán *m* **2 to be a byword for :** estar sinónimo de

C

c [ˈsiː] *n, pl* **c's** *or* **cs :** tercera letra del alfabeto inglés

cab [ˈkæb] *n* **1** TAXI **:** taxi *m* **2 :** cabina *f* (de un camión o una locomotora) **3** CARRIAGE **:** coche *m* de caballos

cabal [kəˈbɑl, -ˈbæl] *n* **1** INTRIGUE, PLOT **:** conspiración *f*, complot *m*, intriga *f* **2 :** grupo *m* de conspiradores

cabaret [ˌkæbəˈreɪ] *n* **:** cabaret *m*

cabbage [ˈkæbɪdʒ] *n* **:** col *f*, repollo *m*

cabbie *or* **cabby** [ˈkæbi] *n* **:** taxista *mf*

cabin [ˈkæbən] *n* **1** HUT **:** cabaña *f*, choza *f*, barraca *f* **2** STATEROOM **:** camarote *m* **3 :** cabina *f* (de un automóvil o avión)

cabinet [ˈkæbnət] *n* **1** CUPBOARD **:** armario *m* **2 :** gabinete *m*, consejo *m* de ministros **3 medicine cabinet :** botiquín *m*

cabinetmaker [ˈkæbnətˌmeɪkər] *n* **:** ebanista *mf*

cabinetmaking [ˈkæbnətˌmeɪkɪŋ] *n* **:** ebanistería *f*

cable¹ [ˈkeɪbəl] *vt* **-bled; -bling :** enviar un cable, telegrafiar

cable² *n* **1 :** cable *m* (para colgar o sostener algo) **2 :** cable *m* eléctrico **3 → cablegram**

cablegram [ˈkeɪbəlˌgræm] *n* **:** telegrama *m*, cable *m*

caboose [kəˈbuːs] *n* **:** furgón *m* de cola, cabús *m Mex*

cabstand [ˈkæbˌstænd] *n* **:** parada *f* de taxis

cacao [kəˈkaʊ, -ˈkeɪo] *n, pl* **cacaos :** cacao *m*

cache¹ [ˈkæʃ] *vt* **cached; caching :** esconder, guardar en un escondrijo

cache² *n* **1 :** escondite *m*, escondrijo *m* <cache of weapons : escondite de armas> **2 :** cache *m* <cache memory : memoria cache>

cachet [kæˈʃeɪ] *n* **:** caché *m*, prestigio *m*

cackle¹ [ˈkækəl] *vi* **-led; -ling 1** CLUCK **:** cacarear **2 :** reírse o carcajearse estridentemente <he was cackling with delight : estaba carcajeándose de gusto>

cackle² *n* **1 :** cacareo *m* (de una polla) **2** LAUGH **:** risa *f* estridente

cacophony [kæˈkɑfəni, -ˈkɔ-] *n, pl* **-nies :** cacofonía *f*

cactus [ˈkæktəs] *n, pl* **cacti** [-ˌtaɪ] *or* **-tuses :** cacto *m*, cactus *m*

cadaver [kəˈdævər] *n* **:** cadáver *m*

cadaverous [kəˈdævərəs] *adj* **:** cadavérico

caddie¹ *or* **caddy** [ˈkædi] *vi* **caddied; caddying :** trabajar de caddie, hacer de caddie

caddie² *or* **caddy** *n, pl* **-dies :** caddie *mf*

caddy [ˈkædi] *n, pl* **-dies :** cajita *f* para té

cadence [ˈkeɪdənts] *n* **:** cadencia *f*, ritmo *m*

cadenced [ˈkeɪdəntst] *adj* **:** cadencioso, rítmico

cadet [kəˈdɛt] *n* **:** cadete *mf*

cadmium [ˈkædmiəm] *n* **:** cadmio *m*

cadre [ˈkæˌdreɪ, ˈkɑ-, -ˌdriː] *n* **:** cuadro *m* (de expertos)

café [kæˈfeɪ, kə-] *n* **:** café *m*, cafetería *f*

cafeteria [ˌkæfəˈtɪriə] *n* **:** cafetería *f*, restaurante *m* de autoservicio

caffeine [kæˈfiːn] *n* **:** cafeína *f*

cage¹ [ˈkeɪdʒ] *vt* **caged; caging :** enjaular

cage² *n* **:** jaula *f*

cagey [ˈkeɪdʒi] *adj* **-gier; -est 1** CAUTIOUS **:** cauteloso, reservado **2** SHREWD **:** astuto, vivo — **cagily** [-dʒəli] *adv*

caisson [ˈkeɪˌsɑn, -sən] *n* **1 :** cajón *m* de municiones **2 :** cajón *m* hidráulico

cajole [kəˈdʒoːl] *vt* **-joled; -joling :** engatusar

cajolery [kəˈdʒoːləri] *n* **:** engatusamiento *m*

cake[1] [ˈkeɪk] *v* **caked; caking** *vt* **:** cubrir <caked with mud : cubierto de barro> — *vi* **:** endurecerse

cake[2] *n* **1 :** torta *f,* bizcocho *m,* pastel *m* **2 :** pastilla *f* (de jabón) **3 to take the cake :** llevarse la palma, ser el colmo

calabash [ˈkæləˌbæʃ] *n* **:** calabaza *f*

calamine [ˈkæləˌmaɪn] *n* **:** calamina *f* <calamine lotion : loción de calamina>

calamitous [kəˈlæmət̬əs] *adj* **:** desastroso, catastrófico, calamitoso — **calamitously** *adv*

calamity [kəˈlæmət̬i] *n, pl* **-ties :** desastre *m,* desgracia *f,* calamidad *f*

calcium [ˈkælsiəm] *n* **:** calcio *m*

calcium carbonate [ˈkɑrbəˌneɪt, -nət] *n* **:** carbonato *m* de calcio

calculable [ˈkælkjələbəl] *adj* **:** calculable, computable

calculate [ˈkælkjəˌleɪt] *v* **-lated; -lating** *vt* **1** COMPUTE **:** calcular, computar **2** ESTIMATE **:** calcular, creer **3** INTEND **:** planear, tener la intención de <I calculated on spending $100 : planeaba gastar $100> — *vi* **:** calcular, hacer cálculos

calculated [ˈkælkjəˌleɪt̬əd] *adj* **1** ESTIMATED **:** calculado **2** DELIBERATE **:** intencional, premeditado, deliberado

calculating [ˈkælkjəˌleɪt̬ɪŋ] *adj* SHREWD **:** calculador, astuto

calculation [ˌkælkjəˈleɪʃən] *n* **:** cálculo *m*

calculator [ˈkælkjəˌleɪt̬ər] *n* **:** calculadora *f*

calculus [ˈkælkjələs] *n, pl* **-li** [-ˌlaɪ] **1 :** cálculo *m* <differential calculus : cálculo diferencial> **2** TARTAR **:** sarro *m* (dental)

caldron [ˈkɔldrən] → **cauldron**

calendar [ˈkæləndər] *n* **1 :** calendario *m* **2** SCHEDULE **:** calendario *m,* programa *m,* agenda *f*

calf [ˈkæf, ˈkaf] *n, pl* **calves** [ˈkævz, ˈkavz] **1 :** becerro *m,* -rra *f;* ternero *m,* -ra *f* (de vacunos) **2 :** cría *f* (de otros mamíferos) **3 :** pantorrilla *f* (de la pierna)

calfskin [ˈkæfˌskɪn] *n* **:** piel *f* de becerro

caliber *or* **calibre** [ˈkæləbər] *n* **1 :** calibre *m* <a .38 caliber gun : una pistola de calibre .38> **2** ABILITY **:** calibre *m,* valor *m,* capacidad *f*

calibrate [ˈkæləˌbreɪt] *vt* **-brated; -brating :** calibrar (armas), graduar (termómetros)

calibration [ˌkæləˈbreɪʃən] *n* **:** calibrado *m,* calibración *f*

calico [ˈkælɪˌkoː] *n, pl* **-coes** *or* **-cos 1 :** calicó *m,* percal *m* **2** *or* **calico cat :** gato *m* manchado

calipers [ˈkæləpərz] *npl* **:** calibrador *m*

caliph *or* **calif** [ˈkeɪləf, ˈkæ-] *n* **:** califa *m*

calisthenics [ˌkæləsˈθɛnɪks] *ns & pl* **:** calistenia *f*

calk [ˈkɔk] → **caulk**

call[1] [ˈkɔl] *vi* **1** CRY, SHOUT **:** gritar, vociferar **2** VISIT **:** hacer (una) visita, visitar **3 to call for :** exigir, requerir, necesitar <it calls for patience : requiere mucha paciencia> — *vt* **1** SUMMON **:** llamar, convocar **2** TELEPHONE **:** llamar por teléfono, telefonear **3** NAME **:** llamar, apodar

call[2] *n* **1** SHOUT **:** grito *m,* llamada *f* **2 :** grito *m* (de un animal), reclamo *m* (de un pájaro) **3** SUMMONS **:** llamada *f* **4** DEMAND **:** llamado *m,* petición *f* **5** VISIT **:** visita *f* **6** DECISION **:** decisión *f* (en deportes) **7** *or* **telephone call :** llamada *f* (telefónica)

call down *vt* REPRIMAND **:** reprender, reñir

caller [ˈkɔlər] *n* **1** VISITOR **:** visita *f* **2 :** persona *f* que llama (por teléfono)

calling [ˈkɔlɪŋ] *n* **:** vocación *f,* profesión *f*

calliope [kəˈlaɪəˌpiː, ˈkæliˌoːp] *n* **:** órgano *m* de vapor

call off *vt* CANCEL **:** cancelar, suspender

callous[1] [ˈkæləs] *vt* **:** encallecer

callous[2] *adj* **1** CALLUSED **:** calloso, encallecido **2** UNFEELING **:** insensible, desalmado, cruel

callously [ˈkæləsli] *adv* **:** cruelmente, insensiblemente

callousness [ˈkæləsnəs] *n* **:** insensibilidad *f,* crueldad *f*

callow [ˈkælo] *adj* **:** inexperto, inmaduro

callus [ˈkæləs] *n* **:** callo m

callused [ˈkæləst] *adj* **:** encallecido, calloso

calm[1] [ˈkɑm, ˈkɑlm] *vt* **:** tranquilizar, calmar, sosegar — *vi* **:** tranquilizarse, calmarse <calm down! : ¡tranquilízate!>

calm[2] *adj* **1** TRANQUIL **:** calmo, tranquilo, sereno, ecuánime **2** STILL **:** en calma (dícese del mar), sin viento (dícese del aire)

calm[3] *n* **:** tranquilidad *f,* calma *f*

calmly [ˈkɑmli, ˈkɑlm-] *adv* **:** con calma, tranquilamente

calmness [ˈkɑmnəs, ˈkɑlm-] *n* **:** calma *f,* tranquilidad *f*

caloric [kəˈlɔrɪk] *adj* **:** calórico (dícese de los alimentos), calorífico (dícese de la energía)

calorie [ˈkæləri] *n* **:** caloría *f*

calumniate [kəˈlʌmniˌeɪt] *vt* **-ated; -ating :** calumniar, difamar

calumny [ˈkæləmni] *n, pl* **-nies :** calumnia *f,* difamación *f*

calve [ˈkæv, ˈkav] *vi* **calved; calving :** parir (dícese de los mamíferos)

calves → **calf**

calypso [kəˈlɪpˌsoː] *n, pl* **-sos :** calipso *m*

calyx [ˈkeɪlɪks, ˈkæ-] *n, pl* **-lyxes** *or* **-lyces** [-ləˌsiːz] : cáliz *m*
cam [ˈkæm] *n* : leva *f*
camaraderie [ˌkɑmˈrɑdəri, ˌkæm-; ˌkɑməˈrɑ-] *n* : compañerismo *m*, camaradería *f*
Cambodian [kæmˈboːdiən] *n* : camboyano *m*, -na *f* — **Cambodian** *adj*
came → **come**
camel [ˈkæməl] *n* : camello *m*
camellia [kəˈmiːljə] *n* : camelia *f*
cameo [ˈkæmiˌoː] *n, pl* **-eos 1** : camafeo *m* **2** *or* **cameo performance** : actuación *f* especial
camera [ˈkæmrə, ˈkæmərə] *n* : cámara *f*, máquina *f* fotográfica
Cameroonian [ˌkæməˈruːniən] *n* : camerunés *m*, -nesa *f*
camouflage[1] [ˈkæməˌflɑʒ, -ˌflɑdʒ] *vt* **-flaged; -flaging** : camuflajear, camuflar
camouflage[2] *n* : camuflaje *m*
camp[1] [ˈkæmp] *vi* : acampar, ir de camping
camp[2] *n* **1** : campamento *m* **2** FACTION : campo *m*, bando *m* <in the same camp : del mismo bando> **3 to pitch camp** : acampar, poner el campamento **4 to break camp** : levantar el campamento
campaign[1] [kæmˈpeɪn] *vi* : hacer (una) campaña
campaign[2] *n* : campaña *f*
campanile [ˌkæmpəˈniːˌliː, -ˈniːl] *n, pl* **-niles** *or* **-nili** [-ˈniːˌliː] : campanario *m*
camper [ˈkæmpər] *n* **1** : campista *mf* (persona) **2** : cámper *m* (vehículo)
campground [ˈkæmpˌgraʊnd] *n* : campamento *m*, camping *m*
camphor [ˈkæmpfər] *n* : alcanfor *m*
campsite [ˈkæmpˌsaɪt] *n* : campamento *m*, camping *m*
campus [ˈkæmpəs] *n* : campus *m*, recinto *m* universitario
can[1] [ˈkæn] *v aux, past* **could** [ˈkʊd]; *present s & pl* **can 1** : poder <could you help me? : ¿podría ayudarme?> **2** : saber <she can't drive yet : todavía no sabe manejar> **3** MAY : poder, tener permiso para <can I sit down? : ¿puedo sentarme?> **4** : poder <it can't be! : ¡no puede ser!> <where can they be? : ¿dónde estarán?>
can[2] [ˈkæn] *vt* **canned; canning 1** : enlatar, envasar <to can tomatoes : enlatar tomates> **2** DISMISS, FIRE : despedir, echar
can[3] *n* : lata *f*, envase *m*, cubo *m* <a can of beer : una lata de cerveza> <garbage can : cubo de basura>
Canadian [kəˈneɪdiən] *n* : canadiense *mf* — **Canadian** *adj*
canal [kəˈnæl] *n* **1** : canal *m*, tubo *m* <alimentary canal : tubo digestivo> **2** : canal *m* <Panama Canal : Canal de Panamá>
canapé [ˈkænəpi, -ˌpeɪ] *n* : canapé *m*
canary [kəˈnɛri] *n, pl* **-naries** : canario *m*
cancel [ˈkæntsəl] *vt* **-celed** *or* **-celled; -celing** *or* **-celling** : cancelar
cancellation [ˌkæntsəˈleɪʃən] *n* : cancelación *f*
cancer [ˈkæntsər] *n* : cáncer *m*
Cancer *n* : Cáncer *mf*
cancerous [ˈkæntsərəs] *adj* : canceroso
candelabrum [ˌkændəˈlɑbrəm, -ˈlæ-] *or* **candelabra** [-brə] *n, pl* **-bra** *or* **-bras** : candelabro *m*
candid [ˈkændɪd] *adj* **1** FRANK : franco, sincero, abierto **2** : natural, espontáneo (en la fotografía)
candidacy [ˈkændədəsi] *n, pl* **-cies** : candidatura *f*
candidate [ˈkændəˌdeɪt, -dət] *n* : candidato *m*, -ta *f*
candidly [ˈkændɪdli] *adv* : con franqueza
candied [ˈkændid] *adj* : confitado
candle [ˈkændəl] *n* : vela *f*, candela *f*, cirio *m* (ceremonial)
candlestick [ˈkændəlˌstɪk] *n* : candelero *m*
candor [ˈkændər] *n* : franqueza *f*
candy [ˈkændi] *n, pl* **-dies** : dulce *m*, caramelo *m*
cane[1] [ˈkeɪn] *vt* **caned; caning 1** : tapizar (muebles) con mimbre **2** FLOG : azotar con una vara
cane[2] *n* **1** : bastón *m* (para andar), vara *f* (para castigar) **2** REED : caña *f*, mimbre *m* (para muebles)
canine[1] [ˈkeɪˌnaɪn] *adj* : canino
canine[2] *n* **1** DOG : canino *m*; perro *m*, -rra *f* **2** *or* **canine tooth** : colmillo *m*, diente *m* canino
canister [ˈkænəstər] *n* : lata *f*, bote *m*
canker [ˈkæŋkər] *n* : úlcera *f* bucal
cannery [ˈkænəri] *n, pl* **-ries** : fábrica *f* de conservas
cannibal [ˈkænəbəl] *n* : caníbal *mf*; antropófago *m*, -ga *f*
cannibalism [ˈkænəbəˌlɪzəm] *n* : canibalismo *m*, antropofagia *f*
cannily [ˈkænəbəˌlaɪz] *adv* : astutamente, sagazmente
cannon [ˈkænən] *n, pl* **-nons** *or* **-non** : cañón *m*
cannot (can not) [ˈkænˌɑt, kəˈnɑt] → **can[1]**
canny [ˈkæni] *adj* **-nier; -est** SHREWD : astuto, sagaz
canoe[1] [kəˈnuː] *vt* **-noed; -noeing** : ir en canoa
canoe[2] *n* : canoa *f*, piragua *f*
canon [ˈkænən] *n* **1** : canon *m* <canon law : derecho canónico> **2** WORKS : canon *m* <the canon of American literature : el canon de la literatura americana> **3** : canónigo *m* (de una catedral) **4** STANDARD : canon *m*, norma *f*
canonize [ˈkænəˌnaɪz] *vt* **-ized; -izing** : canonizar

canopy [ˈkænəpi] *n, pl* **-pies** : dosel *m,* toldo *m*
cant[1] [ˈkænt] *vt* TILT : ladear, inclinar — *vi* **1** SLANT : ladearse, inclinarse, escorar (dícese de un barco) **2** : hablar insinceramente
cant[2] *n* **1** SLANT : plano *m* inclinado **2** JARGON : jerga *f* **3** : palabras *fpl* insinceras
can't [ˈkænt, ˈkant] (*contraction of* **can not**) → **can**[1]
cantaloupe [ˈkæntəl͵oːp] *n* : melón *m,* cantalupo *m*
cantankerous [kænˈtæŋkərəs] *adj* : irritable, irascible — **cantankerously** *adv*
cantankerousness [kænˈtæŋkərəsnəs] *n* : irritabilidad *f,* irascibilidad *f*
cantata [kənˈtɑt̬ə] *n* : cantata *f*
canteen [kænˈtiːn] *n* **1** FLASK : cantimplora *f* **2** CAFETERIA : cantina *f,* comedor *m* **3** : club *m* para actividades sociales y recreativas
canter[1] [ˈkæntər] *vi* : ir a medio galope
canter[2] *n* : medio galope *m*
cantilever [ˈkæntə͵liːvər, -͵lɛvər] *n* **1** : viga *f* voladiza **2 cantilever bridge** : puente *m* voladizo
canto [ˈkæn͵toː] *n, pl* **-tos** : canto *m*
cantor [ˈkæntər] *n* : solista *mf*
canvas [ˈkænvəs] *n* **1** : lona *f* **2** SAILS : velas *fpl* (de un barco) **3** : lienzo *m,* tela *f* (de pintar) **4** PAINTING : pintura *f,* óleo *m,* cuadro *m*
canvass[1] [ˈkænvəs] *vt* **1** SOLICIT : solicitar votos o pedidos de, hacer campaña entre **2** SOUND OUT : sondear (opiniones, etc.)
canvass[2] *n* SURVEY : sondeo *m,* encuesta *f*
canyon [ˈkænjən] *n* : cañón *m*
cap[1] [ˈkæp] *vt* **capped; capping 1** COVER : tapar (un recipiente), enfundar (un diente), cubrir (una montaña) **2** CLIMAX : coronar, ser el punto culminante de <to cap it all off : para colmo> **3** LIMIT : limitar, poner un tope a
cap[2] *n* **1** : gorra *f,* gorro *m,* cachucha *f Mex* <baseball cap : gorra de béisbol> **2** COVER, TOP : tapa *f,* tapón *m* (de botellas), corcholata *f Mex* **3** LIMIT : tope *m,* límite *m*
capability [͵keɪpəˈbɪlət̬i] *n, pl* **-ties** : capacidad *f,* habilidad *f,* competencia *f*
capable [ˈkeɪpəbəl] *adj* : competente, capaz, hábil — **capably** [-bli] *adv*
capacious [kəˈpeɪʃəs] *adj* : amplio, espacioso, de gran capacidad *f*
capacity[1] [kəˈpæsət̬i] *adj* : completo, total <a capacity crowd : un lleno completo>
capacity[2] *n, pl* **-ties 1** ROOM, SPACE : capacidad *f,* cabida *f,* espacio *m* **2** CAPABILITY : habilidad *f,* competencia *f* **3** FUNCTION, ROLE : calidad *f,* función *f* <in his capacity as ambassador : en su calidad de embajador>
cape [ˈkeɪp] *n* **1** : capa *f* **2** : cabo *m* <Cape Horn : el Cabo de Hornos>
caper[1] [ˈkeɪpər] *vi* : dar saltos, correr y brincar
caper[2] *n* **1** : alcaparra *f* <olives and capers : aceitunas y alcaparras> **2** ANTIC, PRANK : broma *f,* travesura *f* **3** LEAP : brinco *m,* salto *m*
Cape Verdean [ˈkeɪpˈvərdiən] *n* : caboverdiano *m,* -na *f* — **Cape Verdean** *adj*
capful [ˈkæp͵fʊl] *n* : tapa *f,* tapita *f*
capillary[1] [ˈkæpə͵lɛri] *adj* : capilar
capillary[2] *n, pl* **-ries** : capilar *m*
capital[1] [ˈkæpət̬əl] *adj* **1** : capital <capital punishment : pena capital> **2** : mayúsculo (dícese de las letras) **3** : de capital <capital assets : activo fijo> <capital gain : ganancia de capital, plusvalía> **4** EXCELLENT : excelente, estupendo
capital[2] *n* **1** *or* **capital city** : capital *f,* sede *f* del gobierno **2** WEALTH : capital *m* **3** *or* **capital letter** : mayúscula *f* **4** : capitel *m* (de una columna)
capitalism [ˈkæpət̬əl͵ɪzəm] *n* : capitalismo *m*
capitalist[1] [ˈkæpət̬əlɪst] *or* **capitalistic** [͵kæpət̬əlˈɪstɪk] *adj* : capitalista
capitalist[2] *n* : capitalista *mf*
capitalization [͵kæpət̬ələˈzeɪʃən] *n* : capitalización *f*
capitalize [ˈkæpət̬əl͵aɪz] *v* **-ized; -izing** *vt* **1** FINANCE : capitalizar, financiar **2** : escribir con mayúscula — *vi* **to capitalize on** : sacar partido de, aprovechar
capitol [ˈkæpət̬əl] *n* : capitolio *m*
capitulate [kəˈpɪtʃə͵leɪt] *vi* **-lated; -lating** : capitular
capitulation [kə͵pɪtʃəˈleɪʃən] *n* : capitulación *f*
capon [ˈkeɪ͵pɑn, -pən] *n* : capón *m*
caprice [kəˈpriːs] *n* : capricho *m,* antojo *m*
capricious [kəˈprɪʃəs, -ˈpriː-] *adj* : caprichoso — **capriciously** *adv*
Capricorn [ˈkæprɪ͵kɔrn] *n* : Capricornio *mf*
capsize [ˈkæp͵saɪz, kæpˈsaɪz] *v* **-sized; -sizing** *vi* : volcar, volcarse — *vt* : hacer volcar
capstan [ˈkæpstən, -͵stæn] *n* : cabrestante *m*
capsule [ˈkæpsəl, -͵suːl] *n* **1** : cápsula *f* (en la farmacéutica y botánica) **2 space capsule** : cápsula *f* espacial
captain[1] [ˈkæptən] *vt* : capitanear
captain[2] *n* **1** : capitán *m,* -tana *f* **2** HEADWAITER : jefe *m,* -fa *f* de comedor **3 captain of industry** : magnate *mf*
caption[1] [ˈkæpʃən] *vt* : ponerle una leyenda a (una ilustración), titular (un artículo), subtitular (una película)
caption[2] *n* **1** HEADING : titular *m,* encabezamiento *m* **2** : leyenda *f* (al pie de una ilustración) **3** SUBTITLE : subtítulo *m*

captivate ['kæptə,veɪt] *vt* **-vated; -vating** CHARM : cautivar, hechizar, encantar
captivating ['kæptə,veɪṭɪŋ] *adj* : cautivador, hechicero, encantador
captive[1] ['kæptɪv] *adj* : cautivo
captive[2] *n* : cautivo *m*, -va *f*
captivity [kæp'tɪvəṭi] *n* : cautiverio *m*
captor ['kæptər] *n* : captor *m*, -tora *f*
capture[1] ['kæpʃər] *vt* **-tured; -turing 1** SEIZE : capturar, apresar **2** CATCH : captar <to capture one's interest : captar el interés de uno>
capture[2] *n* : captura *f*, apresamiento *m*
car ['kɑr] *n* **1** AUTOMOBILE : automóvil *m*, coche *m*, carro *m* **2** : vagón *m*, coche *m* (de un tren) **3** : cabina *f* (de un ascensor)
carafe [kə'ræf, -'rɑf] *n* : garrafa *f*
caramel ['kɑrməl; 'kærəməl, -,mɛl] *n* **1** : caramelo *m*, azúcar *f* quemada **2** *or* **caramel candy** : caramelo *m*, dulce *m* de leche
carat ['kærət] *n* : quilate *m*
caravan ['kærə,væn] *n* : caravana *f*
caraway ['kærə,weɪ] *n* : alcaravea *f*
carbine ['kɑr,baɪn, -,bi:n] *n* : carabina *f*
carbohydrate [,kɑrbo'haɪ,dreɪt, -drət] *n* : carbohidrato *m*, hidrato *m* de carbono
carbon ['kɑrbən] *n* **1** : carbono *m* **2** → **carbon paper 3** → **carbon copy**
carbonated ['kɑrbə,neɪṭəd] *adj* : carbonatado (dícese del agua), gaseoso (dícese de las bebidas)
carbon copy *n* **1** : copia *f* al carbón **2** DUPLICATE : duplicado *m*, copia *f* exacta
carbon paper *n* : papel *m* carbón
carbuncle ['kɑr,bʌŋkəl] *n* : carbunco *m*
carburetor ['kɑrbə,reɪṭər, -bjə-] *n* : carburador *m*
carcass ['kɑrkəs] *n* : cuerpo *m* (de un animal muerto)
carcinogen [kɑr'sɪnədʒən, 'kɑrsənə-,dʒɛn] *n* : carcinógeno *m*, cancerígeno *m*
carcinogenic [,kɑrsəno'dʒɛnɪk] *adj* : carcinogénico
card[1] ['kɑrd] *vt* : cardar (fibras)
card[2] *n* **1** : carta *f*, naipe *m* <to play cards : jugar a las cartas> <a deck of cards : una baraja> **2** : tarjeta *f* <birthday card : tarjeta de cumpleaños> <business card : tarjeta (de visita)> **3** : carda *f* (para cardar fibras)
cardboard ['kɑrd,bord] *n* : cartón *m*, cartulina *f*
cardiac ['kɑrdi,æk] *adj* : cardíaco, cardiaco
cardigan ['kɑrdɪgən] *n* : cárdigan *m*, chaqueta *f* de punto
cardinal[1] ['kɑrdənəl] *adj* FUNDAMENTAL : cardinal, fundamental
cardinal[2] *n* : cardenal *m*
cardinal number *n* : número *m* cardinal
cardinal point *n* : punto *m* cardinal
cardiologist [,kɑrdi'ɑlədʒɪst] *n* : cardiólogo *m*, -ga *f*
cardiology [,kɑrdi'ɑlədʒi] *n* : cardiología *f*
cardiovascular [,kɑrdio'væskjələr] *adj* : cardiovascular
care[1] ['kær] *v* **cared; caring** *vi* **1** : importarle a uno <they don't care : no les importa> **2** : preocuparse, inquietarse <she cares about the poor : se preocupa por los pobres> **3 to care for** TEND : cuidar (de), atender, encargarse de **4 to care for** CHERISH : querer, sentir cariño por **5 to care for** LIKE : gustarle (algo a uno) <I don't care for your attitude : tu actitud no me agrada> — *vt* WISH : desear, querer <if you care to go : si deseas ir>
care[2] *n* **1** ANXIETY : inquietud *f*, preocupación *f* **2** CAREFULNESS : cuidado *m*, atención *f* <handle with care : manejar con cuidado> **3** CHARGE : cargo *m*, cuidado *m* **4 to take care of** : cuidar (de), atender, encargarse de
careen [kə'ri:n] *vi* **1** SWAY : oscilar, balancearse **2** CAREER : ir a toda velocidad
career[1] [kə'rɪr] *vi* : ir a toda velocidad
career[2] *n* VOCATION : vocación *f*, profesión *f*, carrera *f*
carefree ['kær,fri:, ,kær'-] *adj* : despreocupado
careful ['kærfəl] *adj* **1** CAUTIOUS : cuidadoso, cauteloso **2** PAINSTAKING : cuidadoso, esmerado, meticuloso
carefully ['kærfəli] *adv* : con cuidado, cuidadosamente
carefulness ['kærfəlnəs] *n* **1** CAUTION : cuidado *m*, cautela *f* **2** METICULOUSNESS : esmero *m*, meticulosidad *f*
caregiver ['kær,gɪvər] *n* : persona *f* que cuida a niños o enfermos
careless ['kærləs] *adj* : descuidado, negligente — **carelessly** *adv*
carelessness ['kærləsnəs] *n* : descuido *m*, negligencia *f*
caress[1] [kə'rɛs] *vt* : acariciar
caress[2] *n* : caricia *f*
caret ['kærət] *n* : signo *m* de intercalación
caretaker ['kɛr,teɪkər] *n* : conserje *mf*; velador *m*, -dora *f*
cargo ['kɑr,go:] *n*, *pl* **-goes** *or* **-gos** : cargamento *m*, carga *f*
caribou ['kærə,bu:] *n*, *pl* **-bou** *or* **-bous** : caribú *m*
caricature[1] ['kærɪkə,tʃʊr] *vt* **-tured; -turing** : caricaturizar
caricature[2] *n* : caricatura *f*
caricaturist ['kærɪkə,tʃʊrɪst] *n* : caricaturista *mf*
caries ['kær,i:z] *n*, *pl* **caries** : caries *f*
carillon ['kærə,lɑn] *n* : carillón *m*
carmine ['kɑrmən, -,maɪn] *n* : carmín *m*
carnage ['kɑrnɪdʒ] *n* : matanza *f*, carnicería *f*

carnal ['kɑrnəl] *adj* : carnal

carnation [kɑr'neɪʃən] *n* : clavel *m*

carnival ['kɑrnəvəl] *n* : carnaval *m,* feria *f*

carnivore ['kɑrnəˌvor] *n* : carnívoro *m*

carnivorous [kɑr'nɪvərəs] *adj* : carnívoro

carol[1] ['kærəl] *vi* **-oled** *or* **-olled; -oling** *or* **-olling** : cantar villancicos

carol[2] *n* : villancico *m*

caroler *or* **caroller** ['kærələr] *n* : persona *f* que canta villancicos

carom[1] ['kærəm] *vi* **1** REBOUND : rebotar <the bullet caromed off the wall : la bala rebotó contra el muro> **2** : hacer carambola (en billar)

carom[2] *n* : carambola *f*

carouse [kə'raʊz] *vt* **-roused; -rousing** : irse de parranda, irse de juerga

carousel *or* **carrousel** [ˌkærə'sɛl, 'kærəˌ-] *n* : carrusel *m,* tiovivo *m*

carouser [kə'raʊzər] *n* : juerguista *mf*

carp[1] ['kɑrp] *vi* **1** COMPLAIN : quejarse **2 to carp at** : criticar

carp[2] *n, pl* **carp** *or* **carps** : carpa *f*

carpel ['kɑrpəl] *n* : carpelo *m*

carpenter ['kɑrpəntər] *n* : carpintero *m,* -ra *f*

carpentry ['kɑrpəntri] *n* : carpintería *f*

carpet[1] ['kɑrpət] *vt* : alfombrar

carpet[2] *n* : alfombra *f*

carpeting ['kɑrpət̬ɪŋ] *n* : alfombrado *m*

carport ['kɑrˌpɔrt] *n* : cochera *f,* garaje *m* abierto

carriage ['kærɪdʒ] *n* **1** TRANSPORT : transporte *m* **2** POSTURE : porte *m,* postura *f* **3 horse–drawn carriage** : carruaje *m,* coche *m* **4 baby carriage** : cochecito *m*

carrier ['kæriər] *n* **1** : transportista *mf,* empresa *f* de transportes **2** : portador *m,* -dora *f* (de una enfermedad) **3 aircraft carrier** : portaaviones *m*

carrier pigeon : paloma *f* mensajera

carrion ['kæriən] *n* : carroña *f*

carrot ['kærət] *n* : zanahoria *f*

carry ['kæri] *v* **-ried; -rying** *vt* **1** TRANSPORT : llevar, cargar, transportar (cargamento), conducir (electricidad), portar (un virus) <to carry a bag : cargar una bolsa> <to carry money : llevar dinero encima, traer dinero consigo> **2** BEAR : soportar, aguantar, resistir (peso) **3** STOCK : vender, tener en abasto **4** ENTAIL : llevar, implicar, acarrear **5** WIN : ganar (una elección o competición), aprobar (una moción) **6 to carry oneself** : portarse, comportarse <he carried himself honorably : se comportó dignamente> — *vi* : oírse, proyectarse <her voice carries well : su voz se puede oír desde lejos>

carryall ['kæriˌɔl] *n* : bolsa *f* de viaje

carry away *vt* **to get carried away** : exaltarse, entusiasmarse

carry on *vt* CONDUCT : realizar, ejercer, mantener <to carry on research : realizar investigaciones> <to carry on a correspondence : mantener una correspondencia> — *vi* **1** : portarse de manera escandalosa o inapropiada <it's embarrassing how he carries on : su manera de comportarse da vergüenza> **2** CONTINUE : seguir, continuar

carry out *vt* **1** PERFORM : llevar a cabo, realizar **2** FULFILL : cumplir

cart[1] ['kɑrt] *vt* : acarrear, llevar

cart[2] *n* : carreta *f,* carro *m*

cartel [kɑr'tɛl] *n* : cártel *m*

cartilage ['kɑrtəlɪdʒ] *n* : cartílago *m*

cartilaginous [ˌkɑrt̬əl'ædʒənəs] *adj* : cartilaginoso

cartographer [kɑr'tɑgrəfər] *n* : cartógrafo *m,* -fa *f*

cartography [kɑr'tɑgrəfi] *n* : cartografía *f*

carton ['kɑrtən] *n* : caja *f* de cartón

cartoon [kɑr'tuːn] *n* **1** : chiste *m* (gráfico), caricatura *f* <a political cartoon : un chiste político> **2** COMIC STRIP : tira *f* cómica, historieta *f* **3** *or* **animated cartoon** : dibujo *m* animado

cartoonist [kɑr'tuːnɪst] *n* : caricaturista *mf,* dibujante *mf* (de chistes)

cartridge ['kɑrtrɪdʒ] *n* : cartucho *m*

carve ['kɑrv] *vt* **carved; carving 1** : tallar (madera), esculpir (piedra), grabar <he carved his name in the bark : grabó su nombre en la corteza> **2** SLICE : cortar, trinchar (carne)

cascade[1] [kæs'keɪd] *vi* **-caded; -cading** : caer en cascada

cascade[2] *n* : cascada *f,* salto *m* de agua

case[1] ['keɪs] *vt* **cased; casing 1** BOX, PACK : embalar, encajonar **2** INSPECT : observar, inspeccionar (antes de cometer un delito)

case[2] *n* **1** : caso *m* <an unusual case : un caso insólito> <ablative case : caso ablativo> <a case of the flu : un caso de gripe> **2** BOX : caja *f* **3** CONTAINER : funda *f,* estuche *m* **4 in any case** : de todos modos, en cualquier caso **5 in case** : como precaución <just in case : por si acaso> **6 in case of** : en caso de

casement ['keɪsmənt] *n* : ventana *f* con bisagras

cash[1] ['kæʃ] *vt* : convertir en efectivo, cobrar, cambiar (un cheque)

cash[2] *n* : efectivo *m,* dinero *m* en efectivo

cashew ['kæˌʃuː, kə'ʃuː] *n* : anacardo *m*

cashier[1] [kæ'ʃɪr] *vt* : destituir, despedir

cashier[2] *n* : cajero *m,* -ra *f*

cashmere ['kæʒˌmɪr, 'kæʃ-] *n* : cachemir *m*

casino [kə'siːˌnoː] *n, pl* **-nos** : casino *m*

cask ['kæsk] *n* : tonel *m,* barrica *f,* barril *m*

casket ['kæskət] *n* COFFIN : ataúd *m,* féretro *m*

casserole [ˈkæsə,roːl] *n* **1 :** cazuela *f* **2 :** guiso *m,* guisado *m* <tuna casserole : guiso de atún>

cassette [kəˈsɛt, kæ-] *n* **:** cassette *mf*

cassock [ˈkæsək] *n* **:** sotana *f*

cast¹ [ˈkæst] *vt* **cast; casting 1** THROW **:** tirar, echar, arrojar <the die is cast : la suerte está echada> **2 :** depositar (un voto) **3 :** asignar (papeles en una obra de teatro) **4** MOLD **:** moldear, fundir, vaciar **5 to cast off** ABANDON **:** desamparar, abandonar

cast² *n* **1** THROW **:** lance *m,* lanzamiento *m* **2** APPEARANCE **:** aspecto *m,* forma *f* **3 :** elenco *m,* reparto *m* (de una obra de teatro) **4 plaster cast :** molde *m* de yeso, escayola *f*

castanets [,kæstəˈnɛts] *npl* **:** castañuelas *fpl*

castaway¹ [ˈkæstə,weɪ] *adj* **:** náufrago

castaway² *n* **:** náufrago *m,* -ga *f*

caste [ˈkæst] *n* **:** casta *f*

caster [ˈkæstər] *n* **:** ruedita *f* (de un mueble)

castigate [ˈkæstə,geɪt] *vt* **-gated; -gating :** castigar severamente, censurar, reprobar

cast iron *n* **:** hierro *m* fundido

castle [ˈkæsəl] *n* **1 :** castillo *m* **2 :** torre *f* (en ajedrez)

cast–off [ˈkæst,ɔf] *adj* **:** desechado

castoff [ˈkæst,ɔf] *n* **:** desecho *m*

castrate [ˈkæs,treɪt] *vt* **-trated; -trating :** castrar

castration [kæˈstreɪʃən] *n* **:** castración *f*

casual [ˈkæʒʊəl] *adj* **1** FORTUITOUS **:** casual, fortuito **2** INDIFFERENT **:** indiferente, despreocupado **3** INFORMAL **:** informal — **casually** [ˈkæʒʊəli, ˈkæʒəli] *adv*

casualness [ˈkæʒʊəlnəs] *n* **1** FORTUITOUSNESS **:** casualidad *f* **2** INDIFFERENCE **:** indiferencia *f,* despreocupación *f* **3** INFORMALITY **:** informalidad *f*

casualty [ˈkæʒʊəlti, ˈkæʒəl-] *n, pl* **-ties 1** ACCIDENT **:** accidente *m* serio, desastre *m* **2** VICTIM **:** víctima *f;* baja *f;* herido *m,* -da *f*

cat [ˈkæt] *n* **:** gato *m,* -ta *f*

cataclysm [ˈkæt̬ə,klɪzəm] *n* **:** cataclismo *m*

cataclysmal [,kæt̬əˈklɪzməl] *or* **cataclysmic** [,kæt̬əˈklɪzmɪk] *adj* **:** catastrófico

catacombs [ˈkæt̬ə,koːmz] *npl* **:** catacumbas *fpl*

catalog¹ *or* **catalogue** [ˈkæt̬ə,lɔg] *vt* **-loged** *or* **-logued; -loging** *or* **-loguing :** catalogar

catalog² *n* **:** catálogo *m*

catalpa [kəˈtælpə, -ˈtɔl-] *n* **:** catalpa *f*

catalyst [ˈkæt̬ələst] *n* **:** catalizador *m*

catalytic [,kæt̬əlˈɪtɪk] *adj* **:** catalítico

catamaran [,kæt̬əməˈræn, ˈkæt̬əmə,ræn] *n* **:** catamarán *m*

catapult¹ [ˈkæt̬ə,pʌlt, -,pʊlt] *vt* **:** catapultar

catapult² *n* **:** catapulta *f*

cataract [ˈkæt̬ə,rækt] *n* **:** catarata *f*

catarrh [kəˈtɑr] *n* **:** catarro *m*

catastrophe [kəˈtæstrə,fiː] *n* **:** catástrofe *f*

catastrophic [,kæt̬əˈstrɑfɪk] *adj* **:** catastrófico — **catastrophically** [-fɪkli] *adv*

catcall [ˈkæt,kɔl] *n* **:** rechifla *f,* abucheo *m*

catch¹ [ˈkætʃ, ˈkɛtʃ] *v* **caught** [ˈkɔt]; **catching** *vt* **1** CAPTURE, TRAP **:** capturar, agarrar, atrapar, coger **2 :** agarrar, pillar *fam,* tomar de sorpresa <they caught him red-handed : lo pillaron con las manos en la masa> **3** GRASP **:** agarrar, captar **4** ENTANGLE **:** enganchar, enredar **5 :** tomar (un tren, etc.) **6 :** contagiarse de <to catch a cold : contagiarse de un resfriado, resfriarse> — *vi* **1** GRASP **:** agarrar **2** HOOK **:** engancharse **3** IGNITE **:** prender, agarrar

catch² *n* **1** CATCHING **:** captura *f,* atrapada *f,* parada *f* (de una pelota) **2 :** redada *f* (de pescado), presa *f* (de caza) <he's a good catch : es un buen partido> **3** LATCH **:** pestillo *m,* pasador *m* **4** DIFFICULTY, TRICK **:** problema *m,* trampa *f,* truco *m*

catcher [ˈkætʃər, ˈkɛ-] *n* **:** catcher *mf;* receptor *m* , -tora *f* (en béisbol)

catching [ˈkætʃɪŋ, ˈkɛ-] *adj* **:** contagioso

catchup [ˈkætʃəp, ˈkɛ-] → **ketchup**

catchword [ˈkætʃ,wərd, ˈkɛtʃ-] *n* **:** eslogan *m,* lema *m*

catchy [ˈkætʃi, ˈkɛ-] *adj* **catchier; -est :** pegajoso <a catchy song : una canción pegajosa>

catechism [ˈkæt̬ə,kɪzəm] *n* **:** catecismo *m*

categorical [,kæt̬əˈgɔrɪkəl] *adj* **:** categórico, absoluto, rotundo — **categorically** [-kli] *adv*

categorize [ˈkæt̬ɪgə,raɪz] *vt* **-rized; -rizing :** clasificar, catalogar

category [ˈkæt̬ə,gori] *n, pl* **-ries :** categoría *f,* género *m,* clase *f*

cater [ˈkeɪt̬ər] *vi* **1 :** proveer alimentos (para fiestas, bodas, etc.) **2 to cater to :** atender a <to cater to all tastes : atender a todos los gustos>

catercorner¹ [ˈkæt̬i,kɔrnər, ˈkæt̬ə-, ˈkɪti-] *or* **cater–cornered** [-,kɔrnərd] *adv* **:** diagonalmente, en diagonal

catercorner² *or* **cater–cornered** *adj* **:** diagonal

caterer [ˈkeɪt̬ərər] *n* **:** proveedor *m,* -dora *f* de comida

caterpillar [ˈkæt̬ər,pɪlər] *n* **:** oruga *f*

catfish [ˈkæt,fɪʃ] *n* **:** bagre *m*

catgut [ˈkæt,gʌt] *n* **:** cuerda *f* de tripa

catharsis [kəˈθɑrsɪs] *n, pl* **catharses** [-,siːz] **:** catarsis *f*

cathartic¹ [kəˈθɑrtɪk] *adj* **:** catártico

cathartic² *n* **:** purgante *m*

cathedral [kəˈθiːdrəl] *n* **:** catedral *f*

catheter [ˈkæθət̬ər] *n* **:** catéter *m,* sonda *f*

cathode [ˈkæ,θoːd] *n* : cátodo *m*
catholic [ˈkæθəlɪk] *adj* **1** BROAD, UNIVERSAL : liberal, universal **2 Catholic** : católico
Catholic *n* : católico *m*, -ca *f*
Catholicism [kəˈθɑlə,sɪzəm] *n* : catolicismo *m*
catkin [ˈkætkɪn] *n* : amento *m*, candelilla *f*
catlike [ˈkæt,laɪk] *adj* : gatuno, felino
catnap[1] [ˈkæt,næp] *vi* **-napped; -napping** : tomarse una siestecita
catnap[2] *n* : siesta *f* breve, siestecita *f*
catnip [ˈkæt,nɪp] *n* : nébeda *f*
catsup [ˈkɛtʃəp, ˈkætsəp] → **ketchup**
cattail [ˈkæt,teɪl] *n* : espadaña *f*, anea *f*
cattiness [ˈkæt̬inəs] *n* : malicia *f*
cattle [ˈkæt̬əl] *npl* : ganado *m*, reses *mpl*
cattleman [ˈkæt̬əlmən, -,mæn] *n, pl* **-men** [-mən, -,mɛn] : ganadero *m*
catty [ˈkæt̬i] *adj* **-tier; -est** : malicioso, malintencionado
catwalk [ˈkæt,wɔk] *n* : pasarela *f*
Caucasian[1] [kɔˈkeɪʒən] *adj* : caucásico
Caucasian[2] *n* : caucásico *m*, -ca *f*
caucus [ˈkɔkəs] *n* : junta *f* de políticos
caught → **catch**
cauldron [ˈkɔldrən] *n* : caldera *f*
cauliflower [ˈkɑlɪ,flaʊər, ˈkɔ-] *n* : coliflor *f*
caulk[1] [ˈkɔk] *vt* : calafatear (un barco), enmasillar (una grieta)
caulk[2] *n* : masilla *f*
causal [ˈkɔzəl] *adj* : causal
cause[1] [ˈkɔz] *vt* **caused; causing** : causar, provocar, ocasionar
cause[2] *n* **1** ORIGIN : causa *f*, origen *m* **2** REASON : causa *f*, razón *f*, motivo *m* **3** LAWSUIT : litigio *m*, pleito *m* **4** MOVEMENT : causa *f*, movimiento *m*
causeless [ˈkɔzləs] *adj* : sin causa
causeway [ˈkɔz,weɪ] *n* : camino *m* elevado
caustic [ˈkɔstɪk] *adj* **1** CORROSIVE : cáustico, corrosivo **2** BITING : mordaz, sarcástico
cauterize [ˈkɔt̬ə,raɪz] *vt* **-ized; -izing** : cauterizar
caution[1] [ˈkɔʃən] *vt* : advertir
caution[2] *n* **1** WARNING : advertencia *f*, aviso *m* **2** CARE, PRUDENCE : precaución *f*, cuidado *m*, cautela *f*
cautionary [ˈkɔʃə,nɛri] *adv* : admonitorio <cautionary tale : cuento moral>
cautious [ˈkɔʃəs] *adj* : cauteloso, cuidadoso, precavido
cautiously [ˈkɔʃəsli] *adv* : cautelosamente, con precaución
cautiousness [ˈkɔʃəsnəs] *n* : cautela *f*, precaución *f*
cavalcade [,kævəlˈkeɪd, ˈkævəl,-] *n* **1** : cabalgata *f* **2** SERIES : serie *f*
cavalier[1] [,kævəˈlɪr] *adj* : altivo, desdeñoso — **cavalierly** *adv*
cavalier[2] *n* : caballero *m*
cavalry [ˈkævəlri] *n, pl* **-ries** : caballería *f*
cave[1] [ˈkeɪv] *vi* **caved; caving** *or* **to cave in** : derrumbarse
cave[2] *n* : cueva *f*
cavern [ˈkævərn] *n* : caverna *f*
cavernous [ˈkævərnəs] *adj* : cavernoso — **cavernously** *adv*
caviar *or* **caviare** [ˈkævi,ɑr, ˈkɑ-] *n* : caviar *m*
cavity [ˈkævət̬i] *n, pl* **-ties 1** HOLE : cavidad *f*, hueco *m* **2** CARIES : caries *f*
cavort [kəˈvɔrt] *vi* : brincar, hacer cabriolas
caw[1] [ˈkɔ] *vi* : graznar
caw[2] *n* : graznido *m*
cayenne pepper [,kaɪˈɛn, ,keɪ-] *n* : pimienta *f* cayena, pimentón *m*
CD [,siːˈdiː] *n* : CD *m*, disco *m* compacto
cease [ˈsiːs] *v* **ceased; ceasing** *vt* : dejar de <they ceased bickering : dejaron de discutir> — *vi* : cesar, pasarse
ceaseless [ˈsiːsləs] *adj* : incesante, continuo
cedar [ˈsiːdər] *n* : cedro *m*
cede [ˈsiːd] *vt* **ceded; ceding** : ceder, conceder
ceiling [ˈsiːlɪŋ] *n* **1** : techo *m*, cielo *m* **2** LIMIT : límite *m*, tope *m*
celebrant [ˈsɛləbrənt] *n* : celebrante *mf*, oficiante *mf*
celebrate [ˈsɛlə,breɪt] *v* **-brated; -brating** *vt* **1** : celebrar, oficiar <to celebrate Mass : celebrar la misa> **2** : celebrar, festejar <we're celebrating our anniversary : estamos celebrando nuestro aniversario> **3** EXTOL : alabar, ensalzar, exaltar — *vi* : estar de fiesta, divertirse
celebrated [ˈsɛlə,breɪt̬əd] *adj* : célebre, famoso, renombrado
celebration [,sɛləˈbreɪʃən] *n* : celebración *f*, festejos *mpl*
celebrity [səˈlɛbrət̬i] *n, pl* **-ties 1** RENOWN : fama *f*, renombre *m*, celebridad *f* **2** PERSONALITY : celebridad *f*, personaje *m*
celery [ˈsɛləri] *n, pl* **-eries** : apio *m*
celestial [səˈlɛstʃəl, -ˈlɛstiəl] *adj* **1** : celeste **2** HEAVENLY : celestial, paradisiaco
celibacy [ˈsɛləbəsi] *n* : celibato *m*
celibate[1] [ˈsɛləbət] *adj* : célibe
celibate[2] *n* : célibe *mf*
cell [ˈsɛl] *n* **1** : célula *f* (de un organismo) **2** : celda *f* (en una cárcel, etc.) **3** : elemento *m* (de una pila)
cellar [ˈsɛlər] *n* **1** BASEMENT : sótano *m* **2** : bodega *f* (de vinos)
cellist [ˈtʃɛlɪst] *n* : violonchelista *mf*
cello [ˈtʃɛ,loː] *n, pl* **-los** : violonchelo *m*
cellophane [ˈsɛlə,feɪn] *n* : celofán *m*
cellular [ˈsɛljələr] *adj* : celular
cellulose [ˈsɛljə,loːs] *n* : celulosa *f*

Celsius ['sɛlsiəs] *adj* : centígrado <100 degrees Celsius : 100 grados centígrados>

Celt ['kɛlt, 'sɛlt] *n* : celta *mf*

Celtic[1] ['kɛltɪk, 'sɛl-] *adj* : celta

Celtic[2] *n* : celta *m* (idioma)

cement[1] [sɪ'mɛnt] *vi* : unir o cubrir algo con cemento, cementar

cement[2] *n* **1** : cemento *m* **2** GLUE : pegamento *m*

cemetery ['sɛmə,tɛri] *n, pl* **-teries** : cementerio *m,* panteón *m*

censer ['sɛn*t*sər] *n* : incensario *m*

censor[1] ['sɛn*t*sər] *vt* : censurar

censor[2] *n* : censor *m,* -sora *f*

censorious [sɛn'soriəs] *adj* : de censura, crítico

censorship ['sɛn*t*sər,ʃɪp] *n* : censura *f*

censure[1] ['sɛntʃər] *vt* **-sured; -suring** : censurar, criticar, reprobar — **censurable** [-tʃərəbəl] *adj*

censure[2] *n* : censura *f,* reproche *f* oficial

census ['sɛn*t*səs] *n* : censo *m*

cent ['sɛnt] *n* : centavo *m*

centaur ['sɛn,tɔr] *n* : centauro *m*

centennial[1] [sɛn'tɛniəl] *adj* : del centenario

centennial[2] *n* : centenario *m*

center[1] ['sɛntər] *vt* **1** : centrar **2** CONCENTRATE : concentrar, fijar, enfocar — *vi* : centrarse, enfocarse

center[2] *n* **1** : centro *m* <center of gravity : centro de gravedad> **2** : centro *mf* (en futbol americano), pívot *mf* (en basquetbol)

centerpiece ['sɛntər,piːs] *n* : centro *m* de mesa

centigrade ['sɛntə,greɪd, 'sɑn-] *adj* : centígrado

centigram ['sɛntə,græm, 'sɑn-] *n* : centigramo *m*

centimeter ['sɛntə,miːt̬ər, 'sɑn-] *n* : centímetro *m*

centipede ['sɛntə,piːd] *n* : ciempiés *m*

central ['sɛntrəl] *adj* **1** : céntrico, central <in a central location : en un lugar céntrico> **2** MAIN, PRINCIPAL : central, fundamental, principal

Central American[1] *adj* : centroamericano

Central American[2] *n* : centroamericano *m,* -na *f*

centralization [,sɛntrələ'zeɪʃən] *n* : centralización *f*

centralize ['sɛntrə,laɪz] *vt* **-ized; -izing** : centralizar

centrally ['sɛntrəli] *adv* **1 centrally heated** : con calefacción central **2 centrally located** : céntrico, en un lugar céntrico

centre ['sɛntər] → **center**

centrifugal force [sɛn'trɪfjəgəl, -'trɪfɪgəl] *n* : fuerza *f* centrífuga

century ['sɛntʃəri] *n, pl* **-ries** : siglo *m*

ceramic[1] [sə'ræmɪk] *adj* : de cerámica

ceramic[2] *n* **1** : objeto *m* de cerámica, cerámica *f* **2 ceramics** *npl* : cerámica *f*

cereal[1] ['sɪriəl] *adj* : cereal

cereal[2] *n* : cereal *m*

cerebellum [,sɛrə'bɛləm] *n, pl* **-bellums** *or* **-bella** [-'bɛlə] : cerebelo *m*

cerebral [sə'riːbrəl, 'sɛrə-] *adj* : cerebral

cerebral palsy *n* : parálisis *f* cerebral

cerebrum [sə'riːbrəm, 'sɛrə-] *n, pl* **-brums** *or* **-bra** [-brə] : cerebro *m*

ceremonial[1] [,sɛrə'moːniəl] *adj* : ceremonial

ceremonial[2] *n* : ceremonial *m*

ceremonious [,sɛrə'moːniəs] *adj* **1** FORMAL : ceremonioso, formal **2** CEREMONIAL : ceremonial

ceremony ['sɛrə,moːni] *n, pl* **-nies** : ceremonia *f*

cerise [sə'riːs] *n* : rojo *m* cereza

certain[1] ['sərtən] *adj* **1** DEFINITE : cierto, determinado <a certain percentage : un porcentaje determinado> **2** TRUE : cierto, con certeza <I don't know for certain : no sé exactamente> **3** : cierto, alguno <it has a certain charm : tiene cierta gracia> **4** INEVITABLE : seguro, inevitable **5** ASSURED : seguro, asegurado <she's certain to do well : seguro que le irá bien>

certain[2] *pron* : ciertos *pl,* algunos *pl* <certain of my friends : algunos de mis amigos>

certainly ['sərtənli] *adv* **1** DEFINITELY : ciertamente, seguramente **2** OF COURSE : por supuesto

certainty ['sərtənti] *n, pl* **-ties** : certeza *f,* certidumbre *f,* seguridad *f*

certifiable [,sərt̬ə'faɪəbəl] *adj* : certificable

certificate [sər'tɪfɪkət] *n* : certificado *m,* acta *f* <birth certificate : acta de nacimiento>

certification [,sərt̬əfə'keɪʃən] *n* : certificación *f*

certify ['sərt̬ə,faɪ] *vt* **-fied; -fying 1** VERIFY : certificar, verificar, confirmar **2** ENDORSE : endosar, aprobar oficialmente

certitude ['sərt̬ə,tuːd, -,tjuːd] *n* : certeza *f,* certidumbre *f*

cervical ['sərvɪkəl] *adj* **1** : cervical (dícese del cuello) **2** : del cuello del útero

cervix ['sərvɪks] *n, pl* **-vices** [-və-,siːz] *or* **-vixes 1** NECK : cerviz *f* **2** *or* **uterine cervix** : cuello *m* del útero

cesarean[1] [sɪ'zæriən] *adj* : cesáreo

cesarean[2] *n* : cesárea *f*

cesium ['siːziəm] *n* : cesio *m*

cessation [sɛ'seɪʃən] *n* : cesación *f,* cese *m*

cesspool ['sɛs,puːl] *n* : pozo *m* séptico

Chadian ['tʃædiən] *n* : chadiano *m,* -na *f* — **Chadian** *adj*

chafe ['tʃeɪf] *v* **chafed; chafing** *vi* : enojarse, irritarse — *vt* : rozar

chaff ['tʃæf] *n* **1** : barcia *f,* granzas *fpl* **2 to separate the wheat from the chaff** : separar el grano de la paja

chafing dish [ˈtʃeɪfɪŋˌdɪʃ] *n* : escalfador *m*
chagrin[1] [ʃəˈgrɪn] *vt* : desilusionar, avergonzar
chagrin[2] *n* : desilusión *f,* disgusto *m*
chain[1] [ˈtʃeɪn] *vt* : encadenar
chain[2] *n* **1** : cadena *f* <steel chain : cadena de acero> <restaurant chain : cadena de restaurantes> **2** SERIES : serie *f* <chain of events : serie de eventos> **3 chains** *npl* FETTERS : grillos *mpl*
chair[1] [ˈtʃɛr] *vt* : presidir, moderar
chair[2] *n* **1** : silla *f* **2** CHAIRMANSHIP : presidencia *f* **3** → **chairman, chairwoman**
chairman [ˈtʃɛrmən] *n, pl* **-men** [-mən, -ˌmɛn] : presidente *m*
chairmanship [ˈtʃɛrmənˌʃɪp] *n* : presidencia *f*
chairwoman [ˈtʃɛrˌwʊmən] *n, pl* **-women** [-ˌwɪmən] : presidenta *f*
chaise longue [ˈʃeɪzˈlɔŋ] *n, pl* **chaise longues** [-lɔŋ, -ˈlɔŋz] : chaise longue *f*
chalet [ʃæˈleɪ] *n* : chalet *m,* chalé *m*
chalice [ˈtʃælɪs] *n* : cáliz *m*
chalk[1] [ˈtʃɔk] *vt* : escribir con tiza
chalk[2] *n* **1** LIMESTONE : creta *f,* caliza *f* **2** : tiza *f,* gis *m Mex* (para escribir)
chalkboard [ˈtʃɔkˌbord] → **blackboard**
chalk up *vt* **1** ASCRIBE : atribuir, adscribir **2** SCORE : apuntarse, anotarse (una victoria, etc.)
chalky [ˈtʃɔki] *adj* **chalkier; -est** : calcáreo
challenge[1] [ˈtʃælɪndʒ] *vt* **-lenged; -lenging 1** DISPUTE : disputar, cuestionar, poner en duda **2** DARE : desafiar, retar **3** STIMULATE : estimular, incentivar
challenge[2] *n* : reto *m,* desafío *m*
challenger [ˈtʃælɪndʒər] *n* : retador *m,* -dora *f;* contendiente *mf*
chamber [ˈtʃeɪmbər] *n* **1** ROOM : cámara *f,* sala *f* <the senate chamber : la cámara del senado> **2** : recámara *f* (de un arma de fuego), cámara *f* (de combustión) **3** : cámara *f* <chamber of commerce : cámara de comercio> **4 chambers** *npl or* **judge's chambers** : despacho *m* del juez
chambermaid [ˈtʃeɪmbərˌmeɪd] *n* : camarera *f*
chamber music *n* : música *f* de cámara
chameleon [kəˈmiːljən, -liən] *n* : camaleón *m*
chamois [ˈʃæmi] *n, pl* **chamois** [-mi, -miz] : gamuza *f*
champ[1] [ˈtʃæmp, ˈtʃɑmp] *vi* **1** : masticar ruidosamente **2 to champ at the bit** : impacientarse, comerle a uno la impaciencia
champ[2] [ˈtʃæmp] *n* : campeón *m,* -peona *f*
champagne [ʃæmˈpeɪn] *n* : champaña *m,* champán *m*
champion[1] [ˈtʃæmpiən] *vt* : defender, luchar por (una causa)
champion[2] *n* **1** ADVOCATE, DEFENDER : paladín *m;* campeón *m,* -peona *f;* defensor *m,* -sora *f* **2** WINNER : campeón *m,* -peona *f* <world champion : campeón mundial>
championship [ˈtʃæmpiənˌʃɪp] *n* : campeonato *m*
chance[1] [ˈtʃænts] *v* **chanced; chancing** *vi* **1** HAPPEN : ocurrir por casualidad **2 to chance upon** : encontrar por casualidad — *vt* RISK : arriesgar
chance[2] *adj* : fortuito, casual <a chance encounter : un encuentro casual>
chance[3] *n* **1** FATE, LUCK : azar *m,* suerte *f,* fortuna *f* **2** OPPORTUNITY : oportunidad *f,* ocasión *f* **3** PROBABILITY : probabilidad *f,* posibilidad *f* **4** RISK : riesgo *m* **5** : boleto *m* (de una rifa o lotería) **6 by chance** : por casualidad
chancellor [ˈtʃæntsələr] *n* **1** : canciller *m* **2** : rector *m,* -tora *f* (de una universidad)
chancre [ˈʃæŋkər] *n* : chancro *m*
chancy [ˈtʃæntsi] *adj* **chancier; -est** : riesgoso, arriesgado
chandelier [ˌʃændəˈlɪr] *n* : araña *f* de luces
change[1] [ˈtʃeɪndʒ] *v* **changed; changing** *vt* **1** ALTER : cambiar, alterar, modificar **2** EXCHANGE : cambiar de, intercambiar <to change places : cambiar de sitio> — *vi* **1** VARY : cambiar, variar, transformarse <you haven't changed : no has cambiado> **2** *or* **to change clothes** : cambiarse (de ropa)
change[2] *n* **1** ALTERATION : cambio *m* **2** : cambio *m,* vuelto *m* <two dollars change : dos dólares de vuelto> **3** COINS : cambio *m,* monedas *fpl*
changeable [ˈtʃeɪndʒəbəl] *adj* : cambiante, variable
changeless [ˈtʃeɪndʒləs] *adj* : invariable, constante
changer [ˈtʃeɪndʒər] *n* **1** : cambiador *m* <record changer : cambiador de discos> **2** *or* **money changer** : cambista *mf* (de dinero)
channel[1] [ˈtʃænəl] *vt* **-neled** *or* **-nelled; -neling** *or* **-nelling** : encauzar, canalizar
channel[2] *n* **1** RIVERBED : cauce *m* **2** STRAIT : canal *m,* estrecho *m* <English Channel : Canal de la Mancha> **3** COURSE, MEANS : vía *f,* conducto *m* <the usual channels : las vías normales> **4** : canal *m* (de televisión)
chant[1] [ˈtʃænt] *v* : salmodiar, cantar
chant[2] *n* : **1** : salmodia *f* **2 Gregorian chant** : canto *m* gregoriano
Chanukah [ˈxɑnəkə, ˈhɑ-] → **Hanukkah**
chaos [ˈkeɪˌɑs] *n* : caos *m*
chaotic [keɪˈɑtɪk] *adj* : caótico — **chaotically** [-tɪkli] *adv*
chap[1] [ˈtʃæp] *vi* **chapped; chapping** : partirse, agrietarse
chap[2] *n* FELLOW : tipo *m,* hombre *m*
chapel [ˈtʃæpəl] *n* : capilla *f*

chaperon[1] *or* **chaperone** [ˈʃæpəˌroːn] *vt* **-oned; -oning** : ir de chaperón, acompañar
chaperon[2] *or* **chaperone** *n* : chaperón *m,* -rona *f;* acompañante *mf*
chaplain [ˈtʃæplɪn] *n* : capellán *m*
chapter [ˈtʃæptər] *n* **1** : capítulo *m* (de un libro) **2** BRANCH : sección *f,* división *f* (de una organización)
char [ˈtʃɑr] *vt* **charred; charring 1** BURN : carbonizar **2** SCORCH : chamuscar
character [ˈkærɪktər] *n* **1** LETTER, SYMBOL : carácter *m* <Chinese characters : caracteres chinos> **2** DISPOSITION : carácter *m,* personalidad *f* <of good character : de buena reputación> **3** : tipo *m,* personaje *m* peculiar <he's quite a character! : ¡él es algo serio!> **4** : personaje *m* (ficticio)
characteristic[1] [ˌkærɪktəˈrɪstɪk] *adj* : característico, típico — **characteristically** [-tɪkli] *adv*
characteristic[2] *n* : característica *f*
characterization [ˌkærɪktərəˈzeɪʃən] *n* : caracterización *f*
characterize [ˈkærɪktəˌraɪz] *vt* **-ized; -izing** : caracterizar
charades [ʃəˈreɪdz] *ns & pl* : charada *f*
charcoal [ˈtʃɑrˌkoːl] *n* : carbón *m*
chard [ˈtʃɑrd] → **Swiss chard**
charge[1] [ˈtʃɑrdʒ] *v* **charged; charging** *vt* **1** : cargar <to charge the batteries : cargar las pilas> **2** ENTRUST : encomendar, encargar **3** COMMAND : ordenar, mandar **4** ACCUSE : acusar <charged with robbery : acusado de robo> **5** : cargar a una cuenta, comprar a crédito — *vi* **1** : cargar (contra el enemigo) <charge! : ¡a la carga!> **2** : cobrar <they charge too much : cobran demasiado>
charge[2] *n* **1** : carga *f* (eléctrica) **2** BURDEN : carga *f,* peso *m* **3** RESPONSIBILITY : cargo *m,* responsabilidad *f* <to take charge of : hacerse cargo de> **4** ACCUSATION : cargo *m,* acusación *f* **5** COST : costo *m,* cargo *m,* precio *m* **6** ATTACK : carga *f,* ataque *m*
charge card → **credit card**
chargeable [ˈtʃɑrdʒəbəl] *adj* **1** : acusable, perseguible (dícese de un delito) **2 ~ to** : a cargo de (una cuenta)
charger [ˈtʃɑrdʒər] *n* : corcel *m,* caballo *m* (de guerra)
chariot [ˈtʃæriət] *n* : carro *m* (de guerra)
charisma [kəˈrɪzmə] *n* : carisma *m*
charismatic [ˌkærəzˈmætɪk] *adj* : carismático
charitable [ˈtʃærət̬əbəl] *adj* **1** GENEROUS : caritativo <a charitable organization : una organización benéfica> **2** KIND, UNDERSTANDING : generoso, benévolo, comprensivo — **charitably** [-bli] *adv*
charitableness [ˈtʃærət̬əbəlnəs] *n* : caridad *f*
charity [ˈtʃærət̬i] *n, pl* **-ties 1** GENEROSITY : caridad *f* **2** ALMS : caridad *f,* limosna *f* **3** : organización *f* benéfica, obra *f* de beneficencia
charlatan [ˈʃɑrlətən] *n* : charlatán *m,* -tana *f;* farsante *mf*
charley horse [ˈtʃɑrliˌhɔrs] *n* : calambre *m*
charm[1] [ˈtʃɑrm] *vt* : encantar, cautivar, fascinar
charm[2] *n* **1** AMULET : amuleto *m,* talismán *m* **2** ATTRACTION : encanto *m,* atractivo *m* <it has a certain charm : tiene cierto atractivo> **3** : dije *m,* colgante *m* <charm bracelet : pulsera de dijes>
charmer [ˈtʃɑrmər] *n* : persona *f* encantadora
charming [ˈtʃɑrmɪŋ] *adj* : encantador, fascinante
chart[1] [ˈtʃɑrt] *vt* **1** : trazar un mapa de, hacer un gráfico de **2** PLAN : trazar, planear <to chart a course : trazar un derrotero>
chart[2] *n* **1** MAP : carta *f,* mapa *m* **2** DIAGRAM : gráfico *m,* cuadro *m,* tabla *f*
charter[1] [ˈtʃɑrt̬ər] *vt* **1** : establecer los estatutos de (una organización) **2** RENT : alquilar, fletar
charter[2] *n* **1** STATUTES : estatutos *mpl* **2** CONSTITUTION : carta *f,* constitución *f*
chartreuse [ʃɑrˈtruːz, -ˈtruːs] *n* : color *m* verde-amarillo intenso
chary [ˈtʃæri] *adj* **charier; -est 1** WARY : cauteloso, precavido **2** SPARING : parco
chase[1] [ˈtʃeɪs] *vt* **chased; chasing 1** PURSUE : perseguir, ir a la caza de **2** DRIVE : ahuyentar, echar <he chased the dog from the garden : ahuyentó al perro del jardín> **3** : grabar (metales)
chase[2] *n* **1** PURSUIT : persecución *f,* caza *f* **2 the chase** HUNTING : caza *f*
chaser [ˈtʃeɪsər] *n* **1** PURSUER : perseguidor *m,* -dora *f* **2** : bebida *f* que se toma después de un trago de licor
chasm [ˈkæzəm] *n* : abismo *m,* sima *f*
chassis [ˈtʃæsi, ˈʃæsi] *n, pl* **chassis** [-siz] : chasis *m,* armazón *m*
chaste [ˈtʃeɪst] *adj* **chaster; -est 1** : casto **2** MODEST : modesto, puro **3** AUSTERE : austero, sobrio
chastely [ˈtʃeɪstli] *adv* : castamente
chasten [ˈtʃeɪsən] *vt* : castigar, sancionar
chasteness [ˈtʃeɪstnəs] *n* **1** MODESTY : modestia *f,* castidad *f* **2** AUSTERITY : sobriedad *f,* austeridad *f*
chastise [ˈtʃæsˌtaɪz, tʃæsˈ-] *vt* **-tised; -tising 1** REPRIMAND : reprender, corregir, reprobar **2** PUNISH : castigar
chastisement [ˈtʃæsˌtaɪzmənt, tʃæsˈtaɪz-, ˈtʃæstəz-] *n* : castigo *m,* corrección *f*
chastity [ˈtʃæstət̬i] *n* : castidad *f,* decencia *f,* modestia *f*
chat[1] [ˈtʃæt] *vi* **chatted; chatting** : charlar, platicar

chat² *n* **:** charla *f,* plática *f*
château [ʃæˈtoː] *n, pl* **-teaus** [-ˈtoː, -ˈtoːz] *or* **-teaux** [-ˈtoːz] **:** mansión *f* campestre
chattel [ˈtʃætəl] *n* **:** bienes *fpl* muebles, enseres *mpl*
chatter¹ [ˈtʃætər] *vi* **1 :** castañetear (dícese de los dientes) **2** GAB **:** parlotear *fam,* cotorrear *fam*
chatter² *n* **1** CHATTERING **:** castañeteo *m* (de dientes) **2** GABBING **:** parloteo *m fam,* cotorreo *m fam,* cháchara *f fam*
chatterbox [ˈtʃætərˌbɑks] *n* **:** parlanchín *m,* -china *f;* charlatán *m,* -tana *f;* hablador *m,* -dora *f*
chatty [ˈtʃæti] *adj* **chattier; chattiest 1** TALKATIVE **:** parlanchín, charlatán **2** CONVERSATIONAL **:** familiar, conversador <a chatty letter **:** una carta llena de noticias>
chauffeur¹ [ˈʃoːfər, ʃoˈfər] *vi* **:** trabajar de chofer privado — *vt* **:** hacer de chofer para
chauffeur² *n* **:** chofer *m* privado
chauvinism [ˈʃoːvəˌnɪzəm] *n* **:** chauvinismo *m,* patriotería *f*
chauvinist [ˈʃoːvənɪst] *n* **:** chauvinista *mf;* patriotero *m,* -ta *f*
chauvinistic [ˌʃoːvəˈnɪstɪk] *adj* **:** chauvinista, patriotero
cheap¹ [ˈtʃiːp] *adv* **:** barato <to sell cheap **:** vender barato>
cheap² *adj* **1** INEXPENSIVE **:** barato, económico **2** SHODDY **:** barato, mal hecho **3** STINGY **:** tacaño, agarrado *fam,* codo *Mex*
cheapen [ˈtʃiːpən] *vt* **:** degradar, rebajar
cheaply [ˈtʃiːpli] *adv* **:** barato, a precio bajo
cheapness [ˈtʃiːpnəs] *n* **1 :** baratura *f,* precio *m* bajo **2** STINGINESS **:** tacañería *f*
cheapskate [ˈtʃiːpˌskeɪt] *n* **:** tacaño *m,* -ña *f;* codo *m,* -da *f Mex*
cheat¹ [ˈtʃiːt] *vt* **:** defraudar, estafar, engañar — *vi* **:** hacer trampa
cheat² *n* **1** CHEATING **:** engaño *m,* fraude *m,* trampa *f* **2** → **cheater**
cheater [ˈtʃiːtər] *n* **:** estafador *m,* -dora *f;* tramposo *m,* -sa *f*
check¹ [ˈtʃɛk] *vt* **1** HALT **:** frenar, parar, detener **2** RESTRAIN **:** refrenar, contener, reprimir **3** VERIFY **:** verificar, comprobar **4** INSPECT **:** revisar, chequear, inspeccionar **5** MARK **:** marcar, señalar **6 :** chequear, facturar (maletas, equipaje) **7** CHECKER **:** marcar con cuadros **8 to check in :** registrarse en un hotel **9 to check out :** irse de un hotel
check² *n* **1** HALT **:** detención *f* súbita, parada *f* **2** RESTRAINT **:** control *m,* freno *m* **3** INSPECTION **:** inspección *f,* verificación *f,* chequeo *m* **4 :** cheque *m* <to pay by check **:** pagar con cheque> **5** VOUCHER **:** resguardo *m,* comprobante *m* **6** BILL **:** cuenta *f* (en un restaurante) **7** SQUARE **:** cuadro *m* **8** MARK **:** marca *f* **9 :** jaque *m* (en ajedrez)
checker¹ [ˈtʃɛkər] *vt* **:** marcar con cuadros
checker² *n* **1 :** pieza *f* (en el juego de damas) **2 :** verificador *m,* -dora *f;* revisador *m,* -dora *f*
checkerboard [ˈtʃɛkərˌbord] *n* **:** tablero *m* de damas
checkers [ˈtʃɛkərz] *n* **:** damas *fpl*
checkmate¹ [ˈtʃɛkˌmeɪt] *vt* **-mated; -mating 1 :** dar jaque mate a (en ajedrez) **2** THWART **:** frustrar, arruinar
checkmate² *n* **:** jaque mate *m*
checkpoint [ˈtʃɛkˌpɔɪnt] *n* **:** puesto *m* de control
checkup [ˈtʃɛkˌʌp] *n* **:** examen *m* médico, chequeo *m*
cheddar [ˈtʃɛdər] *n* **:** queso *m* Cheddar
cheek [ˈtʃiːk] *n* **1 :** mejilla *f,* cachete *m* **2** IMPUDENCE **:** insolencia *f,* descaro *m*
cheeky [ˈtʃiːki] *adj* **cheekier; -est :** descarado, insolente, atrevido
cheep¹ [ˈtʃiːp] *vi* **:** piar
cheep² *n* **:** pío *m*
cheer¹ [ˈtʃɪr] *vt* **1** ENCOURAGE **:** alentar, animar **2** GLADDEN **:** alegrar, levantar el ánimo a **3** ACCLAIM **:** aclamar, vitorear, echar porras a
cheer² *n* **1** CHEERFULNESS **:** alegría *f,* buen humor *m,* jovialidad *f* **2** APPLAUSE **:** aclamación *f,* ovación *f,* aplausos *mpl* <three cheers for the chief! **:** ¡viva el jefe!> **3 cheers! :** ¡salud!
cheerful [ˈtʃɪrfəl] *adj* **:** alegre, de buen humor
cheerfully [ˈtʃɪrfəli] *adv* **:** alegremente, jovialmente
cheerfulness [ˈtʃɪrfəlnəs] *n* **:** buen humor *m,* alegría *f*
cheerily [ˈtʃɪrəli] *adv* **:** alegremente
cheeriness [ˈtʃɪrinəs] *n* **:** buen humor *m,* alegría *f*
cheerleader [ˈtʃɪrˌliːdər] *n* **:** porrista *mf*
cheerless [ˈtʃɪrləs] *adj* BLEAK **:** triste, sombrío
cheerlessly [ˈtʃɪrləsli] *adv* **:** desanimadamente
cheery [ˈtʃɪri] *adj* **cheerier; -est :** alegre, de buen humor
cheese [ˈtʃiːz] *n* **:** queso *m*
cheesecloth [ˈtʃiːzˌklɔθ] *n* **:** estopilla *f*
cheesy [ˈtʃiːzi] *adj* **cheesier; -est 1 :** a queso **2 :** que contiene queso **3** CHEAP **:** barato, de mala calidad
cheetah [ˈtʃiːtə] *n* **:** guepardo *m*
chef [ˈʃɛf] *n* **:** chef *m*
chemical¹ [ˈkɛmɪkəl] *adj* **:** químico — **chemically** [-mɪkli] *adv*
chemical² *n* **:** sustancia *f* química
chemise [ʃəˈmiːz] *n* **1 :** camiseta *f,* prenda *f* interior de una pieza **2 :** vestido *m* holgado
chemist [ˈkɛmɪst] *n* **:** químico *m,* -ca *f*
chemistry [ˈkɛmɪstri] *n, pl* **-tries :** química *f*
chemotherapy [ˌkiːmoˈθɛrəpi, ˌkɛmo-] *n, pl* **-pies :** quimioterapia *f*

chenille [ʃə'ni:l] *n* **:** felpilla *f*
cherish ['tʃɛrɪʃ] *vt* **1** VALUE **:** apreciar, valorar **2** HARBOR **:** abrigar, albergar
cherry ['tʃɛri] *n, pl* **-ries 1 :** cereza *f* (fruta) **2 :** cerezo *m* (árbol)
cherub ['tʃɛrəb] *n* **1** *pl* **-ubim** ['tʃɛrə,bɪm, 'tʃɛrjə-] ANGEL **:** ángel *m,* querubín *m* **2** *pl* **-ubs :** niño *m* regordete, niña *f* regordeta
cherubic [tʃə'ru:bɪk] *adj* **:** querúbico, angelical
chess ['tʃɛs] *n* **:** ajedrez *m*
chessboard ['tʃɛs,bord] *n* **:** tablero *m* de ajedrez
chessman ['tʃɛsmən, -,mæn] *n, pl* **-men** [-mən, -,mɛn] **:** pieza *f* de ajedrez
chest ['tʃɛst] *n* **1 :** cofre *m,* baúl *m* **2 :** pecho *m* <chest pains : dolores de pecho>
chestnut ['tʃɛs*t*,nʌt] *n* **1 :** castaña *f* (fruto) **2 :** castaño *m* (árbol)
chest of drawers *n* **:** cómoda *f*
chevron ['ʃɛvrən] *n* **:** galón *m* (de un oficial militar)
chew[1] ['tʃu:] *vt* **:** masticar, mascar
chew[2] *n* **:** algo que se masca (como tabaco)
chewable ['tʃu:əbəl] *adj* **:** masticable
chewing gum *n* **:** goma *f* de mascar, chicle *m*
chewy ['tʃu:i] *adj* **chewier; -est 1 :** fibroso (dícese de las carnes o los vegetales) **2 :** pegajoso, chicloso (dícese de los los dulces)
chic[1] ['ʃi:k] *adj* **:** chic, elegante, de moda
chic[2] *n* **:** chic *m,* elegancia *f*
Chicano [tʃɪ'kɑno] *n* **:** chicano *m,* -na *f* **— Chicano** *adj*
chick ['tʃɪk] *n* **:** pollito *m,* -ta *f;* polluelo *m,* -la *f*
chicken ['tʃɪkən] *n* **1** FOWL **:** pollo *m* **2** COWARD **:** cobarde *mf*
chickenhearted ['tʃɪkən,hɑrt̬əd] *n* **:** miedoso, cobarde
chicken pox *n* **:** varicela *f*
chicle ['tʃɪkəl] *n* **:** chicle *m* (resina)
chicory ['tʃɪkəri] *n, pl* **-ries 1 :** endibia *f* (para ensaladas) **2 :** achicoria *f* (aditivo de café)
chide ['tʃaɪd] *vt* **chid** ['tʃɪd] *or* **chided; chid** *or* **chidden** ['tʃɪdən] *or* **chided; chiding** ['tʃaɪdɪŋ] **:** regañar, reprender
chief[1] ['tʃi:f] *adj* **:** principal, capital <chief negotiator : negociador en jefe> **— chiefly** *adv*
chief[2] *n* **:** jefe *m,* -fa *f*
chieftain ['tʃi:ftən] *n* **:** jefe *m,* -fa *f* (de una tribu)
chiffon [ʃɪ'fɑn, 'ʃɪ,-] *n* **:** chifón *m*
chigger ['tʃɪgər] *n* **:** nigua *f*
chignon ['ʃi:n,jɑn, -,jɔn] *n* **:** moño *m,* chongo *m Mex*
chilblain ['tʃɪl,bleɪn] *n* **:** sabañón *m*
child ['tʃaɪld] *n, pl* **children** ['tʃɪldrən] **1** BABY, YOUNGSTER **:** niño *m,* -ña *f;* criatura *f* **2** OFFSPRING **:** hijo *m,* -ja *f;* progenie *f*
childbearing[1] ['tʃaɪlbɛrɪŋ] *adj* **:** relativo al parto <of childbearing age : en edad fértil>
childbearing[2] **→ childbirth**
childbirth ['tʃaɪld,bərθ] *n* **:** parto *m*
childhood ['tʃaɪld,hʊd] *n* **:** infancia *f,* niñez *f*
childish ['tʃaɪldɪʃ] *adj* **:** infantil, inmaduro **— childishly** *adv*
childishness ['tʃaɪldɪʃnəs] *n* **:** infantilismo *m,* inmadurez *f*
childless ['tʃaɪldləs] *adj* **:** sin hijos
childlike ['tʃaɪld,laɪk] *adj* **:** infantil, inocente <a childlike imagination : una imaginación infantil>
childproof ['tʃaɪld,pru:f] *adj* **:** a prueba de niños
Chilean ['tʃɪliən, tʃɪ'leɪən] **:** chileno *m,* -na *f* **— Chilean** *adj*
chili *or* **chile** *or* **chilli** ['tʃɪli] *n, pl* **chilies** *or* **chiles** *or* **chillies 1** *or* **chili pepper :** chile *m,* ají *m* **2 :** chile *m* con carne
chill[1] ['tʃɪl] *v* **:** enfriar
chill[2] *adj* **:** frío, gélido <a chill wind : un viento frío>
chill[3] *n* **1** CHILLINESS **:** fresco *m,* frío *m* **2** SHIVER **:** escalofrío *m* **3** DAMPER **:** enfriamiento *m,* frío *m* <to cast a chill over : enfriar>
chilliness ['tʃɪlinəs] *n* **:** frío *m,* fresco *m*
chilly ['tʃɪli] *adj* **chillier; -est :** frío <it's chilly tonight : hace frío esta noche>
chime[1] ['tʃaɪm] *v* **chimed; chiming** *vt* **:** hacer sonar (una campana) **—** *vi* **:** sonar una campana, dar campanadas
chime[2] *n* **1** BELLS **:** juego *m* de campanitas sintonizadas, carillón *m* **2** PEAL **:** tañido *m,* campanada *f*
chime in *vi* **:** meterse en una conversación
chimera *or* **chimaera** [kaɪ'mɪrə, kə-] *n* **:** quimera *f*
chimney ['tʃɪmni] *n, pl* **-neys :** chimenea *f*
chimney sweep *n* **:** deshollinador *m,* -dora *f*
chimp ['tʃɪmp, 'ʃɪmp] **→ chimpanzee**
chimpanzee [,tʃɪm,pæn'zi:, ,ʃɪm-; tʃɪm'pænzi, ʃɪm-] *n* **:** chimpancé *m*
chin ['tʃɪn] *n* **:** barbilla *f,* mentón *m,* barba *f*
china ['tʃaɪnə] *n* **1** PORCELAIN **:** porcelana *f,* loza *f* **2** CROCKERY, TABLEWARE **:** loza *f,* vajilla *f*
chinchilla [tʃɪn'tʃɪlə] *n* **:** chinchilla *f*
Chinese ['tʃaɪ'ni:z, -'ni:s] *n* **1 :** chino *m,* -na *f* **2 :** chino *m* (idioma) **— Chinese** *adj*
chink ['tʃɪŋk] *n* **:** grieta *f,* abertura *f*
chintz ['tʃɪnts] *n* **:** chintz *m,* chinz *m*
chip[1] ['tʃɪp] *v* **chipped; chipping** *vt* **:** desportillar, desconchar, astillar (madera) **—** *vi* **:** desportillarse, desconcharse, descascararse (dícese de la pintura, etc.)
chip[2] *n* **1 :** astilla *f* (de madera o vidrio), lasca *f* (de piedra) <he's a chip

off the old block : de tal palo, tal astilla> **2** : bocado *m* pequeño (en rodajas o rebanadas) <tortilla chips : totopos, tortillitas tostadas> **3** : ficha *f* (de póker, etc.) **4** NICK : desportilladura *f,* mella *f* **5** : chip *m* <memory chip : chip de memoria>

chip in *v* CONTRIBUTE : contribuir

chipmunk [ˈtʃɪp,mʌŋk] *n* : ardilla *f* listada

chipper [ˈtʃɪpər] *adj* : alegre y vivaz

chiropodist [kəˈrɑpədɪst, ʃə-] *n* : podólogo *m,* -ga *f*

chiropody [kəˈrɑpədi, ʃə-] *n* : podología *f*

chiropractic [ˈkaɪrə,præktɪk] *n* : quiropráctica *f*

chiropractor [ˈkaɪrə,præktər] *n* : quiropráctico *m,* -ca *f*

chirp[1] [ˈtʃərp] *vi* : gorjear (dícese de los pájaros), chirriar (dícese de los grillos)

chirp[2] *n* : gorjeo *m* (de un pájaro), chirrido *m* (de un grillo)

chisel[1] [ˈtʃɪzəl] *vt* **-eled** *or* **-elled; -eling** *or* **-elling 1** : cincelar, tallar, labrar **2** CHEAT : estafar, defraudar

chisel[2] *n* : cincel *m* (para piedras y metales), escoplo *m* (para madera), formón *m*

chiseler [ˈtʃɪzələr] *n* SWINDLER : estafador *m,* -dora *f;* fraude *mf*

chit [ˈtʃɪt] *n* : resguardo *m,* recibo *m*

chitchat [ˈtʃɪt,tʃæt] *n* : cotorreo *m,* charla *f*

chivalric [ʃəˈvælrɪk] → **chivalrous**

chivalrous [ˈʃɪvəlrəs] *adj* **1** KNIGHTLY : caballeresco, relativo a la caballería **2** GENTLEMANLY : caballeroso, honesto, cortés

chivalrousness [ˈʃɪvəlrəsnəs] *n* : caballerosidad *f,* cortesía *f*

chivalry [ˈʃɪvəlri] *n, pl* **-ries 1** KNIGHTHOOD : caballería *f* **2** CHIVALROUSNESS : caballerosidad *f,* nobleza *f,* cortesía *f*

chive [ˈtʃaɪv] *n* : cebollino *m*

chloride [ˈklor,aɪd] *n* : cloruro *m*

chlorinate [ˈklorə,neɪt] *vt* **-nated; -nating** : clorar

chlorination [,klorəˈneɪʃən] *n* : cloración *f*

chlorine [ˈklor,iːn] *n* : cloro *m*

chloroform[1] [ˈklorə,fɔrm] *vt* : cloroformizar

chloroform[2] *n* : cloroformo *m*

chlorophyll [ˈklorə,fɪl] *n* : clorofila *f*

chock–full [ˈtʃɑkˈfʊl, ˈtʃʌk-] *adj* : colmado, repleto

chocolate [ˈtʃɑkələt, ˈtʃɔk-] *n* **1** : chocolate *m* **2** BONBON : bombón *m* **3** : color *m* chocolate, marrón *m*

choice[1] [ˈtʃɔɪs] *adj* **choicer; -est** : selecto, escogido, de primera calidad

choice[2] *n* **1** CHOOSING : elección *f,* selección *f* **2** OPTION : elección *f,* opción *f* <I have no choice : no tengo alternativa> **3** PREFERENCE : preferencia *f,* elección *f* **4** VARIETY : surtido *m,* selección *f* <a wide choice : un gran surtido>

choir [ˈkwaɪr] *n* : coro *m*

choirboy [ˈkwaɪr,bɔɪ] *n* : niño *m* de coro

choke[1] [ˈtʃoːk] *v* **choked; choking** *vt* **1** ASPHYXIATE, STRANGLE : sofocar, asfixiar, ahogar, estrangular **2** BLOCK : tapar, obstruir — *vi* **1** SUFFOCATE : asfixiarse, sofocarse, ahogarse, atragantarse (con comida) **2** CLOG : taparse, obstruirse

choke[2] *n* **1** CHOKING : estrangulación *f* **2** : choke *m* (de un motor)

choker [ˈtʃoːkər] *n* : gargantilla *f*

cholera [ˈkɑlərə] *n* : cólera *m*

cholesterol [kəˈlɛstə,rɔl] *n* : colesterol *m*

choose [ˈtʃuːz] *v* **chose** [ˈtʃoːz]; **chosen** [ˈtʃoːzən]; **choosing** *vt* **1** SELECT : escoger, elegir <choose only one : escoja sólo uno> **2** DECIDE : decidir <he chose to leave : decidió irse> **3** PREFER : preferir <which one do you choose? : ¿cuál prefiere?> — *vi* : escoger <much to choose from : mucho de donde escoger>

choosy *or* **choosey** [ˈtʃuːzi] *adj* **choosier; -est** : exigente, remilgado

chop[1] [ˈtʃɑp] *vt* **chopped; chopping 1** MINCE : picar, cortar, moler (carne) **2 to chop down** : cortar, talar (un árbol)

chop[2] *n* **1** CUT : hachazo *m* (con una hacha), tajo *m* (con una cuchilla) **2** BLOW : golpe *m* (penetrante) <karate chop : golpe de karate> **3** : chuleta *f* <pork chops : chuletas de cerdo>

chopper [ˈtʃɑpər] → **helicopter**

choppy [ˈtʃɑpi] *adj* **choppier; -est 1** : agitado, picado (dícese del mar) **2** DISCONNECTED : incoherente, inconexo

chops [ˈtʃɑps] *npl* **1** : quijada *f,* mandíbula *f,* boca *f* (de una persona) **2 to lick one's chops** : relamerse

chopsticks [ˈtʃɑp,stɪks] *npl* : palillos *mpl*

choral [ˈkorəl] *adj* : coral

chorale [kəˈræl, -ˈrɑl] *n* **1** : coral *f* (composición musical vocal) **2** CHOIR, CHORUS : coral *f,* coro *m*

chord [ˈkɔrd] *n* **1** : acorde *m* (en música) **2** : cuerda *f* (en anatomía o geometría)

chore [ˈtʃor] *n* **1** TASK : tarea *f* rutinaria **2** BOTHER, NUISANCE : lata *f fam,* fastidio *m* **3 chores** *npl* WORK : quehaceres *mpl,* faenas *fpl*

choreograph [ˈkoriə,græf] *vt* : coreografiar

choreographer [,koriˈɑgrəfər] *n* : coreógrafo *m,* -fa *f*

choreographic [,koriəˈgræfɪk] *adj* : coreográfico

choreography [,koriˈɑgrəfi] *n, pl* **-phies** : coreografía *f*

chorister [ˈkorəstər] *n* : corista *mf*

chortle[1] [ˈtʃɔrtəl] *vi* **-tled; -tling** : reírse (con satisfacción o júbilo)

chortle[2] *n* **:** risa *f* (de satisfacción o júbilo)
chorus[1] [ˈkorəs] *vt* **:** corear
chorus[2] *n* **1 :** coro *m* (grupo o composición musical) **2** REFRAIN **:** coro *m,* estribillo *m*
chose *pp* → **choose**
chosen [ˈtʃoːzən] *adj* **:** elegido, selecto
chow [ˈtʃaʊ] *n* **1** FOOD **:** comida *f* **2 :** chow-chow *m* (perro)
chowder [ˈtʃaʊdər] *n* **:** sopa *f* de pescado
christen [ˈkrɪsən] *vt* **1** BAPTIZE **:** bautizar **2** NAME **:** bautizar con el nombre de
Christendom [ˈkrɪsəndəm] *n* **:** cristiandad *f*
christening [ˈkrɪsənɪŋ] *n* **:** bautismo *m,* bautizo *m*
Christian[1] [ˈkrɪstʃən] *adj* **:** cristiano
Christian[2] *n* **:** cristiano *m,* -na *f*
Christianity [ˌkrɪstʃiˈænəṱi, ˌkrɪsˈtʃæ-] *n* **:** cristianismo *m*
Christian name *n* **:** nombre *m* de pila
Christmas [ˈkrɪsməs] *n* **:** Navidad *f* <Christmas season : las Navidades>
chromatic [kroːˈmæṱɪk] *adj* **:** cromático <chromatic scale : escala cromática>
chrome [ˈkroːm] *n* **:** cromo *m* (metal)
chromium [ˈkroːmiəm] *n* **:** cromo *m* (elemento)
chromosome [ˈkroːməˌsoːm, -ˌzoːm] *n* **:** cromosoma *m*
chronic [ˈkrɑnɪk] *adj* **:** crónico — **chronically** [-nɪkli] *adv*
chronicle[1] [ˈkrɑnɪkəl] *vt* **-cled; -cling :** escribir (una crónica o historia)
chronicle[2] *n* **:** crónica *f,* historia *f*
chronicler [ˈkrɑnɪklər] *n* **:** historiador *m,* -dora *f;* cronista *mf*
chronological [ˌkrɑnəlˈɑdʒɪkəl] *adj* **:** cronológico — **chronologically** [-kli] *adv*
chronology [krəˈnɑlədʒi] *n, pl* **-gies :** cronología *f*
chronometer [krəˈnɑməṱər] *n* **:** cronómetro *m*
chrysalis [ˈkrɪsələs] *n, pl* **chrysalides** [krɪˈsæləˌdiːz] *or* **chrysalises :** crisálida *f*
chrysanthemum [krɪˈsæn*t*θəməm] *n* **:** crisantemo *m*
chubbiness [ˈtʃʌbinəs] *n* **:** gordura *f*
chubby [ˈtʃʌbi] *adj* **-bier; -est :** gordito, regordete, rechoncho
chuck[1] [ˈtʃʌk] *vt* **1** TOSS **:** tirar, lanzar, aventar *Col, Mex* **2 to chuck under the chin :** hacer la mamola
chuck[2] *n* **1** PAT **:** mamola *f,* palmada *f* **2** TOSS **:** lanzamiento *m* **3** *or* **chuck steak :** corte *m* de carne de res
chuckle[1] [ˈtʃʌkəl] *vi* **-led; -ling :** reírse entre dientes
chuckle[2] *n* **:** risita *f,* risa *f* ahogada
chug[1] [ˈtʃʌg] *vi* **chugged; chugging :** resoplar, traquetear
chug[2] *n* **:** resoplido *m,* traqueteo *m*
chum[1] [ˈtʃʌm] *vi* **chummed; chumming :** ser camaradas, ser cuates *Mex fam*
chum[2] *n* **:** amigo *m,* -ga *f;* camarada *mf;* compinche *mf fam*
chummy [ˈtʃʌmi] *adj* **-mier; -est :** amistoso <they're very chummy : son muy amigos>
chump [ˈtʃʌmp] *n* **:** tonto *m,* -ta *f;* idiota *mf*
chunk [ˈtʃʌnk] *n* **1** PIECE **:** cacho *m,* pedazo *m,* trozo *m* **2 :** cantidad *f* grande <a chunk of money : mucho dinero>
chunky [ˈtʃʌnki] *adj* **chunkier; -est 1** STOCKY **:** fornido, robusto **2 :** que contiene pedazos
church [ˈtʃərtʃ] *n* **1 :** iglesia *f* <to go to church : ir a la iglesia> **2** CHRISTIANS **:** iglesia *f,* conjunto *m* de fieles cristianos **3** DENOMINATION **:** confesión *f,* secta *f* **4** CONGREGATION **:** feligreses *mpl*, fieles *mpl*
churchgoer [ˈtʃərtʃˌgoːər] *n* **:** practicante *mf*
churchyard [ˈtʃərtʃˌjɑrd] *n* **:** cementerio *m* (junto a una iglesia)
churn[1] [ˈtʃərn] *vt* **1 :** batir (crema), hacer (mantequilla) **2 :** agitar con fuerza, revolver — *vi* **:** agitarse, arremolinarse
churn[2] *n* **:** mantequera *f*
chute [ˈʃuːt] *n* **:** conducto *m* inclinado, vertedero *m* (para basuras)
chutney [ˈtʃʌtni] *n, pl* **-neys :** chutney *m*
chutzpah [ˈhʊtspə, ˈxʊt-, -ˌspɑ] *n* **:** descaro *m,* frescura *f,* cara *f fam*
cicada [səˈkeɪdə, -ˈkɑ-] *n* **:** cigarra *f,* chicharra *f*
cider [ˈsaɪdər] *n* **1 :** jugo *m* (de manzana, etc.) **2 hard cider :** sidra *f*
cigar [sɪˈgɑr] *n* **:** puro *m,* cigarro *m*
cigarette [ˌsɪgəˈrɛt, ˈsɪgəˌrɛt] *n* **:** cigarrillo *m,* cigarro *m*
cinch[1] [ˈsɪntʃ] *vt* **1 :** cinchar (un caballo) **2** ASSURE **:** asegurar
cinch[2] *n* **1 :** cincha *f* (para caballos) **2 :** algo fácil o seguro <it's a cinch : es bien fácil, es pan comido>
cinchona [sɪŋˈkoːnə] *n* **:** quino *m*
cinder [ˈsɪndər] *n* **1** EMBER **:** brasa *f,* ascua *f* **2 cinders** *npl* ASHES **:** cenizas *fpl*
cinema [ˈsɪnəmə] *n* **:** cine *m*
cinematic [ˌsɪnəˈmæṱɪk] *adj* **:** cinematográfico
cinnamon [ˈsɪnəmən] *n* **:** canela *f*
cipher [ˈsaɪfər] *n* **1** ZERO **:** cero *m* **2** CODE **:** cifra *f,* clave *f*
circa [ˈsərkə] *prep* **:** alrededor de, hacia <circa 1800 : hacia el año 1800>
circle[1] [ˈsərkəl] *v* **-cled; -cling** *vt* **1 :** encerrar en un círculo, poner un círculo alrededor de **2 :** girar alrededor de, dar vueltas a <we circled the building twice : le dimos vueltas al edificio dos veces> — *vi* **:** dar vueltas

circle² *n* **1** : círculo *m* **2** CYCLE : ciclo *m* <to come full circle : volver al punto de partida> **3** GROUP : círculo *m,* grupo *m* (social)
circuit [ˈsərkət] *n* **1** BOUNDARY : circuito *m,* perímetro *m* (de una zona o un territorio) **2** TOUR : circuito *m,* recorrido *m,* tour *m* **3** : circuito *m* (eléctrico) <a short circuit : un cortocircuito>
circuitous [ˌsərˈkjuːətəs] *adj* : sinuoso, tortuoso
circuitry [ˈsərkətri] *n, pl* **-ries** : sistema *m* de circuitos
circular¹ [ˈsərkjələr] *adj* ROUND : circular, redondo
circular² *n* : circular *f*
circulate [ˈsərkjəˌleɪt] *v* **-lated; -lating** *vi* : circular — *vt* **1** : circular (noticias, etc.) **2** DISSEMINATE : hacer circular, divulgar
circulation [ˌsərkjəˈleɪʃən] *n* : circulación *f*
circulatory [ˈsərkjələˌtori] *adj* : circulatorio
circumcise [ˈsərkəmˌsaɪz] *vt* **-cised; -cising** : circuncidar
circumcision [ˌsərkəmˈsɪʒən, ˈsərkəmˌ-] *n* : circuncisión *f*
circumference [sərˈkʌmpfrənts] *n* : circunferencia *f*
circumflex [ˈsərkəmˌflɛks] *n* : acento *m* circunflejo
circumlocution [ˌsərkəmloˈkjuːʃən] *n* : circunlocución *f*
circumnavigate [ˌsərkəmˈnævəˌgeɪt] *vt* **-gated; -gating** : circunnavegar
circumscribe [ˈsərkəmˌskraɪb] *vt* **-scribed; -scribing 1** : circunscribir, trazar una figura alrededor de **2** LIMIT : circunscribir, limitar
circumspect [ˈsərkəmˌspɛkt] *adj* : circunspecto, prudente, cauto
circumspection [ˌsərkəmˈspɛkʃən] *n* : circunspección *f,* cautela *f*
circumstance [ˈsərkəmˌstænts] *n* **1** EVENT : circunstancia *f,* acontecimiento *m* **2 circumstances** *npl* SITUATION : circunstancias *fpl,* situación *f* <under the circumstances : dadas las circunstancias> <under no circumstances : de ninguna manera, bajo ningún concepto> **3 circumstances** *npl* : situación *f* económica
circumstantial [ˌsərkəmˈstæntʃəl] *adj* : circunstancial
circumvent [ˌsərkəmˈvɛnt] *vt* : evadir, burlar (una ley o regla), sortear (una responsabilidad o dificultad)
circumvention [ˌsərkəmˈvɛntʃən] *n* : evasión *f*
circus [ˈsərkəs] *n* : circo *m*
cirrhosis [səˈroːsɪs] *n* : cirrosis *f*
cirrus [ˈsɪrəs] *n, pl* **-ri** [ˈsɪrˌaɪ] : cirro *m*
cistern [ˈsɪstərn] *n* : cisterna *f,* aljibe *m*
citadel [ˈsɪtədəl, -ˌdɛl] *n* FORTRESS : ciudadela *f,* fortaleza *f*
citation [saɪˈteɪʃən] *n* **1** SUMMONS : emplazamiento *m,* citación *f,* convocatoria *f* (judicial) **2** QUOTATION : cita *f* **3** COMMENDATION : elogio *m,* mención *f* (de honor)
cite [ˈsaɪt] *vt* **cited; citing 1** ARRAIGN, SUBPOENA : emplazar, citar, hacer comparecer (ante un tribunal) **2** QUOTE : citar **3** COMMEND : elogiar, honrar (oficialmente)
citizen [ˈsɪtəzən] *n* : ciudadano *m,* -na *f*
citizenry [ˈsɪtəzənri] *n, pl* **-ries** : ciudadanía *f,* conjunto *m* de ciudadanos
citizenship [ˈsɪtəzənˌʃɪp] *n* : ciudadanía *f* <Nicaraguan citizenship : ciudadanía nicaragüense>
citron [ˈsɪtrən] *n* : cidra *f*
citrus [ˈsɪtrəs] *n, pl* **-rus** *or* **-ruses** : cítrico *m*
city [ˈsɪti] *n, pl* **cities** : ciudad *f*
civic [ˈsɪvɪk] *adj* : cívico
civics [ˈsɪvɪks] *ns & pl* : civismo *m*
civil [ˈsɪvəl] *adj* **1** : civil <civil law : derecho civil> **2** POLITE : civil, cortés
civilian [səˈvɪljən] *n* : civil *mf* <soldiers and civilians : soldados y civiles>
civility [səˈvɪləti] *n, pl* **-ties** : cortesía *f,* educación *f*
civilization [ˌsɪvələˈzeɪʃən] *n* : civilización *f*
civilize [ˈsɪvəˌlaɪz] *vt* **-lized; -lizing** : civilizar — **civilized** *adj*
civil liberties *npl* : derechos *mpl* civiles
civilly [ˈsɪvəli] *adv* : cortésmente
civil rights *npl* : derechos *mpl* civiles
civil service *n* : administración *f* pública
civil war *n* : guerra *f* civil
clack¹ [ˈklæk] *vi* : tabletear
clack² *n* : tableteo *m*
clad [ˈklæd] *adj* **1** CLOTHED : vestido **2** COVERED : cubierto
claim¹ [ˈkleɪm] *vt* **1** DEMAND : reclamar, reivindicar <she claimed her rights : reclamó sus derechos> **2** MAINTAIN : afirmar, sostener <they claim it's theirs : sostienen que es suyo>
claim² *n* **1** DEMAND : demanda *f,* reclamación *f* **2** DECLARATION : declaración *f,* afirmación *f* **3 to stake a claim** : reclamar, reivindicar
claimant [ˈkleɪmənt] *n* : demandante *mf* (ante un juez), pretendiente *mf* (al trono, etc.)
clairvoyance [klærˈvɔɪənts] *n* : clarividencia *f*
clairvoyant¹ [klærˈvɔɪənt] *adj* : clarividente
clairvoyant² *n* : clarividente *mf*
clam [ˈklæm] *n* : almeja *f*
clamber [ˈklæmbər] *vi* : treparse o subirse torpemente
clammy [ˈklæmi] *adj* **-mier; -est** : húmedo y algo frío
clamor¹ [ˈklæmər] *vi* : gritar, clamar

clamor[2] *n* **:** clamor *m*
clamorous [ˈklæmərəs] *adj* **:** clamoroso, ruidoso, estrepitoso
clamp[1] [ˈklæmp] *vt* **:** sujetar con abrazaderas
clamp[2] *n* **:** abrazadera *f*
clan [ˈklæn] *n* **:** clan *m*
clandestine [klænˈdɛstɪn] *adj* **:** clandestino, secreto
clang[1] [ˈklæŋ] *vi* **:** hacer resonar (dícese de un objeto metálico)
clang[2] *n* **:** ruido *m* metálico fuerte
clangor [ˈklæŋər, -gər] *n* **:** estruendo *m* metálico
clank[1] [ˈklæŋk] *vi* **:** producir un ruido metálico seco
clank[2] *n* **:** ruido *m* metálico seco
clannish [ˈklænɪʃ] *adj* **:** exclusivista
clap[1] [ˈklæp] *v* **clapped; clapping** *vt* **1** SLAP, STRIKE **:** golpear ruidosamente, dar una palmada <to clap one's hands : batir palmas, dar palmadas> **2** APPLAUD **:** aplaudir — *vi* APPLAUD **:** aplaudir
clap[2] *n* **1** SLAP **:** palmada *f,* golpecito *m* **2** NOISE **:** ruido *m* seco <a clap of thunder : un trueno>
clapboard [ˈklæbərd, ˈklæpˌbord] *n* **:** tabla *f* de madera (para revestir muros)
clapper [ˈklæpər] *n* **:** badajo *m* (de una campana)
clarification [ˌklærəfəˈkeɪʃən] *n* **:** clarificación *f*
clarify [ˈklærəˌfaɪ] *vt* **-fied; -fying 1** EXPLAIN **:** aclarar **2 :** clarificar (un líquido)
clarinet [ˌklærəˈnɛt] *n* **:** clarinete *m*
clarinetist *or* **clarinettist** [ˌklærəˈnɛtɪst] *n* **:** clarinetista *mf*
clarion [ˈklæriən] *adj* **:** claro y sonoro
clarity [ˈklærət̬i] *n* **:** claridad *f,* nitidez *f*
clash[1] [ˈklæʃ] *vi* **1 :** sonar, chocarse <the cymbals clashed : los platillos sonaron> **2 :** chocar, enfrentarse <the students clashed with the police : los estudiantes se enfrentaron con la policía> **3** CONFLICT **:** estar en conflicto, oponerse **4 :** desentonar (dícese de los colores), coincidir (dícese de los datos)
clash[2] *n* **1 :** ruido *m* (producido por un choque) **2** CONFLICT, CONFRONTATION **:** enfrentamiento *m,* conflicto *m,* choque *m* **3 :** desentono *m* (de colores), coincidencia *f* (de datos)
clasp[1] [ˈklæsp] *vt* **1** FASTEN **:** sujetar, abrochar **2** EMBRACE, GRASP **:** agarrar, sujetar, abrazar
clasp[2] *n* **1** FASTENING **:** broche *m,* cierre *m* **2** EMBRACE, SQUEEZE **:** apretón *m,* abrazo *m*
class[1] [ˈklæs] *vt* **:** clasificar, catalogar
class[2] *n* **1** KIND, TYPE **:** clase *f,* tipo *m,* especie *f* **2 :** clase *f,* rango *m* social <the working class : la clase obrera> **3** LESSON **:** clase *f,* curso *m* <English class : clase de inglés> **4 :** conjunto *m* de estudiantes, clase *f* <the class of '97 : la promoción del 97>
classic[1] [ˈklæsɪk] *adj* **:** clásico
classic[2] *n* **:** clásico *m,* obra *f* clásica
classical [ˈklæsɪkəl] *adj* **:** clásico — **classically** [-kli] *adv*
classicism [ˈklæsəˌsɪzəm] *n* **:** clasicismo *m*
classification [ˌklæsəfəˈkeɪʃən] *n* **:** clasificación *f*
classified [ˈklæsəˌfaɪd] *adj* **1 :** clasificado <classified ads : avisos clasificados> **2** RESTRICTED **:** confidencial, secreto <classified documents : documentos secretos>
classify [ˈklæsəˌfaɪ] *vt* **-fied; -fying :** clasificar, catalogar
classless [ˈklæsləs] *adj* **:** sin clases
classmate [ˈklæsˌmeɪt] *n* **:** compañero *m,* -ra *f* de clase
classroom [ˈklæsˌruːm] *n* **:** aula *f,* salón *m* de clase
clatter[1] [ˈklæt̬ər] *vi* **:** traquetear, hacer ruido
clatter[2] *n* **:** traqueteo *m,* ruido *m,* estrépito *m*
clause [ˈklɔz] *n* **:** cláusula *f*
claustrophobia [ˌklɔstrəˈfoːbiə] *n* **:** claustrofobia *f*
clavicle [ˈklævɪkəl] *n* **:** clavícula *f*
claw[1] [ˈklɔ] *v* **:** arañar
claw[2] *n* **:** garra *f,* uña *f* (de un gato), pinza *f* (de un crustáceo)
clay [ˈkleɪ] *n* **:** arcilla *f,* barro *m*
clayey [ˈkleɪi] *adj* **:** arcilloso
clean[1] [ˈkliːn] *vt* **:** limpiar, lavar, asear
clean[2] *adv* **:** limpio, limpiamente <to play clean : jugar limpio>
clean[3] *adj* **1 :** limpio **2** UNADULTERATED **:** puro **3** IRREPROACHABLE **:** intachable, sin mancha <to have a clean record : no tener antecedentes penales> **4** DECENT **:** decente **5** COMPLETE **:** completo, absoluto <a clean break with the past : un corte radical con el pasado>
cleaner [ˈkliːnər] *n* **1 :** limpiador *m,* -dora *f* **2 :** producto *m* de limpieza **3** DRY CLEANER **:** tintorería *f* (servicio)
cleanliness [ˈklɛnlinəs] *n* **:** limpieza *f,* aseo *m*
cleanly[1] [ˈkliːnli] *adv* **:** limpiamente, con limpieza
cleanly[2] [ˈklɛnli] *adj* **-lier; -est :** limpio, pulcro
cleanness [ˈkliːnnəs] *n* **:** limpieza *f*
cleanse [ˈklɛnz] *vt* **cleansed; cleansing :** limpiar, purificar
cleanser [ˈklɛnzər] *n* **:** limpiador *m,* purificador *m*
clear[1] [ˈklɪr] *vt* **1** CLARIFY **:** aclarar, clarificar (un líquido) **2 :** despejar (una superficie), desatascar (un tubo), desmontar (una selva) <to clear the table : levantar la mesa> <to clear one's throat : carraspear, aclararse la voz> **3** EXONERATE **:** absolver, limpiar el nombre de **4** EARN **:** ganar, sacar (una ganancia de) **5 :** pasar sin tocar

<he cleared the hurdle : saltó por encima de la valla> **6 to clear up** RESOLVE : aclarar, resolver, esclarecer — *vi* **1** DISPERSE : irse, despejarse, disiparse **2** : ser compensado (dícese de un cheque) **3 to clear up** : despejar (dícese del tiempo), mejorarse (dícese de una enfermedad)

clear[2] *adv* : claro, claramente

clear[3] *adj* **1** BRIGHT : claro, lúcido **2** FAIR : claro, despejado **3** TRANSPARENT : transparente, translúcido **4** EVIDENT, UNMISTAKABLE : evidente, claro, obvio **5** CERTAIN : seguro **6** UNOBSTRUCTED : despejado, libre

clear[4] *n* **1 in the clear** : inocente, libre de toda sospecha **2 in the clear** SAFE : fuera de peligro

clearance [ˈklɪrənts] *n* **1** CLEARING : despeje *m* **2** SPACE : espacio *m* (libre), margen *m* **3** AUTHORIZATION : autorización *f*, despacho *m* (de la aduana)

clearing [ˈklɪrɪŋ] *n* : claro *m* (de un bosque)

clearly [ˈklɪrli] *adv* **1** DISTINCTLY : claramente, directamente **2** OBVIOUSLY : obviamente, evidentemente

cleat [ˈkliːt] *n* **1** : taco *m* **2 cleats** *npl* : zapatos *mpl* deportivos (con tacos)

cleavage [ˈkliːvɪdʒ] *n* **1** CLEFT : hendidura *f*, raja *f* **2** : escote *m* (del busto)

cleave[1] [ˈkliːv] *vi* **cleaved** [ˈkliːvd] *or* **clove** [ˈkloːv]; **cleaving** ADHERE : adherirse, unirse

cleave[2] *vt* **cleaved; cleaving** SPLIT : hender, dividir, partir

cleaver [ˈkliːvər] *n* : cuchilla *f* de carnicero

clef [ˈklɛf] *n* : clave *f*

cleft [ˈklɛft] *n* : hendidura *f*, raja *f*, grieta *f*

clemency [ˈklɛməntsi] *n* : clemencia *f*

clement [ˈklɛmənt] *adj* **1** MERCIFUL : clemente, piadoso **2** MILD : clemente, apacible

clench [ˈklɛntʃ] *vt* **1** CLUTCH : agarrar **2** TIGHTEN : apretar (el puño, los dientes)

clergy [ˈklərdʒi] *n, pl* **-gies** : clero *m*

clergyman [ˈklərdʒimən] *n, pl* **-men** [-mən, -ˌmɛn] : clérigo *m*

cleric [ˈklɛrɪk] *n* : clérigo *m*, -ga *f*

clerical [ˈklɛrɪkəl] *adj* **1** : clerical <a clerical collar : un alzacuello> **2** : de oficina <clerical staff : personal de oficina>

clerk[1] [ˈklərk, *Brit* ˈklɑrk] *vi* : trabajar de oficinista, trabajar de dependiente

clerk[2] *n* **1** : funcionario *m*, -ria *f* (de una oficina gubernamental) **2** : oficinista *mf*, empleado *m*, -da *f* de oficina **3** SALESPERSON : dependiente *m*, -ta *f*

clever [ˈklɛvər] *adj* **1** SKILLFUL : ingenioso, hábil **2** SMART : listo, inteligente, astuto

cleverly [ˈklɛvərli] *adv* **1** SKILLFULLY : ingeniosamente, hábilmente **2** INTELLIGENTLY : inteligentemente

cleverness [ˈklɛvərnəs] *n* **1** SKILL : ingenio *m*, habilidad *f* **2** INTELLIGENCE : inteligencia *f*

clew [ˈkluː] → **clue**

cliché [kliˈʃeɪ] *n* : cliché *m*, tópico *m*

click[1] [ˈklɪk] *vt* : chasquear (la lengua, los dedos) — *vi* **1** : chasquear **2** SUCCEED : tener éxito **3** GET ALONG : congeniar, llevarse bien

click[2] *n* : chasquido *m*

client [ˈklaɪənt] *n* : cliente *m*, -ta *f*

clientele [ˌklaɪənˈtɛl, ˌkliː-] *n* : clientela *f*

cliff [ˈklɪf] *n* : acantilado *m*, precipicio *m*, risco *m*

climate [ˈklaɪmət] *n* : clima *m*

climax[1] [ˈklaɪˌmæks] *vi* : llegar al punto culminante, culminar — *vt* : ser el punto culminante de

climax[2] *n* : clímax *m*, punto *m* culminante

climb[1] [ˈklaɪm] *vt* : escalar, trepar a, subir a <to climb a mountain : escalar una montaña> — *vi* **1** RISE : subir, ascender <prices are climbing : los precios están subiendo> **2** subirse, treparse <to climb up a tree : treparse a un árbol>

climb[2] *n* : ascenso *m*, subida *f*

climber [ˈklaɪmər] *n* **1** : escalador *m*, -dora *f* <a mountain climber : un alpinista> **2** : trepadora *f* (planta)

clinch[1] [ˈklɪntʃ] *vt* **1** FASTEN, SECURE : remachar (un clavo), afianzar, abrochar **2** SETTLE : decidir, cerrar <to clinch the title : ganar el título>

clinch[2] *n* : abrazo *m*, clinch *m* (en el boxeo)

clincher [ˈklɪntʃər] *n* : argumento *m* decisivo

cling [ˈklɪŋ] *vi* **clung** [ˈklʌŋ]; **clinging** **1** STICK : adherirse, pegarse **2** : aferrarse, agarrarse <he clung to the railing : se aferró a la barandilla>

clinic [ˈklɪnɪk] *n* : clínica *f*

clinical [ˈklɪnɪkəl] *adj* : clínico — **clinically** [-kli] *adv*

clink[1] [ˈklɪŋk] *vi* : tintinear

clink[2] *n* : tintineo *m*

clip[1] [ˈklɪp] *vt* **clipped; clipping** **1** CUT : cortar, recortar **2** HIT : golpear, dar un puñetazo a **3** FASTEN : sujetar (con un clip)

clip[2] *n* **1** → **clippers** **2** BLOW : golpe *m*, puñetazo *m* **3** PACE : paso *m* rápido **4** FASTENER : clip *m* <a paper clip : un sujetapapeles>

clipper [ˈklɪpər] *n* **1** : clíper *m* (buque de vela) **2 clippers** *npl* : tijeras *fpl* <nail clippers : cortauñas>

clique [ˈkliːk, ˈklɪk] *n* : grupo *m* exclusivo, camarilla *f* (de políticos)

clitoris [ˈklɪtərəs, klɪˈtɔrəs] *n, pl* **clitorides** [-ˈtɔrəˌdiːz] : clítoris *m*

cloak[1] [ˈkloːk] *vt* : encubrir, envolver (en un manto de)

cloak[2] *n* : capa *f*, capote *m*, manto *m* <under the cloak of darkness : al amparo de la oscuridad>

clobber ['klɑbər] *vt* **:** dar una paliza a
clock¹ ['klɑk] *vt* **:** cronometrar
clock² *n* **1 :** reloj *m* (de pared), cronómetro *m* (en deportes o competencias) **2 around the clock :** las veinticuatro horas
clockwise ['klɑk,waɪz] *adv & adj* **:** en la dirección de las manecillas del reloj
clockwork ['klɑk,wərk] *n* **:** mecanismo *m* de relojería
clod ['klɑd] *n* **1 :** terrón *m* **2** OAF **:** zoquete *mf*
clog¹ ['klɑg] *v* **clogged; clogging** *vt* **1** HINDER **:** estorbar, impedir **2** BLOCK **:** atascar, tapar — *vi* **:** atascarse, taparse
clog² *n* **1** OBSTACLE **:** traba *f,* impedimento *m,* estorbo *m* **2 :** zueco *m* (zapato)
cloister¹ ['klɔɪstər] *vt* **:** enclaustrar
cloister² *n* **:** claustro *m*
clone ['klo:n] *n* **1 :** clon *m* (de un organismo) **2** COPY **:** copia *f,* reproducción *f*
close¹ ['klo:z] *v* **closed; closing** *vt* **:** cerrar — *vi* **1 :** cerrarse, cerrar **2** TERMINATE **:** concluirse, terminar **3 to close in** APPROACH **:** acercarse, aproximarse
close² ['klo:s] *adv* **:** cerca, de cerca
close³ *adj* **closer; closest 1** CONFINING **:** restrictivo, estrecho **2** SECRETIVE **:** reservado **3** STRICT **:** estricto, detallado **4** STUFFY **:** cargado, bochornoso (dícese del tiempo) **5** TIGHT **:** apretado, entallado, ceñido <it's a close fit : es muy apretado> **6** NEAR **:** cercano, próximo **7** INTIMATE **:** íntimo <close friends : amigos íntimos> **8** ACCURATE **:** fiel, exacto **9 :** reñido <a close election : una elección muy reñida>
close⁴ ['klo:z] *n* **:** fin *m,* final *m,* conclusión *f*
closely ['klo:sli] *adv* **:** cerca, de cerca
closeness ['klo:snəs] *n* **1** NEARNESS **:** cercanía *f,* proximidad *f* **2** INTIMACY **:** intimidad *f*
closet¹ ['klɑzət] *vt* **to be closeted with :** estar encerrado con
closet² *n* **:** armario *m,* guardarropa *f,* clóset *m*
closure ['klo:ʒər] *n* **1** CLOSING, END **:** cierre *m,* clausura *f,* fin *m* **2** FASTENER **:** cierre *m*
clot¹ ['klɑt] *v* **clotted; clotting** *vt* **:** coagular, cuajar — *vi* **:** cuajarse, coagularse
clot² *n* **:** coágulo *m*
cloth ['klɔθ] *n, pl* **cloths** ['klɔðz, 'klɔθs] **1** FABRIC **:** tela *f* **2** RAG **:** trapo *m* **3** TABLECLOTH **:** mantel *m*
clothe ['klo:ð] *vt* **clothed** *or* **clad** ['klæd]; **clothing** DRESS **:** vestir, arropar, ataviar
clothes ['klo:z, 'klo:ðz] *npl* **1** CLOTHING **:** ropa *f* **2** BEDCLOTHES **:** ropa *f* de cama
clothespin ['klo:z,pɪn] *n* **:** pinza *f* (para la ropa)
clothing ['klo:ðɪŋ] *n* **:** ropa *f,* indumentaria *f*
cloud¹ ['klaʊd] *vt* **:** nublar, oscurecer — *vi* **to cloud over :** nublarse
cloud² *n* **:** nube *f*
cloudburst ['klaʊd,bərst] *n* **:** chaparrón *m,* aguacero *m*
cloudless ['klaʊdləs] *adj* **:** despejado, claro
cloudy ['klaʊdi] *adj* **cloudier; -est :** nublado, nuboso
clout¹ ['klaʊt] *vt* **:** bofetear, dar un tortazo a
clout² *n* **1** BLOW **:** golpe *m,* tortazo *m fam* **2** INFLUENCE **:** influencia *f,* palanca *f fam*
clove¹ ['klo:v] *n* **1 :** diente *m* (de ajo) **2 :** clavo *m* (especia)
clove² → **cleave**
cloven hoof ['klo:vən] **:** pezuña *f* hendida
clover ['klo:vər] *n* **:** trébol *m*
cloverleaf ['klo:vər,li:f] *n, pl* **-leafs** *or* **-leaves** [-,li:vz] **:** intersección *f* en trébol
clown¹ ['klaʊn] *vi* **:** payasear, bromear <stop clowning around : déjate de payasadas>
clown² *n* **:** payaso *m,* -sa *f*
clownish ['klaʊnɪʃ] *adj* **1 :** de payaso **2** BOORISH **:** grosero — **clownishly** *adv*
cloying ['klɔɪɪŋ] *adj* **:** empalagoso, meloso
club¹ ['klʌb] *vt* **clubbed; clubbing :** aporrear, dar garrotazos a
club² *n* **1** CUDGEL **:** garrote *m,* porra *f* **2 :** palo *m* <golf club : palo de golf> **3 :** trébol *m* (naipe) **4** ASSOCIATION **:** club *m*
clubfoot ['klʌb,fʊt] *n, pl* **-feet :** pie *m* deforme
clubhouse ['klʌb,haʊs] *n* **:** sede *f* de un club
cluck¹ ['klʌk] *vi* **:** cloquear, cacarear
cluck² *n* **:** cloqueo *m,* cacareo *m*
clue¹ ['klu:] *vt* **clued; clueing** *or* **cluing** *or* **to clue in :** dar una pista a, informar
clue² *n* **:** pista *f,* indicio *m*
clump¹ ['klʌmp] *vi* **1 :** caminar con pisadas fuertes **2** LUMP **:** agruparse, aglutinarse — *vt* **:** amontonar
clump² *n* **1 :** grupo *m* (de arbustos o árboles), terrón *m* (de tierra) **2 :** pisada *f* fuerte
clumsily ['klʌmzəli] *adv* **:** torpemente, sin gracia
clumsiness ['klʌmzinəs] *n* **:** torpeza *f*
clumsy ['klʌmzi] *adj* **-sier; -est 1** AWKWARD **:** torpe, desmañado **2** TACTLESS **:** carente de tacto, poco delicado
clung → **cling**
cluster¹ ['klʌstər] *vt* **:** agrupar, juntar — *vi* **:** agruparse, apiñarse, arracimarse
cluster² *n* **:** grupo *m,* conjunto *m,* racimo *m* (de uvas)
clutch¹ ['klʌtʃ] *vt* **:** agarrar, asir — *vi* **to clutch at :** tratar de agarrar

clutch[2] *n* **1** GRASP, GRIP **:** agarre *m,* apretón *m* **2 :** embrague *m,* clutch *m* (de una máquina) **3 clutches** *npl* **:** garras *fpl* <he fell into their clutches : cayó en sus garras>
clutter[1] [ˈklʌtər] *vt* **:** atiborrar o atestar de cosas, llenar desordenadamente
clutter[2] *n* **:** desorden *m,* revoltijo *m*
coach[1] [ˈkoːtʃ] *vt* **:** entrenar (atletas, artistas), preparar (alumnos)
coach[2] *n* **1** CARRIAGE **:** coche *m,* carruaje *m,* carroza *f* **2 :** vagón *m* de pasajeros (de un tren) **3** BUS **:** autobús *m,* ómnibus *m* **4 :** pasaje *m* aéreo de segunda clase **5** TRAINER **:** entrenador *m,* -dora *f*
coagulate [koˈægjəˌleɪt] *v* **-lated; -lating** *vt* **:** coagular, cuajar — *vi* **:** coagularse, cuajarse
coal [ˈkoːl] *n* **1** EMBER **:** ascua *f,* brasa *f* **2 :** carbón *m* <a coal mine : una mina de carbón>
coalesce [ˌkoːəˈlɛs] *vi* **-alesced; -alescing :** unirse
coalition [ˌkoːəˈlɪʃən] *n* **:** coalición *f*
coarse [ˈkors] *adj* **coarser; -est 1 :** grueso (dícese de la arena o la sal), basto (dícese de las telas), áspero (dícese de la piel) **2** CRUDE, ROUGH **:** basto, tosco, ordinario **3** VULGAR **:** grosero — **coarsely** *adv*
coarsen [ˈkorsən] *vt* **:** hacer áspero o basto — *vi* **:** volverse áspero o basto
coarseness [ˈkorsnəs] *n* **:** aspereza *f,* tosquedad *f*
coast[1] [ˈkoːst] *vi* **:** deslizarse, rodar sin impulso
coast[2] *n* **:** costa *f,* litoral *m*
coastal [ˈkoːstəl] *adj* **:** costero
coaster [ˈkoːstər] *n* **:** posavasos *m*
coast guard *n* **:** guardia *f* costera, guardacostas *mpl*
coastline [ˈkoːstˌlaɪn] *n* **:** costa *f*
coat[1] [ˈkoːt] *vt* **:** cubrir, revestir, bañar (en un líquido)
coat[2] *n* **1 :** abrigo *m* <a sport coat : una chaqueta, un saco> **2 :** pelaje *m* (de animales) **3** LAYER **:** capa *f,* mano *f* (de pintura)
coating [ˈkoːtɪŋ] *n* **:** capa *f*
coat of arms *n* **:** escudo *m* de armas
coax [ˈkoːks] *vt* **:** engatusar, persuadir
cob [ˈkɑb] → **corncob**
cobalt [ˈkoːˌbɔlt] *n* **:** cobalto *m*
cobble [ˈkɑbəl] *vt* **cobbled; cobbling 1 :** fabricar o remendar (zapatos) **2 to cobble together :** improvisar, hacer apresuradamente
cobbler [ˈkɑblər] *n* **1** SHOEMAKER **:** zapatero *m,* -ra *f* **2 fruit cobbler :** tarta *f* de fruta
cobblestone [ˈkɑbəlˌstoːn] *n* **:** adoquín *m*
cobra [ˈkoːbrə] *n* **:** cobra *f*
cobweb [ˈkɑbˌwɛb] *n* **:** telaraña *f*
cocaine [koːˈkeɪn, ˈkoːˌkeɪn] *n* **:** cocaína *f*
cock[1] [ˈkɑk] *vt* **1 :** ladear <to cock one's head : ladear la cabeza> **2 :** montar, amartillar (un arma de fuego)
cock[2] *n* **1** ROOSTER **:** gallo *m* **2** FAUCET **:** grifo *m,* llave *f* **3 :** martillo *m* (de un arma de fuego)
cockatoo [ˈkɑkəˌtuː] *n, pl* **-toos :** cacatúa *f*
cockeyed [ˈkɑkˌaɪd] *adj* **1** ASKEW **:** ladeado, torcido, chueco **2** ABSURD **:** disparatado, absurdo
cockfight [ˈkɑkˌfaɪt] *n* **:** pelea *f* de gallos
cockiness [ˈkɑkinəs] *n* **:** arrogancia *f*
cockle [ˈkɑkəl] *n* **:** berberecho *m*
cockpit [ˈkɑkˌpɪt] *n* **:** cabina *f*
cockroach [ˈkɑkˌroːtʃ] *n* **:** cucaracha *f*
cocktail [ˈkɑkˌteɪl] *n* **1 :** coctel *m,* cóctel *m* **2** APPETIZER **:** aperitivo *m*
cocky [ˈkɑki] *adj* **cockier; -est :** creído, engreído
cocoa [ˈkoːˌkoː] *n* **1** CACAO **:** cacao *m* **2 :** cocoa *f,* chocolate *m* (bebida)
coconut [ˈkoːkəˌnʌt] *n* **:** coco *m*
cocoon [kəˈkuːn] *n* **:** capullo *m*
cod [ˈkɑd] *n, pl* **cod :** bacalao *m*
coddle [ˈkɑdəl] *vt* **-dled; -dling :** mimar, consentir
code [ˈkoːd] *n* **1 :** código *m* <civil code : código civil> **2 :** código *m,* clave *f* <secret code : clave secreta>
codeine [ˈkoːˌdiːn] *n* **:** codeína *f*
codger [ˈkɑdʒər] *n* **:** viejo *m,* vejete *m*
codify [ˈkɑdəˌfaɪ, ˈkoː-] *vt* **-fied; -fying :** codificar
coeducation [ˌkoːˌɛdʒəˈkeɪʃən] *n* **:** coeducación *f,* enseñanza *f* mixta
coeducational [ˌkoːˌɛdʒəˈkeɪʃənəl] *adj* **:** mixto
coefficient [ˌkoːəˈfɪʃənt] *n* **:** coeficiente *m*
coerce [koˈərs] *vt* **-erced; -ercing :** coaccionar, forzar, obligar
coercion [koˈərʒən, -ʃən] *n* **:** coacción *f*
coercive [koˈərsɪv] *adj* **:** coactivo
coexist [ˌkoːɪgˈzɪst] *vi* **:** coexistir
coexistence [ˌkoːɪgˈzɪstən*t*s] *n* **:** coexistencia *f*
coffee [ˈkɔfi] *n* **:** café *m*
coffeepot [ˈkɔfiˌpɑt] *n* **:** cafetera *f*
coffer [ˈkɔfər] *n* **:** cofre *m*
coffin [ˈkɔfən] *n* **:** ataúd *m,* féretro *m*
cog [ˈkɑg] *n* **:** diente *m* (de una rueda dentada)
cogent [ˈkoːdʒənt] *adj* **:** convincente, persuasivo
cogitate [ˈkɑdʒəˌteɪt] *vi* **-tated; -tating :** reflexionar, meditar, discurrir
cogitation [ˌkɑdʒəˈteɪʃən] *n* **:** reflexión *f,* meditación *f*
cognac [ˈkoːnˌjæk] *n* **:** coñac *m*
cognate [ˈkɑgˌneɪt] *adj* **:** relacionado, afín
cogwheel [ˈkɑgˌ*h*wiːl] *n* **:** rueda *f* dentada
cohabit [ˌkoːˈhæbət] *vi* **:** cohabitar
cohere [koˈhɪr] *vi* **-hered; -hering 1** ADHERE **:** adherirse, pegarse **2 :** ser coherente o congruente

coherence [koˈhɪrənts] *n* : coherencia *f,* congruencia *f*

coherent [koˈhɪrənt] *adj* : coherente, congruente — **coherently** *adv*

cohesion [koˈhiːʒən] *n* : cohesión *f*

cohort [ˈkoːˌhɔrt] *n* **1** : cohorte *f* (de soldados) **2** COMPANION : compañero *m,* -ra *f;* colega *mf*

coiffure [kwɑˈfjʊr] *n* : peinado *m*

coil[1] [ˈkɔɪl] *vt* : enrollar — *vi* : enrollarse, enroscarse

coil[2] *n* : rollo *m* (de cuerda, etc.), espiral *f* (de humo)

coin[1] [ˈkɔɪn] *vt* **1** MINT : acuñar (moneda) **2** INVENT : acuñar, crear, inventar <to coin a phrase : como se suele decir>

coin[2] *n* : moneda *f*

coincide [ˌkoːɪnˈsaɪd, ˈkoːɪnˌsaɪd] *vi* **-cided; -ciding** : coincidir

coincidence [koˈɪntsədənts] *n* : coincidencia *f,* casualidad *f* <what a coincidence! : ¡qué casualidad!>

coincident [koˈɪntsədənt] *adj* : coincidente, concurrente

coincidental [koˌɪntsəˈdɛntəl] *adj* : casual, accidental, fortuito

coitus [ˈkoːətəs] *n* : coito *m*

coke [ˈkoːk] *n* : coque *m*

colander [ˈkɑləndər, ˈkʌ-] *n* : colador *m*

cold[1] [ˈkoːld] *adj* : frío <it's cold out : hace frío> <a cold reception : una fría recepción> <in cold blood : a sangre fría>

cold[2] *n* **1** : frío *m* <to feel the cold : sentir frío> **2** : resfriado *m,* catarro *m* <to catch a cold : resfriarse>

cold–blooded [ˈkoːldˈblʌdəd] *adj* **1** CRUEL : cruel, despiadado **2** : de sangre fría (dícese de los reptiles, etc.)

coldly [ˈkoːldli] *adv* : fríamente, con frialdad

coldness [ˈkoːldnəs] *n* : frialdad *f* (de una persona o una actitud), frío *m* (de la temperatura)

coleslaw [ˈkoːlˌslɔ] *n* : ensalada *f* de col

colic [ˈkɑlɪk] *n* : cólico *m*

coliseum [ˌkɑləˈsiːəm] *n* : coliseo *m,* arena *f*

collaborate [kəˈlæbəˌreɪt] *vi* **-rated; -rating** : colaborar

collaboration [kəˌlæbəˈreɪʃən] *n* : colaboración *f*

collaborator [kəˈlæbəˌreɪtər] *n* **1** COLLEAGUE : colaborador *m,* -dora *f* **2** TRAITOR : colaboracionista *mf*

collapse[1] [kəˈlæps] *vi* **-lapsed; -lapsing 1** : derrumbarse, desplomarse, hundirse <the building collapsed : el edificio se derrumbó> **2** FALL : desplomarse, caerse <he collapsed on the bed : se desplomó en la cama> <to collapse with laughter : morirse de risa> **3** FAIL : fracasar, quebrar, arruinarse **4** FOLD : plegarse

collapse[2] *n* **1** FALL : derrumbe *m,* desplome *m* **2** BREAKDOWN, FAILURE : fracaso *m,* colapso *m* (físico), quiebra *f* (económica)

collapsible [kəˈlæpsəbəl] *adj* : plegable

collar[1] [ˈkɑlər] *vt* : agarrar, atrapar

collar[2] *n* : cuello *m*

collarbone [ˈkɑlərˌboːn] *n* : clavícula *f*

collate [kəˈleɪt; ˈkɑˌleɪt, ˈkoː-] *vt* **-latcd; -lating 1** COMPARE : cotejar, comparar **2** : ordenar, recopilar (páginas)

collateral[1] [kəˈlætərəl] *adj* : colateral

collateral[2] *n* : garantía *f,* fianza *f,* prenda *f*

colleague [ˈkɑˌliːg] *n* : colega *mf;* compañero *m,* -ra *f*

collect[1] [kəˈlɛkt] *vt* **1** GATHER : recopilar, reunir, recoger <she collected her thoughts : puso en orden sus ideas> **2** : coleccionar, juntar <to collect stamps : coleccionar timbres> **3** : cobrar (una deuda), recaudar (un impuesto) **4** DRAW : cobrar, percibir (un sueldo, etc.) — *vi* **1** ACCUMULATE : acumularse, juntarse **2** CONGREGATE : congregarse, reunirse

collect[2] *adv & adj* : por cobrar, a cobro revertido

collectible *or* **collectable** [kəˈlɛktəbəl] *adj* : coleccionable

collection [kəˈlɛkʃən] *n* **1** COLLECTING : colecta *f* (de contribuciones), cobro *m* (de deudas), recaudación *f* (de impuestos) **2** GROUP : colección *f* (de objetos), grupo *m* (de personas)

collective[1] [kəˈlɛktɪv] *adj* : colectivo — **collectively** *adv*

collective[2] *n* : colectivo *m*

collector [kəˈlɛktər] *n* **1** : coleccionista *mf* (de objetos) **2** : cobrador *m,* -dora *f* (de deudas)

college [ˈkɑlɪdʒ] *n* **1** : universidad *f* **2** : colegio *m* (de electores o profesionales)

collegiate [kəˈliːdʒət] *adj* : universitario

collide [kəˈlaɪd] *vi* **-lided; -liding** : chocar, colisionar, estrellarse

collie [ˈkɑli] *n* : collie *mf*

collision [kəˈlɪʒən] *n* : choque *m,* colisión *f*

colloquial [kəˈloːkwiəl] *adj* : coloquial

colloquialism [kəˈloːkwiəˌlɪzəm] *n* : expresión *f* coloquial

collusion [kəˈluːʒən] *n* : colusión *f*

cologne [kəˈloːn] *n* : colonia *f*

Colombian [kəˈlʌmbiən] *n* : colombiano *m,* -na *f* — **Colombian** *adj*

colon[1] [ˈkoːlən] *n, pl* **colons** *or* **cola** [-lə] : colon *m* (de los intestinos)

colon[2] *n, pl* **colons** : dos puntos *mpl* (signo ortográfico)

colonel [ˈkərnəl] *n* : coronel *m*

colonial[1] [kəˈloːniəl] *adj* : colonial

colonial[2] *n* : colono *m,* -na *f*

colonist [ˈkɑlənɪst] *n* : colono *m,* -na *f;* colonizador *m,* -dora *f*

colonization [ˌkɑlənəˈzeɪʃən] *n* : colonización *f*
colonize [ˈkɑləˌnaɪz] *vt* **-nized; -nizing** **1** : establecer una colonia en **2** SETTLE : colonizar
colonnade [ˌkɑləˈneɪd] *n* : columnata *f*
colony [ˈkɑləni] *n, pl* **-nies** : colonia *f*
color¹ [ˈkʌlər] *vt* **1** : colorear, pintar **2** INFLUENCE : influir en, influenciar — *vi* BLUSH : sonrojarse, ruborizarse
color² *n* **1** : color *m* <primary colors : colores primarios> **2** INTEREST, VIVIDNESS : color *m,* colorido *m* <local color : color local>
color–blind [ˈkʌlərˌblaɪnd] *adj* : daltónico
color blindness *n* : daltonismo *m*
colored [ˈkʌlərd] *adj* **1** : de color (dícese de los objetos) **2** : de color, negro (dícese de las personas)
colorfast [ˈkʌlərˌfæst] *adj* : que no se destiñe
colorful [ˈkʌlərfəl] *adj* **1** : lleno de colorido, de colores vivos **2** PICTURESQUE, STRIKING : pintoresco, llamativo
colorless [ˈkʌlərləs] *adj* **1** : incoloro, sin color **2** DULL : soso, aburrido
colossal [kəˈlɑsəl] *adj* : colosal
colossus [kəˈlɑsəs] *n, pl* **-si** [-ˌsaɪ] : coloso *m*
colt [ˈkoːlt] *n* : potro *m*
column [ˈkɑləm] *n* : columna *f*
columnist [ˈkɑləmnɪst, -ləmɪst] *n* : columnista *mf*
coma [ˈkoːmə] *n* : coma *m,* estado *m* de coma
comatose [ˈkoːməˌtoːs, ˈkɑ-] *adj* : comatoso, en estado de coma
comb¹ [ˈkoːm] *vt* **1** : peinar (el pelo) **2** SEARCH : peinar, rastrear, registrar a fondo
comb² *n* **1** : peine *m* **2** : cresta *f* (de un gallo)
combat¹ [kəmˈbæt, ˈkɑmˌbæt] *vt* **-bated** *or* **-batted; -bating** *or* **-batting** : combatir, luchar contra
combat² [ˈkɑmˌbæt] *n* : combate *m,* lucha *f*
combatant [kəmˈbætənt] *n* : combatiente *mf*
combative [kəmˈbæt̬ɪv] *adj* : combativo
combination [ˌkɑmbəˈneɪʃən] *n* : combinación *f*
combine¹ [kəmˈbaɪn] *v* **-bined; -bining** *vt* : combinar, aunar — *vi* : combinarse, mezclarse
combine² [ˈkɑmˌbaɪn] *n* **1** ALLIANCE : alianza *f* comercial o política **2** HARVESTER : cosechadora *f*
combustible [kəmˈbʌstəbəl] *adj* : inflamable, combustible
combustion [kəmˈbʌstʃən] *n* : combustión *f*
come [ˈkʌm] *vi* **came** [ˈkeɪm]; **come; coming** **1** APPROACH : venir, aproximarse <here they come : acá vienen> **2** ARRIVE : venir, llegar, alcanzar <they came yesterday : vinieron ayer> **3** ORIGINATE : venir, provenir <this wine comes from France : este vino viene de Francia> **4** AMOUNT : llegar, ascender <the investment came to two million : la inversión llegó a dos millones> **5 to come clean** : confesar, desahogar la conciencia **6 to come into** ACQUIRE : adquirir <to come into a fortune : heredar una fortuna> **7 to come off** SUCCEED : tener éxito, ser un éxito **8 to come out** : salir, aparecer, publicarse **9 to come to** REVIVE : recobrar el conocimiento, volver en sí **10 to come to pass** HAPPEN : acontecer **11 to come to terms** : llegar a un acuerdo
comeback [ˈkʌmˌbæk] *n* **1** RETORT : réplica *f,* respuesta *f* **2** RETURN : retorno *m,* regreso *m* <the champion announced his comeback : el campeón anunció su regreso>
come back *vi* **1** RETORT : replicar, contestar **2** RETURN : volver <come back here! : ¡vuelve acá!> <that style's coming back : ese estilo está volviendo>
comedian [kəˈmiːdiən] *n* : cómico *m,* -ca *f;* humorista *mf*
comedienne [kəˌmiːdiˈɛn] *n* : cómica *f,* humorista *f*
comedy [ˈkɑmədi] *n, pl* **-dies** : comedia *f*
comely [ˈkʌmli] *adj* **-lier; -est** : bello, bonito
comet [ˈkɑmət] *n* : cometa *m*
comfort¹ [ˈkʌmpfərt] *vt* **1** CHEER : confortar, alentar **2** CONSOLE : consolar
comfort² *n* **1** CONSOLATION : consuelo *m* **2** WELL-BEING : confort *m,* bienestar *m* **3** CONVENIENCE : comodidad *f* <the comforts of home : las comodidades del hogar>
comfortable [ˈkʌmpfərt̬əbəl, ˈkʌmpftə-] *adj* : cómodo, confortable — **comfortably** [ˈkʌmpfərt̬əbli, ˈkʌmpftə-] *adv*
comforter [ˈkʌmpfərtər] *n* **1** : confortador *m,* -dora *f* **2** QUILT : edredón *m,* cobertor *m*
comic¹ [ˈkɑmɪk] *adj* : cómico, humorístico
comic² *n* **1** COMEDIAN : cómico *m,* -ca *f;* humorista *mf* **2** *or* **comic book** : historieta *f,* cómic *m*
comical [ˈkɑmɪkəl] *adj* : cómico, gracioso, chistoso
comic strip *n* : tira *f* cómica, historieta *f*
coming [ˈkʌmɪŋ] *adj* : siguiente, próximo, que viene
comma [ˈkɑmə] *n* : coma *f*
command¹ [kəˈmænd] *vt* **1** ORDER : ordenar, mandar **2** CONTROL, DIRECT : comandar, tener el mando de — *vi* **1** : dar órdenes **2** GOVERN : estar al mando *m,* gobernar

command[2] *n* **1** CONTROL, LEADERSHIP : mando *m,* control *m,* dirección *f* **2** ORDER : orden *f,* mandato *m* **3** MASTERY : maestría *f,* destreza *f,* dominio *m* **4** : tropa *f* asignada a un comandante

commandant [ˈkɑmənˌdɑnt, -ˌdænt] *n* : comandante *mf*

commandeer [ˌkɑmənˈdɪr] *vt* : piratear, secuestrar (un vehículo, etc.)

commander [kəˈmændər] *n* : comandante *mf*

commandment [kəˈmændmənt] *n* : mandamiento *m,* orden *f* <the Ten Commandments : los diez mandamientos>

commemorate [kəˈmɛməˌreɪt] *vt* **-rated; -rating** : conmemorar

commemoration [kəˌmɛməˈreɪʃən] *n* : conmemoración *f*

commemorative [kəˈmɛmrət̬ɪv, -ˈmɛməˌreɪt̬ɪv] *adj* : conmemorativo

commence [kəˈmɛnts] *v* **-menced; -mencing** *vt* : iniciar, comenzar — *vi* : iniciarse, comenzar

commencement [kəˈmɛntsmənt] *n* **1** BEGINNING : inicio *m,* comienzo *m* **2** : ceremonia *f* de graduación

commend [kəˈmɛnd] *vt* **1** ENTRUST : encomendar **2** RECOMMEND : recomendar **3** PRAISE : elogiar, alabar

commendable [kəˈmɛndəbəl] *adj* : loable, meritorio, encomiable

commendation [ˌkɑmənˈdeɪʃən, -ˌmɛn-] *n* : elogio *m,* encomio *m*

commensurate [kəˈmɛntsərət, -ˈmɛntʃʊrət] *adj* : proporcionado <commensurate with : en proporción a>

comment[1] [ˈkɑˌmɛnt] *vi* **1** : hacer comentarios **2 to comment on** : comentar, hacer observaciones sobre

comment[2] *n* : comentario *m,* observación *f*

commentary [ˈkɑmənˌtɛri] *n, pl* **-taries** : comentario *m,* crónica *f* (deportiva)

commentator [ˈkɑmənˌteɪt̬ər] *n* : comentarista *mf,* cronista *mf* (de deportes)

commerce [ˈkɑmərs] *n* : comercio *m*

commercial[1] [kəˈmərʃəl] *adj* : comercial — **commercially** *adv*

commercial[2] *n* : comercial *m*

commercialize [kəˈmərʃəˌlaɪz] *vt* **-ized; -izing** : comercializar

commiserate [kəˈmɪzəˌreɪt] *vi* **-ated; -ating** : compadecerse, consolarse

commiseration [kəˌmɪzəˈreɪʃən] *n* : conmiseración *f*

commission[1] [kəˈmɪʃən] *vt* **1** : nombrar (un oficial) **2** : comisionar, encargar <to commission a painting : encargar una pintura>

commission[2] *n* **1** : nombramiento *m* (al grado de oficial) **2** COMMITTEE : comisión *f,* comité *m* **3** COMMITTING : comisión *f,* realización *f* (de un acto) **4** PERCENTAGE : comisión *f* <sales commissions : comisiones de venta>

commissioned officer *n* : oficial *mf*

commissioner [kəˈmɪʃənər] *n* **1** : comisionado *m,* -da *f;* miembro *m* de una comisión **2** : comisario *m,* -ria *f* (de policía, etc.)

commit [kəˈmɪt] *vt* **-mitted; -mitting** **1** ENTRUST : encomendar, confiar **2** CONFINE : internar (en un hospital), encarcelar (en una prisión) **3** PERPETRATE : cometer <to commit a crime : cometer un crimen> **4 to commit oneself** : comprometerse

commitment [kəˈmɪtmənt] *n* **1** RESPONSIBILITY : compromiso *m,* responsabilidad *f* **2** DEDICATION : dedicación *f,* devoción *f* <commitment to the cause : devoción a la causa>

committee [kəˈmɪt̬i] *n* : comité *m*

commodious [kəˈmoːdiəs] *adj* SPACIOUS : amplio, espacioso

commodity [kəˈmɑdət̬i] *n, pl* **-ties** : artículo *m* de comercio, mercancía *f,* mercadería *f*

commodore [ˈkɑməˌdor] *n* : comodoro *m*

common[1] [ˈkɑmən] *adj* **1** PUBLIC : común, público <the common good : el bien común> **2** SHARED : común <a common interest : un interés común> **3** GENERAL : común, general <it's common knowledge : todo el mundo lo sabe> **4** ORDINARY : ordinario, común y corriente <the common man : el hombre medio, el hombre de la calle>

common[2] *n* **1** : tierra *f* comunal **2 in ~** : en común

common cold *n* : resfriado *m* común

common denominator *n* : denominador *m* común

commoner [ˈkɑmənər] *n* : plebeyo *m,* -ya *f*

commonly [ˈkɑmənli] *adv* **1** FREQUENTLY : comúnmente, frecuentemente **2** USUALLY : normalmente

common noun *n* : nombre *m* común

commonplace[1] [ˈkɑmənˌpleɪs] *adj* : común, ordinario

commonplace[2] *n* : cliché *m,* tópico *m*

common sense *n* : sentido *m* común

commonwealth [ˈkɑmənˌwɛlθ] *n* : entidad *f* política <the British Commonwealth : la Mancomunidad Británica>

commotion [kəˈmoːʃən] *n* **1** RUCKUS : alboroto *m,* jaleo *m,* escándalo *m* **2** STIR, UPSET : revuelo *m,* conmoción *f*

communal [kəˈmjuːnəl] *adj* : communal

commune[1] [kəˈmjuːn] *vi* **-muned; -muning** : estar en comunión *f*

commune[2] [ˈkɑˌmjuːn, kəˈmjuːn] *n* : comuna *f*

communicable [kəˈmjuːnɪkəbəl] *adj* CONTAGIOUS : transmisible, contagioso

communicate [kəˈmjuːnəˌkeɪt] *v* **-cated; -cating** *vt* **1** CONVEY : comunicar, expresar, hacer saber **2** TRANSMIT : transmitir (una enfermedad), contagiar — *vi* : comunicarse, expresarse

communication [kə,mjuːnəˈkeɪʃən] *n* : comunicación *f*
communicative [kəˈmjuːnɪ,keɪt̬ɪv, -kət̬ɪv] *adj* : comunicativo
communion [kəˈmjuːnjən] *n* **1** SHARING : comunión *f* **2 Communion** : comunión *f*, eucaristía *f*
communiqué [kəˈmjuːnə,keɪ, -,mjuːnəˈkeɪ] *n* : comunicado *m*
communism *or* **Communism** [ˈkɑmjə,nɪzəm] *n* : comunismo *m*
communist[1] *or* **Communist** [ˈkɑmjə,nɪst] *adj* : comunista <the Communist Party : el Partido Comunista>
communist[2] *or* **Communist** *n* : comunista *mf*
communistic *or* **Communistic** [,kɑmjəˈnɪstɪk] *adj* : comunista
community [kəˈmjuːnət̬i] *n, pl* **-ties** : comunidad *f*
commute [kəˈmjuːt] *v* **-muted; -muting** *vt* REDUCE : conmutar, reducir (una sentencia) — *vi* : viajar de la residencia al trabajo
commuter [kəˈmjuːt̬ər] *n* : persona *f* que viaja diariamente al trabajo
compact[1] [kəmˈpækt, ˈkɑm,pækt] *vt* : compactar, consolidar, comprimir
compact[2] [kəmˈpækt, ˈkɑm,pækt] *adj* **1** DENSE, SOLID : compacto, macizo, denso **2** CONCISE : breve, conciso
compact[3] [ˈkɑm,pækt] *n* **1** AGREEMENT : acuerdo *m*, pacto *m* **2** : polvera *f*, estuche *m* de maquillaje **3** *or* **compact car** : auto *m* compacto
compact disc [ˈkɑm,pæktˈdɪsk] *n* : disco *m* compacto, compact disc *m*
compactly [kəmˈpæktli, ˈkɑm,pækt-] *adv* **1** DENSELY : densamente, macizamente **2** CONCISELY : concisamente, brevemente
companion [kəmˈpænjən] *n* **1** COMRADE : compañero *m*, -ra *f*; acompañante *mf* **2** MATE : pareja *f* (de un zapato, etc.)
companionable [kəmˈpænjənəbəl] *adj* : sociable, amigable
companionship [kəmˈpænjən,ʃɪp] *n* : compañerismo *m*, camaradería *f*
company [ˈkʌmpəni] *n, pl* **-nies 1** FIRM : compañía *f*, empresa *f* **2** GROUP : compañía *f* (de actores o soldados) **3** GUESTS : visita *f* <we have company : tenemos visita>
comparable [ˈkɑmpərəbəl] *adj* : comparable, parecido
comparative[1] [kəmˈpærət̬ɪv] *adj* RELATIVE : comparativo, relativo — **comparatively** *adv*
comparative[2] *n* : comparativo *m*
compare[1] [kəmˈpær] *v* **-pared; -paring** *vt* : comparar — *vi* **to compare with** : poder comparar con, tener comparación con
compare[2] *n* : comparación *f* <beyond compare : sin igual, sin par>
comparison [kəmˈpærəsən] *n* : comparación *f*
compartment [kəmˈpɑrtmənt] *n* : compartimento *m*, compartimiento *m*
compass [ˈkʌmpəs, ˈkɑm-] *n* **1** RANGE, SCOPE : alcance *m*, extensión *f*, límites *mpl* **2** : compás *m* (para trazar circunferencias) **3** : compás *m*, brújula *f* <the points of the compass : los puntos cardinales>
compassion [kəmˈpæʃən] *n* : compasión *f*, piedad *f*, misericordia *f*
compassionate [kəmˈpæʃənət] *adj* : compasivo
compatibility [kəm,pæt̬əˈbɪlət̬i] *n* : compatibilidad *f*
compatible [kəmˈpæt̬əbəl] *adj* : compatible, afín
compatriot [kəmˈpeɪtriət, -ˈpæ-] *n* : compatriota *mf*; paisano *m*, -na *f*
compel [kəmˈpɛl] *vt* **-pelled; -pelling** : obligar, compeler
compendium [kəmˈpɛndiəm] *n, pl* **-diums** *or* **-dia** [-diə] : compendio *m*
compensate [ˈkɑmpən,seɪt] *v* **-sated; -sating** *vi* **to compensate for** : compensar — *vt* : indemnizar, compensar
compensation [,kɑmpənˈseɪʃən] *n* : compensación *f*, indemnización *f*
compensatory [kəmˈpɛntsə,tori] *adj* : compensatorio
compete [kəmˈpiːt] *vi* **-peted; -peting** : competir, contender, rivalizar
competence [ˈkɑmpətənts] *n* : competencia *f*, aptitud *f*
competency [ˈkɑmpətəntsi] → **competence**
competent [ˈkɑmpətənt] *adj* : competente, capaz
competition [,kɑmpəˈtɪʃən] *n* : competencia *f*, concurso *m*
competitive [kəmˈpɛt̬ət̬ɪv] *adj* : competitivo
competitor [kəmˈpɛt̬ət̬ər] *n* : competidor *m*, -dora *f*
compile [kəmˈpaɪl] *vt* **-piled; -piling** : compilar, recopilar
complacency [kəmˈpleɪsəntsi] *n* : satisfacción *f* consigo mismo, suficiencia *f*
complacent [kəmˈpleɪsənt] *adj* : satisfecho de sí mismo, suficiente
complain [kəmˈpleɪn] *vi* **1** GRIPE : quejarse, regañar, rezongar **2** PROTEST : reclamar, protestar
complaint [kəmˈpleɪnt] *n* **1** GRIPE : queja *f* **2** AILMENT : afección *f*, dolencia *f* **3** ACCUSATION : reclamo *m*, acusación *f*
complement[1] [ˈkɑmplə,mɛnt] *vt* : complementar
complement[2] [ˈkɑmpləmənt] *n* : complemento *m*
complementary [,kɑmpləˈmɛntəri] *adj* : complementario
complete[1] [kəmˈpliːt] *vt* **-pleted; -pleting 1** : completar, hacer entero <this piece completes the collection : esta pieza completa la colección> **2** FINISH : completar, acabar, terminar

<she completed her studies : completó sus estudios>

complete[2] *adj* **-pleter; -est 1** WHOLE : completo, entero, íntegro **2** FINISHED : terminado, acabado **3** TOTAL : completo, total, absoluto

completely [kəm'pli:tli] *adv* : completamente, totalmente

completion [kəm'pli:ʃən] *n* : finalización *f,* cumplimiento *m*

complex[1] [kɑm'plɛks, kəm-; 'kɑm-ˌplɛks] *adj* : complejo, complicado

complex[2] ['kɑmˌplɛks] *n* : complejo *m*

complexion [kəm'plɛkʃən] *n* : cutis *m,* tez *f* <of dark complexion : de tez morena>

complexity [kəm'plɛksət̬i, kɑm-] *n, pl* **-ties** : complejidad *f*

compliance [kəm'plaɪənts] *n* : conformidad *f* <in compliance with the law : conforme a la ley>

compliant [kəm'plaɪənt] *adj* : dócil, sumiso

complicate ['kɑmpləˌkeɪt] *vt* **-cated; -cating** : complicar

complicated ['kɑmpləˌkeɪt̬əd] *adj* : complicado

complication [ˌkɑmplə'keɪʃən] *n* : complicación *f*

complicity [kəm'plɪsət̬i] *n, pl* **-ties** : complicidad *f*

compliment[1] ['kɑmpləˌmɛnt] *vt* : halagar, florear *Mex*

compliment[2] ['kɑmpləmənt] *n* **1** : halago *m,* cumplido *m* **2 compliments** *npl* : saludos *mpl* <give them my compliments : déles saludos de mi parte>

complimentary [ˌkɑmplə'mɛntəri] *adj* **1** FLATTERING : halagador, halagüeño **2** FREE : de cortesía, gratis

comply [kəm'plaɪ] *vi* **-plied; -plying** : cumplir, acceder, obedecer

component[1] [kəm'po:nənt, 'kɑm-ˌpo:-] *adj* : componente

component[2] *n* : componente *m,* elemento *m,* pieza *f*

compose [kəm'po:z] *vt* **-posed; -posing 1** : componer, crear <to compose a melody : componer una melodía > **2** CALM : calmar, serenar <to compose oneself : serenarse> **3** CONSTITUTE : constar, componer <to be composed of : constar de> **4** : componer (un texto a imprimirse)

composer [kəm'po:zər] *n* : compositor *m,* -tora *f*

composite[1] [kɑm'pɑzət, kəm-; 'kɑmpəzət] *adj* : compuesto (de varias partes)

composite[2] *n* : compuesto *m,* mezcla *f*

composition [ˌkɑmpə'zɪʃən] *n* **1** MAKEUP : composición *f* **2** ESSAY : ensayo *m,* trabajo *m*

compost ['kɑmˌpo:st] *n* : abono *m* vegetal

composure [kəm'po:ʒər] *n* : compostura *f,* serenidad *f*

compound[1] [kɑm'paʊnd, kəm-; 'kɑmˌpaʊnd] *vt* **1** COMBINE, COMPOSE : combinar, componer **2** AUGMENT : agravar, aumentar <to compound a problem : agravar un problema>

compound[2] ['kɑmˌpaʊnd; kɑm-'paʊnd, kəm-] *adj* : compuesto <compound interest : interés compuesto>

compound[3] ['kɑmˌpaʊnd] *n* **1** MIXTURE : compuesto *m,* mezcla *f* **2** ENCLOSURE : recinto *m* (de residencias, etc.)

compound fracture *n* : fractura *f* complicada

comprehend [ˌkɑmprɪ'hɛnd] *vt* **1** UNDERSTAND : comprender, entender **2** INCLUDE : comprender, incluir, abarcar

comprehensible [ˌkɑmprɪ'hɛntsəbəl] *adj* : comprensible

comprehension [ˌkɑmprɪ'hɛntʃən] *n* : comprensión *f*

comprehensive [ˌkɑmprɪ'hɛntsɪv] *adj* **1** INCLUSIVE : inclusivo, exhaustivo **2** BROAD : extenso, amplio

compress[1] [kəm'prɛs] *vt* : comprimir

compress[2] ['kɑmˌprɛs] *n* : compresa *f*

compression [kəm'prɛʃən] *n* : compresión *f*

comprise [kəm'praɪz] *vt* **-prised; -prising 1** INCLUDE : comprender, incluir **2** : componerse de, constar de <the installation comprises several buildings : la instalación está compuesta de varios edificios>

compromise[1] ['kɑmprəˌmaɪz] *v* **-mised; -mising** *vi* : transigir, avenirse — *vt* JEOPARDIZE : comprometer, poner en peligro

compromise[2] *n* : acuerdo *m* mutuo, compromiso *m*

comptroller [kən'tro:lər, 'kɑmp-ˌtro:-] *n* : contralor *m,* -lora *f;* interventor *m,* -tora *f*

compulsion [kəm'pʌlʃən] *n* **1** COERCION : coacción *f* **2** URGE : compulsión *f,* impulso *m*

compulsive [kəm'pʌlsɪv] *adj* : compulsivo

compulsory [kəm'pʌlsəri] *adj* : obligatorio

compunction [kəm'pʌŋkʃən] *n* **1** QUALM : reparo *m,* escrúpulo *m* **2** REMORSE : remordimiento *m*

computation [ˌkɑmpjʊ'teɪʃən] *n* : cálculo *m,* cómputo *m*

compute [kəm'pju:t] *vt* **-puted; -puting** : computar, calcular

computer [kəm'pju:t̬ər] *n* : computadora *f,* computador *m,* ordenador *m Spain*

computerize [kəm'pju:t̬əˌraɪz] *vt* **-ized; -izing** : computarizar, informatizar

comrade ['kɑmˌræd] *n* : camarada *mf;* compañero *m,* -ra *f*

con[1] ['kɑn] *vt* **conned; conning** SWINDLE : estafar, timar

con[2] *adv* : contra

con[3] *n* : contra *m* <the pros and cons : los pros y los contras>
concave [kɑn'keɪv, 'kɑn,keɪv] *adj* : cóncavo
conceal [kən'si:l] *vt* : esconder, ocultar, disimular
concealment [kən'si:lmənt] *n* : escondimiento *m,* ocultación *f*
concede [kən'si:d] *vt* **-ceded; -ceding** **1** ALLOW, GRANT : conceder **2** ADMIT : conceder, reconocer <to concede defeat : reconocer la derrota>
conceit [kən'si:t] *n* : engreimiento *m,* presunción *f*
conceited [kən'si:t̬əd] *adj* : presumido, engreído, presuntuoso
conceivable [kən'si:vəbəl] *adj* : concebible, imaginable
conceivably [kən'si:vəbli] *adv* : posiblemente, de manera concebible
conceive [kən'si:v] *v* **-ceived; -ceiving** *vi* : concebir, embarazarse — *vt* IMAGINE : concebir, imaginar
concentrate[1] ['kɑntsən,treɪt] *v* **-trated; -trating** *vt* : concentrar — *vi* : concentrarse
concentrate[2] *n* : concentrado *m*
concentration [,kɑntsən'treɪʃən] *n* : concentración *f*
concentric [kən'sɛntrɪk] *adj* : concéntrico
concept ['kɑn,sɛpt] *n* : concepto *m,* idea *f*
conception [kən'sɛpʃən] *n* **1** : concepción *f* (de un bebé) **2** IDEA : concepto *m,* idea *f*
concern[1] [kən'sərn] *vt* **1** : tratarse de, tener que ver con <the novel concerns a sailor : la novela se trata de un marinero> **2** INVOLVE : concernir, incumbir a, afectar <that does not concern me : eso no me incumbe>
concern[2] *n* **1** AFFAIR : asunto *m* **2** WORRY : inquietud *f,* preocupación *f* **3** BUSINESS : negocio *m*
concerned [kən'sərnd] *adj* **1** ANXIOUS : preocupado, ansioso **2** INTERESTED, INVOLVED : interesado, afectado
concerning [kən'sərnɪŋ] *prep* REGARDING : con respecto a, acerca de, sobre
concert ['kɑn,sərt] *n* **1** AGREEMENT : concierto *m,* acuerdo *m* **2** : concierto *m* (musical)
concerted [kən'sərt̬əd] *adj* : concertado, coordinado <to make a concerted effort : coordinar los esfuerzos>
concertina [,kɑntsər'ti:nə] *n* : concertina *f*
concerto [kən'tʃɛrt̬o:] *n, pl* **-ti** [-t̬i, -,ti:] *or* **-tos** : concierto *m* <violin concerto : concierto para violín>
concession [kən'sɛʃən] *n* : concesión *f*
conch ['kɑŋk, 'kɑntʃ] *n, pl* **conchs** ['kɑŋks] *or* **conches** ['kɑntʃəz] : caracol *m* (animal), caracola *f* (concha)
conciliatory [kən'sɪliə,tori] *adj* : conciliador, conciliatorio
concise [kən'saɪs] *adj* : conciso, breve — **concisely** *adv*
conclave ['kɑn,kleɪv] *n* : cónclave *m*
conclude [kən'klu:d] *v* **-cluded; -cluding** *vt* **1** END : concluir, finalizar <to conclude a meeting : concluir una reunión> **2** DECIDE : concluir, llegar a la conclusión de — *vi* END : concluir, terminar
conclusion [kən'klu:ʒən] *n* **1** INFERENCE : conclusión *f* **2** END : fin *m,* final *m*
conclusive [kən'klu:sɪv] *adj* : concluyente, decisivo — **conclusively** *adv*
concoct [kən'kɑkt, kɑn-] *vt* **1** PREPARE : preparar, confeccionar **2** DEVISE : inventar, tramar
concoction [kən'kɑkʃən] *n* : invención *f,* mejunje *m,* brebaje *m*
concord ['kɑn,kɔrd, 'kɑŋ-] *n* **1** HARMONY : concordia *f,* armonía *f* **2** AGREEMENT : acuerdo *m*
concordance [kən'kɔrdənts] *n* : concordancia *f*
concourse ['kɑn,kors] *n* : explanada *f,* salón *m* (para pasajeros)
concrete[1] [kɑn'kri:t, 'kɑn,kri:t] *adj* **1** REAL : concreto <concrete objects : objetos concretos> **2** SPECIFIC : determinado, específico **3** : de concreto, de hormigón <concrete walls : paredes de concreto>
concrete[2] ['kɑn,kri:t, kɑn'kri:t] *n* : concreto *m,* hormigón *m*
concur [kən'kər] *vi* **concurred; concurring** **1** COINCIDE : concurrir, coincidir **2** AGREE : concurrir, estar de acuerdo
concurrent [kən'kərənt] *adj* : concurrente, simultáneo
concussion [kən'kʌʃən] *n* : conmoción *f* cerebral
condemn [kən'dɛm] *vt* **1** CENSURE : condenar, reprobar, censurar **2** : declarar insalubre (alimentos), declarar ruinoso (un edificio) **3** SENTENCE : condenar <condemned to death : condenado a muerte>
condemnation [,kɑn,dɛm'neɪʃən] *n* : condena *f,* reprobación *f*
condensation [,kɑn,dɛn'seɪʃən, -dən-] *n* : condensación *f*
condense [kən'dɛnts] *v* **-densed; -densing** *vt* **1** ABRIDGE : condensar, resumir **2** : condensar (vapor, etc.) — *vi* : condensarse
condescend [,kɑndɪ'sɛnd] *vi* **1** DEIGN : condescender, dignarse **2** **to condescend to someone** : tratar a alguien con condescendencia
condescension [,kɑndɪ'sɛntʃən] *n* : condescendencia *f*
condiment ['kɑndəmənt] *n* : condimento *m*
condition[1] [kən'dɪʃən] *vt* **1** DETERMINE : condicionar, determinar **2** : acondicionar (el pelo o el aire), poner en forma (el cuerpo)

condition² *n* **1** STIPULATION : condición *f,* estipulación *f* <on the condition that : a condición de que> **2** STATE : condición *f,* estado *m* <in poor condition : en malas condiciones> **3 conditions** *npl* : condiciones *fpl,* situación *f* <working conditions : condiciones del trabajo>

conditional [kən'dɪʃənəl] *adj* : condicional — **conditionally** *adv*

condolence [kən'doːlən*t*s] *n* **1** SYMPATHY : condolencia *f* **2 condolences** *npl* : pésame *m*

condominium [ˌkandə'mɪniəm] *n, pl* **-ums** : condominio *m*

condone [kən'doːn] *vt* **-doned; -doning** : aprobar, perdonar, tolerar

condor ['kandər, -ˌdɔr] *n* : cóndor *m*

conducive [kən'duːsɪv, -'djuː-] *adj* : propicio, favorable

conduct¹ [kən'dʌkt] *vt* **1** GUIDE : guiar, conducir <to conduct a tour : guiar una visita> **2** DIRECT : conducir, dirigir <to conduct an orchestra : dirigir una orquesta> **3** CARRY OUT : realizar, llevar a cabo <to conduct an investigation : llevar a cabo una investigación> **4** TRANSMIT : conducir, transmitir (calor, electricidad, etc.) **5 to conduct oneself** BEHAVE : conducirse, comportarse

conduct² ['kanˌdʌkt] *n* **1** MANAGEMENT : conducción *f,* dirección *f,* manejo *m* <the conduct of foreign affairs : la conducción de asuntos exteriores> **2** BEHAVIOR : conducta *f,* comportamiento *m*

conduction [kən'dʌkʃən] *n* : conducción *f*

conductivity [ˌkanˌdʌk'tɪvəṭi] *n, pl* **-ties** : conductividad *f*

conductor [kən'dʌktər] *n* **1** : conductor *m,* -tora *f;* revisor *m,* -sora *f* (en un tren); cobrador *m,* -dora *f* (en un bus); director *m,* -tora *f* (de una orquesta) **2** : conductor *m* (de electricidad, etc.)

conduit ['kanˌduːət, -ˌdjuː-] *n* : conducto *m,* canal *m,* vía *f*

cone ['koːn] *n* **1** : piña *f* (fruto de las coníferas) **2** : cono *m* (en geometría) **3 ice–cream cone** : cono *m,* barquillo *m,* cucurucho *m*

confection [kən'fɛkʃən] *n* : dulce *m*

confectioner [kən'fɛkʃənər] *n* : confitero *m,* -ra *f*

confederacy [kən'fɛdərəsi] *n, pl* **-cies** : confederación *f*

confederate¹ [kən'fɛdəˌreɪt] *v* **-ated; -ating** *vt* : unir, confederar — *vi* : confederarse, aliarse

confederate² [kən'fɛdərət] *adj* : confederado

confederate³ *n* : cómplice *mf;* aliado *m,* -da *f*

confederation [kənˌfɛdə'reɪʃən] *n* : confederación *f,* alianza *f*

confer [kən'fər] *v* **-ferred; -ferring** *vt* : conferir, otorgar — *vi* **to confer with** : consultar

conference ['kanfrən*t*s, -fərən*t*s] *n* : conferencia *f* <press conference : conferencia de prensa>

confess [kən'fɛs] *vt* : confesar — *vi* **1** : confesar <the prisoner confessed : el detenido confesó> **2** : confesarse (en religión)

confession [kən'fɛʃən] *n* : confesión *f*

confessional [kən'fɛʃənəl] *n* : confesionario *m*

confetti [kən'fɛṭi] *n* : confeti *m*

confidant ['kanfəˌdant, -ˌdænt] *n* : confidente *mf*

confide [kən'faɪd] *v* **-fided; -fiding** : confiar

confidence ['kanfədən*t*s] *n* **1** TRUST : confianza *f* **2** SELF-ASSURANCE : confianza *f* en sí mismo, seguridad *f* en sí mismo **3** SECRET : confidencia *f,* secreto *m*

confident ['kanfədənt] *adj* **1** SURE : seguro **2** SELF-ASSURED : confiado, seguro de sí mismo

confidential [ˌkanfə'dɛntʃəl] *adj* : confidencial — **confidentially** [ˌkanfə'dɛntʃəli] *adv*

confidently ['kanfədəntli] *adv* : con seguridad, con confianza

configuration [kənˌfɪgjə'reɪʃən] *n* : configuración *f*

confine [kən'faɪn] *vt* **-fined; -fining 1** LIMIT : confinar, restringir, limitar **2** IMPRISON : recluir, encarcelar, encerrar

confinement [kən'faɪnmənt] *n* : confinamiento *m,* reclusión *f,* encierro *m*

confines ['kanˌfaɪnz] *npl* : límites *mpl,* confines *mpl*

confirm [kən'fərm] *vt* **1** RATIFY : ratificar **2** VERIFY : confirmar, verificar **3** : confirmar (en religión)

confirmation [ˌkanfər'meɪʃən] *n* : confirmación *f*

confiscate ['kanfəˌskeɪt] *vt* **-cated; -cating** : confiscar, incautar, decomisar

confiscation [ˌkanfə'skeɪʃən] *n* : confiscación *f,* incautación *f,* decomiso *m*

conflagration [ˌkanflə'greɪʃən] *n* : conflagración *f*

conflict¹ [kən'flɪkt] *vi* : estar en conflicto, oponerse

conflict² ['kanˌflɪkt] *n* : conflicto *m* <to be in conflict : estar en desacuerdo>

conform [kən'fɔrm] *vi* **1** ACCORD, COMPLY : ajustarse, adaptarse, conformarse <it conforms with our standards : se ajusta a nuestras normas> **2** CORRESPOND : corresponder, encajar <to conform to the truth : corresponder a la verdad>

conformity [kən'fɔrməṭi] *n, pl* **-ties** : conformidad *f*

confound [kən'faʊnd, kan-] *vt* : confundir, desconcertar

confront [kən'frʌnt] *vt* : afrontar, enfrentarse a, encarar

confrontation [ˌkanfrən'teɪʃən] *n* : enfrentamiento *m,* confrontación *f*

confuse [kən'fjuːz] *vt* **-fused; -fusing 1** PUZZLE : confundir, enturbiar **2** COMPLICATE : confundir, enredar, complicar <to confuse the issue : complicar las cosas>

confusion [kən'fjuːʒən] *n* **1** PERPLEXITY : confusión *f* **2** MESS, TURMOIL : confusión *f,* embrollo *m,* lío *m fam*

congeal [kən'dʒiːl] *vi* **1** FREEZE : congelarse **2** COAGULATE, CURDLE : coagularse, cuajarse

congenial [kən'dʒiːniəl] *adj* : agradable, simpático

congenital [kən'dʒɛnətəl] *adj* : congénito

congest [kən'dʒɛst] *vt* **1** : congestionar (en la medicina) **2** OVERCROWD : abarrotar, atestar, congestionar (el tráfico) — *vi* : congestionarse

congestion [kən'dʒɛstʃən] *n* : congestión *f*

conglomerate[1] [kən'glɑmərət] *adj* : conglomerado

conglomerate[2] [kən'glɑmərət] *n* : conglomerado *m*

conglomeration [kən,glɑmə'reɪʃən] *n* : conglomerado *m,* acumulación *f*

Congolese [,kɑŋgə'liːz, -'liːs] *n* : congoleño *m,* -ña *f* — **Congolese** *adj*

congratulate [kən'grædʒə,leɪt, -'grætʃə-] *vt* **-lated; -lating** : felicitar

congratulation [kən,grædʒə'leɪʃən, -,grætʃə-] *n* : felicitación *f* <congratulations! : ¡felicidades!, ¡enhorabuena!>

congregate ['kɑŋgrɪ,geɪt] *v* **-gated; -gating** *vt* : congregar, reunir — *vi* : congregarse, reunirse

congregation [,kɑŋgrɪ'geɪʃən] *n* **1** GATHERING : congregación *f,* fieles *mpl* (a un servicio religioso) **2** PARISHIONERS : feligreses *mpl*

congress ['kɑŋgrəs] *n* : congreso *m*

congressional [kən'grɛʃənəl, kɑn-] *adj* : del congreso

congressman ['kɑŋgrəsmən] *n, pl* **-men** [-mən, -,mɛn] : congresista *m,* diputado *m*

congresswoman ['kɑŋgrəs,wʊmən] *n, pl* **-women** [-,wɪmən] : congresista *f,* diputada *f*

congruence [kən'gruːənts, 'kɑŋgrʊənts] *n* : congruencia *f*

congruent [kən'gruːənt, 'kɑŋgrʊənt] *adj* : congruente

conic ['kɑnɪk] → **conical**

conical ['kɑnɪkəl] *adj* : cónico

conifer ['kɑnəfər, 'koː-] *n* : conífera *f*

coniferous [koː'nɪfərəs, kə-] *adj* : conífero

conjecture[1] [kən'dʒɛktʃər] *v* **-tured; -turing** : conjeturar

conjecture[2] *n* : conjetura *f,* presunción *f*

conjugal ['kɑndʒɪgəl, kən'dʒuː-] *adj* : conyugal

conjugate ['kɑndʒə,geɪt] *vt* **-gated; -gating** : conjugar

conjugation [,kɑndʒə'geɪʃən] *n* : conjugación *f*

conjunction [kən'dʒʌŋkʃən] *n* : conjunción *f* <in conjunction with : en combinación con>

conjure ['kɑndʒər, 'kʌn-] *v* **-jured; -juring** *vt* **1** ENTREAT : rogar, suplicar **2 to conjure up** : hacer aparecer (apariciones), evocar (memorias, etc.) — *vi* : practicar la magia

conjurer *or* **conjuror** ['kɑndʒərər, 'kʌn-] *n* : mago *m,* -ga *f;* prestidigitador *m,* -dora *f*

connect [kə'nɛkt] *vi* : conectar, enlazar, empalmar, comunicarse — *vt* **1** JOIN, LINK : conectar, unir, juntar, vincular **2** RELATE : relacionar, asociar (ideas)

connection [kə'nɛkʃən] *n* : conexión *f,* enlace *m* <professional connections : relaciones profesionales>

connective [kə'nɛktɪv] *adj* : conectivo, conjuntivo <connective tissue : tejido conjuntivo>

connector [kə'nɛktər] *n* : conector *m*

connivance [kə'naɪvənts] *n* : connivencia *f,* complicidad *f*

connive [kə'naɪv] *vi* **-nived; -niving** CONSPIRE, PLOT : actuar en connivencia, confabularse, conspirar

connoisseur [,kɑnə'sər, -'sʊr] *n* : conocedor *m,* -dora *f;* entendido *m,* -da *f*

connotation [,kɑnə'teɪʃən] *n* : connotación *f*

connote [kə'noːt] *vt* **-noted; -noting** : connotar

conquer ['kɑŋkər] *vt* : conquistar, vencer

conqueror ['kɑŋkərər] *n* : conquistador *m,* -dora *f*

conquest ['kɑn,kwɛst, 'kɑŋ-] *n* : conquista *f*

conscience ['kɑntʃənts] *n* : conciencia *f,* consciencia *f* <to have a clear conscience : tener la conciencia limpia>

conscientious [,kɑntʃi'ɛntʃəs] *adj* : concienzudo — **conscientiously** *adv*

conscious ['kɑntʃəs] *adj* **1** AWARE : consciente <to become conscious of : darse cuenta de> **2** ALERT, AWAKE : consciente **3** INTENTIONAL : intencional, deliberado

consciously ['kɑntʃəsli] *adv* INTENTIONALLY : intencionalmente, deliberadamente, a propósito

consciousness ['kɑntʃəsnəs] *n* **1** AWARENESS : conciencia *f,* consciencia *f* **2** conocimiento *m* <to lose consciousness : perder el conocimiento>

conscript[1] [kən'skrɪpt] *vt* : reclutar, alistar, enrolar

conscript[2] ['kɑn,skrɪpt] *n* : conscripto *m,* -ta *f;* recluta *mf*

consecrate ['kɑntsə,kreɪt] *vt* **-crated; -crating** : consagrar

consecration [,kɑntsə'kreɪʃən] *n* : consagración *f,* dedicación *f*

consecutive [kən'sɛkjət̬ɪv] *adj* : consecutivo, seguido <on five consecutive days : cinco días seguidos>
consecutively [kən'sɛkjət̬ɪvli] *adv* : consecutivamente
consensus [kən'sɛntsəs] *n* : consenso *m*
consent¹ [kən'sɛnt] *vi* **1** AGREE : acceder, ponerse de acuerdo **2 to consent to do something** : consentir en hacer algo
consent² *n* : consentimiento *m,* permiso *m* <by common consent : de común acuerdo>
consequence ['kɑntsə,kwɛnts, -kwənts] *n* **1** RESULT : consecuencia *f,* secuela *f* **2** IMPORTANCE : importancia *f,* trascendencia *f*
consequent ['kɑntsəkwənt, -,kwɛnt] *adj* : consiguiente
consequential [,kɑntsə'kwɛntʃəl] *adj* **1** CONSEQUENT : consiguiente **2** IMPORTANT : importante, trascendente, trascendental
consequently ['kɑntsəkwəntli, -,kwɛnt-] *adv* : por consiguiente, por ende, por lo tanto
conservation [,kɑntsər'veɪʃən] *n* : conservación *f,* protección *f*
conservationist [,kɑntsər'veɪʃənɪst] *n* : conservacionista *mf*
conservatism [kən'sərvə,tɪzəm] *n* : conservadurismo *m*
conservative¹ [kən'sərvət̬ɪv] *adj* **1** : conservador **2** CAUTIOUS : moderado, cauteloso <a conservative estimate : un cálculo moderado>
conservative² *n* : conservador *m,* -dora *f*
conservatory [kən'sərvə,tori] *n, pl* **-ries** : conservatorio *m*
conserve¹ [kən'sərv] *vt* **-served; -serving** : conservar, preservar
conserve² ['kɑn,sərv] *n* PRESERVES : confitura *f*
consider [kən'sɪdər] *vt* **1** CONTEMPLATE : considerar, pensar en <we'd considered attending : habíamos pensado en asistir> **2** : considerar, tener en cuenta <consider the consequences : considera las consecuencias> **3** JUDGE, REGARD : considerar, estimar
considerable [kən'sɪdərəbəl] *adj* : considerable — **considerably** [-bli] *adv*
considerate [kən'sɪdərət] *adj* : considerado, atento
consideration [kən,sɪdə'reɪʃən] *n* : consideración *f* <to take into consideration : tener en cuenta>
considering [kən'sɪdərɪŋ] *prep* : teniendo en cuenta, visto
consign [kən'saɪn] *vt* **1** COMMIT, ENTRUST : confiar, encomendar **2** TRANSFER : consignar, transferir **3** SEND : consignar, enviar (mercancía)
consignment [kən'saɪnmənt] *n* **1** : envío *m,* remesa *f* **2 on ~** : en consignación
consist [kən'sɪst] *vi* **1** LIE : consistir <success consists in hard work : el éxito consiste en trabajar duro> **2** : constar, componerse <the set consists of 5 pieces : el juego se compone de 5 piezas>
consistency [kən'sɪstəntsi] *n, pl* **-cies 1** : consistencia *f* (de una mezcla o sustancia) **2** COHERENCE : coherencia *f* **3** UNIFORMITY : regularidad *f,* uniformidad *f*
consistent [kən'sɪstənt] *adj* **1** COMPATIBLE : compatible, coincidente <consistent with policy : coincidente con la política> **2** UNIFORM : uniforme, constante, regular — **consistently** [kən'sɪstəntli] *adv*
consolation [,kɑntsə'leɪʃən] *n* **1** : consuelo *m* **2 consolation prize** : premio *m* de consolación
console¹ [kən'so:l] *vt* **-soled; -soling** : consolar
console² ['kɑn,so:l] *n* : consola *f*
consolidate [kən'sɑlə,deɪt] *vt* **-dated; -dating** : consolidar, unir
consolidation [kən,sɑlə'deɪʃən] *n* : consolidación *f*
consommé [,kɑntsə'meɪ] *n* : consomé *m*
consonant ['kɑntsənənt] *n* : consonante *m*
consort¹ [kən'sɔrt] *vi* : asociarse, relacionarse, tener trato <to consort with criminals : tener trato con criminales>
consort² ['kɑn,sɔrt] *n* : consorte *mf*
conspicuous [kən'spɪkjʊəs] *adj* **1** OBVIOUS : visible, evidente **2** STRIKING : llamativo
conspicuously [kən'spɪkjʊəsli] *adv* : de manera llamativa
conspiracy [kən'spɪrəsi] *n, pl* **-cies** : conspiración *f,* complot *m,* confabulación *f*
conspirator [kən'spɪrət̬ər] *n* : conspirador *m,* -dora *f*
conspire [kən'spaɪr] *vi* **-spired; -spiring** : conspirar, confabularse
constable ['kɑntstəbəl, 'kʌntstə-] *n* : agente *mf* de policía (en un pueblo)
constancy ['kɑntstəntsi] *n, pl* **-cies** : constancia *f*
constant¹ ['kɑntstənt] *adj* **1** FAITHFUL : leal, fiel **2** INVARIABLE : constante, invariable **3** CONTINUAL : constante, continuo
constant² *n* : constante *f*
constantly ['kɑntstəntli] *adv* : constantemente, continuamente
constellation [,kɑntstə'leɪʃən] *n* : constelación *f*
consternation [,kɑntstər'neɪʃən] *n* : consternación *f*
constipate ['kɑntstə,peɪt] *vt* **-pated; -pating** : estreñir
constipation [,kɑntstə'peɪʃən] *n* : estreñimiento *m,* constipación *f* (de vientre)

constituency [kən'stɪtʃʊəntsi] *n, pl* **-cies 1 :** distrito *m* electoral **2 :** residentes *mpl* de un distrito electoral

constituent[1] [kən'stɪtʃʊənt] *adj* **1** COMPONENT **:** constituyente, componente **2 :** constituyente, constitutivo <a constituent assembly : una asamblea constituyente>

constituent[2] *n* **1** COMPONENT **:** componente *m* **2** ELECTOR, VOTER **:** elector *m,* -tora *f;* votante *mf*

constitute ['kɑntstə,tu:t, -,tju:t] *vt* **-tuted; -tuting 1** ESTABLISH **:** constituir, establecer **2** COMPOSE, FORM **:** constituir, componer

constitution [,kɑntstə'tu:ʃən, -'tju:-] *n* **:** constitución *f*

constitutional [,kɑntstə'tu:ʃənəl, -'tju:-] *adj* **:** constitucional

constitutionality [,kɑntstə,tu:ʃə'nælət̬i, -,tju:-] *n* **:** constitucionalidad *f*

constrain [kən'streɪn] *vt* **1** COMPEL **:** constreñir, obligar **2** CONFINE **:** constreñir, limitar, restringir **3** RESTRAIN **:** contener, refrenar

constraint [kən'streɪnt] *n* **:** restricción *f,* limitación *f*

constrict [kən'strɪkt] *vt* **:** estrechar, apretar, comprimir

constriction [kən'strɪkʃən] *n* **:** estrechamiento *m,* compresión *f*

construct [kən'strʌkt] *vt* **:** construir

construction [kən'strʌkʃən] *n* **:** construcción *f*

constructive [kən'strʌktɪv] *adj* **:** constructivo

construe [kən'stru:] *vt* **-strued; -struing :** interpretar

consul ['kɑntsəl] *n* **:** cónsul *mf*

consular ['kɑntsələr] *adj* **:** consular

consulate ['kɑntsələt] *n* **:** consulado *m*

consult [kən'sʌlt] *vt* **:** consultar — *vi* **to consult with :** consultar con, solicitar la opinión de

consultant [kən'sʌltənt] *n* **:** consultor *m,* -tora *f;* asesor *m,* -sora *f*

consultation [,kɑntsəl'teɪʃən] *n* **:** consulta *f*

consumable [kən'su:məbəl] *adj* **:** consumible

consume [kən'su:m] *vt* **-sumed; -suming :** consumir, usar, gastar

consumer [kən'su:mər] *n* **:** consumidor *m,* -dora *f*

consummate[1] ['kɑntsə,meɪt] *vt* **-mated; -mating :** consumar

consummate[2] [kən'sʌmət, 'kɑntsəmət] *adj* **:** consumado, perfecto

consummation [,kɑntsə'meɪʃən] *n* **:** consumación *f*

consumption [kən'sʌmpʃən] *n* **1** USE **:** consumo *m,* uso *m* <consumption of electricity : consumo de electricidad> **2** TUBERCULOSIS **:** tisis *f,* consunción *f*

contact[1] ['kɑn,tækt, kən'-] *vt* **:** ponerse en contacto con, contactar (con)

contact[2] ['kɑn,tækt] *n* **1** TOUCHING **:** contacto *m,* tocamiento *m* <to come into contact with : entrar en contacto con> **2** TOUCH **:** contacto *m,* comunicación *f* <to lose contact with : perder contacto con> **3** CONNECTION **:** contacto *m* (en negocios) **4** → **contact lens**

contact lens ['kɑn,tækt'lɛnz] *n* **:** lente *mf* de contacto, pupilente *m Mex*

contagion [kən'teɪdʒən] *n* **:** contagio *m*

contagious [kən'teɪdʒəs] *adj* **:** contagioso

contain [kən'teɪn] *vt* **1 :** contener **2 to contain oneself :** contenerse

container [kən'teɪnər] *n* **:** recipiente *m,* envase *m*

contaminate [kən'tæmə,neɪt] *vt* **-nated; -nating :** contaminar

contamination [kən,tæmə'neɪʃən] *n* **:** contaminación *f*

contemplate ['kɑntəm,pleɪt] *v* **-plated; -plating** *vt* **1** VIEW **:** contemplar **2** PONDER **:** contemplar, considerar **3** CONSIDER, PROPOSE **:** proponerse, proyectar, pensar en <to contemplate a trip : pensar en viajar> — *vi* MEDITATE **:** meditar

contemplation [,kɑntəm'pleɪʃən] *n* **:** contemplación *f*

contemplative [kən'tɛmplət̬ɪv, 'kɑntəm,pleɪt̬ɪv] *adj* **:** contemplativo

contemporaneous [kən,tɛmpə'reɪniəs] → **contemporary[1]**

contemporary[1] [kən'tɛmpə,rɛri] *adj* **:** contemporáneo

contemporary[2] *n, pl* **-raries :** contemporáneo *m,* -nea *f*

contempt [kən'tɛmpt] *n* **1** DISDAIN **:** desprecio *m,* desdén *m* <to hold in contempt : despreciar> **2 :** desacato *m* (ante un tribunal)

contemptible [kən'tɛmptəbəl] *adj* **:** despreciable, vil

contemptuous [kən'tɛmptʃʊəs] *adj* **:** despectivo, despreciativo, desdeñoso

contemptuously [kən'tɛmptʃʊəsli] *adv* **:** despectivamente, con desprecio

contend [kən'tɛnd] *vi* **1** STRUGGLE **:** luchar, lidiar, contender <to contend with a problem : lidiar con un problema> **2** COMPETE **:** competir <to contend for a position : competir por un puesto> — *vt* **1** ARGUE, MAINTAIN **:** argüir, sostener, afirmar <he contended that he was right : afirmó que tenía razón> **2** CONTEST **:** protestar contra (una decisión, etc.), disputar

contender [kən'tɛndər] *n* **:** contendiente *mf;* aspirante *mf;* competidor *m,* -dora *f*

content[1] [kən'tɛnt] *vt* SATISFY **:** contentar, satisfacer

content[2] *adj* **:** conforme, contento, satisfecho

content[3] *n* CONTENTMENT **:** contento *m,* satisfacción *f* <to one's heart's content : hasta quedar satisfecho, a más no poder>

content[4] [ˈkɑnˌtɛnt] *n* **1** MEANING : contenido *m,* significado *m* **2** PROPORTION : contenido *m,* proporción *f* <fat content : contenido de grasa> **3 contents** *npl* : contenido *m,* sumario *m* (de un libro) <table of contents : índice de materias>

contented [kənˈtɛntəd] *adj* : conforme, satisfecho <a contented smile : una sonrisa de satisfacción>

contentedly [kənˈtɛntədli] *adv* : con satisfacción

contention [kənˈtɛntʃən] *n* **1** DISPUTE : disputa *f,* discusión *f* **2** COMPETITION : competencia *f,* contienda *f* **3** OPINION : argumento *m,* opinión *f*

contentious [kənˈtɛntʃəs] *adj* : disputador, pugnaz, combativo

contentment [kənˈtɛntmənt] *n* : satisfacción *f,* contento *m*

contest[1] [kənˈtɛst] *vt* : disputar, cuestionar, impugnar <to contest a will : impugnar un testamento>

contest[2] [ˈkɑnˌtɛst] *n* **1** STRUGGLE : lucha *f,* contienda *f* **2** GAME : concurso *m,* competencia *f*

contestable [kənˈtɛstəbəl] *adj* : discutible, cuestionable

contestant [kənˈtɛstənt] *n* : concursante *mf;* competidor *m,* -dora *f*

context [ˈkɑnˌtɛkst] *n* : contexto *m*

contiguous [kənˈtɪgjʊəs] *adj* : contiguo

continence [ˈkɑntənənts] *n* : continencia *f*

continent[1] [ˈkɑntənənt] *adj* : continente

continent[2] *n* : continente *m* — **continental** [ˌkɑntənˈɛntəl] *adj*

contingency [kənˈtɪndʒəntsi] *n, pl* **-cies** : contingencia *f,* eventualidad *f*

contingent[1] [kənˈtɪndʒənt] *adj* **1** POSSIBLE : contingente, eventual **2** ACCIDENTAL : fortuito, accidental **3 to be contingent on** : depender de, estar sujeto a

contingent[2] *n* : contingente *m*

continual [kənˈtɪnjʊəl] *adj* : continuo, constante — **continually** [kənˈtɪnjʊəli, -ˈtɪnjəli] *adv*

continuance [kənˈtɪnjʊənts] *n* **1** CONTINUATION : continuación *f* **2** DURATION : duración *f* **3** : aplazamiento *m* (de un proceso)

continuation [kənˌtɪnjʊˈeɪʃən] *n* : continuación *f,* prolongación *f*

continue [kənˈtɪnjuː] *v* **-tinued; -tinuing** *vi* **1** CARRY ON : continuar, seguir, proseguir <please continue : continúe, por favor> **2** ENDURE, LAST : continuar, prolongarse, durar **3** RESUME : continuar, reanudarse — *vt* **1** : continuar, seguir <she continued writing : continuó escribiendo> **2** RESUME : continuar, reanudar **3** EXTEND, PROLONG : continuar, prolongar

continuity [ˌkɑntənˈuːəṭi, -ˈjuː-] *n, pl* **-ties** : continuidad *f*

continuous [kənˈtɪnjʊəs] *adj* : continuo — **continuously** *adv*

contort [kənˈtɔrt] *vt* : torcer, retorcer, contraer (el rostro) — *vi* : contraerse, demudarse

contortion [kənˈtɔrʃən] *n* : contorsión *f*

contour [ˈkɑnˌtʊr] *n* **1** OUTLINE : contorno *m* **2 contours** *npl* SHAPE : forma *f,* curvas *fpl* **3 contour map** : mapa *m* topográfico

contraband [ˈkɑntrəˌbænd] *n* : contrabando *m*

contraception [ˌkɑntrəˈsɛpʃən] *n* : anticoncepción *f,* contracepción *f*

contraceptive[1] [ˌkɑntrəˈsɛptɪv] *adj* : anticonceptivo, contraceptivo

contraceptive[2] *n* : anticonceptivo *m,* contraceptivo *m*

contract[1] [kənˈtrækt, 1 *usu* ˈkɑnˌtrækt] *vt* **1** : contratar (servicios profesionales) **2** : contraer (una enfermedad, una deuda) **3** TIGHTEN : contraer (un músculo) **4** SHORTEN : contraer (una palabra) — *vi* : contraerse, reducirse

contract[2] [ˈkɑnˌtrækt] *n* : contrato *m*

contraction [kənˈtrækʃən] *n* : contracción *f*

contractor [ˈkɑnˌtræktər, kənˈtræk-] *n* : contratista *mf*

contractual [kənˈtræktʃʊəl] *adj* : contractual — **contractually** *adv*

contradict [ˌkɑntrəˈdɪkt] *vt* : contradecir, desmentir

contradiction [ˌkɑntrəˈdɪkʃən] *n* : contradicción *f*

contradictory [ˌkɑntrəˈdɪktəri] *adj* : contradictorio

contralto [kənˈtrælˌtoː] *n, pl* **-tos** : contralto *m* (voz), contralto *mf* (vocalista)

contraption [kənˈtræpʃən] *n* DEVICE : aparato *m,* artefacto *m*

contrary[1] [ˈkɑnˌtrɛri, *2 often* kənˈtrɛri] *adj* **1** OPPOSITE : contrario, opuesto **2** BALKY, STUBBORN : terco, testarudo **3 contrary to** : al contrario de, en contra de <contrary to the facts : en contra de los hechos>

contrary[2] [ˈkɑnˌtrɛri] *n, pl* **-traries 1** OPPOSITE : lo contrario, lo opuesto **2 on the contrary** : al contrario, todo lo contrario

contrast[1] [kənˈtræst] *vi* DIFFER : contrastar, diferir — *vt* COMPARE : contrastar, comparar

contrast[2] [ˈkɑnˌtræst] *n* : contraste *m*

contravene [ˌkɑntrəˈviːn] *vt* **-vened; -vening** : contravenir, infringir

contribute [kənˈtrɪbjət] *v* **-uted; -uting** *vt* : contribuir, aportar (dinero, bienes, etc.) — *vi* : contribuir

contribution [ˌkɑntrəˈbjuːʃən] *n* : contribución *f*

contributor [kənˈtrɪbjəṭər] *n* : contribuidor *m,* -dora *f;* colaborador *m,* -dora *f* (en periodismo)

contrite [ˈkɑn͵traɪt, kənˈtraɪt] *adj* REPENTANT : contrito, arrepentido

contrition [kənˈtrɪʃən] *n* : contrición *f*, arrepentimiento *m*

contrivance [kənˈtraɪvən*t*s] *n* **1** DEVICE : aparato *m*, artefacto *m* **2** SCHEME : artimaña *f*, treta *f*, ardid *m*

contrive [kənˈtraɪv] *vt* **-trived; -triving 1** DEVISE : idear, ingeniar, maquinar **2** MANAGE : lograr, ingeniárselas para <she contrived a way out of the mess : se las ingenió para salir del enredo>

control[1] [kənˈtroːl] *vt* **-trolled; -trolling** : controlar, dominar

control[2] *n* **1** : control *m*, dominio *m*, mando *m* <to be under control : estar bajo control> **2** RESTRAINT : control *m*, limitación *f* <birth control : control natal> **3** : control *m*, dispositivo *m* de mando <remote control : control remoto>

controllable [kənˈtroːləbəl] *adj* : controlable

controller [kənˈtroːlər, ˈkɑn͵-] *n* **1** → **comptroller 2** : controlador *m*, -dora *f* <air traffic controller : controlador aéreo>

controversial [͵kɑntrəˈvərʃəl, -siəl] *adj* : controvertido <a controversial decision : una decisión controvertida>

controversy [ˈkɑntrə͵vərsi] *n, pl* **-sies** : controversia *f*

controvert [ˈkɑntrə͵vərt, ͵kɑntrəˈ-] *vt* : controvertir, contradecir

contusion [kənˈtuːʒən, -tjuː-] *n* BRUISE : contusión *f*, moretón *m*

conundrum [kəˈnʌndrəm] *n* RIDDLE : acertijo *m*, adivinanza *f*

convalesce [͵kɑnvəˈlɛs] *vi* **-lesced; -lescing** : convalecer

convalescence [͵kɑnvəˈlɛsən*t*s] *n* : convalecencia *f*

convalescent[1] [͵kɑnvəˈlɛsənt] *adj* : convaleciente

convalescent[2] *n* : convaleciente *mf*

convection [kənˈvɛkʃən] *n* : convección *f*

convene [kənˈviːn] *v* **-vened; -vening** *vt* : convocar — *vi* : reunirse

convenience [kənˈviːnjən*t*s] *n* **1** : conveniencia *f* <at your convenience : cuando le resulte conveniente> **2** AMENITY : comodidad *f* <modern conveniences : comodidades modernas>

convenient [kənˈviːnjənt] *adj* : conveniente, cómodo — **conveniently** *adv*

convent [ˈkɑnvənt, -͵vɛnt] *n* : convento *m*

convention [kənˈvɛntʃən] *n* **1** PACT : convención *f*, convenio *m*, pacto *m* <the Geneva Convention : la Convención de Ginebra> **2** MEETING : convención *f*, congreso *m* **3** CUSTOM : convención *f*, convencionalismo *m*

conventional [kənˈvɛntʃənəl] *adj* : convencional — **conventionally** *adv*

converge [kənˈvərdʒ] *vi* **-verged; -verging** : converger, convergir

conversant [kənˈvərsənt] *adj* **conversant with** : versado con, experto en

conversation [͵kɑnvərˈseɪʃən] *n* : conversación *f*

conversational [͵kɑnvərˈseɪʃənəl] *adj* : familiar <a conversational style : un estilo familiar>

converse[1] [kənˈvərs] *vi* **-versed; -versing** : conversar

converse[2] [kənˈvərs, ˈkɑn͵vɛrs] *adj* : contrario, opuesto, inverso

conversely [kənˈvərsli, ˈkɑn͵vɛrs-] *adv* : a la inversa

conversion [kənˈvərʒən] *n* **1** CHANGE : conversión *f*, transformación *f*, cambio *m* **2** : conversión *f* (a una religión)

convert[1] [kənˈvərt] *vt* **1** : convertir (a una religión o un partido) **2** CHANGE : convertir, cambiar — *vi* : convertirse

convert[2] [ˈkɑn͵vərt] *n* : converso *m*, -sa *f*

converter *or* **convertor** [kənˈvərt̬ər] *n* : convertidor *m*

convertible[1] [kənˈvərt̬əbəl] *adj* : convertible

convertible[2] *n* : convertible *m*, descapotable *m*

convex [kɑnˈvɛks, ˈkɑn͵-, kənˈ-] *adj* : convexo

convey [kənˈveɪ] *vt* **1** TRANSPORT : transportar, conducir **2** TRANSMIT : transmitir, comunicar, expresar (noticias, ideas, etc.)

conveyance [kənˈveɪən*t*s] *n* **1** TRANSPORT : transporte *m*, transportación *f* **2** COMMUNICATION : transmisión *f*, comunicación *f* **3** TRANSFER : transferencia *f*, traspaso *m* (de una propiedad)

conveyor [kənˈveɪər] *n* : transportador *m*, -dora *f* <conveyor belt : cinta transportadora>

convict[1] [kənˈvɪkt] *vt* : declarar culpable

convict[2] [ˈkɑn͵vɪkt] *n* : preso *m*, -sa *f*; presidiario *m*, -ria *f*; recluso *m*, -sa *f*

conviction [kənˈvɪkʃən] *n* **1** : condena *f* (de un acusado) **2** BELIEF : convicción *f*, creencia *f*

convince [kənˈvɪn*t*s] *vt* **-vinced; -vincing** : convencer

convincing [kənˈvɪn*t*sɪŋ] *adj* : convincente, persuasivo

convincingly [kənˈvɪn*t*sɪŋli] *adv* : de forma convincente

convivial [kənˈvɪvjəl, -ˈvɪviəl] *adj* : jovial, festivo, alegre

conviviality [kən͵vɪviˈælət̬i] *n, pl* **-ties** : jovialidad *f*

convoke [kənˈvoːk] *vt* **-voked; -voking** : convocar

convoluted [ˈkɑnvə͵luːt̬əd] *adj* : intrincado, complicado

convoy [ˈkɑn͵vɔɪ] *n* : convoy *m*

convulse [kənˈvʌls] *v* **-vulsed; -vulsing** *vt* : convulsionar <convulsed with laughter : muerto de risa> — *vi* : sufrir convulsiones

convulsion [kən'vʌlʃən] *n* : convulsión *f*

convulsive [kən'vʌlsɪv] *adj* : convulsivo — **convulsively** *adv*

coo[1] ['ku:] *vi* : arrullar

coo[2] *n* : arrullo *m* (de una paloma)

cook[1] ['kʊk] *vi* : cocinar — *vt* **1** : preparar (comida) **2 to cook up** CONCOCT : inventar, tramar

cook[2] *n* : cocinero *m*, -ra *f*

cookbook ['kʊk,bʊk] *n* : libro *m* de cocina

cookery ['kʊkəri] *n, pl* **-eries** : cocina *f*

cookie *or* **cooky** ['kʊki] *n, pl* **-ies** : galleta *f* (dulce)

cookout ['kʊk,aʊt] *n* : comida *f* al aire libre

cool[1] ['ku:l] *vt* : refrescar, enfriar — *vi* **1** : refrescarse, enfriarse <the pie is cooling : el pastel se está enfriando> **2** : calmarse, tranquilizarse <his anger cooled : su ira se calmó>

cool[2] *adj* **1** : fresco, frío <cool weather : tiempo fresco> **2** CALM : tranquilo, sereno **3** ALOOF : frío, distante

cool[3] *n* **1** : fresco *m* <the cool of the evening : el fresco de la tarde> **2** COMPOSURE : calma *f*, serenidad *f*

coolant ['ku:lənt] *n* : refrigerante *m*

cooler ['ku:lər] *n* : nevera *f* portátil

coolie ['ku:li] *n* : culi *m*

coolly ['ku:lli] *adv* **1** CALMLY : con calma, tranquilamente **2** COLDLY : fríamente, con frialdad

coolness ['ku:lnəs] *n* **1** : frescura *f*, frescor *m* <the coolness of the evening : el frescor de la noche> **2** CALMNESS : tranquilidad *f*, serenidad *f* **3** COLDNESS, INDIFFERENCE : frialdad *f*, indiferencia

coop[1] ['ku:p, 'kʊp] *vt or* **to coop up** : encerrar <cooped up in the house : encerrado en la casa>

coop[2] *n* : gallinero *m*

co–op ['ko:,ɑp] → **cooperative**[2]

cooperate [ko'ɑpə,reɪt] *vi* **-ated; -ating** : cooperar, colaborar

cooperation [ko,ɑpə'reɪʃən] *n* : cooperación *f*, colaboración *f*

cooperative[1] [ko'ɑpərət̬iv, -'ɑpə,reɪt̬iv] *adj* : cooperativo

cooperative[2] [ko'ɑpərət̬iv] *n* : cooperativa *f*

co–opt [ko'ɑpt] *vt* **1** : nombrar como miembro, cooptar **2** APPROPRIATE : apropiarse de

coordinate[1] [ko'ɔrdən,eɪt] *v* **-nated; -nating** *vt* : coordinar — *vi* : coordinarse, combinar, acordar

coordinate[2] [ko'ɔrdənət] *adj* **1** COORDINATED : coordinado **2** EQUAL : igual, semejante

coordinate[3] [ko'ɔrdənət] *n* : coordenada *f*

coordination [ko,ɔrdən'eɪʃən] *n* : coordinación *f*

coordinator [ko'ɔrdən,eɪt̬ər] *n* : coordinador *m*, -dora *f*

cop ['kɑp] → **police officer**

cope ['ko:p] *vi* **coped; coping 1** : arreglárselas **2 to cope with** : hacer frente a, poder con <I can't cope with all this! : ¡no puedo con todo esto!>

copier ['kɑpiər] *n* : copiadora *f*, fotocopiadora *f*

copilot ['ko:,paɪlət] *n* : copiloto *m*

copious ['ko:piəs] *adj* : copioso, abundante — **copiously** *adv*

copiousness ['ko:piəsnəs] *n* : abundancia *f*

copper ['kɑpər] *n* : cobre *m*

coppery ['kɑpəri] *adj* : cobrizo

copra ['ko:prə, 'kɑ-] *n* : copra *f*

copse ['kɑps] *n* THICKET : soto *m*, matorral *m*

copulate ['kɑpjə,leɪt] *vi* **-lated; -lating** : copular

copulation [,kɑpjə'leɪʃən] *n* : cópula *f*, relaciones *fpl* sexuales

copy[1] ['kɑpi] *vt* **copied; copying 1** DUPLICATE : hacer una copia de, duplicar, reproducir **2** IMITATE : copiar, imitar

copy[2] *n, pl* **copies 1** : copia *f*, duplicado *m* (de un documento), reproducción *f* (de una obra de arte) **2** : ejemplar *m* (de un libro), número *m* (de una revista) **3** TEXT : manuscrito *m*, texto *m*

copyright[1] ['kɑpi,raɪt] *vt* : registrar los derechos de

copyright[2] *n* : derechos *mpl* de autor

coral[1] ['kɔrəl] *adj* : de coral <a coral reef : un arrecife de coral>

coral[2] *n* : coral *m*

coral snake *n* : serpiente *f* de coral

cord ['kɔrd] *n* **1** ROPE, STRING : cuerda *f*, cordón *m*, cordel *m* **2** : cuerda *f*, cordón *m*, médula *f* (en la anatomía) <vocal cords : cuerdas vocales> **3** : cuerda *f* <a cord of firewood : una cuerda de leña> **4** *or* **electric cord** : cable *m* eléctrico

cordial[1] ['kɔrdʒəl] *adj* : cordial — **cordially** *adv*

cordial[2] *n* : cordial *m*

cordiality [,kɔrdʒi'æləṱi] *n* : cordialidad *f*

cordon[1] ['kɔrdən] *vt* **to cordon off** : acordonar

cordon[2] *n* : cordón *m*

corduroy ['kɔrdə,rɔɪ] *n* **1** : pana *f* **2 corduroys** *npl* : pantalones *mpl* de pana

core[1] ['kor] *vt* **cored; coring** : quitar el corazón a (una fruta)

core[2] *n* **1** : corazón *m*, centro *m* (de algunas frutas) **2** CENTER : núcleo *m*, centro *m* **3** ESSENCE : núcleo *m*, meollo *m* <to the core : hasta la médula>

cork[1] ['kɔrk] *vt* : ponerle un corcho a

cork[2] *n* : corcho *m*

corkscrew ['kɔrk,skru:] *n* : tirabuzón *m*, sacacorchos *m*

cormorant ['kɔrmərənt, -,rænt] *n* : cormorán *m*

corn[1] ['kɔrn] *vt* : conservar en salmuera <corned beef : carne en conserva>

corn[2] *n* **1** GRAIN : grano *m* **2** : maíz *m,* elote *m Mex* <corn tortillas : tortillas de maíz> **3** : callo *m* <corn plaster : emplasto para callos>

corncob [ˈkɔrn,kɑb] *n* : mazorca *f* (de maíz), choclo *m,* elote *m CA, Mex*

cornea [ˈkɔrniə] *n* : córnea *f*

corner[1] [ˈkɔrnər] *vt* **1** TRAP : acorralar, arrinconar **2** MONOPOLIZE : monopolizar, acaparar (un mercado) — *vi* : tomar una curva, doblar una esquina (en un automóvil)

corner[2] *n* **1** ANGLE : rincón *m,* esquina *f,* ángulo *m* <the corner of a room : el rincón de una sala> <all corners of the world : todos los rincones del mundo> <to cut corners : atajar, economizar esfuerzos> **2** INTERSECTION : esquina *f* **3** IMPASSE, PREDICAMENT : aprieto *m,* impasse *m* <to be backed into a corner : estar acorralado>

cornerstone [ˈkɔrnər,stoːn] *n* : piedra *f* angular

cornet [kɔrˈnɛt] *n* : corneta *f*

cornice [ˈkɔrnɪs] *n* : cornisa *f*

cornmeal [ˈkɔrn,miːl] *n* : harina *f* de maíz

cornstalk [ˈkɔrn,stɔk] *n* : tallo *m* del maíz

cornstarch [ˈkɔrn,stɑrtʃ] *n* : maicena *f,* almidón *m* de maíz

cornucopia [,kɔrnəˈkoːpiə, -njə-] *n* : cornucopia *f*

corolla [kəˈrɑlə] *n* : corola *f*

corollary [ˈkɔrə,lɛri] *n, pl* **-laries** : corolario *m*

corona [kəˈroːnə] *n* : corona *f* (del sol)

coronary[1] [ˈkɔrə,nɛri] *adj* : coronario

coronary[2] *n, pl* **-naries 1** : trombosis *f* coronaria **2** HEART ATTACK : infarto *m,* ataque *m* al corazón

coronation [,kɔrəˈneɪʃən] *n* : coronación *f*

coroner [ˈkɔrənər] *n* : médico *m* forense

corporal[1] [ˈkɔrpərəl] *adj* : corporal <corporal punishment : castigos corporales>

corporal[2] *n* : cabo *m*

corporate [ˈkɔrpərət] *adj* : corporativo, empresarial

corporation [,kɔrpəˈreɪʃən] *n* : sociedad *f* anónima, corporación *f,* empresa *f*

corporeal [kɔrˈporiəl] *adj* **1** PHYSICAL : corpóreo **2** MATERIAL : material, tangible — **corporeally** *adv*

corps [ˈkor] *n, pl* **corps** [ˈkorz] : cuerpo *m* <medical corps : cuerpo médico> <diplomatic corps : cuerpo diplomático>

corpse [ˈkɔrps] *n* : cadáver *m*

corpulence [ˈkɔrpjələnts] *n* : obesidad *f,* gordura *f*

corpulent [ˈkɔrpjələnt] *adj* : obeso, gordo

corpuscle [ˈkɔr,pʌsəl] *n* : corpúsculo *m,* glóbulo *m* (sanguíneo)

corral[1] [kəˈræl] *vt* **-ralled; -ralling** : acorralar, encorralar (ganado)

corral[2] *n* : corral *m*

correct[1] [kəˈrɛkt] *vt* **1** RECTIFY : corregir, rectificar **2** REPRIMAND : corregir, reprender

correct[2] *adj* **1** ACCURATE, RIGHT : correcto, exacto <to be correct : estar en lo cierto> **2** PROPER : correcto, apropiado

correction [kəˈrɛkʃən] *n* : corrección *f*

corrective [kəˈrɛktɪv] *adj* : correctivo

correctly [kəˈrɛktli] *adv* : correctamente

correlate [ˈkɔrə,leɪt] *vt* **-lated; -lating** : relacionar, poner en correlación

correlation [,kɔrəˈleɪʃən] *n* : correlación *f*

correspond [,kɔrəˈspɑnd] *vi* **1** MATCH : corresponder, concordar, coincidir **2** WRITE : corresponderse, escribirse

correspondence [,kɔrəˈspɑndənts] *n* : correspondencia *f*

correspondent [,kɔrəˈspɑndənt] *n* : corresponsal *mf*

correspondingly [,kɔrəˈspɑndɪŋli] *adv* : en consecuencia, de la misma manera

corridor [ˈkɔrədər, -,dɔr] *n* : corredor *m,* pasillo *m*

corroborate [kəˈrɑbə,reɪt] *vt* **-rated; -rating** : corroborar

corroboration [kə,rɑbəˈreɪʃən] *n* : corroboración *f*

corrode [kəˈroːd] *v* **-roded; -roding** *vt* : corroer — *vi* : corroerse

corrosion [kəˈroːʒən] *n* : corrosión *f*

corrosive [kəˈroːsɪv] *adj* : corrosivo

corrugate [ˈkɔrə,geɪt] *vt* **-gated; -gating** : ondular, acanalar, corrugar

corrugated [ˈkɔrə,geɪtəd] *adj* : ondulado, acanalado <corrugated cardboard : cartón ondulado>

corrupt[1] [kəˈrʌpt] *vt* **1** PERVERT : corromper, pervertir, degradar (información) **2** BRIBE : sobornar

corrupt[2] *adj* : corrupto, corrompido

corruptible [kəˈrʌptəbəl] *adj* : corruptible

corruption [kəˈrʌpʃən] *n* : corrupción *f*

corsage [kɔrˈsɑʒ, -ˈsɑdʒ] *n* : ramillete *m* que se lleva como adorno

corset [ˈkɔrsət] *n* : corsé *m*

cortex [ˈkɔr,tɛks] *n, pl* **-tices** [ˈkɔrtə,siːz] *or* **-texes** : corteza *f* <cerebral cortex : corteza cerebral>

cortisone [ˈkɔrtə,soːn, -zoːn] *n* : cortisona *f*

cosmetic[1] [kɑzˈmɛtɪk] *adj* : cosmético

cosmetic[2] *n* : cosmético *m*

cosmic [ˈkɑzmɪk] *adj* **1** : cósmico <cosmic ray : rayo cósmico> **2** VAST : grandioso, inmenso, vasto

cosmonaut [ˈkɑzmə,nɔt] *n* : cosmonauta *mf*

cosmopolitan[1] [,kɑzməˈpɑlətən] *adj* : cosmopolita

cosmopolitan[2] *n* : cosmopolita *mf*

cosmos ['kɑzməs, -ˌmoːs, -ˌmɑs] *n* : cosmos *m,* universo *m*
cost[1] ['kɔst] *v* **cost; costing** *vt* : costar <how much does it cost? : ¿cuánto cuesta?, ¿cuánto vale?> — *vi* : costar <these cost more : éstos cuestan más>
cost[2] *n* : costo *m,* precio *m,* coste *m* <cost of living : costo de vida> <victory at all costs : victoria a toda costa>
Costa Rican[1] [ˌkɔstəˈriːkən] *adj* : costarricense
Costa Rican[2] *n* : costarricense *mf*
costly ['kɔstli] *adj* : costoso, caro
costume ['kɑsˌtuːm, -ˌtjuːm] *n* **1** : traje *m* <national costume : traje típico> **2** : disfraz *m* <costume party : fiesta de disfraces> **3** OUTFIT : vestimenta *f,* traje *m,* conjunto *m*
cosy ['koːzi] → **cozy**
cot ['kɑt] *n* : catre *m*
coterie ['koːt̬əˌri, ˌkoːt̬ə'-] *n* : tertulia *f,* círculo *m* (social)
cottage ['kɑt̬ɪdʒ] *n* : casita *f* (de campo)
cottage cheese *n* : requesón *m*
cotton ['kɑtən] *n* : algodón *m*
cottonmouth ['kɑtənˌmaʊθ] → **moccasin**
cottonseed ['kɑtənˌsiːd] *n* : semilla *f* de algodón
cotton swab → **swab**
cottontail ['kɑtənˌteɪl] *n* : conejo *m* de cola blanca
couch[1] ['kaʊtʃ] *vt* : expresar, formular <couched in strong language : expresado en lenguaje enérgico>
couch[2] *n* SOFA : sofá *m*
cougar ['kuːgər] *n* : puma *m*
cough[1] ['kɔf] *vi* : toser
cough[2] *n* : tos *f*
could ['kʊd] → **can**
council ['kaʊntsəl] *n* **1** : concejo *m* <city council : concejo municipal, ayuntamiento> **2** MEETING : concejo *m,* junta *f* **3** BOARD : consejo *m* **4** : concilio *m* (eclesiástico)
councillor *or* **councilor** ['kaʊntsələr] *n* : concejal *m,* -jala *f*
councilman ['kaʊntsəlmən] *n, pl* **-men** [-mən, -ˌmɛn] : concejal *m*
councilwoman ['kaʊntsəlˌwʊmən] *n, pl* **-women** [-ˌwɪmən] : concejala *f*
counsel[1] ['kaʊntsəl] *v* **-seled** *or* **-selled; -seling** *or* **-selling** *vt* ADVISE : aconsejar, asesorar, recomendar — *vi* CONSULT : consultar
counsel[2] *n* **1** ADVICE : consejo *m,* recomendación *f* **2** CONSULTATION : consulta *f* **3 counsel** *ns & pl* LAWYER : abogado *m,* -da *f*
counselor *or* **counsellor** ['kaʊntsələr] *n* : consejero *m,* -ra *f;* consultor *m,* -tora *f;* asesor *m,* -sora *f*
count[1] ['kaʊnt] *vt* : contar, enumerar — *vi* **1** : contar <to count out loud : contar en voz alta> **2** MATTER : contar, valer, importar <that's what counts : eso es lo que cuenta> **3 to count on** : contar con
count[2] *n* **1** COMPUTATION : cómputo *m,* recuento *m,* cuenta *f* <to lose count : perder la cuenta> **2** CHARGE : cargo *m* <two counts of robbery : dos cargos de robo> **3** : conde *m* (noble)
countable ['kaʊntəbəl] *adj* : numerable
countdown ['kaʊntˌdaʊn] *n* : cuenta *f* atrás
countenance[1] ['kaʊntənənts] *vt* **-nanced; -nancing** : permitir, tolerar
countenance[2] *n* FACE : semblante *m,* rostro *m*
counter[1] ['kaʊntər] *vt* **1** → **counteract** **2** OPPOSE : oponerse a, resistir — *vi* RETALIATE : responder, contraatacar
counter[2] *adv* **counter to** : contrario a, en contra de
counter[3] *adj* : contrario, opuesto
counter[4] *n* **1** PIECE : ficha *f* (de un juego) **2** : mostrador *m* (de un negocio), ventanilla *f* (en un banco) **3** : contador *m* (aparato) **4** COUNTERBALANCE : fuerza *f* opuesta, contrapeso *m*
counteract [ˌkaʊntər'ækt] *vt* : contrarrestar
counterattack ['kaʊntərəˌtæk] *n* : contraataque *m*
counterbalance[1] [ˌkaʊntər'bæləntś] *vt* **-anced; -ancing** : contrapesar
counterbalance[2] ['kaʊntərˌbæləntś] *n* : contrapeso *m*
counterclockwise [ˌkaʊntər'klɑkˌwaɪz] *adv & adj* : en el sentido opuesto al de las manecillas del reloj
counterfeit[1] ['kaʊntərˌfɪt] *vt* **1** : falsificar (dinero) **2** PRETEND : fingir, aparentar
counterfeit[2] *adj* : falso, inauténtico
counterfeit[3] *n* : falsificación *f*
counterfeiter ['kaʊntərˌfɪt̬ər] *n* : falsificador *m,* -dora *f*
countermand ['kaʊntərˌmænd, ˌkaʊntər'-] *vt* : contramandar
countermeasure ['kaʊntərˌmɛʒər] *n* : contramedida *f*
counterpart ['kaʊntərˌpɑrt] *n* : homólogo *m,* contraparte *f Mex*
counterpoint ['kaʊntərˌpɔɪnt] *n* : contrapunto *m*
counterproductive [ˌkaʊntərprə'dʌktɪv] *adj* : contraproducente
counterrevolution [ˌkaʊntərˌrɛvə'luːʃən] *n* : contrarrevolución *f*
counterrevolutionary[1] [ˌkaʊntərˌrɛvə'luːʃənˌɛri] *adj* : contrarrevolucionario
counterrevolutionary[2] *n, pl* **-ries** : contrarrevolucionario *m,* -ria *f*
countersign ['kaʊntərˌsaɪn] *n* : contraseña *f*
countess ['kaʊntɪs] *n* : condesa *f*
countless ['kaʊntləs] *adj* : incontable, innumerable
country[1] ['kʌntri] *adj* : campestre, rural
country[2] *n, pl* **-tries** **1** NATION : país *m,* nación *f,* patria *f* <country of origin : país de origen> <love of one's country : amor a la patria> **2** : campo *m*

<they left the city for the country : se fueron de la ciudad al campo>

countryman [ˈkʌntrimən] *n, pl* **-men** [-mən, -ˌmɛn] : compatriota *mf;* paisano *m,* -na *f*

countryside [ˈkʌntriˌsaɪd] *n* : campo *m,* campiña *f*

county [ˈkaʊnti] *n, pl* **-ties** : condado *m*

coup [ˈkuː] *n, pl* **coups** [ˈkuːz] **1** : golpe *m* maestro **2** *or* **coup d'etat** : golpe *m* (de estado), cuartelazo *m*

coupe [ˈkuːp] *n* : cupé *m*

couple[1] [ˈkʌpəl] *vt* **-pled; -pling** : acoplar, enganchar, conectar

couple[2] *n* **1** PAIR : par *m* <a couple of hours : un par de horas, unas dos horas> **2** : pareja *f* <a young couple : una pareja joven>

coupling [ˈkʌplɪŋ] *n* : acoplamiento *m*

coupon [ˈkuːˌpɑn, ˈkjuː-] *n* : cupón *m*

courage [ˈkərɪdʒ] *n* : valor *m,* valentía *f,* coraje *m*

courageous [kəˈreɪdʒəs] *adj* : valiente, valeroso

courier [ˈkʊriər, ˈkəriər] *n* : mensajero *m,* -ra *f*

course[1] [ˈkors] *vi* **coursed; coursing** : correr (a toda velocidad)

course[2] *n* **1** PROGRESS : curso *m,* transcurso *m* <to run its course : seguir su curso> **2** DIRECTION : rumbo *m* (de un avión), derrota *f,* derrotero *m* (de un barco) **3** PATH, WAY : camino *m,* vía *f* <course of action : línea de conducta> **4** : plato *m* (de una cena) <the main course : el plato principal> **5** : curso *m* (académico) **6 of course** : desde luego, por supuesto <yes, of course! : ¡claro que sí!>

court[1] [ˈkort] *vt* WOO : cortejar, galantear

court[2] *n* **1** PALACE : palacio *m* **2** RETINUE : corte *f,* séquito *m* **3** COURTYARD : patio *m* **4** : cancha *f* (de tenis, baloncesto, etc.) **5** TRIBUNAL : corte *f,* tribunal *m* <the Supreme Court : la Corte Suprema>

courteous [ˈkərt̬iəs] *adj* : cortés, atento, educado — **courteously** *adv*

courtesan [ˈkort̬əzən, ˈkər-] *n* : cortesana *f*

courtesy [ˈkərt̬əsi] *n, pl* **-sies** : cortesía *f*

courthouse [ˈkortˌhaʊs] *n* : palacio *m* de justicia, juzgado *m*

courtier [ˈkortiər, ˈkortjər] *n* : cortesano *m,* -na *f*

courtly [ˈkortli] *adj* **-lier; -est** : distinguido, elegante, cortés

court–martial[1] [ˈkortˌmɑrʃəl] *vt* : someter a consejo de guerra

court–martial[2] *n, pl* **courts–martial** [ˈkortsˌmɑrʃəl] : consejo *m* de guerra

court order *n* : mandamiento *m* judicial

courtroom [ˈkortˌruːm] *n* : tribunal *m,* corte *f*

courtship [ˈkortˌʃɪp] *n* : cortejo *m,* noviazgo *m*

courtyard [ˈkortˌjɑrd] *n* : patio *m*

cousin [ˈkʌzən] *n* : primo *m,* -ma *f*

cove [ˈkoːv] *n* : ensenada *f,* cala *f*

covenant [ˈkʌvənənt] *n* : pacto *m,* contrato *m*

cover[1] [ˈkʌvər] *vt* **1** : cubrir, tapar <cover your head : tápate la cabeza> <covered with mud : cubierto de lodo> **2** HIDE, PROTECT : encubrir, proteger **3** TREAT : tratar **4** INSURE : asegurar, cubrir

cover[2] *n* **1** SHELTER : cubierta *f,* abrigo *m,* refugio *m* <to take cover : ponerse a cubierto> <under cover of darkness : al amparo de la oscuridad> **2** LID, TOP : cubierta *f,* tapa *f* **3** : cubierta *f* (de un libro), portada *f* (de una revista) **4 covers** *npl* BEDCLOTHES : ropa *f* de cama, cobijas *fpl,* mantas *fpl*

coverage [ˈkʌvərɪdʒ] *n* : cobertura *f*

coverlet [ˈkʌvərlət] *n* : cobertor *m*

covert[1] [ˈkoːˌvərt, ˈkʌvərt] *adj* : encubierto, secreto <covert operations : operaciones encubiertas>

covert[2] [ˈkʌvərt, ˈkoː-] *n* THICKET : espesura *f,* maleza *f*

cover–up [ˈkʌvərˌʌp] *n* : encubrimiento

covet [ˈkʌvət] *vt* : codiciar

covetous [ˈkʌvət̬əs] *adj* : codicioso

covey [ˈkʌvi] *n, pl* **-eys 1** : bandada *f* pequeña (de codornices, etc.) **2** GROUP : grupo *m*

cow[1] [ˈkaʊ] *vt* : intimidar, acobardar

cow[2] *n* : vaca *f,* hembra *f* (de ciertas especies)

coward [ˈkaʊərd] *n* : cobarde *mf*

cowardice [ˈkaʊərdɪs] *n* : cobardía *f*

cowardly [ˈkaʊərdli] *adj* : cobarde

cowboy [ˈkaʊˌbɔɪ] *n* : vaquero *m,* cowboy *m*

cower [ˈkaʊər] *vi* : encogerse (de miedo), acobardarse

cowgirl [ˈkaʊˌgərl] *n* : vaquera *f*

cowherd [ˈkaʊˌhərd] *n* : vaquero *m,* -ra *f*

cowhide [ˈkaʊˌhaɪd] *n* : cuero *m,* piel *f* de vaca

cowl [ˈkaʊl] *n* : capucha *f* (de un monje)

cowlick [ˈkaʊˌlɪk] *n* : remolino *m*

cowpuncher [ˈkaʊˌpʌntʃər] → **cowboy**

cowslip [ˈkaʊˌslɪp] *n* : prímula *f,* primavera *f*

coxswain [ˈkɑksən, -ˌsweɪn] *n* : timonel *m*

coy [ˈkɔɪ] *adj* **1** SHY : tímido, cohibido **2** COQUETTISH : coqueto

coyote [kaɪˈoːt̬i, ˈkaɪˌoːt] *n, pl* **coyotes** *or* **coyote** : coyote *m*

cozy [ˈkoːzi] *adj* **-zier; -est** : acogedor, cómodo

crab [ˈkræb] *n* : cangrejo *m,* jaiba *f*

crabby [ˈkræbi] *adj* **-bier; -est** : gruñón, malhumorado

crabgrass [ˈkræbˌgræs] *n* : garranchuelo *m*

crack¹ [ˈkræk] *vi* **1** : chasquear, restallar <the whip cracked : el látigo restalló> **2** SPLIT : rajarse, resquebrajarse, agrietarse **3** : quebrarse (dícese de la voz) — *vt* **1** : restallar, chasquear (un látigo, etc.) **2** SPLIT : rajar, agrietar, resquebrajar **3** BREAK : romper (un huevo), cascar (nueces), forzar (una caja fuerte) **4** SOLVE : resolver, descifrar (un código)
crack² *adj* FIRST-RATE : buenísimo, de primera
crack³ *n* **1** : chasquido *m,* restallido *m,* estallido *m* (de un arma de fuego), crujido *m* (de huesos) <a crack of thunder : un trueno> **2** WISECRACK : chiste *m,* ocurrencia *f,* salida *f* **3** CREVICE : raja *f,* grieta *f,* fisura *f* **4** BLOW : golpe *m* **5** ATTEMPT : intento *m*
crackdown [ˈkræk,daʊn] *n* : medidas *fpl* enérgicas
crack down *vt* : tomar medidas enérgicas
cracker [ˈkrækər] *n* : galleta *f* (de soda, etc.)
crackle¹ [ˈkrækəl] *vi* **-led; -ling** : crepitar, chisporrotear
crackle² *n* : crujido *m,* chisporroteo *m*
crackpot [ˈkræk,pɑt] *n* : excéntrico *m,* -ca *f;* chiflado *m,* -da *f*
crack–up [ˈkræk,ʌp] *n* **1** CRASH : choque *m,* estrellamiento *m* **2** BREAKDOWN : crisis *f* nerviosa
crack up *vt* WRECK : estrellar (un vehículo) — *vi* : sufrir una crisis nerviosa
cradle¹ [ˈkreɪdəl] *vt* **-dled; -dling** : acunar, mecer (a un niño)
cradle² *n* : cuna *f*
craft [ˈkræft] *n* **1** TRADE : oficio *m* <the craft of carpentry : el oficio de carpintero> **2** CRAFTSMANSHIP, SKILL : arte *m,* artesanía *f,* destreza *f* **3** CRAFTINESS : astucia *f,* maña *f* **4** *pl usually* **craft** BOAT : barco *m,* embarcación *f* **5** *pl usually* **craft** AIRCRAFT : avión *m,* aeronave *f*
craftiness [ˈkræftinəs] *n* : astucia *f,* maña *f*
craftsman [ˈkræftsmən] *n, pl* **-men** [-mən, -,mɛn] : artesano *m,* -na *f*
craftsmanship [ˈkræftsmən,ʃɪp] *n* : artesanía *f,* destreza *f*
crafty [ˈkræfti] *adj* **craftier; -est** : astuto, taimado
crag [ˈkræg] *n* : peñasco *m*
craggy [ˈkrægi] *adj* **-gier; -est** : peñascoso
cram [ˈkræm] *v* **crammed; cramming** *vt* **1** JAM : embutir, meter **2** STUFF : atiborrar, abarrotar <crammed with people : atiborrado de gente> — *vi* : estudiar a última hora, memorizar (para un examen)
cramp¹ [ˈkræmp] *vt* **1** : dar calambre en **2** RESTRICT : limitar, restringir, entorpecer <to cramp someone's style : cortarle el vuelo a alguien> — *vi or* **to cramp up** : acalambrarse
cramp² *n* **1** SPASM : calambre *m,* espasmo *m* (de los músculos) **2 cramps** *npl* : retorcijones *mpl* <stomach cramps : retorcijones de estómago>
cranberry [ˈkræn,bɛri] *n, pl* **-berries** : arándano *m* (rojo y agrio)
crane¹ [ˈkreɪn] *vi* **craned; craning** : estirar <to crane one's neck : estirar el cuello>
crane² *n* **1** : grulla *f* (ave) **2** : grúa *f* (máquina)
cranial [ˈkreɪniəl] *adj* : craneal, craneano
cranium [ˈkreɪniəm] *n, pl* **-niums** *or* **-nia** [-niə]: cráneo *m*
crank¹ [ˈkræŋk] *vt or* **to crank up** : arrancar (con una manivela)
crank² *n* **1** : manivela *f,* manubrio *m* **2** ECCENTRIC : excéntrico *m,* -ca *f*
cranky [ˈkræŋki] *adj* **crankier; -est** : irritable, malhumorado, enojadizo
cranny [ˈkræni] *n, pl* **-nies** : grieta *f* <every nook and cranny : todos los rincones>
crash¹ [ˈkræʃ] *vi* **1** SMASH : caerse con estrépito, estrellarse **2** COLLIDE : estrellarse, chocar **3** BOOM, RESOUND : retumbar, resonar — *vt* **1** SMASH : estrellar **2 to crash one's car** : tener un accidente
crash² *n* **1** DIN : estrépito *m* **2** COLLISION : choque *m,* colisión *f* <car crash : accidente automovilístico> **3** FAILURE : quiebra *f* (de un negocio), crac *m* (de la bolsa)
crass [ˈkræs] *adj* : grosero, de mal gusto
crate¹ [ˈkreɪt] *vt* **crated; crating** : empacar en un cajón
crate² *n* : cajón *m* (de madera)
crater [ˈkreɪt̬ər] *n* : cráter *m*
cravat [krəˈvæt] *n* : corbata *f*
crave [ˈkreɪv] *vt* **craved; craving** : ansiar, apetecer, tener muchas ganas de
craven [ˈkreɪvən] *adj* : cobarde, pusilánime
craving [ˈkreɪvɪŋ] *n* : ansia *f,* antojo *m,* deseo *m*
crawfish [ˈkrɔ,fɪʃ] → **crayfish**
crawl¹ [ˈkrɔl] *vi* **1** CREEP : arrastrarse, gatear (dícese de un bebé) **2** TEEM : estar plagado
crawl² *n* : paso *m* lento
crayfish [ˈkreɪ,fɪʃ] *n* **1** : ástaco *m* (de agua dulce) **2** : langostino *m* (de mar)
crayon [ˈkreɪ,ɑn, -ən] *n* : crayón *m*
craze [ˈkreɪz] *n* : moda *f* pasajera, manía *f*
crazed [ˈkreɪzd] *adj* : enloquecido
crazily [ˈkreɪzəli] *adv* : locamente, erráticamente, insensatamente
craziness [ˈkreɪzinəs] *n* : locura *f,* demencia *f*
crazy [ˈkreɪzi] *adj* **-zier; -est** **1** INSANE : loco, demente <to go crazy : volverse loco> **2** ABSURD, FOOLISH : loco, insensato, absurdo **3 to be crazy about** : estar loco por

creak[1] ['kriːk] *vi* : chirriar, rechinar, crujir

creak[2] *n* : chirrido *m,* crujido *m*

creaky ['kriːki] *adj* **creakier; -est** : chirriante, que cruje

cream[1] ['kriːm] *vt* **1** BEAT, MIX : batir, mezclar (azúcar y mantequilla, etc.) **2** : preparar (alimentos) con crema

cream[2] *n* **1** : crema *f* (de leche) **2** LOTION : crema *f,* loción *f* **3** ELITE : crema *f,* elite *f* <the cream of the crop : la crema y nata, lo mejor>

creamery ['kriːməri] *n, pl* **-eries** : fábrica *f* de productos lácteos

creamy ['kriːmi] *adj* **creamier; -est** : cremoso

crease[1] ['kriːs] *vt* **creased; creasing 1** : plegar, poner una raya en (pantalones) **2** WRINKLE : arrugar

crease[2] *n* : pliegue *m,* doblez *m,* raya *f* (de pantalones)

create [kri'eɪt] *vt* **-ated; -ating** : crear, hacer

creation [kri'eɪʃən] *n* : creación *f*

creative [kri'eɪtɪv] *adj* : creativo, original <creative people : personas creativas> <a creative work : un obra original>

creatively [kri'eɪtɪvli] *adv* : creativamente, con originalidad

creativity [ˌkriːeɪ'tɪvət̬i] *n* : creatividad *f*

creator [kri'eɪt̬ər] *n* : creador *m,* -dora *f*

creature ['kriːtʃər] *n* : ser *m* viviente, criatura *f,* animal *m*

credence ['kriːdənts] *n* : crédito *m*

credentials [krɪ'dɛntʃəlz] *npl* : referencias *fpl* oficiales, cartas *fpl* credenciales

credibility [ˌkrɛdə'bɪlət̬i] *n* : credibilidad *f*

credible ['krɛdəbəl] *adj* : creíble

credit[1] ['krɛdɪt] *vt* **1** BELIEVE : creer, dar crédito a **2** : ingresar, abonar <to credit $100 to an account : ingresar $100 en (una) cuenta> **3** ATTRIBUTE : atribuir <they credit the invention to him : a él se le atribuye el invento>

credit[2] *n* **1** : saldo *m* positivo, saldo *m* a favor (de una cuenta) **2** : crédito *m* <to buy on credit : comprar a crédito> <credit card : tarjeta de crédito> **3** CREDENCE : crédito *m* <I gave credit to everything he said : di crédito a todo lo que dijo> **4** RECOGNITION : reconocimiento *m* **5** : orgullo *m,* honor *m* <she's a credit to the school : ella es el orgullo de la escuela>

creditable ['krɛdɪt̬əbəl] *adj* : encomiable, loable — **creditably** [-bli] *adv*

credit card *n* : tarjeta de crédito

creditor ['krɛdɪt̬ər] *n* : acreedor *m,* -dora *f*

credulity [krɪ'duːlət̬i, -'djuː-] *n* : credulidad *f*

credulous ['krɛdʒələs] *adj* : crédulo

creed ['kriːd] *n* : credo *m*

creek ['kriːk, 'krɪk] *n* : arroyo *m,* riachuelo *m*

creel ['kriːl] *n* : nasa *f,* cesta *f* (de pescador)

creep[1] ['kriːp] *vi* **crept** ['krɛpt]; **creeping 1** CRAWL : arrastrarse, gatear **2** : moverse lentamente o sigilosamente <he crept out of the house : salió sigilosamente de la casa> **3** SPREAD : trepar (dícese de una planta)

creep[2] *n* **1** CRAWL : paso *m* lento **2** **creeps** *npl* : escalofríos *mpl* <that gives me the creeps : eso me da escalofríos>

creeper ['kriːpər] *n* : planta *f* trepadora, trepadora *f*

cremate ['kriːˌmeɪt] *vt* **-mated; -mating** : cremar

cremation [krɪ'meɪʃən] *n* : cremación *f*

creosote ['kriːəˌsoːt] *n* : creosota *f*

crepe *or* **crêpe** ['kreɪp] *n* **1** : crespón *m* (tela) **2** PANCAKE : crepe *mf,* crepa *f Mex*

crescendo [krɪ'ʃɛnˌdoː] *n, pl* **-dos** *or* **-does** : crescendo *m*

crescent ['krɛsənt] *n* : creciente *m*

crest ['krɛst] *n* **1** : cresta *f,* penacho *m* (de un ave) **2** PEAK, TOP : cresta *f* (de una ola), cima *f* (de una colina) **3** : emblema *m* (sobre un escudo de armas)

crestfallen ['krɛstˌfɔlən] *adj* : alicaído, abatido

cretin ['kriːtən] *n* : cretino *m,* -na *f*

crevasse [krɪ'væs] *n* : grieta *f,* fisura *f*

crevice ['krɛvɪs] *n* : grieta *f,* hendidura *f*

crew ['kruː] *n* **1** : tripulación *f* (de una nave) **2** TEAM : equipo *m* (de trabajadores o atletas)

crib ['krɪb] *n* **1** MANGER : pesebre *m* **2** GRANARY : granero *m* **3** : cuna *f* (de un bebé)

crick ['krɪk] *n* : calambre *m,* espasmo *m* muscular

cricket ['krɪkət] *n* **1** : grillo *m* (insecto) **2** : críquet *m* (juego)

crime ['kraɪm] *n* **1** : crimen *m,* delito *m* <to commit a crime : cometer un delito> **2** : crimen *m,* delincuencia *f* <organized crime : crimen organizado>

criminal[1] ['krɪmənəl] *adj* : criminal

criminal[2] *n* : criminal *mf,* delincuente *mf*

crimp ['krɪmp] *vt* : ondular, rizar (el pelo), arrugar (una tela, etc.)

crimson ['krɪmzən] *n* : carmesí *m*

cringe ['krɪndʒ] *vi* **cringed; cringing** : encogerse

crinkle[1] ['krɪŋkəl] *v* **-kled; -kling** *vt* : arrugar — *vi* : arrugarse

crinkle[2] *n* : arruga *f*

crinkly ['krɪŋkəli] *adj* : arrugado

cripple[1] ['krɪpəl] *vt* **-pled; -pling 1** DISABLE : lisiar, dejar inválido **2** INCAPACITATE : inutilizar, incapacitar

cripple[2] *n* : lisiado *m,* -da *f*

crisis [ˈkraɪsɪs] *n, pl* **crises** [-ˌsiːz] : crisis *f*
crisp[1] [ˈkrɪsp] *vt* : tostar, hacer crujiente
crisp[2] *adj* **1** CRUNCHY : crujiente, crocante **2** FIRM, FRESH : firme, fresco <crisp lettuce : lechuga fresca> **3** LIVELY : vivaz, alegre <a crisp tempo : un ritmo alegre> **4** INVIGORATING : fresco, vigorizante <the crisp autumn air : el fresco aire otoñal> — **crisply** *adv*
crispy [ˈkrɪspi] *adj* **crispier; -est** : crujiente <crispy potato chips : papitas crujientes>
crisscross [ˈkrɪsˌkrɔs] *vt* : entrecruzar
criterion [kraɪˈtɪriən] *n, pl* **-ria** [-iə] : criterio *m*
critic [ˈkrɪtɪk] *n* **1** : crítico *m,* -ca *f* (de las artes) **2** FAULTFINDER : detractor *m,* -tora *f;* criticón *m,* -cona *f*
critical [ˈkrɪtɪkəl] *adj* : crítico
critically [ˈkrɪtɪkli] *adv* : críticamente <critically ill : gravemente enfermo>
criticism [ˈkrɪtəˌsɪzəm] *n* : crítica *f*
criticize [ˈkrɪtəˌsaɪz] *vt* **-cized; -cizing** **1** EVALUATE, JUDGE : criticar, analizar, evaluar **2** CENSURE : criticar, reprobar
critique [krɪˈtiːk] *n* : crítica *f,* evaluación *f*
croak[1] [ˈkroːk] *vi* : croar
croak[2] *n* : croar *m,* canto *m* (de la rana)
Croatian [kroˈeɪʃən] *n* : croata *mf* — **Croatian** *adj*
crochet[1] [kroːˈʃeɪ] *v* : tejer al croché
crochet[2] *n* : croché *m,* crochet *m*
crock [ˈkrɑk] *n* : vasija *f* de barro
crockery [ˈkrɑkəri] *n* : vajilla *f* (de barro)
crocodile [ˈkrɑkəˌdaɪl] *n* : cocodrilo *m*
crocus [ˈkroːkəs] *n, pl* **-cuses** : azafrán *m*
crone [ˈkroːn] *n* : vieja *f* arpía, vieja *f* bruja
crony [ˈkroːni] *n, pl* **-nies** : amigote *m fam;* compinche *mf fam*
crook[1] [ˈkrʊk] *vt* : doblar (el brazo o el dedo)
crook[2] *n* **1** STAFF : cayado *m* (de pastor), báculo *m* (de obispo) **2** THIEF : ratero *m,* -ra *f;* ladrón *m,* -drona *f*
crooked [ˈkrʊkəd] *adj* **1** BENT : chueco, torcido **2** DISHONEST : deshonesto
crookedness [ˈkrʊkədnəs] *n* **1** : lo torcido, lo chueco **2** DISHONESTY : falta *f* de honradez
croon [ˈkruːn] *v* : cantar suavemente
crop[1] [ˈkrɑp] *v* **cropped; cropping** *vt* TRIM : recortar, cortar — *vi* **to crop up** : aparecer, surgir <these problems keep cropping up : estos problemas no cesan de surgir>
crop[2] *n* **1** : buche *m* (de un ave o insecto) **2** WHIP : fusta *f* (de jinete) **3** HARVEST : cosecha *f,* cultivo *m*
croquet [ˌkroːˈkeɪ] *n* : croquet *m*
croquette [ˌkroːˈkɛt] *n* : croqueta *f*
cross[1] [ˈkrɔs] *vt* **1** : cruzar, atravesar <to cross the street : cruzar la calle> <several canals cross the city : varios canales atraviesan la ciudad> **2** CANCEL : tachar, cancelar <he crossed his name off the list : tachó su nombre de la planilla> **3** INTERBREED : cruzar (en genética)
cross[2] *adj* **1** : que atraviesa <cross ventilation : ventilación que atraviesa un cuarto> **2** CONTRARY : contrario, opuesto <cross purposes : objetivos opuestos> **3** ANGRY : enojado, de mal humor
cross[3] *n* **1** : cruz *f* <the sign of the cross : la señal de la cruz> **2** : cruza *f* (en biología)
crossbones [ˈkrɔsˌboːnz] *npl* **1** : huesos *mpl* cruzados **2** → **skull**
crossbow [ˈkrɔsˌboː] *n* : ballesta *f*
crossbreed [ˈkrɔsˌbriːd] *vt* **-bred** [-+bred]; **-breeding** : cruzar
cross–examination [ˌkrɔsɪgˌzæməˈneɪʃən] *n* : repreguntas *fpl,* interrogatorio *m*
cross–examine [ˌkrɔsɪgˈzæmən] *vt* **-ined; -ining** : repreguntar
cross–eyed [ˈkrɔsˌaɪd] *adj* : bizco
crossing [ˈkrɔsɪŋ] *n* **1** INTERSECTION : cruce *m,* paso *m* <pedestrian crossing : paso de peatones> **2** VOYAGE : travesía *f* (del mar)
crossly [ˈkrɔsli] *adv* : con enojo, con enfado
cross–reference [ˌkrɔsˈrɛfrənts, -ˈrɛfərənts] *n* : referencia *f,* remisión *f*
crossroads [ˈkrɔsˌroːdz] *n* : cruce *m,* encrucijada *f,* crucero *m Mex*
cross section *n* **1** SECTION : corte *m* transversal **2** SAMPLE : muestra *f* representativa <a cross section of the population : una muestra representativa de la población>
crosswalk [ˈkrɔsˌwɔk] *n* : cruce *m* peatonal, paso *m* de peatones
crossways [ˈkrɔsˌweɪz] → **crosswise**
crosswise[1] [ˈkrɔsˌwaɪz] *adv* : transversalmente, diagonalmente
crosswise[2] *adj* : transversal, diagonal
crossword puzzle [ˈkrɔsˌwərd] *n* : crucigrama *m*
crotch [ˈkrɑtʃ] *n* : entrepierna *f*
crotchety [ˈkrɑtʃəti] *adj* CRANKY : malhumorado, irritable, enojadizo
crouch [ˈkraʊtʃ] *vi* : agacharse, ponerse de cuclillas
croup [ˈkruːp] *n* : crup *m*
crouton [ˈkruːˌtɑn] *n* : crutón *m*
crow[1] [ˈkroː] *vi* **1** : cacarear, cantar (como un cuervo) **2** BRAG : alardear, presumir
crow[2] *n* **1** : cuervo *m* (ave) **2** : cantar *m* (del gallo)
crowbar [ˈkroːˌbɑr] *n* : palanca *f*
crowd[1] [ˈkraʊd] *vi* : aglomerarse, amontonarse — *vt* : atestar, atiborrar, llenar
crowd[2] *n* : multitud *f,* muchedumbre *f,* gentío *m*
crown[1] [ˈkraʊn] *vt* : coronar
crown[2] *n* : corona *f*

crow's nest *n* : cofa *f*
crucial ['kruːʃəl] *adj* : crucial, decisivo
crucible ['kruːsəbəl] *n* : crisol *m*
crucifix ['kruːsəˌfɪks] *n* : crucifijo *m*
crucifixion [ˌkruːsə'fɪkʃən] *n* : crucifixión *f*
crucify ['kruːsəˌfaɪ] *vt* **-fied; -fying** : crucificar
crude ['kruːd] *adj* **cruder; -est 1** RAW, UNREFINED : crudo, sin refinar <crude oil : petróleo crudo> **2** VULGAR : grosero, de mal gusto **3** ROUGH : tosco, burdo, rudo
crudely ['kruːdli] *adv* **1** VULGARLY : groseramente **2** ROUGHLY : burdamente, de manera rudimentaria
crudity ['kruːdət̬i] *n, pl* **-ties 1** VULGARITY : grosería *f* **2** COARSENESS, ROUGHNESS : tosquedad *f,* rudeza *f*
cruel ['kruːəl] *adj* **-eler** *or* **-eller; -elest** *or* **-ellest** : cruel
cruelly ['kruːəli] *adv* : cruelmente
cruelty ['kruːəlti] *n, pl* **-ties** : crueldad *f*
cruet ['kruːɪt] *n* : vinagrera *f,* aceitera *f*
cruise[1] ['kruːz] *vi* **cruised; cruising 1** : hacer un crucero **2** : navegar o conducir a una velocidad constante <cruising speed : velocidad de crucero>
cruise[2] *n* : crucero *m*
cruiser ['kruːzər] *n* **1** WARSHIP : crucero *m,* buque *m* de guerra **2** : patrulla *f* (de policía)
crumb ['krʌm] *n* : miga *f,* migaja *f*
crumble ['krʌmbəl] *v* **-bled; -bling** *vt* : desmigajar, desmenuzar — *vi* : desmigajarse, desmoronarse, desmenuzarse
crumbly ['krʌmbli] *adj* : que se desmenuza fácilmente, friable
crumple ['krʌmpəl] *v* **-pled; -pling** *vt* RUMPLE : arrugar — *vi* **1** WRINKLE : arrugarse **2** COLLAPSE : desplomarse
crunch[1] ['krʌntʃ] *vt* **1** : ronzar (con los dientes) **2** : hacer crujir (con los pies, etc.) — *vi* : crujir
crunch[2] *n* : crujido *m*
crunchy ['krʌntʃi] *adj* **crunchier; -est** : crujiente
crusade[1] [kruː'seɪd] *vi* **-saded; -sading** : hacer una campaña (a favor de o contra algo)
crusade[2] *n* **1** : campaña *f* (de reforma, etc.) **2 Crusade** : cruzada *f*
crusader [kruː'seɪdər] *n* **1** : cruzado *m* (en la Edad Media) **2** : campeón *m,* -peona *f* (de una causa)
crush[1] ['krʌʃ] *vt* **1** SQUASH : aplastar, apachurrar **2** GRIND, PULVERIZE : triturar, machacar **3** SUPPRESS : aplastar, suprimir
crush[2] *n* **1** CROWD, MOB : gentío *m,* multitud *f,* aglomeración *f* **2** INFATUATION : enamoramiento *m*
crushing ['krʌʃɪŋ] *adj* : aplastante, abrumador
crust ['krʌst] *n* **1** : corteza *f,* costra *f* (de pan) **2** : tapa *f* de masa, pasta *f* (de un pastel) **3** LAYER : capa *f,* corteza *f* <the earth's crust : la corteza terrestre>
crustacean [ˌkrʌs'teɪʃən] *n* : crustáceo *m*
crusty ['krʌsti] *adj* **crustier; -est 1** : de corteza dura **2** CROSS, GRUMPY : enojado, malhumorado
crutch ['krʌtʃ] *n* : muleta *f*
crux ['krʌks, 'krʊks] *n, pl* **cruxes** : quid *m,* esencia *f,* meollo *m* <the crux of the problem : el quid del problema>
cry[1] ['kraɪ] *vi* **cried; crying 1** SHOUT : gritar <they cried for more : a gritos pidieron más> **2** WEEP : llorar
cry[2] *n, pl* **cries 1** SHOUT : grito *m* **2** WEEPING : llanto *m* **3** : chillido *m* (de un animal)
crybaby ['kraɪˌbeɪbi] *n, pl* **-bies** : llorón *m,* -rona *f*
crypt ['krɪpt] *n* : cripta *f*
cryptic ['krɪptɪk] *adj* : enigmático, críptico
crystal ['krɪstəl] *n* : cristal *m*
crystalline ['krɪstələn] *adj* : cristalino
crystallize ['krɪstəˌlaɪz] *v* **-lized; -lizing** *vt* : cristalizar, materializar <to crystallize one's thoughts : cristalizar uno sus pensamientos> — *vi* : cristalizarse
cub ['kʌb] *n* : cachorro *m*
Cuban ['kjuːbən] *n* : cubano *m,* -na *f* — **Cuban** *adj*
cubbyhole ['kʌbiˌhoːl] *n* : chiribitil *m*
cube[1] ['kjuːb] *vt* **cubed; cubing 1** : elevar (un número) al cubo **2** : cortar en cubos
cube[2] *n* **1** : cubo *m* **2 ice cube** : cubito *m* de hielo **3 sugar cube** : terrón *m* de azúcar
cubic ['kjuːbɪk] *adj* : cúbico
cubicle ['kjuːbɪkəl] *n* : cubículo *m*
cuckoo[1] ['kuːˌkuː, 'kʊ-] *adj* : loco, chiflado
cuckoo[2] *n, pl* **-oos** : cuco *m,* cuclillo *m*
cucumber ['kjuːˌkʌmbər] *n* : pepino *m*
cud ['kʌd] *n* **to chew the cud** : rumiar
cuddle ['kʌdəl] *v* **-dled; -dling** *vi* : abrazarse tiernamente, acurrucarse — *vt* : abrazar
cudgel[1] ['kʌdʒəl] *vt* **-geled** *or* **-gelled; -geling** *or* **-gelling** : apalear, aporrear
cudgel[2] *n* : garrote *m,* porra *f*
cue[1] ['kjuː] *vt* **cued; cuing** *or* **cueing** : darle el pie a, darle la señal a
cue[2] *n* **1** SIGNAL : señal *f,* pie *m* (en teatro), entrada *f* (en música) **2** : taco *m* (de billar)
cuff[1] ['kʌf] *vt* : bofetear, cachetear
cuff[2] *n* **1** : puño *m* (de una camisa), vuelta *f* (de pantalones) **2** SLAP : bofetada *f,* cachetada *f* **3 cuffs** *npl* HANDCUFFS : esposas *fpl*
cuisine [kwɪ'ziːn] *n* : cocina *f* <Mexican cuisine : la cocina mexicana>

culinary ['kʌlə,nɛri, 'kjuːlə-] *adj* : culinario
cull ['kʌl] *vt* : seleccionar, entresacar
culminate ['kʌlmə,neɪt] *vi* **-nated; -nating** : culminar
culmination [,kʌlmə'neɪʃən] *n* : culminación *f,* punto *m* culminante
culpable ['kʌlpəbəl] *adj* : culpable
culprit ['kʌlprɪt] *n* : culpable *mf*
cult ['kʌlt] *n* : culto *m*
cultivate ['kʌltə,veɪt] *vt* **-vated; -vating 1** TILL : cultivar, labrar **2** FOSTER : cultivar, fomentar **3** REFINE : cultivar, refinar <to cultivate the mind : cultivar la mente>
cultivation [,kʌltə'veɪʃən] *n* **1** : cultivo *m* <under cultivation : en cultivo> **2** CULTURE, REFINEMENT : cultura *f,* refinamiento *m*
cultural ['kʌltʃərəl] *adj* : cultural — **culturally** *adv*
culture ['kʌltʃər] *n* **1** CULTIVATION : cultivo *m* **2** REFINEMENT : cultura *f,* educación *f,* refinamiento *m* **3** CIVILIZATION : cultura *f,* civilización *f* <the Incan culture : la cultura inca>
cultured ['kʌltʃərd] *adj* **1** EDUCATED, REFINED : culto, educado, refinado **2** : de cultivo, cultivado <cultured pearls : perlas de cultivo>
culvert ['kʌlvərt] *n* : alcantarilla *f*
cumbersome ['kʌmbərsəm] *adj* : torpe y pesado, difícil de manejar
cumulative ['kjuːmjələṭiv, -,leɪṭɪv] *adj* : acumulativo
cumulus ['kjuːmjələs] *n, pl* **-li** [-,laɪ, -,liː] : cúmulo *n*
cunning¹ ['kʌnɪŋ] *adj* **1** CRAFTY : astuto, taimado **2** CLEVER : ingenioso, hábil **3** CUTE : mono, gracioso, lindo
cunning² *n* **1** SKILL : habilidad *f* **2** CRAFTINESS : astucia *f,* maña *f*
cup¹ ['kʌp] *vt* **cupped; cupping** : ahuecar (las manos)
cup² *n* **1** : taza *f* <a cup of coffee : una taza de café> **2** CUPFUL : taza *f* **3** : media pinta *f* (unidad de medida) **4** GOBLET : copa *f* **5** TROPHY : copa *f,* trofeo *m*
cupboard ['kʌbərd] *n* : alacena *f,* armario *m*
cupcake ['kʌp,keɪk] *n* : pastelito *m*
cupful ['kʌp,fʊl] *n* : taza *f*
cupola ['kjuːpələ, -,loː] *n* : cúpula *f*
cur ['kər] *n* : perro *m* callejero, perro *m* corriente *Mex*
curate ['kjʊrət] *n* : cura *m,* párroco *m*
curator ['kjʊr,eɪṭər, kjʊ'reɪṭər] *n* : conservador *m,* -dora *f* (de un museo); director *m,* -tora *f* (de un zoológico)
curb¹ ['kərb] *vt* : refrenar, restringir, controlar
curb² *n* **1** RESTRAINT : freno *m,* control *m* **2** : borde *m* de la acera
curd ['kərd] *n* : cuajada *f*
curdle ['kərdəl] *v* **-dled; -dling** *vi* : cuajarse — *vt* : cuajar <to curdle one's blood : helarle la sangre a uno>
cure¹ ['kjʊr] *vt* **cured; curing 1** HEAL : curar, sanar **2** REMEDY : remediar **3** PROCESS : curar (alimentos, etc.)
cure² *n* **1** RECOVERY : curación *f,* recuperación *f* **2** REMEDY : cura *f,* remedio *m*
curfew ['kər,fjuː] *n* : toque *m* de queda
curio ['kjʊri,oː] *n, pl* **-rios** : curiosidad *f,* objeto *m* curioso
curiosity [,kjʊri'ɑsəṭi] *n, pl* **-ties** : curiosidad *f*
curious ['kjʊriəs] *adj* **1** INQUISITIVE : curioso **2** STRANGE : curioso, raro
curl¹ ['kərl] *vt* **1** : rizar, ondular (el pelo) **2** COIL : enrollar **3** TWIST : torcer <to curl one's lip : hacer una mueca> — *vi* **1** : rizarse, ondularse **2 to curl up** : acurrucarse (con un libro, etc.)
curl² *n* **1** RINGLET : rizo *m* **2** COIL : espiral *f,* rosca *f*
curler ['kərlər] *n* : rulo *m*
curlew ['kər,luː, 'kərl,juː] *n, pl* **-lews** *or* **-lew** : zarapito *m*
curly ['kərli] *adj* **curlier; -est** : rizado, crespo
currant ['kərənt] *n* **1** : grosella *f* (fruta) **2** RAISIN : pasa *f* de Corinto
currency ['kərəntsi] *n, pl* **-cies 1** PREVALENCE, USE : uso *m,* aceptación *f,* difusión *f* <to be in currency : estar en uso> **2** MONEY : moneda *f,* dinero *m*
current¹ ['kərənt] *adj* **1** PRESENT : actual <current events : actualidades> **2** PREVALENT : corriente, común — **currently** *adv*
current² *n* : corriente *f*
curriculum [kə'rɪkjələm] *n, pl* **-la** [-lə] : currículum *m,* currículo *m,* programa *m* de estudio
curriculum vitae ['viː,taɪ, 'vaɪṭi] *n, pl* **curricula vitae** : currículum *m,* currículo *m*
curry¹ ['kəri] *vt* **-ried; -rying 1** GROOM : almohazar (un caballo) **2** : condimentar con curry **3 to curry favor** : congraciarse (con alguien)
curry² *n, pl* **-ries** : curry *m*
curse¹ ['kərs] *v* **cursed; cursing** *vt* **1** DAMN : maldecir **2** INSULT : injuriar, insultar, decir malas palabras a **3** AFFLICT : afligir — *vi* : maldecir, decir malas palabras
curse² *n* **1** : maldición *f* <to put a curse on someone : echarle una maldición a alguien> **2** AFFLICTION : maldición *f,* aflicción *f,* cruz *f*
cursor ['kərsər] *n* : cursor *m*
cursory ['kərsəri] *adj* : rápido, superficial, somero
curt ['kərt] *adj* : cortante, brusco, seco — **curtly** *adv*
curtail [kər'teɪl] *vt* : acortar, limitar, restringir
curtailment [kər'teɪlmənt] *n* : restricción *f,* limitación *f*
curtain ['kərtən] *n* : cortina *f* (de una ventana), telón *m* (en un teatro)
curtness ['kərtnəs] *n* : brusquedad *f,* sequedad *f*

curtsy[1] *or* **curtsey** [ˈkərtsi] *vt* **-sied** *or* **-seyed; -sying** *or* **-seying :** hacer una reverencia
curtsy[2] *or* **curtsey** *n, pl* **-sies** *or* **-seys :** reverencia *f*
curvature [ˈkərvəˌtʃʊr] *n* **:** curvatura *f*
curve[1] [ˈkərv] *v* **curved; curving** *vi* **:** torcerse, describir una curva — *vt* **:** encorvar
curve[2] *n* **:** curva *f*
cushion[1] [ˈkʊʃən] *vt* **1 :** poner cojines o almohadones a **2** SOFTEN **:** amortiguar, mitigar, suavizar <to cushion a blow : amortiguar un golpe>
cushion[2] *n* **1 :** cojín *m,* almohadón *m* **2** PROTECTION **:** colchón *m,* protección *f*
cusp [ˈkʌsp] *n* **:** cúspide *f* (de un diente), cuerno *m* (de la luna)
cuspid [ˈkʌspɪd] *n* **:** diente *m* canino, colmillo *m*
custard [ˈkʌstərd] *n* **:** natillas *fpl*
custodian [ˌkʌˈstoːdiən] *n* **:** custodio *m,* -dia *f;* guardián, -diana *f*
custody [ˈkʌstədi] *n, pl* **-dies :** custodia *f,* cuidado *m* <to be in custody : estar detenido>
custom[1] [ˈkʌstəm] *adj* **:** a la medida, a la orden
custom[2] *n* **1 :** costumbre *f,* tradición *f* **2 customs** *npl* **:** aduana *f*
customarily [ˌkʌstəˈmɛrəli] *adv* **:** habitualmente, normalmente, de costumbre
customary [ˈkʌstəˌmɛri] *adj* **1** TRADITIONAL **:** tradicional **2** USUAL **:** habitual, de costumbre
customer [ˈkʌstəmər] *n* **:** cliente *m,* -ta *f*
custom–made [ˈkʌstəmˈmeɪd] *adj* **:** hecho a la medida
cut[1] [ˈkʌt] *v* **cut; cutting** *vt* **1 :** cortar <to cut paper : cortar papel> **2 :** cortarse <to cut one's finger : cortarse uno el dedo> **3** TRIM **:** cortar, recortar <to have one's hair cut : cortarse el pelo> **4** INTERSECT **:** cruzar, atravesar **5** SHORTEN **:** acortar, abreviar **6** REDUCE **:** reducir, rebajar <to cut prices : rebajar los precios> **7 to cut one's teeth :** salirle los dientes a uno — *vi* **1 :** cortar, cortarse **2 to cut in :** entrometerse
cut[2] *n* **1 :** corte *m* <a cut of meat : un corte de carne> **2** SLASH **:** tajo *m,* corte *m,* cortadura *f* **3** REDUCTION **:** rebaja *f,* reducción *f* <a cut in the rates : una rebaja en las tarifas>
cute [ˈkjuːt] *adj* **cuter; -est :** mono *fam,* lindo
cuticle [ˈkjuːtɪkəl] *n* **:** cutícula *f*
cutlass [ˈkʌtləs] *n* **:** alfanje *m*
cutlery [ˈkʌtləri] *n* **:** cubiertos *mpl*
cutlet [ˈkʌtlət] *n* **:** chuleta *f*
cutter [ˈkʌt̬ər] *n* **1 :** cortadora *f* (implemento) **2 :** cortador *m,* -dora *f* (persona) **3 :** cúter *m* (embarcación)
cutthroat [ˈkʌtˌθroːt] *adj* **:** despiadado, desalmado <cutthroat competition : competencia feroz>
cutting[1] [ˈkʌtɪŋ] *adj* **1 :** cortante <a cutting wind : un viento cortante> **2** CAUSTIC **:** mordaz
cutting[2] *n* **:** esqueje *m* (de una planta)
cuttlefish [ˈkʌt̬əlˌfɪʃ] *n, pl* **-fish** *or* **-fishes :** jibia *f,* sepia *f*
cyanide [ˈsaɪəˌnaɪd, -nɪd] *n* **:** cianuro *m*
cycle[1] [ˈsaɪkəl] *vi* **-cled; -cling :** andar en bicicleta, ir en bicicleta
cycle[2] *n* **1 :** ciclo *m* <life cycle : ciclo de vida, ciclo vital> **2** BICYCLE **:** bicicleta *f* **3** MOTORCYCLE **:** motocicleta *f*
cyclic [ˈsaɪklɪk, ˈsɪ-] *or* **cyclical** [-klɪkəl] *adj* **:** cíclico
cyclist [ˈsaɪklɪst] *n* **:** ciclista *mf*
cyclone [ˈsaɪˌkloːn] *n* **1 :** ciclón *m* **2** TORNADO **:** tornado *m*
cyclopedia *or* **cyclopaedia** [ˌsaɪkləˈpiːdiə] → **encyclopedia**
cylinder [ˈsɪləndər] *n* **:** cilindro *m*
cylindrical [səˈlɪndrɪkəl] *adj* **:** cilíndrico
cymbal [ˈsɪmbəl] *n* **:** platillo *m,* címbalo *m*
cynic [ˈsɪnɪk] *n* **:** cínico *m,* -ca *f*
cynical [ˈsɪnɪkəl] *adj* **:** cínico
cynicism [ˈsɪnəˌsɪzəm] *n* **:** cinismo *m*
cypress [ˈsaɪprəs] *n* **:** ciprés *m*
Cypriot [ˈsɪpriət, -ˌɑt] *n* **:** chipriota *mf* — **Cypriot** *adj*
cyst [ˈsɪst] *n* **:** quiste *m*
cytoplasm [ˈsaɪt̬oˌplæzəm] *n* **:** citoplasma *m*
czar [ˈzɑr, ˈsɑr] *n* **:** zar *m*
czarina [zɑˈriːnə, sɑ-] *n* **:** zarina *f*
Czech [ˈtʃɛk] *n* **1 :** checo *m,* -ca *f* **2 :** checo *m* (idioma) — **Czech** *adj*
Czechoslovak [ˌtʃɛkoˈsloːˌvɑk, -ˌvæk] *or* **Czechoslovakian** [-sloˈvɑkiən, -ˈvæ-] *n* **:** checoslovaco *m,* -ca *f* — **Czechoslovak** *or* **Czechoslovakian** *adj*

D

d [ˈdiː] *n, pl* **d's** *or* **ds** [ˈdiːz] **:** cuarta letra del alfabeto inglés
dab[1] [ˈdæb] *vt* **dabbed; dabbing :** darle toques ligeros a, aplicar suavemente
dab[2] *n* **1** BIT **:** toque *m,* pizca *f,* poco *m* <a dab of ointment : un toque de ungüento> **2** PAT **:** toque *m* ligero, golpecito *m*
dabble [ˈdæbəl] *v* **-bled; -bling** *vt* SPATTER **:** salpicar — *vi* **1** SPLASH **:** chapotear **2** TRIFLE **:** jugar, interesarse superficialmente

dabbler ['dæbələr] *n* : diletante *mf*
dachshund ['dɑks,hʊnt, -,hʊnd; 'dɑksənt, -sənd] *n* : perro *m* salchicha
dad ['dæd] *n* : papá *m fam*
daddy ['dædi] *n, pl* **-dies** : papi *m fam*
daffodil ['dæfə,dɪl] *n* : narciso *m*
daft ['dæft] *adj* : tonto, bobo
dagger ['dægər] *n* : daga *f,* puñal *m*
dahlia ['dæljə, 'dɑl-, 'deɪl-] *n* : dalia *f*
daily[1] ['deɪli] *adv* : a diario, diariamente
daily[2] *adj* : diario, cotidiano
daily[3] *n, pl* **-lies** : diario *m,* periódico *m*
daintily ['deɪntəli] *adv* : delicadamente, con delicadeza
daintiness ['deɪntinəs] *n* : delicadeza *f,* finura *f*
dainty[1] ['deɪnti] *adj* **-tier; -est 1** DELICATE : delicado **2** FASTIDIOUS : remilgado, melindroso **3** DELICIOUS : exquisito, sabroso
dainty[2] *n, pl* **-ties** DELICACY : exquisitez *f,* manjar *m*
dairy ['dæri] *n, pl* **-ies 1** *or* **dairy store** : lechería *f* **2** *or* **dairy farm** : granja *f* lechera
dairymaid ['dæri,meɪd] *n* : lechera *f*
dairyman ['dærimən, -,mæn] *n, pl* **-men** [-mən, -,mɛn] : lechero *m*
dais ['deɪəs] *n* : tarima *f,* estrado *m*
daisy ['deɪzi] *n, pl* **-sies** : margarita *f*
dale ['deɪl] *n* : valle *m*
dally ['dæli] *vi* **-lied; -lying 1** TRIFLE : juguetear **2** DAWDLE : entretenerse, perder tiempo
dalmatian [dæl'meɪʃən, dɔl-] *n* : dálmata *m*
dam[1] ['dæm] *vt* **dammed; damming** : represar, embalsar
dam[2] *n* **1** : represa *f,* dique *m* **2** : madre *f* (de animales domésticos)
damage[1] ['dæmɪdʒ] *vt* **-aged; -aging** : dañar (un objeto o una máquina), perjudicar (la salud o una reputación)
damage[2] *n* **1** : daño *m,* perjuicio *m* **2 damages** *npl* : daños y perjuicios *mpl*
damask ['dæmәsk] *n* : damasco *m*
dame ['deɪm] *n* LADY : dama *f,* señora *f*
damn[1] ['dæm] *vt* **1** CONDEMN : condenar **2** CURSE : maldecir
damn[2] *or* **damned** ['dæmd] *adj* : condenado *fam,* maldito *fam*
damn[3] *n* : pito *m,* bledo *m,* comino *m* <it's not worth a damn : no vale un pito> <I don't give a damn : me importa un comino>
damnable ['dæmnəbəl] *adj* : condenable, detestable
damnation [dæm'neɪʃən] *n* : condenación *f*
damned[1] ['dæmd] *adv* VERY : muy
damned[2] *adj* **1** → **damnable 2** REMARKABLE : extraordinario
damp[1] ['dæmp] *vt* → **dampen**
damp[2] *adj* : húmedo
damp[3] *n* MOISTURE : humedad *f*
dampen ['dæmpən] *vt* **1** MOISTEN : humedecer **2** DISCOURAGE : desalentar, desanimar
damper ['dæmpər] *n* **1** : regulador *m* de tiro (de una chimenea) **2** : sordina *f* (de un piano) **3 to put a damper on** : desanimar, apagar (el entusiasmo), enfriar
dampness ['dæmpnəs] *n* : humedad *f*
damsel ['dæmzəl] *n* : damisela *f*
dance[1] ['dænts] *v* **danced; dancing** : bailar
dance[2] *n* : baile *m*
dancer ['dæntsər] *n* : bailarín *m,* -rina *f*
dandelion ['dændəl,aɪən] *n* : diente *m* de león
dandruff ['dændrəf] *n* : caspa *f*
dandy[1] ['dændi] *adj* **-dier; -est** : excelente, magnífico, macanudo *fam*
dandy[2] *n, pl* **-dies 1** FOP : dandi *m* **2** : algo *m* excelente <this new program is a dandy : este programa nuevo es algo excelente>
Dane ['deɪn] *n* : danés *m,* -nesa *f*
Danish[1] ['deɪnɪʃ] *adj* : danés
Danish[2] *n* : danés *m* (idioma)
danger ['deɪndʒər] *n* : peligro *m*
dangerous ['deɪndʒərəs] *adj* : peligroso
dangle ['dæŋgəl] *v* **-gled; -gling** *vi* HANG : colgar, pender — *vt* **1** SWING : hacer oscilar **2** PROFFER : ofrecer (como incentivo) **3 to keep someone dangling** : dejar a alguien en suspenso
dank ['dæŋk] *adj* : frío y húmedo
dapper ['dæpər] *adj* : pulcro, atildado
dappled ['dæpəld] *adj* : moteado <a dappled horse : un caballo rodado>
dare[1] ['dær] *v* **dared; daring** *vi* : osar, atreverse <how dare you! : ¡cómo te atreves!> — *vt* **1** CHALLENGE : desafiar, retar **2 to dare to do something** : atreverse a hacer algo, osar hacer algo
dare[2] *n* : desafío *m,* reto *m*
daredevil ['dær,dɛvəl] *n* : persona *f* temeraria
daring[1] ['dærɪŋ] *adj* : osado, atrevido, audaz
daring[2] *n* : arrojo *m,* coraje *m,* audacia *f*
dark ['dɑrk] *adj* **1** : oscuro (dícese del ambiente o de los colores), moreno (dícese del pelo o de la piel) **2** SOMBER : sombrío, triste
darken ['dɑrkən] *vt* **1** DIM : oscurecer **2** SADDEN : entristecer — *vi* : ensombrecerse, nublarse
darkly ['dɑrkli] *adv* **1** DIMLY : oscuramente **2** GLOOMILY : tristemente **3** MYSTERIOUSLY : misteriosamente, enigmáticamente
darkness ['dɑrknəs] *n* : oscuridad *f,* tinieblas *f*
darling[1] ['dɑrlɪŋ] *adj* **1** BELOVED : querido, amado **2** CHARMING : encantador, mono *fam*

darling[2] *n* **1** BELOVED **:** querido *m,* -da *f;* amado *m,* -da *f;* cariño *m,* -ña *f* **2** FAVORITE **:** preferido *m,* -da *f;* favorito *m,* -ta *f*

darn[1] [ˈdɑrn] *vt* **:** zurcir

darn[2] *n* **1 :** zurcido *m* **2** → **damn**[3]

dart[1] [ˈdɑrt] *vt* THROW **:** lanzar, tirar — *vi* DASH **:** lanzarse, precipitarse

dart[2] *n* **1 :** dardo *m* **2 darts** *npl* **:** juego *m* de dardos

dash[1] [ˈdæʃ] *vt* **1** SMASH **:** romper, estrellar **2** HURL **:** arrojar, lanzar **3** SPLASH **:** salpicar **4** FRUSTRATE **:** frustrar **5 to dash off :** hacer (algo) rápidamente — *vi* **1** SMASH **:** romperse, estrellarse **2** DART **:** lanzarse, irse apresuradamente

dash[2] *n* **1** BURST, SPLASH **:** arranque *m,* salpicadura *f* (de aguas) **2 :** guión *m* largo (signo de puntuación) **3** DROP **:** gota *f,* pizca *f* **4** VERVE **:** brío *m* **5** RACE **:** carrera *f* <a 100-meter dash : una carrera de 100 metros> **6 to make a dash for it :** precipitarse (hacia), echarse a correr **7** → **dashboard**

dashboard [ˈdæʃˌbord] *n* **:** tablero *m* de instrumentos

dashing [ˈdæʃɪŋ] *adj* **:** gallardo, apuesto

data [ˈdeɪṭə, ˈdæ-, ˈdɑ-] *ns & pl* **:** datos *mpl,* información *f*

database [ˈdeɪṭəˌbeɪs, ˈdæ-, ˈdɑ-] *n* **:** base *f* de datos

date[1] [ˈdeɪt] *v* **dated; dating** *vt* **1 :** fechar (una carta, etc.), datar (un objeto) <it was dated June 9 : estaba fechada el 9 de junio> **2 :** salir con <she's dating my brother : sale con mi hermano> — *vi* **:** datar

date[2] *n* **1 :** fecha *f* <to date : hasta la fecha> **2** EPOCH, PERIOD **:** época *f,* período *m* **3** APPOINTMENT **:** cita *f* **4** COMPANION **:** acompañante *mf* **5 :** dátil *m* (fruta)

dated [ˈdeɪṭəd] *adj* OUT-OF-DATE **:** anticuado, pasado de moda

datum [ˈdeɪṭəm, ˈdæ-, ˈdɑ-] *n, pl* **-ta** [-ṭə] *or* **-tums :** dato *m*

daub[1] [ˈdɔb] *vt* **:** embadurnar

daub[2] *n* **:** mancha *f*

daughter [ˈdɔṭər] *n* **:** hija *f*

daughter–in–law [ˈdɔṭərɪnˌlɔ] *n, pl* **daughters–in–law :** nuera *f,* hija *f* política

daunt [ˈdɔnt] *vt* **:** amilanar, acobardar, intimidar

dauntless [ˈdɔntləs] *adj* **:** intrépido, impávido

davenport [ˈdævənˌport] *n* **:** sofá *m*

dawdle [ˈdɔdəl] *vi* **-dled; -dling 1** DALLY **:** demorarse, entretenerse, perder tiempo **2** LOITER **:** vagar, holgazanear, haraganear

dawn[1] [ˈdɔn] *vi* **1 :** amanecer, alborear, despuntar <Saturday dawned clear and bright : el sábado amaneció claro y luminoso> **2 to dawn on :** hacerse obvio <it dawned on me that she was right : me di cuenta de que tenía razón>

dawn[2] *n* **1** DAYBREAK **:** amanecer *m,* alba *f* **2** BEGINNING **:** albor *m,* comienzo *m* <the dawn of history : los albores de la historia> **3 from dawn to dusk :** de sol a sol

day [ˈdeɪ] *n* **1 :** día *m* **2** DATE **:** fecha *f* **3** TIME **:** día *m,* tiempo *m* <in olden days : antaño> **4** WORKDAY **:** jornada *f* laboral

daybreak [ˈdeɪˌbreɪk] *n* **:** alba *f,* amanecer *m*

day care *n* **:** servicio *m* de guardería infantil

daydream[1] [ˈdeɪˌdriːm] *vi* **:** soñar despierto, fantasear

daydream[2] *n* **:** ensueño *m,* ensoñación *f,* fantasía *f*

daylight [ˈdeɪˌlaɪt] *n* **1 :** luz *f* del día <in broad daylight : a plena luz del día> **2** → **daybreak 3** → **daytime**

daylight saving time *n* **:** hora *f* de verano

daytime [ˈdeɪˌtaɪm] *n* **:** horas *fpl* diurnas, día *m*

daze[1] [ˈdeɪz] *vt* **dazed; dazing 1** STUN **:** aturdir **2** DAZZLE **:** deslumbrar, ofuscar

daze[2] *n* **1 :** aturdimiento *m* **2 in a daze :** aturdido, atonado

dazzle[1] [ˈdæzəl] *vt* **-zled; -zling :** deslumbrar, ofuscar

dazzle[2] *n* **:** resplandor *m,* brillo *m*

DDT [ˌdiːˌdiːˈtiː] *n* **:** DDT *m*

deacon [ˈdiːkən] *n* **:** diácono *m*

dead[1] [ˈdɛd] *adv* **1** ABRUPTLY **:** repentinamente, súbitamente <to stop dead : parar en seco> **2** ABSOLUTELY **:** absolutamente <I'm dead certain : estoy absolutamente seguro> **3** DIRECTLY **:** justo <dead ahead : justo adelante>

dead[2] *adj* **1** LIFELESS **:** muerto **2** NUMB **:** entumecido **3** INDIFFERENT **:** indiferente, frío **4** INACTIVE **:** inactivo <a dead volcano : un volcán inactivo> **5 :** desconectado (dícese del teléfono), descargado (dícese de una batería) **6** EXHAUSTED **:** agotado, derrengado, muerto **7** OBSOLETE **:** obsoleto, muerto <a dead language : una lengua muerta> **8** EXACT **:** exacto <in the dead center : justo en el blanco>

dead[3] *n* **1 the dead :** los muertos **2 in the dead of night :** a las altas horas de la noche **3 in the dead of winter :** en pleno invierno

deadbeat [ˈdɛdˌbiːt] *n* **1** LOAFER **:** vago *m,* -ga *f;* holgazán *m,* -zana *f* **2** FREELOADER **:** gorrón *m,* -rrona *f fam;* gorrero *m,* -ra *f fam*

deaden [ˈdɛdən] *vt* **1 :** atenuar (un dolor), entorpecer (sensaciones) **2** DULL **:** deslustrar **3** DISPIRIT **:** desanimar **4** MUFFLE **:** amortiguar, reducir (sonidos)

dead–end [ˈdɛdˈɛnd] *adj* **1 :** sin salida <dead-end street : calle sin salida> **2 :** sin futuro <a dead-end job : un trabajo sin porvenir>

dead end *n* **:** callejón *m* sin salida

dead heat *n* : empate *m*

deadline [ˈdɛd,laɪn] *n* : fecha *f* límite, fecha *f* tope, plazo *m* (determinado)

deadlock[1] [ˈdɛd,lɑk] *vt* : estancar — *vi* : estancarse, llegar a punto muerto

deadlock[2] *n* : punto *m* muerto, impasse *m*

deadly[1] [ˈdɛdli] *adv* : extremadamente, sumamente <deadly serious : muy en serio>

deadly[2] *adj* **-lier; -est 1** LETHAL : mortal, letal, mortífero **2** ACCURATE : certero, preciso <a deadly aim : una puntería infalible> **3** CAPITAL : capital <the seven deadly sins : los siete pecados capitales> **4** DULL : funesto, aburrido **5** EXTREME : extremo, absoluto <a deadly calm : una calma absoluta>

deadpan[1] [ˈdɛd,pæn] *adv* : de manera inexpresiva, sin expresión

deadpan[2] *adj* : inexpresivo, impasible

deaf [ˈdɛf] *adj* : sordo

deafen [ˈdɛfən] *vt* **-ened; -ening** : ensordecer

deaf–mute [ˈdɛfˈmjuːt] *n* : sordomudo *m*, -da *f*

deafness [ˈdɛfnəs] *n* : sordera *f*

deal[1] [ˈdiːl] *v* **dealt; dealing** *vt* **1** APPORTION : repartir <to deal justice : repartir la justicia> **2** DISTRIBUTE : repartir, dar (naipes) **3** DELIVER : asestar, propinar <to deal a blow : asestar un golpe> — *vi* **1** : dar, repartir (en juegos de naipes) **2 to deal in** : comerciar en, traficar con (drogas) **3 to deal with** CONCERN : tratar de, tener que ver con <the book deals with poverty : el libro trata de la pobreza> **4 to deal with** HANDLE : tratar (con), encargarse de **5 to deal with** TREAT : tratar <the judge dealt with him severely : el juez lo trató con severidad> **6 to deal with** ACCEPT : aceptar (una situación o desgracia)

deal[2] *n* **1** : reparto *m* (de naipes) **2** AGREEMENT, TRANSACTION : trato *m*, acuerdo *m*, transacción *f* **3** TREATMENT : trato *m* <he got a raw deal : le hicieron una injusticia> **4** BARGAIN : ganga *f*, oferta *f* **5 a good deal** *or* **a great deal** : mucho, una gran cantidad

dealer [ˈdiːlər] *n* : comerciante *mf*, traficante *mf*

dealings [ˈdiːlɪŋz] *npl* **1** : relaciones *fpl* (personales) **2** TRANSACTIONS : negocios *mpl*, transacciones *fpl*

dean [ˈdiːn] *n* **1** : deán *m* (del clero) **2** : decano *m*, -na *f* (de una facultad o profesión)

dear[1] [ˈdɪr] *adj* **1** ESTEEMED, LOVED : querido, estimado <a dear friend : un amigo querido> <Dear Sir : Estimado Señor> **2** COSTLY : caro, costoso

dear[2] *n* : querido *m*, -da *f*; amado *m*, -da *f*

dearly [ˈdɪrli] *adv* **1** : mucho <I love them dearly : los quiero mucho> **2** : caro <to pay dearly : pagar caro>

dearth [ˈdərθ] *n* : escasez *f*, carestía *f*

death [ˈdɛθ] *n* **1** : muerte *f*, fallecimiento *m* <to be the death of : matar> **2** FATALITY : víctima *f* (mortal); muerto *m*, -ta *f* **3** END : fin *m* <the death of civilization : el fin de la civilización>

deathbed [ˈdɛθ,bɛd] *n* : lecho *m* de muerte

deathblow [ˈdɛθ,bloː] *n* : golpe *m* mortal

deathless [ˈdɛθləs] *adj* : eterno, inmortal

deathly [ˈdɛθli] *adj* : de muerte, sepulcral (dícese del silencio), cadavérico (dícese de la palidez)

debacle [dɪˈbɑkəl, -ˈbæ-] *n* : desastre *m*, debacle *m*, fiasco *m*

debar [diˈbɑr] *vt* **-barred; -barring** : excluir, prohibir

debase [diˈbeɪs] *vt* **-based; -basing** : degradar, envilecer

debasement [diˈbeɪsmənt] *n* : degradación *f*, envilecimiento *m*

debatable [diˈbeɪt̬əbəl] *adj* : discutible

debate[1] [diˈbeɪt] *vt* **-bated; -bating** : debatir, discutir

debate[2] *n* : debate *m*, discusión *f*

debauch [diˈbɔtʃ] *vt* : pervertir, corromper

debauchery [diˈbɔtʃəri] *n, pl* **-eries** : libertinaje *m*, disipación *f*, intemperancia *f*

debilitate [diˈbɪlə,teɪt] *vt* **-tated; -tating** : debilitar

debility [diˈbɪlət̬i] *n, pl* **-ties** : debilidad *f*

debit[1] [ˈdɛbɪt] *vt* : adeudar, cargar, debitar

debit[2] *n* : débito *m*, cargo *m*, debe *m*

debonair [,dɛbəˈnær] *adj* : elegante y desenvuelto, apuesto

debris [dəˈbriː, deɪ-; ˈdeɪ,briː] *n, pl* **-bris** [-ˈbriːz, -,briːz] **1** RUBBLE, RUINS : escombros *mpl*, ruinas *fpl*, restos *mpl* **2** RUBBISH : basura *f*, deshechos *mpl*

debt [ˈdɛt] *n* **1** : deuda *f* <to pay a debt : saldar una deuda> **2** INDEBTEDNESS : endeudamiento *m*

debtor [ˈdɛt̬ər] *n* : deudor *m*, -dora *f*

debunk [diˈbʌŋk] *vt* DISCREDIT : desacreditar, desprestigiar

debut[1] [deɪˈbjuː, ˈdeɪ,bjuː] *vi* : debutar

debut[2] *n* **1** : debut *m* (de un actor), estreno *m* (de una obra) **2** : debut *m*, presentación *f* (en sociedad)

debutante [ˈdɛbjʊ,tɑnt] *n* : debutante *f*

decade [ˈdɛ,keɪd, dɛˈkeɪd] *n* : década *f*

decadence [ˈdɛkədənts] *n* : decadencia *f*

decadent [ˈdɛkədənt] *adj* : decadente

decal [ˈdiː,kæl, diˈkæl] *n* : calcomanía *f*

decamp [di'kæmp] *vi* : irse, largarse *fam*

decant [di'kænt] *vt* : decantar

decanter [di'kæntər] *n* : licorera *f,* garrafa *f*

decapitate [di'kæpə,teɪt] *vt* **-tated; -tating** : decapitar

decay[1] [di'keɪ] *vi* **1** DECOMPOSE : descomponerse, pudrirse **2** DETERIORATE : deteriorarse **3** : cariarse (dícese de los dientes)

decay[2] *n* **1** DECOMPOSITION : descomposición *f* **2** DECLINE, DETERIORATION : decadencia *f,* deterioro *m* **3** : caries *f* (de los dientes)

decease[1] [di'siːs] *vi* **-ceased; -ceasing** : morir, fallecer

decease[2] *n* : fallecimiento *m,* defunción *f,* deceso *m*

deceit [di'siːt] *n* **1** DECEPTION : engaño *m* **2** DISHONESTY : deshonestidad *f*

deceitful [di'siːtfəl] *adj* : falso, embustero, engañoso, mentiroso

deceitfully [di'siːtfəli] *adv* : con engaño, con falsedad

deceitfulness [di'siːtfəlnəs] *n* : falsedad *f,* engaño *m*

deceive [di'siːv] *vt* **-ceived; -ceiving** : engañar, burlar

deceiver [di'siːvər] *n* : impostor *m,* -tora *f*

decelerate [di'sɛlə,reɪt] *vi* **-ated; -ating** : reducir la velocidad, desacelerar

December [di'sɛmbər] *n* : diciembre *m*

decency ['disəntsi] *n, pl* **-cies** : decencia *f,* decoro *m*

decent ['diːsənt] *adj* **1** CORRECT, PROPER : decente, decoroso, correcto **2** CLOTHED : vestido, presentable **3** MODEST : púdico, modesto **4** ADEQUATE : decente, adecuado <decent wages : paga adecuada>

decently ['diːsəntli] *adv* : decentemente

deception [di'sɛpʃən] *n* : engaño *m*

deceptive [di'sɛptɪv] *adj* : engañoso, falaz — **deceptively** *adv*

decibel ['dɛsəbəl, -,bɛl] *n* : decibelio *m*

decide [di'saɪd] *v* **-cided; -ciding** *vt* **1** CONCLUDE : decidir, llegar a la conclusión de <he decided what to do : decidió qué iba a hacer> **2** DETERMINE : decidir, determinar <one blow decided the fight : un solo golpe determinó la pelea> **3** CONVINCE : decidir <her pleas decided me to help : sus súplicas me decidieron a ayudarla> **4** RESOLVE : resolver — *vi* : decidirse

decided [di'saɪdəd] *adj* **1** UNQUESTIONABLE : indudable **2** RESOLUTE : decidido, resuelto — **decidedly** *adv*

deciduous [di'sɪdʒʊəs] *adj* : caduco, de hoja caduca

decimal[1] ['dɛsəməl] *adj* : decimal

decimal[2] *n* : número *m* decimal

decipher [di'saɪfər] *vt* : descifrar — **decipherable** [-əbəl] *adj*

decision [dɪ'sɪʒən] *n* : decisión *f,* determinación *f* <to make a decision : tomar una decisión>

decisive [dɪ'saɪsɪv] *adj* **1** DECIDING : decisivo <the decisive vote : el voto decisivo> **2** CONCLUSIVE : decisivo, concluyente, contundente <a decisive victory : una victoria contundente> **3** RESOLUTE : decidido, resuelto, firme

decisively [dɪ'saɪsɪvli] *adv* : con decisión, de manera decisiva

decisiveness [dɪ'saɪsɪvnəs] *n* **1** FORCEFULNESS : contundencia *f* **2** RESOLUTION : firmeza *f,* decisión *f,* determinación *f*

deck[1] ['dɛk] *vt* **1** FLOOR : tumbar, derribar <she decked him with one blow : lo tumbó de un solo golpe> **2 to deck out** : adornar, engalanar

deck[2] *n* **1** : cubierta *f* (de un barco) **2** *or* **deck of cards** : baraja *f* (de naipes)

declaim [di'kleɪm] *v* : declamar

declaration [,dɛklə'reɪʃən] *n* : declaración *f,* pronunciamiento *m* (oficial)

declare [di'klær] *vt* **-clared; -claring** : declarar, manifestar <to declare war : declarar la guerra> <they declared their support : manifestaron su apoyo>

decline[1] [di'klaɪn] *v* **-clined; -clining** *vi* **1** DESCEND : descender **2** DETERIORATE : deteriorarse, decaer <her health is declining : su salud se está deteriorando> **3** DECREASE : disminuir, decrecer, decaer **4** REFUSE : rehusar — *vt* **1** INFLECT : declinar **2** REFUSE, TURN DOWN : declinar, rehusar

decline[2] *n* **1** DETERIORATION : decadencia *f,* deterioro *m* **2** DECREASE : disminución *f,* descenso *m* **3** SLOPE : declive *m,* pendiente *f*

decode [di'koːd] *vt* **-coded; -coding** : descifrar (un mensaje), descodificar (una señal)

decompose [,diːkəm'poːz] *v* **-posed; -posing** *vt* **1** BREAK DOWN : descomponer **2** ROT : descomponer, pudrir — *vi* : descomponerse, pudrirse

decomposition [,diː,kɑmpə'zɪʃən] *n* : descomposición *f*

decongestant [,diːkən'dʒɛstənt] *n* : descongestionante *m*

decor *or* **décor** [deɪ'kɔr, 'deɪ,kɔr] *n* : decoración *f*

decorate ['dɛkə,reɪt] *vt* **-rated; -rating 1** ADORN : decorar, adornar **2** : condecorar <he was decorated for bravery : lo condecoraron por valor>

decoration [,dɛkə'reɪʃən] *n* **1** ADORNMENT : decoración *f,* adorno *m* **2** : condecoración *f* (de honor)

decorative ['dɛkərət̬ɪv, -,reɪ-] *adj* : decorativo, ornamental, de adorno

decorator ['dɛkə,reɪt̬ər] *n* : decorador *m,* -dora *f*

decorum [di'korəm] *n* : decoro *m*

decoy[1] [ˈdiːˌkɔɪ, diˈ-] *vt* : atraer (con señuelo)

decoy[2] *n* : señuelo *m*, reclamo *m*, cimbel *m*

decrease[1] [diˈkriːs] *v* **-creased; -creasing** *vi* : decrecer, disminuir, bajar — *vt* : reducir, disminuir

decrease[2] [ˈdiːˌkriːs] *n* : disminución *f*, descenso *m*, bajada *f*

decree[1] [diˈkriː] *vt* **-creed; -creeing** : decretar

decree[2] *n* : decreto *m*

decrepit [diˈkrɛpɪt] *adj* **1** FEEBLE : decrépito, débil **2** DILAPIDATED : deteriorado, ruinoso

decry [diˈkraɪ] *vt* **-cried; -crying** : censurar, criticar

dedicate [ˈdɛdɪˌkeɪt] *vt* **-cated; -cating** **1** : dedicar <she dedicated the book to Carlos : le dedicó el libro a Carlos> **2** : consagrar, dedicar <to dedicate one's life : consagrar uno su vida>

dedication [ˌdɛdɪˈkeɪʃən] *n* **1** DEVOTION : dedicación *f*, devoción *f* **2** : dedicatoria *f* (de un libro, una canción, etc.) **3** CONSECRATION : dedicación *f*

deduce [diˈduːs, -ˈdjuːs] *vt* **-duced; -ducing** : deducir, inferir

deduct [diˈdʌkt] *vt* : deducir, descontar, restar

deductible [diˈdʌktəbəl] *adj* : deducible

deduction [diˈdʌkʃən] *n* : deducción *f*

deed[1] [ˈdiːd] *vt* : ceder, transferir

deed[2] *n* **1** ACT : acto *m*, acción *f*, hecho *m* <a good deed : una buena acción> **2** FEAT : hazaña *f*, proeza *f* **3** TITLE : escritura *f*, título *m*

deem [ˈdiːm] *vt* : considerar, juzgar

deep[1] [ˈdiːp] *adv* : hondo, profundamente <to dig deep : cavar hondo>

deep[2] *adj* **1** : hondo, profundo <the deep end : la parte honda> <a deep wound : una herida profunda> **2** WIDE : ancho **3** INTENSE : profundo, intenso **4** DARK : intenso, subido <deep red : rojo subido> **5** LOW : profundo <a deep tone : un tono profundo> **6** ABSORBED : absorto <deep in thought : absorto en la meditación>

deep[3] *n* **1 the deep** : lo profundo, el piélago **2 the deep of night** : lo más profundo de la noche

deepen [ˈdiːpən] *vt* **1** : ahondar, profundizar **2** INTENSIFY : intensificar — *vi* **1** : hacerse más profundo **2** INTENSIFY : intensificarse

deeply [ˈdiːpli] *adv* : hondo, profundamente <I'm deeply sorry : lo siento sinceramente>

deep–seated [ˈdiːpˈsiːtəd] *adj* : profundamente arraigado, enraizado

deer [ˈdɪr] *ns & pl* : ciervo *m*, venado *m*

deerskin [ˈdɪrˌskɪn] *n* : piel *f* de venado

deface [diˈfeɪs] *vt* **-faced; -facing** MAR : desfigurar

defacement [diˈfeɪsmənt] *n* : desfiguración *f*

defamation [ˌdɛfəˈmeɪʃən] *n* : difamación *f*

defamatory [diˈfæməˌtori] *adj* : difamatorio

defame [diˈfeɪm] *vt* **-famed; -faming** : difamar, calumniar

default[1] [diˈfɔlt, ˈdiːˌfɔlt] *vi* **1** : no cumplir (con una obligación), no pagar **2** : no presentarse (en un tribunal)

default[2] *n* **1** NEGLECT : omisión *f*, negligencia *f* **2** NONPAYMENT : impago *m*, falta *f* de pago **3 to win by default** : ganar por abandono

defaulter [diˈfɔltər] *n* : moroso *m*, -sa *f*; rebelde *mf* (en un tribunal)

defeat[1] [diˈfiːt] *vt* **1** FRUSTRATE : frustrar **2** BEAT : vencer, derrotar

defeat[2] *n* : derrota *f*, rechazo *m* (de legislación), fracaso *m* (de planes, etc.)

defecate [ˈdɛfɪˌkeɪt] *vi* **-cated; -cating** : defecar

defect[1] [diˈfɛkt] *vi* : desertar

defect[2] [ˈdiːˌfɛkt, diˈfɛkt] *n* : defecto *m*

defection [diˈfɛkʃən] *n* : deserción *f*, defección *f*

defective [diˈfɛktɪv] *adj* **1** FAULTY : defectuoso **2** DEFICIENT : deficiente

defector [diˈfɛktər] *n* : desertor *m*, -tora *f*

defend [diˈfɛnd] *vt* : defender

defendant [diˈfɛndənt] *n* : acusado *m*, -da *f*; demandado *m*, -da *f*

defender [diˈfɛndər] *n* **1** ADVOCATE : defensor *m*, -sora *f* **2** : defensa *mf* (en deportes)

defense [diˈfɛnts, ˈdiːˌfɛnts] *n* : defensa *f*

defenseless [diˈfɛntsləs] *adj* : indefenso

defensive[1] [diˈfɛntsɪv] *adj* : defensivo

defensive[2] *n* **on the defensive** : a la defensiva

defer [diˈfər] *v* **-ferred; -ferring** *vt* POSTPONE : diferir, aplazar, posponer — *vi* **to defer to** : deferir a

deference [ˈdɛfərənts] *n* : deferencia *f*

deferential [ˌdɛfəˈrɛntʃəl] *adj* : respetuoso

deferment [diˈfərmənt] *n* : aplazamiento *m*

defiance [diˈfaɪənts] *n* : desafío *m*

defiant [diˈfaɪənt] *adj* : desafiante, insolente

deficiency [diˈfɪʃəntsi] *n, pl* **-cies** : deficiencia *f*, carencia *f*

deficient [diˈfɪʃənt] *adj* : deficiente, carente

deficit [ˈdɛfəsɪt] *n* : déficit *m*

defile [diˈfaɪl] *vt* **-filed; -filing** **1** DIRTY : ensuciar, manchar **2** CORRUPT : corromper **3** DESECRATE, PROFANE : profanar **4** DISHONOR : deshonrar

defilement [diˈfaɪlmənt] *n* **1** DESECRATION : profanación *f* **2** CORRUPTION

: corrupción *f* **3** CONTAMINATION : contaminación *f*

define [di'faɪn] *vt* **-fined; -fining 1** BOUND : delimitar, demarcar **2** CLARIFY : aclarar, definir **3** : definir <to define a word : definir una palabra>

definite ['dɛfənɪt] *adj* **1** CERTAIN : definido, determinado **2** CLEAR : claro, explícito **3** UNQUESTIONABLE : seguro, incuestionable

definite article *n* : artículo *m* definido

definitely ['dɛfənɪtli] *adv* **1** DOUBTLESSLY : indudablemente, sin duda **2** DEFINITIVELY : definitivamente, seguramente

definition [ˌdɛfə'nɪʃən] *n* : definición *f*

definitive [di'fɪnət̬ɪv] *adj* **1** CONCLUSIVE : definitivo, decisivo **2** AUTHORITATIVE : de autoridad, autorizado

deflate [di'fleɪt] *v* **-flated; -flating** *vt* **1** : desinflar (una llanta, etc.) **2** REDUCE : rebajar <to deflate one's ego : bajarle los humos a uno> — *vi* : desinflarse

deflect [di'flɛkt] *vt* : desviar — *vi* : desviarse

defoliant [di'foːliənt] *n* : defoliante *m*

deform [di'fɔrm] *vt* : deformar

deformed [di'fɔrmd] *adj* : deforme

deformity [di'fɔrmət̬i] *n, pl* **-ties** : deformidad *f*

defraud [di'frɔd] *vt* : estafar, defraudar

defray [di'freɪ] *vt* : sufragar, costear

defrost [di'frɔst] *vt* : descongelar, deshelar — *vi* : descongelarse, deshelarse

deft ['dɛft] *adj* : hábil, diestro — **deftly** *adv*

defunct [di'fʌŋkt] *adj* **1** DECEASED : difunto, fallecido **2** EXTINCT : extinto, fenecido

defy [di'faɪ] *vt* **-fied; -fying 1** CHALLENGE : desafiar, retar **2** DISOBEY : desobedecer **3** RESIST : resistir, hacer imposible, hacer inútil

degenerate[1] [di'dʒɛnəˌreɪt] *vi* **-ated; -ating** : degenerar

degenerate[2] [di'dʒɛnərət] *adj* : degenerado

degeneration [diˌdʒɛnə'reɪʃən] *n* : degeneración *f*

degradation [ˌdɛgrə'deɪʃən] *n* : degradación *f*

degrade [di'greɪd] *vt* **-graded; -grading 1** : degradar, envilecer **2 to degrade oneself** : rebajarse

degree [di'griː] *n* **1** EXTENT : grado *m* <a third degree burn : una quemadura de tercer grado> **2** : título *m* (de enseñanza superior) **3** : grado *m* (de un círculo, de la temperatura) **4 by degrees** : gradualmente, poco a poco

dehydrate [di'haɪˌdreɪt] *v* **-drated; -drating** *vt* : deshidratar — *vi* : deshidratarse

dehydration [ˌdiːhaɪ'dreɪʃən] *n* : deshidratación *f*

deice [ˌdiː'aɪs] *vt* **-iced; -icing** : deshelar, descongelar

deify ['diːəˌfaɪ, 'deɪ-] *vt* **-fied; -fying** : deificar

deign ['deɪn] *vi* : dignarse, condescender

deity ['diːət̬i, 'deɪ-] *n, pl* **-ties 1 the Deity** : Dios *m* **2** GOD, GODDESS : deidad *f;* dios *m,* diosa *f*

dejected [di'dʒɛktəd] *adj* : abatido, desalentado, desanimado

dejection [di'dʒɛkʃən] *n* : abatimiento *m,* desaliento *m,* desánimo *m*

delay[1] [di'leɪ] *vt* **1** POSTPONE : posponer, postergar **2** HOLD UP : retrasar, demorar — *vi* : tardar, demorar

delay[2] *n* **1** LATENESS : tardanza *f* **2** HOLDUP : demora *f,* retraso *m*

delectable [di'lɛktəbəl] *adj* **1** DELICIOUS : delicioso, exquisito **2** DELIGHTFUL : encantador

delegate[1] ['dɛlɪˌgeɪt] *v* **-gated; -gating** : delegar

delegate[2] ['dɛlɪgət, -ˌgeɪt] *n* : delegado *m,* -da *f*

delegation [ˌdɛlɪ'geɪʃən] *n* : delegación *f*

delete [di'liːt] *vt* **-leted; -leting** : suprimir, tachar, eliminar

deletion [di'liːʃən] *n* : supresión *f,* tachadura *f,* eliminación *f*

deliberate[1] [dɪ'lɪbəˌreɪt] *v* **-ated; -ating** *vt* : deliberar sobre, reflexionar sobre, considerar — *vi* : deliberar

deliberate[2] [dɪ'lɪbərət] *adj* **1** CONSIDERED : reflexionado, premeditado **2** INTENTIONAL : deliberado, intencional **3** SLOW : lento, pausado

deliberately [dɪ'lɪbərətli] *adv* **1** INTENTIONALLY : adrede, a propósito **2** SLOWLY : pausadamente, lentamente

deliberation [dɪˌlɪbə'reɪʃən] *n* **1** CONSIDERATION : deliberación *f,* consideración *f* **2** SLOWNESS : lentitud *f*

delicacy ['dɛlɪkəsi] *n, pl* **-cies 1** : manjar *m,* exquisitez *f* <caviar is a real delicacy : el caviar es un verdadero manjar> **2** FINENESS : delicadeza *f* **3** FRAGILITY : fragilidad *f*

delicate ['dɛlɪkət] *adj* **1** SUBTLE : delicado <a delicate fragrance : una fragancia delicada> **2** DAINTY : delicado, primoroso, fino **3** FRAGILE : frágil **4** SENSITIVE : delicado <a delicate matter : un asunto delicado>

delicately ['dɛlɪkətli] *adv* : delicadamente, con delicadeza

delicatessen [ˌdɛlɪkə'tɛsən] *n* : charcutería *f,* fiambrería *f,* salchichonería *f Mex*

delicious [di'lɪʃəs] *adj* : delicioso, exquisito, rico — **deliciously** *adv*

delight[1] [dɪ'laɪt] *vt* : deleitar, encantar — *vi* **to delight in** : deleitarse con, complacerse en

delight[2] *n* **1** JOY : placer *m,* deleite *m,* gozo *m* **2** : encanto *m* <your garden is a delight : su jardín es un encanto>

delightful [dɪˈlaɪtfəl] *adj* : delicioso, encantador
delightfully [dɪˈlaɪtfəli] *adv* : de manera encantadora, de maravilla
delineate [diˈlɪni,eɪt] *vt* **-eated; -eating** : delinear, trazar, bosquejar
delinquency [diˈlɪŋkwən*t*si] *n, pl* **-cies** : delincuencia *f*
delinquent[1] [diˈlɪŋkwənt] *adj* **1** : delincuente **2** OVERDUE : vencido y sin pagar, moroso
delinquent[2] *n* : delincuente *mf* <juvenile delinquent : delincuente juvenil>
delirious [diˈlɪriəs] *adj* : delirante <delirious with joy : loco de alegría>
delirium [diˈlɪriəm] *n* : delirio *m,* desvarío *m*
deliver [diˈlɪvər] *vt* **1** FREE : liberar, librar **2** DISTRIBUTE, HAND : entregar, repartir **3** : asistir en el parto de (un niño) **4** : pronunciar <to deliver a speech : pronunciar un discurso> **5** PROJECT : despachar, lanzar <he delivered a fast ball : lanzó un pelota rápida> **6** DEAL : propinar, asestar <to deliver a blow : asestar un golpe>
deliverance [diˈlɪvərən*t*s] *n* : liberación *f,* rescate *m,* salvación *f*
deliverer [diˈlɪvərər] *n* RESCUER : libertador *m,* -dora *f;* salvador *m,* -dora *f*
delivery [diˈlɪvəri] *n, pl* **-eries 1** LIBERATION : liberación *f* **2** : entrega *f,* reparto *m* <cash on delivery : entrega contra reembolso> <home delivery : servicio a domicilio> **3** CHILDBIRTH : parto *m,* alumbramiento *m* **4** SPEECH : expresión *f* oral, modo *m* de hablar **5** THROW : lanzamiento *m*
dell [ˈdɛl] *n* : hondonada *f,* valle *m* pequeño
delta [ˈdɛltə] *n* : delta *m*
delude [diˈluːd] *vt* **-luded; -luding 1** : engañar **2 to delude oneself** : engañarse
deluge[1] [ˈdɛl,juːdʒ, -,juːʒ] *vt* **-uged; -uging 1** FLOOD : inundar **2** OVERWHELM : abrumar <deluged with requests : abrumado de pedidos>
deluge[2] *n* **1** FLOOD : inundación *f* **2** DOWNPOUR : aguacero *m* **3** BARRAGE : aluvión *m*
delusion [diˈluːʒən] *n* **1** : ilusión *f* (falsa) **2 delusions of grandeur** : delirios *mpl* de grandeza
deluxe [diˈlʌks, -ˈlʊks] *adj* : de lujo
delve [ˈdɛlv] *vi* **delved; delving 1** DIG : escarbar **2 to delve into** PROBE : cavar en, ahondar en
demand[1] [diˈmænd] *vt* : demandar, exigir, reclamar
demand[2] *n* **1** REQUEST : petición *f,* pedido *m,* demanda *f* <by popular demand : a petición del público> **2** CLAIM : reclamación *f,* exigencia *f* **3** MARKET : demanda *f* <supply and demand : la oferta y la demanda>
demarcation [,diː,mɑrˈkeɪʃən] *n* : demarcación *f,* deslinde *m*
demean [diˈmiːn] *vt* : degradar, rebajar
demeanor [diˈmiːnər] *n* : comportamiento *m,* conducta *f*
demented [diˈmɛntəd] *adj* : demente, loco
demerit [diˈmɛrət] *n* : demérito *m*
demigod [ˈdɛmi,gɑd, -,gɔd] *n* : semidiós *m*
demise [dɪˈmaɪz] *n* **1** DEATH : fallecimiento *m,* deceso *m* **2** END : hundimiento *m,* desaparición *f* (de una institución, etc.)
demitasse [ˈdɛmi,tæs, -,tɑs] *n* : taza *f* pequeña (de café)
demobilization [di,moːbələˈzeɪʃən] *n* : desmovilización *f*
demobilize [diˈmoːbə,laɪz] *vt* **-lized; -lizing** : desmovilizar
democracy [diˈmɑkrəsi] *n, pl* **-cies** : democracia *f*
democrat [ˈdɛmə,kræt] *n* : demócrata *mf*
democratic [,dɛməˈkræt̬ɪk] *adj* : democrático — **democratically** [-t̬ɪkli] *adv*
demolish [diˈmɑlɪʃ] *vt* **1** RAZE : demoler, derribar, arrasar **2** DESTROY : destruir, destrozar
demolition [,dɛməˈlɪʃən, ,diː-] *n* : demolición *f,* derribo *m*
demon [ˈdiːmən] *n* : demonio *m,* diablo *m*
demonstrably [diˈmɑn*t*strəbli] *adv* : manifiestamente, claramente
demonstrate [ˈdɛmən,streɪt] *vt* **-strated; -strating 1** SHOW : demostrar **2** PROVE : probar, demostrar **3** EXPLAIN : explicar, ilustrar
demonstration [,dɛmənˈstreɪʃən] *n* **1** SHOW : muestra *f,* demostración *f* **2** RALLY : manifestación *f*
demonstrative [diˈmɑn*t*strət̬ɪv] *adj* **1** EFFUSIVE : efusivo, expresivo, demostrativo **2** : demostrativo (en lingüística) <demonstrative pronoun : pronombre demostrativo>
demonstrator [ˈdɛmən,streɪt̬ər] *n* **1** : demostrador *m,* -dora *f* (de productos) **2** PROTESTER : manifestante *mf*
demoralize [diˈmɔrə,laɪz] *vt* **-ized; -izing** : desmoralizar
demote [diˈmoːt] *vt* **-moted; -moting** : degradar, bajar de categoría
demotion [diˈmoːʃən] *n* : degradación *f,* descenso *m* de categoría
demur [diˈmər] *vi* **-murred; -murring 1** OBJECT : oponerse **2 to demur at** : ponerle objeciones a (algo)
demure [diˈmjʊr] *adj* : recatado, modesto — **demurely** *adv*
den [ˈdɛn] *n* **1** LAIR : cubil *m,* madriguera *f* **2** HIDEOUT : guarida *f* **3** STUDY : estudio *m,* gabinete *m*
denature [diˈneɪtʃər] *vt* **-tured; -turing** : desnaturalizar
denial [diˈnaɪəl] *n* **1** REFUSAL : rechazo *m,* denegación *f,* negativa *f* **2** REPUDIATION : negación *f* (de una creencia, etc.), rechazo *m*

denim ['dɛnəm] *n* **1** : tela *f* vaquera, mezclilla *f Chile, Mex* **2 denims** *npl* → **jeans**

denizen ['dɛnəzən] *n* : habitante *mf;* morador *m,* -dora *f*

denomination [dɪˌnɑmə'neɪʃən] *n* **1** FAITH : confesión *f,* fe *f* **2** VALUE : denominación *f,* valor *m* (de una moneda)

denominator [dɪ'nɑməˌneɪt̬ər] *n* : denominador *m*

denote [di'noːt] *vt* **-noted; -noting 1** INDICATE, MARK : indicar, denotar, señalar **2** MEAN : significar

denouement [ˌdeɪˌnuː'mɑ] *n* : desenlace *m*

denounce [di'naʊnts] *vt* **-nounced; -nouncing 1** CENSURE : denunciar, censurar **2** ACCUSE : denunciar, acusar, delatar

dense ['dɛnts] *adj* **denser; -est 1** THICK : espeso, denso <dense vegetation : vegetación densa> <a dense fog : una niebla espesa> **2** STUPID : estúpido, burro *fam*

densely ['dɛntsli] *adv* **1** THICKLY : densamente **2** STUPIDLY : torpemente

denseness ['dɛntsnəs] *n* **1** → **density 2** STUPIDITY : estupidez *f*

density ['dɛntsət̬i] *n, pl* **-ties** : densidad *f*

dent[1] ['dɛnt] *vt* : abollar, mellar

dent[2] *n* : abolladura *f,* mella *f*

dental ['dɛntəl] *adj* : dental

dental floss *n* : hilo *m* dental

dentifrice ['dɛntəfrɪs] *n* : dentífrico *m,* pasta *f* de dientes

dentist ['dɛntɪst] *n* : dentista *mf*

dentistry ['dɛntɪstri] *n* : odontología *f*

dentures ['dɛntʃərz] *npl* : dentadura *f* postiza

denude [di'nuːd, -'njuːd] *vt* **-nuded; -nuding** STRIP : desnudar, despojar

denunciation [diˌnʌntsi'eɪʃən] *n* : denuncia *f,* acusación *f*

deny [di'naɪ] *vt* **-nied; -nying 1** REFUTE : desmentir, negar **2** DISOWN, REPUDIATE : negar, renegar de **3** REFUSE : denegar **4 to deny oneself** : privarse, sacrificarse

deodorant [di'oːdərənt] *n* : desodorante *m*

deodorize [di'oːdəˌraɪz] *vt* **-ized; -izing** : desodorizar

depart [di'pɑrt] *vt* : salirse de — *vi* **1** LEAVE : salir, partir, irse **2** DIE : morir

department [di'pɑrtmənt] *n* **1** DIVISION : sección *f* (de una tienda, una organización, etc.), departamento *m* (de una empresa, una universidad, etc.), ministerio *m* (del gobierno) **2** PROVINCE, SPHERE : esfera *f,* campo *m,* competencia *f*

departmental [diˌpɑrt'mɛntəl, ˌdiː-] *adj* : departamental

department store *n* : grandes almacenes *mpl*

departure [di'pɑrtʃər] *n* **1** LEAVING : salida *f,* partida *f* **2** DEVIATION : desviación *f*

depend [di'pɛnd] *vi* **1** RELY : contar (con), confiar (en) <depend on me! : ¡cuenta conmigo!> **2 to depend on** : depender de <success depends on hard work : el éxito depende de trabajar duro> **3 that depends** : según, eso depende

dependable [di'pɛndəbəl] *adj* : responsable, digno de confianza, fiable

dependence [di'pɛndənts] *n* : dependencia *f*

dependency [di'pɛndəntsi] *n, pl* **-cies 1** → **dependence 2** : posesión *f* (de una unidad política)

dependent[1] [di'pɛndənt] *adj* : dependiente

dependent[2] *n* : persona *f* a cargo de alguien

depict [di'pɪkt] *vt* **1** PORTRAY : representar **2** DESCRIBE : describir

depiction [di'pɪkʃən] *n* : representación *f,* descripción *f*

deplete [di'pliːt] *vt* **-pleted; -pleting 1** EXHAUST : agotar **2** REDUCE : reducir

depletion [di'pliːʃən] *n* **1** EXHAUSTION : agotamiento *m* **2** REDUCTION : reducción *f,* disminución *f*

deplorable [di'plorəbəl] *adj* **1** CONTEMPTIBLE : deplorable, despreciable **2** LAMENTABLE : lamentable

deplore [di'plor] *vt* **-plored; -ploring 1** REGRET : deplorar, lamentar **2** CONDEMN : condenar, deplorar

deploy [di'plɔɪ] *vt* : desplegar

deployment [di'plɔɪmənt] *n* : despliegue *m*

deport [di'port] *vt* **1** EXPEL : deportar, expulsar (de un país) **2 to deport oneself** BEHAVE : comportarse

deportment [di'portmənt] *n* : conducta *f,* comportamiento *f*

depose [di'poːz] *v* **-posed; -posing** *vt* : deponer

deposit[1] [di'pɑzət] *vt* **-ited; -iting** : depositar

deposit[2] *n* **1** : depósito *m* (en el banco) **2** DOWN PAYMENT : entrega *f* inicial **3** : depósito *m,* yacimiento *m* (en geología)

depositor [di'pɑzət̬ər] *n* : depositante *mf*

depository [di'pɑzəˌtori] *n, pl* **-ries** : almacén *m,* depósito *m*

depot [*in sense 1 usu* 'dɛˌpoː, *2 usu* 'diː-] *n* **1** STOREHOUSE : almacén *m,* depósito *m* **2** STATION, TERMINAL : terminal *mf,* estación *f* (de autobuses, ferrocarriles, etc.)

deprave [di'preɪv] *vt* **-praved; -praving** : depravar, pervertir

depraved [di'preɪvd] *adj* : depravado, degenerado

depravity [di'prævət̬i] *n, pl* **-ties** : depravación *f*

depreciate [di'priːʃiˌeɪt] *v* **-ated; -ating** *vt* **1** DEVALUE : depreciar, devaluar **2** DISPARAGE : menospreciar, despreciar — *vi* : depreciarse, devaluarse

depreciation [di͵priːʃi'eɪʃən] *n* : depreciación *f,* devaluación *f*

depress [di'prɛs] *vt* **1** PRESS, PUSH : apretar, presionar, pulsar **2** REDUCE : reducir, hacer bajar (precios, ventas, etc.) **3** SADDEN : deprimir, abatir, entristecer **4** DEVALUE : depreciar

depressant[1] [di'prɛsənt] *adj* : depresivo

depressant[2] *n* : depresivo *m*

depressed [di'prɛst] *adj* **1** DEJECTED : deprimido, abatido **2** : deprimido, en crisis (dícese de la economía)

depressing [di'prɛsɪŋ] *adj* : deprimente, triste

depression [di'prɛʃən] *n* **1** DESPONDENCY : depresión *f,* abatimiento *m* **2** : depresión (en una superficie) **3** RECESSION : depresión *f* económica, crisis *f*

deprivation [͵dɛprə'veɪʃən] *n* : privación *f*

deprive [di'praɪv] *vt* **-prived; -priving** : privar

depth ['dɛpθ] *n, pl* **depths** ['dɛpθs, 'dɛps] : profundidad *f,* fondo *m* <to study in depth : estudiar a fondo> <in the depths of winter : en pleno invierno>

deputize ['dɛpjʊ͵taɪz] *vt* **-tized; -tizing** : nombrar como segundo

deputy ['dɛpjʊt̬i] *n, pl* **-ties** : suplente *mf;* sustituto *m,* -ta *f*

derail [di'reɪl] *v* : descarrilar

derailment [di'reɪlmənt] *n* : descarrilamiento *m*

derange [di'reɪndʒ] *vt* **-ranged; -ranging 1** DISARRANGE : desarreglar, desordenar **2** DISTURB, UPSET : trastornar, perturbar **3** MADDEN : enloquecer, volver loco

derangement [di'reɪndʒmənt] *n* **1** DISTURBANCE, UPSET : trastorno *m* **2** INSANITY : locura *f,* perturbación *f* mental

derby ['dərbi] *n, pl* **-bies 1** : derby *m* <the Kentucky Derby : el Derby de Kentucky> **2** : sombrero *m* hongo

deregulate [di'rɛgjʊ͵leɪt] *vt* **-lated; -lating** : desregular

deregulation [di͵rɛgjʊ'leɪʃən] *n* : desregularización *f*

derelict[1] ['dɛrə͵lɪkt] *adj* **1** ABANDONED : abandonado, en ruinas **2** REMISS : negligente, remiso

derelict[2] *n* **1** : propiedad *f* abandonada **2** VAGRANT : vagabundo *m,* -da *f*

deride [di'raɪd] *vt* **-rided; -riding** : ridiculizar, burlarse de

derision [di'rɪʒən] *n* : escarnio *m,* irrisión *f,* mofa *f*

derisive [di'raɪsɪv] *adj* : burlón

derivative[1] [di'rɪvət̬ɪv] *adj* **1** DERIVED : derivado **2** BANAL : carente de originalidad, banal

derivative[2] *n* : derivado *m*

derive [di'raɪv] *v* **-rived; -riving** *vt* **1** OBTAIN : obtener, sacar **2** DEDUCE : deducir, inferir — *vi* : provenir, derivar, proceder

dermatologist [͵dərmə'tɑlədʒɪst] *n* : dermatólogo *m,* -ga *f*

dermatology [͵dərmə'tɑlədʒi] *n* : dermatología *f*

derogatory [di'rɑgə͵tori] *adj* : despectivo, despreciativo

derrick ['dɛrɪk] *n* **1** CRANE : grúa *f* **2** : torre *f* de perforación (sobre un pozo de petróleo)

descend [di'sɛnd] *vt* : descender, bajar — *vi* **1** : descender, bajar <he descended from the platform : descendió del estrado> **2** DERIVE : descender, provenir **3** STOOP : rebajarse <I descended to his level : me rebajé a su nivel> **4 to descend upon** : caer sobre, invadir

descendant[1] [di'sɛndənt] *adj* : descendente

descendant[2] *n* : descendiente *mf*

descent [di'sɛnt] *n* **1** : bajada *f,* descenso *m* <the descent from the mountain : el descenso de la montaña> **2** ANCESTRY : ascendencia *f,* linaje *f* **3** SLOPE : pendiente *f,* cuesta *f* **4** FALL : caída *f* **5** ATTACK : incursión *f,* ataque *m*

describe [di'skraɪb] *vt* **-scribed; -scribing** : describir

description [di'skrɪpʃən] *n* : descripción *f*

descriptive [di'skrɪptɪv] *adj* : descriptivo <descriptive adjective : adjetivo calificativo>

desecrate ['dɛsɪ͵kreɪt] *vt* **-crated; -crating** : profanar

desecration [͵dɛsɪ'kreɪʃən] *n* : profanación *f*

desegregate [di'sɛgrə͵geɪt] *vt* **-gated; -gating** : eliminar la segregación racial de

desegregation [di͵sɛgrə'geɪʃən] *n* : eliminación *f* de la segregación racial

desert[1] [di'zərt] *vt* : abandonar (una persona o un lugar), desertar de (una causa, etc.) — *vi* : desertar

desert[2] ['dɛzərt] *adj* : desierto <a desert island : una isla desierta>

desert[3] *n* **1** ['dɛzərt] : desierto *m* (en geografía) **2** [di'zərt] → **deserts**

deserter [di'zərt̬ər] *n* : desertor *m,* -tora *f*

desertion [di'zərʃən] *n* : abandono *m,* deserción *f* (militar)

deserts [di'zərts] *npl* : merecido *m* <to get one's just deserts : llevarse uno su merecido>

deserve [di'zərv] *vt* **-served; -serving** : merecer, ser digno de

desiccate ['dɛsɪ͵keɪt] *vt* **-cated; -cating** : desecar, deshidratar

design[1] [di'zaɪn] *vt* **1** DEVISE : diseñar, concebir, idear **2** PLAN : proyectar **3** SKETCH : trazar, bosquejar

design[2] *n* **1** PLAN, SCHEME : plan *m,* proyecto *m* <by design : a propósito, intencionalmente> **2** SKETCH : diseño *m,* bosquejo *m* **3** PATTERN, STYLE : diseño *m,* estilo *m* **4 designs** *npl* INTENTIONS : propósitos *mpl,* designios *mpl*

designate [ˈdɛzɪg,neɪt] *vt* **-nated; -nating 1** INDICATE, SPECIFY : indicar, especificar **2** APPOINT : nombrar, designar

designation [,dɛzɪgˈneɪʃən] *n* **1** NAMING : designación *f* **2** NAME : denominación *f,* nombre *m* **3** APPOINTMENT : designación *f,* nombramiento *m*

designer [diˈzaɪnər] *n* : diseñador *m,* -dora *f*

desirability [di,zaɪrəˈbɪləti] *n, pl* **-ties 1** ADVISABILITY : conveniencia *f* **2** ATTRACTIVENESS : atractivo *m*

desirable [diˈzaɪrəbəl] *adj* **1** ADVISABLE : conveniente, aconsejable **2** ATTRACTIVE : deseable, atractivo

desire[1] [diˈzaɪr] *vt* **-sired; -siring 1** WANT : desear **2** REQUEST : rogar, solicitar

desire[2] *n* : deseo *m,* anhelo *m,* ansia *m*

desist [diˈsɪst, -ˈzɪst] *vi* **to desist from** : desistir de, abstenerse de

desk [ˈdɛsk] *n* : escritorio *m,* pupitre *m* (en la escuela)

desolate[1] [ˈdɛsə,leɪt, -zə-] *vt* **-lated; -lating** : devastar, desolar

desolate[2] [ˈdɛsələt, -zə-] *adj* **1** BARREN : desolado, desierto, yermo **2** DISCONSOLATE : desconsolado, desolado

desolation [,dɛsəˈleɪʃən, -zə-] *n* : desolación *f*

despair[1] [diˈspær] *vi* : desesperar, perder las esperanzas

despair[2] *n* : desesperación *f,* desesperanza *f*

desperate [ˈdɛspərət] *adj* **1** HOPELESS : desesperado, sin esperanzas **2** RASH : desesperado, precipitado **3** SERIOUS, URGENT : grave, urgente, apremiante <a desperate need : una necesidad apremiante>

desperately [ˈdɛspərətli] *adv* : desesperadamente, urgentemente

desperation [,dɛspəˈreɪʃən] *n* : desesperación *f*

despicable [diˈspɪkəbəl, ˈdɛspɪ-] *adj* : vil, despreciable, infame

despise [diˈspaɪz] *vt* **-spised; -spising** : despreciar

despite [dəˈspaɪt] *prep* : a pesar de, aún con

despoil [diˈspɔɪl] *vt* : saquear

despondency [diˈspɑndəntsi] *n* : desaliento *m,* desánimo *m,* depresión *f*

despondent [diˈspɑndənt] *adj* : desalentado, desanimado

despot [ˈdɛspət, -,pɑt] *n* : déspota *mf;* tirano *m,* -na *f*

despotic [dɛsˈpɑtɪk] *adj* : despótico

despotism [ˈdɛspə,tɪzəm] *n* : despotismo *m*

dessert [diˈzərt] *n* : postre *m*

destination [,dɛstəˈneɪʃən] *n* : destino *m,* destinación *f*

destined [ˈdɛstənd] *adj* **1** FATED : predestinado **2** BOUND : destinado, con destino (a), con rumbo (a)

destiny [ˈdɛstəni] *n, pl* **-nies** : destino *m*

destitute [ˈdɛstə,tuːt, -,tjuːt] *adj* **1** LACKING : carente, desprovisto **2** POOR : indigente, en miseria

destitution [,dɛstəˈtuːʃən, -ˈtjuː-] *n* : indigencia *f,* miseria *f*

destroy [diˈstrɔɪ] *vt* **1** KILL : matar **2** DEMOLISH : destruir, destrozar

destroyer [diˈstrɔɪər] *n* : destructor *m* (buque)

destructible [diˈstrʌktəbəl] *adj* : destructible

destruction [diˈstrʌkʃən] *n* : destrucción *f,* ruina *f*

destructive [diˈstrʌktɪv] *adj* : destructor, destructivo

desultory [ˈdɛsəl,tori] *adj* **1** AIMLESS : sin rumbo, sin objeto **2** DISCONNECTED : inconexo

detach [diˈtætʃ] *vt* : separar, quitar, desprender

detached [diˈtætʃt] *adj* **1** SEPARATE : separado, suelto **2** ALOOF : distante, indiferente **3** IMPARTIAL : imparcial, objetivo

detachment [diˈtætʃmənt] *n* **1** SEPARATION : separación *f* **2** DETAIL : destacamento *m* (de tropas) **3** ALOOFNESS : reserva *f,* indiferencia *f* **4** IMPARTIALITY : imparcialidad *f*

detail[1] [diˈteɪl, ˈdiː,teɪl] *vt* : detallar, exponer en detalle

detail[2] *n* **1** : detalle *m,* pormenor *m* **2** : destacamento *m* (de tropas)

detailed [diˈteɪld, ˈdiː,teɪld] *adj* : detallado, minucioso

detain [diˈteɪn] *vt* **1** HOLD : detener **2** DELAY : entretener, demorar, retrasar

detect [diˈtɛkt] *vt* : detectar, descubrir

detection [diˈtɛkʃən] *n* : descubrimiento *m*

detective [diˈtɛktɪv] *n* : detective *mf* <private detective : detective privado>

detention [diˈtɛntʃən] *n* : detención *m*

deter [diˈtər] *vt* **-terred; -terring** : disuadir, impedir

detergent [diˈtərdʒənt] *n* : detergente *m*

deteriorate [diˈtɪriə,reɪt] *vi* **-rated; -rating** : deteriorarse, empeorar

deterioration [di,tɪriəˈreɪʃən] *n* : deterioro *m,* empeoramiento *m*

determination [dɪ,tərməˈneɪʃən] *n* **1** DECISION : determinación *f,* decisión *f* **2** RESOLUTION : resolución *f,* determinación *f* <with grim determination : con una firme resolución>

determine [diˈtərmən] *vt* **-mined; -mining 1** ESTABLISH : determinar, establecer **2** SETTLE : decidir **3** FIND OUT : averiguar **4** BRING ABOUT : determinar

determined [di'tərmənd] *adj* RESOLUTE : decidido, resuelto
deterrent [di'tərənt] *n* : medida *f* disuasiva
detest [di'tɛst] *vt* : detestar, odiar, aborrecer
detestable [di'tɛstəbəl] *adj* : detestable, odioso, aborrecible
dethrone [di'θro:n] *vt* **-throned; -throning** : destronar
detonate ['dɛtən,eɪt] *v* **-nated; -nating** *vt* : hacer detonar — *vi* : detonar, estallar
detonator ['dɛtən,eɪt̬ər] *n* : detonador *m*
detour[1] ['di:,tʊr, di'tʊr] *vi* : desviarse
detour[2] *n* : desvío *m,* rodeo *m*
detract [di'trækt] *vi* **to detract from** : restarle valor a, quitarle méritos a
detriment ['dɛtrəmənt] *n* : detrimento *m,* perjuicio *m*
detrimental [,dɛtrə'mɛntəl] *adj* : perjudicial — **detrimentally** *adv*
devaluation [di,væljʊ'eɪʃən] *n* : devaluación *f*
devalue [di'væl,ju:] *vt* **-ued; -uing** : devaluar, depreciar
devastate ['dɛvə,steɪt] *vt* **-tated; -tating** : devastar, arrasar, asolar
devastation [,dɛvə'steɪʃən] *n* : devastación *f,* estragos *mpl*
develop [di'vɛləp] *vt* **1** FORM, MAKE : desarrollar, elaborar, formar **2** : revelar (en fotografía) **3** FOSTER : desarrollar, fomentar **4** EXPLOIT : explotar (recursos), urbanizar (un área) **5** ACQUIRE : adquirir <to develop an interest : adquirir un interés> **6** CONTRACT : contraer (una enfermedad) — *vi* **1** GROW : desarrollarse **2** ARISE : aparecer, surgir
developed [di'vɛləpt] *adj* : avanzado, desarrollado
development [di'vɛləpmənt] *n* **1** : desarrollo *m* <physical development : desarrollo físico> **2** : urbanización *f* (de un área), explotación *f* (de recursos), creación *f* (de inventos) **3** EVENT : acontecimiento *m,* suceso *m* <to await developments : esperar acontecimientos>
deviant ['di:viənt] *adj* : desviado, anormal
deviate ['di:vi,eɪt] *v* **-ated; -ating** *vi* : desviarse, apartarse — *vt* : desviar
deviation [,di:vi'eɪʃən] *n* : desviación *f*
device [di'vaɪs] *n* **1** MECHANISM : dispositivo *m,* aparato *m,* mecanismo *m* **2** EMBLEM : emblema *m*
devil[1] ['dɛvəl] *vt* **-iled** *or* **-illed; -iling** *or* **-illing 1** : sazonar con picante y especias **2** PESTER : molestar
devil[2] *n* **1** SATAN : el diablo, Satanás *m* **2** DEMON : diablo *m,* demonio *m* **3** FIEND : persona *f* diabólica; malvado *m,* -da *f*
devilish ['dɛvəlɪʃ] *adj* : diabólico
devilry ['dɛvəlri] *n, pl* **-ries** : diabluras *fpl,* travesuras *fpl*
devious ['di:viəs] *adj* **1** CRAFTY : taimado, artero **2** WINDING : tortuoso, sinuoso
devise [di'vaɪz] *vt* **-vised; -vising 1** INVENT : idear, concebir, inventar **2** PLOT : tramar
devoid [di'vɔɪd] *adj* **~ of** : carente de, desprovisto de
devote [di'vo:t] *vt* **-voted; -voting 1** DEDICATE : consagrar, dedicar <to devote one's life : dedicar uno su vida> **2 to devote oneself** : dedicarse
devoted [di'vo:t̬əd] *adj* **1** FAITHFUL : leal, fiel **2 to be devoted to someone** : tenerle mucho cariño a alguien
devotee [,dɛvə'ti:, -'teɪ] *n* : devoto *m,* -ta *f*
devotion [di'vo:ʃən] *n* **1** DEDICATION : dedicación *f,* devoción *f* **2 devotions** PRAYERS : oraciones *fpl,* devociones *fpl*
devour [di'vaʊər] *vt* : devorar
devout [di'vaʊt] *adj* **1** PIOUS : devoto, piadoso **2** EARNEST, SINCERE : sincero, ferviente — **devoutly** *adv*
devoutness [di'vaʊtnəs] *n* : devoción *f,* piedad *f*
dew ['du:, 'dju:] *n* : rocío *m*
dewlap ['du,læp, 'dju-] *n* : papada *f*
dew point *n* : punto *m* de condensación
dewy ['du:i, 'dju:i] *adj* **dewier; -est** : cubierto de rocío
dexterity [dɛk'stɛrət̬i] *n, pl* **-ties** : destreza *f,* habilidad *f*
dexterous ['dɛkstrəs] *adj* : diestro, hábil
dexterously ['dɛkstrəsli] *adv* : con destreza, con habilidad, hábilmente
dextrose ['dɛk,stro:s] *n* : dextrosa *f*
diabetes [,daɪə'bi:t̬iz] *n* : diabetes *f*
diabetic[1] [,daɪə'bɛt̬ɪk] *adj* : diabético
diabetic[2] *n* : diabético *m,* -ca *f*
diabolic [,daɪə'bɑlɪk] *or* **diabolical** [-lɪkəl] *adj* : diabólico, satánico
diacritical mark [,daɪə'krɪt̬ɪkəl] *n* : signo *m* diacrítico
diadem ['daɪə,dɛm, -dəm] *n* : diadema *f*
diagnose ['daɪɪg,no:s, ,daɪɪg'no:s] *vt* **-nosed; -nosing** : diagnosticar
diagnosis [,daɪɪg'no:sɪs] *n, pl* **-noses** [-'no:,si:z] : diagnóstico *m*
diagnostic [,daɪɪg'nɑstɪk] *adj* : diagnóstico
diagonal[1] [daɪ'ægənəl] *adj* : diagonal, en diagonal
diagonal[2] *n* : diagonal *f*
diagonally [daɪ'ægənəli] *adv* : diagonalmente, en diagonal
diagram[1] ['daɪə,græm] *vt* **-gramed** *or* **-grammed; -graming** *or* **-gramming** : hacer un diagrama de
diagram[2] *n* : diagrama *m,* gráfico *m,* esquema *m*
dial[1] ['daɪl] *v* **dialed** *or* **dialled; dialing** *or* **dialling** : marcar, discar

dial[2] *n* : esfera *f* (de un reloj), dial *m* (de un radio), disco *m* (de un teléfono)
dialect [ˈdaɪəˌlɛkt] *n* : dialecto *m*
dialogue [ˈdaɪəˌlɔg] *n* : diálogo *m*
diameter [daɪˈæmət̬ər] *n* : diámetro *m*
diamond [ˈdaɪmənd, ˈdaɪə-] *n* **1** : diamante *m,* brillante *m* <a diamond necklace : un collar de brillantes> **2** : rombo *m,* forma *f* de rombo **3** : diamante *m* (en naipes) **4** INFIELD : cuadro *m,* diamante *m* (en béisbol)
diaper [ˈdaɪpər, ˈdaɪə-] *n* : pañal *m*
diaphragm [ˈdaɪəˌfræm] *n* : diafragma *m*
diarrhea [ˌdaɪəˈriːə] *n* : diarrea *f*
diary [ˈdaɪəri] *n, pl* **-ries:** diario *m*
diatribe [ˈdaɪəˌtraɪb] *n* : diatriba *f*
dice[1] [ˈdaɪs] *vt* **diced; dicing** : cortar en cubos
dice[2] *ns & pl* **1** → **die**[2] **2** : dados *mpl* (juego)
dicker [ˈdɪkər] *vt* : regatear
dictate[1] [ˈdɪkˌteɪt, dɪkˈteɪt] *v* **-tated; -tating** *vt* **1** : dictar <to dictate a letter : dictar una carta> **2** ORDER : mandar, ordenar — *vi* : dar órdenes
dictate[2] [ˈdɪkˌteɪt] *n* **1** : mandato *m,* orden *f* **2 dictates** *npl* : dictados *mpl* <the dictates of conscience : los dictados de la conciencia>
dictation [dɪkˈteɪʃən] *n* : dictado *m*
dictator [ˈdɪkˌteɪt̬ər] *n* : dictador *m,* -dora *f*
dictatorial [ˌdɪktəˈtoriəl] *adj* : dictatorial — **dictatorially** *adv*
dictatorship [dɪkˈteɪt̬ərˌʃɪp, ˈdɪkˌ-] *n* : dictadura *f*
diction [ˈdɪkʃən] *n* **1** : lenguaje *m,* estilo *m* **2** ENUNCIATION : dicción *f,* articulación *f*
dictionary [ˈdɪkʃəˌnɛri] *n, pl* **-naries** : diccionario *m*
did → **do**
didactic [daɪˈdæktɪk] *adj* : didáctico
die[1] [ˈdaɪ] *vi* **died** [ˈdaɪd]; **dying** [ˈdaɪɪŋ] **1** : morir **2** CEASE : morir, morirse <a dying civilization : una civilización moribunda> **3** STOP : apagarse, dejar de funcionar <the motor died : el motor se apagó> **4 to die down** SUBSIDE : amainar, disminuir **5 to die out** : extinguirse **6 to be dying for** *or* **to be dying to** : morirse por <I'm dying to leave : me muero por irme>
die[2] [ˈdaɪ] *n, pl* **dice** [ˈdaɪs] : dado *m*
die[3] *n, pl* **dies** [ˈdaɪz] **1** STAMP : troquel *m,* cuño *m* **2** MOLD : matriz *f,* molde *m*
diesel [ˈdiːzəl, -səl] *n* : diesel *m*
diet[1] [ˈdaɪət] *vi* : ponerse a régimen, hacer dieta
diet[2] *n* : régimen *m,* dieta *f*
dietary [ˈdaɪəˌtɛri] *adj* : alimenticio, dietético
dietitian *or* **dietician** [ˌdaɪəˈtɪʃən] *n* : dietista *mf*
differ [ˈdɪfər] *vi* **-ferred; -ferring 1** : diferir, diferenciarse **2** VARY : variar **3** DISAGREE : discrepar, diferir, no estar de acuerdo
difference [ˈdɪfrənts, ˈdɪfərənts] *n* : diferencia *f*
different [ˈdɪfrənt, ˈdɪfərənt] *adj* : distinto, diferente
differentiate [ˌdɪfəˈrɛntʃiˌeɪt] *v* **-ated; -ating** *vt* **1** : hacer diferente **2** DISTINGUISH : distinguir, diferenciar — *vi* : distinguir
differentiation [ˌdɪfəˌrɛntʃiˈeɪʃən] *n* : diferenciación *f*
differently [ˈdɪfrəntli, ˈdɪfərənt-] *adv* : de otra manera, de otro modo, distintamente
difficult [ˈdɪfɪˌkʌlt] *adj* : difícil
difficulty [ˈdɪfɪˌkʌlti] *n, pl* **-ties 1** : dificultad *f* **2** PROBLEM : problema *f,* dificultad *f*
diffidence [ˈdɪfədənts] *n* **1** SHYNESS : retraimiento *m,* timidez *f,* apocamiento *m* **2** RETICENCE : reticencia *f*
diffident [ˈdɪfədənt] *adj* **1** SHY : tímido, apocado, inseguro **2** RESERVED : reservado
diffuse[1] [dɪˈfjuːz] *v* **-fused; -fusing** *vt* : difundir, esparcir — *vi* : difundirse, esparcirse
diffuse[2] [dɪˈfjuːs] *adj* **1** WORDY : prolijo, verboso **2** WIDESPREAD : difuso
diffusion [dɪˈjuːʒən] *n* : difusión *f*
dig[1] [ˈdɪg] *v* **dug** [ˈdʌg]; **digging** *vt* **1** : cavar, excavar <to dig a hole : cavar un hoyo> **2** EXTRACT : sacar <to dig up potatoes : sacar papas del suelo> **3** POKE, THRUST : clavar, hincar <he dug me in the ribs : me dio un codazo en las costillas> **4 to dig up** DISCOVER : descubrir, sacar a luz — *vi* : cavar, excavar
dig[2] *n* **1** POKE : codazo *m* **2** GIBE : pulla *f* **3** EXCAVATION : excavación *f*
digest[1] [daɪˈdʒɛst, dɪ-] *vt* **1** ASSIMILATE : digerir, asimilar **2** : digerir (comida) **3** SUMMARIZE : compendiar, resumir
digest[2] [ˈdaɪˌdʒɛst] *n* : compendio *m,* resumen *m*
digestible [daɪˈdʒɛstəbəl, dɪ-] *adj* : digerible
digestion [daɪˈdʒɛstʃən, dɪ-] *n* : digestión *f*
digestive [daɪˈdʒɛstɪv, dɪ-] *adj* : digestivo <the digestive system : el sistema digestivo>
digit [ˈdɪdʒət] *n* **1** NUMERAL : dígito *m,* número *m* **2** FINGER, TOE : dedo *m*
digital [ˈdɪdʒət̬əl] *adj* : digital — **digitally** *adv*
dignified [ˈdɪgnəˌfaɪd] *adj* : digno, decoroso
dignify [ˈdɪgnəˌfaɪ] *vt* **-fied; -fying** : dignificar, honrar
dignitary [ˈdɪgnəˌtɛri] *n, pl* **-taries** : dignatario *m,* -ria *f*
dignity [ˈdɪgnət̬i] *n, pl* **-ties** : dignidad *f*
digress [daɪˈgrɛs, də-] *vi* : desviarse del tema, divagar

digression [daɪˈgrɛʃən, də-] *n* : digresión *f*
dike *or* **dyke** [ˈdaɪk] *n* : dique *m*
dilapidated [dəˈlæpəˌdeɪtəd] *adj* : ruinoso, desvencijado, destartalado
dilapidation [dəˌlæpəˈdeɪʃən] *n* : deterioro *m,* estado *m* ruinoso
dilate [daɪˈleɪt, ˈdaɪˌleɪt] *v* **-lated; -lating** *vt* : dilatar — *vi* : dilatarse
dilemma [dɪˈlɛmə] *n* : dilema *m*
dilettante [ˈdɪləˌtɑnt, -ˌtænt] *n, pl* **-tantes** [-ˌtɑnts, -ˌtænts] *or* **-tanti** [ˌdɪləˈtɑnti, -ˈtæn-] : diletante *mf*
diligence [ˈdɪlədʒənts] *n* : diligencia *f,* aplicación *f*
diligent [ˈdɪlədʒənt] *adj* : diligente <a diligent search : una búsqueda minuciosa> — **diligently** *adv*
dill [ˈdɪl] *n* : eneldo *m*
dillydally [ˈdɪliˌdæli] *vi* **-lied; lying** : demorarse, perder tiempo
dilute [daɪˈluːt, də-] *vt* **-luted; -luting** : diluir, aguar
dilution [daɪˈluːʃən, də-] *n* : dilución *f*
dim¹ [ˈdɪm] *v* **dimmed; dimming** *vt* : atenuar (la luz), nublar (la vista), borrar (la memoria), opacar (una superficie) — *vi* : oscurecerse, apagarse
dim² *adj* **dimmer; dimmest 1** FAINT : oscuro, tenue (dícese de la luz), nublado (dícese de la vista), borrado (dícese de la memoria) **2** DULL : deslustrado **3** STUPID : tonto, torpe
dime [ˈdaɪm] *n* : moneda *f* de diez centavos
dimension [dəˈmɛntʃən, daɪ-] *n* **1** : dimensión *f* **2 dimensions** *npl* EXTENT, SCOPE : dimensiones *fpl,* extensión *f,* medida *f*
diminish [dəˈmɪnɪʃ] *vt* LESSEN : disminuir, reducir, amainar — *vi* DWINDLE, WANE : menguar, reducirse
diminutive [dəˈmɪnjʊtɪv] *adj* : diminutivo, minúsculo
dimly [ˈdɪmli] *adv* : indistintamente, débilmente
dimmer [ˈdɪmər] *n* : potenciómetro *m,* conmutador *m* de luces (en automóviles)
dimness [ˈdɪmnəs] *n* : oscuridad *f,* debilidad *f* (de la vista), imprecisión *f* (de la memoria)
dimple [ˈdɪmpəl] *n* : hoyuelo *m*
din [ˈdɪn] *n* : estrépito *m,* estruendo *m*
dine [ˈdaɪn] *vi* **dined; dining** : cenar
diner [ˈdaɪnər] *n* **1** : comensal *mf* (persona) **2** : vagón *m* restaurante (en un tren) **3** : cafetería *f,* restaurante *m* barato
dinghy [ˈdɪŋi, ˈdɪŋgi, ˈdɪŋki] *n, pl* **-ghies** : bote *m*
dinginess [ˈdɪndʒinəs] *n* **1** DIRTINESS : suciedad *f* **2** SHABBINESS : lo gastado, lo deslucido
dingy [ˈdɪndʒi] *adj* **-gier; -est 1** DIRTY : sucio **2** SHABBY : gastado, deslucido
dinner [ˈdɪnər] *n* : cena *f,* comida *f*
dinosaur [ˈdaɪnəˌsɔr] *n* : dinosaurio *m*
dint [ˈdɪnt] *n* **by dint of** : a fuerza de
diocese [ˈdaɪəsəs, -ˌsiːz, -ˌsiːs] *n, pl* **-ceses** [ˈdaɪəsəsəz] : diócesis *f*
dip¹ [ˈdɪp] *v* **dipped; dipping** *vt* **1** DUNK, PLUNGE : sumergir, mojar, meter **2** LADLE : servir con cucharón **3** LOWER : bajar, arriar (una bandera) — *vi* **1** DESCEND, DROP : bajar en picada, descender **2** SLOPE : bajar, inclinarse
dip² *n* **1** SWIM : chapuzón *m* **2** DROP : descenso *m,* caída *f* **3** SLOPE : cuesta *f,* declive *m* **4** SAUCE : salsa *f*
diphtheria [dɪfˈθɪriə] *n* : difteria *f*
diphthong [ˈdɪfˌθɔŋ] *n* : diptongo *m*
diploma [dəˈploːmə] *n, pl* **-mas** : diploma *m*
diplomacy [dəˈploːməsi] *n* **1** : diplomacia *f* **2** TACT : tacto *m,* discreción *f*
diplomat [ˈdɪpləˌmæt] *n* **1** : diplomático *m,* -ca *f* (en relaciones internacionales) **2** : persona *f* diplomática
diplomatic [ˌdɪpləˈmætɪk] *adj* : diplomático <diplomatic immunity : inmunidad diplomática>
dipper [ˈdɪpər] *n* **1** LADLE : cucharón *m,* cazo *m* **2 Big Dipper** : Osa *f* Mayor **3 Little Dipper** : Osa *f* Menor
dire [ˈdaɪr] *adj* **direr; direst 1** HORRIBLE : espantoso, terrible, horrendo **2** EXTREME : extremo <dire poverty : pobreza extrema>
direct¹ [dəˈrɛkt, daɪ-] *vt* **1** ADDRESS : dirigir, mandar **2** AIM, POINT : dirigir **3** GUIDE : indicarle el camino (a alguien), orientar **4** MANAGE : dirigir <to direct a film : dirigir una película> **5** COMMAND : ordenar, mandar
direct² *adv* : directamente
direct³ *adj* **1** STRAIGHT : directo **2** FRANK : franco
direct current *n* : corriente *f* continua
direction [dəˈrɛkʃən, daɪ-] *n* **1** SUPERVISION : dirección *f* **2** INSTRUCTION, ORDER : instrucción *f,* orden *f* **3** COURSE : dirección *f,* rumbo *m* <to change direction : cambiar de dirección> **4 to ask directions** : pedir indicaciones
directly [dəˈrɛktli, daɪ-] *adv* **1** STRAIGHT : directamente <directly north : directamente al norte> **2** FRANKLY : francamente **3** EXACTLY : exactamente, justo <directly opposite : justo enfrente> **4** IMMEDIATELY : en seguida, inmediatamente
directness [dəˈrɛktnəs, daɪ-] *n* : franqueza *f*
director [dəˈrɛktər, daɪ-] *n* **1** : director *m,* -tora *f* **2 board of directors** : junta *f* directiva, directorio *m*
directory [dəˈrɛktəri, daɪ-] *n, pl* **-ries** : guía *f,* directorio *m* <telephone directory : directorio telefónico>
dirge [ˈdərdʒ] *n* : canto *m* fúnebre
dirigible [ˈdɪrədʒəbəl, dəˈrɪdʒə-] *n* : dirigible *m,* zepelín *m*
dirt [ˈdərt] *n* **1** FILTH : suciedad *f,* mugre *f,* porquería *f* **2** SOIL : tierra *f*
dirtiness [ˈdərtinəs] *n* : suciedad *f*
dirty¹ [ˈdərti] *vt* **dirtied; dirtying** : ensuciar, manchar

dirty² *adj* **dirtier; -est 1** SOILED, STAINED : sucio, manchado **2** DISHONEST : sucio, deshonesto <a dirty player : un jugador tramposo> <a dirty trick : una mala pasada> **3** INDECENT : indecente, cochino <a dirty joke : un chiste verde>

disability [ˌdɪsəˈbɪləti] *n, pl* **-ties** : minusvalía *f,* discapacidad *f,* invalidez *f*

disable [dɪsˈeɪbəl] *vt* **-abled; -abling** : dejar inválido, inutilizar, incapacitar

disabled [dɪsˈeɪbəld] *adj* : minusválido, discapacitado

disabuse [ˌdɪsəˈbjuːz] *vt* **-bused; -busing** : desengañar, sacar del error

disadvantage [ˌdɪsədˈvæntɪdʒ] *n* : desventaja *f*

disadvantageous [ˌdɪsˌædˌvænˈteɪdʒəs] *adj* : desventajoso, desfavorable

disagree [ˌdɪsəˈgriː] *vi* **1** DIFFER : discrepar, no coincidir **2** DISSENT : disentir, discrepar, no estar de acuerdo

disagreeable [ˌdɪsəˈgriːəbəl] *adj* : desagradable

disagreement [ˌdɪsəˈgriːmənt] *n* **1** : desacuerdo *m* **2** DISCREPANCY : discrepancia *f* **3** ARGUMENT : discusión *f,* altercado *m,* disputa *f*

disappear [ˌdɪsəˈpɪr] *vi* : desaparecer, desvanecerse <to disappear from view : perderse de vista>

disappearance [ˌdɪsəˈpɪrən*t*s] *n* : desaparición *f*

disappoint [ˌdɪsəˈpɔɪnt] *vt* : decepcionar, defraudar, fallar

disappointment [ˌdɪsəˈpɔɪntmənt] *n* : decepción *f,* desilusión *f,* chasco *m*

disapproval [ˌdɪsəˈpruːvəl] *n* : desaprobación *f*

disapprove [ˌdɪsəˈpruːv] *vi* **-proved; -proving** : desaprobar, estar en contra

disapprovingly [ˌdɪsəˈpruːvɪŋli] *adv* : con desaprobación

disarm [dɪsˈɑrm] *vt* : desarmar

disarmament [dɪsˈɑrməmənt] *n* : desarme *m* <nuclear disarmament : desarme nuclear>

disarrange [ˌdɪsəˈreɪndʒ] *vt* **-ranged; -ranging** : desarreglar, desordenar

disarray [ˌdɪsəˈreɪ] *n* : desorden *m,* confusión *f,* desorganización *f*

disaster [dɪˈzæstər] *n* : desastre *m,* catástrofe *f*

disastrous [dɪˈzæstrəs] *adj* : desastroso

disband [dɪsˈbænd] *vt* : disolver — *vi* : disolverse, dispersarse

disbar [dɪsˈbɑr] *vt* **-barred; -barring** : prohibir de ejercer la abogacía

disbelief [ˌdɪsbɪˈliːf] *n* : incredulidad *f*

disbelieve [ˌdɪsbɪˈliːv] *v* **-lieved; -lieving** : no creer, dudar

disburse [dɪsˈbərs] *vt* **-bursed; -bursing** : desembolsar

disbursement [dɪsˈbərsmənt] *n* : desembolso *m*

disc → **disk**

discard [dɪsˈkɑrd, ˈdɪsˌkɑrd] *vt* : desechar, deshacerse de, botar — *vi* : descartarse (en juegos de naipes)

discern [dɪˈsərn, -ˈzərn] *vt* : discernir, distinguir, percibir

discernible [dɪˈsərnəbəl, -ˈzər-] *adj* : perceptible, visible

discernment [dɪˈsərnmənt, -ˈzərn-] *n* : discernimiento *m,* criterio *m*

discharge¹ [dɪsˈtʃɑrdʒ, ˈdɪsˌ-] *v* **-charged; -charging 1** UNLOAD : descargar (carga), desembarcar (pasajeros) **2** SHOOT : descargar, disparar **3** FREE : liberar, poner en libertad **4** DISMISS : despedir **5** EMIT : despedir (humo, etc.), descargar (electricidad) **6** : cumplir con (una obligación), saldar (una deuda) — *vi* **1** : descargarse (dícese de una batería) **2** OOZE : supurar

discharge² [ˈdɪsˌtʃɑrdʒ, dɪsˈ-] *n* **1** EMISSION : descarga *f* (de electricidad), emisión *f* (de gases) **2** DISMISSAL : despido *m* (del empleo), baja *f* (del ejército) **3** SECRETION : secreción *f*

disciple [dɪˈsaɪpəl] *n* : discípulo *m,* -la *f*

discipline¹ [ˈdɪsəplən] *vt* **-plined; -plining 1** PUNISH : castigar, sancionar (a los empleados) **2** CONTROL : disciplinar **3 to discipline oneself** : disciplinarse

discipline² *n* **1** FIELD : disciplina *f,* campo *m* **2** TRAINING : disciplina *f* **3** PUNISHMENT : castigo *m* **4** SELF-CONTROL : dominio *m* de sí mismo

disc jockey *n* : disc jockey *mf*

disclaim [dɪsˈkleɪm] *vt* DENY : negar

disclose [dɪsˈkloːz] *vt* **-closed; -closing** : revelar, poner en evidencia

disclosure [dɪsˈkloːʒər] *n* : revelación *f*

discolor [dɪsˈkʌlər] *vt* **1** BLEACH : decolorar **2** FADE : desteñir **3** STAIN : manchar — *vi* : decolorarse, desteñirse

discoloration [dɪsˌkʌləˈreɪʃən] *n* **1** FADING : decoloración *f* **2** STAIN : mancha *f*

discomfort [dɪsˈkʌmfərt] *n* **1** PAIN : molestia *f,* malestar *m* **2** UNEASINESS : inquietud *f*

disconcert [ˌdɪskənˈsərt] *vt* : desconcertar

disconnect [ˌdɪskəˈnɛkt] *vt* : desconectar

disconnected [ˌdɪskəˈnɛktəd] *adj* : inconexo

disconsolate [dɪsˈkɑn*t*sələt] *adj* : desconsolado

discontent [ˌdɪskənˈtɛnt] *n* : descontento *m*

discontented [ˌdɪskənˈtɛntəd] *adj* : descontento

discontinue [ˌdɪskənˈtɪnˌjuː] *vt* **-ued; -uing** : suspender, descontinuar

discord [ˈdɪsˌkɔrd] *n* **1** STRIFE : discordia *f,* discordancia *f* **2** : disonancia *f* (en música)

discordant [dɪsˈkɔrdənt] *adj* : discordante, discorde — **discordantly** *adv*
discount¹ [ˈdɪsˌkaʊnt, dɪsˈ-] *vt* **1** REDUCE : descontar, rebajar (precios) **2** DISREGARD : descartar, ignorar
discount² [ˈdɪsˌkaʊnt] *n* : descuento *m,* rebaja *f*
discourage [dɪsˈkərɪdʒ] *vt* **-aged; -aging 1** DISHEARTEN : desalentar, desanimar **2** DISSUADE : disuadir
discouragement [dɪsˈkərɪdʒmənt] *n* : desánimo *m,* desaliento *m*
discourse¹ [dɪsˈkors] *vi* **-coursed; -coursing** : disertar, conversar
discourse² [ˈdɪsˌkors] *n* **1** TALK : conversación *f* **2** SPEECH, TREATISE : discurso *m,* tratado *m*
discourteous [dɪsˈkərt̬iəs] *adj* : descortés — **discourteously** *adv*
discourtesy [dɪsˈkərt̬əsi] *n, pl* **-sies** : descortesía *f*
discover [dɪsˈkʌvər] *vt* : descubrir
discoverer [dɪsˈkʌvərər] *n* : descubridor *m,* -dora *f*
discovery [dɪsˈkʌvəri] *n, pl* **-ries** : descubrimiento *m*
discredit¹ [dɪsˈkrɛdət] *vt* **1** DISBELIEVE : no creer, dudar **2** : desacreditar, desprestigiar, poner en duda <they discredited his research : desacreditaron sus investigaciones>
discredit² *n* **1** DISREPUTE : descrédito *m,* desprestigio *m* **2** DOUBT : duda *f*
discreet [dɪsˈkriːt] *adj* : discreto — **discreetly** *adv*
discrepancy [dɪsˈkrɛpən*t*si] *n, pl* **-cies** : discrepancia *f*
discretion [dɪsˈkrɛʃən] *n* **1** CIRCUMSPECTION : discreción *f,* circunspección *f* **2** JUDGMENT : discernimiento *m,* criterio *m*
discriminate [dɪsˈkrɪməˌneɪt] *v* **-nated; -nating** *vt* DISTINGUISH : distinguir, discriminar, diferenciar — *vi* : discriminar <to discriminate against women : discriminar a las mujeres>
discrimination [dɪsˌkrɪməˈneɪʃən] *n* **1** PREJUDICE : discriminación *f* **2** DISCERNMENT : discernimiento *m*
discriminatory [dɪsˈkrɪmənəˌtori] *adj* : discriminatorio
discus [ˈdɪskəs] *n, pl* **-cuses** [-kəsəz] : disco *m*
discuss [dɪsˈkʌs] *vt* : hablar de, discutir, tratar (de)
discussion [dɪsˈkʌʃən] *n* : discusión *f,* debate *m,* conversación *f*
disdain¹ [dɪsˈdeɪn] *vt* : desdeñar, despreciar <they disdained to reply : no se dignaron a responder>
disdain² *n* : desdén *m*
disdainful [dɪsˈdeɪnfəl] *adj* : desdeñoso — **disdainfully** *adv*
disease [dɪˈziːz] *n* : enfermedad *f,* mal *m,* dolencia *f*
diseased [dɪˈziːzd] *adj* : enfermo
disembark [ˌdɪsɪmˈbɑrk] *v* : desembarcar
disembarkation [dɪsˌɛmˌbɑrˈkeɪʃən] *n* : desembarco *m,* desembarque *m*
disembodied [ˌdɪsɪmˈbɑdid] *adj* : incorpóreo
disenchant [ˌdɪsɪnˈtʃænt] *vt* : desilusionar, desencantar, desengañar
disenchantment [ˌdɪsɪnˈtʃæntmənt] *n* : desencanto *m,* desilusión *f*
disengage [ˌdɪsɪnˈgeɪdʒ] *vt* **-gaged; -gaging 1** : soltar, desconectar (un mecanismo) **2 to disengage the clutch** : desembragar
disentangle [ˌdɪsɪnˈtæŋgəl] *vt* **-gled; -gling** UNTANGLE : desenredar, desenmarañar
disfavor [dɪsˈfeɪvər] *n* : desaprobación *f*
disfigure [dɪsˈfɪgjər] *vt* **-ured; -uring** : desfigurar (a una persona), afear (un edificio, un área)
disfigurement [dɪsˈfɪgjərmənt] *n* : desfiguración *f,* afeamiento *m*
disfranchise [dɪsˈfrænˌtʃaɪz] *vt* **-chised; -chising** : privar del derecho a votar
disgrace¹ [dɪˈskreɪs] *vt* **-graced; -gracing** : deshonrar
disgrace² *n* **1** DISHONOR : desgracia *f,* deshonra *f* **2** SHAME : vergüenza *f* <he's a disgrace to his family : es una vergüenza para su familia>
disgraceful [dɪˈskreɪsfəl] *adj* : vergonzoso, deshonroso, ignominioso
disgracefully [dɪˈskreɪsfəli] *adv* : vergonzosamente
disgruntle [dɪsˈgrʌntəl] *vt* **-tled; -tling** : enfadar, contrariar
disguise¹ [dɪˈskaɪz] *vt* **-guised; -guising 1** : disfrazar, enmascarar (el aspecto) **2** CONCEAL : encubrir, disimular
disguise² *n* : disfraz *m*
disgust¹ [dɪˈskʌst] *vt* : darle asco (a alguien), asquear, repugnar <eso me da asco : that disgusts me>
disgust² *n* : asco *m,* repugnancia *f*
disgusting [dɪˈskʌstɪŋ] *adj* : asqueroso, repugnante — **disgustingly** *adv*
dish¹ [ˈdɪʃ] *vt* SERVE : servir
dish² *n* **1** : plato *m* <the national dish : el plato nacional> **2** PLATE : plato *m* <to wash the dishes : lavar los platos> **3 serving dish** : fuente *f*
dishcloth [ˈdɪʃˌklɔθ] *n* : paño *m* de cocina (para secar), trapo *m* de fregar (para lavar)
dishearten [dɪsˈhɑrtən] *vt* : desanimar, desalentar
dishevel [dɪˈʃɛvəl] *vt* **-eled** *or* **-elled; -eling** *or* **-elling** : desarreglar, despeinar (el pelo)
disheveled *or* **dishevelled** [dɪˈʃɛvəld] *adj* : despeinado (dícese del pelo), desarreglado, desaliñado
dishonest [dɪˈsɑnəst] *adj* : deshonesto, fraudulento — **dishonestly** *adv*
dishonesty [dɪˈsɑnəsti] *n, pl* **-ties** : deshonestidad *f,* falta *f* de honradez
dishonor¹ [dɪˈsɑnər] *vt* : deshonrar

dishonor[2] *n* : deshonra *f*
dishonorable [dɪˈsɑnərəbəl] *adj* : deshonroso — **dishonorably** [-bli] *adv*
dishrag [ˈdɪʃˌræg] → **dishcloth**
dishwasher [ˈdɪʃˌwɔʃər] *n* : lavaplatos *m*, lavavajillas *m*
disillusion [ˌdɪsəˈluːʒən] *vt* : desilusionar, desencantar, desengañar
disillusionment [ˌdɪsəˈluːʒənmənt] *n* : desilusión *f*, desencanto *m*
disinclination [dɪsˌɪnkləˈneɪʃən, -ˌɪŋ-] *n* : aversión *f*
disinclined [ˌdɪsɪnˈklaɪnd] *adv* : poco dispuesto
disinfect [ˌdɪsɪnˈfɛkt] *vt* : desinfectar
disinfectant[1] [ˌdɪsɪnˈfɛktənt] *adj* : desinfectante
disinfectant[2] *n* : desinfectante *m*
disinherit [ˌdɪsɪnˈhɛrət] *vt* : desheredar
disintegrate [dɪsˈɪntəˌgreɪt] *v* **-grated; -grating** *vt* : desintegrar, deshacer — *vi* : desintegrarse, deshacerse
disintegration [dɪsˌɪntəˈgreɪʃən] *n* : desintegración *f*
disinterested [dɪsˈɪntərəstəd, -ˌrɛs-] *adj* **1** INDIFFERENT : indiferente **2** IMPARTIAL : imparcial, desinteresado
disinterestedness [dɪsˈɪntərəstədnəs, -ˌrɛs-] *n* : desinterés *m*
disjointed [dɪsˈdʒɔɪntəd] *adj* : inconexo, incoherente
disk *or* **disc** [ˈdɪsk] *n* : disco *m*
dislike[1] [dɪsˈlaɪk] *vt* **-liked; -liking** : tenerle aversión a (algo), tenerle antipatía (a alguien), no gustarle (algo a uno)
dislike[2] *n* : aversión *f*, antipatía *f*
dislocate [ˈdɪsloˌkeɪt, dɪsˈloː-] *vt* **-cated; -cating** : dislocar
dislocation [ˌdɪsloˈkeɪʃən] *n* : dislocación *f*
dislodge [dɪsˈlɑdʒ] *vt* **-lodged; -lodging** : sacar, desalojar, desplazar
disloyal [dɪsˈlɔɪəl] *adj* : desleal
disloyalty [dɪsˈlɔɪəlti] *n, pl* **-ties** : deslealtad *f*
dismal [ˈdɪzməl] *adj* **1** GLOOMY : sombrío, lúgubre, tétrico **2** DEPRESSING : deprimente, triste
dismantle [dɪsˈmæntəl] *vt* **-tled; -tling** : desmantelar, desmontar, desarmar
dismay[1] [dɪsˈmeɪ] *vt* : consternar
dismay[2] *n* : consternación *f*
dismember [dɪsˈmɛmbər] *vt* : desmembrar
dismiss [dɪsˈmɪs] *vt* **1** : dejar salir, darle permiso (a alguien) para retirarse **2** DISCHARGE : despedir, destituir **3** REJECT : descartar, desechar, rechazar
dismissal [dɪsˈmɪsəl] *n* **1** : permiso *m* para retirarse **2** DISCHARGE : despido *m* (de un empleado), destitución *f* (de un funcionario) **3** REJECTION : rechazo *m*
dismount [dɪsˈmaʊnt] *vi* : desmontar, bajarse, apearse
disobedience [ˌdɪsəˈbiːdiənts] *n* : desobediencia *f* — **disobedient** [-ənt] *adj*
disobey [ˌdɪsəˈbeɪ] *v* : desobedecer
disorder[1] [dɪsˈɔrdər] *vt* : desordenar, desarreglar
disorder[2] *n* **1** DISARRAY : desorden *m* **2** UNREST : disturbios *mpl*, desórdenes *mpl* **3** AILMENT : afección *f*, indisposición *f*, dolencia *f*
disorderly [dɪsˈɔrdərli] *adj* **1** UNTIDY : desordenado, desarreglado **2** UNRULY : indisciplinado, alborotado **3 disorderly conduct** : conducta *f* escandalosa
disorganization [dɪsˌɔrgənəˈzeɪʃən] *n* : desorganización *f*
disorganize [dɪsˈɔrgəˌnaɪz] *vt* **-nized; -nizing** : desorganizar
disown [dɪsˈoːn] *vt* : renegar de, repudiar
disparage [dɪsˈpærɪdʒ] *vt* **-aged; -aging** : menospreciar, denigrar
disparagement [dɪsˈpærɪdʒmənt] *n* : menosprecio *m*
disparate [ˈdɪspərət, dɪsˈpærət] *adj* : dispar, diferente
disparity [dɪsˈpærəṭi] *n, pl* **-ties** : disparidad *f*
dispassionate [dɪsˈpæʃənət] *adj* : desapasionado, imparcial — **dispassionately** *adv*
dispatch[1] [dɪsˈpætʃ] *vt* **1** SEND : despachar, enviar **2** KILL : despachar, matar **3** HANDLE : despachar
dispatch[2] *n* **1** SENDING : envío *m*, despacho *m* **2** MESSAGE : despacho *m*, reportaje *m* (de un periodista), parte *m* (en el ejército) **3** PROMPTNESS : prontitud *f*, rapidez *f*
dispel [dɪsˈpɛl] *vt* **-pelled; -pelling** : disipar, desvanecer
dispensation [ˌdɪspɛnˈseɪʃən] *n* EXEMPTION : exención *m*, dispensa *f*
dispense [dɪsˈpɛnts] *v* **-pensed; -pensing** *vt* **1** DISTRIBUTE : repartir, distribuir, dar **2** ADMINISTER, BESTOW : administrar (justicia), conceder (favores, etc.) **3** : preparar y despachar (medicamentos) — *vi* **to dispense with** : prescindir de
dispenser [dɪsˈpɛntsər] *n* : dispensador *m*, distibuidor *m* automático
dispersal [dɪsˈpərsəl] *n* : dispersión *f*
disperse [dɪsˈpərs] *v* **-persed; -persing** *vt* : dispersar, diseminar — *vi* : dispersarse
dispirit [dɪˈspɪrət] *vt* : desalentar, desanimar
displace [dɪsˈpleɪs] *vt* **-placed; -placing 1** : desplazar (un líquido, etc.) **2** REPLACE : reemplazar
displacement [dɪsˈpleɪsmənt] *n* **1** : desplazamiento *m* (de personas) **2** REPLACEMENT : sustitución *f*, reemplazo *m*
display[1] [dɪsˈpleɪ] *vt* : exponer, exhibir, mostrar
display[2] *n* : muestra *f*, exposición *m*, alarde *m*

displease [dɪs'pliːz] *vt* **-pleased; -pleasing** : desagradar a, disgustar, contrariar
displeasure [dɪs'plɛʒər] *n* : desagrado *m*
disposable [dɪs'poːzəbəl] *adj* **1** : desechable <disposable diapers : pañales desechables> **2** AVAILABLE : disponible
disposal [dɪs'poːzəl] *n* **1** PLACEMENT : disposición *f,* colocación *f* **2** REMOVAL : eliminación *f* **3 to have at one's disposal** : disponer de, tener a su disposición
dispose [dɪs'poːz] *v* **-posed; -posing** *vt* **1** ARRANGE : disponer, colocar **2** INCLINE : predisponer — *vi* **1 to dispose of** DISCARD : desechar, deshacerse de **2 to dispose of** HANDLE : despachar
disposition [ˌdɪspə'zɪʃən] *n* **1** ARRANGEMENT : disposición *f* **2** TENDENCY : predisposición *f,* inclinación *f* **3** TEMPERAMENT : temperamento *m,* carácter *m*
disproportion [ˌdɪsprə'porʃən] *n* : desproporción *f*
disproportionate [ˌdɪsprə'porʃənət] *adj* : desproporcionado — **disproportionately** *adv*
disprove [dɪs'pruːv] *vt* **-proved; -proving** : rebatir, refutar
disputable [dɪs'pjuːtəbəl, 'dɪspjʊtəbəl] *adj* : disputable, discutible
dispute[1] [dɪs'pjuːt] *v* **-puted; -puting** *vt* **1** QUESTION : discutir, cuestionar **2** OPPOSE : combatir, resistir — *vi* ARGUE, DEBATE : discutir
dispute[2] *n* **1** DEBATE : debate *m,* discusión *f* **2** QUARREL : disputa *f,* discusión *f*
disqualification [dɪsˌkwɑləfə'keɪʃən] *n* : descalificación *f*
disqualify [dɪs'kwɑləˌfaɪ] *vt* **-fied; -fying** : descalificar, inhabilitar
disquiet[1] *vt* [dɪs'kwaɪət] : inquietar
disquiet[2] *n* : ansiedad *f,* inquietud *f*
disregard[1] [ˌdɪsrɪ'gɑrd] *vt* : ignorar, no prestar atención a
disregard[2] *n* : indiferencia *f*
disrepair [ˌdɪsrɪ'pær] *n* : mal estado *m*
disreputable [dɪs'rɛpjʊtəbəl] *adj* : de mala fama (dícese de una persona o un lugar), vergonzoso (dícese de la conducta)
disreputably [dɪs'rɛpjʊtəbli] *adv* : vergonzosamente
disrepute [ˌdɪsrɪ'pjuːt] *n* : descrédito *m,* mala fama *f,* deshonra *f*
disrespect [ˌdɪsrɪ'spɛkt] *n* : falta *f* de respeto
disrespectful [ˌdɪsrɪ'spɛktfəl] *adj* : irrespetuoso — **disrespectfully** *adv*
disrobe [dɪs'roːb] *v* **-robed; -robing** *vt* : desvestir, desnudar — *vi* : desvestirse, desnudarse
disrupt [dɪs'rʌpt] *vt* : trastornar, perturbar
disruption [dɪs'rʌpʃən] *n* : trastorno *m*
disruptive [dɪs'rʌptɪv] *adj* : perjudicial, perturbador — **disruptively** *adv*
dissatisfaction [dɪsˌsætəs'fækʃən] *n* : descontento *m,* insatisfacción *f*
dissatisfied [dɪs'sætəsˌfaɪd] *adj* : descontento, insatisfecho
dissatisfy [dɪs'sætəsˌfaɪ] *vt* **-fied; -fying** : no contentar, no satisfacer
dissect [dɪ'sɛkt] *vt* : disecar
dissemble [dɪ'sɛmbəl] *v* **-bled; -bling** *vt* HIDE : ocultar, disimular — *vi* PRETEND : fingir, disimular
disseminate [dɪ'sɛməˌneɪt] *vt* **-nated; -nating** : diseminar, difundir, divulgar
dissemination [dɪˌsɛmə'neɪʃən] *n* : diseminación *f,* difusión *f*
dissension [dɪ'sɛntʃən] *n* : disensión *f,* desacuerdo *m*
dissent[1] [dɪ'sɛnt] *vi* : disentir
dissent[2] *n* : disentimiento *m,* disensión *f*
dissertation [ˌdɪsər'teɪʃən] *n* **1** DISCOURSE : disertación *f,* discurso *m* **2** THESIS : tesis *f*
disservice [dɪs'sərvɪs] *n* : perjuicio *m*
dissident[1] ['dɪsədənt] *adj* : disidente
dissident[2] *n* : disidente *mf*
dissimilar [dɪ'sɪmələr] *adj* : distinto, diferente, disímil
dissipate ['dɪsəˌpeɪt] *vt* **-pated; -pating 1** DISPERSE : disipar, dispersar **2** SQUANDER : malgastar, desperdiciar, derrochar, disipar
dissipation [ˌdɪsə'peɪʃən] *n* : disipación *f,* libertinaje *m*
dissolute ['dɪsəˌluːt] *adj* : disoluto
dissolution [ˌdɪsə'luːʃən] *n* : disolución *f*
dissolve [dɪ'zɑlv] *v* **-solved; -solving** *vt* : disolver — *vi* : disolverse
dissonance ['dɪsənənts] *n* : disonancia *f*
dissuade [dɪ'sweɪd] *vt* **-suaded; -suading** : disuadir
distance ['dɪstənts] *n* **1** : distancia *f* <the distance between two points : la distancia entre dos puntos> <in the distance : a lo lejos> **2** RESERVE : actitud *f* distante, reserva *f* <to keep one's distance : guardar las distancias>
distant ['dɪstənt] *adj* **1** FAR : distante, lejano **2** REMOTE : distante, lejano, remoto **3** ALOOF : distante, frío
distantly ['dɪstəntli] *adv* **1** LOOSELY : aproximadamente, vagamente **2** COLDLY : fríamente, con frialdad
distaste [dɪs'teɪst] *n* : desagrado *m,* aversión *f*
distasteful [dɪs'teɪstfəl] *adj* : desagradable, de mal gusto
distemper [dɪs'tɛmpər] *n* : moquillo *m*
distend [dɪs'tɛnd] *vt* : dilatar, hinchar — *vi* : dilatarse, hincharse
distill [dɪ'stɪl] *vt* : destilar
distillation [ˌdɪstə'leɪʃən] *n* : destilación *f*

distiller [dɪˈstɪlər] *n* **:** destilador *m,* -dora *f*
distinct [dɪˈstɪŋkt] *adj* **1** DIFFERENT **:** distinto, diferente **2** CLEAR, UNMISTAKABLE **:** marcado, claro, evidente <a distinct possibility : una clara posibilidad>
distinction [dɪˈstɪŋkʃən] *n* **1** DIFFERENTIATION **:** distinción *f* **2** DIFFERENCE **:** diferencia *f* **3** EXCELLENCE **:** distinción *f,* excelencia *f* <a writer of distinction : un escritor destacado>
distinctive [dɪˈstɪŋktɪv] *adj* **:** distintivo, característico — **distinctively** *adv*
distinctiveness [dɪˈstɪŋktɪvnəs] *n* **:** peculiaridad *f*
distinctly [dɪˈstɪŋktli] *adv* **:** claramente, con claridad
distinguish [dɪsˈtɪŋgwɪʃ] *vt* **1** DIFFERENTIATE **:** distinguir, diferenciar **2** DISCERN **:** distinguir <he distinguished the sound of the piano : distinguió el sonido del piano> **3 to distinguish oneself :** señalarse, distinguirse — *vi* DISCRIMINATE **:** distinguir
distinguishable [dɪsˈtɪŋgwɪʃəbəl] *adj* **:** distinguible
distinguished [dɪsˈtɪŋgwɪʃt] *adj* **:** distinguido
distort [dɪˈstɔrt] *vt* **1** MISREPRESENT **:** distorsionar, tergiversar **2** DEFORM **:** distorsionar, deformar
distortion [dɪˈstɔrʃən] *n* **:** distorsión *f,* deformación *f,* tergiversación *f*
distract [dɪˈstrækt] *vt* **:** distraer, entretener
distracted [dɪˈstræktəd] *adj* **:** distraído
distraction [dɪˈstrækʃən] *n* **1** INTERRUPTION **:** distracción *f,* interrupción *f* **2** CONFUSION **:** confusión *f* **3** AMUSEMENT **:** diversión *f,* entretenimiento *m,* distracción *f*
distraught [dɪˈstrɔt] *adj* **:** afligido, turbado
distress[1] [dɪˈstrɛs] *vt* **:** afligir, darle pena (a alguien), hacer sufrir
distress[2] *n* **1** SORROW **:** dolor *m,* angustia *f,* aflicción *f* **2** PAIN **:** dolor *m* **3 in ~ :** en peligro
distressful [dɪˈstrɛsfəl] *adj* **:** doloroso, penoso
distribute [dɪˈstrɪˌbjuːt, -bjʊt] *vt* **-uted; -uting :** distribuir, repartir
distribution [ˌdɪstrəˈbjuːʃən] *n* **:** distribución *f,* reparto *m*
distributive [dɪˈstrɪbjʊt̬ɪv] *adj* **:** distributivo
distributor [dɪˈstrɪbjʊt̬ər] *n* **:** distribuidor *m,* -dora *f*
district [ˈdɪsˌtrɪkt] *n* **1** REGION **:** región *f,* zona *f,* barrio *m* (de una ciudad) **2 :** distrito *m* (zona política)
distrust[1] [dɪsˈtrʌst] *vt* **:** desconfiar de
distrust[2] *n* **:** desconfianza *f,* recelo *m*
distrustful [dɪsˈtrʌstfəl] *adj* **:** desconfiado, receloso, suspicaz
disturb [dɪˈstərb] *vt* **1** BOTHER **:** molestar, perturbar <sorry to disturb you : perdone la molestia> **2** DISARRANGE **:** desordenar **3** WORRY **:** inquietar, preocupar **4 to disturb the peace :** alterar el orden público
disturbance [dɪˈstərbənts] *n* **1** COMMOTION **:** alboroto *m,* disturbio *m* **2** INTERRUPTION **:** interrupción *f*
disuse [dɪsˈjuːs] *n* **:** desuso *m*
ditch[1] [ˈdɪtʃ] *vt* **1 :** cavar zanjas en **2** DISCARD **:** deshacerse de, botar
ditch[2] *n* **:** zanja *f,* fosa *f,* cuneta *f* (en una carretera)
dither [ˈdɪðər] *n* **to be in a dither :** estar nervioso, ponerse como loco
ditto [ˈdɪt̬oː] *n, pl* **-tos 1 :** lo mismo, ídem *m* **2 ditto marks :** comillas *fpl*
ditty [ˈdɪt̬i] *n, pl* **-ties :** canción *f* corta y simple
diurnal [daɪˈərnəl] *adj* **1** DAILY **:** diario, cotidiano **2 :** diurno <a diurnal animal : un animal diurno>
divan [ˈdaɪˌvæn, dɪˈ-] *n* **:** diván *m*
dive[1] [ˈdaɪv] *vi* **dived** *or* **dove** [ˈdoːv]; **dived; diving 1** PLUNGE **:** tirarse al agua, zambullirse, dar un clavado **2** SUBMERGE **:** sumergirse **3** DROP **:** bajar en picada (dícese de un avión), caer en picada
dive[2] *n* **1** PLUNGE **:** zambullida *f,* clavado *m* (en el agua) **2** DESCENT **:** descenso *m* en picada **3** BAR, JOINT **:** antro *m*
diver [ˈdaɪvər] *n* **:** saltador *m,* -dora *f;* clavadista *mf*
diverge [dəˈvərdʒ, daɪ-] *vi* **-verged; -verging 1** SEPARATE **:** divergir, separarse **2** DIFFER **:** divergir, discrepar
divergence [dəˈvərdʒənts, daɪ-] *n* **:** divergencia *f* — **divergent** [-ənt] *adj*
diverse [daɪˈvərs, də-, ˈdaɪˌvərs] *adj* **:** diverso, variado
diversify [daɪˈvərsəˌfaɪ, də-] *vt* **-fied; -fying :** diversificar, variar
diversion [daɪˈvərʒən, də-] *n* **1** DEVIATION **:** desviación *f* **2** AMUSEMENT, DISTRACTION **:** diversión *f,* distracción *f,* entretenimiento *m*
diversity [daɪˈvərsət̬i, də-] *n, pl* **-ties :** diversidad *f*
divert [dəˈvərt, daɪ-] *vt* **1** DEVIATE **:** desviar **2** DISTRACT **:** distraer **3** AMUSE **:** divertir, entretener
divest [daɪˈvɛst, də-] *vt* **1** UNDRESS **:** desnudar, desvestir **2 to divest of :** despojar de
divide [dəˈvaɪd] *v* **-vided; -viding** *vt* **1** HALVE **:** dividir, partir por la mitad **2** SHARE **:** repartir, dividir **3 :** dividir (números) — *vi* **:** dividirse, dividir (en matemáticas)
dividend [ˈdɪvəˌdɛnd, -dənd] *n* **1 :** dividendo *m* (en finanzas) **2** BONUS **:** benefício *m,* provecho *m* **3 :** dividendo *m* (en matemáticas)
divider [dɪˈvaɪdər] *n* **1 :** separador *m* (para ficheros, etc.) **2** *or* **room divider :** mampara *f,* biombo *m*

divine[1] [də'vaɪn] *adj* **-viner; -est 1** : divino **2** SUPERB : divino, espléndido — **divinely** *adv*
divine[2] *n* : clérigo *m,* eclesiástico *m*
divinity [də'vɪnəṭi] *n, pl* **-ties** : divinidad *f*
divisible [dɪ'vɪzəbəl] *adj* : divisible
division [dɪ'vɪʒən] *n* **1** DISTRIBUTION : división *f,* reparto *m* <division of labor : distribución del trabajo> **2** PART : división *f,* sección *f* **3** : división *f* (en matemáticas)
divisor [dɪ'vaɪzər] *n* : divisor *m*
divorce[1] [də'vors] *v* **-vorced; -vorcing** *vt* : divorciar — *vi* : divorciarse
divorce[2] *n* : divorcio *m*
divorcé [dɪ,vor'seɪ, -'siː; -'vor,-] *n* : divorciado *m*
divorcée [dɪ,vor'seɪ, -'siː; -'vor,-] *n* : divorciada *f*
divulge [də'vʌldʒ, daɪ-] *vt* **-vulged; -vulging** : revelar, divulgar
dizzily ['dɪzəli] *adv* : vertiginosamente
dizziness ['dɪzinəs] *n* : mareo *m,* vahído *m,* vértigo *m*
dizzy ['dɪzi] *adj* **dizzier; -est 1** : mareado <I feel dizzy : estoy mareado> **2** : vertiginoso <a dizzy speed : una velocidad vertiginosa>
DNA [,diː,ɛn'eɪ] *n* : AND *m*
do ['duː] *v* **did** ['dɪd]; **done** ['dʌn]; **doing; does** ['dʌz] *vt* **1** CARRY OUT, PERFORM : hacer, realizar, llevar a cabo <she did her best : hizo todo lo posible> **2** PREPARE : preparar, hacer <do your homework : haz tu tarea> **3** ARRANGE : arreglar, peinar (el pelo) **4 to do in** RUIN : estropear, arruinar **5 to do in** KILL : matar, liquidar *fam* — *vi* **1** : hacer <you did well : hiciste bien> **2** FARE : estar, ir, andar <how are you doing? : ¿cómo estás?, ¿cómo te va?> **3** FINISH : terminar <now I'm done : ya terminé> **4** SERVE : servir, ser suficiente, alcanzar <this will do for now : esto servirá por el momento> **5 to do away with** ABOLISH : abolir, suprimir **6 to do away with** KILL : eliminar, matar **7 to do by** TREAT : tratar <he does well by her : él la trata bien> — *v aux* **1** (*used in interrogative sentences and negative statements*) <do you know her? : ¿la conoces?> <I don't like that : a mí no me gusta eso> **2** (*used for emphasis*) <I do hope you'll come : espero que vengas> **3** (*used as a substitute verb to avoid repetition*) <do you speak English? yes, I do : ¿habla inglés? sí>
docile ['dɑsəl] *adj* : dócil, sumiso
dock[1] ['dɑk] *vt* **1** CUT : cortar **2** : descontar dinero de (un sueldo) — *vi* ANCHOR, LAND : fondear, atracar
dock[2] *n* **1** PIER : atracadero *m* **2** WHARF : muelle *m* **3** : banquillo *m* de los acusados (en un tribunal)
doctor[1] ['dɑktər] *vt* **1** TREAT : tratar, curar **2** ALTER : adulterar, alterar, falsificar (un documento)
doctor[2] *n* **1** : doctor *m,* -tora *f* <Doctor of Philosophy : doctor en filosofía> **2** PHYSICIAN : médico *m,* -ca *f;* doctor *m,* -tora *f*
doctrine ['dɑktrɪn] *n* : doctrina *f*
document[1] ['dɑkjʊ,mɛnt] *vt* : documentar
document[2] ['dɑkjʊmənt] *n* : documento *m*
documentary[1] [,dɑkjʊ'mɛntəri] *adj* : documental
documentary[2] *n, pl* **-ries** : documental *m*
documentation [,dɑkjʊmən'teɪʃən] *n* : documentación *f*
dodge[1] ['dɑdʒ] *v* **dodged; dodging** *vt* : esquivar, eludir, evadir (impuestos) — *vi* : echarse a un lado
dodge[2] *n* **1** RUSE : truco *m,* treta *f,* artimaña *f* **2** EVASION : regate *m,* evasión *f*
dodo ['doː,doː] *n, pl* **-does** *or* **-dos** : dodo *m*
doe ['doː] *n, pl* **does** *or* **doe** : gama *f,* cierva *f*
doer ['duːər] *n* : hacedor *m,* -dora *f*
does → **do**
doff ['dɑf, 'dɔf] *vt* : quitarse <to doff one's hat : quitarse el sombrero>
dog[1] ['dɔg, 'dɑg] *vt* **dogged; dogging** : seguir de cerca, perseguir, acosar <to dog someone's footsteps : seguir los pasos de alguien> <dogged by bad luck : perseguido por la mala suerte>
dog[2] *n* : perro *m,* -rra *f*
dogcatcher ['dɔg,kætʃər] *n* : perrero *m,* -ra *f*
dog–eared ['dɔg,ɪrd] *adj* : con las esquinas dobladas
dogged ['dɔgəd] *adj* : tenaz, terco, obstinado
doggy ['dɔgi] *n, pl* **doggies** : perrito *m,* -ta *f*
doghouse ['dɔg,haʊs] *n* : casita *f* de perro
dogma ['dɔgmə] *n* : dogma *m*
dogmatic [dɔg'mæṭɪk] *adj* : dogmático
dogmatism ['dɔgmə,tɪzəm] *n* : dogmatismo *m*
dogwood ['dɔg,wʊd] *n* : cornejo *m*
doily ['dɔɪli] *n, pl* **-lies** : pañito *m*
doings ['duːɪŋz] *npl* : eventos *mpl,* actividades *fpl*
doldrums ['doːldrəmz, 'dɑl-] *npl* **1** : zona *f* de las calmas ecuatoriales **2 to be in the doldrums** : estar abatido (dícese de una persona), estar estancado (dícese de una empresa)
dole ['doːl] *n* **1** ALMS : distribución *f* a los necesitados, limosna *f* **2** : subsidios *mpl* de desempleo
doleful ['doːlfəl] *adj* : triste, lúgubre
dolefully ['doːlfəli] *adv* : con pesar, de manera triste
dole out *vt* **doled out; doling out** : repartir
doll ['dɑl, 'dɔl] *n* : muñeco *m,* -ca *f*
dollar ['dɑlər] *n* : dólar *m*

dolly [ˈdɑli] *n, pl* **-lies 1** → **doll 2** : plataforma *f* rodante
dolphin [ˈdɑlfən, ˈdɔl-] *n* : delfín *m*
dolt [ˈdoːlt] *n* : imbécil *mf;* tonto *m,* -ta *f*
domain [doˈmeɪn, də-] *n* **1** TERRITORY : dominio *m,* territorio *m* **2** FIELD : campo *m,* esfera *f,* ámbito *m* <the domain of art : el ámbito de las artes>
dome [ˈdoːm] *n* : cúpula *f,* bóveda *f*
domestic[1] [dəˈmɛstɪk] *adj* **1** HOUSEHOLD : doméstico, casero **2** : nacional, interno <domestic policy : política interna> **3** TAME : domesticado
domestic[2] *n* : empleado *m* doméstico, empleada *f* doméstica
domestically [dəˈmɛstɪkli] *adv* : domésticamente
domesticate [dəˈmɛstɪˌkeɪt] *vt* **-cated; -cating** : domesticar
domicile [ˈdɑməˌsaɪl, ˈdoː-; ˈdɑməsɪl] *n* : domicilio *m*
dominance [ˈdɑmənənts] *n* : dominio *m,* dominación *f*
dominant [ˈdɑmənənt] *adj* : dominante
dominate [ˈdɑməˌneɪt] *v* **-nated; -nating** : dominar
domination [ˌdɑməˈneɪʃən] *n* : dominación *f*
domineer [ˌdɑməˈnɪr] *vt* : dominar sobre, avasallar, tiranizar
Dominican [dəˈmɪnɪkən] *n* : dominicano *m,* -na *f* — **Dominican** *adj*
dominion [dəˈmɪnjən] *n* **1** POWER : dominio *m* **2** DOMAIN, TERRITORY : dominio *m,* territorio *m*
domino [ˈdɑməˌnoː] *n, pl* **-noes** *or* **-nos 1** : dominó *m* **2 dominoes** *npl* : dominó *m* (juego)
don [ˈdɑn] *vt* **donned; donning** : ponerse
donate [ˈdoːˌneɪt, doːˈ-] *vt* **-nated; -nating** : donar, hacer un donativo de
donation [doːˈneɪʃən] *n* : donación *f,* donativo *m*
done[1] [ˈdʌn] → **do**
done[2] *adj* **1** FINISHED : terminado, acabado, concluido **2** COOKED : cocinado
donkey [ˈdɑŋki, ˈdʌŋ-] *n, pl* **-keys** : burro *m,* asno *m*
donor [ˈdoːnər] *n* : donante *mf;* donador *m,* -dora *f*
doodle[1] [ˈduːdəl] *v* **-dled; -dling** : garabatear
doodle[2] *n* : garabato *m*
doom[1] [ˈduːm] *vt* : condenar
doom[2] *n* **1** JUDGMENT : sentencia *f,* condena *f* **2** DEATH : muerte *f* **3** FATE : destino *m* **4** RUIN : perdición *f,* ruina *f*
door [ˈdor] *n* : puerta *f*
doorbell [ˈdorˌbɛl] *n* : timbre *m*
doorknob [ˈdorˌnɑb] *n* : pomo *m,* perilla *f*
doorman [ˈdormən] *n, pl* **-men** [-mən, -ˌmɛn] : portero *m*
doormat [ˈdorˌmæt] *n* : felpudo *m*
doorstep [ˈdorˌstɛp] *n* : umbral *m*
doorway [ˈdorˌweɪ] *n* : entrada *f,* portal *m*
dope[1] [ˈdoːp] *vt* **doped; doping** : drogar, narcotizar
dope[2] *n* **1** DRUG : droga *f,* estupefaciente *m,* narcótico *m* **2** IDIOT : idiota *mf;* tonto *m,* -ta *f* **3** INFORMATION : información *f*
dormant [ˈdɔrmənt] *adj* : inactivo, latente
dormer [ˈdɔrmər] *n* : buhardilla *f*
dormitory [ˈdɔrməˌtori] *n, pl* **-ries** : dormitorio *m,* residencia *f* de estudiantes
dormouse [ˈdɔrˌmaʊs] *n* : lirón *m*
dorsal [ˈdɔrsəl] *adj* : dorsal — **dorsally** *adv*
dory [ˈdori] *n, pl* **-ries** : bote *m* de fondo plano
dosage [ˈdoːsɪdʒ] *n* : dosis *f*
dose[1] [ˈdoːs] *vt* **dosed; dosing** : medicinar
dose[2] *n* : dosis *f*
dot[1] [ˈdɑt] *vt* **dotted; dotting 1** : poner el punto sobre (una letra) **2** SCATTER : esparcir, salpicar
dot[2] *n* : punto *m* <at six on the dot : a las seis en punto> <dots and dashes : puntos y rayas>
dote [ˈdoːt] *vi* **doted; doting** : chochear
double[1] [ˈdʌbəl] *v* **-bled; -bling** *vt* **1** : doblar, duplicar (una cantidad), redoblar (esfuerzos) **2** FOLD : doblar, plegar **3 to double one's fist** : apretar el puño — *vi* **1** : doblarse, duplicarse **2 to double over** : retorcerse
double[2] *adj* : doble — **doubly** *adv*
double[3] *n* : doble *mf*
double bass *n* : contrabajo *m*
double–cross [ˌdʌbəlˈkrɔs] *vt* : traicionar
double–crosser [ˌdʌbəlˈkrɔsər] *n* : traidor *m,* -dora *f*
double–jointed [ˌdʌbəlˈdʒɔintəd] *adj* : con articulaciones dobles
double–talk [ˈdʌbəlˌtɔk] *n* : ambigüedades *fpl,* lenguaje *m* con doble sentido
doubt[1] [ˈdaʊt] *vt* **1** QUESTION : dudar de, cuestionar **2** DISTRUST : desconfiar de **3** : dudar, creer poco probable <I doubt it very much : lo dudo mucho>
doubt[2] *n* **1** UNCERTAINTY : duda *f,* incertidumbre *f* **2** DISTRUST : desconfianza *f* **3** SKEPTICISM : duda *f,* escepticismo *m*
doubtful [ˈdaʊtfəl] *adj* **1** QUESTIONABLE : dudoso **2** UNCERTAIN : dudoso, incierto
doubtfully [ˈdaʊtfəli] *adv* : dudosamente, sin estar convencido
doubtless [ˈdaʊtləs] *or* **doubtlessly** *adv* : sin duda
douche[1] [ˈduːʃ] *vt* **douched; douching** : irrigar
douche[2] *n* : ducha *f,* irrigación *f*
dough [ˈdoː] *n* : masa *f*

doughnut [ˈdoːˌnʌt] *n* : rosquilla *f*, dona *f Mex*
doughty [ˈdaʊṱi] *adj* **-tier; -est** : fuerte, valiente
dour [ˈdaʊər, ˈdʊr] *adj* **1** STERN : severo, adusto **2** SULLEN : hosco, taciturno — **dourly** *adv*
douse [ˈdaʊs, ˈdaʊz] *vt* **doused; dousing 1** DRENCH : empapar, mojar **2** EXTINGUISH : extinguir, apagar
dove[1] [ˈdoːv] → **dive**
dove[2] [ˈdʌv] *n* : paloma *f*
dovetail [ˈdʌvˌteɪl] *vi* : encajar, enlazar
dowdy [ˈdaʊdi] *adj* **dowdier; -est** : sin gracia, poco elegante
dowel [ˈdaʊəl] *n* : clavija *f*
down[1] [ˈdaʊn] *vt* **1** FELL : tumbar, derribar, abatir **2** DEFEAT : derrotar
down[2] *adv* **1** DOWNWARD : hacia abajo **2 to lie down** : acostarse, echarse **3 to put down (money)** : pagar un depósito (de dinero) **4 to sit down** : sentarse **5 to take down, to write down** : apuntar, anotar
down[3] *adj* **1** DESCENDING : de bajada <the down elevator : el ascensor de bajada> **2** REDUCED : reducido, rebajado <attendance is down : la concurrencia ha disminuido> **3** DOWNCAST : abatido, deprimido
down[4] *n* : plumón *m*
down[5] *prep* **1** : (hacia) abajo <down the mountain : montaña abajo> <I walked down the stairs : bajé por la escalera> **2** ALONG : por, a lo largo de <we ran down the beach : corrimos por la playa> **3** : a través de <down the years : a través de los años>
downcast [ˈdaʊnˌkæst] *adj* **1** SAD : triste, abatido **2 with downcast eyes** : con los ojos bajos, con los ojos mirando al suelo
downfall [ˈdaʊnˌfɔl] *n* : ruina *f*, perdición *f*
downgrade[1] [ˈdaʊnˌgreɪd] *vt* **-graded; -grading** : bajar de categoría
downgrade[2] *n* : bajada *f*
downhearted [ˈdaʊnˌhɑrṱəd] *adj* : desanimado, descorazonado
downhill [ˈdaʊnˈhɪl] *adv & adj* : cuesta abajo
down payment *n* : entrega *f* inicial
downpour [ˈdaʊnˌpor] *n* : aguacero *m*, chaparrón *m*
downright[1] [ˈdaʊnˌraɪt] *adv* THOROUGHLY : absolutamente, completamente
downright[2] *adj* : patente, manifiesto, absoluto <a downright refusal : un rechazo categórico>
downstairs[1] [ˈdaʊnˈstærz] *adv* : abajo
downstairs[2] [ˈdaʊnˌstærz] *adj* : del piso de abajo
downstairs[3] [ˈdaʊnˈstærz, -ˌstærz] *n* : planta *f* baja
downstream [ˈdaʊnˈstriːm] *adv* : río abajo
down–to–earth [ˌdaʊntuˈərth] *adj* : práctico, realista
downtown[1] [ˌdaʊnˈtaʊn] *adv* : hacia el centro, al centro, en el centro (de la ciudad)
downtown[2] *adj* : del centro (de la ciudad) <downtown Chicago : el centro de Chicago>
downtown[3] [ˌdaʊnˈtaʊn, ˈdaʊnˌtaʊn] *n* : centro *m* (de la ciudad)
downtrodden [ˈdaʊnˌtrɑdən] *adj* : oprimido
downward [ˈdaʊnwərd] *or* **downwards** [-wərdz] *adv & adj* : hacia abajo
downwind [ˈdaʊnˈwɪnd] *adv & adj* : en la dirección del viento
downy [ˈdaʊni] *adj* **downier; -est 1** : cubierto de plumón, plumoso **2** VELVETY : aterciopelado, velloso
dowry [ˈdaʊri] *n, pl* **-ries** : dote *f*
doze[1] [ˈdoːz] *vi* **dozed; dozing** : dormitar
doze[2] *n* : sueño *m* ligero, cabezada *f*
dozen [ˈdʌzən] *n, pl* **dozens** *or* **dozen** : docena *f*
drab [ˈdræb] *adj* **drabber; drabbest 1** BROWNISH : pardo **2** DULL, LACKLUSTER : monótono, gris, deslustrado
draft[1] [ˈdræft, ˈdraft] *vt* **1** CONSCRIPT : reclutar **2** COMPOSE, SKETCH : hacer el borrador de, redactar
draft[2] *adj* **1** : de barril <draft beer : cerveza de barril> **2** : de tiro <draft horses : caballos de tiro>
draft[3] *n* **1** HAULAGE : tiro *m* **2** DRINK, GULP : trago *m* **3** OUTLINE, SKETCH : bosquejo *m*, borrador *m*, versión *f* **4** : corriente *f* de aire, chiflón *m*, tiro *m* (de una chimenea) **5** CONSCRIPTION : conscripción *f* **6 bank draft** : giro *m* bancario, letra *f* de cambio
draftee [dræfˈtiː] *n* : recluta *mf*
draftsman [ˈdræftsmən] *n, pl* **-men** [-mən, -ˌmɛn] : dibujante *mf*
drafty [ˈdræfti] *adj* **draftier; -est** : con corrientes de aire
drag[1] [ˈdræg] *v* **dragged; dragging** *vt* **1** HAUL : arrastrar, jalar **2** DREDGE : dragar — *vi* **1** TRAIL : arrastrarse **2** LAG : rezagarse **3** : hacerse pesado, hacerse largo <the day dragged on : el día se hizo largo>
drag[2] *n* **1** RESISTANCE : resistencia *f* (aerodinámica) **2** HINDRANCE : traba *f*, estorbo *m* **3** BORE : pesadez *f*, plomo *m fam*
dragnet [ˈdrægˌnɛt] *n* **1** : red *f* barredera (en pesca) **2** : operativo *m* policial de captura
dragon [ˈdrægən] *n* : dragón *m*
dragonfly [ˈdrægənˌflaɪ] *n, pl* **-flies** : libélula *f*
drain[1] [ˈdreɪn] *vt* **1** EMPTY : vaciar, drenar **2** EXHAUST : agotar, consumir — *vi* **1** : escurrir, escurrirse <the dishes are draining : los platos están escurriéndose> **2** EMPTY : desaguar **3 to drain away** : irse agotando

drain[2] *n* **1** : desagüe *m* **2** SEWER : alcantarilla *f* **3** GRATING : sumidero *m*, resumidero *m*, rejilla *f* **4** EXHAUSTION : agotamiento *m*, disminución *f* (de energía, etc.) <to be a drain on : agotar, consumir> **5 to throw down the drain** : tirar por la ventana

drainage [ˈdreɪnɪdʒ] *n* : desagüe *m*, drenaje *m*

drainpipe [ˈdreɪn,paɪp] *n* : tubo *m* de desagüe, caño *m*

drake [ˈdreɪk] *n* : pato *m* (macho)

drama [ˈdrɑmə, ˈdræ-] *n* **1** THEATER : drama *m*, teatro *m* **2** PLAY : obra *f* de teatro, drama *m*

dramatic [drəˈmæt̬ɪk] *adj* : dramático — **dramatically** [-t̬ɪkli] *adv*

dramatist [ˈdræmət̬ɪst, ˈdrɑ-] *n* : dramaturgo *m*, -ga *f*

dramatization [,dræmət̬əˈzeɪʃən, ,drɑ-] *n* : dramatización *f*

dramatize [ˈdræmə,taɪz, ˈdrɑ-] *vt* **-tized; -tizing** : dramatizar

drank → **drink**

drape[1] [ˈdreɪp] *vt* **draped; draping 1** COVER : cubrir (con tela) **2** HANG : drapear, disponer los pliegues de

drape[2] *n* **1** HANG : caída *f* **2 drapes** *npl* : cortinas *fpl*

drapery [ˈdreɪpəri] *n, pl* **-eries 1** CLOTH : pañería *f*, tela *f* para cortinas **2 draperies** *npl* : cortinas *fpl*

drastic [ˈdræstɪk] *adj* **1** HARSH, SEVERE : drástico, severo **2** EXTREME : radical, excepcional — **drastically** [-tɪkli] *adv*

draught [ˈdræft, ˈdraft] → **draft**[3]

draughty [ˈdrafti] → **drafty**

draw[1] [ˈdrɔ] *v* **drew** [ˈdruː]; **drawn** [ˈdrɔn]; **drawing** *vt* **1** PULL : tirar de, jalar, correr (cortinas) **2** ATTRACT : atraer **3** PROVOKE : provocar, suscitar **4** INHALE : aspirar <to draw breath : respirar> **5** EXTRACT : sacar, extraer **6** TAKE : sacar <to draw a number : sacar un número> **7** COLLECT : cobrar, percibir (un sueldo, etc.) **8** BEND : tensar (un arco) **9** TIE : empatar (en deportes) **10** SKETCH : dibujar, trazar **11** FORMULATE : sacar, formular, llegar a <to draw a conclusion : llegar a una conclusión> **12 to draw out** : hacer hablar (sobre algo), hacer salir de sí mismo **13 to draw up** DRAFT : redactar — *vi* **1** SKETCH : dibujar **2** TUG : tirar, jalar **3 to draw near** : acercarse **4 to draw to a close** : terminar, finalizar **5 to draw up** STOP : parar

draw[2] *n* **1** DRAWING, RAFFLE : sorteo *m* **2** TIE : empate *m* **3** ATTRACTION : atracción *f* **4** PUFF : chupada *f* (de un cigarrillo, etc.)

drawback [ˈdrɔ,bæk] *n* : desventaja *f*, inconveniente *m*

drawbridge [ˈdrɔ,bridʒ] *n* : puente *m* levadizo

drawer [ˈdrɔr, ˈdrɔər] *n* **1** ILLUSTRATOR : dibujante *mf* **2** : gaveta *f*, cajón *m* (en un mueble) **3 drawers** *npl* UNDERPANTS : calzones *mpl*

drawing [ˈdrɔɪŋ] *n* **1** LOTTERY : sorteo *m*, lotería *f* **2** SKETCH : dibujo *m*, bosquejo *m*

drawl[1] [ˈdrɔl] *vi* : hablar arrastrando las palabras

drawl[2] *n* : habla *f* lenta y con vocales prolongadas

dread[1] [ˈdrɛd] *vt* : tenerle pavor a, temer

dread[2] *adj* : pavoroso, aterrado

dread[3] *n* : pavor *m*, temor *m*

dreadful [ˈdrɛdfəl] *adj* **1** DREAD : pavoroso **2** TERRIBLE : espantoso, atroz, terrible — **dreadfully** *adv*

dream[1] [ˈdriːm] *v* **dreamed** [ˈdrɛmpt, ˈdriːmd] *or* **dreamt** [ˈdrɛmpt]; **dreaming** *vi* **1** : soñar <to dream about : soñar con> **2** FANTASIZE : fantasear — *vt* **1** : soñar **2** IMAGINE : imaginarse **3 to dream up** : inventar, idear

dream[2] *n* **1** : sueño *m*, ensueño *m* **2 bad dream** NIGHTMARE : pesadilla *f*

dreamer [ˈdriːmər] *n* : soñador *m*, -dora *f*

dreamlike [ˈdriːm,laɪk] *adj* : de ensueño

dreamy [ˈdriːmi] *adj* **dreamier; -est 1** DISTRACTED : soñador, distraído **2** DREAMLIKE : de ensueño **3** MARVELOUS : maravilloso

drearily [ˈdrɪrəli] *adv* : sombríamente

dreary [ˈdrɪri] *adj* **-rier; -est** : deprimente, lóbrego, sombrío

dredge[1] [ˈdrɛdʒ] *vt* **dredged; dredging 1** DIG : dragar **2** COAT : espolvorear, enharinar

dredge[2] *n* : draga *f*

dredger [ˈdrɛdʒər] *n* : draga *f*

dregs [ˈdrɛgz] *npl* **1** LEES : posos *mpl*, heces *fpl* (de un líquido) **2** : heces *fpl*, escoria *f* <the dregs of society : la escoria de la sociedad>

drench [ˈdrɛntʃ] *vt* : empapar, mojar, calar

dress[1] [ˈdrɛs] *vt* **1** CLOTHE : vestir **2** DECORATE : decorar, adornar **3** : preparar (pollo o pescado), aliñar (ensalada) **4** : curar, vendar (una herida) **5** FERTILIZE : abonar (la tierra) — *vi* **1** : vestirse **2 to dress up** : ataviarse, engalanarse, ponerse de etiqueta

dress[2] *n* **1** APPAREL : indumentaria *f*, ropa *f* **2** : vestido *m*, traje *m* (de mujer)

dresser [ˈdrɛsər] *n* : cómoda *f* con espejo

dressing [ˈdrɛsɪŋ] *n* **1** : vestirse *m* **2** : aderezo *m*, aliño *m* (de ensalada), relleno *m* (de pollo) **3** BANDAGE : vendaje *m*, gasa *f*

dressmaker [ˈdrɛs,meɪkər] *n* : modista *mf*

dressmaking [ˈdrɛs,meɪkɪŋ] *n* : costura *f*

dressy [ˈdrɛsi] *adj* **dressier; -est** : de mucho vestir, elegante

drew → **draw**

dribble[1] ['drɪbəl] *vi* **-bled; -bling 1** DRIP : gotear **2** DROOL : babear **3** : driblar (en basquetbol)
dribble[2] *n* **1** TRICKLE : goteo *m,* hilo *m* **2** DROOL : baba *f* **3** : drible *m* (en basquetbol)
drier → **dry**[2], **dryer**
driest → **dry**[2]
drift[1] ['drɪft] *vi* **1** : dejarse llevar por la corriente, ir a la deriva (dícese de un bote), ir sin rumbo (dícese de una persona) **2** ACCUMULATE : amontonarse, acumularse, apilarse
drift[2] *n* **1** DRIFTING : deriva *f* **2** HEAP, MASS : montón *m* (de arena, etc.), ventisquero *m* (de nieve) **3** MEANING : sentido *m*
drifter ['drɪftər] *n* : vagabundo *m,* -da *f*
driftwood ['drɪft,wʊd] *n* : madera *f* flotante
drill[1] ['drɪl] *vt* **1** BORE : perforar, taladrar **2** INSTRUCT : instruir por repetición — *vi* **1** TRAIN : entrenarse **2 to drill for oil** : perforar en busca de petróleo
drill[2] *n* **1** : taladro *m,* barrena *f* **2** EXERCISE, PRACTICE : ejercicio *m,* instrucción *f*
drily → **dryly**
drink[1] ['drɪŋk] *v* **drank** ['dræŋk]; **drunk** ['drʌŋk] *or* **drank; drinking** *vt* **1** IMBIBE : beber, tomar **2 to drink up** ABSORB : absorber — *vi* **1** : beber **2** : beber alcohol, tomar
drink[2] *n* **1** : bebida *f* **2** : bebida *f* alcohólica
drinkable ['drɪŋkəbəl] *adj* : potable
drinker ['drɪŋkər] *n* : bebedor *m,* -dora *f*
drip[1] ['drɪp] *vi* **dripped; dripping** : gotear, chorrear
drip[2] *n* **1** DROP : gota *f* **2** DRIPPING : goteo *m*
drive[1] ['draɪv] *v* **drove** ['dro:v]; **driven** ['drɪvən]; **driving** *vt* **1** IMPEL : impeler, impulsar **2** OPERATE : guiar, conducir, manejar (un vehículo) **3** COMPEL : obligar, forzar **4** : clavar, hincar <to drive a stake : clavar una estaca> **5** *or* **to drive away** : ahuyentar, echar **6 to drive crazy** : volver loco — *vi* : manejar, conducir <do you know how to drive? : ¿sabes manejar?>
drive[2] *n* **1** RIDE : paseo *m* en coche **2** CAMPAIGN : campaña *f* <fund-raising drive : campaña para recaudar fondos> **3** DRIVEWAY : camino *m* de entrada, entrada *f* **4** TRANSMISSION : transmisión *f* <front-wheel drive : tracción delantera> **5** ENERGY : dinamismo *m,* energía *f* **6** INSTINCT, NEED : instinto *m,* necesidad *f* básica
drivel ['drɪvəl] *n* : tontería *f,* estupidez *f*
driver ['draɪvər] *n* : conductor *m,* -tora *f;* chofer *m*
driveway ['draɪv,weɪ] *n* : camino *m* de entrada, entrada *f* (para coches)
drizzle[1] ['drɪzəl] *vi* **-zled; -zling** : lloviznar, garuar
drizzle[2] *n* : llovizna *f,* garúa *f*
droll ['dro:l] *adj* : cómico, gracioso, chistoso — **drolly** *adv*
dromedary ['drɑmə,dɛri] *n, pl* **-daries** : dromedario *m*
drone[1] ['dro:n] *vi* **droned; droning 1** BUZZ : zumbar **2** MURMUR : hablar con monotonía, murmurar
drone[2] *n* **1** : zángano *m* (abeja) **2** FREELOADER : gorrón *m,* -rrona *f fam;* parásito *m,* -ta *f* **3** BUZZ, HUM : zumbido *m,* murmullo *m*
drool[1] ['dru:l] *vi* : babear
drool[2] *n* : baba *f*
droop[1] ['dru:p] *vi* **1** HANG : inclinarse (dícese de la cabeza), encorvarse (dícese de los escombros), marchitarse (dícese de las flores) **2** FLAG : decaer, flaquear <his spirits drooped : se desanimó>
droop[2] *n* : inclinación *f,* caída *f*
drop[1] ['drɑp] *v* **dropped; dropping** *vt* **1** : dejar caer, soltar <she dropped the glass : se le cayó el vaso> <to drop a hint : dejar caer una indirecta> **2** SEND : mandar <drop me a line : mándame unas líneas> **3** ABANDON : abandonar, dejar <to drop the subject : cambiar de tema> **4** LOWER : bajar <he dropped his voice : bajó la voz> **5** OMIT : omitir **6 to drop off** : dejar — *vi* **1** DRIP : gotear **2** FALL : caer(se) **3** DECREASE, DESCEND : bajar, descender <the wind dropped : amainó el viento> **4 to drop back** *or* **to drop behind** : rezagarse, quedarse atrás **5 to drop by** *or* **to drop in** : pasar
drop[2] *n* **1** : gota *f* (de líquido) **2** DECLINE : caída *f,* bajada *f,* descenso *m* **3** INCLINE : caída *f,* pendiente *f* <a 20-foot drop : una caída de 20 pies> **4** SWEET : pastilla *f,* dulce *m* **5 drops** *npl* : gotas *fpl* (de medicina)
droplet ['drɑplət] *n* : gotita *f*
dropper ['drɑpər] *n* : gotero *m,* cuentagotas *m*
dross ['drɑs, 'drɔs] *n* : escoria *f*
drought ['draʊt] *n* : sequía *f*
drove[1] → **drive**
drove[2] ['dro:v] *n* : multitud *f,* gentío *m,* manada *f* (de ganado) <in droves : en manada>
drown ['draʊn] *vt* **1** : ahogar **2** INUNDATE : anegar, inundar **3 to drown out** : ahogar — *vi* : ahogarse
drowse[1] ['draʊz] *vi* **drowsed; drowsing** DOZE : dormitar
drowse[2] *n* : sueño *m* ligero, cabezada *f*
drowsiness ['draʊzinəs] *n* : somnolencia *f,* adormecimiento *m*
drowsy ['draʊzi] *adj* **drowsier; -est** : somnoliento, soñoliento

drub [ˈdrʌb] *vt* **drubbed; drubbing 1** BEAT, THRASH **:** golpear, apalear **2** DEFEAT **:** derrotar por completo
drudge[1] [ˈdrʌdʒ] *vi* **drudged; drudging :** trabajar como esclavo, trabajar duro
drudge[2] *n* **:** esclavo *m*, -va *f* del trabajo
drudgery [ˈdrʌdʒəri] *n, pl* **-eries :** trabajo *m* pesado
drug[1] [ˈdrʌg] *vt* **drugged; drugging :** drogar, narcotizar
drug[2] *n* **1** MEDICATION **:** droga *f*, medicina *f*, medicamento *m* **2** NARCOTIC **:** narcótico *m*, estupefaciente *m*, droga *f*
druggist [ˈdrʌgɪst] *n* **:** farmacéutico *m*, -ca *f*
drugstore [ˈdrʌgˌstor] *n* **:** farmacia *f*, botica *f*, droguería *f*
drum[1] [ˈdrʌm] *v* **drummed; drumming** *vt* **:** meter a fuerza <he drummed it into my head : me lo metió en la cabeza a fuerza> — *vi* **:** tocar el tambor
drum[2] *n* **1 :** tambor *m* **2 :** bidón *m* <oil drum : bidón de petróleo>
drummer [ˈdrʌmər] *n* **:** baterista *mf*
drumstick [ˈdrʌmˌstɪk] *n* **1 :** palillo *m* (de tambor), baqueta *f* **2 :** muslo *m* de pollo
drunk[1] *pp* → **drink**
drunk[2] [ˈdrʌŋk] *adj* **:** borracho, embriagado, ebrio
drunk[3] *n* **:** borracho *m*, -cha *f*
drunkard [ˈdrʌŋkərd] *n* **:** borracho *m*, -cha *f*
drunken [ˈdrʌŋkən] *adj* **:** borracho, ebrio <drunken driver : conductor ebrio> <drunken brawl : pleito de borrachos>
drunkenly [ˈdrʌŋkənli] *adv* **:** como un borracho
drunkenness [ˈdrʌŋkənnəs] *n* **:** borrachera *f*, embriaguez *f*, ebriedad *f*
dry[1] [ˈdraɪ] *v* **dried; drying** *vt* **:** secar — *vi* **:** secarse
dry[2] *adj* **drier; driest 1 :** seco **2** THIRSTY **:** sediento **3 :** donde la venta de bebidas alcohólicas está prohibida <a dry county : un condado seco> **4** DULL **:** aburrido, árido **5 :** seco (dícese del vino), brut (dícese de la champaña)
dry–clean [ˈdraɪˌkliːn] *v* **:** limpiar en seco
dry cleaner *n* **:** tintorería *f* (servicio)
dry cleaning *n* **:** limpieza *f* en seco
dryer [ˈdraɪər] *n* **1 hair dryer :** secador *m* **2 clothes dryer :** secadora *f*
dry goods *npl* **:** artículos *mpl* de confección
dry ice *n* **:** hielo *m* seco
dryly [ˈdraɪli] *adv* **:** secamente
dryness [ˈdraɪnəs] *n* **:** sequedad *f*, aridez *f*
dual [ˈduːəl, ˈdjuː-] *adj* **:** doble
dub [ˈdʌb] *vt* **dubbed; dubbing 1** CALL **:** apodar **2 :** doblar (una película), mezclar (una grabación)
dubious [ˈduːbiəs, ˈdjuː-] *adj* **1** UNCERTAIN **:** dudoso, indeciso **2** QUESTIONABLE **:** sospechoso, dudoso, discutible
dubiously [ˈduːbiəsli, ˈdjuː-] *adv* **1** UNCERTAINLY **:** dudosamente, con desconfianza **2** SUSPICIOUSLY **:** de modo sospechoso, con recelo
duchess [ˈdʌtʃəs] *n* **:** duquesa *f*
duck[1] [ˈdʌk] *vt* **1** LOWER **:** agachar, bajar (la cabeza) **2** PLUNGE **:** zambullir **3** EVADE **:** eludir, evadir — *vi* **to duck down :** agacharse
duck[2] *n, pl* **duck** *or* **ducks :** pato *m*, -ta *f*
duckling [ˈdʌklɪŋ] *n* **:** patito *m*, -ta *f*
duct [ˈdʌkt] *n* **:** conducto *m*
ductile [ˈdʌktəl] *adj* **:** dúctil
dude [ˈduːd, ˈdjuːd] *n* **1** DANDY **:** dandi *m*, dandy *m* **2** GUY **:** tipo *m*
due[1] [ˈduː, ˈdjuː] *adv* **:** justo a, derecho hacia <due north : derecho hacia el norte>
due[2] *adj* **1** PAYABLE **:** pagadero, sin pagar **2** APPROPRIATE **:** debido, apropiado <after due consideration : con las debidas consideraciones> **3** EXPECTED **:** esperado <the train is due soon : esperamos el tren muy pronto, el tren debe llegar pronto> **4 due to :** debido a, por
due[3] *n* **1 to give someone his (her) due :** darle a alguien su merecido **2 dues** *npl* **:** cuota *f*
duel[1] [ˈduːəl, ˈdjuː-] *vi* **:** batirse en duelo
duel[2] *n* **:** duelo *m*
duet [duˈɛt, dju-] *n* **:** dúo *m*
due to *prep* **:** debido a
dug *pp* → **dig**
dugout [ˈdʌgˌaʊt] *n* **1** CANOE **:** piragua *f* **2** SHELTER **:** refugio *m* subterráneo
duke [ˈduːk, ˈdjuːk] *n* **:** duque *m*
dull[1] [ˈdʌl] *vt* **1** DIM **:** opacar, quitar el brillo a, deslustrar **2** BLUNT **:** embotar (un filo), entorpecer (los sentidos), aliviar (el dolor), amortiguar (sonidos)
dull[2] *adj* **1** STUPID **:** torpe, lerdo, lento **2** BLUNT **:** desafilado, despuntado **3** LACKLUSTER **:** sin brillo, deslustrado **4** BORING **:** aburrido, soso, pesado — **dully** *adv*
dullness [ˈdʌlnəs] *n* **1** STUPIDITY **:** estupidez *f* **2 :** embotamiento *m* (de los sentidos) **3** MONOTONY **:** monotonía *f*, insipidez *f* **4 :** falta *f* de brillo **5** BLUNTNESS **:** falta *f* de filo, embotadura *f*
duly [ˈduːli, ˈdjuː-] *adv* PROPERLY **:** debidamente, a su debido tiempo
dumb [ˈdʌm] *adj* **1** MUTE **:** mudo **2** STUPID **:** estúpido, tonto, bobo — **dumbly** *adv*
dumbbell [ˈdʌmˌbɛl] *n* **1** WEIGHT **:** pesa *f* **2 :** estúpido *m*, -da *f*
dumbfound *or* **dumfound** [ˌdʌmˈfaʊnd] *vt* **:** dejar atónito, dejar sin habla
dummy [ˈdʌmi] *n, pl* **-mies 1** SHAM **:** imitación *f*, sustituto *m* **2** PUPPET

: muñeco *m* **3** MANNEQUIN : maniquí *m* **4** IDIOT : tonto *m,* -ta *f;* idiota *mf*
dump[1] ['dʌmp] *vt* : descargar, verter
dump[2] *n* **1** : vertedero *m,* tiradero *m Mex* **2 down in the dumps** : triste, deprimido
dumpling ['dʌmplɪŋ] *n* : bola *f* de masa hervida
dumpy ['dʌmpi] *adj* **dumpier; -est** : rechoncho, regordete
dun[1] ['dʌn] *vt* **dunned; dunning** : apremiar (a un deudor)
dun[2] *adj* : pardo (color)
dunce ['dʌnts] *n* : estúpido *m,* -da *f;* burro *m,* -rra *f fam*
dune ['du:n, 'dju:n] *n* : duna *f*
dung ['dʌŋ] *n* **1** FECES : excrementos *mpl* **2** MANURE : estiércol *m*
dungaree [ˌdʌŋgə'ri:] *n* **1** DENIM : tela *f* vaquera, mezclilla *f Chile, Mex* **2 dungarees** *npl* : pantalones *mpl* de trabajo hechos de tela vaquera
dungeon ['dʌndʒən] *n* : mazmorra *f,* calabozo *m*
dunk ['dʌŋk] *vt* : mojar, ensopar
duo ['du:o:, 'dju:-] *n, pl* **duos** : dúo *m,* par *m*
dupe[1] ['du:p, dju:p] *vt* **duped; duping** : engañar, embaucar
dupe[2] *n* : inocentón *m,* -tona *f;* simple *mf*
duplex[1] ['du:ˌplɛks, 'dju:-] *adj* : doble
duplex[2] *n* : casa *f* de dos viviendas, dúplex *m*
duplicate[1] ['du:plɪˌkeɪt, 'dju:-] *vt* **-cated; -cating 1** COPY : duplicar, hacer copias de **2** REPEAT : repetir, reproducir
duplicate[2] ['du:plɪkət, 'dju:-] *adj* : duplicado <a duplicate invoice : una factura por duplicado>
duplicate[3] ['du:plɪkət, 'dju:-] *n* : duplicado *m,* copia *f*
duplication [ˌdu:plɪ'keɪʃən, ˌdju:-] *n* **1** DUPLICATING : duplicación *f,* repetición *f* (de esfuerzos) **2** DUPLICATE : copia *f,* duplicado *m*
duplicity [dʊ'plɪsət̬i, ˌdju:-] *n, pl* **-ties** : duplicidad *f*
durability [ˌdʊrə'bɪlət̬i, ˌdjʊr-] *n* : durabilidad *f* (de un producto), permanencia *f*
durable ['dʊrəbəl, 'djʊr-] *adj* : duradero
duration [dʊ'reɪʃən, djʊ-] *n* : duración *f*
duress [dʊ'rɛs, djʊ-] *n* : coacción *f*
during ['dʊrɪŋ, 'djʊr-] *prep* : durante
dusk ['dʌsk] *n* : anochecer *m,* crepúsculo *m*
dusky ['dʌski] *adj* **duskier; -est** : oscuro (dícese de los colores)
dust[1] ['dʌst] *vt* **1** : quitar el polvo de **2** SPRINKLE : espolvorear
dust[2] *n* : polvo *m*
duster ['dʌstər] *n* **1** *or* **dust cloth** : trapo *m* de polvo **2** HOUSECOAT : guardapolvo *m* **3 feather duster** : plumero *m*
dustpan ['dʌstˌpæn] *n* : recogedor *m*
dusty ['dʌsti] *adj* **dustier; -est** : cubierto de polvo, polvoriento
Dutch[1] ['dʌtʃ] *adj* : holandés
Dutch[2] *n* **1** : holandés *m* (idioma) **2 the Dutch** *npl* : los holandeses
Dutch treat *n* : invitación *f* o pago *m* a escote
dutiful ['du:t̬ɪfəl, 'dju:-] *adj* : motivado por sus deberes, responsable
duty ['du:t̬i, 'dju:-] *n, pl* **-ties 1** OBLIGATION : deber *m,* obligación *f,* responsabilidad *f* **2** TAX : impuesto *m,* arancel *m*
dwarf[1] ['dwɔrf] *vt* **1** STUNT : arrestar el crecimiento de **2** : hacer parecer pequeño
dwarf[2] *n, pl* **dwarfs** ['dwɔrfs] *or* **dwarves** ['dwɔrvz] : enano *m,* -na *f*
dwell ['dwɛl] *vi* **dwelled** *or* **dwelt** ['dwɛlt]; **dwelling 1** RESIDE : residir, morar, vivir **2 to dwell on** : pensar demasiado en, insistir en
dweller ['dwɛlər] *n* : habitante *mf*
dwelling ['dwɛlɪŋ] *n* : morada *f,* vivienda *f,* residencia *f*
dwindle ['dwɪndəl] *vi* **-dled; -dling** : menguar, reducirse, disminuir
dye[1] ['daɪ] *vt* **dyed; dyeing** : teñir
dye[2] *n* : tintura *f,* tinte *m*
dying → **die**
dyke → **dike**
dynamic [daɪ'næmɪk] *adj* : dinámico
dynamite[1] ['daɪnəˌmaɪt] *vt* **-mited; -miting** : dinamitar
dynamite[2] *n* : dinamita *f*
dynamo ['daɪnəˌmo:] *n, pl* **-mos** : dínamo *m,* generador *m* de electricidad
dynasty ['daɪnəsti, -ˌnæs-] *n, pl* **-ties** : dinastía *f*
dysentery ['dɪsənˌtɛri] *n, pl* **-teries** : disentería *f*
dystrophy ['dɪstrəfi] *n, pl* **-phies 1** : distrofia *f* **2** → **muscular dystrophy**

E

e ['i:] *n, pl* **e's** *or* **es** ['i:z] : quinta letra del alfabeto inglés
each[1] ['i:tʃ] *adv* : cada uno, por persona <they cost $10 each : costaron $10 cada uno>
each[2] *adj* : cada <each student : cada estudiante> <each and every one : todos sin excepción>
each[3] *pron* **1** : cada uno *m,* cada una *f* <each of us : cada uno de nosotros>

2 each other : el uno al otro, mutuamente <we are helping each other : nos ayudamos el uno al otro> <they love each other : se aman>

eager [ˈiːgər] *adj* **1** ENTHUSIASTIC : entusiasta, ávido, deseoso **2** ANXIOUS : ansioso, impaciente

eagerly [ˈiːgərli] *adv* : con entusiasmo, ansiosamente

eagerness [ˈiːgərnəs] *n* : entusiasmo *m,* deseo *m,* impaciencia *f*

eagle [ˈiːgəl] *n* : águila *f*

ear [ˈɪr] *n* **1** : oído *m,* oreja *f* <inner ear : oído interno> <big ears : orejas grandes> **2 ear of corn** : mazorca *f,* choclo *m*

earache [ˈɪrˌeɪk] *n* : dolor *m* de oído

eardrum [ˈɪrˌdrʌm] *n* : tímpano *m*

earl [ˈərl] *n* : conde *m*

earlobe [ˈɪrˌloːb] *n* : lóbulo *m* de la oreja, perilla *f* de la oreja

early[1] [ˈərli] *adv* **earlier; -est** : temprano, pronto <he arrived early : llegó temprano> <as early as possible : lo más pronto posible, cuanto antes> <ten minutes early : diez minutos de adelanto>

early[2] *adj* **earlier; -est 1** (*referring to a beginning*) : primero <the early stages : las primeras etapas> <in early May : a principios de mayo> **2** (*referring to antiquity*) : primitivo, antiguo <early man : el hombre primitivo> <early painting : la pintura antigua> **3** (*referring to a designated time*) : temprano, antes de la hora, prematuro <he was early : llegó temprano> <early fruit : frutas tempraneras> <an early death : una muerte prematura>

earmark [ˈirˌmɑrk] *vt* : destinar <earmarked funds : fondos destinados>

earn [ˈərn] *vt* **1** : ganar <to earn money : ganar dinero> **2** DESERVE : ganarse, merecer

earnest[1] [ˈərnəst] *adj* : serio, sincero

earnest[2] *n* **in ~** : en serio, de verdad <we began in earnest : empezamos de verdad>

earnestly [ˈərnəstli] *adv* **1** SERIOUSLY : con seriedad, en serio **2** FERVENTLY : de todo corazón

earnestness [ˈərnəstnəs] *n* : seriedad *f,* sinceridad *f*

earnings [ˈərnɪŋz] *npl* : ingresos *mpl,* ganancias *fpl,* utilidades *fpl*

earphone [ˈɪrˌfoːn] *n* : audífono *m*

earring [ˈɪrˌrɪŋ] *n* : zarcillo *m,* arete *m,* aro *m Arg, Chile, Uru,* pendiente *m Spain*

earshot [ˈɪrˌʃɑt] *n* : alcance *m* del oído

earth [ˈərθ] *n* **1** LAND, SOIL : tierra *f,* suelo *m* **2 the Earth** : la Tierra

earthen [ˈərθən, -ðən] *adj* : de tierra, de barro

earthenware [ˈərθənˌwær, -ðən-] *n* : loza *f,* vajillas *fpl* de barro

earthly [ˈərθli] *adj* : terrenal, mundano

earthquake [ˈərθˌkweɪk] *n* : terremoto *m,* temblor *m*

earthworm [ˈərθˌwərm] *n* : lombriz *f* (de tierra)

earthy [ˈərθi] *adj* **earthier; -est 1** : terroso <earthy colors : colores terrosos> **2** DOWN-TO-EARTH : realista, práctico, llano **3** COARSE, CRUDE : basto, grosero, tosco <earthy jokes : chistes groseros>

earwax [ˈɪrˌwæks] → **wax**[2]

earwig [ˈɪrˌwɪg] *n* : tijereta *f*

ease[1] [ˈiːz] *v* **eased; easing** *vt* **1** ALLEVIATE : aliviar, calmar, hacer disminuir **2** LOOSEN, RELAX : aflojar (una cuerda), relajar (restricciones), descargar (tensiones) **3** FACILITATE : facilitar — *vi* : calmarse, relajarse

ease[2] *n* **1** CALM, RELIEF : tranquilidad *f,* comodidad *f,* desahogo *m* **2** FACILITY : facilidad *f* **3 at ~** : relajado, cómodo <to put someone at ease : tranquilizar a alguien>

easel [ˈiːzəl] *n* : caballete *m*

easily [ˈiːzəli] *adv* **1** : fácilmente, con facilidad **2** UNQUESTIONABLY : con mucho, de lejos

easiness [ˈiːzinəs] *n* : facilidad *f,* soltura *f*

east[1] [ˈiːst] *adv* : al este

east[2] *adj* : este, del este, oriental <east winds : vientos del este>

east[3] *n* **1** : este *m* **2 the East** : el Oriente

Easter [ˈiːstər] *n* : Pascua *f* (de Resurrección)

easterly [ˈiːstərli] *adv & adj* : del este

eastern [ˈiːstərn] *adj* **1** : Oriental, del Este <Eastern Europe : Europa del Este> **2** : oriental, este

Easterner [ˈiːstərnər] *n* : habitante *mf* del este

eastward [ˈiːstwərd] *adv & adj* : hacia el este

easy [ˈiːzi] *adj* **easier; -est 1** : fácil **2** LENIENT : indulgente

easygoing [ˌiːziˈgoːɪŋ] *adj* : acomodaticio, tolerante, poco exigente

eat [ˈiːt] *v* **ate** [ˈeɪt]; **eaten** [ˈiːtən]; **eating** *vt* **1** : comer **2** CONSUME : consumir, gastar, devorar <expenses ate up profits : los gastos devoraron las ganancias> **3** CORRODE : corroer — *vi* **1** : comer **2 to eat away at** *or* **to eat into** : comerse **3 to eat out** : comer fuera

eatable[1] [ˈiːt̬əbəl] *adj* : comestible, comible *fam*

eatable[2] *n* **1** : algo para comer **2 eatables** *npl* : comestibles *mpl,* alimentos *mpl*

eater [ˈiːt̬ər] *n* : comedor *m,* **-dora** *f*

eaves [ˈiːvz] *npl* : alero *m*

eavesdrop [ˈiːvzˌdrɑp] *vi* **-dropped; -dropping** : escuchar a escondidas

eavesdropper [ˈiːvzˌdrɑpər] *n* : persona *f* que escucha a escondidas

ebb[1] [ˈɛb] *vi* **1** : bajar, menguar (dícese de la marea) **2** DECLINE : decaer, disminuir

ebb[2] *n* **1 :** reflujo *m* (de una marea) **2** DECLINE **:** decadencia *f,* declive *m,* disminución *f*

ebony[1] [ˈɛbəni] *adj* **1 :** de ébano **2** BLACK **:** de color ébano, negro

ebony[2] *n, pl* **-nies :** ébano *m*

ebullience [ɪˈbʊljən*t*s, -ˈbʌl-] *n* **:** efervescencia *f,* vivacidad *f*

ebullient [ɪˈbʊljənt, -ˈbʌl-] *adj* **:** efervescente, vivaz

eccentric[1] [ɪkˈsɛntrɪk] *adj* **1 :** excéntrico <an eccentric wheel : una rueda excéntrica> **2** ODD, SINGULAR **:** excéntrico, extraño, raro — **eccentrically** [-trɪkli] *adv*

eccentric[2] *n* **:** ecéntrico *m,* -ca *f*

eccentricity [ˌɛkˌsɛnˈtrɪsəţi] *n, pl* **-ties :** excentricidad *f*

ecclesiastic [ɪˌkliːziˈæstɪk] *n* **:** eclesiástico *m,* clérigo *m*

ecclesiastical [ɪˌkliːziˈæstɪkəl] *or* **ecclesiastic** *adj* **:** eclesiástico — **ecclesiastically** *adv*

echelon [ˈɛʃəˌlɑn] *n* **1 :** escalón *m* (de tropas o aviones) **2** LEVEL **:** nivel *m,* esfera *f,* estrato *m*

echo[1] [ˈɛˌkoː] *v* **echoed; echoing** *vi* **:** hacer eco, resonar — *vt* **:** repetir

echo[2] *n, pl* **echoes :** eco *m*

éclair [eɪˈklær, i-] *n* **:** pastel *m* relleno de crema

eclectic [ɛˈklɛktɪk, ɪ-] *adj* **:** ecléctico

eclipse[1] [ɪˈklɪps] *vt* **eclipsed; eclipsing :** eclipsar

eclipse[2] *n* **:** eclipse *m*

ecological *adj* [ˌiːkəˈlɑdʒɪkəl, ˌɛkə-] **:** ecológico — **ecologically** *adv*

ecologist [iˈkɑlədʒɪst, ɛ-] *n* **:** ecólogo *m,* -ga *f*

ecology [iˈkɑlədʒi, ɛ-] *n, pl* **-gies :** ecología *f*

economic [ˌiːkəˈnɑmɪk, ˌɛkə-] *adj* **:** económico

economical [ˌiːkəˈnɑmɪkəl, ˌɛkə-] *adj* **:** económico — **economically** *adv*

economics [ˌiːkəˈnɑmɪks, ˌɛkə-] *n* **:** economía *f*

economist [iˈkɑnəmɪst] *n* **:** economista *mf*

economize [iˈkɑnəˌmaɪz] *v* **-mized; -mizing :** economizar, ahorrar

economy [iˈkɑnəmi] *n, pl* **-mies 1 :** economía *f,* sistema *m* económico **2** THRIFT **:** economía *f,* ahorro *m*

ecosystem [ˈiːkoˌsɪstəm] *n* **:** ecosistema *m*

ecru [ˈɛˌkruː, ˈeɪ-] *n* **:** color *m* crudo

ecstasy [ˈɛkstəsi] *n, pl* **-sies :** éxtasis *m*

ecstatic [ɛkˈstæţɪk, ɪk-] *adj* **:** extático

ecstatically [ɛkˈstæţɪkli, ɪk-] *adv* **:** con éxtasis, con gran entusiasmo

Ecuadoran [ˌɛkwəˈdorən] *or* **Ecuadorean** *or* **Ecuadorian** [-ˈdoriən] *n* **:** ecuatoriano *m,* -na *f* — **Ecuadorean** *or* **Ecuadorian** *adj*

ecumenical [ˌɛkjʊˈmɛnɪkəl] *adj* **:** ecuménico

eczema [ɪgˈziːmə, ˈɛgzəmə, ˈɛksə-] *n* **:** eczema *m*

eddy[1] [ˈɛdi] *vi* **eddied; eddying :** arremolinarse, hacer remolinos

eddy[2] *n, pl* **-dies :** remolino *m*

edema [ɪˈdiːmə] *n* **:** edema *m*

Eden [ˈiːdən] *n* **:** Edén *m*

edge[1] [ˈɛdʒ] *v* **edged; edging** *vt* **1** BORDER **:** bordear, ribetear, orlar **2** SHARPEN **:** afilar, aguzar **3** *or* **to edge one's way :** avanzar poco a poco **4 to edge out :** derrotar por muy poco — *vi* ADVANCE **:** ir avanzando (poco a poco)

edge[2] *n* **1 :** filo *m* (de un cuchillo) **2** BORDER **:** borde *m,* orilla *f,* margen *m* **3** ADVANTAGE **:** ventaja *f*

edger [ˈɛdʒər] *n* **:** cortabordes *m*

edgewise [ˈɛdʒˌwaɪz] *adv* SIDEWAYS **:** de lado, de canto

edginess [ˈɛdʒinəs] *n* **:** tensión *f,* nerviosismo *m*

edgy [ˈɛdʒi] *adj* **edgier; -est :** tenso, nervioso

edible [ˈɛdəbəl] *adj* **:** comestible

edict [ˈiːˌdɪkt] *n* **:** edicto *m,* mandato *m,* orden *f*

edification [ˌɛdəfəˈkeɪʃən] *n* **:** edificación *f,* instrucción *f*

edifice [ˈɛdəfɪs] *n* **:** edificio *m*

edify [ˈɛdəˌfaɪ] *vt* **-fied; -fying :** edificar

edit [ˈɛdɪt] *vt* **1 :** editar, redactar, corregir **2** *or* **to edit out** DELETE **:** recortar, cortar

edition [ɪˈdɪʃən] *n* **:** edición *f*

editor [ˈɛdɪţər] *n* **:** editor *m,* -tora *f;* redactor *m,* -tora *f*

editorial[1] [ˌɛdɪˈtoriəl] *adj* **1 :** de redacción **2 :** editorial <an editorial comment : un comentario editorial>

editorial[2] *n* **:** editorial *m*

editorship [ˈɛdəţərˌʃɪp] *n* **:** dirección *f*

educable [ˈɛdʒəkəbəl] *adj* **:** educable

educate [ˈɛdʒəˌkeɪt] *vt* **-cated; -cating 1** TEACH **:** educar, enseñar **2** INSTRUCT **:** formar, educar, instruir **3** INFORM **:** informar, concientizar

education [ˌɛdʒəˈkeɪʃən] *n* **:** educación *f*

educational [ˌɛdʒəˈkeɪʃənəl] *adj* **1 :** docente, de enseñanza <an educational institution : una institución docente> **2** PEDAGOGICAL **:** pedagógico **3** INSTRUCTIONAL **:** educativo, instructivo

educator [ˈɛdʒəˌkeɪţər] *n* **:** educador *m,* -dora *f*

eel [ˈiːl] *n* **:** anguila *f*

eerie [ˈɪri] *adj* **-rier; -est :** extraño, misterioso, fantasmagórico

eerily [ˈɪrəli] *adv* **:** de manera extraña y misteriosa

efface [ɪˈfeɪs, ɛ-] *vt* **-faced; -facing :** borrar

effect[1] [ɪˈfɛkt] *vt* **1** CARRY OUT **:** efectuar, llevar a cabo **2** ACHIEVE **:** lograr, realizar

effect[2] *n* **1** RESULT **:** efecto *m,* resultado *m,* consecuencia *f* <to no effect : sin resultado> **2** MEANING **:** sentido *m* <something to that effect : algo por el estilo> **3** INFLUENCE **:** efecto *m,* influencia *f* **4 effects** *npl* BELONGINGS : efectos *mpl,* pertenencias *fpl* **5 to go into effect** : entrar en vigor **6 in ~** REALLY : en realidad, efectivamente

effective [ɪˈfɛktɪv] *adj* **1** EFFECTUAL : efectivo, eficaz **2** OPERATIVE : vigente — **effectively** *adv*

effectiveness [ɪˈfɛktɪvnəs] *n* : eficacia *f,* efectividad *f*

effectual [ɪˈfɛktʃʊəl] *adj* : eficaz, efectivo — **effectually** *adv*

effeminate [əˈfɛmənət] *adj* : afeminado

effervesce [ˌɛfərˈvɛs] *vi* **-vesced; -vescing 1** : estar en efervescencia, burbujear (dícese de líquidos) **2** : estar eufórico, estar muy animado (dícese de las personas)

effervescence [ˌɛfərˈvɛsənts] *n* **1** : efervescencia *f* **2** LIVELINESS : vivacidad *f*

effervescent [ˌɛfərˈvɛsənt] *adj* **1** : efervescente **2** LIVELY, VIVACIOUS : vivaz, animado

effete [ɛˈfiːt, ɪ-] *adj* **1** WORN- OUT : desgastado, agotado **2** DECADENT : decadente **3** EFFEMINATE : afeminado

efficacious [ˌɛfəˈkeɪʃəs] *adj* : eficaz, efectivo

efficacy [ˈɛfɪkəsi] *n, pl* **-cies** : eficacia *f*

efficiency [ɪˈfɪʃəntsi] *n, pl* **-cies** : eficiencia *f*

efficient [ɪˈfɪʃənt] *adj* : eficiente — **efficiently** *adv*

effigy [ˈɛfədʒi] *n, pl* **-gies** : efigie *f*

effluent [ˈɛˌfluːənt, ɛˈfluː-] *n* : efluente *m* — **effluent** *adj*

effort [ˈɛfərt] *n* **1** EXERTION : esfuerzo *m* **2** ATTEMPT : tentativa *f,* intento *m* <it's not worth the effort : no vale la pena>

effortless [ˈɛfərtləs] *adj* : fácil, sin esfuerzo

effortlessly [ˈɛfərtləsli] *adv* : sin esfuerzo, fácilmente

effrontery [ɪˈfrʌntəri] *n, pl* **-teries** : insolencia *f,* desfachatez *f,* descaro *m*

effusion [ɪˈfjuːʒən, ɛ-] *n* : efusión *f*

effusive [ɪˈfjuːsɪv, ɛ-] *adj* : efusivo — **effusively** *adv*

egg[1] [ˈɛg] *vt* **to egg on** : incitar, azuzar, provocar

egg[2] *n* **1** : huevo *m* **2** OVUM : óvulo *m*

eggbeater [ˈɛgˌbiːt̬ər] *n* : batidor *m* (de huevos)

eggnog [ˈɛgˌnɑg] *n* : ponche *m* de huevo, rompope *m CA, Mex*

eggplant [ˈɛgˌplænt] *n* : berenjena *f*

eggshell [ˈɛgˌʃɛl] *n* : cascarón *m*

ego [ˈiːˌgoː] *n, pl* **egos 1** SELF-ESTEEM : amor *m* propio **2** SELF : ego *m,* yo *m*

egocentric [ˌiːgoˈsɛntrɪk] *adj* : egocéntrico

egoism [ˈiːgoˌwɪzəm] *n* : egoísmo *m*

egoist [ˈiːgowɪst] *n* : egoísta *mf*

egoistic [ˌiːˌgoˈwɪstɪk] *adj* : egoísta

egotism [ˈiːgəˌtɪzəm] *n* : egotismo *m*

egotist [ˈiːgətɪst] *n* : egotista *mf*

egotistic [ˌiːgəˈtɪstɪk] *or* **egotistical** [-ˈtɪstɪkəl] *adj* : egotista — **egotistically** *adv*

egregious [ɪˈgriːdʒəs] *adj* : atroz, flagrante, mayúsculo — **egregiously** *adv*

egress [ˈiːˌgrɛs] *n* : salida *f*

egret [ˈiːgrət, -ˌgrɛt] *n* : garceta *f*

eiderdown [ˈaɪdərˌdaʊn] *n* **1** : plumón *m* **2** COMFORTER : edredón *m*

eight[1] *adj* [ˈeɪt] : ocho

eight[2] *n* : ocho *m*

eight hundred[1] *adj* : ochocientos

eight hundred[2] *n* : ochocientos *m*

eighteen[1] [eitˈtiːn] *adj* : dieciocho

eighteen[2] *n* : dieciocho *m*

eighteenth[1] [eɪtˈtiːnθ] *adj* : decimoctavo

eighteenth[2] *n* **1** : decimoctavo *m,* -va *f* (en una serie) **2** : dieciochoavo *m,* dieciochoava parte *f*

eighth[1] [ˈeɪtθ] *adj* : octavo

eighth[2] *n* **1** : octavo *m,* -va *f* (en una serie) **2** : octavo *m,* octava parte *f*

eightieth[1] [ˈeɪt̬iəθ] *adj* : octagésimo

eightieth[2] *n* **1** : octogésimo *m,* -ma *f* (en una serie) **2** : ochentavo *m,* ochentava parte *f*

eighty[1] [ˈeɪt̬i] *adj* : ochenta

eighty[2] *n, pl* **eighties 1** : ochenta *m* **2 the eighties** : los ochenta *mpl*

either[1] [ˈiːðər, ˈaɪ-] *adj* **1** : cualquiera (de los dos) <we can watch either movie : podemos ver cualquiera de las dos películas> **2** : ninguno de los dos <she wasn't in either room : no estaba en ninguna de las dos salas> **3** EACH : cada <on either side of the street : a cada lado de la calle>

either[2] *pron* **1** : cualquiera *mf* (de los dos) <either is fine : cualquiera de los dos está bien> **2** : ninguno *m,* -na *f* (de los dos) <I don't like either : no me gusta ninguno> **3** : algún *m,* alguna *f* <is either of you interested? : ¿está alguno de ustedes (dos) interesado?>

either[3] *conj* **1** : o, u <either David or Daniel could go : puede ir (o) David o Daniel> **2** : ni <we won't watch either this movie or the other : no veremos ni esta película ni la otra>

ejaculate [iˈdʒækjəˌleɪt] *v* **-lated; -lating** *vt* **1** : eyacular **2** EXCLAIM : exclamar — *vi* : eyacular

ejaculation [iˌdʒækjəˈleɪʃən] *n* **1** : eyaculación *f* (en fisiología) **2** EXCLAMATION : exclamación *f*

eject [iˈdʒɛkt] *vt* : expulsar, expeler

ejection [iˈdʒɛkʃən] *n* : expulsión *f*

eke [ˈiːk] *vt* **eked; eking** *or* **to eke out** : ganar a duras penas

elaborate[1] [iˈlæbəˌreɪt] *v* **-rated; -rating** *vt* : elaborar, idear, desarrollar — *vi* **to elaborate on** : ampliar, entrar en detalles

elaborate[2] [iˈlæbərət] *adj* **1** DETAILED : detallado, minucioso, elaborado **2** COMPLICATED : complicado, intrincado, elaborado — **elaborately** *adv*

elaboration [i,læbə'reɪʃən] *n* : elaboración *f*
elapse [i'læps] *vi* **elapsed; elapsing** : transcurrir, pasar
elastic¹ [i'læstɪk] *adj* : elástico
elastic² *n* **1** : elástico *m* **2** RUBBER BAND : goma *f,* gomita *f,* elástico *m,* liga *f*
elasticity [i,læs'tɪsəti, ,iː,læs-] *n, pl* **-ties** : elasticidad *f*
elate [i'leɪt] *vt* **elated; elating** : alborozar, regocijar
elation [i'leɪʃən] *n* : euforia *f,* júbilo *m,* alborozo *m*
elbow¹ ['ɛl,boː] *vt* : darle un codazo a
elbow² *n* : codo *m*
elder¹ ['ɛldər] *adj* : mayor
elder² *n* **1 to be someone's elder** : ser mayor que alguien **2** : anciano *m,* -na *f* (de un pueblo o una tribu) **3** : miembro *m* del consejo (en varias religiones)
elderberry ['ɛldər,bɛri] *n, pl* **-berries** : baya *f* de saúco (fruta), saúco *m* (árbol)
elderly ['ɛldərli] *adj* : mayor, de edad, anciano
eldest ['ɛldəst] *adj* : mayor, de más edad
elect¹ [i'lɛkt] *vt* : elegir
elect² *adj* : electo <the president-elect : el presidente electo>
elect³ *npl* **the elect** : los elegidos *mpl*
election [i'lɛkʃən] *n* : elección *f*
elective¹ [i'lɛktɪv] *adj* **1** : electivo **2** OPTIONAL : facultativo, optativo
elective² *n* : asignatura *f* electiva
elector [i'lɛktər] *n* : elector *m,* -tora *f*
electoral [i'lɛktərəl] *adj* : electoral
electorate [i'lɛktərət] *n* : electorado *m*
electric [i'lɛktrɪk] *adj* **1** *or* **electrical** [-trɪkəl] : eléctrico **2** THRILLING : electrizante, emocionante
electrician [i,lɛk'trɪʃən] *n* : electricista *mf*
electricity [i,lɛk'trɪsəṭi] *n, pl* **-ties 1** : electricidad *f* **2** CURRENT : corriente *m* eléctrica
electrification [i,lɛktrəfə'keɪʃən] *n* : electrificación *f*
electrify [i'lɛktrə,faɪ] *vt* **-fied; -fying 1** : electrificar **2** THRILL : electrizar, emocionar
electrocardiogram [i,lɛktro'kɑrdiə,græm] *n* : electrocardiograma *m*
electrocardiograph [i,lɛktro'kɑrdiə,græf] *n* : electrocardiógrafo *m*
electrocute [i'lɛktrə,kjuːt] *vt* **-cuted; -cuting** : electrocutar
electrocution [i,lɛktrə'kjuːʃən] *n* : electrocución *f*
electrode [i'lɛk,troːd] *n* : electrodo *m*
electrolysis [i,lɛk'trɑləsɪs] *n* : electrólisis *f*
electrolyte [i'lɛktrə,laɪt] *n* : electrolito *m*
electromagnet [i,lɛktro'mægnət] *n* : electroimán *m*
electromagnetic [i,lɛktromæg'nɛṭɪk] *adj* : electromagnético — **electromagnetically** [-ṭɪkli] *adv*
electromagnetism [i,lɛktro'mægnə,tɪzəm] *n* : electromagnetismo *m*
electron [i'lɛk,trɑn] *n* : electrón *m*
electronic [i,lɛk'trɑnɪk] *adj* : electrónico — **electronically** [-nɪkli] *adv*
electronic mail *n* : correo *m* electrónico
electronics [i,lɛk'trɑnɪks] *n* : electrónica *f*
electroplate [i'lɛktrə,pleɪt] *vt* **-plated; plating** : galvanizar mediante electrólisis
elegance ['ɛlɪgənts] *n* : elegancia *f*
elegant ['ɛlɪgənt] *adj* : elegante — **elegantly** *adv*
elegy ['ɛlədʒi] *n, pl* **-gies** : elegía *f*
element ['ɛləmənt] *n* **1** COMPONENT : elemento *m,* factor *m* **2** : elemento *m* (en la química) **3** MILIEU : elemento *m,* medio *m* <to be in one's element : estar en su elemento> **4 elements** *npl* RUDIMENTS : elementos *mpl,* rudimentos *mpl,* bases *fpl* **5 the elements** WEATHER : los elementos *mpl*
elemental [,ɛlə'mɛntəl] *adj* **1** BASIC : elemental, primario **2** : elemental (dícese de los elementos químicos)
elementary [,ɛlə'mɛntri] *adj* **1** SIMPLE : elemental, simple, fundamental **2** : de enseñanza primaria
elementary school *n* : escuela *f* primaria
elephant ['ɛləfənt] *n* : elefante *m,* -ta *f*
elevate ['ɛlə,veɪt] *vt* **-vated; -vating 1** RAISE : elevar, levantar, alzar **2** EXALT, PROMOTE : elevar, exaltar, ascender **3** ELATE : alborozar, regocijar
elevation [,ɛlə'veɪʃən] *n* **1** : elevación *f* **2** ALTITUDE : altura *f,* altitud *f* **3** PROMOTION : ascenso *m*
elevator ['ɛlə,veɪṭər] *n* : ascensor *m,* elevador *m*
eleven¹ [ɪ'lɛvən] *adj* : once *m*
eleven² *n* : once *m*
eleventh¹ [ɪlɛvəntθ] *adj* : undécimo
eleventh² *n* **1** : undécimo *m,* -ma *f* (en una serie) **2** : onceavo *m,* onceava parte *f*
elf ['ɛlf] *n, pl* **elves** ['ɛlvz] : elfo *m,* geniecillo *m,* duende *m*
elfin ['ɛlfən] *adj* **1** : de elfo, menudo **2** ENCHANTING, MAGIC : mágico, encantador
elfish ['ɛlfɪʃ] *adj* **1** : de elfo **2** MISCHIEVOUS : travieso
elicit [ɪ'lɪsət] *vt* : provocar
eligibility [,ɛlədʒə'bɪləṭi] *n, pl* **-ties** : elegibilidad *f*
eligible ['ɛlədʒəbəl] *adj* **1** QUALIFIED : elegible **2** SUITABLE : idóneo
eliminate [ɪ'lɪmə,neɪt] *vt* **-nated; -nating** : eliminar
elimination [ɪ,lɪmə'neɪʃən] *n* : eliminación *f*
elite [eɪ'liːt, i-] *n* : elite *f*

elixir [iˈlɪksər] *n* : elixir *m*

elk [ˈɛlk] *n* : alce *m* (de Europa), uapití *m* (de América)

ellipse [ɪˈlɪps, ɛ-] *n* : elipse *f*

ellipsis [ɪˈlɪpsəs, ɛ-] *n, pl* **-lipses** [-ˌsiːz] **1** : elipsis *f* **2** : puntos *mpl* suspensivos (en la puntuación)

elliptical [ɪˈlɪptɪkəl, ɛ-] *or* **elliptic** [-tɪk] *adj* : elíptico

elm [ˈɛlm] *n* : olmo *m*

elocution [ˌɛləˈkjuːʃən] *n* : elocución *f*

elongate [iˈlɔŋˌgeɪt] *vt* **-gated; -gating** : alargar

elongation [ˌiːˌlɔŋˈgeɪʃən] *n* : alargamiento *m*

elope [iˈloːp] *vi* **eloped; eloping** : fugarse

elopement [iˈloːpmənt] *n* : fuga *f*

eloquence [ˈɛləkwən*t*s] *n* : elocuencia *f*

eloquent [ˈɛləkwənt] *adj* : elocuente — **eloquently** *adv*

El Salvadoran [ˌɛlˌsælvəˈdorən] *n* : salvadoreño *m*, -ña *f* — **El Salvadoran** *adj*

else[1] [ˈɛls] *adv* **1** DIFFERENTLY : de otro modo, de otra manera <how else? : ¿de qué otro modo?> **2** ELSEWHERE : de otro sitio, de otro lugar <where else? : ¿en qué otro sitio?> **3 or else** OTHERWISE : si no, de lo contrario

else[2] *adj* **1** OTHER : otro <anyone else : cualquier otro> <everyone else : todos los demás> <nobody else : ningún otro, nadie más> <somebody else : otra persona> **2** MORE : más <nothing else : nada más> <what else? : ¿qué más?>

elsewhere [ˈɛlsˌ*h*wɛr] *adv* : en otra parte, en otro sitio, en otro lugar

elucidate [iˈluːsəˌdeɪt] *vt* **-dated; -dating** : dilucidar, elucidar, esclarecer

elucidation [iˌluːsəˈdeɪʃən] *n* : elucidación *f*, esclarecimiento *m*

elude [iˈluːd] *vt* **eluded; eluding** : eludir, evadir

elusive [iˈluːsɪv] *adj* **1** EVASIVE : evasivo, esquivo **2** SLIPPERY : huidizo, escurridizo **3** FLEETING, INTANGIBLE : impalpable, fugaz

elusively [iˈluːsɪvli] *adv* : de manera esquiva

elves → **elf**

emaciate [iˈmeɪʃiˌeɪt] *vt* **-ated; -ating** : enflaquecer

emaciation [iˌmeɪsiˈeɪʃən, -ʃi-] *n* : enflaquecimiento *m*, escualidez *f*, delgadez *f* extrema

E–mail [ˈiːˌmeɪl] → **electronic mail**

emanate [ˈɛməˌneɪt] *v* **-nated; -nating** *vi* : emanar, provenir, proceder — *vt* : emanar

emanation [ˌɛməˈneɪʃən] *n* : emanación *f*

emancipate [iˈmæn*t*səˌpeɪt] *vt* **-pated; -pating** : emancipar

emancipation [iˌmæn*t*səˈpeɪʃən] *n* : emancipación *f*

emasculate [iˈmæskjəˌleɪt] *vt* **-lated; -lating** **1** CASTRATE : castrar, emascular **2** WEAKEN : debilitar

embalm [ɪmˈbɑm, ɛm-, -ˈbɑlm] *vt* : embalsamar

embankment [ɪmˈbæŋkmənt, ɛm-] *n* : terraplén *m*, muro *m* de contención

embargo[1] [ɪmˈbɑrgo, ɛm-] *vt* **-goed; -going** : imponer un embargo sobre

embargo[2] *n, pl* **-goes** : embargo *m*

embark [ɪmˈbɑrk, ɛm-] *vt* : embarcar — *vi* **1** : embarcarse **2 to embark on** START : emprender, embarcarse en

embarkation [ˌɛmˌbɑrˈkeɪʃən] *n* : embarque *m*, embarco *m*

embarrass [ɪmˈbærəs, ɛm-] *vt* : avergonzar, abochornar

embarrassing [ɪmˈbærəsɪŋ, ɛm-] *adj* : embarazoso, violento

embarrassment [ɪmˈbærəsmənt, ɛm-] *n* : vergüenza *f*, pena *f*

embassy [ˈɛmbəsi] *n, pl* **-sies** : embajada *f*

embed [ɪmˈbɛd, ɛm-] *vt* **-bedded; -bedding** : incrustar, empotrar, grabar (en la memoria)

embellish [ɪmˈbɛlɪʃ, ɛm-] *vt* : adornar, embellecer

embellishment [ɪmˈbɛlɪʃmənt, ɛm-] *n* : adorno *m*

ember [ˈɛmbər] *n* : ascua *f*, brasa *f*

embezzle [ɪmˈbɛzəl, ɛm-] *vt* **-zled; -zling** : desfalcar, malversar

embezzlement [ɪmˈbɛzəlmənt, ɛm-] *n* : desfalco *m*, malversación *f*

embezzler [ɪmˈbɛzələr, ɛm-] *n* : desfacador *m*, -dora *f*; malversador *m*, -dora *f*

embitter [ɪmˈbɪt̬ər, ɛm-] *vt* : amargar

emblem [ˈɛmbləm] *n* : emblema *m*, símbolo *m*

emblematic [ˌɛmbləˈmæt̬ɪk] *adj* : emblemático, simbólico

embodiment [ɪmˈbɑdɪmənt, ɛm-] *n* : encarnación *f*, personificación *f*

embody [ɪmˈbɑdi, ɛm-] *vt* **-bodied; -bodying** : encarnar, personificar

emboss [ɪmˈbɑs, ɛm-, -ˈbɔs] *vt* : repujar, grabar en relieve

embrace[1] [ɪmˈbreɪs, ɛm-] *vt* **-braced; -bracing** **1** HUG : abrazar **2** ADOPT, TAKE ON : adoptar, aceptar **3** INCLUDE : abarcar, incluir

embrace[2] *n* : abrazo *m*

embroider [ɪmˈbrɔɪdər, ɛm-] *vt* : bordar (una tela), adornar (una historia)

embroidery [ɪmˈbrɔɪdəri, ɛm-] *n, pl* **-deries** : bordado *m*

embroil [ɪmˈbrɔɪl, ɛm-] *vt* : embrollar, enredar

embryo [ˈɛmbriˌoː] *n, pl* **embryos** : embrión *m*

embryonic [ˌɛmbriˈɑnɪk] *adj* : embrionario

emend [iˈmɛnd] *vt* : enmendar, corregir

emendation [ˌiːˌmɛnˈdeɪʃən] *n* : enmienda *f*
emerald¹ [ˈɛmrəld, ˈɛmə-] *adj* : verde esmeralda
emerald² *n* : esmeralda *f*
emerge [iˈmərdʒ] *vi* **emerged; emerging** : emerger, salir, aparecer, surgir
emergence [iˈmərdʒənts] *n* : aparición *f,* surgimiento *m*
emergency [iˈmərdʒəntsi] *n, pl* **-cies** : emergencia *f*
emergent [iˈmərdʒənt] *adj* : emergente
emery [ˈɛməri] *n, pl* **-eries** : esmeril *m*
emetic¹ [iˈmɛt̬ɪk] *adj* : vomitivo, emético
emetic² *n* : vomitivo *m,* emético *m*
emigrant [ˈɛmɪgrənt] *n* : emigrante *mf*
emigrate [ˈɛməˌgreɪt] *vi* **-grated; -grating** : emigrar
emigration [ˌɛməˈgreɪʃən] *n* : emigración *f*
eminence [ˈɛmənənts] *n* **1** PROMINENCE : eminencia *f,* prestigio *m,* renombre *m* **2** DIGNITARY : eminencia *f;* dignatario *m,* -ria *f* <Your Eminence : Su Eminencia>
eminent [ˈɛmənənt] *adj* : eminente, ilustre
eminently [ˈɛmənəntli] *adv* : sumamente
emissary [ˈɛməˌsɛri] *n, pl* **-saries** : emisario *m,* -ria *f*
emission [iˈmɪʃən] *n* : emisión *f*
emit [iˈmɪt] *vt* **emitted; emitting** : emitir, despedir, producir
emote [iˈmoːt] *vi* **emoted; emoting** : exteriorizar las emociones
emotion [iˈmoːʃən] *n* : emoción *f,* sentimiento *m*
emotional [iˈmoːʃənəl] *adj* **1** : emocional, afectivo <an emotional reaction : una reacción emocional> **2** MOVING : emocionante, emotivo, conmovedor
emotionally [iˈmoːʃənəli] *adv* : emocionalmente
emperor [ˈɛmpərər] *n* : emperador *m*
emphasis [ˈɛmfəsɪs] *n, pl* **-phases** [-ˌsiːz] : énfasis *m,* hincapié *m*
emphasize [ˈɛmfəˌsaɪz] *vt* **-sized; -sizing** : enfatizar, destacar, subrayar, hacer hincapié en
emphatic [ɪmˈfætɪk, ɛm-] *adj* : enfático, enérgico, categórico — **emphatically** [-ɪkli] *adv*
empire [ˈɛmˌpaɪr] *n* : imperio *m*
empirical [ɪmˈpɪrɪkəl, ɛm-] *adj* : empírico — **empirically** [-ɪkli] *adv*
employ¹ [ɪmˈplɔɪ, ɛm-] *vt* **1** USE : usar, utilizar **2** HIRE : contratar, emplear **3** OCCUPY : ocupar, dedicar, emplear
employ² [ɪmˈplɔɪ, ɛm-; ˈɪmˌ-, ˈɛmˌ-] *n* **1** : puesto *m,* cargo *m,* ocupación *f* **2 to be in the employ of** : estar al servicio de, trabajar para
employee [ɪmˌplɔɪˈiː, ɛm-, -ˈplɔɪˌiː] *n* : empleado *m,* -da *f*
employer [ɪmˈplɔɪər, ɛm-] *n* : patrón *m,* -trona *f;* empleador *m,* -dora *f*
employment [ɪmˈplɔɪmənt, ɛm-] *n* : trabajo *m,* empleo *m*
empower [ɪmˈpaʊər, ɛm-] *vt* : facultar, autorizar, conferirle poder a
empowerment [ɪmˈpaʊərmənt, ɛm-] *n* : autorización *f*
empress [ˈɛmprəs] *n* : emperatriz *f*
emptiness [ˈɛmptinəs] *n* : vacío *m,* vacuidad *f*
empty¹ [ˈɛmpti] *v* **-tied; -tying** *vt* : vaciar — *vi* : desaguar (dícese de un río)
empty² *adj* **emptier; -est 1** : vacío **2** VACANT : desocupado, libre **3** MEANINGLESS : vacío, hueco, vano
empty–handed [ˌɛmptiˈhændəd] *adj* : con las manos vacías
empty–headed [ˌɛmptiˈhɛdəd] *adj* : cabeza hueca, tonto
emu [ˈiːˌmjuː] *n* : emú *m*
emulate [ˈɛmjəˌleɪt] *vt* **-lated; -lating** : emular
emulation [ˌɛmjəˈleɪʃən] *n* : emulación *f*
emulsifier [ɪˈmʌlsəˌfaɪər] *n* : emulsionante *m*
emulsify [ɪˈmʌlsəˌfaɪ] *vt* **-fied; -fying** : emulsionar
emulsion [ɪˈmʌlʃən] *n* : emulsión *f*
enable [ɪˈneɪbəl, ɛ-] *vt* **-abled; -abling 1** EMPOWER : habilitar, autorizar, facultar **2** PERMIT : hacer posible, posibilitar, permitar
enact [ɪˈnækt, ɛ-] *vt* **1** : promulgar (un ley o decreto) **2** : representar (un papel en el teatro)
enactment [ɪˈnæktmənt, ɛ-] *n* : promulgación *f*
enamel¹ [ɪˈnæməl] *vt* **-eled** *or* **-elled; -eling** *or* **-elling** : esmaltar
enamel² *n* : esmalte *m*
enamor [ɪˈnæmər] *vt* **1** : enamorar **2 to be enamored of** : estar enamorado de (una persona), estar entusiasmado con (algo)
encamp [ɪnˈkæmp, ɛn-] *vi* : acampar
encampment [ɪnˈkæmpmənt, ɛn-] *n* : campamento *m*
encase [ɪnˈkeɪs, ɛn-] *vt* **-cased; -casing** : encerrar, revestir
encephalitis [ɪnˌsɛfəˈlaɪt̬əs, ɛn-] *n, pl* **-litides** [-ˈlɪt̬əˌdiːz] : encefalitis *f*
enchant [ɪnˈtʃænt, ɛn-] *vt* **1** BEWITCH : hechizar, encantar, embrujar **2** CHARM, FASCINATE : cautivar, fascinar, encantar
enchanting [ɪnˈtʃæntɪŋ, ɛn-] *adj* : encantador
enchanter [ɪnˈtʃæntər, ɛn-] *n* SORCERER : mago *m,* encantador *m*
enchantment [ɪnˈtʃæntmənt, ɛn-] *n* **1** SPELL : encanto *m,* hechizo *m* **2** CHARM : encanto *m*
enchantress [ɪnˈtʃæntrəs, ɛn-] *n* **1** SORCERESS : maga *f,* hechicera *f* **2** CHARMER : mujer *f* cautivadora
encircle [ɪnˈsərkəl, ɛn-] *vt* **-cled; -cling** : rodear, ceñir, cercar
enclose [ɪnˈkloːz, ɛn-] *vt* **-closed; -closing 1** SURROUND : encerrar, cer-

car, rodear 2 INCLUDE : incluir, adjuntar, acompañar <please find enclosed : le enviamos adjunto>
enclosure [ɪnˈkloːʒər, ɛn-] *n* **1** ENCLOSING : encierro *m* **2** : cercado *m* (de terreno), recinto *m* <an enclosure for the press : un recinto para la prensa> **3** ADJUNCT : anexo *m* (con una carta), documento *m* adjunto
encompass [ɪnˈkʌmpəs, ɛn-, -ˈkɑm-] *vt* **1** SURROUND : circundar, rodear **2** INCLUDE : abarcar, comprender
encore [ˈɑnˌkor] *n* : bis *m,* repetición *f*
encounter¹ [ɪnˈkaʊntər, ɛn-] *vt* **1** MEET : encontrar, encontrarse con, toparse con, tropezar con **2** FIGHT : combatir, luchar contra
encounter² *n* : encuentro *m*
encourage [ɪnˈkərɪdʒ, ɛn-] *vt* **-aged; -aging 1** HEARTEN, INSPIRE : animar, alentar **2** FOSTER : fomentar, promover
encouragement [ɪnˈkərɪdʒmənt, ɛn-] *n* : ánimo *m,* aliento *m*
encroach [ɪnˈkroːtʃ, ɛn-] *vi* **to encroach on** : invadir, abusar (derechos), quitar (tiempo)
encroachment [ɪnˈkroːtʃmənt, ɛn-] *n* : invasión *f,* usurpación *f*
encrust [ɪnˈkrʌst, ɛn-] *vt* **1** : recubrir con una costra **2** INLAY : incrustar <encrusted with gems : incrustado de gemas>
encumber [ɪnˈkʌmbər, ɛn-] *vt* **1** BLOCK : obstruir, estorbar **2** BURDEN : cargar, gravar
encumbrance [ɪnˈkʌmbrən*t*s, ɛn-] *n* : estorbo *m,* carga *f,* gravamen *m*
encyclopedia [ɪnˌsaɪkləˈpiːdiə, ɛn-] *n* : enciclopedia *f*
encyclopedic [ɪnˌsaɪkləˈpiːdɪk, ɛn-] *adj* : enciclopédico
end¹ [ˈɛnd] *vt* **1** STOP : terminar, poner fin a **2** CONCLUDE : concluir, terminar — *vi* : terminar(se), acabar, concluir(se)
end² *n* **1** EXTREMITY : extremo *m,* final *m,* punta *f* **2** CONCLUSION : fin *m,* final *m* **3** AIM : fin *m*
endanger [ɪnˈdeɪndʒər, ɛn-] *vt* : poner en peligro
endear [ɪnˈdɪr, ɛn-] *vt* **to endear oneself to** : ganarse la simpatía de, granjearse el cariño de
endearment [ɪnˈdɪrmənt, ɛn-] *n* : expresión *f* de cariño
endeavor¹ [ɪnˈdɛvər, ɛn-] *vt* : intentar, esforzarse por <he endeavored to improve his work : intentó por mejorar su trabajo>
endeavor² *n* : intento *m,* esfuerzo *m*
ending [ˈɛndɪŋ] *n* **1** CONCLUSION : final *m,* desenlace *m* **2** SUFFIX : sufijo *m,* terminación *f*
endive [ˈɛnˌdaɪv, ˌɑnˈdiːv] *n* : endibia *f,* endivia *f*
endless [ˈɛndləs] *adj* **1** INTERMINABLE : interminable, inacabable, sin fin **2** INNUMERABLE : innumerable, incontable
endlessly [ˈɛndləsli] *adv* : interminablemente, eternamente, sin parar
endocrine [ˈɛndəkrən, -ˌkraɪn, -ˌkriːn] *adj* : endocrino
endorse [ɪnˈdɔrs, ɛn-] *vt* **-dorsed; -dorsing 1** SIGN : endosar, firmar **2** APPROVE : aprobar, sancionar
endorsement [ɪnˈdɔrsmənt, ɛn-] *n* **1** SIGNATURE : endoso *m,* firma *f* **2** APPROVAL : aprobación *f,* aval *m*
endow [ɪnˈdaʊ, ɛn-] *vt* : dotar
endowment [ɪnˈdaʊmənt, ɛn-] *n* **1** FUNDING : dotación *f* **2** DONATION : donación *f,* legado *m* **3** ATTRIBUTE, GIFT : atributo *m,* dotes *fpl*
endurable [ɪnˈdʊrəbəl, ɛn-, -ˈdjʊr-] *adj* : tolerable, soportable
endurance [ɪnˈdʊrən*t*s, ɛn-, -ˈdjʊr-] *n* : resistencia *f,* aguante *m*
endure [ɪnˈdʊr, ɛn-, -ˈdjʊr] *v* **-dured; -during** *vt* **1** BEAR : resistir, soportar, aguantar **2** TOLERATE : tolerar, soportar — *vi* LAST : durar, perdurar
enema [ˈɛnəmə] *n* : enema *m,* lavativa *f*
enemy [ˈɛnəmi] *n, pl* **-mies** : enemigo *m,* -ga *f*
energetic [ˌɛnərˈdʒɛtɪk] *adj* : enérgico, vigoroso — **energetically** [-tɪkli] *adv*
energize [ˈɛnərˌdʒaɪz] *vt* **-gized; -gizing 1** ACTIVATE : activar **2** INVIGORATE : vigorizar
energy [ˈɛnərdʒi] *n, pl* **-gies 1** VITALITY : energía *f,* vitalidad *f* **2** EFFORT : esfuerzo *m,* energías *fpl* **3** POWER : energía *f* <atomic energy : energía atómica>
enervate [ˈɛnərˌveɪt] *vt* **-vated; -vating** : enervar, debilitar
enervation [ˌɛnərˈveɪʃən] *n* : enervación *f,* debilidad *f*
enfold [ɪnˈfoːld, ɛn-] *vt* : envolver
enforce [ɪnˈfors, ɛn-] *vt* **-forced; -forcing 1** : hacer respetar, hacer cumplir (una ley, etc.) **2** IMPOSE : imponer <to enforce obedience : imponer la obediencia>
enforcement [ɪnˈforsmənt, ɛn-] *n* : imposición *f*
enfranchise [ɪnˈfrænˌtʃaɪz, ɛn-] *vt* **-chised; -chising** : conceder el voto a
enfranchisement [ɪnˈfrænˌtʃaɪzmənt, ɛn-] *n* : concesión *f* del voto
engage [ɪnˈgeɪdʒ, ɛn-] *v* **-gaged; -gaging** *vt* **1** ATTRACT : captar, atraer, llamar <to engage one's attention : captar la atención> **2** MESH : engranar <to engage the clutch : embragar> **3** COMMIT : comprometer <to get engaged : comprometerse> **4** HIRE : contratar **5** : entablar combate con (un enemigo) — *vi* **1** PARTICIPATE : participar **2 to engage in combat** : entrar en combate

engagement [ɪnˈgeɪdʒmənt, ɛn-] *n* **1** APPOINTMENT : cita *f,* hora *f* **2** BETROTHAL : compromiso *m*
engaging [ɪnˈgeɪdʒɪŋ, ɛn-] *adj* : atractivo, encantador, interesante
engender [ɪnˈdʒɛndər, ɛn-] *vt* **-dered; -dering** : engendrar
engine [ˈɛndʒən] *n* **1** MOTOR : motor *m* **2** LOCOMOTIVE : locomotora *f,* máquina *f*
engineer¹ [ˌɛndʒəˈnɪr] *vt* **1** : diseñar, construir (un sistema, un mecanismo, etc.) **2** CONTRIVE : maquinar, tramar, fraguar
engineer² *n* **1** : ingeniero *m,* -ra *f* **2** : maquinista *mf* (de locomotoras)
engineering [ˌɛndʒəˈnɪrɪŋ] *n* : ingeniería *f*
English¹ [ˈɪŋglɪʃ, ˈŋlɪʃ] *adj* : inglés
English² *n* **1** : inglés *m* (idioma) **2 the English** : los ingleses
Englishman [ˈɪŋglɪʃmən, ˈɪŋlɪʃ-] *n, pl* **-men** [-mən, -ˌmɛn] : inglés *m*
Englishwoman [ˈɪŋglɪʃˌwʊmən, ˈɪŋlɪʃ-] *n, pl* **-women** [-ˌwɪmən] : inglesa *f*
engrave [ɪnˈgreɪv, ɛn-] *vt* **-graved; -graving** : grabar
engraver [ɪnˈgreɪvər, ɛn-] *n* : grabador *m,* -dora *f*
engraving [ɪnˈgreɪvɪŋ, ɛn-] *n* : grabado *m*
engross [ɪnˈgroːs, ɛn-] *vt* : absorber
engrossed [ɪnˈgroːst, ɛn-] *adj* : absorto
engulf [ɪnˈgʌlf, ɛn-] *vt* : envolver, sepultar
enhance [ɪnˈhænts, ɛn-] *vt* **-hanced; -hancing** : realzar, aumentar, mejorar
enhancement [ɪnˈhæntsmənt, ɛn-] *n* : mejora *f,* realce *m,* aumento *m*
enigma [ɪˈnɪgmə] *n* : enigma *m*
enigmatic [ˌɛnɪgˈmæṭɪk, ˌiːnɪg-] *adj* : enigmático — **enigmatically** [-ṭɪkli] *adv*
enjoin [ɪnˈdʒɔɪn, ɛn-] *vt* **1** COMMAND : ordenar, imponer **2** FORBID : prohibir, vedar
enjoy [ɪnˈdʒɔɪ, ɛn-] *vt* **1** : disfrutar, gozar de <did you enjoy the book? : ¿te gustó el libro?> <to enjoy good health : gozar de buena salud> **2 to enjoy oneself** : divertirse, pasarlo bien
enjoyable [ɪnˈdʒɔɪəbəl, ɛn-] *adj* : agradable, placentero, divertido
enjoyment [ɪnˈdʒɔɪmənt, ɛn-] *n* : placer *m,* goce *m,* disfrute *m,* deleite *m*
enlarge [ɪnˈlɑrdʒ, ɛn-] *v* **-larged; -larging** *vt* : extender, agrandar, ampliar — *vi* **1** : ampliarse **2 to enlarge upon** : extenderse sobre, entrar en detalles sobre
enlargement [ɪnˈlɑrdʒmənt, ɛn-] *n* : expansión *f,* ampliación *f* (dícese de fotografías)
enlarger [ɪnˈlɑrdʒər, ɛn-] *n* : ampliadora *f*
enlighten [ɪnˈlaɪtən, ɛn-] *vt* : iluminar, aclarar
enlightenment [ɪnˈlaɪtənmənt, ɛn-] *n* **1** : ilustración *f* <the Enlightenment : la Ilustración> **2** CLARIFICATION : aclaración *f*
enlist [ɪnˈlɪst, ɛn-] *vt* **1** ENROLL : alistar, reclutar **2** SECURE : conseguir <to enlist the support of : conseguir el apoyo de> — *vi* : alistarse
enlisted man [ɪnˈlɪstəd, ɛn-] *n* : soldado *m* raso
enlistment [ɪnˈlɪstmənt, ɛn-] *n* : alistamiento *m,* reclutamiento *m*
enliven [ɪnˈlaɪvən, ɛn-] *vt* : animar, alegrar, darle vida a
enmity [ˈɛnməṭi] *n, pl* **-ties** : enemistad *f,* animadversión *f*
ennoble [ɪˈnoːbəl, ɛ-] *vt* **-bled; -bling** : ennoblecer
ennui [ˌɑnˈwiː] *n* : hastío *m,* tedio *m,* fastidio *m,* aburrimiento *m*
enormity [ɪˈnɔrməṭi] *n, pl* **-ties 1** ATROCITY : atrocidad *f,* barbaridad *f* **2** IMMENSITY : enormidad *f,* inmensidad *f*
enormous [ɪˈnɔrməs] *adj* : enorme, inmenso, tremendo — **enormously** *adv*
enough¹ [ɪˈnʌf] *adv* **1** : bastante, suficientemente **2 fair enough!** : ¡está bien!, ¡de acuerdo! **3 strangely enough** : por extraño que parezca **4 sure enough** : en efecto, sin duda alguna **5 well enough** : muy bien, bastante bien
enough² *adj* : bastante, suficiente <do we have enough chairs? : ¿tenemos suficientes sillas?>
enough³ *pron* : (lo) suficiente, (lo) bastante <enough to eat : lo suficiente para comer> <it's not enough : no basta> <I've had enough! : ¡estoy harto!, ¡está bueno ya!>
enquire [ɪnˈkwaɪr, ɛn-], **enquiry** [ˈɪnˌkwaɪri, ˈɛn-, -kwəri; ɪnˈkwaɪri, ɛnˈ-] → **inquire, inquiry**
enrage [ɪnˈreɪdʒ, ɛn-] *vt* **-raged; -raging** : enfurecer, encolerizar
enraged [ɪnˈreɪdʒd, ɛn-] *adj* : enfurecido, furioso
enrich [ɪnˈrɪtʃ, ɛn-] *vt* : enriquecer
enrichment [ɪnˈrɪtʃmənt, ɛn-] *n* : enriquecimiento *m*
enroll *or* **enrol** [ɪnˈroːl, ɛn-] *v* **-rolled; -rolling** *vt* : matricular, inscribir — *vi* : matricularse, inscribirse
enrollment [ɪnˈroːlmənt, ɛn-] *n* : matrícula *f,* inscripción *f*
en route [ɑˈruːt, ɛnˈraʊt] *adv* : de camino, por el camino
ensconce [ɪnˈskɑnts, ɛn-] *vt* **-sconced; -sconcing** : acomodar, instalar, establecer cómodamente
ensemble [ɑnˈsɑmbəl] *n* : conjunto *m*
enshrine [ɪnˈʃraɪn, ɛn-] *vt* **-shrined; -shrining** : conservar religiosamente, preservar
ensign [ˈɛntsən, ˈɛnˌsaɪn] *n* **1** FLAG : enseña *f,* pabellón *m* **2** : alférez *mf* (de fragata)

enslave [ɪn'sleɪv, ɛn-] *vt* **-slaved; -slaving** : esclavizar

enslavement [ɪn'sleɪvmənt, ɛn-] *n* : esclavización *f*

ensnare [ɪn'snær, ɛn-] *vt* **-snared; -snaring** : atrapar

ensue [ɪn'suː, ɛn-] *vi* **-sued; -suing** : seguir, resultar

ensure [ɪn'ʃʊr, ɛn-] *vt* **-sured; -suring** : asegurar, garantizar

entail [ɪn'teɪl, ɛn-] *vt* : implicar, suponer, conllevar

entangle [ɪn'tæŋgəl, ɛn-] *vt* **-gled; -gling** : enredar

entanglement [ɪn'tæŋgəlmənt, ɛn-] *n* : enredo *m*

enter ['ɛntər] *vt* **1** : entrar en, entrar a **2** BEGIN : entrar en, comenzar, iniciar **3** RECORD : anotar, inscribir, dar entrada a **4** JOIN : entrar en, alistarse en, hacerse socio de — *vi* **1** : entrar **2 to enter into** : entrar en, firmar (un acuerdo), entablar (negociaciones, etc.)

enterprise ['ɛntər,praɪz] *n* **1** UNDERTAKING : empresa *f* **2** BUSINESS : empresa *f,* firma *f* **3** INITIATIVE : iniciativa *f,* empuje *m*

enterprising ['ɛntər,praɪzɪŋ] *adj* : emprendedor

entertain [,ɛntər'teɪn] *vt* **1** : recibir, agasajar <to entertain guests : tener invitados> **2** CONSIDER : considerar, contemplar **3** AMUSE : entretener, divertir

entertainer [,ɛntər'teɪnər] *n* : artista *mf*

entertainment [,ɛntər'teɪnmənt] *n* : entretenimiento *m,* diversión *f*

enthrall *or* **enthral** [ɪn'θrɔl, ɛn-] *vt* **-thralled; -thralling** : cautivar, embelesar

enthusiasm [ɪn'θuːzi,æzəm, ɛn-, -'θjuː-] *n* : entusiasmo *m*

enthusiast [ɪn'θuːzi,æst, ɛn-, -'θjuː-, -əst] *n* : entusiasta *mf;* aficionado *m,* -da *f*

enthusiastic [ɪn,θuːzi'æstɪk, ɛn-, -,θjuː-] *adj* : entusiasta, aficionado

enthusiastically [ɪn,θuːzi'æstɪkli, ɛn-, -,θjuː-] *adv* : con entusiasmo

entice [ɪn'taɪs, ɛn-] *vt* **-ticed; -ticing** : atraer, tentar

enticement [ɪn'taɪsmənt, ɛn-] *n* : tentación *f,* atracción *f,* señuelo *m*

entire [ɪn'taɪr, ɛn-] *adj* : entero, completo

entirely [ɪn'taɪrli, ɛn-] *adv* : completamente, totalmente

entirety [ɪn'taɪrti, ɛn-, -'taɪrəṭi] *n, pl* **-ties** : totalidad *f*

entitle [ɪn'taɪṭəl, ɛn-] *vt* **-tled; -tling 1** NAME : titular, intitular **2** : dar derecho a <it entitles you to enter free : le da derecho a entrar gratis> **3 to be entitled to** : tener derecho a

entitlement [ɪn'taɪṭəlmənt, ɛn-] *n* RIGHT : derecho *m*

entity ['ɛntəṭi] *n, pl* **-ties** : entidad *f,* ente *m*

entomologist [,ɛntə'mɑlədʒɪst] *n* : entomólogo *m,* -ga *f*

entomology [,ɛntə'mɑlədʒi] *n* : entomología *f*

entourage [,ɑntʊ'rɑʒ] *n* : séquito *m*

entrails ['ɛn,treɪlz, -trəlz] *npl* : entrañas *fpl,* vísceras *fpl*

entrance[1] [ɪn'træn*t*s, ɛn-] *vt* **-tranced; -trancing** : encantar, embelesar, fascinar

entrance[2] ['ɛntrən*t*s] *n* **1** ENTERING : entrada *f* <to make an entrance : entrar en escena> **2** ENTRY : entrada *f,* puerta *f* **3** ADMISSION : entrada *f,* ingreso *m* <entrance examination : examen de ingreso>

entrant ['ɛntrənt] *n* : candidato *m,* -ta *f* (en un examen); participante *mf* (en un concurso)

entrap [ɪn'træp, ɛn-] *vt* **-trapped; -trapping** : atrapar, entrampar, hacer caer en una trampa

entrapment [ɪn'træpmənt, ɛn-] *n* : captura *f*

entreat [ɪn'triːt, ɛn-] *vt* : suplicar, rogar

entreaty [ɪn'triːṭi, ɛn-] *n, pl* **-treaties** : ruego *m,* súplica *f*

entrée *or* **entree** ['ɑn,treɪ, ,ɑn'-] *n* : plato *m* principal

entrench [ɪn'trɛntʃ, ɛn-] *vt* **1** FORTIFY : atrincherar (una posición militar) **2** : consolidar, afianzar <firmly entrenched in his job : afianzado en su puesto>

entrepreneur [,ɑntrəprə'nər, -'njʊr] *n* : empresario *m,* -ria *f*

entrust [ɪn'trʌst, ɛn-] *vt* : confiar, encomendar

entry ['ɛntri] *n, pl* **-tries 1** ENTRANCE : entrada *f* **2** NOTATION : entrada *f,* anotación *f*

entwine [ɪn'twaɪn, ɛn-] *vt* **-twined; -twining** : entrelazar, entretejer, entrecruzar

enumerate [ɪ'nuːmə,reɪt, ɛ-, -'njuː-] *vt* **-ated; -ating 1** LIST : enumerar **2** COUNT : contar, enumerar

enumeration [ɪ,nuːmə'reɪʃən, ɛ-, -,njuː-] *n* : enumeración *f,* lista *f*

enunciate [i'nʌn*t*si,eɪt, ɛ-] *vt* **-ated; -ating 1** STATE : enunciar, decir **2** PRONOUNCE : articular, pronunciar

enunciation [i,nʌn*t*si'eɪʃən, ɛ-] *n* **1** STATEMENT : enunciación *f,* declaración *f* **2** ARTICULATION : articulación *f,* pronunciación *f,* dicción *f*

envelop [ɪn'vɛləp, ɛn-] *vt* : envolver, cubrir

envelope ['ɛnvə,loːp, 'ɑn-] *n* : sobre *m*

enviable ['ɛnviəbəl] *adj* : envidiable

envious ['ɛnviəs] *adj* : envidioso — **enviously** *adv*

environment [ɪn'vaɪrənmənt, ɛn-, -'vaɪərn-] *n* : medio *m* (ambiente), ambiente *m,* entorno *m*

environmental [ɪn,vaɪrən'mɛntəl, ɛn-, -,vaɪərn-] *adj* : ambiental

environmentalist [ɪn,vaɪrən'mɛntəlɪst, ɛn-, -,vaɪərn-] *n* : ecologista *mf*
environs [ɪn'vaɪrənz, ɛn-, -'vaɪərnz] *npl* : alrededores *mpl*, entorno *m*, inmediaciones *fpl*
envisage [ɪn'vɪzɪdʒ, ɛn-] *vt* **-aged; -aging 1** IMAGINE : imaginarse, concebir **2** FORESEE : prever
envision [ɪn'vɪʒən, ɛn-] *vt* : imaginar
envoy ['ɛn,vɔɪ, 'ɑn-] *n* : enviado *m*, -da *f*
envy¹ ['ɛnvi] *vt* **-vied; -vying** : envidiar
envy² *n, pl* **envies** : envidia *f*
enzyme ['ɛn,zaɪm] *n* : enzima *f*
eon ['iːən, iː,ɑn] → **aeon**
epaulet [,ɛpə'lɛt] *n* : charretera *f*
ephemeral [ɪ'fɛmərəl, -'fiː-] *adj* : efímero, fugaz
epic¹ ['ɛpɪk] *adj* : épico
epic² *n* : poema *m* épico, epopeya *f*
epicure ['ɛpɪ,kjʊr] *n* : epicúreo *m*, -rea *f*; gastrónomo *m*, -ma *f*
epicurean [,ɛpɪkjʊ'riːən, -'kjʊriən] *adj* : epicúreo
epidemic¹ [,ɛpə'dɛmɪk] *adj* : epidémico
epidemic² *n* : epidemia *f*
epidermis [,ɛpə'dərməs] *n* : epidermis *f*
epigram ['ɛpə,græm] *n* : epigrama *m*
epilepsy ['ɛpə,lɛpsi] *n, pl* **-sies** : epilepsia *f*
epileptic¹ [,ɛpə'lɛptɪk] *adj* : epiléptico
epileptic² *n* : epiléptico *m*, -ca *f*
episcopal [ɪ'pɪskəpəl] *adj* : episcopal
episode ['ɛpə,soːd] *n* : episodio *m*
episodic [,ɛpə'sɑdɪk] *adj* : episódico
epistle [ɪ'pɪsəl] *n* : epístola *f*, carta *f*
epitaph ['ɛpə,tæf] *n* : epitafio *m*
epithet ['ɛpə,θɛt, -θət] *n* : epíteto *m*
epitome [ɪ'pɪtəmi] *n* **1** SUMMARY : epítome *m*, resumen *m* **2** EMBODIMENT : personificación *f*
epitomize [ɪ'pɪtə,maɪz] *vt* **-mized; -mizing 1** SUMMARIZE : resumir **2** EMBODY : ser la personificación de, personificar
epoch ['ɛpək, 'ɛ,pɑk, 'iː,pɑk] *n* : época *f*, era *f*
equable ['ɛkwəbəl, 'iː-] *adj* **1** CALM, STEADY : ecuánime **2** UNIFORM : estable (dícese de la temperatura), constante (dícese del clima), uniforme
equably ['ɛkwəbli, 'iː-] *adv* : con ecuánimidad
equal¹ ['iːkwəl] *vt* **equaled** *or* **equalled; equaling** *or* **equalling 1** : ser igual a <two plus three equals five : dos más tres es igual a cinco> **2** MATCH : igualar
equal² *adj* **1** SAME : igual **2** ADEQUATE : adecuado, capaz
equal³ *n* : igual *mf*
equality [ɪ'kwɑləti] *n, pl* **-ties** : igualdad *f*
equalize ['iːkwə,laɪz] *vt* **-ized; -izing** : igualar, equiparar
equally ['iːkwəli] *adv* : igualmente, por igual
equanimity [,iːkwə'nɪməti, ,ɛ-] *n, pl* **-ties** : ecuanimidad *f*
equate [ɪ'kweɪt] *vt* **equated; equating** : equiparar, identificar
equation [ɪ'kweɪʒən] *n* : ecuación *f*
equator [ɪ'kweɪtər] *n* : ecuador *m*
equatorial [,iːkwə'toriəl, ,ɛ-] *adj* : ecuatorial
equestrian¹ [ɪ'kwɛstriən, ɛ-] *adj* : ecuestre
equestrian² *n* : jinete *mf*, caballista *mf*
equilateral [,iːkwə'lætərəl, ,ɛ-] *adj* : equilátero
equilibrium [,iːkwə'lɪbriəm, ,ɛ-] *n, pl* **-riums** *or* **-ria** [-briə] : equilibrio *m*
equine ['iː,kwaɪn, 'ɛ-] *adj* : equino, hípico
equinox ['iːkwə,nɑks, 'ɛ-] *n* : equinoccio *m*
equip [ɪ'kwɪp] *vt* **equipped; equipping 1** FURNISH : equipar **2** PREPARE : preparar
equipment [ɪ'kwɪpmənt] *n* : equipo *m*
equitable ['ɛkwətəbəl] *adj* : equitativo, justo, imparcial
equity ['ɛkwəti] *n, pl* **-ties 1** FAIRNESS : equidad *f*, imparcialidad *f* **2** VALUE : valor *m* líquido
equivalence [ɪ'kwɪvələnts] *n* : equivalencia *f*
equivalent¹ [ɪ'kwɪvələnt] *adj* : equivalente
equivalent² *n* : equivalente *m*
equivocal [ɪ'kwɪvəkəl] *adj* **1** AMBIGUOUS : equívoco, ambiguo **2** QUESTIONABLE : incierto, dudoso, sospechoso
equivocate [ɪ'kwɪvə,keɪt] *vi* **-cated; -cating** : usar lenguaje equívoco, andarse con evasivas
equivocation [ɪ,kwɪvə'keɪʃən] *n* : evasiva *f*, subterfugio *m*
era ['ɪrə, 'ɛrə, 'iːrə] *n* : era *f*, época *f*
eradicate [ɪ'rædə,keɪt] *vt* **-cated; -cating** : erradicar
erase [ɪ'reɪs] *vt* **erased; erasing** : borrar
eraser [ɪ'reɪsər] *n* : goma *f* de borrar, borrador *m*
erasure [ɪ'reɪʃər] *n* : tachadura *f*
ere¹ ['ɛr] *conj* : antes de que
ere² *prep* **1** : antes de **2 ere long** : dentro de poco
erect¹ [ɪ'rɛkt] *vt* **1** CONSTRUCT : erigir, construir **2** RAISE : levantar **3** ESTABLISH : establecer
erect² *adj* : erguido, derecho, erecto
erection [ɪ'rɛkʃən] *n* **1** : erección *f* (en fisiología) **2** BUILDING : construcción *f*
ermine ['ərmən] *n* : armiño *m*
erode [ɪ'roːd] *vt* **eroded; eroding** : erosionar (el suelo), corroer (metales)
erosion [ɪ'roːʒən] *n* : erosión *f*, corrosión *f*
erotic [ɪ'rɑtɪk] *adj* : erótico — **erotically** [-tɪkli] *adv*

eroticism [ɪˈrɑt̬əˌsɪzəm] *n* : erotismo *m*
err [ˈɛr, ˈər] *vi* : cometer un error, equivocarse, errar
errand [ˈɛrənd] *n* : mandado *m,* encargo *m,* recado *m Spain* <an errand of mercy : una misión de caridad>
errant [ˈɛrənt] *adj* **1** WANDERING : errante **2** ASTRAY : descarriado
erratic [ɪˈræt̬ɪk] *adj* **1** INCONSISTENT : errático, irregular, inconsistente **2** ECCENTRIC : excéntrico, raro
erratically [ɪˈræt̬ɪkli] *adv* : erráticamente, de manera irregular
erroneous [ɪˈroːniəs, ɛ-] *adj* : erróneo — **erroneously** *adv*
error [ˈɛrər] *n* : error *m,* equivocación *f* <to be in error : estar equivocado>
ersatz [ˈɛrˌsɑts, ˈərˌsæts] *adj* : artificial, sustituto
erstwhile [ˈərstˌhwaɪl] *adj* : antiguo
erudite [ˈɛrəˌdaɪt, ˈɛrjʊ-] *adj* : erudito, letrado
erudition [ˌɛrəˈdɪʃən, ˌɛrjʊ-] *n* : erudición *f*
erupt [ɪˈrʌpt] *vi* **1** : hacer erupción (dícese de un volcán o un sarpullido) **2** : estallar (dícese de la cólera o la violencia)
eruption [ɪˈrʌpʃən] *n* : erupción *f,* estallido *m*
eruptive [ɪˈrʌptɪv] *adj* : eruptivo
escalate [ˈɛskəˌleɪt] *v* **-lated; -lating** *vt* : intensificar (un conflicto), aumentar (precios) — *vi* : intensificarse, aumentarse
escalation [ˌɛskəˈleɪʃən] *n* : intensificación *f,* escalada *f,* aumento *m,* subida *f*
escalator [ˈɛskəˌleɪt̬ər] *n* : escalera *f* mecánica
escapade [ˈɛskəˌpeɪd] *n* : aventura *f*
escape[1] [ɪˈskeɪp, ɛ-] *v* **-caped; -caping** *vt* : escaparse de, librarse de, evitar — *vi* : escaparse, fugarse, huir
escape[2] *n* **1** FLIGHT : fuga *f,* huida *f,* escapada *f* **2** LEAKAGE : escape *m,* fuga *f* **3** : escapatoria *f,* evasión *f* <to have no escape : no tener escapatoria> <escape from reality : evasión de la realidad>
escapee [ɪˌskeɪˈpiː, ˌɛ-] *n* : fugitivo *m,* -va *f*
escarole [ˈɛskəˌroːl] *n* : escarola *f*
escarpment [ɪsˈkɑrpmənt, ɛs-] *n* : escarpa *f,* escarpadura *f*
eschew [ɛˈʃuː, ɪsˈtʃuː] *vt* : evitar, rehuir, abstenerse de
escort[1] [ɪˈskɔrt, ɛ-] *vt* **1** : escoltar <to escort a ship : escoltar un barco> **2** ACCOMPANY : acompañar
escort[2] [ˈɛsˌkɔrt] *n* **1** : escolta *f* <armed escort : escolta armada> **2** COMPANION : acompañante *mf;* compañero *m,* -ra *f*
escrow [ˈɛsˌkroː] *n* **in escrow** : en depósito, en custodia de un tercero
esophagus [ɪˈsɑfəgəs, iː-] *n, pl* **-gi** [-ˌgaɪ, -ˌdʒaɪ] : esófago *m*
esoteric [ˌɛsəˈtɛrɪk] *adj* : esotérico, hermético
especially [ɪˈspɛʃəli] *adv* : especialmente, particularmente
espionage [ˈɛspiəˌnɑʒ, -ˌnɑdʒ] *n* : espionaje *m*
espouse [ɪˈspaʊz, ɛ-] *vt* **espoused; espousing 1** MARRY : casarse con **2** ADOPT, ADVOCATE : apoyar, adherirse a, adoptar
espresso [ɛˈsprɛˌsoː] *n, pl* **-sos** : café *m* exprés
essay[1] [ɛˈseɪ, ˈɛˌseɪ] *vt* : intentar, tratar
essay[2] [ˈɛˌseɪ] *n* **1** COMPOSITION : ensayo *m,* trabajo *m* **2** ATTEMPT : intento *m*
essayist [ˈɛˌseɪɪst] *n* : ensayista *mf*
essence [ˈɛsənts] *n* **1** CORE : esencia *f,* núcleo *m,* meollo *m* <in essence : esencialmente> **2** EXTRACT : esencia *f,* extracto *m* **3** PERFUME : esencia *f,* perfume *m*
essential[1] [ɪˈsɛntʃəl] *adj* : esencial, imprescindible, fundamental — **essentially** *adv*
essential[2] *n* : elemento *m* esencial, lo imprescindible
establish [ɪˈstæblɪʃ, ɛ-] *vt* **1** FOUND : establecer, fundar **2** SET UP : establecer, instaurar, instituir **3** PROVE : demostrar, probar
establishment [ɪˈstæblɪʃmənt, ɛ-] *n* **1** ESTABLISHING : establecimiento *m,* fundación *f,* instauración *f* **2** BUSINESS : negocio *m,* establecimiento *m* **3 the Establishment** : la clase dirigente
estate [ɪˈsteɪt, ɛ-] *n* **1** POSSESSIONS : bienes *mpl,* propiedad *f,* patrimonio *m* **2** PROPERTY : hacienda *f,* finca *f,* propiedad *f*
esteem[1] [ɪˈstiːm, ɛ-] *vt* : estimar, apreciar
esteem[2] *n* : estima *f,* aprecio *m*
ester [ˈɛstər] *n* : éster *m*
esthetic [ɛsˈθɛt̬ɪk] → **aesthetic**
estimable [ˈɛstəməbəl] *adj* : estimable
estimate[1] [ˈɛstəˌmeɪt] *vt* **-mated; -mating** : calcular, estimar
estimate[2] [ˈɛstəmət] *n* **1** : cálculo *m* aproximado <to make an estimate : hacer un cálculo> **2** ASSESSMENT : valoración *f,* estimación *f*
estimation [ˌɛstəˈmeɪʃən] *n* **1** JUDGMENT : juicio *m,* opinión *f* <in my estimation : en mi opinión, según mis cálculos> **2** ESTEEM : estima *f,* aprecio *m*
estimator [ˈɛstəˌmeɪt̬ər] *n* : tasador *m,* -dora *f*
Estonian [ɛˈstoːniən] *n* : estonio *m,* -nia *f* — **Estonian** *adj*
estrange [ɪˈstreɪndʒ, ɛ-] *vt* **-tranged; -tranging** : enajenar, apartar, alejar
estrangement [ɪˈstreɪndʒmənt, ɛ-] *n* : alejamiento *m,* distanciamiento *m*
estrogen [ˈɛstrədʒən] *n* : estrógeno *m*
estrus [ˈɛstrəs] *n* : celo *m*
estuary [ˈɛstʃʊˌwɛri] *n, pl* **-aries** : estuario *m,* -ria *f*

et cetera [ɛt'sɛt̬ərə, -'sɛtrə] : etcétera
etch ['ɛtʃ] *v* : grabar al aguafuerte
etching ['ɛtʃɪŋ] *n* : aguafuerte *m,* grabado *m* al aguafuerte
eternal [ɪ'tərnəl, iː-] *adj* **1** EVERLASTING : eterno **2** INTERMINABLE : constante, incesante
eternally [ɪ'tərnəli, iː-] *adv* : eternamente, para siempre
eternity [ɪ'tərnət̬i, iː-] *n, pl* **-ties** : eternidad *f*
ethane ['ɛ,θeɪn] *n* : etano *m*
ethanol ['ɛθə,nɔl, -,noːl] *n* : etanol *m*
ether ['iːθər] *n* : éter *m*
ethereal [ɪ'θiriəl, iː-] *adj* **1** CELESTIAL : etéreo, celeste **2** DELICATE : delicado
ethical ['ɛθɪkəl] *adj* : ético — **ethically** *adv*
ethics ['ɛθɪks] *ns & pl* **1** : ética *f* **2** MORALITY : ética *f,* moral *f,* moralidad *f*
Ethiopian [,iːθi'oːpiən] *n* : etíope *mf* — **Ethiopian** *adj*
ethnic ['ɛθnɪk] *adj* : étnico
ethnologist [ɛθ'nɑlədʒɪst] *n* : etnólogo *m,* **-ga** *f*
ethnology [ɛθ'nɑlədʒi] *n* : etnología *f*
etiquette ['ɛt̬ɪkət, -,kɛt] *n* : etiqueta *f,* protocolo *m*
etymological [,ɛt̬əmə'lɑdʒɪkəl] *adj* : etimológico
etymology [,ɛt̬ə'mɑlədʒi] *n, pl* **-gies** : etimología *f*
eucalyptus [,juːkə'lɪptəs] *n, pl* **-ti** [-,taɪ] *or* **-tuses** [-təsəz] : eucalipto *m*
Eucharist ['juːkərɪst] *n* : Eucaristía *f*
eulogize ['juːlə,dʒaɪz] *vt* **-gized; -gizing** : elogiar, encomiar
eulogy ['juːlədʒi] *n, pl* **-gies** : elogio *m,* encomio *m,* panegírico *m*
eunuch ['juːnək] *n* : eunuco *m*
euphemism ['juːfə,mɪzəm] *n* : eufemismo *m*
euphemistic [,juːfə'mɪstɪk] *adj* : eufemístico
euphony ['juːfəni] *n, pl* **-nies** : eufonía *f*
euphoria [jʊ'foriə] *n* : euforia *f*
euphoric [jʊ'forɪk] *adj* : eufórico
euthanasia [,juːθə'neɪʒə, -ʒiə] *n* : eutanasia *f*
evacuate [ɪ'vækjʊ,eɪt] *v* **-ated; -ating** *vt* VACATE : evacuar, desalojar — *vi* WITHDRAW : retirarse
evacuation [ɪ,vækjʊ'eɪʃən] *n* : evacuación *f,* desalojo *m*
evade [ɪ'veɪd] *vt* **evaded; evading** : evadir, eludir, esquivar
evaluate [ɪ'væljʊ,eɪt] *vt* **-ated; -ating** : evaluar, valorar, tasar
evaluation [ɪ,væljʊ'eɪʃən] *n* : evaluación *f,* valoración *f,* tasación *f*
evangelical [,iː,væn'dʒɛlɪkəl, ,ɛvən-] *adj* : evangélico
evangelist [ɪ'vændʒəlɪst] *n* **1** : evangelista *m* **2** PREACHER : predicador *m,* **-dora** *f*
evaporate [ɪ'væpə,reɪt] *vi* **-rated; -rating 1** VAPORIZE : evaporarse **2** VANISH : evaporarse, desvanecerse, esfumarse
evaporation [ɪ,væpə'reɪʃən] *n* : evaporación *f*
evasion [ɪ'veɪʒən] *n* : evasión *f*
evasive [ɪ'veɪsɪv] *adj* : evasivo
evasiveness [ɪ'veɪsɪvnəs] *n* : carácter *m* evasivo
eve ['iːv] *n* **1** : víspera *f* <on the eve of the festivities : en vísperas de las festividades> **2** → **evening**
even[1] ['iːvən] *vt* **1** LEVEL : allanar, nivelar, emparejar **2** EQUALIZE : igualar, equilibrar — *vi* **to even out** : nivelarse, emparejarse
even[2] *adv* **1** : hasta, incluso <even a child can do it : hasta un niño puede hacerlo> <he looked content, even happy : se le veía satisfecho, incluso feliz> **2** (*in negative constructions*) : ni siquiera <he didn't even try : ni siquiera lo intentó> **3** (*in comparisons*) : aún, todavía <even better : aún mejor, todavía mejor> **4 even if** : aunque **5 even so** : aun así **6 even though** : aun cuando, a pesar de que
even[3] *adj* **1** SMOOTH : uniforme, liso, parejo **2** FLAT : plano, llano **3** EQUAL : igual, igualado <an even score : un marcador igualado> **4** REGULAR : regular, constante <an even pace : un ritmo constante> **5** EXACT : exacto, justo **6** : par <even number : número par> **7 to be even** : estar en paz, estar a mano **8 to get even** : desquitarse, vengarse
evening ['iːvnɪŋ] *n* : tarde *f,* noche *f* <in the evening : por la noche>
evenly ['iːvənli] *adv* **1** UNIFORMLY : de modo uniforme, de manera constante **2** FAIRLY : igualmente, equitativamente
evenness ['iːvənnəs] *n* : uniformidad *f,* igualdad *f,* regularidad *f*
event [ɪ'vɛnt] *n* **1** : acontecimiento *m,* suceso *m,* prueba *f* (en deportes) **2 in the event that** : en caso de que
eventful [ɪ'vɛntfəl] *adj* : lleno de incidentes, memorable
eventual [ɪ'vɛntʃʊəl] *adj* : final, consiguiente
eventuality [ɪ,vɛntʃʊ'ælət̬i] *n, pl* **-ties** : eventualidad *f*
eventually [ɪ'vɛntʃʊəli] *adv* : al fin, con el tiempo, algún día
ever ['ɛvər] *adv* **1** ALWAYS : siempre <as ever : como siempre> <ever since : desde entonces> **2** (*in questions*) : alguna vez, algún día <have you ever been to Mexico? : ¿has estado en México alguna vez?> **3** (*in negative constructions*) : nunca <doesn't he ever work? : ¿es que nunca trabaja?> <nobody ever helps me : nadie nunca me ayuda> **4** (*in comparisons*) : nunca <better than ever : mejor que nunca> **5** (*as intensifier*) <I'm ever so happy! : ¡estoy tan y tan feliz!> <he

looks ever so angry : parece estar muy enojado>
evergreen[1] [ˈɛvərˌgriːn] *adj* : de hoja perenne
evergreen[2] *n* : planta *f* de hoja perenne
everlasting [ˌɛvərˈlæstɪŋ] *adj* : eterno, perpetuo, imperecedero
evermore [ˌɛvərˈmor] *adv* : eternamente
every [ˈɛvri] *adj* **1** EACH : cada <every time : cada vez> <every other house : cada dos casas> **2** ALL : todo <every month : todos los meses> <every woman : toda mujer, todas las mujeres> **3** COMPLETE : pleno, entero <to have every confidence : tener plena confianza>
everybody [ˈɛvriˌbʌdi, -ˌbɑ-] *pron* : todos *mpl*, -das *fpl*; todo el mundo
everyday [ˌɛvriˈdeɪ, ˈɛvriˌ-] *adj* : cotidiano, diario, corriente <everyday clothes : ropa de todos los días>
everyone [ˈɛvri ˌwʌn] → **everybody**
everything [ˈɛvriˌθɪŋ] *pron* : todo
everywhere [ˈɛvriˌ*h*wɛr] *adv* : en todas partes, por todas partes, dondequiera <I looked everywhere : busqué en todas partes> <everywhere we go : dondequiera que vayamos>
evict [ɪˈvɪkt] *vt* : desalojar, desahuciar
eviction [ɪˈvɪkʃən] *n* : desalojo *m*, desahucio *m*
evidence [ˈɛvədən*t*s] *n* **1** INDICATION : indicio *m*, señal *m* <to be in evidence : estar a la vista> **2** PROOF : evidencia *f*, prueba *f* **3** TESTIMONY : testimonio *m*, declaración *f* <to give evidence : declarar como testigo, prestar declaración>
evident [ˈɛvidənt] *adj* : evidente, patente, manifiesto
evidently [ˈɛvidəntli, ˌɛviˈdɛntli] *adv* **1** CLEARLY : claramente, obviamente **2** APPARENTLY : aparentemente, evidentemente, al parecer
evil[1] [ˈiːvəl, -vɪl] *adj* **eviler** *or* **eviller; evilest** *or* **evillest 1** WICKED : malvado, malo, maligno **2** HARMFUL : nocivo, dañino, pernicioso **3** UNPLEASANT : desagradable <an evil odor : un olor horrible>
evil[2] *n* **1** WICKEDNESS : mal *m*, maldad *f* **2** MISFORTUNE : desgracia *f*, mal *m*
evildoer [ˌiːvəlˈduːər, ˌiːvɪl-] *n* : malvado *m*, -da *f*
evince [ɪˈvɪn*t*s] *vt* **evinced; evincing** : mostrar, manifestar, revelar
eviscerate [ɪˈvɪsəˌreɪt] *vt* **-ated; -ating** : eviscerar, destripar (un pollo, etc.)
evocation [ˌiːvoˈkeɪʃən, ˌɛ-] *n* : evocación *f*
evocative [iˈvɑkətɪv] *adj* : evocador
evoke [iˈvoːk] *vt* **evoked; evoking** : evocar, provocar
evolution [ˌɛvəˈluːʃən, ˌiː-] *n* : evolución *f*, desarrollo *m*
evolutionary [ˌɛvəˈluːʃəˌnɛri, ˌiː-] *adj* : evolutivo
evolve [iˈvɑlv] *vi* **evolved; evolving** : evolucionar, desarrollarse
ewe [ˈjuː] *n* : oveja *f*
exact[1] [ɪgˈzækt, ɛ-] *vt* : exigir, imponer, arrancar
exact[2] *adj* : exacto, preciso — **exactly** *adv*
exacting [ɪˈzæktɪŋ, ɛg-] *adj* : exigente, riguroso
exactitude [ɪgˈzæktəˌtuːd, ɛg-, -ˌtjuːd] *n* : exactitud *f*, precisión *f*
exaggerate [ɪgˈzædʒəˌreɪt, ɛg-] *v* **-ated; -ating** : exagerar
exaggerated [ɪgˈzædʒəˌreɪtəd, ɛg-] *adj* : exagerado — **exaggeratedly** *adv*
exaggeration [ɪgˌzædʒəˈreɪʃən, ɛg-] *n* : exageración *f*
exalt [ɪgˈzɔlt, ɛg-] *vt* : exaltar, ensalzar, glorificar
exaltation [ˌɛgˌzɔlˈteɪʃən, ˌɛkˌsɔl-] *n* : exaltación *f*
exam [ɪgˈzæm, ɛg-] → **examination**
examination [ɪgˌzæməˈneɪʃən, ɛg-] *n* **1** TEST : examen *m* **2** INSPECTION : inspección *f*, revisión *f* **3** INVESTIGATION : examen *m*, estudio *m*
examine [ɪgˈzæmən, ɛg-] *vt* **-ined; -ining 1** TEST : examinar **2** INSPECT : inspeccionar, revisar **3** STUDY : examinar
example [ɪgˈzæmpəl, ɛg-] *n* : ejemplo *m* <for example : por ejemplo> <to set an example : dar ejemplo>
exasperate [ɪgˈzæspəˌreɪt, ɛg-] *vt* **-ated; -ating** : exasperar, sacar de quicio
exasperation [ɪgˌzæspəˈreɪʃən, ɛg-] *n* : exasperación *f*
excavate [ˈɛkskəˌveɪt] *vt* **-vated; -vating** : excavar
excavation [ˌɛkskəˈveɪʃən] *n* : excavación *f*
exceed [ɪkˈsiːd, ɛk-] *vt* **1** SURPASS : exceder, rebasar, sobrepasar **2** : exceder de, sobrepasar <not exceeding two months : que no exceda de dos meses>
exceedingly [ɪkˈsiːdɪŋli, ɛk-] *adv* : extremadamente, sumamente
excel [ɪkˈsɛl, ɛk-] *v* **-celled; -celling** *vi* : sobresalir, descollar, lucirse — *vt* : superar
excellence [ˈɛksələn*t*s] *n* : excelencia *f*
excellency [ˈɛksələn*t*si] *n, pl* **-cies** : excelencia *f* <His Excellency : Su Excelencia>
excellent [ˈɛksələnt] *adj* : excelente, sobresaliente — **excellently** *adv*
except[1] [ɪkˈsɛpt] *vt* : exceptuar, excluir
except[2] *conj* : pero, si no fuera por
except[3] *prep* : excepto, menos, salvo <everyone except Carlos : todos menos Carlos>
exception [ɪkˈsɛpʃən] *n* **1** : excepción *f* **2 to take exception to** : ofenderse por, objetar a
exceptional [ɪkˈsɛpʃənəl] *adj* : excepcional, extraordinario — **exceptionally** *adv*

excerpt[1] [ɛk'sərpt, ɛg'zərpt, 'ɛk,-, 'ɛg,-] *vt* : escoger, seleccionar

excerpt[2] ['ɛk,sərpt, 'ɛg,zərpt] *n* : pasaje *m,* selección *f*

excess[1] ['ɛk,sɛs, ɪk'sɛs] *adj* **1** : excesivo, de sobra **2 excess baggage** : exceso *m* de equipaje

excess[2] [ɪk'sɛs, 'ɛk,sɛs] *n* **1** SUPERFLUITY : exceso *m,* superfluidad *f* <an excess of energy : un exceso de energía> **2** SURPLUS : excedente *m,* sobrante *m* <in excess of : superior a>

excessive [ɪk'sɛsɪv, ɛk-] *adj* : excesivo, exagerado, desmesurado — **excessively** *adv*

exchange[1] [ɪks'tʃeɪndʒ, ɛks-; 'ɛks,tʃeɪndʒ] *vt* **-changed; -changing** : cambiar, intercambiar, canjear

exchange[2] *n* **1** : cambio *m,* intercambio *m,* canje *m* **2 stock exchange** : bolsa *f* (de valores)

exchangeable [ɪks'tʃeɪndʒəbəl, ɛks-] *adj* : canjeable

excise[1] [ɪk'saɪz, ɛk-] *vt* **-cised; -cising** : extirpar

excise[2] ['ɛk,saɪz] *n* **excise tax** : impuesto *m* interno, impuesto *m* sobre el consumo

excision [ɪk'sɪʒən, ɛk-] *n* : extirpación *f,* excisión *f*

excitability [ɪk,saɪtə'bɪləţi, ɛk-] *n* : excitabilidad *f*

excitable [ɪk'saɪţəbəl, ɛk-] *adj* : excitable

excitation [,ɛk,saɪ'teɪʃən] *n* : excitación *f*

excite [ɪk'saɪt, ɛk-] *vt* **-cited; -citing 1** AROUSE, STIMULATE : excitar, mover, estimular **2** ANIMATE : entusiasmar, animar **3** EVOKE, PROVOKE : provocar, despertar, suscitar <to excite curiousity : despertar la curiosidad>

excited [ɪk'saɪţəd, ɛk-] *adj* **1** STIMULATED : excitado, estimulado **2** ENTHUSIASTIC : entusiasmado, emocionado

excitedly [ɪk'saɪţədli, ɛk-] *adv* : con excitación, con entusiasmo

excitement [ɪk'saɪtmənt, ɛk-] *n* **1** ENTHUSIASM : entusiasmo *m,* emoción *f* **2** AGITATION : agitación *f,* alboroto *m,* conmoción *f* **3** AROUSAL : excitación *f*

exclaim [ɪks'kleɪm, ɛk-] *v* : exclamar

exclamation [,ɛksklə'meɪʃən] *n* : exclamación *f*

exclamation point *n* : signo *m* de admiración

exclamatory [ɪks'klæmə,tori, ɛks-] *adj* : exclamativo

exclude [ɪks'klu:d, ɛks-] *vt* **-cluded; -cluding 1** BAR : excluir, descartar, no admitir **2** EXPEL : expeler, expulsar

exclusion [ɪks'klu:ʒən, ɛks-] *n* : exclusión *f*

exclusive[1] [ɪks'klu:sɪv, ɛks-] *adj* **1** SOLE : exclusivo, único **2** SELECT : exclusivo, selecto

exclusive[2] *n* : exclusiva *f*

exclusively [ɪks'klu:sɪvli, ɛks-] *adv* : exclusivamente, únicamente

exclusiveness [ɪks'klu:sɪvnəs, ɛks-] *n* : exclusividad *f*

excommunicate [,ɛkskə'mju:nə,keɪt] *vt* **-cated; -cating** : excomulgar

excommunication [,ɛkskə,mju:nə'keɪʃən] *n* : excomunión *f*

excrement ['ɛkskrəmənt] *n* : excremento *m*

excrete [ɪk'skri:t, ɛk-] *vt* **-creted; -creting** : excretar

excretion [ɪk'skri:ʃən, ɛk-] *n* : excreción *f*

excruciating [ɪk'skru:ʃi,eɪţɪŋ, ɛk-] *adj* : insoportable, atroz, terrible — **excruciatingly** *adv*

exculpate ['ɛkskəl,peɪt] *vt* **-pated; -pating** : exculpar

excursion [ɪk'skərʒən, ɛk-] *n* **1** OUTING : excursión *f,* paseo *m* **2** DIGRESSION : digresión *f*

excuse[1] [ɪk'skju:z, ɛk-] *vt* **-cused; -cusing 1** PARDON : disculpar, perdonar <excuse me : con permiso, perdóneme, perdón> **2** EXEMPT : eximir, disculpar **3** JUSTIFY : excusar, justificar

excuse[2] [ɪk'skju:s, ɛk-] *n* **1** JUSTIFICATION : excusa *f,* justificación *f* **2** PRETEXT : pretexto *m* **3 to make one's excuses to someone** : pedirle disculpas a alguien

execute ['ɛksɪ,kju:t] *vt* **-cuted; -cuting 1** CARRY OUT : ejecutar, llevar a cabo, desempeñar **2** ENFORCE : ejecutar, cumplir (un testamento, etc.) **3** KILL : ejecutar, ajusticiar

execution [,ɛksɪ'kju:ʃən] *n* **1** PERFORMANCE : ejecución *f,* desempeño *m* **2** IMPLEMENTATION : cumplimiento *m* **3** : ejecución *f* (por un delito)

executioner [,ɛksɪ'kju:ʃənər] *n* : verdugo *m*

executive[1] [ɪg'zɛkjəţɪv, ɛg-] *adj* : ejecutivo

executive[2] *n* : ejecutivo *m,* -va *f*

executor [ɪg'zɛkjəţər, ɛg-] *n* : albacea *m,* testamentario *m*

executrix [ɪg'zɛkjə,trɪks, ɛg-] *n, pl* **executrices** [-,zɛkjə'traɪ,si:z] *or* **executrixes** [-'zɛkjə,trɪksəz] : albacea *f,* testamentaria *f*

exemplary [ɪg'zɛmpləri, ɛg-] *adj* : ejemplar

exemplify [ɪg'zɛmplə,faɪ, ɛg-] *vt* **-fied; -fying** : ejemplificar, ilustrar, demostrar

exempt[1] [ɪg'zɛmpt, ɛg-] *vt* : eximir, dispensar, exonerar

exempt[2] *adj* : exento, eximido

exemption [ɪg'zɛmpʃən, ɛg-] *n* : exención *f*

exercise[1] ['ɛksər,saɪz] *v* **-cised; -cising** *vt* **1** : ejercitar (el cuerpo) **2** USE : ejercer, hacer uso de — *vi* : hacer ejercicio

exercise[2] *n* **1** : ejercicio *m* **2 exercises** *npl* WORKOUT : ejercicios *mpl* físicos **3 exercises** *npl* CEREMONY : ceremonia *f*

exert [ɪg'zərt, ɛg-] *vt* **1** : ejercer, emplear **2 to exert oneself** : esforzarse

exertion [ɪg'zərʃən, ɛg-] *n* **1** USE : ejercicio *m* (de autoridad, etc.), uso *m* (de fuerza, etc.) **2** EFFORT : esfuerzo *m,* empeño *m*
exhalation [ˌɛksə'leɪʃən, ˌɛkshə-] *n* : exhalación *f,* espiración *f*
exhale [ɛks'heɪl] *v* **-haled; -haling** *vt* **1** : exhalar, espirar **2** EMIT : exhalar, despedir, emitir — *vi* : espirar
exhaust¹ [ɪg'zɔst, ɛg-] *vt* **1** DEPLETE : agotar **2** TIRE : cansar, fatigar, agotar **3** EMPTY : vaciar
exhaust² *n* **1 exhaust fumes** : gases *mpl* de escape **2 exhaust pipe** : tubo *m* de escape **3 exhaust system** : sistema *m* de escape
exhausted [ɪg'zɔstəd, ɛg-] *adj* : agotado, derrengado
exhausting [ɪg'zɔstɪŋ, ɛg-] *adj* : extenuante, agotador
exhaustion [ɪg'zɔstʃən, ɛg-] *n* : agotamiento *m*
exhaustive [ɪg'zɔstɪv, ɛg-] *adj* : exhaustivo
exhibit¹ [ɪg'zɪbət, ɛg-] *vt* **1** DISPLAY : exhibir, exponer **2** PRODUCE, SHOW : mostrar, presentar
exhibit² *n* **1** OBJECT : objeto *m* expuesto **2** EXHIBITION : exposición *f,* exhibición *f* **3** EVIDENCE : prueba *f* instrumental
exhibition [ˌɛksə'bɪʃən] *n* **1** : exposición *f,* exhibición *f* **2 to make an exhibition of oneself** : dar el espectáculo, hacer el ridículo
exhilarate [ɪg'zɪləˌreɪt, ɛg-] *vt* **-rated; -rating** : alegrar, levantar el ánimo de
exhilaration [ɪgˌzɪlə'reɪʃən, ɛg-] *n* : alegría *f,* regocijo *m,* júbilo *m*
exhort [ɪg'zɔrt, ɛg-] *vt* : exhortar
exhortation [ˌɛkˌsɔr'teɪʃən, -sər-; ˌɛgˌzɔr-] *n* : exhortación *f*
exhumation [ˌɛksju'meɪʃən, -hju-; ˌɛgzu-, -zju-] *n* : exhumación *f*
exhume [ɪg'zuːm, -'zjuːm; ɪks'juːm, -'hjuːm] *vt* **-humed; -huming** : exhumar, desenterrar
exigencies ['ɛksɪdʒən*t*siz, ɪg'zɪdʒənˌsiːz] *npl* : exigencias *fpl*
exile¹ ['ɛgˌzaɪl, 'ɛkˌsaɪl] *vt* **exiled; exiling** : exiliar, desterrar
exile² *n* **1** BANISHMENT : exilio *m,* destierro *m* **2** OUTCAST : exiliado *m,* -da *f;* desterrado *m,* -da *f*
exist [ɪg'zɪst, ɛg-] *vi* **1** BE : existir **2** LIVE : subsistir, vivir
existence [ɪg'zɪstən*t*s, ɛg-] *n* : existencia *f*
existent [ɪg'zɪstənt, ɛg-] *adj* : existente
exit¹ ['ɛgzət, 'ɛksət] *vi* : salir, hacer mutis (en el teatro) — *vt* : salir de
exit² *n* **1** DEPARTURE : salida *f,* partida *f* **2** EGRESS : salida *f* <emergency exit : salida de emergencia>
exodus ['ɛksədəs] *n* : éxodo *m*
exonerate [ɪg'zɑnəˌreɪt, ɛg-] *vt* **-ated; -ating** : exonerar, disculpar, absolver
exoneration [ɪgˌzɑnə'reɪʃən, ɛg-] *n* : exoneración *f*
exorbitant [ɪg'zɔrbətənt, ɛg-] *adj* : exorbitante, excesivo
exorcise ['ɛkˌsɔrˌsaɪz, -sər-] *vt* **-cised; -cising** : exorcizar
exorcism ['ɛksərˌsɪzəm] *n* : exorcismo *m*
exotic¹ [ɪg'zɑtɪk, ɛg-] *adj* : exótico — **exotically** [-ɪkli] *adv*
exotic² *n* : planta *f* exótica
expand [ɪk'spænd, ɛk-] *vt* **1** ENLARGE : expandir, dilatar, aumentar, ampliar **2** EXTEND : extender — *vi* **1** ENLARGE : ampliarse, extenderse **2** : expandirse, dilatarse (dícese de los metales, gases, etc.)
expanse [ɪk'spæn*t*s, ɛk-] *n* : extensión *f*
expansion [ɪk'spæntʃən, ɛk-] *n* **1** ENLARGEMENT : expansión *f,* ampliación *f* **2** EXPANSE : extensión *f*
expansive [ɪk'spæn*t*sɪv, ɛk-] *adj* **1** : expansivo **2** OUTGOING : expansivo, comunicativo **3** AMPLE : ancho, amplio — **expansively** *adv*
expansiveness [ɪk'spæn*t*sɪvnəs, ɛk-] *n* : expansibilidad *f*
expatriate¹ [ɛks'peɪtriˌeɪt] *vt* **-ated; -ating** : expatriar
expatriate² [ɛks'peɪtriət, -ˌeɪt] *adj* : expatriado
expatriate³ [ɛks'peɪtriət, -ˌeɪt] *n* : expatriado *m,* -da *f*
expect [ɪk'spɛkt, ɛk-] *vt* **1** SUPPOSE : suponer, imaginarse **2** ANTICIPATE : esperar **3** COUNT ON, REQUIRE : contar con, esperar — *vi* **to be expecting** : estar embarazada
expectancy [ɪk'spɛktən*t*si, ɛk-] *n, pl* **-cies** : expectativa *f,* esperanza *f*
expectant [ɪk'spɛktənt, ɛk-] *adj* **1** ANTICIPATING : expectante **2** EXPECTING : futuro <expectant mother : futura madre>
expectantly [ɪk'spɛktəntli, ɛk-] *adv* : con expectación
expectation [ˌɛkˌspɛk'teɪʃən] *n* **1** ANTICIPATION : expectación *f* **2** EXPECTANCY : expectativa *f*
expedient¹ [ɪk'spiːdiənt, ɛk-] *adj* : conveniente, oportuno
expedient² *n* : expediente *m,* recurso *m*
expedite ['ɛkspəˌdaɪt] *vt* **-dited; -diting 1** FACILITATE : facilitar, dar curso a **2** HASTEN : acelerar
expedition [ˌɛkspə'dɪʃən] *n* : expedición *f*
expeditious [ˌɛkspə'dɪʃəs] *adj* : pronto, rápido
expel [ɪk'spɛl, ɛk-] *vt* **-pelled; -pelling** : expulsar, expeler
expend [ɪk'spɛnd, ɛk-] *vt* **1** DISBURSE : gastar, desembolsar **2** CONSUME : consumir, agotar
expendable [ɪk'spɛndəbəl, ɛk-] *adj* : prescindible
expenditure [ɪk'spɛndɪtʃər, ɛk-, -ˌtʃʊr] *n* : gasto *m*
expense [ɪk'spɛn*t*s, ɛk-] *n* **1** COST : gasto *m* **2 expenses** *npl* : gastos *mpl,*

expensas *fpl* **3 at the expense of :** a expensas de
expensive [ɪk'spɛntsɪv, ɛk-] *adj* **:** costoso, caro — **expensively** *adv*
experience¹ [ɪk'spɪriənts, ɛk-] *vt* **-enced; -encing :** experimentar (sentimientos), tener (dificultades), sufrir (una pérdida)
experience² *n* **:** experiencia *f*
experiment¹ [ɪk'spɛrəmənt, ɛk-, -'spɪr-] *vi* **:** experimentar, hacer experimentos
experiment² *n* **:** experimento *m*
experimental [ɪk,spɛrə'mɛntəl, ɛk-, -,spɪr-] *adj* **:** experimental — **experimentally** *adv*
experimentation [ɪk,spɛrəmən'teɪʃən, ɛk-, -,spɪr-] *n* **:** experimentación *f*
expert¹ ['ɛk,spərt, ɪk'spərt] *adj* **:** experto, de experto, pericial (dícese de un testigo) — **expertly** *adv*
expert² ['ɛk,spərt] *n* **:** experto *m*, -ta *f;* perito *m*, -ta *f;* especialista *mf*
expertise [,ɛkspər'ti:z] *n* **:** pericia *f*, competencia *f*
expiate ['ɛkspi,eɪt] *vt* **-ated; -ating :** expiar
expiation [,ɛkspi'eɪʃən] *n* **:** expiación *f*
expiration [,ɛkspə'reɪʃən] *n* **1** EXHALATION **:** exhalación *f*, espiración *f* **2** DEATH **:** muerte *f* **3** TERMINATION **:** vencimiento *m*, caducidad *f*
expire [ɪk'spaɪr, ɛk-] *vi* **-pired; -piring 1** EXHALE **:** espirar **2** DIE **:** expirar, morir **3** TERMINATE **:** caducar, vencer
explain [ɪk'spleɪn, ɛk-] *vt* **:** explicar
explanation [,ɛksplə'neɪʃən] *n* **:** explicación *f*
explanatory [ɪk'splænə,tori, ɛk-] *adj* **:** explicativo, aclaratorio
expletive ['ɛkspləṭɪv] *n* **:** improperio *m*, palabrota *f fam*, grosería *f*
explicable [ɛk'splɪkəbəl, 'ɛksplɪ-] *adj* **:** explicable
explicit [ɪk'splɪsət, ɛk-] *adj* **:** explícito, claro, categórico, rotundo — **explicitly** *adv*
explicitness [ɪk'splɪsətnəs, ɛk-] *n* **:** claridad *f*, carácter *m* explícito
explode [ɪk'splo:d, ɛk-] *v* **-ploded; -ploding** *vt* **1** BURST **:** explosionar, hacer explotar **2** REFUTE **:** rebatir, refutar, desmentir — *vi* **1** BURST **:** explotar, estallar, reventar **2** SKYROCKET **:** dispararse
exploit¹ [ɪk'splɔɪt, ɛk-] *vt* **:** explotar, aprovecharse de
exploit² ['ɛk,splɔɪt] *n* **:** hazaña *f*, proeza *f*
exploitation [,ɛk,splɔɪ'teɪʃən] *n* **:** explotación *f*
exploration [,ɛksplə'reɪʃən] *n* **:** exploración *f*
exploratory [ɪk'splorə,tori, ɛk-] *adj* **:** exploratorio
explore [ɪk'splor, ɛk-] *vt* **-plored; -ploring :** explorar, investigar, examinar
explorer [ɪk'splorər, ɛk-] *n* **:** explorador *m*, -dora *f*
explosion [ɪk'splo:ʒən, ɛk-] *n* **:** explosión *f*, estallido *m*
explosive¹ [ɪk'splo:sɪv, ɛk-] *adj* **:** explosivo, fulminante — **explosively** *adv*
explosive² *n* **:** explosivo *m*
exponent [ɪk'spo:nənt, 'ɛk,spo:-] *n* **1 :** exponente *m* **2** ADVOCATE **:** defensor *m*, -sora *f;* partidario *m*, -ria *f*
exponential [,ɛkspə'nɛntʃəl] *adj* **:** exponencial — **exponentially** *adv*
export¹ [ɛk'sport, 'ɛk,sport] *vt* **:** exportar
export² ['ɛk,sport] *n* **1 :** artículo *m* de exportación **2** → **exportation**
exportation [,ɛk,spor'teɪʃən] *n* **:** exportación *f*
exporter [ɛk'sporṭər, 'ɛk,spor-] *n* **:** exportador *m*, -dora *f*
expose [ɪk'spo:z, ɛk-] *vt* **-posed; -posing 1 :** exponer (al peligro, a los elementos, a una enfermedad) **2 :** exponer (una película a la luz) **3** DISCLOSE **:** descubrir, revelar, poner en evidencia **4** UNMASK **:** desenmascarar
exposé *or* **expose** [,ɛkspo'zeɪ] *n* **:** exposición *f* (de hechos), relevación *f* (de un escándalo)
exposed [ɪk'spo:zd, ɛk-] *adj* **:** descubierto, sin protección
exposition [,ɛkspə'zɪʃən] *n* **:** exposición *f*
exposure [ɪk'spo:ʒər, ɛk-] *n* **1 :** exposición *f* **2** CONTACT **:** exposición *f*, experiencia *f*, contacto *m* **3** UNMASKING **:** desenmascaramiento *m* **4** ORIENTATION **:** orientación *f* <a room with a northern exposure : una sala orientada al norte>
expound [ɪk'spaʊnd, ɛk-] *vt* **:** exponer, explicar — *vi* **:** hacer comentarios detallados
express¹ [ɪk'sprɛs, ɛk-] *vt* **1** SAY **:** expresar, comunicar **2** SHOW **:** expresar, manifestar, externar *Mex* **3** SQUEEZE **:** exprimir <to express the juice from a lemon : exprimir el jugo de un limón>
express² *adv* **:** por correo exprés, por correo urgente
express³ *adj* **1** EXPLICIT **:** expreso, manifiesto **2** SPECIFIC **:** específico <for that express purpose : con ese fin específico> **3** RAPID **:** expreso, rápido
express⁴ *n* **1 :** correo *m* exprés, correo *m* urgente **2 :** expreso *m* (tren)
expression [ɪk'sprɛʃən, ɛk-] *n* **1** UTTERANCE **:** expresión *f* <freedom of expression : libertad de expresión> **2 :** expresión *f* (en la matemática) **3** PHRASE **:** frase *f*, expresión *f* **4** LOOK **:** expresión *f*, cara *f*, gesto *m* <with a sad expression : con un gesto de tristeza>
expressionless [ɪk'sprɛʃənləs, ɛk-] *adj* **:** inexpresivo

expressive [ɪk'sprɛsɪv, ɛk-] *adj* : expresivo
expressway [ɪk'sprɛs,weɪ, ɛk-] *n* : autopista *f*
expulsion [ɪk'spʌlʃən, ɛk-] *n* : expulsión *f*
expurgate ['ɛkspər,geɪt] *vt* **-gated; -gating** : expurgar
exquisite [ɛk'skwɪzət, 'ɛk,skwɪ-] *adj* **1** FINE : exquisito, delicado, primoroso **2** INTENSE : intenso, extremo
extant ['ɛkstənt, ɛk'stænt] *adj* : existente
extemporaneous [ɛk,stɛmpə'reɪniəs] *adj* : improvisado — **extemporaneously** *adv*
extend [ɪk'stɛnd, ɛk-] *vt* **1** STRETCH : extender, tender **2** PROLONG : prolongar, prorrogar **3** ENLARGE : agrandar, ampliar, aumentar **4** PROFFER : extender, dar, ofrecer — *vi* : extenderse
extended [ɪk'stɛndəd, ɛk-] *adj* LENGTHY : prolongado, largo
extension [ɪk'stɛntʃən, ɛk-] *n* **1** EXTENDING : extensión *f*, ampliación *f*, prórroga *f*, prolongación *f* **2** ANNEX : ampliación *f*, anexo *m* **3** : extensión *f* (de teléfono)
extensive [ɪk'stɛntsɪv, ɛk-] *adj* : extenso, vasto, amplio — **extensively** *adv*
extent [ɪk'stɛnt, ɛk-] *n* **1** SIZE : extensión *f*, magnitud *f* **2** DEGREE, SCOPE : alcance *m*, grado *m* <to a certain extent : hasta cierto punto>
extenuate [ɪk'stɛnjə,weɪt, ɛk-] *vt* **-ated; -ating** : atenuar, aminorar, mitigar <extenuating circumstances : circunstancias atenuantes>
extenuation [ɪk,stɛnjə'weɪʃən, ɛk-] *n* : atenuación *f*, aminoración *f*
exterior¹ [ɛk'stɪriər] *adj* : exterior
exterior² *n* : exterior *m*
exterminate [ɪk'stərmə,neɪt, ɛk-] *vt* **-nated; -nating** : exterminar
extermination [ɪk,stərmə'neɪʃən, ɛk-] *n* : exterminación *f*, exterminio *m*
exterminator [ɪk'stərmə,neɪt̬ər, ɛk-] *n* : exterminador *m*, **-dora** *f*
external [ɪk'stərnəl, ɛk-] *adj* : externo, exterior — **externally** *adv*
extinct [ɪk'stɪŋkt, ɛk-] *adj* : extinto
extinction [ɪk'stɪŋkʃən, ɛk-] *n* : extinción *f*
extinguish [ɪk'stɪŋgwɪʃ, ɛk-] *vt* : extinguir, apagar
extinguisher [ɪk'stɪŋgwɪʃər, ɛk-] *n* : extinguidor *m*, extintor *m*
extirpate ['ɛkstər,peɪt] *vt* **-pated; -pating** : extirpar, exterminar
extol [ɪk'stoːl, ɛk-] *vt* **-tolled; -tolling** : exaltar, ensalzar, alabar
extort [ɪk'stɔrt, ɛk-] *vt* : extorsionar
extortion [ɪk'stɔrʃən, ɛk-] *n* : extorsión *f*
extra¹ ['ɛkstrə] *adv* : extra, más, extremadamente, super <extra special : super especial>
extra² *adj* **1** ADDITIONAL : adicional, suplementario, de más **2** SUPERIOR : superior
extra³ *n* : extra *m*
extract¹ [ɪk'strækt, ɛk-] *vt* : extraer, sacar
extract² ['ɛk,strækt] *n* **1** EXCERPT : pasaje *m*, selección *f*, trozo *m* **2** : extracto *m* <vanilla extract : extracto de vainilla>
extraction [ɪk'strækʃən, ɛk-] *n* : extracción *f*
extractor [ɪk'stræktər, ɛk-] *n* : extractor *m*
extracurricular [,ɛkstrəkə'rɪkjələr] *adj* : extracurricular
extradite ['ɛkstrə,daɪt] *vt* **-dited; -diting** : extraditar
extradition [,ɛkstrə'dɪʃən] *n* : extradición *f*
extramarital [,ɛkstrə'mærət̬əl] *adj* : extramatrimonial
extraneous [ɛk'streɪniəs] *adj* **1** OUTSIDE : extrínseco, externo **2** SUPERFLUOUS : superfluo, ajeno — **extraneously** *adv*
extraordinary [ɪk'strɔrdən,ɛri, ,ɛkstrə'ɔrd-] *adj* : extraordinario, excepcional — **extraordinarily** [ɪk,strɔrdən'ɛrəli, ,ɛkstrə,ɔrd-] *adv*
extrasensory [,ɛkstrə'sɛntsəri] *adj* : extrasensorial
extraterrestrial¹ [,ɛkstrətə'rɛstriəl] *adj* : extraterrestre
extraterrestrial² *n* : extraterrestre *mf*
extravagance [ɪk'strævɪgənts, ɛk-] *n* **1** EXCESS : exceso *m*, extravagancia *f* **2** WASTEFULNESS : derroche *m*, despilfarro *m* **3** LUXURY : lujo *m*
extravagant [ɪk'strævɪgənt, ɛk-] *adj* **1** EXCESSIVE : excesivo, extravagante **2** WASTEFUL : despilfarrador, derrochador, gastador **3** EXORBITANT : costoso, exorbitante
extravagantly [ɪk'strævɪgəntli, ɛk-] *adv* **1** LAVISHLY : a lo grande **2** EXCESSIVELY : exageradamente, desmesuradamente
extravaganza [ɪk,strævə'gænzə, ɛk-] *n* : gran espectáculo *m*
extreme¹ [ɪk'striːm, ɛk-] *adj* **1** UTMOST : extremo, sumo <of extreme importance : de suma importancia> **2** INTENSE : intenso, extremado <extreme cold : frío extremado> **3** EXCESSIVE : excesivo, extremo <extreme views : opiniones extremas> <extreme measures : medidas excepcionales, medidas drásticas> **4** OUTERMOST : extremo <the extreme north : el norte extremo>
extreme² *n* **1** : extremo *m* **2 in the extreme** : en extremo, en sumo grado
extremely [ɪk'striːmli, ɛk-] *adv* : sumamente, extremadamente, terriblemente
extremity [ɪk'strɛmət̬i, ɛk-] *n, pl* **-ties** **1** EXTREME : extremo *m* **2 extremities** *npl* LIMBS : extremidades *fpl*

extricate ['ɛkstrəˌkeɪt] *vt* **-cated; -cating** : librar, sacar
extrinsic [ɪk'strɪnzɪk, -'strɪn*t*sɪk] *adj* : extrínseco
extrovert ['ɛkstrəˌvərt] *n* : extrovertido *m*, -da *f*
extroverted ['ɛkstrəˌvərṱəd] *adj* : extrovertido
extrude [ɪk'struːd, ɛk-] *vt* **-truded; -truding** : extrudir, expulsar
exuberance [ɪg'zuːbərən*t*s, ɛg-] *n* **1** JOYOUSNESS : euforia *f*, exaltación *f* **2** VIGOR : exuberancia *f*, vigor *m*
exuberant [ɪg'zuːbərənt, ɛg-] *adj* **1** JOYOUS : eufórico **2** LUSH : exuberante — **exuberantly** *adv*
exude [ɪg'zuːd, ɛg-] *vt* **-uded; -uding** **1** OOZE : rezumar, exudar **2** EMANATE : emanar, irradiar
exult [ɪg'zʌlt, ɛg-] *vi* : exultar, regocijarse
exultant [ɪg'zʌltənt, ɛg-] *adj* : exultante, jubiloso — **exultantly** *adv*
exultation [ˌɛksəl'teɪʃən, ˌɛgzəl-] *n* : exultación *f*, júbilo *m*, alborozo *m*
eye¹ ['aɪ] *vt* **eyed; eyeing** *or* **eying** : mirar, observar
eye² *n* **1** : ojo *m* **2** VISION : visión *f*, vista *f*, ojo *m* <a good eye for bargains : un buen ojo para las gangas> **3** GLANCE : mirada *f*, ojeada *f* **4** ATTENTION : atención *f* <to catch one's eye : llamar la atención> **5** POINT OF VIEW : punto *m* de vista <in the eyes of the law : según la ley> **6** : ojo *m* (de una aguja, una papa, una tormenta)
eyeball ['aɪˌbɔl] *n* : globo *m* ocular
eyebrow ['aɪˌbraʊ] *n* : ceja *f*
eyedropper ['aɪˌdrɑpər] *n* : cuentagotas *f*
eyeglasses ['aɪˌglæsəz] *npl* : anteojos *mpl*, lentes *mpl*, espejuelos *mpl*, gafas *fpl*
eyelash ['aɪˌlæʃ] *n* : pestaña *f*
eyelet ['aɪlət] *n* : ojete *m*
eyelid ['aɪˌlɪd] *n* : párpado *m*
eye–opener ['aɪˌoːpənər] *n* : revelación *f*, sorpresa *f*
eye–opening ['aɪˌoːpənɪŋ] *adj* : revelador
eyepiece ['aɪˌpiːs] *n* : ocular *m*
eyesight ['aɪˌsaɪt] *n* : vista *f*, visión *f*
eyesore ['aɪˌsor] *n* : monstruosidad *f*, adefesio *m*
eyestrain ['aɪˌstreɪn] *n* : fatiga *f* visual, vista *f* cansada
eyetooth ['aɪˌtuːθ] *n* : colmillo *m*
eyewitness ['aɪ'wɪtnəs] *n* : testigo *mf* ocular, testigo *mf* presencial
eyrie ['aɪri] → **aerie**

F

f ['ɛf] *n, pl* **f's** *or* **fs** ['ɛfs] : sexta letra del alfabeto inglés
fable ['feɪbəl] *n* : fábula *f*
fabled ['feɪbəld] *adj* : legendario, fabuloso
fabric ['fæbrɪk] *n* **1** MATERIAL : tela *f*, tejido *m* **2** STRUCTURE : estructura *f* <the fabric of society : la estructura de la sociedad>
fabricate ['fæbrɪˌkeɪt] *vt* **-cated; -cating** **1** CONSTRUCT, MANUFACTURE : construir, fabricar **2** INVENT : inventar (excusas o mentiras)
fabrication [ˌfæbrɪ'keɪʃən] *n* **1** LIE : mentira *f*, invención *f* **2** MANUFACTURE : fabricación *f*
fabulous ['fæbjələs] *adj* **1** LEGENDARY : fabuloso, legendario **2** INCREDIBLE : increíble, fabuloso <fabulous wealth : riqueza fabulosa> **3** WONDERFUL : magnífico, estupendo, fabuloso — **fabulously** *adv*
facade [fə'sɑd] *n* : fachada *f*
face¹ ['feɪs] *v* **faced; facing** *vt* **1** LINE : recubrir (una superficie), forrar (ropa) **2** CONFRONT : enfrentarse a, afrontar, hacer frente a <to face the music : afrontar las consecuencias> <to face the facts : aceptar la realidad> **3** : estar de cara a, estar enfrente de <she's facing her brother : está de cara a su hermano> **4** OVERLOOK : dar a — *vi* : mirar (hacia), estar orientado (a)
face² *n* **1** : cara *f*, rostro *m* <he told me to my face : me lo dijo a la cara> **2** EXPRESSION : cara *f*, expresión *f* <to pull a long face : poner mala cara> **3** GRIMACE : mueca *f* <to make faces : hacer muecas> **4** APPEARANCE : fisonomía *f*, aspecto *m* <the face of society : la fisonomía de la sociedad> **5** EFFRONTERY : desfachatez *f* **6** PRESTIGE : prestigio *m* <to lose face : desprestigiarse> **7** FRONT, SIDE : cara *f* (de una moneda), esfera *f* (de un reloj), fachada *f* (de un edificio), pared *f* (de una montaña) **8** SURFACE : superficie *f*, faz *f* (de la tierra), cara *f* (de la luna) **9 in the face of** DESPITE : en medio de, en visto de, ante
facedown ['feɪsˌdaʊn] *adv* : boca abajo
faceless ['feɪsləs] *adj* ANONYMOUS : anónimo
face–lift ['feɪsˌlɪft] *n* **1** : estiramiento *m* facial **2** RENOVATION : renovación *f*, remozamiento *m*
facet ['fæsət] *n* **1** : faceta *f* (de una piedra) **2** ASPECT : faceta *f*, aspecto *m*
facetious [fə'siːʃəs] *adj* : gracioso, burlón, bromista
facetiously [fə'siːʃəsli] *adv* : en tono de burla
facetiousness [fə'siːʃəsnəs] *n* : jocosidad *f*
face–to–face *adv & adj* : cara a cara
faceup ['feɪs'ʌp] *adv* : boca arriba

face value *n* **:** valor *m* nominal

facial[1] [ˈfeɪʃəl] *adj* **:** de la cara, facial

facial[2] *n* **:** tratamiento *m* facial, limpieza *f* de cutis

facile [ˈfæsəl] *adj* SUPERFICIAL **:** superficial, simplista

facilitate [fəˈsɪləˌteɪt] *vt* **-tated; -tating :** facilitar

facility [fəˈsɪləṭi] *n, pl* **-ties 1** EASE **:** facilidad *f* **2** CENTER, COMPLEX **:** centro *m,* complejo *m* **3 facilities** *npl* AMENITIES **:** comodidades *fpl*, servicios *mpl*

facing [ˈfeɪsɪŋ] *n* **1** LINING **:** entretela *f* (de una prenda) **2 :** revestimiento *m* (de un edificio)

facsimile [fækˈsɪməli] *n* **:** facsímile *m,* facsímil *m*

fact [ˈfækt] *n* **1 :** hecho *m* <as a matter of fact : de hecho> **2** INFORMATION **:** información *f,* datos *mpl* <facts and figures : datos y cifras> **3** REALITY **:** realidad *f* <in fact : en realidad>

faction [ˈfækʃən] *n* **:** facción *m,* bando *m*

factional [ˈfækʃənəl] *adj* **:** entre facciones

factious [ˈfækʃəs] *adj* **:** faccioso, contencioso

factitious [fækˈtɪʃəs] *adj* **:** artificial, facticio

factor [ˈfæktər] *n* **:** factor *m*

factory [ˈfæktəri] *n, pl* **-ries :** fábrica *f*

factual [ˈfæktʃʊəl] *adj* **:** basado en hechos, objetivo

factually [ˈfæktʃʊəli] *adv* **:** en cuanto a los hechos

faculty [ˈfækəlti] *n, pl* **-ties 1 :** facultad *f* <the faculty of sight : las facultades visuales, el sentido de la vista> **2** APTITUDE **:** aptitud *f,* facilidad *f* **3** TEACHERS **:** cuerpo *m* docente

fad [ˈfæd] *n* **:** moda *f* pasajera, manía *f*

fade [ˈfeɪd] *v* **faded; fading** *vi* **1** WITHER **:** debilitarse (dícese de las personas), marchitarse (dícese de las flores y las plantas) **2** DISCOLOR **:** desteñirse, decolorarse **3** DIM **:** apagarse (dícese de la luz), perderse (dícese de los sonidos), fundirse (dícese de las imágenes) **4** VANISH **:** desvanecerse, decaer — *vt* DISCOLOR **:** desteñir

fag [ˈfæg] *vt* **fagged; fagging** EXHAUST **:** cansar, fatigar

fagot *or* **faggot** [ˈfægət] *n* **:** haz *m* de leña

Fahrenheit [ˈfærənˌhaɪt] *adj* **:** Fahrenheit

fail[1] [ˈfeɪl] *vi* **1** WEAKEN **:** fallar, deteriorarse **2** STOP **:** fallar, detenerse <his heart failed : le falló el corazón> **3 :** fracasar, fallar <her plan failed : su plan fracasó> <the crops failed : se perdió la cosecha> **4 :** quebrar <a business about to fail : una empresa a punto de quebrar> **5 to fail in :** faltar a, no cumplir con <to fail in one's duties : faltar a sus deberes> — *vt* **1** FLUNK **:** reprobar (un examen) **2 :** fallar <words fail me : las palabras me fallan, no encuentro palabras> **3** DISAPPOINT **:** fallar, decepcionar <don't fail me! : ¡no me falles!>

fail[2] *n* **:** fracaso *m*

failing [ˈfeɪlɪŋ] *n* **:** defecto *m*

failure [ˈfeɪljər] *n* **1 :** fracaso *m,* malogro *m* <crop failure : pérdida de la cosecha> <heart failure : insuficiencia cardíaca> <engine failure : falla mecánica> **2** BANKRUPTCY **:** bancarrota *f,* quiebra *f* **3 :** fracaso *m* (persona) <he was a failure as a manager : como gerente, fue un fracaso>

faint[1] [ˈfeɪnt] *vi* **:** desmayarse

faint[2] *adj* **1** COWARDLY, TIMID **:** cobarde, tímido **2** DIZZY **:** mareado <faint with hunger : desfallecido de hambre> **3** SLIGHT **:** leve, ligero, vago <I haven't the faintest idea : no tengo la más mínima idea> **4** INDISTINCT **:** tenue, indistinto, apenas perceptible

faint[3] *n* **:** desmayo *m*

fainthearted [ˈfeɪntˈhɑrṭəd] *adj* **:** cobarde, pusilánime

faintly [ˈfeɪntli] *adv* **:** débilmente, ligeramente, levemente

faintness [ˈfeɪntnəs] *n* **1** INDISTINCTNESS **:** lo débil, falta *f* de claridad **2** FAINTING **:** desmayo *m,* desfallecimiento *m*

fair[1] [ˈfær] *adj* **1** ATTRACTIVE, BEAUTIFUL **:** bello, hermoso, atractivo **2** (*relating to weather*) **:** bueno, despejado <fair weather : tiempo despejado> **3** JUST **:** justo, imparcial **4** ALLOWABLE **:** permisible **5** BLOND, LIGHT **:** rubio (dícese del pelo), blanco (dícese de la tez) **6** ADEQUATE **:** bastante, adecuado <fair to middling : mediano, regular> **7 fair game :** presa *f* fácil **8 to play fair :** jugar limpio

fair[2] *n* **:** feria *f*

fairground [ˈfærˌgraʊnd] *n* **:** parque *m* de diversiones

fairly [ˈfærli] *adv* **1** IMPARTIALLY **:** imparcialmente, limpiamente, equitativamente **2** QUITE **:** bastante **3** MODERATELY **:** medianamente

fairness [ˈfærnəs] *n* **1** IMPARTIALITY **:** imparcialidad *f,* justicia *f* **2** LIGHTNESS **:** blancura *f* (de la piel), lo rubio (del pelo)

fairy [ˈfæri] *n, pl* **fairies 1 :** hada *f* **2 fairy tale :** cuento *m* de hadas

fairyland [ˈfæriˌlænd] *n* **1 :** país *m* de las hadas **2 :** lugar *m* encantador

faith [ˈfeɪθ] *n, pl* **faiths** [ˈfeɪθs, ˈfeɪðz] **1** BELIEF **:** fe *f* **2** ALLEGIANCE **:** lealtad *f* **3** CONFIDENCE, TRUST **:** confianza *f,* fe *f* **4** RELIGION **:** religión *f*

faithful [ˈfeɪθfəl] *adj* **:** fiel — **faithfully** *adv*

faithfulness [ˈfeɪθfəlnəs] *n* **:** fidelidad *f*

faithless [ˈfeɪθləs] *adj* **1** DISLOYAL **:** desleal **2 :** infiel (en la religión) — **faithlessly** *adv*

faithlessness ['feɪθləsnəs] *n* : deslealtad *f*

fake[1] ['feɪk] *v* **faked; faking** *vt* **1** FALSIFY : falsificar, falsear **2** FEIGN : fingir — *vi* **1** PRETEND : fingir **2** : hacer un engaño, hacer una finta (en deportes)

fake[2] *adj* : falso, fingido, postizo

fake[3] *n* **1** IMITATION : imitación *f,* falsificación *f* **2** IMPOSTOR : impostor *m,* -tora *f;* charlatán *m,* -tana *f;* farsante *mf* **3** FEINT : engaño *m,* finta *f* (en deportes)

faker ['feɪkər] *n* : impostor *m,* -tora *f;* charlatán *m,* -tana *f;* farsante *mf*

fakir [fə'kɪr, 'feɪkər] *n* : faquir *m*

falcon ['fælkən, 'fɔl-] *n* : halcón *m*

falconry ['fælkənri, 'fɔl-] *n* : cetrería *f*

fall[1] ['fɔl] *vi* **fell** ['fɛl]; **fallen** [fɔlən]; **falling 1** : caer, caerse <to fall out of bed : caer de la cama> <to fall down : caerse> **2** HANG : caer **3** DESCEND : caer (dícese de la lluvia o de la noche), bajar (dícese de los precios), descender (dícese de la temperatura) **4** : caer (a un enemigo), rendirse <the city fell : la ciudad se rindió> **5** OCCUR : caer <Christmas falls on a Friday : la Navidad cae en viernes> **6 to fall asleep** : dormirse, quedarse dormido **7 to fall from grace** SIN : perder la gracia **8 to fall sick** : caer enfermo, enfermarse **9 to fall through** : fracasar, caer en la nada **10 to fall to** : tocar a, corresponder a <the task fell to him : le tocó hacerlo>

fall[2] *n* **1** TUMBLE : caída *f* <to break one's fall : frenar uno su caída> <a fall of three feet : una caída de tres pies> **2** FALLING : derrumbe *m* (de rocas), aguacero *m* (de lluvia), nevada *f* (de nieve), bajada *f* (de precios), disminución *f* (de cantidades) **3** AUTUMN : otoño *m* **4** DOWNFALL : caída *f,* ruina *f* **5 falls** *npl* WATERFALL : cascada *f,* catarata *f*

fallacious [fə'leɪʃəs] *adj* : erróneo, engañoso, falaz

fallacy ['fæləsi] *n, pl* **-cies** : falacia *f*

fall back *vi* **1** RETREAT : retirarse, replegarse **2 to fall back on** : recurrir a

fall guy *n* SCAPEGOAT : chivo *m* expiatorio

fallible ['fæləbəl] *adj* : falible

fallout ['fɔl,aʊt] *n* **1** : lluvia *f* radioactiva **2** CONSEQUENCES : secuelas *fpl,* consecuencias *fpl*

fallow[1] ['fælo] *vt* : barbechar

fallow[2] *adj* **to lie fallow** : estar en barbecho

fallow[3] *n* : barbecho *m*

false ['fɔls] *adj* **falser; falsest 1** UNTRUE : falso **2** ERRONEOUS : erróneo, equivocado **3** FAKE : falso, postizo **4** UNFAITHFUL : infiel **5** FRAUDULENT : fraudulento <under false pretenses : por fraude>

falsehood ['fɔls,hʊd] *n* : mentira *f,* falsedad *f*

falsely ['fɔlsli] *adv* : falsamente, con falsedad

falseness ['fɔlsnəs] *n* : falsedad *f*

falsetto [fɔl'sɛt̬oː] *n, pl* **-tos** : falsete *m*

falsification [,fɔlsəfə'keɪʃən] *n* : falsificación *f,* falseamiento *m*

falsify ['fɔlsə,faɪ] *vt* **-fied; fying** : falsificar, falsear

falsity ['fɔlsət̬i] *n, pl* **-ties** : falsedad *f*

falter ['fɔltər] *vi* **-tered; -tering 1** TOTTER : tambalearse **2** STAMMER : titubear, tartamudear **3** WAVER : vacilar

faltering ['fɔltərɪŋ] *adj* : titubeante, vacilante

fame ['feɪm] *n* : fama *f*

famed ['feɪmd] *adj* : famoso, célebre, afamado

familial [fə'mɪljəl, -liəl] *adj* : familiar

familiar[1] [fə'mɪljər] *adj* **1** KNOWN : familiar, conocido <to be familiar with : estar familiarizado con> **2** INFORMAL : familiar, informal **3** INTIMATE : íntimo, de confianza **4** FORWARD : confianzudo, atrevido — **familiarly** *adv*

familiar[2] *n* : espíritu *m* guardián

familiarity [fə,mɪli'ærət̬i, -,mɪl'jær-] *n, pl* **-ties 1** KNOWLEDGE : conocimiento *m,* familiaridad *f* **2** INFORMALITY, INTIMACY : confianza *f,* familiaridad *f* **3** FORWARDNESS : exceso *m* de confianza, descaro *m*

familiarize [fə'mɪljə,raɪz] *vt* **-ized; -izing 1** : familiarizar **2 to familiarize oneself** : familiarizarse

family ['fæmli, 'fæmə-] *n, pl* **-lies** : familia *f*

family tree *n* : árbol *m* genealógico

famine ['fæmən] *n* : hambre *f,* hambruna *f*

famish ['fæmɪʃ] *vi* **to be famished** : estar famélico, estar hambriento, morir de hambre *fam*

famous ['feɪməs] *adj* : famoso

famously ['feɪməsli] *adv* **to get on famously** : llevarse de maravilla

fan[1] ['fæn] *vt* **fanned; fanning 1** : abanicar (a una persona), avivar (un fuego) **2** STIMULATE : avivar, estimular

fan[2] *n* **1** : ventilador *m,* abanico *m* **2** ADMIRER, ENTHUSIAST : aficionado *m,* -da *f;* entusiasta *mf;* admirador *m,* -dora *f*

fanatic[1] [fə'næt̬ɪk] *or* **fanatical** [-t̬ɪkəl] *adj* : fanático

fanatic[2] *n* : fanático *m,* -ca *f*

fanaticism [fə'næt̬ə,sɪzəm] *n* : fanatismo *m*

fanciful ['fæntsɪfəl] *adj* **1** CAPRICIOUS : caprichoso, fantástico, extravagante **2** IMAGINATIVE : imaginativo — **fancifully** *adv*

fancy[1] ['fæntsi] *vt* **-cied; -cying 1** IMAGINE : imaginarse, figurarse <fancy that! : ¡figúrate!, ¡imagínate!> **2** CRAVE : apetecer, tener ganas de

fancy[2] *adj* **-cier; -est 1** ELABORATE : elaborado **2** LUXURIOUS : lujoso, elegante — **fancily** ['fæntsəli] *adv*

fancy[3] *n, pl* **-cies 1** LIKING : gusto *m,* afición *f* **2** WHIM : antojo *m,* capricho *m* **3** IMAGINATION : fantasía *f,* imaginación *f*
fandango [fæn'dæŋgo] *n, pl* **-gos** : fandango *m*
fanfare ['fæn,fær] *n* : fanfarria *f*
fang ['fæŋ] *n* : colmillo *m* (de un animal), diente *m* (de una serpiente)
fanlight ['fæn,laɪt] *n* : tragaluz *m*
fantasia [fæn'teɪʒə, -ziə; ,fæntə'zi:ə] *n* : fantasía *f*
fantasize ['fæntə,saɪz] *vi* **-sized; -sizing** : fantasear
fantastic [fæn'tæstɪk] *adj* **1** UNBELIEVABLE : fantástico, increíble, extraño **2** ENORMOUS : fabuloso, inmenso <fantastic sums : sumas fabulosas> **3** WONDERFUL : estupendo, fantástico, bárbaro *fam,* macanudo *fam* — **fantastically** [-tɪkli] *adv*
fantasy ['fæntəsi] *n, pl* **-sies** : fantasía *f*
far[1] ['fɑr] *adv* **farther** ['fɑrðər] *or* **further** ['fər-]; **farthest** *or* **furthest** [-ðəst] **1** : lejos <far from here : lejos de aquí> <to go far : llegar lejos> <as far as Chicago : hasta Chicago> <far away : a lo lejos> **2** MUCH : muy, mucho <far bigger : mucho más grande> <far superior : muy superior> <it's by far the best : es con mucho el mejor> **3** (*expressing degree or extent*) <the results are far off : salieron muy inexactos los resultados> <to go so far as : decir tanto como> <to go far enough : tener el alcance necesario> **4** (*expressing progress*) <the work is far advanced : el trabajo está muy avanzado> <to take (something) too far : llevar (algo) demasiado lejos> **5 far and wide** : por todas partes **6 far from it!** : ¡todo lo contrario! **7 so far** : hasta ahora, todavía
far[2] *adj* **farther** *or* **further; farthest** *or* **furthest 1** REMOTE : lejano, remoto <the Far East : el Lejano Oriente, el Extremo Oriente> <a far country : un país lejano> **2** LONG : largo <a far journey : un viaje largo> **3** EXTREME : extremo <the far right : la extrema derecha> <at the far end of the room : en el otro extremo de la sala>
faraway ['fɑrə,weɪ] *adj* : remoto, lejano
farce ['fɑrs] *n* : farsa *f*
farcical ['fɑrsɪkəl] *adj* : absurdo, ridículo
fare[1] ['fær] *vi* **fared; faring** : ir, salir <how did you fare? : ¿cómo te fue?>
fare[2] *n* **1** : pasaje *m,* billete *m,* boleto *m* <half fare : medio pasaje> **2** FOOD : comida *f*
farewell[1] [fær'wɛl] *adj* : de despedida
farewell[2] *n* : despedida *f*
far–fetched ['fɑr'fɛtʃt] *adj* : improbable, exagerado
farina [fə'ri:nə] *n* : harina *f*
farm[1] ['fɑrm] *vt* **1** : cultivar, labrar **2** : criar (animales) — *vi* : ser agricultor
farm[2] *n* : granja *f,* hacienda *f,* finca *f,* estancia *f*
farmer ['fɑrmər] *n* : agricultor *m,* granjero *m*
farmhand ['fɑrm,hænd] *n* : peón *m*
farmhouse ['fɑrm,haʊs] *n* : granja *f,* vivienda *f* del granjero, casa *f* de hacienda
farming ['fɑrmɪŋ] *n* : labranza *f,* cultivo *m,* crianza *f* (de animales)
farmland ['fɑrm,lænd] *n* : tierras *fpl* de labranza
farmyard ['fɑrm,jɑrd] *n* : corral *m*
far–off ['fɑr,ɔf, -'ɔf] *adj* : remoto, distante, lejano
far–reaching ['fɑr'ri:tʃɪŋ] *adj* : de gran alcance
farsighted ['fɑr,saɪtəd] *adj* **1** : hipermétrope **2** JUDICIOUS : con visión de futuro, previsor, precavido
farsightedness ['fɑr,saɪtədnəs] *n* **1** : hipermetropía *f* **2** PRUDENCE : previsión *f*
farther[1] ['fɑrðər] *adv* **1** AHEAD : más lejos (en el espacio), más adelante (en el tiempo) **2** MORE : más
farther[2] *adj* : más lejano, más remoto
farthermost ['fɑrðər,mo:st] *adj* : (el) más lejano
farthest[1] ['fɑrðəst] *adv* **1** : lo más lejos <I jumped farthest : salté lo más lejos> **2** : lo más avanzado <he progressed farthest : progresó al punto más avanzado> **3** : más <the farthest developed plan : el plan más desarrollado>
farthest[2] *adj* : más lejano
fascicle ['fæsɪkəl] *n* : fascículo *m*
fascinate ['fæsən,eɪt] *vt* **-nated; -nating** : fascinar, cautivar
fascination [,fæsən'eɪʃən] *n* : fascinación *f*
fascism ['fæʃ,ɪzəm] *n* : fascismo *m*
fascist[1] ['fæʃɪst] *adj* : fascista
fascist[2] *n* : fascista *mf*
fashion[1] ['fæʃən] *vt* : formar, moldear
fashion[2] *n* **1** MANNER : manera *f,* modo *m* **2** CUSTOM : costumbre *f* **3** STYLE : moda *f*
fashionable ['fæʃənəbəl] *adj* : de moda, chic
fashionably ['fæʃənəbli] *adv* : a la moda
fast[1] ['fæst] *vi* : ayunar
fast[2] *adv* **1** SECURELY : firmemente, seguramente <to hold fast : agarrarse bien> **2** RAPIDLY : rápidamente, rápido, de prisa **3** SOUNDLY : profundamente <fast asleep : profundamente dormido>
fast[3] *adj* **1** SECURE : firme, seguro <to make fast : amarrar (un barco)> **2** FAITHFUL : leal <fast friends : amigos leales> **3** RAPID : rápido, veloz **4** : adelantado <10 minutes fast : 10 minutos adelantado> **5** DEEP : profundo <a fast sleep : un sueño pro-

fundo> 6 COLORFAST : inalterable, que no destiñe 7 DISSOLUTE : extravagante, disipado, disoluto
fast[4] *n* : ayuno *m*
fasten ['fæsən] *vt* 1 ATTACH : sujetar, atar 2 FIX : fijar <to fasten one's eyes on : fijar los ojos en> 3 SECURE : abrochar (ropa o cinturones), atar (cordones), cerrar (una maleta) — *vi* : abrocharse, cerrar
fastener ['fæsənər] *n* : cierre *m*, sujetador *m*
fastening ['fæsənɪŋ] *n* : cierre *m*, sujetador *m*
fastidious [fæs'tɪdiəs] *adj* : quisquilloso, exigente — **fastidiously** *adv*
fat[1] ['fæt] *adj* **fatter; fattest** 1 OBESE : gordo, obeso 2 THICK : grueso
fat[2] *n* : grasa *f*
fatal ['feɪtəl] *adj* 1 DEADLY : mortal 2 ILL-FATED : malhadado, fatal 3 MOMENTOUS : fatídico
fatalism ['feɪtəl,ɪzəm] *n* : fatalismo *m*
fatalist ['feɪtəlɪst] *n* : fatalista *mf*
fatalistic [,feɪtəl'ɪstɪk] *adj* : fatalista
fatality [feɪ'tæləti, fə-] *n, pl* **-ties** : víctima *f* mortal
fatally ['feɪtəli] *adv* : mortalmente
fate ['feɪt] *n* 1 DESTINY : destino *m* 2 END, LOT : final *m*, suerte *f*
fated ['feɪtəd] *adj* : predestinado
fateful ['feɪtfəl] *adj* 1 MOMENTOUS : fatídico, aciago 2 PROPHETIC : profético — **fatefully** *adv*
father[1] ['fɑðər] *vt* : engendrar
father[2] *n* 1 : padre *m* <my father and my mother : mi padre y mi madre> <Father Smith : el padre Smith> 2 **the Father** GOD : el Padre, Dios *m*
fatherhood ['fɑðər,hʊd] *n* : paternidad *f*
father-in-law ['fɑðərɪn,lɔ] *n, pl* **fathers-in-law** : suegro *m*
fatherland ['fɑðər,lænd] *n* : patria *f*
fatherless ['fɑðərləs] *adj* : huérfano de padre, sin padre
fatherly ['fɑðərli] *adj* : paternal
fathom[1] ['fæðəm] *vt* UNDERSTAND : entender, comprender
fathom[2] *n* : braza *f*
fatigue[1] [fə'ti:g] *vt* **-tigued; -tiguing** : fatigar, cansar
fatigue[2] *n* : fatiga *f*
fatness ['fætnəs] *n* : gordura *f* (de una persona o un animal), grosor *m* (de un objeto)
fatten ['fætən] *vt* : engordar, cebar
fatty ['fæti] *adj* **fattier; -est** : graso, grasoso, adiposo (dícese de los tejidos)
fatuous ['fætʃʊəs] *adj* : necio, fatuo — **fatuously** *adv*
faucet ['fɔsət] *n* : llave *f*, canilla *f Arg,Uru*, grifo *m*
fault[1] ['fɔlt] *vt* : encontrar defectos a
fault[2] *n* 1 SHORTCOMING : defecto *m*, falta *f* 2 DEFECT : falta *f*, defecto *m*, falla *f* 3 BLAME : culpa *f* 4 FRACTURE : falla *f* (geológica)
faultfinder ['fɔlt,faɪndər] *n* : criticón *m*, -cona *f*
faultfinding ['fɔlt,faɪndɪŋ] *n* : crítica *f*
faultless ['fɔltləs] *adj* : sin culpa, sin imperfecciones, impecable
faultlessly ['fɔltləsli] *adv* : impecablemente, perfectamente
faulty ['fɔlti] *adj* **faultier; -est** : defectuoso, imperfecto — **faultily** ['fɔltəli] *adv*
fauna ['fɔnə] *n* : fauna *f*
faux pas [,fo:'pɑ] *n, pl* **faux pas** [*same or* -'pɑz] : metedura *f* de pata *fam*
favor[1] ['feɪvər] *vt* 1 SUPPORT : estar a favor de, ser partidario de, apoyar 2 OBLIGE : hacerle un favor a 3 PREFER : preferir 4 RESEMBLE : parecerse a, salir a
favor[2] *n* : favor *m* <in favor of : a favor de> <an error in his favor : un error a su favor>
favorable ['feɪvərəbəl] *adj* : favorable, propicio
favorably ['feɪvərəbli] *adv* : favorablemente, bien
favorite[1] ['feɪvərət] *adj* : favorito, preferido
favorite[2] *n* : favorito *m*, -ta *f*; preferido *m*, -da *f*
favoritism ['feɪvərə,tɪzəm] *n* : favoritismo *m*
fawn[1] ['fɔn] *vi* : adular, lisonjear
fawn[2] *n* : cervato *m*
fax ['fæks] *n* : facsímil *m*, facsímile *m*
faze ['feɪz] *vt* **fazed; fazing** : desconcertar, perturbar
fear[1] ['fɪr] *vt* : temer, tener miedo de — *vi* : temer
fear[2] *n* : miedo *m*, temor *m* <for fear of : por temor a>
fearful ['fɪrfəl] *adj* 1 FRIGHTENING : espantoso, aterrador, horrible 2 FRIGHTENED : temeroso, miedoso
fearfully ['fɪrfəli] *adv* 1 EXTREMELY : extremadamente, terriblemente 2 TIMIDLY : con temor
fearless ['fɪrləs] *adj* : intrépido, impávido
fearlessly ['fɪrləsli] *adv* : sin temor
fearlessness ['fɪrləsnəs] *n* : intrepidez *f*, impavidez *f*
fearsome ['fɪrsəm] *adj* : aterrador
feasibility [,fi:zə'bɪləti] *n* : viabilidad *f*, factibilidad *f*
feasible ['fi:zəbəl] *adj* : viable, factible, realizable
feast[1] ['fi:st] *vi* : banquetear — *vt* 1 : agasajar, festejar 2 **to feast one's eyes on** : regalarse la vista con
feast[2] *n* 1 BANQUET : banquete *m*, festín *m* 2 FESTIVAL : fiesta *f*
feat ['fi:t] *n* : proeza *f*, hazaña *f*
feather[1] ['fɛðər] *vt* 1 : emplumar 2 **to feather one's nest** : hacer su agosto
feather[2] *n* 1 : pluma *f* 2 **a feather in one's cap** : un triunfo personal
feathered ['fɛðərd] *adj* : con plumas
feathery ['fɛðəri] *adj* 1 DOWNY : plumoso 2 LIGHT : liviano

feature[1] [ˈfiːtʃər] *v* **-tured; -turing** *vt* **1** IMAGINE : imaginarse **2** PRESENT : presentar — *vi* : figurar
feature[2] *n* **1** CHARACTERISTIC : característica *f,* rasgo *m* **2** : largometraje *m* (en el cine), artículo *m* (en un periódico), documental *m* (en la televisión) **3 features** *npl* : rasgos *mpl,* facciones *fpl* <delicate features : facciones delicadas>
February [ˈfɛbjʊˌɛri, ˈfɛbʊ-, ˈfɛbrʊ-] *n* : febrero *m*
fecal [ˈfiːkəl] *adj* : fecal
feces [ˈfiːˌsiːz] *npl* : heces *fpl,* excrementos *mpl*
feckless [ˈfɛkləs] *adj* : irresponsable
fecund [ˈfɛkənd, ˈfiː-] *adj* : fecundo
fecundity [fɪˈkʌndət̬i, fɛ-] *n* : fecundidad *f*
federal [ˈfɛdrəl, -dərəl] *adj* : federal
federalism [ˈfɛdrəˌlɪzəm, -dərə-] *n* : federalismo *m*
federalist[1] [ˈfɛdrəlɪst, -dərə-] *adj* : federalista
federalist[2] *n* : federalista *mf*
federate [ˈfɛdəˌreɪt] *vt* **-ated; -ating** : federar
federation [ˌfɛdəˈreɪʃən] *n* : federación *f*
fedora [fɪˈdorə] *n* : sombrero *m* flexible de fieltro
fed up *adj* : harto
fee [ˈfiː] *n* **1** : honorarios *mpl* (a un médico, un abogado, etc.) **2 entrance fee** : entrada *f*
feeble [ˈfiːbəl] *adj* **-bler; -blest 1** WEAK : débil, endeble **2** INEFFECTIVE : flojo, pobre, poco convincente
feebleminded [ˌfiːbəlˈmaɪndəd] *adj* **1** : débil mental **2** FOOLISH, STUPID : imbécil, tonto
feebleness [ˈfiːbəlnəs] *n* : debilidad *f*
feebly [ˈfiːbli] *adv* : débilmente
feed[1] [ˈfiːd] *v* **fed** [ˈfɛd]; **feeding** *vt* **1** : dar de comer a, nutrir, alimentar (a una persona) **2** : alimentar (un fuego o una máquina), proveer (información), introducir (datos) — *vi* : comer, alimentarse
feed[2] *n* **1** NOURISHMENT : alimento *m* **2** FODDER : pienso *m*
feel[1] [ˈfiːl] *v* **felt** [ˈfɛlt]; **feeling** *vi* **1** : sentirse, encontrarse <I feel tired : me siento cansada> <he feels hungry : tiene hambre> <she feels like a fool : se siente como una idiota> <to feel like doing something : tener ganas de hacer algo> **2** SEEM : parecer <it feels like spring : parece primavera> **3** THINK : parecerse, opinar, pensar <how does he feel about that? : ¿qué opina él de eso?> — *vt* **1** TOUCH : tocar, palpar **2** SENSE : sentir <to feel the cold : sentir el frío> **3** CONSIDER : sentir, creer, considerar <to feel (it) necessary : creer necesario>
feel[2] *n* **1** SENSATION, TOUCH : sensación *f,* tacto *m* **2** ATMOSPHERE : ambiente *m,* atmósfera *f* **3 to have a feel for** : tener un talento especial para
feeler [ˈfiːlər] *n* : antena *f,* tentáculo *m*
feeling [ˈfiːlɪŋ] *n* **1** SENSATION : sensación *f,* sensibilidad *f* **2** EMOTION : sentimiento *m* **3** OPINION : opinión *f* **4 feelings** *npl* SENSIBILITIES : sentimientos *mpl* <to hurt someone's feelings : herir los sentimientos de alguien>
feet → **foot**
feign [ˈfeɪn] *vt* : simular, aparentar, fingir
feint[1] [ˈfeɪnt] *vi* : fintar, fintear
feint[2] *n* : finta *f*
felicitate [fɪˈlɪsəˌteɪt] *vt* **-tated; -tating** : felicitar, congratular
felicitation [fɪˌlɪsəˈteɪʃən] *n* : felicitación *f*
felicitous [fɪˈlɪsət̬əs] *adj* : acertado, oportuno
feline[1] [ˈfiːˌlaɪn] *adj* : felino
feline[2] *n* : felino *m,* -na *f*
fell[1] [ˈfɛl] *vt* : talar (un árbol), derribar (a una persona)
fell[2] → **fall**
fellow [ˈfɛˌloː] *n* **1** COMPANION : compañero *m,* -ra *f;* camarada *mf* **2** ASSOCIATE : socio *m,* -cia *f* **3** MAN : tipo *m,* hombre *m*
fellowman [ˌfɛloˈmæn] *n, pl* **-men** : prójimo *m,* semejante *m*
fellowship [ˈfɛloˌʃɪp] *n* **1** COMPANIONSHIP : camaradería *f,* compañerismo *m* **2** ASSOCIATION : fraternidad *f* **3** GRANT : beca *f* (de investigación)
felon [ˈfɛlən] *n* : malhechor *m,* -chora *f;* criminal *mf*
felonious [fəˈloːniəs] *adj* : criminal
felony [ˈfɛləni] *n, pl* **-nies** : delito *m* grave
felt[1] [ˈfɛlt] *n* : fieltro *m*
felt[2] → **feel**
female[1] [ˈfiːˌmeɪl] *adj* : femenino
female[2] *n* **1** : hembra *f* (de animal) **2** WOMAN : mujer *f*
feminine [ˈfɛmənən] *adj* : femenino
femininity [ˌfɛməˈnɪnət̬i] *n* : feminidad *f,* femineidad *f*
feminism [ˈfɛməˌnɪzəm] *n* : feminismo *m*
feminist[1] [ˈfɛmənɪst] *adj* : feminista
feminist[2] *n* : feminista *mf*
femoral [ˈfɛmərəl] *adj* : femoral
femur [ˈfiːmər] *n, pl* **femurs** *or* **femora** [ˈfɛmərə] : fémur *m*
fence[1] [ˈfɛn*t*s] *v* **fenced; fencing** *vt* : vallar, cercar — *vi* : hacer esgrima
fence[2] *n* : cerca *f,* valla *f,* cerco *m*
fencer [ˈfɛn*t*sər] *n* : esgrimista *mf;* esgrimidor *m,* -dora *f*
fencing [ˈfɛn*t*sɪŋ] *n* **1** : esgrima *m* (deporte) **2** : materiales *mpl* para cercas **3** ENCLOSURE : cercado *m*
fend [ˈfɛnd] *vt* **to fend off** : rechazar (un enemigo), parar (un golpe), eludir (una pregunta) — *vi* **to fend for oneself** : arreglárselas sólo, valerse por sí mismo

fender [ˈfɛndər] *n* : guardabarros *mpl,* salpicadera *f Mex*
fennel [ˈfɛnəl] *n* : hinojo *m*
ferment[1] [fərˈmɛnt] *v* : fermentar
ferment[2] [ˈfərˌmɛnt] *n* **1** : fermento *m* (en la química) **2** TURMOIL : agitación *f,* conmoción *f*
fermentation [ˌfərmənˈteɪʃən, -ˌmɛn-] *n* : fermentación *f*
fern [ˈfərn] *n* : helecho *m*
ferocious [fəˈroːʃəs] *adj* : feroz — **ferociously** *adv*
ferociousness [fəˈroːʃəsnəs] *n* : ferocidad *f*
ferocity [fəˈrɑsət̬i] *n* : ferocidad *f*
ferret[1] [ˈfɛrət] *vi* SNOOP : hurgar, husmear — *vt* **to ferret out** : descubrir
ferret[2] *n* : hurón *m*
ferric [ˈfɛrɪk] *or* **ferrous** [ˈfɛrəs] *adj* : férrico
Ferris wheel [ˈfɛrɪs] *n* : noria *f*
ferry[1] [ˈfɛri] *vt* **-ried; -rying** : llevar, transportar
ferry[2] *n, pl* **-ries** : transbordador *m,* ferry *m*
ferryboat [ˈfɛriˌboːt] *n* : transbordador *m,* ferry *m*
fertile [ˈfərt̬əl] *adj* : fértil, fecundo
fertility [fərˈtɪlət̬i] *n* : fertilidad *f*
fertilization [ˌfərt̬ələˈzeɪʃən] *n* : fertilización *f* (del suelo), fecundación (de un huevo)
fertilize [ˈfərt̬əlˌaɪz] *vt* **-ized; -izing 1** : fecundar (un huevo) **2** : fertilizar, abonar (el suelo)
fertilizer [ˈfərt̬əlˌaɪzər] *n* : fertilizante *m,* abono *m*
fervent [ˈfərvənt] *adj* : ferviente, fervoroso, ardiente — **fervently** *adv*
fervid [ˈfərvɪd] *adj* : ardiente, apasionado — **fervidly** *adv*
fervor [ˈfərvər] *n* : fervor *m,* ardor *m*
fester [ˈfɛstər] *vi* : enconarse, supurar
festival [ˈfɛstəvəl] *n* : fiesta *f,* festividad *f,* festival *m*
festive [ˈfɛstɪv] *adj* : festivo — **festively** *adv*
festivity [fɛsˈtɪvət̬i] *n, pl* **-ties** : festividad *f,* celebración *f*
festoon[1] [fɛsˈtuːn] *vt* : adornar, engalanar
festoon[2] *n* GARLAND : guirnalda *f*
fetal [ˈfiːt̬əl] *adj* : fetal
fetch [ˈfɛtʃ] *vt* **1** BRING : traer, recoger, ir a buscar **2** REALIZE : realizar, venderse por <the jewelry fetched $10,000 : las joyas se vendieron por $10,000>
fetching [ˈfɛtʃɪŋ] *adj* : atractivo, encantador
fête[1] [ˈfeɪt, ˈfɛt] *vt* **fêted; fêting** : festejar, agasajar
fête[2] *n* : fiesta *f*
fetid [ˈfɛt̬əd] *adj* : fétido
fetish [ˈfɛt̬ɪʃ] *n* : fetiche *m*
fetlock [ˈfɛtˌlɑk] *n* : espolón *m*
fetter [ˈfɛt̬ər] *vt* : encadenar, poner grillos a
fetters [ˈfɛt̬ərz] *npl* : grillos *mpl,* grilletes *mpl,* cadenas *fpl*
fettle [ˈfɛt̬əl] *n* **in fine fettle** : en buena forma, en plena forma
fetus [ˈfiːt̬əs] *n* : feto *m*
feud[1] [ˈfjuːd] *vi* : pelear, contender
feud[2] *n* : contienda *f,* enemistad *f* (heredada)
feudal [ˈfjuːdəl] *adj* : feudal
feudalism [ˈfjuːdəlˌɪzəm] *n* : feudalismo *m*
fever [ˈfiːvər] *n* : fiebre *f,* calentura *f*
feverish [ˈfiːvərɪʃ] *adj* **1** : afiebrado, con fiebre, febril **2** FRANTIC : febril, frenético
few[1] [ˈfjuː] *adj* : pocos <with few exceptions : con pocas excepciones> <a few times : varias veces>
few[2] *pron* **1** : pocos <few (of them) were ready : pocos estaban listos> **2 a few** : algunos, unos cuantos **3 few and far between** : contados
fewer [ˈfjuːər] *pron* : menos <the fewer the better : cuantos menos mejor>
fez [ˈfɛz] *n, pl* **fezzes** : fez *m*
fiancé [ˌfiːˌɑnˈseɪ, ˌfiːˈɑnˌseɪ] *n* : prometido *m,* novio *m*
fiancée [ˌfiːˌɑnˈseɪ, ˌfiːˈɑnˌseɪ] *n* : prometida *f,* novia *f*
fiasco [fiˈæsˌkoː] *n, pl* **-coes** : fiasco *m,* fracaso *m*
fiat [ˈfiːˌɑt, -ˌæt, -ət; ˈfaɪət, -ˌæt] *n* : decreto *m,* orden *m*
fib[1] [ˈfɪb] *vi* **fibbed; fibbing** : decir mentirillas
fib[2] *n* : mentirilla *f,* bola *f fam*
fibber [ˈfɪbər] *n* : mentirosillo *m,* -lla *f;* cuentista *mf fam*
fiber *or* **fibre** [ˈfaɪbər] *n* : fibra *f*
fiberboard [ˈfaɪbərˌbord] *n* : cartón *m* madera
fiberglass [ˈfaɪbərˌglæs] *n* : fibra *f* de vidrio
fibrillate [ˈfɪbrəˌleɪt, ˈfaɪ-] *vi* **-lated; -lating** : fibrilar
fibrillation [ˌfɪbrəˈleɪʃən, ˌfaɪ-] *n* : fibrilación *f*
fibrous [ˈfaɪbrəs] *adj* : fibroso
fibula [ˈfɪbjələ] *n, pl* **-lae** [-ˌliː, -ˌlaɪ] *or* **-las** : peroné *m*
fickle [ˈfɪkəl] *adj* : inconstante, voluble, veleidoso
fickleness [ˈfɪkəlnəs] *n* : volubilidad *f,* inconstancia *f,* veleidad *f*
fiction [ˈfɪkʃən] *n* : ficción *f*
fictional [ˈfɪkʃənəl] *adj* : ficticio
fictitious [fɪkˈtɪʃəs] *adj* **1** IMAGINARY : ficticio, imaginario **2** FALSE : falso, ficticio
fiddle[1] [ˈfɪdəl] *vi* **-dled; -dling 1** : tocar el violín **2 to fiddle with** : juguetear con, toquetear
fiddle[2] *n* : violín *m*
fiddler [ˈfɪdlər, ˈfɪdələr] *n* : violinista *mf*
fiddlesticks [ˈfɪdəlˌstɪks] *interj* : ¡tonterías!
fidelity [fəˈdɛlət̬i, faɪ-] *n, pl* **-ties** : fidelidad *f*

fidget[1] [ˈfɪdʒət] *vi* **1 :** moverse, estarse inquieto **2 to fidget with :** juguetear con
fidget[2] *n* **1 :** persona *f* inquieta **2 fidgets** *npl* RESTLESSNESS **:** inquietud *f*
fidgety [ˈfɪdʒəti] *adj* **:** inquieto
fiduciary[1] [fəˈduːʃi,ɛri, -ˈdjuː-, -ʃəri] *adj* **:** fiduciario
fiduciary[2] *n, pl* **-ries :** fiduciario *m,* -ria *f*
field[1] [ˈfiːld] *vt* **:** interceptar y devolver (una pelota), presentar (un candidato), sortear (una pregunta)
field[2] *adj* **:** de campaña, de campo <field hospital : hospital de campaña> <field goal : gol de campo> <field trip : viaje de estudio>
field[3] *n* **1 :** campo *m* (de cosechas, de batalla, de magnetismo) **2 :** campo *m,* cancha *f* (en deportes) **3 :** campo *m* (de trabajo), esfera *f* (de actividades)
fielder [ˈfiːldər] *n* **:** jugador *m,* -dora *f* de campo; fildeador *m,* -dora *f*
field glasses *n* **:** binoculares *mpl,* gemelos *mpl*
fiend [ˈfiːnd] *n* **1** DEMON **:** demonio *m* **2** EVILDOER **:** persona *f* maligna; malvado *m,* -da *f* **3** FANATIC **:** fanático *m,* -ca *f*
fiendish [ˈfiːndɪʃ] *adj* **:** diabólico — **fiendishly** *adv*
fierce [ˈfɪrs] *adj* **fiercer; -est 1** FEROCIOUS **:** fiero, feroz **2** HEATED **:** acalorado **3** INTENSE **:** intenso, violento, fuerte — **fiercely** *adv*
fierceness [ˈfɪrsnəs] *n* **1** FEROCITY **:** ferocidad *f,* fiereza *f* **2** INTENSITY **:** intensidad *f,* violencia *f*
fieriness [ˈfaɪərinəs] *n* **:** pasión *f,* ardor *m*
fiery [ˈfaɪəri] *adj* **fierier; -est 1** BURNING **:** ardiente, llameante **2** GLOWING **:** encendido **3** PASSIONATE **:** acalorado, ardiente, fogoso
fiesta [fiˈɛstə] *n* **:** fiesta *f*
fife [ˈfaɪf] *n* **:** pífano *m*
fifteen[1] [fɪfˈtiːn] *adj* **:** quince
fifteen[2] *n* **:** quince *m*
fifteenth[1] [fɪfˈtiːnθ] *adj* **:** decimoquinto
fifteenth[2] *n* **1 :** decimoquinto *m,* -ta *f* (en una serie) **2 :** quinceavo *m,* quinceava parte *f*
fifth[1] [ˈfɪfθ] *adj* **:** quinto
fifth[2] *n* **1 :** quinto *m,* -ta *f* (en una serie) **2 :** quinto *m,* quinta parte *f* **3 :** quinta *f* (en la música)
fiftieth[1] [ˈfɪftiəθ] *adj* **:** quincuagésimo
fiftieth[2] *n* **1 :** quincuagésimo *m,* -ma *f* (en una serie) **2 :** cincuentavo *m,* cincuentava parte *f*
fifty[1] [ˈfɪfti] *adj* **:** cincuenta
fifty[2] *n, pl* **-ties :** cincuenta *m*
fifty–fifty[1] [,fɪftiˈfɪfti] *adv* **:** a medias, mitad y mitad
fifty–fifty[2] *adj* **to have a fifty–fifty chance :** tener un cincuenta por ciento de posibilidades
fig [ˈfɪg] *n* **:** higo *m*
fight[1] [ˈfaɪt] *v* **fought** [ˈfɔt]; **fighting** *vi* **:** luchar, combatir, pelear — *vt* **:** luchar contra, combatir contra
fight[2] *n* **1** COMBAT **:** lucha *f,* pelea *f,* combate *m* **2** MATCH **:** pelea *f,* combate *m* (en boxeo) **3** QUARREL **:** disputa *f,* pelea *f,* pleito *m*
fighter [ˈfaɪṭər] *n* **1** COMBATANT **:** luchador *m,* -dora *f;* combatiente *mf* **2** BOXER **:** boxeador *m,* -dora *f*
figment [ˈfɪgmənt] *n* **figment of the imagination :** producto *m* de la imaginación
figurative [ˈfɪgjərəṭɪv, -gə-] *adj* **:** figurado, metafórico
figuratively [ˈfɪgjərəṭɪvli, -gə-] *adv* **:** en sentido figurado, de manera metafórica
figure[1] [ˈfɪgjər, -gər] *v* **-ured; -uring** *vt* **1** CALCULATE **:** calcular **2** ESTIMATE **:** figurarse, calcular <he figured it was possible : se figuró que era posible> — *vi* **1** FEATURE, STAND OUT **:** figurar, destacar **2 that figures! :** ¡obvio!, ¡no me extraña nada!
figure[2] *n* **1** DIGIT **:** número *m,* cifra *f* **2** PRICE **:** precio *m,* cifra *f* **3** PERSONAGE **:** figura *f,* personaje *m* **4 :** figura *f,* tipo *m,* físico *m* <to have a good figure : tener buen tipo, tener un buen físico> **5** DESIGN, OUTLINE **:** figura *f* **6 figures** *npl* **:** aritmética *f*
figurehead [ˈfɪgjər,hɛd, -gər-] *n* **:** testaferro *m,* líder *mf* sin poder
figure of speech *n* **:** figura *f* retórica, figura *f* de hablar
figure out *vt* **1** UNDERSTAND **:** entender **2** RESOLVE **:** resolver (un problema, etc.)
figurine [,fɪgjəˈriːn] *n* **:** estatuilla *f*
Fijian [ˈfiːdʒiən, fɪˈjiːən] *n* **:** fijiano *m,* -na *f* — **Fijian** *adj*
filament [ˈfɪləmənt] *n* **:** filamento *m*
filbert [ˈfɪlbərt] *n* **:** avellana *f*
filch [ˈfɪltʃ] *vt* **:** hurtar, birlar *fam*
file[1] [ˈfaɪl] *v* **filed; filing** *vt* **1** CLASSIFY **:** clasificar **2 :** archivar (documentos) **3** SUBMIT **:** presentar <to file charges : presentar cargos> **4** SMOOTH **:** limar — *vi* **:** desfilar, entrar (o salir) en fila
file[2] *n* **1 :** lima *f* <nail file : lima de uñas> **2** DOCUMENTS **:** archivo *m* **3** LINE **:** fila *f*
filial [ˈfɪliəl, ˈfɪljəl] *adj* **:** filial
filibuster[1] [ˈfɪlə,bʌstər] *vi* **:** practicar el obstruccionismo
filibuster[2] *n* **:** obstruccionismo *m*
filibusterer [ˈfɪlə,bʌstərər] *n* **:** obstruccionista *mf*
filigree [ˈfɪlə,griː] *n* **:** filigrana *f*
Filipino [,fɪləˈpiːnoː] *n* **:** filipino *m,* -na *f* — **Filipino** *adj*
fill[1] [ˈfɪl] *vt* **1 :** llenar, ocupar <to fill a cup : llenar una taza> <to fill a room : ocupar una sala> **2** STUFF **:** rellenar **3** PLUG **:** tapar, rellenar, empastar (un diente) **4** SATISFY **:** cumplir con, satisfacer **5** *or* **to fill out :** llenar, re-

llenar <to fill out a form : rellenar un formulario>
fill² *n* **1** FILLING, STUFFING : relleno *m* **2 to eat one's fill :** comer lo suficiente **3 to have one's fill of :** estar harto de
filler ['fɪlər] *n* : relleno *m*
fillet¹ ['fɪlət, fɪ'leɪ, 'fɪ,leɪ] *vt* : cortar en filetes
fillet² *n* : filete *m*
fill in *vt* INFORM : informar, poner al corriente — *vi* **to fill in for** : reemplazar a
filling ['fɪlɪŋ] *n* **1** : relleno *m* **2** : empaste *m* (de un diente)
filling station → **service station**
filly ['fɪli] *n, pl* **-lies** : potra *f*, potranca *f*
film¹ ['fɪlm] *vt* : filmar — *vi* : rodar
film² *n* **1** COATING : capa *f*, película *f* **2** : película *f* (fotográfica) **3** MOVIE : película *f*, filme *m*
filmy ['fɪlmi] *adj* **filmier; -est 1** GAUZY : diáfano, vaporoso **2** : cubierto de una película
filter¹ ['fɪltər] *vt* : filtrar
filter² *n* : filtro *m*
filth ['fɪlθ] *n* : mugre *f*, porquería *f*, roña *f*
filthiness ['fɪlθinəs] *n* : suciedad *f*
filthy ['fɪlθi] *adj* **filthier; -est 1** DIRTY : mugriento, sucio **2** OBSCENE : obsceno, indecente
filtration [fɪl'treɪʃən] *n* : filtración *f*
fin ['fɪn] *n* **1** : aleta *f* **2** : alerón *m* (de un automóvil o un avión)
finagle [fə'neɪgəl] *vt* **-gled; -gling** : arreglárselas para conseguir
final¹ ['faɪnəl] *adj* **1** DEFINITIVE : definitivo, final, inapelable **2** ULTIMATE : final **3** LAST : último, final
final² *n* **1** : final *f* (en deportes) **2 finals** *npl* : exámenes *mpl* finales
finale [fɪ'næli, -'nɑ-] *n* : final *m* <grand finale : final triunfal>
finalist ['faɪnəlɪst] *n* : finalista *mf*
finality [faɪ'nælət̬i, fə-] *n, pl* **-ties** : finalidad *f*
finalize ['faɪnəl,aɪz] *vt* **-ized; -izing** : finalizar
finally ['faɪnəli] *adv* **1** LASTLY : por último, finalmente **2** EVENTUALLY : por fin, al final **3** DEFINITIVELY : definitivamente
finance¹ [fə'nænts, 'faɪ,nænts] *vt* **-nanced; -nancing** : financiar
finance² *n* **1** : finanzas *fpl* **2 finances** *npl* RESOURCES : recursos *mpl* financieros
financial [fə'næntʃəl, faɪ-] *adj* : financiero, económico
financially [fə'næntʃəli, faɪ-] *adv* : económicamente
financier [,fɪnən'sɪr, ,faɪ,næn-] *n* : financiero *m*, -ra *f*; financista *mf*
finch ['fɪntʃ] *n* : pinzón *m*
find¹ ['faɪnd] *vt* **found** ['faʊnd]; **finding 1** LOCATE : encontrar, hallar <I can't find it : no lo encuentro> <to find one's way : encontrar el camino, orientarse> **2** DISCOVER, REALIZE : descubrir, darse cuenta de <he found it difficult : descubrió que era difícil> **3** DECLARE : declarar, hallar <they found him guilty : lo declararon culpable>
find² *n* : hallazgo *m*
finder ['faɪndər] *n* : descubridor *m*, -dora *f*
finding ['faɪndɪŋ] *n* **1** FIND : hallazgo *m* **2 findings** *npl* : conclusiones *fpl*
find out *vt* DISCOVER : descubrir, averiguar — *vi* LEARN : enterarse
fine¹ ['faɪn] *vt* **fined; fining** : multar
fine² *adj* **finer; -est 1** PURE : puro (dícese del oro y de la plata) **2** THIN : fino, delgado **3** : fino <fine sand : arena fina> **4** SMALL : pequeño, minúsculo <fine print : letras minúsculas> **5** SUBTLE : sutil, delicado **6** EXCELLENT : excelente, magnífico, selecto **7** FAIR : bueno <it's a fine day : hace buen tiempo> **8** EXQUISITE : exquisito, delicado, fino **9 fine arts** : bellas artes *fpl*
fine³ *n* : multa *f*
finely ['faɪnli] *adv* **1** EXCELLENTLY : con arte **2** ELEGANTLY : elegantemente **3** PRECISELY : con precisión **4 to chop finely** : picar muy fino, picar en trozos pequeños
fineness ['faɪnnəs] *n* **1** EXCELLENCE : excelencia *f* **2** ELEGANCE : elegancia *f*, refinamiento *m* **3** DELICACY : delicadeza *f*, lo fino **4** PRECISION : precisión *f* **5** SUBTLETY : sutileza *f* **6** PURITY : ley *f* (de oro y plata)
finery ['faɪnəri] *n* : galas *fpl*, adornos *mpl*
finesse¹ [fə'nɛs] *vt* **-nessed; -nessing** : ingeniar
finesse² *n* **1** REFINEMENT : refinamiento *m*, finura *f* **2** TACT : delicadeza *f*, tacto *m*, diplomacia *f* **3** CRAFTINESS : astucia *f*
finger¹ ['fɪŋgər] *vt* **1** HANDLE : tocar, toquetear **2** ACCUSE : acusar, delatar
finger² *n* : dedo *m*
fingerling ['fɪŋgərlɪŋ] *n* : pez *m* pequeño y joven
fingernail ['fɪŋgər,neɪl] *n* : uña *f*
fingerprint¹ ['fɪŋgər,prɪnt] *vt* : tomar las huellas digitales a
fingerprint² *n* : huella *f* digital
fingertip ['fɪŋgər,tɪp] *n* : punta *f* del dedo, yema *f* del dedo
finicky ['fɪnɪki] *adj* : maniático, melindroso, mañoso
finish¹ ['fɪnɪʃ] *vt* **1** COMPLETE : acabar, terminar **2** : aplicar un acabado a (muebles, etc.)
finish² *n* **1** END : fin *m*, final *m* **2** REFINEMENT : refinamiento *m* **3** : acabado *m* <a glossy finish : un acabado brillante>
finite ['faɪ,naɪt] *adj* : finito
fink ['fɪŋk] *n* : mequetrefe *mf fam*
Finn ['fɪn] *n* : finlandés *m*, -desa *f*
Finnish¹ ['fɪnɪʃ] *adj* : finlandés
Finnish² *n* : finlandés *m* (idioma)
fiord [fi'ɔrd] → **fjord**

fir ['fər] *n* : abeto *m*

fire[1] ['faɪr] *vt* **fired; firing 1** IGNITE, KINDLE : encender **2** ENLIVEN : animar, avivar **3** DISMISS : despedir **4** SHOOT : disparar **5** BAKE : cocer (cerámica)

fire[2] *n* **1** : fuego *m* **2** BURNING : incendio *m* <fire alarm : alarma contra incendios> <to be on fire : estar en llamas> **3** ENTHUSIASM : ardor *m,* entusiasmo *m* **4** SHOOTING : disparos *mpl,* fuego *m*

firearm ['faɪr,ɑrm] *n* : arma *f* de fuego

fireball ['faɪr,bɔl] *n* **1** : bola *f* de fuego **2** METEOR : bólido *m*

firebreak ['faɪr,breɪk] *n* : cortafuegos *m*

firebug ['faɪr,bʌg] *n* : pirómano *m,* -na *f;* incendiario *m,* -ria *f*

firecracker ['faɪr,krækər] *n* : petardo *m*

fire escape *n* : escalera *f* de incendios

firefighter ['faɪr,faɪt̬ər] *n* : bombero *m,* -ra *f*

firefly ['faɪr,flaɪ] *n, pl* **-flies** : luciérnaga *f*

fireman ['faɪrmən] *n, pl* **-men** [-mən, -,mɛn] **1** FIREFIGHTER : bombero *m,* -ra *f* **2** STOKER : fogonero *m,* -ra *f*

fireplace ['faɪr,pleɪs] *n* : hogar *m,* chimenea *f*

fireproof[1] ['faɪr,pru:f] *vt* : hacer incombustible

fireproof[2] *adj* : incombustible, ignífugo

fireside[1] ['faɪr,saɪd] *adj* : informal <fireside chat : charla informal>

fireside[2] *n* **1** HEARTH : chimenea *f,* hogar *m* **2** HOME : hogar *m,* casa *f*

firewood ['faɪr,wʊd] *n* : leña *f*

fireworks ['faɪr,wərks] *npl* : fuegos *mpl* artificiales, pirotecnia *f*

firm[1] ['fərm] *vi* : endurecer

firm[2] *adj* **1** VIGOROUS : fuerte, vigoroso **2** SOLID, UNYIELDING : firme, duro, sólido **3** UNCHANGING : firme, inalterable **4** RESOLUTE : firme, resuelto

firm[3] *n* : empresa *f,* firma *f,* compañía *f*

firmament ['fərməmənt] *n* : firmamento *m*

firmly ['fərmli] *adv* : firmemente

firmness ['fərmnəs] *n* : firmeza *f*

first[1] ['fərst] *adv* **1** : primero <finish your homework first : primero termina tu tarea> <first and foremost : ante todo> <first of all : en primer lugar> **2** : por primera vez <I saw it first in Boston : lo vi por primera vez en Boston>

first[2] *adj* **1** : primero <the first time : la primera vez> <at first sight : a primera vista> <in the first place : en primer lugar> <the first ten applicants : los diez primeros candidatos> **2** FOREMOST : principal, primero <first tenor : tenor principal>

first[3] *n* **1** : primero *m,* -ra *f* (en una serie) **2** : primero *m,* primera parte *f* **3** *or* **first gear** : primera *f* **4 at ~** : al principio

first aid *n* : primeros auxilios *mpl*

first–class[1] ['fərst'klæs] *adv* : en primera <to travel first-class : viajar en primera>

first–class[2] *adj* : de primera

first class *n* : primera clase *f*

firsthand[1] ['fərst'hænd] *adv* : directamente

firsthand[2] *adj* : de primera mano

first lieutenant *n* : teniente *mf;* teniente primero *m,* teniente primera *f*

firstly ['fərstli] *adv* : primeramente, principalmente, en primer lugar

first–rate[1] ['fərst'reɪt] *adv* : muy bien

first–rate[2] *adj* : de primera, de primera clase

first sergeant *n* : sargento *mf*

firth ['fərθ] *n* : estuario *m*

fiscal ['fɪskəl] *adj* : fiscal — **fiscally** *adv*

fish[1] ['fɪʃ] *vi* **1** : pescar **2 to fish for** SEEK : buscar, rebuscar <to fish for compliments : andar a la caza de cumplidos> — *vt* : pescar

fish[2] *n, pl* **fish** *or* **fishes** : pez *m* (vivo), pescado *m* (para comer)

fisherman ['fɪʃərmən] *n, pl* **-men** [-mən, -,mɛn] : pescador *m,* -dora *f*

fishery ['fɪʃəri] *n, pl* **-eries 1** → **fishing 2** : zona *f* pesquera, pesquería *f*

fishhook ['fɪʃ,hʊk] *n* : anzuelo *m*

fishing ['fɪʃɪŋ] *n* : pesca *f,* industria *f* pesquera

fishing pole *n* : caña *f* de pescar

fish market *n* : pescadería *f*

fishy ['fɪʃi] *adj* **fishier; -est 1** : a pescado <a fishy taste : un sabor a pescado> **2** QUESTIONABLE : dudoso, sospechoso <there's something fishy going on : aquí hay gato encerrado>

fission ['fɪʃən, -ʒən] *n* : fisión *f*

fissure ['fɪʃər] *n* : fisura *f,* hendidura *f*

fist ['fɪst] *n* : puño *m*

fistful ['fɪst,fʊl] *n* : puñado *m*

fisticuffs ['fɪstɪ,kʌfs] *npl* : lucha *f* a puñetazos

fit[1] ['fɪt] *v* **fitted; fitting** *vt* **1** MATCH : corresponder a, coincidir con <the punishment fits the crime : el castigo corresponde al crimen> **2** : quedar <the dress doesn't fit me : el vestido no me queda> **3** GO : caber, encajar en <her key fits the lock : su llave encaja en la cerradura> **4** INSERT, INSTALL : poner, colocar **5** ADAPT : adecuar, ajustar, adaptar **6** *or* **to fit out** EQUIP : equipar — *vi* **1** : quedar, entallar <these pants don't fit : estos pantalones no me quedan> **2** CONFORM : encajar, cuadrar **3 to fit in** : encajar, estar integrado

fit[2] *adj* **fitter; fittest 1** SUITABLE : adecuado, apropiado, conveniente **2** QUALIFIED : calificado, competente **3** HEALTHY : sano, en forma

fit[3] *n* **1** ATTACK : ataque *m,* acceso *m,* arranque *m* **2 to be a good fit** : quedar bien **3 to be a tight fit** : ser muy entallado (de ropa), estar apretado (de espacios)

fitful [ˈfɪtfəl] *adj* : irregular, intermitente — **fitfully** *adv*

fitness [ˈfɪtnəs] *n* **1** HEALTH : salud *f,* buena forma *f* (física) **2** SUITABILITY : idoneidad *f*

fitting[1] [ˈfɪt̬ɪŋ] *adj* : adecuado, apropiado

fitting[2] *n* : accesorio *m*

five[1] [ˈfaɪv] *adj* : cinco

five[2] *n* : cinco *m*

five hundred[1] *adj* : quinientos

five hundred[2] *n* : quinientos *m*

fix[1] [ˈfɪks] *vt* **1** ATTACH, SECURE : sujetar, asegurar, fijar **2** ESTABLISH : fijar, concretar, establecer **3** REPAIR : arreglar, reparar **4** PREPARE : preparar <to fix dinner : preparar la cena> **5** : arreglar, amañar <to fix a race : arreglar una carrera> **6** RIVET : fijar (los ojos, la mirada, etc.)

fix[2] *n* **1** PREDICAMENT : aprieto *m,* apuro *m* **2** : posición *f* <to get a fix on : establecer la posición de>

fixate [ˈfɪkˌseɪt] *vi* **-ated; -ating** : obsesionarse

fixation [fɪkˈseɪʃən] *n* : fijación *f,* obsesión *f*

fixed [ˈfɪkst] *adj* **1** STATIONARY : estacionario, inmóvil **2** UNCHANGING : fijo, inalterable **3** INTENT : fijo <a fixed stare : una mirada fija> **4 to be comfortably fixed** : estar en posición acomodada

fixedly [ˈfɪksədli] *adv* : fijamente

fixedness [ˈfɪksədnəs, ˈfikst-] *n* : rigidez *f*

fixture [ˈfɪkstʃər] *n* **1** : parte *f* integrante, elemento *m* fijo **2 fixtures** *npl* : instalaciones *fpl* (de una casa)

fizz[1] [ˈfɪz] *vi* : burbujear

fizz[2] *n* : efervescencia *f,* burbujeo *m*

fizzle[1] [ˈfɪzəl] *vi* **-zled; -zling 1** FIZZ : burbujear **2** FAIL : fracasar

fizzle[2] *n* : fracaso *m,* fiasco *m*

fjord [fiˈɔrd] *n* : fiordo *m*

flab [ˈflæb] *n* : gordura *f*

flabbergast [ˈflæbərˌgæst] *vt* : asombrar, pasmar, dejar atónito

flabby [ˈflæbi] *adj* **-bier; -est** : blando, fofo, aguado *CA, Col, Mex*

flaccid [ˈflæksəd, ˈflæsəd] *adj* : fláccido

flag[1] [ˈflæg] *vi* **flagged; flagging 1** : hacer señales con banderas **2** WEAKEN : flaquear, desfallecer

flag[2] *n* : bandera *f,* pabellón *m,* estandarte *m*

flagon [ˈflægən] *n* : jarra *f* grande

flagpole [ˈflægˌpoːl] *n* : asta *f,* mástil *m*

flagrant [ˈfleɪgrənt] *adj* : flagrante — **flagrantly** *adv*

flagship [ˈflægˌʃɪp] *n* : buque *m* insignia

flagstaff [ˈflægˌstæf] → **flagpole**

flagstone [ˈflægˌstoːn] *n* : losa *f,* piedra *f*

flail[1] [ˈfleɪl] *vt* **1** : trillar (grano) **2** : sacudir, agitar (los brazos)

flail[2] *n* : mayal *m*

flair [ˈflær] *n* : don *m,* facilidad *f*

flak [ˈflæk] *ns & pl* **flak 1** : fuego *m* antiaéreo **2** CRITICISM : críticas *fpl*

flake[1] [ˈfleɪk] *vi* **flaked; flaking** : desmenuzarse, pelarse (dícese de la piel)

flake[2] *n* : copo *m* (de nieve), escama *f* (de la piel), astilla *f* (de madera)

flamboyance [flæmˈbɔɪənts] *n* : extravagancia *f,* rimbombancia *f*

flamboyant [flæmˈbɔɪənt] *adj* : exuberante, extravagante, rimbombante

flame[1] [ˈfleɪm] *vi* **flamed; flaming 1** BLAZE : arder, llamear **2** GLOW : brillar, encenderse

flame[2] *n* BLAZE : llama *f* <to burst into flames : estallar en llamas> <to go up in flame : incendiarse>

flamethrower [ˈfleɪmˌθroːər] *n* : lanzallamas *m*

flamingo [fləˈmɪŋgo] *n, pl* **-gos** : flamenco *m*

flammable [ˈflæməbəl] *adj* : inflamable, flamable

flange [ˈflændʒ] *n* : reborde *m,* pestaña *f*

flank[1] [ˈflæŋk] *vt* **1** : flanquear (para defender o atacar) **2** BORDER, LINE : bordear

flank[2] *n* : ijada *f* (de un animal), costado *m* (de una persona), falda *f* (de una colina), flanco *m* (de un cuerpo de soldados)

flannel [ˈflænəl] *n* : franela *f*

flap[1] [ˈflæp] *v* **flapped; flapping** *vi* **1** : aletear <the bird was flapping (its wings) : el pájaro aleteaba> **2** FLUTTER : ondear, agitarse — *vt* : batir, agitar

flap[2] *n* **1** FLAPPING : aleteo *m,* aletazo *m* (de alas) **2** : soplada *f* (de un sobre), hoja *f* (de una mesa), faldón *m* (de una chaqueta)

flapjack [ˈflæpˌdʒæk] → **pancake**

flare[1] [ˈflær] *vi* **flared; flaring 1** FLAME, SHINE : llamear, brillar **2 to flare up** : estallar, explotar (de cólera)

flare[2] *n* **1** FLASH : destello *m* **2** SIGNAL : (luz *f* de) bengala *f* **3 solar flare** : erupción *f* solar

flash[1] [ˈflæʃ] *vi* **1** SHINE, SPARKLE : destellar, brillar, relampaguear **2** : pasar como un relámpago <an idea flashed through my mind : una idea me cruzó la mente como un relámpago> — *vt* : despedir, lanzar (una luz), transmitir (un mensaje)

flash[2] *adj* SUDDEN : repentino

flash[3] *n* **1** : destello *m* (de luz), fogonazo *m* (de una explosión) **2 flash of lightning** : relámpago *m* **3 in a flash** : de repente, de un abrir y cerrar los ojos

flashiness [ˈflæʃinəs] *n* : ostentación *f*

flashlight [ˈflæʃˌlaɪt] *n* : linterna *f*

flashy [ˈflæʃi] *adj* **flashier; -est** : llamativo, ostentoso

flask [ˈflæsk] *n* : frasco *m*

flat[1] ['flæt] *vt* **flatted; flatting 1** FLATTEN : aplanar, achatar **2** : bajar de tono (en música)
flat[2] *adv* **1** EXACTLY : exactamente <in ten minutes flat : en diez minutos exactos> **2** : desafinado, demasiado bajo (en la música)
flat[3] *adj* **flatter; flattest 1** EVEN, LEVEL : plano, llano **2** SMOOTH : liso **3** DEFINITE : categórico, rotundo, explícito <a flat refusal : una negativa categórica> **4** DULL : aburrido, soso, monótono (dícese la voz) **5** DEFLATED : desinflado, pinchado, ponchado *Mex* **6** : bemol (en música) <to sing flat : cantar desafinado>
flat[4] *n* **1** PLAIN : llano *m,* terreno *m* llano **2** : bemol *m* (en la música) **3** APARTMENT : apartamento *m,* departamento *m* **4** *or* **flat tire** : pinchazo *m,* ponchadura *f Mex*
flatbed ['flæt,bɛd] *n* : camión *m* de plataforma
flatcar ['flæt,kɑr] *n* : vagón *m* abierto
flatfish ['flæt,fɪʃ] *n* : platija *f*
flat–footed ['flæt,fʊt̬əd, ,flæt'-] *adj* : de pies planos
flatly ['flætli] *adv* DEFINITELY : categóricamente, rotundamente
flatness ['flætnəs] *n* **1** EVENNESS : lo llano, lisura *f,* uniformidad *f* **2** DULLNESS : monotonía *f*
flat–out ['flæt'aʊt] *adj* **1** : frenético, a toda máquina <a flat-out effort : un esfuerzo frenético> **2** CATEGORICAL : descarado, rotundo, categórico
flatten ['flætən] *vt* : aplanar, achatar
flatter ['flæt̬ər] *vt* **1** OVERPRAISE : adular **2** COMPLIMENT : halagar **3** : favorecer <the photo flatters you : la foto te favorece>
flatterer ['flæt̬ərər] *n* : adulador *m,* -dora *f*
flattering ['flæt̬ərɪŋ] *adj* **1** COMPLIMENTARY : halagador **2** BECOMING : favorecedor
flattery ['flæt̬əri] *n, pl* **-ries** : halagos *mpl*
flatulence ['flætʃələn*t*s] *n* : flatulencia *f,* ventosidad *f*
flatulent ['flætʃələnt] *adj* : flatulento
flatware ['flæt,wær] *n* : cubertería *f,* cubiertos *mpl*
flaunt[1] ['flɔnt] *vt* : alardear, hacer alarde de
flaunt[2] *n* : alarde *m,* ostentación *f*
flavor[1] ['fleɪvər] *vt* : dar sabor a, sazonar
flavor[2] *n* **1** : gusto *m,* sabor *m* **2** FLAVORING : sazón *f,* condimento *m*
flavorful ['fleɪvərfəl] *adj* : sabroso
flavoring ['fleɪvərɪŋ] *n* : condimento *m,* sazón *f*
flavorless ['fleɪvərləs] *adj* : sin sabor
flaw ['flɔ] *n* : falla *f,* defecto *m,* imperfección *f*
flawless ['flɔləs] *adj* : impecable, perfecto — **flawlessly** *adv*
flax ['flæks] *n* : lino *m*
flaxen ['flæksən] *adj* : rubio, blondo (dícese del pelo)
flay ['fleɪ] *vt* **1** SKIN : desollar, despellejar **2** VILIFY : criticar con dureza, vilipendiar
flea ['fli:] *n* : pulga *f*
fleck[1] ['flɛk] *vt* : salpicar
fleck[2] *n* : mota *f,* pinta *f*
fledgling ['flɛdʒlɪŋ] *n* : polluelo *m,* pollito *m*
flee ['fli:] *v* **fled** ['flɛd]; **fleeing** *vi* : huir, escapar(se) — *vt* : huir de
fleece[1] ['fli:s] *vt* **fleeced; fleecing 1** SHEAR : esquilar, trasquilar **2** SWINDLE : estafar, defraudar
fleece[2] *n* : lana *f,* vellón *m*
fleet[1] ['fli:t] *vi* : moverse con rapidez
fleet[2] *adj* SWIFT : rápido, veloz
fleet[3] *n* : flota *f*
fleet admiral *n* : almirante *mf*
fleeting ['fli:t̬ɪŋ] *adj* : fugaz, breve
flesh ['flɛʃ] *n* **1** : carne *f* (de seres humanos y animales) **2** : pulpa *f* (de frutas)
flesh out *vt* : desarrollar, darle cuerpo a
fleshy ['flɛʃi] *adj* **fleshier; -est** : gordo (dícese de las personas), carnoso (dícese de la fruta)
flew → **fly**
flex ['flɛks] *vt* : doblar, flexionar
flexibility [,flɛksə'bɪlət̬i] *n, pl* **-ties** : flexibilidad *f,* elasticidad *f*
flexible ['flɛksəbəl] *adj* : flexible — **flexibly** [-bli] *adv*
flick[1] ['flɪk] *vt* : dar un capirotazo a (con el dedo) <to flick a switch : darle al interruptor> — *vi* **1** FLIT : revolotear **2 to flick through** : hojear (un libro)
flick[2] *n* : coletazo *m* (de una cola), capirotazo *m* (de un dedo)
flicker[1] ['flɪkər] *vi* **1** FLUTTER : revolotear, aletear **2** BLINK, TWINKLE : parpadear, titilar
flicker[2] *n* **1** : parpadeo *m,* titileo *m* **2** HINT, TRACE : indicio *m,* rastro *m* <a flicker of hope : un rayo de esperanza>
flier ['flaɪər] *n* **1** AVIATOR : aviador *m,* -dora *f* **2** CIRCULAR : folleto *m* publicitario, circular *f*
flight ['flaɪt] *n* **1** : vuelo *m* (de aves o aviones), trayectoria *f* (de proyectiles) **2** TRIP : vuelo *m* **3** FLOCK, SQUADRON : bandada *f* (de pájaros), escuadrilla *f* (de aviones) **4** ESCAPE : huida *f,* fuga *f* **5 flight of fancy** : ilusiones *fpl,* fantasía *f* **6 flight of stairs** : tramo *m*
flightless ['flaɪtləs] *adj* : no volador
flighty ['flaɪt̬i] *adj* **flightier; -est** : caprichoso, frívolo
flimsy [flɪmzi] *adj* **flimsier; -est 1** LIGHT, THIN : ligero, fino **2** WEAK : endeble, poco sólido **3** IMPLAUSIBLE : pobre, flojo, poco convincente <a flimsy excuse : una excusa floja>
flinch ['flɪntʃ] *vi* **1** WINCE : estremecerse **2** RECOIL : recular, retroceder

fling[1] [ˈflɪŋ] *vt* **flung** [ˈflʌŋ]; **flinging 1** THROW : lanzar, tirar, arrojar **2 to fling oneself** : lanzarse, tirarse, precipitarse

fling[2] *n* **1** THROW : lanzamiento *m* **2** ATTEMPT : intento *m* **3** AFFAIR : aventura *f* **4** BINGE : juerga *f*

flint [ˈflɪnt] *n* : pedernal *m*

flinty [ˈflɪnti] *adj* **flintier; -est 1** : de pedernal **2** STERN, UNYIELDING : severo, inflexible

flip[1] [ˈflɪp] *v* **flipped; flipping** *vt* **1** TOSS : tirar <to flip a coin : echar a cara o cruz> **2** OVERTURN : dar la vuelta a, voltear — *vi* **1** : moverse bruscamente **2 to flip through** : hojear (un libro)

flip[2] *adj* : insolente, descarado

flip[3] *n* **1** FLICK : capirotazo *m*, golpe *m* ligero **2** SOMERSAULT : voltereta *f*

flippancy [ˈflɪpəntsi] *n, pl* **-cies** : ligereza *f*, falta *f* de seriedad

flippant [ˈflɪpənt] *adj* : ligero, frívolo, poco serio

flipper [ˈflɪpər] *n* : aleta *f*

flirt[1] [ˈflərt] *vi* **1** : coquetear, flirtear **2** TRIFLE : jugar <to flirt with death : jugar con la muerte>

flirt[2] *n* : coqueto *m*, -ta *f*

flirtation [ˌflərˈteɪʃən] *n* : devaneo *m*, coqueteo *m*

flirtatious [ˌflərˈteɪʃəs] *adj* : insinuante, coqueto

flit [ˈflɪt] *vi* **flitted; flitting 1** : revolotear **2 to flit about** : ir y venir rápidamente

float[1] [ˈfloːt] *vi* **1** : flotar **2** WANDER : vagar, errar — *vt* **1** : poner a flote, hacer flotar (un barco) **2** LAUNCH : hacer flotar (una empresa) **3** ISSUE : emitir (acciones en la bolsa)

float[2] *n* **1** : flotador *m*, corcho *m* (para pescar) **2** BUOY : boya *f* **3** : carroza *f* (en un desfile)

flock[1] [ˈflɑk] *vi* **1** : moverse en rebaño **2** CONGREGATE : congregarse, reunirse

flock[2] *n* : rebaño *m* (de ovejas), bandada *f* (de pájaros)

floe [ˈfloː] *n* : témpano *m* de hielo

flog [ˈflɑg] *vt* **flogged; flogging** : azotar, fustigar

flood[1] [ˈflʌd] *vt* : inundar, anegar

flood[2] *n* **1** INUNDATION : inundación *f* **2** TORRENT : avalancha *f*, diluvio *m*, torrente *m* <a flood of tears : un mar de lágrimas>

floodlight [ˈflʌdˌlaɪt] *n* : foco *m*

floodwater [ˈflʌdˌwɔt̬ər] *n* : crecida *f*, creciente *f*

floor[1] [ˈflor] *vt* **1** : solar, poner suelo a (una casa o una sala) **2** KNOCK DOWN : derribar, echar al suelo **3** NONPLUS : desconcertar, confundir, dejar perplejo

floor[2] *n* **1** : suelo *m*, piso *m* <dance floor : pista de baile> **2** STORY : piso *m*, planta *f* <ground floor : planta baja> <second floor : primer piso> **3** : mínimo *m* (de sueldos, precios, etc.)

floorboard [ˈflorˌbord] *n* : tabla *f* del suelo, suelo *m*, piso *m*

flop[1] [ˈflɑp] *vi* **flopped; flopping 1** FLAP : golpearse, agitarse **2** COLLAPSE : dejarse caer, desplomarse **3** FAIL : fracasar

flop[2] *n* **1** FAILURE : fracaso *m* **2 to take a flop** : caerse

floppy [ˈflɑpi] *adj* **-pier; -est 1** : blando, flexible **2 floppy disk** : diskette *m*, disquete *m*

flora [ˈflorə] *n* : flora *f*

floral [ˈflorəl] *adj* : floral, floreado

florid [ˈflorɪd] *adj* **1** FLOWERY : florido **2** REDDISH : rojizo

florist [ˈflorɪst] *n* : florista *mf*

floss[1] [ˈflɔs] *vi* : limpiarse los dientes con hilo dental

floss[2] *n* **1** : hilo *m* de seda (de brodar) **2** → **dental floss**

flotation [floˈteɪʃən] *n* : flotación *f*

flotilla [floˈtɪlə] *n* : flotilla *f*

flotsam [ˈflɑtsəm] *n* **1** : restos *mpl* flotantes (en el mar) **2 flotsam and jetsam** : desechos *mpl*, restos *mpl*

flounce[1] [ˈflaʊnts] *vi* **flounced; flouncing** : moverse haciendo aspavientos <she flounced into the room : entró en la sala haciendo aspavientos>

flounce[2] *n* **1** RUFFLE : volante *m* **2** FLOURISH : aspaviento *m*

flounder[1] [ˈflaʊndər] *vi* **1** STRUGGLE : forcejear **2** STUMBLE : no saber qué hacer o decir, perder el hilo (en un discurso)

flounder[2] *n, pl* **flounder** *or* **flounders** : platija *f*

flour[1] [ˈflaʊər] *vt* : enharinar

flour[2] *n* : harina *f*

flourish[1] [ˈflərɪʃ] *vi* THRIVE : florecer, prosperar, crecer (dícese de las plantas) — *vt* BRANDISH : blandir

flourish[2] *n* : floritura *f*, floreo *m*

flourishing [ˈflərɪʃɪŋ] *adj* : floreciente, próspero

flout [ˈflaʊt] *vt* : desacatar, burlarse de

flow[1] [ˈfloː] *vi* **1** COURSE : fluir, manar, correr **2** CIRCULATE : circular, correr <traffic is flowing smoothly : el tránsito está circulando con fluidez>

flow[2] *n* **1** FLOWING : flujo *m*, circulación *f* **2** STREAM : corriente *f*, chorro *m*

flower[1] [ˈflaʊər] *vi* : florecer, florear

flower[2] *n* : flor *f*

flowered [ˈflaʊərd] *adj* : florido, floreado

floweriness [ˈflaʊərinəs] *n* : floritura *f*

flowering[1] [ˈflaʊərɪŋ] *adj* : floreciente

flowering[2] *n* : floración *f*, florecimiento *m*

flowerpot [ˈflaʊərˌpɑt] *n* : maceta *f*, tiesto *m*, macetero *m*

flowery [ˈflaʊəri] *adj* **1** : florido **2** FLOWERED : floreado, de flores

flowing [ˈfloːɪŋ] *adj* : fluido, corriente

flown → **fly**

flu [ˈfluː] *n* : gripe *f*, gripa *f Col, Mex*

fluctuate [ˈflʌktʃʊˌeɪt] *vi* **-ated; -ating** : fluctuar
fluctuation [ˌflʌktʃʊˈeɪʃən] *n* : fluctuación *f*
flue [ˈfluː] *n* : tiro *m,* salida *f* de humos
fluency [ˈfluːəntsi] *n* : fluidez *f,* soltura *f*
fluent [ˈfluːənt] *adj* : fluido
fluently [ˈfluːəntli] *adv* : con soltura, con fluidez
fluff[1] [ˈflʌf] *vt* **1** : mullir <to fluff up the pillows : mullir las almohadas> **2** BUNGLE : echar a perder, equivocarse
fluff[2] *n* **1** FUZZ : pelusa *f* **2** DOWN : plumón *m*
fluffy [ˈflʌfi] *adj* **fluffier; -est 1** DOWNY : lleno de pelusa, velloso **2** SPONGY : esponjoso
fluid[1] [ˈfluːɪd] *adj* : fluido
fluid[2] *n* : fluido *m,* líquido *m*
fluidity [fluˈɪdət̬i] *n* : fluidez *f*
fluid ounce *n* : onza *f* líquida (29.57 mililitros)
fluke [ˈfluːk] *n* : golpe *m* de suerte, chiripa *f,* casualidad *f*
flung → **fling**
flunk [ˈflʌŋk] *vt* FAIL : reprobar — *vi* : salir reprobando
fluorescence [ˌflʊrˈɛsənts, ˌflɔr-] *n* : fluorescencia *f*
fluorescent [ˌflʊrˈɛsənt, ˌflɔr-] *adj* : fluorescente
fluoridate [ˈflɔrəˌdeɪt, ˈflʊr-] *vt* **-dated; -dating** : fluorizar
fluoridation [ˌflɔrəˈdeɪʃən, ˌflʊr-] *n* : fluorización *f,* fluoración *f*
fluoride [ˈflɔrˌaɪd, ˈflʊr-] *n* : fluoruro *m*
fluorine [ˈflʊrˌiːn] *n* : flúor *m*
fluorocarbon [ˌflɔroˈkɑrbən, ˌflʊr-] *n* : fluorocarbono *m*
flurry [ˈflɔri] *n, pl* **-ries 1** GUST : ráfaga *f* **2** SNOWFALL : nevisca *f* **3** BUSTLE : frenesí *m,* bullicio *m* **4** BARRAGE : aluvión *m,* oleada *f* <a flurry of questions : un aluvión de preguntas>
flush[1] [ˈflʌʃ] *vt* **1** : limpiar con agua <to flush the toilet : jalar la cadena> **2** RAISE : hacer salir, levantar (en la caza) — *vi* BLUSH : ruborizarse, sonrojarse
flush[2] *adv* : al mismo nivel, a ras
flush[3] *adj* **1** *or* **flushed** [ˈflʌʃt] : colorado, rojo, encendido (dícese de la cara) **2** FILLED : lleno a rebosar **3** ABUNDANT : copioso, abundante **4** AFFLUENT : adinerado **5** ALIGNED, SMOOTH : alineado, liso **6 flush against** : pegado a, contra
flush[4] *n* **1** FLOW, JET : chorro *m,* flujo *m* rápido **2** SURGE : arrebato *m,* arranque *m* <a flush of anger : un arrebato de cólera> **3** BLUSH : rubor *m,* sonrojo *m* **4** GLOW : resplandor *m,* flor *f* <the flush of youth : la flor de la juventud> <in the flush of victory : en la euforia del triunfo>
fluster[1] [ˈflʌstər] *vt* : poner nervioso, aturdir
fluster[2] *n* : agitación *f,* confusión *f*
flute [ˈfluːt] *n* : flauta *f*
fluted [ˈfluːt̬əd] *adj* **1** GROOVED : estriado, acanalado **2** WAVY : ondulado
fluting [ˈfluːt̬ɪŋ] *n* : estrías *fpl*
flutist [ˈfluːt̬ɪst] *n* : flautista *mf*
flutter[1] [ˈflʌt̬ər] *vi* **1** : revolotear (dícese de un pájaro), ondear (dícese de una bandera), palpitar con fuerza (dícese del corazón) **2 to flutter about** : ir y venir, revoltear — *vt* : sacudir, batir
flutter[2] *n* **1** FLUTTERING : revoloteo *m,* aleteo *m* **2** COMMOTION, STIR : revuelo *m,* agitación *f*
flux [ˈflʌks] *n* **1** : flujo *m* (en física y medicina) **2** CHANGE : cambio *m* <to be in a state of flux : estar cambiando continuamente>
fly[1] [ˈflaɪ] *v* **flew** [ˈfluː]; **flown** [ˈfloːn]; **flying** *vi* **1** : volar (dícese de los pájaros, etc.) **2** TRAVEL : volar (dícese de los aviones), ir en avión (dícese de los pasajeros) **3** FLOAT : flotar, ondear **4** FLEE : huir, escapar **5** RUSH : correr, irse volando **6** PASS : pasar (volando) <how time flies! : ¡cómo pasa el tiempo!> **7 to fly open** : abrir de golpe — *vt* : pilotar (un avión), hacer volar (una cometa)
fly[2] *n, pl* **flies 1** : mosca *f* <to drop like flies : caer como moscas> **2** : bragueta *f* (de pantalones, etc.)
flyer → **flier**
flying saucer → **UFO**
flypaper [ˈflaɪˌpeɪpər] *n* : papel *m* matamoscas
flyspeck [ˈflaɪˌspɛk] *n* **1** : excremento *m* de mosca **2** SPECK : motita *f,* puntito *m*
flyswatter [ˈflaɪˌswɑt̬ər] *n* : matamoscas *m*
flywheel [ˈflaɪˌhwiːl] *n* : volante *m*
foal[1] [ˈfoːl] *vi* : parir
foal[2] *n* : potro *m,* -tra *f*
foam[1] [ˈfoːm] *vi* : hacer espuma
foam[2] *n* : espuma *f*
foamy [ˈfoːmi] *adj* **foamier; -est** : espumoso
focal [ˈfoːkəl] *adj* **1** : focal, central **2 focal point** : foco *m,* punto *m* de referencia
fo'c'sle [ˈfoːksəl] → **forecastle**
focus[1] [ˈfoːkəs] *v* **-cused** *or* **-cussed; -cusing** *or* **-cussing** *vt* **1** : enfocar (un instrumento) **2** CONCENTRATE : concentrar, centrar — *vi* : enfocar, fijar la vista
focus[2] *n, pl* **-ci** [ˈfoːˌsaɪ, -ˌkaɪ] **1** : foco *m* <to be in focus : estar enfocado> **2** FOCUSING : enfoque *m* **3** CENTER : centro *m,* foco *m*
fodder [ˈfɑdər] *n* : pienso *m,* forraje *m*
foe [ˈfoː] *n* : enemigo *m,* -ga *f*
fog[1] [ˈfɔg, ˈfɑg] *v* **fogged; fogging** *vt* : empañar — *vi* **to fog up** : empañarse
fog[2] *n* : niebla *f,* neblina *f*
foggy [ˈfɔgi, ˈfɑ-] *adj* **foggier; -est** : nebuloso, brumoso

foghorn ['fɔg,hɔrn, 'fɑg-] *n* : sirena *f* de niebla

fogy ['fo:gi] *n, pl* **-gies** : carca *mf fam,* persona *f* chapada a la antigua

foible ['fɔɪbəl] *n* : flaqueza *f,* debilidad *f*

foil[1] ['fɔɪl] *vt* : frustrar, hacer fracasar

foil[2] *n* **1** : lámina *f* de metal, papel *m* de aluminio **2** CONTRAST : contraste *m,* complemento *m* **3** SWORD : florete *m* (en esgrima)

foist ['fɔɪst] *vt* : encajar, endilgar *fam,* colocar

fold[1] ['fo:ld] *vt* **1** BEND : doblar, plegar **2** CLASP : cruzar (brazos), enlazar (manos), plegar (alas) **3** EMBRACE : estrechar, abrazar — *vi* **1** FAIL : fracasar **2 to fold up** : doblarse, plegarse

fold[2] *n* **1** SHEEPFOLD : redil *m* (para ovejas) **2** FLOCK : rebaño *m* <to return to the fold : volver al redil> **3** CREASE : pliegue *m,* doblez *m*

folder ['fo:ldər] *n* **1** CIRCULAR : circular *f,* folleto *m* **2** BINDER : carpeta *f*

foliage ['fo:liɪdʒ, -lɪdʒ] *n* : follaje *m*

folio ['fo:li,o:] *n, pl* **-lios** : folio *m*

folk[1] ['fo:k] *adj* : popular, folklórico <folk customs : costumbres populares> <folk dance : danza folklórica>

folk[2] *n, pl* **folk** *or* **folks 1** PEOPLE : gente *f* **2 folks** *npl* : familia *f,* padres *mpl*

folklore ['fo:k,lor] *n* : folklore *m*

folklorist ['fo:k,lorɪst] *n* : folklorista *mf*

folksy ['fo:ksi] *adj* **folksier; -est** : campechano

follicle ['fɑlɪkəl] *n* : folículo *m*

follow ['fɑlo] *vt* **1** : seguir <follow the guide : siga al guía> <she followed the road : siguió el camino, continuó por el camino> **2** PURSUE : perseguir, seguir **3** OBEY : seguir, cumplir, observar **4** UNDERSTAND : entender — *vi* **1** : seguir **2** UNDERSTAND : entender **3 it follows that...** : se deduce que...

follower ['fɑloər] *n* : seguidor *m,* -dora *f*

following[1] ['fɑloɪŋ] *adj* NEXT : siguiente

following[2] *n* FOLLOWERS : seguidores *mpl*

following[3] *prep* AFTER : después de

follow through *vi* **to follow through with** : continuar con, realizar

follow up *vt* : seguir (una sugerencia, etc.), investigar (una huella)

folly ['fɑli] *n, pl* **-lies** : locura *f,* desatino *m*

foment [fo'mɛnt] *vt* : fomentar

fond ['fɑnd] *adj* **1** LOVING : cariñoso, tierno **2** PARTIAL : aficionado **3** FERVENT : ferviente, fervoroso

fondle ['fɑndəl] *vt* **-dled; -dling** : acariciar

fondly ['fɑndli] *adv* : cariñosamente, afectuosamente

fondness ['fɑndnəs] *n* **1** LOVE : cariño *m* **2** LIKING : afición *f*

fondue [fɑn'du:, -'dju:] *n* : fondue *f*

font ['fɑnt] *n* **1** *or* **baptismal font** : pila *f* bautismal **2** FOUNTAIN : fuente *f*

food ['fu:d] *n* : comida *f,* alimento *m*

food chain *n* : cadena *f* alimenticia

foodstuffs ['fu:d,stʌfs] *npl* : comestibles *mpl*

fool[1] ['fu:l] *vi* **1** JOKE : bromear, hacer el tonto **2** TOY : jugar, juguetear <don't fool with the computer : no juegues con la computadora> **3 to fool around** : perder el tiempo <he fools around instead of working : pierde el tiempo en vez de trabajar> — *vt* DECEIVE : engañar, burlar

fool[2] *n* **1** IDIOT : idiota *mf;* tonto *m,* -ta *f;* bobo *m,* -ba *f* **2** JESTER : bufón *m,* -fona *f*

foolhardiness ['fu:l,hɑrdinəs] *n* : imprudencia *f*

foolhardy ['fu:l,hɑrdi] *adj* RASH : imprudente, temerario, precipitado

foolish ['fu:lɪʃ] *adj* **1** STUPID : insensato, estúpido **2** SILLY : idiota, tonto

foolishly ['fu:lɪʃli] *adv* : tontamente

foolishness ['fu:lɪʃnəs] *n* : insensatez *f,* estupidez *f,* tontería *f*

foolproof ['fu:l,pru:f] *adj* : infalible

foot ['fʊt] *n, pl* **feet** ['fi:t] : pie *m*

footage ['fʊtɪdʒ] *n* : medida *f* en pies, metraje *m* (en el cine)

football ['fʊt,bɔl] *n* : futbol *m* americano, fútbol *m* americano

footbridge ['fʊt,brɪdʒ] *n* : pasarela *f,* puente *m* peatonal

foothills ['fʊt,hɪlz] *npl* : estribaciones *fpl*

foothold ['fʊt,ho:ld] *n* **1** : punto *m* de apoyo **2 to gain a foothold** : afianzarse en una posición

footing ['fʊtɪŋ] *n* **1** BALANCE : equilibrio *m* **2** FOOTHOLD : punto *m* de apoyo **3** BASIS : base *f* <on an equal footing : en igualdad>

footlights ['fʊt,laɪts] *npl* : candilejas *fpl*

footlocker ['fʊt,lɑkər] *n* : baúl *m* pequeño, cofre *m*

footloose ['fʊt,lu:s] *adj* : libre y sin compromiso

footman ['fʊtmən] *n, pl* **-men** [-mən, -,mɛn] : lacayo *m*

footnote ['fʊt,no:t] *n* : nota *f* al pie de la página

footpath ['fʊt,pæθ] *n* : sendero *m,* senda *f,* vereda *f*

footprint ['fʊt,prɪnt] *n* : huella *f*

footrace ['fʊt,reɪs] *n* : carrera *f* pedestre

footrest ['fʊt,rɛst] *n* : apoyapiés *m,* reposapiés *m*

footstep ['fʊt,stɛp] *n* **1** STEP : paso *m* **2** FOOTPRINT : huella *f*

footstool ['fʊt,stu:l] *n* : taburete *m,* escabel *m*

footwear ['fʊt,wær] *n* : calzado *m*

footwork ['fʊt,wɔrk] *n* : juego *m* de piernas, juego *m* de pies

fop ['fɑp] *n* : petimetre *m,* dandi *m*

for[1] ['fɔr] *conj* : puesto que, porque

for[2] *prep* **1** (*indicating purpose*) : para, de <clothes for children : ropa para niños> <it's time for dinner : es la hora de comer> **2** BECAUSE OF : por <for fear of : por miedo de> **3** (*indicating a recipient*) : para, por <a gift for you : un regalo para ti> **4** (*indicating support*) : por <he fought for his country : luchó por su patria> **5** (*indicating a goal*) : por, para <a cure for cancer : una cura para el cáncer> <for your own good : por tu propio bien> **6** (*indicating correspondence or exchange*) : por, para <I bought it for $5 : lo compré por $5> <a lot of trouble for nothing : mucha molestia para nada> **7** AS FOR : para, con respecto a **8** (*indicating duration*) : durante, por <he's going for two years : se va por dos años> <I spoke for ten minutes : hablé (durante) diez minutos> <she has known it for three months : lo sabe desde hace tres meses>

forage[1] ['fɔrɪdʒ] *v* **-aged; -aging** *vi* : hurgar (en busca de alimento) — *vt* : buscar (provisiones)

forage[2] *n* : forraje *m*

foray ['fɔr,eɪ] *n* : incursión *f*

forbear[1] [fɔr'bær] *vi* **-bore** [-'bor]; **-borne** [-'born]; **-bearing 1** ABSTAIN : abstenerse **2** : tener paciencia

forbear[2] → **forebear**

forbearance [fɔr'bærənts] *n* **1** ABSTAINING : abstención *f* **2** PATIENCE : paciencia *f*

forbid [fər'bɪd] *vt* **-bade** [-'bæd, -'beɪd] *or* **-bad** [-'bæd]; **-bidden** [-'bɪdən]; **-bidding 1** PROHIBIT : prohibir **2** PREVENT : impedir

forbidding [fər'bɪdɪŋ] *adj* **1** IMPOSING : imponente **2** DISAGREEABLE : desagradable, ingrato **3** GRIM : severo

force[1] ['fors] *vt* **forced; forcing 1** COMPEL : obligar, forzar **2** : forzar <to force open the window : forzar la ventana> <to force a lock : forzar una cerradura> **3** IMPOSE : imponer, obligar

force[2] *n* **1** : fuerza *f* **2 by force** : por la fuerza **3 in force** : en vigor, en vigencia

forced ['forst] *adj* : forzado, forzoso

forceful ['forsfəl] *adj* : fuerte, energético, contundente

forcefully ['forsfəli] *adv* : con energía, con fuerza

forcefulness ['forsfəlnəs] *n* : contundencia *f*, fuerza *f*

forceps ['fɔrsəps, -,sɛps] *ns & pl* : fórceps *m*

forcible ['forsəbəl] *adj* **1** FORCED : forzoso **2** CONVINCING : contundente, convincente — **forcibly** [-bli] *adv*

ford[1] ['ford] *vt* : vadear

ford[2] *n* : vado *m*

fore[1] ['for] *adv* **1** FORWARD : hacia adelante **2 fore and aft** : de popa a proa

fore[2] *adj* **1** FORWARD : delantero, de adelante **2** FORMER : anterior

fore[3] *n* **1** : frente *m*, delantera *f* **2 to come to the fore** : empezar a destacar, saltar a primera plana

fore–and–aft ['forən'æft, -ənd-] *adj* : longitudinal

forearm ['for,ɑrm] *n* : antebrazo *m*

forebear ['for,bær] *n* : antepasado *m*, -da *f*

foreboding [for'boːdɪŋ] *n* : premonición *f*, presentimiento *m*

forecast[1] ['for,kæst] *vt* **-cast; -casting** : pronosticar, predecir

forecast[2] *n* : predicción *f*, pronóstico *m*

forecastle ['foːksəl] *n* : castillo *m* de proa

foreclose [for'kloːz] *vt* **-closed; -closing** : ejecutar (una hipoteca)

forefather ['for,fɑðər] *n* : antepasado *m*, ancestro *m*

forefinger ['for,fɪŋgər] *n* : índice *m*, dedo *m* índice

forefoot ['for,fʊt] *n* : pata *f* delantera

forefront ['for,frʌnt] *n* : frente *m*, vanguardia *f* <in the forefront : a la vanguardia>

forego [for'goː] *vt* **-went; -gone; -going 1** PRECEDE : preceder **2** → **forgo**

foregoing [for'goːɪŋ] *adj* : precedente, anterior

foregone [for'gɔn] *adj* : previsto <a foregone conclusion : un resultado inevitable>

foreground ['for,graʊnd] *n* : primer plano *m*

forehand[1] ['for,hænd] *adj* : directo, derecho

forehand[2] *n* : golpe *m* del derecho

forehead ['fɔrəd, 'for,hɛd] *n* : frente *f*

foreign ['fɔrən] *adj* **1** : extranjero, exterior <foreign countries : países extranjeros> <foreign trade : comercio exterior> **2** ALIEN : ajeno, extraño <foreign to their nature : ajeno a su carácter> <a foreign body : un cuerpo extraño>

foreigner ['fɔrənər] *n* : extranjero *m*, -ra *f*

foreknowledge [for'nɑlɪdʒ] *n* : conocimiento *m* previo

foreleg ['for,lɛg] *n* : pata *f* delantera

foreman ['formən] *n, pl* **-men** [-mən, -,mɛn] : capataz *mf* <foreman of the jury : presidente del jurado>

foremost[1] ['for,moːst] *adv* : en primer lugar

foremost[2] *adj* : más importante, principal, grande

forenoon ['for,nuːn] *n* : mañana *m*

forensic [fə'rɛntsɪk] *adj* **1** RHETORICAL : retórico, de argumentación **2** : forense <forensic medicine : medicina forense>

foreordain [ˌforɔrˈdeɪn] *vt* : predestinar, predeterminar
forequarter [ˈforˌkwɔrt̬ər] *n* : cuarto *m* delantero
forerunner [ˈforˌrʌnər] *n* : precursor *m,* -sora *f*
foresee [forˈsiː] *vt* **-saw; -seen; -seeing** : prever
foreseeable [forˈsiːəbəl] *adj* : previsible <in the foreseeable future : en el futuro inmediato>
foreshadow [forˈʃædoː] *vt* : anunciar, prefigurar
foresight [ˈforˌsaɪt] *n* : previsión *f*
foresighted [ˈforˌsaɪt̬əd] *adj* : previsto
forest [ˈfɔrəst] *n* : bosque *m* (en zonas templadas), selva *f* (en zonas tropicales)
forestall [forˈstɔl] *vt* **1** PREVENT : prevenir, impedir **2** PREEMPT : adelantarse a
forested [ˈfɔrəstəd] *adj* : arbolado
forester [ˈfɔrəstər] *n* : silvicultor *m,* -tora *f*
forestland [ˈfɔrəstˌlænd] *n* : zona *f* boscosa
forest ranger → **ranger**
forestry [ˈfɔrəstri] *n* : silvicultura *f,* ingeniería *f* forestal
foreswear → **forswear**
foretaste[1] [ˈforˌteɪst] *vt* **-tasted; -tasting** : anticipar
foretaste[2] *n* : anticipo *m*
foretell [forˈtɛl] *vt* **-told; -telling** : predecir, pronosticar, profetizar
forethought [ˈforˌθɔt] *n* : previsión *f,* reflexión *f* previa
forever [fɔrˈɛvər] *adv* **1** PERPETUALLY : para siempre, eternamente **2** CONTINUALLY : siempre, constantemente
forevermore [fɔrˌɛvərˈmor] *adv* : por siempre jamás
forewarn [forˈwɔrn] *vt* : prevenir, advertir
foreword [ˈforwərd] *n* : prólogo *m*
forfeit[1] [ˈfɔrfət] *vt* : perder el derecho a
forfeit[2] *n* **1** FINE, PENALTY : multa *f* **2** : prenda *f* (en un juego)
forge[1] [ˈfordʒ] *v* **forged; forging** *vt* **1** : forjar (metal o un plan) **2** COUNTERFEIT : falsificar — *vi* **to forge ahead** : avanzar, seguir adelante
forge[2] *n* : forja *f*
forger [ˈfordʒər] *n* : falsificador *m,* -dora *f*
forgery [ˈfordʒəri] *n, pl* **-eries** : falsificación *f*
forget [fərˈgɛt] *v* **-got** [-ˈgɑt]; **-gotten** [-ˈgɑtən] *or* **-got; -getting** *vt* : olvidar — *vi* **to forget about** : olvidarse de, no acordarse de
forgetful [fərˈgɛtfəl] *adj* : olvidadizo
forget–me–not [fərˈgɛtmiˌnɑt] *n* : nomeolvides *mf*
forgettable [fərˈgɛt̬əbəl] *adj* : poco memorable
forgivable [fərˈgɪvəbəl] *adj* : perdonable
forgive [fərˈgɪv] *vt* **-gave** [-ˈgeɪv]; **-given** [-ˈgɪvən]; **-giving** : perdonar
forgiveness [fərˈgɪvnəs] *n* : perdón *m*
forgiving [fərˈgɪvɪŋ] *adj* : indulgente, comprensivo, clemente
forgo *or* **forego** [forˈgoː] *vt* **-went; -gone; -going** : privarse de, renunciar a
fork[1] [ˈfɔrk] *vi* : ramificarse, bifurcarse — *vt* **1** : levantar (con un tenedor, una horca, etc.) **2 to fork over** : desembolsar
fork[2] *n* **1** : tenedor *m* (utensilio de cocina) **2** PITCHFORK : horca *f,* horquilla *f* **3** : bifurcación *f* (de un río o camino), horqueta *f* (de un árbol)
forked [ˈfɔrkt, ˈfɔrkəd] *adj* : bífido, ahorquillado
forklift [ˈfɔrkˌlɪft] *n* : carretilla *f* elevadora
forlorn [fɔrˈlɔrn] *adj* **1** DESOLATE : abandonado, desolado, desamparado **2** SAD : triste **3** DESPERATE : desesperado
forlornly [fɔrˈlɔrnli] *adv* **1** SADLY : con tristeza **2** HALFHEARTEDLY : sin ánimo
form[1] [ˈfɔrm] *vt* **1** FASHION, MAKE : formar **2** DEVELOP : moldear, desarrollar **3** CONSTITUTE : constituir, formar **4** ACQUIRE : adquirir (un hábito), formar (una idea) — *vi* : tomar forma, formarse
form[2] *n* **1** SHAPE : forma *f,* figura *f* **2** MANNER : manera *f,* forma *f* **3** DOCUMENT : formulario *m* **4** : forma *f* <in good form : en buena forma> <true to form : en forma consecuente> **5** MOLD : molde *m* **6** KIND, VARIETY : clase *f,* tipo *m* **7** : forma *f* (en gramática) <plural forms : formas plurales>
formal[1] [ˈfɔrməl] *adj* **1** CEREMONIOUS : formal, de etiqueta, ceremonioso **2** OFFICIAL : formal, oficial, de forma
formal[2] *n* **1** BALL : baile *m* formal, baile *m* de etiqueta **2** *or* **formal dress** : traje *m* de etiqueta
formaldehyde [fɔrˈmældəˌhaɪd] *n* : formaldehído *m*
formality [fɔrˈmæləṭi] *n, pl* **-ties** : formalidad *f*
formalize [ˈfɔrməˌlaɪz] *vt* **-ized; -izing** : formalizar
formally [ˈfɔrməli] *adv* : formalmente
format[1] [ˈfɔrˌmæt] *vt* **-matted; -matting** : formatear
format[2] *n* : formato *m*
formation [fɔrˈmeɪʃən] *n* **1** FORMING : formación *f* **2** SHAPE : forma *f* **3 in formation** : en formación
formative [ˈfɔrmət̬ɪv] *adj* : formativo
former [ˈfɔrmər] *adj* **1** PREVIOUS : antiguo, anterior <the former president : el antiguo presidente> **2** : primero (de dos)
formerly [ˈfɔrmərli] *adv* : anteriormente, antes
formidable [ˈfɔrmədəbəl, fɔrˈmɪdə-] *adj* : formidable — **formidably** *adv*

formless [ˈfɔrmləs] *adj* **:** informe, amorfo

formula [ˈfɔrmjələ] *n, pl* **-las** *or* **-lae** [-ˌliː, -ˌlaɪ] **1 :** fórmula *f* **2 baby formula :** preparado *m* para biberón

formulate [ˈfɔrmjəˌleɪt] *vt* **-lated; -lating :** formular, hacer

formulation [ˌfɔrmjəˈleɪʃən] *n* **:** formulación *f*

fornicate [ˈfɔrnəˌkeɪt] *vi* **-cated; -cating :** fornicar

fornication [ˌfɔrnəˈkeɪʃən] *n* **:** fornicación *f*

forsake [fərˈseɪk] *vt* **-sook** [-ˈsʊk]; **-saken** [-ˈseɪkən]; **-saking 1** ABANDON **:** abandonar, desamparar **2** RELINQUISH **:** renunciar a

forswear [fɔrˈswær] *v* **-swore; -sworn; -swearing** *vt* RENOUNCE **:** renunciar a — *vi* **:** perjurar

forsythia [fərˈsɪθiə] *n* **:** forsitia *f*

fort [ˈfort] *n* **1** STRONGHOLD **:** fuerte *m,* fortaleza *f,* fortín *m* **2** BASE **:** base *f* militar

forte [ˈfort, ˈforˌteɪ] *n* **:** fuerte *m*

forth [ˈforθ] *adv* **1 :** adelante <from this day forth : de hoy en adelante> **2 and so forth :** etcétera

forthcoming [forθˈkʌmɪŋ, ˈforθˌ-] *adj* **1** COMING **:** próximo **2** DIRECT, OPEN **:** directo, franco, comunicativo

forthright [ˈforθˌraɪt] *adj* **:** directo, franco — **forthrightly** *adv*

forthrightness [ˈforθˌraɪtnəs] *n* **:** franqueza *f*

forthwith [forθˈwɪθ, -ˈwɪð] *adv* **:** inmediatamente, en el acto, enseguida

fortieth[1] [ˈfɔrt̬iəθ] *adj* **:** cuadragésimo

fortieth[2] *n* **1 :** cuadragésimo *m,* -ma *f* (en una serie) **2 :** cuarentavo *m,* cuarentava parte *f*

fortification [ˌfɔrt̬əfəˈkeɪʃən] *n* **:** fortificación *f*

fortify [ˈfɔrt̬əˌfaɪ] *vt* **-fied; -fying :** fortificar

fortitude [ˈfɔrt̬əˌtuːd, -ˌtjuːd] *n* **:** fortaleza *f,* valor *m*

fortnight [ˈfortˌnaɪt] *n* **:** quince días *mpl,* dos semanas *fpl*

fortnightly[1] [ˈfortˌnaɪtli] *adv* **:** cada quince días

fortnightly[2] *adj* **:** quincenal

fortress [ˈfɔrtrəs] *n* **:** fortaleza *f*

fortuitous [fɔrˈtuːət̬əs, -ˈtjuː-] *adj* **:** fortuito, accidental

fortunate [ˈfɔrtʃənət] *adj* **:** afortunado

fortunately [ˈfɔrtʃənətli] *adv* **:** afortunadamente, con suerte

fortune [ˈfɔrtʃən] *n* **1 :** fortuna *f* <to seek one's fortune : buscar uno su fortuna> **2** LUCK **:** suerte *f,* fortuna *f* **3** DESTINY, FUTURE **:** destino *m,* buenaventura *f* **4 :** dineral *m,* platal *m* <she spent a fortune : se gastó un dineral>

fortune–teller [ˈfɔrtʃənˌtɛlər] *n* **:** adivino *m,* -na *f*

fortune–telling [ˈfɔrtʃənˌtɛlɪŋ] *n* **:** adivinación *f*

forty[1] [ˈfɔrt̬i] *adj* **:** cuarenta

forty[2] *n, pl* **forties :** cuarenta *m*

forum [ˈforəm] *n, pl* **-rums :** foro *m*

forward[1] [ˈfɔrwərd] *vt* **1** PROMOTE **:** promover, adelantar, fomentar **2** SEND **:** remitir, enviar

forward[2] *adv* **1 :** adelante, hacia adelante <to go forward : irse adelante> **2 from this day forward :** de aquí en adelante

forward[3] *adj* **1 :** hacia adelante, delantero **2** BRASH **:** atrevido, descarado

forward[4] *n* **:** delantero *m,* -ra *f* (en deportes)

forwarder [ˈfɔrwərdər] *n* **:** agencia *f* de transportes, agente *mf* expedidor

forwardness [ˈfɔrwərdnəs] *n* **:** atrevimiento *m,* descaro *m*

forwards [ˈfɔrwərdz] → **forward**[2]

fossil[1] [ˈfɑsəl] *adj* **:** fósil

fossil[2] *n* **:** fósil *m*

fossilize [ˈfɑsəˌlaɪz] *vt* **-ized; -izing :** fosilizar — *vi* **:** fosilizarse

foster[1] [ˈfɔstər] *vt* **:** promover, fomentar

foster[2] *adj* **:** adoptivo <foster child : niño adoptivo>

fought → **fight**

foul[1] [ˈfaʊl] *vi* **:** cometer faltas (en deportes) — *vt* **1** DIRTY, POLLUTE **:** contaminar, ensuciar **2** TANGLE **:** enredar

foul[2] *adv* **1** → **foully 2 :** contra las reglas

foul[3] *adj* **1** REPULSIVE **:** asqueroso, repugnante **2** CLOGGED **:** atascado, obstruido **3** TANGLED **:** enredado **4** OBSCENE **:** obsceno **5** BAD **:** malo <foul weather : mal tiempo> **6 :** antirreglamentario (en deportes)

foul[4] *n* **:** falta *f,* faul *m*

foully [ˈfaʊli] *adv* **:** asquerosamente

foulmouthed [ˈfaʊlˌmæʊːðd, -ˌmaʊθt] *adj* **:** malhablado

foulness [ˈfaʊlnəs] *n* **1** DIRTINESS **:** suciedad *f* **2** INCLEMENCY **:** inclemencia *f* **3** OBSCENITY **:** obscenidad *f,* grosería *f*

foul play *n* **:** actos *mpl* criminales

foul–up [ˈfaʊlˌʌp] *n* **:** lío *m,* confusión *f,* desastre *m*

foul up *vt* SPOIL **:** estropear, arruinar — *vi* BUNGLE **:** echar todo a perder

found[1] → **find**

found[2] [ˈfaʊnd] *vt* **:** fundar, establecer

foundation [faʊnˈdeɪʃən] *n* **1** FOUNDING **:** fundación *f* **2** BASIS **:** fundamento *m,* base *f* **3** INSTITUTION **:** fundación *f* **4 :** cimientos *mpl* (de un edificio)

founder[1] [ˈfaʊndər] *vi* SINK **:** hundirse, irse a pique

founder[2] *n* **:** fundador *m,* -dora *f*

foundling [ˈfaʊndlɪŋ] *n* **:** expósito *m,* -ta *f*

foundry [ˈfaʊndri] *n, pl* **-dries :** fundición *f*

fount [ˈfaʊnt] *n* SOURCE **:** fuente *f,* origen *m*

fountain ['faʊntən] *n* **1** SPRING : fuente *f,* manantial *m* **2** SOURCE : fuente *f,* origen *m* **3** JET : chorro *m* (de agua), surtidor *m*
fountain pen *n* : pluma *f* fuente
four[1] ['for] *adj* : cuatro
four[2] *n* : cuatro *m*
fourfold ['for,fo:ld, -'fo:ld] *adj* : cuadruple
four hundred[1] *adj* : cuatrocientos
four hundred[2] *n* : cuatrocientos *m*
fourscore ['for'skor] *adj* EIGHTY : ochenta *m*
fourteen[1] [for'ti:n] *adj* : catorce
fourteen[2] *n* : catorce *m*
fourteenth[1] [for'ti:nθ] *adj* : decimocuarto
fourteenth[2] *n* **1** : decimocuarto *m,* -ta *f* (en una serie) **2** : catorceavo *m,* catorceava parte *f*
fourth[1] ['forθ] *adj* : cuarto
fourth[2] *n* **1** : cuarto *m,* -ta *f* (en una serie) **2** : cuarto *m,* cuarta parte *f*
fowl ['faʊl] *n, pl* **fowl** *or* **fowls 1** BIRD : ave *f* **2** CHICKEN : pollo *m*
fox[1] ['fɑks] *vt* **1** TRICK : engañar **2** BAFFLE : confundir
fox[2] *n, pl* **foxes** : zorro *m,* -ra *f*
foxglove ['fɑks,glʌv] *n* : dedalera *f,* digital *f*
foxhole ['fɑks,ho:l] *n* : hoyo *m* para atrincherarse, trinchera *f* individual
foxy ['fɑksi] *adj* **foxier; -est** SHREWD : astuto
foyer ['fɔɪər, 'fɔɪ,jeɪ] *n* : vestíbulo *m*
fracas ['freɪkəs, 'fræ-] *n, pl* **-cases** [-kəsəz] : altercado *m,* pelea *f,* reyerta *f*
fraction ['frækʃən] *n* **1** : fracción *f,* quebrado *m* **2** PORTION : porción *f,* parte *f*
fractional ['frækʃənəl] *adj* **1** : fraccionario **2** TINY : minúsculo, mínimo, insignificante
fractious ['frækʃəs] *adj* **1** UNRULY : rebelde **2** IRRITABLE : malhumorado, irritable
fracture[1] ['fræktʃər] *vt* **-tured; -turing** : fracturar
fracture[2] *n* **1** : fractura *f* (de un hueso) **2** CRACK : fisura *f,* grieta *f,* falla *f* (geológica)
fragile ['frædʒəl, -,dʒaɪl] *adj* : frágil
fragility [frə'dʒɪləṭi] *n, pl* **-ties** : fragilidad *f*
fragment[1] ['fræg,mɛnt] *vt* : fragmentar — *vi* : fragmentarse, hacerse añicos
fragment[2] ['frægmənt] *n* : fragmento *m,* trozo *m,* pedazo *m*
fragmentary ['frægmən,tɛri] *adj* : fragmentario, incompleto
fragmentation [,frægmən'teɪʃən, -,mɛn-] *n* : fragmentación *f*
fragrance ['freɪgrənts] *n* : fragancia *f,* aroma *m*
fragrant ['freɪgrənt] *adj* : fragante, aromático — **fragrantly** *adv*
frail ['freɪl] *adj* : débil, delicado
frailty ['freɪlti] *n, pl* **-ties** : debilidad *f,* flaqueza *f*
frame[1] ['freɪm] *vt* **framed; framing 1** FORMULATE : formular, elaborar **2** BORDER : enmarcar, encuadrar **3** INCRIMINATE : incriminar
frame[2] *n* **1** BODY : cuerpo *m* **2** : armazón *f* (de un edificio, un barco, o un avión), bastidor *m* (de un automóvil), cuadro *m* (de una bicicleta), marco *m* (de un cuadro, una ventana, una puerta, etc.) **3 frames** *npl* : armazón *mf,* montura *f* (para anteojos) **4 frame of mind** : estado *m* de ánimo
framework ['freɪm,wərk] *n* **1** SKELETON, STRUCTURE : armazón *f,* estructura *f* **2** BASIS : marco *m*
franc ['fræŋk] *n* : franco *m*
franchise ['fræn,tʃaɪz] *n* **1** LICENSE : licencia *f* exclusiva, concesión *f* (en comercio) **2** SUFFRAGE : sufragio *m*
franchisee [,fræn,tʃaɪ'zi:, -tʃə-] *n* : concesionario *m,* -ria *f*
frank[1] ['fræŋk] *vt* : franquear
frank[2] *adj* : franco, sincero, cándido — **frankly** *adv*
frank[3] *n* : franqueo *m* (de correo)
frankfurter ['fræŋkfərtər, -,fər-] *or* **frankfurt** [-fərt] *n* : salchicha *f* (de Frankfurt, de Viena), perro *m* caliente
frankincense ['fræŋkən,sɛnts] *n* : incienso *m*
frankness ['fræŋknəs] *n* : franqueza *f,* sinceridad *f,* candidez *f*
frantic ['fræntɪk] *adj* : frenético, desesperado — **frantically** *adv*
fraternal [frə'tərnəl] *adj* : fraterno, fraternal
fraternity [frə'tərnəṭi] *n, pl* **-ties** : fraternidad *f*
fraternization [,fræṭərnə'zeɪʃən] *n* : fraternización *f,* confraternización *f*
fraternize ['fræṭər,naɪz] *vi* **-nized; -nizing** : fraternizar, confraternizar
fratricidal [,frætrə'saɪdəl] *adj* : fratricida
fratricide ['frætrə,saɪd] *n* : fratricidio *m*
fraud ['frɔd] *n* **1** DECEPTION, SWINDLE : fraude *m,* estafa *f,* engaño *m* **2** IMPOSTOR : impostor *m,* -tora *f;* farsante *mf*
fraudulent ['frɔdʒələnt] *adj* : fraudulento — **fraudulently** *adv*
fraught ['frɔt] *adj* **fraught with** : lleno de, cargado de
fray[1] ['freɪ] *vt* **1** WEAR : desgastar, deshilachar **2** IRRITATE : crispar, irritar (los nervios) — *vi* : desgastarse, deshilacharse
fray[2] *n* : pelea *f,* lucha *f,* refriega *f*
frazzle[1] ['fræzəl] *vt* **-zled; -zling 1** FRAY : desgastar, deshilachar **2** EXHAUST : agotar, fatigar
frazzle[2] *n* EXHAUSTION : agotamiento *m*
freak ['fri:k] *n* **1** ODDITY : ejemplar *m* anormal, fenómeno *m,* rareza *f* **2** ENTHUSIAST : entusiasta *mf*

freakish [ˈfriːkɪʃ] *adj* **:** extraño, estrafalario, raro
freckle[1] [ˈfrɛkəl] *vi* **-led; -ling :** cubrirse de pecas
freckle[2] *n* **:** peca *f*
free[1] [ˈfriː] *vt* **freed; freeing 1** LIBERATE **:** libertar, liberar, poner en libertad **2** RELIEVE, RID **:** librar, eximir **3** RELEASE, UNTIE **:** desatar, soltar **4** UNCLOG **:** desatascar, destapar
free[2] *adv* **1** FREELY **:** libremente **2** GRATIS **:** gratuitamente, gratis
free[3] *adj* **freer; freest 1 :** libre <free as a bird : libre como un pájaro> **2** EXEMPT **:** libre <tax-free : libre de impuestos> **3** GRATIS **:** gratuito, gratis **4** VOLUNTARY **:** espontáneo, voluntario, libre **5** UNOCCUPIED **:** desocupado, libre **6** LOOSE **:** suelto
freebooter [ˈfriːˌbuːt̬ər] *n* **:** pirata *mf*
freeborn [ˈfriːˈbɔrn] *adj* **:** nacido libre
freedom [ˈfriːdəm] *n* **:** libertad *f*
free–for–all [ˈfriːfərˌɔl] *n* **:** pelea *f,* batalla *f* campal
freelance[1] [ˈfriːˌlænts] *vi* **-lanced; -lancing :** trabajar por cuenta propia
freelance[2] *adj* **:** por cuenta propia, independiente
freeload [ˈfriːˌloːd] *vi* **:** gorronear *fam,* gorrear *fam*
freeloader [ˈfriːˌloːdər] *n* **:** gorrón *m,* -rrona *f;* gorrero *m,* -ra *f;* vividor *m,* -dora *f*
freely [ˈfriːli] *adv* **1** FREE **:** libremente **2** GRATIS **:** gratis, gratuitamente
freestanding [ˈfriːˈstændɪŋ] *adj* **:** de pie, no empotrado, independiente
freeway [ˈfriːˌweɪ] *n* **:** autopista *f*
freewill [ˈfriːˌwɪl] *adj* **:** de propia voluntad
free will *n* **:** libre albedrío *m,* propia voluntad *f*
freeze[1] [ˈfriːz] *v* **froze** [ˈfroːz]; **frozen** [ˈfroːzən]; **freezing** *vi* **1 :** congelarse, helarse <the water froze in the lake : el agua se congeló en el lago> <my blood froze : se me heló la sangre> <I'm freezing : me estoy helando> **2** STOP **:** quedarse inmóvil — *vt* **:** helar, congelar (líquidos), congelar (alimentos, precios, activos)
freeze[2] *n* **1** FROST **:** helada *f* **2** FREEZING **:** congelación *f,* congelamiento *m*
freeze–dried [ˈfriːzˈdraɪd] *adj* **:** liofilizado
freeze–dry [ˈfriːzˈdraɪ] *vt* **-dried; -drying :** liofilizar
freezer [ˈfriːzər] *n* **:** congelador *m*
freezing [ˈfriːzɪŋ] *adj* **:** helando <it's freezing! : ¡hace un frío espantoso!>
freezing point *n* **:** punto *m* de congelación
freight[1] [ˈfreɪt] *vt* **:** enviar como carga
freight[2] *n* **1** SHIPPING, TRANSPORT **:** transporte *m,* porte *m,* flete *m* **2** GOODS **:** mercancías *fpl,* carga *f*
freighter [ˈfreɪt̬ər] *n* **:** carguero *m,* buque *m* de carga
French[1] [ˈfrɛntʃ] *adj* **:** francés
French[2] *n* **1 :** francés *m* (idioma) **2 the French** *npl* **:** los franceses
Frenchman [ˈfrɛntʃmən] *n, pl* **-men** [-mən, -ˌmɛn] **:** francés *m*
Frenchwoman [ˈfrɛntʃˌwʊmən] *n, pl* **-women** [-ˌwɪmən] **:** francesa *f*
french fries [ˈfrɛntʃˌfraɪz] *npl* **:** papas *fpl* fritas
frenetic [frɪˈnɛt̬ɪk] *adj* **:** frenético — **frenetically** [-t̬ɪkli] *adv*
frenzied [ˈfrɛnzid] *adj* **:** frenético
frenzy [ˈfrɛnzi] *n, pl* **-zies :** frenesí *m*
frequency [ˈfriːkwəntsi] *n, pl* **-cies :** frecuencia *f*
frequent[1] [friˈkwɛnt, ˈfriːkwənt] *vt* **:** frecuentar
frequent[2] [ˈfriːkwənt] *adj* **:** frecuente — **frequently** *adv*
fresco [ˈfrɛsˌkoː] *n, pl* **-coes :** fresco *m*
fresh [ˈfrɛʃ] *adj* **1 :** dulce <freshwater : agua dulce> **2** PURE **:** puro **3 :** fresco <fresh fruits : frutas frescas> **4** CLEAN, NEW **:** limpio, nuevo <fresh clothes : ropa limpia> <fresh evidence : evidencia nueva> **5** REFRESHED **:** fresco, descansado **6** IMPERTINENT **:** descarado, impertinente
freshen [ˈfrɛʃən] *vt* **:** refrescar, arreglar — *vi* **to freshen up :** arreglarse, lavarse
freshet [ˈfrɛʃət] *n* **:** arroyo *m* desbordado
freshly [ˈfrɛʃli] *adv* **:** recientemente, recién
freshman [ˈfrɛʃmən] *n, pl* **-men** [-mən, -ˌmɛn] **:** estudiante *mf* de primer año universitario
freshness [ˈfrɛʃnəs] *n* **:** frescura *f*
freshwater [ˈfrɛʃˌwɔt̬ər] *n* **:** agua *f* dulce
fret[1] [ˈfrɛt] *vi* **fretted; fretting :** preocuparse, inquietarse
fret[2] *n* **1** VEXATION **:** irritación *f,* molestia *f* **2** WORRY **:** preocupación *f* **3 :** traste *m* (de un instrumento musical)
fretful [ˈfrɛtfəl] *adj* **:** fastidioso, quejoso, neurótico
fretfully [ˈfrɛtfəli] *adv* **:** ansiosamente, fastidiosamente, inquieto
fretfulness [ˈfrɛtfəlnəs] *n* **:** inquietud *f,* irritabilidad *f*
friable [ˈfraɪəbəl] *adj* **:** friable, pulverizable
friar [ˈfraɪər] *n* **:** fraile *m*
fricassee[1] [ˈfrɪkəˌsiː, ˌfrɪkəˈsiː] *vt* **-seed; -seeing :** cocinar al fricasé
fricassee[2] *n* **:** fricasé *m*
friction [ˈfrɪkʃən] *n* **1** RUBBING **:** fricción *f* **2** CONFLICT **:** fricción *f,* roce *m*
Friday [ˈfraɪˌdeɪ, -di] *n* **:** viernes *m*
fridge [ˈfrɪdʒ] → **refrigerator**
friend [ˈfrɛnd] *n* **:** amigo *m,* -ga *f*
friendless [ˈfrɛndləs] *adj* **:** sin amigos
friendliness [ˈfrɛndlinəs] *n* **:** simpatía *f,* amabilidad *f*
friendly [ˈfrɛndli] *adj* **-lier; -est 1 :** simpático, amable, de amigo <a friendly child : un niño simpático> <friendly advice : consejo de amigo>

2 : agradable, acogedor <a friendly atmosphere : un ambiente agradable> 3 GOOD-NATURED : amigable, amistoso <friendly competition : competencia amistosa>

friendship [frɛnd,ʃɪp] *n* : amistad *f*

frieze [ˈfriːz] *n* : friso *m*

frigate [ˈfrɪgət] *n* : fragata *f*

fright [ˈfraɪt] *n* : miedo *m,* susto *m*

frighten [ˈfraitən] *vt* : asustar, espantar

frightened [ˈfraitənd] *adj* : asustado, temeroso

frightening [ˈfraitənɪŋ] *adj* : espantoso, aterrador

frightful [ˈfraɪtfəl] *adj* **1** → **frightening 2** TREMENDOUS : espantoso, tremendo

frightfully [ˈfraɪtfəli] *adv* : terriblemente, tremendamente

frigid [ˈfrɪdʒɪd] *adj* : glacial, extremadamente frío

frigidity [frɪˈdʒɪdəti] *n* **1** COLDNESS : frialdad *f* **2** : frigidez *f* (sexual)

frill [ˈfrɪl] *n* **1** RUFFLE : volante *m* **2** EMBELLISHMENT : floritura *f,* adorno *m*

frilly [ˈfrɪli] *adj* **frillier; -est 1** RUFFLY : con volantes **2** OVERDONE : recargado

fringe[1] [ˈfrɪndʒ] *vt* **fringed; fringing** : orlar, bordear

fringe[2] *n* **1** BORDER : fleco *m,* orla *f* **2** EDGE : periferia *f,* margen *m* **3 fringe benefits** : incentivos *mpl*, extras *mpl*

frisk [ˈfrɪsk] *vi* FROLIC : retozar, juguetear — *vt* SEARCH : cachear, registrar

friskiness [ˈfrɪskinəs] *n* : vivacidad *f*

frisky [ˈfrɪski] *adj* **friskier; -est** : retozón, juguetón

fritter[1] [ˈfrɪtər] *vt* : desperdiciar, malgastar <I frittered away the money : malgasté el dinero>

fritter[2] *n* : buñuelo *m*

frivolity [frɪˈvɑləti] *n, pl* **-ties** : frivolidad *f*

frivolous [ˈfrɪvələs] *adj* : frívolo, de poca importancia

frivolously [ˈfrɪvələsli] *adv* : frívolamente, a la ligera

frizz[1] [ˈfrɪz] *vi* : rizarse, encresparse, ponerse chino *Mex*

frizz[2] *n* : rizos *mpl* muy apretados

frizzy [ˈfrɪzi] *adj* **frizzier; -est** : rizado, crespo, chino *Mex*

fro [ˈfroː] *adv* **to and fro** : de aquí para allá, de un lado para otro

frock [ˈfrɑk] *n* DRESS : vestido *m*

frog [ˈfrɔg, ˈfrɑg] *n* **1** : rana *f* **2** FASTENER : alamar *m* 3 **to have a frog in one's throat** : tener carraspera

frogman [ˈfrɔg,mæn, ˈfrɑg-, -mən] *n, pl* **-men** [-mən, -,mɛn] : hombre *m* rana, submarinista *mf*

frolic[1] [ˈfrɑlɪk] *vi* **-icked; -icking** : retozar, juguetear

frolic[2] *n* FUN : diversión *f*

frolicsome [ˈfrɑlɪksəm] *adj* : juguetón

from [ˈfrʌm, ˈfrɑm] *prep* **1** (*indicating a starting point*) : desde, de, a partir de <from Cali to Bogota : de Cali a Bogotá> <where are you from? : ¿de dónde eres?> <from that time onward : desde entonces> <from tomorrow : a partir de mañana> **2** (*indicating a source or sender*) : de <a letter from my friend : una carta de mi amiga> <a quote from Shakespeare : una cita de Shakespeare> **3** (*indicating distance*) : de <10 feet from the entrance : a 10 pies de la entrada> **4** (*indicating a cause*) : de <red from crying : rojos de llorar> <he died from the cold : murió del frío> **5** OFF, OUT OF : de <she took it from the drawer : lo sacó del cajón> **6** (*with adverbs or adverbial phrases*) : de, desde <from above : desde arriba> <from among : de entre>

frond [ˈfrɑnd] *n* : fronda *f,* hoja *f*

front[1] [ˈfrʌnt] *vi* **1** FACE : dar, estar orientado <the house fronts north : la casa da al norte> **2** : servir de pantalla <he fronts for his boss : sirve de pantalla para su jefe>

front[2] *adj* : delantero, de adelante, primero <the front row : la primera fila>

front[3] *n* **1** : frente *m,* parte *f* de adelante, delantera *f* <the front of the class : el frente de la clase> <at the front of the train : en la parte delantera del tren> **2** AREA, ZONE : frente *m,* zona *f* <the Eastern front : el frente oriental> <on the educational front : en el frente de la enseñanza> **3** FACADE : fachada *f* (de un edificio o una persona> **4** : frente *m* (en meteorología)

frontage [ˈfrʌntɪdʒ] *n* : fachada *f,* frente *m*

frontal [ˈfrʌntəl] *adj* : frontal, de frente

frontier [,frʌnˈtɪr] *n* : frontera *f*

frontiersman [,frʌnˈtɪrzmən] *n, pl* **-men** [-mən, -,mɛn] : hombre *m* de la frontera

frontispiece [ˈfrʌntəs,piːs] *n* : frontispicio *m*

frost[1] [ˈfrɔst] *vt* **1** FREEZE : helar **2** ICE : escarchar (pasteles)

frost[2] *n* **1** : helada *f* (en meteorología) **2** : escarcha *f* <frost on the window : escarcha en la ventana>

frostbite [ˈfrɔst,baɪt] *n* : congelación *f*

frostbitten [ˈfrɔst,bɪtən] *adj* : congelado (dícese de una persona), quemado (dícese de una planta)

frosting [ˈfrɔstɪŋ] *n* ICING : glaseado *m,* betún *m Mex*

frosty [ˈfrɔsti] *adj* **frostier; -est 1** CHILLY : helado, frío **2** COOL, UNFRIENDLY : frío, glacial

froth [ˈfrɔθ] *n, pl* **froths** [ˈfrɔθs, ˈfrɔðz] : espuma *f*

frothy [ˈfrɔθi] *adj* **frothier; -est** : espumoso

frown[1] [ˈfraʊn] *vi* **1** : fruncir el ceño, fruncir el entrecejo **2 to frown at**

: mirar (algo) con ceño, mirar (a alguien) con ceño
frown[2] *n* : ceño *m* (fruncido)
frowsy *or* **frowzy** [ˈfraʊzi] *adj* **frowsier** *or* **frowzier; -est** : desaliñado, desaseado
froze → **freeze**
frozen → **freeze**
frugal [ˈfruːgəl] *adj* : frugal, ahorrativo, parco — **frugally** *adv*
frugality [fruˈgæləṭi] *n* : frugalidad *f*
fruit[1] [ˈfruːt] *vi* : dar fruto
fruit[2] *n* **1** : fruta *f* (término genérico), fruto *m* (término particular) **2 fruits** *npl* REWARDS : frutos *mpl* <the fruits of his labor : los frutos de su trabajo>
fruitcake [ˈfruːtˌkeɪk] *n* : pastel *m* de frutas
fruitful [ˈfruːtfəl] *adj* : fructífero, provechoso
fruition [fruˈɪʃən] *n* **1** : cumplimiento *m,* realización *f* **2 to bring to fruition** : realizar
fruitless [ˈfruːtləs] *adj* : infructuoso, inútil — **fruitlessly** *adv*
fruity [ˈfruːṭi] *adj* **fruitier; -est** : (con sabor) a fruta
frumpy [ˈfrʌmpi] *adj* **frumpier; -est** : anticuado y sin atractivo
frustrate [ˈfrʌsˌtreɪt] *vt* **-trated; -trating** : frustrar
frustrating [ˈfrʌsˌtreɪṭɪŋ] *adj* : frustrante — **frustratingly** *adv*
frustration [ˌfrʌsˈtreɪʃən] *n* : frustración *f*
fry[1] [ˈfraɪ] *vt* **fried; frying** : freír
fry[2] *n, pl* **fries 1** : fritura *f,* plato *m* frito **2** : fiesta *f* en que se sirven frituras **3** *pl* **fry** : alevín *m* (pez)
fuddle [ˈfʌdəl] *vt* **-dled; -dling** : confundir, atontar
fuddy–duddy [ˈfʌdiˌdʌdi] *n, pl* **-dies** : persona *f* chapada a la antigua, carca *mf*
fudge[1] [ˈfʌdʒ] *vt* **fudged; fudging 1** FALSIFY : amañar, falsificar **2** DODGE : esquivar
fudge[2] *n* : dulce *m* blando de chocolate y leche
fuel[1] [ˈfjuːəl] *vt* **-eled** *or* **-elled; -eling** *or* **-elling 1** : abastecer de combustible **2** STIMULATE : estimular
fuel[2] *n* : combustible *m,* carburante *m* (para motores)
fugitive[1] [ˈfjuːdʒəṭɪv] *adj* **1** RUNAWAY : fugitivo **2** FLEETING : efímero, pasajero, fugaz
fugitive[2] *n* : fugitivo *m,* -va *f*
fulcrum [ˈfʊlkrəm, ˈfʌl-] *n, pl* **-crums** *or* **-cra** [-krə] : fulcro *m*
fulfill *or* **fulfil** [fʊlˈfɪl] *vt* **-filled; -filling 1** PERFORM : cumplir con, realizar, llevar a cabo **2** SATISFY : satisfacer
fulfillment [fʊlˈfɪlmənt] *n* **1** PERFORMANCE : cumplimiento *m,* ejecución *f* **2** SATISFACTION : satisfacción *f,* realización *f*
full[1] [ˈfʊl, ˈfʌl] *adv* **1** VERY : muy <full well : muy bien, perfectamente> **2** ENTIRELY : completamente <she swung full around : giró completamente> **3** DIRECTLY : de lleno, directamente <he looked me full in the face : me miró directamente a la cara>
full[2] *adj* **1** FILLED : lleno **2** COMPLETE : completo, detallado **3** MAXIMUM : todo, pleno <at full speed : a toda velocidad> <in full bloom : en plena flor> **4** PLUMP : redondo, llenito *fam,* regordete *fam* <a full face : una cara redonda> <a full figure : un cuerpo llenito> **5** AMPLE : amplio <a full skirt : una falda amplia>
full[3] *n* **1 to pay in full** : pagar en su totalidad **2 to the full** : al máximo
full–fledged [ˈfʊlˈflɛdʒd] *adj* : hecho y derecho
fullness [ˈfʊlnəs] *n* **1** ABUNDANCE : plenitud *f,* abundancia *f* **2** : amplitud *f* (de una falda)
fully [ˈfʊli] *adv* **1** COMPLETELY : completamente, totalmente **2** : al menos, por lo menos <fully half of them : al menos la mitad de ellos>
fulsome [ˈfʊlsəm] *adj* : excesivo, exagerado, efusivo
fumble[1] [ˈfʌmbəl] *v* **-bled; -bling** *vt* **1** : dejar caer, fumblear **2 to fumble one's way** : ir a tientas — *vi* **1** GROPE : hurgar, tantear **2 to fumble with** : manejar con torpeza
fumble[2] *n* : fumble *m* (en futbol americano)
fume[1] [ˈfjuːm] *vi* **fumed; fuming 1** SMOKE : echar humo, humear **2** : enfadarse, enojarse
fume[2] *n* : gas *m,* humo *m,* vapor *m*
fumigate [ˈfjuːməˌgeɪt] *vt* **-gated; -gating** : fumigar
fumigation [ˌfjuːməˈgeɪʃən] *n* : fumigación *m*
fun[1] [ˈfʌn] *adj* : divertido, entretenido
fun[2] *n* **1** AMUSEMENT : diversión *f,* entretenimiento *m* **2** ENJOYMENT : disfrute *m* **3 to have fun** : divertirse **4 to make fun of** : reírse de, burlarse de
function[1] [ˈfʌŋkʃən] *vi* : funcionar, desempeñarse, servir
function[2] *n* **1** PURPOSE : función *f* **2** GATHERING : reunión *f* social, recepción *f* **3** CEREMONY : ceremonia *f,* acto *m*
functional [ˈfʌŋkʃənəl] *adj* : funcional — **functionally** *adv*
functionary [ˈfʌŋkʃəˌnɛri] *n, pl* **-aries** : funcionario *m,* -ria *f*
fund[1] [ˈfʌnd] *vt* : financiar
fund[2] *n* **1** SUPPLY : reserva *f,* cúmulo *m* **2** : fondo *m* <investment fund : fondo de inversiones> **3 funds** *npl* RESOURCES : fondos *mpl*
fundamental[1] [ˌfʌndəˈmɛntəl] *adj* **1** BASIC : fundamental, básico **2** PRINCIPAL : esencial, principal **3** INNATE : innato, intrínseco
fundamental[2] *n* : fundamento *m*

fundamentally [ˌfʌndəˈmɛntəli] *adv* : fundamentalmente, básicamente
funding [ˈfʌndɪŋ] *n* : financiación *f*
funeral¹ [ˈfjuːnərəl] *adj* **1** : funeral, funerario, fúnebre <funeral procession : cortejo fúnebre> **2 funeral home** : funeraria *f*
funeral² *n* : funeral *m,* funerales *mpl*
funereal [fjuːˈnɪriəl] *adj* : fúnebre
fungal [ˈfʌŋgəl] *adj* : de hongos, micótico
fungicidal [ˌfʌndʒəˈsaɪdəl, ˌfʌngə-] *adj* : fungicida
fungicide [ˈfʌndʒəˌsaɪd, ˈfʌŋgə-] *n* : fungicida *m*
fungous [ˈfʌŋgəs] *adj* : fungoso
fungus [ˈfʌŋgəs] *n, pl* **fungi** [ˈfʌnˌdʒaɪ, ˈfʌŋˌgaɪ] : hongo *m*
funk [ˈfʌŋk] *n* **1** FEAR : miedo *m* **2** DEPRESSION : depresión *f*
funky [ˈfʌŋki] *adj* **funkier; -est** ODD, QUAINT : raro, extraño, original
funnel¹ [ˈfʌnəl] *vt* **-neled; -neling** CHANNEL : canalizar, encauzar
funnel² *n* **1** : embudo *m* **2** SMOKESTACK : chimenea *f* (de un barco o vapor)
funnies [ˈfʌniz] *npl* : tiras *fpl* cómicas
funny [ˈfʌni] *adj* **funnier; -est 1** AMUSING : divertido, cómico **2** STRANGE : extraño, raro
fur¹ [ˈfər] *adj* : de piel
fur² *n* **1** : pelaje *m,* piel *f* **2** : prenda *f* de piel
furbish [ˈfərbɪʃ] *vt* : pulir, limpiar
furious [ˈfjʊriəs] *adj* **1** ANGRY : furioso **2** FRANTIC : violento, frenético, vertiginoso (dícese de la velocidad)
furiously [ˈfjʊriəsli] *adv* **1** ANGRILY : furiosamente **2** FRANTICALLY : frenéticamente
furlong [ˈfərˌlɔŋ] *n* : estadio *m* (201.2 m)
furlough¹ [ˈfərˌloː] *vt* : dar permiso a, dar licencia a
furlough² *n* LEAVE : permiso *m,* licencia *f*
furnace [ˈfərnəs] *n* : horno *m*
furnish [ˈfərnɪʃ] *vt* **1** SUPPLY : proveer, suministrar **2** : amueblar <furnished apartment : departamento amueblado>
furnishings [ˈfərnɪʃɪŋz] *npl* **1** ACCESSORIES : accesorios *mpl* **2** FURNITURE : muebles *mpl*, mobiliario *m*
furniture [ˈfərnɪtʃər] *n* : muebles *mpl,* mobiliario *m*
furor [ˈfjʊrˌɔr, -ər] *n* **1** RAGE : furia *f,* rabia *f* **2** UPROAR : escándalo *m,* jaleo *m,* alboroto *m*
furrier [ˈfəriər] *n* : peletero *m,* -ra *f*
furrow¹ [ˈfəroː] *vt* **1** : surcar **2 to furrow one's brow** : fruncir el ceño
furrow² *n* **1** GROOVE : surco *m* **2** WRINKLE : arruga *f,* surco *m*
furry [ˈfəri] *adj* **furrier; -est** : peludo (dícese de un animal), peluche (dícese de un objeto)
further¹ [ˈfərðər] *vt* : promover, fomentar
further² *adv* **1** FARTHER : más lejos, más adelante **2** MOREOVER : además **3** MORE : más <I'll consider it further in the morning : lo consideraré más en la mañana>
further³ *adj* **1** FARTHER : más lejano **2** ADDITIONAL : adicional, más
furtherance [ˈfərðərənts] *n* : promoción *f,* fomento *m,* adelantamiento *m*
furthermore [ˈfərðərˌmor] *adv* : además
furthermost [ˈfərðərˌmoːst] *adj* : más lejano, más distante
furthest [ˈfərðəst] → **farthest¹, farthest²**
furtive [ˈfərṭɪv] *adj* : furtivo, sigiloso — **furtively** *adv*
furtiveness [ˈfərṭɪvnəs] *n* STEALTH : sigilo *m*
fury [ˈfjʊri] *n, pl* **-ries 1** RAGE : furia *f,* ira *f* **2** VIOLENCE : furia *f,* furor *m*
fuse¹ [ˈfjuːz] *or* **fuze** *vt* **fused** *or* **fuzed; fusing** *or* **fuzing** : equipar con un fusible
fuse² *v* **fused; fusing** *vt* **1** SMELT : fundir **2** MERGE : fusionar, fundir — *vi* : fundirse, fusionarse
fuse³ *n* : fusible *m*
fuselage [ˈfjuːsəˌlɑʒ, -zə-] *n* : fuselage *m*
fusillade [ˈfjuːsəˌlɑd, -ˌleɪd, ˌfjuːsəˈ-, -zə-] *n* : descarga *f* de fusilería
fusion [ˈfjuːʒən] *n* : fusión *f*
fuss¹ [ˈfʌs] *vi* **1** WORRY : preocuparse **2 to fuss with** : juguetear con, toquetear **3 to fuss over** : mimar
fuss² *n* **1** COMMOTION : alboroto *m,* escándalo *m* **2** ATTENTION : atenciones *fpl* **3** COMPLAINT : quejas *fpl*
fussbudget [ˈfʌsˌbʌdʒət] *n* : quisquilloso *m,* -sa *f;* melindroso *m,* -sa *f*
fussiness [ˈfʌsinəs] *n* **1** IRRITABILITY : irritabilidad *f* **2** ORNATENESS : lo recargado **3** METICULOUSNESS : meticulosidad *f*
fussy [ˈfʌsi] *adj* **fussier; -est 1** IRRITABLE : irritable, nervioso **2** OVERELABORATE : recargado **3** METICULOUS : meticuloso **4** FASTIDIOUS : quisquilloso, exigente
futile [ˈfjuːṭəl, ˈfjuːˌtaɪl] *adj* : inútil, vano
futility [fjuˈtɪləṭi] *n, pl* **-ties** : inutilidad *f*
future¹ [ˈfjuːtʃər] *adj* : futuro
future² *n* : futuro *m*
futuristic [ˌfjuːtʃəˈrɪstɪk] *adj* : futurista
fuze → **fuse¹**
fuzz [ˈfʌz] *n* : pelusa *f*
fuzziness [ˈfʌzinəs] *n* **1** DOWNINESS : vellosidad *f* **2** INDISTINCTNESS : falta *f* de claridad
fuzzy [ˈfʌzi] *adj* **fuzzier; -est 1** FLUFFY, FURRY : con pelusa, peludo **2** INDISTINCT : indistinto, borroso

G

g [ˈdʒiː] *n, pl* **g's** *or* **gs** [ˈdʒiːz] : séptima letra del alfabeto inglés

gab[1] [ˈgæb] *vi* **gabbed; gabbing** : charlar, cotorrear *fam,* parlotear *fam*

gab[2] *n* CHATTER : cotorreo *m fam,* parloteo *m fam*

gabardine [ˈgæbərˌdiːn] *n* : gabardina *f*

gabby [ˈgæbi] *adj* **gabbier; -est** : hablador, parlanchín

gable [ˈgeɪbəl] *n* : hastial *m,* aguilón *m*

Gabonese [ˌgæbəˈnɪːz, -ˈnɪːs] *n* : gabonés *m,* -nesa *f* — **Gabonese** *adj*

gad [ˈgæd] *vi* **gadded; gadding** WANDER : deambular, vagar, callejear

gadfly [ˈgædˌflaɪ] *n, pl* **-flies 1** : tábano *m* (insecto) **2** FAULTFINDER : criticón *m,* -cona *f fam*

gadget [ˈgædʒət] *n* : artilugio *m,* aparato *m*

gadgetry [ˈgædʒətri] *n* : artilugios *mpl,* aparatos *mpl*

gaff [ˈgæf] *n* **1** : garfio *m* **2** → **gaffe**

gaffe [ˈgæf] *n* : metedura *f* de pata *fam*

gag[1] [ˈgæg] *v* **gagged; gagging** *vt* : amordazar <to tie up and gag : atar y amordazar> — *vi* **1** CHOKE : atragantarse **2** RETCH : hacer arcadas

gag[2] *n* **1** : mordaza *f* (para la boca) **2** JOKE : chiste *m*

gage → **gauge**

gaggle [ˈgægəl] *n* : bandada *f,* manada *f* (de gansos)

gaiety [ˈgeɪəti] *n, pl* **-eties 1** MERRYMAKING : juerga *f* **2** MERRIMENT : alegría *f,* regocijo *m*

gaily [ˈgeɪli] *adv* : alegremente

gain[1] [ˈgeɪn] *vt* **1** ACQUIRE, OBTAIN : ganar, obtener, adquirir, conseguir <to gain knowledge : adquirir conocimientos> <to gain a victory : obtener una victoria> **2** REACH : alcanzar, llegar a **3** INCREASE : ganar, aumentar <to gain weight : aumentar de peso> **4** : adelantarse, ganar <the watch gains two minutes a day : el reloj se adelanta dos minutos por día> — *vi* **1** PROFIT : beneficiarse **2** INCREASE : aumentar

gain[2] *n* **1** PROFIT : beneficio *m,* ganancia *f,* lucro *m,* provecho *m* **2** INCREASE : aumento *m*

gainful [ˈgeɪnfəl] *adj* : lucrativo, beneficioso, provechoso <gainful employment : trabajo remunerado>

gait [ˈgeɪt] *n* : paso *m,* andar *m,* manera *f* de caminar

gal [ˈgæl] *n* : muchacha *f*

gala[1] [ˈgeɪlə, ˈgæ-, ˈgɑ-] *adj* : de gala

gala[2] *n* : gala *f,* fiesta *f*

galactic [gəˈlæktɪk] *adj* : galáctico

galaxy [ˈgæləksi] *n, pl* **-axies** : galaxia *f*

gale [ˈgeɪl] *n* **1** WIND : vendaval *f,* viento *m* fuerte **2 gales of laughter** : carcajadas *fpl*

gall[1] [ˈgɔl] *vt* **1** CHAFE : rozar **2** IRRITATE, VEX : irritar, molestar

gall[2] *n* **1** BILE : bilis *f,* hiel *f* **2** INSOLENCE : audacidad *f,* insolencia *f,* descaro *m* **3** SORE : rozadura *f* (de un caballo) **4** : agalla *f* (de una planta)

gallant [ˈgælənt] *adj* **1** BRAVE : valiente, gallardo **2** CHIVALROUS, POLITE : galante, cortés

gallantry [ˈgæləntri] *n, pl* **-ries** : galantería *f,* caballerosidad *f*

gallbladder [ˈgɔlˌblædər] *n* : vesícula *f* biliar

galleon [ˈgæljən] *n* : galeón *m*

gallery [ˈgæləri] *n, pl* **-leries 1** BALCONY : galería *f* (para espectadores) **2** CORRIDOR : pasillo *m,* galería *f,* corredor *m* **3** : galería *f* (para exposiciones)

galley [ˈgæli] *n, pl* **-leys** : galera *f*

gallium [ˈgæliəm] *n* : galio *m*

gallivant [ˈgæləˌvænt] *vi* : callejear

gallon [ˈgælən] *n* : galón *m*

gallop[1] [ˈgæləp] *vi* : galopar

gallop[2] *n* : galope *m*

gallows [ˈgæˌloːz] *n, pl* **-lows** *or* **-lowses** [-ˌloːzəz] : horca *f*

gallstone [ˈgɔlˌstoːn] *n* : cálculo *m* biliar

galore [gəˈlor] *adj* : en abundancia <bargains galore : muchísimas gangas>

galoshes [gəˈlɑʃəz] *n* : galochas *fpl,* chanclos *mpl*

galvanize [ˈgælvənˌaɪz] *vt* **-nized; -nizing 1** STIMULATE : estimular, excitar, impulsar **2** : galvanizar (metales)

Gambian [ˈgæmbiən] *n* : gambiano *m,* -na *f* — **Gambian** *adj*

gambit [ˈgæmbɪt] *n* **1** : gambito *m* (en ajedrez) **2** STRATAGEM : estratagema *f,* táctica *f*

gamble[1] [ˈgæmbəl] *v* **-bled; -bling** *vi* : jugar, arriesgarse — *vt* **1** BET, WAGER : apostar, jugarse **2** RISK : arriesgar

gamble[2] *n* **1** BET : apuesta *f* **2** RISK : riesga *f*

gambler [ˈgæmbələr] *n* : jugador *m,* -dora *f*

gambol [ˈgæmbəl] *vi* **-boled** *or* **-bolled; -boling** *or* **-bolling** FROLIC : retozar, juguetear

game[1] [ˈgeɪm] *adj* **1** READY : listo, dispuesto <we're game for anything : estamos listos para lo que sea> **2** LAME : cojo

game[2] *n* **1** AMUSEMENT : juego *m,* diversión *f* **2** CONTEST : juego *m,* partido *m,* concurso *m* **3** : caza *f* <big game : caza mayor>

gamecock [ˈgeɪmˌkɑk] *n* : gallo *m* de pelea

gamekeeper [ˈgeɪmˌkiːpər] *n* : guardabosque *mf*

gamely [ˈgeɪmli] *adv* : animosamente

gamma ray [ˈgæmə] *n* : rayo *m* gamma

gamut [ˈgæmət] *n* : gama *f,* espectro *m* <to run the gamut : pasar por toda la gama>

gamy *or* **gamey** [ˈgeɪmi] *adj* **gamier; -est** : con sabor de animal de caza, fuerte

gander [ˈgændər] *n* **1** : ganso *m* (animal) **2** GLANCE : mirada *f,* vistazo *m,* ojeada *f*

gang[1] [ˈgæŋ] *vi* **to gang up** : agruparse, unirse

gang[2] *n* : banda *f,* pandilla *f*

gangling [ˈgæŋglɪŋ] *adj* LANKY : larguirucho *fam*

ganglion [ˈgæŋgliən] *n, pl* **-glia** [-gliə] : ganglio *m*

gangplank [ˈgæŋˌplæŋk] *n* : pasarela *f*

gangrene [ˈgæŋˌgriːn, ˈgæn-; gæŋˈ-, gænˈ-] *n* : gangrena *f*

gangrenous [ˈgæŋgrənəs] *adj* : gangrenoso

gangster [ˈgæŋstər] *n* : gángster *mf*

gangway [ˈgæŋˌweɪ] *n* **1** : pasarela *f* **2** **gangway!** : ¡abran paso!

gap [ˈgæp] *n* **1** BREACH, OPENING : espacio *m,* brecha *f,* abertura *f* **2** GORGE : desfiladero *m,* barranco *m* **3** : laguna *f* <a gap in my education : una laguna en mi educación> **4** INTERVAL : pausa *f,* intervalo *m* **5** DISPARITY : brecha *f,* disparidad *f*

gape[1] [ˈgeɪp] *vi* **gaped; gaping 1** OPEN : abrirse, estar abierto **2** STARE : mirar fijamente con la boca abierta, mirar boquiabierto

gape[2] *n* **1** OPENING : abertura *f,* brecha *f* **2** STARE : mirada *f* boquiabierta

garage[1] [gəˈrɑʒ, -ˈrɑdʒ] *vt* **-raged; -raging** : dejar en un garaje

garage[2] *n* : garaje *m,* cochera *f*

garb[1] [ˈgɑrb] *vt* : vestir, ataviar

garb[2] *n* : vestimenta *f,* atuendo *f*

garbage [ˈgɑrbɪdʒ] *n* : basura *f,* desechos *mpl*

garbageman [ˈgɑrbɪdʒmən] *n, pl* **-men** [-mən, -ˌmɛn] : basurero *m*

garble [ˈgɑrbəl] *vt* **-bled; -bling** : tergiversar, distorsionar

garbled [ˈgɑrbəld] *adj* : incoherente, incomprensible

garden[1] [ˈgɑrdən] *vi* : trabajar en el jardín

garden[2] *n* : jardín *m*

gardener [ˈgɑrdənər] *n* : jardinero *m,* -ra *f*

gardenia [gɑrˈdiːnjə] *n* : gardenia *f*

gargantuan [gɑrˈgæntʃʊən] *adj* : gigantesco, colosal

gargle[1] [ˈgɑrgəl] *vi* **-gled; -gling** : hacer gárgaras, gargarizar

gargle[2] *n* : gárgara *f*

gargoyle [ˈgɑrˌgɔɪl] *n* : gárgola *f*

garish [ˈgærɪʃ] *adj* GAUDY : llamativo, chillón, charro — **garishly** *adv*

garland[1] [ˈgɑrlənd] *vt* : adornar con guirnaldas

garland[2] *n* : guirnalda *f*

garlic [ˈgɑrlɪk] *n* : ajo *m*

garment [ˈgɑrmənt] *n* : prenda *f*

garner [ˈgɑrnər] *vt* : recoger, cosechar

garnet [ˈgɑrnət] *n* : granate *m*

garnish[1] [ˈgɑrnɪʃ] *vt* : aderezar, guarnecer

garnish[2] *n* : aderezo *m,* guarnición *f*

garret [ˈgærət] *n* : buhardilla *f,* desván *m*

garrison[1] [ˈgærəsən] *vt* **1** QUARTER : acuartelar (tropas) **2** OCCUPY : guarnecer, ocupar (con tropas)

garrison[2] *n* **1** : guarnición *f* (ciudad) **2** FORT : fortaleza *f,* poste *m* militar

garrulous [ˈgærələs] *adj* : charlatán, parlanchín, garlero *Col fam*

garter [ˈgɑrtər] *n* : liga *f*

gas[1] [ˈgæs] *v* **gassed; gassing** *vt* : gasear — *vi* **to gas up** : llenar el tanque con gasolina

gas[2] *n, pl* **gases** [ˈgæsəz] **1** : gas *m* <tear gas : gas lacrimógeno> **2** GASOLINE : gasolina *f*

gaseous [ˈgæʃəs, ˈgæsiəs] *adj* : gaseoso

gash[1] [ˈgæʃ] *vt* : hacer un tajo en, cortar

gash[2] *n* : cuchillada *f,* tajo *m*

gasket [ˈgæskət] *n* : junta *f*

gas mask *n* : máscara *f* antigás

gasoline [ˈgæsəˌliːn, ˌgæsəˈ-] *n* : gasolina *f,* nafta *f*

gasp[1] [ˈgæsp] *vi* **1** : boquear <to gasp with surprise : gritar de asombro> **2** PANT : jadear, respirar con dificultad

gasp[2] *n* **1** : boqueada *f* <a gasp of surprise : un grito sofocado> **2** PANTING : jadeo *m*

gas station → **service station**

gastric [ˈgæstrɪk] *adj* : gástrico <gastric juice : jugo gástrico>

gastronomic [ˌgæstrəˈnɑmɪk] *adj* : gastronómico

gastronomy [gæsˈtrɑnəmi] *n* : gastronomía *f*

gate [ˈgeɪt] *n* : portón *m,* verja *f,* puerta *f*

gatekeeper [ˈgeɪtˌkiːpər] *n* : guarda *mf;* guardián *m,* -diana *f*

gateway [ˈgeɪtˌweɪ] *n* : puerta *f* (de acceso), entrada *f*

gather [ˈgæðər] *vt* **1** ASSEMBLE : juntar, recoger, reunir **2** HARVEST : recoger, cosechar **3** : fruncir (una tela) **4** INFER : deducir, suponer

gathering [ˈgæðərɪŋ] *n* : reunión *f*

gauche [ˈgoːʃ] *adj* : torpe, falto de tacto

gaudy [ˈgɔdi] *adj* **gaudier; -est** : chillón, llamativo

gauge[1] [ˈgeɪdʒ] *vt* **gauged; gauging 1** MEASURE : medir **2** ESTIMATE, JUDGE : estimar, evaluar, juzgar

gauge[2] *n* **1** : indicador *m* <pressure gauge : indicador de presión> **2** CALIBER : calibre *m* **3** INDICATION : indicio *m,* muestra *f*

gaunt [ˈgɔnt] *adj* : demacrado, enjuto, descarnado
gauntlet [ˈgɔntlət] *n* : guante *m* <to run the gauntlet of : exponerse a>
gauze [ˈgɔz] *n* : gasa *f*
gauzy [ˈgɔzi] *adj* **gauzier; -est** : diáfano, vaporoso
gave → **give**
gavel [ˈgævəl] *n* : martillo *m* (de un juez, un subastador, etc.)
gawk [ˈgɔk] *vi* GAPE : mirar boquiabierto
gawky [ˈgɔki] *adj* **gawkier; -est** : desmañado, torpe, desgarbado
gay [ˈgeɪ] *adj* **1** MERRY : alegre **2** BRIGHT, COLORFUL : vistoso, vivo **3** HOMOSEXUAL : homosexual
gaze[1] [ˈgeɪz] *vi* **gazed; gazing** : mirar (fijamente)
gaze[2] *n* : mirada *f* (fija)
gazelle [gəˈzɛl] *n* : gacela *f*
gazette [gəˈzɛt] *n* : gaceta *f*
gazetteer [ˌgæzəˈtɪr] *n* : diccionario *m* geográfico
gear[1] [ˈgɪr] *vt* ADAPT, ORIENT : adaptar, ajustar, orientar <a book geared to children : un libro adaptado a los niños> — *vi* **to gear up** : prepararse
gear[2] *n* **1** CLOTHING : ropa *f* **2** BELONGINGS : efectos *mpl* personales **3** EQUIPMENT, TOOLS : equipo *m*, aparejo *m*, herramientas *fpl* <fishing gear : aparejo de pescar> <landing gear : tren de aterrizaje> **4** COGWHEEL : rueda *f* dentada **5** : marcha *f*, velocidad *f* (de un vehículo) <to put in gear : poner en marcha> <to change gear(s) : cambiar de velocidad>
gearshift [ˈgɪrˌʃɪft] *n* : palanca *f* de cambio, palanca *f* de velocidad
geese → **goose**
Geiger counter [ˈgaɪgərˌkaʊntər] *n* : contador *m* Geiger
gelatin [ˈdʒɛlət̬ən] *n* : gelatina *f*
gem [ˈdʒɛm] *n* : joya *f*, gema *f*, alhaja *f*
Gemini [ˈdʒɛməˌnaɪ] *n* : Géminis *mf*
gemstone [ˈdʒɛmˌstoːn] *n* : piedra *f* (semipreciosa o preciosa), gema *f*
gender [ˈdʒɛndər] *n* **1** SEX : sexo *m* **2** : género *m* (en la gramática)
gene [ˈdʒiːn] *n* : gen *m*, gene *m*
genealogical [ˌdʒiːniəˈlɑdʒɪkəl] *adj* : genealógico
genealogy [ˌdʒiːniˈɑlədʒi, ˌdʒɛ-, -ˈæ-] *n, pl* **-gies** : genealogía *f*
genera → **genus**
general[1] [ˈdʒɛnrəl, ˈdʒɛnə-] *adj* : general <in general : en general, por lo general>
general[2] *n* : general *mf*
generality [ˌdʒɛnəˈrælət̬i] *n, pl* **-ties** : generalidad *f*
generalization [ˌdʒɛnrələˈzeɪʃən, ˌdʒɛnərə-] *n* : generalización *f*
generalize [ˈdʒɛnrəˌlaɪz, ˈdʒɛnərə-] *v* **-ized; -izing** : generalizar
generally [ˈdʒɛnrəli, ˈdʒɛnərə-] *adv* : generalmente, por lo general, en general
generate [ˈdʒɛnəˌreɪt] *vt* **-ated; -ating** : generar, producir
generation [ˌdʒɛnəˈreɪʃən] *n* : generación *f*
generator [ˈdʒɛnəˌreɪt̬ər] *n* : generador *m*
generic [dʒəˈnɛrɪk] *adj* : genérico
generosity [ˌdʒɛnəˈrɑsət̬i] *n, pl* **-ties** : generosidad *f*
generous [ˈdʒɛnərəs] *adj* **1** OPENHANDED : generoso, dadivoso, desprendido **2** ABUNDANT, AMPLE : abundante, amplio, generoso — **generously** *adv*
genetic [dʒəˈnɛt̬ɪk] *adj* : genético — **genetically** [-t̬ɪkli] *adv*
geneticist [dʒəˈnɛt̬əsɪst] *n* : genetista *mf*
genetics [dʒəˈnɛt̬ɪks] *n* : genética *f*
genial [ˈdʒiːniəl] *adj* GRACIOUS : simpático, cordial, afable — **genially** *adv*
geniality [ˌdʒiːniˈælət̬i] *n* : simpatía *f*, afabilidad *f*
genie [ˈdʒiːni] *n* : genio *m*
genital [ˈdʒɛnət̬əl] *adj* : genital
genitals [ˈdʒɛnət̬əlz] *npl* : genitales *mpl*
genius [ˈdʒiːnjəs] *n* : genio *m*
genocide [ˈdʒɛnəˌsaɪd] *n* : genocidio *m*
genre [ˈʒɑnrə, ˈʒɑr] *n* : género *m*
genteel [dʒɛnˈtiːl] *adj* : cortés, fino, refinado
gentile[1] [ˈdʒɛnˌtaɪl] *adj* : gentil
gentile[2] *n* : gentil *mf*
gentility [dʒɛnˈtɪlət̬i] *n, pl* **-ties 1** : nobleza *f* (de nacimiento) **2** POLITENESS, REFINEMENT : cortesía *f*, refinamiento *m*
gentle [ˈdʒɛntəl] *adj* **-tler; -tlest 1** NOBLE : bien nacido, noble **2** DOCILE : dócil, manso **3** KINDLY : bondadoso, amable **4** MILD : suave, apacible <a gentle breeze : una brisa suave> **5** SOFT : suave (dícese de un sonido), ligero (dícese del tacto) **6** MODERATE : moderado, gradual <a gentle slope : una cuesta gradual>
gentleman [ˈdʒɛntəlmən] *n, pl* **-men** [-mən, -ˌmɛn] : caballero *m*, señor *m*
gentlemanly [ˈdʒɛntəlmənli] *adj* : caballeroso
gentleness [ˈdʒɛntəlnəs] *n* : delicadeza *f*, suavidad *f*, ternura *f*
gentlewoman [ˈdʒɛntəlˌwʊmən] *n, pl* **-women** [-ˌwɪmən] : dama *f*, señora *f*
gently [ˈdʒɛntli] *adv* **1** CAREFULLY, SOFTLY : con cuidado, suavemente, ligeramente **2** KINDLY : amablemente, con delicadeza
gentry [ˈdʒɛntri] *n, pl* **-tries** : aristocracia *f*
genuflect [ˈdʒɛnjʊˌflɛkt] *vi* : doblar la rodilla, hacer una genuflexión
genuflection [ˌdʒɛnjʊˈflɛkʃən] *n* : genuflexión *f*

genuine [ˈdʒɛnjʊwən] *adj* **1** AUTHENTIC, REAL : genuino, verdadero, auténtico **2** SINCERE : sincero — **genuinely** *adv*
genus [ˈdʒiːnəs] *n, pl* **genera** [ˈdʒɛnərə] : género *m*
geographer [dʒiˈɑgrəfər] *n* : geógrafo *m,* -fa *f*
geographical [ˌdʒiːəˈgræfɪkəl] *or* **geographic** [-fɪk] *adj* : geográfico — **geographically** [-fɪkli] *adv*
geography [dʒiˈɑgrəfi] *n, pl* **-phies** : geografía *f*
geologic [ˌdʒiːəˈlɑdʒɪk] *or* **geological** [-dʒɪkəl] *adj* : geológico — **geologically** [-dʒɪkli] *adv*
geologist [dʒiˈɑlədʒɪst] *n* : geólogo *m,* -ga *f*
geology [dʒiˈɑlədʒi] *n* : geología *f*
geometric [ˌdʒiːəˈmɛtrɪk] *or* **geometrical** [-trɪkəl] *adj* : geométrico
geometry [dʒiˈɑmətri] *n, pl* **-tries** : geometría *f*
geranium [dʒəˈreɪniəm] *n* : geranio *m*
gerbil [ˈdʒərbəl] *n* : jerbo *m,* gerbo *m*
geriatric [ˌdʒɛriˈætrɪk] *adj* : geriátrico
geriatrics [ˌdʒɛriˈætrɪks] *n* : geriatría *f*
germ [ˈdʒərm] *n* **1** MICROORGANISM : microbio *m,* germen *m* **2** BEGINNING : germen *m,* principio *m* <the germ of a plan : el germen de un plan>
German [ˈdʒərmən] *n* **1** : alemán *m,* -mana *f* **2** : alemán *m* (idioma) — **German** *adj*
germane [dʒərˈmeɪn] *adj* : relevante, pertinente
germanium [dʒərˈmeɪniəm] *n* : germanio *m*
germ cell *n* : célula *f* germen
germicide [ˈdʒərməˌsaɪd] *n* : germicida *m*
germinate [ˈdʒərməˌneɪt] *v* **-nated; -nating** *vi* : germinar — *vt* : hacer germinar
germination [ˌdʒərməˈneɪʃən] *n* : germinación *f*
gerund [ˈdʒɛrənd] *n* : gerundio *m*
gestation [dʒɛˈsteɪʃən] *n* : gestación *f*
gesture¹ [ˈdʒɛstʃər] *vi* **-tured; -turing** : gesticular, hacer gestos
gesture² *n* **1** : gesto *m,* ademán *m* **2** SIGN, TOKEN : gesto *m,* señal *f* <a gesture of friendship : una señal de amistad>
get [ˈgɛt] *v* **got** [ˈgɑt]; **got** *or* **gotten** [ˈgɑtən]; **getting** *vt* **1** OBTAIN : conseguir, obtener, adquirir **2** RECEIVE : recibir <to get a letter : recibir una carta> **3** EARN : ganar <he gets $10 an hour : gana $10 por hora> **4** FETCH : traer <get me my book : tráigame el libro> **5** CATCH : tomar (un tren, etc.), agarrar (una pelota, una persona, etc.) **6** CONTRACT : contagiarse de, contraer <she got the measles : le dio el sarampión> **7** PREPARE : preparar (una comida) **8** PERSUADE : persuadir, mandar a hacer <I got him to agree : logré convencerlo> **9** (*to cause to be*) <to get one's hair cut : cortarse el pelo> **10** UNDERSTAND : entender <now I get it! : ¡ya entiendo!> **11 to have got** : tener <I've got a headache : tengo un dolor de cabeza> **12 to have got to** : tener que <you've got to come : tienes que venir> — *vi* **1** BECOME : ponerse, volverse, hacerse <to get angry : ponerse furioso, enojarse> **2** GO, MOVE : ir, avanzar <he didn't get far : no avanzó mucho> **3** ARRIVE : llegar <to get home : llegar a casa> **4 to get to be** : llegar a ser <she got to be the director : llegó a ser directora> **5 to get ahead** : adelantarse, progresar **6 to get along** : llevarse bien (con alguien), congeniar **7 to get by** MANAGE : arreglárselas **8 to get over** OVERCOME : superar, consolarse de **9 to get together** MEET : reunirse **10 to get up** : levantarse
getaway [ˈgɛtəˌweɪ] *n* ESCAPE : fuga *f,* huida *f,* escapada *f*
geyser [ˈgaɪzər] *n* : géiser *m*
Ghanaian [ˈgɑniən, ˈgæ-] *n* : ghanés *m,* -nesa *f* — **Ghanaian** *adj*
ghastly [ˈgæstli] *adj* **-lier; -est 1** HORRIBLE : horrible, espantoso **2** PALE : pálido, cadavérico
gherkin [ˈgərkən] *n* : pepinillo *m*
ghetto [ˈgɛt̬oː] *n, pl* **-tos** *or* **-toes** : gueto *m*
ghost [ˈgoːst] *n* **1** : fantasma *f,* espectro *m* **2 the Holy Ghost** : el Espíritu Santo
ghostly [ˈgoːstli] *adv* : fantasmal
ghoul [ˈguːl] *n* **1** : demonio *m* necrófago **2** : persona *f* de gustos macabros
GI [ˌdʒiːˈaɪ] *n, pl* **GI's** *or* **GIs** : soldado *m* estadounidense
giant¹ [ˈdʒaɪənt] *adj* : gigante, gigantesco, enorme
giant² *n* : gigante *m,* -ta *f*
gibberish [ˈdʒɪbərɪʃ] *n* : galimatías *m,* jerigonza *f*
gibbon [ˈgɪbən] *n* : gibón *m*
gibe¹ [ˈdʒaɪb] *vi* **gibed; gibing** : mofarse, burlarse
gibe² *n* : pulla *f,* burla *f,* mofa *f*
giblets [ˈdʒɪbləts] *npl* : menudos *mpl,* menudencias *fpl*
giddiness [ˈgɪdinəs] *n* **1** DIZZINESS : vértigo *m,* mareo *m* **2** SILLINESS : frivolidad *f,* estupidez *f*
giddy [ˈgɪdi] *adj* **-dier; -est 1** DIZZY : mareado, vertiginoso **2** FRIVOLOUS, SILLY : frívolo, tonto
gift [ˈgɪft] *n* **1** TALENT : don *m,* talento *m,* dotes *fpl* **2** PRESENT : regalo *m,* obsequio *m*
gifted [ˈgɪftəd] *adj* TALENTED : talentoso
gigantic [dʒaɪˈgæntɪk] *adj* : gigantesco, enorme, colosal
giggle¹ [ˈgɪgəl] *vi* **-gled; -gling** : reírse tontamente
giggle² *n* : risita *f,* risa *f* tonta
gild [ˈgɪld] *vt* **gilded** *or* **gilt** [ˈgɪlt]; **gilding** : dorar
gill [ˈgɪl] *n* : agalla *f,* branquia *f*

gilt[1] ['gɪlt] *adj* : dorado

gilt[2] *n* : dorado *m*

gimlet ['gɪmlət] *n* **1** : barrena *f* (herramiento) **2** : bebida *f* de vodka o ginebra y limón

gimmick ['gɪmɪk] *n* **1** GADGET : artilugio *m* **2** CATCH : engaño *m,* trampa *f* **3** SCHEME, TRICK : ardid *m,* truco *m*

gin[1] ['dʒɪn] *vt* **ginned; ginning** : desmotar (algodón)

gin[2] *n* **1** : desmotadora *f* (de algodón) **2** : ginebra *f* (bebida alcohólica)

ginger ['dʒɪndʒər] *n* : jengibre *m*

ginger ale *n* : ginger ale *m,* gaseosa *f* de jengibre

gingerbread ['dʒɪndʒər,brɛd] *n* : pan *m* de jengibre

gingerly ['dʒɪndʒərli] *adv* : con cuidado, cautelosamente

gingham ['gɪŋəm] *n* : guinga *f*

ginseng ['dʒɪn,sɪŋ, -,sɛŋ] *n* : ginseng *m*

giraffe [dʒə'ræf] *n* : jirafa *f*

gird ['gərd] *vt* **girded** *or* **girt** ['gərt]; **girding 1** BIND : ceñir, atar **2** ENCIRCLE : rodear **3 to gird oneself** : prepararse

girder ['gərdər] *n* : viga *f*

girdle[1] ['gərdəl] *vt* **-dled; -dling 1** GIRD : ceñir, atar **2** SURROUND : rodear, circundar

girdle[2] *n* : faja *f*

girl ['gərl] *n* **1** : niña *f,* muchacha *f,* chica *f* **2** SWEETHEART : novia *f* **3** DAUGHTER : hija *f*

girlfriend ['gərl,frɛnd] *n* : novia *f,* amiga *f*

girlhood ['gərl,hʊd] *n* : niñez *f,* juventud *f* (de una muchacha)

girlish ['gərlɪʃ] *adj* : de niña

girth ['gərθ] *n* **1** : circunferencia *f* (de un árbol, etc.), cintura *f* (de una persona) **2** CINCH : cincha *f* (para caballos, etc.)

gist ['dʒɪst] *n* : quid *m,* meollo *m*

give[1] ['gɪv] *v* **gave** ['geɪv]; **given** ['gɪvən]; **giving** *vt* **1** HAND, PRESENT : dar, regalar, obsequiar <give it to me : dámelo> <they gave him a gold watch : le regalaron un reloj de oro> **2** PAY : dar, pagar <I'll give you $10 for this one : te daré $10 por éste> **3** UTTER : dar, pronunciar <to give a shout : dar un grito> <to give a speech : pronunciar un discurso> <to give a verdict : dictar sentencia> **4** PROVIDE : dar <to give one's word : dar uno su palabra> <to give a party : dar una fiesta> **5** CAUSE : dar, causar, ocasionar <to give trouble : causar problemas> <to give someone to understand : darle a entender a alguien> **6** GRANT : dar, otorgar <to give permission : dar permiso> — *vi* **1** : hacer regalos **2** YIELD : ceder, romperse <it gave under the weight of the crowd : cedió bajo el peso de la muchedumbre> **3 to give in** *or* **to give up** SURRENDER : rendirse, entregarse **4 to give out** : agotarse, acabarse <the supplies gave out : las provisiones se agotaron>

give[2] *n* FLEXIBILITY : flexibilidad *f,* elasticidad *f*

giveaway ['gɪvə,weɪ] *n* **1** : revelación *f* involuntaria **2** GIFT : regalo *m,* obsequio *m*

given ['gɪvən] *adj* **1** INCLINED : dado, inclinado <he's given to quarreling : es muy dado a discutir> **2** SPECIFIC : dado, determinado <at a given time : en un momento dado>

given name *n* : nombre *m* de pila

give up *vt* : dejar, renunciar a, abandonar <to give up smoking : dejar de fumar>

gizzard ['gɪzərd] *n* : molleja *f*

glacial ['gleɪʃəl] *adj* : glacial — **glacially** *adv*

glacier ['gleɪʃər] *n* : glaciar *m*

glad ['glæd] *adj* **gladder; gladdest 1** PLEASED : alegre, contento <she was glad I came : se alegró de que haya venido> <glad to meet you! : ¡mucho gusto!> **2** HAPPY, PLEASING : feliz, agradable <glad tidings : buenas nuevas> **3** WILLING : dispuesto, gustoso <I'll be glad to do it : lo haré con mucho gusto>

gladden ['glædən] *vt* : alegrar

glade ['gleɪd] *n* : claro *m*

gladiator ['glædi,eɪtər] *n* : gladiador *m*

gladiolus [,glædi'oːləs] *n, pl* **-li** [-li, -,laɪ] : gladiolo *m,* gladíolo *m*

gladly ['glædli] *adv* : con mucho gusto

gladness ['glædnəs] *n* : alegría *f,* gozo *m*

glamor *or* **glamour** ['glæmər] *n* : atractivo *m,* hechizo *m,* encanto *m*

glamorous ['glæmərəs] *adj* : atractivo, encantador

glance[1] ['glænts] *vi* **glanced; glancing 1** RICOCHET : rebotar <it glanced off the wall : rebotó en la pared> **2 to glance at** : mirar, echar un vistazo a **3 to glance away** : apartar los ojos

glance[2] *n* : mirada *f,* vistazo *m,* ojeada *f*

gland ['glænd] *n* : glándula *f*

glandular ['glændʒʊlər] *adj* : glandular

glare[1] ['glær] *vi* **glared; glaring 1** SHINE : brillar, relumbrar **2** STARE : mirar con ira, lanzar una mirada feroz

glare[2] *n* **1** BRIGHTNESS : resplandor *m,* luz *f* deslumbrante **2** : mirada *f* feroz

glaring ['glærɪŋ] *adj* **1** BRIGHT : deslumbrante, brillante **2** FLAGRANT, OBVIOUS : flagrante, manifiesto <a glaring error : un error que salta a la vista>

glass ['glæs] *n* **1** : vidrio *m,* cristal *m* <stained glass : vidrio de color> **2** : vaso *m* <a glass of milk : un vaso de leche> **3 glasses** *npl* SPECTACLES : gafas *fpl,* anteojos *mpl,* lentes *mpl,* espejuelos *mpl*

glassblowing ['glæs,bloːɪŋ] *n* : soplado *m* del vidrio
glassful ['glæs,fʊl] *n* : vaso *m,* copa *f*
glassware ['glæs,wær] *n* : cristalería *f*
glassy ['glæsi] *adj* **glassier; -est 1** VITREOUS : vítreo **2** : vidrioso <glassy eyes : ojos vidriosos>
glaze¹ ['gleɪz] *vt* **glazed; glazing 1** : ponerle vidrios a (una ventana, etc.) **2** : vidriar (cerámica) **3** : glasear (papel, verduras, etc.)
glaze² *n* : vidriado *m,* glaseado *m,* barniz *m*
glazier ['gleɪʒər] *n* : vidriero *m,* -ra *f*
gleam¹ ['gliːm] *vi* : brillar, destellar, relucir
gleam² *n* **1** LIGHT : luz *f* (oscura) **2** GLINT : destello *m* **3** GLIMMER : rayo *m,* vislumbre *f* <a gleam of hope : un rayo de esperanza>
glean ['gliːn] *vt* : recoger, espigar
glee ['gliː] *n* : alegría *f,* júbilo *m,* regocijo *m*
gleeful ['gliːfəl] *adj* : lleno de alegría
glen ['glɛn] *n* : cañada *f*
glib ['glɪb] *adj* **glibber; glibbest 1** : simplista <a glib reply : una respuesta simplista> **2** : con mucha labia (dícese de una persona)
glibly ['glɪbli] *adv* : con mucha labia
glide¹ ['glaɪd] *vi* **glided; gliding** : deslizarse (en una superficie), planear (en el aire)
glide² *n* : planeo *m*
glider ['glaɪdər] *n* **1** : planeador *m* (aeronave) **2** : mecedor *m* (tipo de columpio)
glimmer¹ ['glɪmər] *vi* : brillar con luz trémula
glimmer² *n* **1** : luz *f* trémula, luz *f* tenue **2** GLEAM : rayo *m,* vislumbre *f* <a glimmer of understanding : un rayo de entendimiento>
glimpse¹ ['glɪmps] *vt* **glimpsed; glimpsing** : vislumbrar, entrever
glimpse² *n* : mirada *f* breve <to catch a glimpse of : alcanzar a ver, vislumbrar>
glint¹ ['glɪnt] *vi* GLEAM, SPARKLE : destellar, fulgurar
glint² *n* **1** SPARKLE : destello *m,* centelleo *m* **2 to have a glint in one's eye** : chispearle los ojos a uno
glisten¹ ['glɪsən] *vi* : brillar, centellear
glisten² *n* : brillo *m,* centelleo *m*
glitter¹ ['glɪt̬ər] *vi* **1** SPARKLE : destellar, relucir, brillar **2** FLASH : relampaguear <his eyes glittered in anger : le relampagueaban los ojos de ira>
glitter² *n* **1** BRIGHTNESS : brillo *m* **2** : purpurina *f* (para decoración)
gloat ['gloːt] *vi* **to gloat over** : regodearse en
glob ['glɑb] *n* : plasta *f,* masa *f,* grumo *m*
global ['gloːbəl] *adj* **1** SPHERICAL : esférico **2** WORLDWIDE : global, mundial **— globally** *adv*
globe ['gloːb] *n* **1** SPHERE : esfera *f,* globo *m* **2** EARTH : globo *m,* Tierra *f* **3** : globo *m* terráqueo (modelo de la Tierra)
globe–trotter ['gloːb,trɑt̬ər] *n* : trotamundos *mf*
globular ['glɑbjʊlər] *adj* : globular
globule ['glɑ,bjuːl] *n* : glóbulo *m*
gloom ['gluːm] *n* **1** DARKNESS : penumbra *f,* oscuridad *f* **2** MELANCHOLY : melancolía *f,* tristeza *f*
gloomily ['gluːməli] *adv* : tristemente
gloomy ['gluːmi] *adj* **gloomier; -est 1** DARK : oscuro, tenebroso <gloomy weather : tiempo gris> **2** MELANCHOLY : melancólico **3** PESSIMISTIC : pesimista **4** DEPRESSING : deprimente, lúgubre
glorification [,glorəfə'keɪʃən] *n* : glorificación *f*
glorify ['glorə,faɪ] *vt* **-fied; -fying** : glorificar
glorious ['gloriəs] *adj* **1** ILLUSTRIOUS : glorioso, ilustre **2** MAGNIFICENT : magnífico, espléndido, maravilloso **— gloriously** *adv*
glory¹ ['glori] *vi* **-ried; -rying** EXULT : exultar, regocijarse
glory² *n, pl* **-ries 1** RENOWN : gloria *f,* fama *f,* honor *m* **2** PRAISE : gloria *f* <glory to God : gloria a Dios> **3** MAGNIFICENCE : magnificencia *f,* esplendor *m,* gloria *f* **4 to be in one's glory** : estar uno en su gloria
gloss¹ ['glɔs, 'glɑs] *vt* **1** EXPLAIN : glosar, explicar **2** POLISH : lustrar, pulir **3 to gloss over** : quitarle importancia a, minimizar
gloss² *n* **1** SHINE : lustre *m,* brillo *m* **2** EXPLANATION : glosa *f,* explicación *f* breve **3 → glossary**
glossary ['glɔsəri, 'glɑ-] *n, pl* **-ries** : glosario *m*
glossy ['glɔsi, 'glɑ-] *adj* **glossier; -est** : brillante, lustroso, satinado (dícese del papel)
glove ['glʌv] *n* : guante *m*
glow¹ ['gloː] *vi* **1** SHINE : brillar, resplandecer **2** BRIM : rebosar <to glow with health : rebosar de salud>
glow² *n* **1** BRIGHTNESS : resplandor *m,* brillo *m,* luminosidad *f* **2** FEELING : sensación *f* (de bienestar), oleada *f* (de sentimiento) **3** INCANDESCENCE : incandescencia *f*
glower ['glaʊər] *vi* : fruncir el ceño
glowworm ['gloː,wərm] *n* : luciérnaga *f*
glucose ['gluː,koːs] *n* : glucosa *f*
glue¹ ['gluː] *vt* **glued; gluing** *or* **glueing** : pegar, encolar
glue² *n* : pegamento *m,* cola *f*
gluey ['gluːi] *adj* **gluier; -est** : pegajoso
glum ['glʌm] *adj* **glummer; glummest 1** SULLEN : hosco, sombrío **2** DREARY, GLOOMY : sombrío, triste, melancólico

glut[1] [ˈglʌt] *vt* **glutted; glutting 1** SATIATE : saciar, hartar **2** : inundar (el mercado)
glut[2] *n* : exceso *m,* superabundancia *f*
glutinous [ˈgluːtənəs] *adj* STICKY : pegajoso, glutinoso
glutton [ˈglʌtən] *n* : glotón *m,* -tona *f*
gluttonous [ˈglʌtənəs] *adj* : glotón
gluttony [ˈglʌtəni] *n, pl* **-tonies** : glotonería *f,* gula *f*
gnarled [ˈnɑrld] *adj* **1** KNOTTY : nudoso **2** TWISTED : retorcido
gnash [ˈnæʃ] *vt* : hacer rechinar (los dientes)
gnat [ˈnæt] *n* : jején *m*
gnaw [ˈnɔ] *vt* : roer
gnome [ˈnoːm] *n* : gnomo *m*
gnu [ˈnuː, ˈnjuː] *n, pl* **gnu** *or* **gnus** : ñu *m*
go[1] [ˈgoː] *v* **went** [ˈwɛnt]; **gone** [ˈgɔn, ˈgɑn]; **going; goes** [ˈgoːz] *vi* **1** PROCEED : ir <to go slow : ir despacio> <to go shopping : ir de compras> **2** LEAVE : irse, marcharse, salir <let's go! : ¡vámonos!> <the train went on time : el tren salió a tiempo> **3** DISAPPEAR : desaparecer, pasarse, irse <her fear is gone : se le ha pasado el miedo> <my pen is gone! : ¡mi pluma desapareció!> **4** EXTEND : ir, extenderse, llegar <this road goes to the river : este camino se extiende hasta el río> <to go from top to bottom : ir de arriba abajo> **5** FUNCTION : funcionar, marchar <the car won't go : el coche no funciona> <to get something going : poner algo en marcha> **6** SELL : venderse <it goes for $15 : se vende por $15> **7** PROGRESS : ir, andar, seguir <my exam went well : me fue bien en el examen> <how did the meeting go? : ¿qué tal la reunión?> **8** BECOME : volverse, quedarse <he's going crazy : está volviéndose loco> <the tire went flat : la llanta se desinfló> **9** FIT : caber <it will go through the door : cabe por la puerta> **10 anything goes!** : ¡todo vale! **11 to go** : faltar <only 10 days to go : faltan sólo 10 días> **12 to go back on** : faltar uno a (su promesa) **13 to go bad** SPOIL : estropearse, echarse a perder **14 to go for** : interesarse uno en, gustarle a uno (algo, alguien) <I don't go for that : eso no me interesa> **15 to go off** EXPLODE : estallar **16 to go with** MATCH : armonizar con, hacer juego con — *v aux* **to be going to** : ir a <I'm going to write a letter : voy a escribir una carta> <it's not going to last : no va a durar>
go[2] *n, pl* **goes 1** ATTEMPT : intento *m* <to have a go at : intentar, probar> **2** SUCCESS : éxito *m* **3** ENERGY : energía *f,* empuje *m* <to be on the go : no parar, no descansar>
goad[1] [ˈgoːd] *vt* : aguijonear (un animal), incitar (a una persona)
goad[2] *n* : aguijón *m*
goal [ˈgoːl] *n* **1** : gol *m* (en deportes) <to score a goal : anotar un gol> **2** *or* **goalposts** : portería *f* **3** AIM, OBJECTIVE : meta *m,* objetivo *m*
goalie [ˈgoːli] → **goalkeeper**
goalkeeper [ˈgoːlˌkiːpər] *n* : portero *m,* -ra *f;* guardameta *mf;* arquero *m,* -ra *f*
goaltender [ˈgoːlˌtɛndər] → **goalkeeper**
goat [ˈgoːt] *n* **1** : cabra *f* (hembra) **2 billy goat** : macho *m* cabrío, chivo *m*
goatee [goːˈtiː] *n* : barbita *f* de chivo, piocha *f Mex*
goatskin [ˈgoːtˌskɪn] *n* : piel *f* de cabra
gob [ˈgɑb] *n* : masa *f,* grumo *m*
gobble [ˈgɑbəl] *v* **-bled; -bling** *vt* **to gobble up** : tragar, engullir — *vi* : hacer ruidos de pavo
gobbledygook [ˈgɑbəldiˌgʊk, -ˌguːk] *n* GIBBERISH : jerigonza *f*
go–between [ˈgoːbɪˌtwiːn] *n* : intermediario *m,* -ria *f;* mediador *m,* -dora *f*
goblet [ˈgɑblət] *n* : copa *f*
goblin [ˈgɑblən] *n* : duende *m,* trasgo *m*
god [ˈgɑd, ˈgɔd] *n* **1** : dios *m* **2 God** : Dios *m*
godchild [ˈgɑdˌtʃaɪld, ˈgɔd-] *n, pl* **-children** : ahijado *m,* -da *f*
goddess [ˈgɑdəs, ˈgɔ-] *n* : diosa *f*
godfather [ˈgɑdˌfɑðər, ˈgɔd-] *n* : padrino *m*
godless [ˈgɑdləs, ˈgɔd-] *adj* : ateo
godlike [ˈgɑdˌlaɪk, ˈgɔd-] *adj* : divino
godly [ˈgɑdli, ˈgɔd-] *adj* **-lier; -est 1** DIVINE : divino **2** DEVOUT, PIOUS : piadoso, devoto, beato
godmother [ˈgɑdˌmʌðər, ˈgɔd-] *n* : madrina *f*
godparents [ˈgɑdˌpærənts, ˈgɔd-] *npl* : padrinos *mpl*
godsend [ˈgɑdˌsɛnd, ˈgɔd-] *n* : bendición *f,* regalo *m* divino
goes → **go**
go–getter [ˈgoːˌgɛtər] *n* : persona *f* ambiciosa, buscavidas *mf fam*
goggle [ˈgɑgəl] *vi* **-gled; -gling** : mirar con ojos desorbitados
goggles [ˈgɑgəlz] *npl* : gafas *fpl* (protectoras), anteojos *mpl*
goings–on [ˌgoːɪŋzˈɑn, -ˈɔn] *npl* : sucesos *mpl,* ocurrencias *fpl*
goiter [ˈgɔɪtər] *n* : bocio *m*
gold [ˈgoːld] *n* : oro *m*
golden [ˈgoːldən] *adj* **1** : (hecho) de oro **2** : dorado, de color oro <golden hair : pelo rubio> **3** FLOURISHING, PROSPEROUS : dorado, próspero <golden years : años dorados> **4** FAVORABLE : favorable, excelente <a golden opportunity : una excelente oportunidad>
goldenrod [ˈgoːldənˌrɑd] *n* : vara *f* de oro
golden rule *n* : regla *f* de oro
goldfinch [ˈgoːldˌfɪntʃ] *n* : jilguero *m*

goldfish [ˈgoːld,fɪʃ] *n* **:** pez *m* de colores
goldsmith [ˈgoːld,smɪθ] *n* **:** orífice *mf,* orfebre *mf*
golf[1] [ˈgɑlf, ˈgɔlf] *vi* **:** jugar (al) golf
golf[2] *n* **:** golf *m*
golfer [ˈgɑlfər, ˈgɔl-] *n* **:** golfista *mf*
gondola [ˈgɑndələ, gɑnˈdoːlə] *n* **:** góndola *f*
gone [ˈgɔn] *adj* **1** DEAD **:** muerto **2** PAST **:** pasado, ido **3** LOST **:** perdido, desaparecido **4 to be far gone :** estar muy avanzado **5 to be gone on :** estar loco por
goner [ˈgɔnər] *n* **to be a goner :** estar en las últimas
gong [ˈgɔŋ, ˈgɑŋ] *n* **:** gong *m*
gonorrhea [,gɑnəˈriːə] *n* **:** gonorrea *f*
good[1] [ˈgʊd] *adv* **1** (*used as an intensifier*) **:** bien <a good strong rope : una cuerda bien fuerte> **2** WELL **:** bien
good[2] *adj* **better** [ˈbɛt̬ər]; **best** [ˈbɛst] **1** PLEASANT **:** bueno, agradable <good news : buenas noticias> <to have a good time : divertirse> **2** BENEFICIAL **:** bueno, beneficioso <good for a cold : beneficioso para los resfriados> <it's good for you : es bueno para uno> **3** FULL **:** completo, entero <a good hour : una hora entera> **4** CONSIDERABLE **:** bueno, bastante <a good many people : muchísima gente, un buen número de gente> **5** ATTRACTIVE, DESIRABLE **:** bueno, bien <a good salary : un buen sueldo> <to look good : quedar bien> **6** KIND, VIRTUOUS **:** bueno, amable <she's a good person : es buena gente> <that's good of you! : ¡qué amable!> <good deeds : buenas obras> **7** SKILLED **:** bueno, hábil <to be good at : tener facilidad para> **8** SOUND **:** bueno, sensato <good advice : buenos consejos> **9** (*in greetings*) **:** bueno <good morning : buenos días> <good afternoon (evening) : buenas tardes> <good night : buenas noches>
good[3] *n* **1** RIGHT **:** bien *m* <to do good : hacer el bien> **2** GOODNESS **:** bondad *f* **3** BENEFIT **:** bien *m,* provecho *m* <it's for your own good : es por tu propio bien> **4 goods** *npl* PROPERTY **:** efectos *mpl* personales, posesiones *fpl* **5 goods** *npl* WARES **:** mercancía *f,* mercadería *f,* artículos *mpl* **6 for ~ :** para siempre
good–bye *or* **good–by** [gʊdˈbaɪ] *n* **:** adiós *m*
good–for–nothing [ˈgʊdfər,nʌθɪŋ] *n* **:** inútil *mf;* haragán *m,* -gana *f;* holgazán *m,* -zana *f*
Good Friday *n* **:** Viernes *m* Santo
good–hearted [ˈgʊdˈhɑrt̬əd] *adj* **:** bondadoso, benévolo, de buen corazón
good–looking [ˈgʊdˈlʊkɪŋ] *adj* **:** bello, bonito, guapo
goodly [ˈgʊdli] *adj* **-lier; -est :** considerable, importante <a goodly number : un número considerable>
good–natured [ˈgʊdˈneɪtʃərd] *adj* **:** amigable, amistoso, bonachón *fam*
goodness [ˈgʊdnəs] *n* **1 :** bondad *f* **2 thank goodness! :** ¡gracias a Dios!, ¡menos mal!
good–tempered [ˈgʊdˈtɛmpərd] *adj* **:** de buen genio
goodwill [,gʊdˈwɪl] *n* **1** BENEVOLENCE **:** benevolencia *f,* buena voluntad *f* **2 :** buen nombre *m* (de comercios), renombre *m* comercial
goody [ˈgʊdi] *n, pl* **goodies :** cosa *f* rica para comer, golosina *f*
gooey [ˈguːi] *adj* **gooier; gooiest :** pegajoso
goof[1] [ˈguːf] *vi* **1 to goof off :** holgazanear **2 to goof around :** hacer tonterías **3 to goof up** BLUNDER **:** cometer un error
goof[2] *n* **1 :** bobo *m,* -ba *f;* tonto *m,* -ta *f* **2** BLUNDER **:** error *m,* planchazo *m fam*
goofy [ˈguːfi] *adj* **goofier; -est** SILLY **:** tonto, bobo
goose [ˈguːs] *n, pl* **geese** [ˈgiːs] **:** ganso *m,* -sa *f;* ánsar *m;* oca *f*
gooseberry [ˈguːs,bɛriː, ˈguːz-] *n, pl* **-berries :** grosella *f* espinosa
goose bumps *npl* **:** carne *f* de gallina
gooseflesh [ˈguːs,flɛʃ] → **goose bumps**
goose pimples → **goose bumps**
gopher [ˈgoːfər] *n* **:** taltuza *f*
gore[1] [ˈgor] *vt* **gored; goring :** cornear
gore[2] *n* BLOOD **:** sangre *f*
gorge[1] [ˈgɔrdʒ] *vt* **gorged; gorging 1** SATIATE **:** saciar, hartar **2 to gorge oneself :** hartarse, atiborrarse, atracarse *fam*
gorge[2] *n* RAVINE **:** desfiladero *m*
gorgeous [ˈgɔrdʒəs] *adj* **:** hermoso, espléndido, magnífico
gorilla [gəˈrɪlə] *n* **:** gorila *m*
gory [ˈgori] *adj* **gorier; -est** BLOODY **:** sangriento
gosling [ˈgɑzlɪŋ, ˈgɔz-] *n* **:** ansarino *m*
gospel [ˈgɑspəl] *n* **1** *or* **Gospel :** evangelio *m* <the four Gospels : los cuatro evangelios> **2 the gospel truth :** el evangelio, la pura verdad
gossamer [ˈgɑsəmər, ˈgɑzə-] *adj* **:** tenue, sutil <gossamer wings : alas tenues>
gossip[1] [ˈgɑsɪp] *vi* **:** chismear, contar chismes
gossip[2] *n* **1 :** chismoso *m,* -sa *f* (persona) **2** RUMOR **:** chisme *m,* rumor *m*
gossipy [ˈgɑsɪpi] *adj* **:** chismoso
got → **get**
Gothic [ˈgɑθɪk] *adj* **:** gótico
gotten → **get**
gouge[1] [ˈgaʊdʒ] *vt* **gouged; gouging 1 :** excavar, escoplear (con una gubia) **2** SWINDLE **:** estafar, extorsionar

gouge[2] *n* **1** CHISEL : gubia *f,* formón *m* **2** GROOVE : ranura *f,* hoyo *m* (hecho por un formón)
goulash [ˈguːˌlɑʃ, -ˌlæʃ] *n* : estofado *m,* guiso *m* al estilo húngaro
gourd [ˈgord, ˈgʊrd] *n* : calabaza *f*
gourmand [ˈgʊrˌmɑnd] *n* **1** GLUTTON : glotón *m,* -tona *f* **2** → **gourmet**
gourmet [ˈgʊrˌmeɪ, gʊrˈmeɪ] *n* : gourmet *mf;* gastrónomo *m,* -ma *f*
gout [ˈgaʊt] *n* : gota *f*
govern [ˈgʌvərn] *vt* **1** RULE : gobernar **2** CONTROL, DETERMINE : determinar, controlar, guiar **3** RESTRAIN : dominar (las emociones, etc.) — *vi* : gobernar
governess [ˈgʌvərnəs] *n* : institutriz *f*
government [ˈgʌvərmənt] *n* : gobierno *m*
governmental [ˌgʌvərˈmɛntəl] *adj* : gubernamental, gubernativo
governor [ˈgʌvənər, ˈgʌvərnər] *n* **1** : gobernador *m,* -dora *f* (de un estado, etc.) **2** : regulador *m* (de una máquina)
governorship [ˈgʌvənərˌʃɪp, ˈgʌvərnər-] *n* : cargo *m* de gobernador
gown [ˈgaʊn] *n* **1** : vestido *m* <evening gown : traje de fiesta> **2** : toga *f* (de magistrados, clérigos, etc.)
grab[1] [ˈgræb] *v* **grabbed; grabbing** *vt* SNATCH : agarrar, arrebatar — *vi* : agarrarse
grab[2] *n* **1 to make a grab for** : tratar de agarrar **2 up for grabs** : disponible, libre
grace[1] [ˈgreɪs] *vt* **graced; gracing 1** HONOR : honrar **2** ADORN : adornar, embellecer
grace[2] *n* **1** : gracia *f* <by the grace of God : por la gracia de Dios> **2** BLESSING : bendición *f* (de la mesa) **3** RESPITE : plazo *m,* gracia *f* <a five days' grace (period) : un plazo de cinco días> **4** GRACIOUSNESS : gentileza *f,* cortesía *f* **5** ELEGANCE : elegancia *f,* gracia *f* **6 to be in the good graces of** : estar en buenas relaciones con **7 with good grace** : de buena gana
graceful [ˈgreɪsfəl] *adj* : lleno de gracia, garboso, grácil
gracefully [ˈgreɪsfəli] *adv* : con gracia, con garbo
gracefulness [ˈgreɪsfəlnəs] *n* : gracilidad *f,* apostura *f,* gallardía *f*
graceless [ˈgreɪsləs] *adj* **1** DISCOURTEOUS : descortés **2** CLUMSY, INELEGANT : torpe, desgarbado, poco elegante
gracious [ˈgreɪʃəs] *adj* : cortés, gentil, cordial
graciously [ˈgreɪʃəsli] *adv* : gentilmente
graciousness [ˈgreɪʃəsnəs] *n* : gentileza *f*
gradation [greɪˈdeɪʃən, grə-] *n* : gradación *f*
grade[1] [ˈgreɪd] *vt* **graded; grading 1** SORT : clasificar **2** LEVEL : nivelar **3** : calificar (exámenes, alumnos)
grade[2] *n* **1** QUALITY : categoría *f,* calidad *f* **2** RANK : grado *m,* rango *m* (militar) **3** YEAR : grado *m,* curso *m,* año *m* <sixth grade : el sexto grado> **4** MARK : nota *f,* calificación *f* (en educación) **5** SLOPE : cuesta *f,* pendiente *f,* gradiente *f*
grade school → **elementary school**
gradual [ˈgrædʒʊəl] *adj* : gradual, paulatino
gradually [ˈgrædʒʊəli, ˈgrædʒəli] *adv* : gradualmente, poco a poco
graduate[1] [ˈgrædʒʊˌeɪt] *v* **-ated; -ating** *vi* : graduarse, licenciarse — *vt* : graduar <a graduated thermometer : un termómetro graduado>
graduate[2] [ˈgrædʒʊət] *adj* : de postgrado <graduate course : curso de postgrado>
graduate[3] *n* **1** : licenciado *m,* -da *f;* graduado *m,* -da *f* (de la universidad) **2** : bachiller *mf* (de la escuela secundaria)
graduate student *n* : postgraduado *m,* -da *f*
graduation [ˌgrædʒʊˈeɪʃən] *n* : graduación *f*
graffiti [grəˈfiːti, græ-] *npl* : pintadas *fpl,* graffiti *mpl*
graft[1] [ˈgræft] *vt* : injertar
graft[2] *n* **1** : injerto *m* <skin graft : injerto cutáneo> **2** CORRUPTION : soborno *m* (político), ganancia *f* ilegal
grain [ˈgreɪn] *n* **1** : grano *m* <a grain of corn : un grano de maíz> <like a grain of sand : como grano de arena> **2** CEREALS : cereales *mpl* **3** : veta *f,* vena *f,* grano *m* (de madera) **4** SPECK, TRACE : pizca *f,* ápice *m* <a grain of truth : una pizca de verdad> **5** : grano *m* (unidad de peso)
gram [ˈgræm] *n* : gramo *m*
grammar [ˈgræmər] *n* : gramática *f*
grammar school → **elementary school**
grammatical [grəˈmætɪkəl] *adj* : gramatical — **grammatically** [-kli] *adv*
granary [ˈgreɪnəri, ˈgræ-] *n, pl* **-ries** : granero *m*
grand [ˈgrænd] *adj* **1** FOREMOST : grande **2** IMPRESSIVE : impresionante, magnífico <a grand view : una vista magnífica> **3** LAVISH : grandioso, suntuoso, lujoso <to live in a grand manner : vivir a lo grande> **4** FABULOUS : fabuloso, magnífico <to have a grand time : pasarlo estupendamente, pasarlo en grande> **5 grand total** : total *m,* suma *f* total
grandchild [ˈgrændˌtʃaɪld] *n, pl* **-children** : nieto *m,* -ta *f*
granddaughter [ˈgrændˌdɔtər] *n* : nieta *f*
grandeur [ˈgrændʒər] *n* : grandiosidad *f,* esplendor *m*
grandfather [ˈgrændˌfɑðər] *n* : abuelo *m*
grandiose [ˈgrændiˌoːs, ˌgrændiˈ-] *adj* **1** IMPOSING : imponente, grandioso **2** POMPOUS : pomposo, presuntuoso

grandmother ['grænd,mʌðər] *n* : abuela *f*
grandparents ['grænd,pærənts] *npl* : abuelos *mpl*
grandson ['grænd,sʌn] *n* : nieto *m*
grandstand ['grænd,stænd] *n* : tribuna *f*
granite ['grænɪt] *n* : granito *m*
grant[1] ['grænt] *vt* **1** ALLOW : conceder <to grant a request : conceder una petición> **2** BESTOW : conceder, dar, otorgar <to grant a favor : otorgar un favor> **3** ADMIT : reconocer, admitir <I'll grant that he's clever : reconozco que es listo> **4 to take for granted** : dar (algo) por sentado
grant[2] *n* **1** GRANTING : concesión *f,* otorgamiento *m* **2** SCHOLARSHIP : beca *f* **3** SUBSIDY : subvención *f*
granular ['grænjʊlər] *adj* : granular
granulated ['grænjʊ,leɪt̬əd] *adj* : granulado
grape ['greɪp] *n* : uva *f*
grapefruit ['greɪp,fruːt] *n* : toronja *f,* pomelo *m*
grapevine ['greɪp,vaɪn] *n* **1** : vid *f,* parra *f* **2 through the grapevine** : por vías secretas <I heard it through the grapevine : me lo contaron>
graph ['græf] *n* : gráfica *f,* gráfico *m*
graphic ['græfɪk] *adj* **1** VIVID : vívido, gráfico **2 graphic arts** : artes gráficas
graphically ['græfɪkli] *adv* : gráficamente
graphite ['græ,faɪt] *n* : grafito *m*
grapnel ['græpnəl] *n* : rezón *m*
grapple ['græpəl] *vi* **-pled; -pling 1** GRIP : agarrar (con un garfio) **2** STRUGGLE : forcejear, luchar (con un problema, etc.)
grasp[1] ['græsp] *vt* **1** GRIP, SEIZE : agarrar, asir **2** COMPREHEND : entender, comprender — *vi* **to grasp at** : aprovechar
grasp[2] *n* **1** GRIP : agarre *m* **2** CONTROL : control *m,* garras *fpl* **3** REACH : alcance *m* <within your grasp : a su alcance> **4** UNDERSTANDING : comprensión *f,* entendimiento *m*
grass ['græs] *n* **1** : hierba *f* (planta) **2** PASTURE : pasto *m,* zacate *m CA, Mex* **3** LAWN : césped *m,* pasto *m*
grasshopper ['græs,hɑpər] *n* : saltamontes *m*
grassland ['græs,lænd] *n* : pradera *f*
grassy ['græsi] *adj* **grassier; -est** : cubierto de hierba
grate[1] ['greɪt] *v* **grated; -ing** *vt* **1** : rallar (en cocina) **2** SCRAPE : rascar **3 to grate one's teeth** : hacer rechinar los dientes — *vi* **1** RASP, SQUEAK : chirriar **2** IRRITATE : irritar <to grate on one's nerves : crisparle los nervios a uno>
grate[2] *n* **1** : parrilla *f* (para cocinar) **2** GRATING : reja *f,* rejilla *f,* verja *f* (en una ventana)
grateful ['greɪtfəl] *adj* : agradecido
gratefully ['greɪtfəli] *adv* : con agradecimiento
gratefulness ['greɪtfəlnəs] *n* : gratitud *f,* agradecimiento *m*
grater ['greɪt̬ər] *n* : rallador *m*
gratification [,græt̬əfə'keɪʃən] *n* : gratificación *f*
gratify ['græt̬ə,faɪ] *vt* **-fied; -fying 1** PLEASE : complacer **2** SATISFY : satisfacer, gratificar
grating ['greɪt̬ɪŋ] *n* : reja *f,* rejilla *f*
gratis[1] ['græt̬əs, 'greɪ-] *adv* : gratis, gratuitamente
gratis[2] *adj* : gratis, gratuito
gratitude ['græt̬ə,tuːd, -,tjuːd] *n* : gratitud *f,* agradecimiento *m*
gratuitous [grə'tuːət̬əs] *adj* : gratuito
gratuity [grə'tuːət̬i] *n, pl* **-ities** TIP : propina *f*
grave[1] ['greɪv] *adj* **graver; -est 1** IMPORTANT : grave, de mucha gravedad **2** SERIOUS, SOLEMN : grave, serio
grave[2] *n* : tumba *f,* sepultura *f*
gravel ['grævəl] *n* : grava *f,* gravilla *f*
gravelly ['grævəli] *adj* **1** : de grava **2** HARSH : áspero (dícese de la voz)
gravely ['greɪvli] *adv* : gravemente
gravestone ['greɪv,stoːn] *n* : lápida *f*
graveyard ['greɪv,jɑrd] *n* CEMETERY : cementerio *m,* panteón *m,* camposanto *m*
gravitate ['grævə,teɪt] *vi* **-tated; -tating** : gravitar
gravitation [,grævə'teɪʃən] *n* : gravitación *f*
gravitational [,grævə'teɪʃənəl] *adj* : gravitacional
gravity ['grævət̬i] *n, pl* **-ties 1** SERIOUSNESS : gravedad *f,* seriedad *f* **2** : gravedad *f* <the law of gravity : la ley de la gravedad>
gravy ['greɪvi] *n, pl* **-vies** : salsa *f* (preparada con el jugo de la carne asada)
gray[1] ['greɪ] *vt* : hacer gris — *vi* : encanecer, ponerse gris
gray[2] *adj* **1** : gris (dícese del color) **2** : cano, canoso <gray hair : pelo canoso> <to go gray : volverse cano> **3** DISMAL, GLOOMY : gris, triste
gray[3] *n* : gris *m*
grayish ['greɪɪʃ] *adj* : grisáceo
graze ['greɪz] *v* **grazed; grazing** *vi* : pastar, pacer — *vt* **1** : pastorear (ganado) **2** BRUSH : rozar **3** SCRATCH : raspar
grease[1] ['griːs, 'griːz] *vt* **greased; greasing** : engrasar, lubricar
grease[2] ['griːs] *n* : grasa *f*
greasy ['griːsi, -zi] *adj* **greasier; -est 1** : grasiento **2** OILY : graso, grasoso
great ['greɪt] *adj* **1** LARGE : grande <a great mountain : una montaña grande> <a great crowd : una gran muchedumbre> **2** INTENSE : intenso, fuerte, grande <great pain : gran dolor> **3** EMINENT : grande, eminente, distinguido <a great poet : un gran poeta> **4** EXCELLENT, TERRIFIC : excelente, estupendo, fabuloso <to have a

great time : pasarlo en grande> **5 a great while :** mucho tiempo
great-aunt [ˌgreɪtˈænt, -ˈant] *n* **:** tía *f* abuela
greater [ˈgreɪtər] (*comparative of* **great**) **:** mayor
greatest [ˈgreɪtəst] (*superlative of* **great**) **:** el mayor, la mayor
great-grandchild [ˌgreɪtˈgrændˌtʃaɪld] *n, pl* **-children** [-ˌtʃɪldrən] **:** bisnieto *m*, -ta *f*
great-grandfather [ˌgreɪtˈgrændˌfɑðər] *n* **:** bisabuelo *m*
great-grandmother [ˌgreɪtˈgrændˌmʌðər] *n* **:** bisabuela *f*
greatly [ˈgreɪtli] *adv* **1** MUCH **:** mucho, sumamente <to be greatly improved : haber mejorado mucho> **2** VERY **:** muy <greatly superior : muy superior>
greatness [ˈgreɪtnəs] *n* **:** grandeza *f*
great-uncle [ˌgreɪtˈʌŋkəl] *n* **:** tío *m* abuelo
grebe [ˈgriːb] *n* **:** somorgujo *m*
greed [ˈgriːd] *n* **1** AVARICE **:** avaricia *f*, codicia *f* **2** GLUTTONY **:** glotonería *f*, gula *f*
greedily [ˈgriːdəli] *adv* **:** con avaricia, con gula
greediness [ˈgriːdinəs] → **greed**
greedy [ˈgriːdi] *adj* **greedier; -est 1** AVARICIOUS **:** codicioso, avaricioso **2** GLUTTONOUS **:** glotón
Greek [ˈgriːk] *n* **1 :** griego *m*, -ga *f* **2 :** griego *m* (idioma) — **Greek** *adj*
green¹ [ˈgriːn] *adj* **1 :** verde (dícese del color) **2** UNRIPE **:** verde, inmaduro **3** INEXPERIENCED **:** verde, novato
green² *n* **1 :** verde *m* **2 greens** *npl* VEGETABLES **:** verduras *fpl*
greenery [ˈgriːnəri] *n, pl* **-eries :** plantas *fpl* verdes, vegetación *f*
greenhorn [ˈgriːnˌhɔrn] *n* **:** novato *m*, -ta *f*
greenhouse [ˈgriːnˌhaʊs] *n* **:** invernadero *m*
greenhouse effect : efecto *m* invernadero
greenish [ˈgriːnɪʃ] *adj* **:** verdoso
Greenlander [ˈgriːnləndər, -ˌlæn-] *n* **:** groenlandés *m*, -desa *f*
greenness [ˈgriːnnəs] *n* **1 :** verdor *m* **2** INEXPERIENCE **:** inexperiencia *f*
green thumb *n* **to have a green thumb :** tener buena mano para las plantas
greet [ˈgriːt] *vt* **1 :** saludar <to greet a friend : saludar a un amigo> **2 :** acoger, recibir <they greeted him with boos : lo recibieron con abucheos>
greeting [ˈgriːtɪŋ] *n* **1 :** saludo *m* **2 greetings** *npl* REGARDS **:** saludos *mpl*, recuerdos *mpl*
gregarious [grɪˈgæriəs] *adj* **:** gregario (dícese de los animales), sociable (dícese de las personas) — **gregariously** *adv*
gregariousness [grɪˈgæriəsnəs] *n* **:** sociabilidad *f*
gremlin [ˈgrɛmlən] *n* **:** duende *m*
grenade [grəˈneɪd] *n* **:** granada *f*
Grenadian [grəˈneɪdiən] *n* **:** granadino *m*, -na *f* — **Grenadian** *adj*
grew → **grow**
grey → **gray**
greyhound [ˈgreɪˌhaʊnd] *n* **:** galgo *m*
grid [ˈgrɪd] *n* **1** GRATING **:** rejilla *f* **2** NETWORK **:** red *f* (de electricidad, etc.) **3 :** cuadriculado *m* (de un mapa)
griddle [ˈgrɪdəl] *n* **:** plancha *f*
griddle cake → **pancake**
gridiron [ˈgrɪdˌaɪərn] *n* **1** GRILL **:** parrilla *f* **2 :** campo *m* de futbol americano
grief [ˈgriːf] *n* **1** SORROW **:** dolor *m*, pena *f* **2** ANNOYANCE, TROUBLE **:** problemas *mpl*, molestia *f*
grievance [ˈgriːvənts] *n* COMPLAINT **:** queja *f*
grieve [ˈgriːv] *v* **grieved; grieving** *vt* DISTRESS **:** afligir, entristecer, apenar — *vi* **1 :** sufrir, afligirse **2 to grieve for** *or* **to grieve over :** llorar, lamentar
grievous [ˈgriːvəs] *adj* **1** OPPRESSIVE **:** gravoso, opresivo, severo **2** GRAVE, SERIOUS **:** grave, severo, doloroso
grievously [ˈgriːvəsli] *adv* **:** gravemente, de gravedad
grill¹ [ˈgrɪl] *vt* **1 :** asar (a la parrilla) **2** INTERROGATE **:** interrogar
grill² *n* **1 :** parrilla *f* (para cocinar) **2 :** parrillada *f* (comida) **3** RESTAURANT **:** grill *m*
grille *or* **grill** [ˈgrɪl] *n* **:** reja *f*, enrejado *m*
grim [ˈgrɪm] *adj* **grimmer; grimmest 1** CRUEL **:** cruel, feroz **2** STERN **:** adusto, severo <a grim expression : un gesto severo> **3** GLOOMY **:** sombrío, deprimente **4** SINISTER **:** macabro, siniestro **5** UNYIELDING **:** inflexible, persistente <with grim determination : con una voluntad de hierro>
grimace¹ [ˈgrɪməs, grɪˈmeɪs] *vi* **-maced; -macing :** hacer muecas
grimace² *n* **:** mueca *f*
grime [ˈgraɪm] *n* **:** mugre *f*, suciedad *f*
grimly [ˈgrɪmli] *adv* **1** STERNLY **:** severamente **2** RESOLUTELY **:** inexorablemente
grimy [ˈgraɪmi] *adj* **grimier; -est :** mugriento, sucio
grin¹ [ˈgrɪn] *vi* **grinned; grinning :** sonreír abiertamente
grin² *n* **:** sonrisa *f* abierta
grind¹ [ˈgraɪnd] *v* **ground** [ˈgraʊnd]; **grinding** *vt* **1** CRUSH **:** moler, machacar, triturar **2** SHARPEN **:** afilar **3** POLISH **:** pulir, esmerilar (lentes, espejos) **4 to grind one's teeth :** rechinarle los dientes a uno **5 to grind down** OPPRESS **:** oprimir, agobiar — *vi* **1 :** funcionar con dificultad, rechinar <to grind to a halt : pararse

poco a poco, llegar a un punto muerto> **2** STUDY **:** estudiar mucho

grind[2] *n* **:** trabajo *m* pesado <the daily grind : la rutina diaria>

grinder ['graɪndər] *n* **:** molinillo *m* <coffee grinder : molinillo de café>

grindstone ['graɪnd,sto:n] *n* **:** piedra *m* de afilar

grip[1] ['grɪp] *vt* **gripped; gripping 1** GRASP **:** agarrar, asir **2** HOLD, INTEREST **:** captar el interés de

grip[2] *n* **1** GRASP **:** agarre *m,* asidero *m* <to have a firm grip on something : agarrarse bien de algo> **2** CONTROL, HOLD **:** control *m,* dominio *m* <to lose one's grip on : perder el control de> <inflation tightened its grip on the economy : la inflación se afianzó en su dominio de la economía> **3** UNDERSTANDING **:** comprensión *f,* entendimiento *m* <to come to grips with : llegar a entender> **4** HANDLE **:** asidero *m,* empuñadura *f* (de un arma)

gripe[1] ['graɪp] *v* **griped; griping** *vt* IRRITATE, VEX **:** irritar, fastidiar, molestar — *vi* COMPLAIN **:** quejarse, rezongar

gripe[2] *n* **:** queja *f*

grippe ['grɪp] *n* **:** influenza *f,* gripe *f,* gripa *f Col, Mex*

grisly ['grɪzli] *adj* **-lier; -est :** horripilante, horroroso, truculento

grist ['grɪst] *n* **:** molienda *f* <it's all grist for the mill : todo ayuda, todo es provechoso>

gristle ['grɪsəl] *n* **:** cartílago *m*

gristly ['grɪsli] *adj* **-tlier; -est :** cartilaginoso

grit[1] ['grɪt] *vt* **gritted; gritting :** hacer rechinar (los dientes, etc.)

grit[2] *n* **1** SAND **:** arena *f* **2** GRAVEL **:** grava *f* **3** COURAGE **:** valor *m,* coraje *m* **4 grits** *npl* **:** sémola *f* de maíz

gritty ['grɪṭi] *adj* **-tier; -est 1 :** arenoso <a gritty surface : una superficie arenosa> **2** PLUCKY **:** valiente

grizzled ['grɪzəld] *adj* **:** entrecano

grizzly bear ['grɪzli] *n* **:** oso *m* pardo

groan[1] ['gro:n] *vi* **1** MOAN **:** gemir, quejarse **2** CREAK **:** crujir

groan[2] *n* **1** MOAN **:** gemido *m,* quejido *m* **2** CREAK **:** crujido *m*

grocer ['gro:sər] *n* **:** tendero *m,* -ra *f*

grocery ['gro:səri, -ʃəri] *n, pl* **-ceries 1** *or* **grocery store :** tienda *f* de comestibles, tienda *f* de abarrotes **2 groceries** *npl* **:** comestibles *mpl,* abarrotes *mpl*

groggy ['grɑgi] *adj* **-gier; -est :** atontado, grogui, tambaleante

groin ['grɔɪn] *n* **:** ingle *f*

grommet ['grɑmət, 'grʌ-] *n* **:** arandela *f*

groom[1] ['gru:m, 'grʊm] *vt* **1 :** cepillar, almohazar (un animal) **2 :** arreglar, cuidar <well-groomed : bien arreglado> **3** PREPARE **:** preparar

groom[2] *n* **1 :** mozo *m,* -za *f* de cuadra **2** BRIDEGROOM **:** novio *m*

groove[1] ['gru:v] *vt* **grooved; grooving :** acanalar, hacer ranuras en, surcar

groove[2] *n* **1** FURROW, SLOT **:** ranura *f,* surco *m* **2** RUT **:** rutina *f*

grope ['gro:p] *v* **groped; groping** *vi* **:** andar a tientas, tantear <he groped for the switch : buscó el interruptor a tientas> — *vt* **to grope one's way :** avanzar a tientas

gross[1] ['gro:s] *vt* **:** tener entrada bruta de, recaudar en bruto

gross[2] *adj* **1** FLAGRANT **:** flagrante, grave <a gross error : un error flagrante> <a gross injustice : una injusticia grave> **2** FAT **:** muy gordo, obeso **3 :** bruto <gross national product : producto nacional bruto> **4** COARSE, VULGAR **:** grosero, basto

gross[3] *n* **1** *pl* **gross :** gruesa *f* (12 docenas) **2** *or* **gross income :** ingresos *mpl* brutos

grossly ['gro:sli] *adv* **1** EXTREMELY **:** extremadamente <grossly unfair : totalmente injusto> **2** CRUDELY **:** groseramente

grotesque [gro:'tɛsk] *adj* **:** grotesco

grotesquely [gro:'tɛskli] *adv* **:** de forma grotesca

grotto ['grɑto:] *n, pl* **-toes :** gruta *f*

grouch[1] ['graʊtʃ] *vi* **:** refunfuñar, rezongar

grouch[2] *n* **1** COMPLAINT **:** queja *f* **2** GRUMBLER **:** gruñón *m,* -ñona *f;* cascarrabias *mf fam*

grouchy ['graʊtʃi] *adj* **grouchier; -est :** malhumorado, gruñón

ground[1] ['graʊnd] *vt* **1** BASE **:** fundar, basar **2** INSTRUCT **:** enseñar los conocimientos básicos a <to be well grounded in : ser muy entendido en> **3 :** conectar a tierra (un aparato eléctrico) **4 :** varar, hacer encallar (un barco) **5 :** restringir (un avión o un piloto) a la tierra

ground[2] *n* **1** EARTH, SOIL **:** suelo *m,* tierra *f* <to dig (in) the ground : cavar la tierra> <to fall to the ground : caerse al suelo> **2** LAND, TERRAIN **:** terreno *m* <hilly ground : terreno alto> <to lose ground : perder terreno> **3** BASIS, REASON **:** razón *f,* motivo *m* <grounds for complaint : motivos de queja> **4** BACKGROUND **:** fondo *m* **5** FIELD **:** campo *m,* plaza *f* <parade ground : plaza de armas> **6 :** tierra *f* (para electricidad) **7 grounds** *npl* PREMISES **:** recinto *m,* terreno *m* **8 grounds** *npl* DREGS **:** posos *mpl* (de café)

ground[3] → **grind**

groundhog ['graʊnd,hɔg] *n* **:** marmota *f* (de América)

groundless ['graʊndləs] *adj* **:** infundado

groundwork ['graʊnd,wərk] *n* **1** FOUNDATION **:** fundamento *m,* base *f* **2** PREPARATION **:** trabajo *m* preparatorio

group[1] ['gru:p] *vt* **:** agrupar

group[2] *n* **:** grupo *m,* agrupación *f,* conjunto *m,* compañía *f*

grouper [ˈgruːpər] *n* : mero *m*
grouse[1] [ˈgraʊs] *vi* **groused; grousing** : quejarse, rezongar, refunfuñar
grouse[2] *n, pl* **grouse** *or* **grouses** : urogallo *m* (ave)
grout [ˈgraʊt] *n* : lechada *f*
grove [ˈgroːv] *n* : bosquecillo *m,* arboleda *f,* soto *m*
grovel [ˈgrɑvəl, ˈgrʌ-] *vi* **-eled** *or* **-elled; -eling** *or* **-elling 1** CRAWL : arrastrarse **2** : humillarse, postrarse <to grovel before someone : postrarse ante alguien>
grow [ˈgroː] *v* **grew** [ˈgruː]; **grown** [ˈgroːn]; **growing** *vi* **1** : crecer <palm trees grow on the islands : las palmas crecen en las islas> <my hair grows very fast : mi pelo crece muy rápido> **2** DEVELOP, MATURE : desarrollarse, madurar **3** INCREASE : crecer, aumentar **4** BECOME : hacerse, volverse, ponerse <she was growing angry : se estaba poniendo furiosa> <to grow dark : oscurecerse> **5 to grow up** : hacerse mayor <grow up! : ¡no seas niño!> — *vt* **1** CULTIVATE, RAISE : cultivar **2** : dejar crecer <to grow one's hair : dejarse crecer el pelo>
grower [ˈgroːər] *n* : cultivador *m,* -dora *f*
growl[1] [ˈgraʊl] *vi* : gruñir (dícese de un animal), refunfuñar (dícese de una persona)
growl[2] *n* : gruñido *m*
grown–up[1] [ˈgroːnˌəp] *adj* : adulto, mayor
grown–up[2] *n* : adulto *m,* -ta *f;* persona *f* mayor
growth [ˈgroːθ] *n* **1** : crecimiento *m* <to stunt one's growth : detener el crecimiento> **2** INCREASE : aumento *m,* crecimiento *m,* expansión *f* **3** DEVELOPMENT : desarrollo *m* <economic growth : desarrollo económico> <a five days' growth of beard : una barba de cinco días> **4** LUMP, TUMOR : bulto *m,* tumor *m*
grub[1] [ˈgrʌb] *vi* **grubbed; grubbing 1** DIG : escarbar **2** RUMMAGE : hurgar, buscar **3** DRUDGE : trabajar duro
grub[2] *n* **1** : larva *f* <beetle grub : larva del escarabajo> **2** DRUDGE : esclavo *m,* -va *f* del trabajo **3** FOOD : comida *f*
grubby [ˈgrʌbi] *adj* **grubbier; -est** : mugriento, sucio
grudge[1] [ˈgrʌdʒ] *vt* **grudged; grudging** : resentir, envidiar
grudge[2] *n* : rencor *m,* resentimiento *m* <to hold a grudge : guardar rencor>
grueling *or* **gruelling** [ˈgruːlɪŋ, ˈgruːə-] *adj* : extenuante, agotador, duro
gruesome [ˈgruːsəm] *adj* : horripilante, truculento, horroroso
gruff [ˈgrʌf] *adj* **1** BRUSQUE : brusco <a gruff reply : una respuesta brusca> **2** HOARSE : ronco — **gruffly** *adv*
grumble[1] [ˈgrʌmbəl] *vi* **-bled; -bling 1** COMPLAIN : refunfuñar, rezongar, quejarse **2** RUMBLE : hacer un ruido sordo, retumbar (dícese del trueno)
grumble[2] *n* **1** COMPLAINT : queja *f* **2** RUMBLE : ruido *m* sordo, estruendo *m*
grumbler [ˈgrʌmbələr] *n* : gruñón *m,* -ñona *f*
grumpy [ˈgrʌmpi] *adj* **grumpier; -est** : malhumorado, gruñón
grunt[1] [ˈgrʌnt] *vi* : gruñir
grunt[2] *n* : gruñido *m*
guacamole [ˌgwɑkəˈmoːli] *n* : guacamole *m,* guacamol *m*
guarantee[1] [ˌgærənˈtiː] *vt* **-teed; -teeing 1** PROMISE : asegurar, prometer **2** : poner bajo garantía, garantizar (un producto o servicio)
guarantee[2] *n* **1** PROMISE : garantía *f,* promesa *f* <lifetime guarantee : garantía de por vida> **2** → **guarantor**
guarantor [ˌgærənˈtɔr] *n* : garante *mf;* fiador *m,* -dora *f*
guaranty [ˌgærənˈtiː] → **guarantee**
guard[1] [ˈgɑrd] *vt* **1** DEFEND, PROTECT : defender, proteger **2** : guardar, vigilar, custodiar <to guard the frontier : vigilar la frontera> <she guarded my secret well : guardó bien mi secreto> — *vi* **to guard against** : protegerse contra, evitar
guard[2] *n* **1** WATCHMAN : guarda *mf* <security guard : guarda de seguridad> **2** VIGILANCE : guardia *f,* vigilancia *f* <to be on guard : estar en guardia> <to let one's guard down : bajar la guardia> **3** SAFEGUARD : salvaguardia *f,* dispositivo *m* de seguridad (en una máquina) **4** PRECAUTION : precaución *f,* protección *f*
guardhouse [ˈgɑrdˌhaʊs] *n* : cuartel *m* de la guardia
guardian [ˈgɑrdiən] *n* **1** PROTECTOR : guardián *m,* -diana *f;* custodio *m,* -dia *f* **2** : tutor *m,* -tora *f* (de un niño)
guardianship [ˈgɑrdiənˌʃɪp] *n* : custodia *f,* tutela *f*
Guatemalan [ˌgwɑtəˈmɑlən] *n* : guatemalteco *m,* -ca *f* — **Guatemalan** *adj*
guava [ˈgwɑvə] *n* : guayaba *f*
gubernatorial [ˌguːbənəˈtoriːəl, ˌgjuː-] *adj* : del gobernador
guerrilla *or* **guerilla** [gəˈrɪlə] *n* : guerrillero *m,* -ra *f*
guess[1] [ˈgɛs] *vt* **1** CONJECTURE : adivinar, conjeturar <guess what happened! : ¡adivina lo que pasó!> **2** SUPPOSE : pensar, creer, suponer <I guess so : supongo que sí> **3** : adivinar correctamente, acertar <to guess the answer : acertar la respuesta> — *vi* : adivinar
guess[2] *n* : conjetura *f,* suposición *f*
guesswork [ˈgɛsˌwərk] *n* : suposiciones *fpl,* conjeturas *fpl*
guest [ˈgɛst] *n* : huésped *mf;* invitado *m,* -da *f*
guffaw[1] [gəˈfɔ] *vi* : reírse a carcajadas, carcajearse *fam*

guffaw[2] [gə'fɔ, 'gʌ,fɔ] *n* : carcajada *f,* risotada *f*
guidance ['gaɪdənts] *n* : orientación *f,* consejos *mpl*
guide[1] ['gaɪd] *vt* **guided; guiding 1** DIRECT, LEAD : guiar, dirigir, conducir **2** ADVISE, COUNSEL : aconsejar, orientar
guide[2] *n* : guía *f*
guidebook ['gaɪd,bʊk] *n* : guía *f* (para viajeros)
guideline ['gaɪd,laɪn] *n* : pauta *f,* directriz *f*
guild ['gɪld] *n* : gremio *m,* sindicato *m,* asociación *f*
guile ['gaɪl] *n* : astucia *f,* engaño *m*
guileless ['gaɪlləs] *adj* : inocente, cándido, sin malicia
guillotine[1] ['gɪlə,ti:n, 'gi:jə,-] *vt* **-tined; -tining** : guillotinar
guillotine[2] *n* : guillotina *f*
guilt ['gɪlt] *n* : culpa *f,* culpabilidad *f*
guilty ['gɪlti] *adj* **guiltier; -est** : culpable
guinea fowl ['gɪni] *n* : gallina *f* de Guinea
guinea pig *n* : conejillo *m* de Indias, cobaya *f*
guise ['gaɪz] *n* : apariencia *f,* aspecto *m,* forma *f*
guitar [gə'tɑr, gɪ-] *n* : guitarra *f*
gulch ['gʌltʃ] *n* : barranco *m,* quebrada *f*
gulf ['gʌlf] *n* **1** : golfo *m* <the Gulf of Mexico : el Golfo de México> **2** GAP : brecha *f* <the gulf between generations : la brecha entre las generaciones> **3** CHASM : abismo *m*
gull ['gʌl] *n* : gaviota *f*
gullet ['gʌlət] *n* : garganta *f*
gullible ['gʌlɪbəl] *adj* : crédulo
gully ['gʌli] *n, pl* **-lies** : barranco *m,* hondonada *f*
gulp[1] ['gʌlp] *vt* **1** : engullir, tragar <he gulped down the whiskey : engulló el whisky> **2** SUPPRESS : suprimir, reprimir, tragar <to gulp down a sob : reprimir un sollozo> — *vi* : tragar saliva, tener un nudo en la garganta
gulp[2] *n* : trago *m*
gum ['gʌm] *n* **1** CHEWING GUM : goma *f* de mascar, chicle *m* **2 gums** *npl* : encías *fpl*
gumbo ['gʌm,bo:] *n* : sopa *f* de quingombó
gumdrop ['gʌm,drɑp] *n* : pastilla *f* de goma
gummy ['gʌmi] *adj* **gummier; -est** : gomoso
gumption ['gʌmpʃən] *n* : iniciativa *f,* agallas *fpl fam*
gun[1] ['gʌn] *vt* **gunned; gunning 1** *or* **to gun down** : matar a tiros, asesinar **2** : acelerar (rápidamente) <to gun the engine : acelerar el motor>
gun[2] *n* **1** CANNON : cañón *m* **2** FIREARM : arma *f* de fuego **3** SPRAY GUN : pistola *f* **4 to jump the gun** : adelantarse, salir antes de tiempo
gunboat ['gʌn,bo:t] *n* : cañonero *m*
gunfight ['gʌn,faɪt] *n* : tiroteo *m,* balacera *f*
gunfire ['gʌn,faɪr] *n* : disparos *mpl*
gunman ['gʌnmən] *n, pl* **-men** [-mən, -,mɛn] : pistolero *m,* gatillero *m Mex*
gunner ['gʌnər] *n* : artillero *m,* -ra *f*
gunnysack ['gʌni,sæk] *n* : saco *m* de yute
gunpowder ['gʌn,paʊdər] *n* : pólvora *f*
gunshot ['gʌn,ʃɑt] *n* : disparo *m,* tiro *m,* balazo *m*
gunwale ['gʌnəl] *n* : borda *f*
guppy ['gʌpi] *n, pl* **-pies** : lebistes *m*
gurgle[1] ['gərgəl] *vi* **-gled; -gling 1** : borbotar, gorgotear (dícese de un líquido) **2** : gorjear (dícese de un niño)
gurgle[2] *n* **1** : borboteo *m,* gorgoteo *m* (de un líquido) **2** : gorjeo *m* (de un niño)
gush ['gʌʃ] *vi* **1** SPOUT : surgir, salir a chorros, chorrear **2** : hablar con entusiasmo efusivo <she gushed with praise : se deshizo en elogios>
gust ['gʌst] *n* : ráfaga *f,* racha *f*
gusto ['gʌs,to:] *n, pl* **gustoes** : entusiasmo *m* <with gusto : con deleite, con ganas>
gusty ['gʌsti] *adj* **gustier; -est** : racheado
gut[1] ['gʌt] *vt* **gutted; gutting 1** EVISCERATE : destripar (un pollo, etc.), limpiar (un pescado) **2** : destruir el interior de (un edificio)
gut[2] *n* **1** INTESTINE : intestino *m* **2 guts** *npl* INNARDS : tripas *fpl fam,* entrañas *fpl* **3 guts** *npl* COURAGE : valentía *f,* agallas *fpl*
gutter ['gʌtər] *n* **1** : canal *mf,* canaleta *f* (de un techo) **2** : cuneta *f,* arroyo *m* (de una calle)
guttural ['gʌtərəl] *adj* : gutural
guy ['gaɪ] *n* **1** *or* **guyline** : cuerda *f* tensora, cable *m* **2** FELLOW : tipo *m,* hombre *m*
guzzle ['gʌzəl] *vt* **-zled; -zling** : chupar, tragarse
gym ['dʒɪm] → **gymnasium**
gymnasium [dʒɪm'neɪziəm, -ʒəm] *n, pl* **-siums** *or* **-sia** [-zi:ə, -ʒə] : gimnasio *m*
gymnast ['dʒɪmnəst, -,næst] *n* : gimnasta *mf*
gymnastic [dʒɪm'næstɪk] *adj* : gimnástico
gymnastics [dʒɪm'næstɪks] *ns & pl* : gimnasia *f*
gynecologist [,gaɪnə'kɑlədʒɪst, ,dʒɪnə-] *n* : ginecólogo *m,* -ga *f*
gynecology [,gaɪnə'kɑlədʒi, ,dʒɪnə-] *n* : ginecología *f*
gyp[1] ['dʒɪp] *vt* **gypped; gypping** : estafar, timar
gyp[2] *n* **1** SWINDLER : estafador *m,* -dora *f* **2** FRAUD, SWINDLE : estafa *f,* timo *m fam*
gypsum ['dʒɪpsəm] *n* : yeso *m*

Gypsy ['dʒɪpsi] *n, pl* **-sies** : gitano *m,* -na *f*

gyrate ['dʒaɪˌreɪt] *vi* **-rated; -rating** : girar, rotar

gyration [dʒaɪ'reɪʃən] *n* : giro *m,* rotación *f*

gyroscope ['dʒaɪrəˌsko:p] *n* : giroscopio *m,* giróscopo *m*

H

h ['eɪtʃ] *n, pl* **h's** *or* **hs** ['eɪtʃəz] : octava letra del alfabeto inglés

haberdashery ['hæbərˌdæʃəri] *n, pl* **-eries** : tienda *f* de ropa para caballeros

habit ['hæbɪt] *n* **1** CUSTOM : hábito *m,* costumbre *f* **2** : hábito *m* (de un monje o una religiosa) **3** ADDICTION : dependencia *f,* adicción *f*

habitable ['hæbɪtəbəl] *adj* : habitable

habitat ['hæbɪˌtæt] *n* : hábitat *m*

habitation [ˌhæbɪ'teɪʃən] *n* **1** OCCUPANCY : habitación *f* **2** RESIDENCE : residencia *f,* morada *f*

habit–forming ['hæbɪtˌfɔrmɪŋ] *adj* : que crea dependencia

habitual [hə'bɪtʃʊəl] *adj* **1** CUSTOMARY : habitual, acostumbrado **2** INVETERATE : incorregible, empedernido — **habitually** *adv*

habituate [hə'bɪtʃʊˌeɪt] *vt* **-ated; -ating** : habituar, acostumbrar

hack[1] ['hæk] *vt* : cortar, tajar <to hack one's way : abrirse paso> — *vi* **1** : hacer tajos **2** COUGH : toser

hack[2] *n* **1** CHOP : hachazo *m,* tajo *m* **2** HORSE : caballo *m* de alquiler **3** WRITER : escritor *m,* -tora *f* a sueldo; escritorzuelo *m,* -la *f* **4** COUGH : tos *f* seca

hackles ['hækəlz] *npl* **1** : pluma *f* erizada (de un ave), pelo *m* erizado (de un perro, etc.) **2 to get one's hackles up** : ponerse furioso

hackney ['hækni] *n, pl* **-neys** : caballo *m* de silla, caballo *m* de tiro

hackneyed ['hæknid] *adj* TRITE : trillado, gastado

hacksaw ['hækˌsɔ] *n* : sierra *f* para metales

had → **have**

haddock ['hædək] *ns & pl* : eglefino *m*

hadn't ['hædənt] (*contraction of* **had not**) → **have**

haft ['hæft] *n* : mango *m,* empuñadura *f*

hag ['hæg] *n* **1** WITCH : bruja *f,* hechicera *f* **2** CRONE : vieja *f* fea

haggard ['hægərd] *adj* : demacrado, macilento — **haggardly** *adv*

haggle ['hægəl] *vi* **-gled; -gling** : regatear

ha–ha [ˌhɑ'hɑ, 'hɑ'hɑ] *interj* : ¡ja, ja!

hail[1] ['heɪl] *vt* **1** GREET : saludar **2** SUMMON : llamar <to hail a taxi : llamar un taxi> — *vi* : granizar (en meteorología)

hail[2] *n* **1** : granizo *m* **2** BARRAGE : aluvión *m,* lluvia *f*

hail[3] *interj* : ¡salve!

hailstone ['heɪlˌsto:n] *n* : granizo *m,* piedra *f* de granizo

hailstorm ['heɪlˌstɔrm] *n* : granizada *f*

hair ['hær] *n* **1** : pelo *m,* cabello *m* <to get one's hair cut : cortarse el pelo> **2** : vello *m* (en las piernas, etc.)

hairbreadth ['hærˌbrɛdθ] *or* **hairsbreadth** ['hærz-] *n* **by a hairbreadth** : por un pelo

hairbrush ['hærˌbrʌʃ] *n* : cepillo *m* (del pelo)

haircut ['hærˌkʌt] *n* : corte *m* de pelo

hairdo ['hærˌdu:] *n, pl* **-dos** : peinado *m*

hairdresser ['hærˌdrɛsər] *n* : peluquero *m,* -ra *f*

hairiness ['hærinəs] *n* : vellosidad *f*

hairless ['hærləs] *adj* : sin pelo, calvo, pelón

hairline ['hærˌlaɪn] *n* **1** : línea *f* delgada **2** : nacimiento *m* del pelo <to have a receding hairline : tener entradas>

hairpin ['hærˌpɪn] *n* : horquilla *f*

hair–raising ['hærˌreɪzɪŋ] *adj* : espeluznante

hairy ['hæri] *adj* **hairier; -est** : peludo, velludo

Haitian ['heɪʃən, 'heɪtiən] *n* : haitiano *m,* -na *f* — **Haitian** *adj*

hake ['heɪk] *n* : merluza *f*

hale[1] ['heɪl] *vt* **haled; haling** : arrastrar, halar <to hale to court : arrastrar al tribunal>

hale[2] *adj* : saludable, robusto

half[1] ['hæf, 'haf] *adv* : medio, a medias <half cooked : medio cocido>

half[2] *adj* : medio, a medias <a half hour : una media hora> <a half truth : una verdad a medias>

half[3] *n, pl* **halves** ['hævz, 'havz] **1** : mitad *f* <half of my friends : la mitad de mis amigos> <in half : por la mitad> **2** : tiempo *m* (en deportes)

half brother *n* : medio hermano *m,* hermanastro *m*

halfhearted ['hæf'hɑrtəd] *adj* : sin ánimo, poco entusiasta

halfheartedly ['hæf'hɑrtədli] *adv* : con poco entusiasmo, sin ánimo

half–life ['hæfˌlaɪf] *n, pl* **half–lives** : media vida *f*

half sister *n* : media hermana *f,* hermanastra *f*

halfway[1] ['hæf'weɪ] *adv* : a medio camino, a mitad de camino

halfway[2] *adj* : medio, intermedio <a halfway point : un punto intermedio>

half-wit ['hæfˌwɪt] *n* : tonto *m,* -ta *f;* imbécil *mf*

half–witted [ˈhæf,wɪt̬əd] *adj* : estúpido
halibut [ˈhælɪbət] *ns & pl* : halibut *m*
hall [ˈhɔl] *n* **1** BUILDING : residencia *f* estudiantil, facultad *f* (de una universidad) **2** VESTIBULE : entrada *f,* vestíbulo *m,* zaguán *m* **3** CORRIDOR : corredor *m,* pasillo *m* **4** AUDITORIUM : sala *f,* salón *m* <concert hall : sala de conciertos> **5 city hall** : ayuntamiento *m*
hallelujah [,hæləˈluːjə, ,hɑ-] *interj* : ¡aleluya!
hallmark [ˈhɔl,mɑrk] *n* : sello *m* (distintivo)
hallow [ˈhæ,loː] *vt* : santificar, consagrar
hallowed [ˈhæ,loːd, ˈhæ,loːəd, ˈhɑ,loːd] *adj* : sagrado
Halloween [,hæləˈwiːn, ,hɑ-] *n* : víspera *f* de Todos los Santos
hallucinate [hæˈluːsən,eɪt] *vi* **-nated; -nating** : alucinar
hallucination [hə,luːsənˈeɪʃən] *n* : alucinación *f*
hallucinatory [həˈluːsənə,tori] *adj* : alucinante
hallucinogen [həˈluːsənədʒən] *n* : alucinógeno *m*
hallucinogenic [hə,luːsənəˈdʒɛnɪk] *adj* : alucinógeno
hallway [ˈhɔl,weɪ] *n* **1** ENTRANCE : entrada *f* **2** CORRIDOR : corredor *m,* pasillo *m*
halo [ˈheɪ,loː] *n, pl* **-los** *or* **-loes** : aureola *f,* halo *m*
halt¹ [ˈhɔlt] *vi* : detenerse, pararse — *vt* **1** STOP : detener, parar (a una persona) **2** INTERRUPT : interrumpir (una actividad)
halt² *n* **1** : alto *m,* parada *f* **2 to come to a halt** : pararse, detenerse
halter [ˈhɔltər] *n* **1** : cabestro *m,* ronzal *m* (para un animal) **2** : blusa *f* sin espalda
halting [ˈhɔltɪŋ] *adj* HESITANT : vacilante, titubeante — **haltingly** *adv*
halve [ˈhæv, ˈhav] *vt* **halved; halving** **1** DIVIDE : partir por la mitad **2** REDUCE : reducir a la mitad
halves → **half**
ham [ˈhæm] *n* **1** : jamón *m* **2** *or* **ham actor** : comicastro *m,* -tra *f* **3** *or* **ham radio operator** : radioaficionado *m,* -da *f* **4 hams** *npl* HAUNCHES : ancas *fpl*
hamburger [ˈhæm,bərgər] *or* **hamburg** [-,bərg] *n* **1** : carne *f* molida **2** : hamburguesa *f* (emparedado)
hamlet [ˈhæmlət] *n* VILLAGE : aldea *f,* poblado *m*
hammer¹ [ˈhæmər] *vt* **1** STRIKE : clavar, golpear **2** NAIL : clavar, martillar **3 to hammer out** NEGOTIATE : elaborar, negociar, llegar a — *vi* : martillar, golpear
hammer² *n* **1** : martillo *m* **2** : percusor *m,* percutor *m* (de un arma de fuego)
hammock [ˈhæmək] *n* : hamaca *f*
hamper¹ [ˈhæmpər] *vt* : obstaculizar, dificultar
hamper² *n* : cesto *m,* canasta *f*
hamster [ˈhæm*p*stər] *n* : hámster *m*
hamstring [ˈhæm,strɪŋ] *vt* **-strung** [-,strʌŋ]; **-stringing** **1** : cortarle el tendón del corvejón a (un animal) **2** INCAPACITATE : incapacitar, inutilizar
hand¹ [ˈhænd] *vt* : pasar, dar, entregar
hand² *n* **1** : mano *f* <made by hand : hecho a mano> **2** POINTER : manecilla *f,* aguja *f* (de un reloj o instrumento) **3** SIDE : lado *m* <on the other hand : por otro lado> **4** HANDWRITING : letra *f,* escritura *f* **5** APPLAUSE : aplauso *m* **6** : mano *f,* cartas *fpl* (en juegos de naipes) **7** WORKER : obrero *m,* -ra *f;* trabajador *m,* -dora *f* **8 to ask for someone's hand (in marriage)** : pedir la mano de alguien **9 to lend a hand** : echar una mano
handbag [ˈhænd,bæg] *n* : cartera *f,* bolso *m,* bolsa *f Mex*
handball [ˈhænd,bɔl] *n* : frontón *m*
handbill [ˈhænd,bɪl] *n* : folleto *m,* volante *m*
handbook [ˈhænd,bʊk] *n* : manual *m*
handcuff [ˈhænd,kʌf] *vt* : esposar, ponerle esposas (a alguien)
handcuffs [ˈhænd,kʌfs] *npl* : esposas *fpl*
handful [ˈhænd,fʊl] *n* : puñado *m*
handgun [ˈhænd,gʌn] *n* : pistola *f,* revólver *m*
handicap¹ [ˈhændi,kæp] *vt* **-capped; -capping** **1** : asignar un handicap a (en deportes) **2** HAMPER : obstaculizar, poner en desventaja
handicap² *n* **1** DISABILITY : minusvalía *f,* discapacidad *f* **2** DISADVANTAGE : desventaja *f,* handicap *m* (en deportes)
handicapped [ˈhændi,kæpt] *adj* DISABLED : minusválido, discapacitado
handicraft [ˈhændi,kræft] *n* : artesanía *f*
handily [ˈhændəli] *adv* EASILY : fácilmente, con facilidad
handiwork [ˈhændi,wərk] *n* **1** WORK : trabajo *m* **2** CRAFTS : artesanías *fpl*
handkerchief [ˈhæŋkərtʃəf, -,tʃiːf] *n, pl* **-chiefs** : pañuelo *m*
handle¹ [ˈhændəl] *v* **-dled; -dling** *vt* **1** TOUCH : tocar **2** MANAGE : tratar, manejar, despachar **3** SELL : comerciar con, vender — *vi* : responder, conducirse (dícese de un vehículo)
handle² *n* : asa *m,* asidero *m,* mango *m* (de un cuchillo, etc.), pomo *m* (de una puerta), tirador *m* (de un cajón)
handlebars [ˈhændəl,bɑrz] *npl* : manubrio *m,* manillar *m*
handler [ˈhændələr] *n* : cuidador *m,* -dora *f*
handmade [ˈhænd,meɪd] *adj* : hecho a mano
hand–me–downs [ˈhæn*d*mi,daʊnz] *npl* : ropa *f* usada

handout [ˈhændˌaʊt] *n* **1** AID : dádiva *f,* limosna *f* **2** LEAFLET : folleto *m*

handpick [ˈhændˈpɪk] *vt* : seleccionar con cuidado

handrail [ˈhændˌreɪl] *n* : pasamanos *m,* barandilla *f,* barandal *m*

handsaw [ˈhændˌsɔ] *n* : serrucho *m*

hands down *adv* **1** EASILY : con facilidad **2** UNQUESTIONABLY : con mucho, de lejos

handshake [ˈhændˌʃeɪk] *n* : apretón *m* de manos

handsome [ˈhæn*t*səm] *adj* **-somer; -est 1** ATTRACTIVE : apuesto, guapo, atractivo **2** GENEROUS : generoso **3** SIZABLE : considerable

handsomely [ˈhæn*t*səmli] *adv* **1** ELEGANTLY : elegantemente **2** GENEROUSLY : con generosidad

handspring [ˈhændˌsprɪŋ] *n* : voltereta *f*

handstand [ˈhændˌstænd] *n* **to do a handstand :** pararse de manos

hand–to–hand [ˈhænd*d*təˈhænd] *adj* : cuerpo a cuerpo

handwriting [ˈhændˌraɪt̬ɪŋ] *n* : letra *f,* escritura *f*

handwritten [ˈhændˌrɪtən] *adj* : escrito a mano

handy [ˈhændi] *adj* **handier; -est 1** NEARBY : a mano, cercano **2** USEFUL : útil, práctico **3** DEXTEROUS : hábil

hang[1] [ˈhæŋ] *v* **hung** [ˈhʌŋ]; **hanging** *vt* **1** SUSPEND : colgar, tender, suspender **2** (*past tense often* **hanged**) EXECUTE : colgar, ahorcar **3 to hang one's head :** bajar la cabeza — *vi* **1** FALL : caer (dícese de las telas y la ropa) **2** DANGLE : colgar **3** HOVER : flotar, sostenerse en el aire **4** : ser ahorcado **5** DROOP : inclinarse **6 to hang up :** colgar <he hung up on me : me colgó>

hang[2] *n* **1** DRAPE : caída *f* **2 to get the hang of something :** colgarle el truco a algo, lograr entender algo

hangar [ˈhæŋər, ˈhæŋgər] *n* : hangar *m*

hanger [ˈhæŋər] *n* : percha *f,* gancho *m* (para ropa)

hangman [ˈhæŋmən] *n, pl* **-men** [-mən, -ˌmɛn] : verdugo *m*

hangnail [ˈhæŋˌneɪl] *n* : padrastro *m*

hangout [ˈhæŋˌaʊt] *n* : lugar *m* popular, sitio *m* muy frecuentado

hangover [ˈhæŋˌoːvər] *n* : resaca *f*

hank [ˈhæŋk] *n* : madeja *f*

hanker [ˈhæŋkər] *vi* **to hanker for** : ansiar, anhelar, tener ganas de

hankering [ˈhæŋkərɪŋ] *n* : ansia *f,* anhelo *m*

hansom [ˈhæn*t*səm] *n* : coche *m* de caballos

Hanukkah [ˈxɑnəkə, ˈhɑ-] *n* : Januká, Hanukkah

haphazard [hæpˈhæzərd] *adj* : casual, fortuito, al azar — **haphazardly** *adv*

hapless [ˈhæpləs] *adj* UNFORTUNATE : desafortunado, desventurado — **haplessly**

happen [ˈhæpən] *vi* **1** OCCUR : pasar, ocurrir, suceder, tener lugar **2** BEFALL : pasar, acontecer <what happened to her? : ¿qué le ha pasado?> **3** CHANCE : resultar, ocurrir por casualidad <it happened that I wasn't home : resulta que estaba fuera de casa> <he happens to be right : da la casualidad de que tiene razón>

happening [ˈhæpənɪŋ] *n* : suceso *m,* acontecimiento *m*

happiness [ˈhæpinəs] *n* : felicidad *f,* dicha *f*

happy [ˈhæpi] *adj* **-pier; -est 1** JOYFUL : feliz, contento, alegre **2** FORTUNATE : afortunado, feliz — **happily** [-pəli] *adv*

happy–go–lucky [ˈhæpigoːˈlʌki] *adj* : despreocupado

harangue[1] [həˈræŋ] *vt* **-rangued; -ranguing** : arengar

harangue[2] *n* : arenga *f*

harass [həˈræs, ˈhærəs] *vt* **1** BESIEGE, HOUND : acosar, asediar, hostigar **2** ANNOY : molestar

harassment [həˈræsmənt, ˈhærəsmənt] *n* : acoso *m,* hostigamiento *m* <sexual harrassment : acoso sexual>

harbinger [ˈhɑrbɪndʒər] *n* **1** HERALD : heraldo *m,* precursor *m* **2** OMEN : presagio *m*

harbor[1] [ˈhɑrbər] *vt* **1** SHELTER : dar refugio a, albergar **2** CHERISH, KEEP : abrigar, guardar, albergar <to harbor doubts : guardar dudas>

harbor[2] *n* **1** REFUGE : refugio *m* **2** PORT : puerto *m*

hard[1] [ˈhɑrd] *adv* **1** FORCEFULLY : fuerte, con fuerza <the wind blew hard : el viento sopló fuerte> **2** STRENUOUSLY : duro, mucho <to work hard : trabajar duro> **3 to take something hard** : tomarse algo muy mal, estar muy afectado por algo

hard[2] *adj* **1** FIRM, SOLID : duro, firme, sólido **2** DIFFICULT : difícil, arduo **3** SEVERE : severo, duro <a hard winter : un invierno severo> **4** UNFEELING : insensible, duro **5** DILIGENT : diligente <to be a hard worker : ser muy trabajador> **6 hard liquor** : bebidas *fpl* fuertes **7 hard water** : agua *f* dura

harden [ˈhɑrdən] *vt* : endurecer

hardheaded [ˌhɑrdˈhɛdəd] *adj* **1** STUBBORN : testarudo, terco **2** REALISTIC : realista, práctico — **hardheadedly** *adv*

hard–hearted [ˌhɑrdˈhɑrt̬əd] *adj* : despiadado, insensible — **hard–heartedly** *adv*

hard–heartedness [ˌhɑrdˈhɑrt̬ədnəs] *n* : dureza *f* de corazón

hardly [ˈhɑrdli] *adv* **1** SCARCELY : apenas, casi <I hardly knew her : apenas la conocía> <hardly ever : casi nunca> **2** NOT : difícilmente, poco, no <they can hardly blame me! : ¡difícilmente pueden echarme la culpa!> <it's hardly likely : es poco probable>

hardness [ˈhɑrdnəs] *n* **1** FIRMNESS : dureza *f* **2** DIFFICULTY : dificultad *f* **3** SEVERITY : severidad *f*

hardship [ˈhɑrdˌʃɪp] *n* : dificultad *f,* privación *f*

hardware [ˈhɑrdˌwær] *n* **1** TOOLS : ferretería *f* **2** : hardware *m* (de una computadora)

hardwood [ˈhɑrdˌwʊd] *n* : madera *f* dura, madera *f* noble

hardy [ˈhɑrdi] *adj* **-dier; -est** : fuerte, robusto, resistente (dícese de las plantas) — **hardily** [-dəli] *adv*

hare [ˈhær] *n, pl* **hare** *or* **hares** : liebre *f*

harebrained [ˈhærˌbreɪnd] *adj* : estúpido, absurdo, disparatado

harelip [ˈhærˌlɪp] *n* : labio *m* leporino

harem [ˈhærəm] *n* : harén *m*

hark [ˈhɑrk] *vi* **1** (*used only in the imperative*) LISTEN : escuchar **2 hark back** RETURN : volver **3 hark back** RECALL : recordar

harlequin [ˈhɑrlɪkən, -kwən] *n* : arlequín *m*

harm[1] [ˈhɑrm] *vt* : hacerle daño a, perjudicar

harm[2] *n* : daño *m,* perjuicio *m*

harmful [ˈhɑrmfəl] *adj* : dañino, perjudicial — **harmfully** *adv*

harmless [ˈhɑrmləs] *adj* : inofensivo, inocuo — **harmlessly** *adv*

harmlessness [ˈhɑrmləsnəs] *n* : inocuidad *f*

harmonic [hɑrˈmɑnɪk] *adj* : armónico — **harmonically** [-nɪkli] *adv*

harmonica [hɑrˈmɑnɪkə] *n* : armónica *f*

harmonious [hɑrˈmoːniəs] *adj* : armonioso — **harmoniously** *adv*

harmonize [ˈhɑrməˌnaɪz] *v* **-nized; -nizing** : armonizar

harmony [ˈhɑrməni] *n, pl* **-nies** : armonía *f*

harness[1] [ˈhɑrnəs] *vt* **1** : enjaezar (un animal) **2** UTILIZE : utilizar, aprovechar

harness[2] *n* : arreos *mpl,* guarniciones *fpl,* arnés *m*

harp[1] [ˈhɑrp] *vi* **to harp on** : insistir sobre, machacar sobre

harp[2] *n* : arpa *m*

harpist [ˈhɑrpɪst] *n* : arpista *mf*

harpoon[1] [hɑrˈpuːn] *vt* : arponear

harpoon[2] *n* : arpón *m*

harpsichord [ˈhɑrpsɪˌkɔrd] *n* : clavicémbalo *m*

harrow[1] [ˈhærˌoː] *vt* **1** CULTIVATE : gradar, labrar (la tierra) **2** TORMENT : atormentar

harrow[2] *n* : grada *f,* rastra *f*

harry [ˈhæri] *vt* **-ried; -rying** HARASS : acosar, hostigar

harsh [ˈhɑrʃ] *adj* **1** ROUGH : áspero **2** SEVERE : duro, severo **3** : discordante (dícese de los sonidos) — **harshly** *adv*

harshness [ˈhɑrʃnəs] *n* **1** ROUGHNESS : aspereza *f* **2** SEVERITY : dureza *f,* severidad *f*

harvest[1] [ˈhɑrvəst] *v* : cosechar

harvest[2] *n* **1** HARVESTING : siega *f,* recolección *f* **2** CROP : cosecha *f*

harvester [ˈhɑrvəstər] *n* : segador *m,* -dora *f;* cosechadora *f* (máquina)

has → **have**

hash[1] [ˈhæʃ] *vt* **1** MINCE : picar **2 to hash over** DISCUSS : discutir, repasar

hash[2] *n* **1** : picadillo *m* (comida) **2** JUMBLE : revoltijo *m,* fárrago *m*

hasn't [ˈhæzənt] (*contraction of* **has not**) → **has**

hasp [ˈhæsp] *n* : picaporte *m,* pestillo *m*

hassle[1] [ˈhæsəl] *vt* **-sled; -sling** : fastidiar, molestar

hassle[2] *n* **1** ARGUMENT : discusión *f,* disputa *f,* bronca *f* **2** FIGHT : pelea *f,* riña *f* **3** BOTHER, TROUBLE : problemas *mpl,* lío *m*

hassock [ˈhæsək] *n* **1** CUSHION : almohadón *m,* cojín *m* **2** FOOTSTOOL : escabel *m*

haste [ˈheɪst] *n* **1** : prisa *f,* apuro *m* **2 to make haste** : darse prisa, apurarse

hasten [ˈheɪsən] *vt* : acelerar, precipitar — *vi* : apresurarse, apurarse

hasty [ˈheɪsti] *adj* **hastier; -est 1** HURRIED, QUICK : rápido, apresurado, apurado **2** RASH : precipitado — **hastily** [-təli] *adv*

hat [ˈhæt] *n* : sombrero *m*

hatch[1] [ˈhætʃ] *vt* **1** : incubar, empollar (huevos) **2** DEVISE : idear, tramar — *vi* : salir del cascarón

hatch[2] *n* : escotilla *f*

hatchery [ˈhætʃəri] *n, pl* **-ries** : criadero *m*

hatchet [ˈhætʃət] *n* : hacha *f*

hatchway [ˈhætʃˌweɪ] *n* : escotilla *f*

hate[1] [ˈheɪt] *vt* **hated; hating** : odiar, aborrecer, detestar

hate[2] *n* : odio *m*

hateful [ˈheɪtfəl] *adj* : odioso, aborrecible, detestable — **hatefully** *adv*

hatred [ˈheɪtrəd] *n* : odio *m*

hatter [ˈhæṭər] *n* : sombrerero *m,* -ra *f*

haughtiness [ˈhɔṭinəs] *n* : altanería *f,* altivez *f*

haughty [ˈhɔṭi] *adj* **-tier; -est** : altanero, altivo — **haughtily** [-ṭəli] *adv*

haul[1] [ˈhɔl] *vt* **1** DRAG, PULL : arrastrar, jalar **2** TRANSPORT : transportar

haul[2] *n* **1** PULL : tirón *m,* jalón *m* **2** CATCH : redada *f* **3** JOURNEY : viaje *m,* trayecto *m* <it's a long haul : es un trayecto largo>

haulage [ˈhɔlɪdʒ] *n* : transporte *m,* tiro *m*

hauler [ˈhɔlər] *n* : transportista *mf*

haunch [ˈhɔntʃ] *n* **1** HIP : cadera *f* **2** **haunches** *npl* HINDQUARTERS : ancas *fpl*, cuartos *mpl* traseros

haunt[1] [ˈhɔnt] *vt* **1** : aparecer en (dícese de un fantasma) **2** FREQUENT : frecuentar, rondar **3** PREOCCUPY : perseguir, obsesionar

haunt[2] *n* : guarida *f* (de animales o ladrones), lugar *m* predilecto

haunting [ˈhɔntɪŋ] *adj* : obsesionante, evocador — **hauntingly** *adv*

have [ˈhæv, *in sense 3 as an auxiliary verb usu* ˈhæf] *v* **had** [ˈhæd]; **having; has** [ˈhæz, *in sense 3 as an auxiliary verb usu* ˈhæs] *vt* **1** POSSESS : tener <do you have change? : ¿tienes cambio?> **2** EXPERIENCE, UNDERGO : tener, experimentar, sufrir <I have a toothache : tengo un dolor de muelas> **3** INCLUDE : tener, incluir <April has 30 days : abril tiene 30 días> **4** CONSUME : comer, tomar **5** RECEIVE : tener, recibir <he had my permission : tenía mi permiso> **6** ALLOW : permitir, dejar <I won't have it! : ¡no lo permitiré!> **7** HOLD : hacer <to have a party : dar una fiesta> <to have a meeting : convocar una reunión> **8** HOLD : tener <he had me in his power : me tenía en su poder> **9** BEAR : tener (niños) **10** (*indicating causation*) <she had a dress made : mandó hacer un vestido> <to have one's hair cut : cortarse el pelo> — *v aux* **1** : haber <she has been very busy : ha estado muy ocupada> <I've lived here three years : hace tres años que vivo aquí> **2** (*used in tags*) <you've finished, haven't you? : ha terminado, ¿no?> **3 to have to** : deber, tener que <we have to leave : tenemos que salir>

haven [ˈheɪvən] *n* : refugio *m*

havoc [ˈhævək] *n* **1** DESTRUCTION : estragos *mpl*, destrucción *f* **2** CHAOS, DISORDER : desorden *m*, caos *m*

Hawaiian[1] [həˈwaɪən] *adj* : hawaiano

Hawaiian[2] *n* : hawaiano *m*, -na *f*

hawk[1] [ˈhɔk] *vt* : pregonar, vender (mercancías) en la calle

hawk[2] *n* : halcón *m*

hawker [ˈhɔkər] *n* : vendedor *m*, -dora *f* ambulante

hawthorn [ˈhɔˌθɔrn] *n* : espino *m*

hay [ˈheɪ] *n* : heno *m*

hay fever *n* : fiebre *f* del heno

hayloft [ˈheɪˌlɔft] *n* : pajar *m*

hayseed [ˈheɪˌsiːd] *n* : palurdo *m*, -da *f*

haystack [ˈheɪˌstæk] *n* : almiar *m*

haywire [ˈheɪˌwaɪr] *adj* : descompuesto, desbaratado <to go haywire : estropearse>

hazard[1] [ˈhæzərd] *vt* : arriesgar, aventurar

hazard[2] *n* **1** DANGER : peligro *m*, riesgo *m* **2** CHANCE : azar *m*

hazardous [ˈhæzərdəs] *adj* : arriesgado, peligroso

haze[1] [ˈheɪz] *vt* **hazed; hazing** : abrumar, acosar

haze[2] *n* : bruma *f*, neblina *f*

hazel [ˈheɪzəl] *n* **1** : avellano *m* (árbol) **2** : color *m* avellana

hazelnut [ˈheɪzəlˌnʌt] *n* : avellana *f*

haziness [ˈheɪzinəs] *n* **1** MISTINESS : nebulosidad *f* **2** VAGUENESS : vaguedad *f*

hazy [ˈheɪzi] *adj* **hazier; -est 1** MISTY : brumoso, neblinoso, nebuloso **2** VAGUE : vago, confuso

he [ˈhiː] *pron* : él

head[1] [ˈhɛd] *vt* **1** LEAD : encabezar **2** DIRECT : dirigir — *vi* : dirigirse

head[2] *adj* MAIN : principal <the head office : la oficina central, la sede>

head[3] *n* **1** : cabeza *f* <from head to foot : de pies a cabeza> **2** MIND : mente *f*, cabeza *f* **3** TIP, TOP : cabeza *f* (de un clavo, un martillo, etc.), cabecera *f* (de una mesa o un río), punta *f* (de una flecha), flor *m* (de un repollo, etc.), encabezamiento *m* (de una carta, etc.), espuma *f* (de cerveza) **4** DIRECTOR, LEADER : director *m*, -tora *f*; jefe *m*, -fa *f*; cabeza *f* (de una familia) **5** : cara *f* (de una moneda) <heads or tails : cara o cruz> **6** : cabeza *f* <500 head of cattle : 500 cabezas de ganado> <$10 a head : $10 por cabeza> **7 to come to a head** : llegar a un punto crítico

headache [ˈhɛdˌeɪk] *n* : dolor *m* de cabeza, jaqueca *f*

headband [ˈhɛdˌbænd] *n* : cinta *f* del pelo

headdress [ˈhɛdˌdrɛs] *n* : tocado *m*

headfirst [ˈhɛdˈfərst] *adv* : de cabeza

headgear [ˈhɛdˌgɪr] *n* : gorro *m*, casco *m*, sombrero *m*

heading [ˈhɛdɪŋ] *n* **1** DIRECTION : dirección *f* **2** TITLE : encabezamiento *m*, título *m* **3** : membrete *m* (de una carta)

headland [ˈhɛdlənd, -ˌlænd] *n* : cabo *m*

headlight [ˈhɛdˌlaɪt] *n* : faro *m*, foco *m*, farol *m Mex*

headline [ˈhɛdˌlaɪn] *n* : titular *m*

headlong[1] [ˈhɛdˈlɔŋ] *adv* **1** HEADFIRST : de cabeza **2** HASTILY : precipitadamente

headlong[2] [ˈhɛdˌlɔŋ] *adj* : precipitado

headmaster [ˈhɛdˌmæstər] *n* : director *m*

headmistress [ˈhɛdˌmɪstrəs, -ˈmɪs-] *n* : directora *f*

head–on [ˈhɛdˈɑn, -ˈɔn] *adv & adj* : de frente

headphones [ˈhɛdˌfoːnz] *npl* : audífonos *mpl*, cascos *mpl*

headquarters [ˈhɛdˌkwɔrtərz] *ns & pl* **1** SEAT : oficina *f* central, sede *f* **2** : cuartel *m* general (de los militares)

headrest [ˈhɛdˌrɛst] *n* : apoyacabezas *m*

headship [ˈhɛdˌʃɪp] *n* : dirección *f*

head start *n* : ventaja *f*

headstone [ˈhɛdˌstoːn] *n* : lápida *f*

headstrong [ˈhɛdˈstrɔŋ] *adj* : testarudo, obstinado, empecinado

headwaiter [ˈhɛdˈweɪt̬ər] *n* : jefe *m*, -fa *f* de comedor

headwaters [ˈhɛd,wɔt̬ərz, -,wɑ-] *npl* : cabecera *f*

headway [ˈhɛd,weɪ] *n* : progreso *m* <to make headway against : avanzar contra>

heady [ˈhɛdi] *adj* **headier; -est 1** INTOXICATING : embriagador, excitante **2** SHREWD : astuto, sagaz

heal [ˈhiːl] *vt* : curar, sanar — *vi* **1** : sanar, curarse **2 to heal up** : cicatrizarse

healer [ˈhiːlər] *n* : curador *m*, -dora *f*

health [ˈhɛlθ] *n* : salud *f*

healthful [ˈhɛlθfəl] *adj* : saludable, salubre — **healthfully** *adv*

healthy [ˈhɛlθi] *adj* **healthier; -est** : sano, bien — **healthily** [-θəli] *adv*

heap[1] [ˈhiːp] *vt* **1** PILE : amontonar, apilar **2** SHOWER : colmar

heap[2] *n* : montón *m*, pila *f*

hear [ˈhɪr] *v* **heard** [ˈhərd]; **hearing** *vt* **1** : oír <do you hear me? : ¿me oyes?> **2** HEED : oír, prestar atención a **3** LEARN : oír, enterarse de — *vi* **1** : oír <to hear about : oír hablar de> **2 to hear from** : tener noticias de

hearing [ˈhɪrɪŋ] *n* **1** : oído *m* <hard of hearing : duro de oído> **2** : vista *f* (en un tribunal) **3** ATTENTION : consideración *f*, oportunidad *f* de expresarse **4** EARSHOT : alcance *m* del oído

hearing aid *n* : audífono *m*

hearken [ˈhɑrkən] *vt* : escuchar

hearsay [ˈhɪr,seɪ] *n* : rumores *mpl*

hearse [ˈhərs] *n* : coche *m* fúnebre

heart [ˈhɑrt] *n* **1** : corazón *m* **2** CENTER, CORE : corazón *m*, centro *m* <the heart of the matter : el meollo del asunto> **3** FEELINGS : corazón *m*, sentimientos *mpl* <a broken heart : un corazón destrozado> <to have a good heart : tener buen corazón> <to take something to heart : tomarse algo a pecho> **4** COURAGE : valor *m*, corazón *m* <to take heart : animarse, cobrar ánimos> **5 hearts** *npl* : corazones *mpl* (en juegos de naipes) **6 by heart** : de memoria

heartache [ˈhɑrt̬,eɪk] *n* : pena *f*, angustia *f*

heart attack *n* : infarto *m*, ataque *m* al corazón

heartbeat [ˈhɑrt,biːt] *n* : latido *m* (del corazón)

heartbreak [ˈhɑrt,breɪk] *n* : congoja *f*, angustia *f*

heartbreaking [ˈhɑrt,breɪkɪŋ] *adj* : desgarrador, que parte el corazón

heartbroken [ˈhɑrt,broːkən] *adj* : desconsolado, destrozado

heartburn [ˈhɑrt,bərn] *n* : acidez *f* estomacal

hearten [ˈhɑrtən] *vt* : alentar, animar

hearth [ˈhɑrθ] *n* : hogar *m*, chimenea *f*

heartily [ˈhɑrt̬əli] *adv* **1** ENTHUSIASTICALLY : de buena gana, con entusiasmo **2** TOTALLY : totalmente, completamente

heartless [ˈhɑrtləs] *adj* : desalmado, despiadado, cruel

heartsick [ˈhɑrt,sɪk] *adj* : abatido, desconsolado

heartstrings [ˈhɑrt,strɪŋz] *npl* : fibras *fpl* del corazón

heartwarming [ˈhɑrt,wɔrmɪŋ] *adj* : conmovedor, emocionante

hearty [ˈhɑrt̬i] *adj* **heartier; -est 1** CORDIAL, WARM : cordial, caluroso **2** STRONG : fuerte <to have a hearty appetite : ser de buen comer> **3** SUBSTANTIAL : abundante, sustancioso <a hearty breakfast : un desayuno abundante>

heat[1] [ˈhiːt] *vt* : calentar

heat[2] *n* **1** WARMTH : calor *m* **2** HEATING : calefacción *f* **3** EXCITEMENT : calor *m*, entusiasmo *m* <in the heat of the moment : en el calor del momento> **4** ESTRUS : celo *m*

heated [ˈhiːt̬əd] *adj* **1** WARMED : calentado **2** IMPASSIONED : acalorado, apasionado

heater [ˈhiːt̬ər] *n* : calentador *m*, estufa *f*, calefactor *m*

heath [ˈhiːθ] *n* **1** MOOR : brezal *m*, páramo *m* **2** HEATHER : brezo *m*

heathen[1] [ˈhiːðən] *adj* : pagano

heathen[2] *n, pl* **-thens** *or* **-then** : pagano *m*, -na *f*; infiel *mf*

heather [ˈhɛðər] *n* : brezo *m*

heave[1] [ˈhiːv] *v* **heaved** *or* **hove** [ˈhoːv]; **heaving** *vt* **1** LIFT, RAISE : levantar con esfuerzo **2** HURL : lanzar, tirar **3 to heave a sigh** : echar un suspiro, suspirar — *vi* **1** : subir y bajar, palpitar (dícese del pecho) **2 to heave up** RISE : levantarse

heave[2] *n* **1** EFFORT : gran esfuerzo *m* (para levantar algo) **2** THROW : lanzamiento *m*

heaven [ˈhɛvən] *n* **1** : cielo *m* <for heaven's sake : por Dios> **2 heavens** *npl* SKY : cielo *m* <the heavens opened up : empezó a llover a cántaros>

heavenly [ˈhɛvənli] *adj* **1** : celestial, celeste **2** DELIGHTFUL : divino, encantador

heavily [ˈhɛvəli] *adv* **1** : pesadamente, con mucho peso **2** LABORIOUSLY : trabajosamente, penosamente **3** : mucho

heaviness [ˈhɛvinəs] *n* : peso *m*, pesadez *f*

heavy [ˈhɛvi] *adj* **heavier; -est 1** WEIGHTY : pesado **2** DENSE, THICK : denso, espeso, grueso **3** BURDENSOME : oneroso, gravoso **4** PROFOUND : profundo **5** SLUGGISH : lento, tardo **6** STOUT : corpulento **7** SEVERE : severo, duro, fuerte

heavy–duty [ˈhɛviˈduːt̬i, -ˈdjuː-] *adj* : muy resistente, fuerte

heavyweight [ˈhɛvi,weɪt] *n* : peso *m* pesado (en deportes)

Hebrew[1] [ˈhiː,bruː] *adj* : hebreo
Hebrew[2] *n* **1** : hebreo *m,* -brea *f* **2** : hebreo *m* (idioma)
heckle [ˈhɛkəl] *vt* **-led; -ling** : interrumpir (a un orador)
hectic [ˈhɛktɪk] *adj* : agitado, ajetreado — **hectically** [-tɪkli] *adv*
he'd [ˈhiːd] (*contraction of* **he had** *or* **he would**) → **have, would**
hedge[1] [ˈhɛdʒ] *v* **hedged; hedging** *vt* **1** : cercar con un seto **2 to hedge one's bet** : cubrirse — *vi* **1** : dar rodeos, contestar con evasivas **2 to hedge against** : cubrirse contra, protegerse contra
hedge[2] *n* **1** : seto *m* vivo **2** SAFEGUARD : salvaguardia *f,* protección *f*
hedgehog [ˈhɛdʒ,hɔg, -hɑg] *n* : erizo *m*
heed[1] [ˈhiːd] *vt* : prestar atención a, hacer caso de
heed[2] *n* : atención *f*
heedless [ˈhiːdləs] *adj* : descuidado, despreocupado, inconsciente <to be heedless of : hacer caso omiso de> — **heedlessly** *adv*
heel[1] [ˈhiːl] *vi* : inclinarse
heel[2] *n* : talón *m* (del pie), tacón *m* (de calzado)
heft [ˈhɛft] *vt* : sopesar
hefty [ˈhɛfti] *adj* **heftier; -est** : robusto, fornido, pesado
heifer [ˈhɛfər] *n* : novilla *f*
height [ˈhaɪt] *n* **1** PEAK : cumbre *f,* cima *f,* punto *m* alto <at the height of her career : en la cumbre de su carrera> <the height of stupidity : el colmo de la estupidez> **2** TALLNESS : estatura *f* (de una persona), altura *f* (de un objeto) **3** ALTITUDE : altura *f*
heighten [ˈhaɪtən] *vt* **1** : hacer más alto **2** INTENSIFY : aumentar, intensificar — *vi* : aumentarse, intensificarse
heinous [ˈheɪnəs] *adj* : atroz, abominable, nefando
heir [ˈær] *n* : heredero *m,* -ra *f*
heiress [ˈærəs] *n* : heredera *f*
heirloom [ˈær,luːm] *n* : reliquia *f* de familia
held → **hold**
helicopter [ˈhɛlə,kɑptər] *n* : helicóptero *m*
helium [ˈhiːliəm] *n* : helio *m*
hell [ˈhɛl] *n* : infierno *m*
he'll [ˈhiːl, ˈhɪl] (*contraction of* **he shall** *or* **he will**) → **shall, will**
hellish [ˈhɛlɪʃ] *adj* : horroroso, infernal
hello [həˈloː, hɛ-] *interj* : ¡hola!
helm [ˈhɛlm] *n* **1** : timón *m* **2 to take the helm** : tomar el mando
helmet [ˈhɛlmət] *n* : casco *m*
help[1] [ˈhɛlp] *vt* **1** AID, ASSIST : ayudar, auxiliar, socorrer, asistir **2** ALLEVIATE : aliviar **3** SERVE : servir <help yourself! : ¡sírvete!> **4** AVOID : evitar <it can't be helped : no lo podemos evitar, no hay más remedio> <I couldn't help smiling : no pude menos que sonreír>
help[2] *n* **1** ASSISTANCE : ayuda *f* <help! : ¡socorro!, ¡auxilio!> **2** STAFF : personal *m* (en una oficina), servicio *m* doméstico
helper [ˈhɛlpər] *n* : ayudante *mf*
helpful [ˈhɛlpfəl] *adj* **1** OBLIGING : servicial, amable, atento **2** USEFUL : útil, práctico — **helpfully** *adv*
helpfulness [ˈhɛlpfəlnəs] *n* **1** KINDNESS : bondad *f,* amabilidad *f* **2** USEFULNESS : utilidad *f*
helping [ˈhɛlpɪŋ] *n* : porción *f*
helpless [ˈhɛlpləs] *adj* **1** POWERLESS : incapaz, impotente **2** DEFENSELESS : indefenso
helplessly [ˈhɛlpləsli] *adv* : en vano, inútilmente
helplessness [ˈhɛlpləsnəs] *n* POWERLESSNESS : incapacidad *f,* impotencia *f*
helter–skelter [,hɛltərˈskɛltər] *adv* : atropelladamente, precipitadamente
hem[1] [ˈhɛm] *vt* **hemmed; hemming 1** : dobladillar **2 to hem in** : encerrar
hem[2] *n* : dobladillo *m,* bastilla *f*
hemisphere [ˈhɛmə,sfɪr] *n* : hemisferio *m*
hemispheric [,hɛməˈsfɪrɪk, -ˈsfɛr-] *or* **hemispherical** [-ɪkəl] *adj* : hemisférico
hemlock [ˈhɛm,lɑk] *n* : cicuta *f*
hemoglobin [ˈhiːmə,gloːbən] *n* : hemoglobina *f*
hemophilia [,hiːməˈfɪliə] *n* : hemofilia *f*
hemorrhage[1] [ˈhɛmərɪdʒ] *vi* **-rhaged; -rhaging** : sufrir una hemorragia
hemorrhage[2] *n* : hemorragia *f*
hemorrhoids [ˈhɛmə,rɔɪdz, ˈhɛm,rɔɪdz] *npl* : hemorroides *fpl,* almorranas *fpl*
hemp [ˈhɛmp] *n* : cáñamo *m*
hen [ˈhɛn] *n* : gallina *f*
hence [ˈhɛnts] *adv* **1** : de aquí, de ahí <10 years hence : de aquí a 10 años> <a dog bit me, hence my dislike of animals : un perro me mordió, de ahí mi aversión a los animales> **2** THEREFORE : por lo tanto, por consiguiente
henceforth [ˈhɛnts,forθ, ,hɛntsˈ-] *adv* : de ahora en adelante
henchman [ˈhɛntʃmən] *n, pl* **-men** [-mən, -,mɛn] : secuaz *mf,* esbirro *m*
henpeck [ˈhɛn,pɛk] *vt* : dominar (al marido)
hepatitis [,hɛpəˈtaɪtəs] *n, pl* **-titides** [-ˈtɪtə,diːz] : hepatitis *f*
her[1] [ˈhər] *adj* : su, sus, de ella <her house : su casa, la casa de ella>
her[2] [ˈhər, ər] *pron* **1** (*used as direct object*) : la <I saw her yesterday : la vi ayer> **2** (*used as indirect object*) : le, se <he gave her the book : le dio el libro> <he sent it to her : se lo mandó> **3** (*used as object of a preposition*) : ella <we did it for her : lo hicimos por ella> <taller than her : más alto que ella>

herald[1] [ˈhɛrəld] *vt* ANNOUNCE : anunciar, proclamar

herald[2] *n* **1** MESSENGER : heraldo *m* **2** HARBINGER : precursor *m*

heraldic [hɛˈrældɪk, hə-] *adj* : heráldico

heraldry [ˈhɛrəldri] *n, pl* **-ries** : heráldica *f*

herb [ˈərb, ˈhərb] *n* : hierba *f*

herbal [ˈərbəl, ˈhər-] *adj* : herbario

herbicide [ˈərbəˌsaɪd, ˈhər-] *n* : herbicida *m*

herbivore [ˈərbəˌvor, ˈhər-] *n* : herbívoro *m*

herbivorous [ˌərˈbɪvərəs, ˌhər-] *adj* : herbívoro

herculean [ˌhərkjəˈliːən, ˌhərˈkjuːliən] *adj* : hercúleo, sobrehumano

herd[1] [ˈhərd] *vt* : reunir en manada, conducir en manada — *vi* : ir en manada (dícese de los animales), apiñarse (dícese de la gente)

herd[2] *n* : manada *f*

herder [ˈhərdər] → **herdsman**

herdsman [ˈhərdzmən] *n, pl* **-men** [-mən, -ˌmɛn] : vaquero *m* (de ganado), pastor *m* (de ovejas)

here [ˈhɪr] *adv* **1** : aquí, acá <come here! : ¡ven acá!> <right here : aquí mismo> **2** NOW : en este momento, ahora, ya <here he comes : ya viene> <here it's three o'clock (already) : ahora son las tres> **3** : en este punto <here we agree : estamos de acuerdo en este punto> **4 here you are!** : ¡toma!

hereabouts [ˈhɪrəˌbaʊts] *or* **hereabout** [-ˌbaʊt] *adv* : por aquí (cerca)

hereafter[1] [hɪrˈæftər] *adv* **1** : de aquí en adelante, a continuación **2** : en el futuro

hereafter[2] *n* **the hereafter** : el más allá

hereby [hɪrˈbaɪ] *adv* : por este medio

hereditary [həˈrɛdəˌtɛri] *adj* : hereditario

heredity [həˈrɛdət̬i] *n* : herencia *f*

herein [hɪrˈɪn] *adv* : aquí

hereof [hɪrˈʌv] *adv* : de aquí

hereon [hɪrˈɑn, -ˈɔn] *adv* : sobre esto

heresy [ˈhɛrəsi] *n, pl* **-sies** : herejía *f*

heretic [ˈhɛrəˌtɪk] *n* : hereje *mf*

heretical [həˈrɛt̬ɪkəl] *adj* : herético

hereto [hɪrˈtuː] *adv* : a esto

heretofore [ˈhɪrt̬əˌfor] *adv* HITHERTO : hasta ahora

hereunder [hɪrˈʌndər] *adv* : a continuación, abajo

hereupon [hɪrəˈpɑn, -ˈpɔn] *adv* : con esto, en ese momento

herewith [hɪrˈwɪθ] *adv* : adjunto

heritage [ˈhɛrət̬ɪdʒ] *n* : patrimonio *m* (nacional)

hermaphrodite [hərˈmæfrəˌdaɪt] *n* : hermafrodita *mf*

hermetic [hərˈmɛt̬ɪk] *adj* : hermético — **hermetically** [-t̬ɪkli] *adv*

hermit [ˈhərmət] *n* : ermitaño *m*, -ña *f*; eremita *mf*

hernia [ˈhərniə] *n, pl* **-nias** *or* **-niae** [-niˌiː, -niˌaɪ] : hernia *f*

hero [ˈhiːˌroː, ˈhɪrˌoː] *n, pl* **-roes** **1** : héroe *m* **2** PROTAGONIST : protagonista *mf*

heroic [hɪˈroːɪk] *adj* : heroico — **heroically** [-ɪkli] *adv*

heroics [hɪˈroːɪks] *npl* : actos *mpl* heroicos

heroin [ˈhɛroən] *n* : heroína *f*

heroine [ˈhɛroən] *n* **1** : heroína *f* **2** PROTAGONIST : protagonista *f*

heroism [ˈhɛroˌɪzəm] *n* : heroísmo *m*

heron [ˈhɛrən] *n* : garza *f*

herpes [ˈhərˌpiːz] *n* : herpes *m*

herpetology [ˌhərpəˈtɑlədʒi] *n* : herpetología *f*

herring [ˈhɛrɪŋ] *n, pl* **-ring** *or* **-rings** : arenque *m*

hers [ˈhərz] *pron* : suyo, -ya; suyos, -yas; de ella <these shoes are hers : estos zapatos son suyos> <hers are bigger : los de ella son más grandes>

herself [hərˈsɛlf] *pron* **1** (*used reflexively*) : se <she dressed herself : se vistió> **2** (*used emphatically*) : ella misma <she fixed it herself : lo arregló ella misma, lo arregló por sí sola>

hertz [ˈhərts, ˈhɛrts] *ns & pl* : hercio *m*

he's [ˈhiːz] (*contraction of* **he is** *or* **he has**) → **be, have**

hesitancy [ˈhɛzət̬əntsi] *n, pl* **-cies** : vacilación *f*, titubeo *m*, indecisión *f*

hesitant [ˈhɛzət̬ənt] *adj* : titubeante, vacilante — **hesitantly** *adv*

hesitate [ˈhɛzəˌteɪt] *vi* **-tated; -tating** : vacilar, titubear

hesitation [ˌhɛzəˈteɪʃən] *n* : vacilación *f*, indecisión *f*, titubeo *m*

heterogeneous [ˌhɛt̬ərəˈdʒiːniəs, -njəs] *adj* : heterogéneo

heterosexual[1] [ˌhɛt̬əroˈsɛkʃʊəl] *adj* : heterosexual

heterosexual[2] *n* : heterosexual *mf*

heterosexuality [ˌhɛt̬əroˌsɛkʃʊˈælət̬i] *n* : heterosexualidad *f*

hew [ˈhjuː] *v* **hewed; hewed** *or* **hewn** [ˈhjuːn]; **hewing** *vt* **1** CUT : cortar, talar (árboles) **2** SHAPE : labrar, tallar — *vi* CONFORM : conformarse, ceñirse

hex[1] [ˈhɛks] *vt* : hacerle un maleficio (a alguien)

hex[2] *n* : maleficio *m*

hexagon [ˈhɛksəˌgɑn] *n* : hexágono *m*

hexagonal [hɛkˈsægənəl] *adj* : hexagonal

hey [ˈheɪ] *interj* : ¡eh!, ¡oye!

heyday [ˈheɪˌdeɪ] *n* : auge *m*, apogeo *m*

hi [ˈhaɪ] *interj* : ¡hola!

hiatus [haɪˈeɪt̬əs] *n* **1** : hiato *m* **2** PAUSE : pausa *f*

hibernate [ˈhaɪbərˌneɪt] *vi* **-nated; -nating** : hibernar, invernar

hibernation [ˌhaɪbərˈneɪʃən] *n* : hibernación *f*

hiccup[1] [ˈhɪkəp] *vi* **-cuped; -cuping** : hipar, tener hipo

hiccup² *n* : hipo *m* <to have the hiccups : tener hipo>
hick [ˈhɪk] *n* BUMPKIN : palurdo *m*, -da *f*
hickory [ˈhɪkəri] *n, pl* **-ries** : nogal *m* americano
hidden [ˈhɪdən] *adj* : oculto
hide¹ [ˈhaɪd] *v* **hid** [ˈhɪd]; **hidden** [ˈhɪdən] *or* **hid; hiding** *vt* **1** CONCEAL : esconder **2** ocultar <to hide one's motives : ocultar uno sus motivos> **3** SCREEN : tapar, no dejar ver — *vi* : esconderse
hide² *n* : piel *f*, cuero *m* <to save one's hide : salvar el pellejo>
hide–and–seek [ˈhaɪdəndˈsiːk] *n* **to play hide–and–seek** : jugar a las escondidas
hidebound [ˈhaɪd,baʊnd] *adj* : rígido, conservador
hideous [ˈhɪdiəs] *adj* : horrible, horroroso, espantoso — **hideously** *adv*
hideout [ˈhaɪd,aʊt] *n* : guarida *f*, escondrijo *m*
hierarchical [,haɪəˈrɑrkɪkəl] *adj* : jerárquico
hierarchy [ˈhaɪə,rɑrki] *n, pl* **-chies** : jerarquía *f*
hieroglyphic [,haɪərəˈglɪfɪk] *n* : jeroglífico *m*
hi–fi [ˈhaɪˈfaɪ] *n* **1** → **high fidelity** **2** : equipo *m* de alta fidelidad
high¹ [ˈhaɪ] *adv* : alto
high² *adj* **1** TALL : alto <a high wall : una pared alta> **2** ELEVATED : alto, elevado <high prices : precios elevados> <high blood pressure : presión alta> **3** GREAT, IMPORTANT : grande, importante, alto <a high number : un número grande> <high society : alta sociedad> <high hopes : grandes esperanzas> **4** : alto (en música) **5** INTOXICATED : borracho, drogado
high³ *n* **1** : récord *m*, punto *m* máximo <to reach an all-time high : batir el récord> **2** : zona *f* de alta presión (en meteorología) **3** *or* **high gear** : directa *f* **4 on high** : en las alturas
highbrow [ˈhaɪ,braʊ] *n* : intelectual *mf*
higher [ˈhaɪər] *adj* : superior
high fidelity *n* : alta fidelidad *f*
high–flown [ˈhaɪˈfloːn] *adj* : altisonante
high–handed [ˈhaɪˈhændəd] *adj* : arbitrario
highlands [ˈhaɪləndz] *npl* : tierras *fpl* altas, altiplano *m*
highlight¹ [ˈhaɪ,laɪt] *vt* **1** EMPHASIZE : destacar, poner en relieve, subrayar **2** : ser el punto culminante de
highlight² *n* : punto *m* culminante
highly [ˈhaɪli] *adv* **1** VERY : muy, sumamente **2** FAVORABLY : muy bien <to speak highly of : hablar muy bien de> <to think highly of : tener en mucho a>
highness [ˈhaɪnəs] *n* **1** HEIGHT : altura *f* **2 Highness** : Alteza *f* <Your Royal Highness : Su Alteza Real>
high–rise [ˈhaɪ,raɪz] *adj* : alto, de muchas plantas
high school *n* : escuela *f* superior, escuela *f* secundaria
high seas *npl* : alta mar *f*
high–spirited [ˈhaɪˈspɪrət̬əd] *adj* : vivaz, muy animado, brioso
high–strung [,haɪˈstrʌŋ] *adj* : nervioso, excitable
highway [ˈhaɪ,weɪ] *n* : carretera *f*
highwayman [ˈhaɪ,weɪmən] *n, pl* **-men** [- mən, -,mɛn] : salteador *m* (de caminos), bandido *m*
hijack¹ [ˈhaɪ,dʒæk] *vt* : secuestrar
hijack² *n* : secuestro *m*
hijacker [ˈhaɪ,dʒækər] *n* : secuestrador *m*, -dora *f*
hike¹ [ˈhaɪk] *v* **hiked; hiking** *vi* : hacer una caminata — *vt* RAISE : subir
hike² *n* **1** : caminata *f*, excursión *f* **2** INCREASE : subida *f* (de precios)
hiker [ˈhaɪkər] *n* : excursionista *mf*
hilarious [hɪˈlæriəs, haɪˈ-] *adj* : muy divertido, hilarante
hilarity [hɪˈlærəti, haɪ-] *n* : hilaridad *f*
hill [ˈhɪl] *n* **1** : colina *f*, cerro *m* **2** SLOPE : cuesta *f*, pendiente *f*
hillbilly [ˈhɪl,bɪli] *n, pl* **-lies** : palurdo *m*, -da *f* (de las montañas)
hillock [ˈhɪlək] *n* : loma *f*, altozano *m*, otero *m*
hillside [ˈhɪl,saɪd] *n* : ladera *f*, cuesta *f*
hilltop [ˈhɪl,tɑp] *n* : cima *f*, cumbre *f*
hilly [ˈhɪli] *adj* **hillier; -est** : montañoso, accidentado
hilt [ˈhɪlt] *n* : puño *m*, empuñadura *f*
him [ˈhɪm, əm] *pron* **1** (*used as direct object*) : lo <I found him : lo encontré> **2** (*used as indirect object*) : le, se <we gave him a present : le dimos un regalo> <I sent it to him : se lo mandé> **3** (*used as object of a preposition*) : él <she was thinking of him : pensaba en él> <younger than him : más joven que él>
himself [hɪmˈsɛlf] *pron* **1** (*used reflexively*) : se <he washed himself : se lavó> **2** (*used emphatically*) : él mismo <he did it himself : lo hizo él mismo, lo hizo por sí solo>
hind¹ [ˈhaɪnd] *adj* : trasero, posterior <hind legs : patas traseras>
hind² *n* : cierva *f*
hinder [ˈhɪndər] *vt* : dificultar, impedir, estorbar
hindquarters [ˈhaɪnd,kwɔrt̬ərz] *npl* : cuartos *mpl* traseros
hindrance [ˈhɪndrənts] *n* : estorbo *m*, obstáculo *m*, impedimento *m*
hindsight [ˈhaɪnd,saɪt] *n* : retrospectiva *f* <with the benefit of hindsight : en retrospectiva, con la perspectiva que da la experiencia>
Hindu¹ [ˈhɪn,duː] *adj* : hindú
Hindu² *n* : hindú *mf*
Hinduism [ˈhɪnduː,ɪzəm] *n* : hinduismo *m*

hinge[1] [ˈhɪndʒ] *v* **hinged; hinging** *vt* : unir con bisagras — *vi* **to hinge on** : depender de

hinge[2] *n* : bisagra *f,* gozne *m*

hint[1] [ˈhɪnt] *vt* : insinuar, dar a entender — *vi* : soltar indirectas

hint[2] *n* **1** INSINUATION : insinuación *f,* indirecta *f* **2** TIP : consejo *m,* sugerencia *f* **3** TRACE : pizca *f,* indicio *m*

hinterland [ˈhɪntərˌlænd, -lənd] *n* : interior *m* (de un país)

hip [ˈhɪp] *n* : cadera *f*

hippopotamus [ˌhɪpəˈpɑt̬əməs] *n, pl* **-muses** *or* **-mi** [-ˌmaɪ] : hipopótamo *m*

hippo [ˈhɪpoː] *n, pl* **hippos** → **hippopotamus**

hire[1] [ˈhaɪr] *vt* **hired; hiring 1** EMPLOY : contratar, emplear **2** RENT : alquilar, arrendar

hire[2] *n* **1** RENT : alquiler *m* <for hire : se alquila> **2** WAGES : paga *f,* sueldo *m* **3** EMPLOYEE : empleado *m,* -da *f*

his[1] [ˈhɪz, ɪz] *adj* : su, sus, de él <his hat : su sombrero, el sombrero de él>

his[2] *pron* : suyo, -ya; suyos, suyas; de él <the decision is his : la decisión es suya> <it's his, not hers : es de él, no de ella>

Hispanic[1] [hɪˈspænɪk] *adj* : hispano, hispánico

Hispanic[2] *n* : hispano *m,* -na *f;* hispánico *m,* -ca *f*

hiss[1] [ˈhɪs] *vi* : sisear, silbar — *vt* : decir entre dientes

hiss[2] *n* : siseo *m,* silbido *m*

historian [hɪˈstɔriən] *n* : historiador *m,* -dora *f*

historic [hɪˈstɔrɪk] *or* **historical** [-ɪkəl] *adj* : histórico — **historically** [-ɪkli] *adv*

history [ˈhɪstəri] *n, pl* **-ries 1** : historia *f* **2** RECORD : historial *m*

histrionics [ˌhɪstriˈɑnɪks] *ns & pl* : histrionismo *m*

hit[1] [ˈhɪt] *v* **hit; hitting** *vt* **1** STRIKE : golpear, pegar, batear (una pelota) <he hit the dog : le pegó al perro> **2** : chocar contra, dar con, dar en (el blanco) <the car hit a tree : el coche chocó contra un árbol> **3** AFFECT : afectar <the news hit us hard : la noticia nos afectó mucho> **4** ENCOUNTER : tropezar con, toparse con <to hit a snag : tropezar con un obstáculo> **5** REACH : llegar a, alcanzar <the price hit $10 a pound : el precio alcanzó los $10 dólares por libra> <to hit town : llegar a la ciudad> <to hit the headlines : ser noticia> **6 to hit on** *or* **to hit upon** : dar con — *vi* : golpear

hit[2] *n* **1** BLOW : golpe *m* **2** : impacto *m* (de un arma) **3** SUCCESS : éxito *m*

hitch[1] [ˈhɪtʃ] *vt* **1** : mover con sacudidas **2** ATTACH : enganchar, atar, amarrar **3** → **hitchhike 4 to hitch up** : subirse (los pantalones, etc.)

hitch[2] *n* **1** JERK : tirón *m,* jalón *m* **2** OBSTACLE : obstáculo *m,* impedimento *m,* tropiezo *m*

hitchhike [ˈhɪtʃˌhaɪk] *vi* **-hiked; -hiking** : hacer autostop, ir de aventón *Col, Mex fam*

hitchhiker [ˈhɪtʃˌhaɪkər] *n* : autostopista *mf*

hither [ˈhɪðər] *adv* : acá, por aquí

hitherto [ˈhɪðərˌtuː, ˌhɪðərˈ-] *adv* : hasta ahora

hitter [ˈhɪt̬ər] *n* BATTER : bateador *m,* -dora *f*

HIV [ˌeɪtʃˌaɪˈviː] *n* : VIH *m,* virus *m* del sida

hive [ˈhaɪv] *n* **1** : colmena *f* **2** SWARM : enjambre *m* **3** : lugar *m* muy activo <a hive of activity : un hervidero de actividad>

hives [ˈhaɪvz] *ns & pl* : urticaria *f*

hoard[1] [ˈhord] *vt* : acumular, atesorar

hoard[2] *n* : tesoro *m,* reserva *f,* provisión *f*

hoarfrost [ˈhorˌfrɔst] *n* : escarcha *f*

hoarse [ˈhors] *adj* **hoarser; -est** : ronco — **hoarsely** *adv*

hoarseness [ˈhorsnəs] *n* : ronquera *f*

hoary [ˈhori] *adj* **hoarier; -est 1** : cano, canoso **2** OLD : vetusto, antiguo

hoax[1] [ˈhoːks] *vt* : engañar, embaucar, bromar

hoax[2] *n* : engaño *m,* broma *f*

hobble[1] [ˈhɑbəl] *v* **-bled; -bling** *vi* LIMP : cojear, renguear — *vt* : manear (un animal)

hobble[2] *n* **1** LIMP : cojera *f,* rengo *m* **2** : maniota *f* (para un animal)

hobby [ˈhɑbi] *n, pl* **-bies** : pasatiempo *m,* afición *f*

hobgoblin [ˈhɑbˌgɑblən] *n* : duende *m*

hobnail [ˈhɑbˌneɪl] *n* : tachuela *f*

hobnob [ˈhɑbˌnɑb] *vi* **-nobbed; -nobbing** : codearse

hobo [ˈhoːˌboː] *n, pl* **-boes** : vagabundo *m,* -da *f*

hock[1] [ˈhɑk] *vt* PAWN : empeñar

hock[2] *n* **in hock** : empeñado

hockey [ˈhɑki] *n* : hockey *m*

hod [ˈhɑd] *n* : capacho *m* (de albañil)

hodgepodge [ˈhɑdʒˌpɑdʒ] *n* : mezcolanza *f*

hoe[1] [ˈhoː] *vt* **hoed; hoeing** : azadonar

hoe[2] *n* : azada *f,* azadón *m*

hog[1] [ˈhɔg, ˈhɑg] *vt* **hogged; hogging** : acaparar, monopolizar

hog[2] *n* **1** PIG : cerdo *m,* -da *f* **2** GLUTTON : glotón *m,* -tona *f*

hogshead [ˈhɔgzˌhɛd, ˈhɑgz-] *n* : tonel *m*

hoist[1] [ˈhɔɪst] *vt* : levantar, alzar, izar (una bandera, una vela)

hoist[2] *n* : grúa *f*

hold[1] [ˈhoːld] *v* **held** [ˈhɛld]; **holding** *vt* **1** POSSESS : tener <to hold office : ocupar un puesto> **2** RESTRAIN : detener, controlar <to hold one's temper : controlar su mal genio> **3** CLASP, GRASP : agarrar, coger <to hold hands : agarrarse de la mano> **4** : sujetar, mantener fijo <hold this nail for me : sujétame este clavo> **5** CONTAIN : contener, dar cabida a **6** SUPPORT : aguantar, sostener **7** REGARD : considerar, tener <he held me responsible : me consideró responsable> **8** CONDUCT : celebrar (una reunión), realizar (un evento), mantener (una conversación) — *vi* **1** : aguantar, resistir <the rope will hold : la cuerda resistirá> **2** : ser válido, valer <my offer still holds : mi oferta todavía es válida> **3 to hold forth** : perorar, arengar **4 to hold to** : mantenerse firme en **5 to hold with** : estar de acuerdo con

hold[2] *n* **1** GRIP : agarre *m,* llave *f* (en deportes) **2** CONTROL : control *m,* dominio *m* <to get hold of oneself : controlarse> **3** DELAY : demora *f* <to put on hold : suspender temporalmente> **4** : bodega *f* (en un barco o un avión) **5 to get hold of** : conseguir, localizar

holder [ˈhoːldər] *n* : poseedor *m,* -dora *f;* titular *mf*

holdings [ˈhoːldɪŋz] *npl* : propiedades *fpl*

hold out *vi* **1** LAST : aguantar, durar **2** RESIST : resistir

holdup [ˈhoːldˌʌp] *n* **1** ROBBERY : atraco *m* **2** DELAY : retraso *m,* demora *f*

hold up *vt* **1** ROB : robarle (a alguien), atracar, asaltar **2** DELAY : retrasar

hole [ˈhoːl] *n* : agujero *m,* hoyo *m*

holiday [ˈhɑləˌdeɪ] *n* **1** : día *m* feriado, fiesta *f* **2** VACATION : vacaciones *fpl*

holiness [ˈhoːlinəs] *n* **1** : santidad *f* **2 His Holiness** : Su Santidad

holistic [hoːˈlɪstɪk] *adj* : holístico

holler[1] [ˈhɑlər] *vi* : gritar, chillar

holler[2] *n* : grito *m,* chillido *m*

hollow[1] [ˈhɑˌloː] *vt or* **to hollow out** : ahuecar

hollow[2] *adj* **-lower; -est** **1** : hueco, hundido (dícese de las mejillas, etc.), cavernoso (dícese de un sonido) **2** EMPTY, FALSE : vacío, falso

hollow[3] *n* **1** CAVITY : hueco *m,* depresión *f,* cavidad *f* **2** VALLEY : hondonada *f,* valle *m*

hollowness [ˈhɑˌloːnəs] *n* **1** HOLLOW : hueco *m,* cavidad *f* **2** FALSENESS : falsedad *f* **3** EMPTINESS : vacuidad *f*

holly [ˈhɑli] *n, pl* **-lies** : acebo *m*

hollyhock [ˈhɑliˌhɑk] *n* : malvarrosa *f*

holocaust [ˈhɑləˌkɔst, ˈhoː-, ˈhɔ-] *n* : holocausto *m*

holster [ˈhoːlstər] *n* : pistolera *f*

holy [ˈhoːli] *adj* **-lier; -est** : santo, sagrado

Holy Ghost → **Holy Spirit**

Holy Spirit *n* **the Holy Spirit** : el Espíritu Santo

homage [ˈɑmɪdʒ, ˈhɑ-] *n* : homenaje *m*

home [ˈhoːm] *n* **1** : casa *f,* hogar *m,* domicilio *m* <to feel at home : sentirse en casa> **2** INSTITUTION : residencia *f,* asilo *m*

homecoming [ˈhoːmˌkʌmɪŋ] *n* : regreso *m* (a casa)

homegrown [ˈhoːmˈgroːn] *adj* **1** : de cosecha propia **2** LOCAL : local

homeland [ˈhoːmˌlænd] *n* : patria *f,* tierra *f* natal, terruño *m*

homeless [ˈhoːmləs] *adj* : sin hogar, sin techo

homely [ˈhoːmli] *adj* **-lier; -est** **1** DOMESTIC : casero, hogareño **2** UGLY : feo, poco atractivo

homemade [ˈhoːmˈmeɪd] *adj* : casero, hecho en casa

homemaker [ˈhoːmˌmeɪkər] *n* : ama *f* de casa, persona *f* que se ocupa de la casa

home plate *n* : base *f* del bateador

home run *n* : jonrón *m*

homesick [ˈhoːmˌsɪk] *adj* : nostálgico <to be homesick : echar de menos a la familia>

homesickness [ˈhoːmˌsɪknəs] *n* : nostalgia *f,* morriña *f*

homespun [ˈhoːmˌspʌn] *adj* : simple, sencillo

homestead [ˈhoːmˌstɛd] *n* : estancia *f,* hacienda *f*

homeward[1] [ˈhoːmwərd] *or* **homewards** [-wərdz] *adv* : de vuelta a casa, hacia casa

homeward[2] *adj* : de vuelta, de regreso

homework [ˈhoːmˌwərk] *n* : tarea *f,* deberes *mpl Spain,* asignación *f PRi*

homey [ˈhoːmi] *adj* **homier; -est** : hogareño

homicidal [ˌhɑməˈsaɪdəl, ˌhoː-] *adj* : homicida

homicide [ˈhɑməˌsaɪd, ˈhoː-] *n* : homicidio *m*

hominy [ˈhɑməni] *n* : maíz *m* descascarillado

homogeneous [ˌhoːməˈdʒiːniəs, -njəs] *adj* : homogéneo — **homogeneously** *adv*

homogenize [hoːˈmɑdʒəˌnaɪz, hə-] *vt* **-nized; -nizing** : homogeneizar

homograph [ˈhɑməˌgræf, ˈhoː-] *n* : homógrafo *m*

homonym [ˈhɑməˌnɪm, ˈhoː-] *n* : homónimo *m*

homophone [ˈhɑməˌfoːn, ˈhoː-] *n* : homófono *m*

homosexual[1] [ˌhoːməˈsɛkʃʊəl] *adj* : homosexual

homosexual[2] *n* : homosexual *mf*

homosexuality [ˌhoːməˌsɛkʃʊˈæləṭi] *n* : homosexualidad *f*

Honduran [hɑnˈdʊrən, -ˈdjʊr-] *n* : hondureño *m,* -ña *f* — **Honduran** *adj*

hone [ˈhoːn] *vt* **honed; honing** : afilar

honest [ˈɑnəst] *adj* : honesto, honrado — **honestly** *adv*

honesty [ˈɑnəsti] *n, pl* **-ties** : honestidad *f,* honradez *f*

honey [ˈhʌni] *n, pl* **-eys** : miel *f*

honeybee [ˈhʌniˌbiː] *n* : abeja *f*

honeycomb [ˈhʌniˌkoːm] *n* : panal *m*

honeymoon[1] [ˈhʌniˌmuːn] *vi* : pasar la luna de miel
honeymoon[2] *n* : luna *f* de miel
honeysuckle [ˈhʌniˌsʌkəl] *n* : madreselva *f*
honk[1] [ˈhɑŋk, ˈhɔŋk] *vi* **1** : graznar (dícese del ganso) **2** : tocar la bocina (dícese de un vehículo), pitar
honk[2] *n* : graznido *m* (del ganso), bocinazo *m* (de un vehículo)
honor[1] [ˈɑnər] *vt* **1** RESPECT : honrar **2** : cumplir con <to honor one's word : cumplir con su palabra> **3** : aceptar (un cheque, etc.)
honor[2] *n* **1** : honor *m* <in honor of : en honor de> **2 honors** *npl* AWARDS : honores *mpl*, condecoraciones *fpl* **3 Your Honor** : Su Señoría
honorable [ˈɑnərəbəl] *adj* : honorable, honroso — **honorably** [-bli] *adv*
honorary [ˈɑnəˌrɛri] *adj* : honorario
hood [ˈhʊd] *n* **1** : capucha *f* **2** : capó *m*, bonete *m Car* (de un automóvil)
hooded [ˈhʊdəd] *adj* : encapuchado
hoodlum [ˈhʊdləm, ˈhuːd-] *n* THUG : maleante *mf*, matón *m*
hoodwink [ˈhʊdˌwɪŋk] *vt* : engañar
hoof [ˈhʊf, ˈhuːf] *n, pl* **hooves** [ˈhʊvz, ˈhuːvz] *or* **hoofs** : pezuña *f*, casco *m*
hoofed [ˈhʊft, ˈhuːft] *adj* : ungulado
hook[1] [ˈhʊk] *vt* : enganchar — *vi* : abrocharse, engancharse
hook[2] *n* : gancho *m*, percha *f*
hookworm [ˈhʊkˌwərm] *n* : anquilostoma *m*
hooligan [ˈhuːlɪgən] *n* : gamberro *m*, -rra *f*
hoop [ˈhuːp] *n* : aro *m*
hooray [hʊˈreɪ] → **hurrah**
hoot[1] [ˈhuːt] *vi* **1** SHOUT : gritar <to hoot with laughter : morirse de risa, reírse a carcajadas> **2** : ulular (dícese de un búho), tocar la bocina (dícese de un vehículo), silbar (dícese de un tren o un barco)
hoot[2] *n* **1** : ululato *m* (de un búho), silbido *m* (de un tren), bocinazo *m* (de un vehículo) **2** GUFFAW : carcajada *f*, risotada *f* **3 I don't give a hoot** : me vale un comino, me importa un pito
hop[1] [ˈhɑp] *vi* **hopped; hopping** : brincar, saltar
hop[2] *n* **1** LEAP : salto *m*, brinco *m* **2** FLIGHT : vuelo *m* corto **3** : lúpulo *m* (planta)
hope[1] [ˈhoːp] *v* **hoped; hoping** *vi* : esperar — *vt* : esperar que <we hope she comes : esperamos que venga> <I hope not : espero que no>
hope[2] *n* : esperanza *f*
hopeful [ˈhoːpfəl] *adj* : esperanzado — **hopefully** *adv*
hopeless [ˈhoːpləs] *adj* **1** DESPAIRING : desesperado **2** IMPOSSIBLE : imposible <a hopeless case : un caso perdido>
hopelessly [ˈhoːpləsli] *adv* **1** : sin esperanzas, desesperadamente **2** COMPLETELY : totalmente, completamente **3** IMPOSSIBLY : imposiblemente
hopelessness [ˈhoːpləsnəs] *n* : desesperanza *f*
hopper [ˈhɑpər] *n* : tolva *f*
hopscotch [ˈhɑpˌskɑtʃ] *n* : tejo *m*
horde [ˈhord] *n* : horda *f*, multitud *f*
horizon [həˈraɪzən] *n* : horizonte *m*
horizontal [ˌhɔrəˈzɑntəl] *adj* : horizontal — **horizontally** *adv*
hormone [ˈhɔrˌmoːn] *n* : hormona *f* — **hormonal** [hɔrˈmoːnəl] *adj*
horn [ˈhɔrn] *n* **1** : cuerno *m* (de un toro, una vaca, etc.) **2** : cuerno *m*, trompa *f* (instrumento musical) **3** : bocina *f*, claxon *m* (de un vehículo)
horned [ˈhɔrnd, ˈhɔrnəd] *adj* : cornudo, astado, con cuernos
hornet [ˈhɔrnət] *n* : avispón *m*
horn of plenty → **cornucopia**
horny [ˈhɔrni] *adj* **hornier; -est** CALLOUS : calloso
horoscope [ˈhɔrəˌskoːp] *n* : horóscopo *m*
horrendous [hɔˈrɛndəs] *adj* : horrendo, horroroso, atroz
horrible [ˈhɔrəbəl] *adj* : horrible, espantoso, horroroso — **horribly** [-bli] *adv*
horrid [ˈhɔrɪd] *adj* : horroroso, horrible — **horridly** *adv*
horrify [ˈhɔrəˌfaɪ] *vt* **-fied; -fying** : horrorizar
horrifying [ˈhɔrəˌfaɪɪŋ] *adj* : horripilante, horroroso
horror [ˈhɔrər] *n* : horror *m*
hors d'oeuvre [ɔrˈdərv] *n, pl* **hors d'oeuvres** [-ˈdərvz] : entremés *m*
horse [ˈhɔrs] *n* : caballo *m*
horseback [ˈhɔrsˌbæk] *n* **on ~** : a caballo
horse chestnut *n* : castaña *f* de Indias
horsefly [ˈhɔrsˌflaɪ] *n, pl* **-flies** : tábano *m*
horsehair [ˈhɔrsˌhær] *n* : crin *f*
horseman [ˈhɔrsmən] *n, pl* **-men** [-mən, -ˌmɛn] : jinete *m*, caballista *m*
horsemanship [ˈhɔrsmənˌʃɪp] *n* : equitación *f*
horseplay [ˈhɔrsˌpleɪ] *n* : payasadas *fpl*
horsepower [ˈhɔrsˌpaʊər] *n* : caballo *m* de fuerza
horseradish [ˈhɔrsˌrædɪʃ] *n* : rábano *m* picante
horseshoe [ˈhɔrsˌʃuː] *n* : herradura *f*
horsewhip [ˈhɔrsˌ*h*wɪp] *vt* **-whipped; -whipping** : azotar, darle fuetazos (a alguien)
horsewoman [ˈhɔrsˌwʊmən] *n, pl* **-women** [-ˌwɪmən] : amazona *f*, jinete *f*, caballista *f*
horsey *or* **horsy** [ˈhɔrsi] *adj* **horsier; -est** : relacionado a los caballos, caballar
horticultural [ˌhɔrt̬əˈkʌltʃərəl] *adj* : hortícola
horticulture [ˈhɔrt̬əˌkʌltʃər] *n* : horticultura *f*

hose[1] [ˈhoːz] *vt* **hosed; hosing :** regar o lavar con manguera

hose[2] *n* **1** *pl* **hose** SOCKS **:** calcetines *mpl*, medias *fpl* **2** *pl* **hose** STOCKINGS **:** medias *fpl* **3** *pl* **hoses :** manguera *f*, manga *f*

hosiery [ˈhoːʒəri, ˈhoːzə-] *n* **:** calcetería *f*, medias *fpl*

hospice [ˈhɑspəs] *n* **:** hospicio *m*

hospitable [hɑˈspɪt̬əbəl, ˈhɑsˌpɪ-] *adj* **:** hospitalario — **hospitably** [-bli] *adv*

hospital [ˈhɑsˌpɪt̬əl] *n* **:** hospital *m*

hospitality [ˌhɑspəˈtæləṯi] *n, pl* **-ties :** hospitalidad *f*

hospitalization [ˌhɑsˌpɪt̬ələˈzeɪʃən] *n* **:** hospitalización *f*

hospitalize [ˈhɑsˌpɪt̬əlˌaɪz] *vt* **-ized; -izing :** hospitalizar

host[1] [ˈhoːst] *vt* **:** presentar (un programa de televisión, etc.)

host[2] *n* **1 :** anfitrión *m*, -triona *f* (en la casa, a un evento); presentador *m*, -dora *f* (de un programa de televisión, etc.) **2** *or* **host organism :** huésped *m* **3** TROOPS **:** huestes *fpl* **4** MULTITUDE **:** multitud *f* <for a host of reasons : por muchas razones> **5** EUCHARIST **:** hostia *f*, Eucaristía *f*

hostage [ˈhɑstɪdʒ] *n* **:** rehén *m*

hostel [ˈhɑstəl] *n* **:** albergue *m* juvenil

hostess [ˈhoːstɪs] *n* **:** anfitriona *f* (en la casa), presentadora *f* (de un programa)

hostile [ˈhɑstəl, -ˌtaɪl] *adj* **:** hostil — **hostilely** *adv*

hostility [hɑsˈtɪləṯi] *n, pl* **-ties :** hostilidad *f*

hot [ˈhɑt] *adj* **hotter; hottest 1 :** caliente, cálido, caluroso <hot water : agua caliente> <a hot climate : un clima cálido> <a hot day : un día caluroso> **2** ARDENT, FIERY **:** ardiente, acalorado <to have a hot temper : tener mal genio> **3** SPICY **:** picante **4** FRESH **:** reciente, nuevo <hot news : noticias de última hora> **5** EAGER **:** ávido **6** STOLEN **:** robado

hot air *n* **:** palabrería *f*

hotbed [ˈhɑtˌbɛd] *n* **1 :** semillero *m* (de plantas) **2 :** hervidero *m*, semillero *m* (de crimen, etc.)

hot dog *n* **:** perro *m* caliente

hotel [hoːˈtɛl] *n* **:** hotel *m*

hothead [ˈhɑtˌhɛd] *n* **:** exaltado *m*, -da *f*

hotheaded [ˈhɑtˈhɛdəd] *adj* **:** exaltado

hothouse [ˈhɑtˌhaʊs] *n* **:** invernadero *m*

hot plate *n* **:** placa *f* (de cocina)

hot rod *n* **:** coche *m* con motor modificado

hot water *n* **to get into hot water :** meterse en un lío

hound[1] [ˈhaʊnd] *vt* **:** acosar, perseguir

hound[2] *n* **:** perro *m* (de caza)

hour [ˈaʊər] *n* **:** hora *f*

hourglass [ˈaʊərˌglæs] *n* **:** reloj *m* de arena

hourly [ˈaʊərli] *adv & adj* **:** cada hora, por hora

house[1] [ˈhaʊz] *vt* **housed; housing :** albergar, alojar, hospedar

house[2] [ˈhaʊs] *n, pl* **houses** [ˈhaʊzəz, -səz] **1** HOME **:** casa *f* **2 :** cámara *f* (del gobierno) **3** BUSINESS **:** casa *f*, empresa *f*

houseboat [ˈhaʊsˌboːt] *n* **:** casa *f* flotante

housebroken [ˈhaʊsˌbroːkən] *adj* **:** enseñado

housefly [ˈhaʊsˌflaɪ] *n, pl* **-flies :** mosca *f* común

household[1] [ˈhaʊsˌhoːld] *adj* **1** DOMESTIC **:** doméstico, de la casa **2** FAMILIAR **:** conocido por todos

household[2] *n* **:** casa *f*, familia *f*

householder [ˈhaʊsˌhoːldər] *n* **:** dueño *m*, -ña *f* de casa

housekeeper [ˈhaʊsˌkiːpər] *n* **:** ama *f* de llaves

housekeeping [ˈhaʊsˌkiːpɪŋ] *n* **:** gobierno *m* de la casa, quehaceres *mpl* domésticos

housemaid [ˈhaʊsˌmeɪd] *n* **:** criada *f*, mucama *f*, muchacha *f*, sirvienta *f*

housewarming [ˈhaʊsˌwɔrmɪŋ] *n* **:** fiesta *f* de estreno de una casa

housewife [ˈhaʊsˌwaɪf] *n, pl* **-wives :** ama *f* de casa

housework [ˈhaʊsˌwərk] *n* **:** faenas *fpl* domésticas, quehaceres *mpl* domésticos

housing [ˈhaʊzɪŋ] *n* **1** HOUSES **:** vivienda *f* **2** COVERING **:** caja *f* protectora

hove → **heave**

hovel [ˈhʌvəl, ˈhɑ-] *n* **:** casucha *f*, tugurio *m*

hover [ˈhʌvər, ˈhɑ-] *vi* **1 :** cernerse, sostenerse en el aire **2 to hover about :** rondar

how [ˈhaʊ] *adv* **1 :** cómo <how are you? : ¿cómo estas?> <I don't know how to fix it : no se cómo arreglarlo> **2 :** qué <how beautiful! : ¡qué bonito!> **3 :** cuánto <how old are you? : ¿cuántos años tienes?> **4 how about...? :** ¿qué te parece...?

however[1] [haʊˈɛvər] *adv* **1 :** por mucho que, por más que <however hot it is : por mucho calor que haga> **2** NEVERTHELESS **:** sin embargo, no obstante

however[2] *conj* **:** comoquiera que, de cualquier manera que

howl[1] [ˈhaʊl] *vi* **:** aullar

howl[2] *n* **:** aullido *m*, alarido *m*

hub [ˈhʌb] *n* **1** CENTER **:** centro *m* **2 :** cubo *m* (de una rueda)

hubbub [ˈhʌˌbʌb] *n* **:** algarabía *f*, alboroto *m*, jaleo *m*

hubcap [ˈhʌbˌkæp] *n* **:** tapacubos *m*

huckster [ˈhʌkstər] *n* **:** buhonero *m*, -ra *f;* vendedor *m*, -dora *f* ambulante

huddle[1] [ˈhʌdəl] *vi* **-dled; -dling 1 :** apiñarse, amontonarse **2 to huddle together :** acurrucarse

huddle[2] *n* : grupo *m* (cerrado) <to go into a huddle : conferenciar en secreto>

hue [ˈhjuː] *n* : color *m,* tono *m*

huff [ˈhʌf] *n* : enojo *m,* enfado *m* <to be in a huff : estar enojado>

huffy [ˈhʌfi] *adj* **huffier; -est** : enojado, enfadado

hug[1] [ˈhʌg] *vt* **hugged; hugging 1** EMBRACE : abrazar **2** : ir pegado a <the road hugs the river : el camino está pegado al río>

hug[2] *n* : abrazo *m*

huge [ˈhjuːdʒ] *adj* **huger; hugest** : inmenso, enorme — **hugely** *adv*

hulk [ˈhʌlk] *n* **1** : persona *f* fornida **2** : casco *m* (barco), armatoste *m* (edificio, etc.)

hulking [ˈhʌlkɪŋ] *adj* : grandote *fam,* pesado

hull[1] [ˈhʌl] *vt* : pelar

hull[2] *n* **1** HUSK : cáscara *f* **2** : casco *m* (de un barco, un avión, etc.)

hullabaloo [ˈhʌləbəˌluː] *n, pl* **-loos** : alboroto *m,* jaleo *m*

hum[1] [ˈhʌm] *v* **hummed; humming** *vi* **1** BUZZ : zumbar **2** : estar muy activo, moverse <to hum with activity : bullir de actividad> — *vt* : tararear (una melodía)

hum[2] *n* : zumbido *m,* murmullo *m*

human[1] [ˈhjuːmən, ˈjuː-] *adj* : humano — **humanly** *adv*

human[2] *n* : ser *m* humano

humane [hjuːˈmeɪn, ˌjuː-] *adj* : humano, humanitario — **humanely** *adv*

humanism [ˈhjuːməˌnɪzəm, ˈjuː-] *n* : humanismo *m*

humanist [ˈhjuːmənɪst, ˈjuː-] *n* : humanista *mf*

humanitarian[1] [hjuːˌmænəˈtɛriən, juː-] *adj* : humanitario

humanitarian[2] *n* : humanitario *m,* -ria *f*

humanity [hjuːˈmænət̬i, juː-] *n, pl* **-ties** : humanidad *f*

humankind [ˈhjuːmənˈkaɪnd, ˈjuː-] *n* : género *m* humano

humble[1] [ˈhʌmbəl] *vt* **-bled; -bling 1** : humillar **2 to humble oneself** : humillarse

humble[2] *adj* **-bler; -blest** : humilde, modesto — **humbly** [ˈhʌmbli] *adv*

humbug [ˈhʌmˌbʌg] *n* **1** FRAUD : charlatán *m,* -tana *f;* farsante *mf* **2** NONSENSE : patrañas *fpl,* tonterías *fpl*

humdrum [ˈhʌmˌdrʌm] *adj* : monótono, rutinario

humid [ˈhjuːməd, ˈjuː-] *adj* : húmedo

humidifier [hjuːˈmɪdəˌfaɪər, juː-] *n* : humidificador *m*

humidify [hjuːˈmɪdəˌfaɪ, juː-] *vt* **-fied; -fying** : humidificar

humidity [hjuːˈmɪdət̬i, juː-] *n, pl* **-ties** : humedad *f*

humiliate [hjuːˈmɪliˌeɪt, juː-] *vt* **-ated; -ating** : humillar

humiliating [hjuːˈmɪliˌeɪt̬ɪŋ, juː-] *adj* : humillante

humiliation [hjuːˌmɪliˈeɪʃən, juː-] *n* : humillación *f*

humility [hjuːˈmɪlət̬i, juː-] *n* : humildad *f*

hummingbird [ˈhʌmɪŋˌbərd] *n* : colibrí *m,* picaflor *m*

hummock [ˈhʌmək] *n* : montículo *m*

humor[1] [ˈhjuːmər, ˈjuː-] *vt* : seguir el humor a, complacer

humor[2] *n* : humor *m*

humorist [ˈhjuːmərɪst, ˈjuː-] *n* : humorista *mf*

humorless [ˈhjuːmərləs, ˈjuː-] *adj* : sin sentido del humor <a humorless smile : una sonrisa forzada>

humorous [ˈhjuːmərəs, ˈjuː-] *adj* : humorístico, cómico — **humorously** *adv*

hump [ˈhʌmp] *n* : joroba *f,* giba *f*

humpback [ˈhʌmpˌbæk] *n* **1** HUMP : joroba *f,* giba *f* **2** HUNCHBACK : jorobado *m,* -da *f;* giboso *m,* -sa *f*

humpbacked [ˈhʌmpˌbækt] *adj* : jorobado, giboso

humus [ˈhjuːməs, ˈjuː-] *n* : humus *m*

hunch[1] [ˈhʌntʃ] *vt* : encorvar — *vi or* **to hunch up** : encorvarse

hunch[2] *n* PREMONITION : presentimiento *m*

hunchback [ˈhʌntʃˌbæk] *n* **1** HUMP : joroba *f,* giba *f* **2** HUMPBACK : jorobado *m,* -da *f;* giboso *m,* -sa *f*

hunchbacked [ˈhʌntʃˌbækt] *adj* : jorobado, giboso

hundred[1] [ˈhʌndrəd] *adj* : cien, ciento

hundred[2] *n, pl* **-dreds** *or* **-dred** : ciento *m*

hundredth[1] [ˈhʌndrədθ] *adj* : centésimo

hundredth[2] *n* **1** : centésimo *m,* -ma *f* (en una serie) **2** : centésimo *m,* centésima parte *f*

hung → **hang**

Hungarian [hʌŋˈgæriən] *n* **1** : húngaro *m,* -ra *f* **2** : húngaro *m* (idioma) — **Hungarian** *adj*

hunger[1] [ˈhʌŋgər] *vi* **1** : tener hambre **2 to hunger for** : ansiar, anhelar

hunger[2] *n* : hambre *m*

hungrily [ˈhʌŋgrəli] *adv* : ávidamente

hungry [ˈhʌŋgri] *adj* **-grier; -est 1** : hambriento **2 to be hungry** : tener hambre

hunk [ˈhʌŋk] *n* : trozo *m,* pedazo *m*

hunt[1] [ˈhʌnt] *vt* **1** PURSUE : cazar **2 to hunt for** : buscar

hunt[2] *n* **1** PURSUIT : caza *f,* cacería *f* **2** SEARCH : búsqueda *f,* busca *f*

hunter [ˈhʌntər] *n* : cazador *m,* -dora *f*

hunting [ˈhʌntɪŋ] *n* : caza *f* <to go hunting : ir de caza>

hurdle[1] [ˈhərdəl] *vt* **-dled; -dling** : saltar, salvar (un obstáculo)

hurdle[2] *n* : valla *f* (en deportes), obstáculo *m*

hurl [ˈhərl] *vt* : arrojar, tirar, lanzar

hurrah [hʊˈrɑ, -ˈrɔ] *interj* : ¡hurra!

hurricane [ˈhərəˌkeɪn] *n* : huracán *m*

hurried [ˈhərid] *adj* : apresurado, precipitado
hurriedly [ˈhərədli] *adv* : apresuradamente, de prisa
hurry[1] [ˈhəri] *v* **-ried; -rying** *vi* : apurarse, darse prisa, apresurarse — *vt* : apurar, darle prisa (a alguien)
hurry[2] *n* : prisa *f,* apuro *f*
hurt[1] [ˈhərt] *v* **hurt; hurting** *vt* **1** INJURE : hacer daño a, herir, lastimar <to hurt oneself : hacerse daño> **2** DISTRESS, OFFEND : hacer sufrir, ofender, herir — *vi* : doler <my foot hurts : me duele el pie>
hurt[2] *n* **1** INJURY : herida *f* **2** DISTRESS, PAIN : dolor *m,* pena *f*
hurtful [ˈhərtfəl] *adj* : hiriente, doloroso
hurtle [ˈhərṭəl] *vi* **-tled; -tling** : lanzarse, precipitarse
husband[1] [ˈhʌzbənd] *vt* : economizar, bien administrar
husband[2] *n* : esposo *m,* marido *m*
husbandry [ˈhʌzbəndri] *n* **1** MANAGEMENT, THRIFT : economía *f,* buena administración *f* **2** AGRICULTURE : agricultura *f* <animal husbandry : cría de animales>
hush[1] [ˈhʌʃ] *vt* **1** SILENCE : hacer callar, acallar **2** CALM : calmar, apaciguar
hush[2] *n* : silencio *m*
hush–hush [ˈhʌʃˌhʌʃ, ˌhʌʃˈhʌʃ] *adj* : muy secreto, confidencial
husk[1] [ˈhʌsk] *vt* : descascarar
husk[2] *n* : cáscara *f*
huskily [ˈhʌskəli] *adv* : con voz ronca
husky[1] [ˈhʌski] *adj* **-kier; -est 1** HOARSE : ronco **2** BURLY : fornido
husky[2] *n, pl* **-kies** : perro *m,* -rra *f* esquimal
hustle[1] [ˈhəsəl] *v* **-tled; -tling** *vt* : darle prisa (a alguien), apurar <they hustled me in : me hicieron entrar a empujones> — *vi* : apurarse, ajetrearse
hustle[2] *n* BUSTLE : ajetreo *m*
hut [ˈhʌt] *n* : cabaña *f,* choza *f,* barraca *f*
hutch [ˈhʌtʃ] *n* **1** CUPBOARD : alacena *f* **2 rabbit hutch** : conejera *f*
hyacinth [ˈhaɪəˌsɪnθ] *n* : jacinto *m*
hybrid[1] [ˈhaɪbrɪd] *adj* : híbrido
hybrid[2] *n* : híbrido *m*
hydrant [ˈhaɪdrənt] *n* : boca *f* de riego, hidrante *m CA, Col* <fire hydrant : boca de incendios>
hydraulic [haɪˈdrɔlɪk] *adj* : hidráulico — **hydraulically** *adv*
hydrocarbon [ˌhaɪdroˈkɑrbən] *n* : hidrocarburo *m*
hydrochloric acid [ˌhaɪdroˈklorɪk] *n* : ácido *m* clorohídrico
hydroelectric [ˌhaɪdroɪˈlɛktrɪk] *adj* : hidroeléctrico
hydrogen [ˈhaɪdrədʒən] *n* : hidrógeno *m*
hydrogen bomb *n* : bomba *f* de hidrógeno
hydrogen peroxide *n* : agua *f* oxigenada, peróxido *m* de hidrógeno
hydrophobia [ˌhaɪdrəˈfoːbiə] *n* : hidrofobia *f,* rabia *f*
hydroplane [ˈhaɪdrəˌpleɪn] *n* : hidroplano *m*
hyena [haɪˈiːnə] *n* : hiena *f*
hygiene [ˈhaɪˌdʒiːn] *n* : higiene *f*
hygienic [haɪˈdʒɛnɪk, -ˈdʒiː-; ˌhaɪdʒiˈɛnɪk] *adj* : higiénico — **hygienically** [-nɪkli] *adv*
hygienist [haɪˈdʒiːnɪst, -ˈdʒɛ-; ˈhaɪˌdʒiː-] *n* : higienista *mf*
hygrometer [haɪˈgrɑməṭər] *n* : higrómetro *m*
hymn [ˈhɪm] *n* : himno *m*
hymnal [ˈhɪmnəl] *n* : himnario *m*
hype [ˈhaɪp] *n* : bombo *m* publicitario
hyperactive [ˌhaɪpərˈæktɪv] *adj* : hiperactivo
hyperbole [haɪˈpərbəli] *n* : hipérbole *f*
hypercritical [ˌhaɪpərˈkrɪṭəkəl] *adj* : hipercrítico
hypersensitivity [ˌhaɪpərˌsɛntsəˈtɪvəṭi] *n* : hipersensibilidad *f*
hypertension [ˈhaɪpərˌtɛntʃən] *n* : hipertensión *f*
hyphen [ˈhaɪfən] *n* : guión *m*
hyphenate [ˈhaɪfənˌeɪt] *vt* **-ated; -ating** : escribir con guión
hypnosis [hɪpˈnoːsɪs] *n, pl* **-noses** [-ˌsiːz] : hipnosis *f*
hypnotic [hɪpˈnɑṭɪk] *adj* : hipnótico, hipnotizador
hypnotism [ˈhɪpnəˌtɪzəm] *n* : hipnotismo *m*
hypnotize [ˈhɪpnəˌtaɪz] *vt* **-tized; -tizing** : hipnotizar
hypochondria [ˌhaɪpəˈkɑndriə] *n* : hipocondría *f*
hypochondriac [ˌhaɪpəˈkɑndriˌæk] *n* : hipocondríaco *m,* -ca *f*
hypocrisy [hɪpˈɑkrəsi] *n, pl* **-sies** : hipocresía *f*
hypocrite [ˈhɪpəˌkrɪt] *n* : hipócrita *mf*
hypocritical [ˌhɪpəˈkrɪṭɪkəl] *adj* : hipócrita
hypodermic[1] [ˌhaɪpəˈdərmɪk] *adj* : hipodérmico
hypodermic[2] *n* : aguja *f* hipodérmica
hypotenuse [haɪˈpɑtənˌuːs, -ˌuːz, -ˌjuːs, -ˌjuːz] *n* : hipotenusa *f*
hypothesis [haɪˈpɑθəsɪs] *n, pl* **-eses** [-ˌsiːz] : hipótesis *f*
hypothetical [ˌhaɪpəˈθɛṭɪkəl] *adj* : hipotético — **hypothetically** [-ṭɪkli] *adv*
hysteria [hɪsˈtɛriə, -tɪr-] *n* : histeria *f,* histerismo *m*
hysterical [hɪsˈtɛrɪkəl] *adj* : histérico — **hysterically** [-ɪkli] *adv*
hysterics [hɪsˈtɛrɪks] *n* : histeria *f,* histerismo *m*

I

i [ˈaɪ] *n, pl* **i's** *or* **is** [ˈaɪz] : novena letra del alfabeto inglés
I [ˈaɪ] *pron* : yo
ibis [ˈaɪbəs] *n, pl* **ibis** *or* **ibises** : ibis *f*
ice[1] [ˈaɪs] *v* **iced; icing** *vt* **1** FREEZE : congelar, helar **2** CHILL : enfriar **3 to ice a cake** : escarchar un pastel — *vi* : helarse, congelarse
ice[2] *n* **1** : hielo *m* **2** SHERBET : sorbete *m*, nieve *f Cuba, Mex, PRi*
iceberg [ˈaɪsˌbərg] *n* : iceberg *m*
icebox [ˈaɪsˌbɑks] → **refrigerator**
icebreaker [ˈaɪsˌbreɪkər] *n* : rompehielos *m*
ice cap *n* : casquete *m* glaciar
ice–cold [ˈaɪsˈkoːld] *adj* : helado
ice cream *n* : helado *m*, mantecado *m PRi*
Icelander [ˈaɪsˌlændər, -lən-] *n* : islandés *m*, -desa *f*
Icelandic[1] [aɪsˈlændɪk] *adj* : islandés
Icelandic[2] *n* : islandés *m* (idioma)
ice–skate [ˈaɪsˌskeɪt] *vi* **-skated; -skating** : patinar
ice skater *n* : patinador *m*, -dora *f*
ichthyology [ˌɪkthiˈɑlədʒi] *n* : ictiología *f*
icicle [ˈaɪˌsɪkəl] *n* : carámbano *m*
icily [ˈaɪsəli] *adv* : fríamente, con frialdad <he stared at me icily : me fijó la mirada con mucha frialdad>
icing [ˈaɪsɪŋ] *n* : glaseado *m*, betún *m Mex*
icon [ˈaɪˌkɑn, -kən] *n* : icono *m*
iconoclasm [aɪˈkɑnəˌklæzəm] *n* : iconoclasia *f*
iconoclast [aɪˈkɑnəˌklæst] *n* : iconoclasta *mf*
icy [ˈaɪsi] *adj* **icier; -est 1** : cubierto de hielo <an icy road : una carretera cubierta de hielo> **2** FREEZING : helado, gélido, glacial **3** ALOOF : frío, distante
id [ˈɪd] *n* : id *m*
I'd [ˈaɪd] (*contraction of* **I should** *or* **I would**) → **should, would**
idea [aɪˈdiːə] *n* : idea *f*
ideal[1] [aɪˈdiːəl] *adj* : ideal
ideal[2] *n* : ideal *m*
idealism [aɪˈdiːəˌlɪzəm] *n* : idealismo *m*
idealist [aɪˈdiːəlɪst] *n* : idealista *mf*
idealistic [aɪˌdiːəˈlɪstɪk] *adj* : idealista
idealistically [aɪˌdiːəˈlɪstɪkli] *adv* : con idealismo
idealization [aɪˌdiːələˈzeɪʃən] *n* : idealización *f*
idealize [aɪˈdiːəˌlaɪz] *vt* **-ized; -izing** : idealizar
ideally [aɪˈdiːəli] *adv* : perfectamente
identical [aɪˈdɛntɪkəl] *adj* : idéntico — **identically** [-tɪkli] *adv*
identifiable [aɪˌdɛntəˈfaɪəbəl] *adj* : identificable
identification [aɪˌdɛntəfəˈkeɪʃən] *n* **1** : identificación *f* **2 identification card** : carnet *m*, cédula *f* de identidad, identificación *f*
identify [aɪˈdɛntəˌfaɪ] *v* **-fied; -fying** *vt* : identificar — *vi* **to identify with** : identificarse con
identity [aɪˈdɛntəṭi] *n, pl* **-ties** : identidad *f*
ideological [ˌaɪdiəˈlɑdʒɪkəl, ˌɪ-] *adj* : ideológico — **ideologically** [-dʒɪkli] *adv*
ideology [ˌaɪdiˈɑlədʒi, ˌɪ-] *n, pl* **-gies** : ideología *f*
idiocy [ˈɪdiəsi] *n, pl* **-cies 1** : idiotez *f* **2** NONSENSE : estupidez *f*, tontería *f*
idiom [ˈɪdiəm] *n* **1** LANGUAGE : lenguaje *m* **2** EXPRESSION : modismo *m*, expresión *f* idiomática
idiomatic [ˌɪdiəˈmæṭɪk] *adj* : idiomático
idiosyncrasy [ˌɪdioˈsɪŋkrəsi] *n, pl* **-sies** : idiosincrasia *f*
idiosyncratic [ˌɪdiosɪnˈkræṭɪk] *adj* : idiosincrásico — **idiosyncratically** [-ṭɪkli] *adv*
idiot [ˈɪdiət] *n* **1** : idiota *mf* (en medicina) **2** FOOL : idiota *mf*; tonto *m*, -ta *f*; imbécil *mf fam*
idiotic [ˌɪdiˈɑṭɪk] *adj* : estúpido, idiota
idiotically [ˌɪdiˈɑṭɪkli] *adv* : estúpidamente
idle[1] [ˈaɪdəl] *v* **idled; idling** *vi* **1** LOAF : holgazanear, flojear, haraganear **2** : andar al ralentí (dícese de un automóvil), marchar en vacío (dícese de una máquina) — *vt* : dejar sin trabajo
idle[2] *adj* **idler; idlest 1** VAIN : frívolo, vano, infundado <idle curiosity : pura curiosidad> **2** INACTIVE : inactivo, parado, desocupado **3** LAZY : holgazán, haragán, perezoso
idleness [ˈaɪdəlnəs] *n* **1** INACTIVITY : inactividad *f*, ociosidad *f* **2** LAZINESS : holgazanería *f*, flojera *f*, pereza *f*
idler [ˈaɪdələr] *n* : haragán *m*, -gana *f*; holgazán *m*, -zana *f*
idly [ˈaɪdəli] *adv* : ociosamente
idol [ˈaɪdəl] *n* : ídolo *m*
idolater *or* **idolator** [aɪˈdɑləṭər] *n* : idólatra *mf*
idolatrous [aɪˈdɑlətrəs] *adj* : idólatra
idolatry [aɪˈdɑlətri] *n, pl* **-tries** : idolatría *f*
idolize [ˈaɪdəlaɪz] *vt* **-ized; -izing** : idolatrar
idyll [ˈaɪdəl] *n* : idilio *m*
idyllic [aɪˈdɪlɪk] *adj* : idílico
if [ˈɪf] *conj* **1** : si <I would do it if I could : lo haría si pudiera> <if so : si es así> <as if : como si> <if I were you : yo que tú> **2** WHETHER : si <I don't know if they're ready : no sé si están listos> **3** THOUGH : aunque, si bien <it's pretty, if somewhat old-fashioned : es lindo aunque algo anticuado>
igloo [ˈɪˌgluː] *n, pl* **-loos** : iglú *m*

ignite [ɪg'naɪt] *v* **-nited; -niting** *vt* : prenderle fuego a, encender — *vi* : prender, encenderse

ignition [ɪg'nɪʃən] *n* **1** IGNITING : ignición *f,* encendido *m* **2** *or* **ignition switch** : encendido *m,* arranque *m* <to turn on the ignition : arrancar el motor>

ignoble [ɪg'noːbəl] *adj* : innoble — **ignobly** *adv*

ignominious [ˌɪgnə'mɪniəs] *adj* : ignominioso, deshonroso — **ignominiously** *adv*

ignominy ['ɪgnəˌmɪni] *n, pl* **-nies** : ignominia *f*

ignoramus [ˌɪgnə'reɪməs] *n* : ignorante *mf;* bestia *mf;* bruto *m,* -ta *f*

ignorance ['ɪgnərən*t*s] *n* : ignorancia *f*

ignorant ['ɪgnərənt] *adj* **1** : ignorante **2 to be ignorant of** : no ser consciente de, desconocer, ignorar

ignorantly ['ɪgnərəntli] *adv* : ignorantemente, con ignorancia

ignore [ɪg'nor] *vt* **-nored; -noring** : ignorar, hacer caso omiso de, no hacer caso de

iguana [ɪ'gwɑnə] *n* : iguana *f,* garrobo *f CA*

ilk ['ɪlk] *n* : tipo *m,* clase *f,* índole *f*

ill[1] ['ɪl] *adv* **worse** ['wərs]; **worst** ['wərst] : mal <to speak ill of : hablar mal de> <he can ill afford to fail : mal puede permitirse el lujo de fracasar>

ill[2] *adj* **worse; worst 1** SICK : enfermo **2** BAD : malo <ill luck : mala suerte>

ill[3] *n* **1** EVIL : mal *m* **2** MISFORTUNE : mal *m,* desgracia *f* **3** AILMENT : enfermedad *f*

I'll ['aɪl] (*contraction of* **I shall** *or* **I will**) → **shall, will**

illegal [ɪl'liːgəl] *adj* : ilegal — **illegally** *adv*

illegality [ɪli'gæləṭi] *n* : ilegalidad *f*

illegibility [ɪlˌlɛdʒə'bɪləṭi] *n, pl* **-ties** : ilegibilidad *f*

illegible [ɪl'lɛdʒəbəl] *adj* : ilegible — **illegibly** [-bli] *adv*

illegitimacy [ˌɪlɪ'dʒɪṭəməsi] *n* : ilegitimidad *f*

illegitimate [ˌɪlɪ'dʒɪṭəmət] *adj* **1** BASTARD : ilegítimo, bastardo **2** UNLAWFUL : ilegítimo, ilegal — **illegitimately** *adv*

ill–fated ['ɪl'feɪṭəd] *adj* : malhadado, infortunado, desventurado

illicit [ɪl'lɪsət] *adj* : ilícito — **illicitly** *adv*

illiteracy [ɪl'lɪṭərəsi] *n, pl* **-cies** : analfabetismo *m*

illiterate[1] [ɪl'lɪṭərət] *adj* : analfabeto

illiterate[2] *n* : analfabeto *m,* -ta *f*

ill–mannered [ˌɪl'manərd] *adj* : descortés, maleducado

ill–natured [ˌɪl'neɪtʃərd] *adj* : desagradable, de mal genio

ill–naturedly [ˌɪl'neɪtʃərdli] *adv* : desagradablemente

illness ['ɪlnəs] *n* : enfermedad *f*

illogical [ɪl'lɑdʒɪkəl] *adj* : ilógico — **illogically** [-kli] *adv*

ill–tempered [ˌɪl'tempərd] → **ill–natured**

ill–treat [ˌɪl'triːt] *vt* : maltratar

ill–treatment [ˌɪl'triːtmənt] *n* : maltrato *m*

illuminate [ɪ'luːməˌneɪt] *vt* **-nated; -nating 1** : iluminar, alumbrar **2** ELUCIDATE : esclarecer, elucidar

illumination [ɪˌluːmə'neɪʃən] *n* **1** LIGHTING : iluminación *f,* luz *f* **2** ELUCIDATION : esclarecimiento *m,* elucidación *f*

ill–use ['ɪl'juːz] → **ill–treat**

illusion [ɪ'luːʒən] *n* : ilusión *f*

illusory [ɪ'luːsəri, -zəri] *adj* : engañoso, ilusorio

illustrate ['ɪləsˌtreɪt] *v* **-trated; -trating** : ilustrar

illustration [ˌɪlə'streɪʃən] *n* **1** PICTURE : ilustración *f* **2** EXAMPLE : ejemplo *m,* ilustración *f*

illustrative [ɪ'lʌstrəṭɪv, 'ɪləˌstreɪṭɪv] *adj* : ilustrativo — **illustratively** *adv*

illustrator ['ɪləˌstreɪṭər] *n* : ilustrador *m,* -dora *f;* dibujante *mf*

illustrious [ɪ'lʌstriəs] *adj* : ilustre, eminente, glorioso

illustriousness [ɪ'lʌstriəsnəs] *n* : eminencia *f,* prestigio *m*

ill will *n* : animosidad *f,* malquerencia *f,* mala voluntad *f*

I'm ['aɪm] (*contraction of* **I am**) → **be**

image[1] ['ɪmɪdʒ] *vt* **-aged; -aging** : imaginar, crear una imagen de

image[2] *n* : imagen *f*

imagery ['ɪmɪdʒri] *n, pl* **-eries 1** IMAGES : imágenes *fpl* **2** : imaginería *f* (en el arte)

imaginable [ɪ'mædʒənəbəl] *adj* : imaginable — **imaginably** [-bli] *adv*

imaginary [ɪ'mædʒəˌnɛri] *adj* : imaginario

imagination [ɪˌmædʒə'neɪʃən] *n* : imaginación *f*

imaginative [ɪ'mædʒənəṭɪv, -əˌneɪṭɪv] *adj* : imaginativo — **imaginatively** *adv*

imagine [ɪ'mædʒən] *vt* **-ined; -ining** : imaginar(se)

imbalance [ɪm'bælən*t*s] *n* : desajuste *m,* desbalance *m,* desequilibrio *m*

imbecile[1] ['ɪmbəsəl, -ˌsɪl] *or* **imbecilic** [ˌɪmbə'sɪlɪk] *adj* : imbécil, estúpido

imbecile[2] *n* **1** : imbécil *mf* (en medicina) **2** FOOL : idiota *mf;* imbécil *mf fam;* estúpido *m,* -da *f*

imbecility [ˌɪmbə'sɪləṭi] *n, pl* **-ties** : imbecilidad *f*

imbibe [ɪm'baɪb] *v* **-bibed; -bibing** *vt* **1** DRINK : beber **2** ABSORB : absorber, embeber — *vi* : beber

imbue [ɪm'bjuː] *vt* **-bued; -buing** : imbuir

imitate ['ɪməˌteɪt] *vt* **-tated; -tating** : imitar, remedar

imitation[1] [ˌɪməˈteɪʃən] *adj* **:** de imitación, artificial
imitation[2] *n* **:** imitación *f*
imitative [ˈɪməˌteɪtɪv] *adj* **:** imitativo, imitador, poco original
imitator [ˈɪməˌteɪt̬ər] *n* **:** imitador *m*, -dora *f*
immaculate [ɪˈmækjələt] *adj* **1** PURE **:** inmaculado, puro **2** FLAWLESS **:** impecable, intachable — **immaculately** *adv*
immaterial [ˌɪməˈtɪriəl] *adj* **1** INCORPOREAL **:** incorpóreo **2** UNIMPORTANT **:** irrelevante, sin importancia
immature [ˌɪməˈtʃʊr, -ˈtjʊr, -ˈtʊr] *adj* **:** inmaduro, verde (dícese de la fruta)
immaturity [ˌɪməˈtʃʊrət̬i, -ˈtjʊr-, -ˈtʊr-] *n, pl* **-ties :** inmadurez *f*, falta *f* de madurez
immeasurable [ɪˈmɛʒərəbəl] *adj* **:** inconmensurable, incalculable — **immeasurably** [-bli] *adv*
immediate [ɪˈmiːdiət] *adj* **1** INSTANT **:** inmediato, instantáneo <immediate relief **:** alivio instantáneo> **2** DIRECT **:** inmediato, directo <the immediate cause of death **:** la causa directa de la muerte> **3** URGENT **:** urgente, apremiante **4** CLOSE **:** cercano, próximo, inmediato <her immediate family **:** sus familiares más cercanos> <in the immediate vicinity **:** en los alrededores, en las inmediaciones>
immediately [ɪˈmiːdiətli] *adv* **:** inmediatamente, enseguida
immemorial [ˌɪməˈmoriəl] *adj* **:** inmemorial
immense [ɪˈmɛnts] *adj* **:** inmenso, enorme — **immensely** *adv*
immensity [ɪˈmɛntsət̬i] *n, pl* **-ties :** inmensidad *f*
immerse [ɪˈmərs] *vt* **-mersed; -mersing 1** SUBMERGE **:** sumergir **2 to immerse oneself in :** enfrascarse en
immersion [ɪˈmərʒən] *n* **1 :** inmersión *f* (en un líquido) **2 :** enfrascamiento *m* (en una actividad)
immigrant [ˈɪmɪgrənt] *n* **:** inmigrante *mf*
immigrate [ˈɪməˌgreɪt] *vi* **-grated; -grating :** inmigrar
immigration [ˌɪməˈgreɪʃən] *n* **:** inmigración *f*
imminence [ˈɪmənənts] *n* **:** inminencia *f*
imminent [ˈɪmənənt] *adj* **:** inminente — **imminently** *adv*
immobile [ɪmˈoːbəl] *adj* **1** FIXED, IMMOVABLE **:** inmovible, fijo **2** MOTIONLESS **:** inmóvil
immobility [ˌɪmoˈbɪlət̬i] *n, pl* **-ties :** inmovilidad *f*
immobilize [ɪˈmoːbəˌlaɪz] *vt* **-lized; -lizing :** inmovilizar, paralizar
immoderate [ɪˈmɑdərət] *adj* **:** inmoderado, desmesurado, desmedido, excesivo — **immoderately** *adv*
immodest [ɪˈmɑdəst] *adj* **1** INDECENT **:** inmodesto, indecente, impúdico **2** CONCEITED **:** inmodesto, presuntuoso, engreído — **immodestly** *adv*
immodesty [ɪˈmɑdəsti] *n* **:** inmodestia *f*
immoral [ɪˈmɔrəl] *adj* **:** inmoral
immorality [ˌɪmɔˈrælət̬i, ˌɪmə-] *n, pl* **-ties :** inmoralidad *f*
immorally [ɪˈmɔrəli] *adv* **:** de manera inmoral
immortal[1] [ɪˈmɔrtəl] *adj* **:** inmortal
immortal[2] *n* **:** inmortal *mf*
immortality [ˌɪˌmɔrˈtælət̬i] *n* **:** inmortalidad *f*
immortalize [ɪˈmɔrtəlˌaɪz] *vt* **-ized; -izing :** inmortalizar
immovable [ɪˈmuːvəbəl] *adj* **1** FIXED **:** fijo, inmovible **2** UNYIELDING **:** inflexible
immune [ɪˈmjuːn] *adj* **1 :** inmune <immune to smallpox **:** inmune a la viruela> **2** EXEMPT **:** exento, inmune
immune system *n* **:** sistema *m* inmunológico
immunity [ɪˈmjuːnət̬i] *n, pl* **-ties 1 :** inmunidad *f* **2** EXEMPTION **:** exención *f*
immunization [ˌɪmjʊnəˈzeɪʃən] *n* **:** inmunización *f*
immunize [ˈɪmjʊˌnaɪz] *vt* **-nized; -nizing :** inmunizar
immunology [ˌɪmjʊˈnɑlədʒi] *n* **:** inmunología *f*
immutable [ɪˈmjuːt̬əbəl] *adj* **:** inmutable
imp [ˈɪmp] *n* RASCAL **:** diablillo *m;* pillo *m*, -lla *f*
impact[1] [ɪmˈpækt] *vt* **1** STRIKE **:** chocar con, impactar **2** AFFECT **:** afectar, impactar, impresionar — *vi* **1** STRIKE **:** hacer impacto, golpear **2 to impact on :** tener un impacto sobre
impact[2] [ˈɪmˌpækt] *n* **1** COLLISION **:** impacto *m*, choque *m*, colisión *f* **2** EFFECT **:** efecto *m*, impacto *m*, consecuencias *fpl*
impacted [ɪmˈpæktəd] *adj* **:** impactado, incrustado (dícese de los dientes)
impair [ɪmˈpær] *vt* **:** perjudicar, dañar, afectar
impairment [ɪmˈpærmənt] *n* **:** perjuicio *m*, daño *m*
impala [ɪmˈpɑlə, -ˈpæ-] *n, pl* **impalas** *or* **impala :** impala *m*
impale [ɪmˈpeɪl] *vt* **-paled; -paling :** empalar
impanel [ɪmˈpænəl] *vt* **-eled** *or* **-elled; eling** *or* **-elling :** elegir (un jurado)
impart [ɪmˈpɑrt] *vt* **1** CONVEY **:** impartir, dar, conferir **2** DISCLOSE **:** revelar, divulgar
impartial [ɪmˈpɑrʃəl] *adj* **:** imparcial — **impartially** *adv*
impartiality [ɪmˌpɑrʃiˈælət̬i] *n, pl* **-ties :** imparcialidad *f*
impassable [ɪmˈpæsəbəl] *adj* **:** infranqueable, intransitable — **impassably** [-bli] *adv*

impasse [ˈɪm,pæs] *n* **1** DEADLOCK : impasse *m,* punto *m* muerto **2** DEAD END : callejón *m* sin salida
impassioned [ɪmˈpæʃənd] *adj* : apasionado, vehemente
impassive [ɪmˈpæsɪv] *adj* : impasible, indiferente
impassively [ɪmˈpæsɪvli] *adv* : impasiblemente, sin emoción
impatience [ɪmˈpeɪʃənts] *n* : impaciencia *f*
impatient [ɪmˈpeɪʃənt] *adj* : impaciente — **impatiently** *adv*
impeach [ɪmˈpiːtʃ] *vt* : destituir (a un funcionario) de su cargo
impeachment [ɪmˈpiːtʃmənt] *n* **1** ACCUSATION : acusación *f* **2** DISMISSAL : destitución *f*
impeccable [ɪmˈpɛkəbəl] *adj* : impecable — **impeccably** [-bli] *adv*
impecunious [,ɪmpɪˈkjuːniəs] *adj* : falto de dinero
impede [ɪmˈpiːd] *vt* **-peded; -peding** : impedir, dificultar, obstaculizar
impediment [ɪmˈpɛdəmənt] *n* **1** HINDRANCE : impedimento *m,* obstáculo *m* **2 speech impediment** : defecto *m* del habla
impel [ɪmˈpɛl] *vt* **-pelled; -pelling** : impeler
impend [ɪmˈpɛnd] *vi* : ser inminente
impenetrable [ɪmˈpɛnətrəbəl] *adj* **1** : impenetrable <an impenetrable forest : una selva impenetrable> **2** INSCRUTABLE : incomprensible, inescrutable, impenetrable — **impenetrably** [-bli] *adv*
impenitent [ɪmˈpɛnətənt] *adj* : impenitente
imperative¹ [ɪmˈpɛrət̬ɪv] *adj* **1** AUTHORITATIVE : imperativo, imperioso **2** NECESSARY : imprescindible — **imperatively** *adv*
imperative² *n* : imperativo *m*
imperceptible [,ɪmpərˈsɛptəbəl] *adj* : imperceptible — **imperceptibly** [-bli] *adv*
imperfect [ɪmˈpərfɪkt] *adj* : imperfecto, defectuoso — **imperfectly** *adv*
imperfection [ɪm,pərˈfɛkʃən] *n* : imperfección *f,* defecto *m*
imperial [ɪmˈpɪriəl] *adj* **1** : imperial **2** SOVEREIGN : soberano **3** IMPERIOUS : imperioso, señorial
imperialism [ɪmˈpɪriə,lɪzəm] *n* : imperialismo *m*
imperialist¹ [ɪmˈpɪriəlɪst] *adj* : imperialista
imperialist² *n* : imperialista *mf*
imperialistic [ɪm,pɪriːəˈlɪstɪk] *adj* : imperialista
imperil [ɪmˈpɛrəl] *vt* **-iled** *or* **-illed; -iling** *or* **-illing** : poner en peligro
imperious [ɪmˈpɪriəs] *adj* : imperioso — **imperiously** *adv*
imperishable [ɪmˈpɛrɪʃəbəl] *adj* : imperecedero
impermanent [ɪmˈpərmənənt] *adj* : pasajero, inestable, efímero — **impermanently** *adv*
impermeable [ɪmˈpərmiəbəl] *adj* : impermeable
impersonal [ɪmˈpərsənəl] *adj* : impersonal — **impersonally** *adv*
impersonate [ɪmˈpərsən,eɪt] *vt* **-ated; -ating** : hacerse pasar por, imitar
impersonation [ɪm,pərsənˈeɪʃən] *n* : imitación *f*
impersonator [ɪmˈpərsən,eɪt̬ər] *n* : imitador *m,* -dora *f*
impertinence [ɪmˈpərtənənts] *n* : impertinencia *f*
impertinent [ɪmˈpərtənənt] *adj* **1** IRRELEVANT : impertinente, irrelevante **2** INSOLENT : impertinente, insolente
impertinently [ɪmˈpərtənəntli] *adv* : con impertinencia, impertinentemente
imperturbable [,ɪmpərˈtərbəbəl] *adj* : imperturbable
impervious [ɪmˈpərviəs] *adj* **1** IMPENETRABLE : impermeable **2** INSENSITIVE : insensible <impervious to criticism : insensible a la crítica>
impetuosity [ɪm,pɛtʃʊˈɑsət̬i] *n, pl* **-ties** : impetuosidad *f*
impetuous [ɪmˈpɛtʃʊəs] *adj* : impetuoso, impulsivo
impetuously [ɪmˈpɛtʃʊəsli] *adv* : de manera impulsiva, impetuosamente
impetus [ˈɪmpət̬əs] *n* : ímpetu *m,* impulso *m*
impiety [ɪmˈpaɪət̬i] *n, pl* **-ties** : impiedad *f*
impinge [ɪmˈpɪndʒ] *vi* **-pinged; -pinging 1 to impinge on** AFFECT : afectar a, incidir en **2 to impinge on** VIOLATE : violar, vulnerar
impious [ˈɪmpiəs, ɪmˈpaɪəs] *adj* : impío, irreverente
impish [ˈɪmpɪʃ] *adj* MISCHIEVOUS : pícaro, travieso
impishly [ˈɪmpɪʃli] *adv* : con picardía
implacable [ɪmˈplækəbəl] *adj* : implacable — **implacably** [-bli] *adv*
implant¹ [ɪmˈplænt] *vt* **1** INCULCATE, INSTILL : inculcar, implantar **2** INSERT : implantar, insertar
implant² [ˈɪm,plænt] *n* : implante *m* (de pelo), injerto *m* (de piel)
implantation [,ɪm,plænˈteɪʃən] *n* : implantación *f*
implausibility [ɪm,plɔzəˈbɪlət̬i] *n, pl* **-ties** : inverosimilitud *f*
implausible [ɪmˈplɔzəbəl] *adj* : inverosímil, poco convincente
implement¹ [ˈɪmplə,mɛnt] *vt* : poner en práctica, implementar
implement² [ˈɪmpləmənt] *n* : utensilio *m,* instrumento *m,* implemento *m*
implementation [,ɪmpləmənˈteɪʃən] *n* : implementación *f,* ejecución *f,* cumplimiento *m*
implicate [ˈɪmplə,keɪt] *vt* **-cated; -cating** : implicar, involucrar

implication [ˌɪmplə'keɪʃən] *n* **1** CONSEQUENCE : implicación *f,* consecuencia *f* **2** INFERENCE : insinuación *f,* inferencia *f*

implicit [ɪm'plɪsət] *adj* **1** IMPLIED : implícito, tácito **2** ABSOLUTE : absoluto, completo <implicit faith : fe ciega> — **implicitly** *adv*

implied [ɪm'plaɪd] *adj* : implícito, tácito

implode [ɪm'ploːd] *vi* **-ploded; -ploding** : implosionar

implore [ɪm'plor] *vt* **-plored; -ploring** : implorar, suplicar

imply [ɪm'plaɪ] *vt* **-plied; -plying 1** SUGGEST : insinuar, dar a entender **2** INVOLVE : implicar, suponer <rights imply obligations : los derechos implican unas obligaciones>

impolite [ˌɪmpə'laɪt] *adj* : descortés, maleducado

impoliteness [ˌɪmpə'laɪtnəs] *n* : descortesía *f,* falta *f* de educación

impolitic [ɪm'pɑləˌtɪk] *adj* : imprudente, poco político

imponderable[1] [ɪm'pɑndərəbəl] *adj* : imponderable

imponderable[2] *n* : imponderable *m*

import[1] [ɪm'port] *vt* **1** SIGNIFY : significar **2** : importar <to import foreign cars : importar autos extranjeros>

import[2] ['ɪmˌport] *n* **1** SIGNIFICANCE : importancia *f,* significación *f* **2** → **importation**

importance [ɪm'portənts] *n* : importancia *f*

important [ɪm'pɔrtənt] *adj* : importante

importantly [ɪm'pɔrtəntli] *adv* **1** : con importancia **2 more importantly** : lo que es más importante

importation [ˌɪmˌpɔr'teɪʃən] *n* : importación *f*

importer [ɪm'portər] *n* : importador *m,* -dora *f*

importunate [ɪm'pɔrtʃənət] *adj* : importuno, insistente

importune [ˌɪmpər'tuːn, -'tjuːn; ɪm'pɔrtʃən] *vt* **-tuned; -tuning** : importunar, implorar

impose [ɪm'poːz] *v* **-posed; -posing** *vt* : imponer <to impose a tax : imponer un impuesto> — *vi* **to impose on** : abusar de, molestar <to impose on her kindness : abusar de su bondad>

imposing [ɪm'poːzɪŋ] *adj* : imponente, impresionante

imposition [ˌɪmpə'zɪʃən] *n* : imposición *f*

impossibility [ɪmˌpɑsə'bɪləṱi] *n, pl* **-ties** : imposibilidad *f*

impossible [ɪm'pɑsəbəl] *adj* **1** : imposible <an impossible task : una tarea imposible> <to make life impossible for : hacerle la vida imposible a> **2** UNACCEPTABLE : inaceptable

impossibly [ɪm'pɑsəbli] *adv* : imposiblemente, increíblemente

impostor *or* **imposter** [ɪm'pɑstər] *n* : impostor *m,* -tora *f*

imposture [ɪm'pɑstʃər] *n* : impostura *f*

impotence ['ɪmpətənts] *n* : impotencia *f*

impotency ['ɪmpətəntsi] → **impotence**

impotent ['ɪmpətənt] *adj* : impotente

impound [ɪm'paʊnd] *vt* : incautar, embargar, confiscar

impoverish [ɪm'pɑvərɪʃ] *vt* : empobrecer

impoverishment [ɪm'pɑvərɪʃmənt] *n* : empobrecimiento *m*

impracticable [ɪm'præktɪkəbəl] *adj* : impracticable

impractical [ɪm'præktɪkəl] *adj* : poco práctico

imprecise [ˌɪmprɪ'saɪs] *adj* : impreciso

imprecisely [ˌɪmprɪ'saɪsli] *adv* : con imprecisión

impreciseness [ˌɪmprɪ'saɪsnəs] → **imprecision**

imprecision [ˌɪmprɪ'sɪʒən] *n* : imprecisión *f,* falta de precisión *f*

impregnable [ɪm'prɛgnəbəl] *adj* : inexpugnable, impenetrable, inconquistable

impregnate [ɪm'prɛgˌneɪt] *vt* **-nated; -nating 1** FERTILIZE : fecundar **2** PERMEATE, SATURATE : impregnar, empapar, saturar

impresario [ˌɪmprə'sɑriˌo, -'sær-] *n, pl* **-rios** : empresario *m,* -ria *f*

impress [ɪm'prɛs] *vt* **1** IMPRINT : imprimir, estampar **2** : impresionar, causar impresión a <I was not impressed : no me hizo buena impresión> **3 to impress (something) on someone** : recalcarle (algo) a alguien — *vi* : impresionar, hacer una impresión

impression [ɪm'prɛʃən] *n* **1** IMPRINT : marca *f,* huella *f,* molde *m* (de los dientes) **2** EFFECT : impresión *f,* efecto *m,* impacto *m* **3** PRINTING : impresión *f* **4** NOTION : impresión *f,* noción *f*

impressionable [ɪm'prɛʃənəbəl] *adj* : impresionable

impressive [ɪm'prɛsɪv] *adj* : impresionante — **impressively** *adv*

impressiveness [ɪm'prɛsɪvnəs] *n* : calidad de ser impresionante

imprint[1] [ɪm'prɪnt, 'ɪmˌ-] *vt* : imprimir, estampar

imprint[2] ['ɪmˌprɪnt] *n* : marca *f,* huella *f*

imprison [ɪm'prɪzən] *vt* **1** JAIL : encarcelar, aprisionar **2** CONFINE : recluir, encerrar

imprisonment [ɪm'prɪzənmənt] *n* : encarcelamiento *m*

improbability [ɪmˌprɑbə'bɪləṱi] *n, pl* **-ties** : improbabilidad *f,* inverosimilitud *f*

improbable [ɪm'prɑbəbəl] *adj* : improbable, inverosímil

impromptu[1] [ɪm'prɑmp,tu:, -,tju:] *adv* : sin preparación, espontáneamente

impromptu[2] *adj* : espontáneo, improvisado

impromptu[3] *n* : improvisación *f*

improper [ɪm'prɑpər] *adj* **1** INCORRECT : incorrecto, impropio **2** INDECOROUS : indecoroso

improperly [ɪm'prɑpərli] *adv* : incorrectamente, indebidamente

impropriety [,ɪmprə'praɪəṭi] *n, pl* **-eties 1** INDECOROUSNESS : indecoro *m,* falta *f* de decoro **2** ERROR : impropiedad *f,* incorrección *f*

improve [ɪm'pru:v] *v* **-proved; -proving** : mejorar

improvement [ɪm'pru:vmənt] *n* : mejoramiento *m,* mejora *f*

improvidence [ɪm'prɑvədənts] *n* : imprevisión *f*

improvident [ɪm'prɑvədənt] *adj* : sin previsión, imprevisor

improvisation [ɪm,prɑvə'zeɪʃən, ,ɪmprəvə-] *n* : improvisación *f*

improvise ['ɪmprə,vaɪz] *v* **-vised; -vising** : improvisar

imprudence [ɪm'pru:dənts] *n* : imprudencia *f,* indiscreción *f*

imprudent [ɪm'pru:dənt] *adj* : imprudente, indiscreto

impudence ['ɪmpjədənts] *n* : insolencia *f,* descaro *m*

impudent ['ɪmpjədənt] *adj* : insolente, descarado — **impudently** *adv*

impugn [ɪm'pju:n] *vt* : impugnar

impulse ['ɪm,pʌls] *n* **1** : impulso *m* **2 on impulse** : sin reflexionar

impulsive [ɪm'pʌlsɪv] *adj* : impulsivo — **impulsively** *adv*

impulsiveness [ɪm'pʌlsɪvnəs] *n* : impulsividad *f*

impunity [ɪm'pju:nəṭi] *n* **1** : impunidad *f* **2 with impunity** : impunemente

impure [ɪm'pjʊr] *adj* **1** : impuro <impure thoughts : pensamientos impuros> **2** CONTAMINATED : con impurezas, impuro

impurity [ɪm'pjʊrəṭi] *n, pl* **-ties** : impureza *f*

impute [ɪm'pju:t] *vt* **-puted; -puting** ATTRIBUTE : imputar, atribuir

in[1] ['ɪn] *adv* **1** INSIDE : dentro, adentro <let's go in : vamos adentro> **2** HARVESTED : recogido <the crops are in : las cosechas ya están recogidas> **3 to be in** : estar <is Linda in? : ¿está Linda?> **4 to be in** : estar en poder <the Democrats are in : los demócratas están en el poder> **5 to be in for** : ser objeto de, estar a punto de <they're in for a treat : los van a agasajar> <he's in for a surprise : se va a llevar una sorpresa> **6 to be in on** : participar en, tomar parte en

in[2] *adj* **1** INSIDE : interior <the in part : la parte interior> **2** FASHIONABLE : de moda

in[3] *prep* **1** (*indicating location or position*) <in the lake : en el lago> <a pain in the leg : un dolor en la pierna> <in the sun : al sol> <in the rain : bajo la lluvia> <the best restaurant in Buenos Aires : el mejor restaurante de Buenos Aires> **2** INTO : en, a <he broke it in pieces : lo rompió en pedazos> <she went in the house : se metió a la casa> **3** DURING : por, durante <in the afternoon : por la tarde> **4** WITHIN : dentro de <I'll be back in a week : vuelvo dentro de una semana> **5** (*indicating manner*) : en, con, de <in Spanish : en español> <written in pencil : escrito con lápiz> <in this way : de esta manera> **6** (*indicating states or circumstances*) <to be in luck : tener suerte> <to be in love : estar enamorado> <to be in a hurry : tener prisa> **7** (*indicating purpose*) : en <in reply : en respuesta, como réplica>

inability [,ɪnə'bɪləṭi] *n, pl* **-ties** : incapacidad *f*

inaccessibility [,ɪnɪk,sɛsə'bɪləṭi] *n, pl* **-ties** : inaccesibilidad *f*

inaccessible [,ɪnɪk'sɛsəbəl] *adj* : inaccesible

inaccuracy [ɪn'ækjərəsi] *n, pl* **-cies 1** : inexactitud *f* **2** MISTAKE : error *m*

inaccurate [ɪn'ækjərət] *n* : inexacto, erróneo, incorrecto

inaccurately [ɪn'ækjərətli] *adv* : incorrectamente, con inexactitud

inaction [ɪn'ækʃən] *n* : inactividad *f,* inacción *f*

inactive [ɪn'æktɪv] *n* : inactivo

inactivity [,ɪn,æk'tɪvəṭi] *n, pl* **-ties** : inactividad *f,* ociosidad *f*

inadequacy [ɪn'ædɪkwəsi] *n, pl* **-cies 1** INSUFFICIENCY : insuficiencia *f* **2** INCOMPETENCE : ineptitud *f,* incompetencia *f*

inadequate [ɪn'ædɪkwət] *adj* **1** INSUFFICIENT : insuficiente, inadecuado **2** INCOMPETENT : inepto, incompetente

inadmissible [,ɪnæd'mɪsəbəl] *adj* : inadmisible

inadvertent [,ɪnəd'vərtənt] *adj* : inadvertido, involuntario — **inadvertently** *adv*

inadvisable [,ɪnæd'vaɪzəbəl] *adj* : desaconsejable

inalienable [ɪn'eɪljənəbəl, -'eɪliənə-] *adj* : inalienable

inane [ɪ'neɪn] *adj* **inaner; -est** : estúpido, idiota, necio

inanimate [ɪn'ænəmət] *adj* : inanimado, exánime

inanity [ɪ'nænəṭi] *n, pl* **-ties 1** STUPIDITY : estupidez *f* **2** NONSENSE : idiotez *f,* disparate *m*

inapplicable [ɪn'æplɪkəbəl, ,ɪnə'plɪkəbəl] *adj* IRRELEVANT : inaplicable, irrelevante

inappreciable [,ɪnə'pri:ʃəbəl] *adj* : inapreciable, imperceptible

inappropriate [,ɪnə'pro:priət] *adj* : inapropiado, inadecuado, impropio

inappropriateness [ˌɪnəˈproːpriətnəs] *n* : lo inapropiado, impropiedad *f*

inapt [ɪnˈæpt] *adj* **1** UNSUITABLE : inadecuado, inapropiado **2** INEPT : inepto

inarticulate [ˌɪnɑrˈtɪkjələt] *adj* : inarticulado, incapaz de expresarse

inarticulately [ˌɪnɑrˈtɪkjələtli] *adv* : inarticuladamente

inasmuch as [ˌɪnæzˈmʌtʃæz] *conj* : ya que, dado que, puesto que

inattention [ˌɪnəˈtɛntʃən] *n* : falta *f* de atención, distracción *f*

inattentive [ˌɪnəˈtɛntɪv] *adj* : distraído, despistado

inattentively [ˌɪnəˈtɛntɪvli] *adv* : distraídamente, sin prestar atención

inaudible [ɪnˈɔdəbəl] *adj* : inaudible

inaudibly [ɪnˈɔdəbli] *adv* : de forma inaudible

inaugural[1] [ɪˈnɔgjərəl, -gərəl] *adj* : inaugural, de investidura

inaugural[2] *n* **1** *or* **inaugural address** : discurso *m* de investidura **2** INAUGURATION : investidura *f* (de una persona)

inaugurate [ɪˈnɔgjəˌreɪt, -gə-] *vt* **-rated; -rating 1** BEGIN : inaugurar **2** INDUCT : investir <to inaugurate the president : investir al presidente>

inauguration [ɪˌnɔgjəˈreɪʃən, -gə-] *n* **1** : inauguración *f* (de un edificio, un sistema, etc.) **2** : investidura *f* (de una persona)

inauspicious [ˌɪnɔˈspɪʃəs] *adj* : desfavorable, poco propicio

inborn [ˈɪnˌbɔrn] *adj* **1** CONGENITAL, INNATE : innato, congénito **2** HEREDITARY : hereditario

inbred [ˈɪnˌbrɛd] *adj* **1** : engendrado por endogamia **2** INNATE : innato

inbreed [ˈɪnˌbriːd] *vt* **-bred; -breeding** : engendrar por endogamia

inbreeding [ˈɪnˌbriːdɪŋ] *n* : endogamia *f*

incalculable [ɪnˈkælkjələbəl] *adj* : incalculable — **incalculably** [-bli] *adv*

incandescence [ˌɪnkənˈdɛsənts] *n* : incandescencia *f*

incandescent [ˌɪnkənˈdɛsənt] *adj* **1** : incandescente **2** BRILLIANT : brillante

incantation [ˌɪnˌkænˈteɪʃən] *n* : conjuro *m,* ensalmo *m*

incapable [ɪnˈkeɪpəbəl] *adj* : incapaz

incapacitate [ˌɪnkəˈpæsəˌteɪt] *vt* **-tated; -tating** : incapacitar

incapacity [ˌɪnkəˈpæsət̮i] *n, pl* **-ties** : incapacidad *f*

incarcerate [ɪnˈkɑrsəˌreɪt] *vt* **-ated; -ating** : encarcelar

incarceration [ɪnˌkɑrsəˈreɪʃən] *n* : encarcelamiento *m,* encarcelación *f*

incarnate[1] [ɪnˈkɑrˌneɪt] *vt* **-nated; -nating** : encarnar

incarnate[2] [ɪnˈkɑrnət, -ˌneɪt] *adj* : encarnado

incarnation [ˌɪnˌkɑrˈneɪʃən] *n* : encarnación *f*

incendiary[1] [ɪnˈsɛndiˌɛri] *adj* : incendiario

incendiary[2] *n, pl* **-aries** : incendiario *m,* -ria *f;* pirómano *m,* -na *f*

incense[1] [ɪnˈsɛnts] *vt* **-censed; -censing** : indignar, enfadar, enfurecer

incense[2] [ˈɪnˌsɛnts] *n* : incienso *m*

incentive [ɪnˈsɛntɪv] *n* : incentivo *m,* aliciente *m,* motivación *f,* acicate *m*

inception [ɪnˈsɛpʃən] *n* : comienzo *m,* principio *m*

incessant [ɪnˈsɛsənt] *adj* : incesante, continuo — **incessantly** *adv*

incest [ˈɪnˌsɛst] *n* : incesto *m*

incestuous [ɪnˈsɛstʃʊəs] *adj* : incestuoso

inch[1] [ˈɪntʃ] *v* : avanzar poco a poco

inch[2] *n* **1** : pulgada *f* **2 every inch** : absoluto, seguro <every inch a winner : un seguro ganador> **3 within an inch of** : a punto de

incidence [ˈɪntsədənts] *n* **1** FREQUENCY : frecuencia *f,* índice *m* <a high incidence of crime : un alto índice de crímenes> **2 angle of incidence** : ángulo *m* de incidencia

incident[1] [ˈɪntsədənt] *adj* : incidente

incident[2] *n* : incidente *m,* incidencia *f,* episodio *m* (en una obra de ficción)

incidental[1] [ˌɪntsəˈdɛntəl] *adj* **1** SECONDARY : incidental, secundario **2** ACCIDENTAL : casual, fortuito

incidental[2] *n* **1** : algo incidental **2 incidentals** *npl* : imprevistos *mpl*

incidentally [ˌɪntsəˈdɛntəli, -ˈdɛntli] *adv* **1** BY CHANCE : incidentalmente, casualmente **2** BY THE WAY : a propósito, por cierto

incinerate [ɪnˈsɪnəˌreɪt] *vt* **-ated; -ating** : incinerar

incinerator [ɪnˈsɪnəˌreɪt̮ər] *n* : incinerador *m*

incipient [ɪnˈsɪpiənt] *adj* : incipiente, naciente

incise [ɪnˈsaɪz] *vt* **-cised; -cising 1** ENGRAVE : grabar, cincelar, inscribir **2** : hacer una incisión en

incision [ɪnˈsɪʒən] *n* : incisión *f*

incisive [ɪnˈsaɪsɪv] *adj* : incisivo, penetrante

incisively [ɪnˈsaɪsɪvli] *adv* : con agudeza

incisor [ɪnˈsaɪzər] *n* : incisivo *m*

incite [ɪnˈsaɪt] *vt* **-cited; -citing** : incitar, instigar

incitement [ɪnˈsaɪtmənt] *n* : incitación *f*

inclemency [ɪnˈklɛməntsi] *n, pl* **-cies** : inclemencia *f*

inclement [ɪnˈklɛmənt] *adj* : inclemente, tormentuoso

inclination [ˌɪnkləˈneɪʃən] *n* **1** PROPENSITY : inclinación *f,* tendencia *f* **2** DESIRE : deseo *m,* ganas *fpl* **3** BOW : inclinación *f*

incline[1] [ɪnˈklaɪn] *v* **-clined; -clining** *vi* **1** SLOPE : inclinarse **2** TEND : inclinarse, tender <he is inclined to be late : tiende a llegar tarde> — *vt* **1** LOWER : inclinar, bajar <to incline one's head

: bajar la cabeza> **2** SLANT : inclinar **3** PREDISPOSE : predisponer
incline[2] [ˈɪn,klaɪn] *n* : inclinación *f*, pendiente *f*
inclined [ɪnˈklaɪnd] *adj* **1** SLOPING : inclinado **2** PRONE : prono, dispuesto, dado
inclose, inclosure → **enclose, enclosure**
include [ɪnˈkluːd] *vt* **-cluded; -cluding** : incluir, comprender
inclusion [ɪnˈkluːʒən] *n* : inclusión *f*
inclusive [ɪnˈkluːsɪv] *adj* : inclusivo
incognito [,ɪn,kɑgˈniːto, ɪnˈkɑgnə,toː] *adv & adj* : de incógnito
incoherence [,ɪnkoˈhɪrənts, -ˈhɛr-] *n* : incoherencia *f*
incoherent [,ɪnkoˈhɪrənt, -ˈhɛr-] *adj* : incoherente — **incoherently** *adv*
incombustible [,ɪnkəmˈbʌstəbəl] *adj* : incombustible
income [ˈɪn,kʌm] *n* : ingresos *mpl*, entradas *fpl*
income tax *n* : impuesto *m* sobre la renta
incoming [ˈɪn,kʌmɪŋ] *adj* **1** ARRIVING : que se recibe (dícese del correo), que llega (dícese de las personas), ascendente (dícese de la marea) **2** NEW : nuevo, entrante <the incoming president : el nuevo presidente> <the incoming year : el año entrante>
incommunicado [,ɪnkə,mjuːnəˈkɑdo] *adj* : incomunicado
incomparable [ɪnˈkɑmpərəbəl] *adj* : incomparable, sin igual
incompatible [,ɪnkəmˈpæt̬əbəl] *adj* : incompatible
incompetence [ɪnˈkɑmpət̬ənts] *n* : incompetencia *f*, impericia *f*, ineptitud *f*
incompetent [ɪnˈkɑmpət̬ənt] *adj* : incompetente, inepto, incapaz
incomplete [,ɪnkəmˈpliːt] *adj* : incompleto — **incompletely** *adv*
incomprehensible [,ɪn,kɑmpriˈhɛntsəbəl] *adj* : incomprensible
inconceivable [,ɪnkənˈsiːvəbəl] *adj* **1** INCOMPREHENSIBLE : incomprensible **2** UNBELIEVABLE : inconcebible, increíble
inconceivably [,ɪnkənˈsiːvəbli] *adv* : inconcebiblemente, increíblemente
inconclusive [,ɪnkənˈkluːsɪv] *adj* : inconcluyente, no decisivo
incongruity [,ɪnkənˈgruːət̬i, -,kɑn-] *n*, *pl* **-ties** : incongruencia *f*
incongruous [ɪnˈkɑŋgrʊəs] *adj* : incongruente, inapropiado, fuera de lugar
incongruously [ɪnˈkɑŋgrʊəsli] *adv* : de manera incongruente, inapropiadamente
inconsequential [,ɪn,kɑnsəˈkwɛntʃəl] *adj* : intrascendente, de poco importancia
inconsiderable [,ɪnkənˈsɪdərəbəl] *adj* : insignificante
inconsiderate [,ɪnkənˈsɪdərət] *adj* : desconsiderado, sin consideración — **inconsiderately** *adv*
inconsistency [,ɪnkənˈsɪstəntsi] *n*, *pl* **-cies** : inconsecuencia *f*, inconsistencia *f*
inconsistent [,ɪnkənˈsɪstənt] *adj* : inconsecuente, inconsistente
inconsolable [,ɪnkənˈsoːləbəl] *adj* : inconsolable — **inconsolably** [-bli] *adv*
inconspicuous [,ɪnkənˈspɪkjʊəs] *adj* : discreto, no conspicuo, que no llama la atención
inconspicuously [,ɪnkənˈspɪkjʊəsli] *adv* : discretamente, sin llamar la atención
incontestable [,ɪnkənˈtɛstəbəl] *adj* : incontestable, indiscutible — **incontestably** [-bli] *adv*
incontinence [ɪnˈkɑntənənts] *n* : incontinencia *f*
incontinent [ɪnˈkɑntənənt] *adj* : incontinente
inconvenience[1] [,ɪnkənˈviːnjənts] **-nienced; -niencing** *vt* : importunar, incomodar, molestar
inconvenience[2] *n* : incomodidad *f*, molestia *f*
inconvenient [,ɪnkənˈviːnjənt] *adj* : inconveniente, importuno, incómodo — **inconveniently** *adv*
incorporate [ɪnˈkɔrpə,reɪt] *vt* **-rated; -rating 1** INCLUDE : incorporar, incluir **2** : incorporar, constituir en sociedad (dícese de un negocio)
incorporation [ɪn,kɔrpəˈreɪʃən] *n* : incorporación *f*
incorporeal [,ɪn,kɔrˈporiəl] *adj* : incorpóreo
incorrect [,ɪnkəˈrɛkt] *adj* **1** INACCURATE : incorrecto **2** WRONG : equivocado, erróneo **3** IMPROPER : impropio — **incorrectly** *adv*
incorrigible [ɪnˈkɔrədʒəbəl] *adj* : incorregible
incorruptible [,ɪnkəˈrʌptəbəl] *adj* : incorruptible
increase[1] [ɪnˈkriːs, ˈɪn,kriːs] *v* **-creased; -creasing** *vi* GROW : aumentar, crecer, subir (dícese de los precios) — *vt* AUGMENT : aumentar, acrecentar
increase[2] [ˈɪn,kriːs, ɪnˈkriːs] *n* : aumento *m*, incremento *m*, subida *f* (de precios)
increasing [ɪnˈkriːsɪŋ, ˈɪn,kriːsɪŋ] *adj* : creciente
increasingly [ɪnˈkriːsɪŋli] *adv* : cada vez más
incredible [ɪnˈkrɛdəbəl] *adj* : increíble — **incredibly** [-bli] *adv*
incredulity [,ɪnkrɪˈduːlət̬i, -ˈdjuː-] *n* : incredulidad *f*
incredulous [ɪnˈkrɛdʒələs] *adj* : incrédulo, escéptico
incredulously [ɪnˈkrɛdʒələsli] *adv* : con incredulidad
increment [ˈɪŋkrəmənt, ˈɪn-] *n* : incremento *m*, aumento *m*
incremental [,ɪŋkrəˈmɛntəl, ,ɪn-] *adj* : de incremento

incriminate [ɪnˈkrɪmə,neɪt] *vt* **-nated; -nating** : incriminar
incrimination [ɪn,krɪməˈneɪʃən] *n* : incriminación *f*
incriminatory [ɪnˈkrɪmənə,tori] *adj* : incriminatorio
incubate [ˈɪŋkjʊ,beɪt, ˈɪn-] *v* **-bated; -bating** *vt* : incubar, empollar — *vi* : incubar(se), empollar
incubation [,ɪŋkjʊˈbeɪʃən, ,ɪn-] *n* : incubación *f*
incubator [ˈɪŋkjʊ,beɪt̬ər, ˈɪn-] *n* : incubadora *f*
inculcate [ɪnˈkʌl,keɪt, ˈɪn,kʌl-] *vt* **-cated; -cating** : inculcar
incumbency [ɪnˈkʌmbəntsi] *n, pl* **-cies** 1 OBLIGATION : incumbencia *f* 2 : mandato *m* (en la política)
incumbent[1] [ɪnˈkʌmbənt] *adj* : obligatorio
incumbent[2] *n* : titular *mf*
incur [ɪnˈkər] *vt* **incurred; incurring** : provocar (al enojo), incurrir en (gastos, obligaciones)
incurable [ɪnˈkjʊrəbəl] *adj* : incurable, sin remedio
incursion [ɪnˈkərʒən] *n* : incursión *f*
indebted [ɪnˈdɛt̬əd] *adj* **1** : endeudado **2 to be indebted to** : estar en deuda con, estarle agracido a
indebtedness [ɪnˈdɛt̬ədnəs] *n* : endeudamiento *m*
indecency [ɪnˈdiːsəntsi] *n, pl* **-cies** : indecencia *f*
indecent [ɪnˈdiːsənt] *adj* : indecente — **indecently** *adv*
indecipherable [,ɪndɪˈsaɪfərəbəl] *adj* : indescifrable
indecision [,ɪndɪˈsɪʒən] *n* : indecisión *f,* irresolución *f*
indecisive [,ɪndɪˈsaɪsɪv] *adj* **1** INCONCLUSIVE : indeciso, que no es decisivo **2** IRRESOLUTE : indeciso, irresoluto, vacilante **3** INDEFINITE : indefinido — **indecisively** *adv*
indecorous [ɪnˈdɛkərəs, ,ɪndɪˈkorəs] *adj* : indecoroso — **indecorously** *adv*
indecorousness [ɪnˈdɛkərəsnəs, ,ɪndɪˈkorəs-] *n* : indecoro *m*
indeed [ɪnˈdiːd] *adv* **1** TRULY : verdaderamente, de veras **2** (*used as intensifier*) <thank you very much indeed : muchísimas gracias> **3** OF COURSE : claro, por supuesto
indefatigable [,ɪndɪˈfæt̬ɪgəbəl] *adj* : incansable, infatigable — **indefatigably** [-bli] *adv*
indefensible [,ɪndɪˈfɛntsəbəl] *adj* **1** VULNERABLE : indefendible, vulnerable **2** INEXCUSABLE : inexcusable
indefinable [,ɪndɪˈfaɪnəbəl] *adj* : indefinible
indefinite [ɪnˈdɛfənət] *adj* **1** : indefinido, indeterminado <indefinite pronouns : pronombres indefinidos> **2** VAGUE : vago, impreciso
indefinitely [ɪnˈdɛfənətli] *adv* : indefinidamente, por un tiempo indefinido
indelible [ɪnˈdɛləbəl] *adj* : indeleble, imborrable — **indelibly** [-bli] *adv*
indelicacy [ɪnˈdɛləkəsi] *n* : falta *f* de delicadeza
indelicate [ɪnˈdɛlɪkət] *adj* **1** IMPROPER : indelicado, indecoroso **2** TACTLESS : indiscreto, falto de tacto
indemnify [ɪnˈdɛmnə,faɪ] *vt* **-fied; -fying 1** INSURE : asegurar **2** COMPENSATE : indemnizar, compensar
indemnity [ɪnˈdɛmnət̬i] *n, pl* **-ties 1** INSURANCE : indemnidad *f* **2** COMPENSATION : indemnización *f*
indent [ɪnˈdɛnt] *vt* : sangrar (un párrafo)
indentation [,ɪn,dɛnˈteɪʃən] *n* **1** NOTCH : muesca *f,* mella *f* **2** INDENTING : sangría *f* (de un párrafo)
indenture[1] [ɪnˈdɛntʃər] *vt* **-tured; -turing** : ligar por contrato
indenture[2] *n* : contrato de aprendizaje
independence [,ɪndəˈpɛndənts] *n* : independencia *f*
Independence Day *n* : día *m* de la Independencia (4 de julio en los EE.UU.)
independent[1] [,ɪndəˈpɛndənt] *adj* : independiente — **independently** *adv*
independent[2] *n* : independiente *mf*
indescribable [,ɪndɪˈskraɪbəbəl] *adj* : indescriptible, incalificable — **indescribably** [-bli] *adv*
indestructibility [,ɪndɪ,strʌktəˈbɪlət̬i] *n* : indestructibilidad *f*
indestructible [,ɪndɪˈstrʌktəbəl] *adj* : indestructible
indeterminate [,ɪndɪˈtərmənət] *adj* **1** VAGUE : vago, impreciso, indeterminado **2** INDEFINITE : indeterminado, indefinido
index[1] [ˈɪn,dɛks] *vt* **1** : ponerle un índice a (un libro o una revista) **2** : incluir en un índice <all proper names are indexed : todos los nombres propios están incluidos en el índice> **3** INDICATE : indicar, señalar **4** REGULATE : indexar, indiciar <to index prices : indiciar los precios>
index[2] *n, pl* **-dexes** *or* **-dices** [ˈɪndə,siːz] **1** : índice *m* (de un libro, de precios) **2** INDICATION : indicio *m,* índice *m,* señal *f* <an index of her character : una señal de su carácter>
index finger *n* FOREFINGER : dedo *m* índice
Indian [ˈɪndiən] *n* **1** : indio *m,* -dia *f* **2** → **American Indian — Indian** *adj*
indicate [ˈɪndə,keɪt] *vt* **-cated; -cating 1** POINT OUT : indicar, señalar **2** SHOW, SUGGEST : ser indicio de, ser señal de **3** EXPRESS : expresar, señalar **4** REGISTER : marcar, poner (una medida, etc.)
indication [,ɪndəˈkeɪʃən] *n* : indicio *m,* señal *f*
indicative [ɪnˈdɪkət̬ɪv] *adj* : indicativo

indicator ['ɪndəˌkeɪt̬ər] *n* : indicador *m*
indict [ɪn'daɪt] *vt* : acusar, procesar (por un crímen)
indictment [ɪn'daɪtmənt] *n* : acusación *f*
indifference [ɪn'dɪfrənts, -'dɪfə-] *n* : indiferencia *f*
indifferent [ɪn'dɪfrənt, -'dɪfə-] *adj* **1** UNCONCERNED : indiferente **2** MEDIOCRE : mediocre
indifferently [ɪn'dɪfrəntli, -'dɪfə-] *adv* **1** : con indiferencia, indiferentemente **2** so-so : de modo regular, más o menos
indigence ['ɪndɪdʒənts] *n* : indigencia *f*
indigenous [ɪn'dɪdʒənəs] *adj* : indígena, nativo
indigent ['ɪndɪdʒənt] *adj* : indigente, pobre
indigestible [ˌɪndaɪ'dʒɛstəbəl, -dɪ-] *adj* : difícil de digerir
indigestion [ˌɪndaɪ'dʒɛstʃən, -dɪ-] *n* : indigestión *f*, empacho *m*
indignant [ɪn'dɪgnənt] *adj* : indignado
indignantly [ɪn'dɪgnəntli] *adv* : con indignación
indignation [ˌɪndɪg'neɪʃən] *n* : indignación *f*
indignity [ɪn'dɪgnət̬i] *n, pl* **-ties** : indignidad *f*
indigo ['ɪndɪˌgoː] *n, pl* **-gos** *or* **-goes** : añil *m*, índigo *m*
indirect [ˌɪndə'rɛkt, -daɪ-] *adj* : indirecto — **indirectly** *adv*
indiscernible [ˌɪndɪ'sərnəbəl, -'zər-] *adj* : imperceptible
indiscreet [ˌɪndɪ'skriːt] *adj* : indiscreto, imprudente — **indiscreetly** *adv*
indiscretion [ˌɪndɪ'skrɛʃən] *n* : indiscreción *f*, imprudencia *f*
indiscriminate [ˌɪndɪ'skrɪmənət] *adj* : indiscriminado
indiscriminately [ˌɪndɪ'skrɪmənətli] *adv* : sin discriminación, sin discernimiento
indispensable [ˌɪndɪ'spɛntsəbəl] *adj* : indispensable, necesario, imprescindible — **indispensably** [-bli] *adv*
indisposed [ˌɪndɪ'spoːzd] *adj* **1** ILL : indispuesto, enfermo **2** AVERSE, DISINCLINED : opuesto, reacio <to be indisposed toward working : no tener ganas de trabajar>
indisputable [ˌɪndɪ'spjuːt̬əbəl, ɪn'dɪspjʊt̬ə-] *adj* : indiscutible, incuestionable, incontestable — **indisputably** [-bli] *adv*
indistinct [ˌɪndɪ'stɪŋkt] *adj* : indistinto — **indistinctly** *adv*
indistinctness [ˌɪndɪ'stɪŋktnəs] *n* : falta *f* de claridad
individual¹ [ˌɪndə'vɪdʒʊəl] *adj* **1** PERSONAL : individual, personal <individual traits : características personales> **2** SEPARATE : individual, separado **3** PARTICULAR : particular, propio
individual² *n* : individuo *m*
individualist [ˌɪndə'vɪdʒʊəlɪst] *n* : individualista *mf*
individuality [ˌɪndəˌvɪdʒʊ'ælət̬i] *n, pl* **-ties** : individualidad *f*
individually [ˌɪndə'vɪdʒʊəli, -dʒəli] *adv* : individualmente
indivisible [ˌɪndɪ'vɪzəbəl] *adj* : indivisible
indoctrinate [ɪn'dɑktrəˌneɪt] *vt* **-nated; -nating 1** TEACH : enseñar, instruir **2** PROPAGANDIZE : adoctrinar
indoctrination [ɪnˌdɑktrə'neɪʃən] *n* : adoctrinamiento *m*
indolence ['ɪndələnts] *n* : indolencia *f*
indolent ['ɪndələnt] *adj* : indolente
indomitable [ɪn'dɑmət̬əbəl] *adj* : invencible, indomable, indómito — **indomitably** [-bli] *adv*
Indonesian [ˌɪndo'niːʒən, -ʃən] *n* : indonesio *m*, -sia *f* — **Indonesian** *adj*
indoor ['ɪn'dor] *adj* : interior (dícese de las plantas), para estar en casa (dícese de la ropa), cubierto (dícese de las piscinas, etc.), bajo techo (dícese de los deportes)
indoors ['ɪn'dorz] *adv* : adentro, dentro
indubitable [ɪn'duːbət̬əbəl, -'djuː-] *adj* : indudable, incuestionable, indiscutible
indubitably [ɪn'duːbət̬əbli, -'djuː-] *adv* : indudablemente
induce [ɪn'duːs, -'djuːs] *vt* **-duced; -ducing 1** PERSUADE : persuadir, inducir **2** CAUSE : inducir, provocar <to induce labor : provocar un parto>
inducement [ɪn'duːsmənt, -'djuːs-] *n* **1** INCENTIVE : incentivo *m*, aliciente *m* **2** : inducción *f*, provocación *f* (de un parto)
induct [ɪn'dʌkt] *vt* **1** INSTALL : instalar, investir **2** ADMIT : admitir (como miembro) **3** CONSCRIPT : reclutar (al servicio militar)
inductee [ˌɪnˌdʌk'tiː] *n* : recluta *mf*, conscripto *m*, -ta *f*
induction [ɪn'dʌkʃən] *n* **1** INTRODUCTION : iniciación *f*, introducción *f* **2** : inducción *f* (en la lógica o la electricidad)
inductive [ɪn'dʌktɪv] *adj* : inductivo
indulge [ɪn'dʌldʒ] *v* **-dulged; -dulging** *vt* **1** GRATIFY : gratificar, satisfacer **2** SPOIL : consentir, mimar — *vi* **to indulge in** : permitirse
indulgence [ɪn'dʌldʒənts] *n* **1** SATISFYING : satisfacción *f*, gratificación *f* **2** HUMORING : complacencia *f*, indulgencia *f* **3** SPOILING : consentimiento *m* **4** : indulgencia *f* (en la religión)
indulgent [ɪŋ'dʌldʒənt] *adj* : indulgente, consentido — **indulgently** *adv*
industrial [ɪn'dʌstriəl] *adj* : industrial — **industrially** *adv*
industrialist [ɪn'dʌstriəlɪst] *n* : industrial *mf*

industrialization [ɪn,dʌstriələ'zeɪʃən] *n* : industrialización *f*
industrialize [ɪn'dʌstriə,laɪz] *vt* **-ized; -izing** : industrializar
industrious [ɪn'dʌstriəs] *adj* : diligente, industrioso, trabajador
industriously [ɪn'dʌstriəsli] *adv* : con diligencia, con aplicación
industriousness [ɪn'dʌstriəsnəs] *n* : diligencia *f,* aplicación *f*
industry ['ɪndəstri] *n, pl* **-tries 1** DILIGENCE : diligencia *f,* aplicación *f* **2** : industria *f* <the steel industry : la industria siderúrgica>
inebriated [ɪ'ni:bri,eɪṭəd] *adj* : ebrio, embriagado
inebriation [ɪ,ni:bri'eɪʃən] *n* : ebriedad *f,* embriaguez *f*
ineffable [ɪn'ɛfəbəl] *adj* : inefable — **ineffably** [-bli] *adv*
ineffective [,ɪnɪ'fɛktɪv] *adj* **1** INEFFECTUAL : ineficaz, inútil **2** INCAPABLE : incompetente, ineficiente, incapaz
ineffectively [,ɪnɪ'fɛktɪvli] *adv* : ineficazmente, infructuosamente
ineffectual [,ɪnɪ'fɛktʃʊəl] *adj* : inútil, ineficaz — **ineffectually** *adv*
inefficiency [,ɪnɪ'fɪʃəntsi] *n, pl* **-cies** : ineficiencia *f,* ineficacia *f*
inefficient [,ɪnɪ'fɪʃənt] *adj* **1** : ineficiente, ineficaz **2** INCAPABLE, INCOMPETENT : incompetente, incapaz — **inefficiently** *adv*
inelegance [ɪn'ɛləgənts] *n* : inelegancia *f*
inelegant [ɪn'ɛləgənt] *adj* : inelegante, poco elegante
ineligibility [ɪn,ɛlədʒə'bɪləṭi] *n* : inelegibilidad *f*
ineligible [ɪn'ɛlədʒəbəl] *adj* : inelegible
inept [ɪ'nɛpt] *adj* : inepto <inept at : incapaz para>
ineptitude [ɪ'nɛptə,tu:d, -,tju:d] *n* : ineptitud *f,* incompetencia *f,* incapacidad *f*
inequality [,ɪnɪ'kwɑləṭi] *n, pl* **-ties** : desigualdad *f*
inert [ɪ'nərt] *adj* **1** INACTIVE : inerte, inactivo **2** SLUGGISH : lento
inertia [ɪ'nərʃə] *n* : inercia *f*
inescapable [,ɪnɪ'skeɪpəbəl] *adj* : inevitable, ineludible — **inescapably** [-bli] *adv*
inessential [,ɪnɪ'sɛntʃəl] *adj* : que no es esencial, innecesario
inestimable [ɪn'ɛstəməbəl] *adj* : inestimable, inapreciable
inevitability [ɪn,ɛvəṭə'bɪləṭi] *n, pl* **-ties** : inevitabilidad *f*
inevitable [ɪn'ɛvəṭəbəl] *adj* : inevitable — **inevitably** [-bli] *adv*
inexact [,ɪnɪg'zækt] *adj* : inexacto
inexactly [,ɪnɪg'zæktli] *adv* : sin exactitud
inexcusable [,ɪnɪk'skju:zəbəl] *adj* : inexcusable, imperdonable — **inexcusably** [-bli] *adv*
inexhaustible [,ɪnɪg'zɔstəbəl] *adj* **1** INDEFATIGABLE : infatigable, incansable **2** ENDLESS : inagotable — **inexhaustibly** [-bli] *adv*
inexorable [ɪn'ɛksərəbəl] *adj* : inexorable — **inexorably** [-bli] *adv*
inexpensive [,ɪnɪk'spɛntsɪv] *adj* : barato, económico
inexperience [,ɪnɪk'spɪriənts] *n* : inexperiencia *f*
inexperienced [,ɪnɪk'spɪriəntst] *adj* : inexperto, novato
inexplicable [,ɪnɪk'splɪkəbəl] *adj* : inexplicable — **inexplicably** [-bli] *adv*
inexpressible [,ɪnɪk'sprɛsəbəl] *adj* : inexpresable, inefable
inextricable [,ɪnɪk'strɪkəbəl, ɪ'nɛk,strɪ-] *adj* : inextricable — **inextricably** [-bli] *adv*
infallibility [ɪn,fælə'bɪləṭi] *n* : infalibilidad *f*
infallible [ɪn'fæləbəl] *adj* : infalible — **infallibly** [-bli] *adv*
infamous ['ɪnfəməs] *adj* : infame — **infamously** *adv*
infamy ['ɪnfəmi] *n, pl* **-mies** : infamia *f*
infancy ['ɪnfəntsi] *n, pl* **-cies** : infancia *f*
infant ['ɪnfənt] *n* : bebé *m;* niño *m,* -ña *f*
infantile ['ɪnfən,taɪl, -təl, -,ti:l] *adj* : infantil, pueril
infantile paralysis → **poliomyelitis**
infantry ['ɪnfəntri] *n, pl* **-tries** : infantería *f*
infatuated [ɪn'fætʃʊ,eɪṭəd] *adj* **to be infatuated with** : estar encaprichado con
infatuation [ɪn,fætʃʊ'eɪʃən] *n* : encaprichamiento *m,* enamoramiento *m*
infect [ɪn'fɛkt] *vt* : infectar, contagiar
infection [ɪn'fɛkʃən] *n* : infección *f,* contagio *m*
infectious [ɪn'fɛkʃəs] *adj* : infeccioso, contagioso
infer [ɪn'fər] *vt* **inferred; inferring 1** DEDUCE : deducir, inferir **2** SURMISE : concluir, suponer, tener entendido **3** IMPLY : sugerir, insinuar
inference ['ɪnfərənts] *n* : deducción *f,* inferencia *f,* conclusión *f*
inferior[1] [ɪn'fɪriər] *adj* : inferior, malo
inferior[2] *n* : inferior *mf*
inferiority [ɪn,fɪri'ɔrəṭi] *n, pl* **-ties** : inferioridad *f* <inferiority complex : complejo de inferioridad>
infernal [ɪn'fərnəl] *adj* **1** : infernal <infernal fires : fuegos infernales> **2** DIABOLICAL : infernal, diabólico **3** DAMNABLE : maldito, condenado
inferno [ɪn'fər,no:] *n, pl* **-nos** : infierno *m*
infertile [ɪn'fərṭəl, -,taɪl] *adj* : estéril, infecundo
infertility [,ɪnfər'tɪləṭi] *n* : esterilidad *f,* infecundidad *f*
infest [ɪn'fɛst] *vt* : infestar, plagar
infidel ['ɪnfədəl, -,dɛl] *n* : infiel *mf*

infidelity [ˌɪnfəˈdɛləṭi, -faɪ-] *n, pl* **-ties 1** UNFAITHFULNESS : infidelidad *f* **2** DISLOYALTY : deslealtad *f*
infield [ˈɪnˌfiːld] *n* : cuadro *m,* diamante *m*
infiltrate [ɪnˈfɪlˌtreɪt, ˈɪnfɪl-] *v* **-trated; -trating** *vt* : infiltrar — *vi* : infiltrarse
infiltration [ˌɪnfɪlˈtreɪʃən] *n* : infiltración *f*
infinite [ˈɪnfənət] *adj* **1** LIMITLESS : infinito, sin límites **2** VAST : infinito, vasto, extenso
infinitely [ˈɪnfənətli] *adv* : infinitamente
infinitesimal [ˌɪnˌfɪnəˈtɛsəməl] *adj* : infinitésimo, infinitesimal — **infinitesimally** *adv*
infinitive [ɪnˈfɪnəṭɪv] *n* : infinitivo *m*
infinitude [ɪnˈfɪnəˌtuːd, -tjuːd] *n* : infinitud *f*
infinity [ɪnˈfɪnəṭi] *n, pl* **-ties 1** : infinito *m* (en matemáticas, etc.) **2** : infinidad *f* <an infinity of stars : una infinidad de estrellas>
infirm [ɪnˈfərm] *adj* **1** FEEBLE : enfermizo, endeble **2** INSECURE : inseguro
infirmary [ɪnˈfərməri] *n, pl* **-ries** : enfermería *f,* hospital *m*
infirmity [ɪnˈfərməṭi] *n, pl* **-ties 1** FRAILTY : debilidad *f,* endeblez *f* **2** AILMENT : enfermedad *f,* dolencia *f* <the infirmities of age : los achaques de la vejez>
inflame [ɪnˈfleɪm] *v* **-flamed; -flaming** *vt* **1** KINDLE : inflamar, encender **2** : inflamar (una herida) **3** STIR UP : encender, provocar, inflamar — *vi* : inflamarse
inflammable [ɪnˈflæməbəl] *adj* **1** FLAMMABLE : inflamable **2** IRASCIBLE : irascible, explosivo
inflammation [ˌɪnfləˈmeɪʃən] *n* : inflamación *f*
inflammatory [ɪnˈflæməˌtori] *adj* : inflamatorio, incendiario
inflatable [ɪnˈfleɪṭəbəl] *adj* : inflable
inflate [ɪnˈfleɪt] *vt* **-flated; -flating** : inflar, hinchar
inflation [ɪnˈfleɪʃən] *n* : inflación *f*
inflationary [ɪnˈfleɪʃəˌnɛri] *adj* : inflacionario, inflacionista
inflect [ɪnˈflɛkt] *vt* **1** CONJUGATE, DECLINE : conjugar, declinar **2** MODULATE : modular (la voz)
inflection [ɪnˈflɛkʃən] *n* : inflexión *f*
inflexibility [ɪnˌflɛksəˈbɪləṭi] *n, pl* **-ties** : inflexibilidad *f*
inflexible [ɪnˈflɛksɪbəl] *adj* : inflexible
inflict [ɪnˈflɪkt] *vt* **1** : infligir, causar, imponer **2 to inflict oneself on** : imponer uno su presencia (a alguien)
infliction [ɪnˈflɪkʃən] *n* : imposición *f*
influence¹ [ˈɪnˌfluːənts, ɪnˈfluːənts] *vt* **-enced; -encing** : influenciar, influir en
influence² *n* **1** : influencia *f,* influjo *m* <to exert influence over : ejercer influencia sobre> <the influence of gravity : el influjo de la gravidad> **2 under the influence** : bajo la influencia del alcohol, embriagado
influential [ˌɪnfluˈɛntʃəl] *adj* : influyente
influenza [ˌɪnfluˈɛnzə] *n* : gripe *f,* influenza *f,* gripa *f Col, Mex*
influx [ˈɪnˌflʌks] *n* : afluencia *f* (de gente), entrada *f* (de mercancías), llegada *f* (de ideas)
inform [ɪnˈfɔrm] *vt* : informar, notificar, avisar — *vi* **to inform on** : delatar, denunciar
informal [ɪnˈfɔrməl] *adj* **1** UNCEREMONIOUS : sin ceremonia, sin etiqueta **2** CASUAL : informal, familiar (dícese del lenguaje) **3** UNOFFICIAL : extraoficial
informality [ˌɪnfɔrˈmæləṭi, -fər-] *n, pl* **-ties** : informalidad *f,* familiaridad *f,* falta *f* de ceremonia
informally [ɪnˈfɔrməli] *adv* : sin ceremonias, de manera informal, informalmente
informant [ɪnˈfɔrmənt] *n* : informante *mf;* informador *m,* -dora *f*
information [ˌɪnfərˈmeɪʃən] *n* : información *f*
informative [ɪnˈfɔrməṭɪv] *adj* : informativo, instructivo
informer [ɪnˈfɔrmər] *n* : informante *mf;* informador *m,* -dora *f*
infraction [ɪnˈfrækʃən] *n* : infracción *f,* violación *f,* transgresión *f*
infrared [ˌɪnfrəˈrɛd] *adj* : infrarrojo
infrastructure [ˈɪnfrəˌstrʌktʃər] *n* : infraestructura *f*
infrequent [ɪnˈfriːkwənt] *adj* : infrecuente, raro
infrequently [ɪnˈfriːkwəntli] *adv* : raramente, con poca frecuencia
infringe [ɪnˈfrɪndʒ] *v* **-fringed; -fringing** *vt* : infringir, violar — *vi* **to infringe on** : abusar de, violar
infringement [ɪnˈfrɪndʒmənt] *n* **1** VIOLATION : violación *f* (de la ley), incumplimiento *m* (de un contrato) **2** ENCROACHMENT : usurpación *f* (de derechos, etc.)
infuriate [ɪnˈfjʊriˌeɪt] *vt* **-ated; -ating** : enfurecer, poner furioso
infuriating [ɪnˈfjʊriˌeɪṭɪŋ] *adj* : indignante, exasperante
infuse [ɪnˈfjuːz] *vt* **-fused; -fusing 1** INSTILL : infundir **2** STEEP : hacer una infusión de
infusion [ɪnˈfjuːʒən] *n* : infusión *f*
ingenious [ɪnˈdʒiːnjəs] *adj* : ingenioso — **ingeniously** *adv*
ingenue *or* **ingénue** [ˈɑndʒəˌnuː, ˈæn-; ˈæʒə-, ˈɑ-] *n* : ingenua *f*
ingenuity [ˌɪndʒəˈnuːəṭi, -ˈnjuː-] *n, pl* **-ities** : ingenio
ingenuous [ɪnˈdʒɛnjʊəs] *adj* **1** FRANK : cándido, franco **2** NAIVE : ingenuo — **ingenuously** *adv*
ingenuousness [ɪnˈdʒɛnjʊəsnəs] *n* **1** FRANKNESS : candidez *f,* candor *m* **2** NAÏVETÉ : ingenuidad *f*

ingest [ɪn'dʒɛst] *vt* : ingerir
inglorious [ɪn'gloriəs] *adj* : deshonroso, ignominioso
ingot ['ɪŋgət] *n* : lingote *m*
ingrained [ɪn'greɪnd] *adj* : arraigado
ingrate ['ɪn,greɪt] *n* : ingrato *m,* -ta *f*
ingratiate [ɪn'greɪʃi,eɪt] *vt* **-ated; -ating** : conseguir la benevolencia de <to ingratiate oneself with someone : congraciarse con alguien>
ingratiating [ɪn'greɪʃi,eɪṭɪŋ] *adj* : halagador, zalamero, obsequioso
ingratitude [ɪn'græṭə,tu:d, -,tju:d] *n* : ingratitud *f*
ingredient [ɪn'gri:diənt] *n* : ingrediente *m,* componente *m*
ingrown ['ɪn,gro:n] *adj* **1** : crecido hacia adentro **2 ingrown toenail** : uña *f* encarnada
inhabit [ɪn'hæbət] *vt* : vivir en, habitar, ocupar
inhabitable [ɪn'hæbəṭəbəl] *adj* : habitable
inhabitant [ɪn'hæbəṭənt] *n* : habitante *mf*
inhalant [ɪn'heɪlənt] *n* : inhalante *m*
inhalation [,ɪnhə'leɪʃən, ,ɪnə-] *n* : inhalación *f*
inhale [ɪn'heɪl] *v* **-haled; -haling** *vt* : inhalar, aspirar — *vi* : inspirar
inhaler [ɪn'heɪlər] *n* : inhalador *m*
inhere [ɪn'hɪr] *vi* **-hered; -hering** : ser inherente
inherent [ɪn'hɪrənt, -'hɛr-] *adj* : inherente, intrínseco — **inherently** *adv*
inherit [ɪn'hɛrət] *vt* : heredar
inheritance [ɪn'hɛrəṭən*t*s] *n* : herencia *f*
inheritor [ɪn'hɛrəṭər] *n* : heredero *m,* -da *f*
inhibit [ɪn'hɪbət] *vt* IMPEDE : inhibir, impedir
inhibition [,ɪnhə'bɪʃən, ,ɪnə-] *n* : inhibición *f,* cohibición *f*
inhuman [ɪn'hju:mən, -'ju:-] *adj* : inhumano, cruel — **inhumanly** *adv*
inhumane [,ɪnhju'meɪn, -ju-] *adj* INHUMAN : inhumano, cruel
inhumanity [,ɪnhju'mænəṭi, -ju-] *n, pl* **-ties** : inhumanidad *f,* crueldad *f*
inimical [ɪ'nɪmɪkəl] *adj* **1** UNFAVORABLE : adverso, desfavorable **2** HOSTILE : hostil — **inimically** *adv*
inimitable [ɪ'nɪməṭəbəl] *adj* : inimitable
iniquitous [ɪ'nɪkwəṭəs] *adj* : inicuo, malvado
iniquity [ɪ'nɪkwəṭi] *n, pl* **-ties** : iniquidad *f*
initial[1] [ɪ'nɪʃəl] *vt* **-tialed** *or* **-tialled; -tialing** *or* **-tialling** : poner las iniciales a, firmar con las iniciales
initial[2] *adj* : inicial, primero — **initially** *adv*
initial[3] *n* : inicial *f*
initiate[1] [ɪ'nɪʃi,eɪt] *vt* **-ated; -ating 1** BEGIN : comenzar, iniciar **2** INDUCT : instruir **3** INTRODUCE : introducir, instruir
initiate[2] [ɪ'nɪʃiət] *n* : iniciado *m,* -da *f*
initiation [ɪ,nɪʃi'eɪʃən] *n* : iniciación *f*
initiative [ɪ'nɪʃəṭɪv] *n* : iniciativa *f*
initiatory [ɪ'nɪʃiə,tori] *adj* **1** INTRODUCTORY : introductorio **2** : de iniciación <initiatory rites : ritos de iniciación>
inject [ɪn'dʒɛkt] *vt* : inyectar
injection [ɪn'dʒɛkʃən] *n* : inyección *f*
injudicious [,ɪndʒʊ'dɪʃəs] *adj* : imprudente, indiscreto, poco juicioso
injunction [ɪn'dʒʌŋkʃən] *n* **1** ORDER : orden *f,* mandato *m* **2** COURT ORDER : mandamiento *m* judicial
injure ['ɪndʒər] *vt* **-jured; -juring 1** WOUND : herir, lesionar **2** HURT : lastimar, dañar, herir **3 to injure oneself** : hacerse daño
injurious [ɪn'dʒʊriəs] *adj* : perjudicial <injurious to one's health : perjudicial a la salud>
injury ['ɪndʒəri] *n, pl* **-ries 1** WRONG : mal *m,* injusticia *f* **2** DAMAGE, HARM : herida *f,* daño *m,* perjuicio *m*
injustice [ɪn'dʒʌstəs] *n* : injusticia *f*
ink[1] ['ɪŋk] *vt* : entintar
ink[2] *n* : tinta *f*
inkling ['ɪŋklɪŋ] *n* : presentimiento *m,* indicio *m,* sospecho *m*
inkwell ['ɪŋk,wɛl] *n* : tintero *m*
inky ['ɪŋki] *adj* **1** : manchado de tinta **2** BLACK : negro, impenetrable <inky darkness : negra oscuridad>
inland[1] ['ɪn,lænd, -lənd] *adv* : hacia el interior, tierra adentro
inland[2] *adj* : interior
inland[3] *n* : interior *m*
in–law ['ɪn,lɔ] *n* **1** : pariente *m* político **2 in–laws** *npl* : suegros *mpl*
inlay[1] [ɪn'leɪ, 'ɪn,leɪ] *vt* **-laid** [-'leɪd, -,leɪd]; **-laying** : incrustar, taracear
inlay[2] ['ɪn,leɪ] *n* **1** : incrustación *f* **2** : empaste *m* (de un diente)
inlet ['ɪn,lɛt, -lət] *n* : cala *f,* ensenada *f*
inmate ['ɪn,meɪt] *n* : paciente *mf* (en un hospital); preso *m,* -sa *f* (en una prisión); interno *m,* -na *f* (en un asilo)
in memoriam [,ɪnmə'moriəm] *prep* : en memoria de
inmost ['ɪn,mo:st] → **innermost**
inn ['ɪn] *n* **1** : posada *f,* hostería *f,* fonda *f* **2** TAVERN : taberna *f*
innards ['ɪnərdz] *npl* : entrañas *fpl,* tripas *fpl fam*
innate [ɪ'neɪt] *adj* **1** INBORN : innato **2** INHERENT : inherente
inner ['ɪnər] *adj* : interior, interno
innermost ['ɪnər,mo:st] *adj* : más íntimo, más profundo
innersole ['ɪnər'so:l] → **insole**
inning ['ɪnɪŋ] *n* : entrada *f*
innkeeper ['ɪn,ki:pər] *n* : posadero *m,* -ra *f*
innocence ['ɪnəsən*t*s] *n* : inocencia *f*
innocent[1] ['ɪnəsənt] *adj* : inocente — **innocently** *adv*
innocent[2] *n* : inocente *mf*

innocuous [ɪˈnɑkjəwəs] *adj* **1** HARMLESS : inocuo **2** INOFFENSIVE : inofensivo
innovate [ˈɪnəˌveɪt] *vi* **-vated; -vating** : innovar
innovation [ˌɪnəˈveɪʃən] *n* : innovación *f,* novedad *f*
innovative [ˈɪnəˌveɪtɪv] *adj* : innovador
innovator [ˈɪnəˌveɪtər] *n* : innovador *m,* -dora *f*
innuendo [ˌɪnjʊˈɛndo] *n, pl* **-dos** *or* **-does** : insinuación *f,* indirecta *f*
innumerable [ɪˈnuːmərəbəl, -ˈnjuː-] *adj* : innumerable
inoculate [ɪˈnɑkjəˌleɪt] *vt* **-lated; -lating** : inocular
inoculation [ɪˌnɑkjəˈleɪʃən] *n* : inoculación *f*
inoffensive [ˌɪnəˈfɛntsɪv] *adj* : inofensivo
inoperable [ɪnˈɑpərəbəl] *adj* : inoperable
inoperative [ɪnˈɑpərətɪv, -ˌreɪ-] *adj* : inoperante
inopportune [ɪnˌɑpərˈtuːn, -ˈtjuːn] *adj* : inoportuno — **inopportunely** *adv*
inordinate [ɪnˈɔrdənət] *adj* : excesivo, inmoderado, desmesurado — **inordinately** *adv*
inorganic [ˌɪnˌɔrˈgænɪk] *adj* : inorgánico
inpatient [ˈɪnˌpeɪʃənt] *n* : paciente *mf* hospitalizado
input[1] [ˈɪnˌpʊt] *vt* **inputted** *or* **input; inputting** : entrar (datos, información)
input[2] *n* **1** CONTRIBUTION : aportación *f,* contribución *f* **2** ENTRY : entrada *f* (de datos) **3** ADVICE, OPINION : consejos *mpl,* opinión *f*
inquest [ˈɪnˌkwɛst] *n* INQUIRY, INVESTIGATION : investigación *f,* averiguación *f,* pesquisa *f* (judicial)
inquire [ɪnˈkwaɪr] *v* **-quired; -quiring** *vt* : preguntar, informarse de, inquirir <he inquired how to get in : preguntó como entrar> — *vi* **1** ASK : preguntar, informarse <to inquire about : informarse sobre> <to inquire after (someone) : preguntar por (alguien)> **2 to inquire into** INVESTIGATE : investigar, inquirir sobre
inquirer [ɪnˈkwaɪrər] *n* : inquiridor *m,* -dora *f;* investigador *m,* -dora *f*
inquiringly [ɪnˈkwaɪrɪŋli] *adv* : inquisitivamente
inquiry [ˈɪnˌkwaɪri, ɪnˈkwaɪri; ˈɪnkwəri, ˈɪŋ-] *n, pl* **-ries 1** QUESTION : pregunta *f* <to make inquiries about : pedir información sobre> **2** INVESTIGATION : investigación *f,* inquisición *f,* pesquisa *f*
inquisition [ˌɪnkwəˈzɪʃən, ˌɪŋ-] *n* **1** : inquisición *f,* interrogatorio *m,* investigación *f* **2 the Inquisition** : la Inquisición *f*
inquisitive [ɪnˈkwɪzətɪv] *adj* : inquisidor, inquisitivo, curioso — **inquisitively** *adv*
inquisitiveness [ɪnˈkwɪzətɪvnəs] *n* : curiosidad *f*
inquisitor [ɪnˈkwɪzətər] *n* : inquisidor *m,* -dora *f;* interrogador *m,* -dora *f*
inroad [ˈɪnˌroːd] *n* **1** ENCROACHMENT, INVASION : invasión *f,* incursión *f* **2 to make inroads into** : ocupar parte de (un tiempo), agotar parte de (ahorros, recursos), invadir (un territorio)
insane [ɪnˈseɪn] *adj* **1** MAD : loco, demente <to go insane : volverse loco> **2** ABSURD : absurdo, insensato <an insane scheme : un proyecto insensato>
insanely [ɪnˈseɪnli] *adv* : como un loco <insanely suspicious : loco de recelo>
insanity [ɪnˈsænəti] *n, pl* **-ties 1** MADNESS : locura *f* **2** FOLLY : locura *f,* insensatez *f*
insatiable [ɪnˈseɪʃəbəl] *adj* : insaciable — **insatiably** [-bli] *adv*
inscribe [ɪnˈskraɪb] *vt* **-scribed; -scribing 1** ENGRAVE : inscribir, grabar **2** ENROLL : inscribir **3** DEDICATE : dedicar (un libro)
inscription [ɪnˈskrɪpʃən] *n* : inscripción *f* (en un monumento), dedicación *f* (en un libro), leyenda *f* (de una ilustración, etc.)
inscrutable [ɪnˈskruːtəbəl] *adj* : inescrutable, misterioso — **inscrutably** [-bli] *adv*
inseam [ˈɪnˌsiːm] *n* : entrepierna *f*
insect [ˈɪnˌsɛkt] *n* : insecto *m*
insecticidal [ɪnˌsɛktəˈsaɪdəl] *adj* : insecticida
insecticide [ɪnˈsɛktəˌsaɪd] *n* : insecticida *m*
insecure [ˌɪnsɪˈkjʊr] *adj* : inseguro, poco seguro — **insecurely** *adv*
insecurely [ˌɪnsɪˈkjʊrli] *adv* : inseguramente
insecurity [ˌɪnsɪˈkjʊrəti] *n, pl* **-ties** : inseguridad *f*
inseminate [ɪnˈsɛməˌneɪt] *vt* **-nated; -nating** : inseminar
insemination [ɪnˌsɛməˈneɪʃən] *n* : inseminación *f*
insensibility [ɪnˌsɛntsəˈbɪləti] *n, pl* **-ties** : insensibilidad *f*
insensible [ɪnˈsɛntsəbəl] *adj* **1** UNCONSCIOUS : inconsciente, sin conocimiento **2** NUMB : insensible, entumecido **3** UNAWARE : inconsciente
insensitive [ɪnˈsɛntsətɪv] *adj* : insensible
insensitivity [ɪnˌsɛntsəˈtɪvəti] *n, pl* **-ties** : insensibilidad *f*
inseparable [ɪnˈsɛpərəbəl] *adj* : inseparable
insert[1] [ɪnˈsərt] *vt* **1** : insertar, introducir, poner, meter <insert your key in the lock : mete tu llave en la cerradura> **2** INTERPOLATE : interpolar, intercalar

insert[2] [ˈɪn,sərt] *n* **:** inserción *f,* hoja *f* insertada (en una revista, etc.)

insertion [ɪnˈsərʃən] *n* **:** inserción *f*

inset [ˈɪn,sɛt] *n* **:** página *f* intercalada (en un libro), entredós *m* (de encaje en la ropa)

inshore[1] [ˈɪnˈʃor] *adv* **:** hacia la costa

inshore[2] *adj* **:** cercano a la costa, costero <inshore fishing : pesca costera>

inside[1] [ɪnˈsaɪd, ˈɪn,saɪd] *adv* **:** adentro, dentro <to run inside : correr para adentro> <inside and out : por dentro y por fuera>

inside[2] *adj* **1 :** interior, de adentro, de dentro <the inside lane : el carril interior> **2 :** confidencial <inside information : información confidencial>

inside[3] *n* **1 :** interior *m,* parte *f* de adentro **2 insides** *npl* BELLY, GUTS **:** tripas *fpl fam* **3 inside out :** al revés

inside[4] *prep* **1** INTO **:** al interior de **2** WITHIN **:** dentro de **3** (*referring to time*) **:** en menos de <inside an hour : en menos de una hora>

inside of *prep* INSIDE **:** dentro de

insider [ɪnˈsaɪdər] *n* **:** persona *f* enterada

insidious [ɪnˈsɪdiəs] *adj* **:** insidioso — **insidiously** *adv*

insidiousness [ɪnˈsɪdiəsnəs] *n* **:** insidia *f*

insight [ˈɪn,saɪt] *n* **:** perspicacia *f,* penetración *f*

insightful [ɪnˈsaɪtfəl] *adj* **:** perspicaz

insignia [ɪnˈsɪgniə] *or* **insigne** [-,niː] *n, pl* **-nia** *or* **-nias :** insignia *f,* enseña *f*

insignificance [,ɪnsɪgˈnɪfɪkənts] *n* **:** insignificancia *f*

insignificant [,ɪnsɪgˈnɪfɪkənt] *adj* **:** insignificante

insincere [,ɪnsɪnˈsɪr] *adj* **:** insincero, poco sincero

insincerely [,ɪnsɪnˈsɪrli] *adv* **:** con poca sinceridad

insincerity [,ɪnsɪnˈsɛrəṱi, -ˈsɪr-] *n, pl* **-ties :** insinceridad *f*

insinuate [ɪnˈsɪnjʊ,eɪt] *vt* **-ated; -ating :** insinuar

insinuation [ɪn,sɪnjʊˈeɪʃən] *n* **:** insinuación *f*

insipid [ɪnˈsɪpəd] *adj* **:** insípido

insist [ɪnˈsɪst] *v* **:** insistir

insistence [ɪnˈsɪstənts] *n* **:** insistencia *f*

insistent [ɪnˈsɪstənt] *adj* **:** insistente — **insistently** *adv*

insofar as [,ɪnsoˈfɑræz] *conj* **:** en la medida en que, en tanto que, en cuanto a

insole [ˈɪn,soːl] *n* **:** plantilla *f*

insolence [ˈɪntsələnts] *n* **:** insolencia *f*

insolent [ˈɪntsələnt] *adj* **:** insolente

insolubility [ɪn,sɑljʊˈbɪləṱi] *n* **:** insolubilidad *f*

insoluble [ɪnˈsɑljʊbəl] *adj* **:** insoluble

insolvency [ɪnˈsɑlvəntsi] *n, pl* **-cies :** insolvencia *f*

insolvent [ɪnˈsɑlvənt] *adj* **:** insolvente

insomnia [ɪnˈsɑmniə] *n* **:** insomnio *m*

insomuch as [,ɪnsoˈmʌtʃæz] → **inasmuch as**

insomuch that *conj* SO **:** así que, de manera que

inspect [ɪnˈspɛkt] *vt* **:** inspeccionar, examinar, revisar

inspection [ɪnˈspɛkʃən] *n* **:** inspección *f,* examen *m,* revisión *f,* revista *f* (de tropas)

inspector [ɪnˈspɛktər] *n* **:** inspector *m,* -tora *f*

inspiration [,ɪntspəˈreɪʃən] *n* **:** inspiración *f*

inspirational [,ɪntspəˈreɪʃənəl] *adj* **:** inspirador

inspire [ɪnˈspaɪr] *v* **-spired; -spiring** *vt* **1** INHALE **:** inhalar, aspirar **2** STIMULATE **:** estimular, animar, inspirar **3** INSTILL **:** inspirar, infundir — *vi* **:** inspirar

instability [,ɪntstəˈbɪləṱi] *n, pl* **-ties :** inestabilidad *f*

install [ɪnˈstɔl] *vt* **-stalled; -stalling 1 :** instalar <to install the new president : instalar el presidente nuevo> <to install a fan : montar un abanico> **2 to install oneself :** instalarse

installation [,ɪntstəˈleɪʃən] *n* **:** instalación *f*

installment [ɪnˈstɔlmənt] *n* **1 :** plazo *m,* cuota *f* <to pay in four installments : pagar a cuatro plazos> **2 :** entrega *f* (de una publicación o telenovela) **3** INSTALLATION **:** instalación *f*

instance [ˈɪntstənts] *n* **1** INSTIGATION **:** instancia *f* **2** EXAMPLE **:** ejemplo *m* <for instance : por ejemplo> **3** OCCASION **:** instancia *f,* caso *m,* ocasión *f* <he prefers, in this instance, to remain anonymous : en este caso prefiere quedarse anónimo>

instant[1] [ˈɪntstənt] *adj* **1** IMMEDIATE **:** inmediato, instantáneo <an instant reply : una respuesta inmediata> **2 :** instantáneo <instant coffee : café instantáneo>

instant[2] *n* **:** momento *m,* instante *m*

instantaneous [,ɪntstənˈteɪniəs] *adj* **:** instantáneo

instantaneously [,ɪntstənˈteɪniəsli] *adv* **:** instantáneamente, al instante

instantly [ˈɪntstəntli] *adv* **:** al instante, instantáneamente

instead [ɪnˈstɛd] *adv* **1 :** en cambio, en lugar de eso, en su lugar <Dad was going, but Mom went instead : papá iba a ir, pero mamá fue en su lugar> **2** RATHER **:** al contrario

instead of *prep* **:** en vez de, en lugar de

instep [ˈɪn,stɛp] *n* **:** empeine *m*

instigate [ˈɪntstə,geɪt] *vt* **-gated; -gating** INCITE, PROVOKE **:** instigar, incitar, provocar, fomentar

instigation [,ɪntstəˈgeɪʃən] *n* **:** instancia *f,* incitación *f*

instigator [ˈɪntstə,geɪṱər] *n* **:** instigador *m,* -dora *f;* incitador *m,* -dora *f*

instill [ɪnˈstɪl] *vt* **-stilled; -stilling** : inculcar, infundir
instinct [ˈɪnˌstɪŋkt] *n* **1** TALENT : instinto *m,* don *m* <an instinct for the right word : un don para escoger la palabra apropiada> **2** : instinto *m* <maternal instincts : instintos maternales>
instinctive [ɪnˈstɪŋktɪv] *adj* : instintivo
instinctively [ɪnˈstɪŋktɪvli] *adv* : instintivamente, por instinto
instinctual [ɪnˈstɪŋktʃʊəl] *adj* : instintivo
institute[1] [ˈɪntstəˌtuːt, -ˌtjuːt] *vt* **-tuted; -tuting 1** ESTABLISH: establecer, instituir, fundar **2** INITIATE : iniciar, empezar, entablar
institute[2] *n* : instituto *m*
institution [ˌɪntstəˈtuːʃən, -ˈtjuː-] *n* **1** ESTABLISHING : institución *f,* establecimiento *m* **2** CUSTOM : institución *f,* tradición *f* <the institution of marriage : la institución del matrimonio> **3** ORGANIZATION : institución *f,* organismo *m* **4** ASYLUM : asilo *m*
institutional [ˌɪntstəˈtuːʃənəl, -ˈtjuː-] *adj* : institucional
institutionalize [ˌɪntstəˈtuːʃənəˌlaɪz, -ˈtjuː-] *vt* **-ized; -izing 1** : institucionalizar <institutionalized values : valores institucionalizados> **2** : internar <institutionalized orphans : huérfanos internados>
instruct [ɪnˈstrʌkt] *vt* **1** TEACH, TRAIN : instruir, adiestrar, enseñar **2** COMMAND : mandar, ordenar, dar instrucciones a
instruction [ɪnˈstrʌkʃən] *n* **1** TEACHING : instrucción *f,* enseñanza *f* **2** COMMAND : orden *f,* instrucción *f* **3 instructions** *npl* DIRECTIONS : instrucciones *fpl,* modo *m* de empleo
instructional [ɪnˈstrʌkʃənəl] *adj* : instructivo, educativo
instructive [ɪnˈstrʌktɪv] *adj* : instructivo
instructor [ɪnˈstrʌktər] *n* : instructor *m,* -tora *f*
instrument [ˈɪntstrəmənt] *n* : instrumento *m*
instrumental [ˌɪntstrəˈmɛntəl] *adj* : instrumental
instrumentalist [ˌɪntstrəˈmɛntəlɪst] *n* : instrumentista *mf*
insubordinate [ˌɪnsəˈbɔrdənət] *adj* : insubordinado
insubordination [ˌɪnsəˌbɔrdənˈeɪʃən] *n* : insubordinación *f*
insubstantial [ˌɪnsəbˈstæntʃəl] *adj* : insustancial, poco nutritivo (dícese de una comida), poco sólido (dícese de una estructura o un argumento)
insufferable [ɪnˈsʌfərəbəl] *adj* UNBEARABLE : insufrible, intolerable, inaguantable, insoportable — **insufferably** [-bli] *adv*
insufficiency [ˌɪnsəˈfɪʃəntsi] *n, pl* **-cies** : insuficiencia *f*
insufficient [ˌɪnsəˈfɪʃənt] *adj* : insuficiente — **insufficiently** *adv*
insular [ˈɪntsʊlər, -sjʊ-] *adj* **1** : isleño (dícese de la gente), insular (dícese del clima) <insular residents : residentes de la isla> **2** NARROW-MINDED : de miras estrechas
insularity [ˌɪntsʊˈlærəṭi, -sjʊ-] *n* : insularidad *f*
insulate [ˈɪntsəˌleɪt] *vt* **-lated; -lating** : aislar
insulation [ˌɪntsəˈleɪʃən] *n* : aislamiento *m*
insulator [ˈɪntsəˌleɪṭər] *n* : aislante *m,* aislador *m*
insulin [ˈɪntsələn] *n* : insulina *f*
insult[1] [ɪnˈsʌlt] *vt* : insultar, ofender, injuriar
insult[2] [ˈɪnˌsʌlt] *n* : insulto *m,* injuria *f,* agravio *m*
insulting [ɪnˈsʌltɪŋ] *adj* : ofensivo, injurioso, insultante
insultingly [ɪnˈsʌltɪŋli] *adv* : ofensivamente, de manera insultante
insuperable [ɪnˈsuːpərəbəl] *adj* : insuperable — **insuperably** [-bli] *adv*
insurable [ɪnˈʃʊrəbəl] *adj* : asegurable
insurance [ɪnˈʃʊrənts, ˈɪnˌʃʊr-] *n* : seguro *m* <life insurance : seguro de vida> <insurance company : compañía de seguros>
insure [ɪnˈʃʊr] *vt* **-sured; -suring 1** UNDERWRITE : asegurar **2** ENSURE : asegurar, garantizar
insured [ɪnˈʃʊrd] *n* : asegurado *m,* -da *f*
insurer [ɪnˈʃʊrər] *n* : asegurador *m,* -dora *f*
insurgent[1] [ɪnˈsərdʒənt] *adj* : insurgente
insurgent[2] *n* : insurgente *mf*
insurmountable [ˌɪnsərˈmaʊntəbəl] *adj* : insuperable, insalvable — **insurmountably** [-bli] *adv*
insurrection [ˌɪnsəˈrɛkʃən] *n* : insurrección *f,* levantamiento *m,* alzamiento *m*
intact [ɪnˈtækt] *adj* : intacto
intake [ˈɪnˌteɪk] *n* **1** OPENING : entrada *f,* toma *f* <fuel intake : toma de combustible> **2** : entrada *f* (de agua o aire), consumo *m* (de sustancias nutritivas) **3 intake of breath** : inhalación *f*
intangible [ɪnˈtændʒəbəl] *adj* : intangible, impalpable — **intangibly** [-bli] *adv*
integer [ˈɪntɪdʒər] *n* : entero *m*
integral [ˈɪntɪgrəl] *adj* : integral, esencial
integrate [ˈɪntəˌgreɪt] *v* **-grated; -grating** *vt* **1** UNITE : integrar, unir **2** DESEGREGATE : eliminar la segregación de — *vi* : integrarse
integration [ˌɪntəˈgreɪʃən] *n* : integración *f*
integrity [ɪnˈtɛgrəṭi] *n* : integridad *f*
intellect [ˈɪntəlˌɛkt] *n* : intelecto *m,* inteligencia *f,* capacidad *f* intelectual

intellectual[1] [ˌɪntəˈlɛktʃuəl] *adj* : intelectual — **intellectually** *adv*
intellectual[2] *n* : intelectual *mf*
intellectualism [ˌɪntəˈlɛktʃuəˌlɪzəm] *n* : intelectualismo *m*
intelligence [ɪnˈtɛlədʒənts] *n* **1** : inteligencia *f* **2** INFORMATION, NEWS : inteligencia *f,* información *f,* noticias *fpl*
intelligent [ɪnˈtɛlədʒənt] *adj* : inteligente — **intelligently** *adv*
intelligibility [ɪnˌtɛlədʒəˈbɪləṭi] *n* : inteligibilidad *f*
intelligible [ɪnˈtɛlədʒəbəl] *adj* : inteligible, comprensible — **intelligibly** [-bli] *adv*
intemperance [ɪnˈtɛmpərənts] *n* : inmoderación *f,* intemperancia *f*
intemperate [ɪnˈtɛmpərət] *adj* : excesivo, inmoderado, desmedido
intend [ɪnˈtɛnd] *vt* **1** MEAN : querer decir <that's not what I intended : eso no es lo que quería decir> **2** PLAN : tener planeado, proyectar, proponerse <I intend to finish by Thursday : me propongo acabar para el jueves>
intended [ɪnˈtɛndəd] *adj* **1** PLANNED : previsto, proyectado **2** INTENTIONAL : intencional, deliberado
intense [ɪnˈtɛnts] *adj* **1** EXTREME : intenso, extremo <intense pain : dolor intenso> **2** : profundo, intenso <to my intense relief : para mi alivio profundo> <intense enthusiasm : entusiasmo ardiente>
intensely [ɪnˈtɛntsli] *adv* : sumamente, profundamente, intensamente
intensification [ɪnˌtɛntsəfəˈkeɪʃən] *n* : intensificación *f*
intensify [ɪnˈtɛntsəˌfaɪ] *v* **-fied; -fying** *vt* **1** STRENGTHEN : intensificar, redoblar <to intensify one's efforts : redoblar uno sus esfuerzos> **2** SHARPEN : intensificar, agudizar (dolor, ansiedad) — *vi* : intensificarse, hacerse más intenso
intensity [ɪnˈtɛntsəṭi] *n, pl* **-ties** : intensidad *f*
intensive [ɪnˈtɛntsɪv] *adj* : intensivo — **intensively** *adv*
intent[1] [ɪnˈtɛnt] *adj* **1** FIXED : concentrado, fijo <an intent stare : una mirada fija> **2 intent on** *or* **intent upon** : resuelto a, atento a
intent[2] *n* **1** PURPOSE : intención *f,* propósito *m* **2 for all intents and purposes** : a todos los efectos, prácticamente
intention [ɪnˈtɛntʃən] *n* : intención *f,* propósito *m*
intentional [ɪnˈtɛntʃənəl] *adj* : intencional, deliberado
intentionally [ɪnˈtɛntʃənəli] *adv* : a propósito, adrede
intently [ɪnˈtɛntli] *adv* : atentamente, fijamente
inter [ɪnˈtər] *vt* **-terred; -terring** : enterrar, inhumar
interact [ˌɪntərˈækt] *vi* : interactuar, actuar recíprocamente, relacionarse
interaction [ˌɪntərˈækʃən] *n* : interacción *f,* interrelación *f*
interactive [ˌɪntərˈæktɪv] *adj* : interactivo
interbreed [ˌɪntərˈbriːd] *v* **-bred** [-ˈbrɛd]; **-breeding** *vt* : cruzar — *vi* : cruzarse
intercalate [ɪnˈtərkəˌleɪt] *vt* **-lated; -lating** : intercalar
intercede [ˌɪntərˈsiːd] *vi* **-ceded; -ceding** : interceder
intercept [ˌɪntərˈsɛpt] *vt* : interceptar
interception [ˌɪntərˈsɛpʃən] *n* : intercepción *f*
intercession [ˌɪntərˈsɛʃən] *n* : intercesión *f*
interchange[1] [ˌɪntərˈtʃeɪndʒ] *vt* **-changed; -changing** : intercambiar
interchange[2] [ˈɪntərˌtʃeɪndʒ] *n* **1** EXCHANGE : intercambio *m,* cambio *m* **2** JUNCTION : empalme *m,* enlace *m* de carreteras
interchangeable [ˌɪntərˈtʃeɪndʒəəl] *adj* : intercambiable
intercity [ˈɪntərˈsɪṭi] *adj* : interurbano
intercollegiate [ˌɪntərkəˈliːdʒət, -dʒiət] *adj* : interuniversitario
intercontinental [ˌɪntərˌkɑntənˈɛntəl] *adj* : intercontinental
intercourse [ˈɪntərˌkors] *n* **1** RELATIONS : relaciones *fpl,* trato *m* **2** COPULATION : acto *m* sexual, relaciones *fpl* sexuales, coito *m*
interdenominational [ˌɪntərdɪˌnɑməˈneɪʃənəl] *adj* : interconfesional
interdepartmental [ˌɪntərdɪˌpɑrtˈmɛntəl, -ˌdiː-] *adj* : interdepartamental
interdependence [ˌɪntərdɪˈpɛndənts] *n* : interdependencia *f*
interdependent [ˌɪntərdɪˈpɛndənt] *adj* : interdependiente
interdict [ˌɪntərˈdɪkt] *vt* **1** PROHIBIT : prohibir **2** : cortar (las líneas de comunicación o provisión del enemigo)
interest[1] [ˈɪntrəst, -təˌrɛst] *vt* : interesar
interest[2] *n* **1** SHARE, STAKE : interés *m,* participación *f* **2** BENEFIT : provecho *m,* beneficio *m,* interés *m* <in the public interest : en el interés público> **3** CHARGE : interés *m,* cargo *m* <compound interest : interés compuesto> **4** CURIOSITY : interés *m,* curiosidad *f* **5** COLOR : color *m,* interés *m* <places of local interest : lugares de color local> **6** HOBBY : afición *f*
interesting [ˈɪntrəstɪŋ, -təˌrɛstɪŋ] *adj* : interesante — **interestingly** *adv*
interface [ˈɪntərˌfeɪs] *n* **1** : punto *m* de contacto <oil-water interface : punto de contacto entre el agua y el aceite> **2** : interfase *f,* interfaz *f* (de una computadora)
interfere [ˌɪntərˈfɪr] *vi* **-fered; -fering** **1** INTERPOSE : interponerse, hacer in-

terferencia <to interfere with a play : obstruir una jugada> 2 MEDDLE : entrometerse, interferir, intervenir 3 **to interfere with** DISRUPT : afectar (una actividad), interferir (la radiotransmisión) 4 **to interfere with** TOUCH : tocar <someone interfered with my papers : alguien tocó mis papeles>

interference [ˌɪntərˈfɪrənts] *n* : interferencia *f*, intromisión *f*

intergalactic [ˌɪntərgəˈlæktɪk] *adj* : intergaláctico

intergovernmental [ˌɪntərˌgʌvərˈmɛntəl, -vərn-] *adj* : intergubernamental

interim[1] [ˈɪntərəm] *adj* : interino, provisional

interim[2] *n* 1 : interín *m*, intervalo *m* 2 **in the interim** : en el interín, mientras tanto

interior[1] [ɪnˈtɪriər] *adj* : interior

interior[2] *n* : interior *m*

interject [ˌɪntərˈdʒɛkt] *vt* : interponer, agregar

interjection [ˌɪntərˈdʒɛkʃən] *n* 1 : interjección *f* (en lingüística) 2 EXCLAMATION : exclamación *f* 3 INTERPOSITION, INTERRUPTION : interposición *f*, interrupción *f*

interlace [ˌɪntərˈleɪs] *vt* **-laced; -lacing** 1 INTERWEAVE : entrelazar 2 INTERSPERSE : intercalar

interlock [ˌɪntərˈlɑk] *vt* 1 UNITE : trabar, unir 2 ENGAGE, MESH : engranar — *vi* : entrelazarse, trabarse

interloper [ˌɪntərˈloːpər] *n* 1 INTRUDER : intruso *m*, -sa *f* 2 MEDDLER : entrometido *m*, -da *f*

interlude [ˈɪntərˌluːd] *n* 1 INTERVAL : intervalo *m*, intermedio *m* (en el teatro) 2 : interludio *m* (en música)

intermarriage [ˌɪntərˈmærɪdʒ] *n* 1 : matrimonio *m* mixto (entre miembros de distintas razas o religiones) 2 : matrimonio *m* entre miembros del mismo grupo

intermarry [ˌɪntərˈmæri] *vi* **-married; -marrying** 1 : casarse (con miembros de otros grupos) 2 : casarse entre sí (con miembros del mismo grupo)

intermediary[1] [ˌɪntərˈmiːdiˌɛri] *adj* : intermediario

intermediary[2] *n, pl* **-aries** : intermediario *m*, -ria *f*

intermediate[1] [ˌɪntərˈmiːdiət] *adj* : intermedio

intermediate[2] *n* GO-BETWEEN : intermediario *m*, -ria *f*; mediador *m*, -dora *f*

interment [ɪnˈtərmənt] *n* : entierro *m*

interminable [ɪnˈtərmənəbəl] *adj* : interminable, constante — **interminably** [-bli] *adv*

intermingle [ˌɪntərˈmɪŋgəl] *vt* **-mingled; -mingling** : entremezclar, mezclar — *vi* : entremezclarse

intermission [ˌɪntərˈmɪʃən] *n* : intermisión *f*, intervalo *m*, intermedio *m*

intermittent [ˌɪntərˈmɪtənt] *adj* : intermitente — **intermittently** *adv*

intermix [ˌɪntərˈmɪks] *vt* : entremezclar

intern[1] [ˈɪnˌtərn, ɪnˈtərn] *vt* : confinar (durante la guerra) — *vi* : servir de interno, hacer las prácticas

intern[2] [ˈɪnˌtərn] *n* : interno *m*, -na *f*

internal [ɪnˈtərnəl] *adj* : interno, interior <internal bleeding : hemorragia interna> <internal affairs : asuntos interiores, asuntos domésticos> — **internally** *adv*

international [ˌɪntərˈnæʃənəl] *adj* : internacional — **internationally** *adv*

internationalize [ˌɪntərˈnæʃənəˌlaɪz] *vt* **-ized; -izing** : internacionalizar

internee [ˌɪnˌtərˈniː] *n* : interno *m*, -na *f*

internist [ˈɪnˌtərnɪst] *n* : internista *mf*

interpersonal [ˌɪntərˈpərsənəl] *adj* : interpersonal

interplay [ˈɪntərˌpleɪ] *n* : interacción *f*, juego *m*

interpolate [ɪnˈtərpəˌleɪt] *vt* **-lated; -lating** : interpolar

interpose [ˌɪntərˈpoːz] *v* **-posed; -posing** *vt* : interponer, interrumpir con — *vi* : interponerse

interposition [ˌɪntərpəˈzɪʃən] *n* : interposición *f*

interpret [ɪnˈtərprət] *vt* : interpretar

interpretation [ɪnˌtərprəˈteɪʃən] *n* : interpretación *f*

interpretative [ɪnˈtərprəˌteɪt̬ɪv] *adj* : interpretativo

interpreter [ɪnˈtərprət̬ər] *n* : intérprete *mf*

interpretive [ɪnˈtərprət̬ɪv] *adj* : interpretativo

interracial [ˌɪntərˈreɪʃəl] *adj* : interracial

interrelate [ˌɪntərɪˈleɪt] *vi* **-related; -relating** : interelacionar

interrelationship [ˌɪntərɪˈleɪʃənˌʃɪp] *n* : interrelación *f*

interrogate [ɪnˈtɛrəˌgeɪt] *vt* **-gated; -gating** : interrogar, someter a un interrogatorio

interrogation [ɪnˌtɛrəˈgeɪʃən] *n* : interrogación *f*

interrogative[1] [ˌɪntəˈrɑgət̬ɪv] *adj* : interrogativo

interrogative[2] *n* : interrogativo *m*

interrogator [ɪnˈtɛrəˌgeɪt̬ər] *n* : interrogador *m*, -dora *f*

interrogatory [ˌɪntəˈrɑgəˌtɔri] → **interrogative**[1]

interrupt [ˌɪntəˈrʌpt] *v* : interrumpir

interruption [ˌɪntəˈrʌpʃən] *n* : interrupción *f*

intersect [ˌɪntərˈsɛkt] *vt* : cruzar, cortar — *vi* : cruzarse (dícese de los caminos), intersectarse (dícese de las líneas o figuras), cortarse

intersection [ˌɪntərˈsɛkʃən] *n* : intersección *f*, cruce *m*

intersperse [ˌɪntərˈspərs] *vt* **-spersed; -spersing** : intercalar, entremezclar

interstate [ˌɪntərˈsteɪt] *adj* : interestatal

interstellar [ˌɪntərˈstɛlər] *adj* : interestelar

interstice [ɪnˈtərstəs] *n, pl* **-stices** [-stəˌsiːz, -stəsəz] : intersticio *m*

intertwine [ˌɪntərˈtwaɪn] *vi* **-twined; -twining** : entrelazarse

interval [ˈɪntərvəl] *n* : intervalo *m*

intervene [ˌɪntərˈviːn] *vi* **-vened; -vening 1** ELAPSE : transcurrir, pasar <the intervening years : los años intermediarios> **2** INTERCEDE : intervenir, interceder, mediar

intervention [ˌɪntərˈvɛntʃən] *n* : intervención *f*

interview¹ [ˈɪntərˌvjuː] *vt* : entrevistar — *vi* : hacer entrevistas

interview² *n* : entrevista *f*

interviewer [ˈɪntərˌvjuːər] *n* : entrevistador *m,* -dora *f*

interweave [ˌɪntərˈwiːv] *v* **-wove** [-ˈwoːv]; **-woven** [-ˈwoːvən]; **-weaving** *vt* : entretejer, entrelazar — *vi* INTERTWINE : entrelazarse, entretejerse

interwoven [ˌɪntərˈwoːvən] *adj* : entretejido

intestate [ɪnˈtɛsˌteɪt, -tət] *adj* : intestado

intestinal [ɪnˈtɛstənəl] *adj* : intestinal

intestine [ɪnˈtɛstən] *n* **1** : intestino *m* **2 small intestine** : intestino *m* delgado **3 large intestine** : intestino *m* grueso

intimacy [ˈɪntəməsi] *n, pl* **-cies 1** CLOSENESS : intimidad *f* **2** FAMILIARITY : familiaridad *f*

intimate¹ [ˈɪntəˌmeɪt] *vt* **-mated; -mating** : insinuar, dar a entender

intimate² [ˈɪntəmət] *adj* **1** CLOSE : íntimo, de confianza <intimate friends : amigos íntimos> **2** PRIVATE : íntimo, privado <intimate clubs : clubes íntimos> **3** INNERMOST, SECRET : íntimo, secreto <intimate fantasies : fantasías secretas>

intimate³ *n* : amigo *m* íntimo, amiga *f* íntima

intimidate [ɪnˈtɪməˌdeɪt] *vt* **-dated; -dating** : intimidar

intimidation [ɪnˌtɪməˈdeɪʃən] *n* : intimidación *f*

into [ˈɪnˌtuː] *prep* **1** (*indicating motion*) : en, a, contra, dentro de <she got into bed : se metió en la cama> <to get into a plane : subir a un avión> <he crashed into the wall : chocó contra la pared> <looking into the sun : mirando al sol> **2** (*indicating state or condition*) : a, en <to burst into tears : echarse a llorar> <the water turned into ice : el agua se convirtió en hielo> <to translate into English : traducir al inglés> **3** (*indicating time*) <far into the night : hasta bien entrada la noche> <he's well into his eighties : tiene los ochenta bien cumplidos> **4** (*in mathematics*) <3 into 12 is 4 : 12 dividido por 3 es 4>

intolerable [ɪnˈtɑlərəbəl] *adj* : intolerable — **intolerably** [-bli] *adv*

intolerance [ɪnˈtɑlərənts] *n* : intolerancia *f*

intolerant [ɪnˈtɑlərənt] *adj* : intolerante

intonation [ˌɪntoˈneɪʃən] *n* : entonación *f*

intone [ɪnˈtoːn] *vt* **-toned; -toning** : entonar

intoxicant [ɪnˈtɑksɪkənt] *n* : bebida *f* alcohólica

intoxicate [ɪnˈtɑksəˌkeɪt] *vt* **-cated; -cating** : emborrachar, embriagar

intoxicated [ɪnˈtɑksəˌkeɪt̬əd] *adj* : borracho, embriagado

intoxicating [ɪnˈtɑksəˌkeɪt̬ɪŋ] *adj* : embriagador

intoxication [ɪnˌtɑksəˈkeɪʃən] *n* : embriaguez *f*

intractable [ɪnˈtræktəbəl] *adj* : obstinado, intratable

intramural [ˌɪntrəˈmjʊrəl] *adj* : interno, dentro de la universidad

intransigence [ɪnˈtræntsədʒənts, -ˈtrænzə-] *n* : intransigencia *f*

intransigent [ɪnˈtræntsədʒənt, -ˈtrænzə-] *adj* : intransigente

intravenous [ˌɪntrəˈviːnəs] *adj* : intravenoso — **intravenously** *adv*

intrepid [ɪnˈtrɛpəd] *adj* : intrépido

intricacy [ˈɪntrɪkəsi] *n, pl* **-cies** : complejidad *f,* lo intrincado

intricate [ˈɪntrɪkət] *adj* : intrincado, complicado — **intricately** *adv*

intrigue¹ [ɪnˈtriːg] *v* **-trigued; -triguing** : intrigar

intrigue² [ˈɪnˌtriːg, ɪnˈtriːg] *n* : intriga *f*

intriguing [ɪnˈtriːgɪŋli] *adj* : intrigante, fascinante

intrinsic [ɪnˈtrɪnzɪk, -ˈtrɪntsɪk] *adj* : intrínseco, esencial — **intrinsically** [-zɪkli, -sɪ-] *adv*

introduce [ˌɪntrəˈduːs, -ˈdjuːs] *vt* **-duced; -ducing 1** : presentar <let me introduce my father : permítame presentar a mi padre> **2** : introducir (algo nuevo), lanzar (un producto), presentar (una ley), proponer (una idea o un tema)

introduction [ˌɪntrəˈdʌkʃən] *n* : introducción *f,* presentación *f*

introductory [ˌɪntrəˈdʌktəri] *adj* : introductorio, preliminar, de introducción

introspection [ˌɪntrəˈspɛkʃən] *n* : introspección *f*

introspective [ˌɪntrəˈspɛktɪv] *adj* : introspectivo — **introspectively** *adv*

introvert [ˈɪntrəˌvərt] *n* : introvertido *m,* -da *f*

introverted [ˈɪntrəˌvərt̬əd] *adj* : introvertido

intrude [ɪnˈtruːd] *v* **-truded; -truding** *vi* **1** INTERFERE : inmiscuirse, entrometerse **2** DISTURB, INTERRUPT : molestar, estorbar, interrumpir — *vt* : introducir por fuerza

intruder [ɪn'tru:dər] *n* : intruso *m,* -sa *f*
intrusion [ɪn'tru:ʒən] *n* : intrusión *f*
intrusive [ɪn'tru:sɪv] *adj* : intruso
intuit [ɪn'tu:ɪt, -'tju:-] *vt* : intuir
intuition [ˌɪntʊ'ɪʃən, -tjʊ-] *n* : intuición *f*
intuitive [ɪn'tu:ət̬ɪv, -'tju:-] *adj* : intuitivo — **intuitively** *adv*
inundate ['ɪnənˌdeɪt] *vt* **-dated; -dating** : inundar
inundation [ˌɪnən'deɪʃən] *n* : inundación *f*
inure [ɪ'nʊr, -'njʊr] *vt* **-ured; -uring** : acostumbrar, habituar
invade [ɪn'veɪd] *vt* **-vaded; -vading** : invadir
invader [ɪn'veɪdər] *n* : invasor *m,* -sora *f*
invalid[1] [ɪn'væləd] *adj* : inválido, nulo
invalid[2] ['ɪnvələd] *adj* : inválido, discapacitado
invalid[3] ['ɪnvələd] *n* : inválido *m,* -da *f*
invalidate [ɪn'væləˌdeɪt] *vt* **-dated; -dating** : invalidar
invalidity [ˌɪnvə'lɪdət̬i] *n, pl* **-ties** : invalidez *f,* falta de validez *f*
invaluable [ɪn'væljəbəl, -'væljʊə-] *adj* : invalorable, inestimable, inapreciable
invariable [ɪn'væriəbəl] *adj* : invariable, constante — **invariably** [-bli] *adv*
invasion [ɪn'veɪʒən] *n* : invasión *f*
invasive [ɪn'veɪsɪv] *adj* : invasivo
invective [ɪn'vɛktɪv] *n* : invectiva *f,* improperio *m,* vituperio *m*
inveigh [ɪn'veɪ] *vi* **to inveigh against** : arremeter contra, lanzar invectivas contra
inveigle [ɪn'veɪgəl, -'vi:-] *vt* **-gled; -gling** : engatusar, embaucar, persuadir con engaños
invent [ɪn'vɛnt] *vt* : inventar
invention [ɪn'vɛntʃən] *n* : invención *f,* invento *m*
inventive [ɪn'vɛntɪv] *adj* : inventivo
inventiveness [ɪn'vɛntɪvnəs] *n* : ingenio *m,* inventiva *f*
inventor [ɪn'vɛntər] *n* : inventor *m,* -tora *f*
inventory[1] ['ɪnvənˌtɔri] *vt* **-ried; -rying** : inventariar
inventory[2] *n, pl* **-ries 1** LIST : inventario *m* **2** STOCK : existencias *fpl*
inverse[1] [ɪn'vərs, 'ɪnˌvərs] *adj* : inverso — **inversely** *adv*
inverse[2] *n* : inverso *m*
inversion [ɪn'vɛrʒən] *n* : inversión *f*
invert [ɪn'vərt] *vt* : invertir
invertebrate[1] [ɪn'vərt̬əbrət, -ˌbreɪt] *adj* : invertebrado
invertebrate[2] *n* : invertebrado *m*
invest [ɪn'vɛst] *vt* **1** AUTHORIZE : investir, autorizar **2** CONFER : conferir **3** : invertir, dedicar <he invested his savings in stocks : invirtió sus ahorros en acciones> <to invest one's time : dedicar uno su tiempo>
investigate [ɪn'vɛstəˌgeɪt] *v* **-gated; -gating** : investigar
investigation [ɪnˌvɛstə'geɪʃən] *n* : investigación *f,* estudio *m*
investigative [ɪn'vɛstəˌgeɪt̬ɪv] *adj* : investigador
investigator [ɪn'vɛstəˌgeɪt̬ər] *n* : investigador *m,* -dora *f*
investiture [ɪn'vɛstəˌtʃʊr, -tʃər] *n* : investidura *f*
investment [ɪn'vɛstmənt] *n* : inversión *f*
investor [ɪn'vɛstər] *n* : inversor *m,* -sora *f;* inversionista *mf*
inveterate [ɪn'vɛt̬ərət] *adj* **1** DEEP-SEATED : inveterado, enraizado **2** HABITUAL : empedernido, incorregible
invidious [ɪn'vɪdiəs] *adj* **1** OBNOXIOUS : repugnante, odioso **2** UNJUST : injusto — **invidiously** *adv*
invigorate [ɪn'vɪgəˌreɪt] *vt* **-rated; -rating** : vigorizar, animar
invigorating [ɪn'vɪgəˌreɪt̬ɪŋ] *adj* : vigorizante, estimulante
invigoration [ɪnˌvɪgə'reɪʃən] *n* : animación *f*
invincibility [ɪnˌvɪntsə'bɪlət̬i] *n* : invencibilidad *f*
invincible [ɪn'vɪntsəbəl] *adj* : invencible — **invincibly** [-bli] *adv*
inviolable [ɪn'vaɪələbəl] *adj* : inviolable
inviolate [ɪn'vaɪələt] *adj* : inviolado, puro
invisibility [ɪnˌvɪzə'bɪlət̬i] *n* : invisibilidad *f*
invisible [ɪn'vɪzəbəl] *adj* : invisible — **invisibly** [-bli] *adv*
invitation [ˌɪnvə'teɪʃən] *n* : invitación *f*
invite [ɪn'vaɪt] *vt* **-vited; -viting 1** ATTRACT : atraer, tentar <a book that invites interest : un libro que atrae el interés> **2** PROVOKE : provocar, buscar <to invite trouble : buscarse problemas> **3** ASK : invitar <we invited them for dinner : los invitamos a cenar> **4** SOLICIT : solicitar, buscar (preguntas, comentarios, etc.)
inviting [ɪn'vaɪt̬ɪŋ] *adj* : atractivo, atrayente
invocation [ˌɪnvə'keɪʃən] *n* : invocación *f*
invoice[1] ['ɪnˌvɔɪs] *vt* **-voiced; -voicing** : facturar
invoice[2] *n* : factura *f*
invoke [ɪn'vo:k] *vt* **-voked; -voking 1** : invocar, apelar a <she invoked our aid : apeló a nuestra ayuda> **2** CITE : invocar, citar <to invoke a precedent : invocar un precedente> **3** CONJURE UP : hacer aparecer, invocar
involuntary [ɪn'vɑlənˌtɛri] *adj* : involuntario — **involuntarily** [ɪnˌvɑlən'tɛrəli] *adv*

involve [ɪn'vɑlv] *vt* **-volved; -volving** **1** ENGAGE **:** ocupar <workers involved in construction **:** trabajadores ocupados con la construcción> **2** IMPLICATE **:** involucrar, enredar, implicar <to be involved in a crime **:** estar involucrado en un crimen> **3** CONCERN **:** concernir, afectar **4** CONNECT **:** conectar, relacionar **5** ENTAIL, INCLUDE **:** suponer, incluir, consistir en <what does the job involve? **:** ¿en qué consiste el trabajo?> **6 to be involved with someone :** tener una relación (amorosa) con alguien

involved [ɪn'vɑlvd] *adj* **1** COMPLEX, INTRICATE **:** complicado, complejo, enrevesado **2** CONCERNED **:** interesado, afectado

involvement [ɪn'vɑlvmənt] *n* **1** PARTICIPATION **:** participación *f,* complicidad *f* **2** RELATIONSHIP **:** relación *f*

invulnerable [ɪn'vʌlnərəbəl] *adj* **:** invulnerable

inward[1] ['ɪnwərd] *or* **inwards** [-wərdz] *adv* **:** hacia adentro, hacia el interior

inward[2] *adj* INSIDE **:** interior, interno

inwardly ['ɪnwərdli] *adv* **1** MENTALLY, SPIRITUALLY **:** por dentro **2** INTERNALLY **:** internamente, interiormente **3** PRIVATELY **:** para sus adentros, para sí

iodide ['aɪəˌdaɪd] *n* **:** yoduro *m*

iodine ['aɪəˌdaɪn, -dən] *n* **:** yodo *m,* tintura *f* de yodo

iodize ['aɪəˌdaɪz] *vt* **-dized; -dizing** **:** yodar

ion ['aɪən, 'aɪˌɑn] *n* **:** ion *m*

ionic [aɪ'ɑnɪk] *adj* **:** iónico

ionize ['aɪəˌnaɪz] *v* **ionized; ionizing** **:** ionizar

ionosphere [aɪ'ɑnəˌsfɪr] *n* **:** ionosfera *f*

iota [aɪ'oːt̬ə] *n* **:** pizca *f,* ápice *m*

IOU [ˌaɪˌo'juː] *n* **:** pagaré *m,* vale *m*

Iranian [ɪ'reɪniən, -'ræ-, -'rɑ-; aɪ'-] *n* **:** iraní *mf* — **Iranian** *adj*

Iraqi [ɪ'rakiː] *n* **:** iraquí *mf* — **Iraqi** *adj*

irascibility [ɪˌræsə'bɪlət̬i] *n* **:** irascibilidad *f*

irascible [ɪ'ræsəbəl] *adj* **:** irascible

irate [aɪ'reɪt] *adj* **:** furioso, airado, iracundo — **irately** *adv*

ire ['aɪr] *n* **:** ira *f,* cólera *f*

iridescence [ˌɪrə'dɛsənts] *n* **:** iridiscencia *f*

iridescent [ˌɪrə'dɛsənt] *adj* **:** iridiscente

iris ['aɪrəs] *n, pl* **irises** *or* **irides** ['aɪrəˌdiːz, 'ɪr-] **1 :** iris *m* (del ojo) **2 :** lirio *m* (planta)

Irish[1] ['aɪrɪʃ] *adj* **:** irlandés

Irish[2] **1 :** irlandés *m* (idioma) **2 the Irish** *npl* **:** los irlandeses

Irishman ['aɪrɪʃmən] *n* **:** irlandés *m*

Irishwoman ['aɪrɪʃˌwʊmən] *n* **:** irlandesa *f*

irk ['ərk] *vt* **:** fastidiar, irritar, preocupar

irksome ['ərksəm] *adj* **:** irritante, fastidioso — **irksomely** *adv*

iron[1] ['aɪərn] *v* **:** planchar

iron[2] *n* **1 :** hierro *m,* fierro *m* <a will of iron **:** una voluntad de hierro, una voluntad férrea> **2 :** plancha *f* (para planchar la ropa)

ironclad ['aɪərn'klæd] *adj* **1 :** acorazado, blindado **2** STRICT **:** riguroso, estricto

ironic [aɪ'rɑnɪk] *or* **ironical** [-nɪkəl] *adj* **:** irónico — **ironically** [-kli] *adv*

ironing ['aɪərnɪŋ] *n* **1** PRESSING **:** planchada *f* **2 :** ropa *f* para planchar

ironing board *n* **:** tabla *f* (de planchar)

ironwork ['aɪərnˌwərk] *n* **1 :** obra *f* de hierro **2 ironworks** *npl* **:** fundición *f*

ironworker ['aɪərnˌwərkər] *n* **:** fundidor *m,* -dora *f*

irony ['aɪrəni] *n, pl* **-nies :** ironía *f*

irradiate [ɪ'reɪdiˌeɪt] *vt* **-ated; -ating** **:** irradiar, radiar

irradiation [ɪˌreɪdi'eɪʃən] *n* **:** irradiación *f,* radiación *f*

irrational [ɪ'ræʃənəl] *adj* **:** irracional — **irrationally** *adv*

irrationality [ɪˌræʃə'nælət̬i] *n, pl* **-ties** **:** irracionalidad *f*

irreconcilable [ɪˌrɛkən'saɪləbəl] *adj* **:** irreconciliable

irrecoverable [ˌɪrɪ'kʌvərəbəl] *adj* **:** irrecuperable — **irrecoverably** [-bli] *adv*

irredeemable [ˌɪrɪ'diːməbəl] *adj* **1 :** irredimible (dícese de un bono) **2** HOPELESS **:** irremediable, irreparable

irreducible [ˌɪrɪ'duːsəbəl, -'djuː-] *adj* **:** irreducible — **irreducibly** [-bli] *adv*

irrefutable [ˌɪrɪ'fjuːt̬əbəl, ɪr'rɛfjə-] *adj* **:** irrefutable

irregular[1] [ɪ'rɛgjələr] *adj* **:** irregular — **irregularly** *adv*

irregular[2] *n* **1 :** soldado *m* irregular **2 irregulars** *npl* **:** artículos *mpl* defectuosos

irregularity [ɪˌrɛgjə'lærət̬i] *n, pl* **-ties** **:** irregularidad *f*

irrelevance [ɪ'rɛləvənts] *n* **:** irrelevancia *f*

irrelevant [ɪ'rɛləvənt] *adj* **:** irrelevante

irreligious [ˌɪrɪ'lɪdʒəs] *adj* **:** irreligioso

irreparable [ɪ'rɛpərəbəl] *adj* **:** irreparable

irreplaceable [ˌɪrɪ'pleɪsəbəl] *adj* **:** irreemplazable, insustituible

irrepressible [ˌɪrɪ'prɛsəbəl] *adj* **:** incontenible, incontrolable

irreproachable [ɪrɪ'proːtʃəbəl] *adj* **:** irreprochable, intachable

irresistible [ˌɪrɪ'zɪstəbəl] *adj* **:** irresistible — **irresistibly** [-bli] *adv*

irresolute [ɪ'rɛzəˌluːt] *adj* **:** irresoluto, indeciso

irresolutely [ɪ'rɛzəˌluːtli, -ˌrɛzə'luːt-] *adv* **:** de manera indecisa

irresolution [ɪˌrɛzə'luːʃən] *n* **:** irresolución *f*

irrespective of [ˌɪrɪˈspɛktɪvəv] *prep* : sin tomar en consideración, sin tener en cuenta

irresponsibility [ˌɪrɪˌspɑntsəˈbɪləṭi] *n, pl* **-ties** : irresponsabilidad *f,* falta *f* de responsabilidad

irresponsible [ˌɪrɪˈspɑntsəbəl] *adj* : irresponsable — **irresponsibly** [-bli] *adv*

irretrievable [ˌɪrɪˈtriːvəbəl] *adj* IRRECOVERABLE : irrecuperable

irreverence [ɪˈrɛvərənts] *n* : irreverencia *f,* falta *f* de respeto

irreverent [ɪˈrɛvərənt] *adj* : irreverente, irrespetuoso

irreversible [ˌɪrɪˈvərsəbəl] *adj* : irreversible

irrevocable [ɪˈrɛvəkəbəl] *adj* : irrevocable — **irrevocably** [-bli] *adv*

irrigate [ˈɪrəˌgeɪt] *vt* **-gated; -gating** : irrigar, regar

irrigation [ˌɪrəˈgeɪʃən] *n* : irrigación *f,* riego *m*

irritability [ˌɪrəṭəˈbɪləṭi] *n, pl* **-ties** : irritabilidad *f*

irritable [ˈɪrəṭəbəl] *adj* : irritable, colérico

irritably [ˈɪrəṭəbli] *adv* : con irritación

irritant¹ [ˈɪrəṭənt] *adj* : irritante

irritant² *n* : agente *m* irritante

irritate [ˈɪrəˌteɪt] *vt* **-tated; -tating 1** ANNOY : irritar, molestar **2** : irritar (en medicina)

irritating [ˈɪrəˌteɪṭɪŋ] *adj* : irritante

irritatingly [ˈɪrəˌteɪṭɪŋli] *adv* : de modo irritante, fastidiosamente

irritation [ˌɪrəˈteɪʃən] *n* : irritación *f*

is → **be**

Islam [ɪsˈlɑm, ɪz-, -ˈlæm; ˈɪsˌlɑm, ˈɪz-, -ˌlæm] *n* : el Islam

Islamic [ɪsˈlɑmɪk, ɪz-, -ˈlæ-] *adj* : islámico

island [ˈaɪlənd] *n* : isla *f*

islander [ˈaɪləndər] *n* : isleño *m,* -ña *f*

isle [ˈaɪl] *n* : isla *f,* islote *m*

islet [ˈaɪlət] *n* : islote *m*

isolate [ˈaɪsəˌleɪt] *vt* **-lated; -lating** : aislar

isolated [ˈaɪsəˌleɪṭəd] *adj* : aislado, solo

isolation [ˌaɪsəˈleɪʃən] *n* : aislamiento *m*

isometric [ˌaɪsəˈmɛtrɪk] *adj* : isométrico

isometrics [ˌaɪsəˈmɛtrɪks] *ns & pl* : isometría *f*

isosceles [aɪˈsɑsəˌliːz] *adj* : isósceles

isotope [ˈaɪsəˌtoːp] *n* : isótopo *m*

Israeli [ɪzˈreɪli] *n* : israelí *mf* — **Israeli** *adj*

issue¹ [ˈɪˌʃuː] *v* **-sued; -suing** *vi* **1** EMERGE : emerger, salir, fluir **2** DESCEND : descender (dícese de los padres o antepasados específicos) **3** EMANATE, RESULT : emanar, surgir, resultar — *vt* **1** EMIT : emitir **2** DISTRIBUTE : emitir, distribuir <to issue a new stamp : emitir un sello nuevo> **3** PUBLISH : publicar

issue² *n* **1** EMERGENCE, FLOW : emergencia *f,* flujo *m* **2** PROGENY : descendencia *f,* progenie *f* **3** OUTCOME, RESULT : desenlace *m,* resultado *m,* consecuencia *f* **4** MATTER, QUESTION : asunto *m,* cuestión *f* **5** PUBLICATION : publicación *f,* distribución *f,* emisión *f* **6** : número *m* (de un periódico o una revista)

isthmus [ˈɪsməs] *n* : istmo *m*

it [ˈɪt] *pron* **1** (*as subject; generally omitted*) : él, ella, ello <it's a big building : es un edificio grande> <who was it? : ¿quién era?> **2** (*as indirect object*) : le <I'll give it some water : voy a darle agua> **3** (*as direct object*) : lo, la <give it to me : dámelo> **4** (*as object of a preposition; generally omitted*) : él, ella, ello <behind it : detrás, detrás de él> **5** (*in impersonal constructions*) <it's raining : está lloviendo> <it's 8 o'clock : son las ocho> **6** (*as the implied subject or object of a verb*) <it is necessary to study : es necesario estudiar> <to give it all one's got : dar lo mejor de sí>

Italian [ɪˈtæliən, aɪ-] *n* **1** : italiano *m,* -na *f* **2** : italiano *m* (idioma) — **Italian** *adj*

italic¹ [ɪˈtælɪk, aɪ-] *adj* : en cursiva, en bastardilla

italic² *n* : cursiva *f,* bastardilla *f*

italicize [ɪˈtæləˌsaɪz, aɪ-] *vt* **-cized; -cizing** : poner en cursiva

itch¹ [ˈɪtʃ] *vi* **1** : picar <her arm itched : le pica el brazo> **2** : morirse <they were itching to go outside : se morían por salir> — *vt* : dar picazón, hacer picar

itch² *n* **1** ITCHING : picazón *f,* picor *m,* comezón *f* **2** RASH : sarpullido *m,* erupción *f* **3** DESIRE : ansia *f,* deseo *m*

itchy [ˈɪtʃi] *adj* **itchier; -est** : que pica, que da comezón

it'd [ˈɪṭəd] (*contraction of* **it had** *or* **it would**) → **have, would**

item [ˈaɪṭəm] *n* **1** OBJECT : artículo *m,* pieza *f* <item of clothing : prenda de vestir> **2** : punto *m* (en una agenda), número *m* (en el teatro), ítem *m* (en un documento) **3 news item** : noticia *f*

itemize [ˈaɪṭəˌmaɪz] *vt* **-ized; -izing** : detallar, enumerar, listar

itinerant [aɪˈtɪnərənt] *adj* : itinerante, ambulante

itinerary [aɪˈtɪnəˌrɛri] *n, pl* **-aries** : itinerario *m*

it'll [ˈɪṭəl] (*contraction of* **it shall** *or* **it will**) → **shall, will**

its [ˈɪts] *adj* : su, sus <its kennel : su perrera> <a city and its inhabitants : una ciudad y sus habitantes>

it's [ˈɪts] (*contraction of* **it is** *or* **it has**) → **be, have**

itself [ɪtˈsɛlf] *pron* **1** (*used reflexively*) : se <the cat gave itself a bath : el gato se bañó> **2** (*used for emphasis*) : (él) mismo, (ella) misma, sí (mismo), solo <he is courtesy itself : es la misma cortesía> <in and of itself : por sí

mismo> <it opened by itself : se abrió solo>
I've [ˈaɪv] (*contraction of* **I have**) → **have**
ivory [ˈaɪvəri] *n, pl* **-ries 1 :** marfil *m* **2 :** color *m* de marfil
ivy [ˈaɪvi] *n, pl* **ivies 1 :** hiedra *f,* yedra *f* **2** → **poison ivy**

J

j [ˈdʒeɪ] *n, pl* **j's** *or* **js** [ˈdʒeɪz] **:** décima letra del alfabeto inglés
jab[1] [ˈdʒæb] *v* **jabbed; jabbing** *vt* **1** PUNCTURE **:** clavar, pinchar **2** POKE **:** dar, golpear (con la punta de algo) <he jabbed me in the ribs : me dio un codazo en las costillas> — *vi* **to jab at :** dar, golpear
jab[2] *n* **1** PRICK **:** pinchazo *m* **2** POKE **:** golpe *m* abrupto
jabber[1] [ˈdʒæbər] *v* **:** farfullar
jabber[2] *n* **:** galimatías *m,* farfulla *f*
jack[1] [ˈdʒæk] *vt* **to jack up 1 :** levantar (con un gato) **2** INCREASE **:** subir, aumentar
jack[2] *n* **1 :** gato *m,* cric *m* <hydraulic jack : gato hidráulico> **2** FLAG **:** pabellón *m* **3** SOCKET **:** enchufe *m* hembra **4 :** jota *f,* valet *m* <jack of hearts : jota de corazones> **5 jacks** *npl* **:** cantillos *mpl*
jackal [ˈdʒækəl] *n* **:** chacal *m*
jackass [ˈdʒækˌæs] *n* **:** asno *m,* burro *m*
jacket [ˈdʒækət] *n* **1 :** chaqueta *f* **2** COVER **:** sobrecubierta *f* (de un libro), carátula *f* (de un disco)
jackhammer [ˈdʒækˌhæmər] *n* **:** martillo *m* neumático
jack–in–the–box [ˈdʒækɪnðəˌbɑks] *n* **:** caja *f* de sorpresa
jackknife[1] [ˈdʒækˌnaɪf] *vi* **-knifed; -knifing :** doblarse como una navaja, plegarse
jackknife[2] *n* **:** navaja *f*
jack–of–all–trades *n* **:** persona *f* que sabe un poco de todo, persona *f* de muchos oficios
jack–o'–lantern [ˈdʒækəˌlæntərn] *n* **:** linterna *f* hecha de una calabaza
jackpot [ˈdʒækˌpɑt] *n* **1 :** primer premio *m,* gordo *m* **2 to hit the jackpot :** sacarse la lotería, sacarse el gordo
jackrabbit [ˈdʒækˌræbət] *n* **:** liebre *f* grande de Norteamérica
jade [ˈdʒeɪd] *n* **:** jade *m*
jaded [ˈdʒeɪdəd] *adj* **1** TIRED **:** agotado **2** BORED **:** hastiado
jagged [ˈdʒægəd] *adj* **:** dentado, mellado
jaguar [ˈdʒægˌwɑr, ˈdʒægjʊˌwɑr] *n* **:** jaguar *m*
jai alai [ˈhaɪˌlaɪ] *n* **:** jai alai *m,* pelota *f* vasca
jail[1] [ˈdʒeɪl] *vt* **:** encarcelar
jail[2] *n* **:** cárcel *f*
jailbreak [ˈdʒeɪlˌbreɪk] *n* **:** fuga *f,* huida *f* (de la cárcel)
jailer *or* **jailor** [ˈdʒeɪlər] *n* **:** carcelero *m,* **-ra** *f*
jalapeño [ˌhɑləˈpeɪnjo, ˌhæ-, -ˈpiːno] *n* **:** jalapeño *m*
jalopy [dʒəˈlɑpi] *n, pl* **-lopies :** cacharro *m fam,* carro *m* destartalado
jalousie [ˈdʒæləsi] *n* **:** celosía *f*
jam[1] [ˈdʒæm] *v* **jammed; jamming** *vt* **1** CRAM **:** apiñar, embutir **2** BLOCK **:** atascar, atorar **3 to jam on the brakes :** frenar en seco — *vi* STICK **:** atascarse, atrancarse
jam[2] *n* **1** *or* **traffic jam :** atasco *m,* embotellamiento *m* (de tráfico) **2** PREDICAMENT **:** lío *m,* aprieto *m,* apuro *m* **3 :** mermelada *f* <strawberry jam : mermelada de fresa>
jamb [ˈdʒæm] *n* **:** jamba *f*
jamboree [ˌdʒæmbəˈriː] *n* **:** fiesta *f* grande
jangle[1] [ˈdʒæŋgəl] *v* **-gled; -gling** *vi* **:** hacer un ruido metálico — *vt* **1 :** hacer sonar **2 to jangle one's nerves :** irritar, crispar
jangle[2] *n* **:** ruido *m* metálico
janitor [ˈdʒænət̬ər] *n* **:** portero *m,* **-ra** *f;* conserje *mf*
January [ˈdʒænjʊˌɛri] *n* **:** enero *m*
Japanese [ˌdʒæpəˈniːz, -ˈniːs] *n* **1 :** japonés *m,* -nesa *f* **2 :** japonés *m* (idioma) — **Japanese** *adj*
jar[1] [ˈdʒɑr] *v* **jarred; jarring** *vi* **1** GRATE **:** chirriar **2** CLASH **:** desentonar **3** SHAKE **:** sacudirse **4 to jar on :** crispar, enervar — *vt* JOLT **:** sacudir
jar[2] *n* **1** GRATING **:** chirrido *m* **2** JOLT **:** vibración *f,* sacudida *f* **3 :** tarro *m,* bote *m,* pote *m* <a jar of honey : un tarro de miel>
jargon [ˈdʒɑrgən] *n* **:** jerga *f*
jasmine [ˈdʒæzmən] *n* **:** jazmín *m*
jasper [ˈdʒæspər] *n* **:** jaspe *m*
jaundice [ˈdʒɔndɪs] *n* **:** ictericia *f*
jaundiced [ˈdʒɔndɪst] *adj* **1 :** ictérico **2** EMBITTERED, RESENTFUL **:** amargado, resentido, negativo <with a jaundiced eye : con una actitud de cinismo>
jaunt [ˈdʒɔnt] *n* **:** excursión *f,* paseo *m*
jauntily [ˈdʒɔntəli] *adv* **:** animadamente
jauntiness [ˈdʒɔntinəs] *n* **:** animación *f,* vivacidad *f*
jaunty [ˈdʒɔnti] *adj* **-tier; -est 1** SPRIGHTLY **:** animado, alegre **2** RAKISH **:** desenvuelto, desenfadado
javelin [ˈdʒævələn] *n* **:** jabalina *f*
jaw[1] [ˈdʒɔ] *vi* GAB **:** cotorrear *fam,* parlotear *fam*
jaw[2] *n* **1 :** mandíbula *f,* quijada *f* **2 :** mordaza *f* (de una herramienta) **3 the jaws of death :** las garras *f* de la muerte

jawbone [ˈdʒɔˌboːn] *n* : mandíbula *f*
jay [ˈdʒeɪ] *n* : arrendajo *m*, chara *f Mex*, azulejo *m Mex*
jaybird [ˈdʒeɪˌbərd] → **jay**
jaywalk [ˈdʒeɪˌwɔk] *vi* : cruzar la calle sin prudencia
jaywalker [ˈdʒeɪˌwɔkər] *n* : peatón *m* imprudente
jazz[1] [ˈdʒæz] *vt* **to jazz up** : animar, alegrar
jazz[2] *n* : jazz *m*
jazzy [ˈdʒæzi] *adj* **jazzier; -est 1** : con ritmo de jazz **2** FLASHY, SHOWY : llamativo, ostentoso
jealous [ˈdʒɛləs] *adj* : celoso, envidioso — **jealously** *adv*
jealousy [ˈdʒɛləsi] *n* : celos *mpl*, envidia *f*
jeans [ˈdʒiːnz] *npl* : jeans *mpl*, vaqueros *mpl*
jeep [ˈdʒiːp] *n* : jeep *m*
jeer[1] [ˈdʒɪr] *vi* **1** BOO : abuchear **2** SCOFF : mofarse, burlarse — *vt* RIDICULE : mofarse de, burlarse de
jeer[2] *n* **1** : abucheo *m* **2** TAUNT : mofa *f*, burla *f*
Jehovah [dʒɪˈhoːvə] *n* : Jehová *m*
jell [ˈdʒɛl] *vi* **1** SET : gelificarse, cuajar **2** FORM : cuajar, formarse (una idea, etc.)
jelly[1] [ˈdʒɛli] *v* **jellied; jellying** *vi* **1** JELL : gelificarse, cuajar **2** : hacer jalea — *vt* : gelificar
jelly[2] *n, pl* **-lies 1** : jalea *f* **2** GELATIN : gelatina *f*
jellyfish [ˈdʒɛliˌfɪʃ] *n* : medusa *f*
jeopardize [ˈdʒɛpərˌdaɪz] *vt* **-dized; -dizing** : arriesgar, poner en peligro
jeopardy [ˈdʒɛpərdi] *n* : peligro *m*, riesgo *m*
jerk[1] [ˈdʒərk] *vt* **1** JOLT : sacudir **2** TUG, YANK : darle un tirón a — *vi* JOLT : dar sacudidas <the train jerked along : el tren iba moviéndose a sacudidas>
jerk[2] *n* **1** TUG : tirón *m*, jalón *m* **2** JOLT : sacudida *f* brusca **3** FOOL : estúpido *m*, -da *f*; idiota *mf*
jerkin [ˈdʒərkən] *n* : chaqueta *f* sin mangas, chaleco *m*
jerky [ˈdʒərki] *adj* **jerkier; -est 1** : espasmódico (dícese de los movimientos) **2** CHOPPY : inconexo (dícese de la prosa) — **jerkily** [-kəli] *adv*
jerry–built [ˈdʒɛriˌbɪlt] *adj* : mal construido, chapucero
jersey [ˈdʒərzi] *n, pl* **-seys** : jersey *m*
jest[1] [ˈdʒɛst] *vi* : bromear
jest[2] *n* : broma *f*, chiste *m*
jester [ˈdʒɛstər] *n* : bufón *m*, -fona *f*
Jesus [ˈdʒiːzəs, -zəz] *n* : Jesús *m*
jet[1] [ˈdʒɛt] *v* **jetted; jetting** *vt* SPOUT : arrojar a chorros — *vi* **1** GUSH : salir a chorros, chorrear **2** FLY : viajar en avión, volar
jet[2] *n* **1** STREAM : chorro *m* **2** *or* **jet airplane** : avión *m* a reacción, reactor *m* **3** : azabache *m* (mineral) **4 jet engine** : reactor *m*, motor *m* a reacción **5 jet lag** : desajuste *m* de horario (debido a un vuelo largo)
jet–propelled *adj* : a reacción
jetsam [ˈdʒɛtsəm] *n* **flotsam and jetsam** : restos *mpl*, desechos *mpl*
jettison [ˈdʒɛtəsən] *vt* **1** : echar al mar **2** DISCARD : desechar, deshacerse de
jetty [ˈdʒɛti] *n, pl* **-ties 1** PIER, WHARF : desembarcadero *m*, muelle *m* **2** BREAKWATER : malecón *m*, rompeolas *m*
Jew [ˈdʒuː] *n* : judío *m*, -día *f*
jewel [ˈdʒuːəl] *n* **1** : joya *f*, alhaja *f* **2** GEM : piedra *f* preciosa, gema *f* **3** : rubí *m* (de un reloj) **4** TREASURE : joya *f*, tesoro *m*
jeweler *or* **jeweller** [ˈdʒuːələr] *n* : joyero *m*, -ra *f*
jewelry [ˈdʒuːəlri] *n* : joyas *fpl*, alhajas *fpl*
Jewish [ˈdʒuːɪʃ] *adj* : judío
jib [ˈdʒɪb] *n* : foque *m* (de un barco)
jibe [ˈdʒaɪb] *vi* **jibed; jibing** AGREE : concordar
jiffy [ˈdʒɪfi] *n, pl* **-fies** : santiamén *m*, segundo *m*, momento *m*
jig[1] [ˈdʒɪg] *vi* **jigged; jigging** : bailar la giga
jig[2] *n* **1** : giga *f* **2 the jig is up** : se acabó la fiesta
jigger [ˈdʒɪgər] *n* : medida de 1 a 2 onzas (para licores)
jiggle[1] [ˈdʒɪgəl] *v* **-gled; -gling** *vt* : agitar o sacudir ligeramente — *vi* : agitarse, vibrar
jiggle[2] *n* : sacudida *f*, vibración *f*
jigsaw [ˈdʒɪgˌsɔ] *n* **1** : sierra *f* de vaivén **2 jigsaw puzzle** : rompecabezas *m*
jilt [ˈdʒɪlt] *vt* : dejar plantado, dar calabazas a
jimmy[1] [ˈdʒɪmi] *vt* **-mied; -mying** : forzar con una palanqueta
jimmy[2] *n, pl* **-mies** : palanqueta *f*
jingle[1] [ˈdʒɪŋgəl] *v* **-gled; -gling** *vi* : tintinear — *vt* : hacer sonar
jingle[2] *n* **1** TINKLE : tintineo *m*, retintín *m* **2** : canción *f* rimada
jingoism [ˈdʒɪŋgoˌɪzəm] *n* : jingoísmo *m*, patriotería *f*
jingoistic [ˌdʒɪŋgoˈɪstɪk] *or* **jingoist** [ˈdʒɪŋgoɪst] *adj* : jingoísta, patriotero
jinx[1] [ˈdʒɪŋks] *vt* : traer mala suerte a, salar *CoRi, Mex*
jinx[2] *n* **1** : cenizo *m*, -za *f* **2 to put a jinx on** : echarle el mal de ojo a
jitters [ˈdʒɪtərz] *npl* : nervios *mpl* <he got the jitters : se puso nervioso>
jittery [ˈdʒɪtəri] *adj* : nervioso
job [ˈdʒɑb] *n* **1** : trabajo *m* <he did odd jobs for her : le hizo algunos trabajos> **2** CHORE, TASK : tarea *f*, quehacer *m* **3** EMPLOYMENT : trabajo *m*, empleo *m*, puesto *m*
jobber [ˈdʒɑbər] *n* MIDDLEMAN : intermediario *m*, -ria *f*
jockey[1] [ˈdʒɑki] *v* **-eyed; -eying** *vt* **1** MANIPULATE : manipular **2** MANEUVER

: maniobrar — *vi* **to jockey for position :** maniobrar para conseguir algo

jockey² *n, pl* **-eys :** jockey *mf*

jocose [dʒoˈkoːs] *adj* : jocoso

jocular [ˈdʒɑkjʊlər] *adj* : jocoso — **jocularly** *adv*

jocularity [ˌdʒɑkjʊˈlærət̬i] *n* : jocosidad *f*

jodhpurs [ˈdʒɑdpərz] *npl* : pantalones *mpl* de montar

jog¹ [ˈdʒɑg] *v* **jogged; jogging** *vt* **1** NUDGE : dar, empujar, codear **2 to jog one's memory :** refrescar la memoria — *vi* **1** RUN : correr despacio, trotar, hacer footing (como ejercicio) **2** TRUDGE : andar a trote corto

jog² *n* **1** PUSH, SHAKE : empujoncito *m,* sacudida *f* leve **2** TROT : trote *m* corto, footing *m* (en deportes) **3** TWIST : recodo *m,* vuelta *f,* curva *f*

jogger [ˈdʒɑgər] *n* : persona *f* que hace footing

join [ˈdʒɔɪn] *vt* **1** CONNECT, LINK : unir, juntar <to join in marriage : unir en matrimonio> **2** ADJOIN : lindar con, colindar con **3** MEET : reunirse con, encontrarse con <we joined them for lunch : nos reunimos con ellos para almorzar> **4** : hacerse socio de (una organización), afiliarse a (un partido), entrar en (una empresa) — *vi* **1** UNITE : unirse **2** MERGE : empalmar (dícese de las carreteras), confluir (dícese de los ríos) **3 to join up :** hacerse socio, enrolarse

joiner [ˈdʒɔɪnər] *n* **1** CARPENTER : carpintero *m,* -ra *f* **2** : persona *f* que se une a varios grupos

joint¹ [ˈdʒɔɪnt] *adj* : conjunto, colectivo, mutuo <a joint effort : un esfuerzo conjunto> — **jointly** *adv*

joint² *n* **1** : articulación *f,* coyuntura *f* <out of joint : dislocado> **2** ROAST : asado *m* **3** JUNCTURE : juntura *f,* unión *f* **4** DIVE : antro *m,* tasca *f*

joist [ˈdʒɔɪst] *n* : viga *f*

joke¹ [ˈdʒoːk] *vi* **joked; joking :** bromear

joke² *n* **1** STORY : chiste *m* **2** PRANK : broma *f*

joker [ˈdʒoːkər] *n* **1** PRANKSTER : bromista *mf* **2** : comodín *m* (en los naipes)

jokingly [ˈdʒoːkɪŋli] *adv* : en broma

jollity [ˈdʒɑlət̬i] *n, pl* **-ties** MERRIMENT : alegría *f,* regocijo *m*

jolly [ˈdʒɑli] *adj* **-lier; -est :** alegre, jovial

jolt¹ [ˈdʒoːlt] *vi* JERK : dar tumbos, dar sacudidas — *vt* : sacudir

jolt² *n* **1** JERK : sacudida *f* brusca **2** SHOCK : golpe *m* (emocional)

jonquil [ˈdʒɑnkwɪl] *n* : junquillo *m*

Jordanian [dʒɔrˈdeɪniən] *n* : jordano *m,* -na *f* — **Jordanian** *adj*

josh [ˈdʒɑʃ] *vt* TEASE : tomarle el pelo (a alguien) — *vi* JOKE : bromear

jostle [ˈdʒɑsəl] *v* **-tled; -tling** *vi* **1** SHOVE : empujar, dar empellones **2** CONTEND : competir — *vt* **1** SHOVE : empujar **2 to jostle one's way :** abrirse paso a empellones

jot¹ [ˈdʒɑt] *vt* **jotted; jotting :** anotar, apuntar <jot it down : apúntalo>

jot² *n* BIT : ápice *m,* jota *f,* pizca *f*

jounce¹ [ˈdʒæʊnts] *v* **jounced; jouncing** *vt* JOLT : sacudir — *vi* : dar tumbos, dar sacudidas

jounce² *n* JOLT : sacudida *f,* tumbo *m*

journal [ˈdʒərnəl] *n* **1** DIARY : diario *m* **2** PERIODICAL : revista *f,* publicación *f* periódica **3** NEWSPAPER : periódico *m,* diario *m*

journalism [ˈdʒərnəlˌɪzəm] *n* : periodismo *m*

journalist [ˈdʒərnəlɪst] *n* : periodista *mf*

journalistic [ˌdʒərnəlˈɪstɪk] *adj* : periodístico

journey¹ [ˈdʒərni] *vi* **-neyed; -neying** : viajar

journey² *n, pl* **-neys :** viaje *m*

journeyman [ˈdʒərnimən] *n, pl* **-men** [-mən, -ˌmɛn] : oficial *m*

joust¹ [ˈdʒæʊst] *vi* : justar

joust² *n* : justa *f*

jovial [ˈdʒoːviəl] *adj* : jovial — **jovially** *adv*

joviality [ˌdʒoːviˈælət̬i] *n* : jovialidad *f*

jowl [ˈdʒæʊl] *n* **1** JAW : mandíbula *f* **2** CHEEK : mejilla *f,* cachete *m*

joy [ˈdʒɔɪ] *n* **1** HAPPINESS : gozo *m,* alegría *f,* felicidad *f* **2** DELIGHT : placer *m,* deleite *m* <the child is a real joy : el niño es un verdadero placer>

joyful [ˈdʒɔɪfəl] *adj* : gozoso, alegre, feliz — **joyfully** *adv*

joyless [ˈdʒɔɪləs] *adj* : sin alegría, triste

joyous [ˈdʒɔɪəs] *adj* : alegre, feliz, eufórico — **joyously** *adv*

joyousness [ˈdʒɔɪəsnəs] *n* : alegría *f,* felicidad *f,* euforia *f*

joyride [ˈdʒɔɪˌraɪd] *n* : paseo *m* temerario e irresponsable (en coche)

jubilant [ˈdʒuːbələnt] *adj* : jubiloso, alborozado — **jubilantly** *adv*

jubilation [ˌdʒuːbəˈleɪʃən] *n* : júbilo *m*

jubilee [ˈdʒuːbəˌliː] *n* **1** : quincuagésimo aniversario *m* **2** CELEBRATION : celebración *f,* festejos *mpl*

Judaic [dʒʊˈdeɪɪk] *adj* : judaico

Judaism [ˈdʒuːdəˌɪzəm, ˈdʒuːdi-, ˈdʒuːˌdeɪ-] *n* : judaísmo *m*

judge¹ [ˈdʒʌdʒ] *vt* **judged; judging 1** ASSESS : evaluar, juzgar **2** DEEM : juzgar, considerar **3** TRY : juzgar (ante el tribuno) **4 judging by :** a juzgar por

judge² *n* **1** : juez *mf,* jueza *f* **2 to be a good judge of :** saber juzgar a, entender mucho de

judgment *or* **judgement** [ˈdʒʌdʒmənt] *n* **1** RULING : fallo *m,* sentencia *f* **2** OPINION : opinión *f* **3** DISCERNMENT : juicio *m,* discernimiento *m*

judgmental [ˌdʒʌdʒˈmɛntəl] *adj* : crítico — **judgmentally** *adv*

judicature [ˈdʒuːdɪkəˌtʃʊr] *n* : judicatura *f*

judicial [dʒʊˈdɪʃəl] *adj* : judicial — **judicially** *adv*

judiciary[1] [dʒʊˈdɪʃiˌɛri, -ˈdɪʃəri] *adj* : judicial

judiciary[2] *n* **1** JUDICATURE : judicatura *f* **2** : poder *m* judicial

judicious [dʒʊˈdɪʃəs] *adj* SOUND, WISE : juicioso, sensato — **judiciously** *adv*

judo [ˈdʒuːˌdoː] *n* : judo *m*

jug [ˈdʒʌg] *n* **1** : jarra *f,* jarro *m,* cántaro *m* **2** JAIL : cárcel *f,* chirona *f fam*

juggernaut [ˈdʒʌgərˌnɔt] *n* : gigante *m,* fuerza *f* irresistible <a political juggernaut : un gigante político>

juggle [ˈdʒʌgəl] *v* **-gled; -gling** *vt* **1** : hacer juegos malabares con **2** MANIPULATE : manipular, jugar con — *vi* : hacer juegos malabares

juggler [ˈdʒʌgələr] *n* : malabarista *mf*

jugular [ˈdʒʌgjʊlər] *adj* : yugular <jugular vein : vena yugular>

juice [ˈdʒuːs] *n* **1** : jugo *m* (de carne, de frutas) *m,* zumo *m* (de frutas) **2** ELECTRICITY : electricidad *f,* luz *f*

juicer [ˈdʒuːsər] *n* : exprimidor *m*

juiciness [ˈdʒuːsinəs] *n* : jugosidad *f*

juicy [ˈdʒuːsi] *adj* **juicier; -est 1** SUCCULENT : jugoso, suculento **2** PROFITABLE : jugoso, lucrativo **3** RACY : picante

jukebox [ˈdʒuːkˌbɑks] *n* : rocola *f,* máquina *f* de discos

julep [ˈdʒuːləp] *n* : bebida *f* hecha con whisky americano y menta

July [dʒʊˈlaɪ] *n* : julio *m*

jumble[1] [ˈdʒʌmbəl] *vt* **-bled; -bling** : mezclar, revolver

jumble[2] *n* : revoltijo *m,* fárrago *m,* embrollo *m*

jumbo[1] [ˈdʒʌmˌboː] *adj* : gigante, enorme, de tamaño extra grande

jumbo[2] *n, pl* **-bos** : coloso *m,* cosa *f* de tamaño extra grande

jump[1] [ˈdʒʌmp] *vi* **1** LEAP : saltar, brincar **2** START : levantarse de un salto, sobresaltarse **3** MOVE, SHIFT : moverse, pasar <to jump from job to job : pasar de un empleo a otro> **4** INCREASE, RISE : dar un salto, aumentarse de golpe, subir bruscamente **5** BUSTLE : animarse, ajetrearse **6 to jump to conclusions** : sacar conclusiones precipitadas — *vt* **1** : saltar <to jump a fence : saltar una valla> **2** SKIP : saltarse **3** ATTACK : atacar, asaltar **4 to jump the gun** : precipitarse

jump[2] *n* **1** LEAP : salto *m* **2** START : sobresalto *m,* respingo *m* **3** INCREASE : subida *f* brusca, aumento *m* **4** ADVANTAGE : ventaja *f* <we got the jump on them : les llevamos la ventaja>

jumper [ˈdʒʌmpər] *n* **1** : saltador *m,* **-dora** *f* (en deportes) **2** : jumper *m,* vestido *m* sin mangas

jumpy [ˈdʒʌmpi] *adj* **jumpier; -est** : asustadizo, nervioso

junction [ˈdʒʌŋkʃən] *n* **1** JOINING : unión *f* **2** : cruce *m* (de calles), empalme *m* (de un ferrocarril), confluencia *f* (de ríos)

juncture [ˈdʒʌŋktʃər] *n* **1** UNION : juntura *f,* unión *f* **2** MOMENT, POINT : coyuntura *f* <at this juncture : en esta coyuntura, en este momento>

June [ˈdʒuːn] *n* : junio *m*

jungle [ˈdʒʌŋgəl] *n* : jungla *f,* selva *f*

junior[1] [ˈdʒuːnjər] *adj* **1** YOUNGER : más joven <John Smith, Junior : John Smith, hijo> **2** SUBORDINATE : subordinado, subalterno

junior[2] *n* **1** : persona *f* de menor edad <she's my junior : es menor que yo> **2** SUBORDINATE : subalterno *m,* **-na** *f;* subordinado *m,* **-da** *f* **3** : estudiante *mf* de penúltimo año

juniper [ˈdʒuːnəpər] *n* : enebro *m*

junk[1] [ˈdʒʌŋk] *vt* : echar a la basura

junk[2] *n* **1** RUBBISH : desechos *mpl,* desperdicios *mpl* **2** STUFF : trastos *mpl fam,* cachivaches *mpl fam* **3 piece of junk** : cacharro *m,* porquería *f*

junket [ˈdʒʌŋkət] *n* : viaje *m* (pagado con dinero público)

junta [ˈhʊntə, ˈdʒʌn-, ˈhʌn-] *n* : junta *f* militar

Jupiter [ˈdʒuːpətər] *n* : Júpiter *m*

jurisdiction [ˌdʒʊ̆rəsˈdɪkʃən] *n* : jurisdicción *f*

jurisprudence [ˌdʒʊrəsˈpruːdənts] *n* : jurisprudencia *f*

jurist [ˈdʒʊrɪst] *n* : jurista *mf;* magistrado *m,* -da *f*

juror [ˈdʒʊrər] *n* : jurado *m,* -da *f*

jury [ˈdʒʊri] *n, pl* **-ries** : jurado *m*

just[1] [ˈdʒʌst] *adv* **1** EXACTLY : justo, precisamente, exactamente **2** POSSIBLY : posiblemente <it just might work : tal vez resulte> **3** BARELY : justo, apenas <just in time : justo a tiempo> **4** ONLY : sólo, solamente, nada más <just us : sólo nosotros> **5** QUITE : muy, simplemente <it's just horrible! : ¡qué horrible!> **6 to have just (done something)** : acabar de (hacer algo) <he just called : acaba de llamar>

just[2] *adj* : justo — **justly** *adv*

justice [ˈdʒʌstɪs] *n* **1** : justicia *f* **2** JUDGE : juez *mf,* jueza *f*

justification [ˌdʒʌstəfəˈkeɪʃən] *n* : justificación *f*

justify [ˈdʒʌstəˌfaɪ] *vt* **-fied; -fying** : justificar — **justifiable** [ˌdʒʌstəˈfaɪəbəl] *adj*

jut [ˈdʒʌt] *vi* **jutted; jutting** : sobresalir

jute [ˈdʒuːt] *n* : yute *m*

juvenile[1] [ˈdʒuːvəˌnaɪl, -vənəl] *adj* **1** : juvenil <juvenile delinquent : delincuente juvenil> <juvenile court : tribunal de menores> **2** CHILDISH : infantil

juvenile[2] *n* : menor *mf*

juxtapose [ˈdʒʌkstəˌpoːz] *vt* **-posed; -posing** : yuxtaponer

juxtaposition [ˌdʒʌkstəpəˈzɪʃən] *n* : yuxtaposición *f*

K

k [ˈkeɪ] *n, pl* **k's** *or* **ks** [ˈkeɪz] : undécima letra del alfabeto inglés
kaiser [ˈkaɪzər] *n* : káiser *m*
kale [ˈkeɪl] *n* : col *f* rizada
kaleidoscope [kəˈlaɪdəˌsko:p] *n* : calidoscopio *m*
kangaroo [ˌkæŋgəˈru:] *n, pl* **-roos** : canguro *m*
kaolin [ˈkeɪələn] *n* : caolín *m*
karat [ˈkærət] *n* : quilate *m*
karate [kəˈrɑti] *n* : karate *m*
katydid [ˈkeɪt̬iˌdɪd] *n* : saltamontes *m*
kayak [ˈkaɪˌæ̆k] *n* : kayac *m,* kayak *m*
keel[1] [ˈki:l] *vi* **to keel over** : volcar (dícese de un barco), desplomarse (dícese de una persona)
keel[2] *n* : quilla *f*
keen [ˈki:n] *adj* **1** SHARP : afilado, filoso <a keen blade : una hoja afilada> **2** PENETRATING : cortante, penetrante <a keen wind : un viento cortante> **3** ENTHUSIASTIC : entusiasta **4** ACUTE : agudo, fino <keen hearing : oído fino> <keen intelligence : inteligencia aguda>
keenly [ˈki:nli] *adv* **1** ENTHUSIASTICALLY : con entusiasmo **2** INTENSELY : vivamente, profundamente <keenly aware of : muy consciente de>
keenness [ˈki:nnəs] *n* **1** SHARPNESS : lo afilado, lo filoso **2** ENTHUSIASM : entusiasmo *m* **3** ACUTENESS : agudeza *f*
keep[1] [ˈki:p] *v* **kept** [ˈkɛpt]; **keeping** *vt* **1** : cumplir (la palabra a uno), acudir a (una cita) **2** OBSERVE : observar (una fiesta) **3** GUARD : guardar, cuidar **4** CONTINUE : mantener <to keep silence : mantener silencio> **5** SUPPORT : mantener (una familia) **6** RAISE : criar (animales) **7** : llevar, escribir (un diario, etc.) **8** RETAIN : guardar, conservar, quedarse con **9** STORE : guardar **10** DETAIN : hacer quedar, detener **11** PRESERVE : guardar <to keep a secret : guardar un secreto> — *vi* **1** : conservarse (dícese de los alimentos) **2** CONTINUE : seguir, no dejar <he keeps on pestering us : no deja de molestarnos> **3 to keep from** : abstenerse de <I couldn't keep from laughing : no podía contener la risa>
keep[2] *n* **1** TOWER : torreón *m* (de un castillo), torre *f* del homenaje **2** SUSTENANCE : manutención *f,* sustento *m* **3 for keeps** : para siempre
keeper [ˈki:pər] *n* **1** : guarda *mf* (en un zoológico); conservador *m,* -dora *f* (en un museo) **2** GAMEKEEPER : guardabosque *mf*
keeping [ˈki:pɪŋ] *n* **1** CONFORMITY : conformidad *f,* acuerdo *m* <in keeping with : de acuerdo con> **2** CARE : cuidado *m* <in the keeping of : al cuidado de>
keepsake [ˈki:pˌseɪk] *n* : recuerdo *m*
keep up *vt* CONTINUE, MAINTAIN : mantener, seguir con — *vi* **1** : mantenerse al corriente <he kept up with the news : se mantenía al tanto de las noticias> **2** CONTINUE : continuar **3 to keep up with someone** : mantener contacto con alguien
keg [ˈkɛg] *n* : barril *m*
kelp [ˈkɛlp] *n* : alga *f* marina
ken [ˈkɛn] *n* **1** SIGHT : vista *f,* alcance *m* de la vista **2** UNDERSTANDING : comprensión *f,* alcance *m* del conocimiento <it's beyond his ken : no lo puede entender>
kennel [ˈkɛnəl] *n* : caseta *f* para perros, perrera *f*
Kenyan [ˈkɛnjən, ˈki:n-] *n* : keniano *m,* -na *f* — **Kenyan** *adj*
kept → **keep**
kerchief [ˈkərtʃəf, -ˌtʃi:f] *n* : pañuelo *m*
kernel [ˈkərnəl] *n* **1** : almendra *f* (de semillas y nueces) **2** : grano *m* (de cereales) **3** CORE : meollo *m* <a kernel of truth : un fondo de verdad>
kerosene *or* **kerosine** [ˈkɛrəˌsi:n, ˌkɛrəˈ-] *n* : queroseno *m,* kerosén *m,* kerosene *m*
ketchup [ˈkɛtʃəp, ˈkæ-] *n* : salsa *f* catsup
kettle [ˈkɛtəl] *n* **1** : hervidor *m,* pava *f Arg, Bol, Chile* **2** → **teakettle**
kettledrum [ˈkɛtəlˌdrʌm] *n* : timbal *m*
key[1] [ˈki:] *vt* **1** ATTUNE : adaptar, adecuar **2 to key up** : poner nervioso, inquietar
key[2] *adj* : clave, fundamental
key[3] *n* **1** : llave *f* **2** SOLUTION : clave *f,* soluciones *fpl* **3** : tecla *f* (de un piano o una máquina) **4** : tono *m,* tonalidad *f* (en la música) **5** ISLET, REEF : cayo *m,* islote *m*
keyboard [ˈki:ˌbord] *n* : teclado *m*
keyhole [ˈki:ˌho:l] *n* : bocallave *f,* ojo *m* (de una cerradura)
keynote[1] [ˈki:ˌno:t] *vt* **-noted; -noting** **1** : establecer la tónica de (en música) **2** : pronunciar el discurso principal de
keynote[2] *n* **1** : tónica *f* (en música) **2** : idea *f* fundamental
keystone [ˈki:ˌsto:n] *n* : clave *f,* dovela *f*
khaki [ˈkæki, ˈkɑ-] *n* : caqui *m*
khan [ˈkɑn, ˈkæn] *n* : kan *m*
kibbutz [kəˈbʊts, -ˈbu:ts] *n, pl* **-butzim** [-ˌbʊtˈsi:m, -ˌbu:t-] : kibutz *m*
kibitz [ˈkɪbɪts] *vi* : dar consejos molestos
kibitzer [ˈkɪbɪtsər, kɪˈbɪt-] *n* : persona *f* que da consejos molestos
kick[1] [ˈkɪk] *vi* **1** : dar patadas (dícese de una persona), cocear (dícese de un animal) **2** PROTEST : patalear, protestar **3** RECOIL : dar un culatazo (dícese de

un arma de fuego) — *vt* : patear, darle una patada (a alguien)
kick[2] *n* **1** : patada *f,* puntapié *m,* coz *f* (de un animal) **2** RECOIL : culatazo *m* (de un arma de fuego) **3** : fuerza *f* <a drink with a kick : una bebida fuerte>
kicker [ˈkɪkər] *n* : pateador *m,* -dora *f* (en deportes)
kickoff [ˈkɪk,ɔf] *n* : saque *m* (inicial)
kick off *vi* **1** : hacer el saque inicial (en deportes) **2** BEGIN : empezar — *vt* : empezar
kid[1] [ˈkɪd] *v* **kidded; kidding** *vt* **1** FOOL : engañar **2** TEASE : tomarle el pelo (a alguien) — *vi* JOKE : bromear <I'm only kidding : lo digo en broma>
kid[2] *n* **1** : chivo *m,* -va *f;* cabrito *m,* -ta *f* **2** CHILD : chico *m,* -ca *f;* niño *m,* -ña *f*
kidder [ˈkɪdər] *n* : bromista *mf*
kiddingly [ˈkɪdɪŋli] *adv* : en broma
kidnap [ˈkɪd,næp] *vt* **-napped** *or* **-naped** [-,næpt]; **-napping** *or* **-naping** [-,næpɪŋ] : secuestrar, raptar
kidnapper *or* **kidnaper** [ˈkɪd,næpər] *n* : secuestrador *m,* -dora *f;* raptor *m,* -tora *f*
kidney [ˈkɪdni] *n, pl* **-neys** : riñón *m*
kidney bean *n* : frijol *m*
kill[1] [ˈkɪl] *vt* **1** : matar **2** END : acabar con, poner fin a **3 to kill time** : matar el tiempo
kill[2] *n* **1** KILLING : matanza *f* **2** PREY : presa *f*
killer [ˈkɪlər] *n* : asesino *m,* -na *f*
kiln [ˈkɪl, ˈkɪln] *n* : horno *m*
kilo [ˈkiː,loː] *n, pl* **-los** : kilo *m*
kilocycle [ˈkɪlə,saɪkəl] *n* : kilociclo *m*
kilogram [ˈkɪlə,græm, ˈkiː-] *n* : kilogramo *m*
kilohertz [ˈkɪlə,hərts] *n* : kilohertzio *m*
kilometer [kɪˈlɑmət̬ər, ˈkɪlə,miː-] *n* : kilómetro *m*
kilowatt [ˈkɪlə,wɑt] *n* : kilovatio *m*
kilt [ˈkɪlt] *n* : falda *f* escocesa
kilter [ˈkɪltər] *n* **1** ORDER : buen estado *m* **2 out of kilter** : descompuesto, estropeado
kimono [kəˈmoːno, -nə] *n, pl* **-nos** : kimono *m,* quimono *m*
kin [ˈkɪn] *n* : familiares *mpl,* parientes *mpl*
kind[1] [ˈkaɪnd] *adj* : amable, bondadoso, benévolo
kind[2] *n* **1** ESSENCE : esencia *f* <a difference in degree, not in kind : una diferencia cuantitativa y no cualitativa> **2** CATEGORY : especie *f,* género *m* **3** TYPE : clase *f,* tipo *m,* índole *f*
kindergarten [ˈkɪndər,gɑrtən, -dən] *n* : kinder *m,* kindergarten *m,* jardín *m* de infantes, jardín *m* de niños *Mex*
kindhearted [,kaɪndˈhɑrt̬əd] *adj* : bondadoso, de buen corazón
kindle [ˈkɪndəl] *v* **-dled; -dling** *vt* **1** IGNITE : encender **2** AROUSE : despertar, suscitar — *vi* : encenderse
kindliness [ˈkaɪndlinəs] *n* : bondad *f*
kindling [ˈkɪndlɪŋ, ˈkɪndlən] *n* : astillas *fpl,* leña *f*
kindly[1] [ˈkaɪndli] *adv* **1** AMIABLY : amablemente, bondadosamente **2** COURTEOUSLY : cortésmente, con cortesía <we kindly ask you not smoke : les rogamos que no fumen> **3** PLEASE : por favor **4 to take kindly to** : aceptar de buena gana
kindly[2] *adj* **-lier; -est** : bondadoso, amable
kindness [ˈkaɪndnəs] *n* : bondad *f*
kind of *adv* SOMEWHAT : un tanto, algo
kindred[1] [ˈkɪndrəd] *adj* SIMILAR : similar, afín <kindred spirits : almas gemelas>
kindred[2] *n* **1** FAMILY : familia *f,* parentela *f* **2** → **kin**
kinfolk [ˈkɪn,foːk] *or* **kinfolks** [-,foːks] *npl* → **kin**
king [ˈkɪŋ] *n* : rey *m*
kingdom [ˈkɪŋdəm] *n* : reino *m*
kingfisher [ˈkɪŋ,fɪʃər] *n* : martín *m* pescador
kingly [ˈkɪŋli] *adj* **-lier; -est** : regio, real
king–size [ˈkɪŋ,saɪz] *or* **king–sized** [-,saɪzd] *adj* : de tamaño muy grande, extra largo (dícese de cigarillos)
kink [ˈkɪŋk] *n* **1** : rizo *m* (en el pelo), vuelta *f* (en una cuerda) **2** CRAMP : calambre *m* <to have a kink in the neck : tener tortícolis>
kinky [ˈkɪŋki] *adj* **-kier; -est** : rizado (dícese del pelo), enroscado (dícese de una cuerda)
kinship [ˈkɪn,ʃɪp] *n* : parentesco *m*
kinsman [ˈkɪnzmən] *n, pl* **-men** [-mən, -,mɛn] : familiar *m,* pariente *m*
kinswoman [ˈkɪnz,wʊmən] *n, pl* **-women** [-,wɪmən] : familiar *f,* pariente *f*
kipper [ˈkɪpər] *n* : arenque *m* ahumado
kiss[1] [ˈkɪs] *vt* : besar — *vi* : besarse
kiss[2] *n* : beso *m*
kit [ˈkɪt] *n* **1** SET : juego *m,* kit *m* **2** CASE : estuche *m,* caja *f* **3 first–aid kit** : botiquín *m* **4 tool kit** : caja *f* de herramientas **5 travel kit** : neceser *m*
kitchen [ˈkɪtʃən] *n* : cocina *f*
kite [ˈkaɪt] *n* **1** : milano *m* (ave) **2** : cometa *f,* papalote *m Mex* <to fly a kite : hacer volar una cometa>
kith [ˈkɪθ] *n* : amigos *mpl* <kith and kin : amigos y parientes>
kitten [ˈkɪtən] *n* : gatito *m,* -ta *f*
kitty [ˈkɪt̬i] *n, pl* **-ties 1** FUND, POOL : bote *m,* fondo *m* común **2** CAT : gato *m,* gatito *m*
kitty–corner [ˈkɪt̬i,kɔrnər] *or* **kitty–cornered** [-nərd] → **catercorner**
kiwi [ˈkiː,wiː] *n* : kiwi *m*
kleptomania [,klɛptəˈmeɪniə] *n* : cleptomanía *f*
kleptomaniac [,klɛptəˈmeɪni,æk] *n* : cleptómano *m,* -na *f*
knack [ˈnæk] *n* : maña *f,* facilidad *f*
knapsack [ˈnæp,sæk] *n* : mochila *f,* morral *m*

knave [ˈneɪv] *n* : bellaco *m,* pícaro *m*
knead [ˈniːd] *vt* **1** : amasar, sobar **2** MASSAGE : masajear
knee [ˈniː] *n* : rodilla *f*
kneecap [ˈniːˌkæp] *n* : rótula *f*
kneel [ˈniːl] *vi* **knelt** [ˈnɛlt] *or* **kneeled** [ˈniːld]; **kneeling** : arrodillarse, ponerse de rodillas
knell [ˈnɛl] *n* : doble *m,* toque *m* <death knell : toque de difuntos>
knew → **know**
knickers [ˈnɪkərz] *npl* : pantalones *mpl* bombachos de media pierna
knickknack [ˈnɪkˌnæk] *n* : chuchería *f,* baratija *f*
knife[1] [ˈnaɪf] *vt* **knifed** [ˈnaɪft]; **knifing** : acuchillar, apuñalar
knife[2] *n, pl* **knives** [ˈnaɪvz] : cuchillo *m*
knight[1] [ˈnaɪt] *vt* : conceder el título de *Sir* a
knight[2] *n* **1** : caballero *m* <knight errant : caballero andante> **2** : caballo *m* (en ajedrez) **3** : uno que tiene el título de *Sir*
knighthood [ˈnaɪtˌhʊd] *n* **1** : caballería *f* **2** : título *m* de *Sir*
knightly [ˈnaɪtli] *adj* : caballeresco
knit[1] [ˈnɪt] *v* **knit** *or* **knitted** [ˈnɪt̬əd]; **knitting** *vt* **1** UNITE : unir, enlazar **2** : tejer <to knit a sweater : tejer un suéter> **3 to knit one's brows** : fruncir el ceño — *vi* **1** : tejer **2** : soldarse (dícese de los huesos)
knit[2] *n* : prenda *f* tejida
knitter [ˈnɪt̬ər] *n* : tejedor *m,* -dora *f*
knob [ˈnɑb] *n* **1** LUMP : bulto *m,* protuberancia *f* **2** HANDLE : perilla *f,* tirador *m,* botón *m*
knobbed [ˈnɑbd] *adj* **1** KNOTTY : nudoso **2** : que tiene perilla o botón
knobby [ˈnɑbi] *adj* **knobbier; -est 1** KNOTTY : nudoso **2 knobby knees** : rodillas *fpl* huesudas
knock[1] [ˈnɑk] *vt* **1** HIT, RAP : golpear, golpetear **2** : hacer chocar <they knocked heads : se dieron en la cabeza> **3** CRITICIZE : criticar — *vi* **1** RAP : dar un golpe, llamar (a la puerta) **2** COLLIDE : darse, chocar
knock[2] *n* : golpe *m,* llamada *f* (a la puerta), golpeteo *m* (de un motor)
knock down *vt* : derribar, echar al suelo
knocker [ˈnɑkər] *n* : aldaba *f,* llamador *m*
knock–kneed [ˈnɑkˈniːd] *adj* : patizambo
knock out *vt* : dejar sin sentido, poner fuera de combate (en el boxeo)
knoll [ˈnoːl] *n* : loma *f,* otero *m,* montículo *m*
knot[1] [ˈnɑt] *v* **knotted; knotting** *vt* : anudar — *vi* : anudarse
knot[2] *n* **1** : nudo *m* (en cordel o madera), nódulo *m* (en los músculos) **2** CLUSTER : grupo *m* **3** : nudo *m* (unidad de velocidad)
knotty [ˈnɑt̬i] *adj* **-tier; -est 1** GNARLED : nudoso **2** COMPLEX : espinoso, enredado, complejo
know [ˈnoː] *v* **knew** [ˈnuː, ˈnjuː]; **known** [ˈnoːn]; **knowing** *vt* **1** : saber <he knows the answer : sabe la respuesta> **2** : conocer (a una persona, un lugar) <do you know Julia? : ¿conoces a Julia?> **3** RECOGNIZE : reconocer **4** DISCERN, DISTINGUISH : distinguir, discernir **5 to know how to** : saber <I don't know how to dance : no sé bailar> — *vi* : saber
knowable [ˈnoːəbəl] *adj* : conocible
knowing [ˈnoːɪŋ] *adj* **1** KNOWLEDGEABLE : informado <a knowing look : una mirada de complicidad> **2** ASTUTE : astuto **3** DELIBERATE : deliberado, intencional
knowingly [ˈnoːɪŋli] *adv* **1** : con complicidad <she smiled knowingly : sonrió con una mirada de complicidad> **2** DELIBERATELY : a sabiendas, adrede, a propósito
know–it–all [ˈnoːɪt̬ˌɔl] *n* : sabelotodo *mf fam*
knowledge [ˈnɑlɪdʒ] *n* **1** AWARENESS : conocimiento *m* **2** LEARNING : conocimientos *mpl,* saber *m*
knowledgeable [ˈnɑlɪdʒəbəl] *adj* : informado, entendido, enterado
known [ˈnoːn] *adj* : conocido, familiar
knuckle [ˈnʌkəl] *n* : nudillo *m*
koala [koˈwɑlə] *n* : koala *m*
kohlrabi [ˌkoːlˈrɑbi, -ˈræ-] *n, pl* **-bies** : colinabo *m*
Koran [kəˈrɑn, -ˈræn] *n* **the Koran** : el Corán
Korean [kəˈriːən] *n* : coreano *m,* -na *f* — **Korean** *adj*
kosher [ˈkoːʃər] *adj* : aprobado por la ley judía
kowtow [ˌkaʊˈtaʊ, ˈkaʊˌtaʊ] *vi* **to kowtow to** : humillarse ante, doblegarse ante
krypton [ˈkrɪpˌtɑn] *n* : criptón *m*
kudos [ˈkjuːˌdɑs, ˈkuː-, -ˌdoːz] *n* : fama *f,* renombre *m*
kumquat [ˈkʌmˌkwɑt] *n* : naranjita *f* china
Kuwaiti [kʊˈweɪt̬i] *n* : kuwaití *mf* — **Kuwaiti** *adj*

L

l [ˈɛl] *n, pl* **l's** *or* **ls** [ˈɛlz] : duodécima letra del alfabeto inglés
lab [ˈlæb] → **laboratory**
label[1] [ˈleɪbəl] *vt* **-beled** *or* **-belled; -beling** *or* **-belling 1** : etiquetar, poner etiqueta a **2** BRAND, CATEGORIZE

: calificar, tildar, tachar <they labeled him as a fraud : lo calificaron de farsante>

label[2] *n* **1** : etiqueta *f*, rótulo *m* **2** DESCRIPTION : calificación *f*, descripción *f* **3** BRAND : marca *f*

labial [ˈleɪbiəl] *adj* : labial

labor[1] [ˈleɪbər] *vi* **1** WORK : trabajar **2** STRUGGLE : avanzar penosamente (dícese de una persona), funcionar con dificultad (dícese de un motor) **3 to labor under a delusion** : hacerse ilusiones, tener una falsa impresión — *vt* BELABOR : insistir en, extenderse sobre

labor[2] *n* **1** EFFORT, WORK : trabajo *m*, esfuerzos *mpl* **2** : parto *m* <to be in labor : estar de parto> **3** TASK : tarea *f*, labor *m* **4** WORKERS : mano *f* de obra

laboratory [ˈlæbrəˌtori, ləˈbɔrə-] *n, pl* **-ries** : laboratorio *m*

Labor Day *n* : Día *m* del Trabajo

laborer [ˈleɪbərər] *n* : peón *m;* trabajador *m*, -dora *f*

laborious [ləˈboriəs] *adj* : laborioso, difícil

laboriously [ləˈboriəsli] *adv* : laboriosamente, trabajosamente

labor union → **union**

labyrinth [ˈlæbəˌrɪnθ] *n* : laberinto *m*

lace[1] [ˈleɪs] *vt* **laced; lacing 1** TIE : acordonar, atar los cordones de **2** : adornar de encaje <I laced the dress in white : adorné el vestido de encaje blanco> **3** SPIKE : echar licor a

lace[2] *n* **1** : encaje *m* **2** SHOELACE : cordón *m* (de zapatos), agujeta *f Mex*

lacerate [ˈlæsəˌreɪt] *vt* **-ated; -ating** : lacerar

laceration [ˌlæsəˈreɪʃən] *n* : laceración *f*

lack[1] [ˈlæk] *vt* : carecer de, no tener <she lacks patience : carece de paciencia> — *vi* : faltar <they lack for nothing : no les falta nada>

lack[2] *n* : falta *f*, carencia *f*

lackadaisical [ˌlækəˈdeɪzɪkəl] *adj* : apático, indiferente, lánguido — **lackadaisically** [-kli] *adv*

lackey [ˈlæki] *n, pl* **-eys 1** FOOTMAN : lacayo *m* **2** TOADY : adulador *m*, -dora *f*

lackluster [ˈlækˌlʌstər] *adj* **1** DULL : sin brillo, apagado, deslustrado **2** MEDIOCRE : deslucido, mediocre

laconic [ləˈkɑnɪk] *adj* : lacónico — **laconically** [-nɪkli] *adv*

lacquer[1] [ˈlækər] *vt* : laquear, pintar con laca

lacquer[2] *n* : laca *f*

lacrosse [ləˈkrɔs] *n* : lacrosse *f*

lactic acid [ˈlæktɪk] *n* : ácido *m* láctico

lacuna [ləˈkuːnə, -ˈkjuː-] *n, pl* **-nae** [-ˌniː, -ˌnaɪ] *or* **-nas** : laguna *f*

lacy [ˈleɪsi] *adj* **lacier; -est** : de encaje, como de encaje

lad [ˈlæd] *n* : muchacho *m*, niño *m*

ladder [ˈlædər] *n* : escalera *f*

laden [ˈleɪdən] *adj* : cargado

ladle[1] [ˈleɪdəl] *vt* **-dled; -dling** : servir con cucharón

ladle[2] *n* : cucharón *m*, cazo *m*

lady [ˈleɪdi] *n, pl* **-dies 1** : señora *f*, dama *f* **2** WOMAN : mujer *f*

ladybird [ˈleɪdiˌbərd] → **ladybug**

ladybug [ˈleɪdiˌbʌg] *n* : mariquita *f*

lag[1] [ˈlæg] *vi* **lagged; lagging** : quedarse atrás, retrasarse, rezagarse

lag[2] *n* **1** DELAY : retraso *m*, demora *f* **2** INTERVAL : lapso *m*, intervalo *m*

lager [ˈlɑgər] *n* : cerveza *f* rubia

laggard[1] [ˈlægərd] *adj* : retardado, retrasado

laggard[2] *n* : rezagado *m*, -da *f*

lagoon [ləˈguːn] *n* : laguna *f*

laid *pp* → **lay**

lain *pp* → **lie**

lair [ˈlær] *n* : guarida *f*, madriguera *f*

laissez–faire [ˌlɛˌseɪˈfær, ˌleɪˌzeɪ-] *n* : liberalismo *m* económico

laity [ˈleɪət̬i] *n* **the laity** : los laicos, el laicado

lake [ˈleɪk] *n* : lago *m*

lama [ˈlɑmə] *n* : lama *m*

lamb [ˈlæm] *n* **1** : cordero *m*, borrego *m* (animal) **2** : carne *f* de cordero

lambaste [læmˈbeɪst] *or* **lambast** [-ˈbæst] *vt* **-basted; -basting 1** BEAT, THRASH : golpear, azotar, darle una paliza (a alguien) **2** CENSURE : arremeter contre, censurar

lame[1] [ˈleɪm] *vt* **lamed; laming** : lisiar, hacer cojo

lame[2] *adj* **lamer; lamest 1** : cojo, renco, rengo **2** WEAK : pobre, débil, poco convincente <a lame excuse : una excusa débil>

lamé [lɑˈmeɪ, læ-] *n* : lamé *m*

lame duck *n* : persona *f* sin poder <a lame-duck President : un presidente saliente>

lamely [ˈleɪmli] *adv* : sin convicción

lameness [ˈleɪmnəs] *n* **1** : cojera *f*, renquera *f* **2** : falta *f* de convicción, debilidad *f*, pobreza *f* <the lameness of her response : la pobreza de su respuesta>

lament[1] [ləˈmɛnt] *vt* **1** MOURN : llorar, llorar por **2** DEPLORE : lamentar, deplorar — *vi* : llorar

lament[2] *n* : lamento *m*

lamentable [ˈlæməntəbəl, ləˈmɛntə-] *adj* : lamentable, deplorable — **lamentably** [-bli] *adv*

lamentation [ˌlæmənˈteɪʃən] *n* : lamentación *f*, lamento *m*

laminate[1] [ˈlæməˌneɪt] *vt* **-nated; -nating** : laminar

laminate[2] [ˈlæmənət] *n* : laminado *m*

laminated [ˈlæməˌneɪt̬əd] *adj* : laminado

lamp [ˈlæmp] *n* : lámpara *f*

lampoon[1] [læmˈpuːn] *vt* : satirizar

lampoon[2] *n* : sátira *f*

lamprey [ˈlæmpri] *n, pl* **-preys** : lamprea *f*

lance[1] [ˈlænts] *vt* **lanced; lancing** : abrir con lanceta, sajar

lance[2] *n* **:** lanza *f*
lance corporal *n* **:** cabo *m* interino, soldado *m* de primera clase
lancet [ˈlæntsət] *n* **:** lanceta *f*
land[1] [ˈlænd] *vt* **1 :** desembarcar (pasajeros de un barco), hacer aterrizar (un avión) **2** CATCH **:** pescar, sacar (un pez) del agua **3** GAIN, SECURE **:** conseguir, ganar <to land a job : conseguir empleo> **4** DELIVER **:** dar, asestar <he landed a punch : asestó un puñetazo> — *vi* **1 :** aterrizar, tomar tierra, atracar <the plane just landed : el avión acaba de aterrizar> <the ship landed an hour ago : el barco atracó hace una hora>**2** ALIGHT **:** posarse, aterrizar <to land on one's feet : caer de pie>
land[2] *n* **1** GROUND **:** tierra *f* <dry land : tierra firme> **2** TERRAIN **:** terreno *m* **3** NATION **:** país *m,* nación *f* **4** DOMAIN **:** mundo *m,* dominio *m* <the land of dreams : el mundo de los sueños>
landfill [ˈlændˌfɪl] *n* **:** vertadero *m* (de basuras)
landing [ˈlændɪŋ] *n* **1 :** aterrizaje *m* (de aviones), desembarco *m* (de barcos) **2 :** descansillo *m* (de una escalera)
landing field *n* **:** campo *m* de aterrizaje
landing strip → airstrip
landlady [ˈlændˌleɪdi] *n, pl* **-dies :** casera *f,* dueña *f,* arrendadora *f*
landless [ˈlændləs] *adj* **:** sin tierra
landlocked [ˈlændˌlɑkt] *adj* **:** sin salida al mar
landlord [ˈlændˌlɔrd] *n* **:** dueño *m,* casero *m,* arrendador *m*
landlubber [ˈlændˌlʌbər] *n* **:** marinero *m* de agua dulce
landmark [ˈlændˌmɑrk] *n* **1 :** señal *f* (geográfica), punto *m* de referencia **2** MILESTONE **:** hito *m* <a landmark in our history : un hito en nuestra historia> **3** MONUMENT **:** monumento *m* histórico
landowner [ˈlændˌoːnər] *n* **:** hacendado *m,* -da *f;* terrateniente *mf*
landscape[1] [ˈlændˌskeɪp] *vt* **-scaped; -scaping :** ajardinar
landscape[2] *n* **:** paisaje *m*
landslide [ˈlændˌslaɪd] *n* **1 :** desprendimiento *m* de tierras, derrumbe *m* **2 landslide victory :** victoria *f* arrolladora
landward [ˈlændwərd] *adv* **:** en dirección de la tierra, hacia tierra
lane [ˈleɪn] *n* **1** PATH, WAY **:** camino *m,* sendero *m* **2 :** carril *m* (de una carretera)
language [ˈlæŋgwɪdʒ] *n* **1 :** idioma *m,* lengua *f* <the English language : el idioma inglés> **2 :** lenguaje *m* <body language : lenguaje corporal>
languid [ˈlæŋgwɪd] *adj* **:** lánguido — **languidly** *adv*
languish [ˈlæŋgwɪʃ] *vi* **1** WEAKEN **:** languidecer, debilitarse **2** PINE **:** consumirse, suspirar (por) <to languish for love : suspirar por el amor> <he languished in prison : estuvo pudriéndose en la cárcel>
languor [ˈlæŋgər] *n* **:** languidez *f*
languorous [ˈlæŋgərəs] *adj* **:** lánguido — **languorously** *adv*
lank [ˈlæŋk] *adj* **1** THIN **:** delgado, larguirucho *fam* **2** LIMP **:** lacio
lanky [ˈlæŋki] *adj* **lankier; -est :** delgado, larguirucho *fam*
lanolin [ˈlænəlɪn] *n* **:** lanolina *f*
lantern [ˈlæntərn] *n* **:** linterna *f,* farol *m*
Laotian [leɪˈoːʃən, ˈlaʊʃən] *n* **:** laosiano *m,* -na *f* — **Laotian** *adj*
lap[1] [ˈlæp] *v* **lapped; lapping** *vt* **1** FOLD **:** plegar, doblar **2** WRAP **:** envolver **3 :** lamer, besar <waves were lapping the shore : las olas lamían la orilla> **4 to lap up :** beber a lengüetadas (como un gato) — *vi* OVERLAP **:** traslaparse
lap[2] *n* **1 :** falda *f,* regazo *m* (del cuerpo) **2** OVERLAP **:** traslapo *m* **3 :** vuelta *f* (en deportes) **4** STAGE **:** etapa *f* (de un viaje)
lapdog [ˈlæpˌdɔg] *n* **:** perro *m* faldero
lapel [ləˈpɛl] *n* **:** solapa *f*
Lapp [ˈlæp] *n* **:** lapón *m,* -pona *f* — **Lapp** *adj*
lapse[1] [ˈlæps] *vi* **lapsed; lapsing 1** FALL, SLIP **:** caer <to lapse into bad habits : caer en malos hábitos> <to lapse into unconsciousness : perder el conocimiento> <to lapse into silence : quedarse callado> **2** FADE **:** decaer, desvanecerse <her dedication lapsed : su dedicación se desvaneció> **3** CEASE **:** cancelarse, perderse **4** ELAPSE **:** transcurrir, pasar **5** EXPIRE **:** caducar
lapse[2] *n* **1** SLIP **:** lapsus *m,* desliz *m,* falla *f* <a lapse of memory : una falla de memoria> **2** INTERVAL **:** lapso *m,* intervalo *m,* período *m* **3** EXPIRATION **:** caducidad *f*
laptop [ˈlæpˌtɑp] *adj* **:** portátil, laptop
larboard [ˈlɑrbərd] *n* **:** babor *m*
larcenous [ˈlɑrsənəs] *adj* **:** de robo
larceny [ˈlɑrsəni] *n, pl* **-nies :** robo *m,* hurto *m*
larch [ˈlɑrtʃ] *n* **:** alerce *f*
lard [ˈlɑrd] *n* **:** manteca *f* de cerdo
larder [ˈlɑrdər] *n* **:** despensa *f,* alacena *f*
large [ˈlɑrdʒ] *adj* **larger; largest 1** BIG **:** grande **2** COMPREHENSIVE **:** amplio, extenso **3 by and large :** por lo general
largely [ˈlɑrdʒli] *adv* **:** en gran parte, en su mayoría
largeness [ˈlɑrdʒnəs] *n* **:** lo grande
largesse *or* **largess** [lɑrˈʒɛs, -ˈdʒɛs] *n* **:** generosidad *f,* largueza *f*
lariat [ˈlæriət] *n* **:** lazo *m*
lark [ˈlɑrk] *n* **1** FUN **:** diversión *f* <what a lark! : ¡qué divertido!> **2 :** alondra *f* (pájaro)
larva [ˈlɑrvə] *n, pl* **-vae** [-ˌviː, -ˌvaɪ] **:** larva *f* — **larval** [-vəl] *adj*
laryngitis [ˌlærənˈdʒaɪtəs] *n* **:** laringitis *f*

larynx [ˈlærɪŋks] *n, pl* **-rynges** [ləˈrɪn,dʒiːz] *or* **-ynxes** [ˈlærɪŋksəz] : laringe *f*
lasagna [ləˈzɑnjə] *n* : lasaña *f*
lascivious [ləˈsɪviəs] *adj* : lascivo
lasciviousness [ləˈsɪviəsnəs] *n* : lascivia *f*, lujuria *f*
laser [ˈleɪzər] *n* : láser *m*
lash[1] [ˈlæʃ] *vt* **1** WHIP : azotar **2** BIND : atar, amarrar
lash[2] *n* **1** WHIP : látigo *m* **2** STROKE : latigazo *m* **3** EYELASH : pestaña *f*
lass [ˈlæs] *or* **lassie** [ˈlæsi] *n* : muchacha *f*, chica *f*
lassitude [ˈlæsə,tuːd, -,tjuːd] *n* : lasitud *f*
lasso[1] [ˈlæ,soː, læˈsuː] *vt* : lazar
lasso[2] *n, pl* **-sos** *or* **-soes** : lazo *m*, reata *f Mex*
last[1] [ˈlæst] *vi* **1** CONTINUE : durar <how long will it last? : ¿cuánto durará?> **2** ENDURE : aguantar, durar **3** SURVIVE : durar, sobrevivir **4** SUFFICE : durar, bastar — *vt* **1** : durar <it will last a lifetime : durará toda la vida> **2 to last out** : aguantar
last[2] *adv* **1** : en último lugar, al último <we came in last : llegamos en último lugar> **2** : por última vez, la última vez <I saw him last in Bogota : lo vi por última vez en Bogotá> **3** FINALLY : por último, en conclusión
last[3] *adj* **1** FINAL : último, final **2** PREVIOUS : pasado <last year : el año pasado>
last[4] *n* **1** : el último, la última, lo último <at last : por fin, al fin, finalmente> **2** : horma *f* (de zapatero)
lasting [ˈlæstɪŋ] *adj* : perdurable, duradero, estable
lastly [ˈlæstli] *adv* : por último, finalmente
latch[1] [ˈlætʃ] *vt* : cerrar con picaporte
latch[2] *n* : picaporte *m*, pestillo *m*, pasador *m*
late[1] [ˈleɪt] *adv* **later; latest 1** : tarde <to arrive late : llegar tarde> <to sleep late : dormir hasta tarde> **2** : a última hora, a finales <late in the month : a finales del mes> **3** RECENTLY : recién, últimamente <as late as last year : todavía en el año pasado>
late[2] *adj* **later; latest 1** TARDY : tardío, de retraso <to be late : llegar tarde> **2** : avanzado <because of the late hour : a causa de la hora avanzada> **3** DECEASED : difunto, fallecido **4** RECENT : reciente, último <our late quarrel : nuestra última pelea>
latecomer [ˈleɪt,kʌmər] *n* : rezagado *m*, -da *f*
lately [ˈleɪtli] *adv* : recientemente, últimamente
lateness [ˈleɪtnəs] *n* **1** DELAY : retraso *m*, atraso *m*, tardanza *f* **2** : lo avanzado (de la hora)
latent [ˈleɪtənt] *adj* : latente — **latently** *adv*
lateral [ˈlæṱərəl] *adj* : lateral — **laterally** *adv*
latex [ˈleɪ,tɛks] *n, pl* **-tices** [ˈleɪṱə,siːz, ˈlæṱə-] *or* **-texes** : látex *m*
lath [ˈlæθ, ˈlæð] *n, pl* **laths** *or* **lath** : listón *m*
lathe [ˈleɪð] *n* : torno *m*
lather[1] [ˈlæðər] *vt* : enjabonar — *vi* : espumar, hacer espuma
lather[2] *n* **1** : espuma *f* (de jabón) **2** : sudor *m* (de caballo) **3 to get into a lather** : ponerse histérico
Latin[1] *adj* : latino
Latin[2] *n* **1** : latín *m* (idioma) **2** → **Latin American**
Latin–American [ˈlætənəˈmɛrikən] *adj* : latinoamericano
Latin American *n* : latinoamericano *m*, -na *f*
latitude [ˈlæṱə,tuːd, -,tjuːd] *n* : latitud *f*
latrine [ləˈtriːn] *n* : letrina *f*
latter[1] [ˈlæṱər] *adj* **1** SECOND : segundo **2** LAST : último
latter[2] *pron* **the latter** : éste, ésta, éstos *pl*, éstas *pl*
lattice [ˈlæṱəs] *n* : enrejado *m*, celosía *f*
Latvian [ˈlætviən] *n* : letón *m*, -tona *f* — **Latvian** *adj*
laud[1] [ˈlɔd] *vt* : alabar, loar
laud[2] *n* : alabanza *f*, loa *f*
laudable [ˈlɔdəbəl] *adj* : loable — **laudably** [-bli] *adv*
laugh[1] [ˈlæf] *vi* : reír, reírse
laugh[2] *n* **1** LAUGHTER : risa *f* **2** JOKE : chiste *m*, broma *f* <he did it for a laugh : lo hizo en broma, lo hizo para divertirse>
laughable [ˈlæfəbəl] *adj* : risible, de risa
laughingstock [ˈlæfɪŋ,stɑk] *n* : hazmerreír *m*
laughter [ˈlæftər] *n* : risa *f*, risas *fpl*
launch[1] [ˈlɔntʃ] *vt* **1** HURL : lanzar **2** : botar (un barco) **3** START : iniciar, empezar
launch[2] *n* **1** : lancha *f* (bote) **2** LAUNCHING : lanzamiento *m*
launder [ˈlɔndər] *vt* **1** : lavar y planchar (ropa) **2** : blanquear, lavar (dinero)
launderer [ˈlɔndərər] *n* : lavandero *m*, -ra *f*
laundress [ˈlɔndrəs] *n* : lavandera *f*
laundry [ˈlɔndri] *n, pl* **laundries 1** : ropa *f* sucia, ropa *f* para lavar <to do the laundry : lavar la ropa> **2** : lavandería *f* (servicio de lavar)
laureate [ˈlɔriət] *n* : laureado *m*, -da *f* <poet laureate : poeta laureado>
laurel [ˈlɔrəl] *n* **1** : laurel *m* (planta) **2 laurels** *npl* : laureles *mpl* <to rest on one's laurels : dormirse uno en sus laureles>
lava [ˈlɑvə, ˈlæ-] *n* : lava *f*
lavatory [ˈlævə,tori] *n, pl* **-ries** : baño *m*, cuarto *m* de baño

lavender ['lævəndər] *n* : lavanda *f,* espliego *m*
lavish[1] ['lævɪʃ] *vt* : prodigar (a), colmar (de)
lavish[2] *adj* **1** EXTRAVAGANT : pródigo, generoso, derrochador **2** ABUNDANT : abundante **3** LUXURIOUS : lujoso, espléndido
lavishly ['lævɪʃli] *adv* : con generosidad, espléndidamente <to live lavishly : vivir a lo grande>
lavishness ['lævɪʃnəs] *n* : generosidad *f,* esplendidez *f*
law ['lɔ] *n* **1** : ley *f* <to break the law : violar la ley> **2** : derecho *m* <criminal law : derecho criminal> **3** : abogacía *f* <to practice law : ejercer la abogacía>
law–abiding ['lɔə,baɪdɪŋ] *adj* : observante de la ley
lawbreaker ['lɔ,breɪkər] *n* : infractor *m,* -tora *f* de la ley
lawful ['lɔfəl] *adj* : legal, legítimo, lícito — **lawfully** *adv*
lawgiver ['lɔ,gɪvər] *n* : legislador *m,* -dora *f*
lawless ['lɔləs] *adj* : anárquico, ingobernable — **lawlessly** *adv*
lawlessness ['lɔləsnəs] *n* : anarquía *f,* desorden *m*
lawmaker ['lɔ,meɪkər] *n* : legislador *m,* -dora *f*
lawman ['lɔmən] *n, pl* **-men** [-mən, -,mɛn] : agente *m* del orden
lawn ['lɔn] *n* : césped *m,* pasto *m*
lawn mower *n* : cortadora *f* de césped
lawsuit ['lɔ,su:t] *n* : pleito *m,* litigio *m,* demanda *f*
lawyer ['lɔɪər, 'lɔjər] *n* : abogado *m,* -da *f*
lax ['læks] *adj* : laxo, relajado — **laxly** *adv*
laxative ['læksətɪv] *n* : laxante *m*
laxity ['læksəti] *n* : relajación *f,* descuido *m,* falta *f* de rigor
lay[1] ['leɪ] *vt* **laid** ['leɪd]; **laying 1** PLACE, PUT : poner, colocar <she laid it on the table : lo puso en la mesa> <to lay eggs : poner huevos> **2** : hacer <to lay a bet : hacer una apuesta> **3** IMPOSE : imponer <to lay a tax : imponer un impuesto> <to lay the blame on : echarle la culpa a> **4 to lay out** PRESENT : presentar, exponer <he laid out his plan : presentó su proyecto> **5 to lay out** DESIGN : diseñar (el trazado de)
lay[2] *pp* → **lie**
lay[3] *adj* SECULAR : laico, lego
lay[4] *n* **1** : disposición *f,* configuración *f* <the lay of the land : la configuración del terreno> **2** BALLAD : romance *m,* balada *f*
layer ['leɪər] *n* **1** : capa *f* (de pintura, etc.), estrato *m* (de roca) **2** : gallina *f* ponedora
layman ['leɪmən] *n, pl* **-men** [-mən, -,mɛn] : laico *m,* lego *m*
layoff ['leɪ,ɔf] *n* : despido *m*
lay off *vt* : despedir
layout ['leɪ,aʊt] *n* : disposición *f,* distribución *f* (de una casa, etc.), trazado *m* (de una ciudad)
lay up *vt* **1** STORE : guardar, almacenar **2 to be laid up** : estar enfermo, tener que guardar cama
laywoman ['leɪ,wʊmən] *n, pl* **-women** [-,wɪmən] : laica *f,* lega *f*
laziness ['leɪzinəs] *n* : pereza *f,* flojera *f*
lazy ['leɪzi] *adj* **-zier; -est** : perezoso, holgazán — **lazily** ['leɪzəli] *adv*
leach ['li:tʃ] *vt* : filtrar
lead[1] ['li:d] *vt* **led** ['lɛd]; **leading 1** GUIDE : conducir, llevar, guiar **2** DIRECT : dirigir **3** HEAD : encabezar, ir al frente de **4 to lead to** : resultar en, llevar a <it only leads to trouble : sólo resulta en problemas>
lead[2] *n* : delantera *f,* primer lugar *m* <to take the lead : tomar la delantera>
lead[3] ['lɛd] *n* **1** : plomo *m* (metal) **2** : mina *f* (de lápiz) **3 lead poisoning** : saturnismo *m*
leaden ['lɛdən] *adj* **1** : plomizo <a leaden sky : un ciel plomizo> **2** HEAVY : pesado
leader ['li:dər] *n* : jefe *m,* -fa *f;* líder *mf;* dirigente *mf;* gobernante *mf*
leadership ['li:dər,ʃɪp] *n* : mando *m,* dirección *f*
leaf[1] ['li:f] *vi* **1** : echar hojas (dícese de un árbol) **2 to leaf through** : hojear (un libro)
leaf[2] *n, pl* **leaves** ['li:vz] **1** : hoja *f* (de plantas o libros) **2 to turn over a new leaf** : hacer borrón y cuenta nueva
leafless ['li:fləs] *adj* : sin hojas, pelado
leaflet ['li:flət] *n* : folleto *m*
leafy ['li:fi] *adj* **leafier; -est** : frondoso
league[1] ['li:g] *v* **leagued; leaguing** *vt* : aliar, unir — *vi* : aliarse, unirse
league[2] *n* **1** : legua *f* (medida de distancia) **2** ASSOCIATION : alianza *f,* sociedad *f,* liga *f*
leak[1] ['li:k] *vt* **1** : perder, dejar escapar (un líquido o un gas) **2** : filtrar (información) — *vi* **1** : gotear, escaparse, fugarse (dícese de un líquido o un gas) **2** : hacer agua (dícese de un bote) **3** : filtrarse, divulgarse (dícese de información)
leak[2] *n* **1** HOLE : agujero *m* (en recipientes), gotera *f* (en un tejado) **2** ESCAPE : fuga *f,* escape *m* **3** : filtración *f* (de información)
leakage ['li:kɪdʒ] *n* : escape *m,* fuga *f*
leaky ['li:ki] *adj* **leakier; -est** : agujereado (dícese de un recipiente), que hace agua (dícese de un bote), con goteras (dícese de un tejado)
lean[1] ['li:n] *vi* **1** BEND : inclinarse, ladearse **2** RECLINE : reclinarse **3** RELY : apoyarse (en), depender (de) **4** INCLINE, TEND : inclinarse, tender — *vt* : apoyar

lean[2] *adj* **1** THIN : delgado, flaco **2** : sin grasa, magro (dícese de la carne)

leanness [ˈliːnnəs] *n* : delgadez *f*

lean–to [ˈliːnˌtuː] *n* : cobertizo *m*

leap[1] [ˈliːp] *vi* **leapt** *or* **leaped** [ˈliːpt, ˈlɛpt]; **leaping** : saltar, brincar

leap[2] *n* : salto *m,* brinco *m*

leap year *n* : año *m* bisiesto

learn [ˈlərn] *vt* **1** : aprender <to learn to sing : aprender a cantar> **2** MEMORIZE : aprender de memoria **3** DISCOVER : saber, enterarse de — *vi* **1** : aprender <to learn from experience : aprender por experiencia> **2** FIND OUT : enterarse, saber

learned [ˈlərnəd] *adj* : erudito

learner [ˈlərnər] *n* : principiante *mf,* estudiante *mf*

learning [ˈlərnɪŋ] *n* : erudición *f,* saber *m*

lease[1] [ˈliːs] *vt* **leased; leasing** : arrendar

lease[2] *n* : contrato *m* de arrendamiento

leash[1] [ˈliːʃ] *vt* : atraillar (un animal)

leash[2] *n* : traílla *f*

least[1] [ˈliːst] *adv* : menos <when least expected : cuando menos se espera>

least[2] *adj* (*superlative of* **little**) : menor, más mínimo

least[3] *n* **1** : lo menos <at least : por lo menos> **2 to say the least** : por no decir más

leather [ˈlɛðər] *n* : cuero *m*

leathery [ˈlɛðəri] *adj* : curtido (dícese de la piel), correoso (dícese de la carne)

leave[1] [ˈliːv] *v* **left** [ˈlɛft]; **leaving** *vt* **1** BEQUEATH : dejar, legar **2** DEPART : dejar, salir(se) de **3** ABANDON : abandonar, dejar **4** FORGET : dejar, olvidarse de <I left the books at the library : dejé los libros en la biblioteca> **5 to be left** : quedar <it's all I have left : es todo lo que me queda> **6 to be left over** : sobrar **7 to leave out** : omitir, excluir — *vi* : irse, salir, partir, marcharse <she left yesterday morning : se fue ayer por la mañana>

leave[2] *n* **1** PERMISSION : permiso *m* <by your leave : con su permiso> **2** *or* **leave of absence** : permiso *m,* licencia *f* <maternity leave : licencia por maternidad> **3 to take one's leave** : despedirse

leaven [ˈlɛvən] *n* : levadura *f*

leaves → **leaf[2]**

leaving [ˈliːvɪŋ] *n* **1** : salida *f,* partida *f* **2 leavings** *npl* : restos *mpl,* sobras *fpl*

Lebanese [ˌlɛbəˈniːz, -ˈniːs] *n* : libanés *m,* -nesa *f* — **Lebanese** *adj*

lecherous [ˈlɛtʃərəs] *adj* : lascivo, libidinoso — **lecherously** *adv*

lechery [ˈlɛtʃəri] *n* : lascivia *f,* lujuria *f*

lecture[1] [ˈlɛktʃər] *v* **-tured; -turing** *vi* : dar clase, dictar clase, dar una conferencia — *vt* SCOLD : sermonear, echar una reprimenda a, regañar

lecture[2] *n* **1** : conferencia *f* **2** REPRIMAND : reprimenda *f*

led *pp* → **lead[1]**

ledge [ˈlɛdʒ] *n* : repisa *f* (de una pared), antepecho *m* (de una ventana), saliente *m* (de una montaña)

ledger [ˈlɛdʒər] *n* : libro *m* mayor, libro *m* de contabilidad

lee[1] [ˈliː] *adj* : de sotavento

lee[2] *n* : sotavento *m*

leech [ˈliːtʃ] *n* : sanguijuela *f*

leek [ˈliːk] *n* : puerro *m*

leer[1] [ˈlɪr] *vi* : mirar con lascivia

leer[2] *n* : mirada *f* lasciva

leery [ˈlɪri] *adj* : receloso

lees [ˈliːz] *npl* : posos *mpl,* heces *fpl*

leeward[1] [ˈliːwərd, ˈluːərd] *adj* : de sotavento

leeward[2] *n* : sotavento *m*

leeway [ˈliːˌweɪ] *n* : libertad *f,* margen *m*

left[1] [ˈlɛft] *adv* : hacia la izquierda

left[2] *pp* → **leave**

left[3] *adj* : izquierdo

left[4] *n* : izquierda *f* <on the left : a la izquierda>

left–hand [ˈlɛftˈhænd] *adj* **1** : de la izquierda **2** → **left–handed**

left–handed [ˈlɛftˈhændəd] *adj* **1** : zurdo (dícese de una persona) **2** : con doble sentido <a left-handed compliment : un cumplido a medias>

leftovers [ˈlɛftˌoːvərz] *npl* : restos *mpl,* sobras *fpl*

left wing *n* **the left wing** : la izquierda

left–winger [ˈlɛftˈwɪŋər] *n* : izquierdista *mf*

leg [ˈlɛg] *n* **1** : pierna *f* (de una persona, de carne, de ropa), pata *f* (de un animal, de muebles) **2** STAGE : etapa *f* (de un viaje), vuelta *f* (de una carrera)

legacy [ˈlɛgəsi] *n, pl* **-cies** : legado *m,* herencia *f*

legal [ˈliːgəl] *adj* **1** : legal, jurídico <legal advisor : asesor jurídico> <the legal profession : la abogacía> **2** LAWFUL : legítimo, legal

legalistic [ˌliːgəˈlɪstɪk] *adj* : legalista

legality [liˈgæləṭi] *n, pl* **-ties** : legalidad *f*

legalize [ˈliːgəˌlaɪz] *vt* **-ized; -izing** : legalizar

legally [ˈliːgəli] *adv* : legalmente

legate [ˈlɛgət] *n* : legado *m*

legation [lɪˈgeɪʃən] *n* : legación *f*

legend [ˈlɛdʒənd] *n* **1** STORY : leyenda *f* **2** INSCRIPTION : leyenda *f,* inscripción *f* **3** : signos *mpl* convencionales (en un mapa)

legendary [ˈlɛdʒənˌdɛri] *adj* : lengendario

legerdemain [ˌlɛdʒərdəˈmeɪn] → **sleight of hand**

leggings [ˈlɛgɪŋz, ˈlɛgənz] *npl* : mallas *fpl*

legibility [ˌlɛdʒəˈbɪləṭi] *n* : legibilidad *f*

legible [ˈlɛdʒəbəl] *adj* : legible

legibly [ˈlɛdʒəbli] *adv* : de manera legible
legion [ˈliːdʒən] *n* : legión *f*
legionnaire [ˌliːdʒəˈnær] *n* : legionario *m,* -ria *f*
legislate [ˈlɛdʒəsˌleɪt] *vi* **-lated; -lating** : legislar
legislation [ˌlɛdʒəsˈleɪʃən] *n* : legislación *f*
legislative [ˈlɛdʒəsˌleɪt̬ɪv] *adj* : legislativo, legislador
legislator [ˈlɛdʒəsˌleɪt̬ər] *n* : legislador *m,* -dora *f*
legislature [ˈlɛdʒəsˌleɪtʃər] *n* : asamblea *f* legislativa
legitimacy [lɪˈdʒɪt̬əməsi] *n* : legitimidad *f*
legitimate [lɪˈdʒɪt̬əmət] *adj* **1** VALID : legítimo, válido, justificado **2** LAWFUL : legítimo, legal
legitimately [lɪˈdʒɪt̬əmətli] *adv* : legítimamente
legitimize [lɪˈdʒɪt̬əˌmaɪz] *vt* **-mized; -mizing** : legitimar, hacer legítimo
legume [ˈlɛˌgjuːm, lɪˈgjuːm] *n* : legumbre *f*
leisure [ˈliːʒər, ˈlɛ-] *n* **1** : ocio *m,* tiempo *m* libre <a life of leisure : una vida de ocio>**2 to take one's leisure** : reposar **3 at your leisure** : cuando te venga bien, cuando tengas tiempo
leisurely [ˈliːʒərli, ˈlɛ-] *adj & adv* : lento, sin prisas
lemming [ˈlɛmɪŋ] *n* : lemming *m*
lemon [ˈlɛmən] *n* : limón *m*
lemonade [ˌlɛməˈneɪd] *n* : limonada *f*
lemony [ˈlɛməni] *adj* : a limón
lend [ˈlɛnd] *vt* **lent** [ˈlɛnt]; **lending 1** : prestar <to lend money : prestar dinero> **2** GIVE : dar <it lends force to his criticism : da fuerza a su crítica> **3 to lend oneself to** : prestarse a
length [ˈlɛŋ*k*θ] *n* **1** : longitud *f,* largo *m* <10 feet in length : 10 pies de largo> **2** DURATION : duración *f* **3** : trozo *m* (de madera), corte *m* (de tela) **4 to go to any lengths** : hacer todo lo posible **5 at ~** : extensamente <to speak at length : hablar largo y tendido>
lengthen [ˈlɛŋ*k*θən] *vt* **1** : alargar <can they lengthen the dress? : ¿se puede alargar el vestido?> **2** EXTEND, PROLONG : prolongar, extender — *vi* : alargarse, crecer <the days are lengthening : los días están creciendo>
lengthways [ˈlɛŋ*k*θˌweɪz] → **lengthwise**
lengthwise [ˈlɛŋ*k*θˌwaɪz] *adv* : a lo largo, longitudinalmente
lengthy [ˈlɛŋ*k*θi] *adj* **lengthier; -est 1** OVERLONG : largo y pesado **2** EXTENDED : prolongado, largo
leniency [ˈliːniən*t*si] *n, pl* **-cies** : lenidad *f,* indulgencia *f*
lenient [ˈliːniənt] *adj* : indulgente, poco severo
leniently [ˈliːniəntli] *adv* : con lenidad, con indulgencia
lens [ˈlɛnz] *n* **1** : cristalino *m* (del ojo) **2** : lente *mf* (de un instrumento o una cámara) **3** → **contact lens**
lent → **lend**
Lent [ˈlɛnt] *n* : Cuaresma *f*
lentil [ˈlɛntəl] *n* : lenteja *f*
Leo [ˈliːoː] *n* : Leo *mf*
leopard [ˈlɛpərd] *n* : leopardo *m*
leotard [ˈliːəˌtɑrd] *n* : leotardo *m,* malla *f*
leper [ˈlɛpər] *n* : leproso *m,* -sa *f*
leprechaun [ˈlɛprəˌkɑn] *n* : duende *m* (irlandés)
leprosy [ˈlɛprəsi] *n* : lepra *f* — **leprous** [ˈlɛprəs] *adj*
lesbian¹ [ˈlɛzbiən] *adj* : lesbiano
lesbian² *n* : lesbiana *f*
lesbianism [ˈlɛzbiəˌnɪzəm] *n* : lesbianismo *m*
lesion [ˈliːʒən] *n* : lesión *f*
less¹ [ˈlɛs] *adv* (*comparative of* **little¹**) : menos <the less you know, the better : cuanto menos sepas, mejor> <less and less : cada vez menos>
less² *adj* (*comparative of* **little²**) : menos <less than three : menos de tres> <less money : menos dinero> <nothing less than perfection : nada menos que la perfección>
less³ *pron* : menos <I'm earning less : estoy ganando menos>
less⁴ *prep* : menos <one month less two days : un mes menos dos días>
lessee [lɛˈsiː] *n* : arrendatario *m,* -ria *f*
lessen [ˈlɛsən] *vt* : disminuir, reducir — *vi* : disminuir, reducirse
lesser [ˈlɛsər] *adj* : menor <to a lesser degree : en menor grado>
lesson [ˈlɛsən] *n* **1** CLASS : clase *f,* curso *m* **2** : lección *f* <the lessons of history : las lecciones de la historia>
lessor [ˈlɛˌsɔr, lɛˈsɔr] *n* : arrendador *m,* -dora *f*
lest [ˈlɛst] *conj* : para (que) no <lest we forget : para que no olvidemos>
let [ˈlɛt] *vt* **let; letting 1** ALLOW : dejar, permitir <let me see it : déjame verlo> **2** MAKE : hacer <let me know : házmelo saber, avísame> <let them wait : que esperen, haz que esperen> **3** RENT : alquilar **4** (*used in the first person plural imperative*) <let's go! : ¡vamos!, ¡vámonos!> <let us pray : oremos> **5 to let down** DISAPPOINT : fallar **6 to let off** FORGIVE : perdonar **7 to let out** REVEAL : revelar **8 to let up** ABATE : amainar, disminuir <the pace never lets up : el ritmo nunca disminuye>
letdown *n* : chasco *m,* decepción *f*
lethal [ˈliːθəl] *adj* : letal — **lethally** *adv*
lethargic [lɪˈθɑrdʒɪk] *adj* : letárgico
lethargy [ˈlɛθərdʒi] *n* : letargo *m*
let on *vi* **1** ADMIT : reconocer <don't let on! : ¡no digas nada!> **2** PRETEND : fingir
let's [ˈlɛts] (*contraction of* **let us**) → **let**

letter[1] [ˈlɛt̬ər] *vt* **:** marcar con letras, inscribir letras en
letter[2] *n* **1 :** letra *f* (del alfabeto) **2 :** carta *f* <a letter to my mother : una carta a mi madre> **3 letters** *npl* ARTS **:** letras *fpl* **4 to the letter :** al pie de la letra
lettering [ˈlɛt̬ərɪŋ] *n* **:** letra *f*
lettuce [ˈlɛt̬əs] *n* **:** lechuga *f*
leukemia [luːˈkiːmiə] *n* **:** leucemia *f*
levee [ˈlɛvi] *n* **:** dique *m*
level[1] [ˈlɛvəl] *vt* **-eled** *or* **-elled; -eling** *or* **-elling 1** FLATTEN **:** nivelar, aplanar **2** AIM **:** apuntar (una pistola), dirigir (una acusación) **3** RAZE **:** rasar, arrasar
level [2] *adj* **1** EVEN **:** llano, plano, parejo **2** CALM **:** tranquilo <to keep a level head : no perder la cabeza>
level [3] *n* **:** nivel *m*
leveler [ˈlɛvələr] *n* **:** nivelador *m*, -dora *f*
levelheaded [ˈlɛvəlˈhɛdəd] *adj* **:** sensato, equilibrado
levelly [ˈlɛvəli] *adv* CALMLY **:** con ecuanimidad *f*, con calma
levelness [ˈlɛvəlnəs] *n* **:** uniformidad *f*
lever [ˈlɛvər, ˈliː-] *n* **:** palanca *f*
leverage [ˈlɛvərɪdʒ, ˈliː-] *n* **1 :** apalancamiento *m* (en física) **2** INFLUENCE **:** influencia *f*, palanca *f fam*
leviathan [lɪˈvaɪəθən] *n* **:** leviatán *m*, gigante *m*
levity [ˈlɛvət̬i] *n* **:** ligereza *f*, frivolidad *f*
levy[1] [ˈlɛvi] *vt* **levied; levying 1** IMPOSE **:** imponer, exigir, gravar (un impuesto) **2** COLLECT **:** recaudar (un impuesto)
levy[2] *n, pl* **levies :** impuesto *m*, gravamen *m*
lewd [ˈluːd] *adj* **:** lascivo — **lewdly** *adv*
lewdness [ˈluːdnəs] *n* **:** lascivia *f*
lexicographer [ˌlɛksəˈkɑgrəfər] *n* **:** lexicógrafo *m*, -fa *f*
lexicographical [ˌlɛksəkoˈgræfɪkəl] *or* **lexicographic** [-ˈgræfɪk] *adj* **:** lexicográfico
lexicography [ˌlɛksəˈkɑgrəfi] *n* **:** lexicografía *f*
lexicon [ˈlɛksɪˌkɑn] *n, pl* **-ica** [-kə] *or* **-icons :** léxico *m*, lexicón *m*
liability [ˌlaɪəˈbɪlət̬i] *n, pl* **-ties 1** RESPONSIBILITY **:** responsabilidad *f* **2** SUSCEPTIBILITY **:** propensión *f* **3** DRAWBACK **:** desventaja *f* **4 liabilities** *npl* DEBTS **:** deudas *fpl*, pasivo *m*
liable [ˈlaɪəbəl] *adj* **1** RESPONSIBLE **:** responsable **2** SUSCEPTIBLE **:** propenso **3** PROBABLE **:** probable <it's liable to happen : es probable que suceda>
liaison [ˈliːəˌzɑn, liˈeɪ-] *n* **1** CONNECTION **:** enlace *m*, relación *f* **2** AFFAIR **:** amorío *m*, aventura *f*
liar [ˈlaɪər] *n* **:** mentiroso *m*, -sa *f*; embustero *m*, -ra *f*
libel[1] [ˈlaɪbəl] *vt* **-beled** *or* **-belled; -beling** *or* **-belling :** difamar, calumniar
libel[2] *n* **:** difamación *f*, calumnia *f*
libeler [ˈlaɪbələr] *n* **:** difamador *m*, -dora *f*; calumniador *m*, -dora *f*; libelista *mf*
libelous *or* **libellous** [ˈlaɪbələs] *adj* **:** difamatorio, calumnioso, injurioso
liberal[1] [ˈlɪbrəl, ˈlɪbərəl] *adj* **1** TOLERANT **:** liberal, tolerante **2** GENEROUS **:** generoso **3** ABUNDANT **:** abundante **4 liberal arts :** humanidades *fpl*, artes *fpl* liberales
liberal[2] *n* **:** liberal *mf*
liberalism [ˈlɪbrəˌlɪzəm, ˈlɪbərə-] *n* **:** liberalismo *m*
liberality [ˌlɪbəˈrælət̬i] *n, pl* **-ties :** liberalidad *f*, generosidad *f*
liberalize [ˈlɪbrəˌlaɪz, ˈlɪbərə-] *vt* **-ized; -izing :** liberalizar
liberally [ˈlɪbrəli, ˈlɪbərə-] *adv* **1** GENEROUSLY **:** generosamente **2** ABUNDANTLY **:** abundantemente **3** FREELY **:** libremente
liberate [ˈlɪbəˌreɪt] *vt* **-ated; -ating :** liberar, libertar
liberation [ˌlɪbəˈreɪʃən] *n* **:** liberación *f*
liberator [ˈlɪbəˌreɪt̬ər] *n* **:** libertador *m*, -dora *f*
Liberian [laɪˈbɪriən] *n* **:** liberiano *m*, -na *f* — **Liberian** *adj*
libertine [ˈlɪbərˌtiːn] *n* **:** libertino *m*, -na *f*
liberty [ˈlɪbərt̬i] *n, pl* **-ties 1 :** libertad *f* **2 to take the liberty of :** tomarse la libertad de **3 to take liberties with :** tomarse confianzas con, tomarse libertades con
libido [ləˈbiːdoː, -ˈbaɪ-] *n, pl* **-dos :** libido *f* — **libidinous** [ləˈbɪdənəs] *adj*
Libra [ˈliːbrə] *n* **:** Libra *mf*
librarian [laɪˈbrɛriən] *n* **:** bibliotecario *m*, -ria *f*
library [ˈlaɪˌbrɛri] *n, pl* **-braries :** biblioteca *f*
librettist [lɪˈbrɛt̬ɪst] *n* **:** libretista *mf*
libretto [lɪˈbrɛt̬o] *n, pl* **-tos** *or* **-ti** [-tiː] **:** libreto *m*
Libyan [ˈlɪbiən] *n* **:** libio *m*, -bia *f* — **Libyan** *adj*
lice → **louse**
license[1] [ˈlaɪsənts] *vt* **licensed; licensing :** licenciar, autorizar, dar permiso a
license[2] *or* **licence** *n* **1** PERMISSION **:** licencia *f*, permiso *m* **2** PERMIT **:** licencia *f*, carnet *m Spain* <driver's license : licencia de conducir> **3** FREEDOM **:** libertad *f* **4** LICENTIOUSNESS **:** libertinaje *m*
licentious [laɪˈsɛntʃəs] *adj* **:** licencioso, disoluto — **licentiously** *adv*
licentiousness [laɪˈsɛntʃəsnəs] *n* **:** libertinaje *m*
lichen [ˈlaɪkən] *n* **:** liquen *m*
licit [ˈlɪsət] *adj* **:** lícito
lick[1] [ˈlɪk] *vt* **1 :** lamer **2** BEAT **:** darle una paliza (a alguien)

lick[2] *n* **:** lamida *f,* lengüetada *f* <a lick of paint **:** una mano de pintura> **2** BIT **:** pizca *f,* ápice *m* **3 a lick and a promise :** una lavada a la carrera

licorice [ˈlɪkərɪʃ, -rəs] *n* **:** regaliz *m,* dulce *m* de regaliz

lid [ˈlɪd] *n* **1** COVER **:** tapa *f* **2** EYELID **:** párpado *m*

lie[1] [ˈlaɪ] *vi* **lay** [ˈleɪ]; **lain** [ˈleɪn]; **lying** [ˈlaɪɪŋ] **1 :** acostarse, echarse <I lay down **:** me acosté> **2 :** estar, estar situado, encontrarse <the book lay on the table **:** el libro estaba en la mesa> <the city lies to the south **:** la ciudad se encuentra al sur> **3** CONSIST **:** consistir **4 to lie in :** residir en <the power lies in the people **:** el poder reside en el pueblo>

lie[2] *vi* **lied; lying** [ˈlaɪɪŋ] **:** mentir

lie[3] *n* **1** UNTRUTH **:** mentira *f* <to tell lies **:** decir mentiras> **2** POSITION **:** posición *f*

liege [ˈliːdʒ] *n* **:** señor *m* feudal

lien [ˈliːn, ˈliːən] *n* **:** derecho *m* de retención

lieutenant [luːˈtɛnənt] *n* **:** teniente *mf*

lieutenant colonel *n* **:** teniente *mf* coronel

lieutenant commander *n* **:** capitán *m,* -tana *f* de corbeta

lieutenant general *n* **:** teniente *mf* general

life [ˈlaɪf] *n, pl* **lives** [ˈlaɪvz] **1 :** vida *f* <plant life **:** la vida vegetal> **2** EXISTENCE **:** vida *f,* existencia *f* **3** BIOGRAPHY **:** biografía *f,* vida *f* **4** DURATION **:** duración *f,* vida *f* **5** LIVELINESS **:** vivacidad *f,* animación *f*

lifeblood [ˈlaɪfˌblʌd] *n* **:** parte *f* vital, sustento *m*

lifeboat [ˈlaɪfˌboːt] *n* **:** bote *m* salvavidas

lifeguard [ˈlaɪfˌgɑrd] *n* **:** socorrista *mf,* salvavidas *mf*

lifeless [ˈlaɪfləs] *adj* **:** sin vida, muerto

lifelike [ˈlaɪfˌlaɪk] *adj* **:** que parece vivo, natural, verosímil

lifelong [ˈlaɪfˈlɔŋ] *adj* **:** de toda la vida <a lifelong friend **:** un amigo de toda la vida>

life preserver *n* **:** salvavidas *m*

lifesaver [ˈlaɪfˌseɪvər] *n* **1 :** salvación *f* **2** → **lifeguard**

lifesaving [ˈlaɪfˌseɪvɪŋ] *n* **:** socorrismo *m*

lifestyle [ˈlaɪfˌstaɪl] *n* **:** estilo *m* de vida

lifetime [ˈlaɪfˌtaɪm] *n* **:** vida *f,* curso *m* de la vida

lift[1] [ˈlɪft] *vt* **1** RAISE **:** levantar, alzar, subir **2** END **:** levantar <to lift a ban **:** levantar una prohibición> — *vi* **1** RISE **:** levantarse, alzarse **2** CLEAR UP **:** despejar <the fog lifted **:** se disipó la niebla>

lift[2] *n* **1** LIFTING **:** levantamiento *m,* alzamiento *m* **2** BOOST **:** impulso *m,* estímulo *m* **3 to give someone a lift :** llevar en coche a alguien

liftoff [ˈlɪftˌɔf] *n* **:** despegue *m*

ligament [ˈlɪgəmənt] *n* **:** ligamento *m*

ligature [ˈlɪgəˌtʃʊr, -tʃər] *n* **:** ligadura *f*

light[1] [ˈlaɪt] *v* **lit** [ˈlɪt] *or* **lighted; lighting** *vt* **1** ILLUMINATE **:** iluminar, alumbrar **2** IGNITE **:** encender, prenderle fuego a — *vi* **:** encenderse, prender

light[2] *vi* **lighted** *or* **lit** [ˈlɪt]; **lighting 1** LAND, SETTLE **:** posarse **2** DISMOUNT **:** bajarse, apearse

light[3] [ˈlaɪt] *adv* **1** LIGHTLY **:** suavemente, ligeramente **2 to travel light :** viajar con poco equipaje

light[4] *adj* **1** LIGHTWEIGHT **:** ligero, liviano, poco pesado **2** EASY **:** fácil, ligero, liviano <light reading **:** lectura fácil> <light work **:** trabajo liviano> **3** GENTLE, MILD **:** fino, suave, leve <a light breeze **:** una brisa suave> <a light rain **:** una lluvia fina> **4** FRIVOLOUS **:** de poca importancia, superficial **5** BRIGHT **:** bien iluminado, claro **6** PALE **:** claro (dícese de los colores), rubio (dícese del pelo)

light[5] *n* **1** ILLUMINATION **:** luz *f* **2** DAYLIGHT **:** luz *f* del día **3** DAWN **:** amanecer *m,* madrugada *f* **4** LAMP **:** lámpara *f* <to turn on off the light **:** apagar la luz> **5** ASPECT **:** aspecto *m* <in a new light **:** con otros ojos> <in the light of **:** en vista de, a la luz de> **6** MATCH **:** fósforo *m,* cerillo *m* **7 to bring to light :** sacar a (la) luz

lightbulb [ˈlaɪtˌbʌlb] *n* **:** bombilla *f,* foco *m,* bombillo *m CA, Col, Ven*

lighten [ˈlaɪtən] *vt* **1** ILLUMINATE **:** iluminar, dar más luz a **2 :** aclararse (el pelo) **3 :** aligerar (una carga, etc.) **4** RELIEVE **:** aliviar **5** GLADDEN **:** alegrar <it lightened his heart **:** alegró su corazón>

lighter [ˈlaɪtər] *n* **:** encendedor *m*

lighthearted [ˈlaɪtˈhɑrtəd] *adj* **:** alegre, despreocupado, desenfadado — **lightheartedly** *adv*

lightheartedness [ˈlaɪtˈhɑrtədnəs] *n* **:** desenfado *m,* alegría *f*

lighthouse [ˈlaɪtˌhaʊs] *n* **:** faro *m*

lighting [ˈlaɪtɪŋ] *n* **:** iluminación *f*

lightly [ˈlaɪtli] *adv* **1** GENTLY **:** suavemente **2** SLIGHTLY **:** ligeramente **3** FRIVOLOUSLY **:** a la ligera **4 to let off lightly :** tratar con indulgencia

lightness [ˈlaɪtnəs] *n* **1** BRIGHTNESS **:** luminosidad *f,* claridad *f* **2** GENTLENESS **:** ligereza *f,* suavidad *f,* delicadeza *f* **3 :** ligereza *f,* liviandad *f* (de peso)

lightning [ˈlaɪtnɪŋ] *n* **:** relámpago *m,* rayo *m*

lightning bug → **firefly**

lightproof [ˈlaɪtˌpruːf] *adj* **:** impenetrable por la luz, opaco

lightweight [ˈlaɪtˈweɪt] *adj* **:** ligero, liviano, de poco peso

light–year [ˈlaɪtˌjɪr] *n* **:** año *m* luz

lignite [ˈlɪgˌnaɪt] *n* **:** lignito *m*

likable *or* **likeable** [ˈlaɪkəbəl] *adj* **:** simpático, agradable

like[1] [ˈlaɪk] *v* **liked; liking** *vt* **1 :** agradar, gustarle (algo a uno) <he likes rice : le gusta el arroz> <she doesn't like flowers : a ella no le gustan las flores> <I like you : me caes bien> **2** WANT **:** querer, desear <I'd like a hamburger : quiero una hamburguesa> <he would like more help : le gustaría tener más ayuda> — *vi* **:** querer <do as you like : haz lo que quieras>

like[2] *adj* **:** parecido, semejante, similar

like[3] *n* **1** PREFERENCE **:** preferencia *f,* gusto *m* **2 the like :** cosa *f* parecida, cosas *fpl* por el estilo <I've never seen the like : nunca he visto cosa parecida>

like[4] *conj* **1** AS IF **:** como si <they looked at me like I was crazy : se me quedaron mirando como si estuviera loca> **2** AS **:** como, igual que <she doesn't love you like I do : ella no te quiere como yo>

like[5] *prep* **1 :** como, parecido a <she acts like my mother : se comporta como mi madre> <he looks like me : se parece a mí> **2 :** propio de, típico de <that's just like her : eso es muy típico de ella> **3 :** como <animals like cows : animales como vacas> **4 like this, like that :** así <do it like that : hazlo así>

likelihood [ˈlaɪkliˌhʊd] *n* **:** probabilidad *f* <in all likelihood : con toda probabilidad>

likely[1] [ˈlaɪkli] *adv* **:** probablemente <most likely he's sick : lo más probable es que esté enfermo> <they're likely to come : es probable que vengan>

likely[2] *adj* **-lier; -est 1** PROBABLE **:** probable <to be likely to : ser muy probable que> **2** SUITABLE **:** apropiado, adecuado **3** BELIEVABLE **:** verosímil, creíble **4** PROMISING **:** prometedor

liken [ˈlaɪkən] *vt* **:** comparar

likeness [ˈlaɪknəs] *n* **1** SIMILARITY **:** semejanza *f,* parecido *m* **2** PORTRAIT **:** retrato *m*

likewise [ˈlaɪkˌwaɪz] *adv* **1** SIMILARLY **:** de la misma manera, asimismo **2** ALSO **:** también, además, asimismo

liking [ˈlaɪkɪŋ] *n* **1** FONDNESS **:** afición *f* (por una cosa), simpatía *f* (por una persona) **2** TASTE **:** gusto *m* <is it to your liking? : ¿te gusta?>

lilac [ˈlaɪlək, -ˌlæk, -ˌlɑk] *n* **:** lila *f*

lilt [ˈlɪlt] *n* **:** cadencia *f,* ritmo *m* alegre

lily [ˈlɪli] *n, pl* **lilies 1 :** lirio *m,* azucena *f* **2 lily of the valley :** lirio *m* de los valles, muguete *m*

lima bean [ˈlaɪmə] *n* **:** frijol *m* de media luna

limb [ˈlɪm] *n* **1** APPENDAGE **:** miembro *m,* extremidad *f* **2** BRANCH **:** rama *f*

limber[1] [ˈlɪmbər] *vi or* **to limber up :** calentarse, prepararse

limber[2] *adj* **:** ágil (dícese de las personas), flexible (dícese de los objetos)

limbo [ˈlɪmˌboː] *n, pl* **-bos 1 :** limbo *m* (en la religión) **2** OBLIVION **:** olvido *m* <the project is in limbo : el proyecto ha caído en el olvido>

lime [ˈlaɪm] *n* **1 :** cal *f* (óxido) **2 :** lima *f* (fruta), limón *m* verde *Mex*

limelight [ˈlaɪmˌlaɪt] *n* **to be in the limelight :** ser el centro de atención, estar en el candelero

limerick [ˈlɪmərɪk] *n* **:** poema *m* jocoso de cinco versos

limestone [ˈlaɪmˌstoːn] *n* **:** piedra *f* caliza, caliza *f*

limit[1] [ˈlɪmət] *vt* **:** limitar, restringir

limit[2] *n* **1** MAXIMUM **:** límite *m,* máximo *m* <speed limit : límite de velocidad> **2 limits** *npl* **:** límites *mpl,* confines *mpl* <city limits : límites de la ciudad> **3 that's the limit! :** ¡eso es el colmo!

limitation [ˌlɪməˈteɪʃən] *n* **:** limitación *f,* restricción *f*

limited [ˈlɪmət̬əd] *adj* **:** limitado, restringido

limitless [ˈlɪmətləs] *adj* **:** ilimitado, sin límites

limousine [ˈlɪməˌziːn, ˌlɪməˈ-] *n* **:** limusina *f*

limp[1] [ˈlɪmp] *vi* **:** cojear

limp[2] *adj* **1** FLACCID **:** fláccido **2** LANK **:** lacio (dícese del pelo) **3** WEAK **:** débil <to feel limp : sentirse desfallecer, sentirse sin fuerzas>

limp[3] *n* **:** cojera *f*

limpid [ˈlɪmpəd] *adj* **:** límpido, claro

limply [ˈlɪmpli] *adv* **:** sin fuerzas

limpness [ˈlɪmpnəs] *n* **:** flaccidez *f,* debilidad *f*

linden [ˈlɪndən] *n* **:** tilo *m*

line[1] [ˈlaɪn] *v* **lined; lining** *vt* **1 :** forrar, cubrir <to line a dress : forrar un vestido> <to line the walls : cubrir las paredes> **2** MARK **:** rayar, trazar líneas en **3** BORDER **:** bordear **4** ALIGN **:** alinear — *vi* **to line up :** ponerse in fila, hacer cola

line[2] *n* **1** CORD, ROPE **:** cuerda *f* **2** WIRE **:** cable *m* <power line : cable eléctrico> **3 :** línea *f* (de teléfono) **4** ROW **:** fila *f,* hilera *f* **5** NOTE **:** nota *f,* líneas *fpl* <drop me a line : mándame unas líneas> **6** COURSE **:** línea *f* <line of inquiry : línea de investigación> **7** AGREEMENT **:** conformidad *f* <to be in line with : ser conforme a> <to fall into line : estar de acuerdo> **8** OCCUPATION **:** ocupación *f,* rama *f,* especialidad *f* **9** LIMIT **:** línea *f,* límite *m* <dividing line : línea divisoria> <to draw the line : fijar límites> **10** SERVICE **:** línea *f* <bus line : línea de autobuses> **11** MARK **:** línea *f,* arruga *f* (de la cara)

lineage [ˈlɪniɪdʒ] *n* **:** linaje *m,* abolengo *m*

lineal [ˈlɪniəl] *adj* **:** en línea directa

lineaments [ˈlɪniəmənts] *npl* **:** facciones *fpl* (de la cara), rasgos *mpl*

linear [ˈlɪniər] *adj* **:** lineal

linen [ˈlɪnən] *n* **:** lino *m*

liner [ˈlaɪnər] *n* **1** LINING **:** forro *m* **2** SHIP **:** buque *m,* transatlántico *m*

lineup [ˈlaɪn,əp] *n* **1 :** fila *f* de sospechosos **2 :** formación *f* (en deportes) **3** ALIGNMENT **:** alineación *f*

linger [ˈlɪŋgər] *vi* **1** TARRY **:** quedarse, entretenerse, rezagarse **2** PERSIST **:** persistir, sobrevivir

lingerie [,lɑndʒəˈreɪ, ,læʒəˈriː] *n* **:** ropa *f* íntima femenina, lencería *f*

lingo [ˈlɪŋgo] *n, pl* **-goes 1** LANGUAGE **:** idioma *m* **2** JARGON **:** jerga *f*

linguist [ˈlɪŋgwɪst] *n* **:** lingüista *mf*

linguistic [lɪŋˈgwɪstɪk] *adj* **:** lingüístico

linguistics [lɪŋˈgwɪstɪks] *n* **:** lingüística *f*

liniment [ˈlɪnəmənt] *n* **:** linimento *m*

lining [ˈlaɪnɪŋ] *n* **:** forro *m*

link[1] [ˈlɪŋk] *vt* **:** unir, enlazar, conectar — *vi* **to link up :** unirse, conectar

link[2] *n* **1 :** eslabón *m* (de una cadena) **2** BOND **:** conexión *f,* lazo *m,* vínculo *m*

linkage [ˈlɪŋkɪdʒ] *n* **:** conexión *f,* unión *f,* enlace *m*

linoleum [ləˈnoːliəm] *n* **:** linóleo *m*

linseed oil [ˈlɪn,siːd] *n* **:** aceite *m* de linaza

lint [ˈlɪnt] *n* **:** pelusa *f*

lintel [ˈlɪntəl] *n* **:** dintel *m*

lion [ˈlaɪən] *n* **:** león *m*

lioness [ˈlaɪənɪs] *n* **:** leona *f*

lionize [ˈlaɪə,naɪz] *vt* **-ized; -izing :** tratar a una persona como muy importante

lip [ˈlɪp] *n* **1 :** labio *m* **2** EDGE, RIM **:** pico *m* (de una jarra), borde *m* (de una taza)

lipreading [ˈlɪp,riːdɪŋ] *n* **:** lectura *f* de los labios

lipstick [ˈlɪp,stɪk] *n* **:** lápiz *m* de labios, barra *f* de labios

liquefy [ˈlɪkwə,faɪ] *v* **-fied; -fying** *vt* **:** licuar — *vi* **:** licuarse

liqueur [lɪˈkʊr, -ˈkər, -ˈkjʊr] *n* **:** licor *m*

liquid[1] [ˈlɪkwəd] *adj* **:** líquido

liquid[2] *n* **:** líquido *m*

liquidate [ˈlɪkwə,deɪt] *vt* **-dated; -dating :** liquidar

liquidation [,lɪkwəˈdeɪʃən] *n* **:** liquidación *f*

liquidity [lɪkˈwɪdəṭi] *n* **:** liquidez *f*

liquor [ˈlɪkər] *n* **:** alcohol *m,* bebidas *fpl* alcohólicas, licor *m*

lisp[1] [ˈlɪsp] *vi* **:** cecear

lisp[2] *n* **:** ceceo *m*

lissome [ˈlɪsəm] *adj* **1** FLEXIBLE **:** flexible **2** LITHE **:** ágil y grácil

list[1] [ˈlɪst] *vt* **1** ENUMERATE **:** hacer una lista de, enumerar **2** INCLUDE **:** poner en una lista, incluir — *vi* **:** escorar (dícese de un barco)

list[2] *n* **1** ENUMERATION **:** lista *f* **2** SLANT **:** escora *f,* inclinación *f*

listen [ˈlɪsən] *vi* **1 :** escuchar, oír **2 to listen to** HEED **:** prestar atención a, hacer caso de, escuchar **3 to listen to reason :** atender a razones

listener [ˈlɪsənər] *n* **:** oyente *mf,* persona *f* que sabe escuchar

listless [ˈlɪstləs] *adj* **:** lánguido, apático — **listlessly** *adv*

listlessness [ˈlɪstləsnəs] *n* **:** apatía *f,* languidez *f,* desgana *f*

lit [ˈlɪt] *pp* → **light**

litany [ˈlɪtəni] *n, pl* **-nies :** letanía *f*

liter [ˈliːṭər] *n* **:** litro *m*

literacy [ˈlɪṭərəsi] *n* **:** alfabetismo *m*

literal [ˈlɪṭərəl] *adj* **:** literal — **literally** *adv*

literary [ˈlɪṭə,rɛri] *adj* **:** literario

literate [ˈlɪṭərət] *adj* **:** alfabetizado

literature [ˈlɪṭərə,tʃʊr, -tʃər] *n* **:** literatura *f*

lithe [ˈlaɪð, ˈlaɪθ] *adj* **:** ágil y grácil

lithesome [ˈlaɪðsəm, ˈlaɪθ-] → **lissome**

lithograph [ˈlɪθə,græf] *n* **:** litografía *f*

lithographer [lɪˈθɑgrəfər, ˈlɪθə,græfər] *n* **:** litógrafo *m,* -fa *f*

lithography [lɪˈθɑgrəfi] *n* **:** litografía *f*

litigant [ˈlɪṭɪgənt] *n* **:** litigante *mf*

litigate [ˈlɪṭə,geɪt] *vi* **-gated; -gating :** litigar

litigation [,lɪṭəˈgeɪʃən] *n* **:** litigio *m*

litmus paper [ˈlɪtməs] *n* **:** papel *m* de tornasol

litter[1] [ˈlɪṭər] *vt* **:** tirar basura en, ensuciar — *vi* **:** tirar basura

litter[2] *n* **1 :** camada *f,* cría *f* <a litter of kittens : una cría de gatitos> **2** STRETCHER **:** camilla *f* **3** RUBBISH **:** basura *f* **4 :** arena *f* higiénica (para gatos)

little[1] [ˈlɪṭəl] *adv* **less** [ˈlɛs]; **least** [ˈliːst] **1 :** poco <she sings very little : canta muy poco> **2 little did I know that... :** no tenía la menor idea de que ... **3 as little as possible :** lo menos posible

little[2] *adj* **littler** *or* **less** [ˈlɛs] *or* **lesser** [ˈlɛsər]; **littlest** *or* **least** [ˈliːst] **1** SMALL **:** pequeño **2 :** poco <they speak little Spanish : hablan poco español> <little by little : poco a poco> **3** TRIVIAL **:** sin importancia, trivial

little[3] *n* **1 :** poco *m* <little has changed : poco ha cambiado> **2 a little :** un poco, algo <it's a little surprising : es algo sorprendente>

Little Dipper → **dipper**

liturgical [ləˈtərdʒɪkəl] *adj* **:** litúrgico — **liturgically** [-kli] *adv*

liturgy [ˈlɪṭərdʒi] *n, pl* **-gies :** liturgia *f*

livable [ˈlɪvəbəl] *adj* **:** habitable

live[1] [ˈlɪv] *vi* **lived; living 1** EXIST **:** vivir <as long as I live : mientras viva> <to live from day to day : vivir al día> **2 :** llevar una vida, vivir <he lived simply : llevó una vida sencilla> **3** SUBSIST **:** mantenerse, vivir **4** RESIDE **:** vivir, residir

live[2] [ˈlaɪv] *adj* **1** LIVING **:** vivo **2** BURNING **:** encendido <a live coal : una brasa> **3 :** con corriente <live wires

: cables con corriente> **4** : cargado, sin estallar <a live bomb : una bomba sin estallar> **5** CURRENT : de actualidad <a live issue : un asunto de actualidad> **6** : en vivo, en directo <a live interview : una entrevista en vivo>
livelihood [ˈlaɪvli,hʊd] *n* : sustento *m,* vida *f,* medio *m* de vida
liveliness [ˈlaɪvlinəs] *n* : animación *f,* vivacidad *f*
livelong [ˈlɪvˈlɔŋ] *adj* : entero, completo
lively [ˈlaɪvli] *adj* **-lier; -est** : animado, vivaz, vivo, enérgico
liven [ˈlaɪvən] *vt* : animar — *vi* : animarse
liver [ˈlɪvər] *n* : hígado *m*
livery [ˈlɪvəri] *n, pl* **-eries** : librea *f*
lives → **life**
livestock [ˈlaɪv,stɑk] *n* : ganado *m*
live wire *n* : persona *f* vivaz y muy activa
livid [ˈlɪvəd] *adj* **1** BLACK-AND-BLUE : amoratado **2** PALE : lívido **3** ENRAGED : furioso
living[1] [ˈlɪvɪŋ] *adj* : vivo
living[2] *n* **to make a living** : ganarse la vida
living room *n* : living *m,* sala *f* de estar
lizard [ˈlɪzərd] *n* : lagarto *m*
llama [ˈlɑmə, ˈjɑ-] *n* : llama *f*
load[1] [ˈloːd] *vt* : cargar, embarcar
load[2] *n* **1** CARGO : carga *f* **2** WEIGHT : peso *m* **3** BURDEN : carga *f,* peso *m* **4** **loads** *npl* : montón *m,* pila *f,* cantidad *f* <loads of work : un montón de trabajo>
loaf[1] [ˈloːf] *vi* : holgazanear, flojear, haraganear
loaf[2] *n, pl* **loaves** [ˈloːvz] **1** : pan *m,* pan *m* de molde, barra *f* de pan **2** **meat loaf** : pan *m* de carne
loafer [ˈloːfər] *n* : holgazán *m,* -zana *f;* haragán *m,* -gana *f;* vago *m,* -ga *f*
loam [ˈloːm] *n* : marga *f,* suelo *m*
loan[1] [ˈloːn] *vt* : prestar
loan[2] *n* : préstamo *m,* empréstito *m* (del banco)
loath [ˈloːθ, ˈloːð] *adj* : poco dispuesto <I am loath to say it : me resisto a decirlo>
loathe [ˈloːð] *vt* **loathed; loathing** : odiar, aborrecer
loathing [ˈloːðɪŋ] *n* : aversión *f,* odio *m,* aborrecimiento *m*
loathsome [ˈloːθsəm, ˈloːð-] *adj* : odioso, repugnante
lob[1] [ˈlɑb] *vt* **lobbed; lobbing** : hacerle un globo (a otro jugador)
lob[2] *n* : globo *m* (en deportes)
lobby[1] [ˈlɑbi] *v* **-bied; -bying** *vt* : presionar, ejercer presión sobre — *vi* **to lobby for** : presionar para (lograr algo)
lobby[2] *n, pl* **-bies** **1** FOYER : vestíbulo *m* **2** LOBBYISTS : grupo *m* de presión, lobby *m*
lobbyist [ˈlɑbiɪst] *n* : miembro *m* de un lobby
lobe [ˈloːb] *n* : lóbulo *m*
lobed [ˈloːbd] *adj* : lobulado
lobotomy [ləˈbɑt̬əmi, lo-] *n, pl* **-mies** : lobotomía *f*
lobster [ˈlɑbstər] *n* : langosta *f*
local[1] [ˈloːkəl] *adj* : local
local[2] *n* **1** : anestesia *f* local **2** **the locals** : los vecinos del lugar, los habitantes
locale [loˈkæl] *n* : lugar *m,* escenario *m*
locality [loˈkæləṭi] *n, pl* **-ties** : localidad *f*
localize [ˈloːkə,laɪz] *vt* **-ized; -izing** : localizar
locally [ˈloːkəli] *adv* : en la localidad, en la zona
locate [ˈloː,keɪt, loˈkeɪt] *v* **-cated; -cating** *vt* **1** POSITION : situar, ubicar **2** FIND : localizar, ubicar — *vi* SETTLE : establecerse
location [loˈkeɪʃən] *n* **1** POSITION : posición *f,* emplazamiento *m,* ubicación *f* **2** PLACE : lugar *m,* sitio *m*
lock[1] [ˈlɑk] *vt* **1** FASTEN : cerrar **2** CONFINE : encerrar <they locked me in the room : me encerraron en la sala> **3** IMMOBILIZE : bloquear (una rueda) — *vi* **1** : cerrarse (dícese de una puerta) **2** : trabarse, bloquearse (dícese de una rueda)
lock[2] *n* **1** : mechón *m* (de pelo) **2** FASTENER : cerradura *f,* cerrojo *m,* chapa *f* **3** : esclusa *f* (de un canal)
locker [ˈlɑkər] *n* : armario *m,* cajón *m* con llave, lócker *m*
locket [ˈlɑkət] *n* : medallón *m,* guardapelo *m,* relicario *m*
lockjaw [ˈlɑk,jɔ] *n* : tétano *m*
lockout [ˈlɑk,aʊt] *n* : cierre *m* patronal, lockout *m*
locksmith [ˈlɑk,smɪθ] *n* : cerrajero *m,* -ra *f*
lockup [ˈlɑk,ʌp] *n* JAIL : cárcel *f*
locomotion [,loːkəˈmoːʃən] *n* : locomoción *f*
locomotive[1] [,loːkəˈmoːṭɪv] *adj* : locomotor
locomotive[2] *n* : locomotora *f*
locust [ˈloːkəst] *n* **1** : langosta *f,* chapulín *m* *CA, Mex* **2** CICADA : cigarra *f,* chicharra *f* **3** : acacia *f* blanca (árbol)
locution [loˈkjuːʃən] *n* : locución *f*
lode [ˈloːd] *n* : veta *f,* vena *f,* filón *m*
lodestar [ˈloːd,stɑr] *n* : estrella *f* polar
lodestone [ˈloːd,stoːn] *n* : piedra *f* imán
lodge[1] [ˈlɑdʒ] *v* **lodged; lodging** *vt* **1** HOUSE : hospedar, alojar **2** FILE : presentar <to lodge a complaint : presentar una demanda> — *vi* **1** : posarse, meterse <the bullet lodged in the door : la bala se incrustó en la puerta> **2** STAY : hospedarse, alojarse
lodge[2] *n* **1** : pabellón *m,* casa *f* de campo <hunting lodge : refugio de caza> **2** : madriguera *f* (de un castor) **3** : logia *f* <Masonic lodge : logia masónica>

lodger [ˈlɑdʒər] *n* : inquilino *m,* -na *f;* huésped *m,* -peda *f*
lodging [ˈlɑdʒɪŋ] *n* **1** : alojamiento *m* **2 lodgings** *npl* ROOMS : habitaciones *fpl*
loft [ˈlɔft] *n* **1** ATTIC : desván *m,* ático *m,* buhardilla *f* **2** : loft *m* (en un depósito comercial) **3** HAYLOFT : pajar *m* **4** : galería *f* <choir loft : galería del coro>
loftily [ˈlɔftəli] *adv* : altaneramente, con altivez
loftiness [ˈlɔftinəs] *n* **1** NOBILITY : nobleza *f* **2** ARROGANCE : altanería *f,* arrogancia *f* **3** HEIGHT : altura *f,* elevación *f*
lofty [ˈlɔfti] *adj* **loftier; -est 1** NOBLE : noble, elevado **2** HAUGHTY : altivo, arrogante, altanero **3** HIGH : majestuoso, elevado
log[1] [ˈlɔg, ˈlɑg] *vi* **logged; logging 1** : talar (árboles) **2** RECORD : registrar, anotar **3 to log on** : entrar (al sistema) **4 to log off** : salir (del sistema)
log[2] *n* **1** : tronco *m,* leño *m* **2** RECORD : diario *m*
logarithm [ˈlɔgəˌrɪðəm, ˈlɑ-] *n* : logaritmo *m*
logger [ˈlɔgər, ˈlɑ-] *n* : leñador *m,* -dora *f*
loggerhead [ˈlɔgərˌhɛd, ˈlɑ-] *n* **1** : tortuga *f* boba **2 to be at loggerheads** : estar en pugna, estar en desacuerdo
logic [ˈlɑdʒɪk] *n* : lógica *f* — **logical** [ˈlɑdʒɪkəl] *adj* — **logically** [-kli] *adv*
logistic [ləˈdʒɪstɪk, lo-] *adj* : logístico
logistics [ləˈdʒɪstɪks, lo-] *ns & pl* : logística *f*
logo [ˈloːˌgoː] *n, pl* **logos** [-ˌgoːz] : logotipo *m*
loin [ˈlɔɪn] *n* **1** : lomo *m* <pork loin : lomo de cerdo> **2 loins** *npl* : lomos *mpl* <to gird one's loins : prepararse para la lucha>
loiter [ˈlɔɪt̬ər] *vi* : vagar, perder el tiempo
loll [ˈlɑl] *vi* **1** SLOUCH : repantigarse **2** IDLE : holgazanear, hacer el vago
lollipop *or* **lollypop** [ˈlɑliˌpɑp] *n* : dulce *m* en palito, chupete *m Chile, Peru,* paleta *f CA, Mex*
lone [ˈloːn] *adj* **1** SOLITARY : solitario **2** ONLY : único
loneliness [ˈloːnlinəs] *n* : soledad *f*
lonely [ˈloːnli] *adj* **-lier; -est 1** SOLITARY : solitario, aislado **2** LONESOME : solo <to feel lonely : sentirse muy solo>
loner [ˈloːnər] *n* : solitario *m,* -ria *f;* recluso *m,* -sa *f*
lonesome [ˈloːnsəm] *adj* : solo, solitario
long[1] [ˈlɔŋ] *vi* **1 to long for** : añorar, desear, anhelar **2 to long to** : anhelar, estar deseando <they longed to see her : estaban deseando verla, tenían muchas ganas de verla>
long[2] *adv* **1** : mucho, mucho tiempo <it didn't take long : no llevó mucho tiempo> <will it last long? : ¿va a durar mucho?> **2 all day long** : todo el día **3 as long as** *or* **so long as** : mientras, con tal que **4 long before** : mucho antes **5 so long!** : ¡hasta luego!, ¡adiós!
long[3] *adj* **longer** [ˈlɔngər]; **longest** [ˈlɔŋgəst] **1** (*indicating length*) : largo <the dress is too long : el vestido es demasiado largo> <a long way from : bastante lejos de> <in the long run : a la larga> **2** (*indicating time*) : largo, prolongado <a long illness : una enfermedad prolongada> <a long walk : un paseo largo> <at long last : por fin> **3 to be long on** : estar cargado de
long[4] *n* **1 before long** : dentro de poco **2 the long and the short** : lo esencial, lo fundamental
longevity [lɑnˈdʒɛvət̬i] *n* : longevidad *f*
longhand [ˈlɔŋˌhænd] *n* : escritura *f* a mano, escritura *f* cursiva
longhorn [ˈlɔŋˌhɔrn] *n* : longhorn *mf*
longing [lɔŋɪŋ] *n* : vivo deseo *m,* ansia *f,* anhelo *m*
longingly [lɔŋɪŋlli] *adv* : ansiosamente, con ansia
longitude [ˈlɑndʒəˌtuːd, -ˌtjuːd] *n* : longitud *f*
longitudinal [ˌlɑndʒəˈtuːdənəl, -ˈtjuː-] *adj* : longitudinal — **longitudinally** *adv*
longshoreman [ˈlɔŋˈʃormən] *n, pl* **-men** [-mən, -ˌmɛn] : estibador *m,* -dora *f*
long–suffering [ˈlɔŋˈsʌfərɪŋ] *adj* : paciente, sufrido
look[1] [ˈlʊk] *vi* **1** GLANCE : mirar <to look out the window : mirar por la ventana> **2** INVESTIGATE : buscar, mirar <look in the closet : busca en el closet> <look before you leap : mira lo que haces> **3** SEEM : parecer <he looks happy : parece estar contento> <I look like my mother : me parezco a mi madre> **4 to look after** : cuidar, cuidar de **5 to look for** EXPECT : esperar **6 to look for** SEEK : buscar — *vt* : mirar
look[2] *n* **1** GLANCE : mirada *f* **2** EXPRESSION : cara *f* <a look of disapproval : una cara de desaprobación> **3** ASPECT : aspecto *m,* apariencia *f,* aire *m*
lookout [ˈlʊkˌaʊt] *n* **1** : centinela *mf,* vigía *mf* **2 to be on the lookout for** : estar al acecho de, andar a la caza de
loom[1] [ˈluːm] *vi* **1** : aparecer, surgir <the city loomed up in the distance : la ciudad surgió en la distancia> **2** IMPEND : amenazar, ser inminente **3 to loom large** : cobrar mucha importancia
loom[2] *n* : telar *m*
loon [ˈluːn] *n* : somorgujo *m,* somormujo *m*
loony *or* **looney** [ˈluːni] *adj* **-nier; -est** : loco, chiflado *fam*

loop[1] [ˈluːp] *vt* **1 :** hacer lazadas con **2 to loop around :** pasar alrededor de — *vi* **1 :** rizar el rizo (dícese de un avión) **2 :** serpentear (dícese de una carretera)

loop[2] *n* **1 :** lazada *f* (en hilo o cuerda) **2** BEND **:** curva *f* **3** CIRCUIT **:** circuito *m* cerrado **4 :** rizo *m* (en la aviación) <to loop the loop : rizar el rizo>

loophole [ˈluːpˌhoːl] *n* **:** escapatoria *f,* pretexto *m*

loose[1] [ˈluːs] *vt* **loosed; loosing 1** RELEASE **:** poner en libertad, soltar **2** UNTIE **:** deshacer, desatar **3** DISCHARGE, UNLEASH **:** descargar, desatar

loose[2] → **loosely**

loose[3] *adj* **looser; -est 1** INSECURE **:** flojo, suelto, poco seguro <a loose tooth : un diente flojo> **2** ROOMY **:** suelto, holgado <loose clothing : ropa holgada> **3** OPEN **:** suelto, abierto <loose soil : suelo suelto> <a loose weave : una tejida abierta> **4** FREE **:** suelto <to break loose : soltarse> **5** SLACK **:** flojo, flexible **6** APPROXIMATE **:** libre, aproximado <a loose translation : una traducción aproximada>

loosely [ˈluːsli] *adv* **1 :** sin apretar **2** ROUGHLY **:** aproximadamente, más o menos

loosen [ˈluːsən] *vt* **:** aflojar

loose–leaf [ˈluːsˈliːf] *adj* **:** de hojas sueltas

looseness [ˈluːsnəs] *n* **1 :** aflojamiento *m,* holgura *f* (de ropa) **2** IMPRECISION **:** imprecisión *f*

loot[1] [ˈluːt] *vt* **:** saquear, robar

loot[2] *n* **:** botín *m*

looter [ˈluːt̬ər] *n* **:** saqueador *m,* -dora *f*

lop [ˈlɑp] *vt* **lopped; lopping :** cortar, podar

lope[1] [ˈloːp] *vi* **loped; loping :** correr a paso largo

lope[2] *n* **:** paso *m* largo

lopsided [ˈlɑpˌsaɪdəd] *adj* **1** CROOKED **:** torcido, chueco, ladeado **2** ASYMETRICAL **:** asimétrico

loquacious [loˈkweɪʃəs] *adj* **:** locuaz

lord [ˈlɔrd] *n* **1 :** señor *m,* noble *m* **2 :** lord *m* (en la Gran Bretaña) **3 the Lord :** el Señor **4 good Lord! :** ¡Dios mío!

lordly [ˈlɔrdli] *adj* **-lier; -est** HAUGHTY **:** arrogante, altanero

lordship [ˈlɔrdˌʃɪp] *n* **:** señoría *f*

Lord's Supper *n* **:** Eucaristía *f*

lore [ˈlor] *n* **:** saber *m* popular, tradición *f*

lose [ˈluːz] *v* **lost** [ˈlɔst]; **losing** [ˈluːzɪŋ] *vt* **1 :** perder <I lost my umbrella : perdí mi paraguas> <to lose blood : perder sangre> <to lose one's voice : quedarse afónico> <to have nothing to lose : no tener nada que perder> <to lose no time : no perder tiempo> <to lose weight : perder peso, adelgazar> <to lose one's temper : perder los estribos, enojarse, enfadarse> <to lose sight of : perder de vista> **2 :** costar, hacer perder <the errors lost him his job : los errores le costaron su empleo> **3 :** atrasar <my watch loses 5 minutes a day : mi reloj atrasa 5 minutos por día> **4 to lose oneself :** perderse, ensimismarse — *vi* **1 :** perder <we lost to the other team : perdimos contra el otro equipo> **2 :** atrasarse <the clock loses time : el reloj se atrasa>

loser [ˈluːzər] *n* **:** perdedor *m,* -dora *f*

loss [ˈlɔs] *n* **1** LOSING **:** pérdida *f* <loss of memory : pérdida de memoria> <to sell at a loss : vender con pérdida> <to be at a loss to : no saber como> **2** DEFEAT **:** derrota *f,* juego *m* perdido **3 losses** *npl* DEATHS **:** muertos *mpl*

lost [ˈlɔst] *adj* **1 :** perdido <a lost cause : una causa perdida> <lost in thought : absorto> **2 to get lost :** perderse **3 to make up for lost time :** recuperar el tiempo perdido

lot [ˈlɑt] *n* **1** DRAWING **:** sorteo *m* <by lot : por sorteo> **2** SHARE **:** parte *f,* porción *f* **3** FATE **:** suerte *f* **4** LAND, PLOT **:** terreno *m,* solar *m,* lote *m,* parcela *f* **5 a lot of** *or* **lots of :** mucho, un montón de, bastante <lots of books : un montón de libros, muchos libros> <a lot of people : mucha gente>

loth [ˈloːθ, ˈloːð] → **loath**

lotion [ˈloːʃən] *n* **:** loción *f*

lottery [ˈlɑt̬əri] *n, pl* **-teries :** lotería *f*

lotus [ˈloːt̬əs] *n* **:** loto *m*

loud[1] [ˈlaʊd] *adv* **:** alto, fuerte <out loud : en voz alta>

loud[2] *adj* **1 :** alto, fuerte <a loud voice : una voz alta> **2** NOISY **:** ruidoso <a loud party : una fiesta ruidosa> **3** FLASHY **:** llamativo, chillón

loudly [ˈlaʊdli] *adv* **:** alto, fuerte, en voz alta

loudness [ˈlaʊdnəs] *n* **:** volumen *m,* fuerza *f* (del ruido)

loudspeaker [ˈlaʊdˌspiːkər] *n* **:** altavoz *m,* altoparlante *m*

lounge[1] [ˈlaʊndʒ] *vi* **lounged; lounging :** holgazanear, gandulear

lounge[2] *n* **:** salón *m,* sala *f* de estar

louse [ˈlaʊs] *n, pl* **lice** [ˈlaɪs] **:** piojo *m*

lousy [ˈlaʊzi] *adj* **lousier; -est 1 :** piojoso, lleno de piojos **2** BAD **:** pésimo, muy malo

lout [ˈlaʊt] *n* **:** bruto *m,* patán *m*

louver *or* **louvre** [ˈluːvər] *n* **:** persiana *f,* listón *m* de persiana

lovable [ˈlʌvəbəl] *adj* **:** adorable, amoroso, encantador

love[1] [ˈlʌv] *v* **loved; loving** *vt* **1 :** querer, amar <I love you : te quiero> **2** ENJOY **:** encantarle a alguien, ser (muy) aficionado a, gustarle mucho a uno (algo) <she loves flowers : le encantan las flores> <he loves golf : es muy aficionado al golf> <I'd love

to go with you : me gustaría mucho acompañarte> — *vi* : querer, amar
love[2] *n* **1** : amor *m,* cariño *m* <to be in love with : estar enamorado de> <to fall in love with : enamorarse de> **2** ENTHUSIASM, INTEREST : amor *m,* afición *m,* gusto *m* <love of music : afición a la música> **3** BELOVED : amor *m;* amado *m,* -da *f;* enamorado *m,* -da *f*
loveless [ˈlʌvləs] *adj* : sin amor
loveliness [ˈlʌvlinəs] *n* : belleza *f,* hermosura *f*
lovelorn [ˈlʌvˌlɔrn] *adj* : herido de amor, perdidamente enamorado
lovely [ˈlʌvli] *adj* **-lier; -est** : hermoso, bello, lindo, precioso
lover [ˈlʌvər] *n* : amante *mf* (de personas); aficionado *m,* -da *f* (a alguna actividad)
loving [ˈlʌvɪŋ] *adj* : amoroso, cariñoso
lovingly [ˈlʌvɪŋli] *adv* : cariñosamente
low[1] [ˈloː] *vi* : mugir
low[2] *adv* : bajo, profundo <to aim low : apuntar bajo> <to lie low : mantenerse escondido> <to turn the lights down low : bajar las luces>
low[3] *adj* **lower** [ˈloːər]; **-est 1** : bajo <a low building : un edificio bajo> <a low bow : una profunda reverencia> **2** SOFT : bajo, suave <in a low voice : en voz baja> **3** SHALLOW : bajo, poco profundo **4** HUMBLE : humilde, modesto **5** DEPRESSED : deprimido, bajo de moral **6** INFERIOR : bajo, inferior **7** UNFAVORABLE : mal <to have a low opinion of him : tener un mal concepto de él> **8 to be low on** : tener poco de, estar escaso de
low[4] *n* **1** : punto *m* bajo <to reach an all-time low : estar más bajo que nunca> **2** *or* **low gear** : primera velocidad *f* **3** : mugido *m* (de una vaca)
lowbrow [ˈloːˌbraʊ] *n* : persona *f* inculta
lower[1] [ˈloːər] *vt* **1** DROP : bajar <to lower one's voice : bajar la voz> **2** : arriar, bajar <to lower the flag : arriar la bandera> **3** REDUCE : reducir, bajar **4 to lower oneself** : rebajarse
lower[2] [ˈloːər] *adj* : inferior, más bajo, de abajo
lowland [ˈloːlənd, -ˌlænd] *n* : tierras *fpl* bajas
lowly [ˈloːli] *adj* **-lier; -est** : humilde, modesto
loyal [ˈlɔɪəl] *adj* : leal, fiel — **loyally** *adv*
loyalist [ˈlɔɪəlɪst] *n* : partidario *m,* -ria *f* del régimen
loyalty [ˈlɔɪəlti] *n, pl* **-ties** : lealtad *f,* fidelidad *f*
lozenge [ˈlɑzəndʒ] *n* : pastilla *f*
LSD [ˌɛlˌɛsˈdiː] *n* : LSD *m*
lubricant [ˈluːbrɪkənt] *n* : lubricante *m*
lubricate [ˈluːbrɪˌkeɪt] *vt* **-cated; -cating** : lubricar — **lubrication** [ˌluːbrɪˈkeɪʃən] *n*
lucid [ˈluːsəd] *adj* : lúcido, claro — **lucidly** *adv*
lucidity [luːˈsɪdət̬i] *n* : lucidez *f*
luck [ˈlʌk] *n* **1** : suerte *f* **2 to have bad luck** : tener mala suerte **3 good luck!** : ¡(buena) suerte!
luckily [ˈlʌkəli] *adv* : afortunadamente, por suerte
luckless [ˈlʌkləs] *adj* : desafortunado
lucky [ˈlʌki] *adj* **luckier; -est 1** : afortunado, que tiene suerte <a lucky woman : una mujer afortunada **2** FORTUITOUS : fortuito, de suerte **3** OPPORTUNE : oportuno **4** : de (la) suerte <lucky number : número de la suerte>
lucrative [ˈluːkrət̬ɪv] *adj* : lucrativo, provechoso — **lucratively** *adv*
ludicrous [ˈluːdəkrəs] *adj* : ridículo, absurdo — **ludicrously** *adv*
ludicrousness [ˈluːdəkrəsnəs] *n* : ridiculez *f,* absurdo *m*
lug [ˈlʌg] *vt* **lugged; lugging** : arrastrar, transportar con dificultad
luggage [ˈlʌgɪdʒ] *n* : equipaje *m*
lugubrious [lʊˈguːbriəs] *adj* : lúgubre — **lugubriously** *adv*
lukewarm [ˈluːkˈwɔrm] *adj* **1** TEPID : tibio **2** HALFHEARTED : poco entusiasta
lull[1] [ˈlʌl] *vt* **1** CALM, SOOTHE : calmar, sosegar **2 to lull to sleep** : arrullar, adormecer
lull[2] *n* : calma *f,* pausa *f*
lullaby [ˈlʌləˌbaɪ] *n, pl* **-bies** : canción *f* de cuna, arrullo *m,* nana *f*
lumbago [ˌlʌmˈbeɪgo] *n* : lumbago *m*
lumber[1] [ˈlʌmbər] *vt* : aserrar (madera) — *vi* : moverse pesadamente
lumber[2] *n* : madera *f*
lumberjack [ˈlʌmbərˌdʒæk] *n* : leñador *m,* -dora *f*
lumberyard [ˈlʌmbərˌjɑrd] *n* : almacén *m* de maderas
luminary [ˈluːməˌnɛri] *n, pl* **-naries** : lumbrera *f,* luminaria *f*
luminescence [ˌluːməˈnɛsənts] *n* : luminiscencia *f* — **luminescent** [-ˈnɛsənt] *adj*
luminosity [ˌluːməˈnɑsət̬i] *n, pl* **-ties** : luminosidad *f*
luminous [ˈluːmənəs] *adj* : luminoso — **luminously** *adv*
lump[1] [ˈlʌmp] *vt or* **to lump together** : juntar, agrupar, amontonar — *vi* CLUMP : agruparse, aglutinarse
lump[2] *n* **1** GLOB : grumo *m* **2** PIECE : pedazo *m,* trozo *m,* terrón *m* <a lump of coal : un trozo de carbón> <a lump of sugar : un terrón de azúcar> **3** SWELLING : bulto *m,* hinchazón *f,* protuberancia *f* **4 to have a lump in one's throat** : tener un nudo en la garganta
lumpy [ˈlʌmpi] *adj* **lumpier; -est 1** : lleno de grumos (dícese de una salsa) **2** UNEVEN : desigual, disparejo
lunacy [ˈluːnəsi] *n, pl* **-cies** : locura *f*
lunar [ˈluːnər] *adj* : lunar
lunatic[1] [ˈluːnəˌtɪk] *adj* : lunático, loco

lunatic[2] *n* : loco *m,* -ca *f*
lunch[1] [ˈlʌntʃ] *vi* : almorzar, comer
lunch[2] *n* : almuerzo *m,* comida *f,* lonche *m*
luncheon [ˈlʌntʃən] *n* **1** : comida *f,* almuerzo *m* **2 luncheon meat** : fiambres *fpl*
lung [ˈlʌŋ] *n* : pulmón *m*
lunge[1] [ˈlʌndʒ] *vi* **lunged; lunging 1** THRUST : atacar (en la esgrima) **2 to lunge forward** : arremeter, lanzarse
lunge[2] *n* **1** : arremetida *f,* embestida *f* **2** : estocada *f* (en la esgrima)
lurch[1] [ˈlərtʃ] *vi* **1** PITCH : cabecear, dar bandazos, dar sacudidas **2** STAGGER : tambalearse
lurch[2] *n* **1** : sacudida *f,* bandazo *m* (de un vehículo) **2** : tambaleo *m* (de una persona)
lure[1] [ˈlʊr] *vt* **lured; luring** : atraer
lure[2] *n* **1** ATTRACTION : atractivo *m* **2** ENTICEMENT : señuelo *m,* aliciente *m* **3** BAIT : cebo *m* artificial (en la pesca)
lurid [ˈlʊrəd] *adj* **1** GRUESOME : espeluznante, horripilante **2** SENSATIONAL : sensacionalista, chocante **3** GAUDY : chillón
lurk [ˈlərk] *vi* : estar al acecho
luscious [ˈlʌʃəs] *adj* **1** DELICIOUS : delicioso, exquisito **2** SEDUCTIVE : seductor, cautivador
lush [ˈlʌʃ] *adj* **1** LUXURIANT : exuberante, lozano **2** LUXURIOUS : suntuoso, lujoso
lust[1] [ˈlʌst] *vi* **to lust after** : desear (a una persona), codiciar (riquezas, etc.)
lust[2] *n* **1** LASCIVIOUSNESS : lujuria *f,* lascivia *f* **2** CRAVING : deseo *m,* ansia *f,* anhelo *m*
luster *or* **lustre** [ˈlʌstər] *n* **1** GLOSS, SHEEN : lustre *m,* brillo *m* **2** SPLENDOR : lustre *m,* esplendor *m*
lusterless [ˈlʌstərləs] *adj* : deslustrado, sin brillo
lustful [ˈlʌstfəl] *adj* : lujurioso, lascivo, lleno de deseo
lustrous [ˈlʌstrəs] *adj* : brillante, brilloso, lustroso
lusty [ˈlʌsti] *adj* **lustier; -est** : fuerte, robusto, vigoroso — **lustily** [ˈlʌstəli] *adv*
lute [ˈluːt] *n* : laúd *m*
luxuriant [ˌlʌgˈʒʊriənt, ˌlʌkˈʃʊr-] *adj* **1** : exuberante, lozano (dícese de las plantas) **2** : abundante y hermoso (dícese del pelo) — **luxuriantly** *adv*
luxuriate [ˌlʌgˈʒʊriˌeɪt, ˌlʌkˈʃʊr-] *vi* **-ated; -ating 1** : disfrutar **2 to luxuriate in** : deleitarse con
luxurious [ˌlʌgˈʒʊriəs, ˌlʌkˈʃʊr-] *adj* : lujoso, suntuoso — **luxuriously** *adv*
luxury [ˈlʌkʃəri, ˈlʌgʒə-] *n, pl* **-ries** : lujo *m*
lye [ˈlaɪ] *n* : lejía *f*
lying → **lie**[1], **lie**[2]
lymph [ˈlɪmpf] *n* : linfa *f*
lymphatic [lɪmˈfæt̬ɪk] *adj* : linfático
lynch [ˈlɪntʃ] *vt* : linchar
lynx [ˈlɪŋks] *n, pl* **lynx** *or* **lynxes** : lince *m*
lyre [ˈlaɪr] *n* : lira *f*
lyric[1] [ˈlɪrɪk] *adj* : lírico
lyric[2] *n* **1** : poema *m* lírico **2 lyrics** *npl* : letra *f* (de una canción)
lyrical [ˈlɪrɪkəl] *adj* : lírico, elocuente

M

m [ˈɛm] *n, pl* **m's** *or* **ms** [ˈɛmz] : decimotercera letra del alfabeto inglés
ma'am [ˈmæm] → **madam**
macabre [məˈkɑb, -ˈkɑbər, -ˈkɑbrə] *adj* : macabro
macadam [məˈkædəm] *n* : macadán *m*
macaroni [ˌmækəˈroːni] *n* : macarrones *mpl*
macaroon [ˌmækəˈruːn] *n* : macarrón *m,* mostachón *m*
macaw [məˈkɔ] *n* : guacamayo *m*
mace [ˈmeɪs] *n* **1** : maza *f* (arma o símbolo) **2** : macis *f* (especia)
machete [məˈʃɛt̬i] *n* : machete *m*
machination [ˌmækəˈneɪʃən, ˌmæʃə-] *n* : maquinación *f,* intriga *f*
machine[1] [məˈʃiːn] *vt* **-chined; -chining** : trabajar a máquina
machine[2] *n* **1** : máquina *f* <machine shop : taller de máquinas> <machine language : lenguaje de la máquina> **2** : aparato *m,* maquinaria *f* (en política)
machine gun *n* : ametralladora *f*
machinery [məˈʃiːnəri] *n, pl* **-eries 1** : maquinaria *f* **2** WORKS : mecanismo *m*
machinist [məˈʃiːnɪst] *n* : maquinista *mf*
mackerel [ˈmækərəl] *n, pl* **-el** *or* **-els** : caballa *f*
mackinaw [ˈmækəˌnɔ] *n* : chaqueta *f* escocesa de lana
mad [ˈmæd] *adj* **madder; maddest 1** INSANE : loco, demente **2** RABID : rabioso **3** FOOLISH : tonto, insensato **4** ANGRY : enojado, furioso **5** CRAZY : loco <I'm mad about you : estoy loco por ti>
Madagascan [ˌmædəˈgæskən] *n* : malgache *mf* — **Madagascan** *adj*
madam [ˈmædəm] *n, pl* **mesdames** [meɪˈdɑm, -ˈdæm] : señora *f*
madcap[1] [ˈmædˌkæp] *adj* ZANY : alocado, disparatado
madcap[2] *n* : alocado *m,* -da *f*
madden [ˈmædən] *vt* : enloquecer, enfurecer
maddeningly [ˈmædənɪŋli] *adv* : irritantemente <maddeningly vague : tan vago que te exaspera>

made → **make**[1]
madhouse ['mæd,haʊs] *n* : manicomio *m* <the office was a madhouse : la oficina parecía una casa de locos>
madly ['mædli] *adv* : como un loco, locamente
madman ['mæd,mæn, -mən] *n, pl* **-men** [-mən, -,mɛn] : loco *m,* demente *m*
madness ['mædnəs] *n* : locura *f,* demencia *f*
madwoman ['mæd,wʊmən] *n, pl* **-women** [-,wɪmən] : loca *f,* demente *f*
maelstrom ['meɪlstrəm] *n* : remolino *m,* vorágine *f*
maestro ['maɪ,stro:] *n, pl* **-stros** *or* **-stri** [-,stri:] : maestro *m*
Mafia ['mɑfiə] *n* : Mafia *f*
magazine ['mægə,zi:n] *n* **1** STOREHOUSE : almacén *m,* polvorín *m* (de explosivos) **2** PERIODICAL : revista *f* **3** : cargador *m* (de un arma de fuego)
magenta [mə'dʒɛntə] *n* : magenta *f,* color *m* magenta
maggot ['mægət] *n* : gusano *m*
magic[1] ['mædʒɪk] *or* **magical** ['mædʒɪkəl] *adj* : mágico
magic[2] *n* : magia *f*
magically ['mædʒɪkli] *adv* : mágicamente <they magically appeared : aparecieron como por arte de magia>
magician [mə'dʒɪʃən] *n* **1** SORCERER : mago *m,* -ga *f* **2** CONJURER : prestidigitador *m,* -dora *f;* mago *m,* -ga *f*
magistrate ['mædʒə,streɪt] *n* : magistrado *m,* -da *f*
magma ['mægmə] *n* : magma *m*
magnanimity [,mægnə'nɪməṯi] *n, pl* **-ties** : magnanimidad *f*
magnanimous [mæg'nænəməs] *adj* : magnánimo, generoso — **magnanimously** *adv*
magnate ['mæg,neɪt, -nət] *n* : magnate *mf*
magnesium [mæg'ni:ziəm, -ʒəm] *n* : magnesio *m*
magnet ['mægnət] *n* : imán *m*
magnetic [mæg'nɛṯɪk] *adj* : magnético — **magnetically** [-ṯɪkli] *adv*
magnetic field *n* : campo *m* magnético
magnetism ['mægnə,tɪzəm] *n* : magnetismo *m*
magnetize ['mægnə,taɪz] *vt* **-tized; -tizing 1** : magnetizar, imantar **2** ATTRACT : magnetizar, atraer
magnification [,mægnəfə'keɪʃən] *n* : aumento *m,* ampliación *f*
magnificence [mæg'nɪfəsənts] *n* : magnificencia *f*
magnificent [mæg'nɪfəsənt] *adj* : magnífico — **magnificently** *adv*
magnify ['mægnə,faɪ] *vt* **-fied; -fying 1** ENLARGE : ampliar **2** EXAGGERATE : magnificar, exagerar
magnifying glass *n* : lupa *f*
magnitude ['mægnə,tu:d, -,tju:d] *n* **1** GREATNESS : magnitud *f,* grandeza *f* **2** QUANTITY : cantidad *f* **3** IMPORTANCE : magnitud *f,* envergadura *f*
magnolia [mæg'no:ljə] *n* : magnolia *f* (flor), magnolio *m* (árbol)
magpie ['mæg,paɪ] *n* : urraca *f*
mahogany [mə'hɑgəni] *n, pl* **-nies** : caoba *f*
maid ['meɪd] *n* **1** MAIDEN : doncella *f* **2** *or* **maidservant** ['meɪd,sərvənt] : sirvienta *f,* muchacha *f,* mucama *f,* criada *f*
maiden[1] ['meɪdən] *adj* **1** UNMARRIED : soltera **2** FIRST : primero <maiden voyage : primera travesía>
maiden[2] *n* : doncella *f*
maidenhood ['meɪdən,hʊd] *n* : doncellez *f*
maiden name *n* : nombre *m* de soltera
mail[1] ['meɪl] *vt* : enviar por correo, echar al correo
mail[2] *n* **1** : correo *m* <airmail : correo aéreo> **2** : malla *f* <coat of mail : cota de malla>
mailbox ['meɪl,bɑks] *n* : buzón *m*
mailman ['meɪl,mæn, -mən] *n, pl* **-men** [-mən, -,mɛn] : cartero *m*
maim ['meɪm] *vt* : mutilar, desfigurar, lisiar
main[1] ['meɪn] *adj* : principal, central <the main office : la oficina central>
main[2] *n* **1** HIGH SEAS : alta mar *f* **2** : tubería *f* principal (de agua o gas), cable *m* principal (de un circuito) **3** **with might and main** : con todas sus fuerzas
mainframe ['meɪn,freɪm] *n* : mainframe *m,* computadora *f* central
mainland ['meɪn,lænd, -lənd] *n* : continente *m*
mainly ['meɪnli] *adv* **1** PRINCIPALLY : principalmente, en primer lugar **2** MOSTLY : principalmente, en la mayor parte
mainstay ['meɪn,steɪ] *n* : pilar *m,* sostén *m* principal
mainstream[1] ['meɪn,stri:m] *adj* : dominante, corriente, convencional
mainstream[2] *n* : corriente *f* principal
maintain [meɪn'teɪn] *vt* **1** SERVICE : dar mantenimiento a (una máquina) **2** PRESERVE : mantener, conservar <to maintain silence : guardar silencio> **3** SUPPORT : mantener, sostener **4** ASSERT : mantener, sostener, afirmar
maintenance ['meɪntənənts] *n* : mantenimiento *m*
maize ['meɪz] *n* : maíz *m*
majestic [mə'dʒɛstɪk] *adj* : majestuoso — **majestically** [-tɪkli] *adv*
majesty ['mædʒəsti] *n, pl* **-ties 1** : majestad *f* <Your Majesty : su Majestad> **2** SPLENDOR : majestuosidad *f,* esplendor *m*
major[1] ['meɪdʒər] *vi* **-jored; -joring** : especializarse

major[2] *adj* **1** GREATER **:** mayor **2** NOTEWORTHY **:** mayor, notable **3** SERIOUS **:** grave **4 :** mayor (en la música)

major[3] *n* **1 :** mayor *mf,* comandante *mf* (en las fuerzas armadas) **2 :** especialidad *f* (universitaria)

Majorcan [mɑˈdʒɔrkən, mə-, -ˈjɔr-] *n* **:** mallorquín *m,* -quina *f* — **Majorcan** *adj*

major general *n* **:** general *mf* de división

majority [məˈdʒɔrət̬i] *n, pl* **-ties 1** ADULTHOOD **:** mayoría *f* de edad **2 :** mayoría *f,* mayor parte *f* <the vast majority : la inmensa mayoría>

make[1] [ˈmeɪk] *v* **made** [ˈmeɪd]; **making** *vt* **1** CREATE **:** hacer <to make noise : hacer ruido> **2** FASHION, MANUFACTURE **:** hacer, fabricar <she made a dress : hizo un vestido> **3** DEVISE, FORM **:** desarrollar, elaborar, formar **4** CONSTITUTE **:** hacer, constituir <made of stone : hecho de piedra> **5** PREPARE **:** hacer, preparar **6** RENDER **:** hacer, poner <it makes him nervous : lo pone nervioso> <to make someone happy : hacer feliz a alguien> <it made me sad : me dio pena> **7** PERFORM **:** hacer <to make a gesture : hacer un gesto> **8** COMPEL **:** hacer, forzar, obligar **9** EARN **:** ganar <to make a living : ganarse la vida> — *vi* **1** HEAD **:** ir, dirigirse <we made for home : nos fuimos a casa> **2 to make do :** arreglárselas **3 to make good** REPAY **:** pagar **4 to make good** SUCCEED **:** tener éxito

make[2] *n* BRAND **:** marca *f*

make–believe[1] [ˌmeɪkbəˈliːv] *adj* **:** imaginario

make–believe[2] *n* **:** fantasía *f,* invención *f* <a world of make-believe : un mundo de ensueño>

make out *vt* **1** WRITE **:** hacer (un cheque) **2** DISCERN **:** distinguir, divisar **3** UNDERSTAND **:** comprender, entender — *vi* **:** arreglárselas <how did you make out? : ¿qué tal te fue?>

maker [ˈmeɪkər] *n* **:** fabricante *mf*

makeshift [ˈmeɪkˌʃɪft] *adj* **:** provisional, improvisado

makeup [ˈmeɪkˌʌp] *n* **1** COMPOSITION **:** composición *f* **2** CHARACTER **:** carácter *m,* temperamento *m* **3** COSMETICS **:** maquillaje *m*

make up *vt* **1** INVENT **:** inventar **2 :** recuperar <she made up the time : recuperó las horas perdidas> — *vi* RECONCILE **:** hacer las paces, reconciliarse

maladjusted [ˌmæləˈdʒʌstəd] *adj* **:** inadaptado

malady [ˈmælədi] *n, pl* **-dies :** dolencia *f,* enfermedad *f,* mal *m*

malaise [məˈleɪz, mæ-] *n* **:** malestar *m*

malapropism [ˈmæləˌprɑˌpɪzəm] *n* **:** uso *m* incorrecto y cómico de una palabra

malaria [məˈlɛriə] *n* **:** malaria *f,* paludismo *m*

malarkey [məˈlɑrki] *n* **:** tonterías *fpl,* estupideces *fpl*

Malawian [məˈlɑwiən] *n* **:** malauiano *m,* -na *f* — **Malawian** *adj*

Malay [məˈleɪ, ˈmeɪˌleɪ] *n* **1** *or* **Malayan** [məˈleɪən, meɪ-; ˈmeɪˌleɪən] **:** malayo *m,* -ya *f* **2 :** malayo *m* (idioma) — **Malay** *or* **Malayan** *adj*

male[1] [ˈmeɪl] *adj* **1 :** macho **2** MASCULINE **:** masculino

male[2] *n* **:** macho *m* (de animales o plantas), varón *m* (de personas)

malefactor [ˈmæləˌfæktər] *n* **:** malhechor *m,* -chora *f*

maleness [ˈmeɪlnəs] *n* **:** masculinidad *f*

malevolence [məˈlɛvələnts] *n* **:** malevolencia *f*

malevolent [məˈlɛvələnt] *adj* **:** malévolo

malformation [ˌmælfɔrˈmeɪʃən] *n* **:** malformación *f*

malformed [mælˈfɔrmd] *adj* **:** mal formado, deforme

malfunction[1] [mælˈfʌŋkʃən] *vi* **:** funcionar mal

malfunction[2] *n* **:** mal funcionamiento *m*

malice [ˈmælɪs] *n* **1 :** malicia *f,* malevolencia *f* **2 with malice aforethought :** con premeditación

malicious [məˈlɪʃəs] *adj* **:** malicioso, malévolo — **maliciously** *adv*

malign[1] [məˈlaɪn] *vt* **:** calumniar, difamar

malign[2] *adj* **:** maligno

malignancy [məˈlɪgnəntsi] *n, pl* **-cies :** malignidad *f*

malignant [məˈlɪgnənt] *adj* **:** maligno

malinger [məˈlɪŋgər] *vi* **:** fingirse enfermo

malingerer [məˈlɪŋgərər] *n* **:** uno que se finge enfermo

mall [ˈmɔl] *n* **1** PROMENADE **:** alameda *f,* paseo *m* (arbolado) **2 :** centro *m* comercial <shopping mall : galería comercial>

mallard [ˈmælərd] *n, pl* **-lard** *or* **-lards :** pato *m* real, ánade *mf* real

malleable [ˈmæliəbəl] *adj* **:** maleable

mallet [ˈmælət] *n* **:** mazo *m*

malnourished [mælˈnərɪʃt] *adj* **:** desnutrido, malnutrido

malnutrition [ˌmælnʊˈtrɪʃən, -njʊ-] *n* **:** desnutrición *f,* malnutrición *f*

malodorous [mælˈoːdərəs] *adj* **:** maloliente

malpractice [ˌmælˈpræktəs] *n* **:** mala práctica *f,* negligencia *f*

malt [ˈmɔlt] *n* **:** malta *f*

maltreat [mælˈtriːt] *vt* **:** maltratar

mama *or* **mamma** [ˈmɑmə] *n* **:** mamá *f*

mammal [ˈmæməl] *n* **:** mamífero *m*

mammalian [məˈmeɪliən, mæ-] *adj* **:** mamífero

mammary [ˈmæməri] *adj* **1 :** mamario **2 mammary gland :** glándula mamaria

mammogram ['mæmə,græm] *n* : mamografía *f*
mammoth[1] ['mæməθ] *adj* : colosal, gigantesco
mammoth[2] *n* : mamut *m*
man[1] ['mæn] *vt* **manned; manning** : tripular (un barco o avión), encargarse de (un servicio)
man[2] *n, pl* **men** ['mɛn] **1** PERSON : hombre *m*, persona *f* **2** MALE : hombre *m* **3** MANKIND : humanidad *f*
manacles ['mænɪkəlz] *npl* HANDCUFFS : esposas *fpl*
manage ['mænɪdʒ] *v* **-aged; -aging** *vt* **1** HANDLE : controlar, manejar **2** DIRECT : administrar, dirigir **3** CONTRIVE : lograr, ingeniárselas para — *vi* COPE : arreglárselas
manageable ['mænɪdʒəbəl] *adj* : manejable
management ['mænɪdʒmənt] *n* **1** DIRECTION : administración *f*, gestión *f*, dirección *f* **2** HANDLING : manejo *m* **3** MANAGERS : dirección *f*, gerencia *f*
manager ['mænɪdʒər] *n* : director *m*, -tora *f*; gerente *mf*; administrador *m*, -dora *f*
managerial [,mænə'dʒɪriəl] *adj* : directivo, gerencial
mandarin ['mændərən] *n* **1** : mandarín *m* **2** *or* **mandarin orange** : mandarina *f*
mandate ['mæn,deɪt] *n* : mandato *m*
mandatory ['mændə,tori] *adj* : obligatorio
mandible ['mændəbəl] *n* : mandíbula *f*
mandolin [,mændə'lɪn, 'mændələn] *n* : mandolina *f*
mane ['meɪn] *n* : crin *f* (de un caballo), melena *f* (de un león o una persona)
maneuver[1] [mə'nuːvər, -'njuː-] *vt* **1** PLACE, POSITION : maniobrar, posicionar, colocar **2** MANIPULATE : manipular, maniobrar — *vi* : maniobrar
maneuver[2] *n* : maniobra *f*
manfully ['mænfəli] *adj* : valientemente
manganese ['mæŋgə,niːz, -,niːs] *n* : manganeso *m*
mange ['meɪndʒ] *n* : sarna *f*
manger ['meɪndʒər] *n* : pesebre *m*
mangle ['mæŋgəl] *vt* **-gled; -gling 1** CRUSH, DESTROY : aplastar, despedazar, destrozar **2** MUTILATE : mutilar <to mangle a text : mutilar un texto>
mango ['mæŋ,goː] *n, pl* **-goes** : mango *m*
mangrove ['mæn,groːv, 'mæŋ-] *n* : mangle *m*
mangy ['meɪndʒi] *adj* **mangier; -est 1** : sarnoso **2** SHABBY : gastoso
manhandle ['mæn,hændəl] *vi* **-dled; -dling** : maltratar, tratar con poco cuidado
manhole ['mæn,hoːl] *n* : boca *f* de alcantarilla
manhood ['mæn,hʊd] *n* **1** : madurez *f* (de un hombre) **2** COURAGE, MANLINESS : hombría *f*, valor *m* **3** MEN : hombres *mpl*
manhunt ['mæn,hʌnt] *n* : búsqueda *f* (de un criminal)
mania ['meɪniə, -njə] *n* : manía *f*
maniac ['meɪni,æk] *n* : maníaco *m*, -ca *f*; maniático *m*, -ca *f*
maniacal [mə'naɪəkəl] *adj* : maníaco, maniaco
manicure[1] ['mænə,kjʊr] *vt* **-cured; -curing 1** : hacer la manicura a **2** TRIM : recortar
manicure[2] *n* : manicura *f*
manicurist ['mænə,kjʊrɪst] *n* : manicuro *m*, -ra *f*
manifest[1] ['mænə,fɛst] *vt* : manifestar
manifest[2] *adj* : manifiesto, patente — **manifestly** *adv*
manifestation [,mænəfə'steɪʃən] *n* : manifestación *f*
manifesto [,mænə'fɛs,toː] *n, pl* **-tos** *or* **-toes** : manifiesto *m*
manifold[1] ['mænə,foːld] *adj* : diverso, variado
manifold[2] *n* : colector *m* (de escape)
manipulate [mə'nɪpjə,leɪt] *vt* **-lated; -lating** : manipular
manipulation [mə,nɪpjə'leɪʃən] *n* : manipulación *f*
manipulative [mə'nɪpjə,leɪt̬ɪv, -lət̬ɪv] *adj* : manipulador
mankind ['mæn'kaɪnd, ,kaɪnd] *n* : género *m* humano, humanidad *f*
manliness ['mænlinəs] *n* : hombría *f*, masculinidad *f*
manly ['mænli] *adj* **-lier; -est** : varonil, viril
man–made ['mæn'meɪd] *adj* : artificial <man-made fabrics : telas sintéticas>
manna ['mænə] *n* : maná *m*
mannequin ['mænɪkən] *n* **1** DUMMY : maniquí *m* **2** MODEL : modelo *mf*
manner ['mænər] *n* **1** KIND, SORT : tipo *m*, clase *f* **2** WAY : manera *f*, modo *m* **3** STYLE : estilo *m* (artístico) **4 manners** *npl* CUSTOMS : costumbres *fpl* <Victorian manners : costumbres victorianas> **5 manners** *npl* ETIQUETTE : modales *mpl*, educación *f*, etiqueta *f* <good manners : buenos modales>
mannered ['mænərd] *adj* **1** AFFECTED, ARTIFICIAL : amanerado, afectado **2 well–mannered** : educado, cortés **3** → **ill–mannered**
mannerism ['mænə,rɪzəm] *n* : peculiaridad *f*, gesto *m* particular
mannerly ['mænərli] *adj* : cortés, bien educado
mannish ['mænɪʃ] *adj* : masculino, hombruno
man–of–war [,mænə'wɔr, -əv'wɔr] *n*, *pl* **men–of–war** [,mɛn-] WARSHIP : buque *m* de guerra
manor ['mænər] *n* **1** : casa *f* solariega, casa *f* señorial **2** ESTATE : señorío *m*

manpower [ˈmæn,pauər] *n* : personal *m,* mano *f* de obra
mansion [ˈmæntʃən] *n* : mansión *f*
manslaughter [ˈmæn,slɔtər] *n* : homicidio *m* sin premeditación
mantel [ˈmæntəl] *n* : repisa *f* de chimenea
mantelpiece [ˈmæntəl,piːs] → **mantel**
mantis [ˈmæntəs] *n, pl* **-tises** *or* **-tes** [ˈmæn,tiːz] : mantis *f* religiosa
mantle [ˈmæntəl] *n* : manto *m*
manual[1] [ˈmænjuəl] *adj* : manual — **manually** *adv*
manual[2] *n* : manual *m*
manufacture[1] [,mænjəˈfæktʃər] *vt* **-tured; -turing** : fabricar, manufacturar, confeccionar (ropa), elaborar (comestibles)
manufacture[2] *n* : manufactura *f,* fabricación *f,* confección *f* (de ropa), elaboración *f* (de comestibles)
manufacturer [,mænjəˈfæktʃərər] *n* : fabricante *m;* manufacturero *m,* -ra *f*
manure [məˈnur, -ˈnjur] *n* : estiércol *m*
manuscript [ˈmænjə,skrɪpt] *n* : manuscrito *m*
many[1] [ˈmɛni] *adj* **more** [ˈmor]; **most** [ˈmoːst] : muchos
many[2] *pron* : muchos *pl,* -chas *pl*
map[1] [ˈmæp] *vt* **mapped; mapping 1** : trazar el mapa de **2** PLAN : planear, proyectar <to map out a program : planear un programa>
map[2] *n* : mapa *m*
maple [ˈmeɪpəl] *n* : arce *m*
mar [ˈmɑr] *vt* **marred; marring 1** SPOIL : estropear, echar a perder **2** DEFACE : desfigurar
maraschino [,mærəˈskiːnoː, -ˈʃiː-] *n, pl* **-nos** : cereza *f* al marrasquino
marathon [ˈmærə,θɑn] *n* **1** RACE : maratón *m* **2** CONTEST : competencia *f* de resistencia
maraud [məˈrɔd] *vi* : merodear
marauder [məˈrɔdər] *n* : merodeador *m,* -dora *f*
marble [ˈmɑrbəl] *n* **1** : mármol *m* **2** : canica *f* <to play marbles : jugar a las canicas>
march[1] [ˈmɑrtʃ] *vi* **1** : marchar, desfilar <they marched past the grandstand : desfilaron ante la tribuna> **2** : caminar con resolución <she marched right up to him : se le acercó sin vacilación>
march[2] *n* **1** MARCHING : marcha *f* **2** PASSAGE : paso *m* (del tiempo) **3** PROGRESS : avance *m,* progreso *m* **4** : marcha *f* (en música)
March [ˈmɑrtʃ] *n* : marzo *m*
marchioness [ˈmɑrʃənɪs] *n* : marquesa *f*
Mardi Gras [ˈmɑrdi,grɑ] *n* : martes *m* de Carnaval
mare [ˈmær] *n* : yegua *f*
margarine [ˈmɑrdʒərən] *n* : margarina *f*
margin [ˈmɑrdʒən] *n* : margen *m*
marginal [ˈmɑrdʒənəl] *adj* **1** : marginal **2** MINIMAL : mínimo — **marginally** *adv*
marigold [ˈmærə,goːld] *n* : maravilla *f,* caléndula *f*
marijuana [,mærəˈhwɑnə] *n* : marihuana *f*
marina [məˈriːnə] *n* : puerto *m* deportivo
marinate [ˈmærə,neɪt] *vt* **-nated; -nating** : marinar
marine[1] [məˈriːn] *adj* **1** : marino <marine life : vida marina> **2** NAUTICAL : náutico, marítimo **3** : de la infantería de marina
marine[2] *n* : soldado *m* de marina
mariner [ˈmærɪnər] *n* : marinero *m,* marino *m*
marionette [,mæriəˈnɛt] *n* : marioneta *f,* títere *m*
marital [ˈmærətəl] *adj* **1** : matrimonial **2 marital status** : estado *m* civil
maritime [ˈmærə,taɪm] *adj* : marítimo
marjoram [ˈmɑrdʒərəm] *n* : mejorana *f*
mark[1] [ˈmɑrk] *vt* **1** : marcar **2** CHARACTERIZE : caracterizar **3** SIGNAL : señalar **4** NOTICE : prestar atención a, hacer caso de **5 to mark off** : demarcar, delimitar
mark[2] *n* **1** TARGET : blanco *m* **2** : marca *f,* señal *f* <put a mark where you left off : pon una señal donde terminaste> **3** INDICATION : señal *f,* indicio *m* **4** GRADE : nota *f* **5** IMPRINT : huella *f,* marca *f* **6** BLEMISH : marca *f,* imperfección *f*
marked [ˈmɑrkt] *adj* : marcado, notable — **markedly** [ˈmɑrkədli] *adv*
marker [ˈmɑrkər] *n* : marcador *m*
market[1] [ˈmɑrkət] *vt* : poner en venta, comercializar
market[2] *n* **1** MARKETPLACE : mercado *m* <the open market : el mercado libre> **2** DEMAND : demanda *f,* mercado *m* **3** STORE : tienda *f* **4** → **stock market**
marketable [ˈmɑrkətəbəl] *adj* : vendible
marketplace [ˈmɑrkət,pleɪs] *n* : mercado *m*
marksman [ˈmɑrksmən] *n, pl* **-men** [-mən, -,mɛn] : tirador *m*
marksmanship [ˈmɑrksmən,ʃɪp] *n* : puntería *f*
marlin [ˈmɑrlɪn] *n* : marlín *m*
marmalade [ˈmɑrmə,leɪd] *n* : mermelada *f*
marmoset [ˈmɑrmə,sɛt] *n* : tití *m*
marmot [ˈmɑrmət] *n* : marmota *f*
maroon[1] [məˈruːn] *vt* : abandonar, aislar
maroon[2] *n* : rojo *m* oscuro, granate *m*
marquee [mɑrˈkiː] *n* : marquesina *f*
marquess [ˈmɑrkwɪs] *or* **marquis** [ˈmɑrkwɪs, mɑrˈkiː] *n, pl* **-quesses** *or* **-quises** [-ˈkiːz, -ˈkiːzəz] *or* **-quis** [-ˈkiː, -ˈkiːz] : marqués *m*
marquise [mɑrˈkiːz] → **marchioness**

marriage ['mærɪdʒ] *n* **1** : matrimonio *m* **2** WEDDING : casamiento *m,* boda *f*
marriageable ['mærɪdʒəbəl] *adj* **of marriageable age** : de edad de casarse
married ['mærid] *adj* **1** : casado **2 to get married** : casarse
marrow ['mæroː] *n* : médula *f,* tuétano *m*
marry ['mæri] *vt* **-ried; -rying 1** : casar <the priest married them : el cura los casó> **2** : casarse con <she married John : se casó con John>
Mars ['mɑrz] *n* : Marte *m*
marsh ['mɑrʃ] *n* **1** : pantano *m* **2 salt marsh** : marisma *f*
marshal¹ ['mɑrʃəl] *vt* **-shaled** *or* **-shalled; -shaling** *or* **-shalling 1** : poner en orden, reunir **2** USHER : conducir
marshal² *n* **1** : maestro *m* de ceremonias **2** : mariscal *m* (en el ejército); jefe *m,* -fa *f* (de la policía, de los bomberos, etc.)
marshmallow ['mɑrʃˌmɛloː, -ˌmæloː] *n* : malvavisco *m*
marshy ['mɑrʃi] *adj* **marshier; -est** : pantanoso
marsupial [mɑr'suːpiəl] *n* : marsupial *m*
mart ['mɑrt] *n* MARKET : mercado *m*
marten ['mɑrtən] *n, pl* **-ten** *or* **-tens** : marta *f*
martial ['mɑrʃəl] *adj* : marcial
martin ['mɑrtən] *n* **1** SWALLOW : golondrina *f* **2** SWIFT : vencejo *m*
martyr¹ ['mɑrtər] *vt* : martirizar
martyr² *n* : mártir *mf*
martyrdom ['mɑrtərdəm] *n* : martirio *m*
marvel¹ ['mɑrvəl] *vi* **-veled** *or* **-velled; -veling** *or* **-velling** : maravillarse
marvel² *n* : maravilla *f*
marvelous ['mɑrvələs] *or* **marvellous** *adj* : maravilloso — **marvelously** *adv*
Marxism ['mɑrkˌsɪzəm] *n* : marxismo *m*
Marxist¹ ['mɑrksɪst] *adj* : marxista
Marxist² *n* : marxista *mf*
mascara [mæs'kærə] *n* : rímel *m,* rimel *m*
mascot ['mæsˌkɑt, -kət] *n* : mascota *f*
masculine ['mæskjələn] *adj* : masculino
masculinity [ˌmæskjə'lɪnəṭi] *n* : masculinidad *f*
mash¹ ['mæʃ] *vt* **1** : hacer puré de (papas, etc.) **2** CRUSH : aplastar, majar
mash² *n* **1** FEED : afrecho *m* **2** : malta *f* (para hacer bebidas alcohólicas) **3** PASTE, PULP : papilla *f,* pasta *f*
mask¹ ['mæsk] *vt* **1** CONCEAL, DISGUISE : enmascarar, ocultar **2** COVER : cubrir, tapar
mask² *n* : máscara *f,* careta *f,* mascarilla *f* (de un cirujano o dentista)
masochism ['mæsəˌkɪzəm, 'mæzə-] *n* : masoquismo *m*
masochist ['mæsəˌkɪst, 'mæzə-] *n* : masoquista *mf*
masochistic [ˌmæsə'kɪstɪk, ˌmæzə-] *adj* : masoquista
mason ['meɪsən] *n* **1** BRICKLAYER : albañil *mf* **2** *or* **stonemason** ['stoːnˌ-] : mampostero *m,* cantero *m*
masonry ['meɪsənri] *n, pl* **-ries 1** BRICKLAYING : albañería *f* **2** *or* **stonemasonry** ['stoːnˌ-] : mampostería *f*
masquerade¹ [ˌmæskə'reɪd] *vi* **-aded; -ading 1** : disfrazarse (de), hacerse pasar (por) **2** : asistir a una mascarada
masquerade² *n* **1** : mascarada *f,* baile *m* de disfraces **2** FACADE : farsa *f,* fachada *f*
mass¹ ['mæs] *vi* : concentrarse, juntarse en masa — *vt* : concentrar
mass² *n* **1** : masa *f* <atomic mass : masa atómica> **2** BULK : mole *f,* volumen *m* **3** MULTITUDE : cantidad *f,* montón *m* (de cosas), multitud *f* (de gente) **4 the masses** : las masas, el pueblo, el populacho
Mass ['mæs] *n* : misa *f*
massacre¹ ['mæsɪkər] *vt* **-cred; -cring** : masacrar
massacre² *n* : masacre *f*
massage¹ [mə'sɑʒ, -'sɑdʒ] *vt* **-saged; -saging** : masajear
massage² *n* : masaje *m*
masseur [mæ'sər] *n* : masajista *m*
masseuse [mæ'søz, -'suːz] *n* : masajista *f*
massive ['mæsɪv] *adj* **1** BULKY : voluminoso, macizo **2** HUGE : masivo, enorme — **massively** *adv*
mast ['mæst] *n* : mástil *m,* palo *m*
master¹ ['mæstər] *vt* **1** SUBDUE : dominar **2** : llegar a dominar <she mastered French : llegó a dominar el francés>
master² *n* **1** TEACHER : maestro *m,* profesor *m* **2** EXPERT : experto *m,* -ta *f;* maestro *m,* -tra *f* **3** : amo *m* (de animales o esclavos), señor *m* (de la casa) **4 master's degree** : maestría *f*
masterful ['mæstərfəl] *adj* **1** IMPERIOUS : autoritario, imperioso, dominante **2** SKILLFUL : magistral — **masterfully** *adv*
masterly ['mæstərli] *adj* : magistral
masterpiece ['mæstərˌpiːs] *n* : obra *f* maestra
masterwork ['mæstərˌwərk] → **masterpiece**
mastery ['mæstəri] *n* **1** DOMINION : dominio *m,* autoridad *f* **2** SUPERIORITY : superioridad *f* **3** EXPERTISE : maestría *f*
masticate ['mæstəˌkeɪt] *v* **-cated; -cating** : masticar
mastiff ['mæstɪf] *n* : mastín *m*
mastodon ['mæstəˌdɑn] *n* : mastodonte *m*
masturbate ['mæstərˌbeɪt] *v* **-bated; bating** *vi* : masturbarse — *vt* : masturbar
masturbation [ˌmæstər'beɪʃən] *n* : masturbación *f*

mat[1] [ˈmæt] *v* **matted; matting** *vt* TANGLE : enmarañar — *vi* : enmarañarse

mat[2] *n* **1** : estera *f* **2** TANGLE : maraña *f* **3** PAD : colchoneta *f* (de gimnasia) **4** *or* **matt** *or* **matte** [ˈmæt] FRAME : marco *m* (de cartón)

mat[3] → **matte**

matador [ˈmæt̬əˌdɔr] *n* : matador *m*

match[1] [ˈmætʃ] *vt* **1** PIT : enfrentar, oponer **2** EQUAL, FIT : igualar, corresponder a, coincidir con **3** : combinar con, hacer juego con <her shoes match her dress : sus zapatos hacen juego con su vestido> — *vi* **1** CORRESPOND : concordar, coincidir **2** : hacer juego <with a tie to match : con una corbata que hace juego>

match[2] *n* **1** EQUAL : igual *mf* <he's no match for her : no puede competir con ella> **2** FIGHT, GAME : partido *m*, combate *m* (en boxeo) **3** MARRIAGE : matrimonio *m*, casamiento *m* **4** : fósforo *m*, cerilla *f*, cerillo *m* (*in various countries*) <he lit a match : encendió un fósforo> **5 to be a good match** : hacer buena pareja (dícese de las personas), hacer juego (dícese de la ropa)

matchless [ˈmætʃləs] *adj* : sin igual, sin par

matchmaker [ˈmætʃˌmeɪkər] *n* : casamentero *m*, -ra *f*

mate[1] [ˈmeɪt] *v* **mated; mating** *vi* **1** FIT : encajar **2** PAIR : emparejarse **3** (*relating to animals*) : aparearse, copular — *vt* : aparear, acoplar (animales)

mate[2] *n* **1** COMPANION : compañero *m*, -ra *f*; camarada *mf* **2** : macho *m*, hembra *f* (de animales) **3** : oficial *mf* (de un barco) <first mate : primer oficial> **4** : compañero *m*, -ra *f*; pareja *f* (de un zapato, etc.)

material[1] [məˈtɪriəl] *adj* **1** PHYSICAL : material, físico <the material world : el mundo material> <material needs : necesidades materiales> **2** IMPORTANT : importante, esencial **3 material evidence** : prueba *f* sustancial

material[2] *n* **1** : material *m* **2** CLOTH : tejido *m*, tela *f*

materialism [məˈtɪriəˌlɪzəm] *n* : materialismo *m*

materialist [məˈtɪriəlɪst] *n* : materialista *mf*

materialistic [məˌtɪriəˈlɪstɪk] *adj* : materialista

materialize [məˈtɪriəˌlaɪz] *v* **-ized; -izing** *vt* : materializar, hacer aparecer — *vi* : materializarse, aparecer

maternal [məˈtərnəl] *adj* MOTHERLY : maternal — **maternally** *adv*

maternity[1] [məˈtərnət̬i] *adj* : de maternidad <maternity clothes : ropa de futura mamá> <maternity leave : licencia por maternidad>

maternity[2] *n, pl* **-ties** : maternidad *f*

math [ˈmæθ] → **mathematics**

mathematical [ˌmæθəˈmæt̬ɪkəl] *adj* : matemático — **mathematically** *adv*

mathematician [ˌmæθəməˈtɪʃən] *n* : matemático *m*, -ca *f*

mathematics [ˌmæθəˈmæt̬ɪks] *ns & pl* : matemáticas *fpl*, matemática *f*

matinee *or* **matinée** [ˌmætənˈeɪ] *n* : matiné *f*

matriarch [ˈmeɪtriˌɑrk] *n* : matriarca *f*

matriarchy [ˈmeɪtriˌɑrki] *n, pl* **-chies** : matriarcado *m*

matriculate [məˈtrɪkjəˌleɪt] *v* **-lated; -lating** *vt* : matricular — *vi* : matricularse

matriculation [məˌtrɪkjəˈleɪʃən] *n* : matrícula *f*, matriculación *f*

matrimony [ˈmætrəˌmoːni] *n* : matrimonio *m* — **matrimonial** [ˌmætrəˈmoːniəl] *adj*

matrix [ˈmeɪtrɪks] *n, pl* **-trices** [ˈmeɪtrəˌsiːz, ˈmæ-] *or* **-trixes** [ˈmeɪtrɪksəz] : matriz *f*

matron [ˈmeɪtrən] *n* : matrona *f*

matronly [ˈmeɪtrənli] *adj* : de matrona, matronal

matte [ˈmæt] *adj* : mate, de acabado mate

matter[1] [ˈmæt̬ər] *vi* : importar <it doesn't matter : no importa>

matter[2] *n* **1** QUESTION : asunto *m*, cuestión *f* <a matter of taste : una cuestión de gusto> **2** SUBSTANCE : materia *f*, sustancia *f* **3 matters** *npl* CIRCUMSTANCES : situación *f*, cosas *fpl* <to make matters worse : para colmo de males> **4 to be the matter** : pasar <what's the matter? : ¿qué pasa?> **5 as a matter of fact** : en efecto, en realidad **6 for that matter** : de hecho **7 no matter how much** : por mucho que

matter–of–fact [ˈmæt̬ərəvˈfækt] *adj* : práctico, realista

mattress [ˈmætrəs] *n* : colchón *m*

mature[1] [məˈtʊr, -ˈtjʊr, -ˈtʃʊr] *vi* **-tured; -turing 1** : madurar **2** : vencer <when does the loan mature? : ¿cuándo vence el préstamo?>

mature[2] *adj* **-turer; -est 1** : maduro **2** DUE : vencido

maturity [məˈtʊrət̬i, -ˈtjʊr-, -ˈtʃʊr-] *n* : madurez *f*

maudlin [ˈmɔdlɪn] *adj* : sensiblero

maul[1] [ˈmɔl] *vt* **1** BEAT : golpear, pegar **2** MANGLE : mutilar **3** MANHANDLE : maltratar

maul[2] *n* MALLET : mazo *m*

Mauritanian [ˌmɔrəˈteɪniən] *n* : mauritano *m*, -na *f* — **Mauritanian** *adj*

mausoleum [ˌmɔsəˈliːəm, ˌmɔzə-] *n, pl* **-leums** *or* **-lea** [-ˈliːə] : mausoleo *m*

mauve [ˈmoːv, ˈmɔv] *n* : malva *m*

maven *or* **mavin** [ˈmeɪvən] *n* EXPERT : experto *m*, -ta *f*

maverick [ˈmævrɪk, ˈmævə-] *n* **1** : ternero *m* sin marcar **2** NONCONFORMIST : inconformista *mf*, disidente *mf*

mawkish [ˈmɔkɪʃ] *adj* : sensiblero

maxim [ˈmæksəm] *n* : máxima *f*

maximize ['mæksə,maɪz] *vt* **-mized; -mizing** : maximizar, llevar al máximo

maximum[1] ['mæksəməm] *adj* : máximo

maximum[2] *n, pl* **-ma** ['mæksəmə] *or* **-mums** : máximo *m*

may ['meɪ] *v aux, past* **might** ['maɪt]; *present s & pl* **may 1** (*expressing permission*) : poder <you may go : puedes ir> **2** (*expressing possibility or probability*) : poder <you may be right : puede que tengas razón> <it may happen occasionally : puede pasar de vez en cuando> **3** (*expressing desires, intentions, or contingencies*) <may the best man win : que gane el mejor> <I laugh that I may not weep : me río para no llorar> <come what may : pase lo que pase>

May ['meɪ] *n* : mayo *m*

maybe ['meɪbi] *adv* PERHAPS : quizás, tal vez

mayfly ['meɪ,flaɪ] *n, pl* **-flies** : efímera *f*

mayhem ['meɪ,hɛm, 'meɪəm] *n* **1** MUTILATION : mutilación *f* **2** DEVASTATION : estragos *mpl*

mayonnaise ['meɪə,neɪz] *n* : mayonesa *f*

mayor ['meɪər, 'mɛr] *n* : alcalde *m*, -desa *f*

mayoral ['meɪərəl, 'mɛrəl] *adj* : de alcalde

maze ['meɪz] *n* : laberinto *m*

me ['mi:] *pron* **1** : me <she called me : me llamó> <give it to me : dámelo> **2** (*after a preposition*) : mí <for me : para mí> <with me : conmigo> **3** (*after conjunctions and verbs*) : yo <it's me : soy yo> <as big as me : tan grande como yo> **4** (*emphatic use*) : yo <me, too! : ¡yo también!> <who, me? : ¿quién, yo?>

meadow ['mɛdo:] *n* : prado *m*, pradera *f*

meadowland ['mɛdo,lænd] *n* : pradera *f*

meadowlark ['mɛdo,lɑrk] *n* : pájaro *m* cantor con el pecho amarillo

meager *or* **meagre** ['mi:gər] *adj* **1** THIN : magro, flaco **2** POOR, SCANTY : exiguo, escaso, pobre

meagerly ['mi:gərli] *adv* : pobremente

meagerness ['mi:gərnəs] *n* : escasez *f*, pobreza *f*

meal ['mi:l] *n* **1** : comida *f* <a hearty meal : una comida sustanciosa> **2** : harina *f* (de maíz, etc.)

mealtime ['mi:l,taɪm] *n* : hora *f* de comer

mean[1] ['mi:n] *vt* **meant** ['mɛnt]; **meaning 1** INTEND : querer, pensar, tener la intención de <I didn't mean to do it : lo hice sin querer> <what do you mean to do? : ¿qué piensas hacer?> **2** SIGNIFY : querer decir, significar <what does that mean? : ¿qué quiere decir eso?> **3** : importar <health means everything : lo que más importa es la salud>

mean[2] *adj* **1** HUMBLE : humilde **2** NEGLIGIBLE : despreciable <it's no mean feat : no es poca cosa> **3** STINGY : mezquino, tacaño **4** CRUEL : malo, cruel <to be mean to someone : tratar mal a alguien> **5** AVERAGE, MEDIAN : medio

mean[3] *n* **1** MIDPOINT : término *m* medio **2** AVERAGE : promedio *m*, media *f* aritmética **3 means** *npl* WAY : medio *m*, manera *f*, vía *f* **4 means** *npl* RESOURCES : medios *mpl*, recursos *mpl* **5 by all means** : por supuesto, cómo no **6 by means of** : por medio de **7 by no means** : de ninguna manera, de ningún modo

meander [mi'ændər] *vi* **-dered; -dering 1** WIND : serpentear **2** WANDER : vagar, andar sin rumbo fijo

meaning ['mi:nɪŋ] *n* **1** : significado *m*, sentido *m* <double meaning : doble sentido> **2** INTENT : intención *f*, propósito *m*

meaningful ['mi:nɪŋfəl] *adj* : significativo — **meaningfully** *adv*

meaningless ['mi:nɪŋləs] *adj* : sin sentido

meanness ['mi:nnəs] *n* **1** CRUELTY : crueldad *f*, mezquindad *f* **2** STINGINESS : tacañería *f*

meantime[1] ['mi:n,taɪm] *adv* → **meanwhile**[1]

meantime[2] *n* **1** : interín *m* **2 in the meantime** : entretanto, mientras tanto

meanwhile[1] ['mi:n,*h*waɪl] *adv* : entretanto, mientras tanto

meanwhile[2] *n* → **meantime**[2]

measles ['mi:zəlz] *ns & pl* : sarampión *m*

measly ['mi:zli] *adj* **-slier; -est** : miserable, mezquino

measurable ['mɛʒərəbəl, 'meɪ-] *adj* : mensurable — **measurably** [-bli] *adv*

measure[1] ['mɛʒər, 'meɪ-] *v* **-sured; -suring** : medir <he measured the table : midió la mesa> <it measures 15 feet tall : mide 15 pies de altura>

measure[2] *n* **1** AMOUNT : medida *f*, cantidad *f* <in large measure : en gran medida> <a full measure : una cantidad exacta> <a measure of proficiency : una cierta competencia> <for good measure : de ñapa, por añadidura> **2** DIMENSIONS, SIZE : medida *f*, tamaño *m* **3** RULER : regla *f* <tape measure : cinta métrica> **4** MEASUREMENT : medida *f* <cubic measure : medida de capacidad> **5** MEASURING : medición *f* **6 measures** *npl* : medidas *fpl* <security measures : medidas de seguridad>

measureless ['mɛʒərləs, 'meɪ-] *adj* : inmensurable

measurement ['mɛʒərmənt, 'meɪ-] *n* **1** MEASURING : medición *f* **2** DIMENSION : medida *f*

measure up *vi* **to measure up to :** estar a la altura de

meat [ˈmiːt] *n* **1** FOOD **:** comida *f* **2 :** carne *f* <meat and fish : carne y pescado> **3** SUBSTANCE **:** sustancia *f*, esencia *f* <the meat of the story : la sustancia del cuento>

meatball [ˈmiːtˌbɔl] *n* **:** albóndiga *f*

meaty [ˈmiːt̬i] *adj* **meatier; -est :** con mucha carne, carnoso

mechanic [mɪˈkænɪk] *n* **:** mecánico *m*, -ca *f*

mechanical [mɪˈkænɪkəl] *adj* **:** mecánico — **mechanically** *adv*

mechanics [mɪˈkænɪks] *ns & pl* **1 :** mecánica *f* <fluid mechanics : la mecánica de fluidos> **2** MECHANISMS **:** mecanismos *mpl*, aspectos *mpl* prácticos

mechanism [ˈmɛkəˌnɪzəm] *n* **:** mecanismo *m*

mechanization [ˌmɛkənəˈzeɪʃən] *n* **:** mecanización *f*

mechanize [ˈmɛkəˌnaɪz] *vt* **-nized; -nizing :** mecanizar

medal [ˈmɛdəl] *n* **:** medalla *f*, condecoración *f*

medalist [ˈmɛdəlɪst] *or* **medallist** *n* **:** medallista *mf*

medallion [məˈdæljən] *n* **:** medallón *m*

meddle [ˈmɛdəl] *vi* **-dled; -dling :** meterse, entrometerse

meddler [ˈmɛdələr] *n* **:** entrometido *m*, -da *f*

meddlesome [ˈmɛdəlsəm] *adj* **:** entrometido

media [ˈmiːdiə] *npl* **:** medios *mpl* de comunicación

median[1] [ˈmiːdiən] *adj* **:** medio

median[2] *n* **:** valor *m* medio

mediate [ˈmiːdiˌeɪt] *vi* **-ated; -ating :** mediar

mediation [ˌmiːdiˈeɪʃən] *n* **:** mediación *f*

mediator [ˈmiːdiˌeɪt̬ər] *n* **:** mediador *m*, -dora *f*

medical [ˈmɛdɪkəl] *adj* **:** médico

medicate [ˈmɛdəˌkeɪt] *vt* **-cated; -cating :** medicar <medicated powder : polvos medicinales>

medication [ˌmɛdəˈkeɪʃən] *n* **1** TREATMENT **:** tratamiento *m*, medicación *f* **2** MEDICINE **:** medicamento *m* <to be on medication : estar medicado>

medicinal [məˈdɪsənəl] *adj* **:** medicinal

medicine [ˈmɛdəsən] *n* **1** MEDICATION **:** medicina *f*, medicamento *m* **2 :** medicina *f* <he's studying medicine : estudia medicina>

medicine man *n* **:** hechicero *m*

medieval *or* **mediaeval** [mɪˈdiːvəl, ˌmiː-, ˌmɛ-, -diˈiːvəl] *adj* **:** medieval

mediocre [ˌmiːdiˈoːkər] *adj* **:** mediocre

mediocrity [ˌmiːdiˈɑkrət̬i] *n, pl* **-ties :** mediocridad *f*

meditate [ˈmɛdəˌteɪt] *vi* **-tated; -tating :** meditar

meditation [ˌmɛdəˈteɪʃən] *n* **:** meditación *f*

meditative [ˈmɛdəˌteɪt̬ɪv] *adj* **:** meditabundo

medium[1] [ˈmiːdiəm] *adj* **:** mediano <of medium height : de estatura mediana, de estatura regular>

medium[2] *n, pl* **-diums** *or* **-dia** [ˈmiːdiə] **1** MEAN **:** punto *m* medio, término *m* medio <happy medium : justo medio> **2** MEANS **:** medio *m* **3** SUBSTANCE **:** medio *m*, sustancia *f* <a viscous medium : un medio viscoso> **4 :** medio *m* de comunicación **5 :** medio *m* (artístico)

medley [ˈmɛdli] *n, pl* **-leys :** popurrí *m* (de canciones)

meek [ˈmiːk] *adj* **1** LONG-SUFFERING **:** paciente, sufrido **2** SUBMISSIVE **:** sumiso, dócil, manso

meekly [ˈmiːkli] *adv* **:** dócilmente

meekness [ˈmiːknəs] *n* **:** mansedumbre *f*, docilidad *f*

meet[1] [ˈmiːt] *v* **met** [ˈmɛt]; **meeting** *vt* **1** ENCOUNTER **:** encontrarse con **2** JOIN **:** unirse con **3** CONFRONT **:** enfrentarse a **4** SATISFY **:** satisfacer, cumplir con <to meet costs : pagar los gastos> **5 :** conocer <I met his sister : conocí a su hermana> — *vi* ASSEMBLE **:** reunirse, congregarse

meet[2] *n* **:** encuentro *m*

meeting [ˈmiːt̬ɪŋ] *n* **1 :** reunión *f* <to open the meeting : abrir la sesión> **2** ENCOUNTER **:** encuentro *m* **3 :** entrevista *f* (formal)

meetinghouse [ˈmiːt̬ɪŋˌhaʊs] *n* **:** iglesia *f* (de ciertas confesiones protestantes)

megabyte [ˈmɛgəˌbaɪt] *n* **:** megabyte *m*

megahertz [ˈmɛgəˌhərts, -ˌhɛrts] *n* **:** megahercio *m*

megaphone [ˈmɛgəˌfoːn] *n* **:** megáfono *m*

melancholy[1] [ˈmɛlənˌkɑli] *adj* **:** melancólico, triste, sombrío

melancholy[2] *n, pl* **-cholies :** melancolía *f*

melanoma [ˌmɛləˈnoːmə] *n, pl* **-mas :** melanoma *m*

melee [ˈmeɪˌleɪ, meɪˈleɪ] *n* BRAWL **:** reyerta *f*, riña *f*, pelea *f*

meliorate [ˈmiːljəˌreɪt, ˈmiːliə-] → **ameliorate**

mellow[1] [ˈmɛloː] *vt* **:** suavizar, endulzar — *vi* **:** suavizarse, endulzarse

mellow[2] *adj* **1** RIPE **:** maduro **2** MILD **:** apacible <a mellow character : un carácter apacible> <mellow wines : vinos añejos> **3 :** suave, dulce <mellow colors : colores suaves> <mellow tones : tonos dulces>

mellowness [ˈmɛlonəs] *n* **:** suavidad *f*, dulzura *f*

melodic [məˈlɑdɪk] *adj* **:** melódico — **melodically** [-dɪkli] *adv*

melodious [məˈloːdiəs] *adj* **:** melodioso — **melodiously** *adv*

melodiousness [mə'lo:diəsnəs] *n* : calidad *f* de melódico
melodrama ['mɛlə,drɑmə, -,dræ-] *n* : melodrama *m*
melodramatic [,mɛlədrə'mæṭɪk] *adj* : melodramático — **melodramatically** [-ṭɪkli] *adv*
melody ['mɛlədi] *n, pl* **-dies** : melodía *f*, tonada *f*
melon ['mɛlən] *n* : melón *m*
melt ['mɛlt] *vt* **1** : derretir, disolver **2** SOFTEN : ablandar <it melted his heart : ablandó su corazón> — *vi* **1** : derretirse, disolverse **2** SOFTEN : ablandarse **3** DISAPPEAR : desvanecerse, esfumarse <the clouds melted away : las nubes se desvanecieron>
melting point *n* : punto *m* de fusión
member ['mɛmbər] *n* **1** LIMB : miembro *m* **2** : miembro *m* (de un grupo); socio *m*, -cia *f* (de un club) **3** PART : miembro *m*, parte *f*
membership ['mɛmbər,ʃɪp] *n* **1** : membresía *f* <application for membership : solicitud de entrada> **2** MEMBERS : membresía *f*, miembros *mpl*, socios *mpl*
membrane ['mɛm,breɪn] *n* : membrana *f* — **membranous** ['mɛmbrənəs] *adj*
memento [mɪ'mɛn,to:] *n, pl* **-tos** *or* **-toes** : recuerdo *m*
memo ['mɛmo:] *n, pl* **memos** : memorándum *m*
memoirs ['mɛm,wɑrz] *npl* : memorias *fpl*, autobiografía *f*
memorabilia [,mɛmərə'biliə, -'bɪljə] *npl* **1** : objetos *mpl* de interés histórico **2** MEMENTOS : recuerdos *mpl*
memorable ['mɛmərəbəl] *adj* : memorable, notable — **memorably** [-bli] *adv*
memorandum [,mɛmə'rændəm] *n, pl* **-dums** *or* **-da** [-də] : memorándum *m*
memorial[1] [mə'moriəl] *adj* : conmemorativo
memorial[2] *n* : monumento *m* conmemorativo
Memorial Day *n* : el último lunes de mayo (observado en Estados Unidos como día feriado para conmemorar a los caídos en guerra)
memorialize [mə'moriə,laɪz] *vt* **-ized; -izing** COMMEMORATE : conmemorar
memorization [,mɛmərə'zeɪʃən] *n* : memorización *f*
memorize ['mɛmə,raɪz] *vt* **-rized; -rizing** : memorizar, aprender de memoria
memory ['mɛmri, 'mɛmə-] *n, pl* **-ries** **1** : memoria *f* <he has a good memory : tiene buena memoria> **2** RECOLLECTION : recuerdo *m* **3** COMMEMORATION : memoria *f*, conmemoración *f*
men → **man**[2]
menace[1] ['mɛnəs] *vt* **-aced; -acing** **1** THREATEN : amenazar **2** ENDANGER : poner en peligro
menace[2] *n* : amenaza *f*
menacing ['mɛnəsɪŋli] *adj* : amenazador, amenazante
menagerie [mə'nædʒəri, -'næʒəri] *n* : colección *f* de animales salvajes
mend[1] ['mɛnd] *vt* **1** CORRECT : enmendar, corregir <to mend one's ways : enmendarse> **2** REPAIR : remendar, arreglar, reparar — *vi* HEAL : curarse
mend[2] *n* : remiendo *m*
mendicant ['mɛndɪkənt] *n* BEGGAR : mendigo *m*, -ga *f*
menhaden [mɛn'heɪdən, mən-] *ns & pl* : pez *m* de la misma familia que los arenques
menial[1] ['mi:niəl] *adj* : servil, bajo
menial[2] *n* : sirviente *m*, -ta *f*
meningitis [,mɛnən'dʒaɪṭəs] *n, pl* **-gitides** [-'dʒɪṭə,di:z] : meningitis *f*
menopause ['mɛnə,pɔz] *n* : menopausia *f*
menorah [mə'norə] *n* : candelabro *m* (usado en los oficios religiosos judíos)
menstrual ['mɛn*t*strʊəl] *adj* : menstrual
menstruate ['mɛn*t*strʊ,eɪt] *vi* **-ated; -ating** : menstruar
menstruation [,mɛn*t*strʊ'eɪʃən] *n* : menstruación *f*
mental ['mɛntəl] *adj* : mental <mental hospital : hospital psiquiátrico> — **mentally** *adv*
mentality [mɛn'tæləṭi] *n, pl* **-ties** : mentalidad *f*
menthol ['mɛn,θɔl, -,θo:l] *n* : mentol *m*
mentholated [,mɛn*t*θə,leɪṭəd] *adj* : mentolado
mention[1] ['mɛntʃən] *vt* : mencionar, mentar, referirse a <don't mention it! : ¡de nada!, ¡no hay de qué!>
mention[2] *n* : mención *f*
mentor ['mɛn,tɔr, 'mɛntər] *n* : mentor *m*
menu ['mɛn,ju:] *n* **1** : menú *m*, carta *f* (en un restaurante) **2** : menú *m* (de computadoras)
meow[1] [mi:'aʊ] *vi* : maullar
meow[2] *n* : maullido *m*, miau *m*
mercantile ['mərkən,ti:l, -,taɪl] *adj* : mercantil
mercenary[1] ['mərsən,ɛri] *adj* : mercenario
mercenary[2] *n, pl* **-naries** : mercenario *m*, -ria *f*
merchandise ['mərtʃən,daɪz, -,daɪs] *n* : mercancía *f*, mercadería *f*
merchandiser ['mərtʃən,daɪzər] *n* : comerciante *mf*; vendedor *m*, -dora *f*
merchant ['mərtʃənt] *n* : comerciante *mf*
merchant marine *n* : marina *f* mercante
merciful ['mərsɪfəl] *adj* : misericordioso, clemente
mercifully ['mərsɪfli] *adv* **1** : con misericordia, con compasión **2** FORTUNATELY : afortunadamente

merciless [ˈmərsɪləs] *adj* : despiadado — **mercilessly** *adv*

mercurial [ˌmərˈkjʊriəl] *adj* TEMPERAMENTAL : temperamental, volátil

mercury [ˈmərkjəri] *n, pl* **-ries** : mercurio *m*

Mercury *n* : Mercurio *m*

mercy [ˈmərsi] *n, pl* **-cies 1** CLEMENCY : misericordia *f,* clemencia *f* **2** BLESSING : bendición *f*

mere [ˈmɪr] *adj, superlative* **merest** : mero, simple

merely [ˈmɪrli] *adv* : solamente, simplemente

merge [ˈmərdʒ] *v* **merged; merging** *vi* : unirse, fusionarse (dícese de las compañías), confluir (dícese de los ríos, las calles, etc.) — *vt* : unir, fusionar, combinar

merger [ˈmərdʒər] *n* : unión *f,* fusión *f*

meridian [məˈrɪdiən] *n* : meridiano *m*

meringue [məˈræŋ] *n* : merengue *m*

merino [məˈriːno] *n, pl* **-nos 1** : merino *m,* -na *f* **2** *or* **merino wool** : lana *f* merino

merit¹ [ˈmɛrət] *vt* : merecer, ser digno de

merit² *n* : mérito *m,* valor *m*

meritorious [ˌmɛrəˈtoriəs] *adj* : meritorio

mermaid [ˈmərˌmeɪd] *n* : sirena *f*

merriment [ˈmɛrɪmənt] *n* : alegría *f,* júbilo *m,* regocijo *m*

merry [ˈmɛri] *adj* **-rier; -est** : alegre — **merrily** [ˈmɛrəli] *adv*

merry-go-round [ˈmɛrigoˌraʊnd] *n* : carrusel *m,* tiovivo *m*

merrymaker [ˈmɛriˌmeɪkər] *n* : juerguista *mf*

merrymaking [ˈmɛriˌmeɪkɪŋ] *n* : juerga *f*

mesa [ˈmeɪsə] *n* : mesa *f*

mesdames → **madam, Mrs.**

mesh¹ [ˈmɛʃ] *vi* **1** ENGAGE : engranar (dícese de las piezas mecánicas) **2** TANGLE : enredarse **3** COORDINATE : coordinarse, combinar

mesh² *n* **1** : malla *f* <wire mesh : malla metálica> **2** NETWORK : red *f* **3** MESHING : engranaje *m* <in mesh : engranado>

mesmerize [ˈmɛzməˌraɪz] *vt* **-ized; -izing 1** HYPNOTIZE : hipnotizar **2** FASCINATE : cautivar, embelesar, fascinar

mess¹ [ˈmɛs] *vt* **1** SOIL : ensuciar **2 to mess up** DISARRANGE : desordenar, desarreglar **3 to mess up** BUNGLE : echar a perder — *vi* **1** PUTTER : entretenerse **2** INTERFERE : meterse, entrometerse <don't mess with me : no te metas conmigo>

mess² *n* **1** : rancho *m* (para soldados, etc.) **2** DISORDER : desorden *m* <your room is a mess : tienes el cuarto hecho un desastre> **3** CONFUSION, TURMOIL : confusión *f,* embrollo *m,* lío *m fam*

message [ˈmɛsɪdʒ] *n* : mensaje *m,* recado *m*

messenger [ˈmɛsəndʒər] *n* : mensajero *m,* -ra *f*

Messiah [məˈsaɪə] *n* : Mesías *m*

Messrs. → **Mr.**

messy [ˈmɛsi] *adj* **messier; -est** UNTIDY : desordenado, sucio

met → **meet**

metabolic [ˌmɛt̬əˈbɑlɪk] *adj* : metabólico

metabolism [məˈtæbəˌlɪzəm] *n* : metabolismo *m*

metabolize [məˈtæbəˌlaɪz] *vt* **-lized; -lizing** : metabolizar

metal [ˈmɛt̬əl] *n* : metal *m*

metallic [məˈtælɪk] *adj* : metálico

metallurgical [ˌmɛt̬əlˈərdʒɪkəl] *adj* : metalúrgico

metallurgy [ˈmɛt̬əlˌərdʒi] *n* : metalurgia *f*

metalwork [ˈmɛt̬əlˌwərk] *n* : objeto *m* de metal

metalworking [ˈmɛt̬əlˌwərkɪŋ] *n* : metalistería *f*

metamorphosis [ˌmɛt̬əˈmɔrfəsɪs] *n, pl* **-phoses** [-ˌsiːz] : metamorfosis *f*

metaphor [ˈmɛt̬əˌfɔr, -fər] *n* : metáfora *f*

metaphoric [ˌmɛt̬əˈfɔrɪk] *or* **metaphorical** [-ɪkəl] *adj* : metafórico

metaphysical [ˌmɛt̬əˈfɪzəkəl] *adj* : metafísico

metaphysics [ˌmɛt̬əˈfɪzɪks] *n* : metafísica *f*

mete [ˈmiːt] *vt* **meted; meting** ALLOT : repartir, distribuir <to mete out punishment : imponer castigos>

meteor [ˈmiːt̬iər, -t̬iːˌɔr] *n* : meteoro *m*

meteoric [ˌmiːt̬iˈɔrɪk] *adj* : meteórico

meteorite [ˈmiːt̬iəˌraɪt] *n* : meteorito *m*

meteorologic [ˌmiːt̬iˌɔrəˈlɑdʒɪk] *or* **meteorological** [-ˈlɑdʒɪkəl] *adj* : meteorológico

meteorologist [ˌmiːt̬iəˈrɑlədʒɪst] *n* : meteorólogo *m,* -ga *f*

meteorology [ˌmiːt̬iəˈrɑlədʒi] *n* : meteorología *f*

meter [ˈmiːt̬ər] *n* **1** : metro *m* <it measures 2 meters : mide 2 metros> **2** : contador *m,* medidor *m* (de electricidad, etc.) <parking meter : parquímetro> **3** : metro *m* (en literatura o música)

methane [ˈmɛˌθeɪn] *n* : metano *m*

method [ˈmɛθəd] *n* : método *m*

methodical [məˈθɑdɪkəl] *adj* : metódico — **methodically** *adv*

meticulous [məˈtɪkjələs] *adj* : meticuloso — **meticulously** *adv*

meticulousness [məˈtɪkjələsnəs] *n* : meticulosidad *f*

metric [ˈmɛtrɪk] *or* **metrical** [-trɪkəl] *adj* : métrico

metric system *n* : sistema *m* métrico

metronome [ˈmɛtrəˌnoːm] *n* : metrónomo *m*

metropolis [məˈtrɑpələs] *n* : metrópoli *f,* metrópolis *f*

metropolitan [ˌmɛtrəˈpɑlətən] *adj* : metropolitano

mettle [ˈmɛtəl] *n* **:** temple *m,* valor *m* <on one's mettle **:** dispuesto a mostrar su valía>

Mexican [ˈmɛksɪkən] *n* **:** mexicano *m,* -na *f* — **Mexican** *adj*

mezzanine [ˈmɛzəˌniːn, ˌmɛzəˈniːn] *n* **1 :** entrepiso *m,* entresuelo *m* **2 :** primer piso *m* (de un teatro)

miasma [maɪˈæzmə] *n* **:** miasma *m*

mica [ˈmaɪkə] *n* **:** mica *f*

mice → **mouse**

micro [ˈmaɪkro] *adj* **:** muy pequeño, microscópico

microbe [ˈmaɪˌkroːb] *n* **:** microbio *m*

microbiology [ˌmaɪkrobaɪˈɑləʤi] *n* **:** microbiología *f*

microcomputer [ˈmaɪkrokəmˌpjuːtər] *n* **:** microcomputadora *f*

microcosm [ˈmaɪkroˌkɑzəm] *n* **:** microcosmo *m*

microfilm [ˈmaɪkroˌfɪlm] *n* **:** microfilm *m*

micrometer [maɪˈkrɑmətər] *n* **:** micrómetro *m*

micron [ˈmaɪˌkrɑn] *n* **:** micrón *m*

microorganism [ˌmaɪkroˈɔrgəˌnɪzəm] *n* **:** microorganismo *m,* microbio *m*

microphone [ˈmaɪkrəˌfoːn] *n* **:** micrófono *m*

microprocessor [ˈmaɪkroˌprɑˌsɛsər] *n* **:** microprocesador *m*

microscope [ˈmaɪkrəˌskoːp] *n* **:** microscopio *m*

microscopic [ˌmaɪkrəˈskɑpɪk] *adj* **:** microscópico

microscopy [maɪˈkrɑskəpi] *n* **:** microscopía *f*

microwave [ˈmaɪkrəˌweɪv] *n* **1 :** microonda *f* **2** *or* **microwave oven :** microondas *m*

mid [ˈmɪd] *adj* **:** medio <mid morning **:** a media mañana> <in mid-August **:** a mediados de agosto> <in mid ocean **:** en alta mar>

midair [ˈmɪdˈær] *n* **in ~ :** en el aire <to catch in midair **:** agarrar al vuelo>

midday [ˈmɪdˈdeɪ] *n* NOON **:** mediodía *m*

middle[1] [ˈmɪdəl] *adj* **1** CENTRAL **:** medio, del medio, de en medio **2** INTERMEDIATE **:** intermedio, mediano <middle age **:** la mediana edad>

middle[2] *n* **1** CENTER **:** medio *m,* centro *m* <fold it down the middle **:** dóblalo por la mitad> **2 in the middle of :** en medio de (un espacio), a mitad de (una actividad) <in the middle of the month **:** a mediados del mes>

Middle Ages *npl* **:** Edad *f* Media

middle class *n* **:** clase *f* media

middleman [ˈmɪdəlˌmæn] *n, pl* **-men** [-mən, -ˌmɛn] **:** intermediario *m,* -ria *f*

middling [ˈmɪdlɪŋ, -lən] *adj* **1** MEDIUM, MIDDLE **:** mediano **2** MEDIOCRE **:** mediocre, regular

midge [ˈmɪʤ] *n* **:** mosca *f* pequeña

midget [ˈmɪʤət] *n* **1 :** enano *m,* -na *f* (persona) **2 :** cosa *f* diminuta

midland [ˈmɪdlənd, -ˌlænd] *n* **:** región *f* central (de un país)

midnight [ˈmɪdˌnaɪt] *n* **:** medianoche *f*

midpoint [ˈmɪdˌpɔɪnt] *n* **:** punto *m* medio, término *m* medio

midriff [ˈmɪdˌrɪf] *n* **:** diafragma *m*

midshipman [ˈmɪdˌʃɪpmən, ˌmɪdˈʃɪp-] *n, pl* **-men** [-mən, -ˌmɛn] **:** guardiamarina *m*

midst[1] [ˈmɪdst] *n* **:** medio *m* <in our midst **:** entre nosotros> <in the midst of **:** en medio de>

midst[2] *prep* **:** entre

midstream [ˈmɪdˈstriːm, -ˌstriːm] *n* **:** medio *m* de la corriente <in the midstream of his career **:** en medio de su carrera>

midsummer [ˈmɪdˈsʌmər, -ˌsʌ-] *n* **:** pleno verano *m*

midtown [ˈmɪdˌtaʊn] *n* **:** centro *m* (de una ciudad)

midway [ˈmɪdˌweɪ] *adv* HALFWAY **:** a mitad de camino

midweek [ˈmɪdˌwiːk] *n* **:** medio *m* de la semana <in midweek **:** a media semana>

midwife [ˈmɪdˌwaɪf] *n, pl* **-wives** [-ˌwaɪvz] **:** partera *f,* comadrona *f*

midwinter [ˈmɪdˈwɪntər, -ˌwin-] *n* **:** pleno invierno *m*

midyear [ˈmɪdˌjɪr] *n* **:** medio *m* del año <at midyear **:** a mediados del año>

mien [ˈmiːn] *n* **:** aspecto *m,* porte *m,* semblante *m*

miff [ˈmɪf] *vt* **:** ofender

might[1] [ˈmaɪt] (*used to express permission or possibility or as a polite alternative to* **may**) → **may** <it might be true **:** podría ser verdad> <might I speak with Sarah? **:** ¿se puede hablar con Sarah?>

might[2] *n* **:** fuerza *f,* poder *m*

mightily [ˈmaɪtəli] *adv* **:** con mucha fuerza, poderosamente

mighty[1] [ˈmaɪti] *adv* VERY **:** muy <mighty good **:** muy bueno, buenísimo>

mighty[2] *adj* **mightier; -est 1** POWERFUL **:** poderoso, potente **2** GREAT **:** grande, imponente

migraine [ˈmaɪˌgreɪn] *n* **:** jaqueca *f,* migraña *f*

migrant [ˈmaɪgrənt] *n* **:** trabajador *m,* -dora *f* ambulante

migrate [ˈmaɪˌgreɪt] *vi* **-grated; -grating :** emigrar

migration [maɪˈgreɪʃən] *n* **:** migración *f*

migratory [ˈmaɪgrəˌtori] *adj* **:** migratorio

mild [ˈmaɪld] *adj* **1** GENTLE **:** apacible, suave <a mild disposition **:** un temperamento suave> **2** LIGHT **:** leve, ligero <a mild punishment **:** un castigo leve, un castigo poco severo> **3** TEMPERATE **:** templado (dícese del clima) — **mildly** *adv*

mildew[1] [ˈmɪl,duː, -,djuː] *vi* : enmohecerse
mildew[2] *n* : moho *m*
mildness [ˈmaɪldnəs] *n* : apacibilidad *f*, suavidad *f*
mile [ˈmaɪl] *n* : milla *f*
mileage [ˈmaɪlɪdʒ] *n* **1** ALLOWANCE : viáticos *mpl* (pagados por milla recorrida) **2** : distancia *f* recorrida (en millas), kilometraje *m*
milestone [ˈmaɪl,stoːn] *n* LANDMARK : hito *m*, jalón *m* <a milestone in his life : un hito en su vida>
milieu [miːlˈjuː, -ˈjø] *n, pl* **-lieus** *or* **-lieux** [-ˈjuːz, -ˈjø] SURROUNDINGS : entorno *m*, medio *m*, ambiente *m*
militant[1] [ˈmɪlətənt] *adj* : militante, combativo
militant[2] *n* : militante *mf*
militarism [ˈmɪlətə,rɪzəm] *n* : militarismo *m*
militaristic [,mɪlətəˈrɪstɪk] *adj* : militarista
military[1] [ˈmɪlə,tɛri] *adj* : militar
military[2] *n* **the military** : las fuerzas armadas
militia [məˈlɪʃə] *n* : milicia *f*
milk[1] [ˈmɪlk] *vt* **1** : ordeñar (una vaca, etc.) **2** EXPLOIT : explotar
milk[2] *n* : leche *f*
milkman [ˈmɪlk,mæn, -mən] *n, pl* **-men** [-mən, -,mɛn] : lechero *m*
milk shake *n* : batido *m*, licuado *m*
milkweed [ˈmɪlk,wiːd] *n* : algodoncillo *m*
milky [ˈmɪlki] *adj* **milkier; -est** : lechoso
Milky Way *n* : Vía *f* Láctea
mill[1] [ˈmɪl] *vt* : moler (granos), fresar (metales), acordonar (monedas) — *vi* **to mill about** : arremolinarse
mill[2] *n* **1** : molino *m* (para moler granos) **2** FACTORY : fábrica *f* <textile mill : fábrica textil> **3** GRINDER : molinillo *m*
millennium [məˈlɛniəm] *n, pl* **-nia** [-niə] *or* **-niums** : milenio *m*
miller [ˈmɪlər] *n* : molinero *m*, -ra *f*
millet [ˈmɪlət] *n* : mijo *m*
milligram [ˈmɪlə,græm] *n* : miligramo *m*
milliliter [ˈmɪlə,liːtər] *n* : mililitro *m*
millimeter [ˈmɪlə,miːtər] *n* : milímetro *m*
milliner [ˈmɪlənər] *n* : sombrerero *m*, -ra *f* (de señoras)
millinery [ˈmɪlə,nɛri] *n* : sombreros *mpl* de señora
million[1] [ˈmɪljən] *adj* **a million** : un millón de
million[2] *n, pl* **millions** *or* **million** : millón *m*
millionaire [,mɪljəˈnær, ˈmɪljə,nær] *n* : millonario *m*, -ria *f*
millionth[1] [ˈmɪljənθ] *adj* : millonésimo
millionth[2] *n* : millonésimo *m*
millipede [ˈmɪlə,piːd] *n* : milpiés *m*
millstone [ˈmɪl,stoːn] *n* : rueda *f* de molino, muela *f*
mime[1] [ˈmaɪm] *v* **mimed; miming** *vt* MIMIC : imitar, remedar — *vi* PANTOMIME : hacer la mímica
mime[2] *n* **1** : mimo *mf* **2** PANTOMIME : pantomima *f*
mimeograph [ˈmɪmiə,græf] *n* : mimeógrafo *m*
mimic[1] [ˈmɪmɪk] *vt* **-icked; -icking** : imitar, remedar
mimic[2] *n* : imitador *m*, -dora *f*
mimicry [ˈmɪmɪkri] *n, pl* **-ries** : mímica *f*, imitación *f*
minaret [,mɪnəˈrɛt] *n* : alminar *m*, minarete *m*
mince [ˈmɪnts] *v* **minced; mincing** *vt* **1** CHOP : picar, moler (carne) **2 not to mince one's words** : no tener uno pelos en la lengua — *vi* : caminar de manera afectada
mincemeat [ˈmɪnts,miːt] *n* : mezcla *f* de fruta picada, sebo, y especias
mind[1] [ˈmaɪnd] *vt* **1** TEND : cuidar, atender <mind the children : cuida a los niños> **2** OBEY : obedecer **3** : preocuparse por, sentirse molestado por <I don't mind his jokes : sus bromas no me molestan> **4** : tener cuidado con <mind the ladder! : ¡cuidado con la escalera!> — *vi* **1** OBEY : obedecer **2** CARE : importarle a uno <I don't mind : no me importa, me es igual>
mind[2] *n* **1** MEMORY : memoria *f*, recuerdo *m* <keep it in mind : téngalo en cuenta> **2** : mente *f* <the mind and the body : la mente y el cuerpo> **3** INTENTION : intención *f*, propósito *m* <to have a mind to do something : tener intención de hacer algo> **4** : razón *f* <he's out of his mind : está loco> **5** OPINION : opinión *f* <to change one's mind : cambiar de opinión> **6** INTELLECT : capacidad *f* intelectual
minded [ˈmaɪndəd] *adj* **1** (*used in combination*) <narrow-minded : de mentalidad cerrada> <health-minded : preocupado por la salud> **2** INCLINED : inclinado
mindful [ˈmaɪndfəl] *adj* AWARE : consciente — **mindfully** *adv*
mindless [ˈmaɪndləs] *adj* **1** SENSELESS : estúpido, sin sentido <mindless violence : violencia sin sentido> **2** HEEDLESS : inconsciente
mindlessly [ˈmaɪndləsli] *adv* **1** SENSELESSLY : sin sentido **2** HEEDLESSLY : inconscientemente
mine[1] [ˈmaɪn] *vt* **mined; mining 1** : extraer (oro, etc.) **2** : minar (con artefactos explosivos)
mine[2] *n* : mina *f* <gold mine : mina de oro>
mine[3] *pron* : mío, mía <that one's mine : ése es el mío> <some friends of mine : unos amigos míos>
minefield [ˈmaɪn,fiːld] *n* : campo *m* de minas
miner [ˈmaɪnər] *n* : minero *m*, -ra *f*

mineral [ˈmɪnərəl] *n* : mineral *m* — **mineral** *adj*
mineralogy [ˌmɪnəˈrɑlədʒi, -ˈræ-] *n* : mineralogía *f*
mingle [ˈmɪŋgəl] *v* **-gled; -gling** *vt* MIX : mezclar — *vi* **1** MIX : mezclarse **2** CIRCULATE : circular
miniature[1] [ˈmɪniəˌtʃʊr, ˈmɪnɪˌtʃʊr, -tʃər] *adj* : en miniatura, diminuto
miniature[2] *n* : miniatura *f*
minibus [ˈmɪniˌbʌs] *n* : microbús *m*, pesera *f Mex*
minicomputer [ˈmɪnikəmˌpjuːt̬ər] *n* : minicomputadora *f*
minimal [ˈmɪnəməl] *adj* : mínimo
minimally [ˈmɪnəməli] *adv* : en grado mínimo
minimize [ˈmɪnəˌmaɪz] *vt* **-mized; -mizing** : minimizar
minimum[1] [ˈmɪnəməm] *adj* : mínimo
minimum[2] *n, pl* **-ma** [ˈmɪnəmə] *or* **-mums** : mínimo *m*
miniskirt [ˈmɪniˌskərt] *n* : minifalda *f*
minister[1] [ˈmɪnəstər] *vi* **to minister to** : cuidar (de), atender a
minister[2] *n* **1** : pastor *m*, -tora *f* (de una iglesia) **2** : ministro *m*, -tra *f* (en política)
ministerial [ˌmɪnəˈstɪriəl] *adj* : ministerial
ministry [ˈmɪnəstri] *n, pl* **-tries 1** : ministerio *m* (en política) **2** : sacerdocio *m* (en el catolicismo), clerecía *f* (en el protestantismo)
minivan [ˈmɪniˌvæn] *n* : minivan *f*
mink [ˈmɪŋk] *n, pl* **mink** *or* **minks** : visón *m*
minnow [ˈmɪnoː] *n, pl* **-nows** : pececillo *m* de agua dulce
minor[1] [ˈmaɪnər] *adj* : menor
minor[2] *n* **1** : menor *mf* (de edad) **2** : asignatura *f* secundaria (de estudios)
minority [məˈnɔrət̬i, maɪ-] *n, pl* **-ties** : minoría *f*
minstrel [ˈmɪnt*s*trəl] *n* : juglar *m*, trovador *m* (en el medioevo)
mint[1] [ˈmɪnt] *vt* : acuñar
mint[2] *adj* : sin usar <in mint condition : como nuevo>
mint[3] *n* **1** : menta *f* <mint tea : té de menta> **2** : pastilla *f* de menta **3** : casa *f* de la moneda <the U.S. Mint : la casa de la moneda de los EE.UU.> **4** FORTUNE : dineral *m*, fortuna *f*
minuet [ˌmɪnjʊˈɛt] *n* : minué *m*
minus[1] [ˈmaɪnəs] *n* **1** : cantidad *f* negativa **2 minus sign** : signo *m* de menos
minus[2] *prep* **1** : menos <four minus two : cuatro menos dos> **2** WITHOUT : sin <minus his hat : sin su sombrero>
minuscule *or* **miniscule** [ˈmɪnəsˌkjuːl, mɪˈnʌs-] *adj* : minúsculo
minute[1] [maɪˈnuːt, mɪ-, -ˈnjuːt] *adj* **-nuter; -est 1** TINY : diminuto, minúsculo **2** DETAILED : minucioso
minute[2] [ˈmɪnət] *n* **1** : minuto *m* <ten minutes late : diez minutos de retraso> **2** MOMENT : momento *m* **3 minutes** *npl* : actas *fpl* (de una reunión)
minutely [maɪˈnuːtli, mɪ-, -ˈnjuːt-] *adv* : minuciosamente
miracle [ˈmɪrɪkəl] *n* : milagro *m*
miraculous [məˈrækjələs] *adj* : milagroso — **miraculously** *adv*
mirage [mɪˈrɑʒ, *chiefly Brit* ˈmɪrˌɑʒ] *n* : espejismo *m*
mire[1] [ˈmaɪr] *vi* **mired; miring** : atascarse
mire[2] *n* : lodo *m*, barro *m*, fango *m*
mirror[1] [ˈmɪrər] *vt* : reflejar
mirror[2] *n* : espejo *m*
mirth [ˈmərθ] *n* : alegría *f*, regocijo *m*
mirthful [ˈmərθfəl] *adj* : alegre, regocijado
misanthrope [ˈmɪsənˌθroːp] *n* : misántropo *m*, -pa *f*
misanthropic [ˌmɪsənˈθrɑpɪk] *adj* : misantrópico
misanthropy [mɪˈsænθrəpi] *n* : misantropía *f*
misapprehend [ˌmɪsˌæprəˈhɛnd] *vt* : entender mal
misapprehension [ˌmɪsˌæprəˈhɛntʃən] *n* : malentendido *m*
misappropriate [ˌmɪsəˈproːpriˌeɪt] *vt* **-ated; -ating** : malversar
misbegotten [ˌmɪsbiˈgɑtən] *adj* **1** ILLEGITIMATE : ilegítimo **2** : mal concebido <misbegotten laws : leyes mal concebidas>
misbehave [ˌmɪsbiˈheɪv] *vi* **-haved; -having** : portarse mal
misbehavior [ˌmɪsbiˈheɪvjər] *n* : mala conducta *f*
miscalculate [mɪsˈkælkjəˌleɪt] *v* **-lated; -lating** : calcular mal
miscalculation [mɪsˌkælkjəˈleɪʃən] *n* : error *m* de cálculo, mal cálculo *m*
miscarriage [ˌmɪsˈkærɪdʒ, ˈmɪsˌkærɪdʒ] *n* **1** : aborto *m* **2** FAILURE : fracaso *m*, malogro *m* <a miscarriage of justice : una injusticia, un error judicial>
miscarry [ˌmɪsˈkæri, ˈmɪsˌkæri] *vi* **-ried; -rying 1** ABORT : abortar **2** FAIL : malograrse, fracasar
miscellaneous [ˌmɪsəˈleɪniəs] *adj* : misceláneo
miscellany [ˈmɪsəˌleɪni] *n, pl* **-nies** : miscelánea *f*
mischance [mɪsˈtʃænt*s*] *n* : desgracia *f*, infortunio *m*, mala suerte *f*
mischief [ˈmɪstʃəf] *n* : diabluras *fpl*, travesuras *fpl*
mischievous [ˈmɪstʃəvəs] *adj* : travieso, pícaro
mischievously [ˈmɪstʃəvəsli] *adv* : de manera traviesa
misconception [ˌmɪskənˈsɛpʃən] *n* : concepto *m* erróneo, idea *f* falsa
misconduct [mɪsˈkɑndəkt] *n* : mala conducta *f*
misconstrue [ˌmɪskənˈstruː] *vt* **-strued; -struing** : malinterpretar
misdeed [mɪsˈdiːd] *n* : fechoría *f*

misdemeanor [ˌmɪsdɪˈmiːnər] *n* : delito *m* menor
miser [ˈmaɪzər] *n* : avaro *m,* -ra *f;* tacaño *m,* -ña *f*
miserable [ˈmɪzərəbəl] *adj* **1** UNHAPPY : triste, desdichado **2** WRETCHED : miserable, desgraciado <a miserable hut : una choza miserable> **3** UNPLEASANT : desagradable, malo <miserable weather : tiempo malísimo> **4** CONTEMPTIBLE : despreciable, mísero <for a miserable $10 : por unos míseros diez dólares>
miserably [ˈmɪzərəbli] *adv* **1** SADLY : tristemente **2** WRETCHEDLY : miserablemente, lamentablemente **3** UNFORTUNATELY : desgraciadamente
miserly [ˈmaɪzərli] *adj* : avaro, tacaño
misery [ˈmɪzəri] *n, pl* **-eries** : miseria *f,* sufrimiento *m*
misfire [mɪsˈfaɪr] *vi* **-fired; -firing** : fallar
misfit [ˈmɪsˌfɪt] *n* : inadaptado *m,* -da *f*
misfortune [mɪsˈfɔrtʃən] *n* : desgracia *f,* desventura *f,* infortunio *m*
misgiving [mɪsˈgɪvɪŋ] *n* : duda *f,* recelo *m*
misguided [mɪsˈgaɪdəd] *adj* : desacertado, equivocado, mal informado
mishap [ˈmɪsˌhæp] *n* : contratiempo *m,* percance *m,* accidente *m*
misinform [ˌmɪsɪnˈfɔrm] *vt* : informar mal
misinterpret [ˌmɪsɪnˈtərprət] *vt* : malinterpretar
misinterpretation [ˌmɪsɪnˌtərprəˈteɪʃən] *n* : mala interpretación *f,* malentendido *m*
misjudge [mɪsˈdʒʌdʒ] *vt* **-judged; -judging** : juzgar mal
mislay [mɪsˈleɪ] *vt* **-laid** [-leɪd]; **-laying** : extraviar, perder
mislead [mɪsˈliːd] *vt* **-led** [-ˈlɛd]; **-leading** : engañar
misleading [mɪsˈliːdɪŋ] *adj* : engañoso
mismanage [mɪsˈmænɪdʒ] *vt* **-aged; -aging** : administrar mal
mismanagement [mɪsˈmænɪdʒmənt] *n* : mala administración *f*
misnomer [mɪsˈnoːmər] *n* : nombre *m* inapropiado
misogynist [mɪˈsɑdʒənɪst] *n* : misógino *m*
misplace [mɪsˈpleɪs] *vt* **-placed; -placing** : extraviar, perder
misprint [ˈmɪsˌprɪnt, mɪsˈ-] *n* : errata *f,* error *m* de imprenta
mispronounce [ˌmɪsprəˈnaʊnts] *vt* **-nounced; -nouncing** : pronunciar mal
mispronunciation [ˌmɪsprəˌnʌntsiˈeɪʃən] *n* : pronunciación *f* incorrecta
misquote [mɪsˈkwoːt] *vt* **-quoted; -quoting** : citar incorrectamente
misread [mɪsˈriːd] *vt* **-read; -reading** **1** : leer mal <she misread the sentence : leyó mal la frase> **2** MISUNDERSTAND : malinterpretar <they misread his intention : malinterpretaron su intención>
misrepresent [ˌmɪsˌrɛprɪˈzɛnt] *vt* : distorsionar, falsear, tergiversar
misrule[1] [mɪsˈruːl] *vt* **-ruled; -ruling** : gobernar mal
misrule[2] *n* : mal gobierno *m*
miss[1] [ˈmɪs] *vt* **1** : errar, faltar <to miss the target : no dar en el blanco> **2** : no encontrar, perder <they missed each other : no se encontraron> <I missed the plane : perdí el avión> **3** : echar de menos, extrañar <we miss him a lot : lo echamos mucho de menos> **4** OVERLOOK : pasar por alto, perder (una oportunidad, etc.) **5** AVOID : evitar <they just missed hitting the tree : por muy poco chocan contra el árbol> **6** OMIT : saltarse <he missed breakfast : se saltó el desayuno>
miss[2] *n* **1** : fallo *m* (de un tiro, etc.) **2** FAILURE : fracaso *m* **3** : señorita *f* <Miss Jones : la señorita Jones> <excuse me, miss : perdone, señorita>
missal [ˈmɪsəl] *n* : misal *m*
misshapen [mɪˈʃeɪpən] *adj* : deforme
missile [ˈmɪsəl] *n* **1** : misil *m* <guided missile : misil guiado> **2** PROJECTILE : proyectil *m*
missing [ˈmɪsɪŋ] *adj* **1** ABSENT : ausente <who's missing? : ¿quién falta?> **2** LOST : perdido, desaparecido <missing persons : los desaparecidos>
mission [ˈmɪʃən] *n* **1** : misión *f* (mandada por una iglesia) **2** DELEGATION : misión *f,* delegación *f,* embajada *f* **3** TASK : misión *f*
missionary[1] [ˈmɪʃəˌnɛri] *adj* : misionero
missionary[2] *n, pl* **-aries** : misionero *m,* -ra *f*
missive [ˈmɪsɪv] *n* : misiva *f*
misspell [mɪsˈspɛl] *vt* : escribir mal
misspelling [mɪsˈspɛlɪŋ] *n* : falta *f* de ortografía
misstep [ˈmɪsˌstɛp] *n* : traspié *m,* tropezón *m*
mist [ˈmɪst] *n* **1** HAZE : neblina *f,* niebla *f* **2** SPRAY : rocío *m*
mistake[1] [mɪˈsteɪk] *vt* **-took** [-ˈstʊk]; **-taken** [-ˈsteɪkən]; **-taking** **1** MISINTERPRET : malinterpretar **2** CONFUSE : confundir <he mistook her for Clara : la confundió con Clara>
mistake[2] *n* **1** MISUNDERSTANDING : malentendido *m,* confusión *f* **2** ERROR : error *m* <I made a mistake : me equivoqué, cometí un error>
mistaken [mɪˈsteɪkən] *adj* WRONG : equivocado — **mistakenly** *adv*
mister [ˈmɪstər] *n* : señor *m* <watch out, mister : cuidado, señor>
mistiness [ˈmɪstinəs] *n* : nebulosidad *f*
mistletoe [ˈmɪsəlˌtoː] *n* : muérdago *m*
mistreat [mɪsˈtriːt] *vt* : maltratar
mistreatment [mɪsˈtriːtmənt] *n* : maltrato *m,* abuso *m*

mistress ['mɪstrəs] *n* **1** : dueña *f,* señora *f* (de una casa) **2** LOVER : amante *f*
mistrust[1] [mɪs'trʌst] *vt* : desconfiar de
mistrust[2] *n* : desconfianza *f*
mistrustful [mɪs'trʌstfəl] *adj* : desconfiado
misty ['mɪsti] *adj* **mistier; -est 1** : neblinoso, nebuloso **2** TEARFUL : lloroso
misunderstand [ˌmɪsˌʌndər'stænd] *vt* **-stood** [-'stʊd]; **-standing 1** : entender mal **2** MISINTERPRET : malinterpretar <don't misunderstand me : no me malinterpretes>
misunderstanding [ˌmɪsˌʌndər'stændɪŋ] *n* **1** MISINTERPRETATION : malentendido *m* **2** DISAGREEMENT, QUARREL : disputa *f,* discusión *f*
misuse[1] [mɪs'ju:z] *vt* **-used; -using 1** : emplear mal **2** ABUSE, MISTREAT : abusar de, maltratar
misuse[2] [mɪs'ju:s] *n* **1** : mal empleo *m,* mal uso *m* **2** WASTE : derroche *m,* despilfarro *m* **3** ABUSE : abuso *m*
mite ['maɪt] *n* **1** : ácaro *m* **2** BIT : poco *m* <a mite tired : un poquito cansado>
miter *or* **mitre** ['maɪt̬ər] *n* **1** : mitra *f* (de un obispo) **2** *or* **miter joint** : inglete *m*
mitigate ['mɪt̬əˌgeɪt] *vt* **-gated; -gating** : mitigar, aliviar
mitigation [ˌmɪt̬ə'geɪʃən] *n* : mitigación *f,* alivio *m*
mitosis [maɪ'to:sɪs] *n, pl* **-toses** [-ˌsi:z] : mitosis *f*
mitt ['mɪt] *n* : manopla *f,* guante *m* (de béisbol)
mitten ['mɪtən] *n* : manopla *f,* mitón *m*
mix[1] ['mɪks] *vt* **1** COMBINE : mezclar **2** STIR : remover, revolver **3 to mix up** CONFUSE : confundir — *vi* : mezclarse
mix[2] *n* : mezcla *f*
mixer ['mɪksər] *n* **1** : batidora *f* (de la cocina) **2 cement mixer** : hormigonera *f*
mixture ['mɪkstʃər] *n* : mezcla *f*
mix–up ['mɪksˌʌp] *n* CONFUSION : confusión *f,* lío *m fam*
mnemonic [nɪ'mɑnɪk] *adj* : mnemónico
moan[1] ['mo:n] *vi* : gemir
moan[2] *n* : gemido *m*
moat ['mo:t] *n* : foso *m*
mob[1] ['mɑb] *vt* **mobbed; mobbing 1** ATTACK : atacar en masa **2** HOUND : acosar, rodear
mob[2] *n* **1** THRONG : multitud *f,* turba *f,* muchedumbre *f* **2** GANG : pandilla *f*
mobile[1] ['mo:bəl, -ˌbi:l, -ˌbaɪl] *adj* : móvil <mobile home : caravana, casa rodante>
mobile[2] ['moˌbi:l] *n* : móvil *m*
mobility [mo'bɪləṭi] *n* : movilidad *f*
mobilize ['mo:bəˌlaɪz] *vt* **-lized; -lizing** : movilizar
moccasin ['mɑkəsən] *n* **1** : mocasín *m* **2** *or* **water moccasin** : serpiente *f* venenosa de Norteamérica
mocha ['mo:kə] *n* **1** : mezcla *f* de café y chocolate **2** : color *m* chocolate
mock[1] ['mɑk, 'mɔk] *vt* **1** RIDICULE : burlarse de, mofarse de **2** MIMIC : imitar, remedar (de manera burlona)
mock[2] *adj* **1** SIMULATED : simulado **2** PHONY : falso
mockery ['mɑkəri, 'mɔ-] *n, pl* **-eries 1** JEER, TAUNT : burla *f,* mofa *f* <to make a mockery of : burlarse de> **2** FAKE : imitación *f* (burlona)
mockingbird ['mɑkɪŋˌbərd, 'mɔ-] *n* : sinsonte *m*
mode ['mo:d] *n* **1** FORM : modo *m,* forma *f* **2** MANNER : modo *m,* manera *f,* estilo *m* **3** FASHION : moda *f*
model[1] ['mɑdəl] *v* **-eled** *or* **-elled; -eling** *or* **-elling** *vt* SHAPE : modelar — *vi* : trabajar de modelo
model[2] *adj* **1** EXEMPLARY : modelo, ejemplar <a model student : un estudiante modelo> **2** MINIATURE : en miniatura
model[3] *n* **1** PATTERN : modelo *m* **2** MINIATURE : modelo *m,* miniatura *f* **3** EXAMPLE : modelo *m,* ejemplo *m* **4** MANNEQUIN : modelo *mf* **5** DESIGN : modelo *m* <the '97 model : el modelo '97>
modem ['mo:dəm, -ˌdɛm] *n* : módem *m*
moderate[1] ['mɑdəˌreɪt] *v* **-ated; -ating** *vt* : moderar, temperar — *vi* **1** CALM : moderarse, calmarse **2** : fungir como moderador (en un debate, etc.)
moderate[2] ['mɑdərət] *adj* : moderado
moderate[3] ['mɑdərət] *n* : moderado *m,* -da *f*
moderately ['mɑdərətli] *adv* **1** : con moderación **2** FAIRLY : medianamente
moderation [ˌmɑdə'reɪʃən] *n* : moderación *f*
moderator ['mɑdəˌreɪt̬ər] *n* : moderador *m,* -dora *f*
modern ['mɑdərn] *adj* : moderno
modernity [mə'dərnəṭi] *n* : modernidad *f*
modernization [ˌmɑdərnə'zeɪʃən] *n* : modernización *f*
modernize ['mɑdərˌnaɪz] *v* **-ized; -izing** *vt* : modernizar — *vi* : modernizarse
modest ['mɑdəst] *adj* **1** HUMBLE : modesto **2** DEMURE : recatado, pudoroso **3** MODERATE : modesto, moderado — **modestly** *adv*
modesty ['mɑdəsti] *n* : modestia *f*
modicum ['mɑdɪkəm] *n* : mínimo *m,* pizca *f*
modification [ˌmɑdəfə'keɪʃən] *n* : modificación *f*
modifier ['mɑdəˌfaɪər] *n* : modificante *m,* modificador *m*
modify ['mɑdəˌfaɪ] *vt* **-fied; -fying** : modificar, calificar (en gramática)
modish ['mo:dɪʃ] *adj* STYLISH : a la moda, de moda
modular ['mɑdʒələr] *adj* : modular
modulate ['mɑdʒəˌleɪt] *vt* **-lated; -lating** : modular

modulation [ˌmɑdʒəˈleɪʃən] *n* : modulación *f*
module [ˈmɑˌdʒuːl] *n* : módulo *m*
mogul [ˈmoːgəl] *n* : magnate *mf;* potentado *m,* -da *f*
mohair [ˈmoːˌhær] *n* : mohair *m*
moist [ˈmɔɪst] *adj* : húmedo
moisten [ˈmɔɪsən] *vt* : humedecer
moistness [ˈmɔɪstnəs] *n* : humedad *f*
moisture [ˈmɔɪstʃər] *n* : humedad *f*
moisturize [ˈmɔɪstʃəˌraɪz] *vt* **-ized; -izing** : humedecer (el aire), humectar (la piel)
moisturizer [ˈmɔɪtʃəˌraɪzər] *n* : crema *f* hidratante, crema *f* humectante
molar [ˈmoːlər] *n* : muela *f,* molar *m*
molasses [məˈlæsəz] *n* : melaza *f*
mold[1] [ˈmoːld] *vt* : moldear, formar (carácter, etc.) — *vi* : enmohecerse <the bread will mold : el pan se enmohecerá>
mold[2] *n* **1** *or* **leaf mold** : mantillo *m* **2** FORM : molde *m* <to break the mold : romper el molde> **3** FUNGUS : moho *m*
molder [ˈmoːldər] *vi* CRUMBLE : desmoronarse
molding [ˈmoːldɪŋ] *n* : moldura *f* (en arquitectura)
moldy [ˈmoːldi] *adj* **moldier; -est** : mohoso
mole [ˈmoːl] *n* **1** : lunar *m* (en la piel) **2** : topo *m* (animal)
molecule [ˈmɑlɪˌkjuːl] *n* : molécula *f* — **molecular** [məˈlɛkjələr] *adj*
molehill [ˈmoːlˌhɪl] *n* : topera *f*
molest [məˈlɛst] *vt* **1** ANNOY, DISTURB : molestar **2** : abusar (sexualmente)
mollify [ˈmɑləˌfaɪ] *vt* **-fied; -fying** : apaciguar, aplacar
mollusk *or* **mollusc** [ˈmɑləsk] *n* : molusco *m*
mollycoddle [ˈmɑliˌkɑdəl] *vt* **-dled; -dling** PAMPER : consentir, mimar
molt [ˈmoːlt] *vi* : mudar, hacer la muda
molten [ˈmoːltən] *adj* : fundido
mom [ˈmɑm, ˈmʌm] *n* : mamá *f*
moment [ˈmoːmənt] *n* **1** INSTANT : momento *m* <one moment, please : un momento, por favor> **2** TIME : momento *m* <at the moment : de momento, actualmente> <from that moment : desde entonces> **3** IMPORTANCE : importancia *f* <of great moment : de gran importancia>
momentarily [ˌmoːmənˈtɛrəli] *adv* **1** : momentáneamente **2** SOON : dentro de poco, pronto
momentary [ˈmoːmənˌtɛri] *adj* : momentáneo
momentous [moˈmɛntəs] *adj* : de suma importancia, fatídico
momentum [moˈmɛntəm] *n, pl* **-ta** [-tə] *or* **-tums 1** : momento *m* (en física) **2** IMPETUS : ímpetu *m,* impulso *m*
monarch [ˈmɑˌnɑrk, -nərk] *n* : monarca *mf*
monarchism [ˈmɑˌnɑrˌkɪzəm, -nər-] *n* : monarquismo *m*
monarchist [ˈmɑˌnɑrkɪst, -nər-] *n* : monárquico *m,* -ca *f*
monarchy [ˈmɑˌnɑrki, -nər-] *n, pl* **-chies** : monarquía *f*
monastery [ˈmɑnəˌstɛri] *n, pl* **-teries** : monasterio *m*
monastic [məˈnæstɪk] *adj* : monástico — **monastically** [-tɪkli] *adv*
Monday [ˈmʌnˌdeɪ, -di] *n* : lunes *m*
monetary [ˈmɑnəˌtɛri, ˈmʌnə-] *adj* : monetario
money [ˈmʌni] *n, pl* **-eys** *or* **-ies** [ˈmʌniz] : dinero *m,* plata *f*
moneyed [ˈmʌnid] *adj* : adinerado
moneylender [ˈmʌniˌlɛndər] *n* : prestamista *mf*
money order *n* : giro *m* postal
Mongolian [mɑnˈgoːliən, mɑŋ-] *n* : mongol *m,* -gola *f* — **Mongolian** *adj*
mongoose [ˈmɑnˌguːs, ˈmɑŋ-] *n, pl* **-gooses** : mangosta *f*
mongrel [ˈmɑŋgrəl, ˈmʌŋ-] *n* **1** : perro *m* mestizo, perro *m* corriente *Mex* **2** HYBRID : híbrido *m*
monitor[1] [ˈmɑnət̬ər] *vt* : controlar, monitorear
monitor[2] *n* **1** : ayudante *mf* (en una escuela) **2** : monitor *m* (de una computadora, etc.)
monk [ˈmʌŋk] *n* : monje *m*
monkey[1] [ˈmʌŋki] *vi* **-keyed; -keying 1 to monkey around** : hacer payasadas, payasear **2 to monkey with** : juguetear con
monkey[2] *n, pl* **-keys** : mono *m,* -na *f*
monkeyshines [ˈmʌŋkiˌʃaɪnz] *npl* PRANKS : picardías *fpl,* travesuras *fpl*
monkey wrench *n* : llave *f* inglesa
monkshood [ˈmʌŋksˌhʊd] *n* : acónito *m*
monocle [ˈmɑnɪkəl] *n* : monóculo *m*
monogamous [məˈnɑgəməs] *adj* : monógamo
monogamy [məˈnɑgəmi] *n* : monogamia *f*
monogram[1] [ˈmɑnəˌgræm] *vt* **-grammed; -gramming** : marcar con monograma <monogrammed towels : toallas con monograma>
monogram[2] *n* : monograma *m*
monograph [ˈmɑnəˌgræf] *n* : monografía *f*
monolingual [ˌmɑnəˈlɪŋgwəl] *adj* : monolingüe
monolith [ˈmɑnəˌlɪθ] *n* : monolito *m*
monolithic [ˌmɑnəˈlɪθɪk] *adj* : monolítico
monologue [ˈmɑnəˌlɔg] *n* : monólogo *m*
monoplane [ˈmɑnəˌpleɪn] *n* : monoplano *m*
monopolize [məˈnɑpəˌlaɪz] *vt* **-lized; -lizing** : monopolizar
monopoly [məˈnɑpəli] *n, pl* **-lies** : monopolio *m*
monosyllabic [ˌmɑnosəˈlæbɪk] *adj* : monosilábico

monosyllable [ˈmɑno,sɪləbəl] *n* : monosílabo *m*
monotheism [ˈmɑnoθiː,ɪzəm] *n* : monoteísmo *m*
monotheistic [,mɑnoθiːˈɪstɪk] *adj* : monoteísta
monotone [ˈmɑnə,toːn] *n* : voz *f* monótona
monotonous [məˈnɑtənəs] *adj* : monótono — **monotonously** *adv*
monotony [məˈnɑtəni] *n* : monotonía *f,* uniformidad *f*
monoxide [məˈnɑk,saɪd] *n* : monóxido *m*
monsoon [mɑnˈsuːn] *n* : monzón *m*
monster [ˈmɑntstər] *n* : monstruo *m*
monstrosity [mɑnˈstrɑsət̬i] *n, pl* **-ties** : monstruosidad *f*
monstrous [ˈmɑntstrəs] *adj* : monstruoso — **monstrously** *adv*
montage [mɑnˈtɑʒ] *n* : montaje *m*
month [ˈmʌnθ] *n* : mes *m*
monthly[1] [ˈmʌnθli] *adv* : mensualmente
monthly[2] *adj* : mensual
monthly[3] *n, pl* **-lies** : publicación *f* mensual
monument [ˈmɑnjəmənt] *n* : monumento *m*
monumental [,mɑnjəˈmɛntəl] *adj* : monumental — **monumentally** *adv*
moo[1] [ˈmuː] *vi* : mugir
moo[2] *n* : mugido *m*
mood [ˈmuːd] *n* : humor *m* <to be in a good mood : estar de buen humor> <to be in the mood for : tener ganas de> <to be in no mood for : no estar para>
moodiness [ˈmuːdinəs] *n* **1** SADNESS : melancolía *f,* tristeza *f* **2** : cambios *mpl* de humor, carácter *m* temperamental
moody [ˈmuːdi] *adj* **moodier; -est 1** GLOOMY : melancólico, deprimido **2** TEMPERAMENTAL : temperamental, de humor variable
moon [ˈmuːn] *n* : luna *f*
moonbeam [ˈmuːn,biːm] *n* : rayo *m* de luna
moonlight[1] [ˈmuːn,laɪt] *vi* : estar pluriempleado
moonlight[2] *n* : claro *m* de luna, luz *f* de la luna
moonlit [ˈmuːn,lɪt] *adj* : iluminado por la luna <a moonlit night : una noche de luna>
moonshine [ˈmuːn,ʃaɪn] *n* **1** MOONLIGHT : luz *f* de la luna **2** NONSENSE : disparates *mpl,* tonterías *fpl* **3** : whiskey *m* destilado ilegalmente
moor[1] [ˈmʊr, ˈmɔr] *vt* : amarrar
moor[2] *n* : brezal *m,* páramo *m*
mooring [ˈmʊrɪŋ, ˈmɔr-] *n* DOCK : atracadero *m*
moose [ˈmuːs] *ns & pl* : alce *m* (norteamericano)
moot [ˈmuːt] *adj* DEBATABLE : discutible
mop[1] [ˈmɑp] *vt* **mopped; mopping** : trapear
mop[2] *n* : trapeador *m*
mope [ˈmoːp] *vi* **moped; moping** : andar deprimido, quedar abatido
moped [ˈmoː,pɛd] *n* : ciclomotor *m*
moral[1] [ˈmɔrəl] *adj* : moral <moral judgment : juicio moral> <moral support : apoyo moral> — **morally** *adv*
moral[2] *n* **1** : moraleja *f* (de un cuento, etc.) **2 morals** *npl* : moral *f,* moralidad *f*
morale [məˈræl] *n* : moral *f*
morality [məˈrælət̬i] *n, pl* **-ties** : moralidad *f*
morass [məˈræs] *n* **1** SWAMP : ciénaga *f,* pantano *m* **2** CONFUSION, MESS : lío *m fam,* embrollo *m*
moratorium [,mɔrəˈtoriəm] *n, pl* **-riums** *or* **-ria** [-iə] : moratoria *f*
moray [ˈmɔr,eɪ, məˈreɪ] *n* : morena *f*
morbid [ˈmɔrbɪd] *adj* **1** : mórbido, morboso (en medicina) **2** GRUESOME : morboso, horripilante
morbidity [mɔrˈbɪdət̬i] *n* : morbosidad *f*
more[1] [ˈmor] *adv* : más <what more can I say? : ¿qué más puedo decir?> <more important : más importante> <once more : una vez más>
more[2] *adj* : más <nothing more than that : nada más que eso> <more work : más trabajo>
more[3] *n* : más *m* <the more you eat, the more you want : cuanto más comes, tanto más quieres>
more[4] *pron* : más <more were found : se encontraron más>
moreover [morˈoːvər] *adv* : además
mores [ˈmɔr,eɪz, -iːz] *npl* CUSTOMS : costumbres *fpl,* tradiciones *fpl*
morgue [ˈmɔrg] *n* : morgue *f*
moribund [ˈmɔrə,bʌnd] *adj* : moribundo
morn [ˈmɔrn] → **morning**
morning [ˈmɔrnɪŋ] *n* : mañana *f* <good morning! : ¡buenos días!>
Moroccan [məˈrɑkən] *n* : marroquí *mf* — **Moroccan** *adj*
moron [ˈmor,ɑn] *n* **1** : retrasado *m,* -da *f* mental **2** DUNCE : estúpido *m,* -da *f;* tonto *m,* -ta *f*
morose [məˈroːs] *adj* : hosco, sombrío — **morosely** *adv*
moroseness [məˈroːsnəs] *n* : malhumor *m*
morphine [ˈmɔr,fiːn] *n* : morfina *f*
morrow [ˈmɑroː] *n* : día *m* siguiente
Morse code [ˈmɔrs] *n* : código *m* morse
morsel [ˈmɔrsəl] *n* **1** BITE : bocado *m* **2** FRAGMENT : pedazo *m*
mortal[1] [ˈmɔrt̬əl] *adj* : mortal <mortal blow : golpe mortal> <mortal fear : miedo mortal> — **mortally** *adv*
mortal[2] *n* : mortal *mf*
mortality [mɔrˈtælət̬i] *n* : mortalidad *f*
mortar [ˈmɔrt̬ər] *n* **1** : mortero *m,* molcajete *m Mex* <mortar and pestle

: mortero y maja> **2** : mortero *m* <mortar shell : granada de mortero> **3** CEMENT : mortero *m,* argamasa *f*

mortgage[1] ['mɔrgɪdʒ] *vt* **-gaged; -gaging** : hipotecar

mortgage[2] *n* : hipoteca *f*

mortification [ˌmɔrt̬əfə'keɪʃən] *n* **1** : mortificación *f* **2** HUMILIATION : humillación *f,* vergüenza *f*

mortify ['mɔrt̬əˌfaɪ] *vt* **-fied; -fying 1** : mortificar (en religión) **2** HUMILIATE : humillar, avergonzar

mortuary ['mɔrtʃəˌwɛri] *n, pl* **-aries** FUNERAL HOME : funeraria *f*

mosaic [mo'zeɪɪk] *n* : mosaico *m*

Moslem ['mɑzləm] → **Muslim**

mosque ['mɑsk] *n* : mezquita *f*

mosquito [mə'skiːt̬o] *n, pl* **-toes** : mosquito *m,* zancudo *m*

moss ['mɔs] *n* : musgo *m*

mossy ['mɔsi] *adj* **-ier; -est** : musgoso

most[1] ['moːst] *adv* : más <the most interesting book : el libro más interesante>

most[2] *adj* **1** : la mayoría de, la mayor parte de <most people : la mayoría de la gente> **2** GREATEST : más (dícese de los números), mayor (dícese de las cantidades) <the most ability : la mayor capacidad>

most[3] *n* : más *m,* máximo *m* <the most I can do : lo más que puedo hacer> <three weeks at the most : tres semanas como máximo>

most[4] *pron* : la mayoría, la mayor parte <most will go : la mayoría irá>

mostly ['moːstli] *adv* MAINLY : en su mayor parte, principalmente

mote ['moːt] *n* SPECK : mota *f*

motel [mo'tɛl] *n* : motel *m*

moth ['mɔθ] *n* : palomilla *f,* polilla *f*

mother[1] ['mʌðər] *vt* **1** BEAR : dar a luz a **2** PROTECT : cuidar de, proteger

mother[2] *n* : madre *f*

motherhood ['mʌðərˌhʊd] *n* : maternidad *f*

mother-in-law ['mʌðərɪnˌlɔ] *n, pl* **mothers-in-law** : suegra *f*

motherland ['mʌðərˌlænd] *n* : patria *f*

motherly ['mʌðərli] *adj* : maternal

mother-of-pearl [ˌmʌðərəv'pərl] *n* : nácar *m,* madreperla *f*

motif [mo'tiːf] *n* : motivo *m*

motion[1] ['moːʃən] *vt* : hacerle señas (a alguien) <she motioned us to come in : nos hizo señas para que entráramos>

motion[2] *n* **1** MOVEMENT : movimiento *m* <to set in motion : poner en marcha> **2** PROPOSAL : moción *f* <to second a motion : apoyar una moción>

motionless ['moːʃənləs] *adj* : inmóvil, quieto

motion picture *n* MOVIE : película *f*

motivate ['moːt̬əˌveɪt] *vt* **-vated; -vating** : motivar, mover, inducir

motivation [ˌmoːt̬ə'veɪʃən] *n* : motivación *f*

motive[1] ['moːtɪv] *adj* : motor <motive power : fuerza motriz>

motive[2] *n* : motivo *m,* móvil *m*

motley ['mɑtli] *adj* : abigarrado, variopinto

motor[1] ['moːt̬ər] *vi* : viajar en coche

motor[2] *n* : motor *m*

motorbike ['moːt̬ərˌbaɪk] *n* : motocicleta *f* (pequeña), moto *f*

motorboat ['moːt̬ərˌboːt] *n* : bote *m* a motor, lancha *f* motora

motorcar ['moːt̬ərˌkɑr] *n* : automóvil *m*

motorcycle ['moːt̬ərˌsaɪkəl] *n* : motocicleta *f*

motorcyclist ['moːt̬ərˌsaɪkəlɪst] *n* : motociclista *mf*

motorist ['moːt̬ərɪst] *n* : automovilista *mf,* motorista *mf*

mottle ['mɑt̬əl] *vt* **-tled; -tling** : manchar, motear <mottled skin : piel manchada> <a mottled surface : una superficie moteada>

motto ['mɑt̬oː] *n, pl* **-toes** : lema *m*

mould ['moːld] → **mold**

mound ['maʊnd] *n* **1** PILE : montón *m* **2** KNOLL : montículo *m* **3 burial mound** : túmulo *m*

mount[1] ['maʊnt] *vt* **1** : montar a (un caballo), montar en (una bicicleta), subir a **2** : montar (artillería, etc.) — *vi* INCREASE : aumentar

mount[2] *n* **1** SUPPORT : soporte *m* **2** HORSE : caballería *f,* montura *f* **3** MOUNTAIN : monte *m,* montaña *f*

mountain ['maʊntən] *n* : montaña *f*

mountaineer [ˌmaʊntən'ɪr] *n* : alpinista *mf;* montañero *m,* -ra *f*

mountainous ['maʊntənəs] *adj* : montañoso

mountaintop ['maʊntənˌtɑp] *n* : cima *f,* cumbre *f*

mourn ['morn] *vt* : llorar (por), lamentar <to mourn the death of : llorar la muerte de> — *vi* : llorar, estar de luto

mourner ['mornər] *n* : doliente *mf*

mournful ['mornfəl] *adj* **1** SORROWFUL : lloroso, plañidero, triste **2** GLOOMY : deprimente, entristecedor — **mournfully** *adv*

mourning ['mornɪŋ] *n* : duelo *m,* luto *m*

mouse ['maʊs] *n, pl* **mice** ['maɪs] **1** : ratón *m,* -tona *f* **2** : ratón *m* (de una computadora)

mousetrap ['maʊsˌtræp] *n* : ratonera *f*

moustache ['mʌˌstæʃ, mə'stæʃ] → **mustache**

mouth[1] ['maʊð] *vt* **1** : decir con poca sinceridad, repetir sin comprensión **2** : articular en silencio <she mouthed the words : formó las palabras con los labios>

mouth[2] ['maʊθ] *n* : boca *f* (de una persona o un animal), entrada *f* (de un túnel), desembocadura *f* (de un río)

mouthful ['maʊθˌfʊl] *n* : bocado *m* (de comida), bocanada *f* (de líquido o humo)

mouthpiece [ˈmaʊθˌpiːs] *n* : boquilla *f* (de un instrumento musical)
movable [ˈmuːvəbəl] *or* **moveable** *adj* : movible, móvil
move[1] [ˈmuːv] *v* **moved; moving** *vi* **1** GO : ir **2** RELOCATE : mudarse, trasladarse **3** STIR : moverse <¡no te muevas! : don't move!> **4** ACT : actuar — *vt* **1** : mover <move it over there : ponlo allí> <he kept moving his feet : no dejaba de mover los pies> **2** INDUCE, PERSUADE : inducir, persuadir, mover **3** TOUCH : conmover <it moved him to tears : lo hizo llorar> **4** PROPOSE : proponer
move[2] *n* **1** MOVEMENT : movimiento *m* **2** RELOCATION : mudanza *f* (de casa), traslado *m* **3** STEP : paso *m* <a good move : un paso acertado>
movement [ˈmuːvmənt] *n* : movimiento *m*
mover [ˈmuːvər] *n* : persona *f* que hace mudanzas
movie [ˈmuːvi] *n* **1** : película *f* **2 movies** *npl* : cine *m*
moving [ˈmuːvɪŋ] *adj* **1** : en movimiento <a moving target : un blanco móvil> **2** TOUCHING : conmovedor, emocionante
mow[1] [ˈmoː] *vt* **mowed; mowed** *or* **mown** [ˈmoːn]; **mowing** : cortar (la hierba)
mow[2] [ˈmaʊ] *n* : pajar *m*
mower [ˈmoːər] → **lawn mower**
Mr. [ˈmɪstər] *n, pl* **Messrs.** [ˈmɛsərz] : señor *m*
Mrs. [ˈmɪsəz, -səs, *esp South* ˈmɪzəz, -zəs] *n, pl* **Mesdames** [meɪ-ˈdɑm, -ˈdæm] : señora *f*
Ms. [ˈmɪz] *n* : señora *f,* señorita *f*
much[1] [ˈmʌtʃ] *adv* **more** [ˈmor]; **most** [ˈmoːst] : mucho <I'm much happier : estoy mucho más contenta> <she talks as much as I do : habla tanto como yo>
much[2] *adj* **more; most** : mucho <it has much validity : tiene mucha validez> <too much time : demasiado tiempo>
much[3] *pron* : mucho, -cha <I don't need much : no necesito mucho>
mucilage [ˈmjuːsəlɪdʒ] *n* : mucílago *m*
muck [ˈmʌk] *n* **1** MANURE : estiércol *m* **2** DIRT, FILTH : mugre *f,* suciedad *f* **3** MIRE, MUD : barro *m,* fango *m,* lodo *m*
mucous [ˈmjuːkəs] *adj* : mucoso <mucous membrane : membrana mucosa>
mucus [ˈmjuːkəs] *n* : mucosidad *f*
mud [ˈmʌd] *n* : barro *m,* fango *m,* lodo *m*
muddle[1] [ˈmʌdəl] *v* **-dled; -dling** *vt* **1** CONFUSE : confundir **2** BUNGLE : echar a perder, malograr — *vi* : andar confundido <to muddle through : arreglárselas>
muddle[2] *n* : confusión *f,* embrollo *m,* lío *m*
muddleheaded [ˌmʌdəlˈhɛdəd, ˈmʌdəlˌ-] *adj* CONFUSED : confuso, despistado
muddy[1] [ˈmʌdi] *vt* **-died; -dying** : llenar de barro
muddy[2] *adj* **-dier; -est** : barroso, fangoso, lodoso, enlodado <you're all muddy : estás cubierto de barro>
muff[1] [ˈmʌf] *vt* BUNGLE : echar a perder, fallar (un tiro, etc.)
muff[2] *n* : manguito *m*
muffin [ˈmʌfən] *n* : magdalena *f,* mantecada *f Mex*
muffle [ˈmʌfəl] *vt* **-fled; -fling 1** ENVELOP : cubrir, tapar **2** DEADEN : amortiguar (un sonido)
muffler [ˈmʌflər] *n* **1** SCARF : bufanda *f* **2** : silenciador *m,* mofle *m CA, Mex* (de un automóvil)
mug[1] [ˈmʌg] *v* **mugged; mugging** *vi* : posar (con afectación), hacer muecas <mugging for the camera : haciendo muecas para la cámara> — *vt* ASSAULT : asaltar, atracar
mug[2] *n* CUP : tazón *m*
mugger [ˈmʌgər] *n* : atracador *m,* -dora *f*
mugginess [ˈmʌginəs] *n* : bochorno *m*
muggy [ˈmʌgi] *adj* **-gier; -est** : bochornoso
mulatto [mʊˈlɑto, -ˈlæ-] *n, pl* **-toes** *or* **-tos** : mulato *m,* -ta *f*
mulberry [ˈmʌlˌbɛri] *n, pl* **-ries** : morera *f* (árbol), mora *f* (fruta)
mulch[1] [ˈmʌltʃ] *vt* : cubrir con pajote
mulch[2] *n* : pajote *m*
mule [ˈmjuːl] *n* **1** : mula *f* **2** : obstinado *m,* -da *f;* terco *m,* -ca *f*
mulish [ˈmjuːlɪʃ] *adj* : obstinado, terco
mull [ˈmʌl] *vt* **to mull over** : reflexionar sobre
mullet [ˈmʌlət] *n, pl* **-let** *or* **-lets** : mújol *m,* múgil *m*
multicolored [ˌmʌltiˈkʌlərd, ˌmʌltaɪ-] *adj* : multicolor, abigarrado
multifaceted [ˌmʌltiˈfæsətəd, ˌmʌltaɪ-] *adj* : multifacético
multifamily [ˌmʌltiˈfæmli, ˌmʌltaɪ-] *adj* : multifamiliar
multifarious [ˌmʌltəˈfæriəs] *adj* DIVERSE : diverso, variado
multilateral [ˌmʌltiˈlætərəl, ˌmʌltaɪ-] *adj* : multilateral
multimedia [ˌmʌltiˈmiːdiə, ˌmʌltaɪ-] *adj* : multimedia
multimillionaire [ˌmʌltiˌmɪljəˈnær, ˌmʌltaɪ-, -ˈmɪljəˌnær] *adj* : multimillonario
multinational [ˌmʌltiˈnæʃənəl, ˌmʌltaɪ-] *adj* : multinacional
multiple[1] [ˈmʌltəpəl] *adj* : múltiple
multiple[2] *n* : múltiplo *m*
multiple sclerosis [skləˈroːsɪs] *n* : esclerosis *f* múltiple
multiplication [ˌmʌltəpləˈkeɪʃən] *n* : multiplicación *f*
multiplicity [ˌmʌltəˈplɪsəti] *n, pl* **-ties** : multiplicidad *f*
multiplier [ˈmʌltəˌplaɪər] *n* : multiplicador *m* (en matemáticas)

multiply [ˈmʌltəˌplaɪ] *v* **-plied; -plying** *vt* : multiplicar — *vi* : multiplicarse

multipurpose [ˌmʌltiˈpərpəs, ˌmʌlˌtaɪ-] *adj* : multiuso

multitude [ˈmʌltəˌtuːd, -ˌtjuːd] *n* **1** CROWD : multitud *f,* muchedumbre *f* **2** HOST : multitud *f,* gran cantidad *f* <a multitude of ideas : numerosas ideas>

multivitamin [ˌmʌltiˈvaɪṭəmən, ˌmʌltaɪ-] *adj* : multivitamínico

mum[1] [ˈmʌm] *adj* SILENT : callado

mum[2] *n* → **chrysanthemum**

mumble[1] [ˈmʌmbəl] *v* **-bled; -bling** *vt* : mascullar, musitar — *vi* : mascullar, hablar entre dientes, murmurar

mumble[2] *n* **to speak in a mumble** : hablar entre dientes

mummy [ˈmʌmi] *n, pl* **-mies** : momia *f*

mumps [ˈmʌmps] *ns & pl* : paperas *fpl*

munch [ˈmʌntʃ] *v* : mascar, masticar

mundane [ˌmʌnˈdeɪn, ˈmʌnˌ-] *adj* **1** EARTHLY, WORLDLY : mundano, terrenal **2** COMMONPLACE : rutinario, ordinario

municipal [mjʊˈnɪsəpəl] *adj* : municipal

municipality [mjʊˌnɪsəˈpæləṭi] *n, pl* **-ties** : municipio *m*

munitions [mjʊˈnɪʃənz] *npl* : municiones *fpl*

mural[1] [ˈmjʊrəl] *adj* : mural

mural[2] [ˈmjʊrəlɪst] *n* : mural *m*

murder[1] [ˈmərdər] *vt* : asesinar, matar — *vi* : matar

murder[2] *n* : asesinato *m,* homicidio *m*

murderer [ˈmərdərər] *n* : asesino *m,* -na *f;* homicida *mf*

murderess [ˈmərdərɪs, -dəˌrɛs, -dərəs] *n* : asesina *f,* homicida *f*

murderous [ˈmərdərəs] *adj* : asesino, homicida

murk [ˈmərk] *n* DARKNESS : oscuridad *f,* tinieblas *fpl*

murkiness [ˈmərkinəs] *n* : oscuridad *f,* tenebrosidad *f*

murky [ˈmərki] *adj* **-kier; -est** : oscuro, tenebroso

murmur[1] [ˈmərmər] *vi* **1** DRONE : murmurar **2** GRUMBLE : refunfuñar, regañar, rezongar — *vt* MUMBLE : murmurar

murmur[2] *n* **1** COMPLAINT : queja *f* **2** DRONE : murmullo *m,* rumor *m*

muscle[1] [ˈmʌsəl] *vi* **-cled; -cling** : meterse <to muscle in on : meterse por la fuerza en, entrometerse en>

muscle[2] *n* **1** : músculo *m* **2** STRENGTH : fuerza *f*

muscular [ˈmʌskjələr] *adj* **1** : muscular <muscular tissue : tejido muscular> **2** BRAWNY : musculoso

muscular dystrophy *n* : distrofia *f* muscular

musculature [ˈmʌskjələˌtʃʊr, -tʃər] *n* : musculatura *f*

muse[1] [ˈmjuːz] *vi* **mused; musing** PONER, REFLECT : cavilar, meditar, reflexionar

muse[2] *n* : musa *f*

museum [mjʊˈziːəm] *n* : museo *m*

mush [ˈmʌʃ] *n* **1** : gachas *fpl* (de maíz) **2** SENTIMENTALITY : sensiblería *f*

mushroom[1] [ˈmʌʃˌruːm, -ˌrʊm] *vi* GROW, MULTIPLY : crecer rápidamente, multiplicarse

mushroom[2] *n* : hongo *m,* champiñón *m,* seta *f*

mushy [ˈmʌʃi] *adj* **mushier; -est 1** SOFT : blando **2** MAWKISH : sensiblero

music [ˈmjuːzɪk] *n* : música *f*

musical[1] [ˈmjuːzɪkəl] *adj* : musical, de música — **musically** *adv*

musical[2] *n* : comedia *f* musical

music box *n* : cajita *f* de música

musician [mjʊˈzɪʃən] *n* : músico *m,* -ca *f*

musk [ˈmʌsk] *n* : almizcle *m*

musket [ˈmʌskət] *n* : mosquete *m*

musketeer [ˌmʌskəˈtɪr] *n* : mosquetero *m*

muskrat [ˈmʌskˌræt] *n, pl* **-rat** *or* **-rats** : rata *f* almizclera

Muslim[1] [ˈmʌzləm, ˈmʊs-, ˈmʊz-] *adj* : musulmán

Muslim[2] *n* : musulmán *m,* -mana *f*

muslin [ˈmʌzlən] *n* : muselina *f*

muss[1] [ˈmʌs] *vt* : desordenar, despeinar (el pelo)

muss[2] *n* : desorden *m*

mussel [ˈmʌsəl] *n* : mejillón *m*

must[1] [ˈmʌst] *v aux* **1** (*expressing obligation or necessity*) : deber, tener que <you must stop : debes parar> <we must obey : tenemos que obedecer> **2** (*expressing probability*) : deber (de), haber de <you must be tired : debes de estar cansado> <it must be late : ha de ser tarde>

must[2] *n* : necesidad *f* <exercise is a must : el ejercicio es imprescindible>

mustache [ˈmʌˌstæʃ, mʌˈstæʃ] *n* : bigote *m,* bigotes *mpl*

mustang [ˈmʌˌstæŋ] *n* : mustang *m*

mustard [ˈmʌstərd] *n* : mostaza *f*

muster[1] [ˈmʌstər] *vt* **1** ASSEMBLE : reunir **2 to muster up** : armarse de, cobrar (valor, fuerzas, etc.)

muster[2] *n* **1** INSPECTION : revista *f* (de tropas) <it didn't pass muster : no resistió un examen minucioso> **2** COLLECTION : colección *f*

mustiness [ˈmʌstinəs] *n* : lo mohoso

musty [ˈmʌsti] *adj* **mustier; -est** : mohoso, que huele a moho, que huele a encerrado

mutant[1] [ˈmjuːtənt] *adj* : mutante

mutant[2] *n* : mutante *m*

mutate [ˈmjuːˌteɪt] *vi* **-tated; -tating 1** : mutar (genéticamente) **2** CHANGE : transformarse

mutation [mjuːˈteɪʃən] *n* : mutación *f* (genética)

mute[1] [ˈmjuːt] *vt* **muted; muting** MUFFLE : amortiguar, ponerle sordina a (un instrumento musical)
mute[2] *adj* **muter; mutest** : mudo — **mutely** *adv*
mute[3] *n* **1** : mudo *m,* -da *f* (persona) **2** : sordina *f* (para un instrumento musical)
mutilate [ˈmjuːt̬ə,leɪt] *vt* **-lated; -lating** : mutilar
mutilation [,mjuːt̬əˈleɪʃən] *n* : mutilación *f*
mutineer [,mjuːtənˈɪr] *n* : amotinado *m,* -da *f*
mutinous [ˈmjuːtənəs] *adj* : amotinado
mutiny[1] [ˈmjuːtəni] *vi* **-nied; -nying** : amotinarse
mutiny[2] *n, pl* **-nies** : amotinamiento *m,* motín *m*
mutt [ˈmʌt] *n* MONGREL : perro *m* mestizo, perro *m* corriente *Mex*
mutter [ˈmʌt̬ər] *vi* **1** MUMBLE : mascullar, hablar entre dientes, murmurar **2** GRUMBLE : refunfuñar, regañar, rezongar
mutton [ˈmʌtən] *n* : carne *f* de carnero
mutual [ˈmjuːtʃʊəl] *adj* **1** : mutuo <mutual respect : respeto mutuo> **2** COMMON : común <a mutual friend : un amigo común>
mutually [ˈmjuːtʃʊəli, -tʃəli] *adv* **1** : mutuamente <mutually beneficial : mutuamente beneficioso> **2** JOINTLY : conjuntamente
muzzle[1] [ˈmʌzəl] *vt* **-zled; -zling** : ponerle un bozal a (un animal), amordazar
muzzle[2] *n* **1** SNOUT : hocico *m* **2** : bozal *m* (para un perro, etc.) **3** : boca *f* (de un arma de fuego)
my[1] [ˈmaɪ] *adj* : mi <my parents : mis padres>
my[2] *interj* : ¡caramba!, ¡Dios mío!
myopia [maɪˈoːpiə] *n* : miopía *f*
myopic [maɪˈoːpɪk, -ˈɑ-] *adj* : miope
myriad[1] [ˈmɪriəd] *adj* INNUMERABLE : innumerable
myriad[2] *n* : miríada *f*
myrrh [ˈmər] *n* : mirra *f*
myrtle [ˈmərt̬əl] *n* : mirto *m,* arrayán *m*
myself [maɪˈsɛlf] *pron* **1** (*used reflexively*) : me <I washed myself : me lavé> **2** (*used for emphasis*) : yo mismo, yo misma <I did it myself : lo hice yo mismo>
mysterious [mɪˈstɪriəs] *adj* : misterioso — **mysteriously** *adv*
mysteriousness [mɪˈstɪriəsnəs] *n* : lo misterioso
mystery [ˈmɪstəri] *n, pl* **-teries** : misterio *m*
mystic[1] [ˈmɪstɪk] *adj* : místico
mystic[2] *n* : místico *m,* -ca *f*
mystical [ˈmɪstɪkəl] *adj* : místico — **mystically** *adv*
mysticism [ˈmɪstə,sɪzəm] *n* : misticismo *m*
mystify [ˈmɪstə,faɪ] *vt* **-fied; -fying** : dejar perplejo, confundir
mystique [mɪˈstiːk] *n* : aura *f* de misterio
myth [ˈmɪθ] *n* : mito *m*
mythical [ˈmɪθɪkəl] *adj* : mítico
mythological [,mɪθəˈlɑdʒɪkəl] *adj* : mitológico
mythology [mɪˈθɑlədʒi] *n, pl* **-gies** : mitología *f*

N

n [ˈɛn] *n, pl* **n's** *or* **ns** [ˈɛnz] : decimocuarta letra del alfabeto inglés
nab [ˈnæb] *vt* **nabbed; nabbing** : prender, pillar *fam,* pescar *fam*
nadir [ˈneɪdər, ˈneɪ,dɪr] *n* : nadir *m,* punto *m* más bajo
nag[1] [ˈnæg] *v* **nagged; nagging** *vi* **1** COMPLAIN : quejarse, rezongar **2 to nag at** HASSLE : molestar, darle (la) lata (a alguien) — *vt* **1** PESTER : molestar, fastidiar **2** SCOLD : regañar, estarle encima a *fam*
nag[2] *n* **1** GRUMBLER : gruñón *m,* -ñona *f* **2** HORSE : jamelgo *m*
naiad [ˈneɪəd, ˈnaɪ-, -,æd] *n, pl* **-iads** *or* **-iades** [-ə,diːz] : náyade *f*
nail[1] [ˈneɪl] *vt* : clavar, sujetar con clavos
nail[2] *n* **1** FINGERNAIL : uña *f* <nail file : lima (de uñas)> <nail polish : laca de uñas> **2** : clavo *m* <to hit the nail on the head : dar en el clavo>
naive *or* **naïve** [nɑˈiːv] *adj* **-iver; -est** **1** INGENUOUS : ingenuo, cándido **2** GULLIBLE : crédulo
naively [nɑˈiːvli] *adv* : ingenuamente
naïveté [,nɑ,iːvəˈteɪ, nɑˈiːvə,-] *n* : ingenuidad *f*
naked [ˈneɪkəd] *adj* **1** UNCLOTHED : desnudo **2** UNCOVERED : desenvainado (dícese de una espada), pelado (dícese de los árboles), expuesto al aire (dícese de una llama) **3** OBVIOUS, PLAIN : manifiesto, puro, desnudo <the naked truth : la pura verdad> **4 to the naked eye** : a simple vista
nakedly [ˈneɪkədli] *adv* : manifiestamente
nakedness [ˈneɪkədnəs] *n* : desnudez *f*
name[1] [ˈneɪm] *vt* **named; naming 1** CALL : llamar, bautizar, ponerle nombre a **2** MENTION : mentar, mencionar, dar el nombre de <they have named a suspect : han dado el nombre de un

sospechoso> **3** APPOINT : nombrar **4 to name a price :** fijar un precio

name[2] *adj* **1** KNOWN : de nombre <name brand : marca conocida> **2** PROMINENT : de renombre, de prestigio

name[3] *n* **1 :** nombre *m* <what is your name : ¿cómo se llama?> **2** SURNAME : apellido *m* **3** EPITHET : epíteto *m* <to call somebody names : llamar a alguien de todo> **4** REPUTATION : fama *f,* reputación *f* <to make a name for oneself : darse a conocer, hacerse famoso>

nameless [ˈneɪmləs] *adj* **1** ANONYMOUS : anónimo **2** INDESCRIBABLE : indecible, indescriptible

namelessly [ˈneɪmləsli] *adv* : anónimamente

namely [ˈneɪmli] *adv* : a saber

namesake [ˈneɪmˌseɪk] *n* : tocayo *m,* -ya *f;* homónimo *m,* -ma *f*

Namibian [nəˈmɪbiən] *n* : namibio *m,* -bia *f* — **Namibian** *adj*

nap[1] [ˈnæp] *vi* **napped; napping 1** : dormir, dormir la siesta **2 to be caught napping :** estar desprevenido

nap[2] *n* **1** SLEEP : siesta *f* <to take a nap : echarse una siesta> **2** FUZZ, PILE : pelo *m,* pelusa *f* (de telas)

nape [ˈneɪp, ˈnæp] *n* : nuca *f,* cerviz *f,* cogote *m*

naphtha [ˈnæfθə] *n* : nafta *f*

napkin [ˈnæpkən] *n* : servilleta *f*

narcissism [ˈnɑrsəˌsɪzəm] *n* : narcisismo *m*

narcissist [ˈnɑrsəsɪst] *n* : narcisista *mf*

narcissistic [ˌnɑrsəˈsɪstɪk] *adj* : narcisista

narcissus [nɑrˈsɪsəs] *n, pl* **-cissus** *or* **-cissuses** *or* **-cissi** [-ˈsɪˌsaɪ, -ˌsiː] : narciso *m*

narcotic[1] [nɑrˈkɑt̬ɪk] *adj* : narcótico

narcotic[2] *n* : narcótico *m,* estupefaciente *m*

narrate [ˈnærˌeɪt] *vt* **-rated; -rating** : narrar, relatar

narration [næˈreɪʃən] *n* : narración *f*

narrative[1] [ˈnærət̬ɪv] *adj* : narrativo

narrative[2] *n* : narración *f,* narrativa *f,* relato *m*

narrator [ˈnærˌeɪt̬ər] *n* : narrador *m,* -dora *f*

narrow[1] [ˈnærˌoː] *vi* : estrecharse, angostarse <the river narrowed : el río se estrechó> — *vt* **1** : estrechar, angostar **2** LIMIT : restringir, limitar <to narrow the search : limitar la búsqueda>

narrow[2] *adj* **1** : estrecho, angosto **2** LIMITED : estricto, limitado <in the narrowest sense of the word : en el sentido más estricto de la palabra> **3 to have a narrow escape** : escapar por un pelo

narrowly [ˈnæroli] *adv* **1** BARELY : por poco **2** CLOSELY : de cerca

narrow-minded [ˌnæroˈmaɪndəd] *adj* : de miras estrechas

narrowness [ˈnæronəs] *n* : estrechez *f*

narrows [ˈnæroːz] *npl* STRAIT : estrecho *m*

narwhal [ˈnɑrˌhwɑl, ˈnɑrwəl] *n* : narval *m*

nasal [ˈneɪzəl] *adj* : nasal, gangoso <a nasal voice : una voz gangosa>

nasally [ˈneɪzəli] *adv* **1** : por la nariz **2** : con voz gangosa

nastily [ˈnæstəli] *adv* : con maldad, cruelmente

nastiness [ˈnæstinəs] *n* : porquería *f*

nasturtium [nəˈstərʃəm, næ-] *n* : capuchina *f*

nasty [ˈnæsti] *adj* **-tier; -est 1** FILTHY : sucio, mugriento **2** OBSCENE : obsceno **3** MEAN, SPITEFUL : malo, malicioso **4** UNPLEASANT : desagradable, feo **5** REPUGNANT : asqueroso, repugnante <a nasty smell : un olor asqueroso>

natal [ˈneɪt̬əl] *adj* : natal

nation [ˈneɪʃən] *n* : nación *f*

national[1] [ˈnæʃənəl] *adj* : nacional

national[2] *n* : ciudadano *m,* -na *f;* nacional *mf*

nationalism [ˈnæʃənəˌlɪzəm] *n* : nacionalismo *m*

nationalist[1] [ˈnæʃənəlɪst] *adj* : nacionalista

nationalist[2] *n* : nacionalista *mf*

nationalistic [ˌnæʃənəˈlɪstɪk] *adj* : nacionalista

nationality [ˌnæʃəˈnælət̬i] *n, pl* **-ties** : nacionalidad *f*

nationalization [ˌnæʃənələˈzeɪʃən] *n* : nacionalización *f*

nationalize [ˈnæʃənəˌlaɪz] *vt* **-ized; -izing** : nacionalizar

nationally [ˈnæʃənəli] *adv* : a escala nacional, a nivel nacional

nationwide [ˈneɪʃənˈwaɪd] *adj* : en toda la nación, por todo el país

native[1] [ˈneɪt̬ɪv] *adj* **1** INNATE : innato **2** : natal <her native city : su ciudad natal> **3** INDIGENOUS : indígeno, autóctono

native[2] *n* **1** ABORIGINE : nativo *m,* -va *f;* indígena *mf* **2** : natural *m* <he's a native of Mexico : es natural de México>

Native American → **American Indian**

nativity [nəˈtɪvət̬i, neɪ-] *n, pl* **-ties 1** BIRTH : navidad *f* **2 the Nativity** : la Natividad, la Navidad

natty [ˈnæt̬i] *adj* **-tier; -est** : elegante, garboso

natural[1] [ˈnætʃərəl] *adj* **1** : natural, de la naturaleza <natural woodlands : bosques naturales> <natural childbirth : parto natural> **2** INNATE : innato, natural **3** UNAFFECTED : natural, sin afectación **4** LIFELIKE : natural, vivo

natural[2] *n* **to be a natural** : tener un talento innato (para algo)

natural gas *n* : gas *m* natural

natural history *n* : historia *f* natural

naturalist [ˈnætʃərəlɪst] *n* **:** naturalista *mf*
naturalization [ˌnætʃərələˈzeɪʃən] *n* **:** naturalización *f*
naturalize [ˈnætʃərəˌlaɪz] *vt* **-ized; -izing :** naturalizar
naturally [ˈnætʃərəli] *adv* **1** INHERENTLY **:** naturalmente, intrínsecamente **2** UNAFFECTEDLY **:** de manera natural **3** OF COURSE **:** por supuesto, naturalmente
naturalness [ˈnætʃərəlnəs] *n* **:** naturalidad *f*
natural science *n* **:** ciencias *fpl* naturales
nature [ˈneɪtʃər] *n* **1 :** naturaleza *f* <the laws of nature : las leyes de la naturaleza> **2** KIND, SORT **:** índole *f,* clase *f* <things of this nature : cosas de esta índole> **3** DISPOSITION **:** carácter *m,* natural *m,* naturaleza *f* <it is his nature to be friendly : es de natural simpático> <human nature : la naturaleza humana>
naught [ˈnɔt] *n* **1 :** nada *f* <to come to naught : reducirse a nada, fracasar> **2** ZERO **:** cero *m*
naughtily [ˈnɔtəli] *adv* **:** traviesamente, con malicia
naughtiness [ˈnɔtinəs] *n* **:** mala conducta *f,* travesuras *fpl*, malicia *f*
naughty [ˈnɔti] *adj* **-tier; -est 1** MISCHIEVOUS **:** travieso, pícaro **2** RISQUÉ **:** picante, subido de tono
nausea [ˈnɔziə, ˈnɔʃə] *n* **1** SICKNESS **:** náuseas *fpl* **2** DISGUST **:** asco *m*
nauseate [ˈnɔziˌeɪt, -ʒi-, -si-, -ʃi-] *vt* **-ated; -ating 1** SICKEN **:** darle náuseas (a alguien) **2** DISGUST **:** asquear, darle asco (a alguien)
nauseating *adj* **:** nauseabundo, repugnante
nauseatingly [ˈnɔziˌeɪtɪŋli, -ʒi-, -si-, -ʃi-] *adv* **:** hasta el punto de dar asco <nauseatingly sweet : tan dulce que da asco>
nauseous [ˈnɔʃəs, -ziəs] *adj* **1** SICK **:** mareado, con náuseas **2** SICKENING **:** nauseabundo
nautical [ˈnɔtɪkəl] *adj* **:** náutico
nautilus [ˈnɔtələs] *n, pl* **-luses** *or* **-li** [-ˌlaɪ, -ˌliː] **:** nautilo *m*
naval [ˈneɪvəl] *adj* **:** naval
nave [ˈneɪv] *n* **:** nave *f*
navel [ˈneɪvəl] *n* **:** ombligo *m*
navigability [ˌnævɪgəˈbɪləti] *n* **:** navegabilidad *f*
navigable [ˈnævɪgəbəl] *adj* **:** navegable
navigate [ˈnævəˌgeɪt] *v* **-gated; -gating** *vi* **:** navegar — *vt* **1** STEER **:** gobernar (un barco), pilotar (un avión) **2 :** navegar por (un río, etc.)
navigation [ˌnævəˈgeɪʃən] *n* **:** navegación *f*
navigator [ˈnævəˌgeɪtər] *n* **:** navegante *mf*
navy [ˈneɪvi] *n, pl* **-vies 1** FLEET **:** flota *f* **2 :** marina *f* de guerra, armada *f* <the United States Navy : la armada de los Estados Unidos> **3** *or* **navy blue :** azul *m* marino
nay[1] [ˈneɪ] *adv* **:** no
nay[2] *n* **:** no *m,* voto *m* en contra
Nazi [ˈnɑtsi, ˈnæt-] *n* **:** nazi *mf*
Nazism [ˈnɑtˌsɪzəm, ˈnæt-] *or* **Naziism** [ˈnɑtsiˌɪzəm, ˈnæt-] *n* **:** nazismo *m*
Neanderthal man [niˈændərˌθɔl, -ˌtɔl] *n* **:** hombre *m* de Neanderthal
near[1] [ˈnɪr] *vt* **1 :** acercarse a <the ship is nearing port : el barco se está acercando al puerto> **2 :** estar a punto de <she is nearing graduation : está a punto de graduarse>
near[2] *adv* **1** CLOSE **:** cerca <my family lives quite near : mi familia vive muy cerca> **2** NEARLY **:** casi <I came near to finishing : casi terminé>
near[3] *adj* **1** CLOSE **:** cercano, próximo **2** SIMILAR **:** parecido, semejante
near[4] *prep* **:** cerca de
nearby[1] [nɪrˈbaɪ, ˈnɪrˌbaɪ] *adv* **:** cerca
nearby[2] *adj* **:** cercano
nearly [ˈnɪrli] *adv* **1** ALMOST **:** casi <nearly asleep : casi dormido> **2 not nearly :** ni con mucho, ni mucho menos <it was not nearly so bad as I had expected : no fue ni con mucho tan malo como esperaba>
nearness [ˈnɪrnəs] *n* **:** proximidad *f*
nearsighted [ˈnɪrˌsaɪtəd] *adj* **:** miope, corto de vista
nearsightedly [ˈnɪrˌsaɪtədli] *adv* **:** con miopía
nearsightedness [ˈnɪrˌsaɪtədnəs] *n* **:** miopía *f*
neat [ˈniːt] *adj* **1** CLEAN, ORDERLY **:** ordenado, pulcro, limpio **2** UNDILUTED **:** solo, sin diluir **3** SIMPLE, TASTEFUL **:** sencillo y de buen gusto **4** CLEVER **:** hábil, ingenioso <a neat trick : un truco ingenioso>
neatly [ˈniːtli] *adv* **1** TIDILY **:** ordenadamente **2** CLEVERLY **:** ingeniosamente
neatness [ˈniːtnəs] *n* **:** pulcritud *f,* limpieza *f,* orden *m*
nebula [ˈnɛbjʊlə] *n, pl* **-lae** [-ˌliː, -ˌlaɪ] **:** nebulosa *f*
nebulous [ˈnɛbjʊləs] *adj* **:** nebuloso, vago
necessarily [ˌnɛsəˈsɛrəli] *adv* **:** necesariamente, forzosamente
necessary[1] [ˈnɛsəˌsɛri] *adj* **1** INEVITABLE **:** inevitable **2** COMPULSORY **:** necesario, obligatorio **3** ESSENTIAL **:** imprescindible, preciso, necesario
necessary[2] *n, pl* **-saries :** lo esencial, lo necesario
necessitate [nɪˈsɛsəˌteɪt] *vt* **-tated; -tating :** necesitar, requerir
necessity [nɪˈsɛsəti] *n, pl* **-ties 1** NEED **:** necesidad *f* **2** REQUIREMENT **:** requisito *m* indispensable **3** POVERTY **:** indigencia *f,* necesidad *f* **4** INEVITABILITY **:** inevitabilitad *f*
neck[1] [ˈnɛk] *vi* **:** besuquearse

neck[2] *n* **1 :** cuello *m* (de una persona), pescuezo *m* (de un animal) **2** COLLAR **:** cuello *m* **3 :** cuello *m* (de una botella), mástil *m* (de una guitarra)
neckerchief [ˈnɛkərtʃəf, -ˌtʃiːf] *n, pl* **-chiefs** [-tʃəfs, -ˌtʃiːfs] **:** pañuelo *m* (para el cuello), mascada *f Mex*
necklace [ˈnɛkləs] *n* **:** collar *m*
neckline [ˈnɛkˌlaɪn] *n* **:** escote *m*
necktie [ˈnɛkˌtaɪ] *n* **:** corbata *f*
nectar [ˈnɛktər] *n* **:** néctar *m*
nectarine [ˌnɛktəˈriːn] *n* **:** nectarina *f*
née *or* **nee** [ˈneɪ] *adj* **:** de soltera <Mrs. Smith, née Whitman : la señora Smith, de soltera Whitman>
need[1] [ˈniːd] *vt* **1 :** necesitar <I need your help : necesito su ayuda> <I need money : me falta dinero> **2** REQUIRE **:** requerir, exigir <that job needs patience : ese trabajo exige paciencia> **3 to need to :** tener que <he needs to study : tiene que estudiar> <they need to be scolded : hay que reprenderlos> — *v aux* **1** MUST **:** tener que, deber <need you shout? : ¿tienes que gritar?> **2 to be needed :** hacer falta <you needn't worry : no hace falta que te preocupes, no hay por qué preocuparse>
need[2] *n* **1** NECESSITY **:** necesidad *f* <in case of need : en caso de necesidad> **2** LACK **:** falta *f* <the need for better training : la falta de mejor capacitación> <to be in need : necesitar> **3** POVERTY **:** necesidad *f,* indigencia *f* **4 needs** *npl* **:** requisitos *mpl*, carencias *fpl*
needful [ˈniːdfəl] *adj* **:** necesario
needle[1] [ˈniːdəl] *vt* **-dled; -dling :** pinchar
needle[2] *n* **1 :** aguja *f* <to thread a needle : enhebrar una aguja> <knitting needle : aguja de tejer> **2** POINTER **:** aguja *f,* indicador *m*
needlepoint [ˈniːdəlˌpɔint] *n* **1** LACE **:** encaje *m* de mano **2** EMBROIDERY **:** bordado *m* en cañamazo
needless [ˈniːdləs] *adj* **:** innecesario
needlessly [ˈniːdləsli] *adv* **:** sin ninguna necesidad, innecesariamente
needlework [ˈniːdəlˌwərk] *n* **:** bordado *m*
needn't [ˈniːdənt] (*contraction of* **need not**) → **need**
needy[1] [ˈniːdi] **needier; -est** *adj* **:** necesitado
needy[2] *n* **the needy :** los necesitados *mpl*
nefarious [nɪˈfæriəs] *adj* **:** nefario, nefando, infame
negate [nɪˈgeɪt] *vt* **-gated; -gating 1** DENY **:** negar **2** NULLIFY **:** invalidar, anular
negation [nɪˈgeɪʃən] *n* **:** negación *f*
negative[1] [ˈnɛgət̬ɪv] *adj* **:** negativo
negative[2] *n* **1 :** negación *f* (en lingüística) **2 :** negativa *f* <to answer in the negative : contestar con una negativa> **3 :** término *m* negativo (en matemáticas) **4 :** negativo *m,* imagen *f* en negativo (en fotografía)
negatively [ˈnɛgət̬ɪvli] *adv* **:** negativamente
neglect[1] [nɪˈglɛkt] *vt* **1 :** desatender, descuidar <to neglect one's health : descuidar la salud> **2 :** no cumplir con, faltar a <to neglect one's obligations : faltar uno a sus obligaciones> <he neglected to tell me : omitió decírmelo>
neglect[2] *n* **1 :** negligencia *f,* descuido *m,* incumplimiento *m* <through neglect : por negligencia> <neglect of duty : incumplimiento del deber> **2 in a state of neglect :** abandonado, descuidado
neglectful [nɪˈglɛktfəl] *adj* **:** descuidado *m*
negligee [ˌnɛgləˈʒeɪ] *n* **:** negligé *m*
negligence [ˈnɛglɪdʒənts] *n* **:** descuido *m,* negligencia *f*
negligent [ˈnɛglɪdʒənt] *adj* **:** negligente, descuidado — **negligently** *adv*
negligible [ˈnɛglɪdʒəbəl] *adj* **:** insignificante, despreciable
negotiable [nɪˈgoːʃəbəl, -ʃiə-] *adj* **:** negociable
negotiate [nɪˈgoːʃiˌeɪt] *v* **-ated; -ating** *vi* **:** negociar — *vt* **1 :** negociar, gestionar <to negotiate a treaty : negociar un trato> **2 :** salvar, franquear <they negotiated the obstacles : salvaron los obstáculos> <to negotiate a turn : tomar una curva>
negotiation [nɪˌgoːʃiˈeɪʃən, -siˈeɪ-] *n* **:** negociación *f*
negotiator [nɪˈgoːʃiˌeɪt̬ər, -siˌeɪ-] *n* **:** negociador *m,* -dora *f*
Negro [ˈniːˌgroː] *n, pl* **-groes :** negro *m,* -gra *f*
neigh[1] [ˈneɪ] *vi* **:** relinchar
neigh[2] *n* **:** relincho *m*
neighbor[1] [ˈneɪbər] *vt* **:** ser vecino de, estar junto a <her house neighbors mine : su casa está junto a la mía> — *vi* **:** estar cercano, lindar, colindar <her land neighbors on mine : sus tierras lindan con las mías>
neighbor[2] *n* **1 :** vecino *m,* -na *f* **2 love thy neighbor :** ama a tu prójimo
neighborhood [ˈneɪbərˌhʊd] *n* **1 :** barrio *m,* vecindad *f,* vecindario *m* **2 in the neighborhood of :** alrededor de, cerca de
neighborly [ˈneɪbərli] *adv* **:** amable, de buena vecindad
neither[1] [ˈniːðər, ˈnaɪ-] *adj* **:** ninguno (de los dos)
neither[2] *conj* **1 :** ni <neither asleep nor awake : ni dormido ni despierto> **2** NOR **:** ni (tampoco) <I'm not asleep — neither am I : no estoy dormido — ni yo tampoco>
neither[3] *pron* **:** ninguno
nemesis [ˈnɛməsɪs] *n, pl* **-eses** [-ˌsiːz] **1** RIVAL **:** rival *mf* **2** RETRIBUTION **:** justo castigo *m*

neologism [niˈɑləˌdʒɪzəm] *n* : neologismo *m*
neon[1] [ˈniːˌɑn] *adj* : de neón <neon sign : letrero de neón>
neon[2] *n* : neón *m*
Nepali [nəˈpɔli, -ˈpɑ-, -ˈpæ-] *n* : nepalés *m,* -lesa *f* — **Nepali** *adj*
neophyte [ˈniːəˌfaɪt] *n* : neófito *m,* -ta *f*
nephew [ˈnɛˌfjuː, *chiefly British* ˈnɛˌvjuː] *n* : sobrino *m*
nepotism [ˈnɛpəˌtɪzəm] *n* : nepotismo *m*
Neptune [ˈnɛpˌtuːn, -ˌtjuːn] *n* : Neptuno *m*
nerd [ˈnərd] *n* : ganso *m,* -sa *f*
nerve [ˈnərv] *n* **1** : nervio *m* **2** COURAGE : coraje *m,* valor *m,* fuerza *f* de la voluntad <to lose one's nerve : perder el valor> **3** AUDACITY, GALL : atrevimiento *m,* descaro *m* <of all the nerve! : ¡qué descaro!> **4 nerves** *npl* : nervios *mpl* <a fit of nerves : un ataque de nervios>
nervous [ˈnərvəs] *adj* **1** : nervioso <the nervous system : el sistema nervioso> **2** EXCITABLE : nervioso, excitable <to get nervous : excitarse, ponerse nervioso> **3** FEARFUL : miedoso, temeroso
nervously [ˈnərvəsli] *adv* : nerviosamente
nervousness [ˈnərvəsnəs] *n* : nerviosismo *m,* nerviosidad *f,* ansiedad *f*
nervy [ˈnərvi] *adj* **nervier; -est 1** COURAGEOUS : valiente **2** IMPUDENT : atrevido, descarado, fresco *fam* **3** NERVOUS : nervioso
nest[1] [ˈnɛst] *vi* : anidar
nest[2] *n* **1** : nido *m* (de un ave), avispero *m* (de una avispa), madriguera *f* (de un animal) **2** REFUGE : nido *m,* refugio *m* **3** SET : juego *m* <a nest of tables : un juego de mesitas>
nestle [ˈnɛsəl] *vi* **-tled; -tling** : acurrucarse, arrimarse cómodamente
net[1] [ˈnɛt] *vt* **netted; netting 1** CATCH : pescar, atrapar con una red **2** CLEAR : ganar neto <they netted $5000 : ganaron $5000 netos> **3** YIELD : producir neto
net[2] *adj* : neto <net weight : peso neto> <net gain : ganancia neta>
net[3] *n* : red *f,* malla *f*
nether [ˈnɛðər] *adj* **1** : inferior, más bajo **2 the nether regions** : el infierno
nettle[1] [ˈnɛtəl] *vt* **-tled; -tling** : irritar, provocar, molestar
nettle[2] *n* : ortiga *f*
network [ˈnɛtˌwərk] *n* **1** SYSTEM : red *f* **2** CHAIN : cadena *f* <a network of supermarkets : una cadena de supermercados>
neural [ˈnʊrəl, ˈnjʊr-] *adj* : neural
neuralgia [nʊˈrældʒə, njʊ-] *n* : neuralgia *f*
neuritis [nʊˈraɪtəs, njʊ-] *n, pl* **-ritides** [-ˈrɪtəˌdiːz] *or* **-ritises** : neuritis *f*
neurological [ˌnʊrəˈlɑdʒɪkəl, ˌnjʊr-] *or* **neurologic** [ˌnʊrəˈlɑdʒɪk, ˌnjʊr-] *adj* : neurológico
neurologist [nʊˈrɑlədʒɪst, njʊ-] *n* : neurólogo *m,* -ga *f*
neurology [nʊˈrɑlədʒi, njʊ-] *n* : neurología *f*
neurosis [nʊˈroːsɪs, njʊ-] *n, pl* **-roses** [-ˌsiːz] : neurosis *f*
neurotic[1] [nʊˈrɑtɪk, njʊ-] *adj* : neurótico
neurotic[2] *n* : neurótico *m,* -ca *f*
neuter[1] [ˈnuːtər, ˈnjuː-] *vt* : castrar
neuter[2] *adj* : neutro
neutral[1] [ˈnuːtrəl, ˈnjuː-] *adj* **1** IMPARTIAL : neutral, imparcial <to remain neutral : permanecer neutral> **2** : neutro <a neutral color : un color neutro> **3** : neutro (en la química o la electricidad)
neutral[2] *n* : punto *m* muerto (de un automóvil)
neutrality [nuːˈtræləti:, njuː-] *n* : neutralidad *f*
neutralization [ˌnuːtrələˈzeɪʃən, ˌnjuː-] *n* : neutralización *f*
neutralize [ˈnuːtrəˌlaɪz, ˈnjuː-] *vt* **-ized; -izing** : neutralizar
neutron [ˈnuːˌtrɑn, ˈnjuː-] *n* : neutrón *m*
never [ˈnɛvər] *adv* **1** : nunca, jamás <he never studies : nunca estudia> **2 never again** : nunca más, nunca jamás **3 never mind** : no importa
nevermore [ˌnɛvərˈmor] *adv* : nunca más
nevertheless [ˌnɛvərðəˈlɛs] *adv* : sin embargo, no obstante
new [ˈnuː, ˈnjuː] *adj* **1** : nuevo <a new dress : un vestido nuevo> **2** RECENT : nuevo, reciente <what's new? : ¿qué hay de nuevo?> <a new arrival : un recién llegado> **3** DIFFERENT : nuevo, distinto <this problem is new : este problema es distinto> <new ideas : ideas nuevas> **4 like new** : como nuevo
newborn [ˈnuːˌbɔrn, ˈnjuː-] *adj* : recién nacido
newcomer [ˈnuːˌkʌmər, ˈnjuː-] *n* : recién llegado *m,* recién llegada *f*
newfangled [ˈnuːˈfæŋgəld, ˈnjuː-] *adj* : novedoso
newfound [ˈnuːˈfaʊnd, ˈnjuː-] *adj* : recién descubierto
newly [ˈnuːli, ˈnjuː-] *adv* : recién, recientemente
newlywed [ˈnuːliˌwɛd, ˈnjuː-] *n* : recién casado *m,* -da *f*
new moon *n* : luna *f* nueva
newness [ˈnuːnəs, ˈnjuː-] *n* : novedad *f*
news [ˈnuːz, ˈnjuːz] *n* : noticias *fpl*
newscast [ˈnuːzˌkæst, ˈnjuːz-] *n* : noticiero *m,* informativo *m*
newscaster [ˈnuːzˌkæstər, ˈnjuːz-] *n* : presentador *m,* -dora *f;* locutor *m,* -tora *f*

newsletter ['nu:z,lɛtər, 'nju:z-] *n* : boletín *m* informativo
newsman ['nu:zmən, 'nju:z-, -,mæn] *n, pl* **-men** [-mən, -,mɛn] : periodista *m,* reportero *m*
newspaper ['nu:z,peɪpər, 'nju:z-] *n* : periódico *m,* diario *m*
newspaperman ['nu:z,peɪpər,mæn, 'nju:z-] *n, pl* **-men** [-mən, -,mɛn] **1** REPORTER : periodista *m,* reportero *m* **2** : dueño *m* de un periódico
newsprint ['nu:z,prɪnt, 'nju:z-] *n* : papel *m* de prensa
newsstand ['nu:z,stænd, 'nju:z-] *n* : quiosco *m,* puesto *m* de periódicos
newswoman ['nu:z,wʊmən, 'nju:z-] *n, pl* **-women** [-,wɪmən] : periodista *f,* reportera *f*
newsworthy ['nu:z,wərði, 'nju:z-] *adj* : de interés periodístico
newsy ['nu:zi:, 'nju:-] *adj* **newsier; -est** : lleno de noticias
newt ['nu:t, 'nju:t] *n* : tritón *m*
New Year *n* : Año *m* Nuevo
New Year's Day *n* : día *m* del Año Nuevo
New Yorker [nu:'jɔrkər, nju:-] *n* : neoyorquino *m,* -na *f*
New Zealander [nu:'zi:ləndər, nju:-] *n* : neozelandés *m,* -desa *f*
next¹ ['nɛkst] *adv* **1** AFTERWARD : después, luego <what will you do next? : ¿qué harás después?> **2** NOW : después, ahora, entonces <next I will sing a song : ahora voy a cantar una canción> **3** : la próxima vez <when next we meet : la próxima vez que nos encontremos>
next² *adj* **1** ADJACENT : contiguo, de al lado **2** COMING : que viene, próximo <next Friday : el viernes que viene> **3** FOLLOWING : siguiente <the next year : el año siguiente>
next-door ['nɛkst'dor] *adj* : de al lado
next to¹ *adv* ALMOST : casi, prácticamente <next to impossible : casi imposible>
next to² *prep* : junto a, al lado de
nib ['nɪb] *n* : plumilla *f*
nibble¹ ['nɪbəl] *v* **-bled; -bling** *vt* : pellizcar, mordisquear, picar — *vi* : picar
nibble² *n* : mordisco *m*
Nicaraguan [,nɪkə'rɑgwən] *n* : nicaragüense *mf* — **Nicaraguan** *adj*
nice ['naɪs] *adj* **nicer; nicest 1** REFINED : pulido, refinado **2** SUBTLE : fino, sutil **3** PLEASING : agradable, bueno, lindo <nice weather : buen tiempo> **4** RESPECTABLE : bueno, decente **5 nice and** : bien, muy <nice and hot : bien caliente> <nice and slow : despacito>
nicely ['naɪsli] *adv* **1** KINDLY : amablemente **2** POLITELY : con buenos modales **3** ATTRACTIVELY : de buen gusto
niceness ['naɪsnəs] *n* : simpatía *f,* amabilidad *f*
nicety ['naɪsəṭi] *n, pl* **-ties 1** DETAIL, SUBTLETY : sutileza *f,* detalle *m* **2 niceties** *npl* : lujos *mpl,* detalles *mpl*
niche ['nɪtʃ] *n* **1** RECESS : nicho *m,* hornacina *f* **2** : nicho *m,* hueco *m* <to make a niche for oneself : hacerse un hueco, encontrarse una buena posición>
nick¹ ['nɪk] *vt* : cortar, hacer una muesca en
nick² *n* **1** CUT : corte *m,* muesca *f* **2 in the nick of time** : en el momento crítico, justo a tiempo
nickel ['nɪkəl] *n* **1** : níquel *m* **2** : moneda *f* de cinco centavos
nickname¹ ['nɪk,neɪm] *vt* **-named; -naming** : apodar
nickname² *n* : apodo *m,* mote *m,* sobrenombre *m*
nicotine ['nɪkə,ti:n] *n* : nicotina *f*
niece ['ni:s] *n* : sobrina *f*
Nigerian [naɪ'dʒɪriən] *n* : nigeriano *m,* -na *f* — **Nigerian** *adj*
niggardly ['nɪgərdli] *adj* : mezquino, tacaño
niggling ['nɪgəlɪŋ] *adj* **1** PETTY : insignificante **2** PERSISTENT : constante, persistente <a niggling doubt : una duda constante>
nigh¹ ['naɪ] *adv* **1** NEARLY : casi **2 to draw nigh** : acercarse, avecinarse
nigh² *adj* : cercano, próximo
night¹ ['naɪt] *adj* : nocturno, de la noche <the night sky : el cielo nocturno> <night shift : turno de la noche>
night² *n* **1** EVENING : noche *f* <at night : de noche> <last night : anoche> <tomorrow night : mañana por la noche> **2** DARKNESS : noche *f,* oscuridad *f* <night fell : cayó la noche>
nightclothes ['naɪt,klo:ðz, -,klo:z] *npl* : ropa *f* de dormir
nightclub ['naɪt,klʌb] *n* : cabaret *m,* club *m* nocturno
night crawler ['naɪt,krɔlər] *n* EARTHWORM : lombriz *f* (de tierra)
nightfall ['naɪt,fɔl] *n* : anochecer *m*
nightgown ['naɪt,gaʊn] *n* : camisón *m* (de noche)
nightingale ['naɪtən,geɪl, 'naɪṭɪŋ-] *n* : ruiseñor *m*
nightly¹ ['naɪtli] *adv* : cada noche, todas las noches
nightly² *adj* : de todas las noches
nightmare ['naɪt,mær] *n* : pesadilla *f*
nightmarish ['naɪt,mærɪʃ] *adj* : de pesadilla
night owl *n* : noctámbulo *m,* -la *f*
nightshade ['naɪt,ʃeɪd] *n* : hierba *f* mora
nightshirt ['naɪt,ʃərt] *n* : camisa *f* de dormir
nightstick ['naɪt,stɪk] *n* : porra *f*
nighttime ['naɪt,taɪm] *n* : noche *f*
nil ['nɪl] *n* : nada *f,* cero *m*
nimble ['nɪmbəl] *adj* **-bler; -blest 1** AGILE : ágil **2** CLEVER : hábil, ingenioso
nimbleness ['nɪmbəlnəs] *n* : agilidad *f*

nimbly ['nɪmbli] *adv* : con agilidad, ágilmente

nincompoop ['nɪnkəm,pu:p, 'nɪŋ-] *n* FOOL : tonto *m*, -ta *f*; bobo *m*, -ba *f*

nine[1] ['naɪn] *adj* **1** : nueve **2 nine times out of ten** : casi siempre

nine[2] *n* : nueve *m*

nine hundred[1] *adj* : novecientos

nine hundred[2] *n* : novecientos *m*

ninepins ['naɪn,pɪnz] *n* : bolos *mpl*

nineteen[1] [naɪn'ti:n] *adj* : diecinueve

nineteen[2] *n* : diecinueve *m*

nineteenth[1] [naɪn'ti:nθ] *adj* : decimonoveno, decimonono <the nineteenth century : el siglo diecinueve>

nineteenth[2] *n* : decimonoveno *m*, -na *f*; decimonono *m*, -na *f* (en una serie) **2** : diecinueveavo *m*, diecinueveava parte *f*

ninetieth[1] ['naɪntiəθ] *adj* : nonagésimo

ninetieth[2] *n* **1** : nonagésimo *m*, -ma *f* (en una serie) **2** : noventavo *m*, noventava parte *f*

ninety[1] ['naɪnti] *adj* : noventa

ninety[2] *n*, *pl* **-ties** : noventa *m*

ninth[1] ['naɪnθ] *adj* : noveno

ninth[2] *n* **1** : noveno *m*, -na *f* (en una serie) **2** : noveno *m*, novena parte *f*

ninny ['nɪni] *n*, *pl* **ninnies** FOOL : tonto *m*, -ta *f*; bobo *m*, -ba *f*

nip[1] ['nɪp] *vt* **nipped; nipping 1** PINCH : pellizcar **2** BITE : morder, mordisquear **3 to nip in the bud** : cortar de raíz

nip[2] *n* **1** TANG : sabor *m* fuerte **2** PINCH : pellizco *m* **3** NIBBLE : mordisco *m* **4** SWALLOW : trago *m*, traguito *m* **5 there's a nip in the air** : hace fresco

nipple ['nɪpəl] *n* : pezón *m* (de una mujer), tetilla *f* (de un hombre)

nippy ['nɪpi] *adj* **-pier; -est 1** SHARP : fuerte, picante **2** CHILLY : frío <it's nippy today : hoy hace frío>

nit ['nɪt] *n* : liendre *f*

nitrate ['naɪ,treɪt] *n* : nitrato *m*

nitric acid ['naɪtrɪk] *n* : ácido *m* nítrico

nitrite ['naɪ,traɪt] *n* : nitrito *m*

nitrogen ['naɪtrədʒən] *n* : nitrógen *m*

nitroglycerin *or* **nitroglycerine** [,naɪtro'glɪsərən] *n* : nitroglicerina *f*

nitwit ['nɪt,wɪt] *n* : zonzo *m*, -za *f*; bobo *m*, -ba *f*

no[1] ['no:] *adv* : no <are you leaving?—no : ¿te vas?—no> <no less than : no menos de> <to say no : decir que no> <like it or no : quieras o no quieras>

no[2] *adj* **1** : ninguno <it's no trouble : no es ningún problema> <she has no money : no tiene dinero> **2** (*indicating a small amount*) <we'll be there in no time : llegamos dentro de poco, no tardamos nada> **3** (*expressing a negation*) <he's no liar : no es mentiroso>

no[3] *n*, *pl* **noes** *or* **nos** ['no:z] **1** DENIAL : no *m* <I won't take no for an answer : no aceptaré un no por respuesta> **2** : vota *f* en contra <the noes have it : se ha rechazado la moción>

nobility [no'bɪləti] *n* : nobleza *f*

noble[1] ['no:bəl] *adj* **-bler; -blest 1** ILLUSTRIOUS : noble, glorioso **2** ARISTOCRATIC : noble **3** STATELY : majestuoso, magnífico **4** LOFTY : noble, elevado <noble sentiments : sentimientos elevados>

noble[2] *n* : noble *mf*, aristócrata *mf*

nobleman ['no:bəlmən] *n*, *pl* **-men** [-mən, -,mɛn] : noble *m*, aristócrata *m*

nobleness ['no:bəlnəs] *n* : nobleza *f*

noblewoman ['no:bəl,wʊmən] *n*, *pl* **-women** [-,wɪmən] : noble *f*, aristócrata *f*

nobly ['no:bli] *adv* : noblemente

nobody[1] ['no:bədi, -,bɑdi] *n*, *pl* **-bodies** : don nadie *m* <he's a mere nobody : es un don nadie>

nobody[2] *pron* : nadie

nocturnal [nɑk'tərnəl] *adj* : nocturno

nocturne ['nɑk,tərn] *n* : nocturno *m*

nod[1] ['nɑd] *v* **nodded; nodding** *vi* **1** : saludar con la cabeza, asentir con la cabeza **2 to nod off** : dormirse, quedarse dormido — *vt* : inclinar (la cabeza) <to nod one's head in agreement : asentir con la cabeza>

nod[2] *n* : saludo *m* con la cabeza, señal *m* con la cabeza, señal *m* de asentimiento

node ['no:d] *n* : nudo *m* (de una planta)

nodule ['nɑ,dʒu:l] *n* : nódulo *m*

noel [no'ɛl] *n* **1** CAROL : villancico *m* de Navidad **2 Noel** CHRISTMAS : Navidad *f*

noes → **no[3]**

noise[1] ['nɔɪz] *vt* **noised; noising** : rumorear, publicar

noise[2] *n* : ruido *m*

noiseless ['nɔɪzləs] *adj* : silencioso, sin ruido

noiselessly ['nɔɪzləsli] *adv* : silenciosamente

noisemaker ['nɔɪz,meɪkər] *n* : matraca *f*

noisiness ['nɔɪzinəs] *n* : ruido *m*

noisome ['nɔɪsəm] *adj* : maloliente, fétido

noisy ['nɔɪzi] *adj* **noisier; -est** : ruidoso — **noisily** ['nɔɪzəli] *adv*

nomad[1] ['no:,mæd] → **nomadic**

nomad[2] *n* : nómada *mf*

nomadic [no'mædɪk] *adj* : nómada

nomenclature ['no:mən,kleɪtʃər] *n* : nomenclatura *f*

nominal ['nɑmənəl] *adj* **1** : nominal <the nominal head of his party : el jefe nominal de su partido> **2** TRIFLING : insignificante

nominally ['nɑmənəli] *adv* : sólo de nombre, nominalmente

nominate ['nɑmə,neɪt] *vt* **-nated; -nating 1** PROPOSE : proponer (como candidato), nominar **2** APPOINT : nombrar

nomination [ˌnɑməˈneɪʃən] *n* **1** PROPOSAL : propuesta *f,* postulación *f* **2** APPOINTMENT : nombramiento *m*
nominative¹ [ˈnɑmənət̬ɪv] *adj* : nominativo
nominative² *n or* **nominative case** : nominativo *m*
nominee [ˌnɑməˈniː] *n* : candidato *m,* -ta *f*
nonaddictive [ˌnɑnəˈdɪktɪv] *adj* : que no crea dependencia
nonalcoholic [ˌnɑnˌælkəˈhɔlɪk] *adj* : sin alcohol, no alcohólico
nonaligned [ˌnɑnəˈlaɪnd] *adj* : no alineado
nonbeliever [ˌnɑnbəˈliːvər] *n* : no creyente *mf*
nonbreakable [ˌnɑnˈbreɪkəbəl] *adj* : irrompible
nonce [ˈnɑnts] *n* **for the nonce** : por el momento
nonchalance [ˌnɑnʃəˈlɑnts] *n* : indiferencia *f,* despreocupación *f*
nonchalant [ˌnɑnʃəˈlɑnt] *adj* : indiferente, despreocupado, impasible
nonchalantly [ˌnɑnʃəˈlɑntli] *adv* : con aire despreocupado, con indiferencia
noncombatant [ˌnɑnkəmˈbætənt, -ˈkɑmbə-] *adj* : no combatiente *mf*
noncommissioned officer [ˌnɑnkəˈmɪʃənd] *n* : suboficial *mf*
noncommittal [ˌnɑnkəˈmɪt̬əl] *adj* : evasivo, que no se compromete
nonconductor [ˌnɑnkənˈdʌktər] *n* : aislante *m*
nonconformist [ˌnɑnkənˈfɔrmɪst] *n* : inconformista *mf,* inconforme *mf*
nonconformity [ˌnɑnkənˈfɔrmət̬i] *n* : inconformidad *f,* no conformidad *f*
noncontagious [ˌnɑnkənˈteɪdʒəs] *adj* : no contagioso
nondenominational [ˌnɑndɪˌnɑməˈneɪʃənəl] *adj* : no sectario
nondescript [ˌnɑndɪˈskrɪpt] *adj* : anodino, soso
nondiscriminatory [ˌnɑndɪˈskrɪmənəˌtori] *adj* : no discriminatorio
nondrinker [ˌnɑnˈdrɪŋkər] *n* : abstemio *m,* -mia *f*
none¹ [ˈnʌn] *adv* : de ninguna manera, de ningún modo, nada <he was none too happy : no se sintió nada contento> <I'm none the worse for it : no estoy peor por ello> <none too soon : a buena hora>
none² *pron* : ninguno, ninguna
nonentity [ˌnɑnˈɛntət̬i] *n, pl* **-ties** : persona *f* insignificante, nulidad *f*
nonessential [ˌnɑnɪˈsɛntʃəl] *adj* : secundario, no esencial
nonessentials [ˌnɑnɪˈsɛntʃəlz] *npl* : cosas *fpl* secundarias, cosas *fpl* accesorias
nonetheless [ˌnʌnðəˈlɛs] *adv* : sin embargo, no obstante
nonexistence [ˌnɑnɪgˈzɪstənts] *n* : inexistencia *f*
nonexistent [ˌnɑnɪgˈzɪstənt] *adj* : inexistente
nonfat [ˌnɑnˈfæt] *adj* : sin grasa
nonfattening [ˌnɑnˈfætənɪŋ] *adj* : que no engorda
nonfiction [ˌnɑnˈfɪkʃən] *n* : no ficción *f*
nonflammable [ˌnɑnˈflæməbəl] *adj* : no inflamable
nonintervention [ˌnɑnˌɪntərˈvɛntʃən] *n* : no intervención *f*
nonmalignant [ˌnɑnməˈlɪgnənt] *adj* : no maligno, benigno
nonnegotiable [ˌnɑnnɪˈgoːʃəbəl, -ʃiə-] *adj* : no negociable
nonpareil¹ [ˌnɑnpəˈrɛl] *adj* : sin parangón, sin par
nonpareil² *n* : persona *f* sin igual, cosa *f* sin par
nonpartisan [ˌnɑnˈpɑrt̬əzən, -sən] *adj* : imparcial
nonpaying [ˌnɑnˈpeɪɪŋ] *adj* : que no paga
nonpayment [ˌnɑnˈpeɪmənt] *n* : impago *m,* falta *f* de pago
nonperson [ˌnɑnˈpərsən] *n* : persona *f* sin derechos
nonplus [ˌnɑnˈplʌs] *vt* **-plussed; -plussing** : confundir, desconcertar, dejar perplejo
nonprescription [ˌnɑnprɪˈskrɪpʃən] *adj* : disponible sin receta del médico
nonproductive [ˌnɑnprəˈdʌktɪv] *adj* : improductivo
nonprofit [ˌnɑnˈprɑfət] *adj* : sin fines lucrativos
nonproliferation [ˌnɑnprəˌlɪfəˈreɪʃən] *adj* : no proliferación
nonresident [ˌnɑnˈrɛzədənt, -ˌdɛnt] *n* : no residente *mf*
nonscheduled [ˌnɑnˈskɛˌdʒuːld] *adj* : no programado, no regular
nonsectarian [ˌnɑnˌsɛkˈtæriən] *adj* : no sectario
nonsense [ˈnɑnˌsɛnts, ˈnɑntsənts] *n* : tonterías *fpl,* disparates *mpl*
nonsensical [nɑnˈsɛntsɪkəl] *adj* ABSURD : absurdo, disparatado — **nonsensically** [-kli] *adv*
nonsmoker [ˌnɑnˈsmoːkər] *n* : no fumador *m,* -dora *f;* persona *f* que no fuma
nonstandard [ˌnɑnˈstændərd] *adj* : no regular, no estándar
nonstick [ˌnɑnˈstɪk] *adj* : antiadherente
nonstop¹ [ˌnɑnˈstɑp] *adv* : sin parar <he talked nonstop : habló sin parar>
nonstop² *adj* : directo, sin escalas <nonstop flight : vuelo directo>
nonsupport [ˌnɑnsəˈpɔrt] *n* : falta *f* de manutención
nontaxable [ˌnɑnˈtæksəbəl] *adj* : exento de impuestos
nontoxic [ˌnɑnˈtɑksɪk] *adj* : no tóxico
nonviolence [ˌnɑnˈvaɪlənts, -ˈvaɪə-] *n* : no violencia *f*
nonviolent [ˌnɑnˈvaɪlənt, -ˈvaɪə-] *adj* : pacífico, no violento
noodle [ˈnuːdəl] *n* : fideo *m,* tallarín *m*

nook [ˈnʊk] *n* : rincón *m,* recoveco *m,* escondrijo *m* <in every nook and cranny : en todos los rincones>
noon [ˈnuːn] *n* : mediodía *m*
noonday [ˈnuːn,deɪ] *n* : mediodía *m* <the noonday sun : el sol de mediodía>
no one *pron* NOBODY : nadie
noontime [ˈnuːn,taɪm] *n* : mediodía *m*
noose [ˈnuːs] *n* **1** LASSO : lazo *m* **2 hangman's noose:** dogal *m,* soga *f*
nor [ˈnɔr] *conj* : ni <neither good nor bad : ni bueno ni malo> <nor I! : ¡ni yo tampoco!>
Nordic [ˈnɔrdɪk] *adj* : nórdico
norm [ˈnɔrm] *n* **1** STANDARD : norma *f,* modelo *m* **2** CUSTOM, RULE : regla *f* general, lo normal
normal [ˈnɔrməl] *adj* : normal — **normally** *adv*
normalcy [ˈnɔrməlsi] *n* : normalidad *f*
normality [nɔrˈmæləṭi] *n* : normalidad *f*
normalize [ˈnɔrmə,laɪz] *vt* : normalizar
Norse [ˈnɔrs] *adj* : nórdico
north¹ [ˈnɔrθ] *adv* : al norte
north² *adj* : norte, del norte <the north coast : la costa del norte>
north³ *n* **1** : norte *m* **2 the North** : el Norte *m*
northbound [ˈnɔrθ,baʊnd] *adv* : con rumbo al norte
North American *n* : norteamericano *m,* -na *f* — **North American** *adj*
northeast¹ [nɔrθˈiːst] *adv* : hacia el nordeste
northeast² *adj* : nordeste, del nordeste
northeast³ *n* : nordeste *m,* noreste *m*
northeasterly¹ [nɔrθˈiːstərli] *adv* : hacia el nordeste
northeasterly² *adj* : nordeste, del nordeste
northeastern [nɔrθˈiːstərn] *adj* : nordeste, del nordeste
northerly¹ [ˈnɔrðərli] *adv* : hacia el norte
northerly² *adj* : del norte <a northerly wind : un viento del norte>
northern [ˈnɔrðərn] *adj* : norte, norteño, septentrional
Northerner [ˈnɔrðərnər] *n* : norteño *m,* -ña *f*
northern lights → **aurora borealis**
North Pole : Polo *m* Norte
North Star *n* : estrella *f* polar
northward [ˈnɔrθwərd] *adv & adj* : hacia el norte
northwest¹ [nɔrθˈwɛst] *adv* : hacia el noroeste
northwest² *adj* : del noroeste
northwest³ *n* : noroeste *m*
northwesterly¹ [nɔrθˈwɛstərli] *adv* : hacia el noroeste
northwesterly² *adj* : del noroeste
northwestern [nɔrθˈwɛstərn] *adj* : noroeste, del noroeste
Norwegian [nɔrˈwiːdʒən] *n* **1** : noruego *m,* -ga *f* **2** : noruego *m* (idioma) — **Norwegian** *adj*
nose¹ [ˈnoːz] *v* **nosed; nosing** *vt* **1** SMELL : olfatear **2** : empujar con el hocico <the dog nosed open the bag : el perro abrió el saco con el hocico> **3** EDGE, MOVE : mover poco a poco — *vi* **1** PRY : entrometerse, meter las narices **2** EDGE : avanzar poco a poco
nose² *n* **1** : nariz *f* (de una persona), hocico *m* (de un animal) <to blow one's nose : sonarse las narices> **2** SMELL : olfato *m,* sentido *m* del olfato **3** FRONT : parte *f* delantera, nariz *f* (de un avión), proa *f* (de un barco) **4 to follow one's nose** : dejarse guiar por el instinto
nosebleed [ˈnoːz,bliːd] *n* : hemorragia *f* nasal
nosedive [ˈnoːz,daɪv] *n* **1** : descenso *m* en picada (de un avión) **2** : caída *f* súbita (de precios, etc.)
nose–dive [ˈnoːz,daɪv] *vi* : descender en picada, caer en picada
nostalgia [nɑˈstældʒə, nə-] *n* : nostalgia *f*
nostalgic [nɑˈstældʒɪk, nə-] *adj* : nostálgico
nostril [ˈnɑstrəl] *n* : ventana *f* de la nariz
nostrum [ˈnɑstrəm] *n* : panacea *f*
nosy *or* **nosey** [ˈnoːzi] *adj* **nosier; -est** : entrometido
not [ˈnɑt] *adv* **1** (*used to form a negative*) : no <she is not tired : no está cansada> <not to say something would be wrong : no decir nada sería injusto> **2** (*used to replace a negative clause*) : no <are we going or not? : ¿vamos a ir o no?> <of course not! : ¡claro que no!>
notable¹ [ˈnoːṭəbəl] *adj* **1** NOTEWORTHY : notable, de notar **2** DISTINGUISHED, PROMINENT : distinguido, destacado
notable² *n* : persona *f* importante, personaje *m*
notably [ˈnoːṭəbli] *adv* : notablemente, particularmente
notarize [ˈnoːṭə,raɪz] *vt* **-rized; -rizing** : autenticar, autorizar
notary public [ˈnoːṭəri] *n, pl* **-ries public** *or* **-ry publics** : notario *m,* -ria *f;* escribano *m,* -na *f*
notation [noˈteɪʃən] *n* **1** NOTE : anotación *f,* nota *f* **2** : notación *f* <musical notation : notación musical>
notch¹ [ˈnɑtʃ] *vt* : hacer una muesca en, cortar
notch² *n* : muesca *f,* corte *m*
note¹ [ˈnoːt] *vt* **noted; noting 1** NOTICE : notar, observar, tomar nota de **2** RECORD : anotar, apuntar
note² *n* **1** : nota *f* (musical) **2** COMMENT : nota *f,* comentario *m* **3** LETTER : nota *f,* cartita *f* **4** PROMINENCE : prestigio *m* <a musician of note : un músico destacado> **5** ATTENTION : atención *f* <to take note of : prestar atención a>

notebook [ˈnoːtˌbʊk] *n* : libreta *f,* cuaderno *m*
noted [ˈnoːtəd] *adj* EMINENT : renombrado, eminente, celebrado
noteworthy [ˈnoːtˌwərði] *adj* : notable, de notar, de interés
nothing[1] [ˈnʌθɪŋ] *adv* **1** : de ninguna manera <nothing daunted, we carried on : sin amilanarnos, seguimos adelante> **2 nothing like** : no...en nada <he's nothing like his brother : no se parece en nada a su hermano>
nothing[2] *n* **1** NOTHINGNESS : nada *f* **2** ZERO : cero *m* **3** : persona *f* de poca importancia, cero *m* **4** TRIFLE : nimiedad *f*
nothing[3] *pron* : nada <there's nothing better : no hay nada mejor> <nothing else : nada más> <nothing but : solamente> <they mean nothing to me : ellos me son indiferentes>
nothingness [ˈnʌθɪŋnəs] *n* **1** VOID : vacío *m,* nada *f* **2** NONEXISTENCE : inexistencia *f* **3** TRIFLE : nimiedad *f*
notice[1] [ˈnoːt̬ɪs] *vt* **-ticed; -ticing** : notar, observar, advertir, darse cuenta de
notice[2] *n* **1** NOTIFICATION : aviso *m,* notificación *f* **2** ATTENTION : atención *f* <to take notice of : prestar atención a>
noticeable [ˈnoːt̬ɪsəbəl] *adj* : evidente, perceptible — **noticeably** [-bli] *adv*
notification [ˌnoːt̬əfəˈkeɪʃən] *n* : notificación *f,* aviso *m*
notify [ˈnoːt̬əˌfaɪ] *vt* **-fied; -fying** : notificar, avisar
notion [ˈnoːʃən] *n* **1** IDEA : idea *f,* noción *f* **2** WHIM : capricho *m,* antojo *m* **3 notions** *npl* : artículos *mpl* de mercería
notoriety [ˌnoːt̬əˈraɪət̬i] *n* : mala fama *f,* notoriedad *f*
notorious [noˈtoːriəs] *adj* : de mala fama, célebre, bien conocido
notwithstanding[1] [ˌnɑtwɪθˈstændɪŋ, -wɪð-] *adv* NEVERTHELESS : no obstante, sin embargo
notwithstanding[2] *conj* : a pesar de que
notwithstanding[3] *prep* : a pesar de, no obstante
nougat [ˈnuːgət] *n* : turrón *m*
nought [ˈnɔt, ˈnɑt] → **naught**
noun [ˈnaʊn] *n* : nombre *m,* sustantivo *m*
nourish [ˈnərɪʃ] *vt* **1** FEED : alimentar, nutrir, sustentar **2** FOSTER : fomentar, alentar
nourishing [ˈnərɪʃɪŋ] *adj* : alimenticio, nutritivo
nourishment [ˈnərɪʃmənt] *n* : nutrición *f,* alimento *m,* sustento *m*
novel[1] [ˈnɑvəl] *adj* : original, novedoso
novel[2] *n* : novela *f*
novelist [ˈnɑvəlɪst] *n* : novelista *mf*
novelty [ˈnɑvəlti] *n, pl* **-ties 1** : novedad *f* **2 novelties** *npl* TRINKETS : baratijas *fpl,* chucherías *fpl*
November [noˈvɛmbər] *n* : noviembre *m*
novice [ˈnɑvɪs] *n* : novato *m,* -ta *f;* principiante *mf;* novicio *m,* -cia *f*
now[1] [ˈnaʊ] *adv* **1** PRESENTLY : ahora, ya, actualmente <from now on : de ahora en adelante> <long before now : ya hace tiempo> <now and then : de vez en cuando> **2** IMMEDIATELY : ahora (mismo), inmediatamente <do it right now! : ¡hazlo ahora mismo!> **3** THEN : ya, entonces <now they were ready : ya estaban listos> **4** (*used to introduce a statement, a question, a command, or a transition*) <now hear this! : ¡presten atención!> <now what do you think of that? : ¿qué piensas de eso?>
now[2] *n* (*indicating the present time*) <until now : hasta ahora> <by now : ya> <ten years from now : dentro de 10 años>
now[3] *conj* **now that** : ahora que, ya que
nowadays [ˈnaʊəˌdeɪz] *adv* : hoy en día, actualmente, en la actualidad
nowhere[1] [ˈnoːˌhwɛr] *adv* **1** : en ninguna parte, a ningún lado <nowhere to be found : en ninguna parte, por ningún lado> <you're going nowhere : no estás yendo a ningún lado, no estás yendo a ninguna parte> **2 nowhere near** : ni con mucho, nada cerca <it's nowhere near here : no está nada cerca de aquí>
nowhere[2] *n* **1** : ninguna parte *f* **2 out of nowhere** : de la nada
noxious [ˈnɑkʃəs] *adj* : nocivo, dañino, tóxico
nozzle [ˈnɑzəl] *n* : boca *f*
nuance [ˈnuːˌɑnts, ˈnjuː-] *n* : matiz *m*
nub [ˈnʌb] *n* **1** KNOB, LUMP : protuberancia *f,* nudo *m* **2** GIST : quid *m,* meollo *m*
nuclear [ˈnuːkliər, ˈnjuː-] *adj* : nuclear
nucleus [ˈnuːkliəs, ˈnjuː-] *n, pl* **-clei** [-kliˌaɪ] : núcleo *m*
nude[1] [ˈnuːd, ˈnjuːd] *adj* **nuder; nudest** : desnudo
nude[2] *n* : desnudo *m*
nudge[1] [ˈnʌʤ] *vt* **nudged; nudging** : darle con el codo (a alguien)
nudge[2] *n* : toque *m* que se da con el codo
nudism [ˈnuːˌdɪzəm, ˈnjuː-] *n* : nudismo *m*
nudist [ˈnuːdɪst, ˈnjuː-] *n* : nudista *mf*
nudity [ˈnuːdət̬i, ˈnjuː-] *n* : desnudez *f*
nugget [ˈnʌgət] *n* : pepita *f*
nuisance [ˈnuːsənts, ˈnjuː-] *n* **1** BOTHER : fastidio *m,* molestia *f,* lata *f* **2** PEST : peste *f;* pesado *m,* -da *f fam*
null [ˈnʌl] *adj* : nulo <null and void : nulo y sin efecto>
nullify [ˈnʌləˌfaɪ] *vt* **-fied; -fying** : invalidar, anular
numb[1] [ˈnʌm] *vt* : entumecer, adormecer

numb[2] *adj* : entumecido, dormido <numb with fear : paralizado de miedo>
number[1] [ˈnʌmbər] *vt* **1** COUNT, INCLUDE : contar, incluir **2** : numerar <number the pages : numera las páginas> **3** TOTAL : ascender a, sumar
number[2] *n* **1** : número *m* <in round numbers : en números redondos> <telephone number : número de teléfono> **2 a number of** : varios, unos pocos, unos cuantos
numberless [ˈnʌmbərləs] *adj* : innumerable, sin número
numbness [ˈnʌmnəs] *n* : entumecimiento *m*
numeral [ˈnuːmərəl, ˈnjuː-] *n* : número *m* <Roman numeral : número romano>
numerator [ˈnuːməˌreɪt̬ər, ˈnjuː-] *n* : numerador *m*
numeric [nʊˈmɛrɪk, njʊ-] *adj* : numérico
numerical [nʊˈmɛrɪkəl, njʊ-] *adj* : numérico — **numerically** [-kli] *adv*
numerous [ˈnuːmərəs, ˈnjuː-] *adj* : numeroso
numismatics [ˌnuːməzˈmæt̬ɪks, ˌnjuː-] *n* : numismática *f*
numskull [ˈnʌmˌskʌl] *n* : tonto *m*, -ta *f*; mentecato *m*, -ta *f*; zoquete *m fam*
nun [ˈnʌn] *n* : monja *f*
nuptial [ˈnʌpʃəl] *adj* : nupcial
nuptials [ˈnʌpʃəlz] *npl* WEDDING : nupcias *fpl*, boda *f*
nurse[1] [ˈnərs] *vt* **nursed; nursing 1** SUCKLE : amamantar **2** : cuidar (de), atender <to nurse the sick : cuidar a los enfermos> <to nurse a cold : curarse de un resfriado>
nurse[2] *n* **1** : enfermero *m*, -ra *f* **2** → **nursemaid**
nursemaid [ˈnərsˌmeɪd] *n* : niñera *f*
nursery [ˈnərsəri] *n, pl* **-eries 1** *or* **day nursery** : guardería *f* **2** : vivero *m* (de plantas)
nursing home *n* : hogar *m* de ancianos, clínica *f* de reposo
nurture[1] [ˈnərtʃər] *vt* **-tured; -turing 1** FEED, NOURISH : nutrir, alimentar **2** EDUCATE : criar, educar **3** FOSTER : alimentar, fomentar
nurture[2] *n* **1** UPBRINGING : crianza *f*, educación *f* **2** FOOD : alimento *m*
nut [ˈnʌt] *n* **1** : nuez *f* **2** : tuerca *f* <nuts and bolts : tuercas y tornillos> **3** LUNATIC : loco *m*, -ca *f*; chiflado *m*, -da *f fam* **4** ENTHUSIAST : fanático *m*, -ca *f*; entusiasta *mf*
nutcracker [ˈnʌtˌkrækər] *n* : cascanueces *m*
nuthatch [ˈnʌtˌhætʃ] *n* : trepador *m*
nutmeg [ˈnʌtˌmɛg] *n* : nuez *f* moscada
nutrient [ˈnuːtriənt, ˈnjuː-] *n* : nutriente *m*, alimento *m* nutritivo
nutriment [ˈnuːtrəmənt, ˈnjuː-] *n* : nutrimento *m*
nutrition [nʊˈtrɪʃən, njʊ-] *n* : nutrición *f*
nutritional [nʊˈtrɪʃənəl, njʊ-] *adj* : alimenticio
nutritious [nʊˈtrɪʃəs, njʊ-] *adj* : nutritivo, alimenticio
nuts [ˈnʌts] *adj* **1** FANATICAL : fanático **2** CRAZY : loco, chiflado *fam*
nutshell [ˈnʌtˌʃɛl] *n* **1** : cáscara *f* de nuez **2 in a nutshell** : en pocas palabras
nutty [ˈnʌt̬i] *adj* **-tier; -tiest** : loco, chiflado *fam*
nuzzle [ˈnʌzəl] *v* **-zled; -zling** *vi* NESTLE : acurrucarse, arrimarse — *vt* : acariciar con el hocico
nylon [ˈnaɪˌlɑn] *n* **1** : nilón *m* **2 nylons** *npl* : medias *fpl* de nilón
nymph [ˈnɪmpf] *n* : ninfa *f*

O

o [ˈoː] *n, pl* **o's** *or* **os** [ˈoːz] **1** : decimoquinta letra del alfabeto inglés **2** ZERO : cero *m*
O [ˈoː] → **oh**
oaf [ˈoːf] *n* : zoquete *m*; bruto *m*, -ta *f*
oafish [ˈoːfɪʃ] *adj* : torpe, lerdo
oak [ˈoːk] *n, pl* **oaks** *or* **oak** : roble *m*
oaken [ˈoːkən] *adj* : de roble
oar [ˈor] *n* : remo *m*
oarlock [ˈorˌlɑk] *n* : tolete *m*, escálamo *m*
oasis [oˈeɪsɪs] *n, pl* **oases** [-ˌsiːz] : oasis *m*
oat [ˈoːt] *n* : avena *f*
oath [ˈoːθ] *n, pl* **oaths** [ˈoːðz, ˈoːθs] **1** : juramento *m* <to take an oath : prestar juramento> **2** SWEARWORD : mala palabra *f*, palabrota *f*
oatmeal [ˈoːtˌmiːl] *n* : avena *f* <instant oatmeal : avena instantánea>
obdurate [ˈɑbdʊrət, -djʊ-] *adj* : inflexible, firme, obstinado
obedience [oˈbiːdiənts] *n* : obediencia *f*
obedient [oˈbiːdiənt] *adj* : obediente — **obediently** *adv*
obelisk [ˈɑbəˌlɪsk] *n* : obelisco *m*
obese [oˈbiːs] *adj* : obeso
obesity [oˈbiːsət̬i] *n* : obesidad *f*
obey [oˈbeɪ] *v* **obeyed; obeying** : obedecer <to obey the law : cumplir la ley>
obfuscate [ˈɑbfəˌskeɪt] *vt* **-cated; -cating** : ofuscar, confundir
obituary [əˈbɪtʃʊˌɛri] *n, pl* **-aries** : obituario *m*, necrología *f*
object[1] [əbˈdʒɛkt] *vt* : objetar — *vi* : oponerse, poner reparos, hacer objeciones
object[2] [ˈɑbdʒɪkt] *n* **1** : objeto *m* **2** OBJECTIVE, PURPOSE : objetivo *m*, pro-

pósito *m* **3** : complemento *m* (en gramática)
objection [əb'dʒɛkʃən] *n* : objeción *f*
objectionable [əb'dʒɛkʃənəbəl] *adj* : ofensivo, indeseable — **objectionably** [-bli] *adv*
objective¹ [əb'dʒɛktɪv] *adj* **1** IMPARTIAL : objetivo, imparcial **2** : de complemento, directo (en gramática)
objective² *n* **1** : objetivo *m* **2** *or* **objective case** : acusativo *m*
objectively [əb'dʒɛktɪvli] *adv* : objetivamente
objectivity [,ɑb,dʒɛk'tɪvət̬i] *n, pl* **-ties** : objetividad *f*
obligate ['ɑblə,geɪt] *vt* **-gated; -gating** : obligar
obligation [,ɑblə'geɪʃən] *n* : obligación *f*
obligatory [ə'blɪgə,tori] *adj* : obligatorio
oblige [ə'blaɪdʒ] *vt* **obliged; obliging** **1** COMPEL : obligar **2** : hacerle un favor (a alguien), complacer <to oblige a friend : hacerle un favor a un amigo> **3 to be much obliged** : estar muy agradecido
obliging [ə'blaɪdʒɪŋ] *adj* : servicial, complaciente — **obligingly** *adv*
oblique [o'bli:k] *adj* **1** SLANTING : oblicuo **2** INDIRECT : indirecto — **obliquely** *adv*
obliterate [ə'blɪt̬ə,reɪt] *vt* **-ated; -ating** **1** ERASE : obliterar, borrar **2** DESTROY : destruir, eliminar
obliteration [ə,blɪt̬ə'reɪʃən] *n* : obliteración *f*
oblivion [ə'blɪviən] *n* : olvido *m*
oblivious [ə'blɪviəs] *adj* : inconsciente — **obliviously** *adv*
oblong¹ ['ɑ,blɔŋ] *adj* : oblongo
oblong² *n* : figura *f* oblonga, rectángulo *m*
obnoxious [ɑb'nɑkʃəs, əb-] *adj* : repugnante, odioso — **obnoxiously** *adv*
oboe ['o:,bo:] *n* : oboe *m*
oboist ['o,boɪst] *n* : oboe *mf*
obscene [ɑb'si:n, əb-] *adj* : obsceno, indecente — **obscenely** *adv*
obscenity [ɑb'sɛnət̬i, əb-] *n, pl* **-ties** : obscenidad *f*
obscure¹ [ɑb'skjʊr, əb-] *vt* **-scured; -scuring** **1** CLOUD, DIM : oscurecer, nublar **2** HIDE : ocultar
obscure² *adj* **1** DIM : oscuro **2** REMOTE, SECLUDED : recóndito **3** VAGUE : oscuro, confuso, vago **4** UNKNOWN : desconocido <an obscure poet : un poeta desconocido> — **obscurely** *adv*
obscurity [ɑb'skjʊrət̬i, əb-] *n, pl* **-ties** : oscuridad *f*
obsequious [əb'si:kwiəs] *adj* : servil, excesivamente atento
observable [əb'zərvəbəl] *adj* : observable, perceptible
observance [əb'zərvənts] *n* **1** FULFILLMENT : observancia *f*, cumplimiento *m* **2** PRACTICE : práctica *f*
observant [əb'zərvənt] *adj* : observador
observation [,ɑbsər'veɪʃən, -zər-] *n* : observación *f*
observatory [əb'zərvə,tori] *n, pl* **-ries** : observatorio *m*
observe [əb'zərv] *v* **-served; -serving** *vt* **1** OBEY : observar, obedecer **2** CELEBRATE : celebrar, guardar (una práctica religiosa) **3** WATCH : observar, mirar **4** REMARK : observar, comentar — *vi* LOOK : mirar
obsess [əb'sɛs] *vt* : obsesionar
obsession [ɑb'sɛʃən, əb-] *n* : obsesión *f*
obsessive [ɑb'sɛsɪv, əb-] *adj* : obsesivo — **obsessively** *adv*
obsolescence [,ɑbsə'lɛsənts] *n* : obsolescencia *f*
obsolescent [,ɑbsə'lɛsənt] *adj* : obsolescente <to become obsolescent : caer en desuso>
obsolete [,ɑbsə'li:t, 'ɑbsə,-] *adj* : obsoleto, anticuado
obstacle ['ɑbstɪkəl] *n* : obstáculo *m*, impedimento *m*
obstetric [əb'stɛtrɪk] *or* **obstetrical** [-trɪkəl] *adj* : obstétrico
obstetrician [,ɑbstə'trɪʃən] *n* : obstetra *mf;* tocólogo *m*, -ga *f*
obstetrics [əb'stɛtrɪks] *ns & pl* : obstetricia *f*, tocología *f*
obstinacy ['ɑbstənəsi] *n, pl* **-cies** : obstinación *f*, terquedad *f*
obstinate ['ɑbstənət] *adj* : obstinado, terco — **obstinately** *adv*
obstreperous [əb'strɛpərəs] *adj* **1** CLAMOROUS : ruidoso, clamoroso **2** UNRULY : rebelde, indisciplinado
obstruct [əb'strʌkt] *vt* : obstruir, bloquear
obstruction [əb'strʌkʃən] *n* : obstrucción *f*, bloqueo *m*
obstructive [əb'strəktɪv] *adj* : obstructor
obtain [əb'teɪn] *vt* : obtener, conseguir — *vi* PREVAIL : imperar, prevalecer
obtainable [əb'teɪnəbəl] *adj* : obtenible, asequible
obtrude [əb'tru:d] *v* **-truded; -truding** *vt* **1** EXTRUDE : expulsar **2** IMPOSE : imponer — *vi* INTRUDE : inmiscuirse, entrometerse
obtrusive [əb'tru:sɪv] *adj* **1** IMPERTINENT, MEDDLESOME : impertinente, entrometido **2** PROTRUDING : prominente
obtuse [ɑb'tu:s, əb-, -'tju:s] *adj* : obtuso, torpe
obtuse angle *n* : ángulo obtuso
obviate ['ɑbvi,eɪt] *vt* **-ated; -ating** : obviar, evitar
obvious ['ɑbviəs] *adj* : obvio, evidente, manifiesto
obviously ['ɑbviəsli] *adv* **1** CLEARLY : obviamente, evidentemente **2** OF COURSE : claro, por supuesto
occasion¹ [ə'keɪʒən] *vt* : ocasionar, causar

occasion[2] *n* **1** OPPORTUNITY : oportunidad *f,* ocasión *f* **2** CAUSE : motivo *m,* razón *f* **3** INSTANCE : ocasión *f* **4** EVENT : ocasión *f,* acontecimiento *m* **5 on ~** : de vez en cuando, ocasionalmente

occasional [ə'keɪʒənəl] *adj* : ocasional

occasionally [ə'keɪʒənəli] *adv* : de vez en cuando, ocasionalmente

occidental [ˌɑksə'dɛntəl] *adj* : oeste, del oeste, occidental

occult[1] [ə'kʌlt, 'ɑˌkʌlt] *adj* **1** HIDDEN, SECRET : oculto, secreto **2** ARCANE : arcano, esotérico

occult[2] *n* **the occult** : las ciencias ocultas

occupancy ['ɑkjəpən*t*si] *n, pl* **-cies** : ocupación *f,* habitación *f*

occupant ['ɑkjəpənt] *n* : ocupante *mf*

occupation [ˌɑkjə'peɪʃən] *n* : ocupación *f,* profesión *f,* oficio *m*

occupational [ˌɑkjə'peɪʃənəl] *adj* : ocupacional

occupy ['ɑkjəˌpaɪ] *vt* **-pied; -pying** : ocupar

occur [ə'kər] *vi* **occurred; occurring** **1** EXIST : encontrarse, existir **2** HAPPEN : ocurrir, acontecer, suceder, tener lugar **3** : ocurrirse <it occurred to him that. . . : se le ocurrió que. . .>

occurrence [ə'kərən*t*s] *n* : acontecimiento *m,* suceso *m,* ocurrencia *f*

ocean ['oːʃən] *n* : océano *m*

oceanic [ˌoːʃi'ænɪk] *adj* : oceánico

oceanography [ˌoːʃə'nɑgrəfi] *n* : oceanografía *f*

ocelot ['ɑsəˌlɑt,'oː-] *n* : ocelote *m*

ocher *or* **ochre** ['oːkər] *n* : ocre *m*

o'clock [ə'klɑk] *adv* (*used in telling time*) <it's ten o'clock : son las diez> <at six o'clock : a las seis>

octagon ['ɑktəˌgɑn] *n* : octágono *m*

octagonal [ɑk'tægənəl] *adj* : octagonal

octave ['ɑktɪv] *n* : octava *f*

October [ɑk'toːbər] *n* : octubre *m*

octopus ['ɑktəˌpʊs, -pəs] *n, pl* **-puses** *or* **-pi** [-ˌpaɪ] : pulpo *m*

ocular ['ɑkjələr] *adj* : ocular

oculist ['ɑkjəlɪst] *n* **1** OPHTHALMOLOGIST : oftalmólogo *m,* -ga *f;* oculista *mf* **2** OPTOMETRIST : optometrista *mf*

odd ['ɑd] *adj* **1** : sin pareja, suelto <an odd sock : un calcetín sin pareja> **2** UNEVEN : impar <odd numbers : números impares> **3** : y pico, y tantos <forty odd years ago : hace cuarenta y pico años> **4** : alguno, uno que otro <odd jobs : algunos trabajos> **5** STRANGE : extraño, raro

oddball ['ɑdˌbɔl] *n* : excéntrico *m,* -ca *f;* persona *f* rara

oddity ['ɑdət̬i] *n, pl* **-ties** : rareza *f,* cosa *f* rara

oddly ['ɑdli] *adv* : de manera extraña

oddness ['ɑdnəs] *n* : rareza *f,* excentricidad *f*

odds ['ɑdz] *npl* **1** CHANCES : probabilidades *fpl* **2** : puntos *mpl* de ventaja (de una apuesta) **3 to be at odds** : estar en desacuerdo

odds and ends *npl* : costillas *fpl,* cosas *fpl* sueltas, cachivaches *mpl*

ode ['oːd] *n* : oda *f*

odious ['oːdiəs] *adj* : odioso — **odiously** *adv*

odor ['oːdər] *n* : olor *m*

odorless ['oːdərləs] *adj* : inodoro, sin olor

odorous ['oːdərəs] *adj* : oloroso

odyssey ['ɑdəsi] *n, pl* **-seys** : odisea *f*

o'er ['or] → **over**

of ['ʌv, 'ɑv] *prep* **1** FROM : de <a man of the city : un hombre de la ciudad> **2** (*indicating character or background*) : de <a woman of great ability : una mujer de gran capacidad> **3** (*indicating cause*) : de <he died of the flu : murió de la gripe> **4** BY : de <the works of Shakespeare : las obras de Shakespeare> **5** (*indicating contents, material or quantity*) : de <a house of wood : una casa de madera> <a glass of water : un vaso de agua> **6** (*indicating belonging or connection*) : de <the front of the house : el frente de la casa> **7** ABOUT : sobre, de <tales of the West : los cuentos del Oeste> **8** (*indicating a particular example*) : de <the city of Caracas : la ciudad de Caracas> **9** FOR : por, a <love of country : amor por la patria> **10** (*indicating time or date*) <five minutes of ten : las diez menos cinco> <the eighth of April : el ocho de abril>

off[1] ['ɔf] *adv* **1** (*indicating change of position or state*) <to march off : marcharse> <he dozed off : se puso a dormir> **2** (*indicating distance in space or time*) <some miles off : a varias millas> <the holiday is three weeks off : faltan tres semanas para la fiesta> **3** (*indicating removal*) <the knob came off : se le cayó el pomo> **4** (*indicating termination*) <shut the television off : apaga la televisión> **5** (*indicating suspension of work*) <to take a day off : tomarse un día de descanso> **6 off and on** : de vez en cuando

off[2] *adj* **1** FARTHER : más remoto, distante <the off side of the building : el lado distante del edificio> **2** STARTED : empezado <to be off on a spree : irse de juerga> **3** OUT : apagado <the light is off : la luz está apagada> **4** CANCELED : cancelado, suspendido **5** INCORRECT : erróneo, incorrecto **6** REMOTE : remoto, lejano <an off chance : una posibilidad remota> **7** FREE : libre <I'm off today : hoy estoy libre> **8 to be well off** : vivir con desahogo, tener bastante dinero

off[3] *prep* **1** (*indicating physical separation*) : de <she took it off the table : lo tomó de la mesa> <a shop off the main street : una tienda al lado de la calle principal> **2** : a la costa de, a expensas de <he lives off his sister : vive a expensas de su hermana> 3 (*indicating the suspension of an activity*) <to be off duty : estar libre> <he's off liquor : ha dejado el alcohol> 4 BELOW : por debajo de <he's off his game : está por debajo de su juego normal>

offal ['ɔfəl] *n* 1 RUBBISH, WASTE : desechos *mpl*, desperdicios *mpl* 2 VISCERA : vísceras *fpl*, asaduras *fpl*

offend [ə'fɛnd] *vt* 1 VIOLATE : violar, atentar contra 2 HURT : ofender <to be easily offended : ser muy susceptible>

offender [ə'fɛndər] *n* : delincuente *mf;* infractor *m*, -tora *f*

offense *or* **offence** [ə'fɛn*t*s, 'ɔ,fɛn*t*s] *n* 1 INSULT : ofensa *f*, injuria *f*, agravio *m* <to take offense : ofenderse> 2 ASSAULT : ataque *m* 3 : ofensiva *f* (en deportes) 4 CRIME, INFRACTION : infracción *f*, delito *m*

offensive[1] [ə'fɛn*t*sɪv, 'ɔ,fɛn*t*-] *adj* : ofensivo — **offensively** *adv*

offensive[2] *n* : ofensiva *f*

offer[1] ['ɔfər] *vt* 1 : ofrecer <they offered him the job : le ofrecieron el puesto> 2 PROPOSE : proponer, sugerir 3 SHOW : ofrecer, mostrar <to offer resistance : ofrecer resistencia>

offer[2] *n* : oferta *f*, ofrecimiento *m*, propuesta *f*

offering ['ɔfərɪŋ] *n* : ofrenda *f*

offhand[1] ['ɔf'hænd] *adv* : sin preparación, sin pensarlo

offhand[2] *adj* 1 IMPROMPTU : improvisado 2 ABRUPT : brusco

office ['ɔfəs] *n* 1 : cargo *m* <to run for office : presentarse como candidato> 2 : oficina *f*, despacho *m*, gabinete *m* (en la casa) <office hours : horas de oficina>

officeholder ['ɔfəs,ho:ldər] *n* : titular *mf*

officer ['ɔfəsər] *n* 1 *or* **police officer** : policía *mf*, agente *mf* de policía 2 OFFICIAL : oficial *mf;* funcionario *m*, -ria *f;* director *m*, -tora *f* (en una empresa) 3 COMMISSIONED OFFICER : oficial *mf*

official[1] [ə'fɪʃəl] *adj* : oficial — **officially** *adv*

official[2] *n* : funcionario *m*, -ria *f;* oficial *mf*

officiate [ə'fɪʃi,eɪt] *v* **-ated; -ating** *vi* 1 : arbitrar (en deportes) 2 **to officiate at** : oficiar, celebrar — *vt* : arbitrar

officious [ə'fɪʃəs] *adj* : oficioso

offing ['ɔfɪŋ] *n* **in the offing** : en perspectiva

offset ['ɔf,sɛt] *vt* **-set; -setting** : compensar

offshoot ['ɔf,ʃu:t] *n* 1 OUTGROWTH : producto *m*, resultado *m* 2 BRANCH, SHOOT : retoño *m*, rama *f*, vástago *m* (de una planta)

offshore[1] ['ɔf'ʃor] *adv* : a una distancia de la costa

offshore[2] *adj* 1 : de (la) tierra <an offshore wind : un viento que sopla de tierra> 2 : (de) costa afuera, cercano a la costa <an offshore island : una isla costera>

offspring ['ɔf,sprɪŋ] *ns* & *pl* 1 YOUNG : crías *fpl* (de los animales) 2 PROGENY : prole *f*, progenie *f*

off-the-road ['ɔfðə'ro:d] *adj* : extraoficial

often ['ɔfən, 'ɔftən] *adv* : muchas veces, a menudo, seguido

oftentimes ['ɔfən,taɪmz, 'ɔftən-] *or* **ofttimes** ['ɔft,taɪms] → **often**

ogle ['o:gəl] *vt* **ogled; ogling** : comerse con los ojos, quedarse mirando a

ogre ['o:gər] *n* : ogro *m*

oh ['o:] *interj* : ¡oh!, ¡ah!, ¡ay! <oh, of course : ah, por supuesto> <oh no! : ¡ay no!> <oh really? : ¿de veras?>

ohm ['o:m] *n* : ohm *m*, ohmio *m*

oil[1] ['ɔɪl] *vt* : lubricar, engrasar, aceitar

oil[2] *n* 1 : aceite *m* 2 PETROLEUM : petróleo *m* 3 *or* **oil painting** : óleo *m*, pintura *f* al óleo 4 *or* **oil paint(s)** : óleo *m*

oilcloth ['ɔɪl,klɔθ] *n* : hule *m*

oiliness ['ɔɪlinəs] *n* : lo aceitoso

oilskin ['ɔɪl,skɪn] *n* 1 : hule *m* 2 **oilskins** *npl* : impermeable *m*

oily ['ɔɪli] *adj* **oilier; -est** : aceitoso, grasiento, grasoso <oily fingers : dedos grasientos>

ointment ['ɔɪntmənt] *n* : ungüento *m*, pomada *f*

OK[1] [,o:'keɪ] *vt* **OK'd** *or* **okayed** [,o:'keɪd]; **OK'ing** *or* **okaying** APPROVE, AUTHORIZE : dar el visto bueno a, autorizar, aprobar

OK[2] *or* **okay** [,o:'keɪ] *adv* 1 WELL : bien 2 YES : sí, por supuesto

OK[3] *adj* : bien <he's OK : está bien> <it's OK with me : estoy de acuerdo>

OK[4] *n* : autorización *f*, visto *m* bueno

okra ['o:krə, *South also* -kri] *n* : quingombó *m*

old[1] ['o:ld] *adj* 1 ANCIENT : antiguo <old civilizations : civilizaciones antiguas> 2 FAMILIAR : viejo <old friends : viejos amigos> <the same old story : el mismo cuento> 3 (*indicating a certain age*) <he's ten years old : tiene diez años (de edad)> 4 AGED : viejo, anciano <an old woman : una anciana> 5 FORMER : antiguo <her old neighborhood : su antiguo barrio> 6 WORN-OUT : viejo, gastado

old[2] *n* 1 **the old** : los viejos, los ancianos 2 **in the days of old** : antaño, en los tiempos antiguos

olden ['o:ldən] *adj* : de antaño, de antigüedad

old–fashioned ['o:ld'fæʃənd] *adj* : anticuado, pasado de moda

old maid *n* 1 SPINSTER : soltera *f* 2 FUSSBUDGET : maniático *m*, -ca *f;* melindroso *m*, -sa *f*

old–time ['o:ld'taɪm] *adj* : antiguo

old–timer ['oːld'taɪmər] *n* **1** VETERAN : veterano *m,* -na *f* **2** *or* **oldster** : anciano *m,* -na *f*
old–world ['oːld'wərld] *adj* : pintoresco (de antaño)
oleander ['oːliˌændər] *n* : adelfa *f*
oleomargarine [ˌoːlio'mɑrdʒərən] → **margarine**
olfactory [ɑl'fæktəri,ol-] *adj* : olfativo
oligarchy ['ɑləˌgɑrki, 'oːlə-] *n, pl* **-chies** : oligarquía *f*
olive ['ɑlɪv, -ləv] *n* **1** : aceituna *f,* oliva *f* (fruta) **2** : olivo *m* (árbol) **3** *or* **olive green** : color *m* aceituna, verde *m* oliva
Olympic Games [o'lɪmpɪk] *npl* : Juegos *mpl* Olímpicos
Omani [o'mɑni, -'mæ-] *n* : omaní *mf* — **Omani** *adj*
ombudsman ['ɑmˌbʊdzmən, ɑm'bʊdz-] *n, pl* **-men** [-mən, -ˌmɛn] : ombudsman *m*
omelet *or* **omelette** ['ɑmlət, 'ɑmə-] *n* : omelette *mf,* tortilla *f* de huevo
omen ['oːmən] *n* : presagio *m,* augurio *m,* agüero *m*
ominous ['ɑmənəs] *adj* : ominoso, agorero, de mal agüero
ominously ['ɑmənəsli] *adv* : de manera amenazadora
omission [o'mɪʃən] *n* : omisión *f*
omit [o'mɪt] *vt* **omitted; omitting 1** LEAVE OUT : omitir, excluir **2** NEGLECT : omitir <they omitted to tell us : omitieron decírnoslo>
omnipotence [ɑm'nɪpətənts] *n* : omnipotencia *f* — **omnipotent** [ɑm'nɪpətənt] *adj*
omnipresent [ˌɑmnɪ'prɛzənt] *adj* : omnipresente
omniscient [ɑm'nɪʃənt] *adj* : omnisciente
omnivorous [ɑm'nɪvərəs] *adj* **1** : omnívoro **2** AVID : ávido, voraz
on[1] ['ɑn, 'ɔn] *adv* **1** (*indicating contact with a surface*) <put the top on : pon la tapa> <he has a hat on : lleva un sombrero puesto> **2** (*indicating forward movement*) <from that moment on : a partir de ese momento> <farther on : más adelante> **3** (*indicating operation or an operating position*) <turn the light on : prende la luz>
on[2] *adj* **1** (*being in operation*) <the radio is on : el radio está prendido> **2** (*taking place*) <the game is on : el juego ha comenzado> **3 to be on to** : estar enterado de
on[3] *prep* **1** (*indicating position*) : en, sobre, encima de <on the table : en (sobre, encima de) la mesa> <shadows on the wall : sombras en la pared> <on horseback : a caballo> **2** AT, TO : a <on the right : a la derecha> **3** ABOARD, IN : en, a <on the plane : en el avión> <he got on the train : subió al tren> **4** (*indicating time*) <she worked on Saturdays : trabajaba los sábados> <every hour on the hour : a la hora en punto> **5** (*indicating means or agency*) : por <he cut himself on a tin can : se cortó con una lata> <to talk on the telephone : hablar por teléfono> **6** (*indicating a state or process*) : en <on fire : en llamas> <on the increase : en aumento> **7** (*indicating connection or membership*) : en <on a committee : en una comisión> **8** (*indicating an activity*) <on vacation : de vacaciones> <on a diet : a dieta> **9** ABOUT, CONCERNING : sobre <a book on insects : un libro sobre insectos> <reflect on that : reflexiona sobre eso>
once[1] ['wʌnts] *adv* **1** : una vez <once a month : una vez al mes> <once and for all : de una vez por todas> **2** EVER : alguna vez **3** FORMERLY : antes, anteriormente
once[2] *adj* FORMER : antiguo
once[3] *n* **1** : una vez **2 at ~** SIMULTANEOUSLY : al mismo tiempo, simultáneamente **3 at ~** IMMEDIATELY : inmediatamente, en seguida
once[4] *conj* : una vez que, tan pronto como
once–over [ˌwʌnts'oːvər, 'wʌntsˌ-] *n* **to give someone the once–over** : echarle un vistazo a alguien
oncoming ['ɑnˌkʌmɪŋ, 'ɔn-] *adj* : que viene
one[1] ['wʌn] *adj* **1** (*being a single unit*) : un, una <he only wants one apple : sólo quiere una manzana> **2** (*being a particular one*) : un, una <he arrived early one morning : llegó temprano una mañana> **3** (*being the same*) : mismo, misma <they're all members of one team : todos son miembros del mismo equipo> <one and the same thing : la misma cosa> **4** SOME : alguno, alguna; un, una <I'll see you again one day : algún día te veré otra vez> <at one time or another : en una u otra ocasión>
one[2] *n* **1** : uno *m* (número) **2** (*indicating the first of a set or series*) <from day one : desde el primer momento> **3** (*indicating a single person or thing*) <the one (girl) on the right : la de la derecha> <he has the one but needs the other : tiene uno pero necesita el otro>
one[3] *pron* **1** : uno, una <one of his friends : una de sus amigas> <one never knows : uno nunca sabe, nunca se sabe> <to cut one's finger : cortarse el dedo> **2 one and all** : todos, todo el mundo **3 one another** : el uno al otro, se <they loved one another : se amaban> **4 that one** : aquél, aquella **5 which one?** : ¿cuál?
onerous ['ɑnərəs, 'oːnə-] *adj* : oneroso, gravoso
oneself [ˌwʌn'sɛlf] *pron* **1** (*used reflexively or for emphasis*) : se, sí mismo, uno mismo <to control oneself : controlarse> <to talk to oneself

: hablarse a sí mismo> <to do it oneself : hacérselo uno mismo> **2 by ~** : solo

one–sided [ˈwʌnˈsaɪdəd] *adj* **1** : de un solo lado **2** LOPSIDED : asimétrico **3** BIASED : parcial, tendencioso **4** UNILATERAL : unilateral

onetime [ˈwʌnˈtaɪm] *adj* FORMER : antiguo

one–way [ˈwʌnˈweɪ] *adj* **1** : de sentido único, de una sola dirección <a one-way street : una calle de sentido único> **2** : de ida, sencillo <a one-way ticket : un boleto de ida>

ongoing [ˈɑnˌgoːɪŋ] *adj* **1** CONTINUING : en curso, corriente **2** DEVELOPING : en desarrollo

onion [ˈʌnjən] *n* : cebolla *f*

only[1] [ˈoːnli] *adv* **1** MERELY : sólo, solamente, nomás <for only two dollars : por tan sólo dos dólares> <only once : sólo una vez, no más de una vez> <I only did it to help : lo hice por ayudar nomás> **2** SOLELY : únicamente, sólo, solamente <only he knows it : solamente él lo sabe> **3** (*indicating a result*) <it will only cause him problems : no hará más que crearle problemas> **4 if only** : ojalá, por lo menos <if only it were true! : ¡ojalá sea cierto!> <if he could only dance : si por lo menos pudiera bailar>

only[2] *adj* : único <an only child : un hijo único> <the only chance : la única oportunidad>

only[3] *conj* BUT : pero <I would go, only I'm sick : iría, pero estoy enfermo>

onset [ˈɑnˌsɛt] *n* : comienzo *m,* llegada *f*

onslaught [ˈɑnˌslɔt, ˈɔn-] *n* : arremetida *f,* embestida *f,* embate *m*

onto [ˈɑnˌtuː, ˈɔn-] *prep* : sobre

onus [ˈoːnəs] *n* : responsabilidad *f,* carga *f*

onward[1] [ˈɑnwərd, ˈɔn-] *or* **onwards** *adv* FORWARD : adelante, hacia adelante

onward[2] *adj* : hacia adelante

onyx [ˈɑnɪks] *n* : ónix *m*

ooze[1] [ˈuːz] *v* **oozed; oozing** *vi* : rezumar — *vt* **1** : rezumar **2** EXUDE : irradiar, rebosar <to ooze confidence : irradiar confianza>

ooze[2] *n* SLIME : cieno *m,* limo *m*

opal [ˈoːpəl] *n* : ópalo *m*

opaque [oˈpeɪk] *adj* **1** : opaco **2** UNCLEAR : poco claro

open[1] [ˈoːpən] *vt* **1** : abrir <open the door : abre la puerta> **2** UNCOVER : destapar **3** UNFOLD : desplegar, abrir **4** CLEAR : abrir (un camino, etc.) **5** INAUGURATE : abrir (una tienda), inaugurar (una exposición, etc.) **6** INITIATE : initiar, entablar, abrir <to open the meeting : abrir la sesión> <to open a discussion : entablar un debate> — *vi* **1** : abrirse **2** BEGIN : empezar, comenzar

open[2] *adj* **1** : abierto <an open window : una ventana abierta> **2** FRANK : abierto, franco, directo **3** UNCOVERED : descubierto, abierto **4** EXTENDED : extendido, abierto <with open arms : con los brazos abiertos> **5** UNRESTRICTED : libre, abierto **6** UNDECIDED : pendiente, por decidir, sin resolver <an open question : una cuestión pendiente> **7** AVAILABLE : vacante, libre <the job is open : el puesto está vacante>

open[3] *n* **in the open 1** OUTDOORS : al aire libre **2** KNOWN : conocido, sacado a la luz

open-air [ˈoːpənˈær] *adj* OUTDOOR : al aire libre

open-and-shut [ˈoːpənənd'ʃʌt] *adj* : claro, evidente <an open-and-shut case : un caso muy claro>

opener [ˈoːpənər] *n* : destapador *m,* abrelatas *m,* abridor *m*

openhanded [ˌoːpənˈhændəd] *adj* : generoso, liberal

openhearted [ˌoːpənˈhɑrt̬əd] *adj* **1** FRANK : franco, sincero **2** : generoso, de gran corazón

opening [ˈoːpənɪŋ] *n* **1** BEGINNING : comienzo *m,* principio *m,* apertura *f* **2** APERTURE : abertura *f,* brecha *f,* claro *m* (en el bosque) **3** OPPORTUNITY : oportunidad *f*

openly [ˈoːpənli] *adv* **1** FRANKLY : abiertamente, francamente **2** PUBLICLY : públicamente, declaradamente

openness [ˈoːpənnəs] *n* : franqueza *f*

opera [ˈɑprə, ˈɑpərə] *n* **1** : ópera *f* **2** → **opus**

opera glasses *npl* : gemelos *mpl* de teatro

operate [ˈɑpəˌreɪt] *v* **-ated; -ating** *vi* **1** ACT, FUNCTION : operar, funcionar, actuar **2 to operate on (someone)** : operar a (alguien) — *vt* **1** WORK : operar, manejar, hacer funcionar (una máquina) **2** MANAGE : manejar, administrar (un negocio)

operatic [ˌɑpəˈrætɪk] *adj* : operístico

operation [ˌɑpəˈreɪʃən] *n* **1** FUNCTIONING : funcionamiento *m* **2** USE : uso *m,* manejo *m* (de máquinas) **3** SURGERY : operación *f,* intervención *f* quirúrgica

operational [ˌɑpəˈreɪʃənəl] *adj* : operacional, de operación

operative [ˈɑpərət̬ɪv, -ˌreɪ-] *adj* **1** OPERATING : vigente, en vigor **2** WORKING : operativo **3** SURGICAL : quirúrgico

operator [ˈɑpəˌreɪt̬ər] *n* : operador *m,* -dora *f*

operetta [ˌɑpəˈrɛt̬ə] *n* : opereta *f*

ophthalmologist [ˌɑfˌθælˈmɑlədʒɪst, -θəˈmɑ-] *n* : oftalmólogo *m,* -ga *f*

ophthalmology [ˌɑfˌθælˈmɑlədʒi, -θəˈmɑ-] *n* : oftalmología *f*

opiate [ˈoːpiət, -piˌeɪt] *n* : opiato *m*

opinion [əˈpɪnjən] *n* : opinión *f*

opinionated [əˈpɪnjəˌneɪt̬əd] *adj* : testarudo, dogmático

opium [ˈoːpiəm] *n* : opio *m*
opossum [əˈpɑsəm] *n* : zarigüeya *f,* oposum *m*
opponent [əˈpoːnənt] *n* : oponente *mf;* opositor *m,* -tora *f;* contrincante *mf* (en deportes)
opportune [ˌɑpərˈtuːn, -ˈtjuːn] *adj* : oportuno — **opportunely** *adv*
opportunist [ˌɑpərˈtuːnɪst, -ˈtjuː-] *n* : oportunista *mf*
opportunity [ˌɑpərˈtuːnəṭi, -ˈtjuː-] *n, pl* **-ties** : oportunidad *f,* ocasión *f,* chance *m,* posibilidades *fpl*
oppose [əˈpoːz] *vt* **-posed; -posing 1** : ir en contra de, oponerse a <good opposes evil : el bien se opone al mal> **2** COMBAT : luchar contra, combatir, resistir
opposite[1] [ˈɑpəzət] *adv* : enfrente
opposite[2] *adj* **1** FACING : de enfrente <the opposite side : el lado de enfrente> **2** CONTRARY : opuesto, contrario <in opposite directions : en direcciones contrarias> <the opposite sex : el sexo opuesto, el otro sexo>
opposite[3] *n* : lo contrario, lo opuesto
opposite[4] *prep* : enfrente de, frente a
opposition [ˌɑpəˈzɪʃən] *n* **1** : oposición *f,* resistencia *f* **2 in opposition to** AGAINST : en contra de
oppress [əˈprɛs] *vt* **1** PERSECUTE : oprimir, perseguir **2** BURDEN : oprimir, agobiar
oppression [əˈprɛʃən] *n* : opresión *f*
oppressive [əˈprɛsɪv] *adj* **1** HARSH : opresivo, severo **2** STIFLING : agobiante, sofocante <oppressive heat : calor sofocante>
oppressor [əˈprɛsər] *n* : opresor *m,* -sora *f*
opprobrium [əˈproːbriəm] *n* : oprobio *m*
opt [ˈɑpt] *vi* : optar
optic [ˈɑptɪk] *or* **optical** [-tɪkəl] *adj* : óptico
optician [ɑpˈtɪʃən] *n* : óptico *m,* -ca *f*
optics [ˈɑptɪks] *npl* : óptica *f*
optimal [ˈɑptəməl] *adj* : óptimo
optimism [ˈɑptəˌmɪzəm] *n* : optimismo *m*
optimist [ˈɑptəmɪst] *n* : optimista *mf*
optimistic [ˌɑptəˈmɪstɪk] *adj* : optimista
optimistically [ˌɑptəˈmɪstɪkli] *adv* : con optimismo, positivamente
optimum[1] [ˈɑptəməm] *adj* → **optimal**
optimum[2] *n, pl* **-ma** [ˈɑptəmə] : lo óptimo, lo ideal
option [ˈɑpʃən] *n* : opción *f* <she has no option : no tiene más remedio>
optional [ˈɑpʃənəl] *adj* : facultativo, optativo
optometrist [ɑpˈtɑmətrɪst] *n* : optometrista *mf*
optometry [ɑpˈtɑmətri] *n* : optometría *f*
opulence [ˈɑpjələnts] *n* : opulencia *f*
opulent [ˈɑpjələnt] *adj* : opulento
opus [ˈoːpəs] *n, pl* **opera** [ˈoːpərə, ˈɑpə-] : opus *m,* obra *f* (de música)
or [ˈɔr] *conj* **1** (*indicating an alternative*) : o (u *before words beginning with* o *or* ho) <coffee or tea : café o té> <one day or another : un día u otro> **2** (*following a negative*) : ni <he didn't have his keys or his wallet : no llevaba ni sus llaves ni su billetera>
oracle [ˈɔrəkəl] *n* : oráculo *m*
oral [ˈorəl] *adj* : oral — **orally** *adv*
orange [ˈɔrɪndʒ] *n* **1** : naranja *f,* china *f PRi* (fruto) **2** : naranja *m* (color), color *m* de china *PRi*
orangeade [ˌɔrɪndʒˈeɪd] *n* : naranjada *f*
orangutan [əˈræŋəˌtæŋ, -ˈræŋgə-, -ˌtæn] *n* : orangután *m*
oration [əˈreɪʃən] *n* : oración *f,* discurso *m*
orator [ˈɔrəṭər] *n* : orador *m,* -dora *f*
oratorio [ˌɔrəˈtoriˌoː] *n, pl* **-rios** : oratorio *m*
oratory [ˈɔrəˌtori] *n, pl* **-ries** : oratoria *f*
orb [ˈɔrb] *n* : orbe *m*
orbit[1] [ˈɔrbət] *vt* **1** CIRCLE : girar alrededor de **2** : poner en órbita (un satélite, etc.) — *vi* : orbitar
orbit[2] *n* : órbita *f*
orbital [ˈɔrbəṭəl] *adj* : orbital
orchard [ˈɔrtʃərd] *n* : huerto *m*
orchestra [ˈɔrkəstrə] *n* : orquesta *f*
orchestral [ɔrˈkɛstrəl] *adj* : orquestal
orchestrate [ˈɔrkəˌstreɪt] *vt* **-trated; -trating 1** : orquestar, instrumentar (en música) **2** ORGANIZE : arreglar, organizar
orchestration [ˌɔrkəˈstreɪʃən] *n* : orquestación *f*
orchid [ˈɔrkɪd] *n* : orquídea *f*
ordain [ɔrˈdeɪn] *vt* **1** : ordenar (en religión) **2** DECREE : decretar, ordenar
ordeal [ɔrˈdiːl, ˈɔrˌdiːl] *n* : prueba *f* dura, experiencia *f* terrible
order[1] [ˈɔrdər] *vt* **1** ORGANIZE : arreglar, ordenar, poner en orden **2** COMMAND : ordenar, mandar **3** REQUEST : pedir, encargar <to order a meal : pedir algo de comer> — *vi* : hacer un pedido
order[2] *n* **1** : orden *f* <a religious order : una orden religiosa> **2** COMMAND : orden *f,* mandato *m* <to give an order : dar una orden> **3** REQUEST : orden *f,* pedido *m* <purchase order : orden de compra> **4** ARRANGEMENT : orden *m* <in chronological order : por orden cronológico> **5** DISCIPLINE : orden *m* <law and order : el orden público> **6 in order to** : para **7 out of order** : descompuesto, averiado **8 orders** *npl or* **holy orders** : órdenes *fpl* sagradas
orderliness [ˈɔrdərlinəs] *n* : orden *m*
orderly[1] [ˈɔrdərli] *adj* **1** METHODICAL : ordenado, metódico **2** PEACEFUL : pacífico, disciplinado
orderly[2] *n, pl* **-lies 1** : ordenanza *m* (en el ejército) **2** : camillero *m* (en un hospital)

ordinal [ˈɔrdənəl] *n or* **ordinal number** : ordinal *m,* número *m* ordinal
ordinance [ˈɔrdənənts] *n* : ordenanza *f,* reglamento *m*
ordinarily [ˌɔrdənˈɛrəli] *adv* : ordinariamente, por lo general
ordinary [ˈɔrdənˌɛri] *adj* **1** NORMAL, USUAL : normal, usual **2** AVERAGE : común y corriente, normal **3** MEDIOCRE : mediocre, ordinario
ordination [ˌɔrdənˈeɪʃən] *n* : ordenación *f*
ordnance [ˈɔrdnənts] *n* : artillería *f*
ore [ˈor] *n* : mineral *m* (metalífero), mena *f*
oregano [əˈrɛgəˌnoː] *n* : orégano *m*
organ [ˈɔrgən] *n* **1** : órgano *m* (instrumento) **2** : órgano *m* (del cuerpo) **3** PERIODICAL : publicación *f* periódica, órgano *m*
organic [ɔrˈgænɪk] *adj* : orgánico — **organically** *adv*
organism [ˈɔrgəˌnɪzəm] *n* : organismo *m*
organist [ˈɔrgənɪst] *n* : organista *mf*
organization [ˌɔrgənəˈzeɪʃən] *n* **1** ORGANIZING : organización *f* **2** BODY : organización *f,* organismo *m*
organizational [ˌɔrgənəˈzeɪʃənəl] *adj* : organizativo
organize [ˈɔrgəˌnaɪz] *vt* **-nized; -nizing** : organizar, arreglar, poner en orden
organizer [ˈɔrgəˌnaɪzər] *n* : organizador *m,* -dora *f*
orgasm [ˈɔrˌgæzəm] *n* : orgasmo *m*
orgy [ˈɔrdʒi] *n, pl* **-gies** : orgía *f*
orient [ˈoriˌɛnt] *vt* : orientar
Orient *n* **the Orient** : el Oriente
oriental [ˌoriˈɛntəl] *adj* : del Oriente, oriental
Oriental *n* : oriental *mf*
orientation [ˌoriənˈteɪʃən] *n* : orientación *f*
orifice [ˈɔrəfəs] *n* : orificio *m*
origin [ˈɔrədʒən] *n* **1** ANCESTRY : origen *m,* ascendencia *f* **2** SOURCE : origen *m,* raíz *f,* fuente *f*
original[1] [əˈrɪdʒənəl] *adj* : original
original[2] *n* : original *m*
originality [əˌrɪdʒəˈnæləṭi] *n* : originalidad *f*
originally [əˈrɪdʒənəli] *adv* **1** AT FIRST : al principio, originariamente **2** CREATIVELY : originalmente, con originalidad
originate [əˈrɪdʒəˌneɪt] *v* **-nated; -nating** *vt* : originar, iniciar, crear — *vi* **1** BEGIN : originarse, empezar **2** COME : provenir, proceder, derivarse
originator [əˈrɪdʒəˌneɪṭər] *n* : creador *m,* -dora *f;* inventor *m,* -tora *f*
oriole [ˈoriˌoːl, -iəl] *n* : oropéndola *f*
ornament[1] [ˈɔrnəmənt] *vt* : adornar, decorar, ornamentar
ornament[2] *n* : ornamento *m,* adorno *m,* decoración *f*
ornamental [ˌɔrnəˈmɛntəl] *adj* : ornamental, de adorno, decorativo
ornamentation [ˌɔrnəmənˈteɪʃən, -mɛn-] *n* : ornamentación *f*
ornate [ɔrˈneɪt] *adj* : elaborado, recargado
ornery [ˈɔrnəri, ˈɑrnəri] *adj* **ornerier; -est** : de mal genio, malhumorado
ornithologist [ˌɔrnəˈθɑlədʒɪst] *n* : ornitólogo *m,* -ga *f*
ornithology [ˌɔrnəˈθɑlədʒi] *n, pl* **-gies** : ornitología *f*
orphan[1] [ˈɔrfən] *vt* : dejar huérfano
orphan[2] *n* : huérfano *m,* -na *f*
orphanage [ˈɔrfənɪdʒ] *n* : orfelinato *m,* orfanato *m*
orthodontics [ˌɔrθəˈdɑntɪks] *n* : ortodoncia *f*
orthodontist [ˌɔrθəˈdɑntɪst] *n* : ortodoncista *mf*
orthodox [ˈɔrθəˌdɑks] *adj* : ortodoxo
orthodoxy [ˈɔrθəˌdɑksi] *n, pl* **-doxies** : ortodoxia *f*
orthographic [ˌɔrθəˈgræfɪk] *adj* : ortográfico
orthography [ɔrˈθɑgrəfi] *n, pl* **-phies** SPELLING : ortografía *f*
orthopedic [ˌɔrθəˈpiːdɪk] *adj* : ortopédico
orthopedics [ˌɔrθəˈpiːdɪks] *ns & pl* : ortopedia *f*
orthopedist [ˌɔrθəˈpiːdɪst] *n* : ortopedista *mf*
oscillate [ˈɑsəˌleɪt] *vi* **-lated; -lating** : oscilar
oscillation [ˌɑsəˈleɪʃən] *n* : oscilación *f*
osmosis [ɑzˈmoːsɪs, ɑs-] *n* : ósmosis *f,* osmosis *f*
ostensible [ɑˈstɛntsəbəl] *adj* APPARENT : aparente, ostensible — **ostensibly** [-bli] *adv*
ostentation [ˌɑstənˈteɪʃən] *n* : ostentación *f,* boato *m*
ostentatious [ˌɑstənˈteɪʃəs] *adj* : ostentoso — **ostentatiously** *adv*
osteopath [ˈɑstiəˌpæθ] *n* : osteópata *f*
osteopathy [ˌɑstiˈɑpəθi] *n* : osteopatía *f*
osteoporosis [ˌɑstiopəˈroːsɪs] *n, pl* **-roses** [-ˌsiːz] : osteoporosis *f*
ostracism [ˈɑstrəˌsɪzəm] *n* : ostracismo *m*
ostracize [ˈɑstrəˌsaɪz] *vt* **-cized; -cizing** : condenar al ostracismo, marginar, aislar
ostrich [ˈɑstrɪtʃ, ˈɔs-] *n* : avestruz *m*
other[1] [ˈʌðər] *adv* **other than** : aparte de, fuera de
other[2] *adj* : otro <the other boys : los otros muchachos> <smarter than other people : más inteligente que los demás> <on the other hand : por otra parte, por otro lado> <every other day : cada dos días>
other[3] *pron* : otro, otra <one in front of the other : uno tras otro> <myself and three others : yo y tres otros, yo y tres más> <somewhere or other : en alguna parte>

otherwise[1] [ˈʌðər͵waɪz] *adv* **1** DIFFERENTLY : de otro modo, de manera distinta <he could not act otherwise : no pudo actuar de manera distinta> **2** : eso aparte, por lo demás <I'm dizzy, but otherwise I'm fine : estoy mareado pero, por lo demás, estoy bien> **3** OR ELSE : de lo contario, si no <do what I tell you, otherwise you'll be sorry : haz lo que te digo, de lo contario, te arrepentirás>

otherwise[2] *adj* : diferente, distinto <the facts are otherwise : la realidad es diferente>

otter [ˈɑt̬ər] *n* : nutria *f*

ought [ˈɔt] *v aux* : deber <you ought to take care of yourself : deberías cuidarte>

oughtn't [ˈɔtənt] (*contraction of* **ought not**) → **ought**

ounce [ˈaʊnts] *n* : onza *f*

our [ˈɑr, ˈaʊr] *adj* : nuestro

ours [ˈaʊrz, ˈɑrz] *pron* : nuestro, nuestra <a cousin of ours : un primo nuestro>

ourselves [ɑrˈsɛlvz, aʊr-] *pron* **1** (*used reflexively*) : nos, nosotros <we amused ourselves : nos divertimos> <we were always thinking of ourselves : siempre pensábamos en nosotros> **2** (*used for emphasis*) : nosotros mismos, nosotras mismas <we did it ourselves : lo hicimos nosotros mismos>

oust [ˈaʊst] *vt* : desbancar, expulsar

ouster [ˈaʊstər] *n* : expulsión *f* (de un país, etc.), destitución *f* (de un puesto)

out[1] [ˈaʊt] *vi* : revelarse, hacerse conocido

out[2] *adv* **1** (*indicating direction or movement*) : para afuera <she opened the door and looked out : abrió la puerta y miró para afuera> **2** (*indicating a location away from home or work*) : fuera, afuera <to eat out : comer afuera> **3** (*indicating loss of control or possession*) <they let the secret out : sacaron el secreto a la luz> **4** (*indicating completion or discontinuance*) <his money ran out : se le acabó el dinero> <to turn out the light : apagar la luz> **5** OUTSIDE : fuera, afuera <out in the garden : afuera en el jardín> **6** ALOUD : en voz alta, en alto <to cry out : gritar>

out[3] *adj* **1** EXTERNAL : externo, exterior **2** OUTLYING : alejado, distante <the out islands : las islas distantes> **3** ABSENT : ausente **4** UNFASHIONABLE : fuera de moda **5** EXTINGUISHED : apagado

out[4] *prep* **1** (*used to indicate an outward movement*) : por <I looked out the window : miré por la ventana> <she ran out the door : corrió por la puerta> **2** → **out of**

out-and-out [ˈaʊtənˈaʊt] *adj* UTTER : redomado, absoluto

outboard motor [ˈaʊt͵bord] *n* : motor *m* fuera de borde

outbound [ˈaʊt͵baʊnd] *adj* : que sale, de salida

outbreak [ˈaʊt͵breɪk] *n* : brote *m* (de una enfermedad), comienzo *m* (de guerra), ola *f* (de violencia), erupción *f* (de granos)

outbuilding [ˈaʊt͵bɪldɪŋ] *n* : edificio *m* anexo

outburst [ˈaʊt͵bərst] *n* : arranque *m*, arrebato *m*

outcast [ˈaʊt͵kæst] *n* : marginado *m*, -da *f*; paria *mf*

outcome [ˈaʊt͵kʌm] *n* : resultado *m*, desenlace *m*, consecuencia *f*

outcrop [ˈaʊt͵krɑp] *n* : afloramiento *m*

outcry [ˈaʊt͵kraɪ] *n, pl* **-cries** : clamor *m*, protesta *f*

outdated [͵aʊtˈdeɪt̬əd] *adj* : anticuado, fuera de moda

outdistance [͵aʊtˈdɪstənts] *vt* **-tanced; -tancing** : aventajar, dejar atrás

outdo [͵aʊtˈduː] *vt* **-did** [-ˈdɪd]; **-done** [-ˈdʌn]; **-doing**; **-does** [-ˈdʌz] : superar

outdoor [ˈaʊtˈdor] *adj* : al aire libre <outdoor sports : deportes al aire libre> <outdoor clothing : ropa de calle>

outdoors[1] [ˈaʊtˈdorz] *adv* : afuera, al aire libre

outdoors[2] *n* : aire *m* libre

outer [ˈaʊt̬ər] *adj* **1** : exterior, externo **2 outer space** : espacio *m* exterior

outermost [ˈaʊt̬ər͵moːst] *adj* : más remoto, más exterior, extremo

outfield [ˈaʊt͵fiːld] *n* **the outfield** : los jardines

outfielder [ˈaʊt͵fiːldər] *n* : jardinero *m*, -ra *f*

outfit[1] [ˈaʊt͵fɪt] *vt* **-fitted; -fitting** EQUIP : equipar

outfit[2] *n* **1** EQUIPMENT : equipo *m* **2** COSTUME, ENSEMBLE : traje *m*, conjunto *m* **3** GROUP : conjunto *m*

outgo [ˈaʊt͵goː] *n, pl* **outgoes** : gasto *m*

outgoing [ˈaʊt͵goːɪŋ] *adj* **1** OUTBOUND : que sale **2** DEPARTING : saliente <an outgoing president : un presidente saliente> **3** EXTROVERTED : extrovertido, expansivo

outgrow [͵aʊtˈgroː] *vt* **-grew** [-ˈgruː]; **-grown** [-ˈgroːn]; **-growing 1** : crecer más que <that tree outgrew all the others : ese árbol creció más que todos los otros> **2 to outgrow one's clothes** : quedarle pequeña la ropa a uno

outgrowth [ˈaʊt͵groːθ] *n* **1** OFFSHOOT : brote *m*, vástago *m* (de una planta) **2** CONSEQUENCE : consecuencia *f*, producto *m*, resultado *m*

outing [ˈaʊt̬ɪŋ] *n* : excursión *f*

outlandish [aʊtˈlændɪʃ] *adj* : descabellado, muy extraño

outlast [͵aʊtˈlæst] *vt* : durar más que

outlaw[1] [ˈaʊt͵lɔ] *vt* : hacerse ilegal, declarar fuera de la ley, prohibir

outlaw[2] *n* : bandido *m*, -da *f*; bandolero *m*, -ra *f*; forajido *m*, -da *f*

outlay [ˈaʊtˌleɪ] *n* : gasto *m*, desembolso *m*

outlet [ˈaʊtˌlɛt, -lət] *n* **1** EXIT : salida *f*, escape *m* <electrical outlet : toma de corriente> **2** RELIEF : desahogo *m* **3** MARKET : mercado *m*, salida *f*

outline[1] [ˈaʊtˌlaɪn] *vt* **-lined; -lining 1** SKETCH : diseñar, esbozar, bosquejar **2** DEFINE, EXPLAIN : perfilar, delinear, explicar <she outlined our responsibilities : delineó nuestras responsabilidades>

outline[2] *n* **1** PROFILE : perfil *m*, silueta *f*, contorno *m* **2** SKETCH : bosquejo *m*, boceto *m* **3** SUMMARY : esquema *m*, resumen *m*, sinopsis *m* <an outline of world history : un esquema de la historia mundial>

outlive [ˌaʊtˈlɪv] *vt* **-lived; -living** : sobrevivir a

outlook [ˈaʊtˌlʊk] *n* **1** VIEW : vista *f*, panorama *f* **2** POINT OF VIEW : punto *m* de vista **3** PROSPECTS : perspectivas *fpl*

outlying [ˈaʊtˌlaɪɪŋ] *adj* : alejado, distante, remoto <the outlying areas : las afueras>

outmoded [ˌaʊtˈmoːdəd] *adj* : pasado de moda, anticuado

outnumber [ˌaʊtˈnʌmbər] *vt* : superar en número a, ser más numeroso de

out of *prep* **1** (*indicating direction or movement from within*) : de, por <we ran out of the house : salimos corriendo de la casa> <to look out of the window : mirar por la ventana> **2** (*being beyond the limits of*) <out of control : fuera de control> <to be out of sight : desaparecer de vista> **3** OF : de <one out of four : uno de cada cuatro> **4** (*indicating absence or loss*) : sin <out of money : sin dinero> <we're out of matches : nos hemos quedado sin fósforos> **5** BECAUSE OF : por <out of curiosity : por curiosidad> **6** FROM : de <made out of plastic : hecho de plástico>

out–of–date [ˌaʊt̬əvˈdeɪt] *adj* : anticuado, obsoleto, pasado de moda

out-of-door [ˌaʊt̬əvˈdor] *or* **out-of-doors** [-ˈdorz] *adj* → **outdoor**

out-of-doors *n* → **outdoors**

outpatient [ˈaʊtˌpeɪʃənt] *n* : paciente *m* externo, paciente *f* externa

outpost [ˈaʊtˌpoːst] *n* : puesto *m* avanzado

output[1] [ˈaʊtˌpʊt] *vt* **-putted** *or* **-put; -putting** : producir

output[2] *n* : producción *f* (de una fábrica), rendimiento *m* (de una máquina), productividad *f* (de una persona)

outrage[1] [ˈaʊtˌreɪdʒ] *vt* **-raged; -raging 1** INSULT : ultrajar, injuriar **2** INFURIATE : indignar, enfurecer

outrage[2] *n* **1** ATROCITY : atropello *m*, atrocidad *f*, atentado *m* **2** SCANDAL : escándalo *m* **3** ANGER : ira *f*, furia *f*

outrageous [ˌaʊtˈreɪdʒəs] *adj* **1** SCANDALOUS : escandaloso, ofensivo, atroz **2** UNCONVENTIONAL : poco convencional, extravagante **3** EXORBITANT : exorbitante, excesivo (dícese de los precios, etc.)

outright[1] [ˌaʊtˈraɪt] *adv* **1** COMPLETELY : por completo, totalmente <to sell outright : vender por completo> <he refused it outright : lo rechazó rotundamente> **2** DIRECTLY : directamente, sin reserva **3** INSTANTLY : al instante, en el acto

outright[2] [ˈaʊtˌraɪt] *adj* **1** COMPLETE : completo, absoluto, categórico <an outright lie : una mentira absoluta> **2** : sin reservas <an outright gift : un regalo sin reservas>

outset [ˈaʊtˌsɛt] *n* : comienzo *m*, principio *m*

outshine [ˌaʊtˈʃaɪn] *vt* **-shone** [-ˈʃoːn, -ˈʃɒn] *or* **-shined; -shining** : eclipsar

outside[1] [ˌaʊtˈsaɪd, ˈaʊtˌ-] *adv* : fuera, afuera

outside[2] *adj* **1** : exterior, externo <the outside edge : el borde exterior> <outside influences : influencias externas> **2** REMOTE : remoto <an outside chance : una posibilidad remota>

outside[3] *n* **1** EXTERIOR : parte *f* de afuera, exterior *m* **2** MOST : máximo *m* <three weeks at the outside : tres semanas como máximo> **3 from the outside** : desde afuera, desde fuera

outside[4] *prep* : fuera de, afuera de <outside my window : fuera de mi ventana> <outside regular hours : fuera del horario normal> <outside the law : afuera de la ley>

outside of *prep* **1** → **outside**[4] **2** → **besides**[2]

outsider [ˌaʊtˈsaɪdər] *n* : forastero *m*, -ra *f*

outskirts [ˈaʊtˌskərts] *npl* : afueras *fpl*, alrededores *mpl*

outsmart [ˌaʊtˈsmɑrt] → **outwit**

outspoken [ˌaʊtˈspoːkən] *adj* : franco, directo

outstanding [ˌaʊtˈstændɪŋ] *adj* **1** UNPAID : pendiente **2** NOTABLE : destacado, notable, excepcional, sobresaliente

outstandingly [ˌaʊtˈstændɪŋli] *adv* : excepcionalmente

outstrip [ˌaʊtˈstrɪp] *vt* **-stripped** *or* **-stript** [-ˈstrɪpt]; **-stripping 1** : aventajar, dejar atrás <he outstripped the other runners : aventajó a los otros corredores> **2** SURPASS : aventajar, sobrepasar

outward[1] [ˈaʊtwərd] *or* **outwards** [-wərdz] *adv* : hacia afuera, hacia el exterior

outward[2] *adj* **1** : hacia afuera <an outward flow : un flujo hacia afuera> **2** : externo, external <outward beauty : belleza externa>

outwardly ['aʊtwərdli] *adv* **1** EXTERNALLY : externalmente **2** APPARENTLY : aparentemente <outwardly friendly : aparentemente simpático>
outwit [ˌaʊt'wɪt] *vt* **-witted; -witting** : ser más listo que
ova → **ovum**
oval[1] ['oːvəl] *adj* : ovalado, oval
oval[2] *n* : óvalo *m*
ovary ['oːvəri] *n, pl* **-ries** : ovario *m*
ovation [o'veɪʃən] *n* : ovación *f*
oven ['ʌvən] *n* : horno *m*
over[1] ['oːvər] *adv* **1** (*indicating movement across*) <he flew over to London : voló a Londres> <come on over! : ¡ven acá!> **2** (*indicating an additional amount*) <the show ran 10 minutes over : el espectáculo terminó 10 minutos de tarde> **3** ABOVE, OVERHEAD : por encima **4** AGAIN : otra vez, de nuevo <over and over : una y otra vez> <to start over : volver a empezar> **5 all over** EVERYWHERE : por todas partes **6 to fall over** : caerse **7 to turn over** : poner boca abajo, voltear
over[2] *adj* **1** HIGHER, UPPER : superior **2** REMAINING : sobrante, que sobra **3** ENDED : terminado, acabado <the work is over : el trabajo está terminado>
over[3] *prep* **1** ABOVE : encima de, arriba de, sobre <over the fireplace : encima de la chimenea> <the hawk flew over the hills : el halcón voló sobre los cerros> **2** : más de <over $50 : más de $50> **3** ALONG : por, sobre <to glide over the ice : deslizarse sobre el hielo> **4** (*indicating motion through a place or thing*) <they showed me over the house : me mostraron la casa> **5** ACROSS : por encima de, sobre <he jumped over the ditch : saltó por encima de la zanja> **6** UPON : sobre <a cape over my shoulders : una capa sobre los hombros> **7** ON : por <to speak over the telephone : hablar por teléfono> **8** DURING : en, durante <over the past 25 years : durante los últimos 25 años> **9** BECAUSE OF : por <they fought over the money : se pelearon por el dinero>
overabundance [ˌoːvərə'bʌndən*t*k] *n* : superabundancia *f*
overabundant [ˌoːvərə'bʌndənt] *adj* : superabundante
overactive [ˌoːvər'æktɪv] *adj* : hiperactivo
overall [ˌoːvər'ɔl] *adj* : total, global, de conjunto
overalls ['oːvərˌɔlz] *npl* : overol *m*
overawe [ˌoːvər'ɔ] *vt* **-awed; -awing** : intimidar, impresionar
overbearing [ˌoːvər'bærɪŋ] *adj* : dominante, imperioso, prepotente
overboard ['oːvərˌbord] *adv* : por la borda, al agua
overburden [ˌoːvər'bərdən] *vt* : sobrecargar, agobiar
overcast ['oːvərˌkæst] *adj* CLOUDY : nublado
overcharge [ˌoːvər'tʃɑrdʒ] *vt* **-charged; -charging** : cobrarle de más (a alguien)
overcoat ['oːvərˌkoːt] *n* : abrigo *m*
overcome [ˌoːvər'kʌm] *v* **-came** [-'keɪm]; **-come; -coming** *vt* **1** CONQUER : vencer, derrotar, superar **2** OVERWHELM : abrumar, agobiar — *vi* : vencer
overconfidence [ˌoːvər'kɑnfədən*t*s] *n* : exceso *m* de confianza
overconfident [ˌoːvər'kɑnfədənt] *adj* : demasiado confiado
overcook [ˌoːvər'kʊk] *vt* : recocer, cocer demasiado
overcrowded [ˌoːvər'kraʊdəd] *adj* **1** PACKED : abarrotado, atestado de gente **2** OVERPOPULATED : superpoblado
overdo [ˌoːvər'duː] *vt* **-did** [-'dɪd]; **-done** [-'dʌn]; **-doing; -does** [-'dʌz] **1** : hacer demasiado **2** EXAGGERATE : exagerar **3** OVERCOOK : recocer
overdose ['oːvərˌdoːs] *n* : sobredosis *f*
overdraft ['oːvərˌdræft] *n* : sobregiro *m,* descubierto *m*
overdraw [ˌoːvər'drɔ] *vt* **-drew** [-'druː]; **-drawn** [-'drɔn]; **-drawing 1** : sobregirar <my account is overdrawn : tengo la cuenta en descubierto> **2** EXAGGERATE : exagerar
overdue [ˌoːvər'duː] *adj* **1** UNPAID : vencido y sin pagar **2** TARDY : de retraso, tardío
overeat [ˌoːvər'iːt] *vi* **-ate** [-'eɪt]; **-eaten** [-'iːtən]; **-eating** : comer demasiado
overelaborate [ˌoːvərɪ'læbərət] *adj* : recargado
overestimate [ˌoːvər'ɛstəˌmeɪt] *vt* **-mated; -mating** : sobreestimar
overexcited [ˌoːvərɪk'saɪt̬əd] *adj* : sobreexcitado
overexpose [ˌoːvərɪk'spoːz] *vt* **-posed; -posing** : sobreexponer
overfeed [ˌoːvər'fiːd] *vt* **-fed** [-'fɛd]; **-feeding** : sobrealimentar
overflow[1] [ˌoːvər'floː] *vt* **1** : desbordar **2** INUNDATE : inundar — *vi* : desbordarse, rebosar
overflow[2] ['oːvərˌfloː] *n* **1** : derrame *m,* desbordamiento *m* (de un río) **2** SURPLUS : exceso *m,* excedente *m*
overfly [ˌoːvər'flaɪ] *vt* **-flew** [-'fluː]; **-flown** [-'floːn]; **-flying** : sobrevolar
overgrown [ˌoːvər'groːn] *adj* **1** : cubierto <overgrown with weeds : cubierto de malas hierbas> **2** : demasiado grande
overhand[1] ['oːvərˌhænd] *adv* : por encima de la cabeza
overhand[2] *adj* : por lo alto (tirada)
overhang[1] [ˌoːvər'hæŋ] *v* **-hung** [-'hʌŋ]; **-hanging** *vt* **1** : sobresalir por encima de **2** THREATEN : amenazar — *vi* : sobresalir
overhang[2] ['oːvərˌhæŋ] *n* : saliente *mf*

overhaul [ˌoːvərˈhɔl] *vt* **1** : revisar <to overhaul an engine : revisar un motor> **2** OVERTAKE : adelantar

overhead[1] [ˌoːvərˈhɛd] *adv* : por encima, arriba, por lo alto

overhead[2] [ˈoːvərˌhɛd] *adj* : de arriba

overhead[3] [ˈoːvərˌhɛd] *n* : gastos *mpl* generales

overhear [ˌoːvərˈhɪr] *vt* **-heard; -hearing** : oír por casualidad

overheat [ˌoːvərˈhiːt] *vt* : recalentar, sobrecalentar, calentar demasiado

overjoyed [ˌoːvərˈdʒɔɪd] *adj* : rebosante de alegría

overkill [ˈoːvərˌkɪl] *n* : exceso *m,* excedente *m*

overland[1] [ˈoːvərˌlænd, -lənd] *adv* : por tierra

overland[2] *adj* : terrestre, por tierra

overlap[1] [ˌoːvərˈlæp] *v* **-lapped; -lapping** *vt* : traslapar — *vi* : traslaparse, solaparse

overlap[2] [ˈoːvərˌlæp] *n* : traslapo *m*

overlay[1] [ˌoːvərˈleɪ] *vt* **-laid** [-ˈleɪd]; **-laying** : recubrir, revestir

overlay[2] [ˈoːvərˌleɪ] *n* : revestimiento *m*

overload [ˌoːvərˈloːd] *vt* : sobrecargar

overlong [ˌoːvərˈlɔŋ] *adj* : excesivamente largo, largo y pesado

overlook [ˌoːvərˈlʊk] *vt* **1** INSPECT : inspeccionar, revisar **2** : tener vista a, dar a <a house overlooking the valley : una casa que tiene vista al valle> **3** MISS : pasar por alto **4** EXCUSE : dejar pasar, disculpar

overly [ˈoːvərli] *adv* : demasiado

overnight[1] [ˌoːvərˈnaɪt] *adv* **1** : por la noche, durante la noche **2** : de la noche a la mañana <we can't do it overnight : no podemos hacerlo de la noche a la mañana>

overnight[2] [ˈoːvərˈnaɪt] *adj* **1** : de noche <an overnight stay : una estancia de una noche> <an overnight bag : una bolsa de viaje> **2** SUDDEN : repentino

overpass [ˈoːvərˌpæs] *n* : paso *m* elevado, paso *m* a desnivel *Mex*

overpopulated [ˌoːvərˈpɑpjəˌleɪṱəd] *adj* : sobrepoblado

overpower [ˌoːvərˈpaʊər] *vt* **1** CONQUER, SUBDUE : vencer, superar **2** OVERWHELM : abrumar, agobiar <overpowered by the heat : sofocado por el calor>

overpraise [ˌoːvərˈpreɪz] *vt* **-praised; -praising** : adular

overrate [ˌoːvərˈreɪt] *vt* **-rated; -rating** : sobrevalorar, sobrevaluar

override [ˌoːvərˈraɪd] *vt* **-rode** [-ˈroːd]; **-ridden** [-ˈrɪdən]; **-riding 1** : predominar sobre, contar más que <hunger overrode our manners : el hambre predominó sobre los modales> **2** ANNUL : anular, invalidar <to override a veto : anular un veto>

overrule [ˌoːvərˈruːl] *vt* **-ruled; -ruling** : anular (una decisión), desautorizar (una persona), denegar (un pedido)

overrun [ˌoːvərˈrʌn] *v* **-ran** [-ˈræn]; **-running** *vt* **1** INVADE : invadir **2** INFEST : infestar, plagar **3** EXCEED : exceder, rebasar — *vi* : rebasar el tiempo previsto

overseas[1] [ˌoːvərˈsiːz] *adv* : en el extranjero <to travel overseas : viajar al extranjero>

overseas[2] [ˈoːvərˌsiːz] *adj* : extranjero, exterior

oversee [ˌoːvərˈsiː] *vt* **-saw** [-ˈsɔ]; **-seen** [-ˈsiːn]; **-seeing** SUPERVISE : supervisar

overseer [ˈoːvərˌsiːər] *n* : supervisor *m,* -sora *f;* capataz *mf*

overshadow [ˌoːvərˈʃæˌdoː] *vt* **1** DARKEN : oscurecer, ensombrecer **2** ECLIPSE, OUTSHINE : eclipsar

overshoe [ˈoːvərˌʃuː] *n* : chanclo *m*

overshoot [ˌoːvərˈʃuːt] *vt* **-shot** [-ˈʃɑt]; **-shooting** : pasarse de <to overshoot the mark : pasarse de la raya>

oversight [ˈoːvərˌsaɪt] *n* : descuido *m,* inadvertencia *f*

oversleep [ˌoːvərˈsliːp] *vi* **-slept** [-ˈslɛpt]; **-sleeping** : no despertarse a tiempo, quedarse dormido

overspread [ˌoːvərˈsprɛd] *vt* **-spread; -spreading** : extenderse sobre

overstaffed [ˌoːvərˈstæft] *adj* : con exceso de personal

overstate [ˌoːvərˈsteɪt] *vt* **-stated; -stating** EXAGGERATE : exagerar

overstatement [ˌoːvərˈsteɪtmənt] *n* : exageración *f*

overstep [ˌoːvərˈstɛp] *vt* **-stepped; -stepping** EXCEED : sobrepasar, traspasar, exceder

overt [oˈvərt, ˈoːˌvərt] *adj* : evidente, manifiesto, patente

overtake [ˌoːvərˈteɪk] *vt* **-took** [-ˈtʊk]; **-taken** [-ˈteɪkən]; **-taking** : pasar, adelantar, rebasar *Mex*

overthrow[1] [ˌoːvərˈθroː] *vt* **-threw** [-ˈθruː]; **-thrown** [-ˈθroːn]; **-throwing 1** OVERTURN : dar la vuelta a, volcar **2** DEFEAT, TOPPLE : derrocar, derribar, deponer

overthrow[2] [ˈoːvərˌθroː] *n* : derrocamiento *m,* caída *f*

overtime [ˈoːvərˌtaɪm] *n* **1** : horas *fpl* extras (de trabajo) **2** : prórroga *f* (en deportes)

overtly [oˈvərtli, ˈoːˌvərt-] *adv* OPENLY : abiertamente

overtone [ˈoːvərˌtoːn] *n* **1** : armónico *m* (en música) **2** HINT, SUGGESTION : tinte *m,* insinuación *f*

overture [ˈoːvərˌtʃʊr, -tʃər] *n* **1** PROPOSAL : propuesta *f* **2** : obertura *f* (en música)

overturn [ˌoːvərˈtərn] *vt* **1** UPSET : dar la vuelta a, volcar **2** NULLIFY : anular, invalidar — *vi* TURN OVER : volcar, dar un vuelco

overuse [ˌoːvərˈjuːz] *vt* **-used; -using** : abusar de

overview [ˈoːvərˌvjuː] *n* : resumen *m,* visión *f* general

overweening [ˌoːvərˈwiːnɪŋ] *adj* **1** ARROGANT : arrogante, soberbio **2** IMMODERATE : desmesurado

overweight [ˌoːvərˈweɪt] *adj* : demasiado gordo, demasiado pesado

overwhelm [ˌoːvərˈ*h*wɛlm] *vt* **1** CRUSH, DEFEAT : aplastar, arrollar **2** SUBMERGE : inundar, sumergir **3** OVERPOWER : abrumar, agobiar <overwhelmed by remorse : abrumado de remordimiento>

overwhelming [ˌoːvərˈ*h*wɛlmɪŋ] *adj* **1** CRUSHING : abrumador, apabullante **2** SWEEPING : arrollador, aplastante <an overwhelming majority : una mayoría aplastante>

overwork [ˌoːvərˈwərk] *vt* **1** : hacer trabajar demasiado **2** OVERUSE : abusar de — *vi* : trabajar demasiado

overwrought [ˌoːvərˈrɔt] *adj* : alterado, sobreexcitado

ovoid [ˈoːˌvɔɪd] *or* **ovoidal** [oˈvɔɪdəl] *adj* : ovoide

ovulate [ˈɑvjəˌleɪt, ˈoː-] *vi* **-lated; -lating** : ovular

ovulation [ˌɑvjəˈleɪʃən, ˌoː-] *n* : ovulación *f*

ovum [ˈoːvəm] *n, pl* **ova** [-və] : óvulo *m*

owe [ˈoː] *vt* **owed; owing** : deber <you owe me $10 : me debes $10> <he owes his wealth to his father : le debe su riqueza a su padre>

owing to *prep* : debido a

owl [ˈaʊl] *n* : búho *m,* lechuza *f,* tecolote *m Mex*

own[1] *v* [ˈoːn] *vt* **1** POSSESS : poseer, tener, ser dueño de **2** ADMIT : reconocer, admitir — *vi* **to own up** : reconocer (algo), admitir (algo)

own[2] *adj* : propio, personal, particular <his own car : su propio coche>

own[3] *pron* **my (your, his/her, our, their) own** : el mío, la mía; el tuyo, la tuya; el suyo, la suya; el nuestro, la nuestra <to each his own : cada uno a lo suyo> <money of my own : mi propio dinero> <to be on one's own : estar solo>

owner [ˈoːnər] *n* : dueño *m,* -ña *f;* propietario *m,* -ria *f*

ownership [ˈoːnərˌʃɪp] *n* : propiedad *f*

ox [ˈɑks] *n, pl* **oxen** [ˈɑksən] : buey *m*

oxidation [ˌɑksəˈdeɪʃən] *n* : oxidación *f*

oxide [ˈɑkˌsaɪd] *n* : óxido *m*

oxidize [ˈɑksəˌdaɪz] *vt* **-dized; -dizing** : oxidar

oxygen [ˈɑksɪdʒən] *n* : oxígeno *m*

oyster [ˈɔɪstər] *n* : ostra *f,* ostión *m Mex*

ozone [ˈoːˌzoːn] *n* : ozono *m*

P

p [ˈpiː] *n, pl* **p's** *or* **ps** [ˈpiːz] : decimosexta letra del alfabeto inglés

pace[1] [ˈpeɪs] *v* **paced; pacing** *vi* : caminar, ir y venir — *vt* **1** : caminar por <she paced the floor : caminaba de un lado a otro del cuarto> **2 to pace a runner** : marcarle el ritmo a un corredor

pace[2] *n* **1** STEP : paso *m* **2** RATE : paso *m,* ritmo *m* <to set the pace : marcar el paso, marcar la pauta>

pacemaker [ˈpeɪsˌmeɪkər] *n* : marcapasos *m*

pacific [pəˈsɪfɪk] *adj* : pacífico

pacifier [ˈpæsəˌfaɪər] *n* : chupete *m,* chupón *m,* mamila *f Mex*

pacifism [ˈpæsəˌfɪzəm] *n* : pacifismo *m*

pacifist [ˈpæsəfɪst] *n* : pacifista *mf*

pacify [ˈpæsəˌfaɪ] *vt* **-fied; -fying 1** SOOTHE : apaciguar, pacificar **2** : pacificar (un país, una región, etc.)

pack[1] [ˈpæk] *vt* **1** PACKAGE : empaquetar, embalar, envasar **2** : empacar, meter (en una maleta) <to pack one's bag : hacer la maleta> **3** FILL : llenar, abarrotar <a packed theater : un teatro abarrotado> **4 to pack off** SEND : mandar — *vi* : empacar, hacer las maletas

pack[2] *n* **1** BUNDLE : bulto *m,* fardo *m* **2** BACKPACK : mochila *f* **3** PACKAGE : paquete *m,* cajetilla *f* (de cigarillos, etc.) **4** : manada *f* (de lobos, etc.), jauría *f* (de perros) <a pack of thieves : una pandilla de ladrones>

package[1] [ˈpækɪdʒ] *vt* **-aged; -aging** : empaquetar, embalar

package[2] *n* : paquete *m,* bulto *m*

packer [ˈpækər] *n* : empacador *m,* -dora *f*

packet [ˈpækət] *n* : paquete *m*

pact [ˈpækt] *n* : pacto *m,* acuerdo *m*

pad[1] [ˈpæd] *vt* **padded; padding 1** FILL, STUFF : rellenar, acolchar (una silla, una pared) **2** : meter paja en, rellenar <to pad a speech : rellenar un discurso>

pad[2] *n* **1** CUSHION : almohadilla *f* <a shoulder pad : una hombrera> **2** TABLET : bloc *m* (de papel) **3** *or* **lily pad** : hoja *f* grande (de un nenúfar) **4 ink pad** : tampón *m* **5 launching pad** : plataforma *f* (de lanzamiento)

padding [ˈpædɪŋ] *n* **1** FILLING : relleno *m* **2** : paja *f* (en un discurso, etc.)

paddle[1] [ˈpædəl] *v* **-dled; -dling** *vt* **1** : hacer avanzar (una canoa) con canalete **2** HIT : azotar, darle nalgadas a (con una pala o paleta) — *vi* **1** : remar (en una canoa) **2** SPLASH : chapotear, mojarse los pies

paddle² *n* **1 :** canalete *m,* zagual *m* (de una canoa, etc.) **2 :** pala *f,* paleta *f* (en deportes)
paddock ['pædək] *n* **1** PASTURE **:** potrero *m* **2 :** paddock *m,* cercado *m* (en un hipódromo)
paddy ['pædi] *n, pl* **-dies :** arrozal *m*
padlock¹ ['pæd,lɑk] *vt* **:** cerrar con candado
padlock² *n* **:** candado *m*
pagan¹ ['peɪgən] *adj* **:** pagano
pagan² *n* **:** pagano *m,* -na *f*
paganism ['peɪgən,ɪzəm] *n* **:** paganismo *m*
page¹ ['peɪdʒ] *vt* **paged; paging :** llamar por altavoz
page² *n* **1** BELLHOP **:** botones *m* **2 :** página *f* (de un libro, etc.)
pageant ['pædʒənt] *n* **1** SPECTACLE **:** espectáculo *m* **2** PROCESSION **:** desfile *m*
pageantry ['pædʒəntri] *n* **:** pompa *f,* fausto *m*
pagoda [pə'goːdə] *n* **:** pagoda *f*
paid → **pay**
pail ['peɪl] *n* **:** balde *m,* cubo *m,* cubeta *f Mex*
pailful ['peɪl,fʊl] *n* **:** balde *m,* cubo *m,* cubeta *f Mex*
pain¹ ['peɪn] *vt* **:** doler
pain² *n* **1** PENALTY **:** pena *f* <under pain of death : so pena de muerte> **2** SUFFERING **:** dolor *m,* malestar *m,* pena *f* (mental) **3 pains** *npl* EFFORT **:** esmero *m,* esfuerzo *m* <to take pains : esmerarse>
painful ['peɪnfəl] *adj* **:** doloroso — **painfully** *adv*
painkiller ['peɪn,kɪlər] *n* **:** analgésico *m*
painless ['peɪnləs] *adj* **:** indoloro, sin dolor
painlessly ['peɪnləsli] *adv* **:** sin dolor
painstaking ['peɪn,steɪkɪŋ] *adj* **:** esmerado, cuidadoso, meticuloso — **painstakingly** *adv*
paint¹ ['peɪnt] *v* **:** pintar
paint² *n* **:** pintura *f*
paintbrush ['peɪnt,brʌʃ] *n* **:** pincel *m* (de un artista), brocha *f* (para pintar casas, etc.)
painter ['peɪntər] *n* **:** pintor *m,* -tora *f*
painting ['peɪntɪŋ] *n* **:** pintura *f*
pair¹ ['pær] *vt* **:** emparejar, poner en parejas — *vi* **:** emparejarse
pair² *n* **:** par *m* (de objetos), pareja *f* (de personas o animales) <a pair of scissors : unas tijeras>
pajamas [pə'dʒɑməz, -'dʒæ-] *npl* **:** pijama *m,* piyama *mf*
Pakistani [,pækɪ'stæni, ,pɑkɪ'stɑni] *n* **:** paquistaní *mf* — **Pakistani** *adj*
pal ['pæl] *n* **:** amigo *m,* -ga *f;* compinche *mf fam;* chamo *m,* -ma *f Ven fam;* cuate *m,* -ta *f Mex*
palace ['pæləs] *n* **:** palacio *m*
palatable ['pælət̬əbəl] *adj* **:** sabroso
palate ['pælət] *n* **1 :** paladar *m* (de la boca) **2** TASTE **:** paladar *m,* gusto *m*
palatial [pə'leɪʃəl] *adj* **:** suntuoso, espléndido
palaver [pə'lævər, -'lɑ-] *n* **:** palabrería *f*
pale¹ ['peɪl] *v* **paled; paling** *vi* **:** palidecer — *vt* **:** hacer pálido
pale² *adj* **paler; palest 1 :** pálido <to turn pale : palidecer, ponerse pálido> **2 :** claro (dícese de los colores)
paleness ['peɪlnəs] *n* **:** palidez *f*
Palestinian [,pælə'stɪniən] *n* **:** palestino *m,* -na *f* — **Palestinian** *adj*
palette ['pælət] *n* **:** paleta *f* (para mezclar pigmentos)
palisade [,pælə'seɪd] *n* **1** FENCE **:** empalizada *f,* estacada *f* **2** CLIFFS **:** acantilado *m*
pall¹ ['pɔl] *vi* **:** perder su sabor, dejar de gustar
pall² *n* **1 :** paño *m* mortuario (sobre un ataúd) **2** COVER **:** cortina *f* (de humo, etc.) **3 to cast a pall over :** ensombrecer
pallbearer ['pɔl,bɛrər] *n* **:** portador *m,* -dora *f* del féretro
pallet ['pælət] *n* **1** BED **:** camastro *m* **2** PLATFORM **:** plataforma *f* de carga
palliative ['pæli,eɪt̬ɪv, 'pæljət̬ɪv] *adj* **:** paliativo
pallid ['pæləd] *adj* **:** pálido
pallor ['pælər] *n* **:** palidez *f*
palm¹ ['pɑm, 'pɑlm] *vt* **1** CONCEAL **:** escamotear (un naipe, etc.) **2 to palm off :** encajar, endilgar *fam* <he palmed it off on me : me lo endilgó>
palm² *n* **1** *or* **palm tree :** palmera *f* **2 :** palma *f* (de la mano)
Palm Sunday *n* **:** Domingo *m* de Ramos
palomino [,pælə'miː,noː] *n, pl* **-nos :** caballo *m* de color dorado
palpable ['pælpəbəl] *adj* **:** palpable — **palpably** [-bli] *adv*
palpitate ['pælpə,teɪt] *vi* **-tated; -tating :** palpitar
palpitation [,pælpə'teɪʃən] *n* **:** palpitación *f*
palsy ['pɔlzi] *n, pl* **-sies 1 :** parálisis *f* **2** → **cerebral palsy**
paltry ['pɔltri] *adj* **-trier; -est :** mísero, mezquino, insignificante <a paltry excuse : una mala excusa>
pampas ['pæmpəz, 'pɑmpəs] *npl* **:** pampa *f*
pamper ['pæmpər] *vt* **:** mimar, consentir, chiquear *Mex*
pamphlet ['pæmpflət] *n* **:** panfleto *m,* folleto *m*
pan¹ ['pæn] *vt* **panned; panning** CRITICIZE **:** poner por los suelos — *vi* **to pan for gold :** cribar el oro con batea, lavar oro
pan² *n* **1 :** cacerola *f,* cazuela *f* **2 frying pan :** sartén *mf,* freidera *f Mex*
panacea [,pænə'siːə] *n* **:** panacea *f*
Panamanian [,pænə'meɪniən] *n* **:** panameño *m,* -ña *f* — **Panamanian** *adj*
pancake ['pæn,keɪk] *n* **:** panqueque *m*

pancreas ['pæŋkriəs, 'pæn-] *n* : páncreas *m*

panda ['pændə] *n* : panda *mf*

pandemonium [ˌpændə'moːniəm] *n* : pandemonio *m,* pandemónium *m*

pander ['pændər] *vi* **to pander to** : satisfacer, complacer (a alguien) <to pander to popular taste : satisfacer el gusto popular>

pane ['peɪn] *n* : cristal *m,* vidrio *m*

panel[1] ['pænəl] *vt* **-eled** *or* **-elled; -eling** *or* **-elling** : adornar con paneles

panel[2] *n* **1** : lista *f* de nombres (de un jurado, etc.) **2** GROUP : panel *m,* grupo *m* <discussion panel : panel de discusión> **3** : panel *m* (de una pared, etc.) **4 instrument panel** : tablero *m* de instrumentos

paneling ['pænəlɪŋ] *n* : paneles *mpl*

pang ['pæŋ] *n* : puntada *f,* punzada *f*

panic[1] ['pænɪk] *v* **-icked; -icking** *vt* : llenar de pánico — *vi* : ser presa de pánico

panic[2] *n* : pánico *m*

panicky ['pænɪki] *adj* : presa de pánico

panorama [ˌpænə'ræmə, -'rɑ-] *n* : panorama *m*

panoramic [ˌpænə'ræmɪk, -'rɑ-] *adj* : panorámico

pansy ['pænzi] *n, pl* **-sies** : pensamiento *m*

pant[1] ['pænt] *vi* : jadear, resoplar

pant[2] *n* : jadeo *m,* resoplo *m*

pantaloons [ˌpæntə'luːnz] → **pants**

panther ['pænθər] *n* : pantera *f*

panties ['pæntiz] *npl* : calzones *mpl,* pantaletas *fpl*

pantomime[1] ['pæntəˌmaɪm] *v* **-mimed; -miming** *vt* : representar mediante la pantomima — *vi* : hacer la mímica

pantomime[2] *n* : pantomima *f*

pantry ['pæntri] *n, pl* **-tries** : despensa *f*

pants ['pænts] *npl* **1** TROUSERS : pantalón *m,* pantalones *mpl* **2** → **panties**

pap ['pæp] *n* : papilla *f* (para bebés, etc.)

papal ['peɪpəl] *adj* : papal

papaya [pə'paɪə] *n* : papaya *f* (fruta)

paper[1] ['peɪpər] *vt* WALLPAPER : empapelar

paper[2] *adj* : de papel

paper[3] *n* **1** : papel *m* <a piece of paper : un papel> **2** DOCUMENT : papel *m,* documento *m* **3** NEWSPAPER : periódico *m,* diario *m*

paperback ['peɪpərˌbæk] *n* : libro *m* en rústica

paper clip *n* : clip *m,* sujetapapeles *m*

paperweight ['peɪpərˌweɪt] *n* : pisapapeles *m*

papery ['peɪpəri] *adj* : parecido al papel

papier–mâché [ˌpeɪpərmə'ʃeɪ, ˌpæˌpjeɪmæ'ʃeɪ] *n* : papel *m* maché

papoose [pæ'puːs, pə-] *n* : niño *m,* -ña *f* de los indios norteamericanos

paprika [pə'priːkə, pæ-] *n* : pimentón *m,* paprika *f*

papyrus [pə'paɪrəs] *n, pl* **-ruses** *or* **-ri** [-ri, -ˌraɪ] : papiro *m*

par ['pɑr] *n* **1** VALUE : valor *m* (nominal), par *f* <below par : debajo de la par> **2** EQUALITY : igualdad *f* <to be on a par with : estar al mismo nivel que> **3** : par *m* (en golf)

parable ['pærəbəl] *n* : parábola *f*

parachute[1] ['pærəˌʃuːt] *vi* **-chuted; -chuting** : lanzarse en paracaídas

parachute[2] *n* : paracaídas *m*

parachutist ['pærəˌʃuːt̬ɪst] *n* : paracaidista *mf*

parade[1] [pə'reɪd] *vi* **-raded; -rading 1** MARCH : desfilar **2** SHOW OFF : pavonearse, lucirse

parade[2] *n* **1** PROCESSION : desfile *m* **2** DISPLAY : alarde *m*

paradigm ['pærəˌdaɪm] *n* : paradigma *m*

paradise ['pærəˌdaɪs, -ˌdaɪz] *n* : paraíso *m*

paradox ['pærəˌdɑks] *n* : paradoja *f*

paradoxical [ˌpærə'dɑksɪkəl] *adj* : paradójico — **paradoxically** *adv*

paraffin ['pærəfən] *n* : parafina *f*

paragraph[1] ['pærəˌgræf] *vt* : dividir en párrafos

paragraph[2] *n* : párrafo *m,* acápite *m*

Paraguayan [ˌpærə'gwaɪən, -'gweɪ-] *n* : paraguayo *m,* -ya *f* — **Paraguayan** *adj*

parakeet ['pærəˌkiːt] *n* : periquito *m*

parallel[1] ['pærəˌlɛl, -ləl] *vt* **1** MATCH, RESEMBLE : ser paralelo a, ser análogo a, corresponder con **2** : extenderse en línea paralela con <the road parallels the river : el camino se extiende a lo largo del río>

parallel[2] *adj* : paralelo

parallel[3] *n* **1** : línea *f* paralela, superficie *f* paralela **2** : paralelo *m* (en geografía) **3** SIMILARITY : paralelismo *m,* semejanza *f*

parallelogram [ˌpærə'lɛləˌgræm] *n* : paralelogramo *m*

paralysis [pə'ræləsɪs] *n, pl* **-yses** [-ˌsiːz] : parálisis *f*

paralyze ['pærəˌlaɪz] *vt* **-lyzed; -lyzing** : paralizar

parameter [pə'ræmət̬ər] *n* : parámetro *m*

paramount ['pærəˌmaʊnt] *adj* : supremo <of paramount importance : de suma importancia>

paranoia [ˌpærə'nɔɪə] *n* : paranoia *f*

paranoid ['pærəˌnɔɪd] *adj* : paranoico

parapet ['pærəpət, -ˌpɛt] *n* : parapeto *m*

paraphernalia [ˌpærəfə'neɪljə, -fər-] *ns & pl* : parafernalia *f*

paraphrase[1] ['pærəˌfreɪz] *vt* **-phrased; -phrasing** : parafrasear

paraphrase[2] *n* : paráfrasis *f*

paraplegic[1] [ˌpærə'pliːdʒɪk] *adj* : parapléjico

paraplegic[2] *n* : parapléjico *m,* -ca *f*

parasite [ˈpærəˌsaɪt] *n* **:** parásito *m*
parasitic [ˌpærəˈsɪtɪk] *adj* **:** parasitario
parasol [ˈpærəˌsɔl] *n* **:** sombrilla *f*, quitasol *m*, parasol *m*
paratrooper [ˈpærəˌtruːpər] *n* **:** paracaidista *mf* (militar)
parboil [ˈpɑrˌbɔɪl] *vt* **:** sancochar, cocer a medias
parcel[1] [ˈpɑrsəl] *vt* **-celed** *or* **-celled; -celing** *or* **-celling** *or* **to parcel out :** repartir, parcelar (tierras)
parcel[2] *n* **1** LOT **:** parcela *f*, lote *m* **2** PACKAGE **:** paquete *m*, bulto *m*
parch [ˈpɑrtʃ] *vt* **:** resecar
parchment [ˈpɑrtʃmənt] *n* **:** pergamino *m*
pardon[1] [ˈpɑrdən] *vt* **1** FORGIVE **:** perdonar, disculpar <pardon me! **:** ¡perdone!, ¡disculpe la molestia!> **2** REPRIEVE **:** indultar (a un delincuente)
pardon[2] *n* **1** FORGIVENESS **:** perdón *m* **2** REPRIEVE **:** indulto *m*
pardonable [ˈpɑrdənəbəl] *adj* **:** perdonable, disculpable
pare [ˈpær] *vt* **pared; paring 1** PEEL **:** pelar **2** TRIM **:** recortar **3** REDUCE **:** reducir <he pared it (down) to 50 pages **:** lo redujo a 50 páginas>
parent [ˈpærənt] *n* **1 :** madre *f*, padre *m* **2 parents** *npl* **:** padres *mpl*
parentage [ˈpærəntɪdʒ] *n* **:** linaje *m*, abolengo *m*, origen *m*
parental [pəˈrɛntəl] *adj* **:** de los padres
parenthesis [pəˈrɛnθəsɪs] *n, pl* **-theses** [-ˌsiːz] **:** paréntesis *m*
parenthetic [ˌpærənˈθɛt̬ɪk] *or* **parenthetical** [-t̬ɪkəl] *adj* **:** parentético — **parenthetically** [-t̬ɪkli] *adv*
parenthood [ˈpærəntˌhʊd] *n* **:** paternidad *f*
parfait [pɑrˈfeɪ] *n* **:** postre *m* elaborado con frutas y helado
pariah [pəˈraɪə] *n* **:** paria *mf*
parish [ˈpærɪʃ] *n* **:** parroquia *f*
parishioner [pəˈrɪʃənər] *n* **:** feligrés *m*, -gresa *f*
parity [ˈpærət̬i] *n, pl* **-ties :** paridad *f*
park[1] [ˈpɑrk] *vt* **:** estacionar, parquear, aparcar *Spain* — *vi* **:** estacionarse, parquearse, aparcar *Spain*
park[2] *n* **:** parque *m*
parka [ˈpɑrkə] *n* **:** parka *f*
parkway [ˈpɑrkˌweɪ] *n* **:** carretera *f* ajardinada, bulevar *m*
parley[1] [ˈpɑrli] *vi* **:** parlamentar, negociar
parley[2] *n, pl* **-leys :** negociación *f*, parlamento *m*
parliament [ˈpɑrləmənt, ˈpɑrljə-] *n* **:** parlamento *m*
parliamentary [ˌpɑrləˈmɛntəri, ˌpɑrljə-] *adj* **:** parlamentario
parlor [ˈpɑrlər] *n* **1 :** sala *f*, salón *m* (en una casa) **2 :** salón *m* <beauty parlor **:** salón de belleza> **3 funeral parlor :** funeraria *f*
parochial [pəˈroːkiəl] *adj* **1 :** parroquial **2** PROVINCIAL **:** pueblerino, de miras estrechas
parody[1] [ˈpærədi] *vt* **-died; -dying :** parodiar
parody[2] *n, pl* **-dies :** parodia *f*
parole [pəˈroːl] *n* **:** libertad *f* condicional
paroxysm [ˈpærəkˌsɪzəm, pəˈrɑk-] *n* **:** paroxismo *m*
parquet [ˈpɑrˌkeɪ, pɑrˈkeɪ] *n* **:** parquet *m*, parqué *m*
parrakeet → **parakeet**
parrot [ˈpærət] *n* **:** loro *m*, papagayo *m*
parry[1] [ˈpæri] *v* **-ried; -rying** *vi* **:** parar un golpe — *vt* EVADE **:** esquivar (una pregunta, etc.)
parry[2] *n, pl* **-ries :** parada *f*
parsimonious [ˌpɑrsəˈmoːniəs] *adj* **:** tacaño, mezquino
parsley [ˈpɑrsli] *n* **:** perejil *m*
parsnip [ˈpɑrsnɪp] *n* **:** chirivía *f*
parson [ˈpɑrsən] *n* **:** pastor *m*, -tora *f*; clérigo *m*
parsonage [ˈpɑrsənɪdʒ] *n* **:** rectoría *f*, casa *f* del párroco
part[1] [ˈpɑrt] *vi* **1** SEPARATE **:** separarse, despedirse <we should part as friends **:** debemos separarnos amistosamente> **2** OPEN **:** abrirse <the curtains parted **:** las cortinas se abrieron> **3 to part with :** dehacerse de — *vt* **1** SEPARATE **:** separar **2 to part one's hair :** hacerse la raya, peinarse con raya
part[2] *n* **1** SECTION, SEGMENT **:** parte *f*, sección *f* **2** PIECE **:** pieza *f* (de una máquina, etc.) **3** ROLE **:** papel *m* **4 :** raya *f* (del pelo)
partake [pɑrˈteɪk, pər-] *vi* **-took** [-ˈtʊk]; **-taken** [-ˈteɪkən]; **-taking 1 to partake of** CONSUME **:** comer, beber, tomar **2 to partake in :** participar en (una actividad, etc.)
partial [ˈpɑrʃəl] *adj* **1** BIASED **:** parcial, tendencioso **2** INCOMPLETE **:** parcial, incompleto **3 to be partial to :** ser aficionado a
partiality [ˌpɑrʃiˈælət̬i] *n, pl* **-ties :** parcialidad *f*
partially [ˈpɑrʃəli] *adv* **:** parcialmente
participant [pərˈtɪsəpənt, pɑr-] *n* **:** participante *mf*
participate [pərˈtɪsəˌpeɪt, pɑr-] *vi* **-pated; -pating :** participar
participation [pərˌtɪsəˈpeɪʃən, pɑr-] *n* **:** participación *f*
participle [ˈpɑrt̬əˌsɪpəl] *n* **:** participio *m*
particle [ˈpɑrt̬ɪkəl] *n* **:** partícula *f*
particular[1] [pɑrˈtɪkjələr] *adj* **1** SPECIFIC **:** particular, en particular <this particular person **:** esta persona en particular> **2** SPECIAL **:** particular, especial <with particular emphasis **:** con un énfasis especial> **3** FUSSY **:** exigente, maniático <to be very particular **:** ser muy especial> <I'm not particular **:** me da igual>
particular[2] *n* **1** DETAIL **:** detalle *m*, sentido *m* **2 in particular :** en particular, en especial

particularly [pɑr'tɪkjələrli] *adv* **1** ESPECIALLY : particularmente, especialmente **2** SPECIFICALLY : específicamente, en especial

partisan ['pɑrtəzən, -sən] *n* **1** ADHERENT : partidario *m,* -ria *f* **2** GUERRILLA : partisano *m,* -na *f;* guerrillero *m,* -ra *f*

partition¹ [pər'tɪʃən, pɑr-] *vt* : dividir <to partition off (a room) : dividir con un tabique>

partition² *n* **1** DISTRIBUTION : partición *f,* división *f,* reparto *m* **2** DIVIDER : tabique *m,* mampara *f,* biombo *m*

partly ['pɑrtli] *adv* : en parte, parcialmente

partner ['pɑrtnər] *n* **1** COMPANION : compañero *m,* -ra *f* **2** : pareja *f* (en un juego, etc.) <dancing partner : pareja de baile> **3** SPOUSE : cónyuge *mf* **4** *or* **business partner** : socio *m,* -cia *f;* asociado *m,* -da *f*

partnership ['pɑrtnər,ʃɪp] *n* **1** ASSOCIATION : asociación *f,* compañerismo *m* **2** : sociedad *f* (de negociantes) <to form a partnership : asociarse>

part of speech : categoría *f* gramatical

partridge ['pɑrtrɪdʒ] *n, pl* **-tridge** *or* **-tridges** : perdiz *f*

party ['pɑrti] *n, pl* **-ties** **1** : partido *m* (político) **2** PARTICIPANT : parte *f,* participante *mf* **3** GROUP : grupo *m* (de personas) **4** GATHERING : fiesta *f* <to throw a party : dar una fiesta>

parvenu ['pɑrvə,nu:, -,nju:] *n* : advenedizo *m,* -za *f*

pass¹ ['pæs] *vi* **1** : pasar, cruzarse <a car passed by : pasó un coche> <we passed in the hallway : nos cruzamos en el pasillo> **2** CEASE : pasarse <the pain passed : se pasó el dolor> **3** ELAPSE : pasar, transcurrir **4** PROCEED : pasar <let me pass : déjame pasar> **5** HAPPEN : pasar, ocurrir **6** : pasar, aprobar (en un examen) **7** RULE : fallar <the jury passed on the case : el jurado falló en el caso> **8** *or* **to pass down** : pasar <the throne passed to his son : el trono pasó a su hijo> **9** **to let pass** OVERLOOK : pasar por alto **10** **to pass as** : pasar por **11** **to pass away** *or* **to pass on** DIE : fallecer, morir — *vt* **1** : pasar por <they passed the house : pasaron por la casa> **2** OVERTAKE : pasar, adelantar **3** SPEND : pasar (tiempo) **4** HAND : pasar <pass me the salt : pásame la sal> **5** : aprobar (un examen, una ley)

pass² *n* **1** CROSSING, GAP : paso *m,* desfiladero *m,* puerto *m* <mountain pass : puerto de montaña> **2** PERMIT : pase *m,* permiso *m* **3** : pase *m* (en deportes) **4** SITUATION : situación *f* (difícil) <things have come to a pretty pass! : ¡hasta dónde hemos llegado!>

passable ['pæsəbəl] *adj* **1** ADEQUATE : adecuado, pasable **2** : transitable (dícese de un camino, etc.)

passably ['pæsəbli] *adv* : pasablemente

passage ['pæsɪdʒ] *n* **1** PASSING : paso *m* <the passage of time : el paso del tiempo> **2** PASSAGEWAY : pasillo *m* (dentro de un edificio), pasaje *m* (entre edificios) **3** VOYAGE : travesía *f* (por el mar), viaje *m* <to grant safe passage : dar un salvoconducto> **4** SECTION : pasaje *m* (en música o literatura)

passageway ['pæsɪdʒ,weɪ] *n* : pasillo *m,* pasadizo *m,* corredor *m*

passbook ['pæs,bʊk] *n* BANKBOOK : libreta *f* de ahorros

passé [pæ'seɪ] *adj* : pasado de moda

passenger ['pæsəndʒər] *n* : pasajero *m,* -ra *f*

passerby [,pæsər'baɪ, 'pæsər,-] *n, pl* **passersby** : transeúnte *mf*

passing ['pæsɪŋ] *n* DEATH : fallecimiento *m*

passion ['pæʃən] *n* : pasión *f,* ardor *m*

passionate ['pæʃənət] *adj* **1** IRASCIBLE : irascible, iracundo **2** ARDENT : apasionado, ardiente, ferviente, fogoso

passionately ['pæʃənətli] *adv* : apasionadamente, fervientemente, con pasión

passive¹ ['pæsɪv] *adj* : pasivo — **passively** *adv*

passive² *n* : voz *f* pasiva (en gramática)

Passover ['pæs,o:vər] *n* : Pascua *f* (en el judaísmo)

passport ['pæs,port] *n* : pasaporte *m*

password ['pæs,wərd] *n* : contraseña *f*

past¹ ['pæst] *adv* : por delante <he drove past : pasamos en coche>

past² *adj* **1** AGO : hace <10 years past : hace 10 años> **2** LAST : último <the past few months : los últimos meses> **3** BYGONE : pasado <in past times : en tiempos pasados> **4** : pasado (en gramática)

past³ *n* : pasado *m*

past⁴ *prep* **1** BY : por, por delante de <he ran past the house : pasó por la casa corriendo> **2** BEYOND : más allá de <just past the corner : un poco más allá de la esquina> <we went past the exit : pasamos la salida> **3** AFTER : después de <past noon : después del mediodía> <half past two : las dos y media>

pasta ['pɑstə, 'pæs-] *n* : pasta *f*

paste¹ ['peɪst] *vt* **pasted; pasting** : pegar (con engrudo)

paste² *n* **1** : pasta *f* <tomato paste : pasta de tomate> **2** : engrudo *m* (para pegar)

pasteboard ['peɪst,bord] *n* : cartón *m,* cartulina *f*

pastel [pæ'stɛl] *n* : pastel *m* — **pastel** *adj*

pasteurization [,pæstʃərə'zeɪʃən, ,pæstjə-] *n* : pasteurización *f*

pasteurize ['pæstʃə,raɪz, 'pæstjə-] *vt* **-ized; -izing** : pasteurizar

pastime ['pæs,taɪm] *n* : pasatiempo *m*

pastor ['pæstər] *n* : pastor *m,* -tora *f*

pastoral [ˈpæstərəl] *adj* : pastoral
past participle *n* : participio *m* pasado
pastry [ˈpeɪstri] *n, pl* **-ries 1** DOUGH : pasta *f*, masa *f* **2 pastries** *npl* : pasteles *mpl*
pasture¹ [ˈpæstʃər] *v* **-tured; -turing** *vi* GRAZE : pacer, pastar — *vt* : apacentar, pastar
pasture² *n* : pastizal *m*, potrero *m*, pasto *m*
pasty [ˈpeɪsti] *adj* **pastier; -est 1** : pastoso (en consistencia) **2** PALLID : pálido
pat¹ [ˈpæt] *vt* **patted; patting** : dar palmaditas a, tocar
pat² *adv* : de memoria <to have down pat : saberse de memoria>
pat³ *adj* **1** APT : apto, apropiado **2** GLIB : fácil **3** UNYIELDING : firme <to stand pat : mantenerse firme>
pat⁴ *n* **1** TAP : golpecito *m*, palmadita *f* <a pat on the back : una palmadita en la espalda> **2** CARESS : caricia *f* **3** : porción *f* <a pat of butter : una porción de mantequilla>
patch¹ [ˈpætʃ] *vt* **1** MEND, REPAIR : remender, parchar, ponerle un parche a **2 to patch together** IMPROVISE : confeccionar, improvisar **3 to patch up** : arreglar <they patched things up : hicieron las paces>
patch² *n* **1** : parche *m*, remiendo *m* (para la ropa) <eye patch : parche para el ojo> **2** PIECE : mancha *f*, trozo *m* <a patch of sky : un trozo de cielo> **3** PLOT : parcela *f*, terreno *m* <cabbage patch : parcela de repollos>
patchwork [ˈpætʃˌwərk] *n* : labor *f* de retazos
patchy [ˈpætʃi] *adj* **patchier; -est 1** IRREGULAR : irregular, desigual **2** INCOMPLETE : parcial, incompleto
patent¹ [ˈpætənt] *vt* : patentar
patent² *adj* [ˈpætənt, ˈpeɪt-] **1** OBVIOUS : patente, evidente **2** [ˈpæt-] PATENTED : patentado
patent³ [ˈpætənt] *n* : patente *f*
patently [ˈpætəntli] *adv* : patentemente, evidentemente
paternal [pəˈtərnəl] *adj* **1** FATHERLY : paternal **2** : paterno <paternal grandfather : abuelo paterno>
paternity [pəˈtərnəti] *n* : paternidad *f*
path [ˈpæθ, ˈpaθ] *n* **1** TRACK, TRAIL : camino *m*, sendero *m*, senda *f* **2** COURSE, ROUTE : recorrido *m*, trayecto *m*, trayectoria *f*
pathetic [pəˈθɛtɪk] *adj* : patético — **pathetically** [-tɪkli] *adv*
pathological [ˌpæθəˈlɑdʒɪkəl] *adj* : patológico
pathologist [pəˈθɑlədʒɪst] *n* : patólogo *m*, -ga *f*
pathology [pəˈθɑlədʒi] *n, pl* **-gies** : patología *f*
pathos [ˈpeɪˌθɑs, ˈpæ-, -ˌθɔs] *n* : patetismo *m*
pathway [ˈpæθˌweɪ] *n* : camino *m*, sendero *m*, senda *f*, vereda *f*
patience [ˈpeɪʃənts] *n* : paciencia *f*
patient¹ [ˈpeɪʃənt] *adj* : paciente — **patiently** *adv*
patient² *n* : paciente *mf*
patio [ˈpætiˌoː] *n, pl* **-tios** : patio *m*
patriarch [ˈpeɪtriˌɑrk] *n* : patriarca *m*
patrimony [ˈpætrəˌmoːni] *n, pl* **-nies** : patrimonio *m*
patriot [ˈpeɪtriət] *n* : patriota *mf*
patriotic [ˌpeɪtriˈɑtɪk] *adj* : patriótico — **patriotically** *adv*
patriotism [ˈpeɪtriəˌtɪzəm] *n* : patriotismo *m*
patrol¹ [pəˈtroːl] *v* **-trolled; -trolling** : patrullar
patrol² *n* : patrulla *f*
patrolman [pəˈtroːlmən] *n, pl* **-men** [-mən, -ˌmɛn] : policía *mf*, guardia *mf*
patron [ˈpeɪtrən] *n* **1** SPONSOR : patrocinador *m*, -dora *f* **2** CUSTOMER : cliente *m*, -ta *f* **3** *or* **patron saint** : patrono *m*, -na *f*
patronage [ˈpeɪtrənɪdʒ, ˈpæ-] *n* **1** SPONSORSHIP : patrocinio *m* **2** CLIENTELE : clientela *f* **3** : influencia *f* (política)
patronize [ˈpeɪtrəˌnaɪz, ˈpæ-] *vt* **-ized; -izing 1** SPONSOR : patrocinar **2** : ser cliente de (un negocio) **3** : tratar con condescendencia
patter¹ [ˈpætər] *vi* **1** TAP : golpetear, tamborilear (dícese de la lluvia) **2 to patter about** : corretear (con pasos ligeros)
patter² *n* **1** TAPPING : golpeteo *m*, tamborileo *m* (de la lluvia), correteo *m* (de pies) **2** CHATTER : palabrería *f*, parloteo *m fam*
pattern¹ [ˈpætərn] *vt* **1** BASE : basar (en un modelo) **2 to pattern after** : hacer imitación de
pattern² *n* **1** MODEL : modelo *m*, patrón *m* (de costura) **2** DESIGN : diseño *m*, dibujo *m*, estampado *m* (de tela) **3** NORM, STANDARD : pauta *f*, norma *f*, patrón *m*
patty [ˈpæti] *n, pl* **-ties** : porción *f* de carne picada (u otro alimento) en forma de ruedita <a hamburger patty : una hamburguesa>
paucity [ˈpɔsəti] *n* : escasez *f*
paunch [ˈpɔntʃ] *n* : panza *f*, barriga *f*
pauper [ˈpɔpər] *n* : pobre *mf*, indigente *mf*
pause¹ [ˈpɔz] *vi* **paused; pausing** : hacer una pausa, pararse (brevemente)
pause² *n* : pausa *f*
pave [ˈpeɪv] *vt* **paved; paving** : pavimentar <to pave with stones : empedrar>
pavement [ˈpeɪvmənt] *n* : pavimento *m*, empedrado *m*
pavilion [pəˈvɪljən] *n* : pabellón *m*
paving [ˈpeɪvɪŋ] → **pavement**
paw¹ [ˈpɔ] *vt* : tocar, manosear, sobar
paw² *n* : pata *f*, garra *f*, zarpa *f*
pawn¹ [ˈpɔn] *vt* : empeñar, prendar

pawn[2] *n* **1** PLEDGE, SECURITY **:** prenda *f* **2** PAWNING **:** empeño *m* **3 :** peón *m* (en ajedrez)

pawnbroker [ˈpɔnˌbroːkər] *n* **:** prestamista *mf*

pawnshop [ˈpɔnˌʃɑp] *n* **:** casa *f* de empeños, monte *m* de piedad

pay[1] [ˈpeɪ] *v* **paid** [ˈpeɪd]; **paying** *vt* **1 :** pagar (una cuenta, a un empleado, etc.) **2 to pay attention :** poner atención, prestar atención, hacer caso **3 to pay back :** pagar, devolver <she paid them back : les devolvió el dinero> <I'll pay you back for what you did! : ¡me las pagarás!> **4 to pay off** SETTLE **:** saldar, cancelar (una deuda, etc.) **5 to pay one's respects :** presentar uno sus respetos **6 to pay a visit :** hacer una visita **—** *vi* **:** valer la pena <crime doesn't pay : no hay crimen sin castigo>

pay[2] *n* **:** paga *f*

payable [ˈpeɪəbəl] *adj* DUE **:** pagadero

paycheck [ˈpeɪˌtʃɛk] *n* **:** sueldo *m,* cheque *m* del sueldo

payee [peɪˈiː] *n* **:** beneficiario *m,* -ria *f* (de un cheque, etc.)

payment [ˈpeɪmənt] *n* **1 :** pago *m* **2** INSTALLMENT **:** plazo *m,* cuota *f* **3** REWARD **:** recompensa *f*

payroll [ˈpeɪˌroːl] *n* **:** nómina *f*

PC [ˌpiːˈsiː] *n, pl* **PCs** *or* **PC's :** PC *mf,* computadora *f* personal

pea [ˈpiː] *n* **:** chícharo *m,* guisante *m,* arveja *f*

peace [ˈpiːs] *n* **1 :** paz *f* <peace treaty : tratado de paz> <peace and tranquillity : paz y tranquilidad> **2** ORDER **:** orden *m* (público)

peaceable [ˈpiːsəbəl] *adj* **:** pacífico **— peaceably** [-bli] *adv*

peaceful [ˈpiːsfəl] *adj* **1** PEACEABLE **:** pacífico **2** CALM, QUIET **:** tranquilo, sosegado **— peacefully** *adv*

peacemaker [ˈpiːsˌmeɪkər] *n* **:** conciliador *m,* -dora *f;* mediador *m,* -dora *f*

peach [ˈpiːtʃ] *n* **:** durazno *m,* melocotón *m*

peacock [ˈpiːˌkɑk] *n* **:** pavo *m* real

peak[1] [ˈpiːk] *vi* **:** alcanzar su nivel máximo

peak[2] *adj* **:** máximo

peak[3] *n* **1** POINT **:** punta *f* **2** CREST, SUMMIT **:** cima *f,* cumbre *f* **3** APEX **:** cúspide *f,* apogeo *m,* nivel *m* máximo

peaked [ˈpiːkəd] *adj* SICKLY **:** pálido

peal[1] [ˈpiːl] *vi* **:** repicar

peal[2] *n* **:** repique *m,* tañido *m* (de campanada) <peals of laughter : carcajadas>

peanut [ˈpiːˌnʌt] *n* **:** maní *m,* cacahuate *m Mex,* cacahuete *m Spain*

pear [ˈpær] *n* **:** pera *f*

pearl [ˈpərl] *n* **:** perla *f*

pearly [ˈpərli] *adj* **pearlier; -est :** nacarado

peasant [ˈpɛzənt] *n* **:** campesino *m,* -na *f*

peat [ˈpiːt] *n* **:** turba *f*

pebble [ˈpɛbəl] *n* **:** piedrita *f,* piedrecita *f,* guijarro *m*

pecan [pɪˈkɑn, -ˈkæn, ˈpiːˌkæn] *n* **:** pacana *f,* nuez *f Mex*

peccadillo [ˌpɛkəˈdɪlo] *n, pl* **-loes** *or* **-los :** pecadillo *m*

peccary [ˈpɛkəri] *n, pl* **-ries :** pécari *m,* pecarí *m*

peck[1] [ˈpɛk] *vt* **:** picar, picotear

peck[2] *n* **1 :** medida *f* de áridos equivalente a 8.810 litros **2 :** picotazo *m* (de un pájaro) <a peck on the cheek : un besito en la mejilla>

pectoral [ˈpɛktərəl] *adj* **:** pectoral

peculiar [pɪˈkjuːljər] *adj* **1** DISTINCTIVE **:** propio, peculiar, característico <peculiar to this area : propio de esta zona> **2** STRANGE **:** extraño, raro **— peculiarly** *adv*

peculiarity [pɪˌkjuːlˈjærət̬i, -ˌkjuːliˈær-] *n, pl* **-ties 1** DISTINCTIVENESS **:** peculiaridad *f* **2** ODDITY, QUIRK **:** rareza *f,* idiosincrasia *f,* excentricidad *f*

pecuniary [pɪˈkjuːniˌɛri] *adj* **:** pecuniario

pedagogical [ˌpɛdəˈgɑdʒɪkəl, -ˈgoː-] *adj* **:** pedagógico

pedagogy [ˈpɛdəˌgoːdʒi, -ˌgɑ-] *n* **:** pedagogía *f*

pedal[1] [ˈpɛdəl] *v* **-aled** *or* **-alled; -aling** *or* **-alling** *vi* **:** pedalear **—** *vt* **:** darle a los pedales de

pedal[2] *n* **:** pedal *m*

pedant [ˈpɛdənt] *n* **:** pedante *mf*

pedantic [pɪˈdæntɪk] *adj* **:** pedante

pedantry [ˈpɛdəntri] *n, pl* **-ries :** pedantería *f*

peddle [ˈpɛdəl] *vt* **-dled; -dling :** vender (en las calles)

peddler [ˈpɛdlər] *n* **:** vendedor *m,* -dora *f* ambulante; mercachifle *m*

pedestal [ˈpɛdəstəl] *n* **:** pedestal *m*

pedestrian[1] [pəˈdɛstriən] *adj* **1** COMMONPLACE **:** pedestre, ordinario **2 :** de peatón <pedestrian crossing : paso de peatones>

pedestrian[2] *n* **:** peatón *m,* -tona *f*

pediatric [ˌpiːdiˈætrɪk] *adj* **:** pediátrico

pediatrician [ˌpiːdiəˈtrɪʃən] *n* **:** pediatra *mf*

pediatrics [ˌpiːdiˈætrɪks] *ns & pl* **:** pediatría *f*

pedigree [ˈpɛdəˌgriː] *n* **1** FAMILY TREE **:** árbol *m* genealógico **2** LINEAGE **:** pedigrí *m* (de un animal), linaje *m* (de una persona)

peek[1] [ˈpiːk] *vi* **1** PEEP **:** espiar, mirar furtivamente **2** GLANCE **:** echar un vistazo

peek[2] *n* **1 :** miradita *f* (furtiva) **2** GLANCE **:** vistazo *m,* ojeada *f*

peel[1] [ˈpiːl] *vt* **1 :** pelar (fruta, etc.) **2** *or* **to peel away :** quitar **—** *vi* **:** pelarse (dícese de la piel), desconcharse (dícese de la pintura)

peel[2] *n* **:** cáscara *f*

peep[1] [ˈpiːp] *vi* **1** PEEK : espiar, mirar furtivamente **2** CHEEP : piar **3 to peep out** SHOW : asomarse
peep[2] *n* **1** CHEEP : pío *m* (de un pajarito) **2** GLANCE : vistazo *m,* ojeada *f*
peer[1] [ˈpɪr] *vi* : mirar detenidamente, mirar con atención
peer[2] *n* **1** EQUAL : par *m,* igual *mf* **2** NOBLE : noble *mf*
peerage [ˈpɪrɪdʒ] *n* : nobleza *f*
peerless [ˈpɪrləs] *adj* : sin par, incomparable
peeve[1] [ˈpiːv] *vt* **peeved; peeving** : fastidiar, irritar, molestar
peeve[2] *n* : queja *f*
peevish [ˈpiːvɪʃ] *adj* : quejoso, fastidioso — **peevishly** *adv*
peevishness [ˈpiːvɪʃnəs] *n* : irritabilidad *f*
peg[1] [ˈpɛg] *vt* **pegged; pegging 1** PLUG : tapar (con una clavija) **2** FASTEN, FIX : sujetar (con estaquillas) **3 to peg out** MARK : marcar (con estaquillas)
peg[2] *n* : estaquilla *f* (para clavar), clavija *f* (para tapar)
pejorative [pɪˈdʒɔrət̬ɪv] *adj* : peyorativo — **pejoratively** *adv*
pelican [ˈpɛlɪkən] *n* : pelícano *m*
pellagra [pəˈlægrə, -ˈleɪ-] *n* : pelagra *f*
pellet [ˈpɛlət] *n* **1** BALL : bolita *f* <food pellet : bolita de comida> **2** SHOT : perdigón *m*
pell–mell [ˈpɛlˈmɛl] *adv* : desordenadamente, atropelladamente
pelt[1] [ˈpɛlt] *vt* **1** THROW : lanzar, tirar (algo a alguien) **2 to pelt with stones** : apedrear — *vi* BEAT : golpear con fuerza <the rain was pelting down : llovía a cántaros>
pelt[2] *n* : piel *f,* pellejo *m*
pelvic [ˈpɛlvɪk] *adj* : pélvico
pelvis [ˈpɛlvɪs] *n, pl* **-vises** *or* **-ves** [ˈpɛlˌviːz] : pelvis *f*
pen[1] [ˈpɛn] *vt* **penned; penning 1** *or* **pen in** : encerrar (animales) **2** WRITE : escribir
pen[2] *n* **1** CORRAL : corral *m,* redil *m* (para ovejas) **2** : pluma *f* <fountain pen : pluma fuente> <ballpoint pen : bolígrafo>
penal [ˈpiːnəl] *adj* : penal
penalize [ˈpiːnəlˌaɪz, ˈpɛn-] *vt* **-ized; -izing** : penalizar, sancionar, penar
penalty [ˈpɛnəlti] *n, pl* **-ties 1** PUNISHMENT : pena *f,* castigo *m* **2** DISADVANTAGE : desventaja *f,* castigo *m,* penalty *m* (en deportes) **3** FINE : multa *f*
penance [ˈpɛnənts] *n* : penitencia *f*
pence → **penny**
penchant [ˈpɛntʃənt] *n* : inclinación *f,* afición *f*
pencil[1] [ˈpɛntsəl] *vt* **-ciled** *or* **-cilled; -ciling** *or* **-cilling** : escribir con lápiz, dibujar con lápiz
pencil[2] *n* : lápiz *m*
pendant [ˈpɛndənt] *n* : colgante *m*
pending[1] [ˈpɛndɪŋ] *adj* : pendiente
pending[2] *prep* **1** DURING : durante **2** AWAITING : en espera de
pendulum [ˈpɛndʒələm, -djʊləm] *n* : péndulo *m*
penetrate [ˈpɛnəˌtreɪt] *vt* **-trated; -trating** : penetrar
penetrating [ˈpɛnəˌtreɪt̬ɪŋ] *adj* : penetrante, cortante
penetration [ˌpɛnəˈtreɪʃən] *n* : penetración *f*
penguin [ˈpɛŋgwɪn, ˈpɛn-] *n* : pingüino *m*
penicillin [ˌpɛnəˈsɪlən] *n* : penicilina *f*
peninsula [pəˈnɪntsələ, -ˈnɪntʃʊlə] *n* : península *f*
penis [ˈpiːnəs] *n, pl* **-nes** [-ˌniːz] *or* **-nises** : pene *m*
penitence [ˈpɛnət̬ənts] *n* : arrepentimiento *m,* penitencia *f*
penitent[1] [ˈpɛnət̬ənt] *adj* : arrepentido, penitente
penitent[2] *n* : penitente *mf*
penitentiary [ˌpɛnəˈtɛntʃəri] *n, pl* **-ries** : penitenciaría *f,* prisión *m,* presidio *m*
penmanship [ˈpɛnmənˌʃɪp] *n* : escritura *f,* caligrafía *f*
pen name *n* : seudónimo *m*
pennant [ˈpɛnənt] *n* : gallardete *m* (de un barco), banderín *m*
penniless [ˈpɛniləs] *adj* : sin un centavo
penny [ˈpɛni] *n, pl* **-nies** *or* **pence** [ˈpɛnts] **1** : penique *m* (del Reino Unido) **2** *pl* **-nies** CENT : centavo *m* (de los Estados Unidos)
pension[1] [ˈpɛntʃən] *vt or* **to pension off** : jubilar
pension[2] *n* : pensión *m,* jubilación *f*
pensive [ˈpɛntsɪv] *adj* : pensativo, meditabundo — **pensively** *adv*
pent [ˈpɛnt] *adj* : encerrado <pent-up feelings : emociones reprimidas>
pentagon [ˈpɛntəˌgɑn] *n* : pentágono *m*
pentagonal [pɛnˈtægənəl] *adj* : pentagonal
penthouse [ˈpɛntˌhaʊs] *n* : ático *m,* penthouse *m*
penury [ˈpɛnjəri] *n* : penuria *f,* miseria *f*
peon [ˈpiːˌɑn, -ən] *n, pl* **-ons** *or* **-ones** [peɪˈoːniːz] : peón *m*
peony [ˈpiːəni] *n, pl* **-nies** : peonía *f*
people[1] [ˈpiːpəl] *vt* **-pled; -pling** : poblar
people[2] *ns & pl* **1 people** *npl* : gente *f,* personas *fpl* <people like him : él le cae bien a la gente> <many people : mucha gente, muchas personas> **2** *pl* **peoples** : pueblo *m* <the Cuban people : el pueblo cubano>
pep[1] [ˈpɛp] *vt* **pepped; pepping** *or* **to pep up** : animar
pep[2] *n* : energía *f,* vigor *m*
pepper[1] [ˈpɛpər] *vt* **1** : añadir pimienta a **2** RIDDLE : acribillar (a balazos) **3** SPRINKLE : salpicar <peppered with quotations : salpicado de citas>

pepper[2] *n* **1 :** pimienta *f* (condimento) **2 :** pimiento *m,* pimentón *m* (fruta) **3** → **chili**

peppermint [ˈpɛpərˌmɪnt] *n* **:** menta *f*

peppery [ˈpɛpəri] *adj* **:** picante

peppy [ˈpɛpi] *adj* **peppier; -est :** lleno de energía, vivaz

peptic [ˈpɛptɪk] *adj* **peptic ulcer :** úlcera *f* estomacal

per [ˈpər] *prep* **1 :** por <miles per hour : millas por hora> **2** ACCORDING TO **:** según <per his specifications : según sus especificaciones>

per annum [pərˈænəm] *adv* **:** al año, por año

percale [ˌpərˈkeɪl, ˈpər-ˌ; ˌpərˈkæl] *n* **:** percal *m*

per capita [pərˈkæpɪṭə] *adv & adj* **:** per cápita

perceive [pərˈsiːv] *vt* **-ceived; -ceiving 1** REALIZE **:** percatarse de, concientizarse de, darse cuenta de **2** NOTE **:** percibir, notar

percent[1] [pərˈsɛnt] *adv* **:** por ciento

percent[2] *n, pl* **-cent** *or* **-cents 1 :** por ciento <10 percent of the population : el 10 por ciento de la población> **2** → **percentage**

percentage [pərˈsɛntɪdʒ] *n* **:** porcentaje *m*

perceptible [pərˈsɛptəbəl] *adj* **:** perceptible — **perceptibly** [-bli] *adv*

perception [pərˈsɛpʃən] *n* **1 :** percepción *f* <color perception : la percepción de los colores> **2** INSIGHT **:** perspicacia *f* **3** IDEA **:** idea *f,* imagen *f*

perceptive [pərˈsɛptɪv] *adj* **:** perspicaz

perceptively [pərˈsɛptɪvli] *adv* **:** con perspicacia

perch[1] [ˈpərtʃ] *vi* **1** ROOST **:** posarse **2** SIT **:** sentarse (en un sitio elevado) — *vt* PLACE **:** posar, colocar

perch[2] *n* **1** ROOST **:** percha *f* (para los pájaros) **2** *pl* **perch** *or* **perches :** perca *f* (pez)

percolate [ˈpərkəˌleɪt] *vi* **-lated; -lating :** colarse, filtrarse <percolated coffee : café filtrado>

percolator [ˈpərkəˌleɪṭər] *n* **:** cafetera *f* de filtro

percussion [pərˈkʌʃən] *n* **1** STRIKING **:** percusión *f* **2** *or* **percussion instruments :** instrumentos *mpl* de percusión

peremptory [pəˈrɛmptəri] *adj* **:** perentorio

perennial[1] [pəˈrɛniəl] *adj* **1 :** perenne, vivaz <perennial flowers : flores perennes> **2** RECURRENT **:** perenne, continuo <a perennial problem : un problema eterno>

perennial[2] *n* **:** planta *f* perenne, planta *f* vivaz

perfect[1] [pərˈfɛkt] *vt* **:** perfeccionar

perfect[2] [ˈpərfɪkt] *adj* **:** perfecto — **perfectly** *adv*

perfection [pərˈfɛkʃən] *n* **:** perfección *f*

perfectionist [pərˈfɛkʃənɪst] *n* **:** perfeccionista *mf*

perfidious [pərˈfɪdiəs] *adj* **:** pérfido

perforate [ˈpərfəˌreɪt] *vt* **-rated; -rating :** perforar

perforation [ˌpərfəˈreɪʃən] *n* **:** perforación *f*

perform [pərˈfɔrm] *vt* **1** CARRY OUT **:** realizar, hacer, desempeñar **2** PRESENT **:** representar, dar (una obra teatral, etc.) — *vi* **:** actuar (en una obra teatral), cantar (en una ópera, etc.), tocar (en un concierto, etc.), bailar (en un ballet, etc.)

performance [pərˈfɔrmənts] *n* **1** EXECUTION **:** ejecución *f,* realización *f,* desempeño *m,* rendimiento *m* **2** INTERPRETATION **:** interpretación *f* <his performance of Hamlet : su interpretación de Hamlet> **3** PRESENTATION **:** representación *f* (de una obra teatral), función *f*

performer [pərˈfɔrmər] *n* **:** artista *mf;* actor *m,* -triz *f;* intérprete *mf* (de música)

perfume[1] [pərˈfjuːm, ˈpərˌ-] *vt* **-fumed; -fuming :** perfumar

perfume[2] [ˈpərˌfjuːm, pərˈ-] *n* **:** perfume *m*

perfunctory [pərˈfʌŋktəri] *adj* **:** mecánico, superficial, somero

perhaps [pərˈhæps] *adv* **:** tal vez, quizá, quizás

peril [ˈpɛrəl] *n* **:** peligro *m*

perilous [ˈpɛrələs] *adj* **:** peligroso — **perilously** *adv*

perimeter [pəˈrɪməṭər] *n* **:** perímetro *m*

period [ˈpɪriəd] *n* **1 :** punto *m* (en puntuación) **2 :** período *m* <a two-hour period : un período de dos horas> **3** STAGE **:** época *f* (histórica), fase *f,* etapa *f*

periodic [ˌpɪriˈɑdɪk] *or* **periodical** [-dɪkəl] *adj* **:** periódico — **periodically** [-dɪkli] *adv*

periodical [ˌpɪriˈɑdɪkəl] *n* **:** publicación *f* periódica, revista *f*

peripheral [pəˈrɪfərəl] *adj* **:** periférico

periphery [pəˈrɪfəri] *n, pl* **-eries :** periferia *f*

periscope [ˈpɛrəˌskoːp] *n* **:** periscopio *m*

perish [ˈpɛrɪʃ] *vi* DIE **:** perecer, morirse

perishable[1] [ˈpɛrɪʃəbəl] *adj* **:** perecedero

perishable[2] *n* **:** producto *m* perecedero

perjure [ˈpərdʒər] *vt* **-jured; -juring** (*used in law*) **to perjure oneself :** perjurar, perjurarse

perjury [ˈpərdʒəri] *n* **:** perjurio *m*

perk[1] [ˈpərk] *vt* **1 :** levantar (las orejas, etc.) **2** *or* **to perk up** FRESHEN **:** arreglar — *vi* **to perk up :** animarse, reanimarse

perk[2] *n* **:** extra *m*

perky [ˈpərki] *adj* **perkier; -est :** animado, alegre, lleno de vida

permanence [ˈpərmənənts] *n* **:** permanencia *f*

permanent[1] [ˈpərmənənt] *adj* : permanente — **permanently** *adv*
permanent[2] *n* : permanente *f*
permeable [ˈpərmiəbəl] *adj* : permeable
permeate [ˈpərmi,eɪt] *v* **-ated; -ating** *vt* **1** PENETRATE : penetrar, impregnar **2** PERVADE : penetrar, difundirse por — *vi* : penetrar
permissible [pərˈmɪsəbəl] *adj* : permisible, lícito
permission [pərˈmɪʃən] *n* : permiso *m*
permissive [pərˈmɪsɪv] *adj* : permisivo
permit[1] [pərˈmɪt] *vt* **-mitted; -mitting** : permitir, dejar <weather permitting : si el tiempo lo permite>
permit[2] [ˈpər,mɪt, pərˈ-] *n* : permiso *m,* licencia *f*
pernicious [pərˈnɪʃəs] *adj* : pernicioso
peroxide [pəˈrɑk,saɪd] *n* **1** : peróxido *m* **2** → **hydrogen peroxide**
perpendicular[1] [,pərpənˈdɪkjələr] *adj* **1** VERTICAL : vertical **2** : perpendicular <perpendicular lines : líneas perpendiculares> — **perpendicularly** *adv*
perpendicular[2] *n* : perpendicular *f*
perpetrate [ˈpərpə,treɪt] *vt* **-trated; -trating** : perpetrar, cometer (un delito)
perpetrator [ˈpərpə,treɪt̬ər] *n* : autor *m,* -tora *f* (de un delito)
perpetual [pərˈpɛtʃʊəl] *adj* **1** EVERLASTING : perpetuo, eterno **2** CONTINUAL : perpetuo, continuo, constante
perpetually [pərˈpɛtʃʊəli, -tʃəli] *adv* : para siempre, eternamente
perpetuate [pərˈpɛtʃʊ,eɪt] *vt* **-ated; -ating** : perpetuar
perpetuity [,pərpəˈtuːət̬i, -ˈtjuː-] *n, pl* **-ties** : perpetuidad *f*
perplex [pərˈplɛks] *vt* : dejar perplejo, confundir
perplexed [pərˈplɛkst] *adj* : perplejo
perplexity [pərˈplɛksət̬i] *n, pl* **-ties** : perplejidad *f,* confusión *f*
persecute [ˈpərsɪ,kjuːt] *vt* **-cuted; -cuting** : perseguir
persecution [,pərsɪˈkjuːʃən] *n* : persecución *f*
perseverance [,pərsəˈvɪrənts] *n* : perseverancia *f*
persevere [,pərsəˈvɪr] *vi* **-vered; -vering** : perseverar
Persian [ˈpərʒən] *n* **1** : persa *mf* **2** : persa *m* (idioma) — **Persian** *adj*
persist [pərˈsɪst] *vi* : persistir
persistence [pərˈsɪstənts] *n* **1** CONTINUATION : persistencia *f* **2** TENACITY : perseverancia *f,* tenacidad *f*
persistent [pərˈsɪstənt] *adj* : persistente — **persistently** *adv*
person [ˈpərsən] *n* **1** HUMAN, INDIVIDUAL : persona *f,* individuo *m,* ser *m* humano **2** : persona *f* (en gramática) **3 in person** : en persona
personable [ˈpərsənəbəl] *adj* : agradable
personage [ˈpərsənɪdʒ] *n* : personaje *m*
personal [ˈpərsənəl] *adj* **1** OWN, PRIVATE : personal, particular, privado <for personal reasons : por razones personales> **2** : en persona <to make a personal appearance : presentarse en persona, hacerse acto de presencia> **3** : íntimo, personal <personal hygiene : higiene personal> **4** INDISCREET, PRYING : indiscreto, personal
personality [,pərsənˈæləti] *n, pl* **-ties** **1** DISPOSITION : personalidad *f,* temperamento *m* **2** CELEBRITY : personalidad *f,* personaje *m,* celebridad *f*
personalize [ˈpərsənə,laɪz] *vt* **-ized; -izing** : personalizar
personally [ˈpərsənəli] *adv* **1** : personalmente, en persona <I'll do it personally : lo haré personalmente> **2** : como persona <personally she's very amiable : como persona es muy amable> **3** : personalmente <personally, I don't believe it : yo, personalmente, no me lo creo>
personification [pər,sɑnəfəˈkeɪʃən] *n* : personificación *f*
personify [pərˈsɑnə,faɪ] *vt* **-fied; -fying** : personificar
personnel [,pərsənˈɛl] *n* : personal *m*
perspective [pərˈspɛktɪv] *n* : perspectiva *f*
perspicacious [,pərspəˈkeɪʃəs] *adj* : perspicaz
perspiration [,pərspəˈreɪʃən] *n* : transpiración *f,* sudor *m*
perspire [pərˈspaɪr] *vi* **-spired; -spiring** : transpirar, sudar
persuade [pərˈsweɪd] *vt* **-suaded; -suading** : persuadir, convencer
persuasion [pərˈsweɪʒən] *n* : persuasión *f*
persuasive [pərˈsweɪsɪv, -zɪv] *adj* : persuasivo — **persuasively** *adv*
persuasiveness [pərˈsweɪsɪvnəs, -zɪv-] *n* : persuasión *f*
pert [ˈpərt] *adj* **1** SAUCY : descarado, impertinente **2** JAUNTY : alegre, animado <a pert little hat : un sombrero coqueto>
pertain [pərˈteɪn] *vi* **1** BELONG : pertenecer (a) **2** RELATE : estar relacionado (con)
pertinence [ˈpərtənənts] *n* : pertinencia *f*
pertinent [ˈpərtənənt] *adj* : pertinente
perturb [pərˈtərb] *vt* : perturbar
perusal [pəˈruːzəl] *n* : lectura *f* cuidadosa
peruse [pəˈruːz] *vt* **-rused; -rusing** **1** READ : leer con cuidado **2** SCAN : recorrer con la vista <he perused the newspaper : echó un vistazo al periódico>
Peruvian [pəˈruːviən] *n* : peruano *m,* -na *f* — **Peruvian** *adj*
pervade [pərˈveɪd] *vt* **-vaded; -vading** : penetrar, difundirse por
pervasive [pərˈveɪsɪv, -zɪv] *adj* : penetrante

perverse [pər'vərs] *adj* **1** CORRUPT : perverso, corrompido **2** STUBBORN : obstinado, porfiado, terco (sin razón) — **perversely** *adv*

perversion [pər'vərʒən] *n* : perversión *f*

perversity [pər'vərsəṭi] *n, pl* **-ties 1** CORRUPTION : corrupción *f* **2** STUBBORNNESS : obstinación *f*, terquedad *f*

pervert[1] [pər'vərt] *vt* **1** DISTORT : pervertir, distorsionar **2** CORRUPT : pervertir, corromper

pervert[2] ['pər,vərt] *n* : pervertido *m*, -da *f*

peso ['peɪ,soː] *n, pl* **-sos** : peso *m*

pessimism ['pɛsə,mɪzəm] *n* : pesimismo *m*

pessimist ['pɛsəmɪst] *n* : pesimista *mf*

pessimistic [,pɛsə'mɪstɪk] *adj* : pesimista

pest ['pɛst] *n* **1** NUISANCE : peste *f*; latoso *m*, -sa *f fam* <to be a pest : dar (la) lata> **2** : insecto *m* nocivo, animal *m* nocivo <the squirrels were pests : las ardillas eran una plaga>

pester ['pɛstər] *vt* **-tered; -tering** : molestar, fastidiar

pesticide ['pɛstə,saɪd] *n* : pesticida *m*

pestilence ['pɛstələn*t*s] *n* : pestilencia *f*, peste *f*

pestle ['pɛsəl, 'pɛstəl] *n* : mano *f* de mortero, mazo *m*, maja *f*

pet[1] ['pɛt] *vt* **petted; petting** : acariciar

pet[2] *n* **1** : animal *m* doméstico **2** FAVORITE : favorito *m*, -ta *f*

petal ['pɛṭəl] *n* : pétalo *m*

petite [pə'tiːt] *adj* : pequeña, menuda, chiquita

petition[1] [pə'tɪʃən] *vt* : peticionar

petition[2] *n* : petición *f*

petitioner [pə'tɪʃənər] *n* : peticionario *m*, -ria *f*

petrify ['pɛtrə,faɪ] *vt* **-fied; -fying** : petrificar

petroleum [pə'troːliəm] *n* : petróleo *m*

petticoat ['pɛṭi,koːt] *n* : enagua *f*, fondo *m Mex*

pettiness ['pɛṭinəs] *n* **1** INSIGNIFICANCE : insignificancia *f* **2** MEANNESS : mezquindad *f*

petty ['pɛṭi] *adj* **-tier; -est 1** MINOR : menor <petty cash : dinero para gastos menores> **2** INSIGNIFICANT : insignificante, trivial, nimio **3** MEAN : mezquino

petty officer *n* : suboficial *mf*

petulance ['pɛtʃələn*t*s] *n* : irritabilidad *f*, mal genio *m*

petulant ['pɛtʃələnt] *adj* : irritable, de mal genio

petunia [pɪ'tuːnjə, -'tjuː-] *n* : petunia *f*

pew ['pjuː] *n* : banco *m* (de iglesia)

pewter ['pjuːṭər] *n* : peltre *m*

pH [,piː'eɪtʃ] *n* : pH *m*

phallic ['fælɪk] *adj* : fálico

phallus ['fæləs] *n, pl* **-li** ['fæ,laɪ] *or* **-luses** : falo *m*

phantasy ['fæntəsi] → **fantasy**

phantom ['fæntəm] *n* : fantasma *m*

pharaoh ['fɛr,oː, 'feɪ,roː] *n* : faraón *m*

pharmaceutical [,fɑrmə'suːṭɪkəl] *adj* : farmacéutico

pharmacist ['fɑrməsɪst] *n* : farmacéutico *m*, -ca *f*

pharmacology [,fɑrmə'kɑlədʒi] *n* : farmacología *f*

pharmacy ['fɑrməsi] *n, pl* **-cies** : farmacia *f*

pharynx ['færɪŋks] *n, pl* **pharynges** [fə'rɪn,dʒiːz] : faringe *f*

phase[1] ['feɪz] *vt* **phased; phasing 1** SYNCHRONIZE : sincronizar, poner en fase **2** STAGGER : escalonar **3 to phase in** : introducir progresivamente **4 to phase out** : retirar progresivamente, dejar de producir

phase[2] *n* **1** : fase *f* (de la luna, etc.) **2** STAGE : fase *f*, etapa *f*

pheasant ['fɛzənt] *n, pl* **-ant** *or* **-ants** : faisán *m*

phenomenal [fɪ'nɑmənəl] *adj* : extraordinario, excepcional

phenomenon [fɪ'nɑmə,nɑn, -nən] *n, pl* **-na** [-nə] *or* **-nons 1** : fenómeno *m* **2** *pl* **-nons** PRODIGY : fenómeno *m*, prodigio *m*

philanthropic [,fɪlən'θrɑpɪk] *adj* : filantrópico

philanthropist [fə'læn*t*θrəpɪst] *n* : filántropo *m*, -pa *f*

philanthropy [fə'læn*t*θrəpi] *n, pl* **-pies** : filantropía *f*

philately [fə'læṭəli] *n* : filatelia *f*

philodendron [,fɪlə'dɛndrən] *n, pl* **-drons** *or* **-dra** [-drə] : arácea *f*

philosopher [fə'lɑsəfər] *n* : filósofo *m*, -fa *f*

philosophic [,fɪlə'sɑfɪk] *or* **philosophical** [-fɪkəl] *adj* : filosófico — **philosophically** [-kli] *adv*

philosophize [fə'lɑsə,faɪz] *vi* **-phized; -phizing** : filosofar

philosophy [fə'lɑsəfi] *n, pl* **-phies** : filosofía *f*

phlebitis [flɪ'baɪṭəs] *n* : flebitis *f*

phlegm ['flɛm] *n* : flema *f*

phlox ['flɑks] *n, pl* **phlox** *or* **phloxes** : polemonio *m*

phobia ['foːbiə] *n* : fobia *f*

phoenix ['fiːnɪks] *n* : fénix *m*

phone[1] ['foːn] *v* → **telephone**[1]

phone[2] *n* → **telephone**[2]

phoneme ['foː,niːm] *n* : fonema *m*

phonetic [fə'nɛṭɪk] *adj* : fonético

phonetics [fə'nɛṭɪks] *n* : fonética *f*

phonics ['fɑnɪks] *n* : método *m* fonético de aprender a leer

phonograph ['foːnə,græf] *n* : fonógrafo *m*, tocadiscos *m*

phony[1] *or* **phoney** ['foːni] *adj* **-nier; -est** : falso

phony[2] *or* **phoney** *n, pl* **-nies** : farsante *mf*; charlatán *m*, -tana *f*

phosphate ['fɑs,feɪt] *n* : fosfato *m*

phosphorescence [,fɑsfə'rɛsən*t*s] *n* : fosforescencia *f*

phosphorescent [ˌfɑsfəˈrɛsənt] *adj* : fosforescente — **phosphorescently** *adv*

phosphorus [ˈfɑsfərəs] *n* : fósforo *m*

photo [ˈfoːt̬oː] *n, pl* **-tos** : foto *f*

photocopier [ˈfoːt̬oˌkɑpiər] *n* : fotocopiadora *f*

photocopy[1] [ˈfoːt̬oˌkɑpi] *vt* **-copied; -copying** : fotocopiar

photocopy[2] *n, pl* **-copies** : fotocopia *f*

photoelectric [ˌfoːt̬oɪˈlɛktrɪk] *adj* : fotoeléctrico

photogenic [ˌfoːt̬əˈdʒɛnɪk] *adj* : fotogénico

photograph[1] [ˈfoːt̬əˌgræf] *vt* : fotografiar

photograph[2] *n* : fotografía *f,* foto *f* <to take a photograph of : tomarle una fotografía a, tomar una fotografía de>

photographer [fəˈtɑgrəfər] *n* : fotógrafo *m,* -fa *f*

photographic [ˌfoːt̬əˈgræfɪk] *adj* : fotográfico — **photographically** [-fɪkli] *adv*

photography [fəˈtɑgrəfi] *n* : fotografía *f*

photosynthesis [ˌfoːt̬oˈsɪntθəsɪs] *n* : fotosíntesis *f*

photosynthetic [ˌfoːtosɪnˈθɛt̬ɪk] *adj* : fotosintético, de fotosíntesis

phrase[1] [ˈfreɪz] *vt* **phrased; phrasing** : expresar

phrase[2] *n* : frase *f,* locución *f* <to coin a phrase : para decirlo así>

phylum [ˈfaɪləm] *n, pl* **-la** [-lə] : phylum *m*

physical[1] [ˈfɪzɪkəl] *adj* **1** : físico <physical laws : leyes físicas> **2** MATERIAL : material, físico **3** BODILY : físico, corpóreo — **physically** [-kli] *adv*

physical[2] *n* CHECKUP : chequeo *m,* reconocimiento *m* médico

physician [fəˈzɪʃən] *n* : médico *m,* -ca *f*

physicist [ˈfɪzəsɪst] *n* : físico *m,* -ca *f*

physics [ˈfɪzɪks] *ns & pl* : física *f*

physiognomy [ˌfɪziˈɑgnəmi] *n, pl* **-mies** : fisonomía *f*

physiological [ˈfɪziəˈlɑdʒɪkəl] *or* **physiologic** [-dʒɪk] *adj* : fisiológico

physiologist [ˌfɪziˈɑlədʒɪst] *n* : fisiólogo *m,* -ga *f*

physiology [ˌfɪziˈɑlədʒi] *n* : fisiología *f*

physique [fəˈziːk] *n* : físico *m*

pi [ˈpaɪ] *n, pl* **pis** [ˈpaɪz] : pi *f*

pianist [piˈænɪst, ˈpiːənɪst] *n* : pianista *mf*

piano [piˈænoː] *n, pl* **-anos** : piano *m*

piazza [piˈæzə, -ˈɑtsə] *n, pl* **-zas** *or* **-ze** [-ˈɑtˌseɪ] : plaza *f*

picayune [ˌpɪkiˈjuːn] *adj* : trivial, nimio, insignificante

piccolo [ˈpɪkəˌloː] *n, pl* **-los** : flautín *m*

pick[1] [ˈpɪk] *vt* **1** : picar, labrar (con un pico) <he picked the hard soil : picó la tierra dura> **2** : quitar, sacar (poco a poco) <to pick meat off the bones : quitar pedazos de carne de los huesos> **3** : recoger, arrancar (frutas, flores, etc.) **4** SELECT : escoger, elegir **5** PROVOKE : provocar <to pick a quarrel : buscar pleito, buscar pelea> **6 to pick a lock** : forzar una cerradura **7 to pick someone's pocket** : robarle algo del bolsillo de alguien <someone picked my pocket! : ¡me robaron la cartera del bolsillo!> — *vi* **1** NIBBLE : picar, picotear **2 to pick and choose** : ser exigente **3 to pick at** : tocar, rascarse (una herida, etc.) **4 to pick on** TEASE : mofarse de, atormentar

pick[2] *n* **1** CHOICE : selección *f* **2** BEST : lo mejor <the pick of the crop : la crema y nata> **3** → **pickax**

pickax [ˈpɪkˌæks] *n* : pico *m,* zapapico *m,* piqueta *f*

pickerel [ˈpɪkərəl] *n, pl* **-el** *or* **-els** : lucio *m* pequeño

picket[1] [ˈpɪkət] *v* : piquetear

picket[2] *n* **1** STAKE : estaca *f* **2** STRIKER : huelguista *mf,* integrante *mf* de un piquete

pickle[1] [ˈpɪkəl] *vt* **-led; -ling** : encurtir, escabechar

pickle[2] *n* **1** BRINE : escabeche *m* **2** GHERKIN : pepinillo *m* (encurtido) **3** JAM, TROUBLE : lío *m,* apuro *m*

pickpocket [ˈpɪkˌpɑkət] *n* : carterista *mf*

pickup [ˈpɪkˌəp] *n* **1** IMPROVEMENT : mejora *f* **2** *or* **pickup truck** : camioneta *f*

pick up *vt* **1** LIFT : levantar **2** TIDY : arreglar, ordenar — *vi* IMPROVE : mejorar

picnic[1] [ˈpɪkˌnɪk] *vi* **-nicked; -nicking** : ir de picnic

picnic[2] *n* : picnic *m*

pictorial [pɪkˈtoriəl] *adj* : pictórico

picture[1] [ˈpɪktʃər] *vt* **-tured; -turing 1** DEPICT : representar **2** IMAGINE : imaginarse <can you picture it? : ¿te lo puedes imaginar?>

picture[2] *n* **1** : cuadro *m* (pintado o dibujado), ilustración *f,* fotografía *f* **2** DESCRIPTION : descripción *f* **3** IMAGE : imagen *f* <he's the picture of his father : es la viva imagen de su padre> **4** MOVIE : película *f*

picturesque [ˌpɪktʃəˈrɛsk] *adj* : pintoresco

pie [ˈpaɪ] *n* : pastel *m* (con fruta o carne), empanada *f* (con carne)

piebald [ˈpaɪˌbɔld] *adj* : picazo, pío

piece[1] [ˈpiːs] *vt* **pieced; piecing 1** PATCH : parchar, arreglar **2 to piece together** : construir pieza por pieza

piece[2] *n* **1** FRAGMENT : trozo *m,* pedazo *m* **2** COMPONENT : pieza *f* <a three-piece suit : un traje de tres piezas> **3** UNIT : pieza *f* <a piece of fruit : una (pieza de) fruta> **4** WORK : obra *f,* pieza *f* (de música, etc.) **5** (*in board games*) : ficha *f,* pieza *f,* figura *f* (en ajedrez)

piecemeal[1] [ˈpiːs,miːl] *adv* : poco a poco, por partes
piecemeal[2] *adj* : hecho poco a poco, poco sistemático
pied [ˈpaɪd] *adj* : pío
pier [ˈpɪr] *n* **1** : pila *f* (de un puente) **2** WHARF : muelle *m,* atracadero *m,* embarcadero *m* **3** PILLAR : pilar *m*
pierce [ˈpɪrs] *vt* **pierced; piercing 1** PENETRATE : atravesar, traspasar, penetrar (en) <the bullet pierced his leg : la bala le atravesó la pierna> <to pierce one's heart : traspasarle el corazón a uno> **2** PERFORATE : perforar, agujerear (las orejas, etc.) **3 to pierce the silence** : desgarrar el silencio
piety [ˈpaɪəti] *n, pl* **-eties** : piedad *f*
pig [ˈpɪg] *n* **1** HOG, SWINE : cerdo *m,* -da *f;* puerco *m,* -ca *f* **2** SLOB : persona *f* desaliñada; cerdo *m,* -da *f* **3** GLUTTON : glotón *m,* -tona *f* **4** *or* **pig iron** : lingote *m* de hierro
pigeon [ˈpɪdʒən] *n* : paloma *f*
pigeonhole [ˈpɪdʒən,hoːl] *n* : casilla *f*
pigeon–toed [ˈpɪdʒən,toːd] *adj* : patituerto
piggish [ˈpɪgɪʃ] *adj* **1** GREEDY : glotón **2** DIRTY : cochino, sucio
piggyback [ˈpɪgi,bæk] *adv & adj* : a cuestas
pigheaded [ˈpɪg,hɛdəd] *adj* : terco, obstinado
piglet [ˈpɪglət] *n* : cochinillo *m;* lechón *m,* -chona *f*
pigment [ˈpɪgmənt] *n* : pigmento *m*
pigmentation [,pɪgmənˈteɪʃən] *n* : pigmentación *f*
pigmy → **pygmy**
pigpen [ˈpɪg,pɛn] *n* : chiquero *m,* pocilga *f*
pigsty [ˈpɪg,staɪ] → **pigpen**
pigtail [ˈpɪg,teɪl] *n* : coleta *f,* trenza *f*
pike [ˈpaɪk] *n, pl* **pike** *or* **pikes 1** : lucio *m* (pez) **2** LANCE : pica *f* **3** → **turnpike**
pile[1] [ˈpaɪl] *v* **piled; piling** *vt* : amontonar, apilar — *vi* **to pile up** : amontonarse, acumularse
pile[2] *n* **1** STAKE : pilote *m* **2** HEAP : montón *m,* pila *f* **3** NAP : pelo *m* (de telas)
piles [ˈpaɪlz] *npl* HEMORRHOIDS : hemorroides *fpl,* almorranas *fpl*
pilfer [ˈpɪlfər] *vt* : robar (cosas pequeñas), ratear
pilgrim [ˈpɪlgrəm] *n* : peregrino *m,* -na *f*
pilgrimage [ˈpɪlgrəmɪdʒ] *n* : peregrinación *f*
pill [ˈpɪl] *n* : pastilla *f,* píldora *f*
pillage[1] [ˈpɪlɪdʒ] *vt* **-laged; -laging** : saquear
pillage[2] *n* : saqueo *m*
pillar [ˈpɪlər] *n* : pilar *m,* columna *f*
pillory [ˈpɪləri] *n, pl* **-ries** : picota *f*
pillow [ˈpɪ,loː] *n* : almohada *f*
pillowcase [ˈpɪ,loː,keɪs] *n* : funda *f*
pilot[1] [ˈpaɪlət] *vt* : pilotar, pilotear
pilot[2] *n* : piloto *mf*
pilot light *n* : piloto *m*
pimento [pəˈmɛn,toː] → **pimiento**
pimiento [pəˈmɛn,toː, -ˈmjɛn-] *n, pl* **-tos** : pimiento *m* morrón
pimp [ˈpɪmp] *n* : proxeneta *m*
pimple [ˈpɪmpəl] *n* : grano *m*
pimply [ˈpɪmpəli] *adj* **-plier; -est** : cubierto de granos
pin[1] [ˈpɪn] *vt* **pinned; pinning 1** FASTEN : prender, sujetar (con alfileres) **2** HOLD, IMMOBILIZE : inmovilizar, sujetar **3 to pin one's hopes on** : poner sus esperanzas en
pin[2] *n* **1** : alfiler *m* <safety pin : alfiler de gancho> <a bobby pin : una horquilla> **2** BROOCH : alfiler *m,* broche *m,* prendedor *m* **3** *or* **bowling pin** : bolo *m*
pinafore [ˈpɪnə,for] *n* : delantal *m*
pincer [ˈpɪntsər] *n* **1** CLAW : pinza *f* (de una langosta, etc.) **2 pincers** *npl* : pinzas *fpl,* tenazas *fpl,* tenaza *f*
pinch[1] [ˈpɪntʃ] *vt* **1** : pellizcar <she pinched my cheek : me pellizcó el cachete> **2** STEAL : robar — *vi* : apretar <my shoes pinch : me aprietan los zapatos>
pinch[2] *n* **1** EMERGENCY : emergencia *f* <in a pinch : en caso necesario> **2** PAIN : dolor *m,* tormento *m* **3** SQUEEZE : pellizco *m* (con los dedos) **4** BIT : pizca *f,* pellizco *m* <a pinch of cinnamon : una pizca de canela>
pinch hitter *n* **1** SUBSTITUTE : sustituto *m,* -ta *f* **2** : bateador *m* emergente (en beisbol)
pincushion [ˈpɪn,kʊʃən] *n* : acerico *m,* alfiletero *m*
pine[1] [ˈpaɪn] *vi* **pined; pining 1 to pine away** : languidecer, consumirse **2 to pine for** : añorar, suspirar por
pine[2] *n* **1** : pino *m* (árbol) **2** : madera *f* de pino
pineapple [ˈpaɪn,æpəl] *n* : piña *f,* ananá *m,* ananás *m*
pinion[1] [ˈpɪnjən] *vt* : sujetar los brazos de, inmovilizar
pinion[2] *n* : piñón *m*
pink[1] [ˈpɪŋk] *adj* : rosa, rosado
pink[2] *n* **1** : clavelito *m* (flor) **2** : rosa *m,* rosado *m* (color) **3 to be in the pink** : estar en plena forma, rebosar de salud
pinkeye [ˈpɪŋk,aɪ] *n* : conjuntivitis *f* aguda
pinkish [ˈpɪŋkɪʃ] *adj* : rosáceo
pinnacle [ˈpɪnɪkəl] *n* **1** : pináculo *m* (de un edificio) **2** PEAK : cima *f,* cumbre *f* (de una montaña) **3** ACME : pináculo *m,* cúspide *f,* apogeo *m*
pinpoint [ˈpɪn,pɔɪnt] *vt* : precisar, localizar con precisión
pint [ˈpaɪnt] *n* : pinta *f*
pinto [ˈpɪn,toː] *n, pl* **pintos** : caballo *m* pinto
pinworm [ˈpɪn,wərm] *n* : oxiuro *m*
pioneer[1] [,paɪəˈnɪr] *vt* : promover, iniciar, introducir
pioneer[2] *n* : pionero *m,* -ra *f*

pious ['paɪəs] *adj* **1** DEVOUT : piadoso, devoto **2** SANCTIMONIOUS : beato
piously ['paɪəsli] *adv* **1** DEVOUTLY : piadosamente **2** SANCTIMONIOUSLY : santurronamente
pipe[1] ['paɪp] *v* **piped; piping** *vi* : hablar en voz chillona — *vt* **1** PLAY : tocar (el caramillo o la flauta) **2** : conducir por tuberías <to pipe water : transportar el agua por tubería>
pipe[2] *n* **1** : caramillo *m* (instrumento musical) **2** BAGPIPE : gaita *f* **3** : tubo *m*, caño *m* <gas pipes : tubería de gas> **4** : pipa *f* (para fumar)
pipeline ['paɪp,laɪn] *n* **1** : conducto *m*, oleoducto *m* (para petróleo), gasoducto *m* (para gas) **2** CONDUIT : vía *f* (de información, etc.)
piper ['paɪpər] *n* : músico *m*, -ca *f* que toca el caramillo o la gaita
piping ['paɪpɪŋ] *n* **1** : música *f* del caramillo o de la gaita **2** TRIM : cordoncillo *m*, ribete *m* con cordón
piquant ['piːkənt, 'pɪkwənt] *adj* **1** SPICY : picante **2** INTRIGUING : intrigante, estimulante
pique[1] ['piːk] *vt* **piqued; piquing 1** IRRITATE : picar, irritar **2** AROUSE : despertar (la curiosidad, etc.)
pique[2] *n* : pique *m*, resentimiento *m*
piracy ['paɪrəsi] *n, pl* **-cies** : piratería *f*
piranha [pə'rɑnə, -'rɑnjə, -'rænjə] *n* : piraña *f*
pirate ['paɪrət] *n* : pirata *mf*
pirouette [,pɪrə'wɛt] *n* : pirueta *f*
pis → **pi**
Pisces ['paɪ,siːz, 'pɪ-; 'pɪs,keɪs] *n* : Piscis *mf*
pistachio [pə'stæʃi,oː, -'stɑ-] *n, pl* **-chios** : pistacho *m*
pistil ['pɪstəl] *n* : pistilo *m*
pistol ['pɪstəl] *n* : pistola *f*
piston ['pɪstən] *n* : pistón *m*, émbolo *m*
pit[1] ['pɪt] *v* **pitted; pitting** *vt* **1** : marcar de hoyos, picar (una superficie) **2** : deshuesar (una fruta) **3 to pit against** : enfrentar a, oponer a — *vi* : quedar marcado
pit[2] *n* **1** HOLE : fosa *f*, hoyo *m* <a bottomless pit : un pozo sin fondo> **2** MINE : mina *f* **3** : foso *m* <orchestra pit : foso orquestal> **4** POCKMARK : marca *f* (en la cara), cicatriz *f* de viruela **5** STONE : hueso *m*, pepa *f* (de una fruta) **6 pit of the stomach** : boca *f* del estómago
pitch[1] ['pɪtʃ] *vt* **1** SET UP : montar, armar (una tienda) **2** THROW : lanzar, arrojar **3** ADJUST, SET : dar el tono de (un discurso, un instrumento musical) — *vi* **1** *or* **pitch forward** FALL : caerse **2** LURCH : cabecear (dícese de un barco o un avión), dar bandazos
pitch[2] *n* **1** LURCHING : cabezada *f*, cabeceo *m* (de un barco o un avión) **2** SLOPE : (grado de) inclinación *f*, pendiente *f* **3** : tono *m* (en música) <perfect pitch : oído absoluto> **4** THROW : lanzamiento *m* **5** DEGREE : grado *m*, nivel *m*, punto *m* <the excitement reached a high pitch : la excitación llegó a un punto culminante> **6** *or* **sales pitch** : presentación *f* (de un vendedor) **7** TAR : pez *f*, brea *f*
pitcher ['pɪtʃər] *n* **1** JUG : jarra *f*, jarro *m*, cántaro *m*, pichel *m* **2** : lanzador *m*, -dora *f* (en béisbol, etc.)
pitchfork ['pɪtʃ,fɔrk] *n* : horquilla *f*, horca *f*
piteous ['pɪt̬iəs] *adj* : lastimoso, lastimero — **piteously** *adv*
pitfall ['pɪt,fɔl] *n* : peligro *m* (poco obvio), dificultad *f*
pith ['pɪθ] *n* **1** : médula *f* (de una planta) **2** CORE : meollo *m*, entraña *f*
pithy ['pɪθi] *adj* **pithier; -est** : conciso y sustancioso <pithy comments : comentarios sucintos>
pitiable ['pɪt̬iəbəl] → **pitiful**
pitiful ['pɪt̬ɪfəl] *adj* **1** LAMENTABLE : lastimero, lastimoso, lamentable **2** CONTEMPTIBLE : despreciable, lamentable — **pitifully** [-fli] *adv*
pitiless ['pɪt̬ɪləs] *adj* : despiadado — **pitilessly** *adv*
pittance ['pɪtənts] *n* : miseria *f*
pituitary [pə'tuːə,tɛri, -'tjuː-] *adj* : pituitario
pity[1] ['pɪt̬i] *vt* **pitied; pitying** : compadecer, compadecerse de
pity[2] *n, pl* **pities 1** COMPASSION : compasión *f*, piedad *f* **2** SHAME : lástima *f*, pena *f* <what a pity! : ¡qué lástima!>
pivot[1] ['pɪvət] *vi* **1** : girar sobre un eje **2 to pivot on** : girar sobre, depender de
pivot[2] *n* : pivote *m*
pivotal ['pɪvət̬əl] *adj* : fundamental, central
pixie *or* **pixy** ['pɪksi] *n, pl* **pixies** : elfo *m*, hada *f*
pizza ['piːtsə] *n* : pizza *f*
pizzazz *or* **pizazz** [pə'zæz] *n* **1** GLAMOR : encanto *m* **2** VITALITY : animación *f*, vitalidad *f*
placard ['plækərd, -,kɑrd] *n* POSTER : cartel *m*, póster *m*, afiche *m*
placate ['pleɪ,keɪt, 'plæ-] *vt* **-cated; -cating** : aplacar, apaciguar
place[1] ['pleɪs] *vt* **placed; placing 1** PUT, SET : poner, colocar **2** SITUATE : situar, ubicar, emplazar <to be well placed : estar bien situado> <to place in a job : colocar en un trabajo> **3** IDENTIFY, RECALL : identificar, ubicar, recordar <I can't place him : no lo ubico> **4 to place an order** : hacer un pedido
place[2] *n* **1** SPACE : sitio *m*, lugar *m* <there's no place to sit : no hay sitio para sentarse> **2** LOCATION, SPOT : lugar *m*, sitio *m*, parte *f* <place of work : lugar de trabajo> <our summer place : nuestra casa de verano> <all over the place : por todas partes> **3** RANK : lugar *m*, puesto *m* <he took first place : ganó el primer lugar> **4**

POSITION : lugar *m* <everything in its place : todo en su debido lugar> <to feel out of place : sentirse fuera de lugar> **5** SEAT : asiento *m,* cubierto *m* (a la mesa) **6** JOB : puesto *m* **7** ROLE : papel *m,* lugar *m* <to change places : cambiarse los papeles> **8 to take place :** tener lugar **9 to take the place of :** sustituir a

placebo [plə'si:ˌbo:] *n, pl* **-bos :** placebo *m*

placement ['pleɪsmənt] *n* **:** colocación *f*

placenta [plə'sɛntə] *n, pl* **-tas** *or* **-tae** [-ti, -ˌtaɪ] **:** placenta *f*

placid ['plæsəd] *adj* **:** plácido, tranquilo — **placidly** *adv*

plagiarism ['pleɪdʒəˌrɪzəm] *n* **:** plagio *m*

plagiarist ['pleɪdʒərɪst] *n* **:** plagiario *m,* -ria *f*

plagiarize ['pleɪdʒəˌraɪz] *vt* **-rized; -rizing :** plagiar

plague[1] ['pleɪg] *vt* **plagued; plaguing 1** AFFLICT **:** plagar, afligir **2** HARASS **:** acosar, atormentar

plague[2] *n* **1 :** plaga *f* (de insectos, etc.) **2 :** peste *f* (en medicina)

plaid[1] ['plæd] *adj* **:** escocés, de cuadros <a plaid skirt : una falda escocesa>

plaid[2] *n* TARTAN **:** tela *f* escocesa, tartán *m*

plain[1] ['pleɪn] *adj* **1** SIMPLE, UNADORNED **:** liso, sencillo, sin adornos **2** CLEAR **:** claro <in plain language : en palabras claras> **3** FRANK **:** franco, puro <the plain truth : la pura verdad> **4** HOMELY **:** ordinario, poco atractivo **5 in plain sight :** a la vista de todos

plain[2] *n* **:** llanura *f,* llano *m,* planicie *f*

plainly ['pleɪnli] *adv* **1** CLEARLY **:** claramente **2** FRANKLY **:** francamente, con franqueza **3** SIMPLY **:** sencillamente

plaintiff ['pleɪntɪf] *n* **:** demandante *mf*

plaintive ['pleɪntɪv] *adj* MOURNFUL **:** lastimero, plañidero

plait[1] ['pleɪt, 'plæt] *vt* **1** PLEAT **:** plisar **2** BRAID **:** trenzar

plait[2] *n* **1** PLEAT **:** pliegue *m* **2** BRAID **:** trenza *f*

plan[1] ['plæn] *v* **planned; planning** *vt* **1 :** planear, proyectar, planificar <to plan a trip : planear un viaje> <to plan a city : planificar una ciudad> **2** INTEND **:** tener planeado, proyectar — *vi* **:** hacer planes

plan[2] *n* **1** DIAGRAM **:** plano *m,* esquema *m* **2** SCHEME **:** plan *m,* proyecto *m,* programa *m* <to draw up a plan : elaborar un proyecto>

plane[1] ['pleɪn] *vt* **planed; planing :** cepillar (madera)

plane[2] *adj* **:** plano

plane[3] *n* **1 :** plano *m* (en matemáticas, etc.) **2** LEVEL **:** nivel *m* **3 :** cepillo *m* (de carpintero) **4** → **airplane**

planet ['plænət] *n* **:** planeta *f*

planetarium [ˌplænə'tɛriəm] *n, pl* **-iums** *or* **-ia** [-iə] **:** planetario *m*

planetary ['plænəˌtɛri] *adj* **:** planetario

plank ['plæŋk] *n* **1** BOARD **:** tablón *m,* tabla *f* **2 :** artículo *m,* punto *m* (de una plataforma política)

plankton ['plæŋktən] *n* **:** plancton *m*

plant[1] ['plænt] *vt* **1 :** plantar (flores, árboles), sembrar (semillas) **2** PLACE **:** plantar, colocar <to plant an idea : inculcar una idea>

plant[2] *n* **1 :** planta *f* <leafy plants : plantas frondosas> **2** FACTORY **:** planta *f,* fábrica *f* <hydroelectric plant : planta hidroeléctrica> **3** MACHINERY **:** maquinaria *f,* equipo *m*

plantain ['plæntən] *n* **1 :** llantén *m* (mala hierba) **2 :** plátano *m,* plátano *m* macho *Mex* (fruta)

plantation [plæn'teɪʃən] *n* **:** plantación *f,* hacienda *f* <a coffee plantation : un cafetal>

planter ['plæntər] *n* **1 :** hacendado *m,* -da *f* (de una hacienda) **2** FLOWERPOT **:** tiesto *m,* maceta *f*

plaque ['plæk] *n* **1** TABLET **:** placa *f* **2 :** placa *f* (dental)

plasma ['plæzmə] *n* **:** plasma *m*

plaster[1] ['plæstər] *vt* **1 :** enyesar, revocar (con yeso) **2** COVER **:** cubrir, llenar <a wall plastered with notices : una pared cubierta de avisos>

plaster[2] *n* **1 :** yeso *m,* revoque *m* (para paredes, etc.) **2 :** escayola *f,* yeso *m* (en medicina) **3 plaster of Paris** ['pærɪs] **:** yeso *m* mate

plaster cast *n* **:** vaciado *m* de yeso

plasterer ['plæstərər] *n* **:** revocador *m,* -dora *f*

plastic[1] ['plæstɪk] *adj* **1 :** de plástico **2** PLIABLE **:** plástico, flexible **3 plastic surgery :** cirugía *f* plástica

plastic[2] *n* **:** plástico *m*

plate[1] ['pleɪt] *vt* **plated; plating :** chapar (en metal)

plate[2] *n* **1** PLAQUE, SHEET **:** placa *f* <a steel plate : una placa de acero> **2** UTENSILS **:** vajilla *f* (de metal) <silver plate : vajilla de plata> **3** DISH **:** plato *m* **4** DENTURES **:** dentadura *f* postiza **5** ILLUSTRATION **:** lámina *f* (en un libro) **6 license plate :** matrícula *f,* placa *f* de matrícula

plateau [plæ'to:] *n, pl* **-teaus** *or* **-teaux** [-'to:z] **:** meseta *f*

platform ['plætˌfɔrm] *n* **1** STAGE **:** plataforma *f,* estrado *m,* tribuna *f* **2 :** andén *m* (de una estación de ferrocarril) **3 political platform :** plataforma *f* política, programa *m* electoral

plating ['pleɪṭɪŋ] *n* **1 :** enchapado *m* **2 silver plating :** plateado *m*

platinum ['plætənəm] *n* **:** platino *m*

platitude ['plæṭəˌtu:d, -ˌtju:d] *n* **:** lugar *m* común, perogrullada *f*

platoon [plə'tu:n] *n* **:** sección *f* (en el ejército)

platter ['plæṭər] *n* **:** fuente *f*

platypus [ˈplætɪpəs, -ˌpʊs] *n, pl* **platypuses** *or* **platypi** [-ˌpaɪ, -ˌpiː] : ornitorrinco *m*

plausibility [ˌplɔzəˈbɪləti] *n, pl* **-ties** : credibilidad *f,* verosimilitud *f*

plausible [ˈplɔzəbəl] *adj* : creíble, convincente, verosímil — **plausibly** [-bli] *adv*

play[1] [ˈpleɪ] *vi* **1** : jugar <to play with a doll : jugar con una muñeca> <to play with an idea : darle vueltas a una idea> **2** FIDDLE, TOY : jugar, juguetear <don't play with your food : no juegues con la comida> **3** : tocar <to play in a band : tocar en un grupo> **4** : actuar (en una obra de teatro) — *vt* **1** : jugar (un deporte, etc.), jugar a (un juego), jugar contra (un contrincante) **2** : tocar (música o un instrumento) **3** PERFORM : interpretar, hacer el papel de (un carácter), representar (una obra de teatro) <she plays the lead : hace el papel principal>

play[2] *n* **1** GAME, RECREATION : juego *m* <children at play : niños jugando> <a play on words : un juego de palabras> **2** ACTION : juego *m* <the ball is in play : la pelota está en juego> <to bring into play : poner en juego> **3** DRAMA : obra *f* de teatro, pieza *f* (de teatro) **4** MOVEMENT : juego *m* (de la luz, una brisa, etc.) **5** SLACK : juego *m* <there's not enough play in the wheel : la rueda no da lo suficiente>

playacting [ˈpleɪˌæktɪŋ] *n* : actuación *f,* teatro *m*

player [ˈpleɪər] *n* **1** : jugador *m,* -dora *f* (en un juego) **2** ACTOR : actor *m,* actriz *f* **3** MUSICIAN : músico *m,* -ca *f*

playful [ˈpleɪfəl] *adj* **1** FROLICSOME : juguetón **2** JOCULAR : jocoso — **playfully** *adv*

playfulness [ˈpleɪfəlnəs] *n* : lo juguetón, jocosidad *f,* alegría *f*

playground [ˈpleɪˌgraʊnd] *n* : patio *m* de recreo, jardín *m* para jugar

playhouse [ˈpleɪˌhaʊs] *n* **1** THEATER : teatro *m* **2** : casita *f* de juguete

playing card *n* : naipe *m,* carta *f*

playmate [ˈpleɪˌmeɪt] *n* : compañero *m,* -ra *f* de juego

play–off [ˈpleɪˌɔf] *n* : desempate *m*

playpen [ˈpleɪˌpɛn] *n* : corral *m* (para niños)

plaything [ˈpleɪˌθɪŋ] *n* : juguete *m*

playwright [ˈpleɪˌraɪt] *n* : dramaturgo *m,* -ga *f*

plaza [ˈplæzə, ˈplɑ-] *n* **1** SQUARE : plaza *f* **2 shopping plaza** MALL : centro *m* comercial

plea [ˈpliː] *n* **1** : acto *m* de declararse <he entered a plea of guilty : se declaró culpable> **2** APPEAL : ruego *m,* súplica *f*

plead [ˈpliːd] *v* **pleaded** *or* **pled** [ˈplɛd]; **pleading** *vi* **1** : declararse (culpable o inocente) **2 to plead for** : suplicar, implorar — *vt* **1** : alegar, pretextar <he pleaded illness : pretextó la enfermedad> **2 to plead a case** : defender un caso

pleasant [ˈplɛzənt] *adj* : agradable, grato, bueno — **pleasantly** *adv*

pleasantness [ˈplɛzəntnəs] *n* : lo agradable, amenidad *f*

pleasantries [ˈplɛzəntriz] *npl* : cumplidos *mpl*, cortesías *fpl* <to exchange pleasantries : intercambiar cumplidos>

please[1] [ˈpliːz] *v* **pleased; pleasing** *vt* **1** GRATIFY : complacer <please yourself! : ¡cómo quieras!> **2** SATISFY : contentar, satisfacer — *vi* **1** SATISFY : complacer, agradar <anxious to please : deseoso de complacer> **2** LIKE : querer <do as you please : haz lo que quieras, haz lo que te parezca>

please[2] *adv* : por favor

pleased [ˈpliːzd] *adj* : contento, satisfecho, alegre

pleasing [ˈpliːzɪŋ] *adj* : agradable — **pleasingly** *adv*

pleasurable [ˈplɛʒərəbəl] *adj* PLEASANT : agradable

pleasure [ˈplɛʒər] *n* **1** WISH : deseo *m,* voluntad *f* <at your pleasure : cuando guste> **2** ENJOYMENT : placer *m,* disfrute *m,* goce *m* <with pleasure : con mucho gusto> **3** : placer *m,* gusto *m* <it's a pleasure to be here : me da gusto estar aquí> <the pleasures of reading : los placeres de leer>

pleat[1] [ˈpliːt] *vt* : plisar

pleat[2] *n* : pliegue *m*

plebeian [plɪˈbiən] *adj* : ordinario, plebeyo

pledge[1] [ˈplɛdʒ] *vt* **pledged; pledging** **1** PAWN : empeñar, prendar **2** PROMISE : prometer, jurar

pledge[2] *n* **1** SECURITY : garantía *f,* prenda *f* **2** PROMISE : promesa *f*

plenteous [ˈplɛntiəs] *adj* : copioso, abundante

plentiful [ˈplɛntɪfəl] *adj* : abundante — **plentifully** [-fli] *adv*

plenty [ˈplɛnti] *n* : abundancia *f* <plenty of time : tiempo de sobra> <plenty of visitors : muchos visitantes>

plethora [ˈplɛθərə] *n* : plétora *f*

pleurisy [ˈplʊrəsi] *n* : pleuresía *f*

pliable [ˈplaɪəbəl] *adj* : flexible, maleable

pliant [ˈplaɪənt] → **pliable**

pliers [ˈplaɪərz] *npl* : alicates *mpl*, pinzas *fpl*

plight [ˈplaɪt] *n* : situación *f* difícil, apuro *m*

plod [ˈplɑd] *vi* **plodded; plodding** **1** TRUDGE : caminar pesadamente y lentamente **2** DRUDGE : trabajar laboriosamente

plot[1] [ˈplɑt] *v* **plotted; plotting** *vt* **1** DEVISE : tramar **2 to plot out** : trazar, determinar (una posición, etc.) — *vi* CONSPIRE : conspirar

plot[2] *n* **1** LOT : terreno *m,* parcela *f,* lote *m* **2** STORY : argumento *m* (en el teatro), trama *f* (en un libro, etc.) **3** CONSPIRACY, INTRIGUE **:** complot *m,* intriga *f*

plotter [ˈplɑt̬ər] *n* **:** conspirador *m,* -dora *f;* intrigante *mf*

plow[1] *or* **plough** [ˈplaʊ] *vt* **1 :** arar (la tierra) **2 to plow the seas :** surcar los mares

plow[2] *or* **plough** *n* **1 :** arado *m* **2** → **snowplow**

plowshare [ˈplaʊˌʃɛr] *n* **:** reja *f* del arado

ploy [ˈplɔɪ] *n* **:** estratagema *f,* maniobra *f*

pluck[1] [ˈplʌk] *vt* **1** PICK **:** arrancar **2 :** desplumar (un pollo, etc.) — *vi* **to pluck at :** tirar de

pluck[2] *n* **1** TUG **:** tirón *m* **2** COURAGE, SPIRIT **:** valor *m,* ánimo *m*

plucky [ˈplʌki] *adj* **pluckier; -est :** valiente, animoso

plug[1] [ˈplʌg] *vt* **plugged; plugging 1** BLOCK **:** tapar **2** PROMOTE **:** hacerle publicidad a, promocionar **3 to plug in :** enchufar

plug[2] *n* **1** STOPPER **:** tapón *m* **2 :** enchufe *m* (eléctrico) **3** ADVERTISEMENT **:** publicidad *f,* propaganda *f*

plum [ˈplʌm] *n* **1 :** ciruela *f* (fruta) **2 :** color *m* ciruela **3** PRIZE **:** premio *m,* algo muy atractivo

plumage [ˈpluːmɪdʒ] *n* **:** plumaje *m*

plumb[1] [ˈplʌm] *vt* **1 :** aplomar <to plumb a wall : aplomar una pared> **2** SOUND **:** sondear, sondar

plumb[2] *adv* **1** VERTICALLY **:** a plomo, verticalmente **2** EXACTLY **:** justo, exactamente **3** COMPLETELY **:** completamente, absolutamente <plumb crazy : loco de remate>

plumb[3] *adj* **:** a plomo

plumb[4] *n or* **plumb line :** plomada *f*

plumber [ˈplʌmər] *n* **:** plomero *m,* -ra *f;* fontanero *m,* -ra *f*

plumbing [ˈplʌmɪŋ] *n* **1 :** plomería *f,* fontanería *f* (trabajo del plomero) **2** PIPES **:** cañería *f,* tubería *f*

plume [ˈpluːm] *n* **1** FEATHER **:** pluma *f* **2** TUFT **:** penacho *m* (en un sombrero, etc.)

plumed [ˈpluːmd] *adj* **:** con plumas <white-plumed birds : aves de plumaje blanco>

plummet [ˈplʌmət] *vi* **:** caer en picada, desplomarse

plump[1] [ˈplʌmp] *vi or* **to plump down :** dejarse caer (pesadamente)

plump[2] *adv* **1** STRAIGHT **:** a plomo **2** DIRECTLY **:** directamente, sin rodeos <he ran plump into the door : dio de cara con la puerta>

plump[3] *adj* **:** llenito *fam,* regordete *fam,* rechoncho *fam*

plumpness [ˈplʌmpnəs] *n* **:** gordura *f*

plunder[1] [ˈplʌndər] *vi* **:** saquear, robar

plunder[2] *n* **:** botín *m*

plunderer [ˈplʌndərər] *n* **:** saqueador *m,* -dora *f*

plunge[1] [ˈplʌndʒ] *v* **plunged; plunging** *vt* **1** IMMERSE **:** sumergir **2** THRUST **:** hundir, clavar — *vi* **1** DIVE **:** zambullirse (en el agua) **2 :** meterse precipitadamente o violentamente <they plunged into war : se enfrascaron en una guerra> <he plunged into depression : cayó en la depresión> **3** DESCEND **:** descender en picada <the road plunges dizzily : la calle desciende vertiginosamente>

plunge[2] *n* **1** DIVE **:** zambullida *f* **2** DROP **:** descenso *m* abrupto <the plunge in prices : el desplome de los precios>

plural[1] [ˈplʊrəl] *adj* **:** plural

plural[2] *n* **:** plural *m*

plurality [plʊˈrælət̬i] *n, pl* **-ties :** pluralidad *f*

pluralize [ˈplʊrəˌlaɪz] *vt* **-ized; -izing :** pluralizar

plus[1] [ˈplʌs] *adj* **1** POSITIVE **:** positivo <a plus factor : un factor positivo> **2** (*indicating a quantity in addition*) <a grade of C plus : una calificación entre C y B> <a salary of $30,000 plus : un sueldo de más de $30,000>

plus[2] *n* **1** *or* **plus sign :** más *m,* signo *m* de más **2** ADVANTAGE **:** ventaja *f*

plus[3] *prep* **:** más (en matemáticas)

plus[4] *conj* AND **:** y

plush[1] [ˈplʌʃ] *adj* **1 :** afelpado **2** LUXURIOUS **:** lujoso

plush[2] *n* **:** felpa *f,* peluche *m*

plushy [ˈplʌʃi] *adj* **plushier; -est :** lujoso

Pluto [ˈpluːt̬oː] *n* **:** Plutón *m*

plutocracy [pluːˈtɑkrəsi] *n, pl* **-cies :** plutocracia *f*

plutonium [pluːˈtoːniəm] *n* **:** plutonio *m*

ply[1] [ˈplaɪ] *v* **plied; plying** *vt* **1** USE, WIELD **:** manejar <to ply an ax : manejar un hacha> **2** PRACTICE **:** ejercer <to ply a trade : ejercer un oficio> **3 to ply with questions :** acosar con preguntas

ply[2] *n, pl* **plies 1** LAYER **:** chapa *f* (de madera), capa *f* (de papel) **2** STRAND **:** cabo *m* (de hilo, etc.)

plywood [ˈplaɪˌwʊd] *n* **:** contrachapado *m*

pneumatic [nʊˈmæt̬ɪk, njʊ-] *adj* **:** neumático

pneumonia [nʊˈmoːnjə, njʊ-] *n* **:** pulmonía *f,* neumonía *f*

poach [ˈpoːtʃ] *vt* **1 :** cocer a fuego lento <to poach an egg : escalfar un huevo> **2 to poach game :** cazar ilegalmente — *vi* **:** cazar ilegalmente

poacher [ˈpoːtʃər] *n* **:** cazador *m* furtivo, cazadora *f* furtiva

pock [ˈpɑk] *n* **1** PUSTULE **:** pústula *f* **2** → **pockmark**

pocket[1] [ˈpɑkət] *vt* **1 :** meterse en el bolsillo <he pocketed the pen : se metió la pluma en el bolsillo> **2** STEAL **:** embolsarse

pocket[2] *n* **1 :** bolsillo *m,* bolsa *f Mex* <a coat pocket : el bolsillo de un abrigo>

<air pockets : bolsas de aire> **2** CENTER : foco *m,* centro *m* <a pocket of resistance : un foco de resistencia>
pocketbook [ˈpɑkət,bʊk] *n* **1** PURSE : cartera *f,* bolso *m,* bolsa *f Mex* **2** MEANS : recursos *mpl*
pocketknife [ˈpɑkət,naɪf] *n, pl* **-knives** : navaja *f*
pocket-size [ˈpɑkətˈsaɪz] *adj* : de bolsillo
pockmark [ˈpɑk,mɑrk] *n* : cicatriz *f* de viruela, viruela *f*
pod [ˈpɑd] *n* : vaina *f* <pea pod : vaina de guisantes>
podiatrist [pəˈdaɪətrɪst, po-] *n* : podólogo *m,* -ga *f*
podiatry [pəˈdaɪətri, po-] *n* : podología *f,* podiatría *f*
podium [ˈpoːdiəm] *n, pl* **-diums** *or* **-dia** [-diə] : podio *m,* estrado *m,* tarima *f*
poem [ˈpoːəm] *n* : poema *m,* poesía *f*
poet [ˈpoːət] *n* : poeta *mf*
poetic [poˈɛt̬ɪk] *or* **poetical** [-t̬ɪkəl] *adj* : poético
poetry [ˈpoːətri] *n* : poesía *f*
pogrom [ˈpoːgrəm, pəˈgrɑm, ˈpɑgrəm] *n* : pogrom *m*
poignancy [ˈpɔɪnjəntsi] *n, pl* **-cies** : lo conmovedor
poignant [ˈpɔɪnjənt] *adj* **1** PAINFUL : penoso, doloroso <poignant grief : profundo dolor> **2** TOUCHING : conmovedor, emocionante
poinsettia [pɔɪnˈsɛt̬iə, -ˈsɛt̬ə] *n* : flor *f* de Nochebuena
point[1] [ˈpɔɪnt] *vt* **1** SHARPEN : afilar (la punta de) **2** INDICATE : señalar, indicar <to point the way : señalar el camino> **3** AIM : apuntar **4 to point out** : señalar, indicar — *vi* **1 to point at** : señalar (con el dedo) **2 to point to** INDICATE : señalar, indicar
point[2] *n* **1** ITEM : punto *m* <the main points : los puntos principales> **2** QUALITY : cualidad *f* <her good points : sus buenas cualidades> <it's not his strong point : no es su (punto) fuerte> **3** (*indicating a chief idea or meaning*) <it's beside the point : no viene al caso> <to get to the point : ir al grano> <to stick to the point : no salirse del tema> **4** PURPOSE : fin *m,* propósito *m* <there's no point to it : no vale la pena, no sirve para nada> **5** PLACE : punto *m,* lugar *m* <points of interest : puntos interesantes> **6** : punto *m* (en una escala) <boiling point : punto de ebullición> **7** MOMENT : momento *m,* coyuntura *f* <at this point : en este momento> **8** TIP : punta *f* **9** HEADLAND : punta *f,* cabo *m* **10** PERIOD : punto *m* (marca de puntuación) **11** UNIT : punto *m* <he scored 15 points : ganó 15 puntos> <shares fell 10 points : las acciones bajaron 10 enteros> **12 compass points** : puntos *mpl* cardinales **13 decimal point** : punto *m* decimal, coma *f*
point–blank[1] [ˈpɔɪntˈblæŋk] *adv* **1** : a quemarropa <to shoot point-blank : disparar a quemarropa> **2** BLUNTLY, DIRECTLY : a bocajarro, sin rodeos, francamente
point–blank[2] *adj* **1** : a quemarropa <point-blank shots : disparos a quemarropa> **2** BLUNT, DIRECT : directo, franco
pointedly [ˈpɔɪntədli] *adv* : intencionadamente, directamente
pointer [ˈpɔɪntər] *n* **1** STICK : puntero *m* (para maestros, etc.) **2** INDICATOR, NEEDLE : indicador *m,* aguja *f* **3** : perro *m* de muestra **4** HINT, TIP : consejo *m*
pointless [ˈpɔɪntləs] *adj* : inútil, ocioso, vano <it's pointless to continue : no tiene sentido continuar>
point of view *n* : perspectiva *f,* punto *m* de vista
poise[1] [ˈpɔɪz] *vt* **poised; poising** BALANCE : equilibrar, balancear
poise[2] *n* : aplomo *m,* compostura *f*
poison[1] [ˈpɔɪzən] *vt* **1** : envenenar, intoxicar **2** CORRUPT : corromper
poison[2] *n* : veneno *m*
poison ivy *n* : hiedra *f* venenosa
poisonous [ˈpɔɪzənəs] *adj* : venenoso, tóxico, ponzoñoso
poke[1] [ˈpoːk] *v* **poked; poking** *vt* **1** JAB : golpear (con la punta de algo), dar <he poked me with his finger : me dio con el dedo> **2** THRUST : introducir, asomar <I poked my head out the window : asomé la cabeza por la ventana> — *vi* **1 to poke around** RUMMAGE : hurgar **2 to poke along** DAWDLE : demorarse, entretenerse
poke[2] *n* : golpe *m* abrupto (con la punta de algo)
poker [ˈpoːkər] *n* **1** : atizador *m* (para el fuego) **2** : póker *m,* poker *m* (juego de naipes)
polar [ˈpoːlər] *adj* : polar
polar bear *n* : oso *m* blanco
Polaris [poˈlærɪs, -ˈlɑr-] → **North Star**
polarize [ˈpoːlə,raɪz] *vt* **-ized; -izing** : polarizar
pole [ˈpoːl] *n* **1** : palo *m,* poste *m,* vara *f* <telephone pole : poste de teléfonos> **2** : polo *m* <the South Pole : el Polo Sur> **3** : polo *m* (eléctrico o magnético)
Pole [ˈpoːl] *n* : polaco *m,* -ca *f*
polecat [ˈpoːl,kæt] *n, pl* **polecats** *or* **polecat 1** : turón *m* (de Europa) **2** SKUNK : mofeta *f,* zorrillo *m*
polemical [pəˈlɛmɪkəl] *adj* : polémico
polemics [pəˈlɛmɪks] *ns & pl* : polémica *f*
polestar [ˈpoːl,stɑr] → **North Star**
police[1] [pəˈliːs] *vt* **-liced; -licing** : mantener el orden en <to police the streets : patrullar las calles>
police[2] *ns & pl* **1** : policía *f* (organización) **2** POLICE OFFICERS : policías *mfpl*
policeman [pəˈliːsmən] *n, pl* **-men** [-mən, -,mɛn] : policía *m*

police officer *n* : policía *mf,* agente *mf* de policía
policewoman [pə'li:s,wʊmən] *n, pl* **-women** [-,wɪmən] : policía *f,* mujer *f* policía
policy ['pɑləsi] *n, pl* **-cies 1** : política *f* <foreign policy : política exterior> **2** *or* **insurance policy** : póliza *f* de seguros, seguro *m*
polio[1] ['po:li,o:] *adj* : de polio <polio vaccine : vacuna contra la polio>
polio[2] *n* → **poliomyelitis**
poliomyelitis [,po:li,o:,maɪə'laɪtəs] *n* : poliomielitis *f,* polio *f*
polish[1] ['pɑlɪʃ] *vt* **1** : pulir, lustrar, sacar brillo a <to polish one's nails : pintarse las uñas> **2** REFINE : pulir, perfeccionar
polish[2] *n* **1** LUSTER : brillo *m,* lustre *m* **2** REFINEMENT : refinamiento *m* **3** : betún *m* (para zapatos), cera *f* (para suelos y muebles), esmalte *m* (para las uñas)
Polish[1] ['po:lɪʃ] *adj* : polaco
Polish[2] *n* : polaco *m* (idioma)
polite [pə'laɪt] *adj* **-liter; -est** : cortés, correcto, educado
politely [pə'laɪtli] *adv* : cortésmente, correctamente, con buenos modales
politeness [pə'laɪtnəs] *n* : cortesía *f*
politic ['pɑlə,tɪk] *adj* : diplomático, prudente
political [pə'lɪtɪkəl] *adj* : político — **politically** [-tɪkli] *adv*
politician [,pɑlə'tɪʃən] *n* : político *m,* -ca *f*
politics ['pɑlə,tɪks] *ns & pl* : política *f*
polka ['po:lkə, 'po:kə] *n* : polka *f*
polka dot ['po:kə,dɑt] *n* : lunar *m* (en un diseño)
poll[1] ['po:l] *vt* **1** : obtener (votos) <she polled over 1000 votes : obtuvo más de 1000 votos> **2** CANVASS : encuestar, sondear — *vi* : obtener votos
poll[2] *n* **1** SURVEY : encuesta *f,* sondeo *m* **2 polls** *npl* : urnas *fpl* <to go to the polls : acudir a las urnas, ir a votar>
pollen ['pɑlən] *n* : polen *m*
pollinate ['pɑlə,neɪt] *vt* **-nated; -nating** : polinizar
pollination [,pɑlə'neɪʃən] *n* : polinización *f*
pollster ['po:lstər] *n* : encuestador *m,* -dora *f*
pollutant [pə'lu:tənt] *n* : contaminante *m*
pollute [pə'lu:t] *vt* **-luted; -luting** : contaminar
pollution [pə'lu:ʃən] *n* : contaminación *f*
pollywog *or* **polliwog** ['pɑli,wɔg] *n* TADPOLE : renacuajo *m*
polo ['po:,lo:] *n* : polo *m*
poltergeist ['po:ltər,gaɪst] *n* : poltergeist *m,* fantasma *m* travieso
polyester ['pɑli,ɛstər, ,pɑli'-] *n* : poliéster *m*
polygamous [pə'lɪgəməs] *adj* : polígamo
polygamy [pə'lɪgəmi] *n* : poligamia *f*
polygon ['pɑli,gɑn] *n* : polígono *m*
polymer ['pɑləmər] *n* : polímero *m*
polyunsaturated [,pɑli,ʌn'sætʃə,reɪtəd] *adj* : poliinsaturado
pomegranate ['pɑmə,grænət, 'pɑm,grænət] *n* : granada *f* (fruta)
pommel[1] ['pʌməl] *vt* → **pummel**
pommel[2] ['pʌməl, 'pɑ-] *n* **1** : pomo *m* (de una espada) **2** : perilla *f* (de una silla de montar)
pomp ['pɑmp] *n* **1** SPLENDOR : pompa *f,* esplendor *m* **2** OSTENTATION : boato *m,* ostentación *f*
pom-pom ['pɑm,pɑm] *n* : borla *f,* pompón *m*
pomposity [pɑm'pɑsəti] *n, pl* **-ties** : pomposidad *f*
pompous ['pɑmpəs] *adj* : pomposo — **pompously** *adv*
poncho ['pɑn,tʃo:] *n, pl* **-chos** : poncho *m*
pond ['pɑnd] *n* : charca *f* (natural), estanque *m* (artificial)
ponder ['pɑndər] *vt* : reflexionar, considerar — *vi* **to ponder over** : reflexionar sobre, sopesar
ponderous ['pɑndərəs] *adj* : pesado
pontiff ['pɑntɪf] *n* POPE : pontífice *m*
pontificate [pɑn'tɪfə,keɪt] *vi* **-cated; -cating** : pontificar
pontoon [pɑn'tu:n] *n* : pontón *m*
pony ['po:ni] *n, pl* **-nies** : poni *m,* poney *m,* jaca *f*
ponytail ['po:ni,teɪl] *n* : cola *f* de caballo, coleta *f*
poodle ['pu:dəl] *n* : caniche *m*
pool[1] ['pu:l] *vt* : mancomunar, hacer un fondo común de
pool[2] *n* **1** : charca *f* <a swimming pool : una piscina> **2** PUDDLE : charco *m* **3** RESERVE, SUPPLY : fondo *m* común (de recursos), reserva *f* **4** : billar *m* (juego)
poor ['pʊr, 'por] *adj* **1** : pobre <poor people : los pobres> **2** SCANTY : pobre, escaso <poor attendance : baja asistencia> **3** UNFORTUNATE : pobre <poor thing! : ¡pobrecito!> **4** BAD : malo <to be in poor health : estar mal de salud>
poorly ['pʊrli, 'por-] *adv* : mal
pop[1] ['pɑp] *v* **popped; popping** *vi* **1** BURST : reventarse, estallar **2** : ir, venir, o aparecer abruptamente <he popped into the house : se metió en la casa> <a menu pops up : aparece un menú> **3 to pop out** PROTRUDE : salirse, saltarse <my eyes popped out of my head : se me saltaban los ojos> — *vt* **1** BURST : reventar **2** : hacer o meter abruptamente <he popped it into his mouth : se lo metió en la boca>
pop[2] *adj* : popular <pop music : música popular>
pop[3] *n* **1** : estallido *m* pequeño (de un globo, etc.) **2** SODA : refresco *m,* gaseosa *f*

popcorn ['pɑp,kɔrn] *n* : palomitas *fpl* (de maíz)
pope ['po:p] *n* : papa *m* <Pope John : el Papa Juan>
poplar ['pɑplər] *n* : álamo *m*
poplin ['pɑplɪn] *n* : popelín *m*, popelina *f*
poppy ['pɑpi] *n, pl* **-pies** : amapola *f*
populace ['pɑpjələs] *n* **1** MASSES : pueblo *m* **2** POPULATION : población *f*
popular ['pɑpjələr] *adj* **1** : popular <the popular vote : el voto popular> **2** COMMON : generalizado, común <popular beliefs : creencias generalizadas> **3** : popular, de gran popularidad <a popular singer : un cantante popular>
popularity [,pɑpjə'lærət̬i] *n* : popularidad *f*
popularize ['pɑpjələ,raɪz] *vt* **-ized; -izing** : popularizar
popularly ['pɑpjələrli] *adv* : popularmente, vulgarmente
populate ['pɑpjə,leɪt] *vt* **-lated; -lating** : poblar
population [,pɑpjə'leɪʃən] *n* : población *f*
populous ['pɑpjələs] *adj* : populoso
porcelain ['porsələn] *n* : porcelana *f*
porch ['portʃ] *n* : porche *m*
porcupine ['pɔrkjə,paɪn] *n* : puerco *m* espín
pore[1] ['por] *vi* **pored; poring 1** GAZE : mirar (con atención) **2 to pore over** : leer detenidamente, estudiar
pore[2] *n* : poro *m*
pork ['pork] *n* : carne *f* de cerdo, carne *f* de puerco
pornographic [,pɔrnə'græfɪk] *adj* : pornográfico
pornography [pɔr'nɑgrəfi] *n* : pornografía *f*
porous ['porəs] *adj* : poroso
porpoise ['pɔrpəs] *n* **1** : marsopa *f* **2** DOLPHIN : delfín *m*
porridge ['pɔrɪdʒ] *n* : sopa *f* espesa de harina, gachas *fpl*
port[1] ['port] *adj* : de babor <on the port side : a babor>
port[2] *n* **1** HARBOR : puerto *m* **2** ORIFICE : orificio *m* (de una válvula, etc.) **3** : puerto *m* (de una computadora) **4** PORTHOLE : portilla *f* **5** *or* **port side** : babor *m* (de un barco) **6** : oporto *m* (vino)
portable ['port̬əbəl] *adj* : portátil
portal ['port̬əl] *n* : portal *m*
portend [pɔr'tɛnd] *vt* : presagiar, augurar
portent ['pɔr,tɛnt] *n* : presagio *m*, augurio *m*
portentous [pɔr'tɛntəs] *adj* : profético, que presagia
porter ['portər] *n* : maletero *m*, mozo *m* (de estación)
portfolio [port'fo:li,o] *n, pl* **-lios 1** FOLDER : cartera *f* (para llevar papeles), carpeta *f* **2** : cartera *f* (diplomática) **3 investment portfolio** : cartera de inversiones
porthole ['port,ho:l] *n* : portilla *f* (de un barco), ventanilla *f* (de un avión)
portico ['port̬ɪ,ko] *n, pl* **-coes** *or* **-cos** : pórtico *m*
portion[1] ['porʃən] *vt* DISTRIBUTE : repartir
portion[2] *n* PART, SHARE : porción *f*, parte *f*
portly ['portli] *adj* **-lier; -est** : corpulento
portrait ['portrət, -,treɪt] *n* : retrato *m*
portray [por'treɪ] *vt* **1** DEPICT : representar, retratar **2** DESCRIBE : describir **3** PLAY : interpretar (un personaje)
portrayal [por'treɪəl] *n* **1** REPRESENTATION : representación *f* **2** PORTRAIT : retrato *m*
Portuguese [,portʃə'gi:z, -'gi:s] *n* **1** : portugués *m*, -guesa *f* (persona) **2** : portugués *m* (idioma) — **Portuguese** *adj*
pose[1] ['po:z] *v* **posed; posing** *vt* PRESENT : plantear (una pregunta, etc.), representar (una amenaza) — *vi* **1** : posar (para una foto, etc.) **2 to pose as** : hacerse pasar por
pose[2] *n* **1** : pose *f* <to strike a pose : asumir una pose> **2** PRETENSE : pose *f*, afectación *f*
posh ['pɑʃ] *adj* : elegante, de lujo
position[1] [pə'zɪʃən] *vt* : colocar, situar, ubicar
position[2] *n* **1** APPROACH, STANCE : posición *f*, postura *f*, planteamiento *m* **2** LOCATION : posición *f*, ubicación *f* **3** STATUS : posición *f* (en una jerarquía) **4** JOB : puesto *m*
positive ['pɑzət̬ɪv] *adj* **1** DEFINITE : incuestionable, inequívoco <positive evidence : pruebas irrefutables> **2** CONFIDENT : seguro **3** : positivo (en gramática, matemáticas, y física) **4** AFFIRMATIVE : positivo, afirmativo <a positive response : una respuesta positiva>
positively ['pɑzət̬ɪvli] *adv* **1** FAVORABLY : favorablemente **2** OPTIMISTICALLY : positivamente **3** DEFINITELY : definitivamente, en forma concluyente **4** (*used for emphasis*) : realmente, verdaderamente <it's positively awful! : ¡es verdaderamente malo!>
possess [pə'zɛs] *vt* **1** HAVE, OWN : poseer, tener **2** SEIZE : apoderarse de <he was possessed by fear : el miedo se apoderó de él>
possession [pə'zɛʃən] *n* **1** POSSESSING : posesión *f* **2** : posesión *f* (por un demonio, etc.) **3 possessions** *npl* PROPERTY : bienes *mpl*, propiedad *f*
possessive[1] [pə'zɛsɪv] *adj* **1** : posesivo (en gramática) **2** JEALOUS : posesivo, celoso
possessive[2] *n or* **possessive case** : posesivo *m*

possessor [pə'zɛsər] *n* **:** poseedor *m,* -dora *f*
possibility [ˌpɑsə'bɪləṭi] *n, pl* **-ties** **:** posibilidad *f*
possible ['pɑsəbəl] *adj* **:** posible
possibly ['pɑsəbli] *adv* **1** CONCEIVABLY **:** posiblemente <it can't possibly be true! : ¡no puede ser!> **2** PERHAPS **:** quizás, posiblemente
possum ['pɑsəm] → **opossum**
post[1] ['po:st] *vt* **1** MAIL **:** echar al correo, mandar por correo **2** ANNOUNCE **:** anunciar <they've posted the grades : han anunciado las notas> **3** AFFIX **:** fijar, poner (noticias, etc.) **4** STATION **:** apostar **5 to keep (someone) posted :** tener al corriente (a alguien)
post[2] *n* **1** POLE **:** poste *m,* palo *m* **2** STATION **:** puesto *m* **3** CAMP **:** puesto *m* (militar) **4** JOB, POSITION **:** puesto *m,* empleo *m,* cargo *m*
postage ['po:stɪdʒ] *n* **:** franqueo *m*
postal ['po:stəl] *adj* **:** postal
postcard ['po:stˌkɑrd] *n* **:** postal *f,* tarjeta *f* postal
poster ['po:stər] *n* **:** póster *m,* cartel *m,* afiche *m*
posterior[1] [pɑ'stɪriər, po-] *adj* **:** posterior
posterior[2] *n* BUTTOCKS **:** trasero *m,* nalgas *fpl,* asentaderas *fpl*
posterity [pɑ'stɛrəṭi] *n* **:** posteridad *f*
postgraduate[1] [ˌpo:st'grædʒʊət] *adj* **:** de postgrado
postgraduate[2] *n* **:** postgraduado *m,* -da *f*
posthaste ['po:st'heɪst] *adv* **:** a toda prisa
posthumous ['pɑstʃəməs] *adj* **:** póstumo **— posthumously** *adv*
postman ['po:stmən, -ˌmæn] → **mailman**
postmark[1] ['po:stˌmɑrk] *vt* **:** matasellar
postmark[2] *n* **:** matasellos *m*
postmaster ['po:stˌmæstər] *n* **:** administrador *m,* -dora *f* de correos
postmortem [ˌpo:st'mɔrṭəm] *n* **:** autopsia *f*
postnatal [ˌpo:st'neɪṭəl] *adj* **:** postnatal <postnatal depression : depresión posparto>
post office *n* **:** correo *m,* oficina *f* de correos
postoperative [ˌpo:st'ɑpərəṭɪv, -ˌreɪ-] *adj* **:** posoperatorio
postpaid [ˌpo:st'peɪd] *adv* **:** con franqueo pagado
postpone [ˌpo:st'po:n] *vt* **-poned; -poning :** postergar, aplazar, posponer
postponement [ˌpo:st'po:nmənt] *n* **:** postergación *f,* aplazamiento *m*
postscript ['po:stˌskrɪpt] *n* **:** postdata *f,* posdata *f*
postulate ['pɑstʃəˌleɪt] *vt* **-lated; -lating :** postular
posture[1] ['pɑstʃər] *vi* **-tured; -turing** **:** posar, asumir una pose
posture[2] *n* **:** postura *f*
postwar [ˌpo:st'wɔr] *adj* **:** de (la) posguerra
posy ['po:zi] *n, pl* **-sies 1** FLOWER **:** flor *f* **2** BOUQUET **:** ramo *m,* ramillete *m*
pot[1] ['pɑt] *vt* **potted; potting :** plantar (en una maceta)
pot[2] *n* **1 :** olla *f* (de cocina) **2 pots and pans :** cacharros *mpl*
potable ['po:ṭəbəl] *adj* **:** potable
potash ['pɑtˌæʃ] *n* **:** potasa *f*
potassium [pə'tæsiəm] *n* **:** potasio *m*
potato [pə'teɪṭo] *n, pl* **-toes :** papa *f,* patata *f Spain*
potato chips *npl* **:** papas *fpl* fritas (de bolsa)
potbellied ['pɑtˌbɛlid] *adj* **:** panzón, barrigón *fam*
potbelly ['pɑtˌbɛli] *n* **:** panza *f,* barriga *f*
potency ['po:tən*t*si] *n, pl* **-cies 1** POWER **:** fuerza *f,* potencia *f* **2** EFFECTIVENESS **:** eficacia *f*
potent ['po:tənt] *adj* **1** POWERFUL **:** potente, poderoso **2** EFFECTIVE **:** eficaz <a potent medicine : una medicina bien fuerte>
potential[1] [pə'tɛntʃəl] *adj* **:** potencial, posible
potential[2] *n* **1 :** potencial *m* <growth potential : potencial de crecimiento> <a child with potential : un niño que promete> **2 :** potencial *m* (eléctrico) **— potentially** *adv*
potful ['pɑtˌfʊl] *n* **:** contenido *m* de una olla <a potful of water : una olla de agua>
pothole ['pɑtˌho:l] *n* **:** bache *m*
potion ['po:ʃən] *n* **:** brebaje *m,* poción *f*
potluck ['pɑtˌlʌk] *n* **to take potluck :** tomar lo que haya
potpourri [ˌpo:pʊ'ri:] *n* **:** popurrí *m*
potshot ['pɑtˌʃɑt] *n* **1 :** tiro *m* al azar <to take potshots at : disparar al azar a> **2** CRITICISM **:** crítica *f* (hecha al azar)
potter ['pɑṭər] *n* **:** alfarero *m,* -ra *f*
pottery ['pɑṭəri] *n, pl* **-teries :** cerámica *f*
pouch ['paʊtʃ] *n* **1** BAG **:** bolsa *f* pequeña **2 :** bolsa *f* (de un animal)
poultice ['po:ltəs] *n* **:** emplasto *m,* cataplasma *f*
poultry ['po:ltri] *n* **:** aves *fpl* de corral
pounce ['paʊn*t*s] *vi* **pounced; pouncing :** abalanzarse
pound[1] ['paʊnd] *vt* **1** CRUSH **:** machacar, machucar, majar **2** BEAT **:** golpear, machacar <she pounded the lessons into them : les machacaba las lecciones> <he pounded home his point : les hizo entender su razonamiento> **—** *vi* **1** BEAT **:** palpitar (dícese del corazón) **2** RESOUND **:** retumbar, resonar **3 :** andar con paso pesado <we pounded through the mud : caminamos pesadamente por el barro>

pound² *n* **1 :** libra *f* (unidad de peso) **2 :** libra *f* (unidad monetaria) **3 dog pound :** perrera *f*
pour ['por] *vt* **1 :** echar, verter, servir (bebidas) <pour it into a pot : viértalo en una olla> **2 :** proveer con abundancia <they poured money into it : le invirtieron mucho dinero> **3 to pour out :** dar salida a <he poured out his feelings to her : se desahogó con ella> — *vi* **1** FLOW **:** manar, fluir, salir <blood was pouring from the wound : la sangre le salía de la herida> **2 it's pouring (outside) :** está lloviendo a cántaros
pout¹ ['paʊt] *vi* **:** hacer pucheros
pout² *n* **:** puchero *m*
poverty ['pɑvərt̬i] *n* **:** pobreza *f,* indigencia *f*
powder¹ ['paʊdər] *vt* **1 :** empolvar <to powder one's face : empolvarse la cara> **2** PULVERIZE **:** pulverizar
powder² *n* **:** polvo *m,* polvos *mpl*
powdery ['paʊdəri] *adj* **:** polvoriento, como polvo
power¹ ['paʊər] *vt* **:** impulsar, propulsar
power² *n* **1** AUTHORITY **:** poder *m,* autoridad *f* <executive powers : poderes ejecutivos> **2** ABILITY **:** capacidad *f,* poder *m* **3 :** potencia *f* (política) <foreign powers : potencias extranjeras> **4** STRENGTH **:** fuerza *f* **5 :** potencia *f* (en física y matemáticas)
powerful ['paʊərfəl] *adj* **:** poderoso, potente — **powerfully** *adv*
powerhouse ['paʊər,haʊs] *n* **:** persona *f* dinámica
powerless ['paʊərləs] *adj* **:** impotente
power plant *n* **:** central *f* eléctrica
powwow ['paʊ,waʊ] *n* **:** conferencia *f*
pox ['pɑks] *n, pl* **pox** *or* **poxes 1** CHICKEN POX **:** varicela *f* **2** SYPHILIS **:** sífilis *f*
practicable ['præktɪkəbəl] *adj* **:** practicable, viable, factible
practical ['præktɪkəl] *adj* **:** práctico
practicality [,præktɪ'kæləti] *n, pl* **-ties :** factibilidad *f,* viabilidad *f*
practical joke *n* **:** broma *f* (pesada)
practically ['præktɪkli] *adv* **1 :** de manera práctica **2** ALMOST **:** casi, prácticamente
practice¹ *or* **practise** ['præktəs] *vt* **-ticed** *or* **-tised; -ticing** *or* **-tising 1 :** practicar <he practiced his German on us : practicó el alemán con nosotros> <to practice politeness : practicar la cortesía> **2 :** ejercer <to practice medicine : ejercer la medicina>
practice² *n* **1** USE **:** práctica *f* <to put into practice : poner en práctica> **2** CUSTOM **:** costumbre *f* <it's a common practice here : por aquí se acostumbra hacerlo> **3** TRAINING **:** práctica *f* **4 :** ejercicio *m* (de una profesión)
practitioner [præk'tɪʃənər] *n* **1 :** profesional *mf* **2 general practitioner :** médico *m,* -ca *f*
pragmatic [præg'mæt̬ɪk] *adj* **:** pragmático — **pragmatically** *adv*
pragmatism ['prægmə,tɪzəm] *n* **:** pragmatismo
prairie ['prɛri] *n* **:** pradera *f,* llanura *f*
praise¹ ['preɪz] *vt* **praised; praising :** elogiar, alabar <to praise God : alabar a Dios>
praise² *n* **:** elogio *m,* alabanza *f*
praiseworthy ['preɪz,wərði] *adj* **:** digno de alabanza, loable
prance¹ ['prænts] *vi* **pranced; prancing 1 :** hacer cabriolas, cabriolar <a prancing horse : un caballo haciendo cabriolas> **2** SWAGGER **:** pavonearse
prance² *n* **:** cabriola *f*
prank ['præŋk] *n* **:** broma *f,* travesura *f*
prankster ['præŋkstər] *n* **:** bromista *mf*
prattle¹ ['prætəl] *vt* **-tled; -tling :** parlotear *fam,* cotorrear *fam,* balbucear (como un niño)
prattle² *n* **:** parloteo *m fam,* cotorreo *m fam,* cháchara *f fam*
prawn ['prɔn] *n* **:** langostino *m,* camarón *m,* gamba *f*
pray ['preɪ] *vt* ENTREAT **:** rogar, suplicar — *vi* **:** rezar
prayer ['prɛr] *n* **1 :** plegaria *f,* oración *f* <to say one's prayers : orar, rezar> <the Lord's Prayer : el Padrenuestro> **2** PRAYING **:** rezo *m,* oración *f* <to kneel in prayer : arrodillarse para rezar>
praying mantis → **mantis**
preach ['pri:tʃ] *vi* **:** predicar — *vt* ADVOCATE **:** abogar por <to preach cooperation : promover la cooperación>
preacher ['pri:tʃər] *n* **1 :** predicador *m,* -dora *f* **2** MINISTER **:** pastor *m,* -tora *f*
preamble ['pri:,æmbəl] *n* **:** preámbulo *m*
prearrange [,pri:ə'reɪndʒ] *vt* **-ranged; -ranging :** arreglar de antemano
precarious [pri'kæriəs] *adj* **:** precario — **precariously** *adv*
precariousness [pri'kæriəsnəs] *n* **:** precariedad *f*
precaution [pri'kɔʃən] *n* **:** precaución *f*
precautionary [pri'kɔʃə,nɛri] *adj* **:** preventivo, cautelar, precautorio
precede [pri'si:d] *v* **-ceded; -ceding :** preceder a
precedence ['prɛsədənts, prɪ'si:dənts] *n* **:** precedencia *f*
precedent ['prɛsədənt] *n* **:** precedente *m*
precept ['pri:,sɛpt] *n* **:** precepto *m*
precinct ['pri:,sɪŋkt] *n* **1** DISTRICT **:** distrito *m* (policial, electoral, etc.) **2 precincts** *npl* PREMISES **:** recinto *m,* predio *m,* límites *mpl* (de una ciudad)
precious ['prɛʃəs] *adj* **1 :** precioso <precious gems : piedras preciosas> **2** DEAR **:** querido **3** AFFECTED **:** afectado
precipice ['prɛsəpəs] *n* **:** precipicio *m*
precipitate [pri'sɪpə,teɪt] *v* **-tated; -tating** *vt* **1** HASTEN, PROVOKE **:** precipitar, provocar **2** HURL **:** arrojar **3**

: precipitar (en química) — *vi* : precipitarse (en química), condensarse (en meteorología)

precipitation [pri,sɪpə'teɪʃən] *n* **1** HASTE : precipitación *f,* prisa *f* **2** : precipitaciones *fpl* (en meteorología)

precipitous [pri'sɪpət̬əs] *adj* **1** HASTY, RASH : precipitado **2** STEEP : escarpado, empinado <a precipitous drop : una caída vertiginosa>

précis [preɪ'siː] *n, pl* **précis** [-'siːz] : resumen *m*

precise [pri'saɪs] *adj* **1** DEFINITE : preciso, explícito **2** EXACT : exacto, preciso <precise calculations : cálculos precisos> — **precisely** *adv*

preciseness [pri'saɪsnəs] *n* : precisión *f,* exactitud *f*

precision [pri'sɪʒən] *n* : precisión *f*

preclude [pri'kluːd] *vt* **-cluded; -cluding** : evitar, impedir, excluir (una posibilidad, etc.)

precocious [pri'koːʃəs] *adj* : precoz — **precociously** *adv*

precocity [pri'kɑsət̬i] *n* : precocidad *f*

preconceive [,priːkən'siːv] *vt* **-ceived; -ceiving** : preconcebir

preconception [,priːkən'sɛpʃən] *n* : idea *f* preconcebida

precondition [,priːkən'dɪʃən] *n* : precondición *f,* condición *f* previa

precook [,priː'kʊk] *vt* : precocinar

precursor [pri'kərsər] *n* : precursor *m,* -sora *f*

predator ['prɛdət̬ər] *n* : depredador *m,* -dora *f*

predatory ['prɛdə,tori] *adj* : depredador

predecessor ['prɛdə,sɛsər, 'priː-] *n* : antecesor *m,* -sora *f;* predecesor *m,* -sora *f*

predestination [pri,dɛstə'neɪʃən] *n* : predestinación *f*

predestine [pri'dɛstən] *vt* **-tined; -tining** : predestinar

predetermine [,priːdɪ'tərmən] *vt* **-mined; -mining** : predeterminar

predicament [pri'dɪkəmənt] *n* : apuro *m,* aprieto *m*

predicate¹ ['prɛdə,keɪt] *vt* **-cated; -cating 1** AFFIRM : afirmar, aseverar **2 to be predicated on** : estar basado en

predicate² ['prɛdɪkət] *n* : predicado *m*

predict [pri'dɪkt] *vt* : pronosticar, predecir

predictable [pri'dɪktəbəl] *adj* : previsible — **predictably** [-bli] *adv*

prediction [pri'dɪkʃən] *n* : pronóstico *m,* predicción *f*

predilection [,prɛdəl'ɛkʃən, ,priː-] *n* : predilección *f*

predispose [,priːdɪ'spoːz] *vt* **-posed; -posing** : predisponer

predominance [pri'dɑmənənts] *n* : predominio *m*

predominant [pri'dɑmənənt] *adj* : predominante — **predominantly** *adv*

predominate [pri'dɑmə,neɪt] *vi* **-nated; -nating 1** : predominar (en cantidad) **2** PREVAIL : prevalecer

preeminence [pri'ɛmənənts] *n* : preeminencia *f*

preeminent [pri'ɛmənənt] *adj* : preeminente

preeminently [pri'ɛmənəntli] *adv* : especialmente

preempt [pri'ɛmpt] *vt* **1** APPROPRIATE : apoderarse de, apropriarse de **2** : reemplazar (un programa de televisión, etc.) **3** FORESTALL : adelantarse a (un ataque, etc.)

preen ['priːn] *vt* : arreglarse (el pelo, las plumas, etc.)

prefabricated [,priː'fæbrə,keɪt̬əd] *adj* : prefabricado

preface ['prɛfəs] *n* : prefacio *m,* prólogo *m*

prefatory ['prɛfə,tori] *adj* : preliminar

prefer [pri'fər] *vt* **-ferred; -ferring 1** : preferir <I prefer coffee : prefiero café> **2 to prefer charges against** : presentar cargos contra

preferable ['prɛfərəbəl] *adj* : preferible

preferably ['prɛfərəbli] *adv* : preferentemente, de preferencia

preference ['prɛfrənts, 'prɛfər-] *n* : preferencia *f,* gusto *m*

preferential [,prɛfə'rɛntʃəl] *adj* : preferencial, preferente

prefigure [pri'fɪgjər] *vt* **-ured; -uring** FORESHADOW : prefigurar, anunciar

prefix ['priː,fɪks] *n* : prefijo *m*

pregnancy ['prɛgnəntsi] *n, pl* **-cies** : embarazo *m,* preñez *f*

pregnant ['prɛgnənt] *adj* **1** : embarazada (dícese de una mujer), preñada (dícese de un animal) **2** MEANINGFUL : significativo

preheat [,priː'hiːt] *vt* : precalentar

prehensile [pri'hɛntsəl, -'hɛn,saɪl] *adj* : prensil

prehistoric [,priːhɪs'tɔrɪk] *or* **prehistorical** [-ɪkəl] *adj* : prehistórico

prejudge [,priː'dʒʌdʒ] *vt* **-judged; -judging** : prejuzgar

prejudice¹ ['prɛdʒədəs] *vt* **-diced; -dicing 1** DAMAGE : perjudicar **2** BIAS : predisponer, influir en

prejudice² *n* **1** DAMAGE : perjuicio *m* (en derecho) **2** BIAS : prejuicio *m*

prelate ['prɛlət] *n* : prelado *m*

preliminary¹ [pri'lɪmə,nɛri] *adj* : preliminar

preliminary² *n, pl* **-naries 1** : preámbulo *m,* preludio *m* **2 preliminaries** *npl* : preliminares *mpl*

prelude ['prɛ,luːd, 'prɛl,juːd; 'preɪ,luːd, 'priː-] *n* : preludio *m*

premarital [,priː'mærət̬əl] *adj* : prematrimonial

premature [,priːmə'tʊr, -'tjʊr, -'tʃʊr] *adj* : prematuro — **prematurely** *adv*

premeditate [pri'mɛdə,teɪt] *vt* **-tated; -tating** : premeditar

premeditation [priˌmɛdəˈteɪʃən] *n* : premeditación *f*
premenstrual [priˈmɛn*t*strʊəl] *adj* : premenstrual
premier[1] [priˈmɪr, -ˈmjɪr; ˈpriːmiər] *adj* : principal
premier[2] *n* PRIME MINISTER : primer ministro *m,* primera ministra *f*
premiere[1] [prɪˈmjɛr, -ˈmɪr] *vt* **-miered; -miering** : estrenar
premiere[2] *n* : estreno *m*
premise [ˈprɛmɪs] *n* **1** : premisa *f* <the premise of his arguments : la premisa de sus argumentos> **2 premises** *npl* : recinto *m,* local *m*
premium [ˈpriːmiəm] *n* **1** BONUS : prima *f* **2** SURCHARGE : recargo *m* <to sell at a premium : vender (algo) muy caro> **3 insurance premium** : prima *f* (de seguros) **4 to set a premium on** : darle un gran valor (a algo)
premonition [ˌpriːməˈnɪʃən, ˌprɛmə-] *n* : presentimiento *m,* premonición *f*
prenatal [ˌpriːˈneɪt̬əl] *adj* : prenatal
preoccupation [priˌɑkjəˈpeɪʃən] *n* : preocupación *f*
preoccupied [priˈɑkjəˌpaɪd] *adj* : abstraído, ensimismado, preocupado
preoccupy [priˈɑkjəˌpaɪ] *vt* **-pied; -pying** : preocupar
preparation [ˌprɛpəˈreɪʃən] *n* **1** PREPARING : preparación *f* **2** MIXTURE : preparado *m* <a preparation for burns : un preparado para quemaduras> **3 preparations** *npl* ARRANGEMENTS : preparativos *mpl*
preparatory [priˈpærəˌtori] *adj* : preparatorio
prepare [priˈpær] *v* **-pared; -paring** *vt* : preparar — *vi* : prepararse
prepay [ˌpriːˈpeɪ] *vt* **-paid; -paying** : pagar por adelantado
preponderance [priˈpɑndərən*t*s] *n* : preponderancia *f*
preponderant [priˈpɑndərənt] *adj* : preponderante — **preponderantly** *adv*
preposition [ˌprɛpəˈzɪʃən] *n* : preposición *f*
prepositional [ˌprɛpəˈzɪʃənəl] *adj* : preposicional
prepossessing [ˌpriːpəˈzɛsɪŋ] *adj* : atractivo, agradable
preposterous [priˈpɑstərəs] *adj* : absurdo, ridículo
prerequisite[1] [priˈrɛkwəzət] *adj* : necesario, esencial
prerequisite[2] *n* : condición *f* necesario, requisito *m* previo
prerogative [priˈrɑgət̬ɪv] *n* : prerrogativa *f*
presage [ˈprɛsɪdʒ, priˈseɪdʒ] *vt* **-saged; -saging** : presagiar
preschool [ˈpriːˌskuːl] *adj* : preescolar <preschool students : estudiantes de preescolar>
prescribe [priˈskraɪb] *vt* **-scribed; -scribing 1** ORDAIN : prescribir, ordenar **2** : recetar (medicinas, etc.)
prescription [priˈskrɪpʃən] *n* : receta *f*
presence [ˈprɛzən*t*s] *n* : presencia *f*
present[1] [priˈzɛnt] *vt* **1** INTRODUCE : presentar <to present oneself : presentarse> **2** : presentar (una obra de teatro, etc.) **3** GIVE : entregar (un regalo, etc.), regalar, obsequiar **4** SHOW : presentar, ofrecer <it presents a lovely view : ofrece una vista muy linda>
present[2] [ˈprɛzənt] *adj* **1** : actual <present conditions : condiciones actuales> **2** : presente <all the students were present : todos los estudiantes estaban presentes>
present[3] [ˈprɛzənt] *n* **1** GIFT : regalo *m,* obsequio *m* **2** : presente *m* <at present : en este momento> **3** *or* **present tense** : presente *m*
presentation [ˌpriːˌzɛnˈteɪʃən, ˌprɛzən-] *n* : presentación *f* <presentation ceremony : ceremonia de entrega>
presentiment [priˈzɛntəmənt] *n* : presentimiento *m,* premonición *f*
presently [ˈprɛzəntli] *adv* **1** SOON : pronto, dentro de poco **2** NOW : actualmente, ahora
present participle *n* : participio *m* presente, participio *m* activo
preservation [ˌprɛzərˈveɪʃən] *n* : conservación *f,* preservación *f*
preservative [priˈzərvət̬ɪv] *n* : conservante *m*
preserve[1] [priˈzərv] *vt* **-served; -serving 1** PROTECT : proteger, preservar **2** : conservar (los alimentos, etc.) **3** MAINTAIN : conservar, mantener
preserve[2] *n* **1** *or* **preserves** *npl* : conserva *f* <peach preserves : duraznos en conserva> **2** : coto *m* <game preserve : coto de caza>
preside [priˈzaɪd] *vi* **-sided; -siding 1 to preside over** : presidir <he presided over the meeting : presidió la reunión> **2 to preside over** : supervisar <she presides over the department : dirige el departamento>
presidency [ˈprɛzədən*t*si] *n, pl* **-cies** : presidencia *f*
president [ˈprɛzədənt] *n* : presidente *m,* -ta *f*
presidential [ˌprɛzəˈdɛntʃəl] *adj* : presidencial
press[1] [ˈprɛs] *vt* **1** PUSH : apretar **2** SQUEEZE : apretar, prensar (frutas, flores, etc.) **3** IRON : planchar (ropa) **4** URGE : instar, apremiar <he pressed me to come : insistió en que viniera> — *vi* **1** PUSH : apretar <press hard : aprieta con fuerza> **2** CROWD : apiñarse **3** : abrirse paso <I pressed through the crowd : me abrí paso entre el gentío> **4** URGE : presionar
press[2] *n* **1** CROWD : multitud *f* **2** : imprenta *f,* prensa *f* <to go to press : entrar en prensa> **3** URGENCY : urgencia *f,* prisa *f* **4** PRINTER, PUBLISHER : imprenta *f,* editorial *f* **5 the press** : la

prensa <freedom of the press : libertad de prensa>
pressing [ˈprɛsɪŋ] *adj* URGENT : urgente
pressure[1] [ˈprɛʃər] *vt* **-sured; -suring** : presionar, apremiar
pressure[2] *n* **1** : presión *f* <to be under pressure : estar bajo presión> **2** → **blood pressure**
pressurize [ˈprɛʃəˌraɪz] *vt* **-ized; -izing** : presurizar
prestige [prɛˈstiːʒ, -ˈstiːdʒ] *n* : prestigio *m*
prestigious [prɛˈstɪdʒəs] *adj* : prestigioso
presto [ˈprɛsˌtoː] *adv* : de pronto
presumably [priˈzuːməbli] *adv* : es de suponer, supuestamente <presumably, he's guilty : supone que es culpable>
presume [priˈzuːm] *vt* **-sumed; -suming 1** ASSUME, SUPPOSE : suponer, asumir, presumir **2 to presume to** : atreverse a, osar
presumption [priˈzʌmpʃən] *n* **1** AUDACITY : atrevimiento *m,* osadía *f* **2** ASSUMPTION : presunción *f,* suposición *f*
presumptuous [priˈzʌmptʃʊəs] *adj* : descarado, atrevido
presuppose [ˌpriːsəˈpoːz] *vt* **-posed; -posing** : presuponer
pretend [priˈtɛnd] *vt* **1** CLAIM : pretender **2** FEIGN : fingir, simular — *vi* : fingir
pretense *or* **pretence** [ˈpriːˌtɛnts, priˈtɛnts] *n* **1** CLAIM : afirmación *f* (falsa), pretensión *f* **2** FEIGNING : fingimiento *m,* simulación *f* <to make a pretense of doing something : fingir hacer algo> <a pretense of order : una apariencia de orden> **3** PRETEXT : pretexto *m* <under false pretenses : con pretextos falsos, de manera fraudulenta>
pretension [priˈtɛntʃən] *n* **1** CLAIM : pretensión *f,* afirmación *f* **2** ASPIRATION : aspiración *f,* ambición *f* **3** PRETENTIOUSNESS : pretensiones *fpl*, presunción *f*
pretentious [priˈtɛntʃəs] *adj* : pretencioso
pretentiousness [priˈtɛntʃəsnəs] *n* : presunción *f,* pretenciones *fpl*
pretext [ˈpriːˌtɛkst] *n* : pretexto *m,* excusa *f*
prettily [ˈprɪtəli] *adv* : atractivamente
prettiness [ˈprɪtinəs] *n* : lindeza *f*
pretty[1] [ˈprɪti] *adv* : bastante, bien <it's pretty obvious : está bien claro> <it's pretty much the same : es más o menos igual>
pretty[2] *adj* **-tier; -est** : bonito, lindo, guapo <a pretty girl : una muchacha guapa> <what a pretty dress! : ¡qué vestido más lindo!>
pretzel [ˈprɛtsəl] *n* : galleta *f* salada (en forma de nudo)
prevail [priˈveɪl] *vi* **1** TRIUMPH : prevalecer **2** PREDOMINATE : predominar **3 to prevail upon** : persuadir, convencer <I prevailed upon her to sing : la convencí para que cantara>
prevalence [ˈprɛvələnts] *n* : preponderancia *f,* predominio *m*
prevalent [ˈprɛvələnt] *adj* **1** COMMON : común y corriente, general **2** WIDESPREAD : extendido
prevaricate [priˈværəˌkeɪt] *vi* **-cated; -cating** LIE : mentir
prevarication [priˌværəˈkeɪʃən] *n* : mentira *f*
prevent [priˈvɛnt] *vt* **1** AVOID : prevenir, evitar <steps to prevent war : medidas para evitar la guerra> **2** HINDER : impedir
preventable [priˈvɛntəbəl] *adj* : evitable
preventative [priˈvɛntət̬ɪv] → **preventive**
prevention [priˈvɛntʃən] *n* : prevención *f*
preventive [priˈvɛntɪv] *adj* : preventivo
preview [ˈpriːˌvju] *n* : preestreno *m*
previous [ˈpriːviəs] *adj* : previo, anterior <previous knowledge : conocimientos previos> <the previous day : el día anterior> <in the previous year : en el año pasado>
previously [ˈpriːviəsli] *adv* : antes
prewar [ˌpriːˈwɔr] *adj* : de antes de la guerra
prey [ˈpreɪ] *n, pl* **preys** : presa *f*
prey on *vt* **1** : cazar, alimentarse de <it preys on fish : se alimenta de peces> **2 to prey on one's mind** : hacer presa en alguien, atormentar a alguien
price[1] [ˈpraɪs] *vt* **priced; pricing** : poner un precio a
price[2] *n* : precio *m* <peace at any price : la paz a toda costa>
priceless [ˈpraɪsləs] *adj* : inestimable, inapreciable
prick[1] [ˈprɪk] *vt* **1** : pinchar **2 to prick up one's ears** : levantar las orejas — *vi* : pinchar
prick[2] *n* **1** STAB : pinchazo *m* <a prick of conscience : un remordimiento> **2** → **pricker**
pricker [ˈprɪkər] *n* THORN : espina *f*
prickle[1] [ˈprɪkəl] *vi* **-led; -ling** : sentir un cosquilleo, tener un hormigueo
prickle[2] *n* **1** : espina *f* (de una planta) **2** TINGLE : cosquilleo *m,* hormigueo *m*
prickly [ˈprɪkəli] *adj* **1** THORNY : espinoso **2** : que pica <a prickly sensation : un hormigueo>
prickly pear *n* : tuna *f*
pride[1] [ˈpraɪd] *vt* **prided; priding** : estar orgulloso de <to pride oneself on : preciarse de, enorgullecerse de>
pride[2] *n* : orgullo *m*
priest [ˈpriːst] *n* : sacerdote *m,* cura *m*
priestess [ˈpriːstɪs] *n* : sacerdotisa *f*
priesthood [ˈpriːstˌhʊd] *n* : sacerdocio *m*
priestly [ˈpriːstli] *adj* : sacerdotal
prig [ˈprɪg] *n* : mojigato *m,* -ta *f;* gazmoño *m,* -ña *f*

prim [ˈprɪm] *adj* **primmer; primmest 1** PRISSY : remilgado **2** PRUDISH : mojigato, gazmoño
primarily [praɪˈmɛrəli] *adv* : principalmente, fundamentalmente
primary[1] [ˈpraɪˌmɛri, ˈpraɪməri] *adj* **1** FIRST : primario **2** PRINCIPAL : principal **3** BASIC : fundamental
primary[2] *n, pl* **-ries** : elección *f* primaria
primary color *n* : color *m* primario
primary school → **elementary school**
primate *n* **1** [ˈpraɪˌmeɪt, -mət] : primado *m* (obispo) **2** [-ˌmeɪt] : primate *m* (animal)
prime[1] [ˈpraɪm] *vt* **primed; priming 1** : cebar <to prime a pump : cebar una bomba> **2** PREPARE : preparar (una superficie para pintar) **3** COACH : preparar (a un testigo, etc.)
prime[2] *adj* **1** CHIEF, MAIN : principal, primero **2** EXCELLENT : de primera (categoría), excelente
prime[3] *n* **the prime of one's life** : la flor de la vida
prime minister *n* : primer ministro *m*, primera ministra *f*
primer[1] [ˈprɪmər] *n* **1** READER : cartilla *f* **2** MANUAL : manual *m*
primer[2] [ˈpraɪmər] *n* **1** : cebo *m* (para explosivos) **2** : base *f* (de pintura)
primeval [praɪˈmiːvəl] *adj* : primitivo, primigenio
primitive [ˈprɪmət̬ɪv] *adj* : primitivo
primly [ˈprɪmli] *adv* : mojigatamente
primness [ˈprɪmnəs] *n* : mojigatería *f*, gazmoñería *f*
primordial [praɪˈmɔrdiəl] *adj* : primordial, fundamental
primp [ˈprɪmp] *vi* : arreglarse, acicalarse
primrose [ˈprɪmˌroːz] *n* : primavera *f*, prímula *f*
prince [ˈprɪnts] *n* : príncipe *m*
princely [ˈprɪntsli] *adj* : principesco
princess [ˈprɪntsəs, ˈprɪnˌsɛs] *n* : princesa *f*
principal[1] [ˈprɪntsəpəl] *adj* : principal — **principally** *adv*
principal[2] *n* **1** PROTAGONIST : protagonista *mf* **2** : director *m*, -tora *f* (de una escuela) **3** CAPITAL : principal *m*, capital *m* (en finanzas)
principality [ˌprɪntsəˈpæləţi] *n, pl* **-ties** : principado *m*
principle [ˈprɪntsəpəl] *n* : principio *m*
print[1] [ˈprɪnt] *vt* : imprimir (libros, etc.) — *vi* : escribir con letra de molde
print[2] *n* **1** IMPRESSION : marca *f*, huella *f*, impresión *f* **2** : texto *m* impreso <to be out of print : estar agotado> **3** LETTERING : letra *f* **4** ENGRAVING : grabado *m* **5** : copia *f* (en fotografía) **6** : estampado *m* (de tela)
printer [ˈprɪntər] *n* **1** : impresor *m*, -sora *f* (persona) **2** : impresora *f* (máquina)
printing [ˈprɪntɪŋ] *n* **1** : impresión *f* (acto) <the third printing : la tercera tirada> **2** : imprenta *f* (profesión) **3** LETTERING : letras *fpl* de molde
printing press *n* : prensa *f*
print out *vt* : imprimir (de una computadora)
printout [ˈprɪntˌaʊt] *n* : copia *f* impresa (de una computadora)
prior [ˈpraɪər] *adj* **1** : previo **2 prior to** : antes de
priority [praɪˈɔrəţi] *n, pl* **-ties** : prioridad *f*
priory [ˈpraɪəri] *n, pl* **-ries** : priorato *m*
prism [ˈprɪzəm] *n* : prisma *m*
prison [ˈprɪzən] *n* : prisión *f*, cárcel *f*
prisoner [ˈprɪzənər] *n* : preso *m*, -sa *f*; recluso *m*, -sa *f* <prisoner of war : prisionero de guerra>
prissy [ˈprɪsi] *adj* **-sier; -est** : remilgado, melindroso
pristine [ˈprɪsˌtiːn, prɪsˈ-] *adj* : puro, prístino
privacy [ˈpraɪvəsi] *n, pl* **-cies** : privacidad *f*
private[1] [ˈpraɪvət] *adj* **1** PERSONAL : privado, particular <private property : propiedad privada> **2** INDEPENDENT : privado, independiente <private studies : estudios privados> **3** SECRET : secreto **4** SECLUDED : aislado, privado — **privately** *adv*
private[2] *n* : soldado *m* raso
privateer [ˌpraɪvəˈtɪr] *n* : corsario *m*
privation [praɪˈveɪʃən] *n* : privación *f*
privilege [ˈprɪvlɪdʒ, ˈprɪvə-] *n* : privilegio *m*
privileged [ˈprɪvlɪdʒd, ˈprɪvə-] *adj* : privilegiado
privy[1] [ˈprɪvi] *adj* **to be privy to** : estar enterado de
privy[2] *n, pl* **privies** : excusado *m*, retrete *m* (exterior)
prize[1] [ˈpraɪz] *vt* **prized; prizing** : valorar, apreciar
prize[2] *adj* **1** : premiado <a prize stallion : un semental premiado> **2** OUTSTANDING : de primera, excepcional
prize[3] *n* **1** AWARD : premio *m* <third prize : el tercer premio> **2** : joya *f*, tesoro *m* <he's a real prize : es un tesoro>
prizefighter [ˈpraɪzˌfaɪţər] *n* : boxeador *m*, -dora *f* profesional
prizewinning [ˈpraɪzˌwɪnɪŋ] *adj* : premiado
pro[1] [ˈproː] *adv* : a favor
pro[2] *adj* → **professional[1]**
pro[3] *n* **1** : pro *m* <the pros and cons : los pros y los contras> **2** → **professional[2]**
probability [ˌprɑbəˈbɪləţi] *n, pl* **-ties** : probabilidad *f*
probable [ˈprɑbəbəl] *adj* : probable — **probably** [-bli] *adv*
probate[1] [ˈproːˌbeɪt] *vt* **-bated; -bating** : autenticar (un testamento)
probate[2] *n* : autenticación *f* (de un testamento)

probation [pro'beɪʃən] *n* **1** : período *m* de prueba (para un empleado, etc.) **2** : libertad *f* condicional (para un preso)
probationary [pro'beɪʃə,nɛri] *adj* : de prueba
probe[1] ['pro:b] *vt* **probed; probing 1** : sondar (en medicina y tecnología) **2** INVESTIGATE : investigar, sondear
probe[2] *n* **1** : sonda *f* (en medicina, etc.) <space probe : sonda espacial> **2** INVESTIGATION : investigación *f,* sondeo *m*
probity ['pro:bəti] *n* : probidad *f*
problem[1] ['prɑbləm] *adj* : difícil
problem[2] *n* : problema *m*
problematic [,prɑblə'mæṭɪk] *or* **problematical** [-ṭɪkəl] *adj* : problemático
proboscis [prə'bɑsɪs] *n, pl* **-cises** *also* **-cides** [-sə,di:z] : probóscide *f*
procedural [prə'si:dʒərəl] *adj* : de procedimiento
procedure [prə'si:dʒər] *n* : procedimiento *m* <administrative procedures : trámites administrativos>
proceed [pro'si:d] *vi* **1** : proceder <to proceed to do something : proceder a hacer algo> **2** CONTINUE : continuar, proseguir, seguir <he proceeded to the next phase : pasó a la segunda fase> **3** ADVANCE : avanzar <as the conference proceeded : mientras seguía avanzando la conferencia> <the road proceeds south : la calle sigue hacia el sur>
proceeding [pro'si:dɪŋ] *n* **1** PROCEDURE : procedimiento *m* **2 proceedings** *npl* EVENTS : acontecimientos *mpl* **3 proceedings** *npl* MINUTES : actas *fpl* (de una reunión, etc.)
proceeds ['pro:,si:dz] *npl* : ganancias *fpl*
process[1] ['prɑ,sɛs, 'pro:-] *vt* : procesar, tratar
process[2] *n, pl* **-cesses** ['prɑ,sɛsəz, 'pro:-, -səsəz, -sə,si:z] **1** : proceso *m* <the process of elimination : el proceso de eliminación> **2** METHOD : proceso *m,* método *m* <manufacturing processes : procesos industriales> **3** : acción *f* judicial <due process of law : el debido proceso (de la ley)> **4** SUMMONS : citación *f* **5** PROJECTION : protuberancia *f* (anatómica) **6 in the process of** : en vías de <in the process of repair : en reparaciones>
procession [prə'sɛʃən] *n* : procesión *f,* desfile *m* <a funeral procession : un cortejo fúnebre>
processional [prə'sɛʃənəl] *n* : himno *m* para una procesión
processor ['prɑ,sɛsər, 'pro:-, -səsər] *n* **1** : procesador *m* (de una computadora) **2 food processor** : procesador *m* de alimentos
proclaim [pro'kleɪm] *vt* : proclamar
proclamation [,prɑklə'meɪʃən] *n* : proclamación *f*
proclivity [pro'klɪvəṭi] *n, pl* **-ties** : proclividad *f*
procrastinate [prə'kræstə,neɪt] *vi* **-nated; -nating** : demorar, aplazar las responsabilidades
procrastination [prə,kræstə'neɪʃən] *n* : aplazamiento *m,* demora *f,* dilación *f*
procreate ['pro:kri,eɪt] *vi* **-ated; -ating** : procrear
procreation [,pro:kri'eɪʃən] *n* : procreación *f*
proctor[1] ['prɑktər] *vt* : supervisar (un examen)
proctor[2] *n* : supervisor *m,* -sora *f* (de un examen)
procure [prə'kjʊr] *vt* **-cured; -curing 1** OBTAIN : procurar, obtener **2** BRING ABOUT : provocar, lograr, conseguir
procurement [prə'kjʊrmənt] *n* : obtención *f*
prod[1] ['prɑd] *vt* **prodded; prodding 1** JAB, POKE : pinchar, golpear (con la punta de algo) **2** GOAD : incitar, estimular
prod[2] *n* **1** JAB, POKE : golpe *m* (con la punta de algo), pinchazo *m* **2** STIMULUS : estímulo *m* **3 cattle prod** : picana *f,* aguijón *m*
prodigal[1] ['prɑdɪgəl] *adj* SPENDTHRIFT : pródigo, despilfarrador, derrochador
prodigal[2] *n* : pródigo *m,* -ga *f;* derrochador *m,* -dora *f*
prodigious [prə'dɪdʒəs] *adj* **1** MARVELOUS : prodigioso, maravilloso **2** HUGE : enorme, vasto <prodigious sums : muchísimo dinero> — **prodigiously** *adv*
prodigy ['prɑdədʒi] *n, pl* **-gies** : prodigio *m* <child prodigy : niño prodigio>
produce[1] [prə'du:s, -'dju:s] *vt* **-duced; -ducing 1** EXHIBIT : presentar, mostrar **2** YIELD : producir **3** CAUSE : producir, causar **4** CREATE : producir <to produce a poem : escribir un poema> **5** : poner en escena (una obra de teatro), producir (una película)
produce[2] ['prɑ,du:s, 'pro:-, -,dju:s] *n* : productos *mpl* agrícolas
producer [prə'du:sər, -'dju:-] *n* : productor *m,* -tora *f*
product ['prɑ,dʌkt] *n* : producto *m*
production [prə'dʌkʃən] *n* : producción *f*
productive [prə'dʌktɪv] *adj* : productivo
productivity [,pro:,dʌk'tɪvəṭi, ,prɑ-] *n* : productividad *f*
profane[1] [pro'feɪn] *vt* **-faned; -faning** : profanar
profane[2] *adj* **1** SECULAR : profano **2** IRREVERENT : irreverente, impío
profanity [pro'fænəṭi] *n, pl* **-ties 1** IRREVERENCE : irreverencia *f,* impiedad *f* **2** : blasfemias *fpl,* obscenidades *fpl* <don't use profanity : no digas blasfemias>
profess [prə'fɛs] *vt* **1** DECLARE : declarar, manifestar **2** CLAIM : pretender **3** : profesar (una religión, etc.)

professedly [prə'fɛsədli] *adv* **1** OPENLY **:** declaradamente **2** ALLEGEDLY **:** supuestamente
profession [prə'fɛʃən] *n* **:** profesión *f*
professional[1] [prə'fɛʃənəl] *adj* **:** profesional — **professionally** *adv*
professional[2] *n* **:** profesional *mf*
professionalism [prə'fɛʃənəˌlizəm] *n* **:** profesionalismo *m*
professor [prə'fɛsər] *n* **:** profesor *m* (universitario), profesora *f* (universitaria); catedrático *m,* -ca *f*
proffer ['prɑfər] *vt* **-fered; -fering** **:** ofrecer, dar
proficiency [prə'fɪʃəntsi] *n* **:** competencia *f,* capacidad *f*
proficient [prə'fɪʃənt] *adj* **:** competente, experto — **proficiently** *adv*
profile ['pro:ˌfaɪl] *n* **:** perfil *m* <a portrait in profile : un retrato de perfil> <to keep a low profile : no llamar la atención, hacerse pasar desapercibido>
profit[1] ['prɑfət] *vi* **:** sacar provecho (de), beneficiarse (de)
profit[2] *n* **1** ADVANTAGE **:** provecho *m,* partido *m,* beneficio *m* **2** GAIN **:** beneficio *m,* utilidad *f,* ganancia *f* <to make a profit : sacar beneficios>
profitable ['prɑfətəbəl] *adj* **:** rentable, lucrativo — **profitably** [-bli] *adv*
profitless ['prɑfətləs] *adj* **:** infructuoso, inútil
profligate ['prɑflɪgət, -ˌgeɪt] *adj* **1** DISSOLUTE **:** disoluto, licencioso **2** SPENDTHRIFT **:** despilfarrador, derrochador, pródigo
profound [prə'faʊnd] *adj* **:** profundo
profoundly [prə'faʊndli] *adv* **:** profundamente, en profundidad
profundity [prə'fʌndəti] *n, pl* **-ties** **:** profundidad *f*
profuse [prə'fju:s] *adj* **1** COPIOUS **:** profuso, copioso **2** LAVISH **:** pródigo — **profusely** *adv*
profusion [prə'fju:ʒən] *n* **:** abundancia *f,* profusión *f*
progeny ['prɑdʒəni] *n, pl* **-nies** **:** progenie *f*
progesterone [pro'dʒɛstəˌro:n] *n* **:** progesterona *f*
prognosis [prɑg'no:sɪs] *n, pl* **-noses** [-ˌsi:z] **:** pronóstico *m* (médico)
program[1] ['pro:ˌgræm, -grəm] *vt* **-grammed** *or* **-gramed; -gramming** *or* **-graming** **:** programar
program[2] *n* **:** programa *m*
programmer ['pro:ˌgræmər] *n* **:** programador *m,* -dora *f*
programming ['pro:ˌgræmɪŋ] *n* **:** programación *f*
progress[1] [prə'grɛs] *vi* **1** PROCEED **:** progresar, adelantar **2** IMPROVE **:** mejorar
progress[2] ['prɑgrəs, -ˌgrɛs] *n* **1** ADVANCE **:** progreso *m,* adelanto *m,* avance *m* <to make progress : hacer progresos> **2** BETTERMENT **:** mejora *f,* mejoramiento *m*
progression [prə'grɛʃən] *n* **1** ADVANCE **:** avance *m* **2** SEQUENCE **:** desarrollo *m* (de eventos)
progressive [prə'grɛsɪv] *adj* **1** **:** progresista <a progressive society : una sociedad progresista> **2** **:** progresivo <a progressive disease : una enfermedad progresiva> **3** *or* **Progressive** **:** progresista (en política) **4** **:** progresivo (en gramática)
progressively [prə'grɛsɪvli] *adv* **:** progresivamente, poco a poco
prohibit [pro'hɪbət] *vt* **:** prohibir
prohibition [ˌpro:ə'bɪʃən, ˌpro:hə-] *n* **:** prohibición *f*
prohibitive [pro'hɪbətɪv] *adj* **:** prohibitivo
project[1] [prə'dʒɛkt] *vt* **1** PLAN **:** proyectar, planear **2** **:** proyectar (imágenes, misiles, etc.) — *vi* PROTRUDE **:** sobresalir, salir
project[2] ['prɑˌdʒɛkt, -dʒɪkt] *n* **:** proyecto *m,* trabajo *m* (de un estudiante) <research project : proyecto de investigación>
projectile [prə'dʒɛktəl, -ˌtaɪl] *n* **:** proyectil *m*
projection [prə'dʒɛkʃən] *n* **1** PLAN **:** plan *m,* proyección *f* **2** **:** proyección *f* (de imágenes, misiles, etc.) **3** PROTRUSION **:** saliente *m*
projector [prə'dʒɛktər] *n* **:** proyector *m*
proletarian[1] [ˌpro:lə'tɛriən] *adj* **:** proletario
proletarian[2] *n* **:** proletario *m,* -ria *f*
proletariat [ˌpro:lə'tɛriət] *n* **:** proletariado *m*
proliferate [prə'lɪfəˌreɪt] *vi* **-ated; -ating** **:** proliferar
proliferation [prəˌlɪfə'reɪʃən] *n* **:** proliferación *f*
prolific [prə'lɪfɪk] *adj* **:** prolífico
prologue ['pro:ˌlɔg] *n* **:** prólogo *m*
prolong [prə'lɔŋ] *vt* **:** prolongar
prolongation [ˌpro:ˌlɔŋ'geɪʃən] *n* **:** prolongación *f*
prom ['prɑm] *n* **:** baile *m* formal (de un colegio)
promenade[1] [ˌprɑmə'neɪd, -'nɑd] *vi* **-naded; -nading** **:** pasear, pasearse, dar un paseo
promenade[2] *n* **:** paseo *m*
prominence ['prɑmənənts] *n* **1** PROJECTION **:** prominencia *f* **2** EMINENCE **:** eminencia *f,* prestigio *m*
prominent ['prɑmənənt] *adj* **1** OUTSTANDING **:** prominente, destacado **2** PROJECTING **:** prominente, saliente
prominently ['prɑmənəntli] *adv* **:** destacadamente, prominentemente
promiscuity [ˌprɑmɪs'kju:əti] *n, pl* **-ties** **:** promiscuidad *f*
promiscuous [prə'mɪskjʊəs] *adj* **:** promiscuo — **promiscuously** *adv*
promise[1] ['prɑməs] *v* **-ised; -ising** **:** prometer

promise[2] *n* **1** : promesa *f* <he kept his promise : cumplió su promesa> **2 to show promise** : prometer

promising ['prɑməsɪŋ] *adj* : prometedor

promissory ['prɑmə,sori] *adj* : que promete <a promissory note : un pagaré>

promontory ['prɑmən,tori] *n, pl* **-ries** : promontorio *m*

promote [prə'mo:t] *vt* **-moted; -moting 1** : ascender (a un alumno o un empleado) **2** ADVERTISE : promocionar, hacerle publicidad a **3** FURTHER : promover, fomentar

promoter [prə'mo:t̬ər] *n* : promotor *m*, -tora *f;* empresario *m*, -ria *f* (en deportes)

promotion [prə'mo:ʃən] *n* **1** : ascenso *m* (de un alumno o un empleado) **2** FURTHERING : promoción *f,* fomento *m* **3** ADVERTISING : publicidad *f,* propaganda *f*

promotional [prə'mo:ʃənəl] *adj* : promocional

prompt[1] ['prɑmpt] *vt* **1** INDUCE : provocar (una cosa), inducir (a una persona) <curiosity prompted me to ask you : la curiosidad me indujo a preguntarle> **2** : apuntar (a un actor, etc.)

prompt[2] *adj* : pronto, rápido <prompt payment : pago puntual>

prompter ['prɑmptər] *n* : apuntador *m*, -dora *f* (en teatro)

promptly ['prɑmptli] *adv* : inmediatamente, rápidamente

promptness ['prɑmptnəs] *n* : prontitud *f,* rapidez *f*

prone ['pro:n] *adj* **1** LIABLE : propenso, proclive <accident-prone : propenso a los accidentes> **2** : boca abajo, decúbito prono <in a prone position : en decúbito prono>

prong ['prɔŋ] *n* : punta *f,* diente *m*

pronoun ['pro:,naʊn] *n* : pronombre *m*

pronounce [prə'naʊnts] *vt* **-nounced; -nouncing 1** : pronunciar <how do you pronounce your name? : ¿cómo se pronuncia su nombre?> **2** DECLARE : declarar **3 to pronounce sentence** : dictar sentencia, pronunciar un fallo

pronounced [prə'naʊntst] *adj* MARKED : pronunciado, marcado

pronouncement [prə'naʊntsmənt] *n* : declaración *f*

pronunciation [prə,nʌntsi'eɪʃən] *n* : pronunciación *f*

proof[1] ['pru:f] *adj* : a prueba <proof against tampering : a prueba de manipulación>

proof[2] *n* : prueba *f*

proofread ['pru:f,ri:d] *v* **-read; -reading** *vt* : corregir — *vi* : corregir pruebas

proofreader ['pru:f,ri:dər] *n* : corrector *m*, -tora *f* (de pruebas)

prop[1] ['prɑp] *vt* **propped; propping 1 to prop against** : apoyar contra **2 to prop up** SUPPORT : apoyar, apuntalar, sostener **3 to prop up** SUSTAIN : alentar (a alguien), darle ánimo (a alguien)

prop[2] *n* **1** SUPPORT : puntal *m*, apoyo *m*, soporte *m* **2** : accesorio *m* (en teatro)

propaganda [,prɑpə'gændə, ,pro:-] *n* : propaganda *f*

propagandize [,prɑpə'gæn,daɪz, ,pro:-] *v* **-dized; -dizing** *vt* : someter a propaganda — *vi* : hacer propaganda

propagate ['prɑpə,geɪt] *v* **-gated; -gating** *vi* : propagarse — *vt* : propagar

propagation [,prɑpə'geɪʃən] *n* : propagación *f*

propane ['pro:,peɪn] *n* : propano *m*

propel [prə'pɛl] *vt* **-pelled; -pelling** : impulsar, propulsar, impeler

propellant *or* **propellent** [prə'pɛlənt] *n* : propulsor *m*

propeller [prə'pɛlər] *n* : hélice *f*

propensity [prə'pɛntsət̬i] *n, pl* **-ties** : propensión *f,* tendencia *f,* inclinación *f*

proper ['prɑpər] *adj* **1** RIGHT, SUITABLE : apropiado, adecuado **2** : propio, mismo <the city proper : la propia ciudad> **3** CORRECT : correcto **4** GENTEEL : fino, refinado, cortés **5** OWN, SPECIAL : propio <proper name : nombre propio> — **properly** *adv*

property ['prɑpərt̬i] *n, pl* **-ties 1** CHARACTERISTIC : característica *f,* propiedad *f* **2** POSSESSIONS : propiedad *f* **3** BUILDING : inmueble *m* **4** LAND, LOT : terreno *m*, lote *m*, parcela *f* **5** PROP : accesorio *m* (en teatro)

prophecy ['prɑfəsi] *n, pl* **-cies** : profecía *f,* vaticinio *m*

prophesy ['prɑfə,saɪ] *v* **-sied; -sying** *vt* **1** FORETELL : profetizar (como profeta) **2** PREDICT : profetizar, predecir, vaticinar — *vi* : hacer profecías

prophet ['prɑfət] *n* : profeta *m*, profetisa *f*

prophetic [prə'fɛt̬ɪk] *or* **prophetical** [-t̬ɪkəl] *adj* : profético — **prophetically** [-t̬ɪkli] *adv*

propitiate [pro'pɪʃi,eɪt] *vt* **-ated; -ating** : propiciar

propitious [prə'pɪʃəs] *adj* : propicio

proponent [prə'po:nənt] *n* : defensor *m*, -sora *f;* partidario *m*, -ria *f*

proportion[1] [prə'porʃən] *vt* : proporcionar <well-proportioned : de buenas proporciones>

proportion[2] *n* **1** RATIO : proporción *f* **2** SYMMETRY : proporción *f,* simetría *f* <out of proportion : desproporcionado> **3** SHARE : parte *f* **4 proportions** *npl* SIZE : dimensiones *fpl*

proportional [prə'porʃənəl] *adj* : proporcional — **proportionally** *adv*

proportionate [prə'porʃənət] *adj* : proporcional — **proportionately** *adv*

proposal [prə'po:zəl] *n* **1** PROPOSITION : propuesta *f,* proposición *f* <marriage

proposal : propuesta de matrimonio> 2 PLAN : proyecto *m,* propuesta *f*

propose [prəˈpoːz] *v* **-posed; -posing** *vi* : proponer matrimonio — *vt* **1** INTEND : pensar, proponerse **2** SUGGEST : proponer

proposition [ˌprɑpəˈzɪʃən] *n* **1** PROPOSAL : proposición *f,* propuesta *f* **2** STATEMENT : proposición *f*

propound [prəˈpaʊnd] *vt* : proponer, exponer

proprietary [prəˈpraɪəˌtɛri] *adj* : propietario, patentado

proprietor [prəˈpraɪət̬ər] *n* : propietario *m,* -ria *f*

propriety [prəˈpraɪət̬i] *n, pl* **-eties 1** DECORUM : decencia *f,* decoro *m* **2 proprieties** *npl* CONVENTIONS : convenciones *fpl,* cánones *mpl* sociales

propulsion [prəˈpʌlʃən] *n* : propulsión *f*

prosaic [proˈzeɪɪk] *adj* : prosaico

proscribe [proˈskraɪb] *vt* **-scribed; -scribing** : proscribir

prose [ˈproːz] *n* : prosa *f*

prosecute [ˈprɑsɪˌkjuːt] *vt* **-cuted; -cuting 1** CARRY OUT : llevar a cabo **2** : procesar, enjuiciar <prosecuted for fraud : procesado por fraude>

prosecution [ˌprɑsɪˈkjuːʃən] *n* **1** : procesamiento *m* <the prosecution of forgers : el procesamiento de falsificadores> **2** PROSECUTORS : acusación *f* <witness for the prosecution : testigo de cargo>

prosecutor [ˈprɑsɪˌkjuːt̬ər] *n* : acusador *m,* -dora *f;* fiscal *mf*

prospect¹ [ˈprɑˌspɛkt] *vi* : prospectar (el terreno) <to prospect for gold : buscar oro>

prospect² *n* **1** VISTA : vista *f,* panorama *m* **2** POSSIBILITY : posibilidad *f* **3** OUTLOOK : perspectiva *f* **4** : posible cliente *m,* -ta *f* <a salesman looking for prospects : un vendedor buscando nuevos clientes>

prospective [prəˈspɛktɪv, ˈprɑˌspɛk-] *adj* **1** EXPECTANT : futuro <prospective mother : futura madre> **2** POTENTIAL : potencial, posible <prospective employee : posible empleado>

prospector [ˈprɑˌspɛktər, prɑˈspɛk-] *n* : prospector *m,* -tora *f;* explorador *m,* -dora *f*

prospectus [prəˈspɛktəs] *n* : prospecto *m*

prosper [ˈprɑspər] *vi* : prosperar

prosperity [prɑˈspɛrət̬i] *n* : prosperidad *f*

prosperous [ˈprɑspərəs] *adj* : próspero

prostate [ˈprɑˌsteɪt] *n* : próstata *f*

prosthesis [prɑsˈθiːsɪs, ˈprɑsθə-] *n, pl* **-theses** [-ˌsiːz] : prótesis *f*

prostitute¹ [ˈprɑstəˌtuːt, -ˌtjuːt] *vt* **-tuted; -tuting 1** : prostituir **2 to prostitute oneself** : prostituirse

prostitute² *n* : prostituto *m,* -ta *f*

prostitution [ˌprɑstəˈtuːʃən, -ˈtjuː-] *n* : prostitución *f*

prostrate¹ [ˈprɑˌstreɪt] *vt* **-trated; -trating 1** : postrar **2 to prostrate oneself** : postrarse

prostrate² *adj* : postrado

prostration [prɑˈstreɪʃən] *n* : postración *f*

protagonist [proˈtægənɪst] *n* : protagonista *mf*

protect [prəˈtɛkt] *vt* : proteger

protection [prəˈtɛkʃən] *n* : protección *f*

protective [prəˈtɛktɪv] *adj* : protector

protector [prəˈtɛktər] *n* **1** : protector *m,* -tora *f* (persona) **2** GUARD : protector *m* (aparato)

protectorate [prəˈtɛktərət] *n* : protectorado *m*

protégé [ˈproːt̬əˌʒeɪ] *n* : protegido *m,* -da *f*

protein [ˈproːˌtiːn] *n* : proteína *f*

protest¹ [proˈtɛst] *vt* **1** ASSERT : afirmar, declarar **2** : protestar <they protested the decision : protestaron (por) la decisión> — *vi* **to protest against** : protestar contra

protest² [ˈproːˌtɛst] *n* **1** DEMONSTRATION : manifestación *f* (de protesta) <a public protest : una manifestación pública> **2** COMPLAINT : queja *f,* protesta *f*

Protestant [ˈprɑt̬əstənt] *n* : protestante *mf*

Protestantism [ˈprɑt̬əstənˌtɪzəm] *n* : protestantismo *m*

protocol [ˈproːt̬əˌkɔl] *n* : protocolo *m*

proton [ˈproˌtɑn] *n* : protón *m*

protoplasm [ˈproːt̬əˌplæzəm] *n* : protoplasma *m*

prototype [ˈproːt̬əˌtaɪp] *n* : prototipo *m*

protozoan [ˌproːt̬əˈzoːən] *n* : protozoario *m,* protozoo *m*

protract [proˈtrækt] *vt* : prolongar

protractor [proˈtræktər] *n* : transportador *m* (instrumento)

protrude [proˈtruːd] *vi* **-truded; -truding** : salir, sobresalir

protrusion [proˈtruːʒən] *n* : protuberancia *f,* saliente *m*

protuberance [proˈtuːbərənts, -ˈtjuː-] *n* : protuberancia *f*

proud [ˈpraʊd] *adj* **1** HAUGHTY : altanero, orgulloso, arrogante **2** : orgulloso <she was proud of her work : estaba orgullosa de su trabajo> <too proud to beg : demasiado orgulloso para rogar> **3** GLORIOUS : glorioso — **proudly** *adv*

prove [ˈpruːv] *v* **proved; proved** *or* **proven** [ˈpruːvən]; **proving** *vt* **1** TEST : probar **2** DEMONSTRATE : probar, demostrar — *vi* : resultar <it proved effective : resultó efectivo>

Provençal [ˌproːvɑnˈsɑl, ˌprɑvən-] *n* **1** : provenzal *mf* **2** : provenzal *m* (idioma) — **Provençal** *adj*

proverb ['prɑ,vərb] *n* : proverbio *m,* refrán *m*
proverbial [prə'vərbiəl] *adj* : proverbial
provide [prə'vaɪd] *v* **-vided; -viding** *vt* **1** STIPULATE : estipular **2 to provide with** : proveer de, proporcionar — *vi* **1** : proveer <the Lord will provide : el Señor proveerá> **2 to provide for** SUPPORT : mantener **3 to provide for** ANTICIPATE : hacer previsiones para, prever
provided [prə'vaɪdəd] *or* **provided that** *conj* : con tal (de) que, siempre que
providence ['prɑvədən*t*s] *n* **1** PRUDENCE : previsión *f,* prudencia *f* **2** *or* **Providence** : providencia *f* <divine providence : la Divina Providencia> **3 Providence** GOD : Providencia *f*
provident ['prɑvədənt] *adj* **1** PRUDENT : previsor, prudente **2** FRUGAL : frugal, ahorrativo
providential [,prɑvə'dɛntʃəl] *adj* : providencial
providing that → **provided**
province ['prɑvɪn*t*s] *n* **1** : provincia *f* (de un país) <to live in the provinces : vivir en las provincias> **2** FIELD, SPHERE : campo *m,* competencia *f* <it's not in my province : no es de mi competencia>
provincial [prə'vɪntʃəl] *adj* **1** : provincial <provincial government : gobierno provincial> **2** : provinciano, pueblerino <a provincial mentality : una mentalidad provinciana>
provision[1] [prə'vɪʒən] *vt* : aprovisionar, abastecer
provision[2] *n* **1** PROVIDING : provisión *f,* suministro *m* **2** STIPULATION : condición *f,* salvedad *f,* estipulación *f* **3 provisions** *npl* : despensa *f,* víveres *mpl,* provisiones *fpl*
provisional [prə'vɪʒənəl] *adj* : provisional, provisorio — **provisionally** *adv*
proviso [prə'vaɪ,zoː] *n, pl* **-sos** *or* **-soes** : condición *f,* salvedad *f,* estipulación *f*
provocation [,prɑvə'keɪʃən] *n* : provocación *f*
provocative [prə'vɑkət̬ɪv] *adj* : provocador, provocativo <a provocative article : un artículo que hace pensar>
provoke [prə'voːk] *vt* **-voked; -voking** : provocar
prow ['praʊ] *n* : proa *f*
prowess ['praʊəs] *n* **1** VALOR : valor *m,* valentía *f* **2** SKILL : habilidad *f,* destreza *f*
prowl ['praʊl] *vi* : merodear, rondar — *vt* : rondar por
prowler ['praʊlər] *n* : merodeador *m,* -dora *f*
proximity [prɑk'sɪmət̬i] *n* : proximidad *f*
proxy ['prɑksi] *n, pl* **proxies 1** : poder *m* (de actuar en nombre de alguien) <by proxy : por poder> **2** AGENT : apoderado *m,* -da *f;* representante *mf*
prude ['pruːd] *n* : mojigato *m,* -ta *f;* gazmoño *m,* -ña *f*
prudence ['pruːdən*t*s] *n* **1** SHREWDNESS : prudencia *f,* sagacidad *f* **2** CAUTION : prudencia *f,* cautela *f* **3** THRIFTINESS : frugalidad *f*
prudent ['pruːdənt] *adj* **1** SHREWD : prudente, sagaz **2** CAUTIOUS, FARSIGHTED : prudente, previsor, precavido **3** THRIFTY : frugal, ahorrativo — **prudently** *adv*
prudery ['pruːdəri] *n, pl* **-eries** : mojigatería *f,* gazmoñería *f*
prudish ['pruːdɪʃ] *adj* : mojigato, gazmoño
prune[1] ['pruːn] *vt* **pruned; pruning** : podar (arbustos, etc.), acortar (un texto), recortar (gastos, etc.)
prune[2] *n* : ciruela *f* pasa
prurient ['prʊriənt] *adj* : lascivo
pry ['praɪ] *v* **pried; prying** *vi* : curiosear, huronear <to pry into other people's business : meterse uno en lo que no le importa> — *vt or* **to pry open** : abrir (con una palanca), apalancar
psalm ['sɑm, 'sɑlm] *n* : salmo *m*
pseudonym ['suːdə,nɪm] *n* : seudónimo *m*
psoriasis [sə'raɪəsɪs] *n* : soriasis *f,* psoriasis *f*
psyche ['saɪki] *n* : psique *f,* psiquis *f*
psychiatric [,saɪki'ætrɪk] *adj* : psiquiátrico, siquiátrico
psychiatrist [sə'kaɪətrɪst, saɪ-] *n* : psiquiatra *mf,* siquiatra *mf*
psychiatry [sə'kaɪətri, saɪ-] *n* : psiquiatría *f,* siquiatría *f*
psychic[1] ['saɪkɪk] *adj* **1** : psíquico, síquico (en psicología) **2** CLAIRVOYANT : clarividente
psychic[2] *n* : vidente *mf,* clarividente *mf*
psychoanalysis [,saɪkoə'næləsɪs] *n, pl* **-yses** : psicoanálisis *m,* sicoanálisis *m*
psychoanalyst [,saɪko'ænəlɪst] *n* : psicoanalista *mf,* sicoanalista *mf*
psychoanalytic [,saɪko,ænəl'ɪt̬ɪk] *adj* : psicoanalítico, sicoanalítico
psychoanalyze [,saɪko'ænəl,aɪz] *vt* **-lyzed; -lyzing** : psicoanalizar, sicoanalizar
psychological [,saɪkə'lɑdʒɪkəl] *adj* : psicológico, sicológico — **psychologically** *adv*
psychologist [saɪ'kɑlədʒɪst] *n* : psicólogo *m,* -ga *f;* sicólogo *m,* -ga *f*
psychology [saɪ'kɑlədʒi] *n, pl* **-gies** : psicología *f,* sicología *f*
psychopath ['saɪkə,pæθ] *n* : psicópata *mf,* sicópata *mf*
psychopathic [,saɪkə'pæθɪk] *adj* : psicopático, sicopático
psychosis [saɪ'koːsɪs] *n, pl* **-choses** [-'koː,siːz] : psicosis *f,* sicosis *f*
psychosomatic [,saɪkəsə'mæt̬ɪk] *adj* : psicosomático, sicosomático
psychotherapist [,saɪko'θɛrəpɪst] *n* : psicoterapeuta *mf,* sicoterapeuta *mf*

psychotherapy [ˌsaɪko'θɛrəpi] *n, pl* **-pies** : psicoterapia *f,* sicoterapia *f*
psychotic[1] [saɪ'kɑṭɪk] *adj* : psicótico, sicótico
psychotic[2] *n* : psicótico *m,* -ca *f;* sicótico *m,* -ca *f*
puberty ['pjuːbərṭi] *n* : pubertad *f*
pubic ['pjuːbɪk] *adj* : pubiano, púbico
public[1] ['pʌblɪk] *adj* : público — **publicly** *adv*
public[2] *n* : público *m*
publication [ˌpʌblə'keɪʃən] *n* : publicación *f*
publicist ['pʌbləsɪst] *n* : publicista *mf*
publicity [pə'blɪsəṭi] *n* : publicidad *f*
publicize ['pʌblə̆ˌsaɪz] *vt* **-cized; -cizing** : publicitar
public school *n* : escuela *f* pública
publish ['pʌblɪʃ] *vt* : publicar
publisher ['pʌblɪʃər] *n* : casa *f* editorial (compañía); editor *m,* -tora *f* (persona)
pucker[1] ['pʌkər] *vt* : fruncir, arrugar — *vi* : arrugarse
pucker[2] *n* : arruga *f,* frunce *m,* fruncido *m*
pudding ['pʊdɪŋ] *n* : budín *m,* pudín *m*
puddle ['pʌdəl] *n* : charco *m*
pudgy ['pʌdʒi] *adj* **pudgier; -est** : regordete *fam,* rechoncho *fam,* gordinflón *fam*
puerile ['pjʊrəl] *adj* : pueril
Puerto Rican[1] [ˌpwɛrṭə'riːkən, ˌporṭə-] *adj* : puertorriqueño
Puerto Rican[2] *n* : puertorriqueño *m,* -ña *f*
puff[1] ['pʌf] *vi* **1** BLOW : soplar **2** PANT : resoplar, jadear **3 to puff up** SWELL : hincharse — *vt* **1** BLOW : soplar <to puff smoke : echar humo> **2** INFLATE : inflar, hinchar <to puff out one's cheeks : inflar las mejillas>
puff[2] *n* **1** GUST : soplo *m,* ráfaga *f,* bocanada *f* (de humo) **2** DRAW : chupada *f* (a un cigarrillo) **3** SWELLING : hinchazón *f* **4 cream puff** : pastelito *m* de crema **5 powder puff** : borla *f*
puffy ['pʌfi] *adj* **puffier; -est 1** SWOLLEN : hinchado, inflado **2** SPONGY : esponjoso, suave
pug ['pʌg] *n* **1** : doguillo *m* (perro) **2** *or* **pug nose** : nariz *f* achatada
pugnacious [ˌpʌg'neɪʃəs] *adj* : pugnaz, agresivo
puke ['pjuːk] *vi* **puked; puking** : vomitar, devolver
pull[1] ['pʊl, 'pʌl] *vt* **1** DRAW, TUG : tirar de, jalar **2** EXTRACT : sacar, extraer <to pull teeth : sacar muelas> <to pull a gun on : amenazar a (alguien) con pistola> **3** TEAR : desgarrarse (un músculo, etc.) **4 to pull down** : bajar, echar abajo, derribar (un edificio) **5 to pull in** ATTRACT : atraer (una muchedumbre, etc.) <to pull in votes : conseguir votos> **6 to pull off** REMOVE : sacar, quitar **7 to pull oneself together** : calmarse, tranquilizarse **8 to pull up** RAISE : levantar, subir — *vi* **1** DRAW, TUG : tirar, jalar **2** (*indicating movement in a specific direction*) <they pulled in front of us : se nos metieron delante> <to pull to a stop : pararse> **3 to pull through** RECOVER : recobrarse, reponerse **4 to pull together** COOPERATE : trabajar juntos, cooperar
pull[2] *n* **1** TUG : tirón *m,* jalón *m* <he gave it a pull : le dio un tirón> **2** ATTRACTION : atracción *f,* fuerza *f* <the pull of gravity : la fuerza de la gravedad> **3** INFLUENCE : influencia *f* **4** HANDLE : tirador *m* (de un cajón, etc.) **5 bell pull** : cuerda *f*
pullet ['pʊlət] *n* : polla *f,* gallina *f* (joven)
pulley ['pʊli] *n, pl* **-leys** : polea *f*
pullover ['pʊlˌoːvər] *n* : suéter *m*
pulmonary ['pʊlməˌnɛri, 'pʌl-] *adj* : pulmonar
pulp ['pʌlp] *n* **1** : pulpa *f* (de una fruta, etc.) **2** MASH : papilla *f,* pasta *f* <wood pulp : pasta de papel, pulpa de papel> <to beat to a pulp : hacer papilla (a alguien)> **3** : pulpa *f* (de los dientes)
pulpit ['pʊlˌpɪt] *n* : púlpito *m*
pulsate ['pʌlˌseɪt] *vi* **-sated; -sating 1** BEAT : latir, palpitar **2** VIBRATE : vibrar
pulsation [ˌpʌl'seɪʃən] *n* : pulsación *f*
pulse ['pʌls] *n* : pulso *m*
pulverize ['pʌlvəˌraɪz] *vt* **-ized; -izing** : pulverizar
puma ['puːmə, 'pjuː-] *n* : puma *m;* león *m,* leona *f* (in various countries)
pumice ['pʌməs] *n* : piedra *f* pómez
pummel ['pʌməl] *vt* **-meled; -meling** : aporrear, apalear
pump[1] ['pʌmp] *vt* **1** : bombear <to pump water : bombear agua> <to pump (up) a tire : inflar una llanta> **2** : mover (una manivela, un pedal, etc.) de arriba abajo <to pump someone's hand : darle un fuerte apretón de manos (a alguien)> **3 to pump out** : sacar, vaciar (con una bomba)
pump[2] *n* **1** : bomba *f* <water pump : bomba de agua> **2** SHOE : zapato *m* de tacón
pumpernickel ['pʌmpərˌnɪkəl] *n* : pan *m* negro de centeno
pumpkin ['pʌmpkɪn, 'pʌŋkən] *n* : calabaza *f,* zapallo *m Arg, Chile, Peru, Uru*
pun[1] ['pʌn] *vi* **punned; punning** : hacer juegos de palabras
pun[2] *n* : juego *m* de palabras, albur *m Mex*
punch[1] ['pʌntʃ] *vt* **1** HIT : darle un puñetazo (a alguien), golpear <she punched him in the nose : le dio un puñetazo en la nariz> **2** PERFORATE : perforar (papel, etc.), picar (un boleto)
punch[2] *n* **1** : perforadora *f* <paper punch : perforadora de papel> **2** BLOW : golpe *m,* puñetazo *m* **3** : ponche *m* <fruit punch : ponche de frutas>

punctilious [pəŋk'tɪliəs] *adj* : puntilloso

punctual ['pʌŋktʃʊəl] *adj* : puntual

punctuality [ˌpʌŋktʃʊ'ælət̬i] *n* : puntualidad *f*

punctually ['pʌŋktʃʊəli] *adv* : puntualmente, a tiempo

punctuate ['pʌŋktʃʊˌeɪt] *vt* **-ated; -ating** : puntuar

punctuation [ˌpʌŋktʃʊ'eɪʃən] *n* : puntuación *f*

puncture[1] ['pʌŋktʃər] *vt* **-tured; -turing** : pinchar, punzar, perforar, ponchar *Mex*

puncture[2] *n* : pinchazo *m,* ponchadura *f Mex*

pundit ['pʌndɪt] *n* : experto *m,* -ta *f*

pungency ['pʌndʒən*t*si] *n* : acritud *f,* acrimonia *f*

pungent ['pʌndʒənt] *adj* : acre

punish ['pʌnɪʃ] *vt* : castigar

punishable ['pʌnɪʃəbəl] *adj* : punible

punishment ['pʌnɪʃmənt] *n* : castigo *m*

punitive ['pju:nət̬ɪv] *adj* : punitivo

punt[1] ['pʌnt] *vt* : impulsar (un barco) con una pértiga — *vi* : despejar (en deportes)

punt[2] *n* **1** : batea *f* (barco) **2** : patada *f* de despeje (en deportes)

puny ['pju:ni] *adj* **-nier; -est** : enclenque, endeble

pup ['pʌp] *n* : cachorro *m,* -rra *f* (de un perro); cría *f* (de otros animales)

pupa ['pju:pə] *n, pl* **-pae** [-pi, -ˌpaɪ] *or* **-pas** : crisálida *f,* pupa *f*

pupil ['pju:pəl] *n* **1** : alumno *m,* -na *f* (de colegio) **2** : pupila *f* (del ojo)

puppet ['pʌpət] *n* : títere *m,* marioneta *f*

puppy ['pʌpi] *n, pl* **-pies** : cachorro *m,* -rra *f*

purchase[1] ['pərtʃəs] *vt* **-chased; -chasing** : comprar

purchase[2] *n* **1** PURCHASING : compra *f,* adquisición *f* **2** : compra *f* <last-minute purchases : compras de última hora> **3** GRIP : agarre *m,* asidero *m* <she got a firm purchase on the wheel : se agarró bien del volante>

purchase order *n* : orden *f* de compra

pure ['pjʊr] *adj* **purer; purest** : puro

puree[1] [pjʊ'reɪ, -'ri:] *vt* **-reed; -reeing** : hacer un puré con

puree[2] *n* : puré *m*

purely ['pjʊrli] *adv* **1** WHOLLY : puramente, completamente <purely by chance : por pura casualidad> **2** SIMPLY : sencillamente, meramente

purgative ['pərgət̬ɪv] *n* : purgante *m*

purgatory ['pərgəˌtori] *n, pl* **-ries** : purgatorio *m*

purge[1] ['pərdʒ] *vt* **purged; purging** : purgar

purge[2] *n* : purga *f*

purification [ˌpjʊrəfə'keɪʃən] *n* : purificación *f*

purify ['pjʊrəˌfaɪ] *vt* **-fied; -fying** : purificar

puritan ['pjʊrətən] *n* : puritano *m,* -na *f*

puritanical [ˌpju:rə'tænɪkəl] *adj* : puritano

purity ['pjʊrət̬i] *n* : pureza *f*

purl[1] ['pərl] *v* : tejer al revés, tejer del revés

purl[2] *n* : punto *m* del revés

purloin [pər'lɔɪn, 'pərˌlɔɪn] *vt* : hurtar, robar

purple ['pərpəl] *n* : morado *m,* color *m* púrpura

purport [pər'port] *vt* : pretender <to purport to be : pretender ser>

purpose ['pərpəs] *n* **1** INTENTION : propósito *m,* intención *f* <on purpose : a propósito, adrede> **2** FUNCTION : función *f* **3** RESOLUTION : resolución *f,* determinación *f*

purposeful ['pərpəsfəl] *adj* : determinado, decidido, resuelto

purposefully ['pərpəsfəli] *adv* : decididamente, resueltamente

purposely ['pərpəsli] *adv* : intencionadamente, a propósito, adrede

purr[1] ['pər] *vi* : ronronear

purr[2] *n* : ronroneo *m*

purse[1] ['pərs] *vt* **pursed; pursing** : fruncir <to purse one's lips : fruncir la boca>

purse[2] *n* **1** HANDBAG : cartera *f,* bolso *m,* bolsa *f Mex* <a change purse : un monedero> **2** FUNDS : fondos *mpl* **3** PRIZE : premio *m*

pursue [pər'su:] *vt* **-sued; -suing 1** CHASE : perseguir **2** SEEK : buscar, tratar de encontrar <to pursue pleasure : buscar el placer> **3** FOLLOW : seguir <the road pursues a northerly course : el camino sigue hacia el norte> **4** : dedicarse a <to pursue a hobby : dedicarse a un pasatiempo>

pursuer [pər'su:ər] *n* : perseguidor *m,* -dora *f*

pursuit [pər'su:t] *n* **1** CHASE : persecución *f* **2** SEARCH : búsqueda *f,* busca *f* **3** ACTIVITY : actividad *f,* pasatiempo *m*

purveyor [pər'veɪər] *n* : proveedor *m,* -dora *f*

pus ['pʌs] *n* : pus *m*

push[1] ['pʊʃ] *vt* **1** SHOVE : empujar **2** PRESS : apretar, pulsar <push that button : aprieta ese botón> **3** PRESSURE, URGE : presionar **4 to push around** BULLY : intimidar, mangonear — *vi* **1** SHOVE : empujar **2** INSIST : insistir, presionar **3 to push off** LEAVE : marcharse, irse, largarse *fam* **4 to push on** PROCEED : seguir

push[2] *n* **1** SHOVE : empujón *m* **2** DRIVE : empuje *m,* energía *f,* dinamismo *m* **3** EFFORT : esfuerzo *m*

push-button ['pʊʃ'bʌt̬ən] *adj* : de botones

pushcart ['pʊʃˌkart] *n* : carretilla *f* de mano

pushy ['pʊʃi] *adj* **pushier; -est** : mandón, prepotente

pussy ['pʊsi] *n, pl* **pussies** : gatito *m,* -ta *f;* minino *m,* -na *f*

pussy willow *n* : sauce *m* blanco

pustule ['pʌsˌtʃuːl] *n* : pústula *f*

put ['pʊt] *v* **put; putting** *vt* **1** PLACE : poner, colocar <put it on the table : ponlo en la mesa> **2** INSERT : meter **3** (*indicating causation of a state or feeling*) : poner <it put her in a good mood : la puso de buen humor> <to put into effect : poner en práctica> **4** IMPOSE : imponer <they put a tax on it : lo gravaron con un impuesto> **5** SUBJECT : someter, poner <to put to the test : poner a prueba> <to put to death : ejecutar> **6** EXPRESS : expresar, decir <he put it simply : lo dijo sencillamente> **7** APPLY : aplicar <to put one's mind to something : proponerse hacer algo> 8 SET : poner <I put him to work : lo puse a trabajar> **9** ATTACH : dar <to put a high value on : dar gran valor a> **10** PRESENT : presentar, exponer <to put a question to someone : hacer una pregunta a alguien> — *vi* **1 to put to sea** : hacerse a la mar **2 to put up with** : aguantar, soportar

put away *vt* **1** KEEP : guardar **2** *or* **to put aside** : dejar a un lado

put by *vt* SAVE : ahorrar

put down *vt* **1** SUPPRESS : aplastar, suprimir **2** ATTRIBUTE : atribuir <she put it down to luck : lo atribuyó a la suerte>

put in *vi* : presentarse <I've put in for the position : me presenté para el puesto> — *vt* DEVOTE : dedicar (unas horas, etc.)

put off *vt* DEFER : aplazar, posponer

put on *vt* **1** ASSUME : afectar, adoptar **2** PRODUCE : presentar (una obra de teatro, etc.) **3** WEAR : ponerse

put out *vt* INCONVENIENCE : importunar, incomodar

putrefy ['pjuːtrəˌfaɪ] *v* **-fied; -fying** *vt* : pudrir — *vi* : pudrirse

putrid ['pjuːtrɪd] *adj* : putrefacto, pútrido

putter ['pʌt̬ər] *vi or* **to putter around** : entretenerse

putty[1] ['pʌt̬i] *vt* **-tied; -tying** : poner masilla en

putty[2] *n, pl* **-ties** : masilla *f*

put up *vt* **1** LODGE : alojar **2** CONTRIBUTE : contribuir, pagar

puzzle[1] ['pʌzəl] *vt* **-zled; -zling 1** CONFUSE : confundir, dejar perplejo **2 to puzzle out** : dar vueltas a, tratar de resolver

puzzle[2] *n* **1** : rompecabezas *m* <a crossword puzzle : un crucigrama> **2** MYSTERY : misterio *m,* enigma *m*

puzzlement ['pʌzəlmənt] *n* : desconcierto *m,* perplejidad *f*

pygmy[1] ['pɪgmi] *adj* : enano, pigmeo

pygmy[2] *n, pl* **-mies 1** DWARF : enano *m,* -na *f* **2 Pygmy** : pigmeo *m,* -mea *f*

pylon ['paɪˌlɑn, -lən] *n* **1** : torre *f* de conducta eléctrica **2** : pilón *m* (de un puente)

pyramid ['pɪrəˌmɪd] *n* : pirámide *f*

pyre ['paɪr] *n* : pira *f*

pyromania [ˌpaɪro'meɪniə] *n* : piromanía *f*

pyromaniac [ˌpaɪro'meɪniˌæk] *n* : pirómano *m,* -na *f*

pyrotechnics [ˌpaɪrə'tɛknɪks] *npl* **1** FIREWORKS : fuegos *mpl* artificiales **2** DISPLAY, SHOW : espectáculo *m,* muestra *f* de virtuosismo <computer pyrotechnics : efectos especiales hechos por computadora>

python ['paɪˌθɑn, -θən] *n* : pitón *f,* serpiente *f* pitón

Q

q ['kjuː] *n, pl* **q's** *or* **qs** ['kjuːz] : decimoséptima letra del alfabeto inglés

quack[1] ['kwæk] *vi* : graznar

quack[2] *n* **1** : graznido *m* (de pato) **2** CHARLATAN : curandero *m,* -ra *f;* matasanos *m fam*

quadrangle ['kwɑˌdræŋgəl] *n* **1** COURTYARD : patio *m* interior **2** → **quadrilateral**

quadrant ['kwɑdrənt] *n* : cuadrante *m*

quadrilateral [ˌkwɑdrə'læt̬ərəl] *n* : cuadrilátero *m*

quadruped ['kwɑdrəˌpɛd] *n* : cuadrúpedo *m*

quadruple [kwɑ'druːpəl, -'drʌ-; 'kwɑdrə-] *v* **-pled; -pling** *vt* : cuadruplicar — *vi* : cuadruplicarse

quadruplet [kwɑ'druːplət, -'drʌ-; 'kwɑdrə-] *-n* : cuatrillizo *m,* -za *f*

quagmire ['kwægˌmaɪr, 'kwɑg-] *n* : cenagal *m,* lodazal *m*

quail[1] ['kweɪl] *vi* : encogerse, acobardarse

quail[2] *n, pl* **quail** *or* **quails** : codorniz *f*

quaint ['kweɪnt] *adj* **1** ODD : extraño, curioso **2** PICTURESQUE : pintoresco — **quaintly** *adv*

quaintness ['kweɪntnəs] *n* : rareza *f,* lo curioso

quake[1] ['kweɪk] *vi* **quaked; quaking** : temblar

quake[2] *n* : temblor *m,* terremoto *m*

qualification [ˌkwɑləfə'keɪʃən] *n* **1** LIMITATION, RESERVATION : reserva *f,* limitación *f* <without qualification : sin reservas> **2** REQUIREMENT : requisito *m* **3 qualifications** *npl* ABILITY : aptitud *f,* capacidad *f*

qualified ['kwɑləˌfaɪd] *adj* : competente, capacitado

qualify ['kwɑləˌfaɪ] *v* **-fied; -fying** *vt* **1** : matizar <to qualify a statement

: matizar una declaración> 2 MODIFY : calificar (en gramática) 3 : habilitar <the certificate qualified her to teach : el certificado la habilitó para enseñar> — *vi* 1 : obtener el título, recibirse <to qualify as an engineer : recibirse de ingeniero> 2 : clasificarse (en deportes)

quality [ˈkwɑləṭi] *n, pl* **-ties** 1 NATURE : carácter *m* 2 ATTRIBUTE : cualidad *f* 3 GRADE : calidad *f* <of good quality : de buena calidad>

qualm [ˈkwɑm, ˈkwɑlm, ˈkwɔm] *n* 1 MISGIVING : duda *f,* aprensión *f* 2 RESERVATION, SCRUPLE : escrúpulo *m,* reparo *m*

quandary [ˈkwɑndri] *n, pl* **-ries** : dilema *m*

quantity [ˈkwɑntəṭi] *n, pl* **-ties** : cantidad *f*

quantum theory [ˈkwɑntəm] *n* : teoría *f* cuántica

quarantine[1] [ˈkwɔrənˌtiːn] *vt* **-tined; -tining** : poner en cuarentena

quarantine[2] *n* : cuarentena *f*

quarrel[1] [ˈkwɔrəl] *vi* **-reled** *or* **-relled; -reling** *or* **-relling** : pelearse, reñir, discutir

quarrel[2] *n* : pelea *f,* riña *f,* disputa *f*

quarrelsome [ˈkwɔrəlsəm] *adj* : pendenciero, discutidor

quarry[1] [ˈkwɔri] *vt* **quarried; quarrying** 1 EXTRACT : extraer, sacar <to quarry marble : extraer mármol> 2 EXCAVATE : excavar <to quarry a hill : excavar un cerro>

quarry[2] *n, pl* **quarries** 1 PREY : presa *f* 2 *or* **stone quarry** : cantera *f*

quart [ˈkwɔrt] *n* : cuarto *m* de galón

quarter[1] [ˈkwɔrṭər] *vt* 1 : dividir en cuatro partes 2 LODGE : alojar, acuartelar (tropas)

quarter[2] *n* 1 : cuarto *m,* cuarta parte *f* <a foot and a quarter : un pie y cuarto> <a quarter after three : las tres y cuarto> 2 : moneda *f* de 25 centavos, cuarto *m* de dólar 3 DISTRICT : barrio *m* <business quarter : barrio comercial> 4 PLACE : parte *f* <from all quarters : de todas partes> <at close quarters : de muy cerca> 5 MERCY : clemencia *f,* cuartel *m* <to give no quarter : no dar cuartel> 6 **quarters** *npl* LODGING : alojamiento *m,* cuartel *m* (militar)

quarterly[1] [ˈkwɔrṭərli] *adv* : cada tres meses, trimestralmente

quarterly[2] *adj* : trimestral

quarterly[3] *n, pl* **-lies** : publicación *f* trimestral

quartermaster [ˈkwɔrṭərˌmæstər] *n* : intendente *mf*

quartet [kwɔrˈtɛt] *n* : cuarteto *m*

quartz [ˈkwɔrts] *n* : cuarzo *m*

quash [ˈkwɑʃ, ˈkwɔʃ] *vt* 1 ANNUL : anular 2 QUELL : sofocar, aplastar

quaver[1] [ˈkweɪvər] *vi* 1 SHAKE : temblar <her voice was quavering : su voz temblaba> 2 TRILL : trinar

quaver[2] *n* : temblor *m* (de la voz)

quay [ˈkiː, ˈkeɪ, ˈkweɪ] *n* : muelle *m*

queasiness [ˈkwiːzinəs] *n* : mareo *m,* náusea *f*

queasy [ˈkwiːzi] *adj* **-sier; -est** : mareado

queen [ˈkwiːn] *n* : reina *f*

queenly [ˈkwiːnli] *adj* **-lier; -est** : de reina, regio

queer [ˈkwɪr] *adj* : extraño, raro, curioso — **queerly** *adv*

quell [ˈkwɛl] *vt* : aplastar, sofocar

quench [ˈkwɛntʃ] *vt* 1 EXTINGUISH : apagar, sofocar 2 SATISFY : saciar, satisfacer (la sed)

querulous [ˈkwɛrələs, ˈkwɛrjələs, ˈkwɪr-] *adj* : quejumbroso, quejoso — **querulously** *adv*

query[1] [ˈkwɪri, ˈkwɛr-] *vt* **-ried; -rying** 1 ASK : preguntar, interrogar <we queried the professor : preguntamos al profesor> 2 QUESTION : cuestionar, poner en duda <to query a matter : cuestionar un asunto>

query[2] *n, pl* **-ries** 1 QUESTION : pregunta *f* 2 DOUBT : duda *f*

quest[1] [ˈkwɛst] *v* : buscar

quest[2] *n* : búsqueda *f*

question[1] [ˈkwɛstʃən] *vt* 1 ASK : preguntar 2 DOUBT : poner en duda, cuestionar 3 INTERROGATE : interrogar — *vi* INQUIRE : inquirir, preguntar

question[2] *n* 1 QUERY : pregunta *f* 2 ISSUE : asunto *m,* problema *f,* cuestión *f* 3 POSSIBILITY : posibilidad *f* <it's out of the question : es indiscutible> 4 DOUBT : duda *f* <to call into question : poner en duda>

questionable [ˈkwɛstʃənəbəl] *adj* : dudoso, discutible, cuestionable <questionable results : resultados discutibles> <questionable motives : motivos sospechosos>

questioner [ˈkwɛstʃənər] *n* : interrogador *m,* -dora *f*

question mark *n* : signo *m* de interrogación

questionnaire [ˌkwɛstʃəˈnær] *n* : cuestionario *m*

queue[1] [ˈkjuː] *vi* **queued; queuing** *or* **queueing** : hacer cola

queue[2] *n* 1 PIGTAIL : coleta *f,* trenza *f* 2 LINE : cola *f,* fila *f*

quibble[1] [ˈkwɪbəl] *vi* **-bled; -bling** : quejarse por nimiedades, andar con sutilezas

quibble[2] *n* : objeción *f* de poca monta, queja *f* insignificante

quick[1] [ˈkwɪk] *adv* : rápidamente

quick[2] *adj* 1 RAPID : rápido 2 ALERT, CLEVER : listo, vivo, agudo 3 **a quick temper** : un genio vivo

quick[3] *n* 1 FLESH : carne *f* viva 2 **to cut someone to the quick** : herir a alguien en lo más vivo

quicken [ˈkwɪkən] *vt* 1 REVIVE : resucitar 2 AROUSE : estimular, despertar 3 HASTEN : acelerar <she quickened her pace : aceleró el paso>

quickly [ˈkwɪkli] *adv* : rápidamente, rápido, de prisa
quickness [ˈkwɪknəs] *n* : rapidez *f*
quicksand [ˈkwɪkˌsænd] *n* : arena *f* movediza
quicksilver [ˈkwɪkˌsɪlvər] *n* : mercurio *m,* azogue *m*
quick–tempered [ˈkwɪkˈtɛmpərd] *adj* : irascible, de genio vivo
quick–witted [ˈkwɪkˈwɪt̬əd] *adj* : agudo
quiet[1] *v* [ˈkwaɪət] *vt* **1** SILENCE : hacer callar, acallar **2** CALM : calmar, tranquilizar — *vi* **to quiet down** : calmarse, tranquilizarse
quiet[2] *adv* : silenciosamente <a quiet-running engine : un motor silencioso>
quiet[3] *adj* **1** CALM : tranquilo, calmoso **2** MILD : sosegado, suave <a quiet disposition : un temperamento sosegado> **3** SILENT : silencioso **4** UNOBTRUSIVE : discreto **5** SECLUDED : aislado <a quiet nook : un rincón aislado> — **quietly** *adv*
quiet[4] *n* **1** CALM : calma *f,* tranquilidad *f* **2** SILENCE : silencio *m*
quietness [ˈkwaɪətnəs] *n* : suavidad *f,* tranquilidad *f,* quietud *f*
quietude [ˈkwaɪəˌtuːd, -ˌtjuːd] *n* : quietud *f,* reposo *m*
quill [ˈkwɪl] *n* **1** SPINE : púa *f* (de un puerco espín) **2** : pluma *f* (para escribir)
quilt[1] [ˈkwɪlt] *vt* : acolchar
quilt[2] *n* : colcha *f,* edredón *m*
quince [ˈkwɪnts] *n* : membrillo *m*
quinine [ˈkwaɪˌnaɪn] *n* : quinina *f*
quintessence [kwɪnˈtɛsənts] *n* : quintaesencia *f*
quintet [kwɪnˈtɛt] *n* : quinteto *m*
quintuple [kwɪnˈtuːpəl, -ˈtjuː-, -ˈtʌ-; ˈkwɪntə-] *adj* : quíntuplo
quintuplet [kwɪnˈtʌplət, -ˈtuː-, -ˈtjuː-; ˈkwɪntə-] *n* : quintillizo *m,* -za *f*
quip[1] [ˈkwɪp] *vi* **quipped; quipping** : bromear
quip[2] *n* : ocurrencia *f,* salida *f*
quirk [ˈkwərk] *n* : peculiaridad *f,* rareza *f* <a quirk of fate : un capricho del destino>
quirky [ˈkwərki] *adj* **-kier; -est** : peculiar, raro
quit [ˈkwɪt] *v* **quit; quitting** *vt* : dejar, abandonar <to quit smoking : dejar de fumar> — *vi* **1** STOP : parar **2** RESIGN : dimitir, renunciar
quite [ˈkwaɪt] *adv* **1** COMPLETELY : completamente, totalmente **2** RATHER : bastante <quite near : bastante cerca>
quits [ˈkwɪts] *adj* **to call it quits** : quedar en paz
quitter [ˈkwɪt̬ər] *n* : derrotista *mf*
quiver[1] [ˈkwɪvər] *vi* : temblar, estremecerse, vibrar
quiver[2] *n* **1** : carcaj *m,* aljaba *f* (para flechas) **2** TREMBLING : temblor *m,* estremecimiento *m*
quixotic [kwɪkˈsɑt̬ɪk] *adj* : quijotesco
quiz[1] [ˈkwɪz] *vt* **quizzed; quizzing** : interrogar, hacer una prueba a (en el colegio)
quiz[2] *n, pl* **quizzes** : examen *m* corto, prueba *f*
quizzical [ˈkwɪzɪkəl] *adj* **1** TEASING : burlón **2** CURIOUS : curioso, interrogativo
quorum [ˈkworəm] *n* : quórum *m*
quota [ˈkwoːt̬ə] *n* : cuota *f,* cupo *m*
quotable [ˈkwoːt̬əbəl] *adj* : citable
quotation [kwoˈteɪʃən] *n* **1** CITATION : cita *f* **2** ESTIMATE : presupuesto *m,* estimación *f* **3** PRICE : cotización *f*
quotation marks *npl* : comillas *fpl*
quote[1] [ˈkwoːt] *vt* **quoted; quoting 1** CITE : citar **2** VALUE : cotizar (en finanzas)
quote[2] *n* **1** → **quotation 2 quotes** *npl* → **quotation marks**
quotient [ˈkwoːʃənt] *n* : cociente *m*

R

r [ˈɑr] *n, pl* **r's** *or* **rs** [ˈɑrz] : decimoctava letra del alfabeto inglés
rabbi [ˈræˌbaɪ] *n* : rabino *m,* -na *f*
rabbit [ˈræbət] *n, pl* **-bit** *or* **-bits** : conejo *m,* -ja *f*
rabble [ˈræbəl] *n* **1** MASSES : populacho *m* **2** RIFFRAFF : chusma *f,* gentuza *f*
rabid [ˈræbɪd] *adj* **1** : rabioso, afectado con la rabia **2** FURIOUS : furioso **3** FANATIC : fanático
rabies [ˈreɪbiːz] *ns & pl* : rabia *f*
raccoon [ræˈkuːn] *n, pl* **-coon** *or* **-coons** : mapache *m*
race[1] [ˈreɪs] *vi* **raced; racing 1** : correr, competir (en una carrera) **2** RUSH : ir a toda prisa, ir corriendo
race[2] *n* **1** CURRENT : corriente *f* (de agua) **2** : carrera *f* <dog race : carrera de perros> <the presidential race : la carrera presidential> **3** : raza *f* <the black race : la raza negra> <the human race : el género humano>
racecourse [ˈreɪsˌkors] *n* : pista *f* (de carreras)
racehorse [ˈreɪsˌhors] *n* : caballo *m* de carreras
racer [ˈreɪsər] *n* : corredor *m,* -dora *f*
racetrack [ˈreɪsˌtræk] *n* : pista *f* (de carreras)
racial [ˈreɪʃəl] *adj* : racial — **racially** *adv*
racism [ˈreɪˌsɪzəm] *n* : racismo *m*
racist [ˈreɪsɪst] *n* : racista *mf*

rack[1] ['ræk] *vt* **1 :** atormentar <racked with pain : atormentado por el dolor> **2 to rack one's brains :** devanarse los sesos

rack[2] *n* **1** SHELF, STAND **:** estante *m* <a luggage rack : un portaequipajes> <a coatrack : un perchero, una percha> **2 :** potro *m* (instrumento de la tortura)

racket ['rækət] *n* **1 :** raqueta *f* (en deportes) **2** DIN **:** estruendo *m,* bulla *f,* jaleo *m fam* **3** SWINDLE **:** estafa *f,* timo *m fam*

racketeer [ˌrækə'tɪr] *n* **:** estafador *m,* -dora *f*

raconteur [ˌræˌkɑn'tər] *n* **:** anecdotista *mf*

racy ['reɪsi] *adj* **racier; -est :** subido de tono, picante

radar ['reɪˌdɑr] *n* **:** radar *m*

radial ['reɪdiəl] *adj* **:** radial

radiance ['reɪdiənts] *n* **:** resplandor *m*

radiant ['reɪdiənt] *adj* **:** radiante — **radiantly** *adv*

radiate ['reɪdiˌeɪt] *v* **-ated; -ating** *vt* **:** irradiar, emitir <to radiate heat : irradiar el calor> <to radiate happiness : rebosar de alegría> — *vi* **1 :** irradiar **2** SPREAD **:** salir, extenderse <to radiate (out) from the center : salir del centro>

radiation [ˌreɪdi'eɪʃən] *n* **:** radiación *f*

radiator ['reɪdiˌeɪtər] *n* **:** radiador *m*

radical[1] ['rædɪkəl] *adj* **:** radical — **radically** [-kli] *adv*

radical[2] *n* **:** radical *mf*

radii → **radius**

radio[1] ['reɪdiˌoː] *v* **:** llamar por radio, transmitir por radio

radio[2] *n, pl* **-dios :** radio *m* (aparato), radio *f* (emisora, radiodifusión)

radioactive [ˌreɪdio'æktɪv] *adj* **:** radiactivo, radioactivo

radioactivity [ˌreɪdioˌæk'tɪvəti] *n, pl* **-ties :** radiactividad *f,* radioactividad *f*

radiologist [ˌreɪdi'ɑlədʒɪst] *n* **:** radiólogo *m,* -ga *f*

radiology [ˌreɪdi'ɑlədʒi] *n* **:** radiología *f*

radish ['rædɪʃ] *n* **:** rábano *m*

radium ['reɪdiəm] *n* **:** radio *m*

radius ['reɪdiəs] *n, pl* **radii** [-diˌaɪ] **:** radio *m*

radon ['reɪˌdɑn] *n* **:** radón *m*

raffle[1] ['ræfəl] *vt* **-fled; -fling :** rifar, sortear

raffle[2] *n* **:** rifa *f,* sorteo *m*

raft ['ræft] *n* **1 :** balsa *f* <rubber rafts : balsas de goma> **2** LOT, SLEW **:** montón *m* <a raft of documents : un montón de documentos>

rafter ['ræftər] *n* **:** par *m,* viga *f*

rag ['ræg] *n* **1** CLOTH **:** trapo *m* **2 rags** *npl* TATTERS **:** harapos *mpl,* andrapos *mpl*

ragamuffin ['rægəˌmʌfən] *n* **:** pilluelo *m,* -la *f*

rage[1] ['reɪdʒ] *vi* **raged; raging 1 :** estar furioso, rabiar <to fly into a rage : enfurecerse> **2 :** bramar, hacer estragos <the wind was raging : el viento bramaba> <flu raged through the school : la gripe hizo estragos por el colegio>

rage[2] *n* **1** ANGER **:** furia *f,* ira *f,* cólera *f* **2** FAD **:** moda *f,* furor *m*

ragged ['rægəd] *adj* **1** UNEVEN **:** irregular, desigual **2** TORN **:** hecho jirones **3** TATTERED **:** andrajoso, harapiento

ragout [ræ'guː] *n* **:** ragú *m,* estofado *m*

ragtime ['rægˌtaɪm] *n* **:** ragtime *m*

ragweed ['rægˌwiːd] *n* **:** ambrosía *f*

raid[1] ['reɪd] *vt* **1 :** invadir, hacer una incursión en <raided by enemy troops : invadido por tropas enemigas> **2 :** asaltar, atracar <the gang raided the warehouse : la pandilla asaltó el almacén> **3 :** allanar, hacer una redada en <police raided the house : la policía allanó la vivienda>

raid[2] *n* **1 :** invasión *f* (militar) **2 :** asalto *m* (por delincuentes) **3 :** redada *f,* allanamiento *m* (por la policía)

raider ['reɪdər] *n* **1** ATTACKER **:** asaltante *mf;* invasor *m,* -sora *f* **2 corporate raider :** tiburón *m*

rail[1] ['reɪl] *vi* **1 to rail against** REVILE **:** denostar contra **2 to rail at** SCOLD **:** regañar, reprender

rail[2] *n* **1** BAR **:** barra *f,* barrera *f* **2** HANDRAIL **:** pasamanos *m,* barandilla *f* **3** TRACK **:** riel *m* (para ferrocarriles) **4** RAILROAD **:** ferrocarril *m*

railing ['reɪlɪŋ] *n* **1 :** baranda *f* (de un balcón, etc.) **2** RAILS **:** verja *f*

raillery ['reɪləri] *n, pl* **-leries :** bromas *fpl*

railroad ['reɪlˌroːd] *n* **:** ferrocarril *m*

railway ['reɪlˌweɪ] → **railroad**

raiment ['reɪmənt] *n* **:** vestiduras *fpl*

rain[1] ['reɪn] *vi* **1 :** llover <it's raining : está lloviendo> **2 to rain down** SHOWER **:** llover <insults rained down on him : le llovieron los insultos>

rain[2] *n* **:** lluvia *f*

rainbow ['reɪnˌboː] *n* **:** arco *m* iris

raincoat ['reɪnˌkoːt] *n* **:** impermeable *m*

raindrop ['reɪnˌdrɑp] *n* **:** gota *f* de lluvia

rainfall ['reɪnˌfɔl] *n* **:** lluvia *f,* precipitación *f*

rainstorm ['reɪnˌstɔrm] *n* **:** temporal *m* (de lluvia)

rainwater ['reɪnˌwɔt̬ər] *n* **:** agua *f* de lluvia

rainy ['reɪni] *adj* **rainier; -est :** lluvioso

raise[1] ['reɪz] *vt* **raised; raising 1** LIFT **:** levantar, subir, alzar <to raise one's spirits : levantarle el ánimo a alguien> **2** ERECT **:** levantar, erigir **3** COLLECT **:** recaudar <to raise money : recaudar dinero> **4** REAR **:** criar <to raise one's children : criar uno a sus niños> **5** GROW **:** cultivar **6** INCREASE **:** aumentar, subir **7** PROMOTE **:** ascender **8** PROVOKE **:** provocar <it raised

a laugh : provocó una risa> 9 BRING UP : sacar (temas, objeciones, etc.)

raise[2] *n* : aumento *m*

raisin [ˈreɪzən] *n* : pasa *f*

raja *or* **rajah** [ˈrɑdʒə, -ˌdʒɑ, -ˌʒɑ] *n* : rajá *m*

rake[1] [ˈreɪk] *v* **raked; raking** *vt* **1** : rastrillar <to rake leaves : rastrillar las hojas> **2** SWEEP : barrer <raked with gunfire : barrido con metralla> — *vi* **to rake through** : revolver, hurgar en

rake[2] *n* **1** : rastrillo *m* **2** LIBERTINE : libertino *m,* -na *f;* calavera *m*

rakish [ˈreɪkɪʃ] *adj* **1** JAUNTY : desenvuelto, desenfadado **2** DISSOLUTE : libertino, disoluto

rally[1] [ˈræli] *v* **-lied; -lying** *vi* **1** MEET, UNITE : reunirse, congregarse **2** RECOVER : recuperarse — *vt* **1** ASSEMBLE : reunir (tropas, etc.) **2** RECOVER : recobrar (la fuerza, el ánimo, etc.)

rally[2] *n, pl* **-lies** : reunión *f,* mitin *m,* manifestación *f*

ram[1] [ˈræm] *v* **rammed; ramming** *vt* **1** DRIVE : hincar, clavar <he rammed it into the ground : lo hincó en la tierra> **2** SMASH : estrellar, embestir — *vi* COLLIDE : chocar (contra), estrellarse

ram[2] *n* **1** : carnero *m* (animal) **2 battering ram** : ariete *m*

RAM [ˈræm] *n* : RAM *f*

ramble[1] [ˈræmbəl] *vi* **-bled; -bling 1** WANDER : pasear, deambular **2 to ramble on** : divagar, perder el hilo **3** SPREAD : trepar (dícese de una planta)

ramble[2] *n* : paseo *m,* excursión *f*

rambler [ˈræmblər] *n* **1** WALKER : excursionista *mf* **2** ROSE : rosa *f* trepadora

rambunctious [ræmˈbʌŋkʃəs] *adj* UNRULY : alborotado

ramification [ˌræməfəˈkeɪʃən] *n* : ramificación *f*

ramify [ˈræməˌfaɪ] *vi* **-fied; -fying** : ramificarse

ramp [ˈræmp] *n* : rampa *f*

rampage[1] [ˈræmˌpeɪdʒ, ræmˈpeɪdʒ] *vi* **-paged; -paging** : andar arrasando todo, correr destrozando

rampage[2] [ˈræmˌpeɪdʒ] *n* : alboroto *m,* frenesí *m* (de violencia)

rampant [ˈræmpənt] *adj* : desenfrenado

rampart [ˈræmˌpɑrt] *n* : terraplén *m,* muralla *f*

ramrod [ˈræmˌrɑd] *n* : baqueta *f*

ramshackle [ˈræmˌʃækəl] *adj* : destartalado

ran → **run**

ranch [ˈræntʃ] *n* **1** : hacienda *f,* rancho *m,* finca *f* ganadera **2** FARM : granja *f* <fruit ranch : granja de frutas>

rancher [ˈræntʃər] *n* : estanciero *m,* -ra *f;* ranchero *m,* -ra *f*

rancid [ˈræntsɪd] *adj* : rancio

rancor [ˈræŋkər] *n* : rencor *m*

random [ˈrændəm] *adj* **1** : fortuito, aleatorio **2 at ~** : al azar — **randomly** *adv*

rang → **ring**

range[1] [ˈreɪndʒ] *v* **ranged; ranging** *vt* ARRANGE : alinear, ordenar, arreglar — *vi* **1** ROAM : deambular <to range through the town : deambular por el pueblo> **2** EXTEND : extenderse <the results range widely : los resultados se extienden mucho> **3** VARY : variar <discounts range from 20% to 40% : los descuentos varían entre 20% y 40%>

range[2] *n* **1** ROW : fila *f,* hilera *f* <a mountain range : una cordillera> **2** GRASSLAND : pradera *f,* pampa *f* **3** STOVE : cocina *f* **4** VARIETY : variedad *f,* gama *f* **5** SPHERE : ámbito *m,* esfera *f,* campo *m* **6** REACH : registro *m* (de la voz), alcance *m* (de un arma de fuego) **7 shooting range** : campo *m* de tiro

ranger [ˈreɪndʒər] *n or* **forest ranger** : guardabosque *mf*

rangy [ˈreɪndʒi] *adj* **rangier; -est** : alto y delgado

rank[1] [ˈræŋk] *vt* **1** RANGE : alinear, ordenar, poner en fila **2** CLASSIFY : clasificar — *vi* **1 to rank above** : ser superior a **2 to rank among** : encontrarse entre, figurar entre

rank[2] *adj* **1** LUXURIANT : lozano, exuberante (dícese de una planta) **2** SMELLY : fétido, maloliente **3** OUTRIGHT : completo, absoluto <a rank injustice : una injusticia manifiesta>

rank[3] *n* **1** LINE, ROW : fila *f* <to close ranks : cerrar filas> **2** GRADE, POSITION : grado *m,* rango *m* (militar) <to pull rank : abusar de su autoridad> **3** CLASS : categoría *f,* clase *f* **4 ranks** *npl* : soldados *mpl* rasos

rank and file *n* **1** RANKS : soldados *mpl* rasos **2** : bases *fpl* (de un partido, etc.)

rankle [ˈræŋkəl] *v* **-kled; -kling** *vi* : doler — *vt* : irritar, herir

ransack [ˈrænˌsæk] *vt* : revolver, desvalijar, registrar de arriba abajo

ransom[1] [ˈræntsəm] *vt* : rescatar, pagar un rescate por

ransom[2] *n* : rescate *m*

rant [ˈrænt] *vi or* **to rant and rave** : despotricar, desvariar

rap[1] [ˈræp] *v* **rapped; rapping** *vt* **1** KNOCK : golpetear, dar un golpe en **2** CRITICIZE : criticar — *vi* **1** CHAT : charlar, cotorrear *fam* **2** KNOCK : dar un golpe

rap[2] *n* **1** BLOW, KNOCK : golpe *m,* golpecito *m* **2** CHAT : charla *f* **3** *or* **rap music** : rap *m* **4 to take the rap** : pagar el pato *fam*

rapacious [rəˈpeɪʃəs] *adj* **1** GREEDY : avaricioso, codicioso **2** PREDATORY : rapaz, de rapiña **3** RAVENOUS : voraz

rape[1] [ˈreɪp] *vt* **raped; raping** : violar

rape[2] *n* **1** : colza *f* (planta) **2** : violación *f* (de una persona)

rapid [ˈræpɪd] *adj* : rápido — **rapidly** *adv*
rapidity [rəˈpɪdəṭi] *n* : rapidez *f*
rapids [ˈræpɪdz] *npl* : rápidos *mpl*
rapier [ˈreɪpiər] *n* : estoque *m*
rapist [ˈreɪpɪst] *n* : violador *m*, -dora *f*
rapport [ræˈpor] *n* : relación *f* armoniosa, entendimiento *m*
rapt [ˈræpt] *adj* : absorto, embelesado
rapture [ˈræptʃər] *n* : éxtasis *m*
rapturous [ˈræptʃərəs] *adj* : extasiado, embelesado
rare [ˈrær] *adj* **rarer; rarest 1** RAREFIED : enrarecido **2** FINE : excelente, excepcional <a rare talent : un talento excepcional> **3** UNCOMMON : raro, poco común **4** : poco cocido (dícese de la carne)
rarefy [ˈrærəˌfaɪ] *vt* **-fied; -fying** : rarificar, enrarecer
rarely [ˈrærli] *adv* SELDOM : pocas veces, rara vez
raring [ˈrærən, -ɪŋ] *adj* : lleno de entusiasmo, con muchas ganas
rarity [ˈrærəṭi] *n, pl* **-ties** : rareza *f*
rascal [ˈræskəl] *n* : pillo *m*, -lla *f*; pícaro *m*, -ra *f*
rash¹ [ˈræʃ] *adj* : imprudente, precipitado — **rashly** *adv*
rash² *n* : sarpullido *m*, erupción *f*
rashness [ˈræʃnəs] *n* : precipitación *f*, impetuosidad *f*
rasp¹ [ˈræsp] *vt* **1** SCRAPE : raspar, escofinar **2 to rasp out** : decir en voz áspera
rasp² *n* : escofina *f*
raspberry [ˈræzˌbɛri] *n, pl* **-ries** : frambuesa *f*
rat [ˈræt] *n* : rata *f*
ratchet [ˈrætʃət] *n* : trinquete *m*
rate¹ [ˈreɪt] *vt* **rated; rating 1** CONSIDER, REGARD : considerar, estimar **2** DESERVE : merecer
rate² *n* **1** PACE, SPEED : velocidad *f*, ritmo *m* <at this rate : a este paso> **2** : índice *m*, tasa *f* <birth rate : índice de natalidad> <interest rate : tasa de interés> **3** CHARGE, PRICE : precio *m*, tarifa *f*
rather [ˈræðər, ˈrʌ-, ˈrɑ-] *adv* **1** (*indicating preference*) <she would rather stay in the house : preferiría quedarse en casa> <I'd rather not : mejor que no> **2** (*indicating preciseness*) <my father, or rather my stepfather : mi padre, o mejor dicho mi padrastro> **3** INSTEAD : sino que, más que, al contrario <I'm not pleased; rather I'm disappointed : no estoy satisfecho, sino desilusionado> **4** SOMEWHAT : algo, un tanto <rather strange : un poco extraño> **5** QUITE : bastante <rather difficult : bastante difícil>
ratification [ˌræṭəfəˈkeɪʃən] *n* : ratificación *f*
ratify [ˈræṭəˌfaɪ] *vt* **-fied; -fying** : ratificar
rating [ˈreɪṭɪŋ] *n* **1** STANDING : clasificación *f*, posición *f* **2 ratings** *npl* : índice *m* de audiencia
ratio [ˈreɪʃio] *n, pl* **-tios** : proporción *f*, relación *f*
ration¹ [ˈræʃən, ˈreɪʃən] *vt* : racionar
ration² *n* **1** : ración *f* **2 rations** *npl* PROVISIONS : víveres *mpl*
rational [ˈræʃənəl] *adj* : racional, razonable, lógico — **rationally** *adv*
rationale [ˌræʃəˈnæl] *n* **1** EXPLANATION : explicación *f* **2** BASIS : base *f*, razones *fpl*
rationalization [ˌræʃənələˈzeɪʃən] *n* : racionalización *f*
rationalize [ˈræʃənəˌlaɪz] *vt* **-ized; -izing** : racionalizar
rattle¹ [ˈræṭəl] *v* **-tled; -tling** *vi* **1** CLATTER : traquetear, hacer ruido **2 to rattle on** CHATTER : parlotear *fam* — *vt* **1** : hacer sonar, agitar <the wind rattled the door : el viento sacudió la puerta> **2** DISCONCERT, WORRY : desconcertar, poner nervioso **3 to rattle off** : despachar, recitar, decir de corrido
rattle² *n* **1** CLATTER : traqueteo *m*, ruido *m* **2** *or* **baby's rattle** : sonajero *m* **3** : cascabel *m* (de una culebra)
rattler [ˈræṭələr] → **rattlesnake**
rattlesnake [ˈræṭəlˌsneɪk] *n* : serpiente *f* de cascabel
ratty [ˈræṭi] *adj* **rattier; -est** : raído, andrajoso
raucous [ˈrɔkəs] *adj* **1** HOARSE : ronco **2** BOISTEROUS : escandaloso, bullicioso — **raucously** *adv*
ravage¹ [ˈrævɪdʒ] *vt* **-aged; -aging** : devastar, arrasar, hacer estragos
ravage² *n* : destrozo *m*, destrucción *f* <the ravages of war : los estragos de la guerra>
rave [ˈreɪv] *vi* **raved; raving 1** : delirar, desvariar <to rave like a maniac : desvariar como un loco> **2 to rave about** : hablar con entusiasmo sobre, entusiasmarse por
ravel [ˈrævəl] *v* **-eled** *or* **-elled; -eling** *or* **-elling** *vt* UNRAVEL : desenredar, desenmarañar — *vi* FRAY : deshilacharse
raven [ˈreɪvən] *n* : cuervo *m*
ravenous [ˈrævənəs] *adj* : hambriento, voraz — **ravenously** *adv*
ravine [rəˈviːn] *n* : barranco *m*, quebrada *f*
ravish [ˈrævɪʃ] *vt* **1** PLUNDER : saquear **2** ENCHANT : embelesar, cautivar, encantar
raw [ˈrɔ] *adj* **rawer; rawest 1** UNCOOKED : crudo **2** UNTREATED : sin tratar, sin refinar, puro <raw data : datos en bruto> <raw materials : materias primas> **3** INEXPERIENCED : novato, inexperto **4** OPEN : abierto, en carne viva <a raw sore : una llaga abierta> **5** : frío y húmedo <a raw day : un día crudo> **6** UNFAIR : injusto <a raw deal : un trato injusto, una injusticia>

rawhide ['rɔ,haɪd] *n* : cuero *m* sin curtir

ray ['reɪ] *n* **1** : rayo *m* (de la luz, etc.) <a ray of hope : un resquicio de esperanza> **2** : raya *f* (pez)

rayon ['reɪ,ɑn] *n* : rayón *m*

raze ['reɪz] *vt* **razed; razing** : arrasar, demoler

razor ['reɪzər] *n* **1 straight razor** : navaja *f* (de afeitar) **2 safety razor** : maquinilla *f* de afeitar, rastrillo *m Mex*

reach[1] ['ri:tʃ] *vt* **1** EXTEND : extender, alargar <to reach out one's hand : extender la mano> **2** : alcanzar <I couldn't reach the apple : no pude alcanzar la manzana> **3** : llegar a, llegar hasta <the shadow reached the wall : la sombra llegó hasta la pared> **4** CONTACT : contactar, ponerse en contacto con — *vi* **1** *or* **to reach out** : extender la mano **2** STRETCH : extenderse **3 to reach for** : tratar de agarrar

reach[2] *n* : alcance *m,* extensión *f*

react [ri'ækt] *vi* : reaccionar

reaction [ri'ækʃən] *n* : reacción *f*

reactionary[1] [ri'ækʃə,nɛri] *adj* : reaccionario

reactionary[2] *n, pl* **-ries** : reaccionario *m,* -ria *f*

reactor [ri'æktər] *n* : reactor *m* <nuclear reactor : reactor nuclear>

read[1] ['ri:d] *v* **read** ['rɛd]; **reading** *vt* **1** : leer <to read a story : leer un cuento> **2** INTERPRET : interpretar <it can be read two ways : se puede interpretar de dos maneras> **3** : decir, poner <the sign read "No smoking" : el letrero decía "No Fumar"> **4** : marcar <the thermometer reads 70° : el termómetro marca 70°> — *vi* **1** : leer <he can read : sabe leer> **2** SAY : decir <the list reads as follows : la lista dice lo siguiente>

read[2] *n* **to be a good read** : ser una lectura amena

readable ['ri:dəbəl] *adj* : legible — **readably** [-bli] *adv*

reader ['ri:dər] *n* : lector *m,* -tora *f*

readily ['rɛdəli] *adv* **1** WILLINGLY : de buena gana, con gusto **2** EASILY : fácilmente, con facilidad

readiness ['rɛdinəs] *n* **1** WILLINGNESS : buena disposición *f* **2 to be in readiness** : estar preparado

reading ['ri:dɪŋ] *n* : lectura *f*

readjust [,ri:ə'dʒʌst] *vt* : reajustar — *vi* : volverse a adaptar

readjustment [,ri:ə'dʒʌstmənt] *n* : reajuste *m*

ready[1] ['rɛdi] *vt* **readied; readying** : preparar

ready[2] *adj* **readier; -est 1** PREPARED : listo, preparado **2** WILLING : dispuesto **3** : a punto de <ready to cry : a punto de llorar> **4** AVAILABLE : disponible <ready cash : efectivo> **5** QUICK : vivo, agudo <a ready wit : un ingenio agudo>

ready–made ['rɛdi'meɪd] *adj* : preparado, confeccionado

reaffirm [,ri:ə'fərm] *vt* : reafirmar

real[1] ['ri:l] *adv* VERY : muy <we had a real good time : lo pasamos muy bien>

real[2] *adj* **1** : inmobilario <real property : bien inmueble, bien raíz> **2** GENUINE : auténtico, genuino **3** ACTUAL, TRUE : real, verdadero <a real friend : un verdadero amigo> **4 for real** SERIOUSLY : de veras, de verdad

real estate *n* : propiedad *f* inmobiliaria, bienes *mpl* raíces

realign [,ri:ə'laɪn] *vt* : realinear

realignment [,ri:ə'laɪnmənt] *n* : realineamiento *m*

realism ['ri:ə,lɪzəm] *n* : realismo *m*

realist ['ri:əlɪst] *n* : realista *mf*

realistic [,ri:ə'lɪstɪk] *adj* : realista

realistically [,ri:ə'lɪstɪkli] *adv* : de manera realista

reality [ri'æləti] *n, pl* **-ties** : realidad *f*

realization [,ri:ələ'zeɪʃən] *n* : realización *f*

realize ['ri:ə,laɪz] *vt* **-ized; -izing 1** ACCOMPLISH : realizar, llevar a cabo **2** GAIN : obtener, realizar, sacar <to realize a profit : realizar beneficios> **3** UNDERSTAND : darse cuenta de, saber

really ['rɪli, 'ri:-] *adv* **1** ACTUALLY : de verdad, en realidad **2** TRULY : verdaderamente, realmente **3** FRANKLY : francamente, en serio

realm ['rɛlm] *n* **1** KINGDOM : reino *m* **2** SPHERE : esfera *f,* campo *m*

ream[1] ['ri:m] *vt* : escariar

ream[2] *n* **1** : resma *f* (de papel) **2 reams** *npl* LOADS : montones *mpl*

reap ['ri:p] *v* : cosechar

reaper ['ri:pər] *n* **1** : cosechador *m,* -dora *f* (persona) **2** : cosechadora *f* (máquina)

reappear [,ri:ə'pɪr] *vi* : reaparecer

reappearance [,ri:ə'pɪrən*t*s] *n* : reaparición *f*

rear[1] ['rɪr] *vt* **1** LIFT, RAISE : levantar **2** BREED, BRING UP : criar — *vi or* **to rear up** : encabritarse

rear[2] *adj* : trasero, posterior, de atrás

rear[3] *n* **1** BACK : parte *f* de atrás <to bring up the rear : cerrar la marcha> **2** *or* **rear end** : trasero *m*

rear admiral *n* : contraalmirante *mf*

rearrange [,ri:ə'reɪndʒ] *vt* **-ranged; -ranging** : colocar de otra manera, volver a arreglar, reorganizar

reason[1] ['ri:zən] *vt* THINK : pensar — *vi* : razonar <I can't reason with her : no puedo razonar con ella>

reason[2] *n* **1** CAUSE, GROUND : razón *f,* motivo *m* <the reason for his trip : el motivo de su viaje> <for this reason : por esta razón, por lo cual> <the reason why : la razón por la cual, el porqué> **2** SENSE : razón *f* <to lose

one's reason : perder los sesos> <to listen to reason : avenirse a razones>

reasonable [ˈriːzənəbəl] *adj* **1** SENSIBLE : razonable **2** INEXPENSIVE : barato, económico

reasonably [ˈriːzənəbli] *adv* **1** SENSIBLY : razonablemente **2** FAIRLY : bastante

reasoning [ˈriːzənɪŋ] *n* : razonamiento *m,* raciocinio *m,* argumentos *mpl*

reassess [ˌriːəˈsɛs] *vt* : revaluar, reconsiderar

reassurance [ˌriːəˈʃʊrən*t*s] *n* : consuelo *m,* palabras *fpl* alentadoras

reassure [ˌriːəˈʃʊr] *vt* **-sured; -suring** : tranquilizar

reawaken [ˌriːəˈweɪkən] *vt* : volver a despertar, reavivar

rebate [ˈriːˌbeɪt] *n* : reembolso *m,* devolución *f*

rebel[1] [rɪˈbɛl] *vi* **-belled; -belling** : rebelarse, sublevarse

rebel[2] [ˈrɛbəl] *adj* : rebelde

rebel[3] [ˈrɛbəl] *n* : rebelde *mf*

rebellion [rɪˈbɛljən] *n* : rebelión *f*

rebellious [rɪˈbɛljəs] *adj* : rebelde

rebelliousness [rɪˈbɛljəsnəs] *n* : rebeldía *f*

rebirth [ˌriːˈbərθ] *n* : renacimiento *m*

rebound[1] [ˈriːˌbaʊnd, ˌriːˈbaʊnd] *vi* : rebotar

rebound[2] [ˈriːˌbaʊnd] *n* : rebote *m*

rebuff[1] [riˈbʌf] *vt* : desairar, rechazar

rebuff[2] *n* : desaire *m,* rechazo *m*

rebuild [ˌriːˈbɪld] *vt* **-built** [-ˈbɪlt]; **-building** : reconstruir

rebuke[1] [riˈbjuːk] *vt* **-buked; -buking** : reprender, regañar

rebuke[2] *n* : reprimenda *f,* reproche *m*

rebut [riˈbʌt] *vt* **-butted; -butting** : rebatir, refutar

rebuttal [riˈbʌtəl] *n* : refutación *f*

recalcitrant [riˈkælsətrənt] *adj* : recalcitrante

recall[1] [riˈkɔl] *vt* **1** : llamar, retirar <recalled to active duty : llamado al servicio activo> **2** REMEMBER : recordar, acordarse de **3** REVOKE : revocar

recall[2] [riˈkɔl, ˈriːˌkɔl] *n* **1** : retirada *f* (de personas o mercancías) **2** MEMORY : memoria *f* <to have total recall : poder recordar todo>

recant [riˈkænt] *vt* : retractarse de — *vi* : retractarse, renegar

recapitulate [ˌriːkəˈpɪtʃəˌleɪt] *v* **-lated; -lating** : resumir, recapitular

recapture [ˌriːˈkæptʃər] *vt* **-tured; -turing 1** REGAIN : volver a tomar, reconquistar **2** RELIVE : revivir (la juventud, etc.)

recede [riˈsiːd] *vi* **-ceded; -ceding 1** WITHDRAW : retirarse, retroceder **2** FADE : desvanecerse, alejarse **3** SLANT : inclinarse **4 to have a receding hairline** : tener entradas

receipt [riˈsiːt] *n* **1** : recibo *m* **2 receipts** *npl* : ingresos *mpl*, entradas *fpl*

receivable [riˈsiːvəbəl] *adj* **accounts receivable** : cuentas por cobrar

receive [riˈsiːv] *vt* **-ceived; -ceiving 1** GET : recibir <to receive a letter : recibir una carta> <to receive a blow : recibir un golpe> **2** WELCOME : acoger, recibir <to receive guests : tener invitados> **3** : recibir, captar (señales de radio)

receiver [riˈsiːvər] *n* **1** : receptor *m,* -tora *f* (en futbol americano) **2** : receptor *m* (de radio o televisión) **3 telephone receiver** : auricular *m*

recent [ˈriːsənt] *adj* : reciente — **recently** *adv*

receptacle [riˈsɛptɪkəl] *n* : receptáculo *m,* recipiente *m*

reception [riˈsɛpʃən] *n* : recepción *f*

receptionist [riˈsɛpʃənɪst] *n* : recepcionista *mf*

receptive [riˈsɛptɪv] *adj* : receptivo

receptivity [ˌriːˌsɛpˈtɪvət̬i] *n* : receptividad *f*

recess[1] [ˈriːˌsɛs, rɪˈsɛs] *vt* **1** : poner en un hueco <recessed lighting : iluminación empotrada> **2** ADJOURN : suspender, levantar

recess[2] *n* **1** ALCOVE : hueco *m,* nicho *m* **2** BREAK : receso *m,* descanso *m,* recreo *m* (en el colegio)

recession [riˈsɛʃən] *n* : recesión *f,* depresión *f* económica

recessive [riˈsɛsɪv] *adj* : recesivo

recharge [ˌriːˈtʃɑrdʒ] *vt* **-charged; -charging** : recargar

rechargeable [ˌriːˈtʃɑrdʒəbəl] *adj* : recargable

recipe [ˈrɛsəˌpiː] *n* : receta *f*

recipient [riˈsɪpiənt] *n* : recipiente *mf*

reciprocal [riˈsɪprəkəl] *adj* : recíproco

reciprocate [riˈsɪprəˌkeɪt] *vi* **-cated; -cating** : reciprocar

reciprocity [ˌrɛsəˈprɑsət̬i] *n, pl* **-ties** : reciprocidad *f*

recital [riˈsaɪt̬əl] *n* **1** PERFORMANCE : recital *m* **2** ENUMERATION : relato *m,* enumeración *f*

recitation [ˌrɛsəˈteɪʃən] *n* : recitación *f*

recite [riˈsaɪt] *vt* **-cited; -citing 1** : recitar (un poema, etc.) **2** RECOUNT : narrar, relatar, enumerar

reckless [ˈrɛkləs] *adj* : imprudente, temerario — **recklessly** *adv*

recklessness [ˈrɛkləsnəs] *n* : imprudencia *f,* temeridad *f*

reckon [ˈrɛkən] *vt* **1** CALCULATE : calcular, contar **2** CONSIDER : considerar

reckoning [ˈrɛkənɪŋ] *n* **1** CALCULATION : cálculo *m* **2** SETTLEMENT : ajuste *m* de cuentas <day of reckoning : día del juicio final>

reclaim [riˈkleɪm] *vt* **1** : ganar, sanear <to reclaim marshy land : sanear las tierras pantanosas> **2** RECOVER : recobrar, reciclar <to reclaim old tires : reciclar llantas desechadas> **3** REGAIN : reclamar, recuperar <to reclaim one's rights : reclamar uno sus derechos>

recline [ri'klaɪn] *vi* **-clined; -clining 1** LEAN : reclinarse **2** REPOSE : recostarse
recluse ['rɛ,klu:s, ri'klu:s] *n* : solitario *m,* -ria *f*
recognition [,rɛkɪg'nɪʃən] *n* : reconocimiento *m*
recognizable ['rɛkəg,naɪzəbəl] *adj* : reconocible
recognize ['rɛkɪg,naɪz] *vt* **-nized; -nizing** : reconocer
recoil[1] [ri'kɔɪl] *vi* : retroceder, dar un culatazo
recoil[2] ['ri:,kɔɪl, ri'-] *n* : retroceso *m,* culatazo *m*
recollect [,rɛkə'lɛkt] *v* : recordar
recollection [,rɛkə'lɛkʃən] *n* : recuerdo *m*
recommend [,rɛkə'mɛnd] *vt* **1** : recomendar <she recommended the medicine : recomendó la medicina> **2** ADVISE, COUNSEL : aconsejar, recomendar
recommendation [,rɛkəmən'deɪʃən] *n* : recomendación *f*
recompense[1] ['rɛkəm,pɛnts] *vt* **-pensed; -pensing** : indemnizar, recompensar
recompense[2] *n* : indemnización *f,* compensación *f*
reconcile ['rɛkən,saɪl] *v* **-ciled; -ciling** *vt* **1** : reconciliar (personas), conciliar (ideas, etc.) **2 to reconcile oneself to** : resignarse a — *vi* MAKE UP : reconciliarse, hacer las paces
reconciliation [,rɛkən,sɪli'eɪʃən] *n* : reconciliación *f* (con personas), conciliación *f* (con ideas, etc.)
recondite ['rɛkən,daɪt, ri'kɑn-] *adj* : recóndito, abstruso
recondition [,ri:kən'dɪʃən] *vt* : reacondicionar
reconnaissance [ri'kɑnəzənts, -sənts] *n* : reconocimiento *m*
reconnoiter *or* **reconnoitre** [,ri:kə'nɔɪtər, ,rɛkə-] *v* **-tered** *or* **-tred; -tering** *or* **-tring** *vt* : reconocer — *vi* : hacer un reconocimiento
reconsider [,ri:kən'sɪdər] *vt* : reconsiderar, repensar
reconsideration [,ri:kən,sɪdə'reɪʃən] *n* : reconsideración *f*
reconstruct [,ri:kən'strʌkt] *vt* : reconstruir
record[1] [ri'kɔrd] *vt* **1** WRITE DOWN : anotar, apuntar **2** REGISTER : registrar, hacer constar **3** INDICATE : marcar (una temperatura, etc.) **4** TAPE : grabar
record[2] ['rɛkərd] *n* **1** DOCUMENT : registro *m,* documento *m* oficial **2** HISTORY : historial *m* <a good academic record : un buen historial académico> <criminal record : antecedentes penales> **3** : récord *m* <the world record : el récord mundial> **4** : disco *m* (de música, etc.) <to make a record : grabar un disco>
recorder [ri'kɔrdər] *n* **1** : flauta *f* dulce (instrumento de viento) **2 tape recorder** : grabadora *f*
recount[1] [ri'kaʊnt] *vt* **1** NARRATE : narrar, relatar **2** : volver a contar (votos, etc.)
recount[2] ['ri:,kaʊnt, ,ri'-] *n* : recuento *m*
recoup [ri'ku:p] *vt* : recuperar, recobrar
recourse ['ri:,kors, ri'-] *n* : recurso *m* <to have recourse to : recurrir a>
recover [ri'kʌvər] *vt* REGAIN : recobrar — *vi* RECUPERATE : recuperarse
recovery [ri'kʌvəri] *n, pl* **-eries** : recuperación *f*
re–create [,ri:kri'eɪt] *vt* **-ated; -ating** : recrear
recreation [,rɛkri'eɪʃən] *n* : recreo *m,* esparcimiento *m,* diversión *f*
recreational [,rɛkri'eɪʃənəl] *adj* : recreativo, de recreo
recrimination [ri,krɪmə'neɪʃən] *n* : recriminación *f*
recruit[1] [ri'kru:t] *vt* : reclutar
recruit[2] *n* : recluta *mf*
recruitment [ri'kru:tmənt] *n* : reclutamiento *m,* alistamiento *m*
rectal ['rɛktəl] *adj* : rectal
rectangle ['rɛk,tæŋgəl] *n* : rectángulo *m*
rectangular [rɛk'tæŋgjələr] *adj* : rectangular
rectify ['rɛktə,faɪ] *vt* **-fied; -fying** : rectificar
rectitude ['rɛktə,tu:d, -,tju:d] *n* : rectitud *f*
rector ['rɛktər] *n* : rector *m,* -tora *f*
rectory ['rɛktəri] *n, pl* **-ries** : rectoría *f*
rectum ['rɛktəm] *n, pl* **-tums** *or* **-ta** [-tə] : recto *m*
recuperate [ri'ku:pə,reɪt, -'kju:-] *v* **-ated; -ating** *vt* : recuperar — *vi* : recuperarse, restablecerse
recuperation [ri,ku:pə'reɪʃən, -,kju:-] *n* : recuperación *f*
recur [ri'kər] *vi* **-curred; -curring** : volver a ocurrir, volver a producirse, repetirse
recurrence [ri'kərənts] *n* : repetición *f,* reaparición *f*
recurrent [ri'kərənt] *adj* : recurrente, que se repite
recycle [ri'saɪkəl] *vt* **-cled; -cling** : reciclar
red[1] ['rɛd] *adj* **1** : rojo, colorado <to be red in the face : ponerse colorado> <to have red hair : ser pelirrojo> **2** COMMUNIST : rojo, comunista
red[2] *n* **1** : rojo *m,* colorado *m* **2 Red** COMMUNIST : comunista *mf*
red blood cell *n* : glóbulo *m* rojo
red–blooded ['rɛd'blʌdəd] *adj* : vigoroso
redcap ['rɛd,kæp] → **porter**
redden ['rɛdən] *vt* : enrojecer — *vi* BLUSH : enrojecerse, ruborizarse
reddish ['rɛdɪʃ] *adj* : rojizo
redecorate [,ri:'dɛkə,reɪt] *vt* **-rated; -rating** : renovar, pintar de nuevo

redeem [ri'di:m] *vt* **1** RESCUE, SAVE : rescatar, salvar **2** : desempeñar <she redeemed it from the pawnshop : lo desempeñó de la casa de empeños> **3** : redimir (en religión) **4** : canjear, vender <to redeem coupons : canjear cupones>
redeemer [ri'di:mər] *n* : redentor *m*, -tora *f*
redemption [ri'dɛmpʃən] *n* : redención *f*
redesign [ˌri:di'zaɪn] *vt* : rediseñar
red–handed ['rɛd'hændəd] *adj* : con las manos en la masa
redhead ['rɛdˌhɛd] *n* : pelirrojo *m*, -ja *f*
red–hot ['rɛd'hɑt] *adj* **1** : candente **2** ARDENT : ardiente, fervoroso
rediscover [ˌri:di'skʌvər] *vt* : redescubrir
redistribute [ˌri:di'strɪˌbju:t] *vt* **-uted; -uting** : redistribuir
red–letter ['rɛd'lɛt̬ər] *adj* **red–letter day** : día *m* memorable
redness ['rɛdnəs] *n* : rojez *f*
redo [ˌri:'du:] *vt* **-did** [-dɪd]; **-done** [-'dʌn]; **-doing 1** : hacer de nuevo **2** → **redecorate**
redolence ['rɛdələnts] *n* : fragancia *f*
redolent ['rɛdələnt] *adj* **1** FRAGRANT : fragante, oloroso **2** SUGGESTIVE : evocador
redouble [ri'dʌbəl] *vt* **-bled; -bling** : redoblar, intensificar (esfuerzos, etc.)
redoubtable [rɛ'daʊt̬əbəl] *adj* : temible
redress [ri'drɛs] *vt* : reparar, remediar, enmendar
red snapper *n* : pargo *m*, huachinango *m Mex*
red tape *n* : papeleo *m*
reduce [ri'du:s, -'dju:s] *v* **-duced; -ducing** *vt* **1** LESSEN : reducir, disminuir, rebajar (precios) **2** DEMOTE : bajar de categoría, degradar **3 to be reduced to** : verse rebajado a, verse forzado a **4 to reduce someone to tears** : hacer llorar a alguien — *vi* SLIM : adelgazar
reduction [ri'dʌkʃən] *n* : reducción *f*, rebaja *f*
redundant [ri'dʌndənt] *adj* : superfluo, redundante
redwood ['rɛdˌwʊd] *n* : secoya *f*
reed ['ri:d] *n* **1** : caña *f*, carrizo *m*, junco *m* **2** : lengüeta *f* (para instrumentos de viento)
reef ['ri:f] *n* : arrecife *m*, escollo *m*
reek[1] ['ri:k] *vi* : apestar
reek[2] *n* : hedor *m*
reel ['ri:l] *vt* **1 to reel in** : enrollar, sacar (un pez) del agua **2 to reel off** : recitar de un tirón — *vi* **1** SPIN, WHIRL : girar, dar vueltas **2** STAGGER : tambalearse
reel[2] *n* **1** : carrete *m* (de pescar etc.), rollo *m* (de fotos) **2** : baile *m* escocés **3** STAGGER : tambaleo *m*
reelect [ˌri:ɪ'lɛkt] *vt* : reelegir
reenact [ˌri:ɪ'nækt] *vt* : representar de nuevo, reconstruir
reenter [ˌri:'ɛntər] *vt* : volver a entrar
reestablish [ˌri:ɪ'stæblɪʃ] *vt* : restablecer
reevaluate [ˌri:ɪ'væljʊˌeɪt] *vt* **-ated; -ating** : revaluar
reevaluation [ˌri:ɪˌvæljʊ'eɪʃən] *n* : revaluación *f*
reexamine [ˌri:ɪg'zæmən, -ɛg-] *vt* **-ined; -ining** : volver a examinar, reexaminar
refer [ri'fər] *v* **-ferred; -ferring** *vt* DIRECT, SEND : remitir, enviar <to refer a patient to a specialist : enviar a un paciente a un especialista> — *vi* **to refer to** MENTION : referirse a, aludir a
referee[1] [ˌrɛfə'ri:] *v* **-eed; -eeing** : arbitrar
referee[2] *n* : árbitro *m*, -tra *f*; réferi *mf*
reference ['rɛfrənts, 'rɛfə-] *n* **1** ALLUSION : referencia *f*, alusión *f* <to make reference to : hacer referencia a> **2** CONSULTATION : consulta *f* <for future reference : para futuras consultas> **3** *or* **reference book** : libro *m* de consulta **4** TESTIMONIAL : informe *m*, referencia *f*, recomendación *f*
referendum [ˌrɛfə'rɛndəm] *n*, *pl* **-da** [-də] *or* **-dums** : referéndum *m*
refill[1] [ˌri:'fɪl] *vt* : rellenar
refill[2] ['ri:ˌfɪl] *n* : recambio *m*
refinance [ˌri:'faɪˌnænts] *vt* **-nanced; -nancing** : refinanciar
refine [ri'faɪn] *vt* **-fined; -fining 1** : refinar (azúcar, petróleo, etc.) **2** PERFECT : perfeccionar, pulir
refined [ri'faɪnd] *adj* **1** : refinado (dícese del azúcar, etc.) **2** CULTURED : culto, educado, refinado
refinement [ri'faɪnmənt] *n* : refinamiento *m*, fineza *f*, finura *f*
refinery [ri'faɪnəri] *n*, *pl* **-eries** : refinería *f*
reflect [ri'flɛkt] *vt* **1** : reflejar <to reflect light : reflejar la luz> <happiness is reflected in her face : la felicidad se refleja en su cara> **2 to reflect that** : pensar que, considerar que — *vi* **1 to reflect on** : reflexionar sobre **2 to reflect badly on** : desacreditar, perjudicar
reflection [ri'flɛkʃən] *n* **1** : reflexión *f*, reflejo *m* (de la luz, de imágenes, etc.) **2** THOUGHT : reflexión *f*, meditación *f*
reflective [ri'flɛktɪv] *adj* **1** THOUGHTFUL : reflexivo, pensativo **2** : reflectante (en física)
reflector [ri'flɛktər] *n* : reflector *m*
reflex ['ri:ˌflɛks] *n* : reflejo *m*
reflexive [ri'flɛksɪv] *adj* : reflexivo <a reflexive verb : un verbo reflexivo>
reform[1] [ri'fɔrm] *vt* : reformar — *vi* : reformarse
reform[2] *n* : reforma *f*
reformation [ˌrɛfər'meɪʃən] *n* : reforma *f* <the Reformation : la Reforma>

reformatory [ri'fɔrmə,tori] *n, pl* **-ries** : reformatorio *m*
reformer [ri'fɔrmər] *n* : reformador *m,* -dora *f*
refract [ri'frækt] *vt* : refractar — *vi* : refractarse
refraction [ri'frækʃən] *n* : refracción *f*
refractory [ri'fræktəri] *adj* OBSTINATE : refractario, obstinado
refrain¹ [ri'freɪn] *vi* **to refrain from** : abstenerse de
refrain² *n* : estribillo *m* (en música)
refresh [ri'frɛʃ] *vt* : refrescar <to refresh one's memory : refrescarle la memoria a uno>
refreshment [ri'frɛʃmənt] *n* **1** : refresco *m* **2 refreshments** *npl* : refrigerio *m*
refrigerate [ri'frɪdʒə,reɪt] *vt* **-ated; -ating** : refrigerar
refrigeration [ri,frɪdʒə'reɪʃən] *n* : refrigeración *f*
refrigerator [ri'frɪdʒə,reɪtər] *n* : refrigerador *mf,* nevera *f*
refuel [ri:'fju:əl] *v* **-eled** *or* **-elled; -eling** *or* **-elling** *vi* : repostar — *vt* : llenar de combustible
refuge ['rɛ,fju:dʒ] *n* : refugio *m*
refugee [,rɛfjʊ'dʒi:] *n* : refugiado *m,* -da *f*
refund¹ [ri'fʌnd, 'ri:,fʌnd] *vt* : reembolsar, devolver
refund² ['ri:,fʌnd] *n* : reembolso *m,* devolución *f*
refundable [ri'fʌndəbəl] *adj* : reembolsable
refurbish [ri'fərbɪʃ] *vt* : renovar, restaurar
refusal [ri'fju:zəl] *n* : negativa *f,* rechazo *m,* denegación *f* (de una petición)
refuse¹ [ri'fju:z] *vt* **-fused; -fusing 1** REJECT : rechazar, rehusar **2** DENY : negar, rehusar, denegar <to refuse permission : negar el permiso> **3 to refuse to** : negarse a
refuse² ['rɛ,fju:s, -,fju:z] *n* : basura *f,* desechos *mpl,* desperdicios *m*
refutation [,rɛfjʊ'teɪʃən] *n* : refutación *f*
refute [ri'fju:t] *vt* **-futed; -futing 1** DENY : desmentir, negar **2** DISPROVE : refutar, rebatir
regain [ri:'geɪn] *vt* **1** RECOVER : recuperar, recobrar **2** REACH : alcanzar <to regain the shore : llegar a la tierra>
regal ['ri:gəl] *adj* : real, regio
regale [ri'geɪl] *vt* **-galed; -galing 1** ENTERTAIN : agasajar, entretener **2** AMUSE, DELIGHT : deleitar, divertir
regalia [ri'geɪljə] *npl* : ropaje *m,* vestiduras *fpl,* adornos *mpl*
regard¹ [ri'gɑrd] *vt* **1** OBSERVE : observar, mirar **2** HEED : tener en cuenta, hacer caso de **3** CONSIDER : considerar **4** RESPECT : respetar <highly regarded : muy estimado> **5 as regards** : en cuanto a, en lo que se refiere a
regard² *n* **1** CONSIDERATION : consideración *f* **2** ESTEEM : respeto *m,* estima *f* **3** PARTICULAR : aspecto *m,* sentido *m* <in this regard : en este sentido> **4 regards** *npl* : saludos *mpl,* recuerdos *mpl* **5 with regard to** : con relación a, con respecto a
regarding [ri'gɑrdɪŋ] *prep* : con respecto a, en cuanto a
regardless [ri'gɑrdləs] *adv* : a pesar de todo
regardless of *prep* : a pesar de, sin tener en cuenta <regardless of our mistakes : a pesar de nuestros errores> <regardless of age : sin tener en cuenta la edad>
regenerate [ri'dʒɛnə,reɪt] *v* **-ated; -ating** *vt* : regenerar — *vi* : regenerarse
regeneration [ri,dʒɛnə'reɪʃən] *n* : regeneración *f*
regent ['ri:dʒənt] *n* **1** RULER : regente *mf* **2** : miembro *m* de la junta directiva (de una universidad, etc.)
regime [reɪ'ʒi:m, rɪ-] *n* : régimen *m*
regimen ['rɛdʒəmən] *n* : régimen *m*
regiment¹ ['rɛdʒə,mɛnt] *vt* : reglamentar
regiment² ['rɛdʒəmənt] *n* : regimiento *m*
region ['ri:dʒən] *n* **1** : región *f* **2 in the region of** : alrededor de
regional ['ri:dʒənəl] *adj* : regional — **regionally** *adv*
register¹ ['rɛdʒəstər] *vt* **1** RECORD : registrar, inscribir **2** INDICATE : marcar (temperatura, medidas, etc.) **3** REVEAL : manifestar, acusar <to register surprise : acusar sorpresa> **4** : certificar (correo) — *vi* ENROLL : inscribirse, matricularse
register² *n* : registro *m*
registrar ['rɛdʒə,strɑr] *n* : registrador *m,* -dora *f* oficial
registration [,rɛdʒə'streɪʃən] *n* **1** REGISTERING : inscripción *f,* matriculación *f,* registro *m* **2** *or* **registration number** : matrícula *f,* número *m* de matrícula
registry ['rɛdʒəstri] *n, pl* **-tries** : registro *m*
regress [ri'grɛs] *vi* : retroceder
regression [ri'grɛʃən] *n* : retroceso *m,* regresión *f*
regressive [ri'grɛsɪv] *adj* : regresivo
regret¹ [ri'grɛt] *vt* **-gretted; -gretting** : arrepentirse de, lamentar <he regrets nothing : no se arrepiente de nada> <I regret to tell you : lamento decirle>
regret² *n* **1** REMORSE : arrepentimiento *m,* remordimientos *mpl* **2** SADNESS : pesar *m,* dolor *m* **3 regrets** *npl* : excusas *fpl* <to send one's regrets : excusarse>
regretful [ri'grɛtfəl] *adj* : arrepentido, pesaroso
regretfully [ri'grɛtfəli] *adv* : con pesar
regrettable [ri'grɛtəbəl] *adj* : lamentable — **regrettably** [-bli] *adv*

regular[1] ['rɛgjələr] *adj* **1** NORMAL : regular, normal, usual **2** STEADY : uniforme, regular <a regular pace : un paso regular> **3** CUSTOMARY, HABITUAL : habitual, de costumbre
regular[2] *n* : cliente *mf* habitual
regularity [ˌrɛgjə'lærəṭi] *n, pl* **-ties** : regularidad *f*
regularly ['rɛgjələrli] *adv* : regularmente, con regularidad
regulate ['rɛgjəˌleɪt] *vt* **-lated; -lating** : regular
regulation [ˌrɛgjə'leɪʃən] *n* **1** REGULATING : regulación *f* **2** RULE : regla *f*, reglamento *m*, norma *f* <safety regulations : reglas de seguridad>
regurgitate [ri'gərdʒəˌteɪt] *v* **-tated; -tating** : regurgitar, vomitar
rehabilitate [ˌriːhə'bɪləˌteɪt, ˌriːə-] *vt* **-tated; -tating** : rehabilitar
rehabilitation [ˌriːhəˌbɪlə'teɪʃən, ˌriːə-] *n* : rehabilitación *f*
rehearsal [ri'hərsəl] *n* : ensayo *m*
rehearse [ri'hərs] *v* **-hearsed; -hearsing** : ensayar
reheat [ˌriː'hiːt] *vt* : recalentar
reign[1] ['reɪn] *vi* **1** RULE : reinar **2** PREVAIL : reinar, predominar
reign[2] *n* : reinado *m*
reimburse [ˌriːəm'bərs] *vt* **-bursed; -bursing** : reembolsar
reimbursement [ˌriːəm'bərsmənt] *n* : reembolso *m*
rein[1] ['reɪn] *vt* : refrenar (un caballo)
rein[2] *n* **1** : rienda *f* <to give free rein to : dar rienda suelta a> **2** CHECK : control *m* <to keep a tight rein on : llevar un estricto control de>
reincarnation [ˌriːɪnˌkɑr'neɪʃən] *n* : reencarnación *f*
reindeer ['reɪnˌdɪr] *n* : reno *m*
reinforce [ˌriːən'fors] *vt* **-forced; -forcing** : reforzar
reinforcement [ˌriːən'forsmənt] *n* : refuerzo *m*
reinstate [ˌriːən'steɪt] *vt* **-stated; -stating** **1** : reintegrar, restituir (una persona) **2** RESTORE : restablecer (un servicio, etc.)
reinstatement [ˌriːən'steɪtmənt] *n* : reintegración *f*, restitución *f*, restablecimiento *m*
reiterate [ri'ɪṭəˌreɪt] *vt* **-ated; -ating** : reiterar, repetir
reiteration [riˌɪṭə'reɪʃən] *n* : reiteración *f*, repetición *f*
reject[1] [ri'dʒɛkt] *vt* : rechazar
reject[2] ['riːˌdʒɛkt] *n* : desecho *m* (cosa), persona *f* rechazada
rejection [ri'dʒɛkʃən] *n* : rechazo *m*
rejoice [ri'dʒɔɪs] *vi* **-joiced; -joicing** : alegrarse, regocijarse
rejoin *vt* [ˌriː'dʒɔɪn] **1** : reincorporarse a, reintegrarse a <he rejoined the firm : se reincorporó a la firma> **2** [ri'-] REPLY, RETORT : replicar
rejoinder [ri'dʒɔɪndər] *n* : réplica *f*
rejuvenate [ri'dʒuːvəˌneɪt] *vt* **-nated; -nating** : rejuvenecer
rejuvenation [riˌdʒuːvə'neɪʃən] *n* : rejuvenecimiento *m*
rekindle [ˌriː'kɪndəl] *vt* **-dled; -dling** : reavivar
relapse[1] [ri'læps] *vi* **-lapsed; -lapsing** : recaer, volver a caer
relapse[2] ['riːˌlæps, ri'læps] *n* : recaída *f*
relate [ri'leɪt] *v* **-lated; -lating** *vt* **1** TELL : relatar, contar **2** ASSOCIATE : relacionar, asociar <to relate crime to poverty : relacionar la delincuencia a la pobreza> — *vi* **1** CONNECT : conectar, estar relacionado (con) **2** INTERACT : relacionarse (con), llevarse bien (con) **3 to relate to** UNDERSTAND : identificarse con, simpatizar con
related [ri'leɪṭəd] *adj* : emparentado <to be related to : ser pariente de>
relation [ri'leɪʃən] *n* **1** NARRATION : relato *m*, narración *f* **2** RELATIVE : pariente *mf*, familiar *mf* **3** RELATIONSHIP : relación *f* <in relation to : en relación con, con relación a> **4 relations** *npl* : relaciones *fpl* <public relations : relaciones públicas>
relationship [ri'leɪʃənˌʃɪp] *n* **1** CONNECTION : relación *f* **2** KINSHIP : parentesco *m*
relative[1] ['rɛləṭɪv] *adj* : relativo — **relatively** *adv*
relative[2] *n* : pariente *mf*, familiar *mf*
relativity [ˌrɛlə'tɪvəṭi] *n, pl* **-ties** : relatividad *f*
relax [ri'læks] *vt* : relajar, aflojar — *vi* : relajarse
relaxation [ˌriːˌlæk'seɪʃən] *n* **1** RELAXING : relajación *f*, aflojamiento *m* **2** DIVERSION : esparcimiento *m*, distracción *f*
relay[1] ['riːˌleɪ, ri'leɪ] *vt* **-layed; -laying** : transmitir
relay[2] ['riːˌleɪ] *n* **1** : relevo *m* **2** *or* **relay race** : carrera de relevos
release[1] [ri'liːs] *vt* **-leased; -leasing** **1** FREE : liberar, poner en libertad **2** LOOSEN : soltar, aflojar <to release the brake : soltar el freno> **3** RELINQUISH : renunciar a, ceder **4** ISSUE : publicar (un libro), estrenar (una película), sacar (un disco)
release[2] *n* **1** LIBERATION : liberación *f*, puesta *f* en libertad **2** RELINQUISHMENT : cesión *f* (de propiedad, etc.) **3** ISSUE : estreno *m* (de una película), puesta *f* en venta (de un disco), publicación *f* (de un libro) **4** ESCAPE : escape *m*, fuga *f* (de un gas)
relegate ['rɛləˌgeɪt] *vt* **-gated; -gating** : relegar
relent [ri'lɛnt] *vi* : ablandarse, ceder
relentless [ri'lɛntləs] *adj* : implacable, sin tregua
relentlessly [ri'lɛntləsli] *adv* : implacablemente
relevance ['rɛləvənts] *n* : pertinencia *f*, relación *f*
relevant ['rɛləvənt] *adj* : pertinente — **relevantly** *adv*

reliability [riˌlaɪəˈbɪləṭi] *n, pl* **-ties 1** : fiabilidad *f,* seguridad *f* (de una cosa) **2** : formalidad *f,* seriedad *f* (de una persona)

reliable [riˈlaɪəbəl] *adj* : confiable, fiable, fidedigno, seguro

reliably [riˈlaɪəbli] *adv* : sin fallar <to be reliably informed : saber (algo) de fuentes fidedignas>

reliance [riˈlaɪən*t*s] *n* **1** DEPENDENCE : dependencia *f* **2** CONFIDENCE : confianza *f*

reliant [riˈlaɪənt] *adj* : confiable, dependente

relic [ˈrɛlɪk] *n* **1** : reliquia *f* **2** VESTIGE : vestigio *m*

relief [riˈliːf] *n* **1** : alivio *m,* desahogo *m* <relief from pain : alivio del dolor> **2** AID, WELFARE : ayuda *f* (benéfica), asistencia *f* social **3** : relieve *m* (en la escultura) <relief map : mapa en relieve> **4** REPLACEMENT : relevo *m*

relieve [riˈliːv] *vt* **-lieved; -lieving 1** ALLEVIATE : aliviar, mitigar <to feel relieved : sentirse aliviado> **2** FREE : liberar, eximir <to relieve someone of responsibility for : eximir a alguien de la responsabilidad de> **3** REPLACE : relevar (a un centinela, etc.) **4** BREAK : romper <to relieve the monotony : romper la monotonía>

religion [riˈlɪdʒən] *n* : religión *f*

religious [riˈlɪdʒəs] *adj* : religioso — **religiously** *adv*

relinquish [riˈlɪŋkwɪʃ, -ˈlɪn-] *vt* **1** GIVE UP : renunciar a, abandonar **2** RELEASE : soltar

relish[1] [ˈrɛlɪʃ] *vt* : saborear (comida), disfrutar con (una idea, una perspectiva, etc.)

relish[2] *n* **1** ENJOYMENT : gusto *m,* deleite *m* **2** : salsa *f* (condimento)

relive [ˌriːˈlɪv] *vt* **-lived; -living** : revivir

relocate [ˌriːˈloːˌkeɪt, ˌriːloˈkeɪt] *v* **-cated; -cating** *vt* : reubicar, trasladar — *vi* : trasladarse

relocation [ˌriːloˈkeɪʃən] *n* : reubicación *f,* traslado *m*

reluctance [riˈlʌktən*t*s] *n* : renuencia *f,* reticencia *f,* desgana *f*

reluctant [riˈlʌktənt] *adj* : renuente, reacio, reticente

reluctantly [riˈlʌktəntli] *adv* : a regañadientes

rely [riˈlaɪ] *vi* **-lied; -lying 1** DEPEND : depender (de), contar (con) **2** TRUST : confiar (en)

remain [riˈmeɪn] *vi* **1** : quedar <very little remains : queda muy poco> <the remaining 10 minutes : los 10 minutos que quedan> **2** STAY : quedarse, permanecer **3** CONTINUE : continuar, seguir <to remain the same : continuar siendo igual> **4 to remain to** : quedar por <to remain to be done : quedar por hacer> <it remains to be seen : está por ver>

remainder [riˈmeɪndər] *n* : resto *m,* remanente *m*

remains [riˈmeɪnz] *npl* : restos *mpl* <mortal remains : restos mortales>

remark[1] [riˈmɑrk] *vt* **1** NOTICE : observar **2** SAY : comentar, observar — *vi* **to remark on** : hacer observaciones sobre

remark[2] *n* : comentario *m,* observación *f*

remarkable [riˈmɑrkəbəl] *adj* : extraordinario, notable — **remarkably** [-bli] *adv*

rematch [ˈriːˌmætʃ] *n* : revancha *f*

remedial [riˈmiːdiəl] *adj* : correctivo <remedial classes : clases para alumnos atrasados>

remedy[1] [ˈrɛmədi] *vt* **-died; -dying** : remediar

remedy[2] *n, pl* **-dies** : remedio *m,* medicamento *m*

remember [riˈmɛmbər] *vt* **1** RECOLLECT : acordarse de, recordar **2** : no olvidar <remember my words : no olvides mis palabras> <to remember to : acordarse de> **3** : dar saludos, dar recuerdos <remember me to her : dale saludos de mi parte> **4** COMMEMORATE : recordar, conmemorar

remembrance [riˈmɛmbrən*t*s] *n* **1** RECOLLECTION : recuerdo *m* <in remembrance of : en conmemoración de> **2** MEMENTO : recuerdo *m*

remind [riˈmaɪnd] *vt* : recordar <remind me to do it : recuérdame que lo haga> <she reminds me of Clara : me recuerda de Clara>

reminder [riˈmaɪndər] *n* : recuerdo *m*

reminisce [ˌrɛməˈnɪs] *vi* **-nisced; -niscing** : rememorar los viejos tiempos

reminiscence [ˌrɛməˈnɪsən*t*s] *n* : recuerdo *m,* reminiscencia *f*

reminiscent [ˌrɛməˈnɪsənt] *adj* **1** NOSTALGIC : reminiscente, nostálgico **2** SUGGESTIVE : evocador, que recuerda — **reminiscently** *adv*

remiss [riˈmɪs] *adj* : negligente, descuidado, remiso

remission [riˈmɪʃən] *n* : remisión *f*

remit [riˈmɪt] *vt* **-mitted; -mitting 1** PARDON : perdonar **2** SEND : remitir, enviar (dinero)

remittance [riˈmɪtən*t*s] *n* : remesa *f*

remnant [ˈrɛmnənt] *n* : restos *mpl,* vestigio *m*

remodel [riˈmɑdəl] *vt* **-eled** *or* **-elled; -eling** *or* **-elling** : remodelar, reformar

remonstrate [riˈmɑnˌstreɪt] *vi* **-strated; -strating** : protestar <to remonstrate with someone : quejarse a alguien>

remorse [riˈmɔrs] *n* : remordimiento *m*

remorseful [riˈmɔrsfəl] *adj* : arrepentido, lleno de remordimiento

remorseless [riˈmɔrsləs] *adj* **1** PITILESS : despiadado **2** RELENTLESS : implacable

remote [ri'mo:t] *adj* **-moter; -est 1** FAR-OFF : lejano, remoto <remote countries : países remotos> <in the remote past : en el pasado lejano> **2** SECLUDED : recóndito **3** : a distancia, remoto <remote control : control remoto> **4** SLIGHT : remoto **5** ALOOF : distante

remotely [ri'mo:tli] *adv* **1** SLIGHTLY : remotamente **2** DISTANTLY : en un lugar remoto, muy lejos

remoteness [ri'mo:tnəs] *n* : lejanía *f*

removable [ri'mu:vəbəl] *adj* : movible, separable

removal [ri'mu:vəl] *n* : separación *f,* extracción *f,* supresión *f* (en algo escrito), eliminación *f* (de problemas, etc.)

remove [ri'mu:v] *vt* **-moved; -moving 1** : quitar, quitarse <remove the lid : quite la tapa> <to remove one's hat : quitarse el sombrero> **2** EXTRACT : sacar, extraer <to remove the contents of : sacar el contenido de> **3** ELIMINATE : eliminar, disipar

remunerate [ri'mju:nə,reɪt] *vt* **-ated; -ating** : remunerar

remuneration [ri,mju:nə'reɪʃən] *n* : remuneración *f*

remunerative [ri'mju:nərət̬ɪv, -,reɪ-] *adj* : remunerativo

renaissance [,rɛnə'sɑnts, -'zɑnts; 'rɛnə,-] *n* : renacimiento *m* <the Renaissance : el Renacimiento>

renal ['ri:nəl] *adj* : renal

rename [,ri:'neɪm] *vt* **-named; -naming** : ponerle un nombre nuevo a

rend ['rɛnd] *vt* **rent** ['rɛnt]; **rending** : desgarrar

render ['rɛndər] *vt* **1** : derretir <to render lard : derretir la manteca> **2** GIVE : prestar, dar <to render aid : prestar ayuda> **3** MAKE : hacer, volver, dejar <it rendered him helpless : lo dejó incapacitado> **4** TRANSLATE : traducir, verter <to render into English : traducir al inglés>

rendezvous ['rɑndɪ,vu:, -deɪ-] *ns & pl* : encuentro *m,* cita *f*

rendition [rɛn'dɪʃən] *n* : interpretación *f*

renegade ['rɛnɪ,geɪd] *n* : renegado *m,* -da *f*

renege [ri'nɪg, -'nɛg] *vi* **-neged; -neging** : no cumplir con (una promesa, etc.)

renew [ri'nu:, -'nju:] *vt* **1** REVIVE : renovar, reavivar <to renew the sentiments of youth : renovar los sentimientos de la juventud> **2** RESUME : reanudar **3** EXTEND : renovar <to renew a subscription : renovar una suscripción>

renewable [ri'nu:əbəl, -'nju:-] *adj* : renovable

renewal [ri'nu:əl, -'nju:-] *n* : renovación *f*

renounce [ri'naʊnts] *vt* **-nounced; -nouncing** : renunciar a

renovate ['rɛnə,veɪt] *vt* **-vated; -vating** : restaurar, renovar

renovation [,rɛnə'veɪʃən] *n* : restauración *f,* renovación *f*

renown [ri'naʊn] *n* : renombre *m,* fama *f,* celebridad *f*

renowned [ri'naʊnd] *adj* : renombrado, célebre, famoso

rent[1] ['rɛnt] *vt* : rentar, alquilar

rent[2] *n* **1** : renta *f,* alquiler *m* <for rent : se alquila> **2** RIP : rasgadura *f*

rental[1] ['rɛntəl] *adj* RENT : de alquiler

rental[2] *n* : alquiler *m*

renter ['rɛntər] *n* : arrendatario *m,* -ria *f*

renunciation [ri,nʌntsi'eɪʃən] *n* : renuncia *f*

reopen [,ri:'o:pən] *vt* : volver a abrir

reorganization [,ri:,ɔrgənə'zeɪʃən] *n* : reorganización *f*

reorganize [,ri:'ɔrgən,aɪz] *vt* **-nized; -nizing** : reorganizar

repair[1] [ri'pær] *vt* : reparar, arreglar, refaccionar

repair[2] *n* **1** : reparación *f,* arreglo *m* **2** CONDITION : estado *m* <in bad repair : en mal estado>

reparation [,rɛpə'reɪʃən] *n* **1** AMENDS : reparación *f* **2 reparations** *npl* COMPENSATION : indemnización *f*

repartee [,rɛpər'ti:, -,pɑr-, -'teɪ] *n* : intercambio *m* de réplicas ingeniosas

repast [ri'pæst, 'ri:,pæst] *n* : comida *f*

repatriate [ri'peɪtri,eɪt] *vt* **-ated; -ating** : repatriar

repay [ri'peɪ] *vt* **-paid; -paying** : pagar, devolver, reembolsar

repeal[1] [ri'pi:l] *vt* : abrogar, revocar

repeal[2] *n* : abrogación *f,* revocación *f*

repeat[1] [ri'pi:t] *vt* : repetir

repeat[2] *n* : repetición *f*

repeatedly [ri'pi:t̬ədli] *adv* : repetidamente, repetidas veces

repel [ri'pɛl] *vt* **-pelled; -pelling 1** REPULSE : repeler (un enemigo, etc.) **2** RESIST : repeler **3** REJECT : rechazar, repeler **4** DISGUST : repugnar, darle asco (a alguien)

repellent *or* **repellant** [ri'pɛlənt] *n* : repelente *m*

repent [ri'pɛnt] *vi* : arrepentirse

repentance [ri'pɛntənts] *n* : arrepentimiento *m*

repentant [ri'pɛntənt] *adj* : arrepentido

repercussion [,ri:pər'kʌʃən, ,rɛpər-] *n* : repercusión *f*

repertoire ['rɛpər,twɑr] *n* : repertorio *m*

repertory ['rɛpər,tori] *n, pl* **-ries** : repertorio *m*

repetition [,rɛpə'tɪʃən] *n* : repetición *f*

repetitious [,rɛpə'tɪʃəs] *adj* : repetitivo, reiterativo — **repetitiously** *adv*

repetitive [riˈpɛtət̬ɪv] *adj* : repetitivo, reiterativo
replace [riˈpleɪs] *vt* **-placed; -placing 1 :** volver a poner <replace it in the drawer : vuelve a ponerlo en el cajón> **2** SUBSTITUTE **:** reemplazar, sustituir **3 :** reponer <to replace the worn carpet : reponer la alfombra raída>
replaceable [riˈpleɪsəbəl] *adj* **:** reemplazable
replacement [riˈpleɪsmənt] *n* **1** SUBSTITUTION **:** reemplazo *m,* sustitución *f* **2** SUBSTITUTE **:** sustituto *m,* -ta *f;* suplente *mf* (persona) **3 replacement part :** repuesto *m,* pieza *f* de recambio
replenish [riˈplɛnɪʃ] *vt* **:** rellenar, llenar de nuevo
replenishment [riˈplɛnɪʃmənt] *n* **:** reabastecimiento *m*
replete [riˈpliːt] *adj* **:** repleto, lleno
replica [ˈrɛplɪkə] *n* **:** réplica *f,* reproducción *f*
reply¹ [riˈplaɪ] *vi* **-plied; -plying :** contestar, responder
reply² *n, pl* **-plies :** respuesta *f,* contestación *f*
report¹ [riˈport] *vt* **1** ANNOUNCE **:** relatar, anunciar **2 :** dar parte de, informar de, reportar <he reported an accident : dio parte de un accidente> <to report a crime : denunciar un delito> **3 :** informar acerca de (en un periódico, la televisión, etc.) — *vi* **1 :** hacer un informe, informar **2 to report for duty :** presentarse, reportarse
report² *n* **1** RUMOR **:** rumor *m* **2** REPUTATION **:** reputación *f* <people of evil report : personas de mala fama> **3** ACCOUNT **:** informe *m,* reportaje *m* (en un periódico, etc.) **4** BANG **:** estallido *m* (de un arma de fuego)
report card *n* **:** boletín *m* de calificaciones, boletín *m* de notas
reportedly [riˈportədli] *adv* **:** según se dice, según se informa
reporter [riˈportər] *n* **:** periodista *mf;* reportero *m,* -ra *f*
repose¹ [riˈpoːz] *vi* **-posed; -posing :** reposar, descansar
repose² *n* **1 :** reposo *m,* descanso *m* **2** CALM **:** calma *f,* tranquilidad *f*
repository [riˈpɑzəˌtori] *n, pl* **-ries :** depósito *m*
repossess [ˌriːpəˈzɛs] *vt* **:** recuperar, recobrar la posesión de
reprehensible [ˌrɛpriˈhɛntsəbəl] *adj* **:** reprensible — **reprehensibly** *adv*
represent [ˌrɛprɪˈzɛnt] *vt* **1** SYMBOLIZE **:** representar <the flag represents our country : la bandera representa a nuestro país> **2 :** representar, ser un representante de <an attorney who represents his client : un abogado que representa su cliente> **3** PORTRAY **:** presentar <he represents himself as a friend : se presenta como amigo>
representation [ˌrɛprɪˌzɛnˈteɪʃən, -zən-] *n* **:** representación *f*
representative¹ [ˌrɛprɪˈzɛntət̬ɪv] *adj* **:** representativo
representative² *n* **1 :** representante *mf* **2 :** diputado *m,* -da *f* (en la política)
repress [riˈprɛs] *vt* **:** reprimir
repression [riˈprɛʃən] *n* **:** represión *f*
repressive [riˈprɛsɪv] *adj* **:** represivo
reprieve¹ [riˈpriːv] *vt* **-prieved; -prieving :** indultar
reprieve² *n* **:** indulto *m*
reprimand¹ [ˈrɛprəˌmænd] *vt* **:** reprender
reprimand² *n* **:** reprimenda *f*
reprint¹ [riˈprɪnt] *vt* **:** reimprimir
reprint² [ˈriːˌprɪnt, riˈprɪnt] *n* **:** reedición *f*
reprisal [riˈpraɪzəl] *n* **:** represalia *f*
reproach¹ [riˈproːtʃ] *vt* **:** reprochar
reproach² *n* **1** DISGRACE **:** deshonra *f* **2** REBUKE **:** reproche *m,* recriminación *f*
reproachful [riˈproːtʃfəl] *adj* **:** de reproche
reproduce [ˌriːprəˈduːs, -ˈdjuːs] *v* **-duced; -ducing** *vt* **:** reproducir — *vi* BREED **:** reproducirse
reproduction [ˌriːprəˈdʌkʃən] *n* **:** reproducción *f*
reproductive [ˌriːprəˈdʌktɪv] *adj* **:** reproductor
reproof [riˈpruːf] *n* **:** reprobación *f,* reprimenda *f,* reproche *m*
reprove [riˈpruːv] *vt* **-proved; -proving :** reprender, censurar
reptile [ˈrɛpˌtaɪl] *n* **:** reptil *m*
republic [riˈpʌblɪk] *n* **:** república *f*
republican¹ [riˈpʌblɪkən] *adj* **:** republicano
republican² *n* **:** republicano *m,* -na *f*
repudiate [riˈpjuːdiˌeɪt] *vt* **-ated; -ating 1** REJECT **:** rechazar **2** DISOWN **:** repudiar, renegar de
repudiation [riˌpjuːdiˈeɪʃən] *n* **:** rechazo *m,* repudio *m*
repugnance [riˈpʌgnənts] *n* **:** repugnancia *f*
repugnant [riˈpʌgnənt] *adj* **:** repugnante, asqueroso
repulse¹ [riˈpʌls] *vt* **-pulsed; -pulsing 1** REPEL **:** repeler **2** REBUFF **:** desairar, rechazar
repulse² *n* **:** rechazo *m*
repulsive [riˈpʌlsɪv] *adj* **:** repulsivo, repugnante, asqueroso — **repulsively** *adv*
reputable [ˈrɛpjət̬əbəl] *adj* **:** acreditado, de buena reputación
reputation [ˌrɛpjəˈteɪʃən] *n* **:** reputación *f,* fama *f*
repute [riˈpjuːt] *n* **:** reputación *f,* fama *f*
reputed [riˈpjuːt̬əd] *adj* **:** reputado, supuesto <she's reputed to be the best : tiene fama de ser la mejor>
reputedly [riˈpjuːt̬ədli] *adv* **:** supuestamente, según se dice
request¹ [riˈkwɛst] *vt* **:** pedir, solicitar, rogar <to request assistance : solicitar asistencia, pedir ayuda> <I requested him to do it : le pedí que lo hiciera>

request[2] *n* **:** petición *f,* solicitud *f,* pedido *m*

requiem [ˈrɛkwiəm, ˈreɪ-] *n* **:** réquiem *m*

require [riˈkwaɪr] *vt* **-quired; -quiring 1** CALL FOR, DEMAND **:** requerir, exigir <if required : si se requiere> <to require that something be done : exigir que algo se haga> **2** NEED **:** necesitar, requerir

requirement [riˈkwaɪrmənt] *n* **1** NECESSITY **:** necesidad *f* **2** DEMAND **:** requisito *m,* demanda *f*

requisite[1] [ˈrɛkwəzɪt] *adj* **:** esencial, necesario

requisite[2] *n* **:** requisito *m,* necesidad *f*

requisition[1] [ˌrɛkwəˈzɪʃən] *vt* **:** requisar

requisition[2] *n* **:** requisición *f,* requisa *f*

reread [ˌriːˈriːd] *vt* **-read; -reading :** releer

reroute [ˌriːˈruːt, -ˈraʊt] *vt* **-routed; -routing :** desviar

resale [ˈriːˌseɪl, ˌriːˈseɪl] *n* **:** reventa *f* <resale price : precio de venta>

rescind [riˈsɪnd] *vt* **1** CANCEL **:** rescindir, cancelar **2** REPEAL **:** abrogar, revocar

rescue[1] [ˈrɛsˌkjuː] *vt* **-cued; -cuing :** rescatar, salvar

rescue[2] *n* **:** rescate *m*

rescuer [ˈrɛskjuər] *n* **:** salvador *m,* -dora *f*

research[1] [riˈsərtʃ, ˈriːˌsərtʃ] *v* **:** investigar

research[2] *n* **:** investigación *f*

researcher [riˈsərtʃər, ˈriːˌ-] *n* **:** investigador *m,* -dora *f*

resemblance [riˈzɛmbləntsʃ] *n* **:** semejanza *f,* parecido *m*

resemble [riˈzɛmbəl] *vt* **-sembled; -sembling :** parecerse a, asemejarse a

resent [riˈzɛnt] *vt* **:** resentirse de, ofenderse por

resentful [riˈzɛntfəl] *adj* **:** resentido, rencoroso **— resentfully** *adv*

resentment [riˈzɛntmənt] *n* **:** resentimiento *m*

reservation [ˌrɛzərˈveɪʃən] *n* **1 :** reservación *f,* reserva *f* <to make a reservation : hacer una reservación> **2** DOUBT, MISGIVING **:** reserva *f,* duda *f* <without reservations : sin reservas> **3 :** reserva *f* (de indios americanos)

reserve[1] [riˈzərv] *vt* **-served; -serving :** reservar

reserve[2] *n* **1** STOCK **:** reserva *f* <to keep in reserve : guardar en reserva> **2** RESTRAINT **:** reserva *f,* moderación *f* **3 reserves** *npl* **:** reservas *fpl* (militares)

reserved [riˈzərvd] *adj* **:** reservado

reservoir [ˈrɛzərˌvwɑr, -ˌvwɔr, -ˌvɔr] *n* **:** embalse *m*

reset [ˌriːˈsɛt] *vt* **-set; -setting :** reajustar, poner en hora (un reloj), reinicializar (una computadora)

reside [riˈzaɪd] *vi* **-sided; -siding 1** DWELL **:** residir **2** LIE **:** radicar, residir <the power resides in the presidency : el poder radica en la presidencia>

residence [ˈrɛzədənts] *n* **:** residencia *f*

resident[1] [ˈrɛzədənt] *adj* **:** residente

resident[2] *n* **:** residente *mf*

residential [ˌrɛzəˈdɛntʃəl] *adj* **:** residencial

residual [riˈzɪdʒʊəl] *adj* **:** residual

residue [ˈrɛzəˌduː, -ˌdjuː] *n* **:** residuo *m,* resto *m*

resign [riˈzaɪn] *vt* **1** QUIT **:** dimitir, renunciar **2 to resign oneself :** aguantarse, resignarse

resignation [ˌrɛzɪgˈneɪʃən] *n* **:** resignación *f*

resignedly [riˈzaɪnədli] *adv* **:** con resignación

resilience [riˈzɪljənts] *n* **1 :** capacidad *f* de recuperación, adaptabilidad *f* **2** ELASTICITY **:** elasticidad *f*

resiliency [riˈzɪljəntsi] → **resilience**

resilient [riˈzɪljənt] *adj* **1** STRONG **:** resistente, fuerte **2** ELASTIC **:** elástico

resin [ˈrɛzən] *n* **:** resina *f*

resist [riˈzɪst] *vt* **1** WITHSTAND **:** resistir <to resist heat : resistir el calor> **2** OPPOSE **:** oponerse a

resistance [riˈzɪstənts] *n* **:** resistencia *f*

resistant [riˈzɪstənt] *adj* **:** resistente

resolute [ˈrɛzəˌluːt] *adj* **:** firme, resuelto, decidido

resolutely [ˈrɛzəˌluːtli, ˌrɛzəˈ-] *adv* **:** resueltamente, firmemente

resolution [ˌrɛzəˈluːʃən] *n* **1** SOLUTION **:** solución *f* **2** RESOLVE **:** resolución *f,* determinación *f* **3** DECISION **:** propósito *m,* decisión *f* <New Year's resolutions : propósitos para el Año Nuevo> **4** MOTION, PROPOSAL **:** moción *f,* resolución *f* (legislativa)

resolve[1] [riˈzɑlv] *vt* **-solved; -solving 1** SOLVE **:** resolver, solucionar **2** DECIDE **:** resolver <she resolved to get more sleep : resolvió dormir más>

resolve[2] *n* **:** resolución *f,* determinación *f*

resonance [ˈrɛzənənts] *n* **:** resonancia *f*

resonant [ˈrɛzənənt] *adj* **:** resonante, retumbante

resort[1] [riˈzɔrt] *vi* **to resort to :** recurrir <to resort to force : recurrir a la fuerza>

resort[2] *n* **1** RECOURSE **:** recurso *m* <as a last resort : como último recurso> **2** HANGOUT **:** lugar *m* popular, lugar *m* muy frecuentado **3 :** lugar *m* de vacaciones <tourist resort : centro turístico>

resound [riˈzaʊnd] *vi* **:** retumbar, resonar

resounding [riˈzaʊndɪŋ] *adj* **1** RESONANT **:** retumbante, resonante **2** ABSOLUTE, CATEGORICAL **:** rotundo, tremendo <a resounding success : un éxito rotundo>

resource [ˈriːˌsors, riˈsors] *n* **1** RESOURCEFULNESS **:** ingenio *m,* recursos *mpl* **2 resources** *npl* **:** recursos *mpl*

<natural resources : recursos naturales> **3 resources** *npl* MEANS : recursos *mpl*, medios *mpl*, fondos *mpl*
resourceful [ri'sorsfəl, -'zors-] *adj* : ingenioso
resourcefulness [ri'sorsfəlnəs, -'zors-] *n* : ingenio *m*, recursos *mpl*, inventiva *f*
respect¹ [ri'spɛkt] *vt* : respetar, estimar
respect² *n* **1** REFERENCE : relación *f*, respeto *m* <with respect to : en lo que respecta a> **2** ESTEEM : respeto *m*, estima *f* **3** DETAIL, PARTICULAR : detalle *m*, sentido *m*, respeto *m* <in some respects : en algunos sentidos> **4 respects** *npl* : respetos *mpl* <to pay one's respects : presentar uno sus respetos>
respectability [ri,spɛktə'bɪləṭi] *n* : respetabilidad *f*
respectable [ri'spɛktəbəl] *adj* **1** PROPER : respetable, decente **2** CONSIDERABLE : considerable, respetable <a respectable amount : una cantidad respetable> — **respectably** [-bli] *adv*
respectful [ri'spɛktfəl] *adj* : respetuoso — **respectfully** *adv*
respectfulness [ri'spɛktfəlnəs] *n* : respetuosidad *f*
respective [ri'spɛktɪv] *adj* : respectivo <their respective homes : sus casas respectivas> — **respectively** *adv*
respiration [,rɛspə'reɪʃən] *n* : respiración *f*
respirator ['rɛspə,reɪṭər] *n* : respirador *m*
respiratory ['rɛspərə,tori, rɪ'spaɪrə-] *adj* : respiratorio
respite ['rɛspɪt, rɪ'spaɪt] *n* : respiro *m*, tregua *f*
resplendent [ri'splɛndənt] *adj* : resplandeciente — **resplendently** *adv*
respond [ri'spɑnd] *vi* **1** ANSWER : contestar, responder **2** REACT : responder, reaccionar <to respond to treatment : responder al tratamiento>
response [ri'spɑnts] *n* : respuesta *f*
responsibility [ri,spɑntsə'bɪləṭi] *n, pl* **-ties** : responsabilidad *f*
responsible [ri'spɑntsəbəl] *adj* : responsable — **responsibly** [-bli] *adv*
responsive [ri'spɑntsɪv] *adj* **1** ANSWERING : que responde **2** SENSITIVE : sensible, receptivo
responsiveness [ri'spɑntsɪvnəs] *n* : receptividad *f*, sensibilidad *f*
rest¹ ['rɛst] *vi* **1** REPOSE : reposar, descansar **2** RELAX : quedarse tranquilo **3** STOP : pararse, detenerse **4** DEPEND : basarse (en), descansar (sobre), depender (de) <the decision rests with her : la decisión pesa sobre ella> **5 to rest on :** apoyarse en, descansar sobre <to rest on one's arm : apoyarse en el brazo> — *vt* **1** RELAX : descansar **2** SUPPORT : apoyar **3 to rest one's eyes on :** fijar la mirada en
rest² *n* **1** RELAXATION, REPOSE : reposo *m*, descanso *m* **2** SUPPORT : soporte *m*, apoyo *m* **3** : silencio *m* (en música) **4** REMAINDER : resto *m* **5 to come to rest** : pararse
restatement [,riː'steɪtmənt] *n* : repetición *f*
restaurant ['rɛstə,rɑnt, -rənt] *n* : restaurante *m*
restful ['rɛstfəl] *adj* **1** RELAXING : relajante **2** PEACEFUL : tranquilo, sosegado
restitution [,rɛstə'tuːʃən, -'tjuː-] *n* : restitución *f*
restive ['rɛstɪv] *adj* : inquieto, nervioso
restless ['rɛstləs] *adj* **1** FIDGETY : inquieto, agitado **2** IMPATIENT : impaciente **3** SLEEPLESS : desvelado <a restless night : una noche en blanco>
restlessly ['rɛstləsli] *adv* : nerviosamente
restlessness ['rɛstləsnəs] *n* : inquietud *f*, agitación *f*
restoration [,rɛstə'reɪʃən] *n* : restauración *f*, restablecimiento *m*
restore [ri'stor] *vt* **-stored; -storing 1** RETURN : volver **2** REESTABLISH : restablecer **3** REPAIR : restaurar
restrain [ri'streɪn] *vt* **1** : refrenar, contener **2 to restrain oneself** : contenerse
restrained [ri'streɪnd] *adj* : comedido, templado, contenido
restraint [ri'streɪnt] *n* **1** RESTRICTION : restricción *f*, limitación *f*, control *m* **2** CONFINEMENT : encierro *m* **3** RESERVE : reserva *f*, control *m* de sí mismo
restrict [ri'strɪkt] *vt* : restringir, limitar, constreñir
restricted [ri'strɪktəd] *adj* **1** LIMITED : limitado, restringido **2** CLASSIFIED : secreto, confidencial
restriction [ri'strɪkʃən] *n* : restricción *f*
restrictive [ri'strɪktɪv] *adj* : restrictivo — **restrictively** *adv*
restructure [ri'strʌktʃər] *vt* **-tured; -turing** : reestructurar
result¹ [ri'zʌlt] *vi* : resultar <to result in : resultar en, tener por resultado>
result² *n* : resultado *m*, consecuencia *f* <as a result of : como consecuencia de>
resultant [ri'zʌltənt] *adj* : resultante
resume [ri'zuːm] *v* **-sumed; -suming** *vt* : reanudar — *vi* : reanudarse
résumé *or* **resume** *or* **resumé** ['rɛzə,meɪ, ,rɛzə'-] *n* **1** SUMMARY : resumen *m* **2** CURRICULUM VITAE : currículum *m*, currículo *m*
resumption [ri'zʌmpʃən] *n* : reanudación *f*
resurface [,riː'sərfəs] *v* **-faced; -facing** *vt* : pavimentar (una carretera) de nuevo — *vi* : volver a salir en la superficie
resurgence [ri'sərdʒənts] *n* : resurgimiento *m*

resurrect [ˌrɛzəˈrɛkt] *vt* : resucitar, desempolvar

resurrection [ˌrɛzəˈrɛkʃən] *n* : resurrección *f*

resuscitate [riˈsʌsəˌteɪt] *vt* **-tated; -tating** : resucitar, revivir

retail[1] [ˈriːˌteɪl] *vt* : vender al por menor, vender al detalle

retail[2] *adv* : al por menor, al detalle

retail[3] *adj* : detallista, minorista

retail[4] *n* : venta *f* al detalle, venta *f* al por menor

retailer [ˈriːˌteɪlər] *n* : detallista *mf,* minorista *mf*

retain [riˈteɪn] *vt* : retener, conservar, guardar

retainer [riˈteɪnər] *n* **1** SERVANT : criado *m,* -da *f* **2** ADVANCE : anticipo *m*

retaliate [riˈtæliˌeɪt] *vi* **-ated; -ating** : responder, contraatacar, tomar represalias

retaliation [riˌtæliˈeɪʃən] *n* : represalia *f,* retaliación *f*

retard [riˈtɑrd] *vt* : retardar, retrasar

retarded [riˈtɑrdəd] *adj* : retrasado

retch [ˈrɛtʃ] *vi* : hacer arcadas

retention [riˈtɛntʃən] *n* : retención *f*

retentive [riˈtɛntɪv] *adj* : retentivo

reticence [ˈrɛtəsənts] *n* : reticencia *f*

reticent [ˈrɛtəsənt] *adj* : reticente

retina [ˈrɛtənə] *n, pl* **-nas** *or* **-nae** [-əni, -ənˌaɪ] : retina *f*

retinue [ˈrɛtənˌuː, -ˌjuː] *n* : séquito *m,* comitiva *f,* cortejo *m*

retire [riˈtaɪr] *vi* **-tired; -tiring** **1** RETREAT, WITHDRAW : retirarse, retraerse **2** : retirarse, jubilarse (de su trabajo) **3** : acostarse, irse a dormir

retiree [riˌtaɪˈriː] *n* : jubilado *m,* -da *f*

retirement [riˈtaɪrmənt] *n* : jubilación *f*

retiring [riˈtaɪrɪŋ] *adj* SHY : retraído

retort[1] [riˈtɔrt] *vt* : replicar

retort[2] *n* : réplica *f*

retrace [ˌriːˈtreɪs] *vt* **-traced; -tracing** : volver sobre, desandar <to retrace one's steps : volver uno sobre sus pasos>

retract [riˈtrækt] *vt* **1** TAKE BACK, WITHDRAW : retirar, retractarse de **2** : retraer (las garras) — *vi* : retractarse

retractable [riˈtræktəbəl] *adj* : retractable

retrain [ˌriːˈtreɪn] *vt* : reciclar, reconvertir

retreat[1] [riˈtriːt] *vi* : retirarse

retreat[2] *n* **1** WITHDRAWAL : retirada *f,* repliegue *m,* retiro *m* <to beat a retreat : batirse en retirada> **2** REFUGE : retiro *m,* refugio *m*

retrench [riˈtrɛntʃ] *vt* : reducir (gastos) — *vi* : economizar

retribution [ˌrɛtrəˈbjuːʃən] *n* PUNISHMENT : castigo *m,* pena *f* merecida

retrieval [riˈtriːvəl] *n* : recuperación *f* <beyond retrieval : irrecuperable> <data retrieval : recuperación de datos>

retrieve [riˈtriːv] *vt* **-trieved; -trieving** **1** : cobrar <to retrieve game : cobrar la caza> **2** RECOVER : recuperar

retriever [riˈtriːvər] *n* : perro *m* cobrador

retroactive [ˌrɛtroˈæktɪv] *adj* : retroactivo — **retroactively** *adv*

retrograde [ˈrɛtrəˌgreɪd] *adj* : retrógrado

retrospect [ˈrɛtrəˌspɛkt] *n* **in retrospect** : mirando hacia atrás, retrospectivamente

retrospective [ˌrɛtrəˈspɛktɪv] *adj* : retrospectivo

return[1] [riˈtərn] *vi* **1** : volver, regresar <to return home : regresar a casa> **2** REAPPEAR : reaparecer, resurgir **3** ANSWER : responder — *vt* **1** REPLACE, RESTORE : devolver, volver (a poner), restituir <to return something to its place : volver a poner algo en su lugar> **2** YIELD : producir, redituar, rendir **3** REPAY : pagar, devolver <to return a compliment : devolver un cumplido>

return[2] *adj* : de vuelta

return[3] *n* **1** RETURNING : regreso *m,* vuelta *f,* retorno *m* **2** *or* **tax return** : declaración *f* de impuestos **3** YIELD : rédito *m,* rendimiento *m,* ganancia *f* **4 returns** *npl* DATA, RESULTS : resultados *mpl,* datos *mpl*

reunion [riˈjuːnjən] *n* : reunión *f,* reencuentro *m*

reunite [ˌriːjʊˈnaɪt] *v* **-nited; -niting** *vt* : (volver a) reunir — *vi* : (volver a) reunirse

reusable [riˈjuːzəbəl] *adj* : reutilizable

reuse [riˈjuːz] *vt* **-used; -using** : reutilizar, usar de nuevo

revamp [ˌriˈvæmp] *vt* : renovar

reveal [riˈviːl] *vt* **1** DIVULGE : revelar, divulgar <to reveal a secret : revelar un secreto> **2** SHOW : manifestar, mostrar, dejar ver

reveille [ˈrɛvəli] *n* : toque *m* de diana

revel[1] [ˈrɛvəl] *vi* **-eled** *or* **-elled; -eling** *or* **-elling** **1** CAROUSE : ir de juerga **2 to revel in** : deleitarse en

revel[2] *n* : juerga *f,* parranda *f fam*

revelation [ˌrɛvəˈleɪʃən] *n* : revelación *f*

reveler *or* **reveller** [ˈrɛvələr] *n* : juerguista *mf*

revelry [ˈrɛvəlri] *n, pl* **–ries** : juerga *f,* parranda *f fam,* jarana *f fam*

revenge[1] [riˈvɛndʒ] *vt* **-venged; -venging** : vengar <to revenge oneself on : vengarse de>

revenge[2] *n* : venganza *f*

revenue [ˈrɛvəˌnuː, -ˌnjuː] *n* : ingresos *mpl,* rentas *fpl*

reverberate [riˈvərbəˌreɪt] *vi* **-ated; -ating** : reverberar

reverberation [riˌvərbəˈreɪʃən] *n* : reverberación *f*

revere [riˈvɪr] *vt* **-vered; -vering** : reverenciar, venerar

reverence ['rɛvərənts] *n* : reverencia *f*, veneración *f*
reverend ['rɛvərənd] *adj* : reverendo <the Reverend John Chapin : el reverendo John Chapin>
reverent ['rɛvərənt] *adj* : reverente — **reverently** *adv*
reverie ['rɛvəri] *n, pl* **-eries** : ensueño *m*
reversal ['rɛvərsəl] *n* **1** INVERSION : inversión *f* (del orden normal) **2** CHANGE : cambio *m* total **3** SETBACK : revés *m*, contratiempo *m*
reverse[1] [ri'vərs] *v* **-versed; -versing** *vt* **1** INVERT : invertir **2** CHANGE : cambiar totalmente **3** ANNUL : anular, revocar — *vi* : dar marcha atrás
reverse[2] *adj* **1** : inverso <in reverse order : en orden inverso> <the reverse side : el reverso> **2** OPPOSITE : contrario, opuesto
reverse[3] *n* **1** OPPOSITE : lo contrario, lo opuesto **2** SETBACK : revés *m*, contratiempo *m* **3** BACK : reverso *m*, dorso *m*, revés *m* **4** *or* **reverse gear** : marcha *f* atrás, reversa *f Col, Mex*
reversible [ri'vərsəbəl] *adj* : reversible
reversion [ri'vərʒən] *n* : reversión *f*, vuelta *f*
revert [ri'vərt] *vi* : revertir
review[1] [ri'vju:] *vt* **1** REEXAMINE : volver a examinar, repasar (una lección) **2** CRITICIZE : reseñar, hacer una crítica de **3** EXAMINE : examinar, analizar <to review one's life : examinar su vida> **4 to review the troops** : pasar revista a las tropas
review[2] *n* **1** INSPECTION : revista *f* (de tropas) **2** ANALYSIS, OVERVIEW : resumen *m*, análisis *m* <a review of current affairs : un análisis de las actualidades> **3** CRITICISM : reseña *f*, crítica *f* (de un libro, etc.) **4** : repaso *m* (para un examen) **5** REVUE : revista *f* (musical)
reviewer [ri'vju:ər] *n* : crítico *m*, -ca *f*
revile [ri'vaɪl] *vt* **-viled; -viling** : injuriar, denostar
revise [ri'vaɪz] *vt* **-vised; -vising** : revisar, corregir, refundir <to revise a dictionary : corregir un diccionario>
revision [ri'vɪʒən] *n* : revisión *f*
revival [ri'vaɪvəl] *n* **1** : renacimiento *m* (de ideas, etc.), restablecimiento *m* (de costumbres, etc.), reactivación *f* (de la economía) **2** : reanimación *f*, resucitación *f* (en medicina) **3** *or* **revival meeting** : asamblea *f* evangelista
revive [ri'vaɪv] *v* **-vived; -viving** *vt* **1** REAWAKEN : reavivar, reanimar, reactivar (la economía), resucitar (a un paciente) **2** REESTABLISH : restablecer — *vi* **1** : renacer, reanimarse, reactivarse **2** COME TO : recobrar el sentido, volver en sí
revoke [ri'vo:k] *vt* **-voked; -voking** : revocar
revolt[1] [ri'vo:lt] *vi* **1** REBEL : rebelarse, sublevarse **2 to revolt at** : sentir repugnancia por — *vt* DISGUST : darle asco (a alguien), repugnar
revolt[2] *n* REBELLION : rebelión *f*, revuelta *f*, sublevación *f*
revolting [ri'vo:ltɪŋ] *adj* : asqueroso, repugnante
revolution [ˌrɛvə'lu:ʃən] *n* : revolución *f*
revolutionary[1] [ˌrɛvə'lu:ʃənˌɛri] *adj* : revolucionario
revolutionary[2] *n, pl* **-aries** : revolucionario *m*, -ria *f*
revolutionize [ˌrɛvə'lu:ʃənˌaɪz] *vt* **-ized; -izing** : cambiar radicalmente, revolucionar
revolve [ri'vɑlv] *v* **-volved; -volving** *vt* ROTATE : hacer girar — *vi* **1** ROTATE : girar <to revolve around : girar alrededor de> **2 to revolve in one's mind** : darle vueltas en la cabeza a alguien
revolver [ri'vɑlvər] *n* : revólver *m*
revue [ri'vju:] *n* : revista *f* (musical)
revulsion [ri'vʌlʃən] *n* : repugnancia *f*
reward[1] [ri'wɔrd] *vt* : recompensar, premiar
reward[2] *n* : recompensa *f*
rewrite [ˌri:'raɪt] *vt* **-wrote; -written; -writing** : escribir de nuevo, volver a escribir
rhapsody ['ræpsədi] *n, pl* **-dies 1** : elogio *m* excesivo <to go into rhapsodies over : extasiarse por> **2** : rapsodia *f* (en música)
rhetoric ['rɛtərɪk] *n* : retórica *f*
rhetorical [rɪ'tɔrɪkəl] *adj* : retórico
rheumatic [rʊ'mætɪk] *adj* : reumático
rheumatism ['ru:məˌtɪzəm, 'rʊ-] *n* : reumatismo *m*
rhinestone ['raɪnˌsto:n] *n* : diamante *m* de imitación
rhino ['raɪˌno:] *n, pl* **rhino** *or* **rhinos** → **rhinoceros**
rhinoceros [raɪ'nɑsərəs] *n, pl* **-eroses** *or* **-eros** *or* **-eri** [-ˌraɪ] : rinoceronte *m*
rhododendron [ˌro:də'dɛndrən] *n* : rododendro *m*
rhombus ['rɑmbəs] *n, pl* **-buses** *or* **-bi** [-ˌbaɪ, -bi] : rombo *m*
rhubarb ['ru:ˌbɑrb] *n* : ruibarbo *m*
rhyme[1] ['raɪm] *vi* **rhymed; rhyming** : rimar
rhyme[2] *n* **1** : rima *f* **2** VERSE : verso *m* (en rima)
rhythm ['rɪðəm] *n* : ritmo *m*
rhythmic ['rɪðmɪk] *or* **rhythmical** [-mɪkəl] *adj* : rítmico — **rhythmically** [-mɪkli] *adv*
rib[1] ['rɪb] *vt* **ribbed; ribbing 1** : hacer en canalé <a ribbed sweater : un suéter en canalé> **2** TEASE : tomarle el pelo (a alguien)
rib[2] *n* **1** : costilla *f* (de una persona o un animal) **2** : nervio *m* (de una bóveda o una hoja), varilla *f* (de un

paraguas), canalé *m* (de una prenda tejida)

ribald [ˈrɪbəld] *adj* **:** escabroso, procaz

ribbon [ˈrɪbən] *n* **1 :** cinta *f* **2 to tear to ribbons :** hacer jirones

rice [ˈraɪs] *n* **:** arroz *m*

rich [ˈrɪtʃ] *adj* **1** WEALTHY **:** rico **2** SUMPTUOUS **:** suntuoso, lujoso **3 :** pesado <rich foods : comida pesada> **4** ABUNDANT **:** abundante **5 :** vivo, intenso <rich colors : colores vivos> **6** FERTILE **:** fértil, rico

riches [ˈrɪtʃəz] *npl* **:** riquezas *fpl*

richly [ˈrɪtʃli] *adv* **1** SUMPTUOUSLY **:** suntuosamente, ricamente **2** ABUNDANTLY **:** abundantemente **3 richly deserved :** bien merecido

richness [ˈrɪtʃnəs] *n* **:** riqueza *f*

rickets [ˈrɪkəts] *n* **:** raquitismo *m*

rickety [ˈrɪkət̬i] *adj* **:** desvencijado, destartalado

ricksha *or* **rickshaw** [ˈrɪkˌʃɔ] *n* **:** cochecillo *m* tirado por un hombre

ricochet[1] [ˈrɪkəˌʃeɪ] *vi* **-cheted** [-ˌʃeɪd] *or* **-chetted** [-ˌʃɛt̬əd]; **-cheting** [-ˌʃeɪɪŋ] *or* **-chetting** [-ˌʃɛt̬ɪŋ] **:** rebotar

ricochet[2] *n* **:** rebote *m*

rid [ˈrɪd] *vt* **rid; ridding 1** FREE **:** librar <to rid the city of thieves : librar la ciudad de ladrones> **2 to rid oneself of :** desembarazarse de

riddance [ˈrɪdənts] *n* **:** libramiento *m* <good riddance! : ¡adiós y buen viaje!, ¡vete con viento fresco!>

riddle[1] [ˈrɪdəl] *vt* **-dled; -dling :** acribillar <riddled with bullets : acribillado a balazos> <riddled with errors : lleno de errores>

riddle[2] *n* **:** acertijo *m,* adivinanza *f*

ride[1] [ˈraɪd] *v* **rode** [ˈroːd]; **ridden** [ˈrɪdən]; **riding** *vt* **1 :** montar, ir, andar <to ride a horse : montar a caballo> <to ride a bicycle : montar en bicicleta, andar en bicicleta> <to ride the bus : ir en autobús> **2** TRAVERSE **:** recorrer <he rode 5 miles : recorrió 5 millas> **3** TEASE **:** burlarse de, ridiculizar **4** CARRY **:** llevar **5** WEATHER **:** capear <they rode out the storm : capearon el temporal> **6 to ride the waves :** surcar los mares — *vi* **1 :** montar a caballo, cabalgar **2** TRAVEL **:** ir, viajar (en coche, en bicicleta, etc.) **3** RUN **:** andar, marchar <the car rides well : el coche anda bien> **4 to ride at anchor :** estar fondeado **5 to let things ride :** dejar pasar las cosas

ride[2] *n* **1 :** paseo *m,* vuelta *f* (en coche, en bicicleta, a caballo) <to go for a ride : dar una vuelta> <to give someone a ride : llevar en coche a alguien> **2 :** aparato *m* (en un parque de diversiones)

rider [ˈraɪdər] *n* **1 :** jinete *mf* <the rider fell off his horse : el jinete se cayó de su caballo> **2** CYCLIST **:** ciclista *mf* **3** MOTORCYCLIST **:** motociclista *mf* **4** CLAUSE **:** cláusula *f* añadida

ridge [ˈrɪdʒ] *n* **1** CHAIN **:** cadena *f* (de montañas o cerros) **2 :** caballete *m* (de un techo), cresta *f* (de una ola o una montaña), cordoncillo *m* (de telas)

ridicule[1] [ˈrɪdəˌkjuːl] *vt* **-culed; -culing :** burlarse de, mofarse de, ridiculizar

ridicule[2] *n* **:** burlas *fpl*

ridiculous [rəˈdɪkjələs] *adj* **:** ridículo, absurdo

ridiculously [rəˈdɪkjələsli] *adv* **:** de forma ridícula

rife [ˈraɪf] *adj* **:** abundante, común <to be rife with : estar plagado de>

riffraff [ˈrɪfˌræf] *n* **:** chusma *f,* gentuza *f*

rifle[1] [ˈraɪfəl] *v* **-fled; -fling** *vt* RANSACK **:** desvalijar, saquear — *vi* **: to rifle through :** revolver

rifle[2] *n* **:** rifle *m,* fusil *m*

rift [ˈrɪft] *n* **1** FISSURE **:** grieta *f,* fisura *f* **2** BREAK **:** ruptura *f* (entre personas), división *f* (dentro de un grupo)

rig[1] [ˈrɪg] *vt* **rigged; rigging 1 :** aparejar (un barco) **2** EQUIP **:** equipar **3** FIX **:** amañar (una elección, etc.) **4 to rig up** CONSTRUCT **:** construir, erigir **5 to rig oneself out as :** vestirse de

rig[2] *n* **1 :** aparejo *m* (de un barco) **2** *or* **oil rig :** torre *f* de perforación, plataforma *f* petrolífera

rigging [ˈrɪgɪŋ, -gən] *n* **:** jarcia *f,* aparejo *m*

right[1] [ˈraɪt] *vt* **1** FIX, RESTORE **:** reparar <to right the economy : reparar la economía> **2** STRAIGHTEN **:** enderezar

right[2] *adv* **1 :** bien <to live right : vivir bien> **2** PRECISELY **:** precisamente, justo <right in the middle : justo en medio> **3** DIRECTLY, STRAIGHT **:** derecho, directamente <he went right home : fue derecho a casa> **4** IMMEDIATELY **:** inmediatamente <right after lunch : inmediatamente después del almuerzo> **5** COMPLETELY **:** completamente <he felt right at home : se sintió completamente cómodo> **6 :** a la derecha <to look left and right : mirar a la izquierda y a la derecha>

right[3] *adj* **1** UPRIGHT **:** bueno, honrado <right conduct : conducta honrada> **2** CORRECT **:** correcto <the right answer : la respuesta correcta> **3** APPROPRIATE **:** apropiado, adecuado, debido <the right man for the job : el hombre perfecto para el trabajo> **4** STRAIGHT **:** recto <a right line : una línea recta> **5 :** derecho <the right hand : la mano derecha> **6** SOUND **:** bien <he's not in his right mind : no está bien de la cabeza>

right[4] *n* **1** GOOD **:** bien *m* <to do right : hacer el bien> **2 :** derecha *f* <on the right : a la derecha> **3** *or* **right hand :** mano *f* derecha **4** ENTITLEMENT **:** derecho *m* <the right to vote : el derecho a votar> <women's rights : los derechos de la mujer> **5 the Right :** la derecha (en la política)

right angle *n* : ángulo *m* recto

right–angled [ˈraɪtˈæŋgəld] *or* **right–angle** [-gəl] *adj* **1** : en ángulo recto **2 right–angled triangle** : triángulo *m* rectángulo

righteous [ˈraɪtʃəs] *adj* : recto, honrado — **righteously** *adv*

righteousness [ˈraɪtʃəsnəs] *n* : rectitud *f*, honradez *f*

rightful [ˈraɪtfəl] *adj* **1** JUST : justo **2** LAWFUL : legítimo — **rightfully** *adv*

right–hand [ˈraɪtˈhænd] *adj* **1** : situado a la derecha **2** RIGHT-HANDED : para la mano derecha, con la mano derecha **3 right–hand man** : brazo *m* derecho

right–handed [ˈraɪtˈhændəd] *adj* **1** : diestro <a right-handed pitcher : un lanzador diestro> **2** : para la mano derecha, con la mano derecha **3** CLOCKWISE : en la dirección de las manecillas del reloj

rightly [ˈraɪtli] *adv* **1** JUSTLY : justamente, con razón **2** PROPERLY : debidamente, apropiadamente **3** CORRECTLY : correctamente

right–of–way [ˈraɪt̬əˈweɪ, -əv-] *n, pl* **rights–of–way 1** : preferencia (del tráfico) **2** ACCESS : derecho *m* de paso

rightward [ˈraɪtwərd] *adj* : a la derecha, hacia la derecha

right–wing [ˈraɪtˈwɪŋ] *adj* : derechista

right wing *n* **the right wing** : la derecha

right–winger [ˈraɪtˈwɪŋər] *n* : derechista *mf*

rigid [ˈrɪdʒɪd] *adj* : rígido — **rigidly** *adv*

rigidity [rɪˈdʒɪdət̬i] *n, pl* **-ties** : rigidez *f*

rigmarole [ˈrɪgməˌroːl, ˈrɪgə-] *n* **1** NONSENSE : galimatías *m*, disparates *mpl* **2** PROCEDURES : trámites *mpl*

rigor [ˈrɪgər] *n* : rigor *m*

rigor mortis [ˌrɪgərˈmɔrt̬əs] *n* : rigidez *f* cadavérica

rigorous [ˈrɪgərəs] *adj* : rigoroso — **rigorously** *adv*

rile [ˈraɪl] *vt* **riled; riling** : irritar

rill [ˈrɪl] *n* : riachuelo *m*

rim [ˈrɪm] *n* **1** EDGE : borde *m* **2** : llanta *f*, rin *m Col, Mex* (de una rueda) **3** FRAME : montura *f* (de anteojos)

rime [ˈraɪm] *n* : escarcha *f*

rind [ˈraɪnd] *n* : corteza *f*

ring[1] [ˈrɪŋ] *v* **rang** [ˈræŋ]; **rung** [ˈrʌŋ]; **ringing** *vi* **1** : sonar <the doorbell rang : el timbre sonó> <to ring for : llamar> **2** RESOUND : resonar **3** SEEM : parecer <to ring true : parecer cierto> — *vt* **1** : tocar, hacer sonar (un timbre, una alarma, etc.) **2** SURROUND : cercar, rodear

ring[2] *n* **1** : anillo *m*, sortija *f* <wedding ring : anillo de matrimonio> **2** BAND : aro *m*, anillo *m* <piston ring : aro de émbolo> **3** CIRCLE : círculo *m* **4** ARENA : arena *f*, ruedo *m* <a boxing ring : un cuadrilátero, un ring> **5** GANG : banda *f* (de ladrones, etc.) **6** SOUND : timbre *m*, sonido *m* **7** CALL : llamada *f* (por teléfono)

ringer [ˈrɪŋər] *n* **to be a dead ringer for** : ser un vivo retrato de

ringleader [ˈrɪŋˌliːdər] *n* : cabecilla *mf*

ringlet [ˈrɪŋlət] *n* : sortija *f*, rizo *m*

ringworm [ˈrɪŋˌwərm] *n* : tiña *f*

rink [ˈrɪŋk] *n* : pista *f* <skating rink : pista de patinaje>

rinse[1] [ˈrɪnts] *vt* **rinsed; rinsing** : enjuagar <to rinse out one's mouth : enjuagarse la boca>

rinse[2] *n* : enjuague *m*

riot[1] [ˈraɪət] *vi* : amotinarse

riot[2] *n* : motín *m*, tumulto *m*, alboroto *m*

rioter [ˈraɪət̬ər] *n* : alborotador *m*, -dora *f*

riotous [ˈraɪət̬əs] *adj* **1** UNRULY, WILD : desenfrenado, alborotado **2** ABUNDANT : abundante

rip[1] [ˈrɪp] *v* **ripped; ripping** *vt* : rasgar, arrancar, desgarrar — *vi* : rasgarse, desgarrarse

rip[2] *n* : rasgón *m*, desgarrón *m*

ripe [ˈraɪp] *adj* **riper; ripest 1** MATURE : maduro <ripe fruit : fruta madura> **2** READY : listo, preparado

ripen [ˈraɪpən] *v* : madurar

ripeness [ˈraɪpnəs] *n* : madurez *f*

rip–off [ˈrɪpˌɔf] *n* **1** THEFT : robo *m* **2** SWINDLE : estafa *f*, timo *m fam*

ripple[1] [ˈrɪpəl] *v* **-pled; -pling** *vi* : rizarse, ondear, ondular — *vt* : rizar

ripple[2] *n* : onda *f*, ondulación *f*

rise[1] [ˈraɪz] *vi* **rose** [ˈroːz]; **risen** [ˈrɪzən]; **rising 1** GET UP : levantarse <to rise to one's feet : ponerse de pie> **2** : elevarse, alzarse <the mountains rose to the west : las montañas se elevaron al oeste> **3** : salir (dícese del sol y de la luna) **4** : subir (dícese de las aguas, del humo, etc.) <the river rose : las aguas subieron de nivel> **5** INCREASE : aumentar, subir **6** ORIGINATE : nacer, proceder **7 to rise in rank** : ascender **8 to rise up** REBEL : sublevarse, rebelarse

rise[2] *n* **1** ASCENT : ascensión *f*, subida *f* **2** ORIGIN : origen *m* **3** ELEVATION : elevación *f* **4** INCREASE : subida *f*, aumento *m*, alzamiento *m* **5** SLOPE : pendiente *f*, cuesta *f*

riser [ˈraɪzər] *n* **1** : contrahuella *f* (de una escalera) **2 early riser** : madrugador *m*, -dora *f* **3 late riser** : dormilón *m*, -lona *f*

risk[1] [ˈrɪsk] *vt* : arriesgar

risk[2] *n* : riesgo *m*, peligro *m* <at risk : en peligro> <at your own risk : por su cuenta y riesgo>

risky [ˈrɪski] *adj* **riskier; -est** : arriesgado, peligroso, riesgoso

risqué [rɪˈskeɪ] *adj* : escabroso, picante, subido de tono

rite [ˈraɪt] *n* : rito *m*

ritual[1] [ˈrɪtʃʊəl] *adj* : ritual — **ritually** *adv*
ritual[2] *n* : ritual *m*
rival[1] [ˈraɪvəl] *vt* **-valed** *or* **-valled; -valing** *or* **-valling** : rivalizar con, competir con
rival[2] *adj* : competidor, rival
rival[3] *n* : rival *mf;* competidor *m,* -dora *f*
rivalry [ˈraɪvəlri] *n, pl* **-ries** : rivalidad *f,* competencia *f*
river [ˈrɪvər] *n* : río *m*
riverbank [ˈrɪvər,bæŋk] *n* : ribera *f,* orilla *f*
riverbed [ˈrɪvər,bɛd] *n* : cauce *m,* lecho *m*
riverside [ˈrɪvər,saɪd] *n* : ribera *f,* orilla *f*
rivet[1] [ˈrɪvət] *vt* **1** : remachar **2** FIX : fijar (los ojos, etc.) **3** FASCINATE : fascinar, cautivar
rivet[2] *n* : remache *m*
rivulet [ˈrɪvjələt] *n* : arroyo *m,* riachuelo *m* <rivulets of sweat : gotas de sudor>
roach [ˈroːtʃ] → **cockroach**
road [ˈroːd] *n* **1** : carretera *f,* calle *f,* camino *m* **2** PATH : camino *m,* sendero *m,* vía *f* <on the road to a solution : en vías de una solución>
roadblock [ˈroːd,blɑk] *n* : control *m*
roadrunner [ˈroːd,rʌnər] *n* : correcaminos *m*
roadside [ˈroːd,saɪd] *n* : borde *m* de la carretera
roadway [ˈroːd,weɪ] *n* : carretera *f,* calzada *f*
roam [ˈroːm] *vi* : vagar, deambular, errar — *vt* : vagar por
roan[1] [ˈroːn] *adj* : ruano
roan[2] *n* : caballo *m* ruano
roar[1] [ˈror] *vi* : rugir, bramar <to roar with laughter : reírse a carcajadas> — *vt* : decir a gritos
roar[2] *n* **1** : rugido *m,* bramido *m* (de un animal) **2** DIN : clamor *m* (de gente), fragor *m* (del trueno), estruendo *m* (del tráfico, etc.)
roast[1] [ˈroːst] *vt* : asar (carne, papas), tostar (café, nueces) — *vi* : asarse
roast[2] *adj* **1** : asado <roast chicken : pollo asado> **2 roast beef** : rosbif *m*
roast[3] *n* : asado *m*
rob [ˈrɑb] *v* **robbed; robbing** *vt* **1** STEAL : robar **2** DEPRIVE : privar, quitar — *vi* : robar
robber [ˈrɑbər] *n* : ladrón *m,* -drona *f*
robbery [ˈrɑbəri] *n, pl* **-beries** : robo *m*
robe[1] [ˈroːb] *vt* **robed; robing** : vestirse
robe[2] *n* **1** : toga *f* (de magistrados, etc.), sotana *f* (de eclesiásticos) <robe of office : traje de ceremonias> **2** BATHROBE : bata *f*
robin [ˈrɑbən] *n* : petirrojo *m*
robot [ˈroː,bɑt, -bət] *n* : robot *m*
robust [roˈbʌst, ˈroː,bʌst] *adj* : robusto, fuerte — **robustly** *adv*
rock[1] [ˈrɑk] *vt* **1** : acunar (a un niño), mecer (una cuna) **2** SHAKE : sacudir — *vi* SWAY : mecerse, balancearse
rock[2] *adj* : de rock
rock[3] *n* **1** ROCKING : balanceo *m* **2** *or* **rock music** : rock *m,* música *f* rock **3** : roca *f* (substancia) **4** STONE : piedra *f*
rock and roll *n* : rock and roll *m*
rocker [ˈrɑkər] *n* **1** : balancín *m* **2** *or* **rocking chair** : mecedora *f,* balancín *m* **3 to be off one's rocker** : estar chiflado, estar loco
rocket[1] [ˈrɑkət] *vi* : dispararse, subir rápidamente
rocket[2] *n* : cohete *m*
rocking horse *n* : caballito *m* (de balancín)
rock salt *n* : sal *f* gema
rocky [ˈrɑki] *adj* **rockier; -est 1** : rocoso, pedregoso **2** UNSTEADY : inestable
rod [ˈrɑd] *n* **1** BAR : barra *f,* varilla *f,* vara *f* (de madera) <a fishing rod : una caña (de pescar)> **2** : medida *f* de longitud equivalente a 5.03 metros (5 yardas)
rode → **ride**[1]
rodent [ˈroːdənt] *n* : roedor *m*
rodeo [ˈroːdi,oː, roˈdeɪ,oː] *n, pl* **-deos** : rodeo *m*
roe [ˈroː] *n* : hueva *f*
roe deer *n* : corzo *m*
rogue [ˈroːg] *n* SCOUNDREL : pícaro *m,* -ra *f;* pillo *m,* -lla *f*
roguish [ˈroːgɪʃ] *adj* : pícaro, travieso
role [ˈroːl] *n* : papel *m,* función *f,* rol *m*
roll[1] [ˈroːl] *vt* **1** : hacer rodar <to roll the ball : hacer rodar la pelota> <to roll one's eyes : poner los ojos en blanco> **2** : liar (un cigarillo) **3** *or* **to roll up** : enrollar <to roll (oneself) up into a ball : hacerse una bola> **4** FLATTEN : estirar (masa), laminar (metales), pasar el rodillo por (el césped) **5 to roll up one's sleeves** : arremangarse — *vi* **1** : rodar <the ball kept on rolling : la pelota siguió rodando> **2** SWAY : balancearse <the ship rolled in the waves : el barco se balanceó en las olas> **3** REVERBERATE, SOUND : tronar (dícese del trueno), redoblar (dícese de un tambor) **4 to roll along** PROCEED : ponerse en marcha **5 to roll around** : revolcarse **6 to roll by** : pasar **7 to roll over** : dar una vuelta
roll[2] *n* **1** LIST : lista *f* <to call the roll : pasar lista> <to have on the roll : tener inscrito> **2** *or* **bread roll** : panecito *m,* bolillo *m Mex* **3** : rollo *m* (de papel, de tela, etc.) <a roll of film : un carrete> <a roll of bills : un fajo> **4** : redoble *m* (de tambores), retumbo *m* (del trueno, etc.) **5** ROLLING, SWAYING : balanceo *m*
roller [ˈroːlər] *n* **1** : rodillo *m* **2** CURLER : rulo *m*
roller coaster [ˈroːlər,koːstər] *n* : montaña *f* rusa

roller–skate ['roːlər,skeɪt] *vi* **-skated; -skating** : patinar (sobre ruedas)
roller skate *n* : patín *m* (de ruedas)
rollicking ['rɑlɪkɪŋ] *adj* : animado, alegre
rolling pin *n* : rodillo *m*
Roman¹ ['roːmən] *adj* : romano
Roman² *n* : romano *m*, -na *f*
Roman Catholic *n* : católico *m*, -ca *f* — **Roman Catholic** *adj*
Roman Catholicism *n* : catolicismo *m*
romance¹ [ro'mænts, 'roː,mænts] *vi* **-manced; -mancing** FANTASIZE : fantasear
romance² *n* **1** : romance *m*, novela *f* de caballerías **2** : novela *f* de amor, novela *f* romántica **3** AFFAIR : romance *m*, amorío *m*
Romanian [rʊ'meɪniən, ro-] *n* **1** : rumano *m*, -na *f* **2** : rumano *m* (idioma) — **Romanian** *adj*
Roman numeral *n* : número *m* romano
romantic [ro'mæntɪk] *adj* : romántico — **romantically** [-tɪkli] *adv*
romp¹ ['rɑmp] *vi* FROLIC : retozar, jugetear
romp² *n* : retozo *m*
roof¹ ['ruːf, 'rʊf] *vt* : techar
roof² *n, pl* **roofs** ['ruːfs, 'rʊfs; 'ruːvz, 'rʊvz] **1** : techo *m*, tejado *m*, techado *m* **2 roof of the mouth** : paladar *m*
roofing ['ruːfɪŋ, 'rʊfɪŋ] *n* : techumbre *f*
rooftop ['ruːf,tɑp, 'rʊf-] *n* ROOF : tejado *m*
rook¹ ['rʊk] *vt* CHEAT : defraudar, estafar, timar
rook² *n* **1** : grajo *m* (ave) **2** : torre *f* (en ajedrez)
rookie ['rʊki] *n* : novato *m*, -ta *f*
room¹ ['ruːm, 'rʊm] *vi* LODGE : alojarse, hospedarse
room² *n* **1** SPACE : espacio *m*, sitio *m*, lugar *m* <to make room for : hacer lugar para> **2** : cuarto *m*, habitación *f* (en una casa), sala *f* (para reuniones, etc.) **3** BEDROOM : dormitorio *m*, habitación *f*, pieza *f* **4** (*indicating possibility or opportunity*) <room for improvement : posibilidad de mejorar> <there's no room for error : no hay lugar para errores>
roomer ['ruːmər, 'rʊmər] *n* : inquilino *m*, -na *f*
rooming house *n* : pensión *f*
roommate ['ruːm,meɪt, 'rʊm-] *n* : compañero *m*, -ra *f* de cuarto
roomy ['ruːmi, 'rʊmi] *adj* **roomier; -est 1** SPACIOUS : espacioso, amplio **2** LOOSE : suelto, holgado <a roomy blouse : una blusa holgada>
roost¹ ['ruːst] *vi* : posarse, dormir (en una percha)
roost² *n* : percha *f*
rooster ['ruːstər, 'rʊs-] *n* : gallo *m*
root¹ ['ruːt, 'rʊt] *vi* **1** : arraigar <the plant rooted easily : la planta arraigó con facilidad> <deeply rooted traditions : tradiciones profundamente arraigadas> **2** : hozar (dícese de los cerdos) <to root around in : hurgar en> **3 to root for** : apoyar a, alentar — *vt* **to root out** *or* **to root up** : desarraigar (plantas), extirpar (problemas, etc.)
root² *n* **1** : raíz *f* (de una planta) **2** ORIGIN : origen *m*, raíz *f* **3** CORE : centro *m*, núcleo *m* <to get to the root of the matter : ir al centro del asunto>
rootless ['ruːtləs, 'rʊt-] *adj* : desarraigado
rope¹ ['roːp] *vt* **roped; roping 1** TIE : amarrar, atar **2** LASSO : lazar **3 to rope off** : acordonar
rope² *n* : soga *f*, cuerda *f*
rosary ['roːzəri] *n, pl* **-ries** : rosario *m*
rose¹ → **rise**¹
rose² ['roːz] *adj* : rosa, color de rosa
rose³ *n* **1** : rosal *m* (planta), rosa *f* (flor) **2** : rosa *m* (color)
rosebush ['roːz,bʊʃ] *n* : rosal *m*
rosemary ['roːz,mɛri] *n, pl* **-maries** : romero *m*
rosette [ro'zɛt] *n* : escarapela *f* (hecho de cintas), roseta *f* (en arquitectura)
Rosh Hashanah [,rɑʃhɑ'ʃɑnə, ,roːʃ-] *n* : el Año Nuevo judío
rosin ['rɑzən] *n* : colofonia *f*
roster ['rɑstər] *n* : lista *f*
rostrum ['rɑstrəm] *n, pl* **-trums** *or* **-tra** [-trə] : tribuna *f*, estrado *m*
rosy ['roːzi] *adj* **rosier; -est 1** : sonrosado, de color rosa **2** PROMISING : prometedor, halagüeno
rot¹ ['rɑt] *v* **rotted; rotting** *vi* : pudrirse, descomponerse — *vt* : pudrir, descomponer
rot² *n* : putrefacción *f*, descomposición *f*, podredumbre *f*
rotary¹ ['roːt̬əri] *adj* : rotativo, rotatorio
rotary² *n, pl* **-ries 1** : máquina *f* rotativa **2** TRAFFIC CIRCLE : rotonda *f*, glorieta *f*
rotate ['roː,teɪt] *v* **-tated; -tating** *vi* REVOLVE : girar, rotar — *vt* **1** TURN : hacer girar, darle vueltas a **2** ALTERNATE : alternar
rotation [ro'teɪʃən] *n* : rotación *f*
rote ['roːt] *n* **to learn by rote** : aprender de memoria
rotor ['roːt̬ər] *n* : rotor *m*
rotten ['rɑtən] *adj* **1** PUTRID : podrido, putrefacto **2** CORRUPT : corrompido **3** BAD : malo <a rotten day : un día malísimo>
rottenness ['rɑtənnəs] *n* : podredumbre *f*
rotund [ro'tʌnd] *adj* **1** ROUNDED : redondeado **2** PLUMP : regordete *fam*, llenito *fam*
rouge ['ruːʒ, 'ruːdʒ] *n* : colorete *m*
rough¹ ['rʌf] *vt* **1** ROUGHEN : poner áspero **2 to rough out** SKETCH : esbozar, bosquejar **3 to rough up** BEAT : darle una paliza (a alguien) **4 to rough it** : vivir sin comodidades

rough[2] *adj* **1** COARSE **:** áspero, basto **2** UNEVEN **:** desigual, escabroso, accidentado (dícese del terreno) **3 :** agitado (dícese del mar), tempestuoso (dícese del tiempo), violento (dícese del viento) **4** VIOLENT **:** violento, brutal <a rough neighborhood : un barrio peligroso> **5** DIFFICULT **:** duro, difícil **6** CRUDE **:** rudo, tosco, burdo <a rough cottage : una casita tosca> <a rough draft : un borrador> <a rough sketch : un bosquejo> **7** APPROXIMATE **:** aproximado <a rough idea : una idea aproximada>

rough[3] *n* **1 the rough :** el rough (en golf) **2 in the rough :** en borrador

roughage [ˈrʌfɪdʒ] *n* **:** fibra *f*

roughen [ˈrʌfən] *vt* **:** poner áspero — *vi* **:** ponerse áspero

roughly [ˈrʌfli] *adv* **1 :** bruscamente <to treat roughly : maltratar> **2** CRUDELY **:** burdamente **3** APPROXIMATELY **:** aproximadamente, más o menos

roughneck [ˈrʌfˌnɛk] *n* **:** matón *m*

roughness [ˈrʌfnəs] *n* **:** rudeza *f,* aspereza *f*

roulette [ruːˈlɛt] *n* **:** ruleta *f*

round[1] [ˈraʊnd] *vt* **1 :** redondear <she rounded the edges : redondeó los bordes> **2** TURN **:** doblar <to round the corner : dar la vuelta a la esquina> **3 to round off :** redondear (un número) **4 to round off** *or* **to round out** COMPLETE **:** rematar, terminar **5 to round up** GATHER **:** reunir

round[2] *adv* → **around**[1]

round[3] *adj* **1 :** redondo <a round table : una mesa redonda> <in round numbers : en números redondos> <round shoulders : espaldas cargadas> **2 round trip :** viaje *m* de ida y vuelta

round[4] *n* **1** CIRCLE **:** círculo *m* **2** SERIES **:** serie *f,* sucesión *f* <a round of talks : una ronda de negociaciones> <the daily round : la rutina cotidiana> **3 :** asalto *m* (en boxeo), recorrido *m* (en golf), vuelta *f* (en varios juegos) **4 :** salva *f* (de aplausos) **5 round of drinks :** ronda *f* **6 round of ammunition :** disparo *m,* cartucho *m* **7 rounds** *npl* **:** recorridos *mpl* (de un cartero), rondas *fpl* (de un vigilante), visitas *fpl* (de un médico) <to make the rounds : hacer visitas>

round[5] *prep* → **around**[2]

roundabout [ˈraʊndəˌbaʊt] *adj* **:** indirecto <to speak in a roundabout way : hablar con rodeos>

roundly [ˈraʊndli] *adv* **1** THOROUGHLY **:** completamente **2** BLUNTLY **:** francamente, rotundamente **3** VIGOROUSLY **:** con vigor

roundness [ˈraʊndnəs] *n* **:** redondez *f*

roundup [ˈraʊndˌʌp] *n* **1 :** rodeo *m* (de animales), redada *f* (de delincuentes, etc.) **2** SUMMARY **:** resumen *m*

round up *vt* **1 :** rodear (ganado), reunir (personas) **2** SUMMARIZE **:** hacer un resumen de

roundworm [ˈraʊndˌwərm] *n* **:** lombriz *f* intestinal

rouse [ˈraʊz] *vt* **roused; rousing 1** AWAKE **:** despertar **2** EXCITE **:** excitar <it roused him to fury : lo enfureció>

rout[1] [ˈraʊt] *vt* **1** DEFEAT **:** derrotar, aplastar **2 to rout out :** hacer salir

rout[2] *n* **1** DISPERSAL **:** desbandada *f,* dispersión *f* **2** DEFEAT **:** derrota *f* aplastante

route[1] [ˈruːt, ˈraʊt] *vt* **routed; routing :** dirigir, enviar, encaminar

route[2] *n* **:** camino *m,* ruta *f,* recorrido *m*

routine[1] [ruːˈtiːn] *adj* **:** rutinario — **routinely** *adv*

routine[2] *n* **:** rutina *f*

rove [ˈroːv] *v* **roved; roving** *vi* **:** vagar, errar — *vt* **:** errar por

rover [ˈroːvər] *n* **:** vagabundo *m,* -da *f*

row[1] [ˈroː] *vt* **1 :** avanzar a remo <to row a boat : remar> **2 :** llevar a remo <he rowed me to shore : me llevó hasta la orilla> — *vi* **:** remar

row[2] [ˈraʊ] *n* **1 :** paseo *m* en barca <to go for a row : salir a remar> **2** LINE, RANK **:** fila *f,* hilera *f* **3** SERIES **:** serie *f* <three days in a row : tres días seguidos> **4** RACKET **:** estruendo *m,* bulla *f* **5** QUARREL **:** pelea *f,* riña *f*

rowboat [ˈroːˌboːt] *n* **:** bote *m* de remos

rowdiness [ˈraʊdinəs] *n* **:** bulla *f*

rowdy[1] [ˈraʊdi] *adj* **-dier; -est :** escandaloso, alborotador

rowdy[2] *n, pl* **-dies :** alborotador *m,* -dora *f*

royal[1] [ˈrɔɪəl] *adj* **:** real — **royally** *adv*

royal[2] *n* **:** persona de linaje real, miembro de la familia real

royalty [ˈrɔɪəlti] *n, pl* **-ties 1 :** realeza *f* (posición) **2 :** miembros *mpl* de la familia real **3 royalties** *npl* **:** derechos *mpl* de autor

rub[1] [ˈrʌb] *v* **rubbed; rubbing** *vt* **1 :** frotar, restregar <to rub one's hands together : frotarse las manos> **2** MASSAGE **:** friccionar, masajear **3** CHAFE **:** rozar **4** POLISH **:** frotar, pulir **5** SCRUB **:** fregar **6 to rub elbows with :** codearse con **7 to rub someone the wrong way :** sacar de quicio a alguien, caerle mal a alguien — *vi* **to rub against :** rozar

rub[2] *n* **1** RUBBING **:** frotamiento *m,* fricción *f* **2** DIFFICULTY **:** problema *m*

rubber [ˈrʌbər] *n* **1 :** goma *f,* caucho *m,* hule *m Mex* **2 rubbers** *npl* OVERSHOES **:** chanclos *mpl*

rubber band *n* **:** goma *f* (elástica), gomita *f*

rubber–stamp [ˈrʌbərˈstæmp] *vt* **1** APPROVE **:** aprobar, autorizar **2** STAMP **:** sellar

rubber stamp *n* **:** sello *m* (de goma)

rubbery [ˈrʌbəri] *adj* **:** gomoso

rubbish ['rʌbɪʃ] *n* : basura *f,* desechos *mpl,* desperdicios *mpl*
rubble ['rʌbəl] *n* : escombros *mpl,* ripio *m*
ruble ['ru:bəl] *n* : rublo *m*
ruby ['ru:bi] *n, pl* **-bies 1** : rubí *m* (gema) **2** : color *m* de rubí
rudder ['rʌdər] *n* : timón *m*
ruddy ['rʌdi] *adj* **-dier; -est** : rubicundo (dícese de la cara, etc.), rojizo (dícese del cielo)
rude ['ru:d] *adj* **ruder; rudest 1** CRUDE : tosco, rústico **2** IMPOLITE : grosero, descortés, maleducado **3** ABRUPT : brusco <a rude awakening : una sorpresa desagradable>
rudely ['ru:dli] *adv* : groseramente
rudeness ['ru:dnəs] *n* **1** IMPOLITENESS : grosería *f,* descortesía *f,* falta *f* de educación **2** ROUGHNESS : tosquedad *f* **3** SUDDENNESS : brusquedad *f*
rudiment ['ru:dəmənt] *n* : rudimento *m,* noción *f* básica <the rudiments of Spanish : los rudimentos del español>
rudimentary [ˌru:də'mɛntəri] *adj* : rudimentario, básico
rue ['ru:] *vt* **rued; ruing** : lamentar, arrepentirse de
rueful ['ru:fəl] *adj* **1** PITIFUL : lastimoso **2** REGRETFUL : arrepentido, pesaroso
ruffian ['rʌfiən] *n* : matón *m*
ruffle[1] ['rʌfəl] *vt* **-fled; -fling 1** AGITATE : agitar, rizar (agua) **2** RUMPLE : arrugar (ropa), despeinar (pelo) **3** ERECT : erizar (plumas) **4** VEX : alterar, irritar, perturbar **5** : fruncir volantes en (tela)
ruffle[2] *n* FLOUNCE : volante *m*
ruffly ['rʌfəli] *adj* : con volantes
rug ['rʌg] *n* : alfombra *f,* tapete *m*
rugged ['rʌgəd] *adj* **1** ROUGH, UNEVEN : accidentado, escabroso <rugged mountains : montañas accidentadas> **2** HARSH : duro, severo **3** ROBUST, STURDY : robusto, fuerte
ruin[1] ['ru:ən] *vt* **1** DESTROY : destruir, arruinar **2** BANKRUPT : arruinar, hacer quebrar
ruin[2] *n* **1** : ruina *f* <to fall into ruin : caer en ruinas> **2** : ruina *f,* perdición *f* <to be the ruin of : ser la perdición de> **3 ruins** *npl* : ruinas *fpl,* restos *mpl* <the ruins of the ancient temple : las ruinas del templo antiguo>
ruinous ['ru:ənəs] *adj* : ruinoso
rule[1] ['ru:l] *v* **ruled; ruling** *vt* **1** CONTROL, GOVERN : gobernar (un país), controlar (las emociones) **2** DECIDE : decidir, fallar <the judge ruled that... : el juez falló que...> **3** DRAW : trazar con una regla — *vi* **1** GOVERN : gobernar, reinar **2** PREVAIL : prevalecer, imperar **3 to rule against** : fallar en contra de
rule[2] *n* **1** REGULATION : regla *f,* norma *f* **2** CUSTOM, HABIT : regla *f* general <as a rule : por lo general> **3** GOVERNMENT : gobierno *m,* dominio *m* **4** RULER : regla *f* (para medir)
ruler ['ru:lər] *n* **1** LEADER, SOVEREIGN : gobernante *mf;* soberano *m,* -na *f* **2** : regla *f* (para medir)
ruling ['ru:lɪŋ] *n* : resolución *f,* fallo *m*
rum ['rʌm] *n* : ron *m*
Rumanian [rʊ'meɪniən] → **Romanian**
rumble[1] ['rʌmbəl] *vi* **-bled; -bling** : retumbar, hacer ruidos (dícese del estómago)
rumble[2] *n* : estruendo *m,* ruido *m* sordo, retumbo *m*
ruminant[1] ['ru:mənənt] *adj* : rumiante
ruminant[2] *n* : rumiante *m*
ruminate ['ru:məˌneɪt] *vi* **-nated; -nating 1** : rumiar (en zoología) **2** REFLECT : reflexionar, rumiar
rummage ['rʌmɪdʒ] *v* **-maged; -maging** *vi* : hurgar — *vt* RANSACK : revolver <they rummaged the attic : revolvieron el ático>
rummy ['rʌmi] *n* : rummy *m* (juego de naipes)
rumor[1] ['ru:mər] *vt* : rumorear <it is rumored that. . . : se rumorea que. . . , se dice que. . .>
rumor[2] *n* : rumor *m*
rump ['rʌmp] *n* **1** : ancas *fpl,* grupa *f* (de un animal) **2** : cadera *f* <rump steak : filete de cadera>
rumple ['rʌmpəl] *vt* **-pled; -pling** : arrugar (ropa, etc.), despeinar (pelo)
rumpus ['rʌmpəs] *n* : lío *m,* jaleo *m fam*
run[1] ['rʌn] *v* **ran** ['ræn]; **run; running** *vi* **1** : correr <she ran to catch the bus : corrió para alcanzar el autobús> <run and fetch the doctor : corre a buscar al médico> **2** : circular, correr <the train runs between Detroit and Chicago : el tren circula entre Detroit y Chicago> <to run on time : ser puntual> **3** FUNCTION : funcionar, ir <the engine runs on gasoline : el motor funciona con gasolina> <to run smoothly : ir bien> **4** FLOW : correr, ir **5** LAST : durar <the movie runs for two hours : la película dura dos horas> <the contract runs for three years : el contrato es válido por tres años> **6** : desteñir, despintar (dícese de los colores) **7** EXTEND : correr, extenderse **8 to run for office** : postularse, presentarse — *vt* **1** : correr <to run 10 miles : correr 10 millas> <to run errands : hacer los mandados> <to run out of town : hacer salir del pueblo> **2** PASS : pasar **3** DRIVE : llevar en coche **4** OPERATE : hacer funcionar (un motor, etc.) **5** : echar <to run water : echar agua> **6** MANAGE : dirigir, llevar (un negocio, etc.) **7** EXTEND : tender (un cable, etc.) **8 to run a risk** : correr un riesgo
run[2] *n* **1** : carrera *f* <at a run : a la carrera, corriendo> <to go for a run : ir a correr> **2** TRIP : vuelta *f,* paseo *m* (en coche), viaje *m* (en avión) **3** SERIES : serie *f* <a run of disappointments : una serie de desilusiones> <in

the long run : a la larga> <in the short run : a corto plazo> 4 DEMAND : gran demanda *f* <a run on the banks : una corrida bancaria> **5** (*used for theatrical productions and films*) <to have a long run : mantenerse mucho tiempo en la cartelera> **6** TYPE : tipo *m* <the average run of students : el tipo más común de estudiante> **7** : carrera *f* (en béisbol) **8** : carrera *f* (en una media) **9 to have the run of** : tener libre acceso de (una casa, etc.) **10 ski run** : pista *f* (de esquí)

runaway[1] [ˈrʌnəˌweɪ] *adj* **1** FUGITIVE : fugitivo **2** UNCONTROLLABLE : incontrolable, fuera de control <runaway inflation : inflación desenfrenada> <a runaway success : un éxito aplastante>

runaway[2] *n* : fugitivo *m*, -va *f*

rundown [ˈrʌnˌdaʊn] *n* SUMMARY : resumen *m*

run–down [ˈrʌnˈdaʊn] *adj* **1** DILAPIDATED : ruinoso, destartalado **2** SICKLY, TIRED : cansado, débil

rung[1] → **ring**[1]

rung[2] [ˈrʌŋ] *n* : peldaño *m*, escalón *m*

run–in [ˈrʌnˌɪn] *n* : disputa *f*, altercado *m*

runner [ˈrʌnər] *n* **1** RACER : corredor *m*, -dora *f* **2** MESSENGER : mensajero *m*, -ra *f* **3** TRACK : riel *m* (de un cajón, etc.) **4** : patín *m* (de un trineo), cuchilla *f* (de un patín) **5** : estolón *m* (planta)

runner–up [ˌrʌnərˈʌp] *n*, *pl* **runners–up** : subcampeón *m*, -peona *f*

running [ˈrʌnɪŋ] *adj* **1** FLOWING : corriente <running water : agua corriente> **2** CONTINUOUS : continuo <a running battle : una lucha continua> **3** CONSECUTIVE : seguido <six days running : por seis días seguidos>

run over *vt* : atropellar — *vi* OVERFLOW : rebosar

runt [ˈrʌnt] *n* : animal *m* pequeño <the runt of the litter : el más pequeño de la camada>

runway [ˈrʌnˌweɪ] *n* : pista *f* de aterrizaje

rupee [ruːˈpiː, ˈruːˌ-] *n* : rupia *f*

rupture[1] [ˈrʌptʃər] *v* **-tured; -turing** *vt* **1** BREAK, BURST : romper, reventar **2** : causar una hernia en — *vi* : reventarse

rupture[2] *n* **1** BREAK : ruptura *f* **2** HERNIA : hernia *f*

rural [ˈrʊrəl] *adj* : rural, campestre

ruse [ˈruːs, ˈruːz] *n* : treta *f*, ardid *m*, estratagema *f*

rush[1] [ˈrʌʃ] *vi* : correr, ir de prisa <to rush around : correr de un lado a otro> <to rush off : irse corriendo> — *vt* **1** HURRY : apresurar, apurar **2** ATTACK : abalanzarse sobre, asaltar

rush[2] *adj* : urgente

rush[3] *n* **1** HASTE : prisa *f*, apuro *m* **2** SURGE : ráfaga *f* (de aire), torrente *m* (de aguas), avalancha *f* (de gente) **3** DEMAND : demanda *f* <a rush on sugar : una gran demanda para el azúcar> **4** : carga *f* (en futbol americano) **5** : junco *m* (planta)

russet [ˈrʌsət] *n* : color *m* rojizo

Russian [ˈrʌʃən] *n* **1** : ruso *m*, -sa *f* **2** : ruso *m* (idioma) — **Russian** *adj*

rust[1] [ˈrʌst] *vi* : oxidarse — *vt* : oxidar

rust[2] *n* **1** : herrumbre *f*, orín *m*, óxido *m* (en los metales) **2** : roya *f* (en las plantas)

rustic[1] [ˈrʌstɪk] *adj* : rústico, campestre — **rustically** [-tɪkli] *adv*

rustic[2] *n* : rústico *m*, -ca *f*; campesino *m*, -na *f*

rustle[1] [ˈrʌsəl] *v* **-tled; -tling** *vt* **1** : hacer susurrar, hacer crujir <to rustle a newspaper : hacer crujir un periódico> **2** STEAL : robar (ganado) — *vi* : susurrar, crujir

rustle[2] *n* : murmullo *m*, susurro *m*, crujido *m*

rustler [ˈrʌsələr] *n* : ladrón *m*, -drona *f* de ganado

rusty [ˈrʌsti] *adj* **rustier; -est** : oxidado, herrumbroso

rut [ˈrʌt] *n* **1** GROOVE, TRACK : rodada *f*, surco *m* **2 to be in a rut** : ser esclavo de la rutina

ruthless [ˈruːθləs] *adj* : despiadado, cruel — **ruthlessly** *adv*

ruthlessness [ˈruːθləsnəs] *n* : crueldad *f*, falta *f* de piedad

Rwandan [rʊˈɑndən] *n* : ruandés *m*, -desa *f* — **Rwandan** *adj*

rye [ˈraɪ] *n* **1** : centeno *m* **2** *or* **rye whiskey** : whisky *m* de centeno

S

s [ˈɛs] *n*, *pl* **s's** *or* **ss** [ˈɛsəz] : decimonovena letra del alfabeto inglés

Sabbath [ˈsæbəθ] *n* **1** : sábado *m* (en el judaísmo) **2** : domingo *m* (en el cristianismo)

saber [ˈseɪbər] *n* : sable *m*

sable [ˈseɪbəl] *n* **1** BLACK : negro *m* **2** : marta *f* cebellina (animal)

sabotage[1] [ˈsæbəˌtɑʒ] *vt* **-taged; -taging** : sabotear

sabotage[2] *n* : sabotaje *m*

sac [ˈsæk] *n* : saco *m* (anatómico)

saccharin [ˈsækərən] *n* : sacarina *f*

saccharine *adj* [ˈsækərən, -ˌriːn, -ˌraɪn] : meloso, empalagoso

sachet [sæˈʃeɪ] *n* : bolsita *f* (perfumada)

sack[1] [ˈsæk] *vt* **1** FIRE : echar (del trabajo), despedir **2** PLUNDER : saquear

sack[2] *n* BAG : saco *m*

sacrament [ˈsækrəmənt] *n* : sacramento *m*

sacramental [ˌsækrəˈmɛntəl] *adj* : sacramental
sacred [ˈseɪkrəd] *adj* **1** RELIGIOUS : sagrado, sacro <sacred texts : textos sagrados> **2** HOLY : sagrado **3 sacred to** : consagrado a
sacrifice[1] [ˈsækrəˌfaɪs] *vt* **-ficed; -ficing 1** : sacrificar **2 to sacrifice oneself** : sacrificarse
sacrifice[2] *n* : sacrificio *m*
sacrilege [ˈsækrəlɪdʒ] *n* : sacrilegio *m*
sacrilegious [ˌsækrəˈlɪdʒəs, -ˈliː-] *adj* : sacrílego
sacrosanct [ˈsækroˌsæŋkt] *adj* : sacrosanto
sad [ˈsæd] *adj* **sadder; saddest** : triste — **sadly** *adv*
sadden [ˈsædən] *vt* : entristecer
saddle[1] [ˈsædəl] *vt* **-dled; -dling** : ensillar
saddle[2] *n* : silla *f* (de montar)
sadism [ˈseɪˌdɪzəm, ˈsæ-] *n* : sadismo *m*
sadist [ˈseɪdɪst, ˈsæ-] *n* : sádico *m*, -ca *f*
sadistic [səˈdɪstɪk] *adj* : sádico — **sadistically** [-tɪkli] *adv*
sadness [ˈsædnəs] *n* : tristeza *f*
safari [səˈfɑri, -ˈfær-] *n* : safari *m*
safe[1] [ˈseɪf] *adj* **safer; safest 1** UNHARMED : ileso <safe and sound : sano y salvo> **2** SECURE : seguro **3 to be on the safe side** : para mayor seguridad **4 to play it safe** : ir a la segura
safe[2] *n* : caja *f* fuerte
safeguard[1] [ˈseɪfˌgɑrd] *vt* : salvaguardar, proteger
safeguard[2] *n* : salvaguarda *f*, protección *f*
safekeeping [ˈseɪfˈkiːpɪŋ] *n* : custodia *f*, protección *f* <to put into safekeeping : poner en buen recaudo>
safely [ˈseɪfli] *adv* **1** UNHARMED : sin incidentes, sin novedades <they landed safely : aterrizaron sin novedades> **2** SECURELY : con toda seguridad, sin peligro
safety [ˈseɪfti] *n, pl* **-ties** : seguridad *f*
safety belt *n* : cinturón *m* de seguridad
safety pin *n* : alfiler *m* de gancho, alfiler *m* de seguridad, imperdible *m Spain*
saffron [ˈsæfrən] *n* : azafrán *m*
sag[1] [ˈsæg] *vi* **sagged; sagging 1** DROOP, SINK : combarse, hundirse, inclinarse **2** : colgar, caer <his jowls sagged : le colgaban las mejillas> **3** FLAG : flaquear, decaer <his spirits sagged : se le flaqueó el ánimo>
sag[2] *n* : combadura *f*
saga [ˈsɑgə, ˈsæ-] *n* : saga *f*
sagacious [səˈgeɪʃəs] *adj* : sagaz
sage[1] [ˈseɪdʒ] *adj* **sager; -est** : sabio — **sagely** *adv*
sage[2] *n* **1** : sabio *m*, -bia *f* **2** : salvia *f* (planta)
sagebrush [ˈseɪdʒˌbrʌʃ] *n* : artemisa *f*
Sagittarius [ˌsædʒəˈtɛriəs] *n* : Sagitario *mf*
said → **say**
sail[1] [ˈseɪl] *vi* **1** : navegar (en un barco) **2** : ir fácilmente <we sailed right in : entramos sin ningún problema> — *vt* **1** : gobernar (un barco) **2 to sail the seas** : cruzar los mares
sail[2] *n* **1** : vela *f* (de un barco) **2** : viaje *m* en velero <to go for a sail : salir a navegar>
sailboat [ˈseɪlˌboːt] *n* : velero *m*, barco *m* de vela
sailfish [ˈseɪlˌfɪʃ] *n* : pez *m* vela
sailor [ˈseɪlər] *n* : marinero *m*
saint [ˈseɪnt, *before a name* ˌseɪnt *or* sənt] *n* : santo *m*, -ta *f* <Saint Francis : San Francisco> <Saint Rose : Santa Rosa>
saintliness [ˈseɪntlinəs] *n* : santidad *f*
saintly [ˈseɪntli] *adj* **saintlier; -est** : santo
sake [ˈseɪk] *n* **1** BENEFIT : bien *m* <for the children's sake : por el bien de los niños> **2** (*indicating an end or a purpose*) <art for art's sake : el arte por el arte> <let's say, for argument's sake, that he's wrong : pongamos que está equivocado> **3 for goodness' sake!** : ¡por (el amor de) Dios!
salable *or* **saleable** [ˈseɪləbəl] *adj* : vendible
salacious [səˈleɪʃəs] *adj* : salaz — **salaciously** *adv*
salad [ˈsæləd] *n* : ensalada *f*
salamander [ˈsæləˌmændər] *n* : salamandra *f*
salami [səˈlɑmi] *n* : salami *m*
salary [ˈsæləri] *n, pl* **-ries** : sueldo *m*
sale [ˈseɪl] *n* **1** SELLING : venta *f* **2** : liquidación *f*, rebajas *fpl* <on sale : de rebaja> **3 sales** *npl* : ventas *fpl* <to work in sales : trabajar en ventas>
salesman [ˈseɪlzmən] *n, pl* **-men** [-mən, -ˌmɛn] **1** : vendedor *m*, dependiente *m* (en una tienda) **2 traveling salesman** : viajante *m*, representante *m*
salesperson [ˈseɪlzˌpərsən] *n* : vendedor *m*, -dora *f*; dependiente *m*, -ta *f* (en una tienda)
saleswoman [ˈseɪlzˌwʊmən] *n, pl* **-women** [-ˌwɪmən] **1** : vendedora *f*, dependienta *f* (en una tienda) **2 traveling saleswoman** : viajante *f*, representante *f*
salient [ˈseɪljənt] *adj* : saliente, sobresaliente
saline [ˈseɪˌliːn, -ˌlaɪn] *adj* : salino
saliva [səˈlaɪvə] *n* : saliva *f*
salivary [ˈsæləˌvɛri] *adj* : salival <salivary gland : glándula salival>
salivate [ˈsæləˌveɪt] *vi* **-vated; -vating** : salivar
sallow [ˈsæloː] *adj* : amarillento, cetrino
sally[1] [ˈsæli] *vi* **-lied; -lying** SET OUT : salir, hacer una salida
sally[2] *n, pl* **-lies 1** : salida *f* (militar), misión *f* **2** QUIP : salida *f*, ocurrencia *f*

salmon [ˈsæmən] *ns & pl* **1 :** salmón *m* (pez) **2 :** color *m* salmón

salon [səˈlɑn, ˈsæˌlɑn, sæˈlɔ̃] *n* **:** salón *m* <beauty salon : salón de belleza>

saloon [səˈluːn] *n* **1** HALL **:** salón *m* (en un barco) **2** BARROOM **:** bar *m*

salsa [ˈsɔlsə, ˈsɑl-] *n* **:** salsa *f* mexicana, salsa *f* picante

salt[1] [ˈsɔlt] *vt* **:** salar, echarle sal a

salt[2] *adj* **:** salado

salt[3] *n* **:** sal *f*

saltwater [ˈsɔltˌwɔt̬ər, -ˌwɑ-] *adj* **:** de agua salada

salty [ˈsɔlt̬i] *adj* **saltier; -est :** salado

salubrious [səˈluːbriəs] *adj* **:** salubre

salutary [ˈsæljəˌtɛri] *adj* **:** saludable, salubre

salutation [ˌsæljəˈteɪʃən] *n* **:** saludo *m,* salutación *f*

salute[1] [səˈluːt] *v* **-luted; -luting** *vt* **1 :** saludar (con gestos o ceremonias) **2** ACCLAIM **:** reconocer, aclamar — *vi* **:** hacer un saludo

salute[2] *n* **1 :** saludo *m* (gesto), salva *f* (de cañonazos) **2** TRIBUTE **:** reconocimiento *m,* homenaje *m*

salvage[1] [ˈsælvɪdʒ] *vt* **-vaged; -vaging :** salvar, rescatar

salvage[2] *n* **1** SALVAGING **:** salvamento *m,* rescate *m* **2 :** objetos *mpl* salvados

salvation [sælˈveɪʃən] *n* **:** salvación *f*

salve[1] [ˈsæv, ˈsav] *vt* **salved; salving :** calmar, apaciguar <to salve one's conscience : aliviarse la conciencia>

salve[2] *n* **:** ungüento *m*

salvo [ˈsælˌvoː] *n, pl* **-vos** *or* **-voes :** salva *f*

same[1] [ˈseɪm] *adj* **:** mismo, igual <the results are the same : los resultados son iguales> <he said the same thing as you : dijo lo mismo que tú>

same[2] *pron* **:** mismo <it's all the same to me : me da lo mismo> <the same to you! : ¡igualmente!>

sameness [ˈseɪmnəs] *n* **1** SIMILARITY **:** identidad *f,* semejanza *f* **2** MONOTONY **:** monotonía *f*

sample[1] [ˈsæmpəl] *vt* **-pled; -pling :** probar

sample[2] *n* **:** muestra *f,* prueba *f*

sampler [ˈsæmplər] *n* **:** dechado *m* (en bordado)

sanatorium [ˌsænəˈtoriəm] *n, pl* **-riums** *or* **-ria** [-iə] **:** sanatorio *m*

sanctify [ˈsæŋktəˌfaɪ] *vt* **-fied; -fying :** santificar

sanctimonious [ˌsæŋktəˈmoːniəs] *adj* **:** beato, santurrón

sanction[1] [ˈsæŋkʃən] *vt* **:** sancionar, aprobar

sanction[2] *n* **1** AUTHORIZATION **:** sanción *f,* autorización *f* **2 sanctions** *npl* **:** sanciones *fpl* <to impose sanctions on : imponer sanciones a>

sanctity [ˈsæŋktət̬i] *n, pl* **-ties :** santidad *f*

sanctuary [ˈsæŋktʃʊˌɛri] *n, pl* **-aries 1 :** presbiterio *m* (en una iglesia) **2** REFUGE **:** refugio *m,* asilo *m*

sand[1] [ˈsænd] *vt* **:** lijar (madera)

sand[2] *n* **:** arena *f*

sandal [ˈsændəl] *n* **:** sandalia *f*

sandbank [ˈsændˌbæŋk] *n* **:** banco *m* de arena

sandpaper *n* **:** papel *m* de lija

sandpiper [ˈsændˌpaɪpər] *n* **:** andarríos *m*

sandstone [ˈsændˌstoːn] *n* **:** arenisca *f*

sandstorm [ˈsændˌstɔrm] *n* **:** tormenta *f* de arena

sandwich[1] [ˈsændˌwɪtʃ] *vt* **:** intercalar, encajonar, meter (entre dos cosas)

sandwich[2] *n* **:** sandwich *m,* emparedado *m,* bocadillo *m Spain*

sandy [ˈsændi] *adj* **sandier; -est :** arenoso

sane [ˈseɪn] *adj* **saner; sanest 1 :** cuerdo **2** SENSIBLE **:** sensato, razonable

sang → **sing**

sanguine [ˈsæŋgwən] *adj* **1** RUDDY **:** sanguíneo, rubicundo **2** HOPEFUL **:** optimista

sanitarium [ˌsænəˈtɛriəm] *n, pl* **-iums** *or* **-ia** [-iə] → **sanatorium**

sanitary [ˈsænətɛri] *adj* **1 :** sanitario <sanitary measures : medidas sanitarias> **2** HYGIENIC **:** higiénico **3 sanitary napkin :** compresa *f,* paño *m* higiénico

sanitation [ˌsænəˈteɪʃən] *n* **:** sanidad *f*

sanity [ˈsænət̬i] *n* **:** cordura *f,* razón *f* <to lose one's sanity : perder el juicio>

sank → **sink**

Santa Claus [ˈsæntəˌklɔz] *n* **:** Papá Noel, San Nicolás

sap[1] [ˈsæp] *vt* **sapped; sapping 1** UNDERMINE **:** socavar **2** WEAKEN **:** minar, debilitar

sap[2] *n* **1 :** savia *f* (de una planta) **2** SUCKER **:** inocentón *m,* -tona *f*

sapling [ˈsæplɪŋ] *n* **:** árbol *m* joven

sapphire [ˈsæˌfaɪr] *n* **:** zafiro *m*

sarcasm [ˈsɑrˌkæzəm] *n* **:** sarcasmo *m*

sarcastic [sɑrˈkæstɪk] *adj* **:** sarcástico — **sarcastically** [-tɪkli] *adv*

sarcophagus [sɑrˈkɑfəgəs] *n, pl* **-gi** [-ˌgaɪ, -ˌdʒaɪ] **:** sarcófago *m*

sardine [sɑrˈdiːn] *n* **:** sardina *f*

sardonic [sɑrˈdɑnɪk] *adj* **:** sardónico — **sardonically** [-nɪkli] *adv*

sarsaparilla [ˌsæspəˈrɪlə, ˌsɑrs-] *n* **:** zarzaparrilla *f*

sash [ˈsæʃ] *n* **1 :** faja *f* (de un vestido), fajín *m* (de un uniforme) **2** *pl* **sash :** marco *m* (de una ventana)

sassafras [ˈsæsəˌfræs] *n* **:** sasafrás *m*

sassy [ˈsæsi] *adj* **sassier; -est** → **saucy**

sat → **sit**

Satan [ˈseɪtən] *n* **:** Satanás *m,* Satán *m*

satanic [səˈtænɪk, seɪ-] *adj* **:** satánico — **satanically** [-nɪkli] *adv*

satchel [ˈsætʃəl] *n* **:** cartera *f,* saco *m*

sate [ˈseɪt] *vt* **sated; sating :** saciar

satellite [ˈsæṭəˌlaɪt] *n* : satélite *m* <spy satellite : satélite espía>
satiate [ˈseɪʃiˌeɪt] *vt* **-ated; -ating** : saciar, hartar
satin [ˈsætən] *n* : raso *m,* satín *m,* satén *m*
satire [ˈsæˌtaɪr] *n* : sátira *f*
satiric [səˈtɪrɪk] *or* **satirical** [-ɪkəl] *adj* : satírico
satirize [ˈsæṭəˌraɪz] *vt* **-rized; -rizing** : satirizar
satisfaction [ˌsæṭəsˈfækʃən] *n* : satisfacción *f*
satisfactory [ˌsæṭəsˈfæktəri] *adj* : satisfactorio, bueno — **satisfactorily** [-rəli] *adv*
satisfy [ˈsæṭəsˌfaɪ] *v* **-fied; -fying** *vt* **1** PLEASE : satisfacer, contentar **2** CONVINCE : convencer **3** FULFILL : satisfacer, cumplir con, llenar **4** SETTLE : pagar, saldar (una cuenta) — *vi* SUFFICE : bastar
saturate [ˈsætʃəˌreɪt] *vt* **-rated; -rating 1** SOAK : empapar **2** FILL : saturar
saturation [ˌsætʃəˈreɪʃən] *n* : saturación *f*
Saturday [ˈsæṭərˌdeɪ, -di] *n* : sábado *m*
Saturn [ˈsæṭərn] *n* : Saturno *m*
satyr [ˈseɪṭər, ˈsæ-] *n* : sátiro *m*
sauce [ˈsɔs] *n* : salsa *f*
saucepan [ˈsɔsˌpæn] *n* : cacerola *f,* cazo *m,* cazuela *f*
saucer [ˈsɔsər] *n* : platillo *m*
sauciness [ˈsɔsinəs] *n* : descaro *m,* frescura *f*
saucy [ˈsɔsi] *adj* **saucier; -est** IMPUDENT : descarado, fresco *fam* — **saucily** *adv*
sauna [ˈsɔnə, ˈsaʊnə] *n* : sauna *mf*
saunter [ˈsɔntər, ˈsɑn-] *vi* : pasear, parsearse
sausage [ˈsɔsɪdʒ] *n* : salchicha *f,* embutido *m*
sauté [sɔˈteɪ, soː-] *vt* **-téed** *or* **-téd; -téing** : saltear, sofreír
savage[1] [ˈsævɪdʒ] *adj* : salvaje, feroz — **savagely** *adv*
savage[2] *n* : salvaje *mf*
savagery [ˈsævɪdʒri, -dʒəri] *n, pl* **-ries 1** FEROCITY : ferocidad *f* **2** WILDNESS : salvajismo *m*
save[1] [ˈseɪv] *vt* **saved; saving 1** RESCUE : salvar, rescatar **2** PRESERVE : preservar, conservar **3** KEEP : guardar, ahorrar (dinero), almacenar (alimentos)
save[2] *prep* EXCEPT : salvo, excepto, menos
savior [ˈseɪvjər] *n* **1** : salvador *m,* -dora *f* **2 the Savior** : el Salvador *m*
savor[1] [ˈseɪvər] *vt* : saborear
savor[2] *n* : sabor *m*
savory [ˈseɪvəri] *adj* : sabroso
saw[1] → **see**
saw[2] [ˈsɔ] *vt* **sawed; sawed** *or* **sawn** [ˈsɔn]; **sawing** : serrar, cortar (con sierra)
saw[3] *n* : sierra *f*
sawdust [ˈsɔˌdʌst] *n* : aserrín *m,* serrín *m*
sawhorse [ˈsɔˌhɔrs] *n* : caballete *m,* burro *m* (en carpintería)
sawmill [ˈsɔˌmɪl] *n* : aserradero *m*
saxophone [ˈsæksəˌfoːn] *n* : saxofón *m*
say[1] [ˈseɪ] *v* **said** [ˈsɛd]; **saying; says** [ˈsɛz] *vt* **1** EXPRESS, UTTER : decir, expresar <to say no : decir que no> <that goes without saying : ni que decir tiene> <no sooner said than done : dicho y hecho> <to say again : repetir> <to say one's prayers : rezar> **2** INDICATE : marcar, poner <my watch says three o'clock : mi reloj marca las tres> <what does the sign say? : ¿qué pone el letrero?> **3** ALLEGE : decir <it's said that she's pretty : se dice que es bonita> — *vi* : decir
say[2] *n, pl* **says** [ˈseɪz] : voz *f,* opinión *f* <to have no say : no tener ni voz ni voto> <to have one's say : dar uno su opinión>
saying [ˈseɪɪŋ] *n* : dicho *m,* refrán *m*
scab [ˈskæb] *n* **1** : costra *f,* postilla *f* (en una herida) **2** STRIKEBREAKER : rompehuelgas *mf,* esquirol *mf*
scabbard [ˈskæbərd] *n* : vaina *f* (de una espada), funda *f* (de un puñal, etc.)
scabby [ˈskæbi] *adj* **scabbier; -est** : lleno de costras
scaffold [ˈskæfəld, -ˌfoːld] *n* **1** *or* **scaffolding** : andamio *m* (para obreros, etc.) **2** : patíbulo *m,* cadalso *m* (para ejecuciones)
scald [ˈskɔld] *vt* **1** BURN : escaldar **2** HEAT : calentar (hasta el punto de ebullición)
scale[1] [ˈskeɪl] *v* **scaled; scaling** *vt* **1** : escamar (un pescado) **2** CLIMB : escalar (un muro, etc.) **3 to scale down** : reducir — *vi* WEIGH : pesar <he scaled in at 200 pounds : pesó 200 libras>
scale[2] *n* **1** *or* **scales** : balanza *f,* báscula *f* (para pesar) **2** : escama *f* (de un pez, etc.) **3** EXTENT : escala *f,* proporción *f* <wage scale : escala salarial> **4** : escala *f* (en música, en cartografía, etc.) <to draw to scale : dibujar a escala>
scallion [ˈskæljən] *n* : cebollino *m,* cebolleta *f*
scallop [ˈskɑləp, ˈskæ-] *n* **1** : vieira *f* (molusco) **2** : festón *m* (decoración)
scalp[1] [ˈskælp] *vt* : arrancar la cabellera a
scalp[2] *n* : cuero *m* cabelludo
scalpel [ˈskælpəl] *n* : bisturí *m,* escalpelo *m*
scaly [ˈskeɪli] *adj* **scalier; -est** : escamoso
scam [ˈskæm] *n* : estafa *f,* timo *m fam,* chanchullo *m fam*
scamp [ˈskæmp] *n* : bribón *m,* -bona *f;* granuja *mf;* travieso *m,* -sa *f*
scamper [ˈskæmpər] *vi* : corretear

scan[1] [ˈskæn] *vt* **scanned; scanning 1** : escandir (versos) **2** SCRUTINIZE : escudriñar, escrutar <to scan the horizon : escudriñar el horizonte> **3** PERUSE : echarle un vistazo a (un periódico, etc.) **4** EXPLORE : explorar (con radar), hacer un escáner de (en ecografía) **5** : escanear (una imagen)
scan[2] *n* **1** : ecografía *f,* examen *m* ultrasónico (en medicina) **2** : imagen *f* escaneada (en una computadora)
scandal [ˈskændəl] *n* **1** DISGRACE, OUTRAGE : escándalo *m* **2** GOSSIP : habladurías *fpl,* chismes *mpl*
scandalize [ˈskændəlˌaɪz] *vt* **-ized; -izing** : escandalizar
scandalous [ˈskændələs] *adj* : de escándalo
Scandinavian[1] [ˌskændəˈneɪviən] *adj* : escandinavo
Scandinavian[2] *n* : escandinavo *m,* -va *f*
scanner [ˈskænər] *n* : escáner *m,* scanner *m*
scant [ˈskænt] *adj* : escaso
scanty [ˈskænti] *adj* **scantier; -est** : exiguo, escaso <a scanty meal : una comida insuficiente> — **scantily** [-təli] *adv*
scapegoat [ˈskeɪpˌgoːt] *n* : chivo *m* expiatorio, cabeza *f* de turco
scapula [ˈskæpjələ] *n, pl* **-lae** [-ˌliː, -ˌlaɪ] *or* **-las** → **shoulder blade**
scar[1] [ˈskɑr] *v* **scarred; scarring** *vt* : dejar una cicatriz en — *vi* : cicatrizar
scar[2] *n* : cicatriz *f,* marca *f*
scarab [ˈskærəb] *n* : escarabajo *m*
scarce [ˈskɛrs] *adj* **scarcer; -est** : escaso
scarcely [ˈskɛrsli] *adv* **1** BARELY : apenas **2** : ni mucho menos, ni nada que se le parezca <he's scarcely an expert : ciertamente no es experto>
scarcity [ˈskɛrsət̬i] *n, pl* **-ties** : escasez *f*
scare[1] [ˈskɛr] *vt* **scared; scaring** : asustar, espantar
scare[2] *n* **1** FRIGHT : susto *m,* sobresalto *m* **2** ALARM : pánico *m*
scarecrow [ˈskɛrˌkroː] *n* : espantapájaros *m,* espantajo *m*
scarf [ˈskɑrf] *n, pl* **scarves** [ˈskɑrvz] *or* **scarfs 1** MUFFLER : bufanda *f* **2** KERCHIEF : pañuelo *m*
scarlet [ˈskɑrlət] *n* : escarlata *f* — **scarlet** *adj*
scarlet fever *n* : escarlatina *f*
scary [ˈskɛri] *adj* **scarier; -est** : espantoso, pavoroso
scathing [ˈskeɪðɪŋ] *adj* : mordaz, cáustico
scatter [ˈskæt̬ər] *vt* : esparcir, desparramar — *vi* DISPERSE : dispersarse
scavenge [ˈskævəndʒ] *v* **-venged; -venging** *vt* : rescatar (de la basura), pepenar *CA, Mex* — *vi* : rebuscar, hurgar en la basura <to scavenge for food : andar buscando comida>
scavenger [ˈskævəndʒər] *n* **1** : persona *f* que rebusca en las basuras; pepenador *m,* -dora *f CA, Mex* **2** : carroñero *m,* -ra *f* (animal)
scenario [səˈnæriˌoː, -ˈnɑr-] *n, pl* **-ios 1** PLOT : argumento *m* (en teatro), guión *m* (en cine) **2** SITUATION : situación *f* hipotética <in the worst-case scenario : en el peor de los casos>
scene [ˈsiːn] *n* **1** : escena *f* (en una obra de teatro) **2** SCENERY : decorado *m* (en el teatro) **3** VIEW : escena *f* **4** LOCALE : escenario *m* **5** COMMOTION, FUSS : escándalo *m,* escena *f* <to make a scene : armar un escándalo>
scenery [ˈsiːnəri] *n, pl* **-eries 1** : decorado *m* (en el teatro) **2** LANDSCAPE : paisaje *m*
scenic [ˈsiːnɪk] *adj* : pintoresco
scent[1] [ˈsɛnt] *vt* **1** SMELL : oler, olfatear **2** PERFUME : perfumar **3** SENSE : sentir, percibir
scent[2] *n* **1** ODOR : olor *m,* aroma *m* **2** : olfato *m* <a dog with a keen scent : un perro con un buen olfato> **3** PERFUME : perfume *m*
scented [ˈsɛntəd] *adj* : perfumado
scepter [ˈsɛptər] *n* : cetro *m*
sceptic [ˈskɛptɪk] → **skeptic**
schedule[1] [ˈskɛˌdʒuːl, -dʒəl, *esp Brit* ˈʃɛdˌjuːl] *vt* **-uled; -uling** : planear, programar
schedule[2] *n* **1** PLAN : programa *m,* plan *m* <on schedule : según lo previsto> <behind schedule : atrasado, con retraso> **2** TIMETABLE : horario *m*
scheme[1] [ˈskiːm] *vi* **schemed; scheming** : intrigar, conspirar
scheme[2] *n* **1** PLAN : plan *m,* proyecto *m* **2** PLOT, TRICK : intriga *f,* ardid *m* **3** FRAMEWORK : esquema *f* <a color scheme : una combinación de colores>
schemer [ˈskiːmər] *n* : intrigante *mf*
schism [ˈsɪzəm, ˈskɪ-] *n* : cisma *m*
schizophrenia [ˌskɪtsəˈfriːniə, ˌskɪzə-, -ˈfrɛ-] *n* : esquizofrenia *f*
schizophrenic [ˌskɪtsəˈfrɛnɪk, ˌskɪzə-] *n* : esquizofrénico *m,* -ca *f* — **schizophrenic** *adj*
scholar [ˈskɑlər] *n* **1** STUDENT : escolar *mf;* alumno *m,* -na *f* **2** EXPERT : especialista *mf*
scholarly [ˈskɑlərli] *adj* : erudito
scholarship [ˈskɑlərˌʃɪp] *n* **1** LEARNING : erudición *f* **2** GRANT : beca *f*
scholastic [skəˈlæstɪk] *adj* : académico
school[1] [ˈskuːl] *vt* : instruir, enseñar
school[2] *n* **1** : escuela *f,* colegio *m* (institución) **2** : estudiantes *mfpl* y profesores *mpl* (de una escuela) **3** : escuela *f* (en pintura, etc.) <the Flemish school : la escuela flamenca> **4** **school of fish** : banco *m,* cardumen *m*
schoolboy [ˈskuːlˌbɔɪ] *n* : escolar *m,* colegial *m*
schoolgirl [ˈskuːlˌgərl] *n* : escolar *f,* colegiala *f*

schoolhouse ['sku:l,haʊs] *n* : escuela *f*
schoolmate ['sku:l,meɪt] *n* : compañero *m,* -ra *f* de escuela
schoolroom ['sku:l,ru:m, -,rʊm] → **classroom**
schoolteacher ['sku:l,ti:tʃər] *n* : maestro *m,* -tra *f;* profesor *m,* -sora *f*
schooner ['sku:nər] *n* : goleta *f*
science ['saɪənts] *n* : ciencia *f*
scientific [,saɪən'tɪfɪk] *adj* : científico — **scientifically** [-fɪkli] *adv*
scientist ['saɪəntɪst] *n* : científico *m,* -ca *f*
scintillating ['sɪntə,leɪtɪŋ] *adj* : chispeante, brillante
scissors ['sɪzərz] *npl* : tijeras *fpl*
scoff ['skɑf] *vi* **to scoff at** : burlarse de, mofarse de
scold ['sko:ld] *vt* : regañar, reprender, reñir
scoop[1] ['sku:p] *vt* **1** : sacar (con pala o cucharón) **2 to scoop out** HOLLOW : vaciar, ahuecar
scoop[2] *n* : pala *f* (para harina, etc.), cucharón *m* (para helado, etc.)
scoot ['sku:t] *vi* : ir rápidamente <she scooted around the corner : volvió la esquina a toda prisa>
scooter ['sku:tər] *n* : patineta *f,* monopatín *m,* patinete *m*
scope ['sko:p] *n* **1** RANGE : alcance *m,* ámbito *m,* extensión *f* **2** OPPORTUNITY : posibilidades *fpl,* libertad *f*
scorch ['skɔrtʃ] *vt* : chamuscar, quemar
score[1] ['skor] *v* **scored; scoring** *vt* **1** RECORD : anotar **2** MARK, SCRATCH : marcar, rayar **3** : marcar, meter (en deportes) **4** GAIN : ganar, apuntarse **5** GRADE : calificar (exámenes, etc.) **6** : instrumentar, orquestar (música) — *vi* **1** : marcar (en deportes) **2** : obtener una puntuación (en un examen)
score[2] *n, pl* **scores 1** *or pl* **score** TWENTY : veintena *f* **2** LINE, SCRATCH : línea *f,* marca *f* **3** : resultado *m* (en deportes) <what's the score? : ¿cómo va el marcador?> **4** GRADE, POINTS : calificación *f* (en un examen), puntuación *f* (en un concurso) **5** ACCOUNT : cuenta *f* <to settle a score : ajustar una cuenta> <on that score : a ese respecto> **6** : partitura *f* (musical)
scorn[1] ['skɔrn] *vt* : despreciar, menospreciar, desdeñar
scorn[2] *n* : desprecio *m,* menosprecio *m,* desdén *m*
scornful ['skɔrnfəl] *adj* : desdeñoso, despreciativo — **scornfully** *adv*
Scorpio ['skɔrpi,o:] *n* : Escorpio *mf,* Escorpión *mf*
scorpion ['skɔrpiən] *n* : alacrán *m,* escorpión *m*
Scot ['skɑt] *n* : escocés *m,* -cesa *f*
Scotch[1] ['skɑtʃ] *adj* → **Scottish**[1]
Scotch[2] *npl* **the Scotch** : los escoceses
scot–free ['skɑt'fri:] *adj* **to get off scot–free** : salir impune, quedar sin castigo
Scots ['skɑts] *n* : escocés *m* (idioma)
Scottish[1] ['skɑtɪʃ] *adj* : escocés
Scottish[2] *n* → **Scots**
scoundrel ['skaʊndrəl] *n* : sinvergüenza *mf;* bellaco *m,* -ca *f*
scour ['skaʊər] *vt* **1** EXAMINE, SEARCH : registrar (un área), revisar (documentos, etc.) **2** SCRUB : fregar, restregar
scourge[1] ['skərdʒ] *vt* **scourged; scourging** : azotar
scourge[2] *n* : azote *m*
scout[1] ['skaʊt] *vi* **1** RECONNOITER : reconocer **2 to scout around for** : explorar en busca de
scout[2] *n* **1** : explorador *m,* -dora *f* **2** *or* **talent scout** : cazatalentos *mf*
scow ['skaʊ] *n* : barcaza *f,* gabarra *f*
scowl[1] ['skaʊl] *vi* : fruncir el ceño
scowl[2] *n* : ceño *m* fruncido
scram ['skræm] *vi* **scrammed; scramming** : largarse
scramble[1] ['skræmbəl] *v* **-bled; -bling** *vi* **1** : trepar, gatear (con torpeza) <he scrambled over the fence : se trepó a la cerca con dificultad> **2** STRUGGLE : pelearse (por) <they scrambled for seats : se pelearon por los asientos> — *vt* **1** JUMBLE : mezclar **2 to scramble eggs** : hacer huevos revueltos
scramble[2] *n* : rebatiña *f,* pelea *f*
scrap[1] ['skræp] *v* **scrapped; scrapping** *vt* DISCARD : desechar — *vi* FIGHT : pelearse
scrap[2] *n* **1** FRAGMENT : pedazo *m,* trozo *m* **2** FIGHT : pelea *f* **3** *or* **scrap metal** : chatarra *f* **4 scraps** *npl* LEFTOVERS : restos *mpl,* sobras *fpl*
scrapbook ['skræp,bʊk] *n* : álbum *m* de recortes
scrape[1] ['skreɪp] *v* **scraped; scraping** *vt* **1** GRAZE, SCRATCH : rozar, rascar <to scrape one's knee : rasparse la rodilla> **2** CLEAN : raspar <to scrape carrots : raspar zanahorias> **3 to scrape off** : raspar (pintura, etc.) **4 to scrape up** *or* **to scrape together** : juntar, reunir poco a poco — *vi* **1** RUB : rozar **2 to scrape by** : arreglárselas, ir tirando
scrape[2] *n* **1** SCRAPING : raspadura *f* **2** SCRATCH : rasguño *m* **3** PREDICAMENT : apuro *m,* aprieto *m*
scratch[1] ['skrætʃ] *vt* **1** : arañar, rasguñar <to scratch an itch : rascarse> **2** MARK : rayar, marcar **3 to scratch out** : tachar
scratch[2] *n* **1** : rasguño *m,* arañazo *m* (en la piel), rayón *m* (en un mueble, etc.) **2** : sonido *m* rasposo <I heard a scratch at the door : oí como que raspaban a la puerta>
scratchy ['skrætʃi] *adj* **scratchier; -est** : áspero, que pica <a scratchy sweater : un suéter que pica>
scrawl[1] ['skrɔl] *v* : garabatear
scrawl[2] *n* : garabato *m*

scrawny [ˈskrɔni] *adj* **scrawnier; -est** : flaco, escuálido

scream[1] [ˈskriːm] *vi* : chillar, gritar

scream[2] *n* : chillido *m,* grito *m*

screech[1] [ˈskriːtʃ] *vi* : chillar (dícese de las personas o de los animales), chirriar (dícese de los frenos, etc.)

screech[2] *n* 1 : chillido *m,* grito *m* (de una persona o un animal) **2** : chirrido *m* (de frenos, etc.)

screen[1] [ˈskriːn] *vt* **1** SHIELD : proteger **2** CONCEAL : tapar, ocultar **3** EXAMINE : someter a una revisión, hacerle un chequeo (a un paciente) **4** SIEVE : cribar

screen[2] *n* **1** PARTITION : biombo *m,* pantalla *f* **2** SIEVE : criba *f* **3** : pantalla *f* (de un televisor, una computadora, etc.) **4** MOVIES : cine *m* **5** *or* **window screen** : ventana *f* de tela metálica

screw[1] [ˈskruː] *vt* : atornillar — *vi* **to screw in** : atornillarse

screw[2] *n* **1** : tornillo *m* (para fijar algo) **2** TWIST : vuelta *f* **3** PROPELLER : hélice *f*

screwdriver [ˈskruːˌdraɪvər] *n* : destornillador *m,* desarmador *m Mex*

scribble[1] [ˈskrɪbəl] *v* **-bled; -bling** : garabatear

scribble[2] *n* : garabato *m*

scribe [ˈskraɪb] *n* : escriba *m*

scrimp [ˈskrɪmp] *vi* **1 to scrimp on** : escatimar **2 to scrimp and save** : hacer economías

script [ˈskrɪpt] *n* **1** HANDWRITING : letra *f,* escritura *f* **2** : guión *m* (de una película, etc.)

scriptural [ˈskrɪptʃərəl] *adj* : bíblico

scripture [ˈskrɪptʃər] *n* **1** : escritos *mpl* sagrados (de una religión) **2 the Scriptures** *npl* : las Sagradas Escrituras

scroll [ˈskroːl] *n* **1** : rollo *m* (de pergamino, etc.) **2** : voluta *f* (adorno en arquitectura)

scrotum [ˈskroːtəm] *n, pl* **scrota** [-tə] *or* **scrotums** : escroto *m*

scrounge [ˈskraʊndʒ] *v* **scrounged; scrounging** *vt* **1** BUM : gorrear *fam,* sablear *fam* (dinero) **2 to scrounge around for** : buscar, andar a la busca de — *vi* **to scrounge off someone** : vivir a costa de alguien

scrub[1] [ˈskrʌb] *vt* **scrubbed; scrubbing** : restregar, fregar

scrub[2] *n* **1** THICKET, UNDERBRUSH : maleza *f,* matorral *m,* matorrales *mpl* **2** SCRUBBING : fregado *m,* restregadura *f*

scrubby [ˈskrʌbi] *adj* **-bier; -est 1** STUNTED : achaparrado **2** : cubierto de maleza

scruff [ˈskrʌf] *n* **by the scruff of the neck** : por el cogote, por el pescuezo

scrumptious [ˈskrʌmpʃəs] *adj* : delicioso, muy rico

scruple [ˈskruːpəl] *n* : escrúpulo *m*

scrupulous [ˈskruːpjələs] *adj* : escrupuloso — **scrupulously** *adv*

scrutinize [ˈskruːtənˌaɪz] *vt* **-nized; -nizing** : escrutar, escudriñar

scrutiny [ˈskruːtəni] *n, pl* **-nies** : escrutinio *m,* inspección *f*

scuff [ˈskʌf] *vt* : rayar, raspar <to scuff one's feet : arrastrar los pies>

scuffle[1] [ˈskʌfəl] *vi* **-fled; -fling 1** TUSSLE : pelearse **2** SHUFFLE : caminar arrastrando los pies

scuffle[2] *n* **1** TUSSLE : refriega *f,* pelea *f* **2** SHUFFLE : arrastre *m* de los pies

scull[1] [ˈskʌl] *vi* : remar (con espadilla)

scull[2] *n* OAR : espadilla *f*

sculpt [ˈskʌlpt] *v* : esculpir

sculptor [ˈskʌlptər] *n* : escultor *m,* -tora *f*

sculpture[1] [ˈskʌlptʃər] *vt* **-tured; -turing** : esculpir

sculpture[2] *n* : escultura *f*

scum [ˈskʌm] *n* **1** FROTH : espuma *f,* nata *f* **2** : verdín *m* (encima de un líquido)

scurrilous [ˈskərələs] *adj* : difamatorio, calumnioso, injurioso

scurry [ˈskəri] *vi* **-ried; -rying** : corretear

scurvy [ˈskərvi] *n* : escorbuto *m*

scuttle[1] [ˈskʌtəl] *v* **-tled; -tling** *vt* : hundir (un barco) — *vi* SCAMPER : corretear

scuttle[2] *n* : cubo *m* (para carbón)

scythe [ˈsaɪð] *n* : guadaña *f*

sea[1] [ˈsiː] *adj* : del mar

sea[2] *n* **1** : mar *mf* <the Black Sea : el Mar Negro> <on the high seas : en alta mar> <heavy seas : mar gruesa, mar agitada> **2** MASS : mar *m,* multitud *f* <a sea of faces : un mar de rostros>

seabird [ˈsiːˌbərd] *n* : ave *f* marina

seacoast [ˈsiːˌkoːst] *n* : costa *f,* litoral *m*

seafarer [ˈsiːˌfærər] *n* : marinero *m*

seafaring[1] [ˈsiːˌfærɪŋ] *adj* : marinero

seafaring[2] *n* : navegación *f*

seafood [ˈsiːˌfuːd] *n* : mariscos *mpl*

seagull [ˈsiːˌgʌl] *n* : gaviota *f*

sea horse [ˈsiːˌhɔrs] *n* : hipocampo *m,* caballito *m* de mar

seal[1] [ˈsiːl] *vt* **1** CLOSE : sellar, cerrar <to seal a letter : cerrar una carta> <to seal an agreement : sellar un acuerdo> **2 to seal up** : tapar, rellenar (una grieta, etc.)

seal[2] *n* **1** : foca *f* (animal) **2** : sello *m* <seal of approval : sello de aprobación> **3** CLOSURE : cierre *m,* precinto *m*

sea level *n* : nivel *m* del mar

sea lion *n* : león *m* marino

sealskin [ˈsiːlˌskɪn] *n* : piel *f* de foca

seam[1] [ˈsiːm] *vt* **1** STITCH : unir con costuras **2** MARK : marcar

seam[2] *n* **1** STITCHING : costura *f* **2** LODE, VEIN : veta *f,* filón *m*

seaman [ˈsiːmən] *n, pl* **-men** [-mən, -ˌmɛn] **1** SAILOR : marinero *m* **2** : marino *m* (en la armada)

seamless [ˈsiːmləs] *adj* **1** : sin costuras, de una pieza **2** : perfecto <a seamless transition : una transición fluida>

seamstress ['siːmpstrəs] *n* : costurera *f*

seamy ['siːmi] *adj* **seamier; -est** : sórdido

séance ['seɪˌɑnts] *n* : sesión *f* de espiritismo

seaplane ['siːˌpleɪn] *n* : hidroavión *m*

seaport ['siːˌport] *n* : puerto *m* marítimo

sear ['sɪr] *vt* **1** PARCH, WITHER : secar, resecar **2** SCORCH : chamuscar, quemar

search¹ ['sərtʃ] *vt* : registrar (un edificio, un área), cachear (a una persona), buscar en — *vi* **to search for** : buscar

search² *n* : búsqueda *f,* registro *m* (de un edificio, etc.), cacheo *m* (de una persona)

searchlight ['sərtʃˌlaɪt] *n* : reflector *m*

seashell ['siːˌʃɛl] *n* : concha *f* (marina)

seashore ['siːˌʃor] *n* : orilla *f* del mar

seasick ['siːˌsɪk] *adj* : mareado <to get seasick : marearse>

seasickness ['siːˌsɪknəs] *n* : mareo *m*

seaside → **seacoast**

season¹ ['siːzən] *vt* **1** FLAVOR, SPICE : sazonar, condimentar **2** CURE : curar, secar <seasoned wood : madera seca> <a seasoned veteran : un veterano avezado>

season² *n* **1** : estación *f* (del año) **2** : temporada *f* (en deportes, etc.) <baseball season : temporada de beisbol>

seasonable ['siːzənəbəl] *adj* **1** : propio de la estación (dícese del tiempo, de las temperaturas, etc.) **2** TIMELY : oportuno

seasonal ['siːzənəl] *adj* : estacional — **seasonally** *adv*

seasoning ['siːzənɪŋ] *n* : condimento *m,* sazón *f*

seat¹ ['siːt] *vt* **1** SIT : sentar <please be seated : siéntense, por favor> **2** HOLD : tener cabida para <the stadium seats 40,000 : el estadio tiene 40,000 asientos>

seat² *n* **1** : asiento *m,* plaza *f* (en un vehículo) <take a seat : tome asiento> **2** BOTTOM : fondillos *mpl* (de la ropa), trasero *m* (del cuerpo) **3** : sede *f* (de un gobierno, etc.)

seat belt *n* : cinturón *m* de seguridad

sea urchin *n* : erizo *m* de mar

seawall ['siːˌwɑl] *n* : rompeolas *m,* dique *m* marítimo

seawater ['siːˌwɔt̬ər, -ˌwɑ-] *n* : agua *f* de mar

seaweed ['siːˌwiːd] *n* : alga *f* marina

seaworthy ['siːˌwərði] *adj* : en condiciones de navegar

secede [sɪ'siːd] *vi* **-ceded; -ceding** : separarse (de una nación, etc.)

seclude [sɪ'kluːd] *vt* **-cluded; -cluding** : aislar

seclusion [sɪ'kluːʒən] *n* : aislamiento *m*

second¹ ['sɛkənd] *vt* : secundar, apoyar (una moción)

second² *or* **secondly** ['sɛkəndli] *adv* : en segundo lugar

second³ *adj* : segundo

second⁴ *n* **1** : segundo *m,* -da *f* (en una serie) **2** : segundo *m,* segunda parte *f* **3** : segundo *m,* ayudante *m* (en deportes) **4** MOMENT : segundo *m,* momento *m*

secondary ['sɛkənˌdɛri] *adj* : secundario

secondhand ['sɛkənd'hænd] *adj* : de segunda mano

second lieutenant *n* : alférez *mf,* subteniente *mf*

second–rate ['sɛkənd'reɪt] *adj* : mediocre, de segunda categoría

secrecy ['siːkrəsi] *n, pl* **-cies** : secreto *m*

secret¹ ['siːkrət] *adj* : secreto — **secretly** *adv*

secret² *n* : secreto *m*

secretarial [ˌsɛkrə'tɛriəl] *adj* : de secretario, de oficina

secretariat [ˌsɛkrə'tɛriət] *n* : secretaría *f,* secretariado *m*

secretary ['sɛkrəˌtɛri] *n, pl* **-taries 1** : secretario *m,* -ria *f* (en una oficina, etc.) **2** : ministro *m,* -tra *f;* secretario *m,* -ria *f* <Secretary of State : Secretario de Estado>

secrete [sɪ'kriːt] *vt* **-creted; -creting 1** : secretar, segregar (en fisiología) **2** HIDE : ocultar

secretion [sɪ'kriːʃən] *n* : secreción *f*

secretive ['siːkrət̬ɪv, sɪ'kriːt̬ɪv] *adj* : reservado, callado, secreto

sect ['sɛkt] *n* : secta *f*

sectarian [sɛk'tɛriən] *adj* : sectario

section ['sɛkʃən] *n* : sección *f,* parte *f* (de un mueble, etc.), sector *m* (de la población), barrio *m* (de una ciudad)

sectional ['sɛkʃənəl] *adj* **1** : en sección, en corte <a sectional diagram : un gráfico en corte> **2** FACTIONAL : de grupo, entre facciones **3** : modular <sectional furniture : muebles modulares>

sector ['sɛktər] *n* : sector *m*

secular ['sɛkjələr] *adj* **1** : secular, laico <secular life : la vida secular> **2** : seglar (dícese de los sacerdotes, etc.)

secure¹ [sɪ'kjʊr] *vt* **-cured; -curing 1** FASTEN : asegurar (una puerta, etc.), sujetar **2** GET : conseguir

secure² *adj* **-curer; -est** : seguro — **securely** *adv*

security [sɪ'kjʊrət̬i] *n, pl* **-ties 1** SAFETY : seguridad *f* **2** GUARANTEE : garantía *f* **3 securities** *npl* : valores *mpl*

sedan [sɪ'dæn] *n* **1** *or* **sedan chair** : silla *f* de manos **2** : sedán *m* (automóvil)

sedate¹ [sɪ'deɪt] *vt* **-dated; -dating** : sedar

sedate² *adj* : sosegado — **sedately** *adv*

sedation [sɪ'deɪʃən] *n* : sedación *f*

sedative¹ ['sɛdət̬ɪv] *adj* : sedante

sedative² *n* : sedante *m,* calmante *m*

sedentary ['sɛdən,tɛri] *adj* : sedentario

sedge ['sɛdʒ] *n* : juncia *f*

sediment ['sɛdəmənt] *n* : sedimento *m* (geológico), poso *m* (en un líquido)

sedimentary [,sɛdə'mɛntəri] *adj* : sedimentario

sedition [sɪ'dɪʃən] *n* : sedición *f*

seditious [sɪ'dɪʃəs] *adj* : sedicioso

seduce [sɪ'du:s, -'dju:s] *vt* **-duced; -ducing** : seducir

seduction [sɪ'dʌkʃən] *n* : seducción *f*

seductive [sɪ'dʌktɪv] *adj* : seductor, seductivo

see[1] ['si:] *v* **saw** ['sɔ]; **seen** ['si:n]; **seeing** *vt* **1** : ver <I saw a dog : vi un perro> <see you later! : ¡hasta luego!> **2** EXPERIENCE : ver, conocer **3** UNDERSTAND : ver, entender **4** ENSURE : asegurarse <see that it's correct : asegúrese de que sea correcto> **5** ACCOMPANY : acompañar **6 to see off** : despedir, despedirse de — *vi* **1** : ver <seeing is believing : ver para creer> **2** UNDERSTAND : entender, ver <now I see! : ¡ya entiendo!> **3** CONSIDER : ver <let's see : vamos a ver> **4 to see to** : ocuparse de

see[2] *n* : sede *f* <the Holy See : la Santa Sede>

seed[1] ['si:d] *vt* **1** SOW : sembrar **2** : despepitar, quitarle las semillas a

seed[2] *n, pl* **seed** *or* **seeds 1** : semilla *f*, pepita *f* (de una fruta) **2** SOURCE : germen *m*, semilla *f*

seedless ['si:dləs] *adj* : sin semillas

seedling ['si:dlɪŋ] *n* : plantón *m*

seedpod ['si:d,pɑd] → **pod**

seedy ['si:di] *adj* **seedier; -est 1** : lleno de semillas **2** SHABBY : raído (dícese de la ropa) **3** RUN-DOWN : ruinoso (dícese de los edificios, etc.), sórdido

seek ['si:k] *v* **sought** ['sɔt]; **seeking** *vt* **1** : buscar <to seek an answer : buscar una solución> **2** REQUEST : solicitar, pedir **3 to seek to** : tratar de, intentar de — *vi* SEARCH : buscar

seem ['si:m] *vi* : parecer

seeming ['si:mɪŋ] *adj* : aparente, ostensible

seemingly ['si:mɪŋli] *adv* : aparentemente, según parece

seemly ['si:mli] *adj* **seemlier; -est** : apropiado, decoroso

seep ['si:p] *vi* : filtrarse

seer ['si:ər] *n* : vidente *mf*, clarividente *mf*

seesaw[1] ['si:,sɔ] *vi* **1** : jugar en un subibaja **2** VACILLATE : vacilar, oscilar

seesaw[2] *n* : balancín *m*, subibaja *m*

seethe ['si:ð] *vi* **seethed; seething 1** : bullir, hervir **2 to seethe with anger** : rabiar, estar furioso

segment ['sɛgmənt] *n* : segmento *m*

segmented ['sɛg,mɛntəd, sɛg'mɛn-] *adj* : segmentado

segregate ['sɛgrɪ,geɪt] *vt* **-gated; -gating** : segregar

segregation [,sɛgrɪ'geɪʃən] *n* : segregación *f*

seismic ['saɪzmɪk, 'saɪs-] *adj* : sísmico

seize ['si:z] *v* **seized; seizing** *vt* **1** CAPTURE : capturar, tomar, apoderarse de **2** ARREST : detener **3** CLUTCH, GRAB : agarrar, coger, aprovechar (una oportunidad) **4 to be seized with** : estar sobrecogido por — *vi or* **to seize up** : agarrotarse

seizure ['si:ʒər] *n* **1** CAPTURE : toma *f*, captura *f* **2** ARREST : detención *f* **3** : ataque *m* <an epileptic seizure : un ataque epiléptico>

seldom ['sɛldəm] *adv* : pocas veces, rara vez, casi nunca

select[1] [sə'lɛkt] *vt* : escoger, elegir, seleccionar (a un candidato, etc.)

select[2] *adj* : selecto

selection [sə'lɛkʃən] *n* : selección *f*, elección *f*

selective [sə'lɛktɪv] *adj* : selectivo

selenium [sə'li:niəm] *n* : selenio *m*

self ['sɛlf] *n, pl* **selves** ['sɛlvz] **1** : ser *m*, persona *f* <the self : el yo> <with his whole self : con todo su ser> <her own self : su propia persona> **2** SIDE : lado (de la personalidad) <his better self : su lado bueno>

self–addressed [,sɛlfə'drɛst] *adj* : con la dirección del remitente <include a self-addressed envelope : incluya un sobre con su nombre y dirección>

self–appointed [,sɛlfə'pɔɪntəd] *adj* : autoproclamado, autonombrado

self–assurance [,sɛlfə'ʃʊrənts] *n* : seguridad *f* en sí mismo

self–assured [,sɛlfə'ʃʊrd] *adj* : seguro de sí mismo

self–centered [,sɛlf'sɛntərd] *adj* : egocéntrico

self–confidence [,sɛlf'kɑnfədənts] *n* : confianza *f* en sí mismo

self–confident [,sɛlf'kɑnfədənt] *adj* : seguro de sí mismo

self–conscious [,sɛlf'kɑntʃəs] *adj* : cohibido, tímido

self–consciously [,sɛlf'kɑntʃəsli] *adv* : de manera cohibida

self–consciousness [,sɛlf'kɑntʃəsnəs] *n* : vergüenza *f*, timidez *f*

self–contained [,sɛlfkən'teɪnd] *adj* **1** INDEPENDENT : independiente **2** RESERVED : reservado

self–control [,sɛlfkən'tro:l] *n* : autocontrol *m*, control *m* de sí mismo

self–defense [,sɛlfdɪ'fɛnts] *n* : defensa *f* propia, defensa *f* personal <to act in self-defense : actuar en defensa propia> <self-defense class : clase de defensa personal>

self–denial [,sɛlfdɪ'naɪəl] *n* : abnegación *f*

self–destructive [,sɛlfdɪ'strʌktɪv] *adj* : autodestructivo

self–determination [,sɛlfdɪ,tərmə'neɪʃən] *n* : autodeterminación *f*

self–discipline [,sɛlf'dɪsəplən] *n* : autodisciplina *f*

self–employed [ˌsɛlfɪm'plɔɪd] *adj* : que trabaja por cuenta propia, autónomo
self–esteem [ˌsɛlfɪ'stiːm] *n* : autoestima *f,* amor *m* propio
self–evident [ˌsɛlf'ɛvədənt] *adj* : evidente, manifiesto
self–explanatory [ˌsɛlfɪk'splænəˌtori] *adj* : fácil de entender, evidente
self–expression [ˌsɛlfɪk'sprɛʃən] *n* : expresión *f* personal
self–government [ˌsɛlf'gʌvərmənt, -vərn-] *n* : autogobierno *m*
self–help [ˌsɛlf'hɛlp] *n* : autoayuda *f*
self–important [ˌsɛlfɪm'pɔrtənt] *adj* **1** VAIN : vanidoso, presumido **2** ARROGANT : arrogante
self–indulgent [ˌsɛlfɪn'dʌldʒənt] *adj* : que se permite excesos
self–inflicted [ˌsɛlfɪn'flɪktəd] *adj* : autoinfligido
self–interest [ˌsɛlf'ɪntrəst, -təˌrɛst] *n* : interés *m* personal
selfish ['sɛlfɪʃ] *adj* : egoísta
selfishly ['sɛlfɪʃli] *adv* : de manera egoísta
selfishness ['sɛlfɪʃnəs] *n* : egoísmo *m*
selfless ['sɛlfləs] *adj* UNSELFISH : desinteresado
self–made [ˌsɛlf'meɪd] *adj* : próspero gracias a sus propios esfuerzos
self–pity [ˌsɛlf'pɪt̬i] *n, pl* **-ties** : autocompasión *f*
self–portrait [ˌsɛlf'pɔrtrət] *n* : autorretrato *m*
self–propelled [ˌsɛlfpro'pɛld] *adj* : autopropulsado
self–reliance [ˌsɛlfri'laɪən*t*s] *n* : independencia *f,* autosuficiencia *f*
self–respect [ˌsɛlfri'spɛkt] *n* : autoestima *f,* amor *m* propio
self–restraint [ˌsɛlfri'streɪnt] *n* : autocontrol *m,* moderación *f*
self–righteous [ˌsɛlf'raɪtʃəs] *adj* : santurrón, moralista
self–sacrifice [ˌsɛlf'sækrəˌfaɪs] *n* : abnegación *f*
selfsame ['sɛlfˌseɪm] *adj* : mismo
self–service [ˌsɛlf'sərvɪs] *adj* **1** : de autoservicio **2 self-service restaurant** : autoservicio *m*
self–sufficiency [ˌsɛlfsə'fɪʃən*t*si] *n* : autosuficiencia *f*
self–sufficient [ˌsɛlfsə'fɪʃənt] *adj* : autosuficiente
self–taught [ˌsɛlf'tɔt] *adj* : autodidacto
sell ['sɛl] *v* **sold** ['soːld]; **selling** *vt* : vender — *vi* : venderse
seller ['sɛlər] *n* : vendedor *m,* -dora *f*
selves → **self**
semantics [sɪ'mæntɪks] *ns & pl* : semántica *f*
semaphore ['sɛməˌfor] *n* : semáforo *m*
semblance ['sɛmblən*t*s] *n* : apariencia *f*
semen ['siːmən] *n* : semen *m*
semester [sə'mɛstər] *n* : semestre *m*
semicolon ['sɛmiˌkoːlən, 'sɛˌmaɪ-] *n* : punto y coma *m*
semiconductor ['sɛmikənˌdʌktər, 'sɛˌmaɪ-] *n* : semiconductor *m*
semifinal ['sɛmiˌfaɪnəl, 'sɛˌmaɪ-] *n* : semifinal *f*
seminar ['sɛməˌnɑr] *n* : seminario *m*
seminary ['sɛməˌnɛri] *n, pl* **-naries** : seminario *m*
senate ['sɛnət] *n* : senado *m*
senator ['sɛnət̬ər] *n* : senador *m,* -dora *f*
send ['sɛnd] *vt* **sent** ['sɛnt]; **sending 1** : mandar, enviar <to send a letter : mandar una carta> <to send word : avisar, mandar decir> **2** PROPEL : mandar, lanzar <he sent it into left field : lo mandó al jardín izquierdo> <to send up dust : alzar polvo> **3 to send into a rage** : poner furioso
sender ['sɛndər] *n* : remitente *mf* (de una carta, etc.)
Senegalese [ˌsɛnəgə'liːz, -'liːs] *n* : senegalés *m,* -lesa *f* — **Senegalese** *adj*
senile ['siːˌnaɪl] *adj* : senil
senility [sɪ'nɪlət̬i] *n* : senilidad *f*
senior[1] ['siːnjər] *adj* **1** ELDER : mayor <John Doe, Senior : John Doe, padre> **2** : superior (en rango), más antiguo (en años de servicio) <a senior official : un alto oficial>
senior[2] *n* **1** : superior *m* (en rango) **2 to be someone's senior** : ser mayor que alguien <she's two years my senior : me lleva dos años>
seniority [ˌsiː'njɔrət̬i] *n* : antigüedad *f* (en años de servicio)
sensation [sɛn'seɪʃən] *n* : sensación *f*
sensational [sɛn'seɪʃənəl] *adj* : que causa sensación <sensational stories : historias sensacionalistas>
sense[1] ['sɛn*t*s] *vt* **sensed; sensing** : sentir <he sensed danger : se dio cuenta del peligro>
sense[2] *n* **1** MEANING : sentido *m,* significado *m* **2** : sentido *m* <the sense of smell : el sentido del olfato> **3 to make sense** : tener sentido
senseless ['sɛn*t*sləs] *adj* **1** MEANINGLESS : sin sentido, sin razón **2** UNCONSCIOUS : inconsciente
senselessly ['sɛn*t*sləsli] *adv* : sin sentido
sensibility [ˌsɛn*t*sə'bɪlət̬i] *n, pl* **-ties** : sensibilidad *f*
sensible ['sɛn*t*səbəl] *adj* **1** PERCEPTIBLE : sensible, perceptible **2** AWARE : consciente **3** REASONABLE : sensato <a sensible man : un hombre sensato> <sensible shoes : zapatos prácticos> — **sensibly** [-bli] *adv*
sensibleness ['sɛn*t*səbəlnəs] *n* : sensatez *f,* solidez *f*
sensitive ['sɛn*t*sət̬ɪv] *adj* **1** : sensible, delicado <sensitive skin : piel sensible> **2** IMPRESSIONABLE : sensible, impresionable **3** TOUCHY : susceptible

sensitiveness [ˈsɛntsət̬ɪvnəs] → **sensitivity**

sensitivity [ˌsɛntsəˈtɪvət̬i] *n, pl* **-ties** : sensibilidad *f*

sensor [ˈsɛnˌsɔr, ˈsɛntsər] *n* : sensor *m*

sensory [ˈsɛntsəri] *adj* : sensorial

sensual [ˈsɛntʃʊəl] *adj* : sensual — **sensually** *adv*

sensuous [ˈsɛntʃʊəs] *adj* : sensual

sent → **send**

sentence1 [ˈsɛntənts, -ənz] *vt* **-tenced; -tencing** : sentenciar

sentence2 *n* **1** JUDGMENT : sentencia *f* **2** : oración *f,* frase *f* (en gramática)

sentiment [ˈsɛntəmənt] *n* **1** BELIEF : opinión *f* **2** FEELING : sentimiento *m* **3** → **sentimentality**

sentimental [ˌsɛntəˈmɛntəl] *adj* : sentimental

sentimentality [ˌsɛntəˌmɛnˈtæləṭi] *n, pl* **-ties** : sentimentalismo *m,* sensiblería *f*

sentinel [ˈsɛntənəl] *n* : centinela *mf,* guardia *mf*

sentry [ˈsɛntri] *n, pl* **-tries** : centinela *mf*

sepal [ˈsiːpəl, ˈsɛ-] *n* : sépalo *m*

separable [ˈsɛpərəbəl] *adj* : separable

separate1 [ˈsɛpəˌreɪt] *v* **-rated; -rating** *vt* **1** DETACH, SEVER : separar **2** DISTINGUISH : diferenciar, distinguir — *vi* PART : separarse

separate2 [ˈsɛprət, ˈsɛpə-] *adj* **1** INDIVIDUAL : separado, aparte <a separate state : un estado separado> <in a separate envelope : en un sobre aparte> **2** DISTINCT : distinto

separately [ˈsɛprətli, ˈsɛpə-] *adv* : por separado, separadamente, aparte

separation [ˌsɛpəˈreɪʃən] *n* : separación *f*

sepia [ˈsiːpiə] *n* : color *m* sepia

September [sɛpˈtɛmbər] *n* : septiembre *m,* setiembre *m*

sepulchre [ˈsɛpəlkər] *n* : sepulcro *m*

sequel [ˈsiːkwəl] *n* **1** CONSEQUENCE : secuela *f,* consecuencia *f* **2** : continuación *f* (de una película, etc.)

sequence [ˈsiːkwənts] *n* **1** SERIES : serie *f,* sucesión *f,* secuencia *f* (matemática o musical) **2** ORDER : orden *m*

sequester [sɪˈkwɛstər] *vt* : aislar

sequin [ˈsiːkwən] *n* : lentejuela *f*

sequoia [sɪˈkwɔɪə] *n* : secoya *f,* secuoya *f*

sera → **serum**

Serb [ˈsərb] *or* **Serbian** [ˈsərbiən] *n* : serbio *m,* -bia *f* — **Serb** *or* **Serbian** *adj*

Serbo-Croatian [ˌsərbokroˈeɪʃən] *n* : serbocroata *m* (idioma) — **Serbo-Croatian** *adj*

serenade1 [ˌsɛrəˈneɪd] *vt* **-naded; -nading** : darle una serenata (a alguien)

serenade2 *n* : serenata *f*

serene [səˈriːn] *adj* : sereno — **serenely** *adv*

serenity [səˈrɛnəṭi] *n* : serenidad *f*

serf [ˈsərf] *n* : siervo *m,* -va *f*

serge [ˈsərdʒ] *n* : sarga *f*

sergeant [ˈsɑrdʒənt] *n* : sargento *mf*

serial1 [ˈsɪriəl] *adj* : seriado

serial2 *n* : serie *f,* serial *m* (de radio o televisión), publicación *f* por entregas

serially [ˈsɪriəli] *adv* : en serie

series [ˈsɪrˌiːz] *n, pl* **series** : serie *f,* sucesión *f*

serious [ˈsɪriəs] *adj* **1** SOBER : serio **2** DEDICATED, EARNEST : serio, dedicado <to be serious about something : tomar algo en serio> **3** GRAVE : serio, grave <serious problems : problemas graves>

seriously [ˈsɪriəsli] *adv* **1** EARNESTLY : seriamente, con seriedad, en serio **2** SEVERELY : gravemente

seriousness [ˈsɪriəsnəs] *n* : seriedad *f,* gravedad *f*

sermon [ˈsərmən] *n* : sermón *m*

serpent [ˈsərpənt] *n* : serpiente *f*

serrated [səˈreɪṭəd, ˈsɛrˌeɪṭəd] *adj* : dentado, serrado

serum [ˈsɪrəm] *n, pl* **serums** *or* **sera** [ˈsɪrə] : suero *m*

servant [ˈsərvənt] *n* : criado *m,* -da *f;* sirviente *m,* -ta *f*

serve [ˈsərv] *v* **served; serving** *vi* **1** : servir <to serve in the navy : servir en la armada> <to serve on a jury : ser miembro de un jurado> **2** DO, FUNCTION : servir <to serve as : servir de, servir como> **3** : sacar (en deportes) — *vt* **1** : servir <to serve God : servir a Dios> **2** HELP : servir <it serves no purpose : no sirve para nada> **3** : servir (comida o bebida) <dinner is served : la cena está servida> **4** SUPPLY : abastecer **5** CARRY OUT : cumplir, hacer <to serve time : servir una pena> **6 to serve a summons** : entregar una citación

server [ˈsərvər] *n* **1** : camarero *m,* -ra *f;* mesero *m,* -ra *f* (en un restaurante) **2** *or* **serving dish** : fuente *f* (para servir comida)

service1 [ˈsərvəs] *vt* **-viced; -vicing 1** MAINTAIN : darle mantenimiento a (una máquina), revisar **2** REPAIR : arreglar, reparar

service2 *n* **1** HELP, USE : servicio *m* <to do someone a service : hacerle un servicio a alguien> <at your service : a sus órdenes> <to be out of service : no funcionar> **2** CEREMONY : oficio *m* (religioso) **3** DEPARTMENT, SYSTEM : servicio *m* <social services : servicios sociales> <train service : servicio de trenes> **4** SET : juego *m,* servicio *m* <tea service : juego de té> **5** MAINTENANCE : mantenimiento *m,* revisión *f,* servicio *m* **6** : saque *m* (en deportes) **7 armed services** : fuerzas *fpl* armadas

serviceable [ˈsərvəsəbəl] *adj* **1** USEFUL : útil **2** DURABLE : duradero

serviceman [ˈsərvəsˌmæn, -mən] *n, pl* **-men** [-mən, -ˌmɛn] : militar *m*

service station *n* **:** estación *f* de servicio

servicewoman [ˈsərvəs,wʊmən] *n, pl* **-women** [-,wɪmən] **:** militar *f*

servile [ˈsərvəl, -,vaɪl] *adj* **:** servil

serving [ˈsərvɪŋ] *n* HELPING **:** porción *f,* ración *f*

servitude [ˈsərvə,tuːd, -,tjuːd] *n* **:** servidumbre *f*

sesame [ˈsɛsəmi] *n* **:** ajonjolí *m,* sésamo *m*

session [ˈsɛʃən] *n* **:** sesión *f*

set[1] [ˈsɛt] *v* **set; setting** *vt* **1** SEAT **:** sentar **2** *or* **to set down** PLACE **:** poner, colocar **3** ARRANGE **:** fijar, establecer <to set the date : poner la fecha> <he set the agenda : estableció la agenda> **4** ADJUST **:** poner (un reloj, etc.) **5** (*indicating the causing of a certain condition*) <to set fire to : prenderle fuego a> <she set it free : lo soltó> **6** MAKE, START **:** poner, hacer <I set them working : los puse a trabajar> — *vi* **1** SOLIDIFY **:** fraguar (dícese del cemento, etc.), cuajar (dícese de la gelatina, etc.) **2 :** ponerse (dícese del sol o de la luna)

set[2] *adj* **1** ESTABLISHED, FIXED **:** fijo, establecido **2** RIGID **:** inflexible <to be set in one's ways : tener costumbres muy arraigadas> **3** READY **:** listo, preparado

set[3] *n* **1** COLLECTION **:** juego *m* <a set of dishes : un juego de platos, una vajilla> <a tool set : una caja de herramientas> **2** *or* **stage set :** decorado *m* (en el teatro), plató *m* (en el cine) **3** APPARATUS **:** aparato *m* <a television set : un televisor> **4 :** conjunto *m* (en matemáticas)

setback [ˈsɛt,bæk] *n* **:** revés *m,* contratiempo *m*

set in *vi* BEGIN **:** comenzar, empezar

set off *vt* **1** PROVOKE **:** provocar **2** EXPLODE **:** hacer estallar (una bomba, etc.) — *vi or* **to set forth :** salir

set out *vi* **:** salir (de viaje) — *vt* INTEND **:** proponerse

settee [sɛˈtiː] *n* **:** sofá *m*

setter [ˈsɛt̬ər] *n* **:** setter *mf* <Irish setter : setter irlandés>

setting [ˈsɛt̬ɪŋ] *n* **1 :** posición *f,* ajuste *m* (de un control) **2 :** engaste *m,* montura *f* (de una gema) **3** SCENE **:** escenario *m* (de una novela, etc.) **4** SURROUNDINGS **:** ambiente *m,* entorno *m,* marco *m*

settle [ˈsɛt̬əl] *v* **settled; settling** *vi* **1** ALIGHT, LAND **:** posarse (dícese de las aves), depositarse (dícese del polvo) **2** SINK **:** asentarse (dícese de los edificios) <he settled into the chair : se arrellanó en la silla> **3 :** instalarse (en una casa), establecerse (en una ciudad o región) **4 to settle down :** calmarse, tranquilizarse <settle down! : ¡tranquilízate!, ¡cálmate!> **5 to settle down :** sentar cabeza, hacerse sensato <to marry and settle down : casarse y sentar cabeza> — *vt* **1** ARRANGE, DECIDE **:** fijar, decidir, acordar (planes, etc.) **2** RESOLVE **:** resolver, solucionar <to settle an argument : resolver una discusión> **3** PAY **:** pagar <to settle an account : saldar una cuenta> **4** CALM **:** calmar (los nervios), asentar (el estómago) **5** COLONIZE **:** colonizar **6 to settle oneself :** acomodarse, hacerse cómodo

settlement [ˈsɛt̬əlmənt] *n* **1** PAYMENT **:** pago *m,* liquidación *f* **2** COLONY **:** asentamiento *m* **3** RESOLUTION **:** acuerdo *m*

settler [ˈsɛt̬ələr] *n* **:** poblador *m,* -dora *f;* colono *m,* -na *f*

set up *vt* **1** ASSEMBLE **:** montar, armar **2** ERECT **:** levantar, erigir **3** ESTABLISH **:** establecer, fundar, montar (un negocio) **4** CAUSE **:** armar <they set up a clamor : armaron un alboroto>

seven[1] [ˈsɛvən] *adj* **:** siete

seven[2] *n* **:** siete *m*

seven hundred[1] *adj* **:** setecientos

seven hundred[2] *n* **:** setecientos *m*

seventeen[1] [,sɛvənˈtiːn] *adj* **:** diecisiete

seventeen[2] *n* **:** diecisiete *m*

seventeenth[1] [,sɛvənˈtiːnθ] *adj* **:** decimoséptimo

seventeenth[2] *n* **1 :** decimoséptimo *m,* -ma *f* (en una serie) **2 :** diecisieteavo *m,* diecisieteava parte *f*

seventh[1] [ˈsɛvənθ] *adj* **:** séptimo

seventh[2] *n* **1 :** séptimo *m,* -ma *f* (en una serie) **2 :** séptimo *m,* séptima parte *f*

seventieth[1] [ˈsɛvəntiəθ] *adj* **:** septuagésimo

seventieth[2] *n* **1 :** septuagésimo *m,* -ma *f* (en una serie) **2 :** setentavo *m,* setentava parte *f,* septuagésima parte *f*

seventy[1] [ˈsɛvənt̬i] *adj* **:** setenta

seventy[2] *n, pl* **-ties :** setenta *m*

sever [ˈsɛvər] *vt* **-ered; -ering :** cortar, romper

several[1] [ˈsɛvrəl, ˈsɛvə-] *adj* **1** DISTINCT **:** distinto **2** SOME **:** varios <several weeks : varias semanas>

several[2] *pron* **:** varios, varias

severance [ˈsɛvrənts, sɛvə-] *n* **1 :** ruptura *f* (de relaciones, etc.) **2 severance pay :** indemnización *f* (por despido)

severe [səˈvɪr] *adj* **severer; -est 1** STRICT **:** severo **2** AUSTERE **:** sobrio, austero **3** SERIOUS **:** grave <a severe wound : una herida grave> <severe aches : dolores fuertes> **4** DIFFICULT **:** duro, difícil — **severely** *adv*

severity [səˈvɛrət̬i] *n* **1** HARSHNESS **:** severidad *f* **2** AUSTERITY **:** sobriedad *f,* austeridad *f* **3** SERIOUSNESS **:** gravedad *f* (de una herida, etc.)

sew [ˈsoː] *v* **sewed; sewn** [ˈsoːn] *or* **sewed; sewing :** coser

sewage [ˈsuːɪdʒ] *n* **:** aguas *fpl* negras, aguas *fpl* residuales

sewer[1] [ˈsoːər] *n* **:** uno que cose

sewer[2] [ˈsuːər] *n* **:** alcantarilla *f,* cloaca *f*

sewing [ˈsoːɪŋ] *n* **:** costura *f*

sex [ˈsɛks] *n* **1 :** sexo *m* <the opposite sex : el sexo opuesto> **2** COPULATION **:** relaciones *fpl* sexuales

sexism [ˈsɛkˌsɪzəm] *n* **:** sexismo *m*

sexist[1] [ˈsɛksɪst] *adj* **:** sexista

sexist[2] *n* **:** sexista *mf*

sextant [ˈsɛkstənt] *n* **:** sextante *m*

sextet [sɛkˈstɛt] *n* **:** sexteto *m*

sexton [ˈsɛkstən] *n* **:** sacristán *m*

sexual [ˈsɛkʃʊəl] *adj* **:** sexual — **sexually** *adv*

sexuality [ˌsɛkʃʊˈælət̬i] *n* **:** sexualidad *f*

sexy [ˈsɛksi] *adj* **sexier; -est :** sexy

shabbily [ˈʃæbəli] *adv* **1 :** pobremente <shabbily dressed : pobremente vestido> **2** UNFAIRLY **:** mal, injustamente

shabbiness [ˈʃæbinəs] *n* **1 :** lo gastado (de ropa, etc.) **2 :** lo mal vestido (de personas) **3** UNFAIRNESS **:** injusticia *f*

shabby [ˈʃæbi] *adj* **shabbier; -est 1 :** gastado (dícese de la ropa, etc.) **2 :** mal vestido (dícese de las personas) **3** UNFAIR **:** malo, injusto <shabby treatment : mal trato>

shack [ˈʃæk] *n* **:** choza *f,* rancho *m*

shackle[1] [ˈʃækəl] *vt* **-led; -ling :** ponerle grilletes (a alguien)

shackle[2] *n* **:** grillete *m*

shad [ˈʃæd] *n* **:** sábalo *m*

shade[1] [ˈʃeɪd] *v* **shaded; shading** *vt* **1** SHELTER **:** proteger (del sol o de la luz) **2** *or* **to shade in :** matizar los colores de — *vi* **:** convertirse gradualmente <his irritation shaded into rage : su irritación iba convirtiéndose en furia>

shade[2] *n* **1 :** sombra *f* <to give shade : dar sombra> **2 :** tono *m* (de un color) **3** NUANCE **:** matiz *m* **4 :** pantalla *f* (de una lámpara), persiana *f* (de una ventana)

shadow[1] [ˈʃædoː] *vt* **1** DARKEN **:** ensombrecer **2** TRAIL **:** seguir de cerca, seguirle la pista (a alguien)

shadow[2] *n* **1 :** sombra *f* **2** DARKNESS **:** oscuridad *f* **3** TRACE **:** sombra *f,* atisbo *m,* indicio *m* <without a shadow of a doubt : sin sombra de duda, sin lugar a dudas> **4 to cast a shadow over :** ensombrecer

shadowy [ˈʃædowi] *adj* **1** INDISTINCT **:** vago, indistinto **2** DARK **:** oscuro

shady [ˈʃeɪdi] *adj* **shadier; -est 1 :** sombreado (dícese de un lugar), que da sombra (dícese de un árbol) **2** DISREPUTABLE **:** sospechoso (dícese de una persona), turbio (dícese de un negocio, etc.)

shaft [ˈʃæft] *n* **1 :** asta *f* (de una lanza), astil *m* (de una flecha), mango *m* (de una herramienta) **2** *or* **mine shaft :** pozo *m*

shaggy [ˈʃægi] *adj* **shaggier; -est 1** HAIRY **:** peludo <a shaggy dog : un perro peludo> **2** UNKEMPT **:** enmarañado, despeinado (dícese del pelo, de las barbas, etc.)

shake[1] [ˈʃeɪk] *v* **shook** [ˈʃʊk]; **shaken** [ˈʃeɪkən]; **shaking** *vt* **1 :** sacudir, agitar, hacer temblar <he shook his head : negó con la cabeza> **2** WEAKEN **:** debilitar, hacer flaquear <it shook her faith : debilitó su confianza> **3** UPSET **:** afectar, alterar **4 to shake hands with someone :** darle la mano a alguien, estrecharle la mano a alguien — *vi* **:** temblar, sacudirse

shake[2] *n* **:** sacudida *f,* apretón *m* (de manos)

shaker [ˈʃeɪkər] *n* **1 salt shaker :** salero *m* **2 pepper shaker :** pimentero *m* **3 cocktail shaker :** coctelera *f*

shake–up [ˈʃeɪkˌʌp] *n* **:** reorganización *f*

shakily [ˈʃeɪkəli] *adv* **:** temblorosamente

shaky [ˈʃeɪki] *adj* **shakier; -est 1** SHAKING **:** tembloroso **2** UNSTABLE **:** poco firme, inestable **3** PRECARIOUS **:** precario, incierto **4** QUESTIONABLE **:** dudoso, cuestionable <shaky arguments : argumentos discutibles>

shale [ˈʃeɪl] *n* **:** esquisto *m*

shall [ˈʃæl] *v aux, past* **should** [ˈʃʊd]; *present s & pl* **shall 1** (*used to express a command*) <you shall do as I say : harás lo que te digo> **2** (*used to express futurity*) <we shall see : ya veremos> <when shall we expect you? : ¿cuándo te podemos esperar?> **3** (*used to express determination*) <you shall have the money : tendrás el dinero> **4** (*used to express a condition*) <if he should die : si muriera> <if they should call, tell me : si llaman, dímelo> **5** (*used to express obligation*) <he should have said it : debería haberlo dicho> **6** (*used to express probability*) <they should arrive soon : deben (de) llegar pronto> <why should he lie? : ¿porqué ha de mentir?>

shallow [ˈʃæloː] *adj* **1 :** poco profundo (dícese del agua, etc.) **2** SUPERFICIAL **:** superficial

shallows [ˈʃæloːz] *npl* **:** bajío *m,* bajos *mpl*

sham[1] [ˈʃæm] *v* **shammed; shamming :** fingir

sham[2] *adj* **:** falso, fingido

sham[3] *n* **1** FAKE, PRETENSE **:** farsa *f,* simulación *f,* imitación *f* **2** FAKER **:** impostor *m,* -tora *f;* farsante *mf*

shamble [ˈʃæmbəl] *vi* **-bled; -bling :** caminar arrastrando los pies

shambles [ˈʃæmbəlz] *ns & pl* **:** caos *m,* desorden *m,* confusión *f*

shame[1] [ˈʃeɪm] *vt* **shamed; shaming 1 :** avergonzar <he was shamed by their words : sus palabras le dieron vergüenza> **2** DISGRACE **:** deshonrar

shame[2] *n* **1 :** vergüenza *f* <to have no shame : no tener vergüenza> **2** DISGRACE **:** vergüenza *f,* deshonra *f* **3** PITY **:** lástima *f,* pena *f* <what a shame! : ¡qué pena!>

shamefaced [ˈʃeɪm,feɪst] *adj* : avergonzado
shameful [ˈʃeɪmfəl] *adj* : vergonzoso — **shamefully** *adv*
shameless [ˈʃeɪmləs] *adj* : descarado, desvergonzado — **shamelessly** *adv*
shampoo[1] [ʃæmˈpuː] *vt* : lavar (el pelo)
shampoo[2] *n, pl* **-poos** : champú *m*
shamrock [ˈʃæm,rɑk] *n* : trébol *m*
shank [ˈʃæŋk] *n* : parte *f* baja de la pierna
shan't [ˈʃænt] (*contraction of* **shall not**) → **shall**
shanty [ˈʃænti] *n, pl* **-ties** : choza *f,* rancho *m*
shape[1] [ˈʃeɪp] *v* **shaped; shaping** *vt* **1** : dar forma a, modelar (arcilla, etc.), tallar (madera, piedra), formar (carácter) <to be shaped like : tener forma de> **2** DETERMINE : decidir, determinar — *vi or* **to shape up** : tomar forma
shape[2] *n* **1** : forma *f,* figura *f* <in the shape of a circle : en forma de círculo> **2** CONDITION : estado *m,* condiciones *fpl,* forma *f* (física) <to get in shape : ponerse en forma>
shapeless [ˈʃeɪpləs] *adj* : informe
shapely [ˈʃeɪpli] *adj* **shapelier; -est** : curvilíneo, bien proporcionado
shard [ˈʃɑrd] *n* : fragmento *m,* casco *m* (de cerámica, etc.)
share[1] [ˈʃɛr] *v* **shared; sharing** *vt* **1** APPORTION : dividir, repartir **2** : compartir <they share a room : comparten una habitación> — *vi* : compartir
share[2] *n* **1** PORTION : parte *f,* porción *f* <one's fair share : lo que le corresponde a uno> **2** : acción *f* (en una compañía) <to hold shares : tener acciones>
sharecropper [ˈʃɛr,krɑpər] *n* : aparcero *m,* -ra *f*
shareholder [ˈʃɛr,hoːldər] *n* : accionista *mf*
shark [ˈʃɑrk] *n* : tiburón *m*
sharp[1] [ˈʃɑrp] *adv* : en punto <at two o'clock sharp : a las dos en punto>
sharp[2] *adj* **1** : afilado, filoso <a sharp knife : un cuchillo afilado> **2** PENETRATING : cortante, fuerte **3** CLEVER : agudo, listo, perspicaz **4** ACUTE : agudo <sharp eyesight : vista aguda> **5** HARSH, SEVERE : duro, severo, agudo <a sharp rebuke : una reprimenda mordaz> **6** STRONG : fuerte <sharp cheese : queso fuerte> **7** ABRUPT : brusco, repentino **8** DISTINCT : nítido, definido <a sharp image : una imagen bien definida> **9** ANGULAR : anguloso (dícese de la cara) **10** : sostenido (en música)
sharp[3] *n* : sostenido *m* (en música)
sharpen [ˈʃɑrpən] *vt* : afilar, aguzar <to sharpen a pencil : sacarle punta a un lápiz> <to sharpen one's wits : aguzar el ingenio>
sharpener [ˈʃɑrpənər] *n* : afilador *m* (para cuchillos, etc.), sacapuntas *m* (para lápices)
sharply [ˈʃɑrpli] *adv* **1** ABRUPTLY : bruscamente **2** DISTINCTLY : claramente, marcadamente
sharpness [ˈʃɑrpnəs] *n* **1** : lo afilado (de un cuchillo, etc.) **2** ACUTENESS : agudeza *f* (de los sentidos o de la mente) **3** INTENSITY : intensidad *f,* agudeza *f* (de dolores, etc.) **4** HARSHNESS : dureza *f,* severidad *f* **5** ABRUPTNESS : brusquedad *f* **6** CLARITY : nitidez *f*
sharpshooter [ˈʃɑrp,ʃuːtər] *n* : tirador *m,* -dora *f* de primera
shatter [ˈʃætər] *vt* **1** : hacer añicos <to shatter the silence : romper el silencio> **2 to be shattered by** : quedar destrozado por — *vi* : hacerse añicos, romperse en pedazos
shave[1] [ˈʃeɪv] *v* **shaved; shaved** *or* **shaven** [ˈʃeɪvən]; **shaving** *vt* **1** : afeitar, rasurar <she shaved her legs : se rasuró las piernas> <they shaved (off) his beard : le afeitaron la barba> **2** SLICE : cortar (en pedazos finos) — *vi* : afeitarse, rasurarse
shave[2] *n* : afeitada *f,* rasurada *f*
shaver [ˈʃeɪvər] *n* : afeitadora *f,* máquina *f* de afeitar, rasuradora *f*
shawl [ˈʃɔl] *n* : chal *m,* mantón *m,* rebozo *m*
she [ˈʃiː] *pron* : ella
sheaf [ˈʃiːf] *n, pl* **sheaves** [ˈʃiːvz] : gavilla *f* (de cereales), haz *m* (de flechas), fajo *m* (de papeles)
shear [ˈʃɪr] *vt* **sheared; sheared** *or* **shorn** [ˈʃorn]; **shearing 1** : esquilar, trasquilar <to shear sheep : trasquilar ovejas> **2** CUT : cortar (el pelo, etc.)
shears [ˈʃɪrz] *npl* : tijeras *fpl* (grandes)
sheath [ˈʃiːθ] *n, pl* **sheaths** [ˈʃiːðz, ˈʃiːθs] : funda *f,* vaina *f*
sheathe [ˈʃiːð] *vt* **sheathed; sheathing** : envainar, enfundar
shed[1] [ˈʃɛd] *vt* **shed; shedding 1** : derramar (sangre o lágrimas) **2** EMIT : emitir (luz) <to shed light on : aclarar> **3** DISCARD : mudar (la piel, etc.) <to shed one's clothes : quitarse uno la ropa>
shed[2] *n* : cobertizo *m*
she'd [ˈʃiːd] (*contraction of* **she had** *or* **she would**) → **have, would**
sheen [ˈʃiːn] *n* : brillo *m,* lustre *m*
sheep [ˈʃiːp] *ns & pl* : oveja *f*
sheepfold [ˈʃiːp,foːld] *n* : redil *m*
sheepish [ˈʃiːpɪʃ] *adj* : avergonzado
sheepskin [ˈʃiːp,skɪn] *n* : piel *f* de oveja, piel *f* de borrego
sheer[1] [ˈʃɪr] *adv* **1** COMPLETELY : completamente, totalmente **2** VERTICALLY : verticalmente
sheer[2] *adj* **1** TRANSPARENT : vaporoso, transparente **2** ABSOLUTE, UTTER : puro <by sheer luck : por pura suerte> **3** STEEP : escarpado, vertical
sheet [ˈʃiːt] *n* **1** *or* **bedsheet** [ˈbɛd,ʃiːt] : sábana *f* **2** : hoja *f* (de papel) **3**

: capa *f* (de hielo, etc.) **4** : lámina *f,* placa *f* (de vidrio, metal, etc.), plancha *f* (de metal, madera, etc.) <baking sheet : placa de horno>

sheikh *or* **sheik** [ˈʃiːk, ˈʃeɪk] *n* : jeque *m*

shelf [ˈʃɛlf] *n, pl* **shelves** [ˈʃɛlvz] **1** : estante *m,* anaquel *m* (en una pared) **2** : banco *m,* arrecife *m* (en geología) <continental shelf : plataforma continental>

shell[1] [ˈʃɛl] *vt* **1** : desvainar (chícharos), pelar (nueces, etc.) **2** BOMBARD : bombardear

shell[2] *n* **1** SEASHELL : concha *f* **2** : cáscara *f* (de huevos, nueces, etc.), vaina *f* (de chícharos, etc.), caparazón *m* (de crustáceos, tortugas, etc.) **3** : cartucho *m,* casquillo *m* <a .45 caliber shell : un cartucho calibre .45> **4** *or* **racing shell** : bote *m* (para hacer regatas de remos)

she'll [ˈʃiːl, ˈʃɪl] (*contraction of* **she shall** *or* **she will**) → **shall, will**

shellac[1] [ʃəˈlæk] *vt* **-lacked; -lacking 1** : laquear (madera, etc.) **2** DEFEAT : darle una paliza (a alguien), derrotar

shellac[2] *n* : laca *f*

shellfish [ˈʃɛl,fɪʃ] *n* : marisco *m*

shelter[1] [ˈʃɛltər] *vt* **1** PROTECT : proteger, abrigar **2** HARBOR : dar refugio a, albergar

shelter[2] *n* : refugio *m,* abrigo *m* <to take shelter : refugiarse>

shelve [ˈʃɛlv] *vt* **shelved; shelving 1** : poner en estantes **2** DEFER : dar carpetazo a

shenanigans [ʃəˈnænɪgənz] *npl* **1** TRICKERY : artimañas *fpl* **2** MISCHIEF : travesuras *fpl*

shepherd[1] [ˈʃɛpərd] *vt* **1** : cuidar (ovejas, etc.) **2** GUIDE : conducir, guiar

shepherd[2] *n* : pastor *m*

shepherdess [ˈʃɛpərdəs] *n* : pastora *f*

sherbet [ˈʃərbət] *or* **sherbert** [-bərt] *n* : sorbete *m,* nieve *f Cuba, Mex, PRi*

sheriff [ˈʃɛrɪf] *n* : sheriff *mf*

sherry [ˈʃɛri] *n, pl* **-ries** : jerez *m*

she's [ˈʃiːz] (*contraction of* **she is** *or* **she has**) → **be, have**

shield[1] [ˈʃiːld] *vt* **1** PROTECT : proteger **2** CONCEAL : ocultar <to shield one's eyes : taparse los ojos>

shield[2] *n* **1** : escudo *m* (armadura) **2** PROTECTION : protección *f,* blindaje *m* (de un cable)

shier, shiest → **shy**

shift[1] [ˈʃɪft] *vt* **1** CHANGE : cambiar <to shift gears : cambiar de velocidad> **2** MOVE : mover **3** TRANSFER : transferir <to shift the blame : echarle la culpa (a otro)> — *vi* **1** CHANGE : cambiar **2** MOVE : moverse **3 to shift for oneself** : arreglárselas solo

shift[2] *n* **1** CHANGE, TRANSFER : cambio *m* <a shift in priorities : un cambio de prioridades> **2** : turno *m* <night shift : turno de noche> **3** DRESS : vestido *m* (suelto) **4** → **gearshift**

shiftless [ˈʃɪftləs] *adj* : perezoso, vago, holgazán

shifty [ˈʃɪfti] *adj* **shiftier; -est** : taimado, artero <a shifty look : una mirada huidiza>

shilling [ˈʃɪlɪŋ] *n* : chelín *m*

shimmer [ˈʃɪmər] *vi* GLIMMER : brillar con luz trémula

shin[1] [ˈʃɪn] *vi* **shinned; shinning** : trepar, subir <she shinned up the pole : subió al poste>

shin[2] *n* : espinilla *f,* canilla *f*

shine[1] [ˈʃaɪn] *v* **shone** [ˈʃoːn, *esp Brit and Canadian* ˈʃɒn] *or* **shined; shining** *vi* **1** : brillar, relucir <the stars were shining : las estrellas brillaban> **2** EXCEL : brillar, lucirse — *vt* **1** : alumbrar <he shined the flashlight at it : lo alumbró con la linterna> **2** POLISH : sacarle brillo a, lustrar

shine[2] *n* : brillo *m,* lustre *m*

shingle[1] [ˈʃɪŋgəl] *vt* **-gled; -gling** : techar

shingle[2] *n* : tablilla *f* (para techar)

shingles [ˈʃɪŋgəlz] *npl* : herpes *m*

shinny [ˈʃɪni] *vi* **-nied; -nying** → **shin**[1]

shiny [ˈʃaɪni] *adj* **shinier; -est** : brillante

ship[1] [ˈʃɪp] *vt* **shipped; shipping 1** LOAD : embarcar (en un barco) **2** SEND : transportar (en barco), enviar <to ship by air : enviar por avión>

ship[2] *n* **1** : barco *m,* buque *m* **2** → **spaceship**

shipboard [ˈʃɪp,bord] *n* **on ~** : a bordo

shipbuilder [ˈʃɪp,bɪldər] *n* : constructor *m,* -tora *f* naval

shipment [ˈʃɪpmənt] *n* **1** SHIPPING : transporte *m,* embarque *m* **2** : envío *m,* remesa *f* <a shipment of medicine : un envío de medicina>

shipping [ˈʃɪpɪŋ] *n* **1** SHIPS : barcos *mpl,* embarcaciones *fpl* **2** TRANSPORTATION : transporte *m* (de mercancías)

shipshape [ˈʃɪpˈʃeɪp] *adj* : ordenado

shipwreck[1] [ˈʃɪp,rɛk] *vt* **to be shipwrecked** : naufragar

shipwreck[2] *n* : naufragio *m*

shipyard [ˈʃɪp,jɑrd] *n* : astillero *m*

shirk [ˈʃərk] *vt* : eludir, rehuir <to shirk one's responsibilities : esquivar uno sus responsabilidades>

shirt [ˈʃərt] *n* : camisa *f*

shiver[1] [ˈʃɪvər] *vi* **1** : tiritar (de frío) **2** TREMBLE : estremecerse, temblar

shiver[2] *n* : escalofrío *m,* estremecimiento *m*

shoal [ˈʃoːl] *n* : banco *m,* bajío *m*

shock[1] [ˈʃɑk] *vt* **1** UPSET : conmover, conmocionar **2** STARTLE : asustar, sobresaltar **3** SCANDALIZE : escandalizar **4** : darle una descarga eléctrica a

shock[2] *n* **1** COLLISION, JOLT : choque *m,* sacudida *f* **2** UPSET : conmoción *f,* golpe *m* emocional **3** : shock *m* (en medicina) **4** *or* **electric shock** : descarga *f* eléctrica **5** SHEAVES : gavillas *fpl* **6 shock of hair** : mata *f* de pelo

shock absorber *n* **:** amortiguador *m*

shoddy [ˈʃɑdi] *adj* **shoddier; -est :** de mala calidad <a shoddy piece of work : un trabajo chapucero>

shoe[1] [ˈʃuː] *vt* **shod** [ˈʃɑd]; **shoeing :** herrar (un caballo)

shoe[2] *n* **1 :** zapato *m* <the shoe industry : la industria del calzado> **2** HORSESHOE **:** herradura *f* **3 brake shoe :** zapata *f*

shoelace [ˈʃuːˌleɪs] *n* **:** cordón *m* (de zapatos)

shoemaker [ˈʃuːˌmeɪkər] *n* **:** zapatero *m,* -ra *f*

shone → **shine**

shook → **shake**

shoot[1] [ˈʃuːt] *v* **shot** [ˈʃɑt]; **shooting** *vt* **1 :** disparar, tirar <to shoot a bullet : tirar una bala> **2 :** pegarle un tiro a, darle un balazo a <he shot her : le pegó un tiro> <they shot and killed him : lo mataron a balazos> **3** THROW **:** lanzar (una pelota, etc.), echar (una mirada) **4** PHOTOGRAPH **:** fotografiar **5** FILM **:** filmar — *vi* **1 :** disparar (con un arma de fuego) **2** DART **:** ir rápidamente <it shot past : pasó como una bala>

shoot[2] *n* **:** brote *m,* retoño *m,* vástago *m*

shooting star *n* **:** estrella *f* fugaz

shop[1] [ˈʃɑp] *vi* **shopped; shopping :** hacer compras <to go shopping : ir de compras>

shop[2] *n* **1** WORKSHOP **:** taller *m* **2** STORE **:** tienda *f*

shopkeeper [ˈʃɑpˌkiːpər] *n* **:** tendero *m,* -ra *f*

shoplift [ˈʃɑpˌlɪft] *vi* **:** hurtar mercancía (de una tienda) — *vt* **:** hurtar (de una tienda)

shoplifter [ˈʃɑpˌlɪftər] *n* **:** ladrón *m,* -drona *f* (que roba en una tienda)

shopper [ˈʃɑpər] *n* **:** comprador *m,* -dora *f*

shore[1] [ˈʃor] *vt* **shored; shoring :** apuntalar <they shored up the wall : apuntalaron la pared>

shore[2] *n* **1 :** orilla *f* (del mar, etc.) **2** PROP **:** puntal *m*

shoreline [ˈʃorˌlaɪn] *n* **:** orilla *f*

shorn → **shear**

short[1] [ˈʃɔrt] *adv* **1** ABRUPTLY **:** repentinamente, súbitamente <the car stopped short : el carro se paró en seco> **2 to fall short :** no alcanzar, quedarse corto

short[2] *adj* **1 :** corto (de medida), bajo (de estatura) **2** BRIEF **:** corto <short and sweet : corto y bueno> <a short time ago : hace poco> **3** CURT **:** brusco, cortante, seco **4 :** corto (de tiempo, de dinero) <I'm one dollar short : me falta un dólar>

short[3] *n* **1 shorts** *npl* **:** shorts *mpl,* pantalones *mpl* cortos **2** → **short circuit**

shortage [ˈʃɔrtɪdʒ] *n* **:** falta *f,* escasez *f,* carencia *f*

shortcake [ˈʃɔrtˌkeɪk] *n* **:** tarta *f* de fruta

shortchange [ˈʃɔrtˈtʃeɪndʒ] *vt* **-changed; -changing :** darle mal el cambio (a alguien)

short circuit *n* **:** cortocircuito *m,* corto *m* (eléctrico)

shortcoming [ˈʃɔrtˌkʌmɪŋ] *n* **:** defecto *m*

shortcut [ˈʃɔrtˌkʌt] *n* **1 :** atajo *m* <to take a shortcut : cortar camino> **2 :** alternativa *f* fácil, método *m* rápido

shorten [ˈʃɔrtən] *vt* **:** acortar — *vi* **:** acortarse

shorthand [ˈʃɔrtˌhænd] *n* **:** taquigrafía *f*

short–lived [ˈʃɔrtˈlɪvd, -ˈlaɪvd] *adj* **:** efímero

shortly [ˈʃɔrtli] *adv* **1** BRIEFLY **:** brevemente <to put it shortly : para decirlo en pocas palabras> **2** SOON **:** dentro de poco

shortness [ˈʃɔrtnəs] *n* **1 :** lo corto <shortness of stature : estatura baja> **2** BREVITY **:** brevedad *f* **3** CURTNESS **:** brusquedad *f* **4** SHORTAGE **:** falta *f,* escasez *f,* carencia *f*

shortsighted [ˈʃɔrtˌsaɪt̬əd] → **nearsighted**

shot [ˈʃɑt] *n* **1 :** disparo *m,* tiro *m* <to fire a shot : disparar> **2** PELLETS **:** perdigones *mpl* **3 :** tiro *m* (en deportes) **4** ATTEMPT **:** intento *m,* tentativa *f* <to have a shot at : hacer un intento por> **5** RANGE **:** alcance *m* <a long shot : una posibilidad remota> **6** PHOTOGRAPH **:** foto *f* **7** INJECTION **:** inyección *f* **8 :** trago *m* (de licor)

shotgun [ˈʃɑtˌgʌn] *n* **:** escopeta *f*

should → **shall**

shoulder[1] [ˈʃoːldər] *vt* **1** JOSTLE **:** empujar (con el hombro) **2 :** ponerse al hombro (una mochila, etc.) **3 :** cargar con (la responsabilidad, etc.)

shoulder[2] *n* **1 :** hombro *m* <to shrug one's shoulders : encogerse los hombros> **2 :** arcén *m* (de una carretera)

shoulder blade *n* **:** omóplato *m,* omoplato *m,* escápula *f*

shouldn't [ˈʃʊdənt] (*contraction of* **should not**) → **should**

shout[1] [ˈʃaʊt] *v* **:** gritar, vocear

shout[2] *n* **:** grito *m*

shove[1] [ˈʃʌv] *v* **shoved; shoving :** empujar bruscamente

shove[2] *n* **:** empujón *m,* empellón *m*

shovel[1] [ˈʃʌvəl] *vt* **-veled** *or* **-velled; -veling** *or* **-velling 1 :** mover con (una) pala <they shoveled the dirt out : sacaron la tierra con palas> **2** DIG **:** cavar (con una pala)

shovel[2] *n* **:** pala *f*

show[1] [ˈʃoː] *v* **showed; shown** [ˈʃoːn] *or* **showed; showing** *vt* **1** DISPLAY **:** mostrar, enseñar **2** REVEAL **:** demostrar, manifestar, revelar <he showed himself to be a coward : se reveló como cobarde> **3** TEACH **:** enseñar **4** PROVE **:** demostrar, probar **5** CON-

DUCT, DIRECT : llevar, acompañar <to show someone the way : indicarle el camino a alguien> **6 :** proyectar (una película), dar (un programa de televisión) — *vi* **1 :** notarse, verse <the stain doesn't show : la mancha no se ve> **2** APPEAR : aparecer, dejarse ver

show[2] *n* **1 :** demostración *f* <a show of force : una demostración de fuerza> **2** EXHIBITION : exposición *f,* exhibición *f* <flower show : exposición de flores> <to be on show : estar expuesto> **3 :** espectáculo *m* (teatral), programa *m* (de televisión, etc.) <to go to a show : ir al teatro>

showcase [ˈʃoːˌkeɪs] *n* **:** vitrina *f*

showdown [ˈʃoːˌdaʊn] *n* **:** confrontación *f* (decisiva)

shower[1] [ˈʃaʊər] *vt* **1** SPRAY : regar, mojar **2** HEAP : colmar <they showered him with gifts : lo colmaron de regalos, le llovieron los regalos> — *vi* **1** BATHE : ducharse, darse una ducha **2** RAIN : llover

shower[2] *n* **1 :** chaparrón *m,* chubasco *m* <a chance of showers : una posibilidad de chaparrones> **2 :** ducha *f* <to take a shower : ducharse> **3** PARTY **:** fiesta *f* <a bridal shower : una despedida de soltera>

show off *vt* **:** hacer alarde de, ostentar — *vi* **:** lucirse

show up *vi* APPEAR **:** aparecer — *vt* EXPOSE **:** revelar

showy [ˈʃoːi] *adj* **showier; -est :** llamativo, ostentoso — **showily** *adv*

shrank → **shrink**

shrapnel [ˈʃræpnəl] *ns & pl* **:** metralla *f*

shred[1] [ˈʃrɛd] *vt* **shredded; shredding :** hacer trizas, desmenuzar (con las manos), triturar (con una máquina) <to shred vegetables : cortar verduras en tiras>

shred[2] *n* **1** STRIP **:** tira *f,* jirón *m* (de tela) **2** BIT **:** pizca *f* <not a shred of evidence : ni la mínima prueba>

shrew [ˈʃruː] *n* **1 :** musaraña *f* (animal) **2 :** mujer *f* regañona, arpía *f*

shrewd [ˈʃruːd] *adj* **:** astuto, inteligente, sagaz — **shrewdly** *adv*

shrewdness [ˈʃruːdnəs] *n* **:** astucia *f*

shriek[1] [ˈʃriːk] *vi* **:** chillar, gritar

shriek[2] *n* **:** chillido *m,* alarido *m,* grito *m*

shrill [ˈʃrɪl] *adj* **:** agudo, estridente

shrilly [ˈʃrɪli] *adv* **:** agudamente

shrimp [ˈʃrɪmp] *n* **:** camarón *m,* langostino *m*

shrine [ˈʃraɪn] *n* **1** TOMB **:** sepulcro *m* (de un santo) **2** SANCTUARY **:** lugar *m* sagrado, santuario *m*

shrink [ˈʃrɪŋk] *vi* **shrank** [ˈʃræŋk]; **shrunk** [ˈʃrʌŋk] *or* **shrunken** [ˈʃrʌŋkən]; **shrinking 1** RECOIL **:** retroceder <he shrank back : se echó para atrás> **2 :** encogerse (dícese de la ropa)

shrinkage [ˈʃrɪŋkɪdʒ] *n* **:** encogimiento *m* (de ropa, etc.), contracción *f,* reducción *f*

shrivel [ˈʃrɪvəl] *vi* **-veled** *or* **-velled; -veling** *or* **-velling :** arrugarse, marchitarse

shroud[1] [ˈʃraʊd] *vt* **:** envolver

shroud[2] *n* **1 :** sudario *m,* mortaja *f* **2** VEIL **:** velo *m* <wrapped in a shroud of mystery : envuelto en un aura de misterio>

shrub [ˈʃrʌb] *n* **:** arbusto *m,* mata *f*

shrubbery [ˈʃrʌbəri] *n, pl* **-beries :** arbustos *mpl,* matas *fpl*

shrug [ˈʃrʌg] *vi* **shrugged; shrugging :** encogerse de hombros

shrunk → **shrink**

shuck[1] [ˈʃʌk] *vt* **:** pelar (mazorcas, etc.), abrir (almejas, etc.)

shuck[2] *n* **1** HUSK **:** cascarilla *f,* cáscara *f* (de una nuez, etc.), hojas *fpl* (de una mazorca) **2** SHELL **:** concha *f* (de una almeja, etc.)

shudder[1] [ˈʃʌdər] *vi* **:** estremecerse

shudder[2] *n* **:** estremecimiento *m,* escalofrío *m*

shuffle[1] [ˈʃʌfəl] *v* **-fled; -fling** *vt* MIX **:** mezclar, revolver, barajar (naipes) — *vi* **:** caminar arrastrando los pies

shuffle[2] *n* **1 :** acto *m* de revolver <each player gets a shuffle : a cada jugador le toca barajar> **2** JUMBLE **:** revoltijo *m* **3 :** arrastramiento *m* de los pies

shun [ˈʃʌn] *vi* **shunned; shunning :** evitar, esquivar, eludir

shunt [ˈʃʌnt] *vt* **:** desviar, cambiar de vía (un tren)

shut [ˈʃʌt] *v* **shut; shutting** *vt* **1** CLOSE **:** cerrar <shut the lid : tápalo> **2 to shut out** EXCLUDE **:** excluir, dejar fuera a (personas), no dejar que entre (luz, ruido, etc.) **3 to shut up** CONFINE **:** encerrar — *vi* **:** cerrarse <the factory shut down : la fábrica cerró sus puertas>

shut–in [ˈʃʌtˌɪn] *n* **:** inválido *m,* -da *f* (que no puede salir de casa)

shutter [ˈʃʌtər] *n* **1 :** contraventana *f,* postigo *m* (de una ventana o puerta) **2 :** obturador *m* (de una cámara)

shuttle[1] [ˈʃʌt̬əl] *v* **-tled; -tling** *vt* **:** transportar <she shuttled him back and forth : lo llevaba de acá para allá> — *vi* **:** ir y venir

shuttle[2] *n* **1 :** lanzadera *f* (para tejer) **2 :** vehículo *m* que hace recorridos cortos **3** → **space shuttle**

shuttlecock [ˈʃʌt̬əlˌkɑk] *n* **:** volante *m*

shut up *vi* **:** callarse <shut up! : ¡cállate (la boca)!>

shy[1] [ˈʃaɪ] *vi* **shied; shying :** retroceder, asustarse

shy[2] *adj* **shier** *or* **shyer** [ˈʃaɪər]; **shiest** *or* **shyest** [ˈʃaɪəst] **1** TIMID **:** tímido **2** WARY **:** cauteloso <he's not shy about asking : no vacila en preguntar> **3** SHORT **:** corto (de dinero, etc.) <I'm two dollars shy : me faltan dos dólares>

shyly ['ʃaɪli] *adv* : tímidamente
shyness ['ʃaɪnəs] *n* : timidez *f*
sibling ['sɪblɪŋ] *n* : hermano *m*, hermana *f*
Sicilian [sə'sɪljən] *n* : siciliano *m*, -na *f* — **Sicilian** *adj*
sick ['sɪk] *adj* **1** : enfermo **2** NAUSEOUS : mareado, con náuseas <to get sick : vomitar> **3** : para uso de enfermos <sick day : día de permiso (por enfermedad)>
sickbed ['sɪk,bɛd] *n* : lecho *m* de enfermo
sicken ['sɪkən] *vt* **1** : poner enfermo **2** REVOLT : darle asco (a alguien) — *vi* : enfermar(se), caer enfermo
sickening ['sɪkənɪŋ] *adj* : asqueroso, repugnante, nauseabundo
sickle ['sɪkəl] *n* : hoz *f*
sickly ['sɪkli] *adj* **sicklier; -est 1** : enfermizo **2** → **sickening**
sickness ['sɪknəs] *n* **1** : enfermedad *f* **2** NAUSEA : náuseas *fpl*
side ['saɪd] *n* **1** : lado *m*, costado *m* (de una persona), ijada *f* (de un animal) **2** : lado *m*, cara *f* (de una moneda, etc.) **3** : lado *m*, parte *f* <he's on my side : está de mi parte> <to take sides : tomar partido>
sideboard ['saɪd,bord] *n* : aparador *m*
sideburns ['saɪd,bərnz] *npl* : patillas *fpl*
sided ['saɪdəd] *adj* : que tiene lados <one-sided : de un lado>
side effect *n* : efecto *m* secundario
sideline ['saɪd,laɪn] *n* **1** : línea *f* de banda (en deportes) **2** : actividad *f* suplementaria (en negocios) **3 to be on the sidelines** : estar al margen
sidelong ['saɪd,lɔŋ] *adj* : de reojo, de soslayo
sideshow ['saɪd,ʃo:] *n* : espectáculo *m* secundario, atracción *f* secundaria
sidestep ['saɪd,stɛp] *v* **-stepped; -stepping** *vi* : dar un paso hacia un lado — *vt* AVOID : esquivar, eludir
sidetrack ['saɪd,træk] *vt* : desviar (una conversación, etc.), distraer (a una persona)
sidewalk ['saɪd,wɔk] *n* : acera *f*, vereda *f*, andén *m CA, Col*, banqueta *f Mex*
sideways¹ ['saɪd,weɪz] *adv* **1** : hacia un lado <it leaned sideways : se inclinaba hacia un lado> **2** : de lado, de costado <lie sideways : acuéstese de costado>
sideways² *adj* : hacia un lado <a sideways glance : una mirada de reojo>
siding ['saɪdɪŋ] *n* **1** : apartadero *m* (para trenes) **2** : revestimiento *m* exterior (de un edificio)
sidle ['saɪdəl] *vi* **-dled; -dling** : moverse furtivamente
siege ['si:dʒ, 'si:ʒ] *n* : sitio *m* <to be under siege : estar sitiado>
siesta [si:'ɛstə] *n* : siesta *f*
sieve ['sɪv] *n* : tamiz *m*, cedazo *m*, criba *f* (en minerología)
sift ['sɪft] *vt* **1** : tamizar, cerner <sift the flour : tamice la harina> **2** *or* **sift through** : examinar cuidadosamente, pasar por el tamiz
sifter ['sɪftər] *n* : tamiz *m*, cedazo *m*
sigh¹ ['saɪ] *vi* : suspirar
sigh² *n* : suspiro *m*
sight¹ ['saɪt] *vt* : ver (a una persona), divisar (la tierra, un barco)
sight² *n* **1** : vista *f* (facultad) <out of sight : fuera de vista> **2** : algo visto <it's a familiar sight : se ve con frecuencia> <she's a sight for sore eyes : da gusto verla> **3** : lugar *m* de interés (para turistas, etc.) **4** : mira *f* (de un rifle, etc.) **5** GLIMPSE : mirada *f* breve <I caught sight of her : la divisé, alcancé a verla>
sightless ['saɪtləs] *adj* : invidente, ciego
sightseer ['saɪt,si:ər] *n* : turista *mf*
sign¹ ['saɪn] *vt* **1** : firmar <to sign a check : firmar un cheque> **2** *or* **to sign on** HIRE : contratar (a un empleado), fichar (a un jugador) — *vi* **1** : hacer una seña <she signed for him to stop : le hizo una seña para que se parara> **2** : comunicarse por señas
sign² *n* **1** SYMBOL : símbolo *m*, signo *m* <minus sign : signo de menos> **2** GESTURE : seña *f*, señal *f*, gesto *m* **3** : letrero *m*, cartel *m* <neon sign : letrero de neón> **4** TRACE : señal *f*, indicio *m*
signal¹ ['sɪgnəl] *vt* **-naled** *or* **-nalled; -naling** *or* **-nalling 1** : hacerle señas (a alguien) <she signaled me to leave : me hizo señas para que saliera> **2** INDICATE : señalar, indicar — *vi* : hacer señas, comunicar por señas
signal² *adj* NOTABLE : señalado, notable
signal³ *n* : señal *f*
signature ['sɪgnə,tʃʊr] *n* : firma *f*
signet ['sɪgnət] *n* : sello *m*
significance [sɪg'nɪfɪkənts] *n* **1** MEANING : significado *m* **2** IMPORTANCE : importancia *f*
significant [sɪg'nɪfɪkənt] *adj* **1** IMPORTANT : importante **2** MEANINGFUL : significativo — **significantly** *adv*
signify ['sɪgnə,faɪ] *vt* **-fied; -fying 1** : indicar <he signified his desire for more : haciendo señas indicó que quería más> **2** MEAN : significar
sign language *n* : lenguaje *m* por señas
signpost ['saɪn,po:st] *n* : poste *m* indicador
silence¹ ['saɪlənts] *vt* **-lenced; -lencing** : silenciar, acallar
silence² *n* : silencio *m*
silent ['saɪlənt] *adj* **1** : callado <to remain silent : quedarse callado, guardar silencio> **2** QUIET, STILL : silencioso **3** MUTE : mudo <a silent letter : una letra muda>
silently ['saɪləntli] *adv* : silenciosamente, calladamente
silhouette¹ [,sɪlə'wɛt] *vt* **-etted; -etting** : destacar la silueta de <it was

silhouetted against the sky : se perfilaba contra el cielo>
silhouette[2] *n* : silueta *f*
silica ['sɪlɪkə] *n* : sílice *f*
silicon ['sɪlɪkən, -ˌkɑn] *n* : silicio *m*
silk ['sɪlk] *n* : seda *f*
silken ['sɪlkən] *adj* **1** : de seda <a silken veil : un velo de seda> **2** SILKY : sedoso <silken hair : cabellos sedosos>
silkworm ['sɪlkˌwərm] *n* : gusano *m* de seda
silky ['sɪlki] *adj* **silkier; -est** : sedoso
sill ['sɪl] *n* : alféizar *m* (de una ventana), umbral *m* (de una puerta)
silliness ['sɪlinəs] *n* : tontería *f*, estupidez *f*
silly ['sɪli] *adj* **sillier; -est** : tonto, estúpido, ridículo
silo ['saɪˌloː] *n, pl* **silos** : silo *m*
silt ['sɪlt] *n* : cieno *m*
silver[1] ['sɪlvər] *adj* **1** : de plata <a silver spoon : una cuchara de plata> **2** → **silvery**
silver[2] *n* **1** : plata *f* **2** COINS : monedas *fpl* **3** → **silverware 4** : color *m* plata
silverware ['sɪlvərˌwær] *n* **1** : artículos *mpl* de plata, platería *f* **2** FLATWARE : cubertería *f*
silvery ['sɪlvəri] *adj* : plateado
similar ['sɪmələr] *adj* : similar, parecido, semejante
similarity [ˌsɪmə'lærəṯi] *n, pl* **-ties** : semejanza *f*, parecido *m*
similarly ['sɪmələrli] *adv* : de manera similar
simile ['sɪməˌliː] *n* : símil *m*
simmer ['sɪmər] *v* : hervir a fuego lento
simper[1] ['sɪmpər] *vi* : sonreír como un tonto
simper[2] *n* : sonrisa *f* tonta
simple ['sɪmpəl] *adj* **simpler; -plest 1** INNOCENT : inocente **2** PLAIN : sencillo, simple **3** EASY : simple, sencillo, fácil **4** STRAIGHTFORWARD : puro, simple <the simple truth : la pura verdad> **5** NAIVE : ingenuo, simple
simpleton ['sɪmpəltən] *n* : bobo *m*, -ba *f*; tonto *m*, -ta *f*
simplicity [sɪm'plɪsəṯi] *n* : simplicidad *f*, sencillez *f*
simplification [ˌsɪmpləfə'keɪʃən] *n* : simplificación *f*
simplify ['sɪmpləˌfaɪ] *vt* **-fied; -fying** : simplificar
simply ['sɪmpli] *adv* **1** PLAINLY : sencillamente **2** SOLELY : simplemente, sólo **3** REALLY : absolutamente
simulate ['sɪmjəˌleɪt] *vt* **-lated; -lating** : simular
simultaneous [ˌsaɪməl'teɪniəs] *adj* : simultáneo — **simultaneously** *adv*
sin[1] ['sɪn] *vi* **sinned; sinning** : pecar
sin[2] *n* : pecado *m*
since[1] ['sɪnts] *adv* **1** : desde entonces <they've been friends ever since : desde entonces han sido amigos> <she's since become mayor : más tarde se hizo alcalde> **2** AGO : hace <he's long since dead : murió hace mucho>
since[2] *conj* **1** : desde que <since he was born : desde que nació> **2** INASMUCH AS : ya que, puesto que, dado que
since[3] *prep* : desde
sincere [sɪn'sɪr] *adj* **-cerer; -est** : sincero — **sincerely** *adv*
sincerity [sɪn'sɛrəṯi] *n* : sinceridad *f*
sinew ['sɪnˌjuː, 'sɪˌnuː] *n* **1** TENDON : tendón *m*, nervio *m* (en la carne) **2** POWER : fuerza *f*
sinewy ['sɪnjʊi, 'sɪnʊi] *adj* **1** STRINGY : fibroso **2** STRONG, WIRY : fuerte, nervudo
sinful ['sɪnfəl] *adj* : pecador (dícese de las personas), pecaminoso
sing ['sɪŋ] *v* **sang** ['sæŋ] *or* **sung** ['sʌŋ]; **sung; singing** : cantar
singe ['sɪndʒ] *vt* **singed; singeing** : chamuscar, quemar
singer ['sɪŋər] *n* : cantante *mf*
single[1] ['sɪŋgəl] *vt* **-gled; -gling** *or* **to single out 1** SELECT : escoger **2** DISTINGUISH : señalar
single[2] *adj* **1** UNMARRIED : soltero **2** SOLE : solo <a single survivor : un solo sobreviviente> <every single one : cada uno, todos>
single[3] *n* **1** : soltero *m*, -ra *f* <for married couples and singles : para los matrimonios y los solteros> **2** *or* **single room** : habitación *f* individual **3** DOLLAR : billete *m* de un dólar
single–handed ['sɪŋgəl'hændəd] *adj* : sin ayuda, solo
singly ['sɪŋgli] *adv* : individualmente, uno por uno
singular[1] ['sɪŋgjələr] *adj* **1** : singular (en gramática) **2** OUTSTANDING : singular, sobresaliente **3** STRANGE : singular, extraño
singular[2] *n* : singular *m*
singularly ['sɪŋgjələrli] *adv* : singularmente
sinister ['sɪnəstər] *adj* : siniestro
sink[1] ['sɪŋk] *v* **sank** ['sæŋk] *or* **sunk** ['sʌŋk]; **sunk; sinking** *vi* **1** : hundirse (dícese de un barco) **2** DROP, FALL : descender, caer <to sink into a chair : dejarse caer en una silla> <her heart sank : se le cayó el alma a los pies> **3** DECREASE : bajar — *vt* **1** : hundir (un barco, etc.) **2** EXCAVATE : excavar (un pozo para minar), perforar (un pozo de agua) **3** PLUNGE, STICK : clavar, hincar **4** INVEST : invertir (fondos)
sink[2] *n* **1 kitchen sink** : fregadero *m*, lavaplatos *m Chile, Col, Mex* **2 bathroom sink** : lavabo *m*, lavamanos *m*
sinner ['sɪnər] *n* : pecador *m*, -dora *f*
sinuous ['sɪnjʊəs] *adj* : sinuoso — **sinuously** *adv*
sinus ['saɪnəs] *n* : seno *m*
sip[1] ['sɪp] *v* **sipped; sipping** *vt* : sorber — *vi* : beber a sorbos
sip[2] *n* : sorbo *m*
siphon[1] ['saɪfən] *vt* : sacar con sifón

siphon² *n* : sifón *m*
sir [ˈsər] *n* **1** (*in titles*) : sir *m* **2** (*as a form of address*) : señor *m* <Dear Sir : Muy señor mío> <yes sir! : ¡sí, señor!>
sire¹ [ˈsaɪr] *vt* **sired; siring** : engendrar, ser el padre de
sire² *n* : padre *m*
siren [ˈsaɪrən] *n* : sirena *f*
sirloin [ˈsər,lɔɪn] *n* : solomillo *m*
sirup → **syrup**
sisal [ˈsaɪsəl, -zəl] *n* : sisal *m*
sissy [ˈsɪsi] *n, pl* **-sies** : mariquita *f fam*
sister [ˈsɪstər] *n* : hermana *f*
sisterhood [ˈsɪstər,hʊd] *n* **1** : condición *f* de ser hermana **2** : sociedad *f* de mujeres
sister–in–law [ˈsɪstərɪn,lɔ] *n, pl* **sisters–in–law** : cuñada *f*
sisterly [ˈsɪstərli] *adj* : de hermana
sit [ˈsɪt] *v* **sat** [ˈsæt]; **sitting** *vi* **1** : sentarse, estar sentado <he sat down : se sentó> **2** ROOST : posarse **3** : sesionar <the legislature is sitting : la legislatura está en sesión> **4** POSE : posar (para un retrato) **5** LIE, REST : estar (ubicado) <the house sits on a hill : la casa está en una colina> — *vt* SEAT : sentar, colocar <I sat him on the sofa : lo senté en el sofá>
site [ˈsaɪt] *n* 1 PLACE : sitio *m,* lugar *m* **2** LOCATION : emplazamiento *m,* ubicación *f*
sitting room → **living room**
sitter [ˈsɪt̬ər] → **baby–sitter**
situated [ˈsɪtʃʊ,eɪt̬əd] *adj* LOCATED : ubicado, situado
situation [,sɪtʃʊˈeɪʃən] *n* **1** LOCATION : situación *f,* ubicación *f,* emplazamiento *m* **2** CIRCUMSTANCES : situación *f* **3** JOB : empleo *m*
six¹ [ˈsɪks] *adj* : seis
six² *n* : seis *m*
six–gun [ˈsɪks,gʌn] *n* : revólver *m* (con seis cámaras)
six hundred¹ *adj* : seiscientos
six hundred² *n* : seiscientos *m*
six–shooter [ˈsɪks,ʃuːt̬ər] → **six–gun**
sixteen¹ [sɪksˈtiːn] *adj* : dieciséis
sixteen² *n* : dieciséis *m*
sixteenth¹ [sɪksˈtiːnθ] *adj* : decimosexto
sixteenth² *n* **1** : decimosexto *m,* -ta *f* (en una serie) **2** : dieciseisavo *m,* dieciseisava parte *f*
sixth¹ [ˈsɪksθ, ˈsɪkst] *adj* : sexto
sixth² *n* **1** : sexto *m,* -ta *f* (en una serie) **2** : sexto *m,* sexta parte *f*
sixtieth¹ [ˈsɪkstiəθ] *adj* : sexagésimo
sixtieth² *n* **1** : sexagésimo *m,* -ma *f* (en una serie) **2** : sesentavo *m,* sesentava parte *f*
sixty¹ [ˈsɪksti] *adj* : sesenta
sixty² *n, pl* **-ties** : sesenta *m*
sizable *or* **sizeable** [ˈsaɪzəbəl] *adj* : considerable
size¹ [ˈsaɪz] *vt* **sized; sizing 1** : clasificar según el tamaño **2 to size up** : evaluar, apreciar
size² *n* **1** DIMENSIONS : tamaño *m,* talla *f* (de ropa), número *m* (de zapatos) **2** MAGNITUDE : magnitud *f*
sizzle [ˈsɪzəl] *vi* **-zled; -zling** : chisporrotear
skate¹ [ˈskeɪt] *vi* **skated; skating** : patinar
skate² *n* **1** : patín *m* <roller skate : patín de ruedas> **2** : raya *f* (pez)
skateboard [ˈskeɪt,bord] *n* : monopatín *m*
skater [ˈskeɪt̬ər] *n* : patinador *m,* -dora *f*
skein [ˈskeɪn] *n* : madeja *f*
skeletal [ˈskɛlət̬əl] *adj* **1** : óseo (en anatomía) **2** EMACIATED : esquelético
skeleton [ˈskɛlət̬ən] *n* **1** : esqueleto *m* (anatómico) **2** FRAMEWORK : armazón *mf*
skeptic [ˈskɛptɪk] *n* : escéptico *m,* -ca *f*
skeptical [ˈskɛptɪkəl] *adj* : escéptico
skepticism [ˈskɛptə,sɪzəm] *n* : escepticismo *m*
sketch¹ [ˈskɛtʃ] *vt* : bosquejar — *vi* : hacer bosquejos
sketch² *n* **1** DRAWING, OUTLINE : esbozo *m,* bosquejo *m* **2** ESSAY : ensayo *m*
sketchy [ˈskɛtʃi] *adj* **sketchier; -est** : incompleto, poco detallado
skewer¹ [ˈskjuːər] *vt* : ensartar (carne, etc.)
skewer² *n* : brocheta *f,* broqueta *f*
ski¹ [ˈskiː] *vi* **skied; skiing** : esquiar
ski² *n, pl* **skis** : esquí *m*
skid¹ [ˈskɪd] *vi* **skidded; skidding** : derrapar, patinar
skid² *n* : derrape *m,* patinazo *m*
skier [ˈskiːər] *n* : esquiador *m,* -dora *f*
skiff [ˈskɪf] *n* : esquife *m*
skill [ˈskɪl] *n* **1** DEXTERITY : habilidad *f,* destreza *f* **2** CAPABILITY : capacidad *f,* arte *m,* técnica *f* <organizational skills : la capacidad para organizar>
skilled [ˈskɪld] *adj* : hábil, experto
skillet [ˈskɪlət] *n* : sartén *mf*
skillful [ˈskɪlfəl] *adj* : hábil, diestro
skillfully [ˈskɪlfəli] *adv* : con habilidad, con destreza
skim¹ [ˈskɪm] *vt* **skimmed; skimming 1** *or* **to skim off** : espumar, descremar (leche) **2** : echarle un vistazo a (un libro, etc.), pasar rozando (un superficie)
skim² *adj* : descremado <skim milk : leche descremada>
skimp [ˈskɪmp] *vi* **to skimp on** : escatimar
skimpy [ˈskɪmpi] *adj* **skimpier; -est** : exiguo, escaso, raquítico
skin¹ [ˈskɪn] *vt* **skinned; skinning** : despellejar, desollar
skin² *n* **1** : piel *f,* cutis *m* (de la cara) <dark skin : piel morena> **2** RIND : piel *f*
skin diving *n* : buceo *m,* submarinismo *m*
skinflint [ˈskɪn,flɪnt] *n* : tacaño *m,* -ña *f*

skinned ['skɪnd] *adj* : de piel <tough-skinned : de piel dura>
skinny ['skɪni] *adj* **skinnier; -est** : flaco
skip[1] ['skɪp] *v* **skipped; skipping** *vi* : ir dando brincos — *vt* : saltarse
skip[2] *n* : brinco *m,* salto *m*
skipper ['skɪpər] *n* : capitán *m,* -tana *f*
skirmish[1] ['skərmɪʃ] *vi* : escaramuzar
skirmish[2] *n* : escaramuza *f,* refriega *f*
skirt[1] ['skərt] *vt* **1** BORDER : bordear **2** EVADE : evadir, esquivar
skirt[2] *n* : falda *f,* pollera *f*
skit ['skɪt] *n* : sketch *m* (teatral)
skittish ['skɪṭɪʃ] *adj* : asustadizo, nervioso
skulk ['skʌlk] *vi* : merodear
skull ['skʌl] *n* **1** : cráneo *m,* calavera *f* **2 skull and crossbones** : calavera *f* (bandera pirata)
skunk ['skʌŋk] *n* : zorrillo *m,* mofeta *f*
sky ['skaɪ] *n, pl* **skies** : cielo *m*
skylark ['skaɪˌlɑrk] *n* : alondra *f*
skylight ['skaɪˌlaɪt] *n* : claraboya *f,* tragaluz *m*
skyline ['skaɪˌlaɪn] *n* : horizonte *m*
skyrocket ['skaɪˌrɑkət] *vi* : dispararse
skyscraper ['skaɪˌskreɪpər] *n* : rascacielos *m*
slab ['slæb] *n* : losa *f* (de piedra), tabla *f* (de madera), pedazo *m* grueso (de pan, etc.)
slack[1] ['slæk] *adj* **1** CARELESS : descuidado, negligente **2** LOOSE : flojo **3** SLOW : de poco movimiento
slack[2] *n* **1** : parte *f* floja <to take up the slack : tensar (una cuerda, etc.)> **2 slacks** *npl* : pantalones *mpl*
slacken ['slækən] *vt* : aflojar — *vi* : aflojarse
slag ['slæg] *n* : escoria *f*
slain → **slay**
slake ['sleɪk] *vt* **slaked; slaking** : saciar (la sed), satisfacer (la curiosidad)
slam[1] ['slæm] *v* **slammed; slamming** *vt* **1** : cerrar de golpe <he slammed the door : dio un portazo> **2** : tirar o dejar caer de golpe <he slammed down the book : dejó caer el libro de un golpe> — *vi* **1** : cerrarse de golpe **2 to slam into** : chocar contra
slam[2] *n* : golpe *m,* portazo *m* (de una puerta)
slander[1] ['slændər] *vt* : calumniar, difamar
slander[2] *n* : calumnia *f,* difamación *f*
slanderous ['slændərəs] *adj* : difamatorio, calumnioso
slang ['slæŋ] *n* : argot *m,* jerga *f*
slant[1] ['slænt] *vi* : inclinarse, ladearse — *vt* **1** SLOPE : inclinar **2** ANGLE : sesgar, orientar, dirigir <a story slanted towards youth : un artículo dirigido a los jóvenes>
slant[2] *n* **1** INCLINE : inclinación *f* **2** PERSPECTIVE : perspectiva *f,* enfoque *m*
slap[1] ['slæp] *vt* **slapped; slapping** : bofetear, cachetear, dar una palmada (en la espalda, etc.)
slap[2] *n* : bofetada *f,* cachetada *f,* palmada *f*
slash[1] ['slæʃ] *vt* **1** GASH : cortar, hacer un tajo en **2** REDUCE : reducir, rebajar (precios)
slash[2] *n* : tajo *m,* corte *m*
slat ['slæt] *n* : tablilla *f,* listón *m*
slate ['sleɪt] *n* **1** : pizarra *f* <a slate roof : un techo de pizarra> **2** : lista *f* de candidatos (políticos)
slaughter[1] ['slɔṭər] *vt* **1** BUTCHER : matar (animales) **2** MASSACRE : masacrar (personas)
slaughter[2] *n* **1** : matanza *f* (de animales) **2** MASSACRE : masacre *f,* carnicería *f*
slaughterhouse ['slɔṭərˌhaʊs] *n* : matadero *m*
Slav ['slɑv, 'slæv] *n* : eslavo *m,* -va *f*
slave[1] ['sleɪv] *vi* **slaved; slaving** : trabajar como un burro
slave[2] *n* : esclavo *m,* -va *f*
slaver ['slævər, 'sleɪ-] *vi* : babear
slavery ['sleɪvəri] *n* : esclavitud *f*
Slavic ['slɑvɪk, 'slæ-] *adj* : eslavo
slavish ['sleɪvɪʃ] *adj* **1** SERVILE : servil **2** IMITATIVE : poco original
slay ['sleɪ] *vt* **slew** ['slu:]; **slain** ['sleɪn]; **slaying** : asesinar, matar
slayer ['sleɪər] *n* : asesino *m,* -na *f*
sleazy ['sli:zi] *adj* **sleazier; -est 1** SHODDY : chapucero, de mala calidad **2** DILAPIDATED : ruinoso **3** DISREPUTABLE : de mala fama
sled[1] ['slɛd] *v* **sledded; sledding** *vi* : ir en trineo — *vt* : transportar en trineo
sled[2] *n* : trineo *m*
sledge ['slɛdʒ] *n* **1** : trineo *m* (grande) **2** → **sledgehammer**
sledgehammer ['slɛdʒˌhæmər] *n* : almádena *f,* combo *m Chile, Peru*
sleek[1] ['sli:k] *vt* SLICK : alisar
sleek[2] *adj* : liso y brillante
sleep[1] ['sli:p] *vi* **slept** ['slɛpt]; **sleeping** : dormir
sleep[2] *n* **1** : sueño *m* **2 to go to sleep** : dormirse
sleeper ['sli:pər] *n* **1** : durmiente *mf* <to be a light sleeper : tener el sueño ligero> **2** *or* **sleeping car** : coche *m* cama, coche *m* dormitorio
sleepily ['sli:pəli] *adv* : de manera somnolienta
sleepiness ['sli:pinəs] *n* : somnolencia *f*
sleepless ['sli:pləs] *adj* : sin dormir, desvelado <to have a sleepless night : pasar la noche en blanco>
sleepwalker ['sli:pˌwɔkər] *n* : sonámbulo *m,* -la *f*
sleepy ['sli:pi] *adj* **sleepier; -est 1** DROWSY : somnoliento, soñoliento <to be sleepy : tener sueño> **2** LETHARGIC : aletargado, letárgico
sleet[1] ['sli:t] *vi* **to be sleeting** : caer aguanieve

sleet² *n* : aguanieve *f*
sleeve ['sli:v] *n* : manga *f* (de una camisa, etc.)
sleeveless ['sli:vləs] *adj* : sin mangas
sleigh¹ ['sleɪ] *vi* : ir en trineo
sleigh² *n* : trineo *m* (tirado por caballos)
sleight of hand [ˌslaɪtəv'hænd] : prestidigitación *f*, juegos *mpl* de manos
slender ['slɛndər] *adj* **1** SLIM : esbelto, delgado **2** SCANTY : exiguo, escaso <a slender hope : una esperanza lejana>
sleuth ['slu:θ] *n* : detective *mf*; sabueso *m*, -sa *f*
slew → **slay**
slice¹ ['slaɪs] *vt* **sliced; slicing** : cortar
slice² *n* : rebanada *f*, tajada *f*, lonja *f* (de carne, etc.), rodaja *f* (de una verdura, fruta, etc.), trozo *m* (de pastel, etc.)
slick¹ ['slɪk] *vt* : alisar
slick² *adj* **1** SLIPPERY : resbaladizo, resbaloso **2** CRAFTY : astuto, taimado
slicker ['slɪkər] *n* : impermeable *m*
slide¹ ['slaɪd] *v* **slid** ['slɪd]; **sliding** ['slaɪdɪŋ] *vi* **1** SLIP : resbalar **2** GLIDE : deslizarse **3** DECLINE : bajar <to let things slide : dejar pasar las cosas> — *vt* : correr, deslizar
slide² *n* **1** SLIDING : deslizamiento *m* **2** SLIP : resbalón *m* **3** : tobogán *m* (para niños) **4** : TRANSPARENCY : diapositiva *f* (fotográfica) **5** DECLINE : descenso *m*
slier, sliest → **sly**
slight¹ ['slaɪt] *vt* : desairar, despreciar
slight² *adj* **1** SLENDER : esbelto, delgado **2** FLIMSY : endeble **3** TRIFLING : leve, insignificante <a slight pain : un leve dolor> **4** SMALL : pequeño, ligero <not in the slightest : en absoluto>
slight³ *n* SNUB : desaire *m*
slightly ['slaɪtli] *adv* : ligeramente, un poco
slim¹ ['slɪm] *v* **slimmed; slimming** : adelgazar
slim² *adj* **slimmer; slimmest 1** SLENDER : esbelto, delgado **2** SCANTY : exiguo, escaso
slime ['slaɪm] *n* **1** : baba *f* (secretado por un animal) **2** MUD, SILT : fango *m*, cieno *m*
slimy ['slaɪmi] *adj* **slimier; -est** : viscoso
sling¹ ['slɪŋ] *vt* **slung** ['slʌŋ]; **slinging 1** THROW : lanzar, tirar **2** HANG : colgar
sling² *n* **1** : honda *f* (arma) **2** : cabestrillo *m* <my arm is in a sling : llevo el brazo en cabestrillo>
slingshot ['slɪŋˌʃɑt] *n* : tiragomas *m*, resortera *f Mex*
slink ['slɪŋk] *vi* **slunk** ['slʌŋk]; **slinking** : caminar furtivamente
slip¹ ['slɪp] *v* **slipped; slipping** *vi* **1** STEAL : ir sigilosamente <to slip away : escabullirse> <to slip out the door : escaparse por la puerta> **2** SLIDE : resbalarse, deslizarse **3** LAPSE : caer <to slip into error : equivocarse> **4 to let slip** : dejar escapar **5 to slip into** PUT ON : ponerse — *vt* **1** PUT : meter, poner **2** PASS : pasar <she slipped me a note : me pasó una nota> **3 to slip one's mind** : olvidársele a uno
slip² *n* **1** PIER : atracadero *m* **2** MISHAP : percance *m*, contratiempo *m* **3** MISTAKE : error *m*, desliz *m* <a slip of the tongue : un lapsus> **4** PETTICOAT : enagua *f* **5** : injerto *m*, esqueje *m* (de una planta) **6 slip of paper** : papelito *m*
slipper ['slɪpər] *n* : zapatilla *f*, pantufla *f*
slipperiness ['slɪpərinəs] *n* **1** : lo resbaloso, lo resbaladizo **2** TRICKINESS : astucia *f*
slippery ['slɪpəri] *adj* **slipperier; -est 1** : resbaloso, resbaladizo <a slippery road : un camino resbaloso> **2** TRICKY : artero, astuto, taimado **3** ELUSIVE : huidizo, escurridizo
slipshod ['slɪpˌʃɑd] *adj* : descuidado, chapucero
slip up *vi* : equivocarse
slit¹ ['slɪt] *vt* **slit; slitting** : cortar, abrir por lo largo
slit² *n* **1** OPENING : abertura *f*, rendija *f* **2** CUT : corte *m*, raja *f*, tajo *m*
slither ['slɪðər] *vi* : deslizarse
sliver ['slɪvər] *n* : astilla *f*
slob ['slɑb] *n* : persona *f* desaliñada <what a slob! : ¡qué cerdo!>
slobber¹ ['slɑbər] *vi* : babear
slobber² *n* : baba *f*
slogan ['slo:gən] *n* : lema *m*, eslogan *m*
sloop ['slu:p] *n* : balandra *f*
slop¹ ['slɑp] *v* **slopped; slopping** *vt* : derramar — *vi* : derramarse
slop² *n* : bazofia *f*
slope¹ ['slo:p] *vi* **sloped; sloping** : inclinarse <the road slopes upward : el camino sube (en pendiente)>
slope² *n* : inclinación *f*, pendiente *f*, declive *m*
sloppy ['slɑpi] *adj* **sloppier; -est 1** MUDDY, SLUSHY : lodoso, fangoso **2** UNTIDY : descuidado (en el trabajo, etc.), desaliñado (de aspecto)
slot ['slɑt] *n* : ranura *f*
sloth ['slɔθ, 'slo:θ] *n* **1** LAZINESS : pereza *f* **2** : perezoso *m* (animal)
slouch¹ ['slaʊtʃ] *vi* : andar con los hombros caídos, repantigarse (en un sillón)
slouch² *n* **1** SLUMPING : mala postura *f* **2** BUNGLER, IDLER : haragán *m*, -gana *f*; inepto *m*, -ta *f* <to be no slouch : no quedarse atrás>
slough¹ ['slʌf] *vt* : mudar de (piel)
slough² ['slu:, 'slaʊ] *n* SWAMP : ciénaga *f*
Slovak ['slo:ˌvɑk, -ˌvæk] *or* **Slovakian** [slo:'vɑkiən, -'væ-] *n* : eslovaco *m*, -ca *f* — **Slovak** *or* **Slovakian** *adj*
Slovene ['slo:ˌvi:n] *or* **Slovenian** [slo:'vi:niən] *n* : esloveno *m*, -na *f* — **Slovene** *or* **Slovenian** *adj*

slovenly ['slɑvənli, 'slʌv-] *adj* : descuidado (en el trabajo, etc.), desaliñado (de aspecto)
slow[1] [slo:] *vt* : retrasar, reducir la marcha de — *vi* : ir más despacio
slow[2] *adv* : despacio, lentamente
slow[3] *adj* **1** : lento <a slow process : un proceso lento> **2** : atrasado <my watch is slow : mi reloj está atrasado, mi reloj se atrasa> **3** SLUGGISH : lento, poco activo **4** STUPID : lento, torpe, corto de alcances
slowly [slo:li] *adv* : lentamente, despacio
slowness [slo:nəs] *n* : lentitud *f,* torpeza *f*
sludge ['slʌdʒ] *n* : aguas *fpl* negras, aguas *fpl* residuales
slug[1] ['slʌg] *vt* **slugged; slugging** : pegarle un porrazo (a alguien)
slug[2] *n* **1** : babosa *f* (molusco) **2** BULLET : bala *f* **3** TOKEN : ficha *f* **4** BLOW : porrazo *m,* puñetazo *m*
sluggish ['slʌgɪʃ] *adj* : aletargado, lento
sluice[1] ['slu:s] *vt* **sluiced; sluicing** : lavar en agua corriente
sluice[2] *n* : canal *m*
slum ['slʌm] *n* : barriada *f,* barrio *m* bajo
slumber[1] ['slʌmbər] *vi* : dormir
slumber[2] *n* : sueño *m*
slump[1] ['slʌmp] *vi* **1** DECLINE, DROP : disminuir, bajar **2** SLOUCH : encorvarse, dejarse caer (en una silla, etc.)
slump[2] *n* : bajón *m,* declive *m* (económico)
slung → **sling**
slunk → **slink**
slur[1] ['slər] *vt* **slurred; slurring** : ligar (notas musicales), tragarse (las palabras)
slur[2] *n* **1** : ligado *m* (en música), mala pronunciación *f* (de las palabras) **2** ASPERSION : calumnia *f,* difamación *f*
slurp[1] ['slərp] *vi* : beber o comer haciendo ruido — *vt* : sorber ruidosamente
slurp[2] *n* : sorbo *m* (ruidoso)
slush ['slʌʃ] *n* : nieve *f* medio derretida
slut ['slʌt] *n* PROSTITUTE : ramera *f,* fulana *f*
sly ['slaɪ] *adj* **slier** ['slaɪər]; **sliest** ['slaɪəst] **1** CUNNING : astuto, taimado **2** UNDERHANDED : soplado — **slyly** *adv*
slyness ['slaɪnəs] *n* : astucia *f*
smack[1] ['smæk] *vi* **to smack of** : oler a, saber a — *vt* **1** KISS : besar, plantarle un beso (a alguien) **2** SLAP : pegarle una bofetada (a alguien) **3 to smack one's lips** : relamerse
smack[2] *adv* : justo, exactamente <smack in the face : en plena cara>
smack[3] *n* **1** TASTE, TRACE : sabor *m,* indicio *m* **2** : chasquido *m* (de los labios) **3** SLAP : bofetada *f* **4** KISS : beso *m*
small ['smɔl] *adj* **1** : pequeño, chico <a small house : una casa pequeña> <small change : monedas de poco valor> **2** TRIVIAL : pequeño, insignificante
smallness ['smɔlnəs] *n* : pequeñez *f*
smallpox ['smɔl,pɑks] *n* : viruela *f*
smart[1] ['smɑrt] *vi* **1** STING : escocer, picar, arder **2** HURT : dolerse, resentirse <to smart under a rejection : dolerse ante un rechazo>
smart[2] *adj* **1** BRIGHT : listo, vivo, inteligente **2** STYLISH : elegante — **smartly** *adv*
smart[3] *n* : escozor *m,* dolor *m*
smartness ['smɑrtnəs] *n* **1** INTELLIGENCE : inteligencia *f* **2** ELEGANCE : elegancia *f*
smash[1] ['smæʃ] *vt* **1** BREAK : romper, quebrar, hacer pedazos **2** WRECK : destrozar, arruinar **3** CRASH : estrellar, chocar — *vi* **1** SHATTER : hacerse pedazos, hacerse añicos **2** COLLIDE, CRASH : estrellarse, chocar
smash[2] *n* **1** BLOW : golpe *m* **2** COLLISION : choque *m* **3** BANG, CRASH : estrépito *m*
smattering ['smæt̬ərɪŋ] *n* **1** : nociones *fpl* <she has a smattering of programming : tiene nociones de programación> **2** : un poco, unos cuantos <a smattering of spectators : unos cuantos espectadores>
smear[1] ['smɪr] *vt* **1** DAUB : embadurnar, untar (mantequilla, etc.) **2** SMUDGE : emborronar **3** SLANDER : calumniar, difamar
smear[2] *n* **1** SMUDGE : mancha *f* **2** SLANDER : calumnia *f*
smell[1] ['smɛl] *v* **smelled** *or* **smelt** ['smɛlt]; **smelling** *vt* : oler, olfatear <to smell danger : olfatear el peligro> — *vi* : oler <to smell good : oler bien>
smell[2] *n* **1** : olfato *m,* sentido *m* del olfato **2** ODOR : olor *m*
smelly ['smɛli] *adj* **smellier; -est** : maloliente
smelt[1] ['smɛlt] *vt* : fundir
smelt[2] *n, pl* **smelts** *or* **smelt** : eperlano *m* (pez)
smile[1] ['smaɪl] *vi* **smiled; smiling** : sonreír
smile[2] *n* : sonrisa *f*
smirk[1] ['smərk] *vi* : sonreír con suficiencia
smirk[2] *n* : sonrisa *f* satisfecha
smite ['smaɪt] *vt* **smote** ['smo:t]; **smitten** ['smɪtən] *or* **smote; smiting 1** STRIKE : golpear **2** AFFLICT : afligir
smith ['smɪθ] *n* : herrero *m,* -ra *f*
smithy ['smɪθi] *n, pl* **smithies** : herrería *f*
smock ['smɑk] *n* : bata *f,* blusón *m*
smog ['smɑg, 'smɔg] *n* : smog *m*
smoke[1] ['smo:k] *v* **smoked; smoking** *vi* **1** : echar humo, humear <a smoking chimney : una chimenea que echa humo> **2** : fumar <I don't smoke : no fumo> — *vt* : ahumar (carne, etc.)
smoke[2] *n* : humo *m*

smoke detector [dɪˈtɛktər] *n* : detector *m* de humo
smoker [ˈsmoːkər] *n* : fumador *m*, -dora *f*
smokestack [ˈsmoːk,stæk] *n* : chimenea *f*
smoky [ˈsmoːki] *adj* **smokier; -est 1** SMOKING : humeante **2** : a humo <a smoky flavor : un sabor a humo> **3** : lleno de humo <a smoky room : un cuarto lleno de humo>
smolder [ˈsmoːldər] *vi* **1** : arder sin llama **2** : arder (en el corazón) <his anger smoldered : su rabia ardía>
smooth¹ [ˈsmuːð] *vt* : alisar
smooth² *adj* **1** : liso (dícese de una superficie) <smooth skin : piel lisa> **2** : suave (dícese de un movimiento) <a smooth landing : un aterrizaje suave> **3** : sin grumos <a smooth sauce : una salsa sin grumos> **4** : fluido <smooth writing : escritura fluida>
smoothly [ˈsmuːðli] *adv* **1** GENTLY, SOFTLY : suavemente **2** EASILY : con facilidad, sin problemas
smoothness [ˈsmuːðnəs] *n* : suavidad *f*
smother [ˈsmʌðər] *vt* **1** SUFFOCATE : ahogar, sofocar **2** COVER : cubrir **3** SUPPRESS : contener — *vi* : asfixiarse
smudge¹ [ˈsmʌdʒ] *v* **smudged; smudging** *vt* : emborronar — *vi* : correrse
smudge² *n* : mancha *f*, borrón *m*
smug [ˈsmʌg] *adj* **smugger; smuggest** : suficiente, pagado de sí mismo
smuggle [ˈsmʌgəl] *vt* **-gled; -gling** : contrabandear, pasar de contrabando
smuggler [ˈsmʌgələr] *n* : contrabandista *mf*
smugly [ˈsmʌgli] *adv* : con suficiencia
smut [ˈsmʌt] *n* **1** SOOT : tizne *m*, hollín *m* **2** FUNGUS : tizón *m* **3** OBSCENITY : obscenidad *f*, inmundicia *f*
smutty [ˈsmʌti] *adj* **smuttier; -est 1** SOOTY : tiznado **2** OBSCENE : obsceno, indecente
snack [ˈsnæk] *n* : refrigerio *m*, bocado *m*, tentempié *m fam* <an afternoon snack : una merienda>
snag¹ [ˈsnæg] *v* **snagged; snagging** *vt* : enganchar — *vi* : engancharse
snag² *n* : problema *m*, inconveniente *m*
snail [ˈsneɪl] *n* : caracol *m*
snake [ˈsneɪk] *n* : culebra *f*, serpiente *f*
snakebite [ˈsneɪk,baɪt] *n* : mordedura *f* de serpiente
snap¹ [ˈsnæp] *v* **snapped; snapping** *vi* **1** : intentar morder (dícese de un perro, etc.), picar (dícese de un pez) **2** : hablar con severidad <he snapped at me! : ¡me gritó!> **3** BREAK : romperse, quebrarse (haciendo un chasquido) — *vt* **1** BREAK : partir (en dos), quebrar **2** : hacer (algo) de un golpe <to snap open : abrir de golpe> **3** RETORT : decir bruscamente **4** CLICK : chasquear <to snap one's fingers : chasquear los dedos>
snap² *n* **1** CLICK, CRACK : chasquido *m* **2** FASTENER : broche *m* **3** CINCH : cosa *f* fácil <it's a snap : es facilísimo>
snapdragon [ˈsnæp,drægən] *n* : dragón *m* (flor)
snapper [ˈsnæpər] → **red snapper**
snappy [ˈsnæpi] *adj* **snappier; -est 1** FAST : rápido <make it snappy! : ¡date prisa!> **2** LIVELY : vivaz **3** CHILLY : frío **4** STYLISH : elegante
snapshot [ˈsnæp,ʃɑt] *n* : instantánea *f*
snare¹ [ˈsnær] *vt* **snared; snaring** : atrapar
snare² *n* : trampa *f*, red *f*
snare drum *n* : tambor *m* con bordón
snarl¹ [ˈsnɑrl] *vi* **1** TANGLE : enmarañar, enredar **2** GROWL : gruñir
snarl² *n* **1** TANGLE : enredo *m*, maraña *f* **2** GROWL : gruñido *m*
snatch¹ [ˈsnætʃ] *vt* : arrebatar
snatch² *n* : fragmento *m*
sneak¹ [ˈsniːk] *vi* : ir a hurtadillas — *vt* : hacer furtivamente <to sneak a look : mirar con disimulo> <he sneaked a smoke : fumó un cigarrillo a escondidas>
sneak² *n* : soplón *m*, -plona *f*
sneakers [ˈsniːkərz] *npl* : tenis *mpl*, zapatillas *fpl*
sneaky [ˈsniːki] *adj* **sneakier; -est** : solapado
sneer¹ [ˈsnɪr] *vi* : sonreír con desprecio
sneer² *n* : sonrisa *f* de desprecio
sneeze¹ [ˈsniːz] *vi* **sneezed; sneezing** : estornudar
sneeze² *n* : estornudo *m*
snicker¹ [ˈsnɪkər] *vi* : reírse disimuladamente
snicker² *n* : risita *f*
snide [ˈsnaɪd] *adj* : sarcástico
sniff¹ [ˈsnɪf] *vi* **1** SMELL : oler, husmear (dícese de los animales) **2 to sniff at** : despreciar, desdeñar — *vt* **1** SMELL : oler **2 to sniff out** : olerse, husmear
sniff² *n* **1** SNIFFING : aspiración *f* por la nariz **2** SMELL : olor *m*
sniffle [ˈsnɪfəl] *vi* **-fled; -fling** : respirar con la nariz congestionada
sniffles [ˈsnɪfəlz] *npl* : resfriado *m*
snip¹ [ˈsnɪp] *vt* **snipped; snipping** : cortar (con tijeras)
snip² *n* : tijeretada *f*, recorte *m*
snipe¹ [ˈsnaɪp] *vi* **sniped; sniping** : disparar
snipe² *n, pl* **snipes** *or* **snipe** : agachadiza *f*
sniper [ˈsnaɪpər] *n* : francotirador *m*, -dora *f*
snivel [ˈsnɪvəl] *vi* **-veled** *or* **-velled; -veling** *or* **-velling 1** → **snuffle 2** WHINE : lloriquear
snob [ˈsnɑb] *n* : esnob *mf*, snob *mf*
snobbery [ˈsnɑbəri] *n, pl* **-beries** : esnobismo *m*
snobbish [ˈsnɑbɪʃ] *adj* : esnob, snob
snobbishness [ˈsnɑbɪʃnəs] *n* : esnobismo *m*
snoop¹ [ˈsnuːp] *vi* : husmear, curiosear
snoop² *n* : fisgón *m*, -gona *f*

snooze[1] ['snuːz] *vi* **snoozed; snoozing** : dormitar
snooze[2] *n* : siestecita *f,* siestita *f*
snore[1] ['snor] *vi* **snored; snoring** : roncar
snore[2] *n* : ronquido *m*
snort[1] ['snɔrt] *vi* : bufar, resoplar
snort[2] *n* : bufido *m,* resoplo *m*
snout ['snaʊt] *n* : hocico *m,* morro *m*
snow[1] ['snoː] *vi* **1** : nevar <I'm snowed in : estoy aislado por la nieve> **2 to be snowed under** : estar inundado
snow[2] *n* : nieve *f*
snowball ['snoːˌbɔl] *n* : bola *f* de nieve
snowdrift ['snoːˌdrɪft] *n* : ventisquero *m*
snowfall ['snoːˌfɔl] *n* : nevada *f*
snowplow ['snoːˌplaʊ] *n* : quitanieves *m*
snowshoe ['snoːˌʃuː] *n* : raqueta *f* (para nieve)
snowstorm ['snoːˌstɔrm] *n* : tormenta *f* de nieve, ventisca *f*
snowy ['snoːi] *adj* **snowier; -est** : nevoso <a snowy road : un camino nevado>
snub[1] ['snʌb] *vi* **snubbed; snubbing** : desairar
snub[2] *n* : desaire *m*
snub–nosed ['snʌbˌnoːzd] *adj* : de nariz respingada
snuff[1] ['snʌf] *vt* **1** : apagar (una vela) **2** : sorber (algo) por la nariz
snuff[2] *n* : rapé *m*
snuffle ['snʌfəl] *vi* **-fled; -fling** : respirar con la nariz congestionada
snug ['snʌg] *adj* **snugger; snuggest 1** COMFORTABLE : cómodo **2** TIGHT : ajustado, ceñido <snug pants : pantalones ajustados>
snuggle ['snʌgəl] *vi* **-gled; -gling** : acurrucarse <to snuggle up to someone : arrimársele a alguien>
snugly ['snʌgli] *adv* **1** COMFORTABLY : cómodamente **2** : de manera ajustada <the shirt fits snugly : la camisa queda ajustada>
so[1] ['soː] *adv* **1** (*referring to something indicated or suggested*) <do you think so? : ¿tú crees?> <so it would seem : eso parece> <I told her so : se lo dije> <he's ready, or so he says : según dice, está listo> <it so happened that. . . : resultó que. . .> <do it like so : hazlo así> <so be it : así sea> **2** ALSO : también <so do I : yo también> **3** THUS : así, de esta manera **4** : tan <he'd never been so happy : nunca había estado tan contento> **5** CONSEQUENTLY : por lo tanto
so[2] *conj* **1** THEREFORE : así que **2** *or* **so that** : para que, así que, de manera que **3 so what?** : ¿y qué?
soak[1] ['soːk] *vi* : estar en remojo — *vt* **1** : poner en remojo **2 to soak up** ABSORB : absorber
soak[2] *n* : remojo *m*
soap[1] ['soːp] *vt* : enjabonar
soap[2] *n* : jabón *m*
soapsuds ['soːpˌsʌdz] → **suds**
soapy ['soːpi] **soapier; -est** *adj* : jabonoso <a soapy taste : un gusto a jabón> <a soapy texture : una textura de jabón>
soar ['sor] *vi* **1** FLY : volar **2** RISE : remontar el vuelo (dícese de las aves) <her hopes soared : su esperanza renació> <prices are soaring : los precios están subiendo vertiginosamente>
sob[1] ['sɑb] *vi* **sobbed; sobbing** : sollozar
sob[2] *n* : sollozo *m*
sober ['soːbər] *adj* **1** : sobrio <he's not sober enough to drive : está demasiado borracho para manejar> **2** SERIOUS : serio
soberly ['soːbərli] *adv* **1** : sobriamente **2** SERIOUSLY : seriamente
sobriety [sə'braɪəti, so-] *n* **1** : sobriedad *f* <sobriety test : prueba de alcoholemia> **2** SERIOUSNESS : seriedad *f*
so–called ['soː'kɔld] *adj* : supuesto, presunto <the so-called experts : los expertos, así llamados>
soccer ['sɑkər] *n* : futbol *m,* fútbol *m*
sociable ['soːʃəbəl] *adj* : sociable
social[1] ['soːʃəl] *adj* : social — **socially** *adv*
social[2] *n* : reunión *f* social
socialism ['soːʃəˌlɪzəm] *n* : socialismo *m*
socialist[1] ['soːʃəlɪst] *adj* : socialista
socialist[2] *n* : socialista *mf*
socialize ['soːʃəˌlaɪz] *v* **-ized; -izing** *vt* **1** NATIONALIZE : nacionalizar **2** : socializar (en psicología) — *vi* : alternar, circular <to socialize with friends : alternar con amigos>
social work *n* : asistencia *f* social
society [sə'saɪəti] *n, pl* **-eties 1** COMPANIONSHIP : compañía *f* **2** : sociedad *f* <a democratic society : una sociedad democrática> <high society : alta sociedad> **3** ASSOCIATION : sociedad *f,* asociación *f*
sociology [ˌsoːsi'ɑlədʒi] *n* : sociología *f*
sociological [ˌsoːsiə'lɑdʒɪkəl] *adj* : sociológico
sociologist [ˌsoːsi'ɑlədʒɪst] *n* : sociólogo *m,* -ga *f*
sock[1] ['sɑk] *vt* : pegar, golpear, darle un puñetazo a
sock[2] *n* **1** *pl* **socks** *or* **sox** ['sɑks] : calcetín *m,* media *f* <shoes and socks : zapatos y calcetines> **2** *pl* **socks** ['sɑks] PUNCH : puñetazo *m*
socket ['sɑkət] *n* **1** *or* **electric socket** : enchufe *m,* toma *f* de corriente **2** : glena *f* (de una articulación) <shoulder socket : glena del hombro> **3 eye socket** : órbita *f,* cuenca *f*
sod[1] ['sɑd] *vt* **sodded; sodding** : cubrir de césped
sod[2] *n* TURF : césped *m,* tepe *m*

soda [ˈsoːdə] *n* **1** *or* **soda water :** soda *f* **2** *or* **soda pop :** gaseosa *f,* refresco *m* **3** *or* **ice–cream soda :** refresco *m* con helado
sodden [ˈsɑdən] *adj* SOGGY **:** empapado
sodium [ˈsoːdiəm] *n* **:** sodio *m*
sodium bicarbonate *n* **:** bicarbonato *m* de soda
sodium chloride → salt
sofa [ˈsoːfə] *n* **:** sofá *m*
soft [ˈsɔft] *adj* **1 :** blando <a soft pillow **:** una almohada blanda> **2** SMOOTH **:** suave (dícese de las texturas, de los sonidos, etc.) **3** NONALCOHOLIC **:** no alcohólico <a soft drink **:** un refresco>
softball [ˈsɔftˌbɔl] *n* **:** softbol *m*
soften [ˈsɔfən] *vt* **:** ablandar (algo sólido), suavizar (la piel, un golpe, etc.), amortiguar (un impacto) — *vi* **:** ablandarse, suavizarse
softly [ˈsɔftli] *adv* **:** suavemente <she spoke softly **:** habló en voz baja>
softness [ˈsɔftnəs] *n* **1 :** blandura *f,* lo blando (de una almohada, de la mantequilla, etc.) **2** SMOOTHNESS **:** suavidad *f*
software [ˈsɔftˌwær] *n* **:** software *m*
soggy [ˈsɑgi] *adj* **soggier; -est :** empapado
soil[1] [ˈsɔɪl] *vt* **:** ensuciar — *vi* **:** ensuciarse
soil[2] *n* **1** DIRTINESS **:** suciedad *f* **2** DIRT, EARTH **:** suelo *m,* tierra *f* **3** COUNTRY **:** patria *f* <her native soil **:** su tierra natal>
sojourn[1] [ˈsoːˌdʒərn, soːˈdʒərn] *vi* **:** pasar una temporada
sojourn[2] *n* **:** estadía *f,* estancia *f,* permanencia *f*
solace [ˈsɑləs] *n* **:** consuelo *m*
solar [ˈsoːlər] *adj* **:** solar <the solar system **:** el sistema solar>
sold → sell
solder[1] [ˈsɑdər, ˈsɔ-] *vt* **:** soldar
solder[2] *n* **:** soldadura *f*
soldier[1] [ˈsoːldʒər] *vi* **:** servir como soldado
soldier[2] *n* **:** soldado *mf*
sole[1] [ˈsoːl] *adj* **:** único
sole[2] *n* **1 :** suela *f* (de un zapato) **2 :** lenguado *m* (pez)
solely [ˈsoːli] *adv* **:** únicamente, sólo
solemn [ˈsɑləm] *adj* **:** solemne, serio — **solemnly** *adv*
solemnity [səˈlɛmnət̬i] *n, pl* **-ties :** solemnidad *f*
solicit [səˈlɪsət] *vt* **:** solicitar
solicitous [səˈlɪsət̬əs] *adj* **:** solícito
solicitude [səˈlɪsəˌtuːd, -ˌtjuːd] *n* **:** solicitud *f*
solid[1] [ˈsɑləd] *adj* **1 :** macizo <a solid rubber ball **:** una bola maciza de caucho> **2** CUBIC **:** tridimensional **3** COMPACT **:** compacto, denso **4** STURDY **:** sólido **5** CONTINUOUS **:** seguido, continuo <two solid hours **:** dos horas seguidas> <a solid line **:** una línea continua> **6** UNANIMOUS **:** unánime **7** DEPENDABLE **:** serio, fiable **8** PURE **:** macizo, puro <solid gold **:** oro macizo>
solid[2] *n* **:** sólido *m*
solidarity [ˌsɑləˈdærət̬i] *n* **:** solidaridad *f*
solidify [səˈlɪdəˌfaɪ] *v* **-fied; -fying** *vt* **:** solidificar — *vi* **:** solidificarse
solidity [səˈlɪdət̬i] *n, pl* **-ties :** solidez *f*
solidly [ˈsɑlədli] *adv* **1 :** sólidamente **2** UNANIMOUSLY **:** unánimemente
soliloquy [səˈlɪləkwi] *n, pl* **-quies :** soliloquio *m*
solitaire [ˈsɑləˌtɛr] *n* **:** solitario *m*
solitary [ˈsɑləˌtɛri] *adj* **1** ALONE **:** solitario **2** SECLUDED **:** apartado, retirado **3** SINGLE **:** solo
solitude [ˈsɑləˌtuːd, -ˌtjuːd] *n* **:** soledad *f*
solo[1] [ˈsoːˌloː] *vi* **:** volar en solitario (dícese de un piloto)
solo[2] *adv & adj* **:** en solitario, a solas
solo[3] *n, pl* **solos :** solo *m*
soloist [ˈsoːloɪst] *n* **:** solista *mf*
solstice [ˈsɑlstɪs] *n* **:** solsticio *m*
soluble [ˈsɑljəbəl] *adj* **:** soluble
solution [səˈluːʃən] *n* **:** solución *f*
solve [ˈsɑlv] *vt* **solved; solving :** resolver, solucionar
solvency [ˈsɑlvəntsi] *n* **:** solvencia *f*
solvent [ˈsɑlvənt] *n* **:** solvente *m*
Somali [soˈmɑli, sə-] *n* **:** somalí *mf* — **Somali** *adj*
somber [ˈsɑmbər] *adj* **1** DARK **:** sombrío, oscuro <somber colors **:** colores oscuros> **2** GRAVE **:** sombrío, serio **3** MELANCHOLY **:** sombrío, lúgubre
sombrero [səmˈbrɛrˌoː] *n, pl* **-ros :** sombrero *m* (mexicano)
some[1] [ˈsʌm] *adj* **1 :** un, algún <some lady stopped me **:** una mujer me detuvo> <some distant galaxy **:** alguna galaxia lejana> **2 :** algo de, un poco de <he drank some water **:** tomó (un poco de) agua> **3 :** unos <do you want some apples? **:** ¿quieres unas manzanas?> <some years ago **:** hace varios años>
some[2] *pron* **1 :** algunos <some went, others stayed **:** algunos se fueron, otros se quedaron> **2 :** un poco, algo <there's some left **:** queda un poco> <I have gum; do you want some? **:** tengo chicle, ¿quieres?>
somebody [ˈsʌmbədi, -ˌbɑdi] *pron* **:** alguien
someday [ˈsʌmˌdeɪ] *adv* **:** algún día
somehow [ˈsʌmˌhaʊ] *adv* **1 :** de alguna manera, de algún modo <I'll do it somehow **:** lo haré de alguna manera> **2 :** por alguna rázon <somehow I don't trust her **:** por alguna razón no me fío de ella>
someone [ˈsʌmˌwʌn] *pron* **:** alguien
somersault[1] [ˈsʌmərˌsɔlt] *vi* **:** dar volteretas, dar un salto mortal
somersault[2] *n* **:** voltereta *f,* salto *m* mortal

something ['sʌmθɪŋ] *pron* : algo <I want something else : quiero otra cosa> <she's writing a novel or something : está escribiendo una novela o no sé qué>
sometime ['sʌm,taɪm] *adv* : algún día, en algún momento <sometime next month : durante el mes que viene>
sometimes ['sʌm,taɪmz] *adv* : a veces, algunas veces, de vez en cuando
somewhat ['sʌm,hwʌt, -,hwɑt] *adv* : algo, un tanto
somewhere ['sʌm,*h*wɛr] *adv* **1** : en alguna parte, a algún lugar **2 somewhere else** : en otro sitio
son ['sʌn] *n* : hijo *m*
sonar ['soː,nɑr] *n* : sonar *m*
sonata [sə'nɑṭə] *n* : sonata *f*
song ['sɔŋ] *n* : canción *f,* canto *m* (de un pájaro)
songbird ['sɔŋ,bərd] *n* : pájaro *m* cantor
sonic ['sɑnɪk] *adj* **1** : sónico **2 sonic boom** : estampido *m* sónico
son–in–law ['sʌnɪn,lɔ] *n, pl* **sons–in–law** : yerno *m,* hijo *m* político
sonnet ['sɑnət] *n* : soneto *m*
sonorous ['sɑnərəs, sə'norəs] *adj* : sonoro
soon ['suːn] *adv* **1** : pronto, dentro de poco <he'll arrive soon : llegará pronto> **2** QUICKLY : pronto <as soon as possible : lo más pronto posible> <the sooner the better : cuanto antes mejor>
soot ['sʊt, 'suːt, 'sʌt] *n* : hollín *m,* tizne *m*
soothe ['suːð] *vt* **soothed; soothing 1** CALM : calmar, tranquilizar **2** RELIEVE : aliviar
soothsayer ['suːθ,seɪər] *n* : adivino *m,* -na *f*
sooty ['sʊṭi, 'suː-, 'sʌ-] *adj* **sootier; -est** : cubierto de hollín, tiznado
sop[1] ['sɑp] *vt* **sopped; sopping 1** DIP : mojar **2** SOAK : empapar **3 to sop up** : rebañar, absorber
sop[2] *n* **1** CONCESSION : concesión *f* **2** BRIBE : soborno *m*
sophisticated [sə'fɪstə,keɪṭəd] *adj* **1** COMPLEX : complejo **2** WORLDLY-WISE : sofisticado
sophistication [sə,fɪstə'keɪʃən] *n* **1** COMPLEXITY : complejidad *f* **2** URBANITY : sofisticación *f*
sophomore ['sɑf,mor, 'sɑfə,mor] *n* : estudiante *mf* de segundo año
soporific [,sɑpə'rɪfɪk, ,soː-] *adj* : soporífero
soprano [sə'præ,noː] *n, pl* **-nos** : soprano *mf*
sorcerer ['sɔrsərər] *n* : hechicero *m,* brujo *m,* mago *m*
sorceress ['sɔrsərəs] *n* : hechicera *f,* bruja *f,* maga *f*
sorcery ['sɔrsəri] *n* : hechicería *f,* brujería *f*
sordid ['sɔrdɪd] *adj* : sórdido
sore[1] ['sor] *adj* **sorer; sorest 1** PAINFUL : dolorido, doloroso <I have a sore throat : me duele la garganta> **2** ACUTE, SEVERE : extremo, grande <in sore straits : en grandes apuros> **3** ANGRY : enojado, enfadado
sore[2] *n* : llaga *f*
sorely ['sorli] *adv* : muchísimo <it was sorely needed : se necesitaba urgentemente> <she was sorely missed : la echaban mucho de menos>
soreness ['sornəs] *n* : dolor *m*
sorghum ['sɔrgəm] *n* : sorgo *m*
sorority [sə'rɔrəṭi] *n, pl* **-ties** : hermandad *f* (de estudiantes femeninas)
sorrel ['sɔrəl] *n* **1** : alazán *m* (color o animal) **2** : acedera *f* (hierba)
sorrow ['sɑr,oː] *n* : pesar *m,* dolor *m,* pena *f*
sorrowful ['sɑrofəl] *adj* : triste, afligido, apenado
sorrowfully ['sɑrofəli] *adv* : con tristeza
sorry ['sɑri] *adj* **sorrier; -est 1** PITIFUL : lastimero, lastimoso **2 to be sorry** : sentir, lamentar <I'm sorry : lo siento> **3 to feel sorry for** : compadecer <I feel sorry for him : me da pena>
sort[1] ['sɔrt] *vt* : clasificar
sort[2] *n* **1** KIND : tipo *m,* clase *f* <a sort of writer : una especie de escritor> **2** NATURE : índole *f* **3 out of sorts** : de mal humor
sortie ['sɔrṭi, sɔr'tiː] *n* : salida *f*
SOS [,ɛs,oː'ɛs] *n* : SOS *m*
so–so ['soː'soː] *adj & adv* : así así, de modo regular
soufflé [suː'fleɪ] *n* : suflé *m*
sought → **seek**
soul ['soːl] *n* **1** SPIRIT : alma *f* **2** ESSENCE : esencia *f* **3** PERSON : persona *f,* alma *f*
soulful ['soːlfəl] *adj* : conmovedor, lleno de emoción
sound[1] ['saʊnd] *vt* **1** : sondar (en navegación) **2** *or* **to sound out** PROBE : sondear **3** : hacer sonar, tocar (una trompeta, etc.) — *vi* **1** : sonar <the alarm sounded : la alarma sonó> **2** SEEM : parecer
sound[2] *adj* **1** HEALTHY : sano <safe and sound : sano y salvo> <of sound mind and body : en pleno uso de sus facultades> **2** FIRM, SOLID : sólido **3** SENSIBLE : lógico, sensato **4** DEEP : profundo <a sound sleep : un sueño profundo>
sound[3] *n* **1** : sonido *m* <the speed of sound : la velocidad del sonido> **2** NOISE : sonido *m,* ruido *m* <I heard a sound : oí un sonido> **3** CHANNEL : brazo *m* de mar, canal *m* (ancho)
soundless ['saʊndləs] *adj* : sordo
soundlessly ['saʊndləsli] *adv* : silenciosamente
soundly ['saʊndli] *adv* **1** SOLIDLY : sólidamente **2** SENSIBLY : lógicamente, sensatamente **3** DEEPLY : profunda-

mente <sleeping soundly : durmiendo profundamente>

soundness ['saʊndnəs] *n* **1** SOLIDITY : solidez *f* **2** SENSIBLENESS : sensatez *f,* solidez *f*

soundproof ['saʊnd,pru:f] *adj* : insonorizado

sound wave *n* : onda *f* sonora

soup ['su:p] *n* : sopa *f*

sour[1] ['saʊər] *vi* : agriarse, cortarse (dícese de la leche) — *vt* : agriar, cortar (leche)

sour[2] *adj* **1** ACID : agrio, ácido (dícese de la fruta, etc.), cortado (dícese de la leche) **2** DISAGREEABLE : desagradable, agrio

source ['sors] *n* : fuente *f,* origen *m,* nacimiento *m* (de un río)

sourness ['saʊərnəs] *n* : acidez *f*

south[1] ['saʊθ] *adv* : al sur, hacia el sur <the window looks south : la ventana mira al sur> <she continued south : continuó hacia el sur>

south[2] *adj* : sur, del sur <the south entrance : la entrada sur> <South America : Sudamérica, América del Sur>

south[3] *n* : sur *m*

South African *n* : sudafricano *m,* -na *f* — **South African** *adj*

South American[1] *adj* : sudamericano, suramericano

South American[2] *n* : sudamericano *m,* -na *f;* suramericano *m,* -na *f*

southbound ['saʊθ,baʊnd] *adj* : con rumbo al sur

southeast[1] [saʊ'θi:st] *adj* : sureste, sudeste, del sureste

southeast[2] *n* : sureste *m,* sudeste *m*

southeasterly [saʊ'θi:stərli] *adv & adj* **1** : del sureste (dícese del viento) **2** : hacia el sureste

southeastern [saʊ'θi:stərn] → **southeast**[1]

southerly ['sʌðərli] *adv & adj* : del sur

southern ['sʌðərn] *adj* : sur, sureño, meridional, austral <a southern city : una ciudad del sur del país, una ciudad meridional> <the southern side : el lado sur>

Southerner ['sʌðərnər] *n* : sureño *m,* -ña *f*

South Pole : Polo *m* Sur

southward ['saʊθwərd] *or* **southwards** [-wərdz] *adv & adj* : hacia el sur

southwest[1] [saʊθ'wɛst, *as a nautical term often* saʊ'wɛst] *adj* : suroeste, sudoeste, del suroeste

southwest[2] *n* : suroeste *m,* sudoeste *m*

southwesterly [saʊθ'wɛstərli] *adv & adj* **1** : del suroeste (dícese del viento) **2** : hacia el suroeste

southwestern [saʊθ'wɛstərn] → **southwest**[1]

souvenir [,su:və'nɪr, 'su:və,-] *n* : recuerdo *m,* souvenir *m*

sovereign[1] ['sɑvərən] *adj* : soberano

sovereign[2] *n* **1** : soberano *m,* -na *f* (monarca) **2** : soberano *m* (moneda)

sovereignty ['sɑvərənti] *n, pl* **-ties** : soberanía *f*

Soviet ['so:vi,ɛt, 'sɑ-, -viət] *adj* : soviético

sow[1] ['so:] *vt* **sowed; sown** ['so:n] *or* **sowed; sowing 1** PLANT : sembrar **2** SCATTER : esparcir

sow[2] ['saʊ] *n* : cerda *f*

sox → **sock**

soybean ['sɔɪ,bi:n] *n* : soya *f,* soja *f*

spa ['spɑ] *n* : balneario *m*

space[1] ['speɪs] *vt* **spaced; spacing** : espaciar

space[2] *n* **1** PERIOD : espacio *m,* lapso *m,* período *m* **2** ROOM : espacio *m,* sitio *m,* lugar *m* <is there space for me? : ¿hay sitio para mí?> **3** : espacio *m* <blank space : espacio en blanco> **4** : espacio *m* (en física) **5** PLACE : plaza *f,* sitio *m* <to reserve space : reservar plazas> <parking space : sitio para estacionarse>

spacecraft ['speɪs,kræft] *n* : nave *f* espacial

spaceflight ['speɪs,flaɪt] *n* : vuelo *m* espacial

spaceman ['speɪsmən, -,mæn] *n, pl* **-men** [-mən, -,mɛn] : astronauta *m,* cosmonauta *m*

spaceship ['speɪs,ʃɪp] *n* : nave *f* espacial

space shuttle *n* : transbordador *m* espacial

space suit *n* : traje *m* espacial

spacious ['speɪʃəs] *adj* : espacioso, amplio

spade[1] ['speɪd] *v* **spaded; spading** *vt* : palear — *vi* : usar una pala

spade[2] *n* **1** SHOVEL : pala *f* **2** : pica *f* (naipe)

spaghetti [spə'gɛti] *n* : espagueti *m,* espaguetis *mpl,* spaghetti *mpl*

span[1] ['spæn] *vt* **spanned; spanning** : abarcar (un período de tiempo), extenderse sobre (un espacio)

span[2] *n* **1** : lapso *m,* espacio *m* (de tiempo) <life span : duración de la vida> **2** : luz *f* (entre dos soportes)

spangle ['spæŋgəl] *n* : lentejuela *f*

Spaniard ['spænjərd] *n* : español *m,* -ñola *f*

spaniel ['spænjəl] *n* : spaniel *m*

Spanish[1] ['spænɪʃ] *adj* : español

Spanish[2] *n* **1** : español *m* (idioma) **2 the Spanish** *npl* : los españoles

spank ['spæŋk] *vt* : darle nalgadas (a alguien)

spar[1] ['spɑr] *vi* **sparred; sparring** : entrenarse (en boxeo)

spar[2] *n* : palo *m,* verga *f* (de un barco)

spare[1] ['spær] *vt* **spared; sparing 1** : perdonar <to spare someone's life : perdonarle la vida a alguien> **2** SAVE : ahorrar, evitar <I'll spare you the trouble : le evitaré la molestia> **3** : prescindir de <I can't spare her : no puedo prescindir de ella> <can you

spare a dollar? : ¿me das un dólar?> **4** STINT : escatimar <they spared no expense : no repararon en gastos> **5** **to spare** : de sobra

spare[2] *adj* **1** : de repuesto, de recambio <spare tire : llanta de repuesto> **2** EXCESS : de más, de sobra <spare time : tiempo libre> **3** LEAN : delgado

spare[3] *n or* **spare part** : repuesto *m,* recambio *m*

sparing [ˈspærɪŋ] *adj* : parco, económico — **sparingly** *adv*

spark[1] [ˈspɑrk] *vi* : chispear, echar chispas — *vt* PROVOKE : despertar, provocar <to spark interest : despertar interés>

spark[2] *n* **1** : chispa *f* <to throw off sparks : echar chispas> **2** GLIMMER, TRACE : destello *m,* pizca *f*

sparkle[1] [ˈspɑrkəl] *vi* **-kled; -kling** **1** FLASH, SHINE : destellar, centellear, brillar **2** : estar muy animado (dícese de una conversación, etc.)

sparkle[2] *n* : destello *m,* centelleo *m*

sparkler [ˈspɑrklər] *n* : luz *f* de bengala

spark plug *n* : bujía *f*

sparrow [ˈspæroː] *n* : gorrión *m*

sparse [ˈspɑrs] *adj* **sparser; -est** : escaso — **sparsely** *adv*

spasm [ˈspæzəm] *n* **1** : espasmo *m* (muscular) **2** BURST, FIT : arrebato *m*

spasmodic [spæzˈmɑdɪk] *adj* **1** : espasmódico **2** SPORADIC : irregular, esporádico — **spasmodically** [-dɪkli] *adv*

spastic [ˈspæstɪk] *adj* : espástico

spat[1] → **spit[1]**

spat[2] [ˈspæt] *n* : discusión *f,* disputa *f,* pelea *f*

spatial [ˈspeɪʃəl] *adj* : espacial

spatter[1] [ˈspæt̬ər] *v* : salpicar

spatter[2] *n* : salpicadura *f*

spatula [ˈspætʃələ] *n* : espátula *f,* paleta *f* (para servir)

spawn[1] [ˈspɔn] *vi* : desovar, frezar — *vt* GENERATE : generar, producir

spawn[2] *n* : hueva *f,* freza *f*

spay [ˈspeɪ] *vt* : esterilizar (una perra, etc.)

speak [ˈspiːk] *v* **spoke** [ˈspoːk]; **spoken** [ˈspoːkən]; **speaking** *vi* **1** TALK : hablar <to speak to someone : hablar con alguien> <who's speaking? : ¿de parte de quien?> <so to speak : por así decirlo> **2** **to speak out** : hablar claramente **3** **to speak out against** : denunciar **4** **to speak up** : hablar en voz alta **5** **to speak up for** : defender — *vt* **1** SAY : decir <she spoke her mind : habló con franqueza> **2** : hablar (un idioma)

speaker [ˈspiːkər] *n* **1** : hablante *mf* <a native speaker : un hablante nativo> **2** : orador *m,* -dora *f* <the keynote speaker : el orador principal> **3** LOUDSPEAKER : altavoz *m,* altoparlante *m*

spear[1] [ˈspɪr] *vt* : atravesar con una lanza

spear[2] *n* : lanza *f*

spearhead[1] [ˈspɪrˌhɛd] *vt* : encabezar

spearhead[2] *n* : punta *f* de lanza

spearmint [ˈspɪrmɪnt] *n* : menta *f* verde

special [ˈspɛʃəl] *adj* : especial <nothing special : nada en especial, nada en particular> — **specially** *adv*

specialist [ˈspɛʃəlɪst] *n* : especialista *mf*

specialization [ˌspɛʃələˈzeɪʃən] *n* : especialización *f*

specialize [ˈspɛʃəˌlaɪz] *vi* **-ized; -izing** : especializarse

specialty [ˈspɛʃəlt̬i] *n, pl* **-ties** : especialidad *f*

species [ˈspiːˌʃiːz, -ˌsiːz] *ns & pl* : especie *f*

specific [spɪˈsɪfɪk] *adj* : específico, determinado — **specifically** [-fɪkli] *adv*

specification [ˌspɛsəfəˈkeɪʃən] *n* : especificación *f*

specify [ˈspɛsəˌfaɪ] *vt* **-fied; -fying** : especificar

specimen [ˈspɛsəmən] *n* **1** SAMPLE : espécimen *m,* muestra *f* **2** EXAMPLE : espécimen *m,* ejemplar *m*

speck [ˈspɛk] *n* **1** SPOT : manchita *f* **2** BIT, TRACE : mota *f,* pizca *f,* ápice *m*

speckled [ˈspɛkəld] *adj* : moteado

spectacle [ˈspɛktɪkəl] *n* **1** : espectáculo *m* **2** **spectacles** *npl* GLASSES : lentes *fpl,* gafas *fpl,* anteojos *mpl,* espejuelos *mpl*

spectacular [spɛkˈtækjələr] *adj* : espectacular

spectator [ˈspɛkˌteɪt̬ər] *n* : espectador *m,* -dora *f*

specter *or* **spectre** [ˈspɛktər] *n* : espectro *m,* fantasma *m*

spectrum [ˈspɛktrəm] *n, pl* **spectra** [-trə] *or* **spectrums** **1** : espectro *m* (de colores, etc.) **2** RANGE : gama *f,* abanico *m*

speculate [ˈspɛkjəˌleɪt] *vi* **-lated; -lating** **1** : especular (en finanza) **2** WONDER : preguntarse, hacer conjeturas

speculation [ˌspɛkjəˈleɪʃən] *n* : especulación *f*

speculative [ˈspɛkjəˌleɪt̬ɪv] *adj* : especulativo

speculator [ˈspɛkjəˌleɪt̬ər] *n* : especulador *m,* -dora *f*

speech [ˈspiːtʃ] *n* **1** : habla *f,* modo *m* de hablar, expresión *f* **2** ADDRESS : discurso *m*

speechless [ˈspiːtʃləs] *adj* : enmudecido, estupefacto

speed[1] [ˈspiːd] *v* **sped** [ˈspɛd] *or* **speeded; speeding** *vi* **1** : ir a toda velocidad, correr a toda prisa <he sped off : se fue a toda velocidad> **2** : conducir a exceso de velocidad <a ticket for speeding : una multa por exceso de velocidad> — *vt* **to speed up** : acelerar

speed[2] *n* **1** SWIFTNESS : rapidez *f* **2** VELOCITY : velocidad *f*

speedboat [ˈspiːd,boːt] *n* : lancha *f* motora
speed bump *n* : badén *m*
speed limit *n* : velocidad *f* máxima, límite *m* de velocidad
speedometer [spɪˈdɑmət̬ər] *n* : velocímetro *m*
speedup [ˈspiːd,ʌp] *n* : aceleracion *f*
speedy [ˈspiːdi] *adj* **speedier, -est** : rápido — **speedily** [-dəli] *adv*
spell[1] [ˈspɛl] *vt* **1** : escribir, deletrear (verbalmente) <how do you spell it? : ¿cómo se escribe?, ¿cómo se deletrea?> **2** MEAN : significar <that could spell trouble : eso puede significar problemas> **3** RELIEVE : relevar
spell[2] *n* **1** TURN : turno *m* **2** PERIOD, TIME : período *m* (de tiempo) **3** ENCHANTMENT : encanto *m,* hechizo *m,* maleficio *m*
spellbound [ˈspɛl,baʊnd] *adj* : embelesado
speller [ˈspɛlər] *n* : persona *f* que escribe <she's a good speller : tiene buena ortografía>
spelling [ˈspɛlɪŋ] *n* : ortografía *f*
spend [ˈspɛnd] *vt* **spent** [ˈspɛnt]; **spending 1** : gastar (dinero, etc.) **2** PASS : pasar (el tiempo) <to spend time on : dedicar tiempo a>
spendthrift [ˈspɛnd,θrɪft] *n* : derrochador *m,* -dora *f;* despilfarrador *m,* -dora *f*
sperm [ˈspərm] *n, pl* **sperm** *or* **sperms** : esperma *mf*
spew [ˈspjuː] *vi* : salir a chorros — *vt* : vomitar, arrojar (lava, etc.)
sphere [ˈsfɪr] *n* : esfera *f*
spherical [ˈsfɪrɪkəl, ˈsfɛr-] *adj* : esférico
spice[1] [ˈspaɪs] *vt* **spiced; spicing 1** SEASON : condimentar, sazonar **2** *or* **to spice up** : salpimentar, hacer más interesante
spice[2] *n* **1** : especia *f* **2** FLAVOR, INTEREST : sabor *m* <the spice of life : la sal de la vida>
spick–and–span [ˈspɪkəndˈspæn] *adj* : limpio y ordenado
spicy [ˈspaɪsi] *adj* **spicier; -est 1** SPICED : condimentado, sazonado **2** HOT : picante **3** RACY : picante
spider [ˈspaɪdər] *n* : araña *f*
spigot [ˈspɪgət, -kət] *n* : llave *f,* grifo *m,* canilla *Arg, Uru*
spike[1] [ˈspaɪk] *vt* **spiked; spiking 1** FASTEN : clavar (con clavos grandes) **2** PIERCE : atravesar **3** : añadir alcohol a <he spiked her drink with rum : le puso ron a la bebida>
spike[2] *n* : clavo *m* grande
spill[1] [ˈspɪl] *vt* **1** SHED : derramar, verter <to spill blood : derrame sangre> **2** DIVULGE : revelar, divulgar — *vi* : derramarse
spill[2] *n* **1** SPILLING : derrame *m,* vertido *m* <oil spill : derrame de petróleo> **2** FALL : caída *f*
spin[1] [ˈspɪn] *v* **spun** [ˈspʌn]; **spinning** *vi* **1** : hilar **2** TURN : girar **3** REEL : dar vueltas <my head is spinning : la cabeza me está dando vueltas> — *vt* **1** : hilar (hilo, etc.) **2** : tejer <to spin a web : tejer una telaraña> **3** TWIRL : hacer girar
spin[2] *n* : vuelta *f,* giro *m* <to go for a spin : dar una vuelta (en coche)>
spinach [ˈspɪnɪtʃ] *n* : espinacas *fpl,* espinaca *f*
spinal column [ˈspaɪnəl] *n* BACKBONE : columna *f* vertebral
spinal cord *n* : médula *f* espinal
spindle [ˈspɪndəl] *n* **1** : huso *m* (para hilar) **2** : eje *m* (de un mecanismo)
spindly [ˈspɪndli] *adj* : larguirucho *fam,* largo y débil (dícese de una planta)
spine [ˈspaɪn] *n* **1** BACKBONE : columna *f* vertebral, espina *f* dorsal **2** QUILL : púa *f* (de un animal) **3** THORN : espina *f* **4** : lomo *m* (de un libro)
spineless [ˈspaɪnləs] *adj* **1** : sin púas, sin espinas **2** INVERTEBRATE : invertebrado **3** WEAK : débil (de carácter)
spinet [ˈspɪnət] *n* : espineta *f*
spinster [ˈspɪntstər] *n* : soltera *f*
spiny [ˈspaɪni] *adj* **spinier; -est** : con púas (dícese de los animales), espinoso (dícese de las plantas)
spiral[1] [ˈspaɪrəl] *vi* **-raled** *or* **-ralled; -raling** *or* **-ralling** : ir en espiral
spiral[2] *adj* : espiral, en espiral <a spiral staircase : una escalera de caracol>
spiral[3] *n* : espiral *f*
spire [ˈspaɪr] *n* : aguja *f*
spirit[1] [ˈspɪrət] *vt* **to spirit away** : hacer desaparecer
spirit[2] *n* **1** : espíritu *m* <body and spirit : cuerpo y espíritu> **2** GHOST : espíritu *m,* fantasma *m* **3** MOOD : espíritu *m,* humor *m* <in the spirit of friendship : en el espíritu de amistad> <to be in good spirits : estar de buen humor> **4** ENTHUSIASM, VIVACITY : espíritu *m,* ánimo *m,* brío *m* **5 spirits** *npl* : licores *mpl*
spirited [ˈspɪrət̬əd] *adj* : animado, energético
spiritless [ˈspɪrətləs] *adj* : desanimado
spiritual[1] [ˈspɪrɪtʃʊəl, -tʃəl] *adj* : espiritual — **spiritually** *adv*
spiritual[2] *n* : espiritual *m* (canción)
spiritualism [ˈspɪrɪtʃʊə,lɪzəm, -tʃə-] *n* : espiritismo *m*
spirituality [,spɪrɪtʃʊˈælət̬i] *n, pl* **-ties** : espiritualidad *f*
spit[1] [ˈspɪt] *v* **spit** *or* **spat** [ˈspæt]; **spitting** : escupir
spit[2] *n* **1** SALIVA : saliva *f* **2** ROTISSERIE : asador *m* **3** POINT : lengua *f* (de tierra)
spite[1] [ˈspaɪt] *vt* **spited; spiting** : fastidiar, molestar
spite[2] *n* **1** : despecho *m,* rencor *m* **2 in spite of** : a pesar de (que), pese a (que)

spiteful ['spaɪtfəl] *adj* **:** malicioso, rencoroso
spitting image *n* **to be the spitting image of :** ser el vivo retrato de
spittle ['spɪtəl] *n* **:** saliva *f*
splash[1] ['splæʃ] *vt* **:** salpicar — *vi* **1 :** salpicar **2 to splash around :** chapotear
splash[2] *n* **1** SPLASHING **:** salpicadura *f* **2** SQUIRT **:** chorrito *m* **3** SPOT **:** mancha *f*
splatter ['splæt̬ər] → **spatter**
splay ['spleɪ] *vt* **:** extender (hacia afuera) <to splay one's fingers **:** abrir los dedos> — *vi* **:** extenderse (hacia afuera)
spleen ['spli:n] *n* **1 :** bazo *m* (órgano) **2** ANGER, SPITE **:** ira *f*, rencor *m*
splendid ['splɛndəd] *adj* **:** espléndido — **splendidly** *adv*
splendor ['splɛndər] *n* **:** esplendor *m*
splice[1] ['splaɪs] *vt* **spliced; splicing :** empalmar, unir
splice[2] *n* **:** empalme *m*, unión *f*
splint ['splɪnt] *n* **:** tablilla *f*
splinter[1] ['splɪntər] *vt* **:** astillar — *vi* **:** astillarse
splinter[2] *n* **:** astilla *f*
split[1] ['splɪt] *v* **split; splitting** *vt* **1** CLEAVE **:** partir, hender <to split wood **:** partir madera> **2** BURST **:** romper, rajar <to split open **:** abrir> **3** DIVIDE, SHARE **:** dividir, repartir — *vi* **1 :** partirse (dícese de la madera, etc.) **2** BURST, CRACK **:** romperse, rajarse **3** *or* **to split up :** dividirse
split[2] *n* **1** CRACK **:** rajadura *f* **2** TEAR **:** rotura *f* **3** DIVISION **:** división *f*, escisión *f*
splurge[1] ['splərdʒ] *v* **splurged; splurging** *vt* **:** derrochar — *vi* **:** derrochar dinero
splurge[2] *n* **:** derroche *m*
spoil[1] ['spɔɪl] *v* **spoiled** *or* **spoilt** ['spɔɪlt]; **spoiling** *vt* **1** PILLAGE **:** saquear **2** RUIN **:** estropear, arruinar **3** PAMPER **:** consentir, mimar — *vi* **:** estropearse, echarse a perder
spoil[2] *n* PLUNDER **:** botín *m*
spoke[1] → **speak**
spoke[2] ['spo:k] *n* **:** rayo *m* (de una rueda)
spoken → **speak**
spokesman ['spo:ksmən] *n, pl* **-men** [-mən, -ˌmɛn] **:** portavoz *mf*; vocero *m*, -ra *f*
spokeswoman ['spo:ksˌwʊmən] *n, pl* **-women** [-ˌwɪmən] **:** portavoz *f*, vocera *f*
sponge[1] ['spʌndʒ] *vt* **sponged; sponging :** limpiar con una esponja
sponge[2] *n* **:** esponja *f*
spongy ['spʌndʒi] *adj* **spongier; -est :** esponjoso
sponsor[1] ['spɑntsər] *vt* **:** patrocinar, auspiciar, apadrinar (a una persona)
sponsor[2] *n* **:** patrocinador *m*, -dora *f*; padrino *m*, madrina *f*
sponsorship ['spɑntsərˌʃɪp] *n* **:** patrocinio *m*, apadrinamiento *m*
spontaneity [ˌspɑntə'ni:ət̬i, -'neɪ-] *n* **:** espontaneidad *f*
spontaneous [spɑn'teɪniəs] *adj* **:** espontáneo — **spontaneously** *adv*
spoof ['spu:f] *n* **:** burla *f*, parodia *f*
spook[1] ['spu:k] *vt* **:** asustar
spook[2] *n* **:** fantasma *m*, espíritu *m*, espectro *m*
spooky ['spu:ki] *adj* **spookier; -est :** que da miedo, espeluzante
spool ['spu:l] *n* **:** carrete *m*
spoon[1] ['spu:n] *vt* **:** comer, servir, o echar con cuchara
spoon[2] *n* **:** cuchara *f*
spoonful ['spu:nˌfʊl] *n* **:** cucharada *f* <by the spoonful **:** a cucharadas>
spoor ['spʊr, 'spor] *n* **:** rastro *m*, pista *f*
sporadic [spə'rædɪk] *adj* **:** esporádico — **sporadically** [-dɪkli] *adv*
spore ['spor] *n* **:** espora *f*
sport[1] ['sport] *vi* FROLIC **:** retozar, juguetear — *vt* SHOW OFF **:** lucir, ostentar
sport[2] *n* **1 :** deporte *m* <outdoor sports **:** deportes al aire libre> **2** JEST **:** broma *f* **3 to be a good sport :** tener espíritu deportivo
sportsman ['sportsmən] *n, pl* **-men** [-mən, -ˌmɛn] **:** deportista *m*
sportsmanship ['sportsmənˌʃɪp] *n* **:** espíritu *m* deportivo, deportividad *f Spain*
sportswoman ['sportsˌwʊmən] *n, pl* **-women** [-ˌwɪmən] **:** deportista *f*
sporty ['sport̬i] *adj* **sportier; -est :** deportivo
spot[1] ['spɑt] *v* **spotted; spotting** *vt* **1** STAIN **:** manchar **2** RECOGNIZE, SEE **:** ver, reconocer <to spot an error **:** descubrir un error> — *vi* **:** mancharse
spot[2] *adj* **:** hecho al azar <a spot check **:** un vistazo, un control aleatorio>
spot[3] *n* **1** STAIN **:** mancha *f* **2** DOT **:** punto *m* **3** PIMPLE **:** grano *m* <to break out in spots **:** salirle granos a alguien> **4** PREDICAMENT **:** apuro *m*, aprieto *m*, lío *m* <in a tight spot **:** en apuros> **5** PLACE **:** lugar *m*, sitio *m* <to be on the spot **:** estar en el lugar>
spotless ['spɑtləs] *adj* **:** impecable, inmaculado — **spotlessly** *adv*
spotlight[1] ['spɑtˌlaɪt] *vt* **-lighted** *or* **-lit** [-ˌlɪt]; **-lighting 1** LIGHT **:** iluminar (con un reflector) **2** HIGHLIGHT **:** destacar, poner en relieve
spotlight[2] *n* **1 :** reflector *m*, foco *m* **2 to be in the spotlight :** ser el centro de atención
spotty ['spɑt̬i] *adj* **spottier; -est :** irregular, desigual
spouse ['spaʊs] *n* **:** cónyuge *mf*
spout[1] ['spaʊt] *vt* **1 :** lanzar chorros de **2** DECLAIM **:** declamar — *vi* **:** salir a chorros
spout[2] *n* **1 :** pico *m* (de una jarra, etc.) **2** STREAM **:** chorro *m*
sprain[1] ['spreɪn] *vt* **:** sufrir un esguince en

sprain[2] *n* : esguince *m,* torcedura *f*
sprawl[1] ['sprɔl] *vi* **1** LIE : tumbarse, echarse, despatarrarse **2** EXTEND : extenderse
sprawl[2] *n* **1** : postura *f* despatarrada **2** SPREAD : extensión *f,* expansión *f*
spray[1] ['spreɪ] *vt* : rociar (una superficie), pulverizar (un líquido)
spray[2] *n* **1** BOUQUET : ramillete *m* **2** MIST : rocío *m* **3** ATOMIZER : atomizador *m,* pulverizador *m*
spray gun *n* : pistola *f*
spread[1] ['sprɛd] *v* **spread; spreading** *vt* **1** *or* **to spread out** : desplegar, extender **2** SCATTER, STREW : esparcir **3** SMEAR : untar (mantequilla, etc.) **4** DISSEMINATE : difundir, sembrar, propagar — *vi* **1** : difundirse, correr, propagarse **2** EXTEND : extenderse
spread[2] *n* **1** EXTENSION : extensión *f,* difusión *f* (de noticias, etc.), propagación *f* (de enfermedades, etc.) **2** : colcha *f* (para una cama), mantel *m* (para una mesa) **3** PASTE : pasta *f* <cheese spread : pasta de queso>
spreadsheet ['sprɛd,ʃiːt] *n* : hoja *f* de cálculo
spree ['spri] *n* **1** : acción *f* desenfrenada <to go on a shopping spree : comprar como loco> **2** BINGE : parranda *f,* juerga *f* <on a spree : de parranda, de juerga>
sprig ['sprɪg] *n* : ramita *f,* ramito *m*
sprightly ['spraɪtli] *adj* **sprightlier; -est** : vivo, animado <with a sprightly step : con paso ligero>
spring[1] ['sprɪŋ] *v* **sprang** ['spræŋ] *or* **sprung** ['sprʌŋ]; **sprung; springing** *vi* **1** LEAP : saltar **2** : mover rápidamente <the lid sprang shut : la tapa se cerró de un golpe> <he sprang to his feet : se paró de un salto> **3 to spring up** : brotar (dícese de las plantas), surgir **4 to spring from** : surgir de — *vt* **1** RELEASE : soltar (de repente) <to spring the news on someone : sorprender a alguien con las noticias> <to spring a trap : hacer saltar una trampa> **2** ACTIVATE : accionar (un mecanismo) **3 to spring a leak** : hacer agua
spring[2] *n* **1** SOURCE : fuente *f,* origen *m* **2** : manantial *m,* fuente *f* <hot spring : fuente termal> **3** : primavera *f* <spring and summer : la primavera y el verano> **4** : resorte *m,* muelle *m* (de metal, etc.) **5** LEAP : salto *m,* brinco *m* **6** RESILIENCE : elasticidad *f*
springboard ['sprɪŋ,bord] *n* : trampolín *m*
springtime ['sprɪŋ,taɪm] *n* : primavera *f*
springy ['sprɪŋi] *adj* **springier; -est 1** RESILIENT : elástico **2** LIVELY : enérgico
sprinkle[1] ['sprɪŋkəl] *vt* **-kled; -kling** : rociar (con agua), espolvorear (con azúcar, etc.), salpicar
sprinkle[2] *n* : llovizna *f*
sprinkler ['sprɪŋkələr] *n* : rociador *m,* aspersor *m*
sprint[1] ['sprɪnt] *vi* : echar la carrera, esprintar (en deportes)
sprint[2] *n* : esprint *m* (en deportes)
sprite ['spraɪt] *n* : hada *f,* elfo *m*
sprocket ['sprɑkət] *n* : diente *m* (de una rueda dentada)
sprout[1] ['spraʊt] *vi* : brotar
sprout[2] *n* : brote *m,* retoño *m,* vástago *m*
spruce[1] ['spruːs] *v* **spruced; sprucing** *vt* : arreglar — *vi or* **to spruce up** : arreglarse, acicalarse
spruce[2] *adj* **sprucer; sprucest** : pulcro, arreglado
spruce[3] *n* : picea *f* (árbol)
spry ['spraɪ] *adj* **sprier** *or* **spryer** ['spraɪər]; **spriest** *or* **spryest** ['spraɪəst] : ágil, activo
spun → **spin**
spunk ['spʌŋk] *n* : valor *m,* coraje *m,* agallas *fpl fam*
spunky ['spʌŋki] *adj* **spunkier; -est** : animoso, corajudo
spur[1] ['spər] *vt* **spurred; spurring** *or* **to spur on** : espolear (un caballo), motivar (a una persona, etc.)
spur[2] *n* **1** : espuela *f,* acicate *m* **2** STIMULUS : acicate *m* **3** : espolón *m* (de aves gallináceas)
spurious ['spjʊriəs] *adj* : espurio
spurn ['spərn] *vt* : desdeñar, rechazar
spurt[1] ['spərt] *vt* SQUIRT : lanzar un chorro de — *vi* SPOUT : salir a chorros
spurt[2] *n* **1** : actividad *f* repentina <a spurt of energy : una explosión de energía> <to do in spurts : hacer por rachas> **2** JET : chorro *m* (de agua, etc.)
sputter[1] ['spʌtər] *vi* **1** JABBER : farfullar **2** : chisporrotear (dícese de la grasa, etc.), petardear (dícese de un motor)
sputter[2] *n* **1** JABBER : farfulla *f* **2** : chisporroteo *m* (de grasa, etc.), petardeo *m* (de un motor)
spy[1] ['spaɪ] *v* **spied; spying** *vt* SEE : ver, divisar — *vi* : espiar <to spy on someone : espiar a alguien>
spy[2] *n* : espía *mf*
squab ['skwɑb] *n, pl* **squabs** *or* **squab** : pichón *m*
squabble[1] ['skwɑbəl] *vi* **-bled; -bling** : reñir, pelearse, discutir
squabble[2] *n* : riña *f,* pelea *f,* discusión *f*
squad ['skwɑd] *n* : pelotón *m* (militar), brigada *f* (de policías), cuadrilla *f* (de obreros, etc.)
squadron ['skwɑdrən] *n* : escuadrón *m* (de militares), escuadrilla *f* (de aviones), escuadra *f* (de naves)
squalid ['skwɑlɪd] *adj* : miserable
squall ['skwɔl] *n* **1** : aguacero *m* tormentoso, chubasco *m* tormentoso **2 snow squall** : tormenta *f* de nieve
squalor ['skwɑlər] *n* : miseria *f*
squander ['skwɑndər] *vt* : derrochar (dinero, etc.), desaprovechar (una

oportunidad, etc.), desperdiciar (talentos, energías, etc.)

square[1] ['skwær] *vt* **squared; squaring 1 :** cuadrar **2 :** elevar al cuadrado (en matemáticas) **3** CONFORM **:** conciliar (con), ajustar (con) **4** SETTLE **:** saldar (una cuenta) <I squared it with him : lo arreglé con él>

square[2] *adj* **squarer; -est 1 :** cuadrado <a square house : una casa cuadrada> **2** RIGHT-ANGLED **:** a escuadra, en ángulo recto **3 :** cuadrado (en matemáticas) <a square mile : una milla cuadrada> **4** HONEST **:** justo <a square deal : un buen acuerdo> <fair and square : en buena lid>

square[3] *n* **1 :** escuadra *f* (instrumento) **2 :** cuadrado *m,* cuadro *m* <to fold into squares : plegar en cuadrados> **3 :** plaza *f* (de una ciudad) **4 :** cuadrado *m* (en matemáticas)

squarely ['skwærli] *adv* **1** EXACTLY **:** exactamente, directamente, justo **2** HONESTLY **:** honradamente, justamente

square root *n* **:** raíz *f* cuadrada

squash[1] ['skwɑʃ, 'skwɔʃ] *vt* **1** CRUSH **:** aplastar **2** SUPPRESS **:** acallar (protestas), sofocar (una rebelión)

squash[2] *n* **1** *pl* **squashes** *or* **squash :** calabaza *f* (vegetal) **2** *or* **squash racquets :** squash *m* (deporte)

squat[1] ['skwɑt] *vi* **squatted; squatting 1** CROUCH **:** agacharse, ponerse en cuclillas **2 :** ocupar un lugar sin derecho

squat[2] *adj* **squatter; squattest :** bajo y ancho, rechoncho *fam* (dícese de una persona)

squat[3] *n* **1 :** posición *f* en cuclillas **2 :** ocupación *f* ilegal (de un lugar)

squaw ['skwɔ] *n* **:** india *f* (norteamericana)

squawk[1] ['skwɔk] *vi* **:** graznar (dícese de las aves), chillar

squawk[2] *n* **:** graznido *m* (de un ave), chillido *m*

squeak[1] ['skwi:k] *vi* **:** chillar (dícese de un animal), chirriar (dícese de un objeto)

squeak[2] *n* **:** chillido *m,* chirrido *m*

squeaky ['skwi:ki] *adj* **squeakier; -est :** chirriante <a squeaky voice : una voz chillona>

squeal[1] ['skwi:l] *vi* **1 :** chillar (dícese de las personas o los animales), chirriar (dícese de los frenos, etc.) **2** PROTEST **:** quejarse

squeal[2] *n* **1 :** chillido *m* (de una persona o un animal) **2** SCREECH **:** chirrido *m* (de frenos, etc.)

squeamish ['skwi:mɪʃ] *adj* **:** impresionable, sensible <he's squeamish about cockroaches : las cucarachas le dan asco>

squeeze[1] ['skwi:z] *vt* **squeezed; squeezing 1** PRESS **:** apretar, exprimir (naranjas, etc.) **2** EXTRACT **:** extraer (jugo, etc.)

squeeze[2] *n* **:** apretón *m*

squelch ['skwɛltʃ] *vt* **:** aplastar (una rebelión, etc.)

squid ['skwɪd] *n, pl* **squid** *or* **squids :** calamar *m*

squint[1] ['skwɪnt] *vi* **:** mirar con los ojos entornados

squint[2] *adj* *or* **squint-eyed** ['skwɪnt,aɪd] **:** bizco

squint[3] *n* **:** ojos *mpl* bizcos, bizquera *f*

squire ['skwaɪr] *n* **:** hacendado *m,* -da *f;* terrateniente *mf*

squirm ['skwərm] *vi* **:** retorcerse

squirrel ['skwərəl] *n* **:** ardilla *f*

squirt[1] ['skwərt] *vt* **:** lanzar un chorro de — *vi* SPURT **:** salir a chorros

squirt[2] *n* **:** chorrito *m*

stab[1] [stæb] *vt* **stabbed; stabbing 1** KNIFE **:** acuchillar, apuñalar **2** STICK **:** clavar (con una aguja, etc.), golpear (con el dedo, etc.)

stab[2] *n* **1 :** puñalada *f,* cuchillada *f* **2** JAB **:** pinchazo *m* (con una aguja, etc.), golpe *m* (con un dedo, etc.) **3 to take a stab at :** intentar

stability [stə'bɪləti] *n, pl* **-ties :** estabilidad *f*

stabilize ['steɪbə,laɪz] *v* **-lized; -lizing** *vt* **:** estabilizar — *vi* **:** estabilizarse

stable[1] ['steɪbəl] *vt* **-bled; -bling :** poner (ganado) en un establo, poner (caballos) en una caballeriza

stable[2] *adj* **-bler; -blest 1** FIXED, STEADY **:** fijo, sólido, estable **2** LASTING **:** estable, perdurable <a stable government : un gobierno estable> **3 :** estacionario (en medicina), equilibrado (en psicología)

stable[3] *n* **:** establo *m* (para ganado), caballeriza *f* o cuadra *f* (para caballos)

staccato [stə'kɑto:] *adj* **:** staccato

stack[1] ['stæk] *vt* **1** PILE **:** amontonar, apilar **2** COVER **:** cubrir, llenar <he stacked the table with books : cubrió la mesa de libros>

stack[2] *n* **1** PILE **:** montón *m,* pila *f* **2** SMOKESTACK **:** chimenea *f*

stadium ['steɪdiəm] *n, pl* **-dia** [-diə] *or* **-diums :** estadio *m*

staff[1] ['stæf] *vt* **:** proveer de personal

staff[2] *n, pl* **staffs** ['stæfs, stævz] *or* **staves** ['stævz, 'steɪvz] **1 :** bastón *m* (de mando), báculo *m* (de obispo) **2** *pl* **staffs** PERSONNEL **:** personal *m* **3** *pl* **staffs :** pentagrama *m* (en música)

stag[1] ['stæg] *adv* **:** solo, sin pareja <to go stag : ir solo>

stag[2] *adj* **:** sólo para hombres

stag[3] *n, pl* **stags** *or* **stag :** ciervo *m,* venado *m*

stage[1] ['steɪdʒ] *vt* **staged; staging :** poner en escena (una obra de teatro)

stage[2] *n* **1** PLATFORM **:** estrado *m,* tablado *m,* escenario *m* (de un teatro) **2** PHASE, STEP **:** fase *f,* etapa *f* <stage of development : fase de desarrollo> <in stages : por etapas> **3 the stage :** el teatro *m*

stagecoach ['steɪdʒ,ko:tʃ] *n* **:** diligencia *f*

stagger[1] [ˈstægər] *vi* TOTTER : tambalearse — *vt* **1** ALTERNATE : alternar, escalonar (turnos de trabajo) **2** : hacer tambalear <to be staggered by : quedarse estupefacto por>

stagger[2] *n* : tambaleo *m*

staggering [ˈstægərɪŋli] *adj* : asombroso

stagnant [ˈstægnənt] *adj* : estancado

stagnate [ˈstægˌneɪt] *vi* **-nated; -nating** : estancarse

staid [ˈsteɪd] *adj* : serio, sobrio

stain[1] [ˈsteɪn] *vt* **1** DISCOLOR : manchar **2** DYE : teñir (madera, etc.) **3** SULLY : manchar, empañar

stain[2] *n* **1** SPOT : mancha *f* **2** DYE : tinte *m,* tintura *f* **3** BLEMISH : mancha *f,* mácula *f*

stainless [ˈsteɪnləs] *adj* : sin mancha <stainless steel : acero inoxidable>

stair [ˈstær] *n* **1** STEP : escalón *m,* peldaño *m* **2 stairs** *npl* : escalera *f,* escaleras *fpl*

staircase [ˈstærˌkeɪs] *n* : escalera *f,* escaleras *fpl*

stairway [ˈstærˌweɪ] *n* : escalera *f,* escaleras *fpl*

stake[1] [ˈsteɪk] *vt* **staked; staking 1** : estacar, marcar con estacas (una propiedad) **2** BET : jugarse, apostar **3 to stake a claim to** : reclamar, reivindicar

stake[2] *n* **1** POST : estaca *f* **2** BET : apuesta *f* <to be at stake : estar en juego> **3** INTEREST, SHARE : interés *m,* participación *f*

stalactite [stəˈlækˌtaɪt] *n* : estalactita *f*

stalagmite [stəˈlægˌmaɪt] *n* : estalagmita *f*

stale [ˈsteɪl] *adj* **staler; stalest** : viejo <stale bread : pan duro> <stale news : viejas noticias>

stalemate [ˈsteɪlˌmeɪt] *n* : punto *m* muerto, impasse *m*

stalk[1] [ˈstɔk] *vt* : acechar — *vi* : caminar rígidamente (por orgullo, ira, etc.)

stalk[2] *n* : tallo *m* (de una planta)

stall[1] [ˈstɔl] *vt* **1** : parar (un motor) **2** DELAY : entretener (a una persona), demorar — *vi* **1** : pararse (dícese de un motor) **2** DELAY : demorar, andar con rodeos

stall[2] *n* **1** : compartimiento *m* (de un establo) **2** : puesto *m* (en un mercado, etc.)

stallion [ˈstæljən] *n* : caballo *m* semental

stalwart [ˈstɔlwərt] *adj* **1** STRONG : fuerte <a stalwart supporter : un firme partidario> **2** BRAVE : valiente, valeroso

stamen [ˈsteɪmən] *n* : estambre *m*

stamina [ˈstæmənə] *n* : resistencia *f*

stammer[1] [ˈstæmər] *vi* : tartamudear, titubear

stammer[2] *n* : tartamudeo *m,* titubeo *m*

stamp[1] [ˈstæmp] *vt* **1** : pisotear (con los pies) <to stamp one's feet : patear, dar una patada> **2** IMPRESS, IMPRINT : sellar (una factura, etc.), acuñar (monedas) **3** : franquear, ponerle estampillas a (correo)

stamp[2] *n* **1** : sello *m* (para documentos, etc.) **2** DIE : cuño *m* (para monedas) **3** *or* **postage stamp** : sello *m,* estampilla *f,* timbre *m CA, Mex*

stampede[1] [stæmˈpiːd] *vi* **-peded; -peding** : salir en estampida

stampede[2] *n* : estampida *f*

stance [ˈstænts] *n* : postura *f*

stanch [ˈstɔntʃ, ˈstɑntʃ] *vt* : detener, estancar (un líquido)

stand[1] [ˈstænd] *v* **stood** [ˈstʊd]; **standing** *vi* **1** : estar de pie, estar parado <I was standing on the corner : estaba parada en la esquina> **2** *or* **to stand up** : levantarse, pararse, ponerse de pie **3** *(indicating a specified position or location)* <they stand third in the country : ocupan el tercer lugar en el país> <the machines are standing idle : las máquinas están paradas> **4** *(referring to an opinion)* <how does he stand on the matter ? : ¿cuál es su postura respecto al asunto?> **5** BE : estar <the house stands on a hill : la casa está en una colina> **6** CONTINUE : seguir <the order still stands : el mandato sigue vigente> — *vt* **1** PLACE, SET : poner, colocar <he stood them in a row : los colocó en hilera> **2** TOLERATE : aguantar, soportar <he can't stand her : no la puede tragar> **3 to stand firm** : mantenerse firme **4 to stand guard** : hacer la guardia

stand[2] *n* **1** RESISTANCE : resistencia *f* <to make a stand against : resistir a> **2** BOOTH, STALL : stand *m,* puesto *m,* kiosko *m* (para vender periódicos, etc.) **3** BASE : pie *m,* base *f* **4** : grupo *m* (de árboles, etc.) **5** POSITION : posición *f,* postura *f* **6 stands** *npl* GRANDSTAND : tribuna *f*

standard[1] [ˈstændərd] *adj* **1** ESTABLISHED : estándar, oficial <standard measures : medidas oficiales> <standard English : el inglés estándar> **2** NORMAL : normal, estándar, común **3** CLASSIC : estándar, clásico <a standard work : una obra clásica>

standard[2] *n* **1** BANNER : estandarte *m* **2** CRITERION : criterio *m* **3** RULE : estándar *m,* norma *f,* regla *f* **4** LEVEL : nivel *m* <standard of living : nivel de vida> **5** SUPPORT : poste *m,* soporte *m*

standardize [ˈstændərˌdaɪz] *vt* **-ized; -izing** : estandarizar

standard time *n* : hora *f* oficial

stand by *vt* : atenerse a, cumplir con (una promesa, etc.) — *vi* **1** : mantenerse aparte <to stand by and do nothing : mirar sin hacer nada> **2** : estar preparado, estar listo (para un anuncio, un ataque, etc.)

stand for *vt* **1** REPRESENT : significar **2** PERMIT, TOLERATE : permitir, tolerar

standing [ˈstændɪŋ] *n* **1** POSITION, RANK : posición *f* **2** DURATION : duración *f*

stand out *vi* **1 :** destacar(se) <she stands out from the rest : se destaca entre los otros> **2 to stand out against** RESIST **:** oponerse a

standpoint [ˈstændˌpɔint] *n* **:** punto *m* de vista

standstill [ˈstændˌstɪl] *n* **1** STOP **:** detención *f,* paro *m* <to come to a standstill : pararse> **2** DEADLOCK **:** punto *m* muerto, impasse *m*

stand up *vt* **:** dejar plantado <he stood me up again : otra vez me dejó plantado> — *vi* **1** ENDURE **:** durar, resistir **2 to stand up for :** defender **3 to stand up to :** hacerle frente (a alguien)

stank → **stink**

stanza [ˈstænzə] *n* **:** estrofa *f*

staple[1] [ˈsteɪpəl] *vt* **-pled; -pling :** engrapar, grapar

staple[2] *adj* **:** principal, básico <a staple food : un alimento básico>

staple[3] *n* **1 :** producto *m* principal **2 :** grapa *f* (para engrapar papeles)

stapler [ˈsteɪplər] *n* **:** engrapadora *f,* grapadora *f*

star[1] [ˈstɑr] *v* **starred; starring** *vt* **1 :** marcar con una estrella o un asterisco **2** FEATURE **:** ser protagonizado por — *vi* **:** tener el papel principal <to star in : protagonizar>

star[2] *n* **:** estrella *f*

starboard [ˈstɑrbərd] *n* **:** estribor *m*

starch[1] [ˈstɑrtʃ] *vt* **:** almidonar

starch[2] *n* **:** almidón *m,* fécula *f* (comida)

starchy [ˈstɑrtʃi] *adj* **starchier; -est :** lleno de almidón <a starchy diet : una dieta feculenta>

stardom [ˈstɑrdəm] *n* **:** estrellato *m*

stare[1] [ˈstær] *vi* **stared; staring :** mirar fijamente

stare[2] *n* **:** mirada *f* fija

starfish [ˈstɑrˌfɪʃ] *n* **:** estrella *f* de mar

stark[1] [ˈstɑrk] *adv* **:** completamente <stark raving mad : loco de remate> <stark naked : completamente desnudo>

stark[2] *adj* **1** ABSOLUTE **:** absoluto **2** BARREN, DESOLATE **:** desolado, desierto **3** BARE **:** desnudo **4** HARSH **:** severo, duro

starlight [ˈstɑrˌlaɪt] *n* **:** luz *f* de las estrellas

starling [ˈstɑrlɪŋ] *n* **:** estornino *m*

starry [ˈstɑri] *adj* **starrier; -est :** estrellado

start[1] [ˈstɑrt] *vi* **1** JUMP **:** levantarse de un salto, sobresaltarse, dar un respingo **2** BEGIN **:** empezar, comenzar **3** SET OUT **:** salir (de viaje, etc.) **4 :** arrancar (dícese de un motor) — *vt* **1** BEGIN **:** empezar, comenzar, iniciar **2** CAUSE **:** provocar, causar **3** ESTABLISH **:** fundar, montar, establecer <to start a business : montar un negocio> **4 :** arrancar, poner en marcha, encender <to start the car : arrancar el motor>

start[2] *n* **1** JUMP **:** sobresalto *m,* respingo *m* **2** BEGINNING **:** principio *m,* comienzo *m* <to get an early start : salir temprano>

starter [ˈstɑrt̬ər] *n* **1** ENTRANT **:** participante *mf* (en deportes) **2** APPETIZER **:** entremés *m,* aperitivo *m* **3 :** motor *m* de arranque (de un vehículo)

startle [ˈstɑrt̬əl] *vt* **-tled; -tling :** asustar, sobresaltar

starvation [stɑrˈveɪʃən] *n* **:** inanición *f,* hambre *f*

starve [ˈstɑrv] *v* **starved; starving** *vi* **:** morirse de hambre — *vt* **:** privar de comida

stash [ˈstæʃ] *vt* **:** esconder, guardar (en un lugar secreto)

state[1] [ˈsteɪt] *vt* **stated; stating 1** REPORT **:** puntualizar, exponer (los hechos, etc.) <state your name : diga su nombre> **2** ESTABLISH, FIX **:** establecer, fijar

state[2] *n* **1** CONDITION **:** estado *m,* condición *f* <a liquid state : un estado líquido> <state of mind : estado de ánimo> <in a bad state : en malas condiciones> **2** NATION **:** estado *m,* nación *f* **3 :** estado *m* (dentro de un país) <the States : los Estados Unidos>

stateliness [ˈsteɪtlinəs] *n* **:** majestuosidad *f*

stately [ˈsteɪtli] *adj* **statelier; -est :** majestuoso

statement [ˈsteɪtmənt] *n* **1** DECLARATION **:** declaración *f,* afirmación *f* **2** *or* **bank statement :** estado *m* de cuenta

stateroom [ˈsteɪtˌruːm, -ˌrʊm] *n* **:** camarote *m*

statesman [ˈsteɪtsmən] *n, pl* **-men** [-mən, -ˌmɛn] **:** estadista *mf*

static[1] [ˈstæt̬ɪk] *adj* **:** estático

static[2] *n* **:** estática *f,* interferencia *f*

station[1] [ˈsteɪʃən] *vt* **:** apostar, estacionar

station[2] *n* **1 :** estación *f* (de trenes, etc.) **2** RANK, STANDING **:** condición *f* (social) **3 :** canal *m* (de televisión), estación *f* o emisora *f* (de radio) **4 police station :** comisaría *f* **5 fire station :** estación *f* de bomberos, cuartel *m* de bomberos

stationary [ˈsteɪʃəˌnɛri] *adj* **1** IMMOBILE **:** estacionario, inmovible **2** UNCHANGING **:** inmutable, inalterable

stationery [ˈsteɪʃəˌnɛri] *n* **:** papel *m* y sobres *mpl* (para correspondencia)

station wagon *n* **:** camioneta *f* guayín, camioneta *f* ranchera

statistic [stəˈtɪstɪk] *n* **:** estadística *f* <according to statistics : según las estadísticas>

statistical [stəˈtɪstɪkəl] *adj* **:** estadístico

statue [ˈstæˌtʃuː] *n* **:** estatua *f*

statuesque [ˌstætʃʊˈɛsk] *adj* **:** escultural

statuette [ˌstætʃʊˈɛt] *n* **:** estatuilla *f*

stature [ˈstætʃər] *n* **1** HEIGHT **:** estatura *f,* talla *f* **2** PRESTIGE **:** talla *f,* prestigio *m*

status [ˈsteɪtəs, ˈstæ-] *n* : condición *f*, situación *f*, estatus *m* (social) <marital status : estado civil>

statute [ˈstæˌtʃuːt] *n* : ley *f*, estatuto *m*

staunch [ˈstɔntʃ] *adj* : acérrimo, incondicional, leal <a staunch supporter : un partidario incondicional> — **staunchly** *adv*

stave[1] [ˈsteɪv] *vt* **staved** *or* **stove** [ˈstoːv]; **staving 1 to stave in** : romper **2 to stave off** : evitar (un ataque), prevenir (un problema)

stave[2] *n* : duela *f* (de un barril)

staves → **staff**

stay[1] [ˈsteɪ] *vi* **1** REMAIN : quedarse, permanecer <to stay in : quedarse en casa> <he stayed in the city : permaneció en la ciudad> **2** CONTINUE : seguir, quedarse <it stayed cloudy : siguió nublado> <to stay awake : mantenerse despierto> **3** LODGE : hospedarse, alojarse (en un hotel, etc.) — *vt* **1** HALT : detener, suspender (una ejecución, etc.) **2 to stay the course** : aguantar hasta el final

stay[2] *n* **1** SOJOURN : estadía *f*, estancia *f*, permanencia *f* **2** SUSPENSION : suspensión *f* (de una sentencia) **3** SUPPORT : soporte *m*

stead [ˈstɛd] *n* **1** : lugar *m* <she went in his stead : fue en su lugar> **2 to stand (someone) in good stead** : ser muy útil a, servir de mucho a

steadfast [ˈstɛdˌfæst] *adj* : firme, resuelto <a steadfast friend : un fiel amigo> <a steadfast refusal : una negativa categórica>

steadily [ˈstɛdəli] *adv* **1** CONSTANTLY : continuamente, sin parar **2** FIRMLY : con firmeza **3** FIXEDLY : fijamente

steady[1] [ˈstɛdi] *v* **steadied; steadying** *vt* : sujetar <she steadied herself : recobró el equilibrio> — *vi* : estabilizarse

steady[2] *adj* **steadier; -est 1** FIRM, SURE : seguro, firme <to have a steady hand : tener buen pulso> **2** FIXED, REGULAR : fijo <a steady income : ingresos fijos> **3** CALM : tranquilo, ecuánime <she has steady nerves : es imperturbable> **4** DEPENDABLE : responsable, fiable **5** CONSTANT : constante

steak [ˈsteɪk] *n* : bistec *m*, filete *m*, churrasco *m*, bife *m Arg, Chile, Uru*

steal [ˈstiːl] *v* **stole** [ˈstoːl]; **stolen** [ˈstoːlən]; **stealing** *vt* : robar, hurtar — *vi* **1** : robar, hurtar **2** : ir sigilosamente <to steal away : escabullirse>

stealth [ˈstɛlθ] *n* : sigilo *m*

stealthily [ˈstɛlθəli] *adv* : furtivamente

stealthy [ˈstɛlθi] *adj* **stealthier; -est** : furtivo, sigiloso

steam[1] [ˈstiːm] *vi* : echar vapor <to steam away : moverse echando vapor> — *vt* **1** : cocer al vapor (en cocina) **2 to steam open** : abrir con vapor

steam[2] *n* **1** : vapor *m* **2 to let off steam** : desahogarse

steamboat [ˈstiːmˌboːt] → **steamship**

steam engine *n* : motor *m* de vapor

steamroller [ˈstiːmˌroːlər] *n* : apisonadora *f*

steamship [ˈstiːmˌʃɪp] *n* : vapor *m*, barco *m* de vapor

steamy [ˈstiːmi] *adj* **steamier; -est 1** : lleno de vapor **2** EROTIC : erótico <a steamy romance : un tórrido romance>

steed [ˈstiːd] *n* : corcel *m*

steel[1] [ˈstiːl] *vt* **to steel oneself** : armarse de valor

steel[2] *adj* : de acero

steel[3] *n* : acero *m*

steely [ˈstiːli] *adj* **steelier; -est** : como acero <a steely gaze : una mirada fría> <steely determination : determinación férrea>

steep[1] [ˈstiːp] *vt* : remojar, dejar (té, etc.) en infusión

steep[2] *adj* **1** : empinado, escarpado <a steep cliff : un precipicio escarpado> **2** CONSIDERABLE : considerable, marcado **3** EXCESSIVE : excesivo <steep prices : precios muy altos>

steeple [ˈstiːpəl] *n* : aguja *f*, campanario *m*

steeplechase [ˈstiːpəlˌtʃeɪs] *n* : carrera *f* de obstáculos

steeply [ˈstiːpli] *adv* : abruptamente

steer[1] [ˈstɪr] *vt* **1** : conducir (un coche), gobernar (un barco) **2** GUIDE : dirigir, guiar

steer[2] *n* : buey *m*

steering wheel *n* : volante *m*

stein [ˈstaɪn] *n* : jarra *f* (para cerveza)

stellar [ˈstɛlər] *adj* : estelar

stem[1] [ˈstɛm] *v* **stemmed; stemming** *vt* : detener, contener, parar <to stem the tide : detener el curso> — *vi* **to stem from** : provenir de, ser el resultado de

stem[2] *n* : tallo *m* (de una planta)

stench [ˈstɛntʃ] *n* : hedor *m*, mal olor *m*

stencil[1] [ˈstɛntsəl] *vt* **-ciled** *or* **-cilled; -ciling** *or* **-cilling** : marcar utilizando una plantilla

stencil[2] *n* : plantilla *f* (para marcar)

stenographer [stəˈnɑgrəfər] *n* : taquígrafo *m*, -fa *f*

stenographic [ˌstɛnəˈgræfɪk] *adj* : taquigráfico

stenography [stəˈnɑgrəfi] *n* : taquigrafía *f*

step[1] [ˈstɛp] *vi* **stepped; stepping 1** : dar un paso <step this way, please : pase por aquí, por favor> <he stepped outside : salió> **2 to step on** : pisar

step[2] *n* **1** : paso *m* <step by step : paso por paso> **2** STAIR : escalón *m*, peldaño *m* **3** RUNG : escalón *m*, travesaño *m* **4** MEASURE, MOVE : medida *f*, paso *m* <to take steps : tomar medidas> **5** STRIDE : paso *m* <with a quick step : con paso rápido>

stepbrother ['stɛp,brʌðər] *n* **:** hermanastro *m*

stepdaughter ['stɛp,dɔt̬ər] *n* **:** hijastra *f*

stepfather ['stɛp,fɑðər, -,fa-] *n* **:** padrastro *m*

stepladder ['stɛp,lædər] *n* **:** escalera *f* de tijera

stepmother ['stɛp,mʌðər] *n* **:** madrastra *f*

steppe ['stɛp] *n* **:** estepa *f*

stepping–stone ['stɛpɪŋ,sto:n] *n* **:** pasadera *f* (en un río, etc.), trampolín *m* (al éxito)

stepsister ['stɛp,sɪstər] *n* **:** hermanastra *f*

stepson ['stɛp,sʌn] *n* **:** hijastro *m*

step up *vt* INCREASE **:** aumentar

stereo[1] ['stɛri,o:, 'stɪr-] *adj* **:** estéreo

stereo[2] *n, pl* **stereos :** estéreo *m*

stereophonic [,stɛrio'fɑnɪk, ,stɪr-] *adj* **:** estereofónico

stereotype[1] ['stɛrio,taɪp, 'stɪr-] *vt* **-typed; -typing :** estereotipar

stereotype[2] *n* **:** estereotipo *m*

sterile ['stɛrəl] *adj* **:** estéril

sterility [stə'rɪlət̬i] *n* **:** esterilidad *f*

sterilization [,stɛrələ'zeɪʃən] *n* **:** esterilización *f*

sterilize ['stɛrə,laɪz] *vt* **-ized; -izing :** esterilizar

sterling ['stərlɪŋ] *adj* **1 :** de ley <sterling silver : plata de ley> **2** EXCELLENT **:** excelente

stern[1] ['stərn] *adj* **:** severo, adusto — **sternly** *adv*

stern[2] *n* **:** popa *f*

sternness ['stərnnəs] *n* **:** severidad *f*

sternum ['stərnəm] *n, pl* **sternums** *or* **sterna** [-nə] **:** esternón *m*

stethoscope ['stɛθə,sko:p] *n* **:** estetoscopio *m*

stevedore ['sti:və,dor] *n* **:** estibador *m*, -dora *f*

stew[1] ['stu:, 'stju:] *vt* **:** estofar, guisar — *vi* **1 :** cocer (dícese de la carne, etc.) **2** FRET **:** preocuparse

stew[2] *n* **1 :** estofado *m*, guiso *m* **2 to be in a stew :** estar agitado

steward ['stu:ərd, 'stju:-] *n* **1** MANAGER **:** administrador *m* **2 :** auxiliar *m* de vuelo (en un avión), camarero *m* (en un barco)

stewardess ['stu:ərdəs, 'stju:-] *n* **1** MANAGER **:** administradora *f* **2 :** camarera *f* (en un barco) **3 :** auxiliar *f* de vuelo, azafata *f*, aeromoza *f* (en un avión)

stick[1] ['stɪk] *v* **stuck** ['stʌk]; **sticking** *vt* **1** STAB **:** clavar **2** ATTACH **:** pegar **3** PUT **:** poner **4 to stick out :** sacar (la lengua, etc.), extender (la mano) — *vi* **1** ADHERE **:** pegarse, adherirse **2** JAM **:** atascarse **3 to stick around :** quedarse **4 to stick out** PROJECT **:** sobresalir (de una superficie), asomar (por detrás o debajo de algo) **5 to stick to :** no abandonar <stick to your guns : manténgase firme> **6 to stick up :** estar parado (dícese del pelo, etc.), sobresalir (de una superficie) **7 to stick with :** serle fiel a (una persona), seguir con (una cosa) <I'll stick with what I know : prefiero lo conocido>

stick[2] *n* **1** BRANCH, TWIG **:** ramita *f* **2 :** palo *m*, vara *f* <a walking stick : un bastón>

sticker ['stɪkər] *n* **:** etiqueta *f* adhesiva

stickler ['stɪklər] *n* **:** persona *f* exigente <to be a stickler for : insistir mucho en>

sticky ['stɪki] *adj* **stickier; -est 1** ADHESIVE **:** pegajoso, adhesivo **2** MUGGY **:** bochornoso **3** DIFFICULT **:** difícil

stiff ['stɪf] *adj* **1** RIGID **:** rígido, tieso <a stiff dough : una masa firme> **2 :** agarrotado, entumecido <stiff muscles : músculos entumecidos> **3** STILTED **:** acartonado, poco natural **4** STRONG **:** fuerte (dícese del viento, etc.) **5** DIFFICULT, SEVERE **:** severo, difícil, duro

stiffen ['stɪfən] *vt* **1** STRENGTHEN **:** fortalecer, reforzar (tela, etc.) **2 :** hacer más duro (un castigo, etc.) — *vi* **1** HARDEN **:** endurecerse **2 :** entumecerse (dícese de los músculos)

stiffly ['stɪfli] *adv* **1** RIGIDLY **:** rígidamente **2** COLDLY **:** con frialdad

stiffness ['stɪfnəs] *n* **1** RIGIDITY **:** rigidez *f* **2** COLDNESS **:** frialdad *f* **3** SEVERITY **:** severidad *f*

stifle ['staɪfəl] *vt* **-fled; -fling** SMOTHER, SUPPRESS **:** sofocar, reprimir, contener <to stifle a yawn : reprimir un bostezo>

stigma ['stɪgmə] *n, pl* **stigmata** [stɪg'mɑt̬ə, 'stɪgmət̬ə] *or* **stigmas :** estigma *m*

stigmatize ['stɪgmə,taɪz] *vt* **-tized; -tizing :** estigmatizar

stile ['staɪl] *n* **:** escalones *mpl* para cruzar un cerco

stiletto [stə'lɛ,t̬o:] *n, pl* **-tos** *or* **-toes :** estilete *m*

still[1] ['stɪl] *vt* CALM **:** pacificar, apaciguar — *vi* **:** pacificarse, apaciguarse

still[2] *adv* **1** QUIETLY **:** quieto <sit still! : ¡quédate quieto!> **2 :** de todos modos, aún, todavía <she still lives there : aún vive allí> <it's still the same : sigue siendo lo mismo> **3** IN ANY CASE **:** de todos modos, aún así <he still has doubts : aún así le quedan dudas> <I still prefer that you stay : de todos modos prefiero que te quedes>

still[3] *adj* **1** MOTIONLESS **:** quieto, inmóvil **2** SILENT **:** callado

still[4] *n* **1** SILENCE **:** quietud *f*, calma *f* **2 :** alambique *m* (para destilar alcohol)

stillborn ['stɪl,bɔrn] *adj* **:** nacido muerto

stillness ['stɪlnəs] *n* **:** calma *f*, silencio *m*

stilt ['stɪlt] *n* **:** zanco *m*

stilted ['stɪltəd] *adj* **:** afectado, poco natural

stimulant [ˈstɪmjələnt] *n* : estimulante *m* — **stimulant** *adj*

stimulate [ˈstɪmjəˌleɪt] *vt* **-lated; -lating** : estimular

stimulation [ˌstɪmjəˈleɪʃən] *n* **1** STIMULATING : estimulación *f* **2** STIMULUS : estímulo *m*

stimulus [ˈstɪmjələs] *n, pl* **-li** [-ˌlaɪ] **1** : estímulo *m* **2** INCENTIVE : acicate *m*

sting¹ [ˈstɪŋ] *v* **stung** [ˈstʌŋ]; **stinging** *vt* **1** : picar <a bee stung him : le picó una abeja> **2** HURT : hacer escocer (físicamente), herir (emocionalmente) — *vi* **1** : picar (dícese de las abejas, etc.) **2** SMART : escocer, arder

sting² *n* : picadura *f* (herida), escozor *m* (sensación)

stinger [ˈstɪŋər] *n* : aguijón *m* (de una abeja, etc.)

stinginess [ˈstɪndʒinəs] *n* : tacañería *f*

stingy [ˈstɪndʒi] *adj* **stingier; -est** **1** MISERLY : tacaño, avaro **2** PALTRY : mezquino, mísero

stink¹ [ˈstɪŋk] *vi* **stank** [ˈstæŋk] *or* **stunk** [ˈstʌŋk]; **stunk; stinking** : apestar, oler mal

stink² *n* : hedor *m,* mal olor *m,* peste *f*

stint¹ [ˈstɪnt] *vt* : escatimar <to stint oneself of : privarse de> — *vi* **to stint on** : escatimar

stint² *n* : período *m*

stipend [ˈstaɪˌpɛnd, -pənd] *n* : estipendio *m*

stipulate [ˈstɪpjəˌleɪt] *vt* **-lated; -lating** : estipular

stipulation [ˌstɪpjəˈleɪʃən] *n* : estipulación *f*

stir¹ [ˈstər] *v* **stirred; stirring** *vt* **1** AGITATE : mover, agitar **2** MIX : revolver, remover **3** INCITE : incitar, impulsar, motivar **4** *or* **to stir up** AROUSE : despertar (memorias, etc.), provocar (ira, etc.) — *vi* : moverse, agitarse

stir² *n* **1** MOTION : movimiento *m* **2** COMMOTION : revuelo *m*

stirrup [ˈstərəp, ˈstɪr-] *n* : estribo *m*

stitch¹ [ˈstɪtʃ] *vt* : coser, bordar (para decorar) — *vi* : coser

stitch² *n* **1** : puntada *f* **2** TWINGE : punzada *f,* puntada *f*

stock¹ [ˈstɑk] *vt* : surtir, abastecer, vender — *vi* **to stock up** : abastecerse

stock² *n* **1** SUPPLY : reserva *f,* existencias *fpl* (en comercio) <to be out of stock : estar agotadas las existencias> **2** SECURITIES : acciones *fpl,* valores *mpl* **3** LIVESTOCK : ganado *m* **4** ANCESTRY : linaje *m,* estirpe *f* **5** BROTH : caldo *m* **6 to take stock** : evaluar

stockade [stɑˈkeɪd] *n* : estacada *f*

stockbroker [ˈstɑkˌbroːkər] *n* : corredor *m,* -dora *f* de bolsa

stockholder [ˈstɑkˌhoːldər] *n* : accionista *mf*

stocking [ˈstɑkɪŋ] *n* : media *f* <a pair of stockings : unas medias>

stock market *n* : bolsa *f*

stockpile¹ [ˈstɑkˌpaɪl] *vt* **-piled; -piling** : acumular, almacenar

stockpile² *n* : reservas *fpl*

stocky [ˈstɑki] *adj* **stockier; -est** : robusto, fornido

stockyard [ˈstɑkˌjɑrd] *n* : corral *m*

stodgy [ˈstɑdʒi] *adj* **stodgier; -est** **1** DULL : aburrido, pesado **2** OLD-FASHIONED : anticuado

stoic¹ [ˈstoːɪk] *or* **stoical** [-ɪkəl] *adj* : estoico — **stoically** [-ɪkli] *adv*

stoic² *n* : estoico *m,* -ca *f*

stoicism [ˈstoːəˌsɪzəm] *n* : estoicismo *m*

stoke [ˈstoːk] *vt* **stoked; stoking** : atizar (un fuego), echarle carbón a (un horno)

stole¹ → **steal**

stole² [ˈstoːl] *n* : estola *f*

stolen → **steal**

stolid [ˈstɑlɪd] *adj* : impasible, imperturbable — **stolidly** *adv*

stomach¹ [ˈstʌmɪk] *vt* : aguantar, soportar

stomach² *n* **1** : estómago *m* **2** BELLY : vientre *m,* barriga *f,* panza *f* **3** DESIRE : ganas *fpl* <he had no stomach for a fight : no quería pelea>

stomachache [ˈstʌmɪkˌeɪk] *n* : dolor *m* de estómago

stomp [ˈstɑmp, ˈstɔmp] *vt* : pisotear — *vi* : pisar fuerte

stone¹ [ˈstoːn] *vt* **stoned; stoning** : apedrear, lapidar

stone² *n* **1** : piedra *f* **2** PIT : hueso *m,* pepa *f* (de una fruta)

Stone Age *n* : Edad *f* de Piedra

stony [ˈstoːni] *adj* **stonier; -est** **1** ROCKY : pedregoso **2** UNFEELING : insensible, frío <a stony stare : una mirada glacial>

stood → **stand**

stool [ˈstuːl] *n* **1** SEAT : taburete *m,* banco *m* **2** FOOTSTOOL : escabel *m* **3** FECES : deposición *f* de heces

stoop¹ [ˈstuːp] *vi* **1** CROUCH : agacharse **2 to stoop to** : rebajarse a

stoop² *n* **1** : espaldas *fpl* encorvadas <to have a stoop : ser encorvado> **2** : entrada *f* (de una casa)

stop¹ [ˈstɑp] *v* **stopped; stopping** *vt* **1** PLUG : tapar **2** PREVENT : impedir, evitar <she stopped me from leaving : me impidió que saliera> **3** HALT : parar, detener **4** CEASE : dejar de <he stopped talking : dejó de hablar> — *vi* **1** HALT : detenerse, parar **2** CEASE : cesar, terminar <the rain won't stop : no deja de llover> **3** STAY : quedarse <she stopped with friends : se quedó en casa de unos amigos> **4 to stop by** : visitar

stop² *n* **1** STOPPER : tapón *m* **2** HALT : parada *f,* alto *m* <to come to a stop : pararse, detenerse> <to put a stop to : poner fin a> **3** : parada *f* <bus stop : parada de autobús>

stopgap [ˈstɑpˌgæp] *n* : arreglo *m* provisorio

stoplight [ˈstɑpˌlaɪt] *n* : semáforo *m*

stoppage [ˈstɑpɪdʒ] *n* : acto *m* de parar <a work stoppage : un paro>
stopper [ˈstɑpər] *n* : tapón *m*
storage [ˈstorɪdʒ] *n* : almacenamiento *m,* almacenaje *m*
storage battery *n* : acumulador *m*
store[1] [ˈstor] *vt* **stored; storing** : guardar, almacenar
store[2] *n* **1** RESERVE, SUPPLY : reserva *f* **2** SHOP : tienda *f* <grocery store : tienda de comestibles>
storehouse [ˈstorˌhaʊs] *n* : almacén *m,* depósito *m*
storekeeper [ˈstorˌkiːpər] *n* : tendero *m,* -ra *f*
storeroom [ˈstorˌruːm, -ˌrʊm] *n* : almacén *m,* depósito *m*
stork [ˈstɔrk] *n* : cigüeña *f*
storm[1] [ˈstɔrm] *vi* **1** : llover o nevar tormentosamente **2** RAGE : ponerse furioso, vociferar **3 to storm out** : salir echando pestes — *vt* ATTACK : asaltar
storm[2] *n* **1** : tormenta *f,* tempestad *f* **2** UPROAR : alboroto *m,* revuelo *m,* escándalo *m* <a storm of abuse : un torrente de abusos>
stormy [ˈstɔrmi] *adj* **stormier; -est** : tormentoso
story [ˈstori] *n, pl* **stories 1** NARRATIVE : cuento *m,* relato *m* **2** ACCOUNT : historia *f,* relato *m* **3** : piso *m,* planta *f* (de un edificio) <first story : planta baja>
stout [ˈstaʊt] *adj* **1** FIRM, RESOLUTE : firme, resuelto **2** STURDY : fuerte, robusto, sólido **3** FAT : corpulento, gordo
stove[1] [ˈstoːv] *n* : cocina *f* (para cocinar), estufa *f* (para calentar)
stove[2] → **stave**[1]
stow [ˈstoː] *vt* **1** STORE : poner, meter, guardar **2** LOAD : cargar — *vi* **to stow away** : viajar de polizón
stowaway [ˈstoːəˌweɪ] *n* : polizón *m*
straddle [ˈstrædəl] *vt* **-dled; -dling** : sentarse a horcajadas sobre
straggle [ˈstrægəl] *vi* **-gled; -gling** : rezagarse, quedarse atrás
straggler [ˈstrægələr] *n* : rezagado *m,* -da *f*
straight[1] [ˈstreɪt] *adv* **1** : derecho, directamente <go straight, then turn right : sigue derecho, luego gira a la derecha> **2** HONESTLY : honestamente <to go straight : enmendarse> **3** CLEARLY : con claridad **4** FRANKLY : francamente, con franqueza
straight[2] *adj* **1** : recto (dícese de las líneas, etc.), derecho (dícese de algo vertical), lacio (dícese del pelo) **2** HONEST, JUST : honesto, justo **3** NEAT, ORDERLY : arreglado, ordenado
straighten [ˈstreɪtən] *vt* **1** : enderezar, poner derecho **2 to straighten up** : arreglar, ordenar <he straightened up the house : arregló la casa>
straightforward [streɪtˈfɔrwərd] *adj* **1** FRANK : franco, sincero **2** CLEAR, PRECISE : puro, simple, claro
straightway [ˈstreɪtˈweɪ, -ˌweɪ] *adv* : inmediatamente
strain[1] [ˈstreɪn] *vt* **1** EXERT : forzar (la vista, la voz) <to strain oneself : hacer un gran esfuerzo> **2** FILTER : colar, filtrar **3** INJURE : lastimarse, hacerse daño en <to strain a muscle : sufrir un esguince>
strain[2] *n* **1** LINEAGE : linaje *m,* abolengo *m* **2** STREAK, TRACE : veta *f* **3** VARIETY : tipo *m,* variedad *f* **4** STRESS : tensión *f,* presión *f* **5** SPRAIN : esguince *m,* torcedura *f* (del tobillo, etc.) **6 strains** *npl* TUNE : melodía *f,* acordes *mpl,* compases *fpl*
strainer [ˈstreɪnər] *n* : colador *m*
strait [ˈstreɪt] *n* **1** : estrecho *m* **2 straits** *npl* DISTRESS : aprietos *mpl,* apuros *mpl* <in dire straits : en serios aprietos>
straitened [ˈstreɪtənd] *adj* **in straitened circumstances** : en apuros económicos
strand[1] [ˈstrænd] *vt* **1** : varar **2 to be left stranded** : quedar(se) varado, quedar colgado <they left me stranded : me dejaron abandonado>
strand[2] *n* **1** : hebra *f* (de hilo, etc.) <a strand of hair : un pelo> **2** BEACH : playa *f*
strange [ˈstreɪndʒ] *adj* **stranger; -est 1** QUEER, UNUSUAL : extraño, raro **2** UNFAMILIAR : desconocido, nuevo
strangely [ˈstreɪndʒli] *adv* ODDLY : de manera extraña <to behave strangely : portarse de una manera rara> <strangely, he didn't call : curiosamente, no llamó>
strangeness [ˈstreɪndʒnəs] *n* **1** ODDNESS : rareza *f* **2** UNFAMILIARITY : lo desconocido
stranger [ˈstreɪndʒər] *n* : desconocido *m,* -da *f;* extraño *m,* -ña *f*
strangle [ˈstræŋgəl] *vt* **-gled; -gling** : estrangular
strangler [ˈstræŋglər] *n* : estrangulador *m,* -dora *f*
strap[1] [ˈstræp] *vt* **strapped; strapping 1** FASTEN : sujetar con una correa **2** FLOG : azotar (con una correa)
strap[2] *n* **1** : correa *f* **2 shoulder strap** : tirante *m*
strapless [ˈstræpləs] *n* : sin tirantes
strapping [ˈstræpɪŋ] *adj* : robusto, fornido
stratagem [ˈstrætədʒəm, -ˌdʒɛm] *n* : estratagema *f,* artimaña *f*
strategic [strəˈtiːdʒɪk] *adj* : estratégico
strategy [ˈstrætədʒi] *n, pl* **-gies** : estrategia *f*
stratified [ˈstrætəˌfaɪd] *adj* : estratificado
stratosphere [ˈstrætəˌsfɪr] *n* : estratosfera *f*
stratum [ˈstreɪtəm, ˈstræ-] *n, pl* **strata** [-tə] : estrato *m,* capa *f*
straw *n* **1** : paja *f* <the last straw : el colmo> **2** *or* **drinking straw** : pajita *f,* popote *m Mex*

strawberry [ˈstrɔˌbɛri] *n, pl* **-ries** : fresa *f*

stray[1] [ˈstreɪ] *vi* **1** WANDER : alejarse, extraviarse <the cattle strayed away : el ganado se descarrió> **2** DIGRESS : desviarse, divagar

stray[2] *adj* : perdido, callejero (dícese de un perro o un gato), descarriado (dícese del ganado)

stray[3] *n* : animal *m* perdido, animal *m* callejero

streak[1] [ˈstriːk] *vt* : hacer rayas en <blue streaked with grey : azul veteado con gris> — *vi* : ir como una flecha

streak[2] *n* **1** : raya *f,* veta *f* (en mármol, queso, etc.), mechón *m* (en el pelo) **2** : rayo *m* (de luz) **3** TRACE : veta *f* **4** : racha *f* <a streak of luck : una racha de suerte>

stream[1] [ˈstriːm] *vi* : correr, salir a chorros <tears streamed from his eyes : las lágrimas brotaban de sus ojos> — *vt* : derramar, dejar correr <to stream blood : derramar sangre>

stream[2] *n* **1** BROOK : arroyo *m,* riachuelo *m* **2** RIVER : río *m* **3** FLOW : corriente *f,* chorro *m*

streamer [ˈstriːmər] *n* **1** PENNANT : banderín *m* **2** RIBBON : serpentina *f* (de papel), cinta *f* (de tela)

streamlined [ˈstriːmˌlaɪnd] *adj* **1** : aerodinámico (dícese de los automóviles, etc.) **2** EFFICIENT : eficiente, racionalizado

street [ˈstriːt] *n* : calle *f*

streetcar [ˈstriːtˌkɑr] *n* : tranvía *m*

strength [ˈstrɛŋ*k*θ] *n* **1** POWER : fuerza *f* **2** SOLIDITY, TOUGHNESS : solidez *f,* resistencia *f,* dureza *f* **3** INTENSITY : intensidad *f* (de emociones, etc.), lo fuerte (de un sabor, etc.) **4** : punto *m* fuerte <strengths and weaknesses : virtudes y defectos> **5** NUMBER : número *m,* complemento *m* <in full strength : en gran número>

strengthen [ˈstrɛŋ*k*θən] *vt* **1** : fortalecer (los músculos, el espíritu, etc.) **2** REINFORCE : reforzar **3** INTENSIFY : intensificar, redoblar (esfuerzos, etc.) — *vi* **1** : fortalecerse, hacerse más fuerte **2** INTENSIFY : intensificarse

strenuous [ˈstrɛnjʊəs] *adj* **1** VIGOROUS : vigoroso, enérgico **2** ARDUOUS : duro, riguroso

strenuously [ˈstrɛnjʊəsli] *adv* : vigorosamente, duro

stress[1] [ˈstrɛs] *vt* **1** : someter a tensión (física) **2** EMPHASIZE : enfatizar, recalcar **3 to stress out** : estresar

stress[2] *n* **1** : tensión *f* (en un material) **2** EMPHASIS : énfasis *m,* acento *m* (en lingüística) **3** TENSION : tensión *f* (nerviosa), estrés *m*

stressful [ˈstrɛsfəl] *adj* : estresante

stretch[1] [ˈstrɛtʃ] *vt* **1** EXTEND : estirar, extender, desplegar (alas) **2 to stretch the truth** : forzar la verdad, exagerar — *vi* : estirarse

stretch[2] *n* **1** STRETCHING : extensión *f,* estiramiento *m* (de músculos) **2** ELASTICITY : elasticidad *f* **3** EXPANSE : tramo *m,* trecho *m* <the home stretch : la recta final> **4** PERIOD : período *m* (de tiempo)

stretcher [ˈstrɛtʃər] *n* : camilla *f*

strew [ˈstruː] *vt* **strewed; strewed** *or* **strewn** [ˈstruːn]; **strewing 1** SCATTER : esparcir (semillas, etc.), desparramar (papeles, etc.) **2 to strew with** : cubrir de

stricken [ˈstrɪkən] *adj* **stricken with** : aquejado de (una enfermedad), afligido por (tristeza, etc.)

strict [ˈstrɪkt] *adj* : estricto — **strictly** *adv*

strictness [ˈstrɪktnəs] *n* : severidad *f,* lo estricto

stricture [ˈstrɪktʃər] *n* : crítica *f,* censura *f*

stride[1] [ˈstraɪd] *vi* **strode** [ˈstroːd]; **stridden** [ˈstrɪdən]; **striding** : ir dando trancos, ir dando zancadas

stride[2] *n* : tranco *m,* zancada *f*

strident [ˈstraɪdənt] *adj* : estridente

strife [ˈstraɪf] *n* : conflictos *mpl,* disensión *f*

strike[1] [ˈstraɪk] *v* **struck** [ˈstrʌk]; **struck; striking** *vt* **1** HIT : golpear (a una persona) <to strike a blow : pegar un golpe> **2** DELETE : suprimir, tachar **3** COIN, MINT : acuñar (monedas) **4** : dar (la hora) **5** AFFLICT : sobrevenir <he was stricken with a fever : le sobrevino una fiebre> **6** IMPRESS : impresionar, parecer <her voice struck me : su voz me impresionó> <it struck him as funny : le pareció chistoso> **7** : encender (un fósforo) **8** FIND : descubrir (oro, petróleo) **9** ADOPT : adoptar (una pose, etc.) — *vi* **1** HIT : golpear <to strike against : chocar contra> **2** ATTACK : atacar **3** : declararse en huelga

strike[2] *n* **1** BLOW : golpe *m* **2** : huelga *f,* paro *m* <to be on strike : estar en huelga> **3** ATTACK : ataque *m*

strikebreaker [ˈstraɪkˌbreɪkər] *n* : rompehuelgas *mf,* esquirol *mf*

strike out *vi* **1** HEAD : salir (para) **2** : ser ponchado (en béisbol) <the batter struck out : poncharon al bateador>

striker [ˈstraɪkər] *n* : huelgista *mf*

strike up *vt* START : entablar, empezar

striking [ˈstraɪkɪŋ] *adj* : notable, sorprendente, llamativo <a striking beauty : una belleza imponente> — **strikingly** *adv*

string[1] [ˈstrɪŋ] *vt* **strung** [ˈstrʌŋ]; **stringing 1** THREAD : ensartar <to string beads : ensartar cuentas> **2** HANG : colgar (con un cordel)

string[2] *n* **1** : cordel *m,* cuerda *f* **2** SERIES : serie *f,* sarta *f* (de insultos, etc.) **3 strings** *npl* : cuerdas *fpl* (en música)

string bean *n* : judía *f,* ejote *m Mex*

stringent [ˈstrɪndʒənt] *adj* : estricto, severo

stringy ['strɪŋi] *adj* **stringier; -est** : fibroso

strip[1] ['strɪp] *v* **stripped; stripping** *vt* : quitar (ropa, pintura, etc.), desnudar, despojar — *vi* UNDRESS : desnudarse

strip[2] *n* : tira *f* <a strip of land : una faja>

stripe[1] ['straɪp] *vt* **striped** ['straɪpt]; **striping** : marcar con rayas o listas

stripe[2] *n* **1** : raya *f,* lista *f* **2** BAND : franja *f*

striped ['straɪpt, 'straɪpəd] *adj* : a rayas, de rayas, rayado, listado

strive ['straɪv] *vi* **strove** ['stro:v]; **striven** ['strɪvən] *or* **strived; striving 1 to strive for** : luchar por lograr **2 to strive to** : esforzarse por

strode → **stride**

stroke[1] ['stro:k] *vt* **stroked; stroking** : acariciar

stroke[2] *n* : golpe *m* <a stroke of luck : un golpe de suerte>

stroll[1] ['stro:l] *vi* : pasear, pasearse, dar un paseo

stroll[2] *n* : paseo *m*

stroller ['stro:lər] *n* : cochecito *m* (para niños)

strong ['strɔŋ] *adj* **1** : fuerte **2** HEALTHY : sano **3** ZEALOUS : ferviente

stronghold ['strɔŋ,ho:ld] *n* : fortaleza *f,* fuerte *m,* bastión *m* <a cultural stronghold : un baluarte de la cultura>

strongly ['strɔŋli] *adv* **1** POWERFULLY : fuerte, con fuerza **2** STURDILY : fuertemente, sólidamente **3** INTENSELY : intensamente, profundamente **4** WHOLEHEARTEDLY : totalmente

struck → **strike[1]**

structural ['strʌktʃərəl] *adj* : estructural

structure[1] ['strʌktʃər] *vt* **-tured; -turing** : estructurar

structure[2] *n* **1** BUILDING : construcción *f* **2** ARRANGEMENT, FRAMEWORK : estructura *f*

struggle[1] ['strʌgəl] *vi* **-gled; -gling 1** CONTEND : forcejear (físicamente), luchar, contender **2** : hacer con dificultad <she struggled forward : avanzó con dificultad>

struggle[2] *n* : lucha *f,* pelea *f* (física)

strum ['strʌm] *vt* **strummed; strumming** : rasguear

strung → **string[1]**

strut[1] ['strʌt] *vi* **strutted; strutting** : pavonearse

strut[2] *n* **1** : pavoneo *m* <he walked with a strut : se pavoneaba> **2** : puntal *m* (en construcción, etc.)

strychnine ['strɪk,naɪn, -nən, -,ni:n] *n* : estricnina *f*

stub[1] ['stʌb] *vt* **stubbed; stubbing 1 to stub one's toe** : darse en el dedo (del pie) **2 to stub out** : apagarse

stub[2] *n* : colilla *f* (de un cigarrillo), cabo *m* (de un lápiz, etc.), talón *m* (de un cheque)

stubble ['stʌbəl] *n* **1** : rastrojo *m* (de plantas) **2** BEARD : barba *f*

stubborn ['stʌbərn] *adj* **1** OBSTINATE : terco, obstinado, empecinado **2** PERSISTENT : pertinaz, persistente — **stubbornly** *adv*

stubbornness ['stʌbərnnəs] *n* **1** OBSTINACY : terquedad *f,* obstinación *f* **2** PERSISTENCE : persistencia *f*

stubby ['stʌbi] *adj* **stubbier; -est** : corto y grueso <stubby fingers : dedos regordetes>

stucco ['stʌko:] *n, pl* **stuccos** *or* **stuccoes** : estuco *m*

stuck → **stick[1]**

stuck–up ['stʌk'ʌp] *adj* : engreído, creído *fam*

stud[1] ['stʌd] *vt* **studded; studding** : tachonar, salpicar

stud[2] *n* **1** *or* **stud horse** : semental *m* **2** : montante *m* (en construcción) **3** HOBNAIL : tachuela *f,* tachón *m*

student ['stu:dənt, 'stju:-] *n* : estudiante *mf;* alumno *m,* -na *f* (de un colegio)

studied ['stʌdid] *adj* : intencionado, premeditado

studio ['stu:di,o:, 'stju:-] *n, pl* **studios** : estudio *m*

studious ['stu:diəs, 'stju:-] *adj* : estudioso — **studiously** *adv*

study[1] ['stʌdi] *v* **studied; studying 1** : estudiar **2** EXAMINE : examinar, estudiar

study[2] *n, pl* **studies 1** STUDYING : estudio *m* **2** OFFICE : estudio *m,* gabinete *m* (en una casa) **3** RESEARCH : investigación *f,* estudio *m*

stuff[1] ['stʌf] *vt* : rellenar, llenar, atiborrar

stuff[2] *n* **1** POSSESSIONS : cosas *fpl* **2** ESSENCE : esencia *f* **3** SUBSTANCE : cosa *f,* cosas *fpl* <some sticky stuff : una cosa pegajosa> <she knows her stuff : es experta>

stuffing ['stʌfɪŋ] *n* : relleno *m*

stuffy ['stʌfi] *adj* **stuffier; -est 1** CLOSE : viciado, cargado <a stuffy room : una sala mal ventilada> <stuffy weather : tiempo bochornoso> **2** : tapado (dícese de la nariz) **3** STODGY : pesado, aburrido

stumble[1] ['stʌmbəl] *vi* **-bled; -bling 1** TRIP : tropezar, dar un traspié **2** FLOUNDER : quedarse sin saber qué hacer o decir **3 to stumble across** *or* **to stumble upon** : dar con, tropezar con

stumble[2] *n* : tropezón *m,* traspié *m*

stump[1] ['stʌmp] *vt* : dejar perplejo <to be stumped : no tener respuesta>

stump[2] *n* **1** : muñón *m* (de un brazo o una pierna) **2** *or* **tree stump** : cepa *f,* tocón *m* **3** STUB : cabo *m*

stun ['stʌn] *vt* **stunned; stunning 1** : aturdir (con un golpe) **2** ASTONISH, SHOCK : dejar estupefacto, dejar atónito, aturdir

stung → **sting[1]**

stunk → **stink[1]**

stunning ['stʌnɪŋ] *adj* **1** ASTONISHING **:** asombroso, pasmoso, increíble **2** STRIKING **:** imponente, impresionante (dícese de la belleza)
stunt[1] ['stʌnt] *vt* **:** atrofiar
stunt[2] *n* **:** proeza *f* (acrobática)
stupefy ['stu:pə,faɪ, 'stju:-] *vt* **-fied; -fying 1 :** aturdir, atontar (con drogas, etc.) **2** AMAZE **:** dejar estupefacto, dejar atónito
stupendous [stʊ'pɛndəs, stjʊ-] *adj* **1** MARVELOUS **:** estupendo, maravilloso **2** TREMENDOUS **:** tremendo — **stupendously** *adv*
stupid ['stu:pəd, 'stju:-] *adj* **1** IDIOTIC, SILLY **:** tonto, bobo, estúpido **2** DULL, OBTUSE **:** lento, torpe, lerdo
stupidity [stʊ'pɪdət̬i, stjʊ-] *n* **:** tontería *f,* estupidez *f*
stupidly ['stu:pədli, 'stju:-] *adv* **1** IDIOTICALLY **:** estúpidamente, tontamente **2** DENSELY **:** torpemente
stupor ['stu:pər, 'stju:-] *n* **:** estupor *m*
sturdily ['stərdəli] *adv* **:** sólidamente
sturdiness ['stərdinəs] *n* **:** solidez *f* (de muebles, etc.), robustez *f* (de una persona)
sturdy ['stərdi] *adj* **sturdier; -est :** fuerte, robusto, sólido
sturgeon ['stərdʒən] *n* **:** esturión *m*
stutter[1] ['stʌt̬ər] *vi* **:** tartamudear
stutter[2] *n* STAMMER **:** tartamudeo *m*
sty ['staɪ] *n* **1** *pl* **sties** PIGPEN **:** chiquero *m,* polcilga *f* **2** *pl* **sties** *or* **styes :** orzuelo *m* (en el ojo)
style[1] ['staɪl] *vt* **styled; styling 1** NAME **:** llamar **2 :** peinar (pelo), diseñar (vestidos, etc.) <carefully styled prose : prosa escrita con gran esmero>
style[2] *n* **1 :** estilo *m* <that's just his style : él es así> <to live in style : vivir a lo grande> **2** FASHION **:** moda *f*
stylish ['staɪlɪʃ] *adj* **:** de moda, elegante, chic
stylishly ['staɪlɪʃli] *adv* **:** con estilo
stylishness ['staɪlɪʃnəs] *n* **:** estilo *m*
stylize ['staɪ,laɪz, 'staɪə-] *vt* **:** estilizar
stylus ['staɪləs] *n, pl* **styli** ['staɪ,laɪ] **1** PEN **:** estilo *m* **2** NEEDLE **:** aguja *f* (de un tocadiscos)
stymie ['staɪmi] *vt* **-mied; -mieing :** obstaculizar
suave ['swɑv] *adj* **:** fino, urbano
sub[1] ['sʌb] *vi* **subbed; subbing** → **substitute**[1]
sub[2] *n* **1** → **substitute**[2] **2** → **submarine**
subcommittee ['sʌbkə,mɪt̬i] *n* **:** subcomité *m*
subconscious[1] [səb'kɑntʃəs] *adj* **:** subconsciente — **subconsciously** *adv*
subconscious[2] *n* **:** subconsciente *m*
subcontract [,sʌb'kɑn,trækt] *vt* **:** subcontratar
subdivide [,sʌbdə'vaɪd, 'sʌbdə,vaɪd] *vt* **-vided; -viding :** subdividir
subdivision ['sʌbdə,vɪʒən] *n* **:** subdivisión *f*
subdue [səb'du:, -'dju:] *vt* **-dued; -duing 1** OVERCOME **:** sojuzgar (a un enemigo), vencer, superar **2** CONTROL **:** dominar **3** SOFTEN **:** suavizar, atenuar (luz, etc.), moderar (lenguaje)
subhead ['sʌb,hɛd] *or* **subheading** [-,hɛdɪŋ] *n* **:** subtítulo *m*
subject[1] [səb'dʒɛkt] *vt* **1** CONTROL, DOMINATE **:** controlar, dominar **2 :** someter <they subjected him to pressure : lo sometieron a presiones>
subject[2] ['sʌbdʒɪkt] *adj* **1 :** subyugado, sometido <a subject nation : una nación subyugada> **2** PRONE **:** sujeto, propenso <subject to colds : sujeto a resfriarse> **3 subject to :** sujeto a <subject to congressional approval : sujeto a la aprobación del congreso>
subject[3] ['sʌbdʒɪkt] *n* **1 :** súbdito *m,* -ta *f* (de un gobierno) **2** TOPIC **:** tema *m* **3 :** sujeto *m* (en gramática)
subjection [səb'dʒɛkʃən] *n* **:** sometimiento *m*
subjective [səb'dʒɛktɪv] *adj* **:** subjetivo — **subjectively** *adv*
subjectivity [,sʌb,dʒɛk'tɪvət̬i] *n* **:** subjetividad *f*
subjugate ['sʌbdʒɪ,geɪt] *vt* **-gated; -gating :** subyugar, someter, sojuzgar
subjunctive [səb'dʒʌŋktɪv] *n* **:** subjuntivo *m* — **subjunctive** *adj*
sublet ['sʌb,lɛt] *vt* **-let; -letting :** subarrendar
sublime [sə'blaɪm] *adj* **:** sublime
sublimely [sə'blaɪmli] *adv* **1 :** de manera sublime **2** UTTERLY **:** absolutamente, completamente
submarine[1] ['sʌbmə,ri:n, ,sʌbmə'-] *adj* **:** submarino
submarine[2] *n* **:** submarino *m*
submerge [səb'mərdʒ] *v* **-merged; -merging** *vt* **:** sumergir — *vi* **:** sumergirse
submission [səb'mɪʃən] *n* **1** YIELDING **:** sumisión *f* **2** PRESENTATION **:** presentación *f*
submissive [səb'mɪsɪv] *adj* **:** sumiso, dócil
submit [səb'mɪt] *v* **-mitted; -mitting** *vi* YIELD **:** rendirse <to submit to : someterse a> — *vt* PRESENT **:** presentar
subnormal [,sʌb'nɔrməl] *adj* **:** por debajo de lo normal
subordinate[1] [sə'bɔrdən,eɪt] *vt* **-nated; -nating :** subordinar
subordinate[2] [sə'bɔrdənət] *adj* **:** subordinado <a subordinate clause : una oración subordinada>
subordinate[3] *n* **:** subordinado *m,* -da *f;* subalterno *m,* -na *f*
subordination [sə,bɔrdən'eɪʃən] *n* **:** subordinación *f*
subpoena[1] [sə'pi:nə] *vt* **-naed; -naing :** citar
subpoena[2] *n* **:** citación *f,* citatorio *m*
subscribe [səb'skraɪb] *vi* **-scribed; -scribing 1 :** suscribirse (a una revista, etc.) **2 to subscribe to :** sus-

cribir (una opinión, etc.), estar de acuerdo con
subscriber [səb'skraɪbər] *n* **:** suscriptor *m,* -tora *f* (de una revista, etc.); abonado *m,* -da *f* (de un servicio)
subscription [səb'skrɪpʃən] *n* **:** suscripción *f*
subsequent ['sʌbsɪkwənt, -sə,kwɛnt] *adj* **:** subsiguiente <subsequent to : posterior a>
subsequently ['sʌb,kwɛntli, -kwənt-] *adv* **:** posteriormente
subservient [səb'sərviənt] *adj* **:** servil
subside [səb'saɪd] *vi* **-sided; -siding 1** SINK **:** hundirse, descender **2** ABATE **:** calmarse (dícese de las emociones), amainar (dícese del viento, etc.)
subsidiary[1] [səb'sɪdi,ɛri] *adj* **:** secundario
subsidiary[2] *n, pl* **-ries :** filial *f,* subsidiaria *f*
subsidize ['sʌbsə,daɪz] *vt* **-dized; -dizing :** subvencionar, subsidiar
subsidy ['sʌbsədi] *n, pl* **-dies :** subvención *f,* subsidio *m*
subsist [səb'sɪst] *vi* **:** subsistir, mantenerse, vivir
subsistence [səb'sɪstənts] *n* **:** subsistencia *f*
substance ['sʌbstənts] *n* **1** ESSENCE **:** sustancia *f,* esencia *f* **2 :** sustancia *f* <a toxic substance : una sustancia tóxica> **3** WEALTH **:** riqueza *f* <a woman of substance : una mujer acaudalada>
substandard [,sʌb'stændərd] *adj* **:** inferior, deficiente
substantial [səb'stæntʃəl] *adj* **1** ABUNDANT **:** sustancioso <a substantial meal : una comida sustanciosa> **2** CONSIDERABLE **:** considerable, apreciable **3** SOLID, STURDY **:** sólido
substantially [səb'stæntʃəli] *adv* **:** considerablemente
substantiate [səb'stæntʃi,eɪt] *vt* **-ated; -ating :** confirmar, probar, justificar
substitute[1] ['sʌbstə,tu:t, -,tju:t] *v* **-tuted; -tuting** *vt* **:** sustituir — *vi* **to substitute for :** sustituir
substitute[2] *n* **1 :** sustituto *m,* -ta *f;* suplente *mf* (persona) **2 :** sucedáneo *m* <sugar substitute : sucedáneo de azúcar>
substitute teacher *n* **:** profesor *m,* -sora *f* suplente
substitution [,sʌbstə'tu:ʃən, -'tju:-] *n* **:** sustitución *f*
subterfuge ['sʌbtər,fju:dʒ] *n* **:** subterfugio *m*
subterranean [,sʌbtə'reɪniən] *adj* **:** subterráneo
subtitle ['sʌb,taɪtəl] *n* **:** subtítulo *m*
subtle ['sʌtəl] *adj* **-tler; -tlest 1** DELICATE, ELUSIVE **:** sutil, delicado **2** CLEVER **:** sutil, ingenioso
subtlety ['sʌtəlti] *n, pl* **-ties :** sutileza *f*
subtly ['sʌtəli] *adv* **:** sutilmente
subtotal ['sʌb,to:təl] *n* **:** subtotal *m*
subtract [səb'trækt] *vt* **:** restar, sustraer
subtraction [səb'trækʃən] *n* **:** resta *f,* sustracción *f*
suburb ['sʌ,bərb] *n* **:** municipio *m* periférico, suburbio *m*
suburban [sə'bərbən] *adj* **:** de las afueras (de una ciudad), suburbano
subversion [səb'vərʒən] *n* **:** subversión *f*
subversive [səb'vərsɪv] *adj* **:** subversivo
subway ['sʌb,weɪ] *n* **:** metro *m,* subterráneo *m Arg, Uru*
succeed [sək'si:d] *vt* FOLLOW **:** suceder a — *vi* **:** tener éxito (dícese de las personas), dar resultado (dícese de los planes, etc.) <she succeeded in finishing : logró terminar>
success [sək'sɛs] *n* **:** éxito *m*
successful [sək'sɛsfəl] *adj* **:** exitoso, logrado — **successfully** *adv*
succession [sək'sɛʃən] *n* **:** sucesión *f* <in succesion : sucesivamente>
successive [sək'sɛsɪv] *adj* **:** sucesivo, consecutivo — **successively** *adv*
successor [sək'sɛsər] *n* **:** sucesor *m,* -sora *f*
succinct [sək'sɪŋkt, sə'sɪŋkt] *adj* **:** sucinto — **succinctly** *adv*
succor[1] ['sʌkər] *vt* **:** socorrer
succor[2] *n* **:** socorro *m*
succotash ['sʌkə,tæʃ] *n* **:** guiso *m* de maíz y frijoles
succulent[1] ['sʌkjələnt] *adj* **:** suculento, jugoso
succulent[2] *n* **:** suculenta *f* (planta)
succumb [sə'kʌm] *vi* **:** sucumbir
such[1] ['sʌtʃ] *adv* **1** SO **:** tan <such tall buildings : edificios tan grandes> **2** VERY **:** muy <he's not in such good shape : anda un poco mal> **3 such that :** de tal manera que
such[2] *adj* **:** tal <there's no such thing : no existe tal cosa> <in such cases : en tales casos> <animals such as cows and sheep : animales como vacas y ovejas>
such[3] *pron* **1 :** tal <such was the result : tal fue el resultado> <he's a child, and acts as such : es un niño, y se porta como tal> **2 :** algo o alguien semejante <books, papers and such : libros, papeles y cosas por el estilo>
suck ['sʌk] *vi* **1 :** chupar (por la boca), aspirar (dícese de las máquinas) **2** SUCKLE **:** mamar — *vt* **:** sorber (bebidas), chupar (dulces, etc.)
sucker ['sʌkər] *n* **1 :** ventosa *f* (de un insecto, etc.) **2 :** chupón *m* (de una planta) **3** → **lollipop 4** FOOL **:** tonto *m,* -ta *f;* idiota *mf*
suckle ['sʌkəl] *v* **-led; -ling** *vt* **:** amamantar — *vi* **:** mamar
suckling ['sʌklɪŋ] *n* **:** lactante *mf*
sucrose ['su:,kro:s, -,kro:z] *n* **:** sacarosa *f*
suction ['sʌkʃən] *n* **:** succión *f*

Sudanese [ˌsuːdənˈiːz, -ˈiːs] *n* : sudanés *m,* -nesa *f* — **Sudanese** *adj*

sudden [ˈsʌdən] *adj* **1** : repentino, súbito <all of a sudden : de pronto, de repente> **2** UNEXPECTED : inesperado, improvisto **3** ABRUPT, HASTY : precipitado, brusco

suddenly [ˈsʌdənli] *adv* **1** : de repente, de pronto **2** ABRUPTLY : bruscamente

suddenness [ˈsʌdənnəs] *n* **1** : lo repentino **2** ABRUPTNESS : brusquedad *f* **3** HASTINESS : lo precipitado

suds [ˈsʌdz] *npl* : espuma *f* (de jabón)

sue [ˈsuː] *v* **sued; suing** *vt* : demandar — *vi* **to sue for** : demandar por (daños, etc.)

suede [ˈsweɪd] *n* : ante *m,* gamuza *f*

suet [ˈsuːət] *n* : sebo *m*

suffer [ˈsʌfər] *vi* : sufrir — *vt* **1** : sufrir, padecer (dolores, etc.) **2** PERMIT : permitir, dejar

sufferer [ˈsʌfərər] *n* : persona que padece (una enfermedad, etc.)

suffering [ˈsʌfərɪŋ] *n* : sufrimiento *m*

suffice [səˈfaɪs] *vi* **-ficed; -ficing** : ser suficiente, bastar

sufficient [səˈfɪʃənt] *adj* : suficiente

sufficiently [səˈfɪʃəntli] *adv* : (lo) suficientemente, bastante

suffix [ˈsʌˌfɪks] *n* : sufijo *m*

suffocate [ˈsʌfəˌkeɪt] *v* **-cated; -cating** *vt* : asfixiar, ahogar — *vi* : asfixiarse, ahogarse

suffocation [ˌsʌfəˈkeɪʃən] *n* : asfixia *f,* ahogo *m*

suffrage [ˈsʌfrɪdʒ] *n* : sufragio *m,* derecho *m* al voto

suffuse [səˈfjuːz] *vt* **-fused; -fusing** : impregnar (de olores, etc.), bañar (de luz), teñir (de colores), llenar (de emociones)

sugar[1] [ˈʃʊgər] *vt* : azucarar

sugar[2] *n* : azúcar *mf*

sugarcane [ˈʃʊgərˌkeɪn] *n* : caña *f* de azúcar

sugary [ˈʃʊgəri] *adj* **1** : azucarado <sugary desserts : postres azucarados> **2** SACCHARINE : empalagoso

suggest [səgˈdʒɛst, sə-] *vt* **1** PROPOSE : sugerir **2** IMPLY : indicar, dar a entender

suggestible [səgˈdʒɛstəbəl, sə-] *adj* : influenciable

suggestion [səgˈdʒɛstʃən, sə-] *n* **1** PROPOSAL : sugerencia *f* **2** INDICATION : indicio *m* **3** INSINUATION : insinuación *f*

suggestive [səgˈdʒɛstɪv, sə-] *adj* : insinuante — **suggestively** *adv*

suicidal [ˌsuːəˈsaɪdəl] *adj* : suicida

suicide [ˈsuːəˌsaɪd] *n* **1** : suicidio *m* (acto) **2** : suicida *mf* (persona)

suit[1] [ˈsuːt] *vt* **1** ADAPT : adaptar **2** BEFIT : convenir a, ser apropiado a **3** BECOME : favorecer, quedarle bien (a alguien) <the dress suits you : el vestido te queda bien> **4** PLEASE : agradecer, satisfacer, convenirle bien (a alguien) <does Friday suit you? : ¿le conviene el viernes?> <suit yourself! : ¡como quieras!>

suit[2] *n* **1** LAWSUIT : pleito *m,* litigio *m* **2** : traje *m* (ropa) **3** : palo *m* (de naipes)

suitability [ˌsuːt̬əˈbɪlət̬i] *n* : idoneidad *f,* lo apropiado

suitable [ˈsuːt̬əbəl] *adj* : apropiado, idóneo — **suitably** [-bli] *adv*

suitcase [ˈsuːtˌkeɪs] *n* : maleta *f,* valija *f,* petaca *f Mex*

suite [ˈswiːt, *for 2 also* ˈsuːt] *n* **1** : suite *f* (de habitaciones) **2** SET : juego *m* (de muebles)

suitor [ˈsuːt̬ər] *n* : pretendiente *m*

sulfur [ˈsʌlfər] *n* : azufre *m*

sulfuric acid [ˌsʌlˈfjʊrɪk] *adj* : ácido *m* sulfúrico

sulfurous [ˌsʌlˈfjʊrəs, ˈsʌlfərəs, ˈsʌlfjə-] *adj* : sulfuroso

sulk[1] [ˈsʌlk] *vi* : estar de mal humor, enfurruñarse *fam*

sulk[2] *n* : mal humor *m*

sulky [ˈsʌlki] *adj* **sulkier; -est** : malhumorado, taimado *Chile*

sullen [ˈsʌlən] *adj* **1** MOROSE : hosco, taciturno **2** DREARY : sombrío, deprimente

sullenly [ˈsʌlənli] *adv* **1** MOROSELY : hoscamente **2** GLOOMILY : sombríamente

sully [ˈsʌli] *vt* **sullied; sullying** : manchar, empañar

sultan [ˈsʌltən] *n* : sultán *m*

sultry [ˈsʌltri] *adj* **sultrier; -est 1** : bochornoso <sultry weather : tiempo sofocante, tiempo bochornoso> **2** SENSUAL : sensual, seductor

sum[1] [ˈsʌm] *vt* **summed; summing 1** : sumar (números) **2** → **sum up**

sum[2] *n* **1** AMOUNT : suma *f,* cantidad *f* **2** TOTAL : suma *f,* total *f* **3** : suma *f,* adición *f* (en matemáticas)

sumac [ˈʃuːˌmæk, ˈsuː-] *n* : zumaque *m*

summarize [ˈsʌməˌraɪz] *v* **-rized; -rizing** : resumir, compendiar

summary[1] [ˈsʌməri] *adj* **1** CONCISE : breve, conciso **2** IMMEDIATE : inmediato <a summary dismissal : un despido inmediato>

summary[2] *n, pl* **-ries** : resumen *m,* compendio *m*

summer [ˈsʌmər] *n* : verano *m*

summery [ˈsʌməri] *adj* : veraniego

summit [ˈsʌmət] *n* **1** : cumbre *f,* cima *f* (de una montaña) **2** *or* **summit conference** : cumbre *f*

summon [ˈsʌmən] *vt* **1** CALL : convocar (una reunión, etc.), llamar (a una persona) **2** : citar (en derecho) **3 to summon up** : armarse de (valor, etc.) <to summon up one's strength : reunir fuerzas>

summons [ˈsʌmənz] *n, pl* **summonses 1** SUBPOENA : citación *f,* citatorio *m Mex* **2** CALL : llamada *f,* llamamiento *m*

sumptuous [ˈsʌmptʃʊəs] *adj* : suntuoso

sum up *vt* **1** SUMMARIZE : resumir **2** EVALUATE : evaluar — *vi* : recapitular
sun[1] ['sʌn] *vt* **sunned; sunning 1** : poner al sol **2 to sun oneself** : asolearse, tomar el sol
sun[2] *n* **1** : sol *m* **2** SUNSHINE : luz *f* del sol
sunbeam ['sʌn,bi:m] *n* : rayo *m* de sol
sunblock ['sʌn,blɑk] *n* : filtro *m* solar
sunburn[1] ['sʌn,bərn] *vi* **-burned** [-,bərnd] *or* **-burnt** [-,bərnt]; **-burning** : quemarse por el sol
sunburn[2] ['sʌn,bərn] *n* : quemadura *f* de sol
sundae ['sʌndi] *n* : sundae *m*
Sunday ['sʌn,deɪ, -di] *n* : domingo *m*
sundial ['sʌn,daɪl] *n* : reloj *m* de sol
sundown ['sʌn,daʊn] → **sunset**
sundries ['sʌndriz] *npl* : artículos *mpl* diversos
sundry ['sʌndri] *adj* : varios, diversos
sunflower ['sʌn,flaʊər] *n* : girasol *m*, mirasol *m*
sung → **sing**
sunglasses ['sʌn,glæsəz] *npl* : gafas *fpl* de sol, lentes *mpl* de sol
sunk → **sink**[1]
sunken ['sʌŋkən] *adj* : hundido
sunlight ['sʌn,laɪt] *n* : sol *m*, luz *f* del sol
sunny ['sʌni] *adj* **sunnier; -est** : soleado
sunrise ['sʌn,raɪz] *n* : salida *f* del sol
sunset ['sʌn,sɛt] *n* : puesta *f* del sol
sunshine ['sʌn,ʃaɪn] *n* : sol *m*, luz *f* del sol
sunspot ['sʌn,spɑt] *n* : mancha *f* solar
sunstroke ['sʌn,stro:k] *n* : insolación *f*
suntan ['sʌn,tæn] *n* : bronceado *m*
sup ['sʌp] *vi* **supped; supping** : cenar
super ['su:pər] *adj* : súper <super! : ¡fantástico!>
superabundance [,su:pərə'bʌndənts] *n* : superabundancia *f*
superb [sʊ'pərb] *adj* : magnífico, espléndido — **superbly** *adv*
supercilious [,su:pər'sɪliəs] *adj* : altivo, altanero, desdeñoso
supercomputer ['su:pərkəm,pju:t̬ər] *n* : supercomputadora *f*
superficial [,su:pər'fɪʃəl] *adj* : superficial — **superficially** *adv*
superfluous [sʊ'pərfluəs] *adj* : superfluo
superhighway ['su:pər,haɪ,weɪ, ,su:pər'-] *n* : autopista *f*
superhuman [,su:pər'*h*ju:mən] *adj* **1** SUPERNATURAL : sobrenatural **2** HERCULEAN : sobrehumano
superimpose [,su:pərɪm'po:z] *vt* **-posed; -posing** : superponer, sobreponer
superintend [,su:pərɪn'tɛnd] *vt* : supervisar
superintendent [,su:pərɪn'tɛndənt] *n* : portero *m*, -ra *f* (de un edificio); director *m*, -tora *f* (de una escuela, etc.); superintendente *mf* (de policía)
superior[1] [sʊ'pɪriər] *adj* **1** BETTER : superior **2** HAUGHTY : altivo, altanero
superior[2] *n* : superior *m*
superiority [sʊ,pɪri'ɔrət̬i] *n, pl* **-ties** : superioridad *f*
superlative[1] [sʊ'pərlət̬ɪv] *adj* **1** : superlativo (en gramática) **2** SUPREME : supremo **3** EXCELLENT : excelente, excepcional
superlative[2] *n* : superlativo *m*
supermarket ['su:pər,mɑrkət] *n* : supermercado *m*
supernatural [,su:pər'nætʃərəl] *adj* : sobrenatural
supernaturally [,su:pər'nætʃərəli] *adv* : de manera sobrenatural
superpower ['su:pər,paʊər] *n* : superpotencia *f*
supersede [,su:pər'si:d] *vt* **-seded; -seding** : suplantar, reemplazar, sustituir
supersonic [,su:pər'sɑnɪk] *adj* : supersónico
superstition [,su:pər'stɪʃən] *n* : superstición *f*
superstitious [,su:pər'stɪʃəs] *adj* : supersticioso
superstructure ['su:pər,strʌktʃər] *n* : superestructura *f*
supervise ['su:pər,vaɪz] *vt* **-vised; -vising** : supervisar, dirigir
supervision [,su:pər'vɪʒən] *n* : supervisión *f*, dirección *f*
supervisor ['su:pər,vaɪzər] *n* : supervisor *m*, -sora *f*
supervisory [,su:pər'vaɪzəri] *adj* : de supervisor
supine [sʊ'paɪn] *adj* **1** : en decúbito supino, en decúbito dorsal **2** ABJECT, INDIFFERENT : indiferente, apático
supper ['sʌpər] *n* : cena *f*, comida *f*
supplant [sə'plænt] *vt* : suplantar
supple ['sʌpəl] *adj* **-pler; -plest** : flexible
supplement[1] ['sʌplə,mɛnt] *vt* : complementar, completar
supplement[2] ['sʌpləmənt] *n* **1** : complemento *m* <dietary supplement : complemento alimenticio> **2** : suplemento *m* (de un libro o periódico)
supplementary [,sʌplə'mɛntəri] *adj* : suplementario
supplicate ['sʌplə,keɪt] *v* **-cated; -cating** *vi* : rezar — *vt* : suplicar
supplier [sə'plaɪər] *n* : proveedor *m*, -dora *f*; abastecedor *m*, -dora *f*
supply[1] [sə'plaɪ] *vt* **-plied; -plying** : suministrar, proveer de, proporcionar
supply[2] *n, pl* **-plies 1** PROVISION : provisión *f*, suministro *m* <supply and demand : la oferta y la demanda> **2** STOCK : reserva *f*, existencias *fpl* (de un negocio) **3 supplies** *npl* PROVISIONS : provisiones *fpl*, víveres *mpl*, despensa *f*
support[1] [sə'port] *vt* **1** BACK : apoyar, respaldar **2** MAINTAIN : mantener, sos-

tener, sustentar **3** PROP UP : sostener, apoyar, apuntalar, soportar

support[2] *n* **1** : apoyo *m* (moral), ayuda *f* (económica) **2** PROP : soporte *m,* apoyo *m*

supporter [sə'port̬ər] *n* : partidario *m,* -ria *f*

suppose [sə'po:z] *vt* **-posed; -posing 1** ASSUME : suponer, imaginarse **2** BELIEVE : suponer, creer **3 to be supposed to** : tener que, deber

supposition [ˌsʌpə'zɪʃən] *n* : suposición *f*

suppository [sə'pɑzəˌtori] *n, pl* **-ries** : supositorio *m*

suppress [sə'prɛs] *vt* **1** SUBDUE : sofocar, suprimir, reprimir (una rebelión, etc.) **2** : suprimir, ocultar (información) **3** REPRESS : reprimir, contener <to suppress a yawn : reprimir un bostezo>

suppression [sə'prɛʃən] *n* **1** SUBDUING : represión *f* **2** : supresión *f* (de información) **3** REPRESSION : represión *f,* inhibición *f*

supremacy [sʊ'prɛməsi] *n, pl* **-cies** : supremacía *f*

supreme [sʊ'pri:m] *adj* : supremo

Supreme Being *n* : Ser *m* Supremo

supremely [sʊ'pri:mli] *adv* : totalmente, sumamente

surcharge ['sərˌtʃɑrdʒ] *n* : recargo *m*

sure[1] ['ʃʊr] *adv* **1** ALL RIGHT : por supuesto, claro **2** *(used as an intensifier)* <it sure is hot! : ¡hace tanto calor!> <she sure is pretty! : ¡qué linda es!>

sure[2] *adj* **surer; -est** : seguro <to be sure about something : estar seguro de algo> <a sure sign : una clara señal> <for sure : seguro, con seguridad>

surely ['ʃʊrli] *adv* **1** CERTAINLY : seguramente **2** (*used as an intensifier*) <you surely don't mean that! : ¡no me digas que estás hablando en serio!>

sureness ['ʃʊrnəs] *n* : certeza *f,* seguridad *f*

surety ['ʃʊrət̬i] *n, pl* **-ties** : fianza *f,* garantía *f*

surf ['sərf] *n* **1** WAVES : oleaje *m* **2** FOAM : espuma *f*

surface[1] ['sərfəs] *v* **-faced; -facing** *vi* : salir a la superficie — *vt* : revestir (una carretera)

surface[2] *n* **1** : superficie *f* **2 on the surface** : en apariencia

surfboard ['sərfˌbord] *n* : tabla *f* de surf, tabla *f* de surfing

surfeit ['sərfət] *n* : exceso *m*

surfing ['sərfɪŋ] *n* : surf *m,* surfing *m*

surge[1] ['sərdʒ] *vi* **surged; surging 1** : hincharse (dícese del mar), levantarse (dícese de las olas) **2** SWARM : salir en tropel (dícese de la gente, etc.)

surge[2] *n* **1** : oleaje *m* (del mar), oleada *f* (de gente) **2** FLUSH : arranque *m,* arrebato *m* (de ira, etc.) **3** INCREASE : aumento *m* (súbito)

surgeon ['sərdʒən] *n* : cirujano *m,* -na *f*

surgery ['sərdʒəri] *n, pl* **-geries** : cirugía *f*

surgical ['sərdʒɪkəl] *adj* : quirúrgico — **surgically** [-kli] *adv*

surly ['sərli] *adj* **surlier; -est** : hosco, arisco

surmise[1] [sər'maɪz] *vt* **-mised; -mising** : conjeturar, suponer, concluir

surmise[2] *n* : conjetura *f*

surmount [sər'maʊnt] *vt* **1** OVERCOME : superar, vencer, salvar **2** CLIMB : escalar **3** CAP, TOP : coronar

surname ['sərˌneɪm] *n* : apellido *m*

surpass [sər'pæs] *vt* : superar, exceder, rebasar, sobrepasar

surplus ['sərˌplʌs] *n* : excedente *m,* sobrante *m,* superávit *m* (de dinero)

surprise[1] [sə'praɪz, sər-] *vt* **-prised; -prising** : sorprender

surprise[2] *n* : sorpresa *f* <to take by surprise : sorprender>

surprising [sə'praɪzɪŋ, sər-] *adj* : sorprendente — **surprisingly** *adv*

surrender[1] [sə'rɛndər] *vt* **1** : entregar, rendir **2 to surrender oneself** : entregarse — *vi* : rendirse

surrender[2] *n* : rendición *m* (de una ciudad, etc.), entrega *f* (de posesiones)

surreptitious [ˌsərəp'tɪʃəs] *adj* : subrepticio — **surreptitiously** *adv*

surrogate ['sərəgət, -ˌgeɪt] *n* : sustituto *m*

surround [sə'raʊnd] *vt* : rodear

surroundings [sə'raʊndɪŋz] *npl* : ambiente *m,* entorno *m*

surveillance [sər'veɪlənts, -'veɪljənts, -'veɪənts] *n* : vigilancia *f*

survey[1] [sər'veɪ] *vt* **-veyed; -veying 1** : medir (un terreno) **2** EXAMINE : inspeccionar, examinar, revisar **3** POLL : hacer una encuesta de, sondear

survey[2] ['sərˌveɪ] *n, pl* **-veys 1** INSPECTION : inspección *f,* revisión *f* **2** : medición *f* (de un terreno) **3** POLL : encuesta *f,* sondeo *m*

surveyor [sər'veɪər] *n* : agrimensor *m,* -sora *f*

survival [sər'vaɪvəl] *n* : supervivencia *f,* sobrevivencia *f*

survive [sər'vaɪv] *v* **-vived; -viving** *vi* : sobrevivir — *vt* OUTLIVE : sobrevivir a

survivor [sər'vaɪvər] *n* : superviviente *mf,* sobreviviente *mf*

susceptibility [səˌsɛptə'bɪlət̬i] *n, pl* **-ties** : vulnerabilidad *f,* propensión *f* (a enfermedades, etc.)

susceptible [sə'sɛptəbəl] *adj* **1** VULNERABLE : vulnerable, sensible <susceptible to flattery : sensible a halagos> **2** PRONE : propenso <susceptible to colds : propenso a resfriarse>

suspect[1] [sə'spɛkt] *vt* **1** DISTRUST : dudar de **2** : sospechar (algo), sospechar de (una persona) **3** IMAGINE, THINK : imaginarse, creer

suspect[2] ['sʌs,pɛkt, sə'spɛkt] *adj* : sospechoso, dudoso, cuestionable

suspect[3] ['sʌs,pɛkt] *n* : sospechoso *m*, -sa *f*

suspend [sə'spɛnd] *vt* : suspender

suspenders [sə'spɛndərz] *npl* : tirantes *mpl*

suspense [sə'spɛnts] *n* : incertidumbre *f*, suspenso *m* (en una película, etc.)

suspenseful [sə'spɛntsfəl] *adj* : de suspenso

suspension [sə'spɛntʃən] *n* : suspensión *f*

suspicion [sə'spɪʃən] *n* **1** : sospecha *f* **2** TRACE : pizca *f*, atisbo *m*

suspicious [sə'spɪʃəs] *adj* **1** QUESTIONABLE : sospechoso, dudoso **2** DISTRUSTFUL : suspicaz, desconfiado

suspiciously [sə'spɪʃəsli] *adv* : de modo sospechoso, con recelo

sustain [sə'steɪn] *vt* **1** NOURISH : sustentar **2** PROLONG : sostener **3** SUFFER : sufrir **4** SUPPORT, UPHOLD : apoyar, respaldar, sostentar

sustenance ['sʌstənənts] *n* **1** NOURISHMENT : sustento *m* **2** SUPPORT : sostén *m*

svelte ['sfɛlt] *adj* : esbelto

swab[1] ['swɑb] *vt* **swabbed; swabbing 1** CLEAN : lavar, limpiar **2** : aplicar a (con hisopo)

swab[2] *n or* **cotton swab** : hisopo *m* (para aplicar medicinas, etc.)

swaddle ['swɑdəl] *vt* **-dled; -dling** ['swɑdəlɪŋ] : envolver (en pañales)

swagger[1] ['swægər] *vi* : pavonearse

swagger[2] *n* : pavoneo *m*

swallow[1] ['swɑloː] *vt* **1** : tragar (comida, etc.) **2** ENGULF : tragarse, envolver **3** REPRESS : tragarse (insultos, etc.) — *vi* : tragar

swallow[2] *n* **1** : golondrina *f* (pájaro) **2** GULP : trago *m*

swam → **swim**[1]

swamp[1] ['swɑmp] *vt* : inundar

swamp[2] *n* : pantano *m*, ciénaga *f*

swampy ['swɑmpi] *adj* **swampier; -est** : pantanoso, cenagoso

swan ['swɑn] *n* : cisne *f*

swap[1] ['swɑp] *vt* **swapped; swapping** : cambiar, intercambiar <to swap places : cambiarse de sitio>

swap[2] *n* : cambio *m*, intercambio *m*

swarm[1] ['swɔrm] *vi* : enjambrar

swarm[2] *n* : enjambre *m*

swarthy ['swɔrði, -θi] *adj* **swarthier; -est** : moreno

swashbuckling ['swɑʃ,bʌklɪŋ] *adj* : de aventurero

swat[1] ['swɑt] *vt* **swatted; swatting** : aplastar (un insecto), darle una palmada (a alguien)

swat[2] *n* : palmada *f* (con la mano), golpe *m* (con un objeto)

swatch ['swɑtʃ] *n* : muestra *f*

swath ['swɑθ, 'swɔθ] *or* **swathe** ['swɑð, 'swɔð, 'sweɪð] *n* : franja *f* (de grano segado)

swathe ['swɑð, 'swɔð, 'sweɪð] *vt* **swathed; swathing** : envolver

swatter ['swɑtər] → **flyswatter**

sway[1] ['sweɪ] *vi* : balancearse, mecerse — *vt* INFLUENCE : influir en, convencer

sway[2] *n* **1** SWINGING : balanceo *m* **2** INFLUENCE : influjo *m*

swear ['swær] *v* **swore** ['swor]; **sworn** ['sworn]; **swearing** *vi* **1** VOW : jurar **2** CURSE : decir palabrotas — *vt* : jurar

swearword ['swær,wərd] *n* : mala palabra *f*, palabrota *f*

sweat[1] ['swɛt] *vi* **sweat** *or* **sweated; sweating 1** PERSPIRE : sudar, transpirar **2** OOZE : rezumar **3 to sweat over** : sudar la gota gorda por

sweat[2] *n* : sudor *m*, transpiración *f*

sweater ['swɛtər] *n* : suéter *m*

sweatshirt ['swɛt,ʃərt] *n* : sudadera *f*

sweaty ['swɛti] *adj* **sweatier; -est** : sudoroso, sudado, transpirado

Swede ['swiːd] *n* : sueco *m*, -ca *f*

Swedish[1] ['swiːdɪʃ] *adj* : sueco

Swedish[2] *n* **1** : sueco *m* (idioma) **2 the Swedish** *npl* : los suecos

sweep[1] ['swiːp] *v* **swept** ['swɛpt]; **sweeping** *vt* **1** : barrer (el suelo, etc.), limpiar (suciedad, etc.) <he swept the books aside : apartó los libros de un manotazo> **2** *or* **to sweep through** : extenderse por (dícese del fuego, etc.), azotar (dícese de una tormenta) — *vi* **1** : barrer, limpiar **2** : extenderse (en una curva), describir una curva <the sun swept across the sky : el sol describía una curva en el cielo>

sweep[2] *n* **1** : barrido *m*, barrida *f* (con una escoba) **2** : movimiento *m* circular **3** SCOPE : alcance *m*

sweeper ['swiːpər] *n* : barrendero *m*, -ra *f*

sweeping ['swiːpɪŋ] *adj* **1** WIDE : amplio (dícese de un movimiento) **2** EXTENSIVE : extenso, radical **3** INDISCRIMINATE : indiscriminado, demasiado general **4** OVERWHELMING : arrollador, aplastante

sweepstakes ['swiːp,steɪks] *ns & pl* **1** : carrera *f* (en que el ganador se lleva el premio entero) **2** LOTTERY : lotería *f*

sweet[1] ['swiːt] *adj* **1** : dulce <sweet desserts : postres dulces> **2** FRESH : fresco **3** : sin sal (dícese de la mantequilla, etc.) **4** PLEASANT : dulce, agradable **5** DEAR : querido

sweet[2] *n* : dulce *m*

sweeten ['swiːtən] *vt* : endulzar

sweetener ['swiːtənər] *n* : endulzante *m*

sweetheart ['swiːt,hɑrt] *n* : novio *m*, -via *f* <thanks, sweetheart : gracias, cariño>

sweetly ['swiːtli] *adv* : dulcemente

sweetness ['swiːtnəs] *n* : dulzura *f*

sweet potato *n* : batata *f*, boniato *m*

swell[1] ['swɛl] *vi* **swelled; swelled** *or* **swollen** ['swoːlən, 'swʌl-]; **swelling 1** *or* **to swell up** : hincharse <her

ankle swelled : se le hinchó el tobillo> **2** *or* **to swell out** : inflarse, hincharse (dícese de las velas, etc.) **3** INCREASE : aumentar, crecer

swell[2] *n* **1** : oleaje *m* (del mar) **2** → **swelling**

swelling ['swɛlɪŋ] *n* : hinchazón *f*

swelter ['swɛltər] *vi* : sofocarse de calor

swept → **sweep**[1]

swerve[1] ['swərv] *vi* **swerved; swerving** : virar bruscamente

swerve[2] *n* : viraje *m* brusco

swift[1] ['swɪft] *adj* **1** FAST : rápido, veloz **2** SUDDEN : repentino, súbito — **swiftly** *adv*

swift[2] *n* : vencejo *m* (pájaro)

swiftness ['swɪftnəs] *n* : rapidez *f*, velocidad *f*

swig[1] ['swɪg] *vi* **swigged; swigging** : tomar a tragos, beber a tragos

swig[2] *n* : trago *m*

swill[1] ['swɪl] *vt* : chupar, beber a tragos grandes

swill[2] *n* **1** SLOP : bazofia *f* **2** GARBAGE : basura *f*

swim[1] ['swɪm] *vi* **swam** ['swæm]; **swum** ['swʌm]; **swimming 1** : nadar **2** FLOAT : flotar **3** REEL : dar vueltas <his head was swimming : la cabeza le daba vueltas>

swim[2] *n* : baño *m*, chapuzón *m* <to go for a swim : ir a nadar>

swimmer ['swɪmər] *n* : nadador *m*, -dora *f*

swindle[1] ['swɪndəl] *vt* **-dled; -dling** : estafar, timar

swindle[2] *n* : estafa *f*, timo *m fam*

swindler ['swɪndələr] *n* : estafador *m*, -dora *f*; timador *m*, -dora *f*

swine ['swaɪn] *ns & pl* : cerdo *m*, -da *f*

swing[1] ['swɪŋ] *v* **swung** ['swʌŋ]; **swinging** *vt* **1** : describir una curva con <he swung the ax at the tree : le dio al arbol con el hacha> **2** : balancear (los brazos, etc.), hacer oscilar **3** SUSPEND : colgar — *vi* **1** SWAY : balancearse (dícese de los brazos, etc.), oscilar (dícese de un objeto), columpiarse, mecerse (en un columpio) **2** SWIVEL : girar (en un pivote) <the door swung shut : la puerta se cerró> **3** CHANGE : virar, cambiar (dícese de las opiniones, etc.)

swing[2] *n* **1** SWINGING : vaivén *m*, balanceo *m* **2** CHANGE, SHIFT : viraje *m*, movimiento *m* **3** : columpio *m* (para niños) **4 to take a swing at someone** : intentar pegarle a alguien

swipe[1] ['swaɪp] *vt* **swiped; swiping 1** STRIKE : dar, pegar (con un movimiento amplio) **2** WIPE : limpiar **3** STEAL : birlar *fam*, robar

swipe[2] *n* BLOW : golpe *m*

swirl[1] ['swərl] *vi* : arremolinarse

swirl[2] *n* **1** EDDY : remolino *m* **2** SPIRAL : espiral *f*

swish[1] ['swɪʃ] *vt* : mover (produciendo un sonido) <she swished her skirt : movía la falda> — *vi* : moverse (produciendo un sonido) <the cars swished by : se oían pasar los coches>

swish[2] *n* : silbido *m* (de un látigo, etc.), susurro *m* (de agua), crujido *m* (de ropa, etc.)

Swiss ['swɪs] *n* : suizo *m*, -za *f* — **Swiss** *adj*

swiss chard *n* : acelga *f*

switch[1] ['swɪtʃ] *vt* **1** LASH, WHIP : azotar **2** CHANGE : cambiar de **3** EXCHANGE : intercambiar **4 to switch on** : encender, prender **5 to switch off** : apagar — *vi* **1** : moverse de un lado al otro **2** CHANGE : cambiar **3** SWAP : intercambiarse

switch[2] *n* **1** WHIP : vara *f* **2** CHANGE, SHIFT : cambio *m* **3** : interruptor *m*, llave *f* (de la luz, etc.)

switchboard ['swɪtʃ,bord] *n* : conmutador *m*, centralita *f*

swivel[1] ['swɪvəl] *vi* **-veled** *or* **-velled; -veling** *or* **-velling** : girar (sobre un pivote)

swivel[2] *n* : base *f* giratoria

swollen → **swell**[1]

swoon[1] ['swu:n] *vi* : desvanecerse, desmayarse

swoon[2] *n* : desvanecimiento *m*, desmayo *m*

swoop[1] ['swu:p] *vi* : abatirse (dícese de las aves), descender en picada (dícese de un avión)

swoop[2] *n* : descenso *m* en picada

sword ['sɔrd] *n* : espada *f*

swordfish ['sɔrd,fɪʃ] *n* : pez *m* espada

swore, sworn → **swear**

swum → **swim**[1]

swung → **swing**[1]

sycamore ['sɪkə,mor] *n* : sicomoro *m*

sycophant ['sɪkəfənt, -,fænt] *n* : adulador *m*, -dora *f*

syllabic [sə'læbɪk] *adj* : silábico

syllable ['sɪləbəl] *n* : sílaba *f*

syllabus ['sɪləbəs] *n*, *pl* **-bi** [-,baɪ] *or* **-buses** : programa *m* (de estudios)

symbol ['sɪmbəl] *n* : símbolo *m*

symbolic [sɪm'bɑlɪk] *adj* : simbólico — **symbolically** [-kli] *adv*

symbolism ['sɪmbə,lɪzəm] *n* : simbolismo *m*

symbolize ['sɪmbə,laɪz] *vt* **-ized; -izing** : simbolizar

symmetrical [sə'mɛtrɪəl] *or* **symmetric** [-trɪk] *adj* : simétrico — **symmetrically** [-trɪkli] *adv*

symmetry ['sɪmətri] *n*, *pl* **-tries** : simetría *f*

sympathetic [,sɪmpə'θɛt̬ɪk] *adj* **1** PLEASING : agradable **2** RECEPTIVE : receptivo, favorable **3** COMPASSIONATE, UNDERSTANDING : comprensivo, compasivo

sympathetically [,sɪmpə'θɛt̬ɪkli] *adv* : con compasión, con comprensión

sympathize [ˈsɪmpəˌθaɪz] *vi* **-thized; -thizing :** compadecer <I sympathize with you : te compadezco>
sympathy [ˈsɪmpəθi] *n, pl* **-thies 1** COMPASSION **:** compasión *f* **2** UNDERSTANDING **:** comprensión *f* **3** AGREEMENT **:** solidaridad *f* <in sympathy with : de acuerdo con> **4** CONDOLENCES **:** pésame *m,* condolencias *fpl*
symphonic [sɪmˈfɑnɪk] *adj* **:** sinfónico
symphony [ˈsɪmpfəni] *n, pl* **-nies :** sinfonía *f*
symposium [sɪmˈpoːziəm] *n, pl* **-sia** [-ziə] *or* **-siums :** simposio *m*
symptom [ˈsɪmptəm] *n* **:** síntoma *m*
symptomatic [ˌsɪmptəˈmæt̬ɪk] *adj* **:** sintomático
synagogue [ˈsɪnəˌgɑg, -ˌgɔg] *n* **:** sinagoga *f*
synchronize [ˈsɪŋkrəˌnaɪz, ˈsɪn-] *v* **-nized; -nizing** *vi* **:** estar sincronizado — *vt* **:** sincronizar
syncopate [ˈsɪŋkəˌpeɪt, ˈsɪn-] *vt* **-pated; -pating :** sincopar
syncopation [ˌsɪŋkəˈpeɪʃən, ˌsɪn-] *n* **:** síncopa *f*
syndicate[1] [ˈsɪndəˌkeɪt] *vi* **-cated; -cating :** formar una asociación
syndicate[2] [ˈsɪndɪkət] *n* **:** asociación *f,* agrupación *f*
syndrome [ˈsɪnˌdroːm] *n* **:** síndrome *m*
synonym [ˈsɪnəˌnɪm] *n* **:** sinónimo *m*
synonymous [səˈnɑnəməs] *adj* **:** sinónimo
synopsis [səˈnɑpsɪs] *n, pl* **-opses** [-ˌsiːz] **:** sinopsis *f*
syntax [ˈsɪnˌtæks] *n* **:** sintaxis *f*
synthesis [ˈsɪnθəsɪs] *n, pl* **-theses** [-ˌsiːz] **:** síntesis *f*
synthesize [ˈsɪnθəˌsaɪz] *vt* **-sized; -sizing :** sintetizar
synthetic[1] [sɪnˈθɛt̬ɪk] *adj* **:** sintético, artificial — **synthetically** [-t̬ɪkli] *adv*
synthetic[2] *n* **:** producto *m* sintético
syphilis [ˈsɪfələs] *n* **:** sífilis *f*
Syrian [ˈsɪriən] *n* **:** sirio *m,* -ria *f* — **Syrian** *adj*
syringe [səˈrɪndʒ, ˈsɪrɪndʒ] *n* **:** jeringa *f,* jeringuilla *f*
syrup [ˈsərəp, ˈsɪrəp] *n* **:** jarabe *m,* almíbar *m* (de azúcar y agua)
system [ˈsɪstəm] *n* **1** METHOD **:** sistema *m,* método *m* **2** APPARATUS **:** sistema *m,* instalación *f,* aparato *m* <electrical system : instalación eléctrica> <digestive system : aparato digestivo> **3** BODY **:** organismo *m,* cuerpo *m* <diseases that affect the whole system : enfermedades que afectan el organismo entero> **4** NETWORK **:** red *f*
systematic [ˌsɪstəˈmæt̬ɪk] *adj* **:** sistemático — **systematically** [-t̬ɪkli] *adv*
systematize [ˈsɪstəməˌtaɪz] *vt* **-tized; -tizing :** sistematizar
systemic [sɪsˈtɛmɪk] *adj* **:** sistémico

T

t [ˈtiː] *n, pl* **t's** *or* **ts** [ˈtiːz] **:** vigésima letra del alfabeto inglés
tab [ˈtæb] *n* **1** FLAP, TAG **:** lengüeta *f* (de un sobre, una caja, etc.), etiqueta *f* (de ropa) **2 → tabulator 3** BILL, CHECK **:** cuenta *f* **4 to keep tabs on :** tener bajo vigilancia
tabby [ˈtæbi] *n, pl* **-bies 1** *or* **tabby cat :** gato *m* atigrado **2 :** gata *f*
tabernacle [ˈtæbərˌnækəl] *n* **:** tabernáculo *m*
table [ˈteɪbəl] *n* **1 :** mesa *f* <a table for two : una mesa para dos> **2** LIST **:** tabla *f* <multiplication table : tabla de multiplicar> **3 table of contents :** índice *m* de materias
tableau [tæˈbloː, ˈtæˌ-] *n, pl* **-leaux** [-ˈbloːz, -ˌbloːz] **:** retablo *m,* cuadro *m* vivo (en teatro)
tablecloth [ˈteɪbəlˌklɔθ] *n* **:** mantel *m*
tablespoon [ˈteɪbəlˌspuːn] *n* **1 :** cuchara *f* (de mesa) **2 → tablespoonful**
tablespoonful [ˈteɪbəlˌspuːnˌfʊl] *n* **:** cucharada *f*
tablet [ˈtæblət] *n* **1** PLAQUE **:** placa *f* **2** PAD **:** bloc *m* (de papel) **3** PILL **:** tableta *f,* pastilla *f,* píldora *f* <an aspirin tablet : una tableta de aspirina>
table tennis *n* **:** tenis *m* de mesa
tableware [ˈteɪbəlˌwær] *n* **:** vajillas *fpl,* cubiertos *mpl* (de mesa)
tabloid [ˈtæˌblɔɪd] *n* **:** tabloide *m*
taboo[1] [təˈbuː, tæ-] *adj* **:** tabú
taboo[2] *n* **:** tabú *m*
tabular [ˈtæbjələr] *adj* **:** tabular
tabulate [ˈtæbjəˌleɪt] *vt* **-lated; -lating :** tabular
tabulator [ˈtæbjəˌleɪt̬ər] *n* **:** tabulador *m*
tacit [ˈtæsɪt] *adj* **:** tácito, implícito — **tacitly** *adv*
taciturn [ˈtæsɪˌtərn] *adj* **:** taciturno
tack[1] [ˈtæk] *vt* **1 :** sujetar con tachuelas **2 to tack on** ADD **:** añadir, agregar
tack[2] *n* **1 :** tachuela *f* **2** COURSE **:** rumbo *m* <to change tack : cambiar de rumbo>
tackle[1] [ˈtækəl] *vt* **-led; -ling 1 :** taclear (en futbol americano) **2** CONFRONT **:** abordar, enfrentar, emprender (un problema, un trabajo, etc.)
tackle[2] *n* **1** EQUIPMENT, GEAR **:** equipo *m,* aparejo *m* **2 :** aparejo *m* (de un buque) **3 :** tacleada *f* (en futbol americano)
tacky [ˈtæki] *adj* **tackier; -est 1** STICKY **:** pegajoso **2** CHEAP, GAUDY **:** de mal gusto, naco *Mex*
tact [ˈtækt] *n* **:** tacto *m,* delicadeza *f,* discreción *f*

tactful ['tæktfəl] *adj* : discreto, diplomático, de mucho tacto

tactfully ['tæktfəli] *adv* : discretamente, con mucho tacto

tactic ['tæktɪk] *n* : táctica *f*

tactical ['tæktɪkəl] *adj* : táctico, estratégico

tactics ['tæktɪks] *ns & pl* : táctica *f,* estrategia *f*

tactile ['tæktəl, -ˌtaɪl] *adj* : táctil

tactless ['tæktləs] *adj* : indiscreto, poco delicado

tactlessly ['tæktləsli] *adv* : rudamente, sin tacto

tadpole ['tædˌpoːl] *n* : renacuajo *m*

taffeta ['tæfətə] *n* : tafetán *m,* tafeta *f Arg, Mex, Uru*

taffy ['tæfi] *n, pl* **-fies** : caramelo *m* de melaza, chicloso *m Mex*

tag[1] ['tæg] *v* **tagged; tagging** *vt* **1** LABEL : etiquetar **2** TAIL : seguir de cerca **3** TOUCH : tocar (en varios juegos) — *vi* **to tag along** : pegarse, acompañar

tag[2] *n* **1** LABEL : etiqueta *f* **2** SAYING : dicho *m,* refrán *m*

tail[1] ['teɪl] *vt* FOLLOW : seguir de cerca, pegarse

tail[2] *n* **1** : cola *f,* rabo *m* (de un animal) **2** : cola *f,* parte *f* posterior <a comet's tail : la cola de un cometa> **3 tails** *npl* : cruz *f* (de una moneda) <heads or tails : cara o cruz>

tailed ['teɪld] *adj* : que tiene cola

tailgate[1] ['teɪlˌgeɪt] *vi* **-gated; -gating** : seguir a un vehículo demasiado de cerca

tailgate[2] *n* : puerta *f* trasera (de un vehículo)

taillight ['teɪlˌlaɪt] *n* : luz *f* trasera (de un vehículo), calavera *f Mex*

tailor[1] ['teɪlər] *vt* **1** : confeccionar o alterar (ropa) **2** ADAPT : adaptar, ajustar

tailor[2] *n* : sastre *m,* -tra *f*

tailpipe ['teɪlˌpaɪp] *n* : tubo *m* de escape

tailspin ['teɪlˌspɪn] *n* : barrena *f*

taint[1] ['teɪnt] *vt* : contaminar, corromper

taint[2] *n* : corrupción *f,* impureza *f*

take[1] ['teɪk] *v* **took** ['tʊk]; **taken** ['teɪkən]; **taking** *vt* **1** CAPTURE : capturar, apresar **2** GRASP : tomar, agarrar <to take the bull by the horns : tomar al toro por los cuernos> **3** CATCH : tomar, agarrar <taken by surprise : tomado por sorpresa> **4** CAPTIVATE : encantar, fascinar **5** INGEST : tomar, ingerir <take two pills : tome dos píldoras> **6** REMOVE : sacar, extraer <take an orange : saca una naranja> **7** : tomar, coger (un tren, un autobús, etc.) **8** NEED, REQUIRE : tomar, requirir <these things take time : estas cosas toman tiempo> **9** BRING, CARRY : llevar, sacar, cargar <take them with you : llévalos contigo> <take the trash out : saca la basura> **10** BEAR, ENDURE : soportar, aguantar (dolores, etc.) **11** ACCEPT : aceptar (un cheque, etc.), seguir (consejos), asumir (la responsabilidad) **12** SUPPOSE : suponer <I take it that... : supongo que...> **13** (*indicating an action or an undertaking*) <to take a walk : dar un paseo> <to take a class : tomar una clase> **14 to take place** HAPPEN : tener lugar, suceder, ocurrir — *vi* : agarrar (dícese de un tinte), prender (dícese de una vacuna)

take[2] *n* **1** PROCEEDS : recaudación *f,* ingresos *mpl,* ganancias *fpl* **2** : toma *f* (de un rodaje o una grabación)

take back *vt* : retirar (palabras, etc.)

take in *vt* **1** : tomarle a, achicar (un vestido, etc.) **2** INCLUDE : incluir, abarcar **3** ATTEND : ir a <to take in a movie : ir al cine> **4** GRASP, UNDERSTAND : captar, entender **5** DECEIVE : engañar

takeoff ['teɪkˌɔf] *n* **1** PARODY : parodia *f* **2** : despegue *m* (de un avión o cohete)

take off *vt* REMOVE : quitar <take off your hat : quítate el sombrero> — *vi* **1** : despegar (dícese de un avión o un cohete) **2** LEAVE : irse, partir

take on *vt* **1** TACKLE : abordar, emprender (problemas, etc.) **2** ACCEPT : aceptar, encargarse de, asumir (una responsabilidad) **3** CONTRACT : contratar (trabajadores) **4** ASSUME : adoptar, asumir, adquirir <the neighborhood took on a dingy look : el barrio asumió una apariencia deprimente>

takeover ['teɪkˌoːvər] *n* : toma *f* (de poder o de control), adquisición *f* (de una empresa por otra)

take over *vt* : tomar el poder de, tomar las riendas de — *vi* : asumir el mando

taker ['teɪkər] *n* : persona *f* interesada <available to all takers : disponible a cuantos estén interesados>

take up *vt* **1** LIFT : levantar **2** SHORTEN : acortar (una falda, etc.) **3** BEGIN : empezar, dedicarse a (un pasatiempo, etc.) **4** OCCUPY : ocupar, llevar (tiempo, espacio) **5** PURSUE : volver a (una cuestión, un asunto) **6** CONTINUE : seguir con

talc ['tælk] *n* : talco *m*

talcum powder ['tælkəm] *n* : talco *m,* polvos *mpl* de talco

tale ['teɪl] *n* **1** ANECDOTE, STORY : cuento *m,* relato *m,* anécdota *f* **2** FALSEHOOD : cuento *m,* mentira *f*

talent ['tælənt] *n* : talento *m,* don *m*

talented ['tæləntəd] *adj* : talentoso

talisman ['tælɪsmən, -lɪz-] *n, pl* **-mans** : talismán *m*

talk[1] ['tɔk] *vi* **1** : hablar <he talks for hours : se pasa horas hablando> **2** CHAT : charlar, platicar — *vt* **1** SPEAK : hablar <to talk French : hablar francés> <to talk business : hablar de negocios> **2** PERSUADE : influenciar, convencer <she talked me out of it : me convenció que no lo hiciera> **3**

to talk over DISCUSS **:** hablar de, discutir
talk² *n* **1** CONVERSATION **:** charla *f,* plática *f,* conversación *f* **2** GOSSIP, RUMOR **:** chisme *m,* rumores *mpl*
talkative [ˈtɔkət̬ɪv] *adj* **:** locuaz, parlanchín, charlatán
talker [ˈtɔkər] *n* **:** conversador *m,* -dora *f;* hablador *m,* -dora *f*
tall [ˈtɔl] *adj* **:** alto <how tall is he? **:** ¿cuánto mide?>
tallness [ˈtɔlnəs] *n* HEIGHT **:** estatura *f* (de una persona), altura *f* (de un objeto)
tallow [ˈtæloː] *n* **:** sebo *m*
tally¹ [ˈtæli] *v* **-lied; -lying** *vt* RECKON **:** contar, hacer una cuenta de — *vi* MATCH **:** concordar, corresponder, cuadrar
tally² *n, pl* **-lies :** cuenta *f* <to keep a tally **:** llevar la cuenta>
talon [ˈtælən] *n* **:** garra *f* (de un ave de rapiña)
tambourine [ˌtæmbəˈriːn] *n* **:** pandero *m,* pandereta *f*
tame¹ [ˈteɪm] *vt* **tamed; taming :** domar, amansar, domesticar
tame² *adj* **tamer; -est 1** DOMESTICATED **:** domesticado, manso **2** DOCILE **:** manso, dócil **3** DULL **:** aburrido, soso
tamely [ˈteɪmli] *adv* **:** mansamente, dócilmente
tamer [ˈteɪmər] *n* **:** domador *m,* -dora *f*
tamp [ˈtæmp] *vt* **:** apisonar
tamper [ˈtæmpər] *vi* **to tamper with :** adulterar (una sustancia), forzar (un sello, una cerradura), falsear (documentos), manipular (una máquina)
tampon [ˈtæmˌpɑn] *n* **:** tampón *m*
tan¹ [ˈtæn] *v* **tanned; tanning** *vt* **1 :** curtir (pieles) **2 :** broncear — *vi* **:** broncearse
tan² *n* **1** SUNTAN **:** bronceado *m* <to get a tan **:** broncearse> **2 :** color *m* canela, color *m* café con leche
tandem¹ [ˈtændəm] *adv or* **in tandem :** en tándem
tandem² *n* **:** tándem *m* (bicicleta)
tang [ˈtæŋ] *n* **:** sabor *m* fuerte
tangent [ˈtændʒənt] *n* **:** tangente *f* <to go off on a tangent **:** irse por la tangente>
tangerine [ˈtændʒəˌriːn, ˌtændʒəˈ-] *n* **:** mandarina *f*
tangible [ˈtændʒəbəl] *adj* **:** tangible, palpable — **tangibly** [-bli] *adv*
tangle¹ [ˈtæŋgəl] *v* **-gled; -gling** *vt* **:** enredar, enmarañar — *vi* **:** enredarse
tangle² *n* **:** enredo *m,* maraña *f*
tango¹ [ˈtæŋˌgoː] *vi* **:** bailar el tango
tango² *n, pl* **-gos :** tango *m*
tangy [ˈtæŋi] *adj* **tangier; -est :** que tiene un sabor fuerte
tank [ˈtæŋk] *n* **:** tanque *m,* depósito *m* <fuel tank **:** depósito de combustibles>
tankard [ˈtæŋkərd] *n* **:** jarra *f*
tanker [ˈtæŋkər] *n* **:** buque *m* cisterna, camión *m* cisterna, avión *m* cisterna <an oil tanker **:** un petrolero>
tanner [ˈtænər] *n* **:** curtidor *m,* -dora *f*
tannery [ˈtænəri] *n, pl* **-neries :** curtiduría *f,* tenería *f*
tannin [ˈtænən] *n* **:** tanino *m*
tantalize [ˈtæntəˌlaɪz] *vt* **-lized; -lizing :** tentar, atormentar (con algo inasequible)
tantalizing [ˈtæntəˌlaɪzɪŋ] *adj* **:** tentador, seductor
tantamount [ˈtæntəˌmaʊnt] *adj* **:** equivalente
tantrum [ˈtæntrəm] *n* **:** rabieta *f,* berrinche *m* <to throw a tantrum **:** hacer un berrinche>
tap¹ [ˈtæp] *vt* **tapped; tapping 1 :** ponerle una espita a, sacar líquido de (un barril, un tanque, etc.) **2 :** intervenir (una línea telefónica) **3** PAT, TOUCH **:** tocar, golpear ligeramente <he tapped me on the shoulder **:** me tocó en el hombro>
tap² *n* **1** FAUCET **:** llave *f,* grifo *m* <beer on tap **:** cerveza de barril> **2 :** extracción *f* (de líquido) <a spinal tap **:** una punción lumbar> **3** PAT, TOUCH **:** golpecito *m,* toque *m*
tape¹ [ˈteɪp] *vt* **taped; taping 1 :** sujetar o mendar con cinta adhesiva **2** RECORD **:** grabar
tape² *n* **1 :** cinta *f* (adhesiva, magnética, etc.) **2** → **tape measure**
tape measure *n* **:** cinta *f* métrica
taper¹ [ˈteɪpər] *vi* **1 :** estrecharse gradualmente <its tail tapers towards the tip **:** su cola va estrechándose hacia la punta> **2** *or* **to taper off :** disminuir gradualmente
taper² *n* **1** CANDLE **:** vela *f* larga y delgada **2** TAPERING **:** estrechamiento *m* gradual
tapestry [ˈtæpəstri] *n, pl* **-tries :** tapiz *m*
tapeworm [ˈteɪpˌwərm] *n* **:** solitaria *f,* tenia *f*
tapioca [ˌtæpiˈoːkə] *n* **:** tapioca *f*
tar¹ [ˈtɑr] *vt* **tarred; tarring :** alquitranar
tar² *n* **:** alquitrán *m,* brea *f,* chapopote *m Mex*
tarantula [təˈræntʃələ, -ˈræntələ] *n* **:** tarántula *f*
tardiness [ˈtɑrdinəs] *n* **:** tardanza *f,* retraso *m*
tardy [ˈtɑrdi] *adj* **-dier; -est** LATE **:** tardío, de retraso
target¹ [ˈtɑrgət] *vt* **:** fijar como objetivo, dirigir, destinar
target² *n* **1 :** blanco *m* <target practice **:** tiro al blanco> **2** GOAL, OBJECTIVE **:** meta *f,* objetivo *m*
tariff [ˈtærɪf] *n* DUTY **:** tarifa *f,* arancel *m*
tarnish¹ [ˈtɑrnɪʃ] *vt* **1** DULL **:** deslustrar **2** SULLY **:** empañar, manchar (una reputación, etc.) — *vi* **:** deslustrarse
tarnish² *n* **:** deslustre *m*

tarpaulin [tɑr'pɔlən, 'tɑrpə-] *n* **:** lona *f* (impermeable)
tarry[1] ['tæri] *vi* **-ried; -rying :** demorarse, entretenerse
tarry[2] ['tɑri] *adj* **1 :** parecido al alquitrán **2 :** cubierto de alquitrán
tart[1] ['tɑrt] *adj* **1** SOUR **:** ácido, agrio **2** CAUSTIC **:** mordaz, acrimonioso — **tartly** *adv*
tart[2] *n* **:** tartaleta *f*
tartan ['tɑrtən] *n* **:** tartán *m*
tartar ['tɑrtər] *n* **1 :** tártaro *m* <tartar sauce : salsa tártara> **2 :** sarro *m* (dental)
tartness ['tɑrtnəs] *n* **1** SOURNESS **:** acidez *f* **2** ACRIMONY, SHARPNESS **:** mordacidad *f,* acrimonia *f,* acritud *f*
task ['tæsk] *n* **:** tarea *f,* trabajo *m*
taskmaster ['tæsk,mæstər] *n* **to be a hard taskmaster :** ser exigente, ser muy estricto
tassel ['tæsəl] *n* **:** borla *f*
taste[1] ['teɪst] *v* **tasted; tasting** *vt* **:** probar (alimentos), degustar, catar (vinos) <taste this soup : prueba esta sopa> — *vi* **:** saber <this tastes good : esto sabe bueno>
taste[2] *n* **1** SAMPLE **:** prueba *f,* bocado *m* (de comida), trago *m* (de bebidas) **2** FLAVOR **:** gusto *m,* sabor *m* **3 :** gusto *m* <she has good taste : tiene buen gusto> <in bad taste : de mal gusto>
taste bud *n* **:** papila *f* gustativa
tasteful ['teɪstfəl] *adj* **:** de buen gusto
tastefully ['teɪstfəli] *adv* **:** con buen gusto
tasteless ['teɪstləs] *adj* **1** FLAVORLESS **:** sin sabor, soso, insípido **2 :** de mal gusto <a tasteless joke : un chiste de mal gusto>
taster ['teɪstər] *n* **:** degustador *m,* -dora *f;* catador *m,* -dora *f* (de vinos)
tastiness ['teɪstinəs] *n* **:** lo sabroso
tasty ['teɪsti] *adj* **tastier; -est :** sabroso, gustoso
tatter ['tæt̬ər] *n* **1** SHRED **:** tira *f,* jirón *m* (de tela) **2 tatters** *npl* **:** andrajos *mpl,* harapos *mpl* <to be in tatters : estar por los suelos>
tattered ['tæt̬ərd] *adj* **:** andrajoso, en jirones
tattle ['tæt̬əl] *vi* **-tled; -tling 1** CHATTER **:** parlotear *fam,* cotorrear *fam* **2 to tattle on someone :** acusar a alguien
tattletale ['tæt̬əl,teɪl] *n* **:** soplón *m,* -plona *f fam*
tattoo[1] [tæ'tuː] *vt* **:** tatuar
tattoo[2] *n* **:** tatuaje *m* <to get a tattoo : tatuarse>
taught → **teach**
taunt[1] ['tɔnt] *vt* MOCK **:** mofarse de, burlarse de
taunt[2] *n* **:** mofa *f,* burla *f*
Taurus ['tɔrəs] *n* **:** Tauro *mf*
taut ['tɔt] *adj* **:** tirante, tenso — **tautly** *adv*
tautness ['tɔtnəs] *n* **:** tirantez *f,* tensión *f*
tavern ['tævərn] *n* **:** taberna *f*
tawdry ['tɔdri] *adj* **-drier; -est :** chabacano, vulgar
tawny ['tɔni] *adj* **-nier; -est :** leonado
tax[1] ['tæks] *vt* **1 :** gravar, cobrar un impuesto sobre **2** CHARGE **:** acusar <they taxed him with neglect : fue acusado de incumplimiento> **3 to tax someone's strength :** ponerle a prueba las fuerzas (a alguien)
tax[2] *n* **1 :** impuesto *m,* tributo *m* **2** BURDEN **:** carga *f*
taxable ['tæksəbəl] *adj* **:** sujeto a un impuesto
taxation [tæk'seɪʃən] *n* **:** impuestos *mpl*
tax–exempt ['tæksɪg'zɛmpt, -ɛg-] *adj* **:** libre de impuestos
taxi[1] ['tæksi] *vi* **taxied; taxiing** *or* **taxying; taxis** *or* **taxies 1 :** ir en taxi **2 :** rodar sobre la pista de aterrizaje (dícese de un avión)
taxi[2] *n, pl* **taxis :** taxi *m,* libre *m Mex*
taxicab ['tæksi,kæb] → **taxi**[2]
taxidermist ['tæksə,dərmɪst] *n* **:** taxidermista *mf*
taxidermy ['tæksə,dərmi] *n* **:** taxidermia *f*
taxpayer ['tæks,peɪər] *n* **:** contribuyente *mf,* causante *mf Mex*
TB [,tiː'biː] → **tuberculosis**
tea ['tiː] *n* **1 :** té *m* (planta y bebida) **2 :** merienda *f,* té *m* (comida)
teach ['tiːtʃ] *v* **taught** ['tɔt]; **teaching** *vt* **:** enseñar, dar clases de <she teaches math : da clases de matemáticas> <she taught me everything I know : me enseñó todo lo que sé> — *vi* **:** enseñar, dar clases
teacher ['tiːtʃər] *n* **:** maestro *m,* -tra *f* (de enseñanza primaria); profesor *m,* -sora *f* (de enseñanza secundaria)
teaching ['tiːtʃɪŋ] *n* **:** enseñanza *f*
teacup ['tiː,kʌp] *n* **:** taza *f* para té
teak ['tiːk] *n* **:** teca *f*
teakettle ['tiː,kɛtəl] *n* **:** tetera *f*
teal ['tiːl] *n, pl* **teal** *or* **teals :** cerceta *f* (pato)
team[1] ['tiːm] *vi or* **to team up 1 :** formar un equipo (en deportes) **2** COLLABORATE **:** asociarse, juntarse, unirse
team[2] *adj* **:** de equipo
team[3] *n* **1 :** tiro *m* (de caballos), yunta *f* (de bueyes o mulas) **2 :** equipo *m* (en deportes, etc.)
teammate ['tiːm,meɪt] *n* **:** compañero *m,* -ra *f* de equipo
teamster ['tiːmstər] *n* **:** camionero *m,* -ra *f*
teamwork ['tiːm,wərk] *n* **:** trabajo *m* en equipo, cooperación *f*
teapot ['tiː,pɑt] *n* **:** tetera *f*
tear[1] ['tær] *v* **tore** ['tor]; **torn** ['torn]; **tearing** *vt* **1** RIP **:** desgarrar, romper, rasgar (tela) <to tear to pieces : hacer pedazos> **2** *or* **to tear apart** DIVIDE **:** dividir **3** REMOVE **:** arrancar <torn from his family : arrancado de su familia> **4 to tear down :** derribar — *vi* **1** RIP **:** desgarrarse, romperse **2** RUSH

: ir a gran velocidad <she went tearing down the street : se fue como rayo por la calle>
tear[2] *n* : desgarradura *f,* rotura *f,* desgarro *m* (muscular)
tear[3] [ˈtɪr] *n* : lágrima *f*
teardrop [ˈtɪrˌdrɑp] → **tear**[3]
tearful [ˈtɪrfəl] *adj* : lloroso, triste — **tearfully** *adv*
tease[1] [ˈtiːz] *vt* **teased; teasing 1** MOCK : burlarse de, mofarse de **2** ANNOY : irritar, fastidiar
tease[2] *n* **1** TEASING : burla *f,* mofa *f* **2** : bromista *mf;* guasón *m,* -sona *f*
teaspoon [ˈtiːˌspuːn] *n* **1** : cucharita *f* **2** → **teaspoonful**
teaspoonful [ˈtiːˌspuːnˌfʊl] *n, pl* **-spoonfuls** [-ˌfʊlz] *or* **-spoonsful** [-ˌspuːnzˌfʊl] : cucharadita *f*
teat [ˈtiːt] *n* : tetilla *f*
technical [ˈtɛknɪkəl] *adj* : técnico — **technically** [-kli] *adv*
technicality [ˌtɛknəˈkæləṭi] *n, pl* **-ties** : detalle *m* técnico
technician [tɛkˈnɪʃən] *n* : técnico *m,* -ca *f*
technique [tɛkˈniːk] *n* : técnica *f*
technological [ˌtɛknəˈlɑdʒɪkəl] *adj* : tecnológico
technology [tɛkˈnɑlədʒi] *n, pl* **-gies** : tecnología *f*
teddy bear [ˈtɛdi] *n* : oso *m* de peluche
tedious [ˈtiːdiəs] *adj* : aburrido, pesado, monótono — **tediously** *adv*
tediousness [ˈtiːdiəsnəs] *n* : lo aburrido, lo pesado
tedium [ˈtiːdiəm] *n* : tedio *m,* pesadez *f*
tee [ˈtiː] *n* : tee *mf*
teem [ˈtiːm] *vi* **to teem with** : estar repleto de, estar lleno de
teenage [ˈtiːnˌeɪdʒ] *or* **teenaged** [-eɪdʒd] *adj* : adolescente, de adolescencia
teenager [ˈtiːnˌeɪdʒər] *n* : adolescente *mf*
teens [ˈtiːnz] *npl* : adolescencia *f*
teepee → **tepee**
teeter[1] [ˈtiːṭər] *vi* : balancearse, tambalearse
teeter[2] *n or* **teeter–totter** [ˈtiːṭərˌtɑṭər] → **seesaw**
teeth → **tooth**
teethe [ˈtiːð] *vi* **teethed; teething** : formársele a uno los dientes <the baby's teething : le están saliendo los dientes al niño>
telecast[1] [ˈtɛləˌkæst] *vt* **-cast; -casting** : televisar, transmitir por televisión
telecast[2] *n* : transmisión *f* por televisión
telecommunication [ˈtɛləkəˌmjuːnəˈkeɪʃən] *n* : telecomunicación *f*
telegram [ˈtɛləˌgræm] *n* : telegrama *m*
telegraph[1] [ˈtɛləˌgræf] *v* : telegrafiar
telegraph[2] *n* : telégrafo *m*
telepathic [ˌtɛləˈpæθɪk] *adj* : telepático — **telepathically** [-θɪkli] *adv*
telepathy [təˈlɛpəθi] *n* : telepatía *f*
telephone[1] [ˈtɛləˌfoːn] *v* **-phoned; -phoning** *vt* : llamar por teléfono a, telefonear — *vi* : telefonear
telephone[2] *n* : teléfono *m*
telescope[1] [ˈtɛləˌskoːp] *vi* **-scoped; -scoping** : plegarse (como un telescopio)
telescope[2] *n* : telescopio *m*
telescopic [ˌtɛləˈskɑpɪk] *adj* : telescópico
televise [ˈtɛləˌvaɪz] *vt* **-vised; -vising** : televisar
television [ˈtɛləˌvɪʒən] *n* : televisión *f*
tell [ˈtɛl] *v* **told** [ˈtoːld]; **telling** *vt* **1** COUNT : contar, enumerar <all told : en total> **2** INSTRUCT : decir <he told me how to fix it : me dijo cómo arreglarlo> <they told her to wait : le dijeron que esperara> **3** RELATE : contar, relatar, narrar <to tell a story : contar una historia> **4** DIVULGE, REVEAL : revelar, divulgar <he told me everything about her : me contó todo acerca de ella> **5** DISCERN : discernir, notar <I can't tell the difference : no noto la diferencia> — *vi* **1** SAY : decir <I won't tell : no voy a decírselo a nadie> **2** KNOW : saber <you never can tell : nunca se sabe> **3** SHOW : notarse, hacerse sentir <the strain is beginning to tell : la tensión se empieza a notar>
teller [ˈtɛlər] *n* **1** NARRATOR : narrador *m,* -dora *f* **2** *or* **bank teller** : cajero *m,* -ra *f*
temerity [təˈmɛrəṭi] *n, pl* **-ties** : temeridad *f*
temp [ˈtɛmp] *n* : empleado *m,* -da *f* temporal
temper[1] [ˈtɛmpər] *vt* **1** MODERATE : moderar, temperar **2** ANNEAL : templar (acero, etc.)
temper[2] *n* **1** DISPOSITION : carácter *m,* genio *m* **2** HARDNESS : temple *m,* dureza *f* (de un metal) **3** COMPOSURE : calma *f,* serenidad *f* <to lose one's temper : perder los estribos> **4** RAGE : furia *f* <to fly into a temper : ponerse furioso>
temperament [ˈtɛmpərmənt, -prə-, -pərə-] *n* : temperamento *m*
temperamental [ˌtɛmpərˈmɛntəl, -prə-, -pərə-] *adj* : temperamental
temperance [ˈtɛmprənts] *n* : templanza *f,* temperancia *f*
temperate [ˈtɛmpərət] *adj* : templado (dícese del clima, etc.), moderado
temperature [ˈtɛmpərˌtʃʊr, -prə-, -pərə-, -tʃər] *n* **1** : temperatura *f* **2** FEVER : calentura *f,* fiebre *f*
tempest [ˈtɛmpəst] *n* : tempestad *f*
tempestuous [tɛmˈpɛstʃʊəs] *adj* : tempestuoso
temple [ˈtɛmpəl] *n* **1** : templo *m* (en religión) **2** : sien *f* (en anatomía)
tempo [ˈtɛmˌpoː] *n, pl* **-pi** [-ˌpiː] *or* **-pos** : ritmo *m,* tempo *m* (en música)
temporal [ˈtɛmpərəl] *adj* : temporal
temporarily [ˌtɛmpəˈrɛrəli] *adv* : temporalmente, provisionalmente

temporary ['tɛmpə,rɛri] *adj* : temporal, provisional, provisorio
tempt ['tɛmpt] *vt* : tentar
temptation [tɛmp'teɪʃən] *n* : tentación *f*
tempter ['tɛmptər] *n* : tentador *m*
temptress ['tɛmptrəs] *n* : tentadora *f*
ten[1] ['tɛn] *adj* : diez
ten[2] *n* **1** : diez *m* (número) **2** : decena *f* <tens of thousands : decenas de millares>
tenable ['tɛnəbəl] *adj* : sostenible, defendible
tenacious [tə'neɪʃəs] *adj* : tenaz
tenacity [tə'næsəṭi] *n* : tenacidad *f*
tenancy ['tɛnən*t*si] *n, pl* **-cies** : tenencia *f,* inquilinato *m* (de un inmueble)
tenant ['tɛnənt] *n* : inquilino *m,* -na *f;* arrendatario *m,* -ria *f*
tend ['tɛnd] *vt* : atender, cuidar (de), ocuparse de — *vi* : tender <it tends to benefit the consumer : tiende a beneficiar al consumidor>
tendency ['tɛndən*t*si] *n, pl* **-cies** : tendencia *f,* proclividad *f,* inclinación *f*
tender[1] ['tɛndər] *vt* : entregar, presentar <I tendered my resignation : presenté mi renuncia>
tender[2] *adj* **1** : tierno, blando <tender steak : bistec tierno> **2** AFFECTIONATE, LOVING : tierno, cariñoso, afectuoso **3** DELICATE : tierno, sensible, delicado
tender[3] *n* **1** OFFER : propuesta *f,* oferta *f* (en negocios) **2 legal tender** : moneda *f* de curso legal
tenderize ['tɛndə,raɪz] *vt* **-ized; -izing** : ablandar (carnes)
tenderloin ['tɛndɛr,lɔɪn] *n* : lomo *f* (de res o de puerco)
tenderly ['tɛndərli] *adv* : tiernamente, con ternura
tenderness ['tɛndərnəs] *n* : ternura *f*
tendon ['tɛndən] *n* : tendón *m*
tendril ['tɛndrɪl] *n* : zarcillo *m*
tenement ['tɛnəmənt] *n* : casa *f* de vecindad
tenet ['tɛnət] *n* : principio *m*
tennis ['tɛnəs] *n* : tenis *m*
tenor ['tɛnər] *n* **1** PURPORT : tenor *m,* significado *m* **2** : tenor *m* (en música)
tenpins ['tɛn,pɪnz] *npl* : bolos *mpl,* boliche *m*
tense[1] ['tɛn*t*s] *v* **tensed; tensing** *vt* : tensar — *vi* : tensarse, ponerse tenso
tense[2] *adj* **tenser; tensest 1** TAUT : tenso, tirante **2** NERVOUS : tenso, nervioso
tense[3] *n* : tiempo *m* (de un verbo)
tensely ['tɛn*t*sli] *adv* : tensamente
tenseness ['tɛn*t*snəs] → **tension**
tension ['tɛntʃən] *n* **1** TAUTNESS : tensión *f,* tirantez *f* **2** STRESS : tensión *f,* nerviosismo *m,* estrés *m*
tent ['tɛnt] *n* : tienda *f* de campaña
tentacle ['tɛntɪkəl] *n* : tentáculo *m*
tentative ['tɛntəṭɪv] *adj* **1** HESITANT : indeciso, vacilante **2** PROVISIONAL : sujeto a cambios, provisional
tentatively ['tɛntəṭɪvli] *adv* : provisionalmente
tenth[1] ['tɛnθ] *adj* : décimo
tenth[2] *n* **1** : décimo *m,* -ma *f* (en una serie) **2** : décimo *m,* décima parte *f*
tenuous ['tɛnjʊəs] *adj* : tenue, débil <tenuous reasons : razones poco convincentes>
tenuously ['tɛnjʊəsli] *adv* : tenuemente, ligeramente
tenure ['tɛnjər] *n* : tenencia *f* (de un cargo o una propiedad), titularidad *f* (de un puesto académico)
tepee ['ti:,pi:] *n* : tipi *m*
tepid ['tɛpɪd] *adj* : tibio
term[1] ['tərm] *vt* : calificar de, llamar, nombrar
term[2] *n* **1** PERIOD : término *m,* plazo *m,* período *m* **2** : término *m* (en matemáticas) **3** WORD : término *m,* vocablo *m* <legal terms : términos legales> **4 terms** *npl* CONDITIONS : términos *mpl,* condiciones *fpl* **5 terms** *npl* RELATIONS : relaciones *fpl* <to be on good terms with : tener buenas relaciones con> **6 in terms of** : con respecto a, en cuanto a
terminal[1] ['tərmənəl] *adj* : terminal
terminal[2] *n* **1** : terminal *m,* polo *m* (en electricidad) **2** : terminal *m* (de una computadora) **3** STATION : terminal *f,* estación *f* (de transporte público)
terminate ['tərmə,neɪt] *v* **-nated; -nating** *vi* : terminar(se), concluirse — *vt* : terminar, poner fin a
termination [,tərmə'neɪʃən] *n* : cese *m,* terminación *f*
terminology [,tərmə'nɑlədʒi] *n, pl* **-gies** : terminología *f*
terminus ['tərmənəs] *n, pl* **-ni** [-,naɪ] *or* **-nuses 1** END : término *m,* fin *m* **2** : terminal *f* (de transporte público)
termite ['tər,maɪt] *n* : termita *f*
tern ['tərn] *n* : golondrina *f* de mar
terrace[1] ['tɛrəs] *vt* **-raced; -racing** : formar en terrazas, disponer en bancales
terrace[2] *n* **1** PATIO : terraza *f,* patio *m* **2** : terraplén *m,* terraza *f,* bancal *m* (en agricultura)
terra–cotta [,tɛrə'kɑṭə] *n* : terracota *f*
terrain [tə'reɪn] *n* : terreno *m*
terrapin ['tɛrəpɪn] *n* : galápago *m* norteamericano
terrarium [tə'ræriəm] *n, pl* **-ia** [-iə] *or* **-iums** : terrario *m*
terrestrial [tə'rɛstriəl] *adj* : terrestre
terrible ['tɛrəbəl] *adj* : atroz, horrible, terrible
terribly ['tɛrəbli] *adv* **1** BADLY : muy mal **2** EXTREMELY : terriblemente, extremadamente
terrier ['tɛriər] *n* : terrier *mf*
terrific [tə'rɪfɪk] *adj* **1** FRIGHTFUL : aterrador **2** EXTRAORDINARY : extraordinario, excepcional **3** EXCELLENT : excelente, estupendo
terrify ['tɛrə,faɪ] *vt* **-fied; -fying** : aterrorizar, aterrar, espantar

terrifying [ˈtɛrəˌfaɪɪŋ] *adj* : espantoso, aterrador

territory [ˈtɛrəˌtori] *n, pl* **-ries** : territorio *m* — **territorial** [ˌtɛrəˈtoriəl] *adj*

terror [ˈtɛrər] *n* : terror *m*

terrorism [ˈtɛrərˌɪzəm] *n* : terrorismo *m*

terrorist1 [ˈtɛrərɪst] *adj* : terrorista

terrorist2 *n* : terrorista *mf*

terrorize [ˈtɛrərˌaɪz] *vt* **-ized; -izing** : aterrorizar

terry [ˈtɛri] *n, pl* **-ries** *or* **terry cloth** : (tela de) toalla *f*

terse [ˈtərs] *adj* **terser; tersest** : lacónico, conciso, seco — **tersely** *adv*

tertiary [ˈtərʃiˌɛri] *adj* : terciario

test1 [ˈtɛst] *vt* : examinar, evaluar — *vi* : hacer pruebas

test2 *n* : prueba *f,* examen *m,* test *m* <to put to the test : poner a prueba>

testament [ˈtɛstəmənt] *n* **1** WILL : testamento *m* **2** : Testamento *m* (en la Biblia) <the Old Testament : el Antiguo Testamento>

testicle [ˈtɛstɪkəl] *n* : testículo *m*

testify [ˈtɛstəˌfaɪ] *v* **-fied; -fying** *vi* : testificar, atestar, testimoniar — *vt* : testificar

testimonial [ˌtɛstəˈmoːniəl] *n* **1** REFERENCE : recomendación *f* **2** TRIBUTE : homenaje *m,* tributo *m*

testimony [ˈtɛstəˌmoːni] *n, pl* **-nies** : testimonio *m,* declaración *f*

test tube *n* : probeta *f,* tubo *m* de ensayo

testy [ˈtɛsti] *adj* **-tier; -est** : irritable

tetanus [ˈtɛtənəs] *n* : tétano *m,* tétanos *m*

tête–à–tête [ˌtɛtəˈtɛt, ˌteɪtəˈteɪt] *n* : conversación *f* en privado

tether1 [ˈtɛðər] *vt* : atar (con una cuerda), amarrar

tether2 *n* : atadura *f,* cadena *f,* correa *f*

text [ˈtɛkst] *n* **1** : texto *m* **2** TOPIC : tema *m* **3** → **textbook**

textbook [ˈtɛkstˌbʊk] *n* : libro *m* de texto

textile [ˈtɛkˌstaɪl, ˈtɛkstəl] *n* : textil *m,* tela *f* <the textile industry : la industria textil>

textual [ˈtɛkstʃʊəl] *adj* : textual

texture [ˈtɛkstʃər] *n* : textura *f*

than1 [ˈðæn] *conj* : que, de <it's worth more than that : vale más que eso> <more than you think : más de lo que piensas>

than2 *prep* : que, de <you're better than he is : eres mejor que él> <more than once : más de una vez>

thank [ˈθæŋk] *vt* : agradecer, darle (las) gracias (a alguien) <thank you! : ¡gracias!> <I thanked her for the present : le di las gracias por el regalo> <I thank you for your help : le agradezco su ayuda>

thankful [ˈθæŋkfəl] *adj* : agradecido

thankfully [ˈθæŋkfəli] *adv* **1** GRATEFULLY : con agradecimiento **2** FORTUNATELY : afortunadamente, por suerte <thankfully, it's over : se acabó, gracias a Dios>

thankfulness [ˈθæŋkfəlnəs] *n* : agradecimiento *m,* gratitud *f*

thankless [ˈθæŋkləs] *adj* : ingrato <a thankless task : un trabajo ingrato>

thanks [ˈθæŋks] *npl* **1** : agradecimiento *m* **2** **thanks!** : ¡gracias!

Thanksgiving [θæŋksˈgɪvɪŋ, ˈθæŋksˌ-] *n* : el día de Acción de Gracias (fiesta estadounidense)

that1 [ˈðæt] *adv* (*in negative constructions*) : tan <it's not that expensive : no es tan caro> <not that much : no tanto>

that2 *adj, pl* **those** : ese, esa, aquel, aquella <do you see those children? : ¿ves a aquellos niños?>

that3 *conj & pron* : que <he said that he was afraid : dijo que tenía miedo> <the book that he wrote : el libro que escribió>

that4 *pron, pl* **those** [ˈðoːz] **1** : ése, ésa, eso <that's my father : ése es mi padre> <those are the ones he likes : ésos son los que le gustan> <what's that? : ¿qué es eso?> **2** (*referring to more distant objects or time*) : aquél, aquélla, aquello <those are maples and these are elms : aquéllos son arces y éstos son olmos> <that came to an end : aquello se acabó>

thatch1 [ˈθætʃ] *vt* : cubrir o techar con paja

thatch2 *n* : paja *f* (usada para techos)

thaw1 [ˈθɔ] *vt* : descongelar — *vi* : derretirse (dícese de la nieve), descongelarse (dícese de los alimentos)

thaw2 *n* : deshielo *m*

the1 [ðə, *before vowel sounds usu* ðiː] *adv* **1** (*used to indicate comparison*) <the sooner the better : cuanto más pronto, mejor> <she likes this one the best : éste es el que más le gusta> **2** (*used as a conjunction*) : cuanto <the more I learn, the less I understand : cuanto más aprendo, menos entiendo>

the2 *art* : el, la, los, las <the gloves : los guantes> <the suitcase : la maleta> <forty cookies to the box : cuarenta galletas por caja>

theater *or* **theatre** [ˈθiːətər] *n* **1** : teatro *m* (edificio) **2** DRAMA : teatro *m,* drama *m*

theatrical [θiˈætrɪkəl] *adj* : teatral, dramático

thee [ˈðiː] *pron* : te, ti

theft [ˈθɛft] *n* : robo *m,* hurto *m*

their [ˈðɛr] *adj* : su <their friends : sus amigos>

theirs [ˈðɛrz] *pron* : (el) suyo, (la) suya, (los) suyos, (las) suyas <they came for theirs : vinieron por el suyo> <theirs is bigger : la suya es más grande, la de ellos es más grande> <a brother of theirs : un hermano suyo, un hermano de ellos>

them [ˈðɛm] *pron* **1** (*as a direct object*) : los (*Spain sometimes* les), las <I know them : los conozco> **2** (*as indirect object*) : les, se <I sent them a letter : les mandé una carta> <give it to them : dáselo (a ellos)> **3** (*as object of a preposition*) : ellos, ellas <go with them : ve con ellos> **4** (*for emphasis*) : ellos, ellas <I wasn't expecting them : no los esperaba a ellos>

theme [ˈθiːm] *n* **1** SUBJECT, TOPIC : tema *m* **2** COMPOSITION : composición *f,* trabajo *m* (escrito) **3** : tema *m* (en música)

themselves [ðəmˈsɛlvz, ðɛm-] *pron* **1** (*as a reflexive*) : se, sí <they enjoyed themselves : se divirtieron> <they divided it among themselves : lo repartieron entre sí, se lo repartieron> **2** (*for emphasis*) : ellos mismos, ellas mismas <they built it themselves : ellas mismas lo construyeron>

then¹ [ˈðɛn] *adv* **1** : entonces, en ese tiempo <I was sixteen then : tenía entonces dieciséis años> <since then : desde entonces> **2** NEXT : después, luego <we'll go to Toronto, then to Winnipeg : iremos a Toronto, y luego a Winnipeg> **3** BESIDES : además, aparte <then there's the tax : y aparte está el impuesto> **4** : entonces, en ese caso <if you like music, then you should attend : si te gusta la música, entonces deberías asistir>

then² *adj* : entonces <the then governor of Georgia : el entonces gobernador de Georgia>

thence [ˈðɛnts, ˈθɛnts] *adv* : de ahí, de ahí en adelante

theologian [ˌθiːəˈloːdʒən] *n* : teólogo *m,* -ga *f*

theological [ˌθiːəˈlɑdʒɪkəl] *adj* : teológico

theology [θiˈɑlədʒi] *n, pl* **-gies** : teología *f*

theorem [ˈθiːərəm, ˈθɪrəm] *n* : teorema *m*

theoretical [ˌθiːəˈrɛtɪkəl] *adj* : teórico — **theoretically** *adv*

theorize [ˈθiːəˌraɪz] *vi* **-rized; -rizing** : teorizar

theory [ˈθiːəri, ˈθɪri] *n, pl* **-ries** : teoría *f*

therapeutic [ˌθɛrəˈpjuːtɪk] *adj* : terapéutico — **therapeutically** *adv*

therapist [ˈθɛrəpɪst] *n* : terapeuta *mf*

therapy [ˈθɛrəpi] *n, pl* **-pies** : terapia *f*

there¹ [ˈðær] *adv* **1** : ahí, allí, allá <stand over there : párate ahí> <over there : por allí, por allá> <who's there? : ¿quién es?> **2** : ahí, en esto, en eso <there is where we disagree : en eso es donde no estamos de acuerdo>

there² *pron* **1** (*introducing a sentence or clause*) <there comes a time to decide : llega un momento en que tiene uno que decidir> **2 there is, there are :** hay <there are many children here : aquí hay muchos niños> <there's a good hotel downtown : hay un buen hotel en el centro>

thereabouts [ðærəˈbaʊts, ˈðærəˌ-] *or* **thereabout** [-ˈbaʊt, -ˌbaʊt] *adv* **or thereabouts :** por ahí, más o menos <at five o'clock or thereabouts : por ahí de las cinco>

thereafter [ðærˈæftər] *adv* : después <shortly thereafter : poco después>

thereby [ðærˈbaɪ, ˈðærˌbaɪ] *adv* : de tal modo, de ese manera, así

therefore [ˈðærˌfor] *adv* : por lo tanto, por consiguiente

therein [ðærˈɪn] *adv* **1** : allí adentro, ahí adentro <the contents therein : lo que allí se contiene> **2** : allí, en ese aspecto <therein lies the problem : allí está el problema>

thereof [ðærˈʌv, -ˈɑv] *adv* : de eso, de esto

thereupon [ˈðærəˌpɑn, -ˌpɔn; ˌðærəˈpɑn, -ˈpɔn] *adv* : acto seguido, inmediatamente (después)

therewith [ðærˈwɪð, -ˈwɪθ] *adv* : con eso, con ello

thermal [ˈθərməl] *adj* **1** : térmico (en física) **2** HOT : termal

thermodynamics [ˌθərmodaɪˈnæmɪks] *ns & pl* : termodinámica *f*

thermometer [θərˈmɑmət̬ər] *n* : termómetro *m*

thermos [ˈθərməs] *n* : termo *m*

thermostat [ˈθərməˌstæt] *n* : termostato *m*

thesaurus [θɪˈsɔrəs] *n, pl* **-sauri** [-ˈsɔrˌaɪ] *or* **-sauruses** [-ˈsɔrəsəz] : diccionario *m* de sinónimos

these → **this**

thesis [ˈθiːsɪs] *n, pl* **theses** [ˈθiːˌsiːz] : tesis *f*

they [ˈðeɪ] *pron* : ellos, ellas <they are here : están aquí> <they don't know : ellos no saben>

they'd [ˈðeɪd] (*contraction of* **they had** *or* **they would**) → **have, would**

they'll [ˈðeɪl, ˈðɛl] (*contraction of* **they shall** *or* **they will**) → **shall, will**

they're [ˈðɛr] (*contraction of* **they are**) → **be**

they've [ˈðeɪv] (*contraction of* **they have**) → **have**

thiamine [ˈθaɪəmɪn, -ˌmiːn] *n* : tiamina *f*

thick¹ [ˈθɪk] *adj* **1** : grueso <a thick plank : una tabla gruesa> **2** : espeso, denso <thick syrup : jarabe espeso> — **thickly** *adv*

thick² *n* **1 in the thick of :** en medio de <in the thick of the battle : en lo más reñido de la batalla> **2 through thick and thin :** a las duras y a las maduras

thicken [ˈθɪkən] *vt* : espesar (un líquido) — *vi* : espesarse

thickener [ˈθɪkənər] *n* : espesante *m*

thicket [ˈθɪkət] *n* : matorral *m,* maleza *f,* espesura *f*

thickness [ˈθɪknəs] *n* : grosor *m,* grueso *m,* espesor *m*
thickset [ˈθɪkˈsɛt] *adj* STOCKY : robusto, fornido
thick–skinned [ˈθɪkˈskɪnd] *adj* : poco sensible, que no se ofende fácilmente
thief [ˈθiːf] *n, pl* **thieves** [ˈθiːvz] : ladrón *m,* -drona *f*
thieve [ˈθiːv] *v* **thieved; thieving** : hurtar, robar
thievery [ˈθiːvəri] *n* : hurto *m,* robo *m,* latrocinio *m*
thigh [ˈθaɪ] *n* : muslo *m*
thighbone [ˈθaɪˌboːn] *n* : fémur *m*
thimble [ˈθɪmbəl] *n* : dedal *m*
thin[1] [ˈθɪn] *v* **thinned; thinning** *vt* : hacer menos denso, diluir, aguar (un líquido), enrarecer (un gas) — *vi* : diluirse, aguarse (dícese de un líquido), enrarecerse (dícese de un gas)
thin[2] *adj* **thinner; -est 1** LEAN, SLIM : delgado, esbelto, flaco **2** SPARSE : ralo, escaso <a thin beard : una barba rala> **3** WATERY : claro, aguado, diluido **4** FINE : delgado, fino <thin slices : rebanadas finas>
thing [ˈθɪŋ] *n* **1** AFFAIR, MATTER : cosa *f,* asunto *m* <don't talk about those things : no hables de esas cosas> <how are things? : ¿cómo van las cosas?> **2** ACT, EVENT : cosa *f,* suceso *m,* evento *m* <the flood was a terrible thing : la inundación fue una cosa terrible> **3** OBJECT : cosa *f,* objeto *m* <don't forget your things : no olvides tus cosas>
think [ˈθɪŋk] *v* **thought** [ˈθɔt]; **thinking** *vt* **1** : pensar <I thought to return early : pensaba regresar temprano> **2** BELIEVE : pensar, creer, opinar **3** PONDER : pensar, reflexionar **4** CONCEIVE : ocurrirse, concebir <we've thought up a plan : se nos ha ocurrido un plan> — *vi* **1** REASON : pensar, razonar **2** CONSIDER : pensar, considerar <think of your family first : primero piensa en tu familia>
thinker [ˈθɪŋkər] *n* : pensador *m,* -dora *f*
thinly [ˈθɪnli] *adv* **1** LIGHTLY : ligeramente **2** SPARSELY : escasamente <thinly populated : poco populado> **3** BARELY : apenas
thinness [ˈθɪnnəs] *n* : delgadez *f*
thin–skinned [ˈθɪnˈskɪnd] *adj* : susceptible, muy sensible
third[1] [ˈθərd] *or* **thirdly** [-li] *adv* : en tercer lugar <she came in third : llegó en tercer lugar>
third[2] *adj* : tercero <the third day : el tercer día>
third[3] *n* **1** : tercero *m,* -ra *f* (en una serie) **2** : tercero *m,* tercera parte *f*
third world *n* **the Third World** : el Tercer Mundo *m*
thirst[1] [ˈθərst] *vi* **1** : tener sed **2 to thirst for** DESIRE : tener sed de, estar sediento de
thirst[2] *n* : sed *f*
thirsty [ˈθərsti] *adj* **thirstier; -est** : sediento, que tiene sed <I'm thirsty : tengo sed>
thirteen[1] [ˌθərˈtiːn] *adj* : trece
thirteen[2] *n* : trece *m*
thirteenth[1] [ˌθərˈtiːnθ] *adj* : décimo tercero
thirteenth[2] *n* **1** : decimotercero *m,* -ra *f* (en una serie) **2** : treceavo *m,* treceava parte *f*
thirtieth[1] [ˈθərtiəθ] *adj* : trigésimo
thirtieth[2] *n* **1** : trigésimo *m,* -ma *f* (en una serie) **2** : treintavo *m,* treintava parte *f*
thirty[1] [ˈθərti] *adj* : treinta
thirty[2] *n, pl* **thirties** : treinta *m*
this[1] [ˈðɪs] *adv* : así, a tal punto <this big : así de grande>
this[2] *adj, pl* **these** [ˈðiːz] : este <these things : estas cosas> <read this book : lee este libro>
this[3] *pron, pl* **these** : esto <what's this? : ¿qué es esto?> <this wasn't here yesterday : esto no estaba aquí ayer>
thistle [ˈθɪsəl] *n* : cardo *m*
thong [ˈθɔŋ] *n* **1** STRAP : correa *f,* tira *f* **2** *or* **thong sandal** : chancla *f,* chancleta *f*
thorax [ˈθorˌæks] *n, pl* **-raxes** *or* **-races** [ˈθorəˌsiːz] : tórax *m*
thorn [ˈθɔrn] *n* : espina *f*
thorny [ˈθɔrni] *adj* **thornier; -est** : espinoso
thorough [ˈθəroː] *adj* **1** CONSCIENTIOUS : concienzudo, meticuloso **2** COMPLETE : absoluto, completo — **thoroughly** *adv*
thoroughbred [ˈθəroˌbrɛd] *adj* : de pura sangre (dícese de un caballo)
Thoroughbred *n or* **Thoroughbred horse** : pura sangre *mf*
thoroughfare [ˈθəroˌfær] *n* : vía *f* pública, carretera *f*
thoroughness [ˈθəronəs] *n* : esmero *m,* meticulosidad *f*
those → **that**
thou [ˈðaʊ] *pron* : tú
though[1] [ˈðoː] *adv* **1** HOWEVER, NEVERTHELESS : sin embargo, no obstante **2 as ∼** : como si <as though nothing had happened : como si nada hubiera pasado>
though[2] *conj* : aunque, a pesar de <though it was raining, we went out : salimos a pesar de la lluvia>
thought[1] → **think**
thought[2] [ˈθɔt] *n* **1** THINKING : pensamiento *m,* ideas *fpl* <Western thought : el pensamiento occidental> **2** COGITATION : pensamiento *m,* reflexión *f,* raciocinio *m* **3** IDEA : idea *f,* ocurrencia *f* <it was just a thought : fue sólo una idea>
thoughtful [ˈθɔtfəl] *adj* **1** PENSIVE : pensativo, meditabundo **2** CONSIDERATE : considerado, atento, cortés — **thoughtfully** *adv*
thoughtfulness [ˈθɔtfəlnəs] *n* : consideración *f,* atención *f,* cortesía *f*

thoughtless ['θɔtləs] *adj* **1** CARELESS : descuidado, negligente **2** INCONSIDERATE : desconsiderado — **thoughtlessly** *adv*
thousand¹ ['θaʊzənd] *adj* : mil
thousand² *n, pl* **-sands** *or* **-sand** : mil *m*
thousandth¹ ['θaʊzəntθ] *adj* : milésimo
thousandth² *n* **1** : milésimo *m*, -ma *f* (en una serie) **2** : milésimo *m*, milésima parte *f*
thrash ['θræʃ] *vt* **1** → **thresh 2** BEAT : golpear, azotar, darle una paliza (a alguien) **3** FLAIL : sacudir, agitar bruscamente
thread¹ ['θrɛd] *vt* **1** : enhilar, enhebrar (una aguja) **2** STRING : ensartar (cuentas en un hilo) **3 to thread one's way** : abrirse paso
thread² *n* **1** : hilo *m*, hebra *f* <needle and thread : aguja e hilo> <the thread of an argument : el hilo de un debate> **2** : rosca *f*, filete *m* (de un tornillo)
threadbare ['θrɛd'bær] *adj* **1** SHABBY, WORN : raído, gastado **2** TRITE : trillado, tópico, manido
threat ['θrɛt] *n* : amenaza *f*
threaten ['θrɛtən] *v* : amenazar
threatening ['θrɛtənɪŋ] *adj* : amenazador — **threateningly** *adv*
three¹ ['θri:] *adj* : tres
three² *n* : tres *m*
threefold ['θri:ˌfo:ld] *adj* TRIPLE : triple
three hundred¹ *adj* : trescientos
three hundred² *n* : trescientos *m*
threescore ['θri:'skor] *adj* SIXTY : sesenta
thresh ['θrɛʃ] *vt* : trillar (grano)
thresher ['θrɛʃər] *n* : trilladora *f*
threshold ['θrɛʃˌho:ld, -ˌo:ld] *n* : umbral *m*
threw → **throw¹**
thrice ['θraɪs] *adv* : tres veces
thrift ['θrɪft] *n* : economía *f*, frugalidad *f*
thriftless ['θrɪftləs] *adj* : despilfarrador, manirroto
thrifty ['θrɪfti] *adj* **thriftier; -est** : económico, frugal — **thriftily** ['θrɪftəli] *adv*
thrill¹ ['θrɪl] *vt* : emocionar — *vi* **to thrill to** : dejarse conmover por, estremecerse con
thrill² *n* : emoción *f*
thriller ['θrɪlər] *n* **1** : evento *m* emocionante **2** : obra *f* de suspenso
thrilling ['θrɪlɪŋ] *adj* : emocionante, excitante
thrive ['θraɪv] *vi* **throve** ['θro:v] *or* **thrived; thriven** ['θrɪvən] **1** FLOURISH : florecer, crecer abundantemente **2** PROSPER : prosperar
throat ['θro:t] *n* : garganta *f*
throaty ['θro:ti] *adj* **throatier; -est** : ronco (dícese de la voz)
throb¹ ['θrɑb] *vi* **throbbed; throbbing** : palpitar, latir (dícese del corazón), vibrar (dícese de un motor, etc.)
throb² *n* : palpitación *f*, latido *m*, vibración *f*
throe ['θro:] *n* **1** PAIN, SPASM : espasmo *m*, dolor *m* <the throes of childbirth : los dolores de parto> **2 throes** *npl* : lucha *f* larga y ardua <in the throes of : en el medio de>
throne ['θro:n] *n* : trono *m*
throng¹ ['θrɔŋ] *vt* CROWD : atestar, atiborrar, llenar — *vi* : aglomerarse, amontonarse
throng² *n* : muchedumbre *f*, gentío *m*, multitud *f*
throttle¹ ['θrɑtəl] *vt* **-tled; -tling 1** STRANGLE : estrangular, ahogar **2 to throttle down** : desacelerar (un motor)
throttle² *n* **1** : válvula *f* reguladora **2 at full throttle** : a toda máquina
through¹ ['θru:] *adv* **1** : a través, de un lado a otro <let them through : déjenlos pasar> **2** : de principio a fin <she read the book through : leyó el libro de principio a fin> **3** COMPLETELY : completamente <soaked through : completamente empapado>
through² *adj* **1** DIRECT : directo <a through train : un tren directo> **2** FINISHED : terminado, acabado <we're through : hemos terminado>
through³ *prep* **1** : a través de, por <through the door : por la puerta> <a road through the woods : un camino que atraviesa el bosque> **2** BETWEEN : entre <a path through the trees : un sendero entre los árboles> **3** BECAUSE OF : a causa de, como consecuencia de **4** (*in expressions of time*) <through the night : durante la noche> <to go through an experience : pasar por una experiencia> **5** : a, hasta <from Monday through Friday : de lunes a viernes>
throughout¹ [θru:'aʊt] *adv* **1** EVERYWHERE : por todas partes **2** THROUGH : desde el principio hasta el fin de (algo)
throughout² *prep* **1** : en todas partes de, a través de <throughout the United States : en todo Estados Unidos> **2** : de principio a fin de, durante <throughout the winter : durante todo el invierno>
throve → **thrive**
throw¹ ['θro:] *vt* **threw** ['θru:]; **thrown** ['θro:n]; **throwing 1** TOSS : tirar, lanzar, echar, arrojar, aventar *Col, Mex* <to throw a ball : tirar una pelota> **2** UNSEAT : desmontar (a un jinete) **3** CAST : proyectar <it threw a long shadow : proyectó una sombra larga> **4 to throw a party** : dar una fiesta **5 to throw into confusion** : desconcertar **6 to throw out** DISCARD : botar, tirar (en la basura)

throw[2] *n* TOSS : tiro *m,* tirada *f,* lanzamiento *m,* lance *m* (de dados)
thrower [ˈθroːər] *n* : lanzador *m,* -dora *f*
throw up *v* VOMIT : vomitar, devolver
thrush [ˈθrʌʃ] *n* : tordo *m,* zorzal *m*
thrust[1] [ˈθrʌst] *vt* **thrust; thrusting 1** SHOVE : empujar bruscamente **2** PLUNGE, STAB : apuñalar, clavar <he thrust a dagger into her heart : la apuñaló en el corazón> **3 to thrust one's way** : abrirse paso **4 to thrust upon** : imponer a
thrust[2] *n* **1** PUSH, SHOVE : empujón *m,* empellón *m* **2** LUNGE : estocada *f* (en esgrima) **3** IMPETUS : ímpetu *m,* impulso *m,* propulsión *f* (de un motor)
thud[1] [ˈθʌd] *vi* **thudded; thudding** : producir un ruido sordo
thud[2] *n* : ruido *m* sordo (que produce un objeto al caer)
thug [ˈθʌg] *n* : matón *m*
thumb[1] [ˈθʌm] *vt* : hojear (con el pulgar)
thumb[2] *n* : pulgar *m,* dedo *m* pulgar
thumbnail [ˈθʌm,neɪl] *n* : uña *f* del pulgar
thumbtack [ˈθʌm,tæk] *n* : tachuela *f,* chinche *f*
thump[1] [ˈθʌmp] *vt* POUND : golpear, aporrear — *vi* : latir con vehemencia (dícese del corazón)
thump[2] *n* THUD : ruido *m* sordo
thunder[1] [ˈθʌndər] *vi* **1** : tronar <it rained and thundered all night : llovió y tronó durante la noche> **2** BOOM : retumbar, bramar, resonar — *vt* ROAR, SHOUT : decir a gritos, vociferar
thunder[2] *n* : truenos *mpl*
thunderbolt [ˈθʌndər,boːlt] *n* : rayo *m*
thunderclap [ˈθʌndər,klæp] *n* : trueno *m*
thunderous [ˈθʌndərəs] *adj* : atronador, ensordecedor, estruendoso
thundershower [ˈθʌndər,ʃaʊər] *n* : lluvia *f* con truenos y relámpagos
thunderstorm [ˈθʌndər,stɔrm] *n* : tormenta *f* con truenos y relámpagos
thunderstruck [ˈθʌndər,strʌk] *adj* : atónito
Thursday [ˈθərz,deɪ, -di] *n* : jueves *m*
thus [ˈðʌs] *adv* **1** : así, de esta manera **2** SO : hasta (cierto punto) <the weather's been nice thus far : hasta ahora ha hecho buen tiempo> **3** HENCE : por consiguiente, por lo tanto
thwart [ˈθwɔrt] *vt* : frustrar
thy [ˈðaɪ] *adj* : tu
thyme [ˈtaɪm, ˈθaɪm] *n* : tomillo *m*
thyroid [ˈθaɪ,rɔɪd] *n or* **thyroid gland** : tiroides *mf,* glándula *f* tiroidea
thyself [ðaɪˈsɛlf] *pron* : ti, ti mismo
tiara [tiˈærə, -ˈɑr-] *n* : diadema *f*
tibia [ˈtɪbiə] *n, pl* **-iae** [-bi,iː] : tibia *f*
tic [ˈtɪk] *n* : tic *m*
tick[1] [ˈtɪk] *vi* **1** : hacer tictac **2** OPERATE, RUN : operar, andar (dícese de un mecanismo) <what makes him tick? : ¿qué es lo que lo mueve?> — *vt or* **to tick off** CHECK : marcar
tick[2] *n* **1** : tictac *m* (de un reloj) **2** CHECK : marca *f* **3** : garrapata *f* (insecto)
ticket[1] [ˈtɪkət] *vt* LABEL : etiquetar
ticket[2] *n* **1** : boleto *m,* entrada *f* (de un espectáculo), pasaje *m* (de avión, tren, etc.) **2** SLATE : lista *f* de candidatos
tickle[1] [ˈtɪkəl] *v* **-led; -ling** *vt* **1** AMUSE : divertir, hacerle gracia (a alguien) **2** : hacerle cosquillas (a alguien) <don't tickle me! : ¡no me hagas cosquillas!> — *vi* : picar
tickle[2] *n* : cosquilla *f*
ticklish [ˈtɪkəlɪʃ] *adj* **1** : cosquilloso (dícese de una persona) **2** DELICATE, TRICKY : delicado, peliagudo
tidal [ˈtaɪdəl] *adj* : de marea, relativo a la marea
tidal wave *n* : maremoto *m*
tidbit [ˈtɪd,bɪt] *n* **1** BITE, SNACK : bocado *m,* golosina *f* **2** : dato *m* o noticia *f* interesante <useful tidbits of information : informaciones útiles>
tide[1] [ˈtaɪd] *vt* **tided; tiding** *or* **to tide over** : proveer lo necesario para aguantar una dificultad <this money will tide you over until you find work : este dinero te mantendrá hasta que encuentres empleo>
tide[2] *n* **1** : marea *f* **2** CURRENT : corriente *f* (de eventos, opiniones, etc.)
tidily [ˈtaɪdəli] *adv* : ordenadamente
tidiness [ˈtaɪdinəs] *n* : aseo *m,* limpieza *f,* orden *m*
tidings [ˈtaɪdɪŋz] *npl* : nuevas *fpl*
tidy[1] [ˈtaɪdi] *vt* **-died; -dying** : asear, limpiar, poner en orden
tidy[2] *adj* **-dier; -est 1** CLEAN, NEAT : limpio, aseado, en orden **2** SUBSTANTIAL : grande, considerable <a tidy sum : una suma considerable>
tie[1] [ˈtaɪ] *v* **tied; tying** *or* **tieing** *vt* **1** : atar, amarrar <to tie a knot : atar un nudo> <to tie one's shoelaces : atarse los cordones> **2** BIND, UNITE : ligar, atar **3** : empatar <they tied the score : empataron el marcador> — *vi* : empatar <the two teams were tied : los dos equipos empataron>
tie[2] *n* **1** : ligadura *f,* cuerda *f,* cordón *m* (para atar algo) **2** BOND, LINK : atadura *f,* ligadura *f,* vínculo *m,* lazo *m* <family ties : lazos familiares> **3** *or* **railroad tie** : traviesa *f* **4** DRAW : empate *m* (en deportes) **5** NECKTIE : corbata *f*
tier [ˈtɪr] *n* : hilera *f,* escalón *m*
tiff [ˈtɪf] *n* : disgusto *m,* disputa *f*
tiger [ˈtaɪgər] *n* : tigre *m*
tight[1] [ˈtaɪt] *adv* TIGHTLY : bien, fuerte <shut it tight : ciérralo bien>
tight[2] *adj* **1** : bien cerrado, hermético <a tight seal : un cierre hermético> **2** STRICT : estricto, severo **3** TAUT : tirante, tenso **4** SNUG : apretado, ajustado, ceñido <a tight dress : un vestido ceñido> **5** DIFFICULT : difícil <to be in a tight spot : estar en un aprieto> **6** STINGY : apretado, avaro, agarrado

fam 7 CLOSE : reñido <a tight game : un juego reñido> 8 SCARCE : escaso <money is tight : escasea el dinero>

tighten ['taɪtən] *vt* : tensar (una cuerda, etc.), apretar (un nudo, un tornillo, etc.), apretarse (el cinturón), reforzar (las reglas)

tightly ['taɪtli] *adv* : bien, fuerte

tightness ['taɪtnəs] *n* : lo apretado, lo tenso, tensión *f*

tightrope ['taɪt,ro:p] *n* : cuerda *f* floja

tights ['taɪts] *npl* : leotardo *m,* malla *f*

tightwad ['taɪt,wɑd] *n* : avaro *m,* -ra *f;* tacaño *m,* -ña *f*

tigress ['taɪgrəs] *n* : tigresa *f*

tile[1] ['taɪl] *vt* **tiled; tiling** : embaldosar (un piso), revestir de azulejos (una pared), tejar (un techo)

tile[2] *n* **1** *or* **floor tile** : losa *f,* baldosa *f,* mosaico *m Mex* (de un piso) **2** : azulejo *m* (de una pared) **3** : teja *f* (de un techo)

till[1] ['tɪl] *vt* : cultivar, labrar

till[2] *n* : caja *f,* caja *f* registradora

till[3] *prep & conj* → **until**

tiller ['tɪlər] *n* **1** : cultivador *m,* -dora *f* (de la tierra) **2** : caña *f* del timón (de un barco)

tilt[1] ['tɪlt] *vt* : ladear, inclinar — *vi* : ladearse, inclinarse

tilt[2] *n* **1** SLANT : inclinación *f* **2 at full tilt** : a toda velocidad

timber ['tɪmbər] *n* **1** : madera *f* (para construcción) **2** BEAM : viga *f*

timberland ['tɪmbər,lænd] *n* : bosque *m* maderero

timbre ['tæmbər, 'tɪm-] *n* : timbre *m*

time[1] ['taɪm] *vt* **timed; timing 1** SCHEDULE : fijar la hora de, calcular el momento oportuno para **2** CLOCK : cronometrar, medir el tiempo de (una competencia, etc.)

time[2] *n* **1** : tiempo *m* <the passing of time : el paso del tiempo> <she doesn't have time : no tiene tiempo> **2** MOMENT : tiempo *m,* momento *m* <this is not the time to bring it up : no es el momento de sacar el tema> **3** : vez *f* <she called you three times : te llamó tres veces> <three times greater : tres veces mayor> **4** AGE : tiempo *m,* era *f* <in your grandparents' time : en el tiempo de tus abuelos> **5** TEMPO : tiempo *m,* ritmo *m* (en música) **6** : hora *f* <what time is it? : ¿qué hora es?> <at the usual time : a la hora acostumbrada> <to keep time : ir a la hora> <to lose time : atrasar> **7** EXPERIENCE : rato *m,* experiencia *f* <we had a nice time together : pasamos juntos un rato agradable> <to have a rough time : pasarlo mal> <have a good time! : ¡que se diviertan!> **8 at times** SOMETIMES : a veces **9 for the time being** : por el momento, de momento **10 from time to time** OCCASIONALLY : de vez en cuando **11 in time** PUNCTUALLY : a tiempo **12 in time** EVENTUALLY : con el tiempo **13 time after time** : una y otra vez

timekeeper ['taɪm,ki:pər] *n* : cronometrador *m,* -dora *f*

timeless ['taɪmləs] *adj* : eterno

timely ['taɪmli] *adj* **-lier; -est** : oportuno

timepiece ['taɪm,pi:s] *n* : reloj *m*

timer ['taɪmər] *n* : temporizador *m,* cronómetro *m*

times ['taɪmz] *prep* : por <3 times 4 is 12 : 3 por 4 son 12>

timetable ['taɪm,teɪbəl] *n* : horario *m*

timid ['tɪmɪd] *adj* : tímido — **timidly** *adv*

timidity [tə'mɪdəti] *n* : timidez *f*

timorous ['tɪmərəs] *adj* : timorato, miedoso

timpani ['tɪmpəni] *npl* : timbales *mpl*

tin ['tɪn] *n* **1** : estaño *m,* hojalata *f* (metal) **2** CAN : lata *f,* bote *m,* envase *m*

tincture ['tɪŋktʃər] *n* : tintura *f*

tinder ['tɪndər] *n* : yesca *f*

tine ['taɪn] *n* : diente *m* (de un tenedor, etc.)

tinfoil ['tɪn,fɔɪl] *n* : papel *m* (de) aluminio

tinge[1] ['tɪndʒ] *vt* **tinged; tingeing** *or* **tinging** ['tɪndʒɪŋ] TINT : matizar, teñir ligeramente

tinge[2] *n* **1** TINT : matiz *m,* tinte *m* sutil **2** TOUCH : dejo *m,* sensación *f* ligera

tingle[1] ['tɪŋgəl] *vi* **-gled; -gling** : sentir (un) hormigueo, sentir (un) cosquilleo

tingle[2] *n* : hormigueo *m,* cosquilleo *m*

tinker ['tɪŋkər] *vi* **to tinker with** : arreglar con pequeños ajustes, toquetear (con intento de arreglar)

tinkle[1] ['tɪŋkəl] *vi* **-kled; -kling** : tintinear

tinkle[2] *n* : tintineo *m*

tinsel ['tɪntsəl] *n* : oropel *m*

tint[1] ['tɪnt] *vt* : teñir, colorar

tint[2] *n* : tinte *m*

tiny ['taɪni] *adj* **-nier; -est** : diminuto, minúsculo

tip[1] ['tɪp] *v* **tipped; tipping** *vt* **1** *or* **to tip over** : volcar, voltear, hacer caer **2** TILT : ladear, inclinar <to tip one's hat : saludar con el sombrero> **3** TAP : tocar, golpear ligeramente **4** : darle una propina (a un mesero, etc.) <I tipped him $5 : le di $5 de propina> **5** : adornar o cubrir la punta de <wings tipped in red : alas que tienen las puntas rojas> **6 to tip off** : dar información a — *vi* TILT : ladearse, inclinarse

tip[2] *n* **1** END, POINT : punta *f,* extremo *m* <on the tip of one's tongue : en la punta de la lengua> **2** GRATUITY : propina *f* **3** ADVICE, INFORMATION : consejo *m,* información *f* (confidencial)

tip-off ['tɪp,ɔf] *n* **1** SIGN : indicación *f,* señal *f* **2** TIP : información *f* (confidencial)

tipple [ˈtɪpəl] *vi* **-pled; -pling** : tomarse unas copas

tipsy [ˈtɪpsi] *adj* **-sier; -est** : achispado

tiptoe[1] [ˈtɪpˌtoː] *vi* **-toed; -toeing** : caminar de puntillas

tiptoe[2] *adv* : de puntillas

tiptoe[3] *n* : punta *f* del pie

tip–top[1] [ˈtɪpˈtɑp, -ˌtɑp] *adj* EXCELLENT : excelente

tip–top[2] *n* SUMMIT : cumbre *f,* cima *f*

tirade [ˈtaɪˌreɪd] *n* : diatriba *f*

tire[1] [ˈtaɪr] *v* **tired; tiring** *vt* : cansar, agotar, fatigar — *vi* : cansarse

tire[2] *n* : llanta *f,* neumático *m,* goma *f*

tired [ˈtaɪrd] *adj* : cansado, agotado, fatigado <to get tired : cansarse>

tireless [ˈtaɪrləs] *adj* : incansable, infatigable — **tirelessly** *adv*

tiresome [ˈtaɪrsəm] *adj* : fastidioso, pesado, tedioso — **tiresomely** *adv*

tissue [ˈtɪˌʃuː] *n* **1** : pañuelo *m* de papel **2** : tejido *m* <lung tissue : tejido pulmonar>

titanic [taɪˈtænɪk, tə-] *adj* GIGANTIC : titánico, gigantesco

titanium [taɪˈteɪniəm, tə-] *n* : titanio *m*

titillate [ˈtɪtəlˌeɪt] *vt* **-lated; -lating** : excitar, estimular placenteramente

title[1] [ˈtaɪtəl] *vt* **-tled; -tling** : titular, intitular

title[2] *n* : título *m*

titter[1] [ˈtɪtər] *vi* GIGGLE : reírse tontamente

titter[2] *n* : risita *f,* risa *f* tonta

tizzy [ˈtɪzi] *n, pl* **tizzies** : estado *m* agitado o nervioso <I'm all in a tizzy : estoy todo alterado>

TNT [ˌtiːˌɛnˈtiː] *n* : TNT *m*

to[1] [ˈtuː] *adv* **1** : a un estado consciente <to come to : volver en sí> **2 to and fro** : de aquí para allá, de un lado para otro

to[2] *prep* **1** (*indicating a place*) : a <to go to the doctor : ir al médico> <I'm going to John's : voy a la casa de John> **2** TOWARD : a, hacia <two miles to the south : dos millas hacia el sur> **3** ON : en, sobre <apply salve to the wound : póngale ungüento a la herida> **4** UP TO : hasta, a <to a degree : hasta cierto grado> <from head to toe : de pies a cabeza> **5** (*in expressions of time*) <it's quarter to seven : son las siete menos cuarto> **6** UNTIL : a, hasta <from May to December : de mayo a diciembre> **7** (*indicating belonging or possession*) : de, a <the key to the lock : la llave del candado> **8** (*indicating response*) : a <dancing to the rhythm : bailando al compás> **9** (*indicating comparison or proportion*) : a <it's similar to mine : es parecido al mío> <they won 4 to 2 : ganaron 4 a 2> **10** (*indicating agreement or conformity*) : a, de acuerdo con <made to order : hecho a la orden> <to my knowledge : a mi saber> **11** (*indicating inclusion*) : en cada, por <twenty to the box : veinte por caja> **12** (*used to form the infinitive*) <to understand : entender> <to go away : irse>

toad [ˈtoːd] *n* : sapo *m*

toadstool [ˈtoːdˌstuːl] *n* : hongo *m* (no comestible)

toady [ˈtoːdi] *n, pl* **toadies** : adulador *m,* -dora *f*

toast[1] [ˈtoːst] *vt* **1** : tostar (pan) **2** : brindar por <to toast the victors : brindar por los vencedores> **3** WARM : calentar <to toast oneself : calentarse>

toast[2] *n* **1** : pan *m* tostado, tostadas *fpl* **2** : brindis *m* <to propose a toast : proponer un brindis>

toaster [ˈtoːstər] *n* : tostador *m*

tobacco [təˈbækoː] *n, pl* **-cos** : tabaco *m*

toboggan[1] [təˈbɑgən] *vi* : deslizarse en tobogán

toboggan[2] *n* : tobogán *m*

today[1] [təˈdeɪ] *adv* **1** : hoy <she arrives today : hoy llega> **2** NOWADAYS : hoy en día

today[2] *n* : hoy *m* <today is a holiday : hoy es día de fiesta>

toddle [ˈtɑdəl] *vi* **-dled; -dling** : hacer pininos, hacer pinitos

toddler [ˈtɑdələr] *n* : niño *m* pequeño, niña *f* pequeña (que comienza a caminar)

to–do [təˈduː] *n, pl* **to–dos** [-ˈduːz] FUSS : lío *m,* alboroto *m*

toe [ˈtoː] *n* : dedo *m* del pie

toenail [ˈtoːˌneɪl] *n* : uña *f* del pie

toffee *or* **toffy** [ˈtɔfi, ˈtɑ-] *n, pl* **toffees** *or* **toffies** : caramelo *m* elaborado con azúcar y mantequilla

toga [ˈtoːgə] *n* : toga *f*

together [təˈgɛðər] *adv* **1** : juntamente, juntos (el uno con el otro) <Susan and Sarah work together : Susan y Sarah trabajan juntas> **2 ~ with** : junto con

togetherness [təˈgɛðərnəs] *n* : unión *f,* compañerismo *m*

togs [ˈtɑgz, ˈtɔgz] *npl* : ropa *f*

toil[1] [ˈtɔɪl] *vi* : trabajar arduamente

toil[2] *n* : trabajo *m* arduo

toilet [ˈtɔɪlət] *n* **1** : arreglo *m* personal **2** BATHROOM : (cuarto de) baño *m,* servicios *mpl* (públicos), sanitario *m Col, Mex, Ven* **3** : inodoro *m* <to flush the toilet : jalar la cadena>

toilet paper *n* : papel *m* higiénico

toiletries [ˈtɔɪlətriz] *npl* : artículos *mpl* de tocador

token [ˈtoːkən] *n* **1** PROOF, SIGN : prueba *f,* muestra *f,* señal *m* **2** SYMBOL : símbolo *m* **3** SOUVENIR : recuerdo *m* **4** : ficha *f* (para transporte público, etc.)

told → **tell**

tolerable [ˈtɑlərəbəl] *adj* : tolerable — **tolerably** [-bli] *adv*

tolerance [ˈtɑlərənts] *n* : tolerancia *f*

tolerant [ˈtɑlərənt] *adj* : tolerante — **tolerantly** *adv*

tolerate ['tɑlə,reɪt] *vt* **-ated; -ating 1** ACCEPT : tolerar, aceptar **2** BEAR, ENDURE : tolerar, aguantar, soportar

toleration [,tɑlə'reɪʃən] *n* : tolerancia *f*

toll[1] ['to:l] *vt* : tañer, sonar (una campana) — *vi* : sonar, doblar (dícese de las campanas)

toll[2] *n* **1** : peaje *m* (de una carretera, un puente, etc.) **2** CASUALTIES : pérdida *f*, número *m* de víctimas **3** TOLLING : tañido *m* (de campanas)

tollbooth ['to:l,bu:θ] *n* : caseta *f* de peaje

tollgate ['to:l,geɪt] *n* : barrera *f* de peaje

tomahawk ['tɑmə,hɔk] *n* : hacha *f* de guerra (de los indígenas norteamericanos)

tomato [tə'meɪt̬o, -'mɑ-] *n, pl* **-toes** : tomate *m*

tomb ['tu:m] *n* : sepulcro *m*, tumba *f*

tomboy ['tɑm,bɔɪ] *n* : marimacho *mf*; niña *f* que se porta como muchacho

tombstone ['tu:m,sto:n] *n* : lápida *f*

tomcat ['tɑm,kæt] *n* : gato *m* (macho)

tome ['to:m] *n* : tomo *m*

tomorrow[1] [tə'mɑro] *adv* : mañana

tomorrow[2] *n* : mañana *m*

tom–tom ['tɑm,tɑm] *n* : tam-tam *m*

ton ['tən] *n* : tonelada *f*

tone[1] ['to:n] *vt* **toned; toning 1** *or* **to tone down** : atenuar, suavizar, moderar **2** *or* **to tone up** STRENGTHEN : tonificar, vigorizar

tone[2] *n* : tono *m* <in a friendly tone : en tono amistoso> <a greyish tone : un tono grisáceo>

tongs ['tɑŋz, 'tɔŋz] *npl* : tenazas *fpl*

tongue ['tʌŋ] *n* **1** : lengua *f* **2** LANGUAGE : lengua *f*, idioma *m*

tongue–tied ['tʌŋ,taɪd] *adj* **to get tongue–tied** : trabársele la lengua a uno

tonic[1] ['tɑnɪk] *adj* : tónico

tonic[2] *n* **1** : tónico *m* **2** *or* **tonic water** : tónica *f*

tonight[1] [tə'naɪt] *adv* : esta noche

tonight[2] *n* : esta noche *f*

tonsil ['tɑn*t*səl] *n* : amígdala *f*, angina *f Mex*

tonsillitis [,tɑn*t*sə'laɪt̬əs] *n* : amigdalitis *f*, anginas *fpl Mex*

too ['tu:] *adv* **1** ALSO : también **2** EXCESSIVELY : demasiado <it's too hot in here : aquí hace demasiado calor>

took → **take**[1]

tool[1] ['tu:l] *vt* **1** : fabricar, confeccionar (con herramientas) **2** EQUIP : instalar maquinaria en (una fábrica)

tool[2] *n* : herramienta *f*

toolbox ['tu:l,bɑks] *n* : caja *f* de herramientas

toot[1] ['tu:t] *vt* : sonar (un claxon o un pito)

toot[2] *n* : pitido *m*, bocinazo *m* (de un claxon)

tooth ['tu:θ] *n, pl* **teeth** ['ti:θ] : diente *m*

toothache ['tu:θ,eɪk] *n* : dolor *m* de muelas

toothbrush ['tu:θ,brʌʃ] *n* : cepillo *m* de dientes

toothless ['tu:θləs] *adj* : desdentado

toothpaste ['tu:θ,peɪst] *n* : pasta *f* de dientes, crema *f* dental, dentífrico *m*

toothpick ['tu:θ,pɪk] *n* : palillo *m* (de dientes), mondadientes *m*

top[1] ['tɑp] *vt* **topped; topping 1** COVER : cubrir, coronar **2** SURPASS : sobrepasar, superar **3** CLEAR : pasar por encima de

top[2] *adj* : superior <the top shelf : la repisa superior> <one of the top lawyers : uno de los mejores abogados>

top[3] *n* **1** : parte *f* superior, cumbre *f*, cima *f* (de un monte, etc.) <to climb to the top : subir a la cumbre> **2** COVER : tapa *f*, cubierta *f* **3** : trompo *m* (juguete) **4 on top of** : encima de

topaz ['to:,pæz] *n* : topacio *m*

topcoat ['tɑp,ko:t] *n* : sobretodo *m*, abrigo *m*

topic ['tɑpɪk] *n* : tema *f*, tópico *m*

topical ['tɑpɪkəl] *adj* : de interés actual

topmost ['tɑp,mo:st] *adj* : más alto

top–notch ['tɑp'nɑtʃ] *adj* : de lo mejor, de primera categoría

topographic [,tɑpə'græfɪk,] *or* **topographical** [-fɪkəl] *adj* : topográfico

topography [tə'pɑgrəfi] *n, pl* **-phies** : topografía *f*

topple ['tɑpəl] *v* **-pled; -pling** *vi* : caerse, venirse abajo — *vt* : volcar, derrocar (un gobierno, etc.)

topsoil ['tɑp,sɔɪl] *n* : capa *f* superior del suelo

topsy–turvy [,tɑpsi'tərvi] *adv & adj* : patas arriba, al revés

torch ['tɔrtʃ] *n* : antorcha *f*

tore → **tear**[1]

torment[1] [tɔr'mɛnt, 'tɔr,-] *vt* : atormentar, torturar, martirizar

torment[2] ['tɔr,mɛnt] *n* : tormento *m*, suplicio *m*, martirio *m*

tormentor [tɔr'mɛntər] *n* : atormentador *m*, -dora *f*

torn → **tear**[1]

tornado [tɔr'neɪdo] *n, pl* **-does** *or* **-dos** : tornado *m*

torpedo[1] [tɔr'pi:do] *vt* : torpedear

torpedo[2] *n, pl* **-does** : torpedo *m*

torpid ['tɔrpɪd] *adj* **1** SLUGGISH : aletargado **2** APATHETIC : apático

torpor ['tɔrpər] *n* : letargo *m*, apatía *f*

torrent ['tɔrənt] *n* : torrente *m*

torrential [tɔ'rɛntʃəl, tə-] *adj* : torrencial

torrid ['tɔrɪd] *adj* : tórrido

torso ['tɔr,so:] *n, pl* **-sos** *or* **-si** [-,si:] : torso *m*

tortilla [tɔr'ti:jə] *n* : tortilla *f*

tortoise ['tɔrt̬əs] *n* : tortuga *f* (terrestre)

tortoiseshell ['tɔrt̬əs,ʃɛl] *n* : carey *m*, concha *f*

tortuous ['tɔrtʃuəs] *adj* : tortuoso

torture[1] [ˈtɔrtʃər] *vt* **-tured; -turing** : torturar, atormentar

torture[2] *n* : tortura *f,* tormento *m* <it was sheer torture! : ¡fue un verdadero suplicio!>

torturer [ˈtɔrtʃərər] *n* : torturador *m,* -dora *f*

toss[1] [ˈtɔs, ˈtɑs] *vt* **1** AGITATE, SHAKE : sacudir, agitar, mezclar (una ensalada) **2** THROW : tirar, echar, lanzar — *vi* : sacudirse, moverse agitadamente <to toss and turn : dar vueltas>

toss[2] *n* THROW : lanzamiento *m,* tiro *m,* tirada *f,* lance *m* (de dados, etc.)

toss–up [ˈtɔsˌʌp] *n* : posibilidad *f* igual <it's a toss-up : quizá sí, quizá no>

tot [ˈtɑt] *n* : pequeño *m,* -ña *f*

total[1] [ˈtoːtəl] *vt* **-taled** *or* **-talled; -taling** *or* **-talling 1** *or* **to total up** ADD : sumar, totalizar **2** AMOUNT TO : ascender a, llegar a

total[2] *adj* : total, completo, absoluto — **totally** *adv*

total[3] *n* : total *m*

totalitarian [toːˌtæləˈtɛriən] *adj* : totalitario

totalitarianism [toːˌtæləˈtɛriəˌnɪzəm] *n* : totalitarismo *m*

totality [toːˈtæləṱi] *n, pl* **-ties** : totalidad *f*

tote [ˈtoːt] *vt* **toted; toting** : cargar, llevar

totem [ˈtoːtəm] *n* : tótem *m*

totter [ˈtɑtər] *vi* : tambalearse

touch[1] [ˈtʌtʃ] *vt* **1** FEEL, HANDLE : tocar, tentar **2** AFFECT, MOVE : conmover, afectar, tocar <his gesture touched our hearts : su gesto nos tocó el corazón> — *vi* : tocarse

touch[2] *n* **1** : tacto *m* (sentido) **2** DETAIL : toque *m,* detalle *m* <a touch of color : un toque de color> **3** BIT : pizca *f,* gota *f,* poco *m* **4** ABILITY : habilidad *f* <to lose one's touch : perder la habilidad> **5** CONTACT : contacto *m,* comunicación *f* <to keep in touch : mantenerse en contacto>

touchdown [ˈtʌtʃˌdaʊn] *n* : touchdown *m* (en futbol americano)

touch up *vt* : retocar

touchy [ˈtʌtʃi] *adj* **touchier; -est 1** : sensible, susceptible (dícese de una persona) **2** : delicado <a touchy subject : un tema delicado>

tough[1] [ˈtʌf] *adj* **1** STRONG : fuerte, resistente (dícese de materiales) **2** LEATHERY : correoso <a tough steak : un bistec duro> **3** HARDY : fuerte, robusto (dícese de una persona) **4** STRICT : severo, exigente **5** DIFFICULT : difícil **6** STUBBORN : terco, obstinado

tough[2] *n* : matón *m,* persona *f* ruda y brusca

toughen [ˈtʌfən] *vt* : fortalecer, endurecer — *vi* : endurecerse, hacerse más fuerte

toughness [ˈtʌfnəs] *n* : dureza *f*

toupee [tuːˈpeɪ] *n* : peluquín *m,* bisoñé *m*

tour[1] [ˈtʊr] *vi* : tomar una excursión, viajar — *vt* : recorrer, hacer una gira por

tour[2] *n* **1** : gira *f,* tour *m,* excursión *f* **2 tour of duty** : período *m* de servicio

tourist [ˈtʊrɪst, ˈtər-] *n* : turista *mf*

tournament [ˈtərnəmənt, ˈtʊr-] *n* : torneo *m*

tourniquet [ˈtərnɪkət, ˈtʊr-] *n* : torniquete *m*

tousle [ˈtaʊzəl] *vt* **-sled; -sling** : desarreglar, despeinar (el cabello)

tout [ˈtaʊt] *vt* : promocionar, elogiar (con exageración)

tow[1] [ˈtoː] *vt* : remolcar

tow[2] *n* : remolque *m*

toward [ˈtord, təˈwɔrd] *or* **towards** [ˈtordz, təˈwɔrdz] *prep* **1** (*indicating direction*) : hacia, rumbo a <heading toward town : dirigiéndose rumbo al pueblo> <efforts towards peace : esfuerzos hacia la paz> **2** (*indicating time*) : alrededor de <toward midnight : alrededor de la medianoche> **3** REGARDING : hacia, con respecto a <his attitude toward life : su actitud hacia la vida> **4** FOR : para, como pago parcial de (una compra o deuda)

towel [ˈtaʊəl] *n* : toalla *f*

tower[1] [ˈtaʊər] *vi* **to tower over** : descollar sobre, elevarse sobre, dominar

tower[2] *n* : torre *f*

towering [ˈtaʊərɪŋ] *adj* : altísimo, imponente

town [ˈtaʊn] *n* : pueblo *m,* ciudad *f* (pequeña)

township [ˈtaʊnˌʃɪp] *n* : municipio *m*

tow truck [ˈtoːˌtrʌk] *n* : grúa *f*

toxic [ˈtɑksɪk] *adj* : tóxico

toxicity [tɑkˈsɪsəṱi] *n, pl* **-ties** : toxicidad *f*

toxin [ˈtɑksɪn] *n* : toxina *f*

toy[1] [ˈtɔɪ] *vi* : juguetear, jugar

toy[2] *adj* : de juguete <a toy rifle : un rifle de juguete>

toy[3] *n* : juguete *m*

trace[1] [ˈtreɪs] *vt* **traced; tracing 1** : calcar (un dibujo, etc.) **2** OUTLINE : delinear, trazar (planes, etc.) **3** TRACK : describir (un curso, una historia) **4** FIND : localizar, ubicar

trace[2] *n* **1** SIGN, TRACK : huella *f,* rastro *m,* indicio *m,* vestigio *m* <he disappeared without a trace : desapareció sin dejar rastro> **2** BIT, HINT : pizca *f,* ápice *m,* dejo *m*

trachea [ˈtreɪkiə] *n, pl* **-cheae** [-kiˌiː] : tráquea *f*

tracing paper *n* : papel *m* de calcar

track[1] [ˈtræk] *vt* **1** TRAIL : seguir la pista de, rastrear **2** : dejar huellas de <he tracked mud all over : dejó huellas de lodo por todas partes>

track[2] *n* **1** : rastro *m,* huella *f* (de animales), pista *f* (de personas) **2** PATH : pista *f,* sendero *m,* camino *m* **3** *or* **railroad track** : vía *f* (férrea) **4** → **racetrack 5** : oruga *f* (de un tanque, etc.) **6 :** pista *f* (deporte) **7 to keep track of :** llevar la cuenta de

track–and–field [ˈtrækənd̩ˈfiːld] *adj* **:** de pista y campo

tract [ˈtrækt] *n* **1** AREA **:** terreno *m,* extensión *f,* área *f* **2 :** tracto *m* <digestive tract : tracto digestivo> **3** PAMPHLET **:** panfleto *m,* folleto *m*

traction [ˈtrækʃən] *n* **:** tracción *f*

tractor [ˈtræktər] *n* **1 :** tractor *m* (vehículo agrícola) **2** TRUCK **:** camión *m* (con remolque)

trade[1] [ˈtreɪd] *v* **traded; trading** *vi* **:** comerciar, negociar — *vt* EXCHANGE **:** intercambiar, canjear

trade[2] *n* **1** OCCUPATION **:** oficio *m,* profesión *f,* ocupación *f* <a carpenter by trade : carpintero de oficio> **2** COMMERCE **:** comercio *m,* industria *f* <free trade : libre comercio> <the book trade : la industria del libro> **3** EXCHANGE **:** intercambio *m,* canje *m*

trade–in [ˈtreɪd,ɪn] *n* **:** artículo *m* que se canjea por otro

trademark [ˈtreɪd,mɑrk] *n* **1 :** marca *f* registrada **2** CHARACTERISTIC **:** sello *m* característico (de un grupo, una persona, etc.)

trader [ˈtreɪdər] *n* **:** negociante *mf,* tratante *mf,* comerciante *mf*

tradesman [ˈtreɪdzmən] *n, pl* **-men** [-mən, -,mɛn] **1** CRAFTSMAN **:** artesano *m,* -na *f* **2** SHOPKEEPER **:** tendero *m,* -ra *f;* comerciante *mf*

trade wind *n* **:** viento *m* alisio

tradition [trəˈdɪʃən] *n* **:** tradición *f*

traditional [trəˈdɪʃənəl] *adj* **:** tradicional — **traditionally** *adv*

traffic[1] [ˈtræfɪk] *vi* **trafficked; trafficking :** traficar (en)

traffic[2] *n* **1** COMMERCE **:** tráfico *m,* comercio *m* <the drug traffic : el narcotráfico> **2 :** tráfico *m,* tránsito *m,* circulación *f* (de vehículos, etc.)

traffic circle *n* **:** rotonda *f,* glorieta *f*

trafficker [ˈtræfɪkər] *n* **:** traficante *mf*

traffic light *n* **:** semáforo *m,* luz *f* (de tránsito)

tragedy [ˈtrædʒədi] *n, pl* **-dies :** tragedia *f*

tragic [ˈtrædʒɪk] *adj* **:** trágico — **tragically** *adv*

trail[1] [ˈtreɪl] *vi* **1** DRAG **:** arrastrarse **2** LAG **:** quedarse atrás, retrasarse **3 to trail away** *or* **to trail off :** disminuir, menguar, desvanecerse — *vt* **1** DRAG **:** arrastrar **2** PURSUE **:** perseguir, seguir la pista de

trail[2] *n* **1** TRACK **:** rastro *m,* huella *f,* pista *f* <a trail of blood : un rastro de sangre> **2 :** cola *f,* estela *f* (de un meteoro) **3** PATH **:** sendero *m,* camino *m,* vereda *f*

trailer [ˈtreɪlər] *n* **1 :** remolque *m,* tráiler *m* (de un camión) **2 :** caravana *f* (vivienda ambulante)

train[1] [ˈtreɪn] *vt* **1 :** entrenar (atletas), capacitar (empleados), adiestrar, amaestrar (animales) **2** POINT **:** apuntar (un arma, etc.) — *vi* **:** entrenar(se) (físicamente), prepararse (profesionalmente) <she's training at the gym : se está entrenando en el gimnasio>

train[2] *n* **1 :** cola *f* (de un vestido) **2** RETINUE **:** cortejo *m,* séquito *m* **3** SERIES **:** serie *f* (de eventos) **4 :** tren *m* <passenger train : tren de pasajeros>

trainee [treɪˈniː] *n* **:** aprendiz *m,* -diza *f*

trainer [ˈtreɪnər] *n* **:** entrenador *m,* -dora *f*

traipse [ˈtreɪps] *vi* **traipsed; traipsing :** andar de un lado para otro, vagar

trait [ˈtreɪt] *n* **:** rasgo *m,* característica *f*

traitor [ˈtreɪt̬ər] *n* **:** traidor *m,* -dora *f*

traitorous [ˈtreɪt̬ərəs] *adj* **:** traidor

trajectory [trəˈdʒɛktəri] *n, pl* **-ries :** trayectoria *f*

tramp[1] [ˈtræmp] *vi* **:** caminar (a paso pesado) — *vt* **:** deambular por, vagar por <to tramp the streets : vagar por las calles>

tramp[2] *n* **1** VAGRANT **:** vagabundo *m,* -da *f* **2** HIKE **:** caminata *f*

trample [ˈtræmpəl] *vt* **-pled; -pling :** pisotear, hollar

trampoline [,træmpəˈliːn, ˈtræmpə,-] *n* **:** trampolín *m,* cama *f* elástica

trance [ˈtræn*t*s] *n* **:** trance *m*

tranquil [ˈtræŋkwəl] *adj* **:** calmo, tranquilo, sereno — **tranquilly** *adv*

tranquilize [ˈtræŋkwə,laɪz] *vt* **-ized; -izing :** tranquilizar

tranquilizer [ˈtræŋkwə,laɪzər] *n* **:** tranquilizante *m*

tranquillity *or* **tranquility** [træŋˈkwɪlət̬i] *n* **:** sosiego *m,* tranquilidad *f*

transact [trænˈzækt] *vt* **:** negociar, gestionar, hacer (negocios)

transaction [trænˈzækʃən] *n* **1 :** transacción *f,* negocio *m,* operación *f* **2 transactions** *npl* RECORDS **:** actas *fpl*

transatlantic [,træn*t*sətˈlæntɪk, ,trænz-] *adj* **:** transatlántico

transcend [trænˈsɛnd] *vt* **:** trascender, sobrepasar

transcribe [trænˈskraɪb] *vt* **-scribed; -scribing :** transcribir

transcript [ˈtræn,skrɪpt] *n* **:** copia *f* oficial

transcription [trænˈskrɪpʃən] *n* **:** transcripción *f*

transfer[1] [træn*t*sˈfər, ˈtræn*t*s,fər] *v* **-ferred; -ferring** *vt* **1 :** trasladar (a una persona), transferir (fondos) **2 :** transferir, traspasar, ceder (propiedad) **3** PRINT **:** imprimir (un diseño) — *vi* **1** MOVE **:** trasladarse, cambiarse **2** CHANGE **:** transbordar, cambiar (de un transporte a otro) <she transferred at E Street : hizo un transborde a la calle E>

transfer[2] [ˈtræn*t*s,fər] *n* **1** TRANSFERRING **:** transferencia *f* (de fondos, de propiedad, etc.), traslado *m* (de una persona) **2** DECAL **:** calcomanía *f* **3** **:** boleto *m* (para cambiar de un avión, etc., a otro)

transferable [trænts'fərəbəl] *adj* **:** transferible

transference [trænts'fərənts] *n* **:** transferencia *f*

transfigure [trænts'fɪgjər] *vt* **-ured; -uring :** transfigurar, transformar

transfix [trænts'fɪks] *vt* **1** PIERCE **:** traspasar, atravesar **2** IMMOBILIZE **:** paralizar

transform [trænts'fɔrm] *vt* **:** transformar

transformation [ˌtræntsfər'meɪʃən] *n* **:** transformación *f*

transformer [trænts'fɔrmər] *n* **:** transformador *m*

transfusion [trænts'fju:ʒən] *n* **:** transfusión *f*

transgress [trænts'grɛs, trænz-] *vt* **:** transgredir, infringir

transgression [trænts'grɛʃən, trænz-] *n* **:** transgresión *f*

transient¹ ['træntʃənt, 'trænsiənt] *adj* **:** pasajero, transitorio **— transiently** *adv*

transient² *n* **:** transeúnte *mf*

transistor [træn'zɪstər, -'sɪs-] *n* **:** transistor *m*

transit ['træntsɪt, 'trænzɪt] *n* **1** PASSAGE **:** pasaje *m*, tránsito *m* <in transit : en tránsito> **2** TRANSPORTATION **:** transporte *m* (público) **3 :** teodolito *m* (instrumento topográfico)

transition [træn'sɪʃən, -'zɪʃ-] *n* **:** transición *f*

transitional [træn'sɪʃənəl, -'zɪʃ-] *adj* **:** de transición

transitive ['træntsətɪv, 'trænzə-] *adj* **:** transitivo

transitory ['træntsəˌtori, 'trænzə-] *adj* **:** transitorio

translate [trænts'leɪt, trænz-; 'træntsˌ-, 'trænsˌ-] *vt* **-lated; -lating :** traducir

translation [trænts'leɪʃən, trænz-] *n* **:** traducción *f*

translator [trænts'leɪtər, trænz-; 'træntsˌ-, 'trænsˌ-] *n* **:** traductor *m*, -tora *f*

translucent [trænts'lu:sənt, trænz-] *adj* **:** translúcido

transmission [trænts'mɪʃən, trænz-] *n* **:** transmisión *f*

transmit [trænts'mɪt, trænz-] *vt* **-mitted; -mitting :** transmitir

transmitter [trænts'mɪtər, trænz-; 'træntsˌ-, 'trænsˌ-] *n* **:** transmisor *m*, emisor *m*

transom ['træntsəm] *n* **:** montante *m* (de una puerta), travesaño *m* (de una ventana)

transparency [trænts'pærəntsi] *n, pl* **-cies :** transparencia *f*

transparent [trænts'pærənt] *adj* **1** **:** transparente, traslúcido <a transparent fabric : una tela transparente> **2** OBVIOUS **:** transparente, obvio, claro **— transparently** *adv*

transpiration [ˌtræntspə'reɪʃən] *n* **:** transpiración *f*

transpire [trænts'paɪr] *vi* **-spired; -spiring 1 :** transpirar (en biología y botanía) **2** TURN OUT **:** resultar **3** HAPPEN **:** suceder, ocurrir, tener lugar

transplant¹ [trænts'plænt] *vt* **:** trasplantar

transplant² ['træntsˌplænt] *n* **:** trasplante *m*

transport¹ [trænts'port, 'træntsˌ-] *vt* **1** CARRY **:** transportar, acarrear **2** ENRAPTURE **:** transportar, extasiar

transport² ['træntsˌport] *n* **1** TRANSPORTATION **:** transporte *m*, transportación *f* **2** RAPTURE **:** éxtasis *m* **3** *or* **transport ship :** buque *m* de transporte (de personal militar)

transportation [ˌtræntspər'teɪʃən] *n* **:** transporte *m*, transportación *f*

transpose [trænts'po:z] *vt* **-posed; -posing :** trasponer, trasladar, transportar (una composición musical)

transverse [trænts'vərs, trænz-] *adj* **:** transversal, transverso, oblicuo **— transversely** *adv*

trap¹ ['træp] *vt* **trapped; trapping :** atrapar, apresar (en una trampa)

trap² *n* **:** trampa *f* <to set a trap : tender una trampa>

trapdoor ['træp'dor] *n* **:** trampilla *f*, escotillón *m*

trapeze [træ'pi:z] *n* **:** trapecio *m*

trapezoid ['træpəˌzɔɪd] *n* **:** trapezoide *m*, trapecio *m*

trapper ['træpər] *n* **:** trampero *m*, -ra *f*; cazador *m*, -dora *f* (que usa trampas)

trappings ['træpɪŋz] *npl* **1 :** arreos *mpl*, jaeces *mpl* (de un caballo) **2** ADORNMENTS **:** adornos *mpl*, pompa *f*

trash ['træʃ] *n* **:** basura *f*

trauma ['trɔmə, 'traʊ-] *n* **:** trauma *m*

traumatic [trə'mætɪk, trɔ-, traʊ-] *adj* **:** traumático

travel¹ ['trævəl] *vi* **-eled** *or* **-elled; -eling** *or* **-elling 1** JOURNEY **:** viajar **2** GO, MOVE **:** desplazarse, moverse, ir <the waves travel at uniform speed : las ondas se desplazan a una velocidad uniforme>

travel² *n* **:** viajes *mpl*

traveler *or* **traveller** ['trævələr] *n* **:** viajero *m*, -ra *f*

traverse [trə'vərs, træ'vərs, 'trævərs] *vt* **-versed; -versing** CROSS **:** atravesar, extenderse a través de, cruzar

travesty ['trævəsti] *n, pl* **-ties :** parodia *f*

trawl¹ ['trɔl] *vi* **:** pescar con red de arrastre, rastrear

trawl² *n or* **trawl net :** red *f* de arrastre

trawler ['trɔlər] *n* **:** barco *m* de pesca (utilizado para rastrear)

tray ['treɪ] *n* **:** bandeja *f*, charola *f Bol, Mex, Peru*

treacherous [ˈtrɛtʃərəs] *adj* **1** TRAITOROUS : traicionero, traidor **2** DANGEROUS : peligroso
treacherously [ˈtrɛtʃərəsli] *adv* : a traición
treachery [ˈtrɛtʃəri] *n, pl* **-eries** : traición *f*
tread[1] [ˈtrɛd] *v* **trod** [ˈtrɑd]; **trodden** [ˈtrɑdən] *or* **trod; treading** *vt* TRAMPLE : pisotear, hollar — *vi* **1** WALK : caminar, andar **2 to tread on** : pisar
tread[2] *n* **1** STEP : paso *m,* andar *m* **2** : banda *f* de rodadura (de un neumático, etc.) **3** : escalón *m* (de una escalera)
treadle [ˈtrɛdəl] *n* : pedal *m* (de una máquina)
treadmill [ˈtrɛd,mɪl] *n* **1** : rueda *f* de andar **2** ROUTINE : rutina *f*
treason [ˈtriːzən] *n* : traición *f* (a la patria, etc.)
treasure[1] [ˈtrɛʒər, ˈtreɪ-] *vt* **-sured; -suring** : apreciar, valorar
treasure[2] *n* : tesoro *m*
treasurer [ˈtrɛʒərər, ˈtreɪ-] *n* : tesorero *m,* -ra *f*
treasury [ˈtrɛʒəri, ˈtreɪ-] *n, pl* **-suries** : tesorería *f,* tesoro *m*
treat[1] [ˈtriːt] *vt* **1** DEAL WITH : tratar (un asunto) <the article treats of poverty : el artículo trata de la pobreza> **2** HANDLE : tratar (a una persona), manejar (un objeto) <to treat something as a joke : tomar(se) algo a broma> **3** INVITE : invitar, convidar <he treated me to a meal : me invitó a comer> **4** : tratar, atender (en medicina) **5** PROCESS : tratar <to treat sewage : tratar las aguas negras>
treat[2] *n* : gusto *m,* placer *m* <it was a treat to see you : fue un placer verte> <it's my treat : yo invito>
treatise [ˈtriːt̬ɪs] *n* : tratado *m,* estudio *m*
treatment [ˈtriːtmənt] *n* : trato *m,* tratamiento *m* (médico)
treaty [ˈtriːt̬i] *n, pl* **-ties** : tratado *m,* convenio *m*
treble[1] [ˈtrɛbəl] *vt* **-bled; -bling** : triplicar
treble[2] *adj* **1** → **triple 2** : de tiple, soprano (en música) **3 treble clef** : clave *f* de sol
treble[3] *n* : tiple *m,* parte *f* soprana
tree [ˈtriː] *n* : árbol *m*
treeless [ˈtriːləs] *adj* : carente de árboles
trek[1] [ˈtrɛk] *vi* **trekked; trekking** : hacer un viaje largo y difícil
trek[2] *n* : viaje *m* largo y difícil
trellis [ˈtrɛlɪs] *n* : enrejado *m,* espaldera *f,* celosía *f*
tremble [ˈtrɛmbəl] *vi* **-bled; -bling** : temblar
tremendous [trɪˈmɛndəs] *adj* : tremendo — **tremendously** *adv*
tremor [ˈtrɛmər] *n* : temblor *m*
tremulous [ˈtrɛmjələs] *adj* : trémulo, tembloroso
trench [ˈtrɛntʃ] *n* **1** DITCH : zanja *f* **2** : trinchera *f* (militar)
trenchant [ˈtrɛntʃənt] *adj* : cortante, mordaz
trend[1] [ˈtrɛnd] *vi* : tender, inclinarse
trend[2] *n* **1** TENDENCY : tendencia *f* **2** FASHION : moda *f*
trendy [ˈtrɛndi] *adj* **trendier; -est** : de moda
trepidation [,trɛpəˈdeɪʃən] *n* : inquietud *f,* ansiedad *f*
trespass[1] [ˈtrɛspəs, -,pæs] *vi* **1** SIN : pecar, transgredir **2** : entrar ilegalmente (en propiedad ajena)
trespass[2] *n* **1** SIN : pecado *m,* transgresión *f* <forgive us our trespasses : perdónanos nuestras deudas> **2** : entrada *f* ilegal (en propiedad ajena)
tress [ˈtrɛs] *n* : mechón *m*
trestle [ˈtrɛsəl] *n* **1** : caballete *m* (armazón) **2** *or* **trestle bridge** : puente *m* de caballete
triad [ˈtraɪ,æd] *n* : tríada *f*
trial[1] [ˈtraɪəl] *adj* : de prueba <trial period : período de prueba>
trial[2] *n* **1** : juicio *m,* proceso *m* <to stand trial : ser sometido a juicio> **2** AFFLICTION : aflicción *f,* tribulación *f* **3** TEST : prueba *f,* ensayo *m*
triangle [ˈtraɪ,æŋgəl] *n* : triángulo *m*
triangular [traɪˈæŋgjələr] *adj* : triangular
tribal [ˈtraɪbəl] *adj* : tribal
tribe [ˈtraɪb] *n* : tribu *f*
tribesman [ˈtraɪbzmən] *n, pl* **-men** [-mən, -,mɛn] : miembro *m* de una tribu
tribulation [,trɪbjəˈleɪʃən] *n* : tribulación *f*
tribunal [traɪˈbjuːnəl, trɪ-] *n* : tribunal *m,* corte *f*
tributary [ˈtrɪbjə,tɛri] *n, pl* **-taries** : afluente *m*
tribute [ˈtrɪb,juːt] *n* : tributo *m*
trick[1] [ˈtrɪk] *vt* : engañar, embaucar
trick[2] *n* **1** RUSE : trampa *f,* treta *f,* artimaña *f* **2** PRANK : broma *f* <we played a trick on her : le gastamos una broma> **3** : truco *m* <magic tricks : trucos de magia> <the trick is to wait five minutes : el truco está en esperar cinco minutos> **4** MANNERISM : peculiaridad *f,* manía *f* **5** : baza *f* (en juegos de naipes)
trickery [ˈtrɪkəri] *n* : engaños *mpl,* trampas *fpl*
trickle[1] [ˈtrɪkəl] *vi* **-led; -ling** : gotear, chorrear
trickle[2] *n* : goteo *m,* hilo *m*
trickster [ˈtrɪkstər] *n* : estafador *m,* -dora *f;* embaucador *m,* -dora *f*
tricky [ˈtrɪki] *adj* **trickier; -est 1** SLY : astuto, taimado **2** DIFFICULT : delicado, peliagudo, difícil
tricycle [ˈtraɪsəkəl, -,sɪkəl] *n* : triciclo *m*
trident [ˈtraɪdənt] *n* : tridente *m*
triennial [ˈtraɪˈɛniəl] *adj* : trienal
trifle[1] [ˈtraɪfəl] *vi* **-fled; -fling** : jugar, juguetear

trifle[2] *n* **:** nimiedad *f,* insignificancia *f*

trifling [ˈtraɪflɪŋ] *adj* **:** trivial, insignificante

trigger[1] [ˈtrɪgər] *vt* **:** causar, provocar

trigger[2] *n* **:** gatillo *m*

trigonometry [ˌtrɪgəˈnɑmətri] *n* **:** trigonometría *f*

trill[1] [ˈtrɪl] *vi* QUAVER **:** trinar, gorjear — *vt* **:** vibrar <to trill the *r* **:** vibrar la *r*>

trill[2] *n* **1** QUAVER **:** trino *m,* gorjeo *m* **2 :** vibración *f* (en fonología)

trillion [ˈtrɪljən] *n* **:** billón *m*

trilogy [ˈtrɪlədʒi] *n, pl* **-gies :** trilogía *f*

trim[1] [ˈtrɪm] *vt* **trimmed; trimming 1** DECORATE **:** adornar, decorar **2** CUT **:** recortar **3** REDUCE **:** recortar, reducir <to trim the excess **:** recortar el exceso>

trim[2] *adj* **trimmer; trimmest 1** SLIM **:** esbelto **2** NEAT **:** limpio y arreglado, bien cuidado

trim[3] *n* **1** CONDITION **:** condición *f,* estado *m* <to keep in trim **:** mantenerse en buena forma> **2** CUT **:** recorte *m* **3** TRIMMING **:** adornos *mpl*

trimming [ˈtrɪmɪŋ] *n* **:** adornos *mpl,* accesorios *mpl*

Trinity [ˈtrɪnəti] *n* **:** Trinidad *f*

trinket [ˈtrɪŋkət] *n* **:** chuchería *f,* baratija *f*

trio [ˈtriːˌoː] *n, pl* **trios :** trío *m*

trip[1] [ˈtrɪp] *v* **tripped; tripping** *vi* **1 :** caminar (a paso ligero) **2** STUMBLE **:** tropezar **3 to trip up** ERR **:** equivocarse, cometer un error — *vt* **1 :** hacerle una zancadilla (a alguien) <you tripped me on purpose! **:** ¡me hiciste la zancadilla a propósito!> **2** ACTIVATE **:** activar (un mecanismo) **3 to trip up :** hacer equivocar (a alguien)

trip[2] *n* **1** JOURNEY **:** viaje *m* <to take a trip **:** hacer un viaje> **2** STUMBLE **:** tropiezo *m,* traspié *m*

tripartite [traɪˈpɑrˌtaɪt] *adj* **:** tripartito

tripe [ˈtraɪp] *n* **1 :** mondongo *m,* callos *mpl,* pancita *f Mex* **2** TRASH **:** porquería *f*

triple[1] [ˈtrɪpəl] *vt* **-pled; -pling :** triplicar

triple[2] *adj* **:** triple

triple[3] *n* **:** triple *m*

triplet [ˈtrɪplət] *n* **1 :** terceto *m* (en poesía, música, etc.) **2 :** trillizo *m,* -za *f* (persona)

triplicate [ˈtrɪplɪkət] *n* **:** triplicado *m*

tripod [ˈtraɪˌpɑd] *n* **:** trípode *m*

trite [ˈtraɪt] *adj* **triter; tritest :** trillado, tópico, manido

triumph[1] [ˈtraɪəmpf] *vi* **:** triunfar

triumph[2] *n* **:** triunfo *m*

triumphal [traɪˈʌmpfəl] *adj* **:** triunfal

triumphant [traɪˈʌmpfənt] *adj* **:** triunfante, triunfal — **triumphantly** *adv*

trivia [ˈtrɪviə] *ns & pl* **:** trivialidades *fpl,* nimiedades *fpl*

trivial [ˈtrɪviəl] *adj* **:** trivial, intrascendente, insignificante

triviality [ˌtrɪviˈæləti] *n, pl* **-ties :** trivialidad *f*

trod, trodden → **tread**[1]

troll [ˈtroːl] *n* **:** duende *m* o gigante *m* de cuentos folklóricos

trolley [ˈtrɑli] *n, pl* **-leys :** tranvía *m*

trombone [trɑmˈboːn] *n* **:** trombón *m*

trombonist [trɑmˈboːnɪst] *n* **:** trombón *m*

troop[1] [ˈtruːp] *vi* **:** desfilar, ir en tropel

troop[2] *n* **1 :** escuadrón *m* (de caballería) **2** GROUP **:** grupo *m,* banda *f* (de personas) **3 troops** *npl* SOLDIERS **:** tropas *fpl,* soldados *mpl*

trooper [ˈtruːpər] *n* **1 :** soldado *m* (de caballería) **2 :** policía *m* montado **3 :** policía *m* (estatal)

trophy [ˈtroːfi] *n, pl* **-phies :** trofeo *m*

tropic[1] [ˈtrɑpɪk] *or* **tropical** [-pɪkəl] *adj* **:** tropical

tropic[2] *n* **1 :** trópico *m* <tropic of Cancer **:** trópico de Cáncer> **2 the tropics :** el trópico

trot[1] [ˈtrɑt] *vi* **trotted; trotting :** trotar

trot[2] *n* **:** trote *m*

trouble[1] [ˈtrʌbəl] *v* **-bled; -bling** *vt* **1** DISTURB, WORRY **:** molestar, perturbar, inquietar **2** AFFLICT **:** afligir, afectar — *vi* **:** molestarse, hacer un esfuerzo <they didn't trouble to come **:** no se molestaron en venir>

trouble[2] *n* **1** PROBLEMS **:** problemas *mpl,* dificultades *fpl* <to be in trouble **:** estar en un aprieto> <heart trouble **:** problemas de corazón> **2** EFFORT **:** molestia *f,* esfuerzo *m* <to take the trouble **:** tomarse la molestia> <it's not worth the trouble **:** no vale la pena>

troublemaker [ˈtrʌbəlˌmeɪkər] *n* **:** agitador *m,* -dora *f;* alborotador *m,* -dora *f*

troublesome [ˈtrʌbəlsəm] *adj* **:** problemático, dificultoso — **troublesomely** *adv*

trough [ˈtrɔf] *n, pl* **troughs** [ˈtrɔfs, ˈtrɔvz] **1 :** comedero *m,* bebedero *m* (de animales) **2** CHANNEL, HOLLOW **:** depresión *f* (en el suelo), seno *m* (de olas)

trounce [ˈtraʊnts] *vt* **trounced; trouncing 1** THRASH **:** apalear, darle una paliza (a alguien) **2** DEFEAT **:** derrotar contundentemente

troupe [ˈtruːp] *n* **:** troupe *f*

trousers [ˈtraʊzərz] *npl* **:** pantalón *m,* pantalones *mpl*

trout [ˈtraʊt] *n, pl* **trout :** trucha *f*

trowel [ˈtraʊəl] *n* **1 :** llana *f,* paleta *f* (de albañil) **2 :** desplantador *m* (de jardinero)

truant [ˈtruːənt] *n* **:** alumno *m,* -na *f* que falta a clase sin permiso

truce [ˈtruːs] *n* **:** tregua *f,* armisticio *m*

truck[1] [ˈtrʌk] *vt* **:** transportar en camión

truck[2] *n* **1 :** camión *m* (vehículo automóvil), carro *m* (manual) **2** DEAL-

INGS : tratos *mpl* <to have no truck with : no tener nada que ver con>

trucker ['trʌkər] *n* : camionero *m,* -ra *f*

truculent ['trʌkjələnt] *adj* : agresivo, beligerante

trudge ['trʌdʒ] *vi* **trudged; trudging** : caminar a paso pesado

true[1] ['tru:] *vt* **trued; trueing** : aplomar (algo vertical), nivelar (algo horizontal), centrar (una rueda)

true[2] *adv* **1** TRUTHFULLY : lealmente, sinceramente **2** ACCURATELY : exactamente, certeramente

true[3] *adj* **truer; truest 1** LOYAL : fiel, leal **2** : cierto, verdadero, verídico <it's true : es cierto, es la verdad> <a true story : una historia verídica> **3** GENUINE : auténtico, genuino — **truly** *adv*

true–blue ['tru:'blu:] *adj* LOYAL : leal, fiel

truffle ['trʌfəl] *n* : trufa *f*

truism ['tru:ˌɪzəm] *n* : perogrullada *f,* verdad *f* obvia

trump[1] ['trʌmp] *vt* : matar (en juegos de naipes)

trump[2] *n* : triunfo *m* (en juegos de naipes)

trumped–up ['trʌmpt'ʌp] *adj* : inventado, fabricado <trumped-up charges : falsas acusaciones>

trumpet[1] ['trʌmpət] *vi* **1** : sonar una trompeta **2** : berrear, bramar (dícese de un animal) — *vt* : proclamar a los cuatro vientos

trumpet[2] *n* : trompeta *f*

trumpeter ['trʌmpət̬ər] *n* : trompetista *mf*

truncate ['trʌŋˌkeɪt, 'trʌn-] *vt* **-cated; -cating** : truncar

trundle ['trʌndəl] *v* **-dled; -dling** *vi* : rodar lentamente — *vt* : hacer rodar, empujar lentamente

trunk ['trʌŋk] *n* **1** : tronco *m* (de un árbol o del cuerpo) **2** : trompa *f* (de un elefante) **3** CHEST : baúl *m* **4** : maletero *m,* cajuela *f Mex* (de un auto) **5 trunks** *npl* : traje *m* de baño (de caballero)

truss[1] ['trʌs] *vt* : atar (con fuerza)

truss[2] *n* **1** FRAMEWORK : armazón *m* (de una estructura) **2** : braguero *m* (en medicina)

trust[1] ['trʌst] *vi* : confiar, esperar <to trust in God : confiar en Dios> — *vt* **1** ENTRUST : confiar, encomendar **2** : confiar en, tenerle confianza a <I trust you : te tengo confianza>

trust[2] *n* **1** CONFIDENCE : confianza *f* **2** HOPE : esperanza *f,* fe *f* **3** CREDIT : crédito *m* <to sell on trust : fiar> **4** : fideicomiso *m* <to hold in trust : guardar en fideicomiso> **5** : trust *m* (consorcio empresarial) **6** CUSTODY : responsabilidad *f,* custodia *f*

trustee [ˌtrʌs'ti:] *n* : fideicomisario *m,* -ria *f;* fiduciario *m,* -ria *f*

trustful ['trʌstfəl] *adj* : confiado — **trustfully** *adv*

trustworthiness ['trəstˌwərðinəs] *n* : integridad *f,* honradez *f*

trustworthy ['trəstˌwərði] *adj* : digno de confianza, confiable

trusty ['trəsti] *adj* **trustier; -est** : fiel, confiable

truth ['tru:θ] *n, pl* **truths** ['tru:ðz, 'tru:θs] : verdad *f*

truthful ['tru:θfəl] *adj* : sincero, veraz — **truthfully** *adv*

truthfulness ['tru:θfəlnəs] *n* : sinceridad *f,* veracidad *f*

try[1] ['traɪ] *v* **tried; trying** *vt* **1** : enjuiciar, juzgar, procesar <he was tried for murder : fue procesado por homicidio> **2** : probar <did you try the salad? : ¿probaste la ensalada?> **3** TEST : tentar, poner a prueba <to try one's patience : tentarle la paciencia a uno> **4** ATTEMPT : tratar (de), intentar **5** *or* **to try on** : probarse (ropa) — *vi* : tratar, intentar

try[2] *n, pl* **tries** : intento *m,* tentativa *f*

tryout ['traɪˌaʊt] *n* : prueba *f*

tsar ['zɑr, 'tsɑr, 'sɑr] → **czar**

T–shirt ['ti:ˌʃərt] *n* : camiseta *f*

tub ['tʌb] *n* **1** CASK : cuba *f,* barril *m,* tonel *m* **2** CONTAINER : envase *m* (de plástico, etc.) <a tub of margarine : un envase de margarina> **3** BATHTUB : tina *f* (de baño), bañera *f*

tuba ['tu:bə, 'tju:-] *n* : tuba *f*

tube ['tu:b, 'tju:b] *n* **1** PIPE : tubo *m* **2** : tubo *m* (de dentífrico, etc.) **3** *or* **inner tube** : cámara *f* **4** : tubo *m* (de un aparato electrónico) **5** : trompa *f* (en anatomía)

tubeless ['tu:bləs, 'tju:b-] *adj* : sin cámara (dícese de una llanta)

tuber ['tu:bər, 'tju:-] *n* : tubérculo *m*

tubercular [tʊ'bərkjələr, tjʊ-] → **tuberculous**

tuberculosis [tʊˌbərkjə'lo:sɪs, tjʊ-] *n, pl* **-loses** [-ˌsi:z] : tuberculosis *f*

tuberculous [tʊ'bərkjələs, tjʊ-] *adj* : tuberculoso

tuberous ['tu:bərəs, 'tju:-] *adj* : tuberoso

tubing ['tu:bɪŋ, 'tju:-] *n* : tubería *f*

tubular ['tu:bjələr, 'tju:-] *adj* : tubular

tuck[1] ['tʌk] *vt* **1** PLACE, PUT : meter, colocar <tuck in your shirt : métete la camisa> **2** : guardar, esconder <to tuck away one's money : guardar uno bien su dinero> **3** COVER : arropar (a un niño en la cama)

tuck[2] *n* : pliegue *m,* alforza *f*

Tuesday ['tu:zˌdeɪ, 'tju:z-, -di] *n* : martes *m*

tuft ['tʌft] *n* : penacho *m* (de plumas), copete *m* (de pelo)

tug[1] ['tʌg] *v* **tugged; tugging** *vi* : tirar, jalar, dar un tirón — *vt* : jalar, arrastrar, remolcar (con un barco)

tug[2] *n* **1** : tirón *m,* jalón *m* **2** → **tugboat**

tugboat ['tʌgˌbo:t] *n* : remolcador *m*

tug–of–war [ˌtʌgə'wɔr] *n, pl* **tugs–of–war** : tira y afloja *m*

tulip ['tu:lɪp, 'tju:-] *n* : tulipán *m*

tumble[1] ['tʌmbəl] *v* **-bled; -bling** *vi* **1** : dar volteretas (en acrobacia) **2** FALL : caerse, venirse abajo — *vt* **1** TOPPLE : volcar **2** TOSS : hacer girar

tumble[2] *n* : voltereta *f,* caída *f*

tumbler ['tʌmblər] *n* **1** ACROBAT : acróbata *mf,* saltimbanqui *mf* **2** GLASS : vaso *m* (de mesa) **3** : clavija *f* (de una cerradura)

tummy ['tʌmi] *n, pl* **-mies** BELLY : panza *f,* vientre *m*

tumor ['tu:mər 'tju:-] *n* : tumor *m*

tumult ['tu:ˌmʌlt 'tju:-] *n* : tumulto *m,* alboroto *m*

tumultuous [tʊ'mʌltʃʊəs, tju:-] *adj* : tumultuoso

tuna ['tu:nə 'tju:-] *n, pl* **-na** *or* **-nas** : atún *m*

tundra ['tʌndrə] *n* : tundra *f*

tune[1] ['tu:n, 'tju:n] *v* **tuned; tuning** *vt* **1** ADJUST : ajustar, hacer más preciso, afinar (un motor) **2** : afinar (un instrumento musical) **3** : sintonizar (un radio o televisor) — *vi* **to tune in** : sintonizar (con una emisora)

tune[2] *n* **1** MELODY : tonada *f,* canción *f,* melodía *f* **2** **in tune** : afinado (dícese de un instrumento o de la voz), sintonizado, en sintonía

tuneful ['tu:nfəl, 'tju:n-] *adj* : armonioso, melódico

tuner ['tu:nər, 'tju:-] *n* : afinador *m,* -dora *f* (de instrumentos); sintonizador *m* (de un radio o un televisior)

tungsten ['tʌŋkstən] *n* : tungsteno *m*

tunic ['tu:nɪk, 'tju:-] *n* : túnica *f*

tuning fork *n* : diapasón *m*

Tunisian [tu:'ni:ʒən, tju:'nɪziən] *n* : tunecino *m,* -na *f* — **Tunisian** *adj*

tunnel[1] ['tʌnəl] *vi* **-neled** *or* **-nelled; -neling** *or* **-nelling** : hacer un túnel

tunnel[2] *n* : túnel *m*

turban ['tərbən] *n* : turbante *m*

turbid ['tərbɪd] *adj* : turbio

turbine ['tərbən, -ˌbaɪn] *n* : turbina *f*

turboprop ['tərbo:ˌprɑp] *n* : turbopropulsor *m* (motor), avión *m* turbopropulsado

turbulence ['tərbjələnts] *n* : turbulencia *f*

turbulent ['tərbjələnt] *adj* : turbulento — **turbulently** *adv*

tureen [tə'ri:n, tjʊ-] *n* : sopera *f*

turf ['tərf] *n* SOD : tepe *m*

turgid ['tərdʒɪd] *adj* **1** SWOLLEN : turgente **2** : ampuloso, hinchado <turgid style : estilo ampuloso>

turkey ['tərki] *n, pl* **-keys** : pavo *m*

turmoil ['tərˌmɔɪl] *n* : agitación *f,* desorden *m,* confusión *f*

turn[1] ['tərn] *vt* **1** : girar, voltear, volver <to turn one's head : voltear la cabeza> <she turned her chair toward the fire : giró su asiento hacia la hoguera> **2** ROTATE : darle vuelta a, hacer girar <turn the handle : dale vuelta a la manivela> **3** SPRAIN, WRENCH : dislocar, torcer **4** UPSET : revolver (el estómago) **5** TRANSFORM : convertir <to turn water into wine : convertir el agua en vino> **6** SHAPE : tornear (en carpintería) — *vi* **1** ROTATE : girar, dar vueltas **2** : girar, doblar, dar una vuelta <turn left : doble a la izquierda> <to turn around : dar la media vuelta> **3** BECOME : hacerse, volverse, ponerse **4** SOUR : agriarse, cortarse (dícese de la leche) **5** **to turn to** : recurrir a <they have no one to turn to : no tienen quien les ayude>

turn[2] *n* **1** : vuelta *f,* giro *m* <a sudden turn : una vuelta repentina> **2** CHANGE : cambio *m* **3** CURVE : curva *f* (en un camino) **4** : turno *m* <they're awaiting their turn : están esperando su turno> <whose turn is it? : ¿a quién le toca?>

turncoat ['tərnˌko:t] *n* : traidor *m,* -dora *f*

turn down *vt* **1** REFUSE : rehusar, rechazar <they turned down our invitation : rehusaron nuestra invitación> **2** LOWER : bajar (el volumen)

turn in *vt* : entregar <to turn in one's work : entregar uno su trabajo> <they turned in the suspect : entregaron al sospechoso> — *vi* : acostarse, irse a la cama

turnip ['tərnəp] *n* : nabo *m*

turn off *vt* : apagar (la luz, la radio, etc.)

turn on *vt* : prender (la luz, etc.), encender (un motor, etc.)

turnout ['tərnˌaʊt] *n* : concurrencia *f*

turn out *vt* **1** EVICT, EXPEL : expulsar, echar, desalojar **2** PRODUCE : producir **3** → **turn off** — *vi* **1** : concurrir, presentarse <many turned out to vote : muchos concurrieron a votar> **2** PROVE, RESULT : resultar

turnover ['tərnˌo:vər] *n* **1** : tarta *f* (rellena de fruta) **2** : volumen *m* (de ventas) **3** : rotación *f* (de personal) <a high turnover : un alto nivel de rotación>

turn over *vt* **1** TRANSFER : entregar, transferir (un cargo o una responsabilidad) **2** : voltear, darle la vuelta a <turn the cassette over : voltea el cassette>

turnpike ['tərnˌpaɪk] *n* : carretera *f* de peaje

turnstile ['tərnˌstaɪl] *n* : torniquete *m* (de acceso)

turntable ['tərnˌteɪbəl] *n* : tornamesa *mf*

turn up *vi* **1** APPEAR : aparecer, presentarse **2** HAPPEN : ocurrir, suceder (inesperadamente) — *vt* : subir (el volumen)

turpentine ['tərpənˌtaɪn] *n* : aguarrás *m,* trementina *f*

turquoise ['tərˌkɔɪz, -ˌkwɔɪz] *n* : turquesa *f*

turret ['tərət] *n* **1** TOWER : torre *f* pequeña **2** : torreta *f* (de un tanque, un avión, etc.)

turtle ['tərt̬əl] *n* : tortuga *f* (marina)

turtledove [ˈtərtəl,dʌv] *n* : tórtola *f*
turtleneck [ˈtərtəl,nɛk] *n* : cuello *m* de tortuga, cuello *m* alto
tusk [ˈtʌsk] *n* : colmillo *m*
tussle[1] [ˈtʌsəl] *vi* **-sled; -sling** SCUFFLE : pelearse, reñir
tussle[2] *n* : riña *f*, pelea *f*
tutor[1] [ˈtuːtər, ˈtjuː-] *vt* : darle clases particulares (a alguien)
tutor[2] *n* : tutor *m*, -tora *f*; maestro *m*, -tra *f* (particular)
tuxedo [,təkˈsiː,doː] *n*, *pl* **-dos** *or* **-does** : esmoquin *m*, smoking *m*
TV [,tiːˈviː, ˈtiː,viː] → **television**
twain [ˈtweɪn] *n* : dos *m*
twang[1] [ˈtwæŋ] *vt* : pulsar la cuerda de (una guitarra) — *vi* : hablar en tono nasal
twang[2] *n* **1** : tañido *m* (de una cuerda de guitarra) **2** : tono *m* nasal (de voz)
tweak[1] [ˈtwiːk] *vt* : pellizcar
tweak[2] *n* : pellizco *m*
tweed [ˈtwiːd] *n* : tweed *m*
tweet[1] [ˈtwiːt] *vi* : piar
tweet[2] *n* : gorjeo *m*, pío *m*
tweezers [ˈtwiːzərz] *npl* : pinzas *fpl*
twelfth[1] [ˈtwɛlfθ] *adj* : duodécimo
twelfth[2] *n* **1** : duodécimo *m*, -ma *f* (en una serie) **2** : doceavo *m*, doceava parte *f*
twelve[1] [ˈtwɛlv] *adj* : doce
twelve[2] *n* : doce *m*
twentieth[1] [ˈtwʌntiəθ, ˈtwɛn-] *adj* : vigésimo
twentieth[2] *n* **1** : vigésimo *m*, -ma *f* (en una serie) **2** : veinteavo *m*, veinteava parte *f*
twenty[1] [ˈtwʌnti, ˈtwɛn-] *adj* : veinte
twenty[2] *n*, *pl* **-ties** : veinte *m*
twice [ˈtwaɪs] *adv* : dos veces <twice a day : dos veces al día> <it costs twice as much : cuesta el doble>
twig [ˈtwɪg] *n* : ramita *f*
twilight [ˈtwaɪ,laɪt] *n* : crepúsculo *m*
twill [ˈtwɪl] *n* : sarga *f*, tela *f* cruzada
twin[1] [ˈtwɪn] *adj* : gemelo, mellizo
twin[2] *n* : gemelo *m*, -la *f*; mellizo *m*, -za *f*
twine[1] [ˈtwaɪn] *v* **twined; twining** *vt* : entrelazar, entrecruzar — *vi* : enroscarse (alrededor de algo)
twine[2] *n* : cordel *m*, cuerda *f*, mecate *m* *CA, Mex, Ven*
twinge[1] [ˈtwɪndʒ] *vi* **twinged; twinging** *or* **twingeing** : sentir punzadas
twinge[2] *n* : punzada *f*, dolor *m* agudo
twinkle[1] [ˈtwɪŋkəl] *vi* **-kled; -kling 1** : centellear, titilar (dícese de las estrellas o de la luz) **2** : chispear, brillar (dícese de los ojos)
twinkle[2] *n* : centelleo *m* (de las estrellas), brillo *m* (de los ojos)
twirl[1] [ˈtwərl] *vt* : girar, darle vueltas a — *vi* : girar, dar vueltas (rápidamente)
twirl[2] *n* : giro *m*, vuelta *f*
twist[1] [ˈtwɪst] *vt* : torcer, retorcer <he twisted my arm : me torció el brazo> — *vi* : retorcerse, enroscarse, serpentear (dícese de un río, un camino, etc.)
twist[2] *n* **1** BEND : vuelta *f*, recodo *m* (en el camino, el río, etc.) **2** TURN : giro *m* <give it a twist : hazlo girar> **3** SPIRAL : espiral *f* <a twist of lemon : una rodajita de limón> **4** : giro *m* inesperado (de eventos, etc.)
twister [ˈtwɪstər] **1** → **tornado 2** → **waterspout**
twitch[1] [ˈtwɪtʃ] *vi* : moverse nerviosamente, contraerse espasmódicamente (dícese de un músculo)
twitch[2] *n* : espasmo *m*, sacudida *f* <a nervous twitch : un tic nervioso>
twitter[1] [ˈtwɪtər] *vi* CHIRP : gorjear, cantar (dícese de los pájaros)
twitter[2] *n* : gorjeo *m*
two[1] [ˈtuː] *adj* : dos
two[2] *n*, *pl* **twos** : dos *m*
twofold[1] [ˈtuːˈfoːld] *adv* : al doble
twofold[2] [ˈtuː,foːld] *adj* : doble
two hundred[1] *adj* : doscientos
two hundred[2] *n* : doscientos *m*
twosome [ˈtuːsəm] *n* COUPLE : pareja *f*
tycoon [taɪˈkuːn] *n* : magnate *mf*
tying → **tie**[1]
type[1] [ˈtaɪp] *v* **typed; typing** *vt* **1** TYPEWRITE : escribir a máquina, pasar (un texto) a máquina **2** CATEGORIZE : categorizar, identificar — *vi* : escribir a máquina
type[2] *n* **1** KIND : tipo *m*, clase *f*, categoría *f* **2** *or* **printing type** : tipo *m*
typewrite [ˈtaɪp,raɪt] *v* **-wrote; -written** : escribir a máquina
typewriter [ˈtaɪp,raɪtər] *n* : máquina *f* de escribir
typhoid[1] [ˈtaɪ,fɔɪd, taɪˈ-] *adj* : relativo al tifus o a la tifoidea
typhoid[2] *n* *or* **typhoid fever** : tifoidea *f*
typhoon [taɪˈfuːn] *n* : tifón *m*
typhus [ˈtaɪfəs] *n* : tifus *m*, tifo *m*
typical [ˈtɪpɪkəl] *adj* : típico, característico — **typically** *adv*
typify [ˈtɪpə,faɪ] *vt* **-fied; -fying** : ser típico o representativo de (un grupo, una clase, etc.)
typist [ˈtaɪpɪst] *n* : mecanógrafo *m*, -fa *f*
typographic [,taɪpəˈgræfɪk] *or* **typographical** [-fɪkəl] *adj* : tipográfico — **typographically** [-fɪkli] *adv*
typography [taɪˈpɑgrəfi] *n* : tipografía *f*
tyrannical [təˈrænɪkəl, taɪ-] *adj* : tiránico — **tyrannically** [-nɪkli] *adv*
tyrannize [ˈtɪrə,naɪz] *vt* **-nized; -nizing** : tiranizar
tyranny [ˈtɪrəni] *n*, *pl* **-nies** : tiranía *f*
tyrant [ˈtaɪrənt] *n* : tirano *m*, -na *f*
tzar [ˈzɑr, ˈtsɑr, ˈsɑr] → **czar**

U

u [ˈjuː] *n, pl* **u's** *or* **us** [ˈjuːz] : vigésima primera letra del alfabeto inglés

ubiquitous [juːˈbɪkwət̬əs] *adj* : ubicuo, omnipresente

udder [ˈʌdər] *n* : ubre *f*

UFO [ˌjuːˌɛfˈoː, ˈjuːˌfoː] *n, pl* **UFO's** *or* **UFOs** (*unidentified flying object*) : ovni *m,* OVNI *m*

Ugandan [juːˈgændən, -ˈgɑn-; uːˈgɑn-] *n* : ugandés *m,* -desa *f* — **Ugandan** *adj*

ugliness [ˈʌglinəs] *n* : fealdad *f*

ugly [ˈʌgli] *adj* **uglier; -est 1** UNATTRACTIVE : feo **2** DISAGREEABLE : desagradable, feo <ugly weather : tiempo feo> <to have an ugly temper : tener mal genio>

Ukrainian [juːˈkreɪniən, -ˈkraɪ-] *n* : ucraniano *m,* -na *f* — **Ukrainian** *adj*

ukulele [ˌjuːkəˈleɪli] *n* : ukelele *m*

ulcer [ˈʌlsər] *n* : úlcera *f* (interna), llaga *f* (externa)

ulcerate [ˈʌlsəˌreɪt] *vi* **-ated; -ating** : ulcerarse

ulceration [ˌʌlsəˈreɪʃən] *n* **1** : ulceración *f* **2** ULCER : úlcera *f,* llaga *f*

ulcerous [ˈʌlsərəs] *adj* : ulceroso

ulna [ˈʌlnə] *n* : cúbito *m*

ulterior [ˌʌlˈtɪriər] *adj* : oculto <ulterior motive : motivo oculto, segunda intención>

ultimate [ˈʌltəmət] *adj* **1** FINAL : último, final **2** SUPREME : supremo, máximo **3** FUNDAMENTAL : fundamental, esencial

ultimately [ˈʌltəmətli] *adv* **1** FINALLY : por último, finalmente **2** EVENTUALLY : a la larga, con el tiempo

ultimatum [ˌʌltəˈmeɪtəm, -ˈmɑ-] *n, pl* **-tums** *or* **-ta** [-tə] : ultimátum *m*

ultraviolet [ˌʌltrəˈvaɪələt] *adj* : ultravioleta

umbilical cord [ˌʌmˈbɪlɪkəl] *adj* : cordón umbilical

umbrage [ˈʌmbrɪdʒ] *n* **to take umbrage at** : ofenderse por

umbrella [ˌʌmˈbrɛlə] *n* **1** : paraguas *m* **2 beach umbrella** : sombrilla *f*

umpire¹ [ˈʌmˌpaɪr] *v* **-pired; -piring** : arbitrar

umpire² *n* : árbitro *m,* -tra *f*

umpteenth [ˌʌmpˈtiːnθ] *adj* : enésimo

unable [ˌʌnˈeɪbəl] *adj* : incapaz <to be unable to : no poder>

unabridged [ˌʌnəˈbrɪdʒd] *adj* : íntegro

unacceptable [ˌʌnɪkˈsɛptəbəl] *adj* : inaceptable

unaccompanied [ˌʌnəˈkʌmpənid] *adj* : solo, sin acompañamiento (en música)

unaccountable [ˌʌnəˈkaʊntəbəl] *adj* : inexplicable, incomprensible — **unaccountably** [-bli] *adv*

unaccustomed [ˌʌnəˈkʌstəmd] *adj* **1** UNUSUAL : desacostumbrado, inusual **2** UNUSED : inhabituado <unaccustomed to noise : inhabituado al ruido>

unacquainted [ˌʌnəˈkweɪntəd] *adj* **to be unacquainted with** : desconocer, ignorar

unadorned [ˌʌnəˈdɔrnd] *adj* : sin adornos, puro y simple

unadulterated [ˌʌnəˈdʌltəˌreɪt̬əd] *adj* **1** PURE : puro <unadulterated food : comida pura> **2** ABSOLUTE : completo, absoluto

unaffected [ˌʌnəˈfɛktəd] *adj* **1** : no afectado, indiferente **2** NATURAL : sin afectación, natural

unaffectedly [ˌʌnəˈfɛktədli] *adv* : de manera natural

unafraid [ˌʌnəˈfreɪd] *adj* : sin miedo

unaided [ˌʌnˈeɪdəd] *adj* : sin ayuda, solo

unambiguous [ˌʌnæmˈbɪgjʊəs] *adj* : inequívoco

unanimity [ˌjuːnəˈnɪmət̬i] *n* : unanimidad *f*

unanimous [jʊˈnænəməs] *adj* : unánime — **unanimously** *adv*

unannounced [ˌʌnəˈnaʊnst] *adj* : sin dar aviso

unanswered [ˌʌnˈæntsərd] *adj* : sin contestar

unappealing [ˌʌnəˈpiːlɪŋ] *adj* : desagradable

unappetizing [ˌʌnˈæpəˌtaɪzɪŋ] *adj* : poco apetitoso, poco apetecible

unarmed [ˌʌnˈɑrmd] *adj* : sin armas, desarmado

unassisted [ˌʌnəˈsɪstəd] *adj* : sin ayuda

unassuming [ˌʌnəˈsuːmɪŋ] *adj* : modesto, sin pretensiones

unattached [ˌʌnəˈtætʃt] *adj* **1** LOOSE : suelto **2** INDEPENDENT : independiente **3** : solo (ni casado ni prometido)

unattractive [ˌʌnəˈtræktɪv] *adj* : poco atractivo

unauthorized [ˌʌnˈɔθəˌraɪzd] *adj* : sin autorización, no autorizado

unavailable [ˌʌnəˈveɪləbəl] *adj* : no disponible

unavoidable [ˌʌnəˈvɔɪdəbəl] *adj* : inevitable, ineludible

unaware¹ [ˌʌnəˈwær] *adv* → **unawares**

unaware² *adj* : inconsciente

unawares [ˌʌnəˈwærz] *adv* **1** : por sorpresa <to catch someone unawares : agarrar a alguien desprevenido> **2** UNINTENTIONALLY : inconscientemente, inadvertidamente

unbalanced [ˌʌnˈbælən*t*st] *adj* : desequilibrado

unbearable [ˌʌnˈbærəbəl] *adj* : insoportable, inaguantable — **unbearably** [-bli] *adv*

unbecoming [ˌʌnbɪˈkʌmɪŋ] *adj* **1** UNSEEMLY : impropio, indecoroso **2** UNFLATTERING : poco favorecedor

unbelievable [ˌʌnbəˈliːvəbəl] *adj* : increíble — **unbelievably** [-bli] *adv*
unbend [ˌʌnˈbɛnd] *vi* **-bent** [-ˈbɛnt]; **-bending** RELAX : relajarse
unbending [ˌʌnˈbɛndɪŋ] *adj* : inflexible
unbiased [ˌʌnˈbaɪəst] *adj* : imparcial, objetivo
unbind [ˌʌnˈbaɪnd] *vt* **-bound** [-ˈbaʊnd]; **-binding 1** UNFASTEN, UNTIE : desatar, desamarrar **2** RELEASE : liberar
unbolt [ˌʌnˈboːlt] *vt* : abrir el cerrojo de, descorrer el pestillo de
unborn [ˌʌnˈbɔrn] *adj* : aún no nacido, que va a nacer
unbosom [ˌʌnˈbʊzəm, -ˈbuː-] *vt* : revelar, divulgar
unbreakable [ˌʌnˈbreɪkəbəl] *adj* : irrompible
unbridled [ˌʌnˈbraɪdəld] *adj* : desenfrenado
unbroken [ˌʌnˈbroːkən] *adj* **1** INTACT : intacto, sano **2** CONTINUOUS : continuo, ininterrumpido
unbuckle [ˌʌnˈbʌkəl] *vt* **-led; -ling** : desabrochar
unburden [ˌʌnˈbərdən] *vt* **1** UNLOAD : descargar **2 to unburden oneself** : desahogarse
unbutton [ˌʌnˈbʌtən] *vt* : desabrochar, desabotonar
uncalled–for [ˌʌnˈkɔldˌfɔr] *adj* : inapropiado, innecesario
uncanny [ənˈkæni] *adj* **-nier; -est 1** STRANGE : extraño **2** EXTRAORDINARY : raro, extraordinario — **uncannily** [-ˈkænəli] *adv*
unceasing [ˌʌnˈsiːsɪŋ] *adj* : incesante, continuo — **unceasingly** *adv*
unceremonious [ˌʌnˌsɛrəˈmoːniəs] *adj* **1** INFORMAL : sin ceremonia, sin pompa **2** ABRUPT : abrupto, brusco — **unceremoniously** *adv*
uncertain [ˌʌnˈsərtən] *adj* **1** INDEFINITE : indeterminado **2** UNSURE : incierto, dudoso **3** CHANGEABLE : inestable, variable <uncertain weather : tiempo inestable> **4** HESITANT : indeciso **5** VAGUE : poco claro
uncertainly [ˌʌnˈsərtənli] *adv* : dudosamente, con desconfianza
uncertainty [ˌʌnˈərtənti] *n, pl* **-ties** : duda *f*, incertidumbre *f*
unchangeable [ˌʌnˈtʃeɪndʒəbəl] *adj* : inalterable, inmutable
unchanged [ˌʌnˈtʃeɪndʒd] *adj* : sin cambiar
unchanging [ˌʌnˈtʃeɪdʒɪŋ] *adj* : inalterable, inmutable, firme
uncharacteristic [ˌʌnˌkærɪktəˈrɪstɪk] *adj* : inusual, desacostumbrado
uncharged [ˌʌnˈtʃɑrdʒd] *adj* : sin carga (eléctrica)
uncivilized [ˌʌnˈsɪvəˌlaɪzd] *adj* **1** BARBAROUS : incivilizado, bárbaro **2** WILD : salvaje
uncle [ˈʌŋkəl] *n* : tío *m*
unclean [ˌʌnˈkliːn] *adj* **1** IMPURE : impuro **2** DIRTY : sucio
unclear [ˌʌnˈklɪr] *adj* : confuso, borroso, poco claro
Uncle Sam [ˈsæm] *n* : el Tío Sam
unclog [ˌʌnˈklɑg] *vt* **-clogged; -clogging** : desatascar, destapar
unclothed [ˌʌnˈkloːðd] *adj* : desnudo
uncomfortable [ˌʌnˈkʌmpfərṭəbəl] *adj* **1** : incómodo (dícese de una silla, etc.) **2** UNEASY : inquieto, incómodo
uncommitted [ˌʌnkəˈmɪṭəd] *adj* : sin compromisos
uncommon [ˌʌnˈkɑmən] *adj* **1** UNUSUAL : raro, poco común **2** REMARKABLE : excepcional, extraordinario
uncommonly [ˌʌnˈkɑmənli] *adv* : extraordinariamente
uncompromising [ˌʌnˈkɑmprəˌmaɪzɪŋ] *adj* : inflexible, intransigente
unconcerned [ˌʌnkənˈsərnd] *adj* : indiferente — **unconcernedly** [-ˈsərnədli] *adv*
unconditional [ˌʌnkənˈdɪʃənəl] *adj* : incondicional — **unconditionally** *adv*
unconscious[1] [ˌʌnˈkɑntʃəs] *adj* : inconsciente — **unconsciously** *adv*
unconscious[2] *n* : inconsciente *m*
unconsciousness [ˌʌnˈkɑntʃəsnəs] *n* : inconsciencia *f*
unconstitutional [ˌʌnˌkɑntstəˈtuːʃənəl, -ˈtjuː-] *adj* : inconstitucional
uncontrollable [ˌʌnkənˈtroːləbəl] *adj* : incontrolable, incontenible — **uncontrollably** [-bli] *adv*
uncontrolled [ˌʌnkənˈtroːld] *adj* : incontrolado
unconventional [ˌʌnkənˈvɛntʃənəl] *adj* : poco convencional
unconvincing [ˌʌnkənˈvɪntsɪŋ] *adj* : poco convincente
uncouth [ˌʌnˈkuːθ] *adj* CRUDE, ROUGH : grosero, rudo
uncover [ˌʌnˈkʌvər] *vt* **1** : destapar (un objeto), dejar al descubierto **2** EXPOSE, REVEAL : descubrir, revelar, exponer
uncultivated [ˌʌnˈkʌltəˌveɪṭəd] *adj* : inculto
uncurl [ˌʌnˈkərl] *vt* UNROLL : desenrollar — *vi* : desenrollarse, desrizarse (dícese del pelo)
uncut [ˌʌnˈkʌt] *adj* **1** : sin cortar <uncut grass : hierba sin cortar> **2** : sin tallar, en bruto <an uncut diamond : un diamante en bruto> **3** UNABRIDGED : completo, íntegro
undaunted [ˌʌnˈdɔntəd] *adj* : impávido
undecided [ˌʌndiˈsaɪdəd] *adj* **1** IRRESOLUTE : indeciso, irresoluto **2** UNRESOLVED : pendiente, no resuelto
undefeated [ˌʌndiˈfiːṭəd] *adj* : invicto
undeniable [ˌʌndiˈnaɪəbəl] *adj* : innegable — **undeniably** [-bli] *adv*
under[1] [ˈʌndər] *adv* **1** LESS : menos <$10 or under : $10 o menos> **2** UNDERWATER : debajo del agua **3** : bajo los efectos de la anestesia

under[2] *adj* **1** LOWER : (más) bajo, inferior **2** SUBORDINATE : inferior **3** : insuficiente <an under dose of medicine : una dosis insuficiente de medicina>

under[3] *prep* **1** BELOW, BENEATH : debajo de, abajo de <under the table : abajo de la mesa> <we walked under the arch : pasamos por debajo del arco> <under the sun : bajo el sol> **2** : menos de <in under 20 minutes : en menos de 20 minutos> **3** (*indicating rank or authority*) : bajo <under the command of : bajo las órdenes de> **4** SUBJECT TO : bajo <under suspicion : bajo sospecha> <under the circumstances : dadas las circunstancias> **5** ACCORDING TO : según, de acuerdo con, conforme a <under the present laws : según las leyes actuales>

underage [ˌʌndərˈeɪdʒ] *adj* : menor de edad

underbrush [ˈʌndərˌbrəʃ] *n* : maleza *f*

underclothes [ˈʌndərˌkloːz, -ˌkloːðz] → **underwear**

underclothing [ˈʌndərˌkloːðɪŋ] → **underwear**

undercover [ˌʌndərˈkʌvər] *adj* : secreto, clandestino

undercurrent [ˈʌndərˌkərənt] *n* **1** : corriente *f* submarina **2** UNDERTONE : corriente *f* oculta, trasfondo *m*

undercut [ˌʌndərˈkʌt] *vt* **-cut; -cutting** : vender más barato que

underdeveloped [ˌʌndərdɪˈvɛləpt] *adj* : subdesarrollado, atrasado

underdog [ˈʌndərˌdɔg] *n* : persona *f* que tiene menos posibilidades

underdone [ˌʌndərˈdʌn] *adj* RARE : poco cocido

underestimate [ˌʌndərˈɛstəˌmeɪt] *vt* **-mated; -mating** : subestimar, menospreciar

underexposed [ˌʌndərɪkˈspoːzd] *adj* : subexpuesto (en fotografía)

underfoot [ˌʌndərˈfʊt] *adv* **1** : bajo los pies <to trample underfoot : pisotear> **2 to be underfoot** : estorbar <they're always underfoot : están siempre estorbando>

undergarment [ˈʌndərˌgɑrmənt] *n* : prenda *f* íntima

undergo [ˌʌndərˈgoː] *vt* **-went** [-ˈwɛnt;]; **-gone** [-ˈgɔn]; **-going** : sufrir, experimentar <to undergo an operation : someterse a una intervención quirúrgica>

undergraduate [ˌʌndərˈgrædʒʊət] *n* : estudiante *m* universitario, estudiante *f* universitaria

underground[1] [ˌʌndərˈgraʊnd] *adv* **1** : bajo tierra **2** SECRETLY : clandestinamente, en secreto <to go underground : pasar a la clandestinidad>

underground[2] [ˈʌndərˌgraʊnd] *adj* **1** SUBTERRANEAN : subterráneo **2** SECRET : secreto, clandestino

underground[3] [ˈʌndərˌgraʊnd] *n* : movimiento *m* o grupo *m* clandestino

undergrowth [ˈʌndərˈgroːθ] *n* : maleza *f*, broza *f*

underhand[1] [ˈʌndərˌhænd] *adv* **1** SECRETLY : de manera clandestina **2** *or* **underhanded** : sin levantar el brazo por encima del hombro (en deportes)

underhand[2] *adj* **1** SLY : solapado **2** : por debajo del hombro (en deportes)

underhanded [ˌʌndərˈhændəd] *adj* **1** SLY : solapado **2** SHADY : turbio, poco limpio

underline [ˈʌndərˌlaɪn] *vt* **-lined; -lining 1** : subrayar **2** EMPHASIZE : subrayar, acentuar, hacer hincapié en

underlying [ˌʌndərˈlaɪɪŋ] *adj* **1** : subyacente <the underlying rock : la roca subyacente> **2** FUNDAMENTAL : fundamental, esencial

undermine [ˌʌndərˈmaɪn] *vt* **-mined; -mining 1** : socavar (una estructura, etc.) **2** SAP, WEAKEN : minar, debilitar

underneath[1] [ˌʌndərˈniːθ] *adv* : debajo, abajo <the part underneath : la parte de abajo>

underneath[2] *prep* : debajo de, abajo de

undernourished [ˌʌndərˈnərɪʃt] *adj* : desnutrido

underpants [ˈʌndərˌpænts] *npl* : calzoncillos *mpl*, calzones *mpl*

underpass [ˈʌndərˌpæs] *n* : paso *m* a desnivel

underprivileged [ˌʌndərˈprɪvlɪdʒd] *adj* : desfavorecido

underrate [ˌʌndərˈreɪt] *vt* **-rated; -rating** : subestimar, menospreciar

underscore [ˈʌndərˌskor] *vt* **-scored; -scoring** → **underline**

undersea[1] [ˌʌndərˈsiː] *or* **underseas** [-ˈsiːz] *adv* : bajo la superficie del mar

undersea[2] *adj* : submarino

undersecretary [ˌʌndərˈsɛkrəˌtɛri] *n, pl* **-ries** : subsecretario *m*, -ria *f*

undersell [ˌʌndərˈsɛl] *vt* **-sold; -selling** : vender más barato que

undershirt [ˈʌndərˌʃərt] *n* : camiseta *f*

undershorts [ˈʌndərˌʃɔrts] *npl* : calzoncillos *mpl*

underside [ˈʌndərˌsaɪd, ˌʌndərˈsaɪd] *n* : parte *f* de abajo

undersized [ˌʌndərˈsaɪzd] *adj* : más pequeño de lo normal

understand [ˌʌndərˈstænd] *v* **-stood** [-ˈstʊd;]; **-standing** *vt* **1** COMPREHEND : comprender, entender <I don't understand it : no lo entiendo> <that's understood : eso se comprende> <to make oneself understood : hacerse entender> **2** BELIEVE : entender <to give someone to understand : dar a alguien a entender> **3** INFER : tener entendido <I understand that she's leaving : tengo entendido que se va> — *vi* : comprender, entender

understandable [ˌʌndərˈstændəbəl] *adj* : comprensible

understanding[1] [ˌʌndərˈstændɪŋ] *adj* : comprensivo, compasivo
understanding[2] *n* **1** GRASP : comprensión *f,* entendimiento *m* **2** SYMPATHY : comprensión *f* (mutua) **3** INTERPRETATION : interpretación *f* <it's my understanding that... : tengo la impresión de que..., tengo entendido que...> **4** AGREEMENT : acuerdo *m,* arreglo *m*
understate [ˌʌndərˈsteɪt] *vt* **-stated; -stating** : minimizar, subestimar
understatement [ˌʌndərˈsteɪtmənt] *n* : atenuación *f* <that's an understatement : decir sólo eso es quedarse corto>
understudy [ˈʌndərˌstʌdi] *n, pl* **-dies** : sobresaliente *mf,* suplente *mf* (en el teatro)
undertake [ˌʌndərˈteɪk] *vt* **-took** [-ˈtʊk]; **-taken** [-ˈteɪkən]; **-taking 1** : emprender (una tarea), asumir (una responsabilidad) **2** PROMISE : comprometerse (a hacer algo)
undertaker [ˈʌndərˌteɪkər] *n* : director *m,* -tora *f* de funeraria
undertaking [ˈʌndərˌteɪkɪŋ, ˌʌndərˈ-] *n* **1** ENTERPRISE, TASK : empresa *f,* tarea *f* **2** PLEDGE : promesa *f,* garantía *f*
undertone [ˈʌndərˌtoːn] *n* **1** : voz *f* baja <to speak in an undertone : hablar en voz baja> **2** HINT, UNDERCURRENT : trasfondo *m,* matiz *m*
undertow [ˈʌndərˌtoː] *n* : resaca *f*
undervalue [ˌʌndərˈvælˌjuː] *vt* **-ued; -uing** : menospreciar, subestimar
underwater[1] [ˌʌndərˈwɔt̬ər, -ˈwɑ-] *adv* : debajo (del agua)
underwater[2] *adj* : submarino
under way [ˌʌndərˈweɪ] *adv* : en marcha, en camino <to get under way : ponerse en marcha>
underwear [ˈʌndərˌwær] *n* : ropa *f* interior, ropa *f* íntima
underworld [ˈʌndərˌwərld] *n* **1** HELL : infierno *m* **2 the underworld** CRIMINALS : la hampa, los bajos fondos
underwrite [ˈʌndərˌraɪt, ˌʌndərˈ-] *vt* **-wrote** [-ˌroːt, -ˈroːt]; **-written** [-ˌrɪtən, -ˈrɪtən]; **-writing 1** INSURE : asegurar **2** FINANCE : financiar **3** BACK, ENDORSE : suscribir, respaldar
underwriter [ˈʌndərˌraɪt̬ər, ˌʌndərˈ-] *n* INSURER : asegurador *m,* -dora *f*
undeserving [ˌʌndiˈzərvɪŋ] *adj* : indigno
undesirable[1] [ˌʌndiˈzaɪrəbəl] *adj* : indeseable
undesirable[2] *n* : indeseable *mf*
undeveloped [ˌʌndiˈvɛləpt] *adj* : sin desarrollar, sin revelar (dícese de una película)
undies [ˈʌndiːz] → **underwear**
undignified [ˌʌnˈdɪgnəfaɪd] *adj* : indecoroso
undiluted [ˌʌndaɪˈluːt̬əd, -də-] *adj* : sin diluir, concentrado
undiscovered [ˌʌndɪˈskʌvərd] *adj* : no descubierto
undisputed [ˌʌndɪˈspjuːt̬əd] *adj* : indiscutible
undisturbed [ˌʌndɪˈstərbd] *adj* : tranquilo (dícese de una persona), sin tocar (dícese de un objeto)
undivided [ˌʌndɪˈvaɪdəd] *adj* : íntegro, completo
undo [ˌʌnˈduː] *vt* **-did** [-ˈdɪd]; **-done** [-ˈdʌn]; **-doing 1** UNFASTEN : desabrochar, desatar, abrir **2** ANNUL : anular **3** REVERSE : deshacer, reparar (daños, etc.) **4** RUIN : arruinar, destruir
undoing [ˌʌnˈduːɪŋ] *n* : ruina *f,* perdición *f*
undoubted [ˌʌnˈdaʊt̬əd] *adj* : cierto, indudable — **undoubtedly** *adv*
undress [ˌʌnˈdrɛs] *vt* : desvestir, desabrigar, desnudar — *vi* : desvestirse, desnudarse
undrinkable [ˌʌnˈdrɪŋkəbəl] *adj* : no potable
undue [ˌʌnˈduː, -ˈdjuː] *adj* : excesivo, indebido — **unduly** *adv*
undulate [ˈʌndʒəˌleɪt] *vi* **-lated; -lating** : ondular
undulation [ˌʌndʒəˈleɪʃən] *n* : ondulación *f*
undying [ˌʌnˈdaɪɪŋ] *adj* : perpetuo, imperecedero
unearth [ˌʌnˈərθ] *vt* **1** EXHUME : desenterrar, exhumar **2** DISCOVER : descubrir
unearthly [ˌʌnˈərθli] *adj* **-lier; -est** : sobrenatural, de otro mundo
uneasily [ˌʌnˈiːzəli] *adv* : inquietamente, con inquietud
uneasiness [ˌʌnˈiːzinəs] *n* : inquietud *f*
uneasy [ˌʌnˈiːzi] *adj* **-easier; -est 1** AWKWARD : incómodo **2** WORRIED : preocupado, inquieto **3** RESTLESS : inquieto, agitado
uneducated [ˌʌnˈɛdʒəˌkeɪt̬əd] *adj* : inculto, sin educación
unemployed [ˌʌnɪmˈplɔɪd] *adj* : desempleado
unemployment [ˌʌnɪmˈplɔɪmənt] *n* : desempleo *m*
unending [ˌʌnˈɛndɪŋ] *adj* : sin fin, interminable
unendurable [ˌʌnɪnˈdʊrəbəl, -ɛn-, -ˈdjʊr-] *adj* : insoportable, intolerable
unequal [ˌʌnˈiːkwəl] *adj* **1** : desigual **2** INADEQUATE : incapaz, incompetente <to be unequal to a task : no estar a la altura de una tarea>
unequaled *or* **unequalled** [ˌʌnˈiːkwəld] *adj* : sin igual
unequivocal [ˌʌnɪˈkwɪvəkəl] *adj* : inequívoco, claro — **unequivocally** *adv*
unerring [ˌʌnˈɛrɪŋ, -ˈər-] *adj* : infalible
unethical [ˌʌnˈɛθɪkəl] *adj* : poco ético
uneven [ˌʌnˈiːvən] *adj* **1** ODD : impar (dícese de un número) **2** : desigual, desnivelado (dícese de una superficie) <uneven terrain : terreno accidentado> **3** IRREGULAR : irregular, poco uniforme **4** UNEQUAL : desigual

unevenly [ˌʌnˈiːvənli] *adv* : desigualmente, irregularmente
uneventful [ˌʌnɪˈvɛntfəl] *adj* : sin incidentes, tranquilo
unexpected [ˌʌnɪkˈspɛktəd] *adj* : imprevisto, inesperado — **unexpectedly** *adv*
unfailing [ˌʌnˈfeɪlɪŋ] *adj* **1** CONSTANT : constante **2** INEXHAUSTIBLE : inagotable **3** SURE : a toda prueba, indefectible
unfair [ˌʌnˈfær] *adj* : injusto — **unfairly** *adv*
unfairness [ˌʌnˈfærnəs] *n* : injusticia *f*
unfaithful [ˌʌnˈfeɪθfəl] *adj* : desleal, infiel — **unfaithfully** *adv*
unfaithfulness [ˌʌnˈfeɪθfəlnəs] *n* : infidelidad *f,* deslealtad *f*
unfamiliar [ˌʌnfəˈmɪljər] *adj* **1** STRANGE : desconocido, extraño <an unfamiliar place : un lugar nuevo> **2 to be unfamiliar with** : no estar familiarizado con, desconocer
unfamiliarity [ˌʌnfəˌmɪliˈærəṱi] *n* : falta *f* de familiaridad
unfashionable [ˌʌnˈfæʃənəbəl] *adj* : fuera de moda
unfasten [ˌʌnˈfæsən] *vt* : desabrochar, desatar (una cuerda, etc.), abrir (una puerta)
unfavorable [ˌʌnˈfeɪvərəbəl] *adj* : desfavorable, mal — **unfavorably** [-bli] *adv*
unfeeling [ˌʌnˈfiːlɪŋ] *adj* : insensible — **unfeelingly** *adv*
unfinished [ˌʌnˈfɪnɪʃd] *adj* : inacabado, incompleto
unfit [ˌʌnˈfɪt] *adj* **1** UNSUITABLE : inadecuado, impropio **2** UNSUITED : no apto, incapaz **3** : incapacitado (físicamente) <to be unfit : no estar en forma>
unflappable [ˌʌnˈflæpəbəl] *adj* : imperturbable
unflattering [ˌʌnˈflæṱərɪŋ] *adj* : poco favorecedor
unfold [ˌʌnˈfoːld] *vt* **1** EXPAND : desplegar, desdoblar, extender <to unfold a map : desplegar un mapa> **2** DISCLOSE, REVEAL : revelar, exponer (un plan, etc.) — *vi* **1** DEVELOP : desarrollarse, desenvolverse <the story unfolded : el cuento se desarrollaba> **2** EXPAND : extenderse, desplegarse
unforeseeable [ˌʌnforˈsiːəbəl] *adj* : imprevisible
unforeseen [ˌʌnforˈsiːn] *adj* : imprevisto
unforgettable [ˌʌnfərˈgɛṱəbəl] *adj* : inolvidable, memorable — **unforgettably** [-bli] *adv*
unforgivable [ˌʌnfərˈgɪvəbəl] *adj* : imperdonable
unfortunate¹ [ˌʌnˈfɔrtʃənət] *adj* **1** UNLUCKY : desgraciado, infortunado, desafortunado <how unfortunate! : ¡qué mala suerte!> **2** INAPPROPRIATE : inoportuno <an unfortunate comment : un comentario poco feliz>
unfortunate² *n* : desgraciado *m,* -da *f*
unfortunately [ˌʌnˈfɔrtʃənətli] *adv* : desafortunadamente
unfounded [ˌʌnˈfaʊndəd] *adj* : infundado
unfreeze [ˌʌnˈfriːz] *v* **-froze** [-ˈfroːz]; **-frozen** [-ˈfroːzən]; **-freezing** *vt* : descongelar — *vi* : descongelarse
unfriendliness [ˌʌnˈfrɛndlinəs] *n* : hostilidad *f,* antipatía *f*
unfriendly [ˌʌnˈfrɛndli] *adj* **-lier; -est** : poco amistoso, hostil
unfurl [ˌʌnˈfərl] *vt* : desplegar, desdoblar — *vi* : desplegarse
unfurnished [ˌʌnˈfərnɪʃt] *adj* : desamueblado
ungainly [ˌʌnˈgeɪnli] *adj* : desgarbado
ungodly [ˌʌnˈgɔdli, -ˈgɑd-] *adj* **1** IMPIOUS : impío **2** OUTRAGEOUS : atroz, terrible <at an ungodly hour : a una hora intempestiva>
ungrateful [ˌʌnˈgreɪtfəl] *adj* : desagradecido, ingrato — **ungratefully** *adv*
ungratefulness [ˌʌnˈgreɪtfəlnəs] *n* : ingratitud *f*
unhappily [ˌʌnˈhæpəli] *adv* **1** SADLY : tristemente **2** UNFORTUNATELY : desafortunadamente, lamentablemente
unhappiness [ˌʌnˈhæpinəs] *n* : infelicidad *f,* tristeza *f,* desdicha *f*
unhappy [ˌʌnˈhæpi] *adj* **-pier; -est 1** UNFORTUNATE : desafortunado, desventurado **2** MISERABLE, SAD : infeliz, triste, desdichado **3** INOPPORTUNE : inoportuno, poco feliz
unharmed [ˌʌnˈhɑrmd] *adj* : salvo, ileso
unhealthy [ˌʌnˈhɛlθi] *adj* **-thier; -est 1** UNWHOLESOME : insalubre, malsano, nocivo a la salud <an unhealthy climate : un clima insalubre> **2** SICKLY : de mala salud, enfermizo
unheard–of [ˌʌnˈhərdəv] *adj* : sin precedente, inaudito, insólito
unhinge [ˌʌnˈhɪndʒ] *vt* **-hinged; -hinging 1** : desquiciar (una puerta, etc.) **2** DISRUPT, UNSETTLE : trastornar, perturbar
unholy [ˌʌnˈhoːli] *adj* **-lier; -est 1** : profano, impío **2** UNGODLY : atroz, terrible
unhook [ˌʌnˈhʊk] *vt* **1** : desenganchar, descolgar (de algo) **2** UNDO : desabrochar
unhurt [ˌʌnˈhərt] *adj* : ileso
unicorn [ˈjuːnəˌkɔrn] *n* : unicornio *m*
unidentified [ˌʌnaɪˈdɛntəˌfaɪd] *adj* : no identificado <unidentified flying object : objeto volador no identificado>
unification [ˌjuːnəfəˈkeɪʃən] *n* : unificación *f*
uniform¹ [ˈjuːnəˌfɔrm] *adj* : uniforme, homogéneo, constante
uniform² *n* : uniforme *m*
uniformity [ˌjuːnəˈfɔrməṱi] *n, pl* **-ties** : uniformidad *f*

unify [ˈjuːnəˌfaɪ] *vt* **-fied; -fying** : unificar, unir
unilateral [ˌjuːnəˈlætərəl] *adj* : unilateral — **unilaterally** *adv*
unimaginable [ˌʌnɪˈmædʒənəbəl] *adj* : inimaginable, inconcebible
unimportant [ˌʌnɪmˈpɔrtənt] *adj* : intrascendente, insignificante, sin importancia
uninhabited [ˌʌnɪnˈhæbət̬əd] *adj* : deshabitado, desierto, despoblado
uninhibited [ˌʌnɪnˈhɪbət̬əd] *adj* : desenfadado, desinhibido, sin reservas
uninjured [ˌʌnˈindʒərd] *adj* : ileso
unintelligent [ˌʌnɪnˈtɛlədʒənt] *adj* : poco inteligente
unintelligible [ˌʌnɪnˈtɛlədʒəbəl] *adj* : ininteligible, incomprensible
unintentional [ˌʌnɪnˈtɛntʃənəl] *adj* : no deliberado, involuntario
unintentionally [ˌʌnɪnˈtɛntʃənəli] *adv* : involuntariamente, sin querer
uninterested [ˌʌnˈɪntəˌrɛstəd, -trəstəd] *adj* : indiferente
uninteresting [ˌʌnˈɪntəˌrɛstɪŋ, -trəstɪŋ] *adj* : poco interesante, sin interés
uninterrupted [ˌʌnˌɪntəˈrʌptəd] *adj* : ininterrumpido, continuo
union [ˈjuːnjən] *n* **1** : unión *f* **2** *or* **labor union** : sindicato *m*, gremio *m*
unionize [ˈjuːnjəˌnaɪz] *v* **-ized; -izing** *vt* : sindicalizar, sindicar — *vi* : sindicalizarse
unique [jʊˈniːk] *adj* **1** SOLE : único, solo **2** UNUSUAL : extraordinario
uniquely [jʊˈniːkli] *adv* **1** EXCLUSIVELY : exclusivamente **2** EXCEPTIONALLY : excepcionalmente
unison [ˈjuːnəsən, -zən] *n* **1** : unísono *m* (en música) **2** CONCORD : acuerdo *m*, armonía *f*, concordia *f* **3 in ~** SIMULTANEOUSLY : simultáneamente, al unísono
unit [ˈjuːnɪt] *n* **1** : unidad *f* **2** : módulo *m* (de un mobiliario)
unite [jʊˈnaɪt] *v* **united; uniting** *vt* : unir, juntar, combinar — *vi* : unirse, juntarse
unity [ˈjuːnət̬i] *n, pl* **-ties 1** UNION : unidad *f*, unión *f* **2** HARMONY : armonía *f*, acuerdo *m*
universal [ˌjuːnəˈvərsəl] *adj* **1** GENERAL : general, universal <a universal rule : una regla universal> **2** WORLDWIDE : universal, mundial — **universally** *adv*
universe [ˈjuːnəˌvərs] *n* : universo *m*
university [ˌjuːnəˈvərsət̬i] *n, pl* **-ties** : universidad *f*
unjust [ˌʌnˈdʒʌst] *adj* : injusto — **unjustly** *adv*
unjustifiable [ˌʌnˌdʒʌstəˈfaɪəbəl] *adj* : injustificable
unjustified [ˌʌnˈdʒʌstəˌfaɪd] *adj* : injustificado
unkempt [ˌʌnˈkɛmpt] *adj* : descuidado, desaliñado, despeinado (dícese del pelo)
unkind [ˌʌnˈkaɪnd] *adj* : poco amable, cruel — **unkindly** *adv*
unkindness [ˌʌnˈkaɪndnəs] *n* : crueldad *f*, falta *f* de amabilidad
unknowing [ˌʌnˈnoːɪŋ] *adj* : inconsciente, ignorante — **unknowingly** *adv*
unknown [ˌʌnˈnoːn] *adj* : desconocido
unlawful [ˌʌnˈlɔfəl] *adj* : ilícito, ilegal — **unlawfully** *adv*
unleash [ˌʌnˈliːʃ] *vt* : soltar, desatar
unless [ənˈlɛs] *conj* : a menos que, salvo que, a no ser que
unlike[1] [ˌʌnˈlaɪk] *adj* **1** DIFFERENT : diferente, distinto **2** UNEQUAL : desigual
unlike[2] *prep* **1** : diferente de, distinto de <unlike the others : distinto a los demás> **2** : a diferencia de <unlike her sister, she is shy : a diferencia de su hermana, es tímida>
unlikelihood [ˌʌnˈlaɪkliˌhʊd] *n* : improbabilidad *f*
unlikely [ˌʌnˈlaɪkli] *adj* **-lier; -est 1** IMPROBABLE : improbable, poco probable **2** UNPROMISING : poco prometedor
unlimited [ˌʌnˈlɪmət̬əd] *adj* : ilimitado
unload [ˌʌnˈloːd] *vt* **1** REMOVE : descargar, desembarcar (mercancías o pasajeros) **2** : descargar (un avión, un camión, etc.) **3** DUMP : deshacerse de — *vi* : descargar (dícese de un avión, un camión, etc.)
unlock [ˌʌnˈlɑk] *vt* **1** : abrir (con llave) **2** DISCLOSE, REVEAL : revelar
unluckily [ˌʌnˈlʌkəli] *adv* : desgraciadamente
unlucky [ˌʌnˈlʌki] *adj* **-luckier; -est 1** : de mala suerte, desgraciado, desafortunado <an unlucky year : un año de mala suerte> **2** INAUSPICIOUS : desfavorable, poco propicio **3** REGRETTABLE : lamentable
unmanageable [ˌʌnˈmænɪdʒəbəl] *adj* : difícil de controlar, poco manejable, ingobernable
unmarried [ˌʌnˈmærid] *adj* : soltero
unmask [ˌʌnˈmæsk] *vt* EXPOSE : desenmascarar
unmerciful [ˌʌnˈmərsɪfəl] *adj* MERCILESS : despiadado — **unmercifully** *adv*
unmistakable [ˌʌnmɪˈsteɪkəbəl] *adj* : evidente, inconfundible, obvio — **unmistakably** [-bli] *adv*
unmoved [ˌʌnˈmuːvd] *adj* : impasible <to be unmoved by : permanecer impasible ante>
unnatural [ˌʌnˈnætʃərəl] *adj* **1** ABNORMAL, UNUSUAL : anormal, poco natural, poco normal **2** AFFECTED : afectado, forzado <an unnatural smile : una sonrisa forzada> **3** PERVERSE : perverso, antinatural
unnecessary [ˌʌnˈnɛsəˌsɛri] *adj* : innecesario — **unnecessarily** [-ˌnɛsəˈsɛrəli] *adv*

unnerve [ˌʌnˈnərv] *vt* **-nerved; -nerving** : turbar, desconcertar, poner nervioso
unnoticed [ˌʌnˈnoːt̬əst] *adj* : inadvertido <to go unnoticed : pasar inadvertido>
unobstructed [ˌʌnəbˈstrʌktəd] *adj* : libre, despejado
unobtainable [ˌʌnəbˈteɪnəbəl] *adj* : inasequible
unobtrusive [ˌʌnəbˈstruːsɪv] *adj* : discreto
unoccupied [ˌʌnˈɑkjəˌpaɪd] *adj* **1** IDLE : desempleado, desocupado **2** EMPTY : desocupado, libre, deshabitado
unofficial [ˌʌnəˈfɪʃəl] *adj* : extraoficial, oficioso, no oficial
unorganized [ˌʌnˈɔrgəˌnaɪzd] *adj* : desorganizado
unorthodox [ˌʌnˈɔrθəˌdɑks] *adj* : poco ortodoxo, poco convencional
unpack [ˌʌnˈpæk] *vt* : desempacar — *vi* : desempacar, deshacer las maletas
unpaid [ˌʌnˈpeɪd] *adj* : no remunerado, no retribuido <an unpaid bill : una cuenta pendiente>
unparalleled [ˌʌnˈpærəˌlɛld] *adj* : sin igual
unpatriotic [ˌʌnˌpeɪtriˈɑt̬ɪk] *adj* : antipatriótico
unpleasant [ˌʌnˈplɛzənt] *adj* : desagradable — **unpleasantly** *adv*
unplug [ˌʌnˈplʌg] *vt* **-plugged; -plugging 1** UNCLOG : destapar, desatascar **2** DISCONNECT : desconectar, desenchufar
unpopular [ˌʌnˈpɑpjələr] *adj* : impopular, poco popular
unpopularity [ˌʌnˌpɑpjəˈlærət̬i] *n* : impopularidad *f*
unprecedented [ˌʌnˈprɛsəˌdɛntəd] *adj* : sin precedentes, inaudito, nuevo
unpredictable [ˌʌnpriˈdɪktəbəl] *adj* : impredecible
unprejudiced [ˌʌnˈprɛdʒədəst] *adj* : imparcial, objetivo
unprepared [ˌʌnpriˈpærd] *adj* : no preparado <an unprepared speech : un discurso improvisado>
unpretentious [ˌʌnpriˈtɛntʃəs] *adj* : modesto, sin pretensiones
unprincipled [ˌʌnˈprɪn*t*səpəld] *adj* : sin principios, carente de escrúpulos
unproductive [ˌʌnprəˈdʌktɪv] *adj* : improductivo
unprofitable [ˌʌnˈprɑfət̬əbəl] *adj* : no rentable, poco provechoso
unpromising [ˌʌnˈprɑməsɪŋ] *adj* : poco prometedor
unprotected [ˌʌnprəˈtɛktəd] *adj* : sin protección, desprotegido
unprovoked [ˌʌnprəˈvoːkt] *adj* : no provocado
unpunished [ˌʌnˈpʌnɪʃt] *adj* : impune <to go unpunished : escapar sin castigo>
unqualified [ˌʌnˈkwɑləˌfaɪd] *adj* **1** : no calificado, sin título **2** COMPLETE : completo, absoluto <an unqualified denial : una negación incondicional>
unquestionable [ˌʌnˈkwɛstʃənəbəl] *adj* : incuestionable, indudable, indiscutible — **unquestionably** [-bli] *adv*
unquestioning [ˌʌnˈkwɛstʃənɪŋ] *adj* : incondicional, absoluto, ciego
unravel [ˌʌnˈrævəl] *v* **-eled** *or* **-elled; -eling** *or* **-elling** *vt* **1** DISENTANGLE : desenmarañar, desenredar **2** SOLVE : aclarar, desenmarañar, desentrañar — *vi* : deshacerse
unreal [ˌʌnˈriːl] *adj* : irreal
unrealistic [ˌʌnˌriːəˈlɪstɪk] *adj* : poco realista
unreasonable [ˌʌnˈriːzənəbəl] *adj* **1** IRRATIONAL : poco razonable, irrazonable, irracional **2** EXCESSIVE : excesivo <unreasonable prices : precios excesivos>
unreasonably [ˌʌnˈriːzənəbli] *adv* **1** IRRATIONALLY : irracionalmente, de manera irrazonable **2** EXCESSIVELY : excesivamente
unrefined [ˌʌnriˈfaɪnd] *adj* **1** : no refinado, sin refinar (dícese del azúcar, de la harina, etc.) **2** : poco refinado, inculto (dícese de una persona)
unrelated [ˌʌnriˈleɪt̬əd] *adj* : no relacionado, inconexo
unrelenting [ˌʌnriˈlɛntɪŋ] *adj* **1** STERN : severo, inexorable **2** CONSTANT, RELENTLESS : constante, implacable
unreliable [ˌʌnriˈlaɪəbəl] *adj* : que no es de fiar, de poca confianza, inestable (dícese del tiempo)
unrepentant [ˌʌnriˈpɛntənt] *adj* : impenitente
unresolved [ˌʌnriˈzɑlvd] *adj* : pendiente, no resuelto
unrest [ˌʌnˈrɛst] *n* : inquietud *f*, malestar *m* <political unrest : disturbios políticos>
unrestrained [ˌʌnriˈstreɪnd] *adj* : desenfrenado, incontrolado
unrestricted [ˌʌnriˈstrɪktəd] *adj* : sin restricción <unrestricted access : libre acceso>
unrewarding [ˌʌnriˈwɔrdɪŋ] *adj* THANKLESS : ingrato
unripe [ˌʌnˈraɪp] *adj* : inmaduro, verde
unrivaled *or* **unrivalled** [ˌʌnˈraɪvəld] *adj* : incomparable
unroll [ˌʌnˈroːl] *vt* : desenrollar — *vi* : desenrollarse
unruffled [ˌʌnˈrʌfəld] *adj* **1** SERENE : sereno, tranquilo **2** SMOOTH : tranquilo, liso <unruffled waters : aguas tranquilas>
unruliness [ˌʌnˈruːlinəs] *n* : indisciplina *f*
unruly [ˌʌnˈruːli] *adj* : indisciplinado, díscolo, rebelde
unsafe [ˌʌnˈseɪf] *adj* : inseguro
unsaid [ˌʌnˈsɛd] *adj* : sin decir <to leave unsaid : quedar por decir>
unsanitary [ˌʌnˈsænəˌtɛri] *adj* : antihigiénico

unsatisfactory [ˌʌnˌsæt̬əsˈfæktəri] *adj* : insatisfactorio
unsatisfied [ˌʌnˈsæt̬əsˌfaɪd] *adj* : insatisfecho
unscathed [ˌʌnˈskeɪðd] *adj* UNHARMED : ileso
unscheduled [ˌʌnˈskɛˌdʒuːld] *adj* : no programado, imprevisto
unscientific [ˌʌnˌsaɪənˈtɪfɪk] *adj* : poco científico
unscrupulous [ˌʌnˈskruːpjələs] *adj* : inescrupuloso, sin escrúpulos — **unscrupulously** *adv*
unseal [ˌʌnˈsiːl] *vt* : abrir, quitarle el sello a
unseasonable [ˌʌnˈsiːzənəbəl] *adj* **1** : extemporáneo <unseasonable rain : lluvia extemporánea> **2** UNTIMELY : extemporáneo, inoportuno
unseemly [ˌʌnˈsiːmli] *adj* **-lier; -est 1** INDECOROUS : indecoroso **2** INAPPROPRIATE : impropio, inapropiado
unseen [ˌʌnˈsiːn] *adj* **1** UNNOTICED : inadvertido **2** INVISIBLE : oculto, invisible
unselfish [ˌʌnˈsɛlfɪʃ] *adj* : generoso, desinteresado — **unselfishly** *adv*
unselfishness [ˌʌnˈsɛlfɪʃnəs] *n* : generosidad *f,* desinterés *m*
unsettle [ˌʌnˈsɛt̬əl] *vt* **-tled; -tling** DISTURB : trastornar, alterar, perturbar
unsettled [ˌʌnˈsɛt̬əld] *adj* **1** CHANGEABLE : inestable, variable <unsettled weather : tiempo inestable> **2** DISTURBED : agitado, inquieto <unsettled waters : aguas agitadas> **3** UNDECIDED : pendiente (dícese de un asunto), indeciso (dícese de una persona) **4** UNPAID : sin saldar, pendiente **5** UNINHABITED : despoblado, no colonizado
unshaped [ˌʌnˈʃeɪpt] *adj* : sin forma, informe
unsightly [ˌʌnˈsaɪtli] *adj* UGLY : feo, de aspecto malo
unskilled [ˌʌnˈskɪld] *adj* : no calificado
unskillful [ˌʌnˈskɪlfəl] *adj* : inexperto, poco hábil
unsnap [ˌʌnˈsnæp] *vt* **-snapped; -snapping** : desabrochar
unsociable *adj* : poco sociable
unsolved [ˌʌnˈsɔlvd] *adj* : no resuelto, sin resolver
unsophisticated [ˌʌnsəˈfɪstəˌkeɪt̬əd] *adj* **1** NAIVE, UNWORLDLY : ingenuo, de poco mundo **2** SIMPLE : simple, poco sofisticado, rudimentario
unsound [ˌʌnˈsaʊnd] *adj* **1** UNHEALTHY : enfermizo, de mala salud **2** : poco sólido, defectuoso (dícese de una estructura, etc.) **3** INVALID : inválido, erróneo **4 of unsound mind** : mentalmente incapacitado
unspeakable [ˌʌnˈspiːkəbəl] *adj* **1** INDESCRIBABLE : indecible, inexpresable, incalificable **2** HEINOUS : atroz, nefando, abominable — **unspeakably** [-bli] *adv*
unspecified [ˌʌnˈspɛsəˌfaɪd] *adj* : indeterminado, sin especificar
unspoiled [ˌʌnˈspɔɪld] *adj* **1** : conservado, sin estropear (dícese de un lugar) **2** : que no está mimado (dícese de un niño)
unstable [ˌʌnˈsteɪbəl] *adj* **1** CHANGEABLE : variable, inestable, cambiable <an unstable pulse : un pulso irregular> **2** UNSTEADY : inestable, poco sólido (dícese de una estructura)
unsteadily [ˌʌnˈstɛdəli] *adv* : de modo inestable
unsteadiness [ˌʌnˈstɛdinəs] *n* : inestabilidad *f,* inseguridad *f*
unsteady [ˌʌnˈstɛdi] *adj* **1** UNSTABLE : inestable, variable **2** SHAKY : tembloroso
unstoppable [ˌʌnˈstɑpəbəl] *adj* : irrefrenable, incontenible
unsubstantiated [ˌʌnsəbˈstæntʃiˌeɪt̬əd] *adj* : no corroborado, no demostrado
unsuccessful [ˌʌnsəkˈsɛsfəl] *adj* : fracasado, infructuoso
unsuitable [ˌʌnˈsuːt̬əbəl] *adj* : inadecuado, impropio, inapropiado <an unsuitable time : una hora inconveniente>
unsuited [ˌʌnˈsuːt̬əd] *adj* : inadecuado, inepto
unsung [ˌʌnˈsʌŋ] *adj* : olvidado
unsure [ˌʌnˈʃʊr] *adj* : incierto, dudoso
unsurpassed [ˌʌnsərˈpæst] *adj* : sin par, sin igual
unsuspecting [ˌʌnsəˈspɛktɪŋ] *adj* : desprevenido, desapercibido, confiado
unsympathetic [ˌʌnˌsɪmpəˈθɛt̬ɪk] *adj* : poco comprensivo, indiferente
untangle [ˌʌnˈteɪŋgəl] *vt* **-gled; -gling** : desenmarañar, desenredar
unthinkable [ˌʌnˈθɪŋkəbəl] *adj* : inconcebible, impensable
unthinking [ˌʌnˈθɪŋkɪŋ] *adj* : irreflexivo, inconsciente — **unthinkingly** *adv*
untidy [ˌʌnˈtaɪdi] *adj* **1** SLOVENLY : desaliñado **2** DISORDERLY : desordenado, desarreglado
untie [ˌʌnˈtaɪ] *vt* **-tied; -tying** *or* **-tieing** : desatar, deshacer
until¹ [ˌʌnˈtɪl] *prep* : hasta <until now : hasta ahora>
until² *conj* : hasta que <until they left : hasta que salieron> <don't answer until you're sure : no contestes hasta que (no) estés seguro>
untimely [ˌʌnˈtaɪmli] *adj* **1** PREMATURE : prematuro <an untimely death : una muerte prematura> **2** INOPPORTUNE : inoportuno, intempestivo
untold [ˌʌnˈtoːld] *adj* **1** : nunca dicho <the untold secret : el secreto sin contar> **2** INCALCULABLE : incalculable, indecible
untouched [ˌʌnˈtʌtʃt] *adj* **1** INTACT : intacto, sin tocar, sin probar (dícese de la comida) **2** UNAFFECTED : insensible, indiferente

untoward [ˌʌn'tɔrd, -'toːərd, -tə'wɔrd] *adj* **1** : indecoroso, impropio (dícese del comportamiento) **2** ADVERSE, UNFORTUNATE : desafortunado, adverso <untoward effects : efectos perjudiciales> **3** UNSEEMLY : indecoroso

untrained [ˌʌn'treɪnd] *adj* : inexperto, no capacitado

untreated [ˌʌn'triːtəd] *adj* : no tratado (dícese de una enfermedad, etc.), sin tratar (dícese de un material)

untroubled [ˌʌn'trʌbəld] *adj* : tranquilo <to be untroubled by : no estar afectado por>

untrue [ˌʌn'truː] *adj* **1** UNFAITHFUL : infiel **2** FALSE : falso

untrustworthy [ˌʌn'trʌstˌwərði] *adj* : de poca confianza (dícese de una persona), no fidedigno (dícese de la información)

untruth [ˌʌn'truːθ, 'ʌnˌ-] *n* : mentira *f,* falsedad *f*

untruthful [ˌʌn'truːθfəl] *adj* : mentiroso, falso

unusable [ˌʌn'juːzəbəl] *adj* : inútil, inservible

unused [ˌʌn'juːzd, *in sense 1 usually* -'juːst] *adj* **1** UNACCUSTOMED : inhabituado **2** NEW : nuevo **3** IDLE : no utilizado (dícese de la tierra) **4** REMAINING : restante <the unused portion : la porción restante>

unusual [ˌʌn'juːʒʊəl] *adj* : inusual, poco común, raro

unusually [ˌʌn'juːʒʊəli, -'juːʒəli] *adv* : excepcionalmente, extraordinariamente, fuera de lo común

unwanted [ˌʌn'wɑntəd] *adj* : superfluo, de sobre

unwarranted [ˌʌn'wɔrəntəd] *adj* : injustificado

unwary [ˌʌn'wæri] *adj* : incauto

unwavering [ˌʌn'weɪvərɪŋ] *adj* : firme, inquebrantable <an unwavering gaze : una mirada fija>

unwelcome [ˌʌn'wɛlkəm] *adj* : importuno, molesto

unwell [ˌʌn'wɛl] *adj* : enfermo, mal

unwholesome [ˌʌn'hoːlsəm] *adj* **1** UNHEALTHY : malsano, insalubre **2** PERNICIOUS : pernicioso **3** LOATHSOME : repugnante, muy desagradable

unwieldy [ˌʌn'wiːldi] *adj* CUMBERSOME : difícil de manejar, torpe y pesado

unwilling [ˌʌn'wɪlɪŋ] *adj* : poco dispuesto <to be unwilling to : no estar dispuesto a>

unwillingly [ˌʌn'wɪlɪŋli] *adv* : a regañadientes, de mala gana

unwind [ˌʌn'waɪnd] *v* **-wound** [-'waʊnd]; **-winding** *vt* **1** UNROLL : desenrollar **2** RELAX : relajar — *vi* : desenrollarse

unwise [ˌʌn'waɪz] *adj* : imprudente, desacertado, poco aconsejable

unwisely [ˌʌn'waɪzli] *adv* : imprudentemente

unwitting [ˌʌn'wɪt̬ɪŋ] *adj* **1** UNAWARE : inconsciente **2** INADVERTENT : involuntario, inadvertido <an unwitting mistake : un error inadvertido> — **unwittingly** *adv*

unworthiness [ˌʌn'wərðinəs] *n* : falta *f* de valía

unworthy [ˌʌn'wərði] *adj* **1** UNDESERVING : indigno <to be unworthy of : no ser digno de> **2** UNMERITED : inmerecido

unwrap [ˌʌn'ræp] *vt* **-wrapped; -wrapping** : desenvolver, deshacer

unwritten [ˌʌn'rɪtən] *adj* : no escrito

unyielding [ˌʌn'jiːldɪŋ] *adj* : firme, inflexible, rígido

unzip [ˌʌn'zɪp] *vt* **-zipped; -zipping** : abrir el cierre de

up[1] ['ʌp] *v* **upped** ['ʌpt]; **upping; ups** *vt* INCREASE : aumentar, subir <they upped the prices : aumentaron los precios> — *vi* **to up and** : agarrar y *fam* <she up and left : agarró y se fue>

up[2] *adv* **1** ABOVE : arriba, en lo alto <up in the mountains : arriba en las montañas> **2** UPWARDS : hacia arriba <push it up : empújalo hacia arriba> <the sun came up : el sol salió> <prices went up : los precios subieron> **3** (*indicating an upright position or waking state*) <to sit up : ponerse derecho> <they got up late : se levantaron tarde> <I stayed up all night : pasé toda la noche sin dormir> **4** (*indicating volume or intensity*) <to speak up : hablar más fuerte> **5** (*indicating a northerly direction*) <the climate up north : el clima del norte> <I'm going up to Canada : voy para Canadá> **6** (*indicating the appearance or existence of something*) <the book turned up : el libro apareció> **7** (*indicating consideration*) <she brought the matter up : mencionó el asunto> **8** COMPLETELY : completamente <eat it up : cómetelo todo> **9** : en pedazos <he tore it up : lo rompió en pedazos> **10** (*indicating a stopping*) <the car pulled up to the curb : el carro paró al borde de la acera> **11** (*indicating an even score*) <the game was 10 up : empataron a 10>

up[3] *adj* **1** (*risen above the horizon*) <the sun is up : ha salido el sol> **2** (*being above a normal or former level*) <prices are up : los precios han aumentado> <the river is up : las aguas están altas> **3** : despierto, levantado <up all night : despierto toda la noche> **4** BUILT : construido <the house is up : la casa está construida> **5** OPEN : abierto <the windows are up : las ventanas están abiertas> **6** (*moving or going upward*) <the up staircase : la escalera para subir> **7** ABREAST : enterado, al día, al corriente <to be up on the news : estar al corriente de las noticias> **8** PREPARED : preparado <we were up for the test

: estuvimos preparados para el examen> 9 FINISHED : terminado, acabado <time is up : se ha terminado el tiempo permitido> 10 **to be up** : pasar <what's up? : ¿qué pasa?>

up[4] *prep* 1 (*to, toward, or at a higher point of*) <he went up the stairs : subió la escalera> 2 (*to or toward the source of*) <to go up the river : ir río arriba> 3 ALONG : a lo largo, por <up the coast : a lo largo de la costa> <just up the way : un poco más adelante> <up and down the city : por toda la ciudad>

upbraid [ˌʌpˈbreɪd] *vt* : reprender, regañar

upbringing [ˈʌpˌbrɪŋɪŋ] *n* : crianza *f*, educación *f*

upcoming [ˌʌpˈkʌmɪŋ] *adj* : próximo

update[1] [ˌʌpˈdeɪt] *vt* **-dated; -dating** : poner al día, poner al corriente, actualizar

update[2] [ˈʌpˌdeɪt] *n* : actualización *f*, puesta *f* al día

upend [ˌʌpˈɛnd] *vt* **1** : poner vertical **2** OVERTURN : volcar

upgrade[1] [ˈʌpˌgreɪd, ˌʌpˈ-] *vt* **-graded; -grading** : elevar la categoría de (un puesto, etc.), implementar mejoras a (una facilidad, etc.)

upgrade[2] [ˈʌpˌgreɪd] *n* **1** SLOPE : cuesta *f*, pendiente *f* **2** RISE : aumento *m* de categoría (de un puesto), ascenso *m* (de un empleado)

upheaval [ˌʌpˈhiːvəl] *n* **1** : levantamiento *m* (en geología) **2** DISTURBANCE, UPSET : trastorno *m*, agitación *f*, conmoción *f*

uphill[1] [ˌʌpˈhɪl] *adv* : cuesta arriba

uphill[2] [ˈʌpˌhɪl] *adj* **1** ASCENDING : en subida **2** DIFFICULT : difícil, arduo

uphold [ˌʌpˈhoːld] *vt* **-held; -holding 1** SUPPORT : sostener, apoyar, mantener **2** RAISE : levantar **3** CONFIRM : confirmar (una decisión judicial)

upholster [ˌʌpˈhoːlstər] *vt* : tapizar

upholsterer [ˌʌpˈhoːlstərər] *n* : tapicero *m*, -ra *f*

upholstery [ˌʌpˈhoːlstəri] *n, pl* **-steries** : tapicería *f*

upkeep [ˈʌpˌkiːp] *n* : mantenimiento *m*

upland [ˈʌplənd, -ˌlænd] *n* : altiplanicie *f*, altiplano *m*

uplift[1] [ˌʌpˈlɪft] *vt* **1** RAISE : elevar, levantar **2** ELEVATE : elevar, animar (el espíritu, la mente, etc.)

uplift[2] [ˈʌpˌlɪft] *n* : elevación *f*

upon [əˈpɔn, əˈpɑn] *prep* : en, sobre <upon the desk : sobre el escritorio> <upon leaving : al salir> <questions upon questions : pregunta tras pregunta>

upper[1] [ˈʌpər] *adj* **1** HIGHER : superior <the upper classes : las clases altas> **2** : alto (en geografía) <the upper Mississippi : el alto Mississippi>

upper[2] *n* : parte *f* superior (del calzado, etc.)

uppercase [ˌʌpərˈkeɪs] *adj* : mayúsculo

upper hand *n* : ventaja *f*, dominio *m*

uppermost [ˈʌpərˌmoːst] *adj* : más alto <it was uppermost in his mind : era lo que más le preocupaba>

upright[1] [ˈʌpˌraɪt] *adj* **1** VERTICAL : vertical **2** ERECT : erguido, derecho <to sit upright : sentarse derecho>**3** JUST : recto, honesto, justo

upright[2] *n* : montante *m*, poste *m*, soporte *m*

uprising [ˈʌpˌraɪzɪŋ] *n* : insurrección *f*, revuelta *f*, alzamiento *m*

uproar [ˈʌpˌror] *n* COMMOTION : alboroto *m*, jaleo *m*, escándalo *m*

uproarious [ˌʌpˈroriəs] *adj* **1** CLAMOROUS : estrepitoso, clamoroso **2** HILARIOUS : muy divertido, hilarante — **uproariously** *adv*

uproot [ˌʌpˈruːt, -ˈrʊt] *vt* : desarraigar

upset[1] [ˌʌpˈsɛt] *vt* **-set; -setting 1** OVERTURN : volcar **2** SPILL : derramar **3** DISTURB : perturbar, disgustar, inquietar, alterar **4** SICKEN : sentar mal a <it upsets my stomach : me sienta mal al estómago> **5** DISRUPT : trastornar, desbaratar (planes, etc.) **6** DEFEAT : derrotar (en deportes)

upset[2] *adj* **1** DISPLEASED, DISTRESSED : disgustado, alterado **2 to have an upset stomach** : estar mal del estómago, estar descompuesto (de estómago)

upset[3] [ˈʌpˌsɛt] *n* **1** OVERTURNING : vuelco *m* **2** DISRUPTION : trastorno *m* (de planes, etc.) **3** DEFEAT : derrota *f* (en deportes)

upshot [ˈʌpˌʃɑt] *n* : resultado *m* final

upside–down [ˌʌpˌsaɪdˈdaʊn] *adj* : al revés

upside down [ˌʌpˌsaɪdˈdaʊn] *adv* **1** : al revés **2** : en confusión, en desorden

upstairs[1] [ˌʌpˈstærz] *adv* : arriba, en el piso superior

upstairs[2] [ˈʌpˌstærz, ˌʌpˈ-] *adj* : de arriba

upstairs[3] [ˈʌpˌstærz, ˌʌpˈ-] *ns & pl* : piso *m* de arriba, planta *f* de arriba

upstanding [ˌʌpˈstændɪŋ, ˈʌpˌ-] *adj* HONEST, UPRIGHT : honesto, íntegro, recto

upstart [ˈʌpˌstɑrt] *n* : advenedizo *m*, -za *f*

upswing [ˈʌpˌswɪŋ] *n* : alza *f*, mejora *f* notable <to be on the upswing : estar mejorándose>

uptight [ˌʌpˈtaɪt] *adj* : tenso, nervioso

up to *prep* **1** : hasta <up to a year : hasta un año> <in mud up to my ankles : en barro hasta los tobillos> **2 to be up to** : estar a la altura de <I'm not up to going : no estoy en condiciones de ir> **3 to be up to** : depender de <it's up to the director : depende del director>

up–to–date [ˌʌptəˈdeɪt] *adj* **1** CURRENT : corriente, al día <to keep up-to-date

: mantenerse al corriente> 2 MODERN : moderno

uptown [ˈʌpˈtaʊn] *adv* : hacia la parte alta de la ciudad, hacia el distrito residencial

upturn [ˈʌpˌtərn] *n* : mejora *f,* auge *m* (económico)

upward¹ [ˈʌpwərd] *or* **upwards** [-wərdz] *adv* : hacia arriba

upward² *adj* : ascendente, hacia arriba

upwind [ˌʌpˈwɪnd] *adv & adj* : contra el viento

uranium [jʊˈreɪniəm] *n* : uranio *m*

Uranus [jʊˈreɪnəs, ˈjʊrənəs] *n* : Urano *m*

urban [ˈərbən] *adj* : urbano

urbane [ˌərˈbeɪn] *adj* : urbano, cortés

urchin [ˈərtʃən] *n* **1** SCAMP : granuja *mf;* pillo *m,* -lla *f* **2 sea urchin** : erizo *m* de mar

urethra [jʊˈriːθrə] *n, pl* **-thras** *or* **-thrae** [-ˌθriː] : uretra *f*

urge¹ [ˈərdʒ] *vt* **urged; urging 1** PRESS : instar, apremiar, insistir <we urged him to come : insistimos en que viniera> **2** ADVOCATE : recomendar, abogar por **3 to urge on** : animar, alentar

urge² *n* : impulso *m,* ganas *fpl,* compulsión *f*

urgency [ˈərdʒən*t*si] *n, pl* **-cies** : urgencia *f*

urgent [ˈərdʒənt] *adj* **1** PRESSING : urgente, apremiante **2** INSISTENT : insistente **3 to be urgent** : urgir

urgently [ˈərdʒəntli] *adv* : urgentemente

urinal [ˈjʊrənəl, *esp Brit* jʊˈraɪnəl] *n* : orinal *m* (recipiente), urinario *m* (lugar)

urinary [ˈjʊrəˌnɛri] *adj* : urinario

urinate [ˈjʊrəˌneɪt] *vi* **-nated; -nating** : orinar

urination [ˌjʊrəˈneɪʃən] *n* : orinación *f*

urine [ˈjʊrən] *n* : orina *f*

urn [ˈərn] *n* **1** VASE : urna *f* **2** : recipiente *m* (para servir café, etc.)

Uruguayan [ˌʊrəˈgwaɪən, ˌjʊr-, -ˈgweɪ-] *n* : uruguayo *m,* -ya *f* — **Uruguayan** *adj*

us [ˈʌs] *pron* **1** (*as direct object*) : nos <they were visiting us : nos visitaban> **2** (*as indirect object*) : nos <he gave us a present : nos dio un regalo> **3** (*as object of preposition*) : nosotros, nosotras <stay with us : quédese con nosotros> <both of us : nosotros dos> **4** (*for emphasis*) : nosotros <it's us! : ¡somos nosotros!>

usable [ˈjuːzəbəl] *adj* : utilizable

usage [ˈjuːsɪdʒ, -zɪdʒ] *n* **1** HABIT : costumbre *f,* hábito *m* **2** USE : uso *m*

use¹ [ˈjuːz] *v* **used** [ˈjuːzd, *in phrase "used to" usually* ˈjuːstuː]; **using** *vt* **1** EMPLOY : emplear, usar **2** CONSUME : consumir, tomar (drogas, etc.) **3** UTILIZE : usar, utilizar <to use tact : usar tacto> <he used his friends to get ahead : usó a sus amigos para mejorar su posición> **4** TREAT : tratar <they used the horse cruelly : maltrataron al caballo> **5 to use up** : agotar, consumir, gastar — *vi* (*used in the past with* **to** *to indicate a former fact or state*) : soler, acostumbrar <winters used to be colder : los inviernos solían ser más fríos, los inviernos eran más fríos> <she used to dance : acostumbraba bailar>

use² [ˈjuːs] *n* **1** APPLICATION, EMPLOYMENT : uso *m,* empleo *m,* utilización *f* <out of use : en desuso> <ready for use : listo para usar> <to be in use : usarse, estar funcionando> <to make use of : servirse de, aprovechar> **2** USEFULNESS : utilidad *f* <to be of no use : no servir (para nada)> <it's no use! : ¡es inútil!> **3 to have the use of** : poder usar, tener acceso a **4 to have no use for** : no necesitar <she has no use for poetry : a ella no le gusta la poesía>

used [ˈjuːzd] *adj* **1** SECONDHAND : usado, de segunda mano <used cars : coches usados> **2 used to** ACCUSTOMED : acostumbrado <used to the heat : acostumbrado al calor>

useful [ˈjuːsfəl] *adj* : útil, práctico — **usefully** *adv*

usefulness [ˈjuːsfəlnəs] *n* : utilidad *f*

useless [ˈjuːsləs] *adj* : inútil — **uselessly** *adv*

uselessness [ˈjuːsləsnəs] *n* : inutilidad *f*

user [ˈjuːzər] *n* : usuario *m,* -ria *f*

usher¹ [ˈʌʃər] *vt* **1** ESCORT : acompañar, conducir **2 to usher in** : hacer pasar (a alguien) <to usher in a new era : anunciar una nueva época>

usher² *n* : acomodador *m,* -dora *f*

usherette [ˌʌʃəˈrɛt] *n* : acomodadora *f*

usual [ˈjuːʒʊəl] *adj* **1** NORMAL : usual, normal **2** CUSTOMARY : acostumbrado, habitual, de costumbre **3** ORDINARY : ordinario, típico

usually [ˈjuːʒʊəli, ˈjuːʒəli] *adv* : usualmente, normalmente

usurp [jʊˈsərp, -ˈzərp] *vt* : usurpar

usurper [jʊˈsərpər, -ˈzər-] *n* : usurpador *m,* -dora *f*

utensil [jʊˈtɛn*t*səl] *n* **1** : utensilio *m* (de cocina) **2** IMPLEMENT : implemento *m,* útil *m* (de labranza, etc.)

uterus [ˈjuːt̬ərəs] *n, pl* **uteri** [-ˌraɪ] : útero *m,* matriz *f*

utilitarian [juːˌtɪləˈtɛriən] *adj* : utilitario

utility [juːˈtɪlət̬i] *n, pl* **-ties 1** USEFULNESS : utilidad *f* **2 public utility** : empresa *f* de servicio público

utilization [ˌjuːt̬ələˈzeɪʃən] *n* : utilización *f*

utilize [ˈjuːt̬əlˌaɪz] *vt* **-lized; -lizing** : utilizar, hacer uso de

utmost¹ [ˈʌtˌmoːst] *adj* **1** FARTHEST : extremo, más lejano **2** GREATEST : sumo, mayor <of the utmost importance : de suma importancia>

utmost² *n* : lo más posible <to the utmost : al máximo>

utopia [jʊ'to:piə] *n* : utopía *f*

utopian [jʊ'to:piən] *adj* : utópico

utter¹ ['ʌtər] *vt* : decir, articular, pronunciar (palabras)

utter² *adj* : absoluto — **utterly** *adv*

utterance ['ʌtərənts] *n* : declaración *f*, articulación *f*

V

v ['vi:] *n, pl* **v's** *or* **vs** ['vi:z] : vigésima segunda letra del alfabeto inglés

vacancy ['veɪkəntsi] *n, pl* **-cies 1** EMPTINESS : vacío *m*, vacuidad *f* **2** : vacante *f*, puesto *m* vacante <to fill a vacancy : ocupar un puesto> **3** : habitación *f* libre (en un hotel) <no vacancies : completo>

vacant ['veɪkənt] *adj* **1** EMPTY : libre, desocupado (dícese de los edificios, etc.) **2** : vacante (dícese de los puestos) **3** BLANK : vacío, ausente <a vacant stare : una mirada ausente>

vacate ['veɪ,keɪt] *vt* **-cated; -cating** : desalojar, desocupar

vacation¹ [veɪ'keɪʃən, və-] *vi* : pasar las vacaciones, vacacionar *Mex*

vacation² *n* : vacaciones *fpl* <to be on vacation : estar de vacaciones>

vacationer [veɪ'keɪʃənər, və-] *n* : turista *mf*, veraneante *mf*, vacacionista *mf CA, Mex*

vaccinate ['væksə,neɪt] *vt* **-nated; -nating** : vacunar

vaccination [,væksə'neɪʃən] *n* : vacunación *f*

vaccine [væk'si:n, 'væk,-] *n* : vacuna *f*

vacillate ['væsə,leɪt] *vi* **-lated; -lating 1** HESITATE : vacilar **2** SWAY : oscilar

vacillation [,væsə'leɪʃən] *n* : indecisión *f*, vacilación *f*

vacuous ['vækjʊəs] *adj* **1** EMPTY : vacío **2** INANE : vacuo, necio, estúpido

vacuum¹ ['væ,kju:m, -kjəm] *vt* : limpiar con aspiradora, pasar la aspiradora por

vacuum² *n, pl* **vacuums** *or* **vacua** ['vækjʊə] : vacío *m*

vacuum cleaner *n* : aspiradora *f*

vagabond¹ ['vægə,bɑnd] *adj* : vagabundo

vagabond² *n* : vagabundo *m*, -da *f*

vagary ['veɪgəri, və'gɛri] *n, pl* **-ries** : capricho *m*

vagina [və'dʒaɪnə] *n, pl* **-nae** [-,ni:, -,naɪ] *or* **-nas** : vagina *f*

vagrancy ['veɪgrəntsi] *n* : vagancia *f*

vagrant¹ ['veɪgrənt] *adj* : vagabundo

vagrant² *n* : vagabundo *m*, -da *f*

vague ['veɪg] *adj* **vaguer; -est 1** IMPRECISE : vago, impreciso <a vague feeling : una sensación indefinida> <I haven't the vaguest idea : no tengo la más remota idea> **2** UNCLEAR : borroso, poco claro <a vague outline : un perfil indistinto> **3** ABSENTMINDED : distraído

vaguely ['veɪgli] *adv* : vagamente, de manera imprecisa

vagueness ['veɪgnəs] *n* : vaguedad *f*, imprecisión *f*

vain ['veɪn] *adj* **1** WORTHLESS : vano **2** FUTILE : vano, inútil <in vain : en vano> **3** CONCEITED : vanidoso, presumido

vainly ['veɪnli] *adv* : en vano, vanamente, inútilmente

valance ['vælənts, 'veɪ-] *n* **1** FLOUNCE : volante *m* (de una cama, etc.) **2** : galería *f* de cortina (sobre una ventana)

vale ['veɪl] *n* : valle *m*

valedictorian [,vælə,dɪk'toriən] *n* : estudiante *mf* que pronuncia el discurso de despedida en ceremonia de graduación

valedictory [,vælə'dɪktəri] *adj* : de despedida

valentine ['vælən,taɪn] *n* : tarjeta *f* que se manda el Día de los Enamorados (el 14 de febrero)

Valentine's Day *n* : Día *m* de los Enamorados

valet ['væ,leɪ, væ'leɪ, 'vælət] *n* : ayuda *m* de cámara

valiant ['væljənt] *adj* : valiente, valeroso

valiantly ['væljəntli] *adv* : con valor, valientemente

valid ['væləd] *adj* : válido

validate ['vælə,deɪt] *vt* **-dated; -dating** : validar, dar validez a

validity [və'lɪdəti, væ-] *n* : validez *f*

valise [və'li:s] *n* : maleta *f* (de mano)

valley ['væli] *n, pl* **-leys** : valle *m*

valor ['vælər] *n* : valor *m*, valentía *f*

valorous ['vælərəs] *adj* : valeroso, valiente

valuable¹ ['væljʊəbəl, 'væljəbəl] *adj* **1** EXPENSIVE : valioso, de valor **2** WORTHWHILE : valioso, apreciable

valuable² *n* : objeto *m* de valor

valuation [,væljʊ'eɪʃən] *n* **1** APPRAISAL : valoración *f*, tasación *f* **2** VALUE : valuación *f*

value¹ ['væl,ju:] *vt* **-ued; -uing 1** APPRAISE : valorar, avaluar, tasar **2** APPRECIATE : valorar, apreciar

value² *n* **1** : valor *m* <of little value : de poco valor> <to be a good value : estar bien de precio, tener buen precio> <at face value : en su sentido literal>

2 values *npl* **:** valores *mpl* (morales), principios *mpl*
valueless [ˈvæljuːləs] *adj* **:** sin valor
valve [ˈvælv] *n* **:** válvula *f*
vampire [ˈvæmˌpaɪr] *n* **1 :** vampiro *m* **2** *or* **vampire bat :** vampiro *m*
van[1] [ˈvæn] → **vanguard**
van[2] *n* **:** furgoneta *f,* camioneta *f*
vanadium [vəˈneɪdiəm] *n* **:** vanadio *m*
vandal [ˈvændəl] *n* **:** vándalo *m*
vandalism [ˈvændəlˌɪzəm] *n* **:** vandalismo *m*
vandalize [ˈvændəlˌaɪz] *vt* **:** destrozar, destruir, estropear
vane [ˈveɪn] *n or* **weather vane :** veleta *f*
vanguard [ˈvænˌgɑrd] *n* **:** vanguardia *f*
vanilla [vəˈnɪlə, -ˈnɛ-] *n* **:** vainilla *f*
vanish [ˈvænɪʃ] *vi* **:** desaparecer, disiparse, desvanecerse
vanity [ˈvænət̬i] *n, pl* **-ties 1 :** vanidad *f* **2** *or* **vanity table :** tocador *m*
vanquish [ˈvæŋkwɪʃ, ˈvæn-] *vt* **:** vencer, conquistar
vantage point [ˈvæntɪdʒ] *n* **:** posición *f* ventajosa
vapid [ˈvæpəd, ˈveɪ-] *adj* **:** insípido, insulso
vapor [ˈveɪpər] *n* **:** vapor *m*
vaporize [ˈveɪpəˌraɪz] *v* **-rized; -rizing** *vt* **:** vaporizar — *vi* **:** vaporizarse, evaporarse
vaporizer [ˈveɪpəˌraɪzər] *n* **:** vaporizador *m*
variability [ˌvɛriəˈbɪlət̬i] *n, pl* **-ties :** variabilidad *f*
variable[1] [ˈvɛriəbəl] *adj* **:** variable <variable cloudiness : nubosidad variable>
variable[2] *n* **:** variable *f,* factor *m*
variance [ˈvɛriənts] *n* **1** DISCREPANCY **:** varianza *f,* discrepancia *f* **2** DISAGREEMENT **:** desacuerdo *m* <at variance with : en desacuerdo con>
variant[1] [ˈvɛriənt] *adj* **:** variante, divergente
variant[2] *n* **:** variante *f*
variation [ˌvɛriˈeɪʃən] *n* **:** variación *f,* diferencias *fpl*
varicose [ˈværəˌkoːs] *adj* **:** varicoso
varicose veins *npl* **:** varices *fpl,* várices *fpl*
varied [ˈvɛrid] *adj* **:** variado, dispar, diferente
variegated [ˈvɛriəˌgeɪt̬ɛd] *adj* **:** abigarrado, multicolor
variety [vəˈraɪət̬i] *n, pl* **-ties 1** DIVERSITY **:** diversidad *f,* variedad *f* **2** ASSORTMENT **:** surtido *m* <for a variety of reasons : por diversas razones> **3** SORT **:** clase *f* **4** BREED **:** variedad *f* (de plantas)
various [ˈvɛriəs] *adj* **:** varios, diversos
varnish[1] [ˈvɑrnɪʃ] *vt* **:** barnizar
varnish[2] *n* **:** barniz *f*
varsity [ˈvɑrsət̬i] *n, pl* **-ties :** equipo *m* universitario
vary [ˈvɛri] *v* **varied; varying** *vt* **:** variar, diversificar — *vi* **1** CHANGE **:** variar, cambiar **2** DEVIATE **:** desviarse
vascular [ˈvæskjələr] *adj* **:** vascular
vase [ˈveɪs, ˈveɪz, ˈvɑz] *n* **:** jarrón *m,* florero *m*
vassal [ˈvæsəl] *n* **:** vasallo *m,* -lla *f*
vast [ˈvæst] *adj* **:** inmenso, enorme, vasto
vastly [ˈvæstli] *adv* **:** enormemente
vastness [ˈvæstnəs] *n* **:** vastedad *f,* inmensidad *f*
vat [ˈvæt] *n* **:** cuba *f,* tina *f*
vaudeville [ˈvɔdvəl, -ˌvɪl; ˈvɔdəˌvɪl] *n* **:** vodevil *m*
vault[1] [ˈvɔlt] *vi* LEAP **:** saltar
vault[2] *n* **1** JUMP **:** salto *m* <pole vault : salto de pértiga, salto con garrocha> **2** DOME **:** bóveda *f* **3 :** bodega *f* (para vino), bóveda *f* de seguridad (de un banco) **4** CRYPT **:** cripta *f*
vaulted [ˈvɔltəd] *adj* **:** abovedado
vaunted [ˈvɔntəd] *adj* **:** cacareado, alardeado <a much vaunted wine : un vino muy alardeado>
VCR [ˌviːˌsiːˈɑr] *n* **:** video *m,* videocasetera *f*
veal [ˈviːl] *n* **:** ternera *f,* carne *f* de ternera
veer [ˈvɪr] *vi* **:** virar (dícese de un barco), girar (dícese de un coche), torcer (dícese de un camino)
vegetable[1] [ˈvɛdʒtəbəl, ˈvɛdʒət̬ə-] *adj* **:** vegetal
vegetable[2] *n* **1 :** vegetal *m* <the vegetable kingdom : el reino vegetal> **2 :** verdura *f,* hortaliza *f* (para comer)
vegetarian [ˌvɛdʒəˈtɛriən] *n* **:** vegetariano *mf*
vegetarianism [ˌvɛdʒəˈtɛriəˌnɪzəm] *n* **:** vegetarianismo *m*
vegetate [ˈvɛdʒəˌteɪt] *vi* **-tated; -tating :** vegetar
vegetation [ˌvɛdʒəˈteɪʃən] *n* **:** vegetación *f*
vehemence [ˈviːəmənts] *n* **:** intensidad *f,* vehemencia *f*
vehement [ˈviːəmənt] *adj* **:** intenso, vehemente
vehemently [ˈviːəməntli] *adv* **:** vehementemente, con vehemencia
vehicle [ˈviːəkəl, ˈviːˌhɪkəl] *n* **1** *or* **motor vehicle :** vehículo *m* **2** MEDIUM **:** vehículo *m,* medio *m*
vehicular [viˈhɪkjələr, və-] *adj* **:** vehicular <vehicular homicide : muerte por atropello>
veil[1] [ˈveɪl] *vt* **1** CONCEAL **:** velar, disimular **2 :** cubrir con un velo <to veil one's face : cubrirse con un velo>
veil[2] *n* **:** velo *m* <bridal veil : velo de novia>
vein [ˈveɪn] *n* **1 :** vena *f* (en anatomía, botánica, etc.) **2** LODE **:** veta *f,* vena *f,* filón *m* **3** STYLE **:** vena *f* <in a humorous vein : en vena humorística>
veined [ˈveɪnd] *adj* **:** veteado (dícese del queso, de los minerales, etc.)

velocity [vəˈlɑsət̬i] *n, pl* **-ties** : velocidad *f*
velour [vəˈlʊr] *or* **velours** [-ˈlʊrz] *n* : velour *m*
velvet[1] [ˈvɛlvət] *adj* **1** : de terciopelo **2** → **velvety**
velvet[2] *n* : terciopelo *m*
velvety [ˈvɛlvət̬i] *adj* : aterciopelado
venal [ˈviːnəl] *adj* : venal, sobornable
vend [ˈvɛnd] *vt* : vender
vendetta [vɛnˈdɛt̬ə] *n* : vendetta *f*
vendor [ˈvɛndər] *n* : vendedor *m*, -dora *f*; puestero *m*, -ra *f*
veneer[1] [vəˈnɪr] *vt* : enchapar, chapar
veneer[2] *n* **1** : enchapado *m*, chapa *f* **2** APPEARANCE : apariencia *f*, barniz *m* <a veneer of culture : un barniz de cultura>
venerable [ˈvɛnərəbəl] *adj* : venerable
venerate [ˈvɛnəˌreɪt] *vt* **-ated; -ating** : venerar
veneration [ˌvɛnəˈreɪʃən] *n* : veneración *f*
venereal disease [vəˈnɪriəl] *n* : enfermedad *f* venérea
venetian blind [vəˈniːʃən] *n* : persiana *f* veneciana
Venezuelan [ˌvɛnəˈzweɪlən, -zʊˈeɪ-] *n* : venezolano *m*, -na *f* — **Venezuelan** *adj*
vengeance [ˈvɛndʒənts] *n* : venganza *f* <to take vengeance on : vengarse de>
vengeful [ˈvɛndʒfəl] *adj* : vengativo
venial [ˈviːniəl] *adj* : venial <a venial sin : un pecado venial>
venison [ˈvɛnəsən, -zən] *n* : venado *m*, carne *f* de venado
venom [ˈvɛnəm] *n* **1** : veneno *m* **2** MALICE : veneno *m*, malevolencia *f*
venomous [ˈvɛnəməs] *adj* : venenoso
vent[1] [ˈvɛnt] *vt* : desahogar, dar salida a <to vent one's feelings : desahogarse>
vent[2] *n* **1** OPENING : abertura *f* (de escape), orificio *m* **2** *or* **air vent** : respiradero *m*, rejilla *f* de ventilación **3** OUTLET : desahogo *m* <to give vent to one's anger : desahogar la ira>
ventilate [ˈvɛntəlˌeɪt] *vt* **-lated; -lating** : ventilar
ventilation [ˌvɛntəlˈeɪʃən] *n* : ventilación *f*
ventilator [ˈvɛntəlˌeɪt̬ər] *n* : ventilador *m*
ventricle [ˈvɛntrɪkəl] *n* : ventrículo *m*
ventriloquism [vɛnˈtrɪləˌkwɪzəm] *n* : ventriloquia *f*
ventriloquist [vɛnˈtrɪləˌkwɪst] *n* : ventrílocuo *m*, -cua *f*
venture[1] [ˈvɛntʃər] *v* **-tured; -turing** *vt* **1** RISK : arriesgar **2** OFFER : aventurar <to venture an opinion : aventurar una opinión> — *vi* : arriesgarse, atreverse, aventurarse
venture[2] *n* **1** UNDERTAKING : empresa *f* **2** GAMBLE, RISK : aventura *f*, riesgo *m*
venturesome [ˈvɛntʃərsəm] *adj* **1** ADVENTUROUS : audaz, atrevido **2** RISKY : arriesgado
venue [ˈvɛnˌjuː] *n* **1** PLACE : lugar *m* **2** : jurisdicción *f* (en derecho)
Venus [ˈviːnəs] *n* : Venus *m*
veracity [vəˈræsət̬i] *n, pl* **-ties** : veracidad *f*
veranda *or* **verandah** [vəˈrændə] *n* : terraza *f*, veranda *f*
verb [ˈvərb] *n* : verbo *m*
verbal [ˈvərbəl] *adj* : verbal
verbalize [ˈvərbəˌlaɪz] *vt* **-ized; -izing** : expresar con palabras, verbalizar
verbally [ˈvərbəli] *adv* : verbalmente, de palabra
verbatim[1] [vərˈbeɪt̬əm] *adv* : palabra por palabra, textualmente
verbatim[2] *adj* : literal, textual
verbose [vərˈboːs] *adj* : verboso, prolijo
verdant [ˈvərdənt] *adj* : verde, verdeante
verdict [ˈvərdɪkt] *n* **1** : veredicto *m* (de un jurado) **2** JUDGMENT, OPINION : juicio *m*, opinión *f*
verge[1] [ˈvərdʒ] *vi* **verged; verging** : estar al borde, rayar <it verges on madness : raya en la locura>
verge[2] *n* **1** EDGE : borde *m* **2 to be on the verge of** : estar a pique de, estar al borde de, estar a punto de
verification [ˌvɛrəfəˈkeɪʃən] *n* : verificación *f*
verify [ˈvɛrəˌfaɪ] *vt* **-fied; -fying** : verificar, comprobar, confirmar
veritable [ˈvɛrət̬əbəl] *adj* : verdadero — **veritably** *adv*
vermicelli [ˌvərməˈtʃɛli, -ˈsɛli] *n* : fideos *mpl* finos
vermin [ˈvərmən] *ns & pl* : alimañas *fpl*, bichos *mpl*, sabandijas *fpl*
vermouth [vərˈmuːθ] *n* : vermut *m*
vernacular[1] [vərˈnækjələr] *adj* : vernáculo
vernacular[2] *n* : lengua *f* vernácula
versatile [ˈvərsət̬əl] *adj* : versátil
versatility [ˌvərsəˈtɪlət̬i] *n* : versatilidad *f*
verse [ˈvərs] *n* **1** LINE, STANZA : verso *m*, estrofa *f* **2** POETRY : poesía *f* **3** : versículo *m* (en la Biblia)
versed [ˈvərst] *adj* : versado <to be well versed in : ser muy versado en>
version [ˈvərʒən] *n* : versión *f*
versus [ˈvərsəs] *prep* : versus
vertebra [ˈvərt̬əbrə] *n, pl* **-brae** [-ˌbreɪ, -ˌbriː] *or* **-bras** : vértebra *f*
vertebrate[1] [ˈvərt̬əbrət, -ˌbreɪt] *adj* : vertebrado
vertebrate[2] *n* : vertebrado *m*
vertex [ˈvərˌtɛks] *n, pl* **vertices** [ˈvərt̬əˌsiːz] **1** : vértice *m* (en matemáticas y anatomía) **2** SUMMIT, TOP : ápice *m*, cumbre *f*, cima *f*
vertical[1] [ˈvərt̬ɪkəl] *adj* : vertical — **verticalmente** *adv*
vertical[2] *n* : vertical *f*
vertigo [ˈvərt̬ɪˌgoː] *n, pl* **-goes** *or* **-gos** : vértigo *m*
verve [ˈvərv] *n* : brío *m*

very[1] [ˈvɛri] *adv* **1** EXTREMELY : muy, sumamente <very few : muy pocos> <I am very sorry : lo siento mucho> **2** (*used for emphasis*) <at the very least : por lo menos, como mínimo> <the same dress : el mismo vestido>
very[2] *adj* **verier; -est 1** EXACT, PRECISE : mismo, exacto <at that very moment : en ese mismo momento> <it's the very thing : es justo lo que hacía falta> **2** BARE, MERE : solo, mero <the very thought of it : sólo pensarlo> **3** EXTREME : extremo, de todo <at the very top : arriba de todo>
vespers [ˈvɛspərz] *npl* : vísperas *fpl*
vessel [ˈvɛsəl] *n* **1** CONTAINER : vasija *f*, recipiente *m* **2** BOAT, CRAFT : nave *f*, barco *m*, buque *m* **3** : vaso *m* <blood vessel : vaso sanguíneo>
vest[1] [ˈvɛst] *vt* **1** CONFER : conferir <to vest authority in : conferirle la autoridad a> **2** CLOTHE : vestir
vest[2] *n* **1** : chaleco *m* **2** UNDERSHIRT : camiseta *f*
vestibule [ˈvɛstəˌbjuːl] *n* : vestíbulo *m*
vestige [ˈvɛstɪdʒ] *n* : vestigio *m*, rastro *m*
vestment [ˈvɛstmənt] *n* : vestidura *f*
vestry [ˈvɛstri] *n, pl* **-tries** : sacristía *f*
vet [ˈvɛt] *n* **1** → **veterinarian 2** → **veteran**[2]
veteran[1] [ˈvɛtərən, ˈvɛtrən] *adj* : veterano
veteran[2] *n* : veterano *m*, -na *f*
Veterans Day *n* : día *m* del Armisticio (celebrado el 11 de noviembre en los Estados Unidos)
veterinarian [ˌvɛtərəˈnɛriən, ˌvɛtəˈnɛr-] *n* : veterinario *m*, -ria *f*
veterinary [ˈvɛtərəˌnɛri] *adj* : veterinario
veto[1] [ˈviːto] *vt* **1** FORBID : prohibir **2** : vetar <to veto a bill : vetar un proyecto de ley>
veto[2] *n, pl* **-toes 1** : veto *m* <the power of veto : el derecho de veto> **2** BAN : veto *m*, prohibición *f*
vex [ˈvɛks] *vt* : contrariar, molestar, irritar
vexation [vɛkˈseɪʃən] *n* : contrariedad *f*, irritación *f*
via [ˈvaɪə, ˈviːə] *prep* : por, vía
viability [ˌvaɪəˈbɪləti] *n* : viabilidad *f*
viable [ˈvaɪəbəl] *adj* : viable
viaduct [ˈvaɪəˌdʌkt] *n* : viaducto *m*
vial [ˈvaɪəl] *n* : frasco *m*
vibrant [ˈvaɪbrənt] *adj* **1** LIVELY : vibrante, animado, dinámico **2** BRIGHT : fuerte, vivo (dícese de los colores)
vibrate [ˈvaɪˌbreɪt] *vi* **-brated; -brating 1** OSCILLATE : vibrar, oscilar **2** THRILL : bullir <to vibrate with excitement : bullir de emoción>
vibration [vaɪˈbreɪʃən] *n* : vibración *f*
vicar [ˈvɪkər] *n* : vicario *m*, -ria *f*
vicarious [vaɪˈkæriːəs, vɪ-] *adj* : indirecto — **vicariously** *adv*
vice [ˈvaɪs] *n* : vicio *m*
vice admiral *n* : vicealmirante *mf*
vice president *n* : vicepresidente *m*, -ta *f*
viceroy [ˈvaɪsˌrɔɪ] *n* : virrey *m*, -rreina *f*
vice versa [ˌvaɪsɪˈvərsə, ˌvaɪsˈvər-] *adv* : viceversa
vicinity [vəˈsɪnəti] *n, pl* **-ties 1** NEIGHBORHOOD : vecindad *f*, inmediaciones *fpl* **2** NEARNESS : proximidad *f*
vicious [ˈvɪʃəs] *adj* **1** DEPRAVED : depravado, malo **2** SAVAGE : malo, fiero, salvaje <a vicious dog : un perro feroz> **3** MALICIOUS : malicioso
viciously [ˈvɪʃəsli] *adv* : con saña, brutalmente
viciousness [ˈvɪʃəsnəs] *n* : brutalidad *f*, ferocidad *f* (de un animal), malevolencia *f* (de un comentario, etc.)
vicissitudes [vəˈsɪsəˌtuːdz, vaɪ-, -ˌtjuːdz] *npl* : vicisitudes *fpl*
victim [ˈvɪktəm] *n* : víctima *f*
victimize [ˈvɪktəˌmaɪz] *vt* **-mized; -mizing** : tomar como víctima, perseguir, victimizar *Arg, Mex*
victor [ˈvɪktər] *n* : vencedor *m*, -dora *f*
Victorian [vɪkˈtoːriən] *adj* : victoriano
victorious [vɪkˈtoːriəs] *adj* : victorioso — **victoriously** *adv*
victory [ˈvɪktəri] *n, pl* **-ries** : victoria *f*, triunfo *m*
victuals [ˈvɪtəlz] *npl* : víveres *mpl*, provisiones *fpl*
video[1] [ˈvɪdiˌoː] *adj* : de video <video recording : grabación de video>
video[2] *n* **1** : video *m* (medio o grabación) **2** → **videotape**[2]
videocassette [ˌvɪdiokəˈsɛt] *n* : videocasete *m*, videocassette *m*
videocassette recorder → **VCR**
videotape[1] [ˈvɪdioˌteɪp] *vt* **-taped; -taping** : grabar en video, videograbar
videotape[2] *n* : videocinta *f*
vie [ˈvaɪ] *vi* **vied; vying** [ˈvaɪɪŋ] : competir, rivalizar
Vietnamese [viˌɛtnəˈmiːz, -ˈmiːs] *n* : vietnamita *mf* — **Vietnamese** *adj*
view[1] [ˈvjuː] *vt* **1** OBSERVE : mirar, ver, observar **2** CONSIDER : considerar, contemplar
view[2] *n* **1** SIGHT : vista *f* <to come into view : aparecer> **2** ATTITUDE, OPINION : opinión *f*, parecer *m*, actitud *f* <in my view : en mi opinión> **3** SCENE : vista *f*, panorama *f* **4** INTENTION : idea *f*, vista *f* <with a view to : con vistas a, con la idea de> **5 in view of** : dado que, en vista de (que)
viewer [ˈvjuːər] *n or* **television viewer** : telespectador *m*, -dora *f*; televidente *mf*
viewpoint [ˈvjuːˌpɔɪnt] *n* : punto *m* de vista
vigil [ˈvɪdʒəl] *n* **1** : vigilia *f*, vela *f* **2 to keep vigil** : velar
vigilance [ˈvɪdʒələnts] *n* : vigilancia *f*
vigilant [ˈvɪdʒələnt] *adj* : vigilante

vigilante [ˌvɪdʒəˈlænˌtiː] *n* : integrante *mf* de un comité de vigilancia (que actúa como policía)

vigilantly [ˈvɪdʒələntli] *adv* : con vigilancia

vigor [ˈvɪgər] *n* : vigor *m,* energía *f,* fuerza *f*

vigorous [ˈvɪgərəs] *adj* : vigoroso, enérgico — **vigorously** *adv*

Viking [ˈvaɪkɪŋ] *n* : vikingo *m,* -ga *f*

vile [ˈvaɪl] *adj* **viler; vilest 1** WICKED : vil, infame **2** REVOLTING : asqueroso, repugnante **3** TERRIBLE : horrible, atroz <vile weather : tiempo horrible> <to be in a vile mood : estar de un humor de perros>

vilify [ˈvɪləˌfaɪ] *vt* **-fied; -fying** : vilipendiar, denigrar, difamar

villa [ˈvɪlə] *n* : casa *f* de campo, quinta *f*

village [ˈvɪlɪdʒ] *n* : pueblo *m* (grande), aldea *f* (pequeña)

villager [ˈvɪlɪdʒər] *n* : vecino *m,* -na *f* (de un pueblo); aldeano *m,* -na *f* (de una aldea)

villain [ˈvɪlən] *n* : villano *m,* -na *f;* malo *m,* -la *f* (en ficción, películas, etc.)

villainess [ˈvɪlənɪs, -nəs] *n* : villana *f*

villainous [ˈvɪlənəs] *adj* : infame, malvado

villainy [ˈvɪləni] *n, pl* **-lainies** : vileza *f,* maldad *f*

vim [ˈvɪm] *n* : brío *m,* vigor *m,* energía *f*

vindicate [ˈvɪndəˌkeɪt] *vt* **-cated; -cating 1** EXONERATE : vindicar, disculpar **2** JUSTIFY : justificar

vindication [ˌvɪndəˈkeɪʃən] *n* : vindicación *f,* justificación *f*

vindictive [vɪnˈdɪktɪv] *adj* : vengativo

vine [ˈvaɪn] *n* **1** GRAPEVINE : vid *f,* parra *f* **2** : planta *f* trepadora, enredadera *f*

vinegar [ˈvɪnɪgər] *n* : vinagre *m*

vinegary [ˈvɪnɪgəri] *adj* : avinagrado

vineyard [ˈvɪnjərd] *n* : viña *f,* viñedo *m*

vintage[1] [ˈvɪntɪdʒ] *adj* **1** : añejo (dícese de un vino) **2** CLASSIC : clásico, de época

vintage[2] *n* **1** : cosecha *f* <the 1947 vintage : la cosecha de 1947> **2** ERA : época *f,* era *f* <slang of recent vintage : argot de la época reciente>

vinyl [ˈvaɪnəl] *n* : vinilo

viola [viːˈoːlə] *n* : viola *f*

violate [ˈvaɪəˌleɪt] *vt* **-lated; -lating 1** BREAK : infringir, violar, quebrantar <to violate the rules : violar las reglas> **2** RAPE : violar **3** DESECRATE : profanar

violation [ˌvaɪəˈleɪʃən] *n* **1** : violación *f,* infracción *f* (de una ley) **2** DESECRATION : profanación *f*

violence [ˈvaɪlənts, ˈvaɪə-] *n* : violencia *f*

violent [ˈvaɪlənt, ˈvaɪə-] *adj* : violento

violently [ˈvaɪləntli, ˈvaɪə-] *adv* : violentamente, con violencia

violet [ˈvaɪlət, ˈvaɪə-] *n* : violeta *f*

violin [ˌvaɪəˈlɪn] *n* : violín *m*

violinist [ˌvaɪəˈlɪnɪst] *n* : violinista *mf*

violoncello [ˌvaɪələnˈtʃɛloː, ˌviː-] → **cello**

VIP [ˌviːˌaɪˈpiː] *n, pl* **VIPs** [-ˈpiːz] : VIP *mf,* persona *f* de categoría

viper [ˈvaɪpər] *n* : víbora *f*

viral [ˈvaɪrəl] *adj* : viral, vírico <viral pneumonia : pulmonía viral>

virgin[1] [ˈvərdʒən] *adj* **1** CHASTE : virginal <the virgin birth : el alumbramiento virginal> **2** : virgen, intacto <a virgin forest : una selva virgen> <virgin wool : lana virgen>

virgin[2] *n* : virgen *mf*

virginity [vərˈdʒɪnəṭi] *n* : virginidad *f*

Virgo [ˈvərˌgoː, ˈvɪr-] *n* : Virgo *mf*

virile [ˈvɪrəl, -ˌaɪl] *adj* : viril, varonil

virility [vəˈrɪləṭi] *n* : virilidad *f*

virtual [ˈvərtʃʊəl] *adj* : virtual <a virtual dictator : un virtual dictador> <virtual reality : realidad virtual>

virtually [ˈvərtʃʊəli, ˈvərtʃəli] *adv* : en realidad, de hecho, casi

virtue [ˈvərˌtʃuː] *n* **1** : virtud *f* **2 by virtue of** : en virtud de, debido a

virtuosity [ˌvərtʃʊˈɑsəṭi] *n, pl* **-ties** : virtuosismo *m*

virtuoso [ˌvərtʃʊˈoːsoː, -zoː] *n, pl* **-sos** *or* **-si** [-ˌsiː, -ˌziː] : virtuoso *m,* -sa *f*

virtuous [ˈvərtʃʊəs] *adj* : virtuoso, bueno — **virtuously** *adv*

virulence [ˈvɪrələnts, ˈvɪrjə-] *n* : virulencia *f*

virulent [ˈvɪrələnt, ˈvɪrjə-] *adj* : virulento

virus [ˈvaɪrəs] *n* : virus *m*

visa [ˈviːzə, -sə] *n* : visa *f*

vis–à–vis [ˌviːzəˈviː, -sə-] *prep* : con relación a, con respecto a

viscera [ˈvɪsərə] *npl* : vísceras *fpl*

visceral [ˈvɪsərəl] *adj* : visceral

viscosity [vɪsˈkɑsəṭi] *n, pl* **-ties** : viscosidad *f*

viscount [ˈvaɪˌkæʊnt] *n* : vizconde *m*

viscountess [ˈvaɪˌkæʊntɪs] *n* : vizcondesa *f*

viscous [ˈvɪskəs] *adj* : viscoso

vise [ˈvaɪs] *n* : torno *m* de banco, tornillo *m* de banco

visibility [ˌvɪzəˈbɪləṭi] *n, pl* **-ties** : visibilidad *f*

visible [ˈvɪzəbəl] *adj* **1** : visible <the visible stars : las estrellas visibles> **2** OBVIOUS : evidente, patente

visibly [ˈvɪzəbli] *adv* : visiblemente

vision [ˈvɪʒən] *n* **1** EYESIGHT : vista *f,* visión *f* **2** APPARITION : visión *f,* aparición *f* **3** FORESIGHT : visión *f* (del futuro), previsión *f* **4** IMAGE : imagen *f* <she had visions of a disaster : se imaginaba un desastre>

visionary[1] [ˈvɪʒəˌnɛri] *adj* **1** FARSIGHTED : visionario, con visión de futuro **2** UTOPIAN : utópico, poco realista

visionary[2] *n, pl* **-ries** : visionario *m,* -ria *f*

visit¹ [ˈvɪzət] *vt* **1** : visitar, ir a ver **2** AFFLICT : azotar, afligir <visited by troubles : afligido con problemas> — *vi* : hacer (una) visita
visit² *n* : visita *f*
visitor [ˈvɪzət̬ər] *n* : visitante *mf* (a una ciudad, etc.), visita *f* (a una casa)
visor [ˈvaɪzər] *n* : visera *f*
vista [ˈvɪstə] *n* : vista *f*
visual [ˈvɪʒʊəl] *adj* : visual <the visual arts : las artes visuales> — **visually** *adv*
visualize [ˈvɪʒʊəˌlaɪz] *vt* **-ized; -izing** : visualizar, imaginarse, hacerse una idea de
vital [ˈvaɪt̬əl] *adj* **1** : vital <vital organs : órganos vitales> **2** CRUCIAL : esencial, crucial, decisivo <of vital importance : de suma importancia> **3** LIVELY : enérgico, lleno de vida, vital
vitality [vaɪˈtæləṭi] *n, pl* **-ties** : vitalidad *f*, energía *f*
vitally [ˈvaɪt̬əli] *adv* : sumamente
vital statistics *npl* : estadísticas *fpl* demográficas
vitamin [ˈvaɪt̬əmən] *n* : vitamina *f* <vitamin deficiency : carencia vitamínica>
vitreous [ˈvɪtriəs] *adj* : vítreo
vitriolic [ˌvɪtriˈɑlɪk] *adj* : mordaz, virulento
vituperation [vaɪˌtuːpəˈreɪʃən, -ˌtjuː-] *n* : vituperio *m*
vivacious [vəˈveɪʃəs, vaɪ-] *adj* : vivaz, animado, lleno de vida
vivaciously [vəˈveɪʃəsli, vaɪ-] *adv* : con vivacidad, animadamente
vivacity [vəˈvæsəṭi, vaɪ-] *n* : vivacidad *f*
vivid [ˈvɪvəd] *adj* **1** LIVELY : lleno de vitalidad **2** BRILLIANT : vivo, intenso <vivid colors : colores vivos> **3** INTENSE, SHARP : vívido, gráfico <a vivid dream : un sueño vívido>
vividly [ˈvɪvədli] *adv* **1** BRIGHTLY : con colores vivos **2** SHARPLY : vívidamente
vividness [ˈvɪvədnəs] *n* **1** BRIGHTNESS : intensidad *f*, viveza *f* **2** SHARPNESS : lo gráfico, nitidez *f*
vivisection [ˌvɪvəˈsɛkʃən, ˈvɪvəˌ-] *n* : vivisección *f*
vixen [ˈvɪksən] *n* : zorra *f*, raposa *f*
vocabulary [voːˈkæbjəˌlɛri] *n, pl* **-laries 1** : vocabulario *m* **2** LEXICON : léxico *m*
vocal [ˈvoːkəl] *adj* **1** : vocal **2** LOUD, OUTSPOKEN : ruidoso, muy franco
vocal cords *npl* : cuerdas *fpl* vocales
vocalist [ˈvoːkəlɪst] *n* : cantante *mf*, vocalista *mf*
vocalize [ˈvoːkəlˌaɪz] *vt* **-ized; -izing** : vocalizar
vocation [voˈkeɪʃən] *n* : vocación *f* <to have a vocation for : tener vocación de>
vocational [voˈkeɪʃənəl] *adj* : profesional <vocational guidance : orientación profesional>
vociferous [voˈsɪfərəs] *adj* : ruidoso, vociferante
vodka [ˈvɑdkə] *n* : vodka *m*
vogue [ˈvoːg] *n* : moda *f*, boga *f* <to be in vogue : estar de moda, estar en boga>
voice¹ [ˈvɔɪs] *vt* **voiced; voicing** : expresar
voice² *n* **1** : voz *f* <in a low voice : en voz baja> <to lose one's voice : quedarse sin voz> <the voice of the people : la voz del pueblo> **2 to make one's voice heard** : hacerse oír
voice box → **larynx**
voiced [ˈvɔɪst] *adj* : sonoro
void¹ [ˈvɔɪd] *vt* : anular, invalidar <to void a contract : anular un contrato>
void² *adj* **1** EMPTY : vacío, desprovisto <void of content : desprovisto de contenido> **2** INVALID : inválido, nulo
void³ *n* : vacío *m*
volatile [ˈvɑləṭəl] *adj* : volátil, inestable
volatility [ˌvɑləˈtɪləṭi] *n* : volatilidad *f*, inestabilidad *f*
volcanic [vɑlˈkænɪk] *adj* : volcánico
volcano [vɑlˈkeɪˌnoː] *n, pl* **-noes** *or* **-nos** : volcán *m*
vole [ˈvoːl] *n* : campañol *m*
volition [voˈlɪʃən] *n* : volición *f*, voluntad *f* <of one's own volition : por voluntad propia>
volley [ˈvɑli] *n, pl* **-leys 1** : descarga *f* (de tiros) **2** : torrente *m*, lluvia *f* (de insultos, etc.) **3** : salva *f* (de aplausos) **4** : volea *f* (en deportes)
volleyball [ˈvɑliˌbɔl] *n* : voleibol *m*
volt [ˈvoːlt] *n* : voltio *m*
voltage [ˈvoːltɪdʒ] *n* : voltaje *m*
volubility [ˌvɑljəˈbɪləṭi] *n* : locuacidad *f*
voluble [ˈvɑljəbəl] *adj* : locuaz
volume [ˈvɑljəm, -ˌjuːm] *n* **1** BOOK : volumen *m*, tomo *m* **2** SPACE : capacidad *f*, volumen *m* (en física) **3** AMOUNT : cantidad *f*, volumen *m* **4** LOUDNESS : volumen *m*
voluminous [vəˈluːmənəs] *adj* : voluminoso
voluntary [ˈvɑlənˌtɛri] *adj* : voluntario — **voluntarily** [ˌvɑlənˈtɛrəli] *adv*
volunteer¹ [ˌvɑlənˈtɪr] *vt* : ofrecer, dar <to volunteer one's assistance : ofrecer la ayuda> — *vi* : ofrecerse, alistarse como voluntario
volunteer² *n* : voluntario *m*, -ria *f*
voluptuous [vəˈlʌptʃʊəs] *adj* : voluptuoso
vomit¹ [ˈvɑmət] *v* : vomitar
vomit² *n* : vómito *m*
voodoo [ˈvuːˌduː] *n, pl* **voodoos** : vudú *m*
voracious [vɔˈreɪʃəs, və-] *adj* : voraz
voraciously [vɔˈreɪʃəsli, və-] *adv* : vorazmente, con voracidad
vortex [ˈvɔrˌtɛks] *n, pl* **vortices** [ˈvɔrtəˌsiːz] : vórtice *m*

vote[1] [ˈvoːt] *vi* **voted; voting :** votar <to vote Democratic : votar por los demócratas>
vote[2] *n* **1 :** voto *m* **2** SUFFRAGE **:** sufragio *m,* derecho *m* al voto
voter [ˈvoːt̬ər] *n* **:** votante *mf*
voting [ˈvoːt̬ɪŋ] *n* **:** votación *f*
vouch [ˈvæʊtʃ] *vi* **to vouch for :** garantizar (algo), responder de (algo), responder por (alguien)
voucher [ˈvæʊtʃər] *n* **1** RECEIPT **:** comprobante *m* **2 :** vale *m* <travel voucher : vale de viajar>
vow[1] [væʊ] *vt* **:** jurar, prometer, hacer voto de
vow[2] *n* **:** promesa *f,* voto *m* (en la religión) <a vow of poverty : un voto de pobreza>
vowel [ˈvæʊəl] *n* **:** vocal *m*
voyage[1] [ˈvɔɪɪdʒ] *vi* **-aged; -aging :** viajar
voyage[2] *n* **:** viaje *m*
voyager [ˈvɔɪɪdʒər] *n* **:** viajero *m,* -ra *f*
vulcanize [ˈvʌlkəˌnaɪz] *vt* **-nized; -nizing :** vulcanizar
vulgar [ˈvʌlgər] *adj* **1** COMMON, PLEBIAN **:** ordinario, populachero, del vulgo **2** COARSE, CRUDE **:** grosero, de mal gusto, majadero *Mex* **3** INDECENT **:** indecente, colorado (dícese de un chiste, etc.)
vulgarity [ˌvʌlˈgærət̬i] *n, pl* **-ties :** grosería *f,* vulgaridad *f*
vulgarly [ˈvʌlgərli] *adv* **:** vulgarmente, groseramente
vulnerability [ˌvʌlnərəˈbɪlət̬i] *n, pl* **-ties :** vulnerabilidad *f*
vulnerable [ˈvʌlnərəbəl] *adj* **:** vulnerable
vulture [ˈvʌltʃər] *n* **:** buitre *m,* zopilote *m CA, Mex*
vying → **vie**

W

w [ˈdʌbəlˌjuː] *n, pl* **w's** *or* **ws** [-ˌjuːz] **:** vigésima tercera letra del alfabeto inglés
wad[1] [ˈwɑd] *vt* **wadded; wadding 1 :** hacer un taco con, formar en una masa **2** STUFF **:** rellenar
wad[2] *n* **:** taco *m* (de papel), bola *f* (de algodón, etc.), fajo *m* (de billetes)
waddle[1] [ˈwɑdəl] *vi* **-dled; -dling :** andar como un pato
waddle[2] *n* **:** andar *m* de pato
wade [ˈweɪd] *v* **waded; wading** *vi* **1 :** caminar por el agua **2 to wade through :** leer (algo) con dificultad — *vt or* **to wade across :** vadear
wading bird *n* **:** zancuda *f,* ave *f* zancuda
wafer [ˈweɪfər] *n* **:** barquillo *m,* galleta *f* de barquillo
waffle [ˈwɑfəl] *n* **1 :** wafle *m* **2 waffle iron :** waflera *f*
waft [ˈwɑft, ˈwæft] *vt* **:** llevar por el aire — *vi* **:** flotar
wag[1] [ˈwæg] *v* **wagged; wagging** *vt* **:** menear — *vi* **:** menearse, moverse
wag[2] *n* **1 :** meneo *m* (de la cola) **2** JOKER, WIT **:** bromista *mf*
wage[1] [ˈweɪdʒ] *vt* **waged; waging :** hacer, librar <to wage war : hacer la guerra>
wage[2] *n or* **wages** *npl* **:** sueldo *m,* salario *m* <minimum wage : salario mínimo>
wager[1] [ˈweɪdʒər] *v* **:** apostar
wager[2] *n* **:** apuesta *f*
waggish [ˈwægɪʃ] *adj* **:** burlón, bromista (dícese de una persona), chistoso (dícese de un comentario)
waggle [ˈwægəl] *vt* **-gled; -gling :** menear, mover (de un lado a otro)
wagon [ˈwægən] *n* **1 :** carro *m* (tirado por caballos) **2** CART **:** carrito *m* **3** → **station wagon**
waif [ˈweɪf] *n* **:** niño *m* abandonado, animal *m* sin hogar
wail[1] [ˈweɪl] *vi* **:** gemir, lamentarse
wail[2] *n* **:** gemido *m,* lamento *m*
wainscot [ˈweɪnskət, -ˌskɑt, -ˌskoːt] *or* **wainscoting** [-skət̬ɪŋ, -ˌskɑ-, -ˌskoː-] *n* **:** boiserie *f,* revestimiento *m* de paneles de madera
waist [ˈweɪst] *n* **:** cintura *f* (del cuerpo humano), talle *m* (de ropa)
waistline [ˈweɪstˌlaɪn] → **waist**
wait[1] [ˈweɪt] *vi* **:** esperar <to wait for something : esperar algo> <wait and see! : ¡espera y verás!> <I can't wait : me muero de ganas> — *vt* **1** AWAIT **:** esperar **2** DELAY **:** retrasar <don't wait lunch : no retrase el almuerzo> **3** SERVE **:** servir, atender <to wait tables : servir (a la mesa)>
wait[2] *n* **1 :** espera *f* **2 to lie in wait :** estar al acecho
waiter [ˈweɪt̬ər] *n* **:** mesero *m,* camarero *m,* mozo *m Arg, Chile, Col, Peru*
waiting room *n* **:** sala *f* de espera
waitress [ˈweɪtrəs] *n* **:** mesera *f,* camarera *f,* moza *f Arg, Chile, Col, Peru*
waive [ˈweɪv] *vt* **waived; waiving :** renunciar a <to waive one's rights : renunciar a sus derechos> <to waive the rules : no aplicar las reglas>
waiver [ˈweɪvər] *n* **:** renuncia *f*
wake[1] [ˈweɪk] *v* **woke** [ˈwoːk]; **woken** [ˈwoːkən] *or* **waked; waking** *vi or* **to wake up :** despertar(se) <he woke at noon : se despertó al mediodía> <wake up! : ¡despiértate!> — *vt* **:** despertar
wake[2] *n* **1** VIGIL **:** velatorio *m,* velorio *m* (de un difunto) **2** TRAIL **:** estela *f* (de un barco, un huracán, etc.) **3** AFTERMATH **:** consecuencias *fpl* <in the wake of : tras, como consecuencia de>

wakeful [ˈweɪkfəl] *adj* **1** SLEEPLESS : desvelado **2** VIGILANT : alerta, vigilante

waken [ˈweɪkən] → **awake**

walk[1] [ˈwɔk] *vi* **1** : caminar, andar, pasear <you're walking too fast : estás caminando demasiado rápido> <to walk around the city : pasearse por la ciudad> **2** : ir andando, ir a pie <we had to walk home : tuvimos que ir a casa a pie> **3** : darle base por bolas (a un bateador) — *vt* **1** : recorrer, caminar <she walked two miles : caminó dos millas> **2** ACCOMPANY : acompañar **3** : sacar a pasear (a un perro)

walk[2] *n* **1** : paseo *m,* caminata *f* <to go for a walk : ir a caminar, dar un paseo> **2** PATH : camino *m* **3** GAIT : andar *m* **4** : marcha *f* (en beisbol) **5 walk of life** : esfera *f,* condición *f*

walker [ˈwɔkər] *n* **1** : paseante *mf;* andador *m,* -dora *f* **2** HIKER : excursionista *mf* **3** *or* **baby walker** : andador *m*

walking stick *n* : bastón *m*

walkout [ˈwɔkˌaʊt] *n* STRIKE : huelga *f*

walk out *vi* **1** STRIKE : declararse en huelga **2** LEAVE : salir, irse **3 to walk out on** : abandonar, dejar

wall[1] [ˈwɔl] *vt* **1 to wall in** : cercar con una pared o un muro, tapiar, amurallar **2 to wall off** : separar con una pared o un muro **3 to wall up** : tapiar, condenar (una ventana, etc.)

wall[2] *n* **1** : muro *m* (exterior) <the walls of the city : las murallas de la ciudad> **2** : pared *f* (interior) **3** BARRIER : barrera *f* <a wall of mountains : una barrera de montañas> **4** : pared *f* (en anatomía)

wallaby [ˈwɑləbi] *n, pl* **-bies** : ualabí *m*

walled [ˈwɔld] *adj* : amurallado

wallet [ˈwɑlət] *n* : billetera *f,* cartera *f*

wallflower [ˈwɔlˌflaʊər] *n* **1** : alhelí *m* (flor) **2 to be a wallflower** : comer pavo

wallop[1] [ˈwɑləp] *vt* **1** TROUNCE : darle una paliza (a alguien) **2** SOCK : pegar fuerte

wallop[2] *n* : golpe *m* fuerte, golpazo *m*

wallow[1] [ˈwɑˌloː] *vi* **1** : revolcarse <to wallow in the mud : revolcarse en el lodo> **2** DELIGHT : deleitarse <to wallow in luxury : nadar en lujos>

wallow[2] *n* : revolcadero *m* (para animales)

wallpaper[1] [ˈwɔlˌpeɪpər] *vt* : empapelar

wallpaper[2] *n* : papel *m* pintado

walnut [ˈwɔlˌnʌt] *n* **1** : nuez *f* (fruta) **2** : nogal *m* (árbol y madera)

walrus [ˈwɔlrəs, ˈwɑl-] *n, pl* **-rus** *or* **-ruses** : morsa *f*

waltz[1] [ˈwɔlts] *vi* **1** : valsar, bailar el vals **2** BREEZE : pasar con ligereza <to waltz in : entrar tan campante>

waltz[2] *n* : vals *m*

wan [ˈwɑn] *adj* **wanner; -est 1** PALLID : pálido **2** DIM : tenue <wan light : luz tenue> **3** LANGUID : lánguido <a wan smile : una sonrisa lánguida> — **wanly** *adv*

wand [ˈwɑnd] *n* : varita *f* (mágica)

wander [ˈwɑndər] *vi* **1** RAMBLE : deambular, vagar, vagabundear **2** STRAY : alejarse, desviarse, divagar <she let her mind wander : dejó vagar la imaginación> — *vt* : recorrer <to wander the streets : vagar por las calles>

wanderer [ˈwɑndərər] *n* : vagabundo *m,* -da *f;* viajero *m,* -ra *f*

wanderlust [ˈwɑndərˌlʌst] *n* : pasión *f* por viajar

wane[1] [ˈweɪn] *vi* **waned; waning 1** : menguar (dícese de la luna) **2** DECLINE : disminuir, decaer, menguar

wane[2] *n* **on the wane** : decayendo, en decadencia

wangle [ˈwæŋgəl] *vt* **-gled; -gling** FINAGLE : arreglárselas para conseguir

want[1] [ˈwɑnt, ˈwɔnt] *vt* **1** LACK : faltar **2** REQUIRE : requerir, necesitar **3** DESIRE : querer, desear

want[2] *n* **1** LACK : falta *f* **2** DESTITUTION : indigencia *f,* miseria *f* **3** DESIRE, NEED : deseo *m,* necesidad *f*

wanting [ˈwɑntɪŋ, ˈwɔn-] *adj* **1** ABSENT : ausente **2** DEFICIENT : deficiente <he's wanting in common sense : le falta sentido común>

wanton [ˈwɑntən, ˈwɔn-] *adj* **1** LEWD, LUSTFUL : lascivo, lujurioso, licencioso **2** INHUMANE, MERCILESS : despiadado <wanton cruelty : crueldad despiadada>

wapiti [ˈwɑpəṭi] *n, pl* **-ti** *or* **-tis** : uapití *m*

war[1] [ˈwɔr] *vi* **warred; warring** : combatir, batallar, hacer la guerra

war[2] *n* : guerra *f* <to go to war : entrar en guerra>

warble[1] [ˈwɔrbəl] *vi* **-bled; -bling** : gorjear, trinar

warble[2] *n* : trino *m,* gorjeo *m*

warbler [ˈwɔrblər] *n* : pájaro *m* gorjeador, curruca *f*

ward[1] [ˈwɔrd] *vt* **to ward off** : desviar, protegerse contra

ward[2] *n* **1** : sala *f* (de un hospital, etc.) <maternity ward : sala de maternidad> **2** : distrito *m* electoral o administrativo (de una ciudad) **3** : pupilo *m,* -la *f* (de un tutor, etc.)

warden [ˈwɔrdən] *n* **1** KEEPER : guarda *mf;* guardián *m,* -diana *f* <game warden : guardabosque> **2** *or* **prison warden** : alcaide *m*

wardrobe [ˈwɔrdˌroːb] *n* **1** CLOSET : armario *m* **2** CLOTHES : vestuario *m,* guardarropa *f*

ware [ˈwær] *n* **1** POTTERY : cerámica *f* **2 wares** *npl* GOODS : mercancía *f,* mercadería *f*

warehouse [ˈwærˌhaʊs] *n* : depósito *m,* almacén *m,* bodega *f Chile, Col, Mex*

warfare [ˈwɔrˌfær] *n* **1** WAR : guerra *f* **2** STRUGGLE : lucha *f* <the warfare against drugs : la lucha contra las drogas>

warhead [ˈwɔrˌhɛd] *n* : ojiva *f,* cabeza *f* (de un misil)

warily [ˈwærəli] *adv* : cautelosamente, con cautela

wariness [ˈwærinəs] *n* : cautela *f*

warlike [ˈwærˌlaɪk] *adj* : belicoso, guerrero

warm[1] [ˈwɔrm] *vt* **1** HEAT : calentar, recalentar **2 to warm one's heart** : reconfortar a uno, alegrar el corazón **3 to warm up** : calentar (los músculos, un automóvil, etc.) — *vi* **1** : calentarse **2 to warm to** : tomarle simpatía (a alguien), entusiasmarse con (algo)

warm[2] *adj* **1** LUKEWARM : tibio, templado **2** : caliente, cálido, caluroso <a warm wind : un viento cálido> <a warm day : un día caluroso, un día de calor> <warm hands : manos calientes> **3** : caliente, que abriga <warm clothes : ropa de abrigo> <I feel warm : tengo calor> **4** CARING, CORDIAL : cariñoso, cordial **5** : cálido (dícese de colores) **6** FRESH : fresco, reciente <a warm trail : un rastro reciente> **7** (*used for riddles*) : caliente

warm–blooded [ˈwɔrmˈblʌdəd] *adj* : de sangre caliente

warmhearted [ˈwɔrmˈhɑrt̬əd] *adj* : cariñoso

warmly [ˈwɔrmli] *adv* **1** AFFECTIONATELY : calurosamente, afectuosamente **2 to dress warmly** : abrigarse

warmonger [ˈwɔrˌmɑŋgər, -ˌmʌŋ-] *n* : belicista *mf*

warmth [ˈwɔrmpθ] *n* **1** : calor *m* **2** AFFECTION : cariño *m,* afecto *m* **3** ENTHUSIASM : ardor *m,* entusiasmo *m*

warm–up [ˈwɔrmˌʌp] *n* : calentamiento *m*

warn [ˈwɔrn] *vt* **1** CAUTION : advertir, alertar **2** INFORM : avisar, informar

warning [ˈwɔrnɪŋ] *n* **1** ADVICE : advertencia *f,* aviso *m* **2** ALERT : alerta *f,* alarma *f*

warp[1] [ˈwɔrp] *vt* **1** : alabear, combar **2** PERVERT : pervertir, deformar — *vi* : pandearse, alabearse, combarse

warp[2] *n* **1** : urdimbre *f* <the warp and the weft : la urdimbre y la trama> **2** : alabeo *m* (en la madera, etc.)

warrant[1] [ˈwɔrənt] *vt* **1** ASSURE : asegurar, garantizar **2** GUARANTEE : garantizar **3** JUSTIFY, MERIT : justificar, merecer

warrant[2] *n* **1** AUTHORIZATION : autorización *f,* permiso *m* <an arrest warrant : una orden de detención> **2** JUSTIFICATION : justificación *f*

warranty [ˈwɔrənti, ˌwɔrənˈtiː] *n, pl* **-ties** : garantía *f*

warren [ˈwɔrən] *n* : madriguera *f* (de conejos)

warrior [ˈwɔriər] *n* : guerrero *m,* -ra *f*

warship [ˈwɔrˌʃɪp] *n* : buque *m* de guerra

wart [ˈwɔrt] *n* : verruga *f*

wartime [ˈwɔrˌtaɪm] *n* : tiempo *m* de guerra

wary [ˈwæri] *adj* **warier; -est** : cauteloso, receloso <to be wary of : desconfiar de>

was → **be**

wash[1] [ˈwɔʃ, ˈwɑʃ] *vt* **1** CLEAN : lavar(se), limpiar, fregar <to wash the dishes : lavar los platos> <to wash one's hands : lavarse las manos> **2** DRENCH : mojar **3** LAP : bañar <waves were washing the shore : las olas bañaban la orilla> **4** CARRY, DRAG : arrastrar **5 to wash away** : llevarse (un puente, etc.) — *vi* **1** : lavarse (dícese de una persona o la ropa) <the dress washes well : el vestido se lava bien> **2 to wash against** *or* **to wash over** : bañar

wash[2] *n* **1** : lavado *m* <to give something a wash : lavar algo> **2** LAUNDRY : artículos *mpl* para lavar, ropa *f* sucia **3** : estela *f* (de un barco)

washable [ˈwɔʃəbəl, ˈwɑ-] *adj* : lavable

washboard [ˈwɔʃˌbord, ˈwɑʃ-] *n* : tabla *f* de lavar

washbowl [ˈwɔʃˌboːl, ˈwɑʃ-] *n* : lavabo *m,* lavamanos *m*

washcloth [ˈwɔʃˌklɔθ, ˈwɑʃ-] *n* : toallita *f* (para lavarse)

washed–out [ˈwɔʃtˈaʊt, ˈwɑʃt-] *adj* **1** : desvaído (dícese de colores) **2** EXHAUSTED : agotado, desanimado

washed–up [ˈwɔʃtˈʌp, ˈwɑʃt-] *adj* : acabado (dícese de una persona), fracasado (dícese de un negocio, etc.)

washer [ˈwɔʃər, ˈwɑ-] *n* **1** → **washing machine 2** : arandela *f* (de una llave, etc.)

washing [ˈwɔʃɪŋ, ˈwɑ-] *n* WASH : ropa *f* para lavar

washing machine *n* : máquina *f* de lavar, lavadora *f*

washout [ˈwɔʃˌaʊt, ˈwɑʃ-] *n* **1** : erosión *f* (de la tierra) **2** FAILURE : fracaso *m* <she's a washout : es un desastre>

washroom [ˈwɔʃˌruːm, ˈwɑʃ-, -ˌrʊm] *n* : servicios *mpl* (públicos), baño *m,* sanitario *m Col, Mex, Ven*

wasn't [ˈwʌzənt] (*contraction of* **was not**) → **be**

wasp [ˈwɑsp] *n* : avispa *f*

waspish [ˈwɑspɪʃ] *adj* **1** IRRITABLE : irritable, irascible **2** CAUSTIC : cáustico, mordaz

waste[1] [ˈweɪst] *v* **wasted; wasting** *vt* **1** DEVASTATE : arrasar, arruinar, devastar **2** SQUANDER : desperdiciar, despilfarrar, malgastar <to waste time : perder tiempo> — *vi or* **to waste away** : consumirse, chuparse

waste[2] *adj* **1** BARREN : yermo, baldío **2** DISCARDED : de desecho **3** EXCESS : sobrante

waste[3] *n* **1** → **wasteland** **2** MISUSE : derroche *m,* desperdicio *m,* despilfarro *m* <a waste of time : una pérdida de tiempo> **3** RUBBISH : basura *f,* desechos *mpl,* desperdicios *mpl* **4** EXCREMENT : excremento *m*

wastebasket [ˈweɪstˌbæskət] *n* : cesto *m* (de basura), papelera *f,* zafacón *m Car*

wasteful [ˈweɪstfəl] *adj* : despilfarrador, derrochador, pródigo

wastefulness [ˈweɪstfəlnəs] *n* : derroche *m,* despilfarro *m*

wasteland [ˈweɪstˌlænd, -lənd] *n* : baldío *m,* yermo *m,* desierto *m*

watch[1] [ˈwɑtʃ] *vi* **1** *or* **to keep watch** : velar **2** OBSERVE : mirar, ver, observar **3** **to watch for** AWAIT : esperar, quedar a la espera de **4** **to watch out** : tener cuidado <watch out! : ¡ten cuidado!, ¡ojo!> — *vt* **1** OBSERVE : mirar, observar **2** *or* **to watch over** : vigilar, cuidar **3** : tener cuidado de <watch what you do : ten cuidado con lo que haces>

watch[2] *n* **1** : guardia *f* <to be on watch : estar de guardia> **2** SURVEILLANCE : vigilancia *f* **3** LOOKOUT : guardia *mf,* centinela *f,* vigía *mf* **4** TIMEPIECE : reloj *m*

watchdog [ˈwɑtʃˌdɔg] *n* : perro *m* guardián

watcher [ˈwɑtʃər] *n* : observador *m,* -dora *f*

watchful [ˈwɑtʃfəl] *adj* : alerta, vigilante, atento

watchfulness [ˈwɑtʃfəlnəs] *n* : vigilancia *f*

watchman [ˈwɑtʃmən] *n, pl* **-men** [-mən, -ˌmɛn] : vigilante *m,* guarda *m*

watchword [ˈwɑtʃˌwərd] *n* **1** PASSWORD : contraseña *f* **2** SLOGAN : lema *m,* eslogan *m*

water[1] [ˈwɔt̬ər, ˈwɑ-] *vt* **1** : regar (el jardín, etc.) **2** **to water down** DILUTE : diluir, aguar — *vi* : lagrimar (dícese de los ojos), hacérsele agua la boca a uno <my mouth is watering : se me hace agua la boca>

water[2] *n* : agua *f*

water buffalo *n* : búfalo *m* de agua

watercolor [ˈwɔt̬ərˌkʌlər, ˈwɑ-] *n* : acuarela *f*

watercourse [ˈwɔt̬ərˌkors, ˈwɑ-] *n* : curso *m* de agua

watercress [ˈwɔt̬ərˌkrɛs, ˈwɑ-] *n* : berro *m*

waterfall [ˈwɔt̬ərˌfɔl, ˈwɑ-] *n* : cascada *f,* salto *m* de agua, catarata *f*

waterfowl [ˈwɔt̬ərˌfaʊl, ˈwɑ-] *n* : ave *f* acuática

waterfront [ˈwɔt̬ərˌfrʌnt, ˈwɑ-] *n* **1** : tierra *f* que bordea un río, un lago, o un mar **2** WHARF : muelle *m*

water lily *n* : nenúfar *m*

waterlogged [ˈwɔt̬ərˌlɔgd, ˈwɑt̬ərˌlɑgd] *adj* : lleno de agua, empapado, inundado (dícese del suelo)

watermark [ˈwɔt̬ərˌmɑrk, ˈwɑ-] *n* **1** : marca *f* del nivel de agua **2** : filigrana *f* (en el papel)

watermelon [ˈwɔt̬ərˌmɛlən, ˈwɑ-] *n* : sandía *f*

water moccasin → **moccasin**

waterpower [ˈwɔt̬ərˌpaʊər, ˈwɑ-] *n* : energía *f* hidráulica

waterproof[1] [ˈwɔt̬ərˌpruːf, ˈwɑ-] *vt* : hacer impermeable, impermeabilizar

waterproof[2] *adj* : impermeable, a prueba de agua

watershed [ˈwɔt̬ərˌʃɛd, ˈwɑ-] *n* **1** : línea *f* divisoria de aguas **2** BASIN : cuenca *f* (de un río)

waterskiing [ˈwɔt̬ərˌskiːɪŋ, ˈwɑ-] *n* : esquí *m* acuático

waterspout [ˈwɔt̬ərˌspaʊt, ˈwɑ-] *n* WHIRLWIND : tromba *f* marina

watertight [ˈwɔt̬ərˌtaɪt, ˈwɑ-] *adj* **1** : hermético **2** IRREFUTABLE : irrebatible, irrefutable <a watertight contract : un contrato sin lagunas>

waterway [ˈwɔt̬ərˌweɪ, ˈwɑ-] *n* : vía *f* navegable

waterworks [ˈwɔt̬ərˌwərks, ˈwɑ-] *npl* : central *f* de abastecimiento de agua

watery [ˈwɔt̬əri, ˈwɑ-] *adj* **1** : acuoso, como agua **2** : aguado, diluido <watery soup : sopa aguada> **3** : lloroso <watery eyes : ojos llorosos> **4** WASHED-OUT : desvaído (dícese de colores)

watt [ˈwɑt] *n* : vatio *m*

wattage [ˈwɑt̬ɪdʒ] *n* : vataje *m*

wattle [ˈwɑt̬əl] *n* : carúncula *f* (de un ave, etc.)

wave[1] [ˈweɪv] *v* **waved; waving** *vi* **1** : saludar con la mano, hacer señas con la mano <she waved at him : lo saludó con la mano> **2** FLUTTER, SHAKE : ondear, agitarse **3** UNDULATE : ondular — *vt* **1** SHAKE : agitar **2** BRANDISH : blandir **3** CURL : ondular, marcar (el pelo) **4** SIGNAL : hacerle señas a (con la mano) <he waved farewell : se despidió con la mano>

wave[2] *n* **1** : ola *f* (de agua) **2** CURL : onda *f* (en el pelo) **3** : onda *f* (en física) **4** SURGE : oleada *f* <a wave of enthusiasm : una oleada de entusiasmo> **5** GESTURE : señal *f* con la mano, saludo *m* con la mano

wavelength [ˈweɪvˌlɛŋkθ] *n* : longitud *f* de onda

waver [ˈweɪvər] *vi* **1** VACILLATE : vacilar, fluctuar **2** FLICKER : parpadear, titilar, oscilar **3** FALTER : flaquear, tambalearse

wavy [ˈweɪvi] *adj* **wavier; -est** : ondulado

wax[1] [ˈwæks] *vi* **1** : crecer (dícese de la luna) **2** BECOME : volverse, ponerse <to wax indignant : indignarse> — *vt* : encerar

wax[2] *n* **1** BEESWAX : cera *f* de abejas **2** : cera *f* <floor wax : cera para el piso>

3 *or* **earwax** [ˈɪrˌwæks] : cerilla *f,* cerumen *m*

waxen [ˈwæksən] *adj* : de cera

waxy [ˈwæksi] *adj* **waxier; -est** : ceroso

way [ˈweɪ] *n* **1** PATH, ROAD : camino *m,* vía *f* **2** ROUTE : camino *m,* ruta *f* <to go the wrong way : equivocarse de camino> <I'm on my way : estoy de camino> **3** : línea *f* de conducta, camino *m* <he chose the easy way : optó por el camino fácil> **4** MANNER, MEANS : manera *f,* modo *m,* forma *f* <in the same way : del mismo modo, igualmente> <there are no two ways about it : no cabe la menor duda> **5** (*indicating a wish*) <have it your way : como tú quieras> <to get one's own way : salirse uno con la suya> **6** STATE : estado *m* <things are in a bad way : las cosas marchan mal> **7** RESPECT : aspecto *m,* sentido *m* **8** CUSTOM : costumbre *f* <to mend one's ways : dejar las malas costumbres> **9** PASSAGE : camino *m* <to get in the way : meterse en el camino> **10** DISTANCE : distancia *f* <to come a long way : hacer grandes progresos> **11** DIRECTION : dirección *f* <come this way : venga por aquí> <which way did he go? : ¿por dónde fue?> **12 by the way** : a propósito, por cierto **13 by way of** VIA : vía, pasando por **14 out of the way** REMOTE : remoto, recóndito **15** → **under way**

wayfarer [ˈweɪˌfærər] *n* : caminante *mf*

waylay [ˈweɪˌleɪ] *vt* **-laid** [-ˌleɪd]; **-laying** ACCOST : abordar

wayside [ˈweɪˌsaɪd] *n* : borde *m* del camino

wayward [ˈweɪwərd] *adj* **1** UNRULY : díscolo, rebelde **2** UNTOWARD : adverso

we [ˈwiː] *pron* : nosotros, nosotras

weak [ˈwiːk] *adj* **1** FEEBLE : débil, endeble **2** : flojo, pobre <a weak excuse : una excusa poco convincente> **3** DILUTED : aguado, diluido <weak tea : té poco cargado> **4** FAINT : tenue (dícese de los colores, las luces, los sonidos, etc.)

weaken [ˈwiːkən] *vt* : debilitar — *vi* : debilitarse, flaquear

weakling [ˈwiːklɪŋ] *n* : alfeñique *m fam;* debilucho *m,* -cha *f*

weakly[1] [ˈwiːkli] *adv* : débilmente

weakly[2] *adj* **weaklier; -est** : débil, enclenque

weakness [ˈwiːknəs] *n* **1** FEEBLENESS : debilidad *f* **2** FAULT, FLAW : flaqueza *f,* punto *m* débil

wealth [ˈwɛlθ] *n* **1** RICHES : riqueza *f* **2** PROFUSION : abundancia *f,* profusión *f*

wealthy [ˈwɛlθi] *adj* **wealthier; -est** : rico, acaudalado, adinerado

wean [ˈwiːn] *vt* **1** : destetar (a los niños o las crías) **2 to wean someone away from** : quitarle a alguien la costumbre de

weapon [ˈwɛpən] *n* : arma *f*

weaponless [ˈwɛpənləs] *adj* : desarmado

wear[1] [ˈwær] *v* **wore** [ˈwor]; **worn** [ˈworn]; **wearing** *vt* **1** : llevar (ropa, un reloj, etc.), calzar (zapatos) <to wear a happy smile : sonreír alegremente> **2** *or* **to wear away** : desgastar, erosionar (rocas, etc.) **3 to wear out** : gastar <he wore out his shoes : gastó sus zapatos> **4 to wear out** EXHAUST : agotar, fatigar <to wear oneself out : agotarse> — *vi* **1** LAST : durar **2 to wear off** DIMINISH : disminuir **3 to wear out** : gastarse

wear[2] *n* **1** USE : uso *m* <for everyday wear : para todos los días> **2** CLOTHING : ropa *f* <children's wear : ropa de niños> **3** DETERIORATION : desgaste *m* <to be the worse for wear : estar deteriorado>

wearable [ˈwærəbəl] *adj* : que puede ponerse (dícese de una prenda)

wear and tear *n* : desgaste *m*

weariness [ˈwɪrinəs] *n* : fatiga *f,* cansancio *m*

wearisome [ˈwɪrisəm] *adj* : aburrido, pesado, cansado

weary[1] [ˈwɪri] *v* **-ried; -rying** *vt* **1** TIRE : cansar, fatigar **2** BORE : hastiar, aburrir — *vi* : cansarse

weary[2] *adj* **-rier; -est 1** TIRED : cansado **2** FED UP : harto **3** BORED : aburrido

weasel [ˈwiːzəl] *n* : comadreja *f*

weather[1] [ˈwɛðər] *vt* **1** WEAR : erosionar, desgastar **2** ENDURE : aguantar, sobrellevar, capear <to weather the storm : capear el temporal>

weather[2] *n* : tiempo *m*

weather–beaten [ˈwɛðərˌbiːtən] *adj* : curtido

weatherman [ˈwɛðərˌmæn] *n, pl* **-men** [-mən, -ˌmɛn] METEOROLOGIST : meteorólogo *m,* -ga *f*

weatherproof [ˈwɛðərˌpruːf] *adj* : que resiste a la intemperie, impermeable

weather vane → **vane**

weave[1] [ˈwiːv] *v* **wove** [ˈwoːv] *or* **weaved; woven** [ˈwoːvən] *or* **weaved; weaving** *vt* **1** : tejer (tela) **2** INTERLACE : entretejer, entrelazar **3 to weave one's way through** : abrirse camino por — *vi* **1** : tejer **2** WIND : serpentear, zigzaguear

weave[2] *n* : tejido *m,* trama *f*

weaver [ˈwiːvər] *n* : tejedor *m,* -dora *f*

web[1] [ˈwɛb] *vt* **webbed; webbing** : cubrir o proveer con una red

web[2] *n* **1** COBWEB, SPIDERWEB : telaraña *f,* tela *f* de araña **2** ENTANGLEMENT, SNARE : red *f,* enredo *m* <a web of intrigue : una red de intriga> **3** : membrana *f* interdigital (de aves) **4** NETWORK : red *f* <a web of highways : una red de carreteras>

webbed [ˈwɛbd] *adj* : palmeado <webbed feet : patas palmeadas>

wed [ˈwɛd] *vt* **wedded; wedding 1** MARRY : casarse con **2** UNITE : ligar, unir

we'd [ˈwiːd] (*contraction of* **we had, we should,** *or* **we would**) → **have, should, would**

wedding [ˈwɛdɪŋ] *n* : boda *f,* casamiento *m*

wedge[1] [ˈwɛdʒ] *vt* **wedged; wedging 1** : apretar (con una cuña) <to wedge open : mantener abierto con una cuña> **2** CRAM : meter, embutir

wedge[2] *n* **1** : cuña *f* **2** PIECE : porción *f,* trozo *m*

wedlock [ˈwɛd,lɑk] → **marriage**

Wednesday [ˈwɛnz,deɪ, -di] *n* : miércoles *m*

wee [ˈwiː] *adj* : pequeño, minúsculo <in the wee hours : a las altas horas>

weed[1] [ˈwiːd] *vt* **1** : desherbar, desyerbar **2 to weed out** : eliminar, quitar

weed[2] *n* : mala hierba *f*

weedy [ˈwiːdi] *adj* **weedier; -est 1** : cubierto de malas hierbas **2** LANKY, SKINNY : flaco, larguirucho *fam*

week [ˈwiːk] *n* : semana *f*

weekday [ˈwiːk,deɪ] *n* : día *m* laborable

weekend [ˈwiːk,ɛnd] *n* : fin *m* de semana

weekly[1] [ˈwiːkli] *adv* : semanalmente

weekly[2] *adj* : semanal

weekly[3] *n, pl* **-lies** : semanario *m*

weep [ˈwiːp] *v* **wept** [ˈwɛpt]; **weeping** : llorar

weeping willow *n* : sauce *m* llorón

weepy [ˈwiːpi] *adj* **weepier; -est** : lloroso, triste

weevil [ˈwiːvəl] *n* : gorgojo *m*

weft [ˈwɛft] *n* : trama *f*

weigh [ˈweɪ] *vt* **1** : pesar **2** CONSIDER : considerar, sopesar **3 to weigh anchor** : levar anclas **4 to weigh down** : sobrecargar (con una carga), abrumar (con preocupaciones, etc.) — *vi* **1** : pesar <it weighs 10 pounds : pesa 10 libras> **2** COUNT : tener importancia, contar **3 to weigh on one's mind** : preocuparle a uno

weight[1] [ˈweɪt] *vt* **1** : poner peso en, sujetar con un peso **2** BURDEN : cargar, oprimir

weight[2] *n* **1** HEAVINESS : peso *m* <to lose weight : bajar de peso, adelgazar> **2** : peso *m* <weights and measures : pesos y medidas> **3** : pesa *f* <to lift weights : levantar pesas> **4** BURDEN : peso *m,* carga *f* <to take a weight off one's mind : quitarle un peso de encima a uno> **5** IMPORTANCE : peso *m* **6** INFLUENCE : influencia *f,* autoridad *f* <to throw one's weight around : hacer sentir su influencia>

weighty [ˈweɪti] *adj* **weightier; -est 1** HEAVY : pesado **2** IMPORTANT : importante, de peso

weird [ˈwɪrd] *adj* **1** MYSTERIOUS : misterioso **2** STRANGE : extraño, raro — **weirdly** *adv*

welcome[1] [ˈwɛlkəm] *vt* **-comed; -coming** : darle la bienvenida a, recibir

welcome[2] *adj* : bienvenido <to make someone welcome : acoger bien a alguien> <you're welcome! : ¡de nada!, ¡no hay de qué!>

welcome[3] *n* : bienvenida *f,* recibimiento *m,* acojida *f*

weld[1] [ˈwɛld] *v* : soldar

weld[2] *n* : soldadura *f*

welder [ˈwɛldər] *n* : soldador *m,* -dora *f*

welfare [ˈwɛl,fær] *n* **1** WELL-BEING : bienestar *m* **2** : asistencia *f* social

well[1] [ˈwɛl] *vi or* **to well up** : brotar, manar

well[2] *adv* **better** [ˈbɛtər]; **best** [ˈbɛst] **1** RIGHTLY : bien, correctamente **2** SATISFACTORILY : bien <to turn out well : resultar bien, salir bien> **3** COMPLETELY : completamente <well-hidden : completamente escondido> **4** INTIMATELY : bien <I knew him well : lo conocía bien> **5** CONSIDERABLY, FAR : muy, bastante <well ahead : muy adelante> <well before the deadline : bastante antes de la fecha> **6 as well** ALSO : también **7** → **as well as**

well[3] *adj* **1** SATISFACTORY : bien <all is well : todo está bien> **2** DESIRABLE : conveniente <it would be well if you left : sería conveniente que te fueras> **3** HEALTHY : bien, sano

well[4] *n* **1** : pozo *m* (de agua, petróleo, gas, etc.), aljibe *m* (de agua) **2** SOURCE : fuente *f* <a well of information : una fuente de información> **3** *or* **stairwell** : caja *f,* hueco *m* (de la escalera)

well[5] *interj* **1** (*used to introduce a remark*) : bueno **2** (*used to express surprise*) : ¡vaya!

we'll [ˈwiːl, wɪl] (*contraction of* **we shall** *or* **we will**) → **shall, will**

well–balanced [ˈwɛlˈbælənst] *adj* : equilibrado

well–being [ˈwɛlˈbiːɪŋ] *n* : bienestar *m*

well–bred [ˈwɛlˈbrɛd] *adj* : fino, bien educado

well–done [ˈwɛlˈdʌn] *adj* **1** : bien hecho <well-done! : ¡bravo!> **2** : bien cocido

well–known [ˈwɛlˈnoːn] *adj* : famoso, bien conocido

well–meaning [ˈwɛlˈmiːnɪŋ] *adj* : bienintencionado, que tiene buenas intenciones

well–nigh [ˈwɛlˈnaɪ] *adv* : casi <well-nigh impossible : casi imposible>

well–off [ˈwɛlˈɔf] → **well–to–do**

well–rounded [ˈwɛlˈraʊndəd] *adj* : completo, equilibrado

well–to–do [,wɛltəˈduː] *adj* : próspero, adinerado, rico

welt [ˈwɛlt] *n* **1 :** vira *f* (de un zapato) **2** WHEAL **:** verdugón *m*
welter [ˈwɛltər] *n* **:** fárrago *m,* revoltijo *m* <a welter of data **:** un fárrago de datos>
wend [ˈwɛnd] *vi* **to wend one's way :** ponerse en camino, encaminar sus pasos
went → **go**
wept → **weep**
were → **be**
we're [ˈwɪr, ˈwər, ˈwiːər] (*contraction of* **we are**) → **be**
werewolf [ˈwɪrˌwʊlf, ˈwɛr-, ˈwər-, -ˌwʌlf] *n, pl* **-wolves** [-ˌwʊlvz, -ˌwʌlvz] **:** hombre *m* lobo
west[1] [ˈwɛst] *adv* **:** al oeste
west[2] *adj* **:** oeste, del oeste, occidental <west winds **:** vientos del oeste>
west[3] *n* **1 :** oeste *m* **2 the West :** el Oeste, el Occidente
westerly [ˈwɛstərli] *adv & adj* **:** del oeste
western [ˈwɛstərn] *adj* **1 :** Occidental, del Oeste **2 :** occidental, oeste
Westerner [ˈwɛstərnər] *n* **:** habitante *mf* del oeste
West Indian *n* **:** antillano *m,* -na *f* — **West Indian** *adj*
westward [ˈwɛstwərd] *adv & adj* **:** hacia el oeste
wet[1] [ˈwɛt] *vt* **wet** *or* **wetted; wetting :** mojar, humedecer
wet[2] *adj* **wetter; wettest 1 :** mojado, húmedo <wet clothes **:** ropa mojada> **2** RAINY **:** lluvioso **3 wet paint :** pintura *f* fresca
wet[3] *n* **1** MOISTURE **:** humedad *f* **2** RAIN **:** lluvia *f*
we've [ˈwiːv] (*contraction of* **we have**) → **have**
whack[1] [ˈhwæk] *vt* **:** golpear (fuertemente), aporrear
whack[2] *n* **1 :** golpe *m* fuerte, porrazo *m* **2** ATTEMPT **:** intento *m,* tentativa *f*
whale[1] [ˈhweɪl] *vi* **whaled; whaling :** cazar ballenas
whale[2] *n, pl* **whales** *or* **whale :** ballena *f*
whaleboat [ˈhweɪlˌboːt] *n* **:** ballenero *m*
whalebone [ˈhweɪlˌboːn] *n* **:** barba *f* de ballena
whaler [ˈhweɪlər] *n* **1 :** ballenero *m,* -ra *f* **2** → **whaleboat**
wharf [ˈhwɔrf] *n, pl* **wharves** [ˈhwɔrvz] **:** muelle *m,* embarcadero *m*
what[1] [ˈhwɑt, ˈhwʌt] *adv* **1** HOW **:** cómo, cúanto <what he suffered! **:** ¡cómo sufría!> **2 what with :** entre <what with one thing and another **:** entre una cosa y otra>
what[2] *adj* **1** (*used in questions*) **:** qué <what more do you want? **:** ¿qué más quieres?> <what color is it? **:** ¿de qué color es?> **2** (*used in exclamations*) **:** qué <what an idea! **:** ¡qué idea!> **3** ANY, WHATEVER **:** cualquier <give what help you can **:** da cualquier contribución que puedas>
what[3] *pron* **1** (*used in direct questions*) **:** qué <what happened? **:** ¿qué pasó?> <what does it cost? **:** ¿cuánto cuesta?> **2** (*used in indirect statements*) **:** lo que, que <I don't know what to do **:** no sé que hacer> <do what I tell you **:** haz lo que te digo> **3 what for** WHY **:** porqué **4 what if :** y si <what if he knows? **:** ¿y si lo sabe?>
whatever[1] [hwɑtˈɛvər, ˌhwʌt-] *adj* **1** ANY **:** cualquier, cualquier...que <whatever way you prefer **:** de cualquier manera que prefiera, como prefiera> **2** (*in negative constructions*) <there's no chance whatever **:** no hay ninguna posibilidad> <nothing whatever **:** nada en absoluto>
whatever[2] *pron* **1** ANYTHING **:** (todo) lo que <I'll do whatever I want **:** haré lo que quiera> **2** (*no matter what*) <whatever it may be **:** sea lo que sea> **3** WHAT **:** qué <whatever do you mean? **:** ¿qué quieres decir?>
whatsoever[1] [ˌhwɑtsoˈɛvər, ˌhwʌt-] *adj* → **whatever**[1]
whatsoever[2] *pron* → **whatever**[2]
wheal [ˈhwiːl] *n* **:** verdugón *m*
wheat [ˈhwiːt] *n* **:** trigo *m*
wheaten [ˈhwiːtən] *adj* **:** de trigo
wheedle [ˈhwiːdəl] *vt* **-dled; -dling** CAJOLE **:** engatusar <to wheedle something out of someone **:** sonsacarle algo a alguien>
wheel[1] [ˈhwiːl] *vt* **:** empujar (una bicicleta, etc.), mover (algo sobre ruedas) — *vi* **1** ROTATE **:** girar, rotar **2 to wheel around** TURN **:** darse la vuelta
wheel[2] *n* **1 :** rueda *f* **2** *or* **steering wheel :** volante *m* (de automóviles, etc.), timón *m* (de barcos o aviones) **3 wheels** *npl* **:** maquinaria *f,* fuerza *f* impulsora <the wheels of government **:** la maquinaria del gobierno>
wheelbarrow [ˈhwiːlˌbærˌoː] *n* **:** carretilla *f*
wheelchair [ˈhwiːlˌtʃær] *n* **:** silla *f* de ruedas
wheeze[1] [ˈhwiːz] *vi* **wheezed; wheezing :** resollar, respirar con dificultad
wheeze[2] *n* **:** resuello *m*
whelk [ˈhwɛlk] *n* **:** buccino *m*
whelp[1] [ˈhwɛlp] *vi* **:** parir
whelp[2] *n* **:** cachorro *m,* -rra *f*
when[1] [ˈhwɛn] *adv* **:** cuándo <when will you return? **:** ¿cuándo volverás?> <he asked me when I would be home **:** me preguntó cuándo estaría en casa>
when[2] *conj* **1** (*referring to a particular time*) **:** cuando, en que <when you are ready **:** cuando estés listo> <the days when I clean the house **:** los días en que limpio la casa> **2** IF **:** cuando, si <how can I go when I have no money? **:** ¿cómo voy a ir si no tengo dinero?> **3** ALTHOUGH **:** cuando <you said it was big when actually it's

small : dijiste que era grande cuando en realidad es pequeño>
when[3] *pron* : cuándo <since when are you the boss? : ¿desde cuándo eres el jefe?>
whence [ˈ*h*wɛnts] *adv* : de donde
whenever[1] [*h*wɛnˈɛvər] *adv* **1** : cuando sea <tomorrow or whenever : manaña o cuando sea> **2** (*in questions*) : cuándo
whenever[2] *conj* **1** : siempre que, cada vez que <whenever I go, I'm disappointed : siempre que voy, quedo desilusionado> **2** WHEN : cuando <whenever you like : cuando quieras>
where[1] [ˈ*h*wɛr] *adv* : dónde, adónde <where is he? : ¿dónde está?> <where did they go? : ¿adónde fueron?>
where[2] *conj* : donde, adonde <she knows where the house is : sabe donde está la casa> <she goes where she likes : va adonde quiera>
where[3] *pron* : donde <Chicago is where I live : Chicago es donde vivo>
whereabouts[1] [ˈ*h*wɛrəˌbaʊts] *adv* : dónde, por dónde <whereabouts is the house? : ¿dónde está la casa?>
whereabouts[2] *ns & pl* : paradero *m*
whereas [*h*wɛrˈæz] *conj* **1** : considerando que (usado en documentos legales) **2** : mientras que <I like the white one whereas she prefers the black : me gusta el blanco mientras que ella prefiere el negro>
whereby [*h*wɛrˈbaɪ] *adv* : por lo cual
wherefore [ˈ*h*wɛrˌfor] *adv* : por qué
wherein [*h*wɛrˈɪn] *adv* : en el cual, en el que
whereof [*h*wɛrˈʌv, -ɑv] *conj* : de lo cual
whereupon [ˈ*h*wɛrəˌpɑn, -ˌpɔn] *conj* : con lo cual, después de lo cual
wherever[1] [*h*wɛrˈɛvər] *adv* **1** WHERE : dónde, adónde **2** : en cualquier parte <or wherever : o donde sea>
wherever[2] *conj* : dondequiera que, donde sea <wherever you go : dondequiera que vayas>
wherewithal [ˈ*h*wɛrwɪˌðɔl, -ˌθɔl] *n* : medios *mpl*, recursos *mpl*
whet [ˈ*h*wɛt] *vt* **whetted; whetting 1** SHARPEN : afilar **2** STIMULATE : estimular <to whet the appetite : estimular el apetito>
whether [ˈ*h*wɛðər] *conj* **1** : si <I don't know whether it is finished : no sé si está acabado> <we doubt whether he'll show up : dudamos que aparezca> **2** (*used in comparisons*) <whether I like it or not : tanto si quiero como si no> <whether he comes or he doesn't : venga o no>
whetstone [ˈ*h*wɛtˌstoːn] *n* : piedra *f* de afilar
whey [ˈ*h*weɪ] *n* : suero *m* (de la leche)
which[1] [ˈ*h*wɪtʃ] *adj* : qué, cuál <which tie do you prefer? : ¿cuál corbata prefieres?> <which ones? : ¿cuáles?> <tell me which house is yours : dime qué casa es la tuya>
which[2] *pron* **1** : cuál <which is the right answer? : ¿cuál es la respuesta correcta?> **2** : que, el (la) cual <the cup which broke : la taza que se quebró> <the house, which is made of brick : la casa, la cual es de ladrillo>
whichever[1] [*h*wɪtʃˈɛvər] *adj* : el (la) que, cualquiera que <whichever book you like : cualquier libro que te guste>
whichever[2] *pron* : el (la) que, cualquiera que <take whichever you want : toma el que quieras> <whichever I choose : cualquiera que elija>
whiff[1] [ˈ*h*wɪf] *v* PUFF : soplar
whiff[2] *n* **1** PUFF : soplo *m*, ráfaga *f* **2** SNIFF : olor *m* **3** HINT : dejo *m*, pizca *f*
while[1] [ˈ*h*waɪl] *vt* **whiled; whiling** : pasar <to while away the time : matar el tiempo>
while[2] *n* **1** TIME : rato *m*, tiempo *m* <after a while : después de un rato> <in a while : dentro de poco> **2 to be worth one's while** : valer la pena
while[3] *conj* **1** : mientras <whistle while you work : silba mientras trabajas> **2** WHEREAS : mientras que **3** ALTHOUGH : aunque <while it's very good, it's not perfect : aunque es muy bueno, no es perfecto>
whim [ˈ*h*wɪm] *n* : capricho *m*, antojo *m*
whimper[1] [ˈ*h*wɪmpər] *vi* : lloriquear, gimotear
whimper[2] *n* : quejido *m*
whimsical [ˈ*h*wɪmzɪkəl] *adj* **1** CAPRICIOUS : caprichoso, fantasioso **2** ERRATIC : errático — **whimsically** *adv*
whine[1] [ˈ*h*waɪn] *vi* **whined; whining 1** : lloriquear, gimotear, gemir **2** COMPLAIN : quejarse
whine[2] *n* : quejido *m*, gemido *m*
whinny[1] [ˈ*h*wɪni] *vi* **-nied; -nying** : relinchar
whinny[2] *n, pl* **-nies** : relincho *m*
whip[1] [ˈ*h*wɪp] *v* **whipped; whipping** *vt* **1** SNATCH : sacar (rápidamente), arrebatar <she whipped the cloth off the table : arrebató el mantel de la mesa> **2** LASH : azotar **3** DEFEAT : vencer, derrotar **4** INCITE : incitar, despertar <to whip up enthusiasm : despertar el entusiasmo> **5** BEAT : batir (huevos, crema, etc.) — *vi* FLAP : agitarse
whip[2] *n* **1** : látigo *m*, azote *m*, fusta *f* (de jinete) **2** : miembro *m* de un cuerpo legislativo encargado de disciplina
whiplash [ˈ*h*wɪpˌlæʃ] *n or* **whiplash injury** : traumatismo *m* cervical
whippet [ˈ*h*wɪpət] *n* : galgo *m* pequeño, galgo *m* inglés
whippoorwill [ˈ*h*wɪpərˌwɪl] *n* : chotacabras *mf*
whir[1] [ˈ*h*wər] *vi* **whirred; whirring** : zumbar
whir[2] *n* : zumbido *m*

whirl[1] ['*h*wərl] *vi* **1** SPIN **:** dar vueltas, girar <my head is whirling **:** la cabeza me está dando vueltas> **2 to whirl about :** arremolinarse, moverse rápidamente

whirl[2] *n* **1** SPIN **:** giro *m,* vuelta *f,* remolino *m* (dícese del polvo, etc.) **2** BUSTLE **:** bullicio *m,* torbellino *m* (de actividad, etc.) **3 to give it a whirl :** intentar hacer, probar

whirlpool ['*h*wərl,pu:l] *n* **:** vorágine *f,* remolino *m*

whirlwind ['*h*wərl,wɪnd] *n* **:** remolino *m,* torbellino *m,* tromba *f*

whisk[1] ['*h*wɪsk] *vt* **1 :** llevar <she whisked the children off to bed **:** llevó a los niños a la cama> **2 :** batir <to whisk eggs **:** batir huevos> **3 to whisk away** *or* **to whisk off :** sacudir

whisk[2] *n* **1** WHISKING **:** sacudida *f* (movimiento) **2 :** batidor *m* (para batir huevos, etc.)

whisk broom *n* **:** escobilla *f*

whisker ['*h*wɪskər] *n* **1 :** pelo *m* (de la barba o el bigote) **2 whiskers** *npl* **:** bigotes *mpl* (de animales)

whiskey *or* **whisky** ['*h*wɪski] *n, pl* **-keys** *or* **-kies :** whisky *m*

whisper[1] ['*h*wɪspər] *vi* **:** cuchichear, susurrar — *vt* **:** decir en voz baja, susurrar

whisper[2] *n* **1** WHISPERING **:** susurro *m,* cuchicheo *m* **2** RUMOR **:** rumor *m* **3** TRACE **:** dejo *m,* pizca *f*

whistle[1] ['*h*wɪsəl] *v* **-tled; -tling** *vi* **:** silbar, chiflar, pitar (dícese de un tren, etc.) — *vt* **:** silbar <to whistle a tune **:** silbar una melodía>

whistle[2] *n* **1** WHISTLING **:** chiflido *m,* silbido *m* **2 :** silbato *m,* pito *m* (instrumento)

whit ['*h*wɪt] *n* BIT **:** ápice *m,* pizca *f*

white[1] ['*h*waɪt] *adj* **whiter; -est :** blanco

white[2] *n* **1 :** blanco *m* (color) **2 :** clara *f* (de huevos) **3** *or* **white person :** blanco *m,* -ca *f*

white blood cell *n* **:** glóbulo *m* blanco

whitecaps ['*h*waɪt,kæps] *npl* **:** cabrillas *fpl*

white–collar ['*h*waɪt'kɑlər] *adj* **1 :** de oficina **2 white–collar worker :** oficinista *mf*

whitefish ['*h*waɪt,fɪʃ] *n* **:** pescado *m* blanco

whiten ['*h*waɪtən] *vt* **:** blanquear — *vi* **:** ponerse blanco

whiteness ['*h*waɪtnəs] *n* **:** blancura *f*

white–tailed deer ['*h*waɪt'teɪld] *n* **:** ciervo *f* de Virginia

whitewash[1] ['*h*waɪt,wɔʃ] *vt* **1 :** enjalbegar, blanquear <to whitewash a fence **:** enjalbegar una valla> **2** CONCEAL **:** encubrir (un escándalo, etc.)

whitewash[2] *n* **1 :** jalbegue *m,* lechada *f* **2** COVER-UP **:** encubrimiento *m*

whither ['*h*wɪðər] *adv* **:** adónde

whiting ['*h*waɪṭɪŋ] *n* **:** merluza *f,* pescadilla *f* (pez)

whitish ['*h*waɪṭɪʃ] *adj* **:** blancuzco

whittle ['*h*wɪṭəl] *vt* **-tled; -tling 1 :** tallar (madera) **2 to whittle down :** reducir, recortar <to whittle down expenses **:** reducir los gastos>

whiz[1] *or* **whizz** ['*h*wɪz] *vi* **whizzed; whizzing 1** BUZZ **:** zumbar **2 to whiz by :** pasar muy rápido, pasar volando

whiz[2] *or* **whizz** *n, pl* **whizzes 1** BUZZ **:** zumbido *m* **2 to be a whiz :** ser un prodigio, ser muy hábil

who ['hu:] *pron* **1** (*used in direct and indirect questions*) **:** quién <who is that? **:** ¿quién es ése?> <who did it? **:** ¿quién lo hizo?> <we know who they are **:** sabemos quiénes son> **2** (*used in relative clauses*) **:** que, quien <the lady who lives there **:** la señora que vive allí> <for those who wait **:** para los que esperan, para quienes esperan>

whodunit [hu:'dʌnɪt] *n* **:** novela *f* policíaca

whoever [hu:'ɛvər] *pron* **1 :** quienquiera que, quien <whoever did it **:** quienquiera que lo hizo> <give it to whoever you want **:** dalo a quien quieras> **2** (*used in questions*) **:** quién <whoever could that be? **:** ¿quién podría ser?>

whole[1] ['ho:l] *adj* **1** UNHURT **:** ileso **2** INTACT **:** intacto, sano **3** ENTIRE **:** entero, íntegro <the whole island **:** toda la isla> <whole milk **:** leche entera> **4 a whole lot :** muchísimo

whole[2] *n* **1 :** todo *m* **2 as a whole :** en conjunto **3 on the whole :** en general

wholehearted ['ho:l'hɑrṭəd] *adj* **:** sin reservas, incondicional

whole number *n* **:** entero *m*

wholesale[1] ['ho:l,seɪl] *v* **-saled; -saling** *vt* **:** vender al por mayor — *vi* **:** venderse al por mayor

wholesale[2] *adv* **:** al por mayor

wholesale[3] *adj* **1 :** al por mayor <wholesale grocer **:** tendero al por mayor> **2** TOTAL **:** total, absoluto <wholesale slaughter **:** matanza sistemática>

wholesale[4] *n* **:** mayoreo *m*

wholesaler ['ho:l,seɪlər] *n* **:** mayorista *mf*

wholesome ['ho:lsəm] *adj* **1 :** sano <wholesome advice **:** consejo sano> **2** HEALTHY **:** sano, saludable

whole wheat *adj* **:** de trigo integral

wholly ['ho:li] *adv* **1** COMPLETELY **:** completamente **2** SOLELY **:** exclusivamente, únicamente

whom ['hu:m] *pron* **1** (*used in direct questions*) **:** a quién <whom did you choose? **:** ¿a quién elegiste?> **2** (*used in indirect questions*) **:** de quién, con quién, en quién <I don't know whom to consult **:** no sé con quién consultar> **3** (*used in relative clauses*) **:** que, a quien <the lawyer whom I recommended to you **:** el abogado que te recomendé>

whomever [huːm'ɛvər] *pron* : a quienquiera que, a quien
whoop[1] ['*h*wuːp, '*h*wʊp] *vi* : gritar, chillar
whoop[2] *n* : grito *m*
whooping cough *n* : tos *f* ferina
whopper ['*h*wɑpər] *n* **1** : cosa *f* enorme **2** LIE : mentira *f* colosal
whopping ['*h*wɑpɪŋ] *adj* : enorme
whore ['hor] *n* : puta *f,* ramera *f*
whorl ['*h*wɔrl, '*h*wərl] *n* : espiral *f,* espira *f* (de una concha), línea *f* (de una huella digital)
whose[1] ['huːz] *adj* **1** (*used in questions*) : de quién <whose truck is that? : ¿de quién es ese camión?> **2** (*used in relative clauses*) : cuyo <the person whose work is finished : la persona cuyo trabajo está terminado>
whose[2] *pron* : de quién <tell me whose it was : dime de quién era>
why[1] ['*h*waɪ] *adv* : por qué <why did you do it? : ¿por qué lo hizo?>
why[2] *n, pl* **whys** REASON : porqué *m,* razón *f*
why[3] *conj* : por qué <I know why he left : yo sé por qué salió> <there's no reason why it should exist : no hay razón para que exista>
why[4] *interj* (*used to express surprise*) : ¡vaya!, ¡mira!
wick ['wɪk] *n* : mecha *f*
wicked ['wɪkəd] *adj* **1** EVIL : malo, malvado **2** MISCHIEVOUS : travieso, pícaro <a wicked grin : una sonrisa traviesa> **3** TERRIBLE : terrible, horrible <a wicked storm : una tormenta horrible>
wickedly ['wɪkədli] *adv* : con maldad
wickedness ['wɪkədnəs] *n* : maldad *f*
wicker[1] ['wɪkər] *adj* : de mimbre
wicker[2] *n* **1** : mimbre *m* **2** → **wickerwork**
wickerwork ['wɪkər,wərk] *n* : artículos *mpl* de mimbre
wicket ['wɪkət] *n* **1** WINDOW : ventanilla *f* **2** *or* **wicket gate** : postigo *m* **3** : aro *m* (en croquet), palos *mpl* (en críquet)
wide[1] ['waɪd] *adv* **wider; widest 1** WIDELY : por todas partes <to travel far and wide : viajar por todas partes> **2** COMPLETELY : completamente, totalmente <wide open : abierto de par en par> **3 wide apart** : muy separados
wide[2] *adj* **wider; widest 1** VAST : vasto, extensivo <a wide area : una área extensiva> **2** : ancho <three meters wide : tres metros de ancho> **3** BROAD : ancho, amplio **4** *or* **wide–open** : muy abierto **5 wide of the mark** : desviado, lejos del blanco
wide–awake ['waɪdə'weɪk] *adj* : (completamente) despierto
wide–eyed ['waɪd'aɪd] *adj* **1** : con los ojos muy abiertos **2** NAIVE : inocente, ingenuo
widely ['waɪdli] *adv* : extensivamente, por todas partes
widen ['waɪdən] *vt* : ampliar, ensanchar — *vi* : ampliarse, ensancharse
widespread ['waɪd'sprɛd] *adj* : extendido, extenso, difuso
widow[1] ['wɪ,doː] *vt* : dejar viuda <to be widowed : enviudar>
widow[2] *n* : viuda *f*
widower ['wɪdowər] *n* : viudo *m*
width ['wɪdθ] *n* : ancho *m,* anchura *f*
wield ['wiːld] *vt* **1** USE : usar, manejar <to wield a broom : usar una escoba> **2** EXERCISE : ejercer <to wield influence : influir>
wiener ['wiːnər] → **frankfurter**
wife ['waɪf] *n, pl* **wives** ['waɪvz] : esposa *f,* mujer *f*
wifely ['waɪfli] *adj* : de esposa, conyugal
wig ['wɪg] *n* : peluca *f*
wiggle[1] ['wɪgəl] *v* **-gled; -gling** *vt* : menear, contonear <to wiggle one's hips : contonearse> — *vi* : menearse
wiggle[2] *n* : meneo *m,* contoneo *m*
wiggly ['wɪgəli] *adj* **-glier; -est 1** : que se menea **2** WAVY : ondulado
wigwag ['wɪg,wæg] *vi* **-wagged; -wagging** : comunicar por señales
wigwam ['wɪg,wɑm] *n* : wigwam *m*
wild[1] ['waɪld] *adv* **1** → **wildly 2 to run wild** : descontrolarse
wild[2] *adj* **1** : salvaje, silvestre, cimarrón <wild horses : caballos salvajes> <wild rice : arroz silvestre> **2** DESOLATE : yermo, agreste **3** UNRULY : desenfrenado **4** CRAZY : loco, fantástico <wild ideas : ideas locas> **5** BARBAROUS : salvaje, bárbaro **6** ERRATIC : errático <a wild throw : un tiro errático>
wild[3] *n* → **wilderness**
wildcat ['waɪld,kæt] *n* **1** : gato *m* montés **2** BOBCAT : lince *m* rojo
wilderness ['wɪldərnəs] *n* : yermo *m,* desierto *m*
wildfire ['waɪld,faɪr] *n* **1** : fuego *m* descontrolado **2 to spread like wildfire** : propagarse como un reguero de pólvora
wildflower ['waɪld,flaʊər] *n* : flor *f* silvestre
wildfowl ['waɪld,faʊl] *n* : ave *f* de caza
wildlife ['waɪld,laɪf] *n* : fauna *f*
wildly ['waɪldli] *adv* **1** FRANTICALLY : frenéticamente, como un loco **2** EXTREMELY : extremadamente <wildly happy : loco de felicidad>
wile[1] ['waɪl] *vt* **wiled; wiling** LURE : atraer
wile[2] *n* : ardid *m,* artimaña *f*
will[1] ['wɪl] *v past* **would** ['wʊd]; *pres sing & pl* **will** *vi* WISH : querer <do what you will : haz lo que quieras> — *v aux* **1** (*expressing willingness*) <no one would take the job : nadie aceptaría el trabajo> <I won't do it : no lo haré> **2** (*expressing habitual action*) <he will get angry over nothing : se pone furioso por cualquier cosa> **3** (*forming the future tense*)

<tomorrow we will go shopping : mañana iremos de compras> **4** (*expressing capacity*) <the couch will hold three people : en el sofá cabrán tres personas> **5** (*expressing determination*) <I will go despite them : iré a pesar de ellos> **6** (*expressing probability*) <that will be the mailman : eso ha de ser el cartero> **7** (*expressing inevitability*) <accidents will happen : los accidentes ocurrirán> **8** (*expressing a command*) <you will do as I say : harás lo que digo>

will[2] *vt* **1** ORDAIN **:** disponer, decretar <if God wills it : si Dios lo dispone, si Dios quiere> **2 :** lograr a fuerza de voluntad <they were willing him to succeed : estaban deseando que tuviera éxito> **3** BEQUEATH **:** legar

will[3] *n* **1** DESIRE **:** deseo *m,* voluntad *f* **2** VOLITION **:** voluntad *f* <free will : libre albedrío> **3** WILLPOWER **:** voluntad *f,* fuerza *f* de voluntad <a will of iron : una voluntad férrea> **4 :** testamento *m* <to make a will : hacer testamento>

willful *or* **wilful** [ˈwɪlfəl] *adj* **1** OBSTINATE **:** obstinado, terco **2** INTENTIONAL **:** intencionado, deliberado — **willfully** *adv*

willing [ˈwɪlɪŋ] *adj* **1** INCLINED, READY **:** listo, dispuesto **2** OBLIGING **:** servicial, complaciente

willingly [ˈwɪlɪŋli] *adv* **:** con gusto

willingness [ˈwɪlɪŋnəs] *n* **:** buena voluntad *f*

willow [ˈwɪˌloː] *n* **:** sauce *m*

willowy [ˈwɪlowi] *adj* **:** esbelto

willpower [ˈwɪlˌpaʊər] *n* **:** voluntad *f,* fuerza *f* de voluntad

wilt [ˈwɪlt] *vi* **1 :** marchitarse (dícese de las flores) **2** LANGUISH **:** debilitarse, languidecer

wily [ˈwaɪli] *adj* **wilier; -est :** artero, astuto

win[1] [ˈwɪn] *v* **won** [ˈwʌn]; **winning** *vi* **:** ganar — *vt* **1 :** ganar, conseguir **2 to win over :** ganarse a **3 to win someone's heart :** conquistar a alguien

win[2] *n* **:** triunfo *m,* victoria *f*

wince[1] [ˈwɪnts] *vi* **winced; wincing :** estremecerse, hacer una mueca de dolor

wince[2] *n* **:** mueca *f* de dolor

winch [ˈwɪntʃ] *n* **:** torno *m*

wind[1] [ˈwɪnd] *vt* **:** dejar sin aliento <to be winded : quedarse sin aliento>

wind[2] [ˈwaɪnd] *v* **wound** [ˈwaʊnd]; **winding** *vi* MEANDER **:** serpentear — *vt* **1** COIL, ROLL **:** envolver, enrollar **2** TURN **:** hacer girar <to wind a clock : darle cuerda a un reloj>

wind[3] [ˈwɪnd] *n* **1 :** viento *m* <against the wind : contra el viento> **2** BREATH **:** aliento *m* **3** FLATULENCE **:** flatulencia *f,* ventosidad *f* **4 to get wind of :** enterarse de

wind[4] [ˈwaɪnd] *n* **1** TURN **:** vuelta *f* **2** BEND **:** recodo *m,* curva *f*

windbreak [ˈwɪndˌbreɪk] *n* **:** barrera *f* contra el viento, abrigadero *m*

windfall [ˈwɪndˌfɔl] *n* **1 :** fruta *f* caída **2 :** beneficio *m* imprevisto

wind instrument *n* **:** instrumento *m* de viento

windlass [ˈwɪndləs] *n* **:** cabrestante *m*

windmill [ˈwɪndˌmɪl] *n* **:** molino *m* de viento

window [ˈwɪnˌdoː] *n* **1 :** ventana *f* (de un edificio o una computadora), ventanilla *f* (de un vehículo o avión), vitrina *f* (de una tienda) **2 → windowpane**

windowpane [ˈwɪnˌdoːˌpeɪn] *n* **:** vidrio *m*

window–shop [ˈwɪndoˌʃɑp] *vi* **-shopped; -shopping :** mirar las vitrinas

windpipe [ˈwɪndˌpaɪp] *n* **:** tráquea *f*

windshield [ˈwɪndˌʃiːld] *n* **1 :** parabrisas *m* **2 windshield wiper :** limpiaparabrisas *m*

windup [ˈwaɪndˌʌp] *n* **:** conclusión *f*

wind up *vt* END **:** terminar, concluir — *vi* **:** terminar, acabar

windward[1] [ˈwɪndwərd] *adj* **:** de barlovento

windward[2] *n* **:** barlovento *m*

windy [ˈwɪndi] *adj* **windier; -est 1 :** ventoso <it's windy : hace viento> **2** VERBOSE **:** verboso, prolijo

wine[1] [ˈwaɪn] *v* **wined; wining** *vi* **:** beber vino — *vt* **to wine and dine :** agasajar

wine[2] *n* **:** vino *m*

wing[1] [ˈwɪŋ] *vi* FLY **:** volar

wing[2] *n* **1 :** ala *f* (de un ave, un avión, o un edificio) **2** FACTION **:** ala *f* <the right wing of the party : el ala derecha del partido> **3 wings** *npl* **:** bastidores *mpl* (de un teatro) **4 on the wing :** al vuelo, volando **5 under one's wing :** bajo el cargo de uno

winged [ˈwɪŋd, ˈwɪŋəd] *adj* **:** alado

wink[1] [ˈwɪŋk] *vi* **1 :** guiñar el ojo **2** BLINK **:** pestañear, parpadear **3** FLICKER **:** parpadear, titilar

wink[2] *n* **1 :** guiño *m* (del ojo) **2** NAP **:** siesta *f* <not to sleep a wink : no pegar el ojo>

winner [ˈwɪnər] *n* **:** ganador *m,* -dora *f*

winning [ˈwɪnɪŋ] *adj* **1** VICTORIOUS **:** ganador **2** CHARMING **:** encantador

winnings [ˈwɪnɪŋz] *npl* **:** ganancias *fpl*

winnow [ˈwɪˌnoː] *vt* **:** aventar (el grano, etc.)

winsome [ˈwɪnsəm] *adj* CHARMING **:** encantador

winter[1] [ˈwɪntər] *adj* **:** invernal, de invierno

winter[2] *n* **:** invierno *m*

wintergreen [ˈwɪntərˌgriːn] *n* **:** gaulteria *f*

wintertime [ˈwɪntərˌtaɪm] *n* **:** invierno *m*

wintry [ˈwɪntri] *adj* **wintrier; -est 1** WINTER **:** invernal, de invierno **2** COLD

: frío <she gave us a wintry greeting : nos saludó fríamente>

wipe[1] [ˈwaɪp] *vt* **wiped; wiping 1** : limpiar, pasarle un trapo a <to wipe one's feet : limpiarse los pies> **2 to wipe away** : enjugar (lágrimas), borrar (una memoria) **3 to wipe out** ANNIHILATE : aniquilar, destruir

wipe[2] *n* : pasada *f* (con un trapo, etc.)

wire[1] [ˈwaɪr] *vt* **-wired; wiring 1** : instalar el cableado en (una casa, etc.) **2** BIND : atar con alambre **3** TELEGRAPH : telegrafiar, mandarle un telegrama (a alguien)

wire[2] *n* **1** : alambre *m* <barbed wire : alambre de púas> **2** : cable *m* (eléctrico o telefónico) **3** CABLEGRAM, TELEGRAM : telegrama *m*, cable *m*

wireless [ˈwaɪrləs] *adj* : inalámbrico

wiretapping [ˈwaɪrˌtæpɪŋ] *n* : intervención *f* electrónica

wiring [ˈwaɪrɪŋ] *n* : cableado *m*

wiry [ˈwaɪri] *adj* **wirier; -est 1** : hirsuto, tieso (dícese del pelo) **2** : esbelto y musculoso (dícese del cuerpo)

wisdom [ˈwɪzdəm] *n* **1** KNOWLEDGE : sabiduría *f* **2** JUDGMENT, SENSE : sensatez *f*

wisdom tooth *n* : muela *f* de juicio

wise[1] [ˈwaɪz] *adj* **wiser; wisest 1** LEARNED : sabio **2** SENSIBLE : sabio, sensato, prudente **3** KNOWLEDGEABLE : entendido, enterado <they're wise to his tricks : conocen muy bien sus mañas>

wise[2] *n* : manera *f*, modo *m* <in no wise : de ninguna manera>

wisecrack [ˈwaɪzˌkræk] *n* : broma *f*, chiste *m*

wisely [ˈwaɪzli] *adv* : sabiamente, sensatamente

wish[1] [ˈwɪʃ] *vt* **1** WANT : desear, querer **2 to wish (something) for** : desear <they wished me well : me desearon lo mejor> — *vi* **1** : pedir (como deseo) **2** : querer <as you wish : como quieras>

wish[2] *n* **1** : deseo *m* <to grant a wish : conceder un deseo> **2 wishes** *npl* : saludos *mpl*, recuerdos *mpl* <to send best wishes : mandar muchos recuerdos>

wishbone [ˈwɪʃˌboːn] *n* : espoleta *f*

wishful [ˈwɪʃfəl] *adj* **1** HOPEFUL : deseoso, lleno de esperanza **2 wishful thinking** : ilusiones *fpl*

wishy–washy [ˈwɪʃiˌwɔʃi, -ˌwɑʃi] *adj* : insípido, soso

wisp [ˈwɪsp] *n* **1** BUNCH : manojo *m* (de paja) **2** STRAND : mechón *m* (de pelo) **3** : voluta *f* (de humo)

wispy [ˈwɪspi] *adj* **wispier; -est** : tenue, ralo (dícese del pelo)

wisteria [wɪsˈtɪriə] *n* : glicinia *f*

wistful [ˈwɪstfəl] *adj* : añorante, anhelante, melancólico — **wistfully** *adv*

wistfulness [ˈwɪstfəlnəs] *n* : añoranza *f*, melancolía *f*

wit [ˈwɪt] *n* **1** INTELLIGENCE : inteligencia *f* **2** CLEVERNESS : ingenio *m*, gracia *f*, agudeza *f* **3** HUMOR : humorismo *m* **4** JOKER : chistoso *m*, -sa *f* **5 wits** *npl* : razón *f*, buen juicio *m* <scared out of one's wits : muerto de miedo> <to be at one's wits' end : estar desesperado>

witch [ˈwɪtʃ] *n* : bruja *f*

witchcraft [ˈwɪtʃˌkræft] *n* : brujería *f*, hechicería *f*

witch doctor *n* : hechicero *m*, -ra *f*

witchery [ˈwɪtʃəri] *n*, *pl* **-eries 1** → **witchcraft 2** CHARM : encanto *m*

witch–hunt [ˈwɪtʃˌhʌnt] *n* : caza *f* de brujas

with [ˈwɪð, ˈwɪθ] *prep* **1** : con <I'm going with you : voy contigo> <coffee with milk : café con leche> **2** AGAINST : con <to argue with someone : discutir con alguien> **3** (*used in descriptions*) : con, de <the girl with red hair : la muchacha de pelo rojo> **4** (*indicating manner, means, or cause*) : con <to cut with a knife : cortar con un cuchillo> <fix it with tape : arréglalo con cinta> <with luck : con suerte> **5** DESPITE : a pesar de, aún con <with all his work, the business failed : a pesar de su trabajo, el negocio fracasó> **6** REGARDING : con respecto a, con <the trouble with your plan : el problema con su plan> **7** ACCORDING TO : según <it varies with the season : varía según la estación> **8** (*indicating support or understanding*) : con <I'm with you all the way : estoy contigo hasta el fin>

withdraw [wɪðˈdrɔ, wɪθ-] *v* **-drew** [-ˈdruː]; **-drawn** [-ˈdrɔn]; **-drawing** *vt* **1** REMOVE : retirar, apartar, sacar (dinero) **2** RETRACT : retractarse de — *vi* : retirarse, recluirse (de la sociedad)

withdrawal [wɪðˈdrɔəl, wɪθ-] *n* **1** : retirada *f*, retiro *m* (de fondos, etc.), retraimiento *m* (social) **2** RETRACTION : retractación *f* **3 withdrawal symptoms** : síndrome *m* de abstinencia

withdrawn [wɪðˈdrɔn, wɪθ-] *adj* : retraído, reservado, introvertido

wither [ˈwɪðər] *vt* : marchitar, agostar — *vi* **1** WILT : marchitarse **2** WEAKEN : decaer, debilitarse

withhold [wɪθˈhoːld, wɪð-] *vt* **-held** [-ˈhɛld]; **-holding** : retener (fondos), aplazar (una decisión), negar (permiso, etc.)

within[1] [wɪðˈɪn, wɪθ-] *adv* : dentro

within[2] *prep* **1** : dentro de <within the limits : dentro de los límites> **2** (*in expressions of distance*) : a menos de <within 10 miles of the ocean : a menos de 10 millas del mar> **3** (*in expressions of time*) : dentro de <within an hour : dentro de una hora> <within a month of her birthday : a poco menos de un mes de su cumpleaños>

without[1] [wɪð'aʊt, wɪθ-] *adv* **1** OUTSIDE : fuera **2 to do without** : pasar sin algo

without[2] *prep* **1** OUTSIDE : fuera de **2** : sin <without fear : sin temor> <he left without his briefcase : se fue sin su portafolios>

withstand [wɪθ'stænd, wɪð-] *vt* **-stood** [-'stʊd]; **-standing 1** BEAR : aguantar, soportar **2** RESIST : resistir, resistirse a

witless ['wɪtləs] *adj* : estúpido, tonto

witness[1] ['wɪtnəs] *vt* **1** SEE : presenciar, ver, ser testigo de **2** : atestiguar (una firma, etc.) — *vi* TESTIFY : atestiguar, testimoniar

witness[2] *n* **1** TESTIMONY : testimonio *m* <to bear witness : atestiguar, testimoniar> **2** : testigo *mf* <witness for the prosecution : testigo de cargo>

witticism ['wɪtə,sɪzəm] *n* : agudeza *f,* ocurrencia *f*

witty ['wɪti] *adj* **-tier; -est** : ingenioso, ocurrente, gracioso

wives → **wife**

wizard ['wɪzərd] *n* **1** SORCERER : mago *m,* brujo *m,* hechicero *m* **2** : genio *m* <a math wizard : un genio en matemáticas>

wizened ['wɪzənd, 'wiː-] *adj* : arrugado, marchito

wobble[1] ['wɑbəl] *vi* **-bled; -bling** : bambolearse, tambalearse, temblar (dícese de la voz)

wobble[2] *n* : tambaleo *m,* bamboleo *m*

wobbly ['wɑbəli] *adj* : bamboleante, tambaleante, inestable

woe ['woː] *n* **1** GRIEF, MISFORTUNE : desgracia *f,* infortunio *m,* aflicción *f* **2 woes** *npl* TROUBLES : penas *fpl,* males *mpl*

woeful ['woːfəl] *adj* **1** SORROWFUL : afligido, apenado, triste **2** UNFORTUNATE : desgraciado, infortunado **3** DEPLORABLE : lamentable

woke, woken → **wake**[1]

wolf[1] ['wʊlf] *vt or* **to wolf down** : engullir

wolf[2] *n, pl* **wolves** ['wʊlvz] : lobo *m,* -ba *f*

wolfram ['wʊlfrəm] → **tungsten**

wolverine [,wʊlvə'riːn] *n* : glotón *m* (animal)

woman ['wʊmən] *n, pl* **women** ['wɪmən] : mujer *f*

womanhood ['wʊmən,hʊd] *n* **1** : condición *f* de mujer **2** WOMEN : mujeres *fpl*

womanly ['wʊmənli] *adj* : femenino

womb ['wuːm] *n* : útero *m,* matriz *f*

won → **win**

wonder[1] ['wʌndər] *vi* **1** SPECULATE : preguntarse, pensar <to wonder about : preguntarse por> **2** MARVEL : asombrarse, maravillarse — *vt* : preguntarse <I wonder if they're coming : me pregunto si vendrán>

wonder[2] *n* **1** MARVEL : maravilla *f,* milagro *m* <to work wonders : hacer maravillas> **2** AMAZEMENT : asombro *m*

wonderful ['wʌndərfəl] *adj* : maravilloso, estupendo

wonderfully ['wʌndərfəli] *adv* : maravillosamente, de maravilla

wonderland ['wʌndər,lænd, -lənd] *n* : país *m* de las maravillas

wonderment ['wʌndərmənt] *n* : asombro *m*

wondrous ['wʌndrəs] → **wonderful**

wont[1] ['wɔnt, 'woːnt, 'wɑnt] *adj* : acostumbrado, habituado

wont[2] *n* : hábito *m,* costumbre *f*

won't ['woːnt] (*contraction of* **will not**) → **will**[1]

woo ['wuː] *vt* **1** COURT : cortejar **2** : buscar el apoyo de (clientes, votantes, etc.)

wood[1] ['wʊd] *adj* : de madera

wood[2] *n* **1** *or* **woods** *npl* FOREST : bosque *m* **2** : madera *f* (materia) **3** FIREWOOD : leña *f*

woodchuck ['wʊd,tʃʌk] *n* : marmota *f* de América

woodcut ['wʊd,kʌt] *n* **1** : plancha *f* de madera (para imprimir imágenes) **2** : grabado *m* en madera

woodcutter ['wʊd,kʌtər] *n* : leñador *m,* -dora *f*

wooded ['wʊdəd] *adj* : arbolado, boscoso

wooden ['wʊdən] *adj* **1** : de madera <a wooden cross : una cruz de madera> **2** STIFF : rígido, inexpresivo (dícese del estilo, de la cara, etc.)

woodland ['wʊdlənd, -,lænd] *n* : bosque *m*

woodpecker ['wʊd,pɛkər] *n* : pájaro *m* carpintero

woodshed ['wʊd,ʃɛd] *n* : leñera *f*

woodsman ['wʊdzmən] → **woodcutter**

woodwind ['wʊd,wɪnd] *n* : instrumento *m* de viento de madera

woodworking ['wʊd,wərkɪŋ] *n* : carpintería *f*

woody ['wʊdi] *adj* **woodier; -est 1** → **wooded 2** : leñoso <woody plants : plantas leñosas> **3** : leñoso (dícese de la textura), a madera (dícese del aroma, etc.)

woof ['wʊf] → **weft**

wool ['wʊl] *n* : lana *f*

woolen[1] *or* **woollen** ['wʊlən] *adj* : de lana

woolen[2] *or* **woollen** *n* **1** : lana *f* (tela) **2 woolens** *npl* : prendas *fpl* de lana

woolly ['wʊli] *adj* **-lier; -est 1** : lanudo **2** CONFUSED : confuso, vago

woozy ['wuːzi] *adj* **-zier; -est** : mareado

word[1] ['wərd] *vt* : expresar, formular, redactar

word[2] *n* **1** : palabra *f,* vocablo *m,* voz *f* <word for word : palabra por palabra> <in one's own words : en sus

propias palabras> <words fail me : me quedo sin habla> **2** REMARK : palabra *f* <by word of mouth : de palabra> <to have a word with : hablar (dos palabras) con> **3** COMMAND : orden *f* <to give the word : dar la orden> <just say the word : no tienes que decirlo> **4** MESSAGE, NEWS : noticias *fpl* <is there any word from her? : ¿hay noticias de ella?> <to send word : mandar un recado> **5** PROMISE : palabra *f* <to keep one's word : cumplir uno su palabra> **6 words** *npl* QUARREL : palabra *f,* riña *f* <to have words with : tener unas palabras con, reñir con> **7 words** *npl* TEXT : letra *f* (de una canción, etc.)

wordiness [ˈwərdinəs] *n* : verbosidad *f*

wording [ˈwərdɪŋ] *n* : redacción *f,* lenguaje *m* (de un documento)

word processing *n* : procesamiento *m* de textos

word processor *n* : procesador *m* de textos

wordy [ˈwərdi] *adj* **wordier; -est** : verboso, prolijo

wore → **wear**[1]

work[1] [ˈwərk] *v* **worked** [ˈwərkt] *or* **wrought** [ˈrɔt]; **working** *vt* **1** OPERATE : trabajar, operar <to work a machine : operar una máquina> **2** : lograr, conseguir (algo) con esfuerzo <to work one's way up : lograr subir por sus propios esfuerzos> **3** EFFECT : efectuar, llevar a cabo, obrar (milagros) **4** MAKE, SHAPE : elaborar, fabricar, formar <a beautifully wrought vase : un florero bellamente elaborado> **5 to work up** : estimular, excitar <don't get worked up : no te agites> — *vi* **1** LABOR : trabajar <to work full-time : trabajar a tiempo completo> **2** FUNCTION : funcionar, servir

work[2] *adj* : laboral

work[3] *n* **1** LABOR : trabajo *m,* labor *f* **2** EMPLOYMENT : trabajo *m,* empleo *m* **3** TASK : tarea *f,* faena *f* **4** DEED : obra *f,* labor *f* <works of charity : obras de caridad> **5** : obra *f* (de arte o literatura) **6** → **workmanship 7 works** *npl* FACTORY : fábrica *f* **8 works** *npl* MECHANISM : mecanismo *m*

workable [ˈwərkəbəl] *adj* **1** : explotable (dícese de una mina, etc.) **2** FEASIBLE : factible, realizable

workaday [ˈwərkəˌdeɪ] *adj* : ordinario, banal

workbench [ˈwərkˌbɛntʃ] *n* : mesa *f* de trabajo

workday [ˈwərkˌdeɪ] *n* **1** : jornada *f* laboral **2** WEEKDAY : día *m* hábil, día *m* laborable

worker [ˈwərkər] *n* : trabajador *m,* -dora *f;* obrero *m,* -ra *f*

working [ˈwərkɪŋ] *adj* **1** : que trabaja <working mothers : madres que trabajan> <the working class : la clase obrera> **2** : de trabajo <working hours : horas de trabajo> **3** FUNCTIONING : que funciona, operativo **4** SUFFICIENT : suficiente <a working majority : una mayoría suficiente> <working knowledge : conocimientos básicos>

workingman [ˈwərkɪŋˌmæn] *n, pl* **-men** [-mən, -ˌmɛn] : obrero *m*

workman [ˈwərkmən] *n, pl* **-men** [-mən, -ˌmɛn] **1** → **workingman 2** ARTISAN : artesano *m*

workmanlike [ˈwərkmənˌlaɪk] *adj* : bien hecho, competente

workmanship [ˈwərkmənˌʃɪp] *n* **1** WORK : ejecución *f,* trabajo *m* **2** CRAFTSMANSHIP : artesanía *f,* destreza *f*

workout [ˈwərkˌaʊt] *n* : ejercicios *mpl* físicos, entrenamiento *m*

work out *vt* **1** DEVELOP, PLAN : idear, planear, desarrollar **2** RESOLVE : solucionar, resolver <to work out the answer : calcular la solución> — *vi* **1** TURN OUT : resultar **2** SUCCEED : lograr, dar resultado, salir bien **3** EXERCISE : hacer ejercicio

workroom [ˈwərkˌruːm, -ˌrʊm] *n* : taller *m*

workshop [ˈwərkˌʃɑp] *n* : taller *m* <ceramics workshop : taller de cerámica>

world[1] [ˈwərld] *adj* : mundial, del mundo <world championship : campeonato mundial>

world[2] *n* : mundo *m* <around the world : alrededor del mundo> <a world of possibilities : un mundo de posibilidades> <to think the world of someone : tener a alguien en alta estima> <to be worlds apart : no tener nada que ver (uno con otro)>

worldly [ˈwərldli] *adj* **1** : mundano <wordly goods : bienes materiales> **2** SOPHISTICATED : sofisticado, de mundo

worldwide[1] [ˈwərldˈwaɪd] *adv* : mundialmente, en todo el mundo

worldwide[2] *adj* : global, mundial

worm[1] [ˈwərm] *vi* **1** CRAWL : arrastrarse, deslizarse (como gusano) <to worm one's way into someone's confidence : ganarse la confianza de alguien> **2 to worm something out of someone** : sonsacarle algo a alguien — *vt* : desparasitar (un animal)

worm[2] *n* **1** : gusano *m,* lombriz *f* **2 worms** *npl* : lombrices *fpl* (parásitos)

wormy [ˈwərmi] *adj* **wormier; -est** : infestado de gusanos

worn → **wear**[1]

worn–out [ˈwornˈaʊt] *adj* **1** USED : gastado, desgastado **2** TIRED : agotado

worried [ˈwərid] *adj* : inquieto, preocupado

worrier [ˈwəriər] *n* : persona *f* que se preocupa mucho

worrisome [ˈwərisəm] *adj* **1** DISTURBING : preocupante, inquietante **2** : que se preocupa mucho (dícese de una persona)

worry[1] [ˈwəri] *v* **-ried; -rying** *vt* : preocupar, inquietar — *vi* : preocuparse, inquietarse, angustiarse

worry[2] *n, pl* **-ries** : preocupación *f,* inquietud *f,* angustia *f*

worse[1] [ˈwərs] *adv* (*comparative of* **bad** *or of* **ill**) : peor <to feel worse : sentirse peor>

worse[2] *adj* (*comparative of* **bad** *or of* **ill**) : peor <from bad to worse : de mal en peor> <to get worse : empeorar>

worse[3] *n* : estado *m* peor <to take a turn for the worse : ponerse peor> <so much the worse : tanto peor>

worsen [ˈwərsən] *vt* : empeorar — *vi* : empeorar(se)

worship[1] [ˈwərʃəp] *v* **-shiped** *or* **-shipped; -shiping** *or* **-shipping** *vt* : adorar, venerar <to worship God : adorar a Dios> — *vi* : practicar una religión

worship[2] *n* : adoración *f,* culto *m*

worshiper *or* **worshipper** [ˈwərʃəpər] *n* : devoto *m,* -ta *f;* adorador *m,* -dora *f*

worst[1] [ˈwərst] *vt* DEFEAT : derrotar

worst[2] *adv* (*superlative of* **ill** *or of* **bad** *or* **badly**) : peor <the worst dressed of all : el peor vestido de todos>

worst[3] *adj* (*superlative of* **bad** *or of* **ill**) : peor <the worst movie : la peor película>

worst[4] *n* **the worst** : lo peor, el (la) peor <the worst is over : ya ha pasado lo peor>

worsted [ˈwʊstəd, ˈwərstəd] *n* : estambre *m*

worth[1] [ˈwərθ] *n* **1** : valor *m* (monetario) <ten dollars' worth of gas : diez dólares de gasolina> **2** MERIT : valor *m,* mérito *m,* valía *f* <an employee of great worth : un empleado de gran valía>

worth[2] *prep* **to be worth** : valer <her holdings are worth a fortune : sus propiedades valen una fortuna> <it's not worth it : no vale la pena>

worthiness [ˈwərðinəs] *n* : mérito *m*

worthless [ˈwərθləs] *adj* **1** : sin valor <worthless trinkets : chucherías sin valor> **2** USELESS : inútil

worthwhile [wərθˈ*h*waɪl] *adj* : que vale la pena

worthy [ˈwərði] *adj* **-thier; -est 1** : digno <worthy of promotion : digno de un ascenso> **2** COMMENDABLE : meritorio, encomiable

would [ˈwʊd] *past of* **will 1** (*expressing preference*) <I would rather go alone than with her : preferiría ir sola que con ella> **2** (*expressing intent*) <those who would ban certain books : aquellos que prohibirían ciertos libros> **3** (*expressing habitual action*) <he would often take his kids to the park : solía llevar a sus hijos al parque> **4** (*expressing contingency*) <I would go if I had the money : iría yo si tuviera el dinero> **5** (*expressing probability*) <she would have won if she hadn't tripped : habría ganado si no hubiera tropezado> **6** (*expressing a request*) <would you kindly help me with this? : ¿tendría la bondad de ayudarme con esto?>

would–be [ˈwʊdˈbiː] *adj* : potencial <a would-be celebrity : un aspirante a celebridad>

wouldn't [ˈwʊdˈənt] (*contraction of* **would not**) → **would**

wound[1] [ˈwuːnd] *vt* : herir

wound[2] *n* : herida *f*

wound[3] [ˈwaʊnd] → **wind**[2]

wove, woven → **weave**[1]

wrangle[1] [ˈræŋgəl] *vi* **-gled; -gling** : discutir, reñir <to wrangle over : discutir por>

wrangle[2] *n* : riña *f,* disputa *f*

wrap[1] [ˈræp] *v* **wrapped; wrapping** *vt* **1** COVER : envolver, cubrir <to wrap a package : envolver un paquete> <wrapped in mystery : envuelto en misterio> **2** ENCIRCLE : rodear, ceñir <to wrap one's arms around someone : estrechar a alguien> **3 to wrap up** FINISH : darle fin a (algo) — *vi* **1** COIL : envolverse, enroscarse **2 to wrap up** DRESS : abrigarse <wrap up warmly : abrígate bien>

wrap[2] *n* **1** WRAPPER : envoltura *f* **2** : prenda *f* que envuelve (como un chal, una bata, etc.)

wrapper [ˈræpər] *n* : envoltura *f,* envoltorio *m*

wrapping [ˈræpɪŋ] *n* : envoltura *f,* envoltorio *m*

wrath [ˈræθ] *n* : ira *f,* cólera *f*

wrathful [ˈræθfəl] *adj* : iracundo

wreak [ˈriːk] *vt* : infligir, causar <to wreak havoc : crear caos, causar estragos>

wreath [ˈriːθ] *n, pl* **wreaths** [ˈriːðz, ˈriːθs] : corona *f* (de flores, etc.)

wreathe [ˈriːð] *vt* **wreathed; wreathing 1** ADORN : coronar (de flores, etc.) **2** ENVELOP : envolver <wreathed in mist : envuelto en niebla>

wreck[1] [ˈrɛk] *vt* : destruir, arruinar, estrellar (un automóvil), naufragar (un barco)

wreck[2] *n* **1** WRECKAGE : restos *mpl* (de un buque naufragado, un avión siniestrado, etc.) **2** RUIN : ruina *f,* desastre *m* <this place is a wreck! : ¡este lugar está hecho un desastre!> <to be a nervous wreck : tener los nervios destrozados>

wreckage [ˈrɛkɪdʒ] *n* : restos *mpl* (de un buque naufragado, un avión siniestrado, etc.), ruinas *fpl* (de un edificio)

wrecker [ˈrɛkər] *n* **1** TOW TRUCK : grúa *f* **2** : desguazador *m* (de autos, barcos, etc.), demoledor *m* (de edificios)

wren [ˈrɛn] *n* : chochín *m*

wrench[1] [ˈrɛntʃ] *vt* **1** PULL : arrancar (de un tirón) **2** SPRAIN, TWIST : torcerse (un tobillo, un músculo, etc.)

wrench[2] *n* **1** TUG : tirón *m,* jalón *m* **2** SPRAIN : torcedura *f* **3** *or* **monkey wrench** : llave *f* inglesa

wrest [ˈrɛst] *vt* : arrancar
wrestle[1] [ˈrɛsəl] *v* **-tled; -tling** *vi* **1** : luchar, practicar la lucha (en deportes) **2** STRUGGLE : luchar <to wrestle with a dilemma : lidiar con un dilema> — *vt* : luchar contra
wrestle[2] *n* STRUGGLE : lucha *f*
wrestler [ˈrɛsələr] *n* : luchador *m,* -dora *f*
wrestling [ˈrɛsəlɪŋ] *n* : lucha *f*
wretch [ˈrɛtʃ] *n* : infeliz *mf;* desgraciado *m,* -da *f*
wretched [ˈrɛtʃəd] *adj* **1** MISERABLE, UNHAPPY : desdichado, afligido <I feel wretched : me siento muy mal> **2** UNFORTUNATE : miserable, desgraciado, lastimoso <wretched weather : tiempo espantoso> **3** INFERIOR : inferior, malo
wretchedly [ˈrɛtʃədli] *adv* : miserablemente, lamentablemente
wriggle [ˈrɪgəl] *vi* **-gled; -gling** : retorcerse, menearse
wring [ˈrɪŋ] *vt* **wrung** [ˈrʌŋ]; **wringing 1** *or* **to wring out** : escurrir, exprimir (el lavado) **2** EXTRACT : arrancar, sacar (por la fuerza) **3** TWIST : torcer, retorcer **4 to wring someone's heart** : partirle el corazón a alguien
wringer [ˈrɪŋər] *n* : escurridor *m*
wrinkle[1] [ˈrɪŋkəl] *v* **-kled; -kling** *vt* : arrugar — *vi* : arrugarse
wrinkle[2] *n* : arruga *f*
wrinkly [ˈrɪŋkəli] *adj* **wrinklier; -est** : arrugado
wrist [ˈrɪst] *n* **1** : muñeca *f* (en anatomía) **2** *or* **wristband** [ˈrɪstˌbænd] CUFF : puño *m*
writ [ˈrɪt] *n* : orden *f* (judicial)
write [ˈraɪt] *v* **wrote** [ˈroːt]; **written** [ˈrɪtən]; **writing** : escribir
write down *vt* : apuntar, anotar
write off *vt* CANCEL : cancelar
writer [ˈraɪt̬ər] *n* : escritor *m,* -tora *f*
writhe [ˈraɪð] *vi* **writhed; writhing** : retorcerse
writing [ˈraɪt̬ɪŋ] *n* : escritura *f*
wrong[1] [ˈrɔŋ] *vt* **wronged; wronging** : ofender, ser injusto con
wrong[2] *adv* : mal, incorrectamente
wrong[3] *adj* **wronger** [ˈrɔŋər]; **wrongest** [ˈrɔŋəst] **1** EVIL, SINFUL : malo, injusto, inmoral **2** IMPROPER, UNSUITABLE : inadecuado, inapropiado, malo **3** INCORRECT : incorrecto, erróneo, malo <a wrong answer : una mala respuesta> **4 to be wrong** : equivocarse, estar equivocado
wrong[4] *n* **1** INJUSTICE : injusticia *f,* mal *m* **2** OFFENSE : ofensa *f,* agravio *m* (en derecho) **3 to be in the wrong** : haber hecho mal, estar equivocado
wrongdoer [ˈrɔŋˌduːər] *n* : malhechor *m,* -chora *f*
wrongdoing [ˈrɔŋˌduːɪŋ] *n* : fechoría *f,* maldad *f*
wrongful [ˈrɔŋfəl] *adj* **1** UNJUST : injusto **2** UNLAWFUL : ilegal
wrongly [ˈrɔŋli] *adv* **1** : injustamente **2** INCORRECTLY : erróneamente, incorrectamente
wrote → **write**
wrought [ˈrɔt] *adj* **1** SHAPED : formado, forjado <wrought iron : hierro forjado> **2** *or* **wrought up** : agitado, excitado
wrung → **wring**
wry [ˈraɪ] *adj* **wrier** [ˈraɪər]; **wriest** [ˈraɪəst] **1** TWISTED : torcido <a wry neck : un cuello torcido> **2** : irónico, sardónico (dícese del humor)

X

x[1] *n, pl* **x's** *or* **xs** [ˈɛksəz] **1** : vigésima cuarta letra del alfabeto inglés **2** : incógnita *f* (en matemáticas)
x[2] [ˈɛks] *vt* **x–ed** [ˈɛkst]; **x–ing** *or* **x'ing** [ˈɛksiŋ] DELETE : tachar
xenon [ˈziːˌnɑn, ˈzɛ-] *n* : xenón *m*
xenophobia [ˌzɛnəˈfoːbiə, ˌziː-] *n* : xenofobia *f*
Xmas [ˈkrɪsməs] *n* : Navidad *f*
x–ray [ˈɛksˌreɪ] *vt* : radiografiar
X ray [ˈɛksˌreɪ] *n* **1** : rayo *m* X **2** *or* **X–ray photograph** : radiografía *f*
xylophone [ˈzaɪləˌfoːn] *n* : xilófono *m*

Y

y [ˈwaɪ] *n, pl* **y's** *or* **ys** [ˈwaɪz] : vigésima quinta letra del alfabeto inglés
yacht[1] [ˈjɑt] *vi* : navegar (a vela), ir en yate <to go yachting : irse a navegar>
yacht[2] *n* : yate *m*
yak [ˈjæk] *n* : yac *m*
yam [ˈjæm] *n* **1** : ñame *m* **2** SWEET POTATO : batata *f,* boniato *m*
yank[1] [ˈjæŋk] *vt* : tirar de, jalar, darle un tirón a
yank[2] *n* : tirón *m*
Yankee [ˈjæŋki] *n* : yanqui *mf*
yap[1] [ˈjæp] *vi* **yapped; yapping 1** BARK, YELP : ladrar, gañir **2** CHATTER : cotorrear *fam,* parlotear *fam*
yap[2] *n* : ladrido *m,* gañido *m*

yard ['jɑrd] *n* **1** : yarda *f* (medida) **2** SPAR : verga *f* (de un barco) **3** COURTYARD : patio *m* **4** : jardín *m* (de una casa) **5** : depósito *m* (de mercancías, etc.)

yardage ['jɑrdɪdʒ] *n* : medida *f* en yardas

yardarm ['jɑrd,ɑrm] *n* : penol *m*

yardstick ['jɑrd,stɪk] *n* **1** : vara *f* **2** CRITERION : criterio *m*, norma *f*

yarn ['jɑrn] *n* **1** : hilado *m* **2** TALE : historia *f*, cuento *m* <to spin a yarn : inventar una historia>

yawl ['jɔl] *n* : yola *f*

yawn[1] ['jɔn] *vi* **1** : bostezar **2** OPEN : abrirse

yawn[2] *n* : bostezo *m*

ye ['ji:] *pron* : vosotros, vosotras

yea[1] ['jeɪ] *adv* YES : sí

yea[2] *n* : voto *m* a favor

year ['jɪr] *n* **1** : año *m* <last year : el año pasado> <he's ten years old : tiene diez años> **2** : curso *m*, año *m* (escolar) **3 years** *npl* AGES : siglos *mpl*, años *mpl* <I haven't seen them in years : hace siglos que no los veo>

yearbook ['jɪr,bʊk] *n* : anuario *m*

yearling ['jɪrlɪŋ, 'jərlən] *n* : animal *m* menor de dos año

yearly[1] ['jɪrli] *adv* : cada año, anualmente

yearly[2] *adj* : anual

yearn ['jərn] *vi* : anhelar, ansiar

yearning ['jərnɪŋ] *n* : anhelo *m*

yeast ['ji:st] *n* : levadura *f*

yell[1] ['jɛl] *vi* : gritar, chillar — *vt* : gritar

yell[2] *n* : grito *m*, alarido *m* <to let out a yell : dar un grito>

yellow[1] ['jɛlo] *vi* : ponerse amarillo, volverse amarillo

yellow[2] *adj* **1** : amarillo **2** COWARDLY : cobarde

yellow[3] *n* : amarillo *m*

yellow fever *n* : fiebre *f* amarilla

yellowish ['jɛloɪʃ] *adj* : amarillento

yellow jacket *n* : avispa *f* (con rayas amarillas)

yelp[1] ['jɛlp] *vi* : dar un gañido (dícese de un animal), dar un grito (dícese de una persona)

yelp[2] *n* : gañido *m* (de un animal), grito *m* (de una persona)

yen ['jɛn] *n* **1** DESIRE : deseo *m*, ganas *fpl* **2** : yen *m* (moneda japonesa)

yeoman ['jo:mən] *n, pl* **-men** [-mən, -mɛn] : suboficial *mf* de marina

yes[1] ['jɛs] *adv* : sí <to say yes : decir que sí>

yes[2] *n* : sí *m*

yesterday[1] ['jɛstər,deɪ, -di] *adv* : ayer

yesterday[2] *n* **1** : ayer *m* **2 the day before yesterday** : anteayer

yet[1] ['jɛt] *adv* **1** BESIDES, EVEN : aún <yet more problems : más problemas aún> <yet again : otra vez> **2** SO FAR : aún, todavía <not yet : todavía no> <as yet : hasta ahora, todavía> **3** : ya <has he come yet? : ¿ya ha venido?> **4** EVENTUALLY : todavía, algún día **5** NEVERTHELESS : sin embargo

yet[2] *conj* : pero

yew ['ju:] *n* : tejo *m*

yield[1] ['ji:ld] *vt* **1** SURRENDER : ceder <to yield the right of way : ceder el paso> **2** PRODUCE : producir, dar, rendir (en finanzas) — *vi* **1** GIVE : ceder <to yield under pressure : ceder por la presión> **2** GIVE IN, SURRENDER : ceder, rendirse, entregarse

yield[2] *n* : rendimiento *m*, rédito *m* (en finanzas)

yodel[1] ['jo:dəl] *vi* **-deled** *or* **-delled; -deling** *or* **-delling** : cantar al estilo tirolés

yodel[2] *n* : canción *f* al estilo tirolés

yoga ['jo:gə] *n* : yoga *m*

yogurt ['jo:gərt] *n* : yogur *m*, yogurt *m*

yoke[1] ['jo:k] *vt* **yoked; yoking** : uncir (animales)

yoke[2] *n* **1** : yugo *m* (para uncir animales) <the yoke of oppression : el yugo de la opresión> **2** TEAM : yunta *f* (de bueyes) **3** : canesú *m* (de ropa)

yokel ['jo:kəl] *n* : palurdo *m*, -da *f*

yolk ['jo:k] *n* : yema *f* (de un huevo)

Yom Kippur [,jo:mkɪ'pʊr, ,jɑm-, -'kɪpər] *n* : el Día *m* del Perdón, Yom Kippur

yon ['jɑn] → **yonder**

yonder[1] ['jɑndər] *adv* : allá <over yonder : allá lejos>

yonder[2] *adj* : aquel <yonder hill : aquella colina>

yore ['jo:r] *n* **in days of yore** : antaño

you ['ju:] *pron* **1** (*used as subject — familiar*) : tú; vos (*in some Latin American countries*); ustedes *pl;* vosotros, vosotras *pl Spain* **2** (*used as subject — formal*) : usted, ustedes *pl* **3** (*used as indirect object — familiar*) : te, les *pl* (se *before lo, la, los, las*), os *pl Spain* <he told it to you : te lo contó> <I gave them to (all of, both of) you : se los di> **4** (*used as indirect object — formal*) : lo (*Spain sometimes* le), la; los (*Spain sometimes* les), las *pl* **5** (*used after a preposition — familiar*) : ti; vos (*in some Latin American countries*); ustedes *pl;* vosotros, vosotras *pl Spain* **6** (*used after a preposition — formal*) : usted, ustedes *pl* **7** (*used as an impersonal subject*) <you never know : nunca se sabe> <you have to be aware : hay que ser consciente> <you mustn't do that : eso no se hace> **8 with you** (*familiar*) : contigo; con ustedes *pl;* con vosotros, con vosotras *pl Spain* **9 with you** (*formal*) : con usted, con ustedes *pl*

you'd ['ju:d, 'jʊd] (*contraction of* **you had** *or* **you would**) → **have, would**

you'll ['ju:l, 'jʊl] (*contraction of* **you shall** *or* **you will**) → **shall, will**

young[1] ['jʌŋ] *adj* **younger** ['jʌŋgər]; **youngest** [-gəst] **1** : joven, pequeño, menor <young people : los jóvenes>

<my younger brother : mi hermano menor> <she is the youngest : es la más pequeña> **2** FRESH, NEW : tierno (dícese de las verduras), joven (dícese del vino) **3** YOUTHFUL : joven, juvenil

young[2] *npl* : jóvenes *mfpl* (de los humanos), crías *fpl* (de los animales)

youngster [ˈjʌŋkstər] *n* **1** YOUTH : joven *mf* **2** CHILD : chico *m,* -ca *f;* niño *m,* -ña *f*

your [ˈjʊr, ˈjoːr, jər] *adj* **1** (*familiar singular*) : tu <your cat : tu gato> <your books : tus libros> <wash your hands : lávate las manos> **2** (*familiar plural*) su, vuestro *Spain* <your car : su coche, el coche de ustedes> **3** (*formal*) : su <your houses : sus casas> **4** (*impersonal*) : el, la, los, las <on your left : a la izquierda>

you're [ˈjʊr, ˈjoːr, ˈjər, ˈjuːər] (*contraction of* **you are**) → **be**

yours [ˈjʊrz, ˈjoːrz] *pron* **1** (*belonging to one person — familiar*) : (el) tuyo, (la) tuya, (los) tuyos, (las) tuyas <those are mine; yours are there : ésas son mías; las tuyas están allí> <is this one yours? : ¿éste es tuyo?> **2** (*belonging to more than one person — familiar*) : (el) suyo, (la) suya, (los) suyos, (las) suyas; (el) vuestro, (la) vuestra, (los) vuestros, (las) vuestras *Spain* <our house and yours : nuestra casa y la suya> **3** (*formal*) : (el) suyo, (la) suya, (los) suyos, (las) suyas

yourself [jərˈsɛlf] *pron, pl* **yourselves** [-ˈsɛlvz] **1** (*used reflexively — familiar*) : te, se *pl,* os *pl Spain* <wash yourself : lávate> <you dressed yourselves : se vistieron, os vestisteis> **2** (*used reflexively — formal*) : se <did you hurt yourself? : ¿se hizo daño?> <you've gotten yourselves dirty : se ensuciaron> **3** (*used for emphasis*) : tú mismo, tú misma; usted mismo, usted misma; ustedes mismos, ustedes mismas *pl;* vosotros mismos, vosotras mismas *pl Spain* <you did it yourselves? : ¿lo hicieron ustedes mismos?, ¿lo hicieron por sí solos?>

youth [ˈjuːθ] *n, pl* **youths** [ˈjuːðz, ˈjuːθs] **1** : juventud *f* <in her youth : en su juventud> **2** BOY : joven *m* **3** : jóvenes *mfpl,* juventud *f* <the youth of our city : los jóvenes de nuestra ciudad>

youthful [ˈjuːθfəl] *adj* **1** : de juventud **2** YOUNG : joven **3** JUVENILE : juvenil

youthfulness [ˈjuːθfəlnəs] *n* : juventud *f*

you've [ˈjuːv] (*contraction of* **you have**) → **have**

yowl[1] [ˈjæʊl] *vi* : aullar

yowl[2] *n* : aullido *m*

yo–yo [ˈjoːˌjoː] *n, pl* **-yos** : yoyo *m,* yoyó *m*

yucca [ˈjʌkə] *n* : yuca *f*

Yugoslavian [ˌjuːgoˈslɑviən] *n* : yugoslavo *m,* -va *f* — **Yugoslavian** *adj*

yule [ˈjuːl] *n* CHRISTMAS : Navidad *f*

yuletide [ˈjuːlˌtaɪd] *n* : Navidades *fpl*

Z

z [ˈziː] *n, pl* **z's** *or* **zs** : vigésima sexta letra del alfabeto inglés

Zambian [ˈzæmbiən] *n* : zambiano *m,* -na *f* — **Zambian** *adj*

zany[1] [ˈzeɪni] *adj* **-nier; -est** : alocado, disparatado

zany[2] *n, pl* **-nies** : bufón *m,* -fona *f*

zeal [ˈziːl] *n* : fervor *m,* celo *m,* entusiasmo *m*

zealot [ˈzɛlət] *n* : fanático *m,* -ca *f*

zealous [ˈzɛləs] *adj* : celoso — **zealously** *adv*

zebra [ˈziːbrə] *n* : cebra *f*

zenith [ˈziːnəθ] *n* **1** : cenit *m* (en astronomía) **2** PEAK : apogeo *m,* cenit *m* <at the zenith of his career : en el apogeo de su carrera>

zephyr [ˈzɛfər] *n* : céfiro *m*

zeppelin [ˈzɛplən, -pəlɪn] *n* : zepelín *m*

zero[1] [ˈziːro, ˈzɪro] *vi* **to zero in on** : apuntar hacia, centrarse en (un problema, etc.)

zero[2] *adj* : cero, nulo <zero degrees : cero grados> <zero opportunities : oportunidades nulas>

zero[3] *n, pl* **-ros** : cero *m* <below zero : bajo cero>

zest [ˈzɛst] *n* **1** GUSTO : entusiasmo *m,* brío *m* **2** FLAVOR : sabor *m,* sazón *f*

zestful [ˈzɛstfəl] *adj* : brioso

zigzag[1] [ˈzɪgˌzæg] *vi* **-zagged; -zagging** : zigzaguear

zigzag[2] *adv & adj* : en zigzag

zigzag[3] *n* : zigzag *m*

Zimbabwean [zɪmˈbɑbwiən, -bweɪ-] *n* : zimbabuense *mf* — **Zimbabwean** *adj*

zinc [ˈzɪŋk] *n* : cinc *m,* zinc *m*

zing [ˈzɪŋ] *n* **1** HISS, HUM : zumbido *m,* silbido *m* **2** ENERGY : brío *m*

zinnia [ˈzɪniə, ˈziː-, -njə] *n* : zinnia *f*

Zionism [ˈzaɪəˌnɪzəm] *n* : sionismo *m*

Zionist [ˈzaɪənɪst] *n* : sionista *mf*

zip[1] [ˈzɪp] *v* **zipped; zipping** *vt or* **to zip up** : cerrar el cierre de — *vi* **1** SPEED : pasarse volando <the day zipped by : el día se pasó volando> **2** HISS, HUM : silbar, zumbar

zip[2] *n* **1** ZING : zumbido *m,* silbido *m* **2** ENERGY : brío *m*

zip code *n* : código *m* postal

zipper [ˈzɪpər] *n* : cierre *m,* cremallera *f,* zíper *m CA, Mex*

zippy [ˈzɪpi] *adj* **-pier; -est** : brioso

zircon ['zər,kɑn] *n* **:** circón *m,* zircón *m*

zirconium [,zər'ko:niəm] *n* **:** circonio *m*

zither ['zɪðər, -θər] *n* **:** cítara *f*

zodiac ['zo:di,æk] *n* **:** zodíaco *m*

zombie ['zɑmbi] *n* **:** zombi *mf,* zombie *mf*

zone[1] ['zo:n] *vt* **zoned; zoning 1 :** dividir en zonas **2** DESIGNATE **:** declarar <to zone for business : declarar como zona comercial>

zone[2] *n* **:** zona *f*

zoo ['zu:] *n, pl* **zoos :** zoológico *m,* zoo *m*

zoological [,zo:ə'lɑdʒɪkəl, ,zu:ə-] *adj* **:** zoológico

zoologist [zo'ɑlədʒɪst, zu:-] *n* **:** zoólogo *m,* -ga *f*

zoology [zo'ɑlədʒi, zu:-] *n* **:** zoología *f*

zoom[1] ['zu:m] *vi* **1 :** zumbar, ir volando <to zoom past : pasar volando> **2** CLIMB **:** elevarse <the plane zoomed up : el avión se elevó>

zoom[2] *n* **1 :** zumbido *m* <the zoom of an engine : el zumbido de un motor> **2 :** subida *f* vertical (de un avión, etc.) **3** *or* **zoom lens :** zoom *m*

zucchini [zʊ'ki:ni] *n, pl* **-ni** *or* **-nis :** calabacín *m,* calabacita *f Mex*

zygote ['zaɪ,go:t] *n* **:** zigoto *m,* cigoto *m*

Common Spanish Abbreviations
Abreviaturas comunes en español

SPANISH ABBREVIATION AND EXPANSION		ENGLISH EQUIVALENT	
abr.	abril	**Apr.**	April
A.C., a.C.	antes de Cristo	**BC**	before Christ
a. de J.C.	antes de Jesucristo	**BC**	before Christ
admon., admón.	administración	—	administration
a/f	a favor	—	in favor
ago.	agosto	**Aug.**	August
Apdo.	apartado (de correos)	—	P.O. box
aprox.	aproximadamente	**approx.**	approximately
Aptdo.	apartado (de correos)	—	P.O. box
Arq.	arquitecto	**arch.**	architect
A.T.	Antiguo Testamento	**O. T.**	Old Testament
atte.	atentamente	—	sincerely
atto., atta.	atento, atenta	—	kind, courteous
av., avda.	avenida	**ave.**	avenue
a/v.	a vista	—	on receipt
BID	Banco Interamericano de Desarrollo	**IDB**	Interamerican Development Bank
B⁰	banco	—	bank
BM	Banco Mundial		World Bank
c/, C/	calle	**st.**	street
C	centígrado, Celsius	**C**	centigrade, Celsius
C.	compañía	**Co.**	company
CA	corriente alterna	**AC**	alternating current
cap.	capítulo	**ch., chap.**	chapter
c/c	cuenta corriente	—	current account, checking account
c.c.	centímetros cúbicos	**cu. cm**	cubic centimeters
CC	corriente continua	**DC**	direct current
c/d	con descuento	—	with discount
Cd.	ciudad	—	city
CE	Comunidad Europea	**EC**	European Community
CEE	Comunidad Económica Europea	**EEC**	European Economic Community
cf.	confróntese	**cf.**	compare
cg.	centígramo	**cg**	centigram
CGT	Confederación General de Trabajadores *or* del Trabajo	—	confederation of workers, workers' union
CI	coeficiente intelectual *or* de inteligencia	**IQ**	intelligence quotient
Cía.	compañía	**Co.**	company
cm.	centímetro	**cm**	centimeter

SPANISH ABBREVIATION AND EXPANSION		ENGLISH EQUIVALENT	
Cnel.	coronel	**Col.**	colonel
col.	columna	**col.**	column
Col. *Mex*	Colonia	—	—
Com.	comandante	**Cmdr.**	commander
comp.	compárese	**comp.**	compare
Cor.	coronel	**Col.**	colonel
C.P.	código postal	—	zip code
CSF, c.s.f.	coste, seguro y flete	**c.i.f.**	cost, insurance, and freight
cta.	cuenta	**ac., acct.**	account
cte.	corriente	**cur.**	current
c/u	cada uno, cada una	**ea.**	each
CV	caballo de vapor	**hp**	horsepower
D.	Don	—	—
Da., D.ª	Doña	—	—
d.C.	después de Cristo	**AD**	anno Domini (in the year of our Lord)
dcha.	derecha	—	right
d. de J.C.	después de Jesucristo	**AD**	anno Domini (in the year of our Lord)
dep.	departamento	**dept.**	department
DF, D.F.	Distrito Federal	—	Federal District
dic.	diciembre	**Dec.**	December
dir.	director, directora	**dir.**	director
dir.	dirección	—	address
Dña.	Doña	—	—
do.	domingo	**Sun.**	Sunday
dpto.	departamento	**dept.**	department
Dr.	doctor	**Dr.**	doctor
Dra.	doctora	**Dr.**	doctor
dto.	descuento	—	discount
E, E.	Este, este	**E**	East, east
Ed.	editorial	—	publishing house
Ed., ed.	edición	**ed.**	edition
edif.	edificio	**bldg.**	building
edo.	estado	**st.**	state
EEUU, EE.UU.	Estados Unidos	**US, U.S.**	United States
ej.	por ejemplo	**e.g.**	for example
E.M.	esclerosis multiple	**MS**	multiple sclerosis
ene.	enero	**Jan.**	January
etc.	etcétera	**etc.**	et cetera
ext.	extensión	**ext.**	extension
F	Fahrenheit	**F**	Fahrenheit
f.a.b.	franco a bordo	**f.o.b.**	free on board
FC	ferrocarril	**RR**	railroad
feb.	febrero	**Feb.**	February
FF AA, FF.AA.	Fuerzas Armadas	—	armed forces
FMI	Fondo Monetario Internacional	**IMF**	International Monetary Fund
g.	gramo	**g., gm, gr.**	gram
G.P.	giro postal	**M.O.**	money order
gr.	gramo	**g., gm, gr.**	gram

SPANISH ABBREVIATION AND EXPANSION		ENGLISH EQUIVALENT	
Gral.	general	**Gen.**	general
h.	hora	**hr.**	hour
Hnos.	hermanos	**Bros.**	brothers
I + D, I & D, I y D	investigación y desarrollo	**R & D**	research and development
i.e.	esto es, es decir	**i.e.**	that is
incl.	inclusive	**incl.**	inclusive, inclusively
Ing.	ingeniero, ingeniera	**eng.**	engineer
IPC	indice de precios al consumo	**CPI**	consumer price index
IVA	impuesto al valor agregado	**VAT**	value-added tax
izq.	izquierda	**l.**	left
juev.	jueves	**Thurs.**	Thursday
jul.	julio	**Jul.**	July
jun.	junio	**Jun.**	June
kg.	kilogramo	**kg**	kilogram
km.	kilómetro	**km**	kilometer
km/h	kilómetros por hora	**kph**	kilometers per hour
kv, kV	kilovatio	**kw, kW**	kilowatt
l.	litro	**l, lit.**	liter
Lic.	licenciado, licenciada	—	*usually indicates a college graduate*
Ltda.	limitada	**Ltd.**	limited
lun.	lunes	**Mon.**	Monday
m	masculino	**m**	masculine
m	metro	**m**	meter
m	minuto	**m**	minute
mar.	marzo	**Mar.**	March
mart.	martes	**Tues.**	Tuesday
mg.	miligramo	**mg**	milligram
miérc.	miércoles	**Wednes.**	Wednesday
min	minuto	**min.**	minute
mm.	milímetro	**mm**	millimeter
M-N, m/n	moneda nacional	—	national currency
Mons.	monseñor	**Msgr.**	monsignor
Mtro.	maestro	—	teacher
Mtra.	maestra	—	teacher
N, N.	Norte, norte	**N, no.**	North, north
n/	nuestro	—	our
n.º	número	**no.**	number
N. de (la) R.	nota de (la) redacción	—	editor's note
NE	nordeste	**NE**	northeast
NN.UU.	Naciones Unidas	**UN**	United Nations
NO	noroeste	**NW**	northwest
nov.	noviembre	**Nov.**	November
N.T.	Nuevo Testamento	**N.T.**	New Testament
ntra., ntro.	nuestra, nuestro	—	our
NU	Naciones Unidas	**UN**	United Nations
núm.	número	**num.**	number
O, O.	Oeste, oeste	**W**	West, west
oct.	octubre	**Oct.**	October
OEA, O.E.A.	Organización de Estados Americanos	**OAS**	Organization of American States

SPANISH ABBREVIATION AND EXPANSION		ENGLISH EQUIVALENT	
OMS	Organización Mundial de la Salud	**WHO**	World Health Organization
ONG	organización no gubernamental	**NGO**	non-governmental organization
ONU	Organización de las Naciones Unidas	**UN**	United Nations
OTAN	Organización del Tratado del Atlántico Norte	**NATO**	North Atlantic Treaty Organization
p.	página	**p.**	page
P, P.	padre (*in religion*)	**Fr.**	father
pág.	página	**pg.**	page
pat.	patente	**pat.**	patent
PCL	pantalla de cristal líquido	**LCD**	liquid crystal display
P.D.	postdata	**P.S.**	postscript
p. ej.	por ejemplo	**e.g.**	for example
PNB	Producto Nacional Bruto	**GNP**	gross national product
P^{0}	paseo	**Ave.**	avenue
p.p.	porte pagado	**ppd.**	postpaid
PP, p.p.	por poder, por poderes	**p.p.**	by proxy
prom.	promedio	**av., avg.**	average
ptas., pts.	pesetas	—	—
q.e.p.d.	que en paz descanse	**R.I.P.**	may he/she rest in peace
R, R/	remite	—	sender
RAE	Real Academia Española	—	—
ref., ref.^{a}	referencia	**ref.**	reference
rep.	república	**rep.**	republic
r.p.m.	revoluciones por minuto	**rpm.**	revolutions per minute
rte.	remite, remitente	—	sender
s.	siglo	**c., cent.**	century
s/	su, sus	—	his, her, your, their
S, S.	Sur, sur	**S, so.**	South, south
S.	san, santo	**St.**	saint
S.A.	sociedad anónima	**Inc.**	incorporated (company)
sáb.	sábado	**Sat.**	Saturday
s/c	su cuenta	—	your account
SE	sudeste, sureste	**SE**	southeast
seg.	segundo, segundos	**sec.**	second, seconds
sep., sept.	septiembre	**Sept.**	September
s.e.u.o.	salvo error u omisión	—	errors and omissions excepted
Sgto.	sargento	**Sgt.**	sergeant
S.L.	sociedad limitada	**Ltd.**	limited (corporation)
S.M.	Su Majestad	**HM**	His Majesty, Her Majesty
s/n	sin número	—	no (street) number
s.n.m.	sobre el nivel de mar	**a.s.l.**	above sea level
SO	sudoeste/suroeste	**SW**	southwest

SPANISH ABBREVIATION AND EXPANSION		ENGLISH EQUIVALENT	
S.R.C.	se ruega contestación	**R.S.V.P.**	please reply
ss.	siguientes	—	the following ones
SS, S.S.	Su Santidad	**H.H.**	His Holiness
Sta.	santa	**St.**	saint
Sto.	santo	**St.**	saint
t, t.	tonelada	**t., tn.**	ton
TAE	tasa anual efectiva	**APR**	annual percentage rate
tb.	también	—	also
tel., Tel.	teléfono	**tel.**	telephone
Tm.	tonelada métrica	**MT**	metric ton
Tn.	tonelada	**t., tn.**	ton
trad.	traducido	**tr., trans., transl.**	translated
UE	Unión Europea	**EU**	European Union
Univ.	universidad	**Univ., U.**	university
UPC	unidad procesadora central	**CPU**	central processing unit
Urb.	urbanización	—	residential area
v	versus	**v., vs.**	versus
v	verso	**v., ver., vs.**	verse
v.	véase	**vid.**	see
Vda.	viuda	—	widow
v.g., v.gr.	verbigracia	**e.g.**	for example
vier., viern.	viernes	**Fri.**	Friday
V.M.	Vuestra Majestad	—	Your Majesty
V⁰B⁰, V.⁰B.⁰	visto bueno	—	OK, approved
vol, vol.	volumen	**vol.**	volume
vra., vro.	vuestra, vuestro	—	your

Common English Abbreviations
Abreviaturas comunes en inglés

ENGLISH ABBREVIATION AND EXPANSION		SPANISH EQUIVALENT	
AAA	American Automobile Association	—	—
AD	anno Domini (in the year of our Lord)	**d.C., d. de J.C.**	después de Cristo, después de Jesucristo
AK	Alaska	—	Alaska
AL, Ala.	Alabama	—	Alabama
Alas.	Alaska	—	Alaska
a.m., AM	ante meridiem (before noon)	**a.m.**	ante meridiem (de la mañana)
Am., Amer.	America, American	—	América, americano
amt.	amount	—	cantidad
anon.	anonymous	—	anónimo
ans.	answer	—	respuesta
Apr.	April	**abr.**	abril
AR	Arkansas	—	Arkansas
Ariz.	Arizona	—	Arizona
Ark.	Arkansas	—	Arkansas
asst.	assistant	**ayte.**	ayudante
atty.	attorney	—	abogado, -da
Aug.	August	**ago.**	agosto
ave.	avenue	**av., avda.**	avenida
AZ	Arizona	—	Arizona
BA	Bachelor of Arts	**Lic.**	Licenciado, -da en Filosofía y Letras
BA	Bachelor of Arts (degree)	—	Licenciatura en Filosofía y Letras
BC	before Christ	**a.C., A.C., a. de J.C.**	antes de Cristo, antes de Jesucristo
BCE	before the Christian Era, before the Common Era	—	antes de la era cristiana, antes de la era común
bet.	between	—	entre
bldg.	building	**edif.**	edificio
blvd.	boulevard	**blvar., br.**	bulevar
Br., Brit.	Britain, British	—	Gran Bretaña, británico
Bro(s).	brother(s)	**Hno(s),**	hermano(s)
BS	Bachelor of Science	**Lic.**	Licenciado, -da en Ciencias
BS	Bachelor of Science (degree)	—	Licenciatura en Ciencias
c	carat	—	quilate
c	cent	—	centavo

ENGLISH ABBREVIATION AND EXPANSION		SPANISH EQUIVALENT	
c	centimeter	**cm.**	centímetro
c	century	**s.**	siglo
c	cup	—	taza
C	Celsius, centigrade	**C**	Celsius, centígrado
CA, Cal., Calif.	California	—	California
Can., Canad.	Canada, Canadian	—	Canadá, canadiense
cap.	capital	—	capital
cap.	capital	—	mayúscula
Capt.	captain	—	capitán
cent.	century	**s.**	siglo
CEO	chief executive officer	—	presidente, -ta (de una corporación)
ch., chap.	chapter	**cap.**	capítulo
CIA	Central Intelligence Agency	—	—
cm	centimeter	**cm.**	centímetro
Co.	company	**C., Cía.**	compañía
co.	county	—	condado
CO	Colorado	—	Colorado
c/o	care of	**a/c**	a cargo de
COD	cash on delivery, collect on delivery	—	(pago) contra reembolso
col.	column	**col.**	columna
Col., Colo.	Colorado	—	Colorado
Conn.	Connecticut	—	Connecticut
corp.	corporation	—	corporación
CPR	cardiopulmonary resuscitation	**RCP**	reanimación cardiopulmonar, resucitación cardiopulmonar
ct.	cent	—	centavo
CT	Connecticut	—	Connecticut
D.A.	district attorney	—	fiscal (del distrito)
DC	District of Columbia	—	—
DDS	Doctor of Dental Surgery	—	doctor de cirugía dental
DE	Delaware	—	Delaware
Dec.	December	**dic.**	diciembre
Del.	Delaware	—	Delaware
DJ	disc jockey		disc-jockey
dept.	department	**dep., dpto.**	departamento
DMD	Doctor of Dental Medicine	—	doctor de medicina dental
doz.	dozen	—	docena
Dr.	doctor	**Dr., Dra.**	doctor, doctora
DST	daylight saving time	—	—
DVM	Doctor of Veterinary Medicine	—	doctor de medicina veterinaria
E	East, east	**E, E.**	Este, este
ea.	each	**c/u**	cada uno, cada una
e.g.	for example	**v.g., v.gr.**	verbigracia

ENGLISH ABBREVIATION	AND EXPANSION	SPANISH EQUIVALENT	
EMT	emergency medical technician	—	técnico, -ca en urgencias médicas
Eng.	England, English	—	Inglaterra, inglés
esp.	especially	—	especialmente
EST	eastern standard time	—	—
etc.	et cetera	**etc.**	etcétera
f	false	—	falso
f	female	**f**	femenino
F	Fahrenheit	**F**	Fahrenheit
FBI	Federal Bureau of Investigation	—	—
Feb.	February	**feb.**	febrero
fem.	feminine	—	femenino
FL, Fla.	Florida	—	Florida
Fri.	Friday	**vier., viern.**	viernes
ft.	feet, foot	—	pie(s)
g	gram	**g., gr.**	gramo
Ga., GA	Georgia	—	Georgia
gal.	gallon	—	galón
Gen.	general	**Gral.**	general
gm	gram	**g., gr.**	gramo
gov.	governor	—	gobernador, -dora
govt.	government	—	gobierno
gr.	gram	**g., gr.**	gramo
HI	Hawaii	—	Hawai, Hawaii
hr.	hour	**h.**	hora
HS	high school	—	colegio secundario
ht.	height	—	altura
Ia., IA	Iowa	—	Iowa
ID	Idaho	—	Idaho
i.e.	id est (that is)	**i.e.**	id est (esto es, es decir)
IL, Ill	Illinois	—	Illinois
in.	inch	—	pulgada
IN	Indiana	—	Indiana
Inc.	incorporated (company)	**S.A.**	sociedad anónima
Ind.	Indian, Indiana	—	Indiana
Jan.	January	**ene.**	enero
Jul.	July	**jul.**	julio
Jun.	June	**jun.**	junio
Jr., Jun.	Junior	**Jr.**	Júnior
Kan., Kans.	Kansas	—	Kansas
kg	kilogram	**kg.**	kilogramo
km	kilometer	**km.**	kilómetro
KS	Kansas	—	Kansas
Ky., KY	Kentucky	—	Kentucky
l	liter	**l.**	litro
l.	left	**izq.**	izquierda
L	large	**G**	(talla) grande
La, LA	Louisiana	—	Luisiana, Louisiana
lb.	pound	—	libra

ENGLISH ABBREVIATION AND EXPANSION		SPANISH EQUIVALENT	
Ltd.	limited (corporation)	**S.L.**	sociedad limitada
m	male	**m**	masculino
m	meter	**m**	metro
m	mile	—	milla
M	medium	**M**	(talla) mediana
MA	Massachusetts	—	Massachusetts
Maj.	major	—	mayor
Mar.	March	**mar.**	marzo
masc.	masculine	—	masculino
Mass.	Massachusetts	—	Massachusetts
Md., MD	Maryland	—	Maryland
M.D.	Doctor of Medicine	—	doctor de medicina
Me., ME	Maine	—	Maine
Mex.	Mexican, Mexico	**Méx.**	mexicano, México
mg	milligram	**mg.**	miligramo
mi.	mile	—	milla
MI, Mich.	Michigan	—	Michigan
min.	minute	**min**	minuto
Minn.	Minnesota	—	Minnesota
Miss.	Mississippi	—	Mississippi, Misisipí
ml	mililiter	**ml.**	mililitro
mm	millimeter	**mm.**	milímetro
MN	Minnesota	—	Minnesota
mo.	month	—	mes
Mo., MO	Missouri	—	Missouri
Mon.	Monday	**lun.**	lunes
Mont.	Montana	—	Montana
mpg	miles per gallon	—	millas por galón
mph	miles per hour	—	millas por hora
MS	Mississippi	—	Mississippi, Misisipí
mt.	mount, mountain	—	monte, montaña
MT	Montana	—	Montana
mtn.	mountain	—	montaña
N	North, north	**N**	Norte, norte
NASA	National Aeronautics and Space Administration	—	—
NC	North Carolina	—	Carolina del Norte, North Carolina
ND, N. Dak.	North Dakota	—	Dakota del Norte, North Dakota
NE	northeast	**NE**	nordeste
NE, Neb., Nebr.	Nebraska	—	Nebraska
Nev.	Nevada	—	Nevada
NH	New Hampshire	—	New Hampshire
NJ	New Jersey	—	Nueva Jersey, New Jersey
NM., N. Mex.	New Mexico	—	Nuevo México, New Mexico
no.	north	**N**	norte
no.	number	**n.º**	número
Nov.	November	**nov.**	noviembre
N.T.	New Testament	**N.T.**	Nuevo Testamento

ENGLISH ABBREVIATION AND EXPANSION		SPANISH EQUIVALENT	
NV	Nevada	—	Nevada
NW	northwest	**NO**	noroeste
NY	New York	**NY**	Nueva York, New York
O	Ohio	—	Ohio
Oct.	October	**oct.**	octubre
OH	Ohio	—	Ohio
OK, Okla.	Oklahoma	—	Oklahoma
OR, Ore., Oreg.	Oregon	—	Oregon
O.T.	Old Testament	**A.T.**	Antiguo Testamento
oz.	ounce, ounces	—	onza, onzas
p.	page	**p.**	página
Pa., PA	Pennsylvania	—	Pennsylvania, Pensilvania
pat.	patent	**pat.**	patente
PD	police department	—	departamento de policía
PE	physical education	—	educación física
Penn., Penna.	Pennsylvania	—	Pennsylvania, Pensilvania
pg.	page	**pág.**	página
PhD	Doctor of Philosophy	—	doctor, -tora (en filosofía)
pkg.	package	—	paquete
p.m., PM	post meridiem (afternoon)	**p.m.**	post meridiem (de la tarde)
P.O.	post office	—	oficina de correos, correo
pp.	pages	**págs.**	páginas
PR	Puerto Rico	**PR**	Puerto Rico
pres.	present	—	presente
pres.	president		presidente, -ta
prof.	professor	—	profesor, -sora
P.S.	postscript	**P.D.**	postdata
P.S.	public school	—	escuela pública
pt.	pint	—	pinta
pt.	point	**pto.**	punto
PTA	Parent-Teacher Association	—	—
PTO	Parent-Teacher Organization	—	—
q, qt.	quart	—	cuarto de galón
r.	right	**dcha.**	derecha
rd.	road	**c/, C/**	calle
RDA	recommended daily allowance	—	consumo diario recomendado
recd.	received	—	recibido
Rev.	reverend	**Rdo.**	reverendo
RI	Rhode Island	—	Rhode Island
rpm	revolutions per minute	**r.p.m.**	revoluciones por minuto
RR	railroad	**FC**	ferrocarril

ENGLISH ABBREVIATION AND EXPANSION		SPANISH EQUIVALENT	
R.S.V.P	please reply (répondez s'il vous plaît)	**S.R.C.**	se ruega contestación
rt.	right	**dcha.**	derecha
rte.	route	—	ruta
S	small	**P**	(talla) pequeña
S	South, south	**S**	Sur, sur
S.A.	South America	—	Sudamérica, América del Sur
Sat.	Saturday	**sáb.**	sábado
SC	South Carolina	—	Carolina del Sur, South Carolina
SD, S. Dak.	South Dakota	—	Dakota del Sur, South Dakota
SE	southeast	**SE**	sudeste, sureste
Sept.	September	**sep., sept.**	septiembre
so.	south	**S**	sur
sq.	square		cuadrado
Sr.	Senior	**Sr.**	Sénior
Sr.	sister (*in religion*)	—	sor
st.	state	—	estado
st.	street	**c/, C/**	calle
St.	saint	**S., Sto., Sta.**	santo, santa
Sun.	Sunday	**dom.**	domingo
SW	southwest	**SO**	sudoeste, suroeste
t.	teaspoon	—	cucharadita
T, tb., tbsp.	tablespoon	—	cucharada (grande)
Tenn.	Tennessee	—	Tennessee
Tex.	Texas	—	Texas
Thu., Thur., Thurs.	Thursday	**juev.**	jueves
TM	trademark	—	marca (de un producto)
TN	Tennessee	—	Tennessee
tsp.	teaspoon	—	cucharadita
Tue., Tues.	Tuesday	**mart.**	martes
TX	Texas	—	Texas
UN	United Nations	**NU, NN.UU.**	Naciones Unidas
US	United States	**EEUU, EE.UU.**	Estados Unidos
USA	United States of America	**EEUU, EE.UU.**	Estados Unidos de América
usu.	usually	—	usualmente
UT	Utah	—	Utah
v.	versus	**v**	versus
Va., VA	Virginia	—	Virginia
vol.	volume	**vol.**	volumen
VP	vice president	—	vicepresidente, -ta
vs.	versus	**v**	versus
Vt., VT	Vermont	—	Vermont

ENGLISH ABBREVIATION AND EXPANSION		SPANISH EQUIVALENT	
W	West, west	**O**	Oeste, oeste
WA, Wash.	Washington (state)	—	Washington
Wed.	Wednesday	**miérc.**	miércoles
WI, Wis., Wisc.	Wisconsin	—	Wisconsin
wt.	weight	—	peso
WV, W. Va.	West Virginia	—	Virginia del Oeste, West Virginia
WY, Wyo.	Wyoming	—	Wyoming
yd.	yard	—	yarda
yr.	year	—	año

Metric System : Conversions
Sistema métrico : conversiones

Length

unit	number of meters	approximate U.S. equivalents	
millimeter	0.001	0.039	inch
centimeter	0.01	0.39	inch
meter	1	39.37	inches
kilometer	1,000	0.62	mile

Longitud

unidad	número de metros	equivalentes aproximados de los EE.UU.	
milímetro	0.001	0.039	pulgada
centímetro	0.01	0.39	pulgada
metro	1	39.37	pulgadas
kilómetro	1,000	0.62	milla

Area

unit	number of square meters	approximate U.S. equivalents	
square centimeter	0.0001	0.155	square inch
square meter	1	10.764	square feet
hectare	10,000	2.47	acres
square kilometer	1,000,000	0.3861	square mile

Superficie

unidad	número de metros cuadrados	equivalentes aproximados de los EE.UU.	
centímetro cuadrado	0.0001	0.155	pulgada cuadrada
metro cuadrado	1	10.764	pies cuadrados
hectárea	10,000	2.47	acres
kilómetro cuadrado	1,000,000	0.3861	milla cuadrada

Volume

unit	number of cubic meters	approximate U.S. equivalents	
cubic centimeter	0.000001	0.061	cubic inch
cubic meter	1	1.307	cubic yards

Volumen

unidad	número de metros cúbicos	equivalentes aproximados de los EE.UU	
centímetro cúbico	0.000001	0.061	pulgada cúbica
metro cúbico	1	1.307	yardas cúbicas

Capacity

unit	number of liters	approximate U.S. equivalents		
		CUBIC	DRY	LIQUID
liter	1	61.02 cubic inches	0.908 quart	1.057 quarts

Capacidad

unidad	número de litros	equivalentes aproximados de los EE.UU.		
		CÚBICO	SECO	LIQUIDO
litro	1	61.02 pulgadas cúbicas	0.908 cuarto	1.057 cuartos

Mass and Weight

unit	number of grams	approximate U.S. equivalents	
milligram	0.001	0.015	grain
centigram	0.01	0.154	grain
gram	1	0.035	ounce
kilogram	1,000	2.2046	pounds
metric ton	1,000,000	1.102	short tons

Masa y peso

unidad	número de gramos	equivalentes aproximados de los EE.UU.	
miligramo	0.001	0.015	grano
centigramo	0.01	0.154	grano
gramo	1	0.035	onza
kilogramo	1.000	2.2046	libras
tonelada métrica	1,000,000	1.102	toneladas cortas